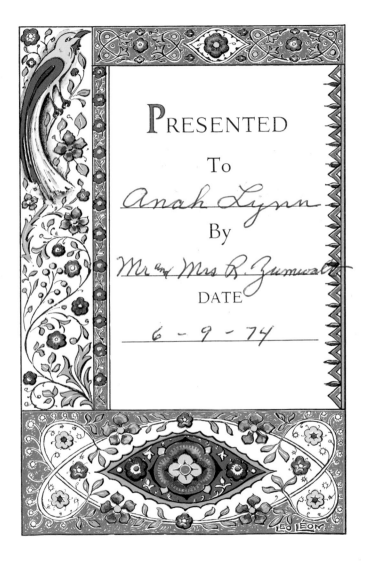

PRESENTED

To

Anah Lynn

By

Mr and Mrs R. Zumwalt

DATE

6 - 9 - 74

SELF-PRONOUNCING EDITION

THE
HOLY BIBLE

REVISED STANDARD VERSION

Containing the

OLD AND NEW TESTAMENTS

TRANSLATED FROM THE ORIGINAL TONGUES
BEING THE VERSION SET FORTH A.D. 1611
REVISED A.D. 1881-1885 AND A.D. 1901
COMPARED WITH THE MOST
ANCIENT AUTHORITIES AND
REVISED A.D. 1952

THE WORLD PUBLISHING COMPANY

CLEVELAND AND NEW YORK

Published by The World Publishing Company
2231 West 110th Street, Cleveland 2, Ohio

Printed in the United States of America

PREFACE

THE Revised Standard Version of the Bible is an authorized revision of the American Standard Version, published in 1901, which was a revision of the King James Version, published in 1611.

The first English version of the Scriptures made by direct translation from the original Hebrew and Greek, and the first to be printed, was the work of William Tyndale. He met bitter opposition. He was accused of willfully perverting the meaning of the Scriptures, and his New Testaments were ordered to be burned as "untrue translations." He was finally betrayed into the hands of his enemies, and in October 1536, was publicly executed and burned at the stake.

Yet Tyndale's work became the foundation of subsequent English versions, notably those of Coverdale, 1535; Thomas Matthew (probably a pseudonym for John Rogers), 1537; the Great Bible, 1539; the Geneva Bible, 1560; and the Bishops' Bible, 1568. In 1582 a translation of the New Testament, made from the Latin Vulgate by Roman Catholic scholars, was published at Rheims.

The translators who made the King James Version took into account all of these preceding versions; and comparison shows that it owes something to each of them. It kept felicitous phrases and apt expressions, from whatever source, which had stood the test of public usage. It owed most, especially in the New Testament, to Tyndale.

The King James Version had to compete with the Geneva Bible in popular use; but in the end it prevailed, and for more than two and a half centuries no other authorized translation of the Bible into English was made. The King James Version became the "Authorized Version" of the English-speaking peoples.

The King James Version has with good reason been termed "the noblest monument of English prose." Its revisers in 1881 expressed admiration for "its simplicity, its dignity, its power, its happy turns of expression . . . the music of its cadences, and the felicities of its rhythm." It entered, as no other book has, into the making of the personal character and the public institutions of the English-speaking peoples. We owe to it an incalculable debt.

Yet the King James Version has grave defects. By the middle of the nineteenth century, the development of Biblical studies and the discovery of many manuscripts more ancient than those upon which the King James Version was based, made it manifest that these defects are so many and so serious as to call for revision of the English translation. The task was undertaken, by authority of the Church of England, in 1870. The English Revised Version of the Bible was published in 1881–1885; and the American Standard Version, its variant embodying the preferences of the American scholars associated in the work, was published in 1901.

Because of unhappy experience with unauthorized publications in the two decades between 1881 and 1901, which tampered with the text of the English Revised Version in the supposed interest of the American public, the American Standard Version was copyrighted, to protect the text from unauthorized changes. In 1928 this copyright was acquired by the International Council of Religious Education, and thus passed into the ownership of the churches of the United States and Canada which were associated in this Council through their boards of education and publication.

The Council appointed a committee of scholars to have charge of the text of the American Standard Version and to undertake inquiry as to whether further revision was necessary. For more than two years the Committee worked upon the problem of whether or not revision should be undertaken; and if so, what should be its nature and extent. In the end the decision was reached that there is need for a thorough revision of the version of 1901, which will stay as close to the Tyndale-King James tradition as it can in the light of our present knowledge of the Hebrew and Greek texts and their meaning on the one hand, and our present understanding of English on the other.

In 1937 the revision was authorized by vote of the Council, which directed that the resulting version should "embody the best results of modern scholarship as to the meaning of the Scriptures, and express this meaning in English diction which is designed for use in public and private worship and preserves those qualities which have given to the King James Version a supreme place in English literature."

Thirty-two scholars have served as members of the Committee charged with making the revision, and they have secured the review and counsel of an Advisory Board of fifty representatives of the co-operating denominations. The Committee has worked in two sections, one dealing with the Old Testament and one with the New Testament. Each section has submitted its work to the scrutiny of the members of the other section; and the charter of the Committee requires that all changes be agreed upon by a two-thirds vote of the total membership of the Committee. The Revised Standard Version of the New Testament was published in 1946. The publication of the Revised Standard Version of the Bible, containing the Old and New Testaments, was authorized by vote of the National Council of the Churches of Christ in the U.S.A. in 1951.

The problem of establishing the correct Hebrew and Aramaic text of the Old Testament is very different from the corresponding problem in the New Testament. For the New Testament we have a large number of Greek manuscripts, preserving many variant forms of the text. Some of them were made only two or three centuries later than the original composition of the books. For the Old Testament only late manuscripts survive, all (with the exception of the Dead Sea texts of Isaiah and Habakkuk and some fragments of other books) based on a standardized form of the text established many centuries after the books were written.

The present revision is based on the consonantal Hebrew and Aramaic text as fixed early in the Christian era and revised by Jewish scholars (the "Masoretes") of the sixth to ninth centuries. The vowel-signs, which were added by the Masoretes, are accepted also in the main, but where a more probable and convincing reading can be ob-

iv

tained by assuming different vowels, this has been done. No notes are given in such cases, because the vowel points are less ancient and reliable than the consonants.

Departures from the consonantal text of the best manuscripts have been made only where it seems clear that errors in copying had been made before the text was standardized. Most of the corrections adopted are based on the ancient versions (translations into Greek, Aramaic, Syriac, and Latin), which were made before the time of the Masoretic revision and therefore reflect earlier forms of the text. In every such instance a footnote specifies the version or versions from which the correction has been derived, and also gives a translation of the Masoretic Text.

Sometimes it is evident that the text has suffered in transmission, but none of the versions provides a satisfactory restoration. Here we can only follow the best judgment of competent scholars as to the most probable reconstruction of the original text. Such corrections are indicated in the footnotes by the abbreviation *Cn*, and a translation of the Masoretic Text is added.

The discovery of the meaning of the text, once the best readings have been established, is aided by many new resources for understanding the original languages. Much progress has been made in the historical and comparative study of these languages. A vast quantity of writings in related Semitic languages, some of them only recently discovered, has greatly enlarged our knowledge of the vocabulary and grammar of Biblical Hebrew and Aramaic. Sometimes the present translation will be found to render a Hebrew word in a sense quite different from that of the traditional interpretation. It has not been felt necessary in such cases to attach a footnote, because no change in the text is involved and it may be assumed that the new rendering was not adopted without convincing evidence. The analysis of religious texts from the ancient Near East has made clearer the significance of ideas and practices recorded in the Old Testament. Many difficulties and obscurities, of course, remain. Where the choice between two meanings is particularly difficult or doubtful, we have given an alternative rendering in a footnote. If in the judgment of the Committee the meaning of a passage is quite uncertain or obscure, either because of corruption in the text or because of the inadequacy of our present knowledge of the language, that fact is indicated by a note. It should not be assumed, however, that the Committee was entirely sure or unanimous concerning every rendering not so indicated. To record all minority views was obviously out of the question.

A major departure from the practice of the American Standard Version is the rendering of the Divine Name, the "Tetragrammaton." The American Standard Version used the term "Jehovah"; the King James Version had employed this in four places, but everywhere else, except in three cases where it was employed as part of a proper name, used the English word LORD (or in certain cases GOD) printed in capitals. The present revision returns to the procedure of the King James Version, which follows the precedent of the ancient Greek and Latin translators and the long established practice in the reading of the Hebrew scriptures in the synagogue. While it is almost if not quite certain that the Name was originally pronounced "Yahweh," this pronunciation was not indicated when the Masoretes added vowel signs to the consonantal Hebrew text. To the four consonants YHWH of the Name, which had come to be regarded as too sacred to be pronounced, they attached vowel signs indicating that in its place should be read the Hebrew word *Adonai* meaning "Lord" (or *Elohim* meaning "God"). The ancient Greek translators substituted the word *Kyrios* (Lord) for the Name. The Vulgate likewise used the Latin word *Dominus*. The form "Jehovah" is of late medieval origin; it is a combination of the consonants of the Divine Name and the vowels attached to it by the Masoretes but belonging to an entirely different word. The sound of Y is represented by J and the sound of W by V, as in Latin. For two reasons the Committee has returned to the more familiar usage of the King James Version: (1) the word "Jehovah" does not accurately represent any form of the Name ever used in Hebrew; and (2) the use of any proper name for the one and only God, as though there were other gods from whom He had to be distinguished, was discontinued in Judaism before the Christian era and is entirely inappropriate for the universal faith of the Christian Church.

The King James Version of the New Testament was based upon a Greek text that was marred by mistakes, containing the accumulated errors of fourteen centuries of manuscript copying. It was essentially the Greek text of the New Testament as edited by Beza, 1589, who closely followed that published by Erasmus, 1516–1535, which was based upon a few medieval manuscripts. The earliest and best of the eight manuscripts which Erasmus consulted was from the tenth century, and he made the least use of it because it differed most from the commonly received text; Beza had access to two manuscripts of great value, dating from the fifth and sixth centuries, but he made very little use of them because they differed from the text published by Erasmus.

We now possess many more ancient manuscripts of the New Testament, and are far better equipped to seek to recover the original wording of the Greek text. The evidence for the text of the books of the New Testament is better than for any other ancient book, both in the number of extant manuscripts and in the nearness of the date of some of these manuscripts to the date when the book was originally written.

The revisers in the 1870's had most of the evidence that we now have for the Greek text, though the most ancient of all extant manuscripts of the Greek New Testament were not discovered until 1931. But they lacked the resources which discoveries within the past eighty years have afforded for understanding the vocabulary, grammar and idioms of the Greek New Testament. An amazing body of Greek papyri has been unearthed in Egypt since the 1870's—private letters, official reports, wills, business accounts, petitions, and other such trivial, everyday recordings of the activities of human beings. In 1895 appeared the first of Adolf Deissmann's studies of these ordinary materials. He proved that many words which had hitherto been assumed to belong to what was called "Biblical Greek" were current in the spoken vernacular of the first century A.D. The New Testament was written in the Koiné, the common Greek which was spoken and understood practically everywhere throughout the Roman Empire in the early centuries of the Christian era. This development in the study of New Testament Greek has come since the work on the English Revised Version and the American Standard Version was done, and at many points sheds new light upon the meaning of the Greek text.

A major reason for revision of the King James Version, which is valid for both the Old Testament and the New Testament, is the change since 1611 in English usage. Many forms of expression have become archaic, while still generally intelligible—the use of thou, thee, thy, thine and the verb endings -est and -edst, the verb endings -eth and -th, it came to pass that, whosoever, whatsoever, insomuch that, because that, for that, unto, howbeit, peradventure, holden, aforetime, must needs, would fain, behooved, to you-ward, etc. Other words are obsolete and no longer understood by the common reader. The greatest problem, however, is presented by the English words which are still in constant use but now convey a different meaning from that which they had in 1611 and in the King James Version. These words were once accurate translations of the Hebrew and Greek Scriptures; but now, having changed in meaning, they have become misleading. They no longer say what the King James translators meant them to say.

The King James Version uses the word "let" in the sense of "hinder," "prevent" to mean "precede," "allow" in the sense of "approve," "communicate" for "share," "conversation" for "conduct," "comprehend" for "overcome," "ghost" for "spirit," "wealth" for "well-being," "allege" for "prove," "demand" for "ask," "take no thought" for "be not anxious," "purchase a good degree" for "gain a good standing," etc. The Greek word for "immediately" is translated in the King James Version not only by "immediately" and "straightway" but also by the terms "anon," "by and by," and "presently." There are more than three hundred such English words which are used in the King James Version in a sense substantially different from that which they now convey. It not only does the King James translators no honor, but it is quite unfair to them and to the truth which they understood and expressed, to retain these words which now convey meanings they did not intend.

The Revised Standard Version of the Bible, containing the Old and New Testaments, was published on September 30, 1952, and has met with wide acceptance. This preface does not undertake to set forth in detail the lines along which the revision proceeded. That is done in pamphlets entitled *An Introduction to the Revised Standard Version of the Old Testament* and *An Introduction to the Revised Standard Version of the New Testament*, written by members of the Committee and designed to help the general public to understand the main principles which have guided this comprehensive revision of the King James and American Standard versions.

These principles were reaffirmed by the Committee in 1959, in connection with a study of criticisms and suggestions from various readers. As a result, a few changes have been authorized for the present and subsequent editions. Most of these are corrections of punctuation, capitalization, or footnotes. Some changes of words or phrases are made in the interest of consistency, clarity or accuracy of translation.

Examples of such changes are "from," Job 19.26; "bread," Matthew 7.9; 1 Corinthians 10.17; "is he," Matthew 21.9 and parallels; "the Son," Matthew 27.54; Mark 15.39; "ask nothing of me," John 16.23; "for this life only," 1 Corinthians 15.19; "the husband of one wife," 1 Timothy 3.2, 12; 5.9; Titus 1.6.

All the reasons which led to the demand for revision of the King James Version in the nineteenth century are still valid, and are even more cogent now than then. We have had a freer charter than our predecessors in the 1870's in that we have not been required, as they were, to limit the language of the English Bible to the vocabulary of the Elizabethan age. But we hope that we have not taken undue advantage of that freedom. The Revised Standard Version is not a new translation in the language of today. It is not a paraphrase which aims at striking idioms. It is a revision which seeks to preserve all that is best in the English Bible as it has been known and used through the years. It is intended for use in public and private worship, not merely for reading and instruction. We have resisted the temptation to use phrases that are merely current usage, and have sought to put the message of the Bible in simple, enduring words that are worthy to stand in the great Tyndale-King James tradition. We are glad to say, with the King James translators: "Truly (good Christian Reader) we never thought from the beginning, that we should need to make a new Translation, nor yet to make of a bad one a good one . . . but to make a good one better."

The Bible is more than a historical document to be preserved. And it is more than a classic of English literature to be cherished and admired. It is a record of God's dealing with men, of God's revelation of Himself and His will. It records the life and work of Him in whom the Word of God became flesh and dwelt among men. The Bible carries its full message, not to those who regard it simply as a heritage of the past or praise its literary style, but to those who read it that they may discern and understand God's Word to men. That Word must not be disguised in phrases that are no longer clear, or hidden under words that have changed or lost their meaning. It must stand forth in language that is direct and plain and meaningful to people today. It is our hope and our earnest prayer that this Revised Standard Version of the Bible may be used by God to speak to men in these momentous times, and to help them to understand and believe and obey His Word.

THE NAMES AND ORDER OF THE BOOKS OF THE

OLD AND NEW TESTAMENTS

THE OLD TESTAMENT

THE NEW TESTAMENT

ABBREVIATIONS AND CROSS REFERENCES

ABBREVIATIONS

References to quoted and parallel passages are given following the notes on pages where these are relevant. The following abbreviations are used for the books of the Bible:

OLD TESTAMENT

Gen	Genesis	Eccles	Ecclesiastes
Ex	Exodus	Song	Song of Solomon
Lev	Leviticus	Is	Isaiah
Num	Numbers	Jer	Jeremiah
Deut	Deuteronomy	Lam	Lamentations
Josh	Joshua	Ezek	Ezekiel
Judg	Judges	Dan	Daniel
Ruth	Ruth	Hos	Hosea
1 Sam	1 Samuel	Joel	Joel
2 Sam	2 Samuel	Amos	Amos
1 Kings	1 Kings	Obad	Obadiah
2 Kings	2 Kings	Jon	Jonah
1 Chron	1 Chronicles	Mic	Micah
2 Chron	2 Chronicles	Nahum	Nahum
Ezra	Ezra	Hab	Habakkuk
Neh	Nehemiah	Zeph	Zephaniah
Esther	Esther	Hag	Haggai
Job	Job	Zech	Zechariah
Ps	Psalms	Mal	Malachi
Prov	Proverbs		

NEW TESTAMENT

Mt	Matthew	1 Tim	1 Timothy
Mk	Mark	2 Tim	2 Timothy
Lk	Luke	Tit	Titus
Jn	John	Philem	Philemon
Acts	Acts of the Apostles	Heb	Hebrews
Rom	Romans	Jas	James
1 Cor	1 Corinthians	1 Pet	1 Peter
2 Cor	2 Corinthians	2 Pet	2 Peter
Gal	Galatians	1 Jn	1 John
Eph	Ephesians	2 Jn	2 John
Phil	Philippians	3 Jn	3 John
Col	Colossians	Jude	Jude
1 Thess	1 Thessalonians	Rev	Revelation
2 Thess	2 Thessalonians		

In the notes to the books of the Old Testament, the following abbreviations are used: Ms for manuscript; Mss for manuscripts. Heb denotes the Hebrew of the consonantal Masoretic Text of the Old Testament; and MT denotes the Hebrew of the pointed Masoretic Text of the Old Testament.

ABBREVIATIONS AND CROSS REFERENCES

The ancient versions of the Old Testament are indicated by:

Gk   Septuagint, Greek Version of Old Testament
Sam   Samaritan Hebrew Text of Old Testament
Syr   Syriac Version of Old Testament
Tg   Targum
Vg   Vulgate, Latin Version of Old Testament

Cn indicates a correction made where the text has suffered in transmission and the versions provide no satisfactory restoration but the Committee agrees with the judgment of competent scholars as to the most probable reconstruction of the original text.

CROSS REFERENCES

Cross references for the thought or theme of an entire verse are given first; further references are put in the order of the words in the verse to which they pertain. These references are kept in the same order as the books of the Bible for each sentence, word, or phrase under consideration. For example: The first reference to Matthew 9.36 (Mk 6.34) refers to the whole verse; the next two references (Mt 14.14; 15.32) apply to the phrase "When he saw the crowds, he had compassion for them"; and the last two references (Num 27.17; Zech 10.2) apply to "helpless, like sheep without a shepherd." The reader is referred to the Preface for a further statement of policy concerning text and notes.

KEY TO PRONUNCIATION

In this edition of the Revised Standard Version of the Holy Bible a pronunciation system has been added so that the reader may easily read and pronounce the proper names. The pronunciation marks are shown in the list below. The names are separated into syllables, and an accent mark (') is placed after the syllable that is to receive the main stress. Pronunciation is shown only for those proper names that are not well known in English. It is not shown for common given names (such as *Benjamin*), common geographical place names (such as *Ethiopia*), or subjects of common reference (such as *Pharaoh*). Each name is pronounced only the first time it appears in any given verse.

a	as in cat		ȯ	as in comply
ā	" " cāke		u	" " up
ä	" " cär		ū	" " ūse
ȧ	" " ȧbout		ü	" " rüle
â	" " câre		u̇	" " focu̇s
e	" " ten		ūr	" " fūrther
ē	" " ēven		y	" " happy
ė	" " agėnt or fathėr		ȳ	" " lȳre
ẽr	" " hẽrd			
i	" " it or sanity		äi	= i as in äisle
ī	" " bīte		ch	= k " " ache
ĩ	" " bĩrd		ċ	= s " " ċite
o	" " lot		ġ	= j " " ġem
ō	" " gō		ṡ	= z " " thoṡe
ô	" " hôrn		ẋ	= z " " ẋylophone

All other consonants are pronounced with their usual sounds in English, as ph = f, c = k, etc.

THE FIRST BOOK OF MOSES

COMMONLY CALLED

GENESIS

In the beginning God created[a] the heavens and the earth. 2 The earth was without form and void, and darkness was upon the face of the deep; and the Spirit[b] of God was moving over the face of the waters.

3 And God said, "Let there be light"; and there was light. 4And God saw that the light was good; and God separated the light from the darkness. 5 God called the light Day, and the darkness he called Night. And there was evening and there was morning, one day.

6 And God said, "Let there be a firmament in the midst of the waters, and let it separate the waters from the waters." 7And God made the firmament and separated the waters which were under the firmament from the waters which were above the firmament. And it was so. 8And God called the firmament Heaven. And there was evening and there was morning, a second day.

9 And God said, "Let the waters under the heavens be gathered together into one place, and let the dry land appear." And it was so. 10 God called the dry land Earth, and the waters that were gathered together he called Seas. And God saw that it was good. 11And God said, "Let the earth put forth vegetation, plants yielding seed, and fruit trees bearing fruit in which is their seed, each according to its kind, upon the earth." And it was so. 12 The earth brought forth vegetation, plants yielding seed according to their own kinds, and trees bearing fruit in which is their seed, each according to its kind. And God saw that it was good. 13And there was evening and there was morning, a third day.

14 And God said, "Let there be lights in the firmament of the heavens to separate the day from the night; and let them be for signs and for seasons and for days and years, 15 and let there be lights in the firmament of the heavens to give light upon the

earth." And it was so. 16And God made the two great lights, the greater light to rule the day, and the lesser light to rule the night; he made the stars also. 17And God set them in the firmament of the heavens to give light upon the earth, 18 to rule over the day and over the night, and to separate the light from the darkness. And God saw that it was good. 19And there was evening and there was morning, a fourth day.

20 And God said, "Let the waters bring forth swarms of living creatures, and let birds fly above the earth across the firmament of the heavens." 21 So God created the great sea monsters and every living creature that moves, with which the waters swarm, according to their kinds, and every winged bird according to its kind. And God saw that it was good. 22And God blessed them, saying, "Be fruitful and multiply and fill the waters in the seas, and let birds multiply on the earth." 23And there was evening and there was morning, a fifth day.

24 And God said, "Let the earth bring forth living creatures according to their kinds: cattle and creeping things and beasts of the earth according to their kinds." And it was so. 25And God made the beasts of the earth according to their kinds and the cattle according to their kinds, and everything that creeps upon the ground according to its kind. And God saw that it was good.

26 Then God said, "Let us make man in our image, after our likeness; and let them have dominion over the fish of the sea, and over the birds of the air, and over the cattle, and over all the earth, and over every creeping thing that creeps upon the earth." 27 So God created man in his own image, in the image of God he created him; male and female he created them. 28And God blessed them, and God said to them, "Be fruitful and multiply, and fill the earth and subdue it; and

a Or *When God began to create*   b Or *wind*

1.1: Jn 1.1.   **1.26-27:** Gen 5.1; Mt 19.4; Mk 10.6; Col 3.10; Jas 3.9.

1

have dominion over the fish of the sea and over the birds of the air and over every living thing that moves upon the earth." [29]And God said, "Behold, I have given you every plant yielding seed which is upon the face of all the earth, and every tree with seed in its fruit; you shall have them for food. [30]And to every beast of the earth, and to every bird of the air, and to everything that creeps on the earth, everything that has the breath of life, I have given every green plant for food." And it was so. [31]And God saw everything that he had made, and behold, it was very good. And there was evening and there was morning, a sixth day.

2 Thus the heavens and the earth were finished, and all the host of them. [2]And on the seventh day God finished his work which he had done, and he rested on the seventh day from all his work which he had done. [3] So God blessed the seventh day and hallowed it, because on it God rested from all his work which he had done in creation.

[4] These are the generations of the heavens and the earth when they were created.

In the day that the LORD God made the earth and the heavens, [5] when no plant of the field was yet in the earth and no herb of the field had yet sprung up—for the LORD God had not caused it to rain upon the earth, and there was no man to till the ground; [6] but a mist[c] went up from the earth and watered the whole face of the ground— [7] then the LORD God formed man of dust from the ground, and breathed into his nostrils the breath of life; and man became a living being. [8]And the LORD God planted a garden in Eden, in the east; and there he put the man whom he had formed. [9]And out of the ground the LORD God made to grow every tree that is pleasant to the sight and good for food, the tree of life also in the midst of the garden, and the tree of the knowledge of good and evil.

[10] A river flowed out of Eden to water the garden, and there it divided and became four rivers. [11] The name of the first is Pi′shon; it is the one which flows around the whole land of Hav′i·lah, where there is gold; [12] and the gold of that land is good; bdellium and onyx stone are there. [13] The name of the second river is Gi′hon; it is the one which flows around the whole land of Cush. [14]And the name of the third

river is Ti′gris, which flows east of Assyria. And the fourth river is the Eū·phra′tēs.

[15] The LORD God took the man and put him in the garden of Eden to till it and keep it. [16]And the LORD God commanded the man, saying, "You may freely eat of every tree of the garden; [17] but of the tree of the knowledge of good and evil you shall not eat, for in the day that you eat of it you shall die."

[18] Then the LORD God said, "It is not good that the man should be alone; I will make him a helper fit for him." [19] So out of the ground the LORD God formed every beast of the field and every bird of the air, and brought them to the man to see what he would call them; and whatever the man called every living creature, that was its name. [20] The man gave names to all cattle, and to the birds of the air, and to every beast of the field; but for the man there was not found a helper fit for him. [21] So the LORD God caused a deep sleep to fall upon the man, and while he slept took one of his ribs and closed up its place with flesh; [22] and the rib which the LORD God had taken from the man he made into a woman and brought her to the man. [23] Then the man said,

"This at last is bone of my bones
    and flesh of my flesh;
she shall be called Woman,[d]
    because she was taken out of
        Man."[e]

[24] Therefore a man leaves his father and his mother and cleaves to his wife, and they become one flesh. [25]And the man and his wife were both naked, and were not ashamed.

3 Now the serpent was more subtle than any other wild creature that the LORD God had made. He said to the woman, "Did God say, 'You shall not eat of any tree of the garden'?" [2]And the woman said to the serpent, "We may eat of the fruit of the trees of the garden; [3] but God said, 'You shall not eat of the fruit of the tree which is in the midst of the garden, neither shall you touch it, lest you die.'" [4] But the serpent said to the woman, "You will not die. [5] For God knows that when you eat of it your eyes will be opened, and you will be like God, knowing good and evil." [6] So when the woman saw that the tree was good for food, and that it was a delight to the eyes, and that the tree was to be

2.1-3: Ex 20.11. **2.2:** Heb 4.4, 10. **2.7:** 1 Cor 15.45, 47. **2.9:** Rev 2.7; 22.2, 14, 19.
2.24: Mt 19.5; Mk 10.7; 1 Cor 6.16; Eph 5.31. **3.1:** Rev 12.9; 20.2. **3.4:** 2 Cor 11.3.

c Or *flood* d Heb *ishshah* e Heb *ish*

desired to make one wise, she took of its fruit and ate; and she also gave some to her husband, and he ate. 7 Then the eyes of both were opened, and they knew that they were naked; and they sewed fig leaves together and made themselves aprons.

8 And they heard the sound of the LORD God walking in the garden in the cool of the day, and the man and his wife hid themselves from the presence of the LORD God among the trees of the garden. 9 But the LORD God called to the man, and said to him, "Where are you?" 10And he said, "I heard the sound of thee in the garden, and I was afraid, because I was naked; and I hid myself." 11 He said, "Who told you that you were naked? Have you eaten of the tree of which I commanded you not to eat?" 12 The man said, "The woman whom thou gavest to be with me, she gave me fruit of the tree, and I ate." 13 Then the LORD God said to the woman, "What is this that you have done?" The woman said, "The serpent beguiled me, and I ate." 14 The LORD God said to the serpent,

"Because you have done this,
    cursed are you above all cattle,
    and above all wild animals;
upon your belly you shall go,
    and dust you shall eat
    all the days of your life.
15 I will put enmity between you and
        the woman,
    and between your seed and her
        seed;
he shall bruise your head,
    and you shall bruise his heel."

16 To the woman he said,
"I will greatly multiply your pain in
        childbearing;
    in pain you shall bring forth
        children,
yet your desire shall be for your
        husband,
    and he shall rule over you."

17 And to Adam he said,
"Because you have listened to the
        voice of your wife,
    and have eaten of the tree
of which I commanded you,
    'You shall not eat of it,'
cursed is the ground because of you;
    in toil you shall eat of it all the
        days of your life;
18 thorns and thistles it shall bring
        forth to you;
    and you shall eat the plants of the
        field.

19 In the sweat of your face
    you shall eat bread
till you return to the ground,
    for out of it you were taken;
you are dust,
    and to dust you shall return."

20 The man called his wife's name Eve,*f* because she was the mother of all living. 21And the LORD God made for Adam and for his wife garments of skins, and clothed them.

22 Then the LORD God said, "Behold, the man has become like one of us, knowing good and evil; and now, lest he put forth his hand and take also of the tree of life, and eat, and live for ever"—23 therefore the LORD God sent him forth from the garden of Eden, to till the ground from which he was taken. 24 He drove out the man; and at the east of the garden of Eden he placed the cherubim, and a flaming sword which turned every way, to guard the way to the tree of life.

4 Now Adam knew Eve his wife, and she conceived and bore Cain, saying, "I have gotten*g* a man with the help of the LORD." 2And again, she bore his brother Abel. Now Abel was a keeper of sheep, and Cain a tiller of the ground. 3 In the course of time Cain brought to the LORD an offering of the fruit of the ground, 4 and Abel brought of the firstlings of his flock and of their fat portions. And the LORD had regard for Abel and his offering, 5 but for Cain and his offering he had no regard. So Cain was very angry, and his countenance fell. 6 The LORD said to Cain, "Why are you angry, and why has your countenance fallen? 7 If you do well, will you not be accepted? And if you do not do well, sin is couching at the door; its desire is for you, but you must master it."

8 Cain said to Abel his brother, "Let us go out to the field."*h* And when they were in the field, Cain rose up against his brother Abel, and killed him. 9 Then the LORD said to Cain, "Where is Abel your brother?" He said, "I do not know; am I my brother's keeper?" 10And the LORD said, "What have you done? The voice of your brother's blood is crying to me from the ground. 11And now you are cursed from the ground, which has opened its mouth to receive your brother's blood from your hand. 12 When you till the ground, it shall no longer yield to you its strength; you

f The name in Hebrew resembles the word for *living*   *g* Heb *qanah*, get
h Sam Gk Syr Compare Vg: Heb lacks *Let us go out to the field*   **3.13**: 2 Cor 11.3.
3.14-15: Rev 12.9; 20.2.   **3.17-18**: Heb 6.8.   **3.22, 24**: Rev 2.7; 22.2, 14, 19.
4.4: Heb 11.4.   **4.8**: 1 Jn 3.12.

shall be a fugitive and a wanderer on the earth." 13 Cain said to the LORD, "My punishment is greater than I can bear. 14 Behold, thou hast driven me this day away from the ground; and from thy face I shall be hidden; and I shall be a fugitive and a wanderer on the earth, and whoever finds me will slay me." 15 Then the LORD said to him, "Not so!*i* If any one slays Cain, vengeance shall be taken on him sevenfold." And the LORD put a mark on Cain, lest any who came upon him should kill him. 16 Then Cain went away from the presence of the LORD, and dwelt in the land of Nod,*j* east of Eden.

17 Cain knew his wife, and she conceived and bore É·nóch; and he built a city, and called the name of the city after the name of his son, Enoch. 18 To É·nóch was born Íʹrad; and Irad was the father of Me·hūʹjà·el, and Mehujael the father of Me·thűʹshà·el, and Methusha-el the father of Lāʹmech. 19And Lāʹmech took two wives; the name of the one was Áʹdàh, and the name of the other Zilʹlàh. 20Áʹdàh bore Jāʹbàl; he was the father of those who dwell in tents and have cattle. 21 His brother's name was Jūʹbàl; he was the father of all those who play the lyre and pipe. 22 Zilʹlàh bore Tūʹbàl-càin; he was the forger of all instruments of bronze and iron. The sister of Tubalcain was Nāʹà·màh.

23 Lāʹmech said to his wives:

"Áʹdàh and Zilʹlàh, hear my voice;
    you wives of Lamech, hearken to
      what I say:
I have slain a man for wounding me,
    a young man for striking me.
24 If Cain is avenged sevenfold,
    truly Lāʹmech seventy-seven-
      fold."

25 And Adam knew his wife again, and she bore a son and called his name Seth, for she said, "God has appointed for me another child instead of Abel, for Cain slew him." 26 To Seth also a son was born, and he called his name É·nósh. At that time men began to call upon the name of the LORD.

5 This is the book of the generations of Adam. When God created man, he made him in the likeness of God. 2 Male and female he created them, and he blessed them and named them Man when they were created. 3 When Adam had lived a hundred and thirty years, he became the father of a son in his own likeness, after his image, and named him Seth. 4 The days of

Adam after he became the father of Seth were eight hundred years; and he had other sons and daughters. 5 Thus all the days that Adam lived were nine hundred and thirty years; and he died.

6 When Seth had lived a hundred and five years, he became the father of É·nósh. 7 Seth lived after the birth of É·nósh eight hundred and seven years, and had other sons and daughters. 8 Thus all the days of Seth were nine hundred and twelve years; and he died.

9 When É·nósh had lived ninety years, he became the father of Kēʹnàn. 10 É·nósh lived after the birth of Kēʹnàn eight hundred and fifteen years, and had other sons and daughters. 11 Thus all the days of É·nósh were nine hundred and five years; and he died.

12 When Kēʹnàn had lived seventy years, he became the father of Ma·halʹà·lel. 13 Kēʹnàn lived after the birth of Ma·halʹà·lel eight hundred and forty years, and had other sons and daughters. 14 Thus all the days of Kēʹnàn were nine hundred and ten years; and he died.

15 When Ma·halʹà·lel had lived sixty-five years, he became the father of Jàrʹéd. 16 Ma·halʹà·lel lived after the birth of Jàrʹéd eight hundred and thirty years, and had other sons and daughters. 17 Thus all the days of Ma·halʹà·lel were eight hundred and ninety-five years; and he died.

18 When Jàrʹéd had lived a hundred and sixty-two years he became the father of É·nóch. 19 Jàrʹéd lived after the birth of É·nóch eight hundred years, and had other sons and daughters. 20 Thus all the days of Jàrʹéd were nine hundred and sixty-two years; and he died.

21 When É·nóch had lived sixty-five years, he became the father of Mé·thűʹsé·làh. 22 É·nóch walked with God after the birth of Mé·thűʹsé·làh three hundred years, and had other sons and daughters. 23 Thus all the days of É·nóch were three hundred and sixty-five years. 24 É·nóch walked with God; and he was not, for God took him.

25 When Mé·thűʹsé·làh had lived a hundred and eighty-seven years, he became the father of Lāʹmech. 26 Mé·thűʹsé·làh lived after the birth of Lāʹmech seven hundred and eighty-two years, and had other sons and daughters. 27 Thus all the days of

i Gk Syr Vg: Heb *Therefore*   *j* That is *Wandering*
5.1: Gen 1.27.   **5.24:** Heb 11.5.

Mė·thü´śė·lăh were nine hundred and sixty-nine years; and he died.

28 When Lā´mech had lived a hundred and eighty-two years, he became the father of a son, 29 and called his name Noah, saying, "Out of the ground which the LORD has cursed this one shall bring us relief from our work and from the toil of our hands." 30 Lā´mech lived after the birth of Noah five hundred and ninety-five years, and had other sons and daughters. 31 Thus all the days of Lā´mech were seven hundred and seventy-seven years; and he died.

32 After Noah was five hundred years old, Noah became the father of Shem, Ham, and Jā´pheth.

6 When men began to multiply on the face of the ground, and daughters were born to them, 2 the sons of God saw that the daughters of men were fair; and they took to wife such of them as they chose. 3 Then the LORD said, "My spirit shall not abide in man for ever, for he is flesh, but his days shall be a hundred and twenty years." 4 The Neph´i·lim were on the earth in those days, and also afterward, when the sons of God came in to the daughters of men, and they bore children to them. These were the mighty men that were of old, the men of renown.

5 The LORD saw that the wickedness of man was great in the earth, and that every imagination of the thoughts of his heart was only evil continually. 6 And the LORD was sorry that he had made man on the earth, and it grieved him to his heart. 7 So the LORD said, "I will blot out man whom I have created from the face of the ground, man and beast and creeping things and birds of the air, for I am sorry that I have made them." 8 But Noah found favor in the eyes of the LORD.

9 These are the generations of Noah. Noah was a righteous man, blameless in his generation; Noah walked with God. 10 And Noah had three sons, Shem, Ham, and Jā´pheth.

11 Now the earth was corrupt in God's sight, and the earth was filled with violence. 12 And God saw the earth, and behold, it was corrupt; for all flesh had corrupted their way upon the earth. 13 And God said to Noah, "I have determined to make an end of all flesh; for the earth is filled with violence through them; behold, I will destroy them with the earth. 14 Make yourself an ark of gopher wood; make

rooms in the ark, and cover it inside and out with pitch. 15 This is how you are to make it: the length of the ark three hundred cubits, its breadth fifty cubits, and its height thirty cubits. 16 Make a roof[k] for the ark, and finish it to a cubit above; and set the door of the ark in its side; make it with lower, second, and third decks. 17 For behold, I will bring a flood of waters upon the earth, to destroy all flesh in which is the breath of life from under heaven; everything that is on the earth shall die. 18 But I will establish my covenant with you; and you shall come into the ark, you, your sons, your wife, and your sons' wives with you. 19 And of every living thing of all flesh, you shall bring two of every sort into the ark, to keep them alive with you; they shall be male and female. 20 Of the birds according to their kinds, and of the animals according to their kinds, of every creeping thing of the ground according to its kind, two of every sort shall come in to you, to keep them alive. 21 Also take with you every sort of food that is eaten, and store it up; and it shall serve as food for you and for them." 22 Noah did this; he did all that God commanded him.

7 Then the LORD said to Noah, "Go into the ark, you and all your household, for I have seen that you are righteous before me in this generation. 2 Take with you seven pairs of all clean animals, the male and his mate; and a pair of the animals that are not clean, the male and his mate; 3 and seven pairs of the birds of the air also, male and female, to keep their kind alive upon the face of all the earth. 4 For in seven days I will send rain upon the earth forty days and forty nights; and every living thing that I have made I will blot out from the face of the ground." 5 And Noah did all that the LORD had commanded him.

6 Noah was six hundred years old when the flood of waters came upon the earth. 7 And Noah and his sons and his wife and his sons' wives with him went into the ark, to escape the waters of the flood. 8 Of clean animals, and of animals that are not clean, and of birds, and of everything that creeps on the ground, 9 two and two, male and female, went into the ark with Noah, as God had commanded Noah. 10 And after seven days the waters of the flood came upon the earth.

11 In the six hundredth year of Noah's life, in the second month, on the seventeenth day of the month, on

k Or window   6.4: Num 13.33.   7.7: Mt 24.38; Lk 17.27.

that day all the fountains of the great deep burst forth, and the windows of the heavens were opened. 12And rain fell upon the earth forty days and forty nights. 13 On the very same day Noah and his sons, Shem and Ham and Jā′pheth, and Noah's wife and the three wives of his sons with them entered the ark, 14 they and every beast according to its kind, and all the cattle according to their kinds, and every creeping thing that creeps on the earth according to its kind, and every bird according to its kind, and every bird of every sort. 15 They went into the ark with Noah, two and two of all flesh in which there was the breath of life. 16And they that entered, male and female of all flesh, went in as God had commanded him; and the LORD shut him in.

17 The flood continued forty days upon the earth; and the waters increased, and bore up the ark, and it rose high above the earth. 18 The waters prevailed and increased greatly upon the earth; and the ark floated on the face of the waters. 19And the waters prevailed so mightily upon the earth that all the high mountains under the whole heaven were covered; 20 the waters prevailed above the mountains, covering them fifteen cubits deep. 21And all flesh died that moved upon the earth, birds, cattle, beasts, all swarming creatures that swarm upon the earth, and every man; 22 everything on the dry land in whose nostrils was the breath of life died. 23 He blotted out every living thing that was upon the face of the ground, man and animals and creeping things and birds of the air; they were blotted out from the earth. Only Noah was left, and those that were with him in the ark. 24And the waters prevailed upon the earth a hundred and fifty days.

8 But God remembered Noah and all the beasts and all the cattle that were with him in the ark. And God made a wind blow over the earth, and the waters subsided; 2 the fountains of the deep and the windows of the heavens were closed, the rain from the heavens was restrained, 3 and the waters receded from the earth continually. At the end of a hundred and fifty days the waters had abated; 4 and in the seventh month, on the seventeenth day of the month, the ark came to rest upon the mountains of Ar′ā·rat. 5And the waters continued to abate until the tenth month; in the tenth month, on the first day of the month, the tops of the mountains were seen.

6 At the end of forty days Noah opened the window of the ark which he had made, 7 and sent forth a raven; and it went to and fro until the waters were dried up from the earth. 8 Then he sent forth a dove from him, to see if the waters had subsided from the face of the ground; 9 but the dove found no place to set her foot, and she returned to him to the ark, for the waters were still on the face of the whole earth. So he put forth his hand and took her and brought her into the ark with him. 10 He waited another seven days, and again he sent forth the dove out of the ark; 11 and the dove came back to him in the evening, and lo, in her mouth a freshly plucked olive leaf; so Noah knew that the waters had subsided from the earth. 12 Then he waited another seven days, and sent forth the dove; and she did not return to him any more.

13 In the six hundred and first year, in the first month, the first day of the month, the waters were dried from off the earth; and Noah removed the covering of the ark, and looked, and behold, the face of the ground was dry. 14 In the second month, on the twenty-seventh day of the month, the earth was dry. 15 Then God said to Noah, 16 "Go forth from the ark, you and your wife, and your sons and your sons' wives with you. 17 Bring forth with you every living thing that is with you of all flesh—birds and animals and every creeping thing that creeps on the earth—that they may breed abundantly on the earth, and be fruitful and multiply upon the earth." 18 So Noah went forth, and his sons and his wife and his sons' wives with him. 19And every beast, every creeping thing, and every bird, everything that moves upon the earth, went forth by families out of the ark.

20 Then Noah built an altar to the LORD, and took of every clean animal and of every clean bird, and offered burnt offerings on the altar. 21And when the LORD smelled the pleasing odor, the LORD said in his heart, "I will never again curse the ground because of man, for the imagination of man's heart is evil from his youth; neither will I ever again destroy every living creature as I have done. 22 While the earth remains, seedtime and harvest, cold and heat, summer and winter, day and night, shall not cease."

9 And God blessed Noah and his sons, and said to them, "Be fruitful and multiply, and fill the earth. 2 The fear of you and the dread of you

shall be upon every beast of the earth, and upon every bird of the air, upon everything that creeps on the ground and all the fish of the sea; into your hand they are delivered. 3 Every moving thing that lives shall be food for you; and as I gave you the green plants, I give you everything. 4 Only you shall not eat flesh with its life, that is, its blood. 5 For your lifeblood I will surely require a reckoning; of every beast I will require it and of man; of every man's brother I will require the life of man. 6 Whoever sheds the blood of man, by man shall his blood be shed; for God made man in his own image. 7 And you, be fruitful and multiply, bring forth abundantly on the earth and multiply in it."

8 Then God said to Noah and to his sons with him, 9 "Behold, I establish my covenant with you and your descendants after you, 10 and with every living creature that is with you, the birds, the cattle, and every beast of the earth with you, as many as came out of the ark.*l* 11 I establish my covenant with you, that never again shall all flesh be cut off by the waters of a flood, and never again shall there be a flood to destroy the earth." 12 And God said, "This is the sign of the covenant which I make between me and you and every living creature that is with you, for all future generations: 13 I set my bow in the cloud, and it shall be a sign of the covenant between me and the earth. 14 When I bring clouds over the earth and the bow is seen in the clouds, 15 I will remember my covenant which is between me and you and every living creature of all flesh; and the waters shall never again become a flood to destroy all flesh. 16 When the bow is in the clouds, I will look upon it and remember the everlasting covenant between God and every living creature of all flesh that is upon the earth." 17 God said to Noah, "This is the sign of the covenant which I have established between me and all flesh that is upon the earth."

18 The sons of Noah who went forth from the ark were Shem, Ham, and Jā′pheth. Ham was the father of Canaan. 19 These three were the sons of Noah; and from these the whole earth was peopled.

20 Noah was the first tiller of the soil. He planted a vineyard; 21 and he drank of the wine, and became drunk,

and lay uncovered in his tent. 22 And Ham, the father of Canaan, saw the nakedness of his father, and told his two brothers outside. 23 Then Shem and Jā′pheth took a garment, laid it upon both their shoulders, and walked backward and covered the nakedness of their father; their faces were turned away, and they did not see their father's nakedness. 24 When Noah awoke from his wine and knew what his youngest son had done to him, 25 he said,

"Cursed be Canaan;
     a slave of slaves shall he be to his
        brothers."
26 He also said,
"Blessed by the LORD my God be
        Shem;*m*
     and let Canaan be his slave.
27 God enlarge Jā′pheth,
     and let him dwell in the tents of
        Shem;
     and let Canaan be his slave."

28 After the flood Noah lived three hundred and fifty years. 29 All the days of Noah were nine hundred and fifty years; and he died.

10 These are the generations of the sons of Noah, Shem, Ham, and Jā′pheth; sons were born to them after the flood.

2 The sons of Jā′pheth: Gō′mer, Mā′gog, Mad′ai, Jā′van, Tū′bal, Mĕ′shech, and Tī′ras. 3 The sons of Gō′mer: Ash′ke·naz, Rī′phath, and Tō·gär′mah. 4 The sons of Jā′van: E·lī′shah, Tär′shish, Kit′tim, and Do′dá·nim. 5 From these the coastland peoples spread. These are the sons of Jā′pheth*n* in their lands, each with his own language, by their families, in their nations.

6 The sons of Ham: Cush, Egypt, Pût, and Canaan. 7 The sons of Cush: Sē′bà, Hav′i·lah, Sab′tah, Rā′á·mah, and Sab′te·cà. The sons of Raamah: Sheba and Dē′dan. 8 Cush became the father of Nimrod; he was the first on earth to be a mighty man. 9 He was a mighty hunter before the LORD; therefore it is said, "Like Nimrod a mighty hunter before the LORD." 10 The beginning of his kingdom was Bā′bel, Ē′rech, and Ac′cad, all of them in the land of Shī′när. 11 From that land he went into Assyria, and built Nin′e·veh, Re·hō′both-Ir, Cā′lah, and 12 Rē′sen between Nin′e·veh and Cā′lah; that is the great city. 13 Egypt became the father of Lü′dim, An′á·mim, Lĕ·hä′bim, Naph′tü·him, 14 Path·rü′sim,

l Gk: Heb repeats *every beast of the earth*   *m* Or *Blessed be the* LORD, *the God of Shem*
n Supplied from verses 20, 31. Heb lacks *These are the sons of Japheth*
9.4: Lev 7.26-27; 17.10-14; Deut 12.16, 23.

Cas·lü'him (whence came the Philistines), and Caph'to·rim.

15 Canaan became the father of Si'don his first-born, and Heth, 16 and the Jeb'u·sites, the Am'o·rites, the Gir'ga·shites, 17 the Hi'vites, the Ärk'-ites, the Si'nites, 18 the Är'vä·dites, the Zem'a·rites, and the Hä'mä·thites. Afterward the families of the Canaanites spread abroad. 19And the territory of the Canaanites extended from Si'don, in the direction of Ge'rär, as far as Gä'zä, and in the direction of Sod'om, Go·môr'räh, Ad'mäh, and Ze·boi'im, as far as Lä'shä. 20 These are the sons of Ham, by their families, their languages, their lands, and their nations.

21 To Shem also, the father of all the children of E'ber, the elder brother of Jä'pheth, children were born. 22 The sons of Shem: E'läm, As'shür, Är-pach'shad, Lüd, and Är'äm. 23 The sons of Är'äm: Uz, Hül, Ge'ther, and Mash. 24Är·pach'shad became the father of She'läh; and Shelah became the father of E'ber. 25 To E'ber were born two sons: the name of the one was Pe'leg,*o* for in his days the earth was divided, and his brother's name was Jok'tan. 26 Jok'tan became the father of Al·mo'dad, She'leph, Hä·zär·mä'-veth, Je'räh, Hä·dôr'äm, U'zäl, Dik'läh, 28 O'bäl, Ä·bim'ä-el, Sheba, 29 O'phir, Hav'i·läh, and Jo'bab; all these were the sons of Jok'tan. 30 The territory in which they lived extended from Me'shä in the direction of Se'phär to the hill country of the east. 31 These are the sons of Shem, by their families, their languages, their lands, and their nations.

32 These are the families of the sons of Noah, according to their genealogies, in their nations; and from these the nations spread abroad on the earth after the flood.

11 Now the whole earth had one language and few words. 2And as men migrated from the east, they found a plain in the land of Shi'när and settled there. 3 And they said to one another, "Come, let us make bricks, and burn them thoroughly." And they had brick for stone, and bitumen for mortar. 4 Then they said, "Come, let us build ourselves a city, and a tower with its top in the heavens, and let us make a name for ourselves, lest we be scattered abroad upon the face of the whole earth." 5And the LORD came down to see the city and the tower, which the sons of men had built. 6And the LORD said, "Behold, they are one people,

and they have all one language; and this is only the beginning of what they will do; and nothing that they propose to do will now be impossible for them. 7 Come, let us go down, and there confuse their language, that they may not understand one another's speech." 8 So the LORD scattered them abroad from there over the face of all the earth, and they left off building the city. 9 Therefore its name was called Bä'bél, because there the LORD confused*p* the language of all the earth; and from there the LORD scattered them abroad over the face of all the earth.

10 These are the descendants of Shem. When Shem was a hundred years old, he became the father of Är·pach'shad two years after the flood; 11 and Shem lived after the birth of Är·pach'shad five hundred years, and had other sons and daughters.

12 When Är·pach'shad had lived thirty-five years, he became the father of She'läh; 13 and Är·pach'shad lived after the birth of She'läh four hundred and three years, and had other sons and daughters.

14 When She'läh had lived thirty years, he became the father of E'ber; 15 and She'läh lived after the birth of E'ber four hundred and three years, and had other sons and daughters.

16 When E'ber had lived thirty-four years, he became the father of Pe'leg; 17 and E'ber lived after the birth of Pe'leg four hundred and thirty years, and had other sons and daughters.

18 When Pe'leg had lived thirty years, he became the father of Re'ü; 19 and Pe'leg lived after the birth of Re'ü two hundred and nine years, and had other sons and daughters.

20 When Re'ü had lived thirty-two years, he became the father of Se'rüg; 21 and Re'ü lived after the birth of Se'rüg two hundred and seven years, and had other sons and daughters.

22 When Se'rüg had lived thirty years, he became the father of Nä'hôr; 23 and Se'rüg lived after the birth of Nä'hôr two hundred years, and had other sons and daughters.

24 When Nä'hôr had lived twenty-nine years, he became the father of Te'räh; 25 and Nä'hôr lived after the birth of Te'räh a hundred and nineteen years, and had other sons and daughters.

26 When Te'räh had lived seventy years, he became the father of Abram, Nä'hôr, and Hâr'än.

o That is *Division*   *p* Compare Heb *balal*, confuse

27 Now these are the descendants of Tē′răh. Terah was the father of Abram, Nā′hôr, and Hâr′ăn; and Haran was the father of Lot. 28 Hâr′ăn died before his father Tē′răh in the land of his birth, in Ŭr of the Chal·dē′ănś. 29And Abram and Nā′hôr took wives; the name of Abram's wife was Sâr′ăi, and the name of Nahor's wife, Mil′căh, the daughter of Hâr′ăn the father of Milcah and Iś′căh. 30 Now Sâr′ăi was barren; she had no child.

31 Tē′răh took Abram his son and Lot the son of Hâr′ăn, his grandson, and Sâr′ăi his daughter-in-law, his son Abram's wife, and they went forth together from Ŭr of the Chal·dē′ănś to go into the land of Canaan; but when they came to Haran, they settled there. 32 The days of Tē′răh were two hundred and five years; and Terah died in Hâr′ăn.

12 Now the LORD said to Abram, "Go from your country and your kindred and your father's house to the land that I will show you. 2And I will make of you a great nation, and I will bless you, and make your name great, so that you will be a blessing. 3 I will bless those who bless you, and him who curses you I will curse; and by you all the families of the earth shall bless themselves."ᵃ

4 So Abram went, as the LORD had told him; and Lot went with him. Abram was seventy-five years old when he departed from Hâr′ăn. 5And Abram took Sâr′ăi his wife, and Lot his brother's son, and all their possessions which they had gathered, and the persons that they had gotten in Hâr′ăn; and they set forth to go to the land of Canaan. When they had come to the land of Canaan, 6Abram passed through the land to the place at Shē′-chem, to the oakʳ of Mō′reh. At that time the Canaanites were in the land. 7 Then the LORD appeared to Abram, and said, "To your descendants I will give this land." So he built there an altar to the LORD, who had appeared to him. 8 Thence he removed to the mountain on the east of Beth′ĕl, and pitched his tent, with Bethel on the west and Äi on the east; and there he built an altar to the LORD and called on the name of the LORD. 9And Abram journeyed on, still going toward the Negeb.

10 Now there was a famine in the land. So Abram went down to Egypt to sojourn there, for the famine was severe in the land. 11When he was about to enter Egypt, he said to Sâr′ăi his wife, "I know that you are a woman beautiful to behold; 12 and when the Egyptians see you, they will say, 'This is his wife'; then they will kill me, but they will let you live. 13 Say you are my sister, that it may go well with me because of you, and that my life may be spared on your account." 14 When Abram entered Egypt the Egyptians saw that the woman was very beautiful. 15And when the princes of Pharaoh saw her, they praised her to Pharaoh. And the woman was taken into Pharaoh's house. 16And for her sake he dealt well with Abram; and he had sheep, oxen, he-asses, menservants, maidservants, she-asses, and camels.

17 But the LORD afflicted Pharaoh and his house with great plagues because of Sâr′ăi, Abram's wife. 18 So Pharaoh called Abram, and said, "What is this you have done to me? Why did you not tell me that she was your wife? 19 Why did you say, 'She is my sister,' so that I took her for my wife? Now then, here is your wife, take her, and be gone." 20And Pharaoh gave men orders concerning him; and they set him on the way, with his wife and all that he had.

13 So Abram went up from Egypt, he and his wife, and all that he had, and Lot with him, into the Negeb. 2 Now Abram was very rich in cattle, in silver, and in gold. 3And he journeyed on from the Negeb as far as Beth′ĕl, to the place where his tent had been at the beginning, between Bethel and Äi, 4 to the place where he had made an altar at the first; and there Abram called on the name of the LORD. 5And Lot, who went with Abram, also had flocks and herds and tents, 6 so that the land could not support both of them dwelling together; for their possessions were so great that they could not dwell together, 7 and there was strife between the herdsmen of Abram's cattle and the herdsmen of Lot's cattle. At that time the Canaanites and the Per′iz·zites dwelt in the land.

8 Then Abram said to Lot, "Let there be no strife between you and me,

ᵃ Or in you all the families of the earth will be blessed   ʳ Or terebinth

12.1: Acts 7.3; Heb 11.8.
12.2: Gen 15.5; 17.4-5; 18.18; 22.17; 28.14; 32.12; 35.11; 46.3.
12.3: Gen 18.18; 22.17-18; 26.4; 28.14; Gal 3.8.
12.7: Gen 13.15; 15.18; 17.8; 24.7; 26.3; 28.4, 13; 35.12; 48.4; Acts 7.5; Gal 3.16.
12.10-20: Gen 20.1-18; 26.7-11.

and between your herdsmen and my herdsmen; for we are kinsmen. ⁹ Is not the whole land before you? Separate yourself from me. If you take the left hand, then I will go to the right; or if you take the right hand, then I will go to the left." ¹⁰And Lot lifted up his eyes, and saw that the Jordan valley was well watered everywhere like the garden of the LORD, like the land of Egypt, in the direction of Zō'är; this was before the LORD destroyed Sod'óm and Gō·môr'räh. ¹¹ So Lot chose for himself all the Jordan valley, and Lot journeyed east; thus they separated from each other. ¹²Abram dwelt in the land of Canaan, while Lot dwelt among the cities of the valley and moved his tent as far as Sod'óm. ¹³ Now the men of Sod'óm were wicked, great sinners against the LORD.

14 The LORD said to Abram, after Lot had separated from him, "Lift up your eyes, and look from the place where you are, northward and southward and eastward and westward; ¹⁵for all the land which you see I will give to you and to your descendants for ever. ¹⁶ I will make your descendants as the dust of the earth; so that if one can count the dust of the earth, your descendants also can be counted. ¹⁷Arise, walk through the length and the breadth of the land, for I will give it to you." ¹⁸ So Abram moved his tent, and came and dwelt by the oaks⁵ of Mam're, which are at Hē'brón; and there he built an altar to the LORD.

14 In the days of Am'rä·phel king of Shi'när, Ar'i·och king of El·lä'sàr, Ched-or-là·ō'mér king of E'läm, and Ti'dàl king of Goi'im, ² these kings made war with Bē'rà king of Sod'óm, Bir'shà king of Gō·môr'räh, Shi'näb king of Ad'màh, Shem·ē'bēr king of Ze·boi'im, and the king of Bē'là (that is, Zō'är). ³And all these joined forces in the Valley of Sid'dim (that is, the Salt Sea). ⁴ Twelve years they had served Ched-or-là·ō'mér, but in the thirteenth year they rebelled. ⁵ In the fourteenth year Ched-or-là·ō'mér and the kings who were with him came and subdued the Reph'à·im in Ash'te·roth-kär·nä'im, the Zū'zim in Ham, the E'mim in Shä'veh-kir·i·à-thä'im, ⁶ and the Hôr'ites in their Mount Sē'ir as far as El-pär'àn on the border of the wilderness; ⁷ then they turned back and came to En·mish'pat (that is, Kä'desh), and subdued all the country of the A·mal'é·kîtes, and also

⁵ Or *terebinths*

the Am'ó·rîtes who dwelt in Haz'à·zon-tä'mär. ⁸ Then the king of Sod'óm, the king of Gō·môr'räh, the king of Ad'màh, the king of Ze·boi'im, and the king of Bē'là (that is, Zō'är) went out, and they joined battle in the Valley of Sid'dim ⁹ with Ched-or-là·ō'mér king of E'läm, Ti'dàl king of Goi'im, Am'rà·phel king of Shi'när, and Ar'i·och king of El·lä'sàr, four kings against five. ¹⁰ Now the Valley of Sid'dim was full of bitumen pits; and as the kings of Sod'óm and Gō·môr'räh fled, some fell into them, and the rest fled to the mountain. ¹¹ So the enemy took all the goods of Sod'óm and Gō·môr'räh, and all their provisions, and went their way; ¹² they also took Lot, the son of Abram's brother, who dwelt in Sod'óm, and his goods, and departed.

13 Then one who had escaped came, and told Abram the Hebrew, who was living by the oaks⁵ of Mam're the Am'ó·rîte, brother of Esh'cól and of A'nér; these were allies of Abram. ¹⁴ When Abram heard that his kinsman had been taken captive, he led forth his trained men, born in his house, three hundred and eighteen of them, and went in pursuit as far as Dan. ¹⁵And he divided his forces against them by night, he and his servants, and routed them and pursued them to Hō'bàh, north of Damascus. ¹⁶ Then he brought back all the goods, and also brought back his kinsman Lot with his goods, and the women and the people.

17 After his return from the defeat of Ched-or-là·ō'mér and the kings who were with him, the king of Sod'óm went out to meet him at the Valley of Shä'veh (that is, the King's Valley). ¹⁸And Mel·chiz'é·dek king of Salem brought out bread and wine; he was priest of God Most High. ¹⁹And he blessed him and said,

"Blessed be Abram by God Most
　　High,
　　maker of heaven and earth;
²⁰ and blessed be God Most High,
　　who has delivered your enemies
　　　into your hand!"

And Abram gave him a tenth of everything. ²¹And the king of Sod'óm said to Abram, "Give me the persons, but take the goods for yourself." ²² But Abram said to the king of Sod'óm, "I have sworn to the LORD God Most High, maker of heaven and earth, ²³ that I would not take a thread or a sandal-thong or anything that is yours,

13.15: Acts 7.5; Gal 3.16.　14.17-20: Heb 7.1-10.

lest you should say, 'I have made Abram rich.' 24 I will take nothing but what the young men have eaten, and the share of the men who went with me; let A´nér, Esh´col, and Mam´re take their share."

15 After these things the word of the LORD came to Abram in a vision, "Fear not, Abram, I am your shield; your reward shall be very great." 2 But Abram said, "O Lord GOD, what wilt thou give me, for I continue childless, and the heir of my house is É·lí·ē´zer of Damascus?" 3And Abram said, "Behold, thou hast given me no offspring; and a slave born in my house will be my heir." 4And behold, the word of the LORD came to him, "This man shall not be your heir; your own son shall be your heir." 5And he brought him outside and said, "Look toward heaven, and number the stars, if you are able to number them." Then he said to him, "So shall your descendants be." 6And he believed the LORD; and he reckoned it to him as righteousness.

7 And he said to him, "I am the LORD who brought you from Ur of the Chal·dē´ans, to give you this land to possess." 8 But he said, "O Lord GOD, how am I to know that I shall possess it?" 9 He said to him, "Bring me a heifer three years old, a she-goat three years old, a ram three years old, a turtledove, and a young pigeon." 10And he brought him all these, cut them in two, and laid each half over against the other; but he did not cut the birds in two. 11And when birds of prey came down upon the carcasses, Abram drove them away.

12 As the sun was going down, a deep sleep fell on Abram; and lo, a dread and great darkness came upon him. 13 Then the LORD said to Abram, "Know of a surety that your descendants will be sojourners in a land that is not theirs, and will be slaves there, and they will be oppressed for four hundred years; 14 but I will bring judgment on the nation which they serve, and afterward they shall come out with great possessions. 15As for yourself, you shall go to your fathers in peace; you shall be buried in a good old age. 16And they shall come back here in the fourth generation; for the iniquity of the Am´o·rites is not yet complete."

17 When the sun had gone down and it was dark, behold, a smoking fire pot and a flaming torch passed between these pieces. 18 On that day the LORD made a covenant with Abram, saying, "To your descendants I give this land, from the river of Egypt to the great river, the river Eū·phrā´tēs, 19 the land of the Ken´ites, the Ken´iz·zites, the Kad´mo·nites, 20 the Hit´tites, the Per´iz·zites, the Reph´a·im, 21 the Am´o·rites, the Canaanites, the Gir´ga·shites and the Jeb´ū·sites."

16 Now Sâr´ai, Abram's wife, bore him no children. She had an Egyptian maid whose name was Hā´gàr; 2 and Sâr´ai said to Abram, "Behold now, the LORD has prevented me from bearing children; go in to my maid; it may be that I shall obtain children by her." And Abram hearkened to the voice of Sarai. 3 So, after Abram had dwelt ten years in the land of Canaan, Sâr´ai, Abram's wife, took Hā´gàr the Egyptian, her maid, and gave her to Abram her husband as a wife. 4And he went in to Hā´gàr, and she conceived; and when she saw that she had conceived, she looked with contempt on her mistress. 5And Sâr´ai said to Abram, "May the wrong done to me be on you! I gave my maid to your embrace, and when she saw that she had conceived, she looked on me with contempt. May the LORD judge between you and me!" 6 But Abram said to Sâr´ai, "Behold, your maid is in your power; do to her as you please." Then Sarai dealt harshly with her, and she fled from her.

7 The angel of the LORD found her by a spring of water in the wilderness, the spring on the way to Shūr. 8And he said, "Hā´gàr, maid of Sâr´ai, where have you come from and where are you going?" She said, "I am fleeing from my mistress Sarai." 9 The angel of the LORD said to her, "Return to your mistress, and submit to her." 10 The angel of the LORD also said to her, "I will so greatly multiply your descendants that they cannot be numbered for multitude." 11And the angel of the LORD said to her, "Behold, you are with child, and shall bear a son; you shall call his name Ish´mà·el;ᶠ because the LORD has given heed to your affliction. 12 He shall be a wild ass of a man, his hand against every man and every man's hand against him; and he shall dwell over against all his kinsmen." 13 So she called the name of the LORD who

ᶠ That is *God hears*

15.4: Gen 17.16, 21; 18.10; 21.2.   **15.5:** Rom 4.18; Heb 11.12.
15.6: Rom 4.3, 9, 22-23; Gal 3.6.   **15.13-14:** Acts 7.6-7.
15.18: Gen 17.2, 7, 9-14, 21.

spoke to her, "Thou art a God of seeing"; for she said, "Have I really seen God and remained alive after seeing him?"[u] 14 Therefore the well was called Bē′ér-lä′häi-roi;[v] it lies between Kä′desh and Bē′red.

15 And Hā′gàr bore Abram a son; and Abram called the name of his son, whom Hagar bore, Ish′mà·el. 16Abram was eighty-six years old when Hā′gàr bore Ish′mà·el to Abram.

17 When Abram was ninety-nine years old the LORD appeared to Abram, and said to him, "I am God Almighty;[w] walk before me, and be blameless. 2And I will make my covenant between me and you, and will multiply you exceedingly." 3 Then Abram fell on his face; and God said to him, 4 "Behold, my covenant is with you, and you shall be the father of a multitude of nations. 5 No longer shall your name be Abram,[x] but your name shall be Abraham;[y] for I have made you the father of a multitude of nations. 6 I will make you exceedingly fruitful; and I will make nations of you, and kings shall come forth from you. 7And I will establish my covenant between me and you and your descendants after you throughout their generations for an everlasting covenant, to be God to you and to your descendants after you. 8And I will give to you, and to your descendants after you, the land of your sojournings, all the land of Canaan, for an everlasting possession; and I will be their God."

9 And God said to Abraham, "As for you, you shall keep my covenant, you and your descendants after you throughout their generations. 10 This is my covenant, which you shall keep, between me and you and your descendants after you: Every male among you shall be circumcised. 11 You shall be circumcised in the flesh of your foreskins, and it shall be a sign of the covenant between me and you. 12 He that is eight days old among you shall be circumcised; every male throughout your generations, whether born in your house, or bought with your money from any foreigner who is not of your offspring, 13 both he that is born in your house and he that is bought with your money, shall be circumcised. So shall my covenant be in your flesh an everlasting covenant. 14Any uncircumcised male who is not

circumcised in the flesh of his foreskin shall be cut off from his people; he has broken my covenant."

15 And God said to Abraham, "As for Sâr′äi your wife, you shall not call her name Sarai, but Sarah shall be her name. 16 I will bless her, and moreover I will give you a son by her; I will bless her, and she shall be a mother of nations; kings of peoples shall come from her." 17 Then Abraham fell on his face and laughed, and said to himself, "Shall a child be born to a man who is a hundred years old? Shall Sarah, who is ninety years old, bear a child?" 18And Abraham said to God, "O that Ish′mà·el might live in thy sight!" 19 God said, "No, but Sarah your wife shall bear you a son, and you shall call his name Isaac.[z] I will establish my covenant with him as an everlasting covenant for his descendants after him. 20As for Ish′mà·el, I have heard you; behold, I will bless him and make him fruitful and multiply him exceedingly; he shall be the father of twelve princes, and I will make him a great nation. 21 But I will establish my covenant with Isaac, whom Sarah shall bear to you at this season next year."

22 When he had finished talking with him, God went up from Abraham. 23 Then Abraham took Ish′mà·el his son and all the slaves born in his house or bought with his money, every male among the men of Abraham's house, and he circumcised the flesh of their foreskins that very day, as God had said to him. 24Abraham was ninety-nine years old when he was circumcised in the flesh of his foreskin. 25And Ish′mà·el his son was thirteen years old when he was circumcised in the flesh of his foreskin. 26 That very day Abraham and his son Ish′mà·el were circumcised; 27 and all the men of his house, those born in the house and those bought with money from a foreigner, were circumcised with him.

18 And the LORD appeared to him by the oaks[a] of Mam′re, as he sat at the door of his tent in the heat of the day. 2 He lifted up his eyes and looked, and behold, three men stood in front of him. When he saw them, he ran from the tent door to meet them, and bowed himself to the earth, 3 and said, "My lord, if I have found favor in your sight, do not pass by

---

[u] Cn: Heb *have I even here seen after him who sees me?*
[v] That is *the well of one who sees and lives*   [w] Heb El Shaddai   [x] That is *exalted father*
[y] Here taken to mean *father of a multitude*   [z] That is *he laughs*   [a] Or terebinths
17.5: Rom 4.17.   **17.7:** Lk 1.55; Gal 3.16.   **17.8:** Acts 7.5.   **17.10:** Acts 7.8.
17.11-14: Gen 17.24; 21.4.

your servant. ⁴ Let a little water be brought, and wash your feet, and rest yourselves under the tree, ⁵ while I fetch a morsel of bread, that you may refresh yourselves, and after that you may pass on—since you have come to your servant." So they said, "Do as you have said." ⁶And Abraham hastened into the tent to Sarah, and said, "Make ready quickly three measures*b* of fine meal, knead it, and make cakes." ⁷And Abraham ran to the herd, and took a calf, tender and good, and gave it to the servant, who hastened to prepare it. ⁸ Then he took curds, and milk, and the calf which he had prepared, and set it before them; and he stood by them under the tree while they ate.

9 They said to him, "Where is Sarah your wife?" And he said, "She is in the tent." ¹⁰ The LORD said, "I will surely return to you in the spring, and Sarah your wife shall have a son." And Sarah was listening at the tent door behind him. ¹¹ Now Abraham and Sarah were old, advanced in age; it had ceased to be with Sarah after the manner of women. ¹² So Sarah laughed to herself, saying, "After I have grown old, and my husband is old, shall I have pleasure?" ¹³ The LORD said to Abraham, "Why did Sarah laugh, and say, 'Shall I indeed bear a child, now that I am old?' ¹⁴ Is anything too hard*c* for the LORD? At the appointed time I will return to you, in the spring, and Sarah shall have a son." ¹⁵ But Sarah denied, saying, "I did not laugh"; for she was afraid. He said, "No, but you did laugh."

16 Then the men set out from there, and they looked toward Sod'ŏm; and Abraham went with them to set them on their way. ¹⁷ The LORD said, "Shall I hide from Abraham what I am about to do, ¹⁸ seeing that Abraham shall become a great and mighty nation, and all the nations of the earth shall bless themselves by him?*d* ¹⁹ No, for I have chosen*e* him, that he may charge his children and his household after him to keep the way of the LORD by doing righteousness and justice; so that the LORD may bring to Abraham what he has promised him." ²⁰ Then the LORD said, "Because the outcry against Sod'ŏm and Gŏ·môr'răh is great and their sin is very grave, ²¹ I will go down to see whether they have done altogether according to the out-

cry which has come to me; and if not, I will know."

22 So the men turned from there, and went toward Sod'ŏm; but Abraham still stood before the LORD. ²³ Then Abraham drew near, and said, "Wilt thou indeed destroy the righteous with the wicked? ²⁴ Suppose there are fifty righteous within the city; wilt thou then destroy the place and not spare it for the fifty righteous who are in it? ²⁵ Far be it from thee to do such a thing, to slay the righteous with the wicked, so that the righteous fare as the wicked! Far be that from thee! Shall not the Judge of all the earth do right?" ²⁶And the LORD said, "If I find at Sod'ŏm fifty righteous in the city, I will spare the whole place for their sake." ²⁷Abraham answered, "Behold, I have taken upon myself to speak to the LORD, I who am but dust and ashes. ²⁸ Suppose five of the fifty righteous are lacking? Wilt thou destroy the whole city for lack of five?" And he said, "I will not destroy it if I find forty-five there." ²⁹Again he spoke to him, and said, "Suppose forty are found there." He answered, "For the sake of forty I will not do it." ³⁰ Then he said, "Oh let not the Lord be angry, and I will speak. Suppose thirty are found there." He answered, "I will not do it, if I find thirty there." ³¹ He said, "Behold, I have taken upon myself to speak to the Lord. Suppose twenty are found there." He answered, "For the sake of twenty I will not destroy it." ³² Then he said, "Oh let not the Lord be angry, and I will speak again but this once. Suppose ten are found there." He answered, "For the sake of ten I will not destroy it." ³³And the LORD went his way, when he had finished speaking to Abraham; and Abraham returned to his place.

19 The two angels came to Sod'ŏm in the evening; and Lot was sitting in the gate of Sodom. When Lot saw them, he rose to meet them, and bowed himself with his face to the earth, ² and said, "My lords, turn aside, I pray you, to your servant's house and spend the night, and wash your feet; then you may rise up early and go on your way." They said, "No; we will spend the night in the street." ³ But he urged them strongly; so they turned aside to him and entered his house; and he made them a feast, and baked unleavened bread, and they ate.

b Heb *seahs* *c* Or *wonderful* *d* Or *in him all the families of the earth shall be blessed*
e Heb *known*

18:10: Rom 9.9. **18:12:** 1 Pet 3.6. **18:14:** Mt 19.26; Mk 10.27; Lk 1.37; Rom 9.9.
18:18: Gal 3.8.

4 But before they lay down, the men of the city, the men of Sŏd′ŏm, both young and old, all the people to the last man, surrounded the house; 5 and they called to Lot, "Where are the men who came to you tonight? Bring them out to us, that we may know them." 6 Lot went out of the door to the men, shut the door after him, 7 and said, "I beg you, my brothers, do not act so wickedly. 8 Behold, I have two daughters who have not known man; let me bring them out to you, and do to them as you please; only do nothing to these men, for they have come under the shelter of my roof." 9 But they said, "Stand back!" And they said, "This fellow came to sojourn, and he would play the judge! Now we will deal worse with you than with them." Then they pressed hard against the man Lot, and drew near to break the door. 10 But the men put forth their hands and brought Lot into the house to them, and shut the door. 11And they struck with blindness the men who were at the door of the house, both small and great, so that they wearied themselves groping for the door.

12 Then the men said to Lot, "Have you any one else here? Sons-in-law, sons, daughters, or any one you have in the city, bring them out of the place; 13 for we are about to destroy this place, because the outcry against its people has become great before the LORD, and the LORD has sent us to destroy it." 14 So Lot went out and said to his sons-in-law, who were to marry his daughters, "Up, get out of this place; for the LORD is about to destroy the city." But he seemed to his sons-in-law to be jesting.

15 When morning dawned, the angels urged Lot, saying, "Arise, take your wife and your two daughters who are here, lest you be consumed in the punishment of the city." 16 But he lingered; so the men seized him and his wife and his two daughters by the hand, the LORD being merciful to him, and they brought him forth and set him outside the city. 17And when they had brought them forth, they*f* said, "Flee for your life; do not look back or stop anywhere in the valley; flee to the hills, lest you be consumed." 18And Lot said to them, "Oh, no, my lords; 19 behold, your servant has found favor in your sight, and you have shown me great kindness in saving my life; but I cannot flee to the hills, lest the disaster overtake me, and I die. 20 Behold,

yonder city is near enough to flee to, and it is a little one. Let me escape there—is it not a little one?—and my life will be saved!" 21 He said to him, "Behold, I grant you this favor also, that I will not overthrow the city of which you have spoken. 22 Make haste, escape there; for I can do nothing till you arrive there." Therefore the name of the city was called Zō′är.*g* 23 The sun had risen on the earth when Lot came to Zō′är.

24 Then the LORD rained on Sŏd′ŏm and Gŏ·môr′räh brimstone and fire from the LORD out of heaven; 25 and he overthrew those cities, and all the valley, and all the inhabitants of the cities, and what grew on the ground. 26 But Lot's wife behind him looked back, and she became a pillar of salt. 27And Abraham went early in the morning to the place where he had stood before the LORD; 28 and he looked down toward Sŏd′ŏm and Gŏ·môr′räh and toward all the land of the valley, and beheld, and lo, the smoke of the land went up like the smoke of a furnace.

29 So it was that, when God destroyed the cities of the valley, God remembered Abraham, and sent Lot out of the midst of the overthrow, when he overthrew the cities in which Lot dwelt.

30 Now Lot went up out of Zō′är, and dwelt in the hills with his two daughters, for he was afraid to dwell in Zoar; so he dwelt in a cave with his two daughters. 31And the first-born said to the younger, "Our father is old, and there is not a man on earth to come in to us after the manner of all the earth. 32 Come, let us make our father drink wine, and we will lie with him, that we may preserve offspring through our father." 33 So they made their father drink wine that night; and the first-born went in, and lay with her father; he did not know when she lay down or when she arose. 34And on the next day, the first-born said to the younger, "Behold, I lay last night with my father; let us make him drink wine tonight also; then you go in and lie with him, that we may preserve offspring through our father." 35 So they made their father drink wine that night also; and the younger arose, and lay with him; and he did not know when she lay down nor when she arose. 36 Thus both the daughters of Lot were with child by their father. 37 The first-born bore a son, and called his

f Gk Syr Vg: Heb *he*   *g* That is *Little*
19.24-25: Lk 17.29.   **19.26:** Lk 17.32.   **19.28:** Rev 9.2.

name Mō′ab; he is the father of the Mō′ab·ites to this day. 38 The younger also bore a son, and called his name Ben-am′mi; he is the father of the Am′mo·nites to this day.

20 From there Abraham journeyed toward the territory of the Negeb, and dwelt between Kā′desh and Shūr; and he sojourned in Gē′rär. 2And Abraham said of Sarah his wife, "She is my sister." And Ā·bim′e·lech king of Gē′rär sent and took Sarah. 3 But God came to Ā·bim′e·lech in a dream by night, and said to him, "Behold, you are a dead man, because of the woman whom you have taken; for she is a man's wife." 4 Now Ā·bim′e·lech had not approached her; so he said, "Lord, wilt thou slay an innocent people? 5 Did he not himself say to me, 'She is my sister'? And she herself said, 'He is my brother.' In the integrity of my heart and the innocence of my hands I have done this." 6 Then God said to him in the dream, "Yes, I know that you have done this in the integrity of your heart, and it was I who kept you from sinning against me; therefore I did not let you touch her. 7 Now then restore the man's wife; for he is a prophet, and he will pray for you, and you shall live. But if you do not restore her, know that you shall surely die, you, and all that are yours."

8 So Ā·bim′e·lech rose early in the morning, and called all his servants, and told them all these things; and the men were very much afraid. 9 Then Ā·bim′e·lech called Abraham, and said to him, "What have you done to us? And how have I sinned against you, that you have brought on me and my kingdom a great sin? You have done to me things that ought not to be done." 10And Ā·bim′e·lech said to Abraham, "What were you thinking of, that you did this thing?" 11Abraham said, "I did it because I thought, There is no fear of God at all in this place, and they will kill me because of my wife. 12 Besides she is indeed my sister, the daughter of my father but not the daughter of my mother; and she became my wife. 13And when God caused me to wander from my father's house, I said to her, 'This is the kindness you must do me: at every place to which we come, say of me, He is my brother.' " 14 Then Ā·bim′e·lech took sheep and oxen, and male and female slaves, and gave them to Abraham, and restored Sarah his wife to him.

15And Ā·bim′e·lech said, "Behold, my land is before you; dwell where it pleases you." 16 To Sarah he said, "Behold, I have given your brother a thousand pieces of silver; it is your vindication in the eyes of all who are with you; and before every one you are righted." 17 Then Abraham prayed to God; and God healed Ā·bim′e·lech, and also healed his wife and female slaves so that they bore children. 18 For the LORD had closed all the wombs of the house of Ā·bim′e·lech because of Sarah, Abraham's wife.

21 The LORD visited Sarah as he had said, and the LORD did to Sarah as he had promised. 2And Sarah conceived, and bore Abraham a son in his old age at the time of which God had spoken to him. 3Abraham called the name of his son who was born to him, whom Sarah bore him, Isaac. 4And Abraham circumcised his son Isaac when he was eight days old, as God had commanded him. 5Abraham was a hundred years old when his son Isaac was born to him. 6And Sarah said, "God has made laughter for me; every one who hears will laugh over me." 7And she said, "Who would have said to Abraham that Sarah would suckle children? Yet I have borne him a son in his old age."

8 And the child grew, and was weaned; and Abraham made a great feast on the day that Isaac was weaned. 9 But Sarah saw the son of Hā′gär the Egyptian, whom she had borne to Abraham, playing with her son Isaac.[h] 10 So she said to Abraham, "Cast out this slave woman with her son; for the son of this slave woman shall not be heir with my son Isaac." 11And the thing was very displeasing to Abraham on account of his son. 12 But God said to Abraham, "Be not displeased because of the lad and because of your slave woman; whatever Sarah says to you, do as she tells you, for through Isaac shall your descendants be named. 13And I will make a nation of the son of the slave woman also, because he is your offspring." 14 So Abraham rose early in the morning, and took bread and a skin of water, and gave it to Hā′gàr, putting it on her shoulder, along with the child, and sent her away. And she departed, and wandered in the wilderness of Beersheba.

15 When the water in the skin was gone, she cast the child under one of

h Gk Vg: Heb lacks *with her son Isaac*

21.4: Acts 7.8.   **21.10:** Gal 4.30.   **21.12:** Rom 9.7; Heb 11.18.

the bushes. [16] Then she went, and sat down over against him a good way off, about the distance of a bowshot; for she said, "Let me not look upon the death of the child." And as she sat over against him, the child lifted up his voice[i] and wept. [17]And God heard the voice of the lad; and the angel of God called to Hā'gàr from heaven, and said to her, "What troubles you, Hagar? Fear not; for God has heard the voice of the lad where he is. [18]Arise, lift up the lad, and hold him fast with your hand; for I will make him a great nation." [19] Then God opened her eyes, and she saw a well of water; and she went, and filled the skin with water, and gave the lad a drink. [20]And God was with the lad, and he grew up; he lived in the wilderness, and became an expert with the bow. [21] He lived in the wilderness of Pâr'an; and his mother took a wife for him from the land of Egypt.

22 At that time À·bim'é·lech and Phi'col the commander of his army said to Abraham, "God is with you in all that you do; [23] now therefore swear to me here by God that you will not deal falsely with me or with my offspring or with my posterity, but as I have dealt loyally with you, you will deal with me and with the land where you have sojourned." [24]And Abraham said, "I will swear."

25 When Abraham complained to À·bim'é·lech about a well of water which Àbimelech's servants had seized, [26]À·bim'é·lech said, "I do not know who has done this thing; you did not tell me, and I have not heard of it until today." [27] So Abraham took sheep and oxen and gave them to À·bim'é·lech, and the two men made a covenant. [28]Abraham set seven ewe lambs of the flock apart. [29]And À·bim'é·lech said to Abraham, "What is the meaning of these seven ewe lambs which you have set apart?" [30] He said, "These seven ewe lambs you will take from my hand, that you may be a witness for me that I dug this well." [31] Therefore that place was called Beer-sheba;[j] because there both of them swore an oath. [32] So they made a covenant at Beer-sheba. Then À·bim'é·lech and Phi'col the commander of his army rose up and returned to the land of the Philistines. [33]Abraham planted a tamarisk tree in Beer-sheba, and called there on the name of the LORD, the Everlasting

God. [34]And Abraham sojourned many days in the land of the Philistines.

22 After these things God tested Abraham, and said to him, "Abraham!" And he said, "Here am I." [2] He said, "Take your son, your only son Isaac, whom you love, and go to the land of Mō·rī'ăh, and offer him there as a burnt offering upon one of the mountains of which I shall tell you." [3] So Abraham rose early in the morning, saddled his ass, and took two of his young men with him, and his son Isaac; and he cut the wood for the burnt offering, and arose and went to the place of which God had told him. [4] On the third day Abraham lifted up his eyes and saw the place afar off. [5] Then Abraham said to his young men, "Stay here with the ass; I and the lad will go yonder and worship, and come again to you." [6]And Abraham took the wood of the burnt offering, and laid it on Isaac his son; and he took in his hand the fire and the knife. So they went both of them together. [7]And Isaac said to his father Abraham, "My father!" And he said, "Here am I, my son." He said, "Behold, the fire and the wood; but where is the lamb for a burnt offering?" [8]Abraham said, "God will provide himself the lamb for a burnt offering, my son." So they went both of them together.

9 When they came to the place of which God had told him, Abraham built an altar there, and laid the wood in order, and bound Isaac his son, and laid him on the altar, upon the wood. [10] Then Abraham put forth his hand, and took the knife to slay his son. [11] But the angel of the LORD called to him from heaven, and said, "Abraham, Abraham!" And he said, "Here am I." [12] He said, "Do not lay your hand on the lad or do anything to him; for now I know that you fear God, seeing you have not withheld your son, your only son, from me." [13]And Abraham lifted up his eyes and looked, and behold, behind him was a ram, caught in a thicket by his horns; and Abraham went and took the ram, and offered it up as a burnt offering instead of his son. [14] So Abraham called the name of that place The LORD will provide;[k] as it is said to this day. "On the mount of the LORD it shall be provided."[l]

15 And the angel of the LORD called to Abraham a second time from heaven, [16] and said, "By myself I have sworn,

*i*Gk: Heb *she lifted up her voice*   *j*That is *Well of seven* or *Well of the oath*   *k*Or *see*   *l*Or *he will be seen*
21.31: Gen 26.33.   22.1-18: Heb 11.17-19.   22.9-10, 12: Jas 2.21.

The Death of Sarah

says the LORD, because you have done
this, and have not withheld your son,
your only son, 17 I will indeed bless
you, and I will multiply your descendants as the stars of heaven and as the
sand which is on the seashore. And
your descendants shall possess the gate
of their enemies, 18 and by your descendants shall all the nations of the
earth bless themselves, because you
have obeyed my voice." 19 So Abraham returned to his young men, and
they arose and went together to Beer-
sheba; and Abraham dwelt at Beer-
sheba.

20 Now after these things it was
told Abraham, "Behold, Mil′cah also
has borne children to your brother
Nā′hôr: 21 Uz the first-born, Buz his
brother, Ke·mū′el the father of Ar′am,
22 Chē′sed, Hā′zō, Pil′dash, Jid′laph,
and Be·thū′el." 23 Be·thū′el became
the father of Rebekah. These eight
Mil′càh bore to Nā′hôr, Abraham's
brother. 24 Moreover, his concubine,
whose name was Reū′māh, bore Tē′-
bàh, Gā′ham, Tā′hash, and Mā′a·cáh.

23 Sarah lived a hundred and
twenty-seven years; these were
the years of the life of Sarah. 2 And
Sarah died at Kír′i·àth ar′bā (that is,
Hē′brón) in the land of Canaan; and
Abraham went in to mourn for Sarah
and to weep for her. 3 And Abraham
rose up from before his dead, and said
to the Hit′tites, 4 "I am a stranger and
a sojourner among you; give me property among you for a burying place,
that I may bury my dead out of my
sight." 5 The Hit′tites answered Abraham, 6 "Hear us, my lord; you are a
mighty prince among us. Bury your
dead in the choicest of our sepulchres;
none of us will withhold from you his
sepulchre, or hinder you from burying
your dead." 7 Abraham rose and bowed
to the Hit′tites, the people of the land.
8 And he said to them, "If you are
willing that I should bury my dead out
of my sight, hear me, and entreat for
me E′phrón the son of Zō′hàr, 9 that
he may give me the cave of Mach-
pē′làh, which he owns; it is at the end
of his field. For the full price let him
give it to me in your presence as a
possession for a burying place." 10 Now
E′phrón was sitting among the Hit′-
tites; and Ephron the Hittite answered
Abraham in the hearing of the Hittites,
of all who went in at the gate of his
city, 11 "No, my lord, hear me; I give
you the field, and I give you the cave
that is in it; in the presence of the sons

of my people I give it to you; bury
your dead." 12 Then Abraham bowed
down before the people of the land.
13 And he said to E′phrón in the hearing of the people of the land, "But if
you will, hear me; I will give the price
of the field; accept it from me, that I
may bury my dead there." 14 E′phrón
answered Abraham, 15 "My lord,
listen to me; a piece of land worth four
hundred shekels of silver, what is that
between you and me? Bury your
dead." 16 Abraham agreed with
E′phrón: and Abraham weighed out
for Ephron the silver which he had
named in the hearing of the Hit′tites,
four hundred shekels of silver, according to the weights current among the
merchants.

17 So the field of E′phrón in Mach-
pē′làh, which was to the east of
Mam′re, the field with the cave which
was in it and all the trees that were in
the field, throughout its whole area,
was made over 18 to Abraham as a
possession in the presence of the Hit′-
tites, before all who went in at the gate
of his city. 19 After this, Abraham
buried Sarah his wife in the cave of
the field of Mach-pē′làh east of Mam′re
(that is, Hē′brón) in the land of
Canaan. 20 The field and the cave that
is in it were made over to Abraham as
a possession for a burying place by the
Hit′tites.

24 Now Abraham was old, well
advanced in years; and the
LORD had blessed Abraham in all
things. 2 And Abraham said to his
servant, the oldest of his house, who
had charge of all that he had, "Put
your hand under my thigh, 3 and I
will make you swear by the LORD, the
God of heaven and of the earth, that
you will not take a wife for my son
from the daughters of the Canaanites,
among whom I dwell, 4 but will go to
my country and to my kindred, and
take a wife for my son Isaac." 5 The
servant said to him, "Perhaps the
woman may not be willing to follow
me to this land; must I then take your
son back to the land from which you
came?" 6 Abraham said to him, "See
to it that you do not take my son back
there. 7 The LORD, the God of heaven,
who took me from my father's house
and from the land of my birth, and
who spoke to me and swore to me, 'To
your descendants I will give this land,'
he will send his angel before you, and
you shall take a wife for my son from
there. 8 But if the woman is not willing

22.16-17: Lk 1.73; Heb 6.13-14; 11.12.   22.18: Acts 3.25; Gal 3.16.
23.4: Heb 11.9, 13.   23.16-17: Acts 7.16.

to follow you, then you will be free from this oath of mine; only you must not take my son back there." 9 So the servant put his hand under the thigh of Abraham his master, and swore to him concerning this matter.

10 Then the servant took ten of his master's camels and departed, taking all sorts of choice gifts from his master; and he arose, and went to Mes·ô·pó·tä´mi·à, to the city of Nä´hôr. 11And he made the camels kneel down outside the city by the well of water at the time of evening, the time when women go out to draw water. 12And he said, "O LORD, God of my master Abraham, grant me success today, I pray thee, and show steadfast love to my master Abraham. 13 Behold, I am standing by the spring of water, and the daughters of the men of the city are coming out to draw water. 14 Let the maiden to whom I shall say, 'Pray let down your jar that I may drink,' and who shall say, 'Drink, and I will water your camels'—let her be the one whom thou hast appointed for thy servant Isaac. By this I shall know that thou hast shown steadfast love to my master."

15 Before he had done speaking, behold, Rebekah, who was born to Be·thū´el the son of Mil´cäh, the wife of Nä´hôr, Abraham's brother, came out with her water jar upon her shoulder. 16 The maiden was very fair to look upon, a virgin, whom no man had known. She went down to the spring, and filled her jar, and came up. 17 Then the servant ran to meet her, and said, "Pray give me a little water to drink from your jar." 18 She said, "Drink, my lord"; and she quickly let down her jar upon her hand, and gave him a drink. 19 When she had finished giving him a drink, she said, "I will draw for your camels also, until they have done drinking." 20 So she quickly emptied her jar into the trough and ran again to the well to draw, and she drew for all his camels. 21 The man gazed at her in silence to learn whether the LORD had prospered his journey or not.

22 When the camels had done drinking, the man took a gold ring weighing a half shekel, and two bracelets for her arms weighing ten gold shekels, 23 and said, "Tell me whose daughter you are. Is there room in your father's house for us to lodge in?" 24 She said to him, "I am the daughter of Be·thū´el the son of Mil´cäh, whom she bore to Nä´hôr." 25 She added, "We have both straw and provender enough, and

room to lodge in." 26 The man bowed his head and worshiped the LORD, 27 and said, "Blessed be the LORD, the God of my master Abraham, who has not forsaken his steadfast love and his faithfulness toward my master. As for me, the LORD has led me in the way to the house of my master's kinsmen." 28 Then the maiden ran and told her mother's household about these things.

29 Rebekah had a brother whose name was Laban; and Laban ran out to the man, to the spring. 30 When he saw the ring, and the bracelets on his sister's arms, and when he heard the words of Rebekah his sister, "Thus the man spoke to me," he went to the man; and behold, he was standing by the camels at the spring. 31 He said, "Come in, O blessed of the LORD; why do you stand outside? For I have prepared the house and a place for the camels." 32 So the man came into the house; and Lä´bän ungirded the camels, and gave him straw and provender for the camels, and water to wash his feet and the feet of the men who were with him. 33 Then food was set before him to eat; but he said, "I will not eat until I have told my errand." He said, "Speak on."

34 So he said, "I am Abraham's servant. 35 The LORD has greatly blessed my master, and he has become great; he has given him flocks and herds, silver and gold, menservants and maidservants, camels and asses. 36And Sarah my master's wife bore a son to my master when she was old; and to him he has given all that he has. 37 My master made me swear, saying, 'You shall not take a wife for my son from the daughters of the Canaanites, in whose land I dwell; 38 but you shall go to my father's house and to my kindred, and take a wife for my son.' 39 I said to my master, 'Perhaps the woman will not follow me.' 40 But he said to me, 'The LORD, before whom I walk, will send his angel with you and prosper your way; and you shall take a wife for my son from my kindred and from my father's house; 41 then you will be free from my oath, when you come to my kindred; and if they will not give her to you, you will be free from my oath.'

42 "I came today to the spring, and said, 'O LORD, the God of my master Abraham, if now thou wilt prosper the way which I go, 43 behold, I am standing by the spring of water; let the young woman who comes out to draw, to whom I shall say, "Pray give me a

ABRAHAM BUILDS AN ALTAR   *Gen. 22:9*

REBEKAH AT THE WELL   *Gen. 24:15*

little water from your jar to drink," ⁴⁴ and who will say to me, "Drink, and I will draw for your camels also," let her be the woman whom the LORD has appointed for my master's son.'

⁴⁵ "Before I had done speaking in my heart, behold, Rebekah came out with her water jar on her shoulder; and she went down to the spring, and drew. I said to her, 'Pray let me drink.' ⁴⁶ She quickly let down her jar from her shoulder, and said, 'Drink, and I will give your camels drink also.' So I drank, and she gave the camels drink also. ⁴⁷ Then I asked her, 'Whose daughter are you?' She said, 'The daughter of Be·thū′el, Nā′hôr's son, whom Mil′cǎh bore to him.' So I put the ring on her nose, and the bracelets on her arms. ⁴⁸ Then I bowed my head and worshiped the LORD, and blessed the LORD, the God of my master Abraham, who had led me by the right way to take the daughter of my master's kinsman for his son. ⁴⁹ Now then, if you will deal loyally and truly with my master, tell me; and if not, tell me; that I may turn to the right hand or to the left."

⁵⁰ Then Lā′bǎn and Be·thū′el answered, "The thing comes from the LORD; we cannot speak to you bad or good. ⁵¹ Behold, Rebekah is before you, take her and go, and let her be the wife of your master's son, as the LORD has spoken."

⁵² When Abraham's servant heard their words, he bowed himself to the earth before the LORD. ⁵³ And the servant brought forth jewelry of silver and of gold, and raiment, and gave them to Rebekah; he also gave to her brother and to her mother costly ornaments. ⁵⁴ And he and the men who were with him ate and drank, and they spent the night there. When they arose in the morning, he said, "Send me back to my master." ⁵⁵ Her brother and her mother said, "Let the maiden remain with us a while, at least ten days; after that she may go." ⁵⁶ But he said to them, "Do not delay me, since the LORD has prospered my way; let me go that I may go to my master." ⁵⁷ They said, "We will call the maiden, and ask her." ⁵⁸ And they called Rebekah, and said to her, "Will you go with this man?" She said, "I will go." ⁵⁹ So they sent away Rebekah their sister and her nurse, and Abraham's servant and his men. ⁶⁰ And they blessed Rebekah, and said to her, "Our sister, be the mother of thousands of ten thousands; and may your descendants possess the gate of those who hate them!" ⁶¹ Then Rebekah and her maids arose, and rode upon the camels and followed the man; thus the servant took Rebekah, and went his way.

⁶² Now Isaac had come fromⁿ Bē′ér-lā′häi-roi, and was dwelling in the Negeb. ⁶³ And Isaac went out to meditate in the field in the evening; and he lifted up his eyes and looked, and behold, there were camels coming. ⁶⁴ And Rebekah lifted up her eyes, and when she saw Isaac, she alighted from the camel, ⁶⁵ and said to the servant, "Who is the man yonder, walking in the field to meet us?" The servant said, "It is my master." So she took her veil and covered herself. ⁶⁶ And the servant told Isaac all the things that he had done. ⁶⁷ Then Isaac brought her into the tent,^o and took Rebekah, and she became his wife; and he loved her. So Isaac was comforted after his mother's death.

25 Abraham took another wife, whose name was Ke·tū′rǎh. ² She bore him Zim′ran, Jok′shǎn, Mē′dan, Mid′i·ǎn, Ish′bak, and Shü′-ǎh. ³ Jok′shǎn was the father of Sheba and Dē′dan. The sons of Dedan were As·shū′rim, Le·tū′shim, and Le·um′-mim. ⁴ The sons of Mid′i·ǎn were Ē′phǎh, Ē′phér, Hā′nŏch, A·bī′dǎ, and El·dā′ǎh. All these were the children of Ke·tū′rǎh. ⁵ Abraham gave all he had to Isaac. ⁶ But to the sons of his concubines Abraham gave gifts, and while he was still living he sent them away from his son Isaac, eastward to the east country.

⁷ These are the days of the years of Abraham's life, a hundred and seventy-five years. ⁸ Abraham breathed his last and died in a good old age, an old man and full of years, and was gathered to his people. ⁹ Isaac and Ish′mā·el his sons buried him in the cave of Mach-pē′lǎh, in the field of Ē′phrŏn the son of Zō′hǎr the Hit′tite, east of Mam′re, ¹⁰ the field which Abraham purchased from the Hit′tites. There Abraham was buried, with Sarah his wife. ¹¹ After the death of Abraham God blessed Isaac his son. And Isaac dwelt at Bē′ér-lā′häi-roi.

¹² These are the descendants of Ish′mā·el, Abraham's son, whom Hā′gǎr the Egyptian, Sarah's maid, bore to Abraham. ¹³ These are the names of the sons of Ish′mā·el, named in the order of their birth: Ne·bā′ioth,

ⁿ Syr Tg: Heb *from coming to* ^o Heb adds *Sarah his mother*
25.13-16: 1 Chron 1.29-31.

the first-born of Ishmael; and Kĕ'där, Ad'bē·el, Mib'săm, ¹⁴ Mish'mă, Dü'mäh, Mas'să, ¹⁵ Hă'dad, Tē'mă, Jē'tūr, Nā'phish, and Ked'e·mäh. ¹⁶ These are the sons of Ish'mà·el and these are their names, by their villages and by their encampments, twelve princes according to their tribes. ¹⁷ (These are the years of the life of Ish'mà·el, a hundred and thirty-seven years; he breathed his last and died, and was gathered to his kindred.) ¹⁸ They dwelt from Hav'ï·läh to Shür, which is opposite Egypt in the direction of Assyria; he settled*ᵖ* over against all his people.

19 These are the descendants of Isaac, Abraham's son: Abraham was the father of Isaac, ²⁰ and Isaac was forty years old when he took to wife Rebekah, the daughter of Be-thü'el the Ar·à·mē'an of Pad'dân-âr'-àm, the sister of Lā'bàn the Aramean. ²¹And Isaac prayed to the LORD for his wife, because she was barren; and the LORD granted his prayer, and Rebekah his wife conceived. ²² The children struggled together within her; and she said, "If it is thus, why do I live?"*q* So she went to inquire of the LORD. ²³And the LORD said to her,

"Two nations are in your womb,
　　and two peoples, born of you,
　　　shall be divided;
the one shall be stronger than the
　　　other,
　　the elder shall serve the younger."

²⁴ When her days to be delivered were fulfilled, behold, there were twins in her womb. ²⁵ The first came forth red, all his body like a hairy mantle; so they called his name Esau. ²⁶Afterward his brother came forth, and his hand had taken hold of Esau's heel; so his name was called Jacob.*r* Isaac was sixty years old when she bore them.

27 When the boys grew up, Esau was a skilful hunter, a man of the field, while Jacob was a quiet man, dwelling in tents. ²⁸ Isaac loved Esau, because he ate of his game; but Rebekah loved Jacob.

29 Once when Jacob was boiling pottage, Esau came in from the field, and he was famished. ³⁰And Esau said to Jacob, "Let me eat some of that red pottage, for I am famished!" (Therefore his name was called E'dòm.*s*) ³¹ Jacob said, "First sell me your birthright." ³² Esau said, "I am about to die; of what use is a birthright to me?" ³³ Jacob said, "Swear to me first."*t* So he swore to him, and sold his birth-

right to Jacob. ³⁴ Then Jacob gave Esau bread and pottage of lentils, and he ate and drank, and rose and went his way. Thus Esau despised his birthright.

26 Now there was a famine in the land, besides the former famine that was in the days of Abraham. And Isaac went to Gē'rär, to A·bim'ē·lech king of the Philistines. ²And the LORD appeared to him, and said, "Do not go down to Egypt; dwell in the land of which I shall tell you. ³ Sojourn in this land, and I will be with you, and will bless you; for to you and to your descendants I will give all these lands, and I will fulfil the oath which I swore to Abraham your father. ⁴ I will multiply your descendants as the stars of heaven, and will give to your descendants all these lands; and by your descendants all the nations of the earth shall bless themselves: ⁵ because Abraham obeyed my voice and kept my charge, my commandments, my statutes, and my laws."

6 So Isaac dwelt in Gē'rär. ⁷ When the men of the place asked him about his wife, he said, "She is my sister"; for he feared to say, "My wife," thinking, "lest the men of the place should kill me for the sake of Rebekah"; because she was fair to look upon. ⁸ When he had been there a long time, A·bim'ē·lech king of the Philistines looked out of a window and saw Isaac fondling Rebekah his wife. ⁹ So A·bim'ē·lech called Isaac, and said, "Behold, she is your wife; how then could you say, 'She is my sister'?" Isaac said to him, "Because I thought, 'Lest I die because of her.'" ¹⁰A·bim'-ē·lech said, "What is this you have done to us? One of the people might easily have lain with your wife, and you would have brought guilt upon us." ¹¹ So A·bim'ē·lech warned all the people, saying, "Whoever touches this man or his wife shall be put to death."

12 And Isaac sowed in that land, and reaped in the same year a hundredfold. The LORD blessed him, ¹³ and the man became rich, and gained more and more until he became very wealthy. ¹⁴ He had possessions of flocks and herds, and a great household, so that the Philistines envied him. ¹⁵ (Now the Philistines had stopped and filled with earth all the wells which his father's servants had dug in the days of Abraham his father.) ¹⁶And A·bim'ē·lech said to Isaac, "Go away

---

p Heb *fell*　　*q* Syr: Heb obscure　　*r* That is *He takes by the heel* or *He supplants*
s That is *Red*　　*t* Heb *today*

from us; for you are much mightier than we."

17 So Isaac departed from there, and encamped in the valley of Gē'rär and dwelt there. 18And Isaac dug again the wells of water which had been dug in the days of Abraham his father; for the Philistines had stopped them after the death of Abraham; and he gave them the names which his father had given them. 19 But when Isaac's servants dug in the valley and found there a well of springing water, 20 the herdsmen of Gē'rär quarreled with Isaac's herdsmen, saying, "The water is ours." So he called the name of the well Ē'sek,*u* because they contended with him. 21 Then they dug another well, and they quarreled over that also; so he called its name Sit'näh.*v* 22And he moved from there and dug another well, and over that they did not quarrel; so he called its name Re·hō'both,*w* saying, "For now the LORD has made room for us, and we shall be fruitful in the land."

23 From there he went up to Beersheba. 24And the LORD appeared to him the same night and said, "I am the God of Abraham your father; fear not, for I am with you and will bless you and multiply your descendants for my servant Abraham's sake." 25 So he built an altar there and called upon the name of the LORD, and pitched his tent there. And there Isaac's servants dug a well.

26 Then A·bim'ė·lech went to him from Gē'rär with A·huz'zath his adviser and Phi'col the commander of his army. 27 Isaac said to them, "Why have you come to me, seeing that you hate me and have sent me away from you?" 28 They said, "We see plainly that the LORD is with you; so we say, let there be an oath between you and us, and let us make a covenant with you, 29 that you will do us no harm, just as we have not touched you and have done to you nothing but good and have sent you away in peace. You are now the blessed of the LORD." 30 So he made them a feast, and they ate and drank. 31 In the morning they rose early and took oath with one another; and Isaac set them on their way, and they departed from him in peace. 32 That same day Isaac's servants came and told him about the well which they had dug, and said to him, "We have found water." 33 He called it Shi'bah; therefore the name of the city is Beer-sheba to this day.

34 When Esau was forty years old, he took to wife Judith the daughter of Be·ē'rï the Hit'tïte, and Bas'ė·math the daughter of Ē'lon the Hittite; 35 and they made life bitter for Isaac and Rebekah.

27 When Isaac was old and his eyes were dim so that he could not see, he called Esau his older son, and said to him, "My son"; and he answered, "Here I am." 2 He said, "Behold, I am old; I do not know the day of my death. 3 Now then, take your weapons, your quiver and your bow, and go out to the field, and hunt game for me, 4 and prepare for me savory food, such as I love, and bring it to me that I may eat; that I may bless you before I die."

5 Now Rebekah was listening when Isaac spoke to his son Esau. So when Esau went to the field to hunt for game and bring it, 6 Rebekah said to her son Jacob, "I heard your father speak to your brother Esau, 7 'Bring me game, and prepare for me savory food, that I may eat it, and bless you before the LORD before I die.' 8 Now therefore, my son, obey my word as I command you. 9 Go to the flock, and fetch me two good kids, that I may prepare from them savory food for your father, such as he loves; 10 and you shall bring it to your father to eat, so that he may bless you before he dies." 11 But Jacob said to Rebekah his mother, "Behold, my brother is a hairy man, and I am a smooth man. 12 Perhaps my father will feel me, and I shall seem to be mocking him, and bring a curse upon myself and not a blessing." 13 His mother said to him, "Upon me be your curse, my son; only obey my word, and go, fetch them to me." 14 So he went and took them and brought them to his mother; and his mother prepared savory food, such as his father loved. 15 Then Rebekah took the best garments of Esau her older son, which were with her in the house, and put them on Jacob her younger son; 16 and the skins of the kids she put upon his hands and upon the smooth part of his neck 17 and she gave the savory food and the bread, which she had prepared, into the hand of her son Jacob.

18 So he went in to his father, and said, "My father"; and he said, "Here I am; who are you, my son?" 19 Jacob said to his father, "I am Esau your first-born. I have done as you told me; now sit up and eat of my game, that

u That is Contention   *v* That is Enmity   *w* That is Broad places or Room
26.33: Gen 21.31.   **27.5:** Gen 12.3; Num 24.9.

you may bless me." 20 But Isaac said to his son, "How is it that you have found it so quickly, my son?" He answered, "Because the LORD your God granted me success." 21 Then Isaac said to Jacob, "Come near, that I may feel you, my son, to know whether you are really my son Esau or not." 22 So Jacob went near to Isaac his father, who felt him and said, "The voice is Jacob's voice, but the hands are the hands of Esau." 23And he did not recognize him, because his hands were hairy like his brother Esau's hands; so he blessed him. 24 He said, "Are you really my son Esau?" He answered, "I am." 25 Then he said, "Bring it to me, that I may eat of my son's game and bless you." So he brought it to him, and he ate; and he brought him wine, and he drank. 26 Then his father Isaac said to him, "Come near and kiss me, my son." 27 So he came near and kissed him; and he smelled the smell of his garments, and blessed him, and said,

"See, the smell of my son
    is as the smell of a field which the
        LORD has blessed!
28 May God give you of the dew of
    heaven,
    and of the fatness of the earth,
    and plenty of grain and wine.
29 Let peoples serve you,
    and nations bow down to you.
Be lord over your brothers,
    and may your mother's sons bow
        down to you.
Cursed be every one who curses you,
    and blessed be every one who blesses
        you!"

30 As soon as Isaac had finished blessing Jacob, when Jacob had scarcely gone out from the presence of Isaac his father, Esau his brother came in from his hunting. 31 He also prepared savory food, and brought it to his father. And he said to his father, "Let my father arise, and eat of his son's game, that you may bless me." 32 His father Isaac said to him, "Who are you?" He answered, "I am your son, your first-born, Esau." 33 Then Isaac trembled violently, and said, "Who was it then that hunted game and brought it to me, and I ate it allˣ before you came, and I have blessed him?—yes, and he shall be blessed." 34 When Esau heard the words of his father, he cried out with an exceedingly great and bitter cry, and said to his father, "Bless me, even me also, O my father!" 35 But he said, "Your brother came with guile, and he has

taken away your blessing." 36 Esau said, "Is he not rightly named Jacob? For he has supplanted me these two times. He took away my birthright; and behold, now he has taken away my blessing." Then he said, "Have you not reserved a blessing for me?" 37 Isaac answered Esau, "Behold, I have made him your lord, and all his brothers I have given to him for servants, and with grain and wine I have sustained him. What then can I do for you, my son?" 38 Esau said to his father, "Have you but one blessing, my father? Bless me, even me also, O my father." And Esau lifted up his voice and wept.

39 Then Isaac his father answered him:

"Behold, away fromʸ the fatness of
    the earth shall your dwelling be,
    and away fromʸ the dew of heaven
        on high.
40 By your sword you shall live,
    and you shall serve your brother;
but when you break loose
    you shall break his yoke from
        your neck."

41 Now Esau hated Jacob because of the blessing with which his father had blessed him, and Esau said to himself, "The days of mourning for my father are approaching; then I will kill my brother Jacob." 42 But the words of Esau her older son were told to Rebekah; so she sent and called Jacob her younger son, and said to him, "Behold, your brother Esau comforts himself by planning to kill you. 43 Now therefore, my son, obey my voice; arise, flee to Lāʹbàn my brother in Hârʹàn, 44 and stay with him a while, until your brother's fury turns away; 45 until your brother's anger turns away, and he forgets what you have done to him; then I will send, and fetch you from there. Why should I be bereft of you both in one day?"

46 Then Rebekah said to Isaac, "I am weary of my life because of the Hitʹtite women. If Jacob marries one of the Hittite women such as these, one of the women of the land, what good will my life be to me?"

28 1 Then Isaac called Jacob and blessed him, and charged him, "You shall not marry one of the Canaanite women. 2Arise, go to Padʹdàn-ârʹàm to the house of Be·thùʹel your mother's father; and take as wife from there one of the daughters of Lāʹbàn your mother's brother. 3 God Almightyᶻ bless you and make you fruitful and multiply you, that you may become a company of peoples. 4 May he give the blessing of Abraham to you and to your descendants with you, that you may take possession of the land of your sojournings which God gave to Abraham!" 5 Thus Isaac sent Jacob away; and he went to Pad'dàn-âr'ám to Lā'bàn, the son of Be·thū'el the Ar·à·mē'án, the brother of Rebekah, Jacob's and Esau's mother.

6 Now Esau saw that Isaac had blessed Jacob and sent him away to Pad'dàn-âr'ám to take a wife from there, and that as he blessed him he charged him, "You shall not marry one of the Canaanite women," 7 and that Jacob had obeyed his father and his mother and gone to Pad'dàn-âr'ám. 8 So when Esau saw that the Canaanite women did not please Isaac his father, 9 Esau went to Ish'mà·el and took to wife, besides the wives he had, Mā'hà·lath the daughter of Ishmael Abraham's son, the sister of Ne·bā'ioth.

10 Jacob left Beer-sheba, and went toward Hâr'àn. 11And he came to a certain place, and stayed there that night, because the sun had set. Taking one of the stones of the place, he put it under his head and lay down in that place to sleep. 12And he dreamed that there was a ladder set up on the earth, and the top of it reached to heaven; and behold, the angels of God were ascending and descending on it! 13And behold, the LORD stood above it*a* and said, "I am the LORD, the God of Abraham your father and the God of Isaac; the land on which you lie I will give to you and to your descendants; 14 and your descendants shall be like the dust of the earth, and you shall spread abroad to the west and to the east and to the north and to the south; and by you and your descendants shall all the families of the earth bless themselves.*b* 15 Behold, I am with you and will keep you wherever you go, and will bring you back to this land; for I will not leave you until I have done that of which I have spoken to you." 16 Then Jacob awoke from his sleep and said, "Surely the LORD is in this place; and I did not know it." 17And he was afraid, and said, "How awesome is this place! This is none other than the house of God, and this is the gate of heaven."

18 So Jacob rose early in the morning and he took the stone which he had put under his head and set it up for a pillar and poured oil on the top of it. 19 He called the name of that place Beth'él;*c* but the name of the city was

Luz at the first. 20 Then Jacob made a vow, saying, "If God will be with me, and will keep me in this way that I go, and will give me bread to eat and clothing to wear, 21 so that I come again to my father's house in peace, then the LORD shall be my God, 22 and this stone, which I have set up for a pillar, shall be God's house; and of all that thou givest me I will give the tenth to thee."

29 Then Jacob went on his journey, and came to the land of the people of the east. 2As he looked, he saw a well in the field, and lo, three flocks of sheep lying beside it; for out of that well the flocks were watered. The stone on the well's mouth was large, 3 and when all the flocks were gathered there, the shepherds would roll the stone from the mouth of the well, and water the sheep, and put the stone back in its place upon the mouth of the well.

4 Jacob said to them, "My brothers, where do you come from?" They said, "We are from Hâr'àn." 5 He said to them, "Do you know Lā'bàn the son of Nā'hôr?" They said, "We know him." 6 He said to them, "Is it well with him?" They said, "It is well; and see, Rachel his daughter is coming with the sheep!" 7 He said, "Behold, it is still high day, it is not time for the animals to be gathered together; water the sheep, and go, pasture them." 8 But they said, "We cannot until all the flocks are gathered together, and the stone is rolled from the mouth of the well; then we water the sheep."

9 While he was still speaking with them, Rachel came with her father's sheep; for she kept them. 10 Now when Jacob saw Rachel the daughter of Lā'bàn his mother's brother, and the sheep of Laban his mother's brother, Jacob went up and rolled the stone from the well's mouth, and watered the flock of Laban his mother's brother. 11 Then Jacob kissed Rachel, and wept aloud. 12And Jacob told Rachel that he was her father's kinsman, and that he was Rebekah's son; and she ran and told her father.

13 When Lā'bàn heard the tidings of Jacob his sister's son, he ran to meet him, and embraced him and kissed him, and brought him to his house. Jacob told Laban all these things, 14 and Lā'bàn said to him, "Surely you are my bone and my flesh!" And he stayed with him a month.

15 Then Lā'bàn said to Jacob, "Because you are my kinsman, should you

a Or *beside him*   *b* Or *be blessed*   *c* That is *The house of God*

therefore serve me for nothing? Tell me, what shall your wages be?" 16 Now Lā′bàn had two daughters; the name of the older was Leah, and the name of the younger was Rachel. 17 Leah's eyes were weak, but Rachel was beautiful and lovely. 18 Jacob loved Rachel; and he said, "I will serve you seven years for your younger daughter Rachel." 19 Lā′bàn said, "It is better that I give her to you than that I should give her to any other man; stay with me." 20 So Jacob served seven years for Rachel, and they seemed to him but a few days because of the love he had for her.

21 Then Jacob said to Lā′bàn, "Give me my wife that I may go in to her, for my time is completed." 22 So Lā′bàn gathered together all the men of the place, and made a feast. 23 But in the evening he took his daughter Leah and brought her to Jacob; and he went in to her. 24 (Lā′bàn gave his maid Zil′pàh to his daughter Leah to be her maid.) 25And in the morning, behold, it was Leah; and Jacob said to Lā′bàn, "What is this you have done to me? Did I not serve with you for Rachel? Why then have you deceived me?" 26 Lā′bàn said, "It is not so done in our country, to give the younger before the first-born. 27 Complete the week of this one, and we will give you the other also in return for serving me another seven years." 28 Jacob did so, and completed her week; then Lā′bàn gave him his daughter Rachel to wife. 29 (Lā′bàn gave his maid Bil′hàh to his daughter Rachel to be her maid.) 30 So Jacob went in to Rachel also, and he loved Rachel more than Leah, and served Lā′bàn for another seven years.

31 When the LORD saw that Leah was hated, he opened her womb; but Rachel was barren. 32And Leah conceived and bore a son, and she called his name Reuben;*d* for she said, "Because the LORD has looked upon my affliction; surely now my husband will love me." 33 She conceived again and bore a son, and said, "Because the LORD has heard*e* that I am hated, he has given me this son also"; and she called his name Simeon. 34Again she conceived and bore a son, and said, "Now this time my husband will be joined*f* to me, because I have borne him three sons"; therefore his name was called Levi. 35And she conceived again and bore a son, and said, "This time I will praise*g* the LORD"; there-

fore she called his name Judah; then she ceased bearing.

30 When Rachel saw that she bore Jacob no children, she envied her sister; and she said to Jacob, "Give me children, or I shall die!" 2 Jacob's anger was kindled against Rachel, and he said, "Am I in the place of God, who has withheld from you the fruit of the womb?" 3 Then she said, "Here is my maid Bil′hàh; go in to her, that she may bear upon my knees, and even I may have children through her." 4 So she gave him her maid Bil′hàh as a wife; and Jacob went in to her. 5And Bil′hàh conceived and bore Jacob a son. 6 Then Rachel said, "God has judged me, and has also heard my voice and given me a son"; therefore she called his name Dan.*h* 7 Rachel's maid Bil′hàh conceived again and bore Jacob a second son. 8 Then Rachel said, "With mighty wrestlings I have wrestled*i* with my sister, and have prevailed"; so she called his name Naph′tà-li.

9 When Leah saw that she had ceased bearing children, she took her maid Zil′pàh and gave her to Jacob as a wife. 10 Then Leah's maid Zil′pàh bore Jacob a son. 11And Leah said, "Good fortune!" so she called his name Gad.*j* 12 Leah's maid Zil′pàh bore Jacob a second son. 13And Leah said, "Happy am I! For the women will call me happy"; so she called his name Ash′ér.*k*

14 In the days of wheat harvest Reuben went and found mandrakes in the field, and brought them to his mother Leah. Then Rachel said to Leah, "Give me, I pray, some of your son's mandrakes." 15 But she said to her, "Is it a small matter that you have taken away my husband? Would you take away my son's mandrakes also?" Rachel said, "Then he may lie with you tonight for your son's mandrakes." 16 When Jacob came from the field in the evening, Leah went out to meet him, and said, "You must come in to me; for I have hired you with my son's mandrakes." So he lay with her that night. 17And God hearkened to Leah, and she conceived and bore Jacob a fifth son. 18 Leah said, "God has given me my hire*l* because I gave my maid to my husband"; so she called his name Is′sà-chär. 19And Leah conceived again, and she bore Jacob a sixth son. 20 Then Leah said, "God has endowed me with a good dowry; now my husband will honor*m* me, because I have

d That is *See, a son*   *e* Heb *shama*   *f* Heb *lawah*   *g* Heb *hodah*   *h* That is *He judged*   *i* Heb *niphtal*   *j* That is *Fortune*   *k* That is *Happy*   *l* Heb *sakar*   *m* Heb *zabal*

borne him six sons"; so she called his name Zeb'u·lun. [21]Afterwards she bore a daughter, and called her name Dinah. [22] Then God remembered Rachel, and God hearkened to her and opened her womb. [23] She conceived and bore a son, and said, "God has taken away my reproach"; [24] and she called his name Joseph,[n] saying, "May the Lord add to me another son!"

25 When Rachel had borne Joseph, Jacob said to La'ban, "Send me away, that I may go to my own home and country. [26] Give me my wives and my children for whom I have served you, and let me go; for you know the service which I have given you." [27] But La'ban said to him, "If you will allow me to say so, I have learned by divination that the Lord has blessed me because of you; [28] name your wages, and I will give it." [29] Jacob said to him, "You yourself know how I have served you, and how your cattle have fared with me. [30] For you had little before I came, and it has increased abundantly; and the Lord has blessed you wherever I turned. But now when shall I provide for my own household also?" [31] He said, "What shall I give you?" Jacob said, "You shall not give me anything; if you will do this for me, I will again feed your flock and keep it: [32] let me pass through all your flock today, removing from it every speckled and spotted sheep and every black lamb, and the spotted and speckled among the goats; and such shall be my wages. [33] So my honesty will answer for me later, when you come to look into my wages with you. Every one that is not speckled and spotted among the goats and black among the lambs, if found with me, shall be counted stolen." [34] La'ban said, "Good! Let it be as you have said." [35] But that day La'ban removed the he-goats that were striped and spotted, and all the she-goats that were speckled and spotted, every one that had white on it, and every lamb that was black, and put them in charge of his sons; [36] and he set a distance of three days' journey between himself and Jacob; and Jacob fed the rest of La'ban's flock.

37 Then Jacob took fresh rods of poplar and almond and plane, and peeled white streaks in them, exposing the white of the rods. [38] He set the rods which he had peeled in front of the flocks in the runnels, that is, the watering troughs, where the flocks came to drink. And since they bred when they came to drink, [39] the flocks bred in front of the rods and so the flocks brought forth striped, speckled, and spotted. [40] And Jacob separated the lambs, and set the faces of the flocks toward the striped and all the black in the flock of La'ban; and he put his own droves apart, and did not put them with Laban's flock. [41] Whenever the stronger of the flock were breeding Jacob laid the rods in the runnels before the eyes of the flock, that they might breed among the rods, [42] but for the feebler of the flock he did not lay them there; so the feebler were La'ban's, and the stronger Jacob's. [43] Thus the man grew exceedingly rich, and had large flocks, maidservants and menservants, and camels and asses.

31 Now Jacob heard that the sons of La'ban were saying, "Jacob has taken all that was our father's; and from what was our father's he has gained all this wealth." [2] And Jacob saw that La'ban did not regard him with favor as before. [3] Then the Lord said to Jacob, "Return to the land of your fathers and to your kindred, and I will be with you." [4] So Jacob sent and called Rachel and Leah into the field where his flock was, [5] and said to them, "I see that your father does not regard me with favor as he did before. But the God of my father has been with me. [6] You know that I have served your father with all my strength; [7] yet your father has cheated me and changed my wages ten times, but God did not permit him to harm me. [8] If he said, 'The spotted shall be your wages,' then all the flock bore spotted; and if he said, 'The striped shall be your wages,' then all the flock bore striped. [9] Thus God has taken away the cattle of your father, and given them to me. [10] In the mating season of the flock I lifted up my eyes, and saw in a dream that the he-goats which leaped upon the flock were striped, spotted, and mottled. [11] Then the angel of God said to me in the dream, 'Jacob,' and I said, 'Here I am!' [12] And he said, 'Lift up your eyes and see, all the goats that leap upon the flock are striped, spotted, and mottled; for I have seen all that La'ban is doing to you. [13] I am the God of Beth'el, where you anointed a pillar and made a vow to me. Now arise, go forth from this land, and return to the land of your birth.'" [14] Then Rachel and Leah answered him, "Is there any portion or inheritance left to us in our father's house? [15] Are we not regarded by him

[n] That is *He adds*

as foreigners? For he has sold us, and he has been using up the money given for us. 16All the property which God has taken away from our father belongs to us and to our children; now then, whatever God has said to you, do."

17 So Jacob arose, and set his sons and his wives on camels, 18 and he drove away all his cattle, all his livestock which he had gained, the cattle in his possession which he had acquired in Pad'dàn-ăr'ăm, to go to the land of Canaan to his father Isaac. 19 Lā'bàn had gone to shear his sheep, and Rachel stole her father's household gods. 20And Jacob outwitted Lā'bàn the Ar-à-mē'àn, in that he did not tell him that he intended to flee. 21 He fled with all that he had, and arose and crossed the Eū'phrā'tēs, and set his face toward the hill country of Gilead.

22 When it was told Lā'bàn on the third day that Jacob had fled, 23 he took his kinsmen with him and pursued him for seven days and followed close after him into the hill country of Gilead. 24 But God came to Lā'bàn the Ar-à-mē'àn in a dream by night, and said to him, "Take heed that you say not a word to Jacob, either good or bad."

25 And Lā'bàn overtook Jacob. Now Jacob had pitched his tent in the hill country, and Laban with his kinsmen encamped in the hill country of Gilead. 26And Lā'bàn said to Jacob, "What have you done, that you have cheated me, and carried away my daughters like captives of the sword? 27 Why did you flee secretly, and cheat me, and did not tell me, so that I might have sent you away with mirth and songs, with tambourine and lyre? 28And why did you not permit me to kiss my sons and my daughters farewell? Now you have done foolishly. 29 It is in my power to do you harm; but the God of your father spoke to me last night, saying, 'Take heed that you speak to Jacob neither good nor bad.' 30And now you have gone away because you longed greatly for your father's house, but why did you steal my gods?" 31 Jacob answered Lā'bàn, "Because I was afraid, for I thought that you would take your daughters from me by force. 32Any one with whom you find your gods shall not live. In the presence of our kinsmen point out what I have that is yours, and take it." Now Jacob did not know that Rachel had stolen them.

33 So Lā'bàn went into Jacob's tent, and into Leah's tent, and into

the tent of the two maidservants, but he did not find them. And he went out of Leah's tent, and entered Rachel's. 34 Now Rachel had taken the household gods and put them in the camel's saddle, and sat upon them. Lā'bàn felt all about the tent, but did not find them. 35And she said to her father, "Let not my lord be angry that I cannot rise before you, for the way of women is upon me." So he searched, but did not find the household gods.

36 Then Jacob became angry, and upbraided Lā'bàn; Jacob said to Laban, "What is my offense? What is my sin, that you have hotly pursued me? 37Although you have felt through all my goods, what have you found of all your household goods? Set it here before my kinsmen and your kinsmen, that they may decide between us two. 38 These twenty years I have been with you; your ewes and your she-goats have not miscarried, and I have not eaten the rams of your flocks. 39 That which was torn by wild beasts I did not bring to you; I bore the loss of it myself; of my hand you required it, whether stolen by day or stolen by night. 40 Thus I was, by day the heat consumed me, and the cold by night, and my sleep fled from my eyes. 41 These twenty years I have been in your house; I served you fourteen years for your two daughters, and six years for your flock, and you have changed my wages ten times. 42 If the God of my father, the God of Abraham and the Fear of Isaac, had not been on my side, surely now you would have sent me away empty-handed. God saw my affliction and the labor of my hands, and rebuked you last night."

43 Then Lā'bàn answered and said to Jacob, "The daughters are my daughters, the children are my children, the flocks are my flocks, and all that you see is mine. But what can I do this day to these my daughters, or to their children whom they have borne? 44 Come now, let us make a covenant, you and I; and let it be a witness between you and me." 45 So Jacob took a stone, and set it up as a pillar. 46And Jacob said to his kinsmen, "Gather stones," and they took stones, and made a heap; and they ate there by the heap. 47 Lā'bàn called it Jē'gàr-sà-hà-dū'thà:o but Jacob called it Gal'ē-ed.p 48 Lā'bàn said, "This heap is a witness between you and me today." Therefore he named it Gal'ē-ed,

o In Aramaic *The heap of witness*   p In Hebrew *The heap of witness*

49 and the pillar*q* Miz′pah,*r* for he said, "The LORD watch between you and me, when we are absent one from the other. 50 If you ill-treat my daughters, or if you take wives besides my daughters, although no man is with us, remember, God is witness between you and me."

51 Then Lā′ban said to Jacob, "See this heap and the pillar, which I have set between you and me. 52 This heap is a witness, and the pillar is a witness, that I will not pass over this heap to you, and you will not pass over this heap and this pillar to me, for harm. 53 The God of Abraham and the God of Nā′hôr, the God of their father, judge between us." So Jacob swore by the Fear of his father Isaac, 54 and Jacob offered a sacrifice on the mountain and called his kinsmen to eat bread; and they ate bread and tarried all night on the mountain.

55*s* Early in the morning Lā′ban arose, and kissed his grandchildren and his daughters and blessed them; then he departed and returned home.

32 Jacob went on his way and the angels of God met him; 2 and when Jacob saw them he said, "This is God's army!" So he called the name of that place Mā·hà·nā′im.*t*

3 And Jacob sent messengers before him to Esau his brother in the land of Sē′ir, the country of E′dom, 4 instructing them, "Thus you shall say to my lord Esau: Thus says your servant Jacob, 'I have sojourned with Lā′ban, and stayed until now; 5 and I have oxen, asses, flocks, menservants, and maidservants; and I have sent to tell my lord, in order that I may find favor in your sight.'"

6 And the messengers returned to Jacob, saying, "We came to your brother Esau, and he is coming to meet you, and four hundred men with him." 7 Then Jacob was greatly afraid and distressed; and he divided the people that were with him, and the flocks and herds and camels, into two companies, 8 thinking, "If Esau comes to the one company and destroys it, then the company which is left will escape."

9 And Jacob said, "O God of my father Abraham and God of my father Isaac, O LORD who didst say to me, 'Return to your country and to your kindred, and I will do you good,' 10 I am not worthy of the least of all the steadfast love and all the faithfulness which thou hast shown to thy servant,

for with only my staff I crossed this Jordan; and now I have become two companies. 11 Deliver me, I pray thee, from the hand of my brother, from the hand of Esau, for I fear him, lest he come and slay us all, the mothers with the children. 12 But thou didst say, 'I will do you good, and make your descendants as the sand of the sea, which cannot be numbered for multitude.'"

13 So he lodged there that night, and took from what he had with him a present for his brother Esau, 14 two hundred she-goats and twenty he-goats, two hundred ewes and twenty rams, 15 thirty milch camels and their colts, forty cows and ten bulls, twenty she-asses and ten he-asses. 16 These he delivered into the hand of his servants, every drove by itself, and said to his servants, "Pass on before me, and put a space between drove and drove." 17 He instructed the foremost, "When Esau my brother meets you, and asks you, 'To whom do you belong? Where are you going? And whose are these before you?' 18 then you shall say, 'They belong to your servant Jacob; they are a present sent to my lord Esau; and moreover he is behind us.'" 19 He likewise instructed the second and the third and all who followed the droves, "You shall say the same thing to Esau when you meet him, 20 and you shall say, 'Moreover your servant Jacob is behind us.'" For he thought, "I may appease him with the present that goes before me, and afterwards I shall see his face; perhaps he will accept me." 21 So the present passed on before him; and he himself lodged that night in the camp.

22 The same night he arose and took his two wives, his two maids, and his eleven children, and crossed the ford of the Jab′bok. 23 He took them and sent them across the stream, and likewise everything that he had. 24 And Jacob was left alone; and a man wrestled with him until the breaking of the day. 25 When the man saw that he did not prevail against Jacob, he touched the hollow of his thigh; and Jacob's thigh was put out of joint as he wrestled with him. 26 Then he said, "Let me go, for the day is breaking." But Jacob said, "I will not let you go, unless you bless me." 27 And he said to him, "What is your name?" And he said, "Jacob." 28 Then he said, "Your name shall no more be called Jacob, but Israel,*u* for you have striven

q Compare Sam: Heb lacks *the pillar*   *r* That is *Watchpost*   *s* Ch 32. 1 in Heb
t Here taken to mean *Two armies*   *u* That is *He who strives with God* or *God strives*

with God and with men, and have prevailed." 29 Then Jacob asked him, "Tell me, I pray, your name." But he said, "Why is it that you ask my name?" And there he blessed him. 30 So Jacob called the name of the place Pe·ni′el,*v* saying, "For I have seen God face to face, and yet my life is preserved." 31 The sun rose upon him as he passed Pe·nu′el, limping because of his thigh. 32 Therefore to this day the Israelites do not eat the sinew of the hip which is upon the hollow of the thigh, because he touched the hollow of Jacob's thigh on the sinew of the hip.

33 And Jacob lifted up his eyes and looked, and behold, Esau was coming, and four hundred men with him. So he divided the children among Leah and Rachel and the two maids. 2 And he put the maids with their children in front, then Leah with her children, and Rachel and Joseph last of all. 3 He himself went on before them, bowing himself to the ground seven times, until he came near to his brother.

4 But Esau ran to meet him, and embraced him, and fell on his neck and kissed him, and they wept. 5 And when Esau raised his eyes and saw the women and children, he said, "Who are these with you?" Jacob said, "The children whom God has graciously given your servant." 6 Then the maids drew near, they and their children, and bowed down; 7 Leah likewise and her children drew near and bowed down; and last Joseph and Rachel drew near, and they bowed down. 8 Esau said, "What do you mean by all this company which I met?" Jacob answered, "To find favor in the sight of my lord." 9 But Esau said, "I have enough, my brother; keep what you have for yourself." 10 Jacob said, "No, I pray you, if I have found favor in your sight, then accept my present from my hand; for truly to see your face is like seeing the face of God, with such favor have you received me. 11 Accept, I pray you, my gift that is brought to you, because God has dealt graciously with me, and because I have enough." Thus he urged him, and he took it.

12 Then Esau said, "Let us journey on our way, and I will go before you." 13 But Jacob said to him, "My lord knows that the children are frail, and that the flocks and herds giving suck are a care to me; and if they are over-

driven for one day, all the flocks will die. 14 Let my lord pass on before his servant, and I will lead on slowly, according to the pace of the cattle which are before me and according to the pace of the children, until I come to my lord in Se′ir."

15 So Esau said, "Let me leave with you some of the men who are with me." But he said, "What need is there? Let me find favor in the sight of my lord." 16 So Esau returned that day on his way to Se′ir. 17 But Jacob journeyed to Suc′coth,*w* and built himself a house, and made booths for his cattle; therefore the name of the place is called Succoth.

18 And Jacob came safely to the city of She′chem, which is in the land of Canaan, on his way from Pad′dan-ar′am; and he camped before the city. 19 And from the sons of Ha′mor, She′chem's father, he bought for a hundred pieces of money*x* the piece of land on which he had pitched his tent. 20 There he erected an altar and called it El-El′o·he-Is′ra·el.*y*

34 Now Dinah the daughter of Leah, whom she had borne to Jacob, went out to visit the women of the land; 2 and when She′chem the son of Ha′mor the Hi′vite, the prince of the land, saw her, he seized her and lay with her and humbled her. 3 And his soul was drawn to Dinah the daughter of Jacob; he loved the maiden and spoke tenderly to her. 4 So She′chem spoke to his father Ha′mor, saying, "Get me this maiden for my wife." 5 Now Jacob heard that he had defiled his daughter Dinah; but his sons were with his cattle in the field, so Jacob held his peace until they came. 6 And Ha′mor the father of She′chem went out to Jacob to speak with him. 7 The sons of Jacob came in from the field when they heard of it; and the men were indignant and very angry, because he had wrought folly in Israel by lying with Jacob's daughter, for such a thing ought not to be done.

8 But Ha′mor spoke with them, saying, "The soul of my son She′chem longs for your daughter; I pray you, give her to him in marriage. 9 Make marriages with us; give your daughters to us, and take our daughters for yourselves. 10 You shall dwell with us; and the land shall be open to you; dwell and trade in it, and get property in it." 11 She′chem also said to her father and to her brothers, "Let me find favor in your eyes, and whatever you say to me

v That is *The face of God*   *w* That is *Booths*   *x* Heb *a hundred qesitas*
y That is *God, the God of Israel*

I will give. 12Ask of me ever so much as marriage present and gift, and I will give according as you say to me; only give me the maiden to be my wife."

13 The sons of Jacob answered Shĕ′chem and his father Hā′mor deceitfully, because he had defiled their sister Dinah. 14 They said to them, "We cannot do this thing, to give our sister to one who is uncircumcised, for that would be a disgrace to us. 15 Only on this condition will we consent to you: that you will become as we are and every male of you be circumcised. 16 Then we will give our daughters to you, and we will take your daughters to ourselves, and we will dwell with you and become one people. 17 But if you will not listen to us and be circumcised, then we will take our daughter, and we will be gone."

18 Their words pleased Hā′mor and Hamor's son Shĕ′chem. 19And the young man did not delay to do the thing, because he had delight in Jacob's daughter. Now he was the most honored of all his family. 20 So Hā′mor and his son Shĕ′chem came to the gate of their city and spoke to the men of their city, saying, 21 "These men are friendly with us; let them dwell in the land and trade in it, for behold, the land is large enough for them; let us take their daughters in marriage, and let us give them our daughters. 22 Only on this condition will the men agree to dwell with us, to become one people: that every male among us be circumcised as they are circumcised. 23 Will not their cattle, their property and all their beasts be ours? Only let us agree with them, and they will dwell with us." 24And all who went out of the gate of his city hearkened to Hā′mor and his son Shĕ′chem; and every male was circumcised, all who went out of the gate of his city.

25 On the third day, when they were sore, two of the sons of Jacob, Simeon and Levi, Dinah's brothers, took their swords and came upon the city unawares, and killed all the males. 26 They slew Hā′mor and his son Shĕ′chem with the sword, and took Dinah out of Shechem's house, and went away. 27And the sons of Jacob came upon the slain, and plundered the city, because their sister had been defiled; 28 they took their flocks and their herds, their asses, and whatever was in the city and in the field; 29 all their wealth, all their little ones and their wives, all that was in the houses, they

captured and made their prey. 30 Then Jacob said to Simeon and Levi, "You have brought trouble on me by making me odious to the inhabitants of the land, the Canaanites and the Per′izzites; my numbers are few, and if they gather themselves against me and attack me, I shall be destroyed, both I and my household." 31 But they said, "Should he treat our sister as a harlot?"

35 God said to Jacob, "Arise, go up to Beth′el, and dwell there; and make there an altar to the God who appeared to you when you fled from your brother Esau." 2 So Jacob said to his household and to all who were with him, "Put away the foreign gods that are among you, and purify yourselves, and change your garments; 3 then let us arise and go up to Beth′el, that I may make there an altar to the God who answered me in the day of my distress and has been with me wherever I have gone." 4 So they gave to Jacob all the foreign gods that they had, and the rings that were in their ears; and Jacob hid them under the oak which was near Shĕ′chem.

5 And as they journeyed, a terror from God fell upon the cities that were round about them, so that they did not pursue the sons of Jacob. 6And Jacob came to Luz (that is, Beth′el), which is in the land of Canaan, he and all the people who were with him, 7 and there he built an altar, and called the place El-beth′el,z because there God had revealed himself to him when he fled from his brother. 8And Deb′o-rah, Rebekah's nurse, died, and she was buried under an oak below Beth′el; so the name of it was called Al′lon-bac′uth.a

9 God appeared to Jacob again, when he came from Pad′dan-âr′âm, and blessed him. 10And God said to him, "Your name is Jacob; no longer shall your name be called Jacob, but Israel shall be your name." So his name was called Israel. 11And God said to him, "I am God Almighty:b be fruitful and multiply; a nation and a company of nations shall come from you, and kings shall spring from you. 12 The land which I gave to Abraham and Isaac I will give to you, and I will give the land to your descendants after you." 13 Then God went up from him in the place where he had spoken with him. 14And Jacob set up a pillar in the place where he had spoken with him, a pillar of stone; and he poured out a drink offering on it, and poured oil on

z That is God of Bethel   a That is Oak of weeping   b Heb El Shaddai it. ¹⁵ So Jacob called the name of the place where God had spoken with him, Beth'él.

16 Then they journeyed from Beth'él; and when they were still some distance from Eph'rath, Rachel travailed, and she had hard labor. ¹⁷And when she was in her hard labor, the midwife said to her, "Fear not; for now you will have another son." ¹⁸And as her soul was departing (for she died), she called his name Ben-o'ni;ᶜ but his father called his name Benjamin.ᵈ ¹⁹ So Rachel died, and she was buried on the way to Eph'rath (that is, Bethlehem), ²⁰ and Jacob set up a pillar upon her grave; it is the pillar of Rachel's tomb, which is there to this day. ²¹ Israel journeyed on, and pitched his tent beyond the tower of E'der.

22 While Israel dwelt in that land Reuben went and lay with Bil'hah his father's concubine; and Israel heard of it.

Now the sons of Jacob were twelve. ²³ The sons of Leah: Reuben (Jacob's first-born), Simeon, Levi, Judah, Is'să-chär, and Zeb'ū-lún. ²⁴ The sons of Rachel: Joseph and Benjamin. ²⁵ The sons of Bil'hah, Rachel's maid: Dan and Naph'tà-li. ²⁶ The sons of Zil'pah, Leah's maid: Gad and Ash'ér. These were the sons of Jacob who were born to him in Pad'dăn-ar'ăm.

27 And Jacob came to his father Isaac at Mam're, or Kir'i-ath-är'bà (that is, He'brŏn), where Abraham and Isaac had sojourned. ²⁸ Now the days of Isaac were a hundred and eighty years. ²⁹And Isaac breathed his last; and he died and was gathered to his people, old and full of days; and his sons Esau and Jacob buried him.

36 These are the descendants of Esau (that is, E'dŏm). ² Esau took his wives from the Canaanites: A'dàh the daughter of E'lon the Hit'-tite, Ō-hol·i·bā'mâh the daughter of An'àh the sonᵉ of Zib'ē·ŏn the Hi'vite, ³ and Bas'é·math, Ish'mà·el's daughter, the sister of Ne·bā'ioth. ⁴And A'dàh bore to Esau, E·li'phaz; Bas'é·math bore Reü'el; ⁵ and Ō-hol·i·bā'-mâh bore Jē'ush, Jā'làm, and Kō'râh. These are the sons of Esau who were born to him in the land of Canaan.

6 Then Esau took his wives, his sons, his daughters, and all the members of his household, his cattle, all his beasts, and all his property which he had acquired in the land of Canaan; and he went into a land away from his brother Jacob. ⁷ For their possessions were too great for them to dwell together; the land of their sojournings could not support them because of their cattle. ⁸ So Esau dwelt in the hill country of Sē'ir; Esau is E'dŏm.

9 These are the descendants of Esau the father of the E'dŏ·mites in the hill country of Sē'ir. ¹⁰ These are the names of Esau's sons: E·li'phaz the son of A'dàh the wife of Esau, Reü'el the son of Bas'é·math the wife of Esau. ¹¹ The sons of E·li'phaz were Tē'màn, Ō'mär, Zē'phō, Gā'tam, and Kē'naz. ¹² (Tim'nà was a concubine of E·li'-phaz, Esau's son; she bore Am'à·lek to Eliphaz.) These are the sons of A'dàh, Esau's wife. ¹³ These are the sons of Reü'el: Nā'hath, Zē'râh, Sham'màh, and Miz'zàh. These are the sons of Bas'é·math, Esau's wife. ¹⁴ These are the sons of Ō·hol·i·bā'màh the daughter of An'àh the sonᶠ of Zib'ē·ŏn, Esau's wife: she bore to Esau Jē'ush, Jā'làm, and Kō'râh.

15 These are the chiefs of the sons of Esau. The sons of E·li'phaz the first-born of Esau: the chiefs Tē'màn, Ō'mär, Zē'phō, Kē'naz, ¹⁶ Kō'râh, Gā'tam, and Am'à·lek; these are the chiefs of E·li'phaz in the land of E'dŏm; they are the sons of A'dàh. ¹⁷ These are the sons of Reü'el, Esau's son: the chiefs Nā'hath, Zē'râh, Sham'màh, and Miz'zàh; these are the chiefs of Reuel in the land of E'dŏm; they are the sons of Bas'é·math, Esau's wife. ¹⁸ These are the sons of Ō·hol·i·bā'-màh, Esau's wife: the chiefs Jē'ush, Jā'làm, and Kō'râh; these are the chiefs born of Oholibamah the daughter of An'àh, Esau's wife. ¹⁹ These are the sons of Esau (that is, E'dŏm), and these are their chiefs.

20 These are the sons of Sē'ir the Hôr'ite, the inhabitants of the land: Lō'tan, Shō'bàl, Zib'ē·ŏn, An'àh, ²¹ Di'shon, E'zèr, and Di'shan; these are the chiefs of the Hôr'ites, the sons of Sē'ir in the land of E'dŏm. ²² The sons of Lō'tan were Hō'ri and Hē'-màn; and Lotan's sister was Tim'nà. ²³ These are the sons of Shō'bàl: Al'-vàn, Man'à·hath, E'bàl, Shē'phō, and Ō'nàm. ²⁴ These are the sons of Zib'ē·ŏn: A'iàh and An'àh; he is the Anah who found the hot springs in the wilderness, as he pastured the asses of Zibeon his father. ²⁵ These are the children of An'àh: Di'shon and Ō·hol·i·bā'màh the daughter of Anah. ²⁶ These are the sons of Di'shon: Hem'dàn,

---

ᶜ That is *Son of my sorrow*   ᵈ That is *Son of the right hand* or *Son of the South*
ᵉ Sam Gk Syr: Heb *daughter*   ᶠ Gk Syr: Heb *daughter*
36.2: Gen 26.34; 28.9.   **36.20-28:** 1 Chron 1.38-42.

Esh'bàn, Ith'ran, and Chē'ràn. 27 These are the sons of Ē'zèr: Bil'han, Zā'à·van, and Ā'kàn. 28 These are the sons of Dī'shan: Uz and Àr'àn. 29 These are the chiefs of the Hôr'ites: the chiefs Lō'tan, Shō'bàl, Zib'ē·ón, An'àh, 30 Dī'shon, Ē'zèr, and Dī'shan; these are the chiefs of the Hôr'ites, according to their clans in the land of Sē'ir.

31 These are the kings who reigned in the land of Ē'dòm, before any king reigned over the Israelites. 32 Bē'là the son of Bē'ôr reigned in Ē'dòm, the name of his city being Din'hà·bàh. 33 Bē'là died, and Jō'bab the son of Zē'ràh of Boz'ràh reigned in his stead. 34 Jō'bab died, and Hū'shàm of the land of the Tē'mà·nïtes reigned in his stead. 35 Hū'shàm died, and Hā'dad the son of Bē'dad, who defeated Mid'-i·àn in the country of Mō'ab, reigned in his stead, the name of his city being Ā'vith. 36 Hā'dad died, and Sam'làh of Mas·rē'kàh reigned in his stead. 37 Sam'làh died, and Shā'ul of Re·hō'-both on the Eū·phrā'tēs reigned in his stead. 38 Shā'ul died, and Bā'al-hā'-nàn the son of Ach'bôr reigned in his stead. 39 Bā'al-hā'nàn the son of Ach'-bôr died, and Hā'dàr reigned in his stead, the name of his city being Pā'ú; his wife's name was Me·het'à·bèl, the daughter of Mā'tred, daughter of Mē'zà·hab.

40 These are the names of the chiefs of Esau, according to their families and their dwelling places, by their names: the chiefs Tim'nà, Al'vàh, Jē'theth, 41 Ō·hol·i·bā'màh, Ē'làh, Pi'non, 42 Kē'-naz, Tē'màn, Mib'zàr, 43 Mag'di·el, and I'ràm; these are the chiefs of Ē'dòm (that is, Esau, the father of Edom), according to their dwelling places in the land of their possession.

37 Jacob dwelt in the land of his father's sojournings, in the land of Canaan. 2 This is the history of the family of Jacob.

Joseph, being seventeen years old, was shepherding the flock with his brothers; he was a lad with the sons of Bil'hàh and Zil'pàh, his father's wives; and Joseph brought an ill report of them to their father. 3 Now Israel loved Joseph more than any other of his children, because he was the son of his old age; and he made him a long robe with sleeves. 4 But when his brothers saw that their father loved him more than all his brothers, they hated him, and could not speak peaceably to him.

5 Now Joseph had a dream, and when he told it to his brothers they only hated him the more. 6 He said to them, "Hear this dream which I have dreamed: 7 behold, we were binding sheaves in the field, and lo, my sheaf arose and stood upright; and behold, your sheaves gathered round it, and bowed down to my sheaf." 8 His brothers said to him, "Are you indeed to reign over us? Or are you indeed to have dominion over us?" So they hated him yet more for his dreams and for his words. 9 Then he dreamed another dream, and told it to his brothers, and said, "Behold, I have dreamed another dream; and behold, the sun, the moon, and eleven stars were bowing down to me." 10 But when he told it to his father and to his brothers, his father rebuked him, and said to him, "What is this dream that you have dreamed? Shall I and your mother and your brothers indeed come to bow ourselves to the ground before you?" 11And his brothers were jealous of him, but his father kept the saying in mind.

12 Now his brothers went to pasture their father's flock near Shē'chem. 13And Israel said to Joseph, "Are not your brothers pasturing the flock at Shē'chem? Come, I will send you to them." And he said to him, "Here I am." 14 So he said to him, "Go now, see if it is well with your brothers, and with the flock; and bring me word again." So he sent him from the valley of Hē'bròn, and he came to Shē'chem. 15And a man found him wandering in the fields; and the man asked him, "What are you seeking?" 16 "I am seeking my brothers," he said, "tell me, I pray you, where they are pasturing the flock." 17And the man said, "They have gone away, for I heard them say, 'Let us go to Dō'than.'" So Joseph went after his brothers, and found them at Dothan. 18 They saw him afar off, and before he came near to them they conspired against him to kill him. 19 They said to one another, "Here comes this dreamer. 20 Come now, let us kill him and throw him into one of the pits; then we shall say that a wild beast has devoured him, and we shall see what will become of his dreams." 21 But when Reuben heard it, he delivered him out of their hands, saying, "Let us not take his life." 22And Reuben said to them, "Shed no blood; cast him into this pit here in the wilderness, but lay no hand upon him"—that he might rescue him out of their hand, to restore him to his father. 23 So when Joseph came to his

36.31-43: 1 Chron 1.43-53.   **37.11, 28:** Acts 7.9.

brothers, they stripped him of his robe, the long robe with sleeves that he wore; 24 and they took him and cast him into a pit. The pit was empty, there was no water in it.

25 Then they sat down to eat; and looking up they saw a caravan of Ish′ma·el·ites coming from Gilead, with their camels bearing gum, balm, and myrrh, on their way to carry it down to Egypt. 26 Then Judah said to his brothers, "What profit is it if we slay our brother and conceal his blood? 27 Come, let us sell him to the Ish′ma·el·ites, and let not our hand be upon him, for he is our brother, our own flesh." And his brothers heeded him. 28 Then Mid′i·a·nīte traders passed by; and they drew Joseph up and lifted him out of the pit, and sold him to the Ish′ma·el·ites for twenty shekels of silver; and they took Joseph to Egypt.

29 When Reuben returned to the pit and saw that Joseph was not in the pit, he rent his clothes 30 and returned to his brothers, and said, "The lad is gone; and I, where shall I go?" 31 Then they took Joseph's robe, and killed a goat, and dipped the robe in the blood; 32 and they sent the long robe with sleeves and brought it to their father, and said, "This we have found; see now whether it is your son's robe or not." 33 And he recognized it, and said, "It is my son's robe; a wild beast has devoured him; Joseph is without doubt torn to pieces." 34 Then Jacob rent his garments, and put sackcloth upon his loins, and mourned for his son many days. 35 All his sons and all his daughters rose up to comfort him; but he refused to be comforted and said, "No, I shall go down to Shē′ōl to my son, mourning." Thus his father wept for him. 36 Meanwhile the Mid′i·a·nītes had sold him in Egypt to Pot′i·phàr, an officer of Pharaoh, the captain of the guard.

38 It happened at that time that Judah went down from his brothers, and turned in to a certain A·dul′la·mīte, whose name was Hī′rah. 2 There Judah saw the daughter of a certain Canaanite whose name was Shü′a; he married her and went in to her, 3 and she conceived and bore a son, and he called his name Ēr. 4 Again she conceived and bore a son, and she called his name Ō′nàn. 5 Yet again she bore a son, and she called his name Shē′lah. She[g] was in Chē′zib when she bore him. 6 And Judah took a wife for Ēr his first-born, and her name was Tā′mär. 7 But Ēr, Judah's first-born,

was wicked in the sight of the Lord; and the Lord slew him. 8 Then Judah said to Ō′nàn, "Go in to your brother's wife, and perform the duty of a brother-in-law to her, and raise up offspring for your brother." 9 But Ō′nàn knew that the offspring would not be his; so when he went in to his brother's wife he spilled the semen on the ground, lest he should give offspring to his brother. 10 And what he did was displeasing in the sight of the Lord, and he slew him also. 11 Then Judah said to Tā′mär his daughter-in-law, "Remain a widow in your father's house, till Shē′lah my son grows up"—for he feared that he would die, like his brothers. So Tamar went and dwelt in her father's house.

12 In course of time the wife of Judah, Shü′a′s daughter, died; and when Judah was comforted, he went up to Tim′nah to his sheepshearers, he and his friend Hī′rah the A·dul′la·mīte. 13 And when Tā′mär was told, "Your father-in-law is going up to Tim′nah to shear his sheep," 14 she put off her widow's garments, and put on a veil, wrapping herself up, and sat at the entrance to E·nā′im, which is on the road to Tim′nah; for she saw that Shē′lah was grown up, and she had not been given to him in marriage. 15 When Judah saw her, he thought her to be a harlot, for she had covered her face. 16 He went over to her at the road side, and said, "Come, let me come in to you," for he did not know that she was his daughter-in-law. She said, "What will you give me, that you may come in to me?" 17 He answered, "I will send you a kid from the flock." And she said, "Will you give me a pledge, till you send it?" 18 He said, "What pledge shall I give you?" She replied, "Your signet and your cord, and your staff that is in your hand." So he gave them to her, and went in to her, and she conceived by him. 19 Then she arose and went away, and taking off her veil she put on the garments of her widowhood.

20 When Judah sent the kid by his friend the A·dul′la·mīte, to receive the pledge from the woman's hand, he could not find her. 21 And he asked the men of the place, "Where is the harlot[h] who was at E·nā′im by the wayside?" And they said, "No harlot[h] has been here." 22 So he returned to Judah, and said, "I have not found her; and also the men of the place said, 'No harlot[h] has been here.'" 23 And Judah replied, "Let her keep the things as her own

g Gk: Heb *He* h Or *cult prostitute*

lest we be laughed at; you see, I sent this kid, and you could not find her."

24 About three months later Judah was told, "Tā'mär your daughter-in-law has played the harlot; and moreover she is with child by harlotry." And Judah said, "Bring her out, and let her be burned." 25As she was being brought out, she sent word to her father-in-law, "By the man to whom these belong, I am with child." And she said, "Mark, I pray you, whose these are, the signet and the cord and the staff." 26 Then Judah acknowledged them and said, "She is more righteous than I, inasmuch as I did not give her to my son Shē'läh." And he did not lie with her again.

27 When the time of her delivery came, there were twins in her womb. 28And when she was in labor, one put out a hand; and the midwife took and bound on his hand a scarlet thread, saying, "This came out first." 29 But as he drew back his hand, behold, his brother came out; and she said, "What a breach you have made for yourself!" Therefore his name was called Per'ez.*i* 30Afterward his brother came out with the scarlet thread upon his hand; and his name was called Zē'räh.

39 Now Joseph was taken down to Egypt, and Pot'i-phär, an officer of Pharaoh, the captain of the guard, an Egyptian, bought him from the Ish'mä-el-ites who had brought him down there. 2 The LORD was with Joseph, and he became a successful man; and he was in the house of his master the Egyptian, 3 and his master saw that the LORD was with him, and that the LORD caused all that he did to prosper in his hands. 4 So Joseph found favor in his sight and attended him, and he made him overseer of his house and put him in charge of all that he had. 5 From the time that he made him overseer in his house and over all that he had the LORD blessed the Egyptian's house for Joseph's sake; the blessing of the LORD was upon all that he had, in house and field. 6 So he left all that he had in Joseph's charge; and having him he had no concern for anything but the food which he ate.

Now Joseph was handsome and good-looking. 7And after a time his master's wife cast her eyes upon Joseph, and said, "Lie with me." 8 But he refused and said to his master's wife, "Lo, having me my master has no concern about anything in the house, and he has put everything that

he has in my hand; 9 he is no greater in this house than I am; nor has he kept back anything from me except yourself, because you are his wife; how then can I do this great wickedness, and sin against God?" 10And although she spoke to Joseph day after day, he would not listen to her, to lie with her or to be with her. 11 But one day, when he went into the house to do his work and none of the men of the house was there in the house, 12 she caught him by his garment, saying, "Lie with me." But he left his garment in her hand, and fled and got out of the house. 13And when she saw that he had left his garment in her hand, and had fled out of the house, 14 she called to the men of her household and said to them, "See, he has brought among us a Hebrew to insult us; he came in to me to lie with me and I cried out with a loud voice; 15 and when he heard that I lifted up my voice and cried, he left his garment with me, and fled and got out of the house." 16 Then she laid up his garment by her until his master came home, 17 and she told him the same story, saying, "The Hebrew servant, whom you have brought among us, came in to me to insult me; 18 but as soon as I lifted up my voice and cried, he left his garment with me, and fled out of the house."

19 When his master heard the words which his wife spoke to him, "This is the way your servant treated me," his anger was kindled. 20And Joseph's master took him and put him into the prison, the place where the king's prisoners were confined, and he was there in prison. 21 But the LORD was with Joseph and showed him steadfast love, and gave him favor in the sight of the keeper of the prison. 22And the keeper of the prison committed to Joseph's care all the prisoners who were in the prison; and whatever was done there, he was the doer of it; 23 the keeper of the prison paid no heed to anything that was in Joseph's care, because the LORD was with him; and whatever he did, the LORD made it prosper.

40 Some time after this, the butler of the king of Egypt and his baker offended their lord the king of Egypt. 2And Pharaoh was angry with his two officers, the chief butler and the chief baker, 3 and he put them in custody in the house of the captain of the guard, in the prison where Joseph was confined. 4 The captain of the

---

i That is *A breach*   **39.1-2, 21:** Acts 7.9.

guard charged Joseph with them, and he waited on them; and they continued for some time in custody. 5And one night they both dreamed—the butler and the baker of the king of Egypt, who were confined in the prison—each his own dream, and each dream with its own meaning. 6 When Joseph came to them in the morning and saw them, they were troubled. 7 So he asked Pharaoh's officers who were with him in custody in his master's house, "Why are your faces downcast today?" 8 They said to him, "We have had dreams, and there is no one to interpret them." And Joseph said to them, "Do not interpretations belong to God? Tell them to me, I pray you."

9 So the chief butler told his dream to Joseph, and said to him, "In my dream there was a vine before me, 10 and on the vine there were three branches; as soon as it budded, its blossoms shot forth, and the clusters ripened into grapes. 11 Pharaoh's cup was in my hand; and I took the grapes and pressed them into Pharaoh's cup, and placed the cup in Pharaoh's hand." 12 Then Joseph said to him, "This is its interpretation: the three branches are three days; 13 within three days Pharaoh will lift up your head and restore you to your office; and you shall place Pharaoh's cup in his hand as formerly, when you were his butler. 14 But remember me, when it is well with you, and do me the kindness, I pray you, to make mention of me to Pharaoh, and so get me out of this house. 15 For I was indeed stolen out of the land of the Hebrews; and here also I have done nothing that they should put me into the dungeon."

16 When the chief baker saw that the interpretation was favorable, he said to Joseph, "I also had a dream: there were three cake baskets on my head, 17 and in the uppermost basket there were all sorts of baked food for Pharaoh, but the birds were eating it out of the basket on my head." 18And Joseph answered, "This is its interpretation: the three baskets are three days; 19 within three days Pharaoh will lift up your head—from you!—and hang you on a tree; and the birds will eat the flesh from you."

20 On the third day, which was Pharaoh's birthday, he made a feast for all his servants, and lifted up the head of the chief butler and the head of the chief baker among his servants. 21 He restored the chief butler to his butlership, and he placed the cup in

Pharaoh's hand; 22 but he hanged the chief baker, as Joseph had interpreted to them. 23 Yet the chief butler did not remember Joseph, but forgot him.

41 After two whole years, Pharaoh dreamed that he was standing by the Nile, 2 and behold, there came up out of the Nile seven cows sleek and fat, and they fed in the reed grass. 3And behold, seven other cows, gaunt and thin, came up out of the Nile after them, and stood by the other cows on the bank of the Nile. 4And the gaunt and thin cows ate up the seven sleek and fat cows. And Pharaoh awoke. 5And he fell asleep and dreamed a second time; and behold, seven ears of grain, plump and good, were growing on one stalk. 6And behold, after them sprouted seven ears, thin and blighted by the east wind. 7And the thin ears swallowed up the seven plump and full ears. And Pharaoh awoke, and behold, it was a dream. 8 So in the morning his spirit was troubled; and he sent and called for all the magicians of Egypt and all its wise men; and Pharaoh told them his dream, but there was none who could interpret it*ʲ* to Pharaoh.

9 Then the chief butler said to Pharaoh, "I remember my faults today. 10 When Pharaoh was angry with his servants, and put me and the chief baker in custody in the house of the captain of the guard, 11 we dreamed on the same night, he and I, each having a dream with its own meaning. 12A young Hebrew was there with us, a servant of the captain of the guard; and when we told him, he interpreted our dreams to us, giving an interpretation to each man according to his dream. 13And as he interpreted to us, so it came to pass; I was restored to my office, and the baker was hanged."

14 Then Pharaoh sent and called Joseph, and they brought him hastily out of the dungeon; and when he had shaved himself and changed his clothes, he came in before Pharaoh. 15And Pharaoh said to Joseph, "I have had a dream, and there is no one who can interpret it; and I have heard it said of you that when you hear a dream you can interpret it." 16 Joseph answered Pharaoh, "It is not in me; God will give Pharaoh a favorable answer." 17 Then Pharaoh said to Joseph, "Behold, in my dream I was standing on the banks of the Nile; 18 and seven cows, fat and sleek, came up out of the Nile and fed in the reed grass; 19 and seven other cows came up after them,

ʲ Gk: Heb *them*

poor and very gaunt and thin, such as I had never seen in all the land of Egypt. 20And the thin and gaunt cows ate up the first seven fat cows, 21 but when they had eaten them no one would have known that they had eaten them, for they were still as gaunt as at the beginning. Then I awoke. 22 I also saw in my dream seven ears growing on one stalk, full and good; 23 and seven ears, withered, thin, and blighted by the east wind, sprouted after them, 24 and the thin ears swallowed up the seven good ears. And I told it to the magicians, but there was no one who could explain it to me."

25 Then Joseph said to Pharaoh, "The dream of Pharaoh is one; God has revealed to Pharaoh what he is about to do. 26 The seven good cows are seven years, and the seven good ears are seven years; the dream is one. 27 The seven lean and gaunt cows that came up after them are seven years, and the seven empty ears blighted by the east wind are also seven years of famine. 28 It is as I told Pharaoh, God has shown to Pharaoh what he is about to do. 29 There will come seven years of great plenty throughout all the land of Egypt, 30 but after them there will arise seven years of famine, and all the plenty will be forgotten in the land of Egypt; the famine will consume the land, 31 and the plenty will be unknown in the land by reason of that famine which will follow, for it will be very grievous. 32And the doubling of Pharaoh's dream means that the thing is fixed by God, and God will shortly bring it to pass. 33 Now therefore let Pharaoh select a man discreet and wise, and set him over the land of Egypt. 34 Let Pharaoh proceed to appoint overseers over the land, and take the fifth part of the produce of the land of Egypt during the seven plenteous years. 35And let them gather all the food of these good years that are coming, and lay up grain under the authority of Pharaoh for food in the cities, and let them keep it. 36 That food shall be a reserve for the land against the seven years of famine which are to befall the land of Egypt, so that the land may not perish through the famine."

37 This proposal seemed good to Pharaoh and to all his servants. 38And Pharaoh said to his servants, "Can we find such a man as this, in whom is the Spirit of God?" 39 So Pharaoh said to Joseph, "Since God has shown you all this, there is none so discreet and wise as you are; 40 you shall be over my house, and all my people shall order themselves as you command; only as regards the throne will I be greater than you." 41And Pharaoh said to Joseph, "Behold, I have set you over all the land of Egypt." 42 Then Pharaoh took his signet ring from his hand, and put it on Joseph's hand, and arrayed him in garments of fine linen, and put a gold chain about his neck; 43 and he made him to ride in his second chariot; and they cried before him, "Bow the knee!"k Thus he set him over all the land of Egypt. 44 Moreover Pharaoh said to Joseph, "I am Pharaoh, and without your consent no man shall lift up hand or foot in all the land of Egypt." 45And Pharaoh called Joseph's name Zaph′é·nath-pà·nē′áh; and he gave him in marriage As′é·nath, the daughter of Pō·ti′phē·rà priest of On. So Joseph went out over the land of Egypt.

46 Joseph was thirty years old when he entered the service of Pharaoh king of Egypt. And Joseph went out from the presence of Pharaoh, and went through all the land of Egypt. 47 During the seven plenteous years the earth brought forth abundantly, 48 and he gathered up all the food of the seven years when there was plentyl in the land of Egypt, and stored up food in the cities; he stored up in every city the food from the fields around it. 49And Joseph stored up grain in great abundance like the sand of the sea, until he ceased to measure it, for it could not be measured.

50 Before the year of famine came, Joseph had two sons, whom As′é·nath, the daughter of Pō·ti′phē·rà priest of On, bore to him. 51 Joseph called the name of the first-born Mà·nas′sèh,m "For," he said, "God has made me forget all my hardship and all my father's house." 52 The name of the second he called E′phrà·im,n "For God has made me fruitful in the land of my affliction."

53 The seven years of plenty that prevailed in the land of Egypt came to an end; 54 and the seven years of famine began to come, as Joseph had said. There was famine in all lands; but in all the land of Egypt there was bread. 55 When all the land of Egypt

k *Abrek*, probably an Egyptian word similar in sound to the Hebrew word meaning *to kneel* l Sam Gk: Heb *which were* m That is *Making to forget* n From a Hebrew word meaning *to be fruitful*
41.38-45: Acts 7.10. **41.54:** Acts 7.11.

was famished, the people cried to Pharaoh for bread; and Pharaoh said to all the Egyptians, "Go to Joseph; what he says to you, do." 56 So when the famine had spread over all the land, Joseph opened all the storehouses,*o* and sold to the Egyptians, for the famine was severe in the land of Egypt. 57 Moreover, all the earth came to Egypt to Joseph to buy grain, because the famine was severe over all the earth.

42 When Jacob learned that there was grain in Egypt, he said to his sons, "Why do you look at one another?" 2And he said, "Behold, I have heard that there is grain in Egypt; go down and buy grain for us there, that we may live, and not die." 3 So ten of Joseph's brothers went down to buy grain in Egypt. 4 But Jacob did not send Benjamin, Joseph's brother, with his brothers, for he feared that harm might befall him. 5 Thus the sons of Israel came to buy among the others who came, for the famine was in the land of Canaan.

6 Now Joseph was governor over the land; he it was who sold to all the people of the land. And Joseph's brothers came, and bowed themselves before him with their faces to the ground. 7 Joseph saw his brothers, and knew them, but he treated them like strangers and spoke roughly to them. "Where do you come from?" he said. They said, "From the land of Canaan, to buy food." 8 Thus Joseph knew his brothers, but they did not know him. 9And Joseph remembered the dreams which he had dreamed of them; and he said to them, "You are spies, you have come to see the weakness of the land." 10 They said to him, "No, my lord, but to buy food have your servants come. 11 We are all sons of one man, we are honest men, your servants are not spies." 12 He said to them, "No, it is the weakness of the land that you have come to see." 13And they said, "We, your servants, are twelve brothers, the sons of one man in the land of Canaan; and behold, the youngest is this day with our father, and one is no more." 14 But Joseph said to them, "It is as I said to you, you are spies. 15 By this you shall be tested: by the life of Pharaoh, you shall not go from this place unless your youngest brother comes here. 16 Send one of you, and let him bring your brother, while you remain in prison, that your words may be tested, whether

there is truth in you; or else, by the life of Pharaoh, surely you are spies." 17And he put them all together in prison for three days.

18 On the third day Joseph said to them, "Do this and you will live, for I fear God: 19 if you are honest men, let one of your brothers remain confined in your prison, and let the rest go and carry grain for the famine of your households, 20 and bring your youngest brother to me; so your words will be verified, and you shall not die." And they did so. 21 Then they said to one another, "In truth we are guilty concerning our brother, in that we saw the distress of his soul, when he besought us and we would not listen; therefore is this distress come upon us." 22And Reuben answered them, "Did I not tell you not to sin against the lad? But you would not listen. So now there comes a reckoning for his blood." 23 They did not know that Joseph understood them, for there was an interpreter between them. 24 Then he turned away from them and wept; and he returned to them and spoke to them. And he took Simeon from them and bound him before their eyes. 25And Joseph gave orders to fill their bags with grain, and to replace every man's money in his sack, and to give them provisions for the journey. This was done for them.

26 Then they loaded their asses with their grain, and departed. 27And as one of them opened his sack to give his ass provender at the lodging place, he saw his money in the mouth of his sack; 28 and he said to his brothers, "My money has been put back; here it is in the mouth of my sack!" At this their hearts failed them, and they turned trembling to one another, saying, "What is this that God has done to us?"

29 When they came to Jacob their father in the land of Canaan, they told him all that had befallen them, saying, 30 "The man, the lord of the land, spoke roughly to us, and took us to be spies of the land. 31 But we said to him, 'We are honest men, we are not spies, 32 we are twelve brothers, sons of our father; one is no more, and the youngest is this day with our father in the land of Canaan.' 33 Then the man, the lord of the land, said to us, 'By this I shall know that you are honest men: leave one of your brothers with me, and take grain for the famine of your households, and go your way.

o Gk Vg Compare Syr: Heb *all that was in them*
42.2: Acts 7.12.   42.5: Acts 7.11.

34 Bring your youngest brother to me; then I shall know that you are not spies but honest men, and I will deliver to you your brother, and you shall trade in the land.' "

35 As they emptied their sacks, behold, every man's bundle of money was in his sack; and when they and their father saw their bundles of money, they were dismayed. 36 And Jacob their father said to them, "You have bereaved me of my children: Joseph is no more, and Simeon is no more, and now you would take Benjamin; all this has come upon me." 37 Then Reuben said to his father, "Slay my two sons if I do not bring him back to you; put him in my hands, and I will bring him back to you." 38 But he said, "My son shall not go down with you, for his brother is dead, and he only is left. If harm should befall him on the journey that you are to make, you would bring down my gray hairs with sorrow to Shē'ōl."

43 Now the famine was severe in the land. 2 And when they had eaten the grain which they had brought from Egypt, their father said to them, "Go again, buy us a little food." 3 But Judah said to him, "The man solemnly warned us, saying, 'You shall not see my face, unless your brother is with you.' 4 If you will send our brother with us, we will go down and buy you food; 5 but if you will not send him, we will not go down, for the man said to us, 'You shall not see my face, unless your brother is with you.'" 6 Israel said, "Why did you treat me so ill as to tell the man that you had another brother?" 7 They replied, "The man questioned us carefully about ourselves and our kindred, saying, 'Is your father still alive? Have you another brother?' What we told him was in answer to these questions; could we in any way know that he would say, 'Bring your brother down'?" 8 And Judah said to Israel his father, "Send the lad with me, and we will arise and go, that we may live and not die, both we and you and also our little ones. 9 I will be surety for him; of my hand you shall require him. If I do not bring him back to you and set him before you, then let me bear the blame for ever; 10 for if we had not delayed, we would now have returned twice."

11 Then their father Israel said to them, "If it must be so, then do this: take some of the choice fruits of the land in your bags, and carry down to the man a present, a little balm and a little honey, gum, myrrh, pistachio nuts, and almonds. 12 Take double the money with you; carry back with you the money that was returned in the mouth of your sacks; perhaps it was an oversight. 13 Take also your brother, and arise, go again to the man; 14 may God Almighty[p] grant you mercy before the man, that he may send back your other brother and Benjamin. If I am bereaved of my children, I am bereaved." 15 So the men took the present, and they took double the money with them, and Benjamin; and they arose and went down to Egypt, and stood before Joseph.

16 When Joseph saw Benjamin with them, he said to the steward of his house, "Bring the men into the house, and slaughter an animal and make ready, for the men are to dine with me at noon." 17 The man did as Joseph bade him, and brought the men to Joseph's house. 18 And the men were afraid because they were brought to Joseph's house, and they said, "It is because of the money, which was replaced in our sacks the first time, that we are brought in, so that he may seek occasion against us and fall upon us, to make slaves of us and seize our asses." 19 So they went up to the steward of Joseph's house, and spoke with him at the door of the house, 20 and said, "Oh, my lord, we came down the first time to buy food; 21 and when we came to the lodging place we opened our sacks, and there was every man's money in the mouth of his sack, our money in full weight; so we have brought it again with us, 22 and we have brought other money down in our hand to buy food. We do not know who put our money in our sacks." 23 He replied, "Rest assured, do not be afraid; your God and the God of your father must have put treasure in your sacks for you; I received your money." Then he brought Simeon out to them. 24 And when the man had brought the men into Joseph's house, and given them water, and they had washed their feet, and when he had given their asses provender, 25 they made ready the present for Joseph's coming at noon, for they heard that they should eat bread there.

26 When Joseph came home, they brought into the house to him the present which they had with them, and bowed down to him to the ground. 27 And he inquired about their welfare,

[p] Heb El Shaddai

and said, "Is your father well, the old man of whom you spoke? Is he still alive?" 28 They said, "Your servant our father is well, he is still alive." And they bowed their heads and made obeisance. 29And he lifted up his eyes, and saw his brother Benjamin, his mother's son, and said, "Is this your youngest brother, of whom you spoke to me? God be gracious to you, my son!" 30 Then Joseph made haste, for his heart yearned for his brother, and he sought a place to weep. And he entered his chamber and wept there. 31 Then he washed his face and came out; and controlling himself he said, "Let food be served." 32 They served him by himself, and them by themselves, and the Egyptians who ate with him by themselves, because the Egyptians might not eat bread with the Hebrews, for that is an abomination to the Egyptians. 33And they sat before him, the first-born according to his birthright and the youngest according to his youth; and the men looked at one another in amazement. 34 Portions were taken to them from Joseph's table, but Benjamin's portion was five times as much as any of theirs. So they drank and were merry with him.

44 Then he commanded the steward of his house, "Fill the men's sacks with food, as much as they can carry, and put each man's money in the mouth of his sack, 2 and put my cup, the silver cup, in the mouth of the sack of the youngest, with his money for the grain." And he did as Joseph told him. 3As soon as the morning was light, the men were sent away with their asses. 4 When they had gone but a short distance from the city, Joseph said to his steward, "Up, follow after the men; and when you overtake them, say to them, 'Why have you returned evil for good? Why have you stolen my silver cup?ᵃ 5 Is it not from this that my lord drinks, and by this that he divines? You have done wrong in so doing.'"

6 When he overtook them, he spoke to them these words. 7 They said to him, "Why does my lord speak such words as these? Far be it from your servants that they should do such a thing! 8 Behold, the money which we found in the mouth of our sacks, we brought back to you from the land of Canaan; how then should we steal silver or gold from your lord's house? 9 With whomever of your servants it be found, let him die, and we also will

be my lord's slaves." 10 He said, "Let it be as you say: he with whom it is found shall be my slave, and the rest of you shall be blameless." 11 Then every man quickly lowered his sack to the ground, and every man opened his sack. 12And he searched, beginning with the eldest and ending with the youngest; and the cup was found in Benjamin's sack. 13 Then they rent their clothes, and every man loaded his ass, and they returned to the city.

14 When Judah and his brothers came to Joseph's house, he was still there; and they fell before him to the ground. 15 Joseph said to them, "What deed is this that you have done? Do you not know that such a man as I can indeed divine?" 16And Judah said, "What shall we say to my lord? What shall we speak? Or how can we clear ourselves? God has found out the guilt of your servants; behold, we are my lord's slaves, both we and he also in whose hand the cup has been found." 17 But he said, "Far be it from me that I should do so! Only the man in whose hand the cup was found shall be my slave; but as for you, go up in peace to your father."

18 Then Judah went up to him and said, "O my lord, let your servant, I pray you, speak a word in my lord's ears, and let not your anger burn against your servant; for you are like Pharaoh himself. 19 My lord asked his servants, saying, 'Have you a father, or a brother?' 20And we said to my lord, 'We have a father, an old man, and a young brother, the child of his old age; and his brother is dead, and he alone is left of his mother's children; and his father loves him.' 21 Then you said to your servants, 'Bring him down to me, that I may set my eyes upon him.' 22 We said to my lord, 'The lad cannot leave his father, for if he should leave his father, his father would die.' 23 Then you said to your servants, 'Unless your youngest brother comes down with you, you shall see my face no more.' 24 When we went back to your servant my father we told him the words of my lord. 25And when our father said, 'Go again, buy us a little food,' 26 we said, 'We cannot go down. If our youngest brother goes with us, then we will go down; for we cannot see the man's face unless our youngest brother is with us.' 27 Then your servant my father said to us, 'You know that my wife bore me two sons; 28 one left me, and I said, Surely he has been torn to pieces; and I have never seen

ᵃ Gk Compare Vg: Heb lacks *Why have you stolen my silver cup?*

him since. 29 If you take this one also from me, and harm befalls him, you will bring down my gray hairs in sorrow to Shĕ'ōl.' 30 Now therefore, when I come to your servant my father, and the lad is not with us, then, as his life is bound up in the lad's life, 31 when he sees that the lad is not with us, he will die; and your servants will bring down the gray hairs of your servant our father with sorrow to Shĕ'ōl. 32 For your servant became surety for the lad to my father, saying, 'If I do not bring him back to you, then I shall bear the blame in the sight of my father all my life.' 33 Now therefore, let your servant, I pray you, remain instead of the lad as a slave to my lord; and let the lad go back with his brothers. 34 For how can I go back to my father if the lad is not with me? I fear to see the evil that would come upon my father."

45 Then Joseph could not control himself before all those who stood by him; and he cried, "Make every one go out from me." So no one stayed with him when Joseph made himself known to his brothers. 2 And he wept aloud, so that the Egyptians heard it, and the household of Pharaoh heard it. 3 And Joseph said to his brothers, "I am Joseph; is my father still alive?" But his brothers could not answer him, for they were dismayed at his presence.

4 So Joseph said to his brothers, "Come near to me, I pray you." And they came near. And he said, "I am your brother, Joseph, whom you sold into Egypt. 5 And now do not be distressed, or angry with yourselves, because you sold me here; for God sent me before you to preserve life. 6 For the famine has been in the land these two years; and there are yet five years in which there will be neither plowing nor harvest. 7 And God sent me before you to preserve for you a remnant on earth, and to keep alive for you many survivors. 8 So it was not you who sent me here, but God; and he has made me a father to Pharaoh, and lord of all his house and ruler over all the land of Egypt. 9 Make haste and go up to my father and say to him, 'Thus says your son Joseph, God has made me lord of all Egypt; come down to me, do not tarry; 10 you shall dwell in the land of Gō'shĕn, and you shall be near me, you and your children and your children's children, and your flocks, your herds, and all that you have; 11 and there I will provide for you, for

there are yet five years of famine to come; lest you and your household, and all that you have, come to poverty.' 12 And now your eyes see, and the eyes of my brother Benjamin see, that it is my mouth that speaks to you. 13 You must tell my father of all my splendor in Egypt, and of all that you have seen. Make haste and bring my father down here." 14 Then he fell upon his brother Benjamin's neck and wept; and Benjamin wept upon his neck. 15 And he kissed all his brothers and wept upon them; and after that his brothers talked with him.

16 When the report was heard in Pharaoh's house, "Joseph's brothers have come," it pleased Pharaoh and his servants well. 17 And Pharaoh said to Joseph, "Say to your brothers, 'Do this: load your beasts and go back to the land of Canaan; 18 and take your father and your households, and come to me, and I will give you the best of the land of Egypt, and you shall eat the fat of the land.' 19 Command them' also, 'Do this: take wagons from the land of Egypt for your little ones and for your wives, and bring your father, and come. 20 Give no thought to your goods, for the best of all the land of Egypt is yours.' "

21 The sons of Israel did so; and Joseph gave them wagons, according to the command of Pharaoh, and gave them provisions for the journey. 22 To each and all of them he gave festal garments; but to Benjamin he gave three hundred shekels of silver and five festal garments. 23 To his father he sent as follows: ten asses loaded with the good things of Egypt, and ten she-asses loaded with grain, bread, and provision for his father on the journey. 24 Then he sent his brothers away, and as they departed, he said to them, "Do not quarrel on the way." 25 So they went up out of Egypt, and came to the land of Canaan to their father Jacob. 26 And they told him, "Joseph is still alive, and he is ruler over all the land of Egypt." And his heart fainted, for he did not believe them. 27 But when they told him all the words of Joseph, which he had said to them, and when he saw the wagons which Joseph had sent to carry him, the spirit of their father Jacob revived; 28 and Israel said, "It is enough; Joseph my son is still alive; I will go and see him before I die."

46 So Israel took his journey with all that he had, and came to Beer-sheba, and offered sacrifices to

---

r Compare Gk Vg: Heb *you are commanded*   45.1: Acts 7.13.

the God of his father Isaac. 2And God spoke to Israel in visions of the night, and said, "Jacob, Jacob." And he said, "Here am I." 3 Then he said, "I am God, the God of your father; do not be afraid to go down to Egypt; for I will there make of you a great nation. 4 I will go down with you to Egypt, and I will also bring you up again; and Joseph's hand shall close your eyes." 5 Then Jacob set out from Beer-sheba; and the sons of Israel carried Jacob their father, their little ones, and their wives, in the wagons which Pharaoh had sent to carry him. 6 They also took their cattle and their goods, which they had gained in the land of Canaan, and came into Egypt, Jacob and all his offspring with him, 7 his sons, and his sons' sons with him, his daughters, and his sons' daughters; all his offspring he brought with him into Egypt.

8 Now these are the names of the descendants of Israel, who came into Egypt, Jacob and his sons. Reuben, Jacob's first-born, 9 and the sons of Reuben: Hā′noch, Pal′lū, Hez′ron, and Cär′mi. 10 The sons of Simeon: Jĕ-mū′el, Jā′min, Ō′had, Jā′chin, Zō′här, and Shā′ul, the son of a Canaanitish woman. 11 The sons of Levi: Gēr′shon, Kō′hath, and Mĕ-râr′ī. 12 The sons of Judah: Ēr, Ō′nàn, Shē′lāh, Per′ez, and Zē′ràh (but Er and Onan died in the land of Canaan); and the sons of Perez were Hez′ron and Hā′múl. 13 The sons of Is′sa-chär: Tō′là, Pū′vàh, Iōb, and Shim′ron. 14 The sons of Zeb′ū-lùn: Sē′rĕd, Ē′lon, and Jäh′lē-ĕl 15 (these are the sons of Leah, whom she bore to Jacob in Pad′dàn-âr′àm, together with his daughter Dinah; altogether his sons and his daughters numbered thirty-three). 16 The sons of Gad: Ziph′i-ȯn, Hag′gi, Shū′ni, Ez′bȯn, Ē′ri, À-rō′di, and À-rē′li. 17 The sons of Ash′ér: Im′nàh, Ish′-vàh, Ish′vi, Bē-ri′àh, with Sē′ràh their sister. And the sons of Beriah: Hē′bér and Mal′chi-el 18 (these are the sons of Zil′pàh, whom Lā′bàn gave to Leah his daughter; and these she bore to Jacob—sixteen persons). 19 The sons of Rachel, Jacob's wife: Joseph and Benjamin. 20And to Joseph in the land of Egypt were born Mà-nas′sĕh and Ē′phrà-im, whom Às′é-nath, the daughter of Pō-ti′phé-rà the priest of Ōn, bore to him. 21And the sons of Benjamin: Bē′là, Bē′chér, Ash′bel, Gē′rà, Nā′à-man, Ē′hi, Rosh, Mup′pim, Hup′pim, and Ārd 22 (these are the sons of Rachel, who were born to

Jacob—fourteen persons in all). 23 The sons of Dan: Hū′shim. 24 The sons of Naph′tà-li: Jäh′zē-ĕl, Gū′ni, Jē′zér, and Shil′lem 25 (these are the sons of Bil′hàh, whom Lā′bàn gave to Rachel his daughter, and these she bore to Jacob—seven persons in all). 26All the persons belonging to Jacob who came into Egypt, who were his own off-spring, not including Jacob's sons' wives, were sixty-six persons in all; 27 and the sons of Joseph, who were born to him in Egypt, were two; all the persons of the house of Jacob, that came into Egypt, were seventy.

28 He sent Judah before him to Joseph, to appears before him in Gō′shĕn; and they came into the land of Goshen. 29 Then Joseph made ready his chariot and went up to meet Israel his father in Gō′shĕn; and he presented himself to him, and fell on his neck, and wept on his neck a good while. 30 Israel said to Joseph, "Now let me die, since I have seen your face and know that you are still alive." 31 Joseph said to his brothers and to his father's household, "I will go up and tell Pharaoh, and will say to him, 'My brothers and my father's household, who were in the land of Canaan, have come to me; 32 and the men are shepherds, for they have been keepers of cattle; and they have brought their flocks, and their herds, and all that they have.' 33 When Pharaoh calls you, and says, 'What is your occupation?' 34 you shall say, 'Your servants have been keepers of cattle from our youth even until now, both we and our fathers,' in order that you may dwell in the land of Gō′shĕn; for every shepherd is an abomination to the Egyptians."

47 So Joseph went in and told Pharaoh, "My father and my brothers, with their flocks and herds and all that they possess, have come from the land of Canaan; they are now in the land of Gō′shĕn." 2And from among his brothers he took five men and presented them to Pharaoh. 3 Pharaoh said to his brothers, "What is your occupation?" And they said to Pharaoh, "Your servants are shepherds, as our fathers were." 4 They said to Pharaoh, "We have come to sojourn in the land; for there is no pasture for your servants' flocks, for the famine is severe in the land of Canaan; and now, we pray you, let your servants dwell in the land of Gō′shĕn." 5 Then Pharaoh said to Joseph, "Your father and

your brothers have come to you. 6 The land of Egypt is before you; settle your father and your brothers in the best of the land; let them dwell in the land of Gō'shĕn; and if you know any able men among them, put them in charge of my cattle."

7 Then Joseph brought in Jacob his father, and set him before Pharaoh, and Jacob blessed Pharaoh. 8And Pharaoh said to Jacob, "How many are the days of the years of your life?" 9And Jacob said to Pharaoh, "The days of the years of my sojourning are a hundred and thirty years; few and evil have been the days of the years of my life, and they have not attained to the days of the years of the life of my fathers in the days of their sojourning." 10And Jacob blessed Pharaoh, and went out from the presence of Pharaoh. 11 Then Joseph settled his father and his brothers, and gave them a possession in the land of Egypt, in the best of the land, in the land of Ram'ĕ-sēs, as Pharaoh had commanded. 12And Joseph provided his father, his brothers, and all his father's household with food, according to the number of their dependents.

13 Now there was no food in all the land; for the famine was very severe, so that the land of Egypt and the land of Canaan languished by reason of the famine. 14And Joseph gathered up all the money that was found in the land of Egypt and in the land of Canaan, for the grain which they bought; and Joseph brought the money into Pharaoh's house. 15And when the money was all spent in the land of Egypt and in the land of Canaan, all the Egyptians came to Joseph, and said, "Give us food; why should we die before your eyes? For our money is gone." 16And Joseph answered, "Give your cattle, and I will give you food in exchange for your cattle, if your money is gone." 17 So they brought their cattle to Joseph; and Joseph gave them food in exchange for the horses, the flocks, the herds, and the asses: and he supplied them with food in exchange for all their cattle that year. 18And when that year was ended, they came to him the following year, and said to him, "We will not hide from my lord that our money is all spent; and the herds of cattle are my lord's; there is nothing left in the sight of my lord but our bodies and our lands. 19 Why should we die before your eyes, both we and our land? Buy us and our land for food, and we with our land will be

slaves to Pharaoh; and give us seed, that we may live, and not die, and that the land may not be desolate."

20 So Joseph bought all the land of Egypt for Pharaoh; for all the Egyptians sold their fields, because the famine was severe upon them. The land became Pharaoh's; 21 and as for the people, he made slaves of them*f* from one end of Egypt to the other. 22 Only the land of the priests he did not buy; for the priests had a fixed allowance from Pharaoh, and lived on the allowance which Pharaoh gave them; therefore they did not sell their land. 23 Then Joseph said to the people, "Behold, I have this day bought you and your land for Pharaoh. Now here is seed for you, and you shall sow the land. 24And at the harvests you shall give a fifth to Pharaoh, and four fifths shall be your own, as seed for the field and as food for yourselves and your households, and as food for your little ones." 25And they said, "You have saved our lives; may it please my lord, we will be slaves to Pharaoh." 26 So Joseph made it a statute concerning the land of Egypt, and it stands to this day, that Pharaoh should have the fifth; the land of the priests alone did not become Pharaoh's.

27 Thus Israel dwelt in the land of Egypt, in the land of Gō'shĕn; and they gained possessions in it, and were fruitful and multiplied exceedingly. 28And Jacob lived in the land of Egypt seventeen years; so the days of Jacob, the years of his life, were a hundred and forty-seven years.

29 And when the time drew near that Israel must die, he called his son Joseph and said to him, "If now I have found favor in your sight, put your hand under my thigh, and promise to deal loyally and truly with me. Do not bury me in Egypt; 30 but let me lie with my fathers; carry me out of Egypt and bury me in their burying place." He answered, "I will do as you have said." 31And he said, "Swear to me"; and he swore to him. Then Israel bowed himself upon the head of his bed.

48 After this Joseph was told, "Behold, your father is ill"; so he took with him his two sons, Mà-nas'sĕh and Ē'phrà-im. 2And it was told to Jacob, "Your son Joseph has come to you"; then Israel summoned his strength, and sat up in bed. 3And Jacob said to Joseph, "God Almighty*u* appeared to me at Luz in the land of Canaan and blessed me, 4 and said to

f Sam Gk Compare Vg: Heb *he removed them to the cities*   *u* Heb *El Shaddai* me, 'Behold, I will make you fruitful, and multiply you, and I will make of you a company of peoples, and will give this land to your descendants after you for an everlasting possession.' 5And now your two sons, who were born to you in the land of Egypt before I came to you in Egypt, are mine; É′phrà·im and Mà·nas′seh shall be mine, as Reuben and Simeon are. 6And the offspring born to you after them shall be yours; they shall be called by the name of their brothers in their inheritance. 7 For when I came from Pad′dàn, Rachel to my sorrow died in the land of Canaan on the way, when there was still some distance to go to Eph′rath; and I buried her there on the way to Ephrath (that is, Bethlehem)."

8 When Israel saw Joseph's sons, he said, "Who are these?" 9 Joseph said to his father, "They are my sons, whom God has given me here." And he said, "Bring them to me, I pray you, that I may bless them." 10 Now the eyes of Israel were dim with age, so that he could not see. So Joseph brought them near him; and he kissed them and embraced them. 11And Israel said to Joseph, "I had not thought to see your face; and lo, God has let me see your children also." 12 Then Joseph removed them from his knees, and he bowed himself with his face to the earth. 13And Joseph took them both, É′phrà·im in his right hand toward Israel's left hand, and Mà·nas′seh in his left hand toward Israel's right hand, and brought them near him. 14And Israel stretched out his right hand and laid it upon the head of É′phrà·im, who was the younger, and his left hand upon the head of Mà·nas′seh, crossing his hands, for Manasseh was the first-born. 15And he blessed Joseph, and said,

"The God before whom my fathers
    Abraham and Isaac walked,
  the God who has led me all my life
    long to this day,
16 the angel who has redeemed me
    from all evil, bless the lads;
  and in them let my name be perpet-
    uated, and the name of my fathers
    Abraham and Isaac;
  and let them grow into a multitude
    in the midst of the earth."

17 When Joseph saw that his father laid his right hand upon the head of É′phrà·im, it displeased him; and he took his father's hand, to remove it from Ephraim's head to Mà·nas′seh's head. 18And Joseph said to his father,

"Not so, my father; for this one is the first-born; put your right hand upon his head." 19 But his father refused, and said, "I know, my son, I know; he also shall become a people, and he also shall be great; nevertheless his younger brother shall be greater than he, and his descendants shall become a multitude of nations." 20 So he blessed them that day, saying,

"By you Israel will pronounce bless-
    ings, saying,
  'God make you as É′phrà·im and as
    Mà·nas′seh' ";
and thus he put Ephraim before Ma-
nasseh. 21 Then Israel said to Joseph, "Behold, I am about to die, but God will be with you, and will bring you again to the land of your fathers. 22 Moreover I have given to you rather than to your brothers one mountain slope[v] which I took from the hand of the Am′ò·rites with my sword and with my bow."

49 Then Jacob called his sons, and said, "Gather yourselves together, that I may tell you what shall befall you in days to come.

2 Assemble and hear, O sons of Jacob,
    and hearken to Israel your father.
3 Reuben, you are my first-born,
    my might, and the first fruits of
      my strength,
  pre-eminent in pride and pre-
    eminent in power.
4 Unstable as water, you shall not
    have pre-eminence
  because you went up to your
    father's bed;
  then you defiled it—you[w] went
    up to my couch!

5 Simeon and Levi are brothers;
    weapons of violence are their
      swords.
6 O my soul, come not into their
    council;
  O my spirit,[x] be not joined to
    their company;
  for in their anger they slay men,
    and in their wantonness they ham-
      string oxen.
7 Cursed be their anger, for it is
    fierce;
  and their wrath, for it is cruel!
  I will divide them in Jacob
    and scatter them in Israel.

8 Judah, your brothers shall praise
    you;
  your hand shall be on the neck of
    your enemies;
  your father's sons shall bow down
    before you.

v Heb *shekem*, shoulder   w Gk Syr Tg: Heb *he*   x Or *glory*

9 Judah is a lion's whelp;
  from the prey, my son, you have
    gone up.
He stooped down, he couched as a
    lion,
  and as a lioness; who dares rouse
    him up?
10 The scepter shall not depart from
    Judah,
  nor the ruler's staff from between
    his feet,
until he comes to whom it belongs;[y]
  and to him shall be the obedience
    of the peoples.
11 Binding his foal to the vine
  and his ass's colt to the choice
    vine,
he washes his garments in wine
  and his vesture in the blood of
    grapes;
12 his eyes shall be red with wine,
  and his teeth white with milk.

13 Zeb'ū·lŭn shall dwell at the shore of
    the sea;
  he shall become a haven for ships,
  and his border shall be at Sī'don.

14 Is'sā·chär is a strong ass,
    crouching between the sheep-
    folds;
15 he saw that a resting place was good,
  and that the land was pleasant;
so he bowed his shoulder to bear,
  and became a slave at forced labor.

16 Dan shall judge his people
  as one of the tribes of Israel.
17 Dan shall be a serpent in the way,
    a viper by the path,
  that bites the horse's heels
    so that his rider falls backward.
18 I wait for thy salvation, O LORD.

19 Raiders[z] shall raid Gad,
  but he shall raid at their heels.

20 Ash'ēr's food shall be rich,
  and he shall yield royal dainties.

21 Naph'tā·lī is a hind let loose,
  that bears comely fawns.[a]

22 Joseph is a fruitful bough,
    a fruitful bough by a spring;
  his branches run over the wall.
23 The archers fiercely attacked him,
    shot at him, and harassed him
    sorely;
24 yet his bow remained unmoved,

his arms[b] were made agile
  by the hands of the Mighty One of
    Jacob
  (by the name of the Shepherd,
    the Rock of Israel),
25 by the God of your father who will
    help you
  by God Almighty[u] who will bless
    you
  with blessings of heaven above,
  blessings of the deep that couches
    beneath,
  blessings of the breasts and of the
    womb.
26 The blessings of your father
  are mighty beyond the blessings
    of the eternal mountains,[c]
  the bounties of the everlasting
    hills;
may they be on the head of Joseph,
  and on the brow of him who was
    separate from his brothers.

27 Benjamin is a ravenous wolf,
    in the morning devouring the
    prey,
  and at even dividing the spoil."

28 All these are the twelve tribes of
Israel; and this is what their father
said to them as he blessed them, blessing each with the blessing suitable to
him. 29 Then he charged them, and
said to them, "I am to be gathered to
my people; bury me with my fathers
in the cave that is in the field of
E'phrŏn the Hit'tite, 30 in the cave
that is in the field at Mach-pē'lah, to
the east of Mam're, in the land of
Canaan, which Abraham bought with
the field from E'phrŏn the Hit'tite to
possess as a burying place. 31 There
they buried Abraham and Sarah his
wife; there they buried Isaac and
Rebekah his wife; and there I buried
Leah—32 the field and the cave that
is in it were purchased from the Hit'-
tites." 33 When Jacob finished charging his sons, he drew up his feet into
the bed, and breathed his last, and
was gathered to his people.

50 Then Joseph fell on his father's
face, and wept over him, and
kissed him. 2 And Joseph commanded
his servants the physicians to embalm
his father. So the physicians embalmed
Israel; 3 forty days were required for
it, for so many are required for embalming. And the Egyptians wept for
him seventy days.

---

[y] Syr Compare Tg: Heb *until Shiloh comes* or *until he comes to Shiloh*
[z] Heb *gedud*, a raiding troop   [a] Or *who gives beautiful words*
[b] Heb *the arms of his hands*   [u] Heb *El Shaddai*
[c] Compare Gk: Heb *of my progenitors to*
49.9-10: Num 24.9; Rev 5.5.

4 And when the days of weeping for him were past, Joseph spoke to the household of Pharaoh, saying, "If now I have found favor in your eyes, speak, I pray you, in the ears of Pharaoh, saying, 5 My father made me swear, saying, 'I am about to die: in my tomb which I hewed out for myself in the land of Canaan, there shall you bury me.' Now therefore let me go up, I pray you, and bury my father; then I will return." 6And Pharaoh answered, "Go up, and bury your father, as he made you swear." 7 So Joseph went up to bury his father; and with him went up all the servants of Pharaoh, the elders of his household, and all the elders of the land of Egypt, 8 as well as all the household of Joseph, his brothers, and his father's household; only their children, their flocks, and their herds were left in the land of Gō'shĕn. 9And there went up with him both chariots and horsemen; it was a very great company. 10 When they came to the threshing floor of Ā'tad, which is beyond the Jordan, they lamented there with a very great and sorrowful lamentation; and he made a mourning for his father seven days. 11 When the inhabitants of the land, the Canaanites, saw the mourning on the threshing floor of Ā'tad, they said, "This is a grievous mourning to the Egyptians." Therefore the place was named Ā'bĕl-miz'ră·im;*d* it is beyond the Jordan. 12 Thus his sons did for him as he had commanded them; 13 for his sons carried him to the land of Canaan, and buried him in the cave of the field at Mach-pē'lăh, to the east of the field of Mam're, which Abraham bought with the field from Ē'phrŏn the Hit'-tīte, to possess as a burying place. 14After he had buried his father, Joseph returned to Egypt with his

d That is meadow (or mourning) of Egypt

brothers and all who had gone up with him to bury his father.

15 When Joseph's brothers saw that their father was dead, they said, "It may be that Joseph will hate us and pay us back for all the evil which we did to him." 16 So they sent a message to Joseph, saying, "Your father gave this command before he died, 17 'Say to Joseph, Forgive, I pray you, the transgression of your brothers and their sin, because they did evil to you.' And now, we pray you, forgive the transgression of the servants of the God of your father." Joseph wept when they spoke to him. 18 His brothers also came and fell down before him, and said, "Behold, we are your servants." 19 But Joseph said to them, "Fear not, for am I in the place of God? 20As for you, you meant evil against me; but God meant it for good, to bring it about that many people should be kept alive, as they are today. 21 So do not fear; I will provide for you and your little ones." Thus he reassured them and comforted them.

22 So Joseph dwelt in Egypt, he and his father's house; and Joseph lived a hundred and ten years. 23And Joseph saw Ē'phră·im's children of the third generation; the children also of Mā'chir the son of Mă·nas'sĕh were born upon Joseph's knees. 24And Joseph said to his brothers, "I am about to die; but God will visit you, and bring you up out of this land to the land which he swore to Abraham, to Isaac, and to Jacob." 25 Then Joseph took an oath of the sons of Israel, saying, "God will visit you, and you shall carry up my bones from here." 26 So Joseph died, being a hundred and ten years old; and they embalmed him, and he was put in a coffin in Egypt.

50.13: Acts 7.16.

THE SECOND BOOK OF MOSES

COMMONLY CALLED

EXODUS

These are the names of the sons of Israel who came to Egypt with Jacob, each with his household: 2 Reuben, Simeon, Levi, and Judah, 3 Is′sachär, Zeb′ū·lún, and Benjamin, 4 Dan and Naph′tà·lĭ, Gad and Ash′ér. 5All the offspring of Jacob were seventy persons; Joseph was already in Egypt. 6 Then Joseph died, and all his brothers, and all that generation. 7 But the descendants of Israel were fruitful and increased greatly; they multiplied and grew exceedingly strong; so that the land was filled with them.

8 Now there arose a new king over Egypt, who did not know Joseph. 9And he said to his people, "Behold, the people of Israel are too many and too mighty for us. 10 Come, let us deal shrewdly with them, lest they multiply, and, if war befall us, they join our enemies and fight against us and escape from the land." 11 Therefore they set taskmasters over them to afflict them with heavy burdens; and they built for Pharaoh store cities, Pi′thom and Rā·am′ses. 12 But the more they were oppressed, the more they multiplied and the more they spread abroad. And the Egyptians were in dread of the people of Israel. 13 So they made the people of Israel serve with rigor, 14 and made their lives bitter with hard service, in mortar and brick, and in all kinds of work in the field; in all their work they made them serve with rigor.

15 Then the king of Egypt said to the Hebrew midwives, one of whom was named Shiph′rah and the other Pū′ah, 16 "When you serve as midwife to the Hebrew women, and see them upon the birthstool, if it is a son, you shall kill him; but if it is a daughter, she shall live." 17 But the midwives feared God, and did not do as the king of Egypt commanded them, but let the male children live. 18 So the king of Egypt called the midwives, and said

to them, "Why have you done this, and let the male children live?" 19 The midwives said to Pharaoh, "Because the Hebrew women are not like the Egyptian women; for they are vigorous and are delivered before the midwife comes to them." 20 So God dealt well with the midwives; and the people multiplied and grew very strong. 21And because the midwives feared God he gave them families. 22 Then Pharaoh commanded all his people, "Every son that is born to the Hebrews*a* you shall cast into the Nile, but you shall let every daughter live."

2 Now a man from the house of Levi went and took to wife a daughter of Levi. 2 The woman conceived and bore a son; and when she saw that he was a goodly child, she hid him three months. 3And when she could hide him no longer she took for him a basket made of bulrushes, and daubed it with bitumen and pitch; and she put the child in it and placed it among the reeds at the river's brink. 4And his sister stood at a distance, to know what would be done to him. 5 Now the daughter of Pharaoh came down to bathe at the river, and her maidens walked beside the river; she saw the basket among the reeds and sent her maid to fetch it. 6 When she opened it she saw the child; and lo, the babe was crying. She took pity on him and said, "This is one of the Hebrews' children." 7 Then his sister said to Pharaoh's daughter, "Shall I go and call you a nurse from the Hebrew women to nurse the child for you?" 8And Pharaoh's daughter said to her, "Go." So the girl went and called the child's mother. 9And Pharaoh's daughter said to her, "Take this child away, and nurse him for me, and I will give you your wages." So the woman took the child and nursed him. 10And the child grew, and she brought him to Pharaoh's daughter, and he became her son; and she named him

---

a Sam Gk Tg: Heb lacks *to the Hebrews*
1.1-4: Gen 46.8-27; Num 26.4-50. **1.5-8:** Acts 7.14-18. **1.10-11, 22:** Acts 7.19.
2.2: Acts 7.20; Heb 11.23. **2.5, 10:** Acts 7.21.

45

Moses,[b] for she said, "Because I drew him out[c] of the water."

11 One day, when Moses had grown up, he went out to his people and looked on their burdens; and he saw an Egyptian beating a Hebrew, one of his people. 12 He looked this way and that, and seeing no one he killed the Egyptian and hid him in the sand. 13 When he went out the next day, behold, two Hebrews were struggling together; and he said to the man that did the wrong, "Why do you strike your fellow?" 14 He answered, "Who made you a prince and a judge over us? Do you mean to kill me as you killed the Egyptian?" Then Moses was afraid, and thought, "Surely the thing is known." 15 When Pharaoh heard of it, he sought to kill Moses.

But Moses fled from Pharaoh, and stayed in the land of Mid'i·an; and he sat down by a well. 16 Now the priest of Mid'i·an had seven daughters; and they came and drew water, and filled the troughs to water their father's flock. 17 The shepherds came and drove them away; but Moses stood up and helped them, and watered their flock. 18 When they came to their father Reü'el, he said, "How is it that you have come so soon today?" 19 They said, "An Egyptian delivered us out of the hand of the shepherds, and even drew water for us and watered the flock." 20 He said to his daughters, "And where is he? Why have you left the man? Call him, that he may eat bread." 21 And Moses was content to dwell with the man, and he gave Moses his daughter Zip·po'rah. 22 She bore a son, and he called his name Ger'shom; for he said, "I have been a sojourner[d] in a foreign land."

23 In the course of those many days the king of Egypt died. And the people of Israel groaned under their bondage, and cried out for help, and their cry under bondage came up to God. 24 And God heard their groaning, and God remembered his covenant with Abraham, with Isaac, and with Jacob. 25 And God saw the people of Israel, and God knew their condition.

3 Now Moses was keeping the flock of his father-in-law, Jethro, the priest of Mid'i·an; and he led his flock to the west side of the wilderness, and came to Hō'reb, the mountain of God. 2 And the angel of the LORD appeared to him in a flame of fire out of the midst of a bush; and he looked, and lo, the bush was burning, yet it was not consumed. 3 And Moses said, "I will turn aside and see this great sight, why the bush is not burnt." 4 When the LORD saw that he turned aside to see, God called to him out of the bush, "Moses, Moses!" And he said, "Here am I." 5 Then he said, "Do not come near; put off your shoes from your feet, for the place on which you are standing is holy ground." 6 And he said, "I am the God of your father, the God of Abraham, the God of Isaac, and the God of Jacob." And Moses hid his face, for he was afraid to look at God.

7 Then the LORD said, "I have seen the affliction of my people who are in Egypt, and have heard their cry because of their taskmasters; I know their sufferings, 8 and I have come down to deliver them out of the hand of the Egyptians, and to bring them up out of that land to a good and broad land, a land flowing with milk and honey, to the place of the Canaanites, the Hit'tites, the Am'ō·rites, the Per'iz·zites, the Hī'vites, and the Jeb'ū·sites. 9 And now, behold, the cry of the people of Israel has come to me, and I have seen the oppression with which the Egyptians oppress them. 10 Come, I will send you to Pharaoh that you may bring forth my people, the sons of Israel, out of Egypt." 11 But Moses said to God, "Who am I that I should go to Pharaoh, and bring the sons of Israel out of Egypt?" 12 He said, "But I will be with you; and this shall be the sign for you, that I have sent you: when you have brought forth the people out of Egypt, you shall serve God upon this mountain."

13 Then Moses said to God, "If I come to the people of Israel and say to them, 'The God of your fathers has sent me to you,' and they ask me, 'What is his name?' what shall I say to them?" 14 God said to Moses, "I AM WHO I AM."[e] And he said, "Say this to the people of Israel, 'I AM has sent me to you.'" 15 God also said to Moses, "Say this to the people of Israel, 'The LORD,[f] the God of your

---

[b] Heb *Mosheh*   [c] Heb *mashah*   [d] Heb *ger*
[e] Or I AM WHAT I AM or I WILL BE WHAT I WILL BE
[f] The word LORD when spelled with capital letters, stands for the divine name, *YHWH*, which is here connected with the verb *hayah*, to be

2.11: Acts 7.23; Heb 11.24.   2.12: Acts 7.24.   2.14: Acts 7.27-28.
2.15, 22: Acts 7.29.   2.24: Acts 7.34.   3.2: Acts 7.30.   3.1-4, 17: Ex 6.2-13.
3.5: Acts 7.33.   3.6: Mt 22.32; Mk 12.26; Lk 20.37; Acts 3-13; 7.32.

fathers, the God of Abraham, the God of Isaac, and the God of Jacob, has sent me to you': this is my name for ever, and thus I am to be remembered throughout all generations. 16 Go and gather the elders of Israel together, and say to them, 'The LORD, the God of your fathers, the God of Abraham, of Isaac, and of Jacob, has appeared to me, saying, "I have observed you and what has been done to you in Egypt; 17 and I promise that I will bring you up out of the affliction of Egypt, to the land of the Canaanites, the Hit´tites, the Am´o·rites, the Per´iz·zites, the Hi´vites, and the Jeb´u·sites, a land flowing with milk and honey." ' 18And they will hearken to your voice; and you and the elders of Israel shall go to the king of Egypt and say to him, 'The LORD, the God of the Hebrews, has met with us; and now, we pray you, let us go a three days' journey into the wilderness, that we may sacrifice to the LORD our God.' 19 I know that the king of Egypt will not let you go unless compelled by a mighty hand.g 20 So I will stretch out my hand and smite Egypt with all the wonders which I will do in it; after that he will let you go. 21And I will give this people favor in the sight of the Egyptians; and when you go, you shall not go empty, 22 but each woman shall ask of her neighbor, and of her who sojourns in her house, jewelry of silver and of gold, and clothing, and you shall put them on your sons and on your daughters; thus you shall despoil the Egyptians."

4 Then Moses answered, "But behold, they will not believe me or listen to my voice, for they will say, 'The LORD did not appear to you.' " 2 The LORD said to him, "What is that in your hand?" He said, "A rod." 3And he said, "Cast it on the ground." So he cast it on the ground, and it became a serpent; and Moses fled from it. 4 But the LORD said to Moses, "Put out your hand, and take it by the tail"— so he put out his hand and caught it, and it became a rod in his hand—5 "that they may believe that the LORD, the God of their fathers, the God of Abraham, the God of Isaac, and the God of Jacob, has appeared to you." 6Again, the LORD said to him, "Put your hand into your bosom." And he put his hand into his bosom; and when he took it out, behold, his hand was leprous, as white as snow. 7 Then God said, "Put your hand back into your bosom." So he put his

hand back into his bosom; and when he took it out, behold, it was restored like the rest of his flesh. 8 "If they will not believe you," God said, "or heed the first sign, they may believe the latter sign. 9 If they will not believe even these two signs or heed your voice, you shall take some water from the Nile and pour it upon the dry ground; and the water which you shall take from the Nile will become blood upon the dry ground."

10 But Moses said to the LORD, "Oh, my Lord, I am not eloquent, either heretofore or since thou hast spoken to thy servant; but I am slow of speech and of tongue." 11 Then the LORD said to him, "Who has made man's mouth? Who makes him dumb, or deaf, or seeing, or blind? Is it not I, the LORD? 12 Now therefore go, and I will be with your mouth and teach you what you shall speak." 13 But he said, "Oh, my Lord, send, I pray, some other person." 14 Then the anger of the LORD was kindled against Moses and he said, "Is there not Aaron, your brother, the Levite? I know that he can speak well; and behold, he is coming out to meet you, and when he sees you he will be glad in his heart. 15And you shall speak to him and put the words in his mouth; and I will be with your mouth and with his mouth, and will teach you what you shall do. 16 He shall speak for you to the people; and he shall be a mouth for you, and you shall be to him as God. 17And you shall take in your hand this rod, with which you shall do the signs."

18 Moses went back to Jethro his father-in-law and said to him, "Let me go back, I pray, to my kinsmen in Egypt and see whether they are still alive." And Jethro said to Moses, "Go in peace." 19And the LORD said to Moses in Mid´i·an, "Go back to Egypt; for all the men who were seeking your life are dead." 20 So Moses took his wife and his sons and set them on an ass, and went back to the land of Egypt; and in his hand Moses took the rod of God.

21 And the LORD said to Moses, "When you go back to Egypt, see that you do before Pharaoh all the miracles which I have put in your power; but I will harden his heart, so that he will not let the people go. 22And you shall say to Pharaoh, 'Thus says the LORD, Israel is my first-born son, 23 and I say to you, "Let my son go that he may serve me"; if you refuse to let him go,

g Gk Vg: Heb no, not by a mighty hand
4.19: Acts 7.34.

behold, I will slay your first-born son.'"

24 At a lodging place on the way the LORD met him and sought to kill him. 25 Then Zip-pō'rāh took a flint and cut off her son's foreskin, and touched Moses' feet with it, and said, "Surely you are a bridegroom of blood to me!" 26 So he let him alone. Then it was that she said, "You are a bridegroom of blood," because of the circumcision.

27 The LORD said to Aaron, "Go into the wilderness to meet Moses." So he went, and met him at the mountain of God and kissed him. 28And Moses told Aaron all the words of the LORD with which he had sent him, and all the signs which he had charged him to do. 29 Then Moses and Aaron went and gathered together all the elders of the people of Israel. 30And Aaron spoke all the words which the LORD had spoken to Moses, and did the signs in the sight of the people. 31And the people believed; and when they heard that the LORD had visited the people of Israel and that he had seen their affliction, they bowed their heads and worshiped.

5 Afterward Moses and Aaron went to Pharaoh and said, "Thus says the LORD, the God of Israel, 'Let my people go, that they may hold a feast to me in the wilderness.'" 2 But Pharaoh said, "Who is the LORD, that I should heed his voice and let Israel go? I do not know the LORD, and moreover I will not let Israel go." 3 Then they said, "The God of the Hebrews has met with us; let us go, we pray, a three days' journey into the wilderness, and sacrifice to the LORD our God, lest he fall upon us with pestilence or with the sword." 4 But the king of Egypt said to them, "Moses and Aaron, why do you take the people away from their work? Get to your burdens." 5And Pharaoh said, "Behold, the people of the land are now many and you make them rest from their burdens!" 6 The same day Pharaoh commanded the taskmasters of the people and their foremen, 7 "You shall no longer give the people straw to make bricks, as heretofore; let them go and gather straw for themselves. 8 But the number of bricks which they made heretofore you shall lay upon them, you shall by no means lessen it; for they are idle; therefore they cry, 'Let us go and offer sacrifice to our God.' 9 Let heavier work be laid upon the men that they may labor at it and pay no regard to lying words."

10 So the taskmasters and the foremen of the people went out and said to the people, "Thus says Pharaoh, 'I will not give you straw. 11 Go yourselves, get your straw wherever you can find it; but your work will not be lessened in the least.'" 12 So the people were scattered abroad throughout all the land of Egypt, to gather stubble for straw. 13 The taskmasters were urgent, saying, "Complete your work, your daily task, as when there was straw." 14And the foremen of the people of Israel, whom Pharaoh's taskmasters had set over them, were beaten, and were asked, "Why have you not done all your task of making bricks today, as hitherto?"

15 Then the foremen of the people of Israel came and cried to Pharaoh, "Why do you deal thus with your servants? 16 No straw is given to your servants, yet they say to us, 'Make bricks!' And behold, your servants are beaten; but the fault is in your own people." 17 But he said, "You are idle, you are idle; therefore you say, 'Let us go and sacrifice to the LORD.' 18 Go now, and work; for no straw shall be given you, yet you shall deliver the same number of bricks." 19 The foremen of the people of Israel saw that they were in evil plight, when they said, "You shall by no means lessen your daily number of bricks." 20 They met Moses and Aaron, who were waiting for them, as they came forth from Pharaoh; 21 and they said to them, "The LORD look upon you and judge, because you have made us offensive in the sight of Pharaoh and his servants, and have put a sword in their hand to kill us."

22 Then Moses turned again to the LORD and said, "O LORD, why hast thou done evil to this people? Why didst thou ever send me? 23 For since I came to Pharaoh to speak in thy name, he has done evil to this people, and thou hast not delivered thy people at all." 1 But the LORD said to

6 Moses, "Now you shall see what I will do to Pharaoh; for with a strong hand he will send them out, yea, with a strong hand he will drive them out of his land."

2 And God said to Moses, "I am the LORD. 3 I appeared to Abraham, to Isaac, and to Jacob, as God Almighty,ʰ but by my name the LORD I did not make myself known to them. 4 I also

ʰ Heb El Shaddai
6.1, 6: Acts 13.17.

established my covenant with them, to give them the land of Canaan, the land in which they dwelt as sojourners. ⁵ Moreover I have heard the groaning of the people of Israel whom the Egyptians hold in bondage and I have remembered my covenant. ⁶ Say therefore to the people of Israel, 'I am the LORD, and I will bring you out from under the burdens of the Egyptians, and I will deliver you from their bondage, and I will redeem you with an outstretched arm and with great acts of judgment, ⁷ and I will take you for my people, and I will be your God; and you shall know that I am the LORD your God, who has brought you out from under the burdens of the Egyptians. ⁸And I will bring you into the land which I swore to give to Abraham, to Isaac, and to Jacob; I will give it to you for a possession. I am the LORD.'"

⁹ Moses spoke thus to the people of Israel; but they did not listen to Moses, because of their broken spirit and their cruel bondage.

10 And the LORD said to Moses, ¹¹ "Go in, tell Pharaoh king of Egypt to let the people of Israel go out of his land." ¹² But Moses said to the LORD, "Behold, the people of Israel have not listened to me; how then shall Pharaoh listen to me, who am a man of uncircumcised lips?" ¹³ But the LORD spoke to Moses and Aaron, and gave them a charge to the people of Israel and to Pharaoh king of Egypt to bring the people of Israel out of the land of Egypt.

14 These are the heads of their fathers' houses: the sons of Reuben, the first-born of Israel: Hā′noch, Pal′lü, Hez′rŏn, and Cär′mï; these are the families of Reuben. ¹⁵ The sons of Simeon: Jē·mū′ĕl, Jā′min, O′had, Jā′chin, Zō′här, and Shā′ŭl, the son of a Canaanite woman; these are the families of Simeon. ¹⁶ These are the names of the sons of Levi according to their generations: Gēr′shŏn, Kō′hath, and Mē·râr′ï, the years of the life of Levi being a hundred and thirty-seven years. ¹⁷ The sons of Gēr′shŏn: Lib′nï and Shim′ē-ï, by their families. ¹⁸ The sons of Kō′hath: Am′ram, Iz′här, Hē′brŏn, and Uz′zi-el, the years of the life of Kohath being a hundred and thirty-three years. ¹⁹ The sons of Mē·râr′ï: Mäh′lï and Mū′shï. These are the families of the Levites according to their generations. ²⁰ Am′ram took to wife Jŏch′ē·bed his father's

sister and she bore him Aaron and Moses, the years of the life of Amram being one hundred and thirty-seven years. ²¹ The sons of Iz′här: Kō′räh, Nē′pheg, and Zĭch′rï. ²²And the sons of Uz′zi-el: Mish′ā-el, El′ză·phan, and Sĭth′rï. ²³Aaron took to wife E·lī′shē·bä, the daughter of Am·mĭn′ă·dab and the sister of Näh′shŏn; and she bore him Nä′dab, À·bï′hū, El·ē·ā′zăr, and Ith′ă·mär. ²⁴ The sons of Kō′räh: As′sir, El·kā′näh, and À·bï′ā·saph; these are the families of the Kō′rähites. ²⁵ El·ē·ā′zăr, Aaron's son, took to wife one of the daughters of Pū′tï-el; and she bore him Phin′ē·häs. These are the heads of the fathers' houses of the Levites by their families.

26 These are the Aaron and Moses to whom the LORD said: "Bring out the people of Israel from the land of Egypt by their hosts." ²⁷ It was they who spoke to Pharaoh king of Egypt about bringing out the people of Israel from Egypt, this Moses and this Aaron.

28 On the day when the LORD spoke to Moses in the land of Egypt, ²⁹ the LORD said to Moses, "I am the LORD; tell Pharaoh king of Egypt all that I say to you." ³⁰ But Moses said to the LORD, "Behold, I am of uncircumcised lips; how then shall Pharaoh listen to me?"

7 ¹And the LORD said to Moses, "See, I make you as God to Pharaoh; and Aaron your brother shall be your prophet. ² You shall speak all that I command you; and Aaron your brother shall tell Pharaoh to let the people of Israel go out of his land. ³ But I will harden Pharaoh's heart, and though I multiply my signs and wonders in the land of Egypt, ⁴ Pharaoh will not listen to you; then I will lay my hand upon Egypt and bring forth my hosts, my people the sons of Israel, out of the land of Egypt by great acts of judgment. ⁵And the Egyptians shall know that I am the LORD, when I stretch forth my hand upon Egypt and bring out the people of Israel from among them." ⁶And Moses and Aaron did so; they did as the LORD commanded them. ⁷ Now Moses was eighty years old, and Aaron eighty-three years old, when they spoke to Pharaoh.

8 And the LORD said to Moses and Aaron, ⁹ "When Pharaoh says to you, 'Prove yourselves by working a miracle,' then you shall say to Aaron, 'Take your rod and cast it down before Pharaoh, that it may become a ser-

6.14-16: Gen 46.8-11; Num 26.5-14.
6.16-19: Num 3.15-20; 26.57-58; 1 Chron 6.1, 16-19. 6.20-23: Num 26.58-60.
7.3: Acts 7.36.

pent.' " 10 So Moses and Aaron went to Pharaoh and did as the LORD commanded; Aaron cast down his rod before Pharaoh and his servants, and it became a serpent. 11 Then Pharaoh summoned the wise men and the sorcerers; and they also, the magicians of Egypt, did the same by their secret arts. 12 For every man cast down his rod, and they became serpents. But Aaron's rod swallowed up their rods. 13 Still Pharaoh's heart was hardened, and he would not listen to them; as the LORD had said.

14 Then the LORD said to Moses, "Pharaoh's heart is hardened, he refuses to let the people go. 15 Go to Pharaoh in the morning, as he is going out to the water; wait for him by the river's brink, and take in your hand the rod which was turned into a serpent. 16And you shall say to him, 'The LORD, the God of the Hebrews, sent me to you, saying, "Let my people go, that they may serve me in the wilderness; and behold, you have not yet obeyed." 17 Thus says the LORD, "By this you shall know that I am the LORD: behold, I will strike the water that is in the Nile with the rod that is in my hand, and it shall be turned to blood, 18 and the fish in the Nile shall die, and the Nile shall become foul, and the Egyptians will loathe to drink water from the Nile." ' " 19And the LORD said to Moses, "Say to Aaron, 'Take your rod and stretch out your hand over the waters of Egypt, over their rivers, their canals, and their ponds, and all their pools of water, that they may become blood; and there shall be blood throughout all the land of Egypt, both in vessels of wood and in vessels of stone.' "

20 Moses and Aaron did as the LORD commanded; in the sight of Pharaoh and in the sight of his servants, he lifted up the rod and struck the water that was in the Nile, and all the water that was in the Nile turned to blood. 21And the fish in the Nile died; and the Nile became foul, so that the Egyptians could not drink water from the Nile; and there was blood throughout all the land of Egypt. 22 But the magicians of Egypt did the same by their secret arts; so Pharaoh's heart remained hardened, and he would not listen to them; as the LORD had said. 23 Pharaoh turned and went into his house, and he did not lay even this to heart. 24And all the Egyptians dug round about the Nile for water to drink, for they could not drink the water of the Nile.

25 Seven days passed after the 8 *i*LORD had struck the Nile. 1 Then the LORD said to Moses, "Go in to Pharaoh and say to him, 'Thus says the LORD, "Let my people go, that they may serve me. 2 But if you refuse to let them go, behold, I will plague all your country with frogs; 3 the Nile shall swarm with frogs which shall come up into your house, and into your bedchamber and on your bed, and into the houses of your servants and of your people,*j* and into your ovens and your kneading bowls; 4 the frogs shall come up on you and on your people and on all your servants." ' " 5 *k*And the LORD said to Moses, "Say to Aaron, 'Stretch out your hand with your rod over the rivers, over the canals, and over the pools, and cause frogs to come upon the land of Egypt!' " 6 So Aaron stretched out his hand over the waters of Egypt; and the frogs came up and covered the land of Egypt. 7 But the magicians did the same by their secret arts, and brought frogs upon the land of Egypt.

8 Then Pharaoh called Moses and Aaron, and said, "Entreat the LORD to take away the frogs from me and from my people; and I will let the people go to sacrifice to the LORD." 9 Moses said to Pharaoh, "Be pleased to command me when I am to entreat, for you and for your servants and for your people, that the frogs be destroyed from you and your houses and be left only in the Nile." 10And he said, "Tomorrow." Moses said, "Be it as you say, that you may know that there is no one like the LORD our God. 11 The frogs shall depart from you and your houses and your servants and your people; they shall be left only in the Nile." 12 So Moses and Aaron went out from Pharaoh; and Moses cried to the LORD concerning the frogs, as he had agreed with Pharaoh.*l* 13And the LORD did according to the word of Moses; the frogs died out of the houses and courtyards and out of the fields. 14And they gathered them together in heaps, and the land stank. 15 But when Pharaoh saw that there was a respite, he hardened his heart, and would not listen to them; as the LORD had said.

16 Then the LORD said to Moses, "Say to Aaron, 'Stretch out your rod and strike the dust of the earth, that it may become gnats throughout all the land of Egypt.' " 17And they did

i Ch 7.26 in Heb   *j* Gk: Heb *upon your people*   *k* Ch 8.1 in Heb
l Or *which he had brought upon Pharaoh*

so; Aaron stretched out his hand with his rod, and struck the dust of the earth, and there came gnats on man and beast; all the dust of the earth became gnats throughout all the land of Egypt. [18] The magicians tried by their secret arts to bring forth gnats, but they could not. So there were gnats on man and beast. [19]And the magicians said to Pharaoh, "This is the finger of God." But Pharaoh's heart was hardened, and he would not listen to them; as the LORD had said.

20 Then the LORD said to Moses, "Rise up early in the morning and wait for Pharaoh, as he goes out to the water, and say to him, 'Thus says the LORD, "Let my people go, that they may serve me. [21] Else, if you will not let my people go, behold, I will send swarms of flies on you and your servants and your people, and into your houses; and the houses of the Egyptians shall be filled with swarms of flies, and also the ground on which they stand. [22] But on that day I will set apart the land of Gō'shen, where my people dwell, so that no swarms of flies shall be there; that you may know that I am the LORD in the midst of the earth. [23] Thus I will put a division[m] between my people and your people. By tomorrow shall this sign be." ' " [24]And the LORD did so; there came great swarms of flies into the house of Pharaoh and into his servants' houses, and in all the land of Egypt the land was ruined by reason of the flies.

25 Then Pharaoh called Moses and Aaron, and said, "Go, sacrifice to your God within the land." [26] But Moses said, "It would not be right to do so; for we shall sacrifice to the LORD our God offerings abominable to the Egyptians. If we sacrifice offerings abominable to the Egyptians before their eyes, will they not stone us? [27] We must go three days' journey into the wilderness and sacrifice to the LORD our God as he will command us." [28] So Pharaoh said, "I will let you go, to sacrifice to the LORD your God in the wilderness; only you shall not go very far away. Make entreaty for me." [29] Then Moses said, "Behold, I am going out from you and I will pray to the LORD that the swarms of flies may depart from Pharaoh, from his servants, and from his people, tomorrow; only let not Pharaoh deal falsely again by not letting the people go to sacrifice to the LORD." [30] So Moses went out from Pharaoh and prayed to the LORD. [31]And the LORD did as Moses asked,

and removed the swarms of flies from Pharaoh, from his servants, and from his people; not one remained. [32] But Pharaoh hardened his heart this time also, and did not let the people go.

9 Then the LORD said to Moses, "Go in to Pharaoh, and say to him, 'Thus says the LORD, the God of the Hebrews, "Let my people go, that they may serve me. [2] For if you refuse to let them go and still hold them, [3] behold, the hand of the LORD will fall with a very severe plague upon your cattle which are in the field, the horses, the asses, the camels, the herds, and the flocks. [4] But the LORD will make a distinction between the cattle of Israel and the cattle of Egypt, so that nothing shall die of all that belongs to the people of Israel." ' " [5]And the LORD set a time, saying, "Tomorrow the LORD will do this thing in the land." [6]And on the morrow the LORD did this thing; all the cattle of the Egyptians died, but of the cattle of the people of Israel not one died. [7]And Pharaoh sent, and behold, not one of the cattle of the Israelites was dead. But the heart of Pharaoh was hardened, and he did not let the people go.

8 And the LORD said to Moses and Aaron, "Take handfuls of ashes from the kiln, and let Moses throw them toward heaven in the sight of Pharaoh. [9]And it shall become fine dust over all the land of Egypt, and become boils breaking out in sores on man and beast throughout all the land of Egypt." [10] So they took ashes from the kiln, and stood before Pharaoh, and Moses threw them toward heaven, and it became boils breaking out in sores on man and beast. [11]And the magicians could not stand before Moses because of the boils, for the boils were upon the magicians and upon all the Egyptians. [12] But the LORD hardened the heart of Pharaoh, and he did not listen to them; as the LORD had spoken to Moses.

13 Then the LORD said to Moses, "Rise up early in the morning and stand before Pharaoh, and say to him, 'Thus says the LORD, the God of the Hebrews, "Let my people go, that they may serve me. [14] For this time I will send all my plagues upon your heart, and upon your servants and your people, that you may know that there is none like me in all the earth. [15] For by now I could have put forth my hand and struck you and your people with pestilence, and you would have been cut off from the earth; [16] but

m Gk Vg: Heb *set redemption*   **9.16:** Rom 9.17.

for this purpose have I let you live, to show you my power, so that my name may be declared throughout all the earth. 17 You are still exalting yourself against my people, and will not let them go. 18 Behold, tomorrow about this time I will cause very heavy hail to fall, such as never has been in Egypt from the day it was founded until now. 19 Now therefore send, get your cattle and all that you have in the field into safe shelter; for the hail shall come down upon every man and beast that is in the field and is not brought home, and they shall die.'' '' 20 Then he who feared the word of the LORD among the servants of Pharaoh made his slaves and his cattle flee into the houses; 21 but he who did not regard the word of the LORD left his slaves and his cattle in the field.

22 And the LORD said to Moses, "Stretch forth your hand toward heaven, that there may be hail in all the land of Egypt, upon man and beast and every plant of the field, throughout the land of Egypt.'' 23 Then Moses stretched forth his rod toward heaven; and the LORD sent thunder and hail, and fire ran down to the earth. And the LORD rained hail upon the land of Egypt; 24 there was hail, and fire flashing continually in the midst of the hail, very heavy hail, such as had never been in all the land of Egypt since it became a nation. 25 The hail struck down everything that was in the field throughout all the land of Egypt, both man and beast; and the hail struck down every plant of the field, and shattered every tree of the field. 26 Only in the land of Gō'shĕn, where the people of Israel were, there was no hail.

27 Then Pharaoh sent, and called Moses and Aaron, and said to them, "I have sinned this time; the LORD is in the right, and I and my people are in the wrong. 28 Entreat the LORD; for there has been enough of this thunder and hail; I will let you go, and you shall stay no longer.'' 29 Moses said to him, "As soon as I have gone out of the city, I will stretch out my hands to the LORD; the thunder will cease, and there will be no more hail, that you may know that the earth is the LORD's. 30 But as for you and your servants, I know that you do not yet fear the LORD God.'' 31 (The flax and the barley were ruined, for the barley was in the ear and the flax was in bud. 32 But the wheat and the spelt were not ruined, for they are late in coming

up.) 33 So Moses went out of the city from Pharaoh, and stretched out his hands to the LORD; and the thunder and the hail ceased, and the rain no longer poured upon the earth. 34 But when Pharaoh saw that the rain and the hail and the thunder had ceased, he sinned yet again, and hardened his heart, he and his servants. 35 So the heart of Pharaoh was hardened, and he did not let the people of Israel go; as the LORD had spoken through Moses.

10 Then the LORD said to Moses, "Go in to Pharaoh; for I have hardened his heart and the heart of his servants, that I may show these signs of mine among them, 2 and that you may tell in the hearing of your son and of your sons' son how I have made sport of the Egyptians and what signs I have done among them; that you may know that I am the LORD.''

3 So Moses and Aaron went in to Pharaoh, and said to him, "Thus says the LORD, the God of the Hebrews, 'How long will you refuse to humble yourself before me? Let my people go, that they may serve me. 4 For if you refuse to let my people go, behold, tomorrow I will bring locusts into your country, 5 and they shall cover the face of the land, so that no one can see the land; and they shall eat what is left to you after the hail, and they shall eat every tree of yours which grows in the field, 6 and they shall fill your houses, and the houses of all your servants and of all the Egyptians; as neither your fathers nor your grandfathers have seen, from the day they came on earth to this day.' '' Then he turned and went out from Pharaoh.

7 And Pharaoh's servants said to him, "How long shall this man be a snare to us? Let the men go, that they may serve the LORD their God; do you not yet understand that Egypt is ruined?'' 8 So Moses and Aaron were brought back to Pharaoh; and he said to them, "Go, serve the LORD your God; but who are to go?'' 9 And Moses said, "We will go with our young and our old; we will go with our sons and daughters and with our flocks and herds, for we must hold a feast to the LORD.'' 10 And he said to them, "The LORD be with you, if ever I let you and your little ones go! Look, you have some evil purpose in mind.^{n} 11 No! Go, the men among you, and serve the LORD, for that is what you desire.'' And they were driven out from Pharaoh's presence.

^{n} Heb *before your face*

12 Then the LORD said to Moses, "Stretch out your hand over the land of Egypt for the locusts, that they may come upon the land of Egypt, and eat every plant in the land, all that the hail has left." 13 So Moses stretched forth his rod over the land of Egypt, and the LORD brought an east wind upon the land all that day and all that night; and when it was morning the east wind had brought the locusts. 14And the locusts came up over all the land of Egypt, and settled on the whole country of Egypt, such a dense swarm of locusts as had never been before, nor ever shall be again. 15 For they covered the face of the whole land, so that the land was darkened, and they ate all the plants in the land and all the fruit of the trees which the hail had left; not a green thing remained, neither tree nor plant of the field, through all the land of Egypt. 16 Then Pharaoh called Moses and Aaron in haste, and said, "I have sinned against the LORD your God, and against you. 17 Now therefore, forgive my sin, I pray you, only this once, and entreat the LORD your God only to remove this death from me." 18 So he went out from Pharaoh, and entreated the LORD. 19And the LORD turned a very strong west wind, which lifted the locusts and drove them into the Red Sea; not a single locust was left in all the country of Egypt. 20 But the LORD hardened Pharaoh's heart, and he did not let the children of Israel go.

21 Then the LORD said to Moses, "Stretch out your hand toward heaven that there may be darkness over the land of Egypt, a darkness to be felt." 22 So Moses stretched out his hand toward heaven, and there was thick darkness in all the land of Egypt three days; 23 they did not see one another, nor did any rise from his place for three days; but all the people of Israel had light where they dwelt. 24 Then Pharaoh called Moses, and said, "Go, serve the LORD; your children also may go with you; only let your flocks and your herds remain behind." 25 But Moses said, "You must also let us have sacrifices and burnt offerings, that we may sacrifice to the LORD our God. 26 Our cattle also must go with us; not a hoof shall be left behind, for we must take of them to serve the LORD our God, and we do not know with what we must serve the LORD until we arrive there." 27 But the LORD hardened Pharaoh's heart, and he would not let them go. 28 Then Pharaoh said to him, "Get away from me; take heed to your-

self; never see my face again; for in the day you see my face you shall die." 29 Moses said, "As you say! I will not see your face again."

11 The LORD said to Moses, "Yet one plague more I will bring upon Pharaoh and upon Egypt; afterwards he will let you go hence; when he lets you go, he will drive you away completely. 2 Speak now in the hearing of the people, that they ask, every man of his neighbor and every woman of her neighbor, jewelry of silver and of gold." 3And the LORD gave the people favor in the sight of the Egyptians. Moreover, the man Moses was very great in the land of Egypt, in the sight of Pharaoh's servants and in the sight of the people.

4 And Moses said, "Thus says the LORD: About midnight I will go forth in the midst of Egypt; 5 and all the first-born in the land of Egypt shall die, from the first-born of Pharaoh who sits upon his throne, even to the first-born of the maidservant who is behind the mill; and all the first-born of the cattle. 6And there shall be a great cry throughout all the land of Egypt, such as there has never been, nor ever shall be again. 7 But against any of the people of Israel, either man or beast, not a dog shall growl; that you may know that the LORD makes a distinction between the Egyptians and Israel. 8And all these your servants shall come down to me, and bow down to me, saying, 'Get you out, and all the people who follow you.' And after that I will go out." And he went out from Pharaoh in hot anger. 9 Then the LORD said to Moses, "Pharaoh will not listen to you; that my wonders may be multiplied in the land of Egypt."

10 Moses and Aaron did all these wonders before Pharaoh; and the LORD hardened Pharaoh's heart, and he did not let the people of Israel go out of his land.

12 The LORD said to Moses and Aaron in the land of Egypt, 2 "This month shall be for you the beginning of months; it shall be the first month of the year for you. 3 Tell all the congregation of Israel that on the tenth day of this month they shall take every man a lamb according to their fathers' houses, a lamb for a household; 4 and if the household is too small for a lamb, then a man and his neighbor next to his house shall take according to the number of persons; according to what each can eat you shall make your count for the lamb. 5 Your lamb shall be without

blemish, a male a year old; you shall take it from the sheep or from the goats; 6 and you shall keep it until the fourteenth day of this month, when the whole assembly of the congregation of Israel shall kill their lambs in the evening.o 7 Then they shall take some of the blood, and put it on the two doorposts and the lintel of the houses in which they eat them. 8 They shall eat the flesh that night, roasted; with unleavened bread and bitter herbs they shall eat it. 9 Do not eat any of it raw or boiled with water, but roasted, its head with its legs and its inner parts. 10And you shall let none of it remain until the morning, anything that remains until the morning you shall burn. 11 In this manner you shall eat it: your loins girded, your sandals on your feet, and your staff in your hand; and you shall eat it in haste. It is the LORD's passover. 12 For I will pass through the land of Egypt that night, and I will smite all the first-born in the land of Egypt, both man and beast; and on all the gods of Egypt I will execute judgments: I am the LORD. 13 The blood shall be a sign for you, upon the houses where you are; and when I see the blood, I will pass over you, and no plague shall fall upon you to destroy you, when I smite the land of Egypt.

14 "This day shall be for you a memorial day, and you shall keep it as a feast to the LORD; throughout your generations you shall observe it as an ordinance for ever. 15 Seven days you shall eat unleavened bread; on the first day you shall put away leaven out of your houses, for if any one eats what is leavened, from the first day until the seventh day, that person shall be cut off from Israel. 16 On the first day you shall hold a holy assembly, and on the seventh day a holy assembly; no work shall be done on those days; but what every one must eat, that only may be prepared by you. 17And you shall observe the feast of unleavened bread, for on this very day I brought your hosts out of the land of Egypt: therefore you shall observe this day, throughout your generations, as an ordinance for ever. 18 In the first month, on the fourteenth day of the month at evening, you shall eat unleavened bread, and so until the twenty-first day of the month at evening. 19 For seven days no leaven shall be found in your houses; for if any one eats what is leavened, that

person shall be cut off from the congregation of Israel, whether he is a sojourner or a native of the land. 20 You shall eat nothing leavened; in all your dwellings you shall eat unleavened bread."

21 Then Moses called all the elders of Israel, and said to them, "Select lambs for yourselves according to your families, and kill the passover lamb. 22 Take a bunch of hyssop and dip it in the blood which is in the basin, and touch the lintel and the two doorposts with the blood which is in the basin; and none of you shall go out of the door of his house until the morning. 23 For the LORD will pass through to slay the Egyptians; and when he sees the blood on the lintel and on the two doorposts, the LORD will pass over the door, and will not allow the destroyer to enter your houses to slay you. 24 You shall observe this rite as an ordinance for you and for your sons for ever. 25And when you come to the land which the LORD will give you, as he has promised, you shall keep this service. 26And when your children say to you, 'What do you mean by this service?' 27 you shall say, 'It is the sacrifice of the LORD's passover, for he passed over the houses of the people of Israel in Egypt, when he slew the Egyptians but spared our houses.'" And the people bowed their heads and worshiped.

28 Then the people of Israel went and did so; as the LORD had commanded Moses and Aaron, so they did.

29 At midnight the LORD smote all the first-born in the land of Egypt, from the first-born of Pharaoh who sat on his throne to the first-born of the captive who was in the dungeon, and all the first-born of the cattle. 30And Pharaoh rose up in the night, he, and all his servants, and all the Egyptians; and there was a great cry in Egypt, for there was not a house where one was not dead. 31And he summoned Moses and Aaron by night, and said, "Rise up, go forth from among my people, both you and the people of Israel; and go, serve the LORD, as you have said. 32 Take your flocks and your herds, as you have said, and be gone; and bless me also!"

33 And the Egyptians were urgent with the people, to send them out of the land in haste; for they said, "We are all dead men." 34 So the people took their dough before it was leavened, their kneading bowls being

o Heb *between the two evenings*
12.13: Heb 11.28.

bound up in their mantles on their shoulders. 35 The people of Israel had also done as Moses told them, for they had asked of the Egyptians jewelry of silver and of gold, and clothing; 36 and the LORD had given the people favor in the sight of the Egyptians, so that they let them have what they asked. Thus they despoiled the Egyptians.

37 And the people of Israel journeyed from Ram´e·ses to Suc´coth, about six hundred thousand men on foot, besides women and children. 38 A mixed multitude also went up with them, and very many cattle, both flocks and herds. 39 And they baked unleavened cakes of the dough which they had brought out of Egypt, for it was not leavened, because they were thrust out of Egypt and could not tarry, neither had they prepared for themselves any provisions.

40 The time that the people of Israel dwelt in Egypt was four hundred and thirty years. 41 And at the end of four hundred and thirty years, on that very day, all the hosts of the LORD went out from the land of Egypt. 42 It was a night of watching by the LORD, to bring them out of the land of Egypt; so this same night is a night of watching kept to the LORD by all the people of Israel throughout their generations.

43 And the LORD said to Moses and Aaron, "This is the ordinance of the passover: no foreigner shall eat of it; 44 but every slave that is bought for money may eat of it after you have circumcised him. 45 No sojourner or hired servant may eat of it. 46 In one house shall it be eaten; you shall not carry forth any of the flesh outside the house; and you shall not break a bone of it. 47 All the congregation of Israel shall keep it. 48 And when a stranger shall sojourn with you and would keep the passover to the LORD, let all his males be circumcised, then he may come near and keep it; he shall be as a native of the land. But no uncircumcised person shall eat of it. 49 There shall be one law for the native and for the stranger who sojourns among you."

50 Thus did all the people of Israel; as the LORD commanded Moses and Aaron, so they did. 51 And on that very day the LORD brought the people of Israel out of the land of Egypt by their hosts.

13 The LORD said to Moses, 2 "Consecrate to me all the first-born; whatever is the first to open the

womb among the people of Israel, both of man and of beast, is mine."

3 And Moses said to the people, "Remember this day, in which you came out from Egypt, out of the house of bondage, for by strength of hand the LORD brought you out from this place; no leavened bread shall be eaten. 4 This day you are to go forth, in the month of A´bib. 5 And when the LORD brings you into the land of the Canaanites, the Hit´tites, the Am´o·rites, the Hi´vites, and the Jeb´u·sites, which he swore to your fathers to give you, a land flowing with milk and honey, you shall keep this service in this month. 6 Seven days you shall eat unleavened bread, and on the seventh day there shall be a feast to the LORD. 7 Unleavened bread shall be eaten for seven days; no leavened bread shall be seen with you, and no leaven shall be seen with you in all your territory. 8 And you shall tell your son on that day, 'It is because of what the LORD did for me when I came out of Egypt.' 9 And it shall be to you as a sign on your hand and as a memorial between your eyes, that the law of the LORD may be in your mouth; for with a strong hand the LORD has brought you out of Egypt. 10 You shall therefore keep this ordinance at its appointed time from year to year.

11 "And when the LORD brings you into the land of the Canaanites, as he swore to you and your fathers, and shall give it to you, 12 you shall set apart to the LORD all that first opens the womb. All the firstlings of your cattle that are males shall be the LORD's. 13 Every firstling of an ass you shall redeem with a lamb, or if you will not redeem it you shall break its neck. Every first-born of man among your sons you shall redeem. 14 And when in time to come your son asks you, 'What does this mean?' you shall say to him, 'By strength of hand the LORD brought us out of Egypt, from the house of bondage. 15 For when Pharaoh stubbornly refused to let us go, the LORD slew all the first-born in the land of Egypt, both the first-born of man and the first-born of cattle. Therefore I sacrifice to the LORD all the males that first open the womb; but all the first-born of my sons I redeem.' 16 It shall be as a mark on your hand or frontlets between your eyes; for by a strong hand the LORD brought us out of Egypt."

17 When Pharaoh let the people go,

12.40: Acts 7.6.   12.46: Num 9.12; Jn 19.36.
12.49: Lev 24.22; Num 9.14; 15.15-16, 29.   13.2, 12, 15: Lk 2.23.

God did not lead them by way of the land of the Philistines, although that was near; for God said, "Lest the people repent when they see war, and return to Egypt." 18 But God led the people round by the way of the wilderness toward the Red Sea. And the people of Israel went up out of the land of Egypt equipped for battle. 19And Moses took the bones of Joseph with him; for Joseph had solemnly sworn the people of Israel, saying, "God will visit you; then you must carry my bones with you from here." 20And they moved on from Suc'coth, and encamped at Ė'thåm, on the edge of the wilderness. 21And the LORD went before them by day in a pillar of cloud to lead them along the way, and by night in a pillar of fire to give them light, that they might travel by day and by night; 22 the pillar of cloud by day and the pillar of fire by night did not depart from before the people.

14 Then the LORD said to Moses, 2 "Tell the people of Israel to turn back and encamp in front of Pī-hå-hī'roth, between Mig'dōl and the sea, in front of Bā'al-zė'phon; you shall encamp over against it, by the sea. 3 For Pharaoh will say of the people of Israel, 'They are entangled in the land; the wilderness has shut them in.' 4And I will harden Pharaoh's heart, and he will pursue them and I will get glory over Pharaoh and all his host; and the Egyptians shall know that I am the LORD." And they did so.

5 When the king of Egypt was told that the people had fled, the mind of Pharaoh and his servants was changed toward the people, and they said, "What is this we have done, that we have let Israel go from serving us?" 6 So he made ready his chariot and took his army with him, 7 and took six hundred picked chariots and all the other chariots of Egypt with officers over all of them. 8And the LORD hardened the heart of Pharaoh king of Egypt and he pursued the people of Israel as they went forth defiantly. 9 The Egyptians pursued them, all Pharaoh's horses and chariots and his horsemen and his army, and overtook them encamped at the sea, by Pī-hå-hī'roth, in front of Bā'al-zė'phon.

10 When Pharaoh drew near, the people of Israel lifted up their eyes, and behold, the Egyptians were marching after them; and they were in great

fear. And the people of Israel cried out to the LORD; 11 and they said to Moses, "Is it because there are no graves in Egypt that you have taken us away to die in the wilderness? What have you done to us, in bringing us out of Egypt? 12 Is not this what we said to you in Egypt, 'Let us alone and let us serve the Egyptians'? For it would have been better for us to serve the Egyptians than to die in the wilderness." 13And Moses said to the people, "Fear not, stand firm, and see the salvation of the LORD, which he will work for you today; for the Egyptians whom you see today, you shall never see again. 14 The LORD will fight for you, and you have only to be still."

15 The LORD said to Moses, "Why do you cry to me? Tell the people of Israel to go forward. 16 Lift up your rod, and stretch out your hand over the sea and divide it, that the people of Israel may go on dry ground through the sea. 17And I will harden the hearts of the Egyptians so that they shall go in after them, and I will get glory over Pharaoh and all his host, his chariots, and his horsemen. 18And the Egyptians shall know that I am the LORD, when I have gotten glory over Pharaoh, his chariots, and his horsemen."

19 Then the angel of God who went before the host of Israel moved and went behind them; and the pillar of cloud moved from before them and stood behind them, 20 coming between the host of Egypt and the host of Israel. And there was the cloud and the darkness; and the night passed[p] without one coming near the other all night.

21 Then Moses stretched out his hand over the sea; and the LORD drove the sea back by a strong east wind all night, and made the sea dry land, and the waters were divided. 22And the people of Israel went into the midst of the sea on dry ground, the waters being a wall to them on their right hand and on their left. 23 The Egyptians pursued, and went in after them into the midst of the sea, all Pharaoh's horses, his chariots, and his horsemen. 24And in the morning watch the LORD in the pillar of fire and of cloud looked down upon the host of the Egyptians, and discomfited the host of the Egyptians, 25 clogging[q] their chariot wheels so that they drove heavily; and the Egyptians said, "Let us flee from before Israel; for the LORD fights for them against the Egyptians."

p Gk: Heb *and it lit up the night*
q Or *binding*. Sam Gk Syr: Heb *removing*
13.19: Gen 50.25.   **14.8:** Acts 13.17.   **14.12:** Ex 16.3; 17.3.

26 Then the LORD said to Moses, "Stretch out your hand over the sea, that the water may come back upon the Egyptians, upon their chariots, and upon their horsemen." 27 So Moses stretched forth his hand over the sea, and the sea returned to its wonted flow when the morning appeared; and the Egyptians fled into it, and the LORD routed[r] the Egyptians in the midst of the sea. 28 The waters returned and covered the chariots and the horsemen and all the host[s] of Pharaoh that had followed them into the sea; not so much as one of them remained. 29 But the people of Israel walked on dry ground through the sea, the waters being a wall to them on their right hand and on their left.

30 Thus the LORD saved Israel that day from the hand of the Egyptians; and Israel saw the Egyptians dead upon the seashore. 31 And Israel saw the great work which the LORD did against the Egyptians, and the people feared the LORD; and they believed in the LORD and in his servant Moses.

15 Then Moses and the people of Israel sang this song to the LORD, saying,
"I will sing to the LORD, for he has triumphed gloriously;
the horse and his rider[t] he has thrown into the sea.
2 The LORD is my strength and my song, and he has become my salvation;
this is my God, and I will praise him, my father's God, and I will exalt him.
3 The LORD is a man of war; the LORD is his name.

4 "Pharaoh's chariots and his host he cast into the sea;
and his picked officers are sunk in the Red Sea.
5 The floods cover them; they went down into the depths like a stone.
6 Thy right hand, O LORD, glorious in power,
thy right hand, O LORD, shatters the enemy.
7 In the greatness of thy majesty thou overthrowest thy adversaries;
thou sendest forth thy fury, it consumes them like stubble.
8 At the blast of thy nostrils the waters piled up,
the floods stood up in a heap, the deeps congealed in the heart of the sea.
9 The enemy said, 'I will pursue, I will overtake,

I will divide the spoil, my desire shall have its fill of them.
I will draw my sword, my hand shall destroy them.'
10 Thou didst blow with thy wind, the sea covered them;
they sank as lead in the mighty waters.

11 "Who is like thee, O LORD, among the gods?
Who is like thee, majestic in holiness,
terrible in glorious deeds, doing wonders?
12 Thou didst stretch out thy right hand,
the earth swallowed them.

13 "Thou hast led in thy steadfast love the people whom thou hast redeemed,
thou hast guided them by thy strength to thy holy abode.
14 The peoples have heard, they tremble;
pangs have seized on the inhabitants of Phi·lis'ti·à.
15 Now are the chiefs of E'dom dismayed;
the leaders of Mō'ab, trembling seizes them;
all the inhabitants of Canaan have melted away.
16 Terror and dread fall upon them; because of the greatness of thy arm, they are as still as a stone,
till thy people, O LORD, pass by, till the people pass by whom thou hast purchased.
17 Thou wilt bring them in, and plant them on thy own mountain,
the place, O LORD, which thou hast made for thy abode,
the sanctuary, O LORD, which thy hands have established.
18 The LORD will reign for ever and ever."

19 For when the horses of Pharaoh with his chariots and his horsemen went into the sea, the LORD brought back the waters of the sea upon them; but the people of Israel walked on dry ground in the midst of the sea. 20 Then Miriam, the prophetess, the sister of Aaron, took a timbrel in her hand; and all the women went out after her with timbrels and dancing. 21 And Miriam sang to them:
"Sing to the LORD, for he has triumphed gloriously;
the horse and his rider he has thrown into the sea."

22 Then Moses led Israel onward

---

[r] Heb *shook off*   [s] Gk Syr: Heb *to all the host*   [t] Or *its chariot*

from the Red Sea, and they went into the wilderness of Shür; they went three days in the wilderness and found no water. 23 When they came to Mâr′äh, they could not drink the water of Marah because it was bitter; therefore it was named Marah.*u* 24And the people murmured against Moses, saying, "What shall we drink?" 25And he cried to the LORD; and the LORD showed him a tree, and he threw it into the water, and the water became sweet.

There the LORD*v* made for them a statute and an ordinance and there he proved them, 26 saying, "If you will diligently hearken to the voice of the LORD your God, and do that which is right in his eyes, and give heed to his commandments and keep all his statutes, I will put none of the diseases upon you which I put upon the Egyptians; for I am the LORD, your healer."

27 Then they came to E′lim, where there were twelve springs of water and seventy palm trees; and they encamped there by the water.

16 They set out from E′lim, and all the congregation of the people of Israel came to the wilderness of Sin, which is between Elim and Sinai, on the fifteenth day of the second month after they had departed from the land of Egypt. 2And the whole congregation of the people of Israel murmured against Moses and Aaron in the wilderness, 3 and said to them, "Would that we had died by the hand of the LORD in the land of Egypt, when we sat by the fleshpots and ate bread to the full; for you have brought us out into this wilderness to kill this whole assembly with hunger."

4 Then the LORD said to Moses, "Behold, I will rain bread from heaven for you; and the people shall go out and gather a day's portion every day, that I may prove them, whether they will walk in my law or not. 5 On the sixth day, when they prepare what they bring in, it will be twice as much as they gather daily." 6 So Moses and Aaron said to all the people of Israel, "At evening you shall know that it was the LORD who brought you out of the land of Egypt, 7 and in the morning you shall see the glory of the LORD, because he has heard your murmurings against the LORD. For what are we, that you murmur against us?" 8And Moses said, "When the LORD gives you in the evening flesh to eat and in the morning bread to the full, because the LORD has heard your

murmurings which you murmur against him—what are we? Your murmurings are not against us but against the LORD."

9 And Moses said to Aaron, "Say to the whole congregation of the people of Israel, 'Come near before the LORD, for he has heard your murmurings.'" 10And as Aaron spoke to the whole congregation of the people of Israel, they looked toward the wilderness, and behold, the glory of the LORD appeared in the cloud. 11And the LORD said to Moses, 12 "I have heard the murmurings of the people of Israel; say to them, 'At twilight you shall eat flesh, and in the morning you shall be filled with bread; then you shall know that I am the LORD your God.'"

13 In the evening quails came up and covered the camp; and in the morning dew lay round about the camp. 14And when the dew had gone up, there was on the face of the wilderness a fine, flake-like thing, fine as hoarfrost on the ground. 15 When the people of Israel saw it, they said to one another, "What is it?"*w* For they did not know what it was. And Moses said to them, "It is the bread which the LORD has given you to eat. 16 This is what the LORD has commanded: 'Gather of it, every man of you, as much as he can eat; you shall take an omer apiece, according to the number of the persons whom each of you has in his tent.'" 17And the people of Israel did so; they gathered, some more, some less. 18 But when they measured it with an omer, he that gathered much had nothing over, and he that gathered little had no lack; each gathered according to what he could eat. 19And Moses said to them, "Let no man leave any of it till the morning." 20 But they did not listen to Moses; some left part of it till the morning, and it bred worms and became foul; and Moses was angry with them. 21 Morning by morning they gathered it, each as much as he could eat; but when the sun grew hot, it melted.

22 On the sixth day they gathered twice as much bread, two omers apiece; and when all the leaders of the congregation came and told Moses, 23 he said to them, "This is what the LORD has commanded: 'Tomorrow is a day of solemn rest, a holy sabbath to the LORD; bake what you will bake and boil what you will boil, and all that is

u That is *Bitterness*   *v* Heb *he*   *w* Or "*It is manna.*" Heb *man hu*
16.3: Ex 14.12; 17.3.   **16.4, 13:** Jn 6.31.   **16.18:** 2 Cor 8.15.

left over lay by to be kept till the morning.'" 24 So they laid it by till the morning, as Moses bade them; and it did not become foul, and there were no worms in it. 25 Moses said, "Eat it today, for today is a sabbath to the LORD; today you will not find it in the field. 26 Six days you shall gather it; but on the seventh day, which is a sabbath, there will be none." 27 On the seventh day some of the people went out to gather, and they found none. 28 And the LORD said to Moses, "How long do you refuse to keep my commandments and my laws? 29 See! The LORD has given you the sabbath, therefore on the sixth day he gives you bread for two days; remain every man of you in his place, let no man go out of his place on the seventh day." 30 So the people rested on the seventh day.

31 Now the house of Israel called its name manna; it was like coriander seed, white, and the taste of it was like wafers made with honey. 32 And Moses said, "This is what the LORD has commanded: 'Let an omer of it be kept throughout your generations, that they may see the bread with which I fed you in the wilderness, when I brought you out of the land of Egypt.'" 33 And Moses said to Aaron, "Take a jar, and put an omer of manna in it, and place it before the LORD, to be kept throughout your generations." 34 As the LORD commanded Moses, so Aaron placed it before the testimony, to be kept. 35 And the people of Israel ate the manna forty years, till they came to a habitable land; they ate the manna, till they came to the border of the land of Canaan. 36 (An omer is the tenth part of an ephah.)

17 All the congregation of the people of Israel moved on from the wilderness of Sin by stages, according to the commandment of the LORD, and camped at Reph'i·dim; but there was no water for the people to drink. 2 Therefore the people found fault with Moses, and said, "Give us water to drink." And Moses said to them, "Why do you find fault with me? Why do you put the LORD to the proof?" 3 But the people thirsted there for water, and the people murmured against Moses, and said, "Why did you bring us up out of Egypt, to kill us and our children and our cattle with thirst?" 4 So Moses cried to the LORD, "What shall I do with this people? They are almost ready to stone me."

5 And the LORD said to Moses, "Pass on before the people, taking with you some of the elders of Israel; and take in your hand the rod with which you struck the Nile, and go. 6 Behold, I will stand before you there on the rock at Hō'reb; and you shall strike the rock, and water shall come out of it, that the people may drink." And Moses did so, in the sight of the elders of Israel. 7 And he called the name of the place Mas'sáh[x] and Mer'i·báh,[y] because of the faultfinding of the children of Israel, and because they put the LORD to the proof by saying, "Is the LORD among us or not?"

8 Then came Am'á·lek and fought with Israel at Reph'i·dim. 9 And Moses said to Joshua, "Choose for us men, and go out, fight with Am'á·lek; tomorrow I will stand on the top of the hill with the rod of God in my hand." 10 So Joshua did as Moses told him, and fought with Am'á·lek; and Moses, Aaron, and Hūr went up to the top of the hill. 11 Whenever Moses held up his hand, Israel prevailed; and whenever he lowered his hand, Am'á·lek prevailed. 12 But Moses' hands grew weary; so they took a stone and put it under him, and he sat upon it, and Aaron and Hūr held up his hands, one on one side, and the other on the other side; so his hands were steady until the going down of the sun. 13 And Joshua mowed down Am'á·lek and his people with the edge of the sword.

14 And the LORD said to Moses, "Write this as a memorial in a book and recite it in the ears of Joshua, that I will utterly blot out the remembrance of Am'á·lek from under heaven." 15 And Moses built an altar and called the name of it, The LORD is my banner, 16 saying, "A hand upon the banner of the LORD![z] The LORD will have war with Am'á·lek from generation to generation."

18 Jethro, the priest of Mid'i·ản, Moses' father-in-law, heard of all that God had done for Moses and for Israel his people, how the LORD had brought Israel out of Egypt. 2 Now Jethro, Moses' father-in-law, had taken Zip·pō'ràh, Moses' wife, after he had sent her away, 3 and her two sons, of whom the name of the one was Gēr'shóm (for he said, "I have been a sojourner[a] in a foreign land"), 4 and the name of the other, E·li·ē'zér[b] (for he said, "The God of my father was my help, and delivered me from the

x That is *Proof*   y That is *Contention*   z Cn: Heb obscure   a Heb ger
b Heb *Eli*, my God, *ezer*, help
17.3: 14.12; 16.3.   **17.14:** Deut 25.17-19; 1 Sam 15.2-9.   **18.3-4:** Acts 7.29.

sword of Pharaoh"). [5]And Jethro, Moses' father-in-law, came with his sons and his wife to Moses in the wilderness where he was encamped at the mountain of God. [6]And when one told Moses, "Lo,[c] your father-in-law Jethro is coming to you with your wife and her two sons with her," [7] Moses went out to meet his father-in-law, and did obeisance and kissed him; and they asked each other of their welfare, and went into the tent. [8] Then Moses told his father-in-law all that the LORD had done to Pharaoh and to the Egyptians for Israel's sake, all the hardship that had come upon them in the way, and how the LORD had delivered them. [9]And Jethro rejoiced for all the good which the LORD had done to Israel, in that he had delivered them out of the hand of the Egyptians.

10 And Jethro said, "Blessed be the LORD, who has delivered you out of the hands of the Egyptians and out of the hand of Pharaoh. [11] Now I know that the LORD is greater than all gods, because he delivered the people from under the hand of the Egyptians,[d] when they dealt arrogantly with them." [12]And Jethro, Moses' father-in-law, offered[e] a burnt offering and sacrifices to God; and Aaron came with all the elders of Israel to eat bread with Moses' father-in-law before God.

13 On the morrow Moses sat to judge the people, and the people stood about Moses from morning till evening. [14] When Moses' father-in-law saw all that he was doing for the people, he said, "What is this that you are doing for the people? Why do you sit alone, and all the people stand about you from morning till evening?" [15]And Moses said to his father-in-law, "Because the people come to me to inquire of God; [16] when they have a dispute, they come to me and I decide between a man and his neighbor, and I make them know the statutes of God and his decisions." [17] Moses' father-in-law said to him, "What you are doing is not good. [18] You and the people with you will wear yourselves out, for the thing is too heavy for you; you are not able to perform it alone. [19] Listen now to my voice; I will give you counsel, and God be with you! You shall represent the people before God, and bring their cases to God; [20] and you shall teach them the statutes and the decisions, and make them know the way in which they must walk and

what they must do.[21] Moreover choose able men from all the people, such as fear God, men who are trustworthy and who hate a bribe; and place such men over the people as rulers of thousands, of hundreds, of fifties, and of tens. [22]And let them judge the people at all times; every great matter they shall bring to you, but any small matter they shall decide themselves; so it will be easier for you, and they will bear the burden with you. [23] If you do this, and God so commands you, then you will be able to endure, and all this people also will go to their place in peace."

24 So Moses gave heed to the voice of his father-in-law and did all that he had said. [25] Moses chose able men out of all Israel, and made them heads over the people, rulers of thousands, of hundreds, of fifties, and of tens. [26]And they judged the people at all times; hard cases they brought to Moses, but any small matter they decided themselves. [27] Then Moses let his father-in-law depart, and he went his way to his own country.

19 On the third new moon after the people of Israel had gone forth out of the land of Egypt, on that day they came into the wilderness of Sinai. [2]And when they set out from Reph'i-dim and came into the wilderness of Sinai, they encamped in the wilderness; and there Israel encamped before the mountain. [3]And Moses went up to God, and the LORD called to him out of the mountain, saying, "Thus you shall say to the house of Jacob, and tell the people of Israel: [4] You have seen what I did to the Egyptians, and how I bore you on 'eagles' wings and brought you to myself. [5] Now therefore, if you will obey my voice and keep my covenant, you shall be my own possession among all peoples; for all the earth is mine, [6] and you shall be to me a kingdom of priests and a holy nation. These are the words which you shall speak to the children of Israel."

7 So Moses came and called the elders of the people, and set before them all these words which the LORD had commanded him. [8]And all the people answered together and said, "All that the LORD has spoken we will do." And Moses reported the words of the people to the LORD. [9]And the LORD said to Moses, "Lo, I am coming to you in a thick cloud, that the people

c Sam Gk Syr: Heb I   d Transposing the last clause of v. 10 to v. 11
e Syr Tg Vg: Heb took
19.5-6: Deut 7.6; 14.2, 21; 26.19; Tit 2.14; 1 Pet 2.9; Rev 1.6; 5.10.

may hear when I speak with you, and may also believe you for ever."

Then Moses told the words of the people to the LORD. 10And the LORD said to Moses, "Go to the people and consecrate them today and tomorrow, and let them wash their garments, 11 and be ready by the third day; for on the third day the LORD will come down upon Mount Sinai in the sight of all the people. 12And you shall set bounds for the people round about, saying, 'Take heed that you do not go up into the mountain or touch the border of it; whoever touches the mountain shall be put to death; 13 no hand shall touch him, but he shall be stoned or shot; whether beast or man, he shall not live.' When the trumpet sounds a long blast, they shall come up to the mountain." 14 So Moses went down from the mountain to the people, and consecrated the people; and they washed their garments. 15And he said to the people, "Be ready by the third day; do not go near a woman."

16 On the morning of the third day there were thunders and lightnings, and a thick cloud upon the mountain, and a very loud trumpet blast, so that all the people who were in the camp trembled. 17 Then Moses brought the people out of the camp to meet God; and they took their stand at the foot of the mountain. 18And Mount Sinai was wrapped in smoke, because the LORD descended upon it in fire; and the smoke of it went up like the smoke of a kiln, and the whole mountain quaked greatly. 19And as the sound of the trumpet grew louder and louder, Moses spoke, and God answered him in thunder. 20And the LORD came down upon Mount Sinai, to the top of the mountain; and the LORD called Moses to the top of the mountain, and Moses went up. 21And the LORD said to Moses, "Go down and warn the people, lest they break through to the LORD to gaze and many of them perish. 22And also let the priests who come near to the LORD consecrate themselves, lest the LORD break out upon them." 23And Moses said to the LORD, "The people cannot come up

to Mount Sinai; for thou thyself didst charge us, saying, 'Set bounds about the mountain, and consecrate it.'" 24And the LORD said to him, "Go down, and come up bringing Aaron with you; but do not let the priests and the people break through to come up to the LORD, lest he break out against them." 25 So Moses went down to the people and told them.

20 And God spoke all these words, saying,

2 "I am the LORD your God, who brought you out of the land of Egypt, out of the house of bondage.

3 "You shall have no other gods before*f* me.

4 "You shall not make for yourself a graven image, or any likeness of anything that is in heaven above, or that is in the earth beneath, or that is in the water under the earth; 5 you shall not bow down to them or serve them; for I the LORD your God am a jealous God, visiting the iniquity of the fathers upon the children to the third and the fourth generation of those who hate me, 6 but showing steadfast love to thousands of those who love me and keep my commandments.

7 "You shall not take the name of the LORD your God in vain; for the LORD will not hold him guiltless who takes his name in vain.

8 "Remember the sabbath day, to keep it holy. 9 Six days you shall labor, and do all your work; 10 but the seventh day is a sabbath to the LORD your God; in it you shall not do any work, you, or your son, or your daughter, your manservant, or your maidservant, or your cattle, or the sojourner who is within your gates; 11 for in six days the LORD made heaven and earth, the sea, and all that is in them, and rested the seventh day; therefore the LORD blessed the sabbath day and hallowed it.

12 "Honor your father and your mother, that your days may be long in the land which the LORD your God gives you.

13 "You shall not kill.

14 "You shall not commit adultery.

15 "You shall not steal.

---

f Or *besides*

19.12-19: Heb 12.18-20.   **20.2-17:** Deut 5.6-21.   **20.3:** Ex 20.23; Deut 5.7.
20.4: Ex 20.23; 34.17; Lev 19.4; 26.1; Deut 4.15-19; 5.8; 27.15.
20.5-6: Ex 23.24; 34.6-7, 14; Deut 4.24; 5.9-10; 7.9.   **20.7:** Lev 19.12; Deut 5.11.
20.8: Ex 23.12; 31.12-17; 34.21; 35.2-3; Lev 19.3; Deut 5.12-15
20.12-16: Mt 19.18-19; Mk 10.19; Lk 18.20.
20.12: Lev 19.3; Deut 5.16; Mt 15.4; Mk 7.10; Eph 6.2.
20.13: Gen 9.6; Ex 21.12; Lev 24.17; Deut 5.17; Mt 5.21; Jas 2.11.
20.13-17: Rom 13.9.   **20.14:** Lev 20.10; Deut 5.18; Mt 5.27; Rom 7.7.
20.15: Lev 19.11; Deut 5.19.

16 "You shall not bear false witness against your neighbor.

17 "You shall not covet your neighbor's house; you shall not covet your neighbor's wife, or his manservant, or his maidservant, or his ox, or his ass, or anything that is your neighbor's."

18 Now when all the people perceived the thunderings and the lightnings and the sound of the trumpet and the mountain smoking, the people were afraid and trembled; and they stood afar off, 19 and said to Moses, "You speak to us, and we will hear; but let not God speak to us, lest we die." 20 And Moses said to the people, "Do not fear; for God has come to prove you, and that the fear of him may be before your eyes, that you may not sin."

21 And the people stood afar off, while Moses drew near to the thick darkness where God was. 22 And the LORD said to Moses, "Thus you shall say to the people of Israel: 'You have seen for yourselves that I have talked with you from heaven. 23 You shall not make gods of silver to be with me, nor shall you make for yourselves gods of gold. 24 An altar of earth you shall make for me and sacrifice on it your burnt offerings and your peace offerings, your sheep and your oxen; in every place where I cause my name to be remembered I will come to you and bless you. 25 And if you make me an altar of stone, you shall not build it of hewn stones; for if you wield your tool upon it you profane it. 26 And you shall not go up by steps to my altar, that your nakedness be not exposed on it.'

21 "Now these are the ordinances which you shall set before them. 2 When you buy a Hebrew slave, he shall serve six years, and in the seventh he shall go out free, for nothing. 3 If he comes in single, he shall go out single; if he comes in married, then his wife shall go out with him. 4 If his master gives him a wife and she bears him sons or daughters, the wife and her children shall be her master's and he shall go out alone. 5 But if the slave plainly says, 'I love my master, my wife, and my children; I will not go out free,' 6 then his master shall bring him to God, and he shall bring him

to the door or the doorpost; and his master shall bore his ear through with an awl; and he shall serve him for life.

7 "When a man sells his daughter as a slave, she shall not go out as the male slaves do. 8 If she does not please her master, who has designated her[g] for himself, then he shall let her be redeemed; he shall have no right to sell her to a foreign people, since he has dealt faithlessly with her. 9 If he designates her for his son, he shall deal with her as with a daughter. 10 If he takes another wife to himself, he shall not diminish her food, her clothing, or her marital rights. 11 And if he does not do these three things for her, she shall go out for nothing, without payment of money.

12 "Whoever strikes a man so that he dies shall be put to death. 13 But if he did not lie in wait for him, but God let him fall into his hand, then I will appoint for you a place to which he may flee. 14 But if a man willfully attacks another to kill him treacherously, you shall take him from my altar, that he may die.

15 "Whoever strikes his father or his mother shall be put to death.

16 "Whoever steals a man, whether he sells him or is found in possession of him, shall be put to death.

17 "Whoever curses his father or his mother shall be put to death.

18 "When men quarrel and one strikes the other with a stone or with his fist and the man does not die but keeps his bed, 19 then if the man rises again and walks abroad with his staff, he that struck him shall be clear; only he shall pay for the loss of his time, and shall have him thoroughly healed.

20 "When a man strikes his slave, male or female, with a rod and the slave dies under his hand, he shall be punished. 21 But if the slave survives a day or two, he is not to be punished; for the slave is his money.

22 "When men strive together, and hurt a woman with child, so that there is a miscarriage, and yet no harm follows, the one who hurt her shall[h] be fined, according as the woman's husband shall lay upon him; and he shall pay as the judges determine. 23 If any harm follows, then you shall give life for life, 24 eye for eye, tooth for

g Another reading is *so that he has not designated her*   h Heb *he shall*

20.16: Ex 23.1; Deut 5.20.   20.17: Deut 5.21; Rom 7.7.
20.23: Ex 20.3-4; 34.17; Deut 27.15.   20.24: Ex 27.1-8; Deut 12.5; 26.2.
20.25: Deut 27.5-6.   21.2-11: Lev 25.39-46; Deut 15.12-18.
21.12: Ex 20.13; Lev 24.17; Deut 5.17; Mt 5.21.
21.13: Num 35.10-34; Deut 19.1-13; Josh 20.1-9.   21.16: Deut 24.7.
21.17: Lev 20.9; Mt 15.4; Mk 7.10.   21.23-25: Lev 24.19-20; Deut 19.21; Mt 5.38.

tooth, hand for hand, foot for foot, 25 burn for burn, wound for wound, stripe for stripe.

26 "When a man strikes the eye of his slave, male or female, and destroys it, he shall let the slave go free for the eye's sake. 27 If he knocks out the tooth of his slave, male or female, he shall let the slave go free for the tooth's sake.

28 "When an ox gores a man or a woman to death, the ox shall be stoned, and its flesh shall not be eaten; but the owner of the ox shall be clear. 29 But if the ox has been accustomed to gore in the past, and its owner has been warned but has not kept it in, and it kills a man or a woman, the ox shall be stoned, and its owner also shall be put to death. 30 If a ransom is laid on him, then he shall give for the redemption of his life whatever is laid upon him. 31 If it gores a man's son or daughter, he shall be dealt with according to this same rule. 32 If the ox gores a slave, male or female, the owner shall give to their master thirty shekels of silver, and the ox shall be stoned.

33 "When a man leaves a pit open, or when a man digs a pit and does not cover it, and an ox or an ass falls into it, 34 the owner of the pit shall make it good; he shall give money to its owner, and the dead beast shall be his.

35 "When one man's ox hurts another's, so that it dies, then they shall sell the live ox and divide the price of it; and the dead beast also they shall divide. 36 Or if it is known that the ox has been accustomed to gore in the past, and its owner has not kept it in, he shall pay ox for ox, and the dead beast shall be his.

22 *i* "If a man steals an ox or a sheep, and kills it or sells it, he shall pay five oxen for an ox, and four sheep for a sheep.*j* He shall make restitution; if he has nothing, then he shall be sold for his theft. 4 If the stolen beast is found alive in his possession, whether it is an ox or an ass or a sheep, he shall pay double.

2*k* "If a thief is found breaking in, and is struck so that he dies, there shall be no bloodguilt for him; 3 but if the sun has risen upon him, there shall be bloodguilt for him.

5 "When a man causes a field or vineyard to be grazed over, or lets his beast loose and it feeds in another man's field, he shall make restitution from the best in his own field and in his own vineyard.

6 "When fire breaks out and catches in thorns so that the stacked grain or the standing grain or the field is consumed, he that kindled the fire shall make full restitution.

7 "If a man delivers to his neighbor money or goods to keep, and it is stolen out of the man's house, then, if the thief is found, he shall pay double. 8 If the thief is not found, the owner of the house shall come near to God, to show whether or not he has put his hand to his neighbor's goods.

9 "For every breach of trust, whether it is for ox, for ass, for sheep, for clothing, or for any kind of lost thing, of which one says, 'This is it,' the case of both parties shall come before God; he whom God shall condemn shall pay double to his neighbor.

10 "If a man delivers to his neighbor an ass or an ox or a sheep or any beast to keep, and it dies or is hurt or is driven away, without any one seeing it, 11 an oath by the LORD shall be between them both to see whether he has not put his hand to his neighbor's property; and the owner shall accept the oath, and he shall not make restitution. 12 But if it is stolen from him, he shall make restitution to its owner. 13 If it is torn by beasts, let him bring it as evidence; he shall not make restitution for what has been torn.

14 "If a man borrows anything of his neighbor, and it is hurt or dies, the owner not being with it, he shall make full restitution. 15 If the owner was with it, he shall not make restitution; if it was hired, it came for its hire.*l*

16 "If a man seduces a virgin who is not betrothed, and lies with her, he shall give the marriage present for her, and make her his wife. 17 If her father utterly refuses to give her to him, he shall pay money equivalent to the marriage present for virgins.

18 "You shall not permit a sorceress to live.

19 "Whoever lies with a beast shall be put to death.

20 "Whoever sacrifices to any god, save to the LORD only, shall be utterly destroyed.

i Ch 21.37 in Heb

j Restoring the second half of verse 3 with 4 to their place immediately following verse 1
k Ch 22.1 in Heb   *l* Or *it is reckoned in* (Heb *comes into*) *its hire*
22.7-15: Lev 5.14-6.7; Num 5.5-8.   **22.16-17:** Deut 22.28-29.
22.18: Lev 20.27; Deut 18.10.   **22.19:** Lev 18.23; 20.15-16; Deut 27.21.

21 "You shall not wrong a stranger or oppress him, for you were strangers in the land of Egypt. 22 You shall not afflict any widow or orphan. 23 If you do afflict them, and they cry out to me, I will surely hear their cry; 24 and my wrath will burn, and I will kill you with the sword, and your wives shall become widows and your children fatherless.

25 "If you lend money to any of my people with you who is poor, you shall not be to him as a creditor, and you shall not exact interest from him. 26 If ever you take your neighbor's garment in pledge, you shall restore it to him before the sun goes down; 27 for that is his only covering, it is his mantle for his body; in what else shall he sleep? And if he cries to me, I will hear, for I am compassionate.

28 "You shall not revile God, nor curse a ruler of your people.

29 "You shall not delay to offer from the fulness of your harvest and from the outflow of your presses.

"The first-born of your sons you shall give to me. 30 You shall do likewise with your oxen and with your sheep: seven days it shall be with its dam; on the eighth day you shall give it to me.

31 "You shall be men consecrated to me; therefore you shall not eat any flesh that is torn by beasts in the field; you shall cast it to the dogs.

23 "You shall not utter a false report. You shall not join hands with a wicked man, to be a malicious witness. 2 You shall not follow a multitude to do evil; nor shall you bear witness in a suit, turning aside after a multitude, so as to pervert justice; 3 nor shall you be partial to a poor man in his suit.

4 "If you meet your enemy's ox or his ass going astray, you shall bring it back to him. 5 If you see the ass of one who hates you lying under its burden, you shall refrain from leaving him with it, you shall help him to lift it up.*m*

6 "You shall not pervert the justice due to your poor in his suit. 7 Keep far from a false charge, and do not

slay the innocent and righteous, for I will not acquit the wicked. 8 And you shall take no bribe, for a bribe blinds the officials, and subverts the cause of those who are in the right.

9 "You shall not oppress a stranger; you know the heart of a stranger, for you were strangers in the land of Egypt.

10 "For six years you shall sow your land and gather in its yield; 11 but the seventh year you shall let it rest and lie fallow, that the poor of your people may eat; and what they leave the wild beasts may eat. You shall do likewise with your vineyard, and with your olive orchard.

12 "Six days you shall do your work, but on the seventh day you shall rest; that your ox and your ass may have rest, and the son of your bond-maid, and the alien, may be refreshed. 13 Take heed to all that I have said to you; and make no mention of the names of other gods, nor let such be heard out of your mouth.

14 "Three times in the year you shall keep a feast to me. 15 You shall keep the feast of unleavened bread; as I commanded you, you shall eat un-leavened bread for seven days at the appointed time in the month of Ā'bib, for in it you came out of Egypt. None shall appear before me empty-handed. 16 You shall keep the feast of harvest, of the first fruits of your labor, of what you sow in the field. You shall keep the feast of ingathering at the end of the year, when you gather in from the field the fruit of your labor. 17 Three times in the year shall all your males appear before the Lord God.

18 "You shall not offer the blood of my sacrifice with leavened bread, or let the fat of my feast remain until the morning.

19 "The first of the first fruits of your ground you shall bring into the house of the Lord your God.

"You shall not boil a kid in its mother's milk.

20 "Behold, I send an angel before you, to guard you on the way and to

---

m Gk: Heb obscure

22.21: Ex 23.9; Lev 19.33-34; Deut 27.19.   **22.22:** Deut 24.17.
22.25-27: Lev 25.36-37; Deut 23.19-20.   **22.28:** Acts 23.5.
22.29: Ex 23.16, 19; Deut 26.2-11; Ex 13.2, 11-16.
22.31: Ex 19.6; Lev 11.44; 19.1; 7.24; 17.15.
23.1: Ex 20.16; 23.7; Deut 5.20; 19.15-21.   **23.3, 6:** Lev 19.15.   **23.7:** Ex 20.16; 23.1.
23.8: Deut 16.19.   **23.9:** Ex 22.21; Lev 19.33-34; Deut 27.19.   **23.10-11:** Lev 25.1-7.
23.12: Ex 20.8-11; 31.15-17; 34.21; 35.2; Deut 5.12-15.
23.14-17: Ex 34.22-24; Lev 23.1-44; Deut 16.1-17.
23.18: Ex 12.10; Lev 2.11; Ex 34.25; Lev 7.15.
23.19: Ex 22.29; 34.26; Deut 26.2-11; 14.21.

bring you to the place which I have prepared. 21 Give heed to him and hearken to his voice, do not rebel against him, for he will not pardon your transgression; for my name is in him.

22 "But if you hearken attentively to his voice and do all that I say, then I will be an enemy to your enemies and an adversary to your adversaries.

23 "When my angel goes before you, and brings you in to the Am′ō-rītes, and the Hit′tītes, and the Per′iz-zītes, and the Canaanites, the Hī′vītes, and the Jeb′ū-sītes, and I blot them out, 24 you shall not bow down to their gods, nor serve them, nor do according to their works, but you shall utterly overthrow them and break their pillars in pieces. 25 You shall serve the LORD your God, and In will bless your bread and your water; and I will take sickness away from the midst of you. 26 None shall cast her young or be barren in your land; I will fulfil the number of your days. 27 I will send my terror before you, and will throw into confusion all the people against whom you shall come, and I will make all your enemies turn their backs to you. 28 And I will send hornets before you, which shall drive out Hī′vīte, Canaanite, and Hit′tīte from before you. 29 I will not drive them out from before you in one year, lest the land become desolate and the wild beasts multiply against you. 30 Little by little I will drive them out from before you, until you are increased and possess the land. 31 And I will set your bounds from the Red Sea to the sea of the Philistines, and from the wilderness to the Eū·phrā′tēs; for I will deliver the inhabitants of the land into your hand, and you shall drive them out before you. 32 You shall make no covenant with them or with their gods. 33 They shall not dwell in your land, lest they make you sin against me; for if you serve their gods, it will surely be a snare to you."

24 And he said to Moses, "Come up to the LORD, you and Aaron, Nā′dab, and Ā·bī′hū, and seventy of the elders of Israel, and worship afar off. 2 Moses alone shall come near to the LORD; but the others shall not come near, and the people shall not come up with him."

3 Moses came and told the people all the words of the LORD and all the ordinances; and all the people answered

with one voice, and said, "All the words which the LORD has spoken we will do." 4 And Moses wrote all the words of the LORD. And he rose early in the morning, and built an altar at the foot of the mountain, and twelve pillars, according to the twelve tribes of Israel. 5 And he sent young men of the people of Israel, who offered burnt offerings and sacrificed peace offerings of oxen to the LORD. 6 And Moses took half of the blood and put it in basins, and half of the blood he threw against the altar. 7 Then he took the book of the covenant, and read it in the hearing of the people; and they said, "All that the LORD has spoken we will do, and we will be obedient." 8 And Moses took the blood and threw it upon the people, and said, "Behold the blood of the covenant which the LORD has made with you in accordance with all these words."

9 Then Moses and Aaron, Nā′dab, and Ā·bī′hū, and seventy of the elders of Israel went up, 10 and they saw the God of Israel; and there was under his feet as it were a pavement of sapphire stone, like the very heaven for clearness. 11 And he did not lay his hand on the chief men of the people of Israel; they beheld God, and ate and drank.

12 The LORD said to Moses, "Come up to me on the mountain, and wait there; and I will give you the tables of stone, with the law and the command-ment, which I have written for their instruction." 13 So Moses rose with his servant Joshua, and Moses went up into the mountain of God. 14 And he said to the elders, "Tarry here for us, until we come to you again; and, behold, Aaron and Hūr are with you; whoever has a cause, let him go to them."

15 Then Moses went up on the mountain, and the cloud covered the mountain. 16 The glory of the LORD settled on Mount Sinai, and the cloud covered it six days; and on the seventh day he called to Moses out of the midst of the cloud. 17 Now the appearance of the glory of the LORD was like a devouring fire on the top of the moun-tain in the sight of the people of Israel. 18 And Moses entered the cloud, and went up on the mountain. And Moses was on the mountain forty days and forty nights.

25 The LORD said to Moses, 2 "Speak to the people of Israel,

n Gk Vg: Heb he

24.8: Mt 26.28; Mk 14.24; Lk 22.20; 1 Cor 11.25; Heb 9.20; 10.29.
24.12: 2 Cor 3.3.   25-31: Ex 35-40.   25.2-8: Ex 35.4-9.

that they take for me an offering; from every man whose heart makes him willing you shall receive the offering for me. ³And this is the offering which you shall receive from them: gold, silver, and bronze, ⁴ blue and purple and scarlet stuff and fine twined linen, goats' hair, ⁵ tanned rams' skins, goat-skins, acacia wood, ⁶ oil for the lamps, spices for the anointing oil and for the fragrant incense, ⁷ onyx stones, and stones for setting, for the ephod and for the breastpiece. ⁸And let them make me a sanctuary, that I may dwell in their midst. ⁹According to all that I show you concerning the pattern of the tabernacle, and of all its furniture, so you shall make it.

10 "They shall make an ark of acacia wood; two cubits and a half shall be its length, a cubit and a half its breadth, and a cubit and a half its height. ¹¹And you shall overlay it with pure gold, within and without shall you overlay it, and you shall make upon it a molding of gold round about. ¹²And you shall cast four rings of gold for it and put them on its four feet, two rings on the one side of it, and two rings on the other side of it. ¹³ You shall make poles of acacia wood, and overlay them with gold. ¹⁴And you shall put the poles into the rings on the sides of the ark, to carry the ark by them. ¹⁵ The poles shall remain in the rings of the ark; they shall not be taken from it. ¹⁶And you shall put into the ark the testimony which I shall give you. ¹⁷ Then you shall make a mercy seatᵒ of pure gold; two cubits and a half shall be its length, and a cubit and a half its breadth. ¹⁸And you shall make two cherubim of gold; of hammered work shall you make them, on the two ends of the mercy seat. ¹⁹ Make one cherub on the one end, and one cherub on the other end; of one piece with the mercy seat shall you make the cherubim on its two ends. ²⁰ The cherubim shall spread out their wings above, overshadowing the mercy seat with their wings, their faces one to another; toward the mercy seat shall the faces of the cherubim be. ²¹And you shall put the mercy seat on the top of the ark; and in the ark you shall put the testimony that I shall give you.²² There I will meet with you, and from above the mercy seat, from between the two cherubim that are upon the ark of the testimony, I will speak with you of all that I will

give you in commandment for the people of Israel.

23 "And you shall make a table of acacia wood; two cubits shall be its length, a cubit its breadth, and a cubit and a half its height. ²⁴ You shall overlay it with pure gold, and make a molding of gold around it. ²⁵And you shall make around it a frame a hand-breadth wide, and a molding of gold around the frame. ²⁶And you shall make for it four rings of gold, and fasten the rings to the four corners at its four legs. ²⁷ Close to the frame the rings shall lie, as holders for the poles to carry the table. ²⁸ You shall make the poles of acacia wood, and overlay them with gold, and the table shall be carried with these. ²⁹And you shall make its plates and dishes for incense, and its flagons and bowls with which to pour libations; of pure gold you shall make them. ³⁰And you shall set the bread of the Presence on the table before me always.

31 "And you shall make a lamp-stand of pure gold. The base and the shaft of the lampstand shall be made of hammered work; its cups, its capitals, and its flowers shall be of one piece with it; ³² and there shall be six branches going out of its sides, three branches of the lampstand out of one side of it and three branches of the lampstand out of the other side of it; ³³ three cups made like almonds, each with capital and flower, on one branch, and three cups made like almonds, each with capital and flower, on the other branch—so for the six branches going out of the lampstand; ³⁴ and on the lampstand itself four cups made like almonds, with their capitals and flowers, ³⁵ and a capital of one piece with it under each pair of the six branches going out from the lamp-stand. ³⁶ Their capitals and their branches shall be of one piece with it, the whole of it one piece of hammered work of pure gold. ³⁷And you shall make the seven lamps for it; and the lamps shall be set up so as to give light upon the space in front of it. ³⁸ Its snuffers and their trays shall be of pure gold. ³⁹ Of a talent of pure gold shall it be made, with all these utensils. ⁴⁰And see that you make them after the pattern for them, which is being shown you on the mountain.

26 "Moreover you shall make the tabernacle with ten curtains of fine twined linen and blue and purple

ᵒ Or *cover*

25.10-22: Ex 37.1-9.   25.23-30: Ex 37.10-15.   25.30: Ex 39.36; 40.23; Lev 24.5-9.
25.31-40: Ex 37.17-24.   25.40: Acts 7.44; Heb 8.5.   26.1-14: Ex 36.8-19.

and scarlet stuff; with cherubim skilfully worked shall you make them. 2 The length of each curtain shall be twenty-eight cubits, and the breadth of each curtain four cubits; all the curtains shall have one measure. 3 Five curtains shall be coupled to one another; and the other five curtains shall be coupled to one another. 4And you shall make loops of blue on the edge of the outmost curtain in the first set; and likewise you shall make loops on the edge of the outmost curtain in the second set. 5 Fifty loops you shall make on the one curtain, and fifty loops you shall make on the edge of the curtain that is in the second set; the loops shall be opposite one another. 6And you shall make fifty clasps of gold, and couple the curtains one to the other with the clasps, that the tabernacle may be one whole.

7 "You shall also make curtains of goats' hair for a tent over the tabernacle; eleven curtains shall you make. 8 The length of each curtain shall be thirty cubits, and the breadth of each curtain four cubits; the eleven curtains shall have the same measure. 9And you shall couple five curtains by themselves, and six curtains by themselves, and the sixth curtain you shall double over at the front of the tent. 10And you shall make fifty loops on the edge of the curtain that is outmost in one set, and fifty loops on the edge of the curtain which is outmost in the second set.

11 "And you shall make fifty clasps of bronze, and put the clasps into the loops, and couple the tent together that it may be one whole. 12And the part that remains of the curtains of the tent, the half curtain that remains, shall hang over the back of the tabernacle. 13And the cubit on the one side, and the cubit on the other side, of what remains in the length of the curtains of the tent shall hang over the sides of the tabernacle, on this side and that side, to cover it. 14And you shall make for the tent a covering of tanned rams' skins and goatskins.

15 "And you shall make upright frames for the tabernacle of acacia wood. 16 Ten cubits shall be the length of a frame, and a cubit and a half the breadth of each frame. 17 There shall be two tenons in each frame, for fitting together; so shall you do for all the frames of the tabernacle. 18 You shall make the frames for the tabernacle: twenty frames for the south side; 19 and forty bases of silver you shall make

under the twenty frames, two bases under one frame for its two tenons, and two bases under another frame for its two tenons; 20 and for the second side of the tabernacle, on the north side twenty frames, 21 and their forty bases of silver, two bases under one frame, and two bases under another frame; 22 and for the rear of the tabernacle westward you shall make six frames. 23And you shall make two frames for corners of the tabernacle in the rear; 24 they shall be separate beneath, but joined at the top, at the first ring; thus shall it be with both of them; they shall form the two corners. 25And there shall be eight frames, with their bases of silver, sixteen bases; two bases under one frame, and two bases under another frame.

26 "And you shall make bars of acacia wood, five for the frames of one side of the tabernacle, 27 and five bars for the frames of the other side of the tabernacle, and five bars for the frames of the side of the tabernacle at the rear westward. 28 The middle bar, halfway up the frames, shall pass through from end to end. 29 You shall overlay the frames with gold, and shall make their rings of gold for holders for the bars; and you shall overlay the bars with gold. 30And you shall erect the tabernacle according to the plan for it which has been shown you on the mountain.

31 "And you shall make a veil of blue and purple and scarlet stuff and fine twined linen; in skilled work shall it be made, with cherubim; 32 and you shall hang it upon four pillars of acacia overlaid with gold, with hooks of gold, upon four bases of silver. 33And you shall hang the veil from the clasps, and bring the ark of the testimony in thither within the veil; and the veil shall separate for you the holy place from the most holy. 34 You shall put the mercy seat upon the ark of the testimony in the most holy place. 35 And you shall set the table outside the veil, and the lampstand on the south side of the tabernacle opposite the table; and you shall put the table on the north side.

36 "And you shall make a screen for the door of the tent, of blue and purple and scarlet stuff and fine twined linen, embroidered with needlework. 37And you shall make for the screen five pillars of acacia, and overlay them with gold; their hooks shall be of gold, and you shall cast five bases of bronze for them.

26.15-29: Ex 36.20-34. **26.31-37:** Ex 36.35-38.

27 "You shall make the altar of acacia wood, five cubits long and five cubits broad; the altar shall be square, and its height shall be three cubits. 2And you shall make horns for it on its four corners; its horns shall be of one piece with it, and you shall overlay it with bronze. 3 You shall make pots for it to receive its ashes, and shovels and basins and forks and firepans; all its utensils you shall make of bronze. 4 You shall also make for it a grating, a network of bronze; and upon the net you shall make four bronze rings at its four corners. 5And you shall set it under the ledge of the altar so that the net shall extend halfway down the altar. 6And you shall make poles for the altar, poles of acacia wood, and overlay them with bronze, 7 and the poles shall be put through the rings, so that the poles shall be upon the two sides of the altar, when it is carried. 8 You shall make it hollow, with boards; as it has been shown you on the mountain, so shall it be made.

9 "You shall make the court of the tabernacle. On the south side the court shall have hangings of fine twined linen a hundred cubits long for one side; 10 their pillars shall be twenty and their bases twenty, of bronze, but the hooks of the pillars and their fillets shall be of silver. 11And likewise for its length on the north side there shall be hangings a hundred cubits long, their pillars twenty and their bases twenty, of bronze, but the hooks of the pillars and their fillets shall be of silver. 12And for the breadth of the court on the west side there shall be hangings for fifty cubits, with ten pillars and ten bases. 13 The breadth of the court on the front to the east shall be fifty cubits. 14 The hangings for the one side of the gate shall be fifteen cubits, with three pillars and three bases. 15 On the other side the hangings shall be fifteen cubits, with three pillars and three bases. 16 For the gate of the court there shall be a screen twenty cubits long, of blue and purple and scarlet stuff and fine twined linen, embroidered with needlework; it shall have four pillars and with them four bases. 17All the pillars around the court shall be filleted with silver; their hooks shall be of silver, and their bases of bronze. 18 The length of the court shall be a hundred cubits, the breadth fifty, and the height five cubits, with hangings of fine twined linen and bases of bronze. 19All the utensils of the tabernacle for every use, and all its pegs and all the pegs of the court, shall be of bronze.

20 "And you shall command the people of Israel that they bring to you pure beaten olive oil for the light, that a lamp may be set up to burn continually. 21 In the tent of meeting, outside the veil which is before the testimony, Aaron and his sons shall tend it from evening to morning before the LORD. It shall be a statute for ever to be observed throughout their generations by the people of Israel.

28 "Then bring near to you Aaron your brother, and his sons with him, from among the people of Israel, to serve me as priests—Aaron and Aaron's sons, Nā′dab and A·bī′hū, El·ē·ā′zär and Ith′á·mär. 2And you shall make holy garments for Aaron your brother, for glory and for beauty. 3And you shall speak to all who have ability, whom I have endowed with an able mind, that they make Aaron's garments to consecrate him for my priesthood. 4 These are the garments which they shall make: a breastpiece, an ephod, a robe, a coat of checker work, a turban, and a girdle; they shall make holy garments for Aaron your brother and his sons to serve me as priests.

5 "They shall receive gold, blue and purple and scarlet stuff, and fine twined linen. 6And they shall make the ephod of gold, of blue and purple and scarlet stuff, and of fine twined linen, skilfully worked. 7 It shall have two shoulder-pieces attached to its two edges, that it may be joined together. 8And the skilfully woven band upon it, to gird it on, shall be of the same workmanship and materials, of gold, blue and purple and scarlet stuff, and fine twined linen. 9And you shall take two onyx stones, and engrave on them the names of the sons of Israel, 10 six of their names on the one stone, and the names of the remaining six on the other stone, in the order of their birth. 11As a jeweler engraves signets, so shall you engrave the two stones with the names of the sons of Israel; you shall enclose them in settings of gold filigree. 12And you shall set the two stones upon the shoulder-pieces of the ephod, as stones of remembrance for the sons of Israel; and Aaron shall bear their names before the LORD upon his two shoulders for remembrance. 13And you shall make settings of gold filigree, 14 and two chains of pure gold, twisted like cords; and you shall attach the corded chains to the settings.

27.1-8: Ex 38.1-7.　　**27.9-19:** Ex 38.9-20.　　**27.20-21:** Lev 24.1-4.　　**28.6-12:** Ex 39.2-7.

15 "And you shall make a breast-piece of judgment, in skilled work; like the work of the ephod you shall make it; of gold, blue and purple and scarlet stuff, and fine twined linen shall you make it. 16 It shall be square and double, a span its length and a span its breadth. 17And you shall set in it four rows of stones. A row of sardius, topaz, and carbuncle shall be the first row; 18 and the second row an emerald, a sapphire, and a diamond; 19 and the third row a jacinth, an agate, and an amethyst; 20 and the fourth row a beryl, an onyx, and a jasper; they shall be set in gold filigree. 21 There shall be twelve stones with their names according to the names of the sons of Israel; they shall be like signets, each engraved with its name, for the twelve tribes. 22And you shall make for the breastpiece twisted chains like cords, of pure gold; 23 and you shall make for the breastpiece two rings of gold, and put the two rings on the two edges of the breastpiece. 24And you shall put the two cords of gold in the two rings at the edges of the breastpiece; 25 the two ends of the two cords you shall attach to the two settings of filigree, and so attach it in front to the shoulder-pieces of the ephod. 26And you shall make two rings of gold, and put them at the two ends of the breastpiece, on its inside edge next to the ephod. 27And you shall make two rings of gold, and attach them in front to the lower part of the two shoulder-pieces of the ephod, at its joining above the skilfully woven band of the ephod. 28And they shall bind the breastpiece by its rings to the rings of the ephod with a lace of blue, that it may lie upon the skilfully woven band of the ephod, and that the breastpiece shall not come loose from the ephod. 29 So Aaron shall bear the names of the sons of Israel in the breastpiece of judgment upon his heart, when he goes into the holy place, to bring them to continual remembrance before the LORD. 30And in the breastpiece of judgment you shall put the U′rim and the Thum′mim, and they shall be upon Aaron's heart, when he goes in before the LORD; thus Aaron shall bear the judgment of the people of Israel upon his heart before the LORD continually.

31 "And you shall make the robe of the ephod all of blue. 32 It shall have at its opening for the head, with a woven binding around the opening, like the opening in a garment,*p* that it may not be torn. 33 On its skirts you shall make pomegranates of blue and purple and scarlet stuff, around its skirts, with bells of gold between them, 34 a golden bell and a pomegranate, a golden bell and a pomegranate, round about on the skirts of the robe. 35And it shall be upon Aaron when he ministers, and its sound shall be heard when he goes into the holy place before the LORD, and when he comes out, lest he die.

36 "And you shall make a plate of pure gold, and engrave on it, like the engraving of a signet, 'Holy to the LORD.' 37And you shall fasten it on the turban by a lace of blue; it shall be on the front of the turban. 38 It shall be upon Aaron's forehead, and Aaron shall take upon himself any guilt incurred in the holy offering which the people of Israel hallow as their holy gifts; it shall always be upon his forehead, that they may be accepted before the LORD.

39 "And you shall weave the coat in checker work of fine linen, and you shall make a turban of fine linen, and you shall make a girdle embroidered with needlework.

40 "And for Aaron's sons you shall make coats and girdles and caps; you shall make them for glory and beauty. 41And you shall put them upon Aaron your brother, and upon his sons with him, and shall anoint them and ordain them and consecrate them, that they may serve me as priests. 42And you shall make for them linen breeches to cover their naked flesh; from the loins to the thighs they shall reach; 43 and they shall be upon Aaron, and upon his sons, when they go into the tent of meeting, or when they come near the altar to minister in the holy place; lest they bring guilt upon themselves and die. This shall be a perpetual statute for him and for his descendants after him.

29 "Now this is what you shall do to them to consecrate them, that they may serve me as priests. Take one young bull and two rams without blemish, 2 and unleavened bread, unleavened cakes mixed with oil, and unleavened wafers spread with oil. You shall make them of fine wheat flour. 3And you shall put them in one basket and bring them in the basket, and bring the bull and the two rams. 4 You

p The Hebrew word is of uncertain meaning

28.15-28: Ex 39.8-21. **28.31-34:** Ex 39.22-26. **28.36-37:** Ex 39.30-31. **28.39-40, 42:** Ex 39.27-29. **29.1-37:** Lev 8.1-34.

shall bring Aaron and his sons to the door of the tent of meeting, and wash them with water. 5And you shall take the garments, and put on Aaron the coat and the robe of the ephod, and the ephod, and the breastpiece, and gird him with the skilfully woven band of the ephod; 6 and you shall set the turban on his head, and put the holy crown upon the turban. 7And you shall take the anointing oil, and pour it on his head and anoint him. 8 Then you shall bring his sons, and put coats on them, 9 and you shall gird them with girdles*q* and bind caps on them; and the priesthood shall be theirs by a perpetual statute. Thus you shall ordain Aaron and his sons.

10 "Then you shall bring the bull before the tent of meeting. Aaron and his sons shall lay their hands upon the head of the bull, 11 and you shall kill the bull before the LORD, at the door of the tent of meeting, 12 and shall take part of the blood of the bull and put it upon the horns of the altar with your finger, and the rest of*r* the blood you shall pour out at the base of the altar. 13And you shall take all the fat that covers the entrails, and the appendage of the liver, and the two kidneys with the fat that is on them, and burn them upon the altar. 14 But the flesh of the bull, and its skin, and its dung, you shall burn with fire outside the camp; it is a sin offering.

15 "Then you shall take one of the rams, and Aaron and his sons shall lay their hands upon the head of the ram, 16 and you shall slaughter the ram, and shall take its blood and throw it against the altar round about. 17 Then you shall cut the ram into pieces, and wash its entrails and its legs, and put them with its pieces and its head, 18 and burn the whole ram upon the altar; it is a burnt offering to the LORD; it is a pleasing odor, an offering by fire to the LORD.

19 "You shall take the other ram; and Aaron and his sons shall lay their hands upon the head of the ram, 20 and you shall kill the ram, and take part of its blood and put it upon the tip of the right ear of Aaron and upon the tips of the right ears of his sons, and upon the thumbs of their right hands, and upon the great toes of their right feet, and throw the rest of the blood against the altar round about. 21 Then you shall take part of the blood that is on the altar, and of the anointing oil, and sprinkle it upon

Aaron and his garments, and upon his sons and his sons' garments with him; and he and his garments shall be holy, and his sons and his sons' garments with him.

22 "You shall also take the fat of the ram, and the fat tail, and the fat that covers the entrails, and the appendage of the liver, and the two kidneys with the fat that is on them, and the right thigh (for it is a ram of ordination), 23 and one loaf of bread, and one cake of bread with oil, and one wafer, out of the basket of unleavened bread that is before the LORD; 24 and you shall put all these in the hands of Aaron and in the hands of his sons, and wave them for a wave offering before the LORD. 25 Then you shall take them from their hands, and burn them on the altar in addition to the burnt offering, as a pleasing odor before the LORD; it is an offering by fire to the LORD.

26 "And you shall take the breast of the ram of Aaron's ordination and wave it for a wave offering before the LORD; and it shall be your portion. 27And you shall consecrate the breast of the wave offering, and the thigh of the priests' portion, which is waved, and which is offered from the ram of ordination, since it is for Aaron and for his sons. 28 It shall be for Aaron and his sons as a perpetual due from the people of Israel, for it is the priests' portion to be offered by the people of Israel from their peace offerings; it is their offering to the LORD.

29 "The holy garments of Aaron shall be for his sons after him, to be anointed in them and ordained in them. 30 The son who is priest in his place shall wear them seven days, when he comes into the tent of meeting to minister in the holy place.

31 "You shall take the ram of ordination, and boil its flesh in a holy place; 32 and Aaron and his sons shall eat the flesh of the ram and the bread that is in the basket, at the door of the tent of meeting. 33 They shall eat those things with which atonement was made, to ordain and consecrate them, but an outsider shall not eat of them, because they are holy. 34And if any of the flesh for the ordination, or of the bread, remain until the morning, then you shall burn the remainder with fire; it shall not be eaten, because it is holy.

35 "Thus you shall do to Aaron and to his sons, according to all that I have commanded you; through seven days

q Gk: Heb *girdles, Aaron and his sons*   *r* Heb *all*
29.18: Eph 5.2; Phil 4.18.

shall you ordain them, 36 and every day you shall offer a bull as a sin offering for atonement. Also you shall offer a sin offering for the altar, when you make atonement for it, and shall anoint it, to consecrate it. 37 Seven days you shall make atonement for the altar, and consecrate it, and the altar shall be most holy; whatever touches the altar shall become holy.

38 "Now this is what you shall offer upon the altar: two lambs a year old day by day continually. 39 One lamb you shall offer in the morning, and the other lamb you shall offer in the evening; 40 and with the first lamb a tenth measure of fine flour mingled with a fourth of a hin of beaten oil, and a fourth of a hin of wine for a libation. 41And the other lamb you shall offer in the evening, and shall offer with it a cereal offering and its libation, as in the morning, for a pleasing odor, an offering by fire to the LORD. 42 It shall be a continual burnt offering throughout your generations at the door of the tent of meeting before the LORD, where I will meet with you, to speak there to you. 43 There I will meet with the people of Israel, and it shall be sanctified by my glory; 44 I will consecrate the tent of meeting and the altar; Aaron also and his sons I will consecrate, to serve me as priests. 45And I will dwell among the people of Israel, and will be their God. 46And they shall know that I am the LORD their God, who brought them forth out of the land of Egypt that I might dwell among them; I am the LORD their God.

30 "You shall make an altar to burn incense upon; of acacia wood shall you make it. 2A cubit shall be its length, and a cubit its breadth; it shall be square, and two cubits shall be its height; its horns shall be of one piece with it. 3And you shall overlay it with pure gold, its top and its side round about and its horns; and you shall make for it a molding of gold round about. 4And two golden rings shall you make for it; under its molding on two opposite sides of it shall you make them, and they shall be holders for poles with which to carry it. 5 You shall make the poles of acacia wood, and overlay them with gold. 6And you shall put it before the veil that is by the ark of the testimony, before the mercy seat that is over the testimony, where I will meet with you. 7And Aaron shall burn fragrant incense on it; every morning when he dresses the

lamps he shall burn it, 8 and when Aaron sets up the lamps in the evening, he shall burn it, a perpetual incense before the LORD throughout your generations. 9 You shall offer no unholy incense thereon, nor burnt offering, nor cereal offering; and you shall pour no libation thereon. 10Aaron shall make atonement upon its horns once a year; with the blood of the sin offering of atonement he shall make atonement for it once in the year throughout your generations; it is most holy to the LORD.

11 The LORD said to Moses, 12 "When you take the census of the people of Israel, then each shall give a ransom for himself to the LORD when you number them, that there be no plague among them when you number them. 13 Each who is numbered in the census shall give this: half a shekel according to the shekel of the sanctuary (the shekel is twenty gerahs), half a shekel as an offering to the LORD. 14 Every one who is numbered in the census, from twenty years old and upward, shall give the LORD's offering. 15 The rich shall not give more, and the poor shall not give less, than the half shekel, when you give the LORD's offering to make atonement for yourselves. 16And you shall take the atonement money from the people of Israel, and shall appoint it for the service of the tent of meeting; that it may bring the people of Israel to remembrance before the LORD, so as to make atonement for yourselves."

17 The LORD said to Moses, 18 "You shall also make a laver of bronze, with its base of bronze, for washing. And you shall put it between the tent of meeting and the altar, and you shall put water in it, 19 with which Aaron and his sons shall wash their hands and their feet. 20 When they go into the tent of meeting, or when they come near the altar to minister, to burn an offering by fire to the LORD, they shall wash with water, lest they die. 21 They shall wash their hands and their feet, lest they die: it shall be a statute for ever to them, even to him and to his descendants throughout their generations."

22 Moreover, the LORD said to Moses, 23 "Take the finest spices: of liquid myrrh five hundred shekels, and of sweet-smelling cinnamon half as much, that is, two hundred and fifty, and of aromatic cane two hundred and fifty, 24 and of cassia five hundred,

according to the shekel of the sanctuary, and of olive oil a hin; 25 and you shall make of these a sacred anointing oil blended as by the perfumer; a holy anointing oil it shall be. 26And you shall anoint with it the tent of meeting and the ark of the testimony, 27 and the table and all its utensils, and the lampstand and its utensils, and the altar of incense, 28 and the altar of burnt offering with all its utensils and the laver and its base; 29 you shall consecrate them, that they may be most holy; whatever touches them will become holy. 30And you shall anoint Aaron and his sons, and consecrate them, that they may serve me as priests. 31And you shall say to the people of Israel, 'This shall be my holy anointing oil throughout your generations. 32 It shall not be poured upon the bodies of ordinary men, and you shall make no other like it in composition; it is holy, and it shall be holy to you. 33 Whoever compounds any like it or whoever puts any of it on an outsider shall be cut off from his people.'"

34 And the LORD said to Moses, "Take sweet spices, stacte, and onycha, and galbanum, sweet spices with pure frankincense (of each shall there be an equal part), 35 and make an incense blended as by the perfumer, seasoned with salt, pure and holy; 36 and you shall beat some of it very small, and put part of it before the testimony in the tent of meeting where I shall meet with you; it shall be for you most holy. 37And the incense which you shall make according to its composition, you shall not make for yourselves; it shall be for you holy to the LORD. 38 Whoever makes any like it to use as perfume shall be cut off from his people."

31 The LORD said to Moses, 2 "See, I have called by name Bez′a·lel the son of U′ri, son of Hūr, of the tribe of Judah; 3 and I have filled him with the Spirit of God, with ability and intelligence, with knowledge and all craftsmanship, 4 to devise artistic designs, to work in gold, silver, and bronze, 5 in cutting stones for setting, and in carving wood, for work in every craft. 6And behold, I have appointed with him Ō·hō′li·ab, the son of A·his′a·mach, of the tribe of Dan; and I have given to all able men ability, that they may make all that I have commanded you: 7 the tent of meeting, and the ark of the testimony, and the mercy seat that is thereon, and all the furnishings

of the tent, 8 the table and its utensils, and the pure lampstand with all its utensils, and the altar of incense, 9 and the altar of burnt offering with all its utensils, and the laver and its base, 10 and the finely worked garments, the holy garments for Aaron the priest and the garments of his sons, for their service as priests, 11 and the anointing oil and the fragrant incense for the holy place. According to all that I have commanded you they shall do."

12 And the LORD said to Moses, 13 "Say to the people of Israel, 'You shall keep my sabbaths, for this is a sign between me and you throughout your generations, that you may know that I, the LORD, sanctify you. 14 You shall keep the sabbath, because it is holy for you; every one who profanes it shall be put to death; whoever does any work on it, that soul shall be cut off from among his people. 15 Six days shall work be done, but the seventh day is a sabbath of solemn rest, holy to the LORD; whoever does any work on the sabbath day shall be put to death. 16 Therefore the people of Israel shall keep the sabbath, observing the sabbath throughout their generations, as a perpetual covenant. 17 It is a sign for ever between me and the people of Israel that in six days the LORD made heaven and earth, and on the seventh day he rested, and was refreshed.'"

18 And he gave to Moses, when he had made an end of speaking with him upon Mount Sinai, the two tables of the testimony, tables of stone, written with the finger of God.

32 When the people saw that Moses delayed to come down from the mountain, the people gathered themselves together to Aaron, and said to him, "Up, make us gods, who shall go before us; as for this Moses, the man who brought us up out of the land of Egypt, we do not know what has become of him." 2And Aaron said to them, "Take off the rings of gold which are in the ears of your wives, your sons, and your daughters, and bring them to me." 3 So all the people took off the rings of gold which were in their ears, and brought them to Aaron. 4And he received the gold at their hand, and fashioned it with a graving tool, and made a molten calf; and they said, "These are your gods, O Israel, who brought you up out of the land of Egypt!" 5 When Aaron saw this, he built an altar before it; and Aaron made proclamation and

31.1-6: Ex 35.30-36.1.　　**31.12-17:** Ex 20.8; 23.12; 35.2; Deut 5.12-15.
32.1-6: Acts 7.40-41.

said, "Tomorrow shall be a feast to the LORD." 6And they rose up early on the morrow, and offered burnt offerings and brought peace offerings; and the people sat down to eat and drink, and rose up to play.

7 And the LORD said to Moses, "Go down; for your people, whom you brought up out of the land of Egypt, have corrupted themselves; 8 they have turned aside quickly out of the way which I commanded them; they have made for themselves a molten calf, and have worshiped it and sacrificed to it, and said, 'These are your gods, O Israel, who brought you up out of the land of Egypt!'" 9And the LORD said to Moses, "I have seen this people, and behold, it is a stiff-necked people; 10 now therefore let me alone, that my wrath may burn hot against them and I may consume them; but of you I will make a great nation."

11 But Moses besought the LORD his God, and said, "O LORD, why does thy wrath burn hot against thy people, whom thou hast brought forth out of the land of Egypt with great power and with a mighty hand? 12 Why should the Egyptians say, 'With evil intent did he bring them forth, to slay them in the mountains, and to consume them from the face of the earth'? Turn from thy fierce wrath, and repent of this evil against thy people. 13 Remember Abraham, Isaac, and Israel, thy servants, to whom thou didst swear by thine own self, and didst say to them, 'I will multiply your descendants as the stars of heaven, and all this land that I have promised I will give to your descendants, and they shall inherit it for ever.'" 14And the LORD repented of the evil which he thought to do to his people.

15 And Moses turned, and went down from the mountain with the two tables of the testimony in his hands, tables that were written on both sides; on the one side and on the other were they written. 16And the tables were the work of God, and the writing was the writing of God, graven upon the tables. 17 When Joshua heard the noise of the people as they shouted, he said to Moses, "There is a noise of war in the camp." 18 But he said, "It is not the sound of shouting for victory, or the sound of the cry of defeat, but the sound of singing that I hear." 19And as soon as he came near the camp and saw the calf and the dancing, Moses'

anger burned hot, and he threw the tables out of his hands and broke them at the foot of the mountain. 20And he took the calf which they had made, and burnt it with fire, and ground it to powder, and scattered it upon the water, and made the people of Israel drink it.

21 And Moses said to Aaron, "What did this people do to you that you have brought a great sin upon them?" 22And Aaron said, "Let not the anger of my lord burn hot; you know the people, that they are set on evil. 23 For they said to me, 'Make us gods, who shall go before us; as for this Moses, the man who brought us up out of the land of Egypt, we do not know what has become of him.' 24And I said to them, 'Let any who have gold take it off'; so they gave it to me, and I threw it into the fire, and there came out this calf."

25 And when Moses saw that the people had broken loose (for Aaron had let them break loose, to their shame among their enemies), 26 then Moses stood in the gate of the camp, and said, "Who is on the LORD's side? Come to me." And all the sons of Levi gathered themselves together to him. 27And he said to them, "Thus says the LORD God of Israel, 'Put every man his sword on his side, and go to and fro from gate to gate throughout the camp, and slay every man his brother, and every man his companion, and every man his neighbor.'" 28And the sons of Levi did according to the word of Moses; and there fell of the people that day about three thousand men. 29And Moses said, "Today you have ordained yourselvesˢ for the service of the LORD, each one at the cost of his son and of his brother, that he may bestow a blessing upon you this day."

30 On the morrow Moses said to the people, "You have sinned a great sin. And now I will go up to the LORD; perhaps I can make atonement for your sin." 31 So Moses returned to the LORD and said, "Alas, this people have sinned a great sin; they have made for themselves gods of gold. 32 But now, if thou wilt forgive their sin—and if not, blot me, I pray thee, out of thy book which thou hast written." 33 But the LORD said to Moses, "Whoever has sinned against me, him will I blot out of my book. 34 But now go, lead the people to the place of which I have spoken to you; behold, my angel shall go before you. Nevertheless, in the

s Gk Vg Tg: Heb *ordain yourselves*
32.6: 1 Cor 10.7.   **32.9-14:** Ex 32.31-35; Num 14.11-25.   **32.23:** Acts 7.40.
32.32-33: Rev 3.5.

day when I visit, I will visit their sin upon them."

35 And the LORD sent a plague upon the people, because they made the calf which Aaron made.

33 The LORD said to Moses, "Depart, go up hence, you and the people whom you have brought up out of the land of Egypt, to the land of which I swore to Abraham, Isaac, and Jacob, saying, 'To your descendants I will give it.' 2 And I will send an angel before you, and I will drive out the Canaanites, the Am'o·rites, the Hit'tites, the Per'iz·zites, the Hi'vites, and the Jeb'ū·sites. 3 Go up to a land flowing with milk and honey; but I will not go up among you, lest I consume you in the way, for you are a stiff-necked people."

4 When the people heard these evil tidings, they mourned; and no man put on his ornaments. 5 For the LORD had said to Moses, "Say to the people of Israel, 'You are a stiff-necked people; if for a single moment I should go up among you, I would consume you. So now put off your ornaments from you, that I may know what to do with you.'" 6 Therefore the people of Israel stripped themselves of their ornaments, from Mount Hō'reb onward.

7 Now Moses used to take the tent and pitch it outside the camp, far off from the camp; and he called it the tent of meeting. And every one who sought the LORD would go out to the tent of meeting, which was outside the camp. 8 Whenever Moses went out to the tent, all the people rose up, and every man stood at his tent door, and looked after Moses, until he had gone into the tent. 9 When Moses entered the tent, the pillar of cloud would descend and stand at the door of the tent, and the LORD would speak with Moses. 10 And when all the people saw the pillar of cloud standing at the door of the tent, all the people would rise up and worship, every man at his tent door. 11 Thus the LORD used to speak to Moses face to face, as a man speaks to his friend. When Moses turned again into the camp, his servant Joshua the son of Nun, a young man, did not depart from the tent.

12 Moses said to the LORD, "See, thou sayest to me, 'Bring up this people'; but thou hast not let me know whom thou wilt send with me. Yet thou hast said, 'I know you by name, and you have also found favor in my

sight.' 13 Now therefore, I pray thee, if I have found favor in thy sight, show me now thy ways, that I may know thee and find favor in thy sight. Consider too that this nation is thy people." 14 And he said, "My presence will go with you, and I will give you rest." 15 And he said to him, "If thy presence will not go with me, do not carry us up from here. 16 For how shall it be known that I have found favor in thy sight, I and thy people? Is it not in thy going with us, so that we are distinct, I and thy people, from all other people that are upon the face of the earth?"

17 And the LORD said to Moses, "This very thing that you have spoken I will do; for you have found favor in my sight, and I know you by name." 18 Moses said, "I pray thee, show me thy glory." 19 And he said, "I will make all my goodness pass before you, and will proclaim before you my name 'The LORD'; and I will be gracious to whom I will be gracious, and will show mercy on whom I will show mercy. 20 But," he said, "you cannot see my face; for man shall not see me and live." 21 And the LORD said, "Behold, there is a place by me where you shall stand upon the rock; 22 and while my glory passes by I will put you in a cleft of the rock, and I will cover you with my hand until I have passed by; 23 then I will take away my hand, and you shall see my back; but my face shall not be seen."

34 The LORD said to Moses, "Cut two tables of stone like the first; and I will write upon the tables the words that were on the first tables, which you broke. 2 Be ready in the morning, and come up in the morning to Mount Sinai, and present yourself there to me on the top of the mountain. 3 No man shall come up with you, and let no man be seen throughout all the mountain; let no flocks or herds feed before that mountain." 4 So Moses cut two tables of stone like the first; and he rose early in the morning and went up on Mount Sinai, as the LORD had commanded him, and took in his hand two tables of stone. 5 And the LORD descended in the cloud and stood with him there, and proclaimed the name of the LORD. 6 The LORD passed before him, and proclaimed, "The LORD, the LORD, a God merciful and gracious, slow to anger, and abounding in steadfast love and faithfulness, 7 keeping steadfast love for thousands, forgiving iniquity and transgression and sin, but who will by no means clear the guilty, visiting the iniquity of the fathers upon the children and the children's children, to the third and the fourth generation." 8And Moses made haste to bow his head toward the earth, and worshiped. 9And he said, "If now I have found favor in thy sight, O LORD, let the LORD, I pray thee, go in the midst of us, although it is a stiff-necked people; and pardon our iniquity and our sin, and take us for thy inheritance."

10 And he said, "Behold, I make a covenant. Before all your people I will do marvels, such as have not been wrought in all the earth or in any nation; and all the people among whom you are shall see the work of the LORD; for it is a terrible thing that I will do with you.

11 "Observe what I command you this day. Behold, I will drive out before you the Am'o·rites, the Canaanites, the Hit'tites, the Per'iz·zites, the Hi'vites, and the Jeb'u·sites. 12 Take heed to yourself, lest you make a covenant with the inhabitants of the land whither you go, lest it become a snare in the midst of you. 13 You shall tear down their altars, and break their pillars, and cut down their A·she'rim 14 (for you shall worship no other god, for the LORD, whose name is Jealous, is a jealous God), 15 lest you make a covenant with the inhabitants of the land, and when they play the harlot after their gods and sacrifice to their gods and one invites you, you eat of his sacrifice, 16 and you take of their daughters for your sons, and their daughters play the harlot after their gods and make your sons play the harlot after their gods.

17 "You shall make for yourself no molten gods.

18 "The feast of unleavened bread you shall keep. Seven days you shall eat unleavened bread, as I commanded you, at the time appointed in the month A'bib; for in the month Abib you came out from Egypt. 19All that opens the womb is mine, all your malex cattle, the firstlings of cow and sheep. 20 The firstling of an ass you shall redeem with a lamb, or if you will not redeem it you shall break its neck. All the first-born of your sons

you shall redeem. And none shall appear before me empty.

21 "Six days you shall work, but on the seventh day you shall rest; in plowing time and in harvest you shall rest. 22And you shall observe the feast of weeks, the first fruits of wheat harvest, and the feast of ingathering at the year's end. 23 Three times in the year shall all your males appear before the LORD God, the God of Israel. 24 For I will cast out nations before you, and enlarge your borders; neither shall any man desire your land, when you go up to appear before the LORD your God three times in the year.

25 "You shall not offer the blood of my sacrifice with leaven; neither shall the sacrifice of the feast of the passover be left until the morning. 26 The first of the first fruits of your ground you shall bring to the house of the LORD your God. You shall not boil a kid in its mother's milk."

27 And the LORD said to Moses, "Write these words; in accordance with these words I have made a covenant with you and with Israel." 28And he was there with the LORD forty days and forty nights; he neither ate bread nor drank water. And he wrote upon the tables the words of the covenant, the ten commandments.t

29 When Moses came down from Mount Sinai, with the two tables of the testimony in his hand as he came down from the mountain, Moses did not know that the skin of his face shone because he had been talking with God. 30And when Aaron and all the people of Israel saw Moses, behold, the skin of his face shone, and they were afraid to come near him. 31 But Moses called to them; and Aaron and all the leaders of the congregation returned to him, and Moses talked with them. 32And afterward all the people of Israel came near, and he gave them in commandment all that the LORD had spoken with him in Mount Sinai. 33And when Moses had finished speaking with them, he put a veil on his face; 34 but whenever Moses went in before the LORD to speak with him, he took the veil off, until he came out; and when he came out, and told the people of Israel what he was commanded, 35 the people of Israel saw the face of Moses, that the skin of Moses' face shone; and

x Gk Theodotion Vg Tg: Heb uncertain   t Heb words

34.14: Ex 20.5; 34.7; Deut 4.24; 5.9.   34.17: Ex 20.4.   34.18: Ex 12.15-20.
34.19-20: Ex 13.2, 11-16.   34.21: Ex 20.8-10; 23.12; 31.12-17; 35.2; Deut 5.12-15.
34.22-24: Ex 23.14-17; Lev 23.1-44; Deut 16.1-17.
34.25: Ex 23.18; Lev 2.11; Ex 12.10.   34.26: Ex 23.19; Deut 14.21; 26.2-11.
34.29-35: 2 Cor 3.7-16.

Moses would put the veil upon his face again, until he went in to speak with him.

35 Moses assembled all the congregation of the people of Israel, and said to them, "These are the things which the LORD has commanded you to do. ² Six days shall work be done, but on the seventh day you shall have a holy sabbath of solemn rest to the LORD; whoever does any work on it shall be put to death; ³ you shall kindle no fire in all your habitations on the sabbath day."

⁴ Moses said to all the congregation of the people of Israel, "This is the thing which the LORD has commanded. ⁵ Take from among you an offering to the LORD; whoever is of a generous heart, let him bring the LORD's offering: gold, silver, and bronze; ⁶ blue and purple and scarlet stuff and fine twined linen; goats' hair, ⁷ tanned rams' skins, and goatskins; acacia wood, ⁸ oil for the light, spices for the anointing oil and for the fragrant incense, ⁹ and onyx stones and stones for setting, for the ephod and for the breastpiece.

10 "And let every able man among you come and make all that the LORD has commanded: the tabernacle, ¹¹ its tent and its covering, its hooks and its frames, its bars, its pillars, and its bases; ¹² the ark with its poles, the mercy seat, and the veil of the screen; ¹³ the table with its poles and all its utensils, and the bread of the Presence; ¹⁴ the lampstand also for the light, with its utensils and its lamps, and the oil for the light; ¹⁵ and the altar of incense, with its poles, and the anointing oil and the fragrant incense, and the screen for the door, at the door of the tabernacle; ¹⁶ the altar of burnt offering, with its grating of bronze, its poles, and all its utensils, the laver and its base; ¹⁷ the hangings of the court, its pillars and its bases, and the screen for the gate of the court; ¹⁸ the pegs of the tabernacle and the pegs of the court, and their cords; ¹⁹ the finely wrought garments for ministering in the holy place, the holy garments for Aaron the priest, and the garments of his sons, for their service as priests."

20 Then all the congregation of the people of Israel departed from the presence of Moses. ²¹And they came, every one whose heart stirred him, and every one whose spirit moved him, and brought the LORD's offering to be used for the tent of meeting, and for

all its service, and for the holy garments. ²² So they came, both men and women; all who were of a willing heart brought brooches and earrings and signet rings and armlets, all sorts of gold objects, every man dedicating an offering of gold to the LORD. ²³And every man with whom was found blue or purple or scarlet stuff or fine linen or goats' hair or tanned rams' skins or goatskins, brought them. ²⁴ Every one who could make an offering of silver or bronze brought it as the LORD's offering; and every man with whom was found acacia wood of any use in the work, brought it. ²⁵And all women who had ability spun with their hands, and brought what they had spun in blue and purple and scarlet stuff and fine twined linen; ²⁶ all the women whose hearts were moved with ability spun the goats' hair. ²⁷And the leaders brought onyx stones and stones to be set, for the ephod and for the breastpiece, ²⁸ and spices and oil for the light, and for the anointing oil, and for the fragrant incense. ²⁹All the men and women, the people of Israel, whose heart moved them to bring anything for the work which the LORD had commanded by Moses to be done, brought it as their freewill offering to the LORD.

30 And Moses said to the people of Israel, "See, the LORD has called by name Bez′a·lel the son of U′ri, son of Hur, of the tribe of Judah; ³¹ and he has filled him with the Spirit of God, with ability, with intelligence, with knowledge, and with all craftsmanship, ³² to devise artistic designs, to work in gold and silver and bronze, ³³ in cutting stones for setting, and in carving wood, for work in every skilled craft. ³⁴And he has inspired him to teach, both him and O·ho′li·ab the son of A·his′a·mach of the tribe of Dan. ³⁵ He has filled them with ability to do every sort of work done by a craftsman or by a designer or by an embroiderer in blue and purple and scarlet stuff and fine twined linen, or by a weaver— by any sort of workman or skilled

36 designer. ¹ Bez′a·lel and O·ho′li·ab and every able man in whom the LORD has put ability and intelligence to know how to do any work in the construction of the sanctuary shall work in accordance with all that the LORD has commanded."

2 And Moses called Bez′a·lel and O·ho′li·ab and every able man in whose mind the LORD had put ability, every

35.2-3: Ex 23.12; 31.12-17; 34.21; Deut 5.12-15.   **35.4-9:** Ex 25.1-9.
35.30–36.1: Ex 31.1-6.

one whose heart stirred him up to come to do the work; 3 and they received from Moses all the freewill offering which the people of Israel had brought for doing the work on the sanctuary. They still kept bringing him freewill offerings every morning, 4 so that all the able men who were doing every sort of task on the sanctuary came, each from the task that he was doing, 5 and said to Moses, "The people bring much more than enough for doing the work which the LORD has commanded us to do." 6 So Moses gave command, and word was proclaimed throughout the camp, "Let neither man nor woman do anything more for the offering for the sanctuary." So the people were restrained from bringing; 7 for the stuff they had was sufficient to do all the work, and more.

8 And all the able men among the workmen made the tabernacle with ten curtains; they were made of fine twined linen and blue and purple and scarlet stuff, with cherubim skilfully worked. 9 The length of each curtain was twenty-eight cubits, and the breadth of each curtain four cubits; all the curtains had the same measure.

10 And he coupled five curtains to one another, and the other five curtains he coupled to one another. 11And he made loops of blue on the edge of the outmost curtain of the first set; likewise he made them on the edge of the outmost curtain of the second set; 12 he made fifty loops on the one curtain, and he made fifty loops on the edge of the curtain that was in the second set; the loops were opposite one another. 13And he made fifty clasps of gold, and coupled the curtains one to the other with clasps; so the tabernacle was one whole.

14 He also made curtains of goats' hair for a tent over the tabernacle; he made eleven curtains. 15 The length of each curtain was thirty cubits, and the breadth of each curtain four cubits; the eleven curtains had the same measure. 16 He coupled five curtains by themselves, and six curtains by themselves. 17And he made fifty loops on the edge of the outmost curtain of the one set, and fifty loops on the edge of the other connecting curtain. 18And he made fifty clasps of bronze to couple the tent together that it might be one whole. 19And he made for the tent a covering of tanned rams' skins and goatskins.

20 Then he made the upright frames for the tabernacle of acacia wood. 21 Ten cubits was the length of a frame, and a cubit and a half the breadth of each frame. 22 Each frame had two tenons, for fitting together; he did this for all the frames of the tabernacle. 23 The frames for the tabernacle he made thus: twenty frames for the south side; 24 and he made forty bases of silver under the twenty frames, two bases under one frame for its two tenons, and two bases under another frame for its two tenons. 25And for the second side of the tabernacle, on the north side, he made twenty frames 26 and their forty bases of silver, two bases under one frame and two bases under another frame. 27And for the rear of the tabernacle westward he made six frames. 28And he made two frames for corners of the tabernacle in the rear. 29And they were separate beneath, but joined at the top, at the first ring; he made two of them thus, for the two corners. 30 There were eight frames with their bases of silver: sixteen bases, under every frame two bases.

31 And he made bars of acacia wood, five for the frames of the one side of the tabernacle, 32 and five bars for the frames of the other side of the tabernacle, and five bars for the frames of the tabernacle at the rear westward. 33And he made the middle bar to pass through from end to end halfway up the frames. 34And he overlaid the frames with gold, and made their rings of gold for holders for the bars, and overlaid the bars with gold.

35 And he made the veil of blue and purple and scarlet stuff and fine twined linen; with cherubim skilfully worked he made it. 36And for it he made four pillars of acacia, and overlaid them with gold; their hooks were of gold, and he cast for them four bases of silver. 37 He also made a screen for the door of the tent, of blue and purple and scarlet stuff and fine twined linen, embroidered with needlework; 38 and its five pillars with their hooks. He overlaid their capitals, and their fillets were of gold, but their five bases were of bronze.

37 Bez′a·lel made the ark of acacia wood; two cubits and a half was its length, a cubit and a half its breadth, and a cubit and a half its height. 2And he overlaid it with pure gold within and without, and made a molding of gold around it. 3And he cast for it four

36.8-19: Ex 26.1-14.   36.20-34: Ex 26.15-29.   36.35-38: Ex 26.31-37.
37.1-9: Ex 25.10-22.

rings of gold for its four corners, two rings on its one side and two rings on its other side. 4And he made poles of acacia wood, and overlaid them with gold, 5 and put the poles into the rings on the sides of the ark, to carry the ark. 6And he made a mercy seat of pure gold; two cubits and a half was its length, and a cubit and a half its breadth. 7And he made two cherubim of hammered gold; on the two ends of the mercy seat he made them, 8 one cherub on the one end, and one cherub on the other end; of one piece with the mercy seat he made the cherubim on its two ends. 9 The cherubim spread out their wings above, overshadowing the mercy seat with their wings, with their faces one to another; toward the mercy seat were the faces of the cherubim.

10 He also made the table of acacia wood; two cubits was its length, a cubit its breadth, and a cubit and a half its height; 11 and he overlaid it with pure gold, and made a molding of gold around it. 12And he made around it a frame a handbreadth wide, and made a molding of gold around the frame. 13 He cast for it four rings of gold, and fastened the rings to the four corners at its four legs. 14 Close to the frame were the rings, as holders for the poles to carry the table. 15 He made the poles of acacia wood to carry the table, and overlaid them with gold. 16And he made the vessels of pure gold which were to be upon the table, its plates and dishes for incense, and its bowls and flagons with which to pour libations.

17 He also made the lampstand of pure gold. The base and the shaft of the lampstand were made of hammered work; its cups, its capitals, and its flowers were of one piece with it. 18And there were six branches going out of its sides, three branches of the lampstand out of one side of it and three branches of the lampstand out of the other side of it; 19 three cups made like almonds, each with capital and flower, on one branch, and three cups made like almonds, each with capital and flower, on the other branch—so for the six branches going out of the lampstand. 20And on the lampstand itself were four cups made like almonds, with their capitals and flowers, 21 and a capital of one piece with it under each pair of the six branches going out of it. 22 Their capitals and their branches were of one

piece with it; the whole of it was one piece of hammered work of pure gold. 23And he made its seven lamps and its snuffers and its trays of pure gold. 24 He made it and all its utensils of a talent of pure gold.

25 He made the altar of incense of acacia wood; its length was a cubit, and its breadth was a cubit; it was square, and two cubits was its height; its horns were of one piece with it. 26 He overlaid it with pure gold, its top, and its sides round about, and its horns; and he made a molding of gold round about it, 27 and made two rings of gold on it under its molding, on two opposite sides of it, as holders for the poles with which to carry it. 28And he made the poles of acacia wood, and overlaid them with gold.

29 He made the holy anointing oil also, and the pure fragrant incense, blended as by the perfumer.

38 He made the altar of burnt offering also of acacia wood; five cubits was its length, and five cubits its breadth; it was square, and three cubits was its height. 2 He made horns for it on its four corners; its horns were of one piece with it, and he overlaid it with bronze. 3And he made all the utensils of the altar, the pots, the shovels, the basins, the forks, and the firepans: all its utensils he made of bronze. 4And he made for the altar a grating, a network of bronze, under its ledge, extending halfway down. 5 He cast four rings on the four corners of the bronze grating as holders for the poles; 6 he made the poles of acacia wood, and overlaid them with bronze. 7And he put the poles through the rings on the sides of the altar, to carry it with them; he made it hollow, with boards.

8 And he made the laver of bronze and its base of bronze, from the mirrors of the ministering women who ministered at the door of the tent of meeting.

9 And he made the court; for the south side the hangings of the court were of fine twined linen, a hundred cubits; 10 their pillars were twenty and their bases twenty, of bronze, but the hooks of the pillars and their fillets were of silver. 11And for the north side a hundred cubits, their pillars twenty, their bases twenty, of bronze, but the hooks of the pillars and their fillets were of silver. 12And for the west side were hangings of fifty cubits, their pillars ten, and their sockets ten; the hooks of the pillars and their fillets

37.10-16: Ex 25.23-29. **37.17-24:** Ex 25.31-39. **37.25-29:** Ex 30.1-5.
38.1-7: Ex 27.1-8. **38.8:** Ex 30.18. **38.9-20:** Ex 27.9-19.

were of silver. 13And for the front to the east, fifty cubits. 14 The hangings for one side of the gate were fifteen cubits, with three pillars and three bases. 15And so for the other side; on this hand and that hand by the gate of the court were hangings of fifteen cubits, with three pillars and three bases. 16All the hangings round about the court were of fine twined linen. 17And the bases for the pillars were of bronze, but the hooks of the pillars and their fillets were of silver; the overlaying of their capitals was also of silver, and all the pillars of the court were filleted with silver. 18And the screen for the gate of the court was embroidered with needlework in blue and purple and scarlet stuff and fine twined linen; it was twenty cubits long and five cubits high in its breadth, corresponding to the hangings of the court. 19And their pillars were four; their four bases were of bronze, their hooks of silver, and the overlaying of their capitals and their fillets of silver. 20And all the pegs for the tabernacle and for the court round about were of bronze.

21 This is the sum of the things for the tabernacle, the tabernacle of the testimony, as they were counted at the commandment of Moses, for the work of the Levites under the direction of Ith′a·mär the son of Aaron the priest. 22 Bez′a·lel the son of U′ri, son of Hur, of the tribe of Judah, made all that the LORD commanded Moses; 23 and with him was O·ho′li·ab the son of A·his′a·mach, of the tribe of Dan, a craftsman and designer and embroiderer in blue and purple and scarlet stuff and fine twined linen.

24 All the gold that was used for the work, in all the construction of the sanctuary, the gold from the offering, was twenty-nine talents and seven hundred and thirty shekels, by the shekel of the sanctuary. 25And the silver from those of the congregation who were numbered was a hundred talents and a thousand seven hundred and seventy-five shekels, by the shekel of the sanctuary: 26 a beka a head (that is, half a shekel, by the shekel of the sanctuary), for every one who was numbered in the census, from twenty years old and upward, for six hundred and three thousand, five hundred and fifty men. 27 The hundred talents of silver were for casting the bases of the sanctuary, and the bases of the veil; a hundred bases for the hundred talents, a talent for a base. 28And of the thou-

sand seven hundred and seventy-five shekels he made hooks for the pillars, and overlaid their capitals and made fillets for them. 29And the bronze that was contributed was seventy talents, and two thousand and four hundred shekels; 30 with it he made the bases for the door of the tent of meeting, the bronze altar and the bronze grating for it and all the utensils of the altar, 31 the bases round about the court, and the bases of the gate of the court, all the pegs of the tabernacle, and all the pegs round about the court.

39 And of the blue and purple and scarlet stuff they made finely wrought garments, for ministering in the holy place; they made the holy garments for Aaron; as the LORD had commanded Moses.

2 And he made the ephod of gold, blue and purple and scarlet stuff, and fine twined linen. 3And gold leaf was hammered out and cut into threads to work into the blue and purple and the scarlet stuff, and into the fine twined linen, in skilled design. 4 They made for the ephod shoulder-pieces, joined to it at its two edges. 5And the skilfully woven band upon it, to gird it on, was of the same materials and workmanship, of gold, blue and purple and scarlet stuff, and fine twined linen; as the LORD had commanded Moses.

6 The onyx stones were prepared, enclosed in settings of gold filigree and engraved like the engravings of a signet, according to the names of the sons of Israel. 7And he set them on the shoulder-pieces of the ephod, to be stones of remembrance for the sons of Israel; as the LORD had commanded Moses.

8 He made the breastpiece, in skilled work, like the work of the ephod, of gold, blue and purple and scarlet stuff, and fine twined linen. 9 It was square; the breastpiece was made double, a span its length and a span its breadth when doubled. 10And they set in it four rows of stones. A row of sardius, topaz, and carbuncle was the first row; 11 and the second row, an emerald, a sapphire, and a diamond; 12 and the third row, a jacinth, an agate, and an amethyst; 13 and the fourth row, a beryl, an onyx, and a jasper; they were enclosed in settings of gold filigree. 14 There were twelve stones with their names according to the names of the sons of Israel; they were like signets, each engraved with its name, for the twelve tribes. 15And they made on the breastpiece twisted

38.25-26: Ex 30.11-16.　39.2-7: Ex 28.6-12.　39.8-21: Ex 28.15-28.

chains like cords, of pure gold; 16 and they made two settings of gold filigree and two gold rings, and put the two rings on the two edges of the breast-piece; 17 and they put the two cords of gold in the two rings at the edges of the breastpiece. 18 Two ends of the two cords they had attached to the two settings of filigree; thus they attached it in front to the shoulder-pieces of the ephod. 19 Then they made two rings of gold, and put them at the two ends of the breastpiece, on its inside edge next to the ephod. 20And they made two rings of gold, and attached them in front to the lower part of the two shoulder-pieces of the ephod, at its joining above the skilfully woven band of the ephod. 21And they bound the breastpiece by its rings to the rings of the ephod with a lace of blue, so that it should lie upon the skilfully woven band of the ephod, and that the breastpiece should not come loose from the ephod; as the LORD had commanded Moses.

22 He also made the robe of the ephod woven all of blue; 23 and the opening of the robe in it was like the opening in a garment, with a binding around the opening, that it might not be torn. 24 On the skirts of the robe they made pomegranates of blue and purple and scarlet stuff and fine twined linen. 25 They also made bells of pure gold, and put the bells between the pomegranates upon the skirts of the robe round about, between the pomegranates; 26 a bell and a pome-granate, a bell and a pomegranate round about upon the skirts of the robe for ministering; as the LORD had commanded Moses.

27 They also made the coats, woven of fine linen, for Aaron and his sons, 28 and the turban of fine linen, and the caps of fine linen, and the linen breeches of fine twined linen, 29 and the girdle of fine twined linen and of blue and purple and scarlet stuff, em-broidered with needlework; as the LORD had commanded Moses.

30 And they made the plate of the holy crown of pure gold, and wrote upon it an inscription, like the engrav-ing of a signet, "Holy to the LORD." 31And they tied to it a lace of blue, to fasten it on the turban above; as the LORD had commanded Moses.

32 Thus all the work of the taber-nacle of the tent of meeting was fin-ished; and the people of Israel had done according to all that the LORD

had commanded Moses; so had they done. 33And they brought the taber-nacle to Moses, the tent and all its utensils, its hooks, its frames, its bars, its pillars, and its bases; 34 the covering of tanned rams' skins and goatskins, and the veil of the screen; 35 the ark of the testimony with its poles and the mercy seat; 36 the table with all its utensils, and the bread of the Presence; 37 the lampstand of pure gold and its lamps with the lamps set and all its utensils, and the oil for the light; 38 the golden altar, the anointing oil and the fragrant incense, and the screen for the door of the tent; 39 the bronze altar, and its grating of bronze, its poles, and all its utensils; the laver and its base; 40 the hangings of the court, its pillars, and its bases, and the screen for the gate of the court, its cords, and its pegs; and all the utensils for the service of the tabernacle, for the tent of meeting; 41 the finely worked gar-ments for ministering in the holy place, the holy garments for Aaron the priest, and the garments of his sons to serve as priests. 42According to all that the LORD had commanded Moses, so the people of Israel had done all the work. 43And Moses saw all the work, and behold, they had done it; as the LORD had commanded, so had they done it. And Moses blessed them.

40

The LORD said to Moses, 2 "On the first day of the first month you shall erect the tabernacle of the tent of meeting. 3And you shall put in it the ark of the testimony, and you shall screen the ark with the veil. 4And you shall bring in the table, and set its arrangements in order; and you shall bring in the lampstand, and set up its lamps. 5And you shall put the golden altar for incense before the ark of the testimony, and set up the screen for the door of the tabernacle. 6 You shall set the altar of burnt offering be-fore the door of the tabernacle of the tent of meeting, 7 and place the laver between the tent of meeting and the altar, and put water in it. 8And you shall set up the court round about, and hang up the screen for the gate of the court. 9 Then you shall take the anoint-ing oil, and anoint the tabernacle and all that is in it, and consecrate it and all its furniture; and it shall become holy. 10 You shall also anoint the altar of burnt offering and all its utensils, and consecrate the altar; and the altar shall be most holy. 11 You shall also anoint the laver and its base, and con-

39.22-26: Ex 28.31-34.   39.27-29: Ex 28.39-40, 42.   39.30-31: Ex 28.36-37.
39.36: Ex 25.30; 40.23; Lev 24.5-9.

secrate it. 12 Then you shall bring Aaron and his sons to the door of the tent of meeting, and shall wash them with water, 13 and put upon Aaron the holy garments, and you shall anoint him and consecrate him, that he may serve me as priest. 14 You shall bring his sons also and put coats on them, 15 and anoint them, as you anointed their father, that they may serve me as priests: and their anointing shall admit them to a perpetual priesthood throughout their generations.''

16 Thus did Moses; according to all that the LORD commanded him, so he did. 17And in the first month in the second year, on the first day of the month, the tabernacle was erected. 18 Moses erected the tabernacle; he laid its bases, and set up its frames, and put in its poles, and raised up its pillars; 19 and he spread the tent over the tabernacle, and put the covering of the tent over it, as the LORD had commanded Moses. 20And he took the testimony and put it into the ark, and put the poles on the ark, and set the mercy seat above on the ark; 21 and he brought the ark into the tabernacle, and set up the veil of the screen, and screened the ark of the testimony; as the LORD had commanded Moses. 22And he put the table in the tent of meeting, on the north side of the tabernacle, outside the veil, 23 and set the bread in order on it before the LORD; as the LORD had commanded Moses. 24And he put the lampstand in the tent of meeting, opposite the table on the south side of the tabernacle, 25 and set up the lamps before the

LORD; as the LORD had commanded Moses. 26And he put the golden altar in the tent of meeting before the veil, 27 and burnt fragrant incense upon it; as the LORD had commanded Moses. 28And he put in place the screen for the door of the tabernacle. 29And he set the altar of burnt offering at the door of the tabernacle of the tent of meeting, and offered upon it the burnt offering and the cereal offering; as the LORD had commanded Moses. 30And he set the laver between the tent of meeting and the altar, and put water in it for washing, 31 with which Moses and Aaron and his sons washed their hands and their feet; 32 when they went into the tent of meeting, and when they approached the altar, they washed; as the LORD commanded Moses. 33And he erected the court round the tabernacle and the altar, and set up the screen of the gate of the court. So Moses finished the work.

34 Then the cloud covered the tent of meeting, and the glory of the LORD filled the tabernacle. 35And Moses was not able to enter the tent of meeting, because the cloud abode upon it, and the glory of the LORD filled the tabernacle. 36 Throughout all their journeys, whenever the cloud was taken up from over the tabernacle, the people of Israel would go onward; 37 but if the cloud was not taken up, then they did not go onward till the day that it was taken up. 38 For throughout all their journeys the cloud of the LORD was upon the tabernacle by day, and fire was in it by night, in the sight of all the house of Israel.

THE THIRD BOOK OF MOSES

COMMONLY CALLED

LEVITICUS

1 The LORD called Moses, and spoke to him from the tent of meeting, saying, 2 "Speak to the people of Israel, and say to them, When any man of you brings an offering to the LORD, you shall bring your offering of cattle from the herd or from the flock.

3 "If his offering is a burnt offering from the herd, he shall offer a male without blemish; he shall offer it at the door of the tent of meeting, that he may be accepted before the LORD; 4 he shall lay his hand upon the head of the burnt offering, and it shall be accepted for him to make atonement for him. 5 Then he shall kill the bull

40.23: Ex 25.30; 39.36; Lev 24.5-9.   **40.30-32:** Ex 30.18-21.   **40.34:** Rev 15.8.

before the LORD; and Aaron's sons the priests shall present the blood, and throw the blood round about against the altar that is at the door of the tent of meeting. 6And he shall flay the burnt offering and cut it into pieces; 7 and the sons of Aaron the priest shall put fire on the altar, and lay wood in order upon the fire; 8 and Aaron's sons the priests shall lay the pieces, the head, and the fat, in order upon the wood that is on the fire upon the altar; 9 but its entrails and its legs he shall wash with water. And the priest shall burn the whole on the altar, as a burnt offering, an offering by fire, a pleasing odor to the LORD.

10 "If his gift for a burnt offering is from the flock, from the sheep or goats, he shall offer a male without blemish; 11 and he shall kill it on the north side of the altar before the LORD, and Aaron's sons the priests shall throw its blood against the altar round about. 12And he shall cut it into pieces, with its head and its fat, and the priest shall lay them in order upon the wood that is on the fire upon the altar; 13 but the entrails and the legs he shall wash with water. And the priest shall offer the whole, and burn it on the altar; it is a burnt offering, an offering by fire, a pleasing odor to the LORD.

14 "If his offering to the LORD is a burnt offering of birds, then he shall bring his offering of turtledoves or of young pigeons. 15And the priest shall bring it to the altar and wring off its head, and burn it on the altar; and its blood shall be drained out on the side of the altar; 16 and he shall take away its crop with the feathers, and cast it beside the altar on the east side, in the place for ashes; 17 he shall tear it by its wings, but shall not divide it asunder. And the priest shall burn it on the altar, upon the wood that is on the fire; it is a burnt offering, an offering by fire, a pleasing odor to the LORD.

2 "When any one brings a cereal offering as an offering to the LORD, his offering shall be of fine flour; he shall pour oil upon it, and put frankincense on it, 2 and bring it to Aaron's sons the priests. And he shall take from it a handful of the fine flour and oil, with all of its frankincense; and the priest shall burn this as its memorial portion upon the altar, an offering by fire, a pleasing odor to the LORD. 3And what is left of the cereal offering shall be for Aaron and his sons; it is a most

holy part of the offerings by fire to the LORD.

4 "When you bring a cereal offering baked in the oven as an offering, it shall be unleavened cakes of fine flour mixed with oil, or unleavened wafers spread with oil. 5And if your offering is a cereal offering baked on a griddle, it shall be of fine flour unleavened, mixed with oil; 6 you shall break it in pieces, and pour oil on it; it is a cereal offering. 7And if your offering is a cereal offering cooked in a pan, it shall be made of fine flour with oil. 8And you shall bring the cereal offering that is made of these things to the LORD; and when it is presented to the priest, he shall bring it to the altar. 9And the priest shall take from the cereal offering its memorial portion and burn this on the altar, an offering by fire, a pleasing odor to the LORD. 10And what is left of the cereal offering shall be for Aaron and his sons; it is a most holy part of the offerings by fire to the LORD.

11 "No cereal offering which you bring to the LORD shall be made with leaven; for you shall burn no leaven nor any honey as an offering by fire to the LORD. 12As an offering of first fruits you may bring them to the LORD, but they shall not be offered on the altar for a pleasing odor. 13 You shall season all your cereal offerings with salt; you shall not let the salt of the covenant with your God be lacking from your cereal offering; with all your offerings you shall offer salt.

14 "If you offer a cereal offering of first fruits to the LORD, you shall offer for the cereal offering of your first fruits crushed new grain from fresh ears, parched with fire. 15And you shall put oil upon it, and lay frankincense on it; it is a cereal offering. 16And the priest shall burn as its memorial portion part of the crushed grain and of the oil with all of its frankincense; it is an offering by fire to the LORD.

3 "If a man's offering is a sacrifice of peace offering, if he offers an animal from the herd, male or female, he shall offer it without blemish before the LORD. 2And he shall lay his hand upon the head of his offering and kill it at the door of the tent of meeting; and Aaron's sons the priests shall throw the blood against the altar round about. 3And from the sacrifice of the peace offering, as an offering by fire to the LORD, he shall offer the fat covering the entrails and all the fat that is

3.1-17: Lev 7.11-18.

JACOB REUNITED WITH JOSEPH *Gen. 46:29*

MOSES ON MOUNT SINAI   *Ex. 19:18*

on the entrails, 4 and the two kidneys with the fat that is on them at the loins, and the appendage of the liver which he shall take away with the kidneys. 5 Then Aaron's sons shall burn it on the altar upon the burnt offering, which is upon the wood on the fire; it is an offering by fire, a pleasing odor to the LORD.

6 "If his offering for a sacrifice of peace offering to the LORD is an animal from the flock, male or female, he shall offer it without blemish. 7 If he offers a lamb for his offering, then he shall offer it before the LORD, 8 laying his hand upon the head of his offering and killing it before the tent of meeting; and Aaron's sons shall throw its blood against the altar round about. 9 Then from the sacrifice of the peace offering as an offering by fire to the LORD he shall offer its fat, the fat tail entire, taking it away close by the backbone, and the fat that covers the entrails, and all the fat that is on the entrails, 10 and the two kidneys with the fat that is on them at the loins, and the appendage of the liver which he shall take away with the kidneys. 11And the priest shall burn it on the altar as food offered by fire to the LORD.

12 "If his offering is a goat, then he shall offer it before the LORD, 13 and lay his hand upon its head, and kill it before the tent of meeting; and the sons of Aaron shall throw its blood against the altar round about. 14 Then he shall offer from it, as his offering for an offering by fire to the LORD, the fat covering the entrails, and all the fat that is on the entrails, 15 and the two kidneys with the fat that is on them at the loins, and the appendage of the liver which he shall take away with the kidneys. 16And the priest shall burn them on the altar as food offered by fire for a pleasing odor. All fat is the LORD'S. 17 It shall be a perpetual statute throughout your generations, in all your dwelling places, that you eat neither fat nor blood."

4 And the LORD said to Moses, 2 "Say to the people of Israel, If any one sins unwittingly in any of the things which the LORD has commanded not to be done, and does any one of them, 3 if it is the anointed priest who sins, thus bringing guilt on the people, then let him offer for the sin which he has committed a young bull without blemish to the LORD for a sin offering. 4 He shall bring the bull to the door of the tent of meeting before the LORD, and lay his hand on the head of the

bull, and kill the bull before the LORD 5And the anointed priest shall take some of the blood of the bull and bring it to the tent of meeting; 6 and the priest shall dip his finger in the blood and sprinkle part of the blood seven times before the LORD in front of the veil of the sanctuary. 7And the priest shall put some of the blood on the horns of the altar of fragrant incense before the LORD which is in the tent of meeting, and the rest of the blood of the bull he shall pour out at the base of the altar of burnt offering which is at the door of the tent of meeting. 8And all the fat of the bull of the sin offering he shall take from it, the fat that covers the entrails and all the fat that is on the entrails, 9 and the two kidneys with the fat that is on them at the loins, and the appendage of the liver which he shall take away with the kidneys 10 (just as these are taken from the ox of the sacrifice of the peace offerings), and the priest shall burn them upon the altar of burnt offering. 11 But the skin of the bull and all its flesh, with its head, its legs, its entrails, and its dung, 12 the whole bull he shall carry forth outside the camp to a clean place, where the ashes are poured out, and shall burn it on a fire of wood; where the ashes are poured out it shall be burned.

13 "If the whole congregation of Israel commits a sin unwittingly and the thing is hidden from the eyes of the assembly, and they do any one of the things which the LORD has commanded not to be done and are guilty; 14 when the sin which they have committed becomes known, the assembly shall offer a young bull for a sin offering and bring it before the tent of meeting; 15 and the elders of the congregation shall lay their hands upon the head of the bull before the LORD, and the bull shall be killed before the LORD. 16 Then the anointed priest shall bring some of the blood of the bull to the tent of meeting, 17 and the priest shall dip his finger in the blood and sprinkle it seven times before the LORD in front of the veil. 18And he shall put some of the blood of the horns of the altar which is in the tent of meeting before the LORD; and the rest of the blood he shall pour out at the base of the altar of burnt offering which is at the door of the tent of meeting. 19And all its fat he shall take from it and burn upon the altar. 20 Thus shall he do with the bull; as he did with the bull of the sin offering,

so shall he do with this; and the priest shall make atonement for them, and they shall be forgiven. 21And he shall carry forth the bull outside the camp, and burn it as he burned the first bull; it is the sin offering for the assembly.

22 "When a ruler sins, doing unwittingly any one of all the things which the LORD his God has commanded not to be done, and is guilty, 23 if the sin which he has committed is made known to him, he shall bring as his offering a goat, a male without blemish, 24 and shall lay his hand upon the head of the goat, and kill it in the place where they kill the burnt offering before the LORD; it is a sin offering. 25 Then the priest shall take some of the blood of the sin offering with his finger and put it on the horns of the altar of burnt offering, and pour out the rest of its blood at the base of the altar of burnt offering. 26And all its fat he shall burn on the altar, like the fat of the sacrifice of peace offerings; so the priest shall make atonement for him for his sin, and he shall be forgiven.

27 "If any one of the common people sins unwittingly in doing any one of the things which the LORD has commanded not to be done, and is guilty, 28 when the sin which he has committed is made known to him he shall bring for his offering a goat, a female without blemish, for his sin which he has committed. 29And he shall lay his hand on the head of the sin offering, and kill the sin offering in the place of burnt offering. 30And the priest shall take some of its blood with his finger and put it on the horns of the altar of burnt offering, and pour out the rest of its blood at the base of the altar. 31And all its fat he shall remove, as the fat is removed from the peace offerings, and the priest shall burn it upon the altar for a pleasing odor to the LORD; and the priest shall make atonement for him, and he shall be forgiven.

32 "If he brings a lamb as his offering for a sin offering, he shall bring a female without blemish, 33 and lay his hand upon the head of the sin offering, and kill it for a sin offering in the place where they kill the burnt offering. 34 Then the priest shall take some of the blood of the sin offering with his finger and put it on the horns of the altar of burnt offering, and pour out the rest of its blood at the base of the altar. 35And all its fat he shall remove as the fat of the lamb is removed from the sacrifice of peace offerings, and the priest shall burn it

on the altar, upon the offerings by fire to the LORD; and the priest shall make atonement for him for the sin which he has committed, and he shall be forgiven.

5 "If any one sins in that he hears a public adjuration to testify and though he is a witness, whether he has seen or come to know the matter, yet does not speak, he shall bear his iniquity. 2 Or if any one touches an unclean thing, whether the carcass of an unclean beast or a carcass of unclean cattle or a carcass of unclean swarming things, and it is hidden from him, and he has become unclean, he shall be guilty. 3 Or if he touches human uncleanness, of whatever sort the uncleanness may be with which one becomes unclean, and it is hidden from him, when he comes to know it he shall be guilty. 4 Or if any one utters with his lips a rash oath to do evil or to do good, any sort of rash oath that men swear, and it is hidden from him, when he comes to know it he shall in any of these be guilty. 5 When a man is guilty in any of these, he shall confess the sin he has committed, 6 and he shall bring his guilt offering to the LORD for the sin which he has committed, a female from the flock, a lamb or a goat, for a sin offering; and the priest shall make atonement for him for his sin.

7 "But if he cannot afford a lamb, then he shall bring, as his guilt offering to the LORD for the sin which he has committed, two turtledoves or two young pigeons, one for a sin offering and the other for a burnt offering. 8 He shall bring them to the priest, who shall offer first the one for the sin offering; he shall wring its head from its neck, but shall not sever it, 9 and he shall sprinkle some of the blood of the sin offering on the side of the altar, while the rest of the blood shall be drained out at the base of the altar; it is a sin offering. 10 Then he shall offer the second for a burnt offering according to the ordinance; and the priest shall make atonement for him for the sin which he has committed, and he shall be forgiven.

11 "But if he cannot afford two turtledoves or two young pigeons, then he shall bring, as his offering for the sin which he has committed, a tenth of an ephah of fine flour for a sin offering; he shall put no oil upon it, and shall put no frankincense on it, for it is a sin offering. 12And he shall bring it to the priest, and the priest shall take a handful of it as its memorial

portion and burn this on the altar, upon the offerings by fire to the LORD; it is a sin offering. 13 Thus the priest shall make atonement for him for the sin which he has committed in any one of these things, and he shall be forgiven. And the remainder shall be for the priest, as in the cereal offering."

14 The LORD said to Moses, 15 "If any one commits a breach of faith and sins unwittingly in any of the holy things of the LORD, he shall bring, as his guilt offering to the LORD, a ram without blemish out of the flock, valued by you in shekels of silver, according to the shekel of the sanctuary; it is a guilt offering. 16 He shall also make restitution for what he has done amiss in the holy thing, and shall add a fifth to it and give it to the priest; and the priest shall make atonement for him with the ram of the guilt offering, and he shall be forgiven.

17 "If any one sins, doing any of the things which the LORD has commanded not to be done, though he does not know it, yet he is guilty and shall bear his iniquity. 18 He shall bring to the priest a ram without blemish out of the flock, valued by you at the price for a guilt offering, and the priest shall make atonement for him for the error which he committed unwittingly, and he shall be forgiven. 19 It is a guilt offering; he is guilty before the LORD."

6 a The LORD said to Moses, 2 "If any one sins and commits a breach of faith against the LORD by deceiving his neighbor in a matter of deposit or security, or through robbery, or if he has oppressed his neighbor 3 or has found what was lost and lied about it, swearing falsely—in any of all the things which men do and sin therein, 4 when one has sinned and become guilty, he shall restore what he took by robbery, or what he got by oppression, or the deposit which was committed to him, or the lost thing which he found, 5 or anything about which he has sworn falsely; he shall restore it in full, and shall add a fifth to it, and give it to him to whom it belongs, on the day of his guilt offering. 6 And he shall bring to the priest his guilt offering to the LORD, a ram without blemish out of the flock, valued by you at the price for a guilt offering; 7 and the priest shall make atonement for him before the LORD, and he shall be forgiven for any of the things which one may do and thereby become guilty."

8b The LORD said to Moses, 9 "Command Aaron and his sons, saying, This is the law of the burnt offering. The burnt offering shall be on the hearth upon the altar all night until the morning, and the fire of the altar shall be kept burning on it. 10 And the priest shall put on his linen garment, and put his linen breeches upon his body, and he shall take up the ashes to which the fire has consumed the burnt offering on the altar, and put them beside the altar. 11 Then he shall put off his garments, and put on other garments, and carry forth the ashes outside the camp to a clean place. 12 The fire on the altar shall be kept burning on it, it shall not go out; the priest shall burn wood on it every morning, and he shall lay the burnt offering in order upon it, and shall burn on it the fat of the peace offerings. 13 Fire shall be kept burning upon the altar continually; it shall not go out.

14 "And this is the law of the cereal offering. The sons of Aaron shall offer it before the LORD, in front of the altar. 15 And one shall take from it a handful of the fine flour of the cereal offering with its oil and all the frankincense which is on the cereal offering, and burn this as its memorial portion on the altar, a pleasing odor to the LORD. 16 And the rest of it Aaron and his sons shall eat; it shall be eaten unleavened in a holy place; in the court of the tent of meeting they shall eat it. 17 It shall not be baked with leaven. I have given it as their portion of my offerings by fire; it is a thing most holy, like the sin offering and the guilt offering. 18 Every male among the children of Aaron may eat of it, as decreed for ever throughout your generations, from the LORD's offerings by fire; whoever touches them shall become holy."

19 The LORD said to Moses, 20 "This is the offering which Aaron and his sons shall offer to the LORD on the day when he is anointed: a tenth of an ephah of fine flour as a regular cereal offering, half of it in the morning and half in the evening. 21 It shall be made with oil on a griddle; you shall bring it well mixed, in baked c pieces like a cereal offering, and offer it for a pleasing odor to the LORD. 22 The priest from among Aaron's sons, who is anointed to succeed him, shall offer it to the LORD as decreed for ever; the whole of it shall be burned. 23 Every cereal offering of

---

a Ch 5.20 in Heb   b Ch 6.1 in Heb   c Meaning of Heb is uncertain
6.1-7: Ex 22.7-15; Num 5.5-8.

a priest shall be wholly burned; it shall not be eaten."

24 The LORD said to Moses, 25 "Say to Aaron and his sons, This is the law of the sin offering. In the place where the burnt offering is killed shall the sin offering be killed before the LORD; it is most holy. 26 The priest who offers it for sin shall eat it; in a holy place it shall be eaten, in the court of the tent of meeting. 27 Whatever*d* touches its flesh shall be holy; and when any of its blood is sprinkled on a garment, you shall wash that on which it was sprinkled in a holy place. 28And the earthen vessel in which it is boiled shall be broken; but if it is boiled in a bronze vessel, that shall be scoured, and rinsed in water. 29 Every male among the priests may eat of it; it is most holy. 30 But no sin offering shall be eaten from which any blood is brought into the tent of meeting to make atonement in the holy place; it shall be burned with fire.

7 "This is the law of the guilt offering. It is most holy; 2 in the place where they kill the burnt offering they shall kill the guilt offering, and its blood shall be thrown on the altar round about. 3And all its fat shall be offered, the fat tail, the fat that covers the entrails, 4 the two kidneys with the fat that is on them at the loins, and the appendage of the liver which he shall take away with the kidneys; 5 the priest shall burn them on the altar as an offering by fire to the LORD; it is a guilt offering. 6 Every male among the priests may eat of it; it shall be eaten in a holy place; it is most holy. 7 The guilt offering is like the sin offering, there is one law for them; the priest who makes atonement with it shall have it. 8And the priest who offers any man's burnt offering shall have for himself the skin of the burnt offering which he has offered. 9And every cereal offering baked in the oven and all that is prepared on a pan or a griddle shall belong to the priest who offers it. 10And every cereal offering, mixed with oil or dry, shall be for all the sons of Aaron, one as well as another.

11 "And this is the law of the sacrifice of peace offerings which one may offer to the LORD. 12 If he offers it for a thanksgiving, then he shall offer with the thank offering unleavened cakes mixed with oil, unleavened wafers spread with oil, and cakes of fine flour well mixed with oil. 13 With the sacrifice of his peace offerings for thanksgiving he shall bring his offering with

d Or *Whoever*

cakes of leavened bread. 14And of such he shall offer one cake from each offering, as an offering to the LORD; it shall belong to the priest who throws the blood of the peace offerings. 15And the flesh of the sacrifice of his peace offerings for thanksgiving shall be eaten on the day of his offering; he shall not leave any of it until the morning. 16 But if the sacrifice of his offering is a votive offering or a freewill offering, it shall be eaten on the day that he offers his sacrifice, and on the morrow what remains of it shall be eaten, 17 but what remains of the flesh of the sacrifice on the third day shall be burned with fire. 18 If any of the flesh of the sacrifice of his peace offering is eaten on the third day, he who offers it shall not be accepted, neither shall it be credited to him; it shall be an abomination, and he who eats of it shall bear his iniquity.

19 "Flesh that touches any unclean thing shall not be eaten; it shall be burned with fire. All who are clean may eat flesh, 20 but the person who eats of the flesh of the sacrifice of the LORD's peace offerings while an uncleanness is on him, that person shall be cut off from his people. 21And if any one touches an unclean thing, whether the uncleanness of man or an unclean beast or any unclean abomination, and then eats of the flesh of the sacrifice of the LORD's peace offerings, that person shall be cut off from his people."

22 The LORD said to Moses, 23 "Say to the people of Israel, You shall eat no fat, of ox, or sheep, or goat. 24 The fat of an animal that dies of itself, and the fat of one that is torn by beasts, may be put to any other use, but on no account shall you eat it. 25 For every person who eats of the fat of an animal of which an offering by fire is made to the LORD shall be cut off from his people. 26 Moreover you shall eat no blood whatever, whether of fowl or of animal, in any of your dwellings. 27 Whoever eats any blood, that person shall be cut off from his people."

28 The LORD said to Moses, 29 "Say to the people of Israel, He that offers the sacrifice of his peace offerings to the LORD shall bring his offering to the LORD; from the sacrifice of his peace offerings 30 he shall bring with his own hands the offerings by fire to the LORD; he shall bring the fat with the breast, that the breast may be waved as a wave offering before the

LORD. 31 The priest shall burn the fat on the altar, but the breast shall be for Aaron and his sons. 32And the right thigh you shall give to the priest as an offering from the sacrifice of your peace offerings; 33 he among the sons of Aaron who offers the blood of the peace offerings and the fat shall have the right thigh for a portion. 34 For the breast that is waved and the thigh that is offered I have taken from the people of Israel, out of the sacrifices of their peace offerings, and have given them to Aaron the priest and to his sons, as a perpetual due from the people of Israel. 35 This is the portion of Aaron and of his sons from the offerings made by fire to the LORD, consecrated to them on the day they were presented to serve as priests of the LORD; 36 the LORD commanded this to be given them by the people of Israel, on the day that they were anointed; it is a perpetual due throughout their generations."

37 This is the law of the burnt offering, of the cereal offering, of the sin offering, of the guilt offering, of the consecration, and of the peace offerings, 38 which the LORD commanded Moses on Mount Sinai, on the day that he commanded the people of Israel to bring their offerings to the LORD, in the wilderness of Sinai.

8 The LORD said to Moses, 2 "Take Aaron and his sons with him, and the garments, and the anointing oil, and the bull of the sin offering, and the two rams, and the basket of unleavened bread; 3 and assemble all the congregation at the door of the tent of meeting." 4And Moses did as the LORD commanded him; and the congregation was assembled at the door of the tent of meeting.

5 And Moses said to the congregation, "This is the thing which the LORD has commanded to be done." 6And Moses brought Aaron and his sons, and washed them with water. 7And he put on him the coat, and girded him with the girdle, and clothed him with the robe, and put the ephod upon him, and girded him with the skilfully woven band of the ephod, binding it to him therewith. 8And he placed the breastpiece on him, and in the breastpiece he put the U'rim and the Thum'mim. 9And he set the turban upon his head, and on the turban, in front, he set the golden plate, the holy crown, as the LORD commanded Moses.

10 Then Moses took the anointing

oil, and anointed the tabernacle and all that was in it, and consecrated them. 11And he sprinkled some of it on the altar seven times, and anointed the altar and all its utensils, and the laver and its base, to consecrate them. 12And he poured some of the anointing oil on Aaron's head, and anointed him, to consecrate him. 13And Moses brought Aaron's sons, and clothed them with coats, and girded them with girdles, and bound caps on them, as the LORD commanded Moses.

14 Then he brought the bull of the sin offering; and Aaron and his sons laid their hands upon the head of the bull of the sin offering. 15And Moses killed it, and took the blood, and with his finger put it on the horns of the altar round about, and purified the altar, and poured out the blood at the base of the altar, and consecrated it, to make atonement for it. 16And he took all the fat that was on the entrails, and the appendage of the liver, and the two kidneys with their fat, and Moses burned them on the altar. 17 But the bull, and its skin, and its flesh, and its dung, he burned with fire outside the camp, as the LORD commanded Moses.

18 Then he presented the ram of the burnt offering; and Aaron and his sons laid their hands on the head of the ram. 19And Moses killed it, and threw the blood upon the altar round about. 20And when the ram was cut into pieces, Moses burned the head and the pieces and the fat. 21And when the entrails and the legs were washed with water, Moses burned the whole ram on the altar, as a burnt offering, a pleasing odor, an offering by fire to the LORD, as the LORD commanded Moses.

22 Then he presented the other ram, the ram of ordination; and Aaron and his sons laid their hands on the head of the ram. 23And Moses killed it, and took some of its blood and put it on the tip of Aaron's right ear and on the thumb of his right hand and on the great toe of his right foot. 24And Aaron's sons were brought, and Moses put some of the blood on the tips of their right ears and on the thumbs of their right hands and on the great toes of their right feet; and Moses threw the blood upon the altar round about. 25 Then he took the fat, and the fat tail, and all the fat that was on the entrails, and the appendage of the liver, and the two kidneys with their fat, and the right thigh; 26 and out of

8.1-36: Ex 29.1-37.

the basket of unleavened bread which was before the Lord he took one unleavened cake, and one cake of bread with oil, and one wafer, and placed them on the fat and on the right thigh; 27 and he put all these in the hands of Aaron and in the hands of his sons, and waved them as a wave offering before the Lord. 28 Then Moses took them from their hands, and burned them on the altar with the burnt offering, as an ordination offering, a pleasing odor, an offering by fire to the Lord. 29And Moses took the breast, and waved it for a wave offering before the Lord; it was Moses' portion of the ram of ordination, as the Lord commanded Moses.

30 Then Moses took some of the anointing oil and of the blood which was on the altar, and sprinkled it upon Aaron and his garments, and also upon his sons and his sons' garments; so he consecrated Aaron and his garments, and his sons and his sons' garments with him.

31 And Moses said to Aaron and his sons, "Boil the flesh at the door of the tent of meeting, and there eat it and the bread that is in the basket of ordination offerings, as I commanded, saying, 'Aaron and his sons shall eat it'; 32 and what remains of the flesh and the bread you shall burn with fire. 33And you shall not go out from the door of the tent of meeting for seven days, until the days of your ordination are completed, for it will take seven days to ordain you. 34As has been done today, the Lord has commanded to be done to make atonement for you. 35At the door of the tent of meeting you shall remain day and night for seven days, performing what the Lord has charged, lest you die; for so I am commanded." 36And Aaron and his sons did all the things which the Lord commanded by Moses.

9 On the eighth day Moses called Aaron and his sons and the elders of Israel; 2 and he said to Aaron, "Take a bull calf for a sin offering, and a ram for a burnt offering, both without blemish, and offer them before the Lord. 3And say to the people of Israel, 'Take a male goat for a sin offering, and a calf and a lamb, both a year old without blemish, for a burnt offering, 4 and an ox and a ram for peace offerings, to sacrifice before the Lord, and a cereal offering mixed with oil; for today the Lord will appear to you.'" 5And they brought what Moses com-

manded before the tent of meeting; and all the congregation drew near and stood before the Lord. 6And Moses said, "This is the thing which the Lord commanded you to do; and the glory of the Lord will appear to you." 7 Then Moses said to Aaron, "Draw near to the altar, and offer your sin offering and your burnt offering, and make atonement for yourself and for the people; and bring the offering of the people, and make atonement for them; as the Lord has commanded."

8 So Aaron drew near to the altar, and killed the calf of the sin offering, which was for himself. 9And the sons of Aaron presented the blood to him, and he dipped his finger in the blood and put it on the horns of the altar, and poured out the blood at the base of the altar; 10 but the fat and the kidneys and the appendage of the liver from the sin offering he burned upon the altar, as the Lord commanded Moses. 11 The flesh and the skin he burned with fire outside the camp.

12 And he killed the burnt offering; and Aaron's sons delivered to him the blood, and he threw it on the altar round about. 13And they delivered the burnt offering to him, piece by piece, and the head; and he burned them upon the altar. 14And he washed the entrails and the legs, and burned them with the burnt offering on the altar.

15 Then he presented the people's offering, and took the goat of the sin offering which was for the people, and killed it, and offered it for sin, like the first sin offering. 16And he presented the burnt offering, and offered it according to the ordinance. 17And he presented the cereal offering, and filled his hand from it, and burned it upon the altar, besides the burnt offering of the morning.

18 He killed the ox also and the ram, the sacrifice of peace offerings for the people; and Aaron's sons delivered to him the blood, which he threw upon the altar round about, 19 and the fat of the ox and of the ram, the fat tail, and that which covers the entrails, and the kidneys, and the appendage of the liver; 20 and they put the fat upon the breasts, and he burned the fat upon the altar, 21 but the breasts and the right thigh Aaron waved for a wave offering before the Lord; as Moses commanded.

22 Then Aaron lifted up his hands toward the people and blessed them; and he came down from offering the sin offering and the burnt offering and

9.18-21: Lev 3.1-11.

the peace offerings. 23And Moses and Aaron went into the tent of meeting; and when they came out they blessed the people, and the glory of the LORD appeared to all the people. 24And fire came forth from before the LORD and consumed the burnt offering and the fat upon the altar; and when all the people saw it, they shouted, and fell on their faces.

10 Now Nā´dab and Ȧ·bī´hū, the sons of Aaron, each took his censer, and put fire in it, and laid incense on it, and offered unholy fire before the LORD, such as he had not commanded them. 2And fire came forth from the presence of the LORD and devoured them, and they died before the LORD. 3 Then Moses said to Aaron, "This is what the LORD has said, 'I will show myself holy among those who are near me, and before all the people I will be glorified.' " And Aaron held his peace.

4 And Moses called Mish´ȧ-el and El´zȧ-phan, the sons of Uz´zi-el the uncle of Aaron, and said to them, "Draw near, carry your brethren from before the sanctuary out of the camp." 5 So they drew near, and carried them in their coats out of the camp, as Moses had said. 6And Moses said to Aaron and to El·ē·ā´zȧr and Ith´ȧ·mär, his sons, "Do not let the hair of your heads hang loose, and do not rend your clothes, lest you die, and lest wrath come upon all the congregation; but your brethren, the whole house of Israel, may bewail the burning which the LORD has kindled. 7And do not go out from the door of the tent of meeting, lest you die; for the anointing oil of the LORD is upon you." And they did according to the word of Moses.

8 And the LORD spoke to Aaron, saying, 9 "Drink no wine nor strong drink, you nor your sons with you, when you go into the tent of meeting, lest you die; it shall be a statute for ever throughout your generations. 10 You are to distinguish between the holy and the common, and between the unclean and the clean; 11 and you are to teach the people of Israel all the statutes which the LORD has spoken to them by Moses."

12 And Moses said to Aaron and to El·ē·ā´zȧr and Ith´ȧ·mär, his sons who were left, "Take the cereal offering that remains of the offerings by fire to the LORD, and eat it unleavened beside the altar, for it is most holy; 13 you shall eat it in a holy place, because it is your due and your sons' due, from the offerings by fire to the LORD; for so I am commanded. 14 But the breast that is waved and the thigh that is offered you shall eat in any clean place, you and your sons and your daughters with you; for they are given as your due and your sons' due, from the sacrifices of the peace offering of the people of Israel. 15 The thigh that is offered and the breast that is waved they shall bring with the offerings by fire of the fat, to wave for a wave offering before the LORD, and it shall be yours, and your sons' with you, as a due for ever; as the LORD has commanded."

16 Now Moses diligently inquired about the goat of the sin offering, and behold, it was burned! And he was angry with El·ē·ā´zȧr and Ith´ȧ·mär, the sons of Aaron who were left, saying, 17 "Why have you not eaten the sin offering in the place of the sanctuary, since it is a thing most holy and has been given to you that you may bear the iniquity of the congregation, to make atonement for them before the LORD? 18 Behold, its blood was not brought into the inner part of the sanctuary. You certainly ought to have eaten it in the sanctuary, as I commanded." 19And Aaron said to Moses, "Behold, today they have offered their sin offering and their burnt offering before the LORD; and yet such things as these have befallen me! If I had eaten the sin offering today, would it have been acceptable in the sight of the LORD?" 20And when Moses heard that, he was content.

11 And the LORD said to Moses and Aaron. 2 "Say to the people of Israel, These are the living things which you may eat among all the beasts that are on the earth. 3 Whatever parts the hoof and is cloven-footed and chews the cud, among the animals, you may eat. 4 Nevertheless among those that chew the cud or part the hoof, you shall not eat these: The camel, because it chews the cud but does not part the hoof, is unclean to you. 5And the rock badger, because it chews the cud but does not part the hoof, is unclean to you. 6And the hare, because it chews the cud but does not part the hoof, is unclean to you. 7And the swine, because it parts the hoof and is cloven-footed but does not chew the cud, is unclean to you. 8 Of their flesh you shall not eat, and their car-

10.8: Ezek 44.21.　10.12-13: Lev 6.14-18.
11.2-47: Deut 14.3-21.

10.14-15: Lev 7.30-34.

casses you shall not touch; they are unclean to you.

9 "These you may eat, of all that are in the waters. Everything in the waters that has fins and scales, whether in the seas or in the rivers, you may eat. 10 But anything in the seas or the rivers that has not fins and scales, of the swarming creatures in the waters and of the living creatures that are in the waters, is an abomination to you. 11 They shall remain an abomination to you; of their flesh you shall not eat, and their carcasses you shall have in abomination. 12 Everything in the waters that has not fins and scales is an abomination to you.

13 "And these you shall have in abomination among the birds, they shall not be eaten, they are an abomination: the eagle, the carrion vulture, the osprey, 14 the kite, the falcon according to its kind, 15 every raven according to its kind, 16 the ostrich, the nighthawk, the sea gull, the hawk according to its kind, 17 the owl, the cormorant, the ibis, 18 the water hen, the pelican, the carrion vulture, 19 the stork, the heron according to its kind, the hoopoe, and the bat.

20 "All winged insects that go upon all fours are an abomination to you. 21 Yet among the winged insects that go on all fours you may eat those which have legs above their feet, with which to leap on the earth. 22 Of them you may eat: the locust according to its kind, the bald locust according to its kind, the cricket according to its kind, and the grasshopper according to its kind. 23 But all other winged insects which have four feet are an abomination to you.

24 "And by these you shall become unclean; whoever touches their carcass shall be unclean until the evening, 25 and whoever carries any part of their carcass shall wash his clothes and be unclean until the evening. 26 Every animal which parts the hoof but is not cloven-footed or does not chew the cud is unclean to you; every one who touches them shall be unclean. 27 And all that go on their paws, among the animals that go on all fours, are unclean to you; whoever touches their carcass shall be unclean until the evening, 28 and he who carries their carcass shall wash his clothes and be unclean until the evening; they are unclean to you.

29 "And these are unclean to you among the swarming things that swarm upon the earth: the weasel, the mouse,

the great lizard according to its kind, 30 the gecko, the land crocodile, the lizard, the sand lizard, and the chameleon. 31 These are unclean to you among all that swarm; whoever touches them when they are dead shall be unclean until the evening. 32 And anything upon which any of them falls when they are dead shall be unclean, whether it is an article of wood or a garment or a skin or a sack, any vessel that is used for any purpose; it must be put into water, and it shall be unclean until the evening; then it shall be clean. 33 And if any of them falls into any earthen vessel, all that is in it shall be unclean, and you shall break it. 34 Any food in it which may be eaten, upon which water may come, shall be unclean; and all drink which may be drunk from every such vessel shall be unclean. 35 And everything upon which any part of their carcass falls shall be unclean; whether oven or stove, it shall be broken in pieces; they are unclean, and shall be unclean to you. 36 Nevertheless a spring or a cistern holding water shall be clean; but whatever touches their carcass shall be unclean. 37 And if any part of their carcass falls upon any seed for sowing that is to be sown, it is clean; 38 but if water is put on the seed and any part of their carcass falls on it, it is unclean to you.

39 "And if any animal of which you may eat dies, he who touches its carcass shall be unclean until the evening, 40 and he who eats of its carcass shall wash his clothes and be unclean until the evening; he also who carries the carcass shall wash his clothes and be unclean until the evening.

41 "Every swarming thing that swarms upon the earth is an abomination; it shall not be eaten. 42 Whatever goes on its belly, and whatever goes on all fours, or whatever has many feet, all the swarming things that swarm upon the earth, you shall not eat; for they are an abomination. 43 You shall not make yourselves abominable with any swarming thing that swarms; and you shall not defile yourselves with them, lest you become unclean. 44 For I am the LORD your God; consecrate yourselves therefore, and be holy, for I am holy. You shall not defile yourselves with any swarming thing that crawls upon the earth. 45 For I am the LORD who brought you up out of the land of Egypt, to be your God; you shall therefore be holy, for I am holy."

46 This is the law pertaining to beast and bird and every living crea-

11.44-45: Lev 19.2; 20.7, 26; 1 Pet 1.16.   **11.46:** Num 5.2-3.

ture that moves through the waters and every creature that swarms upon the earth, [47] to make a distinction between the unclean and the clean and between the living creature that may be eaten and the living creature that may not be eaten.

12 The LORD said to Moses, [2] "Say to the people of Israel, If a woman conceives, and bears a male child, then she shall be unclean seven days; as at the time of her menstruation, she shall be unclean. [3] And on the eighth day the flesh of his foreskin shall be circumcised. [4] Then she shall continue for thirty-three days in the blood of her purifying; she shall not touch any hallowed thing, nor come into the sanctuary, until the days of her purifying are completed. [5] But if she bears a female child, then she shall be unclean two weeks, as in her menstruation; and she shall continue in the blood of her purifying for sixty-six days.

[6] "And when the days of her purifying are completed, whether for a son or for a daughter, she shall bring to the priest at the door of the tent of meeting a lamb a year old for a burnt offering, and a young pigeon or a turtledove for a sin offering, [7] and he shall offer it before the LORD, and make atonement for her; then she shall be clean from the flow of her blood. This is the law for her who bears a child, either male or female. [8] And if she cannot afford a lamb, then she shall take two turtledoves or two young pigeons, one for a burnt offering and the other for a sin offering, and the priest shall make atonement for her, and she shall be clean."

13 The LORD said to Moses and Aaron, [2] "When a man has on the skin of his body a swelling or an eruption or a spot, and it turns into a leprous disease on the skin of his body, then he shall be brought to Aaron the priest or to one of his sons the priests, [3] and the priest shall examine the diseased spot on the skin of his body; and if the hair in the diseased spot has turned white and the disease appears to be deeper than the skin of his body, it is a leprous disease; when the priest has examined him he shall pronounce him unclean. [4] But if the spot is white in the skin of his body, and appears no deeper than the skin, and the hair in it has not turned white, the priest shall shut up the diseased person for seven days; [5] and the priest shall examine him on the seventh day, and if in his

eyes the disease is checked and the disease has not spread in the skin, then the priest shall shut him up seven days more; [6] and the priest shall examine him again on the seventh day, and if the diseased spot is dim and the disease has not spread in the skin, then the priest shall pronounce him clean; it is only an eruption; and he shall wash his clothes, and be clean. [7] But if the eruption spreads in the skin, after he has shown himself to the priest for his cleansing, he shall appear again before the priest; [8] and the priest shall make an examination, and if the eruption has spread in the skin, then the priest shall pronounce him unclean; it is leprosy.

[9] "When a man is afflicted with leprosy, he shall be brought to the priest; [10] and the priest shall make an examination, and if there is a white swelling in the skin, which has turned the hair white, and there is quick raw flesh in the swelling, [11] it is a chronic leprosy in the skin of his body, and the priest shall pronounce him unclean; he shall not shut him up, for he is unclean. [12] And if the leprosy breaks out in the skin, so that the leprosy covers all the skin of the diseased person from head to foot, so far as the priest can see, [13] then the priest shall make an examination, and if the leprosy has covered all his body, he shall pronounce him clean of the disease; it has all turned white, and he is clean. [14] But when raw flesh appears on him, he shall be unclean. [15] And the priest shall examine the raw flesh, and pronounce him unclean; raw flesh is unclean, for it is leprosy. [16] But if the raw flesh turns again and is changed to white, then he shall come to the priest, [17] and the priest shall examine him, and if the disease has turned white, then the priest shall pronounce the diseased person clean; he is clean.

[18] "And when there is in the skin of one's body a boil that has healed, [19] and in the place of the boil there comes a white swelling or a reddish-white spot, then it shall be shown to the priest; [20] and the priest shall make an examination, and if it appears deeper than the skin and its hair has turned white, then the priest shall pronounce him unclean; it is the disease of leprosy, it has broken out in the boil. [21] But if the priest examines it, and the hair on it is not white and it is not deeper than the skin, but is dim, then the priest shall shut him up seven days; [22] and if it spreads in the skin, then

the priest shall pronounce him unclean; it is diseased. 23 But if the spot remains in one place and does not spread, it is the scar of the boil; and the priest shall pronounce him clean.

24 "Or, when the body has a burn on its skin and the raw flesh of the burn becomes a spot, reddish-white or white, 25 the priest shall examine it, and if the hair in the spot has turned white and it appears deeper than the skin, then it is leprosy; it has broken out in the burn, and the priest shall pronounce him unclean; it is a leprous disease. 26 But if the priest examines it, and the hair in the spot is not white and it is no deeper than the skin, but is dim, the priest shall shut him up seven days, 27 and the priest shall examine him the seventh day; if it is spreading in the skin, then the priest shall pronounce him unclean; it is a leprous disease. 28 But if the spot remains in one place and does not spread in the skin, but is dim, it is a swelling from the burn, and the priest shall pronounce him clean; for it is the scar of the burn.

29 "When a man or woman has a disease on the head or the beard, 30 the priest shall examine the disease; and if it appears deeper than the skin, and the hair in it is yellow and thin, then the priest shall pronounce him unclean; it is an itch, a leprosy of the head or the beard. 31And if the priest examines the itching disease, and it appears no deeper than the skin and there is no black hair in it, then the priest shall shut up the person with the itching disease for seven days, 32 and on the seventh day the priest shall examine the disease; and if the itch has not spread, and there is in it no yellow hair, and the itch appears to be no deeper than the skin, 33 then he shall shave himself, but the itch he shall not shave; and the priest shall shut up the person with the itching disease for seven days more; 34 and on the seventh day the priest shall examine the itch, and if the itch has not spread in the skin and it appears to be no deeper than the skin, then the priest shall pronounce him clean; and he shall wash his clothes, and be clean. 35 But if the itch spreads in the skin after his cleansing, 36 then the priest shall examine him, and if the itch has spread in the skin, the priest need not seek for the yellow hair; he is unclean. 37 But if in his eyes the itch is checked, and black hair has grown in it, the itch is healed, he is clean; and the priest shall pronounce him clean.

38 "When a man or a woman has spots on the skin of the body, white spots, 39 the priest shall make an examination, and if the spots on the skin of the body are of a dull white, it is tetter that has broken out in the skin; he is clean.

40 "If a man's hair has fallen from his head, he is bald but he is clean. 41And if a man's hair has fallen from his forehead and temples, he has baldness of the forehead but he is clean. 42 But if there is on the bald head or the bald forehead a reddish-white diseased spot, it is leprosy breaking out on his bald head or his bald forehead. 43 Then the priest shall examine him, and if the diseased swelling is reddish-white on his bald head or on his bald forehead, like the appearance of leprosy in the skin of the body, 44 he is a leprous man, he is unclean; the priest must pronounce him unclean; his disease is on his head.

45 "The leper who has the disease shall wear torn clothes and let the hair of his head hang loose, and he shall cover his upper lip and cry, 'Unclean, unclean.' 46 He shall remain unclean as long as he has the disease; he is unclean; he shall dwell alone in a habitation outside the camp.

47 "When there is a leprous disease in a garment, whether a woolen or a linen garment, 48 in warp or woof of linen or wool, or in a skin or in anything made of skin, 49 if the disease shows greenish or reddish in the garment, whether in warp or woof or in skin or in anything made of skin, it is a leprous disease and shall be shown to the priest. 50And the priest shall examine the disease, and shut up that which has the disease for seven days; 51 then he shall examine the disease on the seventh day. If the disease has spread in the garment, in warp or woof, or in the skin, whatever be the use of the skin, the disease is a malignant leprosy; it is unclean. 52And he shall burn the garment, whether diseased in warp or woof, woolen or linen, or anything of skin, for it is a malignant leprosy; it shall be burned in the fire.

53 "And if the priest examines, and the disease has not spread in the garment in warp or woof or in anything of skin, 54 then the priest shall command that they wash the thing in which is the disease, and he shall shut it up seven days more; 55 and the priest shall examine the diseased thing after it has been washed. And if the diseased spot has not changed color, though the disease has not spread, it is unclean;

you shall burn it in the fire, whether the leprous spot is on the back or on the front.

56 "But if the priest examines, and the disease is dim after it is washed, he shall tear the spot out of the garment or the skin or the warp or woof; 57 then if it appears again in the garment, in warp or woof, or in anything of skin, it is spreading; you shall burn with fire that in which is the disease. 58 But the garment, warp or woof, or anything of skin from which the disease departs when you have washed it, shall then be washed a second time, and be clean."

59 This is the law for a leprous disease in a garment of wool or linen, either in warp or woof, or in anything of skin, to decide whether it is clean or unclean.

14 The LORD said to Moses, 2 "This shall be the law of the leper for the day of his cleansing. He shall be brought to the priest; 3 and the priest shall go out of the camp, and the priest shall make an examination. Then, if the leprous disease is healed in the leper, 4 the priest shall command them to take for him who is to be cleansed two living clean birds and cedarwood and scarlet stuff and hyssop; 5 and the priest shall command them to kill one of the birds in an earthen vessel over running water. 6 He shall take the living bird with the cedarwood and the scarlet stuff and the hyssop, and dip them and the living bird in the blood of the bird that was killed over the running water; 7 and he shall sprinkle it seven times upon him who is to be cleansed of leprosy; then he shall pronounce him clean, and shall let the living bird go into the open field. 8 And he who is to be cleansed shall wash his clothes, and shave off all his hair, and bathe himself in water, and he shall be clean; and after that he shall come into the camp, but shall dwell outside his tent seven days. 9 And on the seventh day he shall shave all his hair off his head; he shall shave off his beard and his eyebrows, all his hair. Then he shall wash his clothes, and bathe his body in water, and he shall be clean.

10 "And on the eighth day he shall take two male lambs without blemish, and one ewe lamb a year old without blemish, and a cereal offering of three tenths of an ephah of fine flour mixed with oil, and one log of oil. 11 And the priest who cleanses him shall set the man who is to be cleansed and these

things before the LORD, at the door of the tent of meeting. 12 And the priest shall take one of the male lambs, and offer it for a guilt offering, along with the log of oil, and wave them for a wave offering before the LORD; 13 and he shall kill the lamb in the place where they kill the sin offering and the burnt offering, in the holy place; for the guilt offering, like the sin offering, belongs to the priest; it is most holy. 14 The priest shall take some of the blood of the guilt offering, and the priest shall put it on the tip of the right ear of him who is to be cleansed, and on the thumb of his right hand, and on the great toe of his right foot. 15 Then the priest shall take some of the log of oil, and pour it into the palm of his own left hand, 16 and dip his right finger in the oil that is in his left hand, and sprinkle some oil with his finger seven times before the LORD. 17 And some of the oil that remains in his hand the priest shall put on the tip of the right ear of him who is to be cleansed, and on the thumb of his right hand, and on the great toe of his right foot, upon the blood of the guilt offering; 18 and the rest of the oil that is in the priest's hand he shall put on the head of him who is to be cleansed. Then the priest shall make atonement for him before the LORD. 19 The priest shall offer the sin offering, to make atonement for him who is to be cleansed from his uncleanness. And afterward he shall kill the burnt offering; 20 and the priest shall offer the burnt offering and the cereal offering on the altar. Thus the priest shall make atonement for him, and he shall be clean.

21 "But if he is poor and cannot afford so much, then he shall take one male lamb for a guilt offering to be waved, to make atonement for him, and a tenth of an ephah of fine flour mixed with oil for a cereal offering, and a log of oil; 22 also two turtledoves or two young pigeons, such as he can afford; the one shall be a sin offering and the other a burnt offering. 23 And on the eighth day he shall bring them for his cleansing to the priest, to the door of the tent of meeting, before the LORD; 24 and the priest shall take the lamb of the guilt offering, and the log of oil, and the priest shall wave them for a wave offering before the LORD. 25 And he shall kill the lamb of the guilt offering; and the priest shall take some of the blood of the guilt offering, and put it on the tip of the right ear

14.2-32: Mt 8.4; Mk 1.44; Lk 5.14; 17.14.

of him who is to be cleansed, and on the thumb of his right hand, and on the great toe of his right foot. 26And the priest shall pour some of the oil into the palm of his own left hand; 27 and shall sprinkle with his right finger some of the oil that is in his left hand seven times before the LORD; 28 and the priest shall put some of the oil that is in his hand on the tip of the right ear of him who is to be cleansed, and on the thumb of his right hand, and the great toe of his right foot, in the place where the blood of the guilt offering was put; 29 and the rest of the oil that is in the priest's hand he shall put on the head of him who is to be cleansed, to make atonement for him before the LORD. 30And he shall offer, of the turtledoves or young pigeons such as he can afford, 31 one*x* for a sin offering and the other for a burnt offering, along with a cereal offering; and the priest shall make atonement before the LORD for him who is being cleansed. 32 This is the law for him in whom is a leprous disease, who cannot afford the offerings for his cleansing."

33 The LORD said to Moses and Aaron, 34 "When you come into the land of Canaan, which I give you for a possession, and I put a leprous disease in a house in the land of your possession, 35 then he who owns the house shall come and tell the priest, 'There seems to me to be some sort of disease in my house.' 36 Then the priest shall command that they empty the house before the priest goes to examine the disease, lest all that is in the house be declared unclean; and afterward the priest shall go in to see the house. 37And he shall examine the disease; and if the disease is in the walls of the house with greenish or reddish spots, and if it appears to be deeper than the surface, 38 then the priest shall go out of the house to the door of the house, and shut up the house seven days. 39And the priest shall come again on the seventh day, and look; and if the disease has spread in the walls of the house, 40 then the priest shall command that they take out the stones in which is the disease and throw them into an unclean place outside the city; 41 and he shall cause the inside of the house to be scraped round about, and the plaster that they scrape off they shall pour into an unclean place outside the city; 42 then they shall take other stones and put them in the place of those stones, and he shall take other plaster and plaster the house.

43 "If the disease breaks out again in the house, after he has taken out the stones and scraped the house and plastered it, 44 then the priest shall go and look; and if the disease has spread in the house, it is a malignant leprosy in the house; it is unclean. 45And he shall break down the house, its stones and timber and all the plaster of the house; and he shall carry them forth out of the city to an unclean place. 46 Moreover he who enters the house while it is shut up shall be unclean until the evening; 47 and he who lies down in the house shall wash his clothes; and he who eats in the house shall wash his clothes.

48 "But if the priest comes and makes an examination, and the disease has not spread in the house after the house was plastered, then the priest shall pronounce the house clean, for the disease is healed. 49And for the cleansing of the house he shall take two small birds, with cedarwood and scarlet stuff and hyssop, 50 and shall kill one of the birds in an earthen vessel over running water, 51 and shall take the cedarwood and the hyssop and the scarlet stuff, along with the living bird, and dip them in the blood of the bird that was killed and in the running water, and sprinkle the house seven times. 52 Thus he shall cleanse the house with the blood of the bird, and with the running water, and with the living bird, and with the cedarwood and hyssop and scarlet stuff; 53 and he shall let the living bird go out of the city into the open field; so he shall make atonement for the house, and it shall be clean."

54 This is the law for any leprous disease: for an itch, 55 for leprosy in a garment or in a house, 56 and for a swelling or an eruption or a spot, 57 to show when it is unclean and when it is clean. This is the law for leprosy.

15 The LORD said to Moses and Aaron, 2 "Say to the people of Israel, When any man has a discharge from his body, his discharge is unclean. 3And this is the law of his uncleanness for a discharge: whether his body runs with his discharge, or his body is stopped from discharge, it is uncleanness in him. 4 Every bed on which he who has the discharge lies shall be unclean; and everything on which he sits shall be unclean. 5And any one who touches his bed shall wash his clothes, and bathe himself in water, and be unclean until the evening. 6And whoever sits on anything

---

x Gk Syr: Heb *afford,* 31 *such as he can afford, one*

on which he who has the discharge has sat shall wash his clothes, and bathe himself in water, and be unclean until the evening. 7And whoever touches the body of him who has the discharge shall wash his clothes, and bathe himself in water, and be unclean until the evening. 8And if he who has the discharge spits on one who is clean, then he shall wash his clothes, and bathe himself in water, and be unclean until the evening. 9And any saddle on which he who has the discharge rides shall be unclean. 10And whoever touches anything that was under him shall be unclean until the evening; and he who carries such a thing shall wash his clothes, and bathe himself in water, and be unclean until the evening. 11Any one whom he that has the discharge touches without having rinsed his hands in water shall wash his clothes, and bathe himself in water, and be unclean until the evening. 12And the earthen vessel which he who has the discharge touches shall be broken; and every vessel of wood shall be rinsed in water.

13 "And when he who has a discharge is cleansed of his discharge, then he shall count for himself seven days for his cleansing, and wash his clothes; and he shall bathe his body in running water, and shall be clean. 14And on the eighth day he shall take two turtledoves or two young pigeons, and come before the LORD to the door of the tent of meeting, and give them to the priest; 15 and the priest shall offer them, one for a sin offering and the other for a burnt offering; and the priest shall make atonement for him before the LORD for his discharge.

16 "And if a man has an emission of semen, he shall bathe his whole body in water, and be unclean until the evening. 17And every garment and every skin on which the semen comes shall be washed with water, and be unclean until the evening. 18 If a man lies with a woman and has an emission of semen, both of them shall bathe themselves in water, and be unclean until the evening.

19 "When a woman has a discharge of blood which is her regular discharge from her body, she shall be in her impurity for seven days, and whoever touches her shall be unclean until the evening. 20And everything upon which she lies during her impurity shall be unclean; everything also upon which she sits shall be unclean. 21And whoever touches her bed shall wash his

clothes, and bathe himself in water, and be unclean until the evening. 22And whoever touches anything upon which she sits shall wash his clothes, and bathe himself in water, and be unclean until the evening; 23 whether it is the bed or anything upon which she sits, when he touches it he shall be unclean until the evening. 24And if any man lies with her, and her impurity is on him, he shall be unclean seven days; and every bed on which he lies shall be unclean.

25 "If a woman has a discharge of blood for many days, not at the time of her impurity, or if she has a discharge beyond the time of her impurity, all the days of the discharge she shall continue in uncleanness; as in the days of her impurity, she shall be unclean. 26 Every bed on which she lies, all the days of her discharge, shall be to her as the bed of her impurity; and everything on which she sits shall be unclean, as in the uncleanness of her impurity. 27And whoever touches these things shall be unclean, and shall wash his clothes, and bathe himself in water, and be unclean until the evening. 28 But if she is cleansed of her discharge, she shall count for herself seven days, and after that she shall be clean. 29And on the eighth day she shall take two turtledoves or two young pigeons, and bring them to the priest, to the door of the tent of meeting. 30And the priest shall offer one for a sin offering and the other for a burnt offering; and the priest shall make atonement for her before the LORD for her unclean discharge.

31 "Thus you shall keep the people of Israel separate from their uncleanness, lest they die in their uncleanness by defiling my tabernacle that is in their midst."

32 This is the law for him who has a discharge and for him who has an emission of semen, becoming unclean thereby; 33 also for her who is sick with her impurity; that is, for any one, male or female, who has a discharge, and for the man who lies with a woman who is unclean.

16 The LORD spoke to Moses, after the death of the two sons of Aaron, when they drew near before the LORD and died; 2 and the LORD said to Moses, "Tell Aaron your brother not to come at all times into the holy place within the veil, before the mercy seat which is upon the ark, lest he die; for I will appear in the cloud upon the mercy seat. 3 But thus shall Aaron

15.24: Lev 18.19; 20.18.   16.2, 12: Heb 6.19; 9.7, 25.

come into the holy place: with a young bull for a sin offering and a ram for a burnt offering. 4 He shall put on the holy linen coat, and shall have the linen breeches on his body, be girded with the linen girdle, and wear the linen turban; these are the holy garments. He shall bathe his body in water, and then put them on. 5And he shall take from the congregation of the people of Israel two male goats for a sin offering, and one ram for a burnt offering.

6 "And Aaron shall offer the bull as a sin offering for himself, and shall make atonement for himself and for his house. 7 Then he shall take the two goats, and set them before the LORD at the door of the tent of meeting; 8 and Aaron shall cast lots upon the two goats, one lot for the LORD and the other lot for Ă·zā′zĕl. 9And Aaron shall present the goat on which the lot fell for the LORD, and offer it as a sin offering; 10 but the goat on which the lot fell for Ă·zā′zĕl shall be presented alive before the LORD to make atonement over it, that it may be sent away into the wilderness to Azazel.

11 "Aaron shall present the bull as a sin offering for himself, and shall make atonement for himself and for his house; he shall kill the bull as a sin offering for himself. 12And he shall take a censer full of coals of fire from the altar before the LORD, and two handfuls of sweet incense beaten small; and he shall bring it within the veil 13 and put the incense on the fire before the LORD, that the cloud of the incense may cover the mercy seat which is upon the testimony, lest he die; 14 and he shall take some of the blood of the bull, and sprinkle it with his finger on the front of the mercy seat, and before the mercy seat he shall sprinkle the blood with his finger seven times.

15 "Then he shall kill the goat of the sin offering which is for the people, and bring its blood within the veil, and do with its blood as he did with the blood of the bull, sprinkling it upon the mercy seat and before the mercy seat; 16 thus he shall make atonement for the holy place, because of the uncleannesses of the people of Israel, and because of their transgressions, all their sins; and so he shall do for the tent of meeting, which abides with them in the midst of their uncleannesses. 17 There shall be no man in the tent of meeting when he enters to make atonement in the holy place until he 16:27: Heb 13.11.

comes out and has made atonement for himself and for his house and for all the assembly of Israel. 18 Then he shall go out to the altar which is before the LORD and make atonement for it, and shall take some of the blood of the bull and of the blood of the goat, and put it on the horns of the altar round about. 19And he shall sprinkle some of the blood upon it with his finger seven times, and cleanse it and hallow it from the uncleannesses of the people of Israel.

20 "And when he has made an end of atoning for the holy place and the tent of meeting and the altar, he shall present the live goat; 21 and Aaron shall lay both his hands upon the head of the live goat, and confess over him all the iniquities of the people of Israel, and all their transgressions, all their sins; and he shall put them upon the head of the goat, and send him away into the wilderness by the hand of a man who is in readiness. 22 The goat shall bear all their iniquities upon him to a solitary land; and he shall let the goat go in the wilderness.

23 "Then Aaron shall come into the tent of meeting, and shall put off the linen garments which he put on when he went into the holy place, and shall leave them there; 24 and he shall bathe his body in water in a holy place, and put on his garments, and come forth, and offer his burnt offering and the burnt offering of the people, and make atonement for himself and for the people. 25And the fat of the sin offering he shall burn upon the altar. 26And he who lets the goat go to Ă·zā′zĕl shall wash his clothes and bathe his body in water, and afterward he may come into the camp. 27And the bull for the sin offering and the goat for the sin offering, whose blood was brought in to make atonement in the holy place, shall be carried forth outside the camp; their skin and their flesh and their dung shall be burned with fire. 28And he who burns them shall wash his clothes and bathe his body in water, and afterward he may come into the camp.

29 "And it shall be a statute to you for ever that in the seventh month, on the tenth day of the month, you shall afflict yourselves, and shall do no work, either the native or the stranger who sojourns among you; 30 for on this day shall atonement be made for you, to cleanse you; from all your sins you shall be clean before the LORD. 31 It is a sabbath of solemn rest to you,

and you shall afflict yourselves; it is a statute for ever. 32And the priest who is anointed and consecrated as priest in his father's place shall make atonement, wearing the holy linen garments; 33 he shall make atonement for the sanctuary, and he shall make atonement for the tent of meeting and for the altar, and he shall make atonement for the priests and for all the people of the assembly. 34And this shall be an everlasting statute for you, that atonement may be made for the people of Israel once in the year because of all their sins." And Moses did as the LORD commanded him.

17 And the LORD said to Moses, 2 "Say to Aaron and his sons, and to all the people of Israel, This is the thing which the LORD has commanded. 3 If any man of the house of Israel kills an ox or a lamb or a goat in the camp, or kills it outside the camp, 4 and does not bring it to the door of the tent of meeting, to offer it as a gift to the LORD before the tabernacle of the LORD, bloodguilt shall be imputed to that man; he has shed blood; and that man shall be cut off from among his people. 5 This is to the end that the people of Israel may bring their sacrifices which they slay in the open field, that they may bring them to the LORD, to the priest at the door of the tent of meeting, and slay them as sacrifices of peace offerings to the LORD; 6 and the priest shall sprinkle the blood on the altar of the LORD at the door of the tent of meeting, and burn the fat for a pleasing odor to the LORD. 7 So they shall no more slay their sacrifices for satyrs, after whom they play the harlot. This shall be a statute for ever to them throughout their generations.

8 "And you shall say to them, Any man of the house of Israel, or of the strangers that sojourn among them, who offers a burnt offering or sacrifice, 9 and does not bring it to the door of the tent of meeting, to sacrifice it to the LORD; that man shall be cut off from his people.

10 "If any man of the house of Israel or of the strangers that sojourn among them eats any blood, I will set my face against that person who eats blood, and will cut him off from among his people. 11 For the life of the flesh is in the blood; and I have given it for you upon the altar to make atonement

for your souls; for it is the blood that makes atonement, by reason of the life. 12 Therefore I have said to the people of Israel, No person among you shall eat blood, neither shall any stranger who sojourns among you eat blood. 13Any man also of the people of Israel, or of the strangers that sojourn among them, who takes in hunting any beast or bird that may be eaten shall pour out its blood and cover it with dust.

14 "For the life of every creature is the blood of it;*e* therefore I have said to the people of Israel, You shall not eat the blood of any creature, for the life of every creature is its blood; whoever eats it shall be cut off. 15And every person that eats what dies of itself or what is torn by beasts, whether he is a native or a sojourner, shall wash his clothes, and bathe himself in water, and be unclean until the evening; then he shall be clean. 16 But if he does not wash them or bathe his flesh, he shall bear his iniquity."

18 And the LORD said to Moses, 2 "Say to the people of Israel, I am the LORD your God. 3 You shall not do as they do in the land of Egypt, where you dwelt, and you shall not do as they do in the land of Canaan, to which I am bringing you. You shall not walk in their statutes. 4 You shall do my ordinances and keep my statutes and walk in them. I am the LORD your God. 5 You shall therefore keep my statutes and my ordinances, by doing which a man shall live: I am the LORD.

6 "None of you shall approach any one near of kin to him to uncover nakedness. I am the LORD. 7 You shall not uncover the nakedness of your father, which is the nakedness of your mother; she is your mother, you shall not uncover her nakedness. 8 You shall not uncover the nakedness of your father's wife; it is your father's nakedness. 9 You shall not uncover the nakedness of your sister, the daughter of your father or the daughter of your mother, whether born at home or born abroad. 10 You shall not uncover the nakedness of your son's daughter or of your daughter's daughter, for their nakedness is your own nakedness. 11 You shall not uncover the nakedness of your father's wife's daughter, begotten by your father, since she is your sister. 12 You shall not uncover the nakedness of your father's sister; she is your father's near kinswoman. 13 You

e Gk Syr Compare Vg: Heb *for the life of all flesh, its blood is in its life*

17.10-16: Lev 3.17; 7.26-27; 19.26; Deut 12.16, 23-25.
18.5: Lk 10.28; Rom 10.5; Gal 3.12. **18.7**: Lev 20.11.
18.9, 11: Lev 20.17; Deut 27.22. **18.12**: Lev 20.19.

shall not uncover the nakedness of your mother's sister, for she is your mother's near kinswoman. 14 You shall not uncover the nakedness of your father's brother, that is, you shall not approach his wife; she is your aunt. 15 You shall not uncover the nakedness of your daughter-in-law; she is your son's wife, you shall not uncover her nakedness. 16 You shall not uncover the nakedness of your brother's wife; she is your brother's nakedness. 17 You shall not uncover the nakedness of a woman and of her daughter, and you shall not take her son's daughter or her daughter's daughter to uncover her nakedness; they are your*f* near kinswomen; it is wickedness. 18 And you shall not take a woman as a rival wife to her sister, uncovering her nakedness while her sister is yet alive.

19 "You shall not approach a woman to uncover her nakedness while she is in her menstrual uncleanness. 20 And you shall not lie carnally with your neighbor's wife, and defile yourself with her. 21 You shall not give any of your children to devote them by fire to Mō'lech, and so profane the name of your God: I am the LORD. 22 You shall not lie with a male as with a woman; it is an abomination. 23 And you shall not lie with any beast and defile yourself with it, neither shall any woman give herself to a beast to lie with it: it is perversion.

24 "Do not defile yourselves by any of these things, for by all these the nations I am casting out before you defiled themselves; 25 and the land became defiled, so that I punished its iniquity, and the land vomited out its inhabitants. 26 But you shall keep my statutes and my ordinances and do none of these abominations, either the native or the stranger who sojourns among you 27 (for all of these abominations the men of the land did, who were before you, so that the land became defiled); 28 lest the land vomit you out, when you defile it, as it vomited out the nation that was before you. 29 For whoever shall do any of these abominations, the persons that do them shall be cut off from among their people. 30 So keep my charge never to practice any of these abomi-

nable customs which were practiced before you, and never to defile yourselves by them: I am the LORD your God."

19 And the LORD said to Moses, 2 "Say to all the congregation of the people of Israel, You shall be holy; for I the LORD your God am holy. 3 Every one of you shall revere his mother and his father, and you shall keep my sabbaths: I am the LORD your God. 4 Do not turn to idols or make for yourselves molten gods: I am the LORD your God.

5 "When you offer a sacrifice of peace offerings to the LORD, you shall offer it so that you may be accepted. 6 It shall be eaten on the same day you offer it, or on the morrow; and anything left over until the third day shall be burned with fire. 7 If it is eaten at all on the third day, it is an abomination; it will not be accepted, 8 and every one who eats it shall bear his iniquity, because he has profaned a holy thing of the LORD; and that person shall be cut off from his people.

9 "When you reap the harvest of your land, you shall not reap your field to its very border, neither shall you gather the gleanings after your harvest. 10 And you shall not strip your vineyard bare, neither shall you gather the fallen grapes of your vineyard; you shall leave them for the poor and for the sojourner: I am the LORD your God.

11 "You shall not steal, nor deal falsely, nor lie to one another. 12 And you shall not swear by my name falsely, and so profane the name of your God: I am the LORD.

13 "You shall not oppress your neighbor or rob him. The wages of a hired servant shall not remain with you all night until the morning. 14 You shall not curse the deaf or put a stumbling block before the blind, but you shall fear your God: I am the LORD.

15 "You shall do no injustice in judgment; you shall not be partial to the poor or defer to the great, but in righteousness shall you judge your neighbor. 16 You shall not go up and down as a slanderer among your people, and you shall not stand forth

f Gk: Heb lacks *your*

18.14: Lev 20.20.   18.15: Lev 20.12.   18.16: Lev 20.21.   18.17: Lev 20.14.
18.19: Lev 15.24; 20.18.   18.21: Lev 20.2-5.   18.22: Lev 20.13; Deut 23.18.
18.23: Ex 22.19; Lev 20.15-16; Deut 27.21.   19.2: Lev 11.44-45; 20.7, 26; 1 Pet 1.16.
19.3, 30: Ex 20.12; Deut 5.16; Ex 20.8; 23.12; 34.21; 35.23; Deut 5.12-15.
19.4: Ex 20.4; Lev 26.1; Deut 4.15-19; 27.15.   19.9-10: Lev 23.22; Deut 24.20-21.
19.11: Ex 20.15-16; Deut 5.19.   19.12: Ex 20.7; Deut 5.11; Mt 5.33.
19.13: Deut 24.15; Jas 5.4.   19.14: Deut 27.18.   19.15: Ex 23.6; Deut 1.17.

against the life*g* of your neighbor: I am the LORD.

17 "You shall not hate your brother in your heart, but you shall reason with your neighbor, lest you bear sin because of him. 18 You shall not take vengeance or bear any grudge against the sons of your own people, but you shall love your neighbor as yourself: I am the LORD.

19 "You shall keep my statutes. You shall not let your cattle breed with a different kind; you shall not sow your field with two kinds of seed; nor shall there come upon you a garment of cloth made of two kinds of stuff.

20 "If a man lies carnally with a woman who is a slave, betrothed to another man and not yet ransomed or given her freedom, an inquiry shall be held. They shall not be put to death, because she was not free; 21 but he shall bring a guilt offering for himself to the LORD, to the door of the tent of meeting, a ram for a guilt offering. 22And the priest shall make atonement for him with the ram of the guilt offering before the LORD for his sin which he has committed; and the sin which he has committed shall be forgiven him.

23 "When you come into the land and plant all kinds of trees for food, then you shall count their fruit as forbidden;*h* three years it shall be forbidden to you, it must not be eaten. 24And in the fourth year all their fruit shall be holy, an offering of praise to the LORD. 25 But in the fifth year you may eat of their fruit, that they may yield more richly for you: I am the LORD your God.

26 "You shall not eat any flesh with the blood in it. You shall not practice augury or witchcraft. 27 You shall not round off the hair on your temples or mar the edges of your beard. 28 You shall not make any cuttings in your flesh on account of the dead or tattoo any marks upon you: I am the LORD. 29 "Do not profane your daughter by making her a harlot, lest the land fall into harlotry and the land become full of wickedness. 30 You shall keep my sabbaths and reverence my sanctuary: I am the LORD.

31 "Do not turn to mediums or wizards; do not seek them out, to be defiled by them: I am the LORD your God.

32 "You shall rise up before the hoary head, and honor the face of an old man, and you shall fear your God: I am the LORD.

33 "When a stranger sojourns with you in your land, you shall not do him wrong. 34 The stranger who sojourns with you shall be to you as the native among you, and you shall love him as yourself; for you were strangers in the land of Egypt: I am the LORD your God.

35 "You shall do no wrong in judgment, in measures of length or weight or quantity. 36 You shall have just balances, just weights, a just ephah, and a just hin: I am the LORD your God, who brought you out of the land of Egypt. 37And you shall observe all my statutes and all my ordinances, and do them: I am the LORD."

20

The LORD said to Moses, 2 "Say to the people of Israel, Any man of the people of Israel, or of the strangers that sojourn in Israel, who gives any of his children to Mō′lech shall be put to death; the people of the land shall stone him with stones. 3 I myself will set my face against that man, and will cut him off from among his people, because he has given one of his children to Mō′lech, defiling my sanctuary and profaning my holy name. 4And if the people of the land do at all hide their eyes from that man, when he gives one of his children to Mō′lech, and do not put him to death, 5 then I will set my face against that man and against his family, and will cut them off from among their people, him and all who follow him in playing the harlot after Mō′lech.

6 "If a person turns to mediums and wizards, playing the harlot after them, I will set my face against that person, and will cut him off from among his people. 7 Consecrate yourselves therefore, and be holy; for I am the LORD your God. 8 Keep my statutes, and do them; I am the LORD who sanctify you. 9 For every one who curses his father or his mother shall be put to death; he has cursed his father or his mother, his blood is upon him.

.18: Mt 5.43; 19.19; 22.39; Mk 12.31; Lk 10.27; Rom 13.9; Gal 5.14; Jas 2.8.
.19: Deut 22.9, 11.
.26: Lev 3.17; 7.26-27; 17.10-16; Deut 12.16, 23-25; 18.10.
.27: Lev 21.5; Deut 14.1.   19.29: Deut 23.17-18.
.30: Ex 20.8-11; 23.12; 34.21; 35.2-3; Lev 19.3; 26.2; Deut 5.12-15.
.31: Lev 20.6, 27.   19.33: Ex 22.21.   20.2-5: Lev 18.21.   20.6: Lev 19.31.
.7: Lev 11.44-45; 19.2; 20.26; 1 Pet 1.16.   20.9: Ex 21.17; Deut 27.16.

10 "If a man commits adultery with the wife of[i] his neighbor, both the adulterer and the adulteress shall be put to death. 11 The man who lies with his father's wife has uncovered his father's nakedness; both of them shall be put to death, their blood is upon them. 12 If a man lies with his daughter-in-law, both of them shall be put to death; they have committed incest, their blood is upon them. 13 If a man lies with a male as with a woman, both of them have committed an abomination; they shall be put to death, their blood is upon them. 14 If a man takes a wife and her mother also, it is wickedness; they shall be burned with fire, both he and they, that there may be no wickedness among you. 15 If a man lies with a beast, he shall be put to death; and you shall kill the beast. 16 If a woman approaches any beast and lies with it, you shall kill the woman and the beast; they shall be put to death, their blood is upon them.

17 "If a man takes his sister, a daughter of his father or a daughter of his mother, and sees her nakedness, and she sees his nakedness, it is a shameful thing, and they shall be cut off in the sight of the children of their people; he has uncovered his sister's nakedness, he shall bear his iniquity. 18 If a man lies with a woman having her sickness, and uncovers her nakedness, he has made naked her fountain, and she has uncovered the fountain of her blood; both of them shall be cut off from among their people. 19 You shall not uncover the nakedness of your mother's sister or of your father's sister, for that is to make naked one's near kin; they shall bear their iniquity. 20 If a man lies with his uncle's wife, he has uncovered his uncle's nakedness; they shall bear their sin, they shall die childless. 21 If a man takes his brother's wife, it is impurity; he has uncovered his brother's nakedness, they shall be childless.

22 "You shall therefore keep all my statutes and all my ordinances, and do them; that the land where I am bringing you to dwell may not vomit you out. 23 And you shall not walk in the customs of the nation which I am casting out before you; for they did all these things, and therefore I abhorred them. 24 But I have said to you, 'You shall inherit their land, and I will give it to you to possess, a land flowing with milk and honey.' I am the LORD your God, who have separated you from the peoples. 25 You shall therefore make a distinction between the clean beast and the unclean, and between the unclean bird and the clean; you shall not make yourselves abominable by beast or by bird or by anything with which the ground teems, which I have set apart for you to hold unclean. 26 You shall be holy to me; for I the LORD am holy, and have separated you from the peoples, that you should be mine.

27 "A man or a woman who is a medium or a wizard shall be put to death; they shall be stoned with stones, their blood shall be upon them."

21 And the LORD said to Moses, "Speak to the priests, the sons of Aaron, and say to them that none of them shall defile himself for the dead among his people, 2 except for his nearest of kin, his mother, his father, his son, his daughter, his brother, 3 or his virgin sister (who is near to him because she has had no husband; for her he may defile himself). 4 He shall not defile himself as a husband among his people and so profane himself. 5 They shall not make tonsures upon their heads, nor shave off the edges of their beards, nor make any cuttings in their flesh. 6 They shall be holy to their God, and not profane the name of their God; for they offer the offerings by fire to the LORD, the bread of their God; therefore they shall be holy. 7 They shall not marry a harlot or a woman who has been defiled; neither shall they marry a woman divorced from her husband; for the priest is holy to his God. 8 You shall consecrate him, for he offers the bread of your God; he shall be holy to you for I the LORD, who sanctify you, am holy. 9 And the daughter of any priest if she profanes herself by playing the harlot, profanes her father; she shall be burned with fire.

10 "The priest who is chief amon[g] his brethren, upon whose head th[e] anointing oil is poured, and who ha[s] been consecrated to wear the garment[s] shall not let the hair of his head han[g] loose, nor rend his clothes; 11 he sha[ll]

iHeb repeats *if a man commits adultery with the wife of*
20.10: Ex 20.14; Lev 18.20; Deut 5.18.   20.11: Lev 18.7-8.   20.12: Lev 18.15.
20.13: Lev 18.22.   20.14: Lev 18.17; Deut 27.23.   20.15-16: Lev 18.23.
20.17: Lev 18.9.   20.18: Lev 15.24; 18.19.   20.19: Lev 18.12-13.   20.20: Lev 18.1
20.21: Lev 18.16.   20.26: Lev 20.7.   20.27: Lev 19.31; 20.6.   21.1-3: Ezek 44.25.
21.5: Lev 19.27; Deut 14.1.

not go in to any dead body, nor defile himself, even for his father or for his mother; [12] neither shall he go out of the sanctuary, nor profane the sanctuary of his God; for the consecration of the anointing oil of his God is upon him: I am the LORD. [13]And he shall take a wife in her virginity. [14]A widow, or one divorced, or a woman who has been defiled, or a harlot, these he shall not marry; but he shall take to wife a virgin of his own people, [15] that he may not profane his children among his people; for I am the LORD who sanctify him."

16 And the LORD said to Moses, [17] "Say to Aaron, None of your descendants throughout their generations who has a blemish may approach to offer the bread of his God. [18] For no one who has a blemish shall draw near, a man blind or lame, or one who has a mutilated face or a limb too long, [19] or a man who has an injured foot or an injured hand, [20] or a hunchback, or a dwarf, or a man with a defect in his sight or an itching disease or scabs or crushed testicles; [21] no man of the descendants of Aaron the priest who has a blemish shall come near to offer the LORD's offerings by fire; since he has a blemish, he shall not come near to offer the bread of his God. [22] He may eat the bread of his God, both of the most holy and of the holy things, [23] but he shall not come near the veil or approach the altar, because he has a blemish, that he may not profane my sanctuaries; for I am the LORD who sanctify them." [24] So Moses spoke to Aaron and to his sons and to all the people of Israel.

22 And the LORD said to Moses, [2] "Tell Aaron and his sons to keep away from the holy things of the people of Israel, which they dedicate to me, so that they may not profane my holy name; I am the LORD. [3] Say to them, 'If any one of all your descendants throughout your generations approaches the holy things, which the people of Israel dedicate to the LORD, while he has an uncleanness, that person shall be cut off from my presence: I am the LORD. [4] None of the line of Aaron who is a leper or suffers a discharge may eat of the holy things until he is clean. Whoever touches anything that is unclean through contact with the dead or a man who has had an emission of semen, [5] and whoever touches a creeping thing by which he may be made unclean or a man from whom he may

take uncleanness, whatever his uncleanness may be—[6] the person who touches any such shall be unclean until the evening and shall not eat of the holy things unless he has bathed his body in water. [7] When the sun is down he shall be clean; and afterward he may eat of the holy things, because such are his food. [8] That which dies of itself or is torn by beasts he shall not eat, defiling himself by it: I am the LORD.' [9] They shall therefore keep my charge, lest they bear sin for it and die thereby when they profane it: I am the LORD who sanctify them.

10 "An outsider shall not eat of a holy thing. A sojourner of the priest's or a hired servant shall not eat of a holy thing; [11] but if a priest buys a slave as his property for money, the slave may eat of it; and those that are born in his house may eat of his food. [12] If a priest's daughter is married to an outsider she shall not eat of the offering of the holy things. [13] But if a priest's daughter is a widow or divorced, and has no child, and returns to her father's house, as in her youth, she may eat of her father's food; yet no outsider shall eat of it. [14]And if a man eats of a holy thing unwittingly, he shall add the fifth of its value to it, and give the holy thing to the priest. [15] The priests shall not profane the holy things of the people of Israel, which they offer to the LORD, [16] and so cause them to bear iniquity and guilt, by eating their holy things: for I am the LORD who sanctify them."

17 And the LORD said to Moses, [18] "Say to Aaron and his sons and all the people of Israel, When any one of the house of Israel or of the sojourners in Israel presents his offering, whether in payment of a vow or as a freewill offering which is offered to the LORD as a burnt offering, [19] to be accepted you shall offer a male without blemish, of the bulls or the sheep or the goats. [20] You shall not offer anything that has a blemish, for it will not be acceptable for you. [21]And when any one offers a sacrifice of peace offerings to the LORD, to fulfil a vow or as a freewill offering, from the herd or from the flock, to be accepted it must be perfect; there shall be no blemish in it. [22]Animals blind or disabled or mutilated or having a discharge or an itch or scabs, you shall not offer to the LORD or make of them an offering by fire upon the altar to the LORD. [23]A bull or a lamb which has a part too long or too short you may present for

22.12: Lev 7.31-36.

a freewill offering; but for a votive offering it cannot be accepted. 24Any animal which has its testicles bruised or crushed or torn or cut, you shall not offer to the LORD or sacrifice within your land; 25 neither shall you offer as the bread of your God any such animals gotten from a foreigner. Since there is a blemish in them, because of their mutilation, they will not be accepted for you."

26 And the LORD said to Moses, 27 "When a bull or sheep or goat is born, it shall remain seven days with its mother; and from the eighth day on it shall be acceptable as an offering by fire to the LORD. 28And whether the mother is a cow or a ewe, you shall not kill both her and her young in one day. 29And when you sacrifice a sacrifice of thanksgiving to the LORD, you shall sacrifice it so that you may be accepted. 30 It shall be eaten on the same day, you shall leave none of it until morning: I am the LORD.

31 "So you shall keep my commandments and do them: I am the LORD. 32And you shall not profane my holy name, but I will be hallowed among the people of Israel; I am the LORD who sanctify you, 33 who brought you out of the land of Egypt to be your God: I am the LORD."

23 The LORD said to Moses, 2 "Say to the people of Israel, The appointed feasts of the LORD which you shall proclaim as holy convocations, my appointed feasts, are these. 3 Six days shall work be done; but on the seventh day is a sabbath of solemn rest, a holy convocation; you shall do no work; it is a sabbath to the LORD in all your dwellings.

4 "These are the appointed feasts of the LORD, the holy convocations, which you shall proclaim at the time appointed for them. 5 In the first month, on the fourteenth day of the month in the evening,*j* is the LORD's passover. 6And on the fifteenth day of the same month is the feast of unleavened bread to the LORD; seven days you shall eat unleavened bread. 7 On the first day you shall have a holy convocation; you shall do no laborious work. 8 But you shall present an offering by fire to the LORD seven days; on the seventh day is a holy convocation; you shall do no laborious work."

9 And the LORD said to Moses, 10 "Say to the people of Israel, When you come into the land which I give you and reap its harvest, you shall bring the sheaf of the first fruits of your harvest to the priest; 11 and he shall wave the sheaf before the LORD, that you may find acceptance; on the morrow after the sabbath the priest shall wave it. 12And on the day when you wave the sheaf, you shall offer a male lamb a year old without blemish as a burnt offering to the LORD. 13And the cereal offering with it shall be two tenths of an ephah of fine flour mixed with oil, to be offered by fire to the LORD, a pleasing odor; and the drink offering with it shall be of wine, a fourth of a hin. 14And you shall eat neither bread nor grain parched or fresh until this same day, until you have brought the offering of your God: it is a statute for ever throughout your generations in all your dwellings.

15 "And you shall count from the morrow after the sabbath, from the day that you brought the sheaf of the wave offering; seven full weeks shall they be, 16 counting fifty days to the morrow after the seventh sabbath; then you shall present a cereal offering of new grain to the LORD. 17 You shall bring from your dwellings two loaves of bread to be waved, made of two tenths of an ephah; they shall be of fine flour, they shall be baked with leaven, as first fruits to the LORD. 18And you shall present with the bread seven lambs a year old without blemish, and one young bull, and two rams; they shall be a burnt offering to the LORD, with their cereal offering and their drink offerings, an offering by fire, a pleasing odor to the LORD. 19And you shall offer one male goat for a sin offering, and two male lambs a year old as a sacrifice of peace offerings. 20And the priest shall wave them with the bread of the first fruits as a wave offering before the LORD, with the two lambs; they shall be holy to the LORD for the priest. 21And you shall make proclamation on the same day; you shall hold a holy convocation; you shall do no laborious work: it is a statute for ever in all your dwellings throughout your generations.

22 "And when you reap the harvest of your land, you shall not reap your field to its very border, nor shall you gather the gleanings after your harvest; you shall leave them for the poor and for the stranger: I am the LORD your God."

23 And the LORD said to Moses, 24 "Say to the people of Israel, In the seventh month, on the first day of

---

j Heb *between the two evenings*
23.1-44: Ex 23.14-17; 34.22-24; Deut 16.1-17.   **23.22:** Lev 19.9-10; Deut 24.20-21.

the month, you shall observe a day of solemn rest, a memorial proclaimed with blast of trumpets, a holy convocation. 25 You shall do no laborious work; and you shall present an offering by fire to the LORD."

26 And the LORD said to Moses, 27 "On the tenth day of this seventh month is the day of atonement; it shall be for you a time of holy convocation, and you shall afflict yourselves and present an offering by fire to the LORD. 28And you shall do no work on this same day; for it is a day of atonement, to make atonement for you before the LORD your God. 29 For whoever is not afflicted on this same day shall be cut off from his people. 30And whoever does any work on this same day, that person I will destroy from among his people. 31 You shall do no work: it is a statute for ever throughout your generations in all your dwellings. 32 It shall be to you a sabbath of solemn rest, and you shall afflict yourselves; on the ninth day of the month beginning at evening, from evening to evening shall you keep your sabbath."

33 And the LORD said to Moses, 34 "Say to the people of Israel, On the fifteenth day of this seventh month and for seven days is the feast of booths*k* to the LORD. 35 On the first day shall be a holy convocation; you shall do no laborious work. 36 Seven days you shall present offerings by fire to the LORD; on the eighth day you shall hold a holy convocation and present an offering by fire to the LORD; it is a solemn assembly; you shall do no laborious work.

37 "These are the appointed feasts of the LORD, which you shall proclaim as times of holy convocation, for presenting to the LORD offerings by fire, burnt offerings and cereal offerings, sacrifices and drink offerings, each on its proper day; 38 besides the sabbaths of the LORD, and besides your gifts, and besides all your votive offerings, and besides all your freewill offerings, which you give to the LORD.

39 "On the fifteenth day of the seventh month, when you have gathered in the produce of the land, you shall keep the feast of the LORD seven days; on the first day shall be a solemn rest, and on the eighth day shall be a solemn rest. 40And you shall take on the first day the fruit of goodly trees, branches of palm trees, and boughs of leafy trees, and willows of the brook; and you shall rejoice before the LORD

your God seven days. 41 You shall keep it as a feast to the LORD seven days in the year; it is a statute for ever throughout your generations; you shall keep it in the seventh month. 42 You shall dwell in booths for seven days; all that are native in Israel shall dwell in booths, 43 that your generations may know that I made the people of Israel dwell in booths when I brought them out of the land of Egypt: I am the LORD your God."

44 Thus Moses declared to the people of Israel the appointed feasts of the LORD.

24 The LORD said to Moses, 2 "Command the people of Israel to bring you pure oil from beaten olives for the lamp, that a light may be kept burning continually. 3 Outside the veil of the testimony, in the tent of meeting, Aaron shall keep it in order from evening to morning before the LORD continually; it shall be a statute for ever throughout your generations. 4 He shall keep the lamps in order upon the lampstand of pure gold before the LORD continually.

5 "And you shall take fine flour, and bake twelve cakes of it; two tenths of an ephah shall be in each cake. 6And you shall set them in two rows, six in a row, upon the table of pure gold. 7And you shall put pure frankincense with each row, that it may go with the bread as a memorial portion to be offered by fire to the LORD. 8 Every sabbath day Aaron shall set it in order before the LORD continually on behalf of the people of Israel as a covenant for ever. 9And it shall be for Aaron and his sons, and they shall eat it in a holy place, since it is for him a most holy portion out of the offerings by fire to the LORD, a perpetual due."

10 Now an Israelite woman's son, whose father was an Egyptian, went out among the people of Israel; and the Israelite woman's son and a man of Israel quarreled in the camp, 11 and the Israelite woman's son blasphemed the Name, and cursed, And they brought him to Moses. His mother's name was She·lo′mith, the daughter of Dib′ri, of the tribe of Dan. 12And they put him in custody, till the will of the LORD should be declared to them.

13 And the LORD said to Moses, 14 "Bring out of the camp him who cursed; and let all who heard him lay their hands upon his head, and let all the congregation stone him. 15And say

k Or *tabernacles*

24.1-4: Ex 27.20-21. **24.5-9:** Ex 25.30; 39.36; 40.23; Mt 12.4; Mk 2.26; Lk 6.4.

to the people of Israel, Whoever curses his God shall bear his sin. ¹⁶ He who blasphemes the name of the LORD shall be put to death; all the congregation shall stone him; the sojourner as well as the native, when he blasphemes the Name, shall be put to death. ¹⁷ He who kills a man shall be put to death. ¹⁸ He who kills a beast shall make it good, life for life. ¹⁹ When a man causes a disfigurement in his neighbor, as he has done it shall be done to him, ²⁰ fracture for fracture, eye for eye, tooth for tooth; as he has disfigured a man, he shall be disfigured. ²¹ He who kills a beast shall make it good; and he who kills a man shall be put to death. ²² You shall have one law for the sojourner and for the native; for I am the LORD your God." ²³ So Moses spoke to the people of Israel; and they brought him who had cursed out of the camp, and stoned him with stones. Thus the people of Israel did as the LORD commanded Moses.

25 The LORD said to Moses on Mount Sinai, ² "Say to the people of Israel, When you come into the land which I give you, the land shall keep a sabbath to the LORD. ³ Six years you shall sow your field, and six years you shall prune your vineyard, and gather in its fruits; ⁴ but in the seventh year there shall be a sabbath of solemn rest for the land, a sabbath to the LORD; you shall not sow your field or prune your vineyard. ⁵ What grows of itself in your harvest you shall not reap, and the grapes of your undressed vine you shall not gather; it shall be a year of solemn rest for the land. ⁶ The sabbath of the land shall provide food for you, for yourself and for your male and female slaves and for your hired servant and the sojourner who lives with you; ⁷ for your cattle also and for the beasts that are in your land all its yield shall be for food.

8 "And you shall count seven weeks*ˡ* of years, seven times seven years, so that the time of the seven weeks of years shall be to you forty-nine years. ⁹ Then you shall send abroad the loud trumpet on the tenth day of the seventh month; on the day of atonement you shall send abroad the trumpet throughout all your land. ¹⁰ And you shall hallow the fiftieth year, and proclaim liberty throughout the land to all its inhabitants; it shall be a jubilee for you, when each of you shall return to his property and each of you shall return

to his family. ¹¹ A jubilee shall that fiftieth year be to you; in it you shall neither sow, nor reap what grows of itself, nor gather the grapes from the undressed vines. ¹² For it is a jubilee; it shall be holy to you; you shall eat what it yields out of the field.

13 "In this year of jubilee each of you shall return to his property. ¹⁴ And if you sell to your neighbor or buy from your neighbor, you shall not wrong one another. ¹⁵ According to the number of years after the jubilee, you shall buy from your neighbor, and according to the number of years for crops he shall sell to you. ¹⁶ If the years are many you shall increase the price, and if the years are few you shall diminish the price, for it is the number of crops that he is selling to you. ¹⁷ You shall not wrong one another, but you shall fear your God; for I am the LORD your God.

18 "Therefore you shall do my statutes, and keep my ordinances and perform them; so you will dwell in the land securely. ¹⁹ The land will yield its fruit, and you will eat your fill, and dwell in it securely. ²⁰ And if you say, 'What shall we eat in the seventh year, if we may not sow or gather in our crop?' ²¹ I will command my blessing upon you in the sixth year, so that it will bring forth fruit for three years. ²² When you sow in the eighth year, you will be eating old produce; until the ninth year, when its produce comes in, you shall eat the old. ²³ The land shall not be sold in perpetuity, for the land is mine; for you are strangers and sojourners with me. ²⁴ And in all the country you possess, you shall grant a redemption of the land.

25 "If your brother becomes poor, and sells part of his property, then his next of kin shall come and redeem what his brother has sold. ²⁶ If a man has no one to redeem it, and then himself becomes prosperous and finds sufficient means to redeem it, ²⁷ let him reckon the years since he sold it and pay back the overpayment to the man to whom he sold it; and he shall return to his property. ²⁸ But if he has not sufficient means to get it back for himself, then what he sold shall remain in the hand of him who bought it until the year of jubilee; in the jubilee it shall be released, and he shall return to his property.

29 "If a man sells a dwelling house in a walled city, he may redeem it

*ˡ*Or *sabbaths*

24:19-20: Ex 21.23-25; Deut 19.21; Mt 5.38.
24.22: Ex 12.49; Num 9.14; 15.15-16, 29.   25.2-7: Ex 23.10-11.

within a whole year after its sale; for a full year he shall have the right of redemption. 30 If it is not redeemed within a full year, then the house that is in the walled city shall be made sure in perpetuity to him who bought it, throughout his generations; it shall not be released in the jubilee. 31 But the houses of the villages which have no wall around them shall be reckoned with the fields of the country; they may be redeemed, and they shall be released in the jubilee. 32 Nevertheless the cities of the Levites, the houses in the cities of their possession, the Levites may redeem at any time. 33And if one of the Levites does not exercise*m* his right of redemption, then the house that was sold in a city of their possession shall be released in the jubilee; for the houses in the cities of the Levites are their possession among the people of Israel. 34 But the fields of common land belonging to their cities may not be sold; for that is their perpetual possession.

35 "And if your brother becomes poor, and cannot maintain himself with you, you shall maintain him; as a stranger and a sojourner he shall live with you. 36 Take no interest from him or increase, but fear your God; that your brother may live beside you. 37 You shall not lend him your money at interest, nor give him your food for profit. 38 I am the LORD your God, who brought you forth out of the land of Egypt to give you the land of Canaan, and to be your God.

39 "And if your brother becomes poor beside you, and sells himself to you, you shall not make him serve as a slave: 40 he shall be with you as a hired servant and as a sojourner. He shall serve with you until the year of the jubilee; 41 then he shall go out from you, he and his children with him, and go back to his own family, and return to the possession of his fathers. 42 For they are my servants, whom I brought forth out of the land of Egypt; they shall not be sold as slaves. 43 You shall not rule over him with harshness, but shall fear your God. 44As for your male and female slaves whom you may have: you may buy male and female slaves from among the nations that are round about you. 45 You may also buy from among the strangers who sojourn

with you and their families that are with you, who have been born in your land; and they may be your property. 46 You may bequeath them to your sons after you, to inherit as a possession for ever; you may make slaves of them, but over your brethren the people of Israel you shall not rule, one over another, with harshness.

47 "If a stranger or sojourner with you becomes rich, and your brother beside him becomes poor and sells himself to the stranger or sojourner with you, or to a member of the stranger's family, 48 then after he is sold he may be redeemed; one of his brothers may redeem him, 49 or his uncle, or his cousin may redeem him, or a near kinsman belonging to his family may redeem him; or if he grows rich he may redeem himself. 50 He shall reckon with him who bought him from the year when he sold himself to him until the year of jubilee, and the price of his release shall be according to the number of years; the time he was with his owner shall be rated as the time of a hired servant. 51 If there are still many years, according to them he shall refund out of the price paid for him the price for his redemption. 52 If there remain but a few years until the year of jubilee, he shall make a reckoning with him; according to the years of service due from him he shall refund the money for his redemption. 53As a servant hired year by year shall he be with him; he shall not rule with harshness over him in your sight. 54And if he is not redeemed by these means, then he shall be released in the year of jubilee, he and his children with him. 55 For to me the people of Israel are servants, they are my servants whom I brought forth out of the land of Egypt: I am the LORD your God.

26 "You shall make for yourselves no idols and erect no graven image or pillar, and you shall not set up a figured stone in your land, to bow down to them; for I am the LORD your God. 2 You shall keep my sabbaths and reverence my sanctuary: I am the LORD.

3 "If you walk in my statutes and observe my commandments and do them, 4 then I will give you your rains in their season, and the land shall

---

m Compare Vg: Heb *exercises*

25.35: Deut 15.7-11.   25.36: Ex 22.25; Deut 23.19-20.
25.39-43: Ex 21.2-6; Deut 15.12-18.
26.1: Lev 19.4; Ex 20.4, 23; Deut 4.15-18; 27.15.
26.2: Ex 20.8; 23.12; 34.21; 35.2-3; Lev 19.3, 30; Deut 5.12-15.
26.3-13: Deut 7.12-26; 28.1-14.

yield its increase, and the trees of the field shall yield their fruit. 5And your threshing shall last to the time of vintage, and the vintage shall last to the time for sowing; and you shall eat your bread to the full, and dwell in your land securely. 6And I will give peace in the land, and you shall lie down, and none shall make you afraid; and I will remove evil beasts from the land, and the sword shall not go through your land. 7And you shall chase your enemies, and they shall fall before you by the sword. 8 Five of you shall chase a hundred, and a hundred of you shall chase ten thousand; and your enemies shall fall before you by the sword. 9And I will have regard for you and make you fruitful and multiply you, and will confirm my covenant with you. 10And you shall eat old store long kept, and you shall clear out the old to make way for the new. 11And I will make my abode among you, and my soul shall not abhor you. 12And I will walk among you, and will be your God, and you shall be my people. 13 I am the LORD your God, who brought you forth out of the land of Egypt, that you should not be their slaves; and I have broken the bars of your yoke and made you walk erect.

14 "But if you will not hearken to me, and will not do all these commandments, 15 if you spurn my statutes, and if your soul abhors my ordinances, so that you will not do all my commandments, but break my covenant, 16 I will do this to you: I will appoint over you sudden terror, consumption, and fever that waste the eyes and cause life to pine away. And you shall sow your seed in vain, for your enemies shall eat it; 17 I will set my face against you, and you shall be smitten before your enemies; those who hate you shall rule over you, and you shall flee when none pursues you. 18And if in spite of this you will not hearken to me, then I will chastise you again sevenfold for your sins, 19 and I will break the pride of your power, and I will make your heavens like iron and your earth like brass; 20 and your strength shall be spent in vain, for your land shall not yield its increase, and the trees of the land shall not yield their fruit.

21 "Then if you walk contrary to me, and will not hearken to me, I will bring more plagues upon you, sevenfold as many as your sins. 22And I will let loose the wild beasts among you,

which shall rob you of your children, and destroy your cattle, and make you few in number, so that your ways shall become desolate.

23 "And if by this discipline you are not turned to me, but walk contrary to me, 24 then I also will walk contrary to you, and I myself will smite you sevenfold for your sins. 25And I will bring a sword upon you, that shall execute vengeance for the covenant; and if you gather within your cities I will send pestilence among you, and you shall be delivered into the hand of the enemy. 26 When I break your staff of bread, ten women shall bake your bread in one oven, and shall deliver your bread again by weight; and you shall eat, and not be satisfied.

27 "And if in spite of this you will not hearken to me, but walk contrary to me, 28 then I will walk contrary to you in fury, and chastise you myself sevenfold for your sins. 29 You shall eat the flesh of your sons, and you shall eat the flesh of your daughters. 30And I will destroy your high places, and cut down your incense altars, and cast your dead bodies upon the dead bodies of your idols; and my soul will abhor you. 31And I will lay your cities waste, and will make your sanctuaries desolate, and I will not smell your pleasing odors. 32And I will devastate the land, so that your enemies who settle in it shall be astonished at it. 33And I will scatter you among the nations, and I will unsheathe the sword after you; and your land shall be desolation, and your cities shall be a waste.

34 "Then the land shall enjoy[n] its sabbaths as long as it lies desolate, while you are in your enemies' land; then the land shall rest, and enjoy[n] its sabbaths. 35As long as it lies desolate it shall have rest, the rest which it had not in your sabbaths when you dwelt upon it. 36And as for those of you that are left, I will send faintness into their hearts in the lands of their enemies; the sound of a driven leaf shall put them to flight, and they shall flee as one flees from the sword, and they shall fall when none pursues. 37 They shall stumble over one another, as if to escape a sword, though none pursues; and you shall have no power to stand before your enemies. 38And you shall perish among the nations, and the land of your enemies shall eat you up. 39And those of you that are left shall pine away in your enemies' lands because of their iniquity; and also because

[n] Or *pay for*

26.11-12: 2 Cor 6.16.　　**26.14-45:** Deut 28.16-68.

of the iniquities of their fathers they shall pine away like them.

40 "But if they confess their iniquity and the iniquity of their fathers in their treachery which they committed against me, and also in walking contrary to me, 41 so that I walked contrary to them and brought them into the land of their enemies; if then their uncircumcised heart is humbled and they make amends for their iniquity; 42 then I will remember my covenant with Jacob, and I will remember my covenant with Isaac and my covenant with Abraham, and I will remember the land. 43 But the land shall be left by them, and enjoy^n its sabbaths while it lies desolate without them; and they shall make amends for their iniquity, because they spurned my ordinances, and their soul abhorred my statutes. 44 Yet for all that, when they are in the land of their enemies, I will not spurn them, neither will I abhor them so as to destroy them utterly and break my covenant with them; for I am the LORD their God; 45 but I will for their sake remember the covenant with their forefathers, whom I brought forth out of the land of Egypt in the sight of the nations, that I might be their God: I am the LORD."

46 These are the statutes and ordinances and laws which the LORD made between him and the people of Israel on Mount Sinai by Moses.

27 The LORD said to Moses, 2 "Say to the people of Israel, When a man makes a special vow of persons to the LORD at your valuation, 3 then your valuation of a male from twenty years old up to sixty years old shall be fifty shekels of silver, according to the shekel of the sanctuary. 4 If the person is a female, your valuation shall be thirty shekels. 5 If the person is from five years old up to twenty years old, your valuation shall be for a male twenty shekels, and for a female ten shekels. 6 If the person is from a month old up to five years old, your valuation shall be for a male five shekels of silver, and for a female your valuation shall be three shekels of silver. 7 And if the person is sixty years old and upward, then your valuation for a male shall be fifteen shekels, and for a female ten shekels. 8 And if a man is too poor to pay your valuation, then he shall bring the person before the priest, and the priest shall value him; according to the ability of him who vowed the priest shall value him.

9 "If it is an animal such as men offer as an offering to the LORD, all of such that any man gives to the LORD is holy. 10 He shall not substitute anything for it or exchange it, a good for a bad, or a bad for a good; and if he makes any exchange of beast for beast, then both it and that for which it is exchanged shall be holy. 11 And if it is an unclean animal such as is not offered as an offering to the LORD, then the man shall bring the animal before the priest, 12 and the priest shall value it as either good or bad; as you, the priest, value it, so it shall be. 13 But if he wishes to redeem it, he shall add a fifth to the valuation.

14 "When a man dedicates his house to be holy to the LORD, the priest shall value it as either good or bad; as the priest values it, so it shall stand. 15 And if he who dedicates it wishes to redeem his house, he shall add a fifth of the valuation in money to it, and it shall be his.

16 "If a man dedicates to the LORD part of the land which is his by inheritance, then your valuation shall be according to the seed for it; a sowing of a homer of barley shall be valued at fifty shekels of silver. 17 If he dedicates his field from the year of jubilee, it shall stand at your full valuation; 18 but if he dedicates his field after the jubilee, then the priest shall compute the money-value for it according to the years that remain until the year of jubilee, and a deduction shall be made from your valuation. 19 And if he who dedicates the field wishes to redeem it, then he shall add a fifth of the valuation in money to it, and it shall remain his. 20 But if he does not wish to redeem the field, or if he has sold the field to another man, it shall not be redeemed any more; 21 but the field, when it is released in the jubilee, shall be holy to the LORD, as a field that has been devoted; the priest shall be in possession of it. 22 If he dedicates to the LORD a field which he has bought, which is not a part of his possession by inheritance, 23 then the priest shall compute the valuation for it up to the year of jubilee, and the man shall give the amount of the valuation on that day as a holy thing to the LORD. 24 In the year of jubilee the field shall return to him from whom it was bought, to whom the land belongs as a possession by inheritance. 25 Every valuation shall be according to the shekel of the sanctuary: twenty gerahs shall make a shekel.

---

^{n} Or pay for   26.40-41: Acts 7.51.

26 "But a firstling of animals, which as a firstling belongs to the LORD, no man may dedicate; whether ox or sheep, it is the LORD's. 27And if it is an unclean animal, then he shall buy it back at your valuation, and add a fifth to it; or, if it is not redeemed, it shall be sold at your valuation.

28 "But no devoted thing that a man devotes to the LORD, of anything that he has, whether of man or beast, or of his inherited field, shall be sold or redeemed; every devoted thing is most holy to the LORD. 29 No one devoted, who is to be utterly destroyed from among men, shall be ransomed; he shall be put to death.

30 "All the tithe of the land, whether of the seed of the land or of the fruit of the trees, is the LORD's; it is holy to the LORD. 31 If a man wishes to redeem any of his tithe, he shall add a fifth to it. 32And all the tithe of herds and flocks, every tenth animal of all that pass under the herdsman's staff, shall be holy to the LORD. 33A man shall not inquire whether it is good or bad, neither shall he exchange it; and if he exchanges it, then both it and that for which it is exchanged shall be holy; it shall not be redeemed."

34 These are the commandments which the LORD commanded Moses for the people of Israel on Mount Sinai.

THE FOURTH BOOK OF MOSES

COMMONLY CALLED

NUMBERS

1 The LORD spoke to Moses in the wilderness of Sinai, in the tent of meeting, on the first day of the second month, in the second year after they had come out of the land of Egypt, saying, 2 "Take a census of all the congregation of the people of Israel, by families, by fathers' houses, according to the number of names, every male, head by head; 3 from twenty years old and upward, all in Israel who are able to go forth to war, you and Aaron shall number them, company by company. 4And there shall be with you a man from each tribe, each man being the head of the house of his fathers. 5And these are the names of the men who shall attend you. From Reuben, E·lī'zūr the son of Shed'ē·ùr; 6 from Simeon, She·lü'mĭ-el the son of Zü·ri·shad'däi; 7 from Judah, Näh'·shŏn the son of Am·min'ȧ·dab; 8 from Is'sȧ·chär, Nē·than'el the son of Zü'är; 9 from Zeb'ū·lùn, E·lī'ab the son of Hē'lon; 10 from the sons of Joseph, from E'phrȧ·im, E·lish'ȧ·mȧ the son of Am·mī'hùd, and from Mȧ·nas'sĕh, Gȧ·mȧ'li·ĕl the son of Pĕ·däh'zŭr; 11 from Benjamin, À·bī'dȧn the son of Gid·ē·ō'ni; 12 from Dan, Ä·hī·ē'zĕr the son of Am·mi·shad'däi; 13 from Ash'ĕr, Pä'gi·el the son of Ŏch'rȧn; 14 from Gad, E·lī'ȧ·saph the son of Deü'el; 15 from Naph'tȧ·li, Ä·hī'rȧ the son of Ē'nan." 16 These were the ones chosen from the congregation, the leaders of their ancestral tribes, the heads of the clans of Israel.

17 Moses and Aaron took these men who have been named, 18 and on the first day of the second month, they assembled the whole congregation together, who registered themselves by families, by fathers' houses, according to the number of names from twenty years old and upward, head by head, 19 as the LORD commanded Moses. So he numbered them in the wilderness of Sinai.

20 The people of Reuben, Israel's first-born, their generations, by their families, by their fathers' houses, according to the number of names, head by head, every male from twenty years old and upward, all who were able to go forth to war; 21 the number of the tribe of Reuben was forty-six thousand five hundred.

22 Of the people of Simeon, their generations, by their families, by their fathers' houses, those of them that were numbered, according to the

27.28: Num 18.14.   1.1-46: Num 26.1-51.

number of names, head by head, every male from twenty years old and upward, all who were able to go forth to war: 23 the number of the tribe of Simeon was fifty-nine thousand three hundred.

24 Of the people of Gad, their generations, by their families, by their fathers' houses, according to the number of the names, from twenty years old and upward, all who were able to go forth to war: 25 the number of the tribe of Gad was forty-five thousand six hundred and fifty.

26 Of the people of Judah, their generations, by their families, by their fathers' houses, according to the number of names, from twenty years old and upward, every man able to go forth to war: 27 the number of the tribe of Judah was seventy-four thousand six hundred.

28 Of the people of Is'sa·chär, their generations, by their families, by their fathers' houses, according to the number of names, from twenty years old and upward, every man able to go forth to war: 29 the number of the tribe of Is'sa·chär was fifty-four thousand four hundred.

30 Of the people of Zeb'ū·lùn, their generations, by their families, by their fathers' houses, according to the number of names, from twenty years old and upward, every man able to go forth to war: 31 the number of the tribe of Zeb'ū·lùn was fifty-seven thousand four hundred.

32 Of the people of Joseph, namely, of the people of E'phrā·im, their generations, by their families, by their fathers' houses, according to the number of names, from twenty years old and upward, every man able to go forth to war: 33 the number of the tribe of E'phrā·im was forty thousand five hundred.

34 Of the people of Mà·nas'sēh, their generations, by their families, by their fathers' houses, according to the number of names, from twenty years old and upward, every man able to go forth to war: 35 the number of the tribe of Mà·nas'sēh was thirty-two thousand two hundred.

36 Of the people of Benjamin, their generations, by their families, by their fathers' houses, according to the number of names, from twenty years old and upward, every man able to go forth to war: 37 the number of the tribe of Benjamin was thirty-five thousand four hundred.

38 Of the people of Dan, their generations, by their families, by their fathers' houses, according to the number of names, from twenty years old and upward, every man able to go forth to war: 39 the number of the tribe of Dan was sixty-two thousand seven hundred.

40 Of the people of Ash'ēr, their generations, by their families, by their fathers' houses, according to the number of names, from twenty years old and upward, every man able to go forth to war: 41 the number of the tribe of Ash'ēr was forty-one thousand five hundred.

42 Of the people of Naph'tà·lï, their generations, by their families, by their fathers' houses, according to the number of names, from twenty years old and upward, every man able to go forth to war: 43 the number of the tribe of Naph'tà·lï was fifty-three thousand four hundred.

44 These are those who were numbered, whom Moses and Aaron numbered with the help of the leaders of Israel, twelve men, each representing his fathers' house. 45 So the whole number of the people of Israel, by their fathers' houses, from twenty years old and upward, every man able to go forth to war in Israel—46 their whole number was six hundred and three thousand five hundred and fifty.

47 But the Levites were not numbered by their ancestral tribe along with them. 48 For the LORD said to Moses, 49 "Only the tribe of Levi you shall not number, and you shall not take a census of them among the people of Israel; 50 but appoint the Levites over the tabernacle of the testimony, and over all its furnishings, and over all that belongs to it; they are to carry the tabernacle and all its furnishings, and they shall tend it, and shall encamp around the tabernacle. 51 When the tabernacle is to set out, the Levites shall take it down; and when the tabernacle is to be pitched, the Levites shall set it up. And if any one else comes near, he shall be put to death. 52 The people of Israel shall pitch their tents by their companies, every man by his own camp and every man by his own standard; 53 but the Levites shall encamp around the tabernacle of the testimony, that there may be no wrath upon the congregation of the people of Israel; and the Levites shall keep charge of the tabernacle of the testimony." 54 Thus did the people of Israel; they did according to all that the LORD commanded Moses.

1.47: Num 2.33.   1.50-53: Num 3.5-8, 21-37; 4.1-33; 8.19; 18.3-4, 23.

2 The LORD said to Moses and Aaron, 2 "The people of Israel shall encamp each by his own standard, with the ensigns of their fathers' houses; they shall encamp facing the tent of meeting on every side. 3 Those to encamp on the east side toward the sunrise shall be of the standard of the camp of Judah by their companies, the leader of the people of Judah being Näh'shŏn the son of Am·min'ă·dab, 4 his host as numbered being seventy-four thousand six hundred. 5 Those to encamp next to him shall be the tribe of Is'să·chär, the leader of the people of Issachar being Né·than'el the son of Zü'ár, 6 his host as numbered being fifty-four thousand four hundred. 7 Then the tribe of Zeb'ū·lùn, the leader of the people of Zebulun being E·li'ab the son of Hē'lon, 8 his host as numbered being fifty-seven thousand four hundred. 9 The whole number of the camp of Judah, by their companies, is a hundred and eighty-six thousand four hundred. They shall set out first on the march.

10 "On the south side shall be the standard of the camp of Reuben by their companies, the leader of the people of Reuben being E·li'zùr the son of Shed'ē·ùr, 11 his host as numbered being forty-six thousand five hundred. 12And those to encamp next to him shall be the tribe of Simeon, the leader of the people of Simeon being She·lū'mi-el the son of Zü·ri·shad'däi, 13 his host as numbered being fifty-nine thousand three hundred. 14 Then the tribe of Gad, the leader of the people of Gad being E·li'ă·saph the son of Reü'el, 15 his host as numbered being forty-five thousand six hundred and fifty. 16 The whole number of the camp of Reuben, by their companies, is a hundred and fifty-one thousand four hundred and fifty. They shall set out second.

17 "Then the tent of meeting shall set out, with the camp of the Levites in the midst of the camps; as they encamp, so shall they set out, each in position, standard by standard.

18 "On the west side shall be the standard of the camp of E'phrà·im by their companies, the leader of the people of Ephraim being E·lish'ă·mà the son of Am·mī'húd, 19 his host as numbered being forty thousand five hundred. 20And next to him shall be the tribe of Mà·nas'sĕh, the leader of the people of Manasseh being Gà·mā'li·ĕl the son of Pĕ·däh'zür, 21 his host as numbered being thirty-two thou-

sand two hundred. 22 Then the tribe of Benjamin, the leader of the people of Benjamin being À·bi'dàn the son of Gid·ē·ō'ni, 23 his host as numbered being thirty-five thousand four hundred. 24 The whole number of the camp of E'phrà·im, by their companies, is a hundred and eight thousand one hundred. They shall set out third on the march.

25 "On the north side shall be the standard of the camp of Dan by their companies, the leader of the people of Dan being À·hi·ē'zĕr the son of Am·mi·shad'däi, 26 his host as numbered being sixty-two thousand seven hundred. 27And those to encamp next to him shall be the tribe of Ash'ĕr, the leader of the people of Asher being Pā'gi·el the son of Ōch'ràn, 28 his host as numbered being forty-one thousand five hundred. 29 Then the tribe of Naph'tà·li, the leader of the people of Naphtali being À·hi'rà the son of E'nan, 30 his host as numbered being fifty-three thousand four hundred. 31 The whole number of the camp of Dan is a hundred and fifty-seven thousand six hundred. They shall set out last, standard by standard."

32 These are the people of Israel as numbered by their fathers' houses; all in the camps who were numbered by their companies were six hundred and three thousand five hundred and fifty. 33 But the Levites were not numbered among the people of Israel, as the LORD commanded Moses.

34 Thus did the people of Israel. According to all that the LORD commanded Moses, so they encamped by their standards, and so they set out, every one in his family, according to his fathers' house.

3 These are the generations of Aaron and Moses at the time when the LORD spoke with Moses on Mount Sinai. 2 These are the names of the sons of Aaron: Nā'dab the first-born, and À·bi'hū, El·ē·ā'zàr, and Ith'ă·mär; 3 these are the names of the sons of Aaron, the anointed priests, whom he ordained to minister in the priest's office. 4 But Nā'dab and À·bi'hū died before the LORD when they offered unholy fire before the LORD in the wilderness of Sinai; and they had no children. So El·ē·ā'zàr and Ith'ă·mär served as priests in the lifetime of Aaron their father.

5 And the LORD said to Moses, 6 "Bring the tribe of Levi near, and set them before Aaron the priest, that they may minister to him. 7 They shall

3.2: Num 26.60.   **3.5-13:** Num 8.6-26.   **3.5-8:** Num 1.50-53; 3.21-37; 4.1-33; 8.19.

perform duties for him and for the whole congregation before the tent of meeting, as they minister at the tabernacle; 8 they shall have charge of all the furnishings of the tent of meeting, and attend to the duties for the people of Israel as they minister at the tabernacle. 9And you shall give the Levites to Aaron and his sons; they are wholly given to him from among the people of Israel. 10And you shall appoint Aaron and his sons, and they shall attend to their priesthood; but if any one else comes near, he shall be put to death."

11 And the LORD said to Moses, 12 "Behold, I have taken the Levites from among the people of Israel instead of every first-born that opens the womb among the people of Israel. The Levites shall be mine, 13 for all the first-born are mine; on the day that I slew all the first-born in the land of Egypt, I consecrated for my own all the first-born in Israel, both of man and of beast; they shall be mine: I am the LORD."

14 And the Lord said to Moses in the wilderness of Sinai, 15 "Number the sons of Levi, by fathers' houses and by families; every male from a month old and upward you shall number." 16 So Moses numbered them according to the word of the LORD, as he was commanded. 17And these were the sons of Levi by their names: Gēr'-shŏn and Kō'hath and Mĕ·râr'ī. 18And these are the names of the sons of Gēr'shŏn by their families: Lib'nī and Shim'ē-ī. 19And the sons of Kō'hath by their families: Am'ram, Iz'här, Hē'-brŏn, and Uz'zi·el. 20And the sons of Mĕ·râr'ī by their families: Mäh'li and Mū'shī. These are the families of the Levites, by their fathers' houses.

21 Of Gēr'shŏn were the family of the Lib'nītes and the family of the Shim'ē·ītes; these were the families of the Gēr'shŏ·nītes. 22 Their number according to the number of all the males from a month old and upward was[a] seven thousand five hundred. 23 The families of the Gēr'shŏ·nītes were to encamp behind the tabernacle on the west, 24 with E·lī'ȧ·saph, the son of Lā'ĕl as head of the fathers' house of the Gēr'shŏ·nītes. 25And the charge of the sons of Gēr'shŏn in the tent of meeting was to be the tabernacle, the tent with its covering, the screen for the door of the tent of meeting, 26 the hangings of the court, the screen for the door of the court which is around

the tabernacle and the altar, and its cords; all the service pertaining to these.

27 Of Kō'hath were the family of the Am'rȧ·mītes, and the family of the Iz·här'ītes, and the family of the Hē'-brŏ·nītes, and the family of the Uz·zī'-ė·lites; these are the families of the Kō'hȧ·thītes. 28According to the number of all the males, from a month old and upward, there were eight thousand six hundred, attending to the duties of the sanctuary. 29 The families of the sons of Kō'hath were to encamp on the south side of the tabernacle, 30 with El·ī·zā'phăn the son of Uz'zi·el as head of the fathers' house of the families of the Kō'hȧ·thītes. 31And their charge was to be the ark, the table, the lampstand, the altars, the vessels of the sanctuary with which the priests minister, and the screen; all the service pertaining to these. 32And El·ē·ā'zär the son of Aaron the priest was to be chief over the leaders of the Levites, and to have oversight of those who had charge of the sanctuary.

33 Of Mĕ·râr'ī were the family of the Mäh'lites and the family of the Mū'shītes: these are the families of Merari. 34 Their number according to the number of all the males from a month old and upward was six thousand two hundred. 35And the head of the fathers' house of the families of Mĕ·râr'ī was Zū'ri·el the son of Ab·ī-hā'il; they were to encamp on the north side of the tabernacle. 36And the appointed charge of the sons of Mĕ·râr'ī was to be the frames of the tabernacle, the bars, the pillars, the bases, and all their accessories; all the service pertaining to these; 37 also the pillars of the court round about, with their bases and pegs and cords.

38 And those to encamp before the tabernacle on the east, before the tent of meeting toward the sunrise, were Moses and Aaron and his sons, having charge of the rites within the sanctuary, whatever had to be done for the people of Israel; and any one else who came near was to be put to death. 39All who were numbered of the Levites, whom Moses and Aaron numbered at the commandment of the LORD, by families, all the males from a month old and upward, were twenty-two thousand.

40 And the LORD said to Moses, "Number all the first-born males of the people of Israel, from a month old and upward, taking their number by

a Heb *their number was*
3.11-13: Num 3.45; 8.18.   3.15-34: Num 4.34-49.   3.17-20: Ex 6.16, 22.

names. 41And you shall take the Levites for me—I am the LORD—instead of all the first-born among the people of Israel, and the cattle of the Levites instead of all the firstlings among the cattle of the people of Israel." 42 So Moses numbered all the first-born among the people of Israel, as the LORD commanded him. 43And all the first-born males, according to the number of names, from a month old and upward as numbered were twenty-two thousand two hundred and seventy-three.

44 And the LORD said to Moses, 45 "Take the Levites instead of all the first-born among the people of Israel, and the cattle of the Levites instead of their cattle; and the Levites shall be mine: I am the LORD. 46And for the redemption of the two hundred and seventy-three of the first-born of the people of Israel, over and above the number of the male Levites, 47 you shall take five shekels apiece; reckoning by the shekel of the sanctuary, the shekel of twenty gerahs, you shall take them, 48 and give the money by which the excess number of them is redeemed to Aaron and his sons." 49 So Moses took the redemption money from those who were over and above those redeemed by the Levites; 50 from the first-born of the people of Israel he took the money, one thousand three hundred and sixty-five shekels, reckoned by the shekel of the sanctuary; 51 and Moses gave the redemption money to Aaron and his sons, according to the word of the LORD, as the LORD commanded Moses.

4 The LORD said to Moses and Aaron, 2 "Take a census of the sons of Kō'hath from among the sons of Levi, by their families and their fathers' houses; 3 from thirty years old up to fifty years old, all who can enter the service, to do the work in the tent of meeting. 4 This is the service of the sons of Kō'hath in the tent of meeting: the most holy things. 5 When the camp is to set out, Aaron and his sons shall go in and take down the veil of the screen, and cover the ark of the testimony with it; 6 then they shall put on it a covering of goatskin, and spread over that a cloth all of blue, and shall put in its poles. 7And over the table of the bread of the Presence they shall spread a cloth of blue, and put upon it the plates, the dishes for incense, the bowls, and the flagons for the drink offering; the continual bread also shall be on it; 8 then they shall spread

over them a cloth of scarlet, and cover the same with a covering of goatskin, and shall put in its poles. 9And they shall take a cloth of blue, and cover the lampstand for the light, with its lamps, its snuffers, its trays, and all the vessels for oil with which it is supplied: 10 and they shall put it with all its utensils in a covering of goatskin and put it upon the carrying frame. 11And over the golden altar they shall spread a cloth of blue, and cover it with a covering of goatskin, and shall put in its poles; 12 and they shall take all the vessels of the service which are used in the sanctuary, and put them in a cloth of blue, and cover them with a covering of goatskin, and put them on the carrying frame. 13And they shall take away the ashes from the altar, and spread a purple cloth over it; 14 and they shall put on it all the utensils of the altar, which are used for the service there, the firepans, the forks, the shovels, and the basins, all the utensils of the altar; and they shall spread upon it a covering of goatskin, and shall put in its poles. 15And when Aaron and his sons have finished covering the sanctuary and all the furnishings of the sanctuary, as the camp sets out, after that the sons of Kō'hath shall come to carry these, but they must not touch the holy things, lest they die. These are the things of the tent of meeting which the sons of Kohath are to carry.

16 "And El·ē·ā'zăr the son of Aaron the priest shall have charge of the oil for the light, the fragrant incense, the continual cereal offering, and the anointing oil, with the oversight of all the tabernacle and all that is in it, of the sanctuary and its vessels."

17 The LORD said to Moses and Aaron, 18 "Let not the tribe of the families of the Kō'hă·thites be destroyed from among the Levites; 19 but deal thus with them, that they may live and not die when they come near to the most holy things: Aaron and his sons shall go in and appoint them each to his task and to his burden, 20 but they shall not go in to look upon the holy things even for a moment, lest they die."

21 The LORD said to Moses, 22 "Take a census of the sons of Gēr'shŏn also, by their families and their fathers' houses; 23 from thirty years old up to fifty years old, you shall number them, all who can enter for service, to do the work in the tent of meeting. 24 This is the service of the

3.45: Num 3.11-13; 8.18.   **4.1-33:** Num 1.50-53; 3.5-8, 21-37; 8.19; 18.3-4, 23.

families of the Gēr′shŏ·nītes, in serving and bearing burdens: 25 they shall carry the curtains of the tabernacle, and the tent of meeting with its covering, and the covering of goatskin that is on top of it, and the screen for the door of the tent of meeting, 26 and the hangings of the court, and the screen for the entrance of the gate of the court which is around the tabernacle and the altar, and their cords, and all the equipment for their service; and they shall do all that needs to be done with regard to them. 27All the service of the sons of the Gēr′shŏ·nītes shall be at the command of Aaron and his sons, in all that they are to carry, and in all that they have to do; and you shall assign to their charge all that they are to carry. 28 This is the service of the families of the sons of the Gēr′shŏ-nītes in the tent of meeting, and their work is to be under the oversight of Ĭth′à·mär the son of Aaron the priest.

29 "As for the sons of Mē·râr′ī, you shall number them by their families and their fathers' houses; 30 from thirty years old up to fifty years old, you shall number them, every one that can enter the service, to do the work of the tent of meeting. 31And this is what they are charged to carry, as the whole of their service in the tent of meeting: the frames of the tabernacle, with its bars, pillars, and bases, 32 and the pillars of the court round about with their bases, pegs, and cords, with all their equipment and all their accessories; and you shall assign by name the objects which they are required to carry. 33 This is the service of the families of the sons of Mē·râr′ī, the whole of their service in the tent of meeting, under the hand of Ĭth′à·mär the son of Aaron the priest."

34 And Moses and Aaron and the leaders of the congregation numbered the sons of the Kō′hà·thītes, by their families and their fathers' houses, 35 from thirty years old up to fifty years old, every one that could enter the service, for work in the tent of meeting; 36 and their number by families was two thousand seven hundred and fifty. 37 This was the number of the families of the Kō′hà·thītes, all who served in the tent of meeting, whom Moses and Aaron numbered according to the commandment of the LORD by Moses.

38 The number of the sons of Gēr′shŏn, by their families and their fathers' houses, 39 from thirty years old up to fifty years old, every one that

could enter the service for work in the tent of meeting—40 their number by their families and their fathers' houses was two thousand six hundred and thirty. 41 This was the number of the families of the sons of Gēr′shŏn, all who served in the tent of meeting, whom Moses and Aaron numbered according to the commandment of the LORD.

42 The number of the families of the sons of Mē·râr′ī, by their families and their fathers' houses, 43 from thirty years old up to fifty years old, every one that could enter the service, for work in the tent of meeting—44 their number by families was three thousand two hundred. 45 These are those who were numbered of the families of the sons of Mē·râr′ī, whom Moses and Aaron numbered according to the commandment of the LORD by Moses.

46 All those who were numbered of the Levites, whom Moses and Aaron and the leaders of Israel numbered, by their families and their fathers' houses, 47 from thirty years old up to fifty years old, every one that could enter to do the work of service and the work of bearing burdens in the tent of meeting, 48 those who were numbered of them were eight thousand five hundred and eighty. 49According to the commandment of the LORD through Moses they were appointed, each to his task of serving or carrying; thus they were numbered by him, as the LORD commanded Moses.

5 The LORD said to Moses, 2 "Command the people of Israel that they put out of the camp every leper, and every one having a discharge, and every one that is unclean through contact with the dead; 3 you shall put out both male and female, putting them outside the camp, that they may not defile their camp, in the midst of which I dwell." 4And the people of Israel did so, and drove them outside the camp; as the LORD said to Moses, so the people of Israel did.

5 And the LORD said to Moses, 6 "Say to the people of Israel, When a man or woman commits any of the sins that men commit by breaking faith with the LORD, and that person is guilty, 7 he shall confess his sin which he has committed; and he shall make full restitution for his wrong, adding a fifth to it, and giving it to him to whom he did the wrong. 8 But if the man has no kinsman to whom restitution may be made for the wrong, the restitution for wrong shall go to

4.34-49: Num 3.15-34.   **5.2-3:** Num 12.14-15.   **5.5-8:** Ex 22.7-15; Lev 6.1-7.

the LORD for the priest, in addition to the ram of atonement with which atonement is made for him. 9And every offering, all the holy things of the people of Israel, which they bring to the priest, shall be his; 10 and every man's holy things shall be his; whatever any man gives to the priest shall be his."

11 And the LORD said to Moses, 12 "Say to the people of Israel, If any man's wife goes astray and acts unfaithfully against him, 13 if a man lies with her carnally, and it is hidden from the eyes of her husband, and she is undetected though she has defiled herself, and there is no witness against her, since she was not taken in the act; 14 and if the spirit of jealousy comes upon him, and he is jealous of his wife who has defiled herself; or if the spirit of jealousy comes upon him, and he is jealous of his wife, though she has not defiled herself; 15 then the man shall bring his wife to the priest, and bring the offering required of her, a tenth of an ephah of barley meal; he shall pour no oil upon it and put no frankincense on it, for it is a cereal offering of jealousy, a cereal offering of remembrance, bringing iniquity to remembrance.

16 "And the priest shall bring her near, and set her before the LORD; 17 and the priest shall take holy water in an earthen vessel, and take some of the dust that is on the floor of the tabernacle and put it into the water. 18And the priest shall set the woman before the LORD, and unbind the hair of the woman's head, and place in her hands the cereal offering of remembrance, which is the cereal offering of jealousy. And in his hand the priest shall have the water of bitterness that brings the curse. 19 Then the priest shall make her take an oath, saying, 'If no man has lain with you, and if you have not turned aside to uncleanness, while you were under your husband's authority, be free from this water of bitterness that brings the curse. 20 But if you have gone astray, though you are under your husband's authority, and if you have defiled yourself, and some man other than your husband has lain with you, 21 then' (let the priest make the woman take the oath of the curse, and say to the woman) 'the LORD make you an execration and an oath among your people, when the LORD makes your thigh fall away and your body swell; 22 may

this water that brings the curse pass into your bowels and make your body swell and your thigh fall away.' And the woman shall say, 'Amen, Amen.'

23 "Then the priest shall write these curses in a book, and wash them off into the water of bitterness; 24 and he shall make the woman drink the water of bitterness that brings the curse, and the water that brings the curse shall enter into her and cause bitter pain. 25And the priest shall take the cereal offering of jealousy out of the woman's hand, and shall wave the cereal offering before the LORD and bring it to the altar; 26 and the priest shall take a handful of the cereal offering, as its memorial portion, and burn it upon the altar, and afterward shall make the woman drink the water. 27And when he has made her drink the water, then, if she has defiled herself and has acted unfaithfully against her husband, the water that brings the curse shall enter into her and cause bitter pain, and her body shall swell, and her thigh shall fall away, and the woman shall become an execration among her people. 28 But if the woman has not defiled herself and is clean, then she shall be free and shall conceive children.

29 "This is the law in cases of jealousy, when a wife, though under her husband's authority, goes astray and defiles herself, 30 or when the spirit of jealousy comes upon a man and he is jealous of his wife; then he shall set the woman before the LORD, and the priest shall execute upon her all this law. 31 The man shall be free from iniquity, but the woman shall bear her iniquity."

6 And the LORD said to Moses, 2 "Say to the people of Israel, When either a man or a woman makes a special vow, the vow of a Naz'i·rite,[b] to separate himself to the LORD, 3 he shall separate himself from wine and strong drink; he shall drink no vinegar made from wine or strong drink, and shall not drink any juice of grapes or eat grapes, fresh or dried. 4All the days of his separation[c] he shall eat nothing that is produced by the grapevine, not even the seeds or the skins.

5 "All the days of his vow of separation no razor shall come upon his head; until the time is completed for which he separates himself to the LORD, he shall be holy; he shall let the locks of hair of his head grow long.

6 "All the days that he separates

b That is *one separated* or *one consecrated*   *c* Or *Naziriteship*
6.3: Lk 1.15.

himself to the LORD he shall not go near a dead body. [7] Neither for his father nor for his mother, nor for brother or sister, if they die, shall he make himself unclean; because his separation to God is upon his head. [8]All the days of his separation he is holy to the LORD.

[9] "And if any man dies very suddenly beside him, and he defiles his consecrated head, then he shall shave his head on the day of his cleansing; on the seventh day he shall shave it. [10] On the eighth day he shall bring two turtledoves or two young pigeons to the priest to the door of the tent of meeting, [11] and the priest shall offer one for a sin offering and the other for a burnt offering, and make atonement for him, because he sinned by reason of the dead body. And he shall consecrate his head that same day, [12] and separate himself to the LORD for the days of his separation, and bring a male lamb a year old for a guilt offering; but the former time shall be void, because his separation was defiled.

[13] "And this is the law for the Naz′i·rite, when the time of his separation has been completed: he shall be brought to the door of the tent of meeting, [14] and he shall offer his gift to the LORD, one male lamb a year old without blemish for a burnt offering, and one ewe lamb a year old without blemish as a sin offering, and one ram without blemish as a peace offering, [15] and a basket of unleavened bread, cakes of fine flour mixed with oil, and unleavened wafers spread with oil, and their cereal offering and their drink offerings. [16]And the priest shall present them before the LORD and offer his sin offering and his burnt offering, [17] and he shall offer the ram as a sacrifice of peace offering to the LORD, with the basket of unleavened bread; the priest shall offer also its cereal offering and its drink offering. [18]And the Naz′i·rite shall shave his consecrated head at the door of the tent of meeting, and shall take the hair from his consecrated head and put it on the fire which is under the sacrifice of the peace offering. [19]And the priest shall take the shoulder of the ram, when it is boiled, and one unleavened cake out of the basket, and one unleavened wafer, and shall put them upon the hands of the Naz′i·rite, after he has shaven the hair of his consecration, [20] and the priest shall wave them for a wave offering before the LORD; they are a holy portion for the priest, to-

6.13-21: Acts 21.24, 26.

gether with the breast that is waved and the thigh that is offered; and after that the Naz′i·rite may drink wine.

[21] "This is the law for the Naz′i·rite who takes a vow. His offering to the LORD shall be according to his vow as a Nazirite, apart from what else he can afford; in accordance with the vow which he takes, so shall he do according to the law for his separation as a Nazirite."

[22] The LORD said to Moses, [23] "Say to Aaron and his sons, Thus you shall bless the people of Israel: you shall say to them,
[24] The LORD bless you and keep
    you:
[25] The LORD make his face to shine
    upon you, and be gracious to
    you:
[26] The LORD lift up his countenance
    upon you, and give you peace.
[27] "So shall they put my name upon the people of Israel, and I will bless them."

7 On the day when Moses had finished setting up the tabernacle, and had anointed and consecrated it with all its furnishings, and had anointed and consecrated the altar with all its utensils, [2] the leaders of Israel, heads of their fathers' houses, the leaders of the tribes, who were over those who were numbered, [3] offered and brought their offerings before the LORD, six covered wagons and twelve oxen, a wagon for every two of the leaders, and for each one an ox; they offered them before the tabernacle. [4] Then the LORD said to Moses, [5] "Accept these from them, that they may be used in doing the service of the tent of meeting, and give them to the Levites, to each man according to his service." [6] So Moses took the wagons and the oxen, and gave them to the Levites. [7] Two wagons and four oxen he gave to the sons of Ger′-shon, according to their service; [8] and four wagons and eight oxen he gave to the sons of Me·rar′i, according to their service, under the direction of Ith′a·mar the son of Aaron the priest. [9] But to the sons of Ko′hath he gave none, because they were charged with the care of the holy things which had to be carried on the shoulder. [10]And the leaders offered offerings for the dedication of the altar on the day it was anointed; and the leaders offered their offering before the altar. [11]And the LORD said to Moses, "They shall offer their offerings, one leader each day, for the dedication of the altar."

12 He who offered his offering the first day was Näh′shŏn the son of Am·min′á·dab, of the tribe of Judah; 13 and his offering was one silver plate whose weight was a hundred and thirty shekels, one silver basin of seventy shekels, according to the shekel of the sanctuary, both of them full of fine flour mixed with oil for a cereal offering; 14 one golden dish of ten shekels, full of incense; 15 one young bull, one ram, one male lamb a year old, for a burnt offering; 16 one male goat for a sin offering; 17 and for the sacrifice of peace offerings, two oxen, five rams, five male goats, and five male lambs a year old. This was the offering of Näh′shŏn the son of Am·min′á·dab.

18 On the second day Nĕ·than′el the son of Zü′ar, the leader of Is′sà·chär, made an offering; 19 he offered for his offering one silver plate, whose weight was a hundred and thirty shekels, one silver basin of seventy shekels, according to the shekel of the sanctuary, both of them full of fine flour mixed with oil for a cereal offering; 20 one golden dish of ten shekels, full of incense; 21 one young bull, one ram, one male lamb a year old, for a burnt offering; 22 one male goat for a sin offering; 23 and for the sacrifice of peace offerings, two oxen, five rams, five male goats, and five male lambs a year old. This was the offering of Nĕ·than′el the son of Zü′ar.

24 On the third day E·li′ab the son of Hē′lon, the leader of the men of Zeb′ū·lùn: 25 his offering was one silver plate, whose weight was a hundred and thirty shekels, one silver basin of seventy shekels, according to the shekel of the sanctuary, both of them full of fine flour mixed with oil for a cereal offering; 26 one golden dish of ten shekels, full of incense; 27 one young bull, one ram, one male lamb a year old, for a burnt offering; 28 one male goat for a sin offering; 29 and for the sacrifice of peace offerings, two oxen, five rams, five male goats, and five male lambs a year old. This was the offering of E·li′ab the son of Hē′lon.

30 On the fourth day E·li′zür the son of Shed′ē·ùr, the leader of the men of Reuben: 31 his offering was one silver plate whose weight was a hundred and thirty shekels, one silver basin of seventy shekels, according to the shekel of the sanctuary, both of them full of fine flour mixed with oil for a cereal offering; 32 one golden dish of ten shekels, full of incense; 33 one young bull, one ram, one male lamb a year old, for a burnt offering; 34 one

male goat for a sin offering; 35 and for the sacrifice of peace offerings, two oxen, five rams, five male goats, and five male lambs a year old. This was the offering of E·li′zür the son of Shed′ē·ùr.

36 On the fifth day She·lü′mi-el the son of Zü·ri·shad′däi, the leader of the men of Simeon: 37 his offering was one silver plate, whose weight was a hundred and thirty shekels, one silver basin of seventy shekels, according to the shekel of the sanctuary, both of them full of fine flour mixed with oil for a cereal offering; 38 one golden dish of ten shekels, full of incense; 39 one young bull, one ram, one male lamb a year old, for a burnt offering; 40 one male goat for a sin offering; 41 and for the sacrifice of peace offerings, two oxen, five rams, five male goats, and five male lambs a year old. This was the offering of She·lü′mi-el the son of Zü·ri·shad′däi.

42 On the sixth day E·li′à·saph the son of Deü′el, the leader of the men of Gad: 43 his offering was one silver plate, whose weight was a hundred and thirty shekels, one silver basin of seventy shekels, according to the shekel of the sanctuary, both of them full of fine flour mixed with oil for a cereal offering; 44 one golden dish of ten shekels, full of incense; 45 one young bull, one ram, one male lamb a year old, for a burnt offering; 46 one male goat for a sin offering; 47 and for the sacrifice of peace offerings, two oxen, five rams, five male goats, and five male lambs a year old. This was the offering of E·li′à·saph the son of Deü′el.

48 On the seventh day E·lish′à·mà the son of Am·mi′hùd, the leader of the men of É′phrà·im: 49 his offering was one silver plate, whose weight was a hundred and thirty shekels, one silver basin of seventy shekels, according to the shekel of the sanctuary, both of them full of fine flour mixed with oil for a cereal offering; 50 one golden dish of ten shekels, full of incense; 51 one young bull, one ram, one male lamb a year old, for a burnt offering; 52 one male goat for a sin offering; 53 and for the sacrifice of peace offerings, two oxen, five rams, five male goats, and five male lambs a year old. This was the offering of E·lish′à·mà the son of Am·mi′hùd.

54 On the eighth day Gà·mā′li·ĕl the son of Pĕ·däh′zùr, the leader of the men of Mà·nas′sĕh: 55 his offering was one silver plate, whose weight was a hundred and thirty shekels, one silver

basin of seventy shekels, according to the shekel of the sanctuary, both of them full of fine flour mixed with oil for a cereal offering; 56 one golden dish of ten shekels, full of incense; 57 one young bull, one ram, one male lamb a year old, for a burnt offering; 58 one male goat for a sin offering; 59 and for the sacrifice of peace offerings, two oxen, five rams, five male goats, and five male lambs a year old. This was the offering of Gà·mā′li·el the son of Pė·däh′zur.

60 On the ninth day À·bī′dàn the son of Gid·ē·ō′ni, the leader of the men of Benjamin: 61 his offering was one silver plate, whose weight was a hundred and thirty shekels, one silver basin of seventy shekels, according to the shekel of the sanctuary, both of them full of fine flour mixed with oil for a cereal offering; 62 one golden dish of ten shekels, full of incense; 63 one young bull, one ram, one male lamb a year old, for a burnt offering; 64 one male goat for a sin offering; 65 and for the sacrifice of peace offerings, two oxen, five rams, five male goats, and five male lambs a year old. This was the offering of À·bī′dàn the son of Gid·ē·ō′ni.

66 On the tenth day Ā·hī·ē′zėr the son of Am·mi·shad′däi, the leader of the men of Dan: 67 his offering was one silver plate, whose weight was a hundred and thirty shekels, one silver basin of seventy shekels, according to the shekel of the sanctuary, both of them full of fine flour mixed with oil for a cereal offering; 68 one golden dish of ten shekels, full of incense; 69 one young bull, one ram, one male lamb a year old, for a burnt offering; 70 one male goat for a sin offering; 71 and for the sacrifice of peace offerings, two oxen, five rams, five male goats, and five male lambs a year old. This was the offering of Ā·hī·ē′zėr the son of Am·mi·shad′däi.

72 On the eleventh day Pā′gi·el the son of Och′rän, the leader of the men of Ash′ėr: 73 his offering was one silver plate, whose weight was a hundred and thirty shekels, one silver basin of seventy shekels, according to the shekel of the sanctuary, both of them full of fine flour mixed with oil for a cereal offering; 74 one golden dish of ten shekels, full of incense; 75 one young bull, one ram, one male lamb a year old, for a burnt offering; 76 one male goat for a sin offering; 77 and for the sacrifice of peace offerings, two oxen, five rams, five male goats, and five male lambs a year old. This was

the offering of Pā′gi·el the son of Och′rän.

78 On the twelfth day À·hī′rà the son of Ē′nan, the leader of the men of Naph′tà·li: 79 his offering was one silver plate, whose weight was a hundred and thirty shekels, one silver basin of seventy shekels, according to the shekel of the sanctuary, both of them full of fine flour mixed with oil for a cereal offering; 80 one golden dish of ten shekels, full of incense; 81 one young bull, one ram, one male lamb a year old, for a burnt offering; 82 one male goat for a sin offering; 83 and for the sacrifice of peace offerings, two oxen, five rams, five male goats, and five male lambs a year old. This was the offering of À·hī′rà the son of Ē′nan.

84 This was the dedication offering for the altar, on the day when it was anointed, from the leaders of Israel: twelve silver plates, twelve silver basins, twelve golden dishes, 85 each silver plate weighing a hundred and thirty shekels and each basin seventy, all the silver of the vessels two thousand four hundred shekels according to the shekel of the sanctuary, 86 the twelve golden dishes, full of incense, weighing ten shekels apiece according to the shekel of the sanctuary, all the gold of the dishes being a hundred and twenty shekels; 87 all the cattle for the burnt offering twelve bulls, twelve rams, twelve male lambs a year old, with their cereal offering; and twelve male goats for a sin offering; 88 and all the cattle for the sacrifice of peace offerings twenty-four bulls, the rams sixty, the male goats sixty, the male lambs a year old sixty. This was the dedication offering for the altar, after it was anointed.

89 And when Moses went into the tent of meeting to speak with the LORD, he heard the voice speaking to him from above the mercy seat that was upon the ark of the testimony, from between the two cherubim; and it spoke to him.

8 Now the LORD said to Moses, 2 "Say to Aaron, When you set up the lamps, the seven lamps shall give light in front of the lampstand." 3 And Aaron did so; he set up its lamps to give light in front of the lampstand, as the LORD commanded Moses. 4 And this was the workmanship of the lampstand, hammered work of gold; from its base to its flowers, it was hammered work; according to the pattern which the LORD had shown Moses, so he made the lampstand.

5 And the LORD said to Moses, 6 "Take the Levites from among the people of Israel, and cleanse them. 7 And thus you shall do to them, to cleanse them: sprinkle the water of expiation upon them, and let them go with a razor over all their body, and wash their clothes and cleanse themselves. 8 Then let them take a young bull and its cereal offering of fine flour mixed with oil, and you shall take another young bull for a sin offering. 9 And you shall present the Levites before the tent of meeting, and assemble the whole congregation of the people of Israel. 10 When you present the Levites before the LORD, the people of Israel shall lay their hands upon the Levites, 11 and Aaron shall offer the Levites before the LORD as a wave offering from the people of Israel, that it may be theirs to do the service of the LORD. 12 Then the Levites shall lay their hands upon the heads of the bulls; and you shall offer the one for a sin offering and the other for a burnt offering to the LORD, to make atonement for the Levites. 13 And you shall cause the Levites to attend Aaron and his sons, and shall offer them as a wave offering to the LORD.

14 "Thus you shall separate the Levites from among the people of Israel, and the Levites shall be mine. 15 And after that the Levites shall go in to do service at the tent of meeting, when you have cleansed them and offered them as a wave offering. 16 For they are wholly given to me from among the people of Israel; instead of all that open the womb, the first-born of all the people of Israel, I have taken them for myself. 17 For all the first-born among the people of Israel are mine, both of man and of beast; on the day that I slew all the first-born in the land of Egypt I consecrated them for myself, 18 and I have taken the Levites instead of all the first-born among the people of Israel. 19 And I have given the Levites as a gift to Aaron and his sons from among the people of Israel, to do the service for the people of Israel at the tent of meeting, and to make atonement for the people of Israel, that there may be no plague among the people of Israel in case the people of Israel should come near the sanctuary."

20 Thus did Moses and Aaron and all the congregation of the people of Israel to the Levites; according to all that the LORD commanded Moses concerning the Levites, the people of Israel did to them. 21 And the Levites purified themselves from sin, and washed their clothes; and Aaron offered them as a wave offering before the LORD, and Aaron made atonement for them to cleanse them. 22 And after that the Levites went in to do their service in the tent of meeting in attendance upon Aaron and his sons; as the LORD had commanded Moses concerning the Levites, so they did to them.

23 And the LORD said to Moses, 24 "This is what pertains to the Levites: from twenty-five years old and upward they shall go in to perform the work in the service of the tent of meeting; 25 and from the age of fifty years they shall withdraw from the work of the service and serve no more, 26 but minister to their brethren in the tent of meeting, to keep the charge, and they shall do no service. Thus shall you do to the Levites in assigning their duties."

9 And the LORD spoke to Moses in the wilderness of Sinai, in the first month of the second year after they had come out of the land of Egypt, saying, 2 "Let the people of Israel keep the passover at its appointed time. 3 On the fourteenth day of this month, in the evening, you shall keep it at its appointed time; according to all its statutes and all its ordinances you shall keep it." 4 So Moses told the people of Israel that they should keep the passover. 5 And they kept the passover in the first month, on the fourteenth day of the month, in the evening, in the wilderness of Sinai; according to all that the LORD commanded Moses, so the people of Israel did. 6 And there were certain men who were unclean through touching the dead body of a man, so that they could not keep the passover on that day; and they came before Moses and Aaron on that day; 7 and those men said to him, "We are unclean through touching the dead body of a man; why are we kept from offering the LORD's offering at its appointed time among the people of Israel?" 8 And Moses said to them, "Wait, that I may hear what the LORD will command concerning you."

9 The LORD said to Moses, 10 "Say to the people of Israel, If any man of you or of your descendants is unclean through touching a dead body, or is afar off on a journey, he shall still keep the passover to the LORD. 11 In the second month on the fourteenth day in the evening they shall keep it; they shall eat it with unleavened bread and

8.6-26: Num 3.5-13.   8.18: Num 3.11-13, 45.   9.1-5: Ex 12.1-14, 21-28.

bitter herbs. 12 They shall leave none of it until the morning, nor break a bone of it; according to all the statute for the passover they shall keep it. 13 But the man who is clean and is not on a journey, yet refrains from keeping the passover, that person shall be cut off from his people, because he did not offer the LORD'S offering at its appointed time; that man shall bear his sin. 14And if a stranger sojourns among you, and will keep the passover to the LORD, according to the statute of the passover and according to its ordinance, so shall he do; you shall have one statute, both for the sojourner and for the native."

15 On the day that the tabernacle was set up, the cloud covered the tabernacle, the tent of the testimony; and at evening it was over the tabernacle like the appearance of fire until morning. 16 So it was continually; the cloud covered it by day,*d* and the appearance of fire by night. 17And whenever the cloud was taken up from over the tent, after that the people of Israel set out; and in the place where the cloud settled down, there the people of Israel encamped. 18At the command of the LORD the people of Israel set out, and at the command of the LORD they encamped; as long as the cloud rested over the tabernacle, they remained in camp. 19 Even when the cloud continued over the tabernacle many days, the people of Israel kept the charge of the LORD, and did not set out. 20 Sometimes the cloud was a few days over the tabernacle, and according to the command of the LORD they remained in camp; then according to the command of the LORD they set out. 21And sometimes the cloud remained from evening until morning; and when the cloud was taken up in the morning, they set out, or if it continued for a day and a night, when the cloud was taken up they set out. 22 Whether it was two days, or a month, or a longer time, that the cloud continued over the tabernacle, abiding there, the people of Israel remained in camp and did not set out; but when it was taken up they set out. 23At the command of the LORD they encamped, and at the command of the LORD they set out; they kept the charge of the LORD, at the command of the LORD by Moses.

10 The LORD said to Moses, 2 "Make two silver trumpets; of hammered work you shall make them; and you shall use them for summoning

the congregation, and for breaking camp. 3And when both are blown, all the congregation shall gather themselves to you at the entrance of the tent of meeting. 4 But if they blow only one, then the leaders, the heads of the tribes of Israel, shall gather themselves to you. 5 When you blow an alarm, the camps that are on the east side shall set out. 6And when you blow an alarm the second time, the camps that are on the south side shall set out. An alarm is to be blown whenever they are to set out. 7 But when the assembly is to be gathered together, you shall blow, but you shall not sound an alarm. 8And the sons of Aaron, the priests, shall blow the trumpets. The trumpets shall be to you for a perpetual statute throughout your generations. 9And when you go to war in your land against the adversary who oppresses you, then you shall sound an alarm with the trumpets, that you may be remembered before the LORD your God, and you shall be saved from your enemies. 10 On the day of your gladness also, and at your appointed feasts, and at the beginnings of your months, you shall blow the trumpets over your burnt offerings and over the sacrifices of your peace offerings; they shall serve you for remembrance before your God; I am the LORD your God."

11 In the second year, in the second month, on the twentieth day of the month, the cloud was taken up from over the tabernacle of the testimony, 12 and the people of Israel set out by stages from the wilderness of Sinai; and the cloud settled down in the wilderness of Pâr'an. 13 They set out for the first time at the command of the LORD by Moses. 14 The standard of the camp of the men of Judah set out first by their companies; and over their host was Näh'shŏn the son of Am·min'ä·dab. 15And over the host of the tribe of the men of Is'sä·chär was Ne·than'el the son of Zü'är. 16And over the host of the tribe of the men of Zeb'ū·lùn was E·lī'ab the son of Hē'lon.

17 And when the tabernacle was taken down, the sons of Gēr'shŏn and the sons of Mė·râr'ĭ, who carried the tabernacle, set out. 18And the standard of the camp of Reuben set out by their companies; and over their host was E·lī'zŭr the son of Shed'ē·ŭr. 19And over the host of the tribe of the men of Simeon was She·lü'mi·el the son of Zü·rī·shad'däi. 20And over the host of

d Gk Syr Vg: Heb lacks *by day*
9.12: Ex 12.46; Jn 19.36. 9.15-23: Ex 40.36-38.

the tribe of the men of Gad was E·lí'a·saph the son of Deü'el.

21 Then the Kō'hȧ·thītes set out, carrying the holy things, and the tabernacle was set up before their arrival. 22And the standard of the camp of the men of Ē'phrȧ·im set out by their companies; and over their host was E·lish'a·mȧ the son of Am·mi'hŭd. 23And over the host of the tribe of the men of Má·nas'seh was Gȧ·má'li·ĕl the son of Pe·däh'zŭr. 24And over the host of the tribe of the men of Benjamin was Ȧ·bī'dȧn the son of Gid·e·ō'ni.

25 Then the standard of the camp of the men of Dan, acting as the rear guard of all the camps, set out by their companies; and over their host was Ā·hī·ē'zĕr the son of Am·mi·shad'däi. 26And over the host of the tribe of the men of Ash'ĕr was Pā'gi·el the son of Öch'rȧn. 27And over the host of the tribe of the men of Naph'tȧ·lī was Ȧ·hī'rȧ the son of Ē'nan. 28 This was the order of march of the people of Israel according to their hosts, when they set out.

29 And Moses said to Hō'bab the son of Reü'el the Mid'i·ȧn·īte, Moses' father-in-law, "We are setting out for the place of which the LORD said, 'I will give it to you'; come with us, and we will do you good; for the LORD has promised good to Israel." 30 But he said to him, "I will not go; I will depart to my own land and to my kindred." 31And he said, "Do not leave us, I pray you, for you know how we are to encamp in the wilderness, and you will serve as eyes for us. 32And if you go with us, whatever good the LORD will do to us, the same will we do to you."

33 So they set out from the mount of the LORD three days' journey; and the ark of the covenant of the LORD went before them three days' journey, to seek out a resting place for them. 34And the cloud of the LORD was over them by day, whenever they set out from the camp.

35 And whenever the ark set out, Moses said, "Arise, O LORD, and let thy enemies be scattered; and let them that hate thee flee before thee." 36And when it rested, he said, "Return, O LORD, to the ten thousand thousands of Israel."

11 And the people complained in the hearing of the LORD about their misfortunes; and when the LORD heard it, his anger was kindled, and the fire of the LORD burned among them, and consumed some outlying parts of the camp. 2 Then the people cried to Moses; and Moses prayed to the LORD, and the fire abated. 3 So the name of that place was called Tab'e·räh,*e* because the fire of the LORD burned among them.

4 Now the rabble that was among them had a strong craving; and the people of Israel also wept again, and said, "O that we had meat to eat! 5 We remember the fish we ate in Egypt for nothing, the cucumbers, the melons, the leeks, the onions, and the garlic; 6 but now our strength is dried up, and there is nothing at all but this manna to look at."

7 Now the manna was like coriander seed, and its appearance like that of bdellium. 8 The people went about and gathered it, and ground it in mills or beat it in mortars, and boiled it in pots, and made cakes of it; and the taste of it was like the taste of cakes baked with oil. 9 When the dew fell upon the camp in the night, the manna fell with it.

10 Moses heard the people weeping throughout their families, every man at the door of his tent; and the anger of the LORD blazed hotly, and Moses was displeased. 11 Moses said to the LORD, "Why hast thou dealt ill with thy servant? And why have I not found favor in thy sight, that thou dost lay the burden of all this people upon me? 12 Did I conceive all this people? Did I bring them forth, that thou shouldst say to me, 'Carry them in your bosom, as a nurse carries the sucking child, to the land which thou didst swear to give their fathers?' 13 Where am I to get meat to give to all this people? For they weep before me and say, 'Give us meat, that we may eat.' 14 I am not able to carry all this people alone, the burden is too heavy for me. 15 If thou wilt deal thus with me, kill me at once, if I find favor in thy sight, that I may not see my wretchedness."

16 And the LORD said to Moses, "Gather for me seventy men of the elders of Israel, whom you know to be the elders of the people and officers over them; and bring them to the tent of meeting, and let them take their stand there with you. 17And I will come down and talk with you there; and I will take some of the spirit which is upon you and put it upon them; and they shall bear the burden of the people with you, that you may not

e That is *Burning*

10.35: Ps 68.1-2.   11.4: 1 Cor 10.6.

bear it yourself alone. 18And say to the people, 'Consecrate yourselves for tomorrow, and you shall eat meat; for you have wept in the hearing of the LORD, saying, "Who will give us meat to eat? For it was well with us in Egypt." Therefore the LORD will give you meat, and you shall eat. 19 You shall not eat one day, or two days, or five days, or ten days, or twenty days, 20 but a whole month, until it comes out at your nostrils and becomes loathsome to you, because you have rejected the LORD who is among you, and have wept before him, saying, "Why did we come forth out of Egypt?"'" 21 But Moses said, "The people among whom I am number six hundred thousand on foot; and thou hast said, 'I will give them meat, that they may eat a whole month!' 22 Shall flocks and herds be slaughtered for them, to suffice them? Or shall all the fish of the sea be gathered together for them, to suffice them?" 23And the LORD said to Moses, "Is the LORD's hand shortened? Now you shall see whether my word will come true for you or not."

24 So Moses went out and told the people the words of the LORD; and he gathered seventy men of the elders of the people, and placed them round about the tent. 25 Then the LORD came down in the cloud and spoke to him, and took some of the spirit that was upon him and put it upon the seventy elders; and when the spirit rested upon them, they prophesied. But they did so no more.

26 Now two men remained in the camp, one named El′dad, and the other named Me′dad, and the spirit rested upon them; they were among those registered, but they had not gone out to the tent, and so they prophesied in the camp. 27And a young man ran and told Moses, "El′dad and Me′dad are prophesying in the camp." 28And Joshua the son of Nun, the minister of Moses, one of his chosen men, said, "My lord Moses, forbid them." 29 But Moses said to him, "Are you jealous for my sake? Would that all the LORD's people were prophets, that the LORD would put his spirit upon them!" 30And Moses and the elders of Israel returned to the camp.

31 And there went forth a wind from the LORD, and it brought quails from the sea, and let them fall beside the camp, about a day's journey on this side and a day's journey on the other side, round about the camp, and

about two cubits above the face of the earth. 32And the people rose all that day, and all night, and all the next day, and gathered the quails; he who gathered least gathered ten homers; and they spread them out for themselves all around the camp. 33 While the meat was yet between their teeth, before it was consumed, the anger of the LORD was kindled against the people, and the LORD smote the people with a very great plague. 34 Therefore the name of that place was called Kib′-roth-hat·ta′a·vah,ᶠ because there they buried the people who had the craving. 35 From Kib′roth-hat·ta′a·vah the people journeyed to Ha·ze′roth; and they remained at Hazeroth.

12 Miriam and Aaron spoke against Moses because of the Cushite woman whom he had married, for he had married a Cushite woman; 2 and they said, "Has the LORD indeed spoken only through Moses? Has he not spoken through us also?" And the LORD heard it. 3 Now the man Moses was very meek, more than all men that were on the face of the earth. 4And suddenly the LORD said to Moses and to Aaron and Miriam, "Come out, you three, to the tent of meeting." And the three of them came out. 5And the LORD came down in a pillar of cloud, and stood at the door of the tent, and called Aaron and Miriam; and they both came forward. 6And he said, "Hear my words: If there is a prophet among you, I the LORD make myself known to him in a vision, I speak with him in a dream. 7 Not so with my servant Moses; he is entrusted with all my house. 8 With him I speak mouth to mouth, clearly, and not in dark speech; and he beholds the form of the LORD. Why then were you not afraid to speak against my servant Moses?"

9 And the anger of the LORD was kindled against them, and he departed; 10 and when the cloud removed from over the tent, behold, Miriam was leprous, as white as snow. And Aaron turned towards Miriam, and behold, she was leprous. 11And Aaron said to Moses, "Oh, my lord, do notᵍ punish us because we have done foolishly and have sinned. 12 Let her not be as one dead, of whom the flesh is half consumed when he comes out of his mother's womb." 13And Moses cried to the LORD, "Heal her, O God, I beseech thee." 14 But the LORD said to Moses, "If her father had but spit in her face, should she not be shamed

ᶠ That is *Graves of craving*   ᵍ Heb *lay not sin upon us*
11.34: 1 Cor 10.6.   **12.7:** Heb 3.2, 5-6.   **12.8:** Ex 33.11; Deut 34.10.

seven days? Let her be shut up outside the camp seven days, and after that she may be brought in again." 15 So Miriam was shut up outside the camp seven days; and the people did not set out on the march till Miriam was brought in again. 16After that the people set out from Hà·zē'roth, and encamped in the wilderness of Pâr'an.

13 The LORD said to Moses, 2 "Send men to spy out the land of Canaan, which I give to the people of Israel; from each tribe of their fathers shall you send a man, every one a leader among them." 3 So Moses sent them from the wilderness of Pâr'an, according to the command of the LORD, all of them men who were heads of the people of Israel. 4And these were their names: From the tribe of Reuben, Sham'mū·à the son of Zac'cūr; 5 from the tribe of Simeon, Shā'phăt the son of Hō'ri; 6 from the tribe of Judah, Caleb the son of Jĕ·phŭn'nĕh; 7 from the tribe of Is'sà·chär, I'gal the son of Joseph; 8 from the tribe of É'phrà·im, Hō·shē'à the son of Nun; 9 from the tribe of Benjamin, Pal'tī the son of Rā'phū; 10 from the tribe of Zeb'ū·lùn, Gad'di·el the son of Sō'dī; 11 from the tribe of Joseph (that is from the tribe of Mà·nas'sĕh), Gad'dī the son of Sü'sī; 12 from the tribe of Dan, Am'mi·el the son of Gĕ·mal'lī; 13 from the tribe of Ash'ĕr, Sē'thŭr the son of Michael; 14 from the tribe of Naph'tà·lī, Näh'bī the son of Voph'sī; 15 from the tribe of Gad, Gĕ·ū'el the son of Mā'chī. 16 These were the names of the men whom Moses sent to spy out the land. And Moses called Hō·shē'à the son of Nun Joshua.

17 Moses sent them to spy out the land of Canaan, and said to them, "Go up into the Negeb yonder, and go up into the hill country. 18 and see what the land is, and whether the people who dwell in it are strong or weak, whether they are few or many, 19 and whether the land that they dwell in is good or bad, and whether the cities that they dwell in are camps or strongholds, 20 and whether the land is rich or poor, and whether there is wood in it or not. Be of good courage, and bring some of the fruit of the land." Now the time was the season of the first ripe grapes.

21 So they went up and spied out the land from the wilderness of Zin to Rē'hob, near the entrance of Hā'math. 22 They went up into the Negeb, and came to Hē'brŏn; and À·hī'màn, Shē'-

shāi, and Tal'mäi, the descendants of A'nak, were there. (Hebron was built seven years before Zō'àn in Egypt.) 23And they came to the Valley of Esh'-còl, and cut down from there a branch with a single cluster of grapes, and they carried it on a pole between two of them; they brought also some pomegranates and figs. 24 That place was called the Valley of Esh'còl,*h* because of the cluster which the men of Israel cut down from there.

25 At the end of forty days they returned from spying out the land. 26And they came to Moses and Aaron and to all the congregation of the people of Israel in the wilderness of Pâr'an, at Kā'desh; they brought back word to them and to all the congregation, and showed them the fruit of the land. 27And they told him, "We came to the land to which you sent us; it flows with milk and honey, and this is its fruit. 28 Yet the people who dwell in the land are strong, and the cities are fortified and very large; and besides, we saw the descendants of A'nak there. 29 The À·mal'ĕ·kites dwell in the land of the Negeb; the Hit'tites, the Jeb'ū·sites, and the Am'ŏ·rites dwell in the hill country; and the Canaanites dwell by the sea, and along the Jordan."

30 But Caleb quieted the people before Moses, and said, "Let us go up at once, and occupy it; for we are well able to overcome it." 31 Then the men who had gone up with him said, "We are not able to go up against the people; for they are stronger than we." 32 So they brought to the people of Israel an evil report of the land which they had spied out, saying, "The land, through which we have gone, to spy it out, is a land that devours its inhabitants; and all the people that we saw in it are men of great stature. 33And there we saw the Neph'i·lim (the sons of A'nak, who come from the Nephilim); and we seemed to ourselves like grasshoppers, and so we seemed to them."

14 Then all the congregation raised a loud cry; and the people wept that night. 2And all the people of Israel murmured against Moses and Aaron; the whole congregation said to them, "Would that we had died in the land of Egypt! Or would that we had died in this wilderness! 3 Why does the LORD bring us into this land, to fall by the sword? Our wives and our little ones will become a prey; would it not be better for us to go back to Egypt?"

h That is *Cluster*

13.33: Gen 6.4.   14.3: Acts 7.39.

4 And they said to one another, "Let us choose a captain, and go back to Egypt." 5 Then Moses and Aaron fell on their faces before all the assembly of the congregation of the people of Israel. 6And Joshua the son of Nun and Caleb the son of Jė-phün′nėh, who were among those who had spied out the land, rent their clothes, 7 and said to all the congregation of the people of Israel, "The land, which we passed through to spy it out, is an exceedingly good land. 8 If the LORD delights in us, he will bring us into this land and give it to us, a land which flows with milk and honey. 9 Only, do not rebel against the LORD; and do not fear the people of the land, for they are bread for us; their protection is removed from them, and the LORD is with us; do not fear them." 10 But all the congregation said to stone them with stones.

Then the glory of the LORD appeared at the tent of meeting to all the people of Israel. 11And the LORD said to Moses, "How long will this people despise me? And how long will they not believe in me, in spite of all the signs which I have wrought among them? 12 I will strike them with the pestilence and disinherit them, and I will make of you a nation greater and mightier than they."

13 But Moses said to the LORD, "Then the Egyptians will hear of it, for thou didst bring up this people in thy might from among them, 14 and they will tell the inhabitants of this land. They have heard that thou, O LORD, art in the midst of this people; for thou, O LORD, art seen face to face, and thy cloud stands over them and thou goest before them, in a pillar of cloud by day and in a pillar of fire by night. 15 Now if thou dost kill this people as one man, then the nations who have heard thy fame will say, 16 'Because the LORD was not able to bring this people into the land which he swore to give to them, therefore he has slain them in the wilderness.' 17And now, I pray thee, let the power of the LORD be great as thou hast promised, saying, 18 'The LORD is slow to anger, and abounding in steadfast love, forgiving iniquity and transgression, but he will by no means clear the guilty, visiting the iniquity of fathers upon children, upon the third and upon the fourth generation.' 19 Pardon the iniquity of this people, I pray thee, according to the greatness

of thy steadfast love, and according as thou hast forgiven this people, from Egypt even until now."

20 Then the LORD said, "I have pardoned, according to your word; 21 but truly, as I live, and as all the earth shall be filled with the glory of the LORD, 22 none of the men who have seen my glory and my signs which I wrought in Egypt and in the wilderness, and yet have put me to the proof these ten times and have not hearkened to my voice, 23 shall see the land which I swore to give to their fathers; and none of those who despised me shall see it. 24 But my servant Caleb, because he has a different spirit and has followed me fully, I will bring into the land into which he went, and his descendants shall possess it. 25 Now, since the A·mal′é·kites and the Canaanites dwell in the valleys, turn tomorrow and set out for the wilderness by the way to the Red Sea."

26 And the LORD said to Moses and to Aaron, 27 "How long shall this wicked congregation murmur against me? I have heard the murmurings of the people of Israel, which they murmur against me. 28 Say to them, 'As I live,' says the LORD, 'what you have said in my hearing I will do to you: 29 your dead bodies shall fall in this wilderness; and of all your number, numbered from twenty years old and upward, who have murmured against me, 30 not one shall come into the land where I swore that I would make you dwell, except Caleb the son of Jė-phün′nėh and Joshua the son of Nun. 31 But your little ones, who you said would become a prey, I will bring in, and they shall know the land which you have despised. 32 But as for you, your dead bodies shall fall in this wilderness. 33And your children shall be shepherds in the wilderness forty years, and shall suffer for your faithlessness, until the last of your dead bodies lies in the wilderness. 34According to the number of the days in which you spied out the land, forty days, for every day a year, you shall bear your iniquity, forty years, and you shall know my displeasure.' 35 I, the LORD, have spoken; surely this will I do to all this wicked congregation that are gathered together against me: in this wilderness they shall come to a full end, and there they shall die."

36 And the men whom Moses sent to spy out the land, and who returned and made all the congregation to mur-

14.11-25: Ex 32.9-14, 31-35. 14.22-23: Heb 3.18. 14.29: Heb 3.17.
14.33: Acts 7.36.

mur against him by bringing up an evil report against the land, 37 the men who brought up an evil report of the land, died by plague before the LORD. 38 But Joshua the son of Nun and Caleb the son of Jé·phün′néh remained alive, of those men who went to spy out the land.

39 And Moses told these words to all the people of Israel, and the people mourned greatly. 40And they rose early in the morning, and went up to the heights of the hill country, saying, "See, we are here, we will go up to the place which the LORD has promised; for we have sinned." 41 But Moses said, "Why now are you transgressing the command of the LORD, for that will not succeed? 42 Do not go up lest you be struck down before your enemies, for the LORD is not among you. 43 For there the Á·mal′é·kites and the Canaanites are before you, and you shall fall by the sword; because you have turned back from following the LORD, the LORD will not be with you." 44 But they presumed to go up to the heights of the hill country, although neither the ark of the covenant of the LORD, nor Moses, departed out of the camp. 45 Then the Á·mal′é·kites and the Canaanites who dwell in that hill country came down, and defeated them and pursued them, even to Hôr′mâh.

15 The LORD said to Moses, 2 "Say to the people of Israel, When you come into the land you are to inhabit, which I give you, 3 and you offer to the LORD from the herd or from the flock an offering by fire or a burnt offering or a sacrifice, to fulfil a vow or as a freewill offering or at your appointed feasts, to make a pleasing odor to the LORD, 4 then he who brings his offering shall offer to the LORD a cereal offering of a tenth of an ephah of fine flour, mixed with a fourth of a hin of oil; 5 and wine for the drink offering, a fourth of a hin, you shall prepare with the burnt offering, or for the sacrifice, for each lamb. 6 Or for a ram, you shall prepare for a cereal offering two tenths of an ephah of fine flour mixed with a third of a hin of oil; 7 and for the drink offering you shall offer a third of a hin of wine, a pleasing odor to the LORD. 8And when you prepare a bull for a burnt offering, or for a sacrifice, to fulfil a vow, or for peace offerings to the LORD, 9 then one shall offer with the bull a cereal offering of three tenths of an ephah of fine

flour, mixed with half a hin of oil, 10 and you shall offer for the drink offering half a hin of wine, as an offering by fire, a pleasing odor to the LORD.

11 "Thus it shall be done for each bull or ram, or for each of the male lambs or the kids. 12According to the number that you prepare, so shall you do with every one according to their number. 13All who are native shall do these things in this way, in offering an offering by fire, a pleasing odor to the LORD. 14And if a stranger is sojourning with you, or any one is among you throughout your generations, and he wishes to offer an offering by fire, a pleasing odor to the LORD, he shall do as you do. 15 For the assembly, there shall be one statute for you and for the stranger who sojourns with you, a perpetual statute throughout your generations; as you are, so shall the sojourner be before the LORD. 16 One law and one ordinance shall be for you and for the stranger who sojourns with you."

17 The LORD said to Moses, 18 "Say to the people of Israel, When you come into the land to which I bring you 19 and when you eat of the food of the land, you shall present an offering to the LORD. 20 Of the first of your coarse meal you shall present a cake as an offering; as an offering from the threshing floor, so shall you present it. 21 Of the first of your coarse meal you shall give to the LORD an offering throughout your generations.

22 "But if you err, and do not observe all these commandments which the LORD has spoken to Moses, 23 all that the LORD has commanded you by Moses, from the day that the LORD gave commandment, and onward throughout your generations, 24 then if it was done unwittingly without the knowledge of the congregation, all the congregation shall offer one young bull for a burnt offering, a pleasing odor to the LORD, with its cereal offering and its drink offering, according to the ordinance, and one male goat for a sin offering. 25And the priest shall make atonement for all the congregation of the people of Israel, and they shall be forgiven; because it was an error, and they have brought their offering, an offering by fire to the LORD, and their sin offering before the LORD, for their error. 26And all the congregation of the people of Israel shall be forgiven, and the stranger who

15.14: Ex 12.49; Lev 24.22; Num 15.15-16, 29.   15.17-21: Ex 34.26; Lev 23.14.
15.22-26: Lev 4.13-21.

sojourns among them, because the whole population was involved in the error. 27 "If one person sins unwittingly, he shall offer a female goat a year old for a sin offering. 28And the priest shall make atonement before the LORD for the person who commits an error, when he sins unwittingly, to make atonement for him; and he shall be forgiven. 29 You shall have one law for him who does anything unwittingly, for him who is native among the people of Israel, and for the stranger who sojourns among them. 30 But the person who does anything with a high hand, whether he is native or a sojourner, reviles the LORD, and that person shall be cut off from among his people. 31 Because he has despised the word of the LORD, and has broken his commandment, that person shall be utterly cut off; his iniquity shall be upon him."

32 While the people of Israel were in the wilderness, they found a man gathering sticks on the sabbath day. 33And those who found him gathering sticks brought him to Moses and Aaron, and to all the congregation. 34 They put him in custody, because it had not been made plain what should be done to him. 35And the LORD said to Moses, "The man shall be put to death; all the congregation shall stone him with stones outside the camp." 36And all the congregation brought him outside the camp, and stoned him to death with stones, as the LORD commanded Moses.

37 The LORD said to Moses, 38 "Speak to the people of Israel, and bid them to make tassels on the corners of their garments throughout their generations, and to put upon the tassel of each corner a cord of blue; 39 and it shall be to you a tassel to look upon and remember all the commandments of the LORD, to do them, not to follow after your own heart and your own eyes, which you are inclined to go after wantonly. 40 So you shall remember and do all my commandments, and be holy to your God. 41 I am the LORD your God, who brought you out of the land of Egypt, to be your God: I am the LORD your God."

16 Now Kōʹrah the son of Izʹhär, son of Kōʹhath, son of Levi, and Dāʹthän and Aʹbiʹräm the sons of E·liʹab, and On the son of Pēʹleth, sons of Reuben, 2 took men; and they rose up before Moses, with a number of the people of Israel, two hundred and fifty leaders of the congregation,

chosen from the assembly, well-known men; 3 and they assembled themselves together against Moses and against Aaron, and said to them, "You have gone too far! For all the congregation are holy, every one of them, and the LORD is among them; why then do you exalt yourselves above the assembly of the LORD?" 4 When Moses heard it, he fell on his face; 5 and he said to Kōʹrah and all his company, "In the morning the LORD will show who is his, and who is holy, and will cause him to come near to him; him whom he will choose he will cause to come near to him. 6 Do this: take censers, Kōʹrah and all his company; 7 put fire in them and put incense upon them before the LORD tomorrow, and the man whom the LORD chooses shall be the holy one. You have gone too far, sons of Levi!" 8And Moses said to Kōʹrah, "Hear now, you sons of Levi: 9 is it too small a thing for you that the God of Israel has separated you from the congregation of Israel, to bring you near to himself, to do service in the tabernacle of the LORD, and to stand before the congregation to minister to them; 10 and that he has brought you near him, and all your brethren the sons of Levi with you? And would you seek the priesthood also? 11 Therefore it is against the LORD that you and all your company have gathered together; what is Aaron that you murmur against him?"

12 And Moses sent to call Dāʹthän and Aʹbiʹräm the sons of E·liʹab; and they said, "We will not come up. 13 Is it a small thing that you have brought us up out of a land flowing with milk and honey, to kill us in the wilderness, that you must also make yourself a prince over us? 14 Moreover you have not brought us into a land flowing with milk and honey, nor given us inheritance of fields and vineyards. Will you put out the eyes of these men? We will not come up."

15 And Moses was very angry, and said to the LORD, "Do not respect their offering. I have not taken one ass from them, and I have not harmed one of them." 16And Moses said to Kōʹrah, "Be present, you and all your company, before the LORD, you and they, and Aaron, tomorrow; 17 and let every one of you take his censer, and put incense upon it, and every one of you bring before the LORD his censer, two hundred and fifty censers; you also, and Aaron, each his censer." 18 So every man took his censer, and they

15.27-29: Lev 4.2-12.   **15.38-40:** Deut 22.12   **16.5:** 2 Tim 2.19.

put fire in them and laid incense upon them, and they stood at the entrance of the tent of meeting with Moses and Aaron. 19 Then Kō′rȧh assembled all the congregation against them at the entrance of the tent of meeting. And the glory of the LORD appeared to all the congregation.

20 And the LORD said to Moses and to Aaron, 21 "Separate yourselves from among this congregation, that I may consume them in a moment." 22And they fell on their faces, and said, "O God, the God of the spirits of all flesh, shall one man sin, and wilt thou be angry with all the congregation?" 23And the LORD said to Moses, 24 "Say to the congregation, Get away from about the dwelling of Kō′rȧh, Dā′thȧn, and Ȧ·bī′rȧm."

25 Then Moses rose and went to Dā′thȧn and Ȧ·bī′rȧm; and the elders of Israel followed him. 26And he said to the congregation, "Depart, I pray you, from the tents of these wicked men, and touch nothing of theirs, lest you be swept away with all their sins." 27 So they got away from about the dwelling of Kō′rȧh, Dā′thȧn, and Ȧ·bī′rȧm; and Dathan and Abiram came out and stood at the door of their tents, together with their wives, their sons, and their little ones. 28And Moses said, "Hereby you shall know that the LORD has sent me to do all these works, and that it has not been of my own accord. 29 If these men die the common death of all men, or if they are visited by the fate of all men, then the LORD has not sent me. 30 But if the LORD creates something new, and the ground opens its mouth, and swallows them up, with all that belongs to them, and they go down alive into Shē′ōl, then you shall know that these men have despised the LORD."

31 And as he finished speaking all these words, the ground under them split asunder; 32 and the earth opened its mouth and swallowed them up, with their households and all the men that belonged to Kō′rȧh and all their goods. 33 So they and all that belonged to them went down alive into Shē′ōl; and the earth closed over them, and they perished from the midst of the assembly. 34And all Israel that were round about them fled at their cry; for they said, "Lest the earth swallow us up!" 35And fire came forth from the LORD, and consumed the two hundred and fifty men offering the incense.

36*i* Then the LORD said to Moses, 37 "Tell El·ē·ā′zȧr the son of Aaron

the priest to take up the censers out of the blaze; then scatter the fire far and wide. For they are holy, 38 the censers of these men who have sinned at the cost of their lives; so let them be made into hammered plates as a covering for the altar, for they offered them before the LORD; therefore they are holy. Thus they shall be a sign to the people of Israel." 39 So El·ē·ā′zȧr the priest took the bronze censers, which those who were burned had offered; and they were hammered out as a covering for the altar, 40 to be a reminder to the people of Israel, so that no one who is not a priest, who is not of the descendants of Aaron, should draw near to burn incense before the LORD, lest he become as Kō′rȧh and as his company —as the LORD said to El·ē·ā′zȧr through Moses.

41 But on the morrow all the congregation of the people of Israel murmured against Moses and against Aaron, saying, "You have killed the people of the LORD." 42And when the congregation had assembled against Moses and against Aaron, they turned toward the tent of meeting; and behold, the cloud covered it, and the glory of the LORD appeared. 43And Moses and Aaron came to the front of the tent of meeting, 44 and the LORD said to Moses, 45 "Get away from the midst of this congregation, that I may consume them in a moment." And they fell on their faces. 46And Moses said to Aaron, "Take your censer, and put fire therein from off the altar, and lay incense on it, and carry it quickly to the congregation, and make atonement for them; for wrath has gone forth from the LORD, the plague has begun." 47 So Aaron took it as Moses said, and ran into the midst of the assembly; and behold, the plague had already begun among the people; and he put on the incense, and made atonement for the people. 48And he stood between the dead and the living; and the plague was stopped. 49 Now those who died by the plague were fourteen thousand seven hundred, besides those who died in the affair of Kō′rȧh. 50And Aaron returned to Moses at the entrance of the tent of meeting, when the plague was stopped.

17*j* The LORD said to Moses, 2 "Speak to the people of Israel, and get from them rods, one for each fathers' house, from all their leaders according to their fathers' houses, twelve rods. Write each man's name upon his rod, 3 and write Aaron's

i Ch 17.1 in Heb   *i* Ch 17.16 in Heb

name upon the rod of Levi. For there shall be one rod for the head of each fathers' house. [4] Then you shall deposit them in the tent of meeting before the testimony, where I meet with you. [5] And the rod of the man whom I choose shall sprout; thus I will make to cease from me the murmurings of the people of Israel, which they murmur against you." [6] Moses spoke to the people of Israel; and all their leaders gave him rods, one for each leader, according to their fathers' houses, twelve rods; and the rod of Aaron was among their rods. [7] And Moses deposited the rods before the LORD in the tent of the testimony.

[8] And on the morrow Moses went into the tent of the testimony; and behold, the rod of Aaron for the house of Levi had sprouted and put forth buds, and produced blossoms, and it bore ripe almonds. [9] Then Moses brought out all the rods from before the LORD to all the people of Israel; and they looked, and each man took his rod. [10] And the LORD said to Moses, "Put back the rod of Aaron before the testimony, to be kept as a sign for the rebels, that you may make an end of their murmurings against me, lest they die." [11] Thus did Moses; as the LORD commanded him, so he did.

[12] And the people of Israel said to Moses, "Behold, we perish, we are undone, we are all undone. [13] Every one who comes near, who comes near to the tabernacle of the LORD, shall die. Are we all to perish?"

18 So the LORD said to Aaron, "You and your sons and your fathers' house with you shall bear iniquity in connection with the sanctuary; and you and your sons with you shall bear iniquity in connection with your priesthood. [2] And with you bring your brethren also, the tribe of Levi, the tribe of your father, that they may join you, and minister to you while you and your sons with you are before the tent of the testimony. [3] They shall attend you and attend to all duties of the tent; but shall not come near to the vessels of the sanctuary or to the altar, lest they, and you, die. [4] They shall join you, and attend to the tent of meeting, for all the service of the tent; and no one else shall come near you. [5] And you shall attend to the duties of the sanctuary and the duties of the altar, that there be wrath no more upon the people of Israel. [6] And

behold, I have taken your brethren the Levites from among the people of Israel; they are a gift to you, given to the LORD, to do the service of the tent of meeting. [7] And you and your sons with you shall attend to your priesthood for all that concerns the altar and that is within the veil; and you shall serve. I give your priesthood as a gift,[k] and any one else who comes near shall be put to death."

[8] Then the LORD said to Aaron, "And behold, I have given you whatever is kept of the offerings made to me, all the consecrated things of the people of Israel; I have given them to you as a portion, and to your sons as a perpetual due. [9] This shall be yours of the most holy things, reserved from the fire; every offering of theirs, every cereal offering of theirs and every sin offering of theirs and every guilt offering of theirs, which they render to me, shall be most holy to you and to your sons. [10] In a most holy place shall you eat of it; every male may eat of it; it is holy to you. [11] This also is yours, the offering of their gift, all the wave offerings of the people of Israel; I have given them to you, and to your sons and daughters with you, as a perpetual due; every one who is clean in your house may eat of it. [12] All the best of the oil, and all the best of the wine and of the grain, the first fruits of what they give to the LORD, I give to you. [13] The first ripe fruits of all that is in their land, which they bring to the LORD, shall be yours; every one who is clean in your house may eat of it. [14] Every devoted thing in Israel shall be yours. [15] Everything that opens the womb of all flesh, whether man or beast, which they offer to the LORD, shall be yours; nevertheless the first-born of man you shall redeem, and the firstling of unclean beasts you shall redeem. [16] And their redemption price (at a month old you shall redeem them) you shall fix at five shekels in silver, according to the shekel of the sanctuary, which is twenty gerahs. [17] But the firstling of a cow, or the firstling of a sheep, or the firstling of a goat, you shall not redeem; they are holy. You shall sprinkle their blood upon the altar, and shall burn their fat as an offering by fire, a pleasing odor to the LORD; [18] but their flesh shall be yours, as the breast that is waved and as the right thigh is yours. [19] All the holy offerings which the people of Israel present to

---

k Heb *service of gift*

18.3-4, 23: Num 1.50-53; 3.5-8, 21-37; 4.1-33; 8.19.   **18.14:** Lev 27.28.
18.19: 2 Chron 13.5.

the LORD I give to you, and to your sons and daughters with you, as a perpetual due; it is a covenant of salt for ever before the LORD for you and for your offspring with you." ²⁰And the LORD said to Aaron, "You shall have no inheritance in their land, neither shall you have any portion among them; I am your portion and your inheritance among the people of Israel.

21 "To the Levites I have given every tithe in Israel for an inheritance, in return for their service which they serve, their service in the tent of meeting. ²²And henceforth the people of Israel shall not come near the tent of meeting, lest they bear sin and die. ²³ But the Levites shall do the service of the tent of meeting, and they shall bear their iniquity; it shall be a perpetual statute throughout your generations; and among the people of Israel they shall have no inheritance. ²⁴ For the tithe of the people of Israel, which they present as an offering to the LORD, I have given to the Levites for an inheritance; therefore I have said of them that they shall have no inheritance among the people of Israel."

25 And the LORD said to Moses, ²⁶ "Moreover you shall say to the Levites, 'When you take from the people of Israel the tithe which I have given you from them for your inheritance, then you shall present an offering from it to the LORD, a tithe of the tithe. ²⁷And your offering shall be reckoned to you as though it were the grain of the threshing floor, and as the fulness of the wine press. ²⁸ So shall you also present an offering to the LORD from all your tithes, which you receive from the people of Israel; and from it you shall give the LORD's offering to Aaron the priest. ²⁹ Out of all the gifts to you, you shall present every offering due to the LORD, from all the best of them, giving the hallowed part from them.' ³⁰ Therefore you shall say to them, 'When you have offered from it the best of it, then the rest shall be reckoned to the Levites as produce of the threshing floor, and as produce of the wine press; ³¹ and you may eat it in any place, you and your households; for it is your reward in return for your service in the tent of meeting. ³²And you shall bear no sin by reason of it, when you have offered the best of it. And you shall not profane the holy things of the people of Israel, lest you die.' "

19 Now the LORD said to Moses and to Aaron, ² "This is the statute of the law which the LORD has commanded: Tell the people of Israel to bring you a red heifer without defect, in which there is no blemish, and upon which a yoke has never come. ³And you shall give her to El·ē·ā′zăr the priest, and she shall be taken outside the camp and slaughtered before him; ⁴ and El·ē·ā′zăr the priest shall take some of her blood with his finger, and sprinkle some of her blood toward the front of the tent of meeting seven times. ⁵And the heifer shall be burned in his sight; her skin, her flesh, and her blood, with her dung, shall be burned; ⁶ and the priest shall take cedarwood and hyssop and scarlet stuff, and cast them into the midst of the burning of the heifer. ⁷ Then the priest shall wash his clothes and bathe his body in water, and afterwards he shall come into the camp; and the priest shall be unclean until evening. ⁸ He who burns the heifer shall wash his clothes in water and bathe his body in water, and shall be unclean until evening. ⁹And a man who is clean shall gather up the ashes of the heifer, and deposit them outside the camp in a clean place; and they shall be kept for the congregation of the people of Israel for the water for impurity, for the removal of sin. ¹⁰And he who gathers the ashes of the heifer shall wash his clothes, and be unclean until evening. And this shall be to the people of Israel, and to the stranger who sojourns among them, a perpetual statute.

11 "He who touches the dead body of any person shall be unclean seven days; ¹² he shall cleanse himself with the water on the third day and on the seventh day, and so be clean; but if he does not cleanse himself on the third day and on the seventh day, he will not become clean. ¹³ Whoever touches a dead person, the body of any man who has died, and does not cleanse himself, defiles the tabernacle of the LORD, and that person shall be cut off from Israel; because the water for impurity was not thrown upon him, he shall be unclean; his uncleanness is still on him.

14 "This is the law when a man dies in a tent: every one who comes into the tent, and every one who is in the tent, shall be unclean seven days. ¹⁵And every open vessel, which has no cover fastened upon it, is unclean. ¹⁶ Whoever in the open field touches one who is slain with a sword, or a dead body, or a bone of a man, or a grave, shall be unclean seven days. ¹⁷ For the unclean they shall take some

ashes of the burnt sin offering, and running water shall be added in a vessel; [18] then a clean person shall take hyssop, and dip it in the water, and sprinkle it upon the tent, and upon all the furnishings, and upon the persons who were there, and upon him who touched the bone, or the slain, or the dead, or the grave; [19] and the clean person shall sprinkle upon the unclean on the third day and on the seventh day; thus on the seventh day he shall cleanse him, and he shall wash his clothes and bathe himself in water, and at evening he shall be clean.

20 "But the man who is unclean and does not cleanse himself, that person shall be cut off from the midst of the assembly, since he has defiled the sanctuary of the LORD; because the water for impurity has not been thrown upon him, he is unclean. [21]And it shall be a perpetual statute for them. He who sprinkles the water for impurity shall wash his clothes; and he who touches the water for impurity shall be unclean until evening. [22]And whatever the unclean person touches shall be unclean; and any one who touches it shall be unclean until evening."

20 And the people of Israel, the whole congregation, came into the wilderness of Zin in the first month, and the people stayed in Kā′desh; and Miriam died there, and was buried there.

2 Now there was no water for the congregation; and they assembled themselves together against Moses and against Aaron. [3]And the people contended with Moses, and said, "Would that we had died when our brethren died before the LORD! [4] Why have you brought the assembly of the LORD into this wilderness, that we should die here, both we and our cattle? [5]And why have you made us come up out of Egypt, to bring us to this evil place? It is no place for grain, or figs, or vines, or pomegranates; and there is no water to drink." [6] Then Moses and Aaron went from the presence of the assembly to the door of the tent of meeting, and fell on their faces. And the glory of the LORD appeared to them, [7] and the LORD said to Moses, [8] "Take the rod, and assemble the congregation, you and Aaron your brother, and tell the rock before their eyes to yield its water; so you shall bring water out of the rock for them; so you shall give drink to the congrega-

tion and their cattle." [9]And Moses took the rod from before the LORD, as he commanded him.

10 And Moses and Aaron gathered the assembly together before the rock, and he said to them, "Hear now, you rebels; shall we bring forth water for you out of this rock?" [11]And Moses lifted up his hand and struck the rock with his rod twice; and water came forth abundantly, and the congregation drank, and their cattle. [12]And the LORD said to Moses and Aaron, "Because you did not believe in me, to sanctify me in the eyes of the people of Israel, therefore you shall not bring this assembly into the land which I have given them." [13] These are the waters of Mer′i·bah,*l* where the people of Israel contended with the LORD, and he showed himself holy among them.

14 Moses sent messengers from Kā′desh to the king of E′dom, "Thus says your brother Israel: You know all the adversity that has befallen us: [15] how our fathers went down to Egypt, and we dwelt in Egypt a long time; and the Egyptians dealt harshly with us and our fathers; [16] and when we cried to the LORD, he heard our voice, and sent an angel and brought us forth out of Egypt; and here we are in Kā′desh, a city on the edge of your territory. [17] Now let us pass through your land. We will not pass through field or vineyard, neither will we drink water from a well; we will go along the King's Highway, we will not turn aside to the right hand or to the left, until we have passed through your territory." [18] But E′dom said to him, "You shall not pass through, lest I come out with the sword against you." [19]And the people of Israel said to him, "We will go up by the highway; and if we drink of your water, I and my cattle, then I will pay for it; let me only pass through on foot, nothing more." [20] But he said, "You shall not pass through." And E′dom came out against them with many men, and with a strong force. [21] Thus E′dom refused to give Israel passage through his territory; so Israel turned away from him.

22 And they journeyed from Kā′-desh, and the people of Israel, the whole congregation, came to Mount Hôr. [23]And the LORD said to Moses and Aaron at Mount Hôr, on the border of the land of E′dom, [24] "Aaron shall be gathered to his people; for he shall not enter the land which I have

l That is *Contention*
20.2-13: Ex 17.2-7.

given to the people of Israel, because you rebelled against my command at the waters of Mer′ĭ·bȧh. 25 Take Aaron and El·ē·ā′zȧr his son, and bring them up to Mount Hôr; 26 and strip Aaron of his garments, and put them upon El·ē·ā′zȧr his son; and Aaron shall be gathered to his people, and shall die there." 27 Moses did as the LORD commanded; and they went up Mount Hôr in the sight of all the congregation. 28And Moses stripped Aaron of his garments, and put them upon El·ē·ā′zȧr his son; and Aaron died there on the top of the mountain. Then Moses and Eleazar came down from the mountain. 29And when all the congregation saw that Aaron was dead, all the house of Israel wept for Aaron thirty days.

21 When the Canaanite, the king of Ar′ad, who dwelt in the Negeb, heard that Israel was coming by the way of Ath′ȧ·rim, he fought against Israel, and took some of them captive. 2And Israel vowed a vow to the LORD, and said, "If thou wilt indeed give this people into my hand, then I will utterly destroy their cities." 3And the LORD hearkened to the voice of Israel, and gave over the Canaanites; and they utterly destroyed them and their cities; so the name of the place was called Hôr′mȧh.ᵐ

4 From Mount Hôr they set out by the way to the Red Sea, to go around the land of E′dŏm; and the people became impatient on the way. 5And the people spoke against God and against Moses, "Why have you brought us up out of Egypt to die in the wilderness? For there is no food and no water, and we loathe this worthless food." 6 Then the LORD sent fiery serpents among the people, and they bit the people, so that many people of Israel died. 7And the people came to Moses, and said, "We have sinned, for we have spoken against the LORD and against you; pray to the LORD, that he take away the serpents from us." So Moses prayed for the people. 8And the LORD said to Moses, "Make a fiery serpent, and set it on a pole; and every one who is bitten, when he sees it, shall live." 9 So Moses made a bronze serpent, and set it on a pole; and if a serpent bit any man, he would look at the bronze serpent and live.

10 And the people of Israel set out, and encamped in Ō′both. 11And they set out from Ō′both, and encamped at

I′ye-ab′ȧ·rim, in the wilderness which is opposite Mō′ab, toward the sunrise. 12 From there they set out, and encamped in the Valley of Zē′red. 13 From there they set out, and encamped on the other side of the Är′non, which is in the wilderness, that extends from the boundary of the Am′ȯ·rītes; for the Arnon is the boundary of Mō′ab, between Moab and the Amorites. 14 Wherefore it is said in the Book of the Wars of the LORD,

"Wä′heb in Sü′phȧh,
    and the valleys of the Är′non,
15 and the slope of the valleys
    that extends to the seat of Är,
    and leans to the border of Mō′ab."

16 And from there they continued to Beer;ⁿ that is the well of which the LORD said to Moses, "Gather the people together, and I will give them water." 17 Then Israel sang this song:

"Spring up, O well!—Sing to it!—
18 the well which the princes dug,
    which the nobles of the people
        delved,
    with the scepter and with their
        staves."

And from the wilderness they went on to Mat′tȧ·nȧh, 19 and from Mat′tȧ·nȧh to Nȧ·hal′ĭ·el, and from Nahaliel to Bā′moth, 20 and from Bā′moth to the valley lying in the region of Mō′ab by the top of Pĭs′gȧh which looks down upon the desert.ᵒ

21 Then Israel sent messengers to Sī′hon king of the Am′ȯ·rītes, saying, 22 "Let me pass through your land; we will not turn aside into field or vineyard; we will not drink the water of a well; we will go by the King's Highway, until we have passed through your territory." 23 But Sī′hon would not allow Israel to pass through his territory. He gathered all his men together, and went out against Israel to the wilderness, and came to Jā′haz, and fought against Israel. 24And Israel slew him with the edge of the sword, and took possession of his land from the Är′non to the Jab′bȯk, as far as to the Am′mȯ·nītes; for Jā′zĕr was the boundary of the Ammonites.ᵖ 25And Israel took all these cities, and Israel settled in all the cities of the Am′ȯ·rītes, in Hesh′bȯn, and in all its villages. 26 For Hesh′bȯn was the city of Sī′hon the king of the Am′ȯ·rītes, who had fought against the former king of Mō′ab and taken all his land out of his hand, as far as the Är′non. 27 Therefore the ballad singers say,

ᵐ Heb *Destruction*   ⁿ That is *Well*   ᵒ Or *Jeshimon*
ᵖ Gk: Heb *the boundary of the Ammonites was strong*
20.25-29: Num 33.38-39.   21.1: Num 33.40.   21.21-30: Deut 2.26-37.

"Come to Hesh'bŏn, let it be
    built,
    let the city of Sī'hŏn be estab-
      lished.
28 For fire went forth from Hesh'bŏn,
    flame from the city of Sī'hŏn.
    It devoured Är of Mō'ab,
      the lords of the heights of the
      Är'non.
29 Woe to you, O Mō'ab!
    You are undone, O people of
      Chē'mosh!
    He has made his sons fugitives,
      and his daughters captives,
    to an Am'ŏ·rīte king, Sī'hŏn.
30 So their posterity perished from
    Hesh'bŏn,*q* as far as Dī'bŏn,
    and we laid waste until fire spread
    to Med'e·bà."*r*
31 Thus Israel dwelt in the land of
the Am'ŏ·rītes. 32 And Moses sent to
spy out Jā'zēr; and they took its villages, and dispossessed the Am'ŏ·rītes
that were there. 33 Then they turned
and went up by the way to Bā'shăn;
and Og the king of Bashan came out
against them, he and all his people, to
battle at Ed'rē-ī. 34 But the LORD said
to Moses, "Do not fear him; for I have
given him into your hand, and all his
people, and his land; and you shall do
to him as you did to Sī'hŏn king of the
Am'ŏ·rītes, who dwelt at Hesh'bŏn."
35 So they slew him, and his sons, and
all his people, until there was not one
survivor left to him; and they possessed
his land.

22 Then the people of Israel set
    out, and encamped in the plains
of Mō'ab beyond the Jordan at
Jericho. 2 And Bā'lak the son of Zip'pŏr
saw all that Israel had done to the
Am'ŏ·rītes. 3 And Mō'ab was in great
dread of the people, because they were
many; Moab was overcome with fear
of the people of Israel. 4 And Mō'ab
said to the elders of Mid'i·àn, "This
horde will now lick up all that is
round about us, as the ox licks up the
grass of the field." So Bā'lak the son
of Zip'pŏr, who was king of Mō'ab at
that time, 5 sent messengers to Balaam the son of Bē'ŏr at Pē'thŏr, which
is near the River, in the land of Am'aw
to call him, saying, "Behold, a people
has come out of Egypt; they cover the
face of the earth, and they are dwelling
opposite me. 6 Come now, curse this
people for me, since they are too
mighty for me; perhaps I shall be able
to defeat them and drive them from
the land; for I know that he whom you

bless is blessed, and he whom you
curse is cursed."
7 So the elders of Mō'ab and the
elders of Mid'i·àn departed with the
fees for divination in their hand; and
they came to Balaam, and gave him
Bā'lak's message. 8 And he said to
them, "Lodge here this night, and I
will bring back word to you, as the
LORD speaks to me"; so the princes of
Mō'ab stayed with Balaam. 9 And God
came to Balaam and said, "Who are
these men with you?" 10 And Balaam
said to God, "Bā'lak the son of Zip'-
pŏr, king of Mō'ab, has sent to me,
saying, 11 'Behold, a people has come
out of Egypt, and it covers the face of
the earth; now come, curse them for
me; perhaps I shall be able to fight
against them and drive them out.'"
12 God said to Balaam, "You shall not
go with them; you shall not curse the
people, for they are blessed." 13 So
Balaam rose in the morning, and said
to the princes of Bā'lak, "Go to your
own land; for the LORD has refused to
let me go with you." 14 So the princes
of Mō'ab rose and went to Bā'lak, and
said, "Balaam refuses to come with
us."
15 Once again Bā'lak sent princes,
more in number and more honorable
than they. 16 And they came to Balaam
and said to him, "Thus says Bā'lak the
son of Zip'pŏr: 'Let nothing hinder
you from coming to me; 17 for I will
surely do you great honor, and whatever you say to me I will do; come,
curse this people for me.'" 18 But
Balaam answered and said to the
servants of Bā'lak, "Though Balak
were to give me his house full of silver
and gold, I could not go beyond the
command of the LORD my God, to do
less or more. 19 Pray, now, tarry here
this night also, that I may know what
more the LORD will say to me." 20 And
God came to Balaam at night and said
to him, "If the men have come to call
you, rise, go with them; but only what
I bid you, that shall you do."
21 So Balaam rose in the morning,
and saddled his ass, and went with the
princes of Mō'ab. 22 But God's anger
was kindled because he went; and the
angel of the LORD took his stand in
the way as his adversary. Now he was
riding on the ass, and his two servants
were with him. 23 And the ass saw the
angel of the LORD standing in the
road, with a drawn sword in his hand;
and the ass turned aside out of the

q Gk: Heb *we have shot at them. Heshbon has perished*
r Compare Sam and Gk: Heb *we have laid waste to Nophah which to Medebah*
21.33-35: Deut 3.1-7.   **22.1:** Num 33.48.

road, and went into the field; and Balaam struck the ass, to turn her into the road. 24 Then the angel of the LORD stood in a narrow path between the vineyards, with a wall on either side. 25And when the ass saw the angel of the LORD, she pushed against the wall, and pressed Balaam's foot against the wall; so he struck her again. 26 Then the angel of the LORD went ahead, and stood in a narrow place, where there was no way to turn either to the right or to the left. 27 When the ass saw the angel of the LORD, she lay down under Balaam; and Balaam's anger was kindled, and he struck the ass with his staff. 28 Then the LORD opened the mouth of the ass, and she said to Balaam, "What have I done to you, that you have struck me these three times?" 29And Balaam said to the ass, "Because you have made sport of me. I wish I had a sword in my hand, for then I would kill you." 30The ass said to Balaam, "Am I not your ass, upon which you have ridden all your life long to this day? Was I ever accustomed to do so to you?" And he said, "No."

31 Then the LORD opened the eyes of Balaam, and he saw the angel of the LORD standing in the way, with his drawn sword in his hand; and he bowed his head, and fell on his face. 32And the angel of the LORD said to him, "Why have you struck your ass these three times? Behold, I have come forth to withstand you, because your way is perverse before me; 33 and the ass saw me, and turned aside before me these three times. If she had not turned aside from me, surely just now I would have slain you and let her live." 34 Then Balaam said to the angel of the LORD, "I have sinned, for I did not know that thou didst stand in the road against me. Now therefore, if it is evil in thy sight, I will go back again." 35And the angel of the LORD said to Balaam, "Go with the men; but only the word which I bid you, that shall you speak." So Balaam went on with the princes of Bā′lak.

36 When Bā′lak heard that Balaam had come, he went out to meet him at the city of Mō′ab, on the boundary formed by the Är′non, at the extremity of the boundary. 37And Bā′lak said to Balaam, "Did I not send to you to call you? Why did you not come to me? Am I not able to honor you?" 38 Balaam said to Bā′lak, "Lo, I have come to you! Have I now any power at all to speak anything? The word that God

puts in my mouth, that must I speak." 39 Then Balaam went with Bā′lak, and they came to Kĭr′i·ath-hū′zŏth. 40And Bā′lak sacrificed oxen and sheep, and sent to Balaam and to the princes who were with him.

41 And on the morrow Bā′lak took Balaam and brought him up to Bā′-mŏth-bā′ăl; and from there he saw the nearest of the people.

23

1And Balaam said to Bā′lak, "Build for me here seven altars, and provide for me here seven bulls and seven rams." 2 Bā′lak did as Balaam had said; and Balak and Balaam offered on each altar a bull and a ram. 3And Balaam said to Bā′lak, "Stand beside your burnt offering, and I will go; perhaps the LORD will come to meet me; and whatever he shows me I will tell you." And he went to a bare height. 4And God met Balaam; and Balaam said to him, "I have prepared the seven altars, and I have offered upon each altar a bull and a ram." 5And the LORD put a word in Balaam's mouth, and said, "Return to Bā′lak, and thus you shall speak." 6And he returned to him, and lo, he and all the princes of Mō′ab were standing beside his burnt offering. 7And Balaam took up his discourse, and said,

"From Âr′am Bā′lak has brought me,
   the king of Mō′ab from the eastern mountains:
'Come, curse Jacob for me,
   and come, denounce Israel!'
8 How can I curse whom God has not cursed?
   How can I denounce whom the LORD has not denounced?
9 For from the top of the mountains I see him,
   from the hills I behold him;
lo, a people dwelling alone,
   and not reckoning itself among the nations!
10 Who can count the dust of Jacob,
   or number the fourth part*s* of Israel?
Let me die the death of the righteous,
   and let my end be like his!"

11 And Bā′lak said to Balaam, "What have you done to me? I took you to curse my enemies, and behold, you have done nothing but bless them." 12And he answered, "Must I not take heed to speak what the LORD puts in my mouth?"

13 And Bā′lak said to him, "Come with me to another place, from which you may see them; you shall see only the nearest of them, and shall not see them all; then curse them for me from

s Or *dust clouds*

there." ¹⁴And he took him to the field of Zō′phim, to the top of Piś′gàh, and built seven altars, and offered a bull and a ram on each altar. ¹⁵ Balaam said to Bā′lak, "Stand here beside your burnt offering, while I meet the LORD yonder." ¹⁶And the LORD met Balaam and put a word in his mouth, and said, "Return to Bā′lak, and thus shall you speak." ¹⁷And he came to him, and, lo, he was standing beside his burnt offering, and the princes of Mō′ab with him. And Bā′lak said to him, "What has the LORD spoken?" ¹⁸And Balaam took up his discourse, and said,

"Rise, Bā′lak, and hear;
　　hearken to me, O son of Zip′pôr:
¹⁹ God is not man, that he should lie,
　　or a son of man, that he should
　　　repent.
Has he said, and will he not do it?
　　Or has he spoken, and will he not
　　　fulfil it?
²⁰ Behold, I received a command to
　　bless:
　　he has blessed, and I cannot re-
　　　voke it.
²¹ He has not beheld misfortune in
　　Jacob;
　　nor has he seen trouble in Israel.
The LORD their God is with them,
　　and the shout of a king is among
　　　them.
²² God brings them out of Egypt;
　　they have as it were the horns of
　　　the wild ox.
²³ For there is no enchantment against
　　Jacob,
　　no divination against Israel;
now it shall be said of Jacob and
　　Israel,
　　'What has God wrought!'
²⁴ Behold, a people! As a lioness it
　　rises up
and as a lion it lifts itself;
　　it does not lie down till it devours
　　　the prey,
　　and drinks the blood of the slain."

25 And Bā′lak said to Balaam, "Neither curse them at all, nor bless them at all." ²⁶ But Balaam answered Bā′lak, "Did I not tell you, 'All that the LORD says, that I must do'?" ²⁷And Bā′lak said to Balaam, "Come now, I will take you to another place; perhaps it will please God that you may curse them for me from there." ²⁸ So Bā′lak took Balaam to the top of Pē′ôr, that overlooks the desert.*ⁱ* ²⁹And Balaam said to Bā′lak, "Build for me here seven altars, and provide for me here seven bulls and seven rams."

³⁰And Bā′lak did as Balaam had said, and offered a bull and a ram on each altar.

24 When Balaam saw that it pleased the LORD to bless Israel, he did not go, as at other times, to look for omens, but set his face toward the wilderness. ²And Balaam lifted up his eyes, and saw Israel encamping tribe by tribe. And the Spirit of God came upon him, ³ and he took up his discourse, and said,

"The oracle of Balaam the son of
　　Bē′ôr,
　　the oracle of the man whose eye
　　　is opened,*ᵘ*
⁴ the oracle of him who hears the
　　words of God,
　　who sees the vision of the Al-
　　　mighty,
　　falling down, but having his eyes
　　　uncovered:
⁵ how fair are your tents, O Jacob,
　　your encampments, O Israel!
⁶ Like valleys that stretch afar,
　　like gardens beside a river,
　　like aloes that the LORD has planted,
　　like cedar trees beside the waters.
⁷ Water shall flow from his buckets,
　　and his seed shall be in many
　　　waters,
his king shall be higher than Ā′gag,
　　and his kingdom shall be exalted.
⁸ God brings him out of Egypt;
　　he has as it were the horns of the
　　　wild ox,
he shall eat up the nations his ad-
　　versaries,
and shall break their bones in
　　pieces,
　　and pierce them through with his
　　　arrows.
⁹ He couched, he lay down like a lion,
　　and like a lioness; who will rouse
　　　him up?
Blessed be every one who blesses
　　you,
　　and cursed be every one who
　　　curses you."

10 And Bā′lak's anger was kindled against Balaam, and he struck his hands together; and Balak said to Balaam, "I called you to curse my enemies, and behold, you have blessed them these three times. ¹¹ Therefore now flee to your place; I said, 'I will certainly honor you,' but the LORD has held you back from honor." ¹²And Balaam said to Bā′lak, "Did I not tell your messengers whom you sent to me, ¹³ 'If Bā′lak should give me his house full of silver and gold, I would not be able to go beyond the word of the

t Or *Jeshimon*　　*u* Or *closed* or *perfect*
24.9: Gen 49.9.

LORD, to do either good or bad of my own will; what the LORD speaks, that will I speak'? 14And now, behold, I am going to my people; come, I will let you know what this people will do to your people in the latter days." 15And he took up his discourse, and said,

"The oracle of Balaam the son of Bē'ôr,
    the oracle of the man whose eye is opened,[y]
16 the oracle of him who hears the words of God,
    and knows the knowledge of the Most High,
    who sees the vision of the Almighty, falling down, but having his eyes uncovered:
17 I see him, but not now;
    I behold him, but not nigh:
a star shall come forth out of Jacob,
    and a scepter shall rise out of Israel;
it shall crush the forehead[w] of Mō'ab,
    and break down all the sons of Sheth.
18 Ē'dôm shall be dispossessed,
    Sē'ir also, his enemies, shall be dispossessed,
    while Israel does valiantly.
19 By Jacob shall dominion be exercised,
    and the survivors of cities be destroyed!"

20 Then he looked on Am'ā.lek, and took up his discourse, and said,

"Amalek was the first of the nations,
    but in the end he shall come to destruction."

21 And he looked on the Ken'ite, and took up his discourse, and said,

"Enduring is your dwelling place,
    and your nest is set in the rock;
22 nevertheless Kāin shall be wasted.
    How long shall As'shür take you away captive?"

23 And he took up his discourse, and said,

"Alas, who shall live when God does this?
24 But ships shall come from Kit'-tim and shall afflict As'shür and Ē'bèr;
    and he also shall come to destruction."

25 Then Balaam rose, and went back to his place; and Bā'lak also went his way.

25 While Israel dwelt in Shit'tim the people began to play the harlot with the daughters of Mō'ab. 2 These invited the people to the sacrifices of their gods, and the people ate,

and bowed down to their gods. 3 So Israel yoked himself to Bā'al of Pē'ôr. And the anger of the LORD was kindled against Israel; 4 and the LORD said to Moses, "Take all the chiefs of the people, and hang them in the sun before the LORD, that the fierce anger of the LORD may turn away from Israel." 5And Moses said to the judges of Israel, "Every one of you slay his men who have yoked themselves to Bā'al of Pē'ôr."

6 And behold, one of the people of Israel came and brought a Mid'i.à.nite woman to his family, in the sight of Moses and in the sight of the whole congregation of the people of Israel, while they were weeping at the door of the tent of meeting. 7 When Phin'ē.hàs the son of El.ē.ā'zàr, son of Aaron the priest, saw it, he rose and left the congregation, and took a spear in his hand 8 and went after the man of Israel into the inner room, and pierced both of them, the man of Israel and the woman, through her body. Thus the plague was stayed from the people of Israel. 9 Nevertheless those that died by the plague were twenty-four thousand.

10 And the LORD said to Moses, 11 "Phin'ē.hàs the son of El.ē.ā'zàr, son of Aaron the priest, has turned back my wrath from the people of Israel, in that he was jealous with my jealousy among them, so that I did not consume the people of Israel in my jealousy. 12 Therefore say, 'Behold, I give to him my covenant of peace; 13 and it shall be to him, and to his descendants after him, the covenant of a perpetual priesthood, because he was jealous for his God, and made atonement for the people of Israel.'"

14 The name of the slain man of Israel, who was slain with the Mid'i.à.nite woman, was Zim'rī the son of Sā'lü, head of a fathers' house belonging to the Simeonites. 15And the name of the Mid'i.à.nite woman who was slain was Coz'bī the daughter of Zür, who was the head of the people of a fathers' house in Mid'i.àn.

16 And the LORD said to Moses, 17 "Harass the Mid'i.à.nites, and smite them; 18 for they have harassed you with their wiles, with which they beguiled you in the matter of Pē'ôr, and in the matter of Coz'bī, the daughter of the prince of Mid'i.àn, their sister, who was slain on the day of the plague on account of Pē'ôr."

26 After the plague the LORD said to Moses and to El.ē.ā'zàr the

[y] Or *closed* or *perfect*   [w] Heb *corners* (of the head)

son of Aaron, the priest, 2 "Take a census of all the congregation of the people of Israel, from twenty years old and upward, by their fathers' houses, all in Israel who are able to go forth to war." 3And Moses and El-ē-ā'zär the priest spoke with them in the plains of Mō'ab by the Jordan at Jericho, saying, 4 "Take a census of the people,ˣ from twenty years old and upward," as the LORD commanded Moses. The people of Israel, who came forth out of the land of Egypt, were:

5 Reuben, the first-born of Israel; the sons of Reuben: of Hā'noch, the family of the Hā'nō-chites; of Pal'lü, the family of the Pal'lü-ites; 6 of Hez'-rŏn, the family of the Hez'rō-nites; of Cär'mi, the family of the Cär'mites. 7 These are the families of the Reubenites; and their number was forty-three thousand seven hundred and thirty. 8And the sons of Pal'lü: E-lī'ab. 9 The sons of E-lī'ab: Nem'ū-el, Dā'than, and Ā-bī'ram. These are the Dathan and Abiram, chosen from the congregation, who contended against Moses and Aaron in the company of Kō'rah, when they contended against the LORD, 10 and the earth opened its mouth and swallowed them up together with Kō'rah, when that company died, when the fire devoured two hundred and fifty men; and they became a warning. 11 Notwithstanding, the sons of Kō'rah did not die.

12 The sons of Simeon according to their families: of Nem'ū-el, the family of the Nem'ū-ė-lites; of Jā'min, the family of the Jā'mi-nites; of Jā'chin, the family of the Jā'chi-nites; 13 of Zē'rah, the family of the Zē'rā-hites; of Shā'ul, the family of the Shā'u-lites. 14 These are the families of the Simeonites, twenty-two thousand two hundred.

15 The sons of Gad according to their families: of Zē'phon, the family of the Zē'phō-nites; of Hag'gi, the family of the Hag'gites; of Shū'ni, the family of the Shū'nites; 16 of Oz'ni, the family of the Oz'nites; of E'ri, the family of the E'rites; 17 of Är'ŏd, the family of the Är'ō-dites; of Ā-rē'li, the family of the Ā-rē'lites. 18 These are the families of the sons of Gad according to their number, forty thousand five hundred.

19 The sons of Judah were Ẽr and Ō'nän; and Er and Onan died in the land of Canaan. 20And the sons of Judah according to their families were: of Shē'lah, the family of the Shē-lā'-

nites; of Per'ez, the family of the Per'ė-zites; of Zē'rah, the family of the Zē'rā-hites. 21And the sons of Per'ez were: of Hez'rŏn, the family of the Hez'rō-nites; of Hā'mŭl, the family of the Hā'mŭ-lites. 22 These are the families of Judah according to their number, seventy-six thousand five hundred.

23 The sons of Is'sà-chär according to their families: of Tō'là, the family of the Tō'là-ites; of Pū'vàh, the family of the Pū'nites; 24 of Jash'ŭb, the family of the Jash'ŭ-bites; of Shim'rŏn, the family of the Shim'rō-nites. 25 These are the families of Is'sà-chär according to their number, sixty-four thousand three hundred.

26 The sons of Zeb'ū-lŭn, according to their families: of Ser'ėd, the family of the Ser'ė-dites; of E'lon, the family of the E'lō-nites; of Jäh'lē-ėl, the family of the Jäh'lē-ė-lites. 27 These are the families of the Ze-bū'lŭ-nites according to their number, sixty thousand five hundred.

28 The sons of Joseph according to their families: Mà-nas'sëh and E'phrà-im. 29 The sons of Mà-nas'sëh: of Mā'chir, the family of the Mā'chi-rites; and Machir was the father of Gilead; of Gilead, the family of the Gil'ē-à-dites. 30 These are the sons of Gilead: of I-ēz'ẽr, the family of the I-ēz'ė-rites; of Hē'lek, the family of the Hē'lė-kites; 31 and of As'ri-el, the family of the As'ri-ė-lites; and of Shē'chem, the family of the Shē'chė-mites; 32 and of She-mī'dà, the family of the She-mī'dà-ites; and of Hē'pher, the family of the Hē'phė-rites. 33 Now Ze-loph'ė-had the son of Hē'pher had no sons, but daughters: and the names of the daughters of Zelophehad were Mäh'-làh, Noah, Hog'làh, Mil'càh, and Tir'zàh. 34 These are the families of Mà-nas'sëh; and their number was fifty-two thousand seven hundred.

35 These are the sons of E'phrà-im according to their families: of Shū'thė-làh, the family of the Shū'thė-lā'hites; of Bē'chër, the family of the Bē'chė-rites; of Tā'han, the family of the Tā'hà-nites. 36And these are the sons of Shū'thė-làh: of E'ràn, the family of the E'rà-nites. 37 These are the families of the sons of E'phrà-im according to their number, thirty-two thousand five hundred. These are the sons of Joseph according to their families.

38 The sons of Benjamin according to their families: of Bē'là, the family of the Bē'là-ites; of Ash'bël, the family

ˣ Supplying *take a census of the people* Compare verse 2
26.5-51: Num 1.22-46.

of the Ash´bē·lites; of Ā·hi´rȧm, the family of the Ā·hi´rȧ·mites; [39] of She-phü´phȧm, the family of the Shü´phȧ-mites; of Hū´pham, the family of the Hū´phȧ·mites. [40]And the sons of Bē´la were Ard and Nā´ȧ·mȧn: of Ard, the family of the Ȧr´dites; of Naaman, the family of the Nā´ȧ·mites. [41] These are the sons of Benjamin according to their families; and their number was forty-five thousand six hundred.

[42] These are the sons of Dan ac-cording to their families: of Shü´hȧm, the family of the Shü´hȧ·mites. These are the families of Dan according to their families. [43]All the families of the Shü´hȧ·mites, according to their num-ber, were sixty-four thousand four hundred.

[44] The sons of Ash´ẽr according to their families: of Im´nah, the family of the Im´nites; of Ish´vī, the family of the Ish´vites; of Bē·rī´ah, the family of the Bē·rī´ites. [45] Of the sons of Bē·rī´ah: of Hē´bẽr, the family of the Hē´bẽ·rites; of Mal´chi-el, the family of the Mal´-chi-ē·lites. [46]And the name of the daughter of Ash´ẽr was Sẽr´ah. [47] These are the families of the sons of Ash´ẽr according to their number, fifty-three thousand four hundred.

[48] The sons of Naph´tȧ·li according to their families: of Jäh´rē·el, the family of the Jäh´rē·ē·lites; of Gū´nī, the family of the Gū´nites; [49] of Jē´zẽr, the family of the Jē´zė·rites; of Shil´lēm, the family of the Shil´lē·mites. [50] These are the families of Naph´tȧ·li according to their families; and their number was forty-five thousand four hundred.

[51] This was the number of the peo-ple of Israel, six hundred and one thousand seven hundred and thirty.

[52] The LORD said to Moses: [53] "To these the land shall be divided for inheritance according to the number of names. [54] To a large tribe you shall give a large inheritance, and to a small tribe you shall give a small inheritance; every tribe shall be given its inherit-ance according to its numbers. [55] But the land shall be divided by lot; according to the names of the tribes of their fathers they shall inherit. [56] Their inheritance shall be divided according to lot between the larger and the smaller."

[57] These are the Levites as num-bered according to their families: of Gẽr´shòn, the family of the Gẽr´shò-nites; of Kō´hath, the family of the Kō´hȧ·thites; of Mė·rär´ī, the family of the Mė·rär´ites. [58] These are the fami-lies of Levi: the family of the Lib´-

nites, the family of the Hē´brò·nites, the family of the Mäh´lites, the family of the Mū´shites, the family of the Kō´rȧ·hites. And Kō´hath was the father of Am´ram. [59] The name of Am´ram's wife was Joch´ė·bed the daughter of Levi, who was born to Levi in Egypt; and she bore to Amram Aaron and Moses and Miriam their sister. [60]And to Aaron were born Nā´-dab, Ȧ·bī´hū, El·ē·ā´zȧr and Ith´ȧ·mär. [61] But Nā´dab and Ȧ·bī´hū died when they offered unholy fire before the LORD. [62]And those numbered of them were twenty-three thousand, every male from a month old and upward; for they were not numbered among the people of Israel, because there was no inheritance given to them among the people of Israel.

[63] These were those numbered by Moses and El·ē·ā´zȧr the priest, who numbered the people of Israel in the plains of Mō´ab by the Jordan at Jericho. [64] But among these there was not a man of those numbered by Moses and Aaron the priest, who had num-bered the people of Israel in the wil-derness of Sinai. [65] For the LORD had said of them, "They shall die in the wilderness." There was not left a man of them, except Caleb the son of Jė·phün´neh and Joshua the son of Nun.

27 Then drew near the daughters of Ze·loph´ė·had the son of Hē´-phẽr, son of Gilead, son of Mā´chir, son of Mȧ·nas´sēh, from the families of Manasseh the son of Joseph. The names of his daughters were: Mäh´lah, Noah, Hog´lah, Mil´cȧh, and Tīr´zȧh. [2]And they stood before Moses, and before El·ē·ā´zȧr the priest, and before the leaders and all the congregation, at the door of the tent of meeting, say-ing, [3] "Our father died in the wilder-ness; he was not among the company of those who gathered themselves to-gether against the LORD in the com-pany of Kō´rȧh, but died for his own sin; and he had no sons. [4] Why should the name of our father be taken away from his family, because he had no son? Give to us a possession among our father's brethren."

[5] Moses brought their case before the LORD. [6]And the LORD said to Moses, [7] "The daughters of Ze·loph´-ė·had are right; you shall give them possession of an inheritance among their father's brethren and cause the inheritance of their father to pass to them. [8]And you shall say to the people of Israel, 'If a man dies, and has no son, then you shall cause his inherit-

26.57-62: Num 1.47-49.   **26.64-65:** Num 14.26-35.   **27.1-11:** Num 36.1-12.

ance to pass to his daughter. 9And if he has no daughter, then you shall give his inheritance to his brothers. 10And if he has no brothers, then you shall give his inheritance to his father's brothers. 11And if his father has no brothers, then you shall give his inheritance to his kinsman that is next to him of his family, and he shall possess it. And it shall be to the people of Israel a statute and ordinance, as the LORD commanded Moses.'"

12 The LORD said to Moses, "Go up into this mountain of Ab′a·rim, and see the land which I have given to the people of Israel. 13And when you have seen it, you also shall be gathered to your people, as your brother Aaron was gathered, 14 because you rebelled against my word in the wilderness of Zin during the strife of the congregation, to sanctify me at the waters before their eyes." (These are the waters of Mer′i·bah of Kā′desh in the wilderness of Zin.) 15 Moses said to the LORD, 16 "Let the LORD, the God of the spirits of all flesh, appoint a man over the congregation, 17 who shall go out before them and come in before them, who shall lead them out and bring them in; that the congregation of the LORD may not be as sheep which have no shepherd." 18And the LORD said to Moses, "Take Joshua the son of Nun, a man in whom is the spirit, and lay your hand upon him; 19 cause him to stand before El·e·ā′zar the priest and all the congregation, and you shall commission him in their sight. 20 You shall invest him with some of your authority, that all the congregation of the people of Israel may obey. 21And he shall stand before El·e·ā′zar the priest, who shall inquire for him by the judgment of the U′rim before the LORD; at his word they shall go out, and at his word they shall come in, both he and all the people of Israel with him, the whole congregation." 22And Moses did as the LORD commanded him; he took Joshua and caused him to stand before El·e·ā′zar the priest and the whole congregation, 23 and he laid his hands upon him, and commissioned him as the LORD directed through Moses.

28 The LORD said to Moses, 2 "Command the people of Israel, and say to them, 'My offering, my food for my offerings by fire, my pleasing odor, you shall take heed to offer to me in its due season.' 3And

you shall say to them, This is the offering by fire which you shall offer to the LORD: two male lambs a year old without blemish, day by day, as a continual offering. 4 The one lamb you shall offer in the morning, and the other lamb you shall offer in the evening; 5 also a tenth of an ephah of fine flour for a cereal offering, mixed with a fourth of a hin of beaten oil. 6 It is a continual burnt offering, which was ordained at Mount Sinai for a pleasing odor, an offering by fire to the LORD. 7 Its drink offering shall be a fourth of a hin for each lamb; in the holy place you shall pour out a drink offering of strong drink to the LORD. 8 The other lamb you shall offer in the evening; like the cereal offering of the morning, and like its drink offering, you shall offer it as an offering by fire, a pleasing odor to the LORD.

9 "On the sabbath day two male lambs a year old without blemish, and two tenths of an ephah of fine flour for a cereal offering, mixed with oil, and its drink offering: 10 this is the burnt offering of every sabbath, besides the continual burnt offering and its drink offering.

11 "At the beginnings of your months you shall offer a burnt offering to the LORD: two young bulls, one ram, seven male lambs a year old without blemish; 12 also three tenths of an ephah of fine flour for a cereal offering, mixed with oil, for each bull; and two tenths of fine flour for a cereal offering, mixed with oil, for the one ram; 13 and a tenth of fine flour mixed with oil as a cereal offering for every lamb; for a burnt offering of pleasing odor, an offering by fire to the LORD. 14 Their drink offerings shall be half a hin of the wine for a bull, a third of a hin for a ram, and a fourth of a hin for a lamb; this is the burnt offering of each month throughout the months of the year. 15Also one male goat for a sin offering to the LORD; it shall be offered besides the continual burnt offering and its drink offering.

16 "On the fourteenth day of the first month is the LORD's passover. 17And on the fifteenth day of this month is a feast; seven days shall unleavened bread be eaten. 18 On the first day there shall be a holy convocation: you shall do no laborious work, 19 but offer an offering by fire, a burnt offering to the LORD: two young bulls, one ram, and seven male lambs a year

27.12-14: Deut 3.23-27; 32.48-52. 27.18-23: Deut 3.28. 28.3-8: Ex 29.38-42.
28.16: Ex 12.1-14, 21-27; Lev 23.5; Deut 16.1-2, 5-7.
28.17-25: Ex 12.15-20; Lev 23.6-8; Deut 16.3-4, 8.

old; see that they are without blemish; 20 also their cereal offering of fine flour mixed with oil; three tenths of an ephah shall you offer for a bull, and two tenths for a ram; 21 a tenth shall you offer for each of the seven lambs, 22 also one male goat for a sin offering, to make atonement for you. 23 You shall offer these besides the burnt offering of the morning, which is for a continual burnt offering. 24 In the same way you shall offer daily, for seven days, the food of an offering by fire, a pleasing odor to the LORD; it shall be offered besides the continual burnt offering and its drink offering. 25 And on the seventh day you shall have a holy convocation; you shall do no laborious work.

26 "On the day of the first fruits, when you offer a cereal offering of new grain to the LORD at your feast of weeks, you shall have a holy convocation; you shall do no laborious work, 27 but offer a burnt offering, a pleasing odor to the LORD: two young bulls, one ram, seven male lambs a year old; 28 also their cereal offering of fine flour mixed with oil, three tenths of an ephah for each bull, two tenths for one ram, 29 a tenth for each of the seven lambs; 30 with one male goat, to make atonement for you. 31 Besides the continual burnt offering and its cereal offering, you shall offer them and their drink offering. See that they are without blemish.

29 "On the first day of the seventh month you shall have a holy convocation; you shall do no laborious work. It is a day for you to blow the trumpets, 2 and you shall offer a burnt offering, a pleasing odor to the LORD: one young bull, one ram, seven male lambs a year old without blemish; 3 also their cereal offering of fine flour mixed with oil, three tenths of an ephah for the bull, two tenths for the ram, 4 and one tenth for each of the seven lambs; 5 with one male goat for a sin offering, to make atonement for you; 6 besides the burnt offering of the new moon, and its cereal offering, and the continual burnt offering and its cereal offering, and their drink offering, according to the ordinance for them, a pleasing odor, an offering by fire to the LORD.

7 "On the tenth day of this seventh month you shall have a holy convocation, and afflict yourselves; you shall do no work, 8 but you shall offer a

burnt offering to the LORD, a pleasing odor: one young bull, one ram, seven male lambs a year old; they shall be to you without blemish; 9 and their cereal offering of fine flour mixed with oil, three tenths of an ephah for the bull, two tenths for the one ram, 10 a tenth for each of the seven lambs: 11 also one male goat for a sin offering, besides the sin offering of atonement, and the continual burnt offering and its cereal offering, and their drink offerings.

12 "On the fifteenth day of the seventh month you shall have a holy convocation; you shall do no laborious work, and you shall keep a feast to the LORD seven days; 13 and you shall offer a burnt offering, an offering by fire, a pleasing odor to the LORD, thirteen young bulls, two rams, fourteen male lambs a year old; they shall be without blemish; 14 and their cereal offering of fine flour mixed with oil, three tenths of an ephah for each of the thirteen bulls, two tenths for each of the two rams, 15 and a tenth for each of the fourteen lambs; 16 also one male goat for a sin offering, besides the continual burnt offering, its cereal offering and its drink offering.

17 "On the second day twelve young bulls, two rams, fourteen male lambs a year old without blemish, 18 with the cereal offering and the drink offerings for the bulls, for the rams, and for the lambs, by number, according to the ordinance; 19 also one male goat for a sin offering, besides the continual burnt offering and its cereal offering, and their drink offerings.

20 "On the third day eleven bulls, two rams, fourteen male lambs a year old without blemish, 21 with the cereal offering and the drink offerings for the bulls, for the rams, and for the lambs, by number, according to the ordinance; 22 also one male goat for a sin offering, besides the continual burnt offering and its cereal offering and its drink offering.

23 "On the fourth day ten bulls, two rams, fourteen male lambs a year old without blemish, 24 with the cereal offering and the drink offerings for the bulls, for the rams, and for the lambs, by number, according to the ordinance; 25 also one male goat for a sin offering, besides the continual burnt offering, its cereal offering and its drink offering.

26 "On the fifth day nine bulls, two

28.26-31: Ex 23.16; 34.22; Lev 23.15-21; Deut 16.9-12.
29.1-6: Ex 23.16; 34.22; Lev 23.23-25.   **29.7-11:** Lev 16.29-34; 23.26-32.
29.12-34: Lev 23.33-35.

rams, fourteen male lambs a year old without blemish, 27 with the cereal offering and the drink offerings for the bulls, for the rams, and for the lambs, by number, according to the ordinance; 28 also one male goat for a sin offering; besides the continual burnt offerings and its cereal offering and its drink offering.

29 "On the sixth day eight bulls, two rams, fourteen male lambs a year old without blemish, 30 with the cereal offering and the drink offerings for the bulls, for the rams, and for the lambs, by number, according to the ordinance; 31 also one male goat for a sin offering; besides the continual burnt offering, its cereal offering, and its drink offerings.

32 "On the seventh day seven bulls, two rams, fourteen male lambs a year old without blemish, 33 with the cereal offering and the drink offerings for the bulls, for the rams, and for the lambs, by number, according to the ordinance; 34 also one male goat for a sin offering; besides the continual burnt offering, its cereal offering, and its drink offering.

35 "On the eighth day you shall have a solemn assembly: you shall do no laborious work, 36 but you shall offer a burnt offering, an offering by fire, a pleasing odor to the LORD: one bull, one ram, seven male lambs a year old without blemish, 37 and the cereal offering and the drink offerings for the bull, for the ram, and for the lambs, by number, according to the ordinance; 38 also one male goat for a sin offering; besides the continual burnt offering and its cereal offering and its drink offering.

39 "These you shall offer to the LORD at your appointed feasts, in addition to your votive offerings and your freewill offerings, for your burnt offerings, and for your cereal offerings, and for your drink offerings, and for your peace offerings."

40ʸ And Moses told the people of Israel everything just as the LORD had commanded Moses.

30 Moses said to the heads of the tribes of the people of Israel, "This is what the LORD has commanded. 2 When a man vows a vow to the LORD, or swears an oath to bind himself by a pledge, he shall not break his word; he shall do according to all that proceeds out of his mouth. 3 Or when a woman vows a vow to the LORD, and binds herself by a pledge,

while within her father's house, in her youth, 4 and her father hears of her vow and of her pledge by which she has bound herself, and says nothing to her; then all her vows shall stand, and every pledge by which she has bound herself shall stand. 5 But if her father expresses disapproval to her on the day that he hears of it, no vow of hers, no pledge by which she has bound herself, shall stand; and the LORD will forgive her, because her father opposed her. 6 And if she is married to a husband, while under her vows or any thoughtless utterance of her lips by which she has bound herself, 7 and her husband hears of it, and says nothing to her on the day that he hears; then her vows shall stand, and her pledges by which she has bound herself shall stand. 8 But if, on the day that her husband comes to hear of it, he expresses disapproval, then he shall make void her vow which was on her, and the thoughtless utterance of her lips, by which she bound herself; and the LORD will forgive her. 9 But any vow of a widow or of a divorced woman, anything by which she has bound herself, shall stand against her. 10 And if she vowed in her husband's house, or bound herself by a pledge with an oath, 11 and her husband heard of it, and said nothing to her, and did not oppose her; then all her vows shall stand, and every pledge by which she bound herself shall stand. 12 But if her husband makes them null and void on the day that he hears them, then whatever proceeds out of her lips concerning her vows, or concerning her pledge of herself, shall not stand: her husband has made them void, and the LORD will forgive her. 13 Any vow and any binding oath to afflict herself, her husband may establish, or her husband may make void. 14 But if her husband says nothing to her from day to day, then he establishes all her vows, or all her pledges, that are upon her; he has established them, because he said nothing to her on the day that he heard of them. 15 But if he makes them null and void after he has heard of them, then he shall bear her iniquity."

16 These are the statutes which the LORD commanded Moses, as between a man and his wife, and between a father and his daughter, while in her youth, within her father's house.

31 The LORD said to Moses, 2 "Avenge the people of Israel on the Mid′i·a·nites; afterward you shall

29.35-38: Lev 23.36.   **30.2-16:** Deut 23.21-23.   **30.2:** Mt 5.33.

be gathered to your people." ³And Moses said to the people, "Arm men from among you for the war, that they may go against Mid′i·an, to execute the LORD'S vengeance on Midian. ⁴ You shall send a thousand from each of the tribes of Israel to the war." ⁵ So there were provided, out of the thousands of Israel, a thousand from each tribe, twelve thousand armed for war. ⁶And Moses sent them to the war, a thousand from each tribe, together with Phin′e·has the son of El·e·a′zar the priest, with the vessels of the sanctuary and the trumpets for the alarm in his hand. ⁷ They warred against Mid′i·an, as the LORD commanded Moses, and slew every male. ⁸ They slew the kings of Mid′i·an with the rest of their slain, E′vi, Re′kem, Zur, Hur, and Re′ba, the five kings of Mid′i·an; and they also slew Balaam the son of Be′or with the sword. ⁹And the people of Israel took captive the women of Mid′i·an and their little ones; and they took as booty all their cattle, their flocks, and all their goods. ¹⁰All their cities in the places where they dwelt, and all their encampments, they burned with fire, ¹¹ and took all the spoil and all the booty, both of man and of beast. ¹² Then they brought the captives and the booty and the spoil to Moses, and to El·e·a′zar the priest, and to the congregation of the people of Israel, at the camp on the plains of Mo′ab by the Jordan at Jericho.

13 Moses, and El·e·a′zar the priest, and all the leaders of the congregation, went forth to meet them outside the camp. ¹⁴And Moses was angry with the officers of the army, the commanders of thousands and the commanders of hundreds, who had come from service in the war. ¹⁵ Moses said to them, "Have you let all the women live? ¹⁶ Behold, these caused the people of Israel, by the counsel of Balaam, to act treacherously against the LORD in the matter of Pe′or, and so the plague came among the congregation of the LORD. ¹⁷ Now therefore, kill every male among the little ones, and kill every woman who has known man by lying with him. ¹⁸ But all the young girls who have not known man by lying with him, keep alive for yourselves. ¹⁹ Encamp outside the camp seven days; whoever of you has killed any person, and whoever has touched any slain, purify yourselves and your captives on the third day and on the seventh day. ²⁰ You shall purify every garment, every article of skin, all work

of goats' hair, and every article of wood."

21 And El·e·a′zar the priest said to the men of war who had gone to battle: "This is the statute of the law which the LORD has commanded Moses: ²² only the gold, the silver, the bronze, the iron, the tin, and the lead, ²³ everything that can stand the fire, you shall pass through the fire, and it shall be clean. Nevertheless it shall also be purified with the water of impurity; and whatever cannot stand the fire, you shall pass through the water. ²⁴ You must wash your clothes on the seventh day, and you shall be clean; and afterward you shall come into the camp."

25 The LORD said to Moses, ²⁶ "Take the count of the booty that was taken, both of man and of beast, you and El·e·a′zar the priest and the heads of the fathers' houses of the congregation; ²⁷ and divide the booty into two parts, between the warriors who went out to battle and all the congregation. ²⁸And levy for the LORD a tribute from the men of war who went out to battle, one out of five hundred, of the persons and of the oxen and of the asses and of the flocks; ²⁹ take it from their half, and give it to El·e·a′zar the priest as an offering to the LORD. ³⁰And from the people of Israel's half you shall take one drawn out of every fifty, of the persons, of the oxen, of the asses, and of the flocks, of all the cattle, and give them to the Levites who have charge of the tabernacle of the LORD." ³¹And Moses and El·e·a′zar the priest did as the LORD commanded Moses.

32 Now the booty remaining of the spoil that the men of war took was: six hundred and seventy-five thousand sheep, ³³ seventy-two thousand cattle, ³⁴ sixty-one thousand asses, ³⁵ and thirty-two thousand persons in all, women who had not known man by lying with him. ³⁶And the half, the portion of those who had gone out to war, was in number three hundred and thirty-seven thousand five hundred sheep, ³⁷ and the LORD'S tribute of sheep was six hundred and seventy-five. ³⁸ The cattle were thirty-six thousand, of which the LORD'S tribute was seventy-two. ³⁹ The asses were thirty thousand five hundred, of which the LORD'S tribute was sixty-one. ⁴⁰ The persons were sixteen thousand, of which the LORD'S tribute was thirty-two persons. ⁴¹And Moses gave the tribute, which was the offering for the

LORD, to El-ē-ā′zàr the priest, as the LORD commanded Moses.

42 From the people of Israel's half, which Moses separated from that of the men who had gone to war—43 now the congregation's half was three hundred and thirty-seven thousand five hundred sheep, 44 thirty-six thousand cattle, 45 and thirty thousand five hundred asses, 46 and sixteen thousand persons—47 from the people of Israel's half Moses took one of every fifty, both of persons and of beasts, and gave them to the Levites who had charge of the tabernacle of the LORD; as the LORD commanded Moses.

48 Then the officers who were over the thousands of the army, the captains of thousands and the captains of hundreds, came near to Moses, 49 and said to Moses, "Your servants have counted the men of war who are under our command, and there is not a man missing from us. 50And we have brought the LORD's offering, what each man found, articles of gold, armlets and bracelets, signet rings, earrings, and beads, to make atonement for ourselves before the LORD." 51And Moses and El-ē-ā′zàr the priest received from them the gold, all wrought articles. 52And all the gold of the offering that they offered to the LORD, from the commanders of thousands and the commanders of hundreds, was sixteen thousand seven hundred and fifty shekels. 53 (The men of war had taken booty, every man for himself.) 54And Moses and El-ē-ā′zàr the priest received the gold from the commanders of thousands and of hundreds, and brought it into the tent of meeting, as a memorial for the people of Israel before the LORD.

32 Now the sons of Reuben and the sons of Gad had a very great multitude of cattle; and they saw the land of Jā′zér and the land of Gilead, and behold, the place was a place for cattle. 2 So the sons of Gad and the sons of Reuben came and said to Moses and to El-ē-ā′zàr the priest and to the leaders of the congregation, 3 "At′à-roth, Dī′bon, Jā′zér, Nim′ràh, Hesh′-bòn, Ē-lē-ā′lēh, Sē′bam, Nē′bō, and Bē′on, 4 the land which the LORD smote before the congregation of Israel, is a land for cattle; and your servants have cattle." 5And they said, "If we have found favor in your sight, let this land be given to your servants for a possession; do not take us across the Jordan."

6 But Moses said to the sons of Gad and to the sons of Reuben, "Shall your brethren go to the war while you sit here? 7 Why will you discourage the heart of the people of Israel from going over into the land which the LORD has given them? 8 Thus did your fathers, when I sent them from Kā′desh-bär′-nē-à to see the land. 9 For when they went up to the Valley of Esh′cōl, and saw the land, they discouraged the heart of the people of Israel from going into the land which the LORD had given them. 10And the LORD's anger was kindled on that day, and he swore, saying, 11 'Surely none of the men who came up out of Egypt, from twenty years old and upward, shall see the land which I swore to give to Abraham, to Isaac, and to Jacob, because they have not wholly followed me; 12 none except Caleb the son of Jē-phün′nēh the Ken′iz-zite and Joshua the son of Nun, for they have wholly followed the LORD.' 13And the LORD's anger was kindled against Israel, and he made them wander in the wilderness forty years, until all the generation that had done evil in the sight of the LORD was consumed. 14And behold, you have risen in your fathers' stead, a brood of sinful men, to increase still more the fierce anger of the LORD against Israel! 15 For if you turn away from following him, he will again abandon them in the wilderness; and you will destroy all this people."

16 Then they came near to him, and said, "We will build sheepfolds here for our flocks, and cities for our little ones, 17 but we will take up arms, ready to go before the people of Israel, until we have brought them to their place; and our little ones shall live in the fortified cities because of the inhabitants of the land. 18 We will not return to our homes until the people of Israel have inherited each his inheritance. 19 For we will not inherit with them on the other side of the Jordan and beyond; because our inheritance has come to us on this side of the Jordan to the east." 20 So Moses said to them, "If you will do this, if you will take up arms to go before the LORD for the war, 21 and every armed man of you will pass over the Jordan before the LORD, until he has driven out his enemies from before him 22 and the land is subdued before the LORD; then after that you shall return and be free of obligation to the LORD and to Israel; and this land shall be your possession before the LORD. 23 But if you will not do so, behold, you have sinned against the LORD; and be sure your sin will find you out. 24 Build cities for

your little ones, and folds for your sheep; and do what you have promised." 25And the sons of Gad and the sons of Reuben said to Moses, "Your servants will do as my lord commands. 26 Our little ones, our wives, our flocks, and all our cattle, shall remain there in the cities of Gilead; 27 but your servants will pass over, every man who is armed for war, before the LORD to battle, as my lord orders."

28 So Moses gave command concerning them to El·ē·ā′zàr the priest, and to Joshua the son of Nun, and to the heads of the fathers' houses of the tribes of the people of Israel. 29And Moses said to them, "If the sons of Gad and the sons of Reuben, every man who is armed to battle before the LORD, will pass with you over the Jordan and the land shall be subdued before you, then you shall give them the land of Gilead for a possession; 30 but if they will not pass over with you armed, they shall have possessions among you in the land of Canaan." 31And the sons of Gad and the sons of Reuben answered, "As the LORD has said to your servants, so we will do. 32 We will pass over armed before the LORD into the land of Canaan, and the possession of our inheritance shall remain with us beyond the Jordan."

33 And Moses gave to them, to the sons of Gad and to the sons of Reuben and to the half-tribe of Mà·nas′sēh the son of Joseph, the kingdom of Si′hon king of the Am′ō·rites and the kingdom of Og king of Bā′shàn, the land and its cities with their territories, the cities of the land throughout the country. 34And the sons of Gad built Dī′bon, At′à·roth, Á·rō′ér, 35At′roth-shō′phàn, Jā′zēr, Jog′be·häh, 36 Beth-nim′ràh and Beth-hâr′àn, fortified cities, and folds for sheep. 37And the sons of Reuben built Hesh′bŏn, Ē·lē·ā′lĕh, Kĭr·i·à·thā′im, 38 Nē′bō, and Bā′al-mē′ŏn (their names to be changed), and Sib′màh; and they gave other names to the cities which they built. 39And the sons of Mā′chir the son of Mà·nas′sēh went to Gilead and took it, and dispossessed the Am′ō·rites who were in it. 40And Moses gave Gilead to Mā′chir the son of Mà·nas′sēh, and he settled in it. 41And Jā′ir the son of Mà·nas′sēh went and took their villages, and called them Hav′vŏth-jā′ir.z 42And Nō′bàh went and took Kē′nath and its villages, and called it Nobah, after his own name.

33 These are the stages of the people of Israel, when they went forth out of the land of Egypt by

z That is *the villages of Jair*

their hosts under the leadership of Moses and Aaron. 2 Moses wrote down their starting places, stage by stage, by command of the LORD; and these are their stages according to their starting places. 3 They set out from Ram′é·sēs in the first month, on the fifteenth day of the first month; on the day after the passover the people of Israel went out triumphantly in the sight of all the Egyptians, 4 while the Egyptians were burying all their firstborn, whom the LORD had struck down among them; upon their gods also the LORD executed judgments.

5 So the people of Israel set out from Ram′é·sēs, and encamped at Suc′coth. 6And they set out from Suc′coth, and encamped at Ē′thàm, which is on the edge of the wilderness. 7And they set out from Ē′thàm, and turned back to Pī-hà·hī′roth, which is east of Bā′àl-zē′phŏn; and they encamped before Mig′dŏl. 8And they set out from before Hà·hī′roth, and passed through the midst of the sea into the wilderness, and they went a three days' journey in the wilderness of Ē′thàm, and encamped at Mâr′àh. 9And they set out from Mâr′àh, and came to Ē′lim; at Elim there were twelve springs of water and seventy palm trees, and they encamped there. 10And they set out from Ē′lim, and encamped by the Red Sea. 11And they set out from the Red Sea, and encamped in the wilderness of Sin. 12And they set out from the wilderness of Sin, and encamped at Doph′kàh. 13And they set out from Doph′kàh, and encamped at Ā′lûsh. 14And they set out from Ā′lûsh, and encamped at Reph′i·dim, where there was no water for the people to drink. 15And they set out from Reph′i·dim, and encamped in the wilderness of Sinai. 16And they set out from the wilderness of Sinai, and encamped at Kib′roth-ha·tā′à·vàh. 17And they set out from Kib′roth-ha·tā′à·vàh, and encamped at Hà·zē′roth. 18And they set out from Hà·zē′roth, and encamped at Rith′màh. 19And they set out from Rith′màh, and encamped at Rim′mon-per′ez. 20And they set out from Rim′mon-per′ez, and encamped at Lib′nàh. 21And they set out from Lib′nàh, and encamped at Ris′sàh. 22And they set out from Ris′sàh, and encamped at Kē·hē·lā′thàh. 23And they set out from Kē·hē·lā′thàh, and encamped at Mount Shē′phér. 24And they set out from Mount Shē′phér, and encamped at Hà·rā′dàh. 25And they set out from Hà·rā′dàh, and encamped at Mak·hē′-

lôth. 26And they set out from Mak-hē′lôth, and encamped at Tā′hath. 27And they set out from Tā′hath, and encamped at Ter′áh. 28And they set out from Ter′áh, and encamped at Mith′kåh. 29And they set out from Mith′kåh, and encamped at Hash-mō′-nåh. 30And they set out from Hash-mō′nåh, and encamped at Mō-sē′rôth. 31And they set out from Mō-sē′rôth, and encamped at Bē′ne-jā′á-kån. 32And they set out from Bē′ne-jā′á-kån, and encamped at Hôr-hág-gid′gad. 33And they set out from Hôr-hág-gid′gad, and encamped at Jot′bá-thåh. 34And they set out from Jot′bá-thåh, and en-camped at Á-brō′nåh. 35And they set out from Á-brō′nåh, and encamped at Ē′zi-on-gē′bér. 36And they set out from Ē′zi-on-gē′bér, and encamped in the wilderness of Zin (that is, Kā′-desh). 37And they set out from Kā′-desh, and encamped at Mount Hôr, on the edge of the land of Ē′dóm.

38 And Aaron the priest went up Mount Hôr at the command of the LORD, and died there, in the fortieth year after the people of Israel had come out of the land of Egypt, on the first day of the fifth month. 39And Aaron was a hundred and twenty-three years old when he died on Mount Hôr.

40 And the Canaanite, the king of Âr′åd, who dwelt in the Negeb in the land of Canaan, heard of the coming of the people of Israel.

41 And they set out from Mount Hôr, and encamped at Zal·mō′nåh. 42And they set out from Zal·mō′nåh, and encamped at Pū′non. 43And they set out from Pū′non, and encamped at Ō′both. 44And they set out from Ō′both, and encamped at Ī′ye-ab′á-rim, in the territory of Mō′ab. 45And they set out from Ī′yim, and encamped at Dī′bon-gad. 46And they set out from Dī′bon-gad, and encamped at Al′mòn-dib-là-thā′im. 47And they set out from Al′mòn-dib-là-thā′im, and encamped in the mountains of Ab′á-rim, before Nē′bō. 48And they set out from the mountains of Ab′á-rim, and encamped in the plains of Mō′ab by the Jordan at Jericho; 49they encamped by the Jordan from Beth-jesh′i-moth as far as Ā′bél-shit′tim in the plains of Mō′ab.

50 And the LORD said to Moses in the plains of Mō′ab by the Jordan at Jericho, 51 "Say to the people of Israel, When you pass over the Jordan into the land of Canaan, 52 then you shall

drive out all the inhabitants of the land from before you, and destroy all their figured stones, and destroy all their molten images, and demolish all their high places; 53 and you shall take possession of the land and settle in it, for I have given the land to you to possess it. 54 You shall inherit the land by lot according to your families; to a large tribe you shall give a large in-heritance, and to a small tribe you shall give a small inheritance; wherever the lot falls to any man, that shall be his; according to the tribes of your fathers you shall inherit. 55 But if you do not drive out the inhabitants of the land from before you, then those of them whom you let remain shall be as pricks in your eyes and thorns in your sides, and they shall trouble you in the land where you dwell. 56And I will do to you as I thought to do to them."

34 The LORD said to Moses, 2 "Command the people of Is-rael, and say to them, When you enter the land of Canaan (this is the land that shall fall to you for an inheritance, the land of Canaan in its full extent), 3 your south side shall be from the wilderness of Zin along the side of Ē′dóm, and your southern boundary shall be from the end of the Salt Sea on the east; 4 and your boundary shall turn south of the ascent of Ak·rab′bim, and cross to Zin, and its end shall be south of Kā′desh-bär′ne-à; then it shall go on to Hā′zär-ad′dàr, and pass along to Az′mòn; 5 and the boundary shall turn from Az′mòn to the Brook of Egypt, and its termination shall be at the sea.

6 "For the western boundary, you shall have the Great Sea and its a coast; this shall be your western boundary.

7 "This shall be your northern boundary: from the Great Sea you shall mark out your line to Mount Hôr; 8 from Mount Hôr you shall mark it out to the entrance of Hā′math, and the end of the boundary shall be at Zē′dad; 9 then the boundary shall ex-tend to Ziph′ron, and its end shall be at Hā′zär-ē′nån; this shall be your northern boundary.

10 "You shall mark out your east-ern boundary from Hā′zär-ē′nån to Shē′pham; 11 and the boundary shall go down from Shē′pham to Rib′låh on the east side of A′in; and the boundary shall go down, and reach to the shoulder of the sea of Chim′nē-reth on the east; 12 and the boundary shall go

---

a Syr: Heb lacks *its*

33.38-39: Num 20.23-29; Deut 10.6.   **33.52:** Ex 23.24; Deut 7.5; 12.3. 34.3-5: Josh 15.1-4.

down to the Jordan, and its end shall be at the Salt Sea. This shall be your land with its boundaries all round."

13 Moses commanded the people of Israel, saying, "This is the land which you shall inherit by lot, which the LORD has commanded to give to the nine tribes and to the half-tribe; 14 for the tribe of the sons of Reuben by fathers' houses and the tribe of the sons of Gad by their fathers' houses have received their inheritance, and also the half-tribe of Ma·nas′seh; 15 the two tribes and the half-tribe have received their inheritance beyond the Jordan at Jericho eastward, toward the sunrise."

16 The LORD said to Moses, 17 "These are the names of the men who shall divide the land to you for inheritance: El·e·a′zar the priest and Joshua the son of Nun. 18 You shall take one leader of every tribe, to divide the land for inheritance. 19 These are the names of the men: Of the tribe of Judah, Caleb the son of Je·phun′neh. 20 Of the tribe of the sons of Simeon, She·mu′el the son of Am·mi′hud. 21 Of the tribe of Benjamin, E·li′dad the son of Chis′lon. 22 Of the tribe of the sons of Dan a leader, Buk′ki the son of Jog′li. 23 Of the sons of Joseph: of the tribe of the sons of Ma·nas′seh a leader, Han′ni·el the son of E′phod. 24 And of the tribe of the sons of E′phra·im a leader, Ke·mu′el the son of Shiph′tan. 25 Of the tribe of the sons of Zeb′u·lun a leader, E·li·za′phan the son of Pär′nach. 26 Of the tribe of the sons of Is′sa·char a leader, Pal′ti·el the son of Az′zan. 27 And of the tribe of the sons of Ash′er a leader, A·hi′hud the son of She·lo′mi. 28 Of the tribe of the sons of Naph′ta·li a leader, Pe·dah′-el the son of Am·mi′hud. 29 These are the men whom the LORD commanded to divide the inheritance for the people of Israel in the land of Canaan."

35 The LORD said to Moses in the plains of Mo′ab by the Jordan at Jericho, 2 "Command the people of Israel, that they give to the Levites, from the inheritance of their possession, cities to dwell in; and you shall give to the Levites pasture lands round about the cities. 3 The cities shall be theirs to dwell in, and their pasture lands shall be for their cattle and for their livestock and for all their beasts. 4 The pasture lands of the cities, which you shall give to the Levites, shall reach from the wall of the city outward a thousand cubits all round.

5 And you shall measure, outside the city, for the east side two thousand cubits, and for the south side two thousand cubits, and for the west side two thousand cubits, and for the north side two thousand cubits, the city being in the middle; this shall belong to them as pasture land for their cities. 6 The cities which you give to the Levites shall be the six cities of refuge, where you shall permit the manslayer to flee, and in addition to them you shall give forty-two cities. 7 All the cities which you give to the Levites shall be forty-eight, with their pasture lands. 8 And as for the cities which you shall give from the possession of the people of Israel, from the larger tribes you shall take many, and from the smaller tribes you shall take few; each, in proportion to the inheritance which it inherits, shall give of its cities to the Levites."

9 And the LORD said to Moses, 10 "Say to the people of Israel, When you cross the Jordan into the land of Canaan, 11 then you shall select cities to be cities of refuge for you, that the manslayer who kills any person without intent may flee there. 12 The cities shall be for you a refuge from the avenger, that the manslayer may not die until he stands before the congregation for judgment. 13 And the cities which you give shall be your six cities of refuge. 14 You shall give three cities beyond the Jordan, and three cities in the land of Canaan, to be cities of refuge. 15 These six cities shall be for refuge for the people of Israel, and for the stranger and for the sojourner among them, that any one who kills any person without intent may flee there.

16 "But if he struck him down with an instrument of iron, so that he died, he is a murderer; the murderer shall be put to death. 17 And if he struck him down with a stone in the hand, by which a man may die, and he died, he is a murderer; the murderer shall be put to death. 18 Or if he struck him down with a weapon of wood in the hand, by which a man may die, and he died, he is a murderer; the murderer shall be put to death. 19 The avenger of blood shall himself put the murderer to death; when he meets him, he shall put him to death. 20 And if he stabbed him from hatred, or hurled at him, lying in wait, so that he died, 21 or in enmity struck him down with his hand, so that he died, then he who struck the

34.13-15: Josh 14.1-5.   35.1-8: Lev 25.32-34; Josh 21.1-42.
35.6, 9-34: Deut 19.1-13.

blow shall be put to death; he is a murderer; the avenger of blood shall put the murderer to death, when he meets him.

22 "But if he stabbed him suddenly without enmity, or hurled anything on him without lying in wait, 23 or used a stone, by which a man may die, and without seeing him cast it upon him, so that he died, though he was not his enemy, and did not seek his harm; 24 then the congregation shall judge between the manslayer and the avenger of blood, in accordance with these ordinances; 25 and the congregation shall rescue the manslayer from the hand of the avenger of blood, and the congregation shall restore him to his city of refuge, to which he had fled, and he shall live in it until the death of the high priest who was anointed with the holy oil. 26 But if the manslayer shall at any time go beyond the bounds of his city of refuge to which he fled, 27 and the avenger of blood finds him outside the bounds of his city of refuge, and the avenger of blood slays the manslayer, he shall not be guilty of blood. 28 For the man must remain in his city of refuge until the death of the high priest; but after the death of the high priest the manslayer may return to the land of his possession.

29 "And these things shall be for a statute and ordinance to you throughout your generations in all your dwellings. 30 If any one kills a person, the murderer shall be put to death on the evidence of witnesses; but no person shall be put to death on the testimony of one witness. 31 Moreover you shall accept no ransom for the life of a murderer, who is guilty of death; but he shall be put to death. 32 And you shall accept no ransom for him who has fled to his city of refuge, that he may return to dwell in the land before the death of the high priest. 33 You shall not thus pollute the land in which you live; for blood pollutes the land, and no expiation can be made for the land, for the blood that is shed in it, except by the blood of him who shed it. 34 You shall not defile the land in which you live, in the midst of which I dwell; for I the LORD dwell in the midst of the people of Israel."

36 The heads of the fathers' houses of the families of the sons of Gilead the son of Má'chir, son of Má·nas'seh, of the fathers' houses

of the sons of Joseph, came near and spoke before Moses and before the leaders, the heads of the fathers' houses of the people of Israel; 2 they said, "The LORD commanded my lord to give the land for inheritance by lot to the people of Israel; and my lord was commanded by the LORD to give the inheritance of Ze·loph'e·had our brother to his daughters. 3 But if they are married to any of the sons of the other tribes of the people of Israel then their inheritance will be taken from the inheritance of our fathers, and added to the inheritance of the tribe to which they belong; so it will be taken away from the lot of our inheritance. 4 And when the jubilee of the people of Israel comes, then their inheritance will be added to the inheritance of the tribe to which they belong; and their inheritance will be taken from the inheritance of the tribe of our fathers."

5 And Moses commanded the people of Israel according to the word of the LORD, saying, "The tribe of the sons of Joseph is right. 6 This is what the LORD commands concerning the daughters of Ze·loph'e·had, 'Let them marry whom they think best; only, they shall marry within the family of the tribe of their father. 7 The inheritance of the people of Israel shall not be transferred from one tribe to another; for every one of the people of Israel shall cleave to the inheritance of the tribe of his fathers. 8 And every daughter who possesses an inheritance in any tribe of the people of Israel shall be wife to one of the family of the tribe of her father, so that every one of the people of Israel may possess the inheritance of his fathers. 9 So no inheritance shall be transferred from one tribe to another; for each of the tribes of the people of Israel shall cleave to its own inheritance.' "

10 The daughters of Ze·loph'e·had did as the LORD commanded Moses; 11 for Mäh'läh, Tïr'zäh, Hog'läh, Mil'càh, and Noah, the daughters of Ze·loph'e·had, were married to sons of their father's brothers. 12 They were married into the families of the sons of Má·nas'seh the son of Joseph, and their inheritance remained in the tribe of the family of their father.

13 These are the commandments and the ordinances which the LORD commanded by Moses to the people of Israel in the plains of Mō'ab by the Jordan at Jericho.

THE FIFTH BOOK OF MOSES

COMMONLY CALLED

DEUTERONOMY

These are the words that Moses spoke to all Israel beyond the Jordan in the wilderness, in the Ar'a·bah over against Süph, between Pâr'an and Tō'phel, Lā'bàn, Hȧ·zē'roth, and Dī'zȧ·hab. 2 It is eleven days' journey from Hō'reb by the way of Mount Sē'ir to Kā'desh-bär'nē·à. 3And in the fortieth year, on the first day of the eleventh month, Moses spoke to the people of Israel according to all that the LORD had given him in commandment to them, 4 after he had defeated Sī'hon the king of the Am'ó·rites, who lived in Hesh'bòn, and Og the king of Bā'shàn, who lived in Ash'tà·roth and in Ed'rē-ī. 5 Beyond the Jordan, in the land of Mō'ab, Moses undertook to explain this law, saying, 6 "The LORD our God said to us in Hō'reb, 'You have stayed long enough at this mountain; 7 turn and take your journey, and go to the hill country of the Am'ó·rites, and to all their neighbors in the Ar'a·bah, in the hill country and in the lowland, and in the Negeb, and by the seacoast, the land of the Canaanites, and Lebanon, as far as the great river, the river Eū·phrā'tēs. 8 Behold, I have set the land before you; go in and take possession of the land which the LORD swore to your fathers, to Abraham, to Isaac, and to Jacob, to give to them and to their descendants after them.

9 "At that time I said to you, 'I am not able alone to bear you; 10 the LORD your God has multiplied you, and behold, you are this day as the stars of heaven for multitude. 11 May the LORD, the God of your fathers, make you a thousand times as many as you are, and bless you, as he has promised you! 12 How can I bear alone the weight and burden of you and your strife? 13 Choose wise, understanding, and experienced men, according to your tribes, and I will appoint them as your heads.' 14And you answered me, 'The thing that you have spoken is good for us to do.' 15 So I took the heads of your tribes, wise and experienced men, and set them as heads

over you, commanders of thousands, commanders of hundreds, commanders of fifties, commanders of tens, and officers, throughout your tribes. 16And I charged your judges at that time, 'Hear the cases between your brethren, and judge righteously between a man and his brother or the alien that is with him. 17 You shall not be partial in judgment; you shall hear the small and the great alike; you shall not be afraid of the face of man, for the judgment is God's; and the case that is too hard for you, you shall bring to me, and I will hear it.' 18And I commanded you at that time all the things that you should do.

19 "And we set out from Hō'reb, and went through all that great and terrible wilderness which you saw, on the way to the hill country of the Am'ó·rites, as the LORD our God commanded us; and we came to Kā'desh-bär'nē·à. 20And I said to you, 'You have come to the hill country of the Am'ó·rites, which the LORD our God gives us. 21 Behold, the LORD your God has set the land before you; go up, take possession, as the LORD, the God of your fathers, has told you; do not fear or be dismayed.' 22 Then all of you came near me, and said, 'Let us send men before us, that they may explore the land for us, and bring us word again of the way by which we must go up and the cities into which we shall come.' 23 The thing seemed good to me, and I took twelve men of you, one man for each tribe; 24 and they turned and went up into the hill country, and came to the Valley of Esh'cŏl and spied it out. 25And they took in their hands some of the fruit of the land and brought it down to us, and brought us word again, and said, 'It is a good land which the LORD our God gives us.'

26 "Yet you would not go up, but rebelled against the command of the LORD your God; 27 and you murmured in your tents, and said, 'Because the LORD hated us he has brought us forth

1.9-15: Num 11.10-25.   1.16-18: Ex 18.25-26.   1.22-46: Num 13.1-14.45; 32.8-13.

146

out of the land of Egypt, to give us into the hand of the Am′o·rites, to destroy us. 28 Whither are we going up? Our brethren have made our hearts melt, saying, "The people are greater and taller than we; the cities are great and fortified up to heaven; and moreover we have seen the sons of the An′a·kim there." ' 29 Then I said to you, 'Do not be in dread or afraid of them. 30 The LORD your God who goes before you will himself fight for you, just as he did for you in Egypt before your eyes, 31 and in the wilderness, where you have seen how the LORD your God bore you, as a man bears his son, in all the way that you went until you came to this place.' 32 Yet in spite of this word you did not believe the LORD your God, 33 who went before you in the way to seek you out a place to pitch your tents, in fire by night, to show you by what way you should go, and in the cloud by day.

34 "And the LORD heard your words, and was angered, and he swore, 35 'Not one of these men of this evil generation shall see the good land which I swore to give to your fathers, 36 except Caleb the son of Jé·phün′neh; he shall see it, and to him and to his children I will give the land upon which he has trodden, because he has wholly followed the LORD!' 37 The LORD was angry with me also on your account, and said, 'You also shall not go in there; 38 Joshua the son of Nun, who stands before you, he shall enter; encourage him, for he shall cause Israel to inherit it. 39 Moreover your little ones, who you said would become a prey, and your children, who this day have no knowledge of good or evil, shall go in there, and to them I will give it, and they shall possess it. 40 But as for you, turn, and journey into the wilderness in the direction of the Red Sea.'

41 "Then you answered me, 'We have sinned against the LORD; we will go up and fight, just as the LORD our God commanded us.' And every man of you girded on his weapons of war, and thought it easy to go up into the hill country. 42And the LORD said to me, 'Say to them, Do not go up or fight, for I am not in the midst of you; lest you be defeated before your enemies.' 43 So I spoke to you, and you would not hearken; but you rebelled against the command of the LORD, and were presumptuous and went up into the hill country. 44 Then the Am′o·rites who lived in that hill

country came out against you and chased you as bees do and beat you down in Sē′ir as far as Hôr′màh. 45And you returned and wept before the LORD; but the LORD did not hearken to your voice or give ear to you. 46 So you remained at Kā′desh many days, the days that you remained there.

2 "Then we turned, and journeyed into the wilderness in the direction of the Red Sea, as the LORD told me; and for many days we went about Mount Sē′ir. 2 Then the LORD said to me, 3 'You have been going about this mountain country long enough; turn northward. 4And command the people, You are about to pass through the territory of your brethren the sons of Esau, who live in Sē′ir; and they will be afraid of you. So take good heed; 5 do not contend with them; for I will not give you any of their land, no, not so much as for the sole of the foot to tread on, because I have given Mount Sē′ir to Esau as a possession. 6 You shall purchase food from them for money, that you may eat; and you shall also buy water of them for money, that you may drink. 7 For the LORD your God has blessed you in all the work of your hands; he knows your going through this great wilderness; these forty years the LORD your God has been with you; you have lacked nothing.' 8 So we went on, away from our brethren the sons of Esau who live in Sē′ir, away from the Ar′a·bàh road from É′lath and É′zi·on·gē′bér.

"And we turned and went in the direction of the wilderness of Mō′ab. 9And the LORD said to me, 'Do not harass Mō′ab or contend with them in battle, for I will not give you any of their land for a possession, because I have given Ar to the sons of Lot for a possession.' 10 (The É′mim formerly lived there, a people great and many, and tall as the An′a·kim; 11 like the An′a·kim they are also known as Reph′a·im, but the Mō′ab·ites call them É′mim. 12 The Hôr′ites also lived in Sē′ir formerly, but the sons of Esau dispossessed them, and destroyed them from before them, and settled in their stead; as Israel did to the land of their possession, which the LORD gave to them.) 13 'Now rise up, and go over the brook Zē′red.' So we went over the brook Zered. 14And the time from our leaving Kā′desh-bär′nē·à until we crossed the brook Zē′red was thirty-eight years, until the entire generation, that is, the men of war, had perished

1.31: Acts 13.18.   **2.1-8:** Num 21.4-20.

from the camp, as the LORD had sworn to them. 15 For indeed the hand of the LORD was against them, to destroy them from the camp, until they had perished.

16 "So when all the men of war had perished and were dead from among the people, 17 the LORD said to me, 18 'This day you are to pass over the boundary of Mō'ab at Är; 19 and when you approach the frontier of the sons of Am'mŏn, do not harass them or contend with them, for I will not give you any of the land of the sons of Ammon as a possession, because I have given it to the sons of Lot for a possession.' 20 (That also is known as a land of Reph'à·im; Rephaim formerly lived there, but the Am'mŏ·nĭtes call them Zam·zum'mim, 21 a people great and many, and tall as the An'á·kim; but the LORD destroyed them before them; and they dispossessed them, and settled in their stead; 22 as he did for the sons of Esau, who live in Sē'ir, when he destroyed the Hŏr'ites before them, and they dispossessed them, and settled in their stead even to this day. 23 As for the Av'vim, who lived in villages as far as Gä'zà, the Caph'tò·rim, who came from Caph'-tor, destroyed them and settled in their stead.) 24 'Rise up, take your journey, and go over the valley of the Är'non; behold, I have given into your hand Sī'hon the Am'ō·rite, king of Hesh'bŏn, and his land; begin to take possession, and contend with him in battle. 25 This day I will begin to put the dread and fear of you upon the peoples that are under the whole heaven, who shall hear the report of you and shall tremble and be in anguish because of you.'

26 "So I sent messengers from the wilderness of Ked'é·moth to Sī'hon the king of Hesh'bŏn, with words of peace, saying, 27 'Let me pass through your land; I will go only by the road, I will turn aside neither to the right nor to the left. 28 You shall sell me food for money, that I may eat, and give me water for money, that I may drink; only let me pass through on foot, 29 as the sons of Esau who live in Sē'ir and the Mō'ab·ites who live in Är did for me, until I go over the Jordan into the land which the LORD our God gives to us.' 30 But Sī'hon the king of Hesh'bŏn would not let us pass by him; for the LORD your God hardened his spirit and made his heart obstinate, that he might give him into your hand, as at this day. 31 And the

LORD said to me, 'Behold, I have begun to give Sī'hon and his land over to you; begin to take possession, that you may occupy his land.' 32 Then Sī'hon came out against us, he and all his people, to battle at Jä'haz. 33 And the LORD our God gave him over to us; and we defeated him and his sons and all his people. 34 And we captured all his cities at that time and utterly destroyed every city, men, women, and children; we left none remaining; 35 only the cattle we took as spoil for ourselves, with the booty of the cities which we captured. 36 From Ä·rō'ér, which is on the edge of the valley of the Är'non, and from the city that is in the valley, as far as Gilead, there was not a city too high for us; the LORD our God gave all into our hands. 37 Only to the land of the sons of Am'mŏn you did not draw near, that is, to all the banks of the river Jab'bŏk and the cities of the hill country, and wherever the LORD our God forbade us.

3 "Then we turned and went up the way to Bā'shàn; and Og the king of Bashan came out against us, he and all his people, to battle at Ed'rē·ī. 2 But the LORD said to me, 'Do not fear him; for I have given him and all his people and his land into your hand; and you shall do to him as you did to Sī'hon the king of the Am'ŏ·rites, who dwelt at Hesh'bŏn.' 3 So the LORD our God gave into our hand Og also, the king of Bā'shàn, and all his people; and we smote him until no survivor was left to him. 4 And we took all his cities at that time—there was not a city which we did not take from them—sixty cities, the whole region of Är'gŏb, the kingdom of Og in Bā'shàn. 5 All these were cities fortified with high walls, gates, and bars, besides very many unwalled villages. 6 And we utterly destroyed them, as we did to Sī'hon the king of Hesh'-bŏn, destroying every city, men, women, and children. 7 But all the cattle and the spoil of the cities we took as our booty. 8 So we took the land at that time out of the hand of the two kings of the Am'ŏ·rites who were beyond the Jordan, from the valley of the Är'non to Mount Hēr'mŏn 9 (the Sĭ·dō'nĭ·ăns call Hēr'mŏn Sir'ĭ·ŏn, while the Am'ŏ·rites call it Sē'nir), 10 all the cities of the tableland and all Gilead and all Bā'shàn, as far as Sal'é-càh and Ed'rē·ī, cities of the kingdom of Og in Bā'shàn. 11 (For only Og the king of Bā'shàn was left of the remnant

2.26–37: Num 21.21–32.   3.1–11: Num 21.33–35.

of the Reph′a·im; behold, his bedstead was a bedstead of iron; is it not in Rab′bah of the Am′mo·nites? Nine cubits was its length, and four cubits its breadth, according to the common cubit.[a])

12 "When we took possession of this land at that time, I gave to the Reubenites and the Gadites the territory beginning at A·ro′er, which is on the edge of the valley of the Ar′non, and half the hill country of Gilead with its cities; 13 the rest of Gilead, and all Ba′shan, the kingdom of Og, that is, all the region of Ar′gob, I gave to the half-tribe of Ma·nas′seh. (The whole of that Bashan is called the land of Reph′a·im. 14 Ja′ir the Ma·nas′site took all the region of Ar′gob, that is, Ba′shan, as far as the border of the Gesh′u·rites and the Ma·ac′a·thites, and called the villages after his own name, Hav′voth-ja′ir, as it is to this day.) 15 To Ma′chir I gave Gilead, 16 and to the Reubenites and the Gadites I gave the territory from Gilead as far as the valley of the Ar′non, with the middle of the valley as a boundary, as far over as the river Jab′bok, the boundary of the Am′mo·nites; 17 the Ar′a·bah also, with the Jordan as the boundary, from Chin′ne·reth as far as the sea of the Arabah, the Salt Sea, under the slopes of Pis′gah on the east.

18 "And I commanded you at that time, saying, 'The LORD your God has given you this land to possess; all your men of valor shall pass over armed before your brethren the people of Israel. 19 But your wives, your little ones, and your cattle (I know that you have many cattle) shall remain in the cities which I have given you, 20 until the LORD gives rest to your brethren, as to you, and they also occupy the land which the LORD your God gives them beyond the Jordan; then you shall return every man to his possession which I have given you.' 21 And I commanded Joshua at that time, 'Your eyes have seen all that the LORD your God has done to these two kings; so will the LORD do to all the kingdoms into which you are going over. 22 You shall not fear them; for it is the LORD your God who fights for you.'

23 "And I besought the LORD at that time, saying, 24 'O Lord GOD, thou hast only begun to show thy servant thy greatness and thy mighty hand; for what god is there in heaven or on earth who can do such works and mighty acts as thine? 25 Let me go over, I pray, and see the good land beyond the Jordan, that goodly hill country, and Lebanon.' 26 But the LORD was angry with me on your account, and would not hearken to me; and the LORD said to me, 'Let it suffice you; speak no more to me of this matter. 27 Go up to the top of Pis′gah, and lift up your eyes westward and northward and southward and eastward, and behold it with your eyes; for you shall not go over this Jordan. 28 But charge Joshua, and encourage and strengthen him; for he shall go over at the head of this people, and he shall put them in possession of the land which you shall see.' 29 So we remained in the valley opposite Beth-pe′or.

4 "And now, O Israel, give heed to the statutes and the ordinances which I teach you, and do them; that you may live, and go in and take possession of the land which the LORD, the God of your fathers, gives you. 2 You shall not add to the word which I command you, nor take from it; that you may keep the commandments of the LORD your God which I command you. 3 Your eyes have seen what the LORD did at Ba′al-pe′or; for the LORD your God destroyed from among you all the men who followed the Ba′al of Pe′or; 4 but you who held fast to the LORD your God are all alive this day. 5 Behold, I have taught you statutes and ordinances, as the LORD my God commanded me, that you should do them in the land which you are entering to take possession of it. 6 Keep them and do them; for that will be your wisdom and your understanding in the sight of the peoples, who, when they hear all these statutes, will say, 'Surely this great nation is a wise and understanding people.' 7 For what great nation is there that has a god so near to it as the LORD our God is to us, whenever we call upon him? 8 And what great nation is there, that has statutes and ordinances so righteous as all this law which I set before you this day?

9 "Only take heed, and keep your soul diligently, lest you forget the things which your eyes have seen, and lest they depart from your heart all the days of your life; make them known to your children and your children's children— 10 how on the day that you stood before the LORD your God at

a Heb cubit of a man

3.12-20: Num 32.   3.23-27: Num 27.12-14; Deut 32.48-52.   4.2: Rev 22.18-19.
4.9-14: Ex 19.1-21.

Hō´reb, the LORD said to me, 'Gather the people to me, that I may let them hear my words, so that they may learn to fear me all the days that they live upon the earth, and that they may teach their children so.' 11And you came near and stood at the foot of the mountain, while the mountain burned with fire to the heart of heaven, wrapped in darkness, cloud, and gloom. 12 Then the LORD spoke to you out of the midst of the fire; you heard the sound of words, but saw no form; there was only a voice. 13And he declared to you his covenant, which he commanded you to perform, that is, the ten commandments;*b* and he wrote them upon two tables of stone. 14And the LORD commanded me at that time to teach you statutes and ordinances, that you might do them in the land which you are going over to possess.

15 "Therefore take good heed to yourselves. Since you saw no form on the day that the LORD spoke to you at Hō´reb out of the midst of the fire, 16 beware lest you act corruptly by making a graven image for yourselves, in the form of any figure, the likeness of male or female, 17 the likeness of any beast that is on the earth, the likeness of any winged bird that flies in the air, 18 the likeness of anything that creeps on the ground, the likeness of any fish that is in the water under the earth. 19And beware lest you lift up your eyes to heaven, and when you see the sun and the moon and the stars, all the host of heaven, you be drawn away and worship them and serve them, things which the LORD your God has allotted to all the peoples under the whole heaven. 20 But the LORD has taken you, and brought you forth out of the iron furnace, out of Egypt, to be a people of his own possession, as at this day. 21 Furthermore the LORD was angry with me on your account, and he swore that I should not cross the Jordan, and that I should not enter the good land which the LORD your God gives you for an inheritance. 22 For I must die in this land, I must not go over the Jordan; but you shall go over and take possession of that good land. 23 Take heed to yourselves, lest you forget the covenant of the LORD your God, which he made with you, and make a graven image in the form of anything which the LORD your God has forbidden you. 24 For the LORD your God is a devouring fire, a jealous God.

25 "When you beget children and children's children, and have grown old in the land, if you act corruptly by making a graven image in the form of anything, and by doing what is evil in the sight of the LORD your God, so as to provoke him to anger, 26 I call heaven and earth to witness against you this day, that you will soon utterly perish from the land which you are going over the Jordan to possess; you will not live long upon it, but will be utterly destroyed. 27And the LORD will scatter you among the peoples, and you will be left few in number among the nations where the LORD will drive you. 28And there you will serve gods of wood and stone, the work of men's hands, that neither see, nor hear, nor eat, nor smell. 29 But from there you will seek the LORD your God, and you will find him, if you search after him with all your heart and with all your soul. 30 When you are in tribulation, and all these things come upon you in the latter days, you will return to the LORD your God and obey his voice, 31 for the LORD your God is a merciful God; he will not fail you or destroy you or forget the covenant with your fathers which he swore to them.

32 "For ask now of the days that are past, which were before you, since the day that God created man upon the earth, and ask from one end of heaven to the other, whether such a great thing as this has ever happened or was ever heard of. 33 Did any people ever hear the voice of a god speaking out of the midst of the fire, as you have heard, and still live? 34 Or has any god ever attempted to go and take a nation for himself from the midst of another nation, by trials, by signs, by wonders, and by war, by a mighty hand and an outstretched arm, and by great terrors, according to all that the LORD your God did for you in Egypt before your eyes? 35 To you it was shown, that you might know that the LORD is God; there is no other besides him. 36 Out of heaven he let you hear his voice, that he might discipline you; and on earth he let you see his great fire, and you heard his words out of the midst of the fire. 37And because he loved your fathers and chose their descendants after them, and brought you out of Egypt with his own presence, by his great power, 38 driving out before you nations greater and mightier than yourselves, to bring you in, to give you their land for an inheritance, as at this

b Heb *words*
4.24: Heb 12.29.   **4.35:** Mk 12.32.

day; 39 know therefore this day, and lay it to your heart, that the LORD is God in heaven above and on the earth beneath; there is no other. 40 Therefore you shall keep his statutes and his commandments, which I command you this day, that it may go well with you, and with your children after you, and that you may prolong your days in the land which the LORD your God gives you for ever."

41 Then Moses set apart three cities in the east beyond the Jordan, 42 that the manslayer might flee there, who kills his neighbor unintentionally, without being at enmity with him in time past, and that by fleeing to one of these cities he might save his life: 43 Bē´zĕr in the wilderness on the tableland for the Reubenites, and Rā´-moth in Gilead for the Gadites, and Gō´lăn in Bā´shăn for the Må·nas´sites.

44 This is the law which Moses set before the children of Israel; 45 these are the testimonies, the statutes, and the ordinances, which Moses spoke to the children of Israel when they came out of Egypt, 46 beyond the Jordan in the valley opposite Beth-pĕ´ôr, in the land of Sī´hŏn the king of the Am´ô-rites, who lived at Hesh´bŏn, whom Moses and the children of Israel defeated when they came out of Egypt. 47And they took possession of his land and the land of Og the king of Bā´shăn, the two kings of the Am´ô·rites, who lived to the east beyond the Jordan; 48 from A·rō´ĕr, which is on the edge of the valley of the Är´non, as far as Mount Sir´i·ônᶜ (that is, Hĕr´mŏn), 49 together with all the Ar´å·bàh on the east side of the Jordan as far as the Sea of the Arabah, under the slopes of Piś´gàh.

5 And Moses summoned all Israel, and said to them, "Hear, O Israel, the statutes and the ordinances which I speak in your hearing this day, and you shall learn them and be careful to do them. 2 The LORD our God made a covenant with us in Hō´rĕb. 3 Not with our fathers did the LORD make this covenant, but with us, who are all of us here alive this day. 4 The LORD spoke with you face to face at the mountain, out of the midst of the fire, 5 while I stood between the LORD and you at that time, to declare to you the word of the LORD; for you were afraid

because of the fire, and you did not go up into the mountain. He said:
6 " 'I am the LORD your God, who brought you out of the land of Egypt, out of the house of bondage.
7 " 'You shall have no other gods beforeᵈ me.
8 " 'You shall not make for yourself a graven image, or any likeness of anything that is in heaven above, or that is on the earth beneath, or that is in the water under the earth; 9 you shall not bow down to them or serve them; for I the LORD your God am a jealous God, visiting the iniquity of the fathers upon the children to the third and fourth generation of those who hate me, 10 but showing steadfast love to thousands of those who love me and keep my commandments.
11 " 'You shall not take the name of the LORD your God in vain: for the LORD will not hold him guiltless who takes his name in vain.
12 " 'Observe the sabbath day, to keep it holy, as the LORD your God commanded you. 13 Six days you shall labor, and do all your work; 14 but the seventh day is a sabbath to the LORD your God; in it you shall not do any work, you, or your son, or your daughter, or your manservant, or your maidservant, or your ox, or your ass, or any of your cattle, or the sojourner who is within your gates, that your manservant and your maidservant may rest as well as you. 15 You shall remember that you were a servant in the land of Egypt, and the LORD your God brought you out thence with a mighty hand and an outstretched arm; therefore the LORD your God commanded you to keep the sabbath day.
16 " 'Honor your father and your mother, as the LORD your God commanded you, that your days may be prolonged, and that it may go well with you, in the land which the LORD your God gives you.
17 " 'You shall not kill.
18 " 'Neither shall you commit adultery.
19 " 'Neither shall you steal.
20 " 'Neither shall you bear false witness against your neighbor.
21 " 'Neither shall you covet your neighbor's wife; and you shall not desire your neighbor's house, his field, or his manservant, or his maidservant,

ᶜ Syr: Heb Sion   ᵈ Or besides

4.41-43: Num 35.6, 9-34; Deut 19.2-13; Josh 20.7-9.
5.6-21: Ex 20.2-17.   5.14: Ex 20.8-11; 23.12.
5.16-20: Mt 19.18-19; Mk 10.19; Lk 18.20.   5.16: Mt 15.4; Mk 7.10; Eph 6.3.
5.17-18: Jas 2.11.   5.17-21: Rom 13.9.   5.18: Mt 5.27; Rom 7.7.
5.21: Rom 7.7.

his ox, or his ass, or anything that is your neighbor's.'

22 "These words the LORD spoke to all your assembly at the mountain out of the midst of the fire, the cloud, and the thick darkness, with a loud voice; and he added no more. And he wrote them upon two tables of stone, and gave them to me. 23And when you heard the voice out of the midst of the darkness, while the mountain was burning with fire, you came near to me, all the heads of your tribes, and your elders; 24 and you said, 'Behold, the LORD our God has shown us his glory and greatness, and we have heard his voice out of the midst of the fire; we have this day seen God speak with man and man still live. 25 Now therefore why should we die? For this great fire will consume us; if we hear the voice of the LORD our God any more, we shall die. 26 For who is there of all flesh, that has heard the voice of the living God speaking out of the midst of fire, as we have, and has still lived? 27 Go near, and hear all that the LORD our God will say; and speak to us all that the LORD our God will speak to you; and we will hear and do it.'

28 "And the LORD heard your words, when you spoke to me; and the LORD said to me, 'I have heard the words of this people, which they have spoken to you; they have rightly said all that they have spoken. 29 Oh that they had such a mind as this always, to fear me and to keep all my commandments, that it might go well with them and with their children for ever! 30 Go and say to them, "Return to your tents." 31 But you, stand here by me, and I will tell you all the commandment and the statutes and the ordinances which you shall teach them, that they may do them in the land which I give them to possess.' 32 You shall be careful to do therefore as the LORD your God has commanded you; you shall not turn aside to the right hand or to the left. 33 You shall walk in all the way which the LORD your God has commanded you, that you may live, and that it may go well with you, and that you may live long in the land which you shall possess.

6 "Now this is the commandment, the statutes, and the ordinances which the LORD your God commanded me to teach you, that you

may do them in the land to which you are going over, to possess it; 2 that you may fear the LORD your God, you and your son and your son's son, by keeping all his statutes and his commandments, which I command you, all the days of your life; and that your days may be prolonged. 3 Hear therefore, O Israel, and be careful to do them; that it may go well with you, and that you may multiply greatly, as the LORD, the God of your fathers, has promised you, in a land flowing with milk and honey.

4 "Hear, O Israel: The LORD our God is one LORD;e 5 and you shall love the LORD your God with all your heart, and with all your soul, and with all your might. 6And these words which I command you this day shall be upon your heart; 7 and you shall teach them diligently to your children, and shall talk of them when you sit in your house, and when you walk by the way, and when you lie down, and when you rise. 8And you shall bind them as a sign upon your hand, and they shall be as frontlets between your eyes. 9And you shall write them on the doorposts of your house and on your gates.

10 "And when the LORD your God brings you into the land which he swore to your fathers, to Abraham, to Isaac, and to Jacob, to give you, with great and goodly cities, which you did not build, 11 and houses full of all good things, which you did not fill, and cisterns hewn out, which you did not hew, and vineyards and olive trees, which you did not plant, and when you eat and are full, 12 then take heed lest you forget the LORD, who brought you out of the land of Egypt, out of the house of bondage. 13 You shall fear the LORD your God; you shall serve him, and swear by his name. 14 You shall not go after other gods, of the gods of the peoples who are round about you; 15 for the LORD your God in the midst of you is a jealous God; lest the anger of the LORD your God be kindled against you, and he destroy you from off the face of the earth.

16 "You shall not put the LORD your God to the test, as you tested him at Mas′sah. 17 You shall diligently keep the commandments of the LORD your God, and his testimonies, and his statutes, which he has commanded you. 18And you shall do what is right

e Or the LORD our God, the LORD is one   Or the LORD is our God, the LORD is one
Or the LORD is our God, the LORD alone

5.22-27: Ex 20.18-21.   6.4-5: Mt 22.37; Mk 12.29-30; Lk 10.27.
6.6-9: Deut 6.20-25; 11.18-20.   6.8: Ex 13.9, 16; Deut 11.18.   6.13: Mt 4.10; Lk 4.8.
6.16: Mt 4.7; Lk 4.12.

and good in the sight of the Lord, that it may go well with you, and that you may go in and take possession of the good land which the Lord swore to give to your fathers 19 by thrusting out all your enemies from before you, as the Lord has promised.

20 "When your son asks you in time to come, 'What is the meaning of the testimonies and the statutes and the ordinances which the Lord our God has commanded you?' 21 then you shall say to your son, 'We were Pharaoh's slaves in Egypt; and the Lord brought us out of Egypt with a mighty hand; 22 and the Lord showed signs and wonders, great and grievous, against Egypt and against Pharaoh and all his household, before our eyes; 23 and he brought us out from there, that he might bring us in and give us the land which he swore to give to our fathers. 24 And the Lord commanded us to do all these statutes, to fear the Lord our God, for our good always, that he might preserve us alive, as at this day. 25 And it will be righteousness for us, if we are careful to do all this commandment before the Lord our God, as he has commanded us.'

7 "When the Lord your God brings you into the land which you are entering to take possession of it, and clears away many nations before you, the Hit′tites, the Gir′ga·shites, the Am′o·rites, the Canaanites, the Per′iz·zites, the Hi′vites, and the Jeb′u·sites, seven nations greater and mightier than yourselves, 2 and when the Lord your God gives them over to you, and you defeat them; then you must utterly destroy them; you shall make no covenant with them, and show no mercy to them. 3 You shall not make marriages with them, giving your daughters to their sons or taking their daughters for your sons. 4 For they would turn away your sons from following me, to serve other gods; then the anger of the Lord would be kindled against you, and he would destroy you quickly. 5 But thus shall you deal with them: you shall break down their altars, and dash in pieces their pillars, and hew down their A·she′rim, and burn their graven images with fire.

6 "For you are a people holy to the Lord your God; the Lord your God has chosen you to be a people for his own possession, out of all the peoples that are on the face of the earth. 7 It was not because you were more in

number than any other people that the Lord set his love upon you and chose you, for you were the fewest of all peoples; 8 but it is because the Lord loves you, and is keeping the oath which he swore to your fathers, that the Lord has brought you out with a mighty hand, and redeemed you from the house of bondage, from the hand of Pharaoh king of Egypt. 9 Know therefore that the Lord your God is God, the faithful God who keeps covenant and steadfast love with those who love him and keep his commandments, to a thousand generations, 10 and requites to their face those who hate him, by destroying them; he will not be slack with him who hates him, he will requite him to his face. 11 You shall therefore be careful to do the commandment, and the statutes, and the ordinances, which I command you this day.

12 "And because you hearken to these ordinances, and keep and do them, the Lord your God will keep with you the covenant and the steadfast love which he swore to your fathers to keep; 13 he will love you, bless you, and multiply you; he will also bless the fruit of your body and the fruit of your ground, your grain and your wine and your oil, the increase of your cattle and the young of your flock, in the land which he swore to your fathers to give you. 14 You shall be blessed above all peoples; there shall not be male or female barren among you, or among your cattle. 15 And the Lord will take away from you all sickness; and none of the evil diseases of Egypt, which you knew, will he inflict upon you, but he will lay them upon all who hate you. 16 And you shall destroy all the peoples that the Lord your God will give over to you, your eye shall not pity them; neither shall you serve their gods, for that would be a snare to you.

17 "If you say in your heart, 'These nations are greater than I; how can I dispossess them?' 18 you shall not be afraid of them, but you shall remember what the Lord your God did to Pharaoh and to all Egypt, 19 the great trials which your eyes saw, the signs, the wonders, the mighty hand, and the outstretched arm, by which the Lord your God brought you out; so will the Lord your God do to all the peoples of whom you are afraid. 20 Moreover the Lord your God will send hornets among them, until those who are left

7.1: Acts 13.19. **7.2-4:** Ex 23.32-33; 34.12, 15-16. **7.3:** Ex 34.15-16.
7.5: Ex 23.24; 34.13; Num 33.52; Deut 12.3.
7.6: Ex 19.5; 22.3; Lev 11.44-45; 19.2; 20.7, 26; Num 15.40; Deut 14.2, 21; 26.19; 28.9.

and hide themselves from you are destroyed. 21 You shall not be in dread of them; for the LORD your God is in the midst of you, a great and terrible God. 22 The LORD your God will clear away these nations before you little by little; you may not make an end of them at once,[f] lest the wild beasts grow too numerous for you. 23 But the LORD your God will give them over to you, and throw them into great confusion, until they are destroyed. 24And he will give their kings into your hand, and you shall make their name perish from under heaven; not a man shall be able to stand against you, until you have destroyed them. 25 The graven images of their gods you shall burn with fire; you shall not covet the silver or the gold that is on them, or take it for yourselves, lest you be ensnared by it; for it is an abomination to the LORD your God. 26And you shall not bring an abominable thing into your house, and become accursed like it; you shall utterly detest and abhor it; for it is an accursed thing.

8 "All the commandment which I command you this day you shall be careful to do, that you may live and multiply, and go in and possess the land which the LORD swore to give to your fathers. 2And you shall remember all the way which the LORD your God has led you these forty years in the wilderness, that he might humble you, testing you to know what was in your heart, whether you would keep his commandments, or not. 3And he humbled you and let you hunger and fed you with manna, which you did not know, nor did your fathers know; that he might make you know that man does not live by bread alone, but that man lives by everything that proceeds out of the mouth of the LORD. 4 Your clothing did not wear out upon you, and your foot did not swell, these forty years. 5 Know then in your heart that, as a man disciplines his son, the LORD your God disciplines you. 6 So you shall keep the commandments of the LORD your God, by walking in his ways and by fearing him. 7 For the LORD your God is bringing you into a good land, a land of brooks of water, of fountains and springs, flowing forth in valleys and hills, 8 a land of wheat and barley, of vines and fig trees and pomegranates, a land of olive trees and honey, 9 a land in which you will eat bread without scarcity, in which you will lack nothing, a land whose stones

are iron, and out of whose hills you can dig copper. 10And you shall eat and be full, and you shall bless the LORD your God for the good land he has given you.

11 "Take heed lest you forget the LORD your God, by not keeping his commandments and his ordinances and his statutes, which I command you this day: 12 lest, when you have eaten and are full, and have built goodly houses and live in them, 13 and when your herds and flocks multiply, and your silver and gold is multiplied, and all that you have is multiplied, 14 then your heart be lifted up, and you forget the LORD your God, who brought you out of the land of Egypt, out of the house of bondage, 15 who led you through the great and terrible wilderness, with its fiery serpents and scorpions and thirsty ground where there was no water, who brought you water out of the flinty rock, 16 who fed you in the wilderness with manna which your fathers did not know, that he might humble you and test you, to do you good in the end. 17 Beware lest you say in your heart, 'My power and the might of my hand have gotten me this wealth.' 18 You shall remember the LORD your God, for it is he who gives you power to get wealth; that he may confirm his covenant which he swore to your fathers, as at this day. 19And if you forget the LORD your God and go after other gods and serve them and worship them, I solemnly warn you this day that you shall surely perish. 20 Like the nations that the LORD makes to perish before you, so shall you perish, because you would not obey the voice of the LORD your God.

9 "Hear, O Israel; you are to pass over the Jordan this day, to go in to dispossess nations greater and mightier than yourselves, cities great and fortified up to heaven, 2 a people great and tall, the sons of the An′a·kim, whom you know, and of whom you have heard it said, 'Who can stand before the sons of A′nak? 3 Know therefore this day that he who goes over before you as a devouring fire is the LORD your God; he will destroy them and subdue them before you; so you shall drive them out, and make them perish quickly, as the LORD has promised you.

4 "Do not say in your heart, after the LORD your God has thrust them out before you, 'It is because of my

[f] Or quickly
8.3: Mt 4.4; Lk 4.4.   **9.3:** Heb 12.29.

righteousness that the LORD has brought me in to possess this land'; whereas it is because of the wickedness of these nations that the LORD is driving them out before you. 5 Not because of your righteousness or the uprightness of your heart are you going in to possess their land; but because of the wickedness of these nations the LORD your God is driving them out from before you, and that he may confirm the word which the Lord swore to your fathers, to Abraham, to Isaac, and to Jacob.

6 "Know therefore, that the LORD your God is not giving you this good land to possess because of your righteousness; for you are a stubborn people. 7 Remember and do not forget how you provoked the LORD your God to wrath in the wilderness; from the day you came out of the land of Egypt, until you came to this place, you have been rebellious against the LORD. 8 Even at Hō′reb you provoked the LORD to wrath, and the LORD was so angry with you that he was ready to destroy you. 9 When I went up the mountain to receive the tables of stone, the tables of the covenant which the LORD made with you, I remained on the mountain forty days and forty nights; I neither ate bread nor drank water. 10And the LORD gave me the two tables of stone written with the finger of God; and on them were all the words which the LORD had spoken with you on the mountain out of the midst of the fire on the day of the assembly. 11And at the end of forty days and forty nights the LORD gave me the two tables of stone, the tables of the covenant. 12 Then the LORD said to me, 'Arise, go down quickly from here; for your people whom you have brought from Egypt have acted corruptly; they have turned aside quickly out of the way which I commanded them; they have made themselves a molten image.'

13 "Furthermore the LORD said to me, 'I have seen this people, and behold, it is a stubborn people; 14 let me alone, that I may destroy them and blot out their name from under heaven; and I will make of you a nation mightier and greater than they.' 15 So I turned and came down from the mountain, and the mountain was burning with fire; and the two tables of the covenant were in my two hands. 16And I looked, and behold, you had sinned against the LORD your God; you had made yourselves a molten calf; you had turned

aside quickly from the way which the LORD had commanded you. 17 So I took hold of the two tables, and cast them out of my two hands, and broke them before your eyes. 18 Then I lay prostrate before the LORD as before, forty days and forty nights; I neither ate bread nor drank water, because of all the sin which you had committed, in doing what was evil in the sight of the LORD, to provoke him to anger. 19 For I was afraid of the anger and hot displeasure which the LORD bore against you, so that he was ready to destroy you. But the LORD hearkened to me that time also. 20And the LORD was so angry with Aaron that he was ready to destroy him; and I prayed for Aaron also at the same time. 21 Then I took the sinful thing, the calf which you had made, and burned it with fire and crushed it, grinding it very small, until it was as fine as dust; and I threw the dust of it into the brook that descended out of the mountain.

22 "At Tab′é·rah also, and at Mas′-sáh, and at Kib′roth-hăt-tă′á·vάh, you provoked the LORD to wrath. 23And when the LORD sent you from Kā′desh-bär′nē·à, saying, 'Go up and take possession of the land which I have given you,' then you rebelled against the commandment of the LORD your God, and did not believe him or obey his voice. 24 You have been rebellious against the LORD from the day that I knew you.

25 "So I lay prostrate before the LORD for these forty days and forty nights, because the LORD had said he would destroy you. 26And I prayed to the LORD, 'O Lord GOD, destroy not thy people and thy heritage, whom thou hast redeemed through thy greatness, whom thou hast brought out of Egypt with a mighty hand. 27 Remember thy servants, Abraham, Isaac, and Jacob; do not regard the stubbornness of this people, or their wickedness, or their sin, 28 lest the land from which thou didst bring us say, "Because the LORD was not able to bring them into the land which he promised them, and because he hated them, he has brought them out to slay them in the wilderness." 29 For they are thy people and thy heritage, whom thou didst bring out by thy great power and by thy outstretched arm.'

10 "At that time the LORD said to me, 'Hew two tables of stone like the first, and come up to me on the mountain, and make an ark of wood. 2And I will write on the tables the

9.8-21: Ex 32.7-20.   9.25-29: Ex 32.11-14.

words that were on the first tables which you broke, and you shall put them in the ark.' ³ So I made an ark of acacia wood, and hewed two tables of stone like the first, and went up the mountain with the two tables in my hand. ⁴And he wrote on the tables, as at the first writing, the ten commandments⁸ which the LORD had spoken to you on the mountain out of the midst of the fire on the day of the assembly; and the LORD gave them to me. ⁵ Then I turned and came down from the mountain, and put the tables in the ark which I had made; and there they are, as the LORD commanded me.

6 (The people of Israel journeyed from Bē-ēr′ŏth Bē′ne-jā′a̱·kàn^h to Mō-sē′rāh. There Aaron died, and there he was buried; and his son El·ē·a′zär ministered as priest in his stead. ⁷ From there they journeyed to Gud′gŏ·dàh, and from Gudgodah to Jŏt′bà·thäh, a land with brooks of water. ⁸At that time the LORD set apart the tribe of Levi to carry the ark of the covenant of the LORD, to stand before the LORD to minister to him and to bless in his name, to this day. ⁹ Therefore Levi has no portion or inheritance with his brothers; the LORD is his inheritance, as the LORD your God said to him.)

10 "I stayed on the mountain, as at the first time, forty days and forty nights, and the LORD hearkened to me that time also; the LORD was unwilling to destroy you. ¹¹And the LORD said to me, 'Arise, go on your journey at the head of the people, that they may go in and possess the land, which I swore to their fathers to give them.'

12 "And now, Israel, what does the LORD our God require of you, but to fear the LORD your God, to walk in all his ways, to love him, to serve the LORD your God with all your heart and with all your soul, ¹³ and to keep the commandments and statutes of the LORD, which I command you this day for your good? ¹⁴ Behold, to the LORD your God belong heaven and the heaven of heavens, the earth with all that is in it; ¹⁵ yet the LORD set his heart in love upon your fathers and chose their descendants after them, you above all peoples, as at this day. ¹⁶ Circumcise therefore the foreskin of your heart, and be no longer stubborn. ¹⁷ For the LORD your God is God of gods and Lord of lords, the great, the mighty, and the terrible God, who is not partial and takes no bribe. ¹⁸ He

executes justice for the fatherless and the widow, and loves the sojourner, giving him food and clothing. ¹⁹ Love the sojourner therefore; for you were sojourners in the land of Egypt. ²⁰ You shall fear the LORD your God; you shall serve him and cleave to him, and by his name you shall swear. ²¹ He is your praise; he is your God, who has done for you these great and terrible things which your eyes have seen. ²² Your fathers went down to Egypt seventy persons; and now the LORD your God has made you as the stars of heaven for multitude.

11 "You shall therefore love the LORD your God, and keep his charge, his statutes, his ordinances, and his commandments always. ²And consider this day (since I am not speaking to your children who have not known or seen it), consider the discipline^i of the LORD your God, his greatness, his mighty hand and his outstretched arm, ³ his signs and his deeds which he did in Egypt to Pharaoh the king of Egypt and to all his land; ⁴ and what he did to the army of Egypt, to their horses and to their chariots; how he made the water of the Red Sea overflow them as they pursued after you, and how the LORD has destroyed them to this day; ⁵ and what he did to you in the wilderness, until you came to this place; ⁶ and what he did to Dā′thàn and Á·bī′ràm the sons of Ē·lī′àb, son of Reuben; how the earth opened its mouth and swallowed them up, with their households, their tents, and every living thing that followed them, in the midst of all Israel; ⁷ for your eyes have seen all the great work of the LORD which he did.

8 "You shall therefore keep all the commandment which I command you this day, that you may be strong, and go in and take possession of the land which you are going over to possess, ⁹ and that you may live long in the land which the LORD swore to your fathers to give to them and to their descendants, a land flowing with milk and honey. ¹⁰ For the land which you are entering to take possession of it is not like the land of Egypt, from which you have come, where you sowed your seed and watered it with your feet, like a garden of vegetables; ¹¹ but the land which you are going over to possess is a land of hills and valleys, which drinks water by the rain from heaven,

12 a land which the LORD your God cares for; the eyes of the LORD your God are always upon it, from the beginning of the year to the end of the year.

13 "And if you will obey my commandments which I command you this day, to love the LORD your God, and to serve him with all your heart and with all your soul, 14 he[j] will give the rain for your land in its season, the early rain and the later rain, that you may gather in your grain and your wine and your oil. 15And he[j] will give grass in your fields for your cattle, and you shall eat and be full. 16 Take heed lest your heart be deceived, and you turn aside and serve other gods and worship them, 17 and the anger of the LORD be kindled against you, and he shut up the heavens, so that there be no rain, and the land yield no fruit, and you perish quickly off the good land which the LORD gives you.

18 "You shall therefore lay up these words of mine in your heart and in your soul; and you shall bind them as a sign upon your hand, and they shall be as frontlets between your eyes. 19And you shall teach them to your children, talking of them when you are sitting in your house, and when you are walking by the way, and when you lie down, and when you rise. 20And you shall write them upon the doorposts of your house and upon your gates, 21 that your days and the days of your children may be multiplied in the land which the LORD swore to your fathers to give them, as long as the heavens are above the earth. 22 For if you will be careful to do all this commandment which I command you to do, loving the LORD your God, walking in all his ways, and cleaving to him, 23 then the LORD will drive out all these nations before you, and you will dispossess nations greater and mightier than yourselves. 24 Every place on which the sole of your foot treads shall be yours; your territory shall be from the wilderness and Lebanon and from the River, the river Eū·phrā′tēs, to the western sea. 25 No man shall be able to stand against you; the LORD your God will lay the fear of you and the dread of you upon all the land that you shall tread, as he promised you.

26 "Behold, I set before you this day a blessing and a curse: 27 the blessing, if you obey the commandments of the LORD your God, which I command you this day, 28 and the curse, if you do not obey the commandments of the LORD your God, but turn aside from the way which I command you this day, to go after other gods which you have not known. 29And when the LORD your God brings you into the land which you are entering to take possession of it, you shall set the blessing on Mount Gĕr′ĭ·zĭm and the curse on Mount Ē′băl. 30Are they not beyond the Jordan, west of the road, toward the going down of the sun, in the land of the Canaanites who live in the Ar′ă·băh, over against Gil′găl, beside the oak[k] of Mŏ′reh? 31 For you are to pass over the Jordan to go in to take possession of the land which the LORD your God gives you; and when you possess it and live in it, 32 you shall be careful to do all the statutes and the ordinances which I set before you this day.

12 "These are the statutes and ordinances which you shall be careful to do in the land which the LORD, the God of your fathers, has given you to possess, all the days that you live upon the earth. 2 You shall surely destroy all the places where the nations whom you shall dispossess served their gods, upon the high mountains and upon the hills and under every green tree; 3 you shall tear down their altars, and dash in pieces their pillars, and burn their Ā·shē′rim with fire; you shall hew down the graven images of their gods, and destroy their name out of that place. 4 You shall not do so to the LORD your God. 5 But you shall seek the place which the LORD your God will choose out of all your tribes to put his name and make his habitation there; thither you shall go, 6 and thither you shall bring your burnt offerings and your sacrifices, your tithes and the offering that you present, your votive offerings, your freewill offerings, and the firstlings of your herd and of your flock; 7 and there you shall eat before the LORD your God, and you shall rejoice, you and your households, in all that you undertake, in which the LORD your God has blessed you. 8 You shall not do according to all that we are doing here this day, every man doing whatever is right in his own eyes; 9 for you have not as yet come to the rest and to the inheritance which the LORD your God gives you. 10 But when you go over the Jordan, and live in the land which the LORD your God

---

[j] Sam Gk Vg: Heb I   [k] Gk Syr: See Gen 12.6. Heb oaks or terebinths

12.1-28: Ex 20.24.

gives you to inherit, and when he gives you rest from all your enemies round about, so that you live in safety, [11] then to the place which the LORD your God will choose, to make his name dwell there, thither you shall bring all that I command you: your burnt offerings and your sacrifices, your tithes and the offering that you present, and all your votive offerings which you vow to the LORD. [12]And you shall rejoice before the LORD your God, you and your sons and your daughters, your menservants and your maidservants, and the Levite that is within your towns, since he has no portion or inheritance with you. [13] Take heed that you do not offer your burnt offerings at every place that you see; [14] but at the place which the LORD will choose in one of your tribes, there you shall offer your burnt offerings, and there you shall do all that I am commanding you.

[15] "However, you may slaughter and eat flesh within any of your towns, as much as you desire, according to the blessing of the LORD your God which he has given you; the unclean and the clean may eat of it, as of the gazelle and as of the hart. [16] Only you shall not eat the blood; you shall pour it out upon the earth like water. [17] You may not eat within your towns the tithe of your grain or of your wine or of your oil, or the firstlings of your herd or of your flock, or any of your votive offerings which you vow, or your freewill offerings, or the offering that you present; [18] but you shall eat them before the LORD your God in the place which the LORD your God will choose, you and your son and your daughter, your manservant and your maidservant, and the Levite who is within your towns; and you shall rejoice before the LORD your God in all that you undertake. [19] Take heed that you do not forsake the Levite as long as you live in your land.

[20] "When the LORD your God enlarges your territory, as he has promised you, and you say, 'I will eat flesh,' because you crave flesh, you may eat as much flesh as you desire. [21] If the place which the LORD your God will choose to put his name there is too far from you, then you may kill any of your herd or your flock, which the LORD has given you, as I have commanded you; and you may eat within your towns as much as you desire. [22] Just as the gazelle or the hart is eaten, so you may eat of it; the

unclean and the clean alike may eat of it. [23] Only be sure that you do not eat the blood; for the blood is the life, and you shall not eat the life with the flesh. [24] You shall not eat it; you shall pour it out upon the earth like water. [25] You shall not eat it; that all may go well with you and with your children after you, when you do what is right in the sight of the LORD. [26] But the holy things which are due from you, and your votive offerings, you shall take, and you shall go to the place which the LORD will choose, [27] and offer your burnt offerings, the flesh and the blood, on the altar of the LORD your God; the blood of your sacrifices shall be poured out on the altar of the LORD your God, but the flesh you may eat. [28] Be careful to heed all these words which I command you, that it may go well with you and with your children after you for ever, when you do what is good and right in the sight of the LORD your God.

[29] "When the LORD your God cuts off before you the nations whom you go in to dispossess, and you dispossess them and dwell in their land, [30] take heed that you be not ensnared to follow them, after they have been destroyed before you, and that you do not inquire about their gods, saying, 'How did these nations serve their gods?'—that I also may do likewise.' [31] You shall not do so to the LORD your God; for every abominable thing which the LORD hates they have done for their gods; for they even burn their sons and their daughters in the fire to their gods.

[32*l*] "Everything that I command you, you shall be careful to do; you shall not add to it or take from it.

13 "If a prophet arises among you, or a dreamer of dreams, and gives you a sign or a wonder, [2] and the sign or wonder which he tells you comes to pass, and if he says, 'Let us go after other gods,' which you have not known, 'and let us serve them,' [3] you shall not listen to the words of that prophet or to that dreamer of dreams; for the LORD your God is testing you, to know whether you love the LORD your God with all your heart and with all your soul. [4] You shall walk after the LORD your God and fear him, and keep his commandments and obey his voice, and you shall serve him and cleave to him. [5] But that prophet or that dreamer of dreams shall be put to death, because he has taught rebel-

l Ch 13.1 in Heb

12.16, 23: Lev 17.10-14; 19.26.   **12.29-32:** Ex 23.24; 34.12-14; Num 33.52.

lion against the LORD your God, who brought you out of the land of Egypt and reedemed you out of the house of bondage, to make you leave the way in which the LORD your God commanded you to walk. So you shall purge the evil from the midst of you.

6 "If your brother, the son of your mother, or your son, or your daughter, or the wife of your bosom, or your friend who is as your own soul, entices you secretly, saying, 'Let us go and serve other gods,' which neither you nor your fathers have known, 7 some of the gods of the peoples that are round about you, whether near you or far off from you, from the one end of the earth to the other, 8 you shall not yield to him or listen to him, nor shall your eye pity him, nor shall you spare him, nor shall you conceal him; 9 but you shall kill him; your hand shall be first against him to put him to death, and afterwards the hand of all the people. 10 You shall stone him to death with stones, because he sought to draw you away from the LORD your God, who brought you out of the land of Egypt, out of the house of bondage. 11And all Israel shall hear, and fear, and never again do any such wickedness as this among you.

12 "If you hear in one of your cities, which the LORD your God gives you to dwell there, 13 that certain base fellows have gone out among you and have drawn away the inhabitants of the city, saying, 'Let us go and serve other gods,' which you have not known, 14 then you shall inquire and make search and ask diligently; and behold, if it be true and certain that such an abominable thing has been done among you, 15 you shall surely put the inhabitants of that city to the sword, destroying it utterly, all who are in it and its cattle, with the edge of the sword. 16 You shall gather all its spoil into the midst of its open square, and burn the city and all its spoil with fire, as a whole burnt offering to the LORD your God; it shall be a heap for ever, it shall not be built again. 17 None of the devoted things shall cleave to your hand; that the LORD may turn from the fierceness of his anger, and show you mercy, and have compassion on you, and multiply you, as he swore to your fathers, 18 if you obey the voice of the LORD your God, keeping all his commandments which I command you

this day, and doing what is right in the sight of the LORD your God.

14 "You are the sons of the LORD your God; you shall not cut yourselves or make any baldness on your foreheads for the dead. 2 For you are a people holy to the LORD your God, and the LORD has chosen you to be a people for his own possession, out of all the peoples that are on the face of the earth.

3 "You shall not eat any abominable thing. 4 These are the animals you may eat: the ox, the sheep, the goat, 5 the hart, the gazelle, the roebuck, the wild goat, the ibex, the antelope, and the mountain-sheep. 6 Every animal that parts the hoof and has the hoof cloven in two, and chews the cud, among the animals, you may eat. 7 Yet of those that chew the cud or have the hoof cloven you shall not eat these: the camel, the hare, and the rock badger, because they chew the cud but do not part the hoof, are unclean for you. 8And the swine, because it parts the hoof but does not chew the cud, is unclean for you. Their flesh you shall not eat, and their carcasses you shall not touch.

9 "Of all that are in the waters you may eat these: whatever has fins and scales you may eat. 10And whatever does not have fins and scales you shall not eat; it is unclean for you.

11 "You may eat all clean birds. 12 But these are the ones which you shall not eat: the eagle, the vulture, the osprey, 13 the buzzard, the kite, after their kinds; 14 every raven after its kind; 15 the ostrich, the nighthawk, the sea gull, the hawk, after their kinds; 16 the little owl and the great owl, the water hen 17 and the pelican, the carrion vulture and the cormorant, 18 the stork, the heron, after their kinds; the hoopoe and the bat. 19And all winged insects are unclean for you; they shall not be eaten. 20All clean winged things you may eat.

21 "You shall not eat anything that dies of itself; you may give it to the alien who is within your towns, that he may eat it, or you may sell it to a foreigner; for you are a people holy to the LORD your God.

"You shall not boil a kid in its mother's milk.

22 "You shall tithe all the yield of your seed, which comes forth from the field year by year. 23And before the LORD your God, in the place which

14.1: Lev 19.28.   **14.2:** Ex 19.5-6; Deut 26.19; Tit 2.14; 1 Pet 2.9; Rev 1.6; **5.10.**
14.3-20: Lev 11.2-23.   **14.21:** Lev 11.39-40; 17.15; Ex 23.19; 34.26.
14.22-29: Lev 27.30-33; Num 18.21-32.

he will choose, to make his name dwell there, you shall eat the tithe of your grain, of your wine, and of your oil, and the firstlings of your herd and flock; that you may learn to fear the LORD your God always. 24And if the way is too long for you, so that you are not able to bring the tithe, when the LORD your God blesses you, because the place is too far from you, which the LORD your God chooses, to set his name there, 25 then you shall turn it into money, and bind up the money in your hand, and go to the place which the LORD your God chooses, 26 and spend the money for whatever you desire, oxen, or sheep, or wine or strong drink, whatever your appetite craves; and you shall eat there before the LORD your God and rejoice, you and your household. 27And you shall not forsake the Levite who is within your towns, for he has no portion or inheritance with you.

28 "At the end of every three years you shall bring forth all the tithe of your produce in the same year, and lay it up within your towns; 29 and the Levite, because he has no portion or inheritance with you, and the sojourner, the fatherless, and the widow, who are within your towns, shall come and eat and be filled; that the LORD your God may bless you in all the work of your hands that you do.

15 "At the end of every seven years you shall grant a release. 2And this is the manner of the release: every creditor shall release what he has lent to his neighbor; he shall not exact it of his neighbor, his brother, because the LORD's release has been proclaimed. 3 Of a foreigner you may exact it; but whatever of yours is with your brother your hand shall release. 4 But there will be no poor among you (for the LORD will bless you in the land which the LORD your God gives you for an inheritance to possess), 5 if only you will obey the voice of the LORD your God, being careful to do all this commandment which I command you this day. 6 For the LORD your God will bless you, as he promised you, and you shall lend to many nations, but you shall not borrow; and you shall rule over many nations, but they shall not rule over you.

7 "If there is among you a poor man, one of your brethren, in any of your towns within your land which the LORD your God gives you, you shall not harden your heart or shut your hand against your poor brother, 8 but you shall open your hand to him, and lend him sufficient for his need, whatever it may be. 9 Take heed lest there be a base thought in your heart, and you say, 'The seventh year, the year of release is near,' and your eye be hostile to your poor brother, and you give him nothing, and he cry to the LORD against you, and it be sin in you. 10 You shall give to him freely, and your heart shall not be grudging when you give to him; because for this the LORD your God will bless you in all your work and in all that you undertake. 11 For the poor will never cease out of the land; therefore I command you, You shall open wide your hand to your brother, to the needy and to the poor, in the land.

12 "If your brother, a Hebrew man, or a Hebrew woman, is sold to you, he shall serve you six years, and in the seventh year you shall let him go free from you. 13And when you let him go free from you, you shall not let him go empty-handed; 14 you shall furnish him liberally out of your flock, out of your threshing floor, and out of your wine press; as the LORD your God has blessed you, you shall give to him. 15 You shall remember that you were a slave in the land of Egypt, and the LORD your God redeemed you; therefore I command you this today. 16 But if he says to you, 'I will not go out from you,' because he loves you and your household, since he fares well with you, 17 then you shall take an awl, and thrust it through his ear into the door, and he shall be your bondman for ever. And to your bondwoman you shall do likewise. 18 It shall not seem hard to you, when you let him go free from you; for at half the cost of a hired servant he has served you six years. So the LORD your God will bless you in all that you do.

19 "All the firstling males that are born of your herd and flock you shall consecrate to the LORD your God; you shall do no work with the firstling of your herd, nor shear the firstling of your flock. 20 You shall eat it, you and your household, before the LORD your God year by year at the place which the LORD will choose. 21 But if it has any blemish, if it is lame or blind, or has any serious blemish whatever, you shall not sacrifice it to the LORD your God. 22 You shall eat it within your towns; the unclean and the clean alike may eat it, as though it were a gazelle

15.12-18: Ex 21.2-11; Lev 25.39-46.
15.19-23: Ex 13.11-12; 22.30; 34.19; Num 18.17-18.

or a hart. 23 Only you shall not eat its blood; you shall pour it out on the ground like water.

16 "Observe the month of A'bib, and keep the passover to the LORD your God; for in the month of Abib the LORD your God brought you out of Egypt by night. 2 And you shall offer the passover sacrifice to the LORD your God, from the flock or the herd, at the place which the LORD will choose, to make his name dwell there. 3 You shall eat no leavened bread with it; seven days you shall eat it with unleavened bread, the bread of affliction —for you came out of the land of Egypt in hurried flight—that all the days of your life you may remember the day when you came out of the land of Egypt. 4 No leaven shall be seen with you in all your territory for seven days; nor shall any of the flesh which you sacrifice on the evening of the first day remain all night until morning. 5 You may not offer the passover sacrifice within any of your towns which the LORD your God gives you; 6 but at the place which the LORD your God will choose, to make his name dwell in it, there you shall offer the passover sacrifice, in the evening at the going down of the sun, at the time you came out of Egypt. 7 And you shall boil it and eat it at the place which the LORD your God will choose; and in the morning you shall turn and go to your tents. 8 For six days you shall eat unleavened bread; and on the seventh day there shall be a solemn assembly to the LORD your God; you shall do no work on it.

9 "You shall count seven weeks; begin to count the seven weeks from the time you first put the sickle to the standing grain. 10 Then you shall keep the feast of weeks to the LORD your God with the tribute of a freewill offering from your hand, which you shall give as the LORD your God blesses you; 11 and you shall rejoice before the LORD your God, you and your son and your daughter, your manservant and your maidservant, the Levite who is within your towns, the sojourner, the fatherless, and the widow who are among you, at the place which the LORD your God will choose, to make his name dwell there. 12 You shall remember that you were a slave in Egypt; and you shall be careful to observe these statutes.

13 "You shall keep the feast of booths seven days, when you make your ingathering from your threshing floor and your wine press; 14 you shall rejoice in your feast, you and your son and your daughter, your manservant and your maidservant, the Levite, the sojourner, the fatherless, and the widow who are within your towns. 15 For seven days you shall keep the feast to the LORD your God at the place which the LORD will choose; because the LORD your God will bless you in all your produce and in all the work of your hands, so that you will be altogether joyful.

16 "Three times a year all your males shall appear before the LORD your God at the place which he will choose: at the feast of unleavened bread, at the feast of weeks, and at the feast of booths. They shall not appear before the LORD empty-handed; 17 every man shall give as he is able, according to the blessing of the LORD your God which he has given you.

18 "You shall appoint judges and officers in all your towns which the LORD your God gives you, according to your tribes; and they shall judge the people with righteous judgment. 19 You shall not pervert justice; you shall not show partiality; and you shall not take a bribe, for a bribe blinds the eyes of the wise and subverts the cause of the righteous. 20 Justice, and only justice, you shall follow, that you may live and inherit the land which the LORD your God gives you.

21 "You shall not plant any tree as an A·she'rah beside the altar of the LORD your God which you shall make. 22 And you shall not set up a pillar, which the LORD your God hates.

17 "You shall not sacrifice to the LORD your God an ox or a sheep in which is a blemish, any defect whatever; for that is an abomination to the LORD your God.

2 "If there is found among you, within any of your towns which the LORD your God gives you, a man or woman who does what is evil in the sight of the LORD your God, in transgressing his covenant, 3 and has gone and served other gods and worshiped them, or the sun or the moon or any of the host of heaven, which I have forbidden, 4 and it is told you and you hear of it; then you shall inquire diligently, and if it is true and certain that such an abominable thing has been done in Israel, 5 then you shall bring forth to your gates that man or woman who has done this evil thing,

and you shall stone that man or woman to death with stones. 6 On the evidence of two witnesses or of three witnesses he that is to die shall be put to death; a person shall not be put to death on the evidence of one witness. 7 The hand of the witnesses shall be first against him to put him to death, and afterward the hand of all the people. So you shall purge the evil from the midst of you.

8 "If any case arises requiring decision between one kind of homicide and another, one kind of legal right and another, or one kind of assault and another, any case within your towns which is too difficult for you, then you shall arise and go up to the place which the LORD your God will choose, 9 and coming to the Levitical priests, and to the judge who is in office in those days, you shall consult them, and they shall declare to you the decision. 10 Then you shall do according to what they declare to you from that place which the LORD will choose; and you shall be careful to do according to all that they direct you; 11 according to the instructions which they give you, and according to the decision which they pronounce to you, you shall do; you shall not turn aside from the verdict which they declare to you, either to the right hand or to the left. 12 The man who acts presumptuously, by not obeying the priest who stands to minister there before the LORD your God, or the judge, that man shall die; so you shall purge the evil from Israel. 13 And all the people shall hear, and fear, and not act presumptuously again.

14 "When you come to the land which the LORD your God gives you, and you possess it and dwell in it, and then say, 'I will set a king over me, like all the nations that are round about me'; 15 you may indeed set as king over you him whom the LORD your God will choose. One from among your brethren you shall set as king over you; you may not put a foreigner over you, who is not your brother. 16 Only he must not multiply horses for himself, or cause the people to return to Egypt in order to multiply horses, since the LORD has said to you, 'You shall never return that way again.' 17 And he shall not multiply wives for himself, lest his heart turn away; nor shall he greatly multiply for himself silver and gold.

18 "And when he sits on the throne of his kingdom, he shall write for himself in a book a copy of this law, from that which is in charge of the Levitical priests; 19 and it shall be with him, and he shall read in it all the days of his life, that he may learn to fear the LORD his God, by keeping all the words of this law and these statutes, and doing them; 20 that his heart may not be lifted up above his brethren, and that he may not turn aside from the commandment, either to the right hand or to the left; so that he may continue long in his kingdom, he and his children, in Israel.

18 "The Levitical priests, that is, all the tribe of Levi, shall have no portion or inheritance with Israel; they shall eat the offerings by fire to the LORD, and his rightful dues. 2 They shall have no inheritance among their brethren; the LORD is their inheritance, as he promised them. 3 And this shall be the priests' due from the people, from those offering a sacrifice, whether it be ox or sheep: they shall give to the priest the shoulder and the two cheeks and the stomach. 4 The first fruits of your grain, of your wine and of your oil, and the first of the fleece of your sheep, you shall give him. 5 For the LORD your God has chosen him out of all your tribes, to stand and minister in the name of the LORD, him and his sons for ever.

6 "And if a Levite comes from any of your towns out of all Israel, where he lives—and he may come when he desires—to the place which the LORD will choose, 7 then he may minister in the name of the LORD his God, like all his fellow-Levites who stand to minister there before the LORD. 8 They shall have equal portions to eat, besides what he receives from the sale of his patrimony.*m*

9 "When you come into the land which the LORD your God gives you, you shall not learn to follow the abominable practices of those nations. 10 There shall not be found among you any one who burns his son or his daughter as an offering,*n* any one who practices divination, a soothsayer, or an augur, or a sorcerer, 11 or a charmer, or a medium, or a wizard, or a necromancer. 12 For whoever does these things is an abomination to the LORD; and because of these abominable practices the LORD your God is driving

m Heb obscure   *n* Heb *makes his son or his daughter pass through the fire*

17.6: Num 35.30; Deut 19.15; Mt 18.16; 2 Cor 13.1; 1 Tim 5.19; Heb 10.28.
17.7: Deut 19.19; 1 Cor 5.13.   **18.1-8:** Num 18.20-24.
18.10-11: Ex 22.18; Lev 19.26, 31; 20.6, 27.

them out before you. 13 You shall be blameless before the LORD your God. 14 For these nations, which you are about to dispossess, give heed to soothsayers and to diviners; but as for you, the LORD your God has not allowed you so to do.

15 "The LORD your God will raise up for you a prophet like me from among you, from your brethren—him you shall heed—16 just as you desired of the LORD your God at Hō'reb on the day of the assembly, when you said, 'Let me not hear again the voice of the LORD my God, or see this great fire any more, lest I die.' 17And the LORD said to me, 'They have rightly said all that they have spoken. 18 I will raise up for them a prophet like you from among their brethren; and I will put my words in his mouth, and he shall speak to them all that I command him. 19And whoever will not give heed to my words which he shall speak in my name, I myself will require it of him. 20 But the prophet who presumes to speak a word in my name which I have not commanded him to speak, or who speaks in the name of other gods, that same prophet shall die.' 21And if you say in your heart, 'How may we know the word which the LORD has not spoken?'—22 when a prophet speaks in the name of the LORD, if the word does not come to pass or come true, that is a word which the LORD has not spoken; the prophet has spoken it presumptuously, you need not be afraid of him.

19 "When the LORD your God cuts off the nations whose land the LORD your God gives you, and you dispossess them and dwell in their cities and in their houses, 2 you shall set apart three cities for you in the land which the LORD your God gives you to possess. 3 You shall prepare the roads, and divide into three parts the area of the land which the LORD your God gives you as a possession, so that any manslayer can flee to them.

4 "This is the provision for the manslayer, who by fleeing there may save his life. If any one kills his neighbor unintentionally without having been at enmity with him in time past—5 as when a man goes into the forest with his neighbor to cut wood, and his hand swings the axe to cut down a tree, and the head slips from

the handle and strikes his neighbor so that he dies—he may flee to one of these cities and save his life; 6 lest the avenger of blood in hot anger pursue the manslayer and overtake him, because the way is long, and wound him mortally, though the man did not deserve to die, since he was not at enmity with his neighbor in time past. 7 Therefore I command you, You shall set apart three cities. 8And if the LORD your God enlarges your border, as he has sworn to your fathers, and gives you all the land which he promised to give to your fathers—9 provided you are careful to keep all this commandment, which I command you this day, by loving the LORD your God and by walking ever in his ways—then you shall add three other cities to these three, 10 lest innocent blood be shed in your land which the LORD your God gives you for an inheritance, and so the guilt of bloodshed be upon you.

11 "But if any man hates his neighbor, and lies in wait for him, and attacks him, and wounds him mortally so that he dies, and the man flees into one of these cities, 12 then the elders of his city shall send and fetch him from there, and hand him over to the avenger of blood, so that he may die. 13 Your eye shall not pity him, but you shall purge the guilt of innocent blood° from Israel, so that it may be well with you.

14 "In the inheritance which you will hold in the land that the LORD your God gives you to possess, you shall not remove your neighbor's landmark, which the men of old have set.

15 "A single witness shall not prevail against a man for any crime or for any wrong in connection with any offense that he has committed; only on the evidence of two witnesses, or of three witnesses, shall a charge be sustained. 16 If a malicious witness rises against any man to accuse him of wrongdoing, 17 then both parties to the dispute shall appear before the LORD, before the priests and the judges who are in office in those days; 18 the judges shall inquire diligently, and if the witness is a false witness and has accused his brother falsely, 19 then you shall do to him as he had meant to do to his brother; so you shall purge the evil from the midst of you. 20And the rest shall hear, and fear, and shall never

° Or *the blood of the innocent* **18.13:** Mt 5.48.
18.15-19: Acts 3.22-23; 7.37.   **19.1-13:** Ex 21.12-14; Num 35.
19.15: Num 35.30; Deut 17.6; Mt 18.16; 2 Cor 13.1; 1 Tim 5.19; Heb 10.28.
19.16-20: Ex 20.16; 23.1; Lev 19.16; Deut 5.20.
19.19: 1 Cor 5.13.

again commit any such evil among you.
21 Your eye shall not pity; it shall be
life for life, eye for eye, tooth for
tooth, hand for hand, foot for foot.

20 "When you go forth to war
against your enemies, and see
horses and chariots and an army larger
than your own, you shall not be afraid
of them; for the LORD your God is
with you, who brought you up out of
the land of Egypt. 2And when you
draw near to the battle, the priest shall
come forward and speak to the people,
3 and shall say to them, 'Hear, O Israel,
you draw near this day to battle against
your enemies: let not your heart faint;
do not fear, or tremble, or be in dread
of them; 4 for the LORD your God is
he that goes with you, to fight for you
against your enemies, to give you the
victory.' 5 Then the officers shall speak
to the people, saying, 'What man is
there that has built a new house and
has not dedicated it? Let him go back
to his house, lest he die in the battle
and another man dedicate it. 6And
what man is there that has planted a
vineyard and has not enjoyed its fruit?
Let him go back to his house, lest he
die in the battle and another man enjoy
its fruit. 7And what man is there that
has betrothed a wife and has not taken
her? Let him go back to his house, lest
he die in the battle and another man
take her.' 8And the officers shall speak
further to the people, and say, 'What
man is there that is fearful and fainthearted? Let him go back to his house,
lest the heart of his fellows melt as his
heart.' 9And when the officers have
made an end of speaking to the people,
then commanders shall be appointed
at the head of the people.
10 "When you draw near to a city
to fight against it, offer terms of peace
to it. 11And if its answer to you is peace
and it opens to you, then all the people
who are found in it shall do forced
labor for you and shall serve you.
12 But if it makes no peace with you,
but makes war against you, then you
shall besiege it; 13 and when the LORD
your God gives it into your hand you
shall put all its males to the sword,
14 but the women and the little ones,
the cattle, and everything else in the
city, all its spoil, you shall take as booty
for yourselves; and you shall enjoy the
spoil of your enemies, which the LORD
your God has given you. 15 Thus you
shall do to all the cities which are very
far from you, which are not cities of
the nations here. 16 But in the cities
of these peoples that the LORD your

19.21: Ex 21.23-26; Lev 24.20; Mt 5.38.

God gives you for an inheritance, you
shall save alive nothing that breathes,
17 but you shall utterly destroy them,
the Hit'tites and the Am'ō·rites, the
Canaanites and the Per'iz·zites, the Hi'-
vites and the Jeb'ū·sites, as the LORD
your God has commanded; 18 that they
may not teach you to do according to
all their abominable practices which
they have done in the service of their
gods, and so to sin against the LORD
your God.
19 "When you besiege a city for a
long time, making war against it in
order to take it, you shall not destroy
its trees by wielding an axe against
them; for you may eat of them, but you
shall not cut them down. Are the trees
in the field men that they should be besieged by you? 20 Only the trees which
you know are not trees for food you
may destroy and cut down that you
may build siegeworks against the city
that makes war with you, until it falls.

21 "If in the land which the LORD
your God gives you to possess,
any one is found slain, lying in the
open country, and it is not known who
killed him, 2 then your elders and your
judges shall come forth, and they shall
measure the distance to the cities
which are around him that is slain;
3 and the elders of the city which is
nearest to the slain man shall take a
heifer which has never been worked
and which has not pulled in the yoke.
4And the elders of that city shall bring
the heifer down to a valley with running water, which is neither plowed
nor sown, and shall break the heifer's
neck there in the valley. 5And the
priests the sons of Levi shall come
forward, for the LORD your God has
chosen them to minister to him and to
bless in the name of the LORD, and by
their word every dispute and every
assault shall be settled. 6And all the
elders of that city nearest to the slain
man shall wash their hands over the
heifer whose neck was broken in the
valley; 7 and they shall testify, 'Our
hands did not shed this blood, neither
did our eyes see it shed. 8 Forgive, O
LORD, thy people Israel, whom thou
hast redeemed, and set not the guilt of
innocent blood in the midst of thy
people Israel; but let the guilt of blood
be forgiven them.' 9 So you shall purge
the guilt of innocent blood from your
midst, when you do what is right in the
sight of the LORD.
10 "When you go forth to war
against your enemies, and the LORD
your God gives them into your hands,

and you take them captive, 11 and see among the captives a beautiful woman, and you have desire for her and would take her for yourself as wife, 12 then you shall bring her home to your house, and she shall shave her head and pare her nails. 13 And she shall put off her captive's garb, and shall remain in your house and bewail her father and her mother a full month; after that you may go in to her, and be her husband, and she shall be your wife. 14 Then, if you have no delight in her, you shall let her go where she will; but you shall not sell her for money, you shall not treat her as a slave, since you have humiliated her.

15 "If a man has two wives, the one loved and the other disliked, and they have borne him children, both the loved and the disliked, and if the first-born son is hers that is disliked, 16 then on the day when he assigns his posses-sions as an inheritance to his sons, he may not treat the son of the loved as the first-born in preference to the son of the disliked, who is the first-born, 17 but he shall acknowledge the first-born, the son of the disliked, by giving him a double portion of all that he has, for he is the first issue of his strength; the right of the first-born is his.

18 "If a man has a stubborn and rebellious son, who will not obey the voice of his father or the voice of his mother, and though they chastise him, will not give heed to them, 19 then his father and his mother shall take hold of him and bring him out to the elders of his city at the gate of the place where he lives, 20 and they shall say to the elders of his city, 'This our son is stubborn and rebellious, he will not obey our voice; he is a glutton and a drunkard.' 21 Then all the men of the city shall stone him to death with stones; so you shall purge the evil from your midst; and all Israel shall hear, and fear.

22 "And if a man has committed a crime punishable by death and he is put to death, and you hang him on a tree, 23 his body shall not remain all night upon the tree, but you shall bury him the same day, for a hanged man is accursed by God; you shall not defile your land which the LORD your God gives you for an inheritance.

22 "You shall not see your broth-er's ox or his sheep go astray, and withhold your help*p* from them; you shall take them back to your

brother. 2 And if he is not near you, or if you do not know him, you shall bring it home to your house, and it shall be with you until your brother seeks it; then you shall restore it to him. 3 And so you shall do with his ass; so you shall do with his garment; so you shall do with any lost thing of your brother's, which he loses and you find; you may not withhold your help. 4 You shall not see your brother's ass or his ox fallen down by the way, and withhold your help*p* from them; you shall help him to lift them up again.

5 "A woman shall not wear any-thing that pertains to a man, nor shall a man put on a woman's garment; for whoever does these things is an abomi-nation to the LORD your God.

6 "If you chance to come upon a bird's nest, in any tree or on the ground, with young ones or eggs and the mother sitting upon the young or upon the eggs, you shall not take the mother with the young; 7 you shall let the mother go, but the young you may take to yourself; that it may go well with you, and that you may live long.

8 "When you build a new house, you shall make a parapet for your roof, that you may not bring the guilt of blood upon your house, if any one fall from it.

9 "You shall not sow your vineyard with two kinds of seed, lest the whole yield be forfeited to the sanctuary,*q* the crop which you have sown and the yield of the vineyard. 10 You shall not plow with an ox and an ass together. 11 You shall not wear a mingled stuff, wool and linen together.

12 "You shall make yourself tassels on the four corners of your cloak with which you cover yourself.

13 "If any man takes a wife, and goes in to her, and then spurns her, 14 and charges her with shameful con-duct, and brings an evil name upon her, saying, 'I took this woman, and when I came near her, I did not find in her the tokens of virginity,' 15 then the father of the young woman and her mother shall take and bring out the tokens of her virginity to the elders of the city in the gate; 16 and the father of the young woman shall say to the elders, 'I gave my daughter to this man to wife, and he spurns her; 17 and lo, he has made shameful charges against her, saying, "I did not find in your daughter the tokens of virginity." And yet these are the tokens of my daugh-

p Heb *hide yourself*   *q* Heb *become holy*
21.18-21: Ex 20.12; 21.15, 17; Lev 20.9; Deut 5.16; 27.16.   **21.22:** Acts 5.30; 10.39.
21.23: Gal 3.13.   **22.1-4:** Ex 23.4-5.   **22.9-11:** Lev 19.19.   **22.12:** Num 15.37-41.

ter's virginity.' And they shall spread the garment before the elders of the city. 18 Then the elders of that city shall take the man and whip him; 19 and they shall fine him a hundred shekels of silver, and give them to the father of the young woman, because he has brought an evil name upon a virgin of Israel; and she shall be his wife; he may not put her away all his days. 20 But if the thing is true, that the tokens of virginity were not found in the young woman, 21 then they shall bring out the young woman to the door of her father's house, and the men of her city shall stone her to death with stones, because she has wrought folly in Israel by playing the harlot in her father's house; so you shall purge the evil from the midst of you.

22 "If a man is found lying with the wife of another man, both of them shall die, the man who lay with the woman, and the woman; so you shall purge the evil from Israel.

23 "If there is a betrothed virgin, and a man meets her in the city and lies with her, 24 then you shall bring them both out to the gate of that city, and you shall stone them to death with stones, the young woman because she did not cry for help though she was in the city, and the man because he violated his neighbor's wife; so you shall purge the evil from the midst of you.

25 "But if in the open country a man meets a young woman who is betrothed, and the man seizes her and lies with her, then only the man who lay with her shall die. 26 But to the young woman you shall do nothing; in the young woman there is no offense punishable by death, for this case is like that of a man attacking and murdering his neighbor; 27 because he came upon her in the open country, and though the betrothed young woman cried for help there was no one to rescue her.

28 "If a man meets a virgin who is not betrothed, and seizes her and lies with her, and they are found, 29 then the man who lay with her shall give to the father of the young woman fifty shekels of silver, and she shall be his wife, because he has violated her; he may not put her away all his days.

30ʳ "A man shall not take his father's wife, nor shall he uncover her who is his father's.ˢ

23 "He whose testicles are crushed or whose male member is cut off shall not enter the assembly of the LORD.

2 "No bastard shall enter the assembly of the LORD; even to the tenth generation none of his descendants shall enter the assembly of the LORD.

3 "No Am′mo·nīte or Mō′ab·īte shall enter the assembly of the LORD; even to the tenth generation none belonging to them shall enter the assembly of the LORD for ever; 4 because they did not meet you with bread and with water on the way, when you came forth out of Egypt, and because they hired against you Balaam the son of Bē′ôr from Pē′thôr of Mes·ô·pô·tā′mi·à, to curse you. 5 Nevertheless the LORD your God would not hearken to Balaam; but the LORD your God turned the curse into a blessing for you, because the LORD your God loved you. 6 You shall not seek their peace or their prosperity all your days for ever.

7 "You shall not abhor an Ē′dôm-īte, for he is your brother; you shall not abhor an Egyptian, because you were a sojourner in his land. 8 The children of the third generation that are born to them may enter the assembly of the LORD.

9 "When you go forth against your enemies and are in camp, then you shall keep yourself from every evil thing.

10 "If there is among you any man who is not clean by reason of what chances to him by night, then he shall go outside the camp, he shall not come within the camp; 11 but when evening comes on, he shall bathe himself in water, and when the sun is down, he may come within the camp.

12 "You shall have a place outside the camp and you shall go out to it; 13 and you shall have a stick with your weapons; and when you sit down outside, you shall dig a hole with it, and turn back and cover up your excrement. 14 Because the LORD your God walks in the midst of your camp, to save you and to give up your enemies before you, therefore your camp must be holy, that he may not see anything indecent among you, and turn away from you.

15 "You shall not give up to his master a slave who has escaped from his master to you; 16 he shall dwell with you, in your midst, in the place which

ʳ Ch 23.1 in Heb   ˢ Heb *uncover his father's skirt*
22.21: 1 Cor 5.13.   22.22-27: Ex 20.14; Lev 18.20; 20.10; Deut 5.18.
22.24: 1 Cor 5.13.   22.28-29: Ex 22.16-17.

he shall choose within one of your towns, where it pleases him best; you shall not oppress him.

17 "There shall be no cult prostitute of the daughters of Israel, neither shall there be a cult prostitute of the sons of Israel. 18 You shall not bring the hire of a harlot, or the wages of a dog,ᶠ into the house of the LORD your God in payment for any vow; for both of these are an abomination to the LORD your God.

19 "You shall not lend upon interest to your brother, interest on money, interest on victuals, interest on anything that is lent for interest. 20 To a foreigner you may lend upon interest, but to your brother you shall not lend upon interest; that the LORD your God may bless you in all that you undertake in the land which you are entering to take possession of it.

21 "When you make a vow to the LORD your God, you shall not be slack to pay it; for the LORD your God will surely require it of you, and it would be sin in you. 22 But if you refrain from vowing, it shall be no sin in you. 23 You shall be careful to perform what has passed your lips, for you have voluntarily vowed to the LORD your God what you have promised with your mouth.

24 "When you go into your neighbor's vineyard, you may eat your fill of grapes, as many as you wish, but you shall not put any in your vessel. 25 When you go into your neighbor's standing grain, you may pluck the ears with your hand, but you shall not put a sickle to your neighbor's standing grain.

24 "When a man takes a wife and marries her, if then she finds no favor in his eyes because he has found some indecency in her, and he writes her a bill of divorce and puts it in her hand and sends her out of his house, and she departs out of his house, 2 and if she goes and becomes another man's wife, 3 and the latter husband dislikes her and writes her a bill of divorce and puts it in her hand and sends her out of his house, or if the latter husband dies, who took her to be his wife, 4 then her former husband, who sent her away, may not take her again to be his wife, after she has been defiled; for that is an abomination before the LORD, and you shall not bring guilt

upon the land which the LORD your God gives you for an inheritance.

5 "When a man is newly married, he shall not go out with the army or be charged with any business; he shall be free at home one year, to be happy with his wife whom he has taken.

6 "No man shall take a mill or an upper millstone in pledge; for he would be taking a life in pledge.

7 "If a man is found stealing one of his brethren, the people of Israel, and if he treats him as a slave or sells him, then that thief shall die; so you shall purge the evil from the midst of you.

8 "Take heed, in an attack of leprosy, to be very careful to do according to all that the Levitical priests shall direct you; as I commanded them, so you shall be careful to do. 9 Remember what the LORD your God did to Miriam on the way as you came forth out of Egypt.

10 "When you make your neighbor a loan of any sort, you shall not go into his house to fetch his pledge. 11 You shall stand outside, and the man to whom you make the loan shall bring the pledge out to you. 12 And if he is a poor man, you shall not sleep in his pledge; 13 when the sun goes down, you shall restore to him the pledge that he may sleep in his cloak and bless you; and it shall be righteousness to you before the LORD your God.

14 "You shall not oppress a hired servant who is poor and needy, whether he is one of your brethren or one of the sojourners who are in your land within your towns; 15 you shall give him his hire on the day he earns it, before the sun goes down (for he is poor, and sets his heart upon it); lest he cry against you to the LORD, and it be sin in you.

16 "The fathers shall not be put to death for the children, nor shall the children be put to death for the fathers; every man shall be put to death for his own sin.

17 "You shall not pervert the justice due to the sojourner or to the fatherless, or take a widow's garment in pledge; 18 but you shall remember that you were a slave in Egypt and the LORD your God redeemed you from there; therefore I command you to do this.

ᶠ Or *sodomite*

23.19: Ex 22.26; Lev 25.35-37. **23.21-23:** Num 30.2-16.
24.1: Mt 5.31; 19.7; Mk 10.4. **24.6, 10-13:** Ex 22.26-27.
24.7: Ex 21.16; 1 Cor 5.13. **24.8-9:** Lev 13-14. **24.14-15:** Lev 19.13; Jas 5.4.
24.17-18: Ex 22.21-24; 23.9; Lev 19.33-34.

19 "When you reap your harvest in your field, and have forgotten a sheaf in the field, you shall not go back to get it; it shall be for the sojourner, the fatherless, and the widow; that the LORD your God may bless you in all the work of your hands. 20 When you beat your olive trees, you shall not go over the boughs again; it shall be for the sojourner, the fatherless, and the widow. 21 When you gather the grapes of your vineyard, you shall not glean it afterward; it shall be for the sojourner, the fatherless, and the widow. 22 You shall remember that you were a slave in the land of Egypt; therefore I command you to do this.

25 "If there is a dispute between men, and they come into court, and the judges decide between them, acquitting the innocent and condemning the guilty, 2 then if the guilty man deserves to be beaten, the judge shall cause him to lie down and be beaten in his presence with a number of stripes in proportion to his offense. 3 Forty stripes may be given him, but not more; lest, if one should go on to beat him with more stripes than these, your brother be degraded in your sight.

4 "You shall not muzzle an ox when it treads out the grain.

5 "If brothers dwell together, and one of them dies and has no son, the wife of the dead shall not be married outside the family to a stranger; her husband's brother shall go in to her, and take her as his wife, and perform the duty of a husband's brother to her. 6 And the first son whom she bears shall succeed to the name of his brother who is dead, that his name may not be blotted out of Israel. 7 And if the man does not wish to take his brother's wife, then his brother's wife shall go up to the gate to the elders, and say, 'My husband's brother refuses to perpetuate his brother's name in Israel; he will not perform the duty of a husband's brother to me.' 8 Then the elders of his city shall call him, and speak to him: and if he persists, saying, 'I do not wish to take her,' 9 then his brother's wife shall go up to him in the presence of the elders, and pull his sandal off his foot, and spit in his face; and she shall answer and say, 'So shall it be done to the man who does not build up his brother's house.' 10 And the name of his house*u* shall be called

in Israel, The house of him that had his sandal pulled off.

11 "When men fight with one another, and the wife of the one draws near to rescue her husband from the hand of him who is beating him, and puts out her hand and seizes him by the private parts, 12 then you shall cut off her hand; your eye shall have no pity.

13 "You shall not have in your bag two kinds of weights, a large and a small. 14 You shall not have in your house two kinds of measures, a large and a small. 15 A full and just weight you shall have, a full and just measure you shall have; that your days may be prolonged in the land which the LORD your God gives you. 16 For all who do such things, all who act dishonestly, are an abomination to the LORD your God.

17 "Remember what Am´a·lek did to you on the way as you came out of Egypt, 18 how he attacked you on the way, when you were faint and weary, and cut off at your rear all who lagged behind you; and he did not fear God. 19 Therefore when the LORD your God has given you rest from all your enemies round about, in the land which the LORD your God gives you for an inheritance to possess, you shall blot out the remembrance of Am´a·lek from under heaven; you shall not forget.

26 "When you come into the land which the LORD your God gives you for an inheritance, and have taken possession of it, and live in it, 2 you shall take some of the first of all the fruit of the ground, which you harvest from your land that the LORD your God gives you, and you shall put it in a basket, and you shall go to the place which the LORD your God will choose, to make his name to dwell there. 3 And you shall go to the priest who is in office at that time, and say to him, 'I declare this day to the LORD your God that I have come into the land which the LORD swore to our fathers to give us.' 4 Then the priest shall take the basket from your hand, and set it down before the altar of the LORD your God.

5 "And you shall make response before the LORD your God, 'A wandering Ar·a·mē´an was my father; and he went down into Egypt and sojourned there, few in number; and there he became a nation, great, mighty, and populous. 6 And the Egyptians treated us harshly,

u Heb *its name*   24.19-22: Lev 19.9-10; 23.22.
25.4: 1 Cor 9.9; 1 Tim 5.18.   25.5-6: Mt 22.24; Mk 12.19; Lk 20.28.
25.13-16: Lev 19.35-36.   25.17-19: Ex 17.14; 1 Sam 15.
26.1-11: Ex 22.29; 23.19; 34.26; Num 18.12-13.

and afflicted us, and laid upon us hard bondage. [7] Then we cried to the LORD the God of our fathers, and the LORD heard our voice, and saw our affliction, our toil, and our oppression; [8] and the LORD brought us out of Egypt with a mighty hand and an outstretched arm, with great terror, with signs and wonders; [9] and he brought us into this place and gave us this land, a land flowing with milk and honey. [10]And behold, now I bring the first of the fruit of the ground, which thou, O LORD, hast given me.' And you shall set it down before the LORD your God, and worship before the LORD your God; [11] and you shall rejoice in all the good which the LORD your God has given to you and to your house, you, and the Levite, and the sojourner who is among you.

[12] "When you have finished paying all the tithe of your produce in the third year, which is the year of tithing, giving it to the Levite, the sojourner, the fatherless, and the widow, that they may eat within your towns and be filled, [13] then you shall say before the LORD your God, 'I have removed the sacred portion out of my house, and moreover I have given it to the Levite, the sojourner, the fatherless, and the widow, according to all thy commandment which thou hast commanded me; I have not transgressed any of thy commandments, neither have I forgotten them; [14] I have not eaten of the tithe while I was mourning, or removed any of it while I was unclean, or offered any of it to the dead; I have obeyed the voice of the LORD my God, I have done according to all that thou hast commanded me. [15] Look down from thy holy habitation, from heaven, and bless thy people Israel and the ground which thou hast given us, as thou didst swear to our fathers, a land flowing with milk and honey.'

[16] "This day the LORD your God commands you to do these statutes and ordinances; you shall therefore be careful to do them with all your heart and with all your soul. [17] You have declared this day concerning the LORD that he is your God, and that you will walk in his ways, and keep his statutes and his commandments and his ordinances, and will obey his voice; [18] and the LORD has declared this day concerning you that you are a people for his own possession, as he has promised you, and that you are to keep all his

commandments, [19] that he will set you high above all nations that he has made, in praise and in fame and in honor, and that you shall be a people holy to the LORD your God, as he has spoken."

27 Now Moses and the elders of Israel commanded the people, saying, "Keep all the commandment which I command you this day. [2]And on the day you pass over the Jordan to the land which the LORD your God gives you, you shall set up large stones, and plaster them with plaster; [3] and you shall write upon them all the words of this law, when you pass over to enter the land which the LORD your God gives you, a land flowing with milk and honey, as the LORD, the God of your fathers, has promised you. [4]And when you have passed over the Jordan, you shall set up these stones, concerning which I command you this day, on Mount E'bal, and you shall plaster them with plaster. [5]And there you shall build an altar to the LORD your God, an altar of stones; you shall lift up no iron tool upon them. [6] You shall build an altar to the LORD your God of unhewn[v] stones; and you shall offer burnt offerings on it to the LORD your God; [7] and you shall sacrifice peace offerings, and shall eat there; and you shall rejoice before the LORD your God. [8]And you shall write upon the stones all the words of this law very plainly."

[9] And Moses and the Levitical priests said to all Israel, "Keep silence and hear, O Israel: this day you have become the people of the LORD your God. [10] You shall therefore obey the voice of the LORD your God, keeping his commandments and his statutes, which I command you this day."

[11] And Moses charged the people the same day, saying, [12] "When you have passed over the Jordan, these shall stand upon Mount Ger'i-zim to bless the people: Simeon, Levi, Judah, Is'sa·char, Joseph, and Benjamin. [13]And these shall stand upon Mount E'bal for the curse: Reuben, Gad, Ash'er, Zeb'u·lun, Dan, and Naph'ta·li. [14]And the Levites shall declare to all the men of Israel with a loud voice:

[15] " 'Cursed be the man who makes a graven or molten image, an abomination to the LORD, a thing made by the hands of a craftsman, and sets it up in secret.' And all the people shall answer and say, 'Amen.'

[16] " 'Cursed be he who dishonors

---

v Heb *whole*

27.15: Ex 20.4, 23; 34.17; Lev 19.4; 26.1; Deut 4.16, 23, 25; 5.8; 7.25.
27.16: Ex 20.12; 21.15, 17; Lev 20.9; Deut 5.16; 21.18-21.

his father or his mother.' And all the people shall say, 'Amen.'

17 " 'Cursed be he who removes his neighbor's landmark.' And all the people shall say, 'Amen.'

18 " 'Cursed be he who misleads a blind man on the road.' And all the people shall say, 'Amen.'

19 " 'Cursed be he who perverts the justice due to the sojourner, the fatherless, and the widow.' And all the people shall say, 'Amen.'

20 " 'Cursed be he who lies with his father's wife, because he has uncovered her who is his father's.'*w* And all the people shall say, 'Amen.'

21 " 'Cursed be he who lies with any kind of beast.' And all the people shall say, 'Amen.'

22 " 'Cursed be he who lies with his sister, whether the daughter of his father or the daughter of his mother.' And all the people shall say, 'Amen.'

23 " 'Cursed be he who lies with his mother-in-law.' And all the people shall say, 'Amen.'

24 " 'Cursed be he who slays his neighbor in secret.' And all the people shall say, 'Amen.'

25 " 'Cursed be he who takes a bribe to slay an innocent person.' And all the people shall say, 'Amen.'

26 " 'Cursed be he who does not confirm the words of this law by doing them.' And all the people shall say, 'Amen.'

28 "And if you obey the voice of the LORD your God, being careful to do all his commandments which I command you this day, the LORD your God will set you high above all the nations of the earth. 2And all these blessings shall come upon you and overtake you, if you obey the voice of the LORD your God. 3 Blessed shall you be in the city, and blessed shall you be in the field. 4 Blessed shall be the fruit of your body, and the fruit of your ground, and the fruit of your beasts, the increase of your cattle, and the young of your flock. 5 Blessed shall be your basket and your kneading-trough. 6 Blessed shall you be when you come in, and blessed shall you be when you go out.

7 "The LORD will cause your enemies who rise against you to be defeated before you; they shall come out against you one way, and flee before you seven ways. 8 The LORD will command the blessing upon you in your

barns, and in all that you undertake; and he will bless you in the land which the LORD your God gives you. 9 The LORD will establish you as a people holy to himself, as he has sworn to you, if you keep the commandments of the LORD your God, and walk in his ways. 10And all the peoples of the earth shall see that you are called by the name of the LORD; and they shall be afraid of you. 11And the LORD will make you abound in prosperity, in the fruit of your body, and in the fruit of your cattle, and in the fruit of your ground, within the land which the LORD swore to your fathers to give you. 12 The LORD will open to you his good treasury the heavens, to give the rain of your land in its season and to bless all the work of your hands; and you shall lend to many nations, but you shall not borrow. 13And the LORD will make you the head, and not the tail; and you shall tend upward only, and not downward; if you obey the commandments of the LORD your God, which I command you this day, being careful to do them, 14 and if you do not turn aside from any of the words which I command you this day, to the right hand or to the left, to go after other gods to serve them.

15 "But if you will not obey the voice of the LORD your God or be careful to do all his commandments and his statutes which I command you this day, then all these curses shall come upon you and overtake you. 16 Cursed shall you be in the city, and cursed shall you be in the field. 17 Cursed shall be your basket and your kneading-trough. 18 Cursed shall be the fruit of your body, and the fruit of your ground, the increase of your cattle, and the young of your flock. 19 Cursed shall you be when you come in, and cursed shall you be when you go out.

20 "The LORD will send upon you curses, confusion, and frustration, in all that you undertake to do, until you are destroyed and perish quickly, on account of the evil of your doings, because you have forsaken me. 21 The LORD will make the pestilence cleave to you until he has consumed you off the land which you are entering to take possession of it. 22 The LORD will smite you with consumption, and with fever, inflammation,*x* and fiery heat, and with drought,*x* and with blasting, and with

w Heb *uncovered his father's skirt*   *x* Another reading is *sword*

27.18: Lev 19.14.   27.19: Ex 22.21-24; 23.9; Lev 19.33-34; Deut 24.17-18.
27.20: Lev 18.8; 20.11; Deut 22.30.   27.21: Ex 22.19; Lev 18.23; 20.15.
27.22: Lev 18.9; 20.17.   27.23: Lev 18.17; 20.14.   27.26: Gal 3.10.   28: Lev 26.3-45.

mildew; they shall pursue you until you perish. 23And the heavens over your head shall be brass, and the earth under you shall be iron. 24 The LORD will make the rain of your land powder and dust; from heaven it shall come down upon you until you are destroyed.

25 "The LORD will cause you to be defeated before your enemies; you shall go out one way against them, and flee seven ways before them; and you shall be a horror to all the kingdoms of the earth. 26And your dead body shall be food for all birds of the air, and for the beasts of the earth; and there shall be no one to frighten them away. 27 The LORD will smite you with the boils of Egypt, and with the ulcers and the scurvy and the itch, of which you cannot be healed. 28 The LORD will smite you with madness and blindness and confusion of mind; 29 and you shall grope at noonday, as the blind grope in darkness, and you shall not prosper in your ways; and you shall be only oppressed and robbed continually, and there shall be no one to help you. 30 You shall betroth a wife, and another man shall lie with her; you shall build a house, and you shall not dwell in it; you shall plant a vineyard, and you shall not use the fruit of it. 31 Your ox shall be slain before your eyes, and you shall not eat of it; your ass shall be violently taken away before your face, and shall not be restored to you; your sheep shall be given to your enemies, and there shall be no one to help you. 32 Your sons and your daughters shall be given to another people, while your eyes look on and fail with longing for them all the day; and it shall not be in the power of your hand to prevent it. 33A nation which you have not known shall eat up the fruit of your ground and of all your labors; and you shall be only oppressed and crushed continually; 34 so that you shall be driven mad by the sight which your eyes shall see. 35 The LORD will smite you on the knees and on the legs with grievous boils of which you cannot be healed, from the sole of your foot to the crown of your head.

36 "The LORD will bring you, and your king whom you set over you, to a nation that neither you nor your fathers have known; and there you shall serve other gods, of wood and stone. 37And you shall become a horror, a proverb, and a byword, among all the peoples where the LORD will lead you away.

38 You shall carry much seed into the field, and shall gather little in; for the locust shall consume it. 39 You shall plant vineyards and dress them, but you shall neither drink of the wine nor gather the grapes; for the worm shall eat them. 40 You shall have olive trees throughout all your territory, but you shall not anoint yourself with the oil; for your olives shall drop off. 41 You shall beget sons and daughters, but they shall not be yours; for they shall go into captivity. 42All your trees and the fruit of your ground the locust shall possess. 43 The sojourner who is among you shall mount above you higher and higher; and you shall come down lower and lower. 44 He shall lend to you, and you shall not lend to him; he shall be the head, and you shall be the tail. 45All these curses shall come upon you and pursue you and overtake you, till you are destroyed, because you did not obey the voice of the LORD your God, to keep his commandments and his statutes which he commanded you. 46 They shall be upon you as a sign and a wonder, and upon your descendants for ever.

47 "Because you did not serve the LORD your God with joyfulness and gladness of heart, by reason of the abundance of all things, 48 therefore you shall serve your enemies whom the LORD will send against you, in hunger and thirst, in nakedness, and in want of all things; and he will put a yoke of iron upon your neck, until he has destroyed you. 49 The LORD will bring a nation against you from afar, from the end of the earth, as swift as the eagle flies, a nation whose language you do not understand, 50 a nation of stern countenance, who shall not regard the person of the old or show favor to the young, 51 and shall eat the offspring of your cattle and the fruit of your ground, until you are destroyed; who also shall not leave you grain, wine, or oil, the increase of your cattle or the young of your flock, until they have caused you to perish. 52 They shall besiege you in all your towns, until your high and fortified walls, in which you trusted, come down throughout all your land; and they shall besiege you in all your towns throughout all your land, which the LORD your God has given you. 53And you shall eat the offspring of your own body, the flesh of your sons and daughters, whom the LORD your God has given you, in the siege and in the distress with which your enemies shall

28.49: 1 Cor 14.21.

distress you. 54 The man who is the most tender and delicately bred among you will grudge food to his brother, to the wife of his bosom, and to the last of the children who remain to him; 55 so that he will not give to any of them any of the flesh of his children whom he is eating, because he has nothing left him, in the siege and in the distress with which your enemy shall distress you in all your towns. 56 The most tender and delicately bred woman among you, who would not venture to set the sole of her foot upon the ground because she is so delicate and tender, will grudge to the husband of her bosom, to her son and to her daughter, 57 her afterbirth that come out from between her feet and her children whom she bears, because she will eat them secretly, for want of all things, in the siege and in the distress with which your enemy shall distress you in your towns.

58 "If you are not careful to do all the words of this law which are written in this book, that you may fear this glorious and awful name, the LORD your God, 59 then the LORD will bring on you and your offspring extraordinary afflictions, afflictions severe and lasting, and sicknesses grievous and lasting. 60 And he will bring upon you again all the diseases of Egypt, which you were afraid of; and they shall cleave to you. 61 Every sickness also, and every affliction which is not recorded in the book of this law, the LORD will bring upon you, until you are destroyed. 62 Whereas you were as the stars of heaven for multitude, you shall be left few in number; because you did not obey the voice of the LORD your God. 63 And as the LORD took delight in doing you good and multiplying you, so the LORD will take delight in bringing ruin upon you and destroying you; and you shall be plucked off the land which you are entering to take possession of it. 64 And the LORD will scatter you among all peoples, from one end of the earth to the other; and there you shall serve other gods, of wood and stone, which neither you nor your fathers have known. 65 And among these nations you shall find no ease, and there shall be no rest for the sole of your foot; but the LORD will give you there a trembling heart, and failing eyes, and a languishing soul; 66 your life shall hang in doubt before you; night and day you shall be in dread, and have no assurance of your life. 67 In the morning you shall say, 'Would it were evening!' and at evening you shall say, 'Would it were morning!' because of the dread which your heart shall fear, and the sights which your eyes shall see. 68 And the LORD will bring you back in ships to Egypt, a journey which I promised that you should never make again; and there you shall offer yourselves for sale to your enemies as male and female slaves, but no man will buy you."

29 These are the words of the covenant which the LORD commanded Moses to make with the people of Israel in the land of Mōʹab, besides the covenant which he had made with them at Hōʹreb.

2z And Moses summoned all Israel and said to them: "You have seen all that the LORD did before your eyes in the land of Egypt, to Pharaoh and to all his servants and to all his land, 3 the great trials which your eyes saw, the signs, and those great wonders; 4 but to this day the LORD has not given you a mind to understand, or eyes to see, or ears to hear. 5 I have led you forty years in the wilderness; your clothes have not worn out upon you, and your sandals have not worn off your feet; 6 you have not eaten bread, and you have not drunk wine or strong drink; that you may know that I am the LORD your God. 7 And when you came to this place, Siʹhon the king of Heshʹbon and Og the king of Bāʹshan came out against us to battle, but we defeated them; 8 we took their land, and gave it for an inheritance to the Reubenites, the Gadites, and the half-tribe of the Mȧ·nasʹsites. 9 Therefore be careful to do the words of this covenant, that you may prosperᵃ in all that you do.

10 "You stand this day all of you before the LORD your God; the heads of your tribes,ᵇ your elders, and your officers, all the men of Israel, 11 your little ones, your wives, and the sojourner who is in your camp, both he who hews your wood and he who draws your water, 12 that you may enter into the sworn covenant of the LORD your God, which the LORD your God makes with you this day; 13 that he may establish you this day as his people, and that he may be your God, as he promised you, and as he swore to your fathers, to Abraham, to Isaac,

y Ch 28.69 in Heb   z Ch 29.1 in Heb   a Or deal wisely
b Gk Syr: Heb your heads, your tribes
29.4: Rom 11.8.

and to Jacob. 14 Nor is it with you only that I make this sworn covenant, 15 but with him who is not here with us this day as well as with him who stands here with us this day before the LORD our God.

16 "You know how we dwelt in the land of Egypt, and how we came through the midst of the nations through which you passed; 17 and you have seen their detestable things, their idols of wood and stone, of silver and gold, which were among them. 18 Beware lest there be among you a man or woman or family or tribe, whose heart turns away this day from the LORD our God to go and serve the gods of those nations; lest there be among you a root bearing poisonous and bitter fruit, 19 one who, when he hears the words of this sworn covenant, blesses himself in his heart, saying, 'I shall be safe, though I walk in the stubbornness of my heart.' This would lead to the sweeping away of moist and dry alike. 20 The LORD would not pardon him, but rather the anger of the LORD and his jealousy would smoke against that man, and the curses written in this book would settle upon him, and the LORD would blot out his name from under heaven. 21And the LORD would single him out from all the tribes of Israel for calamity, in accordance with all the curses of the covenant written in this book of the law. 22And the generation to come, your children who rise up after you, and the foreigner who comes from a far land, would say, when they see the afflictions of that land and the sicknesses with which the LORD has made it sick—23 the whole land brimstone and salt, and a burnt-out waste, unsown, and growing nothing, where no grass can sprout, an overthrow like that of Sod'öm and Gö·mŏr'răh, Ad'măh and Ze·boi'im, which the LORD overthrew in his anger and wrath—24 yea, all the nations would say, 'Why has the LORD done thus to this land? What means the heat of this great anger?' 25 Then men would say, 'It is because they forsook the covenant of the LORD, the God of their fathers, which he made with them when he brought them out of the land of Egypt, 26 and went and served other gods and worshiped them, gods whom they had not known and whom he had not allotted to them; 27 therefore the anger of the LORD was kindled against this land, bringing upon it all the curses written in this book; 28 and the LORD uprooted them

from their land in anger and fury and great wrath, and cast them into another land, as at this day.'

29 "The secret things belong to the LORD our God; but the things that are revealed belong to us and to our children for ever, that we may do all the words of this law.

30 "And when all these things come upon you, the blessing and the curse, which I have set before you, and you call them to mind among all the nations where the LORD your God has driven you, 2 and return to the LORD your God, you and your children, and obey his voice in all that I command you this day, with all your heart and with all your soul; 3 then the LORD your God will restore your fortunes, and have compassion upon you, and he will gather you again from all the peoples where the LORD your God has scattered you. 4 If your outcasts are in the uttermost parts of heaven, from there the LORD your God will gather you, and from there he will fetch you; 5 and the LORD your God will bring you into the land which your fathers possessed, that you may possess it; and he will make you more prosperous and numerous than your fathers. 6And the LORD your God will circumcise your heart and the heart of your offspring, so that you will love the LORD your God with all your heart and with all your soul, that you may live. 7And the LORD your God will put all these curses upon your foes and enemies who persecuted you. 8And you shall again obey the voice of the LORD, and keep all his commandments which I command you this day. 9 The LORD your God will make you abundantly prosperous in all the work of your hand, in the fruit of your body, and in the fruit of your cattle, and in the fruit of your ground; for the LORD will again take delight in prospering you, as he took delight in your fathers, 10 if you obey the voice of the LORD your God, to keep his commandments and his statutes which are written in this book of the law, if you turn to the LORD your God with all your heart and with all your soul.

11 "For this commandment which I command you this day is not too hard for you, neither is it far off. 12 It is not in heaven, that you should say, 'Who will go up for us to heaven, and bring it to us, that we may hear it and do it?' 13 Neither is it beyond the sea, that you should say, 'Who will go over the sea for us, and bring it to us, that

29.18: Acts 8.23; Heb 12.15.   **30.4:** Mt 24.31; Mk 13.27.   **30.12-13:** Rom 10.6-7.

we may hear it and do it?' 14 But the word is very near you; it is in your mouth and in your heart, so that you can do it.

15 "See, I have set before you this day life and good, death and evil. 16 If you obey the commandments of the LORD your God[c] which I command you this day, by loving the LORD your God, by walking in his ways, and by keeping his commandments and his statutes and his ordinances, then you shall live and multiply, and the LORD your God will bless you in the land which you are entering to take possession of it. 17 But if your heart turns away, and you will not hear, but are drawn away to worship other gods and serve them, 18 I declare to you this day, that you shall perish; you shall not live long in the land which you are going over the Jordan to enter and possess. 19 I call heaven and earth to witness against you this day, that I have set before you life and death, blessing and curse; therefore choose life, that you and your descendants may live, 20 loving the LORD your God, obeying his voice, and cleaving to him; for that means life to you and length of days, that you may dwell in the land which the LORD swore to your fathers, to Abraham, to Isaac, and to Jacob, to give them."

31 So Moses continued to speak these words to all Israel. 2 And he said to them, "I am a hundred and twenty years old this day; I am no longer able to go out and come in. The LORD has said to me, 'You shall not go over this Jordan.' 3 The LORD your God himself will go over before you; he will destroy these nations before you, so that you shall dispossess them; and Joshua will go over at your head, as the LORD has spoken. 4 And the LORD will do to them as he did to Si′hon and Og, the kings of the Am′o-rites, and to their land, when he destroyed them. 5 And the LORD will give them over to you, and you shall do to them according to all the commandment which I have commanded you. 6 Be strong and of good courage, do not fear or be in dread of them: for it is the LORD your God who goes with you; he will not fail you or forsake you."

7 Then Moses summoned Joshua, and said to him in the sight of all Israel, "Be strong and of good courage; for you shall go with this people into the land which the LORD has sworn to

their fathers to give them; and you shall put them in possession of it. 8 It is the LORD who goes before you; he will be with you, he will not fail you or forsake you; do not fear or be dismayed."

9 And Moses wrote this law, and gave it to the priests the sons of Levi, who carried the ark of the covenant of the LORD, and to all the elders of Israel. 10 And Moses commanded them, "At the end of every seven years, at the set time of the year of release, at the feast of booths, 11 when all Israel comes to appear before the LORD your God at the place which he will choose, you shall read this law before all Israel in their hearing. 12 Assemble the people, men, women, and little ones, and the sojourner within your towns, that they may hear and learn to fear the LORD your God, and be careful to do all the words of this law, 13 and that their children, who have not known it, may hear and learn to fear the LORD your God, as long as you live in the land which you are going over the Jordan to possess."

14 And the LORD said to Moses, "Behold, the days approach when you must die; call Joshua, and present yourselves in the tent of meeting, that I may commission him." And Moses and Joshua went and presented themselves in the tent of meeting. 15 And the LORD appeared in the tent in a pillar of cloud; and the pillar of cloud stood by the door of the tent.

16 And the LORD said to Moses, "Behold, you are about to sleep with your fathers; then this people will rise and play the harlot after the strange gods of the land, where they go to be among them, and they will forsake me and break my covenant which I have made with them. 17 Then my anger will be kindled against them in that day, and I will forsake them and hide my face from them, and they will be devoured; and many evils and troubles will come upon them, so that they will say in that day, 'Have not these evils come upon us because our God is not among us?' 18 And I will surely hide my face in that day on account of all the evil which they have done, because they have turned to other gods. 19 Now therefore write this song, and teach it to the people of Israel; put it in their mouths, that this song may be a witness for me against the people of Israel. 20 For when I have brought them into the land flowing with milk

c Gk: Heb lacks *If you obey the commandments of the* LORD *your God*
30.14: Rom 10.8.   **31.6, 8:** Heb 13.5.

and honey, which I swore to give to their fathers, and they have eaten and are full and grown fat, they will turn to other gods and serve them, and despise me and break my covenant. 21And when many evils and troubles have come upon them, this song shall confront them as a witness (for it will live unforgotten in the mouths of their descendants); for I know the purposes which they are already forming, before I have brought them into the land that I swore to give." 22 So Moses wrote this song the same day, and taught it to the people of Israel.

23 And the Lord commissioned Joshua the son of Nun and said, "Be strong and of good courage; for you shall bring the children of Israel into the land which I swore to give them: I will be with you."

24 When Moses had finished writing the words of this law in a book, to the very end, 25 Moses commanded the Levites who carried the ark of the covenant of the Lord, 26 "Take this book of the law, and put it by the side of the ark of the covenant of the Lord your God, that it may be there for a witness against you. 27 For I know how rebellious and stubborn you are; behold, while I am yet alive with you, today you have been rebellious against the Lord; how much more after my death! 28Assemble to me all the elders of your tribes, and your officers, that I may speak these words in their ears and call heaven and earth to witness against them. 29 For I know that after my death you will surely act corruptly, and turn aside from the way which I have commanded you; and in the days to come evil will befall you, because you will do what is evil in the sight of the Lord, provoking him to anger through the work of your hands."

30 Then Moses spoke the words of this song until they were finished, in the ears of all the assembly of Israel:

32 "Give ear, O heavens, and I will speak;
   and let the earth hear the words of my mouth.
2 May my teaching drop as the rain,
   my speech distil as the dew,
 as the gentle rain upon the tender grass,
   and as the showers upon the herb.
3 For I will proclaim the name of the Lord.
   Ascribe greatness to our God!

4 "The Rock, his work is perfect;

d Compare Gk: Heb *Israel*
32.5: Phil 2.15.

   for all his ways are justice.
A God of faithfulness and without iniquity,
   just and right is he.
5 They have dealt corruptly with him,
   they are no longer his children because of their blemish;
   they are a perverse and crooked generation.
6 Do you thus requite the Lord,
   you foolish and senseless people?
Is not he your father, who created you,
   who made you and established you?
7 Remember the days of old,
   consider the years of many generations;
 ask your father, and he will show you;
   your elders, and they will tell you.
8 When the Most High gave to the nations their inheritance,
   when he separated the sons of men,
he fixed the bounds of the peoples
   according to the number of the sons of God.*d*
9 For the Lord's portion is his people,
   Jacob his allotted heritage.

10 "He found him in a desert land,
   and in the howling waste of the wilderness;
he encircled him, he cared for him,
   he kept him as the apple of his eye.
11 Like an eagle that stirs up its nest,
   that flutters over its young,
 spreading out its wings, catching them,
   bearing them on its pinions,
12 the Lord alone did lead him,
   and there was no foreign god with him.
13 He made him ride on the high places of the earth,
   and he ate the produce of the field;
and he made him suck honey out of the rock,
   and oil out of the flinty rock.
14 Curds from the herd, and milk from the flock,
   with fat of lambs and rams,
   herds of Bā′shăn and goats—
with the finest of the wheat—
   and of the blood of the grape you drank wine.

15 "But Jesh′ū·rŭn waxed fat, and kicked;

you waxed fat, you grew thick,
   you became sleek;
then he forsook God who made him,
   and scoffed at the Rock of his
   salvation.

16 They stirred him to jealousy with
   strange gods;
   with abominable practices they
   provoked him to anger.

17 They sacrificed to demons which
   were no gods,
   to gods they had never known,
to new gods that had come in of late,
   whom your fathers had never
   dreaded.

18 You were unmindful of the Rock
   that begot*e* you,
   and you forgot the God who gave
   you birth.

19 "The LORD saw it, and spurned
   them,
   because of the provocation of his
   sons and his daughters.

20 And he said, 'I will hide my face
   from them,
   I will see what their end will be,
for they are a perverse generation,
   children in whom is no faithfulness.

21 They have stirred me to jealousy
   with what is no god;
   they have provoked me with their
   idols.
So I will stir them to jealousy with
   those who are no people;
   I will provoke them with a foolish
   nation.

22 For a fire is kindled by my anger,
   and it burns to the depths of
   Shĕ'ōl,
devours the earth and its increase,
   and sets on fire the foundations
   of the mountains.

23 " 'And I will heap evils upon them;
   I will spend my arrows upon them;

24 they shall be wasted with hunger,
   and devoured with burning heat
   and poisonous pestilence;
and I will send the teeth of beasts
   against them,
   with venom of crawling things
   of the dust.

25 In the open the sword shall bereave,
   and in the chambers shall be
   terror,
destroying both young man and
   virgin,
   the sucking child with the man
   of gray hairs.

26 I would have said, "I will scatter
   them afar,

I will make the remembrance of
   them cease from among men,"

27 had I not feared provocation by the
   enemy,
   lest their adversaries should judge
   amiss,
lest they should say, "Our hand is
   triumphant,
   the LORD has not wrought all
   this." '

28 "For they are a nation void of
   counsel,
   and there is no understanding in
   them.

29 If they were wise, they would understand this,
   they would discern their latter
   end!

30 How should one chase a thousand,
   and two put ten thousand to
   flight,
unless their Rock had sold them,
   and the LORD had given them
   up?

31 For their rock is not as our Rock,
   even our enemies themselves being judges.

32 For their vine comes from the vine
   of Sŏd'ŏm,
   and from the fields of Gò·môr'räh;
their grapes are grapes of poison,
   their clusters are bitter;

33 their wine is the poison of serpents,
   and the cruel venom of asps.

34 "Is not this laid up in store with me,
   sealed up in my treasuries?

35 Vengeance is mine, and recompense,
   for the time when their foot shall
   slip;
for the day of their calamity is at
   hand,
   and their doom comes swiftly.

36 For the LORD will vindicate his
   people
   and have compassion on his
   servants,
when he sees that their power is
   gone,
   and there is none remaining, bond
   or free.

37 Then he will say, 'Where are their
   gods,
   the rock in which they took refuge,

38 who ate the fat of their sacrifices,
   and drank the wine of their drink
   offering?
Let them rise up and help you,
   let them be your protection!

39 " 'See now that I, even I, am he,
   and there is no god beside me;

---

e Or *bore*   **32.17:** 1 Cor 10.20.
32.21: Rom 10.19; 11.11; 1 Cor 10.22.   **32.35:** Rom 12.19; Heb 10.30.

I kill and I make alive;
    I wound and I heal;
    and there is none that can deliver
        out of my hand.
40 For I lift up my hand to heaven,
    and swear, As I live for ever,
41 if I whet my glittering sword,[f]
    and my hand takes hold on
        judgment,
    I will take vengeance on my ad-
        versaries,
    and will requite those who hate
        me.
42 I will make my arrows drunk with
        blood,
    and my sword shall devour flesh—
    with the blood of the slain and the
        captives,
    from the long-haired heads of the
        enemy.'

43 "Praise his people, O you nations;[g]
    for he avenges the blood of his
        servants,
    and takes vengeance on his adver-
        saries,
    and makes expiation for the land
        of his people."[g]

44 Moses came and recited all the
words of this song in the hearing of
the people, he and Joshua[h] the son of
Nun. 45And when Moses had finished
speaking all these words to all Israel,
46 he said to them, "Lay to heart all
the words which I enjoin upon you
this day, that you may command them
to your children, that they may be
careful to do all the words of this law.
47 For it is no trifle for you, but it is
your life, and thereby you shall live
long in the land which you are going
over the Jordan to possess."

48 And the LORD said to Moses
that very day, 49 "Ascend this mountain of the Ab'a·rim, Mount Ne'bo,
which is in the land of Mo'ab, opposite
Jericho; and view the land of Canaan,
which I give to the people of Israel for
a possession; 50 and die on the mountain which you ascend, and be gathered
to your people, as Aaron your brother
died in Mount Hor and was gathered
to his people; 51 because you broke
faith with me in the midst of the people
of Israel at the waters of Mer'i·bath-
ka'desh, in the wilderness of Zin; because you did not revere me as holy
in the midst of the people of Israel.
52 For you shall see the land before
you; but you shall not go there, into

the land which I give to the people of
Israel."

33 This is the blessing with which
    Moses the man of God blessed
the children of Israel before his death.
2 He said,
    "The LORD came from Sinai,
        and dawned from Se'ir upon us;[i]
    he shone forth from Mount
        Pa'ran,
    he came from the ten thousands of
        holy ones,
    with flaming fire[j] at his right hand.
3 Yea, he loved his people;[k]
    all those consecrated to him were
        in his[x] hand;
    so they followed[l] in thy steps,
    receiving direction from thee,
4 when Moses commanded us a law,
    as a possession for the assembly
        of Jacob.
5 Thus the LORD became king in
        Jesh'u·run,
    when the heads of the people
        were gathered,
    all the tribes of Israel together.

6 "Let Reuben live, and not die,
    nor let his men be few."

7 And this he said of Judah:
    "Hear, O LORD, the voice of Judah,
        and bring him in to his people.
    With thy hands contend[l] for him,
        and be a help against his adver-
            saries."

8 And of Levi he said,
    "Give to Levi[m] thy Thum'mim,
        and thy U'rim to thy godly one,
    whom thou didst test at Mas'sah,
        with whom thou didst strive at
            the waters of Mer'i·bah;
9 who said of his father and mother,
        'I regard them not';
    he disowned his brothers,
        and ignored his children.
    For they observed thy word,
        and kept thy covenant.
10 They shall teach Jacob thy ordi-
        nances,
    and Israel thy law;
    they shall put incense before thee,
        and whole burnt offering upon
            thy altar.
11 Bless, O LORD, his substance,
        and accept the work of his hands;
    crush the loins of his adversaries,
        of those that hate him, that they
            rise not again."

f Heb *the lightning of my sword*   g Gk Vg: Heb *his land his people*
h Gk Syr Vg: Heb *Hoshea*   i Gk Syr Vg: Heb *them*
j The meaning of the Hebrew word is uncertain   k Gk: Heb *peoples*   x Heb *thy*
l Cn: Heb *with his hands he contended*   m Gk: Heb lacks *Give to Levi*
32.43: Rom 15.10; Heb 1.6 (Septuagint); Rev 6.10; 19.2.

12 Of Benjamin he said,
"The beloved of the LORD,
    he dwells in safety by him;
he encompasses him all the day
        long,
    and makes his dwelling between
        his shoulders."

13 And of Joseph he said,
"Blessed by the LORD be his land,
    with the choicest gifts of heaven
        above,[n]
    and of the deep that couches
        beneath,
14 with the choicest fruits of the sun,
    and the rich yield of the months,
15 with the finest produce of the
        ancient mountains,
    and the abundance of the ever-
        lasting hills,
16 with the best gifts of the earth and
        its fulness,
    and the favor of him that dwelt
        in the bush.
Let these come upon the head of
        Joseph,
    and upon the crown of the head
        of him that is prince among his
        brothers.
17 His firstling bull has majesty,
    and his horns are the horns of a
        wild ox;
with them he shall push the peoples,
    all of them, to the ends of the
        earth;
such are the ten thousands of
        É'phra·im,
    and such are the thousands of
        Ma·nas'seh."

18 And of Zeb'u·lun he said,
"Rejoice, Zebulun, in your going
        out;
    and Is'sa·char, in your tents.
19 They shall call peoples to their
        mountain;
    there they offer right sacrifices;
for they suck the affluence of the seas
    and the hidden treasures of the
        sand."
20 And of Gad he said,
"Blessed be he who enlarges Gad!
Gad couches like a lion,
    he tears the arm, and the crown
        of the head.
21 He chose the best of the land for
        himself,
    for there a commander's portion
        was reserved;
and he came to the heads of the
        people,
    with Israel he executed the com-
        mands
    and just decrees of the LORD."

[n] Two Heb Mss and Tg: Heb *with the dew*

22 And of Dan he said,
"Dan is a lion's whelp,
    that leaps forth from Ba'shan."

23 And of Naph'ta·li he said,
"O Naphtali, satisfied with favor,
    and full of the blessing of the
        LORD,
    possess the lake and the south."

24 And of Ash'er he said,
"Blessed above sons be Asher;
    let him be the favorite of his
        brothers,
    and let him dip his foot in oil.
25 Your bars shall be iron and bronze;
    and as your days, so shall your
        strength be.

26 "There is none like God, O Jesh'ū-
        rùn,
    who rides through the heavens to
        your help,
    and in his majesty through the
        skies.
27 The eternal God is your dwelling
        place,
    and underneath are the everlast-
        ing arms.
And he thrust out the enemy before
        you,
    and said, Destroy.
28 So Israel dwelt in safety,
    the fountain of Jacob alone,
in a land of grain and wine;
    yea, his heavens drop down dew.
29 Happy are you, O Israel! Who is
        like you,
    a people saved by the LORD,
the shield of your help,
    and the sword of your triumph!
Your enemies shall come fawning to
        you;
    and you shall tread upon their
        high places."

34 And Moses went up from the
plains of Mo'ab to Mount
Ne'bo, to the top of Pis'gah, which is
opposite Jericho. And the LORD
showed him all the land, Gilead as far
as Dan, 2 all Naph'ta·li, the land of
É'phra·im and Ma·nas'seh, all the land
of Judah as far as the Western Sea,
3 the Negeb, and the Plain, that is, the
valley of Jericho the city of palm trees,
as far as Zo'ar. 4 And the LORD said to
him, "This is the land of which I
swore to Abraham, to Isaac, and to
Jacob, 'I will give it to your descendants.' I have let you see it with your
eyes, but you shall not go over there."
5 So Moses the servant of the LORD
died there in the land of Mo'ab,
according to the word of the LORD,

6 and he buried him in the valley in the land of Mō'ab opposite Beth-pē'ôr; but no man knows the place of his burial to this day. 7 Moses was a hundred and twenty years old when he died; his eye was not dim, nor his natural force abated. 8 And the people of Israel wept for Moses in the plains of Mō'ab thirty days; then the days of weeping and mourning for Moses were ended.

9 And Joshua the son of Nun was full of the spirit of wisdom, for Moses had laid his hands upon him; so the people of Israel obeyed him, and did as the LORD had commanded Moses. 10 And there has not arisen a prophet since in Israel like Moses, whom the LORD knew face to face, 11 none like him for all the signs and the wonders which the LORD sent him to do in the land of Egypt, to Pharaoh and to all his servants and to all his land, 12 and for all the mighty power and all the great and terrible deeds which Moses wrought in the sight of all Israel.

THE BOOK OF

JOSHUA

1 After the death of Moses the servant of the LORD, the LORD said to Joshua the son of Nun, Moses' minister, 2 "Moses my servant is dead; now therefore arise, go over this Jordan, you and all this people, into the land which I am giving to them, to the people of Israel. 3 Every place that the sole of your foot will tread upon I have given to you, as I promised to Moses. 4 From the wilderness and this Lebanon as far as the great river, the river Eū·phrā'tēs, all the land of the Hit'-tites to the Great Sea toward the going down of the sun shall be your territory. 5 No man shall be able to stand before you all the days of your life; as I was with Moses, so I will be with you; I will not fail you or forsake you. 6 Be strong and of good courage; for you shall cause this people to inherit the land which I swore to their fathers to give them. 7 Only be strong and very courageous, being careful to do according to all the law which Moses my servant commanded you; turn not from it to the right hand or to the left, that you may have good success wherever you go. 8 This book of the law shall not depart out of your mouth, but you shall meditate on it day and night, that you may be careful to do according to all that is written in it; for then you shall make your way prosperous, and then you shall have good success. 9 Have I not commanded you? Be strong and of good courage; be not frightened, neither be

dismayed; for the LORD your God is with you wherever you go."

10 Then Joshua commanded the officers of the people, 11 "Pass through the camp, and command the people, 'Prepare your provisions; for within three days you are to pass over this Jordan, to go in to take possession of the land which the LORD your God gives you to possess.' "

12 And to the Reubenites, the Gadites, and the half-tribe of Má·nas'-sēh Joshua said, 13 "Remember the word which Moses the servant of the LORD commanded you, saying, 'The LORD your God is providing you a place to rest, and will give you this land.' 14 Your wives, your little ones, and your cattle shall remain in the land which Moses gave you beyond the Jordan; but all the men of valor among you shall pass over armed before your brethren and shall help them, 15 until the LORD gives rest to your brethren as well as to you, and they also take possession of the land which the LORD your God is giving them; then you shall return to the land of your possession, and shall possess it, the land which Moses the servant of the LORD gave you beyond the Jordan toward sunrise." 16 And they answered Joshua, "All that you have commanded us we will do, and wherever you send us we will go. 17 Just as we obeyed Moses in all things, so we will obey you; only may the LORD your God be with you, as he was with Moses! 18 Whoever

34.10: Num 12.6-8.   1.5: Heb 13.5.
1.12-18: Josh 22.1-34; Num 32.20-22.

rebels against your commandment and disobeys your words, whatever you command him, shall be put to death. Only be strong and of good courage."

2 And Joshua the son of Nun sent two men secretly from Shit'tim as spies, saying, "Go, view the land, especially Jericho." And they went, and came into the house of a harlot whose name was Rā'hab, and lodged there. 2And it was told the king of Jericho, "Behold, certain men of Israel have come here tonight to search out the land." 3 Then the king of Jericho sent to Rā'hab, saying, "Bring forth the men that have come to you, who entered your house; for they have come to search out all the land." 4 But the woman had taken the two men and hidden them; and she said, "True, men came to me, but I did not know where they came from; 5 and when the gate was to be closed, at dark, the men went out; where the men went I do not know; pursue them quickly, for you will overtake them." 6 But she had brought them up to the roof, and hid them with the stalks of flax which she had laid in order on the roof. 7 So the men pursued after them on the way to the Jordan as far as the fords; and as soon as the pursuers had gone out, the gate was shut.

8 Before they lay down, she came up to them on the roof, 9 and said to the men, "I know that the LORD has given you the land, and that the fear of you has fallen upon us, and that all the inhabitants of the land melt away before you. 10 For we have heard how the LORD dried up the water of the Red Sea before you when you came out of Egypt, and what you did to the two kings of the Am'ō∙rites that were beyond the Jordan, to Si'hon and Og, whom you utterly destroyed. 11And as soon as we heard it, our hearts melted, and there was no courage left in any man, because of you; for the LORD your God is he who is God in heaven above and on earth beneath. 12 Now then, swear to me by the LORD that as I have dealt kindly with you, you also will deal kindly with my father's house, and give me a sure sign, 13 and save alive my father and mother, my brothers and sisters, and all who belong to them, and deliver our lives from death." 14And the men said to her, "Our life for yours! If you do not tell this business of ours, then we will deal kindly and faithfully with you when the LORD gives us the land."

15 Then she let them down by a rope through the window, for her house was built into the city wall, so that she dwelt in the wall. 16And she said to them, "Go into the hills, lest the pursuers meet you; and hide yourselves there three days, until the pursuers have returned; then afterward you may go your way." 17 The men said to her, "We will be guiltless with respect to this oath of yours which you have made us swear. 18 Behold, when we come into the land, you shall bind this scarlet cord in the window through which you let us down; and you shall gather into your house your father and mother, your brothers, and all your father's household. 19 If any one goes out of the doors of your house into the street, his blood shall be upon his head, and we shall be guiltless; but if a hand is laid upon any one who is with you in the house, his blood shall be on our head. 20 But if you tell this business of ours, then we shall be guiltless with respect to your oath which you have made us swear." 21And she said, "According to your words, so be it." Then she sent them away, and they departed; and she bound the scarlet cord in the window.

22 They departed, and went into the hills, and remained there three days, until the pursuers returned; for the pursuers had made search all along the way and found nothing. 23 Then the two men came down again from the hills, and passed over and came to Joshua the son of Nun; and they told him all that had befallen them. 24And they said to Joshua, "Truly the LORD has given all the land into our hands; and moreover all the inhabitants of the land are fainthearted because of us."

3 Early in the morning Joshua rose and set out from Shit'tim, with all the people of Israel; and they came to the Jordan, and lodged there before they passed over. 2At the end of three days the officers went through the camp 3 and commanded the people, "When you see the ark of the covenant of the LORD your God being carried by the Levitical priests, then you shall set out from your place and follow it, 4 that you may know the way you shall go, for you have not passed this way before. Yet there shall be a space between you and it, a distance of about two thousand cubits; do not come near it." 5And Joshua said to the people, "Sanctify yourselves; for tomorrow the LORD will do wonders among you." 6And Joshua said to the priests, "Take up the ark of the covenant, and pass on

before the people." And they took up the ark of the covenant, and went before the people.

7 And the LORD said to Joshua, "This day I will begin to exalt you in the sight of all Israel, that they may know that, as I was with Moses, so I will be with you. 8And you shall command the priests who bear the ark of the covenant, 'When you come to the brink of the waters of the Jordan, you shall stand still in the Jordan.'" 9And Joshua said to the people of Israel, "Come hither, and hear the words of the LORD your God." 10And Joshua said, "Hereby you shall know that the living God is among you, and that he will without fail drive out from before you the Canaanites, the Hit´tites, the Hi´vites, the Per´iz-zites, the Gir´gå-shites, the Am´ó-rites, and the Jeb´u-sites. 11 Behold, the ark of the covenant of the Lord of all the earth is to pass over before you into the Jordan. 12 Now therefore take twelve men from the tribes of Israel, from each tribe a man. 13And when the soles of the feet of the priests who bear the ark of the LORD, the Lord of all the earth, shall rest in the waters of the Jordan, the waters of the Jordan shall be stopped from flowing, and the waters coming down from above shall stand in one heap."

14 So, when the people set out from their tents, to pass over the Jordan with the priests bearing the ark of the covenant before the people, 15 and when those who bore the ark had come to the Jordan, and the feet of the priests bearing the ark were dipped in the brink of the water (the Jordan overflows all its banks throughout the time of harvest), 16 the waters coming down from above stood and rose up in a heap far off, at Adam, the city that is beside Zar´é-than, and those flowing down toward the sea of the Ar´å-bàh, the Salt Sea, were wholly cut off; and the people passed over opposite Jericho. 17And while all Israel were passing over on dry ground, the priests who bore the ark of the covenant of the LORD stood on dry ground in the midst of the Jordan, until all the nation finished passing over the Jordan.

4 When all the nation had finished passing over the Jordan, the LORD said to Joshua, 2 "Take twelve men from the people, from each tribe a man, 3 and command them, 'Take twelve stones from here out of the midst of the Jordan, from the very place where the priests' feet stood, and carry them over with you, and lay them down in the place where you lodge tonight.'" 4 Then Joshua called the twelve men from the people of Israel, whom he had appointed, a man from each tribe; 5 and Joshua said to them, "Pass on before the ark of the LORD your God in the midst of the Jordan, and take up each of you a stone upon his shoulder, according to the number of the tribes of the people of Israel, 6 that this may be a sign among you, when your children ask in time to come, 'What do those stones mean to you?' 7 Then you shall tell them that the waters of the Jordan were cut off before the ark of the covenant of the LORD; when it passed over the Jordan, the waters of the Jordan were cut off. So these stones shall be to the people of Israel a memorial for ever."

8 And the men of Israel did as Joshua commanded, and took up twelve stones out of the midst of the Jordan, according to the number of the tribes of the people of Israel, as the LORD told Joshua; and they carried them over with them to the place where they lodged, and laid them down there. 9And Joshua set up twelve stones in the midst of the Jordan, in the place where the feet of the priests bearing the ark of the covenant had stood; and they are there to this day. 10 For the priests who bore the ark stood in the midst of the Jordan, until everything was finished that the LORD commanded Joshua to tell the people, according to all that Moses had commanded Joshua.

The people passed over in haste; 11 and when all the people had finished passing over, the ark of the LORD and the priests passed over before the people. 12 The sons of Reuben and the sons of Gad and the half-tribe of Må-nas´séh passed over armed before the people of Israel, as Moses had bidden them; 13 about forty thousand ready armed for war passed over before the LORD for battle, to the plains of Jericho. 14 On that day the LORD exalted Joshua in the sight of all Israel; and they stood in awe of him, as they had stood in awe of Moses, all the days of his life.

15 And the LORD said to Joshua, 16 "Command the priests who bear the ark of the testimony to come up out of the Jordan." 17 Joshua therefore commanded the priests, "Come up out of the Jordan." 18And when the priests bearing the ark of the covenant of the LORD came up from the midst of the Jordan, and the soles of the priests' feet were lifted up on dry

ground, the waters of the Jordan returned to their place and overflowed all its banks, as before.

19 The people came up out of the Jordan on the tenth day of the first month, and they encamped in Gil′gǎl on the east border of Jericho. 20And those twelve stones, which they took out of the Jordan, Joshua set up in Gil′gǎl. 21And he said to the people of Israel, "When your children ask their fathers in time to come, 'What do these stones mean?' 22 then you shall let your children know, 'Israel passed over this Jordan on dry ground.' 23 For the LORD your God dried up the waters of the Jordan for you until you passed over, as the LORD your God did to the Red Sea, which he dried up for us until we passed over, 24 so that all the peoples of the earth may know that the hand of the LORD is mighty; that you may fear the LORD your God for ever."

5 When all the kings of the Am′ō-rites that were beyond the Jordan to the west, and all the kings of the Canaanites that were by the sea, heard that the LORD had dried up the waters of the Jordan for the people of Israel until they had crossed over, their heart melted, and there was no longer any spirit in them, because of the people of Israel.

2 At that time the LORD said to Joshua, "Make flint knives and circumcise the people of Israel again the second time." 3 So Joshua made flint knives, and circumcised the people of Israel at Gib′ē-ǎth-hā-ǎr′ā-loth.ᵃ 4And this is the reason why Joshua circumcised them: all the males of the people who came out of Egypt, all the men of war, had died on the way in the wilderness after they had come out of Egypt. 5 Though all the people who came out had been circumcised, yet all the people that were born on the way in the wilderness after they had come out of Egypt had not been circumcised. 6 For the people of Israel walked forty years in the wilderness, till all the nation, the men of war that came forth out of Egypt, perished, because they did not hearken to the voice of the LORD; to them the LORD swore that he would not let them see the land which the LORD had sworn to their fathers to give us, a land flowing with milk and honey. 7 So it was their children, whom he raised up in their stead, that Joshua circumcised; for they were uncircumcised, because they had not been circumcised on the way.

8 When the circumcising of all the

nation was done, they remained in their places in the camp till they were healed. 9And the LORD said to Joshua, "This day I have rolled away the reproach of Egypt from you." And so the name of that place is called Gil′gǎlᵇ to this day.

10 While the people of Israel were encamped in Gil′gǎl they kept the passover on the fourteenth day of the month at evening in the plains of Jericho. 11And on the morrow after the passover, on that very day, they ate of the produce of the land, unleavened cakes and parched grain. 12And the manna ceased on the morrow, when they ate of the produce of the land; and the people of Israel had manna no more, but ate of the fruit of the land of Canaan that year.

13 When Joshua was by Jericho, he lifted up his eyes and looked, and behold, a man stood before him with his drawn sword in his hand; and Joshua went to him and said to him, "Are you for us, or for our adversaries?" 14And he said, "No; but as commander of the army of the LORD I have now come." And Joshua fell on his face to the earth, and worshiped, and said to him, "What does my lord bid his servant?" 15And the commander of the LORD's army said to Joshua, "Put off your shoes from your feet; for the place where you stand is holy." And Joshua did so.

6 Now Jericho was shut up from within and from without because of the people of Israel; none went out, and none came in. 2And the LORD said to Joshua, "See, I have given into your hand Jericho, with its king and mighty men of valor. 3 You shall march around the city, all the men of war going around the city once. Thus shall you do for six days. 4And seven priests shall bear seven trumpets of rams' horns before the ark; and on the seventh day you shall march around the city seven times, the priests blowing the trumpets. 5And when they make a long blast with the ram's horn, as soon as you hear the sound of the trumpet, then all the people shall shout with a great shout; and the wall of the city will fall down flat, and the people shall go up every man straight before him." 6 So Joshua the son of Nun called the priests and said to them, "Take up the ark of the covenant, and let seven priests bear seven trumpets of rams' horns before the ark of the LORD." 7And he said to the people, "Go forward; march around the city,

ᵃ That is *the hill of the foreskins*　　ᵇ From Heb *galal* to roll and let the armed men pass on before the ark of the LORD."

8 And as Joshua had commanded the people, the seven priests bearing the seven trumpets of rams' horns before the LORD went forward, blowing the trumpets, with the ark of the covenant of the LORD following them. 9And the armed men went before the priests who blew the trumpets, and the rear guard came after the ark, while the trumpets blew continually. 10 But Joshua commanded the people, "You shall not shout or let your voice be heard, neither shall any word go out of your mouth, until the day I bid you shout; then you shall shout." 11 So he caused the ark of the LORD to compass the city, going about it once; and they came into the camp, and spent the night in the camp.

12 Then Joshua rose early in the morning, and the priests took up the ark of the LORD. 13And the seven priests bearing the seven trumpets of rams' horns before the ark of the LORD passed on, blowing the trumpets continually; and the armed men went before them, and the rear guard came after the ark of the LORD, while the trumpets blew continually. 14And the second day they marched around the city once, and returned into the camp. So they did for six days.

15 On the seventh day they rose early at the dawn of day, and marched around the city in the same manner seven times: it was only on that day they marched around the city seven times. 16And at the seventh time, when the priests had blown the trumpets, Joshua said to the people, "Shout; for the LORD has given you the city. 17And the city and all that is within it shall be devoted to the LORD for destruction; only Rā′hab the harlot and all who are with her in her house shall live, because she hid the messengers that we sent. 18 But you, keep yourselves from the things devoted to destruction, lest when you have devoted them you take any of the devoted things and make the camp of Israel a thing for destruction, and bring trouble upon it. 19 But all silver and gold, and vessels of bronze and iron, are sacred to the LORD; they shall go into the treasury of the LORD." 20 So the people shouted, and the trumpets were blown. As soon as the people heard the sound of the trumpet, the people raised a great shout, and the wall fell down flat, so that the people went up into the city, every man straight before him, and they took

the city. 21 Then they utterly destroyed all in the city, both men and women, young and old, oxen, sheep, and asses, with the edge of the sword.

22 And Joshua said to the two men who had spied out the land, "Go into the harlot's house, and bring out from it the woman, and all who belong to her, as you swore to her." 23 So the young men who had been spies went in, and brought out Rā′hab, and her father and mother and brothers and all who belonged to her; and they brought all her kindred, and set them outside the camp of Israel. 24And they burned the city with fire, and all within it; only the silver and gold, and the vessels of bronze and of iron, they put into the treasury of the house of the LORD. 25 But Rā′hab the harlot, and her father's household, and all who belonged to her, Joshua saved alive; and she dwelt in Israel to this day, because she hid the messengers whom Joshua sent to spy out Jericho.

26 Joshua laid an oath upon them at that time, saying, "Cursed before the LORD be the man that rises up and rebuilds this city, Jericho.

> At the cost of his first-born shall
>   he lay its foundation,
> and at the cost of his youngest son
>   shall he set up its gates."

27 So the LORD was with Joshua; and his fame was in all the land.

7 But the people of Israel broke faith in regard to the devoted things; for A′chán the son of Cär′mi, son of Zab′di, son of Zē′räh, of the tribe of Judah, took some of the devoted things; and the anger of the LORD burned against the people of Israel.

2 Joshua sent men from Jericho to Ai, which is near Beth-ā′vén, east of Beth′él, and said to them, "Go up and spy out the land." And the men went up and spied out Ai. 3And they returned to Joshua, and said to him, "Let not all the people go up, but let about two or three thousand men go up and attack Ai; do not make the whole people toil up there, for they are but few." 4 So about three thousand went up there from the people; and they fled before the men of Ai, 5 and the men of Ai killed about thirty-six men of them, and chased them before the gate as far as Sheb′á·rim, and slew them at the descent. And the hearts of the people melted, and became as water.

6 Then Joshua rent his clothes, and fell to the earth upon his face before

the ark of the LORD until the evening, he and the elders of Israel; and they put dust upon their heads. 7And Joshua said, "Alas, O Lord GOD, why hast thou brought this people over the Jordan at all, to give us into the hands of the Am′ȯ·rites, to destroy us? Would that we had been content to dwell beyond the Jordan! 8 O Lord, what can I say, when Israel has turned their backs before their enemies! 9 For the Canaanites and all the inhabitants of the land will hear of it, and will surround us, and cut off our name from the earth; and what wilt thou do for thy great name?"

10 The LORD said to Joshua, "Arise, why have you thus fallen upon your face? 11 Israel has sinned; they have transgressed my covenant which I commanded them; they have taken some of the devoted things; they have stolen, and lied, and put them among their own stuff. 12 Therefore the people of Israel cannot stand before their enemies; they turn their backs before their enemies, because they have become a thing for destruction. I will be with you no more, unless you destroy the devoted things from among you. 13 Up, sanctify the people, and say, 'Sanctify yourselves for tomorrow; for thus says the LORD, God of Israel, "There are devoted things in the midst of you, O Israel; you cannot stand before your enemies, until you take away the devoted things from among you." 14 In the morning therefore you shall be brought near by your tribes; and the tribe which the LORD takes shall come near by families; and the family which the LORD takes shall come near by households; and the household which the LORD takes shall come near man by man. 15And he who is taken with the devoted things shall be burned with fire, he and all that he has, because he has transgressed the covenant of the LORD, and because he has done a shameful thing in Israel.'"

16 So Joshua rose early in the morning, and brought Israel near tribe by tribe, and the tribe of Judah was taken; 17 and he brought near the families of Judah, and the family of the Zē′rȧ·hites was taken; and he brought near the family of the Zerahites man by man, and Zab′dī was taken; 18 and he brought near his household man by man, and Ā′chȧn the son of Cär′mī, son of Zab′dī, son of Zē′rȧh of the tribe of Judah, was taken. 19 Then Joshua said to Ā′chȧn, "My son, give glory to the LORD God of Israel, and

c That is Trouble

render praise to him; and tell me now what you have done; do not hide it from me." 20And Ā′chȧn answered Joshua, "Of a truth I have sinned against the LORD God of Israel, and this is what I did: 21 when I saw among the spoil a beautiful mantle from Shī′när, and two hundred shekels of silver, and a bar of gold weighing fifty shekels, then I coveted them, and took them; and behold, they are hidden in the earth inside my tent, with the silver underneath."

22 So Joshua sent messengers, and they ran to the tent; and behold, it was hidden in his tent with the silver underneath. 23And they took them out of the tent and brought them to Joshua and all the people of Israel; and they laid them down before the LORD. 24And Joshua and all Israel with him took Ā′chȧn the son of Zē′rȧh, and the silver and the mantle and the bar of gold, and his sons and daughters, and his oxen and asses and sheep, and his tent, and all that he had; and they brought them up to the Valley of Ā′chȯr. 25And Joshua said, "Why did you bring trouble on us? The LORD brings trouble on you today." And all Israel stoned him with stones; they burned them with fire, and stoned them with stones. 26And they raised over him a great heap of stones that remains to this day; then the LORD turned from his burning anger. Therefore to this day the name of that place is called the Valley of Ā′chȯr.c

8 And the LORD said to Joshua, "Do not fear or be dismayed; take all the fighting men with you, and arise, go up to Äi; see, I have given into your hand the king of Ai, and his people, his city, and his land; 2 and you shall do to Äi and its king as you did to Jericho and its king; only its spoil and its cattle you shall take as booty for yourselves; lay an ambush against the city, behind it."

3 So Joshua arose, and all the fighting men, to go up to Äi; and Joshua chose thirty thousand mighty men of valor, and sent them forth by night. 4And he commanded them, "Behold, you shall lie in ambush against the city, behind it; do not go very far from the city, but hold yourselves all in readiness; 5 and I, and all the people who are with me, will approach the city. And when they come out against us, as before, we shall flee before them; 6 and they will come out after us, till we have drawn them away from the city; for they will say, 'They are fleeing from

us, as before.' So we will flee from them; 7 then you shall rise up from the ambush, and seize the city; for the LORD your God will give it into your hand. 8And when you have taken the city, you shall set the city on fire, doing as the LORD has bidden; see, I have commanded you." 9 So Joshua sent them forth; and they went to the place of ambush, and lay between Beth'el and Ai, to the west of Ai; but Joshua spent that night among the people.

10 And Joshua arose early in the morning and mustered the people, and went up, with the elders of Israel, before the people to Ai. 11And all the fighting men who were with him went up, and drew near before the city, and encamped on the north side of Ai, with a ravine between them and Ai. 12And he took about five thousand men, and set them in ambush between Beth'el and Ai, to the west of the city. 13 So they stationed the forces, the main encampment which was north of the city and its rear guard west of the city. But Joshua spent that night in the valley. 14And when the king of Ai saw this he and all his people, the men of the city, made haste and went out early to the descent*d* toward the Ar'abah to meet Israel in battle; but he did not know that there was an ambush against him behind the city. 15And Joshua and all Israel made a pretense of being beaten before them, and fled in the direction of the wilderness. 16 So all the people who were in the city were called together to pursue them, and as they pursued Joshua they were drawn away from the city. 17 There was not a man left in Ai or Beth'el, who did not go out after Israel; they left the city open, and pursued Israel.

18 Then the LORD said to Joshua, "Stretch out the javelin that is in your hand toward Ai; for I will give it into your hand." And Joshua stretched out the javelin that was in his hand toward the city. 19And the ambush rose quickly out of their place, and as soon as he had stretched out his hand, they ran and entered the city and took it; and they made haste to set the city on fire. 20 So when the men of Ai looked back, behold, the smoke of the city went up to heaven; and they had no power to flee this way or that, for the people that fled to the wilderness turned back upon the pursuers. 21And when Joshua and all Israel saw that

the ambush had taken the city, and that the smoke of the city went up, then they turned back and smote the men of Ai. 22And the others came forth from the city against them; so they were in the midst of Israel, some on this side, and some on that side; and Israel smote them, until there was left none that survived or escaped. 23 But the king of Ai they took alive, and brought him to Joshua.

24 When Israel had finished slaughtering all the inhabitants of Ai in the open wilderness where they pursued them and all of them to the very last had fallen by the edge of the sword, all Israel returned to Ai, and smote it with the edge of the sword. 25And all who fell that day, both men and women, were twelve thousand, all the people of Ai. 26 For Joshua did not draw back his hand, with which he stretched out the javelin, until he had utterly destroyed all the inhabitants of Ai. 27 Only the cattle and the spoil of that city Israel took as their booty, according to the word of the LORD which he commanded Joshua. 28 So Joshua burned Ai, and made it for ever a heap of ruins, as it is to this day. 29And he hanged the king of Ai on a tree until evening; and at the going down of the sun Joshua commanded, and they took his body down from the tree, and cast it at the entrance of the gate of the city, and raised over it a great heap of stones, which stands there to this day.

30 Then Joshua built an altar in Mount E'bal to the LORD, the God of Israel, 31 as Moses the servant of the LORD had commanded the people of Israel, as it is written in the book of the law of Moses, "an altar of unhewn stones, upon which no man has lifted an iron tool"; and they offered on it burnt offerings to the LORD, and sacrificed peace offerings. 32And there, in the presence of the people of Israel, he wrote upon the stones a copy of the law of Moses, which he had written. 33And all Israel, sojourner as well as homeborn, with their elders and officers and their judges, stood on opposite sides of the ark before the Levitical priests who carried the ark of the covenant of the LORD, half of them in front of Mount Ger'i·zim and half of them in front of Mount E'bal, as Moses the servant of the LORD had commanded at the first, that they should bless the people of Israel. 34And afterward he read all the words of the

d Cn: Heb *appointed time*
8.30-35: Deut 27.2-8.

law, the blessing and the curse, according to all that is written in the book of the law. 35 There was not a word of all that Moses commanded which Joshua did not read before all the assembly of Israel, and the women, and the little ones, and the sojourners who lived among them.

9 When all the kings who were beyond the Jordan in the hill country and in the lowland all along the coast of the Great Sea toward Lebanon, the Hit′tites, the Am′ō·rites, the Canaanites, the Per′iz·zites, the Hi′vites, and the Jeb′ū·sites, heard of this, 2 they gathered together with one accord to fight Joshua and Israel.

3 But when the inhabitants of Gib′ē·ŏn heard what Joshua had done to Jericho and to Ai, 4 they on their part acted with cunning, and went and made ready provisions, and took wornout sacks upon their asses, and wineskins, worn-out and torn and mended, 5 with worn-out, patched sandals on their feet, and worn-out clothes; and all their provisions were dry and moldy. 6 And they went to Joshua in the camp at Gil′găl, and said to him and to the men of Israel, "We have come from a far country; so now make a covenant with us." 7 But the men of Israel said to the Hi′vites, "Perhaps you live among us; then how can we make a covenant with you?" 8 They said to Joshua, "We are your servants." And Joshua said to them, "Who are you? And where do you come from?" 9 They said to him, "From a very far country your servants have come, because of the name of the LORD your God; for we have heard a report of him, and all that he did in Egypt, 10 and all that he did to the two kings of the Am′ō·rites who were beyond the Jordan, Si′hon the king of Hesh′bŏn, and Og king of Bā′shàn, who dwelt in Ash′tà·roth. 11 And our elders and all the inhabitants of our country said to us, 'Take provisions in your hand for the journey, and go to meet them, and say to them, "We are your servants; come now, make a covenant with us."' 12 Here is our bread; it was still warm when we took it from our houses as our food for the journey, on the day we set forth to come to you, but now, behold, it is dry and moldy; 13 these wineskins were new when we filled them, and behold, they are burst; and these garments and shoes of ours are worn out from the very long journey." 14 So the men partook of their provisions, and did not ask direction from

ⁿ Heb *they*

the LORD. 15 And Joshua made peace with them, and made a covenant with them, to let them live; and the leaders of the congregation swore to them.

16 At the end of three days after they had made a covenant with them, they heard that they were their neighbors, and that they dwelt among them. 17 And the people of Israel set out and reached their cities on the third day. Now their cities were Gib′ē·ŏn, Chē·phī′răh, Bē·ēr′ŏth, and Kĭr′i·ath-jē′ă·rim. 18 But the people of Israel did not kill them, because the leaders of the congregation had sworn to them by the LORD, the God of Israel. Then all the congregation murmured against the leaders. 19 But all the leaders said to all the congregation, "We have sworn to them by the LORD, the God of Israel, and now we may not touch them. 20 This we will do to them, and let them live, lest wrath be upon us, because of the oath which we swore to them." 21 And the leaders said to them, "Let them live." So they became hewers of wood and drawers of water for all the congregation, as the leaders had said of them.

22 Joshua summoned them, and he said to them, "Why did you deceive us, saying, 'We are very far from you,' when you dwell among us? 23 Now therefore you are cursed, and some of you shall always be slaves, hewers of wood and drawers of water for the house of my God." 24 They answered Joshua, "Because it was told to your servants for a certainty that the LORD your God had commanded his servant Moses to give you all the land, and to destroy all the inhabitants of the land from before you; so we feared greatly for our lives because of you, and did this thing. 25 And now, behold, we are in your hand: do as it seems good and right in your sight to do to us." 26 So he did to them, and delivered them out of the hand of the people of Israel; and they did not kill them. 27 But Joshua made them that day hewers of wood and drawers of water for the congregation and for the altar of the LORD, to continue to this day, in the place which he should choose.

10 When A·dō′ni-zē′dek king of Jerusalem heard how Joshua had taken Ai, and had utterly destroyed it, doing to Ai and its king as he had done to Jericho and its king, and how the inhabitants of Gib′ē·ŏn had made peace with Israel and were among them, 2 heˣ feared greatly, because Gib′ē·ŏn was a great city, like one of

ˣ Heb *they*

the royal cities, and because it was greater than Ai, and all its men were mighty. 3 So Ȧ-dō′ni-zē′dek king of Jerusalem sent to Hō′ham king of Hē′-brŏn, to Pī′rȧm king of Jär′muth, to Jȧ-phī′ȧ king of Lā′chish, and to Dē′-bir king of Eg′lon, saying, 4 "Come up to me, and help me, and let us smite Gib′ē-ŏn; for it has made peace with Joshua and with the people of Israel." 5 Then the five kings of the Am′ō-rites, the king of Jerusalem, the king of Hē′brŏn, the king of Jär′muth, the king of Lā′chish, and the king of Eg′lon, gathered their forces, and went up with all their armies and encamped against Gib′ē-ŏn, and made war against it.

6 And the men of Gib′ē-ŏn sent to Joshua at the camp in Gil′gȧl, saying, "Do not relax your hand from your servants; come up to us quickly, and save us, and help us; for all the kings of the Am′ō-rites that dwell in the hill country are gathered against us." 7 So Joshua went up from Gil′gȧl, he and all the people of war with him, and all the mighty men of valor. 8 And the LORD said to Joshua, "Do not fear them, for I have given them into your hands; there shall not a man of them stand before you." 9 So Joshua came upon them suddenly, having marched up all night from Gil′gȧl. 10 And the LORD threw them into a panic before Israel, who slew them with a great slaughter at Gib′ē-ŏn, and chased them by the way of the ascent of Bēth-hō′-ron, and smote them as far as Ȧ-zē′kȧh and Mak-kē′dȧh. 11 And as they fled before Israel, while they were going down the ascent of Bēth-hō′ron, the LORD threw down great stones from heaven upon them as far as Ȧ-zē′kȧh, and they died; there were more who died because of the hailstones than the men of Israel killed with the sword.

12 Then spoke Joshua to the LORD in the day when the LORD gave the Am′ō-rites over to the men of Israel; and he said in the sight of Israel,

"Sun, stand thou still at Gib′ē-ŏn,
   and thou Moon in the valley of
     Ăi′jȧ-lon."
13 And the sun stood still, and the
   moon stayed,
until the nation took vengeance on
   their enemies.

Is this not written in the Book of Jash′är? The sun stayed in the midst of heaven, and did not hasten to go down for about a whole day. 14 There has been no day like it before or since, when the LORD hearkened to the voice of a man; for the LORD fought for Israel.

15 Then Joshua returned, and all Israel with him, to the camp at Gil′gȧl.

16 These five kings fled, and hid themselves in the cave at Mak-kē′dȧh. 17 And it was told Joshua, "The five kings have been found, hidden in the cave at Mak-kē′dȧh." 18 And Joshua said, "Roll great stones against the mouth of the cave, and set men by it to guard them; 19 but do not stay there yourselves, pursue your enemies, fall upon their rear, do not let them enter their cities; for the LORD your God has given them into your hand." 20 When Joshua and the men of Israel had finished slaying them with a very great slaughter, until they were wiped out, and when the remnant which remained of them had entered into the fortified cities, 21 all the people returned safe to Joshua in the camp at Mak-kē′dȧh; not a man moved his tongue against any of the people of Israel.

22 Then Joshua said, "Open the mouth of the cave, and bring those five kings out to me from the cave." 23 And they did so, and brought those five kings out to him from the cave, the king of Jerusalem, the king of Hē′brŏn, the king of Jär′muth, the king of Lā′chish, and the king of Eg′lon. 24 And when they brought those kings out to Joshua, Joshua summoned all the men of Israel, and said to the chiefs of the men of war who had gone with him, "Come near, put your feet upon the necks of these kings." Then they came near, and put their feet on their necks. 25 And Joshua said to them, "Do not be afraid or dismayed; be strong and of good courage; for thus the LORD will do to all your enemies against whom you fight." 26 And afterward Joshua smote them and put them to death, and he hung them on five trees. And they hung upon the trees until evening; 27 but at the time of the going down of the sun, Joshua commanded, and they took them down from the trees, and threw them into the cave where they had hidden themselves, and they set great stones against the mouth of the cave, which remain to this very day.

28 And Joshua took Mak-kē′dȧh on that day, and smote it and its king with the edge of the sword; he utterly destroyed every person in it, he left none remaining; and he did to the king of Makkedah as he had done to the king of Jericho.

29 Then Joshua passed on from

Mak·kē′dàh, and all Israel with him, to Lib′nàh, and fought against Lib′nah; 30 and the LORD gave it also and its king into the hand of Israel; and he smote it with the edge of the sword, and every person in it; he left none remaining in it; and he did to its king as he had done to the king of Jericho.

31 And Joshua passed on from Lib′nàh, and all Israel with him, to Lā′chish, and laid siege to it, and assaulted it; 32 and the LORD gave Lā′chish into the hand of Israel, and he took it on the second day, and smote it with the edge of the sword, and every person in it, as he had done to Lib′nàh.

33 Then Hō′ram king of Gē′zer came up to help Lā′chish; and Joshua smote him and his people, until he left none remaining.

34 And Joshua passed on with all Israel from Lā′chish to Eg′lon; and they laid siege to it, and assaulted it; 35 and they took it on that day, and smote it with the edge of the sword; and every person in it he utterly destroyed that day, as he had done to Lā′chish.

36 Then Joshua went up with all Israel from Eg′lon to Hē′bròn; and they assaulted it, 37 and took it, and smote it with the edge of the sword, and its king and its towns, and every person in it; he left none remaining, as he had done to Eg′lon, and utterly destroyed it with every person in it.

38 Then Joshua, with all Israel, turned back to Dē′bir and assaulted it, 39 and he took it with its king and all its towns; and they smote them with the edge of the sword, and utterly destroyed every person in it; he left none remaining; as he had done to Hē′bròn and to Lib′nàh and its king, so he did to Dē′bir and to its king.

40 So Joshua defeated the whole land, the hill country and the Negeb and the lowland and the slopes, and all their kings; he left none remaining, but utterly destroyed all that breathed, as the LORD God of Israel commanded. 41And Joshua took them from Kā′desh-bär′nē·à to Gā′za, and all the country of Gō′shén, as far as Gib′ē·òn. 42And Joshua took all these kings and their land at one time, because the LORD God of Israel fought for Israel. 43 Then Joshua returned, and all Israel with him, to the camp at Gil′gàl.

‖ When Jā′bin king of Hā′zôr heard of this, he sent to Jō′bab king of Mā′don, and to the king of Shim′ròn, and to the king of Ach′-shaph, 2 and to the kings who were in the northern hill country, and in the Ar′à·bàh south of Chin′nē·roth, and in the lowland, and in Nā′photh·dôr on the west, 3 to the Canaanites in the east and the west, the Am′ò·rites, the Hit′tites, the Per′iz·zites, and the Jeb′-ū·sites in the hill country, and the Hi′vites under Hēr′mòn in the land of Miz′pàh. 4And they came out, with all their troops, a great host, in number like the sand that is upon the seashore, with very many horses and chariots. 5And all these kings joined their forces and came and encamped together at the waters of Mē′rom, to fight with Israel.

6 And the LORD said to Joshua, "Do not be afraid of them, for to-morrow at this time I will give over all of them, slain, to Israel; you shall hamstring their horses, and burn their chariots with fire." 7 So Joshua came suddenly upon them with all his people of war, by the waters of Mē′rom, and fell upon them. 8And the LORD gave them into the hand of Israel, who smote them and chased them as far as Great Si′don and Mis′rē·photh-mā′im, and eastward as far as the valley of Miz′peh; and they smote them, until they left none remaining. 9And Joshua did to them as the LORD bade him; he hamstrung their horses, and burned their chariots with fire.

10 And Joshua turned back at that time, and took Hā′zôr, and smote its king with the sword; for Hazor formerly was the head of all those kingdoms. 11And they put to the sword all who were in it, utterly destroying them; there was none left that breathed, and he burned Hā′zôr with fire. 12And all the cities of those kings, and all their kings, Joshua took, and smote them with the edge of the sword, utterly destroying them, as Moses the servant of the LORD had commanded. 13 But none of the cities that stood on mounds did Israel burn, except Hā′zôr only; that Joshua burned. 14And all the spoil of these cities and the cattle, the people of Israel took for their booty; but every man they smote with the edge of the sword, until they had destroyed them, and they did not leave any that breathed. 15As the LORD had commanded Moses his servant, so Moses commanded Joshua, and so Joshua did; he left nothing undone of all that the LORD had commanded Moses.

16 So Joshua took all that land, the hill country and all the Negeb and all the land of Gō′shén and the lowland and the Ar′à·bàh and the hill country of Israel and its lowland 17 from Mount

Hā'lak, that rises toward Sē'ir, as far as Bā'al-gad in the valley of Lebanon below Mount Hēr'mŏn. And he took all their kings, and smote them, and put them to death. 18 Joshua made war a long time with all those kings. 19 There was not a city that made peace with the people of Israel, except the Hi'vites, the inhabitants of Gib'ē-ŏn; they took all in battle. 20 For it was the LORD's doing to harden their hearts that they should come against Israel in battle, in order that they should be utterly destroyed, and should receive no mercy but be exterminated, as the LORD commanded Moses.

21 And Joshua came at that time, and wiped out the An'a·kim from the hill country, from Hē'brŏn, from Dē'bir, from Ā'nab, and from all the hill country of Judah, and from all the hill country of Israel; Joshua utterly destroyed them with their cities. 22 There was none of the An'a·kim left in the land of the people of Israel; only in Gä'zà, in Gath, and in Ash'dod, did some remain. 23 So Joshua took the whole land, according to all that the LORD had spoken to Moses; and Joshua gave it for an inheritance to Israel according to their tribal allotments. And the land had rest from war.

12 Now these are the kings of the land, whom the people of Israel defeated, and took possession of their land beyond the Jordan toward the sunrising, from the valley of the Ar'non to Mount Hēr'mŏn, with all the Ar'a·bàh eastward: 2 Si'hon king of the Am'ŏ·rites who dwelt at Hesh'bŏn, and ruled from A·rō'ĕr, which is on the edge of the valley of the Ar'non, and from the middle of the valley as far as the river Jab'bŏk, the boundary of the Am'mŏ·nites, that is, half of Gilead, 3 and the Ar'a·bàh to the Sea of Chin'nĕ·roth eastward, and in the direction of Beth-jesh'i·moth, to the sea of the Arabah, the Salt Sea, southward to the foot of the slopes of Pis'gàh; 4 and Og*e* king of Bā'shàn, one of the remnant of the Reph'a·im, who dwelt at Ash'tà·roth and at Ed'rē-ī 5 and ruled over Mount Hēr'mŏn and Sal'e·càh and all Bā'shàn to the boundary of the Gesh'u·rites and the Mā-ac'a·thites, and over half of Gilead to the boundary of Si'hon king of Hesh'bŏn. 6 Moses, the servant of the LORD, and the people of Israel defeated them; and Moses the servant of the LORD gave their land for a possession to the Reubenites and the Gadites and the half-tribe of Mà·nas'sĕh.

7 And these are the kings of the land whom Joshua and the people of Israel defeated on the west side of the Jordan, from Bā'al-gad in the valley of Lebanon to Mount Hā'lak, that rises toward Sē'ir (and Joshua gave their land to the tribes of Israel as a possession according to their allotments, 8 in the hill country, in the lowland, in the Ar'a·bàh, in the slopes, in the wilderness, and in the Negeb, the land of the Hit'tites, the Am'ŏ·rites, the Canaanites, the Per'iz·zites, the Hi'vites, and the Jeb'ū·sites): 9 the king of Jericho, one; the king of Ai, which is beside Beth'él, one; 10 the king of Jerusalem, one; the king of Hē'brŏn, one; 11 the king of Jär'muth, one; the king of Lā'chish, one; 12 the king of Eg'lon, one; the king of Gē'zĕr, one; 13 the king of Dē'bir, one; the king of Gē'dĕr, one; 14 the king of Hôr'màh, one; the king of Ar'àd, one; 15 the king of Lib'nàh, one; the king of A·dul'làm, one; 16 the king of Mak·kē'dàh, one; the king of Beth'él, one; 17 the king of Tap'pū·àh, one; the king of Hē'phér, one; 18 the king of Ā'phek, one; the king of La·shär'on, one; 19 the king of Mā'don, one; the king of Hā'zŏr, one; 20 the king of Shim'rŏn-mē'ron, one; the king of Ach'shaph, one; 21 the king of Tā'a·nach, one; the king of Mĕgid'dō, one; 22 the king of Kē'desh, one; the king of Jok'nē-am in Cär'mĕl, one; 23 the king of Dôr in Nā'phath-dôr, one; the king of Goi'im in Galilee,*f* one; 24 the king of Tïr'zàh; one: in all, thirty-one kings.

13 Now Joshua was old and advanced in years; and the LORD said to him, "You are old and advanced in years, and there remains yet very much land to be possessed. 2 This is the land that yet remains: all the regions of the Philistines, and all those of the Gesh'ū·rites 3 (from the Shī'hôr, which is east of Egypt, northward to the boundary of Ek'rŏn, it is reckoned as Canaanite; there are five rulers of the Philistines, those of Gä'zà, Ash'dod, Ash'kĕ·lon, Gath, and Ek'rŏn), and those of the Av'vim, 4 in the south, all the land of the Canaanites, and Me-ar'àh which belongs to the Si·dō'ni·àns, to Ā'phek, to the boundary of the Am'ŏ·rites, 5 and the land of the Geb'à·lites, and all Lebanon, toward the sunrising, from Bā'al-gad below Mount Hēr'mŏn to the entrance of Hā'math, 6 all the inhabitants of the hill country from Lebanon to Mis're-photh-mā'im, even all the Si·dō'ni·àns. I will myself drive them out from before the people of Israel; only allot the land to Israel for an inheritance, as I have commanded you. 7 Now therefore divide this land for an inheritance to the nine tribes and half the tribe of Ma·nas´seh."

8 With the other half of the tribe of Ma·nas´seh[g] the Reubenites and the Gadites received their inheritance, which Moses gave them, beyond the Jordan eastward, as Moses the servant of the LORD gave them: 9 from A·rō´er, which is on the edge of the valley of the Ar´non, and the city that is in the middle of the valley, and all the table-land of Med´e·ba as far as Di´bon; 10 and all the cities of Si´hon king of the Am´o·rites, who reigned in Hesh´bon, as far as the boundary of the Am´mo·nites; 11 and Gilead, and the region of the Gesh´u·rites and Ma·ac´a·thites, and all Mount Her´mon, and all Ba´shan to Sal´e·cah; 12 all the kingdom of Og in Ba´shan, who reigned in Ash´ta·roth and in Ed´re-i (he alone was left of the remnant of the Reph´a·im); these Moses had defeated and driven out. 13 Yet the people of Israel did not drive out the Gesh´u·rites or the Ma·ac´a·thites; but Ge´shur and Ma´a·cath dwell in the midst of Israel to this day.

14 To the tribe of Levi alone Moses gave no inheritance; the offerings by fire to the LORD God of Israel are their inheritance, as he said to him.

15 And Moses gave an inheritance to the tribe of the Reubenites according to their families. 16 So their territory was from A·rō´er, which is on the edge of the valley of the Ar´non, and the city that is in the middle of the valley, and all the tableland by Med´e·ba; 17 with Hesh´bon, and all its cities that are in the tableland; Di´bon, and Ba´moth-ba´al, and Beth-ba´al-me´on, 18 and Ja´haz, and Ked´e·moth, and Meph´a·ath, 19 and Kir·i·a·tha´im, and Sib´mah, and Ze´reth-sha´har on the hill of the valley, 20 and Beth-pe´or, and the slopes of Pis´gah, and Beth-jesh´i·moth, 21 that is, all the cities of the tableland, and all the kingdom of Si´hon king of the Am´o·rites, who reigned in Hesh´bon, whom Moses defeated with the leaders of Mid´i·an, E´vi and Re´kem and Zur and Hur and Re´ba, the princes of Sihon, who dwelt in the land. 22 Balaam also, the son of Be´or, the soothsayer, the people of Israel killed with the sword among the rest of their slain. 23 And the border of the people of Reuben was the

Jordan as a boundary. This was the inheritance of the Reubenites, according to their families with their cities and villages.

24 And Moses gave an inheritance also to the tribe of the Gadites, according to their families. 25 Their territory was Ja´zer, and all the cities of Gilead, and half the land of the Am´mo·nites, to A·rō´er, which is east of Rab´bah, 26 and from Hesh´bon to Ra´math-miz´peh and Bet´o·nim, and from Ma·ha·na´im to the territory of De´bir,[h] 27 and in the valley Beth-ha´ram, Beth-nim´rah, Suc´coth, and Za´phon, the rest of the kingdom of Si´hon king of Hesh´bon, having the Jordan as a boundary, to the lower end of the Sea of Chin´ne·reth, eastward beyond the Jordan. 28 This is the inheritance of the Gadites according to their families, with their cities and villages.

29 And Moses gave an inheritance to the half-tribe of Ma·nas´seh; it was allotted to the half-tribe of the Ma·nas´sites according to their families. 30 Their region extended from Ma·ha·na´im, through all Ba´shan, the whole kingdom of Og king of Bashan, and all the towns of Ja´ir, which are in Bashan, sixty cities, 31 and half Gilead, and Ash´ta·roth, and Ed´re-i, the cities of the kingdom of Og in Ba´shan; these were allotted to the people of Ma´chir the son of Ma·nas´seh for the half of the Ma´chi·rites according to their families.

32 These are the inheritances which Moses distributed in the plains of Mō´ab, beyond the Jordan east of Jericho. 33 But to the tribe of Levi Moses gave no inheritance; the LORD God of Israel is their inheritance, as he said to them.

14 And these are the inheritances which the people of Israel received in the land of Canaan, which El·e·a´zar the priest, and Joshua the son of Nun, and the heads of the fathers' houses of the tribes of the people of Israel distributed to them. 2 Their inheritance was by lot, as the LORD had commanded Moses for the nine and one-half tribes. 3 For Moses had given an inheritance to the two and one-half tribes beyond the Jordan; but to the Levites he gave no inheritance among them. 4 For the people of Joseph were two tribes, Ma·nas´seh and E´phra·im; and no portion was given to the Levites in the land, but only cities to dwell in, with their pasture lands for their cattle and their substance. 5 The people of Israel did

g Cn: Heb *With it*   h Gk Syr Vg: Heb *Lidebir*

as the LORD commanded Moses; they allotted the land.

6 Then the people of Judah came to Joshua at Gil′gàl; and Caleb the son of Jè·phün′nĕh the Ken′iz·zìte said to him, "You know what the LORD said to Moses the man of God in Kā′desh-bär′nē·à concerning you and me. 7 I was forty years old when Moses the servant of the LORD sent me from Kā′desh-bär′nē·à to spy out the land; and I brought him word again as it was in my heart. 8 But my brethren who went up with me made the heart of the people melt; yet I wholly followed the LORD my God. 9And Moses swore on that day, saying, 'Surely the land on which your foot has trodden shall be an inheritance for you and your children for ever, because you have wholly followed the LORD my God.' 10And now, behold, the LORD has kept me alive, as he said, these forty-five years since the time that the LORD spoke this word to Moses, while Israel walked in the wilderness; and now, lo, I am this day eighty-five years old. 11 I am still as strong to this day as I was in the day that Moses sent me; my strength now is as my strength was then, for war, and for going and coming. 12 So now give me this hill country of which the LORD spoke on that day; for you heard on that day how the An′à·kim were there, with great fortified cities; it may be that the LORD will be with me, and I shall drive them out as the LORD said."

13 Then Joshua blessed him; and he gave Hē′bron to Caleb the son of Jè·phün′nĕh for an inheritance. 14 So Hē′bron became the inheritance of Caleb the son of Jè·phün′nĕh the Ken′iz·zìte to this day, because he wholly followed the LORD, the God of Israel. 15 Now the name of Hē′bron formerly was Kĭr′i·ath-är′bà;*[i]* Är′bà was the greatest man among the An′à·kim. And the land had rest from war.

15 The lot for the tribe of the people of Judah according to their families reached southward to the boundary of E′dòm, to the wilderness of Zin at the farthest south. 2And their south boundary ran from the end of the Salt Sea, from the bay that faces southward; 3 it goes out southward of the ascent of Ak·rab′bim, passes along to Zin, and goes up south of Kā′desh-bär′nē·à, along by Hez′ron, up to Ad′där, turns about to Kär′kà, 4 passes along to Az′mon, goes out by the Brook

of Egypt, and comes to its end at the sea. This shall be your south boundary. 5And the east boundary is the Salt Sea, to the mouth of the Jordan. And the boundary on the north side runs from the bay of the sea at the mouth of the Jordan; 6 and the boundary goes up to Beth-hog′làh, and passes along north of Beth-ar′à·bàh; and the boundary goes up to the stone of Bō′han the son of Reuben; 7 and the boundary goes up to Dē′bir from the Valley of A′chôr, and so northward, turning toward Gil′gàl, which is opposite the ascent of A·dum′mim, which is on the south side of the valley; and the boundary passes along to the waters of En-shē′mesh, and ends at En-rō′gel; 8 then the boundary goes up by the valley of the son of Hin′nòm at the southern shoulder of the Jeb′ū·sìte (that is, Jerusalem); and the boundary goes up to the top of the mountain that lies over against the valley of Hinnom, on the west, at the northern end of the valley of Reph′à·im; 9 then the boundary extends from the top of the mountain to the spring of the Waters of Neph·tō′àh, and from there to the cities of Mount E′phrŏn; then the boundary bends round to Bā′à·làh (that is, Kĭr′i·ath-jē′à·rim); 10 and the boundary circles west of Bā′à·làh to Mount Sē′ir, passes along to the northern shoulder of Mount Jē′à·rim (that is, Ches′à·lon), and goes down to Beth-shē′mesh, and passes along by Tim′nàh; 11 the boundary goes out to the shoulder of the hill north of Ek′-ròn, then the boundary bends round to Shik′kè·ron, and passes along to Mount Bā′à·làh, and goes out to Jab′-nē·él; then the boundary comes to an end at the sea. 12And the west boundary was the Great Sea with its coast-line. This is the boundary round about the people of Judah according to their families.

13 According to the commandment of the LORD to Joshua, he gave to Caleb the son of Jè·phün′nĕh a portion among the people of Judah, Kĭr′i·ath-är′bà, that is, Hē′bron (Är′bà was the father of A′nak). 14And Caleb drove out from there the three sons of A′nak, Shē′shäi and A·hi′màn and Tal′mĭ, the descendants of Anak. 15And he went up from there against the inhabitants of Dē′bir; now the name of Debir formerly was Kĭr′i·ath-sē′phĕr. 16And Caleb said, "Whoever smites Kĭr′i·ath-sē′phĕr, and takes it, to him will I give Ach′sàh my daughter as wife." 17And

[i] That is The city of Arba

14.6-15: Num 13.6, 30; 14.6, 24, 30.   **15.14-19:** Judg 1.10-15, 20.

Oth'ni-el the son of Kē'naz, the brother of Caleb, took it; and he gave him Ach'sah his daughter as wife. 18 When she came to him, she urged him to ask her father for a field; and she alighted from her ass, and Caleb said to her, "What do you wish?" 19 She said to him, "Give me a present; since you have set me in the land of the Negeb, give me also springs of water." And Caleb gave her the upper springs and the lower springs.

20 This is the inheritance of the tribe of the people of Judah according to their families. 21 The cities belonging to the tribe of the people of Judah in the extreme South, toward the boundary of Ē'dom, were Kab'zē-el, Ē'der, Jā'gŭr, 22 Kī'nah, Di-mō'nah, A-dā'dah, 23 Kē'desh, Hā'zōr, Ith'nan, 24 Ziph, Tē'lem, Be-ā'loth, 25 Hā'zōr-hȧ-dat'tah, Kēr'i-oth-hez'rŏn (that is, Hā'zōr), 26A'mam, Shē'mȧ, Mō'lā-dah, 27 Hā'zär-gad'dah, Hesh'mŏn, Beth-pel'et, 28 Hā'zär-shü'al, Beer-sheba, Biz-i-ȯ-thī'ah, 29 Bā'ȧ-lah, I'im, Ē'zem, 30 El-tō'lad, Chē'sil, Hôr'mah, 31 Zik'lag, Mad-man'nah, San-san'nah, 32 Lē-bā'oth, Shil'him, A'in, and Rim'mon: in all, twenty-nine cities, with their villages.

33 And in the lowland, Esh'tā-ol, Zō'rah, Ash'nah, 34 Zȧ-nō'ah, En-gan'-nim, Tap'pū-ah, E'nam, 35 Jär'muth, A-dul'lam, Sō'cōh, A-zē'kah, 36 Shā-ȧ-rā'im, Ad-i-thā'im, Ge-dē'rah, Ge-dē-roth-ā'im: fourteen cities with their villages.

37 Zē'nan, Hȧ-dash'ah, Mig'dal-gad, 38 Di'lē-an, Miz'peh, Jok'thē-el, 39 Lā'chish, Boz'kath, Eg'lon, 40 Cab'-bon, Läh'mam, Chit'lish, 41 Ge-dē'-roth, Beth-dā'gon, Nā'ȧ-mah, and Mak-kē'dah: sixteen cities with their villages.

42 Lib'nah, Ē'thêr, A'shân, 43 Iph'-tah, Ash'nah, Nē'zib, 44 Kē-i'lah, Ach'-zib, and Mȧ-rē'shah: nine cities with their villages.

45 Ek'rŏn, with its towns and its villages; 46 from Ek'rŏn to the sea, all that were by the side of Ash'dod, with their villages.

47 Ash'dod, its towns and its villages; Gā'zȧ, its towns and its villages; to the Brook of Egypt, and the Great Sea with its coast-line.

48 And in the hill country, Shā'mir, Jat'tir, Sō'cōh, 49 Dan'nah, Kīr'i-ath-san'nah (that is, Dē'bir), 50A'nab, Esh'tē-mōh, A'nim, 51 Gō'shen, Hō'-lon, and Gi'lōh: eleven cities with their villages.

52 Arab, Dü'mah, Ē'shan, 53 Jā'nim,

Beth-tap'pū-ah, A-phē'kah, 54 Hum'-tah, Kīr'i-ath-är'bȧ (that is, Hē'brŏn), and Zī'ôr: nine cities with their villages.

55 Mā'on, Cär'mĕl, Ziph, Jut'tah, 56 Jez'rē-ĕl, Jok'dē-am, Zȧ-nō'ah, 57 Kain, Gib'ē-ah, and Tim'nah: ten cities with their villages.

58 Hal'hul, Beth'-zūr, Gē'dôr, 59 Mā'ȧ-rath, Beth-ā'noth, and El'tē-kon: six cities with their villages.

60 Kīr'i-ath-bā'ȧl (that is, Kīr'i-ath-jē'ȧ-rim), and Rab'bah: two cities with their villages.

61 In the wilderness, Beth-ar'ȧ-bah, Mid'din, Sē-cā'cah, 62 Nib'shan, the City of Salt, and En-gē'dī: six cities with their villages.

63 But the Jeb'ū-sites, the inhabitants of Jerusalem, the people of Judah could not drive out; so the Jebusites dwell with the people of Judah at Jerusalem to this day.

16 The allotment of the descendants of Joseph went from the Jordan by Jericho, east of the waters of Jericho, into the wilderness, going up from Jericho into the hill country to Beth'ĕl; 2 then going from Beth'ĕl to Luz, it passes along to At'ȧ-roth, the territory of the Är'chītes; 3 then it goes down westward to the territory of the Japh'lē-tītes, as far as the territory of Lower Beth-hō'ron, then to Gē'zér, and it ends at the sea.

4 The people of Joseph, Mȧ-nas'-sēh and E'phrȧ-im, received their inheritance.

5 The territory of the E'phrȧ-im-ites by their families was as follows: the boundary of their inheritance on the east was At'ȧ-roth-ad'där as far as Upper Beth-hō'ron, 6 and the boundary goes thence to the sea; on the north is Mich-mē'thath; then on the east the boundary turns round toward Tā'ȧ-nath-shi'lōh, and passes along beyond it on the east to Jȧ-nō'ah, 7 then it goes down from Jȧ-nō'ah to At'ȧ-roth and to Nā'ȧ-rah, and touches Jericho, ending at the Jordan. 8 From Tap'pū-ah the boundary goes westward to the brook Kā'nah, and ends at the sea. Such is the inheritance of the tribe of the E'phrȧ-im-ites by their families, 9 together with the towns which were set apart for the E'phrȧ-im-ites within the inheritance of the Mȧ-nas'sites, all those towns with their villages. 10 However they did not drive out the Canaanites that dwelt in Gē'zér: so the Canaanites have dwelt in the midst of E'phrȧ-im to this day but have become slaves to do forced labor.

15.63: Judg 1.21; 2 Sam 5.6.　16.10: Judg 1.29.

17 Then allotment was made to the tribe of Má·nas′sĕh, for he was the first-born of Joseph. To Mā′chir the first-born of Manasseh, the father of Gilead, were allotted Gilead and Bā′shàn, because he was a man of war. ²And allotments were made to the rest of the tribe of Má·nas′sĕh, by their families, Ā·bi·ē′zĕr, Hē′lĕk, Ăs′ri·el, Shē′chem, Hē′phĕr, and She·mi′dà; these were the male descendants of Manasseh the son of Joseph, by their families.

3 Now Ze·loph′ĕ·had the son of Hē′phĕr, son of Gilead, son of Mā′chir, son of Má·nas′sĕh, had no sons, but only daughters; and these are the names of his daughters: Māh′làh, Noah, Hog′làh, Mil′càh, and Tĭr′zàh. ⁴ They came before El·ē·ā′zàr the priest and Joshua the son of Nun and the leaders, and said, "The LORD commanded Moses to give us an inheritance along with our brethren." So according to the commandment of the LORD he gave them an inheritance among the brethren of their father. ⁵ Thus there fell to Má·nas′sĕh ten portions, besides the land of Gilead and Bā′shàn, which is on the other side of the Jordan; ⁶ because the daughters of Má·nas′sĕh received an inheritance along with his sons. The land of Gilead was allotted to the rest of the Má·nas′sites.

7 The territory of Má·nas′sĕh reached from Ash′er to Mich·mē′thath, which is east of Shē′chem; then the boundary goes along southward to the inhabitants of En·tap′pū·àh. ⁸ The land of Tap′pū·àh belonged to Má·nas′sĕh, but the town of Tappu-ah on the boundary of Manasseh belonged to the sons of Ē′phrà·im. ⁹ Then the boundary went down to the brook Kā′nàh. The cities here, to the south of the brook, among the cities of Má·nas′sĕh, belong to Ē′phrà·im. Then the boundary of Manasseh goes on the north side of the brook and ends at the sea; ¹⁰ the land to the south being Ē′phrà·im′s and that to the north being Má·nas′sĕh′s, with the sea forming its boundary; on the north Ash′er is reached, and on the east Is′sà·chär. ¹¹ Also in Is′sà·chär and in Ash′er Má·nas′sĕh had Beth-shē′àn and its villages, and Ib′lē-am and its villages, and the inhabitants of Dôr and its villages, and the inhabitants of En′-dôr and its villages, and the inhabitants of Tā′á·nach and its villages, and the inhabitants of Mé·gid′dō and

its villages; the third is Nā′phath.ʲ ¹² Yet the sons of Má·nas′sĕh could not take possession of those cities; but the Canaanites persisted in dwelling in that land. ¹³ But when the people of Israel grew strong, they put the Canaanites to forced labor, and did not utterly drive them out.

14 And the tribe of Joseph spoke to Joshua, saying, "Why have you given me but one lot and one portion as an inheritance, although I am a numerous people, since hitherto the LORD has blessed me?" ¹⁵ And Joshua said to them, "If you are a numerous people, go up to the forest, and there clear ground for yourselves in the land of the Per′iz·zites and the Reph′á·im, since the hill country of Ē′phrà·im is too narrow for you." ¹⁶ The tribe of Joseph said, "The hill country is not enough for us; yet all the Canaanites who dwell in the plain have chariots of iron, both those in Beth-shē′àn and its villages and those in the Valley of Jez′rē·ĕl." ¹⁷ Then Joshua said to the house of Joseph, to Ē′phrà·im and Má·nas′sĕh, "You are a numerous people, and have great power; you shall not have one lot only, ¹⁸ but the hill country shall be yours, for though it is a forest, you shall clear it and possess it to its farthest borders; for you shall drive out the Canaanites, though they have chariots of iron, and though they are strong."

18 Then the whole congregation of the people of Israel assembled at Shī′lōh, and set up the tent of meeting there; the land lay subdued before them.

2 There remained among the people of Israel seven tribes whose inheritance had not yet been apportioned. ³ So Joshua said to the people of Israel, "How long will you be slack to go in and take possession of the land, which the LORD, the God of your fathers, has given you? ⁴ Provide three men from each tribe, and I will send them out that they may set out and go up and down the land, writing a description of it with a view to their inheritances, and then come to me. ⁵ They shall divide it into seven portions, Judah continuing in his territory on the south, and the house of Joseph in their territory on the north. ⁶ And you shall describe the land in seven divisions and bring the description here to me; and I will cast lots for you here before the LORD our God. ⁷ The Levites have no portion among you, for the priest-

ʲ Heb obscure

17.3-4: Num 26.33; 27.1-7.   **17.11-13:** Judg 1.27-28.

hood of the LORD is their heritage; and Gad and Reuben and half the tribe of Má·nas'sēh have received their inheritance beyond the Jordan eastward, which Moses the servant of the LORD gave them."

8 So the men started on their way; and Joshua charged those who went to write the description of the land, saying, "Go up and down and write a description of the land, and come again to me; and I will cast lots for you here before the LORD in Shi'lōh."

9 So the men went and passed up and down in the land and set down in a book a description of it by towns in seven divisions; then they came to Joshua in the camp at Shi'lōh, 10 and Joshua cast lots for them in Shi'lōh before the LORD; and there Joshua apportioned the land to the people of Israel, to each his portion.

11 The lot of the tribe of Benjamin according to its families came up, and the territory allotted to it fell between the tribe of Judah and the tribe of Joseph. 12 On the north side their boundary began at the Jordan; then the boundary goes up to the shoulder north of Jericho, then up through the hill country westward; and it ends at the wilderness of Beth-ā'vĕn. 13 From there the boundary passes along southward in the direction of Luz, to the shoulder of Luz (the same is Beth'ĕl), then the boundary goes down to At'a·roth-ad'där, upon the mountain that lies south of Lower Beth-hō'ron. 14 Then the boundary goes in another direction, turning on the western side southward from the mountain that lies to the south, opposite Beth-hō'ron, and it ends at Kīr'i·ath-bā'al (that is, Kīr'i·ath-jē'a·rim), a city belonging to the tribe of Judah. This forms the western side. 15And the southern side begins at the outskirts of Kīr'i·ath-jē'a·rim; and the boundary goes from there to E'phrŏn,^{k} to the spring of the Waters of Neph·tō'áh; 16 then the boundary goes down to the border of the mountain that overlooks the valley of the son of Hin'nŏm, which is at the north end of the valley of Reph'ā·im; and it then goes down the valley of Hinnom, south of the shoulder of the Jeb'ū·sites, and downward to En-rō'gel; 17 then it bends in a northerly direction going on to En-shē'mesh, and thence goes to Ge·li'loth, which is opposite the ascent of A·dum'mim; then it goes down to the Stone of Bō'han the son of Reuben; 18 and

passing on to the north of the shoulder of Beth-ar'a·báh^l it goes down to the Ar'a·bàh; 19 then the boundary passes on to the north of the shoulder of Beth-hog'làh; and the boundary ends at the northern bay of the Salt Sea, at the south end of the Jordan; this is the southern border. 20 The Jordan forms its boundary on the eastern side. This is the inheritance of the tribe of Benjamin, according to its families, boundary by boundary round about.

21 Now the cities of the tribe of Benjamin according to their families were Jericho, Beth-hog'làh, E'mek·kē'ziz, 22 Beth-ar'a·bàh, Zem·á·rā'im, Beth'ĕl, 23Av'vim, Pâr'áh, Oph'ráh, 24 Chē'phär-am'mō·nī, Oph'nī, Gē'ba —twelve cities with their villages: 25Gib'ē·ŏn, Rā'màh, Bē·ēr'ŏth, 26 Miz'-peh, Che·phi'ráh, Mō'záh, 27 Rē'kem, Ir'pē·ĕl, Tar'a·làh, 28 Zē'là, Ha-ē'leph, Jē'bus^m (that is, Jerusalem), Gib'ē·àh^n and Kir'i·ath-jē'a·rim^o—fourteen cities with their villages. This is the inheritance of the tribe of Benjamin according to its families.

19 The second lot came out for Simeon, for the tribe of Simeon, according to its families; and its inheritance was in the midst of the inheritance of the tribe of Judah. 2And it had for its inheritance Beersheba, Sheba, Mō'là·dàh, 3 Hā·zär·shū'ál, Bā'làh, E'zem, 4 El·tō'lad, Bē'thul, Hôr'màh, 5 Zik'lag, Beth-mär'cà·both, Hā'zär-sü'sàh, 6 Beth-lē·bā'oth, and Shà·rü'hen—thirteen cities with their villages; 7 En-rim'mon, E'thĕr, and A'shàn—four cities with their villages; 8 together with all the villages round about these cities as far as Bā'à·lath-bē'ĕr, Rā'màh of the Negeb. This was the inheritance of the tribe of Simeon according to its families. 9 The inheritance of the tribe of Simeon formed part of the territory of Judah; because the portion of the tribe of Judah was too large for them, the tribe of Simeon obtained an inheritance in the midst of their inheritance.

10 The third lot came up for the tribe of Zeb'ū·lùn, according to its families. And the territory of its inheritance reached as far as Sā'rid; 11 then its boundary goes up westward, and on to Mar'ē·ál, and touches Dab'bé·sheth, then the brook which is east of Jok'nē·am; 12 from Sā'rid it goes in the other direction eastward toward the sunrise to the boundary of Chis'loth-tā'bŏr; thence it goes to Dab'é·rath, then up to Jà·phí'à; 13 from

^{k} Cn See 15.9. Heb *westward* ^{l} Gk: Heb *to the shoulder over against the Arabah* ^{m} Gk Syr Vg: Heb *the Jebusite* ^{n} Heb *Gibeath* ^{o} Gk: Heb *Kiriath*

there it passes along on the east toward the sunrise to Gath-he′pher, to Eth-ka′zin, and going on to Rim′mon it bends toward Ne′ah; ¹⁴ then on the north the boundary turns about to Han′na-thon, and it ends at the valley of Iph′tah-el; ¹⁵ and Kat′tath, Na-hal′-al, Shim′ron, I′da-lah, and Bethlehem —twelve cities with their villages. ¹⁶ This is the inheritance of the tribe of Zeb′u-lun, according to its families —these cities with their villages.

17 The fourth lot came out for Is′sa-char, for the tribe of Issachar, according to its families. ¹⁸ Its territory included Jez′re-el, Che-sul′loth, Shu′nem, ¹⁹ Haph′a-ra-im, Shi′on, A-na′ha-rath, ²⁰ Rab′bith, Kish′i-on, E′bez, ²¹ Re′meth, En-gan′nim, En-had′dah, Beth-paz′zez; ²² the boundary also touches Ta′bor, Sha-ha-zu′-mah, and Beth-she′mesh, and its boundary ends at the Jordan—sixteen cities with their villages. ²³ This is the inheritance of the tribe of Is′sa-char, according to its families—the cities with their villages.

24 The fifth lot came out for the tribe of Ash′er according to its families. ²⁵ Its territory included Hel′kath, Ha′li, Be′ten, Ach′shaph, ²⁶Al-lam′me-lech, A′mad, and Mi′shal; on the west it touches Car′mel and Shi-hor-lib′-nath, ²⁷ then it turns eastward, it goes to Beth-da′gon, and touches Zeb′u-lun and the valley of Iph′tah-el northward to Beth-e′mek and Ne-i′el; then it continues in the north to Ca′bul, ²⁸ E′bron, Re′hob, Ham′mon, Ka′nah, as far as Si′don the Great; ²⁹ then the boundary turns to Ra′mah, reaching to the fortified city of Tyre; then the boundary turns to Ho′sah, and it ends at the sea; Ma-ha′lab,ᵖ Ach′zib, ³⁰ Um′mah, A′phek and Re′hob—twenty-two cities with their villages. ³¹ This is the inheritance of the tribe of Ash′er according to its families—these cities with their villages.

32 The sixth lot came out for the tribe of Naph′ta-li, for the tribe of Naphtali, according to its families. ³³And its boundary ran from He′leph, from the oak in Za-a-nan′nim, and Ad′a-mi-nek′eb, and Jab′ne-el, as far as Lak′kum; and it ended at the Jordan; ³⁴ then the boundary turns westward to Az′noth-ta′bor, and goes from there to Huz′kok, touching Zeb′u-lun at the south, and Ash′er on the west, and Judah on the east at the Jordan. ³⁵ The fortified cities are Zid′dim, Zer, Ham′-math, Rak′kath, Chin′ne-reth, ³⁶Ad′a-

mah, Ra′mah, Ha′zor, ³⁷ Ke′desh, Ed′re-i, En-ha′zor, ³⁸ Yi′ron, Mig′dal-el, Ho′rem, Beth-a′nath, and Beth-she′mesh—nineteen cities with their villages. ³⁹ This is the inheritance of the tribe of Naph′ta-li according to its families—the cities with their villages.

40 The seventh lot came out for the tribe of Dan, according to its families. ⁴¹And the territory of its inheritance included Zo′rah, Esh′ta-ol, Ir-she′-mesh, ⁴² Sha-a-lab′bin, Ai′ja-lon, Ith′-lah, ⁴³ E′lon, Tim′nah, Ek′ron, ⁴⁴ El′-te-keh, Gib′be-thon, Ba′a-lath, ⁴⁵ Je′-hud, Ben′e-be′rak, Gath-rim′mon, ⁴⁶ and Me-jar′kon and Rak′kon with the territory over against Jop′pa. ⁴⁷ When the territory of the Danites was lost to them, the Danites went up and fought against Le′shem, and after capturing it and putting it to the sword they took possession of it and settled in it, calling Leshem, Dan, after the name of Dan their ancestor. ⁴⁸ This is the inheritance of the tribe of Dan, according to their families—these cities with their villages.

49 When they had finished distributing the several territories of the land as inheritances, the people of Israel gave an inheritance among them to Joshua the son of Nun. ⁵⁰ By command of the LORD they gave him the city which he asked, Tim′nath-se′rah in the hill country of E′phra-im; and he rebuilt the city, and settled in it.

51 These are the inheritances which El-e-a′zar the priest and Joshua the son of Nun and the heads of the fathers' houses of the tribes of the people of Israel distributed by lot at Shi′loh before the LORD, at the door of the tent of meeting. So they finished dividing the land.

20 Then the LORD said to Joshua, ² "Say to the people of Israel, 'Appoint the cities of refuge, of which I spoke to you through Moses, ³ that the manslayer who kills any person without intent or unwittingly may flee there; they shall be for you a refuge from the avenger of blood. ⁴ He shall flee to one of these cities and shall stand at the entrance of the gate of the city, and explain his case to the elders of that city; then they shall take him into the city, and give him a place, and he shall remain with them. ⁵And if the avenger of blood pursues him, they shall not give up the slayer into his hand; because he killed his neighbor unwittingly, having had no enmity

---

ᵖ Cn Compare Gk: Heb *Mehebel*
19.47: Judg 18.27-31. 20.2-9: Num 35.6-34; Deut 4.41-43; 19.1-13.

against him in times past. 6And he shall remain in that city until he has stood before the congregation for judgment, until the death of him who is high priest at the time: then the slayer may go again to his own town and his own home," to the town from which he fled.' "

7 So they set apart Kē'desh in Galilee in the hill country of Naph'ta·li, and Shē'chem in the hill country of Ē'phra·im, and Kĭr'i·ath-är'bȧ (that is, Hē'bròn) in the hill country of Judah. 8And beyond the Jordan east of Jericho, they appointed Bē'zĕr in the wilderness on the tableland, from the tribe of Reuben, and Rā'moth in Gilead, from the tribe of Gad, and Gō'lan in Bā'shän, from the tribe of Ma·nas'seh. 9 These were the cities designated for all the people of Israel, and for the stranger sojourning among them, that any one who killed a person without intent could flee there, so that he might not die by the hand of the avenger of blood, till he stood before the congregation.

21 Then the heads of the fathers' houses of the Levites came to Ĕl·ē·ā'zȧr the priest and to Joshua the son of Nun and to the heads of the fathers' houses of the tribes of the people of Israel; 2 and they said to them at Shī'lōh in the land of Canaan, "The LORD commanded through Moses that we be given cities to dwell in, along with their pasture lands for our cattle." 3 So by command of the LORD the people of Israel gave to the Levites the following cities and pasture lands out of their inheritance.

4 The lot came out for the families of the Kō'hȧ·thites. So those Levites who were descendants of Aaron the priest received by lot from the tribes of Judah, Simeon, and Benjamin, thirteen cities.

5 And the rest of the Kō'hȧ·thites received by lot from the families of the tribe of Ē'phra·im, from the tribe of Dan and the half-tribe of Ma·nas'seh, ten cities.

6 The Gēr'shō·nites received by lot from the families of the tribe of Is'sȧ·chär, from the tribe of Ash'ĕr, from the tribe of Naph'ta·li, and from the half-tribe of Ma·nas'seh in Bā'shän, thirteen cities.

7 The Mē·râr'ites according to their families received from the tribe of Reuben, the tribe of Gad, and the tribe of Zeb'ū·lùn, twelve cities.

8 These cities and their pasture lands the people of Israel gave by lot

to the Levites, as the LORD had commanded through Moses.

9 Out of the tribe of Judah and the tribe of Simeon they gave the following cities mentioned by name, 10 which went to the descendants of Aaron, one of the families of the Kō'hȧ·thites who belonged to the Levites; since the lot fell to them first. 11 They gave them Kĭr'i·ath-är'bȧ (Är'bȧ being the father of Ā'nak), that is Hē'bròn, in the hill country of Judah, along with the pasture lands round about it. 12 But the fields of the city and its villages had been given to Caleb the son of Jē·phün'neh as his possession.

13 And to the descendants of Aaron the priest they gave Hē'bròn, the city of refuge for the slayer, with its pasture lands, Lib'nȧh with its pasture lands, 14 Jat'tir with its pasture lands, Esh·tē·mō'ȧ with its pasture lands, 15 Hō'lon with its pasture lands, Dē'bir with its pasture lands, 16Ā'in with its pasture lands, Jut'tȧh with its pasture lands, Beth-shē'mesh with its pasture lands—nine cities out of these two tribes; 17 then out of the tribe of Benjamin, Gibeon with its pasture lands, Gē'bȧ with its pasture lands, 18An'ȧ·thoth with its pasture lands, and Al'mon with its pasture lands—four cities. 19 The cities of the descendants of Aaron, the priests, were in all thirteen cities with their pasture lands.

20 As to the rest of the Kō'hȧ·thites belonging to the Kohathite families of the Levites, the cities allotted to them were out of the tribe of Ē'phra·im. 21 To them were given Shē'chem, the city of refuge for the slayer, with its pasture lands in the hill country of Ē'phra·im, Gē'zĕr with its pasture lands, 22 Kib'zȧ-im with its pasture lands, Beth-hō'ron with its pasture lands—four cities; 23 and out of the tribe of Dan, Ĕl'tē·kē with its pasture lands, Gib'bė·thon with its pasture lands, 24Äi'jȧ·lon with its pasture lands, Gath-rim'mon with its pasture lands—four cities; 25 and out of the half-tribe of Ma·nas'seh, Tā'ȧ·nach with its pasture lands, and Gath-rim'mon with its pasture lands—two cities. 26 The cities of the families of the rest of the Kō'hȧ·thites were ten in all with their pasture lands.

27 And to the Gēr'shō·nites, one of the families of the Levites, were given out of the half-tribe of Ma·nas'seh, Gō'lan in Bā'shän with its pasture lands, the city of refuge for the slayer, and Be-esh'tē·rȧh with its pasture lands—two cities; 28 and out of the

tribe of Is′sȧ·chär, Kish′ï·on with its pasture lands, Dab′ë·rath with its pasture lands, ²⁹ Jär′muth with its pasture lands, En-gan′nim with its pasture lands—four cities; ³⁰ and out of the tribe of Ash′ér, Mi′shàl with its pasture lands, Ab′don with its pasture lands, ³¹ Hel′kath with its pasture lands, and Rë′hob with its pasture lands—four cities; ³² and out of the tribe of Naph′tä·lï, Kë′desh in Galilee with its pasture lands, the city of refuge for the slayer, Ham′moth-dôr with its pasture lands, and Kär′tàn with its pasture lands—three cities. ³³ The cities of the several families of the Gër′shö·nïtes were in all thirteen cities with their pasture lands.

34 And to the rest of the Levites, the Mé·râr′ïte families, were given out of the tribe of Zeb′ū·lŭn, Jok′në·am with its pasture lands, Kär′tàh with its pasture lands, ³⁵ Dim′nàh with its pasture lands, Nȧ·hal′ál with its pasture lands—four cities; ³⁶ and out of the tribe of Reuben, Bë′zér with its pasture lands, Jä′haz with its pasture lands, ³⁷ Ked′ë·moth with its pasture lands, and Meph′ȧ-ath with its pasture lands—four cities; ³⁸ and out of the tribe of Gad, Rä′moth in Gilead with its pasture lands, the city of refuge for the slayer, Mä·hȧ·nä′ïm with its pasture lands, ³⁹ Hesh′bön with its pasture lands, Jä′zér with its pasture lands—four cities in all. ⁴⁰ As for the cities of the several Mé·râr′ïte families, that is, the remainder of the families of the Levites, those allotted to them were in all twelve cities.

41 The cities of the Levites in the midst of the possession of the people of Israel were in all forty-eight cities with their pasture lands. ⁴² These cities had each its pasture lands round about it; so it was with all these cities.

43 Thus the LORD gave to Israel all the land which he swore to give to their fathers; and having taken possession of it, they settled there. ⁴⁴ And the LORD gave them rest on every side just as he had sworn to their fathers; not one of all their enemies had withstood them, for the LORD had given all their enemies into their hands. ⁴⁵ Not one of all the good promises which the LORD had made to the house of Israel had failed; all came to pass.

22 Then Joshua summoned the Reubenites, and the Gadites, and the half-tribe of Mȧ·nas′sëh, ² and said to them, "You have kept all that Moses the servant of the LORD commanded you, and have obeyed my

voice in all that I have commanded you; ³ you have not forsaken your brethren these many days, down to this day, but have been careful to keep the charge of the LORD your God. ⁴ And now the LORD your God has given rest to your brethren, as he promised them; therefore turn and go to your home in the land where your possession lies, which Moses the servant of the LORD gave you on the other side of the Jordan. ⁵ Take good care to observe the commandment and the law which Moses the servant of the LORD commanded you, to love the LORD your God, and to walk in all his ways, and to keep his commandments, and to cleave to him, and to serve him with all your heart and with all your soul." ⁶ So Joshua blessed them, and sent them away; and they went to their homes.

7 Now to the one half of the tribe of Mȧ·nas′sëh Moses had given a possession in Bä′shàn; but to the other half Joshua had given a possession beside their brethren in the land west of the Jordan. And when Joshua sent them away to their homes and blessed them, ⁸ he said to them, "Go back to your homes with much wealth, and with very many cattle, with silver, gold, bronze, and iron, and with much clothing; divide the spoil of your enemies with your brethren." ⁹ So the Reubenites and the Gadites and the half-tribe of Mȧ·nas′sëh returned home, parting from the people of Israel at Shi′löh, which is in the land of Canaan, to go to the land of Gilead, their own land of which they had possessed themselves by command of the LORD through Moses.

10 And when they came to the region about the Jordan, that lies in the land of Canaan, the Reubenites and the Gadites and the half-tribe of Mȧ·nas′sëh built there an altar by the Jordan, an altar of great size. ¹¹ And the people of Israel heard say, "Behold, the Reubenites and the Gadites and the half-tribe of Mȧ·nas′sëh have built an altar at the frontier of the land of Canaan, in the region about the Jordan, on the side that belongs to the people of Israel." ¹² And when the people of Israel heard of it, the whole assembly of the people of Israel gathered at Shi′löh, to make war against them.

13 Then the people of Israel sent to the Reubenites and the Gadites and the half-tribe of Mȧ·nas′sëh, in the land of Gilead, Phin′ë·hàs the son of

El·e·a´zar the priest, 14 and with him ten chiefs, one from each of the tribal families of Israel, every one of them the head of a family among the clans of Israel. 15And they came to the Reubenites, the Gadites, and the half-tribe of Ma·nas´seh, in the land of Gilead, and they said to them, 16 "Thus says the whole congregation of the LORD, 'What is this treachery which you have committed against the God of Israel in turning away this day from following the LORD, by building yourselves an altar this day in rebellion against the LORD? 17 Have we not had enough of the sin at Pe´or from which even yet we have not cleansed ourselves, and for which there came a plague upon the congregation of the LORD, 18that you must turn away this day from following the LORD? And if you rebel against the LORD today he will be angry with the whole congregation of Israel tomorrow. 19 But now, if your land is unclean, pass over into the LORD's land where the LORD's tabernacle stands, and take for yourselves a possession among us; only do not rebel against the LORD, or make us as rebels by building yourselves an altar other than the altar of the LORD our God. 20 Did not A´chan the son of Ze´rah break faith in the matter of the devoted things, and wrath fell upon all the congregation of Israel? And he did not perish alone for his iniquity.' "

21 Then the Reubenites, the Gadites, and the half-tribe of Ma·nas´seh said in answer to the heads of the families of Israel, 22 "The Mighty One, God, the LORD! The Mighty One, God, the LORD! He knows; and let Israel itself know! If it was in rebellion or in breach of faith toward the LORD, spare us not today 23 for building an altar to turn away from following the LORD; or if we did so to offer burnt offerings or cereal offerings or peace offerings on it, may the LORD himself take vengeance. 24 Nay, but we did it from fear that in time to come your children might say to our children, 'What have you to do with the LORD, the God of Israel? 25 For the LORD has made the Jordan a boundary between us and you, you Reubenites and Gadites; you have no portion in the LORD.' So your children might make our children cease to worship the LORD. 26 Therefore we said, 'Let us now build an altar, not for burnt offering, nor for sacrifice, 27 but to be a witness between us and you, and between the generations after us, that we do perform the service of the LORD in

his presence with our burnt offerings and sacrifices and peace offerings; lest your children say to our children in time to come, "You have no portion in the LORD." ' 28And we thought, If this should be said to us or to our descendants in time to come, we should say, 'Behold the copy of the altar of the LORD, which our fathers made, not for burnt offerings, nor for sacrifice, but to be a witness between us and you.' 29 Far be it from us that we should rebel against the LORD, and turn away this day from following the LORD by building an altar for burnt offering, cereal offering, or sacrifice, other than the altar of the LORD our God that stands before his tabernacle!"

30 When Phin´e·has the priest and the chiefs of the congregation, the heads of the families of Israel who were with him, heard the words that the Reubenites and the Gadites and the Ma·nas´sites spoke, it pleased them well. 31And Phin´e·has the son of El·e·a´zar the priest said to the Reubenites and the Gadites and the Ma·nas´sites, "Today we know that the LORD is in the midst of us, because you have not committed this treachery against the LORD; now you have saved the people of Israel from the hand of the LORD."

32 Then Phin´e·has the son of El·e·a´zar the priest, and the chiefs, returned from the Reubenites and the Gadites in the land of Gilead to the land of Canaan, to the people of Israel, and brought back word to them. 33And the report pleased the people of Israel; and the people of Israel blessed God and spoke no more of making war against them, to destroy the land where the Reubenites and the Gadites were settled. 34 The Reubenites and the Gadites called the altar Witness; "For," said they, "it is a witness between us that the LORD is God."

23 A long time afterward, when the LORD had given rest to Israel from all their enemies round about, and Joshua was old and well advanced in years, 2 Joshua summoned all Israel, their elders and heads, their judges and officers, and said to them, "I am now old and well advanced in years; 3 and you have seen all that the LORD your God has done to all these nations for your sake, for it is the LORD your God who has fought for you. 4 Behold, I have allotted to you as an inheritance for your tribes those nations that remain, along with all the nations that I have already cut off, from the Jordan to the Great Sea in the west. 5 The LORD your God will push them back

before you, and drive them out of your sight; and you shall possess their land, as the LORD your God promised you. ⁶ Therefore be very steadfast to keep and do all that is written in the book of the law of Moses, turning aside from it neither to the right hand nor to the left, ⁷ that you may not be mixed with these nations left here among you, or make mention of the names of their gods, or swear by them, or serve them, or bow down yourselves to them, ⁸ but cleave to the LORD your God as you have done to this day. ⁹ For the LORD has driven out before you great and strong nations; and as for you, no man has been able to withstand you to this day. ¹⁰ One man of you puts to flight a thousand, since it is the LORD your God who fights for you, as he promised you. ¹¹ Take good heed to yourselves, therefore, to love the LORD your God. ¹² For if you turn back, and join the remnant of these nations left here among you, and make marriages with them, so that you marry their women and they yours, ¹³ know assuredly that the LORD your God will not continue to drive out these nations before you; but they shall be a snare and a trap for you, a scourge on your sides, and thorns in your eyes, till you perish from off this good land which the LORD your God has given you.

14 "And now I am about to go the way of all the earth, and you know in your hearts and souls, all of you, that not one thing has failed of all the good things which the LORD your God promised concerning you; all have come to pass for you, not one of them has failed. ¹⁵ But just as all the good things which the LORD your God promised concerning you have been fulfilled for you, so the LORD will bring upon you all the evil things, until he have destroyed you from off this good land which the LORD your God has given you, ¹⁶ if you transgress the covenant of the LORD your God, which he commanded you, and go and serve other gods and bow down to them. Then the anger of the LORD will be kindled against you, and you shall perish quickly from off the good land which he has given to you."

24 Then Joshua gathered all the tribes of Israel to Shĕ′chem, and summoned the elders, the heads, the judges, and the officers of Israel; and they presented themselves before God. ²And Joshua said to all the people, "Thus says the LORD, the God of Israel, 'Your fathers lived of old beyond the Eū·phrā′tēṣ, Tĕ′ráh, the

father of Abraham and of Nā′hôr; and they served other gods. ³ Then I took your father Abraham from beyond the River and led him through all the land of Canaan, and made his offspring many. I gave him Isaac; ⁴ and to Isaac I gave Jacob and Esau. And I gave Esau the hill country of Sĕ′ir to possess, but Jacob and his children went down to Egypt. ⁵And I sent Moses and Aaron, and I plagued Egypt with what I did in the midst of it; and afterwards I brought you out. ⁶ Then I brought your fathers out of Egypt, and you came to the sea; and the Egyptians pursued your fathers with chariots and horsemen to the Red Sea. ⁷And when they cried to the LORD, he put darkness between you and the Egyptians, and made the sea come upon them and cover them; and your eyes saw what I did to Egypt; and you lived in the wilderness a long time. ⁸ Then I brought you to the land of the Am′ō·rites, who lived on the other side of the Jordan; they fought with you, and I gave them into your hand, and you took possession of their land, and I destroyed them before you. ⁹ Then Bā′lak the son of Zip′pôr, king of Mō′ab, arose and fought against Israel; and he sent and invited Balaam the son of Bĕ′ôr to curse you, ¹⁰ but I would not listen to Balaam; therefore he blessed you; so I delivered you out of his hand. ¹¹And you went over the Jordan and came to Jericho, and the men of Jericho fought against you, and also the Am′ō·rites, the Per′izzites, the Canaanites, the Hit′tites, the Gĭr′gà·shites, the Hī′vites, and the Jeb′ū·sites; and I gave them into your hand. ¹²And I sent the hornet before you, which drove them out before you, the two kings of the Am′ō·rites; it was not by your sword or by your bow. ¹³ I gave you a land on which you had not labored, and cities which you had not built, and you dwell therein; you eat the fruit of vineyards and oliveyards which you did not plant.'

14 "Now therefore fear the LORD, and serve him in sincerity and in faithfulness; put away the gods which your fathers served beyond the River, and in Egypt, and serve the LORD. ¹⁵And if you be unwilling to serve the LORD, choose this day whom you will serve, whether the gods your fathers served in the region beyond the River, or the gods of the Am′ō·rites in whose land you dwell; but as for me and my house, we will serve the LORD."

16 Then the people answered, "Far be it from us that we should forsake the

LORD, to serve other gods; 17 for it is the LORD our God who brought us and our fathers up from the land of Egypt, out of the house of bondage, and who did those great signs in our sight, and preserved us in all the way that we went, and among all the peoples through whom we passed; 18 and the LORD drove out before us all the peoples, the Am′ó·rites who lived in the land; therefore we also will serve the LORD, for he is our God."

19 But Joshua said to the people, "You cannot serve the LORD; for he is a holy God; he is a jealous God; he will not forgive your transgressions or your sins. 20 If you forsake the LORD and serve foreign gods, then he will turn and do you harm, and consume you, after having done you good." 21And the people said to Joshua, "Nay; but we will serve the LORD." 22 Then Joshua said to the people, "You are witnesses against yourselves that you have chosen the LORD, to serve him." And they said, "We are witnesses." 23 He said, "Then put away the foreign gods which are among you, and incline your heart to the LORD, the God of Israel." 24And the people said to Joshua, "The LORD our God we will serve, and his voice we will obey." 25 So Joshua made a covenant with the people that day, and made statutes and ordinances for them at Shĕ′chem. 26And Joshua wrote these words in the book of the law of God; and he took a great stone, and set it up there under the oak in the sanctuary of the LORD. 27And Joshua said to all the people, "Behold, this stone shall be a witness against us; for it has heard all the words of the LORD which he spoke to us; therefore it shall be a witness against you, lest you deal falsely with your God." 28 So Joshua sent the people away, every man to his inheritance.

29 After these things Joshua the son of Nun, the servant of the LORD, died, being a hundred and ten years old. 30And they buried him in his own inheritance at Tim′nath-sē′räh, which is in the hill country of É′phrä·im, north of the mountain of Gä′ash.

31 And Israel served the LORD all the days of Joshua, and all the days of the elders who outlived Joshua and had known all the work which the LORD did for Israel.

32 The bones of Joseph which the people of Israel brought up from Egypt were buried at Shĕ′chem, in the portion of ground which Jacob bought from the sons of Hā′mor the father of Shechem for a hundred pieces of money;*q* it became an inheritance of the descendants of Joseph.

33 And El-ē·ā′zär the son of Aaron died; and they buried him at Gib′ē·äh, the town of Phin′ē·häs his son, which had been given him in the hill country of É′phrä·im.

THE BOOK OF

JUDGES

After the death of Joshua the people of Israel inquired of the LORD, "Who shall go up first for us against the Canaanites, to fight against them?" 2 The LORD said, "Judah shall go up; behold, I have given the land into his hand." 3And Judah said to Simeon his brother, "Come up with me into the territory allotted to me, that we may fight against the Canaanites; and I likewise will go with you into the territory allotted to you." So Simeon went with him. 4 Then Judah went up, and the LORD gave the Canaanites and the Per′iz·zites into their hand; and they defeated ten thousand of them at Bē′zek.

5 They came upon Ȧ·dō′ni-bē′zek at Bē′zek, and fought against him, and defeated the Canaanites and the Per′iz-zites. 6Ȧ·dō′ni-bē′zek fled; but they pursued him, and caught him, and cut off his thumbs and his great toes. 7And Ȧ·dō′ni-bē′zek said, "Seventy kings with their thumbs and their great toes cut off used to pick up scraps under my table; as I have done, so God has requited me." And they brought him to Jerusalem, and he died there.

8 And the men of Judah fought against Jerusalem, and took it, and smote it with the edge of the sword, and set the city on fire. 9And afterward

q Heb *qesitah*
24.32: Gen 50.24-25; Ex 13.19; Acts 7.16.

the men of Judah went down to fight against the Canaanites who dwelt in the hill country, in the Negeb, and in the lowland. ¹⁰And Judah went against the Canaanites who dwelt in Hē′brŏn (now the name of Hebron was formerly Kĭr′ĭ·ăth-är′bå); and they defeated Shē′shäi and Å·hī′măn and Tal′mäi.

11 From there they went against the inhabitants of Dē′bir. The name of Debir was formerly Kĭr′ĭ·ăth-sē′phĕr. ¹²And Caleb said, "He who attacks Kĭr′ĭ·ăth-sē′phĕr and takes it, I will give him Ach′säh my daughter as wife." ¹³And Oth′nĭ-el the son of Kē′naz, Caleb's younger brother, took it; and he gave him Ach′säh his daughter as wife. ¹⁴When she came to him, she urged him to ask her father for a field; and she alighted from her ass, and Caleb said to her, "What do you wish?" ¹⁵ She said to him, "Give me a present; since you have set me in the land of the Negeb, give me also springs of water." And Caleb gave her the upper springs and the lower springs.

16 And the descendants of the Ken′ĭte, Moses' father-in-law, went up with the people of Judah from the city of palms into the wilderness of Judah, which lies in the Negeb near Ăr′ăd; and they went and settled with the people. ¹⁷And Judah went with Simeon his brother, and they defeated the Canaanites who inhabited Zē′-phath, and utterly destroyed it. So the name of the city was called Hŏr′mäh. ¹⁸ Judah also took Gä′zä with its territory, and Ash′kė·lon with its territory, and Ek′rŏn with its territory. ¹⁹And the LORD was with Judah, and he took possession of the hill country, but he could not drive out the inhabitants of the plain, because they had chariots of iron. ²⁰And Hē′brŏn was given to Caleb, as Moses had said; and he drove out from it the three sons of Å′nak. ²¹ But the people of Benjamin did not drive out the Jeb′ū·sites who dwelt in Jerusalem; so the Jebusites have dwelt with the people of Benjamin in Jerusalem to this day.

22 The house of Joseph also went up against Beth′ĕl; and the LORD was with them. ²³And the house of Joseph sent to spy out Beth′ĕl. (Now the name of the city was formerly Luz.) ²⁴And the spies saw a man coming out of the city, and they said to him, "Pray, show us the way into the city, and we will deal kindly with you." ²⁵And he

showed them the way into the city; and they smote the city with the edge of the sword, but they let the man and all his family go. ²⁶And the man went to the land of the Hĭt′tītes and built a city, and called its name Luz; that is its name to this day.

27 Må·nas′sĕh did not drive out the inhabitants of Beth-shē′ăn and its villages, or Tā′å·nach and its villages, or the inhabitants of Dôr and its villages, or the inhabitants of Ib′lē·åm and its villages, or the inhabitants of Mė·gĭd′-dō and its villages; but the Canaanites persisted in dwelling in that land. ²⁸ When Israel grew strong, they put the Canaanites to forced labor, but did not utterly drive them out.

29 And Ē′phrá·im did not drive out the Canaanites who dwelt in Gē′zĕr; but the Canaanites dwelt in Gezer among them.

30 Zeb′ū·lŭn did not drive out the inhabitants of Kit′rŏn, or the inhabitants of Nå·hal′ol; but the Canaanites dwelt among them, and became subject to forced labor.

31 Ash′ĕr did not drive out the inhabitants of Ac′cō, or the inhabitants of Sī′dŏn, or of Äh′lab, or of Ach′zĭb, or of Hel′bäh, or of Å′phik, or of Rē′hob; ³² but the Ash′ĕ·rites dwelt among the Canaanites, the inhabitants of the land; for they did not drive them out.

33 Naph′tå·lī did not drive out the inhabitants of Beth-shē′mesh, or the inhabitants of Beth-ā′nath, but dwelt among the Canaanites, the inhabitants of the land; nevertheless the inhabitants of Beth-shemesh and of Beth-anath became subject to forced labor for them.

34 The Am′ŏ·rites pressed the Danites back into the hill country, for they did not allow them to come down to the plain; ³⁵ the Am′ŏ·rites persisted in dwelling in Här-hē′rĕs, in Ăi′jå·lon, and in Shä-al′bim, but the hand of the house of Joseph rested heavily upon them, and they became subject to forced labor. ³⁶And the border of the Am′ŏ·rites ran from the ascent of Å·krab′bim, from Sē′lå and upward.

2 Now the angel of the LORD went up from Gil′gål to Bō′chim. And he said, "I brought you up from Egypt, and brought you into the land which I swore to give to your fathers. I said 'I will never break my covenant with you, ² and you shall make no covenant with the inhabitants of this land; you shall break down their altars.' But you

1.10: Josh 15.13-19.   **1.10-15:** Josh 15.14-19.   **1.20:** Josh 15.14.   **1.21:** Josh 15.63.
1.27-28: Josh 17.11-13.   **1.29:** Josh 16.10.

have not obeyed my command. What is this you have done? [3] So now I say, I will not drive them out before you; but they shall become adversaries[a] to you, and their gods shall be a snare to you." [4] When the angel of the LORD spoke these words to all the people of Israel, the people lifted up their voices and wept. [5] And they called the name of that place Bō'chim;[b] and they sacrificed there to the LORD.

6 When Joshua dismissed the people, the people of Israel went each to his inheritance to take possession of the land. [7] And the people served the LORD all the days of Joshua, and all the days of the elders who outlived Joshua, who had seen all the great work which the LORD had done for Israel. [8] And Joshua the son of Nun, the servant of the LORD, died at the age of one hundred and ten years. [9] And they buried him within the bounds of his inheritance in Tim'nath-hē'rĕs, in the hill country of Ē'phrà-im, north of the mountain of Gā'ash. [10] And all that generation also were gathered to their fathers; and there arose another generation after them, who did not know the LORD or the work which he had done for Israel.

11 And the people of Israel did what was evil in the sight of the LORD and served the Bā'ăls; [12] and they forsook the LORD, the God of their fathers, who had brought them out of the land of Egypt; they went after other gods, from among the gods of the peoples who were round about them, and bowed down to them; and they provoked the LORD to anger. [13] They forsook the LORD, and served the Bā'ăls and the Ash'tà-roth. [14] So the anger of the LORD was kindled against Israel, and he gave them over to plunderers, who plundered them; and he sold them into the power of their enemies round about, so that they could no longer withstand their enemies. [15] Whenever they marched out, the hand of the LORD was against them for evil, as the LORD had warned, and as the LORD had sworn to them; and they were in sore straits.

16 Then the LORD raised up judges, who saved them out of the power of those who plundered them. [17] And yet they did not listen to their judges; for they played the harlot after other gods and bowed down to them; they soon turned aside from the way in which their fathers had walked, who had obeyed the commandments of the LORD, and they did not do so. [18] Whenever the LORD raised up judges for them, the LORD was with the judge, and he saved them from the hand of their enemies all the days of the judge; for the LORD was moved to pity by their groaning because of those who afflicted and oppressed them. [19] But whenever the judge died, they turned back and behaved worse than their fathers, going after other gods, serving them and bowing down to them; they did not drop any of their practices or their stubborn ways. [20] So the anger of the LORD was kindled against Israel; and he said, "Because this people have transgressed my covenant which I commanded their fathers, and have not obeyed my voice, [21] I will not henceforth drive out before them any of the nations that Joshua left when he died, [22] that by them I may test Israel, whether they will take care to walk in the way of the LORD as their fathers did, or not." [23] So the LORD left those nations, not driving them out at once, and he did not give them into the power of Joshua.

3 Now these are the nations which the LORD left, to test Israel by them, that is, all in Israel who had no experience of any war in Canaan; [2] it was only that the generations of the people of Israel might know war, that he might teach war to such at least as had not known it before. [3] These are the nations: the five lords of the Philistines, and all the Canaanites, and the Sī-dō'ni-ăns, and the Hī'vites who dwelt on Mount Lebanon, from Mount Bā'ăl-hēr'mŏn as far as the entrance of Hā'math. [4] They were for the testing of Israel, to know whether Israel would obey the commandments of the LORD, which he commanded their fathers by Moses. [5] So the people of Israel dwelt among the Canaanites, the Hit'tītes, the Am'ō-rites, the Per'izzītes, the Hī'vites, and the Jĕb'ū-sītes; [6] and they took their daughters to themselves for wives, and their own daughters they gave to their sons; and they served their gods.

7 And the people of Israel did what was evil in the sight of the LORD, forgetting the LORD their God, and serving the Bā'ăls and the A-shē'roth. [8] Therefore the anger of the LORD was kindled against Israel, and he sold them into the hand of Cū'shan-rish-à-thā'im king of Mĕs-ŏ-pŏ-tā'mi-à; and the people of Israel served Cushan-rishathaim eight years. [9] But when the

a Vg Old Latin Compare Gk: Heb *sides*　　*b* That is *Weepers*
2.6-9: Josh 24.28-31.

people of Israel cried to the LORD, the LORD raised up a deliverer for the people of Israel, who delivered them, Oth′ni-el the son of Ke̅′naz, Caleb's younger brother. [10] The Spirit of the LORD came upon him, and he judged Israel; he went out to war, and the LORD gave Cu̅′shan-rish·à·tha̅′im king of Mes·ò·pò·tā′mi·à into his hand; and his hand prevailed over Cushan-rishathaim. [11] So the land had rest forty years. Then Oth′ni-el the son of Ke̅′naz died.

12 And the people of Israel again did what was evil in the sight of the LORD; and the LORD strengthened Eg′lon the king of Mō′ab against Israel, because they had done what was evil in the sight of the LORD. [13] He gathered to himself the Am′mò·nites and the Á·mal′é·kites, and went and defeated Israel; and they took possession of the city of palms. [14] And the people of Israel served Eg′lon the king of Mō′ab eighteen years.

15 But when the people of Israel cried to the LORD, the LORD raised up for them a deliverer, E̅′hud, the son of Ge̅′rà, the Benjaminite, a left-handed man. The people of Israel sent tribute by him to Eg′lon the king of Mō′ab. [16] And E̅′hud made for himself a sword with two edges, a cubit in length; and he girded it on his right thigh under his clothes. [17] And he presented the tribute to Eg′lon king of Mō′ab. Now Eglon was a very fat man. [18] And when E̅′hud had finished presenting the tribute, he sent away the people that carried the tribute. [19] But he himself turned back at the sculptured stones near Gil′gàl, and said, "I have a secret message for you, O king." And he commanded, "Silence." And all his attendants went out from his presence. [20] And E̅′hud came to him, as he was sitting alone in his cool roof chamber. And Ehud said, "I have a message from God for you." And he arose from his seat. [21] And E̅′hud reached with his left hand, took the sword from his right thigh, and thrust it into his belly; [22] and the hilt also went in after the blade, and the fat closed over the blade, for he did not draw the sword out of his belly; and the dirt came out. [23] Then E̅′hud went out into the vestibule,[c] and closed the doors of the roof chamber upon him, and locked them.

24 When he had gone, the servants came; and when they saw that the doors of the roof chamber were locked, they thought, "He is only relieving

himself in the closet of the cool chamber." [25] And they waited till they were utterly at a loss; but when he still did not open the doors of the roof chamber, they took the key and opened them; and there lay their lord dead on the floor.

26 E̅′hud escaped while they delayed, and passed beyond the sculptured stones, and escaped to Se̅·i′ràh. [27] When he arrived, he sounded the trumpet in the hill country of E̅′phrà·im; and the people of Israel went down with him from the hill country, having him at their head. [28] And he said to them, "Follow after me; for the LORD has given your enemies the Mō′ab·ites into your hand." So they went down after him, and seized the fords of the Jordan against the Moabites, and allowed not a man to pass over. [29] And they killed at that time about ten thousand of the Mō′ab·ites, all strong, able-bodied men; not a man escaped. [30] So Mō′ab was subdued that day under the hand of Israel. And the land had rest for eighty years.

31 After him was Sham′gär the son of A′nath, who killed six hundred of the Philistines with an oxgoad; and he too delivered Israel.

4 And the people of Israel again did what was evil in the sight of the LORD, after E̅′hud died. [2] And the LORD sold them into the hand of Jā′bin king of Canaan, who reigned in Hā′zôr; the commander of his army was Sis′ér·à, who dwelt in Hà·rō′sheth-hà-goi′im. [3] Then the people of Israel cried to the LORD for help; for he had nine hundred chariots of iron, and oppressed the people of Israel cruelly for twenty years.

4 Now Deb′ò·ràh, a prophetess, the wife of Lap′pi·doth, was judging Israel at that time. [5] She used to sit under the palm of Deb′ò·ràh between Rā′màh and Beth′ḗl in the hill country of E̅′phrà·im; and the people of Israel came up to her for judgment. [6] She sent and summoned Bâr′ak the son of À·bin′ō-am from Ke̅′desh in Naph′ta-li, and said to him, "The LORD, the God of Israel, commands you, 'Go, gather your men at Mount Tā′bôr, taking ten thousand from the tribe of Naphtali and the tribe of Zeb′u̅·lùn. [7] And I will draw out Sis′ér·à, the general of Jā′bin's army, to meet you by the river Ki′shon with his chariots and his troops; and I will give him into your hand.' " [8] Bâr′ak said to her, "If you will go with me, I will go; but if you will not go with me, I will not

c The meaning of the Hebrew word is unknown

go." ⁹And she said, "I will surely go with you; nevertheless, the road on which you are going will not lead to your glory, for the LORD will sell Sĭs′ĕr·à into the hand of a woman." Then Dĕb′ō·ràh arose, and went with Bâr′àk to Kē′desh. ¹⁰And Bâr′àk summoned Zĕb′ū·lùn and Năph′tà·lī to Kē′desh; and ten thousand men went up at his heels; and Dĕb′ō·ràh went up with him.

11 Now Hē′bĕr the Ken′īte had separated from the Kenites, the descendants of Hō′bab the father-in-law of Moses, and had pitched his tent as far away as the oak in Zā-à·nan′nim, which is near Kē′desh.

12 When Sĭs′ĕr·à was told that Bâr′àk the son of Ă·bin′ō-am had gone up to Mount Tā′bôr, ¹³ Sĭs′ĕr·à called out all his chariots, nine hundred chariots of iron, and all the men who were with him, from Hà·rō′sheth-hà-goi′im to the river Ki′shon. ¹⁴And Dĕb′ō·ràh said to Bâr′àk, "Up! For this is the day in which the LORD has given Sĭs′ĕr·à into your hand. Does not the LORD go out before you?" So Barak went down from Mount Tā′bôr with ten thousand men following him. ¹⁵And the LORD routed Sĭs′ĕr·à and all his chariots and all his army before Bâr′àk at the edge of the sword; and Sisera alighted from his chariot and fled away on foot. ¹⁶And Bâr′àk pursued the chariots and the army to Hà·rō′sheth-hà-goi′im, and all the army of Sĭs′ĕr·à fell by the edge of the sword; not a man was left.

17 But Sĭs′ĕr·à fled away on foot to the tent of Jā′ĕl, the wife of Hē′bĕr the Ken′īte; for there was peace between Jā′bin the king of Hā′zôr and the house of Heber the Kenite. ¹⁸And Jā′ĕl came out to meet Sĭs′ĕr·à, and said to him, "Turn aside, my lord, turn aside to me; have no fear." So he turned aside to her into the tent, and she covered him with a rug. ¹⁹And he said to her, "Pray, give me a little water to drink; for I am thirsty." So she opened a skin of milk and gave him a drink and covered him. ²⁰And he said to her, "Stand at the door of the tent, and if any man comes and asks you, 'Is any one here?' say, No." ²¹ But Jā′ĕl the wife of Hē′bĕr took a tent peg, and took a hammer in her hand, and went softly to him and drove the peg into his temple, till it went down into the ground, as he was lying fast asleep from weariness. So he died. ²²And behold, as Bâr′àk pursued Sĭs′ĕr·à, Jā′ĕl went

out to meet him, and said to him, "Come, and I will show you the man whom you are seeking." So he went in to her tent; and there lay Sisera dead, with the tent peg in his temple.

23 So on that day God subdued Jā′bin the king of Canaan before the people of Israel. ²⁴And the hand of the people of Israel bore harder and harder on Jā′bin the king of Canaan, until they destroyed Jabin king of Canaan.

5   Then sang Dĕb′ō·ràh and Bâr′àk the son of Ă·bin′ō-am on that day:

2 "That the leaders took the lead in Israel,
     that the people offered themselves willingly,
       bless*ᵈ* the LORD!

3 "Hear, O kings; give ear, O princes;
     to the LORD I will sing,
   I will make melody to the LORD,
     the God of Israel.

4 "LORD, when thou didst go forth from Sē′ir,
   when thou didst march from the region of E′dŏm,
the earth trembled,
   and the heavens dropped,
   yea, the clouds dropped water.
5 The mountains quaked before the LORD,
   yon Sinai before the LORD, the God of Israel.

6 "In the days of Sham′gär, son of A′nath,
   in the days of Jā′ĕl, caravans ceased
   and travelers kept to the byways.
7 The peasantry ceased in Israel, they ceased
   until you arose, Dĕb′ō·ràh,
   arose as a mother in Israel.
8 When new gods were chosen,
   then war was in the gates.
Was shield or spear to be seen
   among forty thousand in Israel?
9 My heart goes out to the commanders of Israel
   who offered themselves willingly among the people.
   Bless the LORD.

10 "Tell of it, you who ride on tawny asses,
   you who sit on rich carpets*ᵉ*
   and you who walk by the way.
11 To the sound of musicians*ᵉ* at the watering places,
   there they repeat the triumphs of the LORD,

ᵈ Or You who offered yourselves willingly among the people, bless
ᵉ The meaning of the Hebrew word is uncertain

the triumphs of his peasantry in
  Israel.

"Then down to the gates marched
  the people of the LORD.
12 "Awake, awake, Deb'ó·ráh!
  Awake, awake, utter a song!
Arise, Bâr'âk, lead away your captives,
  O son of Á·bin'ō-am.
13 Then down marched the remnant
  of the noble;
  the people of the LORD marched
  down for him[f] against the
  mighty.
14 From É'phrà·im they set out thither[x]
  into the valley,[g]
  following you, Benjamin, with
  your kinsmen;
  from Mā'chir marched down the
  commanders,
  and from Zeb'ū·lún those who
  bear the marshal's staff;
15 the princes of Is'sà·chär came with
  Deb'ó·ráh,
  and Issachar faithful to Bâr'âk;
  into the valley they rushed forth
  at his heels.
Among the clans of Reuben
  there were great searchings of
  heart.
16 Why did you tarry among the sheepfolds,
  to hear the piping for the flocks?
Among the clans of Reuben
  there were great searchings of
  heart.
17 Gilead stayed beyond the Jordan;
  and Dan, why did he abide with
  the ships?
  Ash'ér sat still at the coast of the sea,
  settling down by his landings.
18 Zeb'ū·lún is a people that jeoparded
  their lives to the death;
  Naph'tà·li too, on the heights of
  the field.

19 "The kings came, they fought;
  then fought the kings of Canaan,
  at Tā'à·nach, by the waters of
  Mè·gid'dō;
  they got no spoils of silver.
20 From heaven fought the stars,
  from their courses they fought
  against Sis'ér·à.
21 The torrent Ki'shon swept them
  away,
  the onrushing torrent, the torrent
  Kishon.
  March on, my soul, with might!

22 "Then loud beat the horses' hoofs

with the galloping, galloping of
  his steeds.

23 "Curse Mě'roz, says the angel of
  the LORD,
  curse bitterly its inhabitants,
  because they came not to the help
  of the LORD,
  to the help of the LORD against
  the mighty.

24 "Most blessed of women be Jā'él,
  the wife of Hě'bér the Ken'ite,
  of tent-dwelling women most
  blessed.
25 He asked water and she gave him
  milk,
  she brought him curds in a lordly
  bowl.
26 She put her hand to the tent peg
  and her right hand to the workmen's mallet;
  she struck Sis'ér·à a blow,
  she crushed his head,
  she shattered and pierced his
  temple.
27 He sank, he fell,
  he lay still at her feet;
  at her feet he sank, he fell;
  where he sank, there he fell dead.

28 "Out of the window she peered,
  the mother of Sis'ér·à gazed[h]
  through the lattice:
'Why is his chariot so long in
  coming?
  Why tarry the hoofbeats of his
  chariots?'
29 Her wisest ladies make answer,
  nay, she gives answer to herself,
30 'Are they not finding and dividing
  the spoil?—
  A maiden or two for every man;
  spoil of dyed stuffs for Sis'ér·à,
  spoil of dyed stuffs embroidered,
  two pieces of dyed work embroidered for my neck as spoil?'

31 "So perish all thine enemies,
  O LORD!
  But thy friends be like the sun as
  he rises in his might."

And the land had rest for forty years.

6 The people of Israel did what was
  evil in the sight of the LORD; and
the LORD gave them into the hand of
Mid'i·àn seven years. 2And the hand
of Mid'i·àn prevailed over Israel; and
because of Midian the people of Israel
made for themselves the dens which
are in the mountains, and the caves

[f] Gk: Heb *me*   [x] Cn: Heb *From Ephraim their root*   [g] Gk: Heb *in Amalek*
[h] Gk Compare Tg: Heb *exclaimed*
5.31: Rev 1.16.

and the strongholds. 3 For whenever the Israelites put in seed the Mid′i·á·nites and the Á·mal′e·kites and the people of the East would come up and attack them; 4 they would encamp against them and destroy the produce of the land, as far as the neighborhood of Gá′zà, and leave no sustenance in Israel, and no sheep or ox or ass. 5 For they would come up with their cattle and their tents, coming like locusts for numbers; both they and their camels could not be counted; so that they wasted the land as they came in. 6And Israel was brought very low because of Mid′i·àn; and the people of Israel cried for help to the LORD.

7 When the people of Israel cried to the LORD on account of the Mid′i·à·nites, 8 the LORD sent a prophet to the people of Israel; and he said to them, "Thus says the LORD, the God of Israel: I led you up from Egypt, and brought you out of the house of bondage; 9 and I delivered you from the hand of the Egyptians, and from the hand of all who oppressed you, and drove them out before you, and gave you their land; 10 and I said to you, 'I am the LORD your God; you shall not pay reverence to the gods of the Am′o·rites, in whose land you dwell.' But you have not given heed to my voice."

11 Now the angel of the LORD came and sat under the oak at Oph′ràh, which belonged to Jō′ash the Ā·bi·ez′-rite, as his son Gideon was beating out wheat in the wine press, to hide it from the Mid′i·à·nites. 12And the angel of the LORD appeared to him and said to him, "The LORD is with you, you mighty man of valor." 13And Gideon said to him, "Pray, sir, if the LORD is with us, why then has all this befallen us? And where are all his wonderful deeds which our fathers recounted to us, saying, 'Did not the LORD bring us up from Egypt?' But now the LORD has cast us off, and given us into the hand of Mid′i·àn." 14And the LORD turned to him and said, "Go in this might of yours and deliver Israel from the hand of Mid′i·àn; do not I send you?" 15And he said to him, "Pray, Lord, how can I deliver Israel? Behold, my clan is the weakest in Mà·nas′sèh, and I am the least in my family." 16And the LORD said to him, "But I will be with you, and you shall smite the Mid′i·à·nites as one man." 17And he said to him, "If now I have found favor with thee, then show me a sign that it is thou who speakest with me. 18 Do not depart from here, I pray thee, until I come to thee, and bring

out my present, and set it before thee." And he said, "I will stay till you return."

19 So Gideon went into his house and prepared a kid, and unleavened cakes from an ephah of flour; the meat he put in a basket, and the broth he put in a pot, and brought them to him under the oak and presented them. 20And the angel of God said to him, "Take the meat and the unleavened cakes, and put them on this rock, and pour the broth over them." And he did so. 21 Then the angel of the LORD reached out the tip of the staff that was in his hand, and touched the meat and the unleavened cakes; and there sprang up fire from the rock and consumed the flesh and the unleavened cakes; and the angel of the LORD vanished from his sight. 22 Then Gideon perceived that he was the angel of the LORD; and Gideon said, "Alas, O Lord GOD! For now I have seen the angel of the LORD face to face." 23 But the LORD said to him, "Peace be to you; do not fear, you shall not die." 24 Then Gideon built an altar there to the LORD, and called it, The LORD is peace. To this day it still stands at Oph′ràh, which belongs to the Ā·bi·ez′rites.

25 That night the LORD said to him, "Take your father's bull, the second bull seven years old, and pull down the altar of Bā′al which your father has, and cut down the Á·shē′ràh that is beside it; 26 and build an altar to the LORD your God on the top of the stronghold here, with stones laid in due order; then take the second bull, and offer it as a burnt offering with the wood of the Á·shē′ràh which you shall cut down." 27 So Gideon took ten men of his servants, and did as the LORD had told him; but because he was too afraid of his family and the men of the town to do it by day, he did it by night.

28 When the men of the town rose early in the morning, behold, the altar of Bā′al was broken down, and the Á·shē′ràh beside it was cut down, and the second bull was offered upon the altar which had been built. 29And they said to one another, "Who has done this thing?" And after they had made search and inquired, they said, "Gideon the son of Jō′ash has done this thing." 30 Then the men of the town said to Jō′ash, "Bring out your son, that he may die, for he has pulled down the altar of Bā′al and cut down the Á·shē′ràh beside it." 31 But Jō′ash said to all who were arrayed against him, "Will you contend for Bā′al? Or will you defend his cause? Whoever

contends for him shall be put to death by morning. If he is a god, let him contend for himself, because his altar has been pulled down." 32 Therefore on that day he was called Jer·ub·bā'al, that is to say, "Let Bā'al contend against him," because he pulled down his altar.

33 Then all the Mid'i·a·nites and the Ā·mal'e·kites and the people of the East came together, and crossing the Jordan they encamped in the Valley of Jez're·el. 34 But the Spirit of the LORD took possession of Gideon; and he sounded the trumpet, and the Ā·bi·ez'rites were called out to follow him. 35And he sent messengers throughout all Mā·nas'seh; and they too were called out to follow him. And he sent messengers to Ash'er, Zeb'u·lun, and Naph'ta·li; and they went up to meet them.

36 Then Gideon said to God, "If thou wilt deliver Israel by my hand, as thou hast said, 37 behold, I am laying a fleece of wool on the threshing floor; if there is dew on the fleece alone, and it is dry on all the ground, then I shall know that thou wilt deliver Israel by my hand, as thou hast said." 38And it was so. When he rose early next morning and squeezed the fleece, he wrung enough dew from the fleece to fill a bowl with water. 39 Then Gideon said to God, "Let not thy anger burn against me, let me speak but this once; pray, let me make trial only this once with the fleece; pray, let it be dry only on the fleece, and on all the ground let there be dew." 40And God did so that night; for it was dry on the fleece only, and on all the ground there was dew.

7 Then Jer·ub·bā'al (that is, Gideon) and all the people who were with him rose early and encamped beside the spring of Hâr'od; and the camp of Mid'i·an was north of them, by the hill of Mō'reh, in the valley.

2 The LORD said to Gideon, "The people with you are too many for me to give the Mid'i·a·nites into their hand, lest Israel vaunt themselves against me, saying, 'My own hand has delivered me.' 3 Now therefore proclaim in the ears of the people, saying, 'Whoever is fearful and trembling, let him return home.'" And Gideon tested them;[i] twenty-two thousand returned, and ten thousand remained.

4 And the LORD said to Gideon, "The people are still too many; take them down to the water and I will test them for you there; and he of whom I

say to you, 'This man shall go with you,' shall go with you; and any of whom I say to you, 'This man shall not go with you,' shall not go." 5 So he brought the people down to the water; and the LORD said to Gideon, "Every one that laps the water with his tongue, as a dog laps, you shall set by himself; likewise every one that kneels down to drink." 6And the number of those that lapped, putting their hands to their mouths, was three hundred men; but all the rest of the people knelt down to drink water. 7And the LORD said to Gideon, "With the three hundred men that lapped I will deliver you, and give the Mid'i·a·nites into your hand; and let all the others go every man to his home." 8 So he took the jars of the people from their hands,[j] and their trumpets; and he sent all the rest of Israel every man to his tent, but retained the three hundred men; and the camp of Mid'i·an was below him in the valley.

9 That same night the LORD said to him, "Arise, go down against the camp; for I have given it into your hand. 10 But if you fear to go down, go down to the camp with Pū'rah your servant; 11 and you shall hear what they say, and afterward your hands shall be strengthened to go down against the camp." Then he went down with Pū'rah his servant to the outposts of the armed men that were in the camp. 12And the Mid'i·a·nites and the Ā·mal'e·kites and all the people of the East lay along the valley like locusts for multitude; and their camels were without number, as the sand which is upon the seashore for multitude. 13 When Gideon came, behold, a man was telling a dream to his comrade; and he said, "Behold, I dreamed a dream; and lo, a cake of barley bread tumbled into the camp of Mid'i·an, and came to the tent, and struck it so that it fell, and turned it upside down, so that the tent lay flat." 14And his comrade answered, "This is no other than the sword of Gideon the son of Jō'ash, a man of Israel; into his hand God has given Mid'i·an and all the host."

15 When Gideon heard the telling of the dream and its interpretation, he worshiped; and he returned to the camp of Israel, and said, "Arise; for the LORD has given the host of Mid'i·an into your hand." 16And he divided the three hundred men into three companies, and put trumpets into the

i Cn: Heb *and depart from Mount Gilead*
j Cn: Heb *the people took provisions in their hands*

hands of all of them and empty jars, with torches inside the jars. [17]And he said to them, "Look at me, and do likewise; when I come to the outskirts of the camp, do as I do. [18] When I blow the trumpet, I and all who are with me, then blow the trumpets also on every side of all the camp, and shout, 'For the LORD and for Gideon.'"

[19] So Gideon and the hundred men who were with him came to the outskirts of the camp at the beginning of the middle watch, when they had just set the watch; and they blew the trumpets and smashed the jars that were in their hands. [20]And the three companies blew the trumpets and broke the jars, holding in their left hands the torches, and in their right hands the trumpets to blow; and they cried, "A sword for the LORD and for Gideon!" [21] They stood every man in his place round about the camp, and all the army ran; they cried out and fled. [22] When they blew the three hundred trumpets, the LORD set every man's sword against his fellow and against all the army; and the army fled as far as Beth-shit′tah toward Zer′e-rah,[k] as far as the border of A′bel-mĕ-hō′lah, by Tab′bath. [23]And the men of Israel were called out from Naph′ta-li and from Ash′er and from all Mȧ-nas′sĕh, and they pursued after Mid′i-an.

24 And Gideon sent messengers throughout all the hill country of E′phrȧ-im, saying, "Come down against the Mid′i-ȧ-nites and seize the waters against them, as far as Beth-bâr′ah, and also the Jordan." So all the men of Ephraim were called out, and they seized the waters as far as Beth-barah, and also the Jordan. [25]And they took the two princes of Mid′i-ȧn, Ŏr′eb and Zē′eb; they killed Oreb at the rock of Oreb, and Zeeb they killed at the wine press of Zeeb, as they pursued Mid′i-ȧn; and they brought the heads of Oreb and Zeeb to Gideon beyond the Jordan.

8 And the men of E′phrȧ-im said to him, "What is this that you have done to us, not to call us when you went to fight with Mid′i-ȧn?" And they upbraided him violently. [2]And he said to them, "What have I done now in comparison with you? Is not the gleaning of the grapes of E′phrȧ-im better than the vintage of Ȧ-bi-e′zẽr? [3] God has given into your hands the princes of Mid′i-ȧn, Ŏr′eb and Zē′eb; what have I been able to do in comparison with you?" Then their anger against

him was abated, when he had said this.

4 And Gideon came to the Jordan and passed over, he and the three hundred men who were with him, faint yet pursuing. [5] So he said to the men of Suc′coth, "Pray, give loaves of bread to the people who follow me; for they are faint, and I am pursuing after Zē′bah and Zal-mun′nȧ, the kings of Mid′i-ȧn." [6]And the officials of Suc′coth said, "Are Zē′bah and Zal-mun′nȧ already in your hand, that we should give bread to your army?" [7]And Gideon said, "Well then, when the LORD has given Zē′bah and Zal-mun′nȧ into my hand, I will flail your flesh with the thorns of the wilderness and with briers." [8]And from there he went up to Pĕ-nū′el, and spoke to them in the same way; and the men of Penuel answered him as the men of Suc′coth had answered. [9]And he said to the men of Pĕ-nū′el, "When I come again in peace, I will break down this tower."

10 Now Zē′bah and Zal-mun′nȧ were in Kär′kŏr with their army, about fifteen thousand men, all who were left of all the army of the people of the East; for there had fallen a hundred and twenty thousand men who drew the sword. [11]And Gideon went up by the caravan route east of Nō′bah and Jog′be-hȧh, and attacked the army; for the army was off its guard. [12]And Zē′bah and Zal-mun′nȧ fled; and he pursued them and took the two kings of Mid′i-ȧn, Zebah and Zalmunna, and he threw all the army into a panic.

13 Then Gideon the son of Jō′ash returned from the battle by the ascent of Hē′rēs. [14]And he caught a young man of Suc′coth, and questioned him; and he wrote down for him the officials and elders of Succoth, seventy-seven men. [15]And he came to the men of Suc′coth, and said, "Behold Zē′bah and Zal-mun′nȧ, about whom you taunted me, saying, 'Are Zebah and Zalmunna already in your hand, that we should give bread to your men who are faint?'" [16]And he took the elders of the city and he took thorns of the wilderness and briers and with them taught the men of Suc′coth. [17]And he broke down the tower of Pĕ-nū′el, and slew the men of the city.

18 Then he said to Zē′bah and Zal-mun′nȧ, "Where are the men whom you slew at Tā′bôr?" They answered, "As you are, so were they, every one of them; they resembled the sons of a king." [19]And he said, "They

[k] Another reading is *Zeredah*

were my brothers, the sons of my mother; as the LORD lives, if you had saved them alive, I would not slay you." 20And he said to Jē´ther his firstborn, "Rise, and slay them." But the youth did not draw his sword; for he was afraid, because he was still a youth. 21 Then Zē´bah and Zal·mun´na said, "Rise yourself, and fall upon us; for as the man is, so is his strength." And Gideon arose and slew Zebah and Zalmunna; and he took the crescents that were on the necks of their camels.

22 Then the men of Israel said to Gideon, "Rule over us, you and your son and your grandson also; for you have delivered us out of the hand of Mid´i·an." 23 Gideon said to them, "I will not rule over you, and my son will not rule over you; the LORD will rule over you." 24And Gideon said to them, "Let me make a request of you; give me every man of you the earrings of his spoil." (For they had golden earrings, because they were Ish´ma·el·ites.) 25And they answered, "We will willingly give them." And they spread a garment, and every man cast in it the earrings of his spoil. 26And the weight of the golden earrings that he requested was one thousand seven hundred shekels of gold; besides the crescents and the pendants and the purple garments worn by the kings of Mid´i·an, and besides the collars that were about the necks of their camels. 27And Gideon made an ephod of it and put it in his city, in Oph´rah; and all Israel played the harlot after it there, and it became a snare to Gideon and to his family. 28 So Mid´i·an was subdued before the people of Israel, and they lifted up their heads no more. And the land had rest forty years in the days of Gideon.

29 Jer·ub·ba´al the son of Jō´ash went and dwelt in his own house. 30 Now Gideon had seventy sons, his own offspring, for he had many wives. 31And his concubine who was in Shē´chem also bore him a son, and he called his name Å·bim´e·lech. 32And Gideon the son of Jō´ash died in a good old age, and was buried in the tomb of Jō´ash his father, at Oph´rah of the Å·bi·ez´rites.

33 As soon as Gideon died, the people of Israel turned again and played the harlot after the Ba´als, and made Bā´al-bē´rith their god. 34And the people of Israel did not remember the LORD their God, who had rescued them from the hand of all their enemies on every side; 35 and they did not show kindness to the family of Jer·ub·ba´al

(that is, Gideon) in return for all the good that he had done to Israel.

9 Now Å·bim´e·lech the son of Jer·ub·ba´al went to Shē´chem to his mother's kinsmen and said to them and to the whole clan of his mother's family, 2 "Say in the ears of all the citizens of Shē´chem, 'Which is better for you, that all seventy of the sons of Jer·ub·ba´al rule over you, or that one rule over you?' Remember also that I am your bone and your flesh." 3And his mother's kinsmen spoke all these words on his behalf in the ears of all the men of Shē´chem; and their hearts inclined to follow Å·bim´e·lech, for they said, "He is our brother." 4And they gave him seventy pieces of silver out of the house of Bā´al-bē´rith with which Å·bim´e·lech hired worthless and reckless fellows, who followed him. 5And he went to his father's house at Oph´rah, and slew his brothers the sons of Jer·ub·ba´al, seventy men, upon one stone; but Jō´tham the youngest son of Jerubbaal was left, for he hid himself. 6And all the citizens of Shē´chem came together, and all Beth-mil´lō, and they went and made Å·bim´e·lech king, by the oak of the pillar at Shechem.

7 When it was told to Jō´tham, he went and stood on the top of Mount Gēr´i·zim, and cried aloud and said to them, "Listen to me, you men of Shē´chem, that God may listen to you. 8 The trees once went forth to anoint a king over them; and they said to the olive tree, 'Reign over us.' 9 But the olive tree said to them, 'Shall I leave my fatness, by which gods and men are honored, and go to sway over the trees?' 10And the trees said to the fig tree, 'Come you, and reign over us.' 11 But the fig tree said to them, 'Shall I leave my sweetness and my good fruit, and go to sway over the trees?' 12And the trees said to the vine, 'Come you, and reign over us.' 13 But the vine said to them, 'Shall I leave my wine which cheers gods and men, and go to sway over the trees?' 14 Then all the trees said to the bramble, 'Come you, and reign over us.' 15And the bramble said to the trees, 'If in good faith you are anointing me king over you, then come and take refuge in my shade; but if not, let fire come out of the bramble and devour the cedars of Lebanon.'

16 "Now therefore, if you acted in good faith and honor when you made Å·bim´e·lech king, and if you have dealt well with Jer·ub·ba´al and his house, and have done to him as his

deeds deserved— 17 for my father fought for you, and risked his life, and rescued you from the hand of Mid′i-àn; 18 and you have risen up against my father's house this day, and have slain his sons, seventy men on one stone, and have made A·bim′e·lech, the son of his maidservant, king over the citizens of She′chem, because he is your kinsman— 19 if you then have acted in good faith and honor with Jer·ub·ba′al and with his house this day, then rejoice in A·bim′e·lech, and let him also rejoice in you; 20 but if not, let fire come out from A·bim′e-lech, and devour the citizens of She′-chem, and Beth-mil′lo; and let fire come out from the citizens of Shechem, and from Beth-millo, and devour Abimelech." 21And Jo′tham ran away and fled, and went to Beer and dwelt there, for fear of A·bim′e·lech his brother.

22 A·bim′e·lech ruled over Israel three years. 23And God sent an evil spirit between A·bim′e·lech and the men of She′chem; and the men of Shechem dealt treacherously with Abimelech; 24 that the violence done to the seventy sons of Jer·ub·ba′al might come and their blood be laid upon A·bim′e·lech their brother, who slew them, and upon the men of She′-chem, who strengthened his hands to slay his brothers. 25And the men of She′chem put men in ambush against him on the mountain tops, and they robbed all who passed by them along the way; and it was told A·bim′e·lech.

26 And Ga′al the son of E′bed moved into She′chem with his kins-men; and the men of Shechem put confidence in him. 27And they went out into the field, and gathered the grapes from their vineyards and trod them, and held festival, and went into the house of their god, and ate and drank and reviled A·bim′e·lech. 28And Ga′al the son of E′bed said, "Who is A·bim′e·lech, and who are we of She′-chem, that we should serve him? Did not the son of Jer·ub·ba′al and Ze′bul his officer serve the men of Ha′mor the father of Shechem? Why then should we serve him? 29 Would that this people were under my hand! then I would remove A·bim′e·lech. I would say*l* to Abimelech, 'Increase your army, and come out.'"

30 When Ze′bul the ruler of the city heard the words of Ga′al the son of E′bed, his anger was kindled. 31And he sent messengers to A·bim′e·lech at A·ru′mah,*m* saying, "Behold, Ga′al the son of E′bed and his kinsmen have come to She′chem, and they are stirring up*n* the city against you. 32 Now therefore, go by night, you and the men that are with you, and lie in wait in the fields. 33 Then in the morning, as soon as the sun is up, rise early and rush upon the city; and when he and the men that are with him come out against you, you may do to them as occasion offers."

34 And A·bim′e·lech and all the men that were with him rose up by night, and laid wait against She′chem in four companies. 35And Ga′al the son of E′bed went out and stood in the entrance of the gate of the city; and A·bim′e·lech and the men that were with him rose from the ambush. 36And when Ga′al saw the men, he said to Ze′bul, "Look, men are coming down from the mountain tops!" And Zebul said to him, "You see the shadow of the mountains as if they were men." 37 Ga′al spoke again and said, "Look, men are coming down from the center of the land, and one company is coming from the direction of the Diviners' Oak." 38 Then Ze′bul said to him, "Where is your mouth now, you who said, 'Who is A·bim′e·lech, that we should serve him'? Are not these the men whom you despised? Go out now and fight with them." 39And Ga′al went out at the head of the men of She′chem, and fought with A·bim′e-lech. 40And A·bim′e·lech chased him, and he fled before him; and many fell wounded, up to the entrance of the gate. 41And A·bim′e·lech dwelt at A·ru′màh; and Ze′bul drove out Ga′al and his kinsmen, so that they could not live on at She′chem.

42 On the following day the men went out into the fields. And A·bim′e-lech was told. 43 He took his men and divided them into three companies, and laid wait in the field; and he looked and saw the men coming out of the city, and he rose against them and slew them. 44A·bim′e·lech and the company*o* that was with him rushed forward and stood at the entrance of the gate of the city, while the two companies rushed upon all who were in the fields and slew them. 45And A·bim′e·lech fought against the city all that day; he took the city, and killed the people that were in it; and he razed the city and sowed it with salt.

46 When all the people of the Tower of She′chem heard of it, they

l Gk: Heb *and he said*   *m* Cn See 9.41. Heb *Tormah*   *n* Cn: Heb *besieging*
o Vg and some Mss of Gk: Heb *companies*

THE WALLS OF JERICHO FALL DOWN   *Josh. 6:20*

DAVID THE SHEPHERD

I Sam. 16:11

entered the stronghold of the house of El-bē′rith. 47Á·bim′ē·lech was told that all the people of the Tower of Shē′chem were gathered together. 48And Á·bim′ē·lech went up to Mount Zal′mon, he and all the men that were with him; and Abimelech took an axe in his hand, and cut down a bundle of brushwood, and took it up and laid it on his shoulder. And he said to the men that were with him, "What you have seen me do, make haste to do, as I have done." 49 So every one of the people cut down his bundle and following Á·bim′ē·lech put it against the stronghold, and they set the stronghold on fire over them, so that all the people of the Tower of Shē′chem also died, about a thousand men and women.

50 Then Á·bim′ē·lech went to Thē′bez, and encamped against Thebez, and took it. 51 But there was a strong tower within the city, and all the people of the city fled to it, all the men and women, and shut themselves in; and they went to the roof of the tower. 52And Á·bim′ē·lech came to the tower, and fought against it, and drew near to the door of the tower to burn it with fire. 53And a certain woman threw an upper millstone upon Á·bim′ē·lech's head, and crushed his skull. 54 Then he called hastily to the young man his armor-bearer, and said to him, "Draw your sword and kill me, lest men say of me, 'A woman killed him.'" And his young man thrust him through, and he died. 55And when the men of Israel saw that Á·bim′ē·lech was dead, they departed every man to his home. 56 Thus God requited the crime of Á·bim′ē·lech, which he committed against his father in killing his seventy brothers; 57 and God also made all the wickedness of the men of Shē′chem fall back upon their heads, and upon them came the curse of Jō′tham the son of Jer·ub·bā′al.

10 After Á·bim′ē·lech there arose to deliver Israel Tō′lä the son of Pū′áh, son of Dō′dō, a man of Is′sa·chär; and he lived at Shā′mir in the hill country of E′phra·im. 2And he judged Israel twenty-three years. Then he died, and was buried at Shā′mir.

3 After him arose Jā′ir the Gileadite, who judged Israel twenty-two years. 4And he had thirty sons who rode on thirty asses; and they had thirty cities, called Hāv′voth-jā′ir to this day, which are in the land of Gilead. 5And Jā′ir died, and was buried in Kā′mon.

6 And the people of Israel again did what was evil in the sight of the LORD, and served the Bā′als and the Ash′ta·roth, the gods of Syria, the gods of Si′don, the gods of Mō′ab, the gods of the Am′mo·nites, and the gods of the Philistines; and they forsook the LORD, and did not serve him. 7And the anger of the LORD was kindled against Israel, and he sold them into the hand of the Philistines and into the hand of the Am′mo·nites, 8 and they crushed and oppressed the children of Israel that year. For eighteen years they oppressed all the people of Israel that were beyond the Jordan in the land of the Am′o·rites, which is in Gilead. 9And the Am′mo·nites crossed the Jordan to fight also against Judah and against Benjamin and against the house of E′phra·im; so that Israel was sorely distressed.

10 And the people of Israel cried to the LORD, saying, "We have sinned against thee, because we have forsaken our God and have served the Bā′als." 11And the LORD said to the people of Israel, "Did I not deliver you from the Egyptians and from the Am′o·rites, from the Am′mo·nites and from the Philistines? 12 The Si·dō′ni·ans also, and the Á·mal′ē·kites, and the Mā′o·nites, oppressed you; and you cried to me, and I delivered you out of their hand. 13 Yet you have forsaken me and served other gods; therefore I will deliver you no more. 14 Go and cry to the gods whom you have chosen; let them deliver you in the time of your distress." 15And the people of Israel said to the LORD, "We have sinned; do to us whatever seems good to thee; only deliver us, we pray thee, this day." 16 So they put away the foreign gods from among them and served the LORD; and he became indignant over the misery of Israel.

17 Then the Am′mo·nites were called to arms, and they encamped in Gilead; and the people of Israel came together, and they encamped at Miz′pah. 18And the people, the leaders of Gilead, said one to another, "Who is the man that will begin to fight against the Am′mo·nites? He shall be head over all the inhabitants of Gilead."

11 Now Jeph′thah the Gileadite was a mighty warrior, but he was the son of a harlot. Gilead was the father of Jephthah. 2And Gilead's wife also bore him sons; and when his wife's sons grew up, they thrust Jeph′thah out, and said to him, "You shall not inherit in our father's house; for you are the son of another woman." 3 Then Jeph′thah fled from his brothers, and dwelt in the land of Tob; and worth-

less fellows collected round Jephthah, and went raiding with him.

4 After a time the Am'mo·nites made war against Israel. 5 And when the Am'mo·nites made war against Israel, the elders of Gilead went to bring Jeph'thah from the land of Tob; 6 and they said to Jeph'thah, "Come and be our leader, that we may fight with the Am'mo·nites." 7 But Jeph'-thah said to the elders of Gilead, "Did you not hate me, and drive me out of my father's house? Why have you come to me now when you are in trouble?" 8 And the elders of Gilead said to Jeph'thah, "That is why we have turned to you now, that you may go with us and fight with the Am'mo·nites, and be our head over all the inhabitants of Gilead." 9 Jeph'thah said to the elders of Gilead, "If you bring me home again to fight with the Am'-mo·nites, and the LORD gives them over to me, I will be your head." 10 And the elders of Gilead said to Jeph'thah, "The LORD will be witness between us; we will surely do as you say." 11 So Jeph'thah went with the elders of Gilead, and the people made him head and leader over them; and Jephthah spoke all his words before the LORD at Miz'pah.

12 Then Jeph'thah sent messengers to the king of the Am'mo·nites and said, "What have you against me, that you have come to me to fight against my land?" 13 And the king of the Am'mo·nites answered the messengers of Jeph'thah, "Because Israel on coming from Egypt took away my land, from the Ar'non to the Jab'bok and to the Jordan; now therefore restore it peaceably." 14 And Jeph'-thah sent messengers again to the king of the Am'mo·nites 15 and said to him, "Thus says Jeph'thah: Israel did not take away the land of Mo'ab or the land of the Am'mo·nites, 16 but when they came up from Egypt, Israel went through the wilderness to the Red Sea and came to Ka'desh. 17 Israel then sent messengers to the king of E'dom, saying, 'Let us pass, we pray, through your land'; but the king of Edom would not listen. And they sent also to the king of Mo'ab, but he would not consent. So Israel remained in Ka'desh. 18 Then they journeyed through the wilderness, and went around the land of E'dom and the land of Mo'ab, and arrived on the east side of the land of Moab, and camped on the other side of the Ar'non; but they did not enter the territory of Moab, for the Arnon was the boundary of Moab. 19 Israel then sent messengers to Si'hon king of the Am'o·rites, king of Hesh'bon; and Israel said to him, 'Let us pass, we pray, through your land to our country.' 20 But Si'hon did not trust Israel to pass through his territory; so Sihon gathered all his people together, and encamped at Ja'haz, and fought with Israel. 21 And the LORD, the God of Israel, gave Si'hon and all his people into the hand of Israel, and they defeated them; so Israel took possession of all the land of the Am'o·rites, who inhabited that country. 22 And they took possession of all the territory of the Am'o·rites from the Ar'non to the Jab'bok and from the wilderness to the Jordan. 23 So then the LORD, the God of Israel, dispossessed the Am'o·rites from before his people Israel; and are you to take possession of them? 24 Will you not possess what Che'mosh your god gives you to possess? And all that the LORD our God has dispossessed before us, we will possess. 25 Now are you any better than Ba'lak the son of Zip'por, king of Mo'ab? Did he ever strive against Israel, or did he ever go to war with them? 26 While Israel dwelt in Hesh'bon and its villages, and in A·ro'er and its villages, and in all the cities that are on the banks of the Ar'non, three hundred years, why did you not recover them within that time? 27 I therefore have not sinned against you, and you do me wrong by making war on me; the LORD, the Judge, decide this day between the people of Israel and the people of Am'mon." 28 But the king of the Am'mo·nites did not heed the message of Jeph'thah which he sent to him.

29 Then the Spirit of the LORD came upon Jeph'thah, and he passed through Gilead and Ma·nas'seh, and passed on to Miz'pah of Gilead, and from Mizpah of Gilead he passed on to the Am'mo·nites. 30 And Jeph'thah made a vow to the LORD, and said, "If thou wilt give the Am'mo·nites into my hand, 31 then whoever comes forth from the doors of my house to meet me, when I return victorious from the Am'mo·nites, shall be the LORD's, and I will offer him up for a burnt offering." 32 So Jeph'thah crossed over to the Am'mo·nites to fight against them; and the LORD gave them into his hand. 33 And he smote them from A·ro'er to the neighborhood of Min'nith, twenty cities, and as far as A·bel-ker'a·mim, with a very great slaughter. So the Am'mo·nites were subdued before the people of Israel.

34 Then Jeph'thàh came to his home at Miz'pàh; and behold, his daughter came out to meet him with timbrels and with dances; she was his only child; beside her he had neither son nor daughter. 35And when he saw her, he rent his clothes, and said, "Alas, my daughter! you have brought me very low, and you have become the cause of great trouble to me; for I have opened my mouth to the LORD, and I cannot take back my vow." 36And she said to him, "My father, if you have opened your mouth to the LORD, do to me according to what has gone forth from your mouth, now that the LORD has avenged you on your enemies, on the Am'mo-nites." 37And she said to her father, "Let this thing be done for me; let me alone two months, that I may go and wander*p* on the mountains, and bewail my virginity, I and my companions." 38And he said, "Go." And he sent her away for two months; and she departed, she and her companions, and bewailed her virginity upon the mountains. 39And at the end of two months, she returned to her father, who did with her according to his vow which he had made. She had never known a man. And it became a custom in Israel 40 that the daughters of Israel went year by year to lament the daughter of Jeph'thàh the Gileadite four days in the year.

12 The men of E'phrà-im were called to arms, and they crossed to Zà'phon and said to Jeph'thàh, "Why did you cross over to fight against the Am'mo-nites, and did not call us to go with you? We will burn your house over you with fire." 2And Jeph'thàh said to them, "I and my people had a great feud with the Am'mo-nites; and when I called you, you did not deliver me from their hand. 3And when I saw that you would not deliver me, I took my life in my hand, and crossed over against the Am'mo-nites, and the LORD gave them into my hand; why then have you come up to me this day, to fight against me?" 4 Then Jeph'thàh gathered all the men of Gilead and fought with E'phrà-im; and the men of Gilead smote Ephraim, because they said, "You are fugitives of Ephraim, you Gileadites, in the midst of Ephraim and Mà-nas'sèh." 5And the Gileadites took the fords of the Jordan against the E'phrà-im-ites. And when any of the fugitives of E'phrà-im said, "Let me go over," the men of Gilead said to

him, "Are you an Ephraimite?" When he said, "No," 6 they said to him, "Then say Shib'bo-lêth," and he said, "Sib'bo-lêth," for he could not pronounce it right; then they seized him and slew him at the fords of the Jordan. And there fell at that time forty-two thousand of the E'phrà-im-ites.

7 Jeph'thàh judged Israel six years. Then Jephthah the Gileadite died, and was buried in his city in Gilead*q*.

8 After him Ib'zàn of Bethlehem judged Israel. 9 He had thirty sons; and thirty daughters he gave in marriage outside his clan, and thirty daughters he brought in from outside for his sons. And he judged Israel seven years. 10 Then Ib'zàn died, and was buried at Bethlehem.

11 After him E'lon the Zeb'u-lù-nite judged Israel; and he judged Israel ten years. 12 Then E'lon the Zeb'u-lù-nite died, and was buried at Äi'jà-lon in the land of Zeb'u-lùn.

13 After him Ab'don the son of Hil'lel the Pir'à-thô-nite judged Israel. 14 He had forty sons and thirty grandsons, who rode on seventy asses; and he judged Israel eight years. 15 Then Ab'don the son of Hil'lel the Pir'à-thô-nite died, and was buried at Pir'à-thon in the land of E'phrà-im, in the hill country of the Á-mal'é-kites.

13 And the people of Israel again did what was evil in the sight of the LORD; and the LORD gave them into the hand of the Philistines for forty years.

2 And there was a certain man of Zo'ràh, of the tribe of the Danites, whose name was Mà-nô'àh; and his wife was barren and had no children. 3And the angel of the LORD appeared to the woman and said to her, "Behold, you are barren and have no children; but you shall conceive and bear a son. 4 Therefore beware, and drink no wine or strong drink, and eat nothing unclean, 5 for lo, you shall conceive and bear a son. No razor shall come upon his head, for the boy shall be a Naz'i-rìte to God from birth; and he shall begin to deliver Israel from the hand of the Philistines." 6 Then the woman came and told her husband, "A man of God came to me, and his countenance was like the countenance of the angel of God, very terrible; I did not ask him whence he was, and he did not tell me his name; 7 but he said to me, 'Behold, you shall conceive and bear a son; so then drink no wine or strong drink, and eat

p Cn: Heb *go down*   *q* Gk: Heb *in the cities of Gilead*
13.4-5: Lk 1.15.

nothing unclean, for the boy shall be a Naz′i·rite to God from birth to the day of his death.' "

8 Then Mȧ·nō′ah entreated the LORD, and said, "O, LORD, I pray thee, let the man of God whom thou didst send come again to us, and teach us what we are to do with the boy that will be born." 9And God listened to the voice of Mȧ·nō′ah, and the angel of God came again to the woman as she sat in the field; but Manoah her husband was not with her. 10And the woman ran in haste and told her husband, "Behold, the man who came to me the other day has appeared to me." 11And Mȧ·nō′ah arose and went after his wife, and came to the man and said to him, "Are you the man who spoke to this woman?" And he said, "I am." 12And Mȧ·nō′ah said, "Now when your words come true, what is to be the boy's manner of life, and what is he to do?" 13And the angel of the LORD said to Mȧ·nō′ah, "Of all that I said to the woman let her beware. 14 She may not eat of anything that comes from the vine, neither let her drink wine or strong drink, or eat any unclean thing; all that I commanded her let her observe."

15 Mȧ·nō′ah said to the angel of the LORD, "Pray, let us detain you, and prepare a kid for you." 16And the angel of the LORD said to Mȧ·nō′ah, "If you detain me, I will not eat of your food; but if you make ready a burnt offering, then offer it to the LORD." (For Manoah did not know that he was the angel of the LORD.) 17And Mȧ·nō′ah said to the angel of the LORD, "What is your name, so that, when your words come true, we may honor you?" 18And the angel of the LORD said to him, "Why do you ask my name, seeing it is wonderful?" 19 So Mȧ·nō′ah took the kid with the cereal offering, and offered it upon the rock to the LORD, to him who works[r] wonders[s]. 20And when the flame went up toward heaven from the altar, the angel of the LORD ascended in the flame of the altar while Mȧ·nō′ah and his wife looked on; and they fell on their faces to the ground.

21 The angel of the LORD appeared no more to Mȧ·nō′ah and to his wife. Then Manoah knew that he was the angel of the LORD. 22And Mȧ·nō′ah said to his wife, "We shall surely die, for we have seen God." 23 But his wife said to him, "If the LORD had meant to kill us, he would not have accepted a burnt offering and a cereal offering

at our hands, or shown us all these things, or now announced to us such things as these." 24And the woman bore a son, and called his name Samson; and the boy grew, and the LORD blessed him. 25And the Spirit of the LORD began to stir him in Mā′hȧ·nḗh-dan, between Zō′rah and Esh′tā-ol.

14 Samson went down to Tim′nah, and at Timnah he saw one of the daughters of the Philistines. 2 Then he came up, and told his father and mother, "I saw one of the daughters of the Philistines at Tim′nah; now get her for me as my wife." 3 But his father and mother said to him, "Is there not a woman among the daughters of your kinsmen, or among all our people, that you must go to take a wife from the uncircumcised Philistines?" But Samson said to his father, "Get her for me; for she pleases me well."

4 His father and mother did not know that it was from the LORD; for he was seeking an occasion against the Philistines. At that time the Philistines had dominion over Israel.

5 Then Samson went down with his father and mother to Tim′nah, and he came to the vineyards of Timnah. And behold, a young lion roared against him; 6 and the Spirit of the LORD came mightily upon him, and he tore the lion asunder as one tears a kid; and he had nothing in his hand. But he did not tell his father or his mother what he had done. 7 Then he went down and talked with the woman; and she pleased Samson well. 8And after a while he returned to take her; and he turned aside to see the carcass of the lion, and behold, there was a swarm of bees in the body of the lion, and honey. 9 He scraped it out into his hands, and went on, eating as he went; and he came to his father and mother, and gave some to them, and they ate. But he did not tell them that he had taken the honey from the carcass of the lion.

10 And his father went down to the woman, and Samson made a feast there; for so the young men used to do. 11And when the people saw him, they brought thirty companions to be with him. 12And Samson said to them, "Let me now put a riddle to you; if you can tell me what it is, within the seven days of the feast, and find it out, then I will give you thirty linen garments and thirty festal garments; 13 but if you cannot tell me what it is, then you shall give me thirty linen

---

r Gk Vg: Heb *and working*   s Heb *wonders, while Manoah and his wife looked on*
13.24: Lk 2.40.

garments and thirty festal garments."
And they said to him, "Put your riddle,
that we may hear it." [14]And he said to
them,

"Out of the eater came something to
eat.
Out of the strong came something
sweet."

And they could not in three days tell
what the riddle was.

15 On the fourth[f] day they said to
Samson's wife, "Entice your husband
to tell us what the riddle is, lest we
burn you and your father's house with
fire. Have you invited us here to
impoverish us?" [16]And Samson's wife
wept before him, and said, "You only
hate me, you do not love me; you have
put a riddle to my countrymen, and
you have not told me what it is." And
he said to her, "Behold, I have not
told my father nor my mother, and
shall I tell you?" [17] She wept before
him the seven days that their feast
lasted; and on the seventh day he told
her, because she pressed him hard.
Then she told the riddle to her countrymen. [18]And the men of the city said to
him on the seventh day before the sun
went down,

"What is sweeter than honey?
What is stronger than a lion?"

And he said to them,

"If you had not plowed with my
heifer,
you would not have found out my
riddle."

[19]And the Spirit of the LORD came
mightily upon him, and he went down
to Ash'ke·lon and killed thirty men of
the town, and took their spoil and gave
the festal garments to those who had
told the riddle. In hot anger he went
back to his father's house. [20]And Samson's wife was given to his companion,
who had been his best man.

15 After a while, at the time of
wheat harvest, Samson went to
visit his wife with a kid; and he said,
"I will go in to my wife in the chamber." But her father would not allow
him to go in. [2]And her father said, "I
really thought that you utterly hated
her; so I gave her to your companion.
Is not her younger sister fairer than
she? Pray take her instead." [3]And Samson said to them, "This time I shall be
blameless in regard to the Philistines,
when I do them mischief." [4] So Samson went and caught three hundred
foxes, and took torches; and he turned
them tail to tail, and put a torch between each pair of tails. [5]And when
he had set fire to the torches, he let the
foxes go into the standing grain of
the Philistines, and burned up the
shocks and the standing grain, as well
as the olive orchards. [6] Then the
Philistines said, "Who has done this?"
And they said, "Samson, the son-in-
law of the Tim'nite, because he has
taken his wife and given her to his
companion." And the Philistines came
up, and burned her and her father with
fire. [7]And Samson said to them, "If
this is what you do, I swear I will be
avenged upon you, and after that I
will quit." [8]And he smote them hip
and thigh with great slaughter; and he
went down and stayed in the cleft of
the rock of E'tam.

9 Then the Philistines came up and
encamped in Judah, and made a raid
on Le'hi. [10]And the men of Judah
said, "Why have you come up against
us?" They said, "We have come up to
bind Samson, to do to him as he did
to us." [11] Then three thousand men
of Judah went down to the cleft of the
rock of E'tam, and said to Samson,
"Do you not know that the Philistines
are rulers over us? What then is this
that you have done to us?" And he
said to them, "As they did to me, so
have I done to them." [12]And they said
to him, "We have come down to bind
you, that we may give you into the
hands of the Philistines." And Samson
said to them, "Swear to me that you
will not fall upon me yourselves."
[13] They said to him, "No; we will only
bind you and give you into their hands;
we will not kill you." So they bound
him with two new ropes, and brought
him up from the rock.

14 When he came to Le'hi, the
Philistines came shouting to meet him;
and the Spirit of the LORD came
mightily upon him, and the ropes
which were on his arms became as
flax that has caught fire, and his bonds
melted off his hands. [15]And he found
a fresh jawbone of an ass, and put out
his hand and seized it, and with it he
slew a thousand men. [16]And Samson
said,

"With the jawbone of an ass,
heaps upon heaps,
with the jawbone of an ass
have I slain a thousand men."

[17] When he had finished speaking, he
threw away the jawbone out of his
hand; and that place was called
Ra'math-le'hi.[u]

18 And he was very thirsty, and he
called on the LORD and said, "Thou
hast granted this great deliverance by
the hand of thy servant; and shall I

---

[f] Gk Syr: Heb *seventh*   [u] That is *The hill of the jawbone*

now die of thirst, and fall into the hands of the uncircumcised?" ¹⁹And God split open the hollow place that is at Lē′hī, and there came water from it; and when he drank, his spirit returned, and he revived. Therefore the name of it was called En-hak-kōr′ē;ᵛ it is at Lehi to this day. ²⁰And he judged Israel in the days of the Philistines twenty years.

16 Samson went to Gä′zà, and there he saw a harlot, and he went in to her. ² The Gä′zites were told, "Samson has come here," and they surrounded the place and lay in wait for him all night at the gate of the city. They kept quiet all night, saying, "Let us wait till the light of the morning; then we will kill him." ³ But Samson lay till midnight, and at midnight he arose and took hold of the doors of the gate of the city and the two posts, and pulled them up, bar and all, and put them on his shoulders and carried them to the top of the hill that is before Hē′brŏn.

4 After this he loved a woman in the valley of Sō′rek, whose name was Dē·lī′làh. ⁵And the lords of the Philistines came to her and said to her, "Entice him, and see wherein his great strength lies, and by what means we may overpower him, that we may bind him to subdue him; and we will each give you eleven hundred pieces of silver." ⁶And Dē·lī′làh said to Samson, "Please tell me wherein your great strength lies, and how you might be bound, that one could subdue you." ⁷And Samson said to her, "If they bind me with seven fresh bowstrings which have not been dried, then I shall become weak, and be like any other man." ⁸ Then the lords of the Philistines brought her seven fresh bowstrings which had not been dried, and she bound him with them. ⁹ Now she had men lying in wait in an inner chamber. And she said to him, "The Philistines are upon you, Samson!" But he snapped the bowstrings, as a string of tow snaps when it touches the fire. So the secret of his strength was not known.

10 And Dē·lī′làh said to Samson, "Behold, you have mocked me, and told me lies; please tell me how you might be bound." ¹¹And he said to her, "If they bind me with new ropes that have not been used, then I shall become weak, and be like any other man." ¹² So Dē·lī′làh took new ropes and bound him with them, and said to

him, "The Philistines are upon you, Samson!" And the men lying in wait were in an inner chamber. But he snapped the ropes off his arms like a thread.

13 And Dē·lī′làh said to Samson, "Until now you have mocked me, and told me lies; tell me how you might be bound." And he said to her, "If you weave the seven locks of my head with the web and make it tight with the pin, then I shall become weak, and be like any other man." ¹⁴ So while he slept, Dē·lī′làh took the seven locks of his head and wove them into the web.ʷ And she made them tight with the pin, and said to him, "The Philistines are upon you, Samson!" But he awoke from his sleep, and pulled away the pin, the loom, and the web.

15 And she said to him, "How can you say, 'I love you,' when your heart is not with me? You have mocked me these three times, and you have not told me wherein your great strength lies." ¹⁶And when she pressed him hard with her words day after day, and urged him, his soul was vexed to death. ¹⁷And he told her all his mind, and said to her, "A razor has never come upon my head; for I have been a Naz′i·rīte to God from my mother's womb. If I be shaved, then my strength will leave me, and I shall become weak, and be like any other man."

18 When Dē·lī′làh saw that he had told her all his mind, she sent and called the lords of the Philistines, saying, "Come up this once, for he has told me all his mind." Then the lords of the Philistines came up to her, and brought the money in their hands. ¹⁹ She made him sleep upon her knees; and she called a man, and had him shave off the seven locks of his head. Then she began to torment him, and his strength left him. ²⁰And she said, "The Philistines are upon you, Samson!" And he awoke from his sleep, and said, "I will go out as at other times, and shake myself free." And he did not know that the LORD had left him. ²¹And the Philistines seized him and gouged out his eyes, and brought him down to Gä′zà, and bound him with bronze fetters; and he ground at the mill in the prison. ²² But the hair of his head began to grow again after it had been shaved.

23 Now the lords of the Philistines gathered to offer a great sacrifice to Dä′gon their god, and to rejoice; for they said, "Our god has given Samson

ᵛ That is *The spring of him who called*
ʷ Compare Gk: Heb lacks *and make it tight . . . into the web*

our enemy into our hand." ²⁴And when the people saw him, they praised their god; for they said, "Our god has given our enemy into our hand, the ravager of our country, who has slain many of us." ²⁵And when their hearts were merry, they said, "Call Samson, that he may make sport for us." So they called Samson out of the prison, and he made sport before them. They made him stand between the pillars; ²⁶ and Samson said to the lad who held him by the hand, "Let me feel the pillars on which the house rests, that I may lean against them." ²⁷ Now the house was full of men and women; all the lords of the Philistines were there, and on the roof there were about three thousand men and women, who looked on while Samson made sport.

²⁸ Then Samson called to the LORD and said, "O Lord GOD, remember me, I pray thee, and strengthen me, I pray thee, only this once, O God, that I may be avenged upon the Philistines for one of my two eyes." ²⁹And Samson grasped the two middle pillars upon which the house rested, and he leaned his weight upon them, his right hand on the one and his left hand on the other. ³⁰And Samson said, "Let me die with the Philistines." Then he bowed with all his might; and the house fell upon the lords and upon all the people that were in it. So the dead whom he slew at his death were more than those whom he had slain during his life. ³¹ Then his brothers and all his family came down and took him and brought him up and buried him between Zō′rah and Esh′tā-ol in the tomb of Mà·nō′áh his father. He had judged Israel twenty years.

17 There was a man of the hill country of E′phrà·im, whose name was Mi′càh. ²And he said to his mother, "The eleven hundred pieces of silver which were taken from you, about which you uttered a curse, and also spoke it in my ears, behold, the silver is with me; I took it." And his mother said, "Blessed be my son by the LORD." ³And he restored the eleven hundred pieces of silver to his mother; and his mother said, "I consecrate the silver to the LORD from my hand for my son, to make a graven image and a molten image; now therefore I will restore it to you." ⁴ So when he restored the money to his mother, his mother took two hundred pieces of silver, and gave it to the silversmith, who made it into a graven image and a

molten image; and it was in the house of Mi′càh. ⁵And the man Mi′càh had a shrine, and he made an ephod and teraphim, and installed one of his sons, who became his priest. ⁶ In those days there was no king in Israel; every man did what was right in his own eyes.

⁷ Now there was a young man of Bethlehem in Judah, of the family of Judah, who was a Levite; and he sojourned there. ⁸And the man departed from the town of Bethlehem in Judah, to live where he could find a place; and as he journeyed, he came to the hill country of E′phrà·im to the house of Mi′càh. ⁹And Mi′càh said to him, "From where do you come?" And he said to him, "I am a Levite of Bethlehem in Judah, and I am going to sojourn where I may find a place." ¹⁰And Mi′càh said to him, "Stay with me, and be to me a father and a priest, and I will give you ten pieces of silver a year, and a suit of apparel, and your living."^w ¹¹And the Levite was content to dwell with the man; and the young man became to him like one of his sons. ¹²And Mi′càh installed the Levite, and the young man became his priest, and was in the house of Mi′càh. ¹³ Then Mi′càh said, "Now I know that the LORD will prosper me, because I have a Levite as priest."

18 In those days there was no king in Israel. And in those days the tribe of the Danites was seeking for itself an inheritance to dwell in; for until then no inheritance among the tribes of Israel had fallen to them. ² So the Danites sent five able men from the whole number of their tribe, from Zō′rah and from Esh′tā-ol, to spy out the land and to explore it; and they said to them, "Go and explore the land." And they came to the hill country of E′phrà·im, to the house of Mi′càh, and lodged there. ³ When they were by the house of Mi′càh, they recognized the voice of the young Levite; and they turned aside and said to him, "Who brought you here? What are you doing in this place? What is your business here?" ⁴And he said to them, "Thus and thus has Mi′càh dealt with me: he has hired me, and I have become his priest." ⁵And they said to him, "Inquire of God, we pray thee, that we may know whether the journey on which we are setting out will succeed." ⁶And the priest said to them, "Go in peace. The journey on which you go is under the eye of the LORD."

⁷ Then the five men departed, and

---

^w Heb *living, and the Levite went*   **18.7:** Judg 18.27-28.

came to Lā'ish, and saw the people who were there, how they dwelt in security, after the manner of the Si-dō'ni·anṣ, quiet and unsuspecting, lacking[x] nothing that is in the earth, and possessing wealth, and how they were far from the Sidonians and had no dealings with any one. [8]And when they came to their brethren at Zō'rah and Esh'tā-ol, their brethren said to them, "What do you report?" [9] They said, "Arise, and let us go up against them; for we have seen the land, and behold, it is very fertile. And will you do nothing? Do not be slow to go, and enter in and possess the land. [10] When you go, you will come to an unsuspecting people. The land is broad; yea, God has given it into your hands, a place where there is no lack of anything that is in the earth."

[11] And six hundred men of the tribe of Dan, armed with weapons of war, set forth from Zō'rah and Esh'tā-ol, [12] and went up and encamped at Kīr'i·ath-jē'a·rim in Judah. On this account that place is called Mā'hā-nēh-dan[y] to this day; behold, it is west of Kiriath-jearim. [13]And they passed on from there to the hill country of E'phra·im, and came to the house of Mi'cáh.

[14] Then the five men who had gone to spy out the country of Lā'ish said to their brethren, "Do you know that in these houses there are an ephod, tera-phim, a graven image, and a molten image? Now therefore consider what you will do." [15]And they turned aside thither, and came to the house of the young Levite, at the home of Mi'cáh, and asked him of his welfare. [16] Now the six hundred men of the Danites, armed with their weapons of war, stood by the entrance of the gate; [17] and the five men who had gone to spy out the land went up, and entered and took the graven image, the ephod, the teraphim, and the molten image, while the priest stood by the entrance of the gate with the six hundred men armed with weapons of war. [18]And when these went into Mi'cáh's house and took the graven image, the ephod, the teraphim, and the molten image, the priest said to them, "What are you doing?" [19]And they said to him, "Keep quiet, put your hand upon your mouth, and come with us, and be to us a father and a priest. Is it better for you to be priest to the house of one man, or to be priest to a tribe and family in Israel?" [20]And the priest's

heart was glad; he took the ephod, and the teraphim, and the graven image, and went in the midst of the people.

[21] So they turned and departed, putting the little ones and the cattle and the goods in front of them. [22] When they were a good way from the home of Mi'cáh, the men who were in the houses near Micah's house were called out, and they overtook the Danites. [23]And they shouted to the Danites, who turned round and said to Mi'cáh, "What ails you that you come with such a company?" [24]And he said, "You take my gods which I made, and the priest, and go away, and what have I left? How then do you ask me, 'What ails you?' " [25]And the Danites said to him, "Do not let your voice be heard among us, lest angry fellows fall upon you, and you lose your life with the lives of your household." [26] Then the Danites went their way; and when Mi'cáh saw that they were too strong for him, he turned and went back to his home.

[27] And taking what Mi'cáh had made, and the priest who belonged to him, the Danites came to Lā'ish, to a people quiet and unsuspecting, and smote them with the edge of the sword, and burned the city with fire. [28]And there was no deliverer because it was far from Si'don, and they had no dealings with any one. It was in the valley which belongs to Beth-rē'hob. And they rebuilt the city, and dwelt in it. [29]And they named the city Dan, after the name of Dan their ancestor, who was born to Israel; but the name of the city was Lā'ish at the first. [30]And the Danites set up the graven image for themselves; and Jonathan the son of Gēr'shŏm, son of Moses,[z] and his sons were priests to the tribe of the Danites until the day of the captivity of the land. [31] So they set up Mi'cáh's graven image which he made, as long as the house of God was at Shī'lōh.

19 In those days, when there was no king in Israel, a certain Levite was sojourning in the remote parts of the hill country of E'phra·im, who took to himself a concubine from Bethlehem in Judah. [2]And his concubine became angry with[a] him, and she went away from him to her father's house at Bethlehem in Judah, and was there some four months. [3] Then her husband arose and went after her, to speak kindly to her and bring her back. He had with him his servant and

[x] Cn Compare 18.10. The Hebrew text is uncertain   [y] That is *Camp of Dan*
[z] Another reading is *Manasseh*   [a] Gk Old Latin: Heb *played the harlot against*

a couple of asses. And he came[b] to her father's house; and when the girl's father saw him, he came with joy to meet him. [4]And his father-in-law, the girl's father, made him stay, and he remained with him three days; so they ate and drank, and lodged there. [5]And on the fourth day they arose early in the morning, and he prepared to go; but the girl's father said to his son-in-law, "Strengthen your heart with a morsel of bread, and after that you may go." [6] So the two men sat and ate and drank together; and the girl's father said to the man, "Be pleased to spend the night, and let your heart be merry." [7]And when the man rose up to go, his father-in-law urged him, till he lodged there again. [8]And on the fifth day he arose early in the morning to depart; and the girl's father said, "Strengthen your heart, and tarry until the day declines." So they ate, both of them. [9]And when the man and his concubine and his servant rose up to depart, his father-in-law, the girl's father, said to him, "Behold, now the day has waned toward evening; pray tarry all night. Behold, the day draws to its close; lodge here and let your heart be merry; and tomorrow you shall arise early in the morning for your journey, and go home."

[10] But the man would not spend the night; he rose up and departed, and arrived opposite Jébus (that is, Jerusalem). He had with him a couple of saddled asses, and his concubine was with him. [11] When they were near Jébus, the day was far spent, and the servant said to his master, "Come now, let us turn aside to this city of the Jebúsites, and spend the night in it." [12]And his master said to him, "We will not turn aside into the city of foreigners, who do not belong to the people of Israel; but we will pass on to Gibéah." [13]And he said to his servant, "Come and let us draw near to one of these places, and spend the night at Gibéah or at Rámah." [14] So they passed on and went their way; and the sun went down on them near Gibéah, which belongs to Benjamin. [15] and they turned aside there, to go in and spend the night at Gibéah. And he went in and sat down in the open square of the city; for no man took them into his house to spend the night.

[16] And behold, an old man was coming from his work in the field at evening; the man was from the hill country of Éphráim, and he was so-

journing in Gibéah; the men of the place were Benjaminites. [17]And he lifted up his eyes, and saw the wayfarer in the open square of the city; and the old man said, "Where are you going? and whence do you come?" [18]And he said to him, "We are passing from Bethlehem in Judah to the remote parts of the hill country of Éphráim, from which I come. I went to Bethlehem in Judah; and I am going to my home;[c] and nobody takes me into his house. [19] We have straw and provender for our asses, with bread and wine for me and your maidservant and the young man with your servants; there is no lack of anything." [20]And the old man said, "Peace be to you; I will care for all your wants; only, do not spend the night in the square." [21] So he brought him into his house, and gave the asses provender; and they washed their feet, and ate and drank.

[22] As they were making their hearts merry, behold, the men of the city, base fellows, beset the house round about, beating on the door; and they said to the old man, the master of the house, "Bring out the man who came into your house, that we may know him." [23]And the man, the master of the house, went out to them and said to them, "No, my brethren, do not act so wickedly; seeing that this man has come into my house, do not do this vile thing. [24] Behold, here are my virgin daughter and his concubine; let me bring them out now. Ravish them and do with them what seems good to you; but against this man do not do so vile a thing." [25] But the men would not listen to him. So the man seized his concubine, and put her out to them; and they knew her, and abused her all night until the morning. And as the dawn began to break, they let her go. [26]And as morning appeared, the woman came and fell down at the door of the man's house where her master was, till it was light.

[27] And her master rose up in the morning, and when he opened the doors of the house and went out to go on his way, behold, there was his concubine lying at the door of the house, with her hands on the threshold. [28] He said to her, "Get up, let us be going." But there was no answer. Then he put her upon the ass; and the man rose up and went away to his home. [29]And when he entered his house, he took a knife, and laying hold of his concubine he divided her, limb by limb, into twelve pieces, and sent

b Gk: Heb *she brought him*   *c* Gk Compare 19.29. Heb *to the house of the* LORD

her throughout all the territory of Israel. 30And all who saw it said, "Such a thing has never happened or been seen from the day that the people of Israel came up out of the land of Egypt until this day; consider it, take counsel, and speak."

20 Then all the people of Israel came out, from Dan to Beer-sheba, including the land of Gilead, and the congregation assembled as one man to the LORD at Miz′pah. 2And the chiefs of all the people, of all the tribes of Israel, presented themselves in the assembly of the people of God, four hundred thousand men on foot that drew the sword. 3 (Now the Benjaminites heard that the people of Israel had gone up to Miz′pah.) And the people of Israel said, "Tell us, how was this wickedness brought to pass?" 4And the Levite, the husband of the woman who was murdered, answered and said, "I came to Gib′e-ah that belongs to Benjamin, I and my concubine, to spend the night. 5And the men of Gib′e-ah rose against me, and beset the house round about me by night; they meant to kill me, and they ravished my concubine, and she is dead. 6And I took my concubine and cut her in pieces, and sent her throughout all the country of the inheritance of Israel; for they have committed abomination and wantonness in Israel. 7 Behold, you people of Israel, all of you, give your advice and counsel here."

8 And all the people arose as one man, saying, "We will not any of us go to his tent, and none of us will return to his house. 9 But now this is what we will do to Gib′e-ah: we will go up against it by lot, 10 and we will take ten men of a hundred throughout all the tribes of Israel, and a hundred of a thousand, and a thousand of ten thousand, to bring provisions for the people, that when they come they may requite Gib′e-ah of Benjamin, for all the wanton crime which they have committed in Israel." 11 So all the men of Israel gathered against the city, united as one man.

12 And the tribes of Israel sent men through all the tribe of Benjamin, saying, "What wickedness is this that has taken place among you? 13 Now therefore give up the men, the base fellows in Gib′e-ah, that we may put them to death, and put away evil from Israel." But the Benjaminites would not listen to the voice of their brethren, the people of Israel. 14And the Benjaminites came together out of the cities to Gib′e-ah, to go out to battle against

the people of Israel. 15And the Benjaminites mustered out of their cities on that day twenty-six thousand men that drew the sword, besides the inhabitants of Gib′e-ah, who mustered seven hundred picked men. 16Among all these were seven hundred picked men who were left-handed; every one could sling a stone at a hair, and not miss; 17And the men of Israel, apart from Benjamin, mustered four hundred thousand men that drew sword; all these were men of war.

18 The people of Israel arose and went up to Beth′el, and inquired of God, "Which of us shall go up first to battle against the Benjaminites?" And the LORD said, "Judah shall go up first."

19 Then the people of Israel rose in the morning, and encamped against Gib′e-ah. 20And the men of Israel went out to battle against Benjamin; and the men of Israel drew up the battle line against them at Gib′e-ah. 21 The Benjaminites came out of Gib′e-ah, and felled to the ground on that day twenty-two thousand men of the Israelites. 22 But the people, the men of Israel, took courage, and again formed the battle line in the same place where they had formed it on the first day. 23And the people of Israel went up and wept before the LORD until the evening; and they inquired of the LORD, "Shall we again draw near to battle against our brethren the Benjaminites?" And the LORD said, "Go up against them."

24 So the people of Israel came near against the Benjaminites the second day. 25And Benjamin went against them out of Gib′e-ah the second day, and felled to the ground eighteen thousand men of the people of Israel; all these were men who drew the sword. 26 Then all the people of Israel, the whole army, went up and came to Beth′el and wept; they sat there before the LORD, and fasted that day until evening, and offered burnt offerings and peace offerings before the LORD. 27And the people of Israel inquired of the LORD (for the ark of the covenant of God was there in those days, 28 and Phin′e-has the son of El-e-a′zar, son of Aaron, ministered before it in those days), saying, "Shall we yet again go out to battle against our brethren the Benjaminites, or shall we cease?" And the LORD said, "Go up; for tomorrow I will give them into your hand."

29 So Israel set men in ambush round about Gib′e-ah. 30And the people of Israel went up against the Ben-

jaminites on the third day, and set themselves in array against Gib′ē-àh, as at other times. 31And the Benjaminites went out against the people, and were drawn away from the city; and as at other times they began to smite and kill some of the people, in the highways, one of which goes up to Beth′el and the other to Gib′ē-àh, and in the open country, about thirty men of Israel. 32And the Benjaminites said, "They are routed before us, as at the first." But the men of Israel said, "Let us flee, and draw them away from the city to the highways." 33And all the men of Israel rose up out of their place, and set themselves in array at Bā′al-tā′mär; and the men of Israel who were in ambush rushed out of their place west*d* of Gē′bà. 34And there came against Gib′ē-àh ten thousand picked men out of all Israel, and the battle was hard; but the Benjaminites did not know that disaster was close upon them. 35And the LORD defeated Benjamin before Israel; and the men of Israel destroyed twenty-five thousand one hundred men of Benjamin that day; all these were men who drew the sword. 36 So the Benjaminites saw that they were defeated.

The men of Israel gave ground to Benjamin, because they trusted to the men in ambush whom they had set against Gib′ē-àh. 37And the men in ambush made haste and rushed upon Gib′ē-àh; the men in ambush moved out and smote all the city with the edge of the sword. 38 Now the appointed signal between the men of Israel and the men in ambush was that when they made a great cloud of smoke rise up out of the city 39 the men of Israel should turn in battle. Now Benjamin had begun to smite and kill about thirty men of Israel; they said, "Surely they are smitten down before us, as in the first battle." 40 But when the signal began to rise out of the city in a column of smoke, the Benjaminites looked behind them; and behold, the whole of the city went up in smoke to heaven. 41 Then the men of Israel turned, and the men of Benjamin were dismayed, for they saw that disaster was close upon them. 42 Therefore they turned their backs before the men of Israel in the direction of the wilderness; but the battle overtook them, and those who came out of the cities destroyed them in the midst of them. 43 Cutting down*e* the Benjaminites, they pursued them and trod them down from Nō′hàh*f* as far as opposite

Gib′ē-àh on the east. 44 Eighteen thousand men of Benjamin fell, all of them men of valor. 45And they turned and fled toward the wilderness to the rock of Rim′mon; five thousand men of them were cut down in the highways, and they were pursued hard to Gi′dom, and two thousand men of them were slain. 46 So all who fell that day of Benjamin were twenty-five thousand men that drew the sword, all of them men of valor. 47 But six hundred men turned and fled toward the wilderness to the rock of Rim′mon, and abode at the rock of Rimmon four months. 48And the men of Israel turned back against the Benjaminites, and smote them with the edge of the sword, men and beasts and all that they found. And all the towns which they found they set on fire.

21 Now the men of Israel had sworn at Miz′pàh, "No one of us shall give his daughter in marriage to Benjamin." 2And the people came to Beth′el, and sat there till evening before God, and they lifted up their voices and wept bitterly. 3And they said, "O LORD, the God of Israel, why has this come to pass in Israel, that there should be today one tribe lacking in Israel?" 4And on the morrow the people rose early, and built there an altar, and offered burnt offerings and peace offerings. 5And the people of Israel said, "Which of all the tribes of Israel did not come up in the assembly to the LORD?" For they had taken a great oath concerning him who did not come up to the LORD to Miz′pàh, saying, "He shall be put to death." 6And the people of Israel had compassion for Benjamin their brother, and said, "One tribe is cut off from Israel this day. 7 What shall we do for wives for those who are left, since we have sworn by the LORD that we will not give them any of our daughters for wives?"

8 And they said, "What one is there of the tribes of Israel that did not come up to the LORD to Miz′pàh?" And behold, no one had come to the camp from Jā′besh-gil′ē-àd, to the assembly. 9 For when the people were mustered, behold, not one of the inhabitants of Jā′besh-gil′ē-àd was there. 10 So the congregation sent thither twelve thousand of their bravest men, and commanded them, "Go and smite the inhabitants of Jā′besh-gil′ē-àd with the edge of the sword; also the women and the little ones. 11 This is what you shall do; every male and every woman

d Gk Vg: Heb *in the plain*   *e* Gk: Heb *surrounding*   *f* Gk: Heb (*at their*) *resting place*

that has lain with a male you shall utterly destroy." [12]And they found among the inhabitants of Jā′besh-gil′e̱·ảd four hundred young virgins who had not known man by lying with him; and they brought them to the camp at Shī′lōh, which is in the land of Canaan.

[13] Then the whole congregation sent word to the Benjaminites who were at the rock of Rim′mon, and proclaimed peace to them. [14]And Benjamin returned at that time; and they gave them the women whom they had saved alive of the women of Jā′besh-gil′e̱·ảd; but they did not suffice for them. [15]And the people had compassion on Benjamin because the LORD had made a breach in the tribes of Israel.

[16] Then the elders of the congregation said, "What shall we do for wives for those who are left, since the women are destroyed out of Benjamin?" [17]And they said, "There must be an inheritance for the survivors of Benjamin, that a tribe be not blotted out from Israel. [18] Yet we cannot give them wives of our daughters." For the people of Israel had sworn, "Cursed be he who gives a wife to Benjamin." [19] So they said, "Behold, there is the yearly feast of the LORD at Shī′lōh, which is north of Beth′ĕl, on the east of the highway that goes up from Bethel to Shē′chem, and south of Lĕ·bō′nảh." [20]And they commanded the Benjaminites, saying, "Go and lie in wait in the vineyards, [21] and watch; if the daughters of Shī′lōh come out to dance in the dances, then come out of the vineyards and seize each man his wife from the daughters of Shiloh, and go to the land of Benjamin. [22]And when their fathers or their brothers come to complain to us, we will say to them, 'Grant them graciously to us; because we did not take for each man of them his wife in battle, neither did you give them to them, else you would now be guilty.' " [23]And the Benjaminites did so, and took their wives, according to their number, from the dancers whom they carried off; then they went and returned to their inheritance, and rebuilt the towns, and dwelt in them. [24]And the people of Israel departed from there at that time, every man to his tribe and family, and they went out from there every man to his inheritance.

[25] In those days there was no king in Israel; every man did what was right in his own eyes.

THE BOOK OF

RUTH

[1] In the days when the judges ruled there was a famine in the land, and a certain man of Bethlehem in Judah went to sojourn in the country of Mō′ab, he and his wife and his two sons. [2] The name of the man was Ė·lim′e̱·lech and the name of his wife Nā′ŏ·mĭ, and the names of his two sons were Mäh′lon and Chil′ĭ·ŏn; they were Eph′rȧ·thĭtes from Bethlehem in Judah. They went into the country of Mō′ab and remained there. [3] But Ė·lim′e̱·lech, the husband of Nā′ŏ·mĭ, died, and she was left with her two sons. [4] These took Mō′ab·ĭte wives; the name of the one was Ŏr′pảh and the name of the other Ruth. They lived there about ten years; [5] and both Mäh′lon and Chil′ĭ·ŏn died, so that the woman was bereft of her two sons and her husband.

[6] Then she started with her daughters-in-law to return from the country of Mō′ab, for she had heard in the country of Moab that the LORD had visited his people and given them food. [7] So she set out from the place where she was, with her two daughters-in-law, and they went on the way to return to the land of Judah. [8] But Nā′ŏ·mĭ said to her two daughters-in-law, "Go, return each of you to her mother's house. May the LORD deal kindly with you, as you have dealt with the dead and with me. [9] The LORD grant that you may find a home, each of you in the house of her husband!" Then she kissed them, and they lifted up their voices and wept. [10]And they said to her, "No, we will return with you to your people." [11] But Nā′ŏ·mĭ said, "Turn back, my daughters, why

will you go with me? Have I yet sons in my womb that they may become your husbands? 12 Turn back, my daughters, go your way, for I am too old to have a husband. If I should say I have hope, even if I should have a husband this night and should bear sons, 13 would you therefore wait till they were grown? Would you therefore refrain from marrying? No, my daughters, for it is exceedingly bitter to me for your sake that the hand of the LORD has gone forth against me." 14 Then they lifted up their voices and wept again; and Ôr'pàh kissed her mother-in-law, but Ruth clung to her.

15 And she said, "See, your sister-in-law has gone back to her people and to her gods; return after your sister-in-law." 16 But Ruth said, "Entreat me not to leave you or to return from following you; for where you go I will go, and where you lodge I will lodge; your people shall be my people, and your God my God; 17 where you die I will die, and there will I be buried. May the LORD do so to me and more also if even death parts me from you." 18 And when Nā'ŏ·mī saw that she was determined to go with her, she said no more.

19 So the two of them went on until they came to Bethlehem. And when they came to Bethlehem, the whole town was stirred because of them; and the women said, "Is this Nā'ŏ·mī?" 20 She said to them, "Do not call me Nā'ŏ·mī,[a] call me Mâr'â,[b] for the Almighty has dealt very bitterly with me. 21 I went away full, and the LORD has brought me back empty. Why call me Nā'ŏ·mī, when the LORD has afflicted[c] me and the Almighty has brought calamity upon me?"

22 So Nā'ŏ·mī returned, and Ruth the Mō'àb·ĭt·ĕss her daughter-in-law with her, who returned from the country of Mō'àb. And they came to Bethlehem at the beginning of barley harvest.

2 Now Nā'ŏ·mī had a kinsman of her husband's, a man of wealth, of the family of Ē·lim'ĕ·lech, whose name was Bō'az. 2 And Ruth the Mō'àb·ĭt·ĕss said to Nā'ŏ·mī, "Let me go to the field, and glean among the ears of grain after him in whose sight I shall find favor." And she said to her, "Go, my daughter." 3 So she set forth and went and gleaned in the field after the reapers; and she happened to come to the part of the field belonging to Bō'az, who was of the family of Ē·lim'ĕ·lech.

4 And behold, Bō'az came from Bethlehem; and he said to the reapers, "The LORD be with you!" And they answered, "The LORD bless you." 5 Then Bō'az said to his servant who was in charge of the reapers, "Whose maiden is this?" 6 And the servant who was in charge of the reapers answered, "It is the Mō'àb·ite maiden, who came back with Nā'ŏ·mī from the country of Mō'àb. 7 She said, 'Pray, let me glean and gather among the sheaves after the reapers.' So she came, and she has continued from early morning until now, without resting even for a moment."[d]

8 Then Bō'az said to Ruth, "Now, listen, my daughter, do not go to glean in another field or leave this one, but keep close to my maidens. 9 Let your eyes be upon the field which they are reaping, and go after them. Have I not charged the young men not to molest you? And when you are thirsty, go to the vessels and drink what the young men have drawn." 10 Then she fell on her face, bowing to the ground, and said to him, "Why have I found favor in your eyes, that you should take notice of me, when I am a foreigner?" 11 But Bō'az answered her, "All that you have done for your mother-in-law since the death of your husband has been fully told me, and how you left your father and mother and your native land and came to a people that you did not know before. 12 The LORD recompense you for what you have done, and a full reward be given you by the LORD, the God of Israel, under whose wings you have come to take refuge!" 13 Then she said, "You are most gracious to me, my lord, for you have comforted me and spoken kindly to your maidservant, though I am not one of your maidservants."

14 And at mealtime Bō'az said to her, "Come here, and eat some bread, and dip your morsel in the wine." So she sat beside the reapers, and he passed to her parched grain; and she ate until she was satisfied, and she had some left over. 15 When she rose to glean, Bō'az instructed his young men, saying, "Let her glean even among the sheaves, and do not reproach her. 16 And also pull out some from the bundles for her, and leave it for her to glean, and do not rebuke her."

17 So she gleaned in the field until evening; then she beat out what she had gleaned, and it was about an ephah of barley. 18 And she took it up and

a That is *Pleasant*   b That is *Bitter*   c Gk Syr Vg: Heb *testified against*
d Compare Gk Vg: the meaning of the Hebrew text is uncertain

went into the city; she showed her mother-in-law what she had gleaned, and she also brought out and gave her what food she had left over after being satisfied. 19And her mother-in-law said to her, "Where did you glean today? And where have you worked? Blessed be the man who took notice of you." So she told her mother-in-law with whom she had worked, and said, "The man's name with whom I worked today is Bō´az." 20And Nā´ŏ·mī said to her daughter-in-law, "Blessed be he by the LORD, whose kindness has not forsaken the living or the dead!" Naomi also said to her, "The man is a relative of ours, one of our nearest kin." 21And Ruth the Mō´ăb·īt·ĕss said, "Besides, he said to me, 'You shall keep close by my servants, till they have finished all my harvest.'" 22And Nā´ŏ·mī said to Ruth, her daughter-in-law, "It is well, my daughter, that you go out with his maidens, lest in another field you be molested." 23 So she kept close to the maidens of Bō´az, gleaning until the end of the barley and wheat harvests; and she lived with her mother-in-law.

3 Then Nā´ŏ·mī her mother-in-law said to her, "My daughter, should I not seek a home for you, that it may be well with you? 2 Now is not Bō´az our kinsman, with whose maidens you were? See, he is winnowing barley tonight at the threshing floor. 3 Wash therefore and anoint yourself, and put on your best clothes and go down to the threshing floor; but do not make yourself known to the man until he has finished eating and drinking. 4 But when he lies down, observe the place where he lies; then, go and uncover his feet and lie down; and he will tell you what to do." 5And she replied, "All that you say I will do."

6 So she went down to the threshing floor and did just as her mother-in-law had told her. 7And when Bō´az had eaten and drunk, and his heart was merry, he went to lie down at the end of the heap of grain. Then she came softly, and uncovered his feet, and lay down. 8At midnight the man was startled, and turned over, and behold, a woman lay at his feet! 9 He said, "Who are you?" And she answered, "I am Ruth, your maidservant; spread your skirt over your maidservant, for you are next of kin." 10And he said, "May you be blessed by the LORD, my daughter; you have made this last kindness greater than the first, in that

you have not gone after young men, whether poor or rich. 11And now, my daughter, do not fear, I will do for you all that you ask, for all my fellow townsmen know that you are a woman of worth. 12And now it is true that I am a near kinsman, yet there is a kinsman nearer than I. 13 Remain this night, and in the morning, if he will do the part of the next of kin for you, well; let him do it; but if he is not willing to do the part of the next of kin for you, then, as the LORD lives, I will do the part of the next of kin for you. Lie down until the morning."

14 So she lay at his feet until the morning, but arose before one could recognize another; and he said, "Let it not be known that the woman came to the threshing floor." 15And he said, "Bring the mantle you are wearing and hold it out." So she held it, and he measured out six measures of barley, and laid it upon her; then she went into the city. 16And when she came to her mother-in-law, she said, "How did you fare, my daughter?" Then she told her all that the man had done for her, 17 saying, "These six measures of barley he gave to me, for he said, 'You must not go back empty-handed to your mother-in-law.'" 18 She replied, "Wait, my daughter, until you learn how the matter turns out, for the man will not rest, but will settle the matter today."

4 And Bō´az went up to the gate and sat down there; and, behold, the next of kin, of whom Boaz had spoken, came by. So Boaz said, "Turn aside, friend; sit down here"; and he turned aside and sat down. 2And he took ten men of the elders of the city, and said, "Sit down here"; so they sat down. 3Then he said to the next of kin, "Nā´ŏ·mī, who has come back from the country of Mō´ab, is selling the parcel of land which belonged to our kinsman Ē·lim´ĕ·lech. 4 So I thought I would tell you of it, and say, Buy it in the presence of those sitting here, and in the presence of the elders of my people. If you will redeem it, redeem it; but if you will not, tell me, that I may know, for there is no one besides you to redeem it, and I come after you." And he said, "I will redeem it." 5 Then Bō´az said, "The day you buy the field from the hand of Nā´ŏ·mī, you are also buying Ruth*e* the Mō´ăb·īt·ĕss, the widow of the dead, in order to restore the name of the dead to his inheritance." 6 Then the next of kin said, "I cannot redeem it for myself,

e Old Latin Vg: Heb *of Naomi and from Ruth*

lest I impair my own inheritance. Take my right of redemption yourself, for I cannot redeem it."

7 Now this was the custom in former times in Israel concerning redeeming and exchanging: to confirm a transaction, the one drew off his sandal and gave it to the other, and this was the manner of attesting in Israel. 8 So when the next of kin said to Bō′az, "Buy it for yourself," he drew off his sandal. 9 Then Bō′az said to the elders and all the people, "You are witnesses this day that I have bought from the hand of Nā′ö·mi all that belonged to Ē·lim′é·lech and all that belonged to Chil′i·ön and to Mäh′lon. 10Also Ruth the Mō′ab·it·ėss, the widow of Mäh′lon, I have bought to be my wife, to perpetuate the name of the dead in his inheritance, that the name of the dead may not be cut off from among his brethren and from the gate of his native place; you are witnesses this day." 11 Then all the people who were at the gate, and the elders, said, "We are witnesses. May the LORD make the woman, who is coming into your house, like Rachel and Leah, who together built up the house of Israel. May you prosper in Eph′rá·thàh and be re-

nowned in Bethlehem; 12 and may your house be like the house of Per′ez, whom Tā′mär bore to Judah, because of the children that the LORD will give you by this young woman."

13 So Bō′az took Ruth and she became his wife; and he went into her, and the LORD gave her conception, and she bore a son. 14 Then the women said to Nā′ö·mi, "Blessed be the LORD, who has not left you this day without next of kin; and may his name be renowned in Israel! 15 He shall be to you a restorer of life and a nourisher of your old age; for your daughter-in-law who loves you, who is more to you than seven sons, has borne him." 16 Then Nā′ö·mi took the child and laid him in her bosom, and became his nurse. 17And the women of the neighborhood gave him a name, saying, "A son has been born to Nā′ö·mi." They named him Ō′bed; he was the father of Jesse, the father of David.

18 Now these are the descendants of Per′ez: Perez was the father of Hez′rön, 19 Hez′rön of Räm, Ram of Am·min′á·dab, 20Am·min′á·dab of Näh′shòn, Nahshon of Sal′mòn, 21Sal′mòn of Bō′az, Boaz of Ō′bed, 22Ō′bed of Jesse, and Jesse of David.

THE FIRST BOOK OF

SAMUEL

I There was a certain man of Rā·má·thā′im·zō′phim of the hill country of Ē′phrá·im, whose name was El·kā′nàh the son of Je·rō′ham, son of E·lī′hū, son of Tō′hū, son of Zuph, an Ē′phrá·im·īte. 2 He had two wives; the name of the one was Hannah, and the name of the other Pĕ·nin′nàh. And Peninnah had children, but Hannah had no children.

3 Now this man used to go up year by year from his city to worship and to sacrifice to the LORD of hosts at Shī′lōh, where the two sons of Eli, Hoph′nī and Phin′é·hàs, were priests of the LORD. 4 On the day when El·kā′nàh sacrificed, he would give portions to Pĕ·nin′nàh his wife and to all her sons and daughters; 5 and, although[a] he loved Hannah, he would

give Hannah only one portion, because the LORD had closed her womb. 6And her rival used to provoke her sorely, to irritate her, because the LORD had closed her womb. 7 So it went on year by year; as often as she went up to the house of the LORD, she used to provoke her. Therefore Hannah wept and would not eat. 8And El·kā′nàh, her husband, said to her, "Hannah, why do you weep? And why do you not eat? And why is your heart sad? Am I not more to you than ten sons?"

9 After they had eaten and drunk in Shī′lōh, Hannah rose. Now Eli the priest was sitting on the seat beside the doorpost of the temple of the LORD. 10 She was deeply distressed and prayed to the LORD, and wept bitterly. 11And she vowed a vow and

a Gk: Heb obscure
4.7: Deut 25.8-10.

said, "O LORD of hosts, if thou wilt indeed look on the affliction of thy maidservant, and remember me, and not forget thy maidservant, but wilt give to thy maidservant a son, then I will give him to the LORD all the days of his life, and no razor shall touch his head."

12 As she continued praying before the LORD, Eli observed her mouth. 13 Hannah was speaking in her heart; only her lips moved, and her voice was not heard; therefore Eli took her to be a drunken woman. 14 And Eli said to her, "How long will you be drunken? Put away your wine from you." 15 But Hannah answered, "No, my lord, I am a woman sorely troubled; I have drunk neither wine nor strong drink, but I have been pouring out my soul before the LORD. 16 Do not regard your maidservant as a base woman, for all along I have been speaking out of my great anxiety and vexation." 17 Then Eli answered, "Go in peace, and the God of Israel grant your petition which you have made to him." 18 And she said, "Let your maidservant find favor in your eyes." Then the woman went her way and ate, and her countenance was no longer sad.

19 They rose early in the morning and worshiped before the LORD; then they went back to their house at Rā′-māh. And El·kā′nàh knew Hannah his wife, and the LORD remembered her; 20 and in due time Hannah conceived and bore a son, and she called his name Samuel, for she said, "I have asked him of the LORD."

21 And the man El·kā′nàh and all his house went up to offer to the LORD the yearly sacrifice, and to pay his vow. 22 But Hannah did not go up, for she said to her husband, "As soon as the child is weaned, I will bring him, that he may appear in the presence of the LORD, and abide there for ever." 23 El·kā′nàh her husband said to her, "Do what seems best to you, wait until you have weaned him; only, may the LORD establish his word." So the woman remained and nursed her son, until she weaned him. 24 And when she had weaned him, she took him up with her, along with a three-year-old bull,*b* an ephah of flour, and a skin of wine; and she brought him to the house of the LORD at Shī′lōh; and the child was young. 25 Then they slew the bull, and they brought the child to Eli. 26 And she said, "Oh, my lord! As you live, my lord, I am the woman who

was standing here in your presence, praying to the LORD. 27 For this child I prayed; and the LORD has granted me my petition which I made to him. 28 Therefore I have lent him to the LORD; as long as he lives, he is lent to the LORD."

And they*x* worshiped the LORD there.

2 Hannah also prayed and said, "My heart exults in the LORD; my strength is exalted in the LORD.
My mouth derides my enemies, because I rejoice in thy salvation.

2 "There is none holy like the LORD, there is none besides thee; there is no rock like our God.
3 Talk no more so very proudly, let not arrogance come from your mouth;
for the LORD is a God of knowledge, and by him actions are weighed.
4 The bows of the mighty are broken, but the feeble gird on strength.
5 Those who were full have hired themselves out for bread, but those who were hungry have ceased to hunger.
The barren has borne seven, but she who has many children is forlorn.
6 The LORD kills and brings to life; he brings down to Shē′ōl and raises up.
7 The LORD makes poor and makes rich; he brings low, he also exalts.
8 He raises up the poor from the dust; he lifts the needy from the ash heap,
to make them sit with princes and inherit a seat of honor.
For the pillars of the earth are the LORD's, and on them he has set the world.

9 "He will guard the feet of his faithful ones; but the wicked shall be cut off in darkness; for not by might shall a man prevail.
10 The adversaries of the LORD shall be broken to pieces; against them he will thunder in heaven.
The LORD will judge the ends of the earth; he will give strength to his king, and exalt the power of his anointed."

b Gk Syr: Heb *three bulls*　*x* Heb *he*
2.1-10: Lk 1.46-55.

11 Then El·kā'nàh went home to Rā'màh. And the boy ministered to the LORD, in the presence of Eli the priest.

12 Now the sons of Eli were worthless men; they had no regard for the LORD. 13 The custom of the priests with the people was that when any man offered sacrifice, the priest's servant would come, while the meat was boiling, with a three-pronged fork in his hand, 14 and he would thrust it into the pan, or kettle, or caldron, or pot; all that the fork brought up the priest would take for himself.c So they did at Shī'lōh to all the Israelites who came there. 15 Moreover, before the fat was burned, the priest's servant would come and say to the man who was sacrificing, "Give meat for the priest to roast; for he will not accept boiled meat from you, but raw." 16And if the man said to him, "Let them burn the fat first, and then take as much as you wish," he would say, "No, you must give it now; and if not, I will take it by force." 17 Thus the sin of the young men was very great in the sight of the LORD; for the men treated the offering of the LORD with contempt.

18 Samuel was ministering before the LORD, a boy girded with a linen ephod. 19And his mother used to make for him a little robe and take it to him each year, when she went up with her husband to offer the yearly sacrifice. 20 Then Eli would bless El·kā'nàh and his wife, and say, "The LORD give you children by this woman for the loan which she lent tod the LORD"; so then they would return to their home.

21 And the LORD visited Hannah, and she conceived and bore three sons and two daughters. And the boy Samuel grew in the presence of the LORD.

22 Now Eli was very old, and he heard all that his sons were doing to all Israel, and how they lay with the women who served at the entrance to the tent of meeting. 23And he said to them, "Why do you do such things? For I hear of your evil dealings from all the people. 24 No, my sons; it is no good report that I hear the people of the LORD spreading abroad. 25 If a man sins against a man, God will mediate for him; but if a man sins against the LORD, who can intercede for him?" But they would not listen to the voice of their father; for it was the will of the LORD to slay them.

26 Now the boy Samuel continued to grow both in stature and in favor with the LORD and with men.

27 And there came a man of God to Eli, and said to him, "Thus the LORD has said, 'I revealede myself to the house of your father when they were in Egypt subject to the house of Pharaoh. 28And I chose him out of all the tribes of Israel to be my priest, to go up to my altar, to burn incense, to wear an ephod before me; and I gave to the house of your father all my offerings by fire from the people of Israel. 29 Why then look with greedy eye atf my sacrifices and my offerings which I commanded, and honor your sons above me by fattening yourselves upon the choicest parts of every offering of my people Israel?' 30 Therefore the LORD the God of Israel declares: 'I promised that your house and the house of your father should go in and out before me for ever'; but now the LORD declares: 'Far be it from me; for those who honor me I will honor, and those who despise me shall be lightly esteemed. 31 Behold, the days are coming, when I will cut off your strength and the strength of your father's house, so that there will not be an old man in your house. 32 Then in distress you will look with envious eye on all the prosperity which shall be bestowed upon Israel; and there shall not be an old man in your house for ever. 33 The man of you whom I shall not cut off from my altar shall be spared to weep out hisg eyes and grieve hisg heart; and all the increase of your house shall die by the sword of men.h 34And this which shall befall your two sons, Hoph'nī and Phin'é·hàs, shall be the sign to you: both of them shall die on the same day. 35And I will raise up for myself a faithful priest, who shall do according to what is in my heart and in my mind; and I will build him a sure house, and he shall go in and out before my anointed for ever. 36And every one who is left in your house shall come to implore him for a piece of silver or a loaf of bread, and shall say, "Put me, I pray you, in one of the priest's places, that I may eat a morsel of bread."'"

3 Now the boy Samuel was ministering to the LORD under Eli. And the word of the LORD was rare in those days; there was no frequent vision.

---

c Gk Syr Vg: Heb *with it*   d Or *for the petition which she asked of*   e Gk Tg: Heb *Did I reveal*   f Or *treat with scorn* Gk: Heb *kick at*   g Gk: Heb *your*   Gk: Heb *die as men*

.26: Lk 2.52.

2 At that time Eli, whose eyesight had begun to grow dim, so that he could not see, was lying down in his own place; ³ the lamp of God had not yet gone out, and Samuel was lying down within the temple of the LORD, where the ark of God was. ⁴ Then the LORD called, "Samuel! Samuel!"*i* and he said, "Here I am!" ⁵ and ran to Eli, and said, "Here I am, for you called me." But he said, "I did not call; lie down again." So he went and lay down. ⁶And the LORD called again, "Samuel!" And Samuel arose and went to Eli and said, "Here I am, for you called me." But he said, "I did not call, my son; lie down again." ⁷ Now Samuel did not yet know the LORD, and the word of the LORD had not yet been revealed to him. ⁸And the LORD called Samuel again the third time. And he arose and went to Eli, and said, "Here I am, for you called me." Then Eli perceived that the LORD was calling the boy. ⁹ Therefore Eli said to Samuel, "Go, lie down; and if he calls you, you shall say, 'Speak, LORD, for thy servant hears.' " So Samuel went and lay down in his place.

10 And the LORD came and stood forth, calling as at other times, "Samuel! Samuel!" And Samuel said, "Speak, for thy servant hears." ¹¹ Then the LORD said to Samuel, "Behold, I am about to do a thing in Israel, at which the two ears of every one that hears it will tingle. ¹² On that day I will fulfil against Eli all that I have spoken concerning his house, from beginning to end. ¹³And I tell him that I am about to punish his house for ever, for the iniquity which he knew, because his sons were blaspheming God,*j* and he did not restrain them. ¹⁴ Therefore I swear to the house of Eli that the iniquity of Eli's house shall not be expiated by sacrifice or offering for ever."

15 Samuel lay until morning; then he opened the doors of the house of the LORD. And Samuel was afraid to tell the vision to Eli. ¹⁶ But Eli called Samuel and said, "Samuel, my son." And he said, "Here I am." ¹⁷And Eli said, "What was it that he told you? Do not hide it from me. May God do so to you and more also, if you hide anything from me of all that he told you." ¹⁸ So Samuel told him everything and hid nothing from him. And he said, "It is the LORD; let him do what seems good to him."

19 And Samuel grew, and the LORD

was with him and let none of his words fall to the ground. ²⁰And all Israel from Dan to Beer-sheba knew that Samuel was established as a prophet of the LORD. ²¹And the LORD appeared again at Shi′lōh, for the LORD revealed himself to Samuel at Shiloh by the word of the LORD.

4 ¹And the word of Samuel came to all Israel.

Now Israel went out to battle against the Philistines; they encamped at Eb-ĕn-ē′zĕr, and the Philistines encamped at A′phek. ² The Philistines drew up in line against Israel, and when the battle spread, Israel was defeated by the Philistines, who slew about four thousand men on the field of battle. ³And when the troops came to the camp, the elders of Israel said, "Why has the LORD put us to rout today before the Philistines? Let us bring the ark of the covenant of the LORD here from Shi′lōh, that he may come among us and save us from the power of our enemies." ⁴ So the people sent to Shi′lōh, and brought from there the ark of the covenant of the LORD of hosts, who is enthroned on the cherubim; and the two sons of Eli, Hoph′nī and Phin′ē-hăs, were there with the ark of the covenant of God.

5 When the ark of the covenant of the LORD came into the camp, all Israel gave a mighty shout, so that the earth resounded. ⁶And when the Philistines heard the noise of the shouting, they said, "What does this great shouting in the camp of the Hebrews mean?" And when they learned that the ark of the LORD had come to the camp, ⁷ the Philistines were afraid; for they said, "A god has come into the camp." And they said, "Woe to us! For nothing like this has happened before. ⁸ Woe to us! Who can deliver us from the power of these mighty gods? These are the gods who smote the Egyptians with every sort of plague in the wilderness. ⁹ Take courage, and acquit yourselves like men, O Philistines, lest you become slaves to the Hebrews as they have been to you; acquit yourselves like men and fight."

10 So the Philistines fought, and Israel was defeated, and they fled, every man to his home; and there was a very great slaughter, for there fell of Israel thirty thousand foot soldiers. ¹¹And the ark of God was captured; and the two sons of Eli, Hoph′nī and Phin′ē-hăs, were slain.

12 A man of Benjamin ran from the battle line, and came to Shi′lōh the

same day, with his clothes rent and with earth upon his head. 13 When he arrived, Eli was sitting upon his seat by the road watching, for his heart trembled for the ark of God. And when the man came into the city and told the news, all the city cried out. 14 When Eli heard the sound of the outcry, he said, "What is this uproar?" Then the man hastened and came and told Eli. 15 Now Eli was ninety-eight years old and his eyes were set, so that he could not see. 16 And the man said to Eli, "I am he who has come from the battle; I fled from the battle today." And he said, "How did it go, my son?" 17 He who brought the tidings answered and said, "Israel has fled before the Philistines, and there has also been a great slaughter among the people; your two sons also, Hoph'ni and Phin'e·has, are dead, and the ark of God has been captured." 18 When he mentioned the ark of God, Eli fell over backward from his seat by the side of the gate; and his neck was broken and he died, for he was an old man, and heavy. He had judged Israel forty years.

19 Now his daughter-in-law, the wife of Phin'e·has, was with child, about to give birth. And when she heard the tidings that the ark of God was captured, and that her father-in-law and her husband were dead, she bowed and gave birth; for her pains came upon her. 20 And about the time of her death the women attending her said to her, "Fear not, for you have borne a son." But she did not answer or give heed. 21 And she named the child Ich'a·bod, saying, "The glory has departed from Israel!" because the ark of God had been captured and because of her father-in-law and her husband. 22 And she said, "The glory has departed from Israel, for the ark of God has been captured."

5 When the Philistines captured the ark of God, they carried it from Eb·en·e'zer to Ash'dod; 2 then the Philistines took the ark of God and brought it into the house of Da'gon and set it up beside Dagon. 3 And when the people of Ash'dod rose early the next day, behold, Da'gon had fallen face downward on the ground before the ark of the LORD. So they took Dagon and put him back in his place. 4 But when they rose early on the next morning, behold, Da'gon had fallen face downward on the ground before the ark of the LORD, and the head of Dagon and both his hands were lying cut off upon the threshold; only the trunk of Dagon was left to him. 5 This is why the priests of Da'gon and all who enter the house of Dagon do not tread on the threshold of Dagon in Ash'dod to this day.

6 The hand of the LORD was heavy upon the people of Ash'dod, and he terrified and afflicted them with tumors, both Ashdod and its territory. 7 And when the men of Ash'dod saw how things were, they said, "The ark of the God of Israel must not remain with us; for his hand is heavy upon us and upon Da'gon our god." 8 So they sent and gathered together all the lords of the Philistines, and said, "What shall we do with the ark of the God of Israel?" They answered, "Let the ark of the God of Israel be brought around to Gath." So they brought the ark of the God of Israel there. 9 But after they had brought it around, the hand of the LORD was against the city, causing a very great panic, and he afflicted the men of the city, both young and old, so that tumors broke out upon them. 10 So they sent the ark of God to Ek'ron. But when the ark of God came to Ekron, the people of Ekron cried out, "They have brought around to us the ark of the God of Israel to slay us and our people." 11 They sent therefore and gathered together all the lords of the Philistines, and said, "Send away the ark of the God of Israel, and let it return to its own place, that it may not slay us and our people." For there was a deathly panic throughout the whole city. The hand of God was very heavy there; 12 the men who did not die were stricken with tumors, and the cry of the city went up to heaven.

6 The ark of the LORD was in the country of the Philistines seven months. 2 And the Philistines called for the priests and the diviners and said, "What shall we do with the ark of the LORD? Tell us with what we shall send it to its place." 3 They said, "If you send away the ark of the God of Israel, do not send it empty, but by all means return him a guilt offering. Then you will be healed, and it will be known to you why his hand does not turn away from you." 4 And they said, "What is the guilt offering that we shall return to him?" They answered, "Five golden tumors and five golden mice, according to the number of the lords of the Philistines; for the same plague was upon all of you and upon your lords. 5 So you must make images of your tumors and images of your mice that ravage the land, and give glory to the God of Israel; perhaps he will lighten his hand

from off you and your gods and your land. 6 Why should you harden your hearts as the Egyptians and Pharaoh hardened their hearts? After he had made sport of them, did not they let the people go, and they departed? 7 Now then, take and prepare a new cart and two milch cows upon which there has never come a yoke, and yoke the cows to the cart, but take their calves home, away from them. 8 And take the ark of the LORD and place it on the cart, and put in a box at its side the figures of gold, which you are returning to him as a guilt offering. Then send it off, and let it go its way. 9 And watch; if it goes up on the way to its own land, to Beth-shĕ′mesh, then it is he who has done us this great harm; but if not, then we shall know that it is not his hand that struck us, it happened to us by chance.

10 The men did so, and took two milch cows and yoked them to the cart, and shut up their calves at home. 11 And they put the ark of the LORD on the cart, and the box with the golden mice and the images of their tumors. 12 And the cows went straight in the direction of Beth-shĕ′mesh along one highway, lowing as they went; they turned neither to the right nor to the left, and the lords of the Philistines went after them as far as the border of Beth-shemesh. 13 Now the people of Beth-shĕ′mesh were reaping their wheat harvest in the valley; and when they lifted up their eyes and saw the ark, they rejoiced to see it. 14 The cart came into the field of Joshua of Beth-shĕ′mesh, and stopped there. A great stone was there; and they split up the wood of the cart and offered the cows as a burnt offering to the LORD. 15 And the Levites took down the ark of the LORD and the box that was beside it, in which were the golden figures, and set them upon the great stone; and the men of Beth-shĕ′mesh offered burnt offerings and sacrificed sacrifices on that day to the LORD. 16 And when the five lords of the Philistines saw it, they returned that day to Ek′rŏn.

17 These are the golden tumors, which the Philistines returned as a guilt offering to the LORD: one for Ash′dod, one for Gā′zȧ, one for Ash′-kė·lon, one for Gath, one for Ek′rŏn; 18 also the golden mice, according to the number of all the cities of the Philistines belonging to the five lords, both fortified cities and unwalled villages. The great stone, beside which they set down the ark of the LORD, is a

witness to this day in the field of Joshua of Beth-shĕ′mesh.

19 And he slew some of the men of Beth-shĕ′mesh, because they looked into the ark of the LORD; he slew seventy men of them,[k] and the people mourned because the LORD had made a great slaughter among the people. 20 Then the men of Beth-shĕ′mesh said, "Who is able to stand before the LORD, this holy God? And to whom shall he go up away from us?" 21 So they sent messengers to the inhabitants of Kĭr′i·ath-jē′a·rim, saying, "The Philistines have returned the ark of the LORD. Come down and take it up to you."

7 And the men of Kĭr′i·ath-jē′a·rim came and took up the ark of the LORD, and brought it to the house of A·bin′a·dab on the hill; and they consecrated his son, El·ē·ā′zȧr, to have charge of the ark of the LORD. 2 From the day that the ark was lodged at Kĭr′i·ath-jē′a·rim, a long time passed, some twenty years, and all the house of Israel lamented after the LORD.

3 Then Samuel said to all the house of Israel, "If you are returning to the LORD with all your heart, then put away the foreign gods and the Ash′tȧ-roth from among you, and direct your heart to the LORD, and serve him only, and he will deliver you out of the hand of the Philistines." 4 So Israel put away the Bā′ȧlş and the Ash′tȧ·roth, and they served the LORD only.

5 Then Samuel said, "Gather all Israel at Mĭz′pȧh, and I will pray to the LORD for you." 6 So they gathered at Mĭz′pȧh, and drew water and poured it out before the LORD, and fasted on that day, and said there, "We have sinned against the LORD." And Samuel judged the people of Israel at Mizpah. 7 Now when the Philistines heard that the people of Israel had gathered at Mĭz′pȧh, the lords of the Philistines went up against Israel. And when the people of Israel heard of it they were afraid of the Philistines. 8 And the people of Israel said to Samuel, "Do not cease to cry to the LORD our God for us, that he may save us from the hand of the Philistines." 9 So Samuel took a sucking lamb and offered it as a whole burnt offering to the LORD; and Samuel cried to the LORD for Israel, and the LORD answered him. 10 As Samuel was offering up the burnt offering, the Philistines drew near to attack Israel; but the LORD thundered with a mighty voice that day against the Philistines and threw them into

k Cn: Heb *of the people seventy men, fifty thousand men*

confusion; and they were routed before Israel. [11]And the men of Israel went out of Miz'pah and pursued the Philistines, and smote them, as far as below Beth'-car.

12 Then Samuel took a stone and set it up between Miz'pah and Je·sha'-nah,[l] and called its name Eb·en·e'zer;[m] for he said, "Hitherto the LORD has helped us." 13 So the Philistines were subdued and did not again enter the territory of Israel. And the hand of the LORD was against the Philistines all the days of Samuel. 14 The cities which the Philistines had taken from Israel were restored to Israel, from Ek'ron to Gath; and Israel rescued their territory from the hand of the Philistines. There was peace also between Israel and the Am'o·rites.

15 Samuel judged Israel all the days of his life. 16And he went on a circuit year by year to Beth'el, Gil'gal, and Miz'pah; and he judged Israel in all these places. 17 Then he would come back to Ra'mah, for his home was there, and there also he administered justice to Israel. And he built there an altar to the LORD.

8 When Samuel became old, he made his sons judges over Israel. 2 The name of his first-born son was Jo'el, and the name of his second, A·bi'jah; they were judges in Beer-sheba. 3 Yet his sons did not walk in his ways, but turned aside after gain; they took bribes and perverted justice.

4 Then all the elders of Israel gathered together and came to Samuel at Ra'-mah, 5 and said to him, "Behold, you are old and your sons do not walk in your ways; now appoint for us a king to govern us like all the nations." 6 But the thing displeased Samuel when they said, "Give us a king to govern us." And Samuel prayed to the LORD. 7And the LORD said to Samuel, "Hearken to the voice of the people in all that they say to you; for they have not rejected you, but they have rejected me from being king over them. 8According to all the deeds which they have done to me,[n] from the day I brought them up out of Egypt even to this day, forsaking me and serving other gods, so they are also doing to you. 9 Now then, hearken to their voice; only, you shall solemnly warn them, and show them the ways of the king who shall reign over them."

10 So Samuel told all the words of the LORD to the people who were asking a king from him. 11 He said,

"These will be the ways of the king who will reign over you: he will take your sons and appoint them to his chariots and to be his horsemen, and to run before his chariots; 12 and he will appoint for himself commanders of thousands and commanders of fifties, and some to plow his ground and to reap his harvest, and to make his implements of war and the equipment of his chariots. 13 He will take your daughters to be perfumers and cooks and bakers. 14 He will take the best of your fields and vineyards and olive orchards and give them to his servants. 15 He will take the tenth of your grain and of your vineyards and give it to his officers and to his servants. 16 He will take your menservants and maidservants, and the best of your cattle[o] and your asses, and put them to his work. 17 He will take the tenth of your flocks, and you shall be his slaves. 18And in that day you will cry out because of your king, whom you have chosen for yourselves; but the LORD will not answer you in that day."

19 But the people refused to listen to the voice of Samuel; and they said, "No! but we will have a king over us, 20 that we also may be like all the nations, and that our king may govern us and go out before us and fight our battles." 21And when Samuel had heard all the words of the people, he repeated them in the ears of the LORD. 22And the LORD said to Samuel, "Hearken to their voice, and make them a king." Samuel then said to the men of Israel, "Go every man to his city."

9 There was a man of Benjamin whose name was Kish, the son of A·bi'el, son of Ze'ror, son of Be·co'-rath, son of A·phi'ah, a Benjaminite, a man of wealth; 2 and he had a son whose name was Saul, a handsome young man. There was not a man among the people of Israel more handsome than he; from his shoulders upward he was taller than any of the people.

3 Now the asses of Kish, Saul's father, were lost. So Kish said to Saul his son, "Take one of the servants with you, and arise, go and look for the asses." 4And they[p] passed through the hill country of E'phra·im and passed through the land of Shal'i·shah, but they did not find them. And they passed through the land of Sha'a·lim, but they were not there. Then they

---

[l] Gk Syr: Heb *Shen*   [m] That is *Stone of help*   [n] Gk: Heb lacks *to me*
[o] Gk: Heb *young men*   [p] Gk Vg: Heb *he*

passed through the land of Benjamin, but did not find them.

5 When they came to the land of Zuph, Saul said to his servant who was with him, "Come, let us go back, lest my father cease to care about the asses and become anxious about us." 6 But he said to him, "Behold, there is a man of God in this city, and he is a man that is held in honor; all that he says comes true. Let us go there; perhaps he can tell us about the journey on which we have set out." 7 Then Saul said to his servant, "But if we go, what can we bring the man? For the bread in our sacks is gone, and there is no present to bring to the man of God. What have we?" 8 The servant answered Saul again, "Here, I have with me the fourth part of a shekel of silver, and I will give it to the man of God, to tell us our way." 9 (Formerly in Israel, when a man went to inquire of God, he said, "Come, let us go to the seer"; for he who is now called a prophet was formerly called a seer.) 10 And Saul said to his servant, "Well said; come, let us go." So they went to the city where the man of God was.

11 As they went up the hill to the city, they met young maidens coming out to draw water, and said to them, "Is the seer here?" 12 They answered, "He is; behold, he is just ahead of you. Make haste; he has come just now to the city, because the people have a sacrifice today on the high place. 13 As soon as you enter the city, you will find him, before he goes up to the high place to eat; for the people will not eat till he comes, since he must bless the sacrifice; afterward those eat who are invited. Now go up, for you will meet him immediately." 14 So they went up to the city. As they were entering the city, they saw Samuel coming out toward them on his way up to the high place.

15 Now the day before Saul came, the LORD had revealed to Samuel: 16 "Tomorrow about this time I will send to you a man from the land of Benjamin, and you shall anoint him to be prince over my people Israel. He shall save my people from the hand of the Philistines; for I have seen the affliction of*a* my people, because their cry has come to me." 17 When Samuel saw Saul, the LORD told him, "Here is the man of whom I spoke to you! He it is who shall rule over my people."

18 Then Saul approached Samuel in the gate, and said, "Tell me where is the house of the seer?" 19 Samuel answered Saul, "I am the seer; go up before me to the high place, for today you shall eat with me, and in the morning I will let you go and will tell you all that is on your mind. 20 As for your asses that were lost three days ago, do not set your mind on them, for they have been found. And for whom is all that is desirable in Israel? Is it not for you and for all your father's house?" 21 Saul answered, "Am I not a Benjaminite, from the least of the tribes of Israel? And is not my family the humblest of all the families of the tribe of Benjamin? Why then have you spoken to me in this way?"

22 Then Samuel took Saul and his servant and brought them into the hall and gave them a place at the head of those who had been invited, who were about thirty persons. 23 And Samuel said to the cook, "Bring the portion I gave you, of which I said to you, 'Put it aside.'" 24 So the cook took up the leg and the upper portion*r* and set them before Saul; and Samuel said, "See, what was kept is set before you. Eat; because it was kept for you until the hour appointed, that you might eat with the guests."*s*

So Saul ate with Samuel that day. 25 And when they came down from the high place into the city, a bed was spread for Saul*t* upon the roof, and he lay down to sleep. 26 Then at the break of dawn*u* Samuel called to Saul upon the roof, "Up, that I may send you on your way." So Saul arose, and both he and Samuel went out into the street.

27 As they were going down to the outskirts of the city, Samuel said to Saul, "Tell the servant to pass on before us, and when he has passed on stop here yourself for a while, that I may make known to you the word of God."

10 Then Samuel took a vial of oil and poured it on his head, and kissed him and said, "Has not the LORD anointed you to be prince over his people Israel? And you shall reign over the people of the LORD and you will save them from the hand of their enemies round about. And this shall be the sign to you that the LORD has anointed you to be prince*w* over his heritage. 2 When you depart from me

a Gk: Heb lacks *the affliction of*   *r* Heb obscure
s Cn: Heb *saying, I have invited the people*   *t* Gk: Heb *and he spoke with Saul*
u Gk: Heb *and they arose early and at break of dawn*
w Gk: Heb lacks *over his people Israel? And you shall . . . to be prince*

today you will meet two men by Rachel's tomb in the territory of Benjamin at Zel′zah, and they will say to you, 'The asses which you went to seek are found, and now your father has ceased to care about the asses and is anxious about you, saying, "What shall I do about my son?"' ³ Then you shall go on from there further and come to the oak of Ta′bor; three men going up to God at Beth′el will meet you there, one carrying three kids, another carrying three loaves of bread, and another carrying a skin of wine. ⁴And they will greet you and give you two loaves of bread, which you shall accept from their hand. ⁵After that you shall come to Gib′e·ath·e·lo′him,ˣ where there is a garrison of the Philistines; and there, as you come to the city, you will meet a band of prophets coming down from the high place with harp, tambourine, flute, and lyre before them, prophesying. ⁶ Then the spirit of the LORD will come mightily upon you, and you shall prophesy with them and be turned into another man. ⁷ Now when these signs meet you, do whatever your hand finds to do, for God is with you. ⁸And you shall go down before me to Gil′gal; and behold, I am coming to you to offer burnt offerings and to sacrifice peace offerings. Seven days you shall wait, until I come to you and show you what you shall do."

9 When he turned his back to leave Samuel, God gave him another heart; and all these signs came to pass that day. ¹⁰ When they came to Gib′e·ah,ᶻ behold, a band of prophets met him; and the spirit of God came mightily upon him, and he prophesied among them. ¹¹And when all who knew him before saw how he prophesied with the prophets, the people said to one another, "What has come over the son of Kish? Is Saul also among the prophets?" ¹²And a man of the place answered, "And who is their father?" Therefore it became a proverb, "Is Saul also among the prophets?" ¹³ When he had finished prophesying, he came to the high place.

14 Saul's uncle said to him and to his servant, "Where did you go?" And he said, "To seek the asses; and when we saw they were not to be found, we went to Samuel." ¹⁵And Saul's uncle said, "Pray, tell me what Samuel said to you." ¹⁶And Saul said to his uncle, 'He told us plainly that the asses had

been found." But about the matter of the kingdom, of which Samuel had spoken, he did not tell him anything.

17 Now Samuel called the people together to the LORD at Miz′pah; ¹⁸ and he said to the people of Israel, "Thus says the LORD, the God of Israel, 'I brought up Israel out of Egypt, and I delivered you from the hand of the Egyptians and from the hand of all the kingdoms that were oppressing you.' ¹⁹ But you have this day rejected your God, who saves you from all your calamities and your distresses; and you have said, 'No! but set a king over us.' Now therefore present yourselves before the LORD by your tribes and by your thousands."

20 Then Samuel brought all the tribes of Israel near, and the tribe of Benjamin was taken by lot. ²¹ He brought the tribe of Benjamin near by its families, and the family of the Ma′trites was taken by lot; finally he brought the family of the Matrites near man by man,ᵃ and Saul the son of Kish was taken by lot. But when they sought him, he could not be found. ²² So they inquired again of the LORD, "Did the man come hither?"ᵇ and the LORD said, "Behold, he has hidden himself among the baggage." ²³ Then they ran and fetched him from there; and when he stood among the people, he was taller than any of the people from his shoulders upward. ²⁴And Samuel said to all the people, "Do you see him whom the LORD has chosen? There is none like him among all the people." And all the people shouted, "Long live the king!"

25 Then Samuel told the people the rights and duties of the kingship; and he wrote them in a book and laid it up before the LORD. Then Samuel sent all the people away, each one to his home. ²⁶ Saul also went to his home at Gib′e·ah, and with him went men of valor whose hearts God had touched. ²⁷ But some worthless fellows said, "How can this man save us?" And they despised him, and brought him no present. But he held his peace.

11 Then Na′hash the Am′mo·nite went up and besieged Ja′besh-gil′e·ad; and all the men of Ja′besh said to Nahash, "Make a treaty with us, and we will serve you." ² But Na′hash the Am′mo·nite said to them, "On this condition I will make a treaty with you, that I gouge out all your right eyes, and thus put disgrace upon all

ˣ Or the hill of God ᶻ Or the hill ᵃ Gk: Heb lacks finally . . . man by man
ᵇ Gk: Heb Is there yet a man to come hither?
¹⁰.11-12: 1 Sam 19.23-24.

Israel." ³ The elders of Jā′besh said to him, "Give us seven days respite that we may send messengers through all the territory of Israel. Then, if there is no one to save us, we will give ourselves up to you." ⁴ When the messengers came to Gib′ē-äh of Saul, they reported the matter in the ears of the people; and all the people wept aloud.

5 Now Saul was coming from the field behind the oxen; and Saul said, "What ails the people, that they are weeping?" So they told him the tidings of the men of Jā′besh. ⁶And the spirit of God came mightily upon Saul when he heard these words, and his anger was greatly kindled. ⁷ He took a yoke of oxen, and cut them in pieces and sent them throughout all the territory of Israel by the hand of messengers, saying, "Whoever does not come out after Saul and Samuel, so shall it be done to his oxen!" Then the dread of the LORD fell upon the people, and they came out as one man. ⁸ When he mustered them at Bē′zek, the men of Israel were three hundred thousand, and the men of Judah thirty thousand. ⁹And they said to the messengers who had come, "Thus shall you say to the men of Jā′besh-gil′ē-àd: 'Tomorrow, by the time the sun is hot, you shall have deliverance.'" When the messengers came and told the men of Jā′besh, they were glad. ¹⁰ Therefore the men of Jā′besh said, "Tomorrow we will give ourselves up to you, and you may do to us whatever seems good to you." ¹¹And on the morrow Saul put the people in three companies; and they came into the midst of the camp in the morning watch, and cut down the Am′mò-nîtes until the heat of the day; and those who survived were scattered, so that no two of them were left together.

12 Then the people said to Samuel, "Who is it that said, 'Shall Saul reign over us?' Bring the men, that we may put them to death." ¹³ But Saul said, "Not a man shall be put to death this day, for today the LORD has wrought deliverance in Israel." ¹⁴ Then Samuel said to the people, "Come, let us go to Gil′gàl and there renew the kingdom." ¹⁵ So all the people went to Gil′gàl, and there they made Saul king before the LORD in Gilgal. There they sacrificed peace offerings before the LORD, and there Saul and all the men of Israel rejoiced greatly.

12 And Samuel said to all Israel, "Behold, I have hearkened to your voice in all that you have said to me, and have made a king over you. ²And now, behold, the king walks before you; and I am old and gray, and behold, my sons are with you; and I have walked before you from my youth until this day. ³ Here I am; testify against me before the LORD and before his anointed. Whose ox have I taken? Or whose ass have I taken? Or whom have I defrauded? Whom have I oppressed? Or from whose hand have I taken a bribe to blind my eyes with it? Testify against me*c* and I will restore it to you." ⁴ They said, "You have not defrauded us or oppressed us or taken anything from any man's hand." ⁵And he said to them, "The LORD is witness against you, and his anointed is witness this day, that you have not found anything in my hand." And they said, "He is witness."

6 And Samuel said to the people, "The LORD is witness,*d* who appointed Moses and Aaron and brought your fathers up out of the land of Egypt. ⁷ Now therefore stand still, that I may plead with you before the LORD concerning all the saving deeds of the LORD which he performed for you and for your fathers. ⁸ When Jacob went into Egypt and the Egyptians oppressed them,*e* then your fathers cried to the LORD and the LORD sent Moses and Aaron, who brought forth your fathers out of Egypt, and made them dwell in this place. ⁹ But they forgot the LORD their God; and he sold them into the hand of Sis′ěr-à, commander of the army of Jā′bin king of*f* Hā′zôr, and into the hand of the Philistines, and into the hand of the king of Mō′ab; and they fought against them. ¹⁰And they cried to the LORD, and said, 'We have sinned, because we have forsaken the LORD, and have served the Bā′àls and the Ash′tē-roth; but now deliver us out of the hand of our enemies, and we will serve thee.' ¹¹And the LORD sent Jer·ub·bā′àl and Bâr′àk,*g* and Jeph′thàh, and Samuel, and delivered you out of the hand of your enemies on every side; and you dwelt in safety. ¹²And when you saw that Nā′hash the king of the Am′mò-nîtes came against you, you said to me, 'No, but a king shall reign over us,' when the LORD your God was your king. ¹³And now behold the king whom you have

---

c Gk: Heb lacks *Testify against me*   *d* Gk: Heb lacks *is witness*
e Gk: Heb lacks *and the Egyptians oppressed them*
f Gk: Heb lacks *Jabin king of*
g Gk Syr: Heb *Bedan*

chosen, for whom you have asked; behold, the LORD has set a king over you. ¹⁴ If you will fear the LORD and serve him and hearken to his voice and not rebel against the commandment of the LORD, and if both you and the king who reigns over you will follow the LORD your God, it will be well; ¹⁵ but if you will not hearken to the voice of the LORD, but rebel against the commandment of the LORD, then the hand of the LORD will be against you and your king.*h* ¹⁶ Now therefore stand still and see this great thing, which the LORD will do before your eyes. ¹⁷ Is it not wheat harvest today? I will call upon the LORD, that he may send thunder and rain; and you shall know and see that your wickedness is great, which you have done in the sight of the LORD, in asking for yourselves a king." ¹⁸ So Samuel called upon the LORD, and the LORD sent thunder and rain that day; and all the people greatly feared the LORD and Samuel.

¹⁹ And all the people said to Samuel, "Pray for your servants to the LORD your God, that we may not die; for we have added to all our sins this evil, to ask for ourselves a king." ²⁰ And Samuel said to the people, "Fear not; you have done all this evil, yet do not turn aside from following the LORD, but serve the LORD with all your heart; ²¹ and do not turn aside after*i* vain things which cannot profit or save, for they are vain. ²² For the LORD will not cast away his people, for his great name's sake, because it has pleased the LORD to make you a people for himself. ²³ Moreover as for me, far be it from me that I should sin against the LORD by ceasing to pray for you; and I will instruct you in the good and the right way. ²⁴ Only fear the LORD, and serve him faithfully with all your heart; for consider what great things he has done for you. ²⁵ But if you still do wickedly, you shall be swept away, both you and your king."

13 Saul was . . .*j* years old when he began to reign; and he reigned . . . and two*k* years over Israel.

² Saul chose three thousand men of Israel; two thousand were with Saul in Mich'mash and the hill country of Beth'el, and a thousand were with Jonathan in Gib'ē-ah of Benjamin; the rest of the people he sent home, every man to his tent. ³ Jonathan defeated

the garrison of the Philistines which was at Gē'ba; and the Philistines heard of it. And Saul blew the trumpet throughout all the land, saying, "Let the Hebrews hear." ⁴ And all Israel heard it said that Saul had defeated the garrison of the Philistines, and also that Israel had become odious to the Philistines. And the people were called out to join Saul at Gil'gal.

⁵ And the Philistines mustered to fight with Israel, thirty thousand chariots, and six thousand horsemen, and troops like the sand on the seashore in multitude; they came up and encamped in Mich'mash, to the east of Beth'-ā'ven. ⁶ When the men of Israel saw that they were in straits (for the people were hard pressed), the people hid themselves in caves and in holes and in rocks and in tombs and in cisterns, ⁷ or crossed the fords of the Jordan*l* to the land of Gad and Gilead. Saul was still at Gil'gal, and all the people followed him trembling.

⁸ He waited seven days, the time appointed by Samuel; but Samuel did not come to Gil'gal, and the people were scattering from him. ⁹ So Saul said, "Bring the burnt offering here to me, and the peace offerings." And he offered the burnt offering. ¹⁰ As soon as he had finished offering the burnt offering, behold, Samuel came; and Saul went out to meet him and salute him. ¹¹ Samuel said, "What have you done?" And Saul said, "When I saw that the people were scattering from me, and that you did not come within the days appointed, and that the Philistines had mustered at Mich'mash, ¹² I said, 'Now the Philistines will come down upon me at Gil'gal, and I have not entreated the favor of the LORD'; so I forced myself, and offered the burnt offering." ¹³ And Samuel said to Saul, "You have done foolishly; you have not kept the commandment of the LORD your God, which he commanded you; for now the LORD would have established your kingdom over Israel for ever. ¹⁴ But now your kingdom shall not continue; the LORD has sought out a man after his own heart; and the LORD has appointed him to be prince over his people, because you have not kept what the LORD commanded you." ¹⁵ And Samuel arose, and went up from Gil'gal to Gib'ē-ah of Benjamin.

h Gk: Heb *fathers*   *i* Gk Syr Tg Vg: Heb *because after*
j The number is lacking in Heb
k *Two* is not the entire number. Something has dropped out.
l Cn: Heb *Hebrews crossed the Jordan*
13.14: Acts 13.22.

And Saul numbered the people who were present with him, about six hundred men. 16 And Saul, and Jonathan his son, and the people who were present with them, stayed in Gē′ba of Benjamin; but the Philistines encamped in Mich′mash. 17 And raiders came out of the camp of the Philistines in three companies; one company turned toward Oph′rah, to the land of Shū′al, 18 another company turned toward Beth-hō′ron, and another company turned toward the border that looks down upon the valley of Ze-bō′im toward the wilderness.

19 Now there was no smith to be found throughout all the land of Israel; for the Philistines said, "Lest the Hebrews make themselves swords or spears"; 20 but every one of the Israelites went down to the Philistines to sharpen his plowshare, his mattock, his axe, or his sickle;*m* 21 and the charge was a pim for the plowshares and for the mattocks, and a third of a shekel for sharpening the axes and for setting the goads.*n* 22 So on the day of the battle there was neither sword nor spear found in the hand of any of the people with Saul and Jonathan; but Saul and Jonathan his son had them. 23 And the garrison of the Philistines went out to the pass of Mich′mash.

14 One day Jonathan the son of Saul said to the young man who bore his armor, "Come, let us go over to the Philistine garrison on yonder side." But he did not tell his father. 2 Saul was staying in the outskirts of Gib′ē-ah under the pomegranate tree which is at Mig′ron; the people who were with him were about six hundred men, 3 and A·hi′jah the son of A·hi′tub, Ich′a·bod's brother, son of Phin′e·has, son of Eli, the priest of the LORD in Shi′loh, wearing an ephod. And the people did not know that Jonathan had gone. 4 In the pass,*o* by which Jonathan sought to go over to the Philistine garrison, there was a rocky crag on the one side and a rocky crag on the other side; the name of the one was Bō′zez, and the name of the other Sē′neh. 5 The one crag rose on the north in front of Mich′mash, and the other on the south in front of Gē′ba.

6 And Jonathan said to the young man who bore his armor, "Come, let us go over to the garrison of these uncircumcised; it may be that the LORD will work for us; for nothing can hinder the LORD from saving by many or by

few." 7 And his armor-bearer said to him, "Do all that your mind inclines to;*p* behold, I am with you, as is your mind so is mine."*q* 8 Then said Jonathan, "Behold, we will cross over to the men, and we will show ourselves to them. 9 If they say to us, 'Wait until we come to you,' then we will stand still in our place, and we will not go up to them. 10 But if they say, 'Come up to us,' then we will go up; for the LORD has given them into our hand. And this shall be the sign to us." 11 So both of them showed themselves to the garrison of the Philistines; and the Philistines said, "Look, Hebrews are coming out of the holes where they have hid themselves." 12 And the men of the garrison hailed Jonathan and his armor-bearer, and said, "Come up to us, and we will show you a thing." And Jonathan said to his armor-bearer, "Come up after me; for the LORD has given them into the hand of Israel." 13 Then Jonathan climbed up on his hands and feet, and his armor-bearer after him. And they fell before Jonathan, and his armor-bearer killed them after him; 14 and that first slaughter, which Jonathan and his armor-bearer made, was of about twenty men within as it were half a furrow's length in an acre*r* of land. 15 And there was a panic in the camp, in the field, and among all the people; the garrison and even the raiders trembled; the earth quaked; and it became a very great panic.

16 And the watchmen of Saul in Gib′ē-ah of Benjamin looked; and behold, the multitude was surging hither and thither.*s* 17 Then Saul said to the people who were with him, "Number and see who has gone from us." And when they had numbered, behold, Jonathan and his armor-bearer were not there. 18 And Saul said to A·hi′jah, "Bring hither the ark of God." For the ark of God went at that time with the people of Israel. 19 And while Saul was talking to the priest, the tumult in the camp of the Philistines increased more and more; and Saul said to the priest, "Withdraw your hand." 20 Then Saul and all the people who were with him rallied and went into the battle; and behold, every man's sword was against his fellow, and there was very great confusion. 21 Now the Hebrews who had been with the Philistines before that time and who had gone up with them into the camp, even they also

m Gk: Heb *plowshare*   *n* The Heb of this verse is obscure   *o* Heb *between the passes*
p Gk: Heb *Do all that is in your mind. Turn*   *q* Gk: Heb lacks *so is mine*   *r* Heb *yoke*
s Gk: Heb *they went and thither*

turned to be with[t] the Israelites who were with Saul and Jonathan. 22 Likewise, when all the men of Israel who had hid themselves in the hill country of É'phră-im heard that the Philistines were fleeing, they too followed hard after them in the battle. 23 So the LORD delivered Israel that day; and the battle passed beyond Beth'-ā'ven.

24 And the men of Israel were distressed that day; for Saul laid an oath on the people, saying, "Cursed be the man who eats food until it is evening and I am avenged on my enemies." So none of the people tasted food. 25And all the people[u] came into the forest; and there was honey on the ground. 26And when the people entered the forest, behold, the honey was dropping, but no man put his hand to his mouth; for the people feared the oath. 27 But Jonathan had not heard his father charge the people with the oath; so he put forth the tip of the staff that was in his hand, and dipped it in the honeycomb, and put his hand to his mouth; and his eyes became bright. 28 Then one of the people said, "Your father strictly charged the people with an oath, saying, 'Cursed be the man who eats food this day.'" And the people were faint. 29 Then Jonathan said, "My father has troubled the land; see how my eyes have become bright, because I tasted a little of this honey. 30 How much better if the people had eaten freely today of the spoil of their enemies which they found; for now the slaughter among the Philistines has not been great."

31 They struck down the Philistines that day from Mich'mash to Ai'jā-lon. And the people were very faint; 32 the people flew upon the spoil, and took sheep and oxen and calves, and slew them on the ground; and the people ate them with the blood. 33 Then they told Saul, "Behold, the people are sinning against the LORD, by eating with the blood." And he said, "You have dealt treacherously; roll a great stone to me here."[v] 34And Saul said, "Disperse yourselves among the people, and say to them, 'Let every man bring his ox or his sheep, and slay them here, and eat; and do not sin against the LORD by eating with the blood.'" So every one of the people brought his ox with him that night, and slew them there. 35And Saul built an altar to the LORD; it was the first altar that he built to the LORD.

36 Then Saul said, "Let us go down after the Philistines by night and despoil them until the morning light; let us not leave a man of them." And they said, "Do whatever seems good to you." But the priest said, "Let us draw near hither to God." 37And Saul inquired of God, "Shall I go down after the Philistines? Wilt thou give them into the hand of Israel?" But he did not answer him that day. 38And Saul said, "Come hither, all you leaders of the people; and know and see how this sin has arisen today. 39 For as the LORD lives who saves Israel, though it be in Jonathan my son, he shall surely die." But there was not a man among all the people that answered him. 40 Then he said to all Israel, "You shall be on one side, and I and Jonathan my son will be on the other side." And the people said to Saul, "Do what seems good to you." 41 Therefore Saul said, "O LORD God of Israel, why hast thou not answered thy servant this day? If this guilt is in me or in Jonathan my son, O LORD, God of Israel, give U'rim; but if this guilt is in thy people Israel,[w] give Thum'mim." And Jonathan and Saul were taken, but the people escaped. 42 Then Saul said, "Cast the lot between me and my son Jonathan." And Jonathan was taken.

43 Then Saul said to Jonathan, "Tell me what you have done." And Jonathan told him, "I tasted a little honey with the tip of the staff that was in my hand; here I am, I will die." 44And Saul said, "God do so to me and more also; you shall surely die, Jonathan." 45 Then the people said to Saul, "Shall Jonathan die, who has wrought this great victory in Israel? Far from it! As the LORD lives, there shall not one hair of his head fall to the ground; for he has wrought with God this day." So the people ransomed Jonathan, that he did not die. 46 Then Saul went up from pursuing the Philistines; and the Philistines went to their own place.

47 When Saul had taken the kingship over Israel, he fought against all his enemies on every side, against Mō'ab, against the Am'mó-nites, against É'dóm, against the kings of Zō'băh, and against the Philistines; wherever he turned he put them to the worse. 48And he did valiantly, and smote the Ả-mal'é-kites, and delivered Israel out of the hands of those who plundered them.

---

t Gk Syr Vg Tg: Heb *round about, they also, to be with*   u Heb *land*

v Gk: Heb *this day*

w Vg Compare Gk: Heb *Saul said to the* LORD, *the God of Israel*

49 Now the sons of Saul were Jonathan, Ish´vi, and Mal´chi·shü´á; and the names of his two daughters were these: the name of the first-born was Mē´reb, and the name of the younger Mi´chàl; 50 and the name of Saul's wife was Á·hin´ō-am the daughter of Á·him´á-az. And the name of the commander of his army was Abner the son of Nĕr, Saul's uncle; 51 Kish was the father of Saul, and Nĕr the father of Abner was the son of Á·bi´ĕl.

52 There was hard fighting against the Philistines all the days of Saul; and when Saul saw any strong man, or any valiant man, he attached him to himself.

15 And Samuel said to Saul, "The LORD sent me to anoint you king over his people Israel; now therefore hearken to the words of the LORD. 2 Thus says the LORD of hosts, 'I will punish what Am´á·lek did to Israel in opposing them on the way, when they came up out of Egypt. 3 Now go and smite Am´á·lek, and utterly destroy all that they have; do not spare them, but kill both man and woman, infant and suckling, ox and sheep, camel and ass.' "

4 So Saul summoned the people, and numbered them in Tĕ·lā´im, two hundred thousand men on foot, and ten thousand men of Judah. 5And Saul came to the city of Am´á·lek, and lay in wait in the valley. 6And Saul said to the Ken´ites, "Go, depart, go down from among the Á·mal´é·kites, lest I destroy you with them; for you showed kindness to all the people of Israel when they came up out of Egypt." So the Kenites departed from among the Amalekites. 7And Saul defeated the Á·mal´é·kites, from Hav´i·làh as far as Shür, which is east of Egypt. 8And he took Ā´gag the king of the Á·mal´é·kites alive, and utterly destroyed all the people with the edge of the sword. 9 But Saul and the people spared Ā´gag, and the best of the sheep and of the oxen and of the fatlings, and the lambs, and all that was good, and would not utterly destroy them; all that was despised and worthless they utterly destroyed.

10 The word of the LORD came to Samuel: 11 "I repent that I have made Saul king; for he has turned back from following me, and has not performed my commandments." And Samuel was angry; and he cried to the LORD all night. 12And Samuel rose early to meet Saul in the morning; and it was told Samuel, "Saul came to Cär´mĕl, and behold, he set up a monument for himself and turned, and passed on, and went down to Gil´gàl." 13And Samuel came to Saul, and Saul said to him, "Blessed be you to the LORD; I have performed the commandment of the LORD." 14And Samuel said, "What then is this bleating of the sheep in my ears, and the lowing of the oxen which I hear?" 15 Saul said, "They have brought them from the Á·mal´é·kites; for the people spared the best of the sheep and of the oxen, to sacrifice to the LORD your God; and the rest we have utterly destroyed." 16 Then Samuel said to Saul, "Stop! I will tell you what the LORD said to me this night." And he said to him, "Say on."

17 And Samuel said, "Though you are little in your own eyes, are you not the head of the tribes of Israel? The LORD anointed you king over Israel. 18And the LORD sent you on a mission, and said, 'Go, utterly destroy the sinners, the Á·mal´é·kites, and fight against them until they are consumed.' 19 Why then did you not obey the voice of the LORD? Why did you swoop on the spoil, and do what was evil in the sight of the LORD?" 20And Saul said to Samuel, "I have obeyed the voice of the LORD, I have gone on the mission on which the LORD sent me, I have brought Ā´gag the king of Am´á·lek, and I have utterly destroyed the Á·mal´é·kites. 21 But the people took of the spoil, sheep and oxen, the best of the things devoted to destruction, to sacrifice to the LORD your God in Gil´gàl." 22And Samuel said,

"Has the LORD as great delight in
    burnt offerings and sacrifices,
as in obeying the voice of the
    LORD?
Behold, to obey is better than
    sacrifice,
    and to hearken than the fat of
    rams.
23 For rebellion is as the sin of
    divination,
    and stubbornness is as iniquity
    and idolatry.
Because you have rejected the word
    of the LORD,
    he has also rejected you from be-
    ing king."

24 And Saul said to Samuel, "I have sinned; for I have transgressed the commandment of the LORD and your words, because I feared the people and obeyed their voice. 25 Now therefore, I pray, pardon my sin, and return with me, that I may worship the LORD." 26And Samuel said to Saul, "I will not return with you; for

14.49: 1 Sam 31.2; 1 Chron 10.2.   15.22: Mk 12.33.

you have rejected the word of the LORD, and the LORD has rejected you from being king over Israel." 27 As Samuel turned to go away, Saul laid hold upon the skirt of his robe, and it tore. 28And Samuel said to him, "The LORD has torn the kingdom of Israel from you this day, and has given it to a neighbor of yours, who is better than you. 29And also the Glory of Israel will not lie or repent; for he is not a man, that he should repent." 30 Then he said, "I have sinned; yet honor me now before the elders of my people and before Israel, and return with me, that I may worship the LORD your God." 31 So Samuel turned back after Saul; and Saul worshiped the LORD.

32 Then Samuel said, "Bring here to me A′gag the king of the Ȧ·mal′ē-kītes." And Agag came to him cheerfully. Agag said, "Surely the bitterness of death is past." 33And Samuel said, "As your sword has made women childless, so shall your mother be childless among women." And Samuel hewed A′gag in pieces before the LORD in Gil′gȧl.

34 Then Samuel went to Rā′mäh; and Saul went up to his house in Gib′ē-ȧh of Saul. 35And Samuel did not see Saul again until the day of his death, but Samuel grieved over Saul. And the LORD repented that he had made Saul king over Israel.

16 The LORD said to Samuel, "How long will you grieve over Saul, seeing I have rejected him from being king over Israel? Fill your horn with oil, and go; I will send you to Jesse the Bethlehemite, for I have provided for myself a king among his sons." 2And Samuel said, "How can I go? If Saul hears it, he will kill me." And the LORD said, "Take a heifer with you, and say, 'I have come to sacrifice to the LORD.' 3And invite Jesse to the sacrifice, and I will show you what you shall do; and you shall anoint for me him whom I name to you." 4 Samuel did what the LORD commanded, and came to Bethlehem. The elders of the city came to meet him trembling, and said, "Do you come peaceably?" 5And he said, "Peaceably; I have come to sacrifice to the LORD; consecrate yourselves, and come with me to the sacrifice." And he consecrated Jesse and his sons, and invited them to the sacrifice.

6 When they came, he looked on E·lī′ab and thought, "Surely the LORD's anointed is before him." 7 But the LORD said to Samuel, "Do not look on his appearance or on the height of his stature, because I have rejected him; for the LORD sees not as man sees; man looks on the outward appearance, but the LORD looks on the heart." 8 Then Jesse called Ȧ·bin′ȧ·dab, and made him pass before Samuel. And he said, "Neither has the LORD chosen this one." 9 Then Jesse made Sham′-mäh pass by. And he said, "Neither has the LORD chosen this one." 10And Jesse made seven of his sons pass before Samuel. And Samuel said to Jesse, "The LORD has not chosen these." 11And Samuel said to Jesse, "Are all your sons here?" And he said, "There remains yet the youngest; but behold, he is keeping the sheep." And Samuel said to Jesse, "Send and fetch him; for we will not sit down till he comes here." 12And he sent, and brought him in. Now he was ruddy, and had beautiful eyes, and was handsome. And the LORD said, "Arise, anoint him; for this is he." 13 Then Samuel took the horn of oil, and anointed him in the midst of his brothers; and the Spirit of the LORD came mightily upon David from that day forward. And Samuel rose up, and went to Rā′mäh.

14 Now the Spirit of the LORD departed from Saul, and an evil spirit from the LORD tormented him. 15And Saul's servants said to him, "Behold now, an evil spirit from God is tormenting you. 16 Let our lord now command your servants, who are before you, to seek out a man who is skilful in playing the lyre; and when the evil spirit from God is upon you, he will play it, and you will be well." 17 So Saul said to his servants, "Provide for me a man who can play well, and bring him to me." 18 One of the young men answered, "Behold, I have seen a son of Jesse the Bethlehemite, who is skilful in playing, a man of valor, a man of war, prudent in speech, and a man of good presence; and the LORD is with him." 19 Therefore Saul sent messengers to Jesse, and said, "Send me David your son, who is with the sheep." 20And Jesse took an ass laden with bread, and a skin of wine and a kid, and sent them by David his son to Saul. 21And David came to Saul, and entered his service. And Saul loved him greatly, and he became his armor-bearer. 22And Saul sent to Jesse, saying, "Let David remain in my service, for he has found favor in my sight." 23And whenever the evil spirit from God was upon Saul, David took the lyre and played it with his hand; so Saul was refreshed, and was well, and the evil spirit departed from him.

17 Now the Philistines gathered their armies for battle; and they were gathered at Sō´cōh, which belongs to Judah, and encamped between Socoh and Ă·zē´kåh, in Ĕ´pheš-dam´mim. ²And Saul and the men of Israel were gathered, and encamped in the valley of Ĕ´lah, and drew up in line of battle against the Philistines. ³And the Philistines stood on the mountain on the one side, and Israel stood on the mountain on the other side, with a valley between them. ⁴And there came out from the camp of the Philistines a champion named Goliath, of Gath, whose height was six cubits and a span. ⁵ He had a helmet of bronze on his head, and he was armed with a coat of mail, and the weight of the coat was five thousand shekels of bronze. ⁶And he had greaves of bronze upon his legs, and a javelin of bronze slung between his shoulders. ⁷And the shaft of his spear was like a weaver's beam, and his spear's head weighed six hundred shekels of iron; and his shield-bearer went before him. ⁸ He stood and shouted to the ranks of Israel, "Why have you come out to draw up for battle? Am I not a Philistine, and are you not servants of Saul? Choose a man for yourselves, and let him come down to me. ⁹ If he is able to fight with me and kill me, then we will be your servants; but if I prevail against him and kill him, then you shall be our servants and serve us." ¹⁰And the Philistine said, "I defy the ranks of Israel this day; give me a man, that we may fight together." ¹¹ When Saul and all Israel heard these words of the Philistine, they were dismayed and greatly afraid.

¹² Now David was the son of an Eph´rà·thite of Bethlehem in Judah, named Jesse, who had eight sons. In the days of Saul the man was already old and advanced in years.ˣ ¹³ The three eldest sons of Jesse had followed Saul to the battle; and the names of his three sons who went to the battle were E·li´ab the first-born, and next to him Ȧ·bin´ȧ·dab, and the third Sham´-mȧh. ¹⁴ David was the youngest; the three eldest followed Saul, ¹⁵ but David went back and forth from Saul to feed his father's sheep at Bethlehem. ¹⁶ For forty days the Philistine came forward and took his stand, morning and evening.

¹⁷ And Jesse said to David his son, "Take for your brothers an ephah of this parched grain, and these ten loaves, and carry them quickly to the camp to your brothers; ¹⁸ also take these ten cheeses to the commander of their thousand. See how your brothers fare, and bring some token from them."

¹⁹ Now Saul, and they, and all the men of Israel, were in the valley of Ĕ´lah, fighting with the Philistines. ²⁰And David rose early in the morning, and left the sheep with a keeper, and took the provisions, and went, as Jesse had commanded him; and he came to the encampment as the host was going forth to the battle line, shouting the war cry. ²¹And Israel and the Philistines drew up for battle, army against army. ²²And David left the things in charge of the keeper of the baggage, and ran to the ranks, and went and greeted his brothers. ²³ As he talked with them, behold, the champion, the Philistine of Gath, Goliath by name, came up out of the ranks of the Philistines, and spoke the same words as before. And David heard him.

²⁴ All the men of Israel, when they saw the man, fled from him, and were much afraid. ²⁵And the men of Israel said, "Have you seen this man who has come up? Surely he has come up to defy Israel; and the man who kills him, the king will enrich with great riches, and will give him his daughter, and make his father's house free in Israel." ²⁶And David said to the men who stood by him, "What shall be done for the man who kills this Philistine, and takes away the reproach from Israel? For who is this uncircumcised Philistine, that he should defy the armies of the living God?" ²⁷And the people answered him in the same way, "So shall it be done to the man who kills him."

²⁸ Now E·li´ab his eldest brother heard when he spoke to the men; and Eliab's anger was kindled against David, and he said, "Why have you come down? And with whom have you left those few sheep in the wilderness? I know your presumption, and the evil of your heart; for you have come down to see the battle." ²⁹And David said, "What have I done now? Was it not but a word?" ³⁰And he turned away from him toward another, and spoke in the same way; and the people answered him again as before.

³¹ When the words which David spoke were heard, they repeated them before Saul; and he sent for him. ³²And David said to Saul, "Let no man's heart fail because of him; your servant will go and fight with this Philistine." ³³And Saul said to David, "You are

ˣ Gk Syr: Heb *among men*

not able to go against this Philistine to fight with him; for you are but a youth, and he has been a man of war from his youth." 34 But David said to Saul, "Your servant used to keep sheep for his father; and when there came a lion, or a bear, and took a lamb from the flock, 35 I went after him and smote him and delivered it out of his mouth; and if he arose against me, I caught him by his beard, and smote him and killed him. 36 Your servant has killed both lions and bears; and this uncircumcised Philistine shall be like one of them, seeing he has defied the armies of the living God." 37 And David said, "The LORD who delivered me from the paw of the lion and from the paw of the bear, will deliver me from the hand of this Philistine." And Saul said to David, "Go, and the LORD be with you!" 38 Then Saul clothed David with his armor; he put a helmet of bronze on his head, and clothed him with a coat of mail. 39 And David girded his sword over his armor, and he tried in vain to go, for he was not used to them. Then David said to Saul, "I cannot go with these; for I am not used to them." And David put them off. 40 Then he took his staff in his hand, and chose five smooth stones from the brook, and put them in his shepherd's bag or wallet; his sling was in his hand, and he drew near to the Philistine.

41 And the Philistine came on and drew near to David, with his shield-bearer in front of him. 42 And when the Philistine looked, and saw David, he disdained him; for he was but a youth, ruddy and comely in appearance. 43 And the Philistine said to David, "Am I a dog, that you come to me with sticks?" And the Philistine cursed David by his gods. 44 The Philistine said to David, "Come to me, and I will give your flesh to the birds of the air and to the beasts of the field." 45 Then David said to the Philistine, "You come to me with a sword and with a spear and with a javelin; but I come to you in the name of the LORD of hosts, the God of the armies of Israel, whom you have defied. 46 This day the LORD will deliver you into my hand, and I will strike you down, and cut off your head; and I will give the dead bodies of the host of the Philistines this day to the birds of the air and to the wild beasts of the earth; that all the earth may know that there is a God in Israel, 47 and that all this assembly may know that the LORD

saves not with sword and spear; for the battle is the LORD's and he will give you into our hand."

48 When the Philistine arose and came and drew near to meet David, David ran quickly toward the battle line to meet the Philistine. 49 And David put his hand in his bag and took out a stone, and slung it, and struck the Philistine on his forehead; the stone sank into his forehead, and he fell on his face to the ground.

50 So David prevailed over the Philistine with a sling and with a stone, and struck the Philistine, and killed him; there was no sword in the hand of David. 51 Then David ran and stood over the Philistine, and took his sword and drew it out of its sheath, and killed him, and cut off his head with it. When the Philistines saw that their champion was dead, they fled. 52 And the men of Israel and Judah rose with a shout and pursued the Philistines as far as Gath^y and the gates of Ek′ron, so that the wounded Philistines fell on the way from Shā-à-rā′im as far as Gath and Ekron. 53 And the Israelites came back from chasing the Philistines, and they plundered their camp. 54 And David took the head of the Philistine and brought it to Jerusalem; but he put his armor in his tent.

55 When Saul saw David go forth against the Philistine, he said to Abner, the commander of the army, "Abner, whose son is this youth?" And Abner said, "As your soul lives, O king, I cannot tell." 56 And the king said, "Inquire whose son the stripling is." 57 And as David returned from the slaughter of the Philistine, Abner took him, and brought him before Saul with the head of the Philistine in his hand. 58 And Saul said to him, "Whose son are you, young man?" And David answered, "I am the son of your servant Jesse the Bethlehemite."

18 When he had finished speaking to Saul, the soul of Jonathan was knit to the soul of David, and Jonathan loved him as his own soul. 2 And Saul took him that day, and would not let him return to his father's house. 3 Then Jonathan made a covenant with David, because he loved him as his own soul. 4 And Jonathan stripped himself of the robe that was upon him, and gave it to David, and his armor, and even his sword and his bow and his girdle. 5 And David went out and was successful wherever Saul sent him; so that Saul set him over the men of war. And this was good in the sight of all the

^y Gk: Heb *Gai*

people and also in the sight of Saul's servants.

6 As they were coming home, when David returned from slaying the Philistine, the women came out of all the cities of Israel, singing and dancing, to meet King Saul, with timbrels, with songs of joy, and with instruments[z] of music. 7And the women sang to one another as they made merry,

"Saul has slain his thousands,
    and David his ten thousands."

8And Saul was very angry, and this saying displeased him; he said, "They have ascribed to David ten thousands, and to me they have ascribed thousands; and what more can he have but the kingdom?" 9And Saul eyed David from that day on.

10 And on the morrow an evil spirit from God rushed upon Saul, and he raved within his house, while David was playing the lyre, as he did day by day. Saul had his spear in his hand; 11and Saul cast the spear, for he thought, "I will pin David to the wall." But David evaded him twice.

12 Saul was afraid of David, because the LORD was with him but had departed from Saul. 13 So Saul removed him from his presence, and made him a commander of a thousand; and he went out and came in before the people. 14And David had success in all his undertakings; for the LORD was with him. 15And when Saul saw that he had great success, he stood in awe of him. 16 But all Israel and Judah loved David; for he went out and came in before them.

17 Then Saul said to David, "Here is my elder daughter Mĕ′rab; I will give her to you for a wife; only be valiant for me and fight the LORD's battles." For Saul thought, "Let not my hand be upon him, but let the hand of the Philistines be upon him." 18And David said to Saul, "Who am I, and who are my kinsfolk, my father's family in Israel, that I should be son-in-law to the king?" 19 But at the time when Mĕ′rab, Saul's daughter, should have been given to David, she was given to A′dri-el the Mĕ-hō′la-thite for a wife.

20 Now Saul's daughter Mi′chal loved David; and they told Saul, and the thing pleased him. 21 Saul thought, "Let me give her to him, that she may be a snare for him, and that the hand of the Philistines may be against him." Therefore Saul said to David a second

time,[a] "You shall now be my son-in-law." 22And Saul commanded his servants, "Speak to David in private and say, 'Behold, the king has delight in you, and all his servants love you; now then become the king's son-in-law.' " 23And Saul's servants spoke those words in the ears of David. And David said, "Does it seem to you a little thing to become the king's son-in-law, seeing that I am a poor man and of no repute?" 24And the servants of Saul told him, "Thus and so did David speak." 25 Then Saul said, "Thus shall you say to David, 'The king desires no marriage present except a hundred foreskins of the Philistines, that he may be avenged of the king's enemies.' " Now Saul thought to make David fall by the hand of the Philistines. 26And when his servants told David these words, it pleased David well to be the king's son-in-law. Before the time had expired. 27 David arose and went, along with his men, and killed two hundred of the Philistines; and David brought their foreskins, which were given in full number to the king, that he might become the king's son-in-law. And Saul gave him his daughter Mi′chal for a wife. 28 But when Saul saw and knew that the LORD was with David, and that all Israel[b] loved him, 29 Saul was still more afraid of David. So Saul was David's enemy continually.

30 Then the princes of the Philistines came out to battle, and as often as they came out David had more success than all the servants of Saul; so that his name was highly esteemed.

19 And Saul spoke to Jonathan his son and to all his servants, that they should kill David. But Jonathan, Saul's son, delighted much in David. 2And Jonathan told David, "Saul my father seeks to kill you; therefore take heed to yourself in the morning, stay in a secret place and hide yourself; 3 and I will go out and stand beside my father in the field where you are, and I will speak to my father about you; and if I learn anything I will tell you." 4And Jonathan spoke well of David to Saul his father, and said to him, "Let not the king sin against his servant David; because he has not sinned against you, and because his deeds have been of good service to you; 5 for he took his life in his hand and he slew the Philistine, and the LORD wrought a great victory for all Israel.

z Or triangles, or three-stringed instruments
b Gk: Heb Michal, Saul's daughter
18.7: 1 Sam 21.11; 29.5.
a Heb by two

You saw it, and rejoiced; why then will you sin against innocent blood by killing David without cause?" 6And Saul hearkened to the voice of Jonathan; Saul swore, "As the LORD lives, he shall not be put to death." 7And Jonathan called David, and Jonathan showed him all these things. And Jonathan brought David to Saul, and he was in his presence as before.

8 And there was war again; and David went out and fought with the Philistines, and made a great slaughter among them, so that they fled before him. 9 Then an evil spirit from the LORD came upon Saul, as he sat in his house with his spear in his hand; and David was playing the lyre. 10And Saul sought to pin David to the wall with the spear; but he eluded Saul, so that he struck the spear into the wall. And David fled, and escaped.

11 That night Saul^x sent messengers to David's house to watch him, that he might kill him in the morning. But Mi'chal, David's wife, told him, "If you do not save your life tonight, tomorrow you will be killed." 12 So Mi'chal let David down through the window; and he fled away and escaped. 13 Mi'chal took an image^c and laid it on the bed and put a pillow^d of goats' hair at its head, and covered it with the clothes. 14And when Saul sent messengers to take David, she said, "He is sick." 15 Then Saul sent the messengers to see David, saying, "Bring him up to me in the bed, that I may kill him." 16And when the messengers came in, behold, the image^c was in the bed, with the pillow^d of goats' hair at its head. 17 Saul said to Mi'chal, "Why have you deceived me thus, and let my enemy go, so that he has escaped?" And Michal answered Saul, "He said to me, 'Let me go; why should I kill you?' "

18 Now David fled and escaped, and he came to Samuel at Rā'mah, and told him all that Saul had done to him. And he and Samuel went and dwelt at Nāi'ōth. 19And it was told Saul, "Behold, David is at Nāi'ōth in Rā'mah." 20 Then Saul sent messengers to take David; and when they saw the company of the prophets prophesying, and Samuel standing as head over them, the Spirit of God came upon the messengers of Saul, and they also prophesied. 21 When it was told Saul, he sent other messengers, and they also prophesied. And Saul sent messengers again the third time, and they also prophesied. 22 Then he himself went to Rā'mah, and came to the great well that is in Sē'cū; and he asked, "Where are Samuel and David?" And one said, "Behold, they are at Nāi'ōth in Ramah." 23And he went from^f there to Nāi'ōth in Rā'mah; and the Spirit of God came upon him also, and as he went he prophesied, until he came to Naioth in Ramah. 24And he too stripped off his clothes, and he too prophesied before Samuel, and lay naked all that day and all that night. Hence it is said, "Is Saul also among the prophets?"

20 Then David fled from Nāi'ōth in Rā'mah, and came and said before Jonathan, "What have I done? What is my guilt? And what is my sin before your father, that he seeks my life?" 2And he said to him, "Far from it! You shall not die. Behold, my father does nothing either great or small without disclosing it to me; and why should my father hide this from me? It is not so." 3 But David replied,^{g} "Your father knows well that I have found favor in your eyes; and he thinks, 'Let not Jonathan know this, lest he be grieved.' But truly, as the LORD lives and as your soul lives, there is but a step between me and death." 4 Then said Jonathan to David, "Whatever you say, I will do for you." 5 David said to Jonathan, "Behold, tomorrow is the new moon, and I should not fail to sit at table with the king; but let me go, that I may hide myself in the field till the third day at evening. 6 If your father misses me at all, then say, 'David earnestly asked leave of me to run to Bethlehem his city; for there is a yearly sacrifice there for all the family.' 7 If he says, 'Good!' it will be well with your servant; but if he is angry, then know that evil is determined by him. 8 Therefore deal kindly with your servant, for you have brought your servant into a sacred covenant^h with you. But if there is guilt in me, slay me yourself; for why should you bring me to your father?" 9And Jonathan said, "Far be it from you! If I knew that it was determined by my father that evil should come upon you, would I not tell you?" 10 Then said David to Jonathan, "Who will tell me if your father answers you roughly?" 11And Jonathan said to David, "Come,

x Gk Old Latin: Heb *escaped that night.* 11 *And Saul* c Heb *teraphim* d The meaning of the Hebrew word is uncertain f Gk: Heb lacks *from* g Gk: Heb *swore again* h Heb *a covenant of the* LORD
19.23-24: 1 Sam 10.10-12.

let us go out into the field." So they both went out into the field.

12 And Jonathan said to David, "The LORD, the God of Israel, be witness![i] When I have sounded my father, about this time tomorrow, or the third day, behold, if he is well disposed toward David, shall I not then send and disclose it to you? [13] But should it please my father to do you harm, the LORD do so to Jonathan, and more also, if I do not disclose it to you, and send you away, that you may go in safety. May the LORD be with you, as he has been with my father. [14] If I am still alive, show me the loyal love of the LORD, that I may not die;[j] [15] and do not cut off your loyalty from my house for ever. When the LORD cuts off every one of the enemies of David from the face of the earth, [16] let not the name of Jonathan be cut off from the house of David.[k] And may the LORD take vengeance on David's enemies." [17]And Jonathan made David swear again by his love for him; for he loved him as he loved his own soul.

18 Then Jonathan said to him, "To-morrow is the new moon; and you will be missed, because your seat will be empty. [19]And on the third day you will be greatly missed;[l] then go to the place where you hid yourself when the matter was in hand, and remain beside yonder stone heap.[m] [20]And I will shoot three arrows to the side of it, as though I shot at a mark. [21]And behold, I will send the lad, saying, 'Go, find the arrows.' If I say to the lad, 'Look, the arrows are on this side of you, take them,' then you are to come, for, as the LORD lives, it is safe for you and there is no danger. [22] But if I say to the youth, 'Look, the arrows are be-yond you,' then go; for the LORD has sent you away. [23]And as for the matter of which you and I have spoken, be-hold, the LORD is between you and me for ever."

24 So David hid himself in the field; and when the new moon came, the king sat down to eat food. [25] The king sat upon his seat, as at other times, upon the seat by the wall; Jonathan sat opposite,[n] and Abner sat by Saul's side, but David's place was empty. [26] Yet Saul did not say anything that day; for he thought, "Something has befallen him; he is not clean, surely he is not clean." [27] But on the

second day, the morrow after the new moon, David's place was empty. And Saul said to Jonathan his son, "Why has not the son of Jesse come to the meal, either yesterday or today?" [28] Jonathan answered Saul, "David earnestly asked leave of me to go to Bethlehem; [29] he said, 'Let me go; for our family holds a sacrifice in the city, and my brother has commanded me to be there. So now, if I have found favor in your eyes, let me get away, and see my brothers.' For this reason he has not come to the king's table."

30 Then Saul's anger was kindled against Jonathan, and he said to him, "You son of a perverse, rebellious woman, do I not know that you have chosen the son of Jesse to your own shame, and to the shame of your mother's nakedness? [31] For as long as the son of Jesse lives upon the earth, neither you nor your kingdom shall be established. Therefore send and fetch him to me, for he shall surely die." [32] Then Jonathan answered Saul his father, "Why should he be put to death? What has he done?" [33] But Saul cast his spear at him to smite him; so Jonathan knew that his father was determined to put David to death. [34]And Jonathan rose from the table in fierce anger and ate no food the second day of the month, for he was grieved for David, because his father had dis-graced him.

35 In the morning Jonathan went out into the field to the appointment with David, and with him a little lad. [36]And he said to his lad, "Run and find the arrows which I shoot." As the lad ran, he shot an arrow beyond him. [37]And when the lad came to the place of the arrow which Jonathan had shot, Jonathan called after the lad and said, "Is not the arrow beyond you?" [38]And Jonathan called after the lad, "Hurry, make haste, stay not." So Jonathan's lad gathered up the arrows, and came to his master. [39] But the lad knew nothing; only Jonathan and David knew the matter. [40]And Jonathan gave his weapons to his lad, and said to him, "Go and carry them to the city." [41]And as soon as the lad had gone, David rose from beside the stone heap[o] and fell on his face to the ground, and bowed three times; and they kissed one another, and wept with one another, until David recovered himself.[p] [42] Then Jonathan said to

---

[i] Heb lacks *be witness* [j] Heb *uncertain*

[k] Gk: Heb *earth, and Jonathan made a covenant with the house of David*

[l] Gk: Heb *go down quickly* [m] Gk: Heb *the stone Ezel* [n] Cn See Gk: Heb *stood up*

[o] Gk: Heb *from beside the south* [p] Or *exceeded*

David, "Go in peace, forasmuch as we have sworn both of us in the name of the LORD, saying, 'The LORD shall be between me and you, and between my descendants and your descendants, for ever.'" And he rose and departed; and Jonathan went into the city.[q]

21 [r] Then came David to Nob to A·him′e·lech the priest; and Ahimelech came to meet David trembling, and said to him, "Why are you alone, and no one with you?" 2And David said to A·him′e·lech the priest, "The king has charged me with a matter, and said to me, 'Let no one know anything of the matter about which I send you, and with which I have charged you.' I have made an appointment with the young men for such and such a place. 3 Now then, what have you at hand? Give me five loaves of bread, or whatever is here." 4And the priest answered David, "I have no common bread at hand, but there is holy bread; if only the young men have kept themselves from women." 5And David answered the priest, "Of a truth women have been kept from us as always when I go on an expedition; the vessels of the young men are holy, even when it is a common journey; how much more today will their vessels be holy?" 6 So the priest gave him the holy bread; for there was no bread there but the bread of the Presence, which is removed from before the LORD, to be replaced by hot bread on the day it is taken away.

7 Now a certain man of the servants of Saul was there that day, detained before the LORD; his name was Dō′eg the E′dom·ite, the chief of Saul's herdsmen.

8 And David said to A·him′e·lech, "And have you not here a spear or a sword at hand? For I have brought neither my sword nor my weapons with me, because the king's business required haste." 9And the priest said, "The sword of Goliath the Philistine, whom you killed in the valley of E′lah, behold, it is here wrapped in a cloth behind the ephod; if you will take that, take it, for there is none but that here." And David said, "There is none like that; give it to me."

10 And David rose and fled that day from Saul, and went to A′chish the king of Gath. 11And the servants of A′chish said to him, "Is not this David the king of the land? Did they not sing to one another of him in dances,

'Saul has slain his thousands, and David his ten thousands'?" 12And David took these words to heart, and was much afraid of A′chish the king of Gath. 13 So he changed his behavior before them, and feigned himself mad in their hands, and made marks on the doors of the gate, and let his spittle run down his beard. 14 Then said A′chish to his servants, "Lo, you see the man is mad; why then have you brought him to me? 15 Do I lack madmen, that you have brought this fellow to play the madman in my presence? Shall this fellow come into my house?"

22 David departed from there and escaped to the cave of A·dul′lam; and when his brothers and all his father's house heard it, they went down there to him. 2And every one who was in distress, and every one who was in debt, and every one who was discontented, gathered to him; and he became captain over them. And there were with him about four hundred men.

3 And David went from there to Miz′peh of Mō′ab; and he said to the king of Moab, "Pray let my father and my mother stay[s] with you, till I know what God will do for me." 4And he left them with the king of Mō′ab, and they stayed with him all the time that David was in the stronghold. 5 Then the prophet Gad said to David, "Do not remain in the stronghold; depart, and go into the land of Judah." So David departed, and went into the forest of Hē′reth.

6 Now Saul heard that David was discovered, and the men who were with him. Saul was sitting at Gib′e·ah, under the tamarisk tree on the height, with his spear in his hand, and all his servants were standing about him. 7And Saul said to his servants who stood about him, "Hear now, you Benjaminites; will the son of Jesse give every one of you fields and vineyards, will he make you all commanders of thousands and commanders of hundreds, 8 that all of you have conspired against me? No one discloses to me when my son makes a league with the son of Jesse, none of you is sorry for me or discloses to me that my son has stirred up my servant against me, to lie in wait, as at this day." 9 Then answered Dō′eg the E′dom·ite, who stood by the servants of Saul, "I saw the son of Jesse coming to Nob, to A·him′e·lech the son of A·hi′tub, 10 and he inquired of the LORD for

---

[q] This sentence is 21.1 in Heb   [r] Ch 21.2 in Heb   [s] Syr Vg: Heb *come out*
21.11: 1 Sam 18.7; 29.5.

him, and gave him provisions, and gave him the sword of Goliath the Philistine."

11 Then the king sent to summon Ả·him′é·lech the priest, the son of Ả·hī′tŭb, and all his father's house, the priests who were at Nob; and all of them came to the king. 12And Saul said, "Hear now, son of Ả·hī′tŭb." And he answered, "Here I am, my lord." 13And Saul said to him, "Why have you conspired against me, you and the son of Jesse, in that you have given him bread and a sword, and have inquired of God for him, so that he has risen against me, to lie in wait, as at this day?" 14 Then Ả·him′é·lech answered the king, "And who among all your servants is so faithful as David, who is the king's son-in-law, and captain over*ᵗ* your bodyguard, and honored in your house? 15 Is today the first time that I have inquired of God for him? No! Let not the king impute anything to his servant or to all the house of my father; for your servant has known nothing of all this, much or little." 16And, the king said, "You shall surely die, Ả·him′é·lech, you and all your father's house." 17And the king said to the guard who stood about him, "Turn and kill the priests of the LORD; because their hand also is with David, and they knew that he fled, and did not disclose it to me." But the servants of the king would not put forth their hand to fall upon the priests of the LORD. 18 Then the king said to Dŏ′eg, "You turn and fall upon the priests." And Doeg the E′dŏm·ite turned and fell upon the priests, and he killed on that day eighty-five persons who wore the linen ephod. 19And Nob, the city of the priests, he put to the sword; both men and women, children and sucklings, oxen, asses and sheep, he put to the sword.

20 But one of the sons of Ả·him′é·lech the son of Ả·hī′tŭb, named Ả·bī′ả·thär, escaped and fled after David. 21And Ả·bī′ả·thär told David that Saul had killed the priests of the LORD. 22And David said to Ả·bī′ả·thär, "I knew on that day, when Dŏ′eg the E′dŏm·ite was there, that he would surely tell Saul. I have occasioned the death of all the persons of your father's house. 23 Stay with me, fear not; for he that seeks my life seeks your life; with me you shall be in safekeeping."

23 Now they told David, "Behold, the Philistines are fighting against Kē·ī′làh, and are robbing the threshing floors." 2 Therefore David

inquired of the LORD, "Shall I go and attack these Philistines?" And the LORD said to David, "Go and attack the Philistines and save Kē·ī′làh." 3 But David's men said to him, "Behold, we are afraid here in Judah; how much more then if we go to Kē·ī′làh against the armies of the Philistines?" 4 Then David inquired of the LORD again. And the LORD answered him, "Arise, go down to Kē·ī′làh; for I will give the Philistines into your hand." 5And David and his men went to Kē·ī′làh, and fought with the Philistines, and brought away their cattle, and made a great slaughter among them. So David delivered the inhabitants of Keilah.

6 When Ả·bī′ả·thär the son of Ả·him′é·lech fled to David to Kē·ī′làh, he came down with an ephod in his hand. 7 Now it was told Saul that David had come to Kē·ī′làh. And Saul said, "God has given him into my hand; for he has shut himself in by entering a town that has gates and bars." 8And Saul summoned all the people to war, to go down to Kē·ī′làh, to besiege David and his men. 9 David knew that Saul was plotting evil against him; and he said to Ả·bī′ả·thär the priest, "Bring the ephod here." 10 Then said David, "O LORD, the God of Israel, thy servant has surely heard that Saul seeks to come to Kē·ī′làh, to destroy the city on my account. 11 Will the men of Kē·ī′làh surrender me into his hand? Will Saul come down, as thy servant has heard? O LORD, the God of Israel, I beseech thee, tell thy servant." And the LORD said, "He will come down." 12 Then said David, "Will the men of Kē·ī′làh surrender me and my men into the hand of Saul?" And the LORD said, "They will surrender you." 13 Then David and his men, who were about six hundred, arose and departed from Kē·ī′làh, and they went wherever they could go. When Saul was told that David had escaped from Keilah, he gave up the expedition. 14And David remained in the strongholds in the wilderness, in the hill country of the Wilderness of Ziph. And Saul sought him every day, but God did not give him into his hand.

15 And David was afraid because*ᵘ* Saul had come out to seek his life. David was in the Wilderness of Ziph at Hō′resh. 16And Jonathan, Saul's son, rose, and went to David at Hō′resh, and strengthened his hand in God. 17And he said to him, "Fear not;

t Gk Tg: Heb *and has turned aside to*   *u* Or *saw that* for the hand of Saul my father shall not find you; you shall be king over Israel, and I shall be next to you; Saul my father also knows this." 18And the two of them made a covenant before the LORD; David remained at Hō'resh, and Jonathan went home.

19 Then the Ziphites went up to Saul at Gib'ē-ăh, saying, "Does not David hide among us in the strongholds at Hō'resh, on the hill of Hă-chī'lăh, which is south of Jē-shī'mon? 20 Now come down, O king, according to all your heart's desire to come down; and our part shall be to surrender him into the king's hand." 21And Saul said, "May you be blessed by the LORD; for you have had compassion on me. 22 Go, make yet more sure; know and see the place where his haunt is, and who has seen him there; for it is told me that he is very cunning. 23 See therefore, and take note of all the lurking places where he hides, and come back to me with sure information. Then I will go with you; and if he is in the land, I will search him out among all the thousands of Judah." 24And they arose, and went to Ziph ahead of Saul.

Now David and his men were in the wilderness of Mā'on, in the Ar'ȧ-bàh to the south of Jē-shī'mon. 25And Saul and his men went to seek him. And David was told; therefore he went down to the rock which is*y* in the wilderness of Mā'on. And when Saul heard that, he pursued after David in the wilderness of Maon. 26 Saul went on one side of the mountain, and David and his men on the other side of the mountain; and David was making haste to get away from Saul, as Saul and his men were closing in upon David and his men to capture them, 27 when a messenger came to Saul, saying, "Make haste and come; for the Philistines have made a raid upon the land." 28 So Saul returned from pursuing after David, and went against the Philistines; therefore that place was called the Rock of Escape. 29 *w*And David went up from there, and dwelt in the strongholds of En-gĕ'dĭ.

24 When Saul returned from following the Philistines, he was told, "Behold, David is in the wilderness of En-gĕ'dĭ." 2 Then Saul took three thousand chosen men out of all Israel, and went to seek David and his men in front of the Wildgoats' Rocks. 3And he came to the sheepfolds by the way, where there was a cave; and

Saul went in to relieve himself. Now David and his men were sitting in the innermost parts of the cave. 4And the men of David said to him, "Here is the day of which the LORD said to you, 'Behold, I will give your enemy into your hand, and you shall do to him as it shall seem good to you.'" Then David arose and stealthily cut off the skirt of Saul's robe. 5And afterward David's heart smote him, because he had cut off Saul's skirt. 6 He said to his men, "The LORD forbid that I should do this thing to my lord, the LORD's anointed, to put forth my hand against him, seeing he is the LORD's anointed." 7 So David persuaded his men with these words, and did not permit them to attack Saul. And Saul rose up and left the cave, and went upon his way.

8 Afterward David also arose, and went out of the cave, and called after Saul, "My lord the king!" And when Saul looked behind him, David bowed with his face to the earth, and did obeisance. 9And David said to Saul, "Why do you listen to the words of men who say, 'Behold, David seeks your hurt'? 10 Lo, this day your eyes have seen how the LORD gave you to-day into my hand in the cave; and some bade me kill you, but I*x* spared you. I said, 'I will not put forth my hand against my lord; for he is the LORD's anointed.' 11 See, my father, see the skirt of your robe in my hand; for by the fact that I cut off the skirt of your robe, and did not kill you, you may know and see that there is no wrong or treason in my hands. I have not sinned against you, though you hunt my life to take it. 12 May the LORD judge between me and you, may the LORD avenge me upon you; but my hand shall not be against you. 13As the proverb of the ancients says, 'Out of the wicked comes forth wickedness'; but my hand shall not be against you. 14After whom has the king of Israel come out? After whom do you pursue? After a dead dog! After a flea! 15 May the LORD therefore be judge, and give sentence between me and you, and see to it, and plead my cause, and deliver me from your hand."

16 When David had finished speaking these words to Saul, Saul said, "Is this your voice, my son David?" And Saul lifted up his voice and wept. 17 He said to David, "You are more righteous than I; for you have repaid

v Gk: Heb *and dwelt*   *w* Ch 24.1 in Heb   *x* Gk Syr Tg: Heb *you*
24.1-22: 1 Sam 26.1-25.

me good, whereas I have repaid you evil. 18And you have declared this day how you have dealt well with me, in that you did not kill me when the LORD put me into your hands. 19 For if a man finds his enemy, will he let him go away safe? So may the LORD reward you with good for what you have done to me this day. 20And now, behold, I know that you shall surely be king, and that the kingdom of Israel shall be established in your hand. 21 Swear to me therefore by the LORD that you will not cut off my descendants after me, and that you will not destroy my name out of my father's house." 22And David swore this to Saul. Then Saul went home; but David and his men went up to the stronghold.

25 Now Samuel died; and all Israel assembled and mourned for him, and they buried him in his house at Rā′mâh.

Then David rose and went down to the wilderness of Pâr′an. 2And there was a man in Mâ′on, whose business was in Cär′mêl. The man was very rich; he had three thousand sheep and a thousand goats. He was shearing his sheep in Carmel. 3 Now the name of the man was Nā′bal, and the name of his wife Ab′i·gâil. The woman was of good understanding and beautiful, but the man was churlish and ill-behaved; he was a Calebite. 4 David heard in the wilderness that Nā′bal was shearing his sheep. 5 So David sent ten young men; and David said to the young men, "Go up to Cär′mêl, and go to Nā′bal, and greet him in my name. 6And thus you shall salute him: 'Peace be to you, and peace be to your house, and peace be to all that you have. 7·I hear that you have shearers; now your shepherds have been with us, and we did them no harm, and they missed nothing, all the time they were in Cär′mêl. 8Ask your young men, and they will tell you. Therefore let my young men find favor in your eyes; for we come on a feast day. Pray, give whatever you have at hand to your servants and to your son David.' "

9 When David's young men came, they said all this to Nā′bal in the name of David; and then they waited. 10And Nā′bal answered David's servants, "Who is David? Who is the son of Jesse? There are many servants nowadays who are breaking away from their masters. 11 Shall I take my bread and my water and my meat that I have killed for my shearers, and give it to

men who come from I do not know where?" 12 So David's young men turned away, and came back and told him all this. 13And David said to his men, "Every man gird on his sword!" And every man of them girded on his sword; David also girded on his sword; and about four hundred men went up after David, while two hundred remained with the baggage.

14 But one of the young men told Ab′i·gâil, Nā′bal's wife, "Behold, David sent messengers out of the wilderness to salute our master; and he railed at them. 15 Yet the men were very good to us, and we suffered no harm, and we did not miss anything when we were in the fields, as long as we went with them; 16 they were a wall to us both by night and by day, all the while we were with them keeping the sheep. 17 Now therefore know this and consider what you should do; for evil is determined against our master and against all his house, and he is so ill-natured that one cannot speak to him."

18 Then Ab′i·gâil made haste, and took two hundred loaves, and two skins of wine, and five sheep ready dressed, and five measures of parched grain, and a hundred clusters of raisins, and two hundred cakes of figs, and laid them on asses. 19And she said to her young men, "Go on before me; behold, I come after you." But she did not tell her husband Nā′bal. 20And as she rode on the ass, and came down under cover of the mountain, behold, David and his men came down toward her; and she met them. 21 Now David had said, "Surely in vain have I guarded all that this fellow has in the wilderness, so that nothing was missed of all that belonged to him; and he has returned me evil for good. 22 God do so to David*y* and more also, if by morning I leave so much as one male of all who belong to him."

23 When Ab′i·gâil saw David, she made haste, and alighted from the ass, and fell before David on her face, and bowed to the ground. 24 She fell at his feet and said, "Upon me alone, my lord, be the guilt; pray let your handmaid speak in your ears, and hear the words of your handmaid. 25 Let not my lord regard this ill-natured fellow, Nā′bal; for as his name is, so is he; Nabal*z* is his name, and folly is with him; but I your handmaid did not see the young men of my lord, whom you sent. 26 Now then, my lord, as the LORD lives, and as your soul lives, seeing the LORD has restrained you from

y Gk Compare Syr: Heb *the enemies of David*   *z* That is *fool*

bloodguilt, and from taking vengeance with your own hand, now then let your enemies and those who seek to do evil to my lord be as Nā′bal. ²⁷And now let this present which your servant has brought to my lord be given to the young men who follow my lord. ²⁸ Pray forgive the trespass of your handmaid; for the LORD will certainly make my lord a sure house, because my lord is fighting the battles of the LORD; and evil shall not be found in you so long as you live. ²⁹ If men rise up to pursue you and to seek your life, the life of my lord shall be bound in the bundle of the living in the care of the LORD your God; and the lives of your enemies he shall sling out as from the hollow of a sling. ³⁰And when the LORD has done to my lord according to all the good that he has spoken concerning you, and has appointed you prince over Israel, ³¹ my lord shall have no cause of grief, or pangs of conscience, for having shed blood without cause or for my lord taking vengeance himself. And when the LORD has dealt well with my lord, then remember your handmaid."

32 And David said to Ab′i·gāil, "Blessed be the LORD, the God of Israel, who sent you this day to meet me! ³³ Blessed be your discretion, and blessed be you, who have kept me this day from bloodguilt and from avenging myself with my own hand! ³⁴ For as surely as the LORD the God of Israel lives, who has restrained me from hurting you, unless you had made haste and come to meet me, truly by morning there had not been left to Nā′bal so much as one male." ³⁵ Then David received from her hand what she had brought him; and he said to her, "Go up in peace to your house; see, I have hearkened to your voice, and I have granted your petition."

36 And Ab′i·gāil came to Nā′bal; and, lo, he was holding a feast in his house, like the feast of a king. And Nabal's heart was merry within him, for he was very drunk; so she told him nothing at all until the morning light. ³⁷And in the morning, when the wine had gone out of Nā′bal, his wife told him these things, and his heart died within him, and he became as a stone. ³⁸And about ten days later the LORD smote Nā′bal; and he died.

39 When David heard that Nā′bal was dead, he said, "Blessed be the LORD who has avenged the insult I received at the hand of Nabal, and has kept back his servant from evil; the

LORD has returned the evil-doing of Nabal upon his own head." Then David sent and wooed Ab′i·gāil, to make her his wife. ⁴⁰And when the servants of David came to Ab′i·gāil at Cär′mĕl, they said to her, "David has sent us to you to take you to him as his wife." ⁴¹And she rose and bowed with her face to the ground, and said, "Behold, your handmaid is a servant to wash the feet of the servants of my lord." ⁴²And Ab′i·gāil made haste and rose and mounted on an ass, and her five maidens attended her; she went after the messengers of David, and became his wife.

43 David also took Å·hin′ō·am of Jez′rē·ĕl; and both of them became his wives. ⁴⁴ Saul had given Mī′chal his daughter, David's wife, to Pal′tī the son of Lā′ish, who was of Gal′lim.

26 Then the Ziphites came to Saul at Gib′ē-ăh, saying, "Is not David hiding himself on the hill of Hå·chi′lăh, which is on the east of Jĕ·shi′mon?" ² So Saul arose and went down to the wilderness of Ziph, with three thousand chosen men of Israel, to seek David in the wilderness of Ziph. ³And Saul encamped on the hill of Hå·chi′lăh, which is beside the road on the east of Jĕ·shi′mon. But David remained in the wilderness; and when he saw that Saul came after him into the wilderness, ⁴ David sent out spies, and learned of a certainty that Saul had come. ⁵ Then David rose and came to the place where Saul had encamped; and David saw the place where Saul lay, with Abner the son of Nĕr, the commander of his army; Saul was lying within the encampment, while the army was encamped around him.

6 Then David said to Å·him′ĕ·lech the Hit′tite, and to Jō′ab's brother Å·bi′shäi the son of Zĕ·rü′i·ăh, "Who will go down with me into the camp to Saul?" And Abishai said, "I will go down with you." ⁷ So David and Å·bi′shäi went to the army by night; and there lay Saul sleeping within the encampment, with his spear stuck in the ground at his head; and Abner and the army lay around him. ⁸ Then said Å·bi′shäi to David, "God has given your enemy into your hand this day; now therefore let me pin him to the earth with one stroke of the spear, and I will not strike him twice." ⁹ But David said to Å·bi′shäi, "Do not destroy him; for who can put forth his hand against the LORD's anointed, and be guiltless?" ¹⁰And David said, "As the LORD lives, the LORD will smite

26.1-25: 1 Sam 24.1-22.

him; or his day shall come to die; or he shall go down into battle and perish. 11 The LORD forbid that I should put forth my hand against the LORD's anointed; but take now the spear that is at his head, and the jar of water, and let us go." 12 So David took the spear and the jar of water from Saul's head; and they went away. No man saw it, or knew it, nor did any awake; for they were all asleep, because a deep sleep from the LORD had fallen upon them.

13 Then David went over to the other side, and stood afar off on the top of the mountain, with a great space between them; 14 and David called to the army, and to Abner the son of Nĕr, saying, "Will you not answer, Abner?" Then Abner answered, "Who are you that calls to the king?" 15 And David said to Abner, "Are you not a man? Who is like you in Israel? Why then have you not kept watch over your lord the king? For one of the people came in to destroy the king your lord. 16 This thing that you have done is not good. As the LORD lives, you deserve to die, because you have not kept watch over your lord, the LORD's anointed. And now see where the king's spear is, and the jar of water that was at his head."

17 Saul recognized David's voice, and said, "Is this your voice, my son David?" And David said, "It is my voice, my lord, O king." 18 And he said, "Why does my lord pursue after his servant? For what have I done? What guilt is on my hands? 19 Now therefore let my lord the king hear the words of his servant. If it is the LORD who has stirred you up against me, may he accept an offering; but if it is men, may they be cursed before the LORD, for they have driven me out this day that I should have no share in the heritage of the LORD, saying, 'Go, serve other gods.' 20 Now therefore, let not my blood fall to the earth away from the presence of the LORD; for the king of Israel has come out to seek my life,*a* like one who hunts a partridge in the mountains."

21 Then Saul said, "I have done wrong; return, my son David, for I will no more do you harm, because my life was precious in your eyes this day; behold, I have played the fool, and have erred exceedingly." 22 And David made answer, "Here is the spear, O king! Let one of the young men come over and fetch it. 23 The LORD rewards every man for his righteousness and his faithfulness; for the LORD gave you

into my hand today, and I would not put forth my hand against the LORD's anointed. 24 Behold, as your life was precious this day in my sight, so may my life be precious in the sight of the LORD, and may he deliver me out of all tribulation." 25 Then Saul said to David, "Blessed be you, my son David! You will do many things and will succeed in them." So David went his way, and Saul returned to his place.

27

And David said in his heart, "I shall now perish one day by the hand of Saul; there is nothing better for me than that I should escape to the land of the Philistines; then Saul will despair of seeking me any longer within the borders of Israel, and I shall escape out of his hand." 2 So David arose and went over, he and the six hundred men who were with him, to Ā'chish the son of Mā'och, king of Gath. 3 And David dwelt with Ā'chish at Gath, he and his men, every man with his household, and David with his two wives, Ā·hin'ō-am of Jez'rē·ĕl, and Ab'i·gāil of Cär'mĕl, Nā'bal's widow. 4 And when it was told Saul that David had fled to Gath, he sought for him no more.

5 Then David said to Ā'chish, "If I have found favor in your eyes, let a place be given me in one of the country towns, that I may dwell there; for why should your servant dwell in the royal city with you?" 6 So that day Ā'chish gave him Zik'lag; therefore Ziklag has belonged to the kings of Judah to this day. 7 And the number of the days that David dwelt in the country of the Philistines was a year and four months.

8 Now David and his men went up, and made raids upon the Gesh'ū·rites, the Gīr'zites, and the Ā·mal'ĕ·kītes; for these were the inhabitants of the land from of old, as far as Shūr, to the land of Egypt. 9 And David smote the land, and left neither man nor woman alive, but took away the sheep, the oxen, the asses, the camels, and the garments, and came back to Ā'chish. 10 When Ā'chish asked, "Against whom*b* have you made a raid today?" David would say, "Against the Negeb of Judah," or "Against the Negeb of the Jé·rāh'mē·ĕ·lītes," or, "Against the Negeb of the Ken'ites." 11 And David saved neither man nor woman alive, to bring tidings to Gath, thinking, "Lest they should tell about us, and say, 'So David has done.'" Such was his custom all the while he

a Gk: Heb *a flea* (as in 24.14)   *b* Gk Vg: Heb lacks *whom* dwelt in the country of the Philistines. [12]And Ā´chish trusted David, thinking, "He has made himself utterly abhorred by his people Israel; therefore he shall be my servant always."

28 In those days the Philistines gathered their forces for war, to fight against Israel. And Ā´chish said to David, "Understand that you and your men are to go out with me in the army." [2] David said to Ā´chish, "Very well, you shall know what your servant can do." And Achish said to David, "Very well, I will make you my body-guard for life."

3 Now Samuel had died, and all Israel had mourned for him and buried him in Rā´mȧh, his own city. And Saul had put the mediums and the wizards out of the land. [4] The Philistines assembled, and came and encamped at Shū´nem; and Saul gathered all Israel, and they encamped at Gil·bō´ȧ. [5] When Saul saw the army of the Philistines, he was afraid, and his heart trembled greatly. [6]And when Saul inquired of the LORD, the LORD did not answer him, either by dreams, or by Ū´rim, or by prophets. [7] Then Saul said to his servants, "Seek out for me a woman who is a medium, that I may go to her and inquire of her." And his servants said to him, "Behold, there is a medium at En´-dŏr."

8 So Saul disguised himself and put on other garments, and went; he and two men with him; and they came to the woman by night. And he said, "Divine for me by a spirit, and bring up for me whomever I shall name to you." [9] The woman said to him, "Surely you know what Saul has done, how he has cut off the mediums and the wizards from the land. Why then are you laying a snare for my life to bring about my death?" [10] But Saul swore to her by the LORD, "As the LORD lives, no punishment shall come upon you for this thing." [11] Then the woman said, "Whom shall I bring up for you?" He said, "Bring up Samuel for me." [12] When the woman saw Samuel, she cried out with a loud voice; and the woman said to Saul, "Why have you deceived me? You are Saul." [13] The king said to her, "Have no fear; what do you see?" And the woman said to Saul, "I see a god coming up out of the earth." [14] He said to her, "What is his appearance?" And she said, "An old man is coming up; and he is wrapped in a robe." And Saul knew that it was Samuel, and he bowed with his face to the ground, and did obeisance.

15 Then Samuel said to Saul, "Why have you disturbed me by bringing me up?" Saul answered, "I am in great distress; for the Philistines are warring against me, and God has turned away from me and answers me no more, either by prophets or by dreams; therefore I have summoned you to tell me what I shall do." [16]And Samuel said, "Why then do you ask me, since the LORD has turned from you and become your enemy? [17] The LORD has done to you as he spoke by me; for the LORD has torn the kingdom out of your hand, and given it to your neighbor, David. [18] Because you did not obey the voice of the LORD, and did not carry out his fierce wrath against Am´ȧ·lek, therefore the LORD has done this thing to you this day. [19] Moreover the LORD will give Israel also with you into the hand of the Philistines; and tomorrow you and your sons shall be with me; the LORD will give the army of Israel also into the hand of the Philistines."

20 Then Saul fell at once full length upon the ground, filled with fear because of the words of Samuel; and there was no strength in him, for he had eaten nothing all day and all night. [21]And the woman came to Saul, and when she saw that he was terrified, she said to him, "Behold, your hand-maid has hearkened to you; I have taken my life in my hand, and have hearkened to what you have said to me. [22] Now therefore, you also hearken to your handmaid; let me set a morsel of bread before you; and eat, that you may have strength when you go on your way." [23] He refused, and said, "I will not eat." But his servants, together with the woman, urged him; and he hearkened to their words. So he arose from the earth, and sat upon the bed. [24] Now the woman had a fatted calf in the house, and she quickly killed it, and she took flour, and kneaded it and baked unleavened bread of it, [25] and she put it before Saul and his servants; and they ate. Then they rose and went away that night.

29 Now the Philistines gathered all their forces at A´phek; and the Israelites were encamped by the fountain which is in Jez´rē·ĕl. [2]As the lords of the Philistines were passing on by hundreds and by thousands, and David and his men were passing on in the rear with A´chish, [3] the commanders of the Philistines said, "What are these Hebrews doing here?" And A´chish said to the commanders of the Philistines, "Is not this David, the servant of Saul, king of Israel, who has been with me now for days and years, and since he deserted to me I have found no fault in him to this day." ⁴ But the commanders of the Philistines were angry with him; and the commanders of the Philistines said to him, "Send the man back, that he may return to the place to which you have assigned him; he shall not go down with us to battle, lest in the battle he become an adversary to us. For how could this fellow reconcile himself to his lord? Would it not be with the heads of the men here? ⁵ Is not this David, of whom they sing to one another in dances,

'Saul has slain his thousands,
    and David his ten thousands'?"

6 Then A′chish called David and said to him, "As the LORD lives, you have been honest, and to me it seems right that you should march out and in with me in the campaign; for I have found nothing wrong in you from the day of your coming to me to this day. Nevertheless the lords do not approve of you. ⁷ So go back now; and go peaceably, that you may not displease the lords of the Philistines." ⁸And David said to A′chish, "But what have I done? What have you found in your servant from the day I entered your service until now, that I may not go and fight against the enemies of my lord the king?" ⁹And A′chish made answer to David, "I know that you are as blameless in my sight as an angel of God; nevertheless the commanders of the Philistines have said, 'He shall not go up with us to the battle.' ¹⁰ Now then rise early in the morning with the servants of your lord who came with you; and start early in the morning, and depart as soon as you have light." ¹¹ So David set out with his men early in the morning, to return to the land of the Philistines. But the Philistines went up to Jez′re·el.

30 Now when David and his men came to Zik′lag on the third day, the A′mal′e·kites had made a raid upon the Negeb and upon Ziklag. They had overcome Ziklag, and burned it with fire, ² and taken captive the women and all*c* who were in it, both small and great; they killed no one, but carried them off, and went their way. ³And when David and his men came to the city, they found it burned with fire, and their wives and sons and daughters taken captive. ⁴ Then David and the people who were with him raised their voices and wept, until they had no

c Gk: Heb lacks *and all*
29.5: 1 Sam 18.7; 21.11.

more strength to weep. ⁵ David's two wives also had been taken captive, A·hin′o-am of Jez′re·el, and Ab′i·gail the widow of Na′bal of Car′mel. ⁶And David was greatly distressed; for the people spoke of stoning him, because all the people were bitter in soul, each for his sons and daughters. But David strengthened himself in the LORD his God.

7 And David said to A·bi′a·thar the priest, the son of A·him′e·lech, "Bring me the ephod." So Abiathar brought the ephod to David. ⁸And David inquired of the LORD, "Shall I pursue after this band? Shall I overtake them?" He answered him, "Pursue; for you shall surely overtake and shall surely rescue." ⁹ So David set out, and the six hundred men who were with him, and they came to the brook Be′sor, where those stayed who were left behind. ¹⁰ But David went on with the pursuit, he and four hundred men; two hundred stayed behind, who were too exhausted to cross the brook Be′sor.

11 They found an Egyptian in the open country, and brought him to David; and they gave him bread and he ate, they gave him water to drink, ¹² and they gave him a piece of a cake of figs and two clusters of raisins. And when he had eaten, his spirit revived; for he had not eaten bread or drunk water for three days and three nights. ¹³And David said to him, "To whom do you belong? And where are you from?" He said, "I am a young man of Egypt, servant to an A·mal′e·kite; and my master left me behind because I fell sick three days ago. ¹⁴ We had made a raid upon the Negeb of the Cher′e·thites and upon that which belongs to Judah and upon the Negeb of Caleb; and we burned Zik′lag with fire." ¹⁵And David said to him, "Will you take me down to this band?" And he said, "Swear to me by God, that you will not kill me, or deliver me into the hands of my master, and I will take you down to this band."

16 And when he had taken him down, behold, they were spread abroad over all the land, eating and drinking and dancing, because of all the great spoil they had taken from the land of the Philistines and from the land of Judah. ¹⁷And David smote them from twilight until the evening of the next day; and not a man of them escaped, except four hundred young men, who mounted camels and fled. ¹⁸ David recovered all that the A·mal′e·kites had

taken; and David rescued his two wives. [19] Nothing was missing, whether small or great, sons or daughters, spoil or anything that had been taken; David brought back all. [20] David also captured all the flocks and herds; and the people drove those cattle before him,[d] and said, "This is David's spoil."

[21] Then David came to the two hundred men, who had been too exhausted to follow David, and who had been left at the brook Bē'sôr; and they went out to meet David and to meet the people who were with him; and when David drew near to the people he saluted them. [22] Then all the wicked and base fellows among the men who had gone with David said, "Because they did not go with us, we will not give them any of the spoil which we have recovered, except that each man may lead away his wife and children, and depart." [23] But David said, "You shall not do so, my brothers, with what the LORD has given us; he has preserved us and given into our hand the band that came against us. [24] Who would listen to you in this matter? For as his share is who goes down into the battle, so shall his share be who stays by the baggage; they shall share alike." [25] And from that day forward he made it a statute and an ordinance for Israel to this day.

[26] When David came to Zik'lag, he sent part of the spoil to his friends, the elders of Judah, saying, "Here is a present for you from the spoil of the enemies of the LORD"; [27] it was for those in Beth'el, in Rā'moth of the Negeb, in Jat'tir, [28] in Ā·rō'ĕr, in Siph'moth, in Esh·tĕ·mō'ă, [29] in Rā'căl, in the cities of the Jĕ·răh'mē·ĕ·lites, in the cities of the Ken'ites, [30] in Hôr'măh, in Bôr·ash'ăn, in Ā'thach, [31] in Hē'brŏn, for all the places where David and his men had roamed.

31 Now the Philistines fought against Israel; and the men of

Israel fled before the Philistines, and fell slain on Mount Gil·bō'ă. [2] And the Philistines overtook Saul and his sons; and the Philistines slew Jonathan and Ā·bin'ă·dab and Mal'chī·shü'ă, the sons of Saul. [3] The battle pressed hard upon Saul, and the archers found him; and he was badly wounded by the archers. [4] Then Saul said to his armor-bearer, "Draw your sword, and thrust me through with it, lest these uncircumcised come and thrust me through, and make sport of me." But his armor-bearer would not; for he feared greatly. Therefore Saul took his own sword, and fell upon it. [5] And when his armor-bearer saw that Saul was dead, he also fell upon his sword, and died with him. [6] Thus Saul died, and his three sons, and his armor-bearer, and all his men, on the same day together. [7] And when the men of Israel who were on the other side of the valley and those beyond the Jordan saw that the men of Israel had fled and that Saul and his sons were dead, they forsook their cities and fled; and the Philistines came and dwelt in them.

[8] On the morrow, when the Philistines came to strip the slain, they found Saul and his three sons fallen on Mount Gil·bō'ă. [9] And they cut off his head, and stripped off his armor, and sent messengers throughout the land of the Philistines, to carry the good news to their idols[e] and to the people. [10] They put his armor in the temple of Ash'tă·roth; and they fastened his body to the wall of Beth'-shan. [11] But when the inhabitants of Jā'besh-gil'ĕ·ăd heard what the Philistines had done to Saul, [12] all the valiant men arose, and went all night, and took the body of Saul and the bodies of his sons from the wall of Beth'-shan; and they came to Jā'besh and burnt them there. [13] And they took their bones and buried them under the tamarisk tree in Jā'besh, and fasted seven days.

[d] Cn: Heb *they drove before those cattle*
[e] Gk Compare 1 Chron 10.9: Heb *to the house of their idols*
31.1-13: 2 Sam 1.6-10; 1 Chron 10.1-12.

THE SECOND BOOK OF

SAMUEL

After the death of Saul, when David had returned from the slaughter of the Ā·mal'ė·kītes, David remained two days in Zĭk'lag; 2 and on the third day, behold, a man came from Saul's camp, with his clothes rent and earth upon his head. And when he came to David, he fell to the ground and did obeisance. 3 David said to him, "Where do you come from?" And he said to him, "I have escaped from the camp of Israel." 4And David said to him, "How did it go? Tell me." And he answered, "The people have fled from the battle, and many of the people also have fallen and are dead; and Saul and his son Jonathan are also dead." 5 Then David said to the young man who told him, "How do you know that Saul and his son Jonathan are dead?" 6And the young man who told him said, "By chance I happened to be on Mount Gĭl·bō'ȧ; and there was Saul leaning upon his spear; and lo, the chariots and the horsemen were close upon him. 7And when he looked behind him, he saw me, and called to me. And I answered, 'Here I am.' 8And he said to me, 'Who are you?' I answered him, 'I am an Ā·mal'ė·kīte.' 9And he said to me, 'Stand beside me and slay me; for anguish has seized me, and yet my life still lingers.' 10 So I stood beside him, and slew him, because I was sure that he could not live after he had fallen; and I took the crown which was on his head and the armlet which was on his arm, and I have brought them here to my lord."

11 Then David took hold of his clothes, and rent them; and so did all the men who were with him; 12 and they mourned and wept and fasted until evening for Saul and for Jonathan his son and for the people of the LORD and for the house of Israel, because they had fallen by the sword. 13And David said to the young man who told him, "Where do you come from?" And he answered, "I am the son of a sojourner, an Ā·mal'ė·kīte." 14 David said to him, "How is it you were not afraid to put forth your hand to destroy the LORD's anointed?" 15 Then David called one of the young men and said, "Go, fall upon him." And he smote him so that he died. 16And David said to him, "Your blood be upon your head; for your own mouth has testified against you, saying, 'I have slain the LORD's anointed.'"

17 And David lamented with this lamentation over Saul and Jonathan his son, 18 and he said it*a* should be taught to the people of Judah; behold, it is written in the Book of Jash'ăr.*b* He said:
19 "Thy glory, O Israel, is slain upon thy high places!
How are the mighty fallen!
20 Tell it not in Gath,
publish it not in the streets of Ash'kė·lon;
lest the daughters of the Philistines rejoice,
lest the daughters of the uncircumcised exult.

21 "Ye mountains of Gĭl·bō'ȧ,
let there be no dew or rain upon you,
nor upsurging of the deep!*c*
For there the shield of the mighty was defiled,
the shield of Saul, not anointed with oil.

22 "From the blood of the slain,
from the fat of the mighty,
the bow of Jonathan turned not back,
and the sword of Saul returned not empty.

23 "Saul and Jonathan, beloved and lovely!
In life and in death they were not divided;
they were swifter than eagles,
they were stronger than lions.

24 "Ye daughters of Israel, weep over Saul,
who clothed you daintily in scarlet,
who put ornaments of gold upon your apparel.

a Gk: Heb the Bow   *b* Or The upright
c Cn: Heb fields of offerings
1.6-10: 1 Sam 31.1-13; 1 Chron 10.1-12.

254

25 "How are the mighty fallen
   in the midst of the battle!

"Jonathan lies slain upon thy high
   places.

26 I am distressed for you, my
   brother Jonathan;
   very pleasant have you been to
   me;
   your love to me was wonderful,
   passing the love of women.

27 "How are the mighty fallen,
   and the weapons of war perished!"

2 After this David inquired of the
LORD, "Shall I go up into any of
the cities of Judah?" And the LORD
said to him, "Go up." David said, "To
which shall I go up?" And he said,
"To Hē′brŏn." 2 So David went up
there, and his two wives also, A·hin′ō-
am of Jez′rē·el, and Ab′i·gāil the widow
of Nā′bal of Cär′mel. 3And David
brought up his men who were with
him, every one with his household; and
they dwelt in the towns of Hē′brŏn.
4And the men of Judah came, and
there they anointed David king over
the house of Judah.

When they told David, "It was the
men of Jā′besh-gil′ē·ȧd who buried
Saul," 5 David sent messengers to the
men of Jā′besh-gil′ē·ȧd, and said to
them, "May you be blessed by the
LORD, because you showed this
loyalty to Saul your lord, and buried
him! 6 Now may the LORD show steadfast love and faithfulness to you! And
I will do good to you because you have
done this thing. 7 Now therefore let
your hands be strong, and be valiant;
for Saul your lord is dead, and the
house of Judah has anointed me king
over them."

8 Now Abner the son of Nĕr, commander of Saul's army, had taken
Ish-bō′sheth the son of Saul, and
brought him over to Mā·hȧ·nā′im;
9 and he made him king over Gilead
and the Ash′ū·rītes and Jez′rē·el and
E′phrȧ·im and Benjamin and all Israel.
10 Ish-bō′sheth, Saul's son, was forty
years old when he began to reign over
Israel, and he reigned two years. But
the house of Judah followed David.
11And the time that David was king in
Hē′brŏn over the house of Judah was
seven years and six months.

12 Abner the son of Nĕr, and the
servants of Ish-bō′sheth the son of
Saul, went out from Mā·hȧ·nā′im to
Gib′ē·ŏn. 13And Jō′ab the son of
Zĕ·rü′i·ȧh, and the servants of David,
went out and met them at the pool of

Gib′ē·ŏn; and they sat down, the one
on the one side of the pool, and the
other on the other side of the pool.
14And Abner said to Jō′ab, "Let the
young men arise and play before us."
And Joab said, "Let them arise."
15 Then they arose and passed over by
number, twelve for Benjamin and Ish-
bō′sheth the son of Saul, and twelve of
the servants of David. 16And each
caught his opponent by the head, and
thrust his sword in his opponent's
side; so they fell down together. Therefore that place was called Hel′kath-
haz-zū′rim,*d* which is at Gib′ē·ŏn.
17And the battle was very fierce that
day; and Abner and the men of Israel
were beaten before the servants of
David.

18 And the three sons of Zĕ·rü′i·ȧh
were there, Jō′ab, A·bi′shäi, and As′ȧ-
hel. Now Asahel was as swift of foot
as a wild gazelle; 19 and as As′ȧ·hel pursued Abner, and as he went he turned
neither to the right hand nor to the
left from following Abner. 20 Then
Abner looked behind him and said,
"Is it you, As′ȧ·hel?" And he answered, "It is I." 21Abner said to him,
"Turn aside to your right hand or to
your left, and seize one of the young
men, and take his spoil." But As′ȧ·hel
would not turn aside from following
him. 22And Abner said again to As′ȧ-
hel, "Turn aside from following me;
why should I smite you to the ground?
How then could I lift up my face to
your brother Jō′ab?" 23 But he refused
to turn aside; therefore Abner smote
him in the belly with the butt of his
spear, so that the spear came out at his
back; and he fell there, and died where
he was. And all who came to the place
where As′ȧ·hel had fallen and died,
stood still.

24 But Jō′ab and A·bi′shäi pursued
Abner; and as the sun was going down
they came to the hill of Am′mäh,
which lies before Gi′äh on the way to
the wilderness of Gib′ē·ŏn. 25And the
Benjaminites gathered themselves together behind Abner, and became one
band, and took their stand on the top
of a hill. 26 Then Abner called to
Jō′ab, "Shall the sword devour for
ever? Do you not know that the end
will be bitter? How long will it be before you bid your people turn from
the pursuit of their brethren?" 27And
Jō′ab said, "As God lives, if you had
not spoken, surely the men would have
given up the pursuit of their brethren
in the morning." 28 So Jō′ab blew the
trumpet; and all the men stopped, and

---

d That is *the field of sword-edges*

pursued Israel no more, nor did they fight any more.

29 And Abner and his men went all that night through the Ar′a·bàh; they crossed the Jordan, and marching the whole forenoon they came to Mā·hà-nā′im. 30 Jō′ab returned from the pursuit of Abner; and when he had gathered all the people together, there were missing of David's servants nineteen men besides As′a·hel. 31 But the servants of David had slain of Benjamin three hundred and sixty of Abner's men. 32And they took up As′a·hel, and buried him in the tomb of his father, which was at Bethlehem. And Jō′ab and his men marched all night, and the day broke upon them at Hē′bròn.

3 There was a long war between the house of Saul and the house of David; and David grew stronger and stronger, while the house of Saul became weaker and weaker.

2 And sons were born to David at Hē′bròn: his first-born was Am′non, of A·hin′ō-am of Jez′rē·èl; 3 and his second, Chil′ē-ab, of Ab′i·gàil the widow of Nā′bal of Cär′mėl; and the third, Ab′sa·lòm the son of Mā·à·càh the daughter of Tal′mäi king of Gĕ′-shŭr; 4 and the fourth, Ad·ȯ·nï′jàh the son of Hag′gith; and the fifth, Sheph-à·tï′àh the son of A·bi′tàl; 5 and the sixth, Ith′rē-am of Eg′làh, David's wife. These were born to David in Hē′bròn.

6 While there was war between the house of Saul and the house of David, Abner was making himself strong in the house of Saul. 7 Now Saul had a concubine, whose name was Riz′pàh, the daughter of Aï′àh; and Ish-bō′-sheth said to Abner, "Why have you gone in to my father's concubine?" 8 Then Abner was very angry over the words of Ish-bō′sheth, and said, "Am I a dog's head of Judah? This day I keep showing loyalty to the house of Saul your father, to his brothers, and to his friends, and have not given you into the hand of David; and yet you charge me today with a fault concerning a woman. 9 God do so to Abner, and more also, if I do not accomplish for David what the LORD has sworn to him, 10 to transfer the kingdom from the house of Saul, and set up the throne of David over Israel and over Judah, from Dan to Beer-sheba." 11And Ish-bō′sheth could not answer Abner another word, because he feared him.

12 And Abner sent messengers to David at Hē′bròn,*e* saying, "To whom does the land belong? Make your covenant with me, and behold, my hand shall be with you to bring over all Israel to you." 13And he said, "Good; I will make a covenant with you; but one thing I require of you; that is, you shall not see my face, unless you first bring Mi′chàl, Saul's daughter, when you come to see my face." 14 Then David sent messengers to Ish-bō′sheth Saul's son, saying, "Give me my wife Michal, whom I betrothed at the price of a hundred foreskins of the Philistines." 15And Ish-bō′sheth sent, and took her from her husband Pal′-ti-el the son of Lā′ish. 16 But her husband went with her, weeping after her all the way to Bà·hū′rim. Then Abner said to him, "Go, return"; and he returned.

17 And Abner conferred with the elders of Israel, saying, "For some time past you have been seeking David as king over you. 18 Now then bring it about; for the LORD has promised David, saying, 'By the hand of my servant David I will save my people Israel from the hand of the Philistines, and from the hand of all their enemies.'" 19Abner also spoke to Benjamin; and then Abner went to tell David at Hē′bròn all that Israel and the whole house of Benjamin thought good to do.

20 When Abner came with twenty men to David at Hē′bròn, David made a feast for Abner and the men who were with him. 21And Abner said to David, "I will arise and go, and will gather all Israel to my lord the king, that they may make a covenant with you, and that you may reign over all that your heart desires." So David sent Abner away; and he went in peace.

22 Just then the servants of David arrived with Jō′ab from a raid, bringing much spoil with them. But Abner was not with David at Hē′bròn, for he had sent him away, and he had gone in peace. 23 When Jō′ab and all the army that was with him came, it was told Joab, "Abner the son of Nĕr came to the king, and he has let him go, and he has gone in peace." 24 Then Jō′ab went to the king and said, "What have you done? Behold, Abner came to you; why is it that you have sent him away, so that he is gone? 25 You know that Abner the son of Nĕr came to deceive you, and to know your going out and your coming in, and to know all that you are doing."

26 When Jō′ab came out from

e Gk: Heb *where he was*   **3.2-5**: 1 Chron 3.1-4.

David's presence, he sent messengers after Abner, and they brought him back from the cistern of Si'rah; but David did not know about it. 27And when Abner returned to He'bron, Jō'ab took him aside into the midst of the gate to speak with him privately, and there he smote him in the belly, so that he died, for the blood of As'a·hel his brother. 28Afterward, when David heard of it, he said, "I and my kingdom are for ever guiltless before the LORD for the blood of Abner the son of Nēr. 29 May it fall upon the head of Jō'ab, and upon all his father's house; and may the house of Joab never be without one who has a discharge, or who is leprous, or who holds a spindle, or who is slain by the sword, or who lacks bread!" 30 So Jō'ab and Ā·bi'shāi his brother slew Abner, because he had killed their brother As'a·hel in the battle at Gib'ē·òn.

31 Then David said to Jō'ab and to all the people who were with him, "Rend your clothes, and gird on sackcloth, and mourn before Abner." And King David followed the bier. 32 The king lifted up his voice and wept at the grave of Abner; and all the people wept. 33And the king lamented for Abner, saying,

"Should Abner die as a fool dies?
34 Your hands were not bound,
   your feet were not fettered;
as one falls before the wicked
   you have fallen."

And all the people wept again over him. 35 Then all the people came to persuade David to eat bread while it was yet day; but David swore, saying, "God do so to me and more also, if I taste bread or anything else till the sun goes down!" 36And all the people took notice of it, and it pleased them; as everything that the king did pleased all the people. 37 So all the people and all Israel understood that day that it had not been the king's will to slay Abner the son of Nēr. 38And the king said to his servants, "Do you not know that a prince and a great man has fallen this day in Israel? 39And I am this day weak, though anointed king; these men the sons of Zě·rù'í·àh are too hard for me. The LORD requite the evildoer according to his wickedness!"

4 When Ish-bō'sheth, Saul's son, heard that Abner had died at He'bron, his courage failed, and all Israel was dismayed. 2 Now Saul's son

had two men who were captains of raiding bands; the name of the one was Bā'a·nah, and the name of the other Rē'chab, sons of Rim'mon a man of Benjamin from Bě·ēr'ŏth (for Be-eroth also is reckoned to Benjamin; 3 the Bě·ēr'ŏ·thītes fled to Git·tā'im, and have been sojourners there to this day).

4 Jonathan, the son of Saul, had a son who was crippled in his feet. He was five years old when the news about Saul and Jonathan came from Jez'rē·ĕl; and his nurse took him up, and fled; and, as she fled in her haste, he fell, and became lame. And his name was Me·phib'ō·sheth.

5 Now the sons of Rim'mon the Bě·ēr'ō·thīte, Rē'chab and Bā'a·nah, set out, and about the heat of the day they came to the house of Ish-bō'sheth, as he was taking his noonday rest. 6And behold, the doorkeeper of the house had been cleaning wheat, but she grew drowsy and slept; so Rē'chab and Bā'a·nah his brother slipped in.ƒ 7 When they came into the house, as he lay on his bed in his bedchamber, they smote him, and slew him, and beheaded him. They took his head, and went by the way of the Ar'a·bàh all night, 8 and brought the head of Ish-bō'sheth to David at He'bron. And they said to the king, "Here is the head of Ish-bosheth, the son of Saul, your enemy, who sought your life; the LORD has avenged my lord the king this day on Saul and on his offspring." 9 But David answered Rē'chab and Bā'a·nah his brother, the sons of Rim'mon the Bě·ēr'ō·thīte, "As the LORD lives, who has redeemed my life out of every adversity, 10 when one told me, 'Behold, Saul is dead,' and thought he was bringing good news, I seized him and slew him at Zik'lag, which was the reward I gave him for his news. 11 How much more, when wicked men have slain a righteous man in his own house upon his bed, shall I not now require his blood at your hand, and destroy you from the earth?" 12And David commanded his young men, and they killed them, and cut off their hands and feet, and hanged them beside the pool at He'bron. But they took the head of Ish-bō'sheth, and buried it in the tomb of Abner at Hebron.

5 Then all the tribes of Israel came to David at He'bron, and said, "Behold, we are your bone and flesh. 2 In times past, when Saul was king over us, it was you that led out and

---

ƒ Gk: Heb 6*And hither they came into the midst of the house fetching wheat; and they smote him in the belly; and Rechab and Baanah his brother escaped*
5.1-3: 1 Chron 11.1-3.

brought in Israel; and the LORD said to you, 'You shall be shepherd of my people Israel, and you shall be prince over Israel.'" ³ So all the elders of Israel came to the king at Hē′brŏn; and King David made a covenant with them at Hebron before the LORD, and they anointed David king over Israel. ⁴ David was thirty years old when he began to reign, and he reigned forty years. ⁵At Hē′brŏn he reigned over Judah seven years and six months; and at Jerusalem he reigned over all Israel and Judah thirty-three years.

6 And the king and his men went to Jerusalem against the Jeb′ū·sītes, the inhabitants of the land, who said to David, "You will not come in here, but the blind and the lame will ward you off"—thinking, "David cannot come in here." ⁷ Nevertheless David took the stronghold of Zion, that is, the city of David. ⁸And David said on that day, "Whoever would smite the Jeb′ū·sītes, let him get up the water shaft to attack the lame and the blind, who are hated by David's soul." Therefore it is said, "The blind and the lame shall not come into the house." ⁹And David dwelt in the stronghold, and called it the city of David. And David built the city round about from the Mil′lō inward. ¹⁰And David became greater and greater, for the LORD, the God of hosts, was with him.

11 And Hiram king of Tȳre sent messengers to David, and cedar trees, also carpenters and masons who built David a house. ¹²And David perceived that the LORD had established him king over Israel, and that he had exalted his kingdom for the sake of his people Israel.

13 And David took more concubines and wives from Jerusalem, after he came from Hē′brŏn; and more sons and daughters were born to David. ¹⁴And these are the names of those who were born to him in Jerusalem: Sham′mū·ȧ, Shō′bab, Nathan, Solomon, ¹⁵ Ib′här, E·lī′shū·ȧ, Nē′pheg, Jȧ·phī′ȧ, ¹⁶ E·lish′ȧ·mȧ, E·lī′ȧ·dȧ, and E·liph′ē·let.

17 When the Philistines heard that David had been anointed king over Israel, all the Philistines went up in search of David; but David heard of it and went down to the stronghold.

18 Now the Philistines had come and spread out in the valley of Reph′ȧ·im. ¹⁹And David inquired of the LORD, "Shall I go up against the Philistines? Wilt thou give them into my hand?" And the LORD said to David, "Go up; for I will certainly give the Philistines into your hand." ²⁰And David came to Bā′al-pe·rā′zim, and David defeated them there; and he said, "The LORD has broken through*ᵍ* my enemies before me, like a bursting flood." Therefore the name of that place is called Baal-perazim.*ʰ* ²¹And the Philistines left their idols there, and David and his men carried them away.

22 And the Philistines came up yet again, and spread out in the valley of Reph′ȧ·im. ²³And when David inquired of the LORD, he said, "You shall not go up; go around to their rear, and come upon them opposite the balsam trees. ²⁴And when you hear the sound of marching in the tops of the balsam trees, then bestir yourself; for then the LORD has gone out before you to smite the army of the Philistines." ²⁵And David did as the LORD commanded him, and smote the Philistines from Gē′bȧ to Gē′zer.

6 David again gathered all the chosen men of Israel, thirty thousand. ²And David arose and went with all the people who were with him from Bā′ȧ·lē-jū′dȧh, to bring up from there the ark of God, which is called by the name of the LORD of hosts who sits enthroned on the cherubim. ³And they carried the ark of God upon a new cart, and brought it out of the house of Ȧ·bin′ȧ·dab which was on the hill; and Uz′zȧh and Ȧ·hi′ō,*ⁱ* the sons of Abinadab, were driving the new cart*ʲ* ⁴ with the ark of God; and Ȧ·hi′ō*ⁱ* went before the ark. ⁵And David and all the house of Israel were making merry before the LORD with all their might, with songs*ᵏ* and lyres and harps and tambourines and castanets and cymbals.

6 And when they came to the threshing floor of Nā′con, Uz′zȧh put out his hand to the ark of God and took hold of it, for the oxen stumbled. ⁷And the anger of the LORD was kindled against Uz′zȧh; and God smote him there because he put forth his hand to the ark;*ˡ* and he died there

---

ᵍ Heb *paraz*   ʰ That is *Lord of breaking through*   ⁱ Or *and his brother*
ʲ Compare Gk: Heb *the new cart, and brought it out of the house of Abinadab which was on the hill*   ᵏ Gk 1 Chron 13.8: Heb *fir-trees*
ˡ 1 Chron 13.10: Heb uncertain

5.4-5: 1 Chron 3.4.   **5.6-10:** 1 Chron 11.4-9.   **5.11-12:** 1 Chron 14.1-2.
5.14-16: 1 Chron 3.5-8; 14.3-7.   **5.17-21:** 1 Chron 14.8-12.
5.22-25: 1 Chron 14.13-16.   **6.1-11:** 1 Chron 13.1-14.

beside the ark of God. 8And David was angry because the LORD had broken forth upon Uz'zàh; and that place is called Per'ez-uz'zàh,[m] to this day. 9And David was afraid of the LORD that day; and he said, "How can the ark of the LORD come to me?" 10 So David was not willing to take the ark of the LORD into the city of David; but David took it aside to the house of O'bed-e'dòm the Git'tite. 11And the ark of the LORD remained in the house of O'bed-e'dòm the Git'-tite three months; and the LORD blessed Obed-edom and all his household.

12 And it was told King David, "The LORD has blessed the household of O'bed-e'dòm and all that belongs to him, because of the ark of God." So David went and brought up the ark of God from the house of Obed-edom to the city of David with rejoicing; 13 and when those who bore the ark of the LORD had gone six paces, he sacrificed an ox and a fatling. 14And David danced before the LORD with all his might; and David was girded with a linen ephod. 15 So David and all the house of Israel brought up the ark of the LORD with shouting, and with the sound of the horn.

16 As the ark of the LORD came into the city of David, Mi'chàl the daughter of Saul looked out of the window, and saw King David leaping and dancing before the LORD; and she despised him in her heart. 17And they brought in the ark of the LORD, and set it in its place, inside the tent which David had pitched for it; and David offered burnt offerings and peace offerings before the LORD. 18And when David had finished offering the burnt offerings and the peace offerings, he blessed the people in the name of the LORD of hosts, 19 and distributed among all the people, the whole multitude of Israel, both men and women, to each a cake of bread, a portion of meat,[n] and a cake of raisins. Then all the people departed, each to his house.

20 And David returned to bless his household. But Mi'chàl the daughter of Saul came out to meet David, and said, "How the king of Israel honored himself today, uncovering himself today before the eyes of his servants' maids, as one of the vulgar fellows shamelessly uncovers himself!" 21And David said to Mi'chàl, "It was before the LORD, who chose me above your

father, and above all his house, to appoint me as prince over Israel, the people of the LORD—and I will make merry before the LORD. 22 I will make myself yet more contemptible than this, and I will be abased in your[o] eyes; but by the maids of whom you have spoken, by them I shall be held in honor." 23And Mi'chàl the daughter of Saul had no child to the day of her death.

7 Now when the king dwelt in his house, and the LORD had given him rest from all his enemies round about, 2 the king said to Nathan the prophet, "See now, I dwell in a house of cedar, but the ark of God dwells in a tent." 3And Nathan said to the king, "Go, do all that is in your heart; for the LORD is with you."

4 But that same night the word of the LORD came to Nathan, 5 "Go and tell my servant David, 'Thus says the LORD: Would you build me a house to dwell in? 6 I have not dwelt in a house since the day I brought up the people of Israel from Egypt to this day, but I have been moving about in a tent for my dwelling. 7 In all places where I have moved with all the people of Israel, did I speak a word with any of the judges[p] of Israel, whom I commanded to shepherd my people Israel, saying, "Why have you not built me a house of cedar?"' 8 Now therefore thus you shall say to my servant David, 'Thus says the LORD of hosts, I took you from the pasture, from following the sheep, that you should be prince over my people Israel; 9 and I have been with you wherever you went, and have cut off all your enemies from before you; and I will make for you a great name, like the name of the great ones of the earth. 10And I will appoint a place for my people Israel, and will plant them, that they may dwell in their own place, and be disturbed no more; and violent men shall afflict them no more, as formerly, 11 from the time that I appointed judges over my people Israel; and I will give you rest from all your enemies. Moreover the LORD declares to you that the LORD will make you a house. 12 When your days are fulfilled and you lie down with your fathers, I will raise up your offspring after you, who shall come forth from your body, and I will establish his kingdom. 13 He shall build a house for my name, and I will establish the throne of his kingdom for

[m] *That is The breaking forth upon Uzzah*   [n] Vg: Heb uncertain   [o] Gk: Heb *my*
[p] 1 Chron 17.6: Heb *tribes*
6.12-19: 1 Chron 15.1-16.3.   7.1-29: 1 Chron 17.1-27.

ever. 14 I will be his father, and he shall be my son. When he commits iniquity, I will chasten him with the rod of men, with the stripes of the sons of men; 15 but I will not take*q* my steadfast love from him, as I took it from Saul, whom I put away from before you. 16 And your house and your kingdom shall be made sure for ever before me; your throne shall be established for ever.'" 17 In accordance with all these words, and in accordance with all this vision, Nathan spoke to David.

18 Then King David went in and sat before the LORD, and said, "Who am I, O Lord GOD, and what is my house, that thou hast brought me thus far? 19 And yet this was a small thing in thy eyes, O Lord GOD; thou hast spoken also of thy servant's house for a great while to come, and hast shown me future generations,*r* O Lord GOD! 20 And what more can David say to thee? For thou knowest thy servant, O Lord GOD! 21 Because of thy promise, and according to thy own heart, thou hast wrought all this greatness, to make thy servant know it. 22 Therefore thou art great, O LORD God; for there is none like thee, and there is no God besides thee, according to all that we have heard with our ears. 23 What other*s* nation on earth is like thy people Israel, whom God went to redeem to be his people, making himself a name, and doing for them*t* great and terrible things, by driving out*u* before his people a nation and its gods?*v* 24 And thou didst establish for thyself thy people Israel to be thy people for ever; and thou, O LORD, didst become their God. 25 And now, O LORD God, confirm for ever the word which thou hast spoken concerning thy servant and concerning his house, and do as thou hast spoken; 26 and thy name will be magnified for ever, saying, 'The LORD of hosts is God over Israel,' and the house of thy servant David will be established before thee. 27 For thou, O LORD of hosts, the God of Israel, hast made this revelation to thy servant, saying, 'I will build you a house'; therefore thy servant has found courage to pray this prayer to thee. 28 And now, O Lord GOD, thou art God, and thy words are true, and thou hast promised this good thing to thy servant; 29 now therefore may it please thee to bless the house of thy servant, that it may continue for ever before thee; for thou, O Lord GOD, hast spoken, and with thy blessing shall the house of thy servant be blessed for ever."

8 After this David defeated the Philistines and subdued them, and David took Meth'eg-am'mah out of the hand of the Philistines.

2 And he defeated Mō'ab, and measured them with a line, making them lie down on the ground; two lines he measured to be put to death, and one full line to be spared. And the Mō'ab·ites became servants to David and brought tribute.

3 David also defeated Had·a·dē'zer the son of Rē'hob, king of Zō'bah, as he went to restore his power at the river Eū·phra'tēs. 4 And David took from him a thousand and seven hundred horsemen, and twenty thousand foot soldiers; and David hamstrung all the chariot horses, but left enough for a hundred chariots. 5 And when the Syrians of Damascus came to help Had·a·dē'zer king of Zō'bah, David slew twenty-two thousand men of the Syrians. 6 Then David put garrisons in Ar'am of Damascus; and the Syrians became servants to David and brought tribute. And the LORD gave victory to David wherever he went. 7 And David took the shields of gold which were carried by the servants of Had·a·dē'zer, and brought them to Jerusalem. 8 And from Bē'tah and from Be·rō'thäi, cities of Had·a·dē'zer, King David took very much bronze.

9 When Tō'i king of Hā'math heard that David had defeated the whole army of Had·a·dē'zer, 10 Tō'i sent his son Jō'ram to King David, to greet him, and to congratulate him because he had fought against Had·a·dē'zer and defeated him; for Hadadezer had often been at war with Toi. And Joram brought with him articles of silver, of gold, and of bronze; 11 these also King David dedicated to the LORD, together with the silver and gold which he dedicated from all the nations he subdued, 12 from E'dom, Mō'ab, the Am'mo·nites, the Philistines, Am'a·lek, and from the spoil of Had·a·dē'zer the son of Rē'hob, king of Zō'bah.

13 And David won a name for himself. When he returned, he slew eighteen thousand E'dom·ites*w* in the Valley of Salt. 14 And he put garrisons in

q Gk Syr Vg 1 Chron 17.13: Heb *shall not depart*   *r* Cn: Heb *this is the law for man*
s Gk: Heb *one*   *t* Heb *you*   *u* Gk 1 Chron 17.21: Heb *for your land*
v Heb *before thy people, whom thou didst redeem for thyself from Egypt, nations and its gods*   *w* Gk: Heb *returned from smiting eighteen thousand Syrians*
7.14: Heb 1.5.   **8.1-14:** 1 Chron 18.1-13.

É'dŏm; throughout all Edom he put garrisons, and all the É'dŏm·ites became David's servants. And the LORD gave victory to David wherever he went.

15 So David reigned over all Israel; and David administered justice and equity to all his people. 16And Jō'ab the son of Zē·rū'i·ah was over the army; and Je·hosh'a·phat the son of Á·hī'lŭd was recorder; 17 and Zā'dok the son of Á·hī'tŭb and Á·hĭm'e·lech the son of Á·bī'a·thär were priests; and Se·räi'ah was secretary; 18 and Be·nā'iăh the son of Je·hoi'a·dá was over[x] the Chĕr'é·thītes and the Pĕl'é·thītes; and David's sons were priests.

9 And David said, "Is there still any one left of the house of Saul, that I may show him kindness for Jonathan's sake?" 2 Now there was a servant of the house of Saul whose name was Zī'bà, and they called him to David; and the king said to him, "Are you Ziba?" And he said, "Your servant is he." 3And the king said, "Is there not still some one of the house of Saul, that I may show the kindness of God to him?" Zī'bà said to the king, "There is still a son of Jonathan; he is crippled in his feet." 4 The king said to him, "Where is he?" And Zī'bà said to the king, "He is in the house of Mā'chir the son of Am'mi·el, at Lō-dē'bär." 5 Then King David sent and brought him from the house of Mā'chir the son of Am'mi·el, at Lō-dē'bär. 6And Me·phib'ŏ·sheth the son of Jonathan, son of Saul, came to David, and fell on his face and did obeisance. And David said, "Mephibosheth!" And he answered, "Behold, your servant." 7And David said to him, "Do not fear; for I will show you kindness for the sake of your father Jonathan, and I will restore to you all the land of Saul your father; and you shall eat at my table always." 8And he did obeisance, and said, "What is your servant, that you should look upon a dead dog such as I?"

9 Then the king called Zī'bà, Saul's servant, and said to him, "All that belonged to Saul and to all his house I have given to your master's son. 10And you and your sons and your servants shall till the land for him, and shall bring in the produce, that your master's son may have bread to eat; but Me·phib'ŏ·sheth your master's son shall always eat at my table." Now Zī'bà had fifteen sons and twenty servants. 11 Then Zī'bà said to the king, "According to all that my lord the king commands his servant, so will your servant do." So Me·phib'ŏ·sheth ate at David's[y] table, like one of the king's sons. 12And Me·phib'ŏ·sheth had a young son, whose name was Mī'cà. And all who dwelt in Zī'bà's house became Mephibosheth's servants. 13 So Me·phib'ŏ·sheth dwelt in Jerusalem; for he ate always at the king's table. Now he was lame in both his feet.

10 After this the king of the Am'mó·nītes died, and Hā'nŭn his son reigned in his stead. 2And David said, "I will deal loyally with Hā'nŭn the son of Nā'hash, as his father dealt loyally with me." So David sent by his servants to console him concerning his father. And David's servants came into the land of the Am'mó·nītes. 3 But the princes of the Am'mó·nītes said to Hā'nŭn their lord, "Do you think, because David has sent comforters to you, that he is honoring your father? Has not David sent his servants to you to search the city, and to spy it out, and to overthrow it?" 4 So Hā'nŭn took David's servants, and shaved off half the beard of each, and cut off their garments in the middle, at their hips, and sent them away. 5 When it was told David, he sent to meet them, for the men were greatly ashamed. And the king said, "Remain at Jericho until your beards have grown, and then return."

6 When the Am'mó·nītes saw that they had become odious to David, the Ammonites sent and hired the Syrians of Beth-rē'hob, and the Syrians of Zō'bàh, twenty thousand foot soldiers, and the king of Mā'à·càh with a thousand men, and the men of Tōb, twelve thousand men. 7And when David heard of it, he sent Jō'ab and all the host of the mighty men. 8And the Am'mó·nītes came out and drew up in battle array at the entrance of the gate; and the Syrians of Zō'bàh and of Rē'hob, and the men of Tōb and Mā'à·càh, were by themselves in the open country.

9 When Jō'ab saw that the battle was set against him both in front and in the rear, he chose some of the picked men of Israel, and arrayed them against the Syrians; 10 the rest of his men he put in the charge of Á·bī'shäi his brother, and he arrayed them against the Am'mó·nītes. 11And he said, "If the Syrians are too strong for me, then you shall help me; but if the Am'mó·nītes are too strong for you,

---

x Syr Tg Vg 20.23; 1 Chron 18.17: Heb lacks *was over*   *y* Gk: Heb *my*
8.15-18: 2 Sam 20.23-26; 1 Chron 18.14-17.   **10.1-19:** 1 Chron 19.1-19.

then I will come and help you. 12 Be of good courage, and let us play the man for our people, and for the cities of our God; and may the LORD do what seems good to him." 13 So Jō′ab and the people who were with him drew near to battle against the Syrians; and they fled before him. 14And when the Am′mo·nites saw that the Syrians fled, they likewise fled before A·bi′-shäi, and entered the city. Then Jō′ab returned from fighting against the Ammonites, and came to Jerusalem.

15 But when the Syrians saw that they had been defeated by Israel, they gathered themselves together. 16And Had·à·dē′zĕr sent, and brought out the Syrians who were beyond the Eū-phrā′tēs;[z] and they came to Hē′lâm, with Shō′bach the commander of the army of Hadadezer at their head. 17And when it was told David, he gathered all Israel together, and crossed the Jordan, and came to Hē′lâm. And the Syrians arrayed themselves against David, and fought with him. 18And the Syrians fled before Israel; and David slew of the Syrians the men of seven hundred chariots, and forty thousand horsemen, and wounded Shō′-bach the commander of their army, so that he died there. 19And when all the kings who were servants of Had·à·dē′-zĕr saw that they had been defeated by Israel, they made peace with Israel, and became subject to them. So the Syrians feared to help the Am′mo-nites any more.

11 In the spring of the year, the time when kings go forth to battle, David sent Jō′ab, and his servants with him, and all Israel; and they ravaged the Am′mo·nites, and besieged Rab′bah. But David remained at Jerusalem.

2 It happened, late one afternoon, when David arose from his couch and was walking upon the roof of the king's house, that he saw from the roof a woman bathing; and the woman was very beautiful. 3And David sent and inquired about the woman. And one said, "Is not this Bath·shē′bà, the daughter of E·lī′am, the wife of U·rī′ah the Hit′tīte?" 4 So David sent messengers, and took her; and she came to him, and he lay with her. (Now she was purifying herself from her uncleanness.) Then she returned to her house. 5And the woman conceived; and she sent and told David, "I am with child."

6 So David sent word to Jō′ab, "Send me U·rī′ah the Hit′tīte." And Joab sent Uriah to David. 7 When U·rī′ah came to him, David asked how Jō′ab was doing, and how the people fared, and how the war prospered. 8 Then David said to U·rī′ah, "Go down to your house, and wash your feet." And Uriah went out of the king's house, and there followed him a present from the king. 9 But U·rī′ah slept at the door of the king's house with all the servants of his lord, and did not go down to his house. 10 When they told David, "U·rī′ah did not go down to his house," David said to Uriah, "Have you not come from a journey? Why did you not go down to your house?" 11 U·rī′ah said to David, "The ark and Israel and Judah dwell in booths; and my lord Jō′ab and the servants of my lord are camping in the open field; shall I then go to my house, to eat and to drink, and to lie with my wife? As you live, and as your soul lives, I will not do this thing." 12 Then David said to U·rī′ah, "Remain here today also, and tomorrow I will let you depart." So Uriah remained in Jerusalem that day, and the next. 13And David invited him, and he ate in his presence and drank, so that he made him drunk; and in the evening he went out to lie on his couch with the servants of his lord, but he did not go down to his house.

14 In the morning David wrote a letter to Jō′ab, and sent it by the hand of U·rī′ah. 15 In the letter he wrote, "Set U·rī′ah in the forefront of the hardest fighting, and then draw back from him, that he may be struck down, and die." 16And as Jō′ab was besieging the city, he assigned U·rī′ah to the place where he knew there were valiant men. 17And the men of the city came out and fought with Jō′ab; among some of the servants of David among the people fell. U·rī′ah the Hit′tīte was slain also. 18 Then Jō′ab sent and told David all the news about the fighting; 19 and he instructed the messenger, "When you have finished telling all the news about the fighting to the king, 20 then, if the king's anger rises, and if he says to you, 'Why did you go so near the city to fight? Did you not know that they would shoot from the wall? 21 Who killed A·bim′e·lech the son of Je·rub′be·sheth? Did not a woman cast an upper millstone upon him from the wall, so that he died at Thē′bez? Why did you go so near the

z Heb *river*
11.1: 1 Chron 20.1

wall?' then you shall say, 'Your servant Ū·ri′ah the Hit′tite is dead also.' "

22 So the messenger went, and came and told David all that Jō′ab had sent him to tell. 23 The messenger said to David, "The men gained an advantage over us, and came out against us in the field; but we drove them back to the entrance of the gate. 24 Then the archers shot at your servants from the wall; some of the king's servants are dead; and your servant Ū·ri′ah the Hit′tite is dead also." 25 David said to the messenger, "Thus shall you say to Jō′ab, 'Do not let this matter trouble you, for the sword devours now one and now another; strengthen your attack upon the city, and overthrow it.' And encourage him."

26 When the wife of Ū·ri′ah heard that Uriah her husband was dead, she made lamentation for her husband. 27And when the mourning was over, David sent and brought her to his house, and she became his wife, and bore him a son. But the thing that David had done displeased the LORD.

12 And the LORD sent Nathan to David. He came to him, and said to him, "There were two men in a certain city, the one rich and the other poor. 2 The rich man had very many flocks and herds; 3 but the poor man had nothing but one little ewe lamb, which he had bought. And he brought it up, and it grew up with him and with his children; it used to eat of his morsel, and drink from his cup, and lie in his bosom, and it was like a daughter to him. 4 Now there came a traveler to the rich man, and he was unwilling to take one of his own flock or herd to prepare for the wayfarer who had come to him, but he took the poor man's lamb, and prepared it for the man who had come to him."

5 Then David's anger was greatly kindled against the man; and he said to Nathan, "As the LORD lives, the man who has done this deserves to die; 6 and he shall restore the lamb fourfold, because he did this thing, and because he had no pity."

7 Nathan said to David, "You are the man. Thus says the LORD, the God of Israel, 'I anointed you king over Israel, and I delivered you out of the hand of Saul; 8 and I gave you your master's house, and your master's wives into your bosom, and gave you the house of Israel and of Judah; and if this were too little, I would add to you as much more. 9 Why have you

despised the word of the LORD, to do what is evil in his sight? You have smitten Ū·ri′ah the Hit′tite with the sword, and have taken his wife to be your wife, and have slain him with the sword of the Am′mō·nites. 10 Now therefore the sword shall never depart from your house, because you have despised me, and have taken the wife of Ū·ri′ah the Hit′tite to be your wife.' 11 Thus says the LORD, 'Behold, I will raise up evil against you out of your own house; and I will take your wives before your eyes, and give them to your neighbor, and he shall lie with your wives in the sight of this sun. 12 For you did it secretly; but I will do this thing before all Israel, and before the sun.' " 13 David said to Nathan, "I have sinned against the LORD." And Nathan said to David, "The LORD also has put away your sin; you shall not die. 14 Nevertheless, because by this deed you have utterly scorned the LORD,*a* the child that is born to you shall die." 15 Then Nathan went to his house.

And the LORD struck the child that Ū·ri′ah′s wife bore to David, and it became sick. 16 David therefore besought God for the child; and David fasted, and went in and lay all night upon the ground. 17And the elders of his house stood beside him, to raise him from the ground; but he would not, nor did he eat food with them. 18 On the seventh day the child died. And the servants of David feared to tell him that the child was dead; for they said, "Behold, while the child was yet alive, we spoke to him, and he did not listen to us; how then can we say to him the child is dead? He may do himself some harm." 19 But when David saw that his servants were whispering together, David perceived that the child was dead; and David said to his servants, "Is the child dead?" They said, "He is dead." 20 Then David arose from the earth, and washed, and anointed himself, and changed his clothes; and he went into the house of the LORD, and worshiped; he then went to his own house; and when he asked, they set food before him, and he ate. 21 Then his servants said to him, "What is this thing that you have done? You fasted and wept for the child while it was alive; but when the child died, you arose and ate food." 22 He said, "While the child was still alive, I fasted and wept; for I said, 'Who knows whether the LORD will be gracious to me, that the child

a Heb *the enemies of the* LORD

may live?' 23 But now he is dead; why should I fast? Can I bring him back again? I shall go to him, but he will not return to me."

24 Then David comforted his wife, Bath·shē′bȧ, and went in to her, and lay with her; and she bore a son, and he called his name Solomon. And the LORD loved him, 25 and sent a message by Nathan the prophet; so he called his name Jed·i·dī′ȧh,[b] because of the LORD.

26 Now Jō′ab fought against Rab′bȧh of the Am′mȯ·nites, and took the royal city. 27 And Jō′ab sent messengers to David, and said, "I have fought against Rab′bȧh; moreover, I have taken the city of waters. 28 Now, then, gather the rest of the people together, and encamp against the city, and take it; lest I take the city, and it be called by my name." 29 So David gathered all the people together and went to Rab′bȧh, and fought against it and took it. 30 And he took the crown of their king[c] from his head; the weight of it was a talent of gold, and in it was a precious stone; and it was placed on David's head. And he brought forth the spoil of the city, a very great amount. 31 And he brought forth the people who were in it, and set them to labor with saws and iron picks and iron axes, and made them toil at[d] the brickkilns; and thus he did to all the cities of the Am′mȯ·nites. Then David and all the people returned to Jerusalem.

13 Now Ab′sȧ·lŏm, David's son, had a beautiful sister, whose name was Tā′mär; and after a time Am′non, David's son, loved her. 2 And Am′non was so tormented that he made himself ill because of his sister Tā′mär; for she was a virgin, and it seemed impossible to Amnon to do anything to her. 3 But Am′non had a friend, whose name was Jon′ȧ·dab, the son of Shim′ē·ȧh, David's brother; and Jonadab was a very crafty man. 4 And he said to him, "O son of the king, why are you so haggard morning after morning? Will you not tell me?" Am′non said to him, "I love Tā′mär, my brother Ab′sȧ·lŏm's sister." 5 Jon′ȧ·dab said to him, "Lie down on your bed, and pretend to be ill; and when your father comes to see you, say to him, 'Let my sister Tā′mär come and give me bread to eat, and prepare the food in my sight, that I may see it,

and eat it from her hand.' " 6 So Am′non lay down, and pretended to be ill; and when the king came to see him, Amnon said to the king, "Pray let my sister Tā′mär come and make a couple of cakes in my sight, that I may eat from her hand."

7 Then David sent home to Tā′mär, saying, "Go to your brother Am′non's house, and prepare food for him." 8 So Tā′mär went to her brother Am′non's house, where he was lying down. And she took dough, and kneaded it, and made cakes in his sight, and baked the cakes. 9 And she took the pan and emptied it out before him, but he refused to eat. And Am′non said, "Send out every one from me." So every one went out from him. 10 Then Am′non said to Tā′mär, "Bring the food into the chamber, that I may eat from your hand." And Tamar took the cakes she had made, and brought them into the chamber to Amnon her brother. 11 But when she brought them near him to eat, he took hold of her, and said to her, "Come, lie with me, my sister." 12 She answered him, "No, my brother, do not force me; for such a thing is not done in Israel; do not do this wanton folly. 13 As for me, where could I carry my shame? And as for you, you would be as one of the wanton fools in Israel. Now therefore, I pray you, speak to the king; for he will not withhold me from you." 14 But he would not listen to her; and being stronger than she, he forced her, and lay with her.

15 Then Am′non hated her with very great hatred; so that the hatred with which he hated her was greater than the love with which he had loved her. And Amnon said to her, "Arise, begone." 16 But she said to him, "No, my brother; for this wrong in sending me away is greater than the other which you did to me."[e] But he would not listen to her. 17 He called the young man who served him and said, "Put this woman out of my presence, and bolt the door after her." 18 Now she was wearing a long robe with sleeves; for thus were the virgin daughters of the king clad of old.[f] So his servant put her out, and bolted the door after her. 19 And Tā′mär put ashes on her head, and rent the long robe which she wore; and she laid her hand on her head, and went away, crying aloud as she went.

---

[b] That is *beloved of the LORD*   [c] Or *Milcom* See Zeph 1.5   [d] Cn: Heb *pass through*
[e] Cn Compare Gk Vg: Heb *No, for this great wrong in sending me away is (worse) than the other which you did to me*   [f] Cn: Heb *clad in robes*
12.26-31: 1 Chron 20.1-3.

20 And her brother Ab′sa·lom said to her, "Has Am′non your brother been with you? Now hold your peace, my sister; he is your brother; do not take this to heart." So Ta′mär dwelt, a desolate woman, in her brother Absalom's house. 21 When King David heard of all these things, he was very angry. 22 But Ab′sa·lom spoke to Am′non neither good nor bad; for Absalom hated Amnon, because he had forced his sister Ta′mär.

23 After two full years Ab′sa·lom had sheepshearers at Ba·al-ha′zôr, which is near E′phra·im, and Absalom invited all the king's sons. 24 And Ab′sa·lom came to the king, and said, "Behold, your servant has sheepshearers; pray let the king and his servants go with your servant." 25 But the king said to Ab′sa·lom, "No, my son, let us not all go, lest we be burdensome to you." He pressed him, but he would not go but gave him his blessing. 26 Then Ab′sa·lom said, "If not, pray let my brother Am′non go with us." And the king said to him, "Why should he go with you?" 27 But Ab′sa·lom pressed him until he let Am′non and all the king's sons go with him. 28 Then Ab′sa·lom commanded his servants, "Mark when Am′non's heart is merry with wine, and when I say to you, 'Strike Amnon,' then kill him. Fear not; have I not commanded you? Be courageous and be valiant." 29 So the servants of Ab′sa·lom did to Am′non as Absalom had commanded. Then all the king's sons arose, and each mounted his mule and fled.

30 While they were on the way, tidings came to David, "Ab′sa·lom has slain all the king's sons, and not one of them is left." 31 Then the king arose, and rent his garments, and lay on the earth; and all his servants who were standing by rent their garments. 32 But Jon′a·dab the son of Shim′e-ah, David's brother, said, "Let not my lord suppose that they have killed all the young men the king's sons; for Am′non alone is dead, for by the command of Ab′sa·lom this has been determined from the day he forced his sister Ta′mär. 33 Now therefore let not my lord the king so take it to heart as to suppose that all the king's sons are dead; for Am′non alone is dead."

34 But Ab′sa·lom fled. And the young man who kept the watch lifted up his eyes, and looked, and behold, many people were coming from the Hor·o·na′im road*g* by the side of the mountain. 35 And Jon′a·dab said to

the king, "Behold, the king's sons have come; as your servant said, so it has come about." 36 And as soon as he had finished speaking, behold, the king's sons came, and lifted up their voice and wept; and the king also and all his servants wept very bitterly.

37 But Ab′sa·lom fled, and went to Tal′mäi the son of Am·mi′hûd, king of Ge′shûr. And David mourned for his son day after day. 38 So Ab′sa·lom fled, and went to Ge′shûr, and was there three years. 39 And the spirit*h* of the king longed to go forth to Ab′sa·lom; for he was comforted about Am′non, seeing he was dead.

14 Now Jo′ab the son of Ze·rü′i·ah perceived that the king's heart went out to Ab′sa·lom. 2 And Jo′ab sent to Te·kô′a, and fetched from there a wise woman, and said to her, "Pretend to be a mourner, and put on mourning garments; do not anoint yourself with oil, but behave like a woman who has been mourning many days for the dead; 3 and go to the king, and speak thus to him." So Jo′ab put the words in her mouth.

4 When the woman of Te·kô′a came to the king, she fell on her face to the ground, and did obeisance, and said, "Help, O king." 5 And the king said to her, "What is your trouble?" She answered, "Alas, I am a widow; my husband is dead. 6 And your handmaid had two sons, and they quarreled with one another in the field; there was no one to part them, and one struck the other and killed him. 7 And now the whole family has risen against your handmaid, and they say, 'Give up the man who struck his brother, that we may kill him for the life of his brother whom he slew'; and so they would destroy the heir also. Thus they would quench my coal which is left, and leave to my husband neither name nor remnant upon the face of the earth."

8 Then the king said to the woman, "Go to your house, and I will give orders concerning you." 9 And the woman of Te·kô′a said to the king, "On me be the guilt, my lord the king, and on my father's house; let the king and his throne be guiltless." 10 The king said, "If any one says anything to you, bring him to me, and he shall never touch you again." 11 Then she said, "Pray let the king invoke the LORD your God, that the avenger of blood slay no more, and my son be not destroyed." He said, "As the LORD lives, not one hair of your son shall fall to the ground."

Cn Compare Gk: Heb *the road behind him*   *h* Gk: Heb *David*

12 Then the woman said, "Pray let your handmaid speak a word to my lord the king." He said, "Speak." 13And the woman said, "Why then have you planned such a thing against the people of God? For in giving this decision the king convicts himself, inasmuch as the king does not bring his banished one home again. 14 We must all die, we are like water spilt on the ground, which cannot be gathered up again; but God will not take away the life of him who devises*ⁱ* means not to keep his banished one an outcast. 15 Now I have come to say this to my lord the king because the people have made me afraid; and your handmaid thought, 'I will speak to the king; it may be that the king will perform the request of his servant. 16 For the king will hear, and deliver his servant from the hand of the man who would destroy me and my son together from the heritage of God.' 17And your handmaid thought, 'The word of my lord the king will set me at rest'; for my lord the king is like the angel of God to discern good and evil. The LORD your God be with you!"

18 Then the king answered the woman, "Do not hide from me anything I ask you." And the woman said, "Let my lord the king speak." 19 The king said, "Is the hand of Jō′ab with you in all this?" The woman answered and said, "As surely as you live, my lord the king, one cannot turn to the right hand or to the left from anything that my lord the king has said. It was your servant Joab who bade me; it was he who put all these words in the mouth of your handmaid. 20 In order to change the course of affairs your servant Jō′ab did this. But my lord has wisdom like the wisdom of the angel of God to know all things that are on the earth."

21 Then the king said to Jō′ab, "Behold now, I grant this; go, bring back the young man Ab′sà·lŏm." 22And Jō′ab fell on his face to the ground, and did obeisance, and blessed the king; and Joab said, "Today your servant knows that I have found favor in your sight, my lord the king, in that the king has granted the request of his servant." 23 So Jō′ab arose and went to Gĕ′shūr, and brought Ab′sà·lŏm to Jerusalem. 24And the king said, "Let him dwell apart in his own house; he is not to come into my presence." So Ab′sà·lŏm dwelt apart in his own house, and did not come into the king's presence.

ⁱ *Cn: Heb* and he devises

25 Now in all Israel there was no one so much to be praised for his beauty as Ab′sà·lŏm; from the sole of his foot to the crown of his head there was no blemish in him. 26And when he cut the hair of his head (for at the end of every year he used to cut it; when it was heavy on him, he cut it), he weighed the hair of his head, two hundred shekels by the king's weight. 27 There were born to Ab′sà·lŏm three sons, and one daughter whose name was Tā′mär; she was a beautiful woman.

28 So Ab′sà·lŏm dwelt two full years in Jerusalem, without coming into the king's presence. 29 Then Ab′sà·lŏm sent for Jō′ab, to send him to the king; but Joab would not come to him. And he sent a second time, but Joab would not come. 30 Then he said to his servants, "See, Jō′ab's field is next to mine, and he has barley there; go and set it on fire." So Ab′sà·lŏm's servants set the field on fire. 31 Then Jō′ab arose and went to Ab′sà·lŏm at his house, and said to him, "Why have your servants set my field on fire?" 32Ab′sà·lŏm answered Jō′ab, "Behold, I sent word to you, 'Come here, that I may send you to the king, to ask, "Why have I come from Gĕ′shūr? It would be better for me to be there still." Now therefore let me go into the presence of the king; and if there is guilt in me, let him kill me.' " 33 Then Jō′ab went to the king, and told him; and he summoned Ab′sà·lŏm. So he came to the king, and bowed himself on his face to the ground before the king; and the king kissed Absalom.

15 After this Ab′sà·lŏm got himself a chariot and horses, and fifty men to run before him. 2And Ab′sà·lŏm used to rise early and stand beside the way of the gate; and when any man had a suit to come before the king for judgment, Absalom would call to him, and say, "From what city are you?" And when he said, "Your servant is of such and such a tribe in Israel," 3Ab′sà·lŏm would say to him, "See, your claims are good and right; but there is no man deputed by the king to hear you." 4Ab′sà·lŏm said moreover, "Oh that I were judge in the land! Then every man with a suit or cause might come to me, and I would give him justice." 5And whenever a man came near to do obeisance to him, he would put out his hand, and take hold of him, and kiss him. 6 Thus Ab′sà·lŏm did to all of Israel who came to the king for judgment; so

Absalom stole the hearts of the men of Israel.

7 And at the end of four[j] years Ab′så·lŏm said to the king, "Pray let me go and pay my vow, which I have vowed to the LORD, in Hē′brŏn. 8 For your servant vowed a vow while I dwelt at Gē′shŭr in Âr′ăm, saying, 'If the LORD will indeed bring me back to Jerusalem, then I will offer worship to the LORD.' " 9 The king said to him, "Go in peace." So he arose, and went to Hē′brŏn. 10 But Ab′så·lŏm sent secret messengers throughout all the tribes of Israel, saying, "As soon as you hear the sound of the trumpet, then say, 'Absalom is king at Hē′brŏn!' " 11 With Ab′så·lŏm went two hundred men from Jerusalem who were invited guests, and they went in their simplicity, and knew nothing. 12 And while Ab′så·lŏm was offering the sacrifices, he sent for[k] A·hĭth′ŏ·phel the Gĭ′lŏ·nĭte, David's counselor, from his city Gĭ′lŏh. And the conspiracy grew strong, and the people with Absalom kept increasing.

13 And a messenger came to David, saying, "The hearts of the men of Israel have gone after Ab′så·lŏm." 14 Then David said to all his servants who were with him at Jerusalem, "Arise, and let us flee; or else there will be no escape for us from Ab′så·lŏm: go in haste, lest he overtake us quickly, and bring down evil upon us, and smite the city with the edge of the sword." 15 And the king's servants said to the king, "Behold, your servants are ready to do whatever my lord the king decides." 16 So the king went forth, and all his household after him. And the king left ten concubines to keep the house. 17 And the king went forth, and all the people after him; and they halted at the last house. 18 And all his servants passed by him; and all the Cher′ē·thites, and all the Pel′ĕ·thites, and all the six hundred Gĭt′tītes who had followed him from Gath, passed on before the king.

19 Then the king said to It′täi the Gĭt′tīte, "Why do you also go with us? Go back, and stay with the king; for you are a foreigner, and also an exile from[l] your home. 20 You came only yesterday, and shall I today make you wander about with us, seeing I go I know not where? Go back, and take your brethren with you; and may the LORD show[m] steadfast love and faithfulness to you." 21 But It′täi answered

the king, "As the LORD lives, and as my lord the king lives, wherever my lord the king shall be, whether for death or for life, there also will your servant be." 22 And David said to It′täi, "Go then, pass on." So Ittai the Gĭt′tīte passed on, with all his men and all the little ones who were with him. 23 And all the country wept aloud as all the people passed by, and the king crossed the brook Kĭd′rŏn, and all the people passed on toward the wilderness.

24 And A·bī′a·thär came up, and lo, Zā′dok came also, with all the Levites, bearing the ark of the covenant of God; and they set down the ark of God, until the people had all passed out of the city. 25 Then the king said to Zā′dok, "Carry the ark of God back into the city. If I find favor in the eyes of the LORD, he will bring me back and let me see both it and his habitation; 26 but if he says, 'I have no pleasure in you,' behold, here I am, let him do to me what seems good to him." 27 The king also said to Zā′dok the priest, "Look,[n] go back to the city in peace, you and A·bī′a·thär,[o] with your two sons, A·hĭm′a-az your son, and Jonathan the son of Abiathar. 28 See, I wait at the fords of the wilderness, until word comes from you to inform me." 29 So Zā′dok and A·bī′a·thär carried the ark of God back to Jerusalem; and they remained there.

30 But David went up the ascent of the Mount of Olives, weeping as he went, barefoot and with his head covered; and all the people who were with him covered their heads, and they went up, weeping as they went. 31 And it was told David, "A·hĭth′ŏ·phel is among the conspirators with Ab′så·lŏm." And David said, "O LORD, I pray thee, turn the counsel of Ahith-ophel into foolishness."

32 When David came to the summit, where God was worshiped, behold, Hū′shäi the Âr′chite came to meet him with his coat rent and earth upon his head. 33 David said to him, "If you go on with me, you will be a burden to me. 34 But if you return to the city, and say to Ab′så·lŏm, 'I will be your servant, O king; as I have been your father's servant in time past, so now I will be your servant,' then you will defeat for me the counsel of A·hĭth′ŏ·phel. 35 Are not Zā′dok and A·bī′a·thär the priests with you there? So whatever you hear from the king's

_____
[j] Gk Syr: Heb forty   [k] Or sent   [l] Gk Syr Vg: Heb to
[m] Gk: Heb lacks may the LORD show   [n] Gk: Heb Are you a seer or Do you see?
[o] Cn: Heb lacks and Abiathar

house, tell it to Zadok and Abiathar
the priests. 36 Behold, their two sons
are with them there, A·him′ȧ-az, Zā′-
dok's son, and Jonathan, A·bī′ȧ·thär's
son; and by them you shall send to me
everything you hear." 37 So Hū′shäi,
David's friend, came into the city, just
as Ab′sȧ·lom was entering Jerusalem.

16 When David had passed a little
beyond the summit, Zī′bȧ the
servant of Me·phib′ō·sheth met him,
with a couple of asses saddled, bearing
two hundred loaves of bread, a hundred bunches of raisins, a hundred of
summer fruits, and a skin of wine.
2 And the king said to Zī′bȧ, "Why
have you brought these?" Ziba answered, "The asses are for the king's
household to ride on, the bread and
summer fruit for the young men to
eat, and the wine for those who faint
in the wilderness to drink." 3 And the
king said, "And where is your master's
son?" Zī′bȧ said to the king, "Behold,
he remains in Jerusalem; for he said,
'Today the house of Israel will give me
back the kingdom of my father.'"
4 Then the king said to Zī′bȧ, "Behold,
all that belonged to Me·phib′ō·sheth is
now yours." And Ziba said, "I do
obeisance; let me ever find favor in
your sight, my lord the king."

5 When King David came to Bȧ-
hū′rim, there came out a man of the
family of the house of Saul, whose
name was Shim′ē-ī, the son of Gē′rȧ;
and as he came he cursed continually.
6 And he threw stones at David, and at
all the servants of King David; and all
the people and all the mighty men
were on his right hand and on his left.
7 And Shim′ē-ī said as he cursed, "Begone, begone, you man of blood, you
worthless fellow! 8 The LORD has
avenged upon you all the blood of the
house of Saul, in whose place you have
reigned; and the LORD has given the
kingdom into the hand of your son
Ab′sȧ·lom. See, your ruin is on you;
for you are a man of blood."

9 Then A·bi′shäi the son of Zė·rü′i-
ȧh said to the king, "Why should this
dead dog curse my lord the king? Let
me go over and take off his head."
10 But the king said, "What have I to
do with you, you sons of Zė·rü′i·ȧh? If
he is cursing because the LORD has
said to him, 'Curse David,' who then
shall say, 'Why have you done so?'"
11 And David said to A·bi′shäi and to
all his servants, "Behold, my own son
seeks my life; how much more now
may this Benjaminite! Let him alone,
and let him curse; for the LORD has
bidden him. 12 It may be that the
LORD will look upon my affliction,[p]
and that the LORD will repay me with
good for this cursing of me today."
13 So David and his men went on the
road, while Shim′ē-ī went along on
the hillside opposite him and cursed
as he went, and threw stones at him
and flung dust. 14 And the king, and
all the people who were with him,
arrived weary at the Jordan;[q] and
there he refreshed himself.

15 Now Ab′sȧ·lom and all the people, the men of Israel, came to Jerusalem, and A·hith′ō·phel with him.
16 And when Hū′shäi the Är′chīte,
David's friend, came to Ab′sȧ·lom,
Hushai said to Absalom, "Long live
the king! Long live the king!" 17 And
Ab′sȧ·lom said to Hū′shäi, "Is this
your loyalty to your friend? Why did
you not go with your friend?" 18 And
Hū′shäi said to Ab′sȧ·lom, "No; for
whom the LORD and this people and
all the men of Israel have chosen, his
I will be, and with him I will remain.
19 And again, whom should I serve?
Should it not be his son? As I have
served your father, so I will serve you."

20 Then Ab′sȧ·lom said to A·hith′-
ō·phel, "Give your counsel; what shall
we do?" 21 A·hith′ō·phel said to Ab′sȧ-
lom, "Go in to your father's concubines, whom he has left to keep the
house; and all Israel will hear that you
have made yourself odious to your
father, and the hands of all who are
with you will be strengthened." 22 So
they pitched a tent for Ab′sȧ·lom upon
the roof; and Absalom went in to his
father's concubines in the sight of all
Israel. 23 Now, in those days the
counsel which A·hith′ō·phel gave was
as if one consulted the oracle[r] of God;
so was all the counsel of Ahithophel
esteemed, both by David and by
Ab′sȧ·lom.

17 Moreover A·hith′ō·phel said to
Ab′sȧ·lom, "Let me choose twelve
thousand men, and I will set out and
pursue David tonight. 2 I will come
upon him while he is weary and discouraged, and throw him into a panic;
and all the people who are with him
will flee. I will strike down the king
only, 3 and I will bring all the people
back to you as a bride comes home to
her husband. You seek the life of only
one man,[s] and all the people will be
at peace." 4 And the advice pleased
Ab′sȧ·lom and all the elders of Israel.

5 Then Ab′sȧ·lom said, "Call Hū′-

[p] Gk Vg: Heb *iniquity* [q] Gk: Heb lacks *at the Jordan* [r] Heb *word*
[s] Gk: Heb *like the return of the whole (is) the man whom you seek*

shāi the Är′chīte also, and let us hear what he has to say." 6And when Hū′shāi came to Ab′sà·lòm, Absalom said to him, "Thus has A·hith′ō·phel spoken; shall we do as he advises? If not, you speak." 7 Then Hū′shāi said to Ab′sà·lòm, "This time the counsel which A·hith′ō·phel has given is not good." 8 Hū′shāi said moreover, "You know that your father and his men are mighty men, and that they are enraged, like a bear robbed of her cubs in the field. Besides, your father is expert in war; he will not spend the night with the people. 9 Behold, even now he has hidden himself in one of the pits, or in some other place. And when some of the people fall*t* at the first attack, whoever hears it will say, 'There has been a slaughter among the people who follow Ab′sà·lòm.' 10 Then even the valiant man, whose heart is like the heart of a lion, will utterly melt with fear; for all Israel knows that your father is a mighty man, and that those who are with him are valiant men. 11 But my counsel is that all Israel be gathered to you, from Dan to Beer-sheba, as the sand by the sea for multitude, and that you go to battle in person. 12 So we shall come upon him in some place where he is to be found, and we shall light upon him as the dew falls on the ground; and of him and all the men with him not one will be left. 13 If he withdraws into a city, then all Israel will bring ropes to that city, and we shall drag it into the valley, until not even a pebble is to be found there." 14And Ab′sà·lòm and all the men of Israel said, "The counsel of Hū′shāi the Är′chīte is better than the counsel of A·hith′ō·phel." For the Lord had ordained to defeat the good counsel of Ahithophel, so that the Lord might bring evil upon Absalom.

15 Then Hū′shāi said to Zā′dok and A·bī′à·thär the priests, "Thus and so did A·hith′ō·phel counsel Ab′sà·lòm and the elders of Israel; and thus and so have I counseled. 16 Now therefore send quickly and tell David, 'Do not lodge tonight at the fords of the wilderness, but by all means pass over; lest the king and all the people who are with him be swallowed up.'" 17 Now Jonathan and A·him′à-az were waiting at En-rō′gel; a maidservant used to go and tell them, and they would go and tell King David; for they must not be seen entering the city. 18 But a lad saw them, and told Ab′sà·lòm; so both of them went away quickly, and came to

the house of a man at Bà·hū′rim, who had a well in his courtyard; and they went down into it. 19And the woman took and spread a covering over the well's mouth, and scattered grain upon it; and nothing was known of it. 20 When Ab′sà·lòm's servants came to the woman at the house, they said "Where are A·him′à-az and Jonathan?" And the woman said to them, "They have gone over the brook*u* of water." And when they had sought and could not find them, they returned to Jerusalem.

21 After they had gone, the men came up out of the well, and went and told King David. They said to David, "Arise, and go quickly over the water; for thus and so has A·hith′ō·phel counseled against you." 22 Then David arose, and all the people who were with him, and they crossed the Jordan; by daybreak not one was left who had not crossed the Jordan.

23 When A·hith′ō·phel saw that his counsel was not followed, he saddled his ass, and went off home to his own city. And he set his house in order, and hanged himself; and he died, and was buried in the tomb of his father.

24 Then David came to Mā·hà·nā′-im. And Ab′sà·lòm crossed the Jordan with all the men of Israel. 25 Now Ab′sà·lòm had set A·mā′sà over the army instead of Jō′ab. Amasa was the son of a man named Ith′rà the Ish′mà-el·ite,*v* who had married Ab′i·gāl the daughter of Nā′hash, sister of Ze·rü′i-àh, Joab's mother. 26And Israel and Ab′sà·lòm encamped in the land of Gilead.

27 When David came to Mā·hà·nā′-im, Shō′bī the son of Nā′hash from Rab′bàh of the Am′mò·nites, and Mā′chir the son of Am′mi-el from Lō-dē′bär, and Bär·zil′lāi the Gilead-ite from Rō′ge·lim, 28 brought beds, basins, and earthen vessels, wheat, barley, meal, parched grain, beans and lentils,*w* 29 honey and curds and sheep and cheese from the herd, for David and the people with him to eat; for they said, "The people are hungry and weary and thirsty in the wilderness."

18 Then David mustered the men who were with him, and set over them commanders of thousands and commanders of hundreds. 2And David sent forth the army, one third under the command of Jō′ab, one third under the command of A·bī′shāi the son of Ze·rü′i·àh, Joab's brother, and one third under the command of It′tāi the

---

t Or *when he falls upon them*   *u* The meaning of the Hebrew word is uncertain
v 1 Chron 2.17: Heb *Israelite*   *w* Heb *lentils and parched grain*

Gitʹtīte. And the king said to the men, "I myself will also go out with you." [3] But the men said, "You shall not go out. For if we flee, they will not care about us. If half of us die, they will not care about us. But you are worth ten thousand of us;[x] therefore it is better that you send us help from the city." [4] The king said to them, "Whatever seems best to you I will do." So the king stood at the side of the gate, while all the army marched out by hundreds and by thousands. [5] And the king ordered Jōʹab and Aʹbi·shäi and Itʹtäi, "Deal gently for my sake with the young man Abʹsa·lŏm." And all the people heard when the king gave orders to all the commanders about Absalom.

[6] So the army went out into the field against Israel; and the battle was fought in the forest of Ēʹphra·im. [7] And the men of Israel were defeated there by the servants of David, and the slaughter there was great on that day, twenty thousand men. [8] The battle spread over the face of all the country; and the forest devoured more people that day than the sword.

[9] And Abʹsa·lŏm chanced to meet the servants of David. Absalom was riding upon his mule, and the mule went under the thick branches of a great oak, and his head caught fast in the oak, and he was left hanging[y] between heaven and earth, while the mule that was under him went on. [10] And a certain man saw it, and told Jōʹab, "Behold, I saw Abʹsa·lŏm hanging in an oak." [11] Jōʹab said to the man who told him, "What, you saw him! Why then did you not strike him there to the ground? I would have been glad to give you ten pieces of silver and a girdle." [12] But the man said to Jōʹab, "Even if I felt in my hand the weight of a thousand pieces of silver, I would not put forth my hand against the king's son; for in our hearing the king commanded you and Aʹbi·shäi and Itʹtäi, 'For my sake protect the young man Abʹsa·lŏm.' [13] On the other hand, if I had dealt treacherously against his life[z] (and there is nothing hidden from the king), then you yourself would have stood aloof." [14] Jōʹab said, "I will not waste time like this with you." And he took three darts in his hand, and thrust them into the heart of Abʹsa·lŏm, while he was still alive in the oak. [15] And ten young men, Jōʹabʹs armor-bearers, surrounded Abʹsa·lŏm and struck him, and killed him.

[16] Then Jōʹab blew the trumpet, and the troops came back from pursuing Israel; for Joab restrained them. [17] And they took Abʹsa·lŏm, and threw him into a great pit in the forest, and raised over him a very great heap of stones; and all Israel fled every one to his own home. [18] Now Abʹsa·lŏm in his lifetime had taken and set up for himself the pillar which is in the King's Valley, for he said, "I have no son to keep my name in remembrance"; he called the pillar after his own name, and it is called Absalom's monument to this day.

[19] Then said A·himʹa·az the son of Zāʹdok, "Let me run, and carry tidings to the king that the LORD has delivered him from the power of his enemies." [20] And Jōʹab said to him, "You are not to carry tidings today; you may carry tidings another day, but today you shall carry no tidings, because the king's son is dead." [21] Then Jōʹab said to the Cushite, "Go, tell the king what you have seen." The Cushite bowed before Joab, and ran. [22] Then A·himʹa·az the son of Zāʹdok said again to Jōʹab, "Come what may, let me also run after the Cushite." And Joab said, "Why will you run, my son, seeing that you will have no reward for the tidings?" [23] "Come what may," he said, "I will run." So he said to him, "Run." Then A·himʹa·az ran by the way of the plain, and outran the Cushite.

[24] Now David was sitting between the two gates; and the watchman went up to the roof of the gate by the wall, and when he lifted up his eyes and looked, he saw a man running alone. [25] And the watchman called out and told the king. And the king said, "If he is alone, there are tidings in his mouth." And he came apace, and drew near. [26] And the watchman saw another man running; and the watchman called to the gate and said, "See, another man running alone!" The king said, "He also brings tidings." [27] And the watchman said, "I think the running of the foremost is like the running of A·himʹa·az the son of Zāʹdok." And the king said, "He is a good man, and comes with good tidings."

[28] Then A·himʹa·az cried out to the king, "All is well." And he bowed before the king with his face to the earth, and said, "Blessed be the LORD your God, who has delivered up the men who raised their hand against my lord the king." [29] And the king said,

"Is it well with the young man Ab'sà·lŏm?" Ă·hĭm'à·az answered, "When Jō'ab sent your servant,*b* I saw a great tumult, but I do not know what it was." 30And the king said, "Turn aside, and stand here." So he turned aside, and stood still.

31 And behold, the Cushite came; and the Cushite said, "Good tidings for my lord the king! For the LORD has delivered you this day from the power of all who rose up against you." 32 The king said to the Cushite, "Is it well with the young man Ab'sà·lŏm?" And the Cushite answered, "May the enemies of my lord the king, and all who rise up against you for evil, be like that young man." 33 *c*And the king was deeply moved, and went up to the chamber over the gate, and wept; and as he went, he said, "O my son Ab'sà·lŏm, my son, my son Absalom! Would I had died instead of you, O Absalom, my son, my son!"

19 It was told Jō'ab, "Behold, the king is weeping and mourning for Ab'sà·lŏm." 2 So the victory that day was turned into mourning for all the people; for the people heard that day, "The king is grieving for his son." 3And the people stole into the city that day as people steal in who are ashamed when they flee in battle. 4 The king covered his face, and the king cried with a loud voice, "O my son Ab'sà·lŏm, O Absalom, my son, my son!" 5 Then Jō'ab came into the house to the king, and said, "You have today covered with shame the faces of all your servants, who have this day saved your life, and the lives of your sons and your daughters, and the lives of your wives and your concubines, 6 because you love those who hate you and hate those who love you. For you have made it clear today that commanders and servants are nothing to you; for today I perceive that if Ab'sà·lŏm were alive and all of us were dead today, then you would be pleased. 7 Now therefore arise, go out and speak kindly to your servants; for I swear by the LORD, if you do not go, not a man will stay with you this night; and this will be worse for you than all the evil that has come upon you from your youth until now." 8 Then the king arose, and took his seat in the gate. And the people were all told, "Behold, the king is sitting in the gate"; and all the people came before the king.

Now Israel had fled every man to his own home. 9And all the people were at strife throughout all the tribes of Israel, saying, "The king delivered us from the hand of our enemies, and saved us from the hand of the Philistines; and now he has fled out of the land from Ab'sà·lŏm. 10 But Ab'sà·lŏm, whom we anointed over us, is dead in battle. Now therefore why do you say nothing about bringing the king back?"

11 And King David sent this message to Zā'dok and Ă·bī'à·thär the priests, "Say to the elders of Judah, 'Why should you be the last to bring the king back to his house, when the word of all Israel has come to the king?*d* 12 You are my kinsmen, you are my bone and my flesh; why then should you be the last to bring back the king?' 13And say to Ă·mā'sà, 'Are you not my bone and my flesh? God do so to me, and more also, if you are not commander of my army henceforth in place of Jō'ab.'" 14And he swayed the heart of all the men of Judah as one man; so that they sent word to the king, "Return, both you and all your servants." 15 So the king came back to the Jordan; and Judah came to Gĭl'gàl to meet the king and to bring the king over the Jordan.

16 And Shĭm'ē·ī the son of Gē'rà, the Benjaminite, from Bà·hū'rim, made haste to come down with the men of Judah to meet King David; 17 and with him were a thousand men from Benjamin. And Zī'bà the servant of the house of Saul, with his fifteen sons and his twenty servants, rushed down to the Jordan before the king, 18 and they crossed the ford*e* to bring over the king's household, and to do his pleasure. And Shĭm'ē·ī the son of Gē'rà fell down before the king, as he was about to cross the Jordan, 19 and said to the king, "Let not my lord hold me guilty or remember how your servant did wrong on the day my lord the king left Jerusalem; let not the king bear it in mind. 20 For your servant knows that I have sinned; therefore, behold, I have come this day, the first of all the house of Joseph to come down to meet my lord the king." 21Ă·bī'shäi the son of Zē·rū'ī·àh answered, "Shall not Shĭm'ē·ī be put to death for this, because he cursed the LORD's anointed?" 22 But David said, "What have I to do with you, you sons of Zē·rū'ī·àh, that you should this day be as an adversary to me? Shall any one be put to death in Israel this day? For do I not know that I am this day king over Israel?" 23And the king said

to Shim′e̅-i, "You shall not die." And the king gave him his oath.

24 And Me·phib′o̅·sheth the son of Saul came down to meet the king; he had neither dressed his feet, nor trimmed his beard, nor washed his clothes, from the day the king departed until the day he came back in safety. 25And when he came from[f] Jerusalem to meet the king, the king said to him, "Why did you not go with me, Me·phib′o̅·sheth?" 26 He answered, "My lord, O king, my servant deceived me; for your servant said to him, 'Saddle an ass for me,[g] that I may ride upon it and go with the king.' For your servant is lame. 27 He has slandered your servant to my lord the king. But my lord the king is like the angel of God; do therefore what seems good to you. 28 For all my father's house were but men doomed to death before my lord the king; but you set your servant among those who eat at your table. What further right have I, then, to cry to the king?" 29And the king said to him, "Why speak any more of your affairs? I have decided: you and Zi′ba shall divide the land." 30And Me·phib′o̅·sheth said to the king, "Oh, let him take it all, since my lord the king has come safely home."

31 Now Bär·zil′lai the Gileadite had come down from Ro̅′ge̅·lim; and he went on with the king to the Jordan, to escort him over the Jordan. 32 Bär·zil′lai was a very aged man, eighty years old; and he had provided the king with food while he stayed at Ma̅·ha·na′im; for he was a very wealthy man. 33And the king said to Bär·zil′lai, "Come over with me, and I will provide for you with me in Jerusalem." 34 But Bär·zil′lai said to the king, "How many years have I still to live, that I should go up with the king to Jerusalem? 35 I am this day eighty years old; can I discern what is pleasant and what is not? Can your servant taste what he eats or what he drinks? Can I still listen to the voice of singing men and singing women? Why then should your servant be an added burden to my lord the king? 36 Your servant will go a little way over the Jordan with the king. Why should the king recompense me with such a reward? 37 Pray let your servant return, that I may die in my own city, near the grave of my father and my mother. But here is your servant Chim′ham; let him go over with my lord the king; and do for him whatever seems good to you." 38And the king answered,

"Chim′ham shall go over with me, and I will do for him whatever seems good to you; and all that you desire of me I will do for you." 39 Then all the people went over the Jordan, and the king went over; and the king kissed Bär·zil′lai and blessed him, and he returned to his own home. 40 The king went on to Gil′gal, and Chim′ham went on with him; all the people of Judah, and also half the people of Israel, brought the king on his way.

41 Then all the men of Israel came to the king, and said to the king, "Why have our brethren the men of Judah stolen you away, and brought the king and his household over the Jordan, and all David's men with him?" 42All the men of Judah answered the men of Israel, "Because the king is near of kin to us. Why then are you angry over this matter? Have we eaten at all at the king's expense? Or has he given us any gift?" 43And the men of Israel answered the men of Judah, "We have ten shares in the king, and in David also we have more than you. Why then did you despise us? Were we not the first to speak of bringing back our king?" But the words of the men of Judah were fiercer than the words of the men of Israel.

20 Now there happened to be there a worthless fellow, whose name was Sheba, the son of Bich′ri, a Benjaminite; and he blew the trumpet, and said,

"We have no portion in David,
  and we have no inheritance in the
    son of Jesse;
every man to his tents, O Israel!"

2 So all the men of Israel withdrew from David, and followed Sheba the son of Bich′ri; but the men of Judah followed their king steadfastly from the Jordan to Jerusalem.

3 And David came to his house at Jerusalem; and the king took the ten concubines whom he had left to care for the house, and put them in a house under guard, and provided for them, but did not go in to them. So they were shut up until the day of their death, living as if in widowhood.

4 Then the king said to A·ma̅′sa, "Call the men of Judah together to me within three days, and be here yourself." 5 So A·ma̅′sa went to summon Judah; but he delayed beyond the set time which had been appointed him. 6And David said to A·bi′shäi, "Now Sheba the son of Bich′ri will do us more harm than Ab′sa·lo̅m; take your lord's servants and pursue him, lest

[f] Heb *to*   [g] Gk Syr Vg: Heb *said, I will saddle an ass for myself*

he get himself fortified cities, and cause us trouble."[h] 7And there went out after A·bi'shäi, Jō'ab[i] and the Cher'ë·thïtes and the Pel'ë·thïtes, and all the mighty men; they went out from Jerusalem to pursue Sheba the son of Bich'ri. 8 When they were at the great stone which is in Gib'ë·òn, A·ma'sà came to meet them. Now Jō'ab was wearing a soldier's garment, and over it was a girdle with a sword in its sheath fastened upon his loins, and as he went forward it fell out. 9And Jō'ab said to A·ma'sà, "Is it well with you, my brother?" And Joab took Amasa by the beard with his right hand to kiss him. 10 But A·ma'sà did not observe the sword which was in Jō'ab's hand; so Joab struck him with it in the body, and shed his bowels to the ground, without striking a second blow; and he died.

Then Joab and A·bi'shäi his brother pursued Sheba the son of Bich'ri. 11And one of Jō'ab's men took his stand by A·ma'sà, and said, "Whoever favors Joab, and whoever is for David, let him follow Joab." 12And A·ma'sà lay wallowing in his blood in the highway. And any one who came by, seeing him, stopped;[j] and when the man saw that all the people stopped, he carried Amasa out of the highway into the field, and threw a garment over him. 13 When he was taken out of the highway, all the people went on after Jō'ab to pursue Sheba the son of Bich'ri.

14 And Sheba passed through all the tribes of Israel to Abel of Beth-ma'à·càh;[k] and all the Bich'rïtes[l] assembled, and followed him in. 15And all the men who were with Jō'ab came and besieged him in Abel of Beth-ma'à·càh; they cast up a mound against the city, and it stood against the rampart; and they were battering the wall, to throw it down. 16 Then a wise woman called from the city, "Hear! Hear! Tell Jō'ab, 'Come here, that I may speak to you.'" 17And he came near her; and the woman said, "Are you Jō'ab?" He answered, "I am." Then she said to him, "Listen to the words of your maidservant." And he answered, "I am listening." 18 Then she said, "They were wont to say in old time, 'Let them but ask counsel at Abel'; and so they settled a matter. 19 I am one of those who are peaceable

and faithful in Israel; you seek to destroy a city which is a mother in Israel; why will you swallow up the heritage of the LORD?" 20 Jō'ab answered, "Far be it from me, far be it, that I should swallow up or destroy! 21 That is not true. But a man of the hill country of E'phra·im, called Sheba the son of Bich'ri, has lifted up his hand against King David; give up him alone, and I will withdraw from the city." And the woman said to Jō'ab, "Behold, his head shall be thrown to you over the wall." 22 Then the woman went to all the people in her wisdom. And they cut off the head of Sheba the son of Bich'ri, and threw it out to Jō'ab. So he blew the trumpet, and they dispersed from the city, every man to his home. And Joab returned to Jerusalem to the king.

23 Now Jō'ab was in command of all the army of Israel; and Be·na'ïàh the son of Je·hoi'à·dà was in command of the Cher'ë·thïtes and the Pel'ë·thïtes; 24 and A·dôr'àm was in charge of the forced labor; and Je·hosh'à·phat the son of A·hi'lùd was the recorder; 25 and Shë'và was secretary; and Zā'dok and A·bi'à·thär were priests; 26 and Ira the Jā'i·rïte was also David's priest.

21 Now there was a famine in the days of David for three years, year after year; and David sought the face of the LORD. And the LORD said, "There is blood guilt on Saul and on his house, because he put the Gib'ë·ò·nïtes to death." 2 So the king called the Gib'ë·ò·nïtes.[m] Now the Gibeonites were not of the people of Israel, but of the remnant of the Am'ò·rïtes; although the people of Israel had sworn to spare them, Saul had sought to slay them in his zeal for the people of Israel and Judah. 3And David said to the Gib'ë·ò·nïtes, "What shall I do for you? And how shall I make expiation, that you may bless the heritage of the LORD?" 4 The Gib'ë·ò·nïtes said to him, "It is not a matter of silver or gold between us and Saul or his house; neither is it for us to put any man to death in Israel." And he said, "What do you say that I shall do for you?" 5 They said to the king, "The man who consumed us and planned to destroy us, so that we should have no place in all the territory of Israel, 6 let seven of his sons be given to us, so

h Tg: Heb snatch away our eyes   i Cn Compare Gk: Heb after him Joab's men
j This clause is transposed from the end of the verse
k With 20.15: Heb and Beth-maacah   l Heb Berites
m Heb the Gibeonites and said to them
20.23-26: 2 Sam 8.15-18; 1 Chron 18.14-17.

that we may hang them up before the LORD at Gib·e·on on the mountain of the LORD."[n] And the king said, "I will give them."

7 But the king spared Me·phib'o·sheth, the son of Saul's son Jonathan, because of the oath of the LORD which was between them, between David and Jonathan the son of Saul. 8 The king took the two sons of Riz'pah the daughter of Ai'ah, whom she bore to Saul, Ar·mo'ni and Me·phib'o·sheth; and the five sons of Me'rab[o] the daughter of Saul, whom she bore to A'dri·el the son of Bar·zil'lai the Me·ho'la·thite; 9 and he gave them into the hands of the Gib'e·o·nites, and they hanged them on the mountain before the LORD, and the seven of them perished together. They were put to death in the first days of harvest, at the beginning of barley harvest.

10 Then Riz'pah the daughter of Ai'ah took sackcloth, and spread it for herself on the rock, from the beginning of harvest until rain fell upon them from the heavens; and she did not allow the birds of the air to come upon them by day, or the beasts of the field by night. 11 When David was told what Riz'pah the daughter of Ai'ah, the concubine of Saul, had done, 12 David went and took the bones of Saul and the bones of his son Jonathan from the men of Ja'besh-gil'e·ad, who had stolen them from the public square of Beth'-shan, where the Philistines had hanged them, on the day the Philistines killed Saul on Gil·bo'a; 13 and he brought up from there the bones of Saul and the bones of his son Jonathan; and they gathered the bones of those who were hanged. 14And they buried the bones of Saul and his son Jonathan in the land of Benjamin in Ze'la, in the tomb of Kish his father; and they did all that the king commanded. And after that God heeded supplications for the land.

15 The Philistines had war again with Israel, and David went down together with his servants, and they fought against the Philistines; and David grew weary. 16And Ish'bi-be'nob, one of the descendants of the giants, whose spear weighed three hundred shekels of bronze, and who was girded with a new sword, thought to kill David. 17 But A·bi'shäi the son of Ze·ru'i·ah came to his aid, and attacked the Philistine and killed him. Then David's men adjured him, "You shall no more go out with us to battle, lest you quench the lamp of Israel."

18 After this there was again war with the Philistines at Gob; then Sib'be·chäi the Hu'sha·thite slew Saph, who was one of the descendants of the giants. 19And there was again war with the Philistines at Gob; and El·ha'nän the son of Ja'a·re·or'e·gim, the Bethlehemite, slew Goliath the Git'tite, the shaft of whose spear was like a weaver's beam. 20And there was again war at Gath, where there was a man of great stature, who had six fingers on each hand, and six toes on each foot, twenty-four in number; and he also was descended from the giants. 21And when he taunted Israel, Jonathan the son of Shim'e·i, David's brother, slew him. 22 These four were descended from the giants in Gath; and they fell by the hand of David and by the hand of his servants.

22

And David spoke to the LORD the words of this song on the day when the LORD delivered him from the hand of all his enemies, and from the hand of Saul. 2 He said,

"The LORD is my rock, and my fortress, and my deliverer,
3 my[p] God, my rock, in whom I take refuge,
my shield and the horn of my salvation,
my stronghold and my refuge,
my savior; thou savest me from violence.
4 I call upon the LORD, who is worthy to be praised,
and I am saved from my enemies.

5 "For the waves of death encompassed me,
the torrents of perdition assailed me;
6 the cords of She'ol entangled me,
the snares of death confronted me.

7 "In my distress I called upon the LORD;
to my God I called.
From his temple he heard my voice,
and my cry came to his ears.

8 "Then the earth reeled and rocked;
the foundations of the heavens trembled
and quaked, because he was angry.
9 Smoke went up from his nostrils,

[n] Cn Compare Gk and 21.9: Heb *at Gibeah of Saul, the chosen of the* LORD
[o] Two Hebrew Mss Gk: Heb *Michal*
[p] Gk Ps 18.2: Heb lacks *my*   **21.18-22:** 1 Chron 20.4-8.   **22.2-51:** Ps 18.2-50.

DAVID BRINGS THE ARK TO JERUSALEM   *II Sam. 6:17*

AMOS, PROPHET OF THE LORD   *Amos 7:14*

and devouring fire from his
mouth;
glowing coals flamed forth from
him.
10 He bowed the heavens, and came
down;
thick darkness was under his feet.
11 He rode on a cherub, and flew;
he was seen upon the wings of
the wind.
12 He made darkness around him
his canopy, thick clouds, a gathering of water.
13 Out of the brightness before him
coals of fire flamed forth.
14 The LORD thundered from heaven,
and the Most High uttered his
voice.
15 And he sent out arrows, and scattered them;
lightning, and routed them.
16 Then the channels of the sea were
seen,
the foundations of the world were
laid bare,
at the rebuke of the LORD,
at the blast of the breath of his
nostrils.

17 "He reached from on high, he took
me,
he drew me out of many waters,
18 He delivered me from my strong
enemy,
from those who hated me;
for they were too mighty for me.
19 They came upon me in the day of
my calamity;
but the LORD was my stay.
20 He brought me forth into a broad
place;
he delivered me, because he
delighted in me.

21 "The LORD rewarded me according
to my righteousness;
according to the cleanness of my
hands he recompensed me.
22 For I have kept the ways of the
LORD,
and have not wickedly departed
from my God.
23 For all his ordinances were before
me,
and from his statutes I did not
turn aside.
24 I was blameless before him,
and I kept myself from guilt.
25 Therefore the LORD has recompensed me according to my
righteousness,
according to my cleanness in his
sight.

26 "With the loyal thou dost show thyself loyal;
with the blameless man thou dost
show thyself blameless;
27 with the pure thou dost show thyself
pure,
and with the crooked thou dost
show thyself perverse.
28 Thou dost deliver a humble people,
but thy eyes are upon the haughty
to bring them down.
29 Yea, thou art my lamp, O LORD,
and my God lightens my darkness.
30 Yea, by thee I can crush a troop,
and by my God I can leap over
a wall.
31 This God—his way is perfect;
the promise of the LORD proves
true;
he is a shield for all those who
take refuge in him.

32 "For who is God, but the LORD?
And who is a rock, except our
God?
33 This God is my strong refuge,
and has made*r* my*s* way safe.
34 He made my*s* feet like hinds' feet,
and set me secure on the heights.
35 He trains my hands for war,
so that my arms can bend a bow
of bronze.
36 Thou hast given me the shield of
thy salvation,
and thy help*t* made me great.
37 Thou didst give a wide place for
my steps under me,
and my feet*u* did not slip;
38 I pursued my enemies and destroyed
them,
and did not turn back until they
were consumed.
39 I consumed them; I thrust them
through, so that they did not
rise;
they fell under my feet.
40 For thou didst gird me with strength
for the battle;
thou didst make my assailants sink
under me.
41 Thou didst make my enemies turn
their backs to me,
those who hated me, and I destroyed them.
42 They looked, but there was none
to save;
they cried to the LORD, but he
did not answer them.
43 I beat them fine as the dust of the
earth,
I crushed them and stamped them
down like the mire of the
streets.

r Ps 18.32: Heb *set free*   *s* Another reading is *his*   *t* Or *gentleness*
u Heb *ankles*

44 "Thou didst deliver me from strife
  with the peoples;*v*
  thou didst keep me as the head of
    the nations;
  people whom I had not known
    served me.
45 Foreigners came cringing to me;
  as soon as they heard of me, they
    obeyed me.
46 Foreigners lost heart,
  and came trembling*w* out of their
    fastnesses.
47 "The LORD lives; and blessed be my
    rock,
  and exalted be my God, the rock
    of my salvation,
48 the God who gave me vengeance
  and brought down peoples under
    me,
49 who brought me out from my
    enemies;
  thou didst exalt me above my
    adversaries,
  thou didst deliver me from men of
    violence.
50 "For this I will extol thee, O LORD,
    among the nations,
  and sing praises to thy name.
51 Great triumphs he gives*x* to his
    king,
  and shows steadfast love to his
    anointed,
  to David, and his descendants for
    ever."

23 Now these are the last words
  of David:
  The oracle of David, the son of
    Jesse,
  the oracle of the man who was
    raised on high,
  the anointed of the God of Jacob,
  the sweet psalmist of Israel:*y*

2 "The Spirit of the LORD speaks by
    me,
  his word is upon my tongue.
3 The God of Israel has spoken,
  the Rock of Israel has said to me:
  When one rules justly over men,
    ruling in the fear of God,
4 he dawns on them like the morning
    light,
  like the sun shining forth upon a
    cloudless morning,
  like rain*z* that makes grass to
    sprout from the earth.
5 Yea, does not my house stand so
    with God?

For he has made with me an ever-
    lasting covenant,
  ordered in all things and secure.
For will he not cause to prosper
  all my help and my desire?
6 But godless men*a* are all like thorns
  that are thrown away;
  for they cannot be taken with the
    hand;
7 but the man who touches them
  arms himself with iron and the
    shaft of a spear,
  and they are utterly consumed
    with fire."*b*

8 These are the names of the mighty
men whom David had: Jŏ'sheb-bas-
shĕ'beth a Täh-chĕ'mŏ·nite; he was
chief of the three;*c* he wielded his
spear*d* against eight hundred whom he
slew at one time.

9 And next to him among the three
mighty men was El·ē·ā'zȧr the son of
Dŏ'dŏ, son of Ȧ·hō'hī. He was with
David when they defied the Philistines
who were gathered there for battle,
and the men of Israel withdrew. 10 He
rose and struck down the Philistines
until his hand was weary, and his hand
cleaved to the sword; and the LORD
wrought a great victory that day; and
the men returned after him only to
strip the slain.

11 And next to him was Shăm'mȧh,
the son of Ā'gee the Hȧr'ȧ·rīte. The
Philistines gathered together at Lē'hī,
where there was a plot of ground full
of lentils; and the men fled from the
Philistines. 12 But he took his stand
in the midst of the plot, and defended
it, and slew the Philistines; and the
LORD wrought a great victory.

13 And three of the thirty chief men
went down, and came about harvest
time to David at the cave of Ȧ·dul'-
lȧm, when a band of Philistines was
encamped in the valley of Reph'ȧ·im.
14 David was then in the stronghold;
and the garrison of the Philistines was
then at Bethlehem. 15 And David said
longingly, "O that some one would
give me water to drink from the well
of Bethlehem which is by the gate!"
16 Then the three mighty men broke
through the camp of the Philistines,
and drew water out of the well of
Bethlehem which was by the gate, and
took and brought it to David. But he
would not drink of it; he poured it out
to the LORD, 17 and said, "Far be it
from me, O LORD, that I should do

---

v Gk: Heb *from strife with my people*   *w* Ps 18.45: Heb *girded themselves*
x Another reading is *He is a tower of salvation*   *y* Or *the favorite of the songs of Israel*
z Heb *from rain*   *a* Heb *worthlessness*   *b* Heb *fire in the sitting*   *c* Or *captains*
d 1 Chron 11.11: Heb obscure
22.50: Rom 15.9.   **23.8-39:** 1 Chron 11.10-41.

this. Shall I drink the blood of the men who went at the risk of their lives?" Therefore he would not drink it. These things did the three mighty men.

18 Now A·bi′shäi, the brother of Jō′ab, the son of Zě·rü′i·äh, was chief of the thirty.[e] And he wielded his spear against three hundred men and slew them, and won a name beside the three. 19 He was the most renowned of the thirty,[f] and became their commander; but he did not attain to the three.

20 And Be·nā′iäh the son of Je·hoi′-ȧ·dȧ was a valiant man[g] of Kab′zě·ěl, a doer of great deeds; he smote two ariels[h] of Mō′ab. He also went down and slew a lion in a pit on a day when snow had fallen. 21And he slew an Egyptian, a handsome man. The Egyptian had a spear in his hand; but Be·nā′iäh went down to him with a staff, and snatched the spear out of the Egyptian's hand, and slew him with his own spear. 22 These things did Be·nā′iäh the son of Je·hoi′ȧ·dȧ, and won a name beside the three mighty men. 23 He was renowned among the thirty, but he did not attain to the three. And David set him over his bodyguard.

24 As′ȧ·hel the brother of Jō′ab was one of the thirty; El·hā′nän the son of Dō′dō of Bethlehem, 25 Sham′mäh of Hâr′od, E·li′kä of Harod, 26 Hě′lez the Pal′tite, Ira the son of Ik′kesh of Te·kō′ȧ, 27Ȧ·bi·e′zěr, of An′ȧ·thoth, Mě·bun′näi the Hü′shȧ·thite, 28 Zal′-mon the Ȧ·hō′hite, Mä′hȧ·räi of Ně-toph′äh, 29 Hē′leb the son of Bā′ȧ·näh of Ně·toph′äh, It′täi the son of Ri′bäi of Gib′e·äh of the Benjaminites, 30 Be-nā′iäh of Pir′ȧ·thon, Hid′däi of the brooks of Gä′ash, 31Ȧ′bi-al′bŏn the Är′bȧ·thite, Az′mȧ·veth of Bȧ·hü′rim, 32 E·li′ȧh·bȧ of Shä-al′bŏn, the sons of Jä′shěn, Jonathan, 33 Sham′mäh the Hâr′ȧ·rite, Ȧ·hī′äm the son of Shâr′ar the Hararite, 34 E·liph′ě·let the son of Ȧ·haś′bäi of Mä′ȧ·cäh, E·li′äm the son of Ȧ·hith′ŏ·phel of Gi′lō, 35 Hez′rō[i] of Cär′měl, Pā′ȧ·räi the Är′bïte, 36 I′gal the son of Nathan of Zō′bäh, Bā′ni the Gad′ite, 37 Zʿ′lek the Am′mŏ·nite, Nä′hȧ·räi of Bě·ěr′ŏth, the armor-bearer of Jō′ab the son of Zě·rü′i·äh, 38 Ira the Ith′rite, Gâr′eb the Ithrite,

39 U′·rī′äh the Hit′tite: thirty-seven in all.

24

Again the anger of the LORD was kindled against Israel, and he incited David against them, saying, "Go, number Israel and Judah." 2 So the king said to Jō′ab and the commanders of the army,[j] who were with him, "Go through all the tribes of Israel, from Dan to Beer-sheba, and number the people, that I may know the number of the people." 3 But Jō′ab said to the king, "May the LORD your God add to the people a hundred times as many as they are, while the eyes of my lord the king still see it; but why does my lord the king delight in this thing?" 4 But the king's word prevailed against Jō′ab and the commanders of the army. So Joab and the commanders of the army went out from the presence of the king to number the people of Israel. 5 They crossed the Jordan, and began from A·rō′ěr,[k] and from the city that is in the middle of the valley, toward Gad and on to Jä′zěr. 6 Then they came to Gilead, and to Kä′desh in the land of the Hit′tites;[l] and they came to Dan, and from Dan[m] they went around to Si′don, 7 and came to the fortress of Tyre and to all the cities of the Hi′vites and Canaanites; and they went out to the Negeb of Judah at Beer-sheba. 8 So when they had gone through all the land, they came to Jerusalem at the end of nine months and twenty days. 9And Jō′ab gave the sum of the numbering of the people to the king: in Israel there were eight hundred thousand valiant men who drew the sword, and the men of Judah were five hundred thousand.

10 But David's heart smote him after he had numbered the people. And David said to the LORD, "I have sinned greatly in what I have done. But now, O LORD, I pray thee, take away the iniquity of thy servant; for I have done very foolishly." 11And when David arose in the morning, the word of the LORD came to the prophet Gad, David's seer, saying, 12 "Go and say to David, 'Thus says the LORD, Three things I offer[n] you; choose one of them, that I may do it to you.'" 13 So Gad came to David and told

---

[e] Two Hebrew Mss Syr: MT *three*
[f] 1 Chron 11.25: Heb *Was he the most renowned of the three?*
[g] Another reading is *the son of Ish-hai*   [h] The meaning of the word *ariel* is unknown
[i] Another reading is *Hezrai*
[j] 1 Chron 21.2 Gk: Heb *to Joab the commander of the army*
[k] Gk: Heb *encamped in Aroer*   [l] Gk: Heb *to the land of Tahtim-hodshi*
[m] Cn Compare Gk: Heb *they came to Dan-jaan and*   [n] Or *hold over*
24.1-25: 1 Chron 21.1-27.

him, and said to him, "Shall three[o] years of famine come to you in your land? Or will you flee three months before your foes while they pursue you? Or shall there be three days' pestilence in your land? Now consider, and decide what answer I shall return to him who sent me." 14 Then David said to Gad, "I am in great distress; let us fall into the hand of the LORD, for his mercy is great; but let me not fall into the hand of man."

15 So the LORD sent a pestilence upon Israel from the morning until the appointed time; and there died of the people from Dan to Beer-sheba seventy thousand men. 16And when the angel stretched forth his hand toward Jerusalem to destroy it, the LORD repented of the evil, and said to the angel who was working destruction among the people, "It is enough; now stay your hand." And the angel of the LORD was by the threshing floor of A·rau′nah the Jeb′ū·site. 17 Then David spoke to the LORD when he saw the angel who was smiting the people, and said, "Lo, I have sinned, and I have done wickedly; but these sheep, what have they done? Let thy hand, I pray thee, be against me and against my father's house."

18 And Gad came that day to David, and said to him, "Go up, rear an altar to the LORD on the threshing floor of A·rau′nah the Jeb′ū·site." 19 So David went up at Gad's word, as the LORD commanded. 20And when A·rau′nah looked down, he saw the king and his servants coming on toward him; and Araunah went forth, and did obeisance to the king with his face to the ground. 21And A·rau′nah said, "Why has my lord the king come to his servant?" David said, "To buy the threshing floor of you, in order to build an altar to the LORD, that the plague may be averted from the people." 22 Then A·rau′nah said to David, "Let my lord the king take and offer up what seems good to him; here are the oxen for the burnt offering, and the threshing sledges and the yokes of the oxen for the wood. 23All this, O king, A·rau′nah gives to the king." And Araunah said to the king, "The LORD your God accept you." 24 But the king said to A·rau′nah, "No, but I will buy it of you for a price; I will not offer burnt offerings to the LORD my God which cost me nothing." So David bought the threshing floor and the oxen for fifty shekels of silver. 25And David built there an altar to the LORD, and offered burnt offerings and peace offerings. So the LORD heeded supplications for the land, and the plague was averted from Israel.

THE FIRST BOOK OF THE

KINGS

Now King David was old and advanced in years; and although they covered him with clothes, he could not get warm. 2 Therefore his servants said to him, "Let a young maiden be sought for my lord the king, and let her wait upon the king, and be his nurse; let her lie in your bosom, that my lord the king may be warm." 3 So they sought for a beautiful maiden throughout all the territory of Israel, and found Ab′i·shag the Shü′nam·mite, and brought her to the king. 4 The maiden was very beautiful; and she became the king's nurse and ministered to him; but the king knew her not.

5 Now Ad·ō·ni′jah the son of Hag′-

gith exalted himself, saying, "I will be king"; and he prepared for himself chariots and horsemen, and fifty men to run before him. 6 His father had never at any time displeased him by asking, "Why have you done thus and so?" He was also a very handsome man; and he was born next after Ab′sà·lôm. 7 He conferred with Jō′ab the son of Ze·rü′i·ah and with A·bi′-à·thär the priest; and they followed Ad·ō·ni′jah and helped him. 8 But Zā′dok the priest, and Be·nā′iàh the son of Je·hoi′à·dä, and Nathan the prophet, and Shim′e·ī, and Re̅′ī, and David's mighty men were not with Ad·ō·ni′jah.

9 Ad·ō·ni′jah sacrificed sheep, oxen,

o 1 Chron 21.12 Gk: Heb *seven*

and fatlings by the Serpent's Stone, which is beside En-rō'gel, and he invited all his brothers, the king's sons, and all the royal officials of Judah, 10 but he did not invite Nathan the prophet or Be-nā'iah or the mighty men or Solomon his brother.

11 Then Nathan said to Bath-shē'ba the mother of Solomon, "Have you not heard that Ad-ō-nī'jah the son of Hag'gith has become king and David our lord does not know it? 12 Now therefore come, let me give you counsel, that you may save your own life and the life of your son Solomon. 13 Go in at once to King David, and say to him, 'Did you not, my lord the king, swear to your maidservant, saying, "Solomon your son shall reign after me, and he shall sit upon my throne"? Why then is Ad-ō-nī'jah king?' 14 Then while you are still speaking with the king, I also will come in after you and confirm your words."

15 So Bath-shē'ba went to the king into his chamber (now the king was very old, and Ab'i-shag the Shü'nam-mite was ministering to the king). 16 Bath-shē'ba bowed and did obeisance to the king, and the king said, "What do you desire?" 17 She said to him, "My lord, you swore to your maidservant by the LORD your God, saying, 'Solomon your son shall reign after me, and he shall sit upon my throne.' 18And now, behold, Ad-ō-nī'jah is king, although you, my lord the king, do not know it. 19 He has sacrificed oxen, fatlings, and sheep in abundance, and has invited all the sons of the king, A-bi'a-thär the priest, and Jō'ab the commander of the army; but Solomon your servant he has not invited. 20And now, my lord the king, the eyes of all Israel are upon you, to tell them who shall sit on the throne of my lord the king after him. 21 Otherwise it will come to pass, when my lord the king sleeps with his fathers, that I and my son Solomon will be counted offenders."

22 While she was still speaking with the king, Nathan the prophet came in. 23And they told the king, "Here is Nathan the prophet." And when he came in before the king, he bowed before the king, with his face to the ground. 24And Nathan said, "My lord the king, have you said, 'Ad-ō-nī'jah shall reign after me, and he shall sit upon my throne'? 25 For he has gone down this day, and has sacrificed oxen, fatlings, and sheep in abundance, and

has invited all the king's sons, Jō'ab the commander*a* of the army, and A-bi'a-thär the priest; and behold, they are eating and drinking before him, and saying, 'Long live King Ad-ō-nī'jäh!' 26 But me, your servant, and Zā'dok the priest, and Be-nā'iah the son of Je-hoi'a-dä, and your servant Solomon, he has not invited. 27 Has this thing been brought about by my lord the king and you have not told your servants who should sit on the throne of my lord the king after him?"

28 Then King David answered, "Call Bath-shē'ba to me." So she came into the king's presence, and stood before the king. 29And the king swore, saying, "As the LORD lives, who has redeemed my soul out of every adversity, 30 as I swore to you by the LORD, the God of Israel, saying, 'Solomon your son shall reign after me, and he shall sit upon my throne in my stead'; even so will I do this day." 31 Then Bath-shē'ba bowed with her face to the ground, and did obeisance to the king, and said, "May my lord King David live for ever!"

32 King David said, "Call to me Zā'dok the priest, Nathan the prophet, and Be-nā'iah the son of Je-hoi'a-dä." So they came before the king. 33And the king said to them, "Take with you the servants of your lord, and cause Solomon my son to ride on my own mule, and bring him down to Gī'hon; 34 and let Zā'dok the priest and Nathan the prophet there anoint him king over Israel; then blow the trumpet, and say, 'Long live King Solomon!' 35 You shall then come up after him, and he shall come and sit upon my throne; for he shall be king in my stead; and I have appointed him to be ruler over Israel and over Judah." 36And Be-nā'iah the son of Je-hoi'a-dä answered the king, "Amen! May the LORD, the God of my lord the king, say so. 37As the LORD has been with my lord the king, even so may he be with Solomon, and make his throne greater than the throne of my lord King David."

38 So Zā'dok the priest, Nathan the prophet, and Be-nā'iah the son of Je-hoi'a-dä, and the Cher'e-thites and the Pel'e-thites, went down and caused Solomon to ride on King David's mule, and brought him to Gī'hon. 39 There Zā'dok the priest took the horn of oil from the tent, and anointed Solomon. Then they blew the trumpet; and all the people said, "Long live King Solomon!" 40And all the people

a Gk: Heb *commanders*

went up after him, playing on pipes, and rejoicing with great joy, so that the earth was split by their noise.

41 Ad·ō·nī′jäh and all the guests who were with him heard it as they finished feasting. And when Jō′ab heard the sound of the trumpet, he said, "What does this uproar in the city mean?" 42 While he was still speaking, behold, Jonathan the son of A·bī′a·thär the priest came; and Ad·ō·nī′jäh said, "Come in, for you are a worthy man and bring good news." 43 Jonathan answered Ad·ō·nī′jäh, "No, for our lord King David has made Solomon king; 44 and the king has sent with him Zā′dok the priest, Nathan the prophet, and Be·nā′iäh the son of Je·hoi′a·dä, and the Cher′ē·thītes and the Pel′ē·thītes; and they have caused him to ride on the king's mule; 45 and Zā′dok the priest and Nathan the prophet have anointed him king at Gī′hon; and they have gone up from there rejoicing, so that the city is in an uproar. This is the noise that you have heard. 46 Solomon sits upon the royal throne. 47 Moreover the king's servants came to congratulate our lord King David, saying, 'Your God make the name of Solomon more famous than yours, and make his throne greater than your throne.' And the king bowed himself upon the bed. 48 And the king also said, "Blessed be the LORD, the God of Israel, who has granted one of my offspring[b] to sit on my throne this day, my own eyes seeing it.' "

49 Then all the guests of Ad·ō·nī′jäh trembled, and rose, and each went his own way. 50 And Ad·ō·nī′jäh feared Solomon; and he arose, and went, and caught hold of the horns of the altar. 51 And it was told Solomon, "Behold, Ad·ō·nī′jäh fears King Solomon; for, lo, he has laid hold of the horns of the altar, saying, 'Let King Solomon swear to me first that he will not slay his servant with the sword.' " 52 And Solomon said, "If he prove to be a worthy man, not one of his hairs shall fall to the earth; but if wickedness is found in him, he shall die." 53 So King Solomon sent, and they brought him down from the altar. And he came and did obeisance to King Solomon; and Solomon said to him, "Go to your house."

2 When David's time to die drew near, he charged Solomon his son, saying, 2 "I am about to go the way of all the earth. Be strong, and show yourself a man, 3 and keep the charge of the LORD your God, walking in his ways and keeping his statutes, his commandments, his ordinances, and his testimonies, as it is written in the law of Moses, that you may prosper in all that you do and wherever you turn; 4 that the LORD may establish his word which he spoke concerning me, saying, 'If your sons take heed to their way, to walk before me in faithfulness with all their heart and with all their soul, there shall not fail you a man on the throne of Israel.'

5 "Moreover you know also what Jō′ab the son of Zĕ·rü′i·äh did to me, how he dealt with the two commanders of the armies of Israel, Abner the son of Nēr, and A·mā′sä the son of Jē′thēr, whom he murdered, avenging[c] in time of peace blood which had been shed in war, and putting innocent blood[d] upon the girdle about my[e] loins, and upon the sandals on my[e] feet. 6 Act therefore according to your wisdom, but do not let his gray head go down to Shē′ōl in peace. 7 But deal loyally with the sons of Bär·zil′läi the Gileadite, and let them be among those who eat at your table; for with such loyalty they met me when I fled from Ab′sà·lòm your brother. 8 And there is also with you Shim′ē·i the son of Gē′rä, the Benjaminite from Bà·hū′rim, who cursed me with a grievous curse on the day when I went to Mä·hà·nā′im; but when he came down to meet me at the Jordan, I swore to him by the LORD, saying, 'I will not put you to death with the sword.' 9 Now therefore hold him not guiltless, for you are a wise man; you will know what you ought to do to him, and you shall bring his gray head down with blood to Shē′ōl."

10 Then David slept with his fathers, and was buried in the city of David. 11 And the time that David reigned over Israel was forty years; he reigned seven years in Hē′brón, and thirty-three years in Jerusalem. 12 So Solomon sat upon the throne of David his father; and his kingdom was firmly established.

13 Then Ad·ō·nī′jäh the son of Hag′gith came to Bath·shē′bà the mother of Solomon. And she said, "Do you come peaceably?" He said, "Peaceably." 14 Then he said, "I have something to say to you." She said, "Say on." 15 He said, "You know that the kingdom was mine, and that all Israel fully expected me to reign; how-

---

b Gk: Heb *one*   c Gk: Heb *placing*   d Gk: Heb *blood of war*   e Gk: Heb *his*
2.12: 1 Chron 29.23.

ever the kingdom has turned about and become my brother's, for it was his from the LORD. ¹⁶And now I have one request to make of you; do not refuse me." She said to him, "Say on." ¹⁷And she said, "Pray ask King Solomon—he will not refuse you—to give me Ab′i·shag the Shü′nam·mite as my wife." ¹⁸ Bath·shē′ba said, "Very well; I will speak for you to the king."

19 So Bath·shē′ba went to King Solomon, to speak to him on behalf of Ad·o·ni′jah. And the king rose to meet her, and bowed down to her; then he sat on his throne, and had a seat brought for the king's mother; and she sat on his right. ²⁰ Then she said, "I have one small request to make of you; do not refuse me." And the king said to her, "Make your request, my mother; for I will not refuse you." ²¹ She said, "Let Ab′i·shag the Shü′nam·mite be given to Ad·o·ni′jah your brother as his wife." ²² King Solomon answered his mother, "And why do you ask Ab′i·shag the Shü′nam·mite for Ad·o·ni′jah? Ask for him the kingdom also; for he is my elder brother, and on his side are A·bi′a·thär′ the priest and Jō′ab the son of Zĕ,rii′-i·ah." ²³ Then King Solomon swore by the LORD, saying, "God do so to me and more also if this word does not cost Ad·o·ni′jah his life! ²⁴ Now therefore as the LORD lives, who has established me, and placed me on the throne of David my father, and who has made me a house, as he promised, Ad·o·ni′jah shall be put to death this day." ²⁵ So King Solomon sent Be·nā′iah the son of Je·hoi′a·dà; and he struck him down, and he died.

26 And to A·bi′a·thär the priest the king said, "Go to An′a·thoth, to your estate; for you deserve death. But I will not at this time put you to death, because you bore the ark of the Lord GOD before David my father, and because you shared in all the affliction of my father." ²⁷ So Solomon expelled A·bi′a·thär from being priest to the LORD, thus fulfilling the word of the LORD which he had spoken concerning the house of Eli in Shi′loh.

28 When the news came to Jō′ab—for Joab had supported Ad·o·ni′jah although he had not supported Ab′sa·lóm—Joab fled to the tent of the LORD and caught hold of the horns of the altar. ²⁹And when it was told King Solomon, "Jō′ab has fled to the tent of the LORD, and behold, he is beside the altar," Solomon sent Be·nā′iah the son of Je·hoi′a·dà, saying, "Go, strike

him down." ³⁰ So Be·nā′iah came to the tent of the LORD, and said to him, "The king commands, 'Come forth.' " But he said, "No, I will die here." Then Benaiah brought the king word again, saying, "Thus said Jō′ab, and thus he answered me." ³¹ The king replied to him, "Do as he has said, strike him down and bury him; and thus take away from me and from my father's house the guilt for the blood which Jō′ab shed without cause. ³² The LORD will bring back his bloody deeds upon his own head, because, without the knowledge of my father David, he attacked and slew with the sword two men more righteous and better than himself, Abner the son of Nĕr, commander of the army of Israel, and A·mā′sà the son of Jĕ′thĕr, commander of the army of Judah. ³³ So shall their blood come back upon the head of Jō′ab and upon the head of his descendants for ever; but to David, and to his descendants, and to his house, and to his throne, there shall be peace from the LORD for evermore." ³⁴ Then Be·nā′iah the son of Je·hoi′a·dà went up, and struck him down and killed him; and he was buried in his own house in the wilderness. ³⁵ The king put Be·nā′iah the son of Je·hoi′a·dà over the army in place of Jō′ab, and the king put Zā′dok the priest in the place of A·bi′a·thär.

36 Then the king sent and summoned Shim′ē·ī, and said to him, "Build yourself a house in Jerusalem, and dwell there, and do not go forth from there to any place whatever. ³⁷ For on the day you go forth, and cross the brook Kid′ron, know for certain that you shall die; your blood shall be upon your own head." ³⁸And Shim′ē·ī said to the king, "What you say is good; as my lord the king has said, so will your servant do." So Shime-i dwelt in Jerusalem many days.

39 But it happened at the end of three years that two of Shim′ē·ī's slaves ran away to A′chish, son of Mā′a·càh, king of Gath. And when it was told Shime-i, "Behold, your slaves are in Gath," ⁴⁰ Shim′ē·ī arose and saddled an ass, and went to Gath to A′chish, to seek his slaves; Shime-i went and brought his slaves from Gath. ⁴¹And when Solomon was told that Shim′ē·ī had gone from Jerusalem to Gath and returned, ⁴² the king sent and summoned Shim′ē·ī, and said to him, "Did I not make you swear by the LORD, and solemnly admonish you, saying, 'Know for certain that

ſ Gk Syr Vg: Heb and for him and for Abiathar

on the day you go forth and go to any place whatever, you shall die'? And you said to me, 'What you say is good; I obey.' 43 Why then have you not kept your oath to the LORD and the commandment with which I charged you?" 44 The king also said to Shim′e-i, "You know in your own heart all the evil that you did to David my father; so the LORD will bring back your evil upon your own head. 45 But King Solomon shall be blessed, and the throne of David shall be established before the LORD for ever." 46 Then the king commanded Be·nā′iäh the son of Je·hoi′a·dä; and he went out and struck him down, and he died.

So the kingdom was established in the hand of Solomon.

3 Solomon made a marriage alliance with Pharaoh king of Egypt; he took Pharaoh's daughter, and brought her into the city of David, until he had finished building his own house and the house of the LORD and the wall around Jerusalem. 2 The people were sacrificing at the high places, however, because no house had yet been built for the name of the LORD.

3 Solomon loved the LORD, walking in the statutes of David his father; only, he sacrificed and burnt incense at the high places. 4And the king went to Gib′e·ón to sacrifice there, for that was the great high place; Solomon used to offer a thousand burnt offerings upon that altar. 5At Gib′e·ón the LORD appeared to Solomon in a dream by night; and God said, "Ask what I shall give you." 6And Solomon said, "Thou hast shown great and steadfast love to thy servant David my father, because he walked before thee in faithfulness, in righteousness, and in uprightness of heart toward thee; and thou hast kept for him this great and steadfast love, and hast given him a son to sit on his throne this day. 7And now, O LORD my God, thou hast made thy servant king in place of David my father, although I am but a little child; I do not know how to go out or come in. 8And thy servant is in the midst of thy people whom thou hast chosen, a great people, that cannot be numbered or counted for multitude. 9 Give thy servant therefore an understanding mind to govern thy people, that I may discern between good and evil; for who is able to govern this thy great people?"

10 It pleased the LORD that Solomon had asked this. 11And God said to him, "Because you have asked this,

and have not asked for yourself long life or riches or the life of your enemies, but have asked for yourself understanding to discern what is right, 12 behold, I now do according to your word. Behold, I give you a wise and discerning mind, so that none like you has been before you and none like you shall arise after you. 13 I give you also what you have not asked, both riches and honor, so that no other king shall compare with you, all your days. 14And if you will walk in my ways, keeping my statutes and my commandments, as your father David walked, then I will lengthen your days."

15 And Solomon awoke, and behold, it was a dream. Then he came to Jerusalem, and stood before the ark of the covenant of the LORD, and offered up burnt offerings and peace offerings, and made a feast for all his servants.

16 Then two harlots came to the king, and stood before him. 17 The one woman said, "Oh, my lord, this woman and I dwell in the same house; and I gave birth to a child while she was in the house. 18 Then on the third day after I was delivered, this woman also gave birth; and we were alone; there was no one else with us in the house, only we two were in the house. 19And this woman's son died in the night, because she lay on it. 20And she arose at midnight, and took my son from beside me, while your maidservant slept, and laid it in her bosom, and laid her dead son in my bosom. 21 When I rose in the morning to nurse my child, behold, it was dead; but when I looked at it closely in the morning, behold, it was not the child that I had borne." 22 But the other woman said, "No, the living child is mine, and the dead child is yours." The first said, "No, the dead child is yours, and the living child is mine." Thus they spoke before the king.

23 Then the king said, "The one says, 'This is my son that is alive, and your son is dead'; and the other says, 'No, but your son is dead, and my son is the living one.'" 24And the king said, "Bring me a sword." So a sword was brought before the king. 25And the king said, "Divide the living child in two, and give half to the one, and half to the other." 26 Then the woman whose son was alive said to the king, because her heart yearned for her son, "Oh, my lord, give her the living child, and by no means slay

3.4-12: 2 Chron 1.3-13.

it." But the other said, "It shall be neither mine nor yours; divide it." 27 Then the king answered and said, "Give the living child to the first woman, and by no means slay it; she is its mother." 28And all Israel heard of the judgment which the king had rendered; and they stood in awe of the king, because they perceived that the wisdom of God was in him, to render justice.

4 King Solomon was king over all Israel, 2 and these were his high officials: Az·a·ri′ah the son of Zā′dok was the priest; 3 El·i·hôr′eph and A·hi′-jäh the sons of Shi′shä were secretaries; Je·hosh′a·phat the son of A·hi′lüd was recorder; 4 Be·nā′iäh the son of Je·hoi′-a·dà was in command of the army; Zā′dok and A·bi′a·thär were priests; 5Az·a·ri′ah the son of Nathan was over the officers; Zā′büd the son of Nathan was priest and king's friend; 6A·hi′shär was in charge of the palace; and Ad·ō-ni′ràm the son of Ab′dà was in charge of the forced labor.

7 Solomon had twelve officers over all Israel, who provided food for the king and his household; each man had to make provision for one month in the year. 8 These were their names: Ben-hûr′, in the hill country of E′phra·im; 9 Ben-dē′kèr, in Mā′kaz, Shā-al′bim, Beth-shē′mesh, and E′lon-beth-hā′nàn; 10 Ben-hē′sed, in A·rüb′-both (to him belonged Sō′côh and all the land of Hē′phèr); 11 Ben-à·bin′à-dab, in all Nā′phath-dôr (he had Tā′phath the daughter of Solomon as his wife); 12 Bā′a·nà the son of A·hi′lüd, in Tā′à·nach, Mè·gid′dō, and all Beth-shē′àn which is beside Zar′è·than below Jez′rē·êl, and from Beth-shean to A′bèl-mè·hō′läh, as far as the other side of Jok′mē·àm; 13 Ben-gē′bèr, in Rā′moth-gil′ē·àd (he had the villages of Jā′ir the son of Mà·nas′sèh, which are in Gilead, and he had the region of Är′gôb, which is in Bā′shàn, sixty great cities with walls and bronze bars); 14 A·hin′à·dab the son of Id′dō, in Mā-hà·nā′im; 15A·him′à-az, in Naph′tà·lī (he had taken Bas′ē·math the daughter of Solomon as his wife); 16 Bā′à·nà the son of Hü′shäi, in Ash′èr and Be·ā′loth; 17 Je·hosh′a·phat the son of Pà·rü′àh, in Is′sà·chär; 18 Shim′ē-ī the son of E′là, in Benjamin; 19 Gē′bèr the son of U′ri, in the land of Gilead, the country of Si′hon king of the Am′ō-rītes and of Og king of Bā′shàn. And there was one officer in the land of Judah.

20 Judah and Israel were as many as the sand by the sea; they ate and drank and were happy. 21g Solomon ruled over all the kingdoms from the Eü·phrā′tēs to the land of the Philistines and to the border of Egypt; they brought tribute and served Solomon all the days of his life.

22 Solomon's provision for one day was thirty cors of fine flour, and sixty cors of meal, 23 ten fat oxen, and twenty pasture-fed cattle, a hundred sheep, besides harts, gazelles, roebucks, and fatted fowl. 24 For he had dominion over all the region west of the Eü·phrā′tēs from Tiph′säh to Gā′zà, over all the kings west of the Euphrates; and he had peace on all sides round about him. 25And Judah and Israel dwelt in safety, from Dan even to Beer-sheba, every man under his vine and under his fig tree, all the days of Solomon. 26 Solomon also had forty thousand stalls of horses for his chariots, and twelve thousand horsemen. 27And those officers supplied provisions for King Solomon, and for all who came to King Solomon's table, each one in his month; they let nothing be lacking. 28 Barley also and straw for the horses and swift steeds they brought to the place where it was required, each according to his charge.

29 And God gave Solomon wisdom and understanding beyond measure, and largeness of mind like the sand on the seashore, 30 so that Solomon's wisdom surpassed the wisdom of all the people of the east, and all the wisdom of Egypt. 31 For he was wiser than all other men, wiser than Ethan the Ez′rà·hite, and Hē′màn, Cal′col, and Där′dà, the sons of Mā′hol; and his fame was in all the nations round about. 32 He also uttered three thousand proverbs; and his songs were a thousand and five. 33 He spoke of trees, from the cedar that is in Lebanon to the hyssop that grows out of the wall; he spoke also of beasts, and of birds, and of reptiles, and of fish. 34And men came from all peoples to hear the wisdom of Solomon, and from all the kings of the earth, who had heard of his wisdom.

5 h Now Hiram king of Tȳre sent his servants to Solomon, when he heard that they had anointed him king in place of his father; for Hiram always loved David. 2And Solomon sent word to Hiram, 3 "You know that David my father could not build a house for the name of the LORD his God because

of the warfare with which his enemies surrounded him, until the LORD put them under the soles of his feet. 4 But now the LORD my God has given me rest on every side; there is neither adversary nor misfortune. 5And so I purpose to build a house for the name of the LORD my God, as the LORD said to David my father, 'Your son, whom I will set upon your throne in your place, shall build the house for my name.' 6 Now therefore command that cedars of Lebanon be cut for me; and my servants will join your servants, and I will pay you for your servants such wages as you set; for you know that there is no one among us who knows how to cut timber like the Si·dō′ni·ans.''

7 When Hiram heard the words of Solomon, he rejoiced greatly, and said, "Blessed be the LORD this day, who has given to David a wise son to be over this great people." 8And Hiram sent to Solomon, saying, "I have heard the message which you have sent to me; I am ready to do all you desire in the matter of cedar and cypress timber. 9 My servants shall bring it down to the sea from Lebanon; and I will make it into rafts to go by sea to the place you direct, and I will have them broken up there, and you shall receive it; and you shall meet my wishes by providing food for my household.'' 10 So Hiram supplied Solomon with all the timber of cedar and cypress that he desired, 11 while Solomon gave Hiram twenty thousand cors of wheat as food for his household, and twenty thousand*i* cors of beaten oil. Solomon gave this to Hiram year by year. 12And the LORD gave Solomon wisdom, as he promised him; and there was peace between Hiram and Solomon; and the two of them made a treaty.

13 King Solomon raised a levy of forced labor out of all Israel; and the levy numbered thirty thousand men. 14And he sent them to Lebanon, ten thousand a month in relays; they would be a month in Lebanon and two months at home; Ad·o·ni′ram was in charge of the levy. 15 Solomon also had seventy thousand burden-bearers and eighty thousand hewers of stone in the hill country, 16 besides Solomon's three thousand three hundred chief officers who were over the work, who had charge of the people who carried on the work. 17At the king's command, they quarried out great,

costly stones in order to lay the foundation of the house with dressed stones. 18 So Solomon's builders and Hiram's builders and the men of Gē′bal did the hewing and prepared the timber and the stone to build the house.

6 In the four hundred and eightieth year after the people of Israel came out of the land of Egypt, in the fourth year of Solomon's reign over Israel, in the month of Ziv, which is the second month, he began to build the house of the LORD. 2 The house which King Solomon built for the LORD was sixty cubits long, twenty cubits wide, and thirty cubits high. 3 The vestibule in front of the nave of the house was twenty cubits long, equal to the width of the house, and ten cubits deep in front of the house. 4And he made for the house windows with recessed frames. 5 He also built a structure against the wall of the house, running round the walls of the house, both the nave and the inner sanctuary; and he made side chambers all around. 6 The lowest story*j* was five cubits broad, the middle one was six cubits broad, and the third was seven cubits broad; for around the outside of the house he made offsets on the wall in order that the supporting beams should not be inserted into the walls of the house.

7 When the house was built, it was with stone prepared at the quarry; so that neither hammer nor axe nor any tool of iron was heard in the temple, while it was being built.

8 The entrance for the lowest*k* story was on the south side of the house; and one went up by stairs to the middle story, and from the middle story to the third. 9 So he built the house, and finished it; and he made the ceiling of the house of beams and planks of cedar. 10 He built the structure against the whole house, each story*l* five cubits high, and it was joined to the house with timbers of cedar.

11 Now the word of the LORD came to Solomon, 12 "Concerning this house which you are building, if you will walk in my statutes and obey my ordinances and keep all my commandments and walk in them, then I will establish my word with you, which I spoke to David your father. 13And I will dwell among the children of Israel, and will not forsake my people Israel.'

14 So Solomon built the house, and finished it. 15 He lined the walls of the house on the inside with boards of

---

i Gk: Heb *twenty*   *j* Gk: Heb *structure*   *k* Gk Tg: Heb *middle*   *l* Heb lacks *each story*
5.5: 2 Chron 2.1.   **5.15-16:** 2 Chron 2.2, 18.   **6.1-28:** 2 Chron 3.1-13; Acts 7.47.

cedar; from the floor of the house to the rafters[m] of the ceiling, he covered them on the inside with wood; and he covered the floor of the house with boards of cypress. 16 He built twenty cubits of the rear of the house with boards of cedar from the floor to the rafters,[m] and he built this within as an inner sanctuary, as the most holy place. 17 The house, that is, the nave in front of the inner sanctuary, was forty cubits long. 18 The cedar within the house was carved in the form of gourds and open flowers; all was cedar, no stone was seen. 19 The inner sanctuary he prepared in the innermost part of the house, to set there the ark of the covenant of the LORD. 20 The inner sanctuary[n] was twenty cubits long, twenty cubits wide, and twenty cubits high; and he overlaid it with pure gold. He also made[o] an altar of cedar. 21And Solomon overlaid the inside of the house with pure gold, and he drew chains of gold across, in front of the inner sanctuary, and overlaid it with gold. 22And he overlaid the whole house with gold, until all the house was finished. Also the whole altar that belonged to the inner sanctuary he overlaid with gold.

23 In the inner sanctuary he made two cherubim of olivewood, each ten cubits high. 24 Five cubits was the length of one wing of the cherub, and five cubits the length of the other wing of the cherub; it was ten cubits from the tip of one wing to the tip of the other. 25 The other cherub also measured ten cubits; both cherubim had the same measure and the same form. 26 The height of one cherub was ten cubits, and so was that of the other cherub. 27 He put the cherubim in the innermost part of the house; and the wings of the cherubim were spread out so that a wing of one touched the one wall, and a wing of the other cherub touched the other wall; their other wings touched each other in the middle of the house. 28And he overlaid the cherubim with gold.

29 He carved all the walls of the house round about with carved figures of cherubim and palm trees and open flowers, in the inner and outer rooms. 30 The floor of the house he overlaid with gold in the inner and outer rooms.

31 For the entrance to the inner sanctuary he made doors of olivewood; the lintel and the doorposts formed a pentagon.[p] 32 He covered the two

doors of olivewood with carvings of cherubim, palm trees, and open flowers; he overlaid them with gold, and spread gold upon the cherubim and upon the palm trees.

33 So also he made for the entrance to the nave doorposts of olivewood, in the form of a square, 34 and two doors of cypress wood; the two leaves of the one door were folding, and the two leaves of the other door were folding. 35 On them he carved cherubim and palm trees and open flowers; and he overlaid them with gold evenly applied upon the carved work. 36 He built the inner court with three courses of hewn stone and one course of cedar beams.

37 In the fourth year the foundation of the house of the LORD was laid, in the month of Ziv. 38And in the eleventh year, in the month of Bul, which is the eighth month, the house was finished in all its parts, and according to all its specifications. He was seven years in building it.

7 Solomon was building his own house thirteen years, and he finished his entire house.

2 He built the House of the Forest of Lebanon; its length was a hundred cubits, and its breadth fifty cubits, and its height thirty cubits, and it was built upon three[q] rows of cedar pillars, with cedar beams upon the pillars. 3And it was covered with cedar above the chambers that were upon the forty-five pillars, fifteen in each row. 4 There were window frames in three rows, and window opposite window in three tiers. 5All the doorways and windows[r] had square frames, and window was opposite window in three tiers.

6 And he made the Hall of Pillars; its length was fifty cubits, and its breadth thirty cubits; there was a porch in front with pillars, and a canopy before them.

7 And he made the Hall of the Throne where he was to pronounce judgment, even the Hall of Judgment; it was finished with cedar from floor to rafters.[s]

8 His own house where he was to dwell, in the other court back of the hall, was of like workmanship. Solomon also made a house like this hall for Pharaoh's daughter whom he had taken in marriage.

9 All these were made of costly stones, hewn according to measure, sawed with saws, back and front, even from the foundation to the coping, and from the court of the house of the

LORD[t] to the great court. [10] The foundation was of costly stones, huge stones, stones of eight and ten cubits. [11]And above were costly stones, hewn according to measurement, and cedar. [12] The great court had three courses of hewn stone round about, and a course of cedar beams; so had the inner court of the house of the LORD, and the vestibule of the house.

[13] And King Solomon sent and brought Hiram from Tȳre. [14] He was the son of a widow of the tribe of Naph′tà·lǐ, and his father was a man of Tȳre, a worker in bronze; and he was full of wisdom, understanding, and skill, for making any work in bronze. He came to King Solomon, and did all his work.

[15] He cast two pillars of bronze. Eighteen cubits was the height of one pillar, and a line of twelve cubits measured its circumference; it was hollow, and its thickness was four fingers; the second pillar was the same.[u] [16] He also made two capitals of molten bronze, to set upon the tops of the pillars; the height of the one capital was five cubits, and the height of the other capital was five cubits. [17] Then he made two[v] nets of checker work with wreaths of chain work for the capitals upon the tops of the pillars; a net[w] for the one capital, and a net[w] for the other capital. [18] Likewise he made pomegranates;[x] in two rows round about upon the one network, to cover the capital that was upon the top of the pillar; and he did the same with the other capital. [19] Now the capitals that were upon the tops of the pillars in the vestibule were of lily-work, four cubits. [20] The capitals were upon the two pillars and also above the rounded projection which was beside the network; there were two hundred pomegranates, in two rows round about; and so with the other capital. [21] He set up the pillars at the vestibule of the temple; he set up the pillar on the south and called its name Jā′chin; and he set up the pillar on the north and called its name Bō′az. [22]And upon the tops of the pillars was lily-work. Thus the work of the pillars was finished.

[23] Then he made the molten sea; it was round, ten cubits from brim to brim, and five cubits high, and a line of thirty cubits measured its circum-ference. [24] Under its brim were gourds, for thirty[y] cubits, compassing the sea round about; the gourds were in two rows, cast with it when it was cast. [25] It stood upon twelve oxen, three facing north, three facing west, three facing south, and three facing east; the sea was set upon them, and all their hinder parts were inward. [26] Its thickness was a handbreadth; and its brim was made like the brim of a cup, like the flower of a lily; it held two thousand baths.

[27] He also made the ten stands of bronze; each stand was four cubits long, four cubits wide, and three cubits high. [28] This was the construction of the stands: they had panels, and the panels were set in the frames [29] and on the panels that were set in the frames were lions, oxen, and cherubim. Upon the frames, both above and below the lions and oxen, there were wreaths of beveled work. [30] Moreover each stand had four bronze wheels and axles of bronze; and at the four corners were supports for a laver. The supports were cast, with wreaths at the side of each. [31] Its opening was within a crown which projected upward one cubit; its opening was round, as a pedestal is made, a cubit and a half deep. At its opening there were carvings; and its panels were square, not round. [32]And the four wheels were underneath the panels; the axles of the wheels were of one piece with the stands; and the height of a wheel was a cubit and a half. [33] The wheels were made like a chariot wheel; their axles, their rims, their spokes, and their hubs, were all cast. [34] There were four supports at the four corners of each stand; the supports were of one piece with the stands. [35]And on the top of the stand there was a round band half a cubit high; and on the top of the stand its stays and its panels were of one piece with it. [36]And on the surfaces of its stays and on its panels, he carved cherubim, lions, and palm trees, according to the space of each, with wreaths round about. [37]After this manner he made the ten stands; all of them were cast alike, of the same measure and the same form.

[38] And he made ten lavers of bronze; each laver held forty baths, each laver measured four cubits, and there was a laver for each of the ten

---

[t] With 7.12. Heb *from the outside*

[u] Tg Syr Compare Gk and Jer 52.21: Heb *and a line of twelve cubits measured the circumference of the second pillar*   [v] Gk: Heb lacks *he made two*   [w] Gk: Heb *seven*

[x] With 2 Mss Compare Gk: Heb *pillars*   [y] Heb *ten*

7.15-21: 2 Chron 3.15-17.   7.23-26: 2 Chron 4.2-5.   7.38-51: 2 Chron 4.6, 5.1.

stands. 39And he set the stands, five on the south side of the house, and five on the north side of the house; and he set the sea on the southeast corner of the house.

40 Hiram also made the pots, the shovels, and the basins. So Hiram finished all the work that he did for King Solomon on the house of the LORD: 41 the two pillars, the two bowls of the capitals that were on the tops of the pillars, and the two networks to cover the two bowls of the capitals that were on the tops of the pillars; 42 and the four hundred pomegranates for the two networks, two rows of pomegranates for each network, to cover the two bowls of the capitals that were upon the pillars; 43 the ten stands, and the ten lavers upon the stands; 44 and the one sea, and the twelve oxen underneath the sea.

45 Now the pots, the shovels, and the basins, all these vessels in the house of the LORD, which Hiram made for King Solomon, were of burnished bronze. 46 In the plain of the Jordan the king cast them, in the clay ground between Suc′coth and Zar′e·than. 47And Solomon left all the vessels unweighed, because there were so many of them; the weight of the bronze was not found out.

48 So Solomon made all the vessels that were in the house of the LORD: the golden altar, the golden table for the bread of the Presence, 49 the lampstands of pure gold, five on the south side and five on the north, before the inner sanctuary; the flowers, the lamps, and the tongs, of gold; 50 the cups, snuffers, basins, dishes for incense, and firepans, of pure gold; and the sockets of gold, for the doors of the innermost part of the house, the most holy place, and for the doors of the nave of the temple.

51 Thus all the work that King Solomon did on the house of the LORD was finished. And Solomon brought in the things which David his father had dedicated, the silver, the gold, and the vessels, and stored them in the treasuries of the house of the LORD.

8 Then Solomon assembled the elders of Israel and all the heads of the tribes, the leaders of the fathers' houses of the people of Israel, before King Solomon in Jerusalem, to bring up the ark of the covenant of the LORD out of the city of David, which is Zion. 2And all the men of Israel assembled to King Solomon at the feast in the

month Eth′a·nim, which is the seventh month. 3And all the elders of Israel came, and the priests took up the ark. 4And they brought up the ark of the LORD, the tent of meeting, and all the holy vessels that were in the tent; the priests and the Levites brought them up. 5And King Solomon and all the congregation of Israel, who had assembled before him, were with him before the ark, sacrificing so many sheep and oxen that they could not be counted or numbered. 6 Then the priests brought the ark of the covenant of the LORD to its place, in the inner sanctuary of the house, in the most holy place, underneath the wings of the cherubim. 7 For the cherubim spread out their wings over the place of the ark, so that the cherubim made a covering above the ark and its poles. 8And the poles were so long that the ends of the poles were seen from the holy place before the inner sanctuary; but they could not be seen from outside; and they are there to this day. 9 There was nothing in the ark except the two tables of stone which Moses put there at Hō′reb, where the LORD made a covenant with the people of Israel, when they came out of the land of Egypt. 10And when the priests came out of the holy place, a cloud filled the house of the LORD, 11 so that the priests could not stand to minister because of the cloud; for the glory of the LORD filled the house of the LORD.

12 Then Solomon said,
"The LORD has set the sun in the heavens,
but² has said that he would dwell in thick darkness.
13 I have built thee an exalted house, a place for thee to dwell in for ever."

14 Then the king faced about, and blessed all the assembly of Israel, while all the assembly of Israel stood. 15And he said, "Blessed be the LORD, the God of Israel, who with his hand has fulfilled what he promised with his mouth to David my father, saying, 16 'Since the day that I brought my people Israel out of Egypt, I chose no city in all the tribes of Israel in which to build a house, that my name might be there; but I chose David to be over my people Israel.' 17 Now it was in the heart of David my father to build a house for the name of the LORD, the God of Israel. 18 But the LORD said to David my father, 'Whereas it was in your heart to build a house for

<hr />

z Gk: Heb lacks *has set the sun in the heavens, but*

8.1-6: Rev 11.19.   **8.10-11:** 2 Chron 5.13-14; Rev 15.8.   **8.12-50:** 2 Chron 6.1-39.

my name, you did well that it was in your heart; [19] nevertheless you shall not build the house, but your son who shall be born to you shall build the house for my name.' [20] Now the LORD has fulfilled his promise which he made; for I have risen in the place of David my father, and sit on the throne of Israel, as the LORD promised, and I have built the house for the name of the LORD, the God of Israel. [21]And there I have provided a place for the ark, in which is the covenant of the LORD which he made with our fathers, when he brought them out of the land of Egypt."

[22] Then Solomon stood before the altar of the LORD in the presence of all the assembly of Israel, and spread forth his hands toward heaven; [23] and said, "O LORD, God of Israel, there is no God like thee, in heaven above or on earth beneath, keeping covenant and showing steadfast love to thy servants who walk before thee with all their heart; [24] who hast kept with thy servant David my father what thou didst declare to him; yea, thou didst speak with thy mouth, and with thy hand hast fulfilled it this day. [25] Now therefore, O LORD, God of Israel, keep with thy servant David my father what thou hast promised him, saying, 'There shall never fail you a man before me to sit upon the throne of Israel, if only your sons take heed to their way, to walk before me as you have walked before me.' [26] Now therefore, O God of Israel, let thy word be confirmed, which thou hast spoken to thy servant David my father.

[27] "But will God indeed dwell on the earth? Behold, heaven and the highest heaven cannot contain thee; how much less this house which I have built! [28] Yet have regard to the prayer of thy servant and to his supplication, O LORD my God, hearkening to the cry and to the prayer which thy servant prays before thee this day; [29] that thy eyes may be open night and day toward this house, the place of which thou hast said, 'My name shall be there,' that thou mayest hearken to the prayer which thy servant offers toward this place. [30]And hearken thou to the supplication of thy servant and of thy people Israel, when they pray toward this place; yea, hear thou in heaven thy dwelling place; and when thou hearest, forgive.

[31] "If a man sins against his neighbor and is made to take an oath, and comes and swears his oath before

thine altar in this house, [32] then hear thou in heaven, and act, and judge thy servants, condemning the guilty by bringing his conduct upon his own head, and vindicating the righteous by rewarding him according to his righteousness.

[33] "When thy people Israel are defeated before the enemy because they have sinned against thee, if they turn again to thee, and acknowledge thy name, and pray and make supplication to thee in this house; [34] then hear thou in heaven, and forgive the sin of thy people Israel, and bring them again to the land which thou gavest to their fathers.

[35] "When heaven is shut up and there is no rain because they have sinned against thee, if they pray toward this place, and acknowledge thy name, and turn from their sin, when thou dost afflict them, [36] then hear thou in heaven, and forgive the sin of thy servants, thy people Israel, when thou dost teach them the good way in which they should walk; and grant rain upon thy land, which thou hast given to thy people as an inheritance.

[37] "If there is famine in the land, if there is pestilence or blight or mildew or locust or caterpillar; if their enemy besieges them in any*a* of their cities; whatever plague, whatever sickness there is; [38] whatever prayer, whatever supplication is made by any man or by all thy people Israel, each knowing the affliction of his own heart and stretching out his hands toward this house; [39] then hear thou in heaven thy dwelling place, and forgive, and act, and render to each whose heart thou knowest, according to all his ways (for thou, thou only, knowest the hearts of all the children of men); [40] that they may fear thee all the days that they live in the land which thou gavest to our fathers.

[41] "Likewise when a foreigner, who is not of thy people Israel, comes from a far country for thy name's sake [42] (for they shall hear of thy great name, and thy mighty hand, and of thy outstretched arm), when he comes and prays toward this house, [43] hear thou in heaven thy dwelling place, and do according to all for which the foreigner calls to thee; in order that all the peoples of the earth may know thy name and fear thee, as do thy people Israel, and that they may know that this house which I have built is called by thy name.

[44] "If thy people go out to battle

a Gk Syr: Heb *the land*

against their enemy, by whatever way thou shalt send them, and they pray to the LORD toward the city which thou hast chosen and the house which I have built for thy name, 45 then hear thou in heaven their prayer and their supplication, and maintain their cause.

46 "If they sin against thee—for there is no man who does not sin—and thou art angry with them, and dost give them to an enemy, so that they are carried away captive to the land of the enemy, far off or near; 47 yet if they lay it to heart in the land to which they have been carried captive, and repent, and make supplication to thee in the land of their captors, saying, 'We have sinned, and have acted perversely and wickedly'; 48 if they repent with all their mind and with all their heart in the land of their enemies, who carried them captive, and pray to thee toward their land, which thou gavest to their fathers, the city which thou hast chosen, and the house which I have built for thy name; 49 then hear thou in heaven thy dwelling place their prayer and their supplication, and maintain their cause 50 and forgive thy people who have sinned against thee, and all their transgressions which they have committed against thee; and grant them compassion in the sight of those who carried them captive, that they may have compassion on them 51 (for they are thy people, and thy heritage, which thou didst bring out of Egypt, from the midst of the iron furnace). 52 Let thy eyes be open to the supplication of thy servant, and to the supplication of thy people Israel, giving ear to them whenever they call to thee. 53 For thou didst separate them from among all the peoples of the earth, to be thy heritage, as thou didst declare through Moses, thy servant, when thou didst bring our fathers out of Egypt, O Lord GOD."

54 Now as Solomon finished offering all this prayer and supplication to the LORD, he arose from before the altar of the LORD, where he had knelt with hands outstretched toward heaven; 55 and he stood, and blessed all the assembly of Israel with a loud voice, saying, 56 "Blessed be the LORD who has given rest to his people Israel, according to all that he promised; not one word has failed of all his good promise, which he uttered by Moses his servant. 57 The LORD our God be with us, as he was with our fathers;

may he not leave us or forsake us; 58 that he may incline our hearts to him, to walk in all his ways, and to keep his commandments, his statutes, and his ordinances, which he commanded our fathers. 59 Let these words of mine, wherewith I have made supplication before the LORD, be near to the LORD our God day and night, and may he maintain the cause of his servant, and the cause of his people Israel, as each day requires; 60 that all the peoples of the earth may know that the LORD is God; there is no other. 61 Let your heart therefore be wholly true to the LORD our God, walking in his statutes and keeping his commandments, as at this day."

62 Then the king, and all Israel with him, offered sacrifice before the LORD. 63 Solomon offered as peace offerings to the LORD twenty-two thousand oxen and a hundred and twenty thousand sheep. So the king and all the people of Israel dedicated the house of the LORD. 64 The same day the king consecrated the middle of the court that was before the house of the LORD; for there he offered the burnt offering and the cereal offering and the fat pieces of the peace offerings, because the bronze altar that was before the LORD was too small to receive the burnt offering and the cereal offering and the fat pieces of the peace offerings.

65 So Solomon held the feast at that time, and all Israel with him, a great assembly, from the entrance of Hā′math to the Brook of Egypt, before the LORD our God, seven days.[b] 66 On the eighth day he sent the people away; and they blessed the king, and went to their homes joyful and glad of heart for all the goodness that the LORD had shown to David his servant and to Israel his people.

9 When Solomon had finished building the house of the LORD and the king's house and all that Solomon desired to build, 2 the LORD appeared to Solomon a second time, as he had appeared to him at Gib′ē·ŏn. 3 And the LORD said to him, "I have heard your prayer and your supplication, which you have made before me; I have consecrated this house which you have built, and put my name there for ever; my eyes and my heart will be there for all time. 4 And as for you, if you will walk before me, as David your father walked, with integrity of heart and uprightness, doing according to all that I have commanded you, and keeping my statutes and my ordinances, 5 then I will establish your royal throne over Israel for ever, as I promised David your father, saying, 'There shall not fail you a man upon the throne of Israel.' 6 But if you turn aside from following me, you or your children, and do not keep my commandments and my statutes which I have set before you, but go and serve other gods and worship them, 7 then I will cut off Israel from the land which I have given them; and the house which I have consecrated for my name I will cast out of my sight; and Israel will become a proverb and a byword among all peoples. 8 And this house will become a heap of ruins;[c] everyone passing by it will be astonished, and will hiss; and they will say, 'Why has the LORD done thus to this land and to this house?' 9 Then they will say, 'Because they forsook the LORD their God who brought their fathers out of the land of Egypt, and laid hold on other gods, and worshiped them and served them; therefore the LORD has brought all this evil upon them.'"

10 At the end of twenty years, in which Solomon had built the two houses, the house of the LORD and the king's house, 11 and Hiram king of Tyre had supplied Solomon with cedar and cypress timber and gold, as much as he desired, King Solomon gave to Hiram twenty cities in the land of Galilee. 12 But when Hiram came from Tyre to see the cities which Solomon had given him, they did not please him. 13 Therefore he said, "What kind of cities are these which you have given me, my brother?" So they are called the land of Cā'būl to this day. 14 Hiram had sent to the king one hundred and twenty talents of gold.

15 And this is the account of the forced labor which King Solomon levied to build the house of the LORD and his own house and the Mil'lō and the wall of Jerusalem and Hā'zôr and Mĕ·gid'dō and Gē'zĕr 16 (Pharaoh king of Egypt had gone up and captured Gē'zĕr and burnt it with fire, and had slain the Canaanites who dwelt in the city, and had given it as dowry to his daughter, Solomon's wife; 17 so Solomon rebuilt Gē'zĕr) and Lower Beth-hō'ron 18 and Bā'ă·lath and Tā'mär in the wilderness, in the land of Judah,[d] 19 and all the store-

cities that Solomon had, and the cities for his chariots, and the cities for his horsemen, and whatever Solomon desired to build in Jerusalem, in Lebanon, and in all the land of his dominion. 20 All the people who were left of the Am'ô·rites, the Hit'tites, the Per'izzites, the Hi'vites, and the Jeb'ū·sites, who were not of the people of Israel— 21 their descendants who were left after them in the land, whom the people of Israel were unable to destroy utterly—these Solomon made a forced levy of slaves, and so they are to this day. 22 But of the people of Israel Solomon made no slaves; they were the soldiers, they were his officials, his commanders, his captains, his chariot commanders and his horsemen.

23 These were the chief officers who were over Solomon's work: five hundred and fifty, who had charge of the people who carried on the work.

24 But Pharaoh's daughter went up from the city of David to her own house which Solomon had built for her; then he built the Mil'lō.

25 Three times a year Solomon used to offer up burnt offerings and peace offerings upon the altar which he built to the LORD, burning incense[e] before the LORD. So he finished the house.

26 King Solomon built a fleet of ships at Ē'zi·on-gē'bĕr, which is near Ē'loth on the shore of the Red Sea, in the land of Ē'dôm. 27 And Hiram sent with the fleet his servants, seamen who were familiar with the sea, together with the servants of Solomon; 28 and they went to Ō'phĭr, and brought from there gold, to the amount of four hundred and twenty talents; and they brought it to King Solomon.

10 Now when the queen of Sheba heard of the fame of Solomon concerning the name of the LORD, she came to test him with hard questions. 2 She came to Jerusalem with a very great retinue, with camels bearing spices, and very much gold, and precious stones; and when she came to Solomon, she told him all that was on her mind. 3 And Solomon answered all her questions; there was nothing hidden from the king which he could not explain to her. 4 And when the queen of Sheba had seen all the wisdom of Solomon, the house that he had built, 5 the food of his table, the seating of his officials, and the attendance of his servants, their clothing, his cup-

---

c Syr Old Latin: Heb *high*   d Heb lacks *of Judah*

e Gk: Heb *burning incense with it which*

9.10-28: 2 Chron 8.8-18.   **10.1-29:** 2 Chron 9.1-28.

bearers, and his burnt offerings which he offered at the house of the LORD, there was no more spirit in her.

6 And she said to the king, "The report was true which I heard in my own land of your affairs and of your wisdom, 7 but I did not believe the reports until I came and my own eyes had seen it; and, behold, the half was not told me; your wisdom and prosperity surpass the report which I heard. 8 Happy are your wives!ᶠ Happy are these your servants, who continually stand before you and hear your wisdom! 9 Blessed be the LORD your God, who has delighted in you and set you on the throne of Israel! Because the LORD loved Israel for ever, he has made you king, that you may execute justice and righteousness." 10 Then she gave the king a hundred and twenty talents of gold, and a very great quantity of spices, and precious stones; never again came such an abundance of spices as these which the queen of Sheba gave to King Solomon.

11 Moreover the fleet of Hiram, which brought gold from Óʹphir, brought from Ophir a very great amount of almug wood and precious stones. 12 And the king made of the almug wood supports for the house of the LORD, and for the king's house, lyres also and harps for the singers; no such almug wood has come or been seen, to this day.

13 And King Solomon gave to the queen of Sheba all that she desired, whatever she asked besides what was given her by the bounty of King Solomon. So she turned and went back to her own land, with her servants.

14 Now the weight of gold that came to Solomon in one year was six hundred and sixty-six talents of gold, 15 besides that which came from the traders and from the traffic of the merchants, and from all the kings of Arabia and from the governors of the land. 16 King Solomon made two hundred large shields of beaten gold; six hundred shekels of gold went into each shield. 17 And he made three hundred shields of beaten gold; three minas of gold went into each shield; and the king put them in the House of the Forest of Lebanon. 18 The king also made a great ivory throne, and overlaid it with the finest gold. 19 The throne had six steps, and at the back of the throne was a calf's head, and on each side of the seat were arm rests and two lions standing beside the arm rests, 20 while twelve lions stood there, one on each end of a step on the six steps. The like of it was never made in any kingdom. 21 All King Solomon's drinking vessels were of gold, and all vessels of the House of the Forest of Lebanon were of pure gold; none were of silver, it was not considered as anything in the days of Solomon. 22 For the king had a fleet of ships of Tärʹshish at sea with the fleet of Hiram. Once every three years the fleet of ships of Tarshish used to come bringing gold, silver, ivory, apes, and peacocks.ᵍ

23 Thus King Solomon excelled all the kings of the earth in riches and in wisdom. 24 And the whole earth sought the presence of Solomon to hear his wisdom, which God had put into his mind. 25 Every one of them brought his present, articles of silver and gold, garments, myrrh, spices, horses, and mules, so much year by year.

26 And Solomon gathered together chariots and horsemen; he had fourteen hundred chariots and twelve thousand horsemen, whom he stationed in the chariot cities and with the king in Jerusalem. 27 And the king made silver as common in Jerusalem as stone, and he made cedar as plentiful as the sycamore of the Sheʹphēʹlàh. 28 And Solomon's import of horses was from Egypt and Küʹe, and the king's traders received them from Kue at a price. 29 A chariot could be imported from Egypt for six hundred shekels of silver, and a horse for a hundred and fifty; and so through the king's traders they were exported to all the kings of the Hitʹtites and the kings of Syria.

11 Now King Solomon loved many foreign women: the daughter of Pharaoh, and Móʹab·ite, Amʹmó·nite, Éʹdóm·ite, Si·dóʹni·àn, and Hitʹtite women, 2 from the nations concerning which the LORD had said to the people of Israel, "You shall not enter into marriage with them, neither shall they with you, for surely they will turn away your heart after their gods"; Solomon clung to these in love. 3 He had seven hundred wives, princesses, and three hundred concubines; and his wives turned away his heart. 4 For when Solomon was old his wives turned away his heart after other gods; and his heart was not wholly true to the LORD his God, as was the heart of David his father. 5 For Solomon went after Ashʹtō·reth the goddess of the Si·dóʹni·àns, and after Milʹcom the abomination of the Amʹmó·nites. 6 So Solomon did what was evil in the

ᶠ Gk Syr: Heb *men*   ᵍ Or *baboons*

sight of the LORD, and did not wholly follow the LORD, as David his father had done. 7 Then Solomon built a high place for Chē′mosh the abomination of Mō′ab, and for Mō′lech the abomination of the Am′mŏ·nĭtes, on the mountain east of Jerusalem. 8And so he did for all his foreign wives, who burned incense and sacrificed to their gods.

9 And the LORD was angry with Solomon, because his heart had turned away from the LORD, the God of Israel, who had appeared to him twice, 10 and had commanded him concerning this thing, that he should not go after other gods; but he did not keep what the LORD commanded. 11 Therefore the LORD said to Solomon, "Since this has been your mind and you have not kept my covenant and my statutes which I have commanded you, I will surely tear the kingdom from you and will give it to your servant. 12 Yet for the sake of David your father I will not do it in your days, but I will tear it out of the hand of your son. 13 However I will not tear away all the kingdom; but I will give one tribe to your son, for the sake of David my servant and for the sake of Jerusalem which I have chosen."

14 And the LORD raised up an adversary against Solomon, Hā′dad the E′dŏm·ĭte; he was of the royal house in E′dŏm. 15 For when David was in E′dŏm, and Jō′ab the commander of the army went up to bury the slain, he slew every male in Edom 16 (for Jō′ab and all Israel remained there six months, until he had cut off every male in E′dŏm); 17 but Hā′dad fled to Egypt, together with certain E′dŏm-ites of his father's servants, Hadad being yet a little child. 18 They set out from Mid′i·ăn and came to Pâr′an, and took men with them from Paran and came to Egypt, to Pharaoh king of Egypt, who gave him a house, and assigned him an allowance of food, and gave him land. 19And Hā′dad found great favor in the sight of Pharaoh, so that he gave him in marriage the sister of his own wife, the sister of Täh′pĕ·nĕš the queen. 20And the sister of Täh′pĕ·nĕš bore him Gĕ·nū′băth his son, whom Tahpenes weaned in Pharaoh's house; and Genubath was in Pharaoh's house among the sons of Pharaoh. 21 But when Hā′dad heard in Egypt that David slept with his fathers and that Jō′ab the commander of the army was dead, Hadad said to Pharaoh, "Let me depart, that I may

go to my own country." 22 But Pharaoh said to him, "What have you lacked with me that you are now seeking to go to your own country?" And he said to him, "Only let me go."

23 God also raised up as an adversary to him, Rē′zon the son of E·lī′ȧ·dȧ, who had fled from his master Hā′dad-ē′zĕr king of Zō′bȧh. 24And he gathered men about him and became leader of a marauding band, after the slaughter by David; and they went to Damascus, and dwelt there, and made him king in Damascus. 25 He was an adversary of Israel all the days of Solomon, doing mischief as Hā′dad did; and he abhorred Israel, and reigned over Syria.

26 Jĕr·ŏ·bō′ăm the son of Nē′bat, an E′phrȧ·ĭm·ĭte of Zer′ē·dȧh, a servant of Solomon, whose mother's name was Zĕ·rū′ȧh, a widow, also lifted up his hand against the king. 27And this was the reason why he lifted up his hand against the king. Solomon built the Mil′lō, and closed up the breach of the city of David his father. 28 The man Jĕr·ŏ·bō′ăm was very able, and when Solomon saw that the young man was industrious he gave him charge over all the forced labor of the house of Joseph. 29And at that time, when Jĕr·ŏ·bō′ăm went out of Jerusalem, the prophet A·hī′jȧh the Shī′lō-nĭte found him on the road. Now Ahijah had clad himself with a new garment; and the two of them were alone in the open country. 30 Then A·hī′jȧh laid hold of the new garment that was on him, and tore it into twelve pieces. 31And he said to Jĕr·ŏ-bō′ăm, "Take for yourself ten pieces; for thus says the LORD, the God of Israel, 'Behold, I am about to tear the kingdom from the hand of Solomon, and will give you ten tribes 32 (but he shall have one tribe, for the sake of my servant David and for the sake of Jerusalem, the city which I have chosen out of all the tribes of Israel), 33 because he has[h] forsaken me, and worshiped Ash′tō·reth the goddess of the Si·dō′ni·ăns, Chē′mosh the god of Mō′ab, and Mil′com the god of the Am′mŏ·nĭtes, and has[h] not walked in my ways, doing what is right in my sight and keeping my statutes and my ordinances, as David his father did. 34 Nevertheless I will not take the whole kingdom out of his hand; but I will make him ruler all the days of his life, for the sake of David my servant whom I chose, who kept my commandments and my statutes; 35 but

h Gk Syr Vg: Heb *they have*

will take the kingdom out of his son's hand, and will give it to you, ten tribes. ³⁶ Yet to his son I will give one tribe, that David my servant may always have a lamp before me in Jerusalem, the city where I have chosen to put my name. ³⁷And I will take you, and you shall reign over all that your soul desires, and you shall be king over Israel. ³⁸And if you will hearken to all that I command you, and will walk in my ways, and do what is right in my eyes by keeping my statutes and my commandments, as David my servant did, I will be with you, and will build you a sure house, as I built for David, and I will give Israel to you. ³⁹And I will for this afflict the descendants of David, but not for ever.' " ⁴⁰ Solomon sought therefore to kill Jer·o·bo′am; but Jeroboam arose, and fled into Egypt, to Shi′shak king of Egypt, and was in Egypt until the death of Solomon.

41 Now the rest of the acts of Solomon, and all that he did, and his wisdom, are they not written in the book of the acts of Solomon? ⁴²And the time that Solomon reigned in Jerusalem over all Israel was forty years. ⁴³And Solomon slept with his fathers, and was buried in the city of David his father; and Rē·hō·bō′am his son reigned in his stead.

12 Rē·hō·bō′am went to She′chem, for all Israel had come to Shechem to make him king. ²And when Jer·o·bo′am the son of Nē′bat heard of it (for he was still in Egypt, whither he had fled from King Solomon), then Jeroboam returned from[f] Egypt. ³ And they sent and called him; and Jer·o·bo′am and all the assembly of Israel came and said to Rē·hō·bō′am, ⁴ "Your father made our yoke heavy. Now therefore lighten the hard service of your father and his heavy yoke upon us, and we will serve you." ⁵ He said to them, "Depart for three days, then come again to me." So the people went away.

6 Then King Rē·hō·bō′am took counsel with the old men, who had stood before Solomon his father while he was yet alive, saying, "How do you advise me to answer this people?" ⁷And they said to him, "If you will be a servant to this people today and serve them, and speak good words to them when you answer them, then they will be your servants for ever." ⁸ But he forsook the counsel which the old men gave him, and took counsel with the young men who had grown up with him and stood before him. ⁹And he said to them, "What do you advise that we answer this people who have said to me, 'Lighten the yoke that your father put upon us'?" ¹⁰And the young men who had grown up with him said to him, "Thus shall you speak to this people who said to you, 'Your father made our yoke heavy, but do you lighten it for us'; thus shall you say to them, 'My little finger is thicker than my father's loins. ¹¹And now, whereas my father laid upon you a heavy yoke, I will add to your yoke. My father chastised you with whips, but I will chastise you with scorpions.' "

12 So Jer·o·bo′am and all the people came to Rē·hō·bō′am the third day, as the king said, "Come to me again the third day." ¹³And the king answered the people harshly, and forsaking the counsel which the old men had given him, ¹⁴ he spoke to them according to the counsel of the young men, saying, "My father made your yoke heavy, but I will add to your yoke; my father chastised you with whips, but I will chastise you with scorpions." ¹⁵ So the king did not hearken to the people; for it was a turn of affairs brought about by the LORD that he might fulfil his word, which the LORD spoke by A·hi′jah the Shi′lo·nite to Jer·o·bo′am the son of Nē′bat.

16 And when all Israel saw that the king did not hearken to them, the people answered the king,

"What portion have we in David?
   We have no inheritance in the son
      of Jesse.
To your tents, O Israel!
   Look now to your own house,
      David."

So Israel departed to their tents. ¹⁷ But Rē·hō·bō′am reigned over the people of Israel who dwelt in the cities of Judah. ¹⁸ Then King Rē·hō·bō′am sent A·dō′ram, who was taskmaster over the forced labor, and all Israel stoned him to death with stones. And King Rehoboam made haste to mount his chariot, to flee to Jerusalem. ¹⁹ So Israel has been in rebellion against the house of David to this day. ²⁰And when all Israel heard that Jer·o·bo′am had returned, they sent and called him to the assembly and made him king over all Israel. There was none that followed the house of David, but the tribe of Judah only.

21 When Rē·hō·bō′am came to Je-

---

[f] Gk Vg Compare 2 Chron 10.2: Heb *dwelt in*
11.42-43: 2 Chron 9.30-31.   **12.1-19:** 2 Chron 10.1-19.

rusalem, he assembled all the house of Judah, and the tribe of Benjamin, a hundred and eighty thousand chosen warriors, to fight against the house of Israel, to restore the kingdom to Rehoboam the son of Solomon. 22 But the word of God came to She·maiʹah the man of God: 23 "Say to Rē·hoʹbō·ʹam the son of Solomon, king of Judah, and to all the house of Judah and Benjamin, and to the rest of the people, 24 'Thus says the LORD, You shall not go up or fight against your kinsmen the people of Israel. Return every man to his home, for this thing is from me.'" So they hearkened to the word of the LORD, and went home again, according to the word of the LORD.

25 Then Jer·o·bōʹam built Shēʹchem in the hill country of Eʹphra·im, and dwelt there; and he went out from there and built Pĕ·nūʹel. 26And Jer·o·bōʹam said in his heart, "Now the kingdom will turn back to the house of David; 27 if this people go up to offer sacrifices in the house of the LORD at Jerusalem, then the heart of this people will turn again to their lord, to Rē·hoʹbō·ʹam king of Judah, and they will kill me and return to Rehoboam king of Judah." 28 So the king took counsel, and made two calves of gold. And he said to the people, "You have gone up to Jerusalem long enough. Behold your gods, O Israel, who brought you up out of the land of Egypt." 29And he set one in Bethʹel, and the other he put in Dan. 30And this thing became a sin, for the people went to the one at Bethʹel and to the other as far as Dan.*j* 31 He also made houses on high places, and appointed priests from among all the people, who were not of the Levites. 32And Jer·o·bōʹam appointed a feast on the fifteenth day of the eighth month like the feast that was in Judah, and he offered sacrifices upon the altar; so he did in Bethʹel, sacrificing to the calves that he had made. And he placed in Bethel the priests of the high places that he had made. 33 He went up to the altar which he had made in Bethʹel on the fifteenth day in the eighth month, in the month which he had devised of his own heart; and he ordained a feast for the people of Israel, and went up to the altar to burn incense.

13 And behold, a man of God came out of Judah by the word of the LORD to Bethʹel. Jer·o·bōʹam was standing by the altar to burn incense.

2And the man cried against the altar by the word of the LORD, and said, "O altar, altar, thus says the LORD: 'Behold, a son shall be born to the house of David, Jō·siʹah by name; and he shall sacrifice upon you the priests of the high places who burn incense upon you, and men's bones shall be burned upon you.'" 3And he gave a sign the same day, saying, "This is the sign that the LORD has spoken: 'Behold, the altar shall be torn down, and the ashes that are upon it shall be poured out.'" 4And when the king heard the saying of the man of God, which he cried against the altar at Bethʹel, Jer·o·bōʹam stretched out his hand from the altar, saying, "Lay hold of him." And his hand, which he stretched out against him, dried up, so that he could not draw it back to himself. 5 The altar also was torn down, and the ashes poured out from the altar, according to the sign which the man of God had given by the word of the LORD. 6And the king said to the man of God, "Entreat now the favor of the LORD your God, and pray for me, that my hand may be restored to me." And the man of God entreated the LORD; and the king's hand was restored to him, and became as it was before. 7And the king said to the man of God, "Come home with me, and refresh yourself, and I will give you a reward." 8And the man of God said to the king, "If you give me half your house, I will not go in with you. And I will not eat bread or drink water in this place; 9 for so was it commanded me by the word of the LORD, saying, 'You shall neither eat bread, nor drink water, nor return by the way that you came.'" 10 So he went another way, and did not return by the way that he came to Bethʹel.

11 Now there dwelt an old prophet in Bethʹel. And his sons*k* came and told him all that the man of God had done that day in Bethel; the words also which he had spoken to the king, they told to their father. 12And their father said to them, "Which way did he go?" And his sons showed him the way which the man of God who came from Judah had gone. 13And he said to his sons, "Saddle the ass for me." So they saddled the ass for him and he mounted it. 14And he went after the man of God, and found him sitting under an oak; and he said to him, "Are you the man of God who came from Judah?" And he said, "I am."

j Gk: Heb *went to the one as far as Dan*   *k* Gk Syr Vg: Heb *son*

12.22-24: 2 Chron 11.1-4.

15 Then he said to him, "Come home with me and eat bread." 16And he said, "I may not return with you, or go in with you; neither will I eat bread nor drink water with you in this place; 17 for it was said to me by the word of the LORD, 'You shall neither eat bread nor drink water there, nor return by the way that you came.'" 18And he said to him, "I also am a prophet as you are, and an angel spoke to me by the word of the LORD, saying, 'Bring him back with you into your house that he may eat bread and drink water.'" But he lied to him. 19 So he went back with him, and ate bread in his house, and drank water.

20 And as they sat at the table, the word of the LORD came to the prophet who had brought him back; 21 and he cried to the man of God who came from Judah, "Thus says the LORD, 'Because you have disobeyed the word of the LORD, and have not kept the commandment which the LORD your God commanded you, 22 but have come back, and have eaten bread and drunk water in the place of which he said to you, "Eat no bread, and drink no water"; your body shall not come to the tomb of your fathers.'" 23And after he had eaten bread and drunk, he saddled the ass for the prophet whom he had brought back. 24And as he went away a lion met him on the road and killed him. And his body was thrown in the road, and the ass stood beside it; the lion also stood beside the body. 25And behold, men passed by, and saw the body thrown in the road, and the lion standing by the body. And they came and told it in the city where the old prophet dwelt.

26 And when the prophet who had brought him back from the way heard of it, he said, "It is the man of God, who disobeyed the word of the LORD; therefore the LORD has given him to the lion, which has torn him and slain him, according to the word which the LORD spoke to him." 27And he said to his sons, "Saddle the ass for me." And they saddled it. 28And he went and found his body thrown in the road, and the ass and the lion standing beside the body. The lion had not eaten the body or torn the ass. 29And the prophet took up the body of the man of God and laid it upon the ass, and brought it back to the city,[j] to mourn and to bury him. 30And he laid the body in his own grave; and they mourned over him, saying, "Alas, my brother!" 31And after he had buried

him, he said to his sons, "When I die, bury me in the grave in which the man of God is buried; lay my bones beside his bones. 32 For the saying which he cried by the word of the LORD against the altar in Beth'el, and against all the houses of the high places which are in the cities of Sa-mâr'i-à, shall surely come to pass."

33 After this thing Jer-ò-bò'àm did not turn from his evil way, but made priests for the high places again from among all the people; any who would, he consecrated to be priests of the high places. 34And this thing became sin to the house of Jer-ò-bò'àm, so as to cut it off and to destroy it from the face of the earth.

14 At that time À-bì'jàh the son of Jer-ò-bò'àm fell sick. 2And Jer-ò-bò'àm said to his wife, "Arise, and disguise yourself, that it be not known that you are the wife of Jeroboam, and go to Shi'lôh; behold, À-hì'jàh the prophet is there, who said of me that I should be king over this people. 3 Take with you ten loaves, some cakes, and a jar of honey, and go to him; he will tell you what shall happen to the child."

4 Jer-ò-bò'àm's wife did so; she arose, and went to Shi'lôh, and came to the house of À-hì'jàh. Now Ahijah could not see, for his eyes were dim because of his age. 5And the LORD said to À-hì'jàh, "Behold, the wife of Jer-ò-bò'àm is coming to inquire of you concerning her son; for he is sick. Thus and thus shall you say to her."

When she came, she pretended to be another woman. 6 But when À-hì'jàh heard the sound of her feet, as she came in at the door, he said, "Come in, wife of Jer-ò-bò'àm; why do you pretend to be another? For I am charged with heavy tidings for you. 7 Go, tell Jer-ò-bò'àm, 'Thus says the LORD, the God of Israel: "Because I exalted you from among the people, and made you leader over my people Israel, 8 and tore the kingdom away from the house of David and gave it to you; and yet you have not been like my servant David, who kept my commandments, and followed me with all his heart, doing only that which was right in my eyes, 9 but you have done evil above all that were before you and have gone and made for yourself other gods, and molten images, provoking me to anger, and have cast me behind your back; 10 therefore behold, I will bring evil upon the house of Jer-ò-

[j] Gk: Heb *he came to the city of the old prophet*

bō′am, and will cut off from Jeroboam every male, both bond and free in Israel, and will utterly consume the house of Jeroboam, as a man burns up dung until it is all gone. ¹¹Any one belonging to Jer·ō·bō′am who dies in the city the dogs shall eat; and any one who dies in the open country the birds of the air shall eat; for the LORD has spoken it." ' ¹²Arise therefore, go to your house. When your feet enter the city, the child shall die. ¹³And all Israel shall mourn for him, and bury him; for he only of Jer·ō·bō′am shall come to the grave, because in him there is found something pleasing to the LORD, the God of Israel, in the house of Jeroboam. ¹⁴ Moreover the LORD will raise up for himself a king over Israel, who shall cut off the house of Jer·ō·bō′am today. And henceforth*m* ¹⁵ the LORD will smite Israel, as a reed is shaken in the water, and root up Israel out of this good land which he gave to their fathers, and scatter them beyond the Eū·phrā′tēš, because they have made their Å·shē′rim, provoking the LORD to anger. ¹⁶And he will give Israel up because of the sins of Jer·ō·bō′am, which he sinned and which he made Israel to sin."

¹⁷ Then Jer·ō·bō′am's wife arose, and departed, and came to Tīr′zäh. And as she came to the threshold of the house, the child died. ¹⁸And all Israel buried him and mourned for him, according to the word of the LORD, which he spoke by his servant Å·hī′jäh the prophet. ¹⁹ Now the rest of the acts of Jer·ō·bō′am, how he warred and how he reigned, behold, they are written in the Book of the Chronicles of the Kings of Israel. ²⁰And the time that Jer·ō·bō′am reigned was twenty-two years; and he slept with his fathers, and Nā′dab his son reigned in his stead.

21 Now Rē·hō·bō·bō′am the son of Solomon reigned in Judah. Rehoboam was forty-one years old when he began to reign, and he reigned seventeen years in Jerusalem, the city which the LORD had chosen out of all the tribes of Israel, to put his name there. His mother's name was Nā′à·mäh the Am′mō·nīt·ĕss. ²²And Judah did what was evil in the sight of the LORD, and they provoked him to jealousy with their sins which they committed, more than all that their fathers had done. 23 For they also built for themselves high places, and pillars, and Å·shē′rim on every high hill and under every green

tree; ²⁴ and there were also male cult prostitutes in the land. They did according to all the abominations of the nations which the LORD drove out before the people of Israel.

25 In the fifth year of King Rē·hō·bō′am, Shi′shak king of Egypt came up against Jerusalem; ²⁶ he took away the treasures of the house of the LORD and the treasures of the king's house; he took away everything. He also took away all the shields of gold which Solomon had made; ²⁷ and King Rē·hō·bō′am made in their stead shields of bronze, and committed them to the hands of the officers of the guard, who kept the door of the king's house. ²⁸And as often as the king went into the house of the LORD, the guard bore them and brought them back to the guardroom.

29 Now the rest of the acts of Rē·hō·bō′am, and all that he did, are they not written in the Book of the Chronicles of the Kings of Judah? ³⁰And there was war between Rē·hō·bō′am and Jer·ō·bō′am continually. ³¹And Rē·hō·bō′am slept with his fathers and was buried with his fathers in the city of David. His mother's name was Nā′à·mäh the Am′mō·nīt·ĕss. And Å·bī′jäm his son reigned in his stead.

15 Now in the eighteenth year of King Jer·ō·bō′am the son of Nē′bat, Å·bī′jäm began to reign over Judah. ² He reigned for three years in Jerusalem. His mother's name was Mā′à·cäh the daughter of Å·bish′à·lom. ³And he walked in all the sins which his father did before him; and his heart was not wholly true to the LORD his God, as the heart of David his father. ⁴ Nevertheless for David's sake the LORD his God gave him a lamp in Jerusalem, setting up his son after him, and establishing Jerusalem; ⁵ because David did what was right in the eyes of the LORD, and did not turn aside from anything that he commanded him all the days of his life, except in the matter of Ū·rī′äh the Hit′tīte. ⁶ Now there was war between Rē·hō·bō′am and Jer·ō·bō′am all the days of his life. ⁷ The rest of the acts of Å·bī′jäm, and all that he did, are they not written in the Book of the Chronicles of the Kings of Judah? And there was war between Å·bī′jäm and Jer·ō·bō′am. ⁸And Å·bī′jäm slept with his fathers; and they buried him in the city of David. And Asa his son reigned in his stead.

9 In the twentieth year of Jer·ō-

---

m Heb obscure

14.25-31: 2 Chron 12.1-16.   **15.1-2, 7:** 2 Chron 13.1-2.   **15.8-12:** 2 Chron 14.1-5.

bō'ăm king of Israel Asa began to reign over Judah, 10 and he reigned forty-one years in Jerusalem. His mother's name was Mā'a·cǎh the daughter of Å·bish'a·lom. 11And Asa did what was right in the eyes of the LORD, as David his father had done. 12 He put away the male cult prostitutes out of the land, and removed all the idols that his fathers had made. 13 He also removed Mā'a·cǎh his mother from being queen mother because she had an abominable image made for Å·shē'rǎh; and Asa cut down her image and burned it at the brook Kid'rŏn. 14 But the high places were not taken away. Nevertheless the heart of Asa was wholly true to the LORD all his days. 15And he brought into the house of the LORD the votive gifts of his father and his own votive gifts, silver, and gold, and vessels.

16 And there was war between Asa and Bā'a·shà king of Israel all their days. 17 Bā'a·shà king of Israel went up against Judah, and built Rā'mǎh, that he might permit no one to go out or come in to Asa king of Judah. 18 Then Asa took all the silver and the gold that were left in the treasures of the house of the LORD and the treasures of the king's house, and gave them into the hands of his servants; and King Asa sent them to Ben-hā'dad the son of Tab·rĭm'mon, the son of Hē'zi-on, king of Syria, who dwelt in Damascus, saying, 19 "Let there be a league between me and you, as between my father and your father: behold, I am sending to you a present of silver and gold; go, break your league with Bā'a·shà king of Israel, that he may withdraw from me." 20And Ben-hā'dad hearkened to King Asa, and sent the commanders of his armies against the cities of Israel, and conquered I'jon, Dan, Å'bĕl-beth-mā'a·cǎh, and all Chin'nê·roth, with all the land of Naph'ta·lĭ. 21And when Bā'a·shà heard of it, he stopped building Rā'mǎh, and he dwelt in Tĭr'zǎh. 22 Then King Asa made a proclamation to all Judah, none was exempt, and they carried away the stones of Rā'mǎh and its timber, with which Bā'a·shà had been building; and with them King Asa built Gē'bà of Benjamin and Miz'pǎh. 23 Now the rest of all the acts of Asa, all his might, and all that he did, and the cities which he built, are they not written in the Book of the Chronicles of the Kings of Judah? But in his old age he was diseased in his feet. 24And Asa slept with his fathers,

and was buried with his fathers in the city of David his father; and Je·hosh'a·phat his son reigned in his stead.

25 Nā'dab the son of Jer·ŏ·bō'ǎm began to reign over Israel in the second year of Asa king of Judah; and he reigned over Israel two years. 26 He did what was evil in the sight of the LORD, and walked in the way of his father, and in his sin which he made Israel to sin.

27 Bā'a·shà the son of Å·hī'jàh, of the house of Is'sà·chär, conspired against him; and Bā'a·shà struck him down at Gib'bè·thon, which belonged to the Philistines; for Nā'dab and all Israel were laying siege to Gibbethon. 28 So Bā'a·shà killed him in the third year of Asa king of Judah, and reigned in his stead. 29And as soon as he was king, he killed all the house of Jer·ŏ·bō'ǎm; he left to the house of Jeroboam not one that breathed, until he had destroyed it, according to the word of the LORD which he spoke by his servant Å·hī'jàh the Shī'lŏ·nìte; 30 it was for the sins of Jer·ŏ·bō'ǎm which he sinned and which he made Israel to sin, and because of the anger to which he provoked the LORD, the God of Israel.

31 Now the rest of the acts of Nā'dab, and all that he did, are they not written in the Book of the Chronicles of the Kings of Israel? 32And there was war between Asa and Bā'a·shà king of Israel all their days.

33 In the third year of Asa king of Judah, Bā'a·shà the son of Å·hī'jàh began to reign over all Israel at Tĭr'zǎh, and reigned twenty-four years. 34 He did what was evil in the sight of the LORD, and walked in the way of Jer·ŏ·bō'ǎm and in his sin which he made Israel to sin.

16 And the word of the LORD came to Jē'hū the son of Hà·nā'nī against Bā'a·shà, saying, 2 "Since I exalted you out of the dust and made you leader over my people Israel, and you have walked in the way of Jer·ŏ·bō'ǎm, and have made my people Israel to sin, provoking me to anger with their sins, 3 behold, I will utterly sweep away Bā'a·shà and his house, and I will make your house like the house of Jer·ŏ·bō'ǎm the son of Nē'bat. 4Any one belonging to Bā'a·shà who dies in the city the dogs shall eat; and any one of his who dies in the field the birds of the air shall eat."

5 Now the rest of the acts of Bā'a·shà, and what he did, and his might, are they not written in the Book of

15.13-22: 2 Chron 15.16-16.6. **15.23-24:** 2 Chron 16.12-14. **15.24:** 2 Chron 17.1.

the Chronicles of the Kings of Israel? 6And Bā'à·shà slept with his fathers, and was buried at Tīr'zàh; and Ē'làh his son reigned in his stead. 7 More-over the word of the LORD came by the prophet Jē'hū the son of Hà·nā'nī against Bā'à·shà and his house, both because of all the evil that he did in the sight of the LORD, provoking him to anger with the work of his hands, in being like the house of Jer·ò·bō'àm, and also because he destroyed it.

8 In the twenty-sixth year of Asa king of Judah, Ē'làh the son of Bā'à·shà began to reign over Israel in Tīr'-zàh, and reigned two years. 9 But his servant Zim'rī, commander of half his chariots, conspired against him. When he was at Tīr'zàh, drinking himself drunk in the house of Är'zà, who was over the household in Tirzah, 10 Zim'rī came in and struck him down and killed him, in the twenty-seventh year of Asa king of Judah, and reigned in his stead.

11 When he began to reign, as soon as he had seated himself on his throne, he killed all the house of Bā'à·shà; he did not leave him a single male of his kinsmen or his friends. 12 Thus Zim'rī destroyed all the house of Bā'à·shà, according to the word of the LORD, which he spoke against Baasha by Jē'hū the prophet, 13 for all the sins of Bā'à·shà and the sins of Ē'làh his son which they sinned, and which they made Israel to sin, provoking the LORD God of Israel to anger with their idols. 14 Now the rest of the acts of Ē'làh, and all that he did, are they not written in the Book of the Chronicles of the Kings of Israel?

15 In the twenty-seventh year of Asa king of Judah, Zim'rī reigned seven days in Tīr'zàh. Now the troops were encamped against Gĭb'bè·thon, which belonged to the Philistines, 16 and the troops who were encamped heard it said, "Zim'rī has conspired, and he has killed the king"; therefore all Israel made Om'rī, the commander of the army, king over Israel that day in the camp. 17 So Om'rī went up from Gĭb'bè·thon, and all Israel with him, and they besieged Tīr'zàh. 18And when Zim'rī saw that the city was taken, he went into the citadel of the king's house, and burned the king's house over him with fire, and died, 19 because of his sins which he committed, doing evil in the sight of the LORD, walking in the way of Jer·ò·bō'àm, and for his sin which he committed, making Israel to sin. 20 Now the rest of the acts of

Zim'rī, and the conspiracy which he made, are they not written in the Book of the Chronicles of the Kings of Israel?

21 Then the people of Israel were divided into two parts; half of the people followed Tĭb'nī the son of Gī'nath, to make him king, and half followed Om'rī. 22 But the people who followed Om'rī overcame the people who followed Tĭb'nī the son of Gī'nath; so Tibni died, and Omri be-came king. 23 In the thirty-first year of Asa king of Judah, Om'rī began to reign over Israel, and reigned for twelve years; six years he reigned in Tīr'zàh. 24 He bought the hill of Sà-mâr'ì·à from Shē'mèr for two talents of silver; and he fortified the hill, and called the name of the city which he built, Samaria, after the name of Shemer, the owner of the hill.

25 Om'rī did what was evil in the sight of the LORD, and did more evil than all who were before him. 26 For he walked in all the way of Jer·ò·bō'àm the son of Nē'bat, and in the sins which he made Israel to sin, provoking the LORD, the God of Israel, to anger by their idols. 27 Now the rest of the acts of Om'rī which he did, and the might that he showed, are they not written in the Book of the Chronicles of the Kings of Israel? 28And Om'rī slept with his fathers, and was buried in Sà·mâr'ì·à; and Ā'hab his son reigned in his stead.

29 In the thirty-eighth year of Asa king of Judah, Ā'hab the son of Om'rī began to reign over Israel, and Ahab the son of Omri reigned over Israel in Sà·mâr'ì·à twenty-two years. 30And Ā'hab the son of Om'rī did evil in the sight of the LORD more than all that were before him. 31And as if it had been a light thing for him to walk in the sins of Jer·ò·bō'àm the son of Nē'bat, he took for wife Jez'é·bél the daughter of Eth·bā'àl king of the Sĭ·dō'nì·àns, and went and served Bā'àl, and worshiped him. 32 He erected an altar for Bā'àl in the house of Baal, which he built in Sà·mâr'ì·à. 33And Ā'hab made an À·shē'ràh. Ahab did more to provoke the LORD, the God of Israel, to anger than all the kings of Israel who were before him. 34 In his days Hī'él of Beth'él built Jericho; he laid its foundation at the cost of À·bī'ràm his first-born, and set up its gates at the cost of his youngest son Sē'gùb, according to the word of the LORD, which he spoke by Joshua the son of Nun.

16.34: Josh 6.26.

17 Now E·lī′jah the Tish′bite, of Tish′be[n] in Gilead, said to A′hab, "As the LORD the God of Israel lives, before whom I stand, there shall be neither dew nor rain these years, except by my word." 2And the word of the LORD came to him. 3 "Depart from here and turn eastward, and hide yourself by the brook Chē′rith, that is east of the Jordan. 4 You shall drink from the brook, and I have commanded the ravens to feed you there." 5 So he went and did according to the word of the LORD; he went and dwelt by the brook Chē′rith that is east of the Jordan. 6And the ravens brought him bread and meat in the morning, and bread and meat in the evening; and he drank from the brook. 7And after a while the brook dried up, because there was no rain in the land.

8 Then the word of the LORD came to him. 9 "Arise, go to Zar′e·phath, which belongs to Si′don, and dwell there. Behold, I have commanded a widow there to feed you." 10 So he arose and went to Zar′e·phath; and when he came to the gate of the city, behold, a widow was there gathering sticks; and he called to her and said, "Bring me a little water in a vessel, that I may drink." 11And as she was going to bring it, he called to her and said, "Bring me a morsel of bread in your hand." 12And she said, "As the LORD your God lives, I have nothing baked, only a handful of meal in a jar, and a little oil in a cruse; and now, I am gathering a couple of sticks, that I may go in and prepare it for myself and my son, that we may eat it, and die." 13And E·lī′jah said to her, "Fear not; go and do as you have said; but first make me a little cake of it and bring it to me, and afterward make for yourself and your son. 14 For thus says the LORD the God of Israel, 'The jar of meal shall not be spent, and the cruse of oil shall not fail, until the day that the LORD sends rain upon the earth.'" 15And she went and did as E·lī′jah said; and she, and he, and her household ate for many days. 16 The jar of meal was not spent, neither did the cruse of oil fail, according to the word of the LORD which he spoke by E·lī′jah.

17 After this the son of the woman, the mistress of the house, became ill; and his illness was so severe that there was no breath left in him. 18And she said to E·lī′jah, "What have you against me, O man of God? You have

come to me to bring my sin to remembrance, and to cause the death of my son!" 19And he said to her, "Give me your son." And he took him from her bosom, and carried him up into the upper chamber, where he lodged, and laid him upon his own bed. 20And he cried to the LORD, "O LORD my God, hast thou brought calamity even upon the widow with whom I sojourn, by slaying her son?" 21 Then he stretched himself upon the child three times, and cried to the LORD, "O LORD my God, let this child's soul come into him again." 22And the LORD hearkened to the voice of E·lī′jah; and the soul of the child came into him again, and he revived. 23And E·lī′jah took the child, and brought him down from the upper chamber into the house, and delivered him to his mother; and Elijah said, "See, your son lives." 24And the woman said to E·lī′jah, "Now I know that you are a man of God, and that the word of the LORD in your mouth is truth."

18 After many days the word of the LORD came to E·lī′jah, in the third year, saying, "Go, show yourself to A′hab; and I will send rain upon the earth." 2 So E·lī′jah went to show himself to A′hab. Now the famine was severe in Sa·mār′i·a. 3And A′hab called Ō·ba·dī′ah, who was over the household. (Now Obadiah revered the LORD greatly; 4 and when Jez′e·bel cut off the prophets of the LORD, Ō·ba·dī′ah took a hundred prophets and hid them by fifties in a cave, and fed them with bread and water.) 5And A′hab said to Ō·ba·dī′ah, "Go through the land to all the springs of water and to all the valleys; perhaps we may find grass and save the horses and mules alive, and not lose some of the animals." 6 So they divided the land between them to pass through it; A′hab went in one direction by himself, and Ō·ba·dī′ah went in another direction by himself.

7 And as Ō·ba·dī′ah was on the way, behold, E·lī′jah met him; and Obadiah recognized him, and fell on his face, and said, "Is it you, my lord Elijah?" 8And he answered him, "It is I. Go, tell your lord, 'Behold, E·lī′jah is here.'" 9And he said, "Wherein have I sinned, that you would give your servant into the hand of A′hab, to kill me? 10As the LORD your God lives, there is no nation or kingdom whither my lord has not sent to seek you; and when they would say, 'He is not here,'

---

[n] Gk: Heb *of the settlers*

17.1: Rev 11.6.   **17.8-16:** Lk 4.25-26.   **17.18:** Mt 8.29; Mk 1.24; Jn 2.4.

he would take an oath of the kingdom or nation, that they had not found you. ¹¹And now you say, 'Go, tell your lord, "Behold, E·li′jah is here." ' ¹²And as soon as I have gone from you, the Spirit of the LORD will carry you whither I know not; and so, when I come and tell A′hab and he cannot find you, he will kill me, although I your servant have revered the LORD from my youth. ¹³ Has it not been told my lord what I did when Jez′e·bel killed the prophets of the LORD, how I hid a hundred men of the LORD's prophets by fifties in a cave, and fed them with bread and water? ¹⁴And now you say, 'Go, tell your lord, "Behold, E·li′jah is here" '; and he will kill me." ¹⁵And E·li′jah said, "As the LORD of hosts lives, before whom I stand, I will surely show myself to him today." ¹⁶ So O·ba·di′ah went to meet A′hab, and told him; and Ahab went to meet E·li′jah.

¹⁷ When A′hab saw E·li′jah, Ahab said to him, "Is it you, you troubler of Israel?" ¹⁸And he answered, "I have not troubled Israel; but you have, and your father's house, because you have forsaken the commandments of the LORD and followed the Ba′als. ¹⁹ Now therefore send and gather all Israel to me at Mount Car′mel, and the four hundred and fifty prophets of Ba′al and the four hundred prophets of A·she′rah, who eat at Jez′e·bel's table."

²⁰ So A′hab sent to all the people of Israel, and gathered the prophets together at Mount Car′mel. ²¹And E·li′jah came near to all the people, and said, "How long will you go limping with two different opinions? If the LORD is God, follow him; but if Ba′al, then follow him." And the people did not answer him a word. ²² Then E·li′jah said to the people, "I, even I only, am left a prophet of the LORD; but Ba′al's prophets are four hundred and fifty men. ²³ Let two bulls be given to us; and let them choose one bull for themselves, and cut it in pieces and lay it on the wood, but put no fire to it; and I will prepare the other bull and lay it on the wood, and put no fire to it. ²⁴And you call on the name of your god and I will call on the name of the LORD; and the God who answers by fire, he is God." And all the people answered, "It is well spoken." ²⁵ Then E·li′jah said to the prophets of Ba′al, "Choose for yourselves one bull and prepare it first, for you are many; and call on the name of your god, but put no fire to it." ²⁶And

they took the bull which was given them, and they prepared it, and called on the name of Ba′al from morning until noon, saying, "O Baal, answer us!" But there was no voice, and no one answered. And they limped about the altar which they had made. ²⁷And at noon E·li′jah mocked them, saying, "Cry aloud, for he is a god; either he is musing, or he has gone aside, or he is on a journey, or perhaps he is asleep and must be awakened." ²⁸And they cried aloud, and cut themselves after their custom with swords and lances, until the blood gushed out upon them. ²⁹And as midday passed, they raved on until the time of the offering of the oblation, but there was no voice; no one answered, no one heeded.

³⁰ Then E·li′jah said to all the people, "Come near to me"; and all the people came near to him. And he repaired the altar of the LORD that had been thrown down; ³¹ E·li′jah took twelve stones, according to the number of the tribes of the sons of Jacob, to whom the word of the LORD came, saying, "Israel shall be your name"; ³² and with the stones he built an altar in the name of the LORD. And he made a trench about the altar, as great as would contain two measures of seed. ³³And he put the wood in order, and cut the bull in pieces and laid it on the wood. And he said, "Fill four jars with water, and pour it on the burnt offering, and on the wood." ³⁴And he said, "Do it a second time"; and they did it a second time. And he said, "Do it a third time"; and they did it a third time. ³⁵And the water ran round about the altar, and filled the trench also with water.

³⁶ And at the time of the offering of the oblation, E·li′jah the prophet came near and said, "O LORD, God of Abraham, Isaac, and Israel, let it be known this day that thou art God in Israel, and that I am thy servant, and that I have done all these things at thy word. ³⁷Answer me, O LORD, answer me, that this people may know that thou, O LORD, art God, and that thou hast turned their hearts back." ³⁸ Then the fire of the LORD fell, and consumed the burnt offering, and the wood, and the stones, and the dust, and licked up the water that was in the trench. ³⁹And when all the people saw it, they fell on their faces; and they said, "The LORD, he is God; the LORD, he is God." ⁴⁰And E·li′jah said to them, "Seize the prophets of Ba′al; let not one of them escape." And they seized them; and Elijah brought them

down to the brook Ki′shon, and killed them there.

41 And E·li′jàh said to A′hab, "Go up, eat and drink; for there is a sound of the rushing of rain." 42 So A′hab went up to eat and to drink. And E·li′jäh went up to the top of Cär′mĕl; and he bowed himself down upon the earth, and put his face between his knees. 43And he said to his servant, "Go up now, look toward the sea." And he went up and looked, and said, "There is nothing." And he said, "Go again seven times." 44And at the seventh time he said, "Behold, a little cloud like a man's hand is rising out of the sea." And he said, "Go up, say to A′hab, 'Prepare your chariot and go down, lest the rain stop you.'" 45And in a little while the heavens grew black with clouds and wind, and there was a great rain. And A′hab rode and went to Jez′rē·ĕl. 46And the hand of the LORD was on E·li′jàh; and he girded up his loins and ran before A′hab to the entrance of Jez′rē·ĕl.

19 A′hab told Jez′é·bĕl all that E·li′jàh had done, and how he had slain all the prophets with the sword. 2 Then Jez′é·bĕl sent a messenger to E·li′jàh, saying, "So may the gods do to me, and more also, if I do not make your life as the life of one of them by this time tomorrow." 3 Then he was afraid, and he arose and went for his life, and came to Beer-sheba, which belongs to Judah, and left his servant there.

4 But he himself went a day's journey into the wilderness, and came and sat down under a broom tree; and he asked that he might die, saying, "It is enough; now, O LORD, take away my life; for I am no better than my fathers." 5And he lay down and slept under a broom tree; and behold, an angel touched him, and said to him, "Arise and eat." 6And he looked, and behold, there was at his head a cake baked on hot stones and a jar of water. And he ate and drank, and lay down again. 7And the angel of the LORD came again a second time, and touched him, and said, "Arise and eat, else the journey will be too great for you." 8And he arose, and ate and drank, and went in the strength of that food forty days and forty nights to Hō′reb the mount of God.

9 And there he came to a cave, and lodged there; and behold, the word of the LORD came to him, and he said to him, "What are you doing here, E·li′jàh?" 10 He said, "I have been

very jealous for the LORD, the God of hosts; for the people of Israel have forsaken thy covenant, thrown down thy altars, and slain thy prophets with the sword; and I, even I only, am left; and they seek my life, to take it away." 11And he said, "Go forth, and stand upon the mount before the LORD." And behold, the LORD passed by, and a great and strong wind rent the mountains, and broke in pieces the rocks before the LORD, but the LORD was not in the wind; and after the wind an earthquake, but the LORD was not in the earthquake; 12 and after the earthquake a fire, but the LORD was not in the fire; and after the fire a still small voice. 13And when E·li′jàh heard it, he wrapped his face in his mantle and went out and stood at the entrance of the cave. And behold, there came a voice to him, and said, "What are you doing here, Elijah?" 14 He said, "I have been very jealous for the LORD, the God of hosts; for the people of Israel have forsaken thy covenant, thrown down thy altars, and slain thy prophets with the sword; and I, even I only, am left; and they seek my life, to take it away." 15And the LORD said to him, "Go, return on your way to the wilderness of Damascus; and when you arrive, you shall anoint Haz′à·el to be king over Syria; 16 and Jē′hū the son of Nim′shi you shall anoint to be king over Israel; and E·li′shà the son of Shā′phàt of A′bĕl-mĕ·hō′làh you shall anoint to be prophet in your place. 17And him who escapes from the sword of Haz′à·el shall Jē′hū slay; and him who escapes from the sword of Jehu shall E·li′shà slay. 18 Yet I will leave seven thousand in Israel, all the knees that have not bowed to Bā′al, and every mouth that has not kissed him."

19 So he departed from there, and found E·li′shà the son of Shā′phàt, who was plowing, with twelve yoke of oxen before him, and he was with the twelfth. E·li′jàh passed by him and cast his mantle upon him. 20And he left the oxen, and ran after E·li′jàh, and said, "Let me kiss my father and my mother, and then I will follow you." And he said to him, "Go back again; for what have I done to you?" 21And he returned from following him, and took the yoke of oxen, and slew them, and boiled their flesh with the yokes of the oxen, and gave it to the people, and they ate. Then he arose and went after E·li′jàh, and ministered to him.

19.10: Rom 11.2-3.   **19.18:** Rom 11.4.

20 Ben-hā′dad the king of Syria gathered all his army together; thirty-two kings were with him, and horses and chariots; and he went up and besieged Sā·mâr′i·à, and fought against it. ²And he sent messengers into the city of Ā′hab king of Israel, and said to him, "Thus says Ben-hā′dad: ³ 'Your silver and your gold are mine; your fairest wives and children also are mine.' " ⁴And the king of Israel answered, "As you say, my lord, O king, I am yours, and all that I have." ⁵ The messengers came again, and said, "Thus says Ben-hā′-dad: 'I sent to you, saying, "Deliver to me your silver and your gold, your wives and your children"; ⁶ neverthe-less I will send my servants to you to-morrow about this time, and they shall search your house and the houses of your servants, and lay hands on what-ever pleases them,ᵒ and take it away.' "

⁷ Then the king of Israel called all the elders of the land, and said, "Mark, now, and see how this man is seeking trouble; for he sent to me for my wives and my children, and for my silver and my gold, and I did not refuse him." ⁸And all the elders and all the people said to him, "Do not heed or consent." ⁹ So he said to the messengers of Ben-hā′dad, "Tell my lord the king, 'All that you first demanded of your servant I will do; but this thing I cannot do.' " And the messengers departed and brought him word again. ¹⁰ Ben-hā′dad sent to him and said, "The gods do so to me, and more also, if the dust of Sā·mâr′i·à shall suffice for handfuls for all the people who follow me." ¹¹And the king of Israel answered, "Tell him, 'Let not him that girds on his armor boast himself as he that puts it off.' " ¹² When Ben-hā′dad heard this mes-sage as he was drinking with the kings in the booths, he said to his men, "Take your positions." And they took their positions against the city.

¹³ And behold, a prophet came near to Ā′hab king of Israel and said, "Thus says the LORD, Have you seen all this great multitude? Behold, I will give it into your hand this day; and you shall know that I am the LORD." ¹⁴And Ā′hab said, "By whom?" He said, "Thus says the LORD, By the servants of the governors of the districts." Then he said, "Who shall begin the battle?" He answered, "You." ¹⁵ Then he mustered the servants of the governors of the dis-tricts, and they were two hundred and thirty-two; and after them he mustered all the people of Israel, seven thousand.

¹⁶ And they went out at noon, while Ben-hā′dad was drinking him-self drunk in the booths, he and the thirty-two kings who helped him. ¹⁷ The servants of the governors of the districts went out first. And Ben-hā′-dad sent out scouts, and they reported to him, "Men are coming out from Sā·mâr′i·à." ¹⁸ He said, "If they have come out for peace, take them alive; or if they have come out for war, take them alive."

¹⁹ So these went out of the city, the servants of the governors of the districts, and the army which followed them. ²⁰And each killed his man; the Syrians fled and Israel pursued them, but Ben-hā′dad king of Syria escaped on a horse with horsemen. ²¹And the king of Israel went out, and capturedᵖ the horses and chariots, and killed the Syrians with a great slaughter.

²² Then the prophet came near to the king of Israel, and said to him, "Come, strengthen yourself, and con-sider well what you have to do; for in the spring the king of Syria will come up against you."

²³ And the servants of the king of Syria said to him, "Their gods are gods of the hills, and so they were stronger than we; but let us fight against them in the plain, and surely we shall be stronger than they. ²⁴And do this: remove the kings, each from his post, and put commanders in their places; ²⁵ and muster an army like the army that you have lost, horse for horse, and chariot for chariot; then we will fight against them in the plain, and surely we shall be stronger than they." And he hearkened to their voice, and did so.

²⁶ In the spring Ben-hā′dad mus-tered the Syrians, and went up to Ā′phek, to fight against Israel. ²⁷And the people of Israel were mustered and were provisioned, and went against them; the people of Israel encamped before them like two little flocks of goats, but the Syrians filled the country. ²⁸And a man of God came near and said to the king of Israel, "Thus says the LORD, 'Because the Syrians have said, "The LORD is a god of the hills but he is not a god of the valleys," therefore I will give all this great multitude into your hand, and you shall know that I am the LORD.' " ²⁹And they encamped opposite one another seven days. Then on the seventh day the battle was joined; and

the people of Israel smote of the Syrians a hundred thousand foot soldiers in one day. ³⁰And the rest fled into the city of A'phek; and the wall fell upon twenty-seven thousand men that were left.

Ben-hā'dad also fled, and entered an inner chamber in the city. ³¹And his servants said to him, "Behold now, we have heard that the kings of the house of Israel are merciful kings; let us put sackcloth on our loins and ropes upon our heads, and go out to the king of Israel; perhaps he will spare your life." ³²So they girded sackcloth on their loins, and put ropes on their heads, and went to the king of Israel and said, "Your servant Ben-hā'dad says, 'Pray, let me live.'" And he said, "Does he still live? He is my brother." ³³Now the men were watching for an omen, and they quickly took it up from him and said, "Yes, your brother Ben-hā'dad." Then he said, "Go and bring him." Then Ben-hadad came forth to him; and he caused him to come up into the chariot. ³⁴And Ben-hā'dad said to him, "The cities which my father took from your father I will restore; and you may establish bazaars for yourself in Damascus, as my father did in Sā·mâr'i·à." And A'hab said, "I will let you go on these terms." So he made a covenant with him and let him go.

35 And a certain man of the sons of the prophets said to his fellow at the command of the LORD, "Strike me, I pray." But the man refused to strike him. ³⁶Then he said to him, "Because you have not obeyed the voice of the LORD, behold, as soon as you have gone from me, a lion shall kill you." And as soon as he had departed from him, a lion met him and killed him. ³⁷Then he found another man, and said, "Strike me, I pray." And the man struck him, smiting and wounding him. ³⁸So the prophet departed, and waited for the king by the way, disguising himself with a bandage over his eyes. ³⁹And as the king passed, he cried to the king and said, "Your servant went out into the midst of the battle; and behold, a soldier turned and brought a man to me, and said, 'Keep this man; if by any means he be missing, your life shall be for his life, or else you shall pay a talent of silver.' ⁴⁰And as your servant was busy here and there, he was gone." The king of Israel said to him, "So shall your judgment be; you yourself have decided it." ⁴¹Then he made haste to take the bandage away from his eyes; and the king of Israel recognized him as one of the prophets. ⁴²And he said to him, "Thus says the LORD, 'Because you have let go out of your hand the man whom I had devoted to destruction, therefore your life shall go for his life, and your people for his people.'" ⁴³And the king of Israel went to his house resentful and sullen, and came to Sā·mâr'i·à.

21 Now Nā'both the Jez'rē·é·lite had a vineyard in Jez'rē·él, beside the palace of A'hab king of Sā·mâr'i·à. ²And after this A'hab said to Nā'both, "Give me your vineyard, that I may have it for a vegetable garden, because it is near my house; and I will give you a better vineyard for it; or, if it seems good to you, I will give you its value in money." ³But Nā'both said to A'hab, "The LORD forbid that I should give you the inheritance of my fathers." ⁴And A'hab went into his house vexed and sullen because of what Nā'both the Jez'rē·é·lite had said to him; for he had said, "I will not give you the inheritance of my fathers." And he lay down on his bed, and turned away his face, and would eat no food.

5 But Jez'é·bĕl his wife came to him, and said to him, "Why is your spirit so vexed that you eat no food?" ⁶And he said to her, "Because I spoke to Nā'both the Jez'rē·é·lite, and said to him, 'Give me your vineyard for money; or else, if it please you, I will give you another vineyard for it'; and he answered, 'I will not give you my vineyard.'" ⁷And Jez'é·bĕl his wife said to him, "Do you now govern Israel? Arise, and eat bread, and let your heart be cheerful; I will give you the vineyard of Nā'both the Jez'rē·é·lite."

8 So she wrote letters in A'hab's name and sealed them with his seal, and she sent the letters to the elders and the nobles who dwelt with Nā'both in his city. ⁹And she wrote in the letters, "Proclaim a fast, and set Nā'both on high among the people; ¹⁰ and set two base fellows opposite him, and let them bring a charge against him, saying, 'You have cursed God and the king.' Then take him out, and stone him to death." ¹¹And the men of his city, the elders and the nobles who dwelt in his city, did as Jez'é·bĕl had sent word to them. As it was written in the letters which she had sent to them, ¹² they proclaimed a fast, and set Nā'both on high among the people. ¹³And the two base fellows came in and sat opposite him; and the base

fellows brought a charge against Nā′-both, in the presence of the people, saying, "Naboth cursed God and the king." So they took him outside the city, and stoned him to death with stones. 14 Then they sent to Jez′e·bĕl, saying, "Nā′both has been stoned; he is dead."

15 As soon as Jez′e·bĕl heard that Nā′both had been stoned and was dead, Jezebel said to A′hab, "Arise, take possession of the vineyard of Naboth the Jez′rē·e·lite, which he refused to give you for money; for Naboth is not alive, but dead." 16And as soon as A′hab heard that Nā′both was dead, Ahab arose to go down to the vineyard of Naboth the Jez′rē·e·lite, to take possession of it.

17 Then the word of the LORD came to E·lī′jah the Tish′bite, saying, 18 "Arise, go down to meet A′hab king of Israel, who is in Sà·mâr′i·à; behold, he is in the vineyard of Nā′both, where he has gone to take possession. 19And you shall say to him, 'Thus says the LORD, "Have you killed, and also taken possession?" ' And you shall say to him, 'Thus says the LORD: "In the place where dogs licked up the blood of Nā′both shall dogs lick your own blood." ' "

20 A′hab said to E·lī′jah, "Have you found me, O my enemy?" He answered, "I have found you, because you have sold yourself to do what is evil in the sight of the LORD. 21 Behold, I will bring evil upon you; I will utterly sweep you away, and will cut off from A′hab every male, bond or free, in Israel; 22 and I will make your house like the house of Jer·ŏ·bō′am the son of Nē′bat, and like the house of Bā′à·shà the son of À·hī′jàh, for the anger to which you have provoked me, and because you have made Israel to sin. 23And of Jez′e·bĕl the LORD also said, 'The dogs shall eat Jezebel within the bounds of Jez′rē·el.' 24Any one belonging to A′hab who dies in the city the dogs shall eat; and any one of his who dies in the open country the birds of the air shall eat."

25 (There was none who sold himself to do what was evil in the sight of the LORD like A′hab, whom Jez′e·bĕl his wife incited. 26 He did very abominably in going after idols, as the Am′ŏ·rites had done, whom the LORD cast out before the people of Israel.)

27 And when A′hab heard those words, he rent his clothes, and put sackcloth upon his flesh, and fasted and lay in sackcloth, and went about

dejectedly. 28And the word of the LORD came to E·lī′jah the Tish′bite, saying, 29 "Have you seen how A′hab has humbled himself before me? Because he has humbled himself before me, I will not bring the evil in his days; but in his son's days I will bring the evil upon his house."

22 For three years Syria and Israel continued without war. 2 But in the third year Je·hosh′à·phat the king of Judah came down to the king of Israel. 3And the king of Israel said to his servants, "Do you know that Rā′moth-gil′ē·àd belongs to us, and we keep quiet and do not take it out of the hand of the king of Syria?" 4And he said to Je·hosh′à·phat, "Will you go with me to battle at Rā′moth-gil′ē·àd?" And Jehoshaphat said to the king of Israel, "I am as you are, my people as your people, my horses as your horses."

5 And Je·hosh′à·phat said to the king of Israel, "Inquire first for the word of the LORD." 6 Then the king of Israel gathered the prophets together, about four hundred men, and said to them, "Shall I go to battle against Rā′moth-gil′ē·àd, or shall I forbear?" And they said, "Go up; for the LORD will give it into the hand of the king." 7 But Je·hosh′à·phat said, "Is there not here another prophet of the LORD of whom we may inquire?" 8And the king of Israel said to Je·hosh′à·phat, "There is yet one man by whom we may inquire of the LORD, Mī·cāi′àh the son of Im′làh; but I hate him, for he never prophesies good concerning me, but evil." And Jehoshaphat said, "Let not the king say so." 9 Then the king of Israel summoned an officer and said, "Bring quickly Mī·cāi′àh the son of Im′làh." 10 Now the king of Israel and Je·hosh′à·phat the king of Judah were sitting on their thrones, arrayed in their robes, at the threshing floor at the entrance of the gate of Sà·mâr′i·à; and all the prophets were prophesying before them. 11And Zed·e·kī′àh the son of Che·nā′à·nàh made for himself horns of iron, and said, "Thus says the LORD, 'With these you shall push the Syrians until they are destroyed.' " 12And all the prophets prophesied so, and said, "Go up to Rā′moth-gil′ē·àd and triumph; the LORD will give it into the hand of the king."

13 And the messenger who went to summon Mī·cāi′àh said to him, "Behold, the words of the prophets with one accord are favorable to the king;

21.19: 2 Kings 9.26.   21.23: 2 Kings 9.36.   22.1-35: 2 Chron 18.1-34.

let your word be like the word of one of them, and speak favorably." 14 But Mī·cāi′ah said, "As the LORD lives, what the LORD says to me, that I will speak." 15And when he had come to the king, the king said to him, "Mī·cāi′ah, shall we go to Rā′moth-gil′ē·ad to battle, or shall we forbear?" And he answered him, "Go up and triumph; the LORD will give it into the hand of the king." 16 But the king said to him, "How many times shall I adjure you that you speak to me nothing but the truth in the name of the LORD?" 17And he said, "I saw all Israel scattered upon the mountains, as sheep that have no shepherd; and the LORD said, 'These have no master; let each return to his home in peace.'" 18And the king of Israel said to Je·hosh′a·phat, "Did I not tell you that he would not prophesy good concerning me, but evil?" 19And Mī·cāi′ah said, "Therefore hear the word of the LORD: I saw the LORD sitting on his throne, and all the host of heaven standing beside him on his right hand and on his left; 20 and the LORD said, 'Who will entice Ā′hab, that he may go up and fall at Rā′moth-gil′ē·ad?' And one said one thing, and another said another. 21 Then a spirit came forward and stood before the LORD, saying, 'I will entice him.' 22And the LORD said to him, 'By what means?' And he said, 'I will go forth, and will be a lying spirit in the mouth of all his prophets.' And he said, 'You are to entice him, and you shall succeed; go forth and do so.' 23 Now therefore behold, the LORD has put a lying spirit in the mouth of all these your prophets; the LORD has spoken evil concerning you."

24 Then Zed·e·kī′ah the son of Che·nā′a·nah came near and struck Mī·cāi′ah on the cheek, and said, "How did the Spirit of the LORD go from me to speak to you?" 25And Mī·cāi′ah said, "Behold, you shall see on that day when you go into an inner chamber to hide yourself." 26And the king of Israel said, "Seize Mī·cāi′ah, and take him back to Ā′mon the governor of the city and to Jō′ash the king's son; 27 and say, 'Thus says the king, "Put this fellow in prison, and feed him with scant fare of bread and water, until I come in peace."'" 28And Mī·cāi′ah said, "If you return in peace, the LORD has not spoken by me." And he said, "Hear, all you peoples!"

29 So the king of Israel and Je·hosh′a·phat the king of Judah went up to Rā′moth-gil′ē·ad. 30And the king of Israel said to Je·hosh′a·phat, "I will disguise myself and go into battle, but you wear your robes." And the king of Israel disguised himself and went into battle. 31 Now the king of Syria had commanded the thirty-two captains of his chariots, "Fight with neither small nor great, but only with the king of Israel." 32And when the captains of the chariots saw Je·hosh′a·phat, they said, "It is surely the king of Israel." So they turned to fight against him; and Jehoshaphat cried out. 33And when the captains of the chariots saw that it was not the king of Israel, they turned back from pursuing him. 34 But a certain man drew his bow at a venture, and struck the king of Israel between the scale armor and the breastplate; therefore he said to the driver of his chariot, "Turn about, and carry me out of the battle, for I am wounded." 35And the battle grew hot that day, and the king was propped up in his chariot facing the Syrians, until at evening he died; and the blood of the wound flowed into the bottom of the chariot. 36And about sunset a cry went through the army, "Every man to his city, and every man to his country!"

37 So the king died, and was brought to Sa·mâr′i·a; and they buried the king in Samaria. 38And they washed the chariot by the pool of Sa·mâr′i·a, and the dogs licked up his blood, and the harlots washed themselves in it, according to the word of the LORD which he had spoken. 39 Now the rest of the acts of Ā′hab, and all that he did, and the ivory house which he built, and all the cities that he built, are they not written in the Book of the Chronicles of the Kings of Israel? 40 So Ā′hab slept with his fathers; and A·hā·zī′ah his son reigned in his stead.

41 Je·hosh′a·phat the son of Asa began to reign over Judah in the fourth year of Ā′hab king of Israel. 42 Je·hosh′a·phat was thirty-five years old when he began to reign, and he reigned twenty-five years in Jerusalem. His mother's name was A·zū′bah the daughter of Shil′hi. 43 He walked in all the way of Asa his father; he did not turn aside from it, doing what was right in the sight of the LORD; yet the high places were not taken away, and the people still sacrificed and burned incense on the high places. 44 Je·hosh′a·phat also made peace with the king of Israel.

45 Now the rest of the acts of Je-

22.17: Mt 9.36.   22.41-43: 2 Chron 20.31-33.

hosh′a·phat, and his might that he showed, and how he warred, are they not written in the Book of the Chronicles of the Kings of Judah? ⁴⁶And the remnant of the male cult prostitutes who remained in the days of his father Asa, he exterminated from the land.

47 There was no king in E′dom; a deputy was king. ⁴⁸ Je·hosh′a·phat made ships of Tär′shish to go to O′phir for gold; but they did not go, for the ships were wrecked at E′zi·on-ge′ber. ⁴⁹ Then A·ha·zi′ah the son of A′hab said to Je·hosh′a·phat, "Let my servants go with your servants in the ships," but Jehoshaphat was not willing. ⁵⁰And Je·hosh′a·phat slept with his fathers, and was buried with his fathers in the city of David his father; and Je·ho′ram his son reigned in his stead.

51 A·ha·zi′ah the son of A′hab began to reign over Israel in Sà·mâr′i·à in the seventeenth year of Je·hosh′a·phat king of Judah, and he reigned two years over Israel. ⁵² He did what was evil in the sight of the LORD, and walked in the way of his father, and in the way of his mother, and in the way of Jer·o·bo′am the son of Ne′bat, who made Israel to sin. ⁵³ He served Ba′al and worshiped him, and provoked the LORD, the God of Israel, to anger in every way that his father had done.

THE SECOND BOOK OF THE

KINGS

I After the death of A′hab, Mō′ab rebelled against Israel.

2 Now A·ha·zi′ah fell through the lattice in his upper chamber in Sà·mâr′i·à, and lay sick; so he sent messengers, telling them, "Go, inquire of Ba′al-ze′bub, the god of Ek′ron, whether I shall recover from this sickness." ³ But the angel of the LORD said to E·li′jah the Tish′bite, "Arise, go up to meet the messengers of the king of Sà·mâr′i·à, and say to them, 'Is it because there is no God in Israel that you are going to inquire of Ba′al-ze′bub, the god of Ek′ron?' ⁴ Now therefore thus says the LORD, 'You shall not come down from the bed to which you have gone, but you shall surely die.'" So E·li′jah went.

5 The messengers returned to the king, and he said to them, "Why have you returned?" ⁶And they said to him, "There came a man to meet us, and said to us, 'Go back to the king who sent you, and say to him, Thus says the LORD, Is it because there is no God in Israel that you are sending to inquire of Ba′al-ze′bub, the god of Ek′ron? Therefore you shall not come down from the bed to which you have gone, but shall surely die.'" ⁷ He said to them, "What kind of man was he who came to meet you and told you these things?" ⁸ They answered him, "He wore a garment of haircloth, with a girdle of leather about his loins." And he said, "It is E·li′jah the Tish′bite."

9 Then the king sent to him a captain of fifty men with his fifty. He went up to E·li′jah, who was sitting on the top of a hill, and said to him, "O man of God, the king says, 'Come down.'" ¹⁰ But E·li′jah answered the captain of fifty, "If I am a man of God, let fire come down from heaven and consume you and your fifty." Then fire came down from heaven, and consumed him and his fifty.

11 Again the king sent to him another captain of fifty men with his fifty. And he went up^a and said to him, "O man of God, this is the king's order, 'Come down quickly!'" ¹² But E·li′jah answered them, "If I am a man of God, let fire come down from heaven and consume you and your fifty." Then the fire of God came down from heaven and consumed him and his fifty.

13 Again the king sent the captain of a third fifty with his fifty. And the third captain of fifty went up, and came and fell on his knees before E·li′jah, and entreated him, "O man

a Gk Compare verses 9, 13: Heb *answered*
22.48-49: 2 Chron 20.35-37.   22.50: 2 Chron 21.1.
1.10-12: Lk 9.54; Rev 11.5; 20.9.

of God, I pray you, let my life, and the life of these fifty servants of yours, be precious in your sight. 14 Lo, fire came down from heaven, and consumed the two former captains of fifty men with their fifties; but now let my life be precious in your sight." 15 Then the angel of the LORD said to E·li′jah, "Go down with him; do not be afraid of him." So he arose and went down with him to the king, 16 and said to him, "Thus says the LORD, 'Because you have sent messengers to inquire of Bā′al-zē′bub, the god of Ek′ron,—is it because there is no God in Israel to inquire of his word?—therefore you shall not come down from the bed to which you have gone, but you shall surely die.' "

17 So he died according to the word of the LORD which E·li′jah had spoken. Je·hō′ram, his brother,[b] became king in his stead in the second year of Jehoram the son of Je·hosh′a·phat, king of Judah, because A·ha·zi′ah had no son. 18 Now the rest of the acts of A·ha·zi′ah which he did, are they not written in the Book of the Chronicles of the Kings of Israel?

2 Now when the LORD was about to take E·li′jah up to heaven by a whirlwind, Elijah and E·li′sha were on their way from Gil′gal. 2 And E·li′jah said to E·li′sha, "Tarry here, I pray you; for the LORD has sent me as far as Beth′el." But Elisha said, "As the LORD lives, and as you yourself live, I will not leave you." So they went down to Bethel. 3 And the sons of the prophets who were in Beth′el came out to E·li′sha, and said to him, "Do you know that today the LORD will take away your master from over you?" And he said, "Yes, I know it; hold your peace."

4 E·li′jah said to him, "E·li′sha, tarry here, I pray you; for the LORD has sent me to Jericho." But he said, "As the LORD lives, and as you yourself live, I will not leave you." So they came to Jericho. 5 The sons of the prophets who were at Jericho drew near to E·li′sha, and said to him, "Do you know that today the LORD will take away your master from over you?" And he answered, "Yes, I know it; hold your peace."

6 Then E·li′jah said to him, "Tarry here, I pray you; for the LORD has sent me to the Jordan." But he said, "As the LORD lives, and as you yourself live, I will not leave you." So the two of them went on. 7 Fifty men of the

sons of the prophets also went, and stood at some distance from them, as they both were standing by the Jordan. 8 Then E·li′jah took his mantle, and rolled it up, and struck the water, and the water was parted to the one side and to the other, till the two of them could go over on dry ground.

9 When they had crossed, E·li′jah said to E·li′sha, "Ask what I shall do for you, before I am taken from you." And Elisha said, "I pray you, let me inherit a double share of your spirit." 10 And he said, "You have asked a hard thing; yet, if you see me as I am being taken from you, it shall be so for you; but if you do not see me, it shall not be so." 11 And as they still went on and talked, behold, a chariot of fire and horses of fire separated the two of them. And E·li′jah went up by a whirlwind into heaven. 12 And E·li′sha saw it and cried, "My father, my father! the chariots of Israel and its horsemen!" And he saw him no more.

Then he took hold of his own clothes and rent them in two pieces. 13 And he took up the mantle of E·li′jah that had fallen from him, and went back and stood on the bank of the Jordan. 14 Then he took the mantle of E·li′jah that had fallen from him, and struck the water, saying, "Where is the LORD, the God of Elijah?" And when he had struck the water, the water was parted to the one side and to the other; and E·li′sha went over.

15 Now when the sons of the prophets who were at Jericho saw him over against them, they said, "The spirit of E·li′jah rests on E·li′sha." And they came to meet him, and bowed to the ground before him. 16 And they said to him, "Behold now, there are with your servants fifty strong men; pray, let them go, and seek your master; it may be that the Spirit of the LORD has caught him up and cast him upon some mountain or into some valley." And he said, "You shall not send." 17 But when they urged him till he was ashamed, he said, "Send." They sent therefore fifty men; and for three days they sought him but did not find him. 18 And they came back to him, while he tarried at Jericho, and he said to them, "Did I not say to you, Do not go?"

19 Now the men of the city said to E·li′sha, "Behold, the situation of this city is pleasant, as my lord sees; but the water is bad, and the land is unfruitful." 20 He said, "Bring me a new

[b] Gk Syr: Heb lacks *his brother*
2.11: Rev 11.12.

bowl, and put salt in it." So they brought it to him. 21 Then he went to the spring of water and threw salt in it, and said, "Thus says the LORD, I have made this water wholesome; henceforth neither death nor miscarriage shall come from it." 22 So the water has been wholesome to this day, according to the word which E·li´shà spoke.

23 He went up from there to Beth´el; and while he was going up on the way, some small boys came out of the city and jeered at him, saying, "Go up, you baldhead! Go up, you baldhead!" 24 And he turned around, and when he saw them, he cursed them in the name of the LORD. And two she-bears came out of the woods and tore forty-two of the boys. 25 From there he went on to Mount Cär´mel, and thence he returned to Sà·mâr´i·à.

3 In the eighteenth year of Je·hosh´à·phat king of Judah, Je·hō´ràm the son of A´hab became king over Israel in Sà·mâr´i·à, and he reigned twelve years. 2 He did what was evil in the sight of the LORD, though not like his father and mother, for he put away the pillar of Bā´ăl which his father had made. 3 Nevertheless he clung to the sin of Jer·ŏ·bō´ăm the son of Nē´bat, which he made Israel to sin; he did not depart from it.

4 Now Mē´shà king of Mō´ab was a sheep breeder; and he had to deliver annually*c* to the king of Israel a hundred thousand lambs, and the wool of a hundred thousand rams. 5 But when A´hab died, the king of Mō´ab rebelled against the king of Israel. 6 So King Je·hō´ràm marched out of Sà·mâr´i·à at that time and mustered all Israel. 7 And he went and sent word to Je·hosh´à·phat king of Judah, "The king of Mō´ab has rebelled against me; will you go with me to battle against Moab?" And he said, "I will go; I am as you are, my people as your people, my horses as your horses." 8 Then he said, "By which way shall we march?" Je·hō´ràm answered, "By the way of the wilderness of E´dóm."

9 So the king of Israel went with the king of Judah and the king of E´dóm. And when they had made a circuitous march of seven days, there was no water for the army or for the beasts which followed them. 10 Then the king of Israel said, "Alas! The LORD has called these three kings to give them into the hand of Mō´ab." 11 And Je·hosh´à·phat said, "Is there no prophet of the LORD here, through

whom we may inquire of the LORD?" Then one of the king of Israel's servants answered, "E·li´shà the son of Shā´phàt is here, who poured water on the hands of E·li´jàh." 12 And Je·hosh´à·phat said, "The word of the LORD is with him." So the king of Israel and Jehoshaphat and the king of E´dóm went down to him.

13 And E·li´shà said to the king of Israel, "What have I to do with you? Go to the prophets of your father and the prophets of your mother." But the king of Israel said to him, "No; it is the LORD who has called these three kings to give them into the hand of Mō´ab." 14 And E·li´shà said, "As the LORD of hosts lives, whom I serve, were it not that I have regard for Je·hosh´à·phat the king of Judah, I would neither look at you, nor see you. 15 But now bring me a minstrel." And when the minstrel played, the power of the LORD came upon him. 16 And he said, "Thus says the LORD, 'I will make this dry stream-bed full of pools.' 17 For thus says the LORD, 'You shall not see wind or rain, but that stream-bed shall be filled with water, so that you shall drink, you, your cattle, and your beasts.' 18 This is a light thing in the sight of the LORD; he will also give the Mō´ab·ites into your hand, 19 and you shall conquer every fortified city, and every choice city, and shall fell every good tree, and stop up all springs of water, and ruin every good piece of land with stones." 20 The next morning, about the time of offering the sacrifice, behold, water came from the direction of E´dóm, till the country was filled with water.

21 When all the Mō´ab·ites heard that the kings had come up to fight against them, all who were able to put on armor, from the youngest to the oldest, were called out, and were drawn up at the frontier. 22 And when they rose early in the morning, and the sun shone upon the water, the Mō´ab·ites saw the water opposite them as red as blood. 23 And they said, "This is blood; the kings have surely fought together, and slain one another. Now then, Mō´ab, to the spoil!" 24 But when they came to the camp of Israel, the Israelites rose and attacked the Mō´ab·ites, till they fled before them; and they went forward, slaughtering the Moabites as they went.*d* 25 And they overthrew the cities, and on every good piece of land every man threw a stone, until it was covered; they stopped every spring of water, and felled all

c Tg: Heb lacks *annually*   *d* Gk: Heb uncertain

the good trees; till only its stones were left in Kĭr-hâr′ĕ·seth, and the slingers surrounded and conquered it. 26 When the king of Mō′ab saw that the battle was going against him, he took with him seven hundred swordsmen to break through, opposite the king of É′dŏm; but they could not. 27 Then he took his eldest son who was to reign in his stead, and offered him for a burnt offering upon the wall. And there came great wrath upon Israel; and they withdrew from him and returned to their own land.

4 Now the wife of one of the sons of the prophets cried to E·lī′shà, "Your servant my husband is dead; and you know that your servant feared the LORD, but the creditor has come to take my two children to be his slaves." 2And E·lī′shà said to her, "What shall I do for you? Tell me; what have you in the house?" And she said, "Your maidservant has nothing in the house, except a jar of oil." 3 Then he said, "Go outside, borrow vessels of all your neighbors, empty vessels and not too few. 4 Then go in, and shut the door upon yourself and your sons, and pour into all these vessels; and when one is full, set it aside." 5 So she went from him and shut the door upon herself and her sons; and as she poured they brought the vessels to her. 6 When the vessels were full, she said to her son, "Bring me another vessel." And he said to her, "There is not another." Then the oil stopped flowing. 7 She came and told the man of God, and he said, "Go, sell the oil and pay your debts, and you and your sons can live on the rest."

8 One day E·lī′shà went on to Shū′nem, where a wealthy woman lived, who urged him to eat some food. So whenever he passed that way, he would turn in there to eat food. 9And she said to her husband, "Behold now, I perceive that this is a holy man of God, who is continually passing our way. 10 Let us make a small roof chamber with walls, and put there for him a bed, a table, a chair, and a lamp, so that whenever he comes to us, he can go in there."

11 One day he came there, and he turned into the chamber and rested there. 12And he said to Ge·hā′zī his servant, "Call this Shū′nàm·mite." When he had called her, she stood before him. 13And he said to him, "Say now to her, See, you have taken all this trouble for us; what is to be done for you? Would you have a word

spoken on your behalf to the king or to the commander of the army?" She answered, "I dwell among my own people." 14And he said, "What then is to be done for her?" Ge·hā′zī answered, "Well, she has no son, and her husband is old." 15 He said, "Call her." And when he had called her, she stood in the doorway. 16And he said, "At this season, when the time comes round, you shall embrace a son." And she said, "No, my lord, O man of God; do not lie to your maidservant." 17 But the woman conceived, and she bore a son about that time the following spring, as E·lī′shà had said to her.

18 When the child had grown, he went out one day to his father among the reapers. 19And he said to his father, "Oh, my head, my head!" The father said to his servant, "Carry him to his mother." 20And when he had lifted him, and brought him to his mother, the child sat on her lap till noon, and then he died. 21And he went up and laid him on the bed of the man of God, and shut the door upon him, and went out. 22 Then she called to her husband, and said, "Send me one of the servants and one of the asses, that I may quickly go to the man of God, and come back again." 23And he said, "Why will you go to him today? It is neither new moon nor sabbath." She said, "It will be well." 24 Then she saddled the ass, and she said to her servant, "Urge the beast on; do not slacken the pace for me unless I tell you." 25 So she set out, and came to the man of God at Mount Cär′mĕl.

When the man of God saw her coming, he said to Ge·hā′zī his servant, "Look, yonder is the Shū′nàm·mite; 26 run at once to meet her, and say to her, Is it well with you? Is it well with your husband? Is it well with the child?" And she answered, "It is well." 27And when she came to the mountain to the man of God, she caught hold of his feet. And Ge·hā′zī came to thrust her away. But the man of God said, "Let her alone, for she is in bitter distress; and the LORD has hidden it from me, and has not told me." 28 Then she said, "Did I ask my lord for a son? Did I not say, Do not deceive me?" 29 He said to Ge·hā′zī, "Gird up your loins, and take my staff in your hand, and go. If you meet any one, do not salute him; and if any one salutes you, do not reply; and lay my staff upon the face of the child." 30 Then the mother of the child said, "As the LORD lives, and as you yourself live, I will not leave you." So he arose and followed her. [31] Ge·hā´zī went on ahead and laid the staff upon the face of the child, but there was no sound or sign of life. Therefore he returned to meet him, and told him, "The child has not awaked."

[32] When E·lī´shà came into the house, he saw the child lying dead on his bed. [33] So he went in and shut the door upon the two of them, and prayed to the LORD. [34] Then he went up and lay upon the child, putting his mouth upon his mouth, his eyes upon his eyes, and his hands upon his hands; and as he stretched himself upon him, the flesh of the child became warm. [35] Then he got up again, and walked once to and fro in the house, and went up, and stretched himself upon him; the child sneezed seven times, and the child opened his eyes. [36] Then he summoned Ge·hā´zī and said, "Call this Shū´nàm·mite." So he called her. And when she came to him, he said, "Take up your son." [37] She came and fell at his feet, bowing to the ground; then she took up her son and went out.

[38] And E·lī´shà came again to Gil´gàl when there was a famine in the land. And as the sons of the prophets were sitting before him, he said to his servant, "Set on the great pot, and boil pottage for the sons of the prophets." [39] One of them went out into the field to gather herbs, and found a wild vine and gathered from it his lap full of wild gourds, and came and cut them up into the pot of pottage, not knowing what they were. [40] And they poured out for the men to eat. But while they were eating of the pottage, they cried out, "O man of God, there is death in the pot!" And they could not eat it. [41] He said, "Then bring meal." And he threw it into the pot, and said, "Pour out for the men, that they may eat." And there was no harm in the pot.

[42] A man came from Bā´àl-shal´i-shàh, bringing the man of God bread of the first fruits, twenty loaves of barley, and fresh ears of grain in his sack. And E·lī´shà said, "Give to the men, that they may eat." [43] But his servant said, "How am I to set this before a hundred men?" So he repeated, "Give them to the men, that they may eat, for thus says the LORD, 'They shall eat and have some left.'" [44] So he set it before them. And they ate, and had some left, according to the word of the LORD.

5 Nā´à·man, commander of the army of the king of Syria, was a great man with his master and in high favor, because by him the LORD had given victory to Syria. He was a mighty man of valor, but he was a leper. [2] Now the Syrians on one of their raids had carried off a little maid from the land of Israel, and she waited on Nā´à·man's wife. [3] She said to her mistress, "Would that my lord were with the prophet who is in Sà·mâr´i·à! He would cure him of his leprosy." [4] So Nā´à·man went in and told his lord, "Thus and so spoke the maiden from the land of Israel." [5] And the king of Syria said, "Go now, and I will send a letter to the king of Israel."

So he went, taking with him ten talents of silver, six thousand shekels of gold, and ten festal garments. [6] And he brought the letter to the king of Israel, which read, "When this letter reaches you, know that I have sent to you Nā´à·man my servant, that you may cure him of his leprosy." [7] And when the king of Israel read the letter, he rent his clothes and said, "Am I God, to kill and to make alive, that this man sends word to me to cure a man of his leprosy? Only consider, and see how he is seeking a quarrel with me."

[8] But when E·lī´shà the man of God heard that the king of Israel had rent his clothes, he sent to the king, saying, "Why have you rent your clothes? Let him come now to me, that he may know that there is a prophet in Israel." [9] So Nā´à·man came with his horses and chariots, and halted at the door of E·lī´shà's house. [10] And E·lī´shà sent a messenger to him, saying, "Go and wash in the Jordan seven times, and your flesh shall be restored, and you shall be clean." [11] But Nā´à·man was angry, and went away, saying, "Behold, I thought that he would surely come out to me, and stand, and call on the name of the LORD his God, and wave his hand over the place, and cure the leper. [12] Are not Â·bā´nàh[e] and Phär´pär, the rivers of Damascus, better than all the waters of Israel? Could I not wash in them, and be clean?" So he turned and went away in a rage. [13] But his servants came near and said to him, "My father, if the prophet had commanded you to do some great thing, would you not have done it? How much rather, then, when he says to you, 'Wash, and be clean?'" [14] So he went down and dipped himself seven times in the Jordan, according to the word of the man of God; and his flesh was restored

_____
[e] Another reading is *Amana*   **4.33:** Mt 6.6.

like the flesh of a little child, and he was clean.

15 Then he returned to the man of God, he and all his company, and he came and stood before him; and he said, "Behold, I know that there is no God in all the earth but in Israel; so accept now a present from your servant." 16 But he said, "As the LORD lives, whom I serve, I will receive none." And he urged him to take it, but he refused. 17 Then Nā'á·man said, "If not, I pray you, let there be given to your servant two mules' burden of earth; for henceforth your servant will not offer burnt offering or sacrifice to any god but the LORD. 18 In this matter may the LORD pardon your servant: when my master goes into the house of Rim'mon to worship there, leaning on my arm, and I bow myself in the house of Rimmon, when I bow myself in the house of Rimmon, the LORD pardon your servant in this matter." 19 He said to him, "Go in peace."

But when Nā'á·man had gone from him a short distance, 20 Ge·hā'zi, the servant of E·lí'shā the man of God, said, "See, my master has spared this Nā'á·man the Syrian, in not accepting from his hand what he brought. As the LORD lives, I will run after him, and get something from him." 21 So Ge·hā'zī followed Nā'á·man. And when Naaman saw some one running after him, he alighted from the chariot to meet him, and said, "Is all well?" 22 And he said, "All is well. My master has sent me to say, 'There have just now come to me from the hill country of E'phrá·im two young men of the sons of the prophets; pray, give them a talent of silver and two festal garments.'" 23 And Nā'á·man said, "Be pleased to accept two talents." And he urged him, and tied up two talents of silver in two bags, with two festal garments, and laid them upon two of his servants; and they carried them before Ge·hā'zī. 24 And when he came to the hill, he took them from their hand, and put them in the house; and he sent the men away, and they departed. 25 He went in, and stood before his master, and E·lí'shā said to him, "Where have you been, Ge·hā'zī?" And he said, "Your servant went nowhere." 26 But he said to him, "Did I not go with you in spirit when the man turned from his chariot to meet you? Was it a time to accept money and garments, olive orchards and vineyards, sheep and oxen, menservants and maidservants? 27 Therefore the

leprosy of Nā'á·man shall cleave to you, and to your descendants for ever." So he went out from his presence a leper, as white as snow.

6 Now the sons of the prophets said to E·lí'shā, "See, the place where we dwell under your charge is too small for us. 2 Let us go to the Jordan and each of us get there a log, and let us make a place for us to dwell there." And he answered, "Go." 3 Then one of them said, "Be pleased to go with your servants." And he answered, "I will go." 4 So he went with them. And when they came to the Jordan, they cut down trees. 5 But as one was felling a log, his axe head fell into the water; and he cried out, "Alas, my master! It was borrowed." 6 Then the man of God said, "Where did it fall?" When he showed him the place, he cut off a stick, and threw it in there, and made the iron float. 7 And he said, "Take it up." So he reached out his hand and took it.

8 Once when the king of Syria was warring against Israel, he took counsel with his servants, saying, "At such and such a place shall be my camp." 9 But the man of God sent word to the king of Israel, "Beware that you do not pass this place, for the Syrians are going down there." 10 And the king of Israel sent to the place of which the man of God told him. Thus he used to warn him, so that he saved himself there more than once or twice.

11 And the mind of the king of Syria was greatly troubled because of this thing; and he called his servants and said to them, "Will you not show me who of us is for the king of Israel?" 12 And one of his servants said, "None, my lord, O king; but E·lí'shā, the prophet who is in Israel, tells the king of Israel the words that you speak in your bedchamber." 13 And he said, "Go and see where he is, that I may send and seize him." It was told him, "Behold, he is in Dō'thăn." 14 So he sent there horses and chariots and a great army; and they came by night, and surrounded the city.

15 When the servant of the man of God rose early in the morning and went out, behold, an army with horses and chariots was round about the city. And the servant said, "Alas, my master! What shall we do?" 16 He said, "Fear not, for those who are with us are more than those who are with them." 17 Then E·lí'shā prayed, and said, "O LORD, I pray thee, open his eyes that he may see." So the LORD opened the eyes of the young man, and he saw;

and behold, the mountain was full of horses and chariots of fire round about Elisha. ¹⁸And when the Syrians came down against him, E·li′shà prayed to the LORD, and said, "Strike this people, I pray thee, with blindness." So he struck them with blindness in accordance with the prayer of Elisha. ¹⁹And E·li′shà said to them, "This is not the way, and this is not the city; follow me, and I will bring you to the man whom you seek." And he led them to Sà·mâr′i·à.

20 As soon as they entered Sà·mâr′i·à, E·li′shà said, "O LORD, open the eyes of these men, that they may see." So the LORD opened their eyes, and they saw; and lo, they were in the midst of Samaria. ²¹ When the king of Israel saw them he said to E·li′shà, "My father, shall I slay them? Shall I slay them?" ²² He answered, "You shall not slay them. Would you slay those whom you have taken captive with your sword and with your bow? Set bread and water before them, that they may eat and drink and go to their master." ²³ So he prepared for them a great feast; and when they had eaten and drunk, he sent them away, and they went to their master. And the Syrians came no more on raids into the land of Israel.

24 Afterward Ben·hā′dad king of Syria mustered his entire army, and went up, and besieged Sà·mâr′i·à. ²⁵And there was a great famine in Sà·mâr′i·à, as they besieged it, until an ass's head was sold for eighty shekels of silver, and the fourth part of a kab of dove's dung for five shekels of silver. ²⁶ Now as the king of Israel was passing by upon the wall, a woman cried out to him, saying, "Help, my lord, O king!" ²⁷And he said, "If the LORD will not help you, whence shall I help you? From the threshing floor, or from the wine press?" ²⁸And the king asked her, "What is your trouble?" She answered, "This woman said to me, 'Give your son, that we may eat him today, and we will eat my son tomorrow.' ²⁹ So we boiled my son, and ate him. And on the next day I said to her, 'Give your son, that we may eat him'; but she has hidden her son." ³⁰ When the king heard the words of the woman he rent his clothes—now he was passing by upon the wall—and the people looked, and behold, he had sackcloth beneath upon his body—³¹ and he said, "May God do so to me, and more also, if the head of E·li′shà the son of

Sha′phàt remains on his shoulders today."

32 E·li′shà was sitting in his house, and the elders were sitting with him. Now the king had dispatched a man from his presence; but before the messenger arrived Elisha said to the elders, "Do you see how this murderer has sent to take off my head? Look, when the messenger comes, shut the door, and hold the door fast against him. Is not the sound of his master's feet behind him?" ³³And while he was still speaking with them, the king*ᶠ* came down to him and said, "This trouble is from the LORD! Why should I wait for the LORD any longer?"

7 ¹ But E·li′shà said, "Hear the word of the LORD: thus says the LORD, Tomorrow about this time a measure of fine meal shall be sold for a shekel, and two measures of barley for a shekel, at the gate of Sà·mâr′i·à." ² Then the captain on whose hand the king leaned said to the man of God, "If the LORD himself should make windows in heaven, could this thing be?" But he said, "You shall see it with your own eyes, but you shall not eat of it."

3 Now there were four men who were lepers at the entrance to the gate; and they said to one another, "Why do we sit here till we die? ⁴ If we say, 'Let us enter the city,' the famine is in the city, and we shall die there; and if we sit here, we die also. So now come, let us go over to the camp of the Syrians; if they spare our lives we shall live, and if they kill us we shall but die." ⁵ So they arose at twilight to go to the camp of the Syrians; but when they came to the edge of the camp of the Syrians, behold, there was no one there. ⁶ For the Lord had made the army of the Syrians hear the sound of chariots, and of horses, the sound of a great army, so that they said to one another, "Behold, the king of Israel has hired against us the kings of the Hit′tites and the kings of Egypt to come upon us." ⁷ So they fled away in the twilight and forsook their tents, their horses, and their asses, leaving the camp as it was, and fled for their lives. ⁸And when these lepers came to the edge of the camp, they went into a tent, and ate and drank, and they carried off silver and gold and clothing, and went and hid them; then they came back, and entered another tent, and carried off things from it, and went and hid them.

9 Then they said to one another,

"We are not doing right. This day is a day of good news; if we are silent and wait until the morning light, punishment will overtake us; now therefore come, let us go and tell the king's household." 10 So they came and called to the gatekeepers of the city, and told them, "We came to the camp of the Syrians, and behold, there was no one to be seen or heard there, nothing but the horses tied, and the asses tied, and the tents as they were." 11 Then the gatekeepers called out, and it was told within the king's household. 12 And the king rose in the night, and said to his servants, "I will tell you what the Syrians have prepared against us. They know that we are hungry; therefore they have gone out of the camp to hide themselves in the open country, thinking, 'When they come out of the city, we shall take them alive and get into the city.'" 13 And one of his servants said, "Let some men take five of the remaining horses, seeing that those who are left here will fare like the whole multitude of Israel that have already perished; let us send and see." 14 So they took two mounted men, and the king sent them after the army of the Syrians, saying, "Go and see." 15 So they went after them as far as the Jordan; and, lo, all the way was littered with garments and equipment which the Syrians had thrown away in their haste. And the messengers returned, and told the king.

16 Then the people went out, and plundered the camp of the Syrians. So a measure of fine meal was sold for a shekel, and two measures of barley for a shekel, according to the word of the LORD. 17 Now the king had appointed the captain on whose hand he leaned to have charge of the gate; and the people trod upon him in the gate, so that he died, as the man of God had said when the king came down to him. 18 For when the man of God had said to the king, "Two measures of barley shall be sold for a shekel, and a measure of fine meal for a shekel, about this time tomorrow in the gate of Sà·mâr′i·à," 19 the captain had answered the man of God, "If the LORD himself should make windows in heaven, could such a thing be?" And he had said, "You shall see it with your own eyes, but you shall not eat of it." 20 And so it happened to him, for the people trod upon him in the gate and he died.

8 Now E·lī′shà had said to the woman whose son he had restored to life, "Arise, and depart with your household, and sojourn wherever you can; for the LORD has called for a famine, and it will come upon the land for seven years." 2 So the woman arose, and did according to the word of the man of God; she went with her household and sojourned in the land of the Philistines seven years. 3 And at the end of the seven years, when the woman returned from the land of the Philistines, she went forth to appeal to the king for her house and her land. 4 Now the king was talking with Ge·hā′zī the servant of the man of God, saying, "Tell me all the great things that E·lī′shà has done." 5 And while he was telling the king how E·lī′shà had restored the dead to life, behold, the woman whose son he had restored to life appealed to the king for her house and her land. And Ge·hā′zī said, "My lord, O king, here is the woman, and here is her son whom Elisha restored to life." 6 And when the king asked the woman, she told him. So the king appointed an official for her, saying, "Restore all that was hers, together with all the produce of the fields from the day that she left the land until now."

7 Now E·lī′shà came to Damascus. Ben-hā′dad the king of Syria was sick; and when it was told him, "The man of God has come here," 8 the king said to Haz′à·el, "Take a present with you and go to meet the man of God, and inquire of the LORD through him, saying, 'Shall I recover from this sickness?'" 9 So Haz′à·el went to meet him, and took a present with him, all kinds of goods of Damascus, forty camel loads. When he came and stood before him, he said, "Your son Ben-hā′dad king of Syria has sent me to you, saying, 'Shall I recover from this sickness?'" 10 And E·lī′shà said to him, "Go, say to him, 'You shall certainly recover'; but the LORD has shown me that he shall certainly die." 11 And he fixed his gaze and stared at him, until he was ashamed. And the man of God wept. 12 And Haz′à·el said, "Why does my lord weep?" He answered, "Because I know the evil that you will do to the people of Israel; you will set on fire their fortresses, and you will slay their young men with the sword, and dash in pieces their little ones, and rip up their women with child." 13 And Haz′à·el said, "What is your servant, who is but a dog, that he should do this great thing?" E·lī′shà answered, "The LORD has shown me that you are to be king over Syria." 14 Then he

departed from E·li'shä, and came to his master, who said to him, "What did Elisha say to you?" And he answered, "He told me that you would certainly recover." ¹⁵ But on the morrow he took the coverlet and dipped it in water and spread it over his face, till he died. And Haz'a·el became king in his stead.

16 In the fifth year of Jō'ràm the son of A'hab, king of Israel,ᵍ Je·hō'-ràm the son of Je·hosh'a·phat, king of Judah, began to reign. ¹⁷ He was thirty-two years old when he became king, and he reigned eight years in Jerusalem. ¹⁸And he walked in the way of the kings of Israel, as the house of A'hab had done, for the daughter of Ahab was his wife. And he did what was evil in the sight of the LORD. ¹⁹ Yet the LORD would not destroy Judah, for the sake of David his servant, since he promised to give a lamp to him and to his sons for ever.

20 In his days E'dom revolted from the rule of Judah, and set up a king of their own. ²¹ Then Jō'ràm passed over to Zā'ir with all his chariots, and rose by night, and he and his chariot commanders smote the E'dom·ites who had surrounded him; but his army fled home. ²² So E'dom revolted from the rule of Judah to this day. Then Lib'-nàh revolted at the same time. ²³ Now the rest of the acts of Jō'ràm, and all that he did, are they not written in the Book of the Chronicles of the Kings of Judah? ²⁴ So Jō'ràm slept with his fathers, and was buried with his fathers in the city of David; and A·hà-zi'àh his son reigned in his stead.

25 In the twelfth year of Jō'ràm the son of A'hab, king of Israel, A·hà-zi'àh the son of Je·hō'ràm, king of Judah, began to reign. ²⁶A·hà·zi'àh was twenty-two years old when he began to reign, and he reigned one year in Jerusalem. His mother's name was Ath·a·li'àh; she was a granddaughter of Om'ri king of Israel. ²⁷ He also walked in the way of the house of A'hab, and did what was evil in the sight of the LORD, as the house of Ahab had done, for he was son-in-law to the house of Ahab.

28 He went with Jō'ràm the son of A'hab to make war against Haz'a·el king of Syria at Rā'moth-gil'ē·àd, where the Syrians wounded Joram. ²⁹And King Jō'ràm returned to be

healed in Jez'rē·èl of the wounds which the Syrians had given him at Rā'màh, when he fought against Haz'-à·el king of Syria. And A·hà·zi'àh the son of Je·hō'ràm king of Judah went down to see Joram the son of A'hab in Jezreel, because he was sick.

9 Then E·li'shà the prophet called one of the sons of the prophets and said to him, "Gird up your loins, and take this flask of oil in your hand, and go to Rā'moth-gil'ē·àd. ²And when you arrive, look there for Jē'hū the son of Je·hosh'à·phat, son of Nim'shî; and go in and bid him rise from among his fellows, and lead him to an inner chamber. ³ Then take the flask of oil, and pour it on his head, and say, 'Thus says the LORD, I anoint you king over Israel.' Then open the door and flee; do not tarry."

4 So the young man, the prophet,ʰ went to Rā'moth-gil'ē·àd. ⁵And when he came, behold, the commanders of the army were in council; and he said, "I have an errand to you, O commander." And Jē'hū said, "To which of us all?" And he said, "To you, O commander." ⁶ So he arose, and went into the house; and the young man poured oil on his head, saying to him, "Thus says the LORD the God of Israel, I anoint you king over the people of the LORD, over Israel. ⁷And you shall strike down the house of A'hab your master, that I may avenge on Jez'e·bèl the blood of my servants the prophets, and the blood of all the servants of the LORD. ⁸ For the whole house of A'hab shall perish; and I will cut off from Ahab every male, bond or free, in Israel. ⁹And I will make the house of A'hab like the house of Jer·ò·bō'àm the son of Nē'bat, and like the house of Bā'à·shà the son of A·hi'jàh. ¹⁰And the dogs shall eat Jez'e·bèl in the territory of Jez'rē·èl, and none shall bury her." Then he opened the door, and fled.

11 When Jē'hū came out to the servants of his master, they said to him, "Is all well? Why did this mad fellow come to you?" And he said to them, "You know the fellow and his talk." ¹²And they said, "That is not true; tell us now." And he said, "Thus and so he spoke to me, saying, 'Thus says the LORD, I anoint you king over Israel.' " ¹³ Then in haste every man of them took his garment, and put it under him on the bareⁱ steps, and they

ᵍ Gk Syr: Heb *Israel, Jehoshaphat being king of Judah*
ʰ Gk Syr: Heb *the young man, the young man, the prophet*
ⁱ The meaning of the Hebrew word is uncertain
8.17-24: 2 Chron 21.5-10, 20.   **8.24-29:** 2 Chron 22.1-6.   **9.1-10, 36:** 2 Chron 22.7-9.

blew the trumpet, and proclaimed, "Jē'hū is king."

14 Thus Jē'hū the son of Je·hosh'a·phat the son of Nim'shi conspired against Jō'ram. (Now Joram with all Israel had been on guard at Rā'moth-gil'ē·ad against Haz'ā·el king of Syria; 15 but King Jō'ram had returned to be healed in Jez'rē·el of the wounds which the Syrians had given him, when he fought with Haz'ā·el king of Syria.) So Jē'hū said, "If this is your mind, then let no one slip out of the city to go and tell the news in Jezreel." 16 Then Jē'hū mounted his chariot, and went to Jez'rē·el, for Jō'ram lay there. And A·hà·zī'ah king of Judah had come down to visit Joram.

17 Now the watchman was standing on the tower in Jez'rē·el, and he spied the company of Jē'hū as he came, and said, "I see a company." And Jō'ram said, "Take a horseman, and send to meet them, and let him say, 'Is it peace?'" 18 So a man on horseback went to meet him, and said, "Thus says the king, 'Is it peace?'" And Jē'hū said, "What have you to do with peace? Turn round and ride behind me." And the watchman reported, saying, "The messenger reached them, but he is not coming back." 19 Then he sent out a second horseman, who came to them, and said, "Thus the king has said, 'Is it peace?'" And Jē'hū answered, "What have you to do with peace? Turn round and ride behind me." 20 Again the watchman reported, "He reached them, but he is not coming back. And the driving is like the driving of Jē'hū the son of Nim'shi; for he drives furiously."

21 Jō'ram said, "Make ready." And they made ready his chariot. Then Joram king of Israel and A·hà·zī'ah king of Judah set out, each in his chariot, and went to meet Jē'hū, and met him at the property of Nā'both the Jez'rē·ē·lite. 22 And when Jō'ram saw Jē'hū, he said, "Is it peace, Jehu?" He answered, "What peace can there be, so long as the harlotries and the sorceries of your mother Jez'ē·bēl are so many?" 23 Then Jō'ram reined about and fled, saying to A·hà·zī'ah, "Treachery, O Ahaziah!" 24 And Jē'hū drew his bow with his full strength, and shot Jō'ram between the shoulders, so that the arrow pierced his heart, and he sank in his chariot. 25 Jē'hū said to Bid'kär his aide, "Take him up, and cast him on the plot of ground belonging to Nā'both the Jez'-

rē·ē·lite; for remember, when you and I rode side by side behind A'hab his father, how the LORD uttered this oracle against him: 26 'As surely as I saw yesterday the blood of Nā'both and the blood of his sons—says the LORD—I will requite you on this plot of ground.' Now therefore take him up and cast him on the plot of ground, in accordance with the word of the LORD."

27 When A·hà·zī'ah the king of Judah saw this, he fled in the direction of Beth-hag'gàn. And Jē'hū pursued him, and said, "Shoot him also"; and they shot him*j* in the chariot at the ascent of Gür, which is by Ib'lē·àm. And he fled to Mè·gid'dō, and died there. 28 His servants carried him in a chariot to Jerusalem, and buried him in his tomb with his fathers in the city of David.

29 In the eleventh year of Jō'ram the son of A'hab, A·hà·zī'ah began to reign over Judah.

30 When Jē'hū came to Jez'rē·el, Jez'ē·bēl heard of it; and she painted her eyes, and adorned her head, and looked out of the window. 31 And as Jē'hū entered the gate, she said, "Is it peace, you Zim'ri, murderer of your master?" 32 And he lifted up his face to the window, and said, "Who is on my side? Who?" Two or three eunuchs looked out at him. 33 He said, "Throw her down." So they threw her down; and some of her blood spattered on the wall and on the horses, and they trampled on her. 34 Then he went in and ate and drank; and he said, "See now to this cursed woman, and bury her; for she is a king's daughter." 35 But when they went to bury her, they found no more of her than the skull and the feet and the palms of her hands. 36 When they came back and told him, he said, "This is the word of the LORD, which he spoke by his servant E·li'jàh the Tish'bīte, 'In the territory of Jez'rē·el the dogs shall eat the flesh of Jez'ē·bēl; 37 and the corpse of Jez'ē·bēl shall be as dung upon the face of the field in the territory of Jez'rē·el, so that no one can say, This is Jezebel."

10 Now A'hab had seventy sons in Sà·mâr'i·à. So Jē'hū wrote letters, and sent them to Samaria, to the rulers of the city,*k* to the elders, and to the guardians of the sons of Ahab, saying, 2 "Now then, as soon as this letter comes to you, seeing your master's sons are with you, and there are with

j Syr Vg Compare Gk: Heb lacks *and they shot him*   *k* Gk Vg: Heb *Jezreel*
9.25: 1 Kings 21.19.   **9.36:** 1 Kings 21.23.

you chariots and horses, fortified cities also, and weapons, 3 select the best and fittest of your master's sons and set him on his father's throne, and fight for your master's house." 4 But they were exceedingly afraid, and said, "Behold, the two kings could not stand before him; how then can we stand?" 5 So he who was over the palace, and he who was over the city, together with the elders and the guardians, sent to Jē′hū, saying, "We are your servants, and we will do all that you bid us. We will not make any one king; do whatever is good in your eyes." 6 Then he wrote to them a second letter, saying, "If you are on my side, and if you are ready to obey me, take the heads of your master's sons, and come to me at Jez′rē·ĕl tomorrow at this time." Now the king's sons, seventy persons, were with the great men of the city, who were bringing them up. 7 And when the letter came to them, they took the king's sons, and slew them, seventy persons, and put their heads in baskets, and sent them to him at Jez′rē·ĕl. 8 When the messenger came and told him, "They have brought the heads of the king's sons," he said, "Lay them in two heaps at the entrance of the gate until the morning." 9 Then in the morning, when he went out, he stood, and said to all the people, "You are innocent. It was I who conspired against my master, and slew him; but who struck down all these? 10 Know then that there shall fall to the earth nothing of the word of the LORD, which the LORD spoke concerning the house of A′hab; for the LORD has done what he said by his servant E.lī′jäh." 11 So Jē′hū slew all that remained of the house of A′hab in Jez′rē·ĕl, all his great men, and his familiar friends, and his priests, until he left him none remaining.

12 Then he set out and went to Sà·mâr′i·à. On the way, when he was at Beth-ek′ed of the Shepherds, 13 Jē′hū met the kinsmen of À·hà·zī′äh king of Judah, and he said, "Who are you?" And they answered, "We are the kinsmen of Ahaziah, and we came down to visit the royal princes and the sons of the queen mother." 14 He said, "Take them alive." And they took them alive, and slew them at the pit of Beth-ek′ed, forty-two persons, and he spared none of them.

15 And when he departed from there, he met Je·hon′à·dab the son of Rē′chab coming to meet him; and he greeted him, and said to him, "Is your heart true to my heart as mine is to yours?"*l* And Je·hon′à·dab answered, "It is." Jē′hū said,*m* "If it is, give me your hand." So he gave him his hand. And Jehu took him up with him into the chariot. 16 And he said, "Come with me, and see my zeal for the LORD." So he*n* had him ride in his chariot. 17 And when he came to Sà·mâr′i·à, he slew all that remained to A′hab in Samaria, till he had wiped them out, according to the word of the LORD which he spoke to E·lī′jäh.

18 Then Jē′hū assembled all the people, and said to them, "A′hab served Bā′ăl a little; but Jehu will serve him much. 19 Now therefore call to me all the prophets of Bā′ăl, all his worshipers and all his priests; let none be missing, for I have a great sacrifice to offer to Baal; whoever is missing shall not live." But Jē′hū did it with cunning in order to destroy the worshipers of Bā′ăl. 20 And Jē′hū ordered, "Sanctify a solemn assembly for Bā′ăl." So they proclaimed it. 21 And Jē′hū sent throughout all Israel; and all the worshipers of Bā′ăl came, so that there was not a man left who did not come. And they entered the house of Baal, and the house of Baal was filled from one end to the other. 22 He said to him who was in charge of the wardrobe, "Bring out the vestments for all the worshipers of Bā′ăl." So he brought out the vestments for them. 23 Then Jē′hū went into the house of Bā′ăl with Je·hon′à·dab the son of Rē′chab; and he said to the worshipers of Baal, "Search, and see that there is no servant of the LORD here among you, but only the worshipers of Baal." 24 Then he*o* went in to offer sacrifices and burnt offerings.

Now Jē′hū had stationed eighty men outside, and said, "The man who allows any of those whom I give into your hands to escape shall forfeit his life." 25 So as soon as he had made an end of offering the burnt offering, Jē′hū said to the guard and to the officers, "Go in and slay them; let not a man escape." So when they put them to the sword, the guard and the officers cast them out and went into the inner room*p* of the house of Bā′ăl 26 and they brought out the pillar that was in the house of Bā′ăl, and burned it. 27 And they demolished the pillar of Bā′ăl,

l Gk: Heb *Is it right with your heart, as my heart is with your heart?*
m Gk: Heb lacks *Jehu said*   *n* Gk Syr Tg: Heb *they*
o Gk Compare verse 25: Heb *they*   *p* Cn: Heb *city*

and demolished the house of Baal, and made it a latrine to this day.

28 Thus Jĕ′hū wiped out Bā′ăl from Israel. 29 But Jĕ′hū did not turn aside from the sins of Jer·o·bō′ăm the son of Nĕ′bat, which he made Israel to sin, the golden calves that were in Beth′ĕl, and in Dan. 30And the LORD said to Jĕ′hū, "Because you have done well in carrying out what is right in my eyes, and have done to the house of Ā′hab according to all that was in my heart, your sons of the fourth generation shall sit on the throne of Israel." 31 But Jĕ′hū was not careful to walk in the law of the LORD the God of Israel with all his heart; he did not turn from the sins of Jer·o·bō′ăm, which he made Israel to sin.

32 In those days the LORD began to cut off parts of Israel. Haz′ă·el defeated them throughout the territory of Israel: 33 from the Jordan eastward, all the land of Gilead, the Gadites, and the Reubenites, and the Mà·nas′sites, from Ā·rō′ĕr, which is by the valley of the Är′non, that is, Gilead and Bā′-shän. 34 Now the rest of the acts of Jĕ′hū, and all that he did, and all his might, are they not written in the Book of the Chronicles of the Kings of Israel? 35 So Jĕ′hū slept with his fathers, and they buried him in Sà-mâr′i·à. And Je·hō′à·haz his son reigned in his stead. 36 The time that Jĕ′hū reigned over Israel in Sà·mâr′i·à was twenty-eight years.

11 Now when Ath·à·lī′ăh the mother of Ā·hà·zī′ăh saw that her son was dead, she arose and destroyed all the royal family. 2 But Je·hosh′ĕ·bà, the daughter of King Jō′răm, sister of Ā·hà·zī′ăh, took Jō′ash the son of Ahaziah, and stole him away from among the king's sons who were about to be slain, and she put*q* him and his nurse in a bedchamber. Thus she*r* hid him from Ath·à·lī′ăh, so that he was not slain; 3 and he remained with her six years, hid in the house of the LORD, while Ath·à·lī′ăh reigned over the land.

4 But in the seventh year Je·hoi′à·dà sent and brought the captains of the Car′i·tēs and of the guards, and had them come to him in the house of the LORD; and he made a covenant with them and put them under oath in the house of the LORD, and he showed them the king's son. 5And he commanded them, "This is the thing that you shall do: one third of you, those

who come off duty on the sabbath and guard the king's house 6 (another third being at the gate Sûr and a third at the gate behind the guards), shall guard the palace; 7 and the two divisions of you, which come on duty in force on the sabbath and guard the house of the LORD,*s* shall surround the king, each with his weapons in his hand; and whoever approaches the ranks is to be slain. Be with the king when he goes out and when he comes in."

9 The captains did according to all that Je·hoi′à·dà the priest commanded, and each brought his men who were to go off duty on the sabbath, with those who were to come on duty on the sabbath, and came to Jehoiada the priest. 10And the priest delivered to the captains the spears and shields that had been King David's, which were in the house of the LORD; 11 and the guards stood, every man with his weapons in his hand, from the south side of the house to the north side of the house, around the altar and the house.*t* 12 Then he brought out the king's son, and put the crown upon him, and gave him the testimony; and they proclaimed him king, and anointed him; and they clapped their hands, and said, "Long live the king!"

13 When Ath·à·lī′ăh heard the noise of the guard and of the people, she went into the house of the LORD to the people; 14 and when she looked, there was the king standing by the pillar, according to the custom, and the captains and the trumpeters beside the king, and all the people of the land rejoicing and blowing trumpets. And Ath·à·lī′ăh rent her clothes, and cried, "Treason! treason!" 15 Then Je·hoi′à-dà the priest commanded the captains who were set over the army, "Bring her out between the ranks; and slay with the sword any one who follows her." For the priest said, "Let her not be slain in the house of the LORD." 16 So they laid hands on her; and she went through the horses' entrance to the king's house, and there she was slain.

17 And Je·hoi′à·dà made a covenant between the LORD and the king and people, that they should be the LORD's people; and also between the king and the people. 18 Then all the people of the land went to the house of the Bā′al, and tore it down; his altars and his

---

q With 2 Chron 22.11: Heb lacks *and she put*
r Gk Syr Vg Compare 2 Chron 22.11: Heb *they*   *s* Heb *the LORD to the king*
t Heb *the house to the king*
11.1-20: 2 Chron 22.10-23.21.

images they broke in pieces, and they slew Mat′tan the priest of Baal before the altars. And the priest posted watchmen over the house of the LORD. ¹⁹And he took the captains, the Car′i-tēs, the guards, and all the people of the land; and they brought the king down from the house of the LORD, marching through the gate of the guards to the king's house. And he took his seat on the throne of the kings. ²⁰ So all the people of the land rejoiced; and the city was quiet after Ath·a·li′ah had been slain with the sword at the king's house.

21ᵘ Je·hō′ash was seven years old when he began to reign.

12 In the seventh year of Jē′hū Je·hō′ash began to reign, and he reigned forty years in Jerusalem. His mother's name was Zib′i·ah of Beer-sheba. ²And Je·hō′ash did what was right in the eyes of the LORD all his days, because Je·hoi′a·dà the priest instructed him. ³ Nevertheless the high places were not taken away; the people continued to sacrifice and burn incense on the high places.

4 Je·hō′ash said to the priests, "All the money of the holy things which is brought into the house of the LORD, the money for which each man is assessed—the money from the assessment of persons—and the money which a man's heart prompts him to bring into the house of the LORD, ⁵ let the priests take, each from his acquaintance; and let them repair the house wherever any need of repairs is discovered." ⁶ But by the twenty-third year of King Je·hō′ash the priests had made no repairs on the house. ⁷ Therefore King Je·hō′ash summoned Je·hoi′a·dà the priest and the other priests and said to them, "Why are you not repairing the house? Now therefore take no more money from your acquaintances, but hand it over for the repair of the house." ⁸ So the priests agreed that they should take no more money from the people, and that they should not repair the house.

9 Then Je·hoi′a·dà the priest took a chest, and bored a hole in the lid of it, and set it beside the altar on the right side as one entered the house of the LORD; and the priests who guarded the threshold put in it all the money that was brought into the house of the LORD. ¹⁰And whenever they saw that there was much money in the chest, the king's secretary and the high priest came up and they counted

and tied up in bags the money that was found in the house of the LORD. ¹¹ Then they would give the money that was weighed out into the hands of the workmen who had the oversight of the house of the LORD; and they paid it out to the carpenters and the builders who worked upon the house of the LORD, ¹² and to the masons and the stonecutters, as well as to buy timber and quarried stone for making repairs on the house of the LORD, and for any outlay upon the repairs of the house. ¹³ But there were not made the the house of the LORD basins of silver, snuffers, bowls, trumpets, or any vessels of gold, or of silver, from the money that was brought into the house of the LORD, ¹⁴ for that was given to the workmen who were repairng the house of the LORD with it. ¹⁵And they did not ask an accounting from the men into whose hand they delivered the money to pay out to the workmen, for they dealt honestly. ¹⁶ The money from the guilt offerings and the money from the sin offerings was not brought into the house of the LORD; it belonged to the priests.

17 At that time Haz′a·el king of Syria went up and fought against Gath, and took it. But when Hazael set his face to go up against Jerusalem, ¹⁸ Je·hō′ash king of Judah took all the votive gifts that Je·hosh′a·phat and Je·hō′ram and A·ha·zi′ah, his fathers, the kings of Judah, had dedicated, and his own votive gifts, and all the gold that was found in the treasuries of the house of the LORD and of the king's house, and sent these to Haz′a·el king of Syria. Then Hazael went away from Jerusalem.

19 Now the rest of the acts of Jō′ash, and all that he did, are they not written in the Book of the Chronicles of the Kings of Judah? ²⁰ His servants arose and made a conspiracy, and slew Jō′ash in the house of Mil′lō, on the way that goes down to Sil′la. ²¹ It was Jō′za·cär the son of Shim′ē-ath and Je·hō′za·bad the son of Shō′mèr, his servants, who struck him down, so that he died. And they buried him with his fathers in the city of David, and Am·a·zi′ah his son reigned in his stead.

13 In the twenty-third year of Jō′ash the son of A·ha·zi′ah, king of Judah, Je·hō′a·haz the son of Jē′hū began to reign over Israel in Sà·már′i·à, and he reigned seventeen years. ² He did what was evil in the sight of the

LORD, and followed the sins of Jer·ŏ-bō′ăm the son of Ne′bat, which he made Israel to sin; he did not depart from them. ³And the anger of the LORD was kindled against Israel, and he gave them continually into the hand of Haz′ȧ·el king of Syria and into the hand of Ben-hā′dad the son of Hazael. ⁴ Then Je·hō′ȧ·haz besought the LORD, and the LORD hearkened to him; for he saw the oppression of Israel, how the king of Syria oppressed them. ⁵ (Therefore the LORD gave Israel a savior, so that they escaped from the hand of the Syrians; and the people of Israel dwelt in their homes as formerly. ⁶ Nevertheless they did not depart from the sins of the house of Jer·ŏ-bō′ăm, which he made Israel to sin, but walked*ʸ* in them; and the Ȧ·shē′-rȧh also remained in Sȧ·mâr′i·ȧ.) ⁷ For there was not left to Je·hō′ȧ·haz an army of more than fifty horsemen and ten chariots and ten thousand footmen; for the king of Syria had destroyed them and made them like the dust at threshing. ⁸ Now the rest of the acts of Je·hō′ȧ·haz and all that he did, and his might, are they not written in the Book of the Chronicles of the Kings of Israel? ⁹ So Je·hō′ȧ·haz slept with his fathers, and they buried him in Sȧ·mâr′i·ȧ; and Jō′ash his son reigned in his stead.

10 In the thirty-seventh year of Jō′ash king of Judah Je·hō′ash the son of Je·hō′ȧ·haz began to reign over Israel in Sȧ·mâr′i·ȧ, and he reigned sixteen years. ¹¹ He also did what was evil in the sight of the LORD; he did not depart from all the sins of Jer·ŏ-bō′ăm the son of Ne′bat, which he made Israel to sin, but he walked in them. ¹² Now the rest of the acts of Jō′ash, and all that he did, and the might with which he fought against Am·a·zī′ah king of Judah, are they not written in the Book of the Chronicles of the Kings of Israel? ¹³ So Jō′ash slept with his fathers, and Jer·ŏ-bō′ăm sat upon his throne; and Joash was buried in Sȧ·mâr′i·ȧ with the kings of Israel.

14 Now when E·lī′shȧ had fallen sick with the illness of which he was to die, Jō′ash king of Israel went down to him, and wept before him, crying, "My father, my father! The chariots of Israel and its horsemen!" ¹⁵And E·lī′shȧ said to him, "Take a bow and arrows"; so he took a bow and arrows. ¹⁶ Then he said to the king of Israel, "Draw the bow"; and he drew it. And

E·lī′shȧ laid his hands upon the king's hands. ¹⁷And he said, "Open the window eastward"; and he opened it. Then E·lī′shȧ said, "Shoot"; and he shot. And he said, "The LORD's arrow of victory, the arrow of victory over Syria! For you shall fight the Syrians in A′phek until you have made an end of them." ¹⁸And he said, "Take the arrows"; and he took them. And he said to the king of Israel, "Strike the ground with them"; and he struck three times, and stopped. ¹⁹ Then the man of God was angry with him, and said, "You should have struck five or six times; then you would have struck down Syria until you had made an end of it, but now you will strike down Syria only three times."

20 So E·lī′shȧ died, and they buried him. Now bands of Mō′ab·ites used to invade the land in the spring of the year. ²¹And as a man was being buried, lo, a marauding band was seen and the man was cast into the grave of E·lī′shȧ; and as soon as the man touched the bones of Elisha, he revived, and stood on his feet.

22 Now Haz′ȧ·el king of Syria oppressed Israel all the days of Je·hō′ȧ-haz. ²³ But the LORD was gracious to them and had compassion on them, and he turned toward them, because of his covenant with Abraham, Isaac, and Jacob, and would not destroy them; nor has he cast them from his presence until now.

24 When Haz′ȧ·el king of Syria died, Ben-hā′dad his son became king in his stead. ²⁵ Then Je·hō′ash the son of Je·hō′ȧ·haz took again from Ben-hā′dad the son of Haz′ȧ·el the cities which he had taken from Jehoahaz his father in war. Three times Jō′ash defeated him and recovered the cities of Israel.

14 In the second year of Jō′ash son of Jō′ȧ·haz, king of Israel, Am·ȧ·zī′ah the son of Joash, king of Judah, began to reign. ² He was twenty-five years old when he began to reign, and he reigned twenty-nine years in Jerusalem. His mother's name was Je·hō·ad′din of Jerusalem. ³And he did what was right in the eyes of the LORD, yet not like David his father; he did in all things as Jō′ash his father had done. ⁴ But the high places were not removed; the people still sacrificed and burned incense on the high places. ⁵And as soon as the royal power was firmly in his hand he killed his servants who had slain the king his father. ⁶ But

---

ʸ Gk Syr Tg Vg: Heb *he walked*
14.2-6: 2 Chron 25.1-4.

he did not put to death the children of the murderers; according to what is written in the book of the law of Moses, where the LORD commanded, "The fathers shall not be put to death for the children, or the children be put to death for the fathers; but every man shall die for his own sin."

7 He killed ten thousand E'dom-ites in the Valley of Salt and took Sē'là by storm, and called it Jok'thē-el, which is its name to this day.

8 Then Am-à-zī'àh sent messengers to Je-hō'ash the son of Je-hō'à-haz, son of Jē'hū, king of Israel, saying, "Come, let us look one another in the face." 9And Je-hō'ash king of Israel sent word to Am-à-zī'àh king of Judah, "A thistle on Lebanon sent to a cedar on Lebanon, saying, 'Give your daughter to my son for a wife'; and a wild beast of Lebanon passed by and trampled down the thistle. 10 You have indeed smitten E'dóm, and your heart has lifted you up. Be content with your glory, and stay at home; for why should you provoke trouble so that you fall, you and Judah with you?"

11 But Am-à-zī'àh would not listen. So Je-hō'ash king of Israel went up, and he and Amaziah king of Judah faced one another in battle at Beth-shē'mesh, which belongs to Judah. 12And Judah was defeated by Israel, and every man fled to his home. 13And Je-hō'ash king of Israel captured Am-à-zī'àh king of Judah, the son of Jehoash, son of À-ha-zī'àh, at Beth-shē'mesh, and came to Jerusalem, and broke down the wall of Jerusalem for four hundred cubits, from the E'phrà-im Gate to the Corner Gate. 14And he seized all the gold and silver, and all the vessels that were found in the house of the LORD and in the treasuries of the king's house, also hostages, and he returned to Sà-mâr'i-à.

15 Now the rest of the acts of Je-hō'ash which he did, and his might, and how he fought with Am-à-zī'àh king of Judah, are they not written in the Book of the Chronicles of the Kings of Israel? 16And Je-hō'ash slept with his fathers, and was buried in Sà-mâr'-i-à with the kings of Israel; and Jer-ó-bō'àm his son reigned in his stead.

17 Am-à-zī'àh the son of Jō'ash, king of Judah, lived fifteen years after the death of Je-hō'ash son of Je-hō'à-haz, king of Israel. 18 Now the rest of the deeds of Am-à-zī'àh, are they not written in the Book of the Chronicles of the Kings of Judah? 19And they

made a conspiracy against him in Jerusalem, and he fled to Lā'chish. But they sent after him to Lachish, and slew him there. 20And they brought him upon horses; and he was buried in Jerusalem with his fathers in the city of David. 21And all the people of Judah took Az-à-rī'àh, who was sixteen years old, and made him king instead of his father Am-à-zī'àh. 22 He built E'lath and restored it to Judah, after the king slept with his fathers.

23 In the fifteenth year of Am-à-zī'àh the son of Jō'ash, king of Judah, Jer-ó-bō'àm the son of Joash, king of Israel, began to reign in Sà-mâr'i-à, and he reigned forty-one years. 24And he did what was evil in the sight of the LORD; he did not depart from all the sins of Jer-ó-bō'àm the son of Nē'bat, which he made Israel to sin. 25 He restored the border of Israel from the entrance of Hā'math as far as the Sea of the Ar'à-bàh, according to the word of the LORD, the God of Israel, which he spoke by his servant Jonah the son of À-mit'tài, the prophet, who was from Gath-hē'phér. 26 For the LORD saw that the affliction of Israel was very bitter, for there was none left, bond or free, and there was none to help Israel. 27 But the LORD had not said that he would |blot out the name of Israel from under heaven, so he saved them by the hand of Jer-ó-bō'àm the son of Jō'ash.

28 Now the rest of the acts of Jer-ó-bō'àm, and all that he did, and his might, how he fought, and how he recovered for Israel Damascus and Hā'math, which had belonged to Judah, are they not written in the Book of the Chronicles of the Kings of Israel? 29And Jer-ó-bō'àm slept with his fathers, the kings of Israel, and Zech-à-rī'àh his son reigned in his stead.

15 In the twenty-seventh year of Jer-ó-bō'àm king of Israel Az-à-rī'àh the son of Am-à-zī'àh, king of Judah, began to reign. 2 He was sixteen years old when he began to reign, and he reigned fifty-two years in Jerusalem. His mother's name was Jec-ó-lī'àh of Jerusalem. 3And he did what was right in the eyes of the LORD, according to all that his father Am-à-zī'àh had done. 4 Nevertheless the high places were not taken away; the people still sacrificed and burned incense on the high places. 5And the LORD smote the king, so that he was a leper to the day of his death, and he dwelt in a

14.7: 2 Chron 25.11.   14.8-14: 2 Chron 25.17-24.   14.17-20: 2 Chron 25.25-28.
14.21-22: 2 Chron 26.1-2.   15.2-3: 2 Chron 26.3-4.   15.5-7: 2 Chron 26.20-23.

separate house. And Jō′thăm the king's son was over the household, governing the people of the land. 6 Now the rest of the acts of Az·à·rī′àh, and all that he did, are they not written in the Book of the Chronicles of the Kings of Judah? 7And Az·à·rī′àh slept with his fathers, and they buried him with his fathers in the city of David, and Jō′thăm his son reigned in his stead.

8 In the thirty-eighth year of Az·à·rī′àh king of Judah Zech·à·rī′àh the son of Jer·ò·bō′àm reigned over Israel in Sà·mâr′i·à six months. 9And he did what was evil in the sight of the LORD, as his fathers had done. He did not depart from the sins of Jer·ò·bō′àm the son of Nē′bat, which he made Israel to sin. 10 Shal′lùm the son of Jā′besh conspired against him, and struck him down at Ib′lē·àm,ʷ and killed him, and reigned in his stead. 11 Now the rest of the deeds of Zech·à·rī′àh, behold, they are written in the Book of the Chronicles of the Kings of Israel. 12 (This was the promise of the LORD which he gave to Jē′hū, "Your sons shall sit upon the throne of Israel to the fourth generation." And so it came to pass.)

13 Shal′lùm the son of Jā′besh began to reign in the thirty-ninth year of Uz·zī′àh king of Judah, and he reigned one month in Sà·mâr′i·à. 14 Then Men′à·hem the son of Gā′di came up from Tîr′zàh and came to Sà·mâr′i·à, and he struck down Shal′lùm the son of Jā′besh in Samaria and slew him, and reigned in his stead. 15 Now the rest of the deeds of Shal′lùm, and the conspiracy which he made, behold, they are written in the Book of the Chronicles of the Kings of Israel. 16 At that time Men′à·hem sacked Tap′pū·àhˣ and all who were in it and its territory from Tîr′zàh on; because they did not open it to him, therefore he sacked it, and he ripped up all the women in it who were with child.

17 In the thirty-ninth year of Az·à·rī′àh king of Judah Men′à·hem the son of Gā′di began to reign over Israel, and he reigned ten years in Sà·mâr′i·à. 18And he did what was evil in the sight of the LORD; he did not depart all his days from all the sins of Jer·ò·bō′àm the son of Nē′bat, which he made Israel to sin. 19 Pül the king of Assyria came against the land; and Men′à·hem gave Pul a thousand talents of silver, that he might help him to

confirm his hold of the royal power. 20 Men′à·hem exacted the money from Israel, that is, from all the wealthy men, fifty shekels of silver from every man, to give to the king of Assyria. So the king of Assyria turned back, and did not stay there in the land. 21 Now the rest of the deeds of Men′à·hem, and all that he did, are they not written in the Book of the Chronicles of the Kings of Israel? 22And Men′à·hem slept with his fathers, and Pek·à·hī′àh his son reigned in his stead.

23 In the fiftieth year of Az·à·rī′àh king of Judah Pek·à·hī′àh the son of Men′à·hem began to reign over Israel in Sà·mâr′i·à, and he reigned two years. 24And he did what was evil in the sight of the LORD; he did not turn away from the sins of Jer·ò·bō′àm the son of Nē′bat, which he made Israel to sin. 25And Pē′kàh the son of Rem·à·lī′àh, his captain, conspired against him with fifty men of the Gileadites, and slew him in Sà·mâr′i·à, in the citadel of the king's house;ʸ he slew him, and reigned in his stead. 26 Now the rest of the deeds of Pek·à·hī′àh, and all that he did, behold, they are written in the Book of the Chronicles of the Kings of Israel.

27 In the fifty-second year of Az·à·rī′àh king of Judah Pē′kàh the son of Rem·à·lī′àh began to reign over Israel in Sà·mâr′i·à, and reigned twenty years. 28And he did what was evil in the sight of the LORD; he did not depart from the sins of Jer·ò·bō′àm the son of Nē′bat, which he made Israel to sin.

29 In the days of Pē′kàh king of Israel Tig′lath-pi·lē′ŝer king of Assyria came and captured I′jon, Ä′bél-beth-mā′à·càh, Jà·nō′àh, Kē′desh, Hā′zôr, Gilead, and Galilee, all the land of Naph′tà·li; and he carried the people captive to Assyria. 30 Then Hō·shē′à the son of Ē′làh made a conspiracy against Pē′kàh the son of Rem·à·lī′àh, and struck him down, and slew him, and reigned in his stead, in the twentieth year of Jō′thăm the son of Uz·zī′àh. 31 Now the rest of the acts of Pē′kàh, and all that he did, behold, they are written in the Book of the Chronicles of the Kings of Israel.

32 In the second year of Pē′kàh the son of Rem·à·lī′àh, king of Israel, Jō′thăm the son of Uz·zī′àh, king of Judah, began to reign. 33 He was twenty-five years old when he began to reign, and he reigned sixteen years

---

ʷ Gk Compare 9.27: Heb *before the people*   ˣ Compare Gk: Heb *Tiphsah*
ʸ Heb adds *Argob and Arieh*, which probably belong to the list of places in verse 29
15.33-35: 2 Chron 27.1-3.

in Jerusalem. His mother's name was Je·rü′shà the daughter of Zā′dok. 34And he did what was right in the eyes of the LORD, according to all that his father Uz·zi′ah had done. 35 Nevertheless the high places were not removed; the people still sacrificed and burned incense on the high places. He built the upper gate of the house of the LORD. 36 Now the rest of the acts of Jō′thàm, and all that he did, are they not written in the Book of the Chronicles of the Kings of Judah? 37 In those days the LORD began to send Rē′zin the king of Syria and Pē′kàh the son of Rem·à·li′àh against Judah. 38 Jō′thàm slept with his fathers, and was buried with his fathers in the city of David his father; and A′haz his son reigned in his stead.

16 In the seventeenth year of Pē′kàh the son of Rem·à·li′àh, A′haz the son of Jō′thàm, king of Judah, began to reign. 2A′haz was twenty years old when he began to reign, and he reigned sixteen years in Jerusalem. And he did not do what was right in the eyes of the LORD his God, as his father David had done, 3 but he walked in the way of the kings of Israel. He even burned his son as an offering,z according to the abominable practices of the nations whom the LORD drove out before the people of Israel. 4And he sacrificed and burned incense on the high places, and on the hills, and under every green tree.

5 Then Rē′zin king of Syria and Pē′kàh the son of Rem·à·li′àh, king of Israel, came up to wage war on Jerusalem, and they besieged A′haz but could not conquer him. 6At that timea the king of E′dòmb recovered E′lath for Edom,b and drove the men of Judah from Elath; and the E′dòm·ites came to Elath, where they dwell to this day. 7 So A′haz sent messengers to Tig′lath-pi·lē′sèr king of Assyria, saying, "I am your servant and your son. Come up, and rescue me from the hand of the king of Syria and from the hand of the king of Israel, who are attacking me." 8A′haz also took the silver and gold that was found in the house of the LORD and in the treasures of the king's house, and sent a present to the king of Assyria. 9And the king of Assyria hearkened to him; the king of Assyria marched up against Damascus, and took it, carrying its people captive to Kīr, and he killed Rē′zin. 10 When King A′haz went to Da-

mascus to meet Tig′lath-pi·lē′sèr king of Assyria, he saw the altar that was at Damascus. And King Ahaz sent to U·ri′áh the priest a model of the altar, and its pattern, exact in all its details. 11And U·ri′áh the priest built the altar; in accordance with all that King A′haz had sent from Damascus, so Uriah the priest made it, before King Ahaz arrived from Damascus. 12And when the king came from Damascus, the king viewed the altar. Then the king drew near to the altar, and went up on it, 13 and burned his burnt offering and his cereal offering, and poured his drink offering, and threw the blood of his peace offerings upon the altar. 14And the bronze altar which was before the LORD he removed from the front of the house, from the place between his altar and the house of the LORD, and put it on the north side of his altar. 15And King A′haz commanded U·ri′áh the priest, saying, "Upon the great altar burn the morning burnt offering, and the evening cereal offering, and the king's burnt offering, and his cereal offering, with the burnt offering of all the people of the land, and their cereal offering, and their drink offering; and throw upon it all the blood of the burnt offering, and all the blood of the sacrifice; but the bronze altar shall be for me to inquire by." 16 U·ri′áh the priest did all this, as King A′haz commanded.

17 And King A′haz cut off the frames of the stands, and removed the laver from them, and he took down the sea from off the bronze oxen that were under it, and put it upon a pediment of stone. 18And the covered way for the sabbath which had been built inside the palace, and the outer entrance for the king he removed fromc the house of the LORD, because of the king of Assyria. 19 Now the rest of the acts of A′haz which he did, are they not written in the Book of the Chronicles of the Kings of Judah? 20And A′haz slept with his fathers, and was buried with his fathers in the city of David; and Hez·é·ki′àh his son reigned in his stead.

17 In the twelfth year of A′haz king of Judah Hō·shē′à the son of E′láh began to reign in Sà·mâr′i·à over Israel, and he reigned nine years. 2And he did what was evil in the sight of the LORD, yet not as the kings of Israel who were before him. 3Against him came up Shal·màn·é′sèr king of

z Or made his son to pass through the fire　a Heb At that time Rezin
b Heb Aram (Syria)　c Cn: Heb turned to
15.38: 2 Chron 27.9.　16.2-4: 2 Chron 28.1-4.　16.20: 2 Chron 28.27.

Assyria; and Hō·shē′å became his vassal, and paid him tribute. 4 But the king of Assyria found treachery in Hō·shē′å; for he had sent messengers to Sō, king of Egypt, and offered no tribute to the king of Assyria, as he had done year by year; therefore the king of Assyria shut him up, and bound him in prison. 5 Then the king of Assyria invaded all the land and came to Så·mâr′i·å, and for three years he besieged it. 6 In the ninth year of Hō·shē′å the king of Assyria captured Så·mâr′i·å, and he carried the Israelites away to Assyria, and placed them in Hā′lǎh, and on the Hā′bôr, the river of Gō′zan, and in the cities of the Medes.

7 And this was so, because the people of Israel had sinned against the LORD their God, who had brought them up out of the land of Egypt from under the hand of Pharaoh king of Egypt, and had feared other gods 8 and walked in the customs of the nations whom the LORD drove out before the people of Israel, and in the customs which the kings of Israel had introduced.ᵈ 9And the people of Israel did secretly against the LORD their God things that were not right. They built for themselves high places at all their towns, from watchtower to fortified city; 10 they set up for themselves pillars and Ā·shē′rim on every high hill and under every green tree; 11 and there they burned incense on all the high places, as the nations did whom the LORD carried away before them. And they did wicked things, provoking the LORD to anger, 12 and they served idols, of which the LORD had said to them, "You shall not do this." 13 Yet the LORD warned Israel and Judah by every prophet and every seer, saying, "Turn from your evil ways and keep my commandments and my statutes, in accordance with all the law which I commanded your fathers, and which I sent to you by my servants the prophets." 14 But they would not listen, but were stubborn, as their fathers had been, who did not believe in the LORD their God. 15 They despised his statutes, and his covenant that he made with their fathers, and the warnings which he gave them. They went after false idols, and became false, and they followed the nations that were round about them, concerning whom the LORD had commanded them that they should not do like them. 16And they forsook all the commandments of the LORD their God, and made for themselves molten images of two calves; and they made an Ā·shē′rǎh, and worshiped all the host of heaven, and served Bā′ǎl. 17And they burned their sons and their daughters as offerings,ᵉ and used divination and sorcery, and sold themselves to do evil in the sight of the LORD, provoking him to anger. 18 Therefore the LORD was very angry with Israel, and removed them out of his sight; none was left but the tribe of Judah only.

19 Judah also did not keep the commandments of the LORD their God, but walked in the customs which Israel had introduced. 20And the LORD rejected all the descendants of Israel, and afflicted them, and gave them into the hand of spoilers, until he had cast them out of his sight.

21 When he had torn Israel from the house of David they made Jer·ŏ-bō′ǎm the son of Nē′bat king. And Jeroboam drove Israel from following the LORD and made them commit great sin. 22 The people of Israel walked in all the sins which Jer·ŏ-bō′ǎm did; they did not depart from them, 23 until the LORD removed Israel out of his sight, as he had spoken by all his servants the prophets. So Israel was exiled from their own land to Assyria until this day.

24 And the king of Assyria brought people from Babylon, Cū′thǎh, Av′vå, Hā′math, and Seph·är·vā′im, and placed them in the cities of Så·mâr′i·å instead of the people of Israel; and they took possession of Samaria, and dwelt in its cities. 25And at the beginning of their dwelling there, they did not fear the LORD; therefore the LORD sent lions among them, which killed some of them. 26 So the king of Assyria was told, "The nations which you have carried away and placed in the cities of Så·mâr′i·å do not know the law of the god of the land; therefore he has sent lions among them, and behold, they are killing them, because they do not know the law of the god of the land." 27 Then the king of Assyria commanded, "Send there one of the priests whom you carried away thence; and let himᶠ go and dwell there, and teach them the law of the god of the land." 28 So one of the priests whom they had carried away from Så·mâr′i·å came and dwelt in Beth′ĕl, and taught them how they should fear the LORD.

29 But every nation still made gods

ᵈ Heb obscure   ᵉ Or *made their sons and their daughters pass through the fire*
ᶠ Syr Vg: Heb *them*

of its own, and put them in the shrines of the high places which the Samaritans had made, every nation in the cities in which they dwelt; 30 the men of Babylon made Suc'coth-bē'noth, the men of Cuth made Něr'gal, the men of Hā'math made A·shi'mà, 31 and the Av'vites made Nib'haz and Tär'tak; and the Sē·phär'vites burned their children in the fire to A·dram'mė-lech and A·nam'mė·lech, the gods of Seph·är·vā'im. 32 They also feared the LORD, and appointed from among themselves all sorts of people as priests of the high places, who sacrificed for them in the shrines of the high places. 33 So they feared the LORD but also served their own gods, after the manner of the nations from among whom they had been carried away. 34 To this day they do according to the former manner.

They do not fear the LORD, and they do not follow the statutes or the ordinances or the law or the commandment which the LORD commanded the children of Jacob, whom he named Israel. 35 The LORD made a covenant with them, and commanded them, "You shall not fear other gods or bow yourselves to them or serve them or sacrifice to them; 36 but you shall fear the LORD, who brought you out of the land of Egypt with great power and with an outstretched arm; you shall bow yourselves to him, and to him you shall sacrifice. 37And the statutes and the ordinances and the law and the commandment which he wrote for you, you shall always be careful to do. You shall not fear other gods, 38 and you shall not forget the covenant that I have made with you. You shall not fear other gods, 39 but you shall fear the LORD your God, and he will deliver you out of the hand of all your enemies." 40 However they would not listen, but they did according to their former manner.

41 So these nations feared the LORD, and also served their graven images; their children likewise, and their children's children—as their fathers did, so they do to this day.

18   In the year of Hō·shē'á son of E'lah, king of Israel, Hez·ė·kī'áh the son of A'haz, king of Judah, began to reign. 2 He was twenty-five years old when he began to reign, and he reigned twenty-nine years in Jerusalem. His mother's name was A'bī the daughter of Zech·à·rī'áh. 3And he did what was right in the eyes of the LORD, according to all that David his

father had done. 4 He removed the high places, and broke the pillars, and cut down the A·shē'ráh. And he broke in pieces the bronze serpent that Moses had made, for until those days the people of Israel had burned incense to it; it was called Ne·hush'tàn. 5 He trusted in the LORD the God of Israel; so that there was none like him among all the kings of Judah after him, nor among those who were before him. 6 For he held fast to the LORD; he did not depart from following him, but kept the commandments which the LORD commanded Moses. 7And the LORD was with him; wherever he went forth, he prospered. He rebelled against the king of Assyria, and would not serve him. 8 He smote the Philistines as far as Gā'zà and its territory, from watchtower to fortified city.

9 In the fourth year of King Hez·ė-kī'áh, which was the seventh year of Hō·shē'á son of E'lah, king of Israel, Shal·màn·ė'sėr king of Assyria came up against Sà·mâr'ï·à and besieged it 10 and at the end of three years he took it. In the sixth year of Hez·ė·kī'áh, which was the ninth year of Hō·shē'á king of Israel, Sà·mâr'ï·à was taken. 11 The king of Assyria carried the Israelites away to Assyria, and put them in Hā'lah, and on the Hā'bôr, the river of Gō'zan, and in the cities of the Medes, 12 because they did not obey the voice of the LORD their God but transgressed his covenant, even all that Moses the servant of the LORD commanded; they neither listened nor obeyed.

13 In the fourteenth year of King Hez·ė·kī'áh Sen·nach'ė·rib king of Assyria came up against all the fortified cities of Judah and took them. 14And Hez·ė·kī'áh king of Judah sent to the king of Assyria at Lā'chish, saying, "I have done wrong; withdraw from me; whatever you impose on me I will bear." And the king of Assyria required of Hezekiah king of Judah three hundred talents of silver and thirty talents of gold. 15And Hez·ė·kī'áh gave him all the silver that was found in the house of the LORD, and in the treasuries of the king's house. 16At that time Hez·ė·kī'áh stripped the gold from the doors of the temple of the LORD, and from the doorposts which Hezekiah king of Judah had overlaid and gave it to the king of Assyria. 17And the king of Assyria sent the Tär'tàn, the Rab'sà·ris, and the Rab'shà·kèh with a great army from Lā'chish to King Hez·ė·kī'áh at Jeru-

18.1-3: 2 Chron 29.1-2.   18.13-19.37: 2 Chron 32.1-21; Is 36.1-37.38.

salem. And they went up and came to Jerusalem. When they arrived, they came and stood by the conduit of the upper pool, which is on the highway to the Fuller's Field. 18And when they called for the king, there came out to them E·li′a·kim the son of Hil·ki′ah, who was over the household, and Sheb′nah the secretary, and Jō′ah the son of A′saph, the recorder.

19 And the Rab′sha·kēh said to them, "Say to Hez·e·ki′ah, 'Thus says the great king, the king of Assyria: On what do you rest this confidence of yours? 20 Do you think that mere words are strategy and power for war? On whom do you now rely, that you have rebelled against me? 21 Behold, you are relying now on Egypt, that broken reed of a staff, which will pierce the hand of any man who leans on it. Such is Pharaoh king of Egypt to all who rely on him. 22 But if you say to me, "We rely on the LORD our God," is it not he whose high places and altars Hez·e·ki′ah has removed, saying to Judah and to Jerusalem, "You shall worship before this altar in Jerusalem"? 23 Come now, make a wager with my master the king of Assyria: I will give you two thousand horses, if you are able on your part to set riders upon them. 24 How then can you repulse a single captain among the least of my master's servants, when you rely on Egypt for chariots and for horsemen? 25 Moreover, is it without the LORD that I have come up against this place to destroy it? The LORD said to me, Go up against this land, and destroy it.' "

26 Then E·li′a·kim the son of Hil·ki′ah, and Sheb′nah, and Jō′ah, said to the Rab′sha·kēh, "Pray, speak to your servants in the Aramaic language, for we understand it; do not speak to us in the language of Judah within the hearing of the people who are on the wall." 27 But the Rab′sha·kēh said to them, "Has my master sent me to speak these words to your master and to you, and not to the men sitting on the wall, who are doomed with you to eat their own dung and to drink their own urine?"

28 Then the Rab′sha·kēh stood and called out in a loud voice in the language of Judah: "Hear the word of the great king, the king of Assyria! 29 Thus says the king: 'Do not let Hez·e·ki′ah deceive you, for he will not be able to deliver you out of my hand. 30 Do not let Hez·e·ki′ah make you to rely on the LORD by saying, The LORD will surely deliver us, and this city will not be given into the hand of the king of Assyria.' 31 Do not listen to Hez·e·ki′ah; for thus says the king of Assyria: 'Make your peace with me and come out to me; then every one of you will eat of his own vine, and every one of his own fig tree, and every one of you will drink the water of his own cistern; 32 until I come and take you away to a land like your own land, a land of grain and wine, a land of bread and vineyards, a land of olive trees and honey, that you may live, and not die. And do not listen to Hez·e·ki′ah when he misleads you by saying, The LORD will deliver us. 33 Has any of the gods of the nations ever delivered his land out of the hand of the king of Assyria? 34 Where are the gods of Hā′math and Ar′pad? Where are the gods of Seph·ar·vā′im, Hē′na, and Iv′vah? Have they delivered Sa·mar′i·a out of my hand? 35 Who among all the gods of the countries have delivered their countries out of my hand, that the LORD should deliver Jerusalem out of my hand?' "

36 But the people were silent and answered him not a word, for the king's command was, "Do not answer him." 37 Then E·li′a·kim the son of Hil·ki′ah, who was over the household, and Sheb′na the secretary, and Jō′ah the son of A′saph, the recorder, came to Hez·e·ki′ah with their clothes rent, and told him the words of the Rab′sha·kēh.

19 When King Hez·e·kī′ah heard it, he rent his clothes, and covered himself with sackcloth, and went into the house of the LORD. 2And he sent E·li′a·kim, who was over the household, and Sheb′na the secretary, and the senior priests, covered with sackcloth, to the prophet I·sāi′ah the son of A′moz. 3 They said to him, "Thus says Hez·e·ki′ah, This day is a day of distress, of rebuke, and of disgrace; children have come to the birth, and there is no strength to bring them forth. 4 It may be that the LORD your God heard all the words of the Rab′-sha·kēh, whom his master the king of Assyria has sent to mock the living God, and will rebuke the words which the LORD your God has heard; therefore lift up your prayer for the remnant that is left." 5 When the servants of King Hez·e·ki′ah came to I·sāi′ah, 6 I·sāi′ah said to them, "Say to your master, 'Thus says the LORD: Do not be afraid because of the words that you have heard, with which the servants of the king of Assyria have reviled me. 7 Behold, I will put a spirit in him,

so that he shall hear a rumor and return to his own land; and I will cause him to fall by the sword in his own land.' "

8 The Răb'shà·kĕh returned, and found the king of Assyria fighting against Lĭb'nàh; for he heard that the king had left Lā'chĭsh. 9And when the king heard concerning Tĭr·hā'kàh king of Ethiopia, "Behold, he has set out to fight against you," he sent messengers again to Hĕz·ė·kī'àh, saying, 10 "Thus shall you speak to Hĕz·ė·kī'àh king of Judah: 'Do not let your God on whom you rely deceive you by promising that Jerusalem will not be given into the hand of the king of Assyria. 11 Behold, you have heard what the kings of Assyria have done to all lands, destroying them utterly. And shall you be delivered? 12 Have the gods of the nations delivered them, the nations which my fathers destroyed, Gō'zan, Hâr'an, Rĕ'zeph, and the people of Eden who were in Tel-as'sàr? 13 Where is the king of Hā'-math, the king of Är'pad, the king of the city of Sĕph·är·vā'ĭm, the king of Hĕ'nà, or the king of Ĭv'vàh?' "

14 Hĕz·ė·kī'àh received the letter from the hand of the messengers, and read it; and Hezekiah went up to the house of the LORD, and spread it before the LORD. 15And Hĕz·ė·kī'àh prayed before the LORD, and said: "O LORD the God of Israel, who art enthroned above the cherubim, thou art the God, thou alone, of all the kingdoms of the earth; thou hast made heaven and earth. 16 Incline thy ear, O LORD, and hear; open thy eyes, O LORD, and see; and hear the words of Sĕn·nach'ė·rĭb, which he has sent to mock the living God. 17 Of a truth, O LORD, the kings of Assyria have laid waste the nations and their lands, 18 and have cast their gods into the fire; for they were no gods, but the work of men's hands, wood and stone; therefore they were destroyed. 19 So now, O LORD our God, save us, I beseech thee, from his hand, that all the kingdoms of the earth may know that thou, O LORD, art God alone."

20 Then Ĭ·śāi'àh the son of Ā'moz sent to Hĕz·ė·kī'àh, saying, "Thus says the LORD, the God of Israel: Your prayer to me about Sĕn·nach'ė·rĭb king of Assyria I have heard. 21 This is the word that the LORD has spoken concerning him:

"She despises you, she scorns you—
    the virgin daughter of Zion;
she wags her head behind you—
    the daughter of Jerusalem.

22 "Whom have you mocked and reviled?
    Against whom have you raised your voice
and haughtily lifted your eyes?
    Against the Holy One of Israel!
23 By your messengers you have mocked the Lord,
    and you have said, 'With my many chariots
I have gone up the heights of the mountains,
    to the far recesses of Lebanon;
I felled its tallest cedars,
    its choicest cypresses;
I entered its farthest retreat,
    its densest forest.
24 I dug wells
    and drank foreign waters,
and I dried up with the sole of my foot
    all the streams of Egypt.'

25 "Have you not heard
    that I determined it long ago?
I planned from days of old
    what now I bring to pass,
that you should turn fortified cities
    into heaps of ruins,
26 while their inhabitants, shorn of strength,
    are dismayed and confounded,
and have become like plants of the field,
    and like tender grass,
like grass on the housetops;
    blighted before it is grown?

27 "But I know your sitting down
    and your going out and coming in,
    and your raging against me.
28 Because you have raged against me
    and your arrogance has come into my ears,
I will put my hook in your nose
    and my bit in your mouth,
and I will turn you back on the way
    by which you came.

29 "And this shall be the sign for you: this year you shall eat what grows of itself, and in the second year what springs of the same; then in the third year sow, and reap, and plant vineyards, and eat their fruit. 30And the surviving remnant of the house of Judah shall again take root downward, and bear fruit upward; 31 for out of Jerusalem shall go forth a remnant, and out of Mount Zion a band of survivors. The zeal of the LORD will do this.

32 "Therefore thus says the LORD concerning the king of Assyria, He

shall not come into this city or shoot an arrow there, or come before it with a shield or cast up a siege mound against it. ³³ By the way that he came, by the same he shall return, and he shall not come into this city, says the LORD. ³⁴ For I will defend this city to save it, for my own sake and for the sake of my servant David."

35 And that night the angel of the LORD went forth, and slew a hundred and eighty-five thousand in the camp of the Assyrians; and when men arose early in the morning, behold, these were all dead bodies. ³⁶ Then Sennach′e·rib king of Assyria departed, and went home, and dwelt at Nin′e·veh. ³⁷And as he was worshiping in the house of Nis′roch his god, A·dram′me·lech and Sha·rē′zĕr, his sons, slew him with the sword, and escaped into the land of Ar′a·rat. And E·sar·had′don his son reigned in his stead.

20 In those days Hez·e·ki′ah became sick and was at the point of death. And I·sāi′ah the prophet the son of A′moz came to him, and said to him, "Thus says the LORD, 'Set your house in order; for you shall die, you shall not recover.'" ² Then Hez·e·ki′ah turned his face to the wall, and prayed to the LORD, saying, ³ "Remember now, O LORD, I beseech thee, how I have walked before thee in faithfulness and with a whole heart, and have done what is good in thy sight." And Hez·e·ki′ah wept bitterly. ⁴And before I·sāi′ah had gone out of the middle court, the word of the LORD came to him: ⁵ "Turn back, and say to Hez·e·ki′ah the prince of my people, Thus says the LORD, the God of David your father: I have heard your prayer, I have seen your tears; behold, I will heal you; on the third day you shall go up to the house of the LORD. ⁶And I will add fifteen years to your life. I will deliver you and this city out of the hand of the king of Assyria, and I will defend this city for my own sake and for my servant David's sake." ⁷And I·sāi′ah said, "Bring a cake of figs. And let them take and lay it on the boil, that he may recover."

8 And Hez·e·ki′ah said to I·sāi′ah, "What shall be the sign that the LORD will heal me, and that I shall go up to the house of the LORD on the third day?" ⁹And I·sāi′ah said, "This is the sign to you from the LORD, that the LORD will do the thing that he has promised: shall the shadow go forward

ten steps, or go back ten steps?" ¹⁰And Hez·e·ki′ah answered, "It is an easy thing for the shadow to lengthen ten steps; rather let the shadow go back ten steps." ¹¹And I·sāi′ah the prophet cried to the LORD; and he brought the shadow back ten steps, by which the sunᵍ had declined on the dial of A′haz.

12 At that time Mer′o·dach-bal′a·dan the son of Bal′a·dan, king of Babylon, sent envoys with letters and a present to Hez·e·ki′ah; for he heard that Hezekiah had been sick. ¹³And Hez·e·ki′ah welcomed them, and he showed them all his treasure house, the silver, the gold, the spices, the precious oil, his armory, all that was found in his storehouses; there was nothing in his house or in all his realm that Hezekiah did not show them. ¹⁴ Then I·sāi′ah the prophet came to King Hez·e·ki′ah, and said to him, "What did these men say? And whence did they come to you?" And Hezekiah said, "They have come from a far country, from Babylon." ¹⁵ He said, "What have they seen in your house?" And Hez·e·ki′ah answered, "They have seen all that is in my house; there is nothing in my storehouses that I did not show them."

16 Then I·sāi′ah said to Hez·e·ki′ah, "Hear the word of the LORD: ¹⁷ Behold, the days are coming, when all that is in your house, and that which your fathers have stored up till this day, shall be carried to Babylon; nothing shall be left, says the LORD. ¹⁸And some of your own sons, who are born to you, shall be taken away; and they shall be eunuchs in the palace of the king of Babylon." ¹⁹ Then said Hez·e·ki′ah to I·sāi′ah, "The word of the LORD which you have spoken is good." For he thought, "Why not, if there will be peace and security in my days?"

20 The rest of the deeds of Hez·e·ki′ah, and all his might, and how he made the pool and the conduit and brought water into the city, are they not written in the Book of the Chronicles of the Kings of Judah? ²¹And Hez·e·ki′ah slept with his fathers; and Ma·nas′seh his son reigned in his stead.

21 Ma·nas′seh was twelve years old when he began to reign, and he reigned fifty-five years in Jerusalem. His mother's name was Heph′zi·bah. ²And he did what was evil in the sight of the LORD, according to the abominable practices of the nations whom the

---

ᵍ Syr See Is. 38.8 and Tg: Heb lacks *the sun*

20.1-21: 2 Chron 32.24-33; Is 38.1-39.8.   **21.1-9:** 2 Chron 33.1-9.

LORD drove out before the people of Israel. [3] For he rebuilt the high places which Hez·e·ki′ah his father had destroyed; and he erected altars for Bā′al, and made an Ā·shē′rah, as Ā′hab king of Israel had done, and worshiped all the host of heaven, and served them. [4] And he built altars in the house of the LORD, of which the LORD had said, "In Jerusalem will I put my name." [5] And he built altars for all the host of heaven in the two courts of the house of the LORD. [6] And he burned his son as an offering, and practiced soothsaying and augury, and dealt with mediums and with wizards. He did much evil in the sight of the LORD, provoking him to anger. [7] And the graven image of Ā·shē′rah that he had made he set in the house of which the LORD said to David and to Solomon his son, "In this house, and in Jerusalem, which I have chosen out of all the tribes of Israel, I will put my name for ever; [8] and I will not cause the feet of Israel to wander any more out of the land which I gave to their fathers, if only they will be careful to do according to all that I have commanded them, and according to all the law that my servant Moses commanded them." [9] But they did not listen, and Mȧ·nas′seh seduced them to do more evil than the nations had done whom the LORD destroyed before the people of Israel.

10 And the LORD said by his servants the prophets, [11] "Because Mȧ·nas′seh king of Judah has committed these abominations, and has done things more wicked than all that the Am′o·rites did, who were before him, and has made Judah also to sin with his idols; [12] therefore thus says the LORD, the God of Israel, Behold, I am bringing upon Jerusalem and Judah such evil that the ears of every one who hears of it will tingle. [13] And I will stretch over Jerusalem the measuring line of Sȧ·mâr′i·ȧ, and the plummet of the house of Ā′hab; and I will wipe Jerusalem as one wipes a dish, wiping it and turning it upside down. [14] And I will cast off the remnant of my heritage, and give them into the hand of their enemies, and they shall become a prey and a spoil to all their enemies, [15] because they have done what is evil in my sight and have provoked me to anger, since the day their fathers came out of Egypt, even to this day."

16 Moreover Mȧ·nas′seh shed very much innocent blood, till he had filled Jerusalem from one end to another, besides the sin which he made Judah to sin so that they did what was evil in the sight of the LORD.

17 Now the rest of the acts of Mȧ·nas′seh, and all that he did, and the sin that he committed, are they not written in the Book of the Chronicles of the Kings of Judah? [18] And Mȧ·nas′seh slept with his fathers, and was buried in the garden of his house, in the garden of Uz′zȧ; and Ā′mon his son reigned in his stead.

19 Ā′mon was twenty-two years old when he began to reign, and he reigned two years in Jerusalem. His mother's name was Me·shul′le·meth the daughter of Hā′rŭz of Jot′bah. [20] And he did what was evil in the sight of the LORD, as Mȧ·nas′seh his father had done. [21] He walked in all the way in which his father walked, and served the idols that his father served, and worshiped them; [22] he forsook the LORD, the God of his fathers, and did not walk in the way of the LORD. [23] And the servants of Ā′mon conspired against him, and killed the king in his house. [24] But the people of the land slew all those who had conspired against King Ā′mon, and the people of the land made Jȯ·si′ah his son king in his stead. [25] Now the rest of the acts of Ā′mon which he did, are they not written in the Book of the Chronicles of the Kings of Judah? [26] And he was buried in his tomb in the garden of Uz′zȧ; and Jȯ·si′ah his son reigned in his stead.

22 Jȯ·si′ah was eight years old when he began to reign, and he reigned thirty-one years in Jerusalem. His mother's name was Je·di′dah the daughter of Ā·dai′ah of Boz′kath. [2] And he did what was right in the eyes of the LORD, and walked in all the way of David his father, and he did not turn aside to the right hand or to the left.

3 In the eighteenth year of King Jȯ·si′ah, the king sent Shā′phan the son of Az·a·li′ah, son of Me·shul′lȧm, the secretary, to the house of the LORD, saying, [4] "Go up to Hil·ki′ah the high priest, that he may reckon the amount of the money which has been brought into the house of the LORD, which the keepers of the threshold have collected from the people; [5] and let it be given into the hand of the workmen who have the oversight of the house of the LORD; and let them give it to the workmen who are at the house of the LORD,

21.18: 2 Chron 33.20.　　21.19-24: 2 Chron 33.21-25.　　22.1-2: 2 Chron 34.1-2.
22.3-7: 2 Chron 34.8-12.

repairing the house, 6 that is, to the carpenters, and to the builders, and to the masons, as well as for buying timber and quarried stone to repair the house. 7 But no accounting shall be asked from them for the money which is delivered into their hand, for they deal honestly."

8 And Hil·ki′ah the high priest said to Sha′phan the secretary, "I have found the book of the law in the house of the LORD." And Hilkiah gave the book to Shaphan, and he read it. 9And Sha′phan the secretary came to the king, and reported to the king, "Your servants have emptied out the money that was found in the house, and have delivered it into the hand of the workmen who have the oversight of the house of the LORD." 10 Then Sha′phan the secretary told the king, "Hil·ki′ah the priest has given me a book." And Shaphan read it before the king.

11 And when the king heard the words of the book of the law, he rent his clothes. 12And the king commanded Hil·ki′ah the priest, and A·hi′kam the son of Sha′phan, and Ach′bor the son of Mi·cai′ah, and Shaphan the secretary, and A·sai′ah the king's servant, saying, 13 "Go, inquire of the LORD for me, and for the people, and for all Judah, concerning the words of this book that has been found; for great is the wrath of the LORD that is kindled against us, because our fathers have not obeyed the words of this book, to do according to all that is written concerning us."

14 So Hil·ki′ah the priest, and A·hi′kam, and Ach′bor, and Sha′phan, and A·sai′ah went to Hul′dah the prophetess, the wife of Shal′lum the son of Tik′vah, son of Har′has, keeper of the wardrobe (now she dwelt in Jerusalem in the Second Quarter); and they talked with her. 15And she said to them, "Thus says the LORD, the God of Israel: 'Tell the man who sent you to me, 16 Thus says the LORD, Behold, I will bring evil upon this place and upon its inhabitants, all the words of the book which the king of Judah has read. 17 Because they have forsaken me and have burned incense to other gods, that they might provoke me to anger with all the work of their hands, therefore my wrath will be kindled against this place, and it will not be quenched. 18 But as to the king of Judah, who sent you to inquire of the LORD, thus shall you say to him, Thus says the LORD, the God of Israel: Regarding the words which you have

23.4-20: 2 Chron 34.3-7.

heard, 19 because your heart was penitent, and you humbled yourself before the LORD, when you heard how I spoke against this place, and against its inhabitants, that they should become a desolation and a curse, and you have rent your clothes and wept before me, I also have heard you, says the LORD. 20 Therefore, behold, I will gather you to your fathers, and you shall be gathered to your grave in peace, and your eyes shall not see all the evil which I will bring upon this place.' " And they brought back word to the king.

23 Then the king sent, and all the elders of Judah and Jerusalem were gathered to him. 2And the king went up to the house of the LORD, and with him all the men of Judah and all the inhabitants of Jerusalem, and the priests and the prophets, all the people, both small and great; and he read in their hearing all the words of the book of the covenant which had been found in the house of the LORD. 3And the king stood by the pillar and made a covenant before the LORD, to walk after the LORD and to keep his commandments and his testimonies and his statutes, with all his heart and all his soul, to perform the words of this covenant that were written in this book; and all the people joined in the covenant.

4 And the king commanded Hil·ki′ah the high priest, and the priests of the second order, and the keepers of the threshold, to bring out of the temple of the LORD all the vessels made for Ba′al, for A·she′rah, and for all the host of heaven; he burned them outside Jerusalem in the fields of the Kid′ron, and carried their ashes to Beth′el. 5And he deposed the idolatrous priests whom the kings of Judah had ordained to burn incense in the high places at the cities of Judah and round about Jerusalem; those also who burned incense to Ba′al, to the sun, and the moon, and the constellations, and all the host of the heavens. 6And he brought out the A·she′rah from the house of the LORD, outside Jerusalem, to the brook Kid′ron, and burned it at the brook Kidron, and beat it to dust and cast the dust of it upon the graves of the common people. 7And he broke down the houses of the male cult prostitutes which were in the house of the LORD, where the women wove hangings for the A·she′rah. 8And he brought all the priests out of the cities of Judah, and defiled the high

places where the priests had burned incense, from Gĕ′bă to Beer-sheba; and he broke down the high places of the gates that were at the entrance of the gate of Joshua the governor of the city, which were on one's left at the gate of the city. 9 However, the priests of the high places did not come up to the altar of the LORD in Jerusalem, but they ate unleavened bread among their brethren. 10And he defiled Tō′-pheth, which is in the valley of the sons of Hin′nŏm, that no one might burn his son or his daughter as an offering to Mō′lech. 11And he removed the horses that the kings of Judah had dedicated to the sun, at the entrance to the house of the LORD, by the chamber of Nā′thăn-mē′lech the chamberlain, which was in the precincts;*h* and he burned the chariots of the sun with fire. 12And the altars on the roof of the upper chamber of Ā′haz, which the kings of Judah had made, and the altars which Mà·nas′sĕh had made in the two courts of the house of the LORD, he pulled down and broke in pieces,*i* and cast the dust of them into the brook Kid′rŏn. 13And the king defiled the high places that were east of Jerusalem, to the south of the mount of corruption, which Solomon the king of Israel had built for Ash′tō·reth the abomination of the Si·dō′ni·ăns, and for Chē′mosh the abomination of Mō′ab, and for Mil′-com the abomination of the Am′mŏ-nites. 14And he broke in pieces the pillars, and cut down the Ā·shē′rim, and filled their places with the bones of men.

15 Moreover the altar at Beth′el, the high place erected by Jer·o·bō′ăm the son of Nē′bat, who made Israel to sin, that altar with the high place he pulled down and he broke in pieces its stones,*j* crushing them to dust; also he burned the Ā·shē′răh. 16And as Jō·sī′ăh turned, he saw the tombs there on the mount; and he sent and took the bones out of the tombs, and burned them upon the altar, and defiled it, according to the word of the LORD which the man of God proclaimed, who had predicted these things. 17 Then he said, "What is yonder monument that I see?" And the men of the city told him, "It is the tomb of the man of God who came from Judah and predicted these things which you have done against the altar at Beth′el." 18And he said, "Let him

be; let no man move his bones." So they let his bones alone, with the bones of the prophet who came out of Sà·mâr′i·à. 19And all the shrines also of the high places that were in the cities of Sà·mâr′i·à, which kings of Israel had made, provoking the LORD to anger, Jō·sī′ăh removed; he did to them according to all that he had done at Beth′el. 20And he slew all the priests of the high places who were there, upon the altars, and burned the bones of men upon them. Then he returned to Jerusalem.

21 And the king commanded all the people, "Keep the passover to the LORD your God, as it is written in this book of the covenant." 22 For no such passover had been kept since the days of the judges who judged Israel, or during all the days of the kings of Israel or of the kings of Judah; 23 but in the eighteenth year of King Jō·sī′ăh this passover was kept to the LORD in Jerusalem.

24 Moreover Jō·sī′ăh put away the mediums and the wizards and the teraphim and the idols and all the abominations that were seen in the land of Judah and in Jerusalem, that he might establish the words of the law which were written in the book that Hil·kī′ăh the priest found in the house of the LORD. 25 Before him there was no king like him, who turned to the LORD with all his heart and with all his soul and with all his might, according to all the law of Moses; nor did any like him arise after him.

26 Still the LORD did not turn from the fierceness of his great wrath, by which his anger was kindled against Judah, because of all the provocations with which Mà·nas′sĕh had provoked him. 27And the LORD said, "I will remove Judah also out of my sight, as I have removed Israel, and I will cast off this city which I have chosen, Jerusalem, and the house of which I said, My name shall be there."

28 Now the rest of the acts of Jō·sī′ăh, and all that he did, are they not written in the Book of the Chronicles of the Kings of Judah? 29 In his days Pharaoh Nē′cō king of Egypt went up to the king of Assyria to the river Eū·phrā′tĕs. King Jō·sī′ăh went to meet him; and Pharaoh Neco slew him at Mĕ·gid′dŏ, when he saw him. 30And his servants carried him dead in a chariot from Mĕ·gid′dŏ, and brought him to Jerusalem, and buried

h The meaning of the Hebrew word is uncertain   *i* Heb *pieces from there*
j Gk: Heb *he burned the high place*
23.21-23: 2 Chron 35.1-19.   **23.30-34:** 2 Chron 36.1-4.

him in his own tomb. And the people of the land took Je·hō′a·haz the son of Jō·si′ah, and anointed him, and made him king in his father's stead.

31 Je·hō′a·haz was twenty-three years old when he began to reign, and he reigned three months in Jerusalem. His mother's name was Hå·mü′tal the daughter of Jeremiah of Lib′nah. 32And he did what was evil in the sight of the LORD, according to all that his fathers had done. 33And Pharaoh Nē′cō put him in bonds at Rib′lah in the land of Hā′math, that he might not reign in Jerusalem, and laid upon the land a tribute of a hundred talents of silver and a talent of gold. 34And Pharaoh Nē′cō made E·li′a·kim the son of Jō·si′ah king in the place of Josiah his father, and changed his name to Je·hoi′a·kim. But he took Je·hō′a·haz away; and he came to Egypt, and died there. 35And Je·hoi′a·kim gave the silver and the gold to Pharaoh, but he taxed the land to give the money according to the command of Pharaoh. He exacted the silver and the gold of the people of the land, from every one according to his assessment, to give it to Pharaoh Nē′cō.

36 Je·hoi′a·kim was twenty-five years old when he began to reign, and he reigned eleven years in Jerusalem. His mother's name was Ze·bi′dah the daughter of Pe·dāi′ah of Rü′mah. 37And he did what was evil in the sight of the LORD, according to all that his fathers had done.

24 In his days Ne·bu·chad·nez′zar king of Babylon came up, and Je·hoi′a·kim became his servant three years; then he turned and rebelled against him. 2And the LORD sent against him bands of the Chal·dē′ans, and bands of the Syrians, and bands of the Mō′ab·ites, and bands of the Am′mo·nites, and sent them against Judah to destroy it, according to the word of the LORD which he spoke by his servants the prophets. 3 Surely this came upon Judah at the command of the LORD, to remove them out of his sight, for the sins of Må·nas′seh, according to all that he had done, 4 and also for the innocent blood that he had shed; for he filled Jerusalem with innocent blood, and the LORD would not pardon. 5 Now the rest of the deeds of Je·hoi′a·kim, and all that he did, are they not written in the Book of the Chronicles of the Kings of Judah? 6 So Je·hoi′a·kim slept with his fathers, and Je·hoi′a·chin his son reigned in his

stead. 7And the king of Egypt did not come again out of his land, for the king of Babylon had taken all that belonged to the king of Egypt from the Brook of Egypt to the river Eū·phrā′tēs.

8 Je·hoi′a·chin was eighteen years old when he became king, and he reigned three months in Jerusalem. His mother's name was Ne·hush′ta the daughter of El·nā′than of Jerusalem. 9And he did what was evil in the sight of the LORD, according to all that his father had done.

10 At that time the servants of Ne·bu·chad·nez′zar king of Babylon came up to Jerusalem, and the city was besieged. 11And Ne·bu·chad·nez′zar king of Babylon came to the city, while his servants were besieging it; 12 and Je·hoi′a·chin the king of Judah gave himself up to the king of Babylon, himself, and his mother, and his servants, and his princes, and his palace officials. The king of Babylon took him prisoner in the eighth year of his reign, 13 and carried off all the treasures of the house of the LORD, and the treasures of the king's house, and cut in pieces all the vessels of gold in the temple of the LORD, which Solomon king of Israel had made, as the LORD had foretold. 14 He carried away all Jerusalem, and all the princes, and all the mighty men of valor, ten thousand captives, and all the craftsmen and the smiths; none remained, except the poorest people of the land. 15And he carried away Je·hoi′a·chin to Babylon; the king's mother, the king's wives, his officials, and the chief men of the land, he took into captivity from Jerusalem to Babylon. 16And the king of Babylon brought captive to Babylon all the men of valor, seven thousand, and the craftsmen and the smiths, one thousand, all of them strong and fit for war. 17And the king of Babylon made Mat·tā·ni′ah, Je·hoi′a·chin's uncle, king in his stead, and changed his name to Zed·e·ki′ah.

18 Zed·e·ki′ah was twenty-one years old when he became king, and he reigned eleven years in Jerusalem. His mother's name was Hå·mü′tal the daughter of Jeremiah of Lib′nah. 19And he did what was evil in the sight of the LORD, according to all that Je·hoi′a·kim had done. 20 For because of the anger of the LORD it came to the point in Jerusalem and Judah that he cast them out from his presence.

23.36–24.6: 2 Chron 36.5-8.   24.8-17: 2 Chron 36.9-10.
24.18-25.21: 2 Chron 36.11-21; Jer 52.1-27.

And Zed·e·ki′ah rebelled against
25 the king of Babylon. [1]And in
the ninth year of his reign, in
the tenth month, on the tenth day of
the month, Ne·bu·chad·nez′zar king
of Babylon came with all his army
against Jerusalem, and laid siege to it;
and they built siegeworks against it
round about. [2] So the city was besieged
till the eleventh year of King Zed·e·
ki′ah. [3] On the ninth day of the fourth
month the famine was so severe in the
city that there was no food for the
people of the land. [4] Then a breach
was made in the city; the king with all
the men of war fled[k] by night by the
way of the gate between the two walls,
by the king's garden, though the Chal-
de′ans were around the city. And they
went in the direction of the Ar′a·bah.
[5] But the army of the Chal·de′ans
pursued the king, and overtook him
in the plains of Jericho; and all his
army was scattered from him. [6] Then
they captured the king, and brought
him up to the king of Babylon at
Rib′lah, who passed sentence upon
him. [7] They slew the sons of Zed·e·
ki′ah before his eyes, and put out the
eyes of Zedekiah, and bound him in
fetters, and took him to Babylon.

8 In the fifth month, on the seventh
day of the month—which was the
nineteenth year of King Ne·bu·chad-
nez′zar, king of Babylon—Ne·bu′za-
rad′an, the captain of the bodyguard,
a servant of the king of Babylon, came
to Jerusalem. [9]And he burned the
house of the LORD, and the king's
house and all the houses of Jerusalem;
every great house he burned down.
[10]And all the army of the Chal·de′ans,
who were with the captain of the guard,
broke down the walls around Jerusalem. [11]And the rest of the people
who were left in the city and the
deserters who had deserted to the king
of Babylon, together with the rest of
the multitude, Ne·bu′za·rad′an the
captain of the guard carried into exile.
[12] But the captain of the guard left
some of the poorest of the land to be
vinedressers and plowmen.

13 And the pillars of bronze that
were in the house of the LORD, and the
stands and the bronze sea that were in
the house of the LORD, the Chal·de′ans
broke in pieces, and carried the bronze
to Babylon. [14]And they took away the
pots, and the shovels, and the snuffers,
and the dishes for incense and all the
vessels of bronze used in the temple

service, [15] the firepans also, and the
bowls. What was of gold the captain
of the guard took away as gold, and
what was of silver, as silver. [16]As for
the two pillars, the one sea, and the
stands, which Solomon had made for
the house of the LORD, the bronze of
all these vessels was beyond weight.
[17] The height of the one pillar was
eighteen cubits, and upon it was a
capital of bronze; the height of the
capital was three cubits; a network
and pomegranates, all of bronze, were
upon the capital round about. And the
second pillar had the like, with the
network.

18 And the captain of the guard took
Se·rai′ah the chief priest, and
Zeph·a·ni′ah the second priest, and
the three keepers of the threshold;
[19] and from the city he took an officer
who had been in command of the men
of war, and five men of the king's
council who were found in the city;
and the secretary of the commander
of the army who mustered the people
of the land; and sixty men of the people of the land who were found in the
city. [20]And Ne·bu′za·rad′an the captain of the guard took them, and
brought them to the king of Babylon
at Rib′lah. [21]And the king of Babylon
smote them, and put them to death at
Rib′lah in the land of Ha′math. So
Judah was taken into exile out of its
land.

22 And over the people who remained in the land of Judah, whom
Ne·bu·chad·nez′zar king of Babylon
had left, he appointed Ged·a·li′ah the
son of A·hi′kam, son of Sha′phan,
governor. [23] Now when all the captains of the forces in the open country[l]
and their men heard that the king of
Babylon had appointed Ged·a·li′ah
governor, they came with their men to
Gedaliah at Miz′pah, namely, Ish′-
ma·el the son of Neth·a·ni′ah, and
Jo·ha′nan the son of Ka·re′ah, and
Se·rai′ah the son of Tan′hu·meth the
Ne·toph′a·thite, and Ja·az·a·ni′ah the
son of the Ma·ac′a·thite. [24]And Ged-
a·li′ah swore to them and their men,
saying, "Do not be afraid because of
the Chal·de′an officials; dwell in the
land, and serve the king of Babylon,
and it shall be well with you." [25] But
in the seventh month, Ish′ma·el the
son of Neth·a·ni′ah, son of E·lish′a-
ma, of the royal family, came with ten
men, and attacked and killed Ged·a·
li′ah and the Jews and the Chal·de′-

k Gk Compare Jer 39.4; 52.7: Heb lacks *the king* and *fled*
l With Jer 40.7: Heb lacks *in the open country*
25.22-26: Jer 40.7-43.7.

ăns̆ who were with him at Miz′păh. 26 Then all the people, both small and great, and the captains of the forces arose, and went to Egypt; for they were afraid of the Chal·dē′ăns.

27 And in the thirty-seventh year of the exile of Je·hoi′ă·chin king of Judah, in the twelfth month, on the twenty-seventh day of the month, E′vil-mer′o·dach king of Babylon, in the year that he began to reign, gra-ciously freed Jehoiachin king of Judah from prison; 28 and he spoke kindly to him, and gave him a seat above the seats of the kings who were with him in Babylon. 29 So Je·hoi′ă·chin put off his prison garments. And every day of his life he dined regularly at the king's table; 30 and for his allowance, a regular allowance was given him by the king, every day a portion, as long as he lived.

THE FIRST BOOK OF THE

CHRONICLES

1 Adam, Seth, E′nosh; 2 Ke′năn, Ma·hal′ă·lel, Jăr′ed; 3 E′noch, Me·thu′se·lăh, Lā′mech; 4 Noah, Shem, Ham, and Jā′pheth.

5 The sons of Jā′pheth: Gō′mĕr, Mā′gog, Mā′dăi, Jā′văn, Tü′băl, Mĕ′shech, and Tī′răs. 6 The sons of Gō′mĕr: Ash′ke·naz, Dī′phath, and Tō·gär′mäh. 7 The sons of Jā′văn: E·lī′shah, Tär′shish, Kit′tim, and Rō′dă·nim.

8 The sons of Ham: Cush, Egypt, Püt, and Canaan. 9 The sons of Cush: Sē′bă, Hav′i·lăh, Sab′tă, Rā′ă·mă, and Sab′te·că. The sons of Rā′ă·măh: Sheba and Dē′dan. 10 Cush was the father of Nim′rod; he began to be a mighty one in the earth.

11 Egypt was the father of Lü′dim, An′ă·mim, Le·hā′bim, Naph′tü·him, 12 Path·rü′sim, Cas·lü′him (whence came the Philistines), and Caph′tŏ·rim.

13 Canaan was the father of Sī′don his first-born, and Heth, 14 and the Jeb′ü·sites, the Am′ŏ·rites, the Gir′gă·shites, 15 the Hī′vites, the Är′kites, the Sī′nites, 16 the Är′vă·dites, the Zem′ă·rites, and the Hā′mă·thites.

17 The sons of Shem: E′lăm, As′shür, Är·pach′shad, Lüd, Är′am, Uz, Hul, Gĕ′thĕr, and Mĕ′shech. 18 Är·pach′shad was the father of Shē′lăh; and Shelah was the father of E′bĕr. 19 To E′bĕr were born two sons: the name of the one was Pē′leg (for in his days the earth was divided), and the name of his brother Jok′tan. 20 Jok′tan was the father of Al·mō′dad, Shē′leph, Hā·zär·mā′veth, Jē′răh, 21 Hă·dôr′ăm, Ū′zăl, Dik′lăh, 22 E′băl, Ā·bim′ă·el, Sheba, 23 O′phīr, Hav′i-lăh, and Jō′bab; all these were the sons of Jok′tan.

24 Shem, Är·pach′shad, Shē′lăh; 25 E′bĕr, Pē′leg, Rē′ü; 26 Sĕ′rŭg, Nā′hôr, Tē′răh; 27 Abram, that is, Abra-ham.

28 The sons of Abraham: Isaac and Ish′mă·el. 29 These are their genealo-gies: the first-born of Ish′mă·el, Ne-bā′ioth; and Kē′där, Ad′bē·ĕl, Mib′-săm, 30 Mish′mă, Dü′măh, Mas′să, Hā′dad, Tē′mă, 31 Jē′tŭr, Nā′phish, and Ked′é·măh. These are the sons of Ish′mă·el. 32 The sons of Ke·tü′răh, Abraham's concubine: she bore Zim′-ran, Jok′shan, Mē′dan, Mid′i·ăn, Ish′bak, and Shü′ăh. The sons of Jokshan: Sheba and Dē′dan. 33 The sons of Mid′i·ăn: E′phăh, E′phĕr, Hā′noch, Ā·bī′dă, and El·dā′ăh. All these were the descendants of Ke·tü′răh.

34 Abraham was the father of Isaac. The sons of Isaac: Esau and Israel. 35 The sons of Esau: E·lī′phaz, Reü′el, Jē′ush, Jā′lăm, and Kō′răh. 36 The sons of E·lī′phaz: Tē′măn, O′mär, Zē′phi, Gā′tăm, Kē′naz, Tim′nă, and Am′ă·lek. 37 The sons of Reü′el: Nā′hath, Zē′răh, Sham′măh, and Miz′zăh.

38 The sons of Sē′ir: Lō′tan, Shō′băl, Zib′con, An′ăh, Dī′shon, E′zĕr, and Dī′shan. 39 The sons of Lō′tan: Hō′rī and Hō′mam; and Lotan's sister was Tim′nă. 40 The sons of Shō′băl: Al′i·an, Man′ă·hath, E′băl, Shĕ′phī, and O′năm. The sons of Zib′ē·ŏn: Ā′iăh and An′ăh. 41 The sons of An′ăh: Dī′shon. The sons of Dishon: Ham′ran, Esh′ban, Ith′ran, and Chē′-ran. 42 The sons of E′zĕr: Bil′han,

25.27-30: Jer 52.31-34.   **1.1-53:** Gen 5; 10; 11; 25; 36.

Zā'à·van, and Jā'à·kan. The sons of Dī'shan: Uz and Ar'àn.

43 These are the kings who reigned in the land of E'dòm before any king reigned over the Israelites: Bē'là the son of Bē'ôr, the name of whose city was Din'hà·bàh. 44 When Bē'là died, Jō'bab the son of Zē'ràh of Boz'ràh reigned in his stead. 45 When Jō'bab died, Hū'sham of the land of the Tē'nà·nites reigned in his stead. 46 When Hū'sham died, Hā'dad the son of Bē'dad, who defeated Mid'i·àn in the country of Mō'ab, reigned in his stead; and the name of his city was A'vith. 47 When Hā'dad died, Sam'làh of Mas·rē'kàh reigned in his stead. 48 When Sam'làh died, Shā'ul of Re·hō'both on the Eū·phrā'tēs reigned in his stead. 49 When Shā'ul died, Bā'àl·hā'nàn, the son of Ach'bôr, reigned in his stead. 50 When Bā'àl·hā'nàn died, Hā'dad reigned in his stead; and the name of his city was Pā'ī, and his wife's name Me·het'à·bēl the daughter of Mā'tred, the daughter of Mē'zà·hab. 51And Hā'dad died.

The chiefs of E'dòm were: chiefs Tim'nà, Al'i·àh, Jē'theth, 52 O·hol·i·bā'màh, E'làh, Pī'non, 53 Kē'naz, Tē'màn, Mib'zàr, 54 Mag'di·el, and I'ram; these are the chiefs of E'dòm.

2 These are the sons of Israel: Reuben, Simeon, Levi, Judah, Is'sà·chär, Zeb'ū·lùn, 2 Dan, Joseph, Benjamin, Naph'tà·li, Gad, and Ash'ér. 3 The sons of Judah: Er, O'nàn, and Shē'làh; these three Bath-shū'à the Canaanitess bore to him. Now Er, Judah's first-born, was wicked in the sight of the LORD, and he slew him. 4 His daughter-in-law Tā'mär also bore him Per'ez and Zē'ràh. Judah had five sons in all.

5 The sons of Per'ez: Hez'ròn and Hā'mùl. 6 The sons of Zē'ràh: Zim'rī, Ethan, Hē'màn, Cal'col, and Dâr'à, five in all. 7 The sons of Cär'mī: A'chär, the troubler of Israel, who transgressed in the matter of the devoted thing; 8 and Ethan's son was Az·à·rī'àh.

9 The sons of Hez'ròn, that were born to him: Jé·räh'mē·ēl, Räm, and Chē·lū'bäi. 10 Räm was the father of Am·min'à·dab, and Amminadab was the father of Näh'shòn, prince of the sons of Judah. 11 Näh'shòn was the father of Sal'mà, Salma of Bō'az, 12 Bō'az of O'bed, Obed of Jesse. 13 Jesse was the father of E·lī'àb his first-born, A·bin'à·dab the second,

Shim'ē·à the third, 14 Nē·than'el the fourth, Rad'däi the fifth, 15 O'zem the sixth, David the seventh; 16 and their sisters were Zē·rū'i·àh and Ab'i·gäil. The sons of Zeruiah: À·bi'shäi, Jō'ab, and As'à·hel, three. 17Ab'i·gäil bore À·mā'sà, and the father of Amasa was Jē'thèr the Ish'mà·el·īte.

18 Caleb the son of Hez'ròn had children by his wife À·zū'bàh, and by Jer'i·oth; and these were her sons: Jē'shèr, Shō'bab, and Ar'dòn. 19 When À·zū'bàh died, Caleb married E'phrath, who bore him Hūr. 20 Hūr was the father of U'rī, and Uri was the father of Bez'à·lel.

21 Afterward Hez'ròn went in to the daughter of Mā'chir the father of Gilead, whom he married when he was sixty years old; and she bore him Se'gùb; 22 and Se'gùb was the father of Jā'ir, who had twenty-three cities in the land of Gilead. 23 But Gē'shūr and Ar'àm took from them Hav·voth·jā'ir, Kē'nath and its villages, sixty towns. All these were descendants of Mā'chir, the father of Gilead. 24After the death of Hez'ròn, Caleb went in to Eph'rà·thàh,*a* the wife of Hezron his father, and she bore him Ash'hūr, the father of Te·kō'à.

25 The sons of Jé·räh'mē·ēl, the first-born of Hez'ròn: Räm, his first-born, Bü'nàh, O'ren, O'zem, and À·hī'jàh. 26 Jé·räh'mē·ēl also had another wife, whose name was At'à·ràh; she was the mother of O'nàm. 27 The sons of Räm, the first-born of Jé·räh'mē·ēl: Mā'az, Jā'min, and E'kér. 28 The sons of O'nàm: Sham'mäi and Jā'dà. The sons of Shammai: Nā'dab and À·bi'shūr. 29 The name of À·bi'shūr's wife was Ab'i·häil, and she bore him Äh'ban and Mō'lid. 30 The sons of Nā'dab: Sē'led and Ap'pà·im; and Seled died childless. 31 The sons of Ap'pà·im: Ish'ī. The sons of Ishi: Shē'shan. The sons of Sheshan: Äh'läi. 32 The sons of Jā'dà, Sham'mäi's brother: Jē'thèr and Jonathan; and Jether died childless. 33 The sons of Jonathan: Pē'leth and Zā'zà. These were the descendants of Jé·räh'mē·ēl. 34 Now Shē'shan had no sons, only daughters; but Sheshan had an Egyptian slave, whose name was Jär'hà. 35 So Shē'shan gave his daughter in marriage to Jär'hà his slave; and she bore him At'täi. 36At'täi was the father of Nathan and Nathan of Zā'bad. 37 Zā'bad was the father of Eph'lal, and Ephlal of O'bed. 38 O'bed was the

---

a Gk Vg: Heb *in Caleb Ephrathah*

2.1-2: Gen 35.23-26.   2.3-4: Gen 38.3-7, 29-30; Num 26.19-20.   2.5: Gen 46.12; Num 26.21.   2.6-8: Josh 7.1; 1 Kings 4.31.

father of Jē′hū, and Jehu of Az·à·rī′ah. ³⁹Az·à·rī′ah was the father of Hē′lez, and Helez of El′e·ā′sàh. ⁴⁰ El′e·ā′sàh was the father of Sis′mäi, and Sismai of Shal′lùm. ⁴¹ Shal′lùm was the father of Jek·à·mī′àh, and Jekamiah of E·lish′à·mà.

42 The sons of Caleb the brother of Je·rāh′mē·ēl: Mà·rē′shàh[b] his first-born, who was the father of Ziph. The sons of Mà·rē′shàh: Hē′brŏn.[c] ⁴³ The sons of Hē′brŏn: Kō′ràh, Tap′pū·àh, Rē′kem, and Shē′mà. ⁴⁴ Shē′mà was the father of Rā′ham, the father of Jŏr′kē·àm; and Rē′kem was the father of Sham′mäi. ⁴⁵ The son of Sham′mäi: Mā′on; and Maon was the father of Beth′zūr. ⁴⁶ É′phàh also, Caleb′s concubine, bore Hàr′àn, Mō′zà, and Gà′zez; and Haran was the father of Gazez. ⁴⁷ The sons of Jäh′däi: Rē′gem, Jō′thàm, Gē′shan, Pē′let, É′phàh, and Shā′aph. ⁴⁸ Mā′à·càh, Caleb′s concubine, bore Shē′bér and Tīr′hà·nàh. ⁴⁹ She also bore Shā′aph the father of Mad·man′nàh, Shē′và the father of Mach·bē′nàh and the father of Gib′ē·à; and the daughter of Caleb was Ach′sàh. ⁵⁰ These were the descendants of Caleb.

The sons[d] of Hūr the first-born of Eph′rà·thàh: Shō′bàl the father of Kĭr′i·ath-jē′à·rim, ⁵¹ Sal′mà, the father of Bethlehem, and Hàr′eph the father of Beth-gā′dér. ⁵² Shō′bàl the father of Kĭr′i·ath-jē′à·rim had other sons: Hà·rō′éh, half of the Me·nū′hoth. ⁵³And the families of Kĭr′i·ath-jē′à·rim: the Ith′rites, the Pū′thites, the Shü′mà·thites, and the Mish′rà·ites; from these came the Zō′rà·thites and the Esh′tā·ò·lites. ⁵⁴ The sons of Sal′mà: Bethlehem, the Ne·toph′à·thites, At′roth-beth-jō′àb, and half of the Man′à·hà′thites, the Zō′rites. ⁵⁵ The families also of the scribes that dwelt at Jā′bez: the Ti′rà·thites, the Shim′ē·à·thites, and the Sü′chà·thites. These are the Ken′ites who came from Ham′math, the father of the house of Rē′chab.

3 These are the sons of David that were born to him in Hē′brŏn: the first-born Am′non, by À·hin′ō·am the Jez′rē·è·līt·èss; the second Daniel, by Ab′i·gàil the Cär′mēl·ît·èss, ² the third Ab′sà·lòm, whose mother was Mā′à·càh, the daughter of Tal′mäi, king of Gē′shūr; the fourth Ad·ò·nī′jàh, whose mother was Hag′gith; ³ the fifth Sheph·à·tī′àh, by À·bī′tal; the sixth Ith′rē·am, by his wife Eg′làh; ⁴ six were born to him in Hē′brŏn, where he reigned for

seven years and six months. And he reigned thirty-three years in Jerusalem. ⁵ These were born to him in Jerusalem: Shim′ē·à, Shō′bab, Nathan, and Solomon, four by Bath-shü′à, the daughter of Am′mi·el; ⁶ then Ib′här, E·lish′à·mà, E·liph′é·let, ⁷ Nō′gàh, Nē′pheg, Jà·phī′à, ⁸ E·lish′à·mà, E·lī′à·dà, and E·liph′é·let, nine. ⁹All these were David′s sons, besides the sons of the concubines; and Tā′mär was their sister.

10 The descendants of Solomon: Rē·hò·bō′àm, À·bī′jàh his son, Asa his son, Je·hosh′à·phat his son, ¹¹ Jō′ràm his son, À·hà·zī′àh his son, Jō′ash his son, ¹²Am·à·zī′àh his son, Az·à·rī′àh his son, Jō′thàm his son, ¹³Ā′haz his son, Hez·é·kī′àh his son, Mà·nas′sèh his son, ¹⁴Ā′mon his son, Jō·sī′àh his son. ¹⁵ The sons of Jō·sī′àh: Jō·hà′nàn the first-born, the second Je·hoi′à·kim, the third Zed·é·kī′àh, the fourth Shal′lúm. ¹⁶ The descendants of Je·hoi′à·kim: Jec·ò·nī′àh his son, Zed·é·kī′àh his son; ¹⁷ and the sons of Jec·ò·nī′àh, the captive: She·al′ti·el his son, ¹⁸ Mal′chi′ràm, Pe·dāi′àh, Shen·az′zàr, Jek·à·mī′àh, Hosh′à·mà, and Ned·à·bī′àh; ¹⁹ and the sons of Pe·dāi′àh: Ze·rub′bà·bel and Shim′ē·ī; and the sons of Ze·rub′bà·bel: Me·shul′làm and Han·à·nī′àh, and She·lō′mith was their sister; ²⁰ and Ha·shü′bàh, Ō′hel, Ber·é·chī′àh, Has·à·dī′àh, and Jü′shab-hē′sed, five. ²¹ The sons of Han·à·nī′àh: Pel·à·tī′àh and Je·shā′iàh, his son[e] Reph·ā′iàh, his son[e] Är′nàn, his son Ō·bà·dī′àh, his son[e] Shec·à·nī′àh. ²² The sons of Shec·à·nī′àh: Shemāi′àh. And the sons of Shemaiah: Hat′tùsh, I′gal, Bà·rī′àh, Nē·à·rī′àh, and Shā′phàt, six. ²³ The sons of Nē·à·rī′àh: El′i·ō·ē′nai, Hiz·kī′àh, and Az·rī′kàm, three. ²⁴ The sons of El′i·ō·ē′nai: Hod′à·vī′àh, E·lī′à·shib, Pe·lā′iàh, Ak′kùb, Jō·hà′nàn, De·lāi′àh, and À·nā′nī, seven.

4 The sons of Judah: Per′ez, Hez′·ròn, Cär′mi, Hūr, and Shō′bàl. ² Rē·āi′àh the son of Shō′bàl was the father of Jā′hath, and Jahath was the father of À·hü′mäi and Lā′had. These were the families of the Zō′rà·thites. ³ These were the sons[f] of É′tam: Jez′rē·ēl, Ish′mà, and Id′bash; and the name of their sister was Haz·zè·lel·pō′nī, ⁴ and Pè·nū′el was the father of Gē′dŏr, and É′zér the father of Hü′shàh. These were the sons of Hūr, the first-born of Eph′rà·thàh, the father of Bethlehem. ⁵Ash′hùr, the father of

b Gk: Heb *Mesha*   c Heb *the father of Hebron*   d Gk Vg: Heb *son*
e Gk Compare Syr Vg: Heb *sons of*   f Gk Compare Vg: Heb *father*
3.1-9: 2 Sam 3.2-5; 5.14-16; 1 Chron 14.3-6.   3.4: 2 Sam 5.4-5.

Te·kō′a, had two wives, Hē′lah and Nā′a·rah; 6 Nā′a·rah bore him A·huz′zam, Hē′pher, Tē′mē·nī, and Hā·a·hash′ta·ri. These were the sons of Naarah. 7 The sons of Hē′lah: Zē′reth, Iz′här, and Eth′nan. 8 Koz was the father of A′nub, Zō·bē′bah, and the families of A·här′hel the son of Hâr′ûm. 9 Jā′bez was more honorable than his brothers; and his mother called his name Jabez, saying, "Because I bore him in pain." 10 Jā′bez called on the God of Israel, saying, "Oh that thou wouldst bless me and enlarge my border, and that thy hand might be with me, and that thou wouldst keep me from harm so that it might not hurt me!" And God granted what he asked. 11 Chē′lub, the brother of Shü′hah, was the father of Mē′hir, who was the father of Esh′ton. 12 Esh′ton was the father of Beth·ra′pha, Pa·sē′ah, and Te·hin′ah the father of Ir·nā′hash. These are the men of Rē′cah. 13 The sons of Kē′naz: Oth′ni·el and Se·räi′ah; and the sons of Othni·el: Hā′thath and Me·ō′nō·thäi.g 14 Me·ō′nō·thäi was the father of Oph′rah; and Se·räi′ah was the father of Jō′ab the father of Ge·hâr′a·shim,h so-called because they were craftsmen. 15 The sons of Caleb the son of Jē·phün′neh: I′rü, Ē′lah, and Nā′am; and the sons of Elah: Kē′naz. 16 The sons of Je·hal′lel: Ziph, Zī′phah, Tir′i·a, and As′a·rel. 17 The sons of Ez′rah: Jē′ther, Mē′red, Ē′pher, and Jā′lon. These are the sons of Bith′i·ah, the daughter of Pharaoh, whom Mered married;i and she conceived and borej Miriam, Sham′mäi, and Ish′bah, the father of Esh·te·mō′a. 18 And his Jewish wife bore Jē′red the father of Gē′dôr, Hē′bēr the father of Sō′cōh, and Je·kü′thi·el the father of Zā·nō′ah. 19 The sons of the wife of Hō·dī′ah, the sister of Nā′ham, were the fathers of Kē·ī′lah the Gär′mite and Esh·te·mō′a the Mā·ac′a·thīte. 20 The sons of Shī′mŏn: Am′non, Rin′nah, Ben-hā′nàn, and Tī′lon. The sons of Ish′ī: Zō′heth and Ben-zō′heth. 21 The sons of Shē′lah the son of Judah: Ēr the father of Lē′cah, Lā′a·dah the father of Ma·rē′shah, and the families of the house of linen workers at Beth-ash·bē′a; 22 and Jō′kim, and the men of Cō·zē′ba, and Jō′ash, and Sâr′aph, who ruled in Mō′ab and returned to Lē′hemk (now the records^l are ancient). 23 These

were the potters and inhabitants of Ne·tā′im and Ge·dē′rah; they dwelt there with the king for his work.

24 The sons of Simeon: Nem′ū·el, Jā′min, Jâr′ib, Zē′rah, Shā′ul; 25 Shal′lüm was his son, Mib′sàm his son, Mish′mà his son. 26 The sons of Mish′mà: Ham′mū·el his son, Zac′cür his son, Shim′ē·ī his son. 27 Shim′ē·ī had sixteen sons and six daughters; but his brothers had not many children, nor did all their family multiply like the men of Judah. 28 They dwelt in Beer-sheba, Mō′la·dah, Hā′zär-shū′al, 29 Bil′hah, Ē′zem, Tō′lad, 30 Be·thū′el, Hôr′mah, Zik′lag, 31 Beth-mär′ca·both, Hā′zär-sü′sim, Beth-bir′ī, and Shā·a·rā′im. These were their cities until David reigned. 32 And their villages were Ē′tam, A′in, Rim′mon, Tō′chen, and A′shàn, five cities, 33 along with all their villages which were round about these cities as far as Bā′al. These were their settlements, and they kept a genealogical record.

34 Me·shō′bab, Jam′lech, Jō′shah the son of Am·a·zī′ah, 35 Jō′el, Jē′hü the son of Josh·i·bī′ah, son of Se·räi′ah, son of As′i·el, 36 El′i·ō·ē′näi, Jā·a·kō′bah, Jesh·ō·hāi′ah, A·säi′ah, Ad′i·el, Je·sim′i·el, Be·nā′iah, 37 Zī′za the son of Shī′phī, son of Al′lon, of Je·dāi′ah, son of Shim′rī, son of She·mäi′ah—38 these mentioned by name were princes in their families, and their fathers' houses increased greatly. 39 They journeyed to the entrance of Gē′dôr, to the east side of the valley, to seek pasture for their flocks, 40 where they found rich, good pasture, and the land was very broad, quiet, and peaceful; for the former inhabitants there belonged to Ham. 41 These, registered by name, came in the days of Hez·ē·kī′ah, king of Judah, and destroyed their tents and the Me·ü′nim who were found there, and exterminated them to this day, and settled in their place, because there was pasture there for their flocks. 42 And some of them, five hundred men of the Simeonites, went to Mount Sē′ir, having as their leaders Pel·a·tī′ah, Nē·a·rī′ah, Reph·a′iah, and Uz′zi·el, the sons of Ish′ī; 43 and they destroyed the remnant of the A·mal′e·kites that had escaped, and they have dwelt there to this day.

5 The sons of Reuben the first-born of Israel (for he was the

g Gk Vg: Heb lacks *Meonothai*   h That is *Valley of craftsmen*
i The clause: *These are . . . married* is transposed from verse 18   j Heb lacks *and bore*
k Vg Compare Gk: Heb *and Jashubi-lahem*   l Or *matters*
4.24: Gen 46.10; Ex 6.15; Num 26.12-13.   **4.28-33:** Josh 19.2-8.
5.1-26: Gen 46.9; Num 26.5-6.

first-born; but because he polluted his father's couch, his birthright was given to the sons of Joseph the son of Israel, so that he is not enrolled in the genealogy according to the birthright; 2 though Judah became strong among his brothers and a prince was from him, yet the birthright belonged to Joseph), 3 the sons of Reuben, the first-born of Israel: Hā´noch, Pal´lü, Hez´ròn, and Cär´mī. 4 The sons of Jō´él: She·māi´ah his son, Gog his son, Shim´ē-ī his son, 5 Mī´cah his son, Rē-āi´ah his son, Bā´al his son. 6 Bē-ēr´ah his son, whom Til´gath-pil·nē´-sèr king of Assyria carried away into exile; he was a chieftain of the Reubenites. 7 And his kinsmen by their families, when the genealogy of their generations was reckoned: the chief, Je-i´el, and Zech·a·rī´ah, 8 and Bē´lā the son of A´zaz, son of Shē´mà, son of Jō´él, who dwelt in A·rō´er, as far as Nē´bō and Bā´al-mē´ón. 9 He also dwelt to the east as far as the entrance of the desert this side of the Eū·phrā´-tēs, because their cattle had multiplied in the land of Gilead. 10 And in the days of Saul they made war on the Hag´rites, who fell by their hand; and they dwelt in their tents throughout all the region east of Gilead.

11 The sons of Gad dwelt over against them in the land of Bā´shàn as far as Sal´é·càh: 12 Jō´él the chief, Shā´phàm the second, Jā´näi, and Shā´phàt in Bā´shàn. 13 And their kinsmen according to their fathers' houses: Michael, Me·shul´làm, Sheba, Jō´räi, Jā´càn, Zī´a, and Ē´bèr, seven. 14 These were the sons of Ab´i·hàil the son of Hū´rī, son of Jà·rō´àh, son of Gilead, son of Michael, son of Je·shish´äi, son of Jäh´dō, son of Buz; 15 A´hī the son of Ab´di-el, son of Gü´nī, was chief in their fathers' houses; 16 and they dwelt in Gilead, in Bā´shàn and in its towns, and in all the pasture lands of Sharon to their limits. 17 All of these were enrolled by genealogies in the days of Jō´thàm king of Judah, and in the days of Jer·ó·bō´am king of Israel.

18 The Reubenites, the Gadites, and the half-tribe of Mà·nas´sēh had valiant men, who carried shield and sword, and drew the bow, expert in war, forty-four thousand seven hundred and sixty, ready for service. 19 They made war upon the Hag´rites, Jē´tūr, Nā´phish, and Nō´dab; 20 and when they received help against them, the Hag´rites and all who were with them were given into their hands, for

they cried to God in the battle, and he granted their entreaty because they trusted in him. 21 They carried off their livestock: fifty thousand of their camels, two hundred and fifty thousand sheep, two thousand asses, and a hundred thousand men alive. 22 For many fell slain, because the war was of God. And they dwelt in their place until the exile.

23 The members of the half-tribe of Mà·nas´sēh dwelt in the land; they were very numerous from Bā´shàn to Bā´al-hēr´mòn, Sē´nir, and Mount Hēr´mòn. 24 These were the heads of their fathers' houses: Ē´phèr,*m* Ish´ī, E·lī´el, Az´ri-el, Jeremiah, Hod·à·vī´àh, and Jäh´dì-el, mighty warriors, famous men, heads of their fathers' houses. 25 But they transgressed against the God of their fathers, and played the harlot after the gods of the peoples of the land, whom God had destroyed before them. 26 So the God of Israel stirred up the spirit of Pül king of Assyria, the spirit of Til´gath-pil·nē´-sèr king of Assyria, and he carried them away, namely, the Reubenites, the Gadites, and the half-tribe of Mà·nas´sēh, and brought them to Hā´làh, Hā´bòr, Hâr´à, and the river Gō´zan, to this day.

6*n* The sons of Levi: Gēr´shòm, Kō´hath, and Mè·rär´ī. 2 The sons of Kō´hath: Am´ram, Iz´här, Hē´bròn, and Uz´zi·el. 3 The children of Am´ram: Aaron, Moses, and Miriam. The sons of Aaron: Nā´dab, A·bī´hū, El·ē-ā´zàr, and Ith´à·mär. 4 El·ē·ā´zàr was the father of Phin´é·hàs, Phinehas the father of Ab·i·shū´à, 5 Ab·i·shū´à of Buk´ki, Bukki of Uz´zī, 6 Uz´zī of Zer·à·hī´àh, Zerahiah of Me·rā´ioth, 7 Me·rā´ioth of Am·à·rī´àh, Amariah of A·hī´tùb, 8 A·hī´-tùb of Zā´dok, Zadok of A·him´à-az, 9 A·him´à-az of Az·à·rī´àh, Azariah of Jō·hā´nàn, 10 and Jō·hā´nàn of Az·à·rī´-àh (it was he who served as priest in the house that Solomon built in Jerusalem). 11 Az·à·rī´àh was the father of Am·à·rī´-àh, Amariah of A·hī´tùb, 12 A·hī´tùb of Zā´dok, Zadok of Shal´lùm, 13 Shal´-lùm of Hil·ki´àh, Hilkiah of Az·à·rī´àh, 14 Az·à·rī´àh of Se·räi´àh, Seraiah of Je·hoz´à·dak; 15 and Je·hoz´à·dak went into exile when the LORD sent Judah and Jerusalem into exile by the hand of Ne·bù·chàd·nez´zàr.

16*o* The sons of Levi: Gēr´shòm, Kō´hath, and Mè·rär´ī. 17 And these are the names of the sons of Gēr´shòm: Lib´nī and Shim´ē-ī. 18 The sons of Kō´hath: Am´ram, Iz´här, Hē´bròn,

---

m Gk Vg: Heb *and Epher*   *n* Ch 5.27 in Heb   *o* Ch 6.1 in Heb
6.1-15: Gen 46.11; Ex 6.16-20; Num 3.2.   **6.16-53:** Ex 6.16-24.

and Uz·zi·el. 19 The sons of Me·râr'ī: Mäh'lī and Mū'shī. These are the families of the Levites according to their fathers. 20 Of Gēr'shŏm: Lib'nī his son, Ja'hath his son, Zim'mäh his son, 21 Jō'äh his son, Id'dō his son, Ze'räh his son, Je·ath'e·räi his son. 22 The sons of Kō'hath: Am·mĭn'a·dab his son, Kō'räh his son, As'sir his son, 23 El·kä'näh his son, E·bi'a·saph his son, As'sir his son, 24 Tä'hath his son, U·rī'el his son, Uz·zi'äh his son, and Shä'ül his son. 25 The sons of El·kä'näh: A·mä'säi and A·hi'moth, 26 El·kä'näh his son, Zō'phäi his son, Nä'hath his son, 27 E·lī'ab his son, Je·rō'ham his son, El·kä'näh his son. 28 The sons of Samuel: Jō'ĕl[p] his first-born, the second A·bi'jäh.[q] 29 The sons of Me·râr'ī: Mäh'lī, Lib'nī his son, Shim'e·ī his son, Uz'zäh his son, 30 Shim'e·ä his son, Hag·gī'äh his son, and A·säi'äh his son.

31 These are the men whom David put in charge of the service of song in the house of the LORD, after the ark rested there. 32 They ministered with song before the tabernacle of the tent of meeting, until Solomon had built the house of the LORD in Jerusalem; and they performed their service in due order. 33 These are the men who served and their sons. Of the sons of the Kō'hath·ītes: Hē'män the singer the son of Jō'ĕl, son of Samuel, 34 son of El·kä'näh, son of Je·rō'ham, son of E·lī'el, son of Tō'äh, 35 son of Zuph, son of El·kä'näh, son of Mä'hath, son of A·mä'säi, 36 son of El·kä'näh, son of Jō'ĕl, son of Az·a·rī'äh, son of Zeph·a·nī'äh, 37 son of Tä'hath, son of As'sir, son of E·bi'a·saph, son of Kō'räh, 38 son of Iz'här, son of Kō'hath, son of Levi, son of Israel; 39 and his brother Ā'saph, who stood on his right hand, namely, Asaph the son of Ber·e·chī'äh, son of Shim'e·ä, 40 son of Michael, son of Bä·a·se'iäh, son of Mal·chi'jäh, 41 son of Eth'nī, son of Ze'räh, son of A·däi'äh, 42 son of Ethan, son of Zim'mäh, son of Shim'e·ī, 43 son of Jä'hath, son of Gēr'shŏm, son of Levi. 44 On the left hand were their brethren the sons of Me·râr'ī: Ethan the son of Kish'ī, son of Ab'dī, son of Mal'lŭch, 45 son of Hash·a·bi'äh, son of Am·a·zī'äh, son of Hil·kī'äh, 46 son of Am'zī, son of Bä'nī, son of She'mĕr, 47 son of Mäh'lī, son of Mū'shī, son of Me·râr'ī, son of Levi; and their brethren the Levites were appointed for all the service of the tabernacle of the house of God.

49 But Aaron and his sons made offerings upon the altar of burnt offering and upon the altar of incense for all the work of the most holy place, and to make atonement for Israel, according to all that Moses the servant of God had commanded. 50 These are the sons of Aaron: El·e·ä'zär his son, Phin'e·hàs his son, Ab·i·shü'a his son, 51 Buk'kī his son, Uz'zī his son, Zer·a·hī'äh his son, 52 Me·rä'ioth his son, Am·a·rī'äh his son, A·hī'tüb his son, 53 Zä'dok his son, A·him'a·az his son.

54 These are their dwelling places according to their settlements within their borders: to the sons of Aaron of the families of Kō'ha·thites, for theirs was the lot, 55 to them they gave Hē'brŏn in the land of Judah and its surrounding pasture lands, 56 but the fields of the city and its villages they gave to Caleb the son of Je·phŭn'neh. 57 To the sons of Aaron they gave the cities of refuge: Hē'brŏn, Lib'näh with its pasture lands, Jat'tir, Esh·tĕ·mō'a with its pasture lands, 58 Hī'len with its pasture lands, Dē'bir with its pasture lands, 59 Ā'shän with its pasture lands, and Beth-she'mesh with its pasture lands; 60 and from the tribe of Benjamin, Ge'bä with its pasture lands, Al'e·meth with its pasture lands, and An'a·thoth with its pasture lands. All their cities throughout their families were thirteen.

61 To the rest of the Kō'ha·thites were given by lot out of the family of the tribe, out of the half-tribe, the half of Mä·nas'seh, ten cities. 62 To the Gēr'shō·mites according to their families were allotted thirteen cities out of the tribes of Is'sa·chär, Ash'ĕr, Naph'ta·lī, and Mä·nas'seh in Bä'shän. 63 To the Me·râr'ītes according to their families were allotted twelve cities out of the tribes of Reuben, Gad, and Zeb'ū·lŭn. 64 So the people of Israel gave the Levites the cities with their pasture lands. 65 They also gave them by lot out of the tribes of Judah, Simeon, and Benjamin these cities which are mentioned by name.

66 And some of the families of the sons of Kō'hath had cities of their territory out of the tribe of E'phra·im. 67 They were given the cities of refuge: She'chem with its pasture lands in the hill country of E'phra·im, Ge'zĕr with its pasture lands, 68 Jok'me·äm with its pasture lands, Beth-hō'ron with its pasture lands, 69 Ai'ja·lon with its pasture lands, Gath-rim'mon with its pasture lands, 70 and out of the half-

p Gk Syr Compare verse 33 and 1 Sam 8.2: Heb lacks *Joel*   q Heb *and Abijah*
6.54-81: Josh 21.1-42.

tribe of Mà·nas'seh, A'ner with its pasture lands, and Bil'e·am with its pasture lands, for the rest of the families of the Kō'hà·thites.

71 To the Gēr'shō·mītes were given out of the half-tribe of Mà·nas'seh: Gō'làn in Bā'shàn with its pasture lands and Ash'tà·roth with its pasture lands; 72 and out of the tribe of Is'sà·chär: Kē'desh with its pasture lands, Dab'e·rath with its pasture lands, 73 Rā'moth with its pasture lands, and A'nem with its pasture lands; 74 out of the tribe of Ash'ēr: Mā'shàl with its pasture lands, Ab'don with its pasture lands, 75 Hū'kok with its pasture lands, and Rē'hob with its pasture lands; 76 and out of the tribe of Naph'tà·lī: Kē'desh in Galilee with its pasture lands, Ham'mòn with its pasture lands, and Kīr'i·à·thā'im with its pasture lands. 77 To the rest of the Mē·râr'ītes were allotted out of the tribe of Zeb'ū·lún: Rim'mó·nō with its pasture lands, Tā'bôr with its pasture lands, 78 and beyond the Jordan at Jericho, on the east side of the Jordan, out of the tribe of Reuben: Bē'zēr in the steppe with its pasture lands, Jäh'zàh with its pasture lands, 79 Kēd'e·moth with its pasture lands, and Meph'à·ath with its pasture lands; 80 and out of the tribe of Gad: Rā'moth in Gilead with its pasture lands, Mā·hà·nā'im with its pasture lands, 81 Hesh'bòn with its pasture lands, and Jā'zēr with its pasture lands.

7 The sons[r] of Is'sà·chär: Tō'là, Pū'àh, Jash'ûb, and Shim'rón, four. 2 The sons of Tō'là: Uz'zī, Reph'ā'iàh, Jē'rī·el, Jäh'mäi, Ib'sàm, and She·mū'el, heads of their fathers' houses, namely of Tola, mighty warriors of their generations, their number in the days of David being twenty-two thousand six hundred. 3 The sons of Uz'zī: Iz·rà·hī'àh. And the sons of Izrahiah: Michael, Ō·bà·dī'àh, Jō'el, and Is·shī'àh, five, all of them chief men; 4 and along with them, by their generations, according to their fathers' houses, were units of the army for war, thirty-six thousand, for they had many wives and sons. 5 Their kinsmen belonging to all the families of Is'sà·chär were in all eighty-seven thousand mighty warriors, enrolled by genealogy.

6 The sons of Benjamin: Bē'là, Bē'chēr, and Je·dī'à·el, three. 7 The sons of Bē'là: Ez'bòn, Uz'zī, Uz'zi·el, Jer'i·moth, and Ī'rī, five, heads of fathers' houses, mighty warriors; and their enrollment by genealogies was twenty-two thousand and thirty-four. 8 The sons of Bē'chēr: Ze·mī'ràh,

Jō'ash, Ē·lī·e'zēr, El·i·ō·e'näi, Om'rī, Jer'e·moth, À·bī'jàh, An'à·thoth, and Al'e·meth. All these were the sons of Becher; 9 and their enrollment by genealogies, according to their generations, as heads of their fathers' houses, mighty warriors, was twenty thousand two hundred. 10 The sons of Je·dī'à·el: Bil'han. And the sons of Bilhan: Jē'ush, Benjamin, Ē'hud, Che·nā'à·nàh, Zē'thàn, Tär'shish, and A·hish'à·här. 11 All these were the sons of Je·dī'à·el according to the heads of their fathers' houses, mighty warriors, seventeen thousand and two hundred, ready for service in war. 12 And Shup'pim and Hup'pim were the sons of Īr, Hū'shim the sons of A'hēr.

13 The sons of Naph'tà·lī: Jäh'zi·el, Gū'nī, Jē'zēr, and Shal'lúm, the offspring of Bil'hàh.

14 The sons of Mà·nas'seh: As'ri·el, whom his Ar·à·mē'àn concubine bore; she bore Mā'chir the father of Gilead. 15 And Mā'chir took a wife for Hup'pim and for Shup'pim. The name of his sister was Mā'à·càh. And the name of the second was Ze·loph'e·had; and Zelophehad had daughters. 16 And Mā'à·càh the wife of Mā'chir bore a son, and she called his name Pē'resh; and the name of his brother was Shē'resh; and his sons were Ū'làm and Rā'kém. 17 The sons of Ū'làm: Bē'dan. These were the sons of Gilead the son of Mā'chir, son of Mà·nas'seh. 18 And his sister Ham·mō'lē·cheth bore Ish'hod, À·bi·e'zēr, and Mäh'làh. 19 The sons of Shē·mī'dà were A·hī'àn, Shē'chem, Lik'hī, and A·nī'àm.

20 The sons of Ē'phrà·im: Shü·thē'làh, and Bē'red his son, Tā'hath his son, E·lē·ā'dàh his son, Tahath his son, 21 Zā'bad his son, Shü·thē'làh his son, and Ē'zēr and Ē'lē·ad, whom the men of Gath who were born in the land slew, because they came down to raid their cattle. 22 And Ē'phrà·im their father mourned many days, and his brothers came to comfort him. 23 And Ē'phrà·im went in to his wife, and she conceived and bore a son; and he called his name Bē·rī'àh, because evil had befallen his house. 24 His daughter was Shē'e·ràh, who built both Lower and Upper Beth·hō'ron, and Uz'zēn·shē'e·ràh. 25 Rē'phàh was his son. Rē'sheph his son, Tē'làh his son, Tā'han his son, 26 Lā'dàn his son, Am·mī'hûd his son, E·lish'à·mà his son, 27 Nun his son, Joshua his son. 28 Their possessions and settlements were Beth'el and its towns, and eastward Nā'à·ran, and westward Gē'zer

and its towns, Shē'chem and its towns, and Ăy'yăh and its towns; 29 also along the borders of the Mà·nas'sites, Beth-shē'an and its towns, Tā'a·nach and its towns, Mĕ·gid'dō and its towns, Dôr and its towns. In these dwelt the sons of Joseph the son of Israel.

30 The sons of Ash'ẽr: Im'năh, Ish'văh, Ish'vī, Bē·rī'ăh, and their sister Sē'răh. 31 The sons of Bē·rī'ăh: Hē'bẽr and Mal'chi-el, who was the father of Bir'zā·ith. 32 Hē'bẽr was the father of Japh'let, Shō'mẽr, Hō'thăm, and their sister Shū'à. 33 The sons of Japh'let: Pā'sach, Bim'hăl, and Ash'-vath. These are the sons of Japhlet. 34 The sons of Shē'mẽr his brother: Rōh'găh, Je·hub'băh, and Ăr'am. 35 The sons of Hē'lem his brother: Zō'phăh, Im'nà, Shē'lesh, and A'măl. 36 The sons of Zō'phăh: Sü'ăh, Här'ne·phẽr, Shü'ăl, Bē'rī, Im'răh, 37 Bē'zẽr, Hod, Sham'mà, Shil'shăh, Ith'ran, and Be·ē'rà. 38 The sons of Jē'thẽr: Jé·phün'neh, Pis'pà, and Ăr'à. 39 The sons of Ul'là: Ä'răh, Han'ni·el, and Ri·zī'à. 40 All of these were men of Ash'ẽr, heads of fathers' houses, approved, mighty warriors, chief of the princes. Their number enrolled by genealogies, for service in war, was twenty-six thousand men.

8 Benjamin was the father of Bē'là his first-born, Ash'bel the second, Ä·hăr'ăh the third, 2 Nō'hăh the fourth, and Rā'phà the fifth. 3 And Bē'là had sons: Ad'där, Gē'rà, Ä·bī'-hüd, 4 Ab·i·shü'à, Nā'a·man, Ä·hō'ăh, 5 Gē'rà, She·phü'phăn, and Hü'răm. 6 These are the sons of Ē'hud (they were heads of fathers' houses of the inhabitants of Gē'bà, and they were carried into exile to Mà·nā'hath): 7 Nā'a·man,ˢ Ä·hī'jăh, and Gē'rà, that is, Heg'lăm,ᵗ who was the father of Uz'zà and Ä·hī'hüd. 8 And Shā·hà·rā'im sons in the country of Mō'ab after he had sent away Hü'shim and Bā'a·rà his wives. 9 He had sons by Hō'desh his wife: Jō'bab, Zib'i·à, Mē'shà, Mal'căm, 10 Jē'üz, Sa·chī'à, and Mir'măh. These were his sons, heads of fathers' houses. 11 He also had sons by Hü'shim: Ä·bī'tüb and El·pā'ăl. 12 The sons of El·pā'ăl: Ē'bẽr, Mi'shăm, and Shē'med, who built O'nō and Lod with its towns, 13 and Bē·rī'ăh and Shē'mà (they were heads of fathers' houses of the inhabitants of Ăī'ja·lon, who put to flight the inhabitants of Gath); 14 and Ä·hī'ō, Shā'shak, and Jer'é·moth. 15 Zeb·à·dī'ăh, Ăr'ăd, Ē'dẽr, 16 Michael, Ish'păh, and Jō'hà

sons of Bē·rī'ăh. 17 Zeb·à·dī'ăh, Me-shul'lăm, Hiz'kī, Hē'bẽr, 18 Ish'mé-räi, Iz·li'ăh, and Jō'bab were the sons of El·pā'ăl. 19 Jā'kim, Zich'rī, Zab'-dī, 20 El'i-ē'näi, Zil'lé·thäi, E·lī'el, 21 Ä·däi'ăh, Be·rā'iăh, and Shim'rath were the sons of Shim'é-ī. 22 Ish'pan, Ē'bẽr, E·lī'el, 23 Ab'don, Zich'rī, Hā'nàn, 24 Han·à·nī'ăh, Ē'lăm, An·thô·thī'jăh, 25 Iph·dē'iăh, and Pé·nū'el were the sons of Shā'shak. 26 Sham'shé·räi, Shē·hà·rī'ăh, Ath·à·lī'ăh, 27 Jä·ăr·é-shī'ăh, E·lī'jăh, and Zich'rī were the sons of Je·rō'ham. 28 These were the heads of fathers' houses, according to their generations, chief men. These dwelt in Jerusalem.

29 Je·ī'elᵘ the father of Gib'ē·ón dwelt in Gibeon, and the name of his wife was Mà'a·căh. 30 His first-born son: Ab'don, then Zŭr, Kish, Bā'ăl, Nā'dab, 31 Gē'dôr, Ä·hī'ō, Zē'chẽr, 32 and Mik'loth (he was the father of Shim'ē-ăh). Now these also dwelt opposite their kinsmen in Jerusalem, with their kinsmen. 33 Nẽr was the father of Kish, Kish of Saul, Saul of Jonathan, Mal'chi-shü'à, Ä·bin'à·dab, and Esh·bā'ăl; 34 and the son of Jonathan was Mer'ib-bā'ăl; and Merib-baal was the father of Mi'căh. 35 The sons of Mi'căh: Pī'thon, Mē'lech, Tà·rē'à, and A'haz. 36 A'haz was the father of Je·hō'ad·dăh; and Jehoaddah was the father of Al'é·meth, Az'mà·veth, and Zim'rī; Zimri was the father of Mō'zà. 37 Mō'zà was the father of Bin'ē-à; Rā'phăh was his son, El·e-ā'săh his son, A'zel his son. 38 A'zel had six sons, and these are their names: Az·rī'kam, Bō'che·rü, Ish'mà·el, Shē·à·rī'ăh, O·bà·dī'ăh, and Hā'nàn. All these were the sons of Azel. 39 The sons of Ē'shek his brother: Ū'lăm his first-born, Jē'ush the second, and E·liph'é·let the third. 40 The sons of Ū'lăm were men who were mighty warriors, bowmen, having many sons and grandsons, one hundred and fifty. All these were Benjaminites.

9 So all Israel was enrolled by genealogies; and these are written in the Book of the Kings of Israel. And Judah was taken into exile in Babylon because of their unfaithfulness. 2 Now the first to dwell again in their possessions in their cities were Israel, the priests, the Levites, and the temple servants. 3 And some of the people of Judah, Benjamin, E'phrà·im, and Mà·nas'seh dwelt in Jerusalem: 4 Ū'thäi the son of Am·mī'hüd, son of Om'rī, son of Im'rī, son of Bā'nī, from

ˢ Heb *and Naaman*   ᵗ Or *he carried them into exile*   ᵘ Compare 9.35: Heb lacks *Jeiel*
9.1-2: Ezra 2.70; Neh 7.73; 11.3.   **9.3-17:** Neh 11.4-19.

the sons of Per′ez the son of Judah. 5 And of the Shi′lo·nites: A·sai′ah the first-born, and his sons. 6 Of the sons of Ze′rah: Je·u′el and their kinsmen, six hundred and ninety. 7 Of the Benjaminites: Sal′lu the son of Me·shul′lam, son of Hod·a·vi′ah, son of Has·se·nu′ah, 8 Ib·ne′iah the son of Je·ro′ham, E′lah the son of Uz′zi, son of Mich′ri, and Me·shul′lam the son of Sheph·a·ti′ah, son of Reü′el, son of Ib·ni′jah; 9 and their kinsmen according to their generations, nine hundred and fifty-six. All these were heads of fathers' houses according to their fathers' houses.

10 Of the priests: Je·dai′ah, Je·hoi′a·rib, Ja′chin, 11 and Az·a·ri′ah the son of Hil·ki′ah, son of Me·shul′lam, son of Za′dok, son of Me·ra′ioth, son of A·hi′tub, the chief officer of the house of God; 12 and A·dai′ah the son of Je·ro′ham, son of Pash′hur, son of Mal·chi′jah, and Ma′a·sai the son of Ad′i-el, son of Jah′ze·rah, son of Me·shul′lam, son of Me·shil′le·mith, son of Im′mer; 13 besides their kinsmen, heads of their fathers' houses, one thousand seven hundred and sixty, very able men for the work of the service of the house of God.

14 Of the Levites: She·mai′ah the son of Has′shub, son of Az·ri′kam, son of Hash·a·bi′ah, of the sons of Me·rar′i; 15 and Bak·bak′kar, He′resh, Ga′lal, and Mat·ta·ni′ah the son of Mi′ca, son of Zich′ri, son of A′saph; 16 and O·ba·di′ah the son of She·mai′ah, son of Ga′lal, son of Je·du′thun, and Ber·e·chi′ah the son of Asa, son of El·ka′nah, who dwelt in the villages of the Ne·toph′a·thites.

17 The gatekeepers were: Shal′lum, Ak′kub, Tal′mon, A·hi′man, and their kinsmen (Shallum being the chief), 18 stationed hitherto in the king's gate on the east side. These were the gatekeepers of the camp of the Levites. 19 Shal′lum the son of Ko′re, son of E·bi′a·saph, son of Ko′rah, and his kinsmen of his fathers' house, the Ko′ra·hites, were in charge of the work of the service, keepers of the thresholds of the tent, as their fathers had been in charge of the camp of the LORD, keepers of the entrance. 20 And Phin′e·has the son of El·e·a′zar was the ruler over them in time past; the LORD was with him. 21 Zech·a·ri′ah the son of Me·shel·e·mi′ah was gatekeeper at the entrance of the tent of meeting. 22 All these, who were chosen as gatekeepers at the thresholds, were two hundred and twelve. They were enrolled by genealogies in their villages. David and Samuel the seer established them in their office of trust. 23 So they and their sons were in charge of the gates of the house of the LORD, that is, the house of the tent, as guards. 24 The gatekeepers were on the four sides, east, west, north, and south; 25 and their kinsmen who were in their villages were obliged to come in every seven days, from time to time, to be with these; 26 for the four chief gatekeepers, who were Levites, were in charge of the chambers and the treasuries of the house of God. 27 And they lodged round about the house of God; for upon them lay the duty of watching, and they had charge of opening it every morning.

28 Some of them had charge of the utensils of service, for they were required to count them when they were brought in and taken out. 29 Others of them were appointed over the furniture, and over all the holy utensils, also over the fine flour, the wine, the oil, the incense, and the spices. 30 Others, of the sons of the priests, prepared the mixing of the spices, 31 and Mat·ti·thi′ah, one of the Levites, the first-born of Shal′lum the Ko′ra·hite, was in charge of making the flat cakes. 32 Also some of their kinsmen of the Ko′ha·thites had charge of the showbread, to prepare it every sabbath.

33 Now these are the singers, the heads of fathers' houses of the Levites, dwelling in the chambers of the temple free from other service, for they were on duty day and night. 34 These were heads of fathers' houses of the Levites, according to their generations, leaders, who lived in Jerusalem.

35 In Gib′e·on dwelt the father of Gibeon, Je·i′el, and the name of his wife was Ma′a·cah, 36 and his first-born son Ab′don, then Zur, Kish, Ba′al, Ner, Na′dab, 37 Ge′dor, A·hi′o, Zech·a·ri′ah, and Mik′loth; 38 and Mikloth was the father of Shim′e·am; and these also dwelt opposite their kinsmen in Jerusalem, with their kinsmen. 39 Ner was the father of Kish, Kish of Saul, Saul of Jonathan, Mal·chi·shu′a, A·bin′a·dab, and Esh·ba′al; 40 and the son of Jonathan was Mer′ib-ba′al; and Merib-baal was the father of Mi′cah. 41 The sons of Mi′cah: Pi′thon, Me′lech, Tah′re·a, and A′haz;ʸ 42 and A′haz was the father of Jar′ah, and Jarah of Al′e·meth, Az′ma·veth, and Zim′ri; and Zimri was the father of Mo′za. 43 Mo′za was the father of

ʸ Compare 8.35: Heb lacks *and Ahaz*

Bin′e-á; and Reph-ā′iáh was his son, El′e-ā′sáh his son, A′zel his son. ⁴⁴A′zel had six sons and these are their names: Az-rī′kam, Bō′che-rü, Ish′má-el, Shē-á-rī′áh, Ō-bá-dī′áh, and Hā′nàn; these were the sons of Azel.

10

Now the Philistines fought against Israel; and the men of Israel fled before the Philistines, and fell slain on Mount Gil-bō′á. ²And the Philistines overtook Saul and his sons; and the Philistines slew Jonathan and Á-bin′á-dab and Mal′chī-shü′á, the sons of Saul. ³ The battle pressed hard upon Saul, and the archers found him; and he was wounded by the archers. ⁴ Then Saul said to his armor-bearer, "Draw your sword, and thrust me through with it, lest these uncircumcised come and make sport of me." But his armor-bearer would not; for he feared greatly. Therefore Saul took his own sword, and fell upon it. ⁵And when his armor-bearer saw that Saul was dead, he also fell upon his sword, and died. ⁶ Thus Saul died; he and his three sons and all his house died together. ⁷And when all the men of Israel who were in the valley saw that the armyʷ had fled and that Saul and his sons were dead, they forsook their cities and fled; and the Philistines came and dwelt in them.

8 On the morrow, when the Philistines came to strip the slain, they found Saul and his sons fallen on Mount Gil-bō′á. ⁹And they stripped him and took his head and his armor, and sent messengers throughout the land of the Philistines, to carry the good news to their idols and to the people. ¹⁰And they put his armor in the temple of their gods, and fastened his head in the temple of Dā′gon. ¹¹ But when all Jā′besh-gil′e-ád heard all that the Philistines had done to Saul, ¹² all the valiant men arose, and took away the body of Saul and the bodies of his sons, and brought them to Jā′besh. And they buried their bones under the oak in Jabesh, and fasted seven days.

13 So Saul died for his unfaithfulness; he was unfaithful to the LORD in that he did not keep the command of the LORD, and also consulted a medium, seeking guidance, ¹⁴ and did not seek guidance from the LORD. Therefore the LORD slew him, and turned the kingdom over to David the son of Jesse.

11

Then all Israel gathered together to David at Hē′brŏn, and said, "Behold, we are your bone and flesh. ² In times past, even when Saul was king, it was you that led out and brought in Israel; and the LORD your God said to you, 'You shall be shepherd of my people Israel, and you shall be prince over my people Israel.'" ³ So all the elders of Israel came to the king at Hē′brŏn; and David made a covenant with them at Hebron before the LORD, and they anointed David king over Israel, according to the word of the LORD by Samuel.

4 And David and all Israel went to Jerusalem, that is Jē′bús, where the Jeb′ū-sītes were, the inhabitants of the land. ⁵ The inhabitants of Jē′bús said to David, "You will not come in here." Nevertheless David took the stronghold of Zion, that is, the city of David. ⁶ David said, "Whoever shall smite the Jeb′ū-sītes first shall be chief and commander." And Jō′ab the son of Zé-rü′i-áh went up first, so he became chief. ⁷And David dwelt in the stronghold; therefore it was called the city of David. ⁸And he built the city round about from the Mil′lō in complete circuit; and Jō′ab repaired the rest of the city. ⁹And David became greater and greater, for the LORD of hosts was with him.

10 Now these are the chiefs of David's mighty men, who gave him strong support in his kingdom, together with all Israel, to make him king, according to the word of the LORD concerning Israel. ¹¹ This is an account of David's mighty men: Jà-shō′bē-àm, a Hach′mó-nīte, was chief of the three;ˣ he wielded his spear against three hundred whom he slew at one time.

12 And next to him among the three mighty men was El-ē-ā′zàr the son of Dō′dō, the Á-hō′hīte. ¹³ He was with David at Pas-dam′mim when the Philistines were gathered there for battle. There was a plot of ground full of barley, and the men fled from the Philistines. ¹⁴ But heʸ took hisʸ stand in the midst of the plot, and defended it, and slew the Philistines; and the LORD saved them by a great victory.

15 Three of the thirty chief men went down to the rock to David at the cave of Á-dul′làm, when the army of Philistines was encamped in the valley

---

ʷ Heb *they*　　ˣ Compare 2 Sam 23.8: Heb *thirty* or *captains*
ʸ Compare 2 Sam 23.12: Heb *they . . . their*
10.1-12: 1 Sam 31.1-13.　　**11.1-3:** 2 Sam 5.1-3.　　**11.4-9:** 2 Sam 5.6-10.
11.10-41: 2 Sam 23.8-39.

of Reph'a·im. ¹⁶David was then in the stronghold; and the garrison of the Philistines was then at Bethlehem. ¹⁷And David said longingly, "O that some one would give me water to drink from the well of Bethlehem which is by the gate!" ¹⁸ Then the three mighty men broke through the camp of the Philistines, and drew water out of the well of Bethlehem which was by the gate, and took and brought it to David. But David would not drink of it; he poured it out to the LORD, ¹⁹ and said, "Far be it from me before my God that I should do this. Shall I drink the lifeblood of these men? For at the risk of their lives they brought it." Therefore he would not drink it. These things did the three mighty men.

20 Now A·bi'shäi, the brother of Jō'ab, was chief of the thirty.ᶻ And he wielded his spear against three hundred men and slew them, and won a name beside the three. ²¹ He was the most renownedᵃ of the thirty,ᶻ and became their commander; but he did not attain to the three.

22 And Be·nä'iäh the son of Je·hoi'a·dä was a valiant manᵇ of Kab'zē·el, a doer of great deeds; he smote two arielsᶜ of Mō'ab. He also went down and slew a lion in a pit on a day when snow had fallen. ²³And he slew an Egyptian, a man of great stature, five cubits tall. The Egyptian had in his hand a spear like a weaver's beam; but Be·nä'iäh went down to him with a staff, and snatched the spear out of the Egyptian's hand, and slew him with his own spear. 24 These things did Be·nä'iäh the son of Je·hoi'a·dä, and won a name beside the three mighty men. 25 He was renowned among the thirty, but he did not attain to the three. And David set him over his bodyguard.

26 The mighty men of the armies were As'a·hel the brother of Jō'ab, El·hä'nän the son of Dō'dō of Bethlehem, 27 Sham'moth of Hâr'od,ᵈ Hē'lez the Pel'ŏ·nite, 28 Ira the son of Ik'kesh of Te·kō'a, A'bi·ē'zĕr of An'a·thoth, 29 Sib'bĕ·cäi the Hū'shä·thite, I'läi the A·hō'hite, 30 Mä'hä·räi of Nĕ·toph'ah, Hē'led the son of Bä'a·näh of Netophah, 31 Ith'äi the son of Ri'bäi of Gib'ē·äh of the Benjaminites, Be·nä'iäh of Pir'a·thon, 32 Hū'räi of the brooks of Gä'ash, A·bi'el the Är'bä-

thite, ³³Az'mä·veth of Bä·hä'rùm, Ĕ·li'ah·bä of Shā·al'bön, ³⁴ Hä'shemᵉ the Gi'zŏ·nite, Jonathan the son of Shä'gee the Hâr'a·rite, ³⁵A·hi'äm the son of Sä'chär the Hararite, E·li'phal the son of Ūr, ³⁶ Hē'phĕr the Me·chē'ra·thite, A·hi'jäh the Pel'ŏ·nite, ³⁷ Hez'rō of Cär'mel, Nä'a·räi the son of Ez'bäi, ³⁸ Jō'el the brother of Nathan, Mib'här the son of Hag'räi, ³⁹Zē'lek the Am'mŏ·nite, Nä'hä·räi of Bē·ēr'öth, the armor-bearer of Jō'ab the son of Zĕ·rü'i·äh, ⁴⁰ Ira the Ith'rite, Gä'reb the Ithrite, ⁴¹ Ū·rī'äh the Hit'tite, Zä'bad the son of Äh'läi, ⁴²Ad'i·nä the son of Shi'zä the Reubenite, a leader of the Reubenites, and thirty with him, ⁴³ Hä'nän the son of Mä'a·cäh, and Josh'a·phat the Mith'nite, ⁴⁴ Uz·zi'ä the Ash'te·ra·thite, Shä'mä and Je·i'el the sons of Hō'thäm the A·rō'e·rite, ⁴⁵ Je·di'a·el the son of Shim'ri, and Jō'hä his brother, the Ti'zīte, ⁴⁶ E·li'el the Mä'hä·vite, and Jer'i·bäi, and Josh·a·vi'äh, the sons of El'nä·äm, and Ith'mäh the Mō'ab·ite, ⁴⁷ E·li'el, and Ō'bed, and Jä·a·si'el the Me·zō'bä·ite.

12 Now these are the men who came to David at Zik'lag, while he could not move about freely because of Saul the son of Kish; and they were among the mighty men who helped him in war. 2 They were bowmen, and could shoot arrows and sling stones with either the right or the left hand; they were Benjaminites, Saul's kinsmen. ³ The chief was A'hi·ē'zĕr, then Jō'ash, both sons of She·mä'äh of Gib'ē·äh; also Jē'zi·el and Pē'let the sons of Az'mä·veth; Bĕr'a·cäh, Jē'hü of An'a·thoth, 4 Ish·mä'iäh of Gib'ē·ŏn, a mighty man among the thirty and a leader over the thirty; Jeremiah,ᶠ Jä·hä'zi·el, Jō·hä'nän, Joz'a·bad of Ge·dē'räh, ⁵ E·lü'zäi,ᵍ Jer'i·moth, Be·a·li'äh, Shem·a·rī'äh, Sheph·a·ti'äh the Hâr'ü·phite; ⁶ El·kä'näh, Is·shi'äh, Az'a·rel, Jō·ē'zĕr, and Jä·sho'bē·äm, the Kō'ra·hites; ⁷ and Jō·ē'läh and Zeb·a·di'äh, the sons of Je·rō'ham of Gē'dor.

8 From the Gadites there went over to David at the stronghold in the wilderness mighty and experienced warriors, expert with shield and spear, whose faces were like the faces of lions, and who were swift as gazelles upon the mountains: 9 Ē'zĕr the chief, Ō·ba·di'äh second, E·li'ab third, 10 Mish-

---

ᶻ Syr: Heb *three*   ᵃ Compare 2 Sam 23.19: Heb *more renowned among the two*
ᵇ Syr: Heb *the son of a valiant man*   ᶜ The meaning of the word *ariel* is unknown
ᵈ Compare 2 Sam 23.25: Heb *the Harorite*
ᵉ Compare Gk and 2 Sam 23.32: Heb *the sons of Hashem*   ᶠ Heb verse 5
ᵍ Heb verse 6

man'náh fourth, Jeremiah fifth, 11At'-täi sixth, E·li'el seventh, 12 Jō·hā'nán eighth, El·zā'bad ninth, 13 Jeremiah tenth, Mach'bán·näi eleventh. 14These Gadites were officers of the army, the lesser over a hundred and the greater over a thousand. 15 These are the men who crossed the Jordan in the first month, when it was overflowing all its banks, and put to flight all those in the valleys, to the east and to the west.

16 And some of the men of Benjamin and Judah came to the stronghold to David. 17 David went out to meet them and said to them, "If you have come to me in friendship to help me, my heart will be knit to you; but if to betray me to my adversaries, although there is no wrong in my hands, then may the God of our fathers see and rebuke you." 18 Then the Spirit came upon Ā·mā'säi, chief of the thirty, and he said,

"We are yours, O David;
    and with you, O son of Jesse!
Peace, peace to you,
    and peace to your helpers!
For your God helps you."

Then David received them, and made them officers of his troops.

19 Some of the men of Mà·nas'sěh deserted to David when he came with the Philistines for the battle against Saul. (Yet he did not help them, for the rulers of the Philistines took counsel and sent him away, saying, "At peril to our heads he will desert to his master Saul.") 20As he went to Zik'lag these men of Mà·nas'sěh deserted to him: Ad'náh, Joz'à·bad, Je·di'à·el, Michael, Jozabad, E·li'hū, and Zil'lé·thäi, chiefs of thousands in Manasseh. 21 They helped David against the band of raiders;h for they were all mighty men of valor, and were commanders in the army. 22 For from day to day men kept coming to David to help him, until there was a great army, like an army of God.

23 These are the numbers of the divisions of the armed troops, who came to David in Hē'brŏn, to turn the kingdom of Saul over to him, according to the word of the LORD. 24 The men of Judah bearing shield and spear were six thousand eight hundred armed troops. 25 Of the Simeonites, mighty men of valor for war, seven thousand one hundred. 26 Of the Levites four thousand six hundred. 27 The prince Je·hoi'à·dà, of the house

of Aaron, and with him three thousand seven hundred. 28 Zā'dok, a young man mighty in valor, and twenty-two commanders from his own father's house. 29 Of the Benjaminites, the kinsmen of Saul, three thousand, of whom the majority had hitherto kept their allegiance to the house of Saul. 30 Of the É'phrà·im·ites twenty thousand eight hundred, mighty men of valor, famous men in their fathers' houses. 31 Of the half-tribe of Mà·nas'sěh eighteen thousand, who were expressly named to come and make David king. 32 Of Is'sà·chär men who had understanding of the times, to know what Israel ought to do, two hundred chiefs, and all their kinsmen under their command. 33 Of Zeb'ū·lùn fifty thousand seasoned troops, equipped for battle with all the weapons of war, to help Davidi with singleness of purpose. 34 Of Naph'tà·li a thousand commanders with whom were thirty-seven thousand men armed with shield and spear. 35 Of the Danites twenty-eight thousand six hundred men equipped for battle. 36 Of Ash'ér forty thousand seasoned troops ready for battle. 37 Of the Reubenites and Gadites and the half-tribe of Mà·nas'sěh from beyond the Jordan, one hundred and twenty thousand men armed with all the weapons of war.

38 All these, men of war, arrayed in battle order, came to Hē'brŏn with full intent to make David king over all Israel; likewise all the rest of Israel were of a single mind to make David king. 39And they were there with David for three days, eating and drinking, for their brethren had made preparation for them. 40And also their neighbors, from as far as Is'sà·chär and Zeb'ū·lùn and Naph'tà·li, came bringing food on asses and on camels and on mules and on oxen, abundant provisions of meal, cakes of figs, clusters of raisins, and wine and oil, oxen and sheep, for there was joy in Israel.

13 David consulted with the commanders of thousands and of hundreds, with every leader. 2And David said to all the assembly of Israel, "If it seems good to you, and if it is the will of the LORD our God, let us send abroad to our brethren who remain in all the land of Israel, and with them to the priests and Levites in the cities that have pasture lands, that they may come together to us. 3 Then let us bring again the ark of our God to us; for we neglected it in the days of Saul." 4All the assembly

h Or as officers of his troops   i Gk: Heb lacks David
13.1–14: 2 Sam 6.1–11.

agreed to do so, for the thing was right in the eyes of all the people.

5 So David assembled all Israel from the Shī'hôr of Egypt to the entrance of Hā'math, to bring the ark of God from Kĭr'ĭ·ath-jē'à·rim. 6And David and all Israel went up to Bā'à·lăh, that is, to Kĭr'ĭ·ath-jē'à·rim which belongs to Judah, to bring up from there the ark of God, which is called by the name of the LORD who sits enthroned above the cherubim. 7And they carried the ark of God upon a new cart, from the house of A·bin'à·dab, and Uz'zàh and A·hī'ō[j] were driving the cart. 8And David and all Israel were making merry before God with all their might, with song and lyres and harps and tambourines and cymbals and trumpets.

9 And when they came to the threshing floor of Chī'don, Uz'zàh put out his hand to hold the ark, for the oxen stumbled. 10And the anger of the LORD was kindled against Uz'zàh; and he smote him because he put forth his hand to the ark; and he died there before God. 11And David was angry because the LORD had broken forth upon Uz'zàh; and that place is called Per'ez-uz'zàh[k] to this day. 12And David was afraid of God that day; and he said, "How can I bring the ark of God home to me?" 13 So David did not take the ark home into the city of David, but took it aside to the house of Ō'bed-ē'dŏm the Gĭt'tite. 14And the ark of God remained with the household of Ō'bed-ē'dŏm in his house three months; and the LORD blessed the household of Obed-edom and all that he had.

14 And Hiram king of Tyre sent messengers to David, and cedar trees, also masons and carpenters to build a house for him. 2And David perceived that the LORD had established him king over Israel, and that his kingdom was highly exalted for the sake of his people Israel.

3 And David took more wives in Jerusalem, and David begot more sons and daughters. 4 These are the names of the children whom he had in Jerusalem: Sham·mū'à, Shō'bab, Nathan, Solomon, 5 Ib'hăr, E·lī'shū-à, El'pe·let, 6 Nō'găh, Ne'pheg, Jà·phī'à, 7 E·lish'à·mà, Bē·ē·lī'à·dà, and E·liph'e·let.

8 When the Philistines heard that David had been anointed king over all

Israel, all the Philistines went up in search of David; and David heard of it and went out against them. 9 Now the Philistines had come and made a raid in the valley of Reph'à·im. 10And David inquired of God, "Shall I go up against the Philistines? Wilt thou give them into my hand?" And the LORD said to him, "Go up, and I will give them into your hand." 11And he went up to Bā'àl-pe·rā'zim, and David defeated them there; and David said, "God has broken through[l] my enemies by my hand, like a bursting flood." Therefore the name of that place is called Baal-perazim.[m] 12And they left their gods there, and David gave command, and they were burned.

13 And the Philistines yet again made a raid in the valley. 14And when David again inquired of God, God said to him, "You shall not go up after them; go around and come upon them opposite the balsam trees. 15And when you hear the sound of marching in the tops of the balsam trees, then go out to battle; for God has gone out before you to smite the army of the Philistines." 16And David did as God commanded him, and they smote the Philistine army from Gĭb'ē·ŏn to Gē'zĕr. 17And the fame of David went out into all lands, and the LORD brought the fear of him upon all nations.

15 David built houses for himself in the city of David; and he prepared a place for the ark of God, and pitched a tent for it. 2 Then David said, "No one but the Levites may carry the ark of God, for the LORD chose them to carry the ark of the LORD and to minister to him for ever." 3And David assembled all Israel at Jerusalem, to bring up the ark of the LORD to its place, which he had prepared for it. 4And David gathered together the sons of Aaron and the Levites: 5 of the sons of Kō'hath, Ū'ri'ēl the chief, with a hundred and twenty of his brethren; 6 of the sons of Mé·râr'ī, À·sāi'àh the chief, with two hundred and twenty of his brethren; 7 of the sons of Gēr'shŏm, Jō'ēl the chief, with a hundred and thirty of his brethren; 8 of the sons of El·ī·zà'phàn, She·māi'àh the chief, with two hundred of his brethren; 9 of the sons of Hē'brŏn, E·lī'el the chief, with eighty of his brethren; 10 of the sons of Uz'zi·el, Am·min'à·dab the chief, with a hundred and twelve of his brethren.

j Or *and his brother*   *k* That is *The breaking forth upon Uzzah*   *l* Heb *paraz*
m That is *Lord of breaking through*

14.1-2: 2 Sam 5.11-12.   **14.3-7:** 1 Chron 3.5-8; 2 Sam 5.14-16.
14.8-12: 2 Sam 5.17-21.   **14.13-16:** 2 Sam 5.22-25.   **15.1-16.3:** 2 Sam 6.12-19.

11 Then David summoned the priests Za′dok and A·bī′a·thär, and the Levites U·rī′el, A·sāi′ah, Jō′el, She·māi′ah, E·lī′el, and Am·min′a·dab, 12 and said to them, "You are the heads of the fathers' houses of the Levites; sanctify yourselves, you and your brethren, so that you may bring up the ark of the LORD, the God of Israel, to the place that I have prepared for it. 13 Because you did not carry it the first time,[n] the LORD our God broke forth upon us, because we did not care for it in the way that is ordained." 14 So the priests and the Levites sanctified themselves to bring up the ark of the LORD, the God of Israel. 15And the Levites carried the ark of God upon their shoulders with the poles, as Moses had commanded according to the word of the LORD.

16 David also commanded the chiefs of the Levites to appoint their brethren as the singers who should play loudly on musical instruments, on harps and lyres and cymbals, to raise sounds of joy. 17 So the Levites appointed Hē′man the son of Jō′el; and of his brethren Ā′saph the son of Ber·e·chī′ah; and of the sons of Me·râr′ī, their brethren, Ethan the son of Kū·shā′iah; 18 and with them their brethren of the second order, Zech·a·rī′ah, Jā·a′zi·el, She·mir′a·moth, Je·hī′el, Un′ni, E·lī′ab, Be·nā′iah, Mā·a·sēī′ah, Mat·ti·thī′ah, E·liph′e·le·hū, and Mik·nē′iah, and the gatekeepers O′bed-ē′dom and Je·ī′el. 19 The singers, Hē′man, Ā′saph, and Ethan, were to sound bronze cymbals; 20 Zech·a·rī′ah, Ā′zi·el, She·mir′a·moth, Je·hī′el, Un′ni, E·lī′ab, Mā·a·sēī′ah, and Be·nā′iah were to play harps according to Al′a·moth; 21 but Mat·ti·thī′ah, E·liph′e·le·hū, Mik·nē′iah, O′bed-ē′dom, Je·ī′el, and Az·a·zī′ah were to lead with lyres according to the Shem·inith. 22 Chen·a·nī′ah, leader of the Levites in music, should direct the music, for he understood it. 23 Ber·e·chī′ah and El·kā′nah were to be gatekeepers for the ark. 24 Sheb·a·nī′ah, Josh′a·phat, Ne·than′el, A·mā′sāi, Zech·a·rī′ah, Be·nā′iah, and E·lī·e′zēr, the priests, should blow the trumpets before the ark of God. O′bed-ē′dom and Je·hī′ah also were to be gatekeepers for the ark.

25 So David and the elders of Israel, and the commanders of thousands, went to bring up the ark of the covenant of the LORD from the house of O′bed-ē′dom with rejoicing. 26 And because God helped the Levites who were carrying the ark of the covenant of the LORD, they sacrificed seven bulls and seven rams. 27 David was clothed with a robe of fine linen, as also were all the Levites who were carrying the ark, and the singers, and Chen·a·nī′ah the leader of the music of the singers; and David wore a linen ephod. 28 So all Israel brought up the ark of the covenant of the LORD with shouting, to the sound of the horn, trumpets, and cymbals, and made loud music on harps and lyres.

29 And as the ark of the covenant of the LORD came to the city of David, Mī′chàl the daughter of Saul looked out of the window, and saw King David dancing and making merry; and she despised him in her heart.

16 And they brought in the ark of God, and set it inside the tent which David had pitched for it; and they offered burnt offerings and peace offerings before God. 2And when David had finished offering the burnt offerings and the peace offerings, he blessed the people in the name of the LORD, 3 and distributed to all Israel, both men and women, to each a loaf of bread, a portion of meat,[o] and a cake of raisins.

4 Moreover he appointed certain of the Levites as ministers before the ark of the LORD, to invoke, to thank, and to praise the LORD, the God of Israel. 5Ā′saph was the chief, and second to him were Zech·a·rī′ah, Je·ī′el, She·mir′a·moth, Je·hī′el, Mat·ti·thī′ah, E·lī′ab, Be·nā′iah, O′bed-ē′dom, and Je·iel, who were to play harps and lyres; Ā′saph was to sound the cymbals, 6 and Be·nā′iah and Jà·hā′zi·el the priests were to blow trumpets continually, before the ark of the covenant of God.

7 Then on that day David first appointed that thanksgiving be sung to the LORD by Ā′saph and his brethren.

8 O give thanks to the LORD, call on his name,
   make known his deeds among the peoples!
9 Sing to him, sing praises to him,
   tell of all his wonderful works!
10 Glory in his holy name;
   let the hearts of those who seek the LORD rejoice!
11 Seek the LORD and his strength,

n The meaning of the Hebrew word is uncertain
o Compare Gk Syr Vg: Heb uncertain
16.8-22: Ps 105.1-15.

seek his presence continually!
12 Remember the wonderful works
   that he has done,
   the wonders he wrought, the
      judgments he uttered,
13 O offspring of Abraham his servant,
   sons of Jacob, his chosen ones!

14 He is the LORD our God;
   his judgments are in all the earth.
15 He is mindful of his covenant for
      ever,
   of the word that he commanded,
      for a thousand generations,
16 the covenant which he made with
      Abraham,
   his sworn promise to Isaac,
17 which he confirmed as a statute to
      Jacob,
   as an everlasting covenant to
      Israel,
18 saying, "To you I will give the land
      of Canaan,
   as your portion for an inherit-
      ance."

19 When they were few in number,
   and of little account, and so-
      journers in it,
20 wandering from nation to nation,
   from one kingdom to another
      people,
21 he allowed no one to oppress them;
   he rebuked kings on their account,
22 saying, "Touch not my anointed
      ones,
   do my prophets no harm!"

23 Sing to the LORD, all the earth!
   Tell of his salvation from day to
      day.
24 Declare his glory among the nations,
   his marvelous works among all
      the peoples!
25 For great is the LORD, and greatly
      to be praised,
   and he is to be held in awe above
      all gods.
26 For all the gods of the peoples are
      idols;
   but the LORD made the heavens.
27 Honor and majesty are before him;
   strength and joy are in his place.

28 Ascribe to the LORD, O families of
      the peoples,
   ascribe to the LORD glory and
      strength!
29 Ascribe to the LORD the glory due
      his name;
   bring an offering, and come be-
      fore him!
   Worship the LORD in holy array;

30 tremble before him, all the earth;
   yea, the world stands firm, never
      to be moved.
31 Let the heavens be glad, and let the
      earth rejoice,
   and let them say among the na-
      tions, "The LORD reigns!"
32 Let the sea roar, and all that fills it,
   let the field exult, and everything
      in it!
33 Then shall the trees of the wood
      sing for joy
   before the LORD, for he comes to
      judge the earth.
34 O give thanks to the LORD, for he
      is good;
   for his steadfast love endures for
      ever!

35 Say also:
   "Deliver us, O God of our salvation,
      and gather and save us from
         among the nations,
   that we may give thanks to thy holy
      name,
   and glory in thy praise.
36 Blessed be the LORD, the God of
      Israel,
   from everlasting to everlasting!"
Then all the people said "Amen!" and
praised the LORD.

37 So David left A'saph and his
brethren there before the ark of the
covenant of the LORD to minister continually before the ark as each day
required, 38 and also O'bed-e'dom and
his^p sixty-eight brethren; while Obed-
edom, the son of Je·dū'thŭn, and
Hō'sah were to be gatekeepers. 39 And
he left Zā'dok the priest and his
brethren the priests before the tabernacle of the LORD in the high place
that was at Gib'e·ŏn, 40 to offer burnt
offerings to the LORD upon the altar
of burnt offering continually morning
and evening, according to all that is
written in the law of the LORD which
he commanded Israel. 41 With them
were Hē'măn and Je·dū'thŭn, and the
rest of those chosen and expressly
named to give thanks to the LORD, for
his steadfast love endures for ever.
42 Hē'măn and Je·dū'thŭn had trumpets and cymbals for the music and
instruments for sacred song. The sons
of Jeduthun were appointed to the
gate.
43 Then all the people departed
each to his house, and David went
home to bless his household.

17 Now when David dwelt in his
house, David said to Nathan the
prophet, "Behold, I dwell in a house

of cedar, but the ark of the covenant of the LORD is under a tent." [2]And Nathan said to David, "Do all that is in your heart, for God is with you."

[3] But that same night the word of the LORD came to Nathan, [4] "Go and tell my servant David, 'Thus says the LORD: You shall not build me a house to dwell in. [5] For I have not dwelt in a house since the day I led up Israel to this day, but I have gone from tent to tent and from dwelling to dwelling. [6] In all places where I have moved with all Israel, did I speak a word with any of the judges of Israel, whom I commanded to shepherd my people, saying, "Why have you not built me a house of cedar?"' [7] Now therefore thus shall you say to my servant David, 'Thus says the LORD of hosts, I took you from the pasture, from following the sheep, that you should be prince over my people Israel; [8] and I have been with you wherever you went, and have cut off all your enemies from before you; and I will make for you a name, like the name of the great ones of the earth. [9] And I will appoint a place for my people Israel, and will plant them, that they may dwell in their own place, and be disturbed no more; and violent men shall waste them no more, as formerly, [10] from the time that I appointed judges over my people Israel; and I will subdue all your enemies. Moreover I declare to you that the LORD will build you a house. [11] When your days are fulfilled to go to be with your fathers, I will raise up your offspring after you, one of your own sons, and I will establish his kingdom. [12] He shall build a house for me, and I will establish his throne for ever. [13] I will be his father, and he shall be my son; I will not take my steadfast love from him, as I took it from him who was before you, [14] but I will confirm him in my house and in my kingdom for ever and his throne shall be established for ever.'" [15] In accordance with all these words, and in accordance with all this vision, Nathan spoke to David.

[16] Then King David went in and sat before the LORD, and said, "Who am I, O LORD God, and what is my house, that thou hast brought me thus far? [17] And this was a small thing in thy eyes, O God; thou hast also spoken of thy servant's house for a great while to come, and hast shown me future generations,[q] O LORD God! [18] And

what more can David say to thee for honoring thy servant? For thou knowest thy servant. [19] For thy servant's sake, O LORD, and according to thy own heart, thou hast wrought all this greatness, in making known all these great things. [20] There is none like thee, O LORD, and there is no God besides thee, according to all that we have heard with our ears. [21] What other[r] nation on earth is like thy people Israel, whom God went to redeem to be his people, making for thyself a name for great and terrible things, in driving out nations before thy people whom thou didst redeem from Egypt? [22] And thou didst make thy people Israel to be thy people for ever; and thou, O LORD, didst become their God. [23] And now, O LORD, let the word which thou hast spoken concerning thy servant and concerning his house be established for ever, and do as thou hast spoken; [24] and thy name will be established and magnified for ever, saying, 'The LORD of hosts, the God of Israel, is Israel's God,' and the house of thy servant David will be established before thee. [25] For thou, my God, hast revealed to thy servant that thou wilt build a house for him; therefore thy servant has found courage to pray before thee. [26] And now, O LORD, thou art God, and thou hast promised this good thing to thy servant; [27] now therefore may it please thee to bless the house of thy servant, that it may continue for ever before thee; for what thou, O LORD, hast blessed is blessed for ever."

18 After this David defeated the Philistines and subdued them, and he took Gath and its villages out of the hand of the Philistines.

[2] And he defeated Mō′ab, and the Mō′ab·ites became servants to David and brought tribute.

[3] David also defeated Had·a·dē′zer king of Zō′bah, toward Hā′math, as he went to set up his monument[s] at the river Eū·phrā′tēs. [4] And David took from him a thousand chariots, seven thousand horsemen, and twenty thousand foot soldiers; and David hamstrung all the chariot horses, but left enough for a hundred chariots. [5] And when the Syrians of Damascus came to help Had·a·dē′zer king of Zō′bah, David slew twenty-two thousand men of the Syrians. [6] Then David put garrisons[t] in Syria of Damascus; and the Syrians became servants to David,

[q] Cn: Heb uncertain   [r] Gk Vg: Heb one   [s] Heb hand
[t] Gk Vg 2 Sam 8.6 Compare Syr: Heb lacks garrisons
18.1-13: 2 Sam 8.1-14.

and brought tribute. And the LORD gave victory to David wherever he went. 7And David took the shields of gold which were carried by the servants of Hăd·ȧ·dē′zĕr, and brought them to Jerusalem. 8And from Tĭb′hath and from Cün, cities of Hăd·ȧ·dē′zĕr, David took very much bronze; with it Solomon made the bronze sea and the pillars and the vessels of bronze.

9 When Tō′ŭ king of Hā′math heard that David had defeated the whole army of Hăd·ȧ·dē′zĕr, king of Zō′bȧh, 10 he sent his son Hȧ·dô′rȧm to King David, to greet him, and to congratulate him because he had fought against Hăd·ȧ·dē′zĕr and defeated him; for Hadadezer had often been at war with Tō′ŭ. And he sent all sorts of articles of gold, of silver, and of bronze; 11 these also King David dedicated to the LORD, together with the silver and gold which he had carried off from all the nations, from Ē′dŏm, Mō′ab, the Am′mō·nites, the Philistines, and Am′ȧ·lek.

12 And Ȧ·bī′shăi, the son of Zĕ·rū′i·ȧh, slew eighteen thousand Ē′dŏm-ites in the Valley of Salt. 13And he put garrisons in Ē′dŏm; and all the Ē′dŏm-ites became David's servants. And the LORD gave victory to David wherever he went.

14 So David reigned over all Israel; and he administered justice and equity to all his people. 15And Jō′ab the son of Zĕ·rū′i·ȧh was over the army; and Je·hŏsh′ȧ·phat the son of Ȧ·hī′lŭd was recorder; 16 and Zā′dŏk the son of Ȧ·hī′tŭb and Ȧ·hĭm′ĕ·lech the son of Ȧ·bī′ȧ·thär were priests; and Shav′shȧ was secretary; 17 and Bĕ·nā′iȧh the son of Je·hoi′ȧ·dȧ was over the Cher′ē-thītes and the Pel′ē·thītes; and David's sons were the chief officials in the service of the king.

19 Now after this Nā′hash the king of the Am′mō·nites died, and his son reigned in his stead. 2And David said, "I will deal loyally with Hā′nŭn the son of Nā′hash, for his father dealt loyally with me." So David sent messengers to console him concerning his father. And David's servants came to Hanun in the land of the Am′mō·nites, to console him. 3 But the princes of the Am′mō·nites said to Hā′nŭn, "Do you think, because David has sent comforters to you, that he is honoring your father? Have not his servants come to you to search and to overthrow and to spy out the land?" 4 So Hā′nŭn took David's servants, and shaved them, and cut off their garments in the

middle, at their hips, and sent them away; 5 and they departed. When David was told concerning the men, he sent to meet them, for the men were greatly ashamed. And the king said, "Remain at Jericho until your beards have grown, and then return."

6 When the Am′mō·nites saw that they had made themselves odious to David, Hā′nŭn and the Ammonites sent a thousand talents of silver to hire chariots and horsemen from Mes·ȯ·pȯ-tā′mi·ȧ, from Âr′ȧm-mā′ȧ·cȧh, and from Zō′bȧh. 7 They hired thirty-two thousand chariots and the king of Mā′ȧ·cȧh with his army, who came and encamped before Mĕd′ĕ·bȧ. And the Am′mō·nites were mustered from their cities and came to battle. 8 When David heard of it, he sent Jō′ab and all the army of the mighty men. 9And the Am′mō·nites came out and drew up in battle array at the entrance of the city, and the kings who had come were by themselves in the open country.

10 When Jō′ab saw that the battle was set against him both in front and in the rear, he chose some of the picked men of Israel, and arrayed them against the Syrians; 11 the rest of his men he put in the charge of Ȧ·bī′shăi his brother, and they were arrayed against the Am′mō·nites. 12And he said, "If the Syrians are too strong for me, then you shall help me; but if the Am′mō-nites are too strong for you, then I will help you. 13 Be of good courage, and let us play the man for our people, and for the cities of our God; and may the LORD do what seems good to him." 14 So Jō′ab and the people who were with him drew near before the Syrians for battle; and they fled before him. 15And when the Am′mō·nites saw that the Syrians fled, they likewise fled before Ȧ·bī′shăi, Jō′ab′s brother, and entered the city. Then Joab came to Jerusalem.

16 But when the Syrians saw that they had been defeated by Israel, they sent messengers and brought out the Syrians who were beyond the Eū-phrā′tēs, with Shō′phach the commander of the army of Hăd·ȧ·dē′zĕr at their head. 17And when it was told David, he gathered all Israel together, and crossed the Jordan, and came to them, and drew up his forces against them. And when David set the battle in array against the Syrians, they fought with him. 18And the Syrians fled before Israel; and David slew of the Syrians the men of seven thousand chariots, and forty thousand foot

8.14-17: 2 Sam 8.15-18.   **19.1-19**: 2 Sam 10.1-19.

soldiers, and killed also Shō′phach the commander of their army. 19And when the servants of Hǎd·à·dē′zěr saw that they had been defeated by Israel, they made peace with David, and became subject to him. So the Syrians were not willing to help the Am′mo·nites any more.

20 In the spring of the year, the time when kings go forth to battle, Jō′ab led out the army, and ravaged the country of the Am′mo·nites, and came and besieged Rab′bȧh. But David remained at Jerusalem. And Jō′ab smote Rabbah, and overthrew it. 2And David took the crown of their king*u* from his head; he found that it weighed a talent of gold, and in it was a precious stone; and it was placed on David's head. And he brought forth the spoil of the city, a very great amount. 3And he brought forth the people who were in it, and set them to labor*v* with saws and iron picks and axes;*w* and thus David did to all the cities of the Am′mo·nites. Then David and all the people returned to Jerusalem.

4 And after this there arose war with the Philistines at Gē′zěr; then Sib′bė·cäi the Hū′shȧ·thite slew Sip′păi, who was one of the descendants of the giants; and the Philistines were subdued. 5And there was again war with the Philistines; and El·hā′nȧn the son of Jā′ir slew Läh′mi the brother of Goliath the Git′tite, the shaft of whose spear was like a weaver's beam. 6And there was again war at Gath, where there was a man of great stature, who had six fingers on each hand, and six toes on each foot, twenty-four in number; and he also was descended from the giants. 7And when he taunted Israel, Jonathan the son of Shim′e·à, David's brother, slew him. 8 These were descended from the giants in Gath; and they fell by the hand of David and by the hand of his servants.

21 Satan stood up against Israel, and incited David to number Israel. 2 So David said to Jō′ab and the commanders of the army, "Go, number Israel, from Beer-sheba to Dan, and bring me a report, that I may know their number." 3 But Jō′ab said, "May the Lord add to his people a hundred times as many as they are! Are they not, my lord the king, all of them my lord's servants? Why then should my lord require this? Why

should he bring guilt upon Israel?" 4 But the king's word prevailed against Jō′ab. So Joab departed and went throughout all Israel, and came back to Jerusalem. 5And Jō′ab gave the sum of the numbering of the people to David. In all Israel there were one million one hundred thousand men who drew the sword, and in Judah four hundred and seventy thousand who drew the sword. 6 But he did not include Levi and Benjamin in the numbering, for the king's command was abhorrent to Jō′ab.

7 But God was displeased with this thing, and he smote Israel. 8And David said to God, "I have sinned greatly in that I have done this thing. But now, I pray thee, take away the iniquity of thy servant; for I have done very foolishly." 9And the Lord spoke to Gad, David's seer, saying, 10 "Go and say to David, 'Thus says the Lord, Three things I offer you; choose one of them, that I may do it to you.'" 11 So Gad came to David and said to him, "Thus says the Lord, 'Take which you will: 12 either three years of famine; or three months of devastation by your foes, while the sword of your enemies overtakes you; or else three days of the sword of the Lord, pestilence upon the land, and the angel of the Lord destroying throughout all the territory of Israel.' Now decide what answer I shall return to him who sent me." 13 Then David said to Gad, "I am in great distress; let me fall into the hand of the Lord, for his mercy is very great; but let me not fall into the hand of man."

14 So the Lord sent a pestilence upon Israel; and there fell seventy thousand men of Israel. 15And God sent the angel to Jerusalem to destroy it; but when he was about to destroy it, the Lord saw, and he repented of the evil; and he said to the destroying angel, "It is enough; now stay your hand." And the angel of the Lord was standing by the threshing floor of Ȯr′nȧn the Jeb′ū·site. 16And David lifted his eyes and saw the angel of the Lord standing between earth and heaven, and in his hand a drawn sword stretched out over Jerusalem. Then David and the elders, clothed in sackcloth, fell upon their faces. 17And David said to God, "Was it not I who gave command to number the people? It is I who have sinned and done ver

u Or *Milcom* See 1 Kings 11.5   *v* Compare 2 Sam 12.31: Heb *he sawed*
w Compare 2 Sam 12.31: Heb *saws*
20.1: 2 Sam 11.1.   **20.1–3:** 2 Sam 12.26–31.   **20.4–8:** 2 Sam 21.18–22.
21.1–27: 2 Sam 24.1–25.

wickedly. But these sheep, what have they done? Let thy hand, I pray thee, O LORD my God, be against me and against my father's house; but let not the plague be upon thy people."

18 Then the angel of the LORD commanded Gad to say to David that David should go up and rear an altar to the LORD on the threshing floor of Ôr′nǎn the Jěb′ū·sïte. 19 So David went up at Gad's word, which he had spoken in the name of the LORD. 20 Now Ôr′nǎn was threshing wheat; he turned and saw the angel, and his four sons who were with him hid themselves. 21As David came to Ôr′nǎn, Ornan looked and saw David and went forth from the threshing floor, and did obeisance to David with his face to the ground. 22And David said to Ôr′nǎn, "Give me the site of the threshing floor that I may build on it an altar to the LORD—give it to me at its full price—that the plague may be averted from the people." 23 Then Ôr′nǎn said to David, "Take it; and let my lord the king do what seems good to him; see, I give the oxen for burnt offerings, and the threshing sledges for the wood, and the wheat for a cereal offering. I give it all." 24 But King David said to Ôr′nǎn, "No, but I will buy it for the full price; I will not take for the LORD what is yours, nor offer burnt offerings which cost me nothing." 25 So David paid Ôr′nǎn six hundred shekels of gold by weight for the site. 26And David built there an altar to the LORD and presented burnt offerings and peace offerings, and called upon the LORD, and he answered him with fire from heaven upon the altar of burnt offering. 27 Then the LORD commanded the angel; and he put his sword back into its sheath.

28 At that time, when David saw that the LORD had answered him at the threshing floor of Ôr′nǎn the Jěb′ū·sïte, he made his sacrifices there. 29 For the tabernacle of the LORD, which Moses had made in the wilderness, and the altar of burnt offering were at that time in the high place at Gĭb′ē·ŏn; 30 but David could not go before it to inquire of God, for he was afraid of the sword of the angel of the LORD.

22 Then David said, "Here shall be the house of the LORD God and here the altar of burnt offering for Israel."

2 David commanded to gather together the aliens who were in the land of Israel, and he set stonecutters to prepare dressed stones for building the house of God. 3 David also provided great stores of iron for nails for the doors of the gates and for clamps, as well as bronze in quantities beyond weighing, 4 and cedar timbers without number; for the Sī·dō′nĭ·ǎns and Tȳ′rĭ·ǎns brought great quantities of cedar to David. 5 For David said, "Solomon my son is young and inexperienced, and the house that is to be built for the LORD must be exceedingly magnificent, of fame and glory throughout all lands; I will therefore make preparation for it." So David provided materials in great quantity before his death.

6 Then he called for Solomon his son, and charged him to build a house for the LORD, the God of Israel. 7 David said to Solomon, "My son, I had it in my heart to build a house to the name of the LORD my God. 8 But the word of the LORD came to me, saying, 'You have shed much blood and have waged great wars; you shall not build a house to my name, because you have shed so much blood before me upon the earth. 9 Behold, a son shall be born to you; he shall be a man of peace. I will give him peace from all his enemies round about; for his name shall be Solomon, and I will give peace and quiet to Israel in his days. 10 He shall build a house for my name. He shall be my son, and I will be his father, and I will establish his royal throne in Israel for ever.' 11 Now, my son, the LORD be with you, so that you may succeed in building the house of the LORD your God, as he has spoken concerning you. 12 Only, may the LORD grant you discretion and understanding, that when he gives you charge over Israel you may keep the law of the LORD your God. 13 Then you will prosper if you are careful to observe the statutes and the ordinances which the LORD commanded Moses for Israel. Be strong, and of good courage. Fear not; be not dismayed. 14 With great pains I have provided for the house of the LORD a hundred thousand talents of gold, a million talents of silver, and bronze and iron beyond weighing, for there is so much of it; timber and stone too I have provided. To these you must add. 15 You have an abundance of workmen: stonecutters, masons, carpenters, and all kinds of craftsmen without number, skilled in working 16 gold, silver, bronze, and iron. Arise and be doing! The LORD be with you!"

17 David also commanded all the leaders of Israel to help Solomon his

son, saying, 18 "Is not the LORD your God with you? And has he not given you peace on every side? For he has delivered the inhabitants of the land into my hand; and the land is subdued before the LORD and his people. 19 Now set your mind and heart to seek the LORD your God. Arise and build the sanctuary of the LORD God, so that the ark of the covenant of the LORD and the holy vessels of God may be brought into a house built for the name of the LORD."

23 When David was old and full of days, he made Solomon his son king over Israel.

2 David assembled all the leaders of Israel and the priests and the Levites. 3 The Levites, thirty years old and upward, were numbered, and the total was thirty-eight thousand men. 4 "Twenty-four thousand of these," David said, "shall have charge of the work in the house of the LORD, six thousand shall be officers and judges, 5 four thousand gatekeepers, and four thousand shall offer praises to the LORD with the instruments which I have made for praise." 6 And David organized them in divisions corresponding to the sons of Levi: Gĕr′shŏm, Kō′hath, and Mĕ·râr′ĭ.

7 The sons of Gĕr′shŏm*x* were Lā′dän and Shĭm′ē-ĭ. 8 The sons of Lā′dän: Je·hī′el the chief, and Zē′thäm, and Jō′el, three. 9 The sons of Shĭm′ē-ĭ: She·lō′moth, Hā′zi-el, and Hâr′ân, three. These were the heads of the fathers' houses of Lā′dän. 10 And the sons of Shĭm′ē-ĭ: Jā′hath, Zĭ′nà, and Jĕ′ush, and Bĕ·rī′ah. These four were the sons of Shime-i. 11 Jā′hath was the chief, and Zĭ′zàh the second; but Jĕ′ush and Bĕ·rī′ah had not many sons, therefore they became a father's house in one reckoning.

12 The sons of Kō′hath: Am′ram, Iz′här, Hē′brŏn, and Uz′zi·el, four. 13 The sons of Am′ram: Aaron and Moses. Aaron was set apart to consecrate the most holy things, that he and his sons for ever should burn incense before the LORD, and minister to him and pronounce blessings in his name for ever. 14 But the sons of Moses the man of God were named among the tribe of Levi. 15 The sons of Moses: Gĕr′shŏm and Ĕ·lĭ·ē′zĕr. 16 The sons of Gĕr′shŏm: She·bū′el the chief. 17 The sons of Ĕ·lĭ·ē′zĕr: Rĕ·hà·bī′ah the chief; Eliezer had no other sons, but the sons of Rĕ·hà·bī′ah were very many. 18 The sons of Iz′här: She·lō′mith the chief. 19 The sons of

Hē′brŏn: Je·rī′ah the chief, Am·à·rī′ah the second, Jà·hā′zi·el the third, and Jek·à·mē′äm the fourth. 20 The sons of Uz′zi·el: Mī′càh the chief and Is·shī′ah the second.

21 The sons of Mĕ·râr′ĭ: Mäh′lĭ and Mū′shĭ. The sons of Mahli: El·ē·ā′zär and Kish. 22 El·ē·ā′zär died having no sons, but only daughters; their kinsmen, the sons of Kish, married them. 23 The sons of Mū′shĭ: Mäh′lĭ, Ĕ′dĕr, and Jer′ĕ·moth, three.

24 These were the sons of Levi by their fathers' houses, the heads of fathers' houses as they were registered according to the number of the names of the individuals from twenty years old and upward who were to do the work for the service of the house of the LORD. 25 For David said, "The LORD, the God of Israel, has given peace to his people; and he dwells in Jerusalem for ever. 26 And so the Levites no longer need to carry the tabernacle or any of the things for its service"— 27 for by the last words of David these were the number of the Levites from twenty years old and upward—28 "but their duty shall be to assist the sons of Aaron for the service of the house of the LORD, having the care of the courts and the chambers, the cleansing of all that is holy, and any work for the service of the house of God; 29 to assist also with the showbread, the flour for the cereal offering, the wafers of unleavened bread, the baked offering, the offering mixed with oil, and all measures of quantity or size. 30 And they shall stand every morning, thanking and praising the LORD, and likewise at evening, 31 and whenever burnt offerings are offered to the LORD on sabbaths, new moons, and feast days, according to the number required of them, continually before the LORD. 32 Thus they shall keep charge of the tent of meeting and the sanctuary, and shall attend the sons of Aaron, their brethren, for the service of the house of the LORD."

24 The divisions of the sons of Aaron were these. The sons of Aaron: Nā′dab, Ā·bī′hū, El·ē·ā′zär, and Ith′à·mär. 2 But Nā′dab and Ā·bī′hū died before their father, and had no children, so El·ē·ā′zär and Ith′à·mär became the priests. 3 With the help of Zā′dok of the sons of El·ē·ā′zär, and Ā·him′ĕ·lech of the sons of Ith′à·mär, David organized them according to the appointed duties in their service. 4 Since more chief men were found among the sons of El·ē·ā′zär than

x Vg Compare Gk Syr: Heb *to the Gershonite*

among the sons of Ith′a·mär, they organized them under sixteen heads of fathers' houses of the sons of Elea-zar, and eight of the sons of Ithamar. 5 They organized them by lot, all alike, for there were officers of the sanctuary and officers of God among both the sons of El·ē·ā′zär and the sons of Ith′a·mär. 6 And the scribe She·mai′-äh the son of Nē·than′el, a Levite, re-corded them in the presence of the king, and the princes, and Zā′dok the priest, and A·him′e·lech the son of A·bi′a·thär, and the heads of the fathers' houses of the priests and of the Levites; one father's house being chosen for El·ē·ā′zär and one chosen for Ith′a·mär.

7 The first lot fell to Je·hoi′a·rib, the second to Je·däi′äh, 8 the third to Hā′rim, the fourth to Se·ō′rim, 9 the fifth to Mal·ē·hi′jäh, the sixth to Mij′-a·min, 10 the seventh to Hak′koz, the eighth to A·bi′jäh, 11 the ninth to Jesh′ü·à, the tenth to Shec·à·ni′äh, 12 the eleventh to E·li′à·shib, the twelfth to Jā′kim, 13 the thirteenth to Hup′päh, the fourteenth to Je·sheb′e-äb, 14 the fifteenth to Bil′gäh, the sixteenth to Im′mêr, 15 the seventeenth to Hē′zir, the eighteenth to Hap′piz-zez, 16 the nineteenth to Peth·à·hi′äh, the twentieth to Je·hez′kel, 17 the twenty-first to Jā′chin, the twenty-second to Gä′mül, 18 the twenty-third to De·läi′äh, the twenty-fourth to Mā·à·zi′äh. 19 These had as their appointed duty in their service to come into the house of the LORD according to the procedure established for them by Aaron their father, as the LORD God of Israel had commanded him.

20 And of the rest of the sons of Levi: of the sons of Am′ram, Shü′bà·el; of the sons of Shuba-el, Jeh·dē′iäh.21 Of Rē·hà·bi′äh: of the sons of Rehabiah, Is·shi′äh the chief. 22 Of the Iz′hà-rites, She·lō′moth; of the sons of Shelo-moth, Jā′hath. 23 The sons of Hē′brön:*y* Je·ri′äh the chief,*z* Am·à·ri′äh the second, Jà·hā′zi·el the third, Jek·à-mē′am the fourth. 24 The sons of Uz′zi·el, Mi′cäh; of the sons of Micah, Shā′mir. 25 The brother of Mi′cäh, Is·shi′äh; of the sons of Isshiah, Zech·à·ri′äh. 26 The sons of Mē·râr′i: Mäh′li and Mü′shi. The sons of Jā-à·zi′äh:*x* Bē′nō. 27 The sons of Mē·râr′i: of Jā·à·zi′äh, Bē′nō, Shō′ham, Zac′cūr, and Ib′ri. 28 Of Mäh′li: El·ē·ā′zär, who had no sons. 29 Of Kish, the sons of Kish: Je·räh′mē·ēl. 30 The sons of

Mü′shi: Mäh′li, E′dêr, and Jer′i·moth. These were the sons of the Levites according to their fathers' houses. 31 These also, the head of each father's house and his younger brother alike, cast lots, just as their brethren the sons of Aaron, in the presence of King David, Zā′dok, A·him′e·lech, and the heads of fathers' houses of the priests and of the Levites.

25 David and the chiefs of the service also set apart for the service certain of the sons of A′saph, and of Hē′mån, and of Je·dü′thün, who should prophesy with lyres, with harps, and with cymbals. The list of those who did the work and of their duties was: 2 Of the sons of A′saph: Zac′cūr, Joseph, Neth·à·ni′äh, and Ash·à·rē′läh, sons of Asaph, under the direction of Asaph, who prophesied under the direction of the king. 3 Of Je·dü′thün, of the sons of Jeduthun: Ged·à·li′äh, Zē′ri, Je·shā′iäh, Shim′ē·i,*a* Hash·à·bi′äh, and Mat·ti·thi′äh, six, under the direction of their father Jeduthun, who prophesied with the lyre in thanksgiving and praise to the LORD. 4 Of Hē′mån, the sons of He-man: Buk·ki′äh, Mat·tà·ni′äh, Uz′zi·el, She·bü′el, and Jer′i·moth, Han·à·ni′äh, Hà·nā′ni, E·li′à·thäh, Gid·dal′ti, and Rō·mam′ti·ē′zêr, Josh·be·kash′äh, Mal-lō′thi, Hō′thir, Mà·hā′zi·oth. 5 All these were the sons of Hē′mån the king's seer, according to the promise of God to exalt him; for God had given Heman fourteen sons and three daughters. 6 They were all under the direction of their father in the music in the house of the LORD with cymbals, harps, and lyres for the service of the house of God. A′saph, Je·dü′thün, and Hē′mån were under the order of the king. 7 The number of them along with their brethren, who were trained in singing to the LORD, all who were skilful, was two hundred and eighty-eight. 8 And they cast lots for their duties, small and great, teacher and pupil alike.

9 The first lot fell for A′saph to Joseph; the second to Ged·à·li′äh, to him and his brethren and his sons, twelve; 10 the third to Zac′cūr, his sons and his brethren, twelve; 11 the fourth to Iz′ri, his sons and his brethren, twelve; 12 the fifth to Neth·à·ni′äh, his sons and his brethren, twelve; 13 the sixth to Buk·ki′äh, his sons and his brethren, twelve; 14 the seventh to Jesh·à·rē′läh, his sons and his brethren, twelve; 15 the eighth to Je·shā′iäh, his

---

y See 23.19: Heb lacks Hebron   z See 23.19: Heb lacks the chief
x One Ms: Gk: Heb lacks Shimei

sons and his brethren, twelve; 16 the ninth to Mat·tà·ni'àh, his sons and his brethren, twelve; 17 the tenth to Shim'ē-ī, his sons and his brethren, twelve; 18 the eleventh to Az'à·rel, his sons and his brethren, twelve; 19 the twelfth to Hash·à·bī'àh, his sons and his brethren, twelve; 20 to the thirteenth, Shū'bà-el, his sons and his brethren, twelve; 21 to the fourteenth, Mat·ti·thī'àh, his sons and his brethren, twelve; 22 to the fifteenth, to Jer'ē·moth, his sons and his brethren, twelve; 23 to the sixteenth, to Han·à·nī'àh, his sons and his brethren, twelve; 24 to the seventeenth, to Josh·be·kash'àh, his sons and his brethren, twelve; 25 to the eighteenth, to Hà·nā'nī, his sons and his brethren, twelve; 26 to the nineteenth, to Mal·lō'thī, his sons and his brethren, twelve; 27 to the twentieth, to E·lī'à·thàh, his sons and his brethren, twelve; 28 to the twenty-first, to Hō'thir, his sons and his brethren, twelve; 29 to the twenty-second, to Gid·dal'tī, his sons and his brethren, twelve; 30 to the twenty-third, to Mà·hā'zi-oth, his sons and his brethren, twelve; 31 to the twenty-fourth, to Rō·mam'ti-ē'zĕr, his sons and his brethren, twelve.

26 As for the divisons of the gate-keepers: of the Kō'rà·hītes, Me-shel·è·mī'àh the son of Kō're, of the sons of A'saph. 2 And Me·shel·è·mī'àh had sons: Zech·à·rī'àh the first-born, Je·dī'à-el the second, Zeb·à·dī'àh the third, Jath'ni-el the fourth, 3 Ē'làm the fifth, Jē'hō-hā'nàn the sixth, El'ī·ē-hō-ē'näi the seventh. 4 And Ō'bed-ē'dóm had sons: She·māī'àh the first-born, Je·hō'zà·bad the second, Jō'àh the third, Sā'chär the fourth, Nē·than'el the fifth, 5 Am'mi-el the sixth, Is'sà-chär the seventh, Pe-ul'lē·thäi the eighth; for God blessed him. 6 Also to his son She·māī'àh were sons born who were rulers in their fathers' houses, for they were men of great ability. 7 The sons of She·māī'àh: Oth'nī, Reph'à-el, Ō'bed, and El·zā'bad, whose brethren were able men, E·lī'hū and Sem·à·chī'àh. 8 All these were of the sons of Ō'bed-ē'dóm with their sons and brethren, able men qualified for the service; sixty-two of Obed-edom. 9 And Me·shel·è·mī'àh had sons and brethren, able men, eighteen. 10 And Hō'sàh, of the sons of Mē·rár'ī, had sons: Shim'rī the chief (for though he was not the first-born, his father made him chief), 11 Hil·kī'àh the second, Teb·à·lī'àh the third, Zech-

à·rī'àh the fourth: all the sons and brethren of Hō'sàh were thirteen.

12 These divisions of the gate-keepers, corresponding to their chief men, had duties, just as their brethren did, ministering in the house of the LORD; 13 and they cast lots by fathers' houses, small and great alike, for their gates. 14 The lot for the east fell to Shel·è·mī'àh. They cast lots also for his son Zech·à·rī'àh, a shrewd counselor, and his lot came out for the north. 15 Ō'bed-ē'dóm's came out for the south, and to his sons was allotted the storehouse. 16 For Shup'pim and Hō'sàh it came out for the west, at the gate of Shal'lē·cheth on the road that goes up. Watch corresponded to watch. 17 On the east there were six each day,[b] on the north four each day, on the south four each day, as well as two and two at the storehouse; 18 and for the parbar[c] on the west there were four at the road and two at the parbar. 19 These were the divisions of the gatekeepers among the Kō'rà·hītes and the sons of Mē·rár'ī.

20 And of the Levites, À·hī'jàh had charge of the treasuries of the house of God and the treasuries of the dedicated gifts. 21 The sons of Lā'dàn, the sons of the Gēr'shò·nītes belonging to Ladan, the heads of the fathers' houses belonging to Ladan the Gershonite: Je·hī'ē·lī.[d]

22 The sons of Je·hī'ē·lī, Zē'thàm and Jō'ĕl his brother, were in charge of the treasuries of the house of the LORD. 23 Of the Am'rà·mites, the Iz'-hà·rites, the Hē'brō·nītes, and the Uz'zi·ē·lītes— 24 and She·bū'el the son of Gēr'shòm, son of Moses, was chief officer in charge of the treasuries. 25 His brethren: from Ē'li·ē'zĕr were his son Rē·hà·bī'àh, and his son Je·shā'-iàh, and his son Jō'ràm, and his son Zich'rī, and his son She·lō'moth. 26 This She·lō'moth and his brethren were in charge of all the treasuries of the dedicated gifts which David the king, and the heads of the fathers' houses, and the officers of the thousands and the hundreds, and the commanders of the army, had dedicated. 27 From spoil won in battles they dedicated gifts for the maintenance of the house of the LORD. 28 Also all that Samuel the seer, and Saul the son of Kish, and Abner the son of Nēr, and Jō'ab the son of Zē·rü'i·àh had dedi-cated—all dedicated gifts were in the care of She·lō'moth[e] and his brethren 29 Of the Iz'hà·rites, Chen·à·nī'àh

and his sons were appointed to outside duties for Israel, as officers and judges. 30 Of the Hē′brŏ·nites, Hash·ă·bī′ah and his brethren, one thousand seven hundred men of ability, had the oversight of Israel westward of the Jordan for all the work of the LORD and for the service of the king. 31 Of the Hē′brŏ·nites, Je·rī′jah was chief of the Hebronites of whatever genealogy or fathers' houses. (In the fortieth year of David's reign search was made and men of great ability among them were found at Jā′zẽr in Gĭlead.) 32 King David appointed him and his brethren, two thousand seven hundred men of ability, heads of fathers' houses, to have the oversight of the Reubenites, the Gadites, and the half-tribe of the Mä·nas′sîtes for everything pertaining to God and for the affairs of the king.

27 This is the list of the people of Israel, the heads of fathers' houses, the commanders of thousands and hundreds, and their officers who served the king in all matters concerning the divisions that came and went, month after month throughout the year, each division numbering twenty-four thousand:

2 Jă·shō′bē·ăm the son of Zăb′di-el was in charge of the first division in the first month; in his divison were twenty-four thousand. 3 He was a descendant of Per′ez, and was chief of all the commanders of the army for the first month. 4 Dō′däi the A·hō′hite′ was in charge of the division of the second month; in his division were twenty-four thousand. 5 The third commander, for the third month, was Be·nā′iäh, the son of Je·hoi′ă·dă the priest, as chief; in his division were twenty-four thousand. 6 This is the Be·nā′iäh who was a mighty man of the thirty and in command of the thirty; Am·miz′ă·bad his son was in charge of his division.ᵍ 7 As′ă·hel the brother of Jō′ab was fourth, for the fourth month, and his son Zeb·ă·dī′ah after him; in his division were twenty-four thousand. 8 The fifth commander, for the fifth month, was Sham′huth, the Iz′rǎ·hite; in his division were twenty-four thousand. 9 Sixth, for the sixth month, was Ira, the son of Ik′kesh the Te·kō′ite; in his division were twenty-four thousand. 10 Seventh, for the seventh month, was Hē′lez the Pel′ŏ·nite, of the sons of É′phrǎ·im; in his division were twenty-four thousand. 11 Eighth, for the eighth month, was Sib′bě·cäi the Hū′shă·thite, of the

Zē′rǎ·hites; in his division were twenty-four thousand. 12 Ninth, for the ninth month, was A′bi·ē′zẽr of An′ă·thoth, a Benjaminite; in his division were twenty-four thousand. 13 Tenth, for the tenth month, was Mā′hă·räi of Nê·toph′äh, of the Zē′rǎ·hites; in his division were twenty-four thousand. 14 Eleventh, for the eleventh month, was Be·nā′iäh of Pir′ă·thon, of the sons of É′phrǎ·im; in his division were twenty-four thousand. 15 Twelfth, for the twelfth month, was Hel′däi the Nê·toph′ă·thïte, of Oth′ni-el; in his division were twenty-four thousand.

16 Over the tribes of Israel, for the Reubenites É·li·ē′zẽr the son of Zich′ri was chief officer; for the Simeonites, Sheph·ă·tī′ah the son of Mā′ă·cäh; 17 for Levi, Hash·ă·bī′ah the son of Ke·mū′el; for Aaron, Zā′dok; 18 for Judah, E·lī′hū, one of David's brothers; for Is′sǎ·chär, Om′ri the son of Michael; 19 for Zeb′ū·lŭn, Ish·mā′iäh the son of Ō·bă·dī′ah; for Naph′tă·li, Jer′ē·moth the son of Az′ri-el; 20 for the É′phrǎ·im·ites, Hō·shē′ă the son of Az·ă·zī′ah; for the half-tribe of Mä·nas′sēh, Jō′ĕl the son of Pe·dāi′ah; 21 for the half-tribe of Mä·nas′sēh in Gilead, Id′dō the son of Zech·ă·rī′ah; for Benjamin, Jā·ă·sī′el, the son of Ab′ner; 22 for Dan, Az′ă·rel the son of Je·rō′ham. These were the leaders of the tribes of Israel. 23 David did not number those below twenty years of age, for the LORD had promised to make Israel as many as the stars of heaven. 24 Jō′ab the son of Zĕ·rü′i·äh began to number, but did not finish; yet wrath came upon Israel for this, and the number was not entered in the chronicles of King David.

25 Over the king's treasuries was Az′mă·veth the son of Ad′i-el; and over the treasuries in the country, in the cities, in the villages and in the towers, was Jonathan the son of Uz·zī′ah; 26 and over those who did the work of the field for tilling the soil was Ez′ri the son of Chē′lŭb, 27 and over the vineyards was Shim′ē-i the Rā′mă·thïte; and over the produce of the vineyards for the wine cellars was Zab′di the Shiph′mite. 28 Over the olive and sycamore trees in the She·phē′läh was Bā′ăl-hā′năn the Ge·dē′rite; and over the stores of oil was Jō′ash. 29 Over the herds that pastured in Sharon was Shit′räi the Shâr′ŏ·nite; over the herds in the valleys was Shā′phät the son of Ad′lā·i. 30 Over the camels was Ō′bil the Ish′mă·el·ite; and over the she-

---

ᶠ Gk: Heb Ahohite and his division and Mikloth the chief officer

ᵍ Gk Vg: Heb was his division

asses was Jeh·dē′iah the Me·ron′ō-thite. Over the flocks was Jā′ziz the Hag′rite. 31All these were stewards of King David's property.

32 Jonathan, David's uncle, was a counselor, being a man of understanding and a scribe; he and Je·hi′el the son of Hach′mō·ni attended the king's sons. 33Ă·hith′ō·phel was the king's counselor, and Hū′shäi the Är′chite was the king's friend. 34Ă·hith′ō·phel was succeeded by Je·hoi′a·dà the son of Be·nä′iàh, and Ă·bī′a·thär. Jō′ab was commander of the king's army.

28 David assembled at Jerusalem all the officials of Israel, the officials of the tribes, the officers of the divisions that served the king, the commanders of thousands, the commanders of hundreds, the stewards of all the property and cattle of the king and his sons, together with the palace officials, the mighty men, and all the seasoned warriors. 2 Then King David rose to his feet and said: "Hear me, my brethren and my people. I had it in my heart to build a house of rest for the ark of the covenant of the LORD, and for the footstool of our God; and I made preparations for building. 3 But God said to me, 'You may not build a house for my name, for you are a warrior and have shed blood.' 4 Yet the LORD God of Israel chose me from all my father's house to be king over Israel for ever; for he chose Judah as leader, and in the house of Judah my father's house, and among my father's sons he took pleasure in me to make me king over all Israel. 5And of all my sons (for the LORD has given me many sons) he has chosen Solomon my son to sit upon the throne of the kingdom of the LORD over Israel. 6 He said to me, 'It is Solomon your son who shall build my house and my courts, for I have chosen him to be my son, and I will be his father. 7 I will establish his kingdom for ever if he continues resolute in keeping my commandments and my ordinances, as he is today.' 8 Now therefore in the sight of all Israel, the assembly of the LORD, and in the hearing of our God, observe and seek out all the commandments of the LORD your God; that you may possess this good land, and leave it for an inheritance to your children after you for ever.

9 "And you, Solomon my son, know the God of your father, and serve him with a whole heart and with a willing mind; for the LORD searches all hearts, and understands every plan

h Cn: Heb upon me

and thought. If you seek him, he will be found by you; but if you forsake him, he will cast you off for ever. 10 Take heed now, for the LORD has chosen you to build a house for the sanctuary; be strong, and do it."

11 Then David gave Solomon his son the plan of the vestibule of the temple, and of its houses, its treasuries, its upper rooms, and its inner chambers, and of the room for the mercy seat; 12 and the plan of all that he had in mind for the courts of the house of the LORD, all the surrounding chambers, the treasuries of the house of God, and the treasuries for dedicated gifts; 13 for the divisions of the priests and of the Levites, and all the work of the service in the house of the LORD; for all the vessels for the service in the house of the LORD, 14 the weight of gold for all golden vessels for each service, the weight of silver vessels for each service, 15 the weight of the golden lampstands and their lamps, the weight of gold for each lampstand and its lamps, the weight of silver for a lampstand and its lamps, according to the use of each lampstand in the service, 16 the weight of gold for each table for the showbread, the silver for the silver tables, 17 and pure gold for the forks, the basins, and the cups; for the golden bowls and the weight of each; for the silver bowls and the weight of each; 18 for the altar of incense made of refined gold, and its weight; also his plan for the golden chariot of the cherubim that spread their wings and covered the ark of the covenant of the LORD. 19All this he made clear by the writing from the hand of the LORD concerning it,h all the work to be done according to the plan.

20 Then David said to Solomon his son, "Be strong and of good courage, and do it. Fear not, be not dismayed; for the LORD God, even my God, is with you. He will not fail you or forsake you, until all the work for the service of the house of the LORD is finished. 21And behold the divisions of the priests and the Levites for all the service of the house of God; and with you in all the work will be every willing man who has skill for any kind of service; also the officers and all the people will be wholly at your command."

29 And David the king said to all the assembly, "Solomon my son, whom alone God has chosen, is young and inexperienced, and the work is great; for the palace will not be for man but for the LORD God. [2] So I have provided for the house of my God, so far as I was able, the gold for the things of gold, the silver for the things of silver, and the bronze for the things of bronze, the iron for the things of iron, and wood for the things of wood, besides great quantities of onyx and stones for setting, antimony, colored stones, all sorts of precious stones, and marble. [3] Moreover, in addition to all that I have provided for the holy house, I have a treasure of my own of gold and silver, and because of my devotion to the house of my God I give it to the house of my God: [4] three thousand talents of gold, of the gold of Ō'phïr, and seven thousand talents of refined silver, for overlaying the walls of the house, [5] and for all the work to be done by craftsmen, gold for the things of gold and silver for the things of silver. Who then will offer willingly, consecrating himself today to the LORD?"

[6] Then the heads of fathers' houses made their freewill offerings, as did also the leaders of the tribes, the commanders of thousands and of hundreds, and the officers over the king's work. [7] They gave for the service of the house of God five thousand talents and ten thousand darics of gold, ten thousand talents of silver, eighteen thousand talents of bronze, and a hundred thousand talents of iron. [8] And whoever had precious stones gave them to the treasury of the house of the LORD, in the care of Je·hī'el the Gēr'shō·nite. [9] Then the people rejoiced because these had given willingly, for with a whole heart they had offered freely to the LORD; David the king also rejoiced greatly.

[10] Therefore David blessed the LORD in the presence of all the assembly; and David said: "Blessed art thou, O LORD, the God of Israel our father, for ever and ever. [11] Thine, O LORD, is the greatness, and the power, and the glory, and the victory, and the majesty; for all that is in the heavens and in the earth is thine; thine is the kingdom, O LORD, and thou art exalted as head above all. [12] Both riches and honor come from thee, and thou rulest over all. In thy hand are power and might; and in thy hand it is to make great and to give strength to all. [13] And now we thank thee, our God, and praise thy glorious name.

[14] "But who am I, and what is my people, that we should be able thus to offer willingly? For all things come from thee, and of thy own have we given thee. [15] For we are strangers before thee, and sojourners, as all our fathers were; our days on the earth are like a shadow, and there is no abiding.[i] [16] O LORD our God, all this abundance that we have provided for building thee a house for thy holy name comes from thy hand and is all thy own. [17] I know, my God, that thou triest the heart, and hast pleasure in uprightness; in the uprightness of my heart I have freely offered all these things, and now I have seen thy people, who are present here, offering freely and joyously to thee. [18] O LORD, the God of Abraham, Isaac, and Israel, our fathers, keep for ever such purposes and thoughts in the hearts of thy people, and direct their hearts toward thee. [19] Grant to Solomon my son that with a whole heart he may keep thy commandments, thy testimonies, and thy statutes, performing all, and that he may build the palace for which I have made provision.

[20] Then David said to all the assembly, "Bless the LORD your God." And all the assembly blessed the LORD, the God of their fathers, and bowed their heads, and worshiped the LORD, and did obeisance to the king. [21] And they performed sacrifices to the LORD, and on the next day offered burnt offerings to the LORD, a thousand bulls, a thousand rams, and a thousand lambs, with their drink offerings, and sacrifices in abundance for all Israel; [22] and they ate and drank before the LORD on that day with great gladness.

And they made Solomon the son of David king the second time, and they anointed him as prince for the LORD, and Zā'dok as priest. [23] Then Solomon sat on the throne of the LORD as king instead of David his father; and he prospered, and all Israel obeyed him. [24] All the leaders and the mighty men, and also all the sons of King David, pledged their allegiance to King Solomon. [25] And the LORD gave Solomon great repute in the sight of all Israel, and bestowed upon him such royal majesty as had not been on any king before him in Israel.

[26] Thus David the son of Jesse reigned over all Israel. [27] The time that he reigned over Israel was forty years; he reigned seven years in Hē'brŏn, and thirty-three years in Jeru-

salem. 28 Then he died in a good old age, full of days, riches, and honor; and Solomon his son reigned in his stead. 29 Now the acts of King David, from first to last, are written in the Chronicles of Samuel the seer, and in the Chronicles of Nathan the prophet, and in the Chronicles of Gad the seer, 30 with accounts of all his rule and his might and of the circumstances that came upon him and upon Israel, and upon all the kingdoms of the countries.

THE SECOND BOOK OF THE

CHRONICLES

1 Solomon the son of David established himself in his kingdom, and the LORD his God was with him and made him exceedingly great.

2 Solomon spoke to all Israel, to the commanders of thousands and of hundreds, to the judges, and to all the leaders in all Israel, the heads of fathers' houses. 3And Solomon, and all the assembly with him, went to the high place that was at Gib'e·ŏn; for the tent of meeting of God, which Moses the servant of the LORD had made in the wilderness, was there. 4 (But David had brought up the ark of God from Kĭr'ĭ·ath-jē'a·rĭm to the place that David had prepared for it, for he had pitched a tent for it in Jerusalem.) 5 Moreover the bronze altar that Bĕz'-a·lĕl the son of Ū'rĭ, son of Hŭr, had made, was there before the tabernacle of the LORD. And Solomon and the assembly sought the LORD. 6And Solomon went up there to the bronze altar before the LORD, which was at the tent of meeting, and offered a thousand burnt offerings upon it.

7 In that night God appeared to Solomon, and said to him, "Ask what I shall give you." 8And Solomon said to God, "Thou hast shown great and steadfast love to David my father, and hast made me king in his stead. 9 O LORD God, let thy promise to David my father be now fulfilled, for thou hast made me king over a people as many as the dust of the earth. 10 Give me now wisdom and knowledge to go out and come in before this people, for who can rule this thy people, that is so great?" 11 God answered Solomon, "Because this was in your heart, and you have not asked possessions, wealth, honor, or the life of those who

hate you, and have not even asked long life, but have asked wisdom and knowledge for yourself that you may rule my people over whom I have made you king, 12 wisdom and knowledge are granted to you. I will also give you riches, possessions, and honor, such as none of the kings had who were before you, and none after you shall have the like." 13 So Solomon came from*a* the high place at Gib'e·ŏn, from before the tent of meeting, to Jerusalem. And he reigned over Israel.

14 Solomon gathered together chariots and horsemen; he had fourteen hundred chariots and twelve thousand horsemen, whom he stationed in the chariot cities and with the king in Jerusalem. 15And the king made silver and gold as common in Jerusalem as stone, and he made cedar as plentiful as the sycamore of the Shĕ·phē'lah. 16And Solomon's import of horses was from Egypt and Kü'e, and the king's traders received them from Kue for a price. 17 They imported a chariot from Egypt for six hundred shekels of silver, and a horse for a hundred and fifty; likewise through them these were exported to all the kings of the Hit'tites and the kings of Syria.

2*b* Now Solomon purposed to build a temple for the name of the LORD, and a royal palace for himself. 2cAnd Solomon assigned seventy thousand men to bear burdens and eighty thousand to quarry in the hill country, and three thousand six hundred to oversee them. 3And Solomon sent word to Hū'răm the king of Tyre: "As you dealt with David my father and sent him cedar to build himself a house to dwell in, so deal with me. 4 Behold, I am about to build a house for the name

a Gk Vg: Heb *to*   *b* Ch 1.18 in Heb   *c* Ch 2.1 in Heb
1.3-13: 1 Kings 3.4-15.   **1.14-17:** 1 Kings 10.26-29.   **2.1:** 1 Kings 5.5.
2.2: 2 Chron 2.18; 1 Kings 5.15-16.   **2.3-16:** 1 Kings 5.2-11.

of the LORD my God and dedicate it to him for the burning of incense of sweet spices before him, and for the continual offering of the showbread, and for burnt offerings morning and evening, on the sabbaths and the new moons and the appointed feasts of the LORD our God, as ordained for ever for Israel. 5 The house which I am to build will be great, for our God is greater than all gods. 6 But who is able to build him a house, since heaven, even highest heaven, cannot contain him? Who am I to build a house for him, except as a place to burn incense before him? 7 So now send me a man skilled to work in gold, silver, bronze, and iron, and in purple, crimson, and blue fabrics, trained also in engraving, to be with the skilled workers who are with me in Judah and Jerusalem, whom David my father provided. 8 Send me also cedar, cypress, and algum timber from Lebanon, for I know that your servants know how to cut timber in Lebanon. And my servants will be with your servants, 9 to prepare timber for me in abundance, for the house I am to build will be great and wonderful. 10 I will give for your servants, the hewers who cut timber, twenty thousand cors of crushed wheat, twenty thousand cors of barley, twenty thousand baths of wine, and twenty thousand baths of oil."

11 Then Hū′ram the king of Tȳre answered in a letter which he sent to Solomon, "Because the LORD loves his people he has made you king over them." 12 Hū′ram also said, "Blessed be the LORD God of Israel, who made heaven and earth, who has given King David a wise son, endued with discretion and understanding, who will build a temple for the LORD, and a royal palace for himself.

13 "Now I have sent a skilled man, endued with understanding, Hū′ram-ā′bi, 14 the son of a woman of the daughters of Dan, and his father was a man of Tȳre. He is trained to work in gold, silver, bronze, iron, stone, and wood, and in purple, blue, and crimson fabrics and fine linen, and to do all sorts of engraving and execute any design that may be assigned him, with your craftsmen, the craftsmen of my lord, David your father. 15 Now therefore the wheat and barley, oil and wine, of which my lord has spoken, let him send to his servants; 16 and we will cut whatever timber you need from

Lebanon, and bring it to you in rafts by sea to Jop′pā, so that you may take it up to Jerusalem."

17 Then Solomon took a census of all the aliens who were in the land of Israel, after the census of them which David his father had taken; and there were found a hundred and fifty-three thousand six hundred. 18 Seventy thousand of them he assigned to bear burdens, eighty thousand to quarry in the hill country, and three thousand six hunded as overseers to make the people work.

3 Then Solomon began to build the house of the LORD in Jerusalem on Mount Mō·rī′ah, where the LORD had appeared to David his father, at the place that David had appointed, on the threshing floor of Ŏr′nan the Jeb′ū-sīte. 2 He began to build in the second month of the fourth year of his reign. 3 These are Solomon's measurements*d* for building the house of God: the length, in cubits of the old standard, was sixty cubits, and the breadth twenty cubits. 4 The vestibule in front of the nave of the house was twenty cubits long, equal to the width of the house;*e* and its height was a hundred and twenty cubits. He overlaid it on the inside with pure gold. 5 The nave he lined with cypress, and covered it with fine gold, and made palms and chains on it. 6 He adorned the house with settings of precious stones. The gold was gold of Pär·vā′im. 7 So he lined the house with gold—its beams, its thresholds, its walls, and its doors; and he carved cherubim on the walls.

8 And he made the most holy place; its length, corresponding to the breadth of the house, was twenty cubits, and its breadth was twenty cubits; he overlaid it with six hundred talents of fine gold. 9 The weight of the nails was one shekel*f* to fifty shekels of gold. And he overlaid the upper chambers with gold.

10 In the most holy place he made two cherubim of wood*g* and overlaid*h* them with gold. 11 The wings of the cherubim together extended twenty cubits: one wing of the one, of five cubits, touched the wall of the house, and its other wing, of five cubits, touched the wing of the other cherub; 12 and of this cherub, one wing, of five cubits, touched the wall of the house, and the other wing, also of five cubits, was joined to the wing of the first cherub. 13 The wings of these

d Syr: Heb *foundations*   *e* 1 Kings 6.3: Heb uncertain
f Compare Gk: Heb lacks *one shekel*   *g* Gk: Heb uncertain   *h* Heb *they overlaid*
3.1-13: 1 Kings 6.1-28.

cherubim extended twenty cubits; the cherubim^l stood on their feet, facing the nave. ^{14}And he made the veil of blue and purple and crimson fabrics and fine linen, and worked cherubim on it.

15 In front of the house he made two pillars thirty-five cubits high, with a capital of five cubits on the top of each. ^{16} He made chains like a necklace^j and put them on the tops of the pillars; and he made a hundred pomegranates, and put them on the chains. ^{17} He set up the pillars in front of the temple, one on the south, the other on the north; that on the south he called Jā′chin, and that on the north Bō′az.

4 He made an altar of bronze, twenty cubits long, and twenty cubits wide, and ten cubits high. ^{2} Then he made the molten sea; it was round, ten cubits from brim to brim, and five cubits high, and a line of thirty cubits measured its circumference. ^{3} Under it were figures of gourds,^{k} for thirty^l cubits, compassing the sea round about; the gourds^k were in two rows, cast with it when it was cast. ^{4} It stood upon twelve oxen, three facing north, three facing west, three facing south, and three facing east; the sea was set upon them, and all their hinder parts were inward. ^{5} Its thickness was a handbreadth; and its brim was made like the brim of a cup, like the flower of a lily; it held over three thousand baths. ^{6} He also made ten lavers in which to wash, and set five on the south side, and five on the north side. In these they were to rinse off what was used for the burnt offering, and the sea was for the priests to wash in.

7 And he made ten golden lampstands as prescribed, and set them in the temple, five on the south side and five on the north. ^{8} He also made ten tables, and placed them in the temple, five on the south side and five on the north. And he made a hundred basins of gold. ^{9} He made the court of the priests, and the great court, and doors for the court, and overlaid their doors with bronze; ^{10} and he set the sea at the southeast corner of the house.

11 Hū′ram also made the pots, the shovels, and the basins. So Huram finished the work that he did for King Solomon on the house of God: ^{12} the two pillars, the bowls, and the two capitals on the top of the pillars; and the two networks to cover the two

bowls of the capitals that were on the top of the pillars; ^{13} and the four hundred pomegranates for the two networks, two rows of pomegranates for each network, to cover the two bowls of the capitals that were upon the pillars. ^{14} He made the stands also, and the lavers upon the stands, ^{15} and the one sea, and the twelve oxen underneath it. ^{16} The pots, the shovels, the forks, and all the equipment for these Hū′ram-ā′bī made of burnished bronze for King Solomon for the house of the LORD. ^{17} In the plain of the Jordan the king cast them, in the clay ground between Suc′coth and Zer′e·dah. ^{18} Solomon made all these things in great quantities, so that the weight of the bronze was not ascertained.

19 So Solomon made all the things that were in the house of God: the golden altar, the tables for the bread of the Presence, ^{20} the lampstands and their lamps of pure gold to burn before the inner sanctuary, as prescribed; ^{21} the flowers, the lamps, and the tongs, of purest gold; ^{22} the snuffers, basins, dishes for incense, and firepans, of pure gold; and the sockets^m of the temple, for the inner doors to the most holy place and for the doors of the nave of the temple were of gold.

5 Thus all the work that Solomon did for the house of the LORD was finished. And Solomon brought in the things which David his father had dedicated, the silver, the gold, and all the vessels in the treasuries of the house of God.

2 Then Solomon assembled the elders of Israel and all the heads of the tribes, the leaders of the fathers' houses of the people of Israel, in Jerusalem, to bring up the ark of the covenant of the LORD out of the city of David, which is Zion. ^{3}And all the men of Israel assembled before the king at the feast which is in the seventh month. ^{4}And all the elders of Israel came, and the Levites took up the ark. ^{5}And they brought up the ark, the tent of meeting, and all the holy vessels that were in the tent; the priests and the Levites brought them up. ^{6}And King Solomon and all the congregation of Israel, who had assembled before him, were before the ark, sacrificing so many sheep and oxen that they could not be counted or numbered. ^{7} So the priests brought the ark of the covenant of the LORD to its place, in the inner sanctuary of the house, in

^{l} Heb *they* ^{j} Cn: Heb *in the inner sanctuary* ^{k} 1 Kings 7.24: Heb *oxen*
^{l} Compare verse 2: Heb *ten* ^{m} 1 Kings 7.50: Heb *the door of the house*
3.15-17: 1 Kings 7.15-21.   **4.2-5:** 1 Kings 7.23-26.   **4.6-5.1:** 1 Kings 7.38-51.

the most holy place, underneath the wings of the cherubim. 8 For the cherubim spread out their wings over the place of the ark, so that the cherubim made a covering above the ark and its poles. 9And the poles were so long that the ends of the poles were seen from the holy place before the inner sanctuary; but they could not be seen from outside; and they are there to this day. 10 There was nothing in the ark except the two tables which Moses put there at Hō′reb, where the LORD made a covenant with the people of Israel, when they came out of Egypt. 11 Now when the priests came out of the holy place (for all the priests who were present had sanctified themselves, without regard to their divisions; 12 and all the Levitical singers, Ā′saph, Hē′mǎn, and Je·dū′thŭn, their sons and kinsmen, arrayed in fine linen, with cymbals, harps and lyres, stood east of the altar with a hundred and twenty priests who were trumpeters; 13 and it was the duty of the trumpeters and singers to make themselves heard in unison in praise and thanksgiving to the LORD), and when the song was raised, with trumpets and cymbals and other musical instruments, in praise to the LORD,

"For he is good,
    for his steadfast love endures for
    ever,"

the house, the house of the LORD, was filled with a cloud, 14 so that the priests could not stand to minister because of the cloud; for the glory of the LORD filled the house of God.

Then Solomon said,
6 "The LORD has said that he would
    dwell in thick darkness.

2 I have built thee an exalted house,
    a place for thee to dwell in for
    ever."

3 Then the king faced about, and blessed all the assembly of Israel, while all the assembly of Israel stood. 4And he said, "Blessed be the LORD, the God of Israel, who with his hand has fulfilled what he promised with his mouth to David my father, saying, 5 'Since the day that I brought my people out of the land of Egypt, I chose no city in all the tribes of Israel in which to build a house, that my name might be there, and I chose no man as prince over my people Israel; 6 but I have chosen Jerusalem that my name may be there and I have chosen David to be over my people Israel.' 7 Now it was in the heart of David my father to build a house for the name

of the LORD, the God of Israel. 8 But the LORD said to David my father, 'Whereas it was in your heart to build a house for my name, you did well that it was in your heart; 9 nevertheless you shall not build the house, but your son who shall be born to you shall build the house for my name.' 10 Now the LORD has fulfilled his promise which he made; for I have risen in the place of David my father, and sit on the throne of Israel, as the LORD promised, and I have built the house for the name of the LORD, the God of Israel. 11And there I have set the ark, in which is the covenant of the LORD which he made with the people of Israel."

12 Then Solomon stood before the altar of the LORD in the presence of all the assembly of Israel, and spread forth his hands. 13 Solomon had made a bronze platform five cubits long, five cubits wide, and three cubits high, and had set it in the court; and he stood upon it. Then he knelt upon his knees in the presence of all the assembly of Israel, and spread forth his hands toward heaven; 14 and said, "O LORD, God of Israel, there is no God like thee, in heaven or on earth, keeping covenant and showing steadfast love to thy servants who walk before thee with all their heart; 15 who hast kept with thy servant David my father what thou didst declare to him; yea, thou didst speak with thy mouth, and with thy hand hast fulfilled it this day. 16 Now therefore, O LORD, God of Israel, keep with thy servant David my father what thou hast promised him, saying, 'There shall never fail you a man before me to sit upon the throne of Israel, if only your sons take heed to their way, to walk in my law as you have walked before me.' 17 Now therefore, O LORD, God of Israel, let thy word be confirmed, which thou hast spoken to thy servant David.

18 "But will God dwell indeed with man on the earth? Behold, heaven and the highest heaven cannot contain thee; how much less this house which I have built! 19 Yet have regard to the prayer of thy servant and to his supplication, O LORD my God, hearkening to the cry and to the prayer which thy servant prays before thee; 20 that thy eyes may be open day and night toward this house, the place where thou hast promised to set thy name, that thou mayest hearken to the prayer which thy servant offers toward this place. 21And hearken thou to the

5.13–14: 1 Kings 8.10–11.   **6.1–39:** 1 Kings 8.12–50.

supplications of thy servant and of thy people Israel, when they pray toward this place; yea, hear thou from heaven thy dwelling place; and when thou hearest, forgive.

22 "If a man sins against his neighbor and is made to take an oath, and comes and swears his oath before thy altar in this house, 23 then hear thou from heaven, and act, and judge thy servants, requiting the guilty by bringing his conduct upon his own head, and vindicating the righteous by rewarding him according to his righteousness.

24 "If thy people Israel are defeated before the enemy because they have sinned against thee, when they turn again and acknowledge thy name, and pray and make supplication to thee in this house, 25 then hear thou from heaven, and forgive the sin of thy people Israel, and bring them again to the land which thou gavest to them and to their fathers.

26 "When heaven is shut up and there is no rain because they have sinned against thee, if they pray toward this place, and acknowledge thy name, and turn from their sin, when thou dost afflict them, 27 then hear thou in heaven, and forgive the sin of thy servants, thy people Israel, when thou dost teach them the good way*n* in which they should walk; and grant rain upon thy land, which thou hast given to thy people as an inheritance.

28 "If there is famine in the land, if there is pestilence or blight or mildew or locust or caterpillar; if their enemies besiege them in any of their cities; whatever plague, whatever sickness there is; 29 whatever prayer, whatever supplication is made by any man or by all thy people Israel, each knowing his own affliction, and his own sorrow and stretching out his hands toward this house; 30 then hear thou from heaven thy dwelling place, and forgive, and render to each whose heart thou knowest, according to all his ways (for thou, thou only, knowest the hearts of the children of men); 31 that they may fear thee and walk in thy ways all the days that they live in the land which thou gavest to our fathers.

32 "Likewise when a foreigner, who is not of thy people Israel, comes from a far country for the sake of thy great name, and thy mighty hand, and thy outstretched arm, when he comes and prays toward this house, 33 hear thou

from heaven thy dwelling place, and do according to all for which the foreigner calls to thee; in order that all the peoples of the earth may know thy name and fear thee, as do thy people Israel, and that they may know that this house which I have built is called by thy name.

34 "If thy people go out to battle against their enemies, by whatever way thou shalt send them, and they pray to thee toward this city which thou hast chosen and the house which I have built for thy name, 35 then hear thou from heaven their prayer and their supplication, and maintain their cause.

36 "If they sin against thee—for there is no man who does not sin—and thou art angry with them, and dost give them to an enemy, so that they are carried away captive to a land far or near; 37 yet if they lay it to heart in the land to which they have been carried captive, and repent, and make supplication to thee in the land of their captivity, saying, 'We have sinned, and have acted perversely and wickedly'; 38 if they repent with all their mind and with all their heart in the land of their captivity, to which they were carried captive, and pray toward their land, which thou gavest to their fathers, the city which thou hast chosen, and the house which I have built for thy name, 39 then hear thou from heaven thy dwelling place their prayer and their supplications, and maintain their cause and forgive thy people who have sinned against thee. 40 Now, O my God, let thy eyes be open and thy ears attentive to a prayer of this place.

41 "And now arise, O LORD God, and go to thy resting place,
   thou and the ark of thy might.
Let thy priests, O LORD God, be clothed with salvation,
   and let thy saints rejoice in thy goodness.
42 O LORD God, do not turn away the face of thy anointed one!
   Remember thy steadfast love for David thy servant."

7 When Solomon had ended his prayer, fire came down from heaven and consumed the burnt offering and the sacrifices, and the glory of the LORD filled the temple. 2 And the priests could not enter the house of the LORD, because the glory of the LORD filled the LORD's house. 3 When all the children of Israel saw the fire

n Gk Syr Vg: Heb *toward the good way*
6.41-42: Ps 132.8-10.

come down and the glory of the LORD upon the temple, they bowed down with their faces to the earth on the pavement, and worshiped and gave thanks to the LORD, saying,

"For he is good,
for his steadfast love endures for ever."

4 Then the king and all the people offered sacrifice before the LORD. 5 King Solomon offered as a sacrifice twenty-two thousand oxen and a hundred and twenty thousand sheep. So the king and all the people dedicated the house of God. 6 The priests stood at their posts; the Levites also, with the instruments for music to the LORD which King David had made for giving thanks to the LORD—for his steadfast love endures for ever—whenever David offered praises by their ministry; opposite them the priests sounded trumpets; and all Israel stood.

7 And Solomon consecrated the middle of the court that was before the house of the LORD; for there he offered the burnt offering and the fat of the peace offerings, because the bronze altar Solomon had made could not hold the burnt offering and the cereal offering and the fat.

8 At that time Solomon held the feast for seven days, and all Israel with him, a very great congregation, from the entrance of Hā'math to the Brook of Egypt. 9 And on the eighth day they held a solemn assembly; for they had kept the dedication of the altar seven days and the feast seven days. 10 On the twenty-third day of the seventh month he sent the people away to their homes, joyful and glad of heart for the goodness that the LORD had shown to David and to Solomon and to Israel his people.

11 Thus Solomon finished the house of the LORD and the king's house; all that Solomon had planned to do in the house of the LORD and in his own house he successfully accomplished. 12 Then the LORD appeared to Solomon in the night and said to him: "I have heard your prayer, and have chosen this place for myself as a house of sacrifice. 13 When I shut up the heavens so that there is no rain, or command the locust to devour the land, or send pestilence among my people, 14 if my people who are called by my name humble themselves, and pray and seek my face, and turn from their wicked ways, then I will hear from heaven, and will forgive their sin

and heal their land. 15 Now my eyes will be open and my ears attentive to the prayer that is made in this place. 16 For now I have chosen and consecrated this house that my name may be there for ever; my eyes and my heart will be there for all time. 17 And as for you, if you walk before me, as David your father walked, doing according to all that I have commanded you and keeping my statutes and my ordinances, 18 then I will establish your royal throne, as I covenanted with David your father, saying, 'There shall not fail you a man to rule Israel.'

19 "But if you*o* turn aside and forsake my statutes and my commandments which I have set before you, and go and serve other gods and worship them, 20 then I will pluck you*p* up from the land which I have given you;*p* and this house, which I have consecrated for my name, I will cast out of my sight, and will make it a proverb and a byword among all peoples. 21 And at this house, which is exalted, every one passing by will be astonished, and say, 'Why has the LORD done thus to this land and to this house?' 22 Then they will say, 'Because they forsook the LORD the God of their fathers who brought them out of the land of Egypt, and laid hold on other gods, and worshiped them and served them; therefore he has brought all this evil upon them.' "

8 At the end of twenty years, in which Solomon had built the house of the LORD and his own house, 2 Solomon rebuilt the cities which Hū'ràm had given to him, and settled the people of Israel in them.

3 And Solomon went to Hā'math-zō'bàh, and took it. 4 He built Tad'-môr in the wilderness and all the store-cities which he built in Hā'math. 5 He also built Upper Beth-hō'ron and Lower Beth-horon, fortified cities with walls, gates, and bars, 6 and Bā'à-lath, and all the store-cities that Solomon had, and all the cities for his chariots, and the cities for his horsemen, and whatever Solomon desired to build in Jerusalem, in Lebanon, and in all the land of his dominion. 7 All the people who were left of the Hit'tites, the Am'ò-rites, the Per'iz-zites, the Hī'vites, and the Jeb'ū-sites, who were not of Israel, 8 from their descendants who were left after them in the land, whom the people of Israel had not destroyed—these Solomon made a forced levy and so they are to this day.

o The word *you* is plural here   *p* Heb *them*

7.4-10: 1 Kings 8.62-66.   **7.11-22:** 1 Kings 9.1-9.   **8.1-18:** 1 Kings 9.10-28.

9 But of the people of Israel Solomon made no slaves for his work; they were soldiers, and his officers, the commanders of his chariots, and his horsemen. 10And these were the chief officers of King Solomon, two hundred and fifty, who exercised authority over the people.

11 Solomon brought Pharaoh's daughter up from the city of David to the house which he had built for her, for he said, "My wife shall not live in the house of David king of Israel, for the places to which the ark of the LORD has come are holy."

12 Then Solomon offered up burnt offerings to the LORD upon the altar of the LORD which he had built before the vestibule, 13 as the duty of each day required, offering according to the commandment of Moses for the sabbaths, the new moons, and the three annual feasts—the feast of unleavened bread, the feast of weeks, and the feast of tabernacles. 14According to the ordinance of David his father, he appointed the divisions of the priests for their service, and the Levites for their offices of praise and ministry before the priests as the duty of each day required, and the gatekeepers in their divisons for the several gates; for so David the man of God had commanded. 15And they did not turn aside from what the king had commanded the priests and Levites concerning any matter and concerning the treasuries.

16 Thus was accomplished all the work of Solomon from*q* the day the foundation of the house of the LORD was laid until it was finished. So the house of the LORD was completed.

17 Then Solomon went to E′zi-on-gē′ber and E′loth on the shore of the sea, in the land of E′dom. 18And Hū′ram sent him by his servants ships and servants familiar with the sea, and they went to O′phir together with the servants of Solomon, and fetched from there four hundred and fifty talents of gold and brought it to King Solomon.

9   Now when the queen of Sheba heard of the fame of Solomon she came to Jerusalem to test him with hard questions, having a very great retinue and camels bearing spices and very much gold and precious stones. When she came to Solomon, she told him all that was on her mind. 2And Solomon answered all her questions; there was nothing hidden from Solo-

mon which he could not explain to her. 3And when the queen of Sheba had seen the wisdom of Solomon, the house that he had built, 4 the food of his table, the seating of his officials, and the attendance of his servants, and their clothing, his cupbearers, and their clothing, and his burnt offerings which he offered at the house of the LORD, there was no more spirit in her.

5 And she said to the king, "The report was true which I heard in my own land of your affairs and of your wisdom, 6 but I did not believe the*r* reports until I came and my own eyes had seen it; and behold, half the greatness of your wisdom was not told me; you surpass the report which I heard. 7 Happy are your wives!*s* Happy are these your servants, who continually stand before you and hear your wisdom! 8 Blessed be the LORD your God, who has delighted in you and set you on his throne as king for the LORD your God! Because your God loved Israel and would establish them for ever, he has made you king over them, that you may execute justice and righteousness." 9 Then she gave the king a hundred and twenty talents of gold, and a very great quantity of spices, and precious stones: there were no spices such as those which the queen of Sheba gave to King Solomon.

10 Moreover the servants of Hū′ram and the servants of Solomon, who brought gold from O′phir, brought algum wood and precious stones. 11And the king made of the algum wood steps*t* for the house of the LORD and for the king's house, lyres also and harps for the singers; there never was seen the like of them before in the land of Judah.

12 And King Solomon gave to the queen of Sheba all that she desired, whatever she asked besides what she had brought to the king. So she turned and went back to her own land, with her servants.

13 Now the weight of gold that came to Solomon in one year was six hundred and sixty-six talents of gold, 14 besides that which the traders and merchants brought; and all the kings of Arabia and the governors of the land brought gold and silver to Solomon. 15 King Solomon made two hundred large shields of beaten gold; six hundred shekels of beaten gold went into each shield. 16And he made three

q Gk Syr Vg: Heb *to*   *r* Heb *their*   *s* Gk Compare 1 Kings 10.8: Heb *men*
t Gk Vg: The meaning of the Hebrew word is uncertain
9.1-28: 1 Kings 10.1-29.

hundred shields of beaten gold; three hundred shekels of gold went into each shield; and the king put them in the House of the Forest of Lebanon. 17 The king also made a great ivory throne, and overlaid it with pure gold. 18 The throne had six steps and a footstool of gold, which were attached to the throne, and on each side of the seat were arm rests and two lions standing beside the arm rests, 19 while twelve lions stood there, one on each end of a step on the six steps. The like of it was never made in any kingdom. 20 All King Solomon's drinking vessels were of gold, and all the vessels of the House of the Forest of Lebanon were of pure gold; silver was not considered as anything in the days of Solomon. 21 For the king's ships went to Tär'-shish with the servants of Hū'ràm; once every three years the ships of Tarshish used to come bringing gold, silver, ivory, apes, and peacocks.*

22 Thus King Solomon excelled all the kings of the earth in riches and in wisdom. 23 And all the kings of the earth sought the presence of Solomon to hear his wisdom, which God had put into his mind. 24 Every one of them brought his present, articles of silver and of gold, garments, myrrh, spices, horses, and mules, so much year by year. 25 And Solomon had four thousand stalls for horses and chariots, and twelve thousand horsemen, whom he stationed in the chariot cities and with the king in Jerusalem. 26 And he ruled over all the kings from the Eū·phrā'tēs to the land of the Philistines, and to the border of Egypt. 27 And the king made silver as common in Jerusalem as stone, and cedar as plentiful as the sycamore of the She-phē'läh. 28 And horses were imported for Solomon from Egypt and from all lands.

29 Now the rest of the acts of Solomon, from first to last, are they not written in the history of Nathan the prophet, and in the prophecy of Ā·hī'jäh the Shī'lô·nīte, and in the visions of Id'dō the seer concerning Jer·ó·bō'äm the son of Ně'bat? 30 Solomon reigned in Jerusalem over all Israel forty years. 31 And Solomon slept with his fathers, and was buried in the city of David his father; and Rē·hó·bō'äm his son reigned in his stead.

10 Rē·hó·bō'äm went to Shē'chem, for all Israel had come to Shechem to make him king. 2 And when

Jer·ó·bō'äm the son of Ně'bat heard of it (for he was in Egypt, whither he had fled from King Solomon), then Jeroboam returned from Egypt. 3 And they sent and called him; and Jer·ó·bō'äm and all Israel came and said to Rē·hó·bō'äm, 4 "Your father made our yoke heavy. Now therefore lighten the hard service of your father and his heavy yoke upon us, and we will serve you." 5 He said to them, "Come to me again in three days." So the people went away.

6 Then King Rē·hó·bō'äm took counsel with the old men, who had stood before Solomon his father while he was yet alive, saying, "How do you advise me to answer this people?" 7 And they said to him, "If you will be kind to this people and please them, and speak good words to them, then they will be your servants for ever." 8 But he forsook the counsel which the old men gave him, and took counsel with the young men who had grown up with him and stood before him. 9 And he said to them, "What do you advise that we answer this people who have said to me, 'Lighten the yoke that your father put upon us'?" 10 And the young men who had grown up with him said to him, "Thus shall you speak to the people who said to you, 'Your father made our yoke heavy, but do you lighten it for us'; thus shall you say to them, 'My little finger is thicker than my father's loins. 11 And now, whereas my father laid upon you a heavy yoke, I will add to your yoke. My father chastised you with whips, but I will chastise you with scorpions.'"

12 So Jer·ó·bō'äm and all the people came to Rē·hó·bō'äm the third day, as the king said, "Come to me again the third day." 13 And the king answered them harshly, and forsaking the counsel of the old men, 14 King Rē·hò·bō'ûm spoke to them according to the counsel of the young men, saying, "My father made your yoke heavy, but I will add to it; my father chastised you with whips, but I will chastise you with scorpions." 15 So the king did not hearken to the people; for it was a turn of affairs brought about by God that the LORD might fulfil his word, which he spoke by Ā·hī'jäh the Shī'lô·nīte to Jer·ó·bō'äm the son of Ně'bat.

16 And when all Israel saw that the king did not hearken to them, the people answered the king,

* Or baboons

9.30-31: 1 Kings 11.42-48.   10.1-19: 1 Kings 12.1-19.

"What portion have we in David?
We have no inheritance in the
son of Jesse.
Each of you to your tents, O Israel!
Look now to your own house,
David."
So all Israel departed to their tents.
[17] But Rē·hȯ·bō'ăm reigned over the
people of Israel who dwelt in the cities
of Judah. [18] Then King Rē·hȯ·bō'ăm
sent Hȧ·dôr'ăm, who was taskmaster
over the forced labor, and the people
of Israel stoned him to death with
stones. And King Rehoboam made
haste to mount his chariot, to flee to
Jerusalem. [19] So Israel has been in
rebellion against the house of David
to this day.

11 When Rē·hȯ·bō'ăm came to Jerusalem, he assembled the house of
Judah, and Benjamin, a hundred and
eighty thousand chosen warriors, to
fight against Israel, to restore the
kingdom to Rehoboam. [2] But the word
of the LORD came to She·māi'ah the
man of God: [3] "Say to Rē·hȯ·bō'ăm
the son of Solomon king of Judah, and
to all Israel in Judah and Benjamin,
[4] 'Thus says the LORD, You shall not
go up or fight against your brethren.
Return every man to his home, for
this thing is from me.'" So they
hearkened to the word of the LORD,
and returned and did not go against
Jer·ȯ·bō'ăm.

[5] Rē·hȯ·bō'ăm dwelt in Jerusalem,
and he built cities for defense in Judah.
[6] He built Bethlehem, E'tam, Te·kō'ȧ,
[7] Beth'-zūr, Sō'cōh, Ȧ·dul'lȧm, [8] Gath,
Mȧ·rē'shȧh, Ziph, [9]Ad·ȯ·rā'im, Lā'-
chish, Ȧ·zē'kȧh, [10] Zō'rȧh, Äi'jȧ·lon,
and Hē'brȯn, fortified cities which are
in Judah and in Benjamin. [11] He made
the fortresses strong, and put commanders in them, and stores of food,
oil, and wine. [12]And he put shields
and spears in all the cities, and made
them very strong. So he held Judah
and Benjamin.

13 And the priests and the Levites
that were in all Israel resorted to him
from all places where they lived. [14] For
the Levites left their common lands
and their holdings and came to Judah
and Jerusalem, because Jer·ȯ·bō'ăm
and his sons cast them out from serving as priests of the LORD, [15] and he
appointed his own priests for the high
places, and for the satyrs, and for the
calves which he had made. [16]And
those who had set their hearts to seek
the LORD God of Israel came after
them from all the tribes of Israel to

Jerusalem to sacrifice to the LORD, the
God of their fathers. [17] They strengthened the kingdom of Judah, and for
three years they made Rē·hȯ·bō'ăm
the son of Solomon secure, for they
walked for three years in the way of
David and Solomon.

18 Rē·hȯ·bō'ăm took as wife Mā'-
hȧ·lath the daughter of Jer'i·moth the
son of David, and of Ab'i·hāil the
daughter of E·li'ab the son of Jesse;
[19] and she bore him sons, Jē'ush,
Shem·ȧ·ri'ăh, and Zā'ham. [20]After her
he took Mā'ȧ·cȧh the daughter of
Ab'sȧ·lŏm, who bore him Ȧ·bi'jȧh,
At'täi, Zī'zȧ, and She·lō'mith. [21] Rē-
hȯ·bō'ăm loved Mā'ȧ·cȧh the daughter
of Ab'sȧ·lŏm above all his wives and
concubines (he took eighteen wives and
sixty concubines, and had twenty-
eight sons and sixty daughters); [22] and
Rē·hȯ·bō'ăm appointed Ȧ·bi'jȧh the
son of Mā'ȧ·cȧh as chief prince among
his brothers, for he intended to make
him king. [23]And he dealt wisely, and
distributed some of his sons through
all the districts of Judah and Benjamin,
in all the fortified cities; and he gave
them abundant provisions, and pro-
cured wives for them.[u]

12 When the rule of Rē·hȯ·bō'ăm
was established and was strong,
he forsook the law of the LORD, and
all Israel with him. [2] In the fifth year
of King Rē·hȯ·bō'ăm, because they
had been unfaithful to the LORD,
Shi'shak king of Egypt came up
against Jerusalem [3] with twelve hundred chariots and sixty thousand
horsemen. And the people were without number who came with him from
Egypt—Libyans, Suk'ki·im, and Ethiopians. [4]And he took the fortified
cities of Judah and came as far as
Jerusalem. [5] Then She·māi'ah the
prophet came to Rē·hȯ·bō'ăm and to
the princes of Judah, who had
gathered at Jerusalem because of
Shi'shak, and said to them, "Thus
says the LORD, 'You abandoned me,
so I have abandoned you to the hand
of Shishak.'" [6] Then the princes of
Israel and the king humbled themselves and said, "The LORD is righteous." [7] When the LORD saw that they
humbled themselves, the word of the
LORD came to She·māi'ah: "They have
humbled themselves; I will not destroy
them, but I will grant them some
deliverance, and my wrath shall not be
poured out upon Jerusalem by the
hand of Shi'shak. [8] Nevertheless they
shall be servants to him, that they may

u Cn: Heb *sought a multitude of wives*
11.1-4: 1 Kings 12.22-24.   **12.1-16:** 1 Kings 14.25-31.

know my service and the service of the kingdoms of the countries."

9 So Shĭ'shak king of Egypt came up against Jerusalem; he took away the treasures of the house of the LORD and the treasures of the king's house; he took away everything. He also took away the shields of gold which Solomon had made; 10 and King Rē·hŏ·bŏ'ăm made in their stead shields of bronze, and committed them to the hands of the officers of the guard, who kept the door of the king's house. 11And as often as the king went into the house of the LORD, the guard came and bore them, and brought them back to the guardroom. 12And when he humbled himself the wrath of the LORD turned from him, so as not to make a complete destruction; moreover, conditions were good in Judah.

13 So King Rē·hŏ·bŏ'ăm established himself in Jerusalem and reigned. Rehoboam was forty-one years old when he began to reign, and he reigned seventeen years in Jerusalem, the city which the LORD had chosen out of all the tribes of Israel to put his name there. His mother's name was Nā'ă·măh the Am'mŏ·nīt·ĕss. 14And he did evil, for he did not set his heart to seek the LORD.

15 Now the acts of Rē·hŏ·bŏ'ăm, from first to last, are they not written in the chronicles of She·māi'ăh the prophet and of Id'dŏ the seer?ᵛ There were continual wars between Rehoboam and Jer·ŏ·bŏ'ăm. 16And Rē·hŏ·bŏ'ăm slept with his fathers, and was buried in the city of David; and Ă·bī'jăh his son reigned in his stead.

13 In the eighteenth year of King Jer·ŏ·bŏ'ăm Ă·bī'jăh began to reign over Judah. 2 He reigned for three years in Jerusalem. His mother's name was Mĭ·cāi'ăh the daughter of Ū'ri·el of Gĭb'ē·ăh.

Now there was war between Ă·bī'jăh and Jer·ŏ·bŏ'ăm. 3Ă·bī'jăh went out to battle having an army of valiant men of war, four hundred thousand picked men; and Jer·ŏ·bŏ'ăm drew up his line of battle against him with eight hundred thousand picked mighty warriors. 4 Then Ă·bī'jăh stood up on Mount Zem·ă·rā'im which is in the hill country of Ē'phrā·im, and said, "Hear me, O Jer·ŏ·bŏ'ăm and all Israel! 5 Ought you not to know that the LORD God of Israel gave the kingship over Israel for ever to David and his sons by a covenant of salt? 6 Yet Jer·ŏ·bŏ'ăm the son of Nē'bat, a servant of

Solomon the son of David, rose up and rebelled against his lord; 7 and certain worthless scoundrels gathered about him and defied Rē·hŏ·bŏ'ăm the son of Solomon, when Rehoboam was young and irresolute and could not withstand them.

8 "And now you think to withstand the kingdom of the LORD in the hand of the sons of David, because you are a great multitude and have with you the golden calves which Jer·ŏ·bŏ'ăm made you for gods. 9 Have you not driven out the priests of the LORD, the sons of Aaron, and the Levites, and made priests for yourselves like the peoples of other lands? Whoever comes to consecrate himself with a young bull or seven rams becomes a priest of what are no gods. 10 But as for us, the LORD is our God, and we have not forsaken him. We have priests ministering to the LORD who are sons of Aaron, and Levites for their service. 11 They offer to the LORD every morning and every evening burnt offerings and incense of sweet spices, set out the showbread on the table of pure gold, and care for the golden lampstand that its lamps may burn every evening; for we keep the charge of the LORD our God, but you have forsaken him. 12 Behold, God is with us at our head, and his priests with their battle trumpets to sound the call to battle against you. O sons of Israel, do not fight against the LORD, the God of your fathers; for you cannot succeed."

13 Jer·ŏ·bŏ'ăm had sent an ambush around to come on them from behind; thus his troopsʷ were in front of Judah, and the ambush was behind them. 14And when Judah looked, behold, the battle was before and behind them; and they cried to the LORD, and the priests blew the trumpets. 15 Then the men of Judah raised the battle shout. And when the men of Judah shouted, God defeated Jer·ŏ·bŏ'ăm and all Israel before Ă·bī'jăh and Judah. 16 The men of Israel fled before Judah, and God gave them into their hand. 17Ă·bī'jăh and his people slew them with a great slaughter; so there fell slain of Israel five hundred thousand picked men. 18 Thus the men of Israel were subdued at that time, and the men of Judah prevailed, because they relied upon the LORD, the God of their fathers. 19And Ă·bī'jăh pursued Jer·ŏ·bŏ'ăm, and took cities from him, Beth'ĕl with its villages and Je·shā'năh with its villages and

ᵛ Heb *seer, to enroll oneself*   ʷ Heb *they*
13.1-2: 1 Kings 15.1-2, 7.

É·phrón[x] with its villages. 20 Jer·ó·bō′am did not recover his power in the days of A·bi′jah; and the LORD smote him, and he died.21 But A·bi′jah grew mighty. And he took fourteen wives, and had twenty-two sons and sixteen daughters. 22 The rest of the acts of A·bi′jah, his ways and his sayings, are written in the story of the prophet Id′dō.

14[y] So A·bi′jah slept with his fathers, and they buried him in the city of David; and Asa his son reigned in his stead. In his days the land had rest for ten years. 2zAnd Asa did what was good and right in the eyes of the LORD his God. 3 He took away the foreign altars and the high places, and broke down the pillars and hewed down the A·she′rim, 4 and commanded Judah to seek the LORD, the God of their fathers, and to keep the law and the commandment. 5 He also took out of all the cities of Judah the high places and the incense altars. And the kingdom had rest under him. 6 He built fortified cities in Judah, for the land had rest. He had no war in those years, for the LORD gave him peace. 7And he said to Judah, "Let us build these cities, and surround them with walls and towers, gates and bars; the land is still ours, because we have sought the LORD our God; we have sought him, and he has given us peace on every side." So they built and prospered. 8And Asa had an army of three hundred thousand from Judah, armed with bucklers and spears, and two hundred and eighty thousand men from Benjamin, that carried shields and drew bows; all these were mighty men of valor.

9 Zé′rah the Ethiopian came out against them with an army of a million men and three hundred chariots, and came as far as Mà·rē′shah. 10And Asa went out to meet him, and they drew up their lines of battle in the valley of Zeph′a·thah at Mà·rē′shah. 11And Asa cried to the LORD his God, "O LORD, there is none like thee to help, between the mighty and the weak. Help us, O LORD our God, for we rely on thee, and in thy name we have come against this multitude. O LORD, thou art our God; let not man prevail against thee." 12 So the LORD defeated the Ethiopians before Asa and before Judah, and the Ethiopians fled. 13Asa and the people that were with him

pursued them as far as Gē′rär, and the Ethiopians fell until none remained alive; for they were broken before the LORD and his army. The men of Judah[a] carried away very much booty. 14And they smote all the cities round about Gē′rär, for the fear of the LORD was upon them. They plundered all the cities, for there was much plunder in them. 15And they smote the tents of those who had cattle,[b] and carried away sheep in abundance and camels. Then they returned to Jerusalem.

15 The Spirit of God came upon Az·a·rī′ah the son of O′ded, 2 and he went out to meet Asa, and said to him, "Hear me, Asa, and all Judah and Benjamin: The LORD is with you, while you are with him. If you seek him, he will be found by you, but if you forsake him, he will forsake you. 3 For a long time Israel was without the true God, and without a teaching priest, and without law; 4 but when in their distress they turned to the LORD, the God of Israel, and sought him, he was found by them. 5 In those times there was no peace to him who went out or to him who came in, for great disturbances afflicted all the inhabitants of the lands. 6 They were broken in pieces, nation against nation and city against city, for God troubled them with every sort of distress. 7 But you, take courage! Do not let your hands be weak, for your work shall be rewarded."

8 When Asa heard these words, the prophecy of Az·a·rī′ah the son of O′ded,[c] he took courage, and put away the abominable idols from all the land of Judah and Benjamin and from the cities which he had taken in the hill country of É′phra·im, and he repaired the altar of the LORD that was in front of the vestibule of the house of the LORD.[d] 9And he gathered all Judah and Benjamin, and those from É′phra·im, Mà·nas′seh, and Simeon who were sojourning with them, for great numbers had deserted to him from Israel when they saw that the LORD his God was with him. 10 They were gathered at Jerusalem in the third month of the fifteenth year of the reign of Asa. 11 They sacrificed to the LORD on that day, from the spoil which they had brought, seven hundred oxen and seven thousand sheep. 12And they entered into a covenant to seek the LORD, the God of their fathers, with

x Another reading is *Ephrain*　y Ch 13.23 in Heb　z Ch 14.1 in Heb　a Heb *they*
b Heb obscure　c Compare Syr Vg: Heb *the prophecy, Oded the prophet*
d Heb *the vestibule of the* LORD
14.1-5: 1 Kings 15.8-12.

all their heart and with all their soul; 13 and that whoever would not seek the Lord, the God of Israel, should be put to death, whether young or old, man or woman. 14 They took oath to the Lord with a loud voice, and with shouting, and with trumpets, and with horns. 15And all Judah rejoiced over the oath; for they had sworn with all their heart, and had sought him with their whole desire, and he was found by them, and the Lord gave them rest round about.

16 Even Māʹá·càh, his mother, King Asa removed from being queen mother because she had made an abominable image for Á·sheʹràh. Asa cut down her image, crushed it, and burned it at the brook Kidʹron. 17 But the high places were not taken out of Israel. Nevertheless the heart of Asa was blameless all his days. 18And he brought into the house of God the votive gifts of his father and his own votive gifts, silver, and gold, and vessels. 19And there was no more war until the thirty-fifth year of the reign of Asa.

16 In the thirty-sixth year of the reign of Asa, Bāʹá·shà king of Israel went up against Judah, and built Rāʹmàh, that he might permit no one to go out or come in to Asa king of Judah. 2 Then Asa took silver and gold from the treasures of the house of the Lord and the king's house, and sent them to Ben-hāʹdad king of Syria, who dwelt in Damascus, saying, 3 "Let there be a league between me and you, as between my father and your father; behold, I am sending to you silver and gold; go, break your league with Bāʹá·shà king of Israel, that he may withdraw from me." 4And Ben-hāʹdad hearkened to King Asa, and sent the commanders of his armies against the cities of Israel, and they conquered Iʹjon, Dan, Āʹbel-māʹim, and all the store-cities of Naphʹtá·li. 5And when Bāʹá·shà heard of it, he stopped building Rāʹmàh, and let his work cease. 6 Then King Asa took all Judah, and they carried away the stones of Rāʹmàh and its timber, with which Bāʹá·shà had been building, and with them he built Gēʹbà and Mizʹpàh.

7 At that time Hăʹnā·nī the seer came to Asa king of Judah, and said to him, "Because you relied on the king of Syria, and did not rely on the Lord your God, the army of the king of Syria has escaped you. 8 Were not the Ethiopians and the Libyans a huge army with exceedingly many chariots

and horsemen? Yet because you relied on the Lord, he gave them into your hand. 9 For the eyes of the Lord run to and fro throughout the whole earth, to show his might in behalf of those whose heart is blameless toward him. You have done foolishly in this; for from now on you will have wars." 10 Then Asa was angry with the seer, and put him in the stocks, in prison, for he was in a rage with him because of this. And Asa inflicted cruelties upon some of the people at the same time.

11 The acts of Asa, from first to last, are written in the Book of the Kings of Judah and Israel. 12 In the thirty-ninth year of his reign Asa was diseased in his feet, and his disease became severe; yet even in his disease he did not seek the Lord, but sought help from physicians. 13And Asa slept with his fathers, dying in the forty-first year of his reign. 14 They buried him in the tomb which he had hewn out for himself in the city of David. They laid him on a bier which had been filled with various kinds of spices prepared by the perfumer's art; and they made a very great fire in his honor.

17 Je·hoshʹá·phat his son reigned in his stead, and strengthened himself against Israel. 2 He placed forces in all the fortified cities of Judah, and set garrisons in the land of Judah, and in the cities of Eʹphra·im which Asa his father had taken. 3 The Lord was with Je·hoshʹá·phat, because he walked in the earlier ways of his father;*e* he did not seek the Bāʹals, 4 but sought the God of his father and walked in his commandments, and not according to the ways of Israel. 5 Therefore the Lord established the kingdom in his hand; and all Judah brought tribute to Je·hoshʹá·phat; and he had great riches and honor. 6 His heart was courageous in the ways of the Lord; and furthermore he took the high places and the Á·sheʹrim out of Judah.

7 In the third year of his reign he sent his princes, Ben-hāʹil, Ō·bá·diʹàh, Zech·á·riʹàh, Né·thanʹel, and Mi·cāiʹàh, to teach in the cities of Judah; 8 and with them the Levites, She·māiʹàh, Neth·à·niʹàh, Zeb·à·diʹàh, Asʹá·hel, She·miʹrà·moth, Je·honʹá·thàn, Ad·ō·niʹjàh, Tō·biʹjàh, and Tob·ad·ō·niʹjàh; and with these Levites, the priests E·lishʹá·mà and Je·hōʹràm. 9And they taught in Judah, having the book of the law of the Lord with them; they

---

e Another reading is *his father David*

15.16-16.6: 1 Kings 15.13-22.   **16.12-14:** 1 Kings 15.23-24.   **17.1:** 1 Kings 15.24.

went about through all the cities of Judah and taught among the people.

10 And the fear of the LORD fell upon all the kingdoms of the lands that were round about Judah, and they made no war against Jĕ·hŏsh′á·phat. 11 Some of the Philistines brought Jĕ·hŏsh′á·phat presents, and silver for tribute; and the Arabs also brought him seven thousand seven hundred rams and seven thousand seven hundred he-goats. 12 And Jĕ·hŏsh′á·phat grew steadily greater. He built in Judah fortresses and store-cities, 13 and he had great stores in the cities of Judah. He had soldiers, mighty men of valor, in Jerusalem. 14 This was the muster of them by fathers' houses: Of Judah, the commanders of thousands: Ad′nàh the commander, with three hundred thousand mighty men of valor, 15 and next to him Jĕ·hō·hā′nán the commander, with two hundred and eighty thousand, 16 and next to him Am·à·sī′áh the son of Zĭch′rī, a volunteer for the service of the LORD, with two hundred thousand mighty men of valor. 17 Of Benjamin: E·lī′á·dà, a mighty man of valor, with two hundred thousand men armed with bow and shield, 18 and next to him Jĕ·hŏ′zà·bad with a hundred and eighty thousand armed for war. 19 These were in the service of the king, besides those whom the king had placed in the fortified cities throughout all Judah.

18 Now Jĕ·hŏsh′á·phat had great riches and honor; and he made a marriage alliance with A′hab. 2 After some years he went down to A′hab in Sà·mâr′ĭ·à. And Ahab killed an abundance of sheep and oxen for him and for the people who were with him, and induced him to go up against Rā′moth-gil′ē·àd. 3 A′hab king of Israel said to Jĕ·hŏsh′á·phat king of Judah, "Will you go with me to Rā′moth-gil′ē·àd?" He answered him, "I am as you are, my people as your people. We will be with you in the war."

4 And Jĕ·hŏsh′á·phat said to the king of Israel, "Inquire first for the word of the LORD." 5 Then the king of Israel gathered the prophets together, four hundred men, and said to them, "Shall we go to battle against Rā′moth-gil′ē·àd, or shall I forbear?" And they said, "Go up; for God will give it into the hand of the king." 6 But Jĕ·hŏsh′á·phat said, "Is there not here another prophet of the LORD of whom we may inquire?" 7 And the king of Israel said to Jĕ·hŏsh′á·phat,

18.1-34: 1 Kings 22.1-35.

"There is yet one man by whom we may inquire of the LORD, Mĭ·cāi′áh the son of Im′làh; but I hate him, for he never prophesies good concerning me, but always evil." And Jehoshaphat said, "Let not the king say so." 8 Then the king of Israel summoned an officer and said, "Bring quickly Mĭ·cāi′áh the son of Im′làh." 9 Now the king of Israel and Jĕ·hŏsh′á·phat the king of Judah were sitting on their thrones, arrayed in their robes; and they were sitting at the threshing floor at the entrance of the gate of Sà·mâr′ĭ·à; and all the prophets were prophesying before them. 10 And Zed·ė·kī′áh the son of Che·nā′á·nàh made for himself horns of iron, and said, "Thus says the LORD, 'With these you shall push the Syrians until they are destroyed.'" 11 And all the prophets prophesied so, and said, "Go up to Rā′moth-gil′ē·àd and triumph; the LORD will give it into the hand of the king."

12 And the messenger who went to summon Mĭ·cāi′áh said to him, "Behold, the words of the prophets with one accord are favorable to the king; let your word be like the word of one of them, and speak favorably." 13 But Mĭ·cāi′áh said, "As the LORD lives, what my God says, that I will speak." 14 And when he had come to the king, the king said to him, "Mĭ·cāi′áh, shall we go to Rā′moth-gil′ē·àd to battle, or shall I forbear?" And he answered, "Go up and triumph; they will be given into your hand." 15 But the king said to him, "How many times shall I adjure you that you speak to me nothing but the truth in the name of the LORD?" 16 And he said, "I saw all Israel scattered upon the mountains, as sheep that have no shepherd; and the LORD said, 'These have no master; let each return to his home in peace.'" 17 And the king of Israel said to Jĕ·hŏsh′á·phat, "Did I not tell you that he would not prophesy good concerning me, but evil?" 18 And Mĭ·cāi′áh said, "Therefore hear the word of the LORD: I saw the LORD sitting on his throne, and all the host of heaven standing on his right hand and on his left; 19 and the LORD said, 'Who will entice A′hab the king of Israel, that he may go up and fall at Rā′moth-gil′ē·àd?' And one said one thing, and another said another. 20 Then a spirit came forward and stood before the LORD, saying, 'I will entice him.' And the LORD said to him, 'By what means?' 21 And he said, 'I will go forth, and will be a lying spirit in the mouth of

all his prophets.' And he said, 'You are to entice him, and you shall succeed; go forth and do so.' ²² Now therefore behold, the LORD has put a lying spirit in the mouth of these your prophets; the LORD has spoken evil concerning you.''

²³ Then Zed·e·kī'ah the son of Che·nā'a·nah came near and struck Mi·cāi'ah on the cheek, and said, "Which way did the Spirit of the LORD go from me to speak to you?" ²⁴And Mi·cāi'ah said, "Behold, you shall see on that day when you go into an inner chamber to hide yourself." ²⁵And the king of Israel said, "Seize Mi·cāi'ah, and take him back to A'mon the governor of the city and to Jō'ash the king's son; ²⁶ and say, 'Thus says the king, Put this fellow in prison, and feed him with scant fare of bread and water, until I return in peace.' " ²⁷And Mi·cāi'ah said, "If you return in peace, the LORD has not spoken by me." And he said, "Hear, all you peoples!"

²⁸ So the king of Israel and Je·hosh'a·phat the king of Judah went up to Rā'moth-gil'ē·ad. ²⁹And the king of Israel said to Je·hosh'a·phat, "I will disguise myself and go into battle, but you wear your robes." And the king of Israel disguised himself; and they went into battle. ³⁰ Now the king of Syria had commanded the captains of his chariots, "Fight with neither small nor great, but only with the king of Israel." ³¹And when the captains of the chariots saw Je·hosh'a·phat, they said, "It is the king of Israel." So they turned to fight against him; and Jehoshaphat cried out, and the LORD helped him. God drew them away from him, ³² for when the captains of the chariots saw that it was not the king of Israel, they turned back from pursuing him. ³³ But a certain man drew his bow at a venture, and struck the king of Israel between the scale armor and the breastplate, therefore he said to the driver of his chariot, "Turn about, and carry me out of the battle, for I am wounded." ³⁴And the battle grew hot that day, and the king of Israel propped himself up in his chariot facing the Syrians until evening; then at sunset he died.

19 Je·hosh'a·phat the king of Judah returned in safety to his house in Jerusalem. ² But Jē'hū the son of Hǎ·nā'ni the seer went out to meet him, and said to king Je·hosh'a·phat, "Should you help the wicked and love those who hate the LORD? Because of this, wrath has gone out against you

from the LORD. ³ Nevertheless some good is found in you, for you destroyed the A·shē'rāhš out of the land, and have set your heart to seek God."

⁴ Je·hosh'a·phat dwelt at Jerusalem; and he went out again among the people, from Beer-sheba to the hill country of E'phrā·im, and brought them back to the LORD, the God of their fathers. ⁵ He appointed judges in the land in all the fortified cities of Judah, city by city, ⁶ and said to the judges, "Consider what you do, for you judge not for man but for the LORD; he is with you in giving judgment. ⁷ Now then, let the fear of the LORD be upon you; take heed what you do, for there is no perversion of justice with the LORD our God, or partiality, or taking bribes."

⁸ Moreover in Jerusalem Je·hosh'a·phat appointed certain Levites and priests and heads of families of Israel, to give judgment for the LORD and to decide disputed cases. They had their seat at Jerusalem. ⁹And he charged them: "Thus you shall do in the fear of the LORD, in faithfulness, and with your whole heart: ¹⁰ wherever a case comes to you from your brethren who live in their cities, concerning bloodshed, law or commandment, statutes or ordinances, then you shall instruct them, that they may not incur guilt before the LORD and wrath may not come upon you and your brethren. Thus you shall do, and you will not incur guilt. ¹¹And behold, Am·a·rī'ah the chief priest is over you in all matters of the LORD; and Zeb·a·dī'ah the son of Ish'mā·el, the governor of the house of Judah, in all the king's matters; and the Levites will serve you as officers. Deal courageously, and may the LORD be with the upright!"

20 After this the Mō'ǎb·ites and Am'mō·nites, and with them some of the Me·ū'nites,ᶠ came against Je·hosh'a·phat for battle. ² Some men came and told Je·hosh'a·phat, "A great multitude is coming against you from E'dom,ᵍ from beyond the sea; and, behold, they are in Haz'a·zon-tā'mär" (that is, En-gē'di). ³ Then Je·hosh'a·phat feared, and set himself to seek the LORD, and proclaimed a fast throughout all Judah. ⁴And Judah assembled to seek help from the LORD; from all the cities of Judah they came to seek the LORD.

⁵ And Je·hosh'a·phat stood in the assembly of Judah and Jerusalem, in the house of the LORD, before the new court, ⁶ and said, "O LORD, God of

---

ᶠ Compare 26.7: Heb *Ammonites*   ᵍ One Ms: Heb *Aram* (Syria)

our fathers, art thou not God in heaven? Dost thou not rule over all the kingdoms of the nations? In thy hand are power and might, so that none is able to withstand thee. ⁷ Didst thou not, O our God, drive out the inhabitants of this land before thy people Israel, and give it for ever to the descendants of Abraham thy friend? ⁸And they have dwelt in it, and have built thee in it a sanctuary for thy name, saying, ⁹ 'If evil comes upon us, the sword, judgment,ʰ or pestilence, or famine, we will stand before this house, and before thee, for thy name is in this house, and cry to thee in our affliction, and thou wilt hear and save.' ¹⁰And now behold, the men of Am′món and Mō′ab and Mount Sē′ir, whom thou wouldest not let Israel invade when they came from the land of Egypt, and whom they avoided and did not destroy—¹¹ behold, they reward us by coming to drive us out of thy possession, which thou hast given us to inherit. ¹² O our God, wilt thou not execute judgment upon them? For we are powerless against this great multitude that is coming against us. We do not know what to do, but our eyes are upon thee."

¹³ Meanwhile all the men of Judah stood before the LORD, with their little ones, their wives, and their children. ¹⁴And the Spirit of the LORD came upon Jà·hā′zi·el the son of Zech·à·rī′áh, son of Be·nā′iáh, son of Je·ī′el, son of Mat·tà·nī′áh, a Levite of the sons of A′saph, in the midst of the assembly. ¹⁵And he said, "Hearken, all Judah and inhabitants of Jerusalem, and King Je·hosh′á·phat: Thus says the LORD to you, 'Fear not, and be not dismayed at this great multitude; for the battle is not yours but God's. ¹⁶ Tomorrow go down against them; behold, they will come up by the ascent of Ziz; you will find them at the end of the valley, east of the wilderness of Je·rü′el. ¹⁷ You will not need to fight in this battle; take your position, stand still, and see the victory of the LORD on your behalf, O Judah and Jerusalem.' Fear not, and be not dismayed; tomorrow go out against them, and the LORD will be with you."

¹⁸ Then Je·hosh′á·phat bowed his head with his face to the ground, and all Judah and the inhabitants of Jerusalem fell down before the LORD, worshiping the LORD. ¹⁹And the Levites, of the Kō′hà·thites and the Kō′rà·hites, stood up to praise the

LORD, the God of Israel, with a very loud voice.

20 And they rose early in the morning and went out into the wilderness of Te·kō′à; and as they went out, Je·hosh′á·phat stood and said, "Hear me, Judah and inhabitants of Jerusalem! Believe in the LORD your God, and you will be established; believe his prophets, and you will succeed." ²¹And when he had taken counsel with the people, he appointed those who were to sing to the LORD and praise him in holy array, as they went before the army, and say,

"Give thanks to the LORD,
    for his steadfast love endures for
    ever."

²²And when they began to sing and praise, the LORD set an ambush against the men of Am′mòn, Mō′ab, and Mount Sē′ir, who had come against Judah, so that they were routed. ²³ For the men of Am′món and Mō′ab rose against the inhabitants of Mount Sē′ir, destroying them utterly, and when they had made an end of the inhabitants of Seir, they all helped to destroy one another.

24 When Judah came to the watchtower of the wilderness, they looked toward the multitude; and behold, they were dead bodies lying on the ground; none had escaped. ²⁵ When Je·hosh′á·phat and his people came to take the spoil from them, they found cattleⁱ in great numbers, goods, clothing, and precious things, which they took for themselves until they could carry no more. They were three days in taking the spoil, it was so much. ²⁶ On the fourth day they assembled in the Valley of Be·rā′càh,ʲ for there they blessed the LORD; therefore the name of that place has been called the Valley of Beracah to this day. ²⁷ Then they returned, every man of Judah and Jerusalem, and Je·hosh′á·phat at their head, returning to Jerusalem with joy, for the LORD had made them rejoice over their enemies. ²⁸ They came to Jerusalem, with harps and lyres and trumpets, to the house of the LORD. ²⁹And the fear of God came on all the kingdoms of the countries when they heard that the LORD had fought against the enemies of Israel. ³⁰ So the realm of Je·hosh′á·phat was quiet, for his God gave him rest round about.

31 Thus Je·hosh′á·phat reigned over Judah. He was thirty-five years old when he began to reign, and he reigned twenty-five years in Jerusalem.

ʰ Or *the sword of judgment*   ⁱ Gk: Heb *among them*   ʲ That is *Blessing*
20.7: Jas 2.23.   **20.31-33:** 1 Kings 22.41-43.

His mother's name was Ā·zü′bah the daughter of Shil′hī. 32 He walked in the way of Asa his father and did not turn aside from it; he did what was right in the sight of the LORD. 33 The high places, however, were not taken away; the people had not yet set their hearts upon the God of their fathers.

34 Now the rest of the acts of Je·hosh′a·phat, from first to last, are written in the chronicles of Jē′hū the son of Hā·nā′nī, which are recorded in the Book of the Kings of Israel.

35 After this Je·hosh′a·phat king of Judah joined with Ā·hà·zī′ah king of Israel, who did wickedly. 36 He joined him in building ships to go to Tär′shish, and they build the ships in Ē′zi·on-gē′ber. 37 Then Ē·lī·ē′zer the son of Dō·dav′a·hū of Mà·rē′shàh prophesied against Je·hosh′a·phat, saying, "Because you have joined with Ā·hà·zī′ah, the LORD will destroy what you have made." And the ships were wrecked and were not able to go to Tär′shish.

21 Je·hosh′a·phat slept with his fathers, and was buried with his fathers in the city of David; and Je·hō′ram his son reigned in his stead. 2 He had brothers, the sons of Je·hosh′a·phat: Az·à·rī′ah, Je·hī′el, Zech·à·rī′ah, Azariah, Michael, and Sheph·à·tī′ah; all these were the sons of Je·hoshaphat king of Judah. 3 Their father gave them great gifts, of silver, gold, and valuable possessions, together with fortified cities in Judah; but he gave the kingdom to Je·hō′ram, because he was the first-born. 4 When Je·hō′ram had ascended the throne of his father and was established, he slew all his brothers with the sword and also some of the princes of Israel. 5 Je·hō′ram was thirty-two years old when he became king, and he reigned eight years in Jerusalem. 6 And he walked in the way of the kings of Israel, as the house of A′hab had done; for the daughter of Ahab was his wife. And he did what was evil in the sight of the LORD. 7 Yet the LORD would not destroy the house of David, because of the covenant which he had made with David, and since he had promised to give a lamp to him and to his sons for ever.

8 In his days E′dom revolted from the rule of Judah, and set up a king of their own. 9 Then Je·hō′ram passed over with his commanders and all his chariots, and he rose by night and smote the E′dom·ites who had surrounded him and his chariot commanders. 10 So E′dom revolted from the rule of Judah to this day. At that time Lib′nàh also revolted from his rule, because he had forsaken the LORD, the God of his fathers.

11 Moreover he made high places in the hill country of Judah, and led the inhabitants of Jerusalem into unfaithfulness, and made Judah go astray. 12 And a letter came to him from E·lī′jàh the prophet saying, "Thus says the LORD, the God of David your father, 'Because you have not walked in the ways of Je·hosh′a·phat your father, or in the ways of Asa king of Judah, 13 but have walked in the way of the kings of Israel, and have led Judah and the inhabitants of Jerusalem into unfaithfulness, as the house of A′hab led Israel into unfaithfulness, and also you have killed your brothers, of your father's house, who were better than yourself; 14 behold, the LORD will bring a great plague on your people, your children, your wives, and all your possessions, 15 and you yourself will have a severe sickness with a disease of your bowels, until your bowels come out because of the disease, day by day.'"

16 And the LORD stirred up against Je·hō′ram the anger of the Philistines and of the Arabs who are near the Ethiopians; 17 and they came up against Judah, and invaded it, and carried away all the possessions they found that belonged to the king's house, and also his sons and his wives, so that no son was left to him except Je·hō′à·haz, his youngest son.

18 And after all this the LORD smote him in his bowels with an incurable disease. 19 In course of time, at the end of two years, his bowels came out because of the disease, and he died in great agony. His people made no fire in his honor, like the fires made for his fathers. 20 He was thirty-two years old when he began to reign, and he reigned eight years in Jerusalem; and he departed with no one's regret. They buried him in the city of David, but not in the tombs of the kings.

22 And the inhabitants of Jerusalem made Ā·hà·zī′ah his youngest son king in his stead; for the band of men that came with the Arabs to the camp had slain all the older sons. So Ahaziah the son of Je·hō′ram king of Judah reigned. 2 Ā·hà·zī′ah was forty-two years old when he began to reign, and he reigned one year in

20.35-37: 1 Kings 22.48-49. 21.1: 1 Kings 22.50. 21.5-10: 2 Kings 8.17-22. 21.20: 2 Kings 8.17, 24. 22.1-6: 2 Kings 8.24-29.

Jerusalem. His mother's name was Ath·à·lī′ah, the granddaughter of Om′rī. 3 He also walked in the ways of the house of A′hab, for his mother was his counselor in doing wickedly. 4 He did what was evil in the sight of the LORD, as the house of A′hab had done; for after the death of his father they were his counselors, to his undoing. 5 He even followed their counsel, and went with Je·hō′ram the son of A′hab king of Israel to make war against Haz′à·el king of Syria at Rā′moth-gil′e·ad. And the Syrians wounded Jō′ram, 6 and he returned to be healed in Jez′rē·el of the wounds which he had received at Rā′mah, when he fought against Haz′à·el king of Syria. And A·hà·zī′ah the son of Je·hō′ram king of Judah went down to see Joram the son of A′hab in Jez′rē·el, because he was sick.

7 But it was ordained by God that the downfall of A·hà·zī′ah should come about through his going to visit Jō′ram. For when he came there he went out with Je·hō′ram to meet Jē′hū the son of Nim′shī, whom the LORD had anointed to destroy the house of A′hab. 8 And when Jē′hū was executing judgment upon the house of A′hab, he met the princes of Judah and the sons of A·hà·zī′ah's brothers, who attended Ahaziah, and he killed them. 9 He searched for A·hà·zī′ah, and he was captured while hiding in Sà·mâr′i·a, and he was brought to Jē′hū and put to death. They buried him, for they said, "He is the grandson of Je·hosh′à·phat, who sought the LORD with all his heart." And the house of A·hà·zī′ah had no one able to rule the kingdom.

10 Now when Ath·à·lī′ah the mother of A·hà·zī′ah saw that her son was dead, she arose and destroyed all the royal family of the house of Judah. 11 But Jē′hō-shab′e-ath, the daughter of the king, took Jō′ash the son of A·hà·zī′ah, and stole him away from among the king's sons who were about to be slain, and she put him and his nurse in a bedchamber. Thus Jehoshabe-ath, the daughter of King Je·hō′ram and wife of Je·hoi′à·dà the priest, because she was a sister of A·hà·zī′ah, hid him from Ath·à·lī′ah, so that she did not slay him; 12 and he remained with them six years, hid in the house of God, while Ath·à·lī′ah reigned over the land.

23 But in the seventh year Je·hoi′à·dà took courage, and entered into a compact with the commanders of hundreds, Az·à·rī′ah the son of Je·rō′ham, Ish′mà·el the son of Jē′hō-hā′nàn, Az·à·rī′ah the son of Ō′bed, Mā-à·sēi′ah the son of A·dāi′ah, and El·i·shā′phat the son of Zich′rī. 2 And they went about through Judah and gathered the Levites from all the cities of Judah, and the heads of fathers' houses of Israel, and they came to Jerusalem. 3 And all the assembly made a covenant with the king in the house of God. And Je·hoi′à·dà′ said to them, "Behold, the king's son! Let him reign, as the LORD spoke concerning the sons of David. 4 This is the thing that you shall do: of you priests and Levites who come off duty on the sabbath, one third shall be gatekeepers, 5 and one third shall be at the king's house and one third at the Gate of the Foundation; and all the people shall be in the courts of the house of the LORD. 6 Let no one enter the house of the LORD except the priests and ministering Levites; they may enter, for they are holy, but all the people shall keep the charge of the LORD. 7 The Levites shall surround the king, each with his weapons in his hand; and whoever enters the house shall be slain. Be with the king when he comes in, and when he goes out."

8 The Levites and all Judah did according to all that Je·hoi′à·dà the priest commanded. They each brought his men, who were to go off duty on the sabbath, with those who were to come on duty on the sabbath; for Jehoiada the priest did not dismiss the divisions. 9 And Je·hoi′à·dà the priest delivered to the captains the spears and the large and small shields that had been King David's, which were in the house of God; 10 and he set all the people as a guard for the king, every man with his weapon in his hand, from the south side of the house to the north side of the house, around the altar and the house. 11 Then he brought out the king's son, and put the crown upon him, and gave him the testimony; and they proclaimed him king, and Je·hoi′à·dà and his sons anointed him, and they said, "Long live the king."

12 When Ath·à·lī′ah heard the noise of the people running and praising the king, she went into the house of the LORD to the people; 13 and when she looked, there was the king standing by his pillar at the entrance, and the captains and the trumpeters beside the king, and all the people of the land

rejoicing and blowing trumpets, and the singers with their musical instruments leading in the celebration. And Ath·a·li′ah rent her clothes, and cried, "Treason! Treason!" ¹⁴ Then Je·hoi′a·da the priest brought out the captains who were set over the army, saying to them, "Bring her out between the ranks; any one who follows her is to be slain with the sword." For the priest said, "Do not slay her in the house of the LORD." ¹⁵ So they laid hands on her; and she went into the entrance of the horse gate of the king's house, and they slew her there.

¹⁶ And Je·hoi′a·da made a covenant between himself and all the people and the king that they should be the LORD's people. ¹⁷ Then all the people went to the house of Ba′al, and tore it down; his altars and his images they broke in pieces, and they slew Mat′tan the priest of Ba′al before the altars. ¹⁸ And Je·hoi′a·da posted watchmen for the house of the LORD under the direction of the Levitical priests and the Levites whom David had organized to be in charge of the house of the LORD, to offer burnt offerings to the LORD, as it is written in the law of Moses, with rejoicing and with singing, according to the order of David. ¹⁹ He stationed the gatekeepers at the gates of the house of the LORD so that no one should enter who was in any way unclean. ²⁰ And he took the captains, the nobles, the governors of the people, and all the people of the land; and they brought the king down from the house of the LORD, marching through the upper gate to the king's house. And they set the king upon the royal throne. ²¹ So all the people of the land rejoiced; and the city was quiet, after Ath·a·li′ah had been slain with the sword.

24 Jo′ash was seven years old when he began to reign, and he reigned forty years in Jerusalem; his mother's name was Zib′i·ah of Beersheba. ² And Jo′ash did what was right in the eyes of the LORD all the days of Je·hoi′a·da the priest. ³ Je·hoi′a·da got for him two wives, and he had sons and daughters.

⁴ After this Jo′ash decided to restore the house of the LORD. ⁵ And he gathered the priests and the Levites, and said to them, "Go out to the cities of Judah, and gather from all Israel money to repair the house of your God from year to year; and see that you hasten the matter." But the Levites

did not hasten it. ⁶ So the king summoned Je·hoi′a·da the chief, and said to him, "Why have you not required the Levites to bring in from Judah and Jerusalem the tax levied by Moses, the servant of the LORD, onᵐ the congregation of Israel for the tent of testimony?" ⁷ For the sons of Ath·a·li′ah, that wicked woman, had broken into the house of God; and had also used all the dedicated things of the house of the LORD for the Ba′als.

⁸ So the king commanded, and they made a chest, and set it outside the gate of the house of the LORD. ⁹ And proclamation was made throughout Judah and Jerusalem, to bring in for the LORD the tax that Moses the servant of God laid upon Israel in the wilderness. ¹⁰ And all the princes and all the people rejoiced and brought their tax and dropped it into the chest until they had finished. ¹¹ And whenever the chest was brought to the king's officers by the Levites, when they saw that there was much money in it, the king's secretary and the officer of the chief priest would come and empty the chest and take it and return it to its place. Thus they did day after day, and collected money in abundance. ¹² And the king and Je·hoi′a·da gave it to those who had charge of the work of the house of the LORD, and they hired masons and carpenters to restore the house of the LORD, and also workers in iron and bronze to repair the house of the LORD. ¹³ So those who were engaged in the work labored, and the repairing went forward in their hands, and they restored the house of God to its proper condition and strengthened it. ¹⁴ And when they had finished, they brought the rest of the money before the king and Je·hoi′a·da, and with it were made utensils for the house of the LORD, both for the service and for the burnt offerings, and dishes for incense, and vessels of gold and silver. And they offered burnt offerings in the house of the LORD continually all the days of Jehoiada.

¹⁵ But Je·hoi′a·da grew old and full of days, and died; he was a hundred and thirty years old at his death. ¹⁶ And they buried him in the city of David among the kings, because he had done good in Israel, and toward God and his house.

¹⁷ Now after the death of Je·hoi′a·da the princes of Judah came and did obeisance to the king; then the king

---

ᵐ Compare Vg: Heb *and*
24.1-14: 2 Kings 11.21-12.14.

hearkened to them. 18And they forsook the house of the LORD, the God of their fathers, and served the A·shē'-rim and the idols. And wrath came upon Judah and Jerusalem for this their guilt. 19 Yet he sent prophets among them to bring them back to the LORD; these testified against them, but they would not give heed.

20 Then the Spirit of God took possession of*n* Zech·a·rī'ah the son of Je·hoi'a·da the priest; and he stood above the people, and said to them, "Thus says God, 'Why do you transgress the commandments of the LORD, so that you cannot prosper? Because you have forsaken the LORD, he has forsaken you.'" 21 But they conspired against him, and by command of the king they stoned him with stones in the court of the house of the LORD. 22 Thus Jō'ash the king did not remember the kindness which Je-hoi'a·da, Zech·a·rī'ah's father, had shown him, but killed his son. And when he was dying, he said, "May the LORD see and avenge!"

23 At the end of the year the army of the Syrians came up against Jō'ash. They came to Judah and Jerusalem, and destroyed all the princes of the people from among the people, and sent all their spoil to the king of Damascus. 24 Though the army of the Syrians had come with few men, the LORD delivered into their hand a very great army, because they had forsaken the LORD, the God of their fathers. Thus they executed judgment on Jō'ash.

25 When they had departed from him, leaving him severely wounded, his servants conspired against him because of the blood of the son*o* of Je·hoi'a·da the priest, and slew him on his bed. So he died; and they buried him in the city of David, but they did not bury him in the tombs of the kings. 26 Those who conspired against him were Zā'bad the son of Shim'ē-ath the Am'mō·nīt·ess, and Je·hō'za·bad the son of Shim'rith the Mō'ab·īt·ess. 27Accounts of his sons, and of the many oracles against him, and of the rebuilding*p* of the house of God are written in the Commentary on the Book of the Kings. And Am·a·zī'ah his son reigned in his stead.

25 Am·a·zī'ah was twenty-five years old when he began to reign, and he reigned twenty-nine years in Jerusalem. His mother's name

was Jē'hō-ad'dan of Jerusalem. 2And he did what was right in the eyes of the LORD, yet not with a blameless heart. 3And as soon as the royal power was firmly in his hand he killed his servants who had slain the king his father. 4 But he did not put their children to death according to what is written in the law, in the book of Moses, where the LORD commanded, "The fathers shall not be put to death for the children, or the children be put to death for the fathers; but every man shall die for his own sin."

5 Then Am·a·zī'ah assembled the men of Judah, and set them by fathers' houses under commanders of thousands and of hundreds for all Judah and Benjamin. He mustered those twenty years old and upward, and found that they were three hundred thousand picked men, fit for war, able to handle spear and shield. 6 He hired also a hundred thousand mighty men of valor from Israel for a hundred talents of silver. 7 But a man of God came to him and said, "O king, do not let the army of Israel go with you, for the LORD is not with Israel, with all these E'phra·im·ītes. 8 But if you suppose that in this way you will be strong for war,*q* God will cast you down before the enemy; for God has power to help or to cast down." 9And Am·a·zī'ah said to the man of God, "But what shall we do about the hundred talents which I have given to the army of Israel?" The man of God answered, "The LORD is able to give you much more than this." 10 Then Am·a·zī'ah discharged the army that had come to him from E'phra·im, to go home again. And they became very angry with Judah, and returned home in fierce anger. 11 But Am·a·zī'ah took courage, and led out his people, and went to the Valley of Salt and smote ten thousand men of Sē'ir. 12 The men of Judah captured another ten thousand alive, and took them to the top of a rock and threw them down from the top of the rock; and they were all dashed to pieces. 13 But the men of the army whom Am·a·zī'ah sent back, not letting them go with him to battle, fell upon the cities of Judah, from Sa·mar'i·a to Beth-hō'ron, and killed three thousand people in them, and took much spoil.

14 After Am·a·zī'ah came from the slaughter of the E'dom·ītes, he brought the gods of the men of Sē'ir, and set them up as his gods, and worshiped

n Heb *clothed itself with*　*o* Gk Vg: Heb *sons*　*p* Heb *founding*
q Gk: Heb *But if you go, act, be strong for the battle*
24.23-26: 2 Kings 12.17-18, 20-21.　**25.1-4:** 2 Kings 14.2-6.　**25.11:** 2 Kings 14.7.

them, making offerings to them. ¹⁵ Therefore the LORD was angry with Am·a·zi′ah and sent to him a prophet, who said to him, "Why have you resorted to the gods of a people, which did not deliver their own people from your hand?" ¹⁶ But as he was speaking the king said to him, "Have we made you a royal counselor? Stop! Why should you be put to death?" So the prophet stopped, but said, "I know that God has determined to destroy you, because you have done this and have not listened to my counsel."

17 Then Am·a·zi′ah king of Judah took counsel and sent to Jō′ash the son of Je·hō′a·haz, son of Jē′hū, king of Israel, saying, "Come, let us look one another in the face." ¹⁸And Jō′ash the king of Israel sent word to Am·a·zi′ah king of Judah, "A thistle on Lebanon sent to a cedar on Lebanon, saying, 'Give your daughter to my son for a wife'; and a wild beast of Lebanon passed by and trampled down the thistle. ¹⁹ You say, 'See, I have smitten Ē′dom,' and your heart has lifted you up in boastfulness. But now stay at home; why should you provoke trouble so that you fall, you and Judah with you?"

20 But Am·a·zi′ah would not listen; for it was of God, in order that he might give them into the hand of their enemies, because they had sought the gods of Ē′dom. ²¹ So Jō′ash king of Israel went up; and he and Am·a·zi′ah king of Judah faced one another in battle at Beth-shē′mesh, which belongs to Judah. ²²And Judah was defeated by Israel, and every man fled to his home. ²³And Jō′ash king of Israel captured Am·a·zi′ah king of Judah, the son of Jō′ash, son of Ā·ha·zi′ah, at Beth-shē′mesh, and brought him to Jerusalem, and broke down the wall of Jerusalem for four hundred cubits, from the Ē′phra·im Gate to the Corner Gate. ²⁴And he seized all the gold and silver, and all the vessels that were found in the house of God, and Ō′bed-ē′dom with them; he seized also the treasuries of the king's house, and hostages, and he returned to Sa·mar′i·a.

25 Am·a·zi′ah the son of Jō′ash king of Judah lived fifteen years after the death of Joash the son of Je·hō′a·haz, king of Israel. ²⁶ Now the rest of the deeds of Am·a·zi′ah, from first to last, are they not written in the Book of the Kings of Judah and Israel? ²⁷ From the time when he turned away from the LORD they made a conspiracy against him in Jerusalem, and he fled to Lā′chish. But they sent after him to Lachish, and slew him there. ²⁸And they brought him upon horses; and he was buried with his fathers in the city of David.

26 And all the people of Judah took Uz·zi′ah, who was sixteen years old, and made him king instead of his father Am·a·zi′ah. ² He built Ē′loth and restored it to Judah, after the king slept with his fathers. ³ Uz·zi′ah was sixteen years old when he began to reign, and he reigned fifty-two years in Jerusalem. His mother's name was Jec·o·li′ah of Jerusalem. ⁴And he did what was right in the eyes of the LORD, according to all that his father Am·a·zi′ah had done. ⁵ He set himself to seek God in the days of Zech·a·ri′ah, who instructed him in the fear of God; and as long as he sought the LORD, God made him prosper.

6 He went out and made war against the Philistines, and broke down the wall of Gath and the wall of Jab′-neh and the wall of Ash′dod; and he built cities in the territory of Ashdod and elsewhere among the Philistines. ⁷ God helped him against the Philistines, and against the Arabs that dwelt in Gūr·bā′al, and against the Me·ū′nītes. ⁸ The Am′mo·nītes paid tribute to Uz·zi′ah, and his fame spread even to the border of Egypt, for he became very strong. ⁹ Moreover Uz·zi′ah built towers in Jerusalem at the Corner Gate and at the Valley Gate and at the Angle, and fortified them. ¹⁰And he built towers in the wilderness, and hewed out many cisterns, for he had large herds, both in the She·phē′lah and in the plain, and he had farmers and vinedressers in the hills and in the fertile lands, for he loved the soil. ¹¹ Moreover Uz·zi′ah had an army of soldiers, fit for war, in divisions according to the numbers in the muster made by Je·i′el the secretary and Mā·a·sēi′ah the officer, under the direction of Han·a·ni′ah, one of the king's commanders. ¹² The whole number of the heads of fathers' houses of mighty men of valor was two thousand six hundred. ¹³ Under their command was an army of three hundred and seven thousand five hundred, who could make war with mighty power, to help the king against the enemy. ¹⁴And Uz·zi′ah prepared for all the army shields, spears, helmets, coats of mail, bows, and stones for slinging.

25.17-20, 21-24: 2 Kings 14.8-14.   25.25-28: 2 Kings 14.17-20.
26.1-4: 2 Kings 14.21-22; 15.2-3.

15 In Jerusalem he made engines, invented by skilful men, to be on the towers and the corners, to shoot arrows and great stones. And his fame spread far, for he was marvelously helped, till he was strong.

16 But when he was strong he grew proud, to his destruction. For he was false to the LORD his God, and entered the temple of the LORD to burn incense on the altar of incense. 17 But Az·à·rī′àh the priest went in after him, with eighty priests of the LORD who were men of valor; 18 and they withstood King Uz·zī′àh, and said to him, "It is not for you, Uzziah, to burn incense to the LORD, but for the priests the sons of Aaron, who are consecrated to burn incense. Go out of the sanctuary; for you have done wrong, and it will bring you no honor from the LORD God." 19 Then Uz·zī′àh was angry. Now he had a censer in his hand to burn incense, and when he became angry with the priests leprosy broke out on his forehead, in the presence of the priests in the house of the LORD, by the altar of incense. 20 And Az·à·rī′àh the chief priest, and all the priests, looked at him, and behold, he was leprous in his forehead! And they thrust him out quickly, and he himself hastened to go out, because the LORD had smitten him. 21 And King Uz·zī′àh was a leper to the day of his death, and being a leper dwelt in a separate house, for he was excluded from the house of the LORD. And Jō′thàm his son was over the king's household, governing the people of the land.

22 Now the rest of the acts of Uz·zī′àh, from first to last, I·sāi′àh the prophet the son of A′moz wrote. 23 And Uz·zī′àh slept with his fathers, and they buried him with his fathers in the burial field which belonged to the kings, for they said, "He is a leper." And Jō′thàm his son reigned in his stead.

27 Jō′thàm was twenty-five years old when he began to reign, and he reigned sixteen years in Jerusalem. His mother's name was Je·rü′shàh the daughter of Zā′dok. 2 And he did what was right in the eyes of the LORD according to all that his father Uz·zī′àh had done—only he did not invade the temple of the LORD. But the people still followed corrupt practices. 3 He built the upper gate of the house of the LORD, and did much building on the wall of O′phel. 4 Moreover he built cities in the hill country of Judah, and forts and towers on the

wooded hills. 5 He fought with the king of the Am′mô·nītes and prevailed against them. And the Ammonites gave him that year a hundred talents of silver, and ten thousand cors of wheat and ten thousand of barley. The Ammonites paid him the same amount in the second and the third years. 6 So Jō′thàm became mighty, because he ordered his ways before the LORD his God. 7 Now the rest of the acts of Jō′thàm, and all his wars, and his ways, behold, they are written in the Book of the Kings of Israel and Judah. 8 He was twenty-five years old when he began to reign, and he reigned sixteen years in Jerusalem. 9 And Jō′thàm slept with his fathers, and they buried him in the city of David; and A′haz his son reigned in his stead.

28 A′haz was twenty years old when he began to reign, and he reigned sixteen years in Jerusalem. And he did not do what was right in the eyes of the LORD, like his father David, 2 but walked in the ways of the kings of Israel. He even made molten images for the Bā′àls; 3 and he burned incense in the valley of the son of Hin′nôm, and burned his sons as an offering, according to the abominable practices of the nations whom the LORD drove out before the people of Israel. 4 And he sacrificed and burned incense on the high places, and on the hills, and under every green tree.

5 Therefore the LORD his God gave him into the hand of the king of Syria, who defeated him and took captive a great number of his people and brought them to Damascus. He was also given into the hand of the king of Israel, who defeated him with great slaughter. 6 For Pē′kàh the son of Rem·à·lī′àh slew a hundred and twenty thousand in Judah in one day, all of them men of valor, because they had forsaken the LORD, the God of their fathers. 7 And Zich′rī, a mighty man of E′phrà·im, slew Mā·à·sēi′àh the king's son and Az·rī′kam the commander of the palace and El·kā′nàh the next in authority to the king.

8 The men of Israel took captive two hundred thousand of their kinsfolk, women, sons, and daughters; they also took much spoil from them and brought the spoil to Sà·mâr′i·à. 9 But a prophet of the LORD was there, whose name was O′bed; and he went out to meet the army that came to Sà·mâr′i·à, and said to them, "Behold, because the LORD, the God of your

26.20-23: 2 Kings 15.5-7.   27.1-3: 2 Kings 15.33-35.   27.9: 2 Kings 15.38.
28.1-4: 2 Kings 16.2-4.

fathers, was angry with Judah, he gave them into your hand, but you have slain them in a rage which has reached up to heaven. 10And now you intend to subjugate the people of Judah and Jerusalem, male and female, as your slaves. Have you not sins of your own against the LORD your God? 11 Now hear me, and send back the captives from your kinsfolk whom you have taken, for the fierce wrath of the LORD is upon you." 12 Certain chiefs also of the men of E'phra·im, Az·a·rī'ah the son of Jō·hā'nan, Ber·e·chi'ah the son of Me·shil'le·moth, Je·hiz·kī'ah the son of Shal'lum, and A·mā'sa the son of Had'lāi, stood up against those who were coming from the war, 13 and said to them, "You shall not bring the captives in here, for you propose to bring upon us guilt against the LORD in addition to our present sins and guilt. For our guilt is already great, and there is fierce wrath against Israel." 14 So the armed men left the captives and the spoil before the princes and all the assembly. 15And the men who have been mentioned by name rose and took the captives, and with the spoil they clothed all that were naked among them; they clothed them, gave them sandals, provided them with food and drink, and anointed them; and carrying all the feeble among them on asses, they brought them to their kinsfolk at Jericho, the city of palm trees. Then they returned to Sa·mār'i·a.

16 At that time King A'haz sent to the king*r* of Assyria for help. 17 For the E'dom·ites had again invaded and defeated Judah, and carried away captives. 18And the Philistines had made raids on the cities in the She·phē'lah and the Negeb of Judah, and had taken Beth-shē'mesh, Ăi'ja·lon, Ge·dē'roth, Sō'cōh with its villages, Tim'nah with its villages, and Gim'zō with its villages; and they settled there. 19 For the LORD brought Judah low because of A'haz king of Israel, for he had dealt wantonly in Judah and had been faithless to the LORD. 20 So Til'gath-pil·nē'ser king of Assyria came against him, and afflicted him instead of strengthening him. 21 For A'haz took from the house of the LORD and the house of the king and of the princes, and gave tribute to the king of Assyria; but it did not help him.

22 In the time of his distress he became yet more faithless to the LORD— this same King A'haz. 23 For he sacri-

ficed to the gods of Damascus which had defeated him, and said, "Because the gods of the kings of Syria helped them, I will sacrifice to them that they may help me." But they were the ruin of him, and of all Israel. 24And A'haz gathered together the vessels of the house of God and cut in pieces the vessels of the house of God, and he shut up the doors of the house of the LORD; and he made himself altars in every corner of Jerusalem. 25 In every city of Judah he made high places to burn incense to other gods, provoking to anger the LORD, the God of his fathers. 26 Now the rest of his acts and all his ways, from first to last, behold, they are written in the Book of the Kings of Judah and Israel. 27And A'haz slept with his fathers, and they buried him in the city, in Jerusalem, for they did not bring him into the tombs of the kings of Israel. And Hez·e·kī'ah his son reigned in his stead.

29 Hez·e·kī'ah began to reign when he was twenty-five years old, and he reigned twenty-nine years in Jerusalem. His mother's name was A·bī'jah the daughter of Zech·a·rī'ah. 2And he did what was right in the eyes of the LORD, according to all that David his father had done.

3 In the first year of his reign, in the first month, he opened the doors of the house of the LORD, and repaired them. 4 He brought in the priests and the Levites, and assembled them in the square on the east, 5 and said to them, "Hear me, Levites! Now sanctify yourselves, and sanctify the house of the LORD, the God of your fathers, and carry out the filth from the holy place. 6 For our fathers have been unfaithful and have done what was evil in the sight of the LORD our God; they have forsaken him, and have turned away their faces from the habitation of the LORD, and turned their backs. 7 They also shut the doors of the vestibule and put out the lamps, and have not burned incense or offered burnt offerings in the holy place to the God of Israel. 8 Therefore the wrath of the LORD came on Judah and Jerusalem, and he has made them an object of horror, of astonishment, and of hissing, as you see with your own eyes. 9 For lo, our fathers have fallen by the sword and our sons and our daughters and our wives are in captivity for this. 10 Now it is in my heart to make a covenant with the LORD, the God of Israel, that his fierce anger

r Gk Syr Vg Compare 2 Kings 16.7: Heb *kings*
28.27: 2 Kings 16.20. **29.1-2**: 2 Kings 18.1-3.

may turn away from us. ¹¹ My sons, do not now be negligent, for the Lord has chosen you to stand in his presence, to minister to him, and to be his ministers and burn incense to him."

¹² Then the Levites arose, Mȧ'-hath the son of Ȧ·mä'säi, and Jō'el the son of Az·a·rī'ah, of the sons of the Kō'hȧ·thītes; and of the sons of Mé-râr'ī, Kish the son of Ab'dī, and Azariah the son of Je·hal'lé·lel; and of the Gēr'shȯ·nītes, Jō'ȧh the son of Zim'mȧh, and Eden the son of Joah; ¹³ and of the sons of El·i·zā'phȧn, Shim'rī and Je·ü'el; and of the sons of Ā'saph, Zech·ȧ·rī'ah and Mat·tȧ-nī'ȧh; ¹⁴ and of the sons of Hē'mȧn, Je·hū'el and Shim'ē·ī; and of the sons of Je·dü'thún, She·mäi'ȧh and Uz'-zi·el. ¹⁵ They gathered their brethren, and sanctified themselves, and went in as the king had commanded, by the words of the Lord, to cleanse the house of the Lord. ¹⁶ The priests went into the inner part of the house of the Lord to cleanse it, and they brought out all the uncleanness that they found in the temple of the Lord into the court of the house of the Lord; and the Levites took it and carried it out to the brook Kid'rȯn. ¹⁷ They began to sanctify on the first day of the first month, and on the eighth day of the month they came to the vestibule of the Lord; then for eight days they sanctified the house of the Lord, and on the sixteenth day of the first month they finished. ¹⁸ Then they went in to Hez·ė·kī'ȧh the king and said, "We have cleansed all the house of the Lord, the altar of burnt offering and all its utensils, and the table for the showbread and all its utensils. ¹⁹ All the utensils which King Ā'haz discarded in his reign when he was faithless, we have made ready and sanctified; and behold, they are before the altar of the Lord."

²⁰ Then Hez·ė·kī'ȧh the king rose early and gathered the officials of the city, and went up to the house of the Lord. ²¹ And they brought seven bulls, seven rams, seven lambs, and seven he-goats for a sin offering for the kingdom and for the sanctuary and for Judah. And he commanded the priests the sons of Aaron to offer them on the altar of the Lord. ²² So they killed the bulls, and the priests received the blood and threw it against the altar; and they killed the rams and their blood was thrown against the altar; and they killed the lambs and their blood was thrown against the altar. ²³ Then the he-goats for the sin offering were

brought to the king and the assembly, and they laid their hands upon them, ²⁴ and the priests killed them and made a sin offering with their blood on the altar, to make atonement for all Israel. For the king commanded that the burnt offering and the sin offering should be made for all Israel.

²⁵ And he stationed the Levites in the house of the Lord with cymbals, harps, and lyres, according to the commandment of David and of Gad the king's seer and of Nathan the prophet; for the commandment was from the Lord through his prophets. ²⁶ The Levites stood with the instruments of David, and the priests with the trumpets. ²⁷ Then Hez·ė·kī'ȧh commanded that the burnt offering be offered on the altar. And when the burnt offering began, the song to the Lord began also, and the trumpets, accompanied by the instruments of David king of Israel. ²⁸ The whole assembly worshiped, and the singers sang, and the trumpeters sounded; all this continued until the burnt offering was finished. ²⁹ When the offering was finished, the king and all who were present with him bowed themselves and worshiped. ³⁰ And Hez·ė·kī'ȧh the king and the princes commanded the Levites to sing praises to the Lord with the words of David and of Ā'saph the seer. And they sang praises with gladness, and they bowed down and worshiped.

³¹ Then Hez·ė·kī'ȧh said, "You have now consecrated yourselves to the Lord; come near, bring sacrifices and thank offerings to the house of the Lord." And the assembly brought sacrifices and thank offerings; and all who were of a willing heart brought burnt offerings. ³² The number of the burnt offerings which the assembly brought was seventy bulls, a hundred rams, and two hundred lambs; all these were for a burnt offering to the Lord. ³³ And the consecrated offerings were six hundred bulls and three thousand sheep. ³⁴ But the priests were too few and could not flay all the burnt offerings, so until other priests had sanctified themselves their brethren the Levites helped them, until the work was finished—for the Levites were more upright in heart than the priests in sanctifying themselves. ³⁵ Besides the great number of burnt offerings there was the fat of the peace offerings, and there were the libations for the burnt offerings. Thus the service of the house of the Lord was restored. ³⁶ And Hez·ė·kī'ȧh and all the people rejoiced

because of what God had done for the people; for the thing came about suddenly.

30 Hez·ė·kī'ah sent to all Israel and Judah, and wrote letters also to Ē'phrà·im and Mà·nas'sēh, that they should come to the house of the LORD at Jerusalem, to keep the passover to the LORD the God of Israel. 2 For the king and his princes and all the assembly in Jerusalem had taken counsel to keep the passover in the second month—3 for they could not keep it in its time because the priests had not sanctified themselves in sufficient number, nor had the people assembled in Jerusalem—4 and the plan seemed right to the king and all the assembly. 5 So they decreed to make a proclamation throughout all Israel, from Beer-sheba to Dan, that the people should come and keep the passover to the LORD the God of Israel, at Jerusalem; for they had not kept it in great numbers as prescribed. 6 So couriers went throughout all Israel and Judah with letters from the king and his princes, as the king had commanded, saying, "O people of Israel, return to the LORD, the God of Abraham, Isaac, and Israel, that he may turn again to the remnant of you who have escaped from the hand of the kings of Assyria. 7 Do not be like your fathers and your brethren, who were faithless to the LORD God of their fathers, so that he made them a desolation, as you see. 8 Do not now be stiffnecked as your fathers were, but yield yourselves to the LORD, and come to his sanctuary, which he has sanctified for ever, and serve the LORD your God, that his fierce anger may turn away from you. 9 For if you return to the LORD, your brethren and your children will find compassion with their captors, and return to this land. For the LORD your God is gracious and merciful, and will not turn away his face from you, if you return to him."

10 So the couriers went from city to city through the country of Ē'phrà·im and Mà·nas'sēh, and as far as Zeb'ū·lùn; but they laughed them to scorn, and mocked them. 11 Only a few men of Ash'ēr, of Mà·nas'sēh, and of Zeb'ū·lùn humbled themselves and came to Jerusalem. 12 The hand of God was also upon Judah to give them one heart to do what the king and the princes commanded by the word of the LORD.

13 And many people came together in Jerusalem to keep the feast of unleavened bread in the second month, a very great assembly. 14 They set to work and removed the altars that were in Jerusalem, and all the altars for burning incense they took away and threw into the Kid'rŏn valley. 15And they killed the passover lamb on the fourteenth day of the second month. And the priests and the Levites were put to shame, so that they sanctified themselves, and brought burnt offerings into the house of the LORD. 16 They took their accustomed posts according to the law of Moses the man of God; the priests sprinkled the blood which they received from the hand of the Levites. 17 For there were many in the assembly who had not sanctified themselves; therefore the Levites had to kill the passover lamb for every one who was not clean, to make it holy to the LORD. 18 For a multitude of the people, many of them from Ē'phrà·im, Mà·nas'sēh, Is'sà·chär, and Zeb'ū·lùn, had not cleansed themselves, yet they ate the passover otherwise than as prescribed. For Hez·ė·kī'ah had prayed for them, saying, "The good LORD pardon every one 19 who sets his heart to seek God, the LORD the God of his fathers, even though not according to the sanctuary's rules of cleanness." 20And the LORD heard Hez·ė·kī'ah, and healed the people. 21And the people of Israel that were present at Jerusalem kept the feast of unleavened bread seven days with great gladness; and the Levites and the priests praised the LORD day by day, singing with all their mights to the LORD. 22And Hez·ė·kī'ah spoke encouragingly to all the Levites who showed good skill in the service of the LORD. So the people ate the food of the festival for seven days, sacrificing peace offerings and giving thanks to the LORD the God of their fathers.

23 Then the whole assembly agreed together to keep the feast for another seven days; so they kept it for another seven days with gladness. 24 For Hez·ė·kī'ah king of Judah gave the assembly a thousand bulls and seven thousand sheep for offerings, and the princes gave the assembly a thousand bulls and ten thousand sheep. And the priests sanctified themselves in great numbers. 25 The whole assembly of Judah, and the priests and the Levites, and the whole assembly that came out of Israel, and the sojourners who came out of the land of Israel, and the sojourners who dwelt in Judah, rejoiced. 26 So there was great joy in Jerusalem,

---

s Compare 1 Chron 13.8: Heb *with instruments of might*

for since the time of Solomon the son of David king of Israel there had been nothing like this in Jerusalem. 27 Then the priests and the Levites arose and blessed the people, and their voice was heard, and their prayer came to his holy habitation in heaven.

31 Now when all this was finished, all Israel who were present went out to the cities of Judah and broke in pieces the pillars and hewed down the Ā·she̅'rim and broke down the high places and the altars throughout all Judah and Benjamin, and in E̅'phrā·im and Mȧ·nas'se̅h, until they had destroyed them all. Then all the people of Israel returned to their cities, every man to his possession.

2 And Hez·ė·ki̅'ȧh appointed the divisions of the priests and of the Levites, division by division, each according to his service, the priests and the Levites, for burnt offerings and peace offerings, to minister in the gates of the camp of the LORD and to give thanks and praise. 3 The contribution of the king from his own possessions was for the burnt offerings: the burnt offerings of morning and evening, and the burnt offerings for the sabbaths, the new moons, and the appointed feasts, as it is written in the law of the LORD. 4 And he commanded the people who lived in Jerusalem to give the portion due to the priests and the Levites, that they might give themselves to the law of the LORD. 5 As soon as the command was spread abroad, the people of Israel gave in abundance the first fruits of grain, wine, oil, honey, and of all the produce of the field; and they brought in abundantly the tithe of everything. 6 And the people of Israel and Judah who lived in the cities of Judah also brought in the tithe of cattle and sheep, and the dedicated things*t* which had been consecrated to the LORD their God, and laid them in heaps. 7 In the third month they began to pile up the heaps, and finished them in the seventh month. 8 When Hez·ė·ki̅'ȧh and the princes came and saw the heaps, they blessed the LORD and his people Israel. 9 And Hez·ė·ki̅'ȧh questioned the priests and the Levites about the heaps. 10 Az·ȧ·ri̅'ȧh the chief priest, who was of the house of Zā'dok, answered him, "Since they began to bring the contributions into the house of the LORD we have eaten and had enough and have plenty left; for the LORD has blessed his people, so that we have this great store left."

11 Then Hez·ė·ki̅'ȧh commanded them to prepare chambers in the house of the LORD; and they prepared them. 12 And they faithfully brought in the contributions, the tithes and the dedicated things. The chief officer in charge of them was Con·ȧ·ni̅'ȧh the Levite, with Shim'e̅-ī his brother as second; 13 while Je·hi̅'el, Az·ȧ·zi̅'ȧh, Nā'hath, Ā·sā'ȧ·hel, Jer'i̅·moth, Jō'zȧ·bad, E·li̅'el, Is·mȧ·chi̅'ȧh, Mā'hath, and Be·nā'iȧh were overseers assisting Con·ȧ·ni̅'ȧh and Shim'e̅-ī his brother, by the appointment of Hez·ė·ki̅'ȧh the king and Az·ȧ·ri̅'ȧh the chief officer of the house of God. 14 And Kō're the son of Im'nȧh the Levite, keeper of the east gate, was over the freewill offerings to God, to apportion the contribution reserved for the LORD and the most holy offerings. 15 Eden, Mi·ni̅'ȧ·min, Jesh'ü·ȧ, She·māi'ȧh, Am·ȧ·ri̅'ȧh, and Shec·ȧ·ni̅'ȧh were faithfully assisting him in the cities of the priests, to distribute the portions to their brethren, old and young alike, by divisions, 16 except those enrolled by genealogy, males from three years old and upwards, all who entered the house of the LORD as the duty of each day required, for their service according to their offices, by their divisions. 17 The enrollment of the priests was according to their fathers' houses; that of the Levites from twenty years old and upwards was according to their offices, by their divisions. 18 The priests were enrolled with all their little children, their wives, their sons, and their daughters, the whole multitude; for they were faithful in keeping themselves holy. 19 And for the sons of Aaron, the priests, who were in the fields of common land belonging to their cities, there were men in the several cities who were designated by name to distribute portions to every male among the priests and to every one among the Levites who was enrolled.

20 Thus Hez·ė·ki̅'ȧh did throughout all Judah; and he did what was good and right and faithful before the LORD his God. 21 And every work that he undertook in the service of the house of God and in accordance with the law and the commandments, seeking his God, he did with all his heart, and prospered.

32 After these things and these acts of faithfulness Sen·nach'e̅-rib king of Assyria came and invaded Judah and encamped against the fortified cities, thinking to win them for

t Heb *the tithe of the dedicated things*   32.1: 2 Kings 18.13.

himself. ²And when Hez·e·kī′ah saw that Sen·nach′e·rib had come and intended to fight against Jerusalem, ³ he planned with his officers and his mighty men to stop the water of the springs that were outside the city; and they helped him. ⁴A great many people were gathered, and they stopped all the springs and the brook that flowed through the land, saying, "Why should the kings of Assyria come and find much water?" ⁵ He set to work resolutely and built up all the wall that was broken down, and raised towers upon it,ᵘ and outside it he built another wall; and he strengthened the Mil′lō in the city of David. He also made weapons and shields in abundance. ⁶And he set combat commanders over the people, and gathered them together to him in the square at the gate of the city and spoke encouragingly to them, saying, ⁷ "Be strong and of good courage. Do not be afraid or dismayed before the king of Assyria and all the horde that is with him; for there is one greater with us than with him. ⁸ With him is an arm of flesh; but with us is the LORD our God, to help us and to fight our battles." And the people took confidence from the words of Hez·e·kī′ah king of Judah.

9 After this Sen·nach′e·rib king of Assyria, who was besieging Lā′chish with all his forces, sent his servants to Jerusalem to Hez·e·kī′ah king of Judah and to all the people of Judah that were in Jerusalem, saying, ¹⁰ "Thus says Sen·nach′e·rib king of Assyria, 'On what are you relying, that you stand siege in Jerusalem? ¹¹ Is not Hez·e·kī′ah misleading you, that he may give you over to die by famine and by thirst, when he tells you, "The LORD our God will deliver us from the hand of the king of Assyria"? ¹² Has not this same Hez·e·kī′ah taken away his high places and his altars and commanded Judah and Jerusalem, "Before one altar you shall worship, and upon it you shall burn your sacrifices"? ¹³ Do you not know what I and my fathers have done to all the peoples of other lands? Were the gods of the nations of those lands at all able to deliver their lands out of my hand? ¹⁴ Who among all the gods of those nations which my fathers utterly destroyed was able to deliver his people from my hand, that your God should be able to deliver you from my hand? ¹⁵ Now therefore do not let Hez·e·kī′ah deceive you or mislead you in this

fashion, and do not believe him, for no god of any nation or kingdom has been able to deliver his people from my hand or from the hand of my fathers. How much less will your God deliver you out of my hand!' "

16 And his servants said still more against the Lord GOD and against his servant Hez·e·kī′ah. ¹⁷And he wrote letters to cast contempt on the LORD the God of Israel and to speak against him, saying, "Like the gods of the nations of the lands who have not delivered their people from my hands, so the God of Hez·e·kī′ah will not deliver his people from my hand." ¹⁸And they shouted it with a loud voice in the language of Judah to the people of Jerusalem who were upon the wall, to frighten and terrify them, in order that they might take the city. ¹⁹And they spoke of the God of Jerusalem as they spoke of the gods of the peoples of the earth, which are the work of men's hands.

20 Then Hez·e·kī′ah the king and I·šāi′ah the prophet, the son of A′moz, prayed because of this and cried to heaven. ²¹And the LORD sent an angel, who cut off all the mighty warriors and commanders and officers in the camp of the king of Assyria. So he returned with shame of face to his own land. And when he came into the house of his god, some of his own sons struck him down there with the sword. ²² So the LORD saved Hez·e·kī′ah and the inhabitants of Jerusalem from the hand of Sen·nach′e·rib king of Assyria and from the hand of all his enemies; and he gave them rest on every side. ²³And many brought gifts to the LORD to Jerusalem and precious things to Hez·e·kī′ah king of Judah, so that he was exalted in the sight of all nations from that time onward.

24 In those days Hez·e·kī′ah became sick and was at the point of death, and he prayed to the LORD; and he answered him and gave him a sign. ²⁵ But Hez·e·kī′ah did not make return according to the benefit done to him, for his heart was proud. Therefore wrath came upon him and Judah and Jerusalem. ²⁶ But Hez·e·kī′ah humbled himself for the pride of his heart, both he and the inhabitants of Jerusalem, so that the wrath of the LORD did not come upon them in the days of Hezekiah.

27 And Hez·e·kī′ah had very great riches and honor; and he made for himself treasuries for silver, for gold,

ᵘ Vg: Heb *and raised upon the towers*

32.9-21: 2 Kings 18.17-19.37. **32.24-33:** 2 Kings 20.1-21.

for precious stones, for spices, for shields, and for all kinds of costly vessels; 28 storehouses also for the yield of grain, wine, and oil; and stalls for all kinds of cattle, and sheepfolds. 29 He likewise provided cities for himself, and flocks and herds in abundance; for God had given him very great possessions. 30 This same Hez-e-ki'ah closed the upper outlet of the waters of Gi'hon and directed them down to the west side of the city of David. And Hezekiah prospered in all his works. 31And so in the matter of the envoys of the princes of Babylon, who had been sent to him to inquire about the sign that had been done in the land, God left him to himself, in order to try him and to know all that was in his heart.

32 Now the rest of the acts of Hez-e-ki'ah, and his good deeds, behold, they are written in the vision of I-śai'ah the prophet the son of A'moz, in the Book of the Kings of Judah and Israel. 33And Hez-e-ki'ah slept with his fathers, and they buried him in the ascent of the tombs of the sons of David; and all Judah and the inhabitants of Jerusalem did him honor at his death. And Ma-nas'seh his son reigned in his stead.

33 Ma-nas'seh was twelve years old when he began to reign, and he reigned fifty-five years in Jerusalem. 2 He did what was evil in the sight of the LORD, according to the abominable practices of the nations whom the LORD drove out before the people of Israel. 3 For he rebuilt the high places which his father Hez-e-ki'ah had broken down, and erected altars to the Ba'als, and made A-she'rahs, and worshiped all the host of heaven, and served them. 4And he built altars in the house of the LORD, of which the LORD had said, "In Jerusalem shall my name be for ever." 5And he built altars for all the host of heaven in the two courts of the house of the LORD. 6And he burned his sons as an offering in the valley of the son of Hin'nom, and practiced soothsaying and augury and sorcery, and dealt with mediums and with wizards. He did much evil in the sight of the LORD, provoking him to anger. 7And the image of the idol which he had made he set in the house of God, of which God said to David and to Solomon his son, "In this house, and in Jerusalem, which I have chosen out of all the tribes of Israel, I will put my name

for ever; 8 and I will no more remove the foot of Israel from the land which I appointed for your fathers, if only they will be careful to do all that I have commanded them, all the law, the statutes, and the ordinances given through Moses." 9 Ma-nas'seh seduced Judah and the inhabitants of Jerusalem, so that they did more evil than the nations whom the LORD destroyed before the people of Israel.

10 The LORD spoke to Ma-nas'seh and to his people, but they gave no heed. 11 Therefore the LORD brought upon them the commanders of the army of the king of Assyria, who took Ma-nas'seh with hooks and bound him with fetters of bronze and brought him to Babylon. 12And when he was in distress he entreated the favor of the LORD his God and humbled himself greatly before the God of his fathers. 13 He prayed to him, and God received his entreaty and heard his supplication and brought him again to Jerusalem into his kingdom. Then Ma-nas'seh knew that the LORD was God.

14 Afterwards he built an outer wall for the city of David west of Gi'hon, in the valley, and for the entrance into the Fish Gate, and carried it round O'phel, and raised it to a very great height; he also put commanders of the army in all the fortified cities in Judah. 15And he took away the foreign gods and the idol from the house of the LORD, and all the altars that he had built on the mountain of the house of the LORD and in Jerusalem, and he threw them outside of the city. 16 He also restored the altar of the LORD and offered upon it sacrifices of peace offerings and of thanksgiving; and he commanded Judah to serve the LORD the God of Israel. 17 Nevertheless the people still sacrificed at the high places, but only to the LORD their God.

18 Now the rest of the acts of Ma-nas'seh, and his prayer to his God, and the words of the seers who spoke to him in the name of the LORD the God of Israel, behold, they are in the Chronicles of the Kings of Israel. 19And his prayer, and how God received his entreaty, and all his sin and his faithlessness, and the sites on which he built high places and set up the A-she'rim and the images, before he humbled himself, behold, they are written in the Chronicles of the Seers.ᵛ 20 So Ma-nas'seh slept with his fathers, and they buried him in his house; and A'mon his son reigned in his stead.

ᵛ One Ms Gk: Heb *of Hozai*
33.1-9: 2 Kings 21.1-9.   33.20: 2 Kings 21.18.

21 Ā′mon was twenty-two years old when he began to reign, and he reigned two years in Jerusalem. 22 He did what was evil in the sight of the LORD, as Má·nas′seh his father had done. Ā′mon sacrificed to all the images that Manasseh his father had made, and served them. 23And he did not humble himself before the LORD, as Má·nas′seh his father had humbled himself, but this Ā′mon incurred guilt more and more. 24And his servants conspired against him and killed him in his house. 25 But the people of the land slew all those who conspired against King Ā′mon; and the people of the land made Jō·sī′ah his son king in his stead.

34 Jō·sī′ah was eight years old when he began to reign, and he reigned thirty-one years in Jerusalem. 2 He did what was right in the eyes of the LORD, and walked in the ways of David his father; and he did not turn aside to the right or to the left. 3 For in the eighth year of his reign, while he was yet a boy, he began to seek the God of David his father; and in the twelfth year he began to purge Judah and Jerusalem of the high places, the Á·shē′rim, and the graven and the molten images. 4And they broke down the altars of the Bā′als in his presence; and he hewed down the incense altars which stood above them; and he broke in pieces the Á·shē′rim and the graven and the molten images, and he made dust of them and strewed it over the graves of those who had sacrificed to them. 5 He also burned the bones of the priests on their altars, and purged Judah and Jerusalem. 6And in the cities of Má·nas′seh, Ē′phra·im, and Simeon, and as far as Naph′ta·li, in their ruins*w* round about, 7 he broke down the altars, and beat the Á·shē′rim and the images into powder, and hewed down all the incense altars throughout all the land of Israel. Then he returned to Jerusalem.

8 Now in the eighteenth year of his reign, when he had purged the land and the house, he sent Shā′phan the son of Az·a·lī′ah, and Mā·a·sēī′ah the governor of the city, and Jō′ah the son of Jō′a·haz, the recorder, to repair the house of the LORD his God. 9 They came to Hil·kī′ah the high priest and delivered the money that had been brought into the house of God, which the Levites, the keepers of the threshold, had collected from Má·nas′seh

w Heb uncertain

and Ē′phra·im and from all the remnant of Israel and from all Judah and Benjamin and from the inhabitants of Jerusalem. 10 They delivered it to the workmen who had the oversight of the house of the LORD; and the workmen who were working in the house of the LORD gave it for repairing and restoring the house. 11 They gave it to the carpenters and the builders to buy quarried stone, and timber for binders and beams for the buildings which the kings of Judah had let go to ruin. 12And the men did the work faithfully. Over them were set Jā′hath and Ō·ba·dī′ah the Levites, of the sons of Mé·rār′ī, and Zech·a·rī′ah and Me·shul′lam, of the sons of the Kō′ha·thites, to have oversight. The Levites, all who were skilful with instruments of music, 13 were over the burden bearers and directed all who did work in every kind of service; and some of the Levites were scribes, and officials, and gatekeepers.

14 While they were bringing out the money that had been brought into the house of the LORD, Hil·kī′ah the priest found the book of the law of the LORD given through Moses. 15 Then Hil·kī′ah said to Shā′phan the secretary, "I have found the book of the law in the house of the LORD"; and Hil·kī′ah gave the book to Shā′phan. 16 Shā′phan brought the book to the king, and further reported to the king, "All that was committed to your servants they are doing. 17 They have emptied out the money that was found in the house of the LORD and have delivered it into the hand of the overseers and the workmen." 18 Then Shā′phan the secretary told the king, "Hil·kī′ah the priest has given me a book." And Shaphan read it before the king.

19 When the king heard the words of the law he rent his clothes. 20And the king commanded Hil·kī′ah, A·hī′kam the son of Shā′phan, Ab′don the son of Mī′cah, Shaphan the secretary, and Á·saī′ah the king's servant, saying, 21 "Go, inquire of the LORD for me and for those who are left in Israel and in Judah, concerning the words of the book that has been found; for great is the wrath of the LORD that is poured out on us, because our fathers have not kept the word of the LORD, to do according to all that is written in this book."

22 So Hil·kī′ah and those whom the

king had sent[x] went to Hul'dàh the prophetess, the wife of Shal'lùm the son of Tok'hath, son of Has'ràh, keeper of the wardrobe (now she dwelt in Jerusalem in the Second Quarter) and spoke to her to that effect. 23And she said to them, "Thus says the LORD, the God of Israel: 'Tell the man who sent you to me, 24 Thus says the LORD, Behold, I will bring evil upon this place and upon its inhabitants, all the curses that are written in the book which was read before the king of Judah. 25 Because they have forsaken me and have burned incense to other gods, that they might provoke me to anger with all the works of their hands, therefore my wrath will be poured out upon this place and will not be quenched. 26 But to the king of Judah, who sent you to inquire of the LORD, thus shall you say to him, Thus says the LORD, the God of Israel: Regarding the words which you have heard, 27 because your heart was penitent and you humbled yourself before God when you heard his words against this place and its inhabitants, and you have humbled yourself before me, and have rent your clothes and wept before me, I also have heard you, says the LORD. 28 Behold, I will gather you to your fathers, and you shall be gathered to your grave in peace, and your eyes shall not see all the evil which I will bring upon this place and its inhabitants.' " And they brought back word to the king.

29 Then the king sent and gathered together all the elders of Judah and Jerusalem. 30And the king went up to the house of the LORD, with all the men of Judah and the inhabitants of Jerusalem and the priests and the Levites, all the people both great and small; and he read in their hearing all the words of the book of the covenant which had been found in the house of the LORD. 31And the king stood in his place and made a covenant before the LORD, to walk after the LORD and to keep his commandments and his testimonies and his statutes, with all his heart and all his soul, to perform the words of the covenant that were written in this book. 32 Then he made all who were present in Jerusalem and in Benjamin stand to it. And the inhabitants of Jerusalem did according to the covenant of God, the God of their fathers. 33And Jō·si'ah took away all the abominations from all the territory that belonged to the people of

Israel, and made all who were in Israel serve the LORD their God. All his days they did not turn away from following the LORD the God of their fathers.

35 Jō·si'ah kept a passover to the LORD in Jerusalem; and they killed the passover lamb on the fourteenth day of the first month. 2 He appointed the priests to their offices and encouraged them in the service of the house of the LORD. 3And he said to the Levites who taught all Israel and who were holy to the LORD, "Put the holy ark in the house which Solomon the son of David, king of Israel, built; you need no longer carry it upon your shoulders. Now serve the LORD your God and his people Israel. 4 Prepare yourselves according to your fathers' houses by your divisions, following the directions of David king of Israel and the directions of Solomon his son. 5And stand in the holy place according to the groupings of the fathers' houses of your brethren the lay people, and let there be for each a part of a father's house of the Levites.[y] 6And kill the passover lamb, and sanctify yourselves, and prepare for your brethren, to do according to the word of the LORD by Moses."

7 Then Jō·si'ah contributed to the lay people, as passover offerings for all that were present, lambs and kids from the flock to the number of thirty thousand, and three thousand bulls; these were from the king's possessions. 8And his princes contributed willingly to the people, to the priests, and to the Levites. Hil·ki'ah, Zech·a·ri'ah, and Je·hi'el, the chief officers of the house of God, gave to the priests for the passover offerings two thousand six hundred lambs and kids and three hundred bulls. 9 Con·a·ni'ah also, and She·mái'ah and Nè·than'el his brothers, and Hash·à·bi'ah and Je·ī'el and Jō'zà·bad, the chiefs of the Levites, gave to the Levites for the passover offerings five thousand lambs and kids and five hundred bulls.

10 When the service had been prepared for, the priests stood in their place, and the Levites in their divisions according to the king's command. 11And they killed the passover lamb, and the priests sprinkled the blood which they received from them while the Levites flayed the victims. 12And they set aside the burnt offerings that they might distribute them according to the groupings of the fathers' houses of the lay people, to offer to the LORD,

---

[x] Syr Vg: Heb lacks *had sent* [y] Heb obscure
35.1-19: 2 Kings 23.21-23.

as it is written in the book of Moses. And so they did with the bulls. 13And they roasted the passover lamb with fire according to the ordinance; and they boiled the holy offerings in pots, in caldrons, and in pans, and carried them quickly to all the lay people. 14And afterward they prepared for themselves and for the priests, because the priests the sons of Aaron were busied in offering the burnt offerings and the fat parts until night; so the Levites prepared for themselves and for the priests the sons of Aaron. 15 The singers, the sons of Ā'saph, were in their place according to the command of David and Asaph, and Hē'man, and Je·dū'thŭn the king's seer; and the gatekeepers were at each gate; they did not need to depart from their service, for their brethren the Levites prepared for them.

16 So all the service of the LORD was prepared that day, to keep the passover and to offer burnt offerings on the altar of the LORD, according to the command of King Jō·sī'ah. 17And the people of Israel who were present kept the passover at that time, and the feast of unleavened bread seven days. 18 No passover like it had been kept in Israel since the days of Samuel the prophet; none of the kings of Israel had kept such a passover as was kept by Jō·sī'ah, and the priests and the Levites, and all Judah and Israel who were present, and the inhabitants of Jerusalem. 19 In the eighteenth year of the reign of Jō·sī'ah this passover was kept.

20 After all this, when Jō·sī'ah had prepared the temple, Nē'cō king of Egypt went up to fight at Cär'chē·mish on the Eū·phrā'tēs and Jō·sī'ah went out against him. 21 But he sent envoys to him, saying, "What have we to do with each other, king of Judah? I am not coming against you this day, but against the house with which I am at war; and God has commanded me to make haste. Cease opposing God, who is with me, lest he destroy you." 22 Nevertheless Jō·sī'ah would not turn away from him, but disguised himself in order to fight with him. He did not listen to the words of Nē'cō from the mouth of God, but joined battle in the plain of Mĕ·gid'dō. 23And the archers shot King Jō·sī'ah; and the king said to his servants, "Take me away, for I am badly wounded." 24 So his servants took him out of the chariot and carried him in his second chariot

and brought him to Jerusalem. And he died, and was buried in the tombs of his fathers. All Judah and Jerusalem mourned for Jō·sī'ah. 25 Jeremiah also uttered a lament for Jō·sī'ah; and all the singing men and singing women have spoken of Josiah in their laments to this day. They made these an ordinance in Israel; behold, they are written in the Laments. 26 Now the rest of the acts of Jō·sī'ah, and his good deeds according to what is written in the law of the LORD, 27 and his acts, first and last, behold, they are written in the Book of the Kings of Israel and Judah.

36 The people of the land took Je·hō'a·haz the son of Jō·sī'ah and made him king in his father's stead in Jerusalem. 2 Je·hō'a·haz was twenty-three years old when he began to reign; and he reigned three months in Jerusalem. 3 Then the king of Egypt deposed him in Jerusalem and laid upon the land a tribute of a hundred talents of silver and a talent of gold. 4And the king of Egypt made E·lī'a·kim his brother king over Judah and Jerusalem, and changed his name to Je·hoi'a·kim; but Nē'cō took Je·hō'a·haz his brother and carried him to Egypt.

5 Je·hoi'a·kim was twenty-five years old when he began to reign, and he reigned eleven years in Jerusalem. He did what was evil in the sight of the LORD his God. 6Against him came up Ne·bu·chăd·nez'zar king of Babylon, and bound him in fetters to take him to Babylon. 7 Ne·bu·chăd·nez'zar also carried part of the vessels of the house of the LORD to Babylon and put them in his palace in Babylon. 8 Now the rest of the acts of Je·hoi'a·kim, and the abominations which he did, and what was found against him, behold, they are written in the Book of the Kings of Israel and Judah; and Je·hoi'a·chin his son reigned in his stead.

9 Je·hoi'a·chin was eight years old when he began to reign, and he reigned three months and ten days in Jerusalem. He did what was evil in the sight of the LORD. 10 In the spring of the year King Ne·bu·chăd·nez'zar sent and brought him to Babylon, with the precious vessels of the house of the LORD, and made his brother Zed·e·kī'ah king over Judah and Jerusalem.

11 Zed·e·kī'ah was twenty-one years old when he began to reign, and he reigned eleven years in Jerusalem.12 He

36.1-4: 2 Kings 23.30-34.   **36.5-8:** 2 Kings 23.36-24.6.   **36.9-10:** 2 Kings 24.8-17. **36.11-21:** 2 Kings 24.18-25.21.

did what was evil in the sight of the LORD his God. He did not humble himself before Jeremiah the prophet, who spoke from the mouth of the LORD. 13 He also rebelled against King Ne·bu·chad·nez'zar, who had made him swear by God; he stiffened his neck and hardened his heart against turning to the LORD, the God of Israel. 14All the leading priests and the people likewise were exceedingly unfaithful, following all the abominations of the nations; and they polluted the house of the LORD which he had hallowed in Jerusalem.

15 The LORD, the God of their fathers, sent persistently to them by his messengers, because he had compassion on his people and on his dwelling place; 16 but they kept mocking the messengers of God, despising his words, and scoffing at his prophets, till the wrath of the LORD rose against his people, till there was no remedy.

17 Therefore he brought up against them the king of the Chal·de'ans, who slew their young men with the sword in the house of their sanctuary, and had no compassion on young man or virgin, old man or aged; he gave them all into his hand. 18And all the vessels of the house of God, great and small, and the treasures of the house of the LORD, and the treasures of the king and of his princes, all these he brought to Babylon. 19And they burned the house of God, and broke down the wall of Jerusalem, and burned all its palaces with fire, and destroyed all its precious vessels. 20 He took into exile in Babylon those who had escaped from the sword, and they became servants to him and to his sons until the establishment of the kingdom of Persia, 21 to fulfil the word of the LORD by the mouth of Jeremiah, until the land had enjoyed its sabbaths. All the days that it lay desolate it kept sabbath, to fulfil seventy years.

22 Now in the first year of Cyrus king of Persia, that the word of the LORD by the mouth of Jeremiah might be accomplished, the LORD stirred up the spirit of Cyrus king of Persia so that he made a proclamation throughout all his kingdom and also put it in writing: 23 "Thus says Cyrus king of Persia, 'The LORD, the God of heaven, has given me all the kingdoms of the earth, and he has charged me to build him a house at Jerusalem, which is in Judah. Whoever is among you of all his people, may the LORD his God be with him. Let him go up.'"

THE BOOK OF

EZRA

I In the first year of Cyrus king of Persia, that the word of the LORD by the mouth of Jeremiah might be accomplished, the LORD stirred up the spirit of Cyrus king of Persia so that he made a proclamation throughout all his kingdom and also put it in writing:

2 "Thus says Cyrus king of Persia: The LORD, the God of heaven, has given me all the kingdoms of the earth, and he has charged me to build him a house at Jerusalem, which is in Judah. 3 Whoever is among you of all his people, may his God be with him, and let him go up to Jerusalem, which is in Judah, and rebuild the house of the LORD, the God of Israel—he is the God who is in Jerusalem; 4 and let each survivor, in whatever place he sojourns, be assisted by the men of his place with silver and gold, with goods and with beasts, besides freewill offerings for the house of God which is in Jerusalem."

5 Then rose up the heads of the fathers' houses of Judah and Benjamin, and the priests and the Levites, every one whose spirit God had stirred to go up to rebuild the house of the LORD which is in Jerusalem; 6 and all who were about them aided them with vessels of silver, with gold, with goods, with beasts, and with costly wares, besides all that was freely offered. 7 Cyrus the king also brought out the vessels of the house of the LORD which Ne·bu·chad·nez'zar had carried away from Jerusalem and placed in the house of his gods. 8 Cyrus king of

36.22-23: Ezra 1.1-3.   1.1-3: 2 Chron 36.22-23; Ezra 5.13; 6.3.

Persia brought these out in charge of Mith'rĕ·dath the treasurer, who counted them out to Shesh-baz'zăr the prince of Judah. 9And this was the number of them: a thousand[a] basins of gold, a thousand basins of silver, twenty-nine censers, 10 thirty bowls of gold, two thousand[b] four hundred and ten bowls of silver, and a thousand other vessels; 11 all the vessels of gold and of silver were five thousand four hundred and sixty-nine.[c] All these did Shesh-baz'zăr bring up, when the exiles were brought up from Babylonia to Jerusalem.

2 Now these were the people of the province who came up out of the captivity of those exiles whom Ne·bù·chăd·nez'zăr the king of Babylon had carried captive to Babylonia; they returned to Jerusalem and Judah, each to his own town. 2 They came with Ze·rub'bà·bel, Jesh'ü·à, Nĕ·hĕ·mī'ăh, Se·räi'ăh, Rē-el·āi'ăh, Môr'de·cäi, Bil'shan, Mis'pår, Big'väi, Rē'hùm, and Bā'à·nàh.

The number of the men of the people of Israel: 3 the sons of Pā'rosh, two thousand one hundred and seventy-two. 4 The sons of Sheph·à·ṭī'ăh, three hundred and seventy-two. 5 The sons of Ā'răh, seven hundred and seventy-five. 6 The sons of Pā'hath-mō'ab, namely the sons of Jesh'ü·à and Jō'ab, two thousand eight hundred and twelve. 7 The sons of Ē'làm, one thousand two hundred and fifty-four. 8 The sons of Zat'tü, nine hundred and forty-five. 9 The sons of Zac'cäi, seven hundred and sixty. 10 The sons of Bā'ni, six hundred and forty-two. 11 The sons of Bē'bäi, six hundred and twenty-three. 12 The sons of Az'gad, one thousand two hundred and twenty-two. 13 The sons of Ad·ò·ni'kăm, six hundred and sixty-six. 14 The sons of Big'väi, two thousand and fifty-six. 15 The sons of Ā'din, four hundred and fifty-four. 16 The sons of Ā'tĕr, namely of Hez·ĕ·kī'ăh, ninety-eight. 17 The sons of Bē'zäi, three hundred and twenty-three. 18 The sons of Jō'răh, one hundred and twelve. 19 The sons of Hā'shùm, two hundred and twenty-three. 20 The sons of Gib'băr, ninety-five. 21 The sons of Bethlehem, one hundred and twenty-three. 22 The men of Nĕ'toph'àh, fifty-six. 23 The men of An'à·thoth, one hundred and twenty-eight. 24 The sons of Az'mà·veth, forty-two. 25 The sons of Kir'i·ath-

âr'im, Che·phi'răh, and Bē-ēr'ôth, seven hundred and forty-three. 26 The sons of Rä'măh and Gē'bà, six hundred and twenty-one. 27 The men of Mich'màs, one hundred and twenty-two. 28 The men of Beth'ĕl and Äi, two hundred and twenty-three. 29 The sons of Nē'bō, fifty-two. 30 The sons of Mag'bish, one hundred and fifty-six. 31 The sons of the other Ē'làm, one thousand two hundred and fifty-four. 32 The sons of Hā'rim, three hundred and twenty. 33 The sons of Lod, Hā'did, and Ō'nō, seven hundred and twenty-five. 34 The sons of Jericho, three hundred and forty-five. 35 The sons of Se·nā'àh, three thousand six hundred and thirty.

36 The priests: the sons of Je·däi'ăh, of the house of Jesh'ü·à, nine hundred and seventy-three. 37 The sons of Im'mĕr, one thousand and fifty-two. 38 The sons of Pash'hür, one thousand two hundred and forty-seven. 39 The sons of Hā'rim, one thousand and seventeen.

40 The Levites: the sons of Jesh'ü·à and Kad'mi-el, of the sons of Hod·à·vī'ăh, seventy-four. 41 The singers: the sons of Ā'saph, one hundred and twenty-eight. 42 The sons of the gatekeepers: the sons of Shal'lùm, the sons of Ā'tĕr, the sons of Tal'mòn, the sons of Ak'kùb, the sons of Hà·ti'tà, and the sons of Shō'bäi, in all one hundred and thirty-nine.

43 The temple servants:[d] the sons of Zi'hà, the sons of Hà·sü'phà, the sons of Tab·bā'oth, 44 the sons of Kē'ros, the sons of Si'à·hà, the sons of Pā'don, 45 the sons of Le·bā'nàh, the sons of Hag'à·bàh, the sons of Ak'kùb, 46 the sons of Hā'gab, the sons of Sham'läi, the sons of Hā'nàn, 47 the sons of Gid'del, the sons of Gā'hàr, the sons of Rē-äi'ăh, 48 the sons of Rē'zin, the sons of Ne·kō'dà, the sons of Gaz'zàm, 49 the sons of Uz'zà, the sons of Pà·sē'ăh, the sons of Bē'säi, 50 the sons of As'nàh, the sons of Me·ü'nim, the sons of Ne·phi'sim, 51 the sons of Bak'bùk, the sons of Hà·kü'phà, the sons of Här'hür, 52 the sons of Baz'lùth, the sons of Me·hi'dà, the sons of Här'shà, 53 the sons of Bär'kos, the sons of Sis'ĕr·à, the sons of Tē'màh, 54 the sons of Ne·zi'ăh, and the sons of Hà·ti'phà.

55 The sons of Solomon's servants: the sons of Sō'täi, the sons of Has·sō'phĕ·reth, the sons of Pe·rü'dà, 56 the

---

a 1 Esdras 2.13: Heb *thirty*

b 1 Esdras 2.13: Heb *of a second sort*

c 1 Esdras 2.14: Heb *five thousand four hundred*   *d* Heb *nethinim*

2.1-70: Neh 7.6-73.

sons of Jā'ȧ·làh, the sons of Där'kon, the sons of Gid'del, 57 the sons of Sheph·ȧ·ti'ȧh, the sons of Hat'til, the sons of Pō'chė·reth-haz·zė·bā'im, and the sons of A'mi.

58 All the temple servants*d* and the sons of Solomon's servants were three hundred and ninety-two.

59 The following were those who came up from Tel-mē'lȧh, Tel-här'shȧ, Chē'rub, Ad'dȧn, and Im'mér, though they could not prove their fathers' houses or their descent, whether they belonged to Israel: 60 the sons of De·läi'ȧh, the sons of Tō·bī'ȧh, and the sons of Ne·kō'dȧ, six hundred and fifty-two. 61Also, of the sons of the priests: the sons of Hȧ·bāi'ȧh, the sons of Hak'koz, and the sons of Bär·zil'läi (who had taken a wife from the daughters of Barzillai the Gileadite, and was called by their name). 62 These sought their registration among those enrolled in the genealogies, but they were not found there, and so they were excluded from the priesthood as unclean; 63 the governor told them that they were not to partake of the most holy food, until there should be a priest to consult U'rim and Thum'mim.

64 The whole assembly together was forty-two thousand three hundred and sixty, 65 besides their menservants and maidservants, of whom there were seven thousand three hundred and thirty-seven; and they had two hundred male and female singers. 66 Their horses were seven hundred and thirty-six, their mules were two hundred and forty-five, 67 their camels were four hundred and thirty-five, and their asses were six thousand seven hundred and twenty.

68 Some of the heads of families, when they came to the house of the LORD which is in Jerusalem, made freewill offerings for the house of God, to erect it on its site; 69 according to their ability they gave to the treasury of the work sixty-one thousand darics of gold, five thousand minas of silver, and one hundred priests' garments.

70 The priests, the Levites, and some of the people lived in Jerusalem and its vicinity;*e* and the singers, the gatekeepers, and the temple servants lived in their towns, and all Israel in their towns.

3 When the seventh month came, and the sons of Israel were in the towns, the people gathered as one man to Jerusalem. 2 Then arose Jesh'ü·ȧ the son of Jō'zȧ·dak, with his fellow priests, and Ze·rub'bȧ·bel the son of

She-al'ti-el with his kinsmen, and they built the altar of the God of Israel, to offer burnt offerings upon it, as it is written in the law of Moses the man of God. 3 They set the altar in its place, for fear was upon them because of the peoples of the lands, and they offered burnt offerings upon it to the LORD, burnt offerings morning and evening. 4And they kept the feast of booths, as it is written, and offered the daily burnt offerings by number according to the ordinance, as each day required, 5 and after that the continual burnt offerings, the offerings at the new moon and at all the appointed feasts of the LORD, and the offerings of every one who made a freewill offering to the LORD. 6 From the first day of the seventh month they began to offer burnt offerings to the LORD. But the foundation of the temple of the LORD was not yet laid. 7 So they gave money to the masons and the carpenters, and food, drink, and oil to the Si·dō'ni·ȧns and the Tyr'i·ȧns to bring cedar trees from Lebanon to the sea, to Jop'pȧ, according to the grant which they had from Cyrus king of Persia.

8 Now in the second year of their coming to the house of God at Jerusalem, in the second month, Ze·rub'bȧ·bel the son of She-al'ti-el and Jesh'ü·ȧ the son of Jō'zȧ·dak made a beginning, together with the rest of their brethren, the priests and the Levites and all who had come to Jerusalem from the captivity. They appointed the Levites, from twenty years old and upward, to have the oversight of the work of the house of the LORD. 9And Jesh'ü·ȧ with his sons and his kinsmen, and Kad'mi-el and his sons, the sons of Judah, together took the oversight of the workmen in the house of God, along with the sons of Hen'ȧ·dad and the Levites, their sons and kinsmen.

10 And when the builders laid the foundation of the temple of the LORD, the priests in their vestments came forward with trumpets, and the Levites, the sons of A'saph, with cymbals, to praise the LORD, according to the directions of David king of Israel; 11 and they sang responsively, praising and giving thanks to the LORD,

"For he is good,
   for his steadfast love endures for
     ever toward Israel."

And all the people shouted with a great shout, when they praised the LORD, because the foundation of the house of the LORD was laid. 12 But many of the priests and Levites and heads of fathers' houses, old men who had seen the first house, wept with a loud voice when they saw the foundation of this house being laid, though many shouted aloud for joy; 13 so that the people could not distinguish the sound of the joyful shout from the sound of the people's weeping, for the people shouted with a great shout, and the sound was heard afar.

4 Now when the adversaries of Judah and Benjamin heard that the returned exiles were building a temple to the LORD, the God of Israel, 2 they approached Ze·rub′ba·bel and the heads of fathers' houses and said to them, "Let us build with you; for we worship your God as you do, and we have been sacrificing to him ever since the days of E′sar-had′don king of Assyria who brought us here." 3 But Ze·rub′ba·bel, Jesh′u·a, and the rest of the heads of fathers' houses in Israel said to them, "You have nothing to do with us in building a house to our God; but we alone will build to the LORD, the God of Israel, as King Cyrus the king of Persia has commanded us."

4 Then the people of the land discouraged the people of Judah, and made them afraid to build, 5 and hired counselors against them to frustrate their purpose, all the days of Cyrus king of Persia, even until the reign of Da·ri′us king of Persia.

6 And in the reign of A·has·u-e′rus, in the beginning of his reign, they wrote an accusation against the inhabitants of Judah and Jerusalem.

7 And in the days of Ar·ta·xerx′es, Bish′lam and Mith′re·dath and Ta′be-el and the rest of their associates wrote to Ar-ta-xerxes king of Persia; the letter was written in Aramaic and translated.*f* 8 Re′hum the commander and Shim′shai the scribe wrote a letter against Jerusalem to Ar·ta·xerx′es the king as follows—9 then wrote Re′hum the commander, Shim′shai the scribe, and the rest of their associates, the judges, the governors, the officials, the Persians, the men of E′rech, the Babylonians, the men of Su′sa, that is, the E′lam·ites, 10 and the rest of the nations whom the great and noble Os·nap′par deported and settled in the cities of Sa·mar′i·a and in the rest of the province Beyond the River, and now 11 this is a copy of the letter that they sent—"To Ar·ta·xerx′es the king: Your servants, the men of the province Beyond the River,

send greeting. And now 12 be it known to the king that the Jews who came up from you to us have gone to Jerusalem. They are rebuilding that rebellious and wicked city; they are finishing the walls and repairing the foundations. 13 Now be it known to the king that, if this city is rebuilt and the walls finished, they will not pay tribute, custom, or toll, and the royal revenue will be impaired. 14 Now because we eat the salt of the palace and it is not fitting for us to witness the king's dishonor, therefore we send and inform the king, 15 in order that search may be made in the book of the records of your fathers. You will find in the book of the records and learn that this city is a rebellious city, hurtful to kings and provinces, and that sedition was stirred up in it from of old. That was why this city was laid waste. 16 We make known to the king that, if this city is rebuilt and its walls finished, you will then have no possession in the province Beyond the River."

17 The king sent an answer: "To Re′hum the commander and Shim′shäi the scribe and the rest of their associates who live in Sa·mar′i·a and in the rest of the province Beyond the River, greeting. And now 18 the letter which you sent to us has been plainly read before me. 19 And I made a decree, and search has been made, and it has been found that this city from of old has risen against kings, and that rebellion and sedition have been made in it. 20 And mighty kings have been over Jerusalem, who ruled over the whole province Beyond the River, to whom tribute, custom, and toll were paid. 21 Therefore make a decree that these men be made to cease, and that this city be not rebuilt, until a decree is made by me. 22 And take care not to be slack in this matter; why should damage grow to the hurt of the king?"

23 Then, when the copy of King Ar·ta·xerx′es' letter was read before Re′hum and Shim′shäi the scribe and their associates, they went in haste to the Jews at Jerusalem and by force and power made them cease. 24 Then the work on the house of God which is in Jerusalem stopped: and it ceased until the second year of the reign of Da·ri′us king of Persia.

5 Now the Prophets, Hag′gai and Zech·a·ri′ah the son of Id′do, prophesied to the Jews who were in Judah and Jerusalem, in the name of the God of Israel who were over them.

---

f Heb adds *in Aramaic*, indicating that 4.8-6.18 is in Aramaic. Another interpretation is *The letter was written in the Aramaic script and set forth in the Aramaic language.*

2 Then Ze·rub′ba·bel the son of She-al′ti-el and Jesh′u·à the son of Jō′za-dak arose and began to rebuild the house of God which is in Jerusalem; and with them were the prophets of God, helping them.

3 At the same time Tat′te·näi the governor[of the province Beyond the River and Shē′thär-boz′é·näi and their associates came to them and spoke to them thus, "Who gave you a decree to build this house and to finish this structure?" 4 They[g] also asked them this, "What are the names of the men who are building this building?" 5 But the eye of their God was upon the elders of the Jews, and they did not stop them till a report should reach Dà·rī′ùs and then answer be returned by letter concerning it.

6 The copy of the letter which Tat′te·näi the governor of the province Beyond the River and Shē′thär-boz′é·näi and his associates the governors who were in the province Beyond the River sent to Dà·rī′ùs the king; 7 they sent him a report, in which was written as follows: "To Dà·rī′ùs the king, all peace. 8 Be it known to the king that we went to the province of Judah, to the house of the great God. It is being built with huge stones, and timber is laid in the walls; this work goes on diligently and prospers in their hands. 9 Then we asked those elders and spoke to them thus, 'Who gave you a decree to build this house and to finish this structure?' 10 We also asked them their names, for your information, that we might write down the names of the men at their head. 11And this was their reply to us: 'We are the servants of the God of heaven and earth, and we are rebuilding the house that was built many years ago, which a great king of Israel built and finished. 12 But because our fathers had angered the God of heaven, he gave them into the hand of Ne·bù·chàd·nez′zàr king of Babylon, the Chal·dē′àn, who destroyed this house and carried away the people to Babylonia. 13 However in the first year of Cyrus king of Babylon, Cyrus the king made a decree that this house of God should be rebuilt. 14And the gold and silver vessels of the house of God, which Ne·bù·chàd·nez′zàr had taken out of the temple that was in Jerusalem and brought into the temple of Baby-lon, these Cyrus the king took out of the temple of Babylon, and they were delivered to one whose name was Shesh-baz′zàr, whom he had made

governor; 15 and he said to him, "Take these vessels, go and put them in the temple which is in Jerusalem, and let the house of God be rebuilt on its site." 16 Then this Shesh-baz′zàr came and laid the foundations of the house of God which is in Jerusalem; and from that time until now it has been in building, and it is not yet finished.'

17 Therefore, if it seem good to the king, let search be made in the royal archives there in Babylon, to see whether a decree was issued by Cyrus the king for the rebuilding of this house of God in Jerusalem. And let the king send us his pleasure in this matter."

6 Then Dà·rī′ùs the king made a decree, and search was made in Babylonia, in the house of the archives where the documents were stored. 2And in Ec·bat′à·nà, the capital which is in the province of Media, a scroll was found on which this was written: "A record. 3 In the first year of Cyrus the king, Cyrus the king issued a decree: Concerning the house of God at Jerusalem, let the house be rebuilt, the place where sacrifices are offered and burnt offerings are brought; its height shall be sixty cubits and its breadth sixty cubits, 4 with three courses of great stones and one course of timber; let the cost be paid from the royal treasury. 5And also let the gold and silver vessels of the house of God, which Ne·bù·chàd·nez′zàr took out of the temple that is in Jerusalem and brought to Babylon, be restored and brought back to the temple which is in Jerusalem, each to its place; you shall put them in the house of God."

6 "Now therefore, Tat′te·näi, gov-ernor of the province Beyond the River, Shē′thär-boz′é·näi, and your associates the governors who are in the province Beyond the River, keep away; 7 let the work on this house of God alone; let the governor of the Jews and the elders of the Jews rebuild this house of God on its site. 8 Moreover I make a decree regarding what you shall do for these elders of the Jews for the rebuilding of this house of God; the cost is to be paid to these men in full and without delay from the royal revenue, the tribute of the province from Beyond the River. 9And what-ever is needed—young bulls, rams, or sheep for burnt offerings to the God of heaven, wheat, salt, wine, or oil, as the priests at Jerusalem require—let

g Gk Syr: Aramaic *We*

5.1: Hag 1.1; Zech 1.1.   5.13: Ezra 1.1; 6.3.   6.3: Ezra 1.1; 5.13.

that be given to them day by day without fail, [10] that they may offer pleasing sacrifices to the God of heaven, and pray for the life of the king and his sons. [11]Also I make a decree that if any one alters this edict, a beam shall be pulled out of his house, and he shall be impaled upon it, and his house shall be made a dunghill. [12] May the God who has caused his name to dwell there overthrow any king or people that shall put forth a hand to alter this, or to destroy this house of God which is in Jerusalem. I Dā·rī'ús make a decree; let it be done with all diligence."

13 Then, according to the word sent by Dā·rī'ús the king, Tat'tē·näi, the governor of the province Beyond the River, Shē'thär-boz'ē·näi, and their associates did with all diligence what Darius the king had ordered. [14]And the elders of the Jews built and prospered, through the prophesying of Hag'gäi the prophet and Zech·à·rī'äh the son of Id'dō. They finished their building by command of the God of Israel and by decree of Cyrus and Dā·rī'ús and Är·tà·xērx'ēş king of Persia; [15] and this house was finished on the third day of the month of Ā·där', in the sixth year of the reign of Dā·rī'ús the king.

16 And the people of Israel, the priests and the Levites, and the rest of the returned exiles, celebrated the dedication of this house of God with joy. [17] They offered at the dedication of this house of God one hundred bulls, two hundred rams, four hundred lambs, and as a sin offering for all Israel twelve he-goats, according to the number of the tribes of Israel. [18]And they set the priests in their divisions and the Levites in their courses, for the service of God at Jerusalem, as it is written in the book of Moses.

19 On the fourteenth day of the first month the returned exiles kept the passover. [20] For the priests and the Levites had purified themselves together; all of them were clean. So they killed the passover lamb for all the returned exiles, for their fellow priests, and for themselves; [21] it was eaten by the people of Israel who had returned from exile, and also by every one who had joined them and separated himself from the pollutions of the peoples of the land to worship the LORD, the God of Israel. [22]And they kept the feast of unleavened bread seven days with joy; for the LORD had made them joyful, and had turned the heart of the king of Assyria to them, so that he aided them in the work of the house of God, the God of Israel.

7 Now after this, in the reign of Är·tà·xērx'ēş king of Persia, Ezra the son of Se·rāi'äh, son of Hil·ki'äh, [2] son of Shal'lŭm, son of Zā'dok, son of Å·hi'tŭb, [3] son of Am·à·rī'äh, son of Az·à·rī'äh, son of Me·rā'ioth, [4] son of Zer·à·hī'äh, son of Uz'zi, son of Buk'ki, [5] son of Ab·i·shü'à, son of Phin'ē·hàs, son of El·ē·à'zär, son of Aaron the chief priest—[6] this Ezra went up from Babylonia. He was a scribe skilled in the law of Moses which the LORD the God of Israel had given; and the king granted him all that he asked, for the hand of the LORD his God was upon him.

7 And there went up also to Jerusalem, in the seventh year of Är·tà·xērx'ēş the king, some of the people of Israel, and some of the priests and Levites, the singers and gatekeepers, and the temple servants. [8]And he came to Jerusalem in the fifth month, which was in the seventh year of the king; [9] for on the first day of the first month he began[h] to go up from Babylonia, and on the first day of the fifth month he came to Jerusalem, for the good hand of his God was upon him. [10] For Ezra had set his heart to study the law of the LORD, and to do it, and to teach his statutes and ordinances in Israel.

11 This is a copy of the letter which King Är·tà·xērx'ēş gave to Ezra the priest, the scribe, learned in matters of the commandments of the LORD and his statutes for Israel: [12] "Är·tà·xērx'ēş, king of kings, to Ezra the priest, the scribe of the law of the God of heaven.[x] And now [13] I make a decree that any one of the people of Israel or the priests or Levites in my kingdom, who freely offers to go to Jerusalem, may go with you. [14] For you are sent by the king and his seven counselors to make inquiries about Judah and Jerusalem according to the law of your God, which is in your hand, [15] and also to convey the silver and gold which the king and his counselors have freely offered to the God of Israel, whose dwelling is in Jerusalem, [16] with all the silver and gold which you shall find in the whole province of Babylonia, and with the freewill offerings of the people and the priests, vowed willingly for the house of their God which is in Jerusalem. [17] With

---

h Vg See Syr: Heb *that was the foundation of the going up*

x Aram adds a word of uncertain meaning

this money, then, you shall with all diligence buy bulls, rams, and lambs, with their cereal offerings and their drink offerings, and you shall offer them upon the altar of the house of your God which is in Jerusalem. ¹⁸ Whatever seems good to you and your brethren to do with the rest of the silver and gold, you may do, according to the will of your God. ¹⁹ The vessels that have been given you for the service of the house of your God, you shall deliver before the God of Jerusalem. ²⁰And whatever else is required for the house of your God, which you have occasion to provide, you may provide it out of the king's treasury.

²¹ "And I, Är-ta-xĕrx′ēś the king, make a decree to all the treasurers in the province Beyond the River: Whatever Ezra the priest, the scribe of the law of the God of heaven, requires of you, be it done with all diligence, ²² up to a hundred talents of silver, a hundred cors of wheat, a hundred baths of wine, a hundred baths of oil, and salt without prescribing how much. ²³ Whatever is commanded by the God of heaven, let it be done in full for the house of the God of heaven, lest his wrath be against the realm of the king and his sons. ²⁴ We also notify you that it shall not be lawful to impose tribute, custom, or toll upon any one of the priests, the Levites, the singers, the doorkeepers, the temple servants, or other servants of this house of God.

²⁵ "And you, Ezra, according to the wisdom of your God which is in your hand, appoint magistrates and judges who may judge all the people in the province Beyond the River, all such as know the laws of your God; and those who do not know them, you shall teach. ²⁶ Whoever will not obey the law of your God and the law of the king, let judgment be strictly executed upon him, whether for death or for banishment or for confiscation of his goods or for imprisonment."

²⁷ Blessed be the Lord, the God of our fathers, who put such a thing as this into the heart of the king, to beautify the house of the Lord which is in Jerusalem, ²⁸ and who extended to me his steadfast love before the king and his counselors, and before all the king's mighty officers. I took courage, for the hand of the Lord my God was upon me, and I gathered leading men from Israel to go up with me.

8 These are the heads of their fathers' houses, and this is the genealogy of those who went up with me from Babylonia, in the reign of Är-ta-xĕrx′ēś the king: ² Of the sons of Phin′e·hàs, Gēr′shŏm. Of the sons of Ith′à·mär, Daniel. Of the sons of David, Hat′tûsh, ³ of the sons of Shec-a·nī′àh. Of the sons of Pā′rosh, Zech-à·rī′àh, with whom were registered one hundred and fifty men. ⁴ Of the sons of Pā′hath-mō′ab, El′i·ē-hō-ē′näi the son of Zer·à·hī′àh, and with him two hundred men. ⁵ Of the sons of Zat′tü,ⁱ Shec-à·nī′àh the son of Jā·hā′zi·el, and with him three hundred men. ⁶ Of the sons of Ā′din, E′bed the son of Jonathan, and with him fifty men. ⁷ Of the sons of Ē′làm, Je·shā′iàh the son of Ath·à·lī′àh, and with him seventy men. ⁸ Of the sons of Sheph·à·tī′àh, Zeb-à·dī′àh the son of Michael, and with him eighty men. ⁹ Of the sons of Jō′ab, Ō·bà·dī′àh the son of Je·hi′el, and with him two hundred and eighteen men. ¹⁰ Of the sons of Bā′nī,^j She·lō′mith the son of Jos·i·phī′àh, and with him a hundred and sixty men. ¹¹ Of the sons of Bē′bäi, Zech·à·rī′àh, the son of Bebai, and with him twenty-eight men. ¹² Of the sons of Az′gad, Jō·hā′nàn the son of Hak′kà·tan, and with him a hundred and ten men. ¹³ Of the sons of Ad·ō·nī′kàm, those who came later, their names being E·liph′e·let, Je·ü′el, and She·māi′àh, and with them sixty men. ¹⁴ Of the sons of Big′väi, Ū′thäi and Zac′cūr, and with them seventy men.

¹⁵ I gathered them to the river that runs to À·hā′và, and there we encamped three days. As I reviewed the people and the priests, I found there none of the sons of Levi. ¹⁶ Then I sent for E·li·ē′zèr, Ar′i·êl, She·māi′àh, El·nā′thàn, Jâr′ib, Elnathan, Nathan, Zech·à·rī′àh, and Me·shul′làm, leading men, and for Joi′à·rib and Elnathan, who were men of insight, ¹⁷ and sent them to Id′dō, the leading man at the place Cas·i·phī′à, telling them what to say to Iddo and his brethren the temple servants^k at the place Casiphia, namely, to send us ministers for the house of our God. ¹⁸ And by the good hand of our God upon us, they brought us a man of discretion, of the sons of Mäh′lī the son of Levi, son of Israel, namely Sher·ê·bi′àh with his sons and kinsmen, eighteen; ¹⁹ also Hash·à·bi′àh and with him Je·shā′iàh of the sons of Mē·râr′ī, with his kinsmen and their sons, twenty; ²⁰ besides two hundred

ⁱ Gk 1 Esdras 8.32: Heb lacks *of Zattu*   ^j Gk 1 Esdras 8.36: Heb lacks *Bani*
^k Heb *nethinim*

and twenty of the temple servants, whom David and his officials had set apart to attend the Levites. These were all mentioned by name.

21 Then I proclaimed a fast there, at the river Ă·hā′vȧ, that we might humble ourselves before our God, to seek from him a straight way for ourselves, our children, and all our goods. 22 For I was ashamed to ask the king for a band of soldiers and horsemen to protect us against the enemy on our way; since we had told the king, "The hand of our God is for good upon all that seek him, and the power of his wrath is against all that forsake him." 23 So we fasted and besought our God for this, and he listened to our entreaty.

24 Then I set apart twelve of the leading priests: Sher·ė·bī′ah, Hash·ȧ·bī′ah, and ten of their kinsmen with them. 25 And I weighed out to them the silver and the gold and the vessels, the offering for the house of our God which the king and his counselors and his lords and all Israel there present had offered; 26 I weighed out into their hand six hundred and fifty talents of silver, and silver vessels worth a hundred talents, and a hundred talents of gold, 27 twenty bowls of gold worth a thousand darics, and two vessels of fine bright bronze as precious as gold. 28 And I said to them, "You are holy to the LORD, and the vessels are holy; and the silver and the gold are a freewill offering to the LORD, the God of your fathers. 29 Guard them and keep them until you weigh them before the chief priests and the Levites and the heads of fathers' houses in Israel at Jerusalem, within the chambers of the house of the LORD." 30 So the priests and the Levites took over the weight of the silver and the gold and the vessels, to bring them to Jerusalem, to the house of our God.

31 Then we departed from the river Ă·hā′vȧ on the twelfth day of the first month, to go to Jerusalem; the hand of our God was upon us, and he delivered us from the hand of the enemy and from ambushes by the way. 32 We came to Jerusalem, and there we remained three days. 33 On the fourth day, within the house of our God, the silver and the gold and the vessels were weighed into the hands of Mer′ė·moth the priest, son of Ū·rī′ah, and with him was El·ė·ā′zȧr the son of Phin′ė·hȧs, and with them were the Levites, Jō′zȧ·bad the son of Jesh′u·ȧ and Nō·ȧ·dī′ah the son of Bin′nu·i. 34 The whole was counted and weighed, and the weight of everything was recorded.

35 At that time those who had come from captivity, the returned exiles, offered burnt offerings to the God of Israel, twelve bulls for all Israel, ninety-six rams, seventy-seven lambs, and as a sin offering twelve he-goats; all this was a burnt offering to the LORD. 36 They also delivered the king's commissions to the king's satraps and to the governors of the province Beyond the River; and they aided the people and the house of God.

9 After these things had been done, the officials approached me and said, "The people of Israel and the priests and the Levites have not separated themselves from the peoples of the lands with their abominations, from the Canaanites, the Hit′tites, the Per′iz·zites, the Jeb′ū·sites, the Am′mŏ·nites, the Mō′ab·ites, the Egyptians, and the Am′ŏ·rites. 2 For they have taken some of their daughters to be wives for themselves and for their sons; so that the holy race has mixed itself with the peoples of the lands. And in this faithlessness the hand of the officials and chief men has been foremost." 3 When I heard this, I rent my garments and my mantle, and pulled hair from my head and beard, and sat appalled. 4 Then all who trembled at the words of the God of Israel, because of the faithlessness of the returned exiles, gathered round me while I sat appalled until the evening sacrifice. 5 And at the evening sacrifice I rose from my fasting, with my garments and my mantle rent, and fell upon my knees and spread out my hands to the LORD my God, 6 saying:

"O my God, I am ashamed and blush to lift my face to thee, my God, for our iniquities have risen higher than our heads, and our guilt has mounted up to the heavens. 7 From the days of our fathers to this day we have been in great guilt; and for our iniquities we, our kings, and our priests have been given into the hand of the kings of the lands, to the sword, to captivity, to plundering, and to utter shame, as at this day. 8 But now for a brief moment favor has been shown by the LORD our God, to leave us a remnant, and to give us a secure hold*¹* within his holy place, that our God may brighten our eyes and grant us a little reviving in our bondage. 9 For we are bondmen; yet our God has not forsaken us in our bondage, but has extended to us his steadfast love before

¹ Heb nail or tent-pin

the kings of Persia, to grant us some reviving to set up the house of our God, to repair its ruins, and to give us protection[m] in Judea and Jerusalem.

10 "And now, O our God, what shall we say after this? For we have forsaken thy commandments, [11] which thou didst command by thy servants the prophets, saying, 'The land which you are entering, to take possession of it, is a land unclean with the pollutions of the peoples of the lands, with their abominations which have filled it from end to end with their uncleanness. [12] Therefore give not your daughters to their sons, neither take their daughters for your sons, and never seek their peace or prosperity, that you may be strong, and eat the good of the land, and leave it for an inheritance to your children for ever.' [13]And after all that has come upon us for our evil deeds and for our great guilt, seeing that thou, our God, hast punished us less than our iniquities deserved and hast given us such a remnant as this, [14] shall we break thy commandments again and intermarry with the peoples who practice these abominations? Wouldst thou not be angry with us till thou wouldst consume us, so that there should be no remnant, nor any to escape? [15] O LORD the God of Israel, thou art just, for we are left a remnant that has escaped, as at this day. Behold, we are before thee in our guilt, for none can stand before thee because of this."

10 While Ezra prayed and made confession, weeping and casting himself down before the house of God, a very great assembly of men, women, and children, gathered to him out of Israel: for the people wept bitterly. [2]And Shec·à·ni′ah the son of Je·hi′el, of the sons of É′lám, addressed Ezra: "We have broken faith with our God and have married foreign women from the peoples of the land, but even now there is hope for Israel in spite of this. [3] Therefore let us make a covenant with our God to put away all these wives and their children, according to the counsel of my lord and of those who tremble at the commandment of our God; and let it be done according to the law. [4]Arise, for it is your task, and we are with you; be strong and do it." [5] Then Ezra arose and made the leading priests and Levites and all Israel take oath that they would do as had been said. So they took the oath.

6 Then Ezra withdrew from before the house of God, and went to the chamber of Jĕ′hō·hā′nàn the son of E·li′à·shib, where he spent the night,[n] neither eating bread nor drinking water; for he was mourning over the faithlessness of the exiles. [7]And a proclamation was made throughout Judah and Jerusalem to all the returned exiles that they should assemble at Jerusalem, [8] and that if any one did not come within three days, by order of the officials and the elders all his property should be forfeited, and he himself banned from the congregation of the exiles.

9 Then all the men of Judah and Benjamin assembled at Jerusalem within the three days; it was the ninth month, on the twentieth day of the month. And all the people sat in the open square before the house of God, trembling because of this matter and because of the heavy rain. [10]And Ezra the priest stood up and said to them, "You have trespassed and married foreign women, and so increased the guilt of Israel. [11] Now then make confession to the LORD the God of your fathers, and do his will; separate yourselves from the peoples of the land and from the foreign wives." [12] Then all the assembly answered with a loud voice, "It is so; we must do as you have said. [13] But the people are many, and it is a time of heavy rain; we cannot stand in the open. Nor is this a work for one day or for two; for we have greatly transgressed in this matter. [14] Let our officials stand for the whole assembly; let all in our cities who have taken foreign wives come at appointed times, and with them the elders and judges of every city, till the fierce wrath of our God over this matter be averted from us." [15] Only Jonathan the son of As′à·hel and Jäh·zēi′ah the son of Tik′vàh opposed this, and Me·shul′làm and Shab′bĕ·thäi the Levite supported them.

16 Then the returned exiles did so. Ezra the priest selected men,[o] heads of fathers' houses, according to their fathers' houses, each of them designated by name. On the first day of the tenth month they sat down to examine the matter; [17] and by the first day of the first month they had come to the end of all the men who had married foreign women.

18 Of the sons of the priests who had married foreign women were found Mā·à·sēi′àh, E·li·ē′zèr, Jâr′ib,

---

[m] Heb *a wall*   [n] 1 Esdras 9.2: Heb *where he went*
[o] 1 Esdras 9.16 Syr: Heb *and there were selected Ezra*, etc.

and Ged·à·lī'ah, of the sons of Jĕsh'ü·å the son of Jō'zȧ·dak and his brethren. ¹⁹ They pledged themselves to put away their wives, and their guilt offering was a ram of the flock for their guilt. ²⁰ Of the sons of Im'mĕr: Hȧ·nā'nī and Zeb·ȧ·dī'ah. ²¹ Of the sons of Hā'rim: Mā·ȧ·sēi'ah, She·māi'ah, Je·hī'el, and Uz·zī'ah. ²² Of the sons of Pash'hŭr: Elī·ō·ē'nāi, Mā·ȧ·sēi'ah, Ish'mȧ·el, Nĕ·than'el, Jō'zȧ·bad, and El·ā'sah.

²³ Of the Levites: Jō'zȧ·bad, Shim'ē·ī, Ke·lāi'ah (that is, Ke·lī'tȧ), Peth·ȧ·hī'ah, Judah, and E·li·ē'zĕr. ²⁴ Of the singers: E.li'ȧ·shib. Of the gatekeepers: Shal'lùm, Tē'lem, and Ŭ'rī.

²⁵ And of Israel: of the sons of Pā'rosh: Rȧ·mī'ah, Iz·zī'ah, Mal·chī'jah, Mī'jȧ·min, El·ē·ā'zar, Hash·ȧ·bī'ah,[p] and Be·nā'iah. ²⁶ Of the sons of Ē'lam: Mat·tȧ·nī'ah, Zech·ȧ·rī'ah, Je·hī'el, Ab'dī, Jer'ê·moth, and E.lī'jah. ²⁷ Of the sons of Zat'tü: Elī·ō·ē'nāi, E.li'ȧ·shib, Mat·tȧ·nī'ah, Jer'ê·moth, Zā'bad, and Ȧ·zī'zȧ. ²⁸ Of the sons of Bē'bäi were Jē'hō·hā'nȧn, Han·ȧ·nī'ah,

Zab'bäi, and Ath'läi. ²⁹ Of the sons of Bā'nī were Me·shul'lȧm, Mal'lüch, Ȧ·dāi'ah, Jash'üb, Shē'al, and Jer'ê·moth. ³⁰ Of the sons of Pā'hath-mō'ab: Ad'nȧ, Chē'lal, Be·nā'iah, Mā·ȧ·sēi'ah, Mat·tȧ·nī'ah, Bez'ȧ·lel, Bin'nü·ī, and Mȧ·nas'sĕh. ³¹ Of the sons of Hā'rim: E.li·ē'zĕr, Is·shī'jah, Mal·chī'jah, She·māi'ah, Shim'ē·on, ³² Benjamin, Mal'lüch, and Shem·ȧ·rī'ah. ³³ Of the sons of Hā'shùm: Mat·tē'näi, Mat'tȧt·tàh, Zā'bad, E.liph'ē·let, Jer'ê·mäi, Mȧ·nas'sĕh, and Shim'ē·ī. ³⁴ Of the sons of Bā'nī: Mā·ȧ·dā'ī, Am'ram, Ū'el, ³⁵ Be·nā'iah, Be·dēi'ah, Chel'ü·hī, ³⁶ Vȧ·nī'ah, Mer'ê·moth, E.li'ȧ·shib, ³⁷ Mat·tȧ·nī'ah, Mat·tē'näi, Jā'ȧ·sü. ³⁸ Of the sons of Bin'nü·ī:[q] Shim'e·ī, ³⁹ Shel·ê·mī'ah, Nathan, Ȧ·dāi'ah, ⁴⁰ Mach·nad'ê·bäi, Shā'shäi, Shā'räi, ⁴¹ Az'ȧ·rel, Shel·ê·mī'ah, Shem·ȧ·rī'ah, ⁴² Shal'lùm, Am·ȧ·rī'ah, and Joseph. ⁴³ Of the sons of Nē'bō: Je·ī'el, Mat·ti·thī'ah, Zā'bad, Ze·bī'nȧ, Jad'däi, Jō'él, and Be·nā'iah. ⁴⁴ All these had married foreign women, and they put them away with their children.[r]

THE BOOK OF

NEHEMIAH

1 The words of Nē·hê·mī'ah the son of Hac·ȧ·lī'ah.

Now it happened in the month of Chis'lev, in the twentieth year, as I was in Su'sà the capital, ² that Hȧ·nā'nī, one of my brethren, came with certain men out of Judah; and I asked them concerning the Jews that survived, who had escaped exile, and concerning Jerusalem. ³ And they said to me, "The survivors there in the province who escaped exile are in great trouble and shame; the wall of Jerusalem is broken down, and its gates are destroyed by fire."

⁴ When I heard these words I sat down and wept, and mourned for days; and I continued fasting and praying before the God of heaven. ⁵ And I said, "O LORD God of heaven, the great and terrible God who keeps covenant and steadfast love with those who love him and keep his commandments; ⁶ let thy ear be attentive, and thy eyes open, to

hear the prayer of thy servant which I now pray before thee day and night for the people of Israel thy servants, confessing the sins of the people of Israel, which we have sinned against thee. Yea, I and my father's house have sinned. ⁷ We have acted very corruptly against thee, and have not kept the commandments, the statutes, and the ordinances which thou didst command thy servant Moses. ⁸ Remember the word which thou didst command thy servant Moses, saying, 'If you are unfaithful, I will scatter you among the peoples; ⁹ but if you return to me and keep my commandments and do them, though your dispersed be under the farthest skies, I will gather them thence and bring them to the place which I have chosen, to make my name dwell there.' ¹⁰ They are thy servants and thy people, whom thou hast redeemed by thy great power and by thy strong hand. ¹¹ O Lord, let thy ear be atten-

p 1 Esdras 9.26 Gk: Heb *Malchijah*   q Gk: Heb *Bani, Binnui*
r 1 Esdras 9.36: Heb obscure

tive to the prayer of thy servant, and to the prayer of thy servants who delight to fear thy name; and give success to thy servant today, and grant him mercy in the sight of this man."

Now I was cupbearer to the king.

2 In the month of Ni′san, in the twentieth year of King Ar-ta-xerx′es, when wine was before him, I took up the wine and gave it to the king. Now I had not been sad in his presence. 2And the king said to me, "Why is your face sad, seeing you are not sick? This is nothing else but sadness of the heart." Then I was very much afraid. 3 I said to the king, "Let the king live for ever! Why should not my face be sad, when the city, the place of my fathers' sepulchres, lies waste, and its gates have been destroyed by fire?" 4 Then the king said to me, "For what do you make request?" So I prayed to the God of heaven. 5And I said to the king, "If it pleases the king, and if your servant has found favor in your sight, that you send me to Judah, to the city of my fathers' sepulchres, that I may rebuild it." 6And the king said to me (the queen sitting beside him), "How long will you be gone, and when will you return?" So it pleased the king to send me; and I set him a time. 7And I said to the king, "If it pleases the king, let letters be given me to the governors of the province Beyond the River, that they may let me pass through until I come to Judah; 8 and a letter to A′saph, the keeper of the king's forest, that he may give me timber to make beams for the gates of the fortress of the temple, and for the wall of the city, and for the house which I shall occupy." And the king granted me what I asked, for the good hand of my God was upon me.

9 Then I came to the governors of the province Beyond the River, and gave them the king's letters. Now the king had sent with me officers of the army and horsemen. 10 But when San·bal′lat the Hor′o·nite and To·bi′ah the servant, the Am′mo·nite, heard this, it displeased them greatly that some one had come to seek the welfare of the children of Israel.

11 So I came to Jerusalem and was there three days. 12 Then I arose in the night, I and a few men with me; and I told no one what my God had put into my heart to do for Jerusalem. There was no beast with me but the beast on which I rode. 13 I went out by night by the Valley Gate to the

Jackal's Well and to the Dung Gate, and I inspected the walls of Jerusalem which were broken down and its gates which had been destroyed by fire. 14 Then I went on to the Fountain Gate and to the King's Pool; but there was no place for the beast that was under me to pass. 15 Then I went up in the night by the valley and inspected the wall; and I turned back and entered by the Valley Gate, and so returned. 16And the officials did not know where I had gone or what I was doing; and I had not yet told the Jews, the priests, the nobles, the officials, and the rest that were to do the work.

17 Then I said to them, "You see the trouble we are in, how Jerusalem lies in ruins with its gates burned. Come, let us build the wall of Jerusalem, that we may no longer suffer disgrace." 18And I told them of the hand of my God which had been upon me for good, and also of the words which the king had spoken to me. And they said, "Let us rise up and build." So they strengthened their hands for the good work. 19 But when San·bal′·lat the Hor′o·nite and To·bi′ah the servant, the Am′mo·nite, and Ge′shem the Arab heard of it, they derided us and despised us and said, "What is this thing that you are doing? Are you rebelling against the king?" 20 Then I replied to them, "The God of heaven will make us prosper, and we his servants will arise and build; but you have no portion or right or memorial in Jerusalem."

3 Then E·li′a·shib the high priest rose up with his brethren the priests and they built the Sheep Gate. They consecrated it and set its doors; they consecrated it as far as the Tower of the Hundred, as far as the Tower of Ha·nan′el. 2And next to him the men of Jericho built. And next to them[a] Zac′cur the son of Im′ri built.

3 And the sons of Has·se·na′ah built the Fish Gate; they laid its beams and set its doors, its bolts, and its bars. 4And next to them Mer′e·moth the son of U·ri′ah, son of Hak′koz repaired. And next to them Me·shul′lam the son of Ber·e·chi′ah, son of Me·shez′a·bel repaired. And next to them Za′dok the son of Ba′a·na repaired. 5And next to them the Te·ko′ites repaired; but their nobles did not put their necks to the work of their Lord.[b]

6 And Joi′a·da the son of Pa·se′ah and Me·shul′lam the son of Bes·o·dei′-ah repaired the Old Gate; they laid its beams and set its doors, its bolts, and

its bars. 7And next to them repaired Mel·à·tī′ah the Gib′ē·ŏ·nīte and Jā′don the Me·rō′nŏ·thite, the men of Gib′ē·ŏn and of Miz′pah, who were under the jurisdiction of the governor of the province Beyond the River. 8 Next to them Uz′zi·el the son of Här·hāi′ah, goldsmiths, repaired. Next to him Han·à·ni′ah, one of the perfumers, repaired; and they restored[c] Jerusalem as far as the Broad Wall. 9 Next to them Reph·ā′iah the son of Hūr, ruler of half the district of[d] Jerusalem, repaired. 10 Next to them Je·dāi′ah the son of Hà·rü′maph repaired opposite his house; and next to him Hat′tüsh the son of Hash·ab·nei′ah repaired. 11 Mal·chī′jäh the son of Hā′rim and Has′shüb the son of Pā′hath-mō′ab repaired another section and the Tower of the Ovens. 12 Next to him Shal′lüm the son of Hal·lō′hesh, ruler of half the district of[d] Jerusalem, repaired, he and his daughters.

13 Hā′nún and the inhabitants of Zà·nō′ah repaired the Valley Gate; they rebuilt it and set its doors, its bolts, and its bars, and repaired a thousand cubits of the wall, as far as the Dung Gate.

14 Mal·chī′jäh the son of Rē′chab, ruler of the district of[d] Beth-hac·chē′-rem, repaired the Dung Gate; he rebuilt it and set its doors, its bolts, and its bars.

15 And Shal′lüm the son of Col-hō′zêh, ruler of the district of[d] Miz′-pah, repaired the Fountain Gate; he rebuilt it and covered it and set its doors, its bolts, and its bars; and he built the wall of the Pool of Shē′läh of the king's garden, as far as the stairs that go down from the City of David. 16After him Nē·hĕ·mi′ah the son of Az′bük, ruler of half the district of[d] Beth′-zür, repaired to a point opposite the sepulchres of David, to the artificial pool, and to the house of the mighty men. 17After him the Levites repaired: Rē′hüm the son of Bā′ni; next to him Hash·à·bi′ah, ruler of half the district of[d] Kē·i′läh, repaired for his district. 18After him their brethren repaired: Bav′väi the son of Hen′à·dad, ruler of half the district of[d] Kē·i′läh; 19 next to him Ē′zĕr the son of Jesh′ü·à, ruler of Miz′pah, repaired another section opposite the ascent to the armory at the Angle. 20After him Bâr′üch the son of Zab′bäi repaired another section from the Angle to the door of the house of E·li′à·shib the high priest. 21After him Mer′ê·moth the son of Ū·ri′ah, son of

Hak′koz repaired another section from the door of the house of E·li′à·shib to the end of the house of Eliashíb. 22After him the priests, the men of the Plain, repaired. 23After them Benjamin and Has′shüb repaired opposite their house. After them Az·à·ri′ah the son of Mā·à·sēi′ah, son of An·à·ni′ah repaired beside his own house. 24After him Bin′nü·i the son of Hen′à·dad repaired another section, from the house of Az·à·ri′ah to the Angle 25 and to the corner. Pā′lal the son of Ū′zäi repaired opposite the Angle and the tower projecting from the upper house of the king at the court of the guard. After him Pe·dāi′ah the son of Pā′rosh 26 and the temple servants living[e] on Ō′phel repaired to a point opposite the Water Gate on the east and the projecting tower. 27After him the Te·kō′ites repaired another section opposite the great projecting tower as far as the wall of Ō′phel.

28 Above the Horse Gate the priests repaired, each one opposite his own house. 29After them Zā′dok the son of Im′mĕr repaired opposite his own house. After him She·māi′ah the son of Shec·à·ni′ah, the keeper of the East Gate, repaired. 30After him Han·à·ni′-äh the son of Shel·ĕ·mi′äh and Hā′nún the sixth son of Zā′laph repaired another section. After him Me·shul′-läm the son of Ber·ĕ·chi′äh repaired opposite his chamber. 31After him Mal·chī′jäh, one of the goldsmiths, repaired as far as the house of the temple servants and of the merchants, opposite the Muster Gate,[f] and to the upper chamber of the corner. 32And between the upper chamber of the corner and the Sheep Gate the goldsmiths and the merchants repaired.

4[g] Now when San·bal′lat heard that we were building the wall, he was angry and greatly enraged, and he ridiculed the Jews. 2And he said in the presence of his brethren and of the army of Sà·mâr′i·à, "What are these feeble Jews doing? Will they restore things? Will they sacrifice? Will they finish up in a day? Will they revive the stones out of the heaps of rubbish, and burned ones at that?" 3 Tō·bī′ah the Am′mò·nīte was by him, and he said, "Yes, what they are building—if a fox goes up on it he will break down their stone wall!" 4 Hear, O our God, for we are despised; turn back their taunt upon their own heads, and give them up to be plundered in a land where they are captives. 5 Do not

c Or abandoned   d Or foreman of half the portion assigned to   e Cn: Heb were living
f Or Hammiphkad Gate   g Ch 3.33 in Heb

cover their guilt, and let not their sin be blotted out from thy sight; for they have provoked thee to anger before the builders.

6 So we built the wall; and all the wall was joined together to half its height. For the people had a mind to work.

7[h] But when San·bal′lat and Tō·bi′ah and the Arabs and the Am′mo·nites and the Ash′do·dites heard that the repairing of the walls of Jerusalem was going forward and that the breaches were beginning to be closed, they were very angry; 8 and they all plotted together to come and fight against Jerusalem and to cause confusion in it. 9And we prayed to our God, and set a guard as a protection against them day and night.

10 But Judah said, "The strength of the burden-bearers is failing, and there is much rubbish; we are not able to work on the wall." 11And our enemies said, "They will not know or see till we come into the midst of them and kill them and stop the work." 12 When the Jews who lived by them came they said to us ten times, "From all the places where they live[j] they will come up against us."[i] 13 So in the lowest parts of the space behind the wall, in open places, I stationed the people according to their families, with their swords, their spears, and their bows. 14And I looked, and arose, and said to the nobles and to the officials and to the rest of the people, "Do not be afraid of them. Remember the Lord, who is great and terrible, and fight for your brethren, your sons, your daughters, your wives, and your homes."

15 When our enemies heard that it was known to us and that God had frustrated their plan, we all returned to the wall, each to his work. 16 From that day on, half of my servants worked on construction, and half held the spears, shields, bows, and coats of mail; and the leaders stood behind all the house of Judah, 17 who were building on the wall. Those who carried burdens were laden in such a way that each with one hand labored on the work and with the other held his weapon. 18And each of the builders had his sword girded at his side while he built. The man who sounded the trumpet was beside me. 19And I said to the nobles and to the officials and to the rest of the people, "The work is great and widely spread, and we are

separated on the wall, far from one another. 20 In the place where you hear the sound of the trumpet, rally to us there. Our God will fight for us."

21 So we labored at the work, and half of them held the spears from the break of dawn till the stars came out. 22 I also said to the people at that time, "Let every man and his servant pass the night within Jerusalem, that they may be a guard for us by night and may labor by day." 23 So neither I nor my brethren nor my servants nor the men of the guard who followed me, none of us took off our clothes; each kept his weapon in his hand.[k]

5 Now there arose a great outcry of the people and of their wives against their Jewish brethren. 2 For there were those who said, "With our sons and our daughters, we are many; let us get grain, that we may eat and keep alive." 3 There were also those who said, "We are mortgaging our fields, our vineyards, and our houses to get grain because of the famine." 4And there were those who said, "We have borrowed money for the king's tax upon our fields and our vineyards. 5 Now our flesh is as the flesh of our brethren, our children are as their children; yet we are forcing our sons and our daughters to be slaves, and some of our daughters have already been enslaved; but it is not in our power to help it, for other men have our fields and our vineyards."

6 I was very angry when I heard their outcry and these words. 7 I took counsel with myself, and I brought charges against the nobles and the officials. I said to them, "You are exacting interest, each from his brother." And I held a great assembly against them, 8 and said to them, "We, as far as we are able, have bought back our Jewish brethren who have been sold to the nations; but you even sell your brethren that they may be sold to us!" They were silent, and could not find a word to say. 9 So I said, "The thing that you are doing is not good. Ought you not to walk in the fear of our God to prevent the taunts of the nations our enemies? 10 Moreover I and my brethren and my servants are lending them money and grain. Let us leave off this interest. 11 Return to them this very day their fields, their vineyards, their olive orchards, and their houses, and the hundredth of money, grain, wine, and oil which you have been exacting of

h Ch 4.1 in Heb   i Cn: Heb you return   l Compare Gk Syr: Heb uncertain
k Cn: Heb each his weapon the water

them." 12 Then they said, "We will restore these and require nothing from them. We will do as you say." And I called the priests, and took an oath of them to do as they had promised. 13 I also shook out my lap and said, "So may God shake out every man from his house and from his labor who does not perform this promise. So may he be shaken out and emptied." And all the assembly said "Amen" and praised the LORD. And the people did as they had promised.

14 Moreover from the time that I was appointed to be their governor in the land of Judah, from the twentieth year to the thirty-second year of Är-tȧ-xẽrx'ẽś the king, twelve years, neither I nor my brethren ate the food allowance of the governor. 15 The former governors who were before me laid heavy burdens upon the people, and took from them food and wine, besides forty shekels of silver. Even their servants lorded it over the people. But I did not do so, because of the fear of God. 16 I also held to the work on this wall, and acquired no land; and all my servants were gathered there for the work. 17 Moreover there were at my table a hundred and fifty men, Jews and officials, besides those who came to us from the nations which were about us. 18 Now that which was prepared for one day was one ox and six choice sheep; fowls likewise were prepared for me, and every ten days skins of wine in abundance; yet with all this I did not demand the food allowance of the governor, because the servitude was heavy upon this people. 19 Remember for my good, O my God, all that I have done for this people.

6 Now when it was reported to San·bal'lȧt and Tō·bī'ȧh and to Gē'shem the Arab and to the rest of our enemies that I had built the wall and that there was no breach left in it (although up to that time I had not set up the doors in the gates), 2 San-bal'lȧt and Gē'shem sent to me, saying, "Come and let us meet together in one of the villages in the plain of Ō'nō." But they intended to do me harm. 3And I sent messengers to them, saying, "I am doing a great work and I cannot come down. Why should the work stop while I leave it and come down to you?" 4And they sent to me four times in this way and I answered them in the same manner. 5 In the same way San·bal'lȧt for the fifth time sent his servant to me with an open letter in his hand. 6 In it was written, "It is reported among the nations, and Gē'shem*ˡ* also says it, that you and the Jews intend to rebel; that is why you are building the wall; and you wish to become their king, according to this report. 7And you have also set up prophets to proclaim concerning you in Jerusalem, 'There is a king in Judah.' And now it will be reported to the king according to these words. So now come, and let us take counsel together." 8 Then I sent to him, saying, "No such things as you say have been done, for you are inventing them out of your own mind." 9 For they all wanted to frighten us, thinking, "Their hands will drop from the work, and it will not be done." But now, O God, strengthen my hands.

10 Now when I went into the house of She·mäī'ȧh the son of De·lāī'ȧh, son of Me·het'ȧ·bĕl, who was shut up, he said, "Let us meet together in the house of God, within the temple, and let us close the doors of the temple; for they are coming to kill you, at night they are coming to kill you." 11 But I said, "Should such a man as I flee? And what man such as I could go into the temple and live?*ᵐ* I will not go in." 12And I understood, and saw that God had not sent him, but he had pronounced the prophecy against me because Tō·bī'ȧh and San·bal'lȧt had hired him. 13 For this purpose he was hired, that I should be afraid and act in this way and sin, and so they could give me an evil name, in order to taunt me. 14 Remember Tō·bī'ȧh and San-bal'lȧt, O my God, according to these things that they did, and also the prophetess Nō·ȧ·dī'ȧh and the rest of the prophets who wanted to make me afraid.

15 So the wall was finished on the twenty-fifth day of the month Ē'lŭl, in fifty-two days. 16And when all our enemies heard of it, all the nations round about us were afraid*ⁿ* and fell greatly in their own esteem; for they perceived that this work had been accomplished with the help of our God. 17 Moreover in those days the nobles of Judah sent many letters to Tō·bī'ȧh, and Tobiah's letters came to them. 18 For many in Judah were bound by oath to him, because he was the son-in-law of Shec·ȧ·nī'ȧh the son of Ā'rȧh: and his son Jē'hō·hā'nȧn had taken the daughter of Me·shul'lȧm the son of Bēr·ē·chī'ȧh as his wife. 19Also they spoke of his good deeds in my presence, and reported my words to

ˡ Heb *Gashmu*   *ᵐ* Or *would go into the temple to save his life*   *ⁿ* Another reading is *saw*

him. And Tō·bī'ah sent letters to make me afraid.

7 Now when the wall had been built and I had set up the doors, and the gatekeepers, the singers, and the Levites had been appointed, 2 I gave my brother Hȧ·nā'nī and Han·ȧ·nī'ah the governor of the castle charge over Jerusalem, for he was a more faithful and God-fearing man than many. 3 And I said to them, "Let not the gates of Jerusalem be opened until the sun is hot; and while they are still standing guard*o* let them shut and bar the doors. Appoint guards from among the inhabitants of Jerusalem, each to his station and each opposite his own house." 4 The city was wide and large, but the people within it were few and no houses had been built.

5 Then God put it into my mind to assemble the nobles and the officials and the people to be enrolled by genealogy. And I found the book of the genealogy of those who came up at the first, and I found written in it:

6 These were the people of the province who came up out of the captivity of those exiles whom Ne·bū·chȧd·nez'zȧr the king of Babylon had carried into exile; they returned to Jerusalem and Judah, each to his town. 7 They came with Ze·rub'bȧ·bel, Jesh'ū·ȧ, Nē·hē·mī'ah, Az·ȧ·rī'ah, Rā·ȧ·mī'ah, Nā·ham'ȧ·nī, Môr'de·cāi, Bil'shan, Mis'pē·reth, Big'vāi, Nē'hum, Bā'ȧ·nȧh.

The number of the men of the people of Israel: 8 the sons of Pā'rosh, two thousand a hundred and seventy-two. 9 The sons of Sheph·ȧ·tī'ah, three hundred and seventy-two. 10 The sons of A'rȧh, six hundred and fifty-two. 11 The sons of Pā'hath-mō'ab, namely the sons of Jesh'ū·ȧ and Jō'ab, two thousand eight hundred and eighteen. 12 The sons of Ē'lȧm, a thousand two hundred and fifty-four. 13 The sons of Zat'tū, eight hundred and forty-five. 14 The sons of Zac'cāi, seven hundred and sixty. 15 The sons of Bin'nū·ī, six hundred and forty-eight. 16 The sons of Bē'bāi, six hundred and twenty-eight. 17 The sons of Az'gad, two thousand three hundred and twenty-two. 18 The sons of Ȧ·dō·nī'kȧm, six hundred and sixty-seven. 19 The sons of Big'vāi, two thousand and sixty-seven. 20 The sons of A'din, six hundred and fifty-five. 21 The sons of A'tēr, namely of Hez·ē·kī'ah, ninety-eight. 22 The sons of Hā'shum, three hundred and twenty-eight. 23 The sons of Bē'zāi, three hundred and twenty-four. 24 The sons of Hā'riph, a hundred and twelve. 25 The sons of Gib'ē·ôn, ninety-five. 26 The men of Bethlehem and Nē·toph'ah, a hundred and eighty-eight. 27 The men of An'ȧ·thoth, a hundred and twenty-eight. 28 The men of Beth-az'mȧ·veth, forty-two. 29 The men of Kīr'i·ath-jē'ȧ·rim, Che·phī'rah, and Bē·ēr'oth, seven hundred and forty-three. 30 The men of Rā'mah and Gē'bȧ, six hundred and twenty-one. 31 The men of Mich'mȧs, a hundred and twenty-two. 32 The men of Beth'ēl and Ai, a hundred and twenty-three. 33 The men of the other Nē'bō, fifty-two. 34 The sons of the other Ē'lȧm, a thousand two hundred and fifty-four. 35 The sons of Hā'rim, three hundred and twenty. 36 The sons of Jericho, three hundred and forty-five. 37 The sons of Lod, Hā'did, and O'nō, seven hundred and twenty-one. 38 The sons of Se·nā'ah, three thousand nine hundred and thirty.

39 The priests: the sons of Je·dāi'ah, namely the house of Jesh'ū·ȧ, nine hundred and seventy-three. 40 The sons of Im'mēr, a thousand and fifty-two. 41 The sons of Pash'hūr, a thousand two hundred and forty-seven. 42 The sons of Hā'rim, a thousand and seventeen.

43 The Levites: the sons of Jesh'ū·ȧ, namely of Kad'mi·el of the sons of Hō'dē·vȧh, seventy-four. 44 The singers: the sons of A'saph, a hundred and forty-eight. 45 The gatekeepers: the sons of Shal'lum, the sons of A'tēr, the sons of Tal'mon, the sons of Ak'kūb, the sons of Hȧ·tī'tȧ, the sons of Shō'bāi, a hundred and thirty-eight.

46 The temple servants:*p* the sons of Zī'hȧ, the sons of Hȧ·sū'phȧ, the sons of Tab·bā'oth, 47 the sons of Kē'ros, the sons of Sī'ȧ, the sons of Pā'don, 48 the sons of Le·bā'nȧ, the sons of Hag'ȧ·bȧ, the sons of Shal'māi, 49 the sons of Hā'nȧn, the sons of Gid'del, the sons of Gā'hȧr, 50 the sons of Rē·āi'ah, the sons of Rē'zin, the sons of Ne·kō'dȧ, 51 the sons of Gaz'zȧm, the sons of Uz'zȧ, the sons of Pȧ·sē'ah, 52 the sons of Bē'sāi, the sons of Me·ü'nim, the sons of Ne·phūsh'ē·sim, 53 the sons of Bak'būk, the sons of Hȧ·kū'phȧ, the sons of Hār'hūr, 54 the sons of Baz'lith, the sons of Me·hī'dȧ, the sons of Hār'shȧ, 55 the sons of Bär'kos, the sons of Sis'ēr·ȧ, the sons of Tē'mah, 56 the sons of Ne·zī'ah, the sons of Hȧ·tī'phȧ.

57 The sons of Solomon's servants: the sons of Sō'tāi, the sons of Sō'phē·reth, the sons of Pe·rī'dȧ, 58 the sons

of Jā´a·lă, the sons of Där´kon, the sons of Gid´del, 59 the sons of Sheph·à·ti´ah, the sons of Hat´til, the sons of Pō´chê-reth-haz·zê·bā´im, the sons of Ā´mon.

60 All the temple servants and the sons of Solomon's servants were three hundred and ninety-two.

61 The following were those who came up from Tel-mē´lah, Tel-här´sha, Chē´rub, Ad´don, and Im´mèr, but they could not prove their fathers' houses nor their descent, whether they belonged to Israel: 62 the sons of De-läi´ah, the sons of Tō·bi´ah, the sons of Ne·kō´dă, six hundred and forty-two.

63 Also, of the priests: the sons of Hō-bāi´ah, the sons of Hak´koz, the sons of Bär·zil´läi (who had taken a wife of the daughters of Barzillai the Gileadite and was called by their name). 64 These sought their registration among those enrolled in the genealogies, but it was not found there, so they were excluded from the priesthood as unclean; 65 the governor told them that they were not to partake of the most holy food, until a priest with U´rim and Thum´mim should arise.

66 The whole assembly together was forty-two thousand three hundred and sixty, 67 besides their menservants and maidservants, of whom there were seven thousand three hundred and thirty-seven; and they had two hundred and forty-five singers, male and female. 68 Their horses were seven hundred and thirty-six, their mules two hundred and forty-five,*q* 69 their camels four hundred and thirty-five, and their asses six thousand seven hundred and twenty.

70 Now some of the heads of fathers' houses gave to the work. The governor gave to the treasury a thousand darics of gold, fifty basins, five hundred and thirty priests' garments. 71 And some of the heads of fathers' houses gave into the treasury of the work twenty thousand darics of gold and two thousand two hundred minas of silver. 72 And what the rest of the people gave was twenty thousand darics of gold, two thousand minas of silver, and sixty-seven priests' garments.

73 So the priests, the Levites, the gatekeepers, the singers, some of the people, the temple servants, and all Israel, lived in their towns.

And when the seventh month had come, the children of Israel were in **8** their towns. 1 And all the people gathered as one man into the

square before the Water Gate; and they told Ezra the scribe to bring the book of the law of Moses which the LORD had given to Israel. 2 And Ezra the priest brought the law before the assembly, both men and women and all who could hear with understanding, on the first day of the seventh month. 3 And he read from it facing the square before the Water Gate from early morning until midday, in the presence of the men and the women and those who could understand; and the ears of all the people were attentive to the book of the law. 4 And Ezra the scribe stood on a wooden pulpit which they had made for the purpose; and beside him stood Mat·ti·thi´ah, Shē´ma, A·nāi´ah, U·ri´ah, Hil·ki´ah, and Mā-à·sēi´ah on his right hand; and Pe-dāi´ah, Mish´a-el, Mal·chi´jah, Hā´-shum, Hash-bad´dà·nah, Zech·a·ri´ah, and Me·shul´làm on his left hand. 5 And Ezra opened the book in the sight of all the people, for he was above all the people; and when he opened it all the people stood. 6 And Ezra blessed the LORD, the great God; and all the people answered, "Amen, Amen," lifting up their hands; and they bowed their heads and worshiped the LORD with their faces to the ground. 7 Also Jesh´u·a, Bā´ni, Sher·è·bi´ah, Jā´min, Ak´kub, Shab´bè·thäi, Hō·di´ah, Mā·à·sēi´ah, Ke·li´tà, Az·à-ri´ah, Jō´za·bad, Hā´nan, Pe·läi´ah, the Levites,*r* helped the people to understand the law, while the people remained in their places. 8 And they read from the book, from the law of God, clearly;*s* and they gave the sense, so that the people understood the reading.

9 And Nē·hē·mi´ah, who was the governor, and Ezra the priest and scribe, and the Levites who taught the people said to all the people, "This day is holy to the LORD your God; do not mourn or weep." For all the people wept when they heard the words of the law. 10 Then he said to them, "Go your way, eat the fat and drink sweet wine and send portions to him for whom nothing is prepared; for this day is holy to our Lord; and do not be grieved, for the joy of the LORD is your strength." 11 So the Levites stilled all the people, saying, "Be quiet, for this day is holy; do not be grieved." 12 And all the people went their way to eat and drink and to send portions and to make great rejoicing, because they had understood the words that were declared to them.

---

q Ezra 2.66 and the margins of some Hebrew Mss: Heb lacks *their horses . . . forty-five*
r 1 Esdras 9.48 Vg: Heb *and the Levites*   *s* Or *with interpretation*

13 On the second day the heads of fathers' houses of all the people, with the priests and the Levites, came together to Ezra the scribe in order to study the words of the law. 14 And they found it written in the law that the LORD had commanded by Moses that the people of Israel should dwell in booths during the feast of the seventh month, 15 and that they should publish and proclaim in all their towns and in Jerusalem, "Go out to the hills and bring branches of olive, wild olive, myrtle, palm, and other leafy trees to make booths, as it is written." 16 So the people went out and brought them and made booths for themselves, each on his roof, and in their courts and in the courts of the house of God, and in the square at the Water Gate and in the square at the Gate of Ē′phrā·im. 17 And all the assembly of those who had returned from the captivity made booths and dwelt in the booths; for from the days of Jesh′ü·à the son of Nun to that day the people of Israel had not done so. And there was very great rejoicing. 18 And day by day, from the first day to the last day, he read from the book of the law of God. They kept the feast seven days; and on the eighth day there was a solemn assembly, according to the ordinance.

9 Now on the twenty-fourth day of this month the people of Israel were assembled with fasting and in sackcloth, and with earth upon their heads. 2 And the Israelites separated themselves from all foreigners, and stood and confessed their sins and the iniquities of their fathers. 3 And they stood up in their place and read from the book of the law of the LORD their God for a fourth of the day; for another fourth of it they made confession and worshiped the LORD their God. 4 Upon the stairs of the Levites stood Jesh′ü·à, Bā′nī, Kad′mi-el, Sheb·à·nī′àh, Bun′nī, Sher·é·bī′àh, Bani, and Che·nā′nī; and they cried with a loud voice to the LORD their God. 5 Then the Levites, Jesh′ü·à, Kad′mi-el, Bā′nī, Hash·ab·nei′àh, Sher·é·bī′àh, Hō·dī′àh, Sheb·à·nī′àh, and Peth·à·hī′àh, said, "Stand up and bless the LORD your God from everlasting to everlasting. Blessed be thy glorious name which is exalted above all blessing and praise."

6 And Ezra said:ᵗ "Thou art the LORD, thou alone; thou hast made heaven, the heaven of heavens, with all their host, the earth and all that is on it, the seas and all that is in them;

ᵗ Gk: Heb lacks *and Ezra said*

and thou preservest all of them; and the host of heaven worships thee. 7 Thou art the LORD, the God who didst choose Abram and bring him forth out of Ur of the Chal·dē′àns and give him the name Abraham;⁸ and thou didst find his heart faithful before thee, and didst make with him the covenant to give to his descendants the land of the Canaanite, the Hit′tite, the Am′ò·rīte, the Per′iz·zīte, the Jeb′ū·sīte, and the Gīr′gà·shīte; and thou hast fulfilled thy promise, for thou art righteous.

9 "And thou didst see the affliction of our fathers in Egypt and hear their cry at the Red Sea, 10 and didst perform signs and wonders against Pharaoh and all his servants and all the people of his land, for thou knewest that they acted insolently against our fathers; and thou didst get thee a name, as it is to this day. 11 And thou didst divide the sea before them, so that they went through the midst of the sea on dry land; and thou didst cast their pursuers into the depths, as a stone into mighty waters. 12 By a pillar of cloud thou didst lead them in the day, and by a pillar of fire in the night to light for them the way in which they should go. 13 Thou didst come down upon Mount Sinai, and speak with them from heaven and give them right ordinances and true laws, good statutes and commandments, 14 and thou didst make known to them thy holy sabbath and command them commandments and statutes and a law by Moses thy servant. 15 Thou didst give them bread from heaven for their hunger and bring forth water for them from the rock for their thirst, and thou didst tell them to go in to possess the land which thou hadst sworn to give them.

16 "But they and our fathers acted presumptuously and stiffened their neck and did not obey thy commandments; 17 they refused to obey, and were not mindful of the wonders which thou didst perform among them; but they stiffened their neck and appointed a leader to return to their bondage in Egypt. But thou art a God ready to forgive, gracious and merciful, slow to anger and abounding in steadfast love, and didst not forsake them. 18 Even when they had made for themselves a molten calf and said, 'This is your God who brought you up out of Egypt,' and had committed great blasphemies, 19 thou in thy great mercies didst not forsake them in the wilderness; the pillar of cloud which

led them in the way did not depart from them by day, nor the pillar of fire by night which lighted for them the way by which they should go. 20 Thou gavest thy good Spirit to instruct them, and didst not withhold thy manna from their mouth, and gavest them water for their thirst. 21 Forty years didst thou sustain them in the wilderness, and they lacked nothing; their clothes did not wear out and their feet did not swell. 22And thou didst give them kingdoms and peoples, and didst allot to them every corner; so they took possession of the land of Si'hon king of Hesh'bon and the land of Og king of Ba'shan. 23 Thou didst multiply their descendants as the stars of heaven, and thou didst bring them into the land which thou hadst told their fathers to enter and possess. 24 So the descendants went in and possessed the land, and thou didst subdue before them the inhabitants of the land, the Canaanites, and didst give them into their hands, with their kings and the peoples of the land, that they might do with them as they would. 25And they captured fortified cities and a rich land, and took possession of houses full of all good things, cisterns hewn out, vineyards, olive orchards and fruit trees in abundance; so they ate, and were filled and became fat, and delighted themselves in thy great goodness.

26 "Nevertheless they were disobedient and rebelled against thee and cast thy law behind their back and killed thy prophets, who had warned them in order to turn them back to thee, and they committed great blasphemies. 27 Therefore thou didst give them into the hand of their enemies, who made them suffer; and in the time of their suffering they cried to thee and thou didst hear them from heaven; and according to thy great mercies thou didst give them saviors who saved them from the hand of their enemies. 28 But after they had rest they did evil again before thee, and thou didst abandon them to the hand of their enemies, so that they had dominion over them; yet when they turned and cried to thee thou didst hear from heaven, and many times thou didst deliver them according to thy mercies. 29And thou didst warn them in order to turn them back to thy law. Yet they acted presumptuously and did not obey thy commandments, but sinned against thy ordinances, by the observance of which a man shall live, and

turned a stubborn shoulder and stiffened their neck and would not obey. 30 Many years thou didst bear with them, and didst warn them by thy Spirit through thy prophets; yet they would not give ear. Therefore thou didst give them into the hand of the peoples of the lands. 31 Nevertheless in thy great mercies thou didst not make an end of them or forsake them; for thou art a gracious and merciful God.

32 "Now therefore, our God, the great and mighty and terrible God, who keepest covenant and steadfast love, let not all the hardship seem little to thee that has come upon us, upon our kings, our princes, our priests, our prophets, our fathers, and all thy people, since the time of the kings of Assyria until this day. 33 Yet thou hast been just in all that has come upon us, for thou hast dealt faithfully and we have acted wickedly; 34 our kings, our princes, our priests, and our fathers have not kept thy law or heeded thy commandments and thy warnings which thou didst give them. 35 They did not serve thee in their kingdom, and in thy great goodness which thou gavest them, and in the large and rich land which thou didst set before them; and they did not turn from their wicked works. 36 Behold, we are slaves this day; in the land that thou gavest to our fathers to enjoy its fruit and its good gifts, behold, we are slaves. 37And its rich yield goes to the kings whom thou hast set over us because of our sins; they have power also over our bodies and over our cattle at their pleasure, and we are in great distress."

38u Because of all this we make a firm covenant and write it, and our princes, our Levites, and our priests set their seal to it.

10v Those who set their seal are Ne·he·mi'ah the governor, the son of Hac·a·li'ah, Zed·e·ki'ah, 2 Se·rai'ah, Az·a·ri'ah, Jeremiah, 3 Pash'hur, Am·a·ri'ah, Mal·chi'jah, 4 Hat'tush, Sheb·a·ni'ah, Mal'luch, 5 Ha'rim, Mer'e·moth, O·ba·di'ah, 6 Daniel, Gin'ne·thon, Bar'uch, 7 Me·shul'lam, A·bi'jah, Mi'ja·min, 8 Ma·a·zi'ah, Bil'gai, She·mai'ah; these are the priests. 9And the Levites: Jesh'u·a the son of Az·a·ni'ah, Bin'nu·i of the sons of Hen'a·dad, Kad'mi·el; 10 and their brethren, Sheb·a·ni'ah, Ho·di'ah, Ke·li'ta, Pe·lai'ah, Ha'nan, 11 Mi'ca, Re'hob, Hash·a·bi'ah, 12 Zac'cur, Sher·e·bi'ah, Sheb·a·ni'ah, 13 Ho·di'ah, Ba'ni, Be·ni'nu. 14 The chiefs of the

u Ch 10.1 in Heb   v Ch 10.2 in Heb

people: Pă′rosh, Pā′hath-mō′ab, Ē′lăm, Zat′tü, Bā′nī, ¹⁵ Bun′nī, Az′gad, Bē′bäi, ¹⁶Ad·ŏ·nī′jăh, Big′väi, Ă′din, ¹⁷Ā′tẽr, Hez·ē·kī′ăh, Az′zŭr, ¹⁸ Hō-dī′ăh, Hā′shúm, Bē′zäi, ¹⁹ Hā′riph, An′ȧ·thoth, Nē′bäi, ²⁰ Mag′pi·ash, Me·shul′lăm, Hē′zir, ²¹ Me·shez′ȧ·bel, Zā′dok, Jad′dü-ȧ, ²² Pel·ȧ·tī′ăh, Hā′nàn, Ȧ·näi′ăh, ²³ Hō·shē′ȧ, Han·ȧ-nī′ăh, Has′shúb, ²⁴ Hal·lō′hesh, Pil′hȧ, Shō′bek, ²⁵ Rē′hùm, Hȧ·shab′năh, Mā-ȧ·sēi′ăh, ²⁶Ȧ·hī′ăh, Hā′nàn, Ā′nan, ²⁷ Mal′lúch, Hā′rim, Bā′ȧ·năh.

28 The rest of the people, the priests, the Levites, the gatekeepers, the singers, the temple servants, and all who have separated themselves from the peoples of the lands to the law of God, their wives, their sons, their daughters, all who have knowledge and understanding, ²⁹ join with their brethren, their nobles, and enter into a curse and an oath to walk in God's law which was given by Moses the servant of God, and to observe and do all the commandments of the LORD our Lord and his ordinances and his statutes. ³⁰ We will not give our daughters to the peoples of the land or take their daughters for our sons; ³¹ and if the peoples of the land bring in wares or any grain on the sabbath day to sell, we will not buy from them on the sabbath or on a holy day; and we will forego the crops of the seventh year and the exaction of every debt.

32 We also lay upon ourselves the obligation to charge ourselves yearly with the third part of a shekel for the service of the house of our God: ³³ for the showbread, the continual cereal offering, the continual burnt offering, the sabbaths, the new moons, the appointed feasts, the holy things, and the sin offerings to make atonement for Israel, and for all the work of the house of our God. ³⁴ We have likewise cast lots, the priests, the Levites, and the people, for the wood offering, to bring it into the house of our God, according to our fathers' houses, at times appointed, year by year, to burn upon the altar of the LORD our God, as it is written in the law. ³⁵ We obligate ourselves to bring the first fruits of our ground and the first fruits of all fruit of every tree, year by year, to the house of the LORD; ³⁶ also to bring to the house of our God, to the priests who minister in the house of our God, the first-born of our sons and of our cattle, as it is written in the law, and the firstlings of our herds and of our flocks; ³⁷ and to bring the first

of our coarse meal, and our contributions, the fruit of every tree, the wine and the oil, to the priests, to the chambers of the house of our God; and to bring to the Levites the tithes from our ground, for it is the Levites who collect the tithes in all our rural towns. ³⁸And the priest, the son of Aaron, shall be with the Levites when the Levites receive the tithes; and the Levites shall bring up the tithe of the tithes to the house of our God, to the chambers, to the storehouse. ³⁹ For the people of Israel and the sons of Levi shall bring the contribution of grain, wine, and oil to the chambers, where are the vessels of the sanctuary, and the priests that minister, and the gatekeepers and the singers. We will not neglect the house of our God.

11 Now the leaders of the people lived in Jerusalem; and the rest of the people cast lots to bring one out of ten to live in Jerusalem the holy city, while nine tenths remained in the other towns. ²And the people blessed all the men who willingly offered to live in Jerusalem.

3 These are the chiefs of the province who lived in Jerusalem; but in the towns of Judah every one lived on his property in their towns: Israel, the priests, the Levites, the temple servants, and the descendants of Solomon's servants. ⁴And in Jerusalem lived certain of the sons of Judah and of the sons of Benjamin. Of the sons of Judah: Ȧ·thäi′ăh the son of Uz·zī′ăh, son of Zech·ȧ·rī′ăh, son of Am·ȧ·rī′ăh, son of Sheph·ȧ·tī′ăh, son of Mȧ·hal′ȧ-lel, of the sons of Per′ez; ⁵ and Mā-ȧ·sēi′ăh the son of Bâr′uch, son of Col·hō′zēh, son of Hȧ·zāi′ăh, son of Ȧ·däi′ăh, son of Joi′ȧ·rib, son of Zech-ȧ·rī′ăh, son of the Shī′lō·nite. ⁶All the sons of Per′ez who lived in Jerusalem were four hundred and sixty-eight valiant men.

7 And these are the sons of Benjamin: Sal′lü the son of Me·shul′lăm, son of Jō′ed, son of Pe·dāi′ăh, son of Kō·läi′ăh, son of Mā·ȧ·sēi′ăh, son of I′thi-el, son of Je·shā′iäh. ⁸And after him Gab·bā′ī, Sal′läi, nine hundred and twenty-eight. ⁹ Jō′ĕl the son of Zich′rī was their overseer; and Judah the son of Has·sē·nü′ăh was second over the city.

10 Of the priests: Je·däi′ăh the son of Joi′ȧ·rib, Jā′chin, ¹¹ Se·räi′ăh the son of Hil·kī′ăh, son of Me·shul′lăm, son of Zā′dok, son of Me·rā′ioth, son of Ȧ·hī′túb, ruler of the house of God, ¹² and their brethren who did the

work of the house, eight hundred and twenty-two; and Ȧ·dāī'ah the son of Je·rō'ham, son of Pel·ȧ·lī'ah, son of Am'zī, son of Zech·ȧ·rī'ah, son of Pash'hūr, son of Mal·chī'jah, 13 and his brethren, heads of fathers' houses, two hundred and forty-two; and Ȧ·mash'säi, the son of Az'ȧ·rel, son of Äh'zäi, son of Me·shil'lė·moth, son of Im'mėr, 14 and their brethren, mighty men of valor, a hundred and twenty-eight; their overseer was Zab'-di·el the son of Hag·gė·dō'lim.

15 And of the Levites: She·māi'ah the son of Has'shûb, son of Az·rī'kam, son of Hash·ȧ·bī'ah, son of Bun'nī; 16 and Shab'bė·thäi and Jō'zȧ·bad, of the chiefs of the Levites, who were over the outside work of the house of God; 17 and Mat·tȧ·nī'ah the son of Mī'că, son of Zab'dī, son of Ā'saph, who was the leader to begin the thanksgiving in prayer, and Bak·bū·kī'ah, the second among his brethren; and Ab'dȧ the son of Sham'mū·ȧ, son of Gā'lal, son of Je·dū'thŭn. 18 All the Levites in the holy city were two hundred and eighty-four.

19 The gatekeepers, Ak'kûb, Tal'-môn and their brethren, who kept watch at the gates, were a hundred and seventy-two. 20 And the rest of Israel, and of the priests and the Levites, were in all the towns of Judah, every one in his inheritance. 21 But the temple servants lived on Ō'phel; and Zī'hȧ and Gish'pȧ were over the temple servants.

22 The overseer of the Levites in Jerusalem was Uz'zī the son of Bā'nī, son of Hash·ȧ·bī'ah, son of Mat·tȧ·nī'ah, son of Mī'că, of the sons of Ā'saph, the singers, over the work of the house of God. 23 For there was a command from the king concerning them, and a settled provision for the singers, as every day required. 24 And Peth·ȧ·hī'ah the son of Me·shez'ȧ·bel, of the sons of Zē'rah the son of Judah, was at the king's hand in all matters concerning the people.

25 And as for the villages, with their fields, some of the people of Judah lived in Kīr'i·ath-är'bȧ and its villages, and in Dī'bon and its villages, and in Je·kab'zē·ėl and its villages, 26 and in Jesh'ū·ȧ and in Mō'lȧ·dah and Beth-pel'et, 27 in Hā'zär-shū'al, in Beer-sheba and its villages, 28 in Zik'lag, in Me·cō'näh and its villages, 29 in En-rim'mon, in Zō'rȧh, in Jär'-muth, 30 Zȧ·nō'ah, Ȧ·dul'lam, and their villages, Lā'chish and its fields, and Ȧ·zē'kah and its villages. So they encamped from Beer-sheba to the valley of Hin'nŏm. 31 The people of Benjamin also lived from Gē'bȧ onward, at Mich'mash, Aï'jȧ, Beth'ėl and its villages, 32 An'ȧ·thoth, Nob, An·ȧ·nī'ah, 33 Hā'zôr, Rā'mah, Gĭt'tȧ·im, 34 Hā'did, Ze·bō'im, Ne·bal'lȧt, 35 Lod, and Ō'nō, the valley of craftsmen. 36 And certain divisions of the Levites in Judah were joined to Benjamin.

12

These are the priests and the Levites who came up with Ze·rub'bȧ·bel the son of She·al'ti·el, and Jesh'ū·ȧ: Se·rāi'ah, Jeremiah, Ezra, 2 Am·ȧ·rī'ah, Mal'lûch, Hat'tûsh, 3 Shec·ȧ·nī'ah, Rē'hŭm, Mer'ė·moth, 4 Id'dō, Gin'nė·thoi, Ȧ·bī'jah, 5 Mī'jȧ·min, Mā·ȧ·dī'ah, Bil'gah, 6 She·māi'ah, Joi'ȧ·rib, Je·dāi'ah, 7 Sal'lū, Ā'mok, Hil·kī'ah, Je·dāi'ah. These were the chiefs of the priests and of their brethren in the days of Jesh'ū·ȧ.

8 And the Levites: Jesh'ū·ȧ, Bin'-nū·ī, Kad'mi·el, Sher·ė·bī'ah, Judah, and Mat·tȧ·nī'ah, who with his brethren was in charge of the songs of thanksgiving. 9 And Bak·bū·kī'ah and Un'nō their brethren stood opposite them in the service. 10 And Jesh'ū·ȧ was the father of Joi'ȧ·kim, Joiakim the father of E·lī'ȧ·shib, Eliashib the father of Joi'ȧ·dȧ, 11 Joi'ȧ·dȧ the father of Jonathan, and Jonathan the father of Jad'dū·ȧ.

12 And in the days of Joi'ȧ·kim were priests, heads of fathers' houses: of Se·rāi'ah, Me·rāi'ah; of Jeremiah, Han·ȧ·nī'ah; 13 of Ezra, Me·shul'lam; of Am·ȧ·rī'ah, Jē'hō-hā'nan; 14 of Mal'-lu·chī, Jonathan; of Sheb·ȧ·nī'ah, Joseph; 15 of Hā'rim, Ad'nȧ; of Me·rā'ioth, Hel'käi; 16 of Id'dō, Zech·ȧ·rī'ah; of Gin'nė·thon, Me·shul'lam; 17 of Ȧ·bī'jah, Zich'ri; of Mi·nī'ȧ·min, of Mō·ȧ·dī'ah, Pil'täi; 18 of Bil'gah, Sham'mū·ȧ; of She·māi'ah, Je·hon'ȧ·thàn; 19 of Joi'ȧ·rib, Mat·tē'näi; of Je·dāi'ah, Uz'zī; 20 of Sal'läi, Kal'läi; of Ā'mok, Ē'bėr; 21 of Hil·kī'ah, Hash·ȧ·bī'ah; of Je·dāi'ah, Nė·than'el.

22 As for the Levites, in the days of E·lī'ȧ·shib, Joi'ȧ·dȧ, Jō·hā'nan, and Jad'dū·ȧ, there were recorded the heads of fathers' houses; also the priests until the reign of Dà·rī'ŭs the Persian. 23 The sons of Levi, heads of fathers' houses, were written in the Book of the Chronicles until the days of Jō·hā'nan the son of E·lī'ȧ·shib. 24 And the chiefs of the Levites: Hash·ȧ·bī'ah, Sher·ė·bī'ah, and Jesh'ū·ȧ the son of Kad'mi·el, with their brethren over against them, to praise and to give thanks, according to the commandment of David the man of God, watch corresponding to watch. 25 Mat·tȧ-

ni′ah, Bak·bū·ki′ah, Ō·ba·di′ah, Me-shul′lam, Tal′mon, and Ak′kub were gatekeepers standing guard at the storehouses of the gates. 26 These were in the days of Joi′a·kim the son of Jesh′u·a son of Jō′za·dak, and in the days of Nē·hē·mi′ah the governor and of Ezra the priest the scribe.

27 And at the dedication of the wall of Jerusalem they sought the Levites in all their places, to bring them to Jerusalem to celebrate the dedication with gladness, with thanksgivings and with singing, with cymbals, harps, and lyres. 28And the sons of the singers gathered together from the circuit round Jerusalem and from the villages of the Nē·toph′a·thites; 29 also from Beth-gil′gal and from the region of Gē′ba and Az′ma·veth; for the singers had built for themselves villages around Jerusalem. 30And the priests and the Levites purified themselves; and they purified the people and the gates and the wall.

31 Then I brought up the princes of Judah upon the wall, and appointed two great companies which gave thanks and went in procession. One went to the right upon the wall to the Dung Gate; 32 and after them went Hō-shäi′ah and half of the princes of Judah, 33 and Az·a·ri′ah, Ezra, Me-shul′lam, 34 Judah, Benjamin, She-māi′ah, and Jeremiah, 35 and certain of the priests' sons with trumpets: Zech·a·ri′ah the son of Jonathan, son of She·māi′ah, son of Mat·ta·ni′ah, son of Mī·cāi′ah, son of Zac′cur, son of Ā′saph; 36 and his kinsmen, She-māi′ah, Az′a·rel, Mil′a·läi, Gil′a·läi, Mā′äi, Nē·than′el, Judah, and Ha·nā′ni, with the musical instruments of David the man of God; and Ezra the scribe went before them. 37At the Fountain Gate they went up straight before them by the stairs of the city of David, at the ascent of the wall, above the house of David, to the Water Gate on the east.

38 The other company of those who gave thanks went to the left, and I followed them with half of the people, upon the wall, above the Tower of the Ovens, to the Broad Wall, 39 and above the Gate of E′phra·im, and by the Old Gate, and by the Fish Gate and the Tower of Ha·nan′el, the Tower of the Hundred, to the Sheep Gate; and they came to a halt at the Gate of the Guard. 40 So both companies of those who gave thanks stood in the house of God, and I and half of the officials with me; 41 and the priests

E·li′a·kim, Mā·a·sēi′ah, Mi·ni′a·min, Mī·cāi′ah, El·i·ō-ē′näi, Zech·a·ri′ah, and Han·a·ni′ah, with trumpets; 42 and Mā·a·sēi′ah, She·māi′ah, El·ē·ā′zàr, Uz′zi, Jē′hō-hā′nàn, Mal·chi′jàh, E′làm, and E′zér. And the singers sang with Jez·ra·hi′ah as their leader. 43And they offered great sacrifices that day and rejoiced, for God had made them rejoice with great joy; the women and children also rejoiced. And the joy of Jerusalem was heard afar off.

44 On that day men were appointed over the chambers for the stores, the contributions, the first fruits, and the tithes, to gather into them the portions required by the law for the priests and for the Levites according to the fields of the towns; for Judah rejoiced over the priests and the Levites who minis-tered. 45And they performed the service of their God and the service of purification, as did the singers and the gatekeepers, according to the com-mand of David and his son Solomon. 46 For in the days of David and Ā′saph of old there was a chief of the singers, and there were songs of praise and thanksgiving to God. 47And all Israel in the days of Ze·rub′ba·bel and in the days of Nē·hē·mi′ah gave the daily portions for the singers and the gate-keepers; and they set apart that which was for the Levites; and the Levites set apart that which was for the sons of Aaron.

13 On that day they read from the book of Moses in the hearing of the people; and in it was found written that no Am′mo·nīte or Mō′ab·ite should ever enter the assembly of God; 2 for they did not meet the children of Israel with bread and water, but hired Balaam against them to curse them— yet our God turned the curse into a blessing. 3 When the people heard the law, they separated from Israel all those of foreign descent.

4 Now before this, E·li′a·shib the priest, who was appointed over the chambers of the house of our God, and who was connected with Tō·bi′ah, 5 prepared for Tō·bi′ah a large chamber where they had previously put the cereal offering, the frankincense, the vessels, and the tithes of grain, wine, and oil, which were given by com-mandment to the Levites, singers, and gatekeepers, and the contributions for the priests. 6 While this was taking place I was not in Jerusalem, for in the thirty-second year of Ar·ta·xĕrx′ēs king of Babylon I went to the king. And after some time I asked leave of

the king 7 and came to Jerusalem, and I then discovered the evil that E·li′a·shib had done for Tō·bi′ah, preparing for him a chamber in the courts of the house of God. 8 And I was very angry, and I threw all the household furniture of Tō·bi′ah out of the chamber. 9 Then I gave orders and they cleansed the chambers; and I brought back thither the vessels of the house of God, with the cereal offering and the frankincense.

10 I also found out that the portions of the Levites had not been given to them; so that the Levites and the singers, who did the work, had fled each to his field. 11 So I remonstrated with the officials and said, "Why is the house of God forsaken?" And I gathered them together and set them in their stations. 12 Then all Judah brought the tithe of the grain, wine, and oil into the storehouses. 13 And I appointed as treasurers over the storehouses Shel·e·mi′ah the priest, Zā′dok the scribe, and Pe·dāi′ah of the Levites, and as their assistant Hā′nan the son of Zac′cur, son of Mat·ta·ni′ah, for they were counted faithful; and their duty was to distribute to their brethren. 14 Remember me, O my God, concerning this, and wipe not out my good deeds that I have done for the house of my God and for his service.

15 In those days I saw in Judah men treading wine presses on the sabbath, and bringing in heaps of grain and loading them on asses; and also wine, grapes, figs, and all kinds of burdens, which they brought into Jerusalem on the sabbath day; and I warned them on the day when they sold food. 16 Men of Tȳre also, who lived in the city, brought in fish and all kinds of wares and sold them on the sabbath to the people of Judah, and in Jerusalem. 17 Then I remonstrated with the nobles of Judah and said to them, "What is this evil thing which you are doing, profaning the sabbath day? 18 Did not your fathers act in this way, and did not our God bring all this evil on us and on this city? Yet you bring more wrath upon Israel by profaning the sabbath."

19 When it began to be dark at the gates of Jerusalem before the sabbath, I commanded that the doors should be shut and gave orders that they should not be opened until after the sabbath. And I set some of my servants over the gates, that no burden might be brought in on the sabbath day. 20 Then the merchants and sellers of all kinds of wares lodged outside Jerusalem once or twice. 21 But I warned them and said to them, "Why do you lodge before the wall? If you do so again I will lay hands on you." From that time on they did not come on the sabbath. 22 And I commanded the Levites that they should purify themselves and come and guard the gates, to keep the sabbath day holy. Remember this also in my favor, O my God, and spare me according to the greatness of thy steadfast love.

23 In those days also I saw the Jews who had married women of Ash′dod, Am′mon, and Mō′ab; 24 and half of their children spoke the language of Ash′dod, and they could not speak the language of Judah, but the language of each people. 25 And I contended with them and cursed them and beat some of them and pulled out their hair; and I made them take oath in the name of God, saying, "You shall not give your daughters to their sons, or take their daughters for your sons or for yourselves. 26 Did not Solomon king of Israel sin on account of such women? Among the many nations there was no king like him, and he was beloved by his God, and God made him king over all Israel; nevertheless foreign women made even him to sin. 27 Shall we then listen to you and do all this great evil and act treacherously against our God by marrying foreign women?"

28 And one of the sons of Je·hoi′a·da, the son of E·li′a·shib the high priest, was the son-in-law of San·bal′lat the Hôr′ŏ·nīte; therefore I chased him from me. 29 Remember them, O my God, because they have defiled the priesthood and the covenant of the priesthood and the Levites.

30 Thus I cleansed them from everything foreign, and I established the duties of the priests and Levites, each in his work; 31 and I provided for the wood offering, at appointed times, and for the first fruits. Remember me, O my God, for good.

THE BOOK OF

ESTHER

1 In the days of Å·haś'ū-ē'rŭs, the Ahasu-erus who reigned from India to Ethiopia over one hundred and twenty-seven provinces, 2 in those days when King Å·haś'ū-ē'rŭs sat on his royal throne in Su'să the capital, 3 in the third year of his reign he gave a banquet for all his princes and servants, the army chiefs[a] of Persia and Media and the nobles and governors of the provinces being before him, 4 while he showed the riches of his royal glory and the splendor and pomp of his majesty for many days, a hundred and eighty days. 5 And when these days were completed, the king gave for all the people present in Su'să the capital, both great and small, a banquet lasting for seven days, in the court of the garden of the king's palace. 6 There were white cotton curtains and blue hangings caught up with cords of fine linen and purple to silver rings[b] and marble pillars, and also couches of gold and silver on a mosaic pavement of porphyry, marble, mother-of-pearl and precious stones. 7 Drinks were served in golden goblets, goblets of different kinds, and the royal wine was lavished according to the bounty of the king. 8 And drinking was according to the law, no one was compelled; for the king had given orders to all the officials of his palace to do as every man desired. 9 Queen Vash'tī also gave a banquet for the women in the palace which belonged to King Å·haś'ū-ē'rŭs.

10 On the seventh day, when the heart of the king was merry with wine, he commanded Me·hü'măn, Biz'thă, Här·bō'nă, Big'thă and Å·bag'thă, Zē'thär and Cär'kas, the seven eunuchs who served King Å·haś'ū-ē'rŭs as chamberlains, 11 to bring Queen Vash'tī before the king with her royal crown, in order to show the peoples and the princes her beauty; for she was fair to behold. 12 But Queen Vash'tī refused to come at the king's command conveyed by the eunuchs. At this the king was enraged, and his anger burned within him.

13 Then the king said to the wise men who knew the times—for this was the king's procedure toward all who were versed in law and judgment, 14 the men next to him being Cär·shē'nă, Shē'thär, Ad·mā'thă, Tär'shish, Mē'rĕś, Mär·sē'nă, and Me·mū'căn, the seven princes of Persia and Media, who saw the king's face, and sat first in the kingdom—: 15 "According to the law, what is to be done to Queen Vash'tī, because she has not performed the command of King Å·haś'ū-ē'rŭs conveyed by the eunuchs?" 16 Then Me·mū'căn said in presence of the king and the princes, "Not only to the king has Queen Vash'tī done wrong, but also to all the princes and all the peoples who are in all the provinces of King Å·haś'ū-ē'rŭs. 17 For this deed of the queen will be made known to all women, causing them to look with contempt upon their husbands, since they will say, 'King Å·haś'ū-ē'rŭs commanded Queen Vash'tī to be brought before him, and she did not come.' 18 This very day the ladies of Persia and Media who have heard of the queen's behavior will be telling it to all the king's princes, and there will be contempt and wrath in plenty. 19 If it please the king, let a royal order go forth from him, and let it be written among the laws of the Persians and the Medes so that it may not be altered, that Vash'tī is to come no more before King Å·haś'ū-ē'rŭs; and let the king give her royal position to another who is better than she. 20 So when the decree made by the king is proclaimed throughout all his kingdom, vast as it is, all women will give honor to their husbands, high and low." 21 This advice pleased the king and the princes, and the king did as Me·mū'căn proposed; 22 he sent letters to all the royal provinces, to every province in its own script and to every people in its own language, that every man be lord in his own house and speak according to the language of his people.

2 After these things, when the anger of King Å·haś'ū-ē'rŭs had abated, he remembered Vash'tī and what she had done and what had been

a Heb *the army*
b Or *rods*

410

decreed against her. 2 Then the king's servants who attended him said, "Let beautiful young virgins be sought out for the king. 3 And let the king appoint officers in all the provinces of his kingdom to gather all the beautiful young virgins to the harem in Su'sà the capital, under custody of Heg'äi the king's eunuch who is in charge of the women; let their ointments be given them. 4 And let the maiden who pleases the king be queen instead of Vash'ti." This pleased the king, and he did so.

5 Now there was a Jew in Su'sà the capital whose name was Môr'de·cäi, the son of Jä'ir, son of Shim'e·ī, son of Kish, a Benjaminite, 6 who had been carried away from Jerusalem among the captives carried away with Jec·o·nī'äh king of Judah, whom Ne·bù·chàd·nez'zàr king of Babylon had carried away. 7 He had brought up Hà·das'sàh, that is Esther, the daughter of his uncle, for she had neither father nor mother; the maiden was beautiful and lovely, and when her father and her mother died, Môr'de·cäi adopted her as his own daughter. 8 So when the king's order and his edict were proclaimed, and when many maidens were gathered in Su'sà the capital in custody of Heg'äi, Esther also was taken into the king's palace and put in custody of Hegai who had charge of the women. 9 And the maiden pleased him and won his favor; and he quickly provided her with her ointments and her portion of food, and with seven chosen maids from the king's palace, and advanced her and her maids to the best place in the harem. 10 Esther had not made known her people or kindred, for Môr'de·cäi had charged her not to make it known. 11 And every day Môr'de·cäi walked in front of the court of the harem, to learn how Esther was and how she fared.

12 Now when the turn came for each maiden to go in to King Á·hàs'ū·ē'rùs, after being twelve months under the regulations for the women, since this was the regular period of their beautifying, six months with oil of myrrh and six months with spices and ointments for women—13 when the maiden went in to the king in this way she was given whatever she desired to take with her from the harem to the king's palace. 14 In the evening she went, and in the morning she came back to the second harem in custody of Shà·ash'gaz the king's eunuch who was in charge of the concubines; she

did not go in to the king again, unless the king delighted in her and she was summoned by name.

15 When the turn came for Esther the daughter of Ab'i·häil the uncle of Môr'de·cäi, who had adopted her as his own daughter, to go in to the king, she asked for nothing except what Heg'äi the king's eunuch, who had charge of the women, advised. Now Esther found favor in the eyes of all who saw her. 16 And when Esther was taken to King Á·hàs'ū·ē'rùs into his royal palace in the tenth month, which is the month of Tē'beth, in the seventh year of his reign, 17 the king loved Esther more than all the women, and she found grace and favor in his sight more than all the virgins, so that he set the royal crown on her head and made her queen instead of Vash'ti. 18 Then the king gave a great banquet to all his princes and servants; it was Esther's banquet. He also granted a remission of taxes[c] to the provinces, and gave gifts with royal liberality.

19 When the virgins were gathered together the second time, Môr'de·cäi was sitting at the king's gate. 20 Now Esther had not made known her kindred or her people, as Môr'de·cäi had charged her; for Esther obeyed Mordecai just as when she was brought up by him. 21 And in those days, as Môr'de·cäi was sitting at the king's gate, Big'than and Tē'resh, two of the king's eunuchs, who guarded the threshold, became angry and sought to lay hands on King Á·hàs'ū·ē'rùs. 22 And this came to the knowledge of Môr'de·cäi, and he told it to Queen Esther, and Esther told the king in the name of Mordecai. 23 When the affair was investigated and found to be so, the men were both hanged on the gallows. And it was recorded in the Book of the Chronicles in the presence of the king.

3 After these things King Á·hàs'ū·ē'rùs promoted Hä'màn the Ag'à·gite, the son of Ham·mė·dā'thà, and advanced him and set his seat above all the princes who were with him. 2 And all the king's servants who were at the king's gate bowed down and did obeisance to Hä'màn; for the king had so commanded concerning him. But Môr'de·cäi did not bow down or do obeisance. 3 Then the king's servants who were at the king's gate said to Môr'de·cäi, "Why do you transgress the king's command?" 4 And when they spoke to him day after day and he would not listen to them, they told

Or *a holiday*

Hā′màn, in order to see whether Môr′de·cäi′š words would avail; for he had told them that he was a Jew. ⁵And when Hā′màn saw that Môr′de·cäi did not bow down or do obeisance to him, Haman was filled with fury. ⁶ But he disdained to lay hands on Môr′de·cäi alone. So, as they had made known to him the people of Môr′de·cäi, Hā′màn sought to destroy all the Jews, the people of Mordecai, throughout the whole kingdom of Å·haš′ū-ē′rùs.

7 In the first month, which is the month of Ni′sàn, in the twelfth year of King Å·haš′ū-ē′rùs, they cast Pür, that is the lot, before Hā′màn day after day; and they cast it month after month till the twelfth month, which is the month of Å·där′. ⁸ Then Hā′màn said to King Å·haš′ū-ē′rùs, "There is a certain people scattered abroad and dispersed among the peoples in all the provinces of your kingdom; their laws are different from those of every other people, and they do not keep the king's laws, so that it is not for the king's profit to tolerate them. ⁹ If it please the king, let it be decreed that they be destroyed, and I will pay ten thousand talents of silver into the hands of those who have charge of the king's business, that they may put it into the king's treasuries." ¹⁰ So the king took his signet ring from his hand and gave it to Hā′màn the Ag′à·gite, the son of Ham·mè·dā′thà, the enemy of the Jews. ¹¹And the king said to Hā′màn, "The money is given to you, the people also, to do with them as it seems good to you."

12 Then the king's secretaries were summoned on the thirteenth day of the first month, and an edict, according to all that Hā′màn commanded, was written to the king's satraps and to the governors over all the provinces and to the princes of all the peoples, to every province in its own script and every people in its own language; it was written in the name of King Å·haš′ū-ē′rùs and sealed with the king's ring. ¹³ Letters were sent by couriers to all the king's provinces, to destroy, to slay, and to annihilate all Jews, young and old, women and children, in one day, the thirteenth day of the twelfth month, which is the month of Å·där′, and to plunder their goods. ¹⁴A copy of the document was to be issued as a decree in every province by proclamation to all the peoples to be ready for that day. ¹⁵ The couriers went in haste by order of the king, and the decree was issued in Su′sà the capital. And the king and

Hā′màn sat down to drink; but the city of Susa was perplexed.

4 When Môr′de·cäi learned all that had been done, Mordecai rent his clothes and put on sackcloth and ashes, and went out into the midst of the city, wailing with a loud and bitter cry; ² he went up to the entrance of the king's gate, for no one might enter the king's gate clothed with sackcloth. ³And in every province, wherever the king's command and his decree came, there was great mourning among the Jews, with fasting and weeping and lamenting, and most of them lay in sackcloth and ashes.

4 When Esther's maids and her eunuchs came and told her, the queen was deeply distressed; she sent garments to clothe Môr′de·cäi, so that he might take off his sackcloth, but he would not accept them. ⁵ Then Esther called for Hā′thach, one of the king's eunuchs, who had been appointed to attend her, and ordered him to go to Môr′de·cäi to learn what this was and why it was. ⁶ Hā′thach went out to Môr′de·cäi in the open square of the city in front of the king's gate, ⁷ and Môr′de·cäi told him all that had happened to him, and the exact sum of money that Hā′màn had promised to pay into the king's treasuries for the destruction of the Jews. ⁸ Môr′de·cäi also gave him a copy of the written decree issued in Su′sà for their destruction, that he might show it to Esther and explain it to her and charge her to go to the king to make supplication to him and entreat him for her people. ⁹And Hā′thach went and told Esther what Môr′de·cäi had said. ¹⁰ Then Esther spoke to Hā′thach and gave him a message for Môr′de·cäi, saying, ¹¹ "All the king's servants and the people of the king's provinces know that if any man or woman goes to the king inside the inner court without being called, there is but one law; all alike are to be put to death, except the one to whom the king holds out the golden scepter that he may live. And I have not been called to come in to the king these thirty days." ¹²And they told Môr′de·cäi what Esther had said. ¹³ Then Môr′de·cäi told them to return answer to Esther, "Think not that in the king's palace you will escape any more than all the other Jews. ¹⁴ For if you keep silence at such a time as this, relief and deliverance will rise for the Jews from another quarter, but you and your father's house will perish. And who knows whether you have not come to the

kingdom for such a time as this?" [15] Then Esther told them to reply to Môr′de·cäi, [16] "Go, gather all the Jews to be found in Su′sà, and hold a fast on my behalf, and neither eat nor drink for three days, night or day. I and my maids will also fast as you do. Then I will go to the king, though it is against the law; and if I perish, I perish." [17] Môr′de·cäi then went away and did everything as Esther had ordered him.

5 On the third day Esther put on her royal robes and stood in the inner court of the king's palace, opposite the king's hall. The king was sitting on his royal throne inside the palace opposite the entrance to the palace; [2] and when the king saw Queen Esther standing in the court, she found favor in his sight and he held out to Esther the golden scepter that was in his hand. Then Esther approached and touched the top of the scepter. [3] And the king said to her, "What is it, Queen Esther? What is your request? It shall be given you, even to the half of my kingdom." [4] And Esther said, "If it please the king, let the king and Hä′màn come this day to a dinner that I have prepared for the king." [5] Then said the king, "Bring Hä′màn quickly, that we may do as Esther desires." So the king and Haman came to the dinner that Esther had prepared. [6] And as they were drinking wine, the king said to Esther, "What is your petition? It shall be granted you. And what is your request? Even to the half of my kingdom, it shall be fulfilled." [7] But Esther said, "My petition and my request is: [8] If I have found favor in the sight of the king, and if it please the king to grant my petition and fulfil my request, let the king and Hä′màn come tomorrow[d] to the dinner which I will prepare for them, and tomorrow I will do as the king has said."

[9] And Hä′màn went out that day joyful and glad of heart. But when Haman saw Môr′de·cäi in the king's gate, that he neither rose nor trembled before him, he was filled with wrath against Mordecai. [10] Nevertheless Hä′màn restrained himself, and went home; and he sent and fetched his friends and his wife Zē′resh. [11] And Hä′màn recounted to them the splendor of his riches, the number of his sons, all the promotions with which the king had honored him, and how he had advanced him above the princes and the servants of the king. [12] And

Hä′màn added, "Even Queen Esther let no one come with the king to the banquet she prepared but myself. And tomorrow also I am invited by her together with the king. [13] Yet all this does me no good, so long as I see Môr′de·cäi the Jew sitting at the king's gate." [14] Then his wife Zē′resh and all his friends said to him, "Let a gallows fifty cubits high be made, and in the morning tell the king to have Môr′de·cäi hanged upon it; then go merrily with the king to the dinner." This counsel pleased Hä′màn, and he had the gallows made.

6 On that night the king could not sleep; and he gave orders to bring the book of memorable deeds, the chronicles, and they were read before the king. [2] And it was found written how Môr′de·cäi had told about Big·thä′nà and Tē′resh, two of the king's eunuchs, who guarded the threshold, and who had sought to lay hands upon King À·has′ū·ē′rùs. [3] And the king said, "What honor or dignity has been bestowed on Môr′de·cäi for this?" The king's servants who had attended him said, "Nothing has been done for him." [4] And the king said, "Who is in the court?" Now Hä′màn had just entered the outer court of the king's palace to speak to the king about having Môr′de·cäi hanged on the gallows that he had prepared for him. [5] So the king's servants told him, "Hä′màn is there, standing in the court." And the king said, "Let him come in." [6] So Hä′màn came in, and the king said to him, "What shall be done to the man whom the king delights to honor?" And Haman said to himself, "Whom would the king delight to honor more than me?" [7] And Hä′màn said to the king, "For the man whom the king delights to honor, [8] let royal robes be brought, which the king has worn, and the horse which the king has ridden, and on whose head a royal crown is set; [9] and let the robes and the horse be handed over to one of the king's most noble princes; let him[e] array the man whom the king delights to honor, and let him[e] conduct the man on horseback through the open square of the city, proclaiming before him: 'Thus shall it be done to the man whom the king delights to honor.'" [10] Then the king said to Hä′màn, "Make haste, take the robes and the horse, as you have said, and do so to Môr′de·cäi the Jew who sits at the king's gate. Leave out nothing that you have mentioned." [11] So Hä′màn took the robes and the

---

d Gk: Heb lacks *tomorrow*   *e* Heb *them*   **5.3, 6:** Mk 6.23.

horse, and he arrayed Môr′de·cäi and made him ride through the open square of the city, proclaiming, "Thus shall it be done to the man whom the king delights to honor."

12 Then Môr′de·cäi returned to the king's gate. But Hā′màn hurried to his house, mourning and with his head covered. ¹³And Hā′màn told his wife Ze′resh and all his friends everything that had befallen him. Then his wise men and his wife Zeresh said to him, "If Môr′de·cäi, before whom you have begun to fall, is of the Jewish people, you will not prevail against him but will surely fall before him."

14 While they were yet talking with him, the king's eunuchs arrived and brought Hā′màn in haste to the banquet that Esther had prepared.

7 So the king and Hā′màn went in to feast with Queen Esther. ²And on the second day, as they were drinking wine, the king again said to Esther, "What is your petition, Queen Esther? It shall be granted you. And what is your request? Even to the half of my kingdom, it shall be fulfilled." ³ Then Queen Esther answered, "If I have found favor in your sight, O king, and if it please the king, let my life be given me at my petition, and my people at my request. ⁴ For we are sold, I and my people, to be destroyed, to be slain, and to be annihilated. If we had been sold merely as slaves, men and women, I would have held my peace; for our affliction is not to be compared with the loss to the king." ⁵ Then King Ā·haś′ū-ē′rùs said to Queen Esther, "Who is he, and where is he, that would presume to do this?" ⁶And Esther said, "A foe and enemy! This wicked Hā′màn!" Then Haman was in terror before the king and the queen. ⁷And the king rose from the feast in wrath and went into the palace garden; but Hā′màn stayed to beg his life from Queen Esther, for he saw that evil was determined against him by the king. ⁸And the king returned from the palace garden to the place where they were drinking wine, where Hā′màn was falling on the couch where Esther was; and the king said, "Will he even assault the queen in my presence, in my own house?" As the words left the mouth of the king, they covered Haman's face. ⁹ Then said Här·bō′nà, one of the eunuchs in attendance on the king, "Moreover, the gallows which Hā′màn has prepared for Môr′de·cäi, whose word saved the king, is standing in Haman's house, fifty cubits

7.2: Mk 6.23.

high." ¹⁰And the king said, "Hang him on that." So they hanged Hā′màn on the gallows which he had prepared for Môr′de·cäi. Then the anger of the king abated.

8 On that day King Ā·haś′ū-ē′rùs gave to Queen Esther the house of Hā′màn, the enemy of the Jews. And Môr′de·cäi came before the king, for Esther had told what he was to her; ² and the king took off his signet ring, which he had taken from Hā′màn, and gave it to Môr′de·cäi. And Esther set Mordecai over the house of Haman.

3 Then Esther spoke again to the king; she fell at his feet and besought him with tears to avert the evil design of Hā′màn the Ag′à·gïte and the plot which he had devised against the Jews. ⁴And the king held out the golden scepter to Esther, ⁵ and Esther rose and stood before the king. And she said, "If it please the king, and if I have found favor in his sight, and if the thing seem right before the king, and I be pleasing in his eyes, let an order be written to revoke the letters devised by Hā′màn the Ag′à·gïte, the son of Ham·mé·dä′thà, which he wrote to destroy the Jews who are in all the provinces of the king. ⁶ For how can I endure to see the calamity that is coming to my people? Or how can I endure to see the destruction of my kindred?" ⁷ Then King Ā·haś′ū-ē′rùs said to Queen Esther and to Môr′de·cäi the Jew, "Behold, I have given Esther the house of Hā′màn, and they have hanged him on the gallows, because he would lay hands on the Jews. ⁸And you may write as you please with regard to the Jews, in the name of the king, and seal it with the king's ring; for an edict written in the name of the king and sealed with the king's ring cannot be revoked."

9 The king's secretaries were summoned at that time, in the third month, which is the month of Sī′vàn, on the twenty-third day; and an edict was written according to all that Môr′de·cäi commanded concerning the Jews to the satraps and the governors and the princes of the provinces from India to Ethiopia, a hundred and twenty-seven provinces, to every province in its own script and to every people in its own language, and also to the Jews in their script and their language. ¹⁰ The writing was in the name of King Ā·haś′ū-ē′rùs and sealed with the king's ring, and letters were sent by mounted couriers riding on swift

horses that were used in the king's service, bred from the royal stud. 11 By these the king allowed the Jews who were in every city to gather and defend their lives, to destroy, to slay, and to annihilate any armed force of any people or province that might attack them, with their children and women, and to plunder their goods, 12 upon one day throughout all the provinces of King Ȧ·hȧs´ū–ē´rŭs, on the thirteenth day of the twelfth month, which is the month of Ȧ·där´. 13 A copy of what was written was to be issued as a decree in every province, and by proclamation to all peoples, and the Jews were to be ready on that day to avenge themselves upon their enemies. 14 So the couriers, mounted on their swift horses that were used in the king's service, rode out in haste, urged by the king's command; and the decree was issued in Su´sȧ the capital.

15 Then Môr´de·cȧi went out from the presence of the king in royal robes of blue and white, with a great golden crown and a mantle of fine linen and purple, while the city of Su´sȧ shouted and rejoiced. 16 The Jews had light and gladness and joy and honor. 17 And in every province and in every city, wherever the king's command and his edict came, there was gladness and joy among the Jews, a feast and a holiday. And many from the peoples of the country declared themselves Jews, for the fear of the Jews had fallen upon them.

9 Now in the twelfth month, which is the month of Ȧ·där´, on the thirteenth day of the same, when the king's command and edict were about to be executed, on the very day when the enemies of the Jews hoped to get the mastery over them, but which had been changed to a day when the Jews should get the mastery over their foes, the Jews gathered in their cities throughout all the provinces of King Ȧ·hȧs´ū–ē´rŭs to lay hands on such as ought their hurt. And no one could make a stand against them, for the fear of them had fallen upon all peoples. All the princes of the provinces and the satraps and the governors and the royal officials also helped the Jews, for the fear of Môr´de·cȧi had fallen upon them. 4 For Môr´de·cȧi was great in the king's house, and his fame spread throughout all the provinces; for the man Mordecai grew more and more powerful. 5 So the Jews smote all their enemies with the sword, slaughtering, and destroying them, and did as they pleased to those who hated them. 6 In

Su´sȧ the capital itself the Jews slew and destroyed five hundred men, 7 and also slew Pär·shȧn·dä´thȧ and Dal´phon and As·pä´thȧ 8 and Pō·rä´thȧ and Ȧ·dä´li·ȧ and Ȧr·i·dä´thȧ 9 and Pȧr·mash´tȧ and Ȧr´i·säi and Ȧr´i·däi and Väi·zä´thȧ, 10 the ten sons of Hä´mȧn the son of Ham·mė·dä´thȧ, the enemy of the Jews; but they laid no hand on the plunder.

11 That very day the number of those slain in Su´sȧ the capital was reported to the king. 12 And the king said to Queen Esther. "In Su´sȧ the capital the Jews have slain five hundred men and also the ten sons of Hä´mȧn. What then have they done in the rest of the king's provinces! Now what is your petition? It shall be granted you. And what further is your request? It shall be fulfilled." 13 And Esther said, "If it please the king, let the Jews who are in Su´sȧ be allowed tomorrow also to do according to this day's edict. And let the ten sons of Hä´mȧn be hanged on the gallows." 14 So the king commanded this to be done; a decree was issued in Su´sȧ, and the ten sons of Hä´mȧn were hanged. 15 The Jews who were in Su´sȧ gathered also on the fourteenth day of the month of Ȧ·där´ and they slew three hundred men in Susa; but they laid no hands on the plunder.

16 Now the other Jews who were in the king's provinces also gathered to defend their lives, and got relief from their enemies, and slew seventy-five thousand of those who hated them; but they laid no hands on the plunder. 17 This was on the thirteenth day of the month of Ȧ·där´, and on the fourteenth day they rested and made that a day of feasting and gladness. 18 But the Jews who were in Su´sȧ gathered on the thirteenth day and on the fourteenth, and rested on the fifteenth day, making that a day of feasting and gladness. 19 Therefore the Jews of the villages, who live in the open towns, hold the fourteenth day of the month of Ȧ·där´ as a day for gladness and feasting and holiday-making, and a day on which they send choice portions to one another.

20 And Môr´de·cȧi recorded these things, and sent letters to all the Jews who were in all the provinces of King Ȧ·hȧs´ū–ē´rŭs, both near and far, 21 enjoining them that they should keep the fourteenth day of the month Ȧ·där´ and also the fifteenth day of the same, year by year, 22 as the days on which the Jews got relief from their enemies, and as the month that had

been turned for them from sorrow into gladness and from mourning into a holiday; that they should make them days of feasting and gladness, days for sending choice portions to one another and gifts to the poor.

23 So the Jews undertook to do as they had begun, and as Môr′de·cäi had written to them. 24 For Hä′man the Ag′á·gite, the son of Ham·mé·dä′thá, the enemy of all the Jews, had plotted against the Jews to destroy them, and had cast Pür, that is the lot, to crush and destroy them; 25 but when Esther came before the king, he gave orders in writing that his wicked plot which he had devised against the Jews should come upon his own head, and that he and his sons should be hanged on the gallows. 26 Therefore they called these days Pür′im, after the term Pür. And therefore, because of all that was written in this letter, and of what they had faced in this matter, and of what had befallen them, 27 the Jews ordained and took it upon themselves and their descendants and all who joined them, that without fail they would keep these two days according to what was written and at the time appointed every year, 28 that these days should be remembered and kept throughout every generation, in every family, province, and city, and that these days of Pür′im should never fall into disuse among

the Jews, nor should the commemoration of these days cease among their descendants.

29 Then Queen Esther, the daughter of Ab′i·häil, and Môr′de·cäi the Jew gave full written authority, confirming this second letter about Pür′im. 30 Letters were sent to all the Jews, to the hundred and twenty-seven provinces of the kingdom of Á·has̄′ū̇-ē′rùs, in words of peace and truth, 31 that these days of Pür′im should be observed at their appointed seasons, as Môr′de·cäi the Jew and Queen Esther enjoined upon the Jews, and as they had laid down for themselves and for their descendants, with regard to their fasts and their lamenting. 32 The command of Queen Esther fixed these practices of Pür′im, and it was recorded in writing.

10 King Á·has̄′ū̇-ē′rùs laid tribute on the land and on the coastlands of the sea. 2 And all the acts of his power and might, and the full account of the high honor of Môr′de·cäi, to which the king advanced him, are they not written in the Book of the Chronicles of the kings of Media and Persia? 3 For Môr′de·cäi the Jew was next in rank to King Á·has̄′ū̇-ē′rùs, and he was great among the Jews and popular with the multitude of his brethren, for he sought the welfare of his people and spoke peace to all his people.

THE BOOK OF

JOB

1 There was a man in the land of Uz, whose name was Jōb; and that man was blameless and upright, one who feared God, and turned away from evil. 2 There were born to him seven sons and three daughters. 3 He had seven thousand sheep, three thousand camels, five hundred yoke of oxen, and five hundred she-asses, and very many servants; so that this man was the greatest of all the people of the east. 4 His sons used to go and hold a feast in the house of each on his day; and they would send and invite their three sisters to eat and drink with them. 5 And when the days of the feast had run their course, Jōb would send and

sanctify them, and he would rise early in the morning and offer burnt offerings according to the number of them all; for Jōb said, "It may be that my sons have sinned, and cursed God in their hearts." Thus Jōb did continually.

6 Now there was a day when the sons of God came to present themselves before the Lord, and Satan*a* also came among them. 7 The Lord said to Satan, "Whence have you come?" Satan answered the Lord, "From going to and fro on the earth, and from walking up and down on it." 8 And the Lord said to Satan, "Have you considered my servant Jōb, that there i

a Heb *the adversary*

none like him on the earth, a blameless and upright man, who fears God and turns away from evil?" 9 Then Satan answered the LORD, "Does Jōb fear God for nought? 10 Hast thou not put a hedge about him and his house and all that he has, on every side? Thou hast blessed the work of his hands, and his possessions have increased in the land. 11 But put forth thy hand now, and touch all that he has, and he will curse thee to thy face." 12And the LORD said to Satan, "Behold, all that he has is in your power; only upon himself do not put forth your hand." So Satan went forth from the presence of the LORD.

13 Now there was a day when his sons and daughters were eating and drinking wine in their eldest brother's house; 14 and there came a messenger to Jōb, and said, "The oxen were plowing and the asses feeding beside them; 15 and the Sà·bē'ăns fell upon them and took them, and slew the servants with the edge of the sword; and I alone have escaped to tell you." 16 While he was yet speaking, there came another, and said, "The fire of God fell from heaven and burned up the sheep and the servants, and consumed them; and I alone have escaped to tell you." 17 While he was yet speaking, there came another, and said, "The Chăl·dē'ăns formed three companies, and made a raid upon the camels and took them, and slew the servants with the edge of the sword; and I alone have escaped to tell you." 18 While he was yet speaking, there came another, and said, "Your sons and daughters were eating and drinking wine in their eldest brother's house; 19 and behold, a great wind came across the wilderness, and struck the four corners of the house, and it fell upon the young people, and they are dead; and I alone have escaped to tell you."

20 Then Jōb arose, and rent his robe, and shaved his head, and fell upon the ground, and worshiped. 1And he said, "Naked I came from my mother's womb, and naked shall I return; the LORD gave, and the LORD has taken away; blessed be the name of the LORD."

22 In all this Jōb did not sin or charge God with wrong.

2 Again there was a day when the sons of God came to present themselves before the LORD, and Satan also came among them to present himself before the LORD. 2And the LORD said

.3-19: Jer 20.14-18.

to Satan, "Whence have you come?" Satan answered the LORD, "From going to and fro on the earth, and from walking up and down on it." 3And the LORD said to Satan, "Have you considered my servant Jōb, that there is none like him on the earth, a blameless and upright man, who fears God and turns away from evil? He still holds fast his integrity, although you moved me against him, to destroy him without cause." 4 Then Satan answered the LORD, "Skin for skin! All that a man has he will give for his life. 5 But put forth thy hand now, and touch his bone and his flesh, and he will curse thee to thy face." 6And the LORD said to Satan, "Behold, he is in your power; only spare his life."

7 So Satan went forth from the presence of the LORD, and afflicted Jōb with loathsome sores from the sole of his foot to the crown of his head. 8And he took a potsherd with which to scrape himself, and sat among the ashes.

9 Then his wife said to him, "Do you still hold fast your integrity? Curse God, and die." 10 But he said to her, "You speak as one of the foolish women would speak. Shall we receive good at the hand of God, and shall we not receive evil?" In all this Jōb did not sin with his lips.

11 Now when Jōb's three friends heard of all this evil that had come upon him, they came each from his own place, E·lī'phaz the Tē'mà·nīte, Bĭl'dad the Shū'hīte, and Zō'phär the Nā'á·mà·thīte. They made an appointment together to come to condole with him and comfort him. 12And when they saw him from afar, they did not recognize him; and they raised their voices and wept; and they rent their robes and sprinkled dust upon their heads toward heaven. 13And they sat with him on the ground seven days and seven nights, and no one spoke a word to him, for they saw that his suffering was very great.

3 After this Jōb opened his mouth and cursed the day of his birth. 2 And Jōb said:
3 "Let the day perish wherein I was born,
  and the night which said,
  'A man-child is conceived.'
4 Let that day be darkness!
  May God above not seek it,
  nor light shine upon it.
5 Let gloom and deep darkness claim it.
  Let clouds dwell upon it;

let the blackness of the day terrify
it.

6 That night—let thick darkness seize
it!
let it not rejoice among the days
of the year,
let it not come into the number
of the months.

7 Yea, let that night be barren;
let no joyful cry be heard[b] in it.

8 Let those curse it who curse the
day,
who are skilled to rouse up
Le·vi'a·than.

9 Let the stars of its dawn be dark;
let it hope for light, but have
none,
nor see the eyelids of the morning;

10 because it did not shut the doors of
my mother's womb,
nor hide trouble from my eyes.

11 "Why did I not die at birth,
come forth from the womb and
expire?

12 Why did the knees receive me?
Or why the breasts, that I should
suck?

13 For then I should have lain down
and been quiet;
I should have slept; then I should
have been at rest,

14 with kings and counselors of the
earth
who rebuilt ruins for themselves,

15 or with princes who had gold,
who filled their houses with silver.

16 Or why was I not as a hidden untimely birth,
as infants that never see the light?

17 There the wicked cease from
troubling,
and there the weary are at rest.

18 There the prisoners are at ease
together;
they hear not the voice of the
taskmaster.

19 The small and the great are there,
and the slave is free from his
master.

20 "Why is light given to him that is
in misery,
and life to the bitter in soul,

21 who long for death, but it comes not,
and dig for it more than for hid
treasures;

22 who rejoice exceedingly,
and are glad, when they find the
grave?

23 Why is light given to a man whose
way is hid,
whom God has hedged in?

24 For my sighing comes as[c] my bread,

and my groanings are poured out
like water.

25 For the thing that I fear comes upon
me,
and what I dread befalls me.

26 I am not at ease, nor am I quiet;
I have no rest; but trouble comes."

4 Then E·li'phaz the Te'ma·nite
answered:

2 "If one ventures a word with you,
will you be offended?
Yet who can keep from speaking?

3 Behold, you have instructed many,
and you have strengthened the
weak hands.

4 Your words have upheld him who
was stumbling,
and you have made firm the
feeble knees.

5 But now it has come to you, and you
are impatient;
it touches you, and you are dismayed.

6 Is not your fear of God your confidence,
and the integrity of your ways
your hope?

7 "Think now, who that was innocent
ever perished?
Or where were the upright cut
off?

8 As I have seen, those who plow
iniquity
and sow trouble reap the same.

9 By the breath of God they perish,
and by the blast of his anger they
are consumed.

10 The roar of the lion, the voice of
the fierce lion,
the teeth of the young lions, are
broken.

11 The strong lion perishes for lack of
prey,
and the whelps of the lioness are
scattered.

12 "Now a word was brought to me
stealthily,
my ear received the whisper of it

13 Amid thoughts from visions of the
night,
when deep sleep falls on men,

14 dread came upon me, and trembling
which made all my bones shake.

15 A spirit glided past my face;
the hair of my flesh stood up.

16 It stood still,
but I could not discern its appearance.
A form was before my eyes;
there was silence, then I heard
voice:

b Heb *come*   *c* Heb *before*

17 'Can mortal man be righteous before[d] God?
Can a man be pure before[d] his Maker?
18 Even in his servants he puts no trust, and his angels he charges with error;
19 how much more those who dwell in houses of clay,
whose foundation is in the dust, who are crushed before the moth.
20 Between morning and evening they are destroyed;
they perish for ever without any regarding it.
21 If their tent-cord is plucked up within them,
do they not die, and that without wisdom?'

5   "Call now; is there any one who will answer you?
To which of the holy ones will you turn?
2 Surely vexation kills the fool,
and jealousy slays the simple.
3 I have seen the fool taking root,
but suddenly I cursed his dwelling.
4 His sons are far from safety,
they are crushed in the gate,
and there is no one to deliver them.
5 His harvest the hungry eat,
and he takes it even out of thorns;[e]
and the thirsty[f] pant after his[g] wealth.
6 For affliction does not come from the dust,
nor does trouble sprout from the ground;
7 but man is born to trouble
as the sparks fly upward.

8 "As for me, I would seek God,
and to God would I commit my cause;
9 who does great things and unsearchable,
marvelous things without number:
10 he gives rain upon the earth
and sends waters upon the fields;
11 he sets on high those who are lowly,
and those who mourn are lifted to safety.
12 He frustrates the devices of the crafty,
so that their hands achieve no success.
13 He takes the wise in their own craftiness;

and the schemes of the wily are brought to a quick end.
14 They meet with darkness in the daytime,
and grope at noonday as in the night.
15 But he saves the fatherless from their mouth,[h]
the needy from the hand of the mighty.
16 So the poor have hope,
and injustice shuts her mouth.

17 "Behold, happy is the man whom God reproves;
therefore despise not the chastening of the Almighty.
18 For he wounds, but he binds up;
he smites, but his hands heal.
19 He will deliver you from six troubles;
in seven there shall no evil touch you.
20 In famine he will redeem you from death,
and in war from the power of the sword.
21 You shall be hid from the scourge of the tongue,
and shall not fear destruction when it comes.
22 At destruction and famine you shall laugh,
and shall not fear the beasts of the earth.
23 For you shall be in league with the stones of the field,
and the beasts of the field shall be at peace with you.
24 You shall know that your tent is safe,
and you shall inspect your fold and miss nothing.
25 You shall know also that your descendants shall be many,
and your offspring as the grass of the earth.
26 You shall come to your grave in ripe old age,
as a shock of grain comes up to the threshing floor in its season.
27 Lo, this we have searched out; it is true.
Hear, and know it for your good."[i]

6   Then Jōb answered:
2 "O that my vexation were weighed,
and all my calamity laid in the balances!
3 For then it would be heavier than the sand of the sea;

---

[d] Or more than   [e] Heb obscure
[f] Aquila Symmachus Syr Vg: Heb snare   [g] Heb their   [h] Cn: Heb uncertain
[i] Heb for yourself
5.12–13: 1 Cor 3.19.

therefore my words have been rash.

4 For the arrows of the Almighty are in me;
    my spirit drinks their poison;
    the terrors of God are arrayed against me.
5 Does the wild ass bray when he has grass,
    or the ox low over his fodder?
6 Can that which is tasteless be eaten without salt,
    or is there any taste in the slime of the purslane?[j]
7 My appetite refuses to touch them,
    they are as food that is loathsome to me.[k]

8 "O that I might have my request,
    and that God would grant my desire;
9 that it would please God to crush me,
    that he would let loose his hand and cut me off!
10 This would be my consolation;
    I would even exult[l] in pain unsparing;
    for I have not denied the words of the Holy One.
11 What is my strength, that I should wait?
    And what is my end, that I should be patient?
12 Is my strength the strength of stones,
    or is my flesh bronze?
13 In truth I have no help in me,
    and any resource is driven from me.

14 "He who withholds[m] kindness from a friend
    forsakes the fear of the Almighty.
15 My brethren are treacherous as a torrent-bed
    as freshets that pass away,
16 which are dark with ice,
    and where the snow hides itself.
17 In time of heat they disappear;
    when it is hot, they vanish from their place.
18 The caravans turn aside from their course;
    they go up into the waste, and perish.
19 The caravans of Tē'mà look,
    the travelers of Sheba hope.
20 They are disappointed because they were confident;
    they come thither and are confounded.
21 Such you have now become to me;[n]

you see my calamity, and are afraid.
22 Have I said, 'Make me a gift'?
    Or, 'From your wealth offer a bribe for me'?
23 Or, 'Deliver me from the adversary's hand'?
    Or, 'Ransom me from the hand of oppressors'?

24 "Teach me, and I will be silent;
    make me understand how I have erred.
25 How forceful are honest words!
    But what does reproof from you reprove?
26 Do you think that you can reprove words,
    when the speech of a despairing man is wind?
27 You would even cast lots over the fatherless,
    and bargain over your friend.

28 "But now, be pleased to look at me;
    for I will not lie to your face.
29 Turn, I pray, let no wrong be done.
    Turn now, my vindication is at stake.
30 Is there any wrong on my tongue?
    Cannot my taste discern calamity?

7 "Has not man a hard service upon earth,
    and are not his days like the days of a hireling?
2 Like a slave who longs for the shadow,
    and like a hireling who looks for his wages,
3 so I am allotted months of emptiness,
    and nights of misery are apportioned to me.
4 When I lie down I say, 'When shall I arise?'
    But the night is long,
    and I am full of tossing till the dawn.
5 My flesh is clothed with worms and dirt;
    my skin hardens, then breaks out afresh.
6 My days are swifter than a weaver's shuttle,
    and come to their end without hope.

7 "Remember that my life is a breath;
    my eye will never again see good.
8 The eye of him who sees me will behold me no more;

j The meaning of the Hebrew word is uncertain *k* Heb obscure
l The meaning of the Hebrew word is uncertain
m Syr Vg Compare Tg: Heb obscure *n* Cn Compare Gk Syr: Heb obscure

while thy eyes are upon me, I
shall be gone.
9 As the cloud fades and vanishes,
so he who goes down to Shĕ′ōl
does not come up;
10 he returns no more to his house,
nor does his place know him any
more.

11 "Therefore I will not restrain my
mouth;
I will speak in the anguish of my
spirit;
I will complain in the bitterness
of my soul.
12 Am I the sea, or a sea monster,
that thou settest a guard over me?
13 When I say, 'My bed will comfort
me,
my couch will ease my complaint,'
14 then thou dost scare me with dreams
and terrify me with visions,
15 so that I would choose strangling
and death rather than my bones.
16 I loathe my life; I would not live
for ever.
Let me alone, for my days are a
breath.
17 What is man, that thou dost make
so much of him,
and that thou dost set thy mind
upon him,
18 dost visit him every morning,
and test him every moment?
19 How long wilt thou not look away
from me,
nor let me alone till I swallow
my spittle?
20 If I sin, what do I do to thee, thou
watcher of men?
Why hast thou made me thy
mark?
Why have I become a burden to
thee?
21 Why dost thou not pardon my
transgression
and take away my iniquity?
For now I shall lie in the earth;
thou wilt seek me, but I shall
not be."

8 Then Bil′dad the Shū′hite answered:
2 "How long will you say these things,
and the words of your mouth be
a great wind?
3 Does God pervert justice?
Or does the Almighty pervert the
right?
4 If your children have sinned against
him,
he has delivered them into the
power of their transgression.

5 If you will seek God
and make supplication to the
Almighty,
6 if you are pure and upright,
surely then he will rouse himself
for you
and reward you with a rightful
habitation.
7 And though your beginning was
small,
your latter days will be very great.

8 "For inquire, I pray you, of bygone
ages,
and consider what the fathers
have found;
9 for we are but of yesterday, and
know nothing,
for our days on earth are a
shadow.
10 Will they not teach you, and tell you,
and utter words out of their
understanding?

11 "Can papyrus grow where there is
no marsh?
Can reeds flourish where there is
no water?
12 While yet in flower and not cut
down,
they wither before any other
plant.
13 Such are the paths of all who forget
God;
the hope of the godless man shall
perish.
14 His confidence breaks in sunder,
and his trust is a spider's web.*o*
15 He leans against his house, but it
does not stand;
he lays hold of it, but it does not
endure.
16 He thrives before the sun,
and his shoots spread over his
garden.
17 His roots twine about the stone-
heap;
he lives among the rocks.*p*
18 If he is destroyed from his place,
then it will deny him, saying, 'I
have never seen you.'
19 Behold, this is the joy of his way;
and out of the earth others will
spring.

20 "Behold, God will not reject a
blameless man,
nor take the hand of evildoers.
21 He will yet fill your mouth with
laughter,
and your lips with shouting.
22 Those who hate you will be clothed
with shame,

o Heb *house*   *p* Gk Vg: Heb uncertain
7.17: Ps 8.4.

and the tent of the wicked will be no more."

9 Then Jōb answered:

2 "Truly I know that it is so:
  But how can a man be just before God?

3 If one wished to contend with him,
  one could not answer him once in a thousand times.

4 He is wise in heart, and mighty in strength
  —who has hardened himself against him, and succeeded?—

5 he who removes mountains, and they know it not,
  when he overturns them in his anger;

6 who shakes the earth out of its place,
  and its pillars tremble;

7 who commands the sun, and it does not rise;
  who seals up the stars;

8 who alone stretched out the heavens,
  and trampled the waves of the sea;q

9 who made the Bear and Ō·rī′ŏn,
  the Plēi′ȧ·dēs and the chambers of the south;

10 who does great things beyond understanding,
  and marvelous things without number.

11 Lo, he passes by me, and I see him not;
  he moves on, but I do not perceive him.

12 Behold, he snatches away; who can hinder him?
  Who will say to him, 'What doest thou'?

13 "God will not turn back his anger;
  beneath him bowed the helpers of Rā′hab.

14 How then can I answer him,
  choosing my words with him?

15 Though I am innocent, I cannot answer him;
  I must appeal for mercy to my accuser.r

16 If I summoned him and he answered me,
  I would not believe that he was listening to my voice.

17 For he crushes me with a tempest,
  and multiplies my wounds without cause;

18 he will not let me get my breath,
  but fills me with bitterness.

19 If it is a contest of strength, behold him!
  If it is a matter of justice, who can summon him?s

20 Though I am innocent, my own mouth would condemn me;
  though I am blameless, he would prove me perverse.

21 I am blameless; I regard not myself;
  I loathe my life.

22 It is all one; therefore I say,
  he destroys both the blameless and the wicked.

23 When disaster brings sudden death,
  he mocks at the calamity$t$ of the innocent.

24 The earth is given into the hand of the wicked;
  he covers the faces of its judges—
  if it is not he, who then is it?

25 "My days are swifter than a runner;
  they flee away, they see no good.

26 They go by like skiffs of reed,
  like an eagle swooping on the prey.

27 If I say, 'I will forget my complaint,
  I will put off my sad countenance, and be of good cheer,'

28 I become afraid of all my suffering,
  for I know thou wilt not hold me innocent.

29 I shall be condemned;
  why then do I labor in vain?

30 If I wash myself with snow,
  and cleanse my hands with lye,

31 yet thou wilt plunge me into a pit,
  and my own clothes will abhor me.

32 For he is not a man, as I am, that I might answer him,
  that we should come to trial together.

33 There is no$u$ umpire between us,
  who might lay his hand upon us both.

34 Let him take his rod away from me,
  and let not dread of him terrify me.

35 Then I would speak without fear of him,
  for I am not so in myself.

10 "I loathe my life;
  I will give free utterance to my complaint;
  I will speak in the bitterness of my soul.

2 I will say to God, Do not condemn me;

---

q Or *trampled the back of the sea dragon*
r Or *for my right*
s Compare Gk: Heb *me*. The text of the verse is uncertain
t The meaning of the Hebrew word is uncertain
u Another reading is *Would that there were*

let me know why thou dost contend against me.

3 Does it seem good to thee to oppress,
  to despise the work of thy hands
  and favor the designs of the wicked?
4 Hast thou eyes of flesh?
  Dost thou see as man sees?
5 Are thy days as the days of man,
  or thy years as man's years,
6 that thou dost seek out my iniquity
  and search for my sin,
7 although thou knowest that I am not guilty,
  and there is none to deliver out of thy hand?
8 Thy hands fashioned and made me;
  and now thou dost turn about and destroy me.^{v}
9 Remember that thou hast made me of clay;^{w}
  and wilt thou turn me to dust again?
10 Didst thou not pour me out like milk
  and curdle me like cheese?
11 Thou didst clothe me with skin and flesh,
  and knit me together with bones and sinews.
12 Thou hast granted me life and steadfast love;
  and thy care has preserved my spirit.
13 Yet these things thou didst hide in thy heart;
  I know that this was thy purpose.
14 If I sin, thou dost mark me,
  and dost not acquit me of my iniquity.
15 If I am wicked, woe to me!
  If I am righteous, I cannot lift up my head,
  for I am filled with disgrace
  and look upon my affliction.
16 And if I lift myself up,^{x} thou dost hunt me like a lion,
  and again work wonders against me;
17 thou dost renew thy witnesses against me,
  and increase thy vexation toward me;
  thou dost bring fresh hosts against me.^{y}

18 "Why didst thou bring me forth from the womb?
  Would that I had died before any eye had seen me,
19 and were as though I had not been,
  carried from the womb to the grave.
20 Are not the days of my life few?^{z}
  Let me alone, that I may find a little comfort^a
21 before I go whence I shall not return,
  to the land of gloom and deep darkness,
22 the land of gloom^b and chaos,
  where light is as darkness."

11 Then Zŏ′phär the Nā′à·mà·thīte answered:
2 "Should a multitude of words go unanswered,
  and a man full of talk be vindicated?
3 Should your babble silence men,
  and when you mock, shall no one shame you?
4 For you say, 'My doctrine is pure,
  and I am clean in God's eyes.'
5 But oh, that God would speak,
  and open his lips to you,
6 and that he would tell you the secrets of wisdom!
  For he is manifold in understanding.^{c}
  Know then that God exacts of you less than your guilt deserves.

7 "Can you find out the deep things of God?
  Can you find out the limit of the Almighty?
8 It is higher than heaven^d—what can you do?
  Deeper than Shĕ′ōl—what can you know?
9 Its measure is longer than the earth,
  and broader than the sea.
10 If he passes through, and imprisons,
  and calls to judgment, who can hinder him?
11 For he knows worthless men;
  when he sees iniquity, will he not consider it?
12 But a stupid man will get understanding,
  when a wild ass's colt is born a man.

13 "If you set your heart aright,
  you will stretch out your hands toward him.
14 If iniquity is in your hand, put it far away,

^{v} Cn Compare Gk Syr: Heb *made me together round about and thou dost destroy me*
^{w} Gk: Heb *like clay* ^{x} Syr: Heb *he lifts himself up*
^{y} Cn Compare Gk: Heb *changes and a host are with me*
^{z} Cn Compare Gk Syr: Heb *Are not my days few? Let him cease* ^{a} Heb *brighten up*
^{b} Heb *gloom as darkness, deep darkness* ^{c} Heb *obscure* ^{d} Heb *The heights of heaven*

and let not wickedness dwell in your tents.

15 Surely then you will lift up your face without blemish;
you will be secure, and will not fear.

16 You will forget your misery;
you will remember it as waters that have passed away.

17 And your life will be brighter than the noonday;
its darkness will be like the morning.

18 And you will have confidence, because there is hope;
you will be protected[e] and take your rest in safety.

19 You will lie down, and none will make you afraid;
many will entreat your favor.

20 But the eyes of the wicked will fail;
all way of escape will be lost to them,
and their hope is to breathe their last."

12 Then Jōb answered:

2 "No doubt you are the people,
and wisdom will die with you.

3 But I have understanding as well as you;
I am not inferior to you.
Who does not know such things as these?

4 I am a laughingstock to my friends;
I, who called upon God and he answered me,
a just and blameless man, am a laughingstock.

5 In the thought of one who is at ease there is contempt for misfortune;
it is ready for those whose feet slip.

6 The tents of robbers are at peace,
and those who provoke God are secure,
who bring their god in their hand.[f]

7 "But ask the beasts, and they will teach you;
the birds of the air, and they will tell you;

8 or the plants of the earth,[g] and they will teach you;
and the fish of the sea will declare to you.

9 Who among all these does not know that the hand of the LORD has done this?

10 In his hand is the life of every living thing
and the breath of all mankind.

11 Does not the ear try words

as the palate tastes food?

12 Wisdom is with the aged,
and understanding in length of days.

13 "With God[h] are wisdom and might;
he has counsel and understanding.

14 If he tears down, none can rebuild;
if he shuts a man in, none can open.

15 If he withholds the waters, they dry up;
if he sends them out, they overwhelm the land.

16 With him are strength and wisdom;
the deceived and the deceiver are his.

17 He leads counselors away stripped,
and judges he makes fools.

18 He looses the bonds of kings,
and binds a waistcloth on their loins.

19 He leads priests away stripped,
and overthrows the mighty.

20 He deprives of speech those who are trusted,
and takes away the discernment of the elders.

21 He pours contempt on princes,
and looses the belt of the strong.

22 He uncovers the deeps out of darkness,
and brings deep darkness to light.

23 He makes nations great, and he destroys them:
he enlarges nations, and leads them away.

24 He takes away understanding from the chiefs of the people of the earth,
and makes them wander in a pathless waste.

25 They grope in the dark without light;
and he makes them stagger like a drunken man.

13 "Lo, my eye has seen all this,
my ear has heard and understood it.

2 What you know, I also know;
I am not inferior to you.

3 But I would speak to the Almighty,
and I desire to argue my case with God.

4 As for you, you whitewash with lies;
worthless physicians are you all.

5 Oh that you would keep silent,
and it would be your wisdom!

6 Hear now my reasoning,
and listen to the pleadings of my lips.

7 Will you speak falsely for God,
and speak deceitfully for him?

e Or you will look around   f Hebrew uncertain   g Or speak to the earth   h Heb him

8 Will you show partiality toward him,
 will you plead the case for God?
9 Will it be well with you when he
 searches you out?
 Or can you deceive him, as one
 deceives a man?
10 He will surely rebuke you
 if in secret you show partiality.
11 Will not his majesty terrify you,
 and the dread of him fall upon you?
12 Your maxims are proverbs of ashes,
 your defenses are defenses of clay.

13 "Let me have silence, and I will
 speak,
 and let come on me what may.
14 I will take*i* my flesh in my teeth,
 and put my life in my hand.
15 Behold, he will slay me; I have no
 hope;
 yet I will defend my ways to his
 face.
16 This will be my salvation,
 that a godless man shall not come
 before him.
17 Listen carefully to my words,
 and let my declaration be in your
 ears.
18 Behold, I have prepared my case;
 I know that I shall be vindicated.
19 Who is there that will contend with
 me?
 For then I would be silent and die.
20 Only grant two things to me,
 then I will not hide myself from
 thy face:
21 withdraw thy hand far from me,
 and let not dread of thee terrify
 me.
22 Then call, and I will answer;
 or let me speak, and do thou reply
 to me.
23 How many are my iniquities and
 my sins?
 Make me know my transgression
 and my sin.
24 Why dost thou hide thy face,
 and count me as thy enemy?
25 Wilt thou frighten a driven leaf
 and pursue dry chaff?
26 For thou writest bitter things against
 me,
 and makest me inherit the iniquities of my youth.
27 Thou puttest my feet in the stocks,
 and watchest all my paths;
 thou settest a bound to the soles
 of my feet.
28 Man*j* wastes away like a rotten thing,
 like a garment that is moth-eaten.

14 "Man that is born of a woman is
 of few days, and full of trouble.

2 He comes forth like a flower, and
 withers;
 he flees like a shadow, and continues not.
3 And dost thou open thy eyes upon
 such a one
 and bring him*k* into judgment
 with thee?
4 Who can bring a clean thing out of
 an unclean?
 There is not one.
5 Since his days are determined,
 and the number of his months is
 with thee,
 and thou hast appointed his
 bounds that he cannot pass,
6 look away from him, and desist,*l*
 that he may enjoy, like a hireling,
 his day.

7 "For there is hope for a tree,
 if it be cut down, that it will
 sprout again,
 and that its shoots will not cease.
8 Though its root grow old in the
 earth,
 and its stump die in the ground,
9 yet at the scent of water it will bud
 and put forth branches like a
 young plant.
10 But man dies, and is laid low;
 man breathes his last, and where
 is he?
11 As waters fail from a lake,
 and a river wastes away and dries
 up,
12 so man lies down and rises not again;
 till the heavens are no more he
 will not awake,
 or be roused out of his sleep.
13 Oh that thou wouldest hide me in
 Shē'ōl,
 that thou wouldest conceal me
 until thy wrath be past,
 that thou wouldest appoint me a
 set time, and remember me!
14 If a man die, shall he live again?
 All the days of my service I
 would wait,
 till my release should come.
15 Thou wouldest call, and I would
 answer thee;
 thou wouldest long for the work
 of thy hands.
16 For then thou wouldest number my
 steps,
 thou wouldest not keep watch
 over my sin;
17 my transgression would be sealed
 up in a bag,
 and thou wouldest cover over my
 iniquity.

i Gk: Heb *Why should I take?*
j Heb *He*   *k* Gk Syr Vg: Heb *me*
l Cn: Heb *that he may desist*

18 "But the mountain falls and
        crumbles away,
    and the rock is removed from its
        place;
19 the waters wear away the stones;
    the torrents wash away the soil of
        the earth;
    so thou destroyest the hope of
        man.
20 Thou prevailest for ever against
        him, and he passes;
    thou changest his countenance,
        and sendest him away.
21 His sons come to honor, and he does
        not know it;
    they are brought low, and he
        perceives it not.
22 He feels only the pain of his own
        body,
    and he mourns only for himself."

15 Then E·li′phaz the Tē′mà·nīte
    answered:
2 "Should a wise man answer with
        windy knowledge,
    and fill himself with the east
        wind?
3 Should he argue in unprofitable
        talk,
    or in words with which he can
        do no good?
4 But you are doing away with the
        fear of God,
    and hindering meditation before
        God.
5 For your iniquity teaches your
        mouth,
    and you choose the tongue of the
        crafty.
6 Your own mouth condemns you,
        and not I;
    your own lips testify against you.

7 "Are you the first man that was
        born?
    Or were you brought forth before
        the hills?
8 Have you listened in the council of
        God?
    And do you limit wisdom to
        yourself?
9 What do you know that we do not
        know?
    What do you understand that is
        not clear to us?
10 Both the gray-haired and the aged
        are among us,
    older than your father.
11 Are the consolations of God too
        small for you,
    or the word that deals gently with
        you?
12 Why does your heart carry you away,
    and why do your eyes flash,

13 that you turn your spirit against
        God,
    and let such words go out of your
        mouth?
14 What is man, that he can be clean?
    Or he that is born of a woman,
        that he can be righteous?
15 Behold, God puts no trust in his
        holy ones,
    and the heavens are not clean in
        his sight;
16 how much less one who is abomi-
        nable and corrupt,
    a man who drinks iniquity like
        water!

17 "I will show you, hear me;
    and what I have seen I will de-
        clare
18 (what wise men have told,
    and their fathers have not hidden,
19 to whom alone the land was given,
    and no stranger passed among
        them).
20 The wicked man writhes in pain all
        his days,
    through all the years that are laid
        up for the ruthless.
21 Terrifying sounds are in his ears;
    in prosperity the destroyer will
        come upon him.
22 He does not believe that he will
        return out of darkness,
    and he is destined for the sword.
23 He wanders abroad for bread, say-
        ing, 'Where is it?'
    He knows that a day of darkness
        is ready at his hand;
24 distress and anguish terrify him;
    they prevail against him, like a
        king prepared for battle.
25 Because he has stretched forth his
        hand against God,
    and bids defiance to the Almighty,
26 running stubbornly against him
    with a thick-bossed shield;
27 because he has covered his face with
        his fat,
    and gathered fat upon his loins,
28 and has lived in desolate cities,
    in houses which no man should
        inhabit,
    which were destined to become
        heaps of ruins;
29 he will not be rich, and his wealth
        will not endure,
    nor will he strike root in the
        earth;^{m}
30 he will not escape from darkness;
    the flame will dry up his shoots,
    and his blossom^n will be swept
        away^o by the wind.
31 Let him not trust in emptiness,
        deceiving himself;

m Vg: Heb obscure n Gk: Heb mouth o Cn: Heb will depart

for emptiness will be his recompense.

32 It will be paid in full before his time,
and his branch will not be green.

33 He will shake off his unripe grape, like the vine,
and cast off his blossom, like the olive tree.

34 For the company of the godless is barren,
and fire consumes the tents of bribery.

35 They conceive mischief and bring forth evil
and their heart prepares deceit."

16 Then Jōb answered:
2 "I have heard many such things;
miserable comforters are you all.

3 Shall windy words have an end?
Or what provokes you that you answer?

4 I also could speak as you do,
if you were in my place;
I could join words together against you,
and shake my head at you.

5 I could strengthen you with my mouth,
and the solace of my lips would assuage your pain.

6 "If I speak, my pain is not assuaged,
and if I forbear, how much of it leaves me?

7 Surely now God has worn me out;
he has[p] made desolate all my company.

8 And he has[p] shriveled me up,
which is a witness against me;
and my leanness has risen up against me,
it testifies to my face.

9 He has torn me in his wrath, and hated me;
he has gnashed his teeth at me;
my adversary sharpens his eyes against me.

10 Men have gaped at me with their mouth,
they have struck me insolently upon the cheek,
they mass themselves together against me.

11 God gives me up to the ungodly,
and casts me into the hands of the wicked.

12 I was at ease, and he broke me asunder;
he seized me by the neck and dashed me to pieces;
he set me up as his target,

13 his archers surround me.

He slashes open my kidneys, and does not spare;
he pours out my gall on the ground.

14 He breaks me with breach upon breach;
he runs upon me like a warrior.

15 I have sewed sackcloth upon my skin,
and have laid my strength in the dust.

16 My face is red with weeping,
and on my eyelids is deep darkness;

17 although there is no violence in my hands,
and my prayer is pure.

18 "O earth, cover not my blood,
and let my cry find no resting place.

19 Even now, behold, my witness is in heaven,
and he that vouches for me is on high.

20 My friends scorn me;
my eye pours out tears to God,

21 that he would maintain the right of a man with God,
like[q] that of a man with his neighbor.

22 For when a few years have come
I shall go the way whence I shall not return.

17 My spirit is broken, my days are extinct,
the grave is ready for me.

2 Surely there are mockers about me,
and my eye dwells on their provocation.

3 "Lay down a pledge for me with thyself;
who is there that will give surety for me?

4 Since thou hast closed their minds to understanding,
therefore thou wilt not let them triumph.

5 He who informs against his friends to get a share of their property,
the eyes of his children will fail.

6 "He has made me a byword of the peoples,
and I am one before whom men spit.

7 My eye has grown dim from grief,
and all my members are like a shadow.

8 Upright men are appalled at this,
and the innocent stirs himself up against the godless.

9 Yet the righteous holds to his way,

[p] Heb thou hast   [q] Syr Vg Tg: Heb and

and he that has clean hands grows
    stronger and stronger.
10 But you, come on again, all of you,
    and I shall not find a wise man
    among you.
11 My days are past, my plans are
    broken off,
    the desires of my heart.
12 They make night into day;
    'The light,' they say, 'is near to
    the darkness.'ʳ
13 If I look for Shē′ōl as my house,
    if I spread my couch in darkness,
14 if I say to the pit, 'You are my
    father,'
    and to the worm, 'My mother,' or
    'My sister,'
15 where then is my hope?
    Who will see my hope?
16 Will it go down to the bars of Shē′ōl?
    Shall we descend together into
    the dust?''

18 Then Bil′dad the Shü′hite answered:
2 "How long will you hunt for words?
    Consider, and then we will speak.
3 Why are we counted as cattle?
    Why are we stupid in your sight?
4 You who tear yourself in your anger,
    shall the earth be forsaken for
    you,
    or the rock be removed out of its
    place?

5 "Yea, the light of the wicked is put
    out,
    and the flame of his fire does not
    shine.
6 The light is dark in his tent,
    and his lamp above him is put
    out.
7 His strong steps are shortened
    and his own schemes throw him
    down.
8 For he is cast into a net by his own
    feet,
    and he walks on a pitfall.
9 A trap seizes him by the heel,
    a snare lays hold of him.
10 A rope is hid for him in the ground,
    a trap for him in the path.
11 Terrors frighten him on every side,
    and chase him at his heels.
12 His strength is hunger-bitten,
    and calamity is ready for his
    stumbling.
13 By disease his skin is consumed,ˢ
    the first-born of death consumes
    his limbs.
14 He is torn from the tent in which
    he trusted,
    and is brought to the king of
    terrors.

15 In his tent dwells that which is none
    of his;
    brimstone is scattered upon his
    habitation.
16 His roots dry up beneath,
    and his branches wither above.
17 His memory perishes from the
    earth,
    and he has no name in the street.
18 He is thrust from light into darkness,
    and driven out of the world.
19 He has no offspring or descendant
    among his people,
    and no survivor where he used
    to live.
20 They of the west are appalled at his
    day,
    and horror seizes them of the
    east.
21 Surely such are the dwellings of the
    ungodly,
    such is the place of him who
    knows not God.''

19 Then Jōb answered:
2 "How long will you torment
    me,
    and break me in pieces with
    words?
3 These ten times you have cast re-
    proach upon me;
    are you not ashamed to wrong
    me?
4 And even if it be true that I have
    erred,
    my error remains with myself.
5 If indeed you magnify yourselves
    against me,
    and make my humiliation an
    argument against me,
6 know then that God has put me in
    the wrong,
    and closed his net about me.
7 Behold, I cry out, 'Violence!' but
    I am not answered;
    I call aloud, but there is no justice.
8 He has walled up my way, so that
    I cannot pass,
    and he has set darkness upon my
    paths.
9 He has stripped from me my glory,
    and taken the crown from my
    head.
10 He breaks me down on every side,
    and I am gone,
    and my hope has he pulled up
    like a tree.
11 He has kindled his wrath against
    me,
    and counts me as his adversary.
12 His troops come on together;
    they have cast up siegeworksᵗ
    against me,
    and encamp round about my tent.

ʳ Heb obscure   ˢ Cn: Heb *it consumes the limbs of his skin*   ᵗ Heb *their way*

13 "He has put my brethren far from me,
and my acquaintances are wholly estranged from me.

14 My kinsfolk and my close friends have failed me;

15 the guests in my house have forgotten me;
my maidservants count me as a stranger;
I have become an alien in their eyes.

16 I call to my servant, but he gives me no answer;
I must beseech him with my mouth.

17 I am repulsive to my wife,
loathsome to the sons of my own mother.

18 Even young children despise me;
when I rise they talk against me.

19 All my intimate friends abhor me,
and those whom I loved have turned against me.

20 My bones cleave to my skin and to my flesh,
and I have escaped by the skin of my teeth.

21 Have pity on me, have pity on me,
O you my friends,
for the hand of God has touched me!

22 Why do you, like God, pursue me?
Why are you not satisfied with my flesh?

23 "Oh that my words were written!
Oh that they were inscribed in a book!

24 Oh that with an iron pen and lead they were graven in the rock for ever!

25 For I know that my Redeemer^u lives,
and at last he will stand upon the earth;^{v}

26 and after my skin has been thus destroyed,
then from^w my flesh I shall see God,^{x}

27 whom I shall see on my side,^{y}
and my eyes shall behold, and not another.
My heart faints within me!

28 If you say, 'How we will pursue him!'
and, 'The root of the matter is found in him';

29 be afraid of the sword,
for wrath brings the punishment of the sword,
that you may know there is a judgment."

20 Then Zō'phär the Nā'à·ma·thite answered:

2 "Therefore my thoughts answer me,
because of my haste within me.

3 I hear censure which insults me,
and out of my understanding a spirit answers me.

4 Do you not know this from of old,
since man was placed upon earth,

5 that the exulting of the wicked is short,
and the joy of the godless but for a moment?

6 Though his height mount up to the heavens,
and his head reach to the clouds,

7 he will perish for ever like his own dung;
those who have seen him will say, 'Where is he?'

8 He will fly away like a dream, and not be found;
he will be chased away like a vision of the night.

9 The eye which saw him will see him no more,
nor will his place any more behold him.

10 His children will seek the favor of the poor,
and his hands will give back his wealth.

11 His bones are full of youthful vigor,
but it will lie down with him in the dust.

12 "Though wickedness is sweet in his mouth,
though he hides it under his tongue,

13 though he is loath to let it go,
and holds it in his mouth,

14 yet his food is turned in his stomach;
it is the gall of asps within him.

15 He swallows down riches and vomits them up again;
God casts them out of his belly.

16 He will suck the poison of asps;
the tongue of a viper will kill him.

17 He will not look upon the rivers,
the streams flowing with honey and curds.

18 He will give back the fruit of his toil,
and will not swallow it down;
from the profit of his trading he will get no enjoyment.

19 For he has crushed and abandoned the poor,
he has seized a house which he did not build.

20 "Because his greed knew no rest,

^{u} Or *Vindicator* ^{v} Or *dust* ^{w} Or *without* ^{x} The meaning of this verse is uncertain ^{y} Or *for myself*

he will not save anything in which
he delights.
21 There was nothing left after he had
eaten;
therefore his prosperity will not
endure.
22 In the fulness of his sufficiency he
will be in straits;
all the force of misery will come
upon him.
23 To fill his belly to the full
God[z] will send his fierce anger
into him,
and rain it upon him as his food.[a]
24 He will flee from an iron weapon;
a bronze arrow will strike him
through.
25 It is drawn forth and comes out of
his body,
the glittering point comes out of
his gall;
terrors come upon him.
26 Utter darkness is laid up for his
treasures;
a fire not blown upon will devour
him;
what is left in his tent will be
consumed.
27 The heavens will reveal his iniquity,
and the earth will rise up against
him.
28 The possessions of his house will
be carried away,
dragged off in the day of God's[b]
wrath.
29 This is the wicked man's portion
from God,
the heritage decreed for him by
God."

21   Then Jōb answered:
2 "Listen carefully to my words,
and let this be your consolation.
3 Bear with me, and I will speak,
and after I have spoken, mock on.
4 As for me, is my complaint against
man?
Why should I not be impatient?
5 Look at me, and be appalled,
and lay your hand upon your
mouth.
6 When I think of it I am dismayed,
and shuddering seizes my flesh.
7 Why do the wicked live,
reach old age, and grow mighty
in power?
8 Their children are established in
their presence,
and their offspring before their
eyes.
9 Their houses are safe from fear,
and no rod of God is upon them.
10 Their bull breeds without fail;

their cow calves, and does not
cast her calf.
11 They send forth their little ones like
a flock,
and their children dance.
12 They sing to the tambourine and
the lyre,
and rejoice to the sound of the
pipe.
13 They spend their days in prosperity,
and in peace they go down to
Shē'ōl.
14 They say to God, 'Depart from us!
We do not desire the knowledge
of thy ways.
15 What is the Almighty, that we
should serve him?
And what profit do we get if we
pray to him?'
16 Behold, is not their prosperity in
their hand?
The counsel of the wicked is far
from me.

17 "How often is it that the lamp of
the wicked is put out?
That their calamity comes upon
them?
That God[c] distributes pains in
his anger?
18 That they are like straw before the
wind,
and like chaff that the storm
carries away?
19 You say, 'God stores up their iniquity for his sons.'
Let him recompense it to themselves, that they may know it.
20 Let their own eyes see their destruction,
and let them drink of the wrath
of the Almighty.
21 For what do they care for their
houses after them,
when the number of their months
is cut off?
22 Will any teach God knowledge,
seeing that he judges those that
are on high?
23 One dies in full prosperity,
being wholly at ease and secure,
24 his body[d] full of fat
and the marrow of his bones
moist.
25 Another dies in bitterness of soul,
never having tasted of good.
26 They lie down alike in the dust,
and the worms cover them.

27 "Behold, I know your thoughts,
and your schemes to wrong me.
28 For you say, 'Where is the house
of the prince?

---

[z] Heb *he*   [a] Cn: Heb *in his flesh*   [b] Heb *his*   [c] Heb *he*
[d] The meaning of the Hebrew word is uncertain

Where is the tent in which the wicked dwelt?'

29 Have you not asked those who travel the roads,
and do you not accept their testimony

30 that the wicked man is spared in the day of calamity,
that he is rescued in the day of wrath?

31 Who declares his way to his face,
and who requites him for what he has done?

32 When he is borne to the grave,
watch is kept over his tomb.

33 The clods of the valley are sweet to him;
all men follow after him,
and those who go before him are innumerable.

34 How then will you comfort me with empty nothings?
There is nothing left of your answers but falsehood."

22 Then E·li′phaz the Tē′ma·nīte answered:

2 "Can a man be profitable to God?
Surely he who is wise is profitable to himself.

3 Is it any pleasure to the Almighty if you are righteous,
or is it gain to him if you make your ways blameless?

4 Is it for your fear of him that he reproves you,
and enters into judgment with you?

5 Is not your wickedness great?
There is no end to your iniquities.

6 For you have exacted pledges of your brothers for nothing,
and stripped the naked of their clothing.

7 You have given no water to the weary to drink,
and you have withheld bread from the hungry.

8 The man with power possessed the land,
and the favored man dwelt in it.

9 You have sent widows away empty,
and the arms of the fatherless were crushed.

10 Therefore snares are round about you,
and sudden terror overwhelms you;

11 your light is darkened, so that[e] you cannot see,
and a flood of water covers you.

12 "Is not God high in the heavens?
See the highest stars, how lofty they are!

13 Therefore you say, 'What does God know?
Can he judge through the deep darkness?

14 Thick clouds enwrap him, so that he does not see,
and he walks on the vault of heaven.'

15 Will you keep to the old way which wicked men have trod?

16 They were snatched away before their time;
their foundation was washed away.

17 They said to God, 'Depart from us,'
and 'What can the Almighty do to us?'[f]

18 Yet he filled their houses with good things—
but the counsel of the wicked is far from me.

19 The righteous see it and are glad;
the innocent laugh them to scorn,

20 saying, 'Surely our adversaries are cut off,
and what they left the fire has consumed.'

21 "Agree with God, and be at peace;
thereby good will come to you.

22 Receive instruction from his mouth,
and lay up his words in your heart.

23 If you return to the Almighty and humble yourself,[g]
if you remove unrighteousness far from your tents,

24 if you lay gold in the dust,
and gold of O′phir among the stones of the torrent bed,

25 and if the Almighty is your gold,
and your precious silver;

26 then you will delight yourself in the Almighty,
and lift up your face to God.

27 You will make your prayer to him,
and he will hear you;
and you will pay your vows.

28 You will decide on a matter, and it will be established for you,
and light will shine on your ways.

29 For God abases the proud,[h]
but he saves the lowly.

30 He delivers the innocent man;[i]
you will be delivered through the cleanness of your hands."

---

e Cn Compare Gk: Heb *or darkness*   f Gk Syr: Heb *them*
g Cn: Heb *you will be built up*   h Cn: Heb *when they abased you said, Proud*
i Gk Syr Vg: Heb *him that is not innocent*
22.2-3: Job 35.6-8.

23 Then Jōb answered:
2 "Today also my complaint is bitter,[j]
  his[k] hand is heavy in spite of my groaning.
3 Oh, that I knew where I might find him,
  that I might come even to his seat!
4 I would lay my case before him
  and fill my mouth with arguments.
5 I would learn what he would answer me,
  and understand what he would say to me.
6 Would he contend with me in the greatness of his power?
  No; he would give heed to me.
7 There an upright man could reason with him,
  and I should be acquitted for ever by my judge.

8 "Behold, I go forward, but he is not there;
  and backward, but I cannot perceive him;
9 on the left hand I seek him,[l] but I cannot behold him;
  I[m] turn to the right hand, but I cannot see him.
10 But he knows the way that I take;
  when he has tried me, I shall come forth as gold.
11 My foot has held fast to his steps;
  I have kept his way and have not turned aside.
12 I have not departed from the commandment of his lips;
  I have treasured in[n] my bosom the words of his mouth.
13 But he is unchangeable and who can turn him?
  What he desires, that he does.
14 For he will complete what he appoints for me;
  and many such things are in his mind.
15 Therefore I am terrified at his presence;
  when I consider, I am in dread of him.
16 God has made my heart faint;
  the Almighty has terrified me;
17 for I am[o] hemmed in by darkness,
  and thick darkness covers my face.[p]

24 "Why are not times of judgment kept by the Almighty,
  and why do those who know him never see his days?

2 Men remove landmarks;
  they seize flocks and pasture them.
3 They drive away the ass of the fatherless;
  they take the widow's ox for a pledge.
4 They thrust the poor off the road;
  the poor of the earth all hide themselves.
5 Behold, like wild asses in the desert they go forth to their toil,
  seeking prey in the wilderness as food[q] for their children.
6 They gather their[r] fodder in the field
  and they glean the vineyard of the wicked man.
7 They lie all night naked, without clothing,
  and have no covering in the cold.
8 They are wet with the rain of the mountains,
  and cling to the rock for want of shelter.
9 (There are those who snatch the fatherless child from the breast,
  and take in pledge the infant of the poor.)
10 They go about naked, without clothing;
  hungry, they carry the sheaves;
11 among the olive rows of the wicked[s] they make oil;
  they tread the wine presses, but suffer thirst.
12 From out of the city the dying groan,
  and the soul of the wounded cries for help;
  yet God pays no attention to their prayer.

13 "There are those who rebel against the light,
  who are not acquainted with its ways,
  and do not stay in its paths.
14 The murderer rises in the dark,[t]
  that he may kill the poor and needy;
  and in the night he is as a thief.
15 The eye of the adulterer also waits for the twilight,
  saying, 'No eye will see me';
  and he disguises his face.
16 In the dark they dig through houses;
  by day they shut themselves up;
  they do not know the light.
17 For deep darkness is morning to all of them;

[j] Syr Vg Tg: Heb *rebellious*   [k] Gk Syr: Heb *my*
[l] Compare Syr: Heb *on the left hand when he works*   [m] Syr Vg: Heb *he*
[n] Gk Vg: Heb *from*   [o] With one Ms: Heb *am not*   [p] Vg: Heb *from my face*
[q] Heb *food to him*   [r] Heb *his*   [s] Heb *their olive rows*   [t] Cn: Heb *at the light*

for they are friends with the terrors of deep darkness.

18 "You say, 'They are swiftly carried
    away upon the face of the
    waters;
  their portion is cursed in the land;
  no treader turns toward their
    vineyards.

19 Drought and heat snatch away the
    snow waters;
  so does Shĕ'ōl those who have
    sinned.

20 The squares of the town[u] forget
    them;
  their name[v] is no longer remembered;
  so wickedness is broken like a
    tree.'

21 "They feed on the barren childless
    woman,
  and do no good to the widow.

22 Yet God[w] prolongs the life of the
    mighty by his power;
  they rise up when they despair of
    life.

23 He gives them security, and they
    are supported;
  and his eyes are upon their ways.

24 They are exalted a little while, and
    then are gone;
  they wither and fade like the
    mallow;[x]
  they are cut off like the heads of
    grain.

25 If it is not so, who will prove me a
    liar,
  and show that there is nothing
    in what I say?

25 Then Bil'dad the Shü'hite answered:
2 "Dominion and fear are with God;[y]
  he makes peace in his high heaven.
3 Is there any number to his armies?
  Upon whom does his light not
    arise?
4 How then can man be righteous before God?
  How can he who is born of woman
    be clean?
5 Behold, even the moon is not bright
  and the stars are not clean in his
    sight;
6 how much less man, who is a
    maggot,
  and the son of man, who is a
    worm!"

26 Then Jōb answered:
2 "How you have helped him
    who has no power!

How you have saved the arm that
  has no strength!
3 How you have counseled him who
    has no wisdom,
  and plentifully declared sound
    knowledge!
4 With whose help have you uttered
    words,
  and whose spirit has come forth
    from you?
5 The shades below tremble,
  the waters and their inhabitants.
6 Shĕ'ōl is naked before God,
  and A·bad'dŏn has no covering.
7 He stretches out the north over the
    void,
  and hangs the earth upon nothing.
8 He binds up the waters in his thick
    clouds,
  and the cloud is not rent under
    them.
9 He covers the face of the moon,[z]
  and spreads over it his cloud.
10 And has described a circle upon the
    face of the waters
  at the boundary between light and
    darkness.
11 The pillars of heaven tremble,
  and are astounded at his rebuke.
12 By his power he stilled the sea;
  by his understanding he smote
    Rā'hab.
13 By his wind the heavens were made
    fair;
  his hand pierced the fleeing
    serpent.
14 Lo, these are but the outskirts of
    his ways;
  and how small a whisper do we
    hear of him!
  But the thunder of his power who
    can understand?"

27 And Jōb again took up his
    discourse, and said:
2 "As God lives, who has taken away
    my right,
  and the Almighty, who has made
    my soul bitter;
3 as long as my breath is in me,
  and the spirit of God is in my
    nostrils;
4 my lips will not speak falsehood,
  and my tongue will not utter
    deceit.
5 Far be it from me to say that you
    are right;
  till I die I will not put away my
    integrity from me.
6 I hold fast my righteousness, and
    will not let it go;
  my heart does not reproach me
    for any of my days.

---

u Cn: Heb obscure   v Cn: Heb *a worm*   w Heb *he*   x Gk: Heb *all*   y Heb *him*
z Or *his throne*

7 "Let my enemy be as the wicked,
    and let him that rises up against
       me be as the unrighteous.
8 For what is the hope of the godless
    when God cuts him off,
    when God takes away his life?
9 Will God hear his cry,
    when trouble comes upon him?
10 Will he take delight in the Almighty?
    Will he call upon God at all times?
11 I will teach you concerning the
    hand of God;
    what is with the Almighty I will
      not conceal.
12 Behold, all of you have seen it
    yourselves;
    why then have you become alto-
      gether vain?

13 "This is the portion of a wicked man
    with God,
    and the heritage which oppressors
      receive from the Almighty:
14 If his children are multiplied, it is
    for the sword;
    and his offspring have not enough
      to eat.
15 Those who survive him the pesti-
    lence buries,
    and their widows make no lam-
      entation.
16 Though he heap up silver like dust,
    and pile up clothing like clay;
17 he may pile it up, but the just will
    wear it,
    and the innocent will divide the
      silver.
18 The house which he builds is like a
    spider's web,^{a}
    like a booth which a watchman
      makes.
19 He goes to bed rich, but will do so
    no more;^{b}
    he opens his eyes, and his wealth
      is gone.
20 Terrors overtake him like a flood;
    in the night a whirlwind carries
      him off.
21 The east wind lifts him up and he
    is gone;
    it sweeps him out of his place.
22 It^c hurls at him without pity;
    he flees from its^d power in head-
      long flight.
23 It^c claps its^d hands at him,
    and hisses at him from its^d place.

28 "Surely there is a mine for
    silver,
    and a place for gold which they
      refine.
2 Iron is taken out of the earth,

and copper is smelted from the
    ore.
3 Men put an end to darkness,
    and search out to the farthest
      bound
    the ore in gloom and deep dark-
      ness.
4 They open shafts in a valley away
    from where men live;
    they are forgotten by travelers,
    they hang afar from men, they
      swing to and fro.
5 As for the earth, out of it comes
    bread;
    but underneath it is turned up
      as by fire.
6 Its stones are the place of sapphires,^{e}
    and it has dust of gold.

7 "That path no bird of prey knows,
    and the falcon's eye has not seen
      it.
8 The proud beasts have not trodden
    it;
    the lion has not passed over it.

9 "Man puts his hand to the flinty
    rock,
    and overturns mountains by the
      roots.
10 He cuts out channels in the rocks,
    and his eye sees every precious
      thing.
11 He binds up the streams so that
    they do not trickle,
    and the thing that is hid he brings
      forth to light.

12 "But where shall wisdom be found?
    And where is the place of under-
      standing?
13 Man does not know the way to it,^{f}
    and it is not found in the land of
      the living.
14 The deep says, 'It is not in me,'
    and the sea says, 'It is not with
      me.'
15 It cannot be gotten for gold,
    and silver cannot be weighed as
      its price.
16 It cannot be valued in the gold of
    Ō′phĭr,
    in precious onyx or sapphire.^{g}
17 Gold and glass cannot equal it,
    nor can it be exchanged for jewels
      of fine gold.
18 No mention shall be made of coral
    or of crystal;
    the price of wisdom is above
      pearls.
19 The topaz of Ethiopia cannot com-
    pare with it,

---

^{a} Cn Compare Gk Syr: Heb *He builds his house like the moth*
^{b} Gk Compare Syr: Heb *shall not be gathered* ^{c} Or *he* (that is God) ^{d} Or *his*
^{e} Or *lapis lazuli* ^{f} Gk: Heb *its price* ^{g} Or *lapis lazuli*

nor can it be valued in pure
    gold.
20 "Whence then comes wisdom?
    And where is the place of under-
       standing?
21 It is hid from the eyes of all living,
    and concealed from the birds of
       the air.
22 A·bad'don and Death say,
    'We have heard a rumor of it with
       our ears.'

23 "God understands the way to it,
    and he knows its place.
24 For he looks to the ends of the earth,
    and sees everything under the
       heavens.
25 When he gave to the wind its
       weight,
    and meted out the waters by
       measure;
26 when he made a decree for the
       rain,
    and a way for the lightning of the
       thunder;
27 then he saw it and declared it;
    he established it, and searched it
       out.
28 And he said to man,
    'Behold, the fear of the Lord, that
       is wisdom;
    and to depart from evil is under-
       standing.'"

29 And Jōb again took up his dis-
       course, and said:
2 "Oh, that I were as in the months
       of old,
    as in the days when God watched
       over me;
3 when his lamp shone upon my
       head,
    and by his light I walked through
       darkness;
4 as I was in my autumn days,
    when the friendship of God was
       upon my tent;
5 when the Almighty was yet with
       me,
    when my children were about me;
6 when my steps were washed with
       milk,
    and the rock poured out for me
       streams of oil!
7 When I went out to the gate of the
       city,
    when I prepared my seat in the
       square,
8 the young men saw me and with-
       drew,
    and the aged rose and stood;
9 the princes refrained from talking,
    and laid their hand on their
       mouth;

10 the voice of the nobles was hushed,
    and their tongue cleaved to the
       roof of their mouth.
11 When the ear heard, it called me
       blessed,
    and when the eye saw, it approved;
12 because I delivered the poor who
       cried,
    and the fatherless who had none
       to help him.
13 The blessing of him who was about
       to perish came upon me,
    and I caused the widow's heart to
       sing for joy.
14 I put on righteousness, and it
       clothed me;
    my justice was like a robe and a
       turban.
15 I was eyes to the blind,
    and feet to the lame.
16 I was a father to the poor,
    and I searched out the cause of
       him whom I did not know.
17 I broke the fangs of the unrighteous,
    and made him drop his prey from
       his teeth.
18 Then I thought, 'I shall die in my
       nest,
    and I shall multiply my days as
       the sand,
19 my roots spread out to the waters,
    with the dew all night on my
       branches,
20 my glory fresh with me,
    and my bow ever new in my
       hand.'

21 "Men listened to me, and waited,
    and kept silence for my counsel.
22 After I spoke they did not speak
       again,
    and my word dropped upon them.
23 They waited for me as for the
       rain;
    and they opened their mouths as
       for the spring rain.
24 I smiled on them when they had no
       confidence;
    and the light of my countenance
       they did not cast down.
25 I chose their way, and sat as chief,
    and I dwelt like a king among his
       troops,
    like one who comforts mourners.

30 "But now they make sport of
       me,
    men who are younger than I,
    whose fathers I would have dis-
       dained
    to set with the dogs of my flock.
2 What could I gain from the strength
       of their hands,
    men whose vigor is gone?
3 Through want and hard hunger

they gnaw the dry and desolate
ground;[h]

4 they pick mallow and the leaves of
bushes,
and to warm themselves the roots
of the broom.

5 They are driven out from among men;
they shout after them as after a
thief.

6 In the gullies of the torrents they
must dwell,
in holes of the earth and of the
rocks.

7 Among the bushes they bray;
under the nettles they huddle together.

8 A senseless, a disreputable brood,
they have been whipped out of
the land.

9 "And now I have become their song,
I am a byword to them.

10 They abhor me, they keep aloof
from me;
they do not hesitate to spit at the
sight of me.

11 Because God has loosed my cord
and humbled me,
they have cast off restraint in my
presence.

12 On my right hand the rabble rise,
they drive me[i] forth,
they cast up against me their ways
of destruction.

13 They break up my path,
they promote my calamity;
no one restrains[j] them.

14 As through[k] a wide breach they come;
amid the crash they roll on.

15 Terrors are turned upon me;
my honor is pursued as by the wind,
and my prosperity has passed
away like a cloud.

16 "And now my soul is poured out
within me;
days of affliction have taken hold
of me.

17 The night racks my bones,
and the pain that gnaws me takes
no rest.

18 With violence it seizes my garment;[l]
it binds me about like the collar
of my tunic.

19 God has cast me into the mire,
and I have become like dust and
ashes.

20 I cry to thee and thou dost not
answer me;
I stand, and thou dost not[m] heed
me.

21 Thou hast turned cruel to me;

with the might of thy hand thou
dost persecute me.

22 Thou liftest me up on the wind,
thou makest me ride on it,
and thou tossest me about in the
roar of the storm.

23 Yea, I know that thou wilt bring me
to death,
and to the house appointed for
all living.

24 "Yet does not one in a heap of ruins
stretch out his hand,
and in his disaster cry for help?[n]

25 Did not I weep for him whose day
was hard?
Was not my soul grieved for the
poor?

26 But when I looked for good, evil
came;
and when I waited for light, darkness came.

27 My heart is in turmoil, and is never
still;
days of affliction come to meet me.

28 I go about blackened, but not by
the sun;
I stand up in the assembly, and
cry for help.

29 I am a brother of jackals,
and a companion of ostriches.

30 My skin turns black and falls from
me,
and my bones burn with heat.

31 My lyre is turned to mourning,
and my pipe to the voice of those
who weep.

31

"I have made a covenant with
my eyes;
how then could I look upon a
virgin?

2 What would be my portion from
God above,
and my heritage from the Almighty on high?

3 Does not calamity befall the unrighteous,
and disaster the workers of iniquity?

4 Does not he see my ways,
and number all my steps?

5 "If I have walked with falsehood,
and my foot has hastened to
deceit;

6 (Let me be weighed in a just balance,
and let God know my integrity!)

7 if my step has turned aside from
the way,
and my heart has gone after my
eyes,

---

[h] Heb *ground yesterday waste*   [i] Heb *my feet*   [j] Cn: Heb *helps*   [k] Cn: Heb *like*
[l] Gk: Heb *my garment is disfigured*   [m] One Heb Ms and Vg: Heb lacks *not*
[n] Cn: Heb *obscure*

and if any spot has cleaved to my hands;

8 then let me sow, and another eat;
and let what grows for me be rooted out.

9 "If my heart has been enticed to a woman,
and I have lain in wait at my neighbor's door;

10 then let my wife grind for another,
and let others bow down upon her.

11 For that would be a heinous crime;
that would be an iniquity to be punished by the judges;

12 for that would be a fire which consumes unto A·bad'don,
and it would burn to the root all my increase.

13 "If I have rejected the cause of my manservant or my maidservant,
when they brought a complaint against me;

14 what then shall I do when God rises up?
When he makes inquiry, what shall I answer him?

15 Did not he who made me in the womb make him?
And did not one fashion us in the womb?

16 "If I have withheld anything that the poor desired,
or have caused the eyes of the widow to fail,

17 or have eaten my morsel alone,
and the fatherless has not eaten of it

18 (for from his youth I reared him as a father,
and from his mother's womb I guided him[o]);

19 if I have seen any one perish for lack of clothing,
or a poor man without covering;

20 if his loins have not blessed me,
and if he was not warmed with the fleece of my sheep;

21 if I have raised my hand against the fatherless,
because I saw help in the gate;

22 then let my shoulder blade fall from my shoulder,
and let my arm be broken from its socket.

23 For I was in terror of calamity from God,
and I could not have faced his majesty.

24 "If I have made gold my trust,
or called fine gold my confidence;

25 if I have rejoiced because my wealth was great,
or because my hand had gotten much;

26 if I have looked at the sun[p] when it shone,
or the moon moving in splendor,

27 and my heart has been secretly enticed,
and my mouth has kissed my hand;

28 this also would be an iniquity to be punished by the judges,
for I should have been false to God above.

29 "If I have rejoiced at the ruin of him that hated me,
or exulted when evil overtook him

30 (I have not let my mouth sin
by asking for his life with a curse);

31 if the men of my tent have not said,
'Who is there that has not been filled with his meat?'

32 (the sojourner has not lodged in the street;
I have opened my doors to the wayfarer);

33 if I have concealed my transgressions from men,[q]
by hiding my iniquity in my bosom,

34 because I stood in great fear of the multitude,
and the contempt of families terrified me,
so that I kept silence, and did not go out of doors—

35 Oh, that I had one to hear me!
(Here is my signature! let the Almighty answer me!)
Oh, that I had the indictment written by my adversary!

36 Surely I would carry it on my shoulder;
I would bind it on me as a crown;

37 I would give him an account of all my steps;
like a prince I would approach him.

38 "If my land has cried out against me,
and its furrows have wept together;

39 if I have eaten its yield without payment,
and caused the death of its owners;

---

o Cn: Heb *for from my youth he grew up to me as a father, and from my mother's womb I guided her*   *p* Heb *the light*
q Cn: Heb *like men* or *like Adam*

40 let thorns grow instead of wheat,
and foul weeds instead of barley.''

The words of Jōb are ended.

32 So these three men ceased to
answer Jōb, because he was
righteous in his own eyes. 2 Then
E·li′hū the son of Bär′ă·chel the Buzite,
of the family of Räm, became angry.
He was angry at Jōb because he justified himself rather than God; 3 he was
angry also at Jōb's three friends because they had found no answer,
although they had declared Job to be
in the wrong. 4 Now E·li′hū had waited
to speak to Jōb because they were
older than he. 5 And when E·li′hū saw
that there was no answer in the mouth
of these three men, he became angry.
6 And E·li′hū the son of Bär′ă·chel
the Buzite answered:
"I am young in years,
and you are aged;
therefore I was timid and afraid
to declare my opinion to you.
7 I said, 'Let days speak,
and many years teach wisdom.'
8 But it is the spirit in a man,
the breath of the Almighty,
that makes him understand.
9 It is not the old*r* that are wise,
nor the aged that understand what
is right.
10 Therefore I say, 'Listen to me;
let me also declare my opinion.'

11 "Behold, I waited for your words,
I listened for your wise sayings,
while you searched out what to
say.
12 I gave you my attention,
and, behold, there was none that
confuted Jōb,
or that answered his words,
among you.
13 Beware lest you say, 'We have
found wisdom;
God may vanquish him, not man.'
14 He has not directed his words
against me,
and I will not answer him with
your speeches.

15 "They are discomfited, they answer
no more;
they have not a word to say.
16 And shall I wait, because they do
not speak,
because they stand there, and
answer no more?
17 I also will give my answer;
I also will declare my opinion.

18 For I am full of words,
the spirit within me constrains
me.
19 Behold, my heart is like wine that
has no vent;
like new wineskins, it is ready to
burst.
20 I must speak, that I may find relief;
I must open my lips and answer.
21 I will not show partiality to any
person
or use flattery toward any man.
22 For I do not know how to flatter,
else would my Maker soon put
an end to me.

33 "But now, hear my speech,
O Jōb,
and listen to all my words.
2 Behold, I open my mouth;
the tongue in my mouth speaks.
3 My words declare the uprightness
of my heart,
and what my lips know they speak
sincerely.
4 The spirit of God has made me,
and the breath of the Almighty
gives me life.
5 Answer me, if you can;
set your words in order before
me; take your stand.
6 Behold, I am toward God as you are;
I too was formed from a piece of
clay.
7 Behold, no fear of me need terrify
you;
my pressure will not be heavy
upon you.

8 "Surely, you have spoken in my
hearing,
and I have heard the sound of
your words.
9 You say, 'I am clean, without
transgression;
I am pure, and there is no iniquity in me.
10 Behold, he finds occasions against
me,
he counts me as his enemy;
11 he puts my feet in the stocks,
and watches all my paths.'

12 "Behold, in this you are not right.
I will answer you.
God is greater than man.
13 Why do you contend against him,
saying, 'He will answer none of
my*s* words'?
14 For God speaks in one way,
and in two, though man does not
perceive it.
15 In a dream, in a vision of the night,

r Gk Syr Vg: Heb *many*
s Compare Gk: Heb *his*

when deep sleep falls upon men,
while they slumber on their beds,

16 then he opens the ears of men,
and terrifies them with warnings,

17 that he may turn man aside from
his deed,
and cut off[t] pride from man;

18 he keeps back his soul from the Pit,
his life from perishing by the
sword.

19 "Man is also chastened with pain
upon his bed,
and with continual strife in his
bones;

20 so that his life loathes bread,
and his appetite dainty food.

21 His flesh is so wasted away that it
cannot be seen;
and his bones which were not
seen stick out.

22 His soul draws near the Pit,
and his life to those who bring
death.

23 If there be for him an angel,
a mediator, one of the thousand,
to declare to man what is right
for him;

24 and he is gracious to him, and says,
'Deliver him from going down
into the Pit,
I have found a ransom;

25 let his flesh become fresh with
youth;
let him return to the days of his
youthful vigor;'

26 then man prays to God, and he
accepts him,
he comes into his presence with
joy.
He recounts[u] to men his salvation,

27 and he sings before men, and
says:
'I sinned, and perverted what was
right,
and it was not requited to me.

28 He has redeemed my soul from
going down into the Pit,
and my life shall see the light.'

29 "Behold, God does all these things,
twice, three times, with a man,

30 to bring back his soul from the Pit,
that he may see the light of
life.[v]

31 Give heed, O Jōb, listen to me;
be silent, and I will speak.

32 If you have anything to say, answer
me;
speak, for I desire to justify you.

33 If not, listen to me;
be silent, and I will teach you
wisdom."

34

Then E·li′hū said:

2 "Hear my words, you wise
men,
and give ear to me, you who
know;

3 for the ear tests words
as the palate tastes food.

4 Let us choose what is right;
let us determine among ourselves
what is good.

5 For Jōb has said, 'I am innocent,
and God has taken away my right;

6 in spite of my right I am counted
a liar;
my wound is incurable, though
I am without transgression.'

7 What man is like Jōb,
who drinks up scoffing like water,

8 who goes in company with evildoers
and walks with wicked men?

9 For he has said, 'It profits a man
nothing
that he should take delight in
God.'

10 "Therefore, hear me, you men of
understanding,
far be it from God that he should
do wickedness,
and from the Almighty that he
should do wrong.

11 For according to the work of a man
he will requite him,
and according to his ways he will
make it befall him.

12 Of a truth, God will not do wickedly,
and the Almighty will not pervert
justice.

13 Who gave him charge over the earth
and who laid on him[w] the whole
world?

14 If he should take back his spirit[x] to
himself,
and gather to himself his breath,

15 all flesh would perish together,
and man would return to dust.

16 "If you have understanding, hear
this;
listen to what I say.

17 Shall one who hates justice govern?
Will you condemn him who is
righteous and mighty,

18 who says to a king, 'Worthless one,'
and to nobles, 'Wicked man';

19 who shows no partiality to princes,
nor regards the rich more than
the poor,
for they are all the work of his
hands?

20 In a moment they die;
at midnight the people are shaken
and pass away,

---

t Cn: Heb *hide*   u Cn: Heb *returns*   v Syr: Heb *to be lighted with the light of life*
w Heb lacks *on him*   x Heb *his heart his spirit*

and the mighty are taken away
　　by no human hand.

21 "For his eyes are upon the ways of
　　a man,
　　and he sees all his steps.
22 There is no gloom or deep dark-
　　ness
　　where evildoers may hide them-
　　selves.
23 For he has not appointed a time[y] for
　　any man
　　to go before God in judgment.
24 He shatters the mighty without in-
　　vestigation,
　　and sets others in their place.
25 Thus, knowing their works,
　　he overturns them in the night,
　　and they are crushed.
26 He strikes them for their wickedness
　　in the sight of men,
27 because they turned aside from
　　following him,
　　and had no regard for any of his
　　ways,
28 so that they caused the cry of the
　　poor to come to him,
　　and he heard the cry of the
　　afflicted—
29 When he is quiet, who can condemn?
　　When he hides his face, who can
　　behold him,
　　whether it be a nation or a man?—
30 that a godless man should not reign,
　　that he should not ensnare the
　　people.

31 "For has any one said to God,
　　'I have borne chastisement; I will
　　not offend any more;
32 teach me what I do not see;
　　if I have done iniquity, I will do
　　it no more'?
33 Will he then make requital to suit
　　you,
　　because you reject it?
For you must choose, and not I;
　　therefore declare what you know.[z]
34 Men of understanding will say to
　　me,
　　and the wise man who hears me
　　will say:
35 'Jōb speaks without knowledge,
　　his words are without insight.'
36 Would that Jōb were tried to the
　　end,
　　because he answers like wicked
　　men.
37 For he adds rebellion to his sin;
　　he claps his hands among us,
　　and multiplies his words against
　　God."

35 And E·li′hū said:
2 "Do you think this to be just?
　　Do you say, 'It is my right before
　　God,'
3 that you ask, 'What advantage have
　　I?
　　How am I better off than if I had
　　sinned?'
4 I will answer you
　　and your friends with you.
5 Look at the heavens, and see;
　　and behold the clouds, which are
　　higher than you.
6 If you have sinned, what do you
　　accomplish against him?
　　And if your transgressions are
　　multiplied, what do you do to
　　him?
7 If you are righteous, what do you
　　give to him;
　　or what does he receive from
　　your hand?
8 Your wickedness concerns a man
　　like yourself,
　　and your righteousness a son of
　　man.

9 "Because of the multitude of oppres-
　　sions people cry out;
　　they call for help because of the
　　arm of the mighty.
10 But none says, 'Where is God my
　　Maker,
　　who gives songs in the night,
11 who teaches us more than the beasts
　　of the earth,
　　and makes us wiser than the birds
　　of the air?'
12 There they cry out, but he does not
　　answer,
　　because of the pride of evil men.
13 Surely God does not hear an empty
　　cry,
　　nor does the Almighty regard it.
14 How much less when you say that
　　you do not see him,
　　that the case is before him, and
　　you are waiting for him!
15 And now, because his anger does
　　not punish,
　　and he does not greatly heed
　　transgression,[a]
16 Jōb opens his mouth in empty talk,
　　he multiplies words without
　　knowledge."

36 And E·li′hū continued, and
said:
2 "Bear with me a little, and I will
　　show you,
　　for I have yet something to say
　　on God's behalf.

---

[y] Cn: Heb *yet*　　[z] The Hebrew of verses 29-33 is obscure
[a] Theodotion Symmachus Compare Vg: The meaning of the Hebrew word is uncertain
35.6-8: Job 22.2-3.

3 I will fetch my knowledge from afar,
and ascribe righteousness to my
Maker.
4 For truly my words are not false;
one who is perfect in knowledge
is with you.

5 "Behold, God is mighty, and does
not despise any;
he is mighty in strength of understanding.
6 He does not keep the wicked alive,
but gives the afflicted their right.
7 He does not withdraw his eyes from
the righteous,
but with kings upon the throne
he sets them for ever, and they
are exalted.
8 And if they are bound in fetters
and caught in the cords of affliction,
9 then he declares to them their work
and their transgressions, that they
are behaving arrogantly.
10 He opens their ears to instruction,
and commands that they return
from iniquity.
11 If they hearken and serve him,
they complete their days in
prosperity,
and their years in pleasantness.
12 But if they do not hearken, they
perish by the sword,
and die without knowledge.

13 "The godless in heart cherish anger;
they do not cry for help when he
binds them.
14 They die in youth,
and their life ends in shame.*b*
15 He delivers the afflicted by their
affliction,
and opens their ear by adversity.
16 He also allured you out of distress
into a broad place where there
was no cramping,
and what was set on your table
was full of fatness.

17 "But you are full of the judgment
on the wicked;
judgment and justice seize you.
18 Beware lest wrath entice you into
scoffing;
and let not the greatness of the
ransom turn you aside.
19 Will your cry avail to keep you from
distress,
or all the force of your strength?
20 Do not long for the night,
when peoples are cut off in their
place.
21 Take heed, do not turn to iniquity,

for this you have chosen rather
than affliction.
22 Behold, God is exalted in his power;
who is a teacher like him?
23 Who has prescribed for him his
way,
or who can say, 'Thou hast done
wrong?'

24 "Remember to extol his work,
of which men have sung.
25 All men have looked on it;
man beholds it from afar.
26 Behold, God is great, and we know
him not;
the number of his years is unsearchable.
27 For he draws up the drops of water,
he*c* distils his mist in rain
28 which the skies pour down,
and drop upon man abundantly.
29 Can any one understand the spreading of the clouds,
the thunderings of his pavilion?
30 Behold, he scatters his lightning
about him,
and covers the roots of the sea.
31 For by these he judges peoples;
he gives food in abundance.
32 He covers his hands with the
lightning,
and commands it to strike the
mark.
33 Its crashing declares concerning
him,
who is jealous with anger against
iniquity.

37 "At this also my heart
trembles,
and leaps out of its place.
2 Hearken to the thunder of his voice
and the rumbling that comes from
his mouth.
3 Under the whole heaven he lets it
go,
and his lightning to the corners
of the earth.
4 After it his voice roars;
he thunders with his majestic
voice
and he does not restrain the
lightnings*d* when his voice is
heard.
5 God thunders wondrously with his
voice;
he does great things which we
cannot comprehend.
6 For to the snow he says, 'Fall on
the earth';
and to the shower and the rain,*e*
'Be strong.'
7 He seals up the hand of every man,

b Heb *among the cult prostitutes*   *c* Cn: Heb *they distil*   *d* Heb *them*
e Cn Compare Syr: Heb *shower of rain and shower of rains*

that all men may know his work.*

8 Then the beasts go into their lairs,
and remain in their dens.

9 From its chamber comes the whirlwind,
and cold from the scattering
winds.

10 By the breath of God ice is given,
and the broad waters are frozen
fast.

11 He loads the thick cloud with
moisture;
the clouds scatter his lightning.

12 They turn round and round by his
guidance,
to accomplish all that he commands them
on the face of the habitable world.

13 Whether for correction, or for his
land,
or for love, he causes it to happen.

14 "Hear this, O Jōb;
stop and consider the wondrous
works of God.

15 Do you know how God lays his
command upon them,
and causes the lightning of his
cloud to shine?

16 Do you know the balancings of the
clouds,
the wondrous works of him who
is perfect in knowledge,

17 you whose garments are hot
when the earth is still because of
the south wind?

18 Can you, like him, spread out the
skies,
hard as a molten mirror?

19 Teach us what we shall say to him;
we cannot draw up our case because of darkness.

20 Shall it be told him that I would
speak?
Did a man ever wish that he
would be swallowed up?

21 "And now men cannot look on the
light
when it is bright in the skies,
when the wind has passed and
cleared them.

22 Out of the north comes golden
splendor;
God is clothed with terrible
majesty.

23 The Almighty—we cannot find
him;
he is great in power and justice,
and abundant righteousness he
will not violate.

24 Therefore men fear him;

he does not regard any who are
wise in their own conceit."

38 Then the LORD answered Jōb
out of the whirlwind:

2 "Who is this that darkens counsel
by words without knowledge?

3 Gird up your loins like a man,
I will question you, and you shall
declare to me.

4 "Where were you when I laid the
foundation of the earth?
Tell me, if you have understanding.

5 Who determined its measurements
—surely you know!
Or who stretched the line upon it?

6 On what were its bases sunk,
or who laid its cornerstone,

7 when the morning stars sang together,
and all the sons of God shouted
for joy?

8 "Or who shut in the sea with doors,
when it burst forth from the
womb;

9 when I made clouds its garment,
and thick darkness its swaddling
band,

10 and prescribed bounds for it,
and set bars and doors,

11 and said, 'Thus far shall you come,
and no farther,
and here shall your proud waves
be stayed'?

12 'Have you commanded the morning
since your days began,
and caused the dawn to know its
place,

13 that it might take hold of the skirts
of the earth,
and the wicked be shaken out of it?

14 It is changed like clay under the seal,
and it is dyed* like a garment.

15 From the wicked their light is withheld,
and their uplifted arm is broken.

16 "Have you entered into the springs
of the sea,
or walked in the recesses of the
deep?

17 Have the gates of death been revealed to you,
or have you seen the gates of deep
darkness?

18 Have you comprehended the ex-
panse of the earth?
Declare, if you know all this.

---

f Vg Compare Syr Tg: Heb *that all men whom he has made may know it*
g Cn: Heb *they stand forth*
38.10: Jer 5.22.

19 "Where is the way to the dwelling
of light,
and where is the place of darkness,
20 that you may take it to its territory
and that you may discern the
paths to its home?
21 You know, for you were born then,
and the number of your days is
great!

22 "Have you entered the storehouses
of the snow,
or have you seen the storehouses
of the hail,
23 which I have reserved for the time
of trouble,
for the day of battle and war?
24 What is the way to the place where
the light is distributed,
or where the east wind is scattered
upon the earth?

25 "Who has cleft a channel for the
torrents of rain,
and a way for the thunderbolt,
26 to bring rain on a land where no
man is,
on the desert in which there is
no man;
27 to satisfy the waste and desolate land,
and to make the ground put forth
grass?

28 "Has the rain a father,
or who has begotten the drops of
dew?
29 From whose womb did the ice come
forth,
and who has given birth to the
hoarfrost of heaven?
30 The waters become hard like stone,
and the face of the deep is frozen.

31 "Can you bind the chains of the
Plēĭ'a·dēs,
or loose the cords of O·rĭ'ŏn?
32 Can you lead forth the Măz'zȧ·roth
in their season,
or can you guide the Bear with
its children?
33 Do you know the ordinances of the
heavens?
Can you establish their rule on
the earth?

34 "Can you lift up your voice to the
clouds,
that a flood of waters may cover
you?
35 Can you send forth lightnings, that
they may go
and say to you, 'Here we are'?
36 Who has put wisdom in the clouds,[h]

or given understanding to the
mists?[h]
37 Who can number the clouds by
wisdom?
Or who can tilt the waterskins of
the heavens,
38 when the dust runs into a mass
and the clods cleave fast together?

39 "Can you hunt the prey for the lion,
or satisfy the appetite of the young
lions,
40 when they crouch in their dens,
or lie in wait in their covert?
41 Who provides for the raven its prey,
when its young ones cry to God,
and wander about for lack of food?

39

"Do you know when the
mountain goats bring forth?
Do you observe the calving of
the hinds?
2 Can you number the months that
they fulfil,
and do you know the time when
they bring forth,
3 when they crouch, bring forth their
offspring,
and are delivered of their young?
4 Their young ones become strong,
they grow up in the open;
they go forth, and do not return
to them.

5 "Who has let the wild ass go free?
Who has loosed the bonds of the
swift ass,
6 to whom I have given the steppe for
his home,
and the salt land for his dwelling
place?
7 He scorns the tumult of the city;
he hears not the shouts of the
driver.
8 He ranges the mountains as his
pasture,
and he searches after every green
thing.

9 "Is the wild ox willing to serve
you?
Will he spend the night at your
crib?
10 Can you bind him in the furrow
with ropes,
or will he harrow the valleys after
you?
11 Will you depend on him because
his strength is great,
and will you leave to him your
labor?
12 Do you have faith in him that he
will return,

[h] The meaning of the Hebrew word is uncertain

and bring your grain to your threshing floor?[i]

13 "The wings of the ostrich wave proudly;
but are they the pinions and plumage of love?[j]
14 For she leaves her eggs to the earth,
and lets them be warmed on the ground,
15 forgetting that a foot may crush them,
and that the wild beast may trample them.
16 She deals cruelly with her young, as if they were not hers;
though her labor be in vain, yet she has no fear;
17 because God has made her forget wisdom,
and given her no share in understanding.
18 When she rouses herself to flee,[k]
she laughs at the horse and his rider.

19 "Do you give the horse his might?
Do you clothe his neck with strength?[l]
20 Do you make him leap like the locust?
His majestic snorting is terrible.
21 He paws[m] in the valley, and exults in his strength;
he goes out to meet the weapons.
22 He laughs at fear, and is not dismayed;
he does not turn back from the sword.
23 Upon him rattle the quiver,
the flashing spear and the javelin.
24 With fierceness and rage he swallows the ground;
he cannot stand still at the sound of the trumpet.
25 When the trumpet sounds, he says 'Aha!'
He smells the battle from afar,
the thunder of the captains, and the shouting.

26 "Is it by your wisdom that the hawk soars,
and spreads his wings toward the south?
27 Is it at your command that the eagle mounts up
and makes his nest on high?
28 On the rock he dwells and makes his home
in the fastness of the rocky crag.

29 Thence he spies out the prey;
his eyes behold it afar off.
30 His young ones suck up blood;
and where the slain are, there is he."

40

And the LORD said to Jōb:
2 "Shall a faultfinder contend with the Almighty?
He who argues with God, let him answer it."

3 Then Jōb answered the LORD:
4 "Behold, I am of small account;
what shall I answer thee?
I lay my hand on my mouth.
5 I have spoken once, and I will not answer;
twice, but I will proceed no further."

6 Then the LORD answered Jōb out of the whirlwind:
7 "Gird up your loins like a man;
I will question you, and you declare to me.
8 Will you even put me in the wrong?
Will you condemn me that you may be justified?
9 Have you an arm like God,
and can you thunder with a voice like his?

10 Deck yourself with majesty and dignity;
clothe yourself with glory and splendor.
11 Pour forth the overflowings of your anger,
and look on every one that is proud, and abase him.
12 Look on every one that is proud, and bring him low;
and tread down the wicked where they stand.
13 Hide them all in the dust together;
bind their faces in the world below.[n]
14 Then will I also acknowledge to you,
that your own right hand can give you victory.

15 "Behold, Bē′hê·mŏth,[o]
which I made as I made you;
he eats grass like an ox.
16 Behold, his strength in his loins,
and his power in the muscles of his belly.
17 He makes his tail stiff like a cedar;
the sinews of his thighs are knit together.

---

[i] Heb *your grain and your threshing floor*   [j] Heb obscure   [k] Heb obscure
[l] Tg: The meaning of the Hebrew word is obscure   [m] Gk Syr Vg: Heb *they dig*
[n] Heb *hidden place*   [o] Or *the hippopotamus*

18 His bones are tubes of bronze,
   his limbs like bars of iron.

19 "He is the first of the works*p* of God;
   let him who made him bring near
   his sword!
20 For the mountains yield food for
   him
   where all the wild beasts play.
21 Under the lotus plants he lies,
   in the covert of the reeds and in
   the marsh.
22 For his shade the lotus trees cover
   him;
   the willows of the brook surround
   him.
23 Behold, if the river is turbulent he
   is not frightened;
   he is confident though Jordan
   rushes against his mouth.
24 Can one take him with hooks,*q*
   or pierce his nose with a snare?

41 "Can you draw out Lē·vī'a-
   thān*s* with a fishhook,
   or press down his tongue with a
   cord?
2 Can you put a rope in his nose,
   or pierce his jaw with a hook?
3 Will he make many supplications to
   you?
   Will he speak to you soft words?
4 Will he make a covenant with
   you
   to take him for your servant for
   ever?
5 Will you play with him as with a
   bird,
   or will you put him on leash for
   your maidens?
6 Will traders bargain over him?
   Will they divide him up among
   the merchants?
7 Can you fill his skin with harpoons,
   or his head with fishing spears?
8 Lay hands on him;
   think of the battle; you will not
   do it again!
9 *t* Behold, the hope of a man is
   disappointed;
   he is laid low even at the sight of
   him.
10 No one is so fierce that he dares to
   stir him up.
   Who then is he that can stand
   before me?
11 Who has given to me,*u* that I should
   repay him?
   Whatever is under the whole
   heaven is mine.

12 "I will not keep silence concerning
   his limbs,
   or his mighty strength, or his
   goodly frame.
13 Who can strip off his outer garment?
   Who can penetrate his double
   coat of mail?*v*
14 Who can open the doors of his face?
   Round about his teeth is terror.
15 His back*w* is made of rows of shields,
   shut up closely as with a seal.
16 One is so near to another
   that no air can come between
   them.
17 They are joined one to another;
   they clasp each other and cannot
   be separated.
18 His sneezings flash forth light,
   and his eyes are like the eyelids
   of the dawn.
19 Out of his mouth go flaming torches;
   sparks of fire leap forth.
20 Out of his nostrils comes forth
   smoke,
   as from a boiling pot and burning
   rushes.
21 His breath kindles coals,
   and a flame comes forth from his
   mouth.
22 In his neck abides strength,
   and terror dances before him.
23 The folds of his flesh cleave together,
   firmly cast upon him and immovable.
24 His heart is hard as a stone,
   hard as the nether millstone.
25 When he raises himself up the
   mighty*x* are afraid;
   at the crashing they are beside
   themselves.
26 Though the sword reaches him, it
   does not avail;
   nor the spear, the dart, or the
   javelin.
27 He counts iron as straw,
   and bronze as rotten wood.
28 The arrow cannot make him flee;
   for him slingstones are turned to
   stubble.
29 Clubs are counted as stubble;
   he laughs at the rattle of javelins.
30 His underparts are like sharp potsherds;
   he spreads himself like a threshing
   sledge on the mire.
31 He makes the deep boil like a pot;
   he makes the sea like a pot of
   ointment.
32 Behind him he leaves a shining
   wake;

p Heb *ways*   *q* Cn: Heb *in his eyes*   *r* Ch 40.25 in Heb
s Or *the crocodile*   *t* Ch 41.1 in Heb   *u* The meaning of the Hebrew is uncertain
v Gk: Heb *bridle*   *w* Cn Compare Gk Vg: Heb *pride*
x Or *gods*
41.11: Rom 11.35.

one would think the deep to be
hoary.
33 Upon earth there is not his like,
a creature without fear.
34 He beholds everything that is high;
he is king over all the sons of
pride."

42 Then Jōb answered the LORD:
2 "I know that thou canst do all
things,
and that no purpose of thine can
be thwarted.
3 'Who is this that hides counsel
without knowledge?'
Therefore I have uttered what I did
not understand,
things too wonderful for me,
which I did not know.
4 'Hear, and I will speak;
I will question you, and you declare to me.'
5 I had heard of thee by the hearing
of the ear,
but now my eye sees thee;
6 therefore I despise myself,
and repent in dust and ashes."

7 After the LORD had spoken these
words to Jōb, the LORD said to E·lī´-
phaz the Tē´mà·nite: "My wrath is
kindled against you and against your
two friends; for you have not spoken
of me what is right, as my servant Jōb
has. 8 Now therefore take seven bulls
and seven rams, and go to my servant
Jōb, and offer up for yourselves a
burnt offering; and my servant Job

ʸ Heb qesitah

shall pray for you, for I will accept his
prayer not to deal with you according
to your folly; for you have not spoken
of me what is right, as my servant Job
has." 9 So E·lī´phaz the Tē´mà·nite
and Bil´dad the Shü´hite and Zō´phär
the Nā´à·mà·thīte went and did what
the LORD had told them; and the LORD
accepted Jōb's prayer.

10 And the LORD restored the fortunes of Jōb, when he had prayed for
his friends; and the LORD gave Job
twice as much as he had before.
11 Then came to him all his brothers
and sisters and all who had known him
before, and ate bread with him in his
house; and they showed him sympathy
and comforted him for all the evil that
the LORD had brought upon him; and
each of them gave him a piece of
moneyʸ and a ring of gold. 12 And the
LORD blessed the latter days of Jōb
more than his beginning; and he had
fourteen thousand sheep, six thousand
camels, a thousand yoke of oxen, and
a thousand she-asses. 13 He had also
seven sons and three daughters. 14 And
he called the name of the first Je·mī´-
màh; and the name of the second
Ke·zī´àh; and the name of the third
Ker´èn-hap´pūch. 15 And in all the
land there were no women so fair as
Jōb's daughters; and their father gave
them inheritance among their brothers.
16 And after this Jōb lived a hundred
and forty years, and saw his sons, and
his sons' sons, four generations. 17 And
Jōb died, an old man, and full of days.

THE PSALMS

BOOK I

1 Blessed is the man
   who walks not in the counsel of
      the wicked,
   nor stands in the way of sinners,
      nor sits in the seat of scoffers;
2 but his delight is in the law of the
      LORD,
   and on his law he meditates day
      and night.
3 He is like a tree
   planted by streams of water,
   that yields its fruit in its season,
      and its leaf does not wither.
   In all that he does, he prospers.

4 The wicked are not so,
   but are like chaff which the wind
      drives away.
5 Therefore the wicked will not stand
      in the judgment,
   nor sinners in the congregation
      of the righteous;
6 for the LORD knows the way of the
      righteous,
   but the way of the wicked will
      perish.

2 Why do the nations conspire, and
   the peoples plot in vain?
2 The kings of the earth set them-
      selves,
   and the rulers take counsel to-
      gether,
   against the LORD and his anointed,
      saying,
3 "Let us burst their bonds asunder,
   and cast their cords from us."

4 He who sits in the heavens laughs;
   the LORD has them in derision.
5 Then he will speak to them in his
      wrath,
   and terrify them in his fury,
      saying,
6 "I have set my king
   on Zion, my holy hill."

7 I will tell of the decree of the
      LORD:
   He said to me, "You are my son,
      today I have begotten you.
8 Ask of me, and I will make the na-
      tions your heritage,

and the ends of the earth your
      possession.
9 You shall break them with a rod
      of iron,
   and dash them in pieces like a
      potter's vessel."

10 Now therefore, O kings, be wise;
   be warned, O rulers of the
      earth.
11 Serve the LORD with fear,
   with trembling 12 kiss his feet,*a*
   lest he be angry, and you perish in
      the way;
   for his wrath is quickly kindled.

   Blessed are all who take refuge in
      him.

A Psalm of David, when he fled from
   Ab'sà·lóm his son.

3 O LORD, how many are my foes!
   Many are rising against me;
2 many are saying of me,
   there is no help for him in
      God.   *Selah*

3 But thou, O LORD, art a shield
      about me,
   my glory, and the lifter of my
      head.
4 I cry aloud to the LORD,
   and he answers me from his holy
      hill.   *Selah*

5 I lie down and sleep;
   I wake again, for the LORD sus-
      tains me.
6 I am not afraid of ten thousands of
      people
   who have set themselves against
      me round about.

7 Arise, O LORD!
   Deliver me, O my God!
   For thou dost smite all my enemies
      on the cheek,
   thou dost break the teeth of the
      wicked.

8 Deliverance belongs to the LORD;
   thy blessing be upon thy people!
                              Selah

a Cn: The Hebrew of 11b and 12a is uncertain
1.1-3: Jer 17.7-8. **2.1-2:** Acts 4.25-26.
2.7: Mt 3.17; Acts 13.33; Heb 1.5; 5.5; 2 Pet 1.17.
2.8-9: Rev 2.26; 12.5; 19.15.

To the choirmaster: with stringed instruments. A Psalm of David.

4 Answer me when I call, O God of my right!
Thou hast given me room when I was in distress.
Be gracious to me, and hear my prayer.

2 O men, how long shall my honor suffer shame?
How long will you love vain words, and seek after lies?
Selah

3 But know that the LORD has set apart the godly for himself;
the LORD hears when I call to him.

4 Be angry, but sin not;
commune with your own hearts on your beds, and be silent.
Selah

5 Offer right sacrifices,
and put your trust in the LORD.

6 There are many who say, "O that we might see some good!
Lift up the light of thy countenance upon us, O LORD!"

7 Thou hast put more joy in my heart than they have when their grain and wine abound.

8 In peace I will both lie down and sleep;
for thou alone, O LORD, makest me dwell in safety.

To the choirmaster: for the flutes. A Psalm of David.

5 Give ear to my words, O LORD;
give heed to my groaning.

2 Hearken to the sound of my cry,
my King and my God,
for to thee do I pray.

3 O LORD, in the morning thou dost hear my voice;
in the morning I prepare a sacrifice for thee, and watch.

4 For thou art not a God who delights in wickedness;
evil may not sojourn with thee.

5 The boastful may not stand before thy eyes;
thou hatest all evildoers.

6 Thou destroyest those who speak lies;
the LORD abhors bloodthirsty and deceitful men.

4.4: Eph 4.26.   5.9: Rom 3.13.

7 But I through the abundance of thy steadfast love
will enter thy house,
I will worship toward thy holy temple
in the fear of thee.

8 Lead me, O LORD, in thy righteousness
because of my enemies;
make thy way straight before me.

9 For there is no truth in their mouth;
their heart is destruction,
their throat is an open sepulchre,
they flatter with their tongue.

10 Make them bear their guilt, O God;
let them fall by their own counsels;
because of their many transgressions cast them out,
for they have rebelled against thee.

11 But let all who take refuge in thee rejoice,
let them ever sing for joy;
and do thou defend them,
that those who love thy name may exult in thee.

12 For thou dost bless the righteous, O LORD;
thou dost cover him with favor as with a shield.

To the choirmaster: with stringed instruments; according to The Sheminith. A Psalm of David.

6 O LORD, rebuke me not in thy anger,
nor chasten me in thy wrath.

2 Be gracious to me, O LORD, for I am languishing;
O LORD, heal me, for my bones are troubled.

3 My soul also is sorely troubled.
But thou, O LORD—how long?

4 Turn, O LORD, save my life;
deliver me for the sake of thy steadfast love.

5 For in death there is no remembrance of thee;
in She′ōl who can give thee praise?

6 I am weary with my moaning;
every night I flood my bed with tears;
I drench my couch with my weeping.

7 My eye wastes away because of grief,
it grows weak because of all my foes.

8 Depart from me, all you workers of evil;
  for the LORD has heard the sound of my weeping.
9 The LORD has heard my supplication;
  the LORD accepts my prayer.
10 All my enemies shall be ashamed and sorely troubled;
  they shall turn back, and be put to shame in a moment.

A Shiggaion of David, which he sang to the LORD concerning Cush a Benjaminite.

7 O LORD my God, in thee do I take refuge;
  save me from all my pursuers, and deliver me,
2 lest like a lion they rend me,
  dragging me away, with none to rescue.

3 O LORD my God, if I have done this,
  if there is wrong in my hands,
4 if I have requited my friend with evil or plundered my enemy without cause,
5 let the enemy pursue me and overtake me,
  and let him trample my life to the ground,
  and lay my soul in the dust. *Selah*

6 Arise, O LORD, in thy anger,
  lift thyself up against the fury of my enemies;
  awake, O my God;[b] thou hast appointed a judgment.
7 Let the assembly of the peoples be gathered about thee;
  and over it take thy seat[c] on high.
8 The LORD judges the peoples;
  judge me, O LORD, according to my righteousness
  and according to the integrity that is in me.

9 O let the evil of the wicked come to an end,
  but establish thou the righteous,
  thou who triest the minds and hearts,
  thou righteous God.
10 My shield is with God,
  who saves the upright in heart.
11 God is a righteous judge,
  and a God who has indignation every day.

12 If a man[d] does not repent, God[d] will whet his sword;
  he has bent and strung his bow;
13 he has prepared his deadly weapons,
  making his arrows fiery shafts.
14 Behold, the wicked man conceives evil,
  and is pregnant with mischief, and brings forth lies.
15 He makes a pit, digging it out,
  and falls into the hole which he has made.
16 His mischief returns upon his own head,
  and on his own pate his violence descends.

17 I will give to the LORD the thanks due to his righteousness,
  and I will sing praise to the name of the LORD, the Most High.

To the choirmaster: according to The Gittith. A Psalm of David.

8 O LORD, our Lord,
  how majestic is thy name in all the earth!

Thou whose glory above the heavens is chanted
2 by the mouth of babes and infants,
  thou hast founded a bulwark because of thy foes,
  to still the enemy and the avenger.

3 When I look at thy heavens, the work of thy fingers,
  the moon and the stars which thou hast established;
4 what is man that thou art mindful of him,
  and the son of man that thou dost care for him?

5 Yet thou hast made him little less than God,
  and dost crown him with glory and honor.
6 Thou hast given him dominion over the works of thy hands;
  thou hast put all things under his feet,
7 all sheep and oxen,
  and also the beasts of the field,
8 the birds of the air, and the fish of the sea,
  whatever passes along the paths of the sea.

9 O LORD, our Lord,

b Or *for me*   *c* Cn: Heb *return*   *d* Heb *he*
6.8: Mt 7.23; Lk 13.27.   **7.9:** Rev 2.23.   **8.2:** Mt 21.16.
8.4-6: Job 7.17-18; Ps 144.3; Heb 2.6-8.   **8.6:** 1 Cor 15.27; Eph 1.22.

how majestic is thy name in all
the earth!

To the choirmaster: according to
Muth-labben. A Psalm of David.

9 I will give thanks to the LORD
with my whole heart;
I will tell of all thy wonderful
deeds.
2 I will be glad and exult in thee,
I will sing praise to thy name,
O Most High.

3 When my enemies turned back,
they stumbled and perished before thee.
4 For thou hast maintained my just
cause;
thou hast sat on the throne giving
righteous judgment.

5 Thou hast rebuked the nations, thou
hast destroyed the wicked;
thou hast blotted out their name
for ever and ever.
6 The enemy have vanished in everlasting ruins;
their cities thou hast rooted out;
the very memory of them has
perished.

7 But the LORD sits enthroned for
ever,
he has established his throne for
judgment;
8 and he judges the world with righteousness,
he judges the peoples with equity.

9 The LORD is a stronghold for the
oppressed,
a stronghold in times of trouble.
10 And those who know thy name put
their trust in thee,
for thou, O LORD, hast not forsaken those who seek thee.

11 Sing praises to the LORD, who dwells
in Zion!
Tell among the peoples his deeds!
12 For he who avenges blood is mindful
of them;
he does not forget the cry of the
afflicted.

13 Be gracious to me, O LORD!
Behold what I suffer from those
who hate me,
O thou who liftest me up from
the gates of death,
14 that I may recount all thy praises,

9.8: Acts 17.31.
10.7: Rom 3.14.

that in the gates of the daughter
of Zion
I may rejoice in thy deliverance.

15 The nations have sunk in the pit
which they made;
in the net which they hid has
their own foot been caught.
16 The LORD has made himself known,
he has executed judgment;
the wicked are snared in the work
of their own hands.

Higgaion. Selah

17 The wicked shall depart to Shē'ōl,
all the nations that forget God.

18 For the needy shall not always be
forgotten,
and the hope of the poor shall not
perish for ever.

19 Arise, O LORD! Let not man prevail;
let the nations be judged before
thee!
20 Put them in fear, O LORD!
Let the nations know that they
are but men!   *Selah*

10 Why dost thou stand afar off,
O LORD?
Why dost thou hide thyself in
times of trouble?
2 In arrogance the wicked hotly pursue the poor;
let them be caught in the schemes
which they have devised.

3 For the wicked boasts of the desires
of his heart,
and the man greedy for gain
curses and renounces the LORD.
4 In the pride of his countenance the
wicked does not seek him;
all his thoughts are, "There is no
God."

5 His ways prosper at all times;
thy judgments are on high, out
of his sight;
as for all his foes, he puffs at them.
6 He thinks in his heart, "I shall not
be moved;
throughout all generations I shall
not meet adversity."

7 His mouth is filled with cursing and
deceit and oppression;
under his tongue are mischief and
iniquity.
8 He sits in ambush in the villages;
in hiding places he murders the
innocent.

His eyes stealthily watch for the
  hapless,
9 he lurks in secret like a lion in his
  covert;
he lurks that he may seize the poor,
  he seizes the poor when he draws
  him into his net.

10 The hapless is crushed, sinks down,
  and falls by his might.
11 He thinks in his heart, "God has
  forgotten,
he has hidden his face, he will
  never see it."

12 Arise, O LORD; O God, lift up thy
  hand;
forget not the afflicted.
13 Why does the wicked renounce God,
  and say in his heart, "Thou wilt
  not call to account"?

14 Thou dost see; yea, thou dost note
  trouble and vexation,
that thou mayst take it into thy
  hands;
the hapless commits himself to thee;
  thou hast been the helper of the
  fatherless.

15 Break thou the arm of the wicked
  and evildoer;
seek out his wickedness till thou
  find none.
16 The LORD is king for ever and ever;
  the nations shall perish from his
  land.

17 O LORD, thou wilt hear the desire
  of the meek;
thou wilt strengthen their heart,
  thou wilt incline thy ear
18 to do justice to the fatherless and
  the oppressed,
so that man who is of the earth
  may strike terror no more.

To the choirmaster. Of David.

11   In the LORD I take refuge;
  how can you say to me,
"Flee like a bird to the mountains;[e]
2 for lo, the wicked bend the bow, they
  have fitted their arrow to the string,
to shoot in the dark at the upright
  in heart;
3 if the foundations are destroyed,
  what can the righteous do"?

4 The LORD is in his holy temple,
  the LORD's throne is in heaven;
his eyes behold, his eyelids test,
  the children of men.

5 The LORD tests the righteous and
  the wicked,
and his soul hates him that loves
  violence.
6 On the wicked he will rain coals of
  fire and brimstone;
a scorching wind shall be the
  portion of their cup.
7 For the LORD is righteous, he loves
  righteous deeds;
the upright shall behold his face.

To the choirmaster: according to The
  Sheminith. A Psalm of David.

12   Help, LORD; for there is no
  longer any that is godly;
for the faithful have vanished
  from among the sons of men.
2 Every one utters lies to his neighbor;
  with flattering lips and a double
  heart they speak.

3 May the LORD cut off all flattering lips,
  the tongue that makes great boasts,
4 those who say, "With our tongue
  we will prevail,
our lips are with us; who is our
  master?"

5 "Because the poor are despoiled,
  because the needy groan,
I will now arise," says the LORD;
"I will place him in the safety
  for which he longs."
6 The promises of the LORD are promises that are pure,
silver refined in a furnace on the
  ground,
purified seven times.

7 Do thou, O LORD, protect us,
  guard us ever from this generation.
8 On every side the wicked prowl,
  as vileness is exalted among the
  sons of men.

To the choirmaster. A Psalm of David.

13   How long, O LORD? Wilt thou
  forget me for ever?
How long wilt thou hide thy face
  from me?
2 How long must I bear pain[f] in my
  soul,
and have sorrow in my heart all
  the day?
How long shall my enemy be exalted
  over me?

3 Consider and answer me, O LORD
  my God;

e Gk Syr Jerome Tg: Heb *flee to your mountain, O bird*   f Syr: Heb *hold counsels*

lighten my eyes, lest I sleep the
sleep of death;
4 lest my enemy say, "I have prevailed
over him";
lest my foes rejoice because I am
shaken.

5 But I have trusted in thy steadfast
love;
my heart shall rejoice in thy
salvation.
6 I will sing to the LORD,
because he has dealt bountifully
with me.

To the choirmaster. Of David.

14 The fool says in his heart,
"There is no God."
They are corrupt, they do
abominable deeds,
there is none that does good.

2 The LORD looks down from heaven
upon the children of men,
to see if there are any that act
wisely,
that seek after God.

3 They have all gone astray, they are
all alike corrupt;
there is none that does good,
no, not one.

4 Have they no knowledge, all the
evildoers
who eat up my people as they eat
bread,
and do not call upon the LORD?

5 There they shall be in great terror,
for God is with the generation of
the righteous.
6 You would confound the plans of
the poor,
but the LORD is his refuge.

7 O that deliverance for Israel would
come out of Zion!
When the LORD restores the
fortunes of his people,
Jacob shall rejoice, Israel shall be
glad.

A Psalm of David.

15 O LORD, who shall sojourn in
thy tent?
Who shall dwell on thy holy hill?

2 He who walks blamelessly, and does
what is right,
and speaks truth from his heart;
3 who does not slander with his
tongue,
and does no evil to his friend,
nor takes up a reproach against
his neighbor;
4 in whose eyes a reprobate is despised,
but who honors those who fear
the LORD;
who swears to his own hurt and
does not change;
5 who does not put out his money at
interest,
and does not take a bribe against
the innocent.

He who does these things shall never
be moved.

A Miktam of David.

16 Preserve me, O God, for in thee
I take refuge.
2 I say to the LORD, "Thou art my
Lord;
I have no good apart from thee."*g*

3 As for the saints in the land, they
are the noble,
in whom is all my delight.

4 Those who choose another god
multiply their sorrows;*h*
their libations of blood I will not
pour out
or take their names upon my lips.

5 The LORD is my chosen portion and
my cup;
thou holdest my lot.
6 The lines have fallen for me in
pleasant places;
yea, I have a goodly heritage.

7 I bless the LORD who gives me
counsel;
in the night also my heart instructs me.
8 I keep the LORD always before me;
because he is at my right hand,
I shall not be moved.

9 Therefore my heart is glad, and my
soul rejoices;
my body also dwells secure.
10 For thou dost not give me up to
Shĕ'ōl,

g Jerome Tg: The meaning of the Hebrew is uncertain
h Cn: The meaning of the Hebrew is uncertain
14.1-3: Rom 3.10-12.   **14.1-7**: Ps 53.1-6.
16.8-11: Acts 2.25-28, 31.   **16.10**: Acts 13.35.

or let thy godly one see the Pit.

11 Thou dost show me the path of life;
   in thy presence there is fulness of
     joy,
   in thy right hand are pleasures
     for evermore.

A Prayer of David.

17 Hear a just cause, O LORD;
     attend to my cry!
   Give ear to my prayer from lips
     free of deceit!
2 From thee let my vindication come!
   Let thy eyes see the right!

3 If thou triest my heart, if thou
     visitest me by night,
   if thou testest me, thou wilt find
     no wickedness in me;
   my mouth does not transgress.
4 With regard to the works of men,
     by the word of thy lips
   I have avoided the ways of the
     violent.
5 My steps have held fast to thy paths,
   my feet have not slipped.

6 I call upon thee, for thou wilt an-
     swer me, O God;
   incline thy ear to me, hear my
     words.
7 Wondrously show thy steadfast love,
   O savior of those who seek refuge
   from their adversaries at thy right
     hand.

8 Keep me as the apple of the eye;
   hide me in the shadow of thy wings,
9 from the wicked who despoil me,
   my deadly enemies who surround
     me.
10 They close their hearts to pity;
   with their mouths they speak
     arrogantly.
11 They track me down; now they
     surround me;
   they set their eyes to cast me to
     the ground.
12 They are like a lion eager to tear,
   as a young lion lurking in ambush.

13 Arise, O LORD! confront them, over-
     throw them!
   Deliver my life from the wicked
     by thy sword,
14 from men by thy hand, O LORD,
   from men whose portion in life
     is of the world.
   May their belly be filled with what
     thou hast stored up for them;

18.1-50: 2 Sam 22.2-51.

may their children have more
    than enough;
   may they leave something over to
    their babes.

15 As for me, I shall behold thy face
    in righteousness;
   when I awake, I shall be satisfied
    with beholding thy form.

To the choirmaster. A Psalm of David
the servant of the LORD, who addressed
the words of this song to the LORD on
the day when the LORD delivered him
from the hand of all his enemies, and
from the hand of Saul. He said:

18 I love thee, O LORD, my
     strength.
2 The LORD is my rock, and my
     fortress, and my deliverer,
   my God, my rock, in whom I
     take refuge,
   my shield, and the horn of my
     salvation, my stronghold.
3 I call upon the LORD, who is worthy
     to be praised,
   and I am saved from my enemies.

4 The cords of death encompassed me,
   the torrents of perdition assailed
     me;
5 the cords of Shē′ol entangled me,
   the snares of death confronted me.

6 In my distress I called upon the
     LORD;
   to my God I cried for help.
   From his temple he heard my voice,
   and my cry to him reached his ears.

7 Then the earth reeled and rocked;
   the foundations also of the moun-
     tains trembled
   and quaked, because he was
     angry.
8 Smoke went up from his nostrils,
   and devouring fire from his mouth;
   glowing coals flamed forth from
     him.
9 He bowed the heavens, and came
     down;
   thick darkness was under his feet.
10 He rode on a cherub, and flew;
   he came swiftly upon the wings
     of the wind.
11 He made darkness his covering
     around him,
   his canopy thick clouds dark with
     water.
12 Out of the brightness before him
   there broke through his clouds
   hailstones and coals of fire.

13 The LORD also thundered in the heavens,
 and the Most High uttered his voice,
 hailstones and coals of fire.
14 And he sent out his arrows, and scattered them;
 he flashed forth lightnings, and routed them.
15 Then the channels of the sea were seen,
 and the foundations of the world were laid bare,
 at thy rebuke, O LORD,
 at the blast of the breath of thy nostrils.

16 He reached from on high, he took me,
 he drew me out of many waters.
17 He delivered me from my strong enemy,
 and from those who hated me;
 for they were too mighty for me.
18 They came upon me in the day of my calamity;
 but the LORD was my stay.
19 He brought me forth into a broad place;
 he delivered me, because he delighted in me.

20 The LORD rewarded me according to my righteousness;
 according to the cleanness of my hands he recompensed me.
21 For I have kept the ways of the LORD,
 and have not wickedly departed from my God.
22 For all his ordinances were before me,
 and his statutes I did not put away from me.
23 I was blameless before him,
 and I kept myself from guilt.
24 Therefore the LORD has recompensed me according to my righteousness,
 according to the cleanness of my hands in his sight.

25 With the loyal thou dost show thyself loyal;
 with the blameless man thou dost show thyself blameless;
26 with the pure thou dost show thyself pure;
 and with the crooked thou dost show thyself perverse.
27 For thou dost deliver a humble people;
 but the haughty eyes thou dost bring down.

28 Yea, thou dost light my lamp;
 the LORD my God lightens my darkness.
29 Yea, by thee I can crush a troop;
 and by my God I can leap over a wall.
30 This God—his way is perfect;
 the promise of the LORD proves true;
 he is a shield for all those who take refuge in him.

31 For who is God, but the LORD?
 And who is a rock, except our God?—
32 the God who girded me with strength,
 and made my way safe.
33 He made my feet like hinds' feet,
 and set me secure on the heights.
34 He trains my hands for war,
 so that my arms can bend a bow of bronze.
35 Thou hast given me the shield of thy salvation,
 and thy right hand supported me,
 and thy help[i] made me great.
36 Thou didst give a wide place for my steps under me,
 and my feet did not slip.
37 I pursued my enemies and overtook them;
 and did not turn back till they were consumed.
38 I thrust them through, so that they were not able to rise;
 they fell under my feet.
39 For thou didst gird me with strength for the battle;
 thou didst make my assailants sink under me.
40 Thou didst make my enemies turn their backs to me,
 and those who hated me I destroyed.
41 They cried for help, but there was none to save,
 they cried to the LORD, but he did not answer them.
42 I beat them fine as dust before the wind;
 I cast them out like the mire of the streets.

43 Thou didst deliver me from strife with the peoples;[j]
 thou didst make me the head of the nations;
 people whom I had not known served me.
44 As soon as they heard of me they obeyed me;
 foreigners came cringing to me.
45 Foreigners lost heart,

i Or gentleness *j* Gk Tg: Heb *people*

and came trembling out of their fastnesses.

46 The LORD lives; and blessed be my rock,
and exalted be the God of my salvation,
47 the God who gave me vengeance
and subdued peoples under me;
48 who delivered me from my enemies;
yea, thou didst exalt me above my adversaries;
thou didst deliver me from men of violence.

49 For this I will extol thee, O LORD, among the nations,
and sing praises to thy name.
50 Great triumphs he gives to his king,
and shows steadfast love to his anointed,
to David and his descendants for ever.

To the choirmaster. A Psalm of David.

19 The heavens are telling the glory of God;
and the firmament proclaims his handiwork.
2 Day to day pours forth speech,
and night to night declares knowledge.
3 There is no speech, nor are there words;
their voice is not heard;
4 yet their voice[k] goes out through all the earth,
and their words to the end of the world.

In them he has set a tent for the sun,
5 which comes forth like a bridegroom leaving his chamber,
and like a strong man runs its course with joy.
6 Its rising is from the end of the heavens,
and its circuit to the end of them;
and there is nothing hid from its heat.

7 The law of the LORD is perfect, reviving the soul;
the testimony of the LORD is sure, making wise the simple;
8 the precepts of the LORD are right, rejoicing the heart;
the commandment of the LORD is pure, enlightening the eyes;
9 the fear of the LORD is clean, enduring for ever;

the ordinances of the LORD are true, and righteous altogether.
10 More to be desired are they than gold, even much fine gold;
sweeter also than honey and drippings of the honeycomb.

11 Moreover by them is thy servant warned;
in keeping them there is great reward.
12 But who can discern his errors? Clear thou me from hidden faults.
13 Keep back thy servant also from presumptuous sins;
let them not have dominion over me!
Then I shall be blameless, and innocent of great transgression.

14 Let the words of my mouth and the meditation of my heart
be acceptable in thy sight,
O LORD, my rock and my redeemer.

To the choirmaster. A Psalm of David.

20 The LORD answer you in the day of trouble!
The name of the God of Jacob protect you!
2 May he send you help from the sanctuary,
and give you support from Zion!
3 May he remember all your offerings,
and regard with favor your burnt sacrifices! *Selah*

4 May he grant you your heart's desire,
and fulfil all your plans!
5 May we shout for joy over your victory,
and in the name of our God set up our banners!
May the LORD fulfil all your petitions!

6 Now I know that the LORD will help his anointed;
he will answer him from his holy heaven
with mighty victories by his right hand.
7 Some boast of chariots, and some of horses;
but we boast of the name of the LORD our God.
8 They will collapse and fall;
but we shall rise and stand upright.

k Gk Jerome Compare Syr: Heb *line*   18.49: Rom 15.9.   19.4: Rom 10.18.

9 Give victory to the king, O LORD;
　　answer us when we call.[l]

To the choirmaster. A Psalm of David.

21 In thy strength the king rejoices, O LORD;
　　and in thy help how greatly he exults!
2 Thou hast given him his heart's desire,
　　and hast not withheld the request of his lips.　　　　*Selah*
3 For thou dost meet him with goodly blessings;
　　thou dost set a crown of fine gold upon his head.
4 He asked life of thee; thou gavest it to him,
　　length of days for ever and ever.
5 His glory is great through thy help;
　　splendor and majesty thou dost bestow upon him.
6 Yea, thou dost make him most blessed for ever;
　　thou dost make him glad with the joy of thy presence.
7 For the king trusts in the LORD;
　　and through the steadfast love of the Most High he shall not be moved.

8 Your hand will find out all your enemies;
　　your right hand will find out those who hate you.
9 You will make them as a blazing oven when you appear.
　　The LORD will swallow them up in his wrath;
　　and fire will consume them.
10 You will destroy their offspring from the earth,
　　and their children from among the sons of men.
11 If they plan evil against you,
　　if they devise mischief, they will not succeed.
12 For you will put them to flight;
　　you will aim at their faces with your bows.

13 Be exalted, O LORD, in thy strength!
　　We will sing and praise thy power.

To the choirmaster: according to The Hind of the Dawn. A Psalm of David.

22 My God, my God, why hast thou forsaken me?

Why art thou so far from helping me, from the words of my groaning?
2 O my God, I cry by day, but thou dost not answer;
　　and by night, but find no rest.

3 Yet thou art holy,
　　enthroned on the praises of Israel.
4 In thee our fathers trusted;
　　they trusted, and thou didst deliver them.
5 To thee they cried, and were saved;
　　in thee they trusted, and were not disappointed.

6 But I am a worm, and no man;
　　scorned by men, and despised by the people.
7 All who see me mock at me,
　　they make mouths at me, they wag their heads;
8 "He committed his cause to the LORD; let him deliver him,
　　let him rescue him, for he delights in him!"

9 Yet thou art he who took me from the womb;
　　thou didst keep me safe upon my mother's breasts.
10 Upon thee was I cast from my birth,
　　and since my mother bore me thou hast been my God.
11 Be not far from me,
　　for trouble is near
　　and there is none to help.

12 Many bulls encompass me,
　　strong bulls of Bā'shān surround me;
13 they open wide their mouths at me,
　　like a ravening and roaring lion.

14 I am poured out like water,
　　and all my bones are out of joint;
　　my heart is like wax,
　　it is melted within my breast;
15 my strength is dried up like a potsherd,
　　and my tongue cleaves to my jaws;
　　thou dost lay me in the dust of death.

16 Yea, dogs are round about me;
　　a company of evildoers encircle me;
　　they have pierced[m] my hands and feet—
17 I can count all my bones—
　　they stare and gloat over me;

l Gk: Heb *give victory, O* LORD, *let the King answer us when we call*
m Gk Syr Jerome: Heb *like a lion*
22.1: Mt 27.46; Mk 15.34.　　**22.7-8:** Mt 27.39, 43; Mk 15.29; Lk 23.35.

18 they divide my garments among
   them,
   and for my raiment they cast lots.

19 But thou, O Lord, be not far off!
   O thou my help, hasten to my
   aid!
20 Deliver my soul from the sword,
   my life[n] from the power of the
   dog!
21 Save me from the mouth of the
   lion,
   my afflicted soul[o] from the horns
   of the wild oxen!

22 I will tell of thy name to my
   brethren;
   in the midst of the congregation
   I will praise thee:
23 You who fear the Lord, praise him!
   all you sons of Jacob, glorify him,
   and stand in awe of him, all you
   sons of Israel!
24 For he has not despised or abhorred
   the affliction of the afflicted;
   and he has not hid his face from him,
   but has heard, when he cried to
   him.

25 From thee comes my praise in the
   great congregation;
   my vows I will pay before those
   who fear him.
26 The afflicted[p] shall eat and be
   satisfied;
   those who seek him shall praise
   the Lord!
   May your hearts live for ever!

27 All the ends of the earth shall remember
   and turn to the Lord;
   and all the families of the nations
   shall worship before him.[q]
28 For dominion belongs to the Lord,
   and he rules over the nations.

29 Yea, to him[r] shall all the proud of
   the earth bow down;
   before him shall bow all who go
   down to the dust,
   and he who cannot keep himself
   alive.
30 Posterity shall serve him;
   men shall tell of the Lord to the
   coming generation,
31 and proclaim his deliverance to a
   people yet unborn,
   that he has wrought it.

A Psalm of David.

23 The Lord is my shepherd,
   I shall not want;
2   he makes me lie down in green
   pastures.
   He leads me beside still waters;[s]
3   he restores my soul.[t]
   He leads me in paths of righteousness[u]
   for his name's sake.

4 Even though I walk through the
   valley of the shadow of death,[v]
   I fear no evil;
   for thou art with me;
   thy rod and thy staff,
   they comfort me.

5 Thou preparest a table before me
   in the presence of my enemies;
   thou anointest my head with oil,
   my cup overflows.
6 Surely[w] goodness and mercy[x] shall
   follow me
   all the days of my life;
   and I shall dwell in the house of the
   Lord
   for ever.[y]

A Psalm of David.

24 The earth is the Lord's and
   the fulness thereof,
   the world and those who dwell
   therein;
2 for he has founded it upon the seas,
   and established it upon the rivers.

3 Who shall ascend the hill of the
   Lord?
   And who shall stand in his holy
   place?
4 He who has clean hands and a pure
   heart,
   who does not lift up his soul to
   what is false,
   and does not swear deceitfully.
5 He will receive blessing from the
   Lord,
   and vindication from the God of
   his salvation.
6 Such is the generation of those who
   seek him,
   who seek the face of the God of
   Jacob.[z]   *Selah*

7 Lift up your heads, O gates!
   and be lifted up, O ancient doors!

n Heb *my only one*   *o* Gk Syr: Heb *thou hast answered me*   *p* Or *poor*
q Gk Syr Jerome: Heb *thee*   *r* Cn: Heb *they have eaten and*   *s* Heb *the waters of rest*
t Or *life*   *u* Or *right paths*   *v* Or *the valley of deep darkness*   *w* Or *Only*
x Or *kindness*   *y* Or *as long as I live*   *z* Gk Syr: Heb *thy face, O Jacob*
22.18: Mt 27.35; Mk 15.24; Lk 23.34; Jn 19.24.   **22.22:** Heb 2.12.
23.2: Rev 7.17.   **24.1:** 1 Cor 10.26.   **24.4:** Mt 5.8.

that the King of glory may come
in.
8 Who is the King of glory?
The LORD, strong and mighty,
the LORD, mighty in battle!
9 Lift up your heads, O gates!
and be lifted up,[a] O ancient doors!
that the King of glory may come
in.
10 Who is this King of glory?
The LORD of hosts,
he is the King of glory!   Selah

A Psalm of David.

25 To thee, O LORD, I lift up my
soul.
2 O my God, in thee I trust,
let me not be put to shame;
let not my enemies exult over me.
3 Yea, let none that wait for thee be
put to shame;
let them be ashamed who are
wantonly treacherous.

4 Make me to know thy ways, O LORD;
teach me thy paths.
5 Lead me in thy truth, and teach me,
for thou art the God of my
salvation;
for thee I wait all the day long.

6 Be mindful of thy mercy, O LORD,
and of thy steadfast love,
for they have been from of old.
7 Remember not the sins of my youth,
or my transgressions;
according to thy steadfast love
remember me,
for thy goodness' sake, O LORD!

8 Good and upright is the LORD;
therefore he instructs sinners in
the way.
9 He leads the humble in what is
right,
and teaches the humble his way.
10 All the paths of the LORD are steadfast love and faithfulness,
for those who keep his covenant
and his testimonies.

11 For thy name's sake, O LORD,
pardon my guilt, for it is great.
12 Who is the man that fears the LORD?
Him will he instruct in the way
that he should choose.
13 He himself shall abide in prosperity,
and his children shall possess the
land.
14 The friendship of the LORD is for
those who fear him,

and he makes known to them his
covenant.
15 My eyes are ever toward the LORD,
for he will pluck my feet out of
the net.

16 Turn thou to me, and be gracious
to me;
for I am lonely and afflicted.
17 Relieve the troubles of my heart,
and bring me[b] out of my distresses.
18 Consider my affliction and my
trouble,
and forgive all my sins.

19 Consider how many are my foes,
and with what violent hatred they
hate me.
20 Oh guard my life, and deliver me;
let me not be put to shame, for
I take refuge in thee.
21 May integrity and uprightness preserve me,
for I wait for thee.

22 Redeem Israel, O God,
out of all his troubles.

A Psalm of David.

26 Vindicate me, O LORD,
for I have walked in my integrity,
and I have trusted in the LORD
without wavering.
2 Prove me, O LORD, and try me;
test my heart and my mind.
3 For thy steadfast love is before my
eyes,
and I walk in faithfulness to thee.[c]

4 I do not sit with false men,
nor do I consort with dissemblers;
5 I hate the company of evildoers,
and I will not sit with the wicked.

6 I wash my hands in innocence,
and go about thy altar, O LORD,
7 singing aloud a song of thanksgiving,
and telling all thy wondrous deeds.

8 O LORD, I love the habitation of
thy house,
and the place where thy glory
dwells.
9 Sweep me not away with sinners,
nor my life with bloodthirsty
men,
10 men in whose hands are evil devices,
and whose right hands are full of
bribes.

a Gk Syr Jerome Tg. Compare verse 7: Heb *lift up*
b Or *The troubles of my heart are enlarged; bring me*   c Or *in thy faithfulness*

11 But as for me, I walk in my integrity;
   redeem me, and be gracious to me.
12 My foot stands on level ground;
   in the great congregation I will
     bless the LORD.

A Psalm of David.

27 The LORD is my light and my
     salvation;
   whom shall I fear?
   The LORD is the stronghold[d] of my
     life;
   of whom shall I be afraid?

2 When evildoers assail me,
   uttering slanders against me,[e]
   my adversaries and foes,
     they shall stumble and fall.

3 Though a host encamp against me,
   my heart shall not fear;
   though war arise against me,
     yet I will be confident.

4 One thing have I asked of the LORD,
   that will I seek after;
   that I may dwell in the house of
     the LORD
   all the days of my life,
   to behold the beauty of the LORD,
     and to inquire in his temple.

5 For he will hide me in his shelter
   in the day of trouble;
   he will conceal me under the cover
     of his tent,
   he will set me high upon a rock.

6 And now my head shall be lifted
     up above my enemies round
     about me;
   and I will offer in his tent
   sacrifices with shouts of joy;
   I will sing and make melody to the
     LORD.

7 Hear, O LORD, when I cry aloud,
   be gracious to me and answer me!
8 Thou hast said, "Seek ye my face."
   My heart says to thee,
   "Thy face, LORD, do I seek."
9 Hide not thy face from me.

   Turn not thy servant away in anger,
     thou who hast been my help.
   Cast me not off, forsake me not,
     O God of my salvation!
10 For my father and my mother have
     forsaken me,
   but the LORD will take me up.

11 Teach me thy way, O LORD;

and lead me on a level path
   because of my enemies.
12 Give me not up to the will of my
     adversaries;
   for false witnesses have risen
     against me,
   and they breathe out violence.

13 I believe that I shall see the goodness
     of the LORD
   in the land of the living!
14 Wait for the LORD;
   be strong, and let your heart take
     courage;
   yea, wait for the LORD!

A Psalm of David.

28 To thee, O LORD, I call;
     my rock, be not deaf to me,
   lest, if thou be silent to me,
   I become like those who go down
     to the Pit.
2 Hear the voice of my supplication,
     as I cry to thee for help,
   as I lift up my hands
   toward thy most holy sanctuary.[f]

3 Take me not off with the wicked,
   with those who are workers of
     evil,
   who speak peace with their neigh-
     bors,
   while mischief is in their hearts.
4 Requite them according to their
     work,
   and according to the evil of their
     deeds;
   requite them according to the work
     of their hands;
   render them their due reward.
5 Because they do not regard the
     works of the LORD,
   or the work of his hands,
   he will break them down and build
     them up no more.

6 Blessed be the LORD!
   for he has heard the voice of my
     supplications.
7 The LORD is my strength and my
     shield;
   in him my heart trusts;
   so I am helped, and my heart exults,
   and with my song I give thanks
     to him.

8 The LORD is the strength of his
     people,
   he is the saving refuge of his
     anointed.
9 O save thy people, and bless thy
     heritage;

---

[d] Or *refuge*   [e] Heb *to eat up my flesh*   [f] Heb *thy innermost sanctuary*

be thou their shepherd, and carry
them for ever.

A Psalm of David.

29 Ascribe to the LORD, O
heavenly beings,[g]
ascribe to the LORD glory and
strength.
2 Ascribe to the LORD the glory of his
name;
worship the LORD in holy array.

3 The voice of the LORD is upon the
waters;
the God of glory thunders,
the LORD, upon many waters.
4 The voice of the LORD is powerful,
the voice of the LORD is full of
majesty.

5 The voice of the LORD breaks the
cedars,
the LORD breaks the cedars of
Lebanon.
6 He makes Lebanon to skip like a
calf,
and Sir′i·on like a young wild ox.

7 The voice of the LORD flashes forth
flames of fire.
8 The voice of the LORD shakes the
wilderness,
the LORD shakes the wilderness
of Ka′desh.

9 The voice of the LORD makes the
oaks to whirl,[h]
and strips the forests bare;
and in his temple all cry, "Glory!"

10 The LORD sits enthroned over the
flood;
the LORD sits enthroned as king
for ever.
11 May the LORD give strength to his
people!
May the LORD bless his people
with peace!

A Psalm of David. A Song at the
dedication of the Temple.

30 I will extol thee, O LORD, for
thou hast drawn me up,
and hast not let my foes rejoice
over me.
2 O LORD my God, I cried to thee
for help,
and thou hast healed me.

3 O LORD, thou hast brought up my
soul from Shē′ōl,
restored me to life from among
those gone down to the Pit.[i]

4 Sing praises to the LORD, O you his
saints,
and give thanks to his holy name.
5 For his anger is but for a moment,
and his favor is for a lifetime.
Weeping may tarry for the night,
but joy comes with the morning.

6 As for me, I said in my prosperity,
"I shall never be moved."
7 By thy favor, O LORD,
thou hadst established me as a
strong mountain;
thou didst hide thy face,
I was dismayed.

8 To thee, O LORD, I cried;
and to the LORD I made supplication:
9 "What profit is there in my death,
if I go down to the Pit?
Will the dust praise thee?
Will it tell of thy faithfulness?
10 Hear, O LORD, and be gracious to
me!
O LORD, be thou my helper!"

11 Thou hast turned for me my mourning into dancing;
thou hast loosed my sackcloth
and girded me with gladness,
12 that my soul[j] may praise thee and
not be silent.
O LORD my God, I will give
thanks to thee for ever.

To the choirmaster. A Psalm of David.

31 In thee, O LORD, do I seek
refuge;
let me never be put to shame;
in thy righteousness deliver me!
2 Incline thy ear to me,
rescue me speedily!
Be thou a rock of refuge for me,
a strong fortress to save me!

3 Yea, thou art my rock and my
fortress;
for thy name's sake lead me and
guide me,
4 take me out of the net which is
hidden for me,
for thou art my refuge.
5 Into thy hand I commit my spirit;

g Heb sons of gods   h Or makes the hinds to calve
i Or that I should not go down to the Pit   j Heb that glory
31:5: Lk 23.46.

thou hast redeemed me, O LORD,
faithful God.

6 Thou hatest[k] those who pay regard
to vain idols;
but I trust in the LORD.
7 I will rejoice and be glad for thy
steadfast love,
because thou hast seen my affliction,
thou hast taken heed of my ad-
versities,
8 and hast not delivered me into the
hand of the enemy;
thou hast set my feet in a broad
place.

9 Be gracious to me, O LORD, for I
am in distress;
my eye is wasted from grief,
my soul and my body also.
10 For my life is spent with sorrow,
and my years with sighing;
my strength fails because of my
misery,[l]
and my bones waste away.

11 I am the scorn of all my adversaries,
a horror[m] to my neighbors,
an object of dread to my acquaintances;
those who see me in the street
flee from me.
12 I have passed out of mind like one
who is dead;
I have become like a broken vessel.
13 Yea, I hear the whispering of many—
terror on every side!—
as they scheme together against me,
as they plot to take my life.

14 But I trust in thee, O LORD,
I say, "Thou art my God."
15 My times are in thy hand;
deliver me from the hand of my
enemies and persecutors!
16 Let thy face shine on thy servant;
save me in thy steadfast love!
17 Let me not be put to shame, O LORD,
for I call on thee;
let the wicked be put to shame,
let them go dumbfounded to
Shĕ′ōl.
18 Let the lying lips be dumb,
which speak insolently against the
righteous
in pride and contempt.

19 O how abundant is thy goodness,
which thou hast laid up for those
who fear thee,

and wrought for those who take
refuge in thee,
in the sight of the sons of men!
20 In the covert of thy presence thou
hidest them
from the plots of men;
thou holdest them safe under thy
shelter
from the strife of tongues.

21 Blessed be the LORD,
for he has wondrously shown his
steadfast love to me
when I was beset as in a besieged
city.
22 I had said in my alarm,
"I am driven far[n] from thy
sight."
But thou didst hear my supplications,
when I cried to thee for help.

23 Love the LORD, all you his saints!
The LORD preserves the faithful,
but abundantly requites him who
acts haughtily.
24 Be strong, and let your heart take
courage,
all you who wait for the LORD!

A Psalm of David. A Maskil.

32   Blessed is he whose transgression is forgiven,
whose sin is covered.
2 Blessed is the man to whom the
LORD imputes no iniquity,
and in whose spirit there is no
deceit.

3 When I declared not my sin, my
body wasted away
through my groaning all day long.
4 For day and night thy hand was
heavy upon me;
my strength was dried up[o] as by
the heat of summer.   *Selah*

5 I acknowledged my sin to thee,
and I did not hide my iniquity;
I said, "I will confess my transgressions to the LORD";
then thou didst forgive the guilt
of my sin.   *Selah*

6 Therefore let every one who is godly
offer prayer to thee;
at a time of distress,[p] in the rush of
great waters,
they shall not reach him.
7 Thou art a hiding place for me,

k With one Heb Ms Gk Syr Jerome: Heb *I hate*   l Gk Syr:*Heb iniquity*
m Cn: Heb *exceedingly*   n Another reading is *cut off*   o Heb obscure
p Cn: Heb *at a time of finding only*
31.13: Jer 6.25; 20.3, 10; 46.5; 49.29.   **32.1-2:** Rom 4.7-8.

thou preservest me from trouble;
thou dost encompass me with
deliverance.*q*   *Selah*

8 I will instruct you and teach you the
    way you should go;
  I will counsel you with my eye
    upon you.
9 Be not like a horse or a mule, with-
    out understanding,
  which must be curbed with bit
    and bridle,
  else it will not keep with you.

10 Many are the pangs of the wicked;
  but steadfast love surrounds him
    who trusts in the LORD.
11 Be glad in the LORD, and rejoice,
    O righteous,
  and shout for joy, all you upright
    in heart!

33 Rejoice in the LORD, O you
    righteous!
  Praise befits the upright.
2 Praise the LORD with the lyre,
  make melody to him with the
    harp of ten strings!
3 Sing to him a new song,
  play skilfully on the strings, with
    loud shouts.

4 For the word of the LORD is up-
    right;
  and all his work is done in faith-
    fulness.
5 He loves righteousness and justice;
  the earth is full of the steadfast love
    of the LORD.

6 By the word of the LORD the heavens
    were made,
  and all their host by the breath
    of his mouth.
7 He gathered the waters of the sea
    as in a bottle;
  he put the deeps in storehouses.

8 Let all the earth fear the LORD,
  let all the inhabitants of the world
    stand in awe of him!
9 For he spoke, and it came to be;
  he commanded, and it stood forth.

10 The LORD brings the counsel of the
    nations to nought;
  he frustrates the plans of the
    peoples.
11 The counsel of the LORD stands for
    ever,
  the thoughts of his heart to all
    generations.
12 Blessed is the nation whose God is
    the LORD,

the people whom he has chosen
    as his heritage!

13 The LORD looks down from heaven,
  he sees all the sons of men;
14 from where he sits enthroned he
    looks forth
  on all the inhabitants of the earth,
15 he who fashions the hearts of them
    all,
  and observes all their deeds.
16 A king is not saved by his great army;
  a warrior is not delivered by his
    great strength.
17 The war horse is a vain hope for
    victory,
  and by its great might it cannot
    save.

18 Behold, the eye of the LORD is on
    those who fear him,
  on those who hope in his steadfast
    love,
19 that he may deliver their soul from
    death,
  and keep them alive in famine.

20 Our soul waits for the LORD;
  he is our help and shield.
21 Yea, our heart is glad in him,
  because we trust in his holy name.
22 Let thy steadfast love, O LORD, be
    upon us,
  even as we hope in thee.

A Psalm of David, when he feigned
madness before A·bim′e·lech, so that
he drove him out, and he went away.

34 I will bless the LORD at all
    times;
  his praise shall continually be in
    my mouth.
2 My soul makes its boast in the
    LORD;
  let the afflicted hear and be glad.
3 O magnify the LORD with me,
  and let us exalt his name together!

4 I sought the LORD, and he answered
    me,
  and delivered me from all my
    fears.
5 Look to him, and be radiant;
  so your*r* faces shall never be
    ashamed.
6 This poor man cried, and the LORD
    heard him,
  and saved him out of all his
    troubles.
7 The angel of the LORD encamps
  around those who fear him, and
    delivers them.

q Cn: Heb *shouts of deliverance*   *r* Gk Syr Jerome: Heb *their*

8 O taste and see that the LORD is good!
  Happy is the man who takes
    refuge in him!
9 O fear the LORD, you his saints,
  for those who fear him have no
    want!
10 The young lions suffer want and
    hunger;
  but those who seek the LORD lack
    no good thing.

11 Come, O sons, listen to me,
  I will teach you the fear of the
    LORD.
12 What man is there who desires life,
  and covets many days, that he
    may enjoy good?
13 Keep your tongue from evil,
  and your lips from speaking
    deceit.
14 Depart from evil, and do good;
  seek peace, and pursue it.

15 The eyes of the LORD are toward
    the righteous,
  and his ears toward their cry.
16 The face of the LORD is against
    evildoers,
  to cut off the remembrance of
    them from the earth.
17 When the righteous cry for help,
    the LORD hears,
  and delivers them out of all their
    troubles.
18 The LORD is near to the broken-
    hearted,
  and saves the crushed in spirit.

19 Many are the afflictions of the
    righteous;
  but the LORD delivers him out of
    them all.
20 He keeps all his bones;
  not one of them is broken.
21 Evil shall slay the wicked;
  and those who hate the righteous
    will be condemned.
22 The LORD redeems the life of his
    servants;
  none of those who take refuge in
    him will be condemned.

A Psalm of David.

35 Contend, O LORD, with
  those who contend with me;
  fight against those who fight
    against me!
2 Take hold of shield and buckler,
  and rise for my help!
3 Draw the spear and javelin

against my pursuers!
Say to my soul,
  "I am your deliverance!"

4 Let them be put to shame and dis-
    honor
  who seek after my life!
  Let them be turned back and con-
    founded
  who devise evil against me!
5 Let them be like chaff before the
    wind,
  with the angel of the LORD driving
    them on!
6 Let their way be dark and slippery,
  with the angel of the LORD pur-
    suing them!

7 For without cause they hid their
    net for me;
  without cause they dug a pit[s] for
    my life.
8 Let ruin come upon them unawares!
  And let the net which they hid en-
    snare them;
  let them fall therein to ruin!

9 Then my soul shall rejoice in the
    LORD,
  exulting in his deliverance.
10 All my bones shall say,
  "O LORD, who is like thee,
  thou who deliverest the weak
    from him who is too strong for
    him,
  the weak and needy from him
    who despoils him?"

11 Malicious witnesses rise up;
  they ask me of things that I know
    not.
12 They requite me evil for good;
  my soul is forlorn.
13 But I, when they were sick—
  I wore sackcloth,
  I afflicted myself with fasting.
  I prayed with head bowed[t] on my
    bosom,
14 as though I grieved for my friend
    or my brother;
  I went about as one who laments
    his mother,
  bowed down and in mourning.

15 But at my stumbling they gathered
    in glee,
  they gathered together against me;
cripples whom I knew not
  slandered me without ceasing;
16 they impiously mocked more and
    more,[u]
  gnashing at me with their teeth.

[s] The word *pit* is transposed from the preceding line   [t] Or *My prayer turned back*
[u] Cn Compare Gk: Heb *like the profanest of mockers of a cake*
34.8: 1 Pet 2.3.   **34.12-16:** 1 Pet 3.10-12.

17 How long, O LORD, wilt thou look
    on?
    Rescue me from their ravages,
      my life from the lions!
18 Then I will thank thee in the great
    congregation;
    in the mighty throng I will praise
    thee.

19 Let not those rejoice over me
    who are wrongfully my foes,
  and let not those wink the eye
    who hate me without cause.
20 For they do not speak peace,
    but against those who are quiet
      in the land
  they conceive words of deceit.
21 They open wide their mouths
    against me;
  they say, "Aha, Aha!
    our eyes have seen it!"

22 Thou hast seen, O LORD; be not
    silent!
  O Lord, be not far from me!
23 Bestir thyself, and awake for my
    right,
  for my cause, my God and my
    Lord!
24 Vindicate me, O LORD, my God,
    according to thy righteousness;
  and let them not rejoice over me!
25 Let them not say to themselves,
    "Aha, we have our heart's desire!"
  Let them not say, "We have swal-
    lowed him up."

26 Let them be put to shame and con-
    fusion altogether
  who rejoice at my calamity!
  Let them be clothed with shame and
    dishonor
  who magnify themselves against
    me!

27 Let those who desire my vindication
    shout for joy and be glad,
  and say evermore,
  "Great is the LORD,
    who delights in the welfare of his
    servant!"
28 Then my tongue shall tell of thy
    righteousness
  and of thy praise all the day long.

To the choirmaster. A Psalm of David,
    the servant of the LORD.

36 Transgression speaks to the
    wicked
  deep in his heart;
  there is no fear of God
    before his eyes.

2 For he flatters himself in his own
    eyes
  that his iniquity cannot be found
    out and hated.
3 The words of his mouth are mischief
    and deceit;
  he has ceased to act wisely and do
    good.
4 He plots mischief while on his bed;
  he sets himself in a way that is
    not good;
  he spurns not evil.

5 Thy steadfast love, O LORD, extends
    to the heavens,
  thy faithfulness to the clouds.
6 Thy righteousness is like the moun-
    tains of God,
  thy judgments are like the great
    deep;
  man and beast thou savest, O
    LORD.

7 How precious is thy steadfast love,
    O God!
  The children of men take refuge
    in the shadow of thy wings.
8 They feast on the abundance of thy
    house,
  and thou givest them drink from
    the river of thy delights.
9 For with thee is the fountain of life;
  in thy light do we see light.

10 O continue thy steadfast love to
    those who know thee,
  and thy salvation to the upright
    of heart!
11 Let not the foot of arrogance come
    upon me,
  nor the hand of the wicked drive
    me away.
12 There the evildoers lie prostrate,
  they are thrust down, unable to
    rise.

A Psalm of David.

37 Fret not yourself because of
    the wicked,
  be not envious of wrongdoers!
2 For they will soon fade like the
    grass,
  and wither like the green herb.

3 Trust in the LORD, and do good;
  so you will dwell in the land, and
    enjoy security.
4 Take delight in the LORD,
  and he will give you the desires
    of your heart.

5 Commit your way to the LORD;

35.19: Ps 69.4; Jn 15.25.   36.1: Rom 3.18.

trust in him, and he will act.

6 He will bring forth your vindication
  as the light,
  and your right as the noonday.

7 Be still before the LORD, and wait
  patiently for him;
  fret not yourself over him who
  prospers in his way,
  over the man who carries out evil
  devices!

8 Refrain from anger, and forsake
  wrath!
  Fret not yourself; it tends only
  to evil.

9 For the wicked shall be cut off;
  but those who wait for the LORD
  shall possess the land.

10 Yet a little while, and the wicked
  will be no more;
  though you look well at his place,
  he will not be there.

11 But the meek shall possess the
  land,
  and delight themselves in abundant prosperity.

12 The wicked plots against the righteous,
  and gnashes his teeth at him;

13 but the LORD laughs at the wicked,
  for he sees that his day is coming.

14 The wicked draw the sword and
  bend their bows,
  to bring down the poor and needy,
  to slay those who walk uprightly;

15 their sword shall enter their own
  heart,
  and their bows shall be broken.

16 Better is a little that the righteous
  has
  than the abundance of many
  wicked.

17 For the arms of the wicked shall be
  broken;
  but the LORD upholds the righteous.

18 The LORD knows the days of the
  blameless,
  and their heritage will abide for
  ever;

19 they are not put to shame in evil
  times,
  in the days of famine they have
  abundance.

20 But the wicked perish;
  the enemies of the LORD are like
  the glory of the pastures,

they vanish—like smoke they
  vanish away.

21 The wicked borrows, and cannot
  pay back,
  but the righteous is generous and
  gives;

22 for those blessed by the LORD shall
  possess the land,
  but those cursed by him shall be
  cut off.

23 The steps of a man are from the
  LORD,
  and he establishes him in whose
  way he delights;

24 though he fall, he shall not be cast
  headlong,
  for the LORD is the stay of his
  hand.

25 I have been young, and now am old;
  yet I have not seen the righteous
  forsaken
  or his children begging bread.

26 He is ever giving liberally and
  lending,
  and his children become a blessing.

27 Depart from evil, and do good;
  so shall you abide for ever.

28 For the LORD loves justice;
  he will not forsake his saints.

The righteous shall be preserved for
  ever,
  but the children of the wicked
  shall be cut off.

29 The righteous shall possess the land,
  and dwell upon it for ever.

30 The mouth of the righteous utters
  wisdom,
  and his tongue speaks justice.

31 The law of his God is in his heart;
  his steps do not slip.

32 The wicked watches the righteous,
  and seeks to slay him.

33 The LORD will not abandon him to
  his power,
  or let him be condemned when he
  is brought to trial.

34 Wait for the LORD, and keep to his
  way,
  and he will exalt you to possess
  the land;
  you will look on the destruction
  of the wicked.

35 I have seen a wicked man overbearing,

and towering like a cedar of
Lebanon.ᵛ
36 Again Iʷ passed by, and, lo, he was
no more;
though I sought him, he could not
be found.

37 Mark the blameless man, and behold
the upright,
for there is posterity for the man
of peace.
38 But transgressors shall be altogether
destroyed;
the posterity of the wicked shall
be cut off.

39 The salvation of the righteous is
from the LORD;
he is their refuge in the time of
trouble.
40 The LORD helps them and delivers
them;
he delivers them from the wicked,
and saves them,
because they take refuge in him.

A Psalm of David, for the memorial
offering.

38 O LORD, rebuke me not in
thy anger,
nor chasten me in thy wrath!
2 For thy arrows have sunk into me,
and thy hand has come down
on me.

3 There is no soundness in my flesh
because of thy indignation;
there is no health in my bones
because of my sin.
4 For my iniquities have gone over
my head;
they weigh like a burden too
heavy for me.

5 My wounds grow foul and fester
because of my foolishness,
6 I am utterly bowed down and
prostrate;
all the day I go about mourning.
7 For my loins are filled with burning,
and there is no soundness in my
flesh.
8 I am utterly spent and crushed;
I groan because of the tumult of
my heart.

9 Lord, all my longing is known to thee,
my sighing is not hidden from
thee.
10 My heart throbs, my strength fails
me;

and the light of my eyes—it also
has gone from me.
11 My friends and companions stand
aloof from my plague,
and my kinsmen stand afar off.

12 Those who seek my life lay their
snares,
those who seek my hurt speak of
ruin,
and meditate treachery all the day
long.
13 But I am like a deaf man, I do not
hear,
like a dumb man who does not
open his mouth.
14 Yea, I am like a man who does not
hear,
and in whose mouth are no rebukes.

15 But for thee, O LORD, do I wait;
it is thou, O LORD my God, who
wilt answer.
16 For I pray, "Only let them not rejoice over me,
who boast against me when my
foot slips!"

17 For I am ready to fall,
and my pain is ever with me,
18 I confess my iniquity,
I am sorry for my sin.
19 Those who are my foes without
causeˣ are mighty,
and many are those who hate me
wrongfully.
20 Those who render me evil for good
are my adversaries because I
follow after good.

21 Do not forsake me, O LORD!
O my God, be not far from me!
22 Make haste to help me,
O Lord, my salvation!

To the choirmaster: to Je·dü′thŭn.
A Psalm of David.

39 I said, "I will guard my ways,
that I may not sin with tongue;
I will bridleʸ my mouth,
so long as the wicked are in my
presence."
2 I was dumb and silent,
I held my peace to no avail;
my distress grew worse,
3 my heart became hot within me.
As I mused, the fire burned;
then I spoke with my tongue:

4 "LORD, let me know my end,

ᵛ Gk: Heb obscure   ʷ Gk Syr Jerome: Heb *he*   ˣ Cn: Heb *living*
ʸ Heb *muzzle*

and what is the measure of my
days;
let me know how fleeting my life is!

5 Behold, thou hast made my days a
few handbreadths,
and my lifetime is as nothing in
thy sight.
Surely every man stands as a mere
breath!   *Selah*

6   Surely man goes about as a
shadow!
Surely for nought are they in turmoil;
man heaps up, and knows not
who will gather!

7 "And now, Lord, for what do I
wait?
My hope is in thee.

8 Deliver me from all my transgressions.
Make me not the scorn of the fool!

9 I am dumb, I do not open my mouth;
for it is thou who hast done it.

10 Remove thy stroke from me;
I am spent by the blows[z] of thy
hand.

11 When thou dost chasten man
with rebukes for sin,
thou dost consume like a moth what
is dear to him;
surely every man is a mere breath!
    Selah

12 "Hear my prayer, O LORD,
and give ear to my cry;
hold not thy peace at my tears!
for I am thy passing guest,
a sojourner, like all my fathers.

13 Look away from me, that I may
know gladness,
before I depart and be no more!"

To the choirmaster. A Psalm of David.

40 I waited patiently for the
LORD;
he inclined to me and heard my
cry.

2 He drew me up from the desolate
pit,[a]
out of the miry bog,
and set my feet upon a rock,
making my steps secure.

3 He put a new song in my mouth,
a song of praise to our God.
Many will see and fear,
and put their trust in the LORD.

4 Blessed is the man who makes
the LORD his trust,
who does not turn to the proud,

to those who go astray after false
gods!

5 Thou hast multiplied, O LORD my
God,
thy wondrous deeds and thy
thoughts toward us;
none can compare with thee!
Were I to proclaim and tell of them,
they would be more than can be
numbered.

6 Sacrifice and offering thou dost not
desire;
but thou hast given me an open
ear.[b]
Burnt offering and sin offering
thou hast not required.

7 Then I said, "Lo, I come;
in the roll of the book it is written
of me;

8 I delight to do thy will, O my God;
thy law is within my heart."

9 I have told the glad news of deliverance
in the great congregation;
lo, I have not restrained my lips,
as thou knowest, O LORD.

10 I have not hid thy saving help within my heart,
I have spoken of thy faithfulness
and thy salvation;
I have not concealed thy steadfast
love and thy faithfulness
from the great congregation.

11 Do not thou, O LORD, withhold
thy mercy from me,
let thy steadfast love and thy faithfulness
ever preserve me!

12 For evils have encompassed me
without number;
my iniquities have overtaken me,
till I cannot see;
they are more than the hairs of my
head;
my heart fails me.

13 Be pleased, O LORD, to deliver me!
O LORD, make haste to help me!

14 Let them be put to shame and confusion altogether
who seek to snatch away my life;
let them be turned back and brought
to dishonor
who desire my hurt!

15 Let them be appalled because of
their shame
who say to me, "Aha, Aha!"

16 But may all who seek thee
rejoice and be glad in thee;

[z] Heb *hostility*   [a] Cn: Heb *pit of tumult*   [b] Heb *ears thou hast dug for me*
40.6-8: Heb 10.5-9.   **40.13-17:** Ps 70.1-5.

may those who love thy salvation
  say continually, "Great is the
  LORD!"
17 As for me, I am poor and needy;
  but the Lord takes thought for me.
  Thou art my help and my deliverer;
  do not tarry, O my God!

To the choirmaster. A Psalm of David.

41 Blessed is he who considers
  the poor!*c*
  The LORD delivers him in the day
    of trouble;
2 the LORD protects him and keeps
    him alive;
  he is called blessed in the land;
  thou dost not give him up to the
    will of his enemies.
3 The LORD sustains him on his sick-
    bed;
  in his illness thou healest all his
    infirmities.*d*

4 As for me, I said, "O LORD, be
    gracious to me;
  heal me, for I have sinned against
    thee!"
5 My enemies say of me in malice,
  "When will he die, and his name
    perish?"
6 And when one comes to see me, he
    utters empty words,
  while his heart gathers mischief;
  when he goes out, he tells it abroad.
7 All who hate me whisper together
    about me;
  they imagine the worst for me.

8 They say, "A deadly thing has
    fastened upon him;
  he will not rise again from where
    he lies."
9 Even my bosom friend in whom I
    trusted,
  who ate of my bread, has lifted
    his heel against me.
10 But do thou, O LORD, be gracious
    to me,
  and raise me up, that I may re-
    quite them!

11 By this I know that thou art pleased
    with me,
  in that my enemy has not tri-
    umphed over me.
12 But thou hast upheld me because of
    my integrity,
  and set me in thy presence for ever.

13 Blessed be the LORD, the God of
    Israel,

c Or *weak*   *d* Heb *thou changest all his bed*
41.9: Jn 13.18.

from everlasting to everlasting!
  Amen and Amen.

BOOK II

To the choirmaster. A Maskil of the
  Sons of Kō'räh.

42 As a hart longs
  for flowing streams,
so longs my soul
  for thee, O God.
2 My soul thirsts for God,
  for the living God.
  When shall I come and behold
    the face of God?
3 My tears have been my food
    day and night,
  while men say to me continually,
  "Where is your God?"

4 These things I remember,
    as I pour out my soul:
  how I went with the throng,
    and led them in procession to the
    house of God,
  with glad shouts and songs of
    thanksgiving,
  a multitude keeping festival.
5 Why are you cast down, O my
    soul,
  and why are you disquieted with-
    in me?
  Hope in God; for I shall again praise
    him,
  my help 6 and my God.

My soul is cast down within me,
  therefore I remember thee
from the land of Jordan and of
    Hēr'mòn,
  from Mount Mī'zär.
7 Deep calls to deep
    at the thunder of thy cataracts;
  all thy waves and thy billows
    have gone over me.
8 By day the LORD commands his
    steadfast love;
  and at night his song is with me,
  a prayer to the God of my life.

9 I say to God, my rock:
  "Why hast thou forgotten me?
  Why go I mourning
    because of the oppression of the
    enemy?"
10 As with a deadly wound in my body,
    my adversaries taunt me,
  while they say to me continually,
  "Where is your God?"

11 Why are you cast down, O my soul,
  and why are you disquieted with-
    in me?
Hope in God; for I shall again praise
    him,
  my help and my God.

43 Vindicate me, O God, and
  defend my cause
  against an ungodly people;
from deceitful and unjust men
    deliver me!
2 For thou art the God in whom I
    take refuge;
  why hast thou cast me off?
Why go I mourning
  because of the oppression of the
    enemy?

3 Oh send out thy light and thy truth;
    let them lead me,
  let them bring me to thy holy hill
    and to thy dwelling!
4 Then I will go to the altar of God,
    to God my exceeding joy;
  and I will praise thee with the lyre,
    O God, my God.

5 Why are you cast down, O my
    soul,
  and why are you disquieted with-
    in me?
Hope in God; for I shall again praise
    him,
  my help and my God.

*To the choirmaster. A Maskil of the
    Sons of Korah.*

44 We have heard with our ears,
  O God,
  our fathers have told us,
what deeds thou didst perform in
    their days,
  in the days of old:
2 thou with thy own hand didst drive
    out the nations,
  but them thou didst plant;
thou didst afflict the peoples,
  but them thou didst set free;
3 for not by their own sword did they
    win the land,
  nor did their own arm give them
    victory;
but thy right hand, and thy arm,
  and the light of thy countenance;
  for thou didst delight in them.

4 Thou art my King and my God,
  who ordainest[e] victories for Jacob.
5 Through thee we push down our
    foes;

through thy name we tread down
    our assailants.
6 For not in my bow do I trust,
  nor can my sword save me.
7 But thou hast saved us from our foes,
  and hast put to confusion those
    who hate us.
8 In God we have boasted continually,
  and we will give thanks to thy
    name for ever.   *Selah*

9 Yet thou hast cast us off and abased
    us, and hast not gone out with
    our armies.
10 Thou hast made us turn back from
    the foe;
  and our enemies have gotten spoil.
11 Thou hast made us like sheep for
    slaughter,
  and hast scattered us among the
    nations.
12 Thou hast sold thy people for a
    trifle,
  demanding no high price for
    them.

13 Thou hast made us the taunt of our
    neighbors;
  the derision and scorn of those
    about us.
14 Thou hast made us a byword among
    the nations,
  a laughingstock[f] among the
    peoples.
15 All day long my disgrace is before
    me,
  and shame has covered my face,
16 at the words of the taunters and
    revilers,
  at the sight of the enemy and the
    avenger.

17 All this has come upon us,
  though we have not forgotten
    thee,
  or been false to thy covenant.
18 Our heart has not turned back,
  nor have our steps departed from
    thy way,
19 that thou shouldst have broken us
    in the place of jackals,
  and covered us with deep dark-
    ness.

20 If we had forgotten the name of our
    God,
  or spread forth our hands to a
    strange god,
21 would not God discover this?
  For he knows the secrets of the
    heart.
22 Nay, for thy sake we are slain all
    the day long,

and accounted as sheep for the
slaughter.

23 Rouse thyself! Why sleepest thou,
O Lord?
Awake! Do not cast us off for ever!
24 Why dost thou hide thy face?
Why dost thou forget our affliction and oppression?
25 For our soul is bowed down to the
dust;
our body cleaves to the ground.
26 Rise up, come to our help!
Deliver us for the sake of thy
steadfast love!

To the choirmaster: according to
Lilies. A Maskil of the Sons of
Kō′rǎh; a love song.

45   My heart overflows with a
goodly theme;
I address my verses to the king;
my tongue is like the pen of a
ready scribe.

2 You are the fairest of the sons of men;
grace is poured upon your lips;
therefore God has blessed you
for ever.
3 Gird your sword upon your thigh,
O mighty one,
in your glory and majesty!

4 In your majesty ride forth victori-
ously
for the cause of the truth and to
defend^g the right;
let your right hand teach you
dread deeds!
5 Your arrows are sharp
in the heart of the king's enemies;
the peoples fall under you.

6 Your divine throne^h endures for
ever and ever.
Your royal scepter is a scepter of
equity;
7 you love righteousness and hate
wickedness.
Therefore God, your God, has
anointed you
with the oil of gladness above
your fellows;
8 your robes are all fragrant with
myrrh and aloes and cassia.
From ivory palaces stringed instruments make you glad;
9 daughters of kings are among
your ladies of honor;

at your right hand stands the
queen in gold of Ō′phǐr.

10 Hear, O daughter, consider, and
incline your ear;
forget your people and your
father's house;
11 and the king will desire your
beauty.
Since he is your lord, bow to
him;
12 the people^i of Tȳre will sue your
favor with gifts,
the richest of the people 13 with
all kinds of wealth.

The princess is decked in her chamber with gold-woven robes;^{j}
14 in many-colored robes she is led
to the king,
with her virgin companions, her
escort,^{k} in her train.
15 With joy and gladness they are led
along
as they enter the palace of the
king.

16 Instead of your fathers shall be your
sons;
you will make them princes in all
the earth.
17 I will cause your name to be celebrated in all generations;
therefore the peoples will praise
you for ever and ever.

To the choirmaster. A Psalm of the
Sons of Kō′rǎh. According to
Alamoth. A Song.

46   God is our refuge and
strength,
a very present^l help in trouble.
2 Therefore we will not fear though
the earth should change,
though the mountains shake in
the heart of the sea;
3 though its waters roar and foam,
though the mountains tremble
with its tumult.   Selah

4 There is a river whose streams make
glad the city of God,
the holy habitation of the Most
High.
5 God is in the midst of her, she shall
not be moved;
God will help her right early.
6 The nations rage, the kingdoms
totter;

^{g} Cn: Heb and the meekness of
^{h} Or Your throne is a throne of God, or Thy throne, O God ^{i} Heb daughter
^{j} Or people. All glorious is the princess within, gold embroidery is her clothing
^{k} Heb those brought to you ^{l} Or well proved   **45.6-7:** Heb 1.8-9.

he utters his voice, the earth melts.

7 The LORD of hosts is with us;
  the God of Jacob is our
    refuge.^m   *Selah*

8 Come, behold the works of the
    LORD,
  how he has wrought desolations
    in the earth.
9 He makes wars cease to the end of
    the earth;
  he breaks the bow, and shatters
    the spear,
  he burns the chariots with fire!
10 "Be still, and know that I am
    God.
  I am exalted among the nations,
  I am exalted in the earth!"
11 The LORD of hosts is with us;
  the God of Jacob is our
    refuge.^m   *Selah*

To the choirmaster. A Psalm of the
    Sons of Kō′rah.

47 Clap your hands, all peoples!
  Shout to God with loud songs
    of joy!
2 For the LORD, the Most High, is
    terrible,
  a great king over all the earth.
3 He subdued peoples under us,
  and nations under our feet.
4 He chose our heritage for us,
  the pride of Jacob whom he loves.
                                        Selah

5 God has gone up with a shout,
  the LORD with the sound of a
    trumpet.
6 Sing praises to God, sing praises!
  Sing praises to our King, sing
    praises!
7 For God is the king of all the earth;
  sing praises with a psalm!^n

8 God reigns over the nations;
  God sits on his holy throne.
9 The princes of the peoples gather
    as the people of the God of
    Abraham.
  For the shields of the earth belong
    to God;
  he is highly exalted!

A song. A Psalm of the Sons of Kō′rah.

48 Great is the LORD and greatly
  to be praised
    in the city of our God!

His holy mountain, 2 beautiful in
    elevation,
  is the joy of all the earth,
Mount Zion, in the far north,
  the city of the great King.
3 Within her citadels God
  has shown himself a sure de-
    fense.

4 For lo, the kings assembled,
  they came on together.
5 As soon as they saw it, they were
    astounded,
  they were in panic, they took to
    flight;
6 trembling took hold of them there,
  anguish as of a woman in travail.
7 By the east wind thou didst shatter
  the ships of Tär′shish.
8 As we have heard, so have we seen
  in the city of the LORD of
    hosts,
in the city of our God,
  which God establishes for ever.
                                        Selah

9 We have thought on thy steadfast
    love, O God,
  in the midst of thy temple.
10 As thy name, O God,
  so thy praise reaches to the ends
    of the earth.
  Thy right hand is filled with victory;
11 let Mount Zion be glad!
  Let the daughters of Judah rejoice
    because of thy judgments!

12 Walk about Zion, go round about
    her,
  number her towers,
13 consider well her ramparts,
  go through her citadels;
  that you may tell the next genera-
    tion
14 that this is God,
  our God for ever and ever.
  He will be our guide for ever.

To the choirmaster. A Psalm of the
    Sons of Kō′rah.

49 Hear this, all peoples!
  Give ear, all inhabitants of the
    world,
2 both low and high,
  rich and poor together!
3 My mouth shall speak wisdom;
  the meditation of my heart shall
    be understanding.
4 I will incline my ear to a proverb;
  I will solve my riddle to the music
    of the lyre.

^m Or *fortress*   ^n Heb *Maskil*
48.2: Mt 5.35.

5 Why should I fear in times of
trouble,
  when the iniquity of my persecutors surrounds me,
6 men who trust in their wealth
  and boast of the abundance of
  their riches?
7 Truly no man can ransom himself,[o]
  or give to God the price of his
  life,
8 for the ransom of his[p] life is costly,
  and can never suffice,
9 that he should continue to live on
  for ever,
  and never see the Pit.

10 Yea, he shall see that even the wise
die,
  the fool and the stupid alike must
  perish
  and leave their wealth to others.
11 Their graves[q] are their homes for
ever,
  their dwelling places to all generations,
  though they named lands their
  own.
12 Man cannot abide in his pomp,
  he is like the beasts that perish.

13 This is the fate of those who have
foolish confidence,
  the end of those[r] who are pleased
  with their portion.   *Selah*
14 Like sheep they are appointed for
Shĕ'ōl;
  Death shall be their shepherd;
  straight to the grave they descend,[s]
  and their form shall waste away;
  Sheol shall be their home.[t]
15 But God will ransom my soul from
the power of Shĕ'ōl,
  for he will receive me.   *Selah*

16 Be not afraid when one becomes
rich,
  when the glory[u] of his house
  increases.
17 For when he dies he will carry
nothing away;
  his glory[u] will not go down after
  him.
18 Though, while he lives, he counts
himself happy,
  and though a man gets praise
  when he does well for himself,
19 he will go to the generation of his
fathers,
  who will never more see the light.
20 Man cannot abide in his pomp,
  he is like the beasts that perish.

A Psalm of Ā'saph.

50 The Mighty One, God the
LORD,
  speaks and summons the earth
  from the rising of the sun to its
  setting.
2 Out of Zion, the perfection of
beauty,
  God shines forth.

3 Our God comes, he does not keep
silence,
  before him is a devouring fire,
  round about him a mighty tempest.
4 He calls to the heavens above
  and to the earth, that he may
  judge his people:
5 "Gather to me my faithful ones,
  who made a covenant with me by
  sacrifice!"
6 The heavens declare his righteousness,
  for God himself is judge!   *Selah*

7 "Hear, O my people, and I will
speak,
  O Israel, I will testify against you.
  I am God, your God.
8 I do not reprove you for your
sacrifices;
  your burnt offerings are continually before me.
9 I will accept no bull from your
house,
  nor he-goat from your folds.
10 For every beast of the forest is mine,
  the cattle on a thousand hills.
11 I know all the birds of the air,[v]
  and all that moves in the field is
  mine.

12 "If I were hungry, I would not tell
you;
  for the world and all that is in it
  is mine.
13 Do I eat the flesh of bulls,
  or drink the blood of goats?
14 Offer to God a sacrifice of thanksgiving,[w]
  and pay your vows to the Most
  High;
15 and call upon me in the day of
trouble;
  I will deliver you, and you shall
  glorify me."

16 But to the wicked God says:
  "What right have you to recite
  my statutes,

---

o Another reading is *no man can ransom his brother*   p Gk: Heb *their*
q Gk Syr Compare Tg: Heb *their inward* (thought)   r Tg: Heb *after them*
s Cn: Heb *the upright shall have dominion over them in the morning*   t Heb uncertain
u Or *wealth*   v Gk Syr Tg: Heb *mountains*   w Or *make thanksgiving your sacrifice to God*

or take my covenant on your lips?
17 For you hate discipline,
   and you cast my words behind you.
18 If you see a thief, you are a friend
     of his;
   and you keep company with
     adulterers.

19 "You give your mouth free rein for
     evil,
   and your tongue frames deceit.
20 You sit and speak against your
     brother;
   you slander your own mother's
     son.
21 These things you have done and
     I have been silent;
   you thought that I was one like
     yourself.
   But now I rebuke you, and lay the
     charge before you.

22 "Mark this, then, you who forget
     God,
   lest I rend, and there be none to
     deliver!
23 He who brings thanksgiving as his
     sacrifice honors me;
   to him who orders his way aright
   I will show the salvation of God!"

To the choirmaster. A Psalm of David,
when Nathan the prophet came to him,
after he had gone in to Bath·she′ba.

51   Have mercy on me, O God,
    according to thy steadfast love;
   according to thy abundant mercy
   blot out my transgressions.
2 Wash me thoroughly from my in-
     iquity,
   and cleanse me from my sin!

3 For I know my transgressions,
   and my sin is ever before me.
4 Against thee, thee only, have I
     sinned,
   and done that which is evil in thy
     sight,
  so that thou art justified in thy
     sentence
   and blameless in thy judgment.
5 Behold, I was brought forth in in-
     iquity,
   and in sin did my mother con-
     ceive me.

6 Behold, thou desirest truth in the
     inward being;
   therefore teach me wisdom in my
     secret heart.

7 Purge me with hyssop, and I shall
     be clean;
   wash me, and I shall be whiter
     than snow.
8 Fill^x me with joy and gladness;
   let the bones which thou hast
     broken rejoice.
9 Hide thy face from my sins,
   and blot out all my iniquities.

10 Create in me a clean heart, O God,
   and put a new and right^y spirit
     within me.
11 Cast me not away from thy presence,
   and take not thy holy Spirit from
     me.
12 Restore to me the joy of thy salva-
     tion,
   and uphold me with a willing
     spirit.

13 Then I will teach transgressors thy
     ways,
   and sinners will return to thee.
14 Deliver me from bloodguiltiness,^{z}
     O God,
   thou God of my salvation,
   and my tongue will sing aloud of
     thy deliverance.

15 O Lord, open thou my lips,
   and my mouth shall show forth
     thy praise.
16 For thou hast no delight in sacri-
     fice;
   were I to give a burnt offering,
     thou wouldst not be pleased.
17 The sacrifice acceptable to God^a is
     a broken spirit;
   a broken and contrite heart, O
     God, thou wilt not despise.

18 Do good to Zion in thy good
     pleasure;
   rebuild the walls of Jerusalem,
19 then wilt thou delight in right
     sacrifices,
   in burnt offerings and whole burnt
     offerings;
   then bulls will be offered on thy
     altar.

To the choirmaster. A Maskil of
David, when Do′eg, the E′dom·ite,
came and told Saul, "David has come
to the house of A·him′e·lech."

52   Why do you boast, O mighty
    man,
   of mischief done against the
     godly?^{b}

x Syr: Heb *Make to hear*   y Or *steadfast*   z Or *death*   a Or *My sacrifice, O God*
b Cn Compare Syr: Heb *the kindness of God*
51.4: Rom 3.4.

All the day [2] you are plotting
destruction.
Your tongue is like a sharp razor,
you worker of treachery.
[3] You love evil more than good,
and lying more than speaking the
truth.   *Selah*
[4] You love all words that devour,
O deceitful tongue.

[5] But God will break you down for ever;
he will snatch and tear you from
your tent;
he will uproot you from the land
of the living.   *Selah*
[6] The righteous shall see, and fear,
and shall laugh at him, saying,
[7] "See the man who would not make
God his refuge,
but trusted in the abundance of his
riches,
and sought refuge in his wealth!"[c]

[8] But I am like a green olive tree
in the house of God.
I trust in the steadfast love of God
for ever and ever.
[9] I will thank thee for ever,
because thou hast done it.
I will proclaim[d] thy name, for it is
good,
in the presence of the godly.

To the choirmaster: according to
Mahalath. A Maskil of David.

53 The fool says in his heart,
"There is no God."
They are corrupt, doing abominable
iniquity;
there is none that does good.

[2] God looks down from heaven
upon the sons of men
to see if there are any that are wise,
that seek after God.

[3] They have all fallen away;
they are all alike depraved;
there is none that does good,
no, not one.

[4] Have those who work evil no understanding,
who eat up my people as they eat
bread,
and do not call upon God?

[5] There they are, in great terror,
in terror such as has not been!
For God will scatter the bones of
the ungodly;[e]
they will be put to shame,[f] for
God has rejected them.

[6] O that deliverance for Israel would
come from Zion!
When God restores the fortunes
of his people,
Jacob will rejoice and Israel be
glad.

To the choirmaster: with stringed
instruments. A Maskil of David, when
the Ziphites went and told Saul,
"David is in hiding among us."

54 Save me, O God, by thy
name,
and vindicate me by thy might.
[2] Hear my prayer, O God;
give ear to the words of my
mouth.

[3] For insolent[g] men have risen against
me,
ruthless men seek my life;
they do not set God before them.
Selah

[4] Behold, God is my helper;
the Lord is the upholder[h] of my
life.
[5] He will requite my enemies with evil;
in thy faithfulness put an end to
them.

[6] With a freewill offering I will sacrifice to thee;
I will give thanks to thy name,
O LORD, for it is good.
[7] For thou hast delivered me from
every trouble,
and my eye has looked in triumph
on my enemies.

To the choirmaster: with stringed
instruments. A Maskil of David.

55 Give ear to my prayer, O
God;
and hide not thyself from my
supplication!
[2] Attend to me, and answer me;
I am overcome by my trouble.
I am distraught [3] by the noise of
the enemy,

---

[c] Syr Tg: Heb *his destruction*   [d] Cn: Heb *wait for*
[e] Cn Compare Gk Syr: Heb *him who encamps against you*
[f] Gk: Heb *you will put to shame*   [g] Another reading is *strangers*
[h] Gk Syr Jerome: Heb *of* or *with those who uphold*
53.1-3: Rom 3.10-12.   **53.1-6:** Ps 14.1-7.

because of the oppression of the
wicked.
For they bring[i] trouble upon me,
and in anger they cherish enmity
against me.

4 My heart is in anguish within me,
the terrors of death have fallen
upon me.
5 Fear and trembling come upon me,
and horror overwhelms me.
6 And I say, "O that I had wings like
a dove!
I would fly away and be at rest;
7 yea, I would wander afar,
I would lodge in the wilderness,
                    Selah
8 I would haste to find me a shelter
from the raging wind and tempest."

9 Destroy their plans,[j] O Lord, confuse their tongues;
for I see violence and strife in
the city.
10 Day and night they go around it
on its walls;
and mischief and trouble are within
it,
11   ruin is in its midst;
oppression and fraud
do not depart from its market
place.

12 It is not an enemy who taunts me—
then I could bear it;
it is not an adversary who deals
insolently with me—
then I could hide from him.
13 But it is you, my equal,
my companion, my familiar friend.
14 We used to hold sweet converse together;
within God's house we walked in
fellowship.
15 Let death[k] come upon them;
let them go down to Shē'ōl alive;
let them go away in terror into
their graves.[l]

16 But I call upon God;
and the LORD will save me.
17 Evening and morning and at noon
I utter my complaint and moan,
and he will hear my voice.
18 He will deliver my soul in safety
from the battle that I wage,
for many are arrayed against
me.
19 God will give ear, and humble them,
he who is enthroned from of old;

because they keep no law,[m]
and do not fear God.   Selah

20 My companion stretched out his
hand against his friends,
he violated his covenant.
21 His speech was smoother than
butter,
yet war was in his heart;
his words were softer than oil,
yet they were drawn swords.

22 Cast your burden[n] on the LORD,
and he will sustain you;
he will never permit
the righteous to be moved.

23 But thou, O God, wilt cast them
down
into the lowest pit;
men of blood and treachery
shall not live out half their days.
But I will trust in thee.

To the choirmaster: according to The
Dove on Far-off Terebinths. A Miktam of David, when the Philistines
seized him in Gath.

56   Be gracious to me, O God,
for men trample upon me;
all day long foemen oppress me;
2 my enemies trample upon me all
day long,
for many fight against me proudly.
3 When I am afraid,
I put my trust in thee.
4 In God, whose word I praise,
in God I trust without a fear.
What can flesh do to me?

5 All day long they seek to injure my
cause;
all their thoughts are against me
for evil.
6 They band themselves together, they
lurk,
they watch my steps.
As they have waited for my life,
7 so recompense[o] them for their
crime,
in wrath cast down the peoples,
O God!

8 Thou hast kept count of my tossings;
put thou my tears in thy bottle!
Are they not in thy book?
9 Then my enemies will be turned
back
in the day when I call.

i Cn Compare Gk: Heb they cause to totter   j Tg: Heb lacks their plans
k Or desolations   l Cn: Heb evils are in their habitation, in their midst
m Or do not change   n Or what he has given you   o Cn: Heb deliver
55.22: 1 Pet 5.7.

This I know, that[p] God is for me.
10 In God, whose word I praise,
  in the LORD, whose word I praise,
11 in God I trust without a fear.
  What can man do to me?

12 My vows to thee I must perform
    O God;
  I will render thank offerings to
    thee.
13 For thou hast delivered my soul
    from death,
  yea, my feet from falling,
  that I may walk before God
    in the light of life.

To the choirmaster: according to Do
Not Destroy. A Miktam of David,
when he fled from Saul, in the cave.

57 Be merciful to me, O God,
    be merciful to me,
  for in thee my soul takes refuge;
  in the shadow of thy wings I will
    take refuge,
    till the storms of destruction pass
    by.
2 I cry to God Most High,
  to God who fulfils his purpose for
    me.
3 He will send from heaven and save
    me,
  he will put to shame those who
    trample upon me.   *Selah*
God will send forth his steadfast
  love and his faithfulness!

4 I lie in the midst of lions
  that greedily devour[q] the sons of
    men;
  their teeth are spears and arrows,
    their tongues sharp swords.

5 Be exalted, O God, above the
    heavens!
  Let thy glory be over all the earth!

6 They set a net for my steps;
  my soul was bowed down.
They dug a pit in my way,
  but they have fallen into it them-
    selves.   *Selah*

7 My heart is steadfast, O God,
  my heart is steadfast!
I will sing and make melody!
8   Awake, my soul!
Awake, O harp and lyre!
  I will awake the dawn!
9 I will give thanks to thee, O Lord,
  among the peoples;

I will sing praises to thee among
  the nations.
10 For thy steadfast love is great to the
    heavens,
  thy faithfulness to the clouds.

11 Be exalted, O God, above the
    heavens!
  Let thy glory be over all the
    earth!

To the choirmaster: according to
Do Not Destroy. A Miktam of
David.

58 Do you indeed decree what is
    right, you gods?[s]
  Do you judge the sons of men
    uprightly?
2 Nay, in your hearts you devise
    wrongs;
  your hands deal out violence on
    earth.

3 The wicked go astray from the
    womb,
  they err from their birth, speaking
    lies.
4 They have venom like the venom of
    a serpent,
  like the deaf adder that stops its
    ear,
5 so that it does not hear the voice of
    charmers
  or of the cunning enchanter.

6 O God, break the teeth in their
    mouths;
  tear out the fangs of the young
    lions, O LORD!
7 Let them vanish like water that runs
    away;
  like grass let them be trodden
    down and wither.[t]
8 Let them be like the snail which
    dissolves into slime,
  like the untimely birth that never
    sees the sun.
9 Sooner than your pots can feel the
    heat of thorns,
  whether green or ablaze, may he
    sweep them away!

10 The righteous will rejoice when he
    sees the vengeance;
  he will bathe his feet in the blood
    of the wicked.
11 Men will say, "Surely there is a re-
    ward for the righteous;
  surely there is a God who judges
    on earth."

p Or *because*   q Cn: Heb *are aflame*   s Or *mighty lords*
t Cn: Heb uncertain
57.7-11: Ps 108.1-5.

To the choirmaster: according to Do Not Destroy. A Miktam of David, when Saul sent men to watch his house in order to kill him.

59 Deliver me from my enemies, O my God,
protect me from those who rise up against me,
2 deliver me from those who work evil,
    and save me from bloodthirsty men.

3 For, lo, they lie in wait for my life;
    fierce men band themselves against me.
For no transgression or sin of mine, O LORD,
4   for no fault of mine, they run and make ready.

Rouse thyself, come to my help, and see!
5 Thou, LORD God of hosts, art God of Israel.
Awake to punish all the nations;
    spare none of those who treacherously plot evil.   *Selah*

6 Each evening they come back,
    howling like dogs
    and prowling about the city.
7 There they are, bellowing with their mouths,
    and snarling with[u] their lips—
for "Who," they think, "will hear us?"

8 But thou, O LORD, dost laugh at them;
    thou dost hold all the nations in derision.
9 O my Strength, I will sing praises to thee;[v]
    for thou, O God, art my fortress.
10 My God in his steadfast love will meet me;
    my God will let me look in triumph on my enemies.

11 Slay them not, lest my people forget;
    make them totter by thy power,
    and bring them down,
    O Lord, our shield!
12 For the sin of their mouths, the words of their lips,
    let them be trapped in their pride.
For the cursing and lies which they utter,
13   consume them in wrath,
    consume them till they are no more,

that men may know that God rules over Jacob
    to the ends of the earth.   *Selah*

14 Each evening they come back,
    howling like dogs
    and prowling about the city.
15 They roam about for food,
    and growl if they do not get their fill.

16 But I will sing of thy might;
    I will sing aloud of thy steadfast love in the morning.
For thou hast been to me a fortress
    and a refuge in the day of my distress.
17 O my Strength, I will sing praises to thee,
    for thou, O God, art my fortress,
    the God who shows me steadfast love.

To the choirmaster: according to Shushan Eduth. A Miktam of David; for instruction; when he strove with Ărʹ·ăm-nāʹhă·rāʹim and with Ărʹ·ăm-zōʹbăh, and when Jōʹab on his return killed twelve thousand of Eʹdŏm in the Valley of Salt.

60 O God, thou hast rejected us, broken our defenses;
    thou hast been angry; oh, restore us.
2 Thou hast made the land to quake, thou hast rent it open;
    repair its breaches, for it totters.
3 Thou hast made thy people suffer hard things;
    thou hast given us wine to drink that made us reel.

4 Thou hast set up a banner for those who fear thee,
    to rally to it from the bow.[w] *Selah*
5 That thy beloved may be delivered,
    give victory by thy right hand and answer us!

6 God has spoken in his sanctuary:[x]
"With exultation I will divide up Shēʹchem
    and portion out the Vale of Sucʹcoth.
7 Gilead is mine; Măˑnăsʹsĕh is mine;
    Eʹphră·im is my helmet;
    Judah is my scepter.
8 Mōʹab is my washbasin;
    upon Eʹdŏm I cast my shoe;
    over Phiˑlisʹtiˑă I shout in triumph.''

---

u Cn: Heb *swords in*   *v* Syr: Heb *I will watch for thee*   *w* Gk Syr Jerome: Heb *truth*
Or *by his holiness*   **60.5-12:** Ps 108.6-13.

9 Who will bring me to the fortified
   city?
   Who will lead me to E´dom?
10 Hast thou not rejected us, O God?
   Thou dost not go forth, O God,
   with our armies.
11 O grant us help against the foe,
   for vain is the help of man!
12 With God we shall do valiantly;
   it is he who will tread down our
   foes.

To the choirmaster: with stringed
instruments. A Psalm of David.

61 Hear my cry, O God,
   listen to my prayer;
2 from the end of the earth I call to
   thee,
   when my heart is faint.

   Lead thou me
   to the rock that is higher than I;
3 for thou art my refuge,
   a strong tower against the enemy.

4 Let me dwell in thy tent for ever!
   Oh to be safe under the shelter of
   thy wings!   *Selah*
5 For thou, O God, hast heard my
   vows,
   thou hast given me the heritage
   of those who fear thy name.

6 Prolong the life of the king;
   may his years endure to all generations!
7 May he be enthroned for ever before God;
   bid steadfast love and faithfulness
   watch over him!

8 So will I ever sing praises to thy
   name,
   as I pay my vows day after day.

To the choirmaster: according to
Je·dü´thün. A Psalm of David.

62 For God alone my soul waits
   in silence;
   from him comes my salvation.
2 He only is my rock and my salvation,
   my fortress; I shall not be greatly
   moved.

3 How long will you set upon a man
   to shatter him, all of you,
   like a leaning wall, a tottering
   fence?
4 They only plan to thrust him down
   from his eminence.

62.12: Jer 17.10; Rev 2.23; 22.12.

They take pleasure in falsehood.
They bless with their mouths,
   but inwardly they curse.   *Selah*

5 For God alone my soul waits in
   silence,
   for my hope is from him.
6 He only is my rock and my salvation,
   my fortress; I shall not be shaken.
7 On God rests my deliverance and
   my honor;
   my mighty **rock**, my refuge is
   God.

8 Trust in him at all times, O people;
   pour out your heart before him;
   God is a refuge for us.   *Selah*

9 Men of low estate are but a breath,
   men of high estate are a delusion;
   in the balances they go up;
   they are together lighter than a
   breath.
10 Put no confidence in extortion,
   set no vain hopes on robbery;
   if riches increase, set not your
   heart on them.

11 Once God has spoken;
   twice have I heard this:
   that power belongs to God;
12   and that to thee, O Lord, belongs
   steadfast love.
   For thou dost requite a man
   according to his work.

A Psalm of David, when he was in the
Wilderness of Judah.

63 O God, thou art my God, I
   seek thee,
   my soul thirsts for thee;
   my flesh faints for thee,
   as in a dry and weary land where
   no water is.
2 So I have looked upon thee in the
   sanctuary,
   beholding thy power and glory.
3 Because thy steadfast love is better
   than life,
   my lips will praise thee.
4 So I will bless thee as long as I
   live;
   I will lift up my hands and call
   on thy name.

5 My soul is feasted as with marrow
   and fat,
   and my mouth praises thee with
   joyful lips,
6 when I think of thee upon my bed,
   and meditate on thee in the
   watches of the night;

7 for thou hast been my help,
  and in the shadow of thy wings
    I sing for joy.
8 My soul clings to thee;
  thy right hand upholds me.

9 But those who seek to destroy my
    life
  shall go down into the depths of
    the earth;
10 they shall be given over to the
    power of the sword,
  they shall be prey for jackals.
11 But the king shall rejoice in
    God;
  all who swear by him shall glory;
  for the mouths of liars will be
    stopped.

To the choirmaster. A Psalm of David.

64 Hear my voice, O God, in my
    complaint;
  preserve my life from dread of
    the enemy.
2 hide me from the secret plots of the
    wicked,
  from the scheming of evildoers,
3 who whet their tongues like swords,
  who aim bitter words like arrows,
4 shooting from ambush at the
    blameless,
  shooting at him suddenly and
    without fear.
5 They hold fast to their evil pur-
    pose;
  they talk of laying snares secretly,
  thinking, "Who can see us?"[y]
6 Who can search out our crimes?[z]
  We have thought out a cunningly
    conceived plot.
  For the inward mind and heart of
    a man are deep!

7 But God will shoot his arrow at
    them;
  they will be wounded suddenly.
8 Because of their tongue he will
    bring them to ruin;[a]
  all who see them will wag their
    heads.
9 Then all men will fear;
  they will tell what God has
    wrought,
  and ponder what he has done.

10 Let the righteous rejoice in the
    LORD,
  and take refuge in him!
  Let all the upright in heart glory!

To the choirmaster. A Psalm of David.
  A Song.

65 Praise is due to thee,
    O God, in Zion;
  and to thee shall vows be performed,
2 O thou who hearest prayer!
  To thee shall all flesh come
3 on account of sins.
  When our transgressions prevail
    over us,[b]
  thou dost forgive them.
4 Blessed is he whom thou dost choose
    and bring near,
  to dwell in thy courts!
  We shall be satisfied with the good-
    ness of thy house,
  thy holy temple!

5 By dread deeds thou dost answer us
    with deliverance,
  O God of our salvation,
  who art the hope of all the ends of
    the earth,
  and of the farthest seas;
6 who by thy strength hast established
    the mountains,
  being girded with might;
7 who dost still the roaring of the seas,
  the roaring of their waves,
  the tumult of the peoples;
8 so that those who dwell at earth's
    farthest bounds
  are afraid at thy signs;
  thou makest the outgoings of the
    morning and the evening
  to shout for joy.

9 Thou visitest the earth and waterest
    it,
  thou greatly enrichest it;
  the river of God is full of water;
  thou providest their grain,
  for so thou hast prepared it.
10 Thou waterest its furrows abun-
    dantly,
  settling its ridges,
  softening it with showers,
  and blessing its growth.
11 Thou crownest the year with thy
    bounty;
  the tracks of thy chariot drip
    with fatness.
12 The pastures of the wilderness drip,
  the hills gird themselves with joy,
13 the meadows clothe themselves with
    flocks,
  the valleys deck themselves with
    grain,
  they shout and sing together for
    joy.

Syr: Heb *them*
Cn: Heb *they search out crimes*
Cn: Heb *They will bring him to ruin, their tongue being against them*
Gk: Heb *me*

To the choirmaster. A Song. A Psalm.

66 Make a joyful noise to God,
all the earth;
2 sing the glory of his name;
give to him glorious praise!
3 Say to God, "How terrible are thy
deeds!
So great is thy power that thy
enemies cringe before thee.
4 All the earth worships thee;
they sing praises to thee,
sing praises to thy name."
Selah

5 Come and see what God has done:
he is terrible in his deeds among
men.
6 He turned the sea into dry land;
men passed through the river on
foot.
There did we rejoice in him,
7 who rules by his might for ever,
whose eyes keep watch on the nations—
let not the rebellious exalt themselves.   *Selah*

8 Bless our God, O peoples,
let the sound of his praise be
heard,
9 who has kept us among the living,
and has not let our feet slip.
10 For thou, O God, hast tested us;
thou hast tried us as silver is
tried.
11 Thou didst bring us into the net;
thou didst lay affliction on our
loins;
12 thou didst let men ride over our
heads;
we went through fire and through
water;
yet thou hast brought us forth to a
spacious place.*c*

13 I will come into thy house with
burnt offerings;
I will pay thee my vows,
14 that which my lips uttered
and my mouth promised when I
was in trouble.
15 I will offer to thee burnt offerings
of fatlings,
with the smoke of the sacrifice of
rams;
I will make an offering of bulls and
goats.   *Selah*

16 Come and hear, all you who fear
God,
and I will tell what he has done
for me.
17 I cried aloud to him,

and he was extolled with my
tongue.
18 If I had cherished iniquity in my
heart,
the Lord would not have listened.
19 But truly God has listened;
he has given heed to the voice of
my prayer.

20 Blessed be God,
because he has not rejected my
prayer
or removed his steadfast love from
me!

To the choirmaster: with stringed
instruments. A Psalm. A Song.

67 May God be gracious to us
and bless us
and make his face to shine upon
us,   *Selah*
2 that thy way may be known upon
earth,
thy saving power among all nations.
3 Let the peoples praise thee, O
God;
let all the peoples praise thee!

4 Let the nations be glad and sing for
joy,
for thou dost judge the peoples
with equity
and guide the nations upon earth.
Selah
5 Let the peoples praise thee, O God;
let all the peoples praise thee!

6 The earth has yielded its increase;
God, our God, has blessed us.
7 God has blessed us;
let all the ends of the earth fear
him!

To the choirmaster. A Psalm of David.
A Song.

68 Let God arise, let his enemies
be scattered;
let those who hate him flee before
him!
2 As smoke is driven away, so drive
them away;
as wax melts before fire,
let the wicked perish before God!
3 But let the righteous be joyful;
let them exult before God;
let them be jubilant with joy!

4 Sing to God, sing praises to his
name;

c Cn Compare Gk Syr Jerome Tg: Heb *saturation*

lift up a song to him who rides
upon the clouds;[d]
his name is the LORD, exult before
him!

5 Father of the fatherless and pro-
tector of widows
is God in his holy habitation.
6 God gives the desolate a home to
dwell in;
he leads out the prisoners to
prosperity;
but the rebellious dwell in a
parched land.

7 O God, when thou didst go forth
before thy people,
when thou didst march through
the wilderness, *Selah*
8 the earth quaked, the heavens
poured down rain,
at the presence of God;
yon Sinai quaked at the presence of
God,
the God of Israel.
9 Rain in abundance, O God, thou
didst shed abroad;
thou didst restore thy heritage as
it languished;
10 thy flock found a dwelling in it;
in thy goodness, O God, thou
didst provide for the needy.

11 The Lord gives the command;
great is the host of those who bore
the tidings:
12 "The kings of the armies, they
flee, they flee!"
The women at home divide the spoil,
13 though they stay among the
sheepfolds—
the wings of a dove covered with
silver,
its pinions with green gold.
14 When the Almighty scattered kings
there,
snow fell on Zal'mon.

15 O mighty mountain, mountain of
Bā'shän;
O many-peaked mountain,
mountain of Bashan!
16 Why look you with envy, O many-
peaked mountain,
at the mount which God desired
for his abode,
yea, where the LORD will dwell
for ever?

17 With mighty chariotry, twice ten
thousand,
thousands upon thousands,
the Lord came from Sinai into
the holy place.[e]
18 Thou didst ascend the high mount,
leading captives in thy train,
and receiving gifts among men,
even among the rebellious, that the
LORD God may dwell there.

19 Blessed be the Lord,
who daily bears us up;
God is our salvation. *Selah*
20 Our God is a God of salvation;
and to GOD, the Lord, belongs
escape from death.

21 But God will shatter the heads of
his enemies,
the hairy crown of him who walks
in his guilty ways.
22 The Lord said,
"I will bring them back from
Bā'shăn,
I will bring them back from the
depths of the sea,
23 that you may bathe[f] your feet in
blood,
that the tongues of your dogs
may have their portion from
the foe."

24 Thy solemn processions are seen,[g]
O God,
the processions of my God, my
King, into the sanctuary—
25 the singers in front, the minstrels
last,
between them maidens playing
timbrels:
26 "Bless God in the great congregation,
the LORD, O you who are of Israel's fountain!"
27 There is Benjamin, the least of
them, in the lead,
the princes of Judah in their
throng,
the princes of Zeb'ū·lŭn, the
princes of Naph'tā·lī.

28 Summon thy might, O God;
show thy strength, O God, thou
who hast wrought for us.
29 Because of thy temple at Jerusalem
kings bear gifts to thee.
30 Rebuke the beasts that dwell among
the reeds,
the herd of bulls with the calves
of the peoples.
Trample[h] under foot those who lust
after tribute;

---

[d] Or *cast up a highway for him who rides through the deserts*
[e] Cn: Heb *The Lord among them Sinai in the holy place*   [f] Gk Syr Tg: Heb *shatter*
[g] Or *have been seen*   [h] Cn: Heb *trampling*
68.18: Eph 4.8.

scatter the peoples who delight in war.[i]

31 Let bronze be brought from Egypt;
   let Ethiopia hasten to stretch out
      her hands to God.

32 Sing to God, O kingdoms of the
      earth;
   sing praises to the Lord,   *Selah*
33 to him who rides in the heavens, the
      ancient heavens;
   lo, he sends forth his voice, his
      mighty voice.
34 Ascribe power to God,
   whose majesty is over Israel,
      and his power is in the skies.
35 Terrible is God in his[j] sanctuary,
      the God of Israel,
   he gives power and strength to
      his people.

Blessed be God!

To the choirmaster: according to
Lilies. A Psalm of David.

69 Save me, O God!
    For the waters have come up
       to my neck.
2 I sink in deep mire,
   where there is no foothold;
I have come into deep waters,
   and the flood sweeps over me.
3 I am weary with my crying;
   my throat is parched.
My eyes grow dim
   with waiting for my God.

4 More in number than the hairs of
      my head
   are those who hate me without
      cause;
mighty are those who would destroy
      me,
   those who attack me with lies.
What I did not steal
   must I now restore?
5 O God, thou knowest my folly;
   the wrongs I have done are not
      hidden from thee.

6 Let not those who hope in thee be
      put to shame through me,
   O Lord GOD of hosts;
let not those who seek thee be
      brought to dishonor through
      me,
   O God of Israel.
7 For it is for thy sake that I have
      borne reproach,

that shame has covered my face.
8 I have become a stranger to my
      brethren,
   an alien to my mother's sons.

9 For zeal for thy house has consumed
      me,
   and the insults of those who insult
      thee have fallen on me.
10 When I humbled[k] my soul with
      fasting,
   it became my reproach.
11 When I made sackcloth my clothing,
   I became a byword to them.
12 I am the talk of those who sit in the
      gate,
   and the drunkards make songs
      about me.

13 But as for me, my prayer is to thee,
      O LORD.
   At an acceptable time, O God,
   in the abundance of thy steadfast
      love answer me.
With thy faithful help 14 rescue me
      from sinking in the mire;
   let me be delivered from my enemies
      and from the deep waters.
15 Let not the flood sweep over me,
   or the deep swallow me up,
   or the pit close its mouth over me.

16 Answer me, O LORD, for thy stead-
      fast love is good;
   according to thy abundant mercy,
      turn to me.
17 Hide not thy face from thy servant;
   for I am in distress, make haste
      to answer me.
18 Draw near to me, redeem me,
   set me free because of my enemies!

19 Thou knowest my reproach,
   and my shame and my dishonor;
   my foes are all known to thee.
20 Insults have broken my heart,
   so that I am in despair.
I looked for pity, but there was
      none;
   and for comforters, but I found
      none.
21 They gave me poison for food,
   and for my thirst they gave me
      vinegar to drink.
22 Let their own table before them be-
      come a snare;
   let their sacrificial feasts[l] be a
      trap.
23 Let their eyes be darkened, so that
      they cannot see;

i The Hebrew of verse 30 is obscure   *j* Gk: Heb *from thy*
k Gk Syr: Heb *I wept with fasting my soul* or *I made my soul mourn with fasting*
l Tg: Heb *for security*   **69.4:** Ps 35.19; Jn 15.25.   **69.9:** Jn 2.17; Rom 15.3.
69.21: Mt 27.34, 48; Mk 15.36; Lk 23.36; Jn 19.29.   **69.22-23:** Rom 11.9-10.

and make their loins tremble continually.

24 Pour out thy indignation upon them,
    and let thy burning anger overtake them.

25 May their camp be a desolation,
    let no one dwell in their tents.

26 For they persecute him whom thou hast smitten,
    and him[m] whom thou hast wounded, they afflict still more.[n]

27 Add to them punishment upon punishment;
    may they have no acquittal from thee.

28 Let them be blotted out of the book of the living;
    let them not be enrolled among the righteous.

29 But I am afflicted and in pain;
    let thy salvation, O God, set me on high!

30 I will praise the name of God with a song;
    I will magnify him with thanksgiving.

31 This will please the LORD more than an ox
    or a bull with horns and hoofs.

32 Let the oppressed see it and be glad;
    you who seek God, let your hearts revive.

33 For the LORD hears the needy,
    and does not despise his own that are in bonds.

34 Let heaven and earth praise him,
    the seas and everything that moves therein.

35 For God will save Zion
    and rebuild the cities of Judah;
    and his servants shall dwell[o] there and possess it;

36 the children of his servants shall inherit it,
    and those who love his name shall dwell in it.

To the choirmaster. A Psalm of David, for the memorial offering.

70 Be pleased, O God, to deliver me!
    O LORD, make haste to help me!
2 Let them be put to shame and confusion
    who seek my life!

Let them be turned back and brought to dishonor
    who desire my hurt!
3 Let them be appalled because of their shame
    who say, "Aha, Aha!"

4 May all who seek thee
    rejoice and be glad in thee!
May those who love thy salvation
    say evermore, "God is great!"
5 But I am poor and needy;
    hasten to me, O God!
Thou art my help and my deliverer;
    O LORD, do not tarry!

71 In thee, O LORD, do I take refuge;
    let me never be put to shame!
2 In thy righteousness deliver me and rescue me;
    incline thy ear to me, and save me!
3 Be thou to me a rock of refuge,
    a strong fortress,[p] to save me,
    for thou art my rock and my fortress.

4 Rescue me, O my God, from the hand of the wicked,
    from the grasp of the unjust and cruel man.
5 For thou, O Lord, art my hope,
    my trust, O LORD, from my youth.
6 Upon thee I have leaned from my birth;
    thou art he who took me from my mother's womb.
My praise is continually of thee.

7 I have been as a portent to many;
    but thou art my strong refuge.
8 My mouth is filled with thy praise,
    and with thy glory all the day.
9 Do not cast me off in the time of old age;
    forsake me not when my strength is spent.
10 For my enemies speak concerning me,
    those who watch for my life consult together,
11 and say, "God has forsaken him;
    pursue and seize him,
    for there is none to deliver him."

12 O God, be not far from me;
    O my God, make haste to help me!
13 May my accusers be put to shame and consumed;
    with scorn and disgrace may they be covered
    who seek my hurt.

---

[m] One Ms Tg Compare Syr: Heb *those*   [n] Gk Syr: Heb *recount the pain of*
Syr: Heb *and they shall dwell*
   [o] Gk Compare 31.3: Heb *to come continually thou hast commanded*   **69.24:** Rev 16.1.
69.25: Acts 1.20.   **69.28:** Rev 3.5; 13.8; 17.8; 20.12, 15; 21.27.   **70.1-5:** Ps 40.13-17.

14 But I will hope continually,
   and will praise thee yet more and
      more.
15 My mouth will tell of thy righteous
      acts,
   of thy deeds of salvation all the
      day,
   for their number is past my
      knowledge.
16 With the mighty deeds of the Lord
      GOD I will come,
   I will praise thy righteousness,
      thine alone.

17 O God, from my youth thou hast
      taught me,
   and I still proclaim thy wondrous
      deeds.
18 So even to old age and gray hairs,
   O God, do not forsake me,
   till I proclaim thy might
      to all the generations to come.*q*
   Thy power 19 and thy righteousness,
      O God,
   reach the high heavens.

   Thou who hast done great things,
      O God, who is like thee?
20 Thou who hast made me see many
      sore troubles
   wilt revive me again;
   from the depths of the earth
      thou wilt bring me up again.
21 Thou wilt increase my honor,
   and comfort me again.

22 I will also praise thee with the harp
      for thy faithfulness, O my God;
   I will sing praises to thee with the lyre,
      O Holy One of Israel.
23 My lips will shout for joy,
   when I sing praises to thee;
   my soul also, which thou hast
      rescued.
24 And my tongue will talk of thy
      righteous help
   all the day long,
   for they have been put to shame and
      disgraced
   who sought to do me hurt.

A Psalm to Solomon.

72 Give the king thy justice, O
   God,
   and thy righteousness to the royal
      son!
2 May he judge thy people with
      righteousness,
   and thy poor with justice!
3 Let the mountains bear prosperity
      for the people,

and the hills, in righteousness!
4 May he defend the cause of the poor
      of the people,
   give deliverance to the needy,
   and crush the oppressor!

5 May he live*r* while the sun endures,
   and as long as the moon, through-
      out all generations!
6 May he be like rain that falls on the
      mown grass,
   like showers that water the earth!
7 In his days may righteousness
      flourish,
   and peace abound, till the moon
      be no more!

8 May he have dominion from sea to
      sea,
   and from the River to the ends
      of the earth!
9 May his foes*s* bow down before him,
   and his enemies lick the dust!
10 May the kings of Tär′shish and of
      the isles
   render him tribute,
   may the kings of Sheba and Sē′bà
      bring gifts!
11 May all kings fall down before him,
   all nations serve him!

12 For he delivers the needy when he
      calls,
   the poor and him who has no
      helper.
13 He has pity on the weak and the
      needy,
   and saves the lives of the needy.
14 From oppression and violence he
      redeems their life;
   and precious is their blood in his
      sight.

15 Long may he live,
   may gold of Sheba be given to
      him!
   May prayer be made for him con-
      tinually,
   and blessings invoked for him all
      the day!
16 May there be abundance of grain in
      the land;
   on the tops of the mountains may
      it wave;
   may its fruit be like Lebanon;
   and may men blossom forth from
      the cities
   like the grass of the field!
17 May his name endure for ever,
   his fame continue as long as the
      sun!
   May men bless themselves by him,
   all nations call him blessed!

q Gk Compare Syr: Heb *to a generation, to all that come*
r Gk: Heb *may they fear thee*   *s* Cn: Heb *those who dwell in the wilderness*

18 Blessed be the LORD, the God of
     Israel,
     who alone does wondrous things.
19 Blessed be his glorious name for
     ever;
     may his glory fill the whole earth!
     Amen and Amen!

20 The prayers of David, the son of
   Jesse, are ended.

BOOK III

A Psalm of Ā′saph.

73 Truly God is good to the up-
     right,
     to those who are pure in heart.^{l}
2 But as for me, my feet had almost
     stumbled,
     my steps had well nigh slipped.
3 For I was envious of the arrogant,
     when I saw the prosperity of the
     wicked.

4 For they have no pangs;
     their bodies are sound and sleek.
5 They are not in trouble as other
     men are;
     they are not stricken like other
     men.
6 Therefore pride is their necklace;
     violence covers them as a garment.
7 Their eyes swell out with fatness,
     their hearts overflow with follies.
8 They scoff and speak with malice;
     loftily they threaten oppression.
9 They set their mouths against the
     heavens,
     and their tongue struts through
     the earth.

10 Therefore the people turn and praise
     them;^{u}
     and find no fault in them.^{y}
11 And they say, "How can God know?
     Is there knowledge in the Most
     High?"
12 Behold, these are the wicked;
     always at ease, they increase in
     riches.
13 All in vain have I kept my heart
     clean
     and washed my hands in inno-
     cence.
14 For all the day long I have been
     stricken,
     and chastened every morning.

15 If I had said, "I will speak thus,"

I would have been untrue to the
   generation of thy children.
16 But when I thought how to understand this,
   it seemed to me a wearisome task,
17 until I went into the sanctuary of
   God;
   then I perceived their end.
18 Truly thou dost set them in slippery
   places;
   thou dost make them fall to ruin.
19 How they are destroyed in a moment,
   swept away utterly by terrors!
20 They are^w like a dream when one
   awakes,
   on awaking you despise their
   phantoms.

21 When my soul was embittered,
   when I was pricked in heart,
22 I was stupid and ignorant,
   I was like a beast toward thee.
23 Nevertheless I am continually with
   thee;
   thou dost hold my right hand.
24 Thou dost guide me with thy
   counsel,
   and afterward thou wilt receive
   me to glory.^{x}
25 Whom have I in heaven but thee?
   And there is nothing upon earth
   that I desire besides thee.
26 My flesh and my heart may fail,
   but God is the strength^y of my
   heart and my portion for ever.

27 For lo, those who are far from thee
   shall perish;
   thou dost put an end to those who
   are false to thee.
28 But for me it is good to be near God;
   I have made the Lord GOD my
   refuge,
   that I may tell of all thy works.

A Maskil of Ā′saph.

74 O God, why dost thou cast us
     off for ever?
   Why does thy anger smoke against
   the sheep of thy pasture?
2 Remember thy congregation, which
   thou hast gotten of old,
   which thou hast redeemed to be
   the tribe of thy heritage!
   Remember Mount Zion, where
   thou hast dwelt.
3 Direct thy steps to the perpetual
   ruins;
   the enemy has destroyed everything in the sanctuary!

---

^{t} Or *Truly God is good to Israel, to those who are pure in heart*
^{u} Cn: Heb *his people return hither* ^{v} Cn: Heb *abundant waters are drained by them*
^{w} Cn: Heb *Lord* ^{x} Or *honor* ^{y} Heb *rock*

4 Thy foes have roared in the midst
    of thy holy place;
  they set up their own signs for
    signs.
5 At the upper entrance they hacked
    the wooden trellis with axes.z
6 And then all its carved wood
    they broke down with hatchets
      and hammers.
7 They set thy sanctuary on fire;
  to the ground they desecrated the
    dwelling place of thy name.
8 They said to themselves, "We will
    utterly subdue them";
  they burned all the meeting places
    of God in the land.

9 We do not see our signs;
  there is no longer any prophet,
  and there is none among us who
    knows how long.
10 How long, O God, is the foe to
    scoff?
  Is the enemy to revile thy name
    for ever?
11 Why dost thou hold back thy hand,
  why dost thou keep thy right
    hand ina thy bosom?

12 Yet God my King is from of old,
  working salvation in the midst of
    the earth.
13 Thou didst divide the sea by thy
    might;
  thou didst break the heads of the
    dragons on the waters.
14 Thou didst crush the heads of
    Lē·vī′a·thăn,
  thou didst give him as foodb for
    the creatures of the wilderness.
15 Thou didst cleave open springs and
    brooks;
  thou didst dry up ever-flowing
    streams.
16 Thine is the day, thine also the
    night;
  thou hast established the lumi-
    naries and the sun.
17 Thou hast fixed all the bounds of
    the earth;
  thou hast made summer and
    winter.

18 Remember this, O LORD, how the
    enemy scoffs,
  and an impious people reviles thy
    name.
19 Do not deliver the soul of thy dove
    to the wild beasts;
  do not forget the life of thy poor
    for ever.

20 Have regard for thyc covenant;
  for the dark places of the land are
    full of the habitations of
      violence.
21 Let not the downtrodden be put to
    shame;
  let the poor and needy praise thy
    name.

22 Arise, O God, plead thy cause;
  remember how the impious scoff
    at thee all the day!
23 Do not forget the clamor of thy foes,
  the uproar of thy adversaries
    which goes up continually!

To the choirmaster: according to Do
Not Destroy. A Psalm of Ā′saph.
A Song.

75 We give thanks to thee, O
    God; we give thanks;
  we call on thy name and recountd
    thy wondrous deeds.

2 At the set time which I appoint
  I will judge with equity.
3 When the earth totters, and all its
    inhabitants,
  it is I who keep steady its pillars.
                                    Selah
4 I say to the boastful, "Do not
    boast,"
  and to the wicked, "Do not lift
    up your horn;
5 do not lift up your horn on high,
  or speak with insolent neck."

6 For not from the east or from the
    west
  and not from the wilderness comes
    lifting up;
7 but it is God who executes judg-
    ment,
  putting down one and lifting up
    another.
8 For in the hand of the LORD there
    is a cup,
  with foaming wine, well mixed;
  and he will pour a draught from it,
  and all the wicked of the earth
    shall drain it down to the dregs.

9 But I will rejoicee for ever,
  I will sing praises to the God of
    Jacob.
10 All the horns of the wicked hef will
    cut off,
  but the horns of the righteous
    shall be exalted.

z Cn Compare Gk Syr: Heb uncertain
a Cn: Heb *consume thy right hand from*   b Heb *food for the people*   c Gk Syr: Heb *the*
d Syr Compare Gk: Heb *and near is thy name. They recount*   e Gk: Heb *declare*
f Heb *I*

To the choirmaster: with stringed instruments. A Psalm of A′saph. A Song.

76   In Judah God is known,
    his name is great in Israel.
2 His abode has been established in Salem,
    his dwelling place in Zion.
3 There he broke the flashing arrows,
    the shield, the sword, and the
    weapons of war.   *Selah*

4 Glorious art thou, more majestic
    than the everlasting mountains.^g
5 The stouthearted were stripped of their spoil;
    they sank into sleep;
    all the men of war
    were unable to use their hands.
6 At thy rebuke, O God of Jacob,
    both rider and horse lay stunned.

7 But thou, terrible art thou!
    Who can stand before thee
    when once thy anger is roused?
8 From the heavens thou didst utter judgment;
    the earth feared and was still,
9 when God arose to establish judgment
    to save all the oppressed of the earth.   *Selah*

10 Surely the wrath of men shall praise thee;
    the residue of wrath thou wilt gird upon thee.
11 Make your vows to the Lord your God, and perform them;
    let all around him bring gifts
    to him who is to be feared,
12 who cuts off the spirit of princes,
    who is terrible to the kings of the earth.

To the choirmaster: according to Je·dü′thun. A Psalm of A′saph.

77   I cry aloud to God,
    aloud to God, that he may hear me.
2 In the day of my trouble I seek the Lord;
    in the night my hand is stretched out without wearying;
    my soul refuses to be comforted.

3 I think of God, and I moan;
    I meditate, and my spirit faints.   *Selah*
4 Thou dost hold my eyelids from closing;

I am so troubled that I cannot speak.
5 I consider the days of old,
    I remember the years long ago.
6 I commune^h with my heart in the night;
    I meditate and search my spirit:ⁱ
7 "Will the Lord spurn for ever,
    and never again be favorable?
8 Has his steadfast love for ever ceased?
    Are his promises at an end for all time?
9 Has God forgotten to be gracious?
    Has he in anger shut up his compassion?"   *Selah*
10 And I say, "It is my grief
    that the right hand of the Most High has changed."

11 I will call to mind the deeds of the Lord;
    yea, I will remember thy wonders of old.
12 I will meditate on all thy work,
    and muse on thy mighty deeds.
13 Thy way, O God, is holy.
    What god is great like our God?
14 Thou are the God who workest wonders,
    who has manifested thy might among the peoples.
15 Thou didst with thy arm redeem thy people,
    the sons of Jacob and Joseph.   *Selah*

16 When the waters saw thee, O God,
    when the waters saw thee, they were afraid,
    yea, the deep trembled.
17 The clouds poured out water;
    the skies gave forth thunder;
    thy arrows flashed on every side.
18 The crash of thy thunder was in the whirlwind;
    thy lightnings lighted up the world;
    the earth trembled and shook.
19 Thy way was through the sea,
    thy path through the great waters;
    yet thy footprints were unseen.
20 Thou didst lead thy people like a flock
    by the hand of Moses and Aaron.

A Maskil of A′saph.

78   Give ear, O my people, to my teaching;
    incline your ears to the words of my mouth!

^g Gk Heb *the mountains of prey*   ^h Gk Syr: Heb *my music*
ⁱ Syr Jerome: Heb *my spirit searches*

2 I will open my mouth in a parable;
  I will utter dark sayings from of
    old,
3 things that we have heard and
    known,
  that our fathers have told us.
4 We will not hide them from their
    children,
  but tell to the coming generation
  the glorious deeds of the LORD, and
    his might,
  and the wonders which he has
    wrought.

5 He established a testimony in Jacob,
  and appointed a law in Israel,
  which he commanded our fathers
    to teach to their children;
6 that the next generation might know
    them,
  the children yet unborn,
  and arise and tell them to their
    children,
7 so that they should set their hope
    in God,
  and not forget the works of God,
  but keep his commandments;
8 and that they should not be like
    their fathers,
  a stubborn and rebellious gen-
    eration,
  a generation whose heart was not
    steadfast,
  whose spirit was not faithful to
    God.

9 The E´phra·im·ites, armed with[j]
    the bow,
  turned back on the day of battle.
10 They did not keep God's covenant,
  but refused to walk according to
    his law.
11 They forgot what he had done,
  and the miracles that he had
    shown them.
12 In the sight of their fathers he
    wrought marvels
  in the land of Egypt, in the fields
    of Zo´an.
13 He divided the sea and let them
    pass through it,
  and made the waters stand like a
    heap.
14 In the daytime he led them with a
    cloud,
  and all the night with a fiery light.
15 He cleft rocks in the wilderness,
  and gave them drink abundantly
    as from the deep.
16 He made streams come out of the
    rock,
  and caused waters to flow down
    like rivers.

17 Yet they sinned still more against
    him,
  rebelling against the Most High
    in the desert.
18 They tested God in their heart
  by demanding the food they
    craved.
19 They spoke against God, saying,
  "Can God spread a table in the
    wilderness?
20 He smote the rock so that water
    gushed out
  and streams overflowed.
  Can he also give bread,
  or provide meat for his people?"

21 Therefore, when the LORD heard,
    he was full of wrath;
  a fire was kindled against Jacob,
  his anger mounted against Israel;
22 because they had no faith in God,
  and did not trust his saving power.
23 Yet he commanded the skies above,
  and opened the doors of heaven;
24 and he rained down upon them
    manna to eat,
  and gave them the grain of heaven.
25 Man ate of the bread of the angels;
  he sent them food in abundance.
26 He caused the east wind to blow in
    the heavens,
  and by his power he led out the
    south wind;
27 he rained flesh upon them like dust,
  winged birds like the sand of the
    seas;
28 he let them fall in the midst of their
    camp,
  all around their habitations.
29 And they ate and were well filled,
  for he gave them what they
    craved.
30 But before they had sated their
    craving,
  while the food was still in their
    mouths,
31 the anger of God rose against them
  and he slew the strongest of them,
  and laid low the picked men of
    Israel.

32 In spite of all this they still sinned;
  despite his wonders they did not
    believe.
33 So he made their days vanish like a
    breath,
  and their years in terror.
34 When he slew them, they sought
    for him;
  they repented and sought God
    earnestly.
35 They remembered that God was
    their rock,

j Heb armed with shooting
78.2: Mt 13.35.   **78.24:** Jn 6.31.

the Most High God their redeemer.

36 But they flattered him with their
mouths;
they lied to him with their
tongues.

37 Their heart was not steadfast toward him;
they were not true to his covenant.

38 Yet he, being compassionate,
forgave their iniquity,
and did not destroy them;
he restrained his anger often,
and did not stir up all his wrath.

39 He remembered that they were but
flesh,
a wind that passes and comes not
again.

40 How often they rebelled against him
in the wilderness
and grieved him in the desert!

41 They tested him again and again,
and provoked the Holy One of
Israel.

42 They did not keep in mind his
power,
or the day when he redeemed
them from the foe;

43 when he wrought his signs in Egypt,
and his miracles in the fields of
Zŏ'an.

44 He turned their rivers to blood,
so that they could not drink of
their streams.

45 He sent among them swarms of flies,
which devoured them,
and frogs, which destroyed them.

46 He gave their crops to the caterpillar,
and the fruit of their labor to the
locust.

47 He destroyed their vines with hail,
and their sycamores with frost.

48 He gave over their cattle to the hail,
and their flocks to thunderbolts.

49 He let loose on them his fierce anger,
wrath, indignation, and distress,
a company of destroying angels.

50 He made a path for his anger;
he did not spare them from death,
but gave their lives over to the
plague.

51 He smote all the first-born in Egypt,
the first issue of their strength in
the tents of Ham.

52 Then he led forth his people like
sheep,
and guided them in the wilderness
like a flock.

53 He led them in safety, so that they
were not afraid;
but the sea overwhelmed their
enemies.

54 And he brought them to his holy
land,

to the mountain which his right
hand had won.

55 He drove out nations before them;
he apportioned them for a possession
and settled the tribes of Israel in
their tents.

56 Yet they tested and rebelled against
the Most High God,
and did not observe his testimonies,

57 but turned away and acted treacherously like their fathers;
they twisted like a deceitful
bow.

58 For they provoked him to anger
with their high places;
they moved him to jealousy with
their graven images.

59 When God heard, he was full of
wrath,
and he utterly rejected Israel.

60 He forsook his dwelling at Shi'lōh,
the tent where he dwelt among
men,

61 and delivered his power to captivity,
his glory to the hand of the foe.

62 He gave his people over to the
sword,
and vented his wrath on his
heritage.

63 Fire devoured their young men,
and their maidens had no marriage song.

64 Their priests fell by the sword,
and their widows made no lamentation.

65 Then the Lord awoke as from sleep,
like a strong man shouting because of wine.

66 And he put his adversaries to rout;
he put them to everlasting shame.

67 He rejected the tent of Joseph,
he did not choose the tribe of
E'phrā·im;

68 but he chose the tribe of Judah,
Mount Zion, which he loves.

69 He built his sanctuary like the high
heavens,
like the earth, which he has
founded for ever.

70 He chose David his servant,
and took him from the sheepfolds;

71 from tending the ewes that had
young he brought him
to be the shepherd of Jacob his
people,
of Israel his inheritance.

72 With upright heart he tended them,
and guided them with skilful
hand.

78.37: Acts 8.21.

A Psalm of A'saph.

79 O God, the heathen have come into thy inheritance;
they have defiled thy holy temple;
they have laid Jerusalem in ruins.

2 They have given the bodies of thy servants
to the birds of the air for food,
the flesh of thy saints to the beasts of the earth.

3 They have poured out their blood like water
round about Jerusalem,
and there was none to bury them.

4 We have become a taunt to our neighbors,
mocked and derided by those round about us.

5 How long, O LORD? Wilt thou be angry for ever?
Will thy jealous wrath burn like fire?

6 Pour out thy anger on the nations that do not know thee,
and on the kingdoms
that do not call on thy name!

7 For they have devoured Jacob,
and laid waste his habitation.

8 Do not remember against us the iniquities of our forefathers;
let thy compassion come speedily to meet us,
for we are brought very low.

9 Help us, O God of our salvation,
for the glory of thy name;
deliver us, and forgive our sins,
for thy name's sake!

10 Why should the nations say,
"Where is their God?"
Let the avenging of the outpoured blood of thy servants
be known among the nations before our eyes!

11 Let the groans of the prisoners come before thee;
according to thy great power preserve those doomed to die!

12 Return sevenfold into the bosom of our neighbors
the taunts with which they have taunted thee, O Lord!

13 Then we thy people, the flock of thy pasture,
will give thanks to thee for ever;
from generation to generation we will recount thy praise.

To the choirmaster: according to Lilies. A Testimony of A'saph.
A Psalm.

80 Give ear, O Shepherd of Israel,
thou who leadest Joseph like a flock!
Thou who art enthroned upon the cherubim, shine forth

2 before E'phra·im and Benjamin and Ma·nas'seh!
Stir up thy might,
and come to save us!

3 Restore us, O God;
let thy face shine, that we may be saved!

4 O LORD God of hosts,
how long wilt thou be angry with thy people's prayers?

5 Thou hast fed them with the bread of tears,
and given them tears to drink in full measure.

6 Thou dost make us the scorn[k] of our neighbors;
and our enemies laugh among themselves.

7 Restore us, O God of hosts;
let thy face shine, that we may be saved!

8 Thou didst bring a vine out of Egypt;
thou didst drive out the nations and plant it.

9 Thou didst clear the ground for it;
it took deep root and filled the land.

10 The mountains were covered with its shade,
the mighty cedars with its branches;

11 it sent out its branches to the sea,
and its shoots to the River.

12 Why then hast thou broken down its walls,
so that all who pass along the way pluck its fruit?

13 The boar from the forest ravages it,
and all that move in the field feed on it.

14 Turn again, O God of hosts!
Look down from heaven, and see;
have regard for this vine,

15 the stock which thy right hand planted.[l]

16 They have burned it with fire, they have cut it down;

---

k Syr: Heb strife
l Heb planted and upon the son whom thou hast reared for thyself

may they perish at the rebuke of
thy countenance!
17 But let thy hand be upon the man
of thy right hand,
the son of man whom thou hast
made strong for thyself!
18 Then we will never turn back from
thee;
give us life, and we will call on
thy name!

19 Restore us, O LORD God of hosts!
let thy face shine, that we may be
saved!

To the choirmaster: according to The
Gittith. A Psalm of A'saph.

81 Sing aloud to God our
strength;
shout for joy to the God of Jacob!
2 Raise a song, sound the timbrel,
the sweet lyre with the harp.
3 Blow the trumpet at the new moon,
at the full moon, on our feast day.
4 For it is a statute for Israel,
an ordinance of the God of Jacob.
5 He made it a decree in Joseph,
when he went out over^m the land
of Egypt.

I hear a voice I had not known:
6 "I relieved your^n shoulder of the
burden;
your^n hands were freed from the
basket.
7 In distress you called, and I delivered you;
I answered you in the secret place
of thunder;
I tested you at the waters of
Mer'i·bah.   *Selah*
8 Hear, O my people, while I admonish you!
O Israel, if you would but listen
to me!
9 There shall be no strange god
among you;
you shall not bow down to a
foreign god.
10 I am the LORD your God,
who brought you up out of the
land of Egypt.
Open your mouth wide, and I
will fill it.

11 "But my people did not listen to my
voice;
Israel would have none of me.
12 So I gave them over to their stubborn hearts,
to follow their own counsels.
13 O that my people would listen to
me,
that Israel would walk in my ways!
14 I would soon subdue their enemies,
and turn my hand against their
foes.
15 Those who hate the LORD would
cringe toward him,
and their fate would last for ever.
16 I would feed you^o with the finest
of the wheat,
and with honey from the rock I
would satisfy you."

A Psalm of A'saph.

82 God has taken his place in the
divine council;
in the midst of the gods he holds
judgment:
2 "How long will you judge unjustly
and show partiality to the wicked?
Selah
3 Give justice to the weak and the
fatherless;
maintain the right of the afflicted
and the destitute.
4 Rescue the weak and the needy;
deliver them from the hand of the
wicked."

5 They have neither knowledge nor
understanding,
they walk about in darkness;
all the foundations of the earth
are shaken.

6 I say, "You are gods,
sons of the Most High, all of you;
7 nevertheless, you shall die like men,
and fall like any prince."^p

8 Arise, O God, judge the earth;
for to thee belong all the nations!

A Song. A Psalm of A'saph.

83 O God, do not keep silence;
do not hold thy peace or be
still, O God!
2 For lo, thy enemies are in tumult;
those who hate thee have raised
their heads.
3 They lay crafty plans against thy
people;
they consult together against thy
protected ones.
4 They say, "Come, let us wipe them
out as a nation;

m Or against   n Heb his   o Cn Compare verse 16b: Heb he would feed him
p Or fall as one man, O princes
82.6: Jn 10.34.

let the name of Israel be remembered no more!"

5 Yea, they conspire with one accord;
   against thee they make a covenant—

6 the tents of Ē′dŏm and the Ĭsh′mȧ-
   el·ītes,
   Mō′ab and the Hăg′rītes,

7 Gē′bȧl and Ăm′mŏn and Ăm′ȧ·lĕk,
   Phĭ·lĭs′tĭ·ȧ with the inhabitants of
   Tyre;

8 Assyria also has joined them;
   they are the strong arm of the
   children of Lot.   *Selah*

9 Do to them as thou didst to Mid′-
   ĭ·ȧn,
   as to Sĭs′ĕr·ȧ and Jā′bĭn at the
   river Kī′shon,

10 who were destroyed at Ēn′-dŏr,
   who became dung for the ground.

11 Make their nobles like Ōr′ĕb and
   Zē′ĕb,
   all their princes like Zē′bȧh and
   Zȧl·mŭn′nȧ,

12 who said, "Let us take possession
   for ourselves
   of the pastures of God."

13 O my God, make them like whirling
   dust,*q*
   like chaff before the wind.

14 As fire consumes the forest,
   as the flame sets the mountains
   ablaze,

15 so do thou pursue them with thy
   tempest
   and terrify them with thy hur-
   ricane!

16 Fill their faces with shame,
   that they may seek thy name, O
   LORD.

17 Let them be put to shame and dismayed for ever;
   let them perish in disgrace.

18 Let them know that thou alone,
   whose name is the LORD,
   art the Most High over all the
   earth.

To the choirmaster: according to The
      Gittith. A Psalm of the
            Sons of Kō′rȧh.

84 How lovely is thy dwelling
      place,
      O LORD of hosts!

2 My soul longs, yea, faints
   for the courts of the LORD;
   my heart and flesh sing for joy
   to the living God.

3 Even the sparrow finds a home,

q Or a tumbleweed   r Heb lacks to Zion

and the swallow a nest for herself,
   where she may lay her young,
at thy altars, O LORD of hosts,
   my King and my God.

4 Blessed are those who dwell in thy
   house,
   ever singing thy praise!   *Selah*

5 Blessed are the men whose strength
   is in thee,
   in whose heart are the highways
   to Zion.*r*

6 As they go through the valley of Bā′cȧ
   they make it a place of springs;
   the early rain also covers it with
   pools.

7 They go from strength to strength;
   the God of gods will be seen in
   Zion.

8 O LORD God of hosts, hear my
   prayer;
   give ear, O God of Jacob!
                              Selah

9 Behold our shield, O God;
   look upon the face of thine
   anointed!

10 For a day in thy courts is better
   than a thousand elsewhere.
I would rather be a doorkeeper in
   the house of my God
   than dwell in the tents of wickedness.

11 For the LORD God is a sun and shield;
   he bestows favor and honor.
No good thing does the LORD withhold
   from those who walk uprightly.

12 O LORD of hosts,
   blessed is the man who trusts in
   thee!

To the choirmaster. A Psalm of the
         Sons of Kō′rȧh.

85 LORD, thou wast favorable to
      thy land;
      thou didst restore the fortunes of
      Jacob.

2 Thou didst forgive the iniquity of
   thy people;
   thou didst pardon all their sin.
                              Selah

3 Thou didst withdraw all thy wrath;
   thou didst turn from thy hot
   anger.

4 Restore us again, O God of our
   salvation,
   and put away thy indignation toward us!

5 Wilt thou be angry with us for ever?

Wilt thou prolong thy anger to all generations?

6 Wilt thou not revive us again,
that thy people may rejoice in thee?

7 Show us thy steadfast love, O LORD,
and grant us thy salvation.

8 Let me hear what God the LORD will speak,
for he will speak peace to his people,
to his saints, to those who turn to him in their hearts.[s]

9 Surely his salvation is at hand for those who fear him,
that glory may dwell in our land.

10 Steadfast love and faithfulness will meet;
righteousness and peace will kiss each other.

11 Faithfulness will spring up from the ground,
and righteousness will look down from the sky.

12 Yea, the LORD will give what is good,
and our land will yield its increase.

13 Righteousness will go before him,
and make his footsteps a way.

A Prayer of David.

86 Incline thy ear, O LORD, and answer me,
for I am poor and needy.

2 Preserve my life, for I am godly;
save thy servant who trusts in thee.
Thou art my God; 3 be gracious to me, O Lord,
for to thee do I cry all the day.

4 Gladden the soul of thy servant,
for to thee, O Lord, do I lift up my soul.

5 For thou, O Lord, art good and forgiving,
abounding in steadfast love to all who call on thee.

6 Give ear, O LORD, to my prayer;
hearken to my cry of supplication.

7 In the day of my trouble I call on thee,
for thou dost answer me.

8 There is none like thee among the gods, O Lord,
nor are there any works like thine.

9 All the nations thou hast made shall come
and bow down before thee, O Lord,

s Gk: Heb but let them not turn back to folly

and shall glorify thy name.

10 For thou art great and doest wondrous things,
thou alone art God.

11 Teach me thy way, O LORD,
that I may walk in thy truth;
unite my heart to fear thy name.

12 I give thanks to thee, O Lord my God, with my whole heart,
and I will glorify thy name for ever.

13 For great is thy steadfast love toward me;
thou hast delivered my soul from the depths of She'ol.

14 O God, insolent men have risen up against me;
a band of ruthless men seek my life,
and they do not set thee before them.

15 But thou, O Lord, art a God merciful and gracious,
slow to anger and abounding in steadfast love and faithfulness.

16 Turn to me and take pity on me;
give thy strength to thy servant,
and save the son of thy handmaid.

17 Show me a sign of thy favor,
that those who hate me may see and be put to shame
because thou, LORD, hast helped me and comforted me.

A Psalm of the Sons of Kō'rah.
A Song.

87 On the holy mount stands the city he founded;

2 the LORD loves the gates of Zion
more than all the dwelling places of Jacob.

3 Glorious things are spoken of you, O city of God.   *Selah*

4 Among those who know me I mention Rā'hab and Babylon;
behold, Phi·lis'ti·a and Tȳre, with Ethiopia—
"This one was born there," they say.

5 And of Zion it shall be said,
"This one and that one were born in her";
for the Most High himself will establish her.

6 The LORD records as he registers the peoples,
"This one was born there."   *Selah*

7 Singers and dancers alike say,
"All my springs are in you."

A Song. A Psalm of the Sons of Kō'rȧh. To the choirmaster: according to Mahalath Leannoth. A Maskil of Hē'mȧn the Ez'rȧ·hīte.

88

O LORD, my God, I call for help[f] by day;
    I cry out in the night before thee.

2 Let my prayer come before thee,
    incline thy ear to my cry!

3 For my soul is full of troubles,
    and my life draws near to Shē'ōl.
4 I am reckoned among those who go down to the Pit;
    I am a man who has no strength,
5 like one forsaken among the dead,
    like the slain that lie in the grave,
like those whom thou dost remember no more,
    for they are cut off from thy hand.
6 Thou hast put me in the depths of the Pit,
    in the regions dark and deep.
7 Thy wrath lies heavy upon me,
    and thou dost overwhelm me with all thy waves.   *Selah*
8 Thou hast caused my companions to shun me;
    thou hast made me a thing of horror to them.
I am shut in so that I cannot escape;
9   my eye grows dim through sorrow.
Every day I call upon thee, O LORD;
    I spread out my hands to thee.
10 Dost thou work wonders for the dead?
    Do the shades rise up to praise thee?   *Selah*
11 Is thy steadfast love declared in the grave,
    or thy faithfulness in A·bad'don?
12 Are thy wonders known in the darkness,
    or thy saving help in the land of forgetfulness?

13 But I, O LORD, cry to thee;
    in the morning my prayer comes before thee.
14 O LORD, why dost thou cast me off?
    Why dost thou hide thy face from me?
15 Afflicted and close to death from my youth up,
    I suffer thy terrors; I am helpless.[u]
16 Thy wrath has swept over me;
    thy dread assaults destroy me.
17 They surround me like a flood all day long;
    they close in upon me together.
18 Thou hast caused lover and friend to shun me;
    my companions are in darkness.

A Maskil of Ethan the Ez'rȧ·hīte.

89

I will sing of thy steadfast love, O LORD,[v] for ever;
    with my mouth I will proclaim thy faithfulness to all generations.
2 For thy steadfast love was established for ever,
    thy faithfulness is firm as the heavens.
3 Thou hast said, "I have made a covenant with my chosen one,
    I have sworn to David my servant:
4 'I will establish your descendants for ever,
    and build your throne for all generations.'"   *Selah*

5 Let the heavens praise thy wonders, O LORD,
    thy faithfulness in the assembly of the holy ones!
6 For who in the skies can be compared to the LORD?
    Who among the heavenly beings[w] is like the LORD,
7 a God feared in the council of the holy ones,
    great and terrible[x] above all that are round about him?
8 O LORD God of hosts,
    who is mighty as thou art, O LORD,
    with thy faithfulness round about thee?
9 Thou dost rule the raging of the sea;
    when its waves rise, thou stillest them.
10 Thou didst crush Rā'hab like a carcass,
    thou didst scatter thy enemies with thy mighty arm.
11 The heavens are thine, the earth also is thine;
    the world and all that is in it, thou hast founded them.
12 The north and the south, thou hast created them;
    Tā'bor and Hēr'mon joyously praise thy name.
13 Thou hast a mighty arm;
    strong is thy hand, high thy right hand.
14 Righteousness and justice are the foundation of thy throne;

---

[f] Cn: Heb O LORD, *God of my salvation*
[u] The meaning of the Hebrew word is uncertain
[v] Gk: Heb *the steadfast love of the* LORD   [w] Or *sons of gods*
[x] Gk Syr: Heb *greatly terrible*   **89.3-4:** Ps 132.11; Acts 2.30.

steadfast love and faithfulness go
before thee.

15 Blessed are the people who know
the festal shout,
who walk, O LORD, in the light of
thy countenance,

16 who exult in thy name all the day,
and extol[y] thy righteousness.

17 For thou art the glory of their
strength;
by thy favor our horn is exalted.

18 For our shield belongs to the LORD,
our king to the Holy One of Israel.

19 Of old thou didst speak in a vision
to thy faithful one, and say:
"I have set the crown[z] upon one
who is mighty,
I have exalted one chosen from
the people.

20 I have found David, my servant;
with my holy oil I have anointed
him;

21 so that my hand shall ever abide
with him,
my arm also shall strengthen him.

22 The enemy shall not outwit him,
the wicked shall not humble him.

23 I will crush his foes before him
and strike down those who hate
him.

24 My faithfulness and my steadfast
love shall be with him,
and in my name shall his horn be
exalted.

25 I will set his hand on the sea
and his right hand on the rivers.

26 He shall cry to me, 'Thou art my
Father,
my God, and the Rock of my
salvation.'

27 And I will make him the first-born,
the highest of the kings of the
earth.

28 My steadfast love I will keep for
him for ever,
and my covenant will stand firm
for him.

29 I will establish his line for ever
and his throne as the days of the
heavens.

30 If his children forsake my law
and do not walk according to my
ordinances,

31 if they violate my statutes
and do not keep my commandments,

32 then I will punish their transgression with the rod
and their iniquity with scourges;

33 but I will not remove from him my
steadfast love,

or be false to my faithfulness.

34 I will not violate my covenant,
or alter the word that went forth
from my lips.

35 Once for all I have sworn by my
holiness;
I will not lie to David.

36 His line shall endure for ever,
his throne as long as the sun before me.

37 Like the moon it shall be established
for ever;
it shall stand firm while the skies
endure."[a]   Selah

38 But now thou hast cast off and
rejected,
thou art full of wrath against thy
anointed.

39 Thou hast renounced the covenant
with thy servant;
thou hast defiled his crown in the
dust.

40 Thou hast breached all his walls;
thou hast laid his strongholds in
ruins.

41 All that pass by despoil him;
he has become the scorn of his
neighbors.

42 Thou hast exalted the right hand of
his foes;
thou hast made all his enemies
rejoice.

43 Yea, thou hast turned back the edge
of his sword,
and thou hast not made him stand
in battle.

44 Thou hast removed the scepter from
his hand,[b]
and cast his throne to the ground.

45 Thou hast cut short the days of his
youth;
thou hast covered him with shame.
Selah

46 How long, O LORD? Wilt thou hide
thyself for ever?
How long will thy wrath burn
like fire?

47 Remember, O Lord,[c] what the
measure of life is,
for what vanity thou hast created
all the sons of men!

48 What man can live and never see
death?
Who can deliver his soul from
the power of She´ol?   Selah

49 Lord, where is thy steadfast love of
old,
which by thy faithfulness thou
didst swear to David?

y Cn: Heb *are exalted in*   z Cn: Heb *help*   a Cn: Heb *the witness in the skies is sure*
b Cn: Heb *removed his cleanness*   c Cn: Heb *I*
89.20: Acts 13.22.   **89.27:** Rev 1.5.   **89.37:** Rev 1.5; 3.14.

50 Remember, O Lord, how thy servant is scorned;
how I bear in my bosom the
insults[d] of the peoples,
51 with which thy enemies taunt, O
Lord,
with which they mock the footsteps of thy anointed.

52   Blessed be the Lord for ever!
Amen and Amen.

BOOK IV

A Prayer of Moses, the man of God.

90   Lord, thou hast been our
dwelling place[e]
in all generations.
2 Before the mountains were brought
forth,
or ever thou hadst formed the
earth and the world,
from everlasting to everlasting
thou art God.

3 Thou turnest man back to the dust,
and sayest, "Turn back, O children of men!"
4 For a thousand years in thy sight
are but as yesterday when it is
past,
or as a watch in the night.

5 Thou dost sweep men away; they
are like a dream,
like grass which is renewed in the
morning:
6 in the morning it flourishes and is
renewed;
in the evening it fades and
withers.

7 For we are consumed by thy anger;
by thy wrath we are overwhelmed.
8 Thou hast set our iniquities before
thee,
our secret sins in the light of thy
countenance.

9 For all our days pass away under thy
wrath,
our years come to an end[f] like a
sigh.
10 The years of our life are threescore
and ten,
or even by reason of strength
fourscore;
yet their span[g] is but toil and
trouble;

they are soon gone, and we fly
away.

11 Who considers the power of thy
anger,
and thy wrath according to the
fear of thee?
12 So teach us to number our days
that we may get a heart of wisdom.

13 Return, O Lord! How long?
Have pity on thy servants!
14 Satisfy us in the morning with thy
steadfast love,
that we may rejoice and be glad
all our days.
15 Make us glad as many days as thou
hast afflicted us,
and as many years as we have
seen evil.
16 Let thy work be manifest to thy
servants,
and thy glorious power to their
children.
17 Let the favor of the Lord our God
be upon us,
and establish thou the work of
our hands upon us,
yea, the work of our hands establish thou it.

91   He who dwells in the shelter
of the Most High,
who abides in the shadow of the
Almighty,
2 will say to the Lord, "My refuge
and my fortress;
my God, in whom I trust."
3 For he will deliver you from the
snare of the fowler
and from the deadly pestilence;
4 he will cover you with his pinions,
and under his wings you will find
refuge;
his faithfulness is a shield and
buckler.
5 You will not fear the terror of the
night,
nor the arrow that flies by day,
6 nor the pestilence that stalks in
darkness,
nor the destruction that wastes
at noonday.

7 A thousand may fall at your
side,
ten thousand at your right hand;
but it will not come near you.
8 You will only look with your eyes
and see the recompense of the
wicked.

---

[d] Cn: Heb *all of many*   [e] Another reading is *refuge*
[f] Syr: Heb *we bring our years to an end*   [g] Cn Compare Gk Syr Jerome Tg: Heb *pride*
90.4: 2 Pet 3.8.

9 Because you have made the LORD
    your refuge,^h
    the Most High your habitation,
10 no evil shall befall you,
    no scourge come near your tent.

11 For he will give his angels charge
    of you
    to guard you in all your ways.
12 On their hands they will bear you
    up,
    lest you dash your foot against a
    stone.
13 You will tread on the lion and the
    adder,
    the young lion and the serpent
    you will trample under foot.

14 Because he cleaves to me in love,
    I will deliver him;
    I will protect him, because he
    knows my name.
15 When he calls to me, I will answer
    him;
    I will be with him in trouble,
    I will rescue him and honor
    him.
16 With long life I will satisfy him,
    and show him my salvation.

A Psalm. A Song for the Sabbath.

92 It is good to give thanks to
    the LORD,
    to sing praises to thy name, O
    Most High;
2 to declare thy steadfast love in the
    morning,
    and thy faithfulness by night,
3 to the music of the lute and the harp,
    to the melody of the lyre.
4 For thou, O LORD, hast made me
    glad by thy work;
    at the works of thy hands I sing
    for joy.

5 How great are thy works, O LORD!
    Thy thoughts are very deep!
6 The dull man cannot know,
    the stupid cannot understand
    this:
7 that, though the wicked sprout like
    grass
    and all evildoers flourish,
    they are doomed to destruction for
    ever,
8 but thou, O LORD, art on high for
    ever.
9 For, lo, thy enemies, O LORD,
    for, lo, thy enemies shall perish;
    all evildoers shall be scattered.

10 But thou hast exalted my horn like
    that of the wild ox;
    thou hast poured over meⁱ fresh
    oil.
11 My eyes have seen the downfall of
    my enemies,
    my ears have heard the doom of
    my evil assailants.

12 The righteous flourish like the palm
    tree,
    and grow like a cedar in Lebanon.
13 They are planted in the house of
    the LORD,
    they flourish in the courts of our
    God.
14 They still bring forth fruit in old
    age,
    they are ever full of sap and green,
15 to show that the LORD is upright;
    he is my rock, and there is no
    unrighteousness in him.

93 The LORD reigns; he is robed
    in majesty;
    the LORD is robed, he is girded
    with strength.
    Yea, the world is established; it
    shall never be moved;
2   thy throne is established from of
    old;
    thou art from everlasting.

3 The floods have lifted up, O LORD,
    the floods have lifted up their
    voice,
    the floods lift up their roaring.
4 Mightier than the thunders of many
    waters,
    mightier than the waves^j of the
    sea,
    the LORD on high is mighty!

5 Thy decrees are very sure;
    holiness befits thy house,
    O LORD, for evermore.

94 O LORD, thou God of venge-
    ance,
    thou God of vengeance, shine
    forth!
2 Rise up, O judge of the earth;
    render to the proud their deserts!
3 O LORD, how long shall the wicked,
    how long shall the wicked exult?

4 They pour out their arrogant words,
    they boast, all the evildoers.
5 They crush thy people, O LORD,
    and afflict thy heritage.
6 They slay the widow and the so-
    journer,

h Cn: Heb Because thou, LORD, art my refuge; you have made   i Syr: Heb uncertain
j Cn: Heb mighty the waves
91.11-12: Mt 4.6; Lk 4.10-11.   **91.13:** Lk 10.19.

and murder the fatherless;
7 and they say, "The LORD does not
 see;
 the God of Jacob does not perceive."

8 Understand, O dullest of the people!
 Fools, when will you be wise?
9 He who planted the ear, does he not
 hear?
 He who formed the eye, does he
 not see?
10 He who chastens the nations, does
 he not chastise?
 He who teaches men knowledge,
11 the LORD, knows the thoughts of
 man,
 that they are but a breath.

12 Blessed is the man whom thou dost
 chasten, O LORD,
 and whom thou dost teach out of
 thy law
13 to give him respite from days of
 trouble,
 until a pit is dug for the wicked.
14 For the LORD will not forsake his
 people;
 he will not abandon his heritage;
15 for justice will return to the righteous,
 and all the upright in heart will
 follow it.

16 Who rises up for me against the
 wicked?
 Who stands up for me against
 evildoers?
17 If the LORD had not been my help,
 my soul would soon have dwelt
 in the land of silence.
18 When I thought, "My foot slips,"
 thy steadfast love, O LORD, held
 me up.
19 When the cares of my heart are
 many,
 thy consolations cheer my soul.
20 Can wicked rulers be allied with
 thee,
 who frame mischief by statute?
21 They band together against the life
 of the righteous,
 and condemn the innocent to
 death.
22 But the LORD has become my
 stronghold,
 and my God the rock of my
 refuge.
23 He will bring back on them their
 iniquity
 and wipe them out for their
 wickedness;
 the LORD our God will wipe them
 out.

95 O come, let us sing to the
 LORD;
 let us make a joyful noise to the
 rock of our salvation!
2 Let us come into his presence with
 thanksgiving;
 let us make a joyful noise to him
 with songs of praise!
3 For the LORD is a great God,
 and a great King above all gods.
4 In his hand are the depths of the
 earth;
 the heights of the mountains are
 his also.
5 The sea is his, for he made it;
 for his hands formed the dry land.

6 O come, let us worship and bow
 down,
 let us kneel before the LORD, our
 Maker!
7 For he is our God,
 and we are the people of his
 pasture,
 and the sheep of his hand.

O that today you would hearken to
 his voice!
8 Harden not your hearts, as at
 Mer'i·bah,
 as on the day at Mas'sah in the
 wilderness,
9 when your fathers tested me,
 and put me to the proof, though
 they had seen my work.
10 For forty years I loathed that generation
 and said, "They are a people who
 err in heart,
 and they do not regard my ways."
11 Therefore I swore in my anger
 that they should not enter my rest.

96 O sing to the LORD a new
 song;
 sing to the LORD, all the earth!
2 Sing to the LORD, bless his name;
 tell of his salvation from day to
 day.
3 Declare his glory among the nations,
 his marvelous works among all
 the peoples!
4 For great is the LORD, and greatly
 to be praised;
 he is to be feared above all gods.
5 For all the gods of the peoples are
 idols;
 but the LORD made the heavens.
6 Honor and majesty are before him;
 strength and beauty are in his
 sanctuary.

7 Ascribe to the LORD, O families of
 the peoples,

94.11: 1 Cor 3.20.   **95.7-11:** Heb 3.7-11; 4.3-11.   **96.1-13:** 1 Chron 16.23-33.

ascribe to the LORD glory and
strength!
8 Ascribe to the LORD the glory due
his name;
bring an offering, and come into
his courts!
9 Worship the LORD in holy array;
tremble before him, all the earth!

10 Say among the nations, "The LORD
reigns!
Yea, the world is established, it
shall never be moved;
he will judge the peoples with
equity."
11 Let the heavens be glad, and let the
earth rejoice;
let the sea roar, and all that fills it;
12 let the field exult, and everything
in it!
Then shall all the trees of the wood
sing for joy
13 before the LORD, for he comes,
for he comes to judge the earth.
He will judge the world with righteousness,
and the peoples with his truth.

97 The LORD reigns; let the earth
rejoice;
let the many coastlands be glad!
2 Clouds and thick darkness are round
about him;
righteousness and justice are the
foundation of his throne.
3 Fire goes before him,
and burns up his adversaries
round about.
4 His lightnings lighten the world;
the earth sees and trembles.
5 The mountains melt like wax before
the LORD,
before the Lord of all the earth.

6 The heavens proclaim his righteousness;
and all the peoples behold his
glory.
7 All worshipers of images are put to
shame,
who make their boast in worthless
idols;
all gods bow down before him.
8 Zion hears and is glad,
and the daughters of Judah rejoice,
because of thy judgments, O God.
9 For thou, O LORD, art most high
over all the earth;
thou art exalted far above all gods.

10 The LORD loves those who hate
evil;[k]

he preserves the lives of his saints;
he delivers them from the hand
of the wicked.
11 Light dawns[l] for the righteous,
and joy for the upright in heart.
12 Rejoice in the LORD, O you righteous,
and give thanks to his holy name!

A Psalm.

98 O sing to the LORD a new
song,
for he has done marvelous things!
His right hand and his holy arm
have gotten him victory.
2 The LORD has made known his
victory,
he has revealed his vindication in
the sight of the nations.
3 He has remembered his steadfast
love and faithfulness
to the house of Israel.
All the ends of the earth have seen
the victory of our God.

4 Make a joyful noise to the LORD, all
the earth;
break forth into joyous song and
sing praises!
5 Sing praises to the LORD with the
lyre,
with the lyre and the sound of
melody!
6 With trumpets and the sound of the
horn
make a joyful noise before the
King, the LORD!

7 Let the sea roar, and all that fills it;
the world and those who dwell
in it!
8 Let the floods clap their hands;
let the hills sing for joy together
9 before the LORD, for he comes
to judge the earth.
He will judge the world with
righteousness,
and the peoples with equity.

99 The LORD reigns; let the peoples tremble!
He sits enthroned upon the
cherubim; let the earth quake!
2 The LORD is great in Zion;
he is exalted over all the peoples.
3 Let them praise thy great and terrible name!
Holy is he!
4 Mighty King,[m] lover of justice,
thou hast established equity;

k Cn: Heb You who love the LORD hate evil
m Cn: Heb and the king's strength
97.7: Heb 1.6.

l Gk Syr Jerome: Heb is sown

thou hast executed justice
   and righteousness in Jacob.
5 Extol the LORD our God;
   worship at his footstool!
   Holy is he!

6 Moses and Aaron were among his
   priests,
   Samuel also was among those who
     called on his name.
   They cried to the LORD, and he
     answered them.
7 He spoke to them in the pillar of
   cloud;
   they kept his testimonies,
   and the statutes that he gave them.

8 O LORD our God, thou didst answer
   them;
   thou wast a forgiving God to
   them,
   but an avenger of their wrong-
   doings.
9 Extol the LORD our God,
   and worship at his holy mountain;
   for the LORD our God is holy!

A Psalm for the thank offering.

100 Make a joyful noise to the
     LORD, all the lands!*n*
2 Serve the LORD with gladness!
   Come into his presence with
   singing!

3 Know that the LORD is God!
   It is he that made us, and we are
   his;*o*
   we are his people, and the sheep
   of his pasture.

4 Enter his gates with thanksgiving,
   and his courts with praise!
   Give thanks to him, bless his
   name!

5 For the LORD is good;
   his steadfast love endures for ever,
   and his faithfulness to all generations.

A Psalm of David.

101 I will sing of loyalty and of
     justice;
   to thee, O LORD, I will sing.
2 I will give heed to the way that is
   blameless.
   Oh when wilt thou come to me?

I will walk with integrity of heart

within my house;
3 I will not set before my eyes
   anything that is base.

I hate the work of those who fall
   away;
   it shall not cleave to me.
4 Perverseness of heart shall be far
   from me;
   I will know nothing of evil.

5 Him who slanders his neighbor
   secretly
   I will destroy.
   The man of haughty looks and
   arrogant heart
   I will not endure.

6 I will look with favor on the faithful
   in the land,
   that they may dwell with me;
   he who walks in the way that is
   blameless
   shall minister to me.

7 No man who practices deceit
   shall dwell in my house;
   no man who utters lies
   shall continue in my presence.

8 Morning by morning I will destroy
   all the wicked in the land,
   cutting off all the evildoers
   from the city of the LORD.

*A prayer of one afflicted, when he is
faint and pours out his complaint
before the LORD.*

102 Hear my prayer, O LORD;
     let my cry come to thee!
2 Do not hide thy face from me
   in the day of my distress!
   Incline thy ear to me;
   answer me speedily in the day
   when I call!

3 For my days pass away like smoke,
   and my bones burn like a furnace.
4 My heart is smitten like grass, and
   withered;
   I forgot to eat my bread.
5 Because of my loud groaning
   my bones cleave to my flesh.
6 I am like a vulture*p* of the wilderness,
   like an owl of the waste places;
7 I lie awake,
   I am like a lonely bird on the
   housetop.
8 All the day my enemies taunt me,
   those who deride me use my
   name for a curse.

n Heb *land* or *earth*   *o* Another reading is *and not we ourselves*
p The meaning of the Hebrew word is uncertain

9 For I eat ashes like bread,
   and mingle tears with my drink,
10 because of thy indignation and anger;
   for thou hast taken me up and thrown me away.
11 My days are like an evening shadow;
   I wither away like grass.

12 But thou, O LORD, art enthroned for ever;
   thy name endures to all generations.
13 Thou wilt arise and have pity on Zion;
   it is the time to favor her;
   the appointed time has come.
14 For thy servants hold her stones dear,
   and have pity on her dust.
15 The nations will fear the name of the LORD,
   and all the kings of the earth thy glory.
16 For the LORD will build up Zion,
   he will appear in his glory;
17 he will regard the prayer of the destitute,
   and will not despise their supplication.

18 Let this be recorded for a generation to come,
   so that a people yet unborn may praise the LORD:
19 that he looked down from his holy height,
   from heaven the LORD looked at the earth,
20 to hear the groans of the prisoners,
   to set free those who were doomed to die;
21 that men may declare in Zion the name of the LORD,
   and in Jerusalem his praise,
22 when peoples gather together,
   and kingdoms, to worship the LORD.

23 He has broken my strength in midcourse;
   he has shortened my days.
24 "O my God," I say, "take me not hence
   in the midst of my days,
   thou whose years endure throughout all generations!"

25 Of old thou didst lay the foundation of the earth,
   and the heavens are the work of thy hands.

26 They will perish, but thou dost endure;
   they will all wear out like a garment.
   Thou changest them like raiment, and they pass away;
27 but thou art the same, and thy years have no end.
28 The children of thy servants shall dwell secure;
   their posterity shall be established before thee.

A Psalm of David.

103 Bless the LORD, O my soul;
   and all that is within me, bless his holy name!
2 Bless the LORD, O my soul,
   and forget not all his benefits,
3 who forgives all your iniquity,
   who heals all your diseases,
4 who redeems your life from the Pit,
   who crowns you with steadfast love and mercy,
5 who satisfies you with good as long as you live*q*
   so that your youth is renewed like the eagle's.

6 The LORD works vindication
   and justice for all who are oppressed.
7 He made known his ways to Moses,
   his acts to the people of Israel.
8 The LORD is merciful and gracious,
   slow to anger and abounding in steadfast love.
9 He will not always chide,
   nor will he keep his anger for ever.
10 He does not deal with us according to our sins,
   nor requite us according to our iniquities.
11 For as the heavens are high above the earth,
   so great is his steadfast love toward those who fear him;
12 as far as the east is from the west,
   so far does he remove our transgressions from us.
13 As a father pities his children,
   so the LORD pities those who fear him.
14 For he knows our frame;
   he remembers that we are dust.

15 As for man, his days are like grass;
   he flourishes like a flower of the field;
16 for the wind passes over it, and it is gone,

q Heb uncertain
102.25-27: Heb 1.10-12.   **103.8:** Jas 5.11.

and its place knows it no more.

17 But the steadfast love of the LORD
is from everlasting to everlasting
upon those who fear him,
and his righteousness to children's
children,

18 to those who keep his covenant
and remember to do his commandments.

19 The LORD has established his throne
in the heavens,
and his kingdom rules over
all.

20 Bless the LORD, O you his angels,
you mighty ones who do his
word,
hearkening to the voice of his
word!

21 Bless the LORD, all his hosts,
his ministers that do his will!

22 Bless the LORD, all his works,
in all places of his dominion.
Bless the LORD, O my soul!

104 Bless the LORD, O my soul!
O LORD my God, thou art
very great!
Thou art clothed with honor and
majesty,

2 who coverest thyself with light
as with a garment,
who hast stretched out the heavens
like a tent,

3 who hast laid the beams of thy
chambers on the waters,
who makest the clouds thy chariot,
who ridest on the wings of the
wind,

4 who makest the winds thy messengers,
fire and flame thy ministers.

5 Thou didst set the earth on its
foundations,
so that it should never be shaken.

6 Thou didst cover it with the deep
as with a garment;
the waters stood above the
mountains.

7 At thy rebuke they fled;
at the sound of thy thunder they
took to flight.

8 The mountains rose, the valleys
sank down
to the place which thou didst
appoint for them.

9 Thou didst set a bound which they
should not pass,
so that they might not again cover
the earth.

10 Thou makest springs gush forth in
the valleys;
they flow between the hills,

11 they give drink to every beast of
the field;
the wild asses quench their thirst.

12 By them the birds of the air have
their habitation;
they sing among the branches.

13 From thy lofty abode thou waterest
the mountains;
the earth is satisfied with the fruit
of thy work.

14 Thou dost cause the grass to grow
for the cattle,
and plants for man to cultivate,[r]
that he may bring forth food from
the earth,

15 and wine to gladden the heart of
man,
oil to make his face shine,
and bread to strengthen man's
heart.

16 The trees of the LORD are watered
abundantly,
the cedars of Lebanon which he
planted.

17 In them the birds build their nests;
the stork has her home in the fir
trees.

18 The high mountains are for the
wild goats;
the rocks are a refuge for the
badgers.

19 Thou hast made the moon to mark
the seasons;
the sun knows its time for setting.

20 Thou makest darkness, and it is
night,
when all the beasts of the forest
creep forth.

21 The young lions roar for their prey,
seeking their food from God.

22 When the sun rises, they get them
away
and lie down in their dens.

23 Man goes forth to his work
and to his labor until the evening.

24 O LORD, how manifold are thy
works!
In wisdom hast thou made them
all;
the earth is full of thy creatures.

25 Yonder is the sea, great and wide,
which teems with things innumerable,
living things both small and great.

26 There go the ships,
and Le·vi′a·than which thou didst
form to sport in it.

---

r Or *fodder for the animals that serve man*
103.17: Lk 1.50.   **104.4:** Heb 1.7.
104.12: Mt 13.32; Mk 4.32; Lk 13.19.

27 These all look to thee,
   to give them their food in due
      season.
28 When thou givest to them, they
      gather it up;
   when thou openest thy hand,
      they are filled with good things.
29 When thou hidest thy face, they are
      dismayed;
   when thou takest away their
      breath, they die
   and return to their dust.
30 When thou sendest forth thy Spirit,[s]
   they are created;
   and thou renewest the face of the
      ground.

31 May the glory of the LORD endure
      for ever,
   may the LORD rejoice in his
      works,
32 who looks on the earth and it
      trembles,
   who touches the mountains and
      they smoke!
33 I will sing to the LORD as long as
      I live;
   I will sing praise to my God
      while I have being.
34 May my meditation be pleasing to
      him,
   for I rejoice in the LORD.
35 Let sinners be consumed from the
      earth,
   and let the wicked be no more!
   Bless the LORD, O my soul!
   Praise the LORD!

105 O give thanks to the LORD,
      call on his name,
   make known his deeds among the
      peoples!
2 Sing to him, sing praises to him,
   tell of all his wonderful works!
3 Glory in his holy name;
   let the hearts of those who seek
      the LORD rejoice!
4 Seek the LORD and his strength,
   seek his presence continually!
5 Remember the wonderful works
      that he has done,
   his miracles, and the judgments
      he uttered,
6 O offspring of Abraham his servant,
   sons of Jacob, his chosen ones!

7 He is the LORD our God;
   his judgments are in all the earth.
8 He is mindful of his covenant for
      ever,
   of the word that he commanded,
      for a thousand generations,

9 the covenant which he made with
      Abraham,
   his sworn promise to Isaac,
10 which he confirmed to Jacob as a
      statute,
   to Israel as an everlasting cove-
      nant,
11 saying, "To you I will give the land
      of Canaan
   as your portion for an inherit-
      ance."

12 When they were few in number,
   of little account, and sojourners
      in it,
13 wandering from nation to nation,
   from one kingdom to another
      people,
14 he allowed no one to oppress them;
   he rebuked kings on their account,
15 saying, "Touch not my anointed
      ones,
   do my prophets no harm!"

16 When he summoned a famine on
      the land,
   and broke every staff of bread,
17 he had sent a man ahead of them,
   Joseph, who was sold as a slave.
18 His feet were hurt with fetters,
   his neck was put in a collar of
      iron;
19 until what he had said came to pass
   the word of the LORD tested him.
20 The king sent and released him,
   the ruler of the peoples set him
      free;
21 he made him lord of his house,
   and ruler of all his possessions,
22 to instruct[t] his princes at his pleas-
      ure,
   and to teach his elders wisdom.

23 Then Israel came to Egypt;
   Jacob sojourned in the land of
      Ham.
24 And the LORD made his people very
      fruitful,
   and made them stronger than
      their foes.
25 He turned their hearts to hate his
      people,
   to deal craftily with his servants.

26 He sent Moses his servant,
   and Aaron whom he had chosen.
27 They wrought his signs among them,
   and miracles in the land of Ham.
28 He sent darkness, and made the
      land dark;
   they rebelled[u] against his words.
29 He turned their waters into blood,

s Or breath   t Gk Syr Jerome: Heb to bind
u Cn Compare Gk Syr: Heb they did not rebel
105.1-15: 1 Chron 16.8-22.   105.8-9: Lk 1.72-73.

and caused their fish to die.
³⁰ Their land swarmed with frogs,
even in the chambers of their kings.
³¹ He spoke, and there came swarms
of flies,
and gnats throughout their
country.
³² He gave them hail for rain,
and lightning that flashed through
their land.
³³ He smote their vines and fig trees,
and shattered the trees of their
country.
³⁴ He spoke, and the locusts came,
and young locusts without number;
³⁵ which devoured all the vegetation
in their land,
and ate up the fruit of their
ground.
³⁶ He smote all the first-born in their
land,
the first issue of all their strength.

³⁷ Then he led forth Israel with silver
and gold,
and there was none among his
tribes who stumbled.
³⁸ Egypt was glad when they departed,
for dread of them had fallen upon
it.
³⁹ He spread a cloud for a covering,
and fire to give light by night.
⁴⁰ They asked, and he brought quails
and gave them bread from heaven
in abundance.
⁴¹ He opened the rock, and water
gushed forth;
it flowed through the desert like
a river.
⁴² For he remembered his holy
promise,
and Abraham his servant.

⁴³ So he led forth his people with joy,
his chosen ones with singing.
⁴⁴ And he gave them the lands of the
nations;
and they took possession of the
fruit of the peoples' toil,
⁴⁵ to the end that they should keep his
statutes,
and observe his laws.
Praise the LORD!

106 Praise the LORD!
O give thanks to the LORD, for
he is good;
for his steadfast love endures for
ever!
² Who can utter the mighty doings
of the LORD,
or show forth all his praise?

³ Blessed are they who observe justice,
who do righteousness at all times!

⁴ Remember me, O LORD, when thou
showest favor to thy people;
help me when thou deliverest
them;
⁵ that I may see the prosperity of thy
chosen ones,
that I may rejoice in the gladness
of thy nation,
that I may glory with thy heritage.

⁶ Both we and our fathers have
sinned;
we have committed iniquity, we
have done wickedly.
⁷ Our fathers, when they were in
Egypt,
did not consider thy wonderful
works;
they did not remember the
abundance of thy steadfast
love,
but rebelled against the Most
Highʸ at the Red Sea.
⁸ Yet he saved them for his name's
sake,
that he might make known his
mighty power.
⁹ He rebuked the Red Sea, and it
became dry;
and he led them through the deep
as through a desert.
¹⁰ So he saved them from the hand of
the foe,
and delivered them from the
power of the enemy.
¹¹ And the waters covered their adversaries;
not one of them was left.
¹² Then they believed his words;
they sang his praise.

¹³ But they soon forgot his works;
they did not wait for his counsel.
¹⁴ But they had a wanton craving in
the wilderness,
and put God to the test in the
desert;
¹⁵ he gave them what they asked,
but sent a wasting disease among
them.

¹⁶ When men in the camp were jealous
of Moses
and Aaron, the holy one of the
LORD,
¹⁷ the earth opened and swallowed up
Dā´thăn,
and covered the company of
Ă·bī´răm.

18 Fire also broke out in their company;
  the flame burned up the wicked.

19 They made a calf in Hō'reb
  and worshiped a molten image.
20 They exchanged the glory of God
  for the image of an ox that eats
  grass.
21 They forgot God, their Savior,
  who had done great things in
  Egypt,
22 wondrous works in the land of Ham,
  and terrible things by the Red
  Sea.
23 Therefore he said he would destroy
  them—
  had not Moses, his chosen one,
  stood in the breach before him,
  to turn away his wrath from destroying them.

24 Then they despised the pleasant
  land,
  having no faith in his promise.
25 They murmured in their tents,
  and did not obey the voice of the
  LORD.
26 Therefore he raised his hand and
  swore to them
  that he would make them fall in
  the wilderness,
27 and would disperse[w] their descendants among the nations,
  scattering them over the lands.

28 Then they attached themselves to
  the Bā'al of Pē'ôr,
  and ate sacrifices offered to the
  dead;
29 they provoked the LORD to anger
  with their doings,
  and a plague broke out among
  them.
30 Then Phin'ē·hăs stood up and interposed,
  and the plague was stayed.
31 And that has been reckoned to him
  as righteousness
  from generation to generation for
  ever.

32 They angered him at the waters of
  Mer'ĭ·băh,
  and it went ill with Moses on
  their account;
33 for they made his spirit bitter,
  and he spoke words that were
  rash.

34 They did not destroy the peoples,
  as the LORD commanded them,
35 but they mingled with the nations
  and learned to do as they did.

36 They served their idols,
  which became a snare to them.
37 They sacrificed their sons
  and their daughters to the demons;
38 they poured out innocent blood,
  the blood of their sons and
  daughters,
  whom they sacrificed to the idols
  of Canaan;
  and the land was polluted with
  blood.
39 Thus they became unclean by their
  acts,
  and played the harlot in their
  doings.

40 Then the anger of the LORD was
  kindled against his people,
  and he abhorred his heritage;
41 he gave them into the hand of the
  nations,
  so that those who hated them
  ruled over them.
42 Their enemies oppressed them,
  and they were brought into subjection under their power.
43 Many times he delivered them,
  but they were rebellious in their
  purposes,
  and were brought low through
  their iniquity.
44 Nevertheless he regarded their
  distress,
  when he heard their cry.
45 He remembered for their sake his
  covenant,
  and relented according to the
  abundance of his steadfast love.
46 He caused them to be pitied
  by all those who held them captive.

47 Save us, O LORD our God,
  and gather us from among the
  nations,
  that we may give thanks to thy holy
  name
  and glory in thy praise.

48 Blessed be the LORD, the God of
  Israel,
  from everlasting to everlasting!
  And let all the people say, "Amen!"
  Praise the LORD!

BOOK V

107 O give thanks to the LORD,
  for he is good;
  for his steadfast love endures for
  ever!

---

w Syr Compare Ezek 20.23: Heb *cause to fall*
106.47-48: 1 Chron 16.35-36.

2 Let the redeemed of the LORD say
    so,
     whom he has redeemed from
       trouble
3 and gathered in from the lands,
     from the east and from the west,
     from the north and from the
       south.

4 Some wandered in desert wastes,
     finding no way to a city to dwell
       in;
5 hungry and thirsty,
     their soul fainted within them.
6 Then they cried to the LORD in their
       trouble,
     and he delivered them from their
       distress;
7 he led them by a straight way,
     till they reached a city to dwell in.
8 Let them thank the LORD for his
       steadfast love,
     for his wonderful works to the
       sons of men!
9 For he satisfies him who is thirsty,
     and the hungry he fills with good
       things.

10 Some sat in darkness and in gloom,
      prisoners in affliction and in irons,
11 for they had rebelled against the
       words of God,
      and spurned the counsel of the
        Most High.
12 Their hearts were bowed down with
       hard labor;
      they fell down, with none to help.
13 Then they cried to the LORD in their
       trouble,
      and he delivered them from their
        distress;
14 he brought them out of darkness
       and gloom,
      and broke their bonds asunder.
15 Let them thank the LORD for his
       steadfast love,
      for his wonderful works to the
        sons of men!
16 For he shatters the doors of bronze,
      and cuts in two the bars of iron.

17 Some were sick[x] through their sinful
       ways,
      and because of their iniquities
        suffered affliction;
18 they loathed any kind of food,
      and they drew near to the gates
        of death.
19 Then they cried to the LORD in
       their trouble,
      and he delivered them from their
        distress;
20 he sent forth his word, and healed
       them,

x Cn: Heb *fools*

and delivered them from de-
       struction.
21 Let them thank the LORD for his
       steadfast love,
      for his wonderful works to the
        sons of men!
22 And let them offer sacrifices of
       thanksgiving,
      and tell of his deeds in songs of
        joy!

23 Some went down to the sea in
       ships,
      doing business on the great waters;
24 they saw the deeds of the LORD,
      his wondrous works in the deep.
25 For he commanded, and raised the
       stormy wind,
      which lifted up the waves of the
        sea.
26 They mounted up to heaven, they
       went down to the depths;
      their courage melted away in their
        evil plight;
27 they reeled and staggered like
       drunken men,
      and were at their wits' end.
28 Then they cried to the LORD in their
       trouble,
      and he delivered them from their
        distress;
29 he made the storm be still,
      and the waves of the sea were
        hushed.
30 Then they were glad because they
       had quiet,
      and he brought them to their
        desired haven.
31 Let them thank the LORD for his
       steadfast love,
      for his wonderful works to the
        sons of men!
32 Let them extol him in the congrega-
       tion of the people,
      and praise him in the assembly of
        the elders.

33 He turns rivers into a desert,
      springs of water into thirsty
        ground,
34 a fruitful land into a salty waste,
      because of the wickedness of its
        inhabitants.
35 He turns a desert into pools of water,
      a parched land into springs of
        water.
36 And there he lets the hungry dwell,
      and they establish a city to live
        in;
37 they sow fields, and plant vineyards,
      and get a fruitful yield.
38 By his blessing they multiply greatly;
      and he does not let their cattle
        decrease.

39 When they are diminished and
brought low
through oppression, trouble, and
sorrow,
40 he pours contempt upon princes
and makes them wander in track-
less wastes;
41 but he raises up the needy out of
affliction,
and makes their families like flocks.
42 The upright see it and are glad;
and all wickedness stops its
mouth.
43 Whoever is wise, let him give heed
to these things;
let men consider the steadfast love
of the LORD.

A Song. A Psalm of David.

108 My heart is steadfast, O God,
my heart is steadfast!
I will sing and make melody!
Awake, my soul!
2 Awake, O harp and lyre!
I will awake the dawn!
3 I will give thanks to thee, O LORD,
among the peoples,
I will sing praises to thee among
the nations.
4 For thy steadfast love is great above
the heavens,
thy faithfulness reaches to the
clouds.

5 Be exalted, O God, above the
heavens!
Let thy glory be over all the earth!
6 That thy beloved may be delivered,
give help by thy right hand, and
answer me!

7 God has promised in his sanctuary:[y]
"With exultation I will divide up
Shē′chem,
and portion out the Vale of
Suc′coth.
8 Gilead is mine; Mà·nas′sĕh is mine;
E′phrā·im is my helmet;
Judah my scepter.
9 Mō′ab is my washbasin;
upon E′dŏm I cast my shoe;
over Phi·lis′ti·à I shout in triumph."

10 Who will bring me to the fortified
city?
Who will lead me to E′dŏm?
11 Hast thou not rejected us, O God?

Thou dost not go forth, O God,
with our armies.
12 O grant us help against the foe,
for vain is the help of man!
13 With God we shall do valiantly;
it is he who will tread down our
foes.

To the choirmaster. A Psalm of David.

109 Be not silent, O God of my
praise!
2 For wicked and deceitful mouths
are opened against me,
speaking against me with lying
tongues.
3 They beset me with words of hate,
and attack me without cause.
4 In return for my love they accuse
me,
even as I make prayer for them.[z]
5 So they reward me evil for good,
and hatred for my love.

6 Appoint a wicked man against him;
let an accuser bring him to trial.[a]
7 When he is tried, let him come forth
guilty;
let his prayer be counted as sin!
8 May his days be few;
may another seize his goods!
9 May his children be fatherless,
and his wife a widow!
10 May his children wander about and
beg;
may they be driven out of[b] the
ruins they inhabit!
11 May the creditor seize all that he
has;
may strangers plunder the fruits
of his toil!
12 Let there be none to extend kindness
to him,
nor any to pity his fatherless
children!
13 May his posterity be cut off;
may his name be blotted out in
the second generation!
14 May the iniquity of his fathers be
remembered before the LORD,
and let not the sin of his mother
be blotted out!
15 Let them be before the LORD continually;
and may his[c] memory be cut off
from the earth!
16 For he did not remember to show
kindness,
but pursued the poor and needy

y Or *by his holiness*   *z* Syr: Heb *I prayer*
a Heb *stand at his right hand*
b Gk: Heb *and seek*   *c* Gk: Heb *their*
108.1-5: Ps 57.7-11.   **108.6-13:** Ps 60.5-12.
109.8: Acts 1.20.

and the brokenhearted to their
death.

17 He loved to curse; let curses come
on him!
He did not like blessing; may it
be far from him!

18 He clothed himself with cursing as
his coat,
may it soak into his body like
water,
like oil into his bones!

19 May it be like a garment which he
wraps round him,
like a belt with which he daily
girds himself!

20 May this be the reward of my accusers from the LORD,
of those who speak evil against
my life!

21 But thou, O GOD my Lord,
deal on my behalf for thy name's
sake;
because thy steadfast love is good,
deliver me!

22 For I am poor and needy,
and my heart is stricken within
me.

23 I am gone, like a shadow at evening;
I am shaken off like a locust.

24 My knees are weak through fasting;
my body has become gaunt.

25 I am an object of scorn to my accusers;
when they see me, they wag their
heads.

26 Help me, O LORD my God!
Save me according to thy steadfast love!

27 Let them know that this is thy hand;
thou, O LORD, hast done it!

28 Let them curse, but do thou bless!
Let my assailants be put to
shame;[d] may thy servant be
glad!

29 May my accusers be clothed with
dishonor;
may they be wrapped in their own
shame as in a mantle!

30 With my mouth I will give great
thanks to the LORD;
I will praise him in the midst of
the throng.

31 For he stands at the right hand of
the needy,
to save him from those who condemn him to death.

A Psalm of David.

110 The LORD says to my lord:
"Sit at my right hand,
till I make your enemies
your footstool."

2 The LORD sends forth from Zion
your mighty scepter.
Rule in the midst of your foes!

3 Your people will offer themselves
freely
on the day you lead your host
upon the holy mountains.[e]
From the womb of the morning
like dew your youth[f] will come to
you.

4 The LORD has sworn
and will not change his mind,
"You are a priest for ever
after the order of Mel·chiz'e·dek."

5 The Lord is at your right hand;
he will shatter kings on the day of
his wrath.

6 He will execute judgment among
the nations,
filling them with corpses;
he will shatter chiefs[g]
over the wide earth.

7 He will drink from the brook by the
way;
therefore he will lift up his head.

111 Praise the LORD.
I will give thanks to the LORD
with my whole heart,
in the company of the upright,
in the congregation.

2 Great are the works of the LORD,
studied by all who have pleasure
in them.

3 Full of honor and majesty is his
work,
and his righteousness endures for
ever.

4 He has caused his wonderful works
to be remembered;
the LORD is gracious and merciful.

5 He provides food for those who fear
him;
he is ever mindful of his covenant.

6 He has shown his people the power
of his works,
in giving them the heritage of the
nations.

7 The works of his hands are faithful
and just;
all his precepts are trustworthy,

d Gk: Heb *they have arisen and have been put to shame*
e Another reading is *in holy array*   *f* Cn: Heb *the dew of your youth*   *g* Or *the head*
109.25: Mt 27.39; Mk 15.29.
110.1: Mt 22.44; 26.64; Mk 12.36; 14.62; 16.19; Lk 20.42-43; 22.69; Acts 2.34; 1 Cor
15.25; Eph 1.20; Col 3.1; Heb 1.3, 13; 10.12-13; 12.2.
110.4: Heb 5.6, 10; 6.20; 7.11, 15, 21.

8 they are established for ever and
ever,
to be performed with faithfulness
and uprightness.
9 He sent redemption to his people;
he has commanded his covenant
for ever.
Holy and terrible is his name!
10 The fear of the LORD is the beginning of wisdom;
a good understanding have all
those who practice it.
His praise endures for ever!

112 Praise the LORD.
Blessed is the man who fears
the LORD,
who greatly delights in his commandments!
2 His descendants will be mighty in
the land;
the generation of the upright will
be blessed.
3 Wealth and riches are in his house;
and his righteousness endures for
ever.
4 Light rises in the darkness for the
upright;
the LORD[h] is gracious, merciful,
and righteous.
5 It is well with the man who deals
generously and lends,
who conducts his affairs with
justice.
6 For the righteous will never be
moved;
he will be remembered for ever.
7 He is not afraid of evil tidings;
his heart is firm, trusting in the
LORD.
8 His heart is steady, he will not be
afraid,
until he sees his desire on his
adversaries.
9 He has distributed freely, he has
given to the poor;
his righteousness endures for
ever;
his horn is exalted in honor.
10 The wicked man sees it and is
angry;
he gnashes his teeth and melts
away;
the desire of the wicked man
comes to nought.

113 Praise the LORD!
Praise, O servants of the LORD,
praise the name of the LORD!

2 Blessed be the name of the LORD
from this time forth and for evermore!

3 From the rising of the sun to its
setting
the name of the LORD is to be
praised!
4 The LORD is high above all nations,
and his glory above the heavens!
5 Who is like the LORD our God,
who is seated on high,
6 who looks far down
upon the heavens and the earth?
7 He raises the poor from the dust,
and lifts the needy from the ash
heap,
8 to make them sit with princes,
with the princes of his people.
9 He gives the barren woman a home,
making her the joyous mother of
children.
Praise the LORD!

114 When Israel went forth from
Egypt,
the house of Jacob from a people
of strange language,
2 Judah became his sanctuary,
Israel his dominion.

3 The sea looked and fled,
Jordan turned back.
4 The mountains skipped like rams,
the hills like lambs.

5 What ails you, O sea, that you
flee?
O Jordan, that you turn back?
6 O mountains, that you skip like
rams?
O hills, like lambs?

7 Tremble, O earth, at the presence of
the LORD,
at the presence of the God of
Jacob,
8 who turns the rock into a pool of
water,
the flint into a spring of water.

115 Not to us, O LORD, not to
us,
but to thy name give glory,
for the sake of thy steadfast love
and thy faithfulness!
2 Why should the nations say,
"Where is their God?"

3 Our God is in the heavens;
he does whatever he pleases.
4 Their idols are silver and gold,
the work of men's hands.
5 They have mouths, but do not
speak;
eyes, but do not see.

h Gk: Heb lacks the LORD
112.9: 2 Cor 9.9.   115.4-8: Ps 135.15-18.

6 They have ears, but do not hear;
  noses, but do not smell.
7 They have hands, but do not feel;
  feet, but do not walk;
  and they do not make a sound in
  their throat.
8 Those who make them are like them;
  so are all who trust in them.

9 O Israel, trust in the LORD!
  He is their help and their shield.
10 O house of Aaron, put your trust
  in the LORD!
  He is their help and their shield.
11 You who fear the LORD, trust in the
  LORD!
  He is their help and their shield.

12 The LORD has been mindful of us;
  he will bless us;
  he will bless the house of Israel;
  he will bless the house of Aaron;
13 he will bless those who fear the
  LORD,
  both small and great.

14 May the LORD give you increase,
  you and your children!
15 May you be blessed by the LORD,
  who made heaven and earth!

16 The heavens are the LORD'S heavens,
  but the earth he has given to the
  sons of men.
17 The dead do not praise the LORD,
  nor do any that go down into
  silence.
18 But we will bless the LORD
  from this time forth and for evermore.
  Praise the LORD!

116 I love the LORD, because he
  has heard
  my voice and my supplications.
2 Because he inclined his ear to me,
  therefore I will call on him as
  long as I live.
3 The snares of death encompassed
  me;
  the pangs of Shē'ōl laid hold on
  me;
  I suffered distress and anguish.
4 Then I called on the name of the
  LORD:
  "O LORD, I beseech thee, save
  my life!"

5 Gracious is the LORD, and righteous;
  our God is merciful.
6 The LORD preserves the simple;
  when I was brought low, he
  saved me.
7 Return, O my soul, to your rest;

for the LORD has dealt bountifully
  with you.

8 For thou hast delivered my soul
  from death,
  my eyes from tears,
  my feet from stumbling;
9 I walk before the LORD
  in the land of the living.
10 I kept my faith, even when I said,
  "I am greatly afflicted";
11 I said in my consternation,
  "Men are all a vain hope."

12 What shall I render to the LORD
  for all his bounty to me?
13 I will lift up the cup of salvation
  and call on the name of the LORD,
14 I will pay my vows to the LORD
  in the presence of all his people.
15 Precious in the sight of the LORD
  is the death of his saints.
16 O LORD, I am thy servant;
  I am thy servant, the son of thy
  handmaid.
  Thou hast loosed my bonds.
17 I will offer to thee the sacrifice of
  thanksgiving
  and call on the name of the LORD.
18 I will pay my vows to the LORD
  in the presence of all his people,
19 in the courts of the house of the
  LORD,
  in your midst, O Jerusalem.
  Praise the LORD!

117 Praise the LORD, all nations!
  Extol him, all peoples!
2 For great is his steadfast love toward
  us;
  and the faithfulness of the LORD
  endures for ever.
  Praise the LORD!

118 O give thanks to the LORD, for
  he is good;
  his steadfast love endures for ever!

2 Let Israel say,
  "His steadfast love endures for
  ever."
3 Let the house of Aaron say,
  "His steadfast love endures for
  ever."
4 Let those who fear the LORD say,
  "His steadfast love endures for
  ever."

5 Out of my distress I called on the
  LORD;
  the LORD answered me and set
  me free.
6 With the LORD on my side I do not
  fear.

115.13: Rev 11.18; 19.5.   **116.10:** 2 Cor 4.13.   **117.1:** Rom 15.11.   **118.6:** Heb 13.6.

What can man do to me?

7 The LORD is on my side to help me;
   I shall look in triumph on those
      who hate me.

8 It is better to take refuge in the
      LORD
   than to put confidence in man.

9 It is better to take refuge in the LORD
   than to put confidence in princes.

10 All nations surrounded me;
   in the name of the LORD I cut
      them off!

11 They surrounded me, surrounded
      me on every side;
   in the name of the LORD I cut
      them off!

12 They surrounded me like bees,
   they blazed*i* like a fire of thorns;
   in the name of the LORD I cut
      them off!

13 I was pushed hard,*j* so that I was
      falling,
   but the LORD helped me.

14 The LORD is my strength and my
      song;
   he has become my salvation.

15 Hark, glad songs of victory
   in the tents of the righteous:
   "The right hand of the LORD does
      valiantly,

16 the right hand of the LORD is
      exalted,
   the right hand of the LORD does
      valiantly!"

17 I shall not die, but I shall live,
   and recount the deeds of the
      LORD.

18 The LORD has chastened me sorely,
   but he has not given me over to
      death.

19 Open to me the gates of righteous-
      ness,
   that I may enter through them
   and give thanks to the LORD.

20 This is the gate of the LORD;
   the righteous shall enter through
      it.

21 I thank thee that thou hast answered
      me
   and hast become my salvation.

22 The stone which the builders re-
      jected
   has become the head of the corner.

23 This is the LORD'S doing;
   it is marvelous in our eyes.

24 This is the day which the LORD has
      made;

let us rejoice and be glad in it.

25 Save us, we beseech thee, O LORD!
   O LORD, we beseech thee, give us
      success!

26 Blessed be he who enters in the
      name of the LORD!
   We bless you from the house of
      the LORD.

27 The LORD is God,
   and he has given us light.
   Bind the festal procession with
      branches,
   up to the horns of the altar!

28 Thou art my God, and I will give
      thanks to thee;
   thou art my God, I will extol
      thee.

29 O give thanks to the LORD, for he
      is good;
   for his steadfast love endures for
      ever!

119   Blessed are those whose way is
         blameless,
   who walk in the law of the LORD!

2 Blessed are those who keep his
      testimonies,
   who seek him with their whole
      heart,

3 who also do no wrong,
   but walk in his ways!

4 Thou hast commanded thy precepts
   to be kept diligently.

5 O that my ways may be steadfast
   in keeping thy statutes!

6 Then I shall not be put to shame,
   having my eyes fixed on all thy
      commandments.

7 I will praise thee with an upright
      heart,
   when I learn thy righteous ordi-
      nances.

8 I will observe thy statutes;
   O forsake me not utterly!

9 How can a young man keep his way
      pure?
   By guarding it according to thy
      word.

10 With my whole heart I seek thee;
   let me not wander from thy
      commandments!

11 I have laid up thy word in my
      heart,
   that I might not sin against thee.

12 Blessed be thou, O LORD;
   teach me thy statutes!

13 With my lips I declare
   all the ordinances of thy mouth.

i Gk: Heb *were extinguished*   *j* Gk Syr Jerome: Heb *thou didst push me hard*
118.22-23: Mt 21.42; Mk 12.10-11; Lk 20.17; Acts 4.11; 1 Pet 2.7.
118:25-26: Mt 21.9; 23.39; Mk 11.9-10; Lk 13.35; 19.38; Jn 12.13.

14 In the way of thy testimonies I
    delight
        as much as in all riches.
15 I will meditate on thy precepts,
    and fix my eyes on thy ways.
16 I will delight in thy statutes;
    I will not forget thy word.

17 Deal bountifully with thy servant,
    that I may live and observe thy
    word.
18 Open my eyes, that I may behold
    wondrous things out of thy law.
19 I am a sojourner on earth;
    hide not thy commandments from
    me!
20 My soul is consumed with longing
    for thy ordinances at all times.
21 Thou dost rebuke the insolent, ac-
    cursed ones,
        who wander from thy command-
        ments;
22 take away from me their scorn and
    contempt,
        for I have kept thy testimonies.
23 Even though princes sit plotting
    against me,
        thy servant will meditate on thy
        statutes.
24 Thy testimonies are my delight,
    they are my counselors.

25 My soul cleaves to the dust;
    revive me according to thy word!
26 When I told of my ways, thou didst
    answer me;
        teach me thy statutes!
27 Make me understand the way of thy
    precepts,
        and I will meditate on thy won-
        drous works.
28 My soul melts away for sorrow;
    strengthen me according to thy
    word!
29 Put false ways far from me;
    and graciously teach me thy law!
30 I have chosen the way of faithfulness,
    I set thy ordinances before me.
31 I cleave to thy testimonies, O LORD;
    let me not be put to shame!
32 I will run in the way of thy com-
    mandments
        when thou enlargest my under-
        standing!

33 Teach me, O LORD, the way of thy
    statutes;
        and I will keep it to the end.
34 Give me understanding, that I may
    keep thy law
        and observe it with my whole
        heart.
35 Lead me in the path of thy com-
    mandments,
        for I delight in it.

36 Incline my heart to thy testimonies,
    and not to gain!
37 Turn my eyes from looking at
    vanities;
        and give me life in thy ways.
38 Confirm to thy servant thy promise,
    which is for those who fear thee.
39 Turn away the reproach which I
    dread;
        for thy ordinances are good.
40 Behold, I long for thy precepts;
    in thy righteousness give me life!

41 Let thy steadfast love come to me,
    O LORD,
        thy salvation according to thy
        promise;
42 then shall I have an answer for those
    who taunt me,
        for I trust in thy word.
43 And take not the word of truth
    utterly out of my mouth,
        for my hope is in thy ordinances.
44 I will keep thy law continually,
    for ever and ever;
45 and I shall walk at liberty,
    for I have sought thy precepts.
46 I will also speak of thy testimonies
    before kings,
        and shall not be put to shame;
47 for I find my delight in thy com-
    mandments,
        which I love.
48 I revere thy commandments, which
    I love,
        and I will meditate on thy statutes.

49 Remember thy word to thy servant,
    in which thou hast made me hope.
50 This is my comfort in my affliction
    that thy promise gives me life.
51 Godless men utterly deride me,
    but I do not turn away from thy
    law.
52 When I think of thy ordinances
    from of old,
        I take comfort, O LORD.
53 Hot indignation seizes me because
    of the wicked,
        who forsake thy law.
54 Thy statutes have been my songs
    in the house of my pilgrimage.
55 I remember thy name in the night,
    O LORD,
        and keep thy law.
56 This blessing has fallen to me,
    that I have kept thy precepts.

57 The LORD is my portion;
    I promise to keep thy words.
58 I entreat thy favor with all my heart;
    be gracious to me according to
    thy promise.
59 When I think of thy ways,
    I turn my feet to thy testimonies;

60 I hasten and do not delay
    to keep thy commandments.
61 Though the cords of the wicked en-
    snare me,
    I do not forget thy law.
62 At midnight I rise to praise thee,
    because of thy righteous ordi-
    nances.
63 I am a companion of all who fear
    thee,
    of those who keep thy precepts.
64 The earth, O LORD, is full of thy
    steadfast love;
    teach me thy statutes!

65 Thou hast dealt well with thy ser-
    vant,
    O LORD, according to thy word.
66 Teach me good judgment and
    knowledge,
    for I believe in thy command-
    ments.
67 Before I was afflicted I went astray;
    but now I keep thy word.
68 Thou art good and doest good;
    teach me thy statutes.
69 The godless besmear me with lies,
    but with my whole heart I keep
    thy precepts;
70 their heart is gross like fat,
    but I delight in thy law.
71 It is good for me that I was afflicted,
    that I might learn thy statutes.
72 The law of thy mouth is better to me
    than thousands of gold and silver
    pieces.

73 Thy hands have made and fashioned
    me;
    give me understanding that I may
    learn thy commandments.
74 Those who fear thee shall see me
    and rejoice,
    because I have hoped in thy word.
75 I know, O LORD, that thy judgments
    are right,
    and that in faithfulness thou hast
    afflicted me.
76 Let thy steadfast love be ready to
    comfort me
    according to thy promise to thy
    servant.
77 Let thy mercy come to me, that I
    may live;
    for thy law is my delight.
78 Let the godless be put to shame,
    because they have subverted me
    with guile;
    as for me, I will meditate on thy
    precepts.
79 Let those who fear thee turn to me,
    that they may know thy testi-
    monies.
80 May my heart be blameless in thy
    statutes,
    that I may not be put to shame!

81 My soul languishes for thy salvation;
    I hope in thy word.
82 My eyes fail with watching for thy
    promise;
    I ask, "When wilt thou comfort
    me?"
83 For I have become like a wineskin
    in the smoke,
    yet I have not forgotten thy
    statutes.
84 How long must thy servant endure?
    When wilt thou judge those who
    persecute me?
85 Godless men have dug pitfalls for
    me,
    men who do not conform to thy
    law.
86 All thy commandments are sure;
    they persecute me with falsehood;
    help me!
87 They have almost made an end of
    me on earth;
    but I have not forsaken thy
    precepts.
88 In thy steadfast love spare my life,
    that I may keep the testimonies
    of thy mouth.

89 For ever, O LORD, thy word
    is firmly fixed in the heavens.
90 Thy faithfulness endures to all gen-
    erations;
    thou hast established the earth,
    and it stands fast.
91 By thy appointment they stand this
    day;
    for all things are thy servants.
92 If thy law had not been my delight,
    I should have perished in my
    affliction.
93 I will never forget thy precepts;
    for by them thou hast given me life.
94 I am thine, save me;
    for I have sought thy precepts.
95 The wicked lie in wait to destroy me;
    but I consider thy testimonies.
96 I have seen a limit to all perfection,
    but thy commandment is ex-
    ceedingly broad.

97 Oh, how I love thy law!
    It is my meditation all the day.
98 Thy commandment makes me wiser
    than my enemies,
    for it is ever with me.
99 I have more understanding than all
    my teachers,
    for thy testimonies are my medi-
    tation.
100 I understand more than the aged,
    for I keep thy precepts.
101 I hold back my feet from every evil
    way,

in order to keep thy word.
102 I do not turn aside from thy ordinances,
    for thou hast taught me.
103 How sweet are thy words to my taste,
    sweeter than honey to my mouth!
104 Through thy precepts I get understanding;
    therefore I hate every false way.

105 Thy word is a lamp to my feet
    and a light to my path.
106 I have sworn an oath and confirmed it,
    to observe thy righteous ordinances.
107 I am sorely afflicted;
    give me life, O LORD, according to thy word!
108 Accept my offerings of praise, O LORD,
    and teach me thy ordinances.
109 I hold my life in my hand continually,
    but I do not forget thy law.
110 The wicked have laid a snare for me,
    but I do not stray from thy precepts.
111 Thy testimonies are my heritage for ever;
    yea, they are the joy of my heart.
112 I incline my heart to perform thy statutes
    for ever, to the end.

113 I hate double-minded men,
    but I love thy law.
114 Thou art my hiding place and my shield;
    I hope in thy word.
115 Depart from me, you evildoers,
    that I may keep the commandments of my God.
116 Uphold me according to thy promise, that I may live,
    and let me not be put to shame in my hope!
117 Hold me up, that I may be safe
    and have regard for thy statutes continually!
118 Thou dost spurn all who go astray from thy statutes;
    yea, their cunning is in vain.
119 All the wicked of the earth thou dost count as dross;
    therefore I love thy testimonies.
120 My flesh trembles for fear of thee,
    and I am afraid of thy judgments.

121 I have done what is just and right;
    do not leave me to my oppressors.
122 Be surety for thy servant for good;

k Gk Jerome: Heb uncertain

let not the godless oppress me.
123 My eyes fail with watching for thy salvation,
    and for the fulfilment of thy righteous promise.
124 Deal with thy servant according to thy steadfast love,
    and teach me thy statutes.
125 I am thy servant; give me understanding,
    that I may know thy testimonies!
126 It is time for the LORD to act,
    for thy law has been broken.
127 Therefore I love thy commandments
    above gold, above fine gold.
128 Therefore I direct my steps by all thy precepts;*k*
    I hate every false way.

129 Thy testimonies are wonderful;
    therefore my soul keeps them.
130 The unfolding of thy words gives light;
    it imparts understanding to the simple.
131 With open mouth I pant,
    because I long for thy commandments.
132 Turn to me and be gracious to me,
    as is thy wont toward those who love thy name.
133 Keep steady my steps according to thy promise,
    and let no iniquity get dominion over me.
134 Redeem me from man's oppression,
    that I may keep thy precepts.
135 Make thy face shine upon thy servant,
    and teach me thy statutes.
136 My eyes shed streams of tears,
    because men do not keep thy law.

137 Righteous art thou, O LORD,
    and right are thy judgments.
138 Thou hast appointed thy testimonies in righteousness
    and in all faithfulness.
139 My zeal consumes me,
    because my foes forget thy words.
140 Thy promise is well tried,
    and thy servant loves it.
141 I am small and despised,
    yet I do not forget thy precepts.
142 Thy righteousness is righteous for ever,
    and thy law is true.
143 Trouble and anguish have come upon me,
    but thy commandments are my delight.
144 Thy testimonies are righteous for ever;

give me understanding that I
may live.

145 With my whole heart I cry; answer
me, O LORD!
I will keep thy statutes.
146 I cry to thee; save me,
that I may observe thy testimonies.
147 I rise before dawn and cry for help;
I hope in thy words.
148 My eyes are awake before the
watches of the night,
that I may meditate upon thy
promise.
149 Hear my voice in thy steadfast love;
O LORD, in thy justice preserve
my life.
150 They draw near who persecute me
with evil purpose;
they are far from thy law.
151 But thou art near, O LORD,
and all thy commandments are
true.
152 Long have I known from thy
testimonies
that thou hast founded them for
ever.

153 Look on my affliction and deliver me,
for I do not forget thy law.
154 Plead my cause and redeem me;
give me life according to thy
promise!
155 Salvation is far from the wicked,
for they do not seek thy statutes.
156 Great is thy mercy, O LORD;
give me life according to thy
justice.
157 Many are my persecutors and my
adversaries,
but I do not swerve from thy
testimonies.
158 I look at the faithless with disgust,
because they do not keep thy
commands.
159 Consider how I love thy precepts!
Preserve my life according to thy
steadfast love.
160 The sum of thy word is truth;
and every one of thy righteous
ordinances endures for ever.

161 Princes persecute me without cause,
but my heart stands in awe of
thy words.
162 I rejoice at thy word
like one who finds great spoil.
163 I hate and abhor falsehood,
but I love thy law.
164 Seven times a day I praise thee
for thy righteous ordinances.
165 Great peace have those who love
thy law;
nothing can make them stumble.

166 I hope for thy salvation, O LORD,
and I do thy commandments.
167 My soul keeps thy testimonies;
I love them exceedingly.
168 I keep thy precepts and testimonies,
for all my ways are before thee.

169 Let my cry come before thee, O
LORD;
give me understanding according
to thy word!
170 Let my supplication come before
thee;
deliver me according to thy word.
171 My lips will pour forth praise
that thou dost teach me thy
statutes.
172 My tongue will sing of thy word,
for all thy commandments are
right.
173 Let thy hand be ready to help me,
for I have chosen thy precepts.
174 I long for thy salvation, O LORD,
and thy law is my delight.
175 Let me live, that I may praise thee,
and let thy ordinances help me.
176 I have gone astray like a lost sheep;
seek thy servant,
for I do not forget thy commandments.

A Song of Ascents.

120 In my distress I cry to the
LORD,
that he may answer me:
2 "Deliver me, O LORD,
from lying lips,
from a deceitful tongue."

3 What shall be given to you?
And what more shall be done to
you,
you deceitful tongue?
4 A warrior's sharp arrows,
with glowing coals of the broom
tree!

5 Woe is me, that I sojourn in
Mĕ'shech,
that I dwell among the tents of
Kĕ'där!
6 Too long have I had my dwelling
among those who hate peace.
7 I am for peace;
but when I speak,
they are for war!

A Song of Ascents.

121 I lift up my eyes to the hills.
From whence does my help
come?

2 My help comes from the LORD,
  who made heaven and earth.

3 He will not let your foot be moved,
  he who keeps you will not
    slumber.
4 Behold, he who keeps Israel
  will neither slumber nor sleep.

5 The LORD is your keeper;
  the LORD is your shade
    on your right hand.
6 The sun shall not smite you by day,
  nor the moon by night.

7 The LORD will keep you from all
    evil;
  he will keep your life.
8 The LORD will keep
  your going out and your coming
    in
  from this time forth and for ever-
    more.

A Song of Ascents. Of David.

122 I was glad when they said to
        me,
  "Let us go to the house of the
    LORD!"
2 Our feet have been standing
  within your gates, O Jerusalem!

3 Jerusalem, built as a city
  which is bound firmly together,
4 to which the tribes go up,
  the tribes of the LORD,
  as was decreed for Israel,
  to give thanks to the name of the
    LORD.
5 There thrones for judgment were
    set,
  the thrones of the house of David.

6 Pray for the peace of Jerusalem!
  "May they prosper who love you!
7 Peace be within your walls,
  and security within your towers!"
8 For my brethren and companions'
    sake
  I will say, "Peace be within you!"
9 For the sake of the house of the
    LORD our God,
  I will seek your good.

A Song of Ascents.

123 To thee I lift up my eyes,
        O thou who art enthroned
  in the heavens!
2 Behold, as the eyes of servants
  look to the hand of their master,
  as the eyes of a maid

to the hand of her mistress,
  so our eyes look to the LORD our
    God,
  till he have mercy upon us.

3 Have mercy upon us, O LORD, have
    mercy upon us,
  for we have had more than
    enough of contempt.
4 Too long our soul has been sated
  with the scorn of those who are at
    ease,
  the contempt of the proud.

A Song of Ascents. Of David.

124 If it had not been the LORD
        who was on our side,
  let Israel now say—
2 if it had not been the LORD who was
    on our side,
  when men rose up against us,
3 then they would have swallowed us
    up alive,
  when their anger was kindled
    against us;
4 then the flood would have swept us
    away,
  the torrent would have gone over
    us;
5 then over us would have gone the
    raging waters.

6 Blessed be the LORD,
  who has not given us
  as prey to their teeth!
7 We have escaped as a bird
  from the snare of the fowlers;
  the snare is broken,
  and we have escaped!

8 Our help is in the name of the
    LORD,
  who made heaven and earth.

A Song of Ascents.

125 Those who trust in the LORD
        are like Mount Zion,
  which cannot be moved, but
    abides for ever.
2 As the mountains are round about
    Jerusalem,
  so the LORD is round about his
    people,
  from this time forth and for ever-
    more.
3 For the scepter of wickedness shall
    not rest
  upon the land allotted to the
    righteous,
  lest the righteous put forth
    their hands to do wrong.

4 Do good, O LORD, to those who are
   good,
      and to those who are upright in
      their hearts!
5 But those who turn aside upon their
   crooked ways
      the LORD will lead away with
      evildoers!
   Peace be in Israel!

A Song of Ascents.

126 When the LORD restored the
   fortunes of Zion,*l*
      we were like those who dream.
2 Then our mouth was filled with
   laughter,
      and our tongue with shouts of
      joy;
   then they said among the nations,
      "The LORD has done great things
      for them."
3 The LORD has done great things for
   us;
      we are glad.

4 Restore our fortunes, O LORD,
      like the watercourses in the
      Negeb!
5 May those who sow in tears
      reap with shouts of joy!
6 He that goes forth weeping,
      bearing the seed for sowing,
   shall come home with shouts of
   joy,
      bringing his sheaves with him.

A Song of Ascents. Of Solomon.

127 Unless the LORD builds the
   house,
      those who build it labor in vain.
   Unless the LORD watches over the
   city,
      the watchman stays awake in
      vain.
2 It is in vain that you rise up early
   and go late to rest,
      eating the bread of anxious toil;
         for*m* he gives to his beloved
         sleep.

3 Lo, sons are a heritage from the
   LORD,
      the fruit of the womb a reward.
4 Like arrows in the hand of a warrior
      are the sons of one's youth.
5 Happy is the man who has
      his quiver full of them!
   He shall not be put to shame
      when he speaks with his enemies
      in the gate.

A Song of Ascents.

128 Blessed is every one who fears
   the LORD,
      who walks in his ways!
2 You shall eat the fruit of the labor
   of your hands;
      you shall be happy, and it shall
      be well with you.

3 Your wife will be like a fruitful vine
      within your house;
   your children will be like olive
   shoots
      around your table.
4 Lo, thus shall the man be blessed
      who fears the LORD.

5 The LORD bless you from Zion!
   May you see the prosperity of
   Jerusalem
      all the days of your life!
6 May you see your children's children!
      Peace be upon Israel!

A Song of Ascents.

129 "Sorely have they afflicted
   me from my youth,"
      let Israel now say—
2 "Sorely have they afflicted me from
   my youth,
      yet they have not prevailed against
      me.
3 The plowers plowed upon my back;
      they made long their furrows."
4 The LORD is righteous;
      he has cut the cords of the wicked.
5 May all who hate Zion
      be put to shame and turned back-
      ward!
6 Let them be like the grass on the
   housetops,
      which withers before it grows up,
7 with which the reaper does not fill
   his hand
      or the binder of sheaves his
      bosom,
8 while those who pass by do not say,
      "The blessing of the LORD be
      upon you!
   We bless you in the name of the
   LORD!"

A Song of Ascents.

130 Out of the depths I cry to
   thee, O LORD!
2 Lord, hear my voice!
   Let thy ears be attentive
      to the voice of my supplications!

l Or *brought back those who returned to Zion*   *m* Another reading is *so*

3 If thou, O LORD, shouldst mark
    iniquities,
  Lord, who could stand?
4 But there is forgiveness with thee,
    that thou mayest be feared.

5 I wait for the LORD, my soul waits,
    and in his word I hope;
6 my soul waits for the LORD
    more than watchmen for the
      morning,
    more than watchmen for the
      morning.

7 O Israel, hope in the LORD!
  For with the LORD there is stead-
    fast love,
  and with him is plenteous re-
    demption.
8 And he will redeem Israel
  from all his iniquities.

A Song of Ascents. Of David.

131 O LORD, my heart is not lifted
    up,
  my eyes are not raised too
    high;
  I do not occupy myself with things
    too great and too marvelous for
    me.
2 But I have calmed and quieted my
    soul,
  like a child quieted at its mother's
    breast;
  like a child that is quieted is my
    soul.

3 O Israel, hope in the LORD
  from this time forth and for ever-
    more.

A Song of Ascents.

132 Remember, O LORD, in
    David's favor,
  all the hardships he endured;
2 how he swore to the LORD
  and vowed to the Mighty One of
    Jacob,
3 "I will not enter my house
  or get into my bed;
4 I will not give sleep to my eyes
  or slumber to my eyelids,
5 until I find a place for the LORD,
  a dwelling place for the Mighty
    One of Jacob."

6 Lo, we heard of it in Eph′ra·thah,
  we found it in the fields of Jā′ar.
7 "Let us go to his dwelling place;
  let us worship at his footstool!"

8 Arise, O LORD, and go to thy resting
    place,
  thou and the ark of thy might.
9 Let thy priests be clothed with
    righteousness,
  and let thy saints shout for joy.
10 For thy servant David's sake
  do not turn away the face of thy
    anointed one.

11 The LORD swore to David a sure oath
  from which he will not turn back:
  "One of the sons of your body
  I will set on your throne.
12 If your sons keep my covenant
  and my testimonies which I shall
    teach them,
  their sons also for ever
    shall sit upon your throne."

13 For the LORD has chosen Zion;
  he has desired it for his habitation:
14 "This is my resting place for ever;
  here I will dwell, for I have de-
    sired it.
15 I will abundantly bless her provi-
    sions;
  I will satisfy her poor with bread.
16 Her priests I will clothe with sal-
    vation,
  and her saints will shout for joy.
17 There I will make a horn to sprout
    for David;
  I have prepared a lamp for my
    anointed.
18 His enemies I will clothe with
    shame,
  but upon himself his crown will
    shed its luster."

A Song of Ascents.

133 Behold, how good and pleas-
    ant it is
  when brothers dwell in unity!
2 It is like the precious oil upon the
    head,
  running down upon the beard,
  upon the beard of Aaron,
  running down on the collar of
    his robes!
3 It is like the dew of Hĕr′mòn,
  which falls on the mountains of
    Zion!
  For there the LORD has commanded
    the blessing,
  life for evermore.

A Song of Ascents.

134 Come, bless the LORD,
  all you servants of the LORD,

who stand by night in the house
  of the LORD!
2 Lift up your hands to the holy place,
  and bless the LORD!

3 May the LORD bless you from Zion,
  he who made heaven and earth!

135 Praise the LORD.
    Praise the name of the LORD,
  give praise, O servants of the
    LORD,
2 you that stand in the house of the
    LORD,
  in the courts of the house of our
    God!
3 Praise the LORD, for the LORD is
    good;
  sing to his name, for he is gracious!
4 For the LORD has chosen Jacob for
    himself,
  Israel as his own possession.

5 For I know that the LORD is great,
  and that our Lord is above all
    gods.
6 Whatever the LORD pleases he does,
  in heaven and on earth,
  in the seas and all deeps.
7 He it is who makes the clouds rise
    at the end of the earth,
  who makes lightnings for the rain
  and brings forth the wind from
    his storehouses.

8 He it was who smote the first-born
    of Egypt,
  both of man and of beast;
9 who in thy midst, O Egypt,
  sent signs and wonders
  against Pharaoh and all his
    servants;
10 who smote many nations
  and slew mighty kings,
11 Si'hon, king of the Am'ō·rites,
  and Og, king of Bā'shăn,
  and all the kingdoms of Canaan,
12 and gave their land as a heritage,
  a heritage to his people Israel.

13 Thy name, O LORD, endures for
    ever,
  thy renown, O LORD, throughout
    all ages.
14 For the LORD will vindicate his
    people,
  and have compassion on his
    servants.

15 The idols of the nations are silver
    and gold,
  the work of men's hands.
16 They have mouths, but they speak
    not,

they have eyes, but they see not,
17 they have ears, but they hear not,
  nor is there any breath in their
    mouths.
18 Like them be those who make
    them!—
  yea, every one who trusts in them!

19 O house of Israel, bless the LORD!
  O house of Aaron, bless the LORD!
20 O house of Levi, bless the LORD!
  You that fear the LORD, bless the
    LORD!
21 Blessed be the LORD from Zion,
  he who dwells in Jerusalem!
  Praise the LORD!

136 O give thanks to the LORD,
    for he is good,
  for his steadfast love endures for
    ever.
2 O give thanks to the God of gods,
  for his steadfast love endures for
    ever.
3 O give thanks to the Lord of lords,
  for his steadfast love endures for
    ever;

4 to him who alone does great wonders,
  for his steadfast love endures for
    ever;
5 to him who by understanding made
    the heavens,
  for his steadfast love endures for
    ever;
6 to him who spread out the earth
    upon the waters,
  for his steadfast love endures for
    ever;
7 to him who made the great lights,
  for his steadfast love endures for
    ever;
8 the sun to rule over the day,
  for his steadfast love endures for
    ever;
9 the moon and stars to rule over the
    night,
  for his steadfast love endures for
    ever;

10 to him who smote the first-born of
    Egypt,
  for his steadfast love endures for
    ever;
11 and brought Israel out from among
    them,
  for his steadfast love endures for
    ever;
12 with a strong hand and an out-
    stretched arm,
  for his steadfast love endures for
    ever;
13 to him who divided the Red Sea in
    sunder,

135.14: Heb 10.30.   **135.15-18:** Ps 115.4-8.

for his steadfast love endures for ever;

14 and made Israel pass through the midst of it,
    for his steadfast love endures for ever;

15 but overthrew Pharaoh and his host in the Red Sea,
    for his steadfast love endures for ever;

16 to him who led his people through the wilderness,
    for his steadfast love endures for ever;

17 to him who smote great kings,
    for his steadfast love endures for ever;

18 and slew famous kings,
    for his steadfast love endures for ever;

19 Sī'hon, king of the Am'ō·rites,
    for his steadfast love endures for ever;

20 and Og, king of Bā'shăn,
    for his steadfast love endures for ever;

21 and gave their land as a heritage,
    for his steadfast love endures for ever;

22 a heritage to Israel his servant,
    for his steadfast love endures for ever.

23 It is he who remembered us in our low estate,
    for his steadfast love endures for ever;

24 and rescued us from our foes,
    for his steadfast love endures for ever;

25 he who gives food to all flesh,
    for his steadfast love endures for ever.

26 O give thanks to the God of heaven,
    for his steadfast love endures for ever.

137 By the waters*ᵒ* of Babylon,
there we sat down and wept,
when we remembered Zion.
2 On the willows*ᵖ* there
    we hung up our lyres.
3 For there our captors
required of us songs,
and our tormentors, mirth, saying,
    "Sing us one of the songs of Zion!"

4 How shall we sing the LORD's song in a foreign land?
5 If I forget you, O Jerusalem,

let my right hand wither!
6 Let my tongue cleave to the roof of my mouth,
if I do not remember you,
if I do not set Jerusalem
    above my highest joy!

7 Remember, O LORD, against the Ē'dŏm·ites
the day of Jerusalem,
how they said, "Rase it, rase it!
    Down to its foundations!"
8 O daughter of Babylon, you devastator!*�q*
Happy shall he be who requites you
    with what you have done to us!
9 Happy shall he be who takes your little ones
    and dashes them against the rock!

A Psalm of David.

138 I give thee thanks, O LORD, with my whole heart;
before the gods I sing thy praise;
2 I bow down toward thy holy temple
and give thanks to thy name for thy steadfast love and thy faithfulness;
for thou hast exalted above everything
    thy name and thy word.*ʳ*
3 On the day I called, thou didst answer me,
my strength of soul thou didst increase.*ˢ*

4 All the kings of the earth shall praise thee, O LORD,
for they have heard the words of thy mouth;
5 and they shall sing of the ways of the LORD,
for great is the glory of the LORD.
6 For though the LORD is high, he regards the lowly;
but the haughty he knows from afar.

7 Though I walk in the midst of trouble,
thou dost preserve my life;
thou dost stretch out thy hand against the wrath of my enemies,
and thy right hand delivers me.
8 The LORD will fulfil his purpose for me;
thy steadfast love, O LORD, endures for ever.

ᵒ Heb streams   ᵖ Or poplars   q Or you who are devastated
ʳ Cn: Heb thou hast exalted thy word above all thy name
ˢ Syr Compare Gk Tg: Heb thou didst make me arrogant in my soul with strength

Do not forsake the work of thy
  hands.

To the choirmaster. A Psalm of David.

139 O LORD, thou hast searched
  me and known me!
2 Thou knowest when I sit down and
  when I rise up;
    thou discernest my thoughts from
    afar.
3 Thou searchest out my path and my
  lying down,
    and art acquainted with all my
    ways.
4 Even before a word is on my
  tongue,
    lo, O LORD, thou knowest it al-
    together.
5 Thou dost beset me behind and
  before,
    and layest thy hand upon me.
6 Such knowledge is too wonderful
  for me;
    it is high, I cannot attain it.

7 Whither shall I go from thy Spirit?
    Or whither shall I flee from thy
    presence?
8 If I ascend to heaven, thou art
  there!
    If I make my bed in Shē′ōl, thou
    art there!
9 If I take the wings of the morning
    and dwell in the uttermost parts
    of the sea,
10 even there thy hand shall lead me,
    and thy right hand shall hold me.
11 If I say, "Let only darkness cover me,
    and the light about me be night,"
12 even the darkness is not dark to
  thee,
    the night is bright as the day;
    for darkness is as light with
    thee.

13 For thou didst form my inward
  parts,
    thou didst knit me together in my
    mother's womb.
14 I praise thee, for thou art fearful
  and wonderful.ᵗ
    Wonderful are thy works!
    Thou knowest me right well;
15 my frame was not hidden from
  thee,
    when I was being made in secret,
    intricately wrought in the depths
    of the earth.

16 Thy eyes beheld my unformed
  substance;
    in thy book were written, every
    one of them,
    the days that were formed for me,
    when as yet there was none of
    them.
17 How precious to me are thy
  thoughts, O God!
    How vast is the sum of them!
18 If I would count them, they are
  more than the sand.
    When I awake, I am still with
    thee.ᵘ

19 O that thou wouldst slay the wicked,
  O God,
    and that men of blood would
    depart from me,
20 men who maliciously defy thee,
    who lift themselves up against
    thee for evil!ᵛ
21 Do I not hate them that hate thee,
  O LORD?
    And do I not loathe them that
    rise up against thee?
22 I hate them with perfect hatred;
    I count them my enemies.
23 Search me, O God, and know my
  heart!
    Try me and know my thoughts!
24 And see if there be any wickedʷ way
  in me,
    and lead me in the way ever-
    lasting!ˣ

To the choirmaster. A Psalm of David.

140 Deliver me, O LORD, from
  evil men;
    preserve me from violent men,
2 who plan evil things in their heart,
    and stir up wars continually.
3 They make their tongue sharp as a
    serpent's,
    and under their lips is the poison
    of vipers.   *Selah*

4 Guard me, O LORD, from the hands
    of the wicked;
    preserve me from violent men,
    who have planned to trip up my
    feet.
5 Arrogant men have hidden a trap for
  me,
    and with cords they have spread
    a net,ʸ
    by the wayside they have set
    snares for me.   *Selah*

ᵗ Cn Compare Gk Syr Jerome: Heb *fearful things I am wonderful*
ᵘ Or *were I to come to the end I would still be with thee*   ᵛ Cn: Heb uncertain
ʷ Heb *hurtful*   ˣ Or *the ancient way*. Compare Jer 6.16.
ʸ Or *they have spread cords as a net*
140.3: Rom 3.13.

6 I say to the LORD, Thou art my
    God;
    give ear to the voice of my sup-
      plications, O LORD!
7 O LORD, my Lord, my strong
    deliverer,
    thou hast covered my head in the
      day of battle.
8 Grant not, O LORD, the desires of
    the wicked;
    do not further his evil plot!
                    Selah

9 Those who surround me lift up their
    head,[z]
    let the mischief of their lips over-
      whelm them!
10 Let burning coals fall upon them!
    Let them be cast into pits, no
      more to rise!
11 Let not the slanderer be established
    in the land;
    let evil hunt down the violent man
      speedily!

12 I know that the LORD maintains the
    cause of the afflicted,
    and executes justice for the needy.
13 Surely the righteous shall give
    thanks to thy name;
    the upright shall dwell in thy
      presence.

A Psalm of David.

141 I call upon thee, O LORD; make
    haste to me!
    Give ear to my voice, when I call
    to thee!
2 Let my prayer be counted as incense
    before thee,
    and the lifting up of my hands as
    an evening sacrifice!

3 Set a guard over my mouth, O
    LORD,
    keep watch over the door of my
    lips!
4 Incline not my heart to any evil,
    to busy myself with wicked deeds
    in company with men who work
      iniquity;
    and let me not eat of their dainties!

5 Let a good man strike or rebuke me
    in kindness,
    but let the oil of the wicked never
    anoint my head;[a]
    for my prayer is continually[b]
      against their wicked deeds.

6 When they are given over to those
    who shall condemn them,
    then they shall learn that the
      word of the LORD is true.
7 As a rock which one cleaves and
    shatters on the land,
    so shall their bones be strewn at
      the mouth of Shĕ′ŏl.[c]

8 But my eyes are toward thee, O
    LORD God;
    in thee I seek refuge; leave me
      not defenseless!
9 Keep me from the trap which they
    have laid for me,
    and from the snares of evildoers!
10 Let the wicked together fall into
    their own nets,
    while I escape.

A Maskil of David, when he was in the cave. A Prayer.

142 I cry with my voice to the
    LORD,
    with my voice I make supplication
    to the LORD,
2 I pour out my complaint before him,
    I tell my trouble before him.
3 When my spirit is faint,
    thou knowest my way!

In the path where I walk
    they have hidden a trap for me.
4 I look to the right and watch,[d]
    but there is none who takes notice
    of me;
no refuge remains to me,
    no man cares for me.

5 I cry to thee, O LORD;
    I say, Thou art my refuge,
    my portion in the land of the
      living.
6 Give heed to my cry;
    for I am brought very low!

Deliver me from my persecutors;
    for they are too strong for me!
7 Bring me out of prison,
    that I may give thanks to thy name!
The righteous will surround me;
    for thou wilt deal bountifully with
    me.

A Psalm of David.

143 Hear my prayer, O LORD;
    give ear to my supplications!

---

z Cn Compare Gk: Heb *those who surround me are uplifted in head*
a Gk: Heb obscure   b Cn: Heb *for continually and my prayer*
c The Hebrew of verses 5-7 is obscure   d Or *Look to the right and watch*
141.2: Rev 5.8; 8.3-4.

In thy faithfulness answer me, in
    thy righteousness!
2 Enter not into judgment with thy
        servant;
    for no man living is righteous be-
        fore thee.

3 For the enemy has pursued me;
    he has crushed my life to the
        ground;
    he has made me sit in darkness
        like those long dead.
4 Therefore my spirit faints within me;
    my heart within me is appalled.

5 I remember the days of old,
    I meditate on all that thou hast
        done;
    I muse on what thy hands have
        wrought.
6 I stretch out my hands to thee;
    my soul thirsts for thee like a
        parched land.   *Selah*

7 Make haste to answer me, O LORD!
    My spirit fails!
    Hide not thy face from me,
    lest I be like those who go down
        to the Pit.
8 Let me hear in the morning of thy
        steadfast love,
    for in thee I put my trust.
    Teach me the way I should go,
    for to thee I lift up my soul.

9 Deliver me, O LORD, from my
        enemies!
    I have fled to thee for refuge!*e*
10 Teach me to do thy will,
    for thou art my God!
    Let thy good spirit lead me
    on a level path!

11 For thy name's sake, O LORD, pre-
        serve my life!
    In thy righteousness bring me out
        of trouble!
12 And in thy steadfast love cut off my
        enemies,
    and destroy all my adversaries,
    for I am thy servant.

A Psalm of David.

144 Blessed be the LORD, my
    rock,
    who trains my hands for war,
    and my fingers for battle;
2 my rock*f* and my fortress,

my stronghold and my deliverer,
my shield and he in whom I take
    refuge,
who subdues the peoples under
    him.*g*

3 O LORD, what is man that thou dost
        regard him,
    or the son of man that thou dost
        think of him?
4 Man is like a breath,
    his days are like a passing shadow.

5 Bow thy heavens, O LORD, and
        come down!
    Touch the mountains that they
        smoke!
6 Flash forth the lightning and scatter
        them,
    send out thy arrows and rout
        them!
7 Stretch forth thy hand from on
        high,
    rescue me and deliver me from
        the many waters,
    from the hand of aliens,
8 whose mouths speak lies,
    and whose right hand is a right
        hand of falsehood.

9 I will sing a new song to thee, O God;
    upon a ten-stringed harp I will
        play to thee,
10 who givest victory to kings,
    who rescuest David thy*h* servant.
11 Rescue me from the cruel sword,
    and deliver me from the hand of
        aliens,
    whose mouths speak lies,
    and whose right hand is a right
        hand of falsehood.

12 May our sons in their youth
    be like plants full grown,
    our daughters like corner pillars
    cut for the structure of a palace;
13 may our garners be full,
    providing all manner of store;
    may our sheep bring forth thou-
        sands
    and ten thousands in our fields;
14 may our cattle be heavy with young,
    suffering no mischance or failure
        in bearing;
    may there be no cry of distress in
        our streets!
15 Happy the people to whom such
        blessings fall!
    Happy the people whose God is
        the LORD!

e One Heb Ms Gk: Heb *to thee I have hidden*
f With 18.2 2 Sam 22.2: Heb *my steadfast love*
g Another reading is *my people under me*
h Heb *his*
143.2: Ps 130.3; Rom 3.20; Gal 2.16.

A Song of Praise. Of David.

145 I will extol thee, my God and King,
  and bless thy name for ever and ever.
2 Every day I will bless thee,
  and praise thy name for ever and ever.
3 Great is the LORD, and greatly to be praised,
  and his greatness is unsearchable.

4 One generation shall laud thy works to another,
  and shall declare thy mighty acts.
5 On the glorious splendor of thy majesty,
  and on thy wondrous works, I will meditate.
6 Men shall proclaim the might of thy terrible acts,
  and I will declare thy greatness.
7 They shall pour forth the fame of thy abundant goodness,
  and shall sing aloud of thy righteousness.

8 The LORD is gracious and merciful,
  slow to anger and abounding in steadfast love.
9 The LORD is good to all,
  and his compassion is over all that he has made.

10 All thy works shall give thanks to thee, O LORD,
  and all thy saints shall bless thee!
11 They shall speak of the glory of thy kingdom,
  and tell of thy power,
12 to make known to the sons of men thy[h] mighty deeds,
  and the glorious splendor of thy[h] kingdom.
13 Thy kingdom is an everlasting kingdom,
  and thy dominion endures throughout all generations.

  The LORD is faithful in all his words,
  and gracious in all his deeds.[i]
14 The LORD upholds all who are falling,
  and raises up all who are bowed down.
15 The eyes of all look to thee,
  and thou givest them their food in due season.
16 Thou openest thy hand,
  thou satisfiest the desire of every living thing.
17 The LORD is just in all his ways,
  and kind in all his doings.

18 The LORD is near to all who call upon him,
  to all who call upon him in truth.
19 He fulfils the desire of all who fear him,
  he also hears their cry, and saves them.
20 The LORD preserves all who love him;
  but all the wicked he will destroy.
21 My mouth will speak the praise of the LORD,
  and let all flesh bless his holy name for ever and ever.

146 Praise the LORD!
  Praise the LORD, O my soul!
2 I will praise the LORD as long as I live;
  I will sing praises to my God while I have being.

3 Put not your trust in princes,
  in a son of man, in whom there is no help.
4 When his breath departs he returns to his earth;
  on that very day his plans perish.

5 Happy is he whose help is the God of Jacob,
  whose hope is in the LORD his God,
6 who made heaven and earth,
  the sea, and all that is in them;
  who keeps faith for ever;
7 who executes justice for the oppressed;
  who gives food to the hungry.

  The LORD sets the prisoners free;
8 the LORD opens the eyes of the blind.
  The LORD lifts up those who are bowed down;
  the LORD loves the righteous.
9 The LORD watches over the sojourners,
  he upholds the widow and the fatherless;
  but the way of the wicked he brings to ruin.

10 The LORD will reign for ever,
  thy God, O Zion, to all generations.
  Praise the LORD!

147 Praise the LORD!
  For it is good to sing praises to our God;
  for he is gracious, and a song of praise is seemly.
2 The LORD builds up Jerusalem;

h Heb *his*   i These two lines are supplied by one Hebrew Ms, Gk and Syr

he gathers the outcasts of Israel.
3 He heals the brokenhearted,
  and binds up their wounds.
4 He determines the number of the
    stars,
  he gives to all of them their names.
5 Great is our LORD, and abundant
    in power;
  his understanding is beyond
    measure.
6 The LORD lifts up the downtrodden,
  he casts the wicked to the ground.

7 Sing to the LORD with thanksgiving;
  make melody to our God upon
    the lyre!
8 He covers the heavens with clouds,
  he prepares rain for the earth,
  he makes grass grow upon the
    hills.
9 He gives to the beasts their food,
  and to the young ravens which
    cry.
10 His delight is not in the strength of
    the horse,
  nor his pleasure in the legs of a
    man;
11 but the LORD takes pleasure in those
    who fear him,
  in those who hope in his steadfast
    love.

12 Praise the LORD, O Jerusalem!
  Praise your God, O Zion!
13 For he strengthens the bars of your
    gates;
  he blesses your sons within
    you.
14 He makes peace in your borders;
  he fills you with the finest of the
    wheat.
15 He sends forth his command to the
    earth;
  his word runs swiftly.
16 He gives snow like wool;
  he scatters hoarfrost like ashes.
17 He casts forth his ice like morsels;
  who can stand before his cold?
18 He sends forth his word, and melts
    them;
  he makes his wind blow, and the
    waters flow.
19 He declares his word to Jacob,
  his statutes and ordinances to
    Israel.
20 He has not dealt thus with any other
    nation;
  they do not know his ordinances.
  Praise the LORD!

148 Praise the LORD!
  Praise the LORD from the
    heavens,
  praise him in the heights!

j Or he set a law which cannot pass away

2 Praise him, all his angels,
  praise him, all his host!

3 Praise him, sun and moon,
  praise him, all you shining stars!
4 Praise him, you highest heavens,
  and you waters above the heavens!

5 Let them praise the name of the
    LORD!
  For he commanded and they were
    created.
6 And he established them for ever
    and ever;
  he fixed their bounds which can-
    not be passed.*j*

7 Praise the LORD from the earth,
  you sea monsters and all deeps,
8 fire and hail, snow and frost,
  stormy wind fulfilling his com-
    mand!

9 Mountains and all hills,
  fruit trees and all cedars!
10 Beasts and all cattle,
  creeping things and flying birds!

11 Kings of the earth and all peoples,
  princes and all rulers of the earth!
12 Young men and maidens together,
  old men and children!

13 Let them praise the name of the
    LORD,
  for his name alone is exalted;
  his glory is above earth and
    heaven.
14 He has raised up a horn for his
    people,
  praise for all his saints,
  for the people of Israel who are
    near to him.
  Praise the LORD!

149 Praise the LORD!
  Sing to the LORD a new song,
  his praise in the assembly of the
    faithful!
2 Let Israel be glad in his Maker,
  let the sons of Zion rejoice in
    their King!
3 Let them praise his name with
    dancing,
  making melody to him with
    timbrel and lyre!
4 For the LORD takes pleasure in his
    people;
  he adorns the humble with victory.
5 Let the faithful exult in glory;
  let them sing for joy on their
    couches.
6 Let the high praises of God be in
    their throats

and two-edged swords in their hands,

7 to wreak vengeance on the nations
and chastisement on the peoples,

8 to bind their kings with chains
and their nobles with fetters of iron,

9 to execute on them the judgment written!
This is glory for all his faithful ones.
Praise the LORD!

150 Praise the LORD!
Praise God in his sanctuary;

praise him in his mighty firmament!

2 Praise him for his mighty deeds;
praise him according to his exceeding greatness!

3 Praise him with trumpet sound;
praise him with lute and harp!

4 Praise him with timbrel and dance;
praise him with strings and pipe!

5 Praise him with sounding cymbals;
praise him with loud clashing cymbals!

6 Let everything that breathes praise the LORD!
Praise the LORD!

THE PROVERBS

1 The proverbs of Solomon, son of David, king of Israel:

2 That men may know wisdom and instruction,
understanding words of insight,
3 receive instruction in wise dealing,
righteousness, justice, and equity;
4 that prudence may be given to the simple,
knowledge and discretion to the youth—
5 the wise man also may hear and increase in learning,
and the man of understanding acquire skill,
6 to understand a proverb and a figure,
the words of the wise and their riddles.

7 The fear of the LORD is the beginning of knowledge;
fools despise wisdom and instruction.

8 Hear, my son, your father's instruction,
and reject not your mother's teaching;
9 for they are a fair garland for your head,
and pendants for your neck.
10 My son, if sinners entice you,
do not consent.
11 If they say, "Come with us, let us lie in wait for blood,
let us wantonly ambush the innocent;
12 like Shĕ'ōl let us swallow them alive and whole,
like those who go down to the Pit;
13 we shall find all precious goods,
we shall fill our houses with spoil;
14 throw in your lot among us,
we will all have one purse"—
15 my son, do not walk in the way with them,
hold back your foot from their paths;
16 for their feet run to evil,
and they make haste to shed blood.
17 For in vain is a net spread
in the sight of any bird;
18 but these men lie in wait for their own blood,
they set an ambush for their own lives.
19 Such are the ways of all who get gain by violence;
it takes away the life of its possessors.

20 Wisdom cries aloud in the street;
in the markets she raises her voice;
21 on the top of the walls[a] she cries out;
at the entrance of the city gates she speaks:
22 "How long, O simple ones, will you love being simple?
How long will scoffers delight in their scoffing
and fools hate knowledge?
23 Give heed[b] to my reproof;
behold, I will pour out my thoughts[c] to you;
I will make my words known to you.
24 Because I have called and you refused to listen,
have stretched out my hand and no one has heeded,
25 and you have ignored all my counsel
and would have none of my reproof,
26 I also will laugh at your calamity;
I will mock when panic strikes you,
27 when panic strikes you like a storm,
and your calamity comes like a whirlwind,
when distress and anguish come upon you.
28 Then they will call upon me, but I will not answer;
they will seek me diligently but will not find me.
29 Because they hated knowledge
and did not choose the fear of the LORD,
30 would have none of my counsel,
and despised all my reproof,
31 therefore they shall eat the fruit of their way
and be sated with their own devices.
32 For the simple are killed by their turning away,
and the complacence of fools destroys them;

a Heb uncertain   b Heb Turn   c Heb spirit
1.20-21: Prov 8.1-3.

33 but he who listens to me will dwell
    secure
    and will be at ease, without dread
    of evil."

2 My son, if you receive my words
    and treasure up my command-
    ments with you,
2 making your ear attentive to wisdom
    and inclining your heart to un-
    derstanding;
3 yes, if you cry out for insight
    and raise your voice for under-
    standing,
4 if you seek it like silver
    and search for it as for hidden
    treasures;
5 then you will understand the fear
    of the LORD
    and find the knowledge of God.
6 For the LORD gives wisdom;
    from his mouth come knowledge
    and understanding;
7 he stores up sound wisdom for the
    upright;
    he is a shield to those who walk
    in integrity,
8 guarding the paths of justice
    and preserving the way of his
    saints.
9 Then you will understand right-
    eousness and justice
    and equity, every good path;
10 for wisdom will come into your
    heart,
    and knowledge will be pleasant to
    your soul;
11 discretion will watch over you;
    understanding will guard you;
12 delivering you from the way of evil,
    from men of perverted speech,
13 who forsake the paths of uprightness
    to walk in the ways of darkness,
14 who rejoice in doing evil
    and delight in the perverseness of
    evil;
15 men whose paths are crooked,
    and who are devious in their ways.

16 You will be saved from the loose[d]
    woman,
    from the adventuress[e] with her
    smooth words,
17 who forsakes the companion of her
    youth
    and forgets the covenant of her
    God;
18 for her house sinks down to death,
    and her paths to the shades;
19 none who go to her come back
    nor do they regain the paths of life.

20 So you will walk in the way of good
    men
    and keep to the paths of the
    righteous.
21 For the upright will inhabit the land,
    and men of integrity will remain
    in it;
22 but the wicked will be cut off from
    the land,
    and the treacherous will be rooted
    out of it.

3 My son, do not forget my teach-
    ing,
    but let your heart keep my com-
    mandments;
2 for length of days and years of life
    and abundant welfare will they
    give you.
3 Let not loyalty and faithfulness for-
    sake you;
    bind them about your neck,
    write them on the tablet of your
    heart.
4 So you will find favor and good
    repute[f]
    in the sight of God and man.

5 Trust in the LORD with all your
    heart,
    and do not rely on your own
    insight.
6 In all your ways acknowledge him,
    and he will make straight your
    paths.
7 Be not wise in your own eyes;
    fear the LORD, and turn away
    from evil.
8 It will be healing to your flesh[g]
    and refreshment[h] to your bones.

9 Honor the LORD with your sub-
    stance
    and with the first fruits of all
    your produce;
10 then your barns will be filled with
    plenty,
    and your vats will be bursting
    with wine.

11 My son, do not despise the LORD's
    discipline
    or be weary of his reproof,
12 for the LORD reproves him whom
    he loves,
    as a father the son in whom he
    delights.

13 Happy is the man who finds wisdom,
    and the man who gets under-
    standing,

d Heb *strange*   *e* Heb *foreign woman*   *f* Cn: Heb *understanding*   *g* Heb *navel*
h Or *medicine*
3.4: Rom 12.17.   **3.7:** Rom 12.16.
3.11-12: Heb 12.5-6.

14 for the gain from it is better than
     gain from silver
     and its profit better than gold.
15 She is more precious than jewels,
     and nothing you desire can com-
     pare with her.
16 Long life is in her right hand;
     in her left hand are riches and
     honor.
17 Her ways are ways of pleasantness,
     and all her paths are peace.
18 She is a tree of life to those who lay
     hold of her;
     those who hold her fast are called
     happy.

19 The LORD by wisdom founded the
     earth;
     by understanding he established
     the heavens;
20 by his knowledge the deeps broke
     forth,
     and the clouds drop down the
     dew.

21 My son, keep sound wisdom and
     discretion;
     let them not escape from your
     sight,[i]
22 and they will be life for your soul
     and adornment for your neck.
23 Then you will walk on your way
     securely
     and your foot will not stumble.
24 If you sit down,[j] you will not be
     afraid;
     when you lie down, your sleep
     will be sweet.
25 Do not be afraid of sudden panic,
     or of the ruin[k] of the wicked,
     when it comes;
26 for the LORD will be your confidence
     and will keep your foot from be-
     ing caught.

27 Do not withhold good from those
     to whom it[l] is due,
     when it is in your power to do it.
28 Do not say to your neighbor, "Go,
     and come again,
     tomorrow I will give it"—when
     you have it with you.
29 Do not plan evil against your
     neighbor
     who dwells trustingly beside you.
30 Do not contend with a man for no
     reason,
     when he has done you no harm.
31 Do not envy a man of violence
     and do not choose any of his
     ways;

32 for the perverse man is an abomi-
     nation to the LORD,
     but the upright are in his con-
     fidence.
33 The LORD's curse is on the house of
     the wicked,
     but he blesses the abode of the
     righteous.
34 Toward the scorners he is scornful,
     but to the humble he shows favor.
35 The wise will inherit honor,
     but fools get[m] disgrace.

4 Hear, O sons, a father's instruc-
     tion,
     and be attentive, that you may
     gain[n] insight;
2 for I give you good precepts;
     do not forsake my teaching.
3 When I was a son with my father,
     tender, the only one in the sight
     of my mother,
4 he taught me, and said to me,
     "Let your heart hold fast my words;
     keep my commandments, and
     live;
5 do not forget, and do not turn away
     from the words of my mouth.
     Get wisdom; get insight.[o]
6 Do not forsake her, and she will
     keep you;
     love her, and she will guard you.
7 The beginning of wisdom is this:
     Get wisdom,
     and whatever you get, get insight.
8 Prize her highly,[p] and she will exalt
     you;
     she will honor you if you embrace
     her.
9 She will place on your head a fair
     garland;
     she will bestow on you a beautiful
     crown."

10 Hear, my son, and accept my words,
     that the years of your life may be
     many.
11 I have taught you the way of wisdom;
     I have led you in the paths of
     uprightness.
12 When you walk, your step will not
     be hampered;
     and if you run, you will not
     stumble.
13 Keep hold of instruction, do not let
     go;
     guard her, for she is your life.
14 Do not enter the path of the wicked,
     and do not walk in the way of
     evil men.
15 Avoid it; do not go on it;

[i] Reversing the order of the clauses   [j] Gk: Heb *lie down*   [k] Heb *storm*
[l] Heb *Do not withhold good from its owners*   [m] Cn: Heb *exalt*   [n] Heb *know*
[o] Reversing the order of the lines   [p] The meaning of the Hebrew is uncertain
3.34 (Gk): Jas 4.6; 1 Pet 5.5.

turn away from it and pass on.

16 For they cannot sleep unless they
    have done wrong;
    they are robbed of sleep unless
        they have made some one
        stumble.
17 For they eat the bread of wickedness
        and drink the wine of violence.
18 But the path of the righteous is like
        the light of dawn,
    which shines brighter and brighter
        until full day.
19 The way of the wicked is like deep
        darkness;
    they do not know over what they
        stumble.

20 My son, be attentive to my words;
    incline your ear to my sayings.
21 Let them not escape from your
        sight;
    keep them within your heart.
22 For they are life to him who finds
        them,
    and healing to all his flesh.
23 Keep your heart with all vigilance;
    for from it flow the springs of life.
24 Put away from you crooked speech,
    and put devious talk far from you.
25 Let your eyes look directly forward,
    and your gaze be straight before
        you.
26 Take heed to^q the path of your feet,
    then all your ways will be sure.
27 Do not swerve to the right or to the
        left;
    turn your foot away from evil.

5 My son, be attentive to my wisdom,
    incline your ear to my under-
        standing;
2 that you may keep discretion,
    and your lips may guard knowl-
        edge.
3 For the lips of a loose woman drip
        honey,
    and her speech^r is smoother than
        oil;
4 but in the end she is bitter as worm-
        wood,
    sharp as a two-edged sword.
5 Her feet go down to death;
    her steps follow the path to^s Shĕ′ōl;
6 she does not take heed to^t the path
        of life;
    her ways wander, and she does
        not know it.

7 And now, O sons, listen to me,

and do not depart from the words
    of my mouth.
8 Keep your way far from her,
    and do not go near the door of
        her house;
9 lest you give your honor to others
    and your years to the merciless;
10 lest strangers take their fill of your
        strength,^{u}
    and your labors go to the house
        of an alien;
11 and at the end of your life you groan,
    when your flesh and body are
        consumed,
12 and you say, "How I hated disci-
        pline,
    and my heart despised reproof!
13 I did not listen to the voice of my
        teachers
    or incline my ear to my instruc-
        tors.
14 I was at the point of utter ruin
    in the assembled congregation."

15 Drink water from your own cistern,
    flowing water from your own well.
16 Should your springs be scattered
        abroad,
    streams of water in the streets?
17 Let them be for yourself alone,
    and not for strangers with you.
18 Let your fountain be blessed,
    and rejoice in the wife of your
        youth,
19   a lovely hind, a graceful doe.
    Let her affection fill you at all times
        with delight,
    be infatuated always with her love.
20 Why should you be infatuated,
        my son, with a loose woman
    and embrace the bosom of an
        adventuress?
21 For a man's ways are before the
        eyes of the LORD,
    and he watches^v all his paths.
22 The iniquities of the wicked en-
        snare him,
    and he is caught in the toils of
        his sin.
23 He dies for lack of discipline,
    and because of his great folly he
        is lost.

6 My son, if you have become surety
    for your neighbor,
    have given your pledge for a
        stranger,
2 if you are snared in the utterance of
    your lips,^{w}

^{q} The meaning of the Hebrew word is uncertain
^{r} Heb *palate* ^{s} Heb *lay hold of*
^{t} The meaning of the Hebrew word is uncertain ^{u} Or *wealth*
^{v} The meaning of the Hebrew word is uncertain
^{w} Cn Compare Gk Syr: Heb *the words of your mouth*
4.26 (Gk): Heb 12.13.

caught in the words of your mouth;

3 then do this, my son, and save yourself,
for you have come into your neighbor's power:
go, hasten,[x] and importune your neighbor.

4 Give your eyes no sleep
and your eyelids no slumber;

5 save yourself like a gazelle from the hunter,[y]
like a bird from the hand of the fowler.

6 Go to the ant, O sluggard;
consider her ways, and be wise.

7 Without having any chief,
officer or ruler,

8 she prepares her food in summer,
and gathers her sustenance in harvest.

9 How long will you lie there, O sluggard?
When will you arise from your sleep?

10 A little sleep, a little slumber,
a little folding of the hands to rest,

11 and poverty will come upon you like a vagabond,
and want like an armed man.

12 A worthless person, a wicked man, goes about with crooked speech,

13 winks with his eyes, scrapes[z] with his feet,
points with his finger,

14 with perverted heart devises evil, continually sowing discord;

15 therefore calamity will come upon him suddenly;
in a moment he will be broken beyond healing.

16 There are six things which the LORD hates,
seven which are an abomination to him:

17 haughty eyes, a lying tongue,
and hands that shed innocent blood,

18 a heart that devises wicked plans,
feet that make haste to run to evil,

19 a false witness who breathes out lies,
and a man who sows discord among brothers.

20 My son, keep your father's commandment,
and forsake not your mother's teaching.

21 Bind them upon your heart always;
tie them about your neck.

22 When you walk, they[a] will lead you;
when you lie down, they[a] will watch over you;
and when you awake, they[a] will talk with you.

23 For the commandment is a lamp and the teaching a light,
and the reproofs of discipline are the way of life,

24 to preserve you from the evil woman,
from the smooth tongue of the adventuress.

25 Do not desire her beauty in your heart,
and do not let her capture you with her eyelashes;

26 for a harlot may be hired for a loaf of bread,[b]
but an adulteress[c] stalks a man's very life.

27 Can a man carry fire in his bosom and his clothes not be burned?

28 Or can one walk upon hot coals and his feet not be scorched?

29 So is he who goes in to his neighbor's wife;
none who touches her will go unpunished.

30 Do not men despise[d] a thief if he steals
to satisfy his appetite when he is hungry?

31 And if he is caught, he will pay sevenfold;
he will give all the goods of his house.

32 He who commits adultery has no sense;
he who does it destroys himself.

33 Wounds and dishonor will he get,
and his disgrace will not be wiped away.

34 For jealousy makes a man furious,
and he will not spare when he takes revenge.

35 He will accept no compensation,
nor be appeased though you multiply gifts.

7 My son, keep my words
and treasure up my commandments with you;

2 keep my commandments and live,
keep my teachings as the apple of your eye;

3 bind them on your fingers,

[x] Or *humble yourself*   [y] Cn: Heb *hand*   [z] Or *taps*
[a] Heb *it*
[b] Cn Compare Gk Syr Vg Tg: Heb *for because of a harlot to a piece of bread*
[c] Heb *a man's wife*   [d] Or *Men do not despise*

write them on the tablet of your
heart.
4 Say to wisdom, "You are my sister,"
and call insight your intimate
friend;
5 to preserve you from the loose
woman,
from the adventuress with her
smooth words.

6 For at the window of my house
I have looked out through my
lattice,
7 and I have seen among the simple,
I have perceived among the
youths,
a young man without sense,
8 passing along the street near her
corner,
taking the road to her house
9 in the twilight, in the evening,
at the time of night and darkness.

10 And lo, a woman meets him,
dressed as a harlot, wily of heart.*e*
11 She is loud and wayward,
her feet do not stay at home;
12 now in the street, now in the market,
and at every corner she lies in
wait.
13 She seizes him and kisses him,
and with impudent face she says
to him:
14 "I had to offer sacrifices,
and today I have paid my vows;
15 so now I have come out to meet you,
to seek you eagerly, and I have
found you.
16 I have decked my couch with
coverings,
colored spreads of Egyptian linen;
17 I have perfumed my bed with myrrh,
aloes, and cinnamon.
18 Come, let us take our fill of love till
morning;
let us delight ourselves with love.
19 For my husband is not at home;
he has gone on a long journey;
20 he took a bag of money with him;
at full moon he will come home."

21 With much seductive speech she
persuades him;
with her smooth talk she compels
him.
22 All at once he follows her,
as an ox goes to the slaughter,
or as a stag is caught fast*f*
23   till an arrow pierces its entrails;
as a bird rushes into a snare;
he does not know that it will cost
him his life.

24 And now, O sons, listen to me,
and be attentive to the words of
my mouth.
25 Let not your heart turn aside to her
ways,
do not stray into her paths;
26 for many a victim has she laid low;
yea, all her slain are a mighty host.
27 Her house is the way to Shĕ'ōl,
going down to the chambers of
death.

8 Does not wisdom call,
does not understanding raise her
voice?
2 On the heights beside the way,
in the paths she takes her stand;
3 beside the gates in front of the town,
at the entrance of the portals she
cries aloud:
4 "To you, O men, I call,
and my cry is to the sons of men.
5 O simple ones, learn prudence;
O foolish men, pay attention.
6 Hear, for I will speak noble things,
and from my lips will come what
is right;
7 for my mouth will utter truth;
wickedness is an abomination to
my lips.
8 All the words of my mouth are
righteous;
there is nothing twisted or
crooked in them.
9 They are all straight to him who
understands
and right to those who find
knowledge.
10 Take my instruction instead of
silver,
and knowledge rather than choice
gold;
11 for wisdom is better than jewels,
and all that you may desire cannot compare with her.
12 I, wisdom, dwell in prudence,*g*
and I find knowledge and discretion.
13 The fear of the Lord is hatred of evil.
Pride and arrogance and the way of
evil
and perverted speech I hate.
14 I have counsel and sound wisdom,
I have insight, I have strength.
15 By me kings reign,
and rulers decree what is just;
16 by me princes rule,
and nobles govern*h* the earth.
17 I love those who love me,
and those who seek me diligently
find me.
18 Riches and honor are with me,

e The meaning of the Hebrew is uncertain   *f* Cn Compare Gk: Heb uncertain
g Heb obscure   *h* Gk: Heb *all the governors of*
8.1-3: Prov 1.20-21.

enduring wealth and prosperity.

19 My fruit is better than gold, even
fine gold,
and my yield than choice silver.

20 I walk in the way of righteousness,
in the paths of justice,

21 endowing with wealth those who
love me,
and filling their treasuries.

22 The LORD created me at the beginning of his work,[i]
the first of his acts of old.

23 Ages ago I was set up,
at the first, before the beginning
of the earth.

24 When there were no depths I was
brought forth,
when there were no springs
abounding with water.

25 Before the mountains had been
shaped,
before the hills, I was brought
forth;

26 before he had made the earth with
its fields,[i]
or the first of the dust[i] of the
world.

27 When he established the heavens,
I was there,
when he drew a circle on the face
of the deep,

28 when he made firm the skies above,
when he established[i] the fountains of the deep,

29 when he assigned to the sea its limit,
so that the waters might not
transgress his command,
when he marked out the foundations
of the earth,

30 then I was beside him, like a
master workman;[l]
and I was daily his[m] delight,
rejoicing before him always,

31 rejoicing in his inhabited world
and delighting in the sons of men.

32 And now, my sons, listen to me:
happy are those who keep my
ways.

33 Hear instruction and be wise,
and do not neglect it.

34 Happy is the man who listens to me,
watching daily at my gates,
waiting beside my doors.

35 For he who finds me finds life
and obtains favor from the LORD;

36 but he who misses me injures himself;
all who hate me love death."

9 Wisdom has built her house,
she has set up[n] her seven pillars.

2 She has slaughtered her beasts,
she has mixed her wine,
she has also set her table.

3 She has sent out her maids to call
from the highest places in the
town,

4 "Whoever is simple, let him turn in
here!"
To him who is without sense she
says,

5 "Come, eat of my bread
and drink of the wine I have
mixed.

6 Leave simpleness,[o] and live,
and walk in the way of insight."

7 He who corrects a scoffer gets himself abuse,
and he who reproves a wicked
man incurs injury.

8 Do not reprove a scoffer, or he will
hate you;
reprove a wise man, and he will
love you.

9 Give instruction[p] to a wise man, and
he will be still wiser;
teach a righteous man and he will
increase in learning.

10 The fear of the LORD is the beginning of wisdom,
and the knowledge of the Holy
One is insight.

11 For by me your days will be multiplied,
and years will be added to your
life.

12 If you are wise, you are wise for
yourself;
if you scoff, you alone will bear it.

13 A foolish woman is noisy;
she is wanton[q] and knows no
shame.[r]

14 She sits at the door of her house,
she takes a seat on the high places
of the town,

15 calling to those who pass by,
who are going straight on their
way,

16 "Whoever is simple, let him turn
in here!"
And to him who is without sense
she says,

17 "Stolen water is sweet,
and bread eaten in secret is
pleasant."

18 But he does not know that the dead[s]
are there,

i Heb *way*   j The meaning of the Hebrew is uncertain
l Another reading is *little child*   m Gk: Heb lacks *his*   n Gk Syr Tg: Heb *hewn*
o Gk Syr Vg Tg: Heb *simple ones*   p Heb lacks *instruction*
q Cn Compare Syr Vg: The meaning of the Hebrew is uncertain
r Gk Syr: The meaning of the Hebrew is uncertain   s Heb *shades*

that her guests are in the depths of Shĕ'ōl.

10 The proverbs of Solomon.

A wise son makes a glad father,
but a foolish son is a sorrow to his mother.

2 Treasures gained by wickedness do not profit,
but righteousness delivers from death.

3 The LORD does not let the righteous go hungry,
but he thwarts the craving of the wicked.

4 A slack hand causes poverty,
but the hand of the diligent makes rich.

5 A son who gathers in summer is prudent,
but a son who sleeps in harvest brings shame.

6 Blessings are on the head of the righteous,
but the mouth of the wicked conceals violence.

7 The memory of the righteous is a blessing,
but the name of the wicked will rot.

8 The wise of heart will heed commandments,
but a prating fool will come to ruin.

9 He who walks in integrity walks securely,
but he who perverts his ways will be found out.

10 He who winks the eye causes trouble,
but he who boldly reproves makes peace.*f*

11 The mouth of the righteous is a fountain of life,
but the mouth of the wicked conceals violence.

12 Hatred stirs up strife,
but love covers all offenses.

13 On the lips of him who has understanding wisdom is found,
but a rod is for the back of him who lacks sense.

14 Wise men lay up knowledge,
but the babbling of a fool brings ruin near.

15 A rich man's wealth is his strong city;
the poverty of the poor is their ruin.

16 The wage of the righteous leads to life,
the gain of the wicked to sin.

17 He who heeds instruction is on the path to life,
but he who rejects reproof goes astray.

18 He who conceals hatred has lying lips,
and he who utters slander is a fool.

19 When words are many, transgression is not lacking,
but he who restrains his lips is prudent.

20 The tongue of the righteous is choice silver;
the mind of the wicked is of little worth.

21 The lips of the righteous feed many,
but fools die for lack of sense.

22 The blessing of the LORD makes rich,
and he adds no sorrow with it.*u*

23 It is like sport to a fool to do wrong,
but wise conduct is pleasure to a man of understanding.

24 What the wicked dreads will come upon him,
but the desire of the righteous will be granted.

25 When the tempest passes, the wicked is no more,
but the righteous is established for ever.

26 Like vinegar to the teeth, and smoke to the eyes,
so is the sluggard to those who send him.

27 The fear of the LORD prolongs life,
but the years of the wicked will be short.

28 The hope of the righteous ends in gladness,
but the expectation of the wicked comes to nought.

29 The LORD is a stronghold to him whose way is upright,
but destruction to evildoers.

30 The righteous will never be removed,
but the wicked will not dwell in the land.

31 The mouth of the righteous brings forth wisdom,
but the perverse tongue will be cut off.

32 The lips of the righteous know what is acceptable,
but the mouth of the wicked, what is perverse.

11 A false balance is an abomination to the LORD,
but a just weight is his delight.

2 When pride comes, then comes disgrace;

f Gk: Heb *but a prating fool will come to ruin*   *u* Or *and toil adds nothing to it*
10.12: Jas 5.20; 1 Pet 4.8.

but with the humble is wisdom.

3 The integrity of the upright guides
  them,
  but the crookedness of the treach-
    erous destroys them.

4 Riches do not profit in the day of
    wrath,
  but righteousness delivers from
    death.

5 The righteousness of the blameless
    keeps his way straight,
  but the wicked falls by his own
    wickedness.

6 The righteousness of the upright
    delivers them,
  but the treacherous are taken
    captive by their lust.

7 When the wicked dies, his hope
    perishes,
  and the expectation of the godless
    comes to nought.

8 The righteous is delivered from
    trouble,
  and the wicked gets into it instead.

9 With his mouth the godless man
    would destroy his neighbor,
  but by knowledge the righteous
    are delivered.

10 When it goes well with the right-
    eous, the city rejoices;
  and when the wicked perish there
    are shouts of gladness.

11 By the blessing of the upright a city
    is exalted,
  but it is overthrown by the mouth
    of the wicked.

12 He who belittles his neighbor lacks
    sense,
  but a man of understanding re-
    mains silent.

13 He who goes about as a talebearer
    reveals secrets,
  but he who is trustworthy in
    spirit keeps a thing hidden.

14 Where there is no guidance, a peo-
    ple falls;
  but in an abundance of counselors
    there is safety.

15 He who gives surety for a stranger
    will smart for it,
  but he who hates suretyship is
    secure.

16 A gracious woman gets honor,
  and violent men get riches.

17 A man who is kind benefits himself,
  but a cruel man hurts himself.

18 A wicked man earns deceptive wages,
  but one who sows righteousness
    gets a sure reward.

19 He who is steadfast in righteousness
    will live,
  but he who pursues evil will die.

20 Men of perverse mind are an abom-
    ination to the LORD,
  but those of blameless ways are
    his delight.

21 Be assured, an evil man will not go
    unpunished,
  but those who are righteous will
    be delivered.

22 Like a gold ring in a swine's snout
  is a beautiful woman without
    discretion.

23 The desire of the righteous ends
    only in good;
  the expectation of the wicked in
    wrath.

24 One man gives freely, yet grows all
    the richer;
  another withholds what he should
    give, and only suffers want.

25 A liberal man will be enriched,
  and one who waters will himself
    be watered.

26 The people curse him who holds
    back grain,
  but a blessing is on the head of
    him who sells it.

27 He who diligently seeks good seeks
    favor,
  but evil comes to him who
    searches for it.

28 He who trusts in his riches will
    wither,[v]
  but the righteous will flourish like
    a green leaf.

29 He who troubles his household will
    inherit wind,
  and the fool will be servant to the
    wise.

30 The fruit of the righteous is a tree
    of life,
  but lawlessness[w] takes away lives.

31 If the righteous is requited on earth,
  how much more the wicked and
    the sinner!

12 Whoever loves discipline loves
    knowledge,
  but he who hates reproof is
    stupid.

2 A good man obtains favor from the
    LORD,
  but a man of evil devices he
    condemns.

3 A man is not established by wicked-
    ness,
  but the root of the righteous will
    never be moved.

4 A good wife is the crown of her
    husband,
  but she who brings shame is like
    rottenness in his bones.

5 The thoughts of the righteous are
    just;

v Cn: Heb *fall*
w Cn Compare Gk Syr: Heb *a wise man*
11.31 (Gk): 1 Pet 4.18.

the counsels of the wicked are treacherous.

6 The words of the wicked lie in wait for blood,
but the mouth of the upright delivers men.

7 The wicked are overthrown and are no more,
but the house of the righteous will stand.

8 A man is commended according to his good sense,
but one of perverse mind is despised.

9 Better is a man of humble standing who works for himself
than one who plays the great man but lacks bread.

10 A righteous man has regard for the life of his beast,
but the mercy of the wicked is cruel.

11 He who tills his land will have plenty of bread,
but he who follows worthless pursuits has no sense.

12 The strong tower of the wicked comes to ruin,
but the root of the righteous stands firm.^{x}

13 An evil man is ensnared by the transgression of his lips,
but the righteous escapes from trouble.

14 From the fruit of his words a man is satisfied with good,
and the work of a man's hand comes back to him.

15 The way of a fool is right in his own eyes,
but a wise man listens to advice.

16 The vexation of a fool is known at once,
but the prudent man ignores an insult.

17 He who speaks the truth gives honest evidence,
but a false witness utters deceit.

18 There is one whose rash words are like sword thrusts,
but the tongue of the wise brings healing.

19 Truthful lips endure for ever,
but a lying tongue is but for a moment.

20 Deceit is in the heart of those who devise evil,
but those who plan good have joy.

21 No ill befalls the righteous,
but the wicked are filled with trouble.

22 Lying lips are an abomination to the LORD,
but those who act faithfully are his delight.

23 A prudent man conceals his knowledge,
but fools^y proclaim their folly.

24 The hand of the diligent will rule,
while the slothful will be put to forced labor.

25 Anxiety in a man's heart weighs him down,
but a good word makes him glad.

26 A righteous man turns away from evil,^{z}
but the way of the wicked leads them astray.

27 A slothful man will not catch his prey,^{a}
but the diligent man will get precious wealth.^{b}

28 In the path of righteousness is life,
but the way of error leads to death.^{c}

13 A wise son hears his father's instruction,
but a scoffer does not listen to rebuke.

2 From the fruit of his mouth a good man eats good,
but the desire of the treacherous is for violence.

3 He who guards his mouth preserves his life;
he who opens wide his lips comes to ruin.

4 The soul of the sluggard craves, and gets nothing,
while the soul of the diligent is richly supplied.

5 A righteous man hates falsehood,
but a wicked man acts shamefully and disgracefully.

6 Righteousness guards him whose way is upright,
but sin overthrows the wicked.

7 One man pretends to be rich, yet has nothing;
another pretends to be poor, yet has great wealth.

8 The ransom of a man's life is his wealth,
but a poor man has no means of redemption.^{d}

9 The light of the righteous rejoices,
but the lamp of the wicked will be put out.

x Cn: The Hebrew of verse 12 is obscure y Heb *the heart of fools*
z Cn: The meaning of the Hebrew is uncertain
a Cn Compare Gk Syr: The meaning of the Hebrew is uncertain
b Cn: The meaning of the Hebrew is uncertain
c Cn: The meaning of the Hebrew is uncertain
d Cn: Heb *does not hear rebuke*

10 By insolence the heedless make strife,
   but with those who take advice is wisdom.

11 Wealth hastily gotten[e] will dwindle,
   but he who gathers little by little will increase it.

12 Hope deferred makes the heart sick,
   but a desire fulfilled is a tree of life.

13 He who despises the word brings destruction on himself,
   but he who respects the commandment will be rewarded.

14 The teaching of the wise is a fountain of life,
   that one may avoid the snares of death.

15 Good sense wins favor,
   but the way of the faithless is their ruin.[f]

16 In everything a prudent man acts with knowledge,
   but a fool flaunts his folly.

17 A bad messenger plunges men into trouble,
   but a faithful envoy brings healing.

18 Poverty and disgrace come to him who ignores instruction,
   but he who heeds reproof is honored.

19 A desire fulfilled is sweet to the soul;
   but to turn away from evil is an abomination to fools.

20 He who walks with wise men becomes wise,
   but the companion of fools will suffer harm.

21 Misfortune pursues sinners,
   but prosperity rewards the righteous.

22 A good man leaves an inheritance to his children's children,
   but the sinner's wealth is laid up for the righteous.

23 The fallow ground of the poor yields much food,
   but it is swept away through injustice.

24 He who spares the rod hates his son,
   but he who loves him is diligent to discipline him.

25 The righteous has enough to satisfy his appetite,
   but the belly of the wicked suffers want.

14 Wisdom[g] builds her house,
   but folly with her own hands tears it down.

2 He who walks in uprightness fears the LORD,
   but he who is devious in his ways despises him.

3 The talk of a fool is a rod for his back,[h]
   but the lips of the wise will preserve them.

4 Where there are no oxen, there is no[i] grain;
   but abundant crops come by the strength of the ox.

5 A faithful witness does not lie,
   but a false witness breathes out lies.

6 A scoffer seeks wisdom in vain,
   but knowledge is easy for a man of understanding.

7 Leave the presence of a fool,
   for there you do not meet words of knowledge.

8 The wisdom of a prudent man is to discern his way,
   but the folly of fools is deceiving.

9 God scorns the wicked,[j]
   but the upright enjoy his favor.

10 The heart knows its own bitterness,
   and no stranger shares its joy.

11 The house of the wicked will be destroyed,
   but the tent of the upright will flourish.

12 There is a way which seems right to a man,
   but its end is the way to death.[k]

13 Even in laughter the heart is sad,
   and the end of joy is grief.

14 A perverse man will be filled with the fruit of his ways,
   and a good man with the fruit of his deeds.[l]

15 The simple believes everything,
   but the prudent looks where he is going.

16 A wise man is cautious and turns away from evil,
   but a fool throws off restraint and is careless.

17 A man of quick temper acts foolishly,
   but a man of discretion is patient.[m]

18 The simple acquire folly,
   but the prudent are crowned with knowledge.

19 The evil bow down before the good,
   the wicked at the gates of the righteous.

20 The poor is disliked even by his neighbor,
   but the rich has many friends.

---

e Gk Vg: Heb *from vanity*   *f* Cn Compare Gk Syr Vg Tg: Heb *is enduring*
g Heb *Wisdom of women*   *h* Cn: Heb *a rod of pride*   *i* Cn: Heb *a manger of*
l Cn: Heb *obscure*   *k* Heb *ways of death*   *l* Cn: Heb *from upon him*
m Gk: Heb *is hated*

21 He who despises his neighbor is a
  sinner,
  but happy is he who is kind to
  the poor.
22 Do they not err that devise evil?
  Those who devise good meet
  loyalty and faithfulness.
23 In all toil there is profit,
  but mere talk tends only to want.
24 The crown of the wise is their
  wisdom,[n]
  but folly is the garland[o] of fools.
25 A truthful witness saves lives,
  but one who utters lies is a betrayer.
26 In the fear of the LORD one has
  strong confidence,
  and his children will have a
  refuge.
27 The fear of the LORD is a fountain
  of life,
  that one may avoid the snares of
  death.
28 In a multitude of people is the glory
  of a king,
  but without people a prince is
  ruined.
29 He who is slow to anger has great
  understanding,
  but he who has a hasty temper
  exalts folly.
30 A tranquil mind gives life to the
  flesh,
  but passion makes the bones
  rot.
31 He who oppresses a poor man insults his Maker,
  but he who is kind to the needy
  honors him.
32 The wicked is overthrown through
  his evil-doing,
  but the righteous finds refuge
  through his integrity.[p]
33 Wisdom abides in the mind of a man
  of understanding,
  but it is not[q] known in the heart
  of fools.
34 Righteousness exalts a nation,
  but sin is a reproach to any
  people.
35 A servant who deals wisely has the
  king's favor,
  but his wrath falls on one who
  acts shamefully.

15 A soft answer turns away
    wrath,
    but a harsh word stirs up anger.
2 The tongue of the wise dispenses
  knowledge,[r]
  but the mouths of fools pour out
  folly.
3 The eyes of the LORD are in every
  place,

keeping watch on the evil and the
  good.
4 A gentle tongue is a tree of life,
  but perverseness in it breaks the
  spirit.
5 A fool despises his father's instruction,
  but he who heeds admonition is
  prudent.
6 In the house of the righteous there
  is much treasure,
  but trouble befalls the income of
  the wicked.
7 The lips of the wise spread knowledge;
  not so the minds of fools.
8 The sacrifice of the wicked is an
  abomination to the LORD,
  but the prayer of the upright is
  his delight.
9 The way of the wicked is an
  abomination to the LORD,
  but he loves him who pursues
  righteousness.
10 There is severe discipline for him
  who forsakes the way;
  he who hates reproof will die.
11 Shē'ōl and Ă·bad'don lie open before the LORD,
  how much more the hearts of
  men!
12 A scoffer does not like to be reproved;
  he will not go to the wise.
13 A glad heart makes a cheerful
  countenance,
  but by sorrow of heart the spirit
  is broken.
14 The mind of him who has understanding seeks knowledge,
  but the mouths of fools feed on
  folly.
15 All the days of the afflicted are evil,
  but a cheerful heart has a continual feast.
16 Better is a little with the fear of the
  LORD
  than great treasure and trouble
  with it.
17 Better is a dinner of herbs where
  love is
  than a fatted ox and hatred with
  it.
18 A hot-tempered man stirs up strife,
  but he who is slow to anger quiets
  contention.
19 The way of a sluggard is overgrown
  with thorns,
  but the path of the upright is a
  level highway.
20 A wise son makes a glad father,
  but a foolish man despises his
  mother.

[n] Cn Compare Gk: Heb *riches*   [o] Cn: Heb *folly*   [p] Gk Syr: Heb *in his death*
[q] Gk Syr: Heb lacks *not*   [r] Cn: Heb *makes knowledge good*

21 Folly is a joy to him who has no sense,
   but a man of understanding walks aright.

22 Without counsel plans go wrong,
   but with many advisers they succeed.

23 To make an apt answer is a joy to a man,
   and a word in season, how good it is!

24 The wise man's path leads upward to life,
   that he may avoid Shē′ōl beneath.

25 The LORD tears down the house of the proud,
   but maintains the widow's boundaries.

26 The thoughts of the wicked are an abomination to the LORD,
   the words of the pure are pleasing to him.[s]

27 He who is greedy for unjust gain makes trouble for his household,
   but he who hates bribes will live.

28 The mind of the righteous ponders how to answer,
   but the mouth of the wicked pours out evil things.

29 The LORD is far from the wicked,
   but he hears the prayer of the righteous.

30 The light of the eyes rejoices the heart,
   and good news refreshes[t] the bones.

31 He whose ear heeds wholesome admonition
   will abide among the wise.

32 He who ignores instruction despises himself,
   but he who heeds admonition gains understanding.

33 The fear of the LORD is instruction in wisdom,
   and humility goes before honor.

16 The plans of the mind belong to man,
   but the answer of the tongue is from the LORD.

2 All the ways of a man are pure in his own eyes,
   but the LORD weighs the spirit.

3 Commit your work to the LORD,
   and your plans will be established.

4 The LORD has made everything for its purpose,
   even the wicked for the day of trouble.

5 Every one who is arrogant is an abomination to the LORD;

be assured, he will not go unpunished.

6 By loyalty and faithfulness iniquity is atoned for,
   and by the fear of the LORD a man avoids evil.

7 When a man's ways please the LORD,
   he makes even his enemies to be at peace with him.

8 Better is a little with righteousness than great revenues with injustice.

9 A man's mind plans his way,
   but the LORD directs his steps.

10 Inspired decisions are on the lips of a king;
   his mouth does not sin in judgment.

11 A just balance and scales are the LORD's;
   all the weights in the bag are his work.

12 It is an abomination to kings to do evil,
   for the throne is established by righteousness.

13 Righteous lips are the delight of a king,
   and he loves him who speaks what is right.

14 A king's wrath is a messenger of death,
   and a wise man will appease it.

15 In the light of a king's face there is life,
   and his favor is like the clouds that bring the spring rain.

16 To get wisdom is better[u] than gold;
   to get understanding is to be chosen rather than silver.

17 The highway of the upright turns aside from evil;
   he who guards his way preserves his life.

18 Pride goes before destruction,
   and a haughty spirit before a fall.

19 It is better to be of a lowly spirit with the poor
   than to divide the spoil with the proud.

20 He who gives heed to the word will prosper,
   and happy is he who trusts in the LORD.

21 The wise of heart is called a man of discernment,
   and pleasant speech increases persuasiveness.

22 Wisdom is a fountain of life to him who has it,
   but folly is the chastisement of fools.

23 The mind of the wise makes his speech judicious,

---

[s] Cn Compare Gk: Heb *pleasant words are pure*   [t] Heb *makes fat*
[u] Gk Syr Vg Tg: Heb *how much better*

and adds persuasiveness to his lips.

24 Pleasant words are like a honey-comb,
    sweetness to the soul and health to the body.

25 There is a way which seems right to a man,
    but its end is the way to death.*v*

26 A worker's appetite works for him;
    his mouth urges him on.

27 A worthless man plots evil,
    and his speech is like a scorching fire.

28 A perverse man spreads strife,
    and a whisperer separates close friends.

29 A man of violence entices his neighbor
    and leads him in a way that is not good.

30 He who winks his eyes plans*w* per-verse things,
    he who compresses his lips brings evil to pass.

31 A hoary head is a crown of glory;
    it is gained in a righteous life.

32 He who is slow to anger is better than the mighty,
    and he who rules his spirit than he who takes a city.

33 The lot is cast into the lap,
    but the decision is wholly from the LORD.

17 Better is a dry morsel with quiet
    than a house full of feasting with strife.

2 A slave who deals wisely will rule over a son who acts shamefully,
    and will share the inheritance as one of the brothers.

3 The crucible is for silver, and the furnace is for gold,
    and the LORD tries hearts.

4 An evildoer listens to wicked lips;
    and a liar gives heed to a mis-chievous tongue.

5 He who mocks the poor insults his Maker;
    he who is glad at calamity will not go unpunished.

6 Grandchildren are the crown of the aged,
    and the glory of sons is their fathers.

7 Fine speech is not becoming to a fool;
    still less is false speech to a prince.

8 A bribe is like a magic stone in the eyes of him who gives it;
    wherever he turns he prospers.

9 He who forgives an offense seeks love,
    but he who repeats a matter alienates a friend.

10 A rebuke goes deeper into a man of understanding
    than a hundred blows into a fool.

11 An evil man seeks only rebellion,
    and a cruel messenger will be sent against him.

12 Let a man meet a she-bear robbed of her cubs,
    rather than a fool in his folly.

13 If a man returns evil for good,
    evil will not depart from his house.

14 The beginning of strife is like let-ting out water;
    so quit before the quarrel breaks out.

15 He who justifies the wicked and he who condemns the righteous
    are both alike an abomination to the LORD.

16 Why should a fool have a price in his hand to buy wisdom,
    when he has no mind?

17 A friend loves at all times,
    and a brother is born for adversity.

18 A man without sense gives a pledge,
    and becomes surety in the pres-ence of his neighbor.

19 He who loves transgression loves strife;
    he who makes his door high seeks destruction.

20 A man of crooked mind does not prosper,
    and one with a perverse tongue falls into calamity.

21 A stupid son is a grief to a father;
    and the father of a fool has no joy.

22 A cheerful heart is a good medicine,
    but a downcast spirit dries up the bones.

23 A wicked man accepts a bribe from the bosom
    to pervert the ways of justice.

24 A man of understanding sets his face toward wisdom,
    but the eyes of a fool are on the ends of the earth.

25 A foolish son is a grief to his father
    and bitterness to her who bore him.

26 To impose a fine on a righteous man is not good;
    to flog noble men is wrong.

27 He who restrains his words has knowledge,
    and he who has a cool spirit is a man of understanding.

28 Even a fool who keeps silent is con-sidered wise;
    when he closes his lips, he is deemed intelligent.

v Heb *ways of death*   *w* Gk Syr Vg Tg: Heb *to plan*

18 He who is estranged^x seeks pretexts^y
   to break out against all sound judgment.

2 A fool takes no pleasure in understanding,
   but only in expressing his opinion.

3 When wickedness comes, contempt comes also;
   and with dishonor comes disgrace.

4 The words of a man's mouth are deep waters;
   the fountain of wisdom is a gushing stream.

5 It is not good to be partial to a wicked man,
   or to deprive a righteous man of justice.

6 A fool's lips bring strife,
   and his mouth invites a flogging.

7 A fool's mouth is his ruin,
   and his lips are a snare to himself.

8 The words of a whisperer are like delicious morsels;
   they go down into the inner parts of the body.

9 He who is slack in his work
   is a brother to him who destroys.

10 The name of the LORD is a strong tower;
   the righteous man runs into it and is safe.

11 A rich man's wealth is his strong city,
   and like a high wall protecting him.^z

12 Before destruction a man's heart is haughty,
   but humility goes before honor.

13 If one gives answer before he hears,
   it is his folly and shame.

14 A man's spirit will endure sickness;
   but a broken spirit who can bear?

15 An intelligent mind acquires knowledge,
   and the ear of the wise seeks knowledge.

16 A man's gift makes room for him
   and brings him before great men.

17 He who states his case first seems right,
   until the other comes and examines him.

18 The lot puts an end to disputes
   and decides between powerful contenders.

19 A brother helped is like a strong city,^a
   but quarreling is like the bars of a castle.

20 From the fruit of his mouth a man is satisfied;
   he is satisfied by the yield of his lips.

21 Death and life are in the power of the tongue,
   and those who love it will eat its fruits.

22 He who finds a wife finds a good thing,
   and obtains favor from the LORD.

23 The poor use entreaties,
   but the rich answer roughly.

24 There are^b friends who pretend to be friends,^c
   but there is a friend who sticks closer than a brother.

19 Better is a poor man who walks in his integrity
   than a man who is perverse in speech, and is a fool.

2 It is not good for a man to be without knowledge,
   and he who makes haste with his feet misses his way.

3 When a man's folly brings his way to ruin,
   his heart rages against the LORD.

4 Wealth brings many new friends,
   but a poor man is deserted by his friend.

5 A false witness will not go unpunished,
   and he who utters lies will not escape.

6 Many seek the favor of a generous man,
   and every one is a friend to a man who gives gifts.

7 All a poor man's brothers hate him;
   how much more do his friends go far from him!
He pursues them with words, but does not have them.^d

8 He who gets wisdom loves himself;
   he who keeps understanding will prosper.

9 A false witness will not go unpunished,
   and he who utters lies will perish.

10 It is not fitting for a fool to live in luxury,
   much less for a slave to rule over princes.

11 Good sense makes a man slow to anger,
   and it is his glory to overlook an offense.

12 A king's wrath is like the growling of a lion,
   but his favor is like dew upon the grass.

13 A foolish son is ruin to his father,

---

^x Heb *separated*   ^y Gk Vg: Heb *desire*   ^z Or *in his imagination*
^a Gk Syr Vg Tg: The meaning of the Hebrew is uncertain   ^b Syr Tg: Heb *A man of*
^c Cn Compare Syr Vg Tg: Heb *to be broken*   ^d Heb uncertain

and a wife's quarreling is a continual dripping of rain.

14 House and wealth are inherited from fathers,
    but a prudent wife is from the LORD.

15 Slothfulness casts into a deep sleep,
    and an idle person will suffer hunger.

16 He who keeps the commandment keeps his life;
    he who despises the word^e will die.

17 He who is kind to the poor lends to the LORD,
    and he will repay him for his deed.

18 Discipline your son while there is hope;
    do not set your heart on his destruction.

19 A man of great wrath will pay the penalty;
    for if you deliver him, you will only have to do it again.^f

20 Listen to advice and accept instruction,
    that you may gain wisdom for the future.

21 Many are the plans in the mind of a man,
    but it is the purpose of the LORD that will be established.

22 What is desired in a man is loyalty,
    and a poor man is better than a liar.

23 The fear of the LORD leads to life;
    and he who has it rests satisfied;
    he will not be visited by harm.

24 The sluggard buries his hand in the dish,
    and will not even bring it back to his mouth.

25 Strike a scoffer, and the simple will learn prudence;
    reprove a man of understanding, and he will gain knowledge.

26 He who does violence to his father and chases away his mother
    is a son who causes shame and brings reproach.

27 Cease, my son, to hear instruction only to stray from the words of knowledge.

28 A worthless witness mocks at justice,
    and the mouth of the wicked devours iniquity.

29 Condemnation is ready for scoffers,
    and flogging for the backs of fools.

20 Wine is a mocker, strong drink a brawler;
    and whoever is led astray by it is not wise.

2 The dread wrath of a king is like the growling of a lion;
    he who provokes him to anger forfeits his life.

3 It is an honor for a man to keep aloof from strife;
    but every fool will be quarreling.

4 The sluggard does not plow in the autumn;
    he will seek at harvest and have nothing.

5 The purpose in a man's mind is like deep water,
    but a man of understanding will draw it out.

6 Many a man proclaims his own loyalty,
    but a faithful man who can find?

7 A righteous man who walks in his integrity—
    blessed are his sons after him!

8 A king who sits on the throne of judgment
    winnows all evil with his eyes.

9 Who can say, "I have made my heart clean;
    I am pure from my sin"?

10 Diverse weights and diverse measures
    are both alike an abomination to the LORD.

11 Even a child makes himself known by his acts,
    whether what he does is pure and right.

12 The hearing ear and the seeing eye,
    the LORD has made them both.

13 Love not sleep, lest you come to poverty;
    open your eyes, and you will have plenty of bread.

14 "It is bad, it is bad," says the buyer;
    but when he goes away, then he boasts.

15 There is gold, and abundance of costly stones;
    but the lips of knowledge are a precious jewel.

16 Take a man's garment when he has given surety for a stranger,
    and hold him in pledge when he gives surety for foreigners.

17 Bread gained by deceit is sweet to a man,
    but afterward his mouth will be full of gravel.

18 Plans are established by counsel;
    by wise guidance wage war.

19 He who goes about gossiping reveals secrets;
    therefore do not associate with one who speaks foolishly.

20 If one curses his father or his mother,

^e Cn Compare 13.13: Heb *his ways*   ^f Heb obscure

his lamp will be put out in utter
darkness.

21 An inheritance gotten hastily in the
beginning
will in the end not be blessed.

22 Do not say, "I will repay evil";
wait for the LORD, and he will
help you.

23 Diverse weights are an abomination
to the LORD,
and false scales are not good.

24 A man's steps are ordered by the
LORD;
how then can man understand
his way?

25 It is a snare for a man to say rashly,
"It is holy,"
and to reflect only after making
his vows.

26 A wise king winnows the wicked,
and drives the wheel over them.

27 The spirit of man is the lamp of the
LORD,
searching all his innermost parts.

28 Loyalty and faithfulness preserve
the king,
and his throne is upheld by righteousness.*g*

29 The glory of young men is their
strength,
but the beauty of old men is their
gray hair.

30 Blows that wound cleanse away evil;
strokes make clean the innermost
parts.

21 The king's heart is a stream of
water in the hand of the LORD;
he turns it wherever he will.

2 Every way of a man is right in his
own eyes,
but the LORD weighs the heart.

3 To do righeousness and justice
is more acceptable to the LORD
than sacrifice.

4 Haughty eyes and a proud heart,
the lamp of the wicked, are sin.

5 The plans of the diligent lead surely
to abundance,
but every one who is hasty comes
only to want.

6 The getting of treasures by a lying
tongue
is a fleeting vapor and a snare of
death.

7 The violence of the wicked will
sweep them away,
because they refuse to do what
is just.

8 The way of the guilty is crooked,
but the conduct of the pure is
right.

9 It is better to live in a corner of the
housetop

than in a house shared with a
contentious woman.

10 The soul of the wicked desires evil;
his neighbor finds no mercy in
his eyes.

11 When a scoffer is punished, the
simple becomes wise;
when a wise man is instructed, he
gains knowledge.

12 The righteous observes the house
of the wicked;
the wicked are cast down to ruin.

13 He who closes his ear to the cry of
the poor
will himself cry out and not be
heard.

14 A gift in secret averts anger;
and a bribe in the bosom, strong
wrath.

15 When justice is done, it is a joy to
the righteous,
but dismay to evildoers.

16 A man who wanders from the way
of understanding
will rest in the assembly of the
dead.

17 He who loves pleasure will be a
poor man;
he who loves wine and oil will
not be rich.

18 The wicked is a ransom for the
righteous,
and the faithless for the upright.

19 It is better to live in a desert land
than with a contentious and fret-
ful woman.

20 Precious treasure remains*h* in a
wise man's dwelling,
but a foolish man devours it.

21 He who pursues righteousness and
kindness
will find life*i* and honor.

22 A wise man scales the city of the
mighty
and brings down the stronghold
in which they trust.

23 He who keeps his mouth and his
tongue
keeps himself out of trouble.

24 "Scoffer" is the name of the proud,
haughty man
who acts with arrogant pride.

25 The desire of the sluggard kills him
for his hands refuse to labor.

26 All day long the wicked covets,*j*
but the righteous gives and does
not hold back.

27 The sacrifice of the wicked is an
abomination;
how much more when he brings
it with evil intent.

28 A false witness will perish,

g Gk: Heb *loyalty*   *h* Gk: Heb *and oil*   *i* Gk: Heb *life and righteousness*
j Gk: Heb *all day long he covets covetously*

but the word of a man who hears
will endure.

29 A wicked man puts on a bold face,
but an upright man considers[k]
his ways.

30 No wisdom, no understanding, no
counsel,
can avail against the LORD.

31 The horse is made ready for the day
of battle,
but the victory belongs to the
LORD.

22 A good name is to be chosen
rather than great riches,
and favor is better than silver or
gold.

2 The rich and the poor meet together;
the LORD is the maker of them all.

3 A prudent man sees danger and
hides himself;
but the simple go on, and suffer
for it.

4 The reward for humility and fear of
the LORD
is riches and honor and life.

5 Thorns and snares are in the way of
the perverse;
he who guards himself will keep
far from them.

6 Train up a child in the way he
should go,
and when he is old he will not
depart from it.

7 The rich rules over the poor,
and the borrower is the slave of
the lender.

8 He who sows injustice will reap
calamity,
and the rod of his fury will fail.

9 He who has a bountiful eye will be
blessed,
for he shares his bread with the
poor.

10 Drive out a scoffer, and strife will
go out,
and quarreling and abuse will
cease.

11 He who loves purity of heart,
and whose speech is gracious,
will have the king as his friend.

12 The eyes of the LORD keep watch
over knowledge,
but he overthrows the words of
the faithless.

13 The sluggard says, "There is a lion
outside!
I shall be slain in the streets!"

14 The mouth of a loose woman is a
deep pit;
he with whom the LORD is angry
will fall into it.

15 Folly is bound up in the heart of a
child,

but the rod of discipline drives it
far from him.

16 He who oppresses the poor to increase his own wealth,
or gives to the rich, will only
come to want.

17 Incline your ear, and hear the words
of the wise,
and apply your mind to my
knowledge;

18 for it will be pleasant if you keep
them within you,
if all of them are ready on your
lips.

19 That your trust may be in the LORD,
I have made them known to you
today, even to you.

20 Have I not written for you thirty
sayings
of admonition and knowledge,

21 to show you what is right and true,
that you may give a true answer
to those who sent you?

22 Do not rob the poor, because he is
poor,
or crush the afflicted at the gate;

23 for the LORD will plead their cause
and despoil of life those who
despoil them.

24 Make no friendship with a man
given to anger,
nor go with a wrathful man,

25 lest you learn his ways
and entangle yourself in a snare.

26 Be not one of those who give pledges,
who become surety for debts.

27 If you have nothing with which to
pay,
why should your bed be taken
from under you?

28 Remove not the ancient landmark
which your fathers have set.

29 Do you see a man skilful in his
work?
he will stand before kings;
he will not stand before obscure
men.

23 When you sit down to eat with
a ruler,
observe carefully what[l] is before
you;

2 and put a knife to your throat
if you are a man given to appetite.

3 Do not desire his delicacies,
for they are deceptive food.

4 Do not toil to acquire wealth;
be wise enough to desist.

5 When your eyes light upon it, it is
gone;

[k] Another reading is *establishes* [l] Or *who*
22.8 (Gk): 1 Cor 9.7.

for suddenly it takes to itself
   wings,
flying like an eagle toward heaven.
6 Do not eat the bread of a man who
   is stingy;
do not desire his delicacies;
7 for he is like one who is inwardly
   reckoning.*m*
"Eat and drink!" he says to you;
but his heart is not with you.
8 You will vomit up the morsels
   which you have eaten,
and waste your pleasant words.
9 Do not speak in the hearing of a
   fool,
for he will despise the wisdom of
   your words.
10 Do not remove an ancient landmark
or enter the fields of the fatherless;
11 for their Redeemer is strong;
he will plead their cause against
   you.
12 Apply your mind to instruction
and your ear to words of knowledge.
13 Do not withhold discipline from a
   child;
if you beat him with a rod, he
   will not die.
14 If you beat him with the rod
you will save his life from Shē'ōl.
15 My son, if your heart is wise,
my heart too will be glad.
16 My soul will rejoice
when your lips speak what is
   right.
17 Let not your heart envy sinners,
but continue in the fear of the
   LORD all the day.
18 Surely there is a future,
and your hope will not be cut off.

19 Hear, my son, and be wise,
and direct your mind in the way.
20 Be not among winebibbers,
or among gluttonous eaters of
   meat;
21 for the drunkard and the glutton
will come to poverty,
and drowsiness will clothe a man
   with rags.

22 Hearken to your father who begot
   you,
and do not despise your mother
   when she is old.
23 Buy truth, and do not sell it;
buy wisdom, instruction, and
   understanding.
24 The father of the righteous will
   greatly rejoice;
he who begets a wise son will be
   glad in him.

25 Let your father and mother be glad,
let her who bore you rejoice.

26 My son, give me your heart,
and let your eyes observe*n* my ways.
27 For a harlot is a deep pit;
an adventuress is a narrow well.
28 She lies in wait like a robber
and increases the faithless among
   men.

29 Who has woe? Who has sorrow?
Who has strife? Who has com-
   plaining?
Who has wounds without cause?
Who has redness of eyes?
30 Those who tarry long over wine,
those who go to try mixed wine.
31 Do not look at wine when it is red,
when it sparkles in the cup
and goes down smoothly.
32 At the last it bites like a serpent,
and stings like an adder.
33 Your eyes will see strange things,
and your mind utter perverse
   things.
34 You will be like one who lies down
in the midst of the sea,
like one who lies on the top of a
   mast.*o*
35 "They struck me," you will say,*p*
"but I was not hurt;
they beat me, but I did not feel it.
When shall I awake?
I will seek another drink."

24 Be not envious of evil men,
   nor desire to be with them;
2 for their minds devise violence,
and their lips talk of mischief.

3 By wisdom a house is built,
and by understanding it is established;
4 by knowledge the rooms are filled
with all precious and pleasant
   riches.
5 A wise man is mightier than a
   strong man,*q*
and a man of knowledge than he
   who has strength;
6 for by wise guidance you can wage
   your war,
and in abundance of counselors
   there is victory.
7 Wisdom is too high for a fool;
in the gate he does not open his
   mouth.

8 He who plans to do evil
will be called a mischief-maker.
9 The devising of folly is sin,
and the scoffer is an abomination
   to men.

m Heb obscure   *n* Another reading is *delight in*   *o* Heb obscure
p Gk Syr Vg Tg: Heb lacks *you will say*   *q* Gk Compare Syr Tg: Heb *is in strength*

10 If you faint in the day of adversity,
 your strength is small.
11 Rescue those who are being taken
 away to death;
 hold back those who are stumbling
 to the slaughter.
12 If you say, "Behold, we did not
 know this,"
 does not he who weighs the heart
 perceive it?
 Does not he who keeps watch over
 your soul know it,
 and will he not requite man according to his work?

13 My son, eat honey, for it is good,
 and the drippings of the honeycomb are sweet to your taste.
14 Know that wisdom is such to your
 soul;
 if you find it, there will be a
 future,
 and your hope will not be cut off.

15 Lie not in wait as a wicked man
 against the dwelling of the
 righteous;
 do not violence to his home;
16 for a righteous man falls seven
 times, and rises again;
 but the wicked are overthrown by
 calamity.

17 Do not rejoice when your enemy
 falls,
 and let not your heart be glad
 when he stumbles;
18 lest the LORD see it, and be displeased,
 and turn away his anger from
 him.

19 Fret not yourself because of evildoers,
 and be not envious of the wicked;
20 for the evil man has no future;
 the lamp of the wicked will be
 put out.

21 My son, fear the LORD and the king,
 and do not disobey either of
 them;*r*
22 for disaster from them will rise
 suddenly,
 and who knows the ruin that will
 come from them both?

23 These also are sayings of the wise.

 Partiality in judging is not good.
24 He who says to the wicked, "You
 are innocent,"
 will be cursed by peoples, abhorred by nations;

25 but those who rebuke the wicked
 will have delight,
 and a good blessing will be upon
 them.
26 He who gives a right answer
 kisses the lips.

27 Prepare your work outside,
 get everything ready for you in
 the field;
 and after that build your house.

28 Be not a witness against your
 neighbor without cause,
 and do not deceive with your lips.
29 Do not say, "I will do to him as he
 has done to me;
 I will pay the man back for what
 he has done."

30 I passed by the field of a sluggard,
 by the vineyard of a man without
 sense;
31 and lo, it was all overgrown with
 thorns;
 the ground was covered with
 nettles,
 and its stone wall was broken
 down.
32 Then I saw and considered it;
 I looked and received instruction.
33 A little sleep, a little slumber,
 a little folding of the hands to
 rest,
34 and poverty will come upon you
 like a robber,
 and want like an armed man.

25 These also are proverbs of
 Solomon which the men of Hez-
 e·ki′ah king of Judah copied.

2 It is the glory of God to conceal
 things,
 but the glory of kings is to search
 things out.
3 As the heavens for height, and the
 earth for depth,
 so the mind of kings is unsearchable.
4 Take away the dross from the silver,
 and the smith has material for a
 vessel;
5 take away the wicked from the
 presence of the king,
 and his throne will be established
 in righteousness.
6 Do not put yourself forward in the
 king's presence
 or stand in the place of the great;
7 for it is better to be told, "Come up
 here,"
 than to be put lower in the
 presence of the prince.

r Gk: Heb *do not associate with those who change*

What your eyes have seen

8 do not hastily bring into court;
for⁵ what will you do in the end,
when your neighbor puts you to
shame?

9 Argue your case with your neighbor
himself,
and do not disclose another's
secret;

10 lest he who hears you bring shame
upon you,
and your ill repute have no end.

11 A word fitly spoken
is like apples of gold in a setting
of silver.

12 Like a gold ring or an ornament of
gold
is a wise reprover to a listening
ear.

13 Like the cold of snow in the time of
harvest
is a faithful messenger to those
who send him,
he refreshes the spirit of his
masters.

14 Like clouds and wind without rain
is a man who boasts of a gift he
does not give.

15 With patience a ruler may be persuaded,
and a soft tongue will break a
bone.

16 If you have found honey, eat only
enough for you,
lest you be sated with it and
vomit it.

17 Let your foot be seldom in your
neighbor's house,
lest he become weary of you and
hate you.

18 A man who bears false witness
against his neighbor
is like a war club, or a sword, or
a sharp arrow.

19 Trust in a faithless man in time of
trouble
is like a bad tooth or a foot that
slips.

20 He who sings songs to a heavy heart
is like one who takes off a garment
on a cold day,
and like vinegar on a wound.ᵗ

21 If your enemy is hungry, give him
bread to eat;
and if he is thirsty, give him water
to drink;

22 for you will heap coals of fire on his
head,
and the LORD will reward you.

23 The north wind brings forth rain;
and a backbiting tongue, angry
looks.

24 It is better to live in a corner of the
housetop
than in a house shared with a
contentious woman.

25 Like cold water to a thirsty soul,
so is good news from a far country.

26 Like a muddied spring or a polluted
fountain
is a righteous man who gives way
before the wicked.

27 It is not good to eat much honey,
so be sparing of complimentary
words.ᵘ

28 A man without self-control
is like a city broken into and left
without walls.

26 Like snow in summer or rain
in harvest,
so honor is not fitting for a fool.

2 Like a sparrow in its flitting, like a
swallow in its flying,
a curse that is causeless does not
alight.

3 A whip for the horse, a bridle for
the ass,
and a rod for the back of fools.

4 Answer not a fool according to his
folly,
lest you be like him yourself.

5 Answer a fool according to his folly,
lest he be wise in his own eyes.

6 He who sends a message by the
hand of a fool
cuts off his own feet and drinks
violence.

7 Like a lame man's legs, which hang
useless,
is a proverb in the mouth of fools.

8 Like one who binds the stone in
the sling
is he who gives honor to a fool.

9 Like a thorn that goes up into the
hand of a drunkard
is a proverb in the mouth of fools.

10 Like an archer who wounds every-
body
is he who hires a passing fool or
drunkard.ᵛ

11 Like a dog that returns to his vomit
is a fool that repeats his folly.

12 Do you see a man who is wise in
his own eyes?
There is more hope for a fool than
for him.

13 The sluggard says, "There is a lion
in the road!
There is a lion in the streets!"

14 As a door turns on its hinges,

---

⁵ Cn: Heb *lest*   ᵗ Gk: Heb *lye*
ᵘ Cn Compare Gk Syr Tg: Heb *searching out their glory is glory*
ᵛ The Hebrew text of this verse is uncertain
25.21-22: Rom 12.20.   **26.11:** 2 Pet 2.22.

so does a sluggard on his bed.

15 The sluggard buries his hand in the
   dish;
   it wears him out to bring it back
      to his mouth.

16 The sluggard is wiser in his own
      eyes
   than seven men who can answer
      discreetly.

17 He who meddles in a quarrel not
      his own
   is like one who takes a passing
      dog by the ears.

18 Like a madman who throws fire-
      brands,
   arrows, and death,

19 is the man who deceives his neighbor
   and says, "I am only joking!"

20 For lack of wood the fire goes out;
   and where there is no whisperer,
      quarreling ceases.

21 As charcoal to hot embers and wood
      to fire,
   so is a quarrelsome man for
      kindling strife.

22 The words of a whisperer are like
      delicious morsels;
   they go down into the inner parts
      of the body.

23 Like the glaze*w* covering an earthen
      vessel
   are smooth*x* lips with an evil heart.

24 He who hates, dissembles with his
      lips
   and harbors deceit in his heart;

25 when he speaks graciously, believe
      him not,
   for there are seven abominations
      in his heart;

26 though his hatred be covered with
      guile,
   his wickedness will be exposed
      in the assembly.

27 He who digs a pit will fall into it,
   and a stone will come back upon
      him who starts it rolling.

28 A lying tongue hates its victims,
   and a flattering mouth works
      ruin.

27 Do not boast about tomorrow,
   for you do not know what a
      day may bring forth.

2 Let another praise you, and not your
      own mouth;
   a stranger, and not your own lips.

3 A stone is heavy, and sand is
      weighty,
   but a fool's provocation is heavier
      than both.

4 Wrath is cruel, anger is over-
      whelming;
   but who can stand before jealousy?

5 Better is open rebuke
   than hidden love.

6 Faithful are the wounds of a friend;
   profuse are the kisses of an enemy.

7 He who is sated loathes honey,
   but to one who is hungry every-
      thing bitter is sweet.

8 Like a bird that strays from its nest,
   is a man who strays from his
      home.

9 Oil and perfume make the heart
      glad,
   but the soul is torn by trouble.*y*

10 Your friend, and your father's
      friend, do not forsake;
   and do not go to your brother's
      house in the day of your
      calamity.
   Better is a neighbor who is near
      than a brother who is far away.

11 Be wise, my son, and make my
      heart glad,
   that I may answer him who re-
      proaches me.

12 A prudent man sees danger and
      hides himself;
   but the simple go on, and suffer
      for it.

13 Take a man's garment when he has
      given surety for a stranger,
   and hold him in pledge when he
      gives surety for foreigners.*z*

14 He who blesses his neighbor with
      a loud voice,
   rising early in the morning,
   will be counted as cursing.

15 A continual drippping on a rainy
      day
   and a contentious woman are
      alike;

16 to restrain her is to restrain the
      wind*a*
   or to grasp oil in his right hand.

17 Iron sharpens iron,
   and one man sharpens another.

18 He who tends a fig tree will eat its
      fruit,
   and he who guards his master
      will be honored.

19 As in water face answers to face,
   so the mind of man reflects the
      man.

20 She'ol and A·bad'don are never
      satisfied,
   and never satisfied are the eyes of
      man.

21 The crucible is for silver, and the
      furnace is for gold,
   and a man is judged by his praise.

22 Crush a fool in a mortar with a
      pestle
   along with crushed grain,

w Cn: Heb *silver of dross*   *x* Gk: Heb *burning*
y Gk: Heb *the sweetness of his friend from hearty counsel*
z Vg and 20.16: Heb *a foreign woman*   *a* Heb *obscure*

yet his folly will not depart from
him.

23 Know well the condition of your
   flocks,
   and give attention to your herds;
24 for riches do not last for ever;
   and does a crown endure to all
   generations?
25 When the grass is gone, and the
   new growth appears,
   and the herbage of the mountains
   is gathered;
26 the lambs will provide your clothing,
   and the goats the price of a field;
27 there will be enough goats' milk for
   your food,
   for the food of your household
   and   maintenance   for   your
   maidens.

28 The wicked flee when no one
   pursues,
   but the righteous are bold as a
   lion.
2 When a land transgresses
   it has many rulers;
   but with men of understanding and
   knowledge
   its stability will long continue.
3 A poor man who oppresses the poor
   is a beating rain that leaves no
   food.
4 Those who forsake the law praise
   the wicked,
   but those who keep the law strive
   against them.
5 Evil men do not understand justice,
   but those who seek the LORD
   understand it completely.
6 Better is a poor man who walks in
   his integrity
   than a rich man who is perverse
   in his ways.
7 He who keeps the law is a wise son,
   but a companion of gluttons
   shames his father.
8 He who augments his wealth by
   interest and increase
   gathers it for him who is kind to
   the poor.
9 If one turns away his ear from hearing the law,
   even his prayer is an abomination.
10 He who misleads the upright into
   an evil way
   will fall into his own pit;
   but the blameless will have a
   goodly inheritance.
11 A rich man is wise in his own eyes,
   but a poor man who has understanding will find him out.
12 When the righteous triumph, there
   is great glory;

but when the wicked rise, men
hide themselves.
13 He who conceals his transgressions
   will not prosper,
   but he who confesses and forsakes,
   them will obtain mercy.
14 Blessed is the man who fears the
   LORD always;
   but he who hardens his heart will
   fall into calamity.
15 Like a roaring lion or a charging
   bear
   is a wicked ruler over a poor
   people.
16 A ruler who lacks understanding is
   a cruel oppressor;
   but he who hates unjust gain will
   prolong his days.
17 If a man is burdened with the blood
   of another,
   let him be a fugitive until
   death;
   let no one help him.
18 He who walks in integrity will be
   delivered,
   but he who is perverse in his ways
   will fall into a pit.[b]
19 He who tills his land will have
   plenty of bread,
   but he who follows worthless
   pursuits will have plenty of
   poverty.
20 A faithful man will abound with
   blessings,
   but he who hastens to be rich
   will not go unpunished.
21 To show partiality is not good;
   but for a piece of bread a man
   will do wrong.
22 A miserly man hastens after wealth,
   and does not know that want will
   come upon him.
23 He who rebukes a man will afterward find more favor
   than he who flatters with his
   tongue.
24 He who robs his father or his mother
   and says, "That is no transgression,"
   is the companion of a man who
   destroys.
25 A greedy man stirs up strife,
   but he who trusts in the LORD
   will be enriched.
26 He who trusts in his own mind is
   a fool;
   but he who walks in wisdom will
   be delivered.
27 He who gives to the poor will not
   want,
   but he who hides his eyes will get
   many a curse.
28 When the wicked rise, men hide
   themselves,

but when they perish, the righteous increase.

29 He who is often reproved, yet
stiffens his neck
will suddenly be broken beyond
healing.

2 When the righteous are in authority,
the people rejoice;
but when the wicked rule, the
people groan.

3 He who loves wisdom makes his
father glad,
but one who keeps company with
harlots squanders his substance.

4 By justice a king gives stability to
the land,
but one who exacts gifts ruins it.

5 A man who flatters his neighbor
spreads a net for his feet.

6 An evil man is ensnared in his
transgression,
but a righteous man sings and
rejoices.

7 A righteous man knows the rights
of the poor;
a wicked man does not understand
such knowledge.

8 Scoffers set a city aflame,
but wise men turn away wrath.

9 If a wise man has an argument with
a fool,
the fool only rages and laughs,
and there is no quiet.

10 Bloodthirsty men hate one who is
blameless,
and the wicked*c* seek his life.

11 A fool gives full vent to his anger,
but a wise man quietly holds it
back.

12 If a ruler listens to falsehood,
all his officials will be wicked.

13 The poor man and the oppressor
meet together;
the LORD gives light to the eyes
of both.

14 If a king judges the poor with equity
his throne will be established for
ever.

15 The rod and reproof give wisdom,
but a child left to himself brings
shame to his mother.

16 When the wicked are in authority,
transgression increases;
but the righteous will look upon
their downfall.

17 Discipline your son, and he will
give you rest;
he will give delight to your heart.

18 Where there is no prophecy the
people cast off restraint,
but blessed is he who keeps the law.

19 By mere words a servant is not
disciplined,

for though he understands, he
will not give heed.

20 Do you see a man who is hasty in
his words?
There is more hope for a fool
than for him.

21 He who pampers his servant from
childhood,
will in the end find him his heir.*d*

22 A man of wrath stirs up strife,
and a man given to anger causes
much transgression.

23 A man's pride will bring him low,
but he who is lowly in spirit will
obtain honor.

24 The partner of a thief hates his own
life;
he hears the curse, but discloses
nothing.

25 The fear of man lays a snare,
but he who trusts in the LORD is
safe.

26 Many seek the favor of a ruler,
but from the LORD a man gets
justice.

27 An unjust man is an abomination to
the righteous,
but he whose way is straight is an
abomination to the wicked.

30 The words of A'gŭr son of
Jā'keh of Mas'să.*e*

The man says to Ith'i-el,
to Ithi-el and U'căl:*f*

2 Surely I am too stupid to be a man.
I have not the understanding of
a man.

3 I have not learned wisdom,
nor have I knowledge of the Holy
One.

4 Who has ascended to heaven and
come down?
Who has gathered the wind in
his fists?
Who has wrapped up the waters in
a garment?
Who has established all the ends
of the earth?
What is his name, and what is his
son's name?
Surely you know!

5 Every word of God proves true;
he is a shield to those who take
refuge in him.

6 Do not add to his words,
lest he rebuke you, and you be
found a liar.

7 Two things I ask of thee;
deny them not to me before I
die:

c Cn: Heb *upright*   *d* The meaning of the Hebrew word is uncertain   *e* Or *the oracle*
f The Hebrew of this verse is obscure

8 Remove far from me falsehood and
    lying;
  give me neither poverty nor
    riches;
  feed me with the food that is
    needful for me,
9 lest I be full, and deny thee,
  and say, "Who is the LORD?"
  or lest I be poor, and steal,
  and profane the name of my God.

10 Do not slander a servant to his master,
  lest he curse you, and you be held
    guilty.

11 There are those who curse their
    fathers
  and do not bless their mothers.
12 There are those who are pure in
    their own eyes
  but are not cleansed of their filth.
13 There are those—how lofty are
    their eyes,
  how high their eyelids lift!
14 There are those whose teeth are
    swords,
  whose teeth are knives,
to devour the poor from off the
    earth,
  the needy from among men.

15 The leech[g] has two daughters;
  "Give, give," they cry.
Three things are never satisfied;
  four never say, "Enough":
16 She'ōl, the barren womb,
  the earth ever thirsty for water,
  and the fire which never says,
    "Enough."[h]

17 The eye that mocks a father
  and scorns to obey a mother
will be picked out by the ravens of
    the valley
  and eaten by the vultures.

18 Three things are too wonderful for
    me;
  four I do not understand:
19 the way of an eagle in the sky,
  the way of a serpent on a rock,
the way of a ship on the high seas,
  and the way of a man with a
    maiden.

20 This is the way of an adulteress:
  she eats, and wipes her mouth,
  and says, "I have done no wrong."

21 Under three things the earth
    trembles;
  under four it cannot bear up:

22 a slave when he becomes king,
  and a fool when he is filled with
    food;
23 an unloved woman when she gets a
    husband,
  and a maid when she succeeds her
    mistress.

24 Four things on earth are small,
  but they are exceedingly wise:
25 the ants are a people not strong,
  yet they provide their food in the
    summer;
26 the badgers are a people not mighty,
  yet they make their homes in the
    rocks;
27 the locusts have no king,
  yet all of them march in rank;
28 the lizard you can take in your
    hands,
  yet it is in kings' palaces.

29 Three things are stately in their
    tread;
  four are stately in their stride:
30 the lion, which is mightiest among
    beasts
  and does not turn back before any;
31 the strutting cock,[i] the he-goat,
  and a king striding before[j] his
    people.

32 If you have been foolish, exalting
    yourself,
  or if you have been devising evil,
  put your hand on your mouth.
33 For pressing milk produces curds,
  pressing the nose produces blood,
  and pressing anger produces strife.

31

The words of Lem'ū·el, king of
Mas'sà,[k] which his mother taught
him:

2 What, my son? What, son of my
    womb?
  What, son of my vows?
3 Give not your strength to women,
  your ways to those who destroy
    kings.
4 It is not for kings, O Lem'ū·el,
  it is not for kings to drink wine,
  or for rulers to desire[l] strong
    drink;
5 lest they drink and forget what has
    been decreed,
  and pervert the rights of all the
    afflicted.
6 Give strong drink to him who is
    perishing,
  and wine to those in bitter dis-
    tress;

---

[g] The meaning of the Hebrew word is uncertain   [h] Heb obscure
[i] Gk Syr Tg Compare Vg: Heb obscure   [j] The meaning of the Hebrew is uncertain
[k] Or *King Lemuel, the oracle*   [l] Cn: Heb *where*

7 let them drink and forget their
poverty,
and remember their misery no
more.
8 Open your mouth for the dumb,
for the rights of all who are left
desolate.[m]
9 Open your mouth, judge righteously,
maintain the rights of the poor
and needy.

10 A good wife who can find?
She is far more precious than
jewels.
11 The heart of her husband trusts in
her,
and he will have no lack of gain.
12 She does him good, and not harm,
all the days of her life.
13 She seeks wool and flax,
and works with willing hands.
14 She is like the ships of the merchant,
she brings her food from afar.
15 She rises while it is yet night
and provides food for her household
and tasks for her maidens.
16 She considers a field and buys it;
with the fruit of her hands she
plants a vineyard.
17 She girds her loins with strength
and makes her arms strong.
18 She perceives that her merchandise
is profitable.
Her lamp does not go out at night.
19 She puts her hands to the distaff,
and her hands hold the spindle.
20 She opens her hand to the poor,
and reaches out her hands to the
needy.

21 She is not afraid of snow for her
household,
for all her household are clothed
in scarlet.
22 She makes herself coverings;
her clothing is fine linen and
purple.
23 Her husband is known in the
gates,
when he sits among the elders of
the land.
24 She makes linen garments and sells
them;
she delivers girdles to the merchant.
25 Strength and dignity are her clothing,
and she laughs at the time to
come.
26 She opens her mouth with wisdom,
and the teaching of kindness is on
her tongue.
27 She looks well to the ways of her
household,
and does not eat the bread of
idleness.
28 Her children rise up and call her
blessed;
her husband also, and he praises
her:
29 "Many women have done excel-
lently,
but you surpass them all."
30 Charm is deceitful, and beauty is
vain,
but a woman who fears the LORD
is to be praised.
31 Give her of the fruit of her hands,
and let her works praise her in
the gates.

m Heb *are sons of passing away*

ECCLESIASTES

OR THE PREACHER

The words of the Preacher,[a] the son of David, king in Jerusalem.
2 Vanity of vanities, says the Preacher,
vanity of vanities! All is vanity.
3 What does man gain by all the toil
at which he toils under the sun?
4 A generation goes, and a generation
comes,
but the earth remains for ever.
5 The sun rises and the sun goes
down,
and hastens to the place where it
rises.
6 The wind blows to the south,
and goes round to the north;
round and round goes the wind,
and on its circuits the wind returns.
7 All streams run to the sea,
but the sea is not full;
to the place where the streams flow,
there they flow again.
8 All things are full of weariness;
a man cannot utter it;
the eye is not satisfied with seeing,
nor the ear filled with hearing.
9 What has been is what will be,
and what has been done is what
will be done;
and there is nothing new under
the sun.
10 Is there a thing of which it is said,
"See, this is new"?
It has been already,
in the ages before us.
11 There is no remembrance of former
things,
nor will there be any remembrance
of later things yet to happen
among those who come after.
12 I the Preacher have been king
over Israel in Jerusalem. 13 And I applied my mind to seek and to search
out by wisdom all that is done under
heaven; it is an unhappy business that
God has given to the sons of men to
be busy with. 14 I have seen everything that is done under the sun; and
behold, all is vanity and a striving after
wind.[b]
15 What is crooked cannot be made
straight,
and what is lacking cannot be
numbered.

16 I said to myself, "I have acquired great wisdom, surpassing all
who were over Jerusalem before me;
and my mind has had great experience
of wisdom and knowledge." 17 And I
applied my mind to know wisdom and
to know madness and folly. I perceived
that this also is but a striving after
wind.
18 For in much wisdom is much vexation,
and he who increases knowledge
increases sorrow.

2 I said to myself, "Come now, I
will make a test of pleasure; enjoy
yourself." But behold, this also was
vanity. 2 I said of laughter, "It is
mad," and of pleasure, "What use is
it?" 3 I searched with my mind how
to cheer my body with wine—my mind
still guiding me with wisdom—and
how to lay hold on folly, till I might
see what was good for the sons of men
to do under heaven during the few
days of their life. 4 I made great works;
I built houses and planted vineyards
for myself; 5 I made myself gardens
and parks, and planted in them all
kinds of fruit trees. 6 I made myself
pools from which to water the forest
of growing trees. 7 I bought male and
female slaves, and had slaves who
were born in my house; I had also
great possessions of herds and flocks,
more than any who had been before
me in Jerusalem. 8 I also gathered for
myself silver and gold and the treasure
of kings and provinces; I got singers,
both men and women, and many
concubines,[c] man's delight.

9 So I became great and surpassed
all who were before me in Jerusalem;
also my wisdom remained with me.
10 And whatever my eyes desired I did
not keep from them; I kept my heart
from no pleasure, for my heart found
pleasure in all my toil, and this was
my reward for all my toil. 11 Then I
considered all that my hands had done
and the toil I had spent in doing it,
and behold, all was vanity and a
striving after wind, and there was
nothing to be gained under the sun.

12 So I turned to consider wisdom

a Heb Koheleth   b Or a feeding on wind. See Hos 12.1
c The meaning of the Hebrew word is uncertain

and madness and folly; for what can the man do who comes after the king? Only what he has already done. 13 Then I saw that wisdom excels folly as light excels darkness. 14 The wise man has his eyes in his head, but the fool walks in darkness; and yet I perceived that one fate comes to all of them. 15 Then I said to myself, "What befalls the fool will befall me also; why then have I been so very wise?" And I said to myself that this also is vanity. 16 For of the wise man as of the fool there is no enduring remembrance, seeing that in the days to come all will have been long forgotten. How the wise man dies just like the fool! 17 So I hated life, because what is done under the sun was grievous to me; for all is vanity and a striving after wind.

18 I hated all my toil in which I had toiled under the sun, seeing that I must leave it to the man who will come after me; 19 and who knows whether he will be a wise man or a fool? Yet he will be master of all for which I toiled and used my wisdom under the sun. This also is vanity. 20 So I turned about and gave my heart up to despair over all the toil of my labors under the sun, 21 because sometimes a man who has toiled with wisdom and knowledge and skill must leave all to be enjoyed by a man who did not toil for it. This also is vanity and a great evil. 22 What has a man from all the toil and strain with which he toils beneath the sun? 23 For all his days are full of pain, and his work is a vexation; even in the night his mind does not rest. This also is vanity.

24 There is nothing better for a man than that he should eat and drink, and find enjoyment in his toil. This also, I saw, is from the hand of God; 25 for apart from him*d* who can eat or who can have enjoyment? 26 For to the man who pleases him God gives wisdom and knowledge and joy; but to the sinner he gives the work of gathering and heaping, only to give to one who pleases God. This also is vanity and a striving after wind.

3 For everything there is a season and a time for every matter under heaven:

2 a time to be born, and a time to die;
a time to plant, and a time to pluck up what is planted:
3 a time to kill, and a time to heal;
a time to break down, and a time to build up;
4 a time to weep, and a time to laugh;

d Gk Syr: Heb *apart from me*

a time to mourn, and a time to dance;
5 a time to cast away stones, and a time to gather stones together;
a time to embrace, and a time to refrain from embracing;
6 a time to seek, and a time to lose;
a time to keep, and a time to cast away;
7 a time to rend, and a time to sew;
a time to keep silence, and a time to speak;
8 a time to love, and a time to hate;
a time for war, and a time for peace.
9 What gain has the worker from his toil?

10 I have seen the business that God has given to the sons of men to be busy with. 11 He has made everything beautiful in its time; also he has put eternity into man's mind, yet so that he cannot find out what God has done from the beginning to the end. 12 I know that there is nothing better for them than to be happy and enjoy themselves as long as they live; 13 also that it is God's gift to man that every one should eat and drink and take pleasure in all his toil. 14 I know that whatever God does endures for ever; nothing can be added to it, nor anything taken from it; God has made it so, in order that men should fear before him. 15 That which is, already has been; that which is to be, already has been; and God seeks what has been driven away.

16 Moreover I saw under the sun that in the place of justice, even there was wickedness, and in the place of righteousness, even there was wickedness. 17 I said in my heart, God will judge the righteous and the wicked, for he has appointed a time for every matter, and for every work. 18 I said in my heart with regard to the sons of men that God is testing them to show them that they are but beasts. 19 For the fate of the sons of men and the fate of beasts is the same; as one dies, so dies the other. They all have the same breath, and man has no advantage over the beasts; for all is vanity. 20 All go to one place; all are from the dust, and all turn to dust again. 21 Who knows whether the spirit of man goes upward and the spirit of the beast goes down to the earth? 22 So I saw that there is nothing better than that a man should enjoy his work, for that is his lot; who can bring him to see what will be after him?

4 Again I saw all the oppressions that are practiced under the sun.

And behold, the tears of the oppressed, and they had no one to comfort them! On the side of their oppressors there was power, and there was no one to comfort them. 2 And I thought the dead who are already dead more fortunate than the living who are still alive; 3 but better than both is he who has not yet been, and has not seen the evil deeds that are done under the sun.

4 Then I saw that all toil and all skill in work come from a man's envy of his neighbor. This also is vanity and a striving after wind.

5 The fool folds his hands, and eats his own flesh.

6 Better is a handful of quietness than two hands full of toil and a striving after wind.

7 Again, I saw vanity under the sun: 8 a person who has no one, either son or brother, yet there is no end to all his toil, and his eyes are never satisfied with riches, so that he never asks, "For whom am I toiling and depriving myself of pleasure?" This also is vanity and an unhappy business.

9 Two are better than one, because they have a good reward for their toil. 10 For if they fall, one will lift up his fellow; but woe to him who is alone when he falls and has not another to lift him up. 11 Again, if two lie together, they are warm; but how can one be warm alone? 12 And though a man might prevail against one who is alone, two will withstand him. A threefold cord is not quickly broken.

13 Better is a poor and wise youth than an old and foolish king, who will no longer take advice, 14 even though he had gone from prison to the throne or in his own kingdom had been born poor. 15 I saw all the living who move about under the sun, as well as that*f* youth, who was to stand in his place; 16 there was no end of all the people; he was over all of them. Yet those who come later will not rejoice in him. Surely this also is vanity and a striving after wind.

5 *g* Guard your steps when you go to the house of God; to draw near to listen is better than to offer the sacrifice of fools; for they do not know that they are doing evil. 2*h* Be not rash with your mouth, nor let your heart be hasty to utter a word before God, for God is in heaven, and you upon earth; therefore let your words be few.

3 For a dream comes with much business, and a fool's voice with many words.

4 When you vow a vow to God, do not delay paying it; for he has no pleasure in fools. Pay what you vow. 5 It is better that you should not vow than that you should vow and not pay. 6 Let not your mouth lead you into sin, and do not say before the messenger*i* that it was a mistake; why should God be angry at your voice, and destroy the work of your hands?

7 For when dreams increase, empty words grow many:*j* but do you fear God.

8 If you see in a province the poor oppressed and justice and right violently taken away, do not be amazed at the matter; for the high official is watched by a higher, and there are yet higher ones over them. 9 But in all, a king is an advantage to a land with cultivated fields.*k*

10 He who loves money will not be satisfied with money; nor he who loves wealth, with gain: this also is vanity.

11 When goods increase, they increase who eat them; and what gain has their owner but to see them with his eyes?

12 Sweet is the sleep of a laborer, whether he eats little or much; but the surfeit of the rich will not let him sleep.

13 There is a grievous evil which I have seen under the sun: riches were kept by their owner to his hurt, 14 and those riches were lost in a bad venture; and he is father of a son, but he has nothing in his hand. 15 As he came from his mother's womb shall he go again, naked as he came, and shall take nothing for his toil, which he may carry away in his hand. 16 This also is a grievous evil: just as he came, so shall he go; and what gain has he that he toiled for the wind, 17 and spent all his days in darkness and grief,*l* in much vexation and sickness and resentment?

18 Behold, what I have seen to be good and to be fitting is to eat and drink and find enjoyment in all the toil with which one toils under the sun the few days of his life which God has given him, for this is his lot. 19 Every man also to whom God has given wealth and possessions and power to enjoy them, and to accept his lot and find enjoyment in his toil—this is the gift of God. 20 For he will not much remember the days of his life because

---

f Heb *the second*   *g* Ch 4.17 in Heb   *h* Ch 5.1 in Heb   *i* Or *angel*
j Or *For in a multitude of dreams there is futility, and ruin in a flood of words*
k Or *The profit of the land is among all of them; a cultivated field has a king*
l Gk: Heb *all his days also he eats in darkness*

God keeps him occupied with joy in his heart.

6 There is an evil which I have seen under the sun, and it lies heavy upon men: 2 a man to whom God gives wealth, possessions, and honor, so that he lacks nothing of all that he desires, yet God does not give him power to enjoy them, but a stranger enjoys them; this is vanity; it is a sore affliction. 3 If a man begets a hundred children, and lives many years, so that the days of his years are many, but he does not enjoy life's good things, and also has no burial, I say that an untimely birth is better off than he. 4 For it comes into vanity and goes into darkness, and in darkness its name is covered; 5 moreover it has not seen the sun or known anything; yet it finds rest rather than he. 6 Even though he should live a thousand years twice told, yet enjoy no good—do not all go to the one place?

7 All the toil of man is for his mouth, yet his appetite is not satisfied. 8 For what advantage has the wise man over the fool? And what does the poor man have who knows how to conduct himself before the living? 9 Better is the sight of the eyes than the wandering of desire; this also is vanity and a striving after wind.

10 Whatever has come to be has already been named, and it is known what man is, and that he is not able to dispute with one stronger than he. 11 The more words, the more vanity, and what is man the better? 12 For who knows what is good for man while he lives the few days of his vain life, which he passes like a shadow? For who can tell man what will be after him under the sun?

7 A good name is better than precious ointment;
    and the day of death, than the day of birth.
2 It is better to go to the house of mourning
    than to go to the house of feasting; for this is the end of all men,
    and the living will lay it to heart.
3 Sorrow is better than laughter,
    for by sadness of countenance the heart is made glad.
4 The heart of the wise is in the house of mourning;
    but the heart of fools is in the house of mirth.
5 It is better for a man to hear the rebuke of the wise
    than to hear the song of fools.
6 For as the crackling of thorns under a pot,

so is the laughter of the fools;
    this also is vanity.
7 Surely oppression makes the wise man foolish,
    and a bribe corrupts the mind.
8 Better is the end of a thing than its beginning;
    and the patient in spirit is better than the proud in spirit.
9 Be not quick to anger,
    for anger lodges in the bosom of fools.
10 Say not, "Why were the former days better than these?"
    For it is not from wisdom that you ask this.
11 Wisdom is good with an inheritance,
    and advantage to those who see the sun.
12 For the protection of wisdom is like the protection of money;
    and the advantage of knowledge is that wisdom preserves the life of him who has it.
13 Consider the work of God;
    who can make straight what he has made crooked?

14 In the day of prosperity be joyful, and in the day of adversity consider; God has made the one as well as the other, so that man may not find out anything that will be after him.

15 In my vain life I have seen everything; there is a righteous man who perishes in his righteousness, and there is a wicked man who prolongs his life in his evil-doing. 16 Be not righteous overmuch, and do not make yourself overwise; why should you destroy yourself? 17 Be not wicked overmuch, neither be a fool; why should you die before your time? 18 It is good that you should take hold of this, and from that withhold not your hand; for he who fears God shall come forth from them all.

19 Wisdom gives strength to the wise man more than ten rulers that are in a city.

20 Surely there is not a righteous man on earth who does good and never sins.

21 Do not give heed to all the things that men say, lest you hear your servant cursing you; 22 your heart knows that many times you have yourself cursed others.

23 All this I have tested by wisdom; I said, "I will be wise"; but it was far from me. 24 That which is, is far off, and deep, very deep; who can find it out? 25 I turned my mind to know and to search out and to seek wisdom and the sum of things, and to know the wickedness of folly and the foolishness

which is madness. 26And I found more bitter than death the woman whose heart is snares and nets, and whose hands are fetters; he who pleases God escapes her, but the sinner is taken by her. 27 Behold, this is what I found, says the Preacher, adding one thing to another to find the sum, 28 which my mind has sought repeatedly, but I have not found. One man among a thousand I found, but a woman among all these I have not found. 29 Behold, this alone I found, that God made man upright, but they have sought out many devices.

8 Who is like the wise man?
And who knows the interpretation of a thing?
A man's wisdom makes his face shine,
   and the hardness of his countenance is changed.

2 Keep[m] the king's command, and because of your sacred oath be not dismayed; 3 go from his presence, do not delay when the matter is unpleasant, for he does whatever he pleases. 4 For the word of the king is supreme, and who may say to him, "What are you doing?" 5 He who obeys a command will meet no harm, and the mind of a wise man will know the time and way. 6 For every matter has its time and way, although man's trouble lies heavy upon him. 7 For he does not know what is to be, for who can tell him how it will be? 8 No man has power to retain the spirit, or authority over the day of death; there is no discharge from war, nor will wickedness deliver those who are given to it. 9All this I observed while applying my mind to all that is done under the sun, while man lords it over man to his hurt.

10 Then I saw the wicked buried; they used to go in and out of the holy place, and were praised in the city where they had done such things. This also is vanity. 11 Because sentence against an evil deed is not executed speedily, the heart of the sons of men is fully set to do evil. 12 Though a sinner does evil a hundred times and prolongs his life, yet I know that it will be well with those who fear God, because they fear before him; 13 but it will not be well with the wicked, neither will he prolong his days like a shadow, because he does not fear before God.

14 There is a vanity which takes place on earth, that there are righteous men to whom it happens according to

the deeds of the wicked, and there are wicked men to whom it happens according to the deeds of the righteous. I said that this also is vanity. 15And I commend enjoyment, for man has no good thing under the sun but to eat, and drink, and enjoy himself, for this will go with him in his toil through the days of life which God gives him under the sun.

16 When I applied my mind to know wisdom, and to see the business that is done on earth, how neither day nor night one's eyes see sleep; 17 then I saw all the work of God, that man cannot find out the work that is done under the sun. However much man may toil in seeking, he will not find it out; even though a wise man claims to know, he cannot find it out.

9 But all this I laid to heart, examining it all, how the righteous and the wise and their deeds are in the hand of God; whether it is love or hate man does not know. Everything before them is vanity,[n] 2 since one fate comes to all, to the righteous and the wicked, to the good and the evil,[o] to the clean and the unclean, to him who sacrifices and him who does not sacrifice. As is the good man, so is the sinner; and he who swears is as he who shuns an oath. 3 This is an evil in all that is done under the sun, that one fate comes to all; also the hearts of men are full of evil, and madness is in their hearts while they live, and after that they go to the dead. 4 But he who is joined with all the living has hope, for a living dog is better than a dead lion. 5 For the living know that they will die, but the dead know nothing, and they have no more reward; but the memory of them is lost. 6 Their love and their hate and their envy have already perished, and they have no more for ever any share in all that is done under the sun.

7 Go, eat your bread with enjoyment, and drink your wine with a merry heart; for God has already approved what you do.

8 Let your garments be always white; let not oil be lacking on your head.

9 Enjoy life with the wife whom you love, all the days of your vain life which he has given you under the sun, because that is your portion in life and in your toil at which you toil under the sun. 10 Whatever your hand finds to do, do it with your might; for there is no work or thought or knowledge or

m Heb inserts an I   n Syr Compare Gk: Heb Everything before them is everything
o Gk Syr Vg: Heb lacks and the evil

wisdom in Shĕ'ōl, to which you are going.

11 Again I saw that under the sun the race is not to the swift, nor the battle to the strong, nor bread to the wise, nor riches to the intelligent, nor favor to the men of skill; but time and chance happen to them all. 12 For man does not know his time. Like fish which are taken in an evil net, and like birds which are caught in a snare, so the sons of men are snared at an evil time, when it suddenly falls upon them.

13 I have also seen this example of wisdom under the sun, and it seemed great to me. 14 There was a little city with few men in it; and a great king came against it and besieged it, building great siegeworks against it. 15 But there was found in it a poor wise man, and he by his wisdom delivered the city. Yet no one remembered that poor man. 16 But I say that wisdom is better than might, though the poor man's wisdom is despised, and his words are not heeded.

17 The words of the wise heard in quiet are better than the shouting of a ruler among fools. 18 Wisdom is better than weapons of war, but one sinner destroys much good.

10 Dead flies make the perfumer's ointment give off an evil odor; so a little folly outweighs wisdom and honor.

2 A wise man's heart inclines him toward the right,
    but a fool's heart toward the left.
3 Even when the fool walks on the road, he lacks sense,
    and he says to every one that he is a fool.
4 If the anger of the ruler rises against you, do not leave your place,
    for deference will make amends for great offenses.

5 There is an evil which I have seen under the sun, as it were an error proceeding from the ruler: 6 folly is set in many high places, and the rich sit in a low place. 7 I have seen slaves on horses, and princes walking on foot like slaves.

8 He who digs a pit will fall into it;
    and a serpent will bite him who breaks through a wall.
9 He who quarries stones is hurt by them;
    and he who splits logs is endangered by them.
10 If the iron is blunt, and one does not whet the edge,
    he must put forth more strength; but wisdom helps one to succeed.

11 If the serpent bites before it is charmed,
    there is no advantage in a charmer.

12 The words of a wise man's mouth win him favor,
    but the lips of a fool consume him.
13 The beginning of the words of his mouth is foolishness,
    and the end of his talk is wicked madness.
14 A fool multiplies words,
    though no man knows what is to be,
    and who can tell him what will be after him?
15 The toil of a fool wearies him,
    so that he does not know the way to the city.

16 Woe to you, O land, when your king is a child,
    and your princes feast in the morning!
17 Happy are you, O land, when your king is the son of free men,
    and your princes feast at the proper time,
    for strength, and not for drunkenness!
18 Through sloth the roof sinks in,
    and through indolence the house leaks.
19 Bread is made for laughter,
    and wine gladdens life,
    and money answers everything.
20 Even in your thought, do not curse the king,
    nor in your bedchamber curse the rich;
    for a bird of the air will carry your voice,
    or some winged creature tell the matter.

11 Cast your bread upon the waters,
    for you will find it after many days.
2 Give a portion to seven, or even to eight,
    for you know not what evil may happen on earth.
3 If the clouds are full of rain,
    they empty themselves on the earth;
    and if a tree falls to the south or to the north,
    in the place where the tree falls, there it will lie.
4 He who observes the wind will not sow;
    and he who regards the clouds will not reap.
5 As you do not know how the spirit comes to the bones in the womb*p* of a woman with child, so you do not

p Or *As you do not know the way of the wind, or how the bones grow in the womb*

know the work of God who makes everything.

6 In the morning sow your seed, and at evening withhold not your hand; for you do not know which will prosper, this or that, or whether both alike will be good.

7 Light is sweet, and it is pleasant for the eyes to behold the sun.

8 For if a man lives many years, let him rejoice in them all; but let him remember that the days of darkness will be many. All that comes is vanity.

9 Rejoice, O young man, in your youth, and let your heart cheer you in the days of your youth; walk in the ways of your heart and the sight of your eyes. But know that for all these things God will bring you into judgment.

10 Remove vexation from your mind, and put away pain from your body; for youth and the dawn of life are vanity.

12 Remember also your Creator in the days of your youth, before the evil days come, and the years draw nigh, when you will say, "I have no pleasure in them"; 2 before the sun and the light and the moon and the stars are darkened and the clouds return after the rain; 3 in the day when the keepers of the house tremble, and the strong men are bent, and the grinders cease because they are few, and those that look through the windows are dimmed, 4 and the doors

on the street are shut; when the sound of the grinding is low, and one rises up at the voice of a bird, and all the daughters of song are brought low; 5 they are afraid also of what is high, and terrors are in the way; the almond tree blossoms, the grasshopper drags itself along*q* and desire fails; because man goes to his eternal home, and the mourners go about the streets; 6 before the silver cord is snapped,*r* or the golden bowl is broken, or the pitcher is broken at the fountain, or the wheel broken at the cistern, 7 and the dust returns to the earth as it was, and the spirit returns to God who gave it. 8 Vanity of vanities, says the Preacher; all is vanity.

9 Besides being wise, the Preacher also taught the people knowledge, weighing and studying and arranging proverbs with great care. 10 The Preacher sought to find pleasing words, and uprightly he wrote words of truth.

11 The sayings of the wise are like goads, and like nails firmly fixed are the collected sayings which are given by one Shepherd. 12 My son, beware of anything beyond these. Of making many books there is no end, and much study is a weariness of the flesh.

13 The end of the matter; all has been heard. Fear God, and keep his commandments; for this is the whole duty of man.*s* 14 For God will bring every deed into judgment, with*t* every secret thing, whether good or evil.

THE SONG OF SOLOMON

1 The Song of Songs, which is Solomon's.

2 O that you*a* would kiss me with the kisses of your*b* mouth!
For your love is better than wine,
3 your anointing oils are fragrant,
your name is oil poured out;
therefore the maidens love you.
4 Draw me after you, let us make haste.
The king has brought me into his chambers.
We will exult and rejoice in you;

we will extol your love more than wine;
rightly do they love you.

5 I am very dark, but comely,
O daughters of Jerusalem,
like the tents of Ke̅da̅r,
like the curtains of Solomon.
6 Do not gaze at me because I am swarthy,
because the sun has scorched me.
My mother's sons were angry with me,
they made me keeper of the vineyards;

*q Or is a burden   r Syr Vg Compare Gk: Heb is removed   s Or the duty of all men
t Or into the judgment on   a Heb he   b Heb his*

but, my own vineyard I have not
    kept!

7 Tell me, you whom my soul loves,
    where you pasture your flock,
    where you make it lie down at
      noon;
for why should I be like one who
      wanders*c*
beside the flocks of your com-
    panions?

8 If you do not know,
    O fairest among women,
follow in the tracks of the flock,
    and pasture your kids
    beside the shepherds' tents.

9 I compare you, my love,
    to a mare of Pharaoh's chariots.
10 Your cheeks are comely with
    ornaments,
    your neck with strings of jewels.
11 We will make you ornaments of
    gold,
    studded with silver.

12 While the king was on his couch,
    my nard gave forth its fragrance.
13 My beloved is to me a bag of myrrh,
    that lies between my breasts.
14 My beloved is to me a cluster of
    henna blossoms
    in the vineyards of En·ge′di.

15 Behold, you are beautiful, my love;
    behold, you are beautiful;
    your eyes are doves.
16 Behold, you are beautiful, my be-
    loved,
    truly lovely.
Our couch is green;
17   the beams of our house are cedar,
    our rafters*d* are pine.

2 I am a rose*e* of Sharon,
    a lily of the valleys.

2 As a lily among brambles,
    so is my love among maidens.

3 As an apple tree among the trees of
    the wood,
    so is my beloved among young
      men.
With great delight I sat in his
    shadow,
    and his fruit was sweet to my taste.
4 He brought me to the banqueting
    house,
    and his banner over me was love.
5 Sustain me with raisins,
    refresh me with apples;

for I am sick with love.
6 O that his left hand were under my
    head,
    and that his right hand embraced
    me!
7 I adjure you, O daughters of Jeru-
    salem,
    by the gazelles or the hinds of
    the field,
that you stir not up nor awaken love
    until it please.

8 The voice of my beloved!
    Behold, he comes,
leaping upon the mountains,
    bounding over the hills.
9 My beloved is like a gazelle,
    or a young stag.
Behold, there he stands
    behind our wall,
gazing in at the windows,
    looking through the lattice.
10 My beloved speaks and says to me:
    "Arise, my love, my fair one,
    and come away;
11 for lo, the winter is past,
    the rain is over and gone.
12 The flowers appear on the earth,
    the time of singing has come,
and the voice of the turtledove
    is heard in our land.
13 The fig tree puts forth its figs,
    and the vines are in blossom;
    they give forth fragrance.
Arise, my love, my fair one,
    and come away.
14 O my dove, in the clefts of the rock,
    in the covert of the cliff,
let me see your face,
    let me hear your voice,
for your voice is sweet,
    and your face is comely.
15 Catch us the foxes,
    the little foxes,
that spoil the vineyards,
    for our vineyards are in blossom."

16 My beloved is mine and I am his,
    he pastures his flock among the
    lilies.
17 Until the day breathes
    and the shadows flee,
turn, my beloved, be like a gazelle,
    or a young stag upon rugged*f*
    mountains.

3 Upon my bed by night
    I sought him whom my soul
    loves;
I sought him, but found him not;
    I called him, but he gave no
    answer.*g*

c Gk Syr Vg: Heb *is veiled*   *d* The meaning of the Hebrew word is uncertain
e Heb *crocus*   *f* The meaning of the Hebrew word is unknown
g Gk: Heb lacks this line

2 "I will rise now and go about the
    city,
    in the streets and in the squares;
I will seek him whom my soul
    loves."
    I sought him, but found him
    not.
3 The watchmen found me,
    as they went about in the city.
"Have you seen him whom my soul
    loves?"
4 Scarcely had I passed them,
    when I found him whom my soul
    loves.
I held him, and would not let him
    go
    until I had brought him into my
    mother's house,
    and into the chamber of her that
    conceived me.
5 I adjure you, O daughters of Jeru-
    salem,
    by the gazelles or the hinds of the
    field,
that you stir not up nor awaken love
    until it please.

6 What is that coming up from the
    wilderness,
    like a column of smoke,
perfumed with myrrh and frank-
    incense,
    with all the fragrant powders of
    the merchant?
7 Behold, it is the litter of Solomon!
About it are sixty mighty men
    of the mighty men of Israel,
8 all girt with swords
    and expert in war,
each with his sword at his thigh,
    against alarms by night.
9 King Solomon made himself a
    palanquin
    from the wood of Lebanon.
10 He made its posts of silver,
    its back of gold, its seat of purple;
it was lovingly wrought within*h*
    by the daughters of Jerusalem.
11 Go forth, O daughters of Zion,
    and behold King Solomon,
with the crown with which his
    mother crowned him
    on the day of his wedding,
    on the day of the gladness of his
    heart.

4 Behold, you are beautiful, my
    love,
    behold, you are beautiful!
Your eyes are doves
    behind your veil.
Your hair is like a flock of goats,
    moving down the slopes of Gilead.

2 Your teeth are like a flock of shorn
    ewes
    that have come up from the
    washing,
all of which bear twins,
    and not one among them is be-
    reaved.
3 Your lips are like a scarlet thread,
    and your mouth is lovely.
Your cheeks are like halves of a
    pomegranate
    behind your veil.
4 Your neck is like the tower of David,
    built for an arsenal,*i*
whereon hang a thousand bucklers,
    all of them shields of warriors.
5 Your two breasts are like two fawns,
    twins of a gazelle,
    that feed among the lilies.
6 Until the day breathes
    and the shadows flee,
I will hie me to the mountain of
    myrrh
    and the hill of frankincense.
7 You are all fair, my love;
    there is no flaw in you.
8 Come with me from Lebanon, my
    bride;
    come with me from Lebanon.
Depart from the peak of Ă·mä′nä,
    from the peak of Sē′nir and
    Hĕr′mŏn,
    from the dens of lions,
    from the mountains of leopards.

9 You have ravished my heart, my
    sister, my bride,
    you have ravished my heart with
    a glance of your eyes,
    with one jewel of your necklace.
10 How sweet is your love, my sister,
    my bride!
    how much better is your love
    than wine,
    and the fragrance of your oils
    than any spice!
11 Your lips distil nectar, my bride;
    honey and milk are under your
    tongue;
    the scent of your garments is like
    the scent of Lebanon.
12 A garden locked is my sister, my
    bride,
    a garden locked, a fountain sealed.
13 Your shoots are an orchard of
    pomegranates
    with all choicest fruits,
    henna with nard,
14 nard and saffron, calamus and
    cinnamon,
    with all trees of frankincense,
    myrrh and aloes,
    with all chief spices—

---

h The meaning of the Hebrew is uncertain
i The meaning of the Hebrew word is uncertain *j* Or *Look*

15 a garden fountain, a well of living
water,
and flowing streams from Lebanon.

16 Awake, O north wind,
and come, O south wind!
Blow upon my garden,
let its fragrance be wafted abroad.
Let my beloved come to his garden,
and eat its choicest fruits.

5 I come to my garden, my sister,
my bride,
I gather my myrrh with my spice,
I eat my honeycomb with my
honey,
I drink my wine with my milk.

Eat, O friends, and drink;
drink deeply, O lovers!

2 I slept, but my heart was awake.
Hark! my beloved is knocking.
"Open to me, my sister, my love,
my dove, my perfect one;
for my head is wet with dew,
my locks with the drops of the
night."
3 I had put off my garment,
how could I put it on?
I had bathed my feet,
how could I soil them?
4 My beloved put his hand to the
latch,
and my heart was thrilled within
me.
5 I arose to open to my beloved,
and my hands dripped with
myrrh,
my fingers with liquid myrrh,
upon the handles of the bolt.
6 I opened to my beloved,
but my beloved had turned and
gone.
My soul failed me when he spoke.
I sought him, but found him not;
I called him, but he gave no
answer.
7 The watchmen found me,
as they went about in the city;
they beat me, they wounded me,
they took away my mantle,
those watchmen of the walls.
8 I adjure you, O daughters of Jerusalem,
if you find my beloved,
that you tell him
I am sick with love.

9 What is your beloved more than
another beloved,
O fairest among women?

What is your beloved more than
another beloved,
that you thus adjure us?

10 My beloved is all radiant and ruddy,
distinguished among ten thousand.
11 His head is the finest gold;
his locks are wavy,
black as a raven.
12 His eyes are like doves
beside springs of water,
bathed in milk,
fitly set.*k*
13 His cheeks are like beds of spices,
yielding fragrance.
His lips are lilies,
distilling liquid myrrh.
14 His arms are rounded gold,
set with jewels.
His body is ivory work,*l*
encrusted with sapphires.*m*
15 His legs are alabaster columns,
set upon bases of gold.
His appearance is like Lebanon,
choice as the cedars.
16 His speech is most sweet,
and he is altogether desirable.
This is my beloved and this is my
friend,
O daughters of Jerusalem.

6 Whither has your beloved gone,
O fairest among women?
Whither has your beloved turned,
that we may seek him with you?

2 My beloved has gone down to his
garden,
to the beds of spices,
to pasture his flock in the gardens,
and to gather lilies.
3 I am my beloved's and my beloved
is mine;
he pastures his flock among the
lilies.

4 You are beautiful as Tĭr'zàh, my
love,
comely as Jerusalem,
terrible as an army with banners.
5 Turn away your eyes from me,
for they disturb me—
Your hair is like a flock of goats,
moving down the slopes of Gilead.
6 Your teeth are like a flock of ewes,
that have come up from the washing,
all of them bear twins,
not one among them is bereaved.
7 Your cheeks are like halves of a
pomegranate
behind your veil.

k The meaning of the Hebrew is uncertain
l The meaning of the Hebrew word is uncertain   *m* Heb *lapis lazuli*

8 There are sixty queens and eighty
    concubines,
  and maidens without number.
9 My dove, my perfect one, is only
    one,
    the darling of her mother,
  flawless to her that bore her.
  The maidens saw her and called her
    happy;
    the queens and concubines also,
    and they praised her.
10 "Who is this that looks forth like
    the dawn,
    fair as the moon, bright as the
    sun,
  terrible as an army with banners?"

11 I went down to the nut orchard,
    to look at the blossoms of the
    valley,
  to see whether the vines had budded,
    whether the pomegranates were
    in bloom.
12 Before I was aware, my fancy set
    me
  in a chariot beside my prince.[n]

13[o] Return, return, O Shü′lăm·mĭte,
  return, return, that we may look
    upon you.

  Why should you look upon the
    Shulammite,
  as upon a dance before two
    armies?[p]

7 How graceful are your feet in
    sandals,
  O queenly maiden!
  Your rounded thighs are like jewels,
    the work of a master hand.
2 Your navel is a rounded bowl
    that never lacks mixed wine.
  Your belly is a heap of wheat,
    encircled with lilies.
3 Your two breasts are like two fawns,
    twins of a gazelle.
4 Your neck is like an ivory tower.
  Your eyes are pools in Hesh′bŏn,
    by the gate of Bath-rab′bim.
  Your nose is like a tower of Leb-
    anon,
    overlooking Damascus.
5 Your head crowns you like Cär′mĕl,
    and your flowing locks are like
    purple;
  a king is held captive in the
    tresses.[q]

6 How fair and pleasant you are,

  O loved one, delectable maiden![r]
7 You are stately[s] as a palm tree,
    and your breasts are like its
    clusters.
8 I say I will climb the palm tree
    and lay hold of its branches.
  Oh, may your breasts be like clusters
    of the vine,
    and the scent of your breath like
    apples,
9 and your kisses[t] like the best wine
    that goes down[u] smoothly,
    gliding over lips and teeth.[v]

10 I am my beloved's,
    and his desire is for me.
11 Come, my beloved,
    let us go forth into the fields,
    and lodge in the villages;
12 let us go out early to the vineyards,
    and see whether the vines have
    budded,
  whether the grape blossoms have
    opened
    and the pomegranates are in
    bloom.
  There I will give you my love.
13 The mandrakes give forth fragrance,
    and over our doors are all choice
    fruits,
  new as well as old,
    which I have laid up for you, O
    my beloved.

8 O that you were like a brother to
    me,
    that nursed at my mother's breast!
  If I met you outside, I would kiss
    you,
    and none would despise me.
2 I would lead you and bring you
    into the house of my mother,
    and into the chamber of her that
    conceived me.[w]
  I would give you spiced wine to
    drink,
    the juice of my pomegranates.
3 O that his left hand were under my
    head,
    and that his right hand embraced
    me!
4 I adjure you, O daughters of Jeru-
    salem,
    that you stir not up nor awaken
    love
    until it please.

5 Who is that coming up from the
    wilderness,
    leaning upon her beloved?

n The meaning of the Hebrew is uncertain   *o* Ch 7.1 in Heb
p Or *dance of Mahanaim*   *q* The meaning of the Hebrew word is uncertain
r Syr: Heb *in delights*   *s* Heb *This your stature is*   *t* Heb *palate*
u Heb *down for my lover*   *v* Gk Syr Vg: Heb *lips of sleepers*
w Gk Syr: Heb *mother; she* (or *you*) *will teach me*

Under the apple tree I awakened
    you.
There your mother was in travail
    with you,
    there she who bore you was in
       travail.

6 Set me as a seal upon your heart,
    as a seal upon your arm;
for love is strong as death,
    jealousy is cruel as the grave.
Its flashes are flashes of fire,
    a most vehement flame.
7 Many waters cannot quench love,
    neither can floods drown it.
If a man offered for love
    all the wealth of his house,
    it would be utterly scorned.

8 We have a little sister,
    and she has no breasts.
What shall we do for our sister,
    on the day when she is spoken
      for?
9 If she is a wall,
    we will build upon her a battle-
      ment of silver;
but if she is a door,

we will enclose her with boards
    of cedar.
10 I was a wall,
    and my breasts were like towers;
then I was in his eyes
    as one who brings*x* peace.

11 Solomon had a vineyard at Bā'ăl-
    hā'mon;
he let out the vineyard to keepers;
    each one was to bring for its fruit
      a thousand pieces of silver.
12 My vineyard, my very own, is for
    myself;
you, O Solomon, may have the
      thousand,
and the keepers of the fruit two
      hundred.

13 O you who dwell in the gardens,
    my companions are listening for
      your voice;
    let me hear it.

14 Make haste, my beloved,
    and be like a gazelle
or a young stag
    upon the mountains of spices.

THE BOOK OF

ISAIAH

1 The vision of I·ṣăi'ăh the son of
  A'moz, which he saw concerning
Judah and Jerusalem in the days of
Uz·zĭ'ăh, Jō'thăm, A'haz, and Hez·ĕ-
kĭ'ăh, kings of Judah.
2 Hear, O heavens, and give ear, O
    earth;
    for the LORD has spoken:
"Sons have I reared and brought up,
    but they have rebelled against me.
3 The ox knows its owner,
    and the ass its master's crib;
but Israel does not know,
    my people does not understand."

4 Ah, sinful nation,
    a people laden with iniquity,
    offspring of evildoers,
    sons who deal corruptly!
They have forsaken the LORD,
    they have despised the Holy One
      of Israel,
    they are utterly estranged.

5 Why will you still be smitten,
    that you continue to rebel?

The whole head is sick,
    and the whole heart faint.
6 From the sole of the foot even to the
    head,
    there is no soundness in it,
but bruises and sores
    and bleeding wounds;
they are not pressed out, or bound
    up,
    or softened with oil.

7 Your country lies desolate,
    your cities are burned with fire;
in your very presence
    aliens devour your land;
    it is desolate, as overthrown by
      aliens.
8 And the daughter of Zion is left
    like a booth in a vineyard,
like a lodge in a cucumber field,
    like a besieged city.

9 If the LORD of hosts
    had not left us a few survivors,
we should have been like Sŏd'ŏm,
    and become like Gŏ·môr'răh.

x Or *finds*   **1.9:** Rom 9.29.

10 Hear the word of the LORD,
  you rulers of Sod'óm!
Give ear to the teaching of our God,
  you people of Gò·mòr'ràh!
11 "What to me is the multitude of
    your sacrifices?
  says the LORD;
I have had enough of burnt offerings
    of rams
  and the fat of fed beasts;
I do not delight in the blood of bulls,
  or of lambs, or of he-goats.

12 "When you come to appear before me,
  who requires of you
    this trampling of my courts?
13 Bring no more vain offerings;
  incense is an abomination to me.
New moon and sabbath and the
    calling of assemblies—
  I cannot endure iniquity and
    solemn assembly.
14 Your new moons and your ap-
    pointed feasts
  my soul hates;
they have become a burden to me,
  I am weary of bearing them.
15 When you spread forth your hands,
  I will hide my eyes from you;
even though you make many
    prayers,
  I will not listen;
your hands are full of blood.
16 Wash yourselves; make yourselves
    clean;
  remove the evil of your doings
    from before my eyes;
cease to do evil,
17   learn to do good;
seek justice,
  correct oppression;
defend the fatherless,
  plead for the widow.

18 "Come now, let us reason together,
  says the LORD:
though your sins are like scarlet,
  they shall be as white as snow;
though they are red like crimson,
  they shall become like wool.
19 If you are willing and obedient,
  you shall eat the good of the land;
20 But if you refuse and rebel,
  you shall be devoured by the
    sword;
  for the mouth of the LORD has
    spoken."

21 How the faithful city
  has become a harlot,
  she that was full of justice!
Righteousness lodged in her,
  but now murderers.
22 Your silver has become dross,
  your wine mixed with water.
23 Your princes are rebels
  and companions of thieves.
Every one loves a bribe
  and runs after gifts.
They do not defend the fatherless,
  and the widow's cause does not
    come to them.

24 Therefore the Lord says,
  the LORD of hosts,
  the Mighty One of Israel:
"Ah, I will vent my wrath on my
    enemies,
  and avenge myself on my foes.
25 I will turn my hand against you
  and will smelt away your dross as
    with lye
  and remove all your alloy.
26 And I will restore your judges as at
    the first,
  and your counselors as at the
    beginning.
Afterward you shall be called the
    city of righteousness,
  the faithful city."

27 Zion shall be redeemed by justice,
  and those in her who repent, by
    righteousness.
28 But rebels and sinners shall be de-
    stroyed together,
  and those who forsake the LORD
    shall be consumed.
29 For you shall be ashamed of the oaks
  in which you delighted;
and you shall blush for the gardens
  which you have chosen.
30 For you shall be like an oak
  whose leaf withers,
  and like a garden without water.
31 And the strong shall become tow,
  and his work a spark,
and both of them shall burn together,
  with none to quench them.

2 The word which I·şāi'áh the son
   of Ā'moz saw concerning Judah
and Jerusalem.
2 It shall come to pass in the latter days
  that the mountain of the house of
    the LORD
shall be established as the highest
    of the mountains,
  and shall be raised above the hills;
and all the nations shall flow to it,
3   and many peoples shall come, and
    say:
"Come, let us go up to the moun-
    tain of the LORD,
  to the house of the God of Jacob;
that he may teach us his ways
  and that we may walk in his
    paths."

2.2-4: Mic 4.1-3.

For out of Zion shall go forth the
    law,
  and the word of the LORD from
    Jerusalem.
4 He shall judge between the nations,
    and shall decide for many peoples;
  and they shall beat their swords into
    plowshares,
    and their spears into pruning
     hooks;
  nation shall not lift up sword against
    nation,
    neither shall they learn war any
     more.

5 O house of Jacob,
  come, let us walk
  in the light of the LORD.

6 For thou hast rejected thy people,
  the house of Jacob,
  because they are full of diviners*a*
    from the east
    and of soothsayers like the
     Philistines,
  and they strike hands with for-
    eigners.
7 Their land is filled with silver and
    gold,
    and there is no end to their
     treasures;
  their land is filled with horses,
    and there is no end to their
     chariots.
8 Their land is filled with idols;
    they bow down to the work of
     their hands,
    to what their own fingers have
     made.
9 So man is humbled,
  and men are brought low—
    forgive them not!
10 Enter into the rock,
  and hide in the dust
  from before the terror of the LORD,
  and from the glory of his majesty.
11 The haughty looks of man shall be
    brought low,
    and the pride of men shall be
     humbled;
  and the LORD alone will be exalted
    in that day.

12 For the LORD of hosts has a day
    against all that is proud and lofty,
    against all that is lifted up and
     high;*b*
13 against all the cedars of Lebanon,
    lofty and lifted up;
    and against all the oaks of Bā'shăn;
14 against all the high mountains,
    and against all the lofty hills;
15 against every high tower,
    and against every fortified wall;

16 against all the ships of Tär'shĭsh,
    and against all the beautiful craft.
17 And the haughtiness of man shall be
    humbled,
    and the pride of men shall be
     brought low;
    and the LORD alone will be ex-
     alted in that day.
18 And the idols shall utterly pass away.
19 And men shall enter the caves of the
    rocks
    and the holes of the ground,
  from before the terror of the LORD,
    and from the glory of his majesty,
    when he rises to terrify the earth.

20 In that day men will cast forth
    their idols of silver and their idols
     of gold,
  which they made for themselves to
    worship,
    to the moles and to the bats,
21 to enter the caverns of the rocks
    and the clefts of the cliffs,
  from before the terror of the LORD,
    and from the glory of his majesty,
    when he rises to terrify the earth.
22 Turn away from man
  in whose nostrils is breath,
  for of what account is he?

3 For, behold, the Lord, the LORD
   of hosts,
  is taking away from Jerusalem
    and from Judah
stay and staff,
  the whole stay of bread,
  and the whole stay of water;
2 the mighty man and the soldier,
  the judge and the prophet,
  the diviner and the elder,
3 the captain of fifty
  and the man of rank,
  the counselor and the skilful ma-
    gician
  and the expert in charms.
4 And I will make boys their princes,
  and babes shall rule over them.
5 And the people will oppress one
    another,
  every man his fellow
  and every man his neighbor;
  the youth will be insolent to the
    elder,
    and the base fellow to the hon-
     orable.

6 When a man takes hold of his
    brother
  in the house of his father, saying:
"You have a mantle;
  you shall be our leader,
  and this heap of ruins
    shall be under your rule";

a Cn: Heb lacks *of diviners* *b* Cn Compare Gk: Heb *low*

7 in that day he will speak out, saying:
"I will not be a healer;
  in my house there is neither bread
    nor mantle;
you shall not make me
  leader of the people."
8 For Jerusalem has stumbled,
    and Judah has fallen;
because their speech and their deeds
    are against the LORD,
  defying his glorious presence.

9 Their partiality witnesses against
    them;
  they proclaim their sin like
    Sod′om,
  they do not hide it.
Woe to them!
  For they have brought evil upon
    themselves.
10 Tell the righteous that it shall be
    well with them,
  for they shall eat the fruit of their
    deeds.
11 Woe to the wicked! It shall be ill
    with him,
  for what his hands have done
    shall be done to him.
12 My people—children are their op-
    pressors,
  and women rule over them.
O my people, your leaders mislead
    you,
  and confuse the course of your
    paths.

13 The LORD has taken his place to
    contend,
  he stands to judge his people.*d*
14 The LORD enters into judgment
  with the elders and princes of his
    people:
"It is you who have devoured the
    vineyard,
  the spoil of the poor is in your
    houses.
15 What do you mean by crushing my
    people,
  by grinding the face of the poor?"
    says the Lord GOD of hosts.

16 The LORD said:
Because the daughters of Zion are
    haughty
  and walk with outstretched necks,
    glancing wantonly with their eyes,
  mincing along as they go,
    tinkling with their feet;
17 the Lord will smite with a scab
  the heads of the daughters of
    Zion,
  and the LORD will lay bare their
    secret parts.

18 In that day the Lord will take
away the finery of the anklets, the
headbands, and the crescents; 19 the
pendants, the bracelets, and the scarfs;
20 the headdresses, the armlets, the
sashes, the perfume boxes, and the
amulets; 21 the signet rings and nose
rings; 22 the festal robes, the mantles,
the cloaks, and the handbags; 23 the
garments of gauze, the linen garments,
the turbans, and the veils.
24 Instead of perfume there will be
    rottenness;
  and instead of a girdle, a rope;
  and instead of well-set hair, bald-
    ness;
  and instead of a rich robe, a gird-
    ing of sackcloth;
  instead of beauty, shame.*e*
25 Your men shall fall by the sword
  and your mighty men in battle.
26 And her gates shall lament and
    mourn;
  ravaged, she shall sit upon the
    ground.

4 And seven women shall take hold
of one man in that day, saying,
"We will eat our own bread and wear
our own clothes, only let us be called
by your name; take away our reproach."

2 In that day the branch of the
LORD shall be beautiful and glorious,
and the fruit of the land shall be the
pride and glory of the survivors of
Israel. 3 And he who is left in Zion and
remains in Jerusalem will be called
holy, every one who has been recorded
for life in Jerusalem, 4 when the Lord
shall have washed away the filth of the
daughters of Zion and cleansed the
bloodstains of Jerusalem from its midst
by a spirit of judgment and by a spirit
of burning. 5 Then the LORD will
create over the whole site of Mount
Zion and over her assemblies a cloud
by day, and smoke and the shining of
a flaming fire by night; for over all the
glory there will be a canopy and a
pavilion. 6 It will be for a shade by
day from the heat, and for a refuge and
a shelter from the storm and rain.

5 Let me sing for my beloved
a love song concerning his vine-
    yard:
My beloved had a vineyard
  on a very fertile hill.
2 He digged it and cleared it of stones,
  and planted it with choice vines;
he built a watchtower in the midst
  of it,
  and hewed out a wine vat in it;

d Gk Syr: Heb *judge peoples*   *e* One ancient Ms: Heb lacks *shame*
4.2: Jer 23.5; 33.15; Zech 3.8; 6.12.   **5.1-7:** Mt 21.33-46; Mk 12.1-12; Lk 20.9-19.

and he looked for it to yield grapes,
but it yielded wild grapes.

3 And now, O inhabitants of Jerusalem
and men of Judah,
judge, I pray you, between me
and my vineyard.
4 What more was there to do for my
vineyard,
that I have not done in it?
When I looked for it to yield grapes,
why did it yield wild grapes?

5 And now I will tell you
what I will do to my vineyard.
I will remove its hedge,
and it shall be devoured;
I will break down its wall,
and it shall be trampled down.
6 I will make it a waste;
it shall not be pruned or hoed,
and briers and thorns shall grow
up;
I will also command the clouds
that they rain no rain upon it.

7 For the vineyard of the LORD of
hosts
is the house of Israel,
and the men of Judah
are his pleasant planting;
and he looked for justice,
but behold, bloodshed;
for righteousness,
but behold, a cry!

8 Woe to those who join house to house,
who add field to field,
until there is no more room,
and you are made to dwell alone
in the midst of the land.
9 The LORD of hosts has sworn in my
hearing:
"Surely many houses shall be
desolate,
large and beautiful houses, without inhabitant.
10 For ten acres of vineyard shall yield
but one bath,
and a homer of seed shall yield but
an ephah."

11 Woe to those who rise early in the
morning,
that they may run after strong
drink,
who tarry late into the evening
till wine inflames them!
12 They have lyre and harp,
timbrel and flute and wine at
their feasts;
but they do not regard the deeds of
the LORD,
or see the work of his hands.

13 Therefore my people go into exile
for want of knowledge;
their honored men are dying of
hunger,
and their multitude is parched
with thirst.
14 Therefore Shĕ′ōl has enlarged its
appetite
and opened its mouth beyond
measure,
and the nobility of Jerusalem*f* and
her multitude go down,
her throng and he who exults in
her.
15 Man is bowed down, and men are
brought low,
and the eyes of the haughty are
humbled.
16 But the LORD of hosts is exalted in
justice,
and the Holy God shows himself
holy in righteousness.
17 Then shall the lambs graze as in
their pasture,
fatlings and kids*g* shall feed among
the ruins.

18 Woe to those who draw iniquity
with cords of falsehood,
who draw sin as with cart ropes,
19 who say: "Let him make haste,
let him speed his work
that we may see it;
let the purpose of the Holy One of
Israel draw near,
and let it come, that we may know
it!"
20 Woe to those who call evil good
and good evil,
who put darkness for light
and light for darkness,
who put bitter for sweet
and sweet for bitter!
21 Woe to those who are wise in their
own eyes,
and shrewd in their own sight!
22 Woe to those who are heroes at
drinking wine,
and valiant men in mixing strong
drink,
23 who acquit the guilty for a bribe,
and deprive the innocent of his
right!

24 Therefore, as the tongue of fire
devours the stubble,
and as dry grass sinks down in
the flame,
so their root will be as rottenness,
and their blossom go up like dust;
for they have rejected the law of
the LORD of hosts,
and have despised the word of
the Holy One of Israel.

f Heb *her nobility*   *g* Cn Compare Gk: Heb *aliens*

25 Therefore the anger of the LORD
        was kindled against his people,
    and he stretched out his hand
        against them and smote them,
    and the mountains quaked;
and their corpses were as refuse
    in the midst of the streets.
For all this his anger is not turned
    away
    and his hand is stretched out still.

26 He will raise a signal for a nation
        afar off,
    and whistle for it from the ends
        of the earth;
    and lo, swiftly, speedily it comes!
27 None is weary, none stumbles,
        none slumbers or sleeps,
    not a waistcloth is loose,
        not a sandal-thong broken;
28 their arrows are sharp,
        all their bows bent,
    their horses' hoofs seem like flint,
        and their wheels like the whirlwind.
29 Their roaring is like a lion,
        like young lions they roar;
    they growl and seize their prey,
        they carry it off, and none can
            rescue.
30 They will growl over it on that day,
        like the roaring of the sea.
    And if one look to the land,
        behold, darkness and distress;
    and the light is darkened by its clouds.

6   In the year that King Uz·zi′ah
    died I saw the Lord sitting upon
a throne, high and lifted up; and his
train filled the temple. 2Above him
stood the seraphim; each had six
wings: with two he covered his face,
and with two he covered his feet, and
with two he flew. 3And one called to
another and said:

    "Holy, holy, holy is the LORD of hosts;
        the whole earth is full of his glory."

4And the foundations of the thresholds
shook at the voice of him who called,
and the house was filled with smoke.
5And I said: "Woe is me! For I am
lost; for I am a man of unclean lips,
and I dwell in the midst of a people of
unclean lips; for my eyes have seen
the King, the LORD of hosts!"
   6 Then flew one of the seraphim to
me, having in his hand a burning coal
which he had taken with tongs from
the altar. 7And he touched my mouth,
and said: "Behold, this has touched
your lips; your guilt is taken away, and
your sin forgiven." 8And I heard the
voice of the Lord saying, "Whom shall
I send, and who will go for us?" Then

I said, "Here am I! Send me." 9And
he said, "Go and say to this people:
    'Hear and hear, but do not under-
        stand;
    see and see, but do not perceive.'
10 Make the heart of this people fat,
        and their ears heavy,
        and shut their eyes;
    lest they see with their eyes,
        and hear with their ears,
    and understand with their hearts,
        and turn and be healed."
11 Then I said, "How long, O Lord?"
And he said:
    "Until cities lie waste
        without inhabitant,
    and houses without men,
        and the land is utterly desolate,
12 and the LORD removes men far
        away,
    and the forsaken places are many
        in the midst of the land.
13 And though a tenth remain in it,
        it will be burned again,
    like a terebinth or an oak,
        whose stump remains standing
            when it is felled."
    The holy seed is its stump.

7   In the days of A′haz the son of
    Jo′tham, son of Uz·zi′ah, king of
Judah, Re′zin the king of Syria and
Pe′kah the son of Rem·a·li′ah the king
of Israel came up to Jerusalem to wage
war against it, but they could not conquer it. 2 When the house of David
was told, "Syria is in league with
E′phra·im," his heart and the heart of
his people shook as the trees of the
forest shake before the wind.

   3 And the LORD said to I·sai′ah,
"Go forth to meet A′haz, you and
She′ar-jash′ub[h] your son, at the end of
the conduit of the upper pool on the
highway to the Fuller's Field, 4 and
say to him, 'Take heed, be quiet, do
not fear, and do not let your heart be
faint because of these two smoldering
stumps of firebrands, at the fierce
anger of Re′zin and Syria and the son
of Rem·a·li′ah. 5 Because Syria, with
E′phra·im and the son of Rem·a·li′ah,
has devised evil against you, saying,
6 "Let us go up against Judah and
terrify it, and let us conquer it for ourselves, and set up the son of Ta′be-el
as king in the midst of it," 7 thus says
the Lord GOD:
    It shall not stand,
        and it shall not come to pass.
8 For the head of Syria is Damascus,
    and the head of Damascus is
        Re′zin.

h That is *A remnant shall return*   **6.3:** Rev 4.8.   **6.4:** Rev 15.8.
6.9-10: Mt 13.14-15; Mk 4.12; Lk 8.10; Jn 12.39-41; Acts 28.26-27.

(Within sixty-five years Ē'phrā·im will be broken to pieces so that it will no longer be a people.)

9 And the head of Ē'phrā·im is
  Să·mâr'i·à,
  and the head of Samaria is the son
  of Rem·à·lī'àh.
  If you will not believe,
  surely you shall not be estab-
    lished.' "

10 Again the LORD spoke to A'haz, 11 "Ask a sign of the LORD your God; let it be deep as Shē'ōl or high as heaven." 12 But A'haz said, "I will not ask, and I will not put the LORD to the test." 13 And he said, "Hear then, O house of David! Is it too little for you to weary men, that you weary my God also? 14 Therefore the Lord himself will give you a sign. Behold, a young woman*i* shall conceive and bear*j* a son, and shall call his name Im·man'-ū·ĕl.*k* 15 He shall eat curds and honey when he knows how to refuse the evil and choose the good. 16 For before the child knows how to refuse the evil and choose the good, the land before whose two kings you are in dread will be deserted. 17 The LORD will bring upon you and upon your people and upon your father's house such days as have not come since the day that Ē'phrā·im departed from Judah—the king of Assyria."

18 In that day the LORD will whistle for the fly which is at the sources of the streams of Egypt, and for the bee which is in the land of Assyria. 19 And they will all come and settle in the steep ravines, and in the clefts of the rocks, and on all the thorn-bushes, and on all the pastures.

20 In that day the Lord will shave with a razor which is hired beyond the River—with the kings of Assyria—the head and the hair of the feet, and it will sweep away the beard also.

21 In that day a man will keep alive a young cow and two sheep; 22 and because of the abundance of milk which they give, he will eat curds; for every one that is left in the land will eat curds and honey.

23 In that day every place where there used to be a thousand vines, worth a thousand shekels of silver, will become briers and thorns. 24 With bow and arrows men will come there, for all the land will be briers and thorns; 25 and as for all the hills which used to be hoed with a hoe, you will not come there for fear of briers and

thorns; but they will become a place where cattle are let loose and where sheep tread.

8 Then the LORD said to me, "Take a large tablet and write upon it in common characters, 'Belonging to Mā'hĕr-shal'al-hash'baz.' "*l* 2 And I got reliable witnesses, Ū'rī·àh the priest and Zech·à·rī'àh the son of Je·ber·ĕ-chī'àh, to attest for me. 3 And I went to the prophetess, and she conceived and bore a son. Then the LORD said to me, "Call his name Mā'hĕr-shal'al-hash'baz; 4 for before the child knows how to cry 'My father' or 'My mother,' the wealth of Damascus and the spoil of Să·mâr'i·à will be carried away before the king of Assyria."

5 The LORD spoke to me again: 6 "Because this people have refused the waters of Shi·lō'àh that flow gently, and melt in fear before*m* Rē'zin and the son of Rem·à·lī'àh; 7 therefore, behold, the Lord is bringing up against them the waters of the River, mighty and many, the king of Assyria and all his glory; and it will rise over all its channels and go over all its banks; 8 and it will sweep on into Judah, it will overflow and pass on, reaching even to the neck; and its outspread wings will fill the breadth of your land, O Im·man'ū·ĕl."

9 Be broken, you peoples, and be dismayed;
  give ear, all you far countries;
  gird yourselves and be dismayed;
  gird yourselves and be dismayed.
10 Take counsel together, but it will
    come to nought;
  speak a word, but it will not
    stand,
  for God is with us.*x*

11 For the LORD spoke thus to me with his strong hand upon me, and warned me not to walk in the way of this people, saying: 12 "Do not call conspiracy all that this people call conspiracy, and do not fear what they fear, nor be in dread. 13 But the LORD of hosts, him you shall regard as holy; let him be your fear, and let him be your dread. 14 And he will become a sanctuary, and a stone of offense, and a rock of stumbling to both houses of Israel, a trap and a snare to the inhabitants of Jerusalem. 15 And many shall stumble thereon; they shall fall and be broken; they shall be snared and taken."

---

i Or *virgin*   *j* Or *is with child and shall bear*   *k* That is *God is with us*
l That is *The spoil speeds, the prey hastes*   *m* Cn: Heb *rejoices in*   *x* Heb *immanu el*
7.14: Mt 1.23.   8.12-13: 1 Pet 3.14-15.   8.14: Rom 9.32-33; 1 Pet 2.8.

16 Bind up the testimony, seal the teaching among my disciples. 17 I will wait for the LORD, who is hiding his face from the house of Jacob, and I will hope in him. 18 Behold, I and the children whom the LORD has given me are signs and portents in Israel from the LORD of hosts, who dwells on Mount Zion. 19 And when they say to you, "Consult the mediums and the wizards who chirp and mutter," should not a people consult their God? Should they consult the dead on behalf of the living? 20 To the teaching and to the testimony! Surely for this word which they speak there is no dawn. 21 They will pass through the land,[n] greatly distressed and hungry; and when they are hungry, they will be enraged and will curse[o] their king and their God, and turn their faces upward; 22 and they will look to the earth, but behold, distress and darkness, the gloom of anguish; and they will be thrust into thick darkness.

9 [p] But there will be no gloom for her that was in anguish. In the former time he brought into contempt the land of Zeb′u·lun and the land of Naph′ta·li, but in the latter time he will make glorious the way of the sea, the land beyond the Jordan, Galilee of the nations.
2 [q] The people who walked in darkness have seen a great light;
  those who dwelt in a land of deep darkness,
  on them has light shined.
3 Thou hast multiplied the nation,
  thou hast increased its joy;
they rejoice before thee
  as with joy at the harvest,
  as men rejoice when they divide the spoil.
4 For the yoke of his burden,
  and the staff for his shoulder,
  the rod of his oppressor,
  thou hast broken as on the day of Mid′i·an.
5 For every boot of the tramping warrior in battle tumult
  and every garment rolled in blood
  will be burned as fuel for the fire.
6 For to us a child is born,
  to us a son is given;
and the government will be upon his shoulder,
  and his name will be called
  "Wonderful Counselor, Mighty God,
  Everlasting Father, Prince of Peace."

7 Of the increase of his government and of peace
  there will be no end,
upon the throne of David, and over his kingdom,
  to establish it, and to uphold it
with justice and with righteousness
  from this time forth and for evermore.
The zeal of the LORD of hosts will do this.

8 The Lord has sent a word against Jacob,
  and it will light upon Israel;
9 and all the people will know,
  E′phra·im and the inhabitants of Sa·mar′i·a,
  who say in pride and in arrogance of heart:
10 "The bricks have fallen,
  but we will build with dressed stones;
  the sycamores have been cut down,
  but we will put cedars in their place."
11 So the LORD raises adversaries[r] against them,
  and stirs up their enemies.
12 The Syrians on the east and the Philistines on the west
  devour Israel with open mouth.
For all this his anger is not turned away
  and his hand is stretched out still.

13 The people did not turn to him who smote them,
  nor seek the LORD of hosts.
14 So the LORD cut off from Israel head and tail,
  palm branch and reed in one day—
15 the elder and honored man is the head,
  and the prophet who teaches lies is the tail;
16 for those who lead this people lead them astray,
  and those who are led by them are swallowed up.
17 Therefore the Lord does not rejoice over their young men,
  and has no compassion on their fatherless and widows;
for every one is godless and an evildoer,
  and every mouth speaks folly.
For all this his anger is not turned away
  and his hand is stretched out still.

18 For wickedness burns like a fire,

n Heb it   o Or curse by   p Ch 8.23 in Heb
r Cn: Heb the adversaries of Rezin   q Ch 9.1 in Heb
8.17-18: Heb 2.13.   9.1-2: Mt 4.15-16; Lk 1.79.

it consumes briers and thorns;
it kindles the thickets of the forest,
  and they roll upward in a column
    of smoke.
19 Through the wrath of the LORD of
  hosts
  the land is burned,
and the people are like fuel for the
  fire;
no man spares his brother.
20 They snatch on the right, but are
  still hungry,
  and they devour on the left, but
    are not satisfied;
each devours his neighbor's[s] flesh,
21 Mà·nas′sĕh E′phrà·im, and Ephraim
  Manasseh,
  and together they are against
    Judah.
For all this his anger is not turned
  away
  and his hand is stretched out still.

10 Woe to those who decree in-
  iquitous decrees,
  and the writers who keep writing
    oppression,
2 to turn aside the needy from justice
  and to rob the poor of my people
    of their right,
that widows may be their spoil,
  and that they may make the
    fatherless their prey!
3 What will you do on the day of
  punishment,
  in the storm which will come
    from afar?
To whom will you flee for help,
  and where will you leave your
    wealth?
4 Nothing remains but to crouch
  among the prisoners
or fall among the slain.
For all this his anger is not turned
  away
  and his hand is stretched out still.

5 Ah, Assyria, the rod of my anger,
  the staff of my fury![t]
6 Against a godless nation I send him,
  and against the people of my
    wrath I command him,
to take spoil and seize plunder,
  and to tread them down like the
    mire of the streets.
7 But he does not so intend,
  and his mind does not so think;
but it is in his mind to destroy,
  and to cut off nations not a few;
8 for he says:
  "Are not my commanders all kings?
9 Is not Cal′nō like Cär′chē·mish?
  Is not Hä′math like Är′pad?

Is not Sà·mâr′i·à like Damascus?
10 As my hand has reached to the kingdoms of the idols
  whose graven images were greater
    than those of Jerusalem and
    Sà·mâr′i·à,
11 shall I not do to Jerusalem and her
  idols
  as I have done to Sà·mâr′i·à and
    her images?"

12 When the Lord has finished all
his work on Mount Zion and on Jerusalem he[u] will punish the arrogant
boasting of the king of Assyria and his
haughty pride. 13 For he says:
"By the strength of my hand I have
  done it,
  and by my wisdom, for I have
    understanding;
I have removed the boundaries of
  peoples,
  and have plundered their treas-
    ures;
like a bull I have brought down
  those who sat on thrones.
14 My hand has found like a nest
  the wealth of the peoples;
and as men gather eggs that have
  been forsaken
so I have gathered all the earth;
and there was none that moved a
  wing,
  or opened the mouth, or chirped."

15 Shall the axe vaunt itself over him
  who hews with it,
  or the saw magnify itself against
    him who wields it?
As if a rod should wield him who
  lifts it,
  or as if a staff should lift him who
    is not wood!
16 Therefore the Lord, the LORD of
  hosts,
  will send wasting sickness among
    his stout warriors,
and under his glory a burning will
  be kindled,
  like the burning of fire.
17 The light of Israel will become a fire,
  and his Holy One a flame;
and it will burn and devour
  his thorns and briers in one day.
18 The glory of his forest and of his
  fruitful land
  the LORD will destroy, both soul
    and body,
and it will be as when a sick man
  wastes away.
19 The remnant of the trees of his
  forest will be so few
  that a child can write them down.

---

[s] Tg Compare Gk: Heb *the flesh of his arm*
[u] Heb *I*   **10.5-34**: Nahum; Zeph 2.13-15.
[t] Heb *a staff it is in their hand my fury*

20 In that day the remnant of Israel and the survivors of the house of Jacob will no more lean upon him that smote them, but will lean upon the LORD, the Holy One of Israel, in truth. 21A remnant will return, the remnant of Jacob, to the mighty God. 22 For though your people Israel be as the sand of the sea, only a remant of them will return. Destruction is decreed, overflowing with righteousness. 23 For the Lord, the LORD of hosts, will make a full end, as decreed, in the midst of all the earth.

24 Therefore thus says the Lord, the LORD of hosts: "O my people, who dwell in Zion, be not afraid of the Assyrians when they smite with the rod and lift up their staff against you as the Egyptians did. 25 For in a very little while my indignation will come to an end, and my anger will be directed to their destruction. 26And the LORD of hosts will wield against them a scourge, as when he smote Mid′i·ăn at the rock of Ŏr′eb; and his rod will be over the sea, and he will lift it as he did in Egypt. 27And in that day his burden will depart from your shoulder, and his yoke will be destroyed from your neck."

He has gone up from Rim′mon,ᵛ
28   he has come to Ăi′ath;
he has passed through Mig′ron,
    at Mich′mash he stores his baggage;
29 they have crossed over the pass,
    at Gĕ′bà they lodge for the night;
Rā′màh trembles,
    Gĭb′ē-àh of Saul has fled.
30 Cry aloud, O daughter of Gal′lim!
    Hearken, O Lā′i·shàh!
    Answer her, O An′à·thoth!
31 Mad·mē′nàh is in flight,
    the inhabitants of Gĕ′bim flee for
      safety.
32 This very day he will halt at Nob,
    he will shake his fist
    at the mount of the daughter of
      Zion,
    the hill of Jerusalem.

33 Behold, the Lord, the LORD of hosts
    will lop the boughs with terrify-
      ing power;
the great in height will be hewn down,
    and the lofty will be brought low.
34 He will cut down the thickets of the
    forest with an axe,
    and Lebanon with its majestic
      treesʷ will fall.

11 There shall come forth a shoot
    from the stump of Jesse,
    and a branch shall grow out of his
      roots.
2 And the Spirit of the LORD shall
    rest upon him,
    the spirit of wisdom and under-
      standing,
    the spirit of counsel and might,
    the spirit of knowledge and the
      fear of the LORD.
3 And his delight shall be in the fear
    of the LORD.

He shall not judge by what his eyes
    see,
    or decide by what his ears hear;
4 but with righteousness he shall
    judge the poor,
    and decide with equity for the
      meek of the earth;
    and he shall smite the earth with
      the rod of his mouth,
    and with the breath of his lips
      he shall slay the wicked.
5 Righteousness shall be the girdle of
    his waist,
    and faithfulness the girdle of his
      loins.

6 The wolf shall dwell with the lamb,
    and the leopard shall lie down
      with the kid,
    and the calf and the lion and the
      fatling together,
    and a little child shall lead them.
7 The cow and the bear shall feed;
    their young shall lie down together;
    and the lion shall eat straw like
      the ox.
8 The sucking child shall play over
    the hole of the asp,
    and the weaned child shall put
      his hand on the adder's den.
9 They shall not hurt or destroy
    in all my holy mountain;
    for the earth shall be full of the
      knowledge of the LORD
    as the waters cover the sea.

10 In that day the root of Jesse shall stand as an ensign to the peoples; him shall the nations seek, and his dwellings shall be glorious.

11 In that day the Lord will extend his hand yet a second time to recover the remnant which is left of his people, from Assyria, from Egypt, from Path′ros, from Ethiopia, from Ē′làm, from Shi′när, from Hā′math, and from the coastlands of the sea.

ᵛ Cn: Heb *and his yoke from your neck, and a yoke will be destroyed because of fatness*
ʷ Cn Compare Gk Vg: Heb *with a majestic one*
10.22-23: Rom 9.27-28.   11.1: Is 11.10; Rom 15.12.   11.2: 1 Pet 4.14.
11.5: Eph 6.14.   11.6-9: Is 65.25; Hab 2.14.   11.10: Is 11.1; Rom 15.12.

12 He will raise an ensign for the nations,
and will assemble the outcasts of Israel,
and gather the dispersed of Judah from the four corners of the earth.

13 The jealousy of É'phrá·im shall depart,
and those who harass Judah shall be cut off;
Ephraim shall not be jealous of Judah,
and Judah shall not harass Ephraim.

14 But they shall swoop down upon the shoulder of the Philistines in the west,
and together they shall plunder the people of the east.
They shall put forth their hand against É'dóm and Mó'ab,
and the Am'mó·nites shall obey them.

15 And the LORD will utterly destroy the tongue of the sea of Egypt;
and will wave his hand over the River with his scorching wind,
and smite it into seven channels that men may cross dryshod.

16 And there will be a highway from Assyria
for the remnant which is left of his people,
as there was for Israel
when they came up from the land of Egypt.

12 You will say in that day:
"I will give thanks to thee, O LORD,
for though thou wast angry with me,
thy anger turned away,
and thou didst comfort me.

2 "Behold, God is my salvation;
I will trust, and will not be afraid;
for the LORD GOD is my strength and my song,
and he has become my salvation."

3 With joy you will draw water from the wells of salvation. 4 And you will say in that day:
"Give thanks to the LORD,
call upon his name;
make known his deeds among the nations,
proclaim that his name is exalted.

5 "Sing praises to the LORD, for he has done gloriously;
let this be known[x] in all the earth.

6 Shout, and sing for joy, O inhabitant of Zion,
for great in your midst is the Holy One of Israel."

13 The oracle concerning Babylon which I·sāi'áh the son of Ā'moz saw.

2 On a bare hill raise a signal,
cry aloud to them;
wave the hand for them to enter the gates of the nobles.

3 I myself have commanded my consecrated ones,
have summoned my mighty men to execute my anger,
my proudly exulting ones.

4 Hark, a tumult on the mountains as of a great multitude!
Hark, an uproar of kingdoms, of nations gathering together!
The LORD of hosts is mustering a host for battle.

5 They come from a distant land, from the end of the heavens,
the LORD and the weapons of his indignation,
to destroy the whole earth.

6 Wail, for the day of the LORD is near;
as destruction from the Almighty it will come!

7 Therefore all hands will be feeble, and every man's heart will melt,
8 and they will be dismayed.
Pangs and agony will seize them;
they will be in anguish like a woman in travail.
They will look aghast at one another; their faces will be aflame.

9 Behold, the day of the LORD comes, cruel, with wrath and fierce anger,
to make the earth a desolation and to destroy its sinners from it.
10 For the stars of the heavens and their constellations
will not give their light;
the sun will be dark at its rising and the moon will not shed its light.
11 I will punish the world for its evil, and the wicked for their iniquity;
I will put an end to the pride of the arrogant,
and lay low the haughtiness of the ruthless.
12 I will make men more rare than fine gold,
and mankind than the gold of Ó'phir.
13 Therefore I will make the heavens tremble,

x Or *this is made known*

13.1-14.23: Is 47; Jer 50-51; Hab 1-2.   13.10: Mt 24.29; Mk 13.24; Rev 6.12; 8.12.

and the earth will be shaken out
of its place,
at the wrath of the LORD of hosts
in the day of his fierce anger.
14 And like a hunted gazelle,
or like sheep with none to gather
them,
every man will turn to his own
people,
and every man will flee to his
own land.
15 Whoever is found will be thrust
through,
and whoever is caught will fall
by the sword.
16 Their infants will be dashed in
pieces
before their eyes;
their houses will be plundered
and their wives ravished.

17 Behold, I am stirring up the Medes
against them,
who have no regard for silver
and do not delight in gold.
18 Their bows will slaughter the young
men;
they will have no mercy on the
fruit of the womb;
their eyes will not pity children.
19 And Babylon, the glory of kingdoms,
the splendor and pride of the
Chal·dē′ans,
will be like Sod′om and Go·mor′rah
when God overthrew them.
20 It will never be inhabited
or dwelt in for all generations;
no Arab will pitch his tent there,
no shepherds will make their
flocks lie down there.
21 But wild beasts will lie down there,
and its houses will be full of
howling creatures;
there ostriches will dwell,
and there satyrs will dance.
22 Hyenas will cry in its towers,
and jackals in the pleasant palaces;
its time is close at hand
and its days will not be prolonged.

14 The LORD will have compassion
on Jacob and will again choose
Israel, and will set them in their own
land, and aliens will join them and
will cleave to the house of Jacob. 2 And
the peoples will take them and bring
them to their place, and the house of
Israel will possess them in the LORD's
land as male and female slaves; they
will take captive those who were their
captors, and rule over those who
oppressed them.
3 When the LORD has given you

rest from your pain and turmoil and
the hard service with which you were
made to serve, 4 you will take up this
taunt against the king of Babylon:
"How the oppressor has ceased,
the insolent fury[y] ceased!
5 The LORD has broken the staff of
the wicked,
the scepter of rulers,
6 that smote the peoples in wrath
with unceasing blows,
that ruled the nations in anger
with unrelenting persecution.
7 The whole earth is at rest and quiet;
they break forth into singing.
8 The cypresses rejoice at you,
the cedars of Lebanon, saying,
'Since you were laid low,
no hewer comes up against us.'
9 Shē′ōl beneath is stirred up
to meet you when you come,
it rouses the shades to greet you,
all who were leaders of the earth;
it raises from their thrones
all who were kings of the nations.
10 All of them will speak
and say to you:
'You too have become as weak as we!
You have become like us!'
11 Your pomp is brought down to
Shē′ōl,
the sound of your harps;
maggots are the bed beneath you,
and worms are your covering.

12 "How you are fallen from heaven,
O Day Star, son of Dawn!
How you are cut down to the
ground,
you who laid the nations low!
13 You said in your heart,
'I will ascend to heaven;
above the stars of God
I will set my throne on high;
I will sit on the mount of assembly
in the far north;
14 I will ascend above the heights of
the clouds,
I will make myself like the Most
High.'
15 But you are brought down to Shē′ōl,
to the depths of the Pit.
16 Those who see you will stare at you,
and ponder over you:
'Is this the man who made the earth
tremble,
who shook kingdoms,
17 who made the world like a desert
and overthrew its cities,
who did not let his prisoners go
home?'
18 All the kings of the nations lie in
glory,

---

[y] One ancient Ms Compare Gk Syr Vg: The meaning of the Hebrew word is uncertain
13.21: Rev 18.2.

each in his own tomb;
19 but you are cast out, away from
your sepulchre,
like a loathed untimely birth,z
clothed with the slain, those pierced
by the sword,
who go down to the stones of the
Pit,
like a dead body trodden under
foot.
20 You will not be joined with them
in burial,
because you have destroyed your
land,
you have slain your people.

"May the descendants of evildoers
nevermore be named!
21 Prepare slaughter for his sons
because of the guilt of their
fathers,
lest they rise and possess the earth,
and fill the face of the world with
cities."

22 "I will rise up against them,"
says the LORD of hosts, "and will cut
off from Babylon name and remnant,
offspring and posterity, says the LORD.
23 And I will make it a possession of
the hedgehog, and pools of water, and
I will sweep it with the broom of
destruction, says the LORD of hosts."

24 The LORD of hosts has sworn:
"As I have planned,
so shall it be,
and as I have purposed,
so shall it stand,
25 that I will break the Assyrian in my
land,
and upon my mountains trample
him under foot;
and his yoke shall depart from them,
and his burden from their
shoulder."
26 This is the purpose that is purposed
concerning the whole earth;
and this is the hand that is stretched
out
over all the nations.
27 For the LORD of hosts has purposed,
and who will annul it?
His hand is stretched out,
and who will turn it back?

28 In the year that King Ā'haz died
came this oracle:
29 "Rejoice not, O Phi·lis'ti·à, all of
you,

that the rod which smote you is
broken,
for from the serpent's root will come
forth an adder,
and its fruit will be a flying serpent.
30 And the first-born of the poor will
feed,
and the needy lie down in safety;
but I will kill your root with famine,
and your remnant Ia will slay.
31 Wail, O gate; cry, O city;
melt in fear, O Phi·lis'ti·à, all of
you!
For smoke comes out of the north,
and there is no straggler in his
ranks."

32 What will one answer the messengers
of the nation?
"The LORD has founded Zion,
and in her the afflicted of his people find refuge."

15 An oracle concerning Mō'ab.
Because Ār is laid waste in a night
Moab is undone;
because Kĭr is laid waste in a night
Moab is undone.
2 The daughter of Dĭ'bonb has gone
up
to the high places to weep;
over Nē'bō and over Med'é·bà
Mō'ab wails.
On every head is baldness,
every beard is shorn;
3 in the streets they gird on sackcloth;
on the housetops and in the
squares
every one wails and melts in tears.
4 Hesh'bón and É·lé·ā'léh cry out,
their voice is heard as far as
Jā'haz;
therefore the armed men of Mō'ab
cry aloud;
his soul trembles.
5 My heart cries out for Mō'ab;
his fugitives flee to Zō'är,
to Eg'làth-she·lish'i·yàh.
For at the ascent of Lū'hith
they go up weeping;
on the road to Hor·ō·nā'im
they raise a cry of destruction;
6 the waters of Nim'rim
are a desolation;
the grass is withered, the new
growth fails,
the verdure is no more.
7 Therefore the abundance they have
gained
and what they have laid up

z Cn Compare Tg Symmachus: Heb *a loathed branch*
a One ancient Ms Vg: Heb *he*　　b Cn: Heb *the house and Dibon*
14.29-31: Jer 47; Ezek 25.15-17; Joel 3.4-8; Amos 1.6-8; Zeph 2.4-7; Zech 9.5-7.
15-16: Is 25.10-12; Jer 48; Ezek 25.8-11; Amos 2.1-3; Zeph 2.8-11.

they carry away
  over the brook of the Willows.
8 For a cry has gone
  round the land of Mō'ab;
the wailing reaches to Eg.lā'im,
  the wailing reaches to Bē'ér-ē'lim.
9 For the waters of Di'bon*c* are full of
  blood;
  yet I will bring upon Dibon*c* even
  more,
a lion for those of Mō'ab who escape,
  for the remnant of the land.

16 They have sent lambs
  to the ruler of the land,
from Sē'là, by way of the desert,
  to the mount of the daughter of
  Zion.
2 Like fluttering birds,
  like scattered nestlings,
so are the daughters of Mō'ab
  at the fords of the Är'non.
3 "Give counsel,
  grant justice;
make your shade like night
  at the height of noon;
hide the outcasts,
  betray not the fugitive;
4 let the outcasts of Mō'ab
  sojourn among you;
be a refuge to them
  from the destroyer.
When the oppressor is no more,
  and destruction has ceased,
and he who tramples under foot
  has vanished from the land,
5 then a throne will be established in
  steadfast love
and on it will sit in faithfulness
  in the tent of David
one who judges and seeks justice
  and is swift to do righteousness."

6 We have heard of the pride of
  Mō'ab,
  how proud he was;
of his arrogance, his pride, and his
  insolence—
  his boasts are false.
7 Therefore let Mō'ab wail,
  let every one wail for Moab.
Mourn, utterly stricken,
  for the raisin-cakes of Kĭr-hâr'-
  é·seth.

8 For the fields of Hesh'bon languish,
  and the vine of Sib'màh;
the lords of the nations
  have struck down its branches,
which reached to Jā'zèr
  and strayed to the desert;
its shoots spread abroad

and passed over the sea.
9 Therefore I weep with the weeping
  of Jā'zèr
  for the vine of Sib'màh;
I drench you with my tears,
  O Hesh'bòn and E·lé·ā'léh;
for upon your fruit and your harvest
  the battle shout has fallen.
10 And joy and gladness are taken
  away
  from the fruitful field;
and in the vineyards no songs are
  sung,
  no shouts are raised;
no treader treads out wine in the
  presses;
  the vintage shout is hushed.*d*
11 Therefore my soul moans like a lyre
  for Mō'ab,
  and my heart for Kĭr-hē'res.
12 And when Mō'ab presents himself, when he wearies himself upon the
high place, when he comes to his
sanctuary to pray, he will not prevail.
13 This is the word which the LORD
spoke concerning Mō'ab in the past.
14 But now the LORD says, "In three
years, like the years of a hireling, the
glory of Mō'ab will be brought into
contempt, in spite of all his great
multitude, and those who survive will
be very few and feeble."

17 An oracle concerning Damascus.
  Behold, Damascus will cease to
  be a city,
  and will become a heap of ruins.
2 Her cities will be deserted for ever;*e*
  they will be for flocks,
which will lie down, and none will
  make them afraid.
3 The fortress will disappear from
  E'phrà·im,
  and the kingdom from Damascus;
and the remnant of Syria will be
  like the glory of the children of
  Israel,
  says the LORD of hosts.

4 And in that day
  the glory of Jacob will be brought
  low,
  and the fat of his flesh will grow
  lean.
5 And it shall be as when the reaper
  gathers standing grain
  and his arm harvests the ears,
and as when one gleans the ears of
  grain
  in the Valley of Reph'à·im.
6 Gleanings will be left in it,
  as when an olive tree is beaten—

c One ancient Ms Vg Compare Syr: Heb *Dimon*   *d* Gk: Heb *I have hushed*
e Cn Compare Gk: Heb *the cities of Aroer are deserted*
17.1-3: Jer 49.23-27; Amos 1.3-5; Zech 9.1.

two or three berries
  in the top of the highest bough,
four or five
  on the branches of a fruit tree,
    says the LORD God of Israel.

7 In that day men will regard their Maker, and their eyes will look to the Holy One of Israel; 8 they will not have regard for the altars, the work of their hands, and they will not look to what their own fingers have made, either the Á·she′rim or the altars of incense. 9 In that day their strong cities will be like the deserted places of the Hi′vites and the Am′ó·rites,*f* which they deserted because of the children of Israel, and there will be desolation.

10 For you have forgotten the God of
    your salvation,
  and have not remembered the
    Rock of your refuge;
therefore, though you plant pleasant
    plants
  and set out slips of an alien god,
11 though you make them grow on the
    day that you plant them,
  and make them blossom in the
    morning that you sow;
yet the harvest will flee away
  in a day of grief and incurable
    pain.

12 Ah, the thunder of many peoples,
  they thunder like the thundering
    of the sea!
Ah, the roar of nations,
  they roar like the roaring of
    mighty waters!
13 The nations roar like the roaring of
    many waters,
  but he will rebuke them, and they
    will flee far away,
chased like chaff on the mountains
    before the wind
  and whirling dust before the storm.
14 At evening time, behold, terror!
  Before morning, they are no more!
This is the portion of those who
    despoil us,
  and the lot of those who plunder
    us.

18 Ah, land of whirring wings
    which is beyond the rivers of
    Ethiopia;
2 which sends ambassadors by the
    Nile,
  in vessels of papyrus upon the
    waters!
Go, you swift messengers,

to a nation, tall and smooth,
to a people feared near and far,
  a nation mighty and conquering,
    whose land the rivers divide.

3 All you inhabitants of the world,
  you who dwell on the earth,
when a signal is raised on the moun-
    tains, look!
  When a trumpet is blown, hear!
4 For thus the LORD said to me:
"I will quietly look from my
    dwelling
  like clear heat in sunshine,
  like a cloud of dew in the heat of
    harvest."
5 For before the harvest, when the
    blossom is over,
  and the flower becomes a ripening
    grape,
he will cut off the shoots with
    pruning hooks,
  and the spreading branches he
    will hew away.
6 They shall all of them be left
  to the birds of prey of the
    mountains
  and to the beasts of the earth.
And the birds of prey will summer
    upon them,
  and all the beasts of the earth will
    winter upon them.

7 At that time gifts will be brought to the LORD of hosts
from a people tall and smooth,
  from a people feared near and far,
a nation mighty and conquering,
  whose land the rivers divide,
to Mount Zion, the place of the name of the LORD of hosts.

19 An oracle concerning Egypt.
    Behold, the LORD is riding on a
    swift cloud
  and comes to Egypt;
and the idols of Egypt will tremble
    at his presence,
  and the heart of the Egyptians
    will melt within them.
2 And I will stir up Egyptians against
    Egyptians,
  and they will fight, every man
    against his brother
  and every man against his
    neighbor,
  city against city, kingdom against
    kingdom;
3 and the spirit of the Egyptians with-
    in them will be emptied out,
  and I will confound their plans;
and they will consult the idols and
    the sorcerers,

f Cn Compare Gk: Heb *the wood and the highest bough*
18: Zeph 2.12.   **19:** Jer 46; Ezek 29–32; Zech 14.18–19.

and the mediums and the wizards;
4 and I will give over the Egyptians
  into the hand of a hard master;
and a fierce king will rule over them,
  says the Lord, the LORD of hosts.

5 And the waters of the Nile will be
  dried up,
  and the river will be parched and
    dry;
6 and its canals will become foul,
  and the branches of Egypt's Nile
    will diminish and dry up,
  reeds and rushes will rot away.
7 There will be bare places by the
    Nile,
  on the brink of the Nile,
  and all that is sown by the Nile will
    dry up,
  be driven away, and be no more.
8 The fishermen will mourn and
    lament,
  all who cast hook in the Nile;
  and they will languish
  who spread nets upon the water.
9 The workers in combed flax will be
    in despair,
  and the weavers of white cotton.
10 Those who are the pillars of the
    land will be crushed,
  and all who work for hire will be
    grieved.

11 The princes of Zō'an are utterly
    foolish;
  the wise counselors of Pharaoh
    give stupid counsel.
How can you say to Pharaoh,
"I am a son of the wise,
a son of ancient kings"?
12 Where then are your wise men?
  Let them tell you and make known
    what the LORD of hosts has
    purposed against Egypt.
13 The princes of Zō'an have become
    fools,
  and the princes of Memphis are
    deluded;
  those who are the cornerstones of
    her tribes
  have led Egypt astray.
14 The LORD has mingled within her
    a spirit of confusion;
  and they have made Egypt stagger
    in all her doings
  as a drunken man staggers in his
    vomit.
15 And there will be nothing for Egypt
    which head or tail, palm branch
    or reed, may do.

16 In that day the Egyptians will be
like women, and tremble with fear before the hand which the LORD of hosts
shakes over them. 17And the land of
Judah will become a terror to the
Egyptians; every one to whom it is
mentioned will fear because of the
purpose which the LORD of hosts has
purposed against them.
18 In that day there will be five
cities in the land of Egypt which speak
the language of Canaan and swear
allegiance to the LORD of hosts. One of
these will be called the City of the Sun.
19 In that day there will be an altar
to the LORD in the midst of the land of
Egypt, and a pillar to the LORD at its
border. 20 It will be a sign and a
witness to the LORD of hosts in the
land of Egypt; when they cry to the
LORD because of oppressors he will
send them a savior, and will defend
and deliver them. 21And the LORD will
make himself known to the Egyptians;
and the Egyptians will know the LORD
in that day and worship with sacrifice
and burnt offering, and they will make
vows to the LORD and perform them.
22And the LORD will smite Egypt,
smiting and healing, and they will return to the LORD, and he will heed
their supplications and heal them.
23 In that day there will be a highway from Egypt to Assyria, and the
Assyrian will come into Egypt, and the
Egyptian into Assyria, and the Egyptians will worship with the Assyrians.
24 In that day Israel will be the
third with Egypt and Assyria, a blessing in the midst of the earth, 25 whom
the LORD of hosts has blessed, saying,
"Blessed be Egypt my people, and
Assyria the work of my hands, and
Israel my heritage."

20 In the year that the commander in chief, who was sent
by Sär'gon the king of Assyria, came
to Ash'dod and fought against it and
took it,—2 at that time the LORD had
spoken by I-sāi'ah the son of A'moz,
saying, "Go, and loose the sackcloth
from your loins and take off your shoes
from your feet," and he had done so,
walking naked and barefoot—3 the
LORD said, "As my servant I-sāi'ah has
walked naked and barefoot for three
years as a sign and a portent against
Egypt and Ethiopia, 4 so shall the king
of Assyria lead away the Egyptians
captives and the Ethiopians exiles,
both the young and the old, naked and
barefoot, with buttocks uncovered, to
the shame of Egypt. 5 Then they shall
be dismayed and confounded because
of Ethiopia their hope and of Egypt
their boast. 6And the inhabitants of
this coastland will say in that day,
'Behold, this is what has happened to

those in whom we hoped and to whom
we fled for help to be delivered from
the king of Assyria! And we, how shall
we escape?'"

21 The oracle concerning the
wilderness of the sea.
As whirlwinds in the Negeb sweep
on,
it comes from the desert,
from a terrible land.
2 A stern vision is told to me;
the plunderer plunders,
and the destroyer destroys.
Go up, O É'lăm,
lay siege, O Media;
all the sighing she has caused
I bring to an end.
3 Therefore my loins are filled with
anguish;
pangs have seized me,
like the pangs of a woman in
travail;
I am bowed down so that I cannot
hear,
I am dismayed so that I cannot see.
4 My mind reels, horror has appalled
me;
the twilight I longed for
has been turned for me into
trembling.
5 They prepare the table,
they spread the rugs,
they eat, they drink.
Arise, O princes,
oil the shield!
6 For thus the Lord said to me:
"Go, set a watchman,
let him announce what he sees.
7 When he sees riders, horsemen in
pairs,
riders on asses, riders on camels,
let him listen diligently,
very diligently."
8 Then he who saw[g] cried:
"Upon a watchtower I stand, O
Lord,
continually by day,
and at my post I am stationed
whole nights.
9 And, behold, here come riders,
horsemen in pairs!"
And he answered,
"Fallen, fallen is Babylon;
and all the images of her gods
he has shattered to the ground."
10 O my threshed and winnowed one,
what I have heard from the Lord
of hosts,
the God of Israel, I announce to
you.

11 The oracle concerning Dü'mah.

One is calling to me from Sē'ir,
"Watchman, what of the night?
Watchman, what of the night?"
12 The watchman says:
"Morning comes, and also the night.
If you will inquire, inquire;
come back again."

13 The oracle concerning Arabia.
In the thickets in Arabia you will
lodge,
O caravans of Dē'da·nītes.
14 To the thirsty bring water,
meet the fugitive with bread,
O inhabitants of the land of
Tē'mà.
15 For they have fled from the swords,
from the drawn sword,
from the bent bow,
and from the press of battle.
16 For thus the Lord said to me,
"Within a year, according to the years
of a hireling, all the glory of Kē'där
will come to an end; 17 and the remainder of the archers of the mighty
men of the sons of Kē'där will be few;
for the Lord, the God of Israel, has
spoken."

22 The oracle concerning the
valley of vision.
What do you mean that you have
gone up,
all of you, to the housetops,
2 you who are full of shoutings,
tumultuous city, exultant town?
Your slain are not slain with the
sword
or dead in battle.
3 All your rulers have fled together,
without the bow they were captured.
All of you who were found were
captured,
though they had fled far away.[h]
4 Therefore I said:
"Look away from me,
let me weep bitter tears;
do not labor to comfort me
for the destruction of the daughter
of my people."

5 For the Lord God of hosts has a day
of tumult and trampling and
confusion
in the valley of vision,
a battering down of walls
and a shouting to the mountains.
6 And É'làm bore the quiver
with chariots and horsemen,[i]
and Kir uncovered the shield.
7 Your choicest valleys were full of
chariots,

g One ancient Ms: Heb a lion   h Gk Syr Vg: Heb from far away
i The Hebrew of this line is obscure

and the horsemen took their stand at the gates.

8 He has taken away the covering of Judah.

In that day you looked to the weapons of the House of the Forest, 9 and you saw that the breaches of the city of David were many, and you collected the waters of the lower pool, 10 and you counted the houses of Jerusalem, and you broke down the houses to fortify the wall. 11 You made a reservoir between the two walls for the water of the old pool. But you did not look to him who did it, or have regard for him who planned it long ago.

12 In that day the Lord GOD of hosts
    called to weeping and mourning,
    to baldness and girding with sack
       cloth;
13 and behold, joy and gladness,
    slaying oxen and killing sheep,
    eating flesh and drinking wine.
 "Let us eat and drink,
    for tomorrow we die."
14 The LORD of hosts has revealed him-
       self in my ears;
 "Surely this inquity will not be for-
       given you
    till you die,"
 says the Lord GOD of hosts.

15 Thus says the Lord GOD of hosts, "Come, go to this steward, to Sheb′nà, who is over the household, and say to him: 16 What have you to do here and whom have you here, that you have hewn here a tomb for yourself, you who hew a tomb on the height, and carve a habitation for yourself in the rock? 17 Behold, the LORD will hurl you away violently, O you strong man. He will seize firm hold on you, 18 and whirl you round and round, and throw you like a ball into a wide land; there you shall die, and there shall be your splendid chariots, you shame of your master's house. 19 I will thrust you from your office, and you will be cast down from your station. 20 In that day I will call my servant E-li′á-kim the son of Hil-ki′áh, 21 and I will clothe him with your robe, and will bind your girdle on him, and will commit your authority to his hand; and he shall be a father to the inhabitants of Jerusalem and to the house of Judah. 22 And I will place on his shoulder the key of the house of David; he shall open, and none shall shut; and he shall shut, and none shall

open. 23 And I will fasten him like a peg in a sure place, and he will become a throne of honor to his father's house. 24 And they will hang on him the whole weight of his father's house, the off-spring and issue, every small vessel, from the cups to all the flagons. 25 In that day, says the LORD of hosts, the peg that was fastened in a sure place will give way; and it will be cut down and fall, and the burden that was upon it will be cut off, for the LORD has spoken."

23 The oracle concerning Tȳre.
    Wail, O ships of Tär′shish,
 for Tyre is laid waste, without
       house or haven!
 From the land of Cyprus
    it is revealed to them.
2 Be still, O inhabitants of the coast,
    O merchants of Si′don;
 your messengers passed over the sea[j]
3   and were on many waters;
 your revenue was the grain of
       Shi′hôr,
    the harvest of the Nile;
 you were the merchant of the
       nations.
4 Be ashamed, O Si′don, for the sea
       has spoken,
    the stronghold of the sea, saying:
 "I have neither travailed nor given
       birth,
 I have neither reared young men
    nor brought up virgins."
5 When the report comes to Egypt,
    they will be in anguish over the
       report about Tȳre.
6 Pass over to Tär′shish,
    wail, O inhabitants of the coast!
7 Is this your exultant city
    whose origin is from days of old,
 whose feet carried her
    to settle afar?
8 Who has purposed this
    against Tȳre, the bestower of
       crowns,
 whose merchants were princes,
    whose traders were the honored
       of the earth?
9 The LORD of hosts has purposed it,
    to defile the pride of all glory,
    to dishonor all the honored of the
       earth.
10 Overflow your land like the Nile,
    O daughter of Tär′shish;
 there is no restraint any more.
11 He has stretched out his hand over
       the sea,
    he has shaken the kingdoms;
 the LORD has given command con-
       cerning Canaan

j One ancient Ms: Heb *who passed over the sea, they replenished you*

22.22: Rev 3.7. **23:** Ezek 26.1-28.19; Joel 3.4-8; Amos 1.9-10; Zech 9.3-4.

to destroy its strongholds.

12 And he said:
"You will no more exult,
　O oppressed virgin daughter of
　　Si′don;
arise, pass over to Cyprus,
　even there you will have no rest."

13 Behold the land of the Chal·dē′-
ănš! This is the people; it was not
Assyria. They destined Tyre for wild
beasts. They erected their siege-
towers, they razed her palaces, they
made her a ruin.*k*
14 Wail, O ships of Tär′shish,
　for your stronghold is laid waste.
15 In that day Tyre will be forgotten
for seventy years, like the days of one
king. At the end of seventy years, it
will happen to Tyre as in the song of
the harlot:
16 "Take a harp,
　go about the city,
　　O forgotten harlot!
Make sweet melody,
　sing many songs,
　that you may be remembered."
17 At the end of seventy years, the
LORD will visit Tyre, and she will return to her hire, and will play the harlot with all the kingdoms of the world
upon the face of the earth. 18 Her
merchandise and her hire will be
dedicated to the LORD; it will not be
stored or hoarded, but her merchandise will supply abundant food and
fine clothing for those who dwell before the LORD.

24 Behold, the LORD will lay
waste the earth and make it
desolate,
and he will twist its surface and
　scatter its inhabitants.
2 And it shall be, as with the people,
　so with the priest;
　as with the slave, so with his
　　master;
　as with the maid, so with her
　　mistress;
as with the buyer, so with the seller;
　as with the lender, so with the
　　borrower;
　as with the creditor, so with the
　　debtor.
3 The earth shall be utterly laid waste,
　and utterly despoiled;
for the LORD has spoken this
　word.

4 The earth mourns and withers,
　the world languishes and withers;
　the heavens languish together
　　with the earth.

5 The earth lies polluted
　under its inhabitants;
for they have transgressed the laws,
　violated the statutes,
　broken the everlasting covenant.
6 Therefore a curse devours the earth,
　and its inhabitants suffer for their
　　guilt;
therefore the inhabitants of the earth
　are scorched,
　and few men are left.
7 The wine mourns,
　the vine languishes,
　all the merry-hearted sigh.
8 The mirth of the timbrels is stilled,
　the noise of the jubilant has
　　ceased,
　the mirth of the lyre is stilled.
9 No more do they drink wine with
　singing;
　strong drink is bitter to those who
　　drink it.
10 The city of chaos is broken down,
　every house is shut up so that
　　none can enter.
11 There is an outcry in the streets for
　lack of wine;
　all joy has reached its eventide;
　the gladness of the earth is
　　banished.
12 Desolation is left in the city,
　the gates are battered into ruins.
13 For thus it shall be in the midst of
　the earth
　among the nations,
as when an olive tree is beaten,
　as at the gleaning when the
　　vintage is done.

14 They lift up their voices, they sing
　for joy;
　over the majesty of the LORD they
　　shout from the west.
15 Therefore in the east give glory to
　the LORD;
　in the coastlands of the sea, to the
　　name of the LORD, the God of
　　Israel.
16 From the ends of the earth we hear
　songs of praise,
　of glory to the Righteous One.
But I say, "I pine away,
　I pine away. Woe is me!
For the treacherous deal treach-
　erously,
　the treacherous deal very treach-
　　erously."

17 Terror, and the pit, and the snare
　are upon you, O inhabitant of the
　　earth!
18 He who flees at the sound of the
　terror
　shall fall into the pit;

k The Hebrew of this verse is obscure   **23.17:** Rev 17.2.   **24.8:** Rev 18.22.

and he who climbs out of the pit
 shall be caught in the snare.
For the windows of heaven are
 opened,
 and the foundations of the earth
 tremble.
19 The earth is utterly broken,
 the earth is rent asunder,
 the earth is violently shaken.
20 The earth staggers like a drunken
 man,
 it sways like a hut;
its transgression lies heavy upon it,
 and it falls, and will not rise again.

21 On that day the LORD will punish
 the host of heaven, in heaven,
 and the kings of the earth, on the
 earth.
22 They will be gathered together
 as prisoners in a pit;
they will be shut up in a prison,
 and after many days they will be
 punished.
23 Then the moon will be confounded,
 and the sun ashamed;
for the LORD of hosts will reign
 on Mount Zion and in Jerusalem
and before his elders he will manifest his glory.

25 O LORD, thou art my God;
 I will exalt thee, I will praise
 thy name;
for thou hast done wonderful things,
 plans formed of old, faithful and
 sure.
2 For thou hast made the city a heap,
 the fortified city a ruin;
the palace of aliens is a city no more,
 it will never be rebuilt.
3 Therefore strong peoples will glorify thee;
cities of ruthless nations will fear
 thee.
4 For thou hast been a stronghold to
 the poor,
 a stronghold to the needy in his
 distress,
 a shelter from the storm and a
 shade from the heat;
for the blast of the ruthless is like a
 storm against a wall,
5   like heat in a dry place.
Thou dost subdue the noise of the
 aliens;
 as heat by the shade of a cloud,
 so the song of the ruthless is
 stilled.

6 On this mountain the LORD of

hosts will make for all peoples a feast of
fat things, a feast of wine on the lees,
of fat things full of marrow, of wine on
the lees well refined. 7 And he will destroy on this mountain the covering
that is cast over all peoples, the veil
that is spread over all nations. 8 He
will swallow up death for ever, and
the Lord GOD will wipe away tears
from all faces, and the reproach of his
people he will take away from all the
earth, for the LORD has spoken.
9 It will be said on that day, "Lo,
this is our God; we have waited for
him, that he might save us. This is the
LORD; we have waited for him; let us
be glad and rejoice in his salvation."
10 For the hand of the LORD will
rest on this mountain, and Mō´ab shall
be trodden down in his place, as straw
is trodden down in a dungpit. 11 And
he will spread out his hands in the
midst of it as a swimmer spreads his
hands out to swim; but the LORD will
lay low his pride together with the
skill*l* of his hands. 12 And the high
fortifications of his walls he will bring
down, lay low, and cast to the ground,
even to the dust.

26 In that day this song will be
 sung in the land of Judah:
"We have a strong city;
 he sets up salvation
 as walls and bulwarks.
2 Open the gates,
 that the righteous nation which
 keeps faith
 may enter in.
3 Thou dost keep him in perfect
 peace,
 whose mind is stayed on thee,
 because he trusts in thee.
4 Trust in the LORD for ever,
 for the LORD GOD
 is an everlasting rock.
5 For he has brought low
 the inhabitants of the height,
 the lofty city.
He lays it low, lays it low to the
 ground,
 casts it to the dust.
6 The foot tramples it,
 the feet of the poor,
 the steps of the needy."

7 The way of the righteous is level;
 thou*m* dost make smooth the path
 of the righteous.
8 In the path of thy judgments,
 O LORD, we wait for thee;

l The meaning of the Hebrew word is uncertain
m Cn Compare Gk: Heb *thou (that art) upright*
25.8: 1 Cor 15.54; Rev 7.17; 21.4.
25.10-12: Is 15-16; Jer 48; Ezek 25.8-11; Amos 2.1-3; Zeph 2.8-11.

thy memorial name
   is the desire of our soul.
9 My soul yearns for thee in the night,
   my spirit within me earnestly
      seeks thee.
For when thy judgments are in the
      earth,
   the inhabitants of the world learn
      righteousness.
10 If favor is shown to the wicked,
   he does not learn righteousness;
in the land of uprightness he deals
      perversely
   and does not see the majesty of
      the LORD.
11 O LORD, thy hand is lifted up,
   but they see it not.
Let them see thy zeal for thy people,
      and be ashamed.
Let the fire for thy adversaries
      consume them.
12 O LORD, thou wilt ordain peace for
      us,
   thou hast wrought for us all our
      works.
13 O LORD our God,
   other lords besides thee have
      ruled over us,
   but thy name alone we acknowl-
      edge.
14 They are dead, they will not live;
   they are shades, they will not
      arise;
to that end thou hast visited them
      with destruction
   and wiped out all remembrance
      of them.
15 But thou hast increased the nation,
      O LORD,
   thou hast increased the nation;
      thou art glorified;
   thou hast enlarged all the borders
      of the land.

16 O LORD, in distress they sought
      thee,
   they poured out a prayer[n]
   when thy chastening was upon
      them.
17 Like a woman with child,
   who writhes and cries out in her
      pangs,
   when she is near her time,
so were we because of thee, O LORD;
18   we were with child, we writhed,
   we have as it were brought forth
      wind.
We have wrought no deliverance in
      the earth,
   and the inhabitants of the world
      have not fallen.
19 Thy dead shall live, their bodies[o]
      shall rise.

O dwellers in the dust, awake and
      sing for joy!
For thy dew is a dew of light,
   and on the land of the shades thou
      wilt let it fall.
20 Come, my people, enter your
      chambers,
   and shut your doors behind you;
hide yourselves for a little while
   until the wrath is past.
21 For behold, the LORD is coming
      forth out of his place
   to punish the inhabitants of the
      earth for their iniquity,
and the earth will disclose the blood
      shed upon her,
   and will no more cover her slain.

27 In that day the LORD with his
      hard and great and strong
sword will punish Lě·vī'a·thăn the
fleeing serpent, Leviathan the twisting
serpent, and he will slay the dragon
that is in the sea.

2 In that day:
   "A pleasant vineyard, sing of it!
3   I, the LORD, am its keeper;
      every moment I water it.
   Lest any one harm it,
      I guard it night and day;
4   I have no wrath.
   Would that I had thorns and briers
         to battle!
   I would set out against them,
      I would burn them up together.
5 Or let them lay hold of my protection,
      let them make peace with me,
      let them make peace with me."

6 In days to come[q] Jacob shall take root,
   Israel shall blossom and put forth
      shoots,
   and fill the whole world with fruit.

7 Has he smitten them as he smote
      those who smote them?
   Or have they been slain as their
      slayers were slain?
8 Measure by measure,[r] by exile thou
      didst contend with them;
   he removed them with his fierce
      blast in the day of the east wind.
9 Therefore by this the guilt of Jacob
      will be expiated,
   and this will be the full fruit of
      the removal of his sin:
when he makes all the stones of the
      altars
   like chalkstones crushed to pieces,
   no A·shē'rim or incense altars will
      remain standing.

n Heb uncertain   o Cn Compare Syr Tg: Heb *my body*   q Heb *Those to come*
r Compare Syr Vg Tg: The meaning of the Hebrew word is unknown

10 For the fortified city is solitary,
    a habitation deserted and for-
    saken, like the wilderness;
there the calf grazes,
    there he lies down, and strips its
    branches.
11 When its boughs are dry, they are
    broken;
    women come and make a fire of
    them.
For this is a people without dis-
    cernment;
    therefore he who made them will
    not have compassion on them,
he who formed them will show
    them no favor.

12 In that day from the river Eū-
phrā′tēs to the Brook of Egypt the
LORD will thresh out the grain, and
you will be gathered one by one, O
people of Israel. 13And in that day a
great trumpet will be blown, and those
who were lost in the land of Assyria and
those who were driven out to the land of
Egypt will come and worship the LORD
on the holy mountain at Jerusalem.

28   Woe to the proud crown of
    the drunkards of E′phrà·im,
and to the fading flower of its
    glorious beauty,
which is on the head of the rich
    valley of those overcome with
    wine!
2 Behold, the Lord has one who is
    mighty and strong;
like a storm of hail, a destroying
    tempest,
like a storm of mighty, overflowing
    waters,
he will cast down to the earth
    with violence.
3 The proud crown of the drunkards
    of E′phrà·im
will be trodden under foot;
4 and the fading flower of its glorious
    beauty,
which is on the head of the rich
    valley,
will be like a first-ripe fig before the
    summer:
when a man sees it, he eats it up
    as soon as it is in his hand.

5 In that day the LORD of hosts will
    be a crown of glory,
and a diadem of beauty, to the
    remnant of his people;
6 and a spirit of justice to him who
    sits in judgment,
and strength to those who turn
    back the battle at the gate.

7 These also reel with wine
    and stagger with strong drink;
the priest and the prophet reel with
    strong drink,
they are confused with wine,
    they stagger with strong drink;
they err in vision,
    they stumble in giving judgment.
8 For all tables are full of vomit,
    no place is without filthiness.

9 "Whom will he teach knowledge,
    and to whom will he explain the
    message?
Those who are weaned from the
    milk,
    those taken from the breast?
10 For it is precept upon precept, pre-
    cept upon precept,
line upon line, line upon line,
    here a little, there a little."

11 Nay, but by men of strange lips
    and with an alien tongue
the LORD will speak to this people,
12   to whom he has said,
"This is rest;
    give rest to the weary;
and this is repose";
    yet they would not hear.
13 Therefore the word of the LORD
    will be to them
precept upon precept, precept
    upon precept,
line upon line, line upon line,
    here a little, there a little;
that they may go, and fall backward,
    and be broken, and snared, and
    taken.

14 Therefore hear the word of the
    LORD, you scoffers,
who rule this people in Jerusalem!
15 Because you have said, "We have
    made a covenant with death,
and with Shē′ōl we have an
    agreement;
when the overwhelming scourge
    passes through
it will not come to us;
for we have made lies our refuge,
    and in falsehood we have taken
    shelter";
16 therefore thus says the Lord GOD,
    "Behold, I am laying in Zion for a
    foundation
a stone, a tested stone,
a precious cornerstone, of a sure
    foundation:
'He who believes will not be in
    haste.'
17 And I will make justice the line,
    and righteousness the plummet;

27.13: Mt. 24.31; 1 Cor 15.52; 1 Thess 4.16.   28.11-12: 1 Cor 14.21.   28.12: Mt 11.29.
28.16: Rom 9.33; 10.11; 1 Pet 2.4-6.

and hail will sweep away the refuge
of lies,
and waters will overwhelm the
shelter."
18 Then your covenant with death will
be annulled,
and your agreement with Shē′ōl
will not stand;
when the overwhelming scourge
passes through
you shall be beaten down by it.
19 As often as it passes through it will
take you;
for morning by morning it will
pass through,
by day and by night;
and it will be sheer terror to understand the message.
20 For the bed is too short to stretch
oneself on it,
and the covering too narrow to
wrap oneself in it.
21 For the LORD will rise up as on
Mount Pe·rā′zim,
he will be wroth as in the valley
of Gib′ē·ŏn;
to do his deed—strange is his deed!
and to work his work—alien is
his work!
22 Now therefore do not scoff,
lest your bonds be made strong;
for I have heard a decree of destruction
from the Lord GOD of hosts upon
the whole land.

23 Give ear, and hear my voice;
hearken, and hear my speech.
24 Does he who plows for sowing plow
continually?
does he continually open and
harrow his ground?
25 When he has leveled its surface,
does he not scatter dill, sow
cummin,
and put in wheat in rows
and barley in its proper place,
and spelt as the border?
26 For he is instructed aright;
his God teaches him.

27 Dill is not threshed with a threshing
sledge,
nor is a cart wheel rolled over
cummin;
but dill is beaten out with a stick,
and cummin with a rod.
28 Does one crush bread grain?
No, he does not thresh it for ever;
when he drives his cart wheel over it
with his horses, he does not crush it.
29 This also comes from the LORD of
hosts;
he is wonderful in counsel,

s Cn: Heb *strangers*

and excellent in wisdom.

29 Ho Ăr′i·ĕl, Ariel,
the city where David encamped!
Add year to year;
let the feasts run their round.
2 Yet I will distress Ăr′i·ĕl,
and there shall be moaning and
lamentation,
and she shall be to me like an Ariel.
3 And I will encamp against you
round about,
and will besiege you with towers
and I will raise siegeworks
against you.
4 Then deep from the earth you shall
speak,
from low in the dust your word
shall come;
your voice shall come from the
ground like the voice of a ghost,
and your speech shall whisper out
of the dust.

5 But the multitude of your foes[s] shall
be like small dust,
and the multitude of the ruthless
like passing chaff.
And in an instant, suddenly,
6   you will be visited by the LORD
of hosts
with thunder and with earthquake
and great noise,
with whirlwind and tempest, and
the flame of a devouring fire.
7 And the multitude of all the nations
that fight against Ăr′i·ĕl,
all that fight against her and her
stronghold and distress her,
shall be like a dream, a vision of
the night.
8 As when a hungry man dreams he
is eating
and awakes with his hunger not
satisfied,
or as when a thirsty man dreams he
is drinking
and awakes faint, with his thirst
not quenched,
so shall the multitude of all the
nations be
that fight against Mount Zion.

9 Stupefy yourselves and be in a
stupor,
blind yourselves and be blind!
Be drunk, but not with wine;
stagger, but not with strong drink!
10 For the LORD has poured out upon
you
a spirit of deep sleep,
and has closed your eyes, the
prophets,
and covered your heads, the seers.

11 And the vision of all this has become to you like the words of a book that is sealed. When men give it to one who can read, saying, "Read this," he says, "I cannot, for it is sealed." 12And when they give the book to one who cannot read, saying, "Read this," he says, "I cannot read."

13 And the Lord said:
"Because this people draw near with their mouth
and honor me with their lips,
while their hearts are far from me,
and their fear of me is a commandment of men learned by rote;
14therefore, behold, I will again
do marvelous things with this people,
wonderful and marvelous;
and the wisdom of their wise men shall perish,
and the discernment of their discerning men shall be hid."

15 Woe to those who hide deep from the LORD their counsel,
whose deeds are in the dark,
and who say, "Who sees us? Who knows us?"
16 You turn things upside down!
Shall the potter be regarded as the clay;
that the thing made should say of its maker,
"He did not make me";
or the thing formed say of him who formed it,
"He has no understanding"?

17 Is it not yet a very little while
until Lebanon shall be turned into a fruitful field,
and the fruitful field shall be regarded as a forest?
18 In that day the deaf shall hear the words of a book,
and out of their gloom and darkness the eyes of the blind shall see.
19 The meek shall obtain fresh joy in the LORD,
and the poor among men shall exult in the Holy One of Israel.
20 For the ruthless shall come to nought and the scoffer cease,
and all who watch to do evil shall be cut off,
21 who by a word make a man out to be an offender,
and lay a snare for him who reproves in the gate,

and with an empty plea turn aside him who is in the right.

22 Therefore thus says the LORD, who redeemed Abraham, concerning the house of Jacob:
"Jacob shall no more be ashamed,
no more shall his face grow pale.
23 For when he sees his children,
the work of my hands, in his midst,
they will sanctify my name;
they will sanctify the Holy One of Jacob,
and will stand in awe of the God of Israel.
24 And those who err in spirit will come to understanding,
and those who murmur will accept instruction."

30 "Woe to the rebellious children," says the LORD,
"who carry out a plan, but not mine;
and who make a league, but not of my spirit,
that they may add sin to sin;
2 who set out to go down to Egypt,
without asking for my counsel,
to take refuge in the protection of Pharaoh,
and to seek shelter in the shadow of Egypt!
3 Therefore shall the protection of Pharaoh turn to your shame,
and the shelter in the shadow of Egypt to your humiliation.
4 For though his officials are at Zō′an
and his envoys reach Hā′nēs,
5 every one comes to shame
through a people that cannot profit them,
that brings neither help nor profit, but shame and disgrace."

6 An oracle on the beasts of the Negeb.
Through a land of trouble and anguish,
from where come the lioness and the lion,
the viper and the flying serpent,
they carry their riches on the backs of asses,
and their treasures on the humps of camels,
to a people that cannot profit them.
7 For Egypt's help is worthless and empty,
therefore I have called her
"Rā′hab who sits still."

29.13: Mt 15.8-9; Mk 7.6-7.   29.14: 1 Cor 1.19.   29.16: Is 45.9; Rom 9.20.
29.18-19: Mt 11.5.

8 And now, go, write it before them
on a tablet,
and inscribe it in a book,
that it may be for the time to come
as a witness for ever.
9 For they are a rebellious people,
lying sons,
sons who will not hear
the instruction of the LORD;
10 who say to the seers, "See not";
and to the prophets, "Prophesy
not to us what is right;
speak to us smooth things,
prophesy illusions,
11 leave the way, turn aside from the
path,
let us hear no more of the Holy
One of Israel."
12 Therefore thus says the Holy One
of Israel,
"Because you despise this word,
and trust in oppression and perverseness,
and rely on them;
13 therefore this iniquity shall be to you
like a break in a high wall, bulging
out, and about to collapse,
whose crash comes suddenly, in
an instant;
14 and its breaking is like that of a
potter's vessel
which is smashed so ruthlessly
that among its fragments not a sherd
is found
with which to take fire from the
hearth,
or to dip up water out of the
cistern."

15 For thus said the Lord GOD, the
Holy One of Israel,
"In returning and rest you shall
be saved;
in quietness and in trust shall be
your strength."
And you would not, 16 but you said,
"No! We will speed upon horses,"
therefore you shall speed away;
and, "We will ride upon swift
steeds,"
therefore your pursuers shall be
swift.
17 A thousand shall flee at the threat
of one,
at the threat of five you shall flee,
till you are left
like a flagstaff on the top of a
mountain,
like a signal on a hill.

18 Therefore the LORD waits to be
gracious to you;
therefore he exalts himself to
show mercy to you.
For the LORD is a God of justice;

blessed are all those who wait for
him.
19 Yea, O people in Zion who dwell
at Jerusalem; you shall weep no more.
He will surely be gracious to you at
the sound of your cry; when he hears
it, he will answer you. 20And though
the Lord give you the bread of adversity and the water of affliction, yet your
Teacher will not hide himself any
more, but your eyes shall see your
Teacher. 21And your ears shall hear a
word behind you, saying, "This is the
way, walk in it," when you turn to the
right or when you turn to the left.
22 Then you will defile your silver-
covered graven images and your gold-
plated molten images. You will scatter
them as unclean things; you will say
to them, "Begone!"
23 And he will give rain for the seed
with which you sow the ground, and
grain, the produce of the ground,
which will be rich and plenteous. In
that day your cattle will graze in large
pastures; 24 and the oxen and the asses
that till the ground will eat salted
provender, which has been winnowed
with shovel and fork. 25And upon
every lofty mountain and every high
hill there will be brooks running with
water, in the day of the great slaughter,
when the towers fall. 26 Moreover the
light of the moon will be as the light
of the sun, and the light of the sun will
be sevenfold, as the light of seven days,
in the day when the LORD binds up
the hurt of his people, and heals the
wounds inflicted by his blow.

27 Behold, the name of the LORD comes
from far,
burning with his anger, and in
thick rising smoke;
his lips are full of indignation,
and his tongue is like a devouring
fire;
28 his breath is like an overflowing
stream
that reaches up to the neck;
to sift the nations with the sieve of
destruction,
and to place on the jaws of the
peoples a bridle that leads
astray.

29 You shall have a song as in the
night when a holy feast is kept; and
gladness of heart, as when one sets out
to the sound of the flute to go to the
mountain of the LORD, to the Rock of
Israel. 30And the LORD will cause his
majestic voice to be heard and the
descending blow of his arm to be seen,
in furious anger and a flame of devour-

ing fire, with a cloudburst and tempest and hailstones. 31 The Assyrians will be terror-stricken at the voice of the LORD, when he smites with his rod. 32And every stroke of the staff of punishment which the LORD lays upon them will be to the sound of timbrels and lyres; battling with brandished arm he will fight with them. 33 For a burning place*t* has long been prepared; yea, for the king*u* it is made ready, its pyre made deep and wide, with fire and wood in abundance; the breath of the LORD, like a stream of brimstone, kindles it.

31

Woe to those who go down to Egypt for help
and rely on horses,
who trust in chariots because they
are many
and in horsemen because they are
very strong,
but do not look to the Holy One of
Israel
or consult the LORD!
2 And yet he is wise and brings disaster,
he does not call back his words,
but will arise against the house of
the evildoers,
and against the helpers of those
who work iniquity.
3 The Egyptians are men, and not God;
and their horses are flesh, and not
spirit.
When the LORD stretches out his
hand,
the helper will stumble, and he
who is helped will fall,
and they will all perish together.

4 For thus the LORD said to me,
As a lion or a young lion growls
over his prey,
and when a band of shepherds is
called forth against him
is not terrified by their shouting
or daunted at their noise,
so the LORD of hosts will come down
to fight upon Mount Zion and
upon its hill.
5 Like birds hovering, so the LORD of
hosts
will protect Jerusalem;
he will protect and deliver it,
he will spare and rescue it.

6 Turn to him from whom you*v*
have deeply revolted, O people of
Israel. 7 For in that day every one shall
cast away his idols of silver and his
idols of gold, which your hands have
sinfully made for you.

8 "And the Assyrian shall fall by a
sword, not of man;
and a sword, not of man, shall
devour him;
and he shall flee from the sword,
and his young men shall be put
to forced labor.
9 His rock shall pass away in terror,
and his officers desert the standard in panic,"
says the LORD, whose fire is in Zion,
and whose furnace is in Jerusalem.

32

Behold, a king will reign in
righteousness,
and princes will rule in justice.
2 Each will be like a hiding place from
the wind,
a covert from the tempest,
like streams of water in a dry place,
like the shade of a great rock in a
weary land.
3 Then the eyes of those who see will
not be closed,
and the ears of those who hear
will hearken.
4 The mind of the rash will have good
judgment,
and the tongue of the stammerers
will speak readily and distinctly.
5 The fool will no more be called
noble,
nor the knave said to be honorable.
6 For the fool speaks folly,
and his mind plots iniquity:
to practice ungodliness,
to utter error concerning the
LORD,
to leave the craving of the hungry
unsatisfied,
and to deprive the thirsty of drink.
7 The knaveries of the knave are evil;
he devises wicked devices
to ruin the poor with lying words,
even when the plea of the needy
is right.
8 But he who is noble devises noble
things,
and by noble things he stands.

9 Rise up, you women who are at
ease, hear my voice;
you complacent daughters, give
ear to my speech.
10 In little more than a year
you will shudder, you complacent women;
for the vintage will fail,
the fruit harvest will not come.
11 Tremble, you women who are at
ease,
shudder, you complacent ones;
strip, and make yourselves bare,

t Or Topheth   u Or Molech   v Heb they

and gird sackcloth upon your loins.

12 Beat upon your breasts for the pleasant fields,
   for the fruitful vine,

13 for the soil of my people
   growing up in thorns and briers;
   yea, for all the joyous houses
   in the joyful city.

14 For the palace will be forsaken,
   the populous city deserted;
   the hill and the watchtower
   will become dens for ever,
   a joy of wild asses,
   a pasture of flocks;

15 until the Spirit is poured upon us
   from on high,
   and the wilderness becomes a fruitful field,
   and the fruitful field is deemed a forest.

16 Then justice will dwell in the wilderness,
   and righteousness abide in the fruitful field.

17 And the effect of righteousness will be peace,
   and the result of righteousness, quietness and trust for ever.

18 My people will abide in a peaceful habitation,
   in secure dwellings, and in quiet resting places.

19 And the forest will utterly go down,[w]
   and the city will be utterly laid low.

20 Happy are you who sow beside all waters,
   who let the feet of the ox and the ass range free.

33 Woe to you, destroyer,
   who yourself have not been destroyed;
   you treacherous one,
   with whom none has dealt treacherously!
   When you have ceased to destroy,
   you will be destroyed;
   and when you have made an end of dealing treacherously,
   you will be dealt with treacherously.

2 O LORD, be gracious to us; we wait for thee.
   Be our arm every morning,
   our salvation in the time of trouble.

3 At the thunderous noise peoples flee,
   at the lifting up of thyself nations are scattered;

4 and spoil is gathered as the caterpillar gathers;
   as locusts leap, men leap upon it.

5 The LORD is exalted, for he dwells on high;
   he will fill Zion with justice and righteousness;

6 and he will be the stability of your times,
   abundance of salvation, wisdom, and knowledge;
   the fear of the LORD is his treasure.

7 Behold, the valiant ones[y] cry without;
   the envoys of peace weep bitterly.

8 The highways lie waste,
   the wayfaring man ceases.
   Covenants are broken,
   witnesses[z] are despised,
   there is no regard for man.

9 The land mourns and languishes;
   Lebanon is confounded and withers away;
   Sharon is like a desert;
   and Bā′shăn and Cär′mĕl shake off their leaves.

10 "Now I will arise," says the LORD,
   "now I will lift myself up;
   now I will be exalted.

11 You conceive chaff, you bring forth stubble;
   your breath is a fire that will consume you.

12 And the peoples will be as if burned to lime,
   like thorns cut down, that are burned in the fire."

13 Hear, you who are far off, what I have done;
   and you who are near, acknowledge my might.

14 The sinners in Zion are afraid;
   trembling has seized the godless:
   "Who among us can dwell with the devouring fire?
   Who among us can dwell with everlasting burnings?"

15 He who walks righteously and speaks uprightly,
   who despises the gain of oppressions,
   who shakes his hands, lest they hold a bribe,
   who stops his ears from hearing of bloodshed
   and shuts his eyes from looking upon evil,

16 he will dwell on the heights;
   his place of defense will be the fortresses of rocks;

---

w Cn: Heb *And it will hail when the forest comes down*
y The meaning of the Hebrew word is uncertain   z One ancient Ms: Heb *cities*

his bread will be given him, his
water will be sure.

17 Your eyes will see the king in his
beauty;
they will behold a land that
stretches afar.
18 Your mind will muse on the terror:
"Where is he who counted,
where is he who weighed the
tribute?
Where is he who counted the
towers?"
19 You will see no more the insolent
people,
the people of an obscure speech
which you cannot comprehend,
stammering in a tongue which
you cannot understand.
20 Look upon Zion, the city of our
appointed feasts!
Your eyes will see Jerusalem,
a quiet habitation, an immovable
tent,
whose stakes will never be plucked up,
nor will any of its cords be
broken.
21 But there the LORD in majesty will
be for us
a place of broad rivers and
streams,
where no galley with oars can go,
nor stately ship can pass.
22 For the LORD is our judge, the LORD
is our ruler,
the LORD is our king; he will save
us.

23 Your tackle hangs loose;
it cannot hold the mast firm in
its place,
or keep the sail spread out.

Then prey and spoil in abundance
will be divided;
even the lame will take the prey.
24 And no inhabitant will say, "I am
sick";
the people who dwell there will
be forgiven their iniquity.

34 Draw near, O nations, to hear,
and hearken, O peoples!
Let the earth listen, and all that fills
it;
the world, and all that comes
from it.
2 For the LORD is enraged against all
the nations,
and furious against all their host,
he has doomed them, has given
them over for slaughter.

3 Their slain shall be cast out,
and the stench of their corpses
shall rise;
the mountains shall flow with
their blood.
4 All the host of heaven shall rot
away,
and the skies roll up like a scroll.
All their host shall fall,
as leaves fall from the vine,
like leaves falling from the fig
tree.

5 For my sword has drunk its fill in
the heavens;
behold, it descends for judgment
upon E´dom,
upon the people I have doomed.
6 The LORD has a sword; it is sated
with blood,
it is gorged with fat,
with the blood of lambs and goats,
with the fat of the kidneys of
rams.
For the LORD has a sacrifice in
Boz´rah,
a great slaughter in the land of
E´dom.
7 Wild oxen shall fall with them,
and young steers with the mighty
bulls.
Their land shall be soaked with
blood,
and their soil made rich with fat.

8 For the LORD has a day of vengeance,
a year of recompense for the
cause of Zion.
9 And the streams of E´dom*a* shall be
turned into pitch,
and her soil into brimstone;
her land shall become burning
pitch.
10 Night and day it shall not be
quenched;
its smoke shall go up for ever.
From generation to generation it
shall lie waste;
none shall pass through it for
ever and ever.
11 But the hawk and the porcupine
shall possess it,
the owl and the raven shall dwell
in it.
He shall stretch the line of confusion over it,
and the plummet of chaos over*b*
its nobles.
12 They shall name it No Kingdom
There,
and all its princes shall be nothing.

---

a Heb *her streams*   *b* Heb lacks *over*

34: Is 63.1-6; Jer 49.7-22; Ezek 25.12-14; 35; Amos 1.11-12; Obad; Mal 1.2-5.
34.4: Rev 6.13-14.   **34.9-10:** Rev 19.3.

13 Thorns shall grow over its strongholds,
  nettles and thistles in its fortresses.
It shall be the haunt of jackals,
  an abode for ostriches.
14 And wild beasts shall meet with
hyenas,
  the satyr shall cry to his fellow;
yea, there shall the night hag alight,
  and find for herself a resting place.

15 There shall the owl nest and lay
  and hatch and gather her young
in her shadow;
yea, there shall the kites be gathered,
  each one with her mate.
16 Seek and read from the book of the
LORD:
  Not one of these shall be missing;
none shall be without her mate.
For the mouth of the LORD has
commanded,
  and his Spirit has gathered them.
17 He has cast the lot for them,
  his hand has portioned it out to
them with the line;
they shall possess it for ever,
  from generation to generation
they shall dwell in it.

35 The wilderness and the dry
land shall be glad,
  the desert shall rejoice and
blossom;
like the crocus 2 it shall blossom
abundantly,
  and rejoice with joy and singing.
The glory of Lebanon shall be given
to it,
  the majesty of Cär'mĕl and
Sharon.
They shall see the glory of the LORD,
  the majesty of our God.

3 Strengthen the weak hands,
  and make firm the feeble knees.
4 Say to those who are of a fearful
heart,
  "Be strong, fear not!
Behold, your God
  will come with vengeance,
with the recompense of God.
  He will come and save you."

5 Then the eyes of the blind shall be
opened,
  and the ears of the deaf unstopped;
6 then shall the lame man leap like a
hart,
  and the tongue of the dumb sing
for joy.

For waters shall break forth in the
wilderness,
  and streams in the desert;
7 the burning sand shall become a
pool,
  and the thirsty ground springs of
water;
the haunt of jackals shall become a
swamp,*c*
  the grass shall become reeds and
rushes.

8 And a highway shall be there,
  and it shall be called the Holy
Way;
the unclean shall not pass over it,*d*
  and fools shall not err therein.
9 No lion shall be there,
  nor shall any ravenous beast come
up on it;
they shall not be found there,
  but the redeemed shall walk there.
10 And the ransomed of the LORD shall
return,
  and come to Zion with singing;
everlasting joy shall be upon their
heads;
  they shall obtain joy and gladness,
and sorrow and sighing shall flee
away.

36 In the fourteenth year of King
Hĕz·ė·kī'ăh, Sĕn·nach'ė·rĭb king
of Assyria came up against all the
fortified cities of Judah and took them.
2 And the king of Assyria sent the
Rab'shȧ·kĕh from Lā'chish to King
Hĕz·ė·kī'ăh at Jerusalem, with a great
army. And he stood by the conduit of
the upper pool on the highway to the
Fuller's Field. 3 And there came out to
him E·lī'ȧ·kim the son of Hil·kī'ăh,
who was over the household, and
Sheb'nȧ the secretary, and Jō'äh the
son of Ā'saph, the recorder.
4 And the Rab'shȧ·kĕh said to
them, "Say to Hĕz·ė·kī'ăh, 'Thus says
the great king, the king of Assyria: On
what do you rest this confidence of
yours? 5 Do you think that mere words
are strategy and power for war? On
whom do you now rely, that you have
rebelled against me? 6 Behold, you are
relying on Egypt, that broken reed of
a staff, which will pierce the hand of
any man who leans on it. Such is
Pharaoh king of Egypt to all who rely
on him. 7 But if you say to me, "We
rely on the LORD our God," is it not
he whose high places and altars Hĕz·ė·
kī'ăh has removed, saying to Judah
and to Jerusalem, "You shall worship

c Cn: Heb *in the haunt of jackals is her resting place*
d Heb *it and he is for them a wayfarer*   **35.3:** Heb 12.12.   **35.5–6:** Mt 11.5; Lk 7.22.
36.1–38.8, 21–22: 2 Kings 18.13–20.11; 2 Chron 32.1–24.

before this altar"? 8 Come now, make a wager with my master the king of Assyria: I will give you two thousand horses, if you are able on your part to set riders upon them. 9 How then can you repulse a single captain among the least of my master's servants, when you rely on Egypt for chariots and for horsemen? 10 Moreover, is it without the LORD that I have come up against this land to destroy it? The LORD said to me, Go up against this land, and destroy it.' "

11 Then E·li′å·kim, Sheb′nå, and Jō′åh said to the Rab′shå·kéh, "Pray, speak to your servants in Aramaic, for we understand it; do not speak to us in the language of Judah within the hearing of the people who are on the wall." 12 But the Rab′shå·kéh said, "Has my master sent me to speak these words to your master and to you, and not to the men sitting on the wall, who are doomed with you to eat their own dung and drink their own urine?"

13 Then the Rab′shå·kéh stood and called out in a loud voice in the language of Judah: "Hear the words of the great king, the king of Assyria! 14 Thus says the king: 'Do not let Hez·é·kī′åh deceive you, for he will not be able to deliver you. 15 Do not let Hez·é·kī′åh make you rely on the LORD by saying, "The LORD will surely deliver us; this city will not be given into the hand of the king of Assyria." 16 Do not listen to Hez·é·kī′åh; for thus says the king of Assyria: Make your peace with me and come out to me; then every one of you will eat of his own vine, and every one of his own fig tree, and every one of you will drink the water of his own cistern; 17 until I come and take you away to a land like your own land, a land of grain and wine, a land of bread and vineyards. 18 Beware lest Hez·é·kī′åh mislead you by saying, "The LORD will deliver us." Has any of the gods of the nations delivered his land out of the hand of the king of Assyria? 19 Where are the gods of Hā′math and Är′pad? Where are the gods of Seph·är·vā′im? Have they delivered Så·mâr′i·å out of my hand? 20 Who among all the gods of these countries have delivered their countries out of my hand, that the LORD should deliver Jerusalem out of my hand?' "

21 But they were silent and answered him not a word, for the king's command was, "Do not answer him." 22 Then E·li′å·kim the son of Hil·kī′åh, who was over the household, and Sheb′nå the secretary, and Jō′åh the

son of A′saph, the recorder, came to Hez·é·kī′åh with their clothes rent, and told him the words of the Rab′shå·kéh.

37 When King Hez·é·kī′åh heard it, he rent his clothes, and covered himself with sackcloth, and went into the house of the LORD. 2 And he sent E·li′å·kim, who was over the household, and Sheb′nå the secretary, and the senior priests, clothed with sackcloth, to the prophet I·šāi′åh the son of A′moz. 3 They said to him, "Thus says Hez·é·kī′åh, 'This day is a day of distress, of rebuke, and of disgrace; children have come to the birth, and there is no strength to bring them forth. 4 It may be that the LORD your God heard the words of the Rab′shå·kéh, whom his master the king of Assyria has sent to mock the living God, and will rebuke the words which the LORD your God has heard; therefore lift up your prayer for the remnant that is left.' "

5 When the servants of King Hez·é·kī′åh came to I·šāi′åh, 6 I·šāi′åh said to them, "Say to your master, 'Thus says the LORD: Do not be afraid because of the words that you have heard, with which the servants of the king of Assyria have reviled me. 7 Behold, I will put a spirit in him, so that he shall hear a rumor, and return to his own land; and I will make him fall by the sword in his own land.' "

8 The Rab′shå·kéh returned, and found the king of Assyria fighting against Lib′nåh; for he had heard that the king had left Lā′chish. 9 Now the king heard concerning Tĭr·hā′kåh king of Ethiopia, "He has set out to fight against you." And when he heard it, he sent messengers to Hez·é·kī′åh, saying, 10 "Thus shall you speak to Hez·é·kī′åh king of Judah: 'Do not let your God on whom you rely deceive you by promising that Jerusalem will not be given into the hand of the king of Assyria. 11 Behold, you have heard what the kings of Assyria have done to all lands, destroying them utterly. And shall you be delivered? 12 Have the gods of the nations delivered them, the nations which my fathers destroyed, Gō′zån, Hâr′ån, Rē′zeph, and the people of Eden who were in Te·las′sår? 13 Where is the king of Hā′math, the king of Är′pad, the king of the city of Seph·är·vā′im, the king of Hē′nå, or the king of Iv′våh?' "

14 Hez·é·kī′åh received the letter from the hand of the messengers, and read it; and Hezekiah went up to the house of the LORD, and spread it be-

fore the LORD. 15And Hez·e·ki'ah prayed to the LORD; 16 "O LORD of hosts, God of Israel, who art enthroned above the cherubim, thou art the God, thou alone, of all the kingdoms of the earth; thou hast made heaven and earth. 17 Incline thy ear, O LORD, and hear; open thy eyes, O LORD, and see; and hear all the words of Sen·nach'e·rib, which he has sent to mock the living God. 18 Of a truth, O LORD, the kings of Assyria have laid waste all the nations and their lands, 19 and have cast their gods into the fire; for they were no gods, but the work of men's hands, wood and stone; therefore they were destroyed. 20 So now, O LORD our God, save us from his hand, that all the kingdoms of the earth may know that thou alone art the LORD."

21 Then I·sai'ah the son of A'moz sent to Hez·e·ki'ah, saying, "Thus says the LORD, the God of Israel: Because you have prayed to me concerning Sen·nach'e·rib king of Assyria, 22 this is the word that the LORD has spoken concerning him:

'She despises you, she scorns you—
    the virgin daughter of Zion;
she wags her head behind you—
    the daughter of Jerusalem.

23 'Whom have you mocked and reviled?
    Against whom have you raised your voice
and haughtily lifted your eyes?
    Against the Holy One of Israel!
24 By your servants you have mocked the Lord,
    and you have said, With my many chariots
I have gone up the heights of the mountains,
    to the far recesses of Lebanon;
I felled its tallest cedars,
    its choicest cypresses;
I came to its remotest height,
    its densest forest.
25 I dug wells
    and drank waters,
and I dried up with the sole of my foot
    all the streams of Egypt.

26 'Have you not heard
    that I determined it long ago?
I planned from days of old
    what now I bring to pass,
that you should make fortified cities
    crash into heaps of ruins,
27 while their inhabitants, shorn of strength,
    are dismayed and confounded,

and have become like plants of the field
    and like tender grass,
like grass on the housetops,
    blighted*e* before it is grown.

28 'I know your sitting down
    and your going out and coming in,
    and your raging against me.
29 Because you have raged against me
    and your arrogance has come to my ears,
I will put my hook in your nose
    and my bit in your mouth,
and I will turn you back on the way
    by which you came.'

30 "And this shall be the sign for you: this year eat what grows of itself, and in the second year what springs of the same; then in the third year sow and reap, and plant vineyards, and eat their fruit. 31And the surviving remnant of the house of Judah shall again take root downward, and bear fruit upward; 32 for out of Jerusalem shall go forth a remnant, and out of Mount Zion a band of survivors. The zeal of the LORD of hosts will accomplish this.

33 "Therefore thus says the LORD concerning the king of Assyria: He shall not come into this city, or shoot an arrow there, or come before it with a shield, or cast up a siege mound against it. 34 By the way that he came, by the same he shall return, and he shall not come into this city, says the LORD. 35 For I will defend this city to save it, for my own sake and for the sake of my servant David."

36 And the angel of the LORD went forth, and slew a hundred and eighty-five thousand in the camp of the Assyrians; and when men arose early in the morning, behold, these were all dead bodies. 37 Then Sen·nach'e·rib king of Assyria departed, and went home and dwelt at Nin'e·veh. 38And as he was worshiping in the house of Nis'roch his god, A·dram'me·lech and Sha·re'zer, his sons, slew him with the sword, and escaped into the land of Ar'a·rat. And E'sar-had'don his son reigned in his stead.

38 In those days Hez·e·ki'ah became sick and was at the point of death. And I·sai'ah the prophet the son of A'moz came to him, and said to him, "Thus says the LORD: Set your house in order; for you shall die, you shall not recover." 2 Then Hez·e·ki'ah turned his face to the wall, and prayed to the LORD, 3 and said, "Re-

e With 2 Kings 19.26: Heb *field*

member now, O LORD, I beseech thee, how I have walked before thee in faithfulness and with a whole heart, and have done what is good in thy sight." And Hez·e·ki′ah wept bitterly. 4 Then the word of the LORD came to I·sāi′ah: 5 "Go and say to Hez·e·ki′ah, Thus says the LORD, the God of David your father: I have heard your prayer, I have seen your tears; behold, I will add fifteen years to your life. 6 I will deliver you and this city out of the hand of the king of Assyria, and defend this city.

7 "This is the sign to you from the LORD, that the LORD will do this thing that he has promised: 8 Behold, I will make the shadow cast by the declining sun on the dial of A′haz turn back ten steps." So the sun turned back on the dial the ten steps by which it had declined.[f]

9 A writing of Hez·e·ki′ah king of Judah, after he had been sick and had recovered from his sickness:

10 I said, In the noontide of my days I must depart;
    I am consigned to the gates of Shē′ol
      for the rest of my years.
11 I said, I shall not see the LORD in the land of the living;
    I shall look upon man no more among the inhabitants of the world.
12 My dwelling is plucked up and removed from me like a shepherd's tent;
    like a weaver I have rolled up my life;
    he cuts me off from the loom;
    from day to night thou dost bring me to an end;[g]
13 I cry for help[h] until morning;
    like a lion he breaks all my bones;
    from day to night thou dost bring me to an end.[g]
14 Like a swallow or a crane[i] I clamor, I moan like a dove.
    My eyes are weary with looking upward.
    O Lord, I am oppressed; be thou my security!
15 But what can I say? For he has spoken to me,
    and he himself has done it.
    All my sleep has fled[j]
    because of the bitterness of my soul.

16 O Lord, by these things men live, and in all these is the life of my spirit.[k]
    Oh, restore me to health and make me live!
17 Lo, it was for my welfare that I had great bitterness;
    but thou hast held back[l] my life from the pit of destruction,
    for thou hast cast all my sins behind thy back.
18 For Shē′ol cannot thank thee, death cannot praise thee;
    those who go down to the pit cannot hope
      for thy faithfulness.
19 The living, the living, he thanks thee,
    as I do this day;
    the father makes known to the children
      thy faithfulness.

20 The LORD will save me,
    and we will sing to stringed instruments[m]
    all the days of our life,
    at the house of the LORD.

21 Now I·sāi′ah had said, 'Let them take a cake of figs, and apply it to the boil, that he may recover." 22 Hez·e·ki′ah also had said, "What is the sign that I shall go up to the house of the LORD?"

39 At that time Mer′o·dach-bal′a·dan the son of Bal′a·dan, king of Babylon, sent envoys with letters and a present to Hez·e·ki′ah, for he heard that he had been sick and had recovered. 2 And Hez·e·ki′ah welcomed them; and he showed them his treasure house, the silver, the gold, the spices, the precious oil, his whole armory, all that was found in his storehouses. There was nothing in his house or in all his realm that Hezekiah did not show them. 3 Then I·sāi′ah the prophet came to King Hez·e·ki′ah, and said to him, "What did these men say? And whence did they come to you?" Hezekiah said, "They have come to me from a far country, from Babylon." 4 He said, "What have they seen in your house?" Hez·e·ki′ah answered, "They have seen all that is in my house; there is nothing in my storehouses that I did not show them."

5 Then I·sāi′ah said to Hez·e·ki′ah, "Hear the word of the LORD of hosts: 6 Behold, the days are coming, when

f The Hebrew of this verse is obscure   g Heb uncertain   h Cn: Heb obscure
i Heb uncertain   j Cn Compare Syr: Heb *I will walk slowly all my years*
k Heb uncertain   l Cn Compare Gk Vg: Heb *loved*   m Heb *my stringed instruments*
39.1-8: 2 Kings 20.12-19; 2 Chron 32.31.

all that is in your house, and that which
your fathers have stored up till this
day, shall be carried to Babylon;
nothing shall be left, says the LORD.
7 And some of your own sons, who are
born to you, shall be taken away; and
they shall be eunuchs in the palace of
the king of Babylon." 8 Then said
Hez·e·ki′ah to I·sai′ah, "The word of
the LORD which you have spoken is
good." For he thought, "There will
be peace and security in my days."

40 Comfort, comfort my people,
says your God.
2 Speak tenderly to Jerusalem,
and cry to her
that her warfare[n] is ended,
that her iniquity is pardoned,
that she has received from the
LORD's hand
double for all her sins.

3 A voice cries:
"In the wilderness prepare the way
of the LORD,
make straight in the desert a
highway for our God.
4 Every valley shall be lifted up,
and every mountain and hill be
made low;
the uneven ground shall become
level,
and the rough places a plain.
5 And the glory of the LORD shall be
revealed,
and all flesh shall see it together,
for the mouth of the LORD has
spoken."

6 A voice says, "Cry!"
And I said, "What shall I cry?"
All flesh is grass,
and all its beauty is like the flower
of the field.
7 The grass withers, the flower fades,
when the breath of the LORD
blows upon it;
surely the people is grass.
8 The grass withers, the flower fades;
but the word of our God will
stand for ever.

9 Get you up to a high mountain,
O Zion, herald of good tidings;[o]
lift up your voice with strength,
O Jerusalem, herald of good
tidings,[p]
lift it up, fear not;
say to the cities of Judah,
"Behold your God!"
10 Behold, the Lord GOD comes with
might,
and his arm rules for him;
behold, his reward is with him,
and his recompense before him.
11 He will feed his flock like a shepherd,
he will gather the lambs in his
arms,
he will carry them in his bosom,
and gently lead those that are
with young.

12 Who has measured the waters in the
hollow of his hand
and marked off the heavens with
a span,
enclosed the dust of the earth in a
measure
and weighed the mountains in
scales
and the hills in a balance?
13 Who has directed the Spirit of the
LORD,
or as his counselor has instructed
him?
14 Whom did he consult for his en-
lightenment,
and who taught him the path of
justice,
and taught him knowledge,
and showed him the way of understanding?
15 Behold, the nations are like a drop
from a bucket,
and are accounted as the dust on
the scales;
behold, he takes up the isles like
fine dust.
16 Lebanon would not suffice for fuel,
nor are its beasts enough for a
burnt offering.
17 All the nations are as nothing before
him,
they are accounted by him as less
than nothing and emptiness.

18 To whom then will you liken God,
or what likeness compare with
him?
19 The idol! a workman casts it,
and a goldsmith overlays it with
gold,
and casts for it silver chains.
20 He who is impoverished[q] chooses
for an offering
wood that will not rot;
he seeks out a skilful craftsman
to set up an image that will not
move.

n Or *time of service*   o Or *O herald of good tidings to Zion*
p Or *O herald of good tidings to Jerusalem*   q Heb uncertain
40.3: Mt 3.3; Mk 1.3; Lk 3.4; Jn 1.23.   **40.4-5:** Lk 3.5-6.   **40.6-8:** 1 Pet 1.24-25.
40.9: Is 52.7; Nahum 1.15; Acts 10.36; Rom 10.15.   **40.10:** Rev 22.7, 12.
40.13: Rom 11.34; 1 Cor 2.16.

21 Have you not known? Have you not
heard?
Has it not been told you from the
beginning?
Have you not understood from
the foundations of the earth?
22 It is he who sits above the circle of
the earth,
and its inhabitants are like grasshoppers;
who stretches out the heavens like
a curtain,
and spreads them like a tent to
dwell in;
23 who brings princes to nought,
and makes the rulers of the earth
as nothing.

24 Scarcely are they planted, scarcely
sown,
scarcely has their stem taken root
in the earth,
when he blows upon them, and they
wither,
and the tempest carries them off
like stubble.

25 To whom then will you compare
me,
that I should be like him?
says the Holy One.
26 Lift up your eyes on high and see:
who created these?
He who brings out their host by
number,
calling them all by name;
by the greatness of his might,
and because he is strong in power
not one is missing.

27 Why do you say, O Jacob,
and speak, O Israel,
"My way is hid from the LORD,
and my right is disregarded by
my God"?
28 Have you not known? Have you not
heard?
The LORD is the everlasting God,
the Creator of the ends of the
earth.
He does not faint or grow weary,
his understanding is unsearchable.
29 He gives power to the faint,
and to him who has no might he
increases strength.
30 Even youths shall faint and be
weary,
and young men shall fall exhausted;
31 but they who wait for the LORD
shall renew their strength,
they shall mount up with wings
like eagles,

they shall run and not be weary,
they shall walk and not faint.

41 Listen to me in silence, O coastlands;
let the peoples renew their
strength;
let them approach, then let them
speak;
let us together draw near for
judgment.

2 Who stirred up one from the east
whom victory meets at every step?
He gives up nations before him,
so that he tramples kings under
foot;
he makes them like dust with his
sword,
like driven stubble with his bow.
3 He pursues them and passes on
safely,
by paths his feet have not trod.
4 Who has performed and done this,
calling the generations from the
beginning?
I, the LORD, the first,
and with the last; I am He.

5 The coastlands have seen and are
afraid,
the ends of the earth tremble;
they have drawn near and come.
6 Every one helps his neighbor,
and says to his brother, "Take
courage!"
7 The craftsman encourages the goldsmith,
and he who smooths with the
hammer him who strikes the
anvil,
saying of the soldering, "It is
good";
and they fasten it with nails so
that it cannot be moved.

8 But you, Israel, my servant,
Jacob, whom I have chosen,
the offspring of Abraham, my
friend;
9 you whom I took from the ends of
the earth,
and called from its farthest corners,
saying to you, "You are my servant,
I have chosen you and not cast
you off";
10 fear not, for I am with you,
be not dismayed, for I am your
God;
I will strengthen you, I will help
you,
I will uphold you with my victorious right hand.

41.8: Jas 2.23. **41.8-9:** Lk 1.54; Heb 2.16. **41.10:** Acts 18.10.

11 Behold, all who are incensed against
you
    shall be put to shame and con-
founded;
those who strive against you
    shall be as nothing and shall
perish.
12 You shall seek those who contend
with you,
    but you shall not find them;
those who war against you
    shall be as nothing at all.
13 For I, the LORD your God,
    hold your right hand;
it is I who say to you, "Fear not,
    I will help you."

14 Fear not, you worm Jacob,
    you men of Israel!
I will help you, says the LORD;
    your Redeemer is the Holy One
of Israel.
15 Behold, I will make of you a threshing sledge,
    new, sharp, and having teeth;
you shall thresh the mountains and
crush them,
    and you shall make the hills like
chaff;
16 you shall winnow them and the
wind shall carry them away,
    and the tempest shall scatter them.
And you shall rejoice in the LORD;
    in the Holy One of Israel you
shall glory.

17 When the poor and needy seek water,
    and there is none,
and their tongue is parched with
thirst,
I the LORD will answer them,
    I the God of Israel will not for-
sake them.
18 I will open rivers on the bare heights,
    and fountains in the midst of the
valleys;
I will make the wilderness a pool of
water,
    and the dry land springs of water.
19 I will put in the wilderness the
cedar,
    the acacia, the myrtle, and the
olive;
I will set in the desert the cypress,
    the plane and the pine together;
20 that men may see and know,
    may consider and understand to-
gether,
that the hand of the LORD has done
this,
    the Holy One of Israel has cre-
ated it.

21 Set forth your case, says the LORD;
    bring your proofs, says the King
of Jacob.
22 Let them bring them, and tell us
    what is to happen.
Tell us the former things, what they
are,
    that we may consider them,
that we may know their outcome;
    or declare to us the things to
come.
23 Tell us what is to come hereafter,
    that we may know that you are
gods;
do good, or do harm,
    that we may be dismayed and
terrified.
24 Behold, you are nothing,
    and your work is nought;
an abomination is he who chooses
    you.

25 I stirred up one from the north, and
he has come,
    from the rising of the sun, and he
shall call on my name;
he shall trample^r on rulers as on
mortar,
    as the potter treads clay.
26 Who declared it from the beginning,
    that we might know,
and beforetime, that we might
say, "He is right"?
There was none who declared it,
    none who proclaimed,
    none who heard your words.
27 I first have declared it to Zion,^s
    and I give to Jerusalem a herald
of good tidings.
28 But when I look there is no one;
    among these there is no counselor
who, when I ask, gives an answer.
29 Behold, they are all a delusion;
    their works are nothing;
their molten images are empty
wind.

42 Behold my servant, whom I
uphold,
    my chosen, in whom my soul
delights;
I have put my Spirit upon him,
    he will bring forth justice to the
nations.
2 He will not cry or lift up his voice,
    or make it heard in the street;
3 a bruised reed he will not break,
    and a dimly burning wick he will
not quench;
he will faithfully bring forth
justice.
4 He will not fail^t or be discouraged^u

---

^r Cn: Heb *come*   ^s Cn: Heb *first to Zion, Behold, behold them*   ^t Or *burn dimly*
^u Or *bruised*
42.1-4: Mt 12.18-21.

till he has established justice in
the earth;
and the coastlands wait for his
law.

5 Thus says God, the LORD,
who created the heavens and
stretched them out,
who spread forth the earth and
what comes from it,
who gives breath to the people upon
it
and spirit to those who walk in
it;
6 "I am the LORD, I have called you
in righteousness,
I have taken you by the hand and
kept you;
I have given you as a covenant to
the people,
a light to the nations,
7 to open the eyes that are blind,
to bring out the prisoners from the
dungeon,
from the prison those who sit in
darkness.
8 I am the LORD, that is my name;
my glory I give to no other,
nor my praise to graven images.
9 Behold, the former things have come
to pass,
and new things I now declare;
before they spring forth
I tell you of them."

10 Sing to the LORD a new song,
his praise from the end of the
earth!
Let the sea roar^v and all that fills it,
the coastlands and their inhabitants.
11 Let the desert and its cities lift up
their voice,
the villages that Kē'där inhabits;
let the inhabitants of Sē'là sing for
joy,
let them shout from the top of
the mountains.
12 Let them give glory to the LORD,
and declare his praise in the
coastlands.
13 The LORD goes forth like a mighty
man,
like a man of war he stirs up his
fury;
he cries out, he shouts aloud,
he shows himself mighty against
his foes.

14 For a long time I have held my
peace,
I have kept still and restrained
myself;

now I will cry out like a woman in
travail,
I will gasp and pant.
15 I will lay waste mountains and
hills,
and dry up all their herbage;
I will turn the rivers into islands,
and dry up the pools.
16 And I will lead the blind
in a way that they know not,
in paths that they have not known
I will guide them.
I will turn the darkness before them
into light,
the rough places into level ground.
These are the things I will do,
and I will not forsake them.
17 They shall be turned back and
utterly put to shame,
who trust in graven images,
who say to molten images,
"You are our gods."

18 Hear, you deaf;
and look, you blind, that you may
see!
19 Who is blind but my servant,
or deaf as my messenger whom
I send?
Who is blind as my dedicated one,
or blind as the servant of the
LORD?
20 He sees^w many things, but does not
observe them;
his ears are open, but he does not
hear.
21 The LORD was pleased, for his
righteousness' sake,
to magnify his law and make it
glorious.
22 But this is a people robbed and
plundered,
they are all of them trapped in
holes
and hidden in prisons;
they have become a prey with none
to rescue,
a spoil with none to say, "Restore!"
23 Who among you will give ear to
this,
will attend and listen for the time
to come?
24 Who gave up Jacob to the spoiler,
and Israel to the robbers?
Was it not the LORD, against whom
we have sinned,
in whose ways they would not
walk,
and whose law they would not
obey?
25 So he poured upon him the heat of
his anger

^{v} Cn Compare Ps 96.11; 98.7: Heb *Those who go down to the sea* ^{w} Heb *you see*
42.5: Acts 17.24-25.   **42.6**: Is 49.6; Lk 2.32; Acts 13.47; 26.23.   **42.7, 16**: Acts 26.18.

and the might of battle;
it set him on fire round about, but
he did not understand;
it burned him, but he did not
take it to heart.

43 But now thus says the LORD,
who created you, O Jacob,
he who formed you, O Israel:
"Fear not, for I have redeemed you;
I have called you by name, you
are mine.
2 When you pass through the waters
I will be with you;
and through the rivers, they shall
not overwhelm you;
when you walk through fire you
shall not be burned,
and the flame shall not consume
you.
3 For I am the LORD your God,
the Holy One of Israel, your
Savior.
I give Egypt as your ransom,
Ethiopia and Sē′bà in exchange
for you.
4 Because you are precious in my
eyes,
and honored, and I love you,
I give men in return for you,
peoples in exchange for your life.
5 Fear not, for I am with you;
I will bring your offspring from
the east,
and from the west I will gather
you;
6 I will say to the north, Give up,
and to the south, Do not withhold;
bring my sons from afar
and my daughters from the end
of the earth,
7 every one who is called by my name,
whom I created for my glory,
whom I formed and made."

8 Bring forth the people who are
blind, yet have eyes,
who are deaf, yet have ears!
9 Let all the nations gather together,
and let the peoples assemble.
Who among them can declare this,
and show us the former things?
Let them bring their witnesses to
justify them,
and let them hear and say, It is
true.
10 "You are my witnesses," says the
LORD,
"and my servant whom I have
chosen,
that you may know and believe me
and understand that I am He.
Before me no god was formed,

nor shall there be any after me.
11 I, I am the LORD,
and besides me there is no savior.
12 I declared and saved and proclaimed,
when there was no strange god
among you;
and you are my witnesses," says
the LORD.
13 "I am God, and also henceforth I
am He;
there is none who can deliver
from my hand;
I work and who can hinder it?"

14 Thus says the LORD,
your Redeemer, the Holy One of
Israel:
"For your sake I will send to
Babylon
and break down all the bars,
and the shouting of the Chal·dē′-
áns will be turned to lamentations.*x*
15 I am the LORD, your Holy One,
the Creator of Israel, your King."
16 Thus says the LORD,
who makes a way in the sea,
a path in the mighty waters,
17 who brings forth chariot and horse,
army and warrior;
they lie down, they cannot rise,
they are extinguished,
quenched like a wick:
18 "Remember not the former things,
nor consider the things of old.
19 Behold, I am doing a new thing;
now it springs forth, do you not
perceive it?
I will make a way in the wilderness
and rivers in the desert.
20 The wild beasts will honor me,
the jackals and the ostriches;
for I give water in the wilderness,
rivers in the desert,
to give drink to my chosen people,
21 the people whom I formed for
myself
that they might declare my praise.

22 "Yet you did not call upon me, O
Jacob;
but you have been weary of me,
O Israel!
23 You have not brought me your
sheep for burnt offerings,
or honored me with your sacrifices.
I have not burdened you with offerings,
or wearied you with frankincense.
24 You have not bought me sweet
cane with money,
or satisfied me with the fat of
your sacrifices.

x Heb obscure   **43.5:** Acts 18.10.

But you have burdened me with
    your sins,
you have wearied me with your
    iniquities.

25 "I, I am He
    who blots out your transgressions
      for my own sake,
    and I will not remember your sins.
26 Put me in remembrance, let us argue
    together;
    set forth your case, that you may
      be proved right.
27 Your first father sinned,
    and your mediators transgressed
      against me.
28 Therefore I profaned the princes of
    the sanctuary,
    I delivered Jacob to utter de-
      struction
    and Israel to reviling.

44   "But now hear, O Jacob my
    servant,
    Israel whom I have chosen!
2 Thus says the LORD who made you,
    who formed you from the womb
      and will help you:
Fear not, O Jacob my servant,
    Jesh′u·run whom I have chosen.
3 For I will pour water on the thirsty
    land,
    and streams on the dry ground;
I will pour my Spirit upon your
    descendants,
    and my blessing on your offspring.
4 They shall spring up like grass amid
    waters,ʸ
    like willows by flowing streams.
5 This one will say, 'I am the LORD's,'
    another will call himself by the
      name of Jacob,
and another will write on his hand,
    'The LORD's,'
    and surname himself by the name
      of Israel."

6 Thus says the LORD, the King of
    Israel
    and his Redeemer, the LORD of
      hosts:
"I am the first and I am the last;
    besides me there is no god.
7 Who is like me? Let him proclaim
    it,
    let him declare and set it forth
      before me.
Who has announced from of old the
    things to come?ᶻ
    Let them tell usᵃ what is yet to
      be.

8 Fear not, nor be afraid;
    have I not told you from of old
      and declared it?
    And you are my witnesses!
Is there a God besides me?
    There is no Rock; I know not
      any."

9 All who make idols are nothing,
and the things they delight in do not
profit; their witnesses neither see nor
know, that they may be put to shame.
10 Who fashions a god or casts an
image, that is profitable for nothing?
11 Behold, all his fellows shall be put
to shame, and the craftsmen are but
men; let them all assemble, let them
stand forth, they shall be terrified,
they shall be put to shame together.

12 The ironsmith fashions itᵇ and
works it over the coals; he shapes it
with hammers, and forges it with his
strong arm; he becomes hungry and
his strength fails, he drinks no water
and is faint. 13 The carpenter stretches
a line, he marks it out with a pencil;
he fashions it with planes, and marks
it with a compass; he shapes it into
the figure of a man, with the beauty
of a man, to dwell in a house. 14 He
cuts down cedars; or he chooses a
holm tree or an oak and lets it grow
strong among the trees of the forest;
he plants a cedar and the rain nourishes
it. 15 Then it becomes fuel for a man;
he takes a part of it and warms himself,
he kindles a fire and bakes bread; also
he makes a god and worships it, he
makes it a graven image and falls down
before it. 16 Half of it he burns in the
fire; over the half he eats flesh, he
roasts meat and is satisfied; also he
warms himself and says, "Aha, I am
warm, I have seen the fire!" 17 And the
rest of it he makes into a god, his idol;
and falls down to it and worships it;
he prays to it and says, "Deliver me,
for thou art my god!"

18 They know not, nor do they
discern; for he has shut their eyes, so
that they cannot see, and their minds,
so that they cannot understand. 19 No
one considers, nor is there knowledge
or discernment to say, "Half of it I
burned in the fire, I also baked bread
on its coals, I roasted flesh and have
eaten; and shall I make the residue of
it an abomination? Shall I fall down
before a block of wood?" 20 He feeds
on ashes; a deluded mind has led him
astray, and he cannot deliver himself

ʸ Gk Compare Tg: Heb *They shall spring up in among grass*
ᶻ Cn: Heb *from my placing an eternal people and things to come*   ᵃ Tg: Heb *them*
ᵇ Cn: Heb *an axe*
44.6: Is 48.12; Rev 1.17; 2.8; 22.13.

or say, "Is there not a lie in my right hand?"

21 Remember these things, O Jacob,
  and Israel, for you are my servant;
 I formed you, you are my servant;
  O Israel, you will not be forgotten by me.
22 I have swept away your transgressions like a cloud,
  and your sins like mist;
 return to me, for I have redeemed you.

23 Sing, O heavens, for the LORD has done it;
  shout, O depths of the earth;
 break forth into singing, O mountains,
  O forest, and every tree in it!
 For the LORD has redeemed Jacob,
  and will be glorified in Israel.

24 Thus says the LORD, your Redeemer,
  who formed you from the womb:
 "I am the LORD, who made all things,
  who stretched out the heavens alone,
  who spread out the earth—Who was with me?c
25 who frustrates the omens of liars,
  and makes fools of diviners;
 who turns wise men back,
  and makes their knowledge foolish;
26 who confirms the word of his servant,
  and performs the counsel of his messengers;
 who says of Jerusalem, 'She shall be inhabited,'
  and of the cities of Judah, 'They shall be built,
  and I will raise up their ruins';
27 who says to the deep, 'Be dry,
  I will dry up your rivers';
28 who says of Cyrus, 'He is my shepherd,
  and he shall fulfil all my purpose';
 saying of Jerusalem, 'She shall be built,'
  and of the temple, 'Your foundation shall be laid.'"

45 Thus says the LORD to his anointed, to Cyrus,
  whose right hand I have grasped,
 to subdue nations before him
  and ungird the loins of kings,

to open doors before him
  that gates may not be closed:
2 "I will go before you
  and level the mountains,d
 I will break in pieces the doors of bronze
  and cut asunder the bars of iron,
3 I will give you the treasures of darkness
  and the hoards in secret places,
 that you may know that it is I, the LORD,
  the God of Israel, who call you by your name.
4 For the sake of my servant Jacob,
  and Israel my chosen,
 I call you by your name,
  I surname you, though you do not know me.
5 I am the LORD, and there is no other,
  besides me there is no God;
 I gird you, though you do not know me,
6 that men may know, from the rising of the sun
  and from the west, that there is none besides me;
 I am the LORD, and there is no other.
7 I form light and create darkness,
  I make weal and create woe,
 I am the LORD, who do all these things.

8 "Shower, O heavens, from above,
  and let the skies rain down righteousness;
 let the earth open, that salvation may sprout forth,e
  and let it cause righteousness to spring up also;
 I the LORD have created it.

9 "Woe to him who strives with his Maker,
  an earthen vessel with the potter!f
 Does the clay say to him who fashions it, 'What are you making'?
  or 'Your work has no handles'?
10 Woe to him who says to a father, 'What are you begetting?'
  or to a woman, 'With what are you in travail?'"
11 Thus says the LORD,
  the Holy One of Israel, and his Maker:
 "Will you question meg about my children,
  or command me concerning the work of my hands?

c Another reading is *who spread out the earth by myself*
d One ancient Ms Gk: Heb *the swellings*
e One ancient Ms: Heb *that they may bring forth salvation*
f Cn: Heb *potsherds* or *potters*   g Cn: Heb *Ask me of things to come*
44.23: Jer 51.48; Rev 12.12; 18.20.   **44.25:** 1 Cor 1.20.   **45.9:** Is 29.16; Rom 9. 20.

12 I made the earth,
  and created man upon it;
it was my hands that stretched out
    the heavens,
  and I commanded all their host.
13 I have aroused him in righteousness,
  and I will make straight all his
    ways;
he shall build my city
  and set my exiles free,
not for price or reward,"
  says the LORD of hosts.

14 Thus says the LORD:
"The wealth of Egypt and the mer-
    chandise of Ethiopia,
  and the Sà-bē'àns̄, men of stature,
shall come over to you and be yours,
  they shall follow you;
  they shall come over in chains
    and bow down to you.
They will make supplication to you,
    saying:
'God is with you only, and there
    is no other,
no god besides him.' "
15 Truly, thou art a God who hidest
    thyself,
  O God of Israel, the Savior.
16 All of them are put to shame and
    confounded,
  the makers of idols go in con-
    fusion together.
17 But Israel is saved by the LORD
  with everlasting salvation;
you shall not be put to shame or
    confounded
  to all eternity.

18 For thus says the LORD,
  who created the heavens
    (he is God!),
who formed the earth and made it
    (he established it;
he did not create it a chaos,
  he formed it to be inhabited!):
"I am the LORD, and there is no
    other.
19 I did not speak in secret,
  in a land of darkness;
I did not say to the offspring of
    Jacob,
  'Seek me in chaos.'
I the LORD speak the truth,
  I declare what is right.

20 "Assemble yourselves and come,
  draw near together,
  you survivors of the nations!
They have no knowledge
  who carry about their wooden
    idols,
and keep on praying to a god

  that cannot save.
21 Declare and present your case;
  let them take counsel together!
Who told this long ago?
  Who declared it of old?
Was it not I, the LORD?
  And there is no other god besides
    me,
a righteous God and a Savior;
  there is none besides me.

22 "Turn to me and be saved,
  all the ends of the earth!
For I am God, and there is no
    other.
23 By myself I have sworn,
  from my mouth has gone forth in
    righteousness
a word that shall not return:
'To me every knee shall bow,
  every tongue shall swear.'
24 "Only in the LORD, it shall be said
    of me,
  are righteousness and strength;
to him shall come and be ashamed,
  all who were incensed against
    him.
25 In the LORD all the offspring of
    Israel
  shall triumph and glory."

46 Bel bows down, Nē'bō stoops,
  their idols are on beasts and
    cattle;
these things you carry are loaded
  as burdens on weary beasts.
2 They stoop, they bow down to-
    gether,
  they cannot save the burden,
but themselves go into captivity.

3 "Hearken to me, O house of Jacob,
  all the remnant of the house of
    Israel,
who have been borne by me from
    your birth,
  carried from the womb;
4 even to your old age I am He,
  and to gray hairs I will carry you.
I have made, and I will bear;
  I will carry and will save.

5 "To whom will you liken me and
    make me equal,
  and compare me, that we may be
    alike?
6 Those who lavish gold from the
    purse,
  and weigh out silver in the scales,
hire a goldsmith, and he makes it
    into a god;
then they fall down and worship!

45.14: 1 Cor 14.25.   45.17: Heb 5.9.   45.21: Acts 15.18.
45.23: Rom 14.11; Phil 2.10-11.

7 They lift it upon their shoulders,
     they carry it,
   they set it in its place, and it
     stands there;
   it cannot move from its place.
 If one cries to it, it does not answer
   or save him from his trouble.

8 "Remember this and consider,
   recall it to mind, you transgres-
     sors,
9 remember the former things of
     old;
   for I am God, and there is no other;
   I am God, and there is none like
     me,
10 declaring the end from the begin-
     ning
   and from ancient times things not
     yet done,
 saying, 'My counsel shall stand,
   and I will accomplish all my
     purpose,'
11 calling a bird of prey from the east,
   the man of my counsel from a far
     country.
 I have spoken, and I will bring it
   to pass;
   I have purposed, and I will do it.

12 "Hearken to me, you stubborn of
     heart,
   you who are far from deliverance:
13 I bring near my deliverance, it is
     not far off,
   and my salvation will not tarry;
 I will put salvation in Zion,
   for Israel my glory."

47 Come down and sit in the
     dust,
   O virgin daughter of Babylon;
 sit on the ground without a throne,
   O daughter of the Chal·dē′ans!
 For you shall no more be called
   tender and delicate.
2 Take the millstones and grind meal,
   put off your veil,
 strip off your robe, uncover your
     legs,
   pass through the rivers.
3 Your nakedness shall be uncovered,
   and your shame shall be seen.
 I will take vengeance,
   and I will spare no man.
4 Our Redeemer—the LORD of hosts
   is his name—
   is the Holy One of Israel.

5 Sit in silence, and go into darkness,
   O daughter of the Chal·dē′ans;
 for you shall no more be called
   the mistress of kingdoms.

6 I was angry with my people,
   I profaned my heritage;
 I gave them into your hand,
   you showed them no mercy;
 on the aged you made your yoke
   exceedingly heavy.
7 You said, "I shall be mistress for
     ever,"
   so that you did not lay these
     things to heart
   or remember their end.

8 Now therefore hear this, you lover
     of pleasures,
   who sit securely,
 who say in your heart,
   "I am, and there is no one besides
     me;
 I shall not sit as a widow
   or know the loss of children":
9 These two things shall come to you
   in a moment, in one day;
 the loss of children and widowhood
   shall come upon you in full
     measure,
 in spite of your many sorceries
   and the great power of your
     enchantments.

10 You felt secure in your wickedness,
   you said, "No one sees me";
 your wisdom and your knowledge
   led you astray,
 and you said in your heart,
   "I am, and there is no one besides
     me."
11 But evil shall come upon you,
   for which you cannot atone;
 disaster shall fall upon you,
   which you will not be able to
     expiate;
 and ruin shall come on you sud-
     denly,
   of which you know nothing.

12 Stand fast in your enchantments
   and your many sorceries,
   with which you have labored
     from your youth;
 perhaps you may be able to succeed,
   perhaps you may inspire terror.
13 You are wearied with your many
     counsels;
   let them stand forth and save you,
 those who divide the heavens,
   who gaze at the stars,
 who at the new moons predict
   what[h] shall befall you.

14 Behold, they are like stubble,
   the fire consumes them;
 they cannot deliver themselves
   from the power of the flame.

h Gk Syr Compare Vg: Heb *from what*
47: Is 13.1-14.23; Jer 50-51; Hab 1-2.   47.8: Rev 18.7.   47.9: Rev 18.8.

No coal for warming oneself is this,
no fire to sit before!
15 Such to you are those with whom
you have labored,
who have trafficked with you from
your youth;
they wander about each in his own
direction;
there is no one to save you.

48 Hear this, O house of Jacob,
who are called by the name of
Israel,
and who came forth from the
loins[j] of Judah;
who swear by the name of the LORD,
and confess the God of Israel,
but not in truth or right.
2 For they call themselves after the
holy city,
and stay themselves on the God
of Israel;
the LORD of hosts is his name.

3 "The former things I declared of old,
they went forth from my mouth
and I made them known;
then suddenly I did them and
they came to pass.
4 Because I know that you are obstinate,
and your neck is an iron sinew
and your forehead brass,
5 I declared them to you from of old,
before they came to pass I announced them to you,
lest you should say, 'My idol did
them,
my graven image and my molten
image commanded them.'
6 "You have heard; now see all this;
and will you not declare it?
From this time forth I make you
hear new things,
hidden things which you have
not known.
7 They are created now, not long ago;
before today you have never
heard of them,
lest you should say, 'Behold, I
knew them.'
8 You have never heard, you have
never known,
from of old your ear has not been
opened.
For I knew that you would deal very
treacherously,
and that from birth you were
called a rebel.

9 "For my name's sake I defer my
anger,

for the sake of my praise I restrain
it for you,
that I may not cut you off.
10 Behold, I have refined you, but not
like[j] silver;
I have tried you in the furnace of
affliction.
11 For my own sake, for my own sake,
I do it,
for how should my name[k] be
profaned?
My glory I will not give to another.

12 "Hearken to me, O Jacob,
and Israel, whom I called!
I am He, I am the first,
and I am the last.
13 My hand laid the foundation of the
earth,
and my right hand spread out the
heavens;
when I call to them,
they stand forth together.

14 Assemble, all of you, and hear!
Who among them has declared
these things?
The LORD loves him;
he shall perform his purpose on
Babylon,
and his arm shall be against the
Chal·dē′ans.
15 I, even I, have spoken and called him,
I have brought him, and he will
prosper in his way.
16 Draw near to me, hear this:
from the beginning I have not
spoken in secret,
from the time it came to be I
have been there."
And now the Lord GOD has sent me
and his Spirit.

17 Thus says the LORD,
your Redeemer, the Holy One of
Israel:
"I am the LORD your God,
who teaches you to profit,
who leads you in the way you
should go.
18 O that you had hearkened to my
commandments!
Then your peace would have been
like a river,
and your righteousness like the
waves of the sea;
19 your offspring would have been like
the sand,
and your descendants like its
grains;
their name would never be cut off
or destroyed from before me."

Cn: Heb *waters*   *j* Cn: Heb *with*   *k* Gk Old Latin: Heb lacks *my name*
48.12: Is 44.6; Rev 1.17; 2.8; 22.13.

20 Go forth from Babylon, flee from
  Chal·dē´ȧ,
  declare this with a shout of joy,
    proclaim it,
  send it forth to the end of the earth;
  say, "The LORD has redeemed
    his servant Jacob!"
21 They thirsted not when he led them
    through the deserts;
  he made water flow for them from
    the rock;
  he cleft the rock and the water
    gushed out.
22 "There is no peace," says the LORD,
  "for the wicked."

49 Listen to me, O coastlands,
  and hearken, you peoples from
    afar.
  The LORD called me from the
    womb,
  from the body of my mother he
    named my name.
2 He made my mouth like a sharp
    sword,
  in the shadow of his hand he hid
    me;
  he made me a polished arrow,
  in his quiver he hid me away.
3 And he said to me, "You are my
    servant,
  Israel, in whom I will be glori-
    fied."
4 But I said, "I have labored in vain,
  I have spent my strength for
    nothing and vanity;
  yet surely my right is with the LORD,
  and my recompense with my
    God."

5 And now the LORD says,
  who formed me from the womb
    to be his servant,
  to bring Jacob back to him,
  and that Israel might be gathered
    to him,
  for I am honored in the eyes of the
    LORD,
  and my God has become my
    strength—
6 he says:
  "It is too light a thing that you
    should be my servant
  to raise up the tribes of Jacob
  and to restore the preserved of
    Israel;
  I will give you as a light to the
    nations,
  that my salvation may reach to
    the end of the earth."

7 Thus says the LORD,

the Redeemer of Israel and his
    Holy One,
to one deeply despised, abhorred
    by the nations,
  the servant of rulers:
"Kings shall see and arise;
  princes, and they shall prostrate
    themselves;
because of the LORD, who is faithful,
  the Holy One of Israel, who has
    chosen you."

8 Thus says the LORD:
"In a time of favor I have answered
    you,
  in a day of salvation I have helped
    you;
I have kept you and given you
  as a covenant to the people,
to establish the land,
  to apportion the desolate herit-
    ages;
9 saying to the prisoners, 'Come
    forth,'
  to those who are in darkness,
    'Appear.'
They shall feed along the ways,
  on all bare heights shall be their
    pasture;
10 they shall not hunger or thirst,
  neither scorching wind nor sun
    shall smite them,
for he who has pity on them will
    lead them,
  and by springs of water will guide
    them.
11 And I will make all my mountains
    a way,
  and my highways shall be raised
    up.
12 Lo, these shall come from afar,
  and lo, these from the north and
    from the west,
  and these from the land of
    Sў·ē´nē."ˡ
13 Sing for joy, O heavens, and exult,
    O earth;
  break forth, O mountains, into
    singing!
For the LORD has comforted his
    people,
  and will have compassion on his
    afflicted.

14 But Zion said, "The LORD has for-
    saken me,
  my Lord has forgotten me."
15 "Can a woman forget her sucking
    child,
  that she should have no com-
    passion on the son of her
    womb?"

ˡCn: Heb *Sinim*
49.1: Jer 1.5; Gal 1.15.   49.4: Phil 2.16.   49.6: Is 42.6; Lk 2.32; Acts 13.47; 26.23.
49.8: 2 Cor 6.2.   49.10: Rev 7.16.   49.13: Is 44.23; Jer 51.48; Rev 12.12; 18.20.

Even these may forget,
    yet I will not forget you.
16 Behold, I have graven you on the
    palms of my hands;
    your walls are continually before
    me.
17 Your builders outstrip your de-
    stroyers,
    and those who laid you waste go
    forth from you.
18 Lift up your eyes round about and see;
    they all gather, they come to you.
    As I live, says the LORD,
    you shall put them all on as an
    ornament,
    you shall bind them on as a bride
    does.

19 "Surely your waste and your deso-
    late places
    and your devastated land—
surely now you will be too narrow
    for your inhabitants,
    and those who swallowed you up
    will be far away.
20 The children born in the time of
    your bereavement
    will yet say in your ears:
    'The place is too narrow for me;
    make room for me to dwell in.'
21 Then you will say in your heart:
    'Who has borne me these?
    I was bereaved and barren,
    exiled and put away,
    but who has brought up these?
    Behold, I was left alone;
    whence then have these come?'"

22 Thus says the Lord GOD:
    "Behold, I will lift up my hand to
    the nations,
    and raise my signal to the peoples;
    and they shall bring your sons in
    their bosom,
    and your daughters shall be car-
    ried on their shoulders.
23 Kings shall be your foster fathers,
    and their queens your nursing
    mothers.
    With their faces to the ground they
    shall bow down to you,
    and lick the dust of your feet.
    Then you will know that I am the
    LORD;
    those who wait for me shall not
    be put to shame."

24 Can the prey be taken from the
    mighty,
    or the captives of a tyrant[m] be
    rescued?
25 Surely, thus says the LORD:
    "Even the captives of the mighty
    shall be taken,

and the prey of the tyrant be
    rescued,
for I will contend with those who
    contend with you,
    and I will save your children.
26 I will make your oppressors eat
    their own flesh,
    and they shall be drunk with their
    own blood as with wine.
    Then all flesh shall know
    that I am the LORD your Savior,
    and your Redeemer, the Mighty
    One of Jacob."

50 Thus says the LORD:
    "Where is your mother's bill of
    divorce,
    with which I put her away?
    Or which of my creditors is it
    to whom I have sold you?
    Behold, for your iniquities you
    were sold,
    and for your transgressions your
    mother was put away.
2 Why, when I came, was there no
    man?
    When I called, was there no one
    to answer?
    Is my hand shortened, that it can-
    not redeem?
    Or have I no power to deliver?
    Behold, by my rebuke I dry up the
    sea,
    I make the rivers a desert;
    their fish stink for lack of water,
    and die of thirst.
3 I clothe the heavens with blackness,
    and make sackcloth their cover-
    ing."

4 The Lord GOD has given me
    the tongue of those who are
    taught,
    that I may know how to sustain with
    a word
    him that is weary.
    Morning by morning he wakens,
    he wakens my ear
    to hear as those who are taught.
5 The Lord GOD has opened my
    ear,
    and I was not rebellious,
    I turned not backward.
6 I gave my back to the smiters,
    and my cheeks to those who
    pulled out the beard;
    I hid not my face
    from shame and spitting.

7 For the Lord GOD helps me;
    therefore I have not been con-
    founded;
    therefore I have set my face like a
    flint,

[m] One ancient Ms Syr Vg: Heb *righteous man*

and I know that I shall not be
put to shame;
8 he who vindicates me is near.
Who will contend with me?
Let us stand up together.
Who is my adversary?
Let him come near to me.
9 Behold, the Lord GOD helps me;
who will declare me guilty?
Behold, all of them will wear out
like a garment;
the moth will eat them up.

10 Who among you fears the LORD
and obeys the voice of his servant,
who walks in darkness
and has no light,
yet trusts in the name of the LORD
and relies upon his God?
11 Behold, all you who kindle a fire,
who set brands alight![n]
Walk by the light of your fire,
and by the brands which you
have kindled!
This shall you have from my hand:
you shall lie down in torment.

51 "Hearken to me, you who pursue deliverance,
you who seek the LORD;
look to the rock from which you
were hewn,
and to the quarry from which you
were digged.
2 Look to Abraham your father
and to Sarah who bore you;
for when he was but one I called
him,
and I blessed him and made him
many.
3 For the LORD will comfort Zion;
he will comfort all her waste
places,
and will make her wilderness like
Eden,
her desert like the garden of the
LORD;
joy and gladness will be found in
her,
thanksgiving and the voice of
song.

4 "Listen to me, my people,
and give ear to me, my nation;
for a law will go forth from me,
and my justice for a light to the
peoples.
5 My deliverance draws near speedily,
my salvation has gone forth,
and my arms will rule the peoples;
the coastlands wait for me,
and for my arm they hope.
6 Lift up your eyes to the heavens,

and look at the earth beneath;
for the heavens will vanish like
smoke,
the earth will wear out like a
garment,
and they who dwell in it will die
like gnats;[o]
but my salvation will be for ever,
and my deliverance will never be
ended.

7 "Hearken to me, you who know
righteousness,
the people in whose heart is my
law;
fear not the reproach of men,
and be not dismayed at their
revilings.
8 For the moth will eat them up like
a garment,
and the worm will eat them like
wool;
but my deliverance will be for
ever,
and my salvation to all generations."

9 Awake, awake, put on strength,
O arm of the LORD;
awake, as in days of old,
the generations of long ago.
Was it not thou that didst cut Rā′hab
in pieces,
that didst pierce the dragon?
10 Was it not thou that didst dry up
the sea,
the waters of the great deep;
that didst make the depths of the
sea a way
for the redeemed to pass over?
11 And the ransomed of the LORD shall
return,
and come to Zion with singing;
everlasting joy shall be upon their
heads;
they shall obtain joy and gladness,
and sorrow and sighing shall flee
away.

12 "I, I am he that comforts you;
who are you that you are afraid
of man who dies,
of the son of man who is made
like grass,
13 and have forgotten the LORD, your
Maker,
who stretched out the heavens
and laid the foundations of the
earth,
and fear continually all the day
because of the fury of the oppressor,
when he sets himself to destroy?

n Syr: Heb gird yourselves with brands   o Or in like manner
50.8-9: Rom 8.33; Heb 1.11.   51.6: Heb 1.11.

And where is the fury of the oppressor?

14 He who is bowed down shall
speedily be released;
  he shall not die and go down to
    the Pit,
  neither shall his bread fail.

15 For I am the LORD your God,
  who stirs up the sea so that its
    waves roar—
  the LORD of hosts is his name.

16 And I have put my words in your
    mouth,
  and hid you in the shadow of my
    hand,
stretching out[p] the heavens
  and laying the foundations of the
    earth,
  and saying to Zion, 'You are my
    people.'"

17 Rouse yourself, rouse yourself,
    stand up, O Jerusalem,
  you who have drunk at the hand of
    the LORD
  the cup of his wrath,
  who have drunk to the dregs
    the bowl of staggering.

18 There is none to guide her
  among all the sons she has borne;
  there is none to take her by the hand
  among all the sons she has
    brought up.

19 These two things have befallen
    you—
  who will condole with you?—
  devastation and destruction, famine
    and sword;
  who will comfort you?[q]

20 Your sons have fainted,
  they lie at the head of every street
    like an antelope in a net;
  they are full of the wrath of the
    LORD,
  the rebuke of your God.

21 Therefore hear this, you who are
    afflicted,
  who are drunk, but not with
    wine:

22 Thus says your Lord, the LORD,
  your God who pleads the cause
    of his people:
"Behold, I have taken from your
    hand
  the cup of staggering;
  the bowl of my wrath
  you shall drink no more;

23 and I will put it into the hand of
    your tormentors,
  who have said to you,

'Bow down, that we may pass over';
  and you have made your back like
    the ground
  and like the street for them to
    pass over.'"

52

Awake, awake,
  put on your strength, O Zion;
put on your beautiful garments,
  O Jerusalem, the holy city;
for there shall no more come into you
  the uncircumcised and the un-
    clean.

2 Shake yourself from the dust, arise,
  O captive[r] Jerusalem;
loose the bonds from your neck,
  O captive daughter of Zion.

3 For thus says the LORD: "You
were sold for nothing, and you shall
be redeemed without money. 4 For
thus says the Lord GOD: My people
went down at the first into Egypt to
sojourn there, and the Assyrian oppressed them for nothing. 5 Now
therefore what have I here, says the
LORD, seeing that my people are taken
away for nothing? Their rulers wail,
says the LORD, and continually all the
day my name is despised. 6 Therefore
my people shall know my name; therefore in that day they shall know that
it is I who speak; here am I."

7 How beautiful upon the mountains
  are the feet of him who brings
    good tidings,
  who publishes peace, who brings
    good tidings of good,
  who publishes salvation,
  who says to Zion, "Your God
    reigns."

8 Hark, your watchmen lift up their
    voice,
  together they sing for joy;
for eye to eye they see
  the return of the LORD to Zion.

9 Break forth together into singing,
  you waste places of Jerusalem;
for the LORD has comforted his
    people,
  he has redeemed Jerusalem.

10 The LORD has bared his holy arm
  before the eyes of all the nations;
  and all the ends of the earth shall see
    the salvation of our God.

11 Depart, depart, go out thence,
    touch no unclean thing;
  go out from the midst of her, purify
    yourselves,

---

[p] Syr: Heb *plant*   [q] One ancient Ms Gk Syr Vg: Heb *how may I comfort you*
[r] Cn: Heb *sit*

52.1: Rev 21.27.   **52.5:** Rom 2.24.   **52.7:** Acts 10.36; Rom 10.15; Eph 6.15.
52.10: Lk 2.30; 3.6.   **52.11:** 2 Cor 6.17.

you who bear the vessels of the
LORD.
12 For you shall not go out in haste,
and you shall not go in flight,
for the LORD will go before you,
and the God of Israel will be your
rear guard.

13 Behold, my servant shall prosper,
he shall be exalted and lifted up,
and shall be very high.
14 As many were astonished at him[s]—
his appearance was so marred,
beyond human semblance,
and his form beyond that of the
sons of men—
15 so shall he startle[t] many nations;
kings shall shut their mouths because of him;
for that which has not been told
them they shall see,
and that which they have not
heard they shall understand.

53

Who has believed what we
have heard?
And to whom has the arm of the
LORD been revealed?
2 For he grew up before him like a
young plant,
and like a root out of dry ground;
he had no form or comeliness that
we should look at him,
and no beauty that we should
desire him.
3 He was despised and rejected[u] by men;
a man of sorrows,[v] and acquainted
with grief;[w]
and as one from whom men hide
their faces
he was despised, and we esteemed
him not.

4 Surely he has borne our griefs[x]
and carried our sorrows;[y]
yet we esteemed him stricken,
smitten by God, and afflicted.
5 But he was wounded for our transgressions,
he was bruised for our iniquities;
upon him was the chastisement that
made us whole,
and with his stripes we are healed.
6 All we like sheep have gone astray;
we have turned every one to his
own way;
and the LORD has laid on him
the iniquity of us all.

7 He was oppressed, and he was
afflicted,
yet he opened not his mouth;
like a lamb that is led to the
slaughter,
and like a sheep that before its
shearers is dumb,
so he opened not his mouth.
8 By oppression and judgment he was
taken away;
and as for his generation, who
considered
that he was cut off out of the land of
the living,
stricken for the transgression of
my people?
9 And they made his grave with the
wicked
and with a rich man in his death,
although he had done no violence,
and there was no deceit in his
mouth.

10 Yet it was the will of the LORD to
bruise him;
he has put him to grief;[z]
when he makes himself[a] an offering
for sin,
he shall see his offspring, he shall
prolong his days;
the will of the LORD shall prosper
in his hand;
11 he shall see the fruit of the travail
of his soul and be satisfied;
by his knowledge shall the righteous
one, my servant,
make many to be accounted
righteous;
and he shall bear their iniquities.
12 Therefore I will divide him a portion with the great,
and he shall divide the spoil with
the strong;
because he poured out his soul to
death,
and was numbered with the
transgressors;
yet he bore the sin of many,
and made intercession for the
transgressors.

54

"Sing, O barren one, who did
not bear;
break forth into singing and cry
aloud,
you who have not been in travail!
For the children of the desolate one
will be more

s Syr Tg: Heb *you*
t The meaning of the Hebrew word is uncertain   u Or *forsaken*
v Or *pains*   w Or *sickness*   x Or *sicknesses*   y Or *pains*   z Heb *made him sick*
a Vg: Heb *thou makest his soul*
52.15: Rom 15.21.   53.1: Jn 12.38; Rom 10.16.   53.4: Mt 8.17.
53.5-6: 1 Pet 2.24-25.   53.7-8: Acts 8.32-33.   53.9: 1 Pet 2.22.   53.12: Lk 22.37.
54.1: Gal 4.27.

than the children of her that is
married, says the LORD.
2 Enlarge the place of your tent,
and let the curtains of your
habitations be stretched out;
hold not back, lengthen your cords
and strengthen your stakes.
3 For you will spread abroad to the
right and to the left,
and your descendants will possess
the nations
and will people the desolate cities.

4 "Fear not, for you will not be
ashamed;
be not confounded, for you will
not be put to shame;
for you will forget the shame of your
youth,
and the reproach of your widowhood you will remember no
more.
5 For your Maker is your husband,
the LORD of hosts is his name;
and the Holy One of Israel is your
Redeemer,
the God of the whole earth he is
called.
6 For the LORD has called you
like a wife forsaken and grieved
in spirit,
like a wife of youth when she is cast
off,
says your God.
7 For a brief moment I forsook you,
but with great compassion I will
gather you.
8 In overflowing wrath for a moment
I hid my face from you,
but with everlasting love I will have
compassion on you,
says the LORD, your Redeemer.

9 "For this is like the days of Noah
to me:
as I swore that the waters of
Noah
should no more go over the earth,
so I have sworn that I will not be
angry with you
and will not rebuke you.
10 For the mountains may depart
and the hills be removed,
but my steadfast love shall not
depart from you,
and my covenant of peace shall
not be removed,
says the LORD, who has compassion on you.

11 "O afflicted one, storm-tossed, and
not comforted,

behold, I will set your stones in
antimony,
and lay your foundations with
sapphires.[b]
12 I will make your pinnacles of agate,
your gates of carbuncles,
and all your wall of precious
stones.
13 All your sons shall be taught by the
LORD,
and great shall be the prosperity
of your sons.
14 In righteousness you shall be
established;
you shall be far from oppression,
for you shall not fear;
and from terror, for it shall not
come near you.
15 If any one stirs up strife,
it is not from me;
whoever stirs up strife with you
shall fall because of you.
16 Behold, I have created the smith
who blows the fire of coals,
and produces a weapon for its
purpose.
I have also created the ravager to
destroy;
17 no weapon that is fashioned
against you shall prosper,
and you shall confute every
tongue that rises against you in
judgment.
This is the heritage of the servants
of the LORD
and their vindication from me,
says the LORD."

55 "Ho, every one who thirsts,
come to the waters;
and he who has no money,
come, buy and eat!
Come, buy wine and milk
without money and without price.
2 Why do you spend your money for
that which is not bread,
and your labor for that which
does not satisfy?
Hearken diligently to me, and eat
what is good,
and delight yourselves in fatness.
3 Incline your ear, and come to me;
hear, that your soul may live;
and I will make with you an everlasting covenant,
my steadfast, sure love for David.
4 Behold, I made him a witness to
the peoples,
a leader and commander for the
peoples.
5 Behold, you shall call nations that
you know not,

Or *lapis lazuli*
4.11-12: Rev 21.19.   54.13: Jn 6.45.   55.1: Rev 21.6; 22.17.
5.3: Acts 13.34; Heb 13.20.

and nations that knew you not
    shall run to you,
because of the LORD your God, and
    of the Holy One of Israel,
    for he has glorified you.

6 "Seek the LORD while he may be
    found,
    call upon him while he is near;
7 let the wicked forsake his way,
    and the unrighteous man his
        thoughts;
let him return to the LORD, that he
    may have mercy on him,
    and to our God, for he will
        abundantly pardon.
8 For my thoughts are not your
    thoughts,
    neither are your ways my ways,
        says the LORD.
9 For as the heavens are higher than
    the earth,
    so are my ways higher than your
        ways
    and my thoughts than your
        thoughts.

10 "For as the rain and the snow come
    down from heaven,
    and return not thither but water
        the earth,
making it bring forth and sprout,
    giving seed to the sower and bread
        to the eater,
11 so shall my word be that goes forth
    from my mouth;
    it shall not return to me empty,
but it shall accomplish that which
    I purpose,
    and prosper in the thing for which
        I sent it.

12 "For you shall go out in joy,
    and be led forth in peace;
the mountains and the hills before
    you
    shall break forth into singing,
    and all the trees of the field shall
        clap their hands.
13 Instead of the thorn shall come up
    the cypress;
instead of the brier shall come up
    the myrtle;
and it shall be to the LORD for a
    memorial,
    for an everlasting sign which shall
        not be cut off."

56   Thus says the LORD:
    "Keep justice, and do right-
        eousness,
for soon my salvation will come,
    and my deliverance be revealed.

2 Blessed is the man who does this,
    and the son of man who holds it fast,
who keeps the sabbath, not pro-
    faning it,
    and keeps his hand from doing
        any evil."

3 Let not the foreigner who has joined
    himself to the LORD say,
    "The LORD will surely separate
        me from his people";
and let not the eunuch say,
    "Behold, I am a dry tree."
4 For thus says the LORD:
    "To the eunuchs who keep my
        sabbaths,
who choose the things that please me
    and hold fast my covenant,
5 I will give in my house and within
    my walls
    a monument and a name
    better than sons and daughters;
I will give them an everlasting name
    which shall not be cut off.

6 "And the foreigners who join them-
    selves to the LORD,
    to minister to him, to love the
        name of the LORD,
    and to be his servants,
every one who keeps the sabbath,
    and does not profane it,
    and holds fast my covenant—
7 these I will bring to my holy
    mountain,
    and make them joyful in my
        house of prayer;
their burnt offerings and their
    sacrifices
    will be accepted on my altar;
for my house shall be called a house
    of prayer
    for all peoples.
8 Thus says the Lord GOD,
    who gathers the outcasts of Israel,
I will gather yet others to him
    besides those already gathered."[c]

9 All you beasts of the field, come to
    devour—
    all you beasts in the forest.
10 His watchmen are blind,
    they are all without knowledge;
they are all dumb dogs,
    they cannot bark;
dreaming, lying down,
    loving to slumber.
11 The dogs have a mighty appetite;
    they never have enough.
The shepherds also have no under-
    standing;
    they have all turned to their own
        way,

Heb his gathered ones
55.10: 2 Cor 9.10.   **56.7:** Mt 21.13; Mk 11.17; Lk 19.46.

each to his own gain, one and all.

12 "Come," they say, "let us*d* get wine,
let us fill ourselves with strong
drink;
and tomorrow will be like this day,
great beyond measure."

57 The righteous man perishes,
and no one lays it to heart;
devout men are taken away,
while no one understands.
For the righteous man is taken away
from calamity,

2 he enters into peace;
they rest in their beds
who walk in their uprightness.

3 But you, draw near hither,
sons of the sorceress,
offspring of the adulterer and the
harlot.

4 Of whom are you making sport?
Against whom do you open your
mouth wide
and put out your tongue?
Are you not children of transgression,
the offspring of deceit,

5 you who burn with lust among the
oaks,
under every green tree;
who slay your children in the valleys,
under the clefts of the rocks?

6 Among the smooth stones of the
valley is your portion;
they, they, are your lot;
to them you have poured out a
drink offering,
you have brought a cereal offering.
Shall I be appeased for these
things?

7 Upon a high and lofty mountain
you have set your bed,
and thither you went up to offer
sacrifice.

8 Behind the door and the doorpost
you have set up your symbol;
for, deserting me, you have uncovered your bed,
you have gone up to it,
you have made it wide;
and you have made a bargain for
yourself with them,
you have loved their bed,
you have looked on nakedness.*e*

9 You journeyed to Mē′loch*f* with oil
and multiplied your perfumes;
you sent your envoys far off,
and sent down even to Shē′ol.

10 You were wearied with the length
of your way,
but you did not say, "It is hopeless";

you found new life for your strength,
and so you were not faint.

11 Whom did you dread and fear,
so that you lied,
and did not remember me,
did not give me a thought?
Have I not held my peace, even for
a long time,
and so you do not fear me?

12 I will tell of your righteousness and
your doings,
but they will not help you.

13 When you cry out, let your collection of idols deliver you!
The wind will carry them off,
a breath will take them away.
But he who takes refuge in me shall
possess the land,
and shall inherit my holy mountain.

14 And it shall be said,
"Build up, build up, prepare the
way,
remove every obstruction from
my people's way."

15 For thus says the high and lofty One
who inhabits eternity, whose
name is Holy:
"I dwell in the high and holy
place,
and also with him who is of a
contrite and humble spirit,
to revive the spirit of the humble,
and to revive the heart of the
contrite.

16 For I will not contend for ever,
nor will I always be angry;
for from me proceeds the spirit,
and I have made the breath of life.

17 Because of the iniquity of his covetousness I was angry,
I smote him, I hid my face and
was angry;
but he went on backsliding in the
way of his own heart.

18 I have seen his ways, but I will heal
him;
I will lead him and requite him
with comfort,
creating for his mourners the
fruit of the lips.

19 Peace, peace, to the far and to the
near, says the LORD;
and I will heal him.

20 But the wicked are like the tossing
sea;
for it cannot rest,
and its waters toss up mire and
dirt.

21 There is no peace, says my God,
for the wicked."

d One ancient Ms Syr Vg Tg: Heb *me*   *e* The meaning of the Hebrew is uncertain
f Or *the king*

57.15: Mt 5.3.   57.19: Acts 2.39; Eph 2.13, 17.

58 "Cry aloud, spare not,
lift up your voice like a trumpet;
declare to my people their transgression,
to the house of Jacob their sins.
2 Yet they seek me daily,
and delight to know my ways,
as if they were a nation that did righteousness
and did not forsake the ordinance of their God;
they ask of me righteous judgments,
they delight to draw near to God.
3 'Why have we fasted, and thou seest it not?
Why have we humbled ourselves,
and thou takest no knowledge of it?'
Behold, in the day of your fast you
seek your own pleasure,[g]
and oppress all your workers.
4 Behold, you fast only to quarrel and to fight
and to hit with wicked fist.
Fasting like yours this day
will not make your voice to be heard on high.
5 Is such the fast that I choose,
a day for a man to humble himself?
Is it to bow down his head like a rush,
and to spread sackcloth and ashes under him?
Will you call this a fast,
and a day acceptable to the LORD?

6 "Is not this the fast that I choose:
to loose the bonds of wickedness,
to undo the thongs of the yoke,
to let the oppressed go free,
and to break every yoke?
7 Is it not to share your bread with the hungry,
and bring the homeless poor into your house;
when you see the naked, to cover him,
and not to hide yourself from your own flesh?
8 Then shall your light break forth like the dawn,
and your healing shall spring up speedily;
your righteousness shall go before you,
the glory of the LORD shall be your rear guard.
9 Then you shall call, and the LORD will answer;
you shall cry, and he will say, Here I am.

"If you take away from the midst of you the yoke,
the pointing of the finger, and speaking wickedness,
10 if you pour yourself out for the hungry
and satisfy the desire of the afflicted,
then shall your light rise in the darkness
and your gloom be as the noonday.
11 And the LORD will guide you continually,
and satisfy your desire with good things,[h]
and make your bones strong;
and you shall be like a watered garden,
like a spring of water,
whose waters fail not.
12 And your ancient ruins shall be rebuilt;
you shall raise up the foundations of many generations;
you shall be called the repairer of the breach,
the restorer of streets to dwell in.

13 "If you turn back your foot from the sabbath,
from doing your pleasure[i] on my holy day,
and call the sabbath a delight
and the holy day of the LORD honorable;
if you honor it, not going your own ways,
or seeking your own pleasure,[j] or talking idly;
14 then you shall take delight in the LORD,
and I will make you ride upon the heights of the earth;
I will feed you with the heritage of Jacob your father,
for the mouth of the LORD has spoken."

59 Behold, the LORD's hand is not
shortened, that it cannot save,
or his ear dull, that it cannot hear;
2 but your iniquities have made a separation
between you and your God,
and your sins have hid his face from you
so that he does not hear.
3 For your hands are defiled with blood
and your fingers with iniquity;
your lips have spoken lies,

---

g Or *pursue your own business*   *h* The meaning of the Hebrew word is uncertain
i Or *business*   *j* Or *pursuing your own business*
58.6: Acts 8.23.

your tongue mutters wickedness.

4 No one enters suit justly,
> no one goes to law honestly;
they rely on empty pleas, they speak lies,
> they conceive mischief and bring forth iniquity.

5 They hatch adders' eggs,
> they weave the spider's web;
he who eats their eggs dies,
> and from one which is crushed a viper is hatched.

6 Their webs will not serve as clothing;
> men will not cover themselves with what they make.
Their works are works of iniquity,
> and deeds of violence are in their hands.

7 Their feet run to evil,
> and they make haste to shed innocent blood;
their thoughts are thoughts of iniquity,
> desolation and destruction are in their highways.

8 The way of peace they know not,
> and there is no justice in their paths;
they have made their roads crooked,
> no one who goes in them knows peace.

9 Therefore justice is far from us,
> and righteousness does not overtake us;
we look for light, and behold, darkness,
> and for brightness, but we walk in gloom.

10 We grope for the wall like the blind,
> we grope like those who have no eyes;
we stumble at noon as in the twilight,
> among those in full vigor we are like dead men.

11 We all growl like bears,
> we moan and moan like doves;
we look for justice, but there is none;
> for salvation, but it is far from us.

12 For our transgressions are multiplied before thee,
> and our sins testify against us;
for our transgressions are with us,
> and we know our iniquities:

13 transgressing, and denying the LORD,
> and turning away from following our God,
speaking oppression and revolt,
> conceiving and uttering from the heart lying words.

14 Justice is turned back,
> and righteousness stands afar off;
for truth has fallen in the public squares,
> and uprightness cannot enter.

15 Truth is lacking,
> and he who departs from evil makes himself a prey.

The LORD saw it, and it displeased him
> that there was no justice.

16 He saw that there was no man,
> and wondered that there was no one to intervene;
then his own arm brought him victory,
> and his righteousness upheld him.

17 He put on righteousness as a breastplate,
> and a helmet of salvation upon his head;
he put on garments of vengeance for clothing,
> and wrapped himself in fury as a mantle.

18 According to their deeds, so will he repay,
> wrath to his adversaries, requital to his enemies;
to the coastlands he will render requital.

19 So they shall fear the name of the LORD from the west,
> and his glory from the rising of the sun;
for he will come like a rushing stream,
> which the wind of the LORD drives.

20 "And he will come to Zion as Redeemer,
> to those in Jacob who turn from transgression, says the LORD.

21 "And as for me, this is my covenant with them, says the LORD: my spirit which is upon you, and my words which I have put in your mouth, shall not depart out of your mouth, or out of the mouth of your children, or out of the mouth of your children's children, says the LORD, from this time forth and for evermore."

60

Arise, shine; for your light has come,
> and the glory of the LORD has risen upon you.

2 For behold, darkness shall cover the earth,
> and thick darkness the peoples;
but the LORD will arise upon you,

59.7-8: Rom 3.15-17.   **59.17:** Eph 6.14, 17; 1 Thess 5.8.   **59.19:** Mt 8.11; Lk 13.29.
59.20-21: Rom 11.26-27.

and his glory will be seen upon you.
3 And nations shall come to your
light,
    and kings to the brightness of
    your rising.

4 Lift up your eyes round about, and
see;
    they all gather together, they
    come to you;
your sons shall come from far,
    and your daughters shall be car-
    ried in the arms.
5 Then you shall see and be radiant,
    your heart shall thrill and re-
    joice;[k]
because the abundance of the sea
    shall be turned to you,
    the wealth of the nations shall
    come to you.
6 A multitude of camels shall cover
you,
    the young camels of Mid′i·an and
    E′phah;
all those from Sheba shall come.
    They shall bring gold and frank-
    incense,
    and shall proclaim the praise of
    the LORD.
7 All the flocks of Kē′där shall be
    gathered to you,
    the rams of Ne·bā′ioth shall
    minister to you;
they shall come up with acceptance
    on my altar,
    and I will glorify my glorious
    house.

8 Who are these that fly like a cloud,
    and like doves to their windows?
9 For the coastlands shall wait for me,
    the ships of Tär′shish first,
to bring your sons from far,
    their silver and gold with them,
for the name of the LORD your God,
    and for the Holy One of Israel,
    because he has glorified you.

10 Foreigners shall build up your walls,
    and their kings shall minister to
    you;
for in my wrath I smote you,
    but in my favor I have had mercy
    on you.
11 Your gates shall be open continually;
    day and night they shall not be
    shut;
that men may bring to you the
    wealth of the nations,
    with their kings led in procession.
12 For the nation and kingdom
    that will not serve you shall
    perish;

those nations shall be utterly laid
    waste.
13 The glory of Lebanon shall come to
    you,
    the cypress, the plane, and the
    pine,
to beautify the place of my sanctuary;
    and I will make the place of my
    feet glorious.
14 The sons of those who oppressed you
    shall come bending low to you;
and all who despised you
    shall bow down at your feet;
they shall call you the City of the
    LORD,
    the Zion of the Holy One of
    Israel.

15 Whereas you have been forsaken
    and hated,
    with no one passing through,
I will make you majestic for ever,
    a joy from age to age.
16 You shall suck the milk of nations,
    you shall suck the breast of kings;
and you shall know that I, the LORD,
    am your Savior
    and your Redeemer, the Mighty
    One of Jacob.

17 Instead of bronze I will bring gold,
    and instead of iron I will bring
    silver;
instead of wood, bronze,
    instead of stones, iron.
I will make your overseers peace
    and your taskmasters righteous-
    ness.
18 Violence shall no more be heard in
    your land,
    devastation or destruction within
    your borders;
you shall call your walls Salvation,
    and your gates Praise.

19 The sun shall be no more
    your light by day,
    nor for brightness shall the moon
    give light to you by night;[l]
but the LORD will be your everlast-
    ing light,
    and your God will be your glory.
20 Your sun shall no more go down,
    nor your moon withdraw itself;
for the LORD will be your everlast-
    ing light,
    and your days of mourning shall
    be ended.
21 Your people shall all be righteous;
    they shall possess the land for ever,
the shoot of my planting, the work
    of my hands,
    that I might be glorified.

---

k Heb *be enlarged*　l One ancient Ms Gk Old Latin Tg: Heb lacks *by night*
60.6: Mt 2.11.　**60.11:** Rev 21.25-26.　**60.14:** Rev 3.9.　**60.19:** Rev 21.23; 22.5.

22 The least one shall become a clan,
   and the smallest one a mighty
      nation;
   I am the LORD;
      in its time I will hasten it.

61 The Spirit of the Lord GOD is
      upon me,
   because the LORD has anointed
      me
to bring good tidings to the af-
      flicted;*m*
   he has sent me to bind up the
      brokenhearted,
to proclaim liberty to the cap-
      tives,
   and the opening of the prison*n* to
      those who are bound;
2 to proclaim the year of the LORD's
      favor,
   and the day of vengeance of our
      God;
   to comfort all who mourn;
3 to grant to those who mourn in
      Zion—
   to give them a garland instead of
      ashes,
the oil of gladness instead of mourn-
      ing,
   the mantle of praise instead of a
      faint spirit;
that they may be called oaks of
      righteousness,
   the planting of the LORD, that he
      may be glorified.
4 They shall build up the ancient
      ruins,
   they shall raise up the former
      devastations;
they shall repair the ruined cities,
   the devastations of many genera-
      tions.

5 Aliens shall stand and feed your
      flocks,
   foreigners shall be your plowmen
      and vinedressers;
6 but you shall be called the priests
      of the LORD,
   men shall speak of you as the
      ministers of our God;
   you shall eat the wealth of the
      nations,
   and in their riches you shall glory.
7 Instead of your shame you shall
      have a double portion,
   instead of dishonor you*o* shall re-
      joice in your*p* lot;
therefore in your*p* land you*o* shall
      possess a double portion;

yours*q* shall be everlasting joy.

8 For I the LORD love justice,
   I hate robbery and wrong;*r*
   I will faithfully give them their
      recompense,
   and I will make an everlasting
      covenant with them.
9 Their descendants shall be known
      among the nations,
   and their offspring in the midst of
      the peoples;
all who see them shall acknowledge
      them,
   that they are a people whom the
      LORD has blessed.

10 I will greatly rejoice in the LORD,
   my soul shall exult in my God;
for he has clothed me with the gar-
      ments of salvation,
   he has covered me with the robe
      of righteousness,
as a bridegroom decks himself with
      a garland,
   and as a bride adorns herself with
      her jewels.
11 For as the earth brings forth its
      shoots,
   and as a garden causes what is
      sown in it to spring up,
so the Lord GOD will cause right-
      eousness and praise
   to spring forth before all the
      nations.

62 For Zion's sake I will not
      keep silent,
   and for Jerusalem's sake I will
      not rest,
until her vindication goes forth as
      brightness,
   and her salvation as a burning
      torch.
2 The nations shall see your vindi-
      cation,
   and all the kings your glory;
and you shall be called by a new
      name which the mouth of the
      LORD will give.
3 You shall be a crown of beauty in
      the hand of the LORD,
   and a royal diadem in the hand
      of your God.
4 You shall no more be termed For-
      saken,*s*
   and your land shall no more be
      termed Desolate;*t*
but you shall be called My delight
      is in her,*u*

---

m Or *poor*   *n* Or *the opening of the eyes:* Heb *the opening*   *o* Heb *they*   *p* Heb *their*
q Heb *theirs*   *r* Or *robbery with a burnt offering*   *s* Heb *Azubah*   *t* Heb *Shemamah*
u Heb *Hephzibah*
61.1-2: Mt 11.5; Lk 4.18-19; 7.22.   **61.6:** Ex 19.6; 1 Pet 2.5; Rev 1.6; 5.10; 20.6.
62.2: Rev 2.17.

and your land Married;^{v}
for the LORD delights in you,
and your land shall be married.
5 For as a young man marries a virgin,
so shall your sons marry you,
and as the bridegroom rejoices over
the bride,
so shall your God rejoice over you.

6 Upon your walls, O Jerusalem,
I have set watchmen;
all the day and all the night
they shall never be silent.
You who put the LORD in remembrance,
take no rest,
7 and give him no rest
until he establishes Jerusalem
and makes it a praise in the earth.
8 The LORD has sworn by his right
hand
and by his mighty arm:
"I will not again give your grain
to be food for your enemies,
and foreigners shall not drink your
wine
for which you have labored;
9 but those who garner it shall eat it
and praise the LORD,
and those who gather it shall drink
it
in the courts of my sanctuary."

10 Go through, go through the gates,
prepare the way for the people;
build up, build up the highway,
clear it of stones,
lift up an ensign over the peoples.
11 Behold, the LORD has proclaimed
to the end of the earth:
Say to the daughter of Zion,
"Behold, your salvation comes;
behold, his reward is with him,
and his recompense before him."
12 And they shall be called The holy
people,
The redeemed of the LORD;
and you shall be called Sought out,
a city not forsaken.

63 Who is this that comes from
E′dom,
in crimsoned garments from
Boz′rah,
he that is glorious in his apparel,
marching in the greatness of his
strength?

"It is I, announcing vindication,
mighty to save."

2 Why is thy apparel red,

and thy garments like his that
treads in the wine press?

3 "I have trodden the wine press alone,
and from the peoples no one was
with me;
I trod them in my anger
and trampled them in my wrath;
their lifeblood is sprinkled upon my
garments,
and I have stained all my raiment.
4 For the day of vengeance was in my
heart,
and my year of redemption^w has
come.
5 I looked, but there was no one to
help;
I was appalled, but there was no
one to uphold;
so my own arm brought me victory,
and my wrath upheld me.
6 I trod down the peoples in my anger,
I made them drunk in my wrath
and I poured out their lifeblood
on the earth."

7 I will recount the steadfast love of
the LORD,
the praises of the LORD,
according to all that the LORD has
granted us,
and the great goodness to the
house of Israel
which he has granted them according to his mercy,
according to the abundance of his
steadfast love.
8 For he said, Surely they are my
people,
sons who will not deal falsely;
and he became their Savior.
9 In all their affliction he was afflicted,^{x}
and the angel of his presence
saved them;
in his love and in his pity he redeemed them;
he lifted them up and carried
them all the days of old.

10 But they rebelled
and grieved his holy Spirit;
therefore he turned to be their
enemy,
and himself fought against them.
11 Then he remembered the days of
old,
of Moses his servant.
Where is he who brought up out
of the sea
the shepherds of his flock?
Where is he who put in the midst
of them

^{v} Heb *Beulah* ^{w} Or *the year of my redeemed* ^{x} Another reading is *he did not afflict*
63.1-6: Is 34; Jer 49.7-22; Ezek 25.12-14; 35; Amos 1.11-12; Obad; Mal 1.2-5.
63.3: Rev 19.15. **63.11:** Heb 13.20.

his holy Spirit,
12 who caused his glorious arm
    to go at the right hand of Moses,
who divided the waters before them
    to make for himself an everlasting
        name,
13 who led them through the depths?
Like a horse in the desert,
    they did not stumble.
14 Like cattle that go down into the
        valley,
    the Spirit of the LORD gave them
        rest.
So thou didst lead thy people,
    to make for thyself a glorious
        name.

15 Look down from heaven and see,
    from thy holy and glorious
        habitation.
Where are thy zeal and thy might?
    The yearning of thy heart and thy
        compassion
    are withheld from me.
16 For thou art our Father,
    though Abraham does not know us
    and Israel does not acknowledge
        us;
thou, O LORD, art our Father,
    our Redeemer from of old is thy
        name.
17 O LORD, why dost thou make us err
        from thy ways
    and harden our heart, so that we
        fear thee not?
Return for the sake of thy servants,
    the tribes of thy heritage.
18 Thy holy people possessed thy
        sanctuary a little while;
    our adversaries have trodden it
        down.
19 We have become like those over
        whom thou hast never ruled,
    like those who are not called by
        thy name.

64 O that thou wouldst rend the
        heavens and come down,
    that the mountains might quake
        at thy presence—
2y as when fire kindles brushwood
    and the fire causes water to boil—
to make thy name known to thy
        adversaries,
    and that the nations might
        tremble at thy presence!
3 When thou didst terrible things
        which we looked not for,
    thou camest down, the mountains
        quaked at thy presence.
4 From of old no one has heard
    or perceived by the ear,
no eye has seen a God besides thee,

who works for those who wait for
        him.
5 Thou meetest him that joyfully
        works righteousness,
    those that remember thee in thy
        ways.
Behold, thou wast angry, and we
        sinned;
    in our sins we have been a long
        time, and shall we be saved?z
6 We have all become like one who is
        unclean,
    and all our righteous deeds are
        like a polluted garment.
We all fade like a leaf,
    and our iniquities, like the wind,
        take us away.
7 There is no one that calls upon thy
        name,
    that bestirs himself to take hold
        of thee;
for thou hast hid thy face from us,
    and hast delivereda us into the
        hand of our iniquities.

8 Yet, O LORD, thou art our Father;
    we are the clay, and thou art our
        potter;
    we are all the work of thy hand.
9 Be not exceedingly angry, O LORD,
    and remember not iniquity for
        ever.
Behold, consider, we are all thy
        people.
10 Thy holy cities have become a
        wilderness,
    Zion has become a wilderness,
        Jerusalem a desolation.
11 Our holy and beautiful house,
    where our fathers praised thee,
has been burned by fire,
    and all our pleasant places have
        become ruins.
12 Wilt thou restrain thyself at these
        things, O LORD?
    Wilt thou keep silent, and afflict
        us sorely?

65 I was ready to be sought by
        those who did not ask for me;
    I was ready to be found by those
        who did not seek me.
I said, "Here am I, here am I,"
    to a nation that did not call on my
        name.
2 I spread out my hands all the day
    to a rebellious people,
who walk in a way that is not good,
    following their own devices;
3 a people who provoke me
    to my face continually,
sacrificing in gardens
    and burning incense upon bricks;

y Ch 64.1 in Heb   z Hebrew obscure   a Gk Syr Old Latin Tg: Heb melted
64.4: 1 Cor 2.9.   65.1-2: Rom 10.20-21.

4 who sit in tombs,
   and spend the night in secret
      places;
who eat swine's flesh,
   and broth of abominable things
      is in their vessels!
5 who say, "Keep to yourself,
   do not come near me, for I am
      set apart from you."
These are a smoke in my nostrils,
   a fire that burns all the day.
6 Behold, it is written before me:
   "I will not keep silent, but I will
      repay,
yea, I will repay into their bosom
7   their[b] iniquities and their[b] fa-
      thers' iniquities together,
               says the LORD;
because they burned incense upon
      the mountains
   and reviled me upon the hills,
I will measure into their bosom
   payment for their former doings."

8 Thus says the LORD:
   "As the wine is found in the cluster,
      and they say, 'Do not destroy it,
      for there is a blessing in it,'
so I will do for my servants' sake,
   and not destroy them all.
9 I will bring forth descendants from
      Jacob,
   and from Judah inheritors of my
      mountains;
my chosen shall inherit it,
   and my servants shall dwell there.
10 Sharon shall become a pasture for
      flocks,
   and the Valley of A'chôr a place
      for herds to lie down,
   for my people who have sought
      me.
11 But you who forsake the LORD,
   who forget my holy mountain,
who set a table for Fortune
   and fill cups of mixed wine for
      Destiny;
12 I will destine you to the sword,
   and all of you shall bow down to
      the slaughter;
because, when I called, you did not
      answer,
   when I spoke, you did not listen,
but you did what was evil in my
      eyes,
   and chose what I did not delight
      in."

13 Therefore thus says the Lord GOD:
   "Behold, my servants shall eat,
      but you shall be hungry;
behold, my servants shall drink,
   but you shall be thirsty;

behold, my servants shall rejoice,
   but you shall be put to shame;
14 behold, my servants shall sing for
      gladness of heart,
   but you shall cry out for pain of
      heart,
   and shall wail for anguish of
      spirit.
15 You shall leave your name to my
      chosen for a curse,
   and the Lord GOD will slay you;
but his servants he will call by a
      different name.
16 So that he who blesses himself in
      the land
   shall bless himself by the God of
      truth,
and he who takes an oath in the land
   shall swear by the God of truth;
because the former troubles are for-
      gotten
   and are hid from my eyes.

17 "For behold, I create new heavens
      and a new earth;
   and the former things shall not be
      remembered
   or come into mind.
18 But be glad and rejoice for ever
   in that which I create;
for behold, I create Jerusalem a
      rejoicing,
   and her people a joy.
19 I will rejoice in Jerusalem,
   and be glad in my people;
no more shall be heard in it the
      sound of weeping
   and the cry of distress.
20 No more shall there be in it
   an infant that lives but a few days,
   or an old man who does not fill
      out his days,
for the child shall die a hundred
      years old,
   and the sinner a hundred years
      old shall be accursed.
21 They shall build houses and inhabit
      them;
   they shall plant vineyards and eat
      their fruit.
22 They shall not build and another
      inhabit;
   they shall not plant and another
      eat;
for like the days of a tree shall the
      days of my people be,
   and my chosen shall long enjoy
      the work of their hands.
23 They shall not labor in vain,
   or bear children for calamity;[c]
for they shall be the offspring of the
      blessed of the LORD,
   and their children with them.

b Gk Syr: Heb *your*   *c* Or *sudden terror*
65:17: Is 66.22; 2 Pet 3.13; Rev 21.1.

24 Before they call I will answer,
    while they are yet speaking I will
    hear.
25 The wolf and the lamb shall feed
    together,
    the lion shall eat straw like the ox;
    and dust shall be the serpent's food.
They shall not hurt or destroy
    in all my holy mountain,
              says the LORD."

66   Thus says the LORD:
     "Heaven is my throne
    and the earth is my footstool;
what is the house which you would
    build for me,
    and what is the place of my rest?
2 All these things my hand has made,
    and so all these things are mine,*d*
            says the LORD.
But this is the man to whom I will
    look,
    he that is humble and contrite in
    spirit,
    and trembles at my word.

3 "He who slaughters an ox is like
    him who kills a man;
    he who sacrifices a lamb, like him
    who breaks a dog's neck;
    he who presents a cereal offering,
    like him who offers swine's
    blood;
    he who makes a memorial offering
    of frankincense, like him who
    blesses an idol.
These have chosen their own ways,
    and their soul delights in their
    abominations;
4 I also will choose affliction for them,
    and bring their fears upon them;
because, when I called, no one
    answered,
    when I spoke they did not listen;
but they did what was evil in my
    eyes,
    and chose that in which I did not
    delight."

5 Hear the word of the LORD,
    you who tremble at his word:
"Your brethren who hate you
    and cast you out for my name's
    sake
have said, 'Let the LORD be glori-
    fied,
    that we may see your joy';
but it is they who shall be put to
    shame.

6 "Hark, an uproar from the city!
    A voice from the temple!

The voice of the LORD,
    rendering recompense to his
    enemies!

7 "Before she was in labor
    she gave birth;
before her pain came upon her
    she was delivered of a son.
8 Who has heard such a thing?
    Who has seen such things?
Shall a land be born in one day?
    Shall a nation be brought forth
    in one moment?
For as soon as Zion was in labor
    she brought forth her sons.
9 Shall I bring to the birth and not
    cause to bring forth?
    says the LORD;
shall I, who cause to bring forth,
    shut the womb?
    says your God.

10 "Rejoice with Jerusalem, and be
    glad for her,
    all you who love her;
rejoice with her in joy,
    all you who mourn over her;
11 that you may suck and be satisfied
    with her consoling breasts;
    that you may drink deeply with
    delight
    from the abundance of her glory."

12 For thus says the LORD:
"Behold, I will extend prosperity to
    her like a river,
    and the wealth of the nations like
    an overflowing stream;
and you shall suck, you shall be
    carried upon her hip,
    and dandled upon her knees.
13 As one whom his mother comforts,
    so I will comfort you;
    you shall be comforted in Jeru-
    salem.
14 You shall see, and your heart shall
    rejoice;
    your bones shall flourish like the
    grass;
and it shall be known that the hand
    of the LORD is with his servants,
    and his indignation is against his
    enemies.

15 "For behold, the LORD will come in
    fire,
    and his chariots like the storm-
    wind,
to render his anger in fury,
    and his rebuke with flames of fire.
16 For by fire will the LORD execute
    judgment;

d Gk Syr: Heb *came to be*

65.25: Is 11.6-9.   66.1-2: Mt 5.34; Acts 7.49-50.   66.6: Rev 16.1, 17.
66.7: Rev 12.5.

and by his sword, upon all flesh; and those slain by the LORD shall be many.

17 "Those who sanctify and purify themselves to go into the gardens, following one in the midst, eating swine's flesh and the abomination and mice, shall come to an end together, says the LORD.

18 "For I know[e] their works and their thoughts, and I am[f] coming to gather all nations and tongues; and they shall come and shall see my glory, 19 and I will set a sign among them. And from them I will send survivors to the nations, to Tär'shish, Püt,[g] and Lüd, who draw the bow, to Tü'bal and Jä'van, to the coastlands afar off, that have not heard my fame or seen my glory; and they shall declare my glory among the nations. 20And they shall bring all your brethren from all the nations as an offering to the LORD, upon horses, and in chariots, and in litters, and upon mules, and upon dromedaries, to my holy mountain Jerusalem, says the LORD, just as the Israelites bring their cereal offering in a clean vessel to the house of the LORD. 21And some of them also I will take for priests and for Levites, says the LORD.

22 "For as the new heavens and the
    new earth
    which I will make
shall remain before me, says the
    LORD;
    so shall your descendants and
    your name remain.
23 From new moon to new moon,
    and from sabbath to sabbath,
all flesh shall come to worship be-
    fore me,
says the LORD.

24 "And they shall go forth and look on the dead bodies of the men that have rebelled against me; for their worm shall not die, their fire shall not be quenched, and they shall be an abhorrence to all flesh."

THE BOOK OF

JEREMIAH

I The words of Jeremiah, the son of Hil·ki'ah, of the priests who were in An'a·thoth in the land of Benjamin, 2 to whom the word of the LORD came in the days of Jō·si'ah the son of A'mon, king of Judah, in the thirteenth year of his reign. 3 It came also in the days of Je·hoi'a·kim the son of Jō·si'ah, king of Judah, and until the end of the eleventh year of Zed·e·ki'ah, the son of Josiah, king of Judah, until the captivity of Jerusalem in the fifth month.

4 Now the word of the LORD came to me saying,
5 "Before I formed you in the womb
    I knew you,
and before you were born I conse-
    crated you;
I appointed you a prophet to the
    nations."
6 Then I said, "Ah, Lord GOD! Behold, I do not know how to speak, for I am only a youth." 7 But the LORD said to me,
"Do not say, 'I am only a youth';
for to all to whom I send you you
    shall go,
and whatever I command you you
    shall speak.
8 Be not afraid of them,
for I am with you to deliver you,
      says the LORD."
9 Then the LORD put forth his hand and touched my mouth; and the LORD said to me,
"Behold, I have put my words in
    your mouth.
10 See, I have set you this day over
    nations and over kingdoms,
to pluck up and to break down,
to destroy and to overthrow,
to build and to plant."
11 And the word of the LORD came to me, saying, "Jeremiah, what do you see?" And I said, "I see a rod of

[e] Gk Syr: Heb lacks *know*   [f] Gk Syr Vg Tg: Heb *it is*   [g] Gk: Heb *Pul*
66.22: Is 65.17; 2 Pet 3.13; Rev 21.1.   **66.24:** Mk 9.48.   **1.5:** Is 49.1; Gal 1.15.
1.8: Is 43.5; Acts 18.9-10.   **1.10:** Rev 10.11.

almond." [a] 12 Then the LORD said to me, "You have seen well, for I am watching[b] over my word to perform it."

13 The word of the LORD came to me a second time, saying, "What do you see?" And I said, "I see a boiling pot, facing away from the north." 14 Then the LORD said to me, "Out of the north evil shall break forth upon all the inhabitants of the land. 15 For, lo, I am calling all the tribes of the kingdoms of the north, says the LORD; and they shall come and every one shall set his throne at the entrance of the gates of Jerusalem, against all its walls round about, and against all the cities of Judah. 16And I will utter my judgments against them, for all their wickedness in forsaking me; they have burned incense to other gods, and worshiped the works of their own hands. 17 But you, gird up your loins; arise, and say to them everything that I command you. Do not be dismayed by them, lest I dismay you before them. 18And I, behold, I make you this day a fortified city, an iron pillar, and bronze walls, against the whole land, against the kings of Judah, its princes, its priests, and the people of the land. 19 They will fight against you; but they shall not prevail against you, for I am with you, says the LORD, to deliver you."

2 The word of the LORD came to me, saying, 2 "Go and proclaim in the hearing of Jerusalem, Thus says the LORD,

I remember the devotion of your youth,
    your love as a bride,
how you followed me in the wilderness,
    in a land not sown.
3 Israel was holy to the LORD,
    the first fruits of his harvest.
All who ate of it became guilty;
    evil came upon them,
            says the LORD."

4 Hear the word of the LORD, O house of Jacob, and all the families of the house of Israel. 5 Thus says the LORD:
"What wrong did your fathers find in me
    that they went far from me,
and went after worthlessness, and became worthless?
6 They did not say, 'Where is the LORD
    who brought us up from the land of Egypt,

who led us in the wilderness,
    in a land of deserts and pits,
in a land of drought and deep darkness,
in a land that none passes through,
    where no man dwells?'
7 And I brought you into a plentiful land
    to enjoy its fruits and its good things.
But when you came in you defiled my land,
    and made my heritage an abomination.
8 The priests did not say, 'Where is the LORD?'
    Those who handle the law did not know me;
the rulers[c] transgressed against me;
    the prophets prophesied by Ba'al,
    and went after things that do not profit.

9 "Therefore I still contend with you,
            says the LORD,
    and with your children's children I will contend.
10 For cross to the coasts of Cyprus and see,
    or send to Ke'där and examine with care;
    see if there has been such a thing.
11 Has a nation changed its gods,
    even though they are no gods?
But my people have changed their glory
    for that which does not profit.
12 Be appalled, O heavens, at this,
    be shocked, be utterly desolate,
            says the LORD,
13 for my people have committed two evils:
    they have forsaken me,
the fountain of living waters,
    and hewed out cisterns for themselves,
broken cisterns,
    that can hold no water.

14 "Is Israel a slave? Is he a homeborn servant?
    Why then has he become a prey?
15 The lions have roared against him,
    they have roared loudly.
They have made his land a waste;
    his cities are in ruins, without inhabitant.
16 Moreover, the men of Memphis and Täh'păn·hēs
    have broken the crown of your head.
17 Have you not brought this upon yourself
    by forsaking the LORD your God,

---

[a] Heb shaqed [b] Heb shoqed [c] Heb shepherds

when he led you in the way?
18 And now what do you gain by going to Egypt,
to drink the waters of the Nile?
Or what do you gain by going to
Assyria,
to drink the waters of the Eū-
phrā'tēs?
19 Your wickedness will chasten you,
and your apostasy will reprove
you.
Know and see that it is evil and
bitter
for you to forsake the LORD your
God;
the fear of me is not in you,
says the Lord GOD of hosts.

20 "For long ago you broke your yoke
and burst your bonds;
and you said, 'I will not serve.'
Yea, upon every high hill
and under every green tree
you bowed down as a harlot.
21 Yet I planted you a choice vine,
wholly of pure seed.
How then have you turned de-
generate
and become a wild vine?
22 Though you wash yourself with lye
and use much soap,
the stain of your guilt is still before me,
says the Lord GOD.
23 How can you say, 'I am not defiled,
I have not gone after the Bā'alṣ'?
Look at your way in the valley;
know what you have done—
a restive young camel interlacing
her tracks,
24   a wild ass used to the wilderness,
in her heat sniffing the wind!
Who can restrain her lust?
None who seek her need weary
themselves;
in her month they will find her.
25 Keep your feet from going unshod
and your throat from thirst.
But you said, 'It is hopeless,
for I have loved strangers,
and after them I will go.'

26 "As a thief is shamed when caught,
so the house of Israel shall be
shamed:
they, their kings, their princes,
their priests, and their prophets,
27 who say to a tree, 'You are my
father,'
and to a stone, 'You gave me
birth.'
For they have turned their back to
me,
and not their face.

But in the time of their trouble they
say,
'Arise and save us!'
28 But where are your gods
that you made for yourself?
Let them arise, if they can save you,
in your time of trouble;
for as many as your cities
are your gods, O Judah.

29 "Why do you complain against me?
You have all rebelled against me,
says the LORD.
30 In vain have I smitten your children,
they took no correction;
your own sword devoured your
prophets
like a ravening lion.
31 And you, O generation, heed the
word of the LORD.
Have I been a wilderness to Israel,
or a land of thick darkness?
Why then do my people say, 'We
are free,
we will come no more to thee'?
32 Can a maiden forget her ornaments,
or a bride her attire?
Yet my people have forgotten me
days without number.

33 "How well you direct your course
to seek lovers!
So that even to wicked women
you have taught your ways.
34 Also on your skirts is found
the lifeblood of guiltless poor;
you did not find them breaking in.
Yet in spite of all these things
35 you say, 'I am innocent;
surely his anger has turned from
me.'
Behold, I will bring you to judgment
for saying, 'I have not sinned.'
36 How lightly you gad about,
changing your way!
You shall be put to shame by Egypt
as you were put to shame by
Assyria.
37 From it too you will come away
with your hands upon your head,
for the LORD has rejected those in
whom you trust,
and you will not prosper by them.

3 "If^d a man divorces his wife and
she goes from him
and becomes another man's wife,
will he return to her?
Would not that land be greatly
polluted?
You have played the harlot with
many lovers;
and would you return to me?
says the LORD.

^{d} Gk Syr: Heb *Saying, If*

2 Lift up your eyes to the bare heights,
and see!
Where have you not been lain
with?
By the waysides you have sat awaiting lovers
like an Arab in the wilderness.
You have polluted the land
with your vile harlotry.
3 Therefore the showers have been
withheld,
and the spring rain has not come;
yet you have a harlot's brow,
you refuse to be ashamed.
4 Have you not just now called to me,
'My father, thou art the friend of
my youth—
5 will he be angry for ever,
will he be indignant to the end?'
Behold, you have spoken,
but you have done all the evil
that you could."

6 The LORD said to me in the days
of King Jō·sī′ah: "Have you seen what
she did, that faithless one, Israel, how
she went up on every high hill and
under every green tree, and there
played the harlot? 7And I thought,
'After she has done all this she will
return to me'; but she did not return,
and her false sister Judah saw it. 8 She
saw that for all the adulteries of that
faithless one, Israel, I had sent her
away with a decree of divorce; yet her
false sister Judah did not fear, but she
too went and played the harlot. 9 Because harlotry was so light to her, she
polluted the land, committing adultery
with stone and tree. 10 Yet for all this
her false sister Judah did not return to
me with her whole heart, but in pretense, says the LORD."

11 And the LORD said to me,
"Faithless Israel has shown herself less
guilty than false Judah. 12 Go, and
proclaim these words toward the north,
and say,
'Return, faithless Israel,
says the LORD.
I will not look on you in anger,
for I am merciful,
says the LORD;
I will not be angry for ever.
13 Only acknowledge your guilt,
that you rebelled against the
LORD your God
and scattered your favors among
strangers under every green
tree,
and that you have not obeyed my
voice,
says the LORD.
14 Return, O faithless children,
says the LORD;

for I am your master;
I will take you, one from a city and
two from a family,
and I will bring you to Zion.
15 " 'And I will give you shepherds
after my own heart, who will feed you
with knowledge and understanding.
16And when you have multiplied and
increased in the land, in those days,
says the LORD, they shall no more say,
"The ark of the covenant of the LORD."
It shall not come to mind, or be remembered, or missed; it shall not be
made again. 17At that time Jerusalem
shall be called the throne of the LORD,
and all nations shall gather to it, to the
presence of the LORD in Jerusalem,
and they shall no more stubbornly
follow their own evil heart. 18 In those
days the house of Judah shall join the
house of Israel, and together they shall
come from the land of the north to the
land that I gave your fathers for a
heritage.
19 " 'I thought
how I would set you among my
sons,
and give you a pleasant land,
a heritage most beauteous of all
nations.
And I thought you would call me,
My Father,
and would not turn from following me.
20 Surely, as a faithless wife leaves her
husband,
so have you been faithless to me,
O house of Israel,
says the LORD.' "

21 A voice on the bare heights is heard,
the weeping and pleading of
Israel's sons,
because they have perverted their
way,
they have forgotten the LORD
their God.
22 "Return, O faithless sons,
I will heal your faithlessness."
"Behold, we come to thee;
for thou art the LORD our
God.
23 Truly the hills are a delusion,
the orgies on the mountains.
Truly in the LORD our God
is the salvation of Israel.
24 "But from our youth the shameful thing has devoured all for which
our fathers labored, their flocks and
their herds, their sons and their
daughters. 25 Let us lie down in our
shame, and let our dishonor cover us;
for we have sinned against the LORD
our God, we and our fathers, from our
youth even to this day; and we have

not obeyed the voice of the LORD our God."

4 "If you return, O Israel,
                 says the LORD,
to me you should return.
If you remove your abominations
   from my presence,
and do not waver,
2 and if you swear, 'As the LORD
   lives,'
   in truth, in justice, and in up-
     rightness,
then nations shall bless themselves
   in him,
and in him shall they glory."

3 For thus says the LORD to the men of Judah and to the inhabitants of Jerusalem:
"Break up your fallow ground,
   and sow not among thorns.
4 Circumcise yourselves to the LORD,
   remove the foreskin of your hearts,
   O men of Judah and inhabitants
     of Jerusalem;
lest my wrath go forth like fire,
   and burn with none to quench it,
   because of the evil of your do-
     ings."

5 Declare in Judah, and proclaim in Jerusalem, and say,
"Blow the trumpet through the
   land;
   cry aloud and say,
'Assemble, and let us go
   into the fortified cities!'
6 Raise a standard toward Zion,
   flee for safety, stay not,
for I bring evil from the north,
   and great destruction.
7 A lion has gone up from his thicket,
   a destroyer of nations has set out;
   he has gone forth from his place
to make your land a waste;
   your cities will be ruins
   without inhabitant.
8 For this gird you with sackcloth,
   lament and wail;
for the fierce anger of the LORD
   has not turned back from us."

9 "In that day, says the LORD, courage shall fail both king and princes; the priests shall be appalled and the prophets astounded." 10 Then I said, "Ah, Lord GOD, surely thou hast utterly deceived this people and Jerusalem, saying, 'It shall be well with you'; whereas the sword has reached their very life."

11 At that time it will be said to this people and to Jerusalem, "A hot wind from the bare heights in the desert toward the daughter of my people, not to winnow or cleanse, 12 a wind too full for this comes for me. Now it is I who speak in judgment upon them."

13 Behold, he comes up like clouds,
   his chariots like the whirlwind;
his horses are swifter than eagles—
   woe to us, for we are ruined!
14 O Jerusalem, wash your heart from
     wickedness,
   that you may be saved.
How long shall your evil thoughts
   lodge within you?
15 For a voice declares from Dan
   and proclaims evil from Mount
     Ē′phrà·im.
16 Warn the nations that he is coming;
   announce to Jerusalem,
"Besiegers come from a distant land;
   they shout against the cities of
     Judah.
17 Like keepers of a field are they
   against her round about,
   because she has rebelled against
     me,
                 says the LORD.
18 Your ways and your doings
   have brought this upon you.
This is your doom, and it is bitter;
   it has reached your very heart."

19 My anguish, my anguish! I writhe
   in pain!
Oh, the walls of my heart!
My heart is beating wildly;
   I cannot keep silent;
for I hear the sound of the trumpet,
   the alarm of war.
20 Disaster follows hard on disaster,
   the whole land is laid waste.
Suddenly my tents are destroyed,
   my curtains in a moment.
21 How long must I see the standard,
   and hear the sound of the trum-
     pet?
22 "For my people are foolish,
   they know me not;
they are stupid children,
   they have no understanding.
They are skilled in doing evil,
   but how to do good they know
     not."

23 I looked on the earth, and lo, it was
     waste and void;
   and to the heavens, and they had
     no light.
24 I looked on the mountains, and lo,
     they were quaking,
   and all the hills moved to and fro.
25 I looked, and lo, there was no man,
   and all the birds of the air had fled.
26 I looked, and lo, the fruitful land
     was a desert,

and all its cities were laid in ruins
    before the LORD, before his fierce
    anger.
27 For thus says the LORD, "The
whole land shall be a desolation; yet I
will not make a full end.
28 For this the earth shall mourn,
    and the heavens above be black;
for I have spoken, I have purposed;
    I have not relented nor will I
    turn back."

29 At the noise of horseman and archer
    every city takes to flight;
    they enter thickets; they climb
    among rocks;
    all the cities are forsaken,
    and no man dwells in them.
30 And you, O desolate one,
    what do you mean that you dress
    in scarlet,
    that you deck yourself with orna-
    ments of gold,
    that you enlarge your eyes with
    paint?
In vain you beautify yourself.
    Your lovers despise you;
    they seek your life.
31 For I heard a cry as of a woman in
    travail,
    anguish as of one bringing forth
    her first child,
the cry of the daughter of Zion
    gasping for breath,
    stretching out her hands,
"Woe is me! I am fainting before
    murderers."

5 Run to and fro through the streets
    of Jerusalem,
    look and take note!
Search her squares to see
    if you can find a man,
one who does justice
    and seeks truth;
    that I may pardon her.
2 Though they say, "As the LORD
    lives,"
    yet they swear falsely.
3 O LORD, do not thy eyes look for
    truth?
Thou hast smitten them,
    but they felt no anguish;
thou hast consumed them,
    but they refused to take correction.
They have made their faces harder
    than rock;
    they have refused to repent.

4 Then I said, "These are only the
    poor,
    they have no sense;
for they do not know the way of the
    LORD,

the law of their God.
5 I will go to the great,
    and will speak to them;
for they know the way of the
    LORD,
    the law of their God."
But they all alike had broken the
    yoke,
    they had burst the bonds.

6 Therefore a lion from the forest shall
    slay them,
    a wolf from the desert shall de-
    stroy them.
A leopard is watching against their
    cities,
    every one who goes out of them
    shall be torn in pieces;
because their transgressions are
    many,
    their apostasies are great.

7 "How can I pardon you?
    Your children have forsaken me,
    and have sworn by those who are
    no gods.
When I fed them to the full,
    they committed adultery
    and trooped to the houses of
    harlots.
8 They were well-fed lusty stallions,
    each neighing for his neighbor's
    wife.
9 Shall I not punish them for these
    things?
                    says the LORD;
    and shall I not avenge myself
    on a nation such as this?

10 "Go up through her vine-rows and
    destroy,
    but make not a full end;
strip away her branches,
    for they are not the LORD's.
11 For the house of Israel and the
    house of Judah
    have been utterly faithless to me,
                    says the LORD.
12 They have spoken falsely of the
    LORD,
    and have said, 'He will do noth-
    ing;
no evil will come upon us,
    nor shall we see sword or famine.
13 The prophets will become wind;
    the word is not in them.
Thus shall it be done to them!' "

14 Therefore thus says the LORD, the
    God of hosts:
"Because they*e* have spoken this
    word,
    behold, I am making my words in
    your mouth a fire,

e Heb *you*

and this people wood, and the fire
shall devour them.

15 Behold, I am bringing upon you
a nation from afar, O house of
Israel,
says the LORD.
It is an enduring nation,
it is an ancient nation,
a nation whose language you do not
know,
nor can you understand what they
say.
16 Their quiver is like an open tomb,
they are all mighty men.
17 They shall eat up your harvest and
your food;
they shall eat up your sons and
your daughters;
they shall eat up your flocks and
your herds;
they shall eat up your vines and
your fig trees;
your fortified cities in which you trust
they shall destroy with the sword."

18 "But even in those days, says the
LORD, I will not make a full end of
you. 19And when your people say,
'Why has the LORD our God done all
these things to us?' you shall say to
them, 'As you have forsaken me and
served foreign gods in your land, so
you shall serve strangers in a land that
is not yours.' "

20 Declare this in the house of Jacob,
proclaim it in Judah:
21 "Hear this, O foolish and senseless
people,
who have eyes, but see not,
who have ears, but hear not.
22 Do you not fear me? says the LORD;
Do you not tremble before me?
I placed the sand as the bound for
the sea,
a perpetual barrier which it cannot
pass;
though the waves toss, they cannot
prevail,
though they roar, they cannot
pass over it.
23 But this people has a stubborn and
rebellious heart;
they have turned aside and gone
away.
24 They do not say in their hearts,
'Let us fear the LORD our God,
who gives the rain in its season,
the autumn rain and the spring
rain,
and keeps for us
the weeks appointed for the
harvest.'

f Heb uncertain
5.21: Is 6.9-10; Mt 13.10-15; Mk 8.17-18.

25 Your iniquities have turned these
away,
and your sins have kept good from
you.
26 For wicked men are found among
my people;
they lurk like fowlers lying in
wait.f
They set a trap;
they catch men.
27 Like a basket full of birds,
their houses are full of treachery;
therefore they have become great
and rich,
28 they have grown fat and sleek.
They know no bounds in deeds of
wickedness;
they judge not with justice
the cause of the fatherless, to make
it prosper,
and they do not defend the rights
of the needy.
29 Shall I not punish them for these
things?
says the LORD,
and shall I not avenge myself
on a nation such as this?"

30 An appalling and horrible thing
has happened in the land:
31 the prophets prophesy falsely,
and the priests rule at their
direction;
my people love to have it so,
but what will you do when the
end comes?

6 Flee for safety, O people of Benjamin,
from the midst of Jerusalem!
Blow the trumpet in Te·kōʹa,
and raise a signal on Beth-hac-
cheʹrem;
for evil looms out of the north,
and great destruction.
2 The comely and delicately bred I
will destroy,
the daughter of Zion.
3 Shepherds with their flocks shall
come against her;
they shall pitch their tents
around her,
they shall pasture, each in his
place.
4 "Prepare war against her;
up, and let us attack at noon!"
"Woe to us, for the day declines,
for the shadows of evening
lengthen!"
5 "Up, and let us attack by night,
and destroy her palaces!"

6 For thus says the LORD of hosts:

"Hew down her trees;
   cast up a siege mound against
     Jerusalem.
This is the city which must be
   punished;
   there is nothing but oppression
     within her.
7 As a well keeps its water fresh,
   so she keeps fresh her wickedness;
violence and destruction are heard
   within her;
   sickness and wounds are ever be-
     fore me.
8 Be warned, O Jerusalem,
   lest I be alienated from you;
lest I make you a desolation,
   an uninhabited land."

9 Thus says the LORD of hosts:
"Glean^g thoroughly as a vine
   the remnant of Israel;
like a grape-gatherer pass your hand
   again
   over its branches."
10 To whom shall I speak and give
   warning,
   that they may hear?
Behold, their ears are closed,^{h}
   they cannot listen;
behold, the word of the LORD is to
   them an object of scorn,
   they take no pleasure in it.
11 Therefore I am full of the wrath of
   the LORD;
   I am weary of holding it in.
"Pour it out upon the children in
   the street,
and upon the gatherings of young
   men, also;
both husband and wife shall be
   taken,
   the old folk and the very aged.
12 Their houses shall be turned over
   to others,
   their fields and wives together;
for I will stretch out my hand
   against the inhabitants of the
     land,"
               says the LORD.
13 "For from the least to the greatest
   of them,
   every one is greedy for unjust
     gain;
and from prophet to priest,
   every one deals falsely.
14 They have healed the wound of my
   people lightly,
   saying, 'Peace, peace,'
   when there is no peace.
15 Were they ashamed when they committed abomination?
No, they were not at all ashamed;
   they did not know how to blush.

Therefore they shall fall among
   those who fall;
at the time that I punish them,
   they shall be overthrown,"
               says the LORD.

16 Thus says the LORD:
"Stand by the roads, and look,
   and ask for the ancient paths,
where the good way is; and walk in
   it,
   and find rest for your souls.
But they said, 'We will not walk in
   it.'
17 I set watchmen over you, saying,
   'Give heed to the sound of the
     trumpet!'
But they said, 'We will not give
   heed.'
18 Therefore hear, O nations,
   and know, O congregation, what
     will happen to them.
19 Hear, O earth; behold, I am bringing
   evil upon this people,
   the fruit of their devices;
because they have not given heed to
   my words;
   and as for my law, they have re-
     jected it.
20 To what purpose does frankincense
   come to me from Sheba,
   or sweet cane from a distant land?
Your burnt offerings are not acceptable,
   nor your sacrifices pleasing to me.
21 Therefore thus says the LORD:
'Behold, I will lay before this people
   stumbling blocks against which
     they shall stumble;
fathers and sons together,
   neighbor and friend shall per-
     ish.'"

22 Thus says the LORD:
"Behold, a people is coming from
   the north country,
a great nation is stirring from the
   farthest parts of the earth.
23 They lay hold on bow and spear,
   they are cruel and have no mercy,
   the sound of them is like the roar-
     ing sea;
they ride upon horses,
   set in array as a man for battle,
   against you, O daughter of Zion!"
24 We have heard the report of it,
   our hands fall helpless;
anguish has taken hold of us,
   pain as of a woman in travail.
25 Go not forth into the field,
   nor walk on the road;
for the enemy has a sword,
   terror is on every side.

^{g} Cn: Heb *they shall glean* ^{h} Heb *uncircumcised*
6.16: Mt 11.29.   **6.25:** Jer 20.3, 10; 46.5; 49.29; Ps 31.13.

26 O daughter of my people, gird on
    sackcloth,
    and roll in ashes;
make mourning as for an only son,
    most bitter lamentation;
for suddenly the destroyer
    will come upon us.

27 "I have made you an assayer and
    tester among my people,
    that you may know and assay
    their ways.
28 They are all stubbornly rebellious,
    going about with slanders;
they are bronze and iron,
    all of them act corruptly.
29 The bellows blow fiercely,
    the lead is consumed by the fire;
in vain the refining goes on,
    for the wicked are not removed.
30 Refuse silver they are called,
    for the LORD has rejected them."

7 The word that came to Jeremiah
from the LORD: 2 Stand in the gate
of the LORD's house, and proclaim
there this word, and say, Hear the
word of the LORD, all you men of
Judah who enter these gates to worship the LORD. 3 Thus says the LORD
of hosts, the God of Israel, Amend
your ways and your doings, and I will
let you dwell in this place. 4 Do not
trust in these deceptive words: 'This
is the temple of the LORD, the temple
of the LORD, the temple of the LORD.'
5 "For if you truly amend your
ways and your doings, if you truly
execute justice one with another, 6 if
you do not oppress the alien, the
fatherless or the widow, or shed innocent blood in this place, and if you
do not go after other gods to your own
hurt, 7 then I will let you dwell in this
place, in the land that I gave of old to
your fathers for ever.
8 "Behold, you trust in deceptive
words to no avail. 9 Will you steal,
murder, commit adultery, swear
falsely, burn incense to Bā´al, and go
after other gods that you have not
known, 10 and then come and stand
before me in this house, which is
called by my name, and say, 'We are
delivered!'—only to go on doing all
these abominations? 11 Has this house,
which is called by my name, become a
den of robbers in your eyes? Behold,
I myself have seen it, says the LORD.
12 Go now to my place that was in
Shi´lōh, where I made my name dwell
at first, and see what I did to it for the
wickedness of my people Israel. 13 And
now, because you have done all these

7.11: Mt 21.13; Mk 11.17; Lk 19.46.

things, says the LORD, and when I
spoke to you persistently you did not
listen, and when I called you, you did
not answer, 14 therefore I will do to
the house which is called by my name,
and in which you trust, and to the
place which I gave to you and to your
fathers, as I did to Shi´lōh. 15 And I
will cast you out of my sight, as I cast
out all your kinsmen, all the offspring
of E´phra·im.
16 "As for you, do not pray for this
people, or lift up cry or prayer for
them, and do not intercede with me,
for I do not hear you. 17 Do you not
see what they are doing in the cities of
Judah and in the streets of Jerusalem?
18 The children gather wood, the
fathers kindle fire, and the women
knead dough, to make cakes for the
queen of heaven; and they pour out
drink offerings to other gods, to provoke me to anger. 19 Is it I whom they
provoke? says the LORD. Is it not themselves, to their own confusion?
20 Therefore thus says the Lord GOD:
Behold, my anger and my wrath will
be poured out on this place, upon man
and beast, upon the trees of the field
and the fruit of the ground; it will burn
and not be quenched."
21 Thus says the LORD of hosts, the
God of Israel: "Add your burnt offerings to your sacrifices, and eat the
flesh. 22 For in the day that I brought
them out of the land of Egypt, I did
not speak to your fathers or command
them concerning burnt offerings and
sacrifices. 23 But this command I gave
them, 'Obey my voice, and I will be
your God, and you shall be my people;
and walk in all the way that I command
you, that it may be well with you.'
24 But they did not obey or incline
their ear, but walked in their own
counsels and the stubbornness of their
evil hearts, and went backward and
not forward. 25 From the day that
your fathers came out of the land of
Egypt to this day, I have persistently
sent all my servants the prophets to
them, day after day; 26 yet they did
not listen to me, or incline their ear,
but stiffened their neck. They did
worse than their fathers.
27 "So you shall speak all these
words to them, but they will not listen
to you. You shall call to them, but
they will not answer you. 28 And you
shall say to them, 'This is the nation
that did not obey the voice of the
LORD their God, and did not accept
discipline; truth has perished; it is cut
off from their lips.

29 Cut off your hair and cast it away;
  raise a lamentation on the bare
      heights,
for the LORD has rejected and for-
      saken
    the generation of his wrath.'
30 "For the sons of Judah have
done evil in my sight, says the LORD;
they have set their abominations in the
house which is called by my name, to
defile it. 31And they have built the
high place*i* of To'pheth, which is in
the valley of the son of Hin'nom, to
burn their sons and their daughters in
the fire; which I did not command, nor
did it come into my mind. 32 Therefore, behold, the days are coming, says
the LORD, when it will no more be
called To'pheth, or the valley of the
son of Hin'nom, but the valley of
Slaughter: for they will bury in Topheth, because there is no room elsewhere. 33And the dead bodies of this
people will be food for the birds of the
air, and for the beasts of the earth;
and none will frighten them away.
34And I will make to cease from the
cities of Judah and from the streets of
Jerusalem the voice of mirth and the
voice of gladness, the voice of the
bridegroom and the voice of the bride;
for the land shall become a waste.

8 "At that time, says the LORD, the
  bones of the kings of Judah, the
bones of its princes, the bones of the
priests, the bones of the prophets, and
the bones of the inhabitants of Jerusalem shall be brought out of their
tombs; 2 and they shall be spread before the sun and the moon and all the
host of heaven, which they have loved
and served, which they have gone
after, and which they have sought and
worshiped; and they shall not be
gathered or buried; they shall be as
dung on the surface of the ground.
3 Death shall be preferred to life by
all the remnant that remains of this
evil family in all the places where I
have driven them, says the LORD of
hosts.

4 "You shall say to them, Thus says
      the LORD:
  When men fall, do they not rise
      again?
    If one turns away, does he not
        return?
5 Why then has this people turned
      away
    in perpetual backsliding?
  They hold fast to deceit,

they refuse to return.
6 I have given heed and listened,
    but they have not spoken aright;
no man repents of his wickedness,
    saying, 'What have I done?'
Every one turns to his own course,
    like a horse plunging headlong
        into battle.
7 Even the stork in the heavens
      knows her times;
and the turtledove, swallow, and
      crane*j*
    keep the time of their coming;
but my people know not
    the ordinance of the LORD.

8 "How can you say, 'We are wise,
    and the law of the LORD is with
        us'?
But, behold, the false pen of the
      scribes
    has made it into a lie.
9 The wise men shall be put to shame,
    they shall be dismayed and taken;
lo, they have rejected the word of
      the LORD,
    and what wisdom is in them?
10 Therefore I will give their wives to
      others
    and their fields to conquerors,
because from the least to the
      greatest
    every one is greedy for unjust gain;
from prophet to priest
    every one deals falsely.
11 They have healed the wound of my
      people lightly,
    saying, 'Peace, peace,'
    when there is no peace.
12 Were they ashamed when they com-
      mitted abomination?
No, they were not at all ashamed;
    they did not know how to blush.
Therefore they shall fall among the
      fallen;
    when I punish them, they shall
        be overthrown,
                    says the LORD.
13 When I would gather them, says the
      LORD,
    there are no grapes on the vine,
    nor figs on the fig tree;
even the leaves are withered,
    and what I gave them has passed
        away from them."*k*

14 Why do we sit still?
  Gather together, let us go into the
      fortified cities
    and perish there;
  for the LORD our God has doomed
      us to perish,

---

i Gk Tg: Heb *high places*   *j* The meaning of the Hebrew word is uncertain
k Heb uncertain
7.34: Rev 18.23.

and has given us poisoned water
   to drink,
because we have sinned against
   the LORD.
15 We looked for peace, but no good
   came,
   for a time of healing, but behold,
      terror.

16 "The snorting of their horses is
      heard from Dan;
   at the sound of the neighing of
      their stallions
   the whole land quakes.
They come and devour the land and
   all that fills it,
   the city and those who dwell in it.
17 For behold, I am sending among
      you serpents,
   adders which cannot be charmed,
   and they shall bite you,"
                           says the LORD.

18 My grief is beyond healing,[l]
   my heart is sick within me.
19 Hark, the cry of the daughter of my
      people
   from the length and breadth of
      the land:
"Is the LORD not in Zion?
   Is her King not in her?"
"Why have they provoked me to
      anger with their graven images,
   and with their foreign idols?"
20 "The harvest is past, the summer is
      ended,
   and we are not saved."
21 For the wound of the daughter of
      my people is my heart wounded,
   I mourn, and dismay has taken
      hold on me.

22 Is there no balm in Gilead?
   Is there no physician there?
Why then has the health of the
      daughter of my people
   not been restored?

9[m] O that my head were waters, and
   my eyes a fountain of tears,
that I might weep day and night
   for the slain of the daughter of
      my people!
2[n] O that I had in the desert
   a wayfarers' lodging place,
that I might leave my people
   and go away from them!
For they are all adulterers,
   a company of treacherous men.
3 They bend their tongue like a bow;
   falsehood and not truth has grown
      strong[o] in the land;
   for they proceed from evil to evil,

and they do not know me, says
   the LORD.

4 Let every one beware of his
      neighbor,
   and put no trust in any brother;
for every brother is a supplanter,
   and every neighbor goes about as
      a slanderer.
5 Every one deceives his neighbor,
   and no one speaks the truth;
they have taught their tongue to
      speak lies;
   they commit iniquity and are too
      weary to repent.[p]
6 Heaping oppression upon oppres-
      sion, and deceit upon deceit,
   they refuse to know me, says the
      LORD.

7 Therefore thus says the LORD of
      hosts:
"Behold, I will refine them and test
      them,
   for what else can I do, because of
      my people?
8 Their tongue is a deadly arrow;
   it speaks deceitfully;
with his mouth each speaks peace-
      ably to his neighbor,
   but in his heart he plans an
      ambush for him.
9 Shall I not punish them for these
      things? says the LORD;
   and shall I not avenge myself
      on a nation such as this?

10 "Take up[q] weeping and wailing for
      the mountains,
   and a lamentation for the pastures
      of the wilderness,
because they are laid waste so that
      no one passes through,
   and the lowing of cattle is not
      heard;
both the birds of the air and the
      beasts
   have fled and are gone.
11 I will make Jerusalem a heap of
      ruins,
   a lair of jackals;
and I will make the cities of Judah
      a desolation,
   without inhabitant."

12 Who is the man so wise that he
can understand this? To whom has
the mouth of the LORD spoken, that
he may declare it? Why is the land
ruined and laid waste like a wilderness,
so that no one passes through? 13 And
the LORD says: "Because they have

[l] Cn Compare Gk: Heb uncertain   [m] Ch 8.23 in Heb   [n] Ch 9.1 in Heb
[o] Gk: Heb and not for truth they have grown strong
[p] Cn Compare Gk: Heb your dwelling   [q] Gk Syr: Heb I will take up

forsaken my law which I set before them, and have not obeyed my voice, or walked in accord with it, 14 but have stubbornly followed their own hearts and have gone after the Bā´als̆, as their fathers taught them. 15 Therefore thus says the LORD of hosts, the God of Israel: Behold, I will feed this people with wormwood, and give them poisonous water to drink. 16 I will scatter them among the nations whom neither they nor their fathers have known; and I will send the sword after them, until I have consumed them."

17 Thus says the LORD of hosts:
"Consider, and call for the mourn-
    ing women to come;
    send for the skilful women to
      come;
18 let them make haste and raise a wail-
    ing over us,
that our eyes may run down with
    tears,
and our eyelids gush with water.
19 For a sound of wailing is heard from
    Zion:
'How we are ruined!
We are utterly shamed,
because we have left the land,
    because they have cast down our
      dwellings.' "

20 Hear, O women, the word of the
    LORD,
and let your ear receive the word
    of his mouth;
teach to your daughters a lament,
    and each to her neighbor a dirge.
21 For death has come up into our
    windows,
it has entered our palaces,
cutting off the children from the
    streets
and the young men from the
    squares.
22 Speak, "Thus says the LORD:
'The dead bodies of men shall fall
    like dung upon the open field,
like sheaves after the reaper,
    and none shall gather them.' "

23 Thus says the LORD: "Let not the wise man glory in his wisdom, let not the mighty man glory in his might, let not the rich man glory in his riches; 24 but let him who glories glory in this, that he understands and knows me, that I am the LORD who practice stead-fast love, justice, and righteousness in the earth; for in these things I delight, says the LORD."

r Heb They

9.24: 1 Cor 1.31; 2 Cor 10.17.   9.26: Acts 7.51.

25 "Behold, the days are coming, says the LORD, when I will punish all those who are circumcised but yet un-circumcised—26 Egypt, Judah, E´dom, the sons of Am´mon, Mō´ab, and all who dwell in the desert that cut the corners of their hair; for all these nations are uncircumcised, and all the house of Israel is uncircumcised in heart."

10 Hear the word which the LORD speaks to you, O house of Israel. 2 Thus says the LORD:
"Learn not the way of the nations,
    nor be dismayed at the signs of
      the heavens
because the nations are dismayed
    at them,
3 for the customs of the peoples are
    false.
A tree from the forest is cut down,
    and worked with an axe by the
      hands of a craftsman.
4 Men deck it with silver and gold;
    they fasten it with hammer and
      nails
so that it cannot move.
5 Their idols^r are like scarecrows in
    a cucumber field,
and they cannot speak;
they have to be carried,
    for they cannot walk.
Be not afraid of them,
    for they cannot do evil,
neither is it in them to do good."

6 There is none like thee, O LORD;
    thou art great, and thy name is
      great in might.
7 Who would not fear thee, O King
    of the nations?
For this is thy due;
for among all the wise ones of the
    nations
and in all their kingdoms
    there is none like thee.
8 They are both stupid and foolish;
    the instruction of idols is but
      wood!
9 Beaten silver is brought from Tär´-
    shish,
and gold from Ū´phaz.
They are the work of the craftsman
    and of the hands of the gold-
      smith;
their clothing is violet and purple;
they are all the work of skilled
    men.
10 But the LORD is the true God;
    he is the living God and the ever-
      lasting King.
At his wrath the earth quakes,

and the nations cannot endure his indignation.

11 Thus shall you say to them: "The gods who did not make the heavens and the earth shall perish from the earth and from under the heavens."[s]

12 It is he who made the earth by his power,
who established the world by his wisdom,
and by his understanding stretched out the heavens.
13 When he utters his voice there is a tumult of waters in the heavens,
and he makes the mist rise from the ends of the earth.
He makes lightnings for the rain,
and he brings forth the wind from his storehouses.
14 Every man is stupid and without knowledge;
every goldsmith is put to shame by his idols;
for his images are false,
and there is no breath in them.
15 They are worthless, a work of delusion;
at the time of their punishment they shall perish.
16 Not like these is he who is the portion of Jacob,
for he is the one who formed all things,
and Israel is the tribe of his inheritance;
the LORD of hosts is his name.

17 Gather up your bundle from the ground,
O you who dwell under siege!
18 For thus says the LORD:
"Behold, I am slinging out the inhabitants of the land
at this time,
and I will bring distress on them,
that they may feel it."

19 Woe is me because of my hurt!
My wound is grievous.
But I said, "Truly this is an affliction,
and I must bear it."
20 My tent is destroyed,
and all my cords are broken;
my children have gone from me,
and they are not;
there is no one to spread my tent again,
and to set up my curtains.
21 For the shepherds are stupid,
and do not inquire of the LORD;

therefore they have not prospered,
and all their flock is scattered.

22 Hark, a rumor! Behold, it comes!—
a great commotion out of the north country
to make the cities of Judah a desolation,
a lair of jackals.

23 I know, O LORD, that the way of man is not in himself,
that it is not in man who walks to direct his steps.
24 Correct me, O LORD, but in just measure;
not in thy anger, lest thou bring me to nothing.

25 Pour out thy wrath upon the nations that know thee not,
and upon the peoples that call not on thy name;
for they have devoured Jacob;
they have devoured him and consumed him,
and have laid waste his habitation.

11 The word that came to Jeremiah from the LORD: 2 "Hear the words of this covenant, and speak to the men of Judah and the inhabitants of Jerusalem. 3 You shall say to them, Thus says the LORD, the God of Israel: Cursed be the man who does not heed the words of this covenant 4 which I commanded your fathers when I brought them out of the land of Egypt, from the iron furnace, saying, Listen to my voice, and do all that I command you. So shall you be my people, and I will be your God, 5 that I may perform the oath which I swore to your fathers, to give them a land flowing with milk and honey, as at this day." Then I answered, "So be it, LORD."

6 And the LORD said to me, "Proclaim all these words in the cities of Judah, and in the streets of Jerusalem: Hear the words of this covenant and do them. 7 For I solemnly warned your fathers when I brought them up out of the land of Egypt, warning them persistently, even to this day, saying, Obey my voice. 8 Yet they did not obey or incline their ear, but every one walked in the stubbornness of his evil heart. Therefore I brought upon them all the words of this covenant, which I commanded them to do, but they did not."

9 Again the LORD said to me, "There is revolt among the men of Judah and

[s] This verse is in Aramaic
10.25: 1 Thess 4.5; Rev 16.1.

the inhabitants of Jerusalem. ¹⁰ They have turned back to the iniquities of their forefathers, who refused to hear my words; they have gone after other gods to serve them; the house of Israel and the house of Judah have broken my covenant which I made with their fathers. ¹¹ Therefore, thus says the LORD, Behold, I am bringing evil upon them which they cannot escape; though they cry to me, I will not listen to them. ¹² Then the cities of Judah and the inhabitants of Jerusalem will go and cry to the gods to whom they burn incense, but they cannot save them in the time of their trouble. ¹³ For your gods have become as many as your cities, O Judah; and as many as the streets of Jerusalem are the altars you have set up to shame, altars to burn incense to Bā'ál.

14 "Therefore do not pray for this people, or lift up a cry or prayer on their behalf, for I will not listen when they call to me in the time of their trouble. ¹⁵ What right has my beloved in my house, when she has done vile deeds? Can vows*ᵗ* and sacrificial flesh avert your doom? Can you then exult? ¹⁶ The LORD once called you, 'A green olive tree, fair with goodly fruit'; but with the roar of a great tempest he will set fire to it, and its branches will be consumed. ¹⁷ The LORD of hosts, who planted you, has pronounced evil against you, because of the evil which the house of Israel and the house of Judah have done, provoking me to anger by burning incense to Bā'ál."

18 The LORD made it known to me and I knew;
    then thou didst show me their evil deeds.
19 But I was like a gentle lamb led to the slaughter.
I did not know it was against me they devised schemes, saying,
"Let us destroy the tree with its fruit,
    let us cut him off from the land of the living,
    that his name be remembered no more."
20 But, O LORD of hosts, who judgest righteously,
    who tries the heart and the mind,
let me see thy vengeance upon them,
    for to thee have I committed my cause.
21 Therefore thus says the LORD concerning the men of An'á·thoth, who seek your life, and say, "Do not prophesy in the name of the LORD, or

t Gk: Heb *many*

you will die by our hand"—²²therefore thus says the LORD of hosts: "Behold, I will punish them; the young men shall die by the sword; their sons and their daughters shall die by famine; ²³ and none of them shall be left. For I will bring evil upon the men of An'á·thoth, the year of their punishment."

12 Righteous art thou, O LORD,
    when I complain to thee;
    yet I would plead my case before thee.
Why does the way of the wicked prosper?
    Why do all who are treacherous thrive?
2 Thou plantest them, and they take root;
    they grow and bring forth fruit;
thou art near in their mouth
    and far from their heart.
3 But thou, O LORD, knowest me;
    thou seest me, and triest my mind toward thee.
Pull them out like sheep for the slaughter,
    and set them apart for the day of slaughter.
4 How long will the land mourn,
    and the grass of every field wither?
For the wickedness of those who dwell in it
    the beasts and the birds are swept away,
because men said, "He will not see our latter end."

5 "If you have raced with men on foot, and they have wearied you,
    how will you compete with horses?
And if in a safe land you fall down,
    how will you do in the jungle of the Jordan?
6 For even your brothers and the house of your father,
    even they have dealt treacherously with you;
    they are in full cry after you;
believe them not,
    though they speak fair words to you."

7 "I have forsaken my house,
    I have abandoned my heritage;
I have given the beloved of my soul
    into the hands of her enemies.
8 My heritage has become to me
    like a lion in the forest,

she has lifted up her voice against
me;
therefore I hate her.
9 Is my heritage to me like a speckled
bird of prey?
Are the birds of prey against her
round about?
Go, assemble all the wild beasts;
bring them to devour.
10 Many shepherds have destroyed my
vineyard,
they have trampled down my
portion,
they have made my pleasant portion
a desolate wilderness.
11 They have made it a desolation;
desolate, it mourns to me.
The whole land is made desolate,
but no man lays it to heart.
12 Upon all the bare heights in the
desert
destroyers have come;
for the sword of the LORD devours
from one end of the land to the
other;
no flesh has peace.
13 They have sown wheat and have
reaped thorns,
they have tired themselves out
but profit nothing.
They shall be ashamed of their[u]
harvests
because of the fierce anger of the
LORD.”

14 Thus says the LORD concerning
all my evil neighbors who touch the
heritage which I have given my people
Israel to inherit: “Behold, I will pluck
them up from their land, and I will
pluck up the house of Judah from
among them. 15 And after I have
plucked them up, I will again have
compassion on them, and I will bring
them again each to his heritage and
each to his land. 16 And it shall come
to pass, if they will diligently learn the
ways of my people, to swear by my
name, ‘As the LORD lives,’ even as they
taught my people to swear by Bā′al,
then they shall be built up in the midst
of my people. 17 But if any nation
will not listen, then I will utterly
pluck it up and destroy it, says the
LORD.”

13 Thus said the LORD to me, “Go
and buy a linen waistcloth, and
put it on your loins, and do not dip it
in water.” 2 So I bought a waistcloth
according to the word of the LORD,
and put it on my loins. 3 And the word
of the LORD came to me a second time,
4 “Take the waistcloth which you have

bought, which is upon your loins, and
arise, go to the Eū·phrā′tēs, and hide
it there in a cleft of the rock.” 5 So I
went, and hid it by the Eū·phrā′tēs, as
the LORD commanded me. 6 And after
many days the LORD said to me, “Arise,
go to the Eū·phrā′tēs, and take from
there the waistcloth which I commanded you to hide there.” 7 Then I
went to the Eū·phrā′tēs, and dug, and
I took the waistcloth from the place
where I had hidden it. And behold,
the waistcloth was spoiled, it was good
for nothing.

8 Then the word of the LORD came
to me: 9 “Thus says the LORD: Even
so will I spoil the pride of Judah and
the great pride of Jerusalem. 10 This
evil people, who refuse to hear my
words, who stubbornly follow their
own heart and have gone after other
gods to serve them and worship them,
shall be like this waistcloth, which is
good for nothing. 11 For as the waistcloth clings to the loins of a man, so I
made the whole house of Israel and
the whole house of Judah cling to me,
says the LORD, that they might be for
me a people, a name, a praise, and a
glory, but they would not listen.

12 “You shall speak to them this
word: ‘Thus says the LORD, the God
of Israel, “Every jar shall be filled with
wine.” ’ And they will say to you, ‘Do
we not indeed know that every jar will
be filled with wine?’ 13 Then you shall
say to them, ‘Thus says the LORD: Behold, I will fill with drunkenness all
the inhabitants of this land: the kings
who sit on David’s throne, the priests,
the prophets, and all the inhabitants of
Jerusalem. 14 And I will dash them one
against another, fathers and sons together, says the LORD. I will not pity
or spare or have compassion, that I
should not destroy them.’ ”

15 Hear and give ear; be not proud,
for the LORD has spoken.
16 Give glory to the LORD your God
before he brings darkness,
before your feet stumble
on the twilight mountains,
and while you look for light
he turns it into gloom
and makes it deep darkness.
17 But if you will not listen,
my soul will weep in secret for
your pride;
my eyes will weep bitterly and run
down with tears,
because the LORD’s flock has been
taken captive.

[u] Heb *your*

18 Say to the king and the queen
mother:
"Take a lowly seat,
for your beautiful crown
has come down from your head."^{v}
19 The cities of the Negeb are shut up,
with none to open them;
all Judah is taken into exile,
wholly taken into exile.

20 "Lift up your eyes and see
those who come from the north.
Where is the flock that was given
you,
your beautiful flock?
21 What will you say when they set as
head over you
those whom you yourself have
taught
to be friends to you?
Will not pangs take hold of you,
like those of a woman in travail?
22 And if you say in your heart,
'Why have these things come
upon me?'
it is for the greatness of your iniquity
that your skirts are lifted up,
and you suffer violence.
23 Can the Ethiopian change his skin
or the leopard his spots?
Then also you can do good
who are accustomed to do evil.
24 I will scatter you^w like chaff
driven by the wind from the
desert.
25 This is your lot,
the portion I have measured out
to you, says the LORD,
because you have forgotten me
and trusted in lies.
26 I myself will lift up your skirts over
your face,
and your shame will be seen.
27 I have seen your abominations,
your adulteries and neighings,
your lewd harlotries,
on the hills in the field.
Woe to you, O Jerusalem!
How long will it be
before you are made clean?"

14 The word of the LORD which
came to Jeremiah concerning the
drought:
2 "Judah mourns
and her gates languish;
her people lament on the ground,
and the cry of Jerusalem goes
up.
3 Her nobles send their servants for
water;
they come to the cisterns,
they find no water,

they return with their vessels
empty;
they are ashamed and confounded
and cover their heads.
4 Because of the ground which is dismayed,
since there is no rain on the land,
the farmers are ashamed,
they cover their heads.
5 Even the hind in the field forsakes
her newborn calf
because there is no grass.
6 The wild asses stand on the bare
heights,
they pant for air like jackals;
their eyes fail
because there is no herbage.

7 "Though our iniquities testify
against us,
act, O LORD, for thy name's sake;
for our backslidings are many,
we have sinned against thee.
8 O thou hope of Israel,
its savior in time of trouble,
why shouldst thou be like a stranger
in the land,
like a wayfarer who turns aside to
tarry for a night?
9 Why shouldst thou be like a man
confused?
like a mighty man who cannot
save?
Yet thou, O LORD, art in the midst
of us,
and we are called by thy name;
leave us not."

10 Thus says the LORD concerning this
people:
"They have loved to wander thus,
they have not restrained their feet;
therefore the LORD does not accept
them,
now he will remember their iniquity
and punish their sins."

11 The LORD said to me: "Do not
pray for the welfare of this people.
12 Though they fast, I will not hear
their cry, and though they offer burnt
offering and cereal offering I will not
accept them; but I will consume them
by the sword, by famine, and by
pestilence."
13 Then I said: "Ah, Lord GOD,
behold, the prophets say to them, 'You
shall not see the sword, nor shall you
have famine, but I will give you
assured peace in this place.'" 14 And
the LORD said to me: "The prophets
are prophesying lies in my name; I did

^{v} Gk Syr Vg: Heb obscure ^{w} Heb *them*
14.12: Rev 6.8.

not send them, nor did I command them or speak to them. They are prophesying to you a lying vision, worthless divination, and the deceit of their own minds. 15 Therefore thus says the LORD concerning the prophets who prophesy in my name although I did not send them, and who say, 'Sword and famine shall not come on this land': By sword and famine those prophets shall be consumed. 16 And the people to whom they prophesy shall be cast out in the streets of Jerusalem, victims of famine and sword, with none to bury them—them, their wives, their sons, and their daughters. For I will pour out their wickedness upon them.

17 "You shall say to them this word:
'Let my eyes run down with tears
    night and day,
  and let them not cease,
for the virgin daughter of my people
    is smitten with a great wound,
  with a very grievous blow.
18 If I go out into the field,
  behold, those slain by the sword!
And if I enter the city,
  behold, the diseases of famine!
For both prophet and priest ply
    their trade through the land,
  and have no knowledge.' "

19 Hast thou utterly rejected Judah?
  Does thy soul loathe Zion?
Why hast thou smitten us
  so that there is no healing for us?
We looked for peace, but no good
    came;
  for a time of healing, but behold,
    terror.
20 We acknowledge our wickedness, O
    LORD,
  and the iniquity of our fathers,
  for we have sinned against thee.
21 Do not spurn us, for thy name's
    sake;
  do not dishonor thy glorious
    throne;
  remember and do not break thy
    covenant with us.
22 Are there any among the false gods
  of the nations that can bring
    rain?
  Or can the heavens give showers?
Art thou not he, O LORD our God?
  We set our hope on thee,
  for thou doest all these things.

15 Then the LORD said to me, "Though Moses and Samuel stood before me, yet my heart would not turn toward this people. Send them

out of my sight, and let them go! 2 And when they ask you, 'Where shall we go?' you shall say to them, 'Thus says the LORD:

"Those who are for pestilence, to
    pestilence,
  and those who are for the sword,
    to the sword;
those who are for famine, to famine,
  and those who are for captivity,
    to captivity." '

3 "I will appoint over them four kinds of destroyers, says the LORD: the sword to slay, the dogs to tear, and the birds of the air and the beasts of the earth to devour and destroy. 4 And I will make them a horror to all the kingdoms of the earth because of what Má·nas′sĕh the son of Hez·ĕ·ki′ăh, king of Judah, did in Jerusalem.

5 "Who will have pity on you, O
    Jerusalem,
  or who will bemoan you?
Who will turn aside
  to ask about your welfare?
6 You have rejected me, says the
    LORD,
  you keep going backward;
so I have stretched out my hand
    against you and destroyed
    you;—
  I am weary of relenting.
7 I have winnowed them with a
    winnowing fork
  in the gates of the land;
I have bereaved them, I have de-
    stroyed my people;
  they did not turn from their ways.
8 I have made their widows more in
    number
  than the sand of the seas;
I have brought against the mothers
    of young men
  a destroyer at noonday;
I have made anguish and terror
  fall upon them suddenly.
9 She who bore seven has languished;
  she has swooned away;
her sun went down while it was yet
    day;
  she has been shamed and dis-
    graced.
And the rest of them I will give to
    the sword
  before their enemies,
          says the LORD."

10 Woe is me, my mother, that you bore me, a man of strife and contention to the whole land! I have not lent, nor have I borrowed, yet all of them curse me. 11 So let it be, O LORD,ˣ if I have

not entreated[y] thee for their good, if I have not pleaded with thee on behalf of the enemy in the time of trouble and in the time of distress! 12 Can one break iron, iron from the north, and bronze?

13 "Your wealth and your treasures I will give as spoil, without price, for all your sins, throughout all your territory. 14 I will make you serve your enemies in a land which you do not know, for in my anger a fire is kindled which shall burn for ever."

15 O LORD, thou knowest;
remember me and visit me,
and take vengeance for me on my persecutors.
In thy forbearance take me not away;
know that for thy sake I bear reproach.
16 Thy words were found, and I ate them,
and thy words became to me a joy
and the delight of my heart;
for I am called by thy name,
O LORD, God of hosts.
17 I did not sit in the company of merrymakers,
nor did I rejoice;
I sat alone, because thy hand was upon me,
for thou hadst filled me with indignation.
18 Why is my pain unceasing,
my wound incurable,
refusing to be healed?
Wilt thou be to me like a deceitful brook,
like waters that fail?

19 Therefore thus says the LORD:
"If you return, I will restore you,
and you shall stand before me.
If you utter what is precious, and not what is worthless,
you shall be as my mouth.
They shall turn to you,
but you shall not turn to them.
20 And I will make you to this people a fortified wall of bronze;
they shall fight against you,
but they shall not prevail over you,
for I am with you
to save you and deliver you,
says the LORD.
21 I will deliver you out of the hand of the wicked,
and redeem you from the grasp of the ruthless."

[y] Cn: Heb obscure
16.9: Jer 7.34; 25.10; Rev 18.23.

16 The word of the LORD came to me: 2 "You shall not take a wife, nor shall you have sons or daughters in this place. 3 For thus says the LORD concerning the sons and daughters who are born in this place, and concerning the mothers who bore them and the fathers who begot them in this land: 4 They shall die of deadly diseases. They shall not be lamented, nor shall they be buried; they shall be as dung on the surface of the ground. They shall perish by the sword and by famine, and their dead bodies shall be food for the birds of the air and for the beasts of the earth.

5 "For thus says the LORD: Do not enter the house of mourning, or go to lament, or bemoan them; for I have taken away my peace from this people, says the LORD, my steadfast love and mercy. 6 Both great and small shall die in this land; they shall not be buried, and no one shall lament for them or cut himself or make himself bald for them. 7 No one shall break bread for the mourner, to comfort him for the dead; nor shall any one give him the cup of consolation to drink for his father or his mother. 8 You shall not go into the house of feasting to sit with them, to eat and drink. 9 For thus says the LORD of hosts, the God of Israel: Behold, I will make to cease from this place, before your eyes and in your days, the voice of mirth and the voice of gladness, the voice of the bridegroom and the voice of the bride.

10 "And when you tell this people all these words, and they say to you, 'Why has the LORD pronounced all this great evil against us? What is our iniquity? What is the sin that we have committed against the LORD our God?' 11 then you shall say to them: 'Because your fathers have forsaken me, says the LORD, and have gone after other gods and have served and worshiped them, and have forsaken me and have not kept my law, 12 and because you have done worse than your fathers, for behold, every one of you follows his stubborn evil will, refusing to listen to me; 13 therefore I will hurl you out of this land into a land which neither you nor your fathers have known, and there you shall serve other gods day and night, for I will show you no favor.'

14 "Therefore, behold, the days are coming, says the LORD, when it shall no longer be said, 'As the LORD lives

who brought up the people of Israel out of the land of Egypt,' 15 but 'As the LORD lives who brought up the people of Israel out of the north country and out of all the countries where he had driven them.' For I will bring them back to their own land which I gave to their fathers.

16 "Behold, I am sending for many fishers, says the LORD, and they shall catch them; and afterwards I will send for many hunters, and they shall hunt them from every mountain and every hill, and out of the clefts of the rocks. 17 For my eyes are upon all their ways; they are not hid from me, nor is their iniquity concealed from my eyes. 18 And[z] I will doubly recompense their iniquity and their sin, because they have polluted my land with the carcasses of their detestable idols, and have filled my inheritance with their abominations."

19 O LORD, my strength and my stronghold,
  my refuge in the day of trouble,
to thee shall the nations come
    from the ends of the earth and say:
"Our fathers have inherited nought but lies,
  worthless things in which there is no profit.
20 Can man make for himself gods?
  Such are no gods!"

21 "Therefore, behold, I will make them know, this once I will make them know my power and my might, and they shall know that my name is the LORD."

17 "The sin of Judah is written with a pen of iron; with a point of diamond it is engraved on the tablet of their heart, and on the horns of their altars, 2 while their children remember their altars and their Á·shē′rim, beside every green tree, and on the high hills, 3 on the mountains in the open country. Your wealth and all your treasures I will give for spoil as the price of your sin[a] throughout all your territory. 4 You shall loosen your hand[b] from your heritage which I gave to you, and I will make you serve your enemies in a land which you do not know, for in my anger a fire is kindled which shall burn for ever."

5 Thus says the LORD:

"Cursed is the man who trusts in man
  and makes flesh his arm,
  whose heart turns away from the LORD.
6 He is like a shrub in the desert,
  and shall not see any good come.
He shall dwell in the parched places of the wilderness,
  in an uninhabited salt land.

7 "Blessed is the man who trusts in the LORD,
  whose trust is the LORD.
8 He is like a tree planted by water,
  that sends out its roots by the stream,
and does not fear when heat comes,
  for its leaves remain green,
and is not anxious in the year of drought,
  for it does not cease to bear fruit."

9 The heart is deceitful above all things,
  and desperately corrupt;
  who can understand it?
10 "I the LORD search the mind
  and try the heart,
to give to every man according to his ways,
  according to the fruit of his doings."

11 Like the partridge that gathers a brood which she did not hatch,
  so is he who gets riches but not by right;
in the midst of his days they will leave him,
  and at his end he will be a fool.

12 A glorious throne set on high from the beginning
  is the place of our sanctuary.
13 O LORD, the hope of Israel,
  all who forsake thee shall be put to shame;
those who turn away from thee[c]
  shall be written in the earth,
for they have forsaken the LORD,
  the fountain of living water.

14 Heal me, O LORD, and I shall be healed;
  save me, and I shall be saved;
  for thou art my praise.
15 Behold, they say to me,
  "Where is the word of the LORD?
  Let it come!"
16 I have not pressed thee to send evil,
  nor have I desired the day of disaster,

---

z Gk: Heb *And first*   a Cn: Heb *your high places for sin*   b Cn: Heb *and in you*
c Heb *me*
17.7-8: Ps 1.1-3.   17.10: Ps 62.12; Rev 2.23; 22.12.

thou knowest;
that which came out of my lips
    was before thy face.
17 Be not a terror to me;
    thou art my refuge in the day of
    evil.
18 Let those be put to shame who
    persecute me,
    but let me not be put to shame;
let them be dismayed,
    but let me not be dismayed;
bring upon them the day of evil;
    destroy them with double de-
    struction!

19 Thus said the LORD to me: "Go
and stand in the Benjamin[d] Gate, by
which the kings of Judah enter and
by which they go out, and in all the
gates of Jerusalem, 20 and say: 'Hear
the word of the LORD, you kings of
Judah, and all Judah, and all the inhabitants of Jerusalem, who enter by
these gates. 21 Thus says the LORD:
Take heed for the sake of your lives,
and do not bear a burden on the sabbath day or bring it in by the gates of
Jerusalem. 22 And do not carry a
burden out of your houses on the
sabbath or do any work, but keep the
sabbath day holy, as I commanded
your fathers. 23 Yet they did not listen
or incline their ear, but stiffened their
neck, that they might not hear and
receive instruction.

24 " 'But if you listen to me, says
the LORD, and bring in no burden by
the gates of this city on the sabbath
day, but keep the sabbath day holy and
do no work on it, 25 then there shall
enter by the gates of this city kings[e]
who sit on the throne of David, riding
in chariots and on horses, they and
their princes, the men of Judah and
the inhabitants of Jerusalem; and this
city shall be inhabited for ever. 26 And
people shall come from the cities of
Judah and the places round about
Jerusalem, from the land of Benjamin,
from the She·phe'lah, from the hill
country, and from the Negeb, bringing burnt offerings and sacrifices,
cereal offerings and frankincense, and
bringing thank offerings to the house
of the LORD. 27 But if you do not listen
to me, to keep the sabbath day holy,
and not to bear a burden and enter by
the gates of Jerusalem on the sabbath
day, then I will kindle a fire in its gates,
and it shall devour the palaces of Jerusalem and shall not be quenched.' "

18 The word that came to Jeremiah
    from the LORD: 2 "Arise, and go
down to the potter's house, and there
I will let you hear my words." 3 So I
went down to the potter's house, and
there he was working at his wheel.
4 And the vessel he was making of clay
was spoiled in the potter's hand, and
he reworked it into another vessel, as
it seemed good to the potter to do.

5 Then the word of the LORD came
to me: 6 "O house of Israel, can I not
do with you as this potter has done?
says the LORD. Behold, like the clay
in the potter's hand, so are you in my
hand, O house of Israel. 7 If at any
time I declare concerning a nation or
a kingdom, that I will pluck up and
break down and destroy it, 8 and if
that nation, concerning which I have
spoken, turns from its evil, I will repent of the evil that I intended to do
to it. 9 And if at any time I declare concerning a nation or a kingdom that I
will build and plant it, 10 and if it does
evil in my sight, not listening to my
voice, then I will repent of the good
which I had intended to do to it.
11 Now, therefore, say to the men of
Judah and the inhabitants of Jerusalem: 'Thus says the LORD, Behold,
I am shaping evil against you and
devising a plan against you. Return,
every one from his evil way, and amend
your ways and your doings.'

12 "But they say, 'That is in vain!
We will follow our own plans, and will
every one act according to the stubbornness of his evil heart.'

13 "Therefore thus says the LORD:
    Ask among the nations,
        who has heard the like of this?
    The virgin Israel
        has done a very horrible thing.
14 Does the snow of Lebanon leave
        the crags of Sir'i·on?[f]
    Do the mountain[g] waters run dry,[h]
        the cold flowing streams?
15 But my people have forgotten me,
        they burn incense to false gods;
    they have stumbled[i] in their ways,
        in the ancient roads,
    and have gone into bypaths,
        not the highway,
16 making their land a horror,
        a thing to be hissed at for ever.
    Every one who passes by it is hor-
        rified
        and shakes his head.
17 Like the east wind I will scatter them
        before the enemy.

[d] Cn: Heb *sons of people*   [e] Cn: *kings and princes*   [f] Cn: Heb *the field*   [g] Cn: Heb *foreign*
[h] Cn: Heb *Are . . . plucked up?*   [i] Gk Syr Vg: Heb *they made them stumble*
18.6: Rom 9.21.

I will show them my back, not my
face,
in the day of their calamity."

18 Then they said, "Come, let us
make plots against Jeremiah, for the
law shall not perish from the priest,
nor counsel from the wise, nor the
word from the prophet. Come, let us
smite him with the tongue, and let us
not heed any of his words."

19 Give heed to me, O LORD,
and hearken to my plea.[j]
20 Is evil a recompense for good?
Yet they have dug a pit for my
life.
Remember how I stood before thee
to speak good for them,
to turn away thy wrath from
them.
21 Therefore deliver up their children
to famine;
give them over to the power of
the sword,
let their wives become childless and
widowed.
May their men meet death by
pestilence,
their youths be slain by the
sword in battle.
22 May a cry be heard from their
houses,
when thou bringest the marauder
suddenly upon them!
For they have dug a pit to take me,
and laid snares for my feet.
23 Yet, thou, O LORD, knowest
all their plotting to slay me.
Forgive not their iniquity,
nor blot out their sin from thy
sight.
Let them be overthrown before thee;
deal with them in the time of
thine anger.

19 Thus said the LORD, "Go, buy
a potter's earthen flask, and take
some of the elders of the people and
some of the senior priests, 2 and go
out to the valley of the son of Hin'nóm
at the entry of the Potsherd Gate, and
proclaim there the words that I tell
you. 3 You shall say, 'Hear the word
of the LORD, O kings of Judah and
inhabitants of Jerusalem. Thus says
the LORD of hosts, the God of Israel,
Behold, I am bringing such evil upon
this place that the ears of every one
who hears of it will tingle. 4 Because
the people have forsaken me, and have
profaned this place by burning incense
in it to other gods whom neither they
nor their fathers nor the kings of
Judah have known; and because they
[j] Gk Compare Syr Tg: Heb *my adversaries*

have filled this place with the blood of
innocents, 5 and have built the high
places of Bā'ál to burn their sons in
the fire as burnt offerings to Baal,
which I did not command or decree,
nor did it come into my mind; 6 therefore, behold, days are coming, says the
LORD, when this place shall no more
be called Tō'pheth, or the valley of
the son of Hin'nóm, but the valley of
Slaughter. 7 And in this place I will
make void the plans of Judah and
Jerusalem, and will cause their people
to fall by the sword before their
enemies, and by the hand of those who
seek their life. I will give their dead
bodies for food to the birds of the air
and to the beasts of the earth. 8 And I
will make this city a horror, a thing to
be hissed at; every one who passes by
it will be horrified and will hiss because of all its disasters. 9 And I will
make them eat the flesh of their sons
and their daughters, and every one
shall eat the flesh of his neighbor in the
siege and in the distress, with which
their enemies and those who seek their
life afflict them.'

10 "Then you shall break the flask
in the sight of the men who go with
you, 11 and shall say to them, 'Thus
says the LORD of hosts: So will I break
this people and this city, as one breaks
a potter's vessel, so that it can never
be mended. Men shall bury in Tō'-
pheth because there will be no place
else to bury. 12 Thus will I do to this
place, says the LORD, and to its inhabitants, making this city like Tō'-
pheth. 13 The houses of Jerusalem and
the houses of the kings of Judah—all
the houses upon whose roofs incense
has been burned to all the host of
heaven, and drink offerings have been
poured out to other gods—shall be
defiled like the place of Tō'pheth.' "

14 Then Jeremiah came from Tō'-
pheth, where the LORD had sent him
to prophesy, and he stood in the court
of the LORD's house, and said to all
the people: 15 "Thus says the LORD
of hosts, the God of Israel, Behold, I
am bringing upon this city and upon
all its towns all the evil that I have
pronounced against it, because they
have stiffened their neck, refusing to
hear my words."

20 Now Pash'húr the priest, the
son of Im'mér, who was chief
officer in the house of the LORD, heard
Jeremiah prophesying these things.
2 Then Pash'húr beat Jeremiah the
prophet, and put him in the stocks that
were in the upper Benjamin Gate of

19.13: Acts 7.42.

the house of the Lord. 3 On the morrow, when Pash'hŭr released Jeremiah from the stocks, Jeremiah said to him, "The Lord does not call your name Pash'hŭr, but Terror on every side. 4 For thus says the Lord: Behold, I will make you a terror to yourself and to all your friends. They shall fall by the sword of their enemies while you look on. And I will give all Judah into the hand of the king of Babylon; he shall carry them captive to Babylon, and shall slay them with the sword. 5 Moreover, I will give all the wealth of the city, all its gains, all its prized belongings, and all the treasures of the kings of Judah into the hand of their enemies, who shall plunder them, and seize them, and carry them to Babylon. 6 And you, Pash'hŭr, and all who dwell in your house, shall go into captivity; to Babylon you shall go; and there you shall die, and there you shall be buried, you and all your friends, to whom you have prophesied falsely."

7 O Lord, thou hast deceived me,
  and I was deceived;
thou art stronger than I,
  and thou hast prevailed.
I have become a laughingstock all
    the day;
  every one mocks me.
8 For whenever I speak, I cry out,
  I shout, "Violence and destruction!"
For the word of the Lord has become for me
  a reproach and derision all day long.
9 If I say, "I will not mention him,
    or speak any more in his name,"
there is in my heart as it were a
    burning fire
  shut up in my bones,
and I am weary with holding it in,
  and I cannot.
10 For I hear many whispering.
    Terror is on every side!
"Denounce him! Let us denounce
    him!"
  say all my familiar friends,
  watching for my fall.
"Perhaps he will be deceived,
  then we can overcome him,
  and take our revenge on him."
11 But the Lord is with me as a dread
    warrior;
  therefore my persecutors will
    stumble,
  they will not overcome me.
They will be greatly shamed,
  for they will not succeed.
Their eternal dishonor

will never be forgotten.
12 O Lord of hosts, who triest the
    righteous,
  who seest the heart and the mind,
let me see thy vengeance upon
    them,
  for to thee have I committed my
    cause.

13 Sing to the Lord;
  praise the Lord!
For he has delivered the life of the
    needy
  from the hand of evildoers.

14 Cursed be the day
  on which I was born!
The day when my mother bore me,
  let it not be blessed!
15 Cursed be the man
  who brought the news to my
    father,
"A son is born to you,"
  making him very glad.
16 Let that man be like the cities
  which the Lord overthrew without pity;
let him hear a cry in the morning
  and an alarm at noon,
17 because he did not kill me in the
    womb;
  so my mother would have been
    my grave,
  and her womb for ever great.
18 Why did I come forth from the
    womb
  to see toil and sorrow,
  and spend my days in shame?

21 This is the word which came to Jeremiah from the Lord, when King Zed·e·kī'ah sent to him Pash'hŭr the son of Mal·chī'ah and Zeph·a·nī'ah the priest, the son of Mā·a·sēi'ah, saying, 2 "Inquire of the Lord for us, for Ne·bu·chăd·rez'zar king of Babylon is making war against us; perhaps the Lord will deal with us according to all his wonderful deeds, and will make him withdraw from us."

3 Then Jeremiah said to them: 4 "Thus you shall say to Zed·e·kī'ah, 'Thus says the Lord, the God of Israel: Behold, I will turn back the weapons of war which are in your hands and with which you are fighting against the king of Babylon and against the Chal·dē'ans who are besieging you outside the walls; and I will bring them together into the midst of this city. 5 I myself will fight against you with outstretched hand and strong arm, in anger, and in fury, and in great wrath. 6 And I will smite the inhabit-

20.3, 10: Jer 6.25; 46.5; 49.29; Ps 31.13. 20.14-18: Job 3.3-13.

ants of this city, both man and beast;
they shall die of a great pestilence.
⁷Afterward, says the LORD, I will give
Zed·e·ki′ah king of Judah, and his
servants, and the people in this city
who survive the pestilence, sword, and
famine, into the hand of Ne·bu·chad-
rez′zar king of Babylon and into the
hand of their enemies, into the hand
of those who seek their lives. He shall
smite them with the edge of the sword;
he shall not pity them, or spare them,
or have compassion.'

8 "And to this people you shall say:
'Thus says the LORD: Behold, I set
before you the way of life and the way
of death. ⁹ He who stays in this city
shall die by the sword, by famine, and
by pestilence; but he who goes out
and surrenders to the Chal·de′ans who
are besieging you shall live and shall
have his life as a prize of war. ¹⁰ For
I have set my face against this city for
evil and not for good, says the LORD:
it shall be given into the hand of the
king of Babylon, and he shall burn it
with fire.'

11 "And to the house of the king
of Judah say, 'Hear the word of the
LORD, ¹² O house of David! Thus says
the LORD:

"'Execute justice in the morning,
    and deliver from the hand of the
        oppressor
    him who has been robbed,
lest my wrath go forth like fire,
    and burn with none to quench it,
    because of your evil doings.'"

13 "Behold, I am against you, O in-
    habitant of the valley,
O rock of the plain,
                    says the LORD;
you who say, 'Who shall come down
    against us,
    or who shall enter our habita-
        tions?'
14 I will punish you according to the
    fruit of your doings,
                    says the LORD;
I will kindle a fire in her forest,
    and it shall devour all that is
    round about her."

22 Thus says the LORD: "Go
down to the house of the king
of Judah, and speak there this word,
² and say, 'Hear the word of the LORD,
O King of Judah, who sit on the throne
of David, you, and your servants, and
your people who enter these gates.
³ Thus says the LORD: Do justice and
righteousness, and deliver from the

hand of the oppressor him who has
been robbed. And do no wrong or
violence to the alien, the fatherless,
and the widow, nor shed innocent
blood in this place. ⁴ For if you will
indeed obey this word, then there shall
enter the gates of this house kings who
sit on the throne of David, riding in
chariots and on horses, they, and their
servants, and their people. ⁵ But if you
will not heed these words, I swear by
myself, says the LORD, that this house
shall become a desolation. ⁶ For thus
says the LORD concerning the house
of the king of Judah:

"'You are as Gilead to me,
    as the summit of Lebanon,
yet surely I will make you a desert,
    an uninhabited city.ᵏ

7 I will prepare destroyers against you,
    each with his weapons;
and they shall cut down your
        choicest cedars,
    and cast them into the fire.

8 "'And many nations will pass by
this city, and every man will say to his
neighbor, "Why has the LORD dealt
thus with this great city?" ⁹And they
will answer, "Because they forsook the
covenant of the LORD their God, and
worshiped other gods and served
them."'"

10 Weep not for him who is dead,
    nor bemoan him;
but weep bitterly for him who goes
        away,
    for he shall return no more
        to see his native land.

11 For thus says the LORD concerning Shal′lum the son of Jo·si′ah,
king of Judah, who reigned instead of
Josiah his father, and who went away
from this place: "He shall return here
no more, ¹² but in the place where they
have carried him captive, there shall
he die, and he shall never see this land
again."

13 "Woe to him who builds his house
        by unrighteousness,
    and his upper rooms by injustice;
who makes his neighbor serve him
        for nothing,
    and does not give him his wages;
14 who says, 'I will build myself a
        great house
    with spacious upper rooms,'
and cuts out windows for it,
    paneling it with cedar,
    and painting it with vermilion.
15 Do you think you are a king
    because you compete in cedar?

ᵏ Cn: Heb *cities*
22.5: Mt 23.38; Lk 13.35.

Did not your father eat and drink
    and do justice and righteousness?
    Then it was well with him.
16 He judged the cause of the poor and
    needy;
        then it was well.
    Is not this to know me?
        says the LORD.
17 But you have eyes and heart
        only for your dishonest gain,
    for shedding innocent blood,
        and for practicing oppression and
            violence."
18 Therefore thus says the LORD
concerning Je·hoi′a·kim the son of
Jō·si′ah, king of Judah:
    "They shall not lament for him,
        saying,
    'Ah my brother!' or 'Ah sister!'
    They shall not lament for him, say-
        ing,
    'Ah lord!' or 'Ah his majesty!'
19 With the burial of an ass he shall be
    buried,
        dragged and cast forth beyond the
            gates of Jerusalem."

20 "Go up to Lebanon, and cry out,
        and lift up your voice in Ba′shan;
    cry from Ab′a·rim,
        for all your lovers are destroyed:
21 I spoke to you in your prosperity,
        but you said, 'I will not listen.'
    This has been your way from your
        youth,
        that you have not obeyed my
            voice.
22 The wind shall shepherd all your
        shepherds,
        and your lovers shall go into
            captivity;
    then you will be ashamed and con-
        founded
        because of all your wickedness.
23 O inhabitants of Lebanon,
        nested among the cedars,
    how you will groan[l] when pangs
        come upon you,
    pain as of a woman in travail!"

24 "As I live, says the LORD,
though Cō·ni′ah the son of Je·hoi′a-
kim, king of Judah, were the signet
ring on my right hand, yet I would
tear you off 25 and give you into the
hand of those who seek your life, into
the hand of those of whom you are
afraid, even into the hand of Ne·bu-
chad·rez′zar king of Babylon and into
the hand of the Chal·dē′ans. 26 I will
hurl you and the mother who bore
you into another country, where you
were not born, and there you shall die.

27 But to the land to which they will
long to return, there they shall not
return."
28 Is this man Cō·ni′ah a despised,
        broken pot,
    a vessel no one cares for?
    Why are he and his children hurled
        and cast
        into a land which they do not
            know?
29 O land, land, land,
        hear the word of the LORD!
30 Thus says the LORD:
    "Write this man down as childless,
        a man who shall not succeed in
            his days;
    for none of his offspring shall suc-
        ceed
        in sitting on the throne of David,
        and ruling again in Judah."

23

"Woe to the shepherds who
destroy and scatter the sheep of
my pasture!" says the LORD. 2 Therefore thus says the LORD, the God of
Israel, concerning the shepherds who
care for my people: "You have
scattered my flock, and have driven
them away, and you have not attended
to them. Behold, I will attend to you
for your evil doings, says the LORD.
3 Then I will gather the remnant of
my flock out of all the countries where
I have driven them, and I will bring
them back to their fold, and they shall
be fruitful and multiply. 4 I will set
shepherds over them who will care for
them, and they shall fear no more, nor
be dismayed, neither shall any be
missing, says the LORD.

5 "Behold, the days are coming,
says the LORD, when I will raise up for
David a righteous Branch, and he
shall reign as king and deal wisely, and
shall execute justice and righteousness
in the land. 6 In his days Judah will
be saved, and Israel will dwell
securely. And this is the name by
which he will be called. 'The LORD is
our righteousness.'

7 "Therefore, behold, the days are
coming, says the LORD, when men
shall no longer say, 'As the LORD lives
who brought up the people of Israel
out of the land of Egypt,' 8 but 'As the
LORD lives who brought up and led
the descendants of the house of Israel
out of the north country and out of all
the countries where he[m] had driven
them.' Then they shall dwell in their
own land."

[l] Gk Vg Syr: Heb be pitied   [m] Gk: Heb I
23.5: Jer 33.15; Is 4.2; Zech 3.8; 6.12.

9 Concerning the prophets:
My heart is broken within me,
    all my bones shake;
I am like a drunken man,
    like a man overcome by wine,
because of the LORD
    and because of his holy words.
10 For the land is full of adulterers;
    because of the curse the land
      mourns,
    and the pastures of the wilderness
      are dried up.
Their course is evil,
    and their might is not right.
11 "Both prophet and priest are un-
    godly;
    even in my house I have found
      their wickedness,
              says the LORD.
12 Therefore their way shall be to
    them
    like slippery paths in the darkness,
    into which they shall be driven
      and fall;
for I will bring evil upon them
    in the year of their punishment,
              says the LORD.
13 In the prophets of Sà·mâr′i·à
    I saw an unsavory thing:
they prophesied by Bā′ăl
    and led my people Israel astray.
14 But in the prophets of Jerusalem
    I have seen a horrible thing:
they commit adultery and walk in
    lies;
they strengthen the hands of evil-
    doers,
    so that no one turns from his
      wickedness;
all of them have become like Sod′ŏm
    to me,
    and its inhabitants like Gò·môr′-
      ràh."
15 Therefore thus says the LORD of
hosts concerning the prophets:
"Behold, I will feed them with
    wormwood,
    and give them poisoned water to
      drink;
for from the prophets of Jerusalem
    ungodliness has gone forth into
      all the land."

16 Thus says the LORD of hosts:
"Do not listen to the words of the
prophets who prophesy to you, filling
you with vain hopes; they speak visions
of their own minds, not from the
mouth of the LORD. 17 They say continually to those who despise the word
of the LORD, 'It shall be well with you';
and to every one who stubbornly
follows his own heart, they say, 'No
evil shall come upon you.'"

n Cn Compare Syr: Heb obscure

18 For who among them has stood in
    the council of the LORD
    to perceive and to hear his
      word,
    or who has given heed to his word
      and listened?
19 Behold, the storm of the LORD!
    Wrath has gone forth,
a whirling tempest;
    it will burst upon the head of the
      wicked.
20 The anger of the LORD will not
    turn back
    until he has executed and ac-
      complished
    the intents of his mind.
In the latter days you will under-
    stand it clearly.

21 "I did not send the prophets,
    yet they ran;
I did not speak to them,
    yet they prophesied.
22 But if they had stood in my council,
    then they would have proclaimed
      my words to my people,
    and they would have turned them
      from their evil way,
    and from the evil of their doings.

23 "Am I a God at hand, says the
LORD, and not a God afar off? 24 Can
a man hide himself in secret places so
that I cannot see him? says the LORD.
Do I not fill heaven and earth? says
the LORD. 25 I have heard what the
prophets have said who prophesy lies
in my name, saying, 'I have dreamed,
I have dreamed!' 26 How long shall
there be lies[n] in the heart of the
prophets who prophesy lies, and who
prophesy the deceit of their own heart,
27 who think to make my people forget
my name by their dreams which they
tell one another, even as their fathers
forgot my name for Bā′ăl? 28 Let the
prophet who has a dream tell the
dream, but let him who has my word
speak my word faithfully. What has
straw in common with wheat? says the
LORD. 29 Is not my word like fire, says
the LORD, and like a hammer which
breaks the rock in pieces? 30 Therefore, behold, I am against the prophets,
says the LORD, who steal my words
from one another. 31 Behold, I am
against the prophets, says the LORD,
who use their tongues and say, 'Says
the LORD.' 32 Behold, I am against
those who prophesy lying dreams,
says the LORD, and who tell them and
lead my people astray by their lies and
their recklessness, when I did not
send them or charge them; so they do

not profit this people at all, says the LORD:

33 "When one of this people, or a prophet, or a priest asks you, 'What is the burden of the LORD?' you shall say to them, 'You are the burden,^{o} and I will cast you off, says the LORD.' 34And as for the prophet, priest, or one of the people who says, 'The burden of the LORD,' I will punish that man and his household. 35 Thus shall you say, every one to his neighbor and every one to his brother, 'What has the LORD answered?' or 'What has the LORD spoken?' 36 But 'the burden of the LORD' you shall mention no more, for the burden is every man's own word, and you pervert the words of the living God, the LORD of hosts, our God. 37 Thus you shall say to the prophet, 'What has the LORD answered you?' or 'What has the LORD spoken?' 38 But if you say, 'The burden of the LORD,' thus says the LORD, 'Because you have said these words, "The burden of the LORD," when I sent to you, saying, "You shall not say, 'The burden of the LORD,' " ' 39 therefore, behold, I will surely lift you up and cast you away from my presence, you and the city which I gave to you and your fathers. 40And I will bring upon you everlasting reproach and perpetual shame, which shall not be forgotten.' "

24 After Ne·bu·chad·rez'zar king of Babylon had taken into exile from Jerusalem Jec·o·ni'ah the son of Je·hoi'a·kim, king of Judah, together with the princes of Judah, the craftsmen, and the smiths, and had brought them to Babylon, the LORD showed me this vision: Behold, two baskets of figs placed before the temple of the LORD. 2 One basket had very good figs, like first-ripe figs, but the other basket had very bad figs, so bad that they could not be eaten. 3And the LORD said to me, "What do you see, Jeremiah?" I said, "Figs, the good figs very good, and the bad figs very bad, so bad that they cannot be eaten."

4 Then the word of the LORD came to me: 5 "Thus says the LORD, the God of Israel: Like these good figs, so I will regard as good the exiles from Judah, whom I have sent away from this place to the land of the Chal·de'ans. 6 I will set my eyes upon them for good, and I will bring them back to this land. I will build them up, and not tear them down; I will plant them,

o Gk Vg: Heb *What burden*
p Compare Gk: Heb *horror for evil*

and not uproot them. 7 I will give them a heart to know that I am the LORD; and they shall be my people and I will be their God, for they shall return to me with their whole heart.

8 "But thus says the LORD: Like the bad figs which are so bad they cannot be eaten, so will I treat Zed·e·ki'ah the king of Judah, his princes, the remnant of Jerusalem who remain in this land, and those who dwell in the land of Egypt. 9 I will make them a horror^p to all the kingdoms of the earth, to be a reproach, a byword, a taunt, and a curse in all the places where I shall drive them. 10And I will send sword, famine, and pestilence upon them, until they shall be utterly destroyed from the land which I gave to them and their fathers."

25 The word that came to Jeremiah concerning all the people of Judah, in the fourth year of Je·hoi'a·kim the son of Jo·si'ah, king of Judah (that was the first year of Ne·bu·chad·rez'zar king of Babylon), 2 which Jeremiah the prophet spoke to all the people of Judah and all the inhabitants of Jerusalem: 3 "For twenty-three years, from the thirteenth year of Jo·si'ah the son of A'mon, king of Judah, to this day, the word of the LORD has come to me, and I have spoken persistently to you, but you have not listened. 4 You have neither listened nor inclined your ears to hear, although the LORD persistently sent to you all his servants the prophets, 5 saying, 'Turn now, every one of you, from his evil way and wrong doings, and dwell upon the land which the LORD has given to you and your fathers from of old and for ever; 6 do not go after other gods to serve and worship them, or provoke me to anger with the work of your hands. Then I will do you no harm.' 7 Yet you have not listened to me, says the LORD, that you might provoke me to anger with the work of your hands to your own harm.

8 "Therefore thus says the LORD of hosts: Because you have not obeyed my words, 9 behold, I will send for all the tribes of the north, says the LORD, and for Ne·bu·chad·rez'zar the king of Babylon, my servant, and I will bring them against this land and its inhabitants, and against all these nations round about; I will utterly destroy them, and make them a horror, a

hissing, and an everlasting reproach.*q*
10 Moreover, I will banish from them the voice of mirth and the voice of gladness, the voice of the bridegroom and the voice of the bride, the grinding of the millstones and the light of the lamp. 11 This whole land shall become a ruin and a waste, and these nations shall serve the king of Babylon seventy years. 12 Then after seventy years are completed, I will punish the king of Babylon and that nation, the land of the Chal-dē′ăns, for their iniquity, says the LORD, making the land an everlasting waste. 13 I will bring upon that land all the words which I have uttered against it, everything written in this book, which Jeremiah prophesied against all the nations. 14 For many nations and great kings shall make slaves even of them; and I will recompense them according to their deeds and the work of their hands.''

15 Thus the LORD, the God of Israel, said to me: "Take from my hand this cup of the wine of wrath, and make all the nations to whom I send you drink it. 16 They shall drink and stagger and be crazed because of the sword which I am sending among them.''

17 So I took the cup from the LORD's hand, and made all the nations to whom the LORD sent me drink it: 18 Jerusalem and the cities of Judah, its kings and princes, to make them a desolation and a waste, a hissing and a curse, as at this day; 19 Pharaoh king of Egypt, his servants, his princes, all his people, 20 and all the foreign folk among them; all the kings of the land of Uz and all the kings of the land of the Philistines (Ash′ke-lon, Gā′zà, Ek′rŏn, and the remnant of Ash′dod); 21 Ē′dŏm, Mō′ab, and the sons of Am′mŏn; 22 all the kings of Tўre, all the kings of Si′don, and the kings of the coastland across the sea; 23 Dē′dan, Tē′mà, Buz, and all who cut the corners of their hair; 24 all the kings of Arabia and all the kings of the mixed tribes that dwell in the desert; 25 all the kings of Zim′ri, all the kings of Ē′lăm, and all the kings of Media; 26 all the kings of the north, far and near, one after another, and all the kingdoms of the world which are on the face of the earth. And after them the king of Babylon*r* shall drink.

27 "Then you shall say to them, 'Thus says the LORD of hosts, the God of Israel: Drink, be drunk and vomit, fall and rise no more, because of the sword which I am sending among you.'

28 "And if they refuse to accept the cup from your hand to drink, then you shall say to them, 'Thus says the LORD of hosts: You must drink! 29 For behold, I begin to work evil at the city which is called by my name, and shall you go unpunished? You shall not go unpunished, for I am summoning a sword against all the inhabitants of the earth, says the LORD of hosts.'

30 "You, therefore, shall prophesy against them all these words, and say to them:

'The LORD will roar from on high,
    and from his holy habitation utter
    his voice;
he will roar mightily against his fold,
    and shout, like those who tread
    grapes,
    against all the inhabitants of the
    earth.
31 The clamor will resound to the ends
    of the earth,
    for the LORD has an indictment
    against the nations;
he is entering into judgment with all
    flesh,
    and the wicked he will put to the
    sword,
                    says the LORD.'

32 "Thus says the LORD of hosts:
Behold, evil is going forth
    from nation to nation,
and a great tempest is stirring
    from the farthest parts of the
    earth!
33 "And those slain by the LORD on that day shall extend from one end of the earth to the other. They shall not be lamented, or gathered, or buried; they shall be dung on the surface of the ground.
34 "Wail, you shepherds, and cry,
    and roll in ashes, you lords of the
    flock,
for the days of your slaughter and
    dispersion have come,
    and you shall fall like choice rams.*s*
35 No refuge will remain for the
    shepherds,
    nor escape for the lords of the
    flock.
36 Hark, the cry of the shepherds,
    and the wail of the lords of the
    flock!
For the LORD is despoiling their
    pasture,
37   and the peaceful folds are dev-
    astated,

q Gk Compare Syr: Heb *desolations*
r Heb *Sheshach*, a cipher for Babylon   *s* Gk: Heb *a choice vessel*
25.10: Jer 7.34; 16.9; Rev 18.23.   **25.15:** Jer 51.7; Rev 14.8, 10; 16.19; 17.4; 18.3.

because of the fierce anger of the
LORD.
38 Like a lion he has left his covert,
   for their land has become a waste
because of the sword of the
   oppressor,
   and because of his fierce anger."

26 In the beginning of the reign
of Je·hoi′a·kim the son of
Jō·si′ah, king of Judah, this word came
from the LORD, 2 "Thus says the
LORD: Stand in the court of the LORD's
house, and speak to all the cities of
Judah which come to worship in the
house of the LORD all the words that
I command you to speak to them; do
not hold back a word. 3 It may be they
will listen, and every one turn from
his evil way, that I may repent of the
evil which I intend to do to them because of their evil doings. 4 You shall
say to them, 'Thus says the LORD: If
you will not listen to me, to walk in
my law which I have set before you,
5 and to heed the words of my servants
the prophets whom I send to you
urgently, though you have not heeded,
6 then I will make this house like
Shi′loh, and I will make this city a
curse for all the nations of the earth.' "

7 The priests and the prophets and
all the people heard Jeremiah speaking
these words in the house of the LORD.
8 And when Jeremiah had finished
speaking all that the LORD had commanded him to speak to all the people,
then the priests and the prophets and
all the people laid hold of him, saying,
"You shall die! 9 Why have you
prophesied in the name of the LORD,
saying, 'This house shall be like Shi′-
loh, and this city shall be desolate,
without inhabitant'?" And all the
people gathered about Jeremiah in the
house of the LORD.

10 When the princes of Judah
heard these things, they came up from
the king's house to the house of the
LORD and took their seat in the entry
of the New Gate of the house of the
LORD. 11 Then the priests and the
prophets said to the princes and to all
the people, "This man deserves the
sentence of death, because he has
prophesied against this city, as you
have heard with your own ears."

12 Then Jeremiah spoke to all the
princes and all the people, saying,
"The LORD sent me to prophesy
against this house and this city all the
words you have heard. 13 Now therefore amend your ways and your doings, and obey the voice of the LORD

your God, and the LORD will repent
of the evil which he has pronounced
against you. 14 But as for me, behold,
I am in your hands. Do with me as
seems good and right to you. 15 Only
know for certain that if you put me to
death, you will bring innocent blood
upon yourselves and upon this city
and its inhabitants, for in truth the
LORD sent me to you to speak all these
words in your ears."

16 Then the princes and all the
people said to the priests and the
prophets, "This man does not deserve
the sentence of death, for he has
spoken to us in the name of the LORD
our God." 17 And certain of the elders
of the land arose and spoke to all the
assembled people, saying, 18 "Mi′cah
of Mō′re·sheth prophesied in the days
of Hez·e·ki′ah king of Judah, and said
to all the people of Judah: 'Thus says
the LORD of hosts,
Zion shall be plowed as a field;
   Jerusalem shall become a heap of
   ruins,
   and the mountain of the house a
   wooded height.'
19 Did Hez·e·ki′ah king of Judah and
all Judah put him to death? Did he not
fear the LORD and entreat the favor of
the LORD, and did not the LORD repent
of the evil which he had pronounced
against them? But we are about to
bring great evil upon ourselves."

20 There was another man who
prophesied in the name of the LORD,
U·ri′ah the son of She·mai′ah from
Kir′i·ath-je′a·rim. He prophesied
against this city and against this land
in words like those of Jeremiah. 21 And
when King Je·hoi′a·kim, with all his
warriors and all the princes, heard his
words, the king sought to put him to
death; but when U·ri′ah heard of it, he
was afraid and fled and escaped to
Egypt. 22 Then King Je·hoi′a·kim
sent to Egypt certain men, El·na′than
the son of Ach′bor and others with
him, 23 and they fetched U·ri′ah from
Egypt and brought him to King
Je·hoi′a·kim, who slew him with the
sword and cast his dead body into the
burial place of the common people.

24 But the hand of A·hi′kam the son
of Sha′phan was with Jeremiah so that
he was not given over to the people to
be put to death.

27 In the beginning of the reign of
Zed·e·ki′ah[u] the son of Jō·si′ah,
king of Judah, this word came to
Jeremiah from the LORD. 2 Thus the
LORD said to me: "Make yourself

---

[u] Another reading is *Jehoiakim*

thongs and yoke-bars, and put them on your neck. 3 Send word^v to the king of E´dom, the king of Mō´ab, the king of the sons of Am´mon, the king of Tyre, and the king of Si´don by the hand of the envoys who have come to Jerusalem to Zed·e·ki´ah king of Judah. 4 Give them this charge for their masters: 'Thus says the LORD of hosts, the God of Israel: This is what you shall say to your masters: 5 "It is I who by my great power and my outstretched arm have made the earth, with the men and animals that are on the earth, and I give it to whomever it seems right to me. 6 Now I have given all these lands into the hand of Ne·bu·chad·nez´zar, the king of Babylon, my servant, and I have given him also the beasts of the field to serve him. 7 All the nations shall serve him and his son and his grandson, until the time of his own land comes; then many nations and great kings shall make him their slave.

8 " " "But if any nation or kingdom will not serve this Ne·bu·chad·nez´zar king of Babylon, and put its neck under the yoke of the king of Babylon, I will punish that nation with the sword, with famine, and with pestilence, says the LORD, until I have consumed it by his hand. 9 So do not listen to your prophets, your diviners, your dreamers,^{w} your soothsayers, or your sorcerers, who are saying to you, 'You shall not serve the king of Babylon.' 10 For it is a lie which they are prophesying to you, with the result that you will be removed far from your land, and I will drive you out, and you will perish. 11 But any nation which will bring its neck under the yoke of the king of Babylon and serve him, I will leave on its own land, to till it and dwell there, says the LORD." ' "

12 To Zed·e·ki´ah king of Judah I spoke in like manner: "Bring your necks under the yoke of the king of Babylon, and serve him and his people, and live. 13 Why will you and your people die by the sword, by famine, and by pestilence, as the LORD has spoken concerning any nation which will not serve the king of Babylon? 14 Do not listen to the words of the prophets who are saying to you, 'You shall not serve the king of Babylon,' for it is a lie which they are prophesying to you. 15 I have not sent them, says the LORD, but they are prophesying falsely in my name, with the result that I will drive you out and you will perish, you and the

prophets who are prophesying to you."

16 Then I spoke to the priests and to all this people, saying, "Thus says the LORD: Do not listen to the words of your prophets who are prophesying to you, saying, 'Behold, the vessels of the LORD's house will now shortly be brought back from Babylon,' for it is a lie which they are prophesying to you. 17 Do not listen to them; serve the king of Babylon and live. Why should this city become a desolation? 18 If they are prophets, and if the word of the LORD is with them, then let them intercede with the LORD of hosts, that the vessels which are left in the house of the LORD, in the house of the king of Judah, and in Jerusalem may not go to Babylon. 19 For thus says the LORD of hosts concerning the pillars, the sea, the stands, and the rest of the vessels which are left in this city, 20 which Ne·bu·chad·nez´zar king of Babylon did not take away, when he took into exile from Jerusalem to Babylon Jec·o·ni´ah the son of Je·hoi´a·kim, king of Judah, and all the nobles of Judah and Jerusalem—21 thus says the LORD of hosts, the God of Israel, concerning the vessels which are left in the house of the LORD, in the house of the king of Judah, and in Jerusalem: 22 They shall be carried to Babylon and remain there until the day when I give attention to them, says the LORD. Then I will bring them back and restore them to this place."

28 In that same year, at the beginning of the reign of Zed·e·ki´ah king of Judah, in the fifth month of the fourth year, Han·a·ni´ah the son of Az´zur, the prophet from Gib´e·on, spoke to me in the house of the LORD, in the presence of the priests and all the people, saying, 2 "Thus says the LORD of hosts, the God of Israel: I have broken the yoke of the king of Babylon. 3 Within two years I will bring back to this place all the vessels of the LORD's house, which Ne·bu·chad·nez´zar king of Babylon took away from this place and carried to Babylon. 4 I will also bring back to this place Jec·o·ni´ah the son of Je·hoi´a·kim, king of Judah, and all the exiles from Judah who went to Babylon, says the LORD, for I will break the yoke of the king of Babylon."

5 Then the prophet Jeremiah spoke to Han·a·ni´ah the prophet in the presence of the priests and all the people who were standing in the house of

^{v} Cn: Heb *send them* ^{w} Gk Syr Vg: Heb *dreams*

the LORD; ⁶ and the prophet Jeremiah said, "Amen! May the LORD do so; may the LORD make the words which you have prophesied come true, and bring back to this place from Babylon the vessels of the house of the LORD, and all the exiles. ⁷ Yet hear now this word which I speak in your hearing and in the hearing of all the people. ⁸ The prophets who preceded you and me from ancient times prophesied war, famine, and pestilence against many countries and great kingdoms. ⁹As for the prophet who prophesies peace, when the word of that prophet comes to pass, then it will be known that the LORD has truly sent the prophet."

10 Then the prophet Han·a·ni′ah took the yoke-bars from the neck of Jeremiah the prophet, and broke them. ¹¹And Han·a·ni′ah spoke in the presence of all the people, saying, "Thus says the LORD: Even so will I break the yoke of Ne·bu·chad·nez′zar king of Babylon from the neck of all the nations within two years." But Jeremiah the prophet went his way.

12 Sometime after the prophet Han·a·ni′ah had broken the yoke-bars from off the neck of Jeremiah the prophet, the word of the LORD came to Jeremiah: ¹³ "Go, tell Han·a·ni′ah, 'Thus says the LORD: You have broken wooden bars, but Iˣ will make in their place bars of iron. ¹⁴ For thus says the LORD of hosts, the God of Israel: I have put upon the neck of all these nations an iron yoke of servitude to Ne·bu·chad·nez′zar king of Babylon, and they shall serve him, for I have given to him even the beasts of the field.'" ¹⁵And Jeremiah the prophet said to the prophet Han·a·ni′ah, "Listen, Hananiah, the LORD has not sent you, and you have made this people trust in a lie. ¹⁶ Therefore thus says the LORD: 'Behold, I will remove you from the face of the earth. This very year you shall die, because you have uttered rebellion against the LORD.'"

17 In that same year, in the seventh month, the prophet Han·a·ni′ah died.

29 These are the words of the letter which Jeremiah the prophet sent from Jerusalem to the eldersʸ of the exiles, and to the priests, the prophets, and all the people, whom Ne·bu·chad·nez′zar had taken into exile from Jerusalem to Babylon. ² This was after King Jec·o·ni′ah, and the queen mother, the eunuchs, the princes of Judah and Jerusalem, the craftsmen, and the smiths had departed from Jerusalem. ³ The letter was sent by the hand of El·a′sah the son of Sha′phan and Gem·a·ri′ah the son of Hil·ki′ah, whom Zed·e·ki′ah king of Judah sent to Babylon to Ne·bu·chad·nez′zar king of Babylon. It said: ⁴ "Thus says the LORD of hosts, the God of Israel, to all the exiles whom I have sent into exile from Jerusalem to Babylon: ⁵ Build houses and live in them; plant gardens and eat their produce. ⁶ Take wives and have sons and daughters; take wives for your sons, and give your daughters in marriage, that they may bear sons and daughters; multiply there, and do not decrease. ⁷ But seek the welfare of the city where I have sent you into exile, and pray to the LORD on its behalf, for in its welfare you will find your welfare. ⁸ For thus says the LORD of hosts, the God of Israel: Do not let your prophets and your diviners who are among you deceive you, and do not listen to the dreams which they dream,ᶻ ⁹ for it is a lie which they are prophesying to you in my name; I did not send them, says the LORD.

10 "For thus says the LORD: When seventy years are completed for Babylon, I will visit you, and I will fulfil to you my promise and bring you back to this place. ¹¹ For I know the plans I have for you, says the LORD, plans for welfare and not for evil, to give you a future and a hope. ¹² Then you will call upon me and come and pray to me, and I will hear you. ¹³ You will seek me and find me; when you seek me with all your heart, ¹⁴ I will be found by you, says the LORD, and I will restore your fortunes and gather you from all the nations and all the places where I have driven you, says the LORD, and I will bring you back to the place from which I sent you into exile.

15 "Because you have said, 'The LORD has raised up prophets for us in Babylon,'—¹⁶ Thus says the LORD concerning the king who sits on the throne of David, and concerning all the people who dwell in this city, your kinsmen who did not go out with you into exile: ¹⁷ 'Thus says the LORD of hosts, Behold, I am sending on them sword, famine, and pestilence, and I will make them like vile figs which are so bad they cannot be eaten. ¹⁸ I will pursue them with sword, famine, and pestilence, and will make them a

---

ˣ Gk: Heb *you* ʸ Gk: Heb *the rest of the elders*
ᶻ Cn: Heb *your dreams which you cause to dream*

horror to all the kingdoms of the earth, to be a curse, a terror, a hissing, and a reproach among all the nations where I have driven them, 19 because they did not heed my words, says the LORD, which I persistently sent to you by my servants the prophets, but you would not listen, says the LORD.'— 20 Hear the word of the LORD, all you exiles whom I sent away from Jerusalem to Babylon: 21 'Thus says the LORD of hosts, the God of Israel, concerning A'hab the son of Kō·lǎi'ǎh and Zed·ē·kī'ǎh the son of Mā·ā·sēi'ǎh, who are prophesying a lie to you in my name: Behold, I will deliver them into the hand of Ne·bū·chǎd·rez'zǎr king of Babylon, and he shall slay them before your eyes. 22 Because of them this curse shall be used by all the exiles from Judah in Babylon: "The LORD make you like Zed·ē·kī'ǎh and A'hab, whom the king of Babylon roasted in the fire," 23 because they have committed folly in Israel, they have committed adultery with their neighbors' wives, and they have spoken in my name lying words which I did not command them. I am the one who knows, and I am witness, says the LORD.'"

24 To She·māi'ǎh of Ne·hel'ǎm you shall say: 25 'Thus says the LORD of hosts, the God of Israel: You have sent letters in your name to all the people who are in Jerusalem, and to Zeph·à·nī'ǎh the son of Mā·ā·sēi'ǎh the priest, and to all the priests, saying, 26 'The LORD has made you priest instead of Je·hoi'ā·dà the priest, to have charge in the house of the LORD over every madman who prophesies, to put him in the stocks and collar. 27 Now why have you not rebuked Jeremiah of An'ā·thoth who is prophesying to you? 28 For he has sent to us in Babylon, saying, "Your exile will be long; build houses and live in them, and plant gardens and eat their produce." '''

29 Zeph·à·nī'ǎh the priest read this letter in the hearing of Jeremiah the prophet. 30 Then the word of the LORD came to Jeremiah: 31 "Send to all the exiles, saying, 'Thus says the LORD concerning She·māi'ǎh of Ne·hel'ǎm: Because Shemaiah has prophesied to you when I did not send him, and has made you trust in a lie, 32 therefore thus says the LORD: Behold, I will punish She·māi'ǎh of Ne·hel'ǎm and his descendants; he shall not have any one living among this people to see*a*

the good that I will do to my people, says the LORD, for he has talked rebellion against the LORD.' "

30 The word that came to Jeremiah from the LORD: 2 "Thus says the LORD, the God of Israel: Write in a book all the words that I have spoken to you. 3 For behold, days are coming, says the LORD, when I will restore the fortunes of my people, Israel and Judah, says the LORD, and I will bring them back to the land which I gave to their fathers, and they shall take possession of it."

4 These are the words which the LORD spoke concerning Israel and Judah:

5 "Thus says the LORD:
We have heard a cry of panic,
   of terror, and no peace.
6 Ask now, and see,
   can a man bear a child?
Why then do I see every man
   with his hands on his loins like a
    woman in labor?
Why has every face turned pale?
7 Alas! that day is so great
   there is none like it;
it is a time of distress for Jacob;
   yet he shall be saved out of it.

8 "And it shall come to pass in that day, says the LORD of hosts, that I will break the yoke from off their*b* neck, and I will burst their*b* bonds, and strangers shall no more make servants of them.*c* 9 But they shall serve the LORD their God and David their king, whom I will raise up for them.

10 "Then fear not, O Jacob my servant, says the LORD,
   nor be dismayed, O Israel;
for lo, I will save you from afar,
   and your offspring from the land
    of their captivity.
Jacob shall return and have quiet
   and ease,
   and none shall make him afraid.
11 For I am with you to save you,
             says the LORD;
I will make a full end of all the
   nations
   among whom I scattered you,
but of you I will not make a full
   end.
I will chasten you in just measure,
   and I will by no means leave you
   unpunished.

12 "For thus says the LORD:
Your hurt is incurable,
   and your wound is grievous.

---

a Gk: Heb *and he shall not see*   *b* Gk Old Latin: Heb *your*
c Heb *make a servant of him*

13 There is none to uphold your cause,
    no medicine for your wound,
    no healing for you.
14 All your lovers have forgotten you;
    they care nothing for you;
for I have dealt you the blow of an
        enemy,
    the punishment of a merciless foe,
because your guilt is great,
    because your sins are flagrant.
15 Why do you cry out over your hurt?
    Your pain is incurable.
Because your guilt is great,
    because your sins are flagrant,
I have done these things to you.
16 Therefore all who devour you shall
        be devoured,
    and all your foes, every one of
        them, shall go into captivity;
those who despoil you shall become
        a spoil,
    and all who prey on you I will
        make a prey.
17 For I will restore health to you,
    and your wounds I will heal,
                    says the LORD,
because they have called you an
        outcast:
    'It is Zion, for whom no one cares!'

18 "Thus says the LORD:
Behold, I will restore the fortunes
        of the tents of Jacob,
    and have compassion on his
        dwellings;
the city shall be rebuilt upon its
        mound,
    and the palace shall stand where
        it used to be.
19 Out of them shall come songs of
        thanksgiving,
    and the voices of those who make
        merry.
I will multiply them, and they shall
        not be few;
    I will make them honored, and
        they shall not be small.
20 Their children shall be as they were
        of old,
    and their congregation shall be
        established before me;
    and I will punish all who oppress
        them.
21 Their prince shall be one of them-
        selves,
    their ruler shall come forth from
        their midst;
I will make him draw near, and he
        shall approach me,
    for who would dare of himself to
        approach me?
                    says the LORD.
22 And you shall be my people,
    and I will be your God."

23 Behold the storm of the LORD!
    Wrath has gone forth,
a whirling tempest;
    it will burst upon the head of the
        wicked.
24 The fierce anger of the LORD will
        not turn back
    until he has executed and ac-
        complished
    the intents of his mind.
In the latter days you will under-
        stand this.

31 "At that time, says the LORD,
    I will be the God of all the
families of Israel, and they shall be
my people."

2 Thus says the LORD:
"The people who survived the
        sword
    found grace in the wilderness;
when Israel sought for rest,
3   the LORD appeared to him[d] from
            afar.
I have loved you with an everlasting
        love;
    therefore I have continued my
        faithfulness to you.
4 Again I will build you, and you
        shall be built,
    O virgin Israel!
Again you shall adorn yourself with
        timbrels,
    and shall go forth in the dance of
        the merrymakers.
5 Again you shall plant vineyards
    upon the mountains of Sa·mar'i·à;
the planters shall plant,
    and shall enjoy the fruit.
6 For there shall be a day when
        watchmen will call
    in the hill country of E'phra·im:
'Arise, and let us go up to Zion,
    to the LORD our God.'"

7 For thus says the LORD:
"Sing aloud with gladness for
        Jacob,
    and raise shouts for the chief of
        the nations;
proclaim, give praise, and say,
    'The LORD has saved his people,
    the remnant of Israel.'
8 Behold, I will bring them from the
        north country,
    and gather them from the farthest
        parts of the earth,
among them the blind and the lame,
    the woman with child and her
        who is in travail, together;
    a great company, they shall re-
        turn here.
9 With weeping they shall come,
    and with consolations[e] I will lead
        them back,

d Gk: Heb me   e Gk Compare Vg Tg: Heb *supplications*

I will make them walk by brooks of
  water,
 in a straight path in which they
  shall not stumble;
for I am a father to Israel,
 and E′phrȧ·im is my first-born.

10 "Hear the word of the LORD, O
  nations,
 and declare it in the coastlands
  afar off;
say, 'He who scattered Israel will
  gather him,
 and will keep him as a shepherd
  keeps his flock.'
11 For the LORD has ransomed Jacob,
 and has redeemed him from hands
  too strong for him.
12 They shall come and sing aloud on
  the height of Zion,
 and they shall be radiant over the
  goodness of the LORD,
over the grain, the wine, and the oil,
 and over the young of the flock
  and the herd;
their life shall be like a watered
  garden,
 and they shall languish no more.
13 Then shall the maidens rejoice in
  the dance,
 and the young men and the old
  shall be merry.
I will turn their mourning into joy,
 I will comfort them, and give
  them gladness for sorrow.
14 I will feast the soul of the priests
  with abundance,
 and my people shall be satisfied
  with my goodness,
     says the LORD."

15 Thus says the LORD:
"A voice is heard in Rā′mȧh,
 lamentation and bitter weeping.
Rachel is weeping for her children;
 she refuses to be comforted for
  her children,
 because they are not."

16 Thus says the LORD:
"Keep your voice from weeping,
 and your eyes from tears;
for your work shall be rewarded,
     says the LORD,
 and they shall come back from
  the land of the enemy.
17 There is hope for your future,
     says the LORD,
 and your children shall come
  back to their own country.
18 I have heard E′phrȧ·im bemoaning,
'Thou hast chastened me, and I was
  chastened,

like an untrained calf;
bring me back that I may be restored,
 for thou art the LORD my God.
19 For after I had turned away I
  repented;
 and after I was instructed, I
  smote upon my thigh;
I was ashamed, and I was confounded,
 because I bore the disgrace of
  my youth.'
20 Is E′phrȧ·im my dear son?
 Is he my darling child?
For as often as I speak against
  him,
 I do remember him still.
Therefore my heart yearns for him;
 I will surely have mercy on him,
     says the LORD.

21 "Set up waymarks for yourself,
 make yourself guideposts;
consider well the highway,
 the road by which you went.
Return, O virgin Israel,
 return to these your cities.
22 How long will you waver,
 O faithless daughter?
For the LORD has created a new
  thing on the earth:
 a woman protects a man."

23 Thus says the LORD of hosts,
the God of Israel: "Once more they
shall use these words in the land of
Judah and in its cities, when I restore
their fortunes:
'The LORD bless you, O habitation
  of righteousness,
 O holy hill!'
24 And Judah and all its cities shall
dwell there together, and the farmers
and those who wander*f* with their
flocks. 25 For I will satisfy the weary
soul, and every languishing soul I will
replenish."
26 Thereupon I awoke and looked,
and my sleep was pleasant to me.
27 "Behold, the days are coming,
says the LORD, when I will sow the
house of Israel and the house of Judah
with the seed of man and the seed of
beast. 28 And it shall come to pass that
as I have watched over them to pluck
up and break down, to overthrow,
destroy, and bring evil, so I will watch
over them to build and to plant, says
the LORD. 29 In those days they shall
no longer say:
'The fathers have eaten sour grapes,
 and the children's teeth are set
  on edge.'

f Cn Compare Syr Vg Tg: Heb *and they shall wander*
31.15: Mt 2.18.

30 But every one shall die for his own sin; each man who eats sour grapes, his teeth shall be set on edge.

31 "Behold, the days are coming, says the LORD, when I will make a new covenant with the house of Israel and the house of Judah, 32 not like the covenant which I made with their fathers when I took them by the hand to bring them out of the land of Egypt, my covenant which they broke, though I was their husband, says the LORD. 33 But this is the covenant which I will make with the house of Israel after those days, says the LORD: I will put my law within them, and I will write it upon their hearts; and I will be their God, and they shall be my people. 34 And no longer shall each man teach his neighbor and each his brother, saying, 'Know the LORD,' for they shall all know me, from the least of them to the greatest, says the LORD; for I will forgive their iniquity, and I will remember their sin no more."

35 Thus says the LORD,
who gives the sun for light by day
and the fixed order of the moon
and the stars for light by night,
who stirs up the sea so that its waves
roar—
the LORD of hosts is his name:
36 "If this fixed order departs
from before me, says the LORD,
then shall the descendants of Israel
cease
from being a nation before me for
ever."

37 Thus says the LORD:
"If the heavens above can be
measured,
and the foundations of the earth
below can be explored,
then I will cast off all the descendants of Israel
for all that they have done,
says the LORD."

38 "Behold, the days are coming, says the LORD, when the city shall be rebuilt for the LORD from the tower of Hà·nan'el to the Corner Gate. 39 And the measuring line shall go out farther, straight to the hill Gā'reb, and shall then turn to Gō'áh. 40 The whole valley of the dead bodies and the ashes, and all the fields as far as the brook Kid'ron, to the corner of the Horse Gate toward the east, shall be sacred to the LORD. It shall not be uprooted or overthrown any more for ever."

32 The word that came to Jere-
miah from the LORD in the tenth year of Zed·e·ki'áh king of Ju-dah, which was the eighteenth year of Ne·bu·chàd·rez'zàr. 2 At that time the army of the king of Babylon was besieging Jerusalem, and Jeremiah the prophet was shut up in the court of the guard which was in the palace of the king of Judah. 3 For Zed·e·ki'áh king of Judah had imprisoned him, saying, "Why do you prophesy and say, 'Thus says the LORD: Behold, I am giving this city into the hand of the king of Babylon, and he shall take it; 4 Zed·e·ki'áh king of Judah shall not escape out of the hand of the Chal-dē'áns, but shall surely be given into the hand of the king of Babylon, and shall speak with him face to face and see him eye to eye; 5 and he shall take Zed·e·ki'áh to Babylon, and there he shall remain until I visit him, says the LORD; though you fight against the Chal·dē'áns, you shall not succeed'?"

6 Jeremiah said, "The word of the LORD came to me: 7 Behold, Han'á·mel the son of Shal'lùm your uncle will come to you and say, 'Buy my field which is at An'á·thoth, for the right of redemption by purchase is yours.' 8 Then Han'á·mel my cousin came to me in the court of the guard, in accordance with the word of the LORD, and said to me, 'Buy my field which is at An'à·thoth in the land of Benja-min, for the right of possession and redemption is yours; buy it for your-self. Then I knew that this was the word of the LORD.'

9 "And I bought the field at An'á·thoth from Han'á·mel my cousin, and weighed out the money to him, seventeen shekels of silver. 10 I signed the deed, sealed it, got witnesses, and weighed the money on scales. 11 Then I took the sealed deed of purchase, containing the terms and conditions, and the open copy; 12 and I gave the deed of purchase to Bâr'úch the son of Ne·ri'áh son of Mäh·sēi'áh, in the presence of Han'á·mel my cousin, in the presence of the witnesses who signed the deed of purchase, and in the presence of all the Jews who were sitting in the court of the guard. 13 I charged Bâr'úch in their presence, saying, 14 'Thus says the LORD of hosts, the God of Israel: Take these deeds, both this sealed deed of pur-chase and this open deed, and put them in an earthenware vessel, that they may last for a long time. 15 For thus says the LORD of hosts, the God

31.31: Lk 22.20; 1 Cor 11.25. **31.31–34:** Jer 32.38-40; Heb 8.8-12; 10.16-17.

of Israel: Houses and fields and vineyards shall again be bought in this land.'

16 "After I had given the deed of purchase to Bâr'uch the son of Ne-ri'ah, I prayed to the LORD, saying: 17 'Ah Lord GOD! It is thou who hast made the heavens and the earth by thy great power and by thy outstretched arm! Nothing is too hard for thee, 18 who showest steadfast love to thousands, but dost requite the guilt of fathers to their children after them, O great and mighty God whose name is the LORD of hosts, 19 great in counsel and mighty in deed; whose eyes are open to all the ways of men, rewarding every man according to his ways and according to the fruit of his doings; 20 who hast shown signs and wonders in the land of Egypt, and to this day in Israel and among all mankind, and hast made thee a name, as at this day. 21 Thou didst bring thy people Israel out of the land of Egypt with signs and wonders, with a strong hand and outstretched arm, and with great terror; 22 and thou gavest them this land, which thou didst swear to their fathers to give them, a land flowing with milk and honey; 23 and they entered and took possession of it. But they did not obey thy voice or walk in thy law; they did nothing of all thou didst command them to do. Therefore thou hast made all this evil come upon them. 24 Behold, the siege mounds have come up to the city to take it, and because of sword and famine and pestilence the city is given into the hands of the Chal·dē'ans who are fighting against it. What thou didst speak has come to pass, and behold, thou seest it. 25 Yet thou, O Lord GOD, hast said to me, "Buy the field for money and get witnesses"— though the city is given into the hands of the Chal·dē'ans.' "

26 The word of the LORD came to Jeremiah: 27 "Behold, I am the LORD, the God of all flesh; is anything too hard for me? 28 Therefore, thus says the LORD: Behold, I am giving this city into the hands of the Chal·dē'ans and into the hands of Ne·bu·chad·rez'-zar king of Babylon, and he shall take it. 29 The Chal·dē'ans who are fighting against this city shall come and set this city on fire, and burn it, with the houses on whose roofs incense has been offered to Bâ'al and drink offerings have been poured out to other gods, to provoke me to anger. 30 For the sons of Israel and the sons of

Judah have done nothing but evil in my sight from their youth; the sons of Israel have done nothing but provoke me to anger by the work of their hands, says the LORD. 31 This city has aroused my anger and wrath, from the day it was built to this day, so that I will remove it from my sight 32 because of all the evil of the sons of Israel and the sons of Judah which they did to provoke me to anger—their kings and their princes, their priests and their prophets, the men of Judah and the inhabitants of Jerusalem. 33 They have turned to me their back and not their face; and though I have taught them persistently they have not listened to receive instruction. 34 They set up their abominations in the house which is called by my name, to defile it. 35 They built the high places of Bâ'al in the valley of the son of Hin'-nom, to offer up their sons and daughters to Mō'lech, though I did not command them, nor did it enter into my mind, that they should do this abomination, to cause Judah to sin.

36 "Now therefore thus says the LORD, the God of Israel, concerning this city of which you say, 'It is given into the hand of the king of Babylon by sword, by famine, and by pestilence': 37 Behold, I will gather them from all the countries to which I drove them in my anger and my wrath and in great indignation; I will bring them back to this place, and I will make them dwell in safety. 38 And they shall be my people, and I will be their God. 39 I will give them one heart and one way, that they may fear me for ever, for their own good and the good of their children after them. 40 I will make with them an everlasting covenant, that I will not turn away from doing good to them; and I will put the fear of me in their hearts, that they may not turn from me. 41 I will rejoice in doing them good, and I will plant them in this land in faithfulness, with all my heart and all my soul.

42 "For thus says the LORD: Just as I have brought all this great evil upon this people, so I will bring upon them all the good that I promise them. 43 Fields shall be bought in this land of which you are saying, It is a desolation, without man or beast; it is given into the hands of the Chal·dē'ans. 44 Fields shall be bought for money, and deeds shall be signed and sealed and witnessed, in the land of Benjamin, in the places about Jerusalem,

32.38-40: Jer 31.31-34.

and in the cities of Judah, in the cities of the hill country, in the cities of the She·phē′lah, and in the cities of the Negeb; for I will restore their fortunes, says the LORD."

33 The word of the LORD came to Jeremiah a second time, while he was still shut up in the court of the guard: 2 "Thus says the LORD who made the earth,[g] the LORD who formed it to establish it—the LORD is his name: 3 Call to me and I will answer you, and will tell you great and hidden things which you have not known. 4 For thus says the LORD, the God of Israel, concerning the houses of this city and the houses of the kings of Judah which were torn down to make a defense against the siege mounds and before the sword:[h] 5 The Chal·dē′ans are coming in to fight[i] and to fill them with the dead bodies of men whom I shall smite in my anger and my wrath, for I have hidden my face from this city because of all their wickedness. 6 Behold, I will bring to it health and healing, and I will heal them and reveal to them abundance[j] of prosperity and security. 7 I will restore the fortunes of Judah and the fortunes of Israel, and rebuild them as they were at first. 8 I will cleanse them from all the guilt of their sin against me, and I will forgive all the guilt of their sin and rebellion against me. 9And this city[k] shall be to me a name of joy, a praise and a glory before all the nations of the earth who shall hear of all the good that I do for them; they shall fear and tremble because of all the good and all the prosperity I provide for it.

10 "Thus says the LORD: In this place of which you say, 'It is a waste without man or beast,' in the cities of Judah and the streets of Jerusalem that are desolate, without man or inhabitant or beast, there shall be heard again 11 the voice of mirth and the voice of gladness, the voice of the bridegroom and the voice of the bride, the voices of those who sing, as they bring thank offerings to the house of the LORD:

'Give thanks to the LORD of hosts,
      for the LORD is good,
   for his steadfast love endures for
         ever!'

For I will restore the fortunes of the land as at first, says the LORD.

12 "Thus says the LORD of hosts:

In this place which is waste, without man or beast, and in all of its cities, there shall again be habitations of shepherds resting their flocks. 13 In the cities of the hill country, in the cities of the She·phē′lah, and in the cities of the Negeb, in the land of Benjamin, the places about Jerusalem, and in the cities of Judah, flocks shall again pass under the hands of the one who counts them, says the LORD.

14 "Behold, the days are coming, says the LORD, when I will fulfil the promise I made to the house of Israel and the house of Judah. 15 In those days and at that time I will cause a righteous Branch to spring forth for David; and he shall execute justice and righteousness in the land. 16 In those days Judah will be saved and Jerusalem will dwell securely. And this is the name by which it will be called: 'The LORD is our righteousness.'

17 "For thus says the LORD: David shall never lack a man to sit on the throne of the house of Israel, 18 and the Levitical priests shall never lack a man in my presence to offer burnt offerings, to burn cereal offerings, and to make sacrifices for ever."

19 The word of the LORD came to Jeremiah: 20 "Thus says the LORD: If you can break my covenant with the day and my covenant with the night, so that day and night will not come at their appointed time, 21 then also my covenant with David my servant may be broken, so that he shall not have a son to reign on his throne, and my covenant with the Levitical priests my ministers. 22As the host of heaven cannot be numbered and the sands of the sea cannot be measured, so I will multiply the descendants of David my servant, and the Levitical priests who minister to me."

23 The word of the LORD came to Jeremiah: 24 "Have you not observed what these people are saying, 'The LORD has rejected the two families which he chose'? Thus they have despised my people so that they are no longer a nation in their sight. 25 Thus says the LORD: If I have not established my covenant with day and night and the ordinances of heaven and earth, 26 then I will reject the descendants of Jacob and David my servant and will not choose one of his descendants to rule over the seed of Abraham, Isaac, and Jacob. For I will restore their

_g_ Gk: Heb _it_   _h_ Heb obscure
_i_ Cn: Heb _They are coming in to fight against the Chaldeans_   _l_ Heb uncertain
_k_ Heb _and it_
33.15: Jer 23.5; Is 4.2; Zech 3.8; 6.12.

fortunes, and will have mercy upon them."

34 The word which came to Jeremiah from the LORD, when Ne·bu·chad·rez′zar king of Babylon and all his army and all the kingdoms of the earth under his dominion and all the peoples were fighting against Jerusalem and all of its cities: 2 "Thus says the LORD, the God of Israel: Go and speak to Zed·e·ki′ah king of Judah and say to him, 'Thus says the LORD: Behold, I am giving this city into the hand of the king of Babylon, and he shall burn it with fire. 3 You shall not escape from his hand, but shall surely be captured and delivered into his hand; you shall see the king of Babylon eye to eye and speak with him face to face; and you shall go to Babylon.' 4 Yet hear the word of the LORD, O Zed·e·ki′ah king of Judah! Thus says the LORD concerning you: 'You shall not die by the sword. 5 You shall die in peace. And as spices were burned for your fathers, the former kings who were before you, so men shall burn spices for you and lament for you, saying, "Alas, lord!" ' For I have spoken the word, says the LORD."

6 Then Jeremiah the prophet spoke all these words to Zed·e·ki′ah king of Judah, in Jerusalem, 7 when the army of the king of Babylon was fighting against Jerusalem and against all the cities of Judah that were left, La′chish and A·ze′kah; for these were the only fortified cities of Judah that remained.

8 The word which came to Jeremiah from the LORD, after King Zed·e·ki′ah had made a covenant with all the people in Jerusalem to make a proclamation of liberty to them, 9 that every one should set free his Hebrew slaves, male and female, so that no one should enslave a Jew, his brother. 10And all the people obeyed, all the princes and all the people who had entered into the covenant that every one would set free his slave, male or female, so that they would not be enslaved again; they obeyed and set them free. 11 But afterward they turned around and took back the male and female slaves they had set free, and brought them into subjection as slaves. 12 The word of the LORD came to Jeremiah from the LORD: 13 "Thus says the LORD, the God of Israel: I made a covenant with your fathers when I brought them out of the land of Egypt, out of the house of bondage, saying, 14 'At the end of six*l* years each of you must set free

the fellow Hebrew who has been sold to you and has served you six years; you must set him free from your service.' But your fathers did not listen to me or incline their ears to me. 15 You recently repented and did what was right in my eyes by proclaiming liberty, each to his neighbor, and you made a covenant before me in the house which is called by my name; 16 but then you turned around and profaned my name when each of you took back his male and female slaves, whom you had set free according to their desire, and you brought them into subjection to be your slaves. 17 Therefore, thus says the LORD: You have not obeyed me by proclaiming liberty, every one to his brother and to his neighbor; behold, I proclaim to you liberty to the sword, to pestilence, and to famine, says the LORD. I will make you a horror to all the kingdoms of the earth. 18And the men who transgressed my covenant and did not keep the terms of the covenant which they made before me, I will make like*m* the calf which they cut in two and passed between its parts—19 the princes of Judah, the princes of Jerusalem, the eunuchs, the priests, and all the people of the land who passed between the parts of the calf; 20 and I will give them into the hand of their enemies and into the hand of those who seek their lives. Their dead bodies shall be food for the birds of the air and the beasts of the earth. 21And Zed·e·ki′ah king of Judah, and his princes I will give into the hand of their enemies and into the hand of those who seek their lives, into the hand of the army of the king of Babylon which has withdrawn from you. 22 Behold, I will command, says the LORD, and will bring them back to this city; and they will fight against it, and take it, and burn it with fire. I will make the cities of Judah a desolation without inhabitant."

35 The word which came to Jeremiah from the LORD in the days of Je·hoi′a·kim the son of Jo·si′ah, king of Judah: 2 "Go to the house of the Re′cha·bites, and speak with them, and bring them to the house of the LORD, into one of the chambers; then offer them wine to drink." 3 So I took Ja·az·a·ni′ah the son of Jeremiah, son of Ha·baz·zi·ni′ah, and his brothers, and all his sons, and the whole house of the Re′cha·bites. 4 I brought them to the house of the LORD into the chamber of the sons of Ha′nan the son

l Gk: Heb *seven*   *m* Cn: Heb lacks *like*

of Ig·dà·lī′ah, the man of God, which was near the chamber of the princes, above the chamber of Mā·à·sēī′ah the son of Shal′lùm, keeper of the threshold. ⁵ Then I set before the Rē′chà·bites pitchers full of wine, and cups; and I said to them, "Drink wine." ⁶ But they answered, "We will drink no wine, for Jon′à·dab the son of Rē′chab, our father, commanded us, 'You shall not drink wine, neither you nor your sons for ever; ⁷ you shall not build a house; you shall not sow seed; you shall not plant or have a vineyard; but you shall live in tents all your days, that you may live many days in the land where you sojourn.' ⁸ We have obeyed the voice of Jon′à·dab the son of Rē′chab, our father, in all that he commanded us, to drink no wine all our days, ourselves, our wives, our sons, or our daughters, ⁹ and not to build houses to dwell in. We have no vineyard or field or seed; ¹⁰ but we have lived in tents, and have obeyed and done all that Jon′à·dab our father commanded us. ¹¹ But when Ne·bù·chàd·rez′zàr king of Babylon came up against the land, we said, 'Come, and let us go to Jerusalem for fear of the army of the Chal·dē′àns and the army of the Syrians.' So we are living in Jerusalem."

12 Then the word of the LORD came to Jeremiah: ¹³ "Thus says the LORD of hosts, the God of Israel: Go and say to the men of Judah and the inhabitants of Jerusalem, Will you not receive instruction and listen to my words? says the LORD. ¹⁴ The command which Jon′à·dab the son of Rē′chab gave to his sons, to drink no wine, has been kept; and they drink none to this day, for they have obeyed their father's command. I have spoken to you persistently, but you have not listened to me. ¹⁵ I have sent to you all my servants the prophets, sending them persistently, saying, 'Turn now every one of you from his evil way, and amend your doings, and do not go after other gods to serve them, and then you shall dwell in the land which I gave to you and your fathers.' But you did not incline your ear or listen to me. ¹⁶ The sons of Jon′à·dab the son of Rē′chab have kept the command which their father gave them, but this people has not obeyed me. ¹⁷ Therefore, thus says the LORD, the God of hosts, the God of Israel: Behold, I am bringing on Judah and all the inhabitants of Jerusalem all the evil that I have pronounced against them; because I have spoken to them and they

have not listened, I have called to them and they have not answered."

18 But to the house of the Rē′chà·bites Jeremiah said, "Thus says the LORD of hosts, the God of Israel: Because you have obeyed the command of Jon′à·dab your father, and kept all his precepts, and done all that he commanded you, ¹⁹ therefore thus says the LORD of hosts, the God of Israel: Jon′à·dab the son of Rē′chab shall never lack a man to stand before me."

36 In the fourth year of Je·hoi′à·kim the son of Jō·si′àh, king of Judah, this word came to Jeremiah from the LORD: ² "Take a scroll and write on it all the words that I have spoken to you against Israel and Judah and all the nations, from the day I spoke to you, from the days of Jō·si′àh until today. ³ It may be that the house of Judah will hear all the evil which I intend to do to them, so that every one may turn from his evil way, and that I may forgive their iniquity and their sin."

4 Then Jeremiah called Bâr′ùch the son of Ne·rī′àh, and Baruch wrote upon a scroll at the dictation of Jeremiah all the words of the LORD which he had spoken to him. ⁵ And Jeremiah ordered Bâr′ùch, saying, "I am debarred from going to the house of the LORD; ⁶ so you are to go, and on a fast day in the hearing of all the people in the LORD's house you shall read the words of the LORD from the scroll which you have written at my dictation. You shall read them also in the hearing of all the men of Judah who come out of their cities. ⁷ It may be that their supplication will come before the LORD, and that every one will turn from his evil way, for great is the anger and wrath that the LORD has pronounced against this people." ⁸ And Bâr′ùch the son of Ne·rī′àh did all that Jeremiah the prophet ordered him about reading from the scroll the words of the LORD in the LORD's house.

9 In the fifth year of Je·hoi′à·kim the son of Jō·si′àh, king of Judah, in the ninth month, all the people in Jerusalem and all the people who came from the cities of Judah to Jerusalem proclaimed a fast before the LORD. ¹⁰ Then, in the hearing of all the people, Bâr′ùch read the words of Jeremiah from the scroll, in the house of the LORD, in the chamber of Gem·à·rī′àh the son of Shā′phàn the secretary, which was in the upper court, at the

entry of the New Gate of the LORD's house.

11 When Mĭ·cāi'ah the son of Gem·à·rī'ah, son of Shā'phan, heard all the words of the LORD from the scroll, 12 he went down to the king's house, into the secretary's chamber; and all the princes were sitting there: E·lish'à·mà the secretary, De·lāi'ah the son of She·māi'ah, El·nā'than the son of Ach'bôr, Gem·à·rī'ah the son of Shā'phan, Zed·ĕ·kī'ah the son of Han·à·nī'ah, and all the princes. 13And Mĭ·cāi'ah told them all the words that he had heard, when Bâr'uch read the scroll in the hearing of the people. 14 Then all the princes sent Je·hū'di the son of Neth·à·nī'ah, son of Shel·ĕ·mī'ah, son of Cü'shi, to say to Bâr'uch, "Take in your hand the scroll that you read in the hearing of the people, and come." So Baruch the son of Ne·rī'ah took the scroll in his hand and came to them. 15And they said to him, "Sit down and read it." So Bâr'uch read it to them. 16 When they heard all the words, they turned one to another in fear; and they said to Bâr'uch, "We must report all these words to the king." 17 Then they asked Bâr'uch, "Tell us, how did you write all these words? Was it at his dictation?" 18 Bâr'uch answered them, "He dictated all these words to me, while I wrote them with ink on the scroll." 19 Then the princes said to Bâr'uch, "Go and hide, you and Jeremiah, and let no one know where you are."

20 So they went into the court to the king, having put the scroll in the chamber of E·lish'à·mà the secretary; and they reported all the words to the king. 21 Then the king sent Je·hū'di to get the scroll, and he took it from the chamber of E·lish'à·mà the secretary; and Je·hū'di read it to the king and all the princes who stood beside the king. 22 It was the ninth month, and the king was sitting in the winter house and there was a fire burning in the brazier before him. 23As Je·hū'di read three or four columns, the king would cut them off with a penknife and throw them into the fire in the brazier, until the entire scroll was consumed in the fire that was in the brazier. 24 Yet neither the king, nor any of his servants who heard all these words, was afraid, nor did they rend their garments. 25 Even when El·nā'than and De·lāi'ah and Gem·à·rī'ah urged the king not to burn the scroll, he would not listen to them. 26And the king commanded Jĕ·rǎh'mē·ĕl the king's son and Se·rāi'ah the son of Az'ri·el and Shel·ĕ·mī'ah the son of Ab'dĕ·ĕl to seize Bâr'uch the secretary and Jeremiah the prophet, but the LORD hid them.

27 Now, after the king had burned the scroll with the words which Bâr'uch wrote at Jeremiah's dictation, the word of the LORD came to Jeremiah: 28 "Take another scroll and write on it all the former words that were in the first scroll, which Je·hoi'à·kim king of Judah has burned. 29And concerning Je·hoi'à·kim king of Judah you shall say, 'Thus says the LORD, You have burned this scroll, saying, "Why have you written in it that the king of Babylon will certainly come and destroy this land, and will cut off from it man and beast?" 30 Therefore thus says the LORD concerning Je·hoi'à·kim king of Judah, He shall have none to sit upon the throne of David, and his dead body shall be cast out to the heat by day and the frost by night. 31And I will punish him and his offspring and his servants for their iniquity; I will bring upon the inhabitants of Jerusalem, and upon the men of Judah, all the evil that I have pronounced against them, but they would not hear.'"

32 Then Jeremiah took another scroll and gave it to Bâr'uch the scribe, the son of Ne·rī'ah, who wrote on it at the dictation of Jeremiah all the words of the scroll which Je·hoi'à·kim king of Judah had burned in the fire; and many similar words were added to them.

37 Zed·ĕ·kī'ah the son of Jō·sī'ah, whom Ne·bù·chàd·rez'zàr king of Babylon made king in the land of Judah, reigned instead of Cō·nī'ah the son of Je·hoi'à·kim. 2 But neither he nor his servants nor the people of the land listened to the words of the LORD which he spoke through Jeremiah the prophet.

3 King Zed·ĕ·kī'ah sent Je·hū'cal the son of Shel·ĕ·mī'ah, and Zeph·à·nī'ah the priest, the son of Mā·à·sēi'ah, to Jeremiah the prophet, saying, "Pray for us to the LORD our God." 4 Now Jeremiah was still going in and out among the people, for he had not yet been put in prison. 5 The army of Pharaoh had come out of Egypt; and when the Chal·dē'àns who were besieging Jerusalem heard news of them, they withdrew from Jerusalem.

6 Then the word of the LORD came to Jeremiah the prophet: 7 "Thus says the LORD, God of Israel: Thus shall you say to the king of Judah who sent

you to me to inquire of me, 'Behold, Pharaoh's army which came to help you is about to return to Egypt, to its own land. [8] And the Chal·dē´ans shall come back and fight against this city; they shall take it and burn it with fire. [9] Thus says the LORD, Do not deceive yourselves, saying, "The Chal·dē´ans will surely stay away from us," for they will not stay away. [10] For even if you should defeat the whole army of Chal·dē´ans who are fighting against you, and there remained of them only wounded men, every man in his tent, they would rise up and burn this city with fire.'"

[11] Now when the Chal·dē´an army had withdrawn from Jerusalem at the approach of Pharaoh's army, [12] Jeremiah set out from Jerusalem to go to the land of Benjamin to receive his portion[n] there among the people. [13] When he was at the Benjamin Gate, a sentry there named I·ri´jah the son of Shel·e·mi´ah, son of Han·a·ni´ah, seized Jeremiah the prophet, saying, "You are deserting to the Chal·dē´ans." [14] And Jeremiah said, "It is false; I am not deserting to the Chal·dē´ans." But I·ri´jah would not listen to him, and seized Jeremiah and brought him to the princes. [15] And the princes were enraged at Jeremiah, and they beat him and imprisoned him in the house of Jonathan the secretary, for it had been made a prison.

[16] When Jeremiah had come to the dungeon cells, and remained there many days, [17] King Zed·e·ki´ah sent for him, and received him. The king questioned him secretly in his house, and said, "Is there any word from the LORD?" Jeremiah said, "There is." Then he said, "You shall be delivered into the hand of the king of Babylon." [18] Jeremiah also said to King Zed·e·ki´ah, "What wrong have I done to you or your servants or this people, that you have put me in prison? [19] Where are your prophets who prophesied to you, saying, 'The king of Babylon will not come against you and against this land'? [20] Now hear, I pray you, O my lord the king: let my humble plea come before you, and do not send me back to the house of Jonathan the secretary, lest I die there." [21] So King Zed·e·ki´ah gave orders, and they committed Jeremiah to the court of the guard; and a loaf of bread was given him daily from the bakers' street, until all the bread of the city was gone. So Jeremiah remained in the court of the guard.

38 Now Sheph·a·ti´ah the son of Mat´tan, Ged·a·li´ah the son of Pash´hur, Ju´cal the son of Shel·e·mi´ah, and Pash´hur the son of Mal·chi´ah heard the words that Jeremiah was saying to all the people, [2] "Thus says the LORD, He who stays in this city shall die by the sword, by famine, and by pestilence; but he who goes out to the Chal·dē´ans shall live; he shall have his life as a prize of war, and live. [3] Thus says the LORD, This city shall surely be given into the hand of the army of the king of Babylon and be taken." [4] Then the princes said to the king, "Let this man be put to death, for he is weakening the hands of the soldiers who are left in this city, and the hands of all the people, by speaking such words to them. For this man is not seeking the welfare of this people, but their harm." [5] King Zed·e·ki´ah said, "Behold, he is in your hands; for the king can do nothing against you." [6] So they took Jeremiah and cast him into the cistern of Mal·chi´ah, the king's son, which was in the court of the guard, letting Jeremiah down by ropes. And there was no water in the cistern, but only mire, and Jeremiah sank in the mire.

[7] When E´bed-mel´ech the Ethiopian, a eunuch, who was in the king's house, heard that they had put Jeremiah into the cistern—the king was sitting in the Benjamin Gate— [8] E´bed-mel´ech went from the king's house and said to the king, [9] "My lord the king, these men have done evil in all that they did to Jeremiah the prophet by casting him into the cistern, and he will die there of hunger, for there is no bread left in the city." [10] Then the king commanded E´bed-mel´ech, the Ethiopian, "Take three men with you from here, and lift Jeremiah the prophet out of the cistern before he dies." [11] So E´bed-mel´ech took the men with him and went to the house of the king, to a wardrobe of[o] the storehouse, and took from there old rags and worn-out clothes, which he let down to Jeremiah in the cistern by ropes. [12] Then E´bed-mel´ech the Ethiopian said to Jeremiah, "Put the rags and clothes between your armpits and the ropes." Jeremiah did so. [13] Then they drew Jeremiah up with ropes and lifted him out of the cistern. And Jeremiah remained in the court of the guard.

[14] King Zed·e·ki´ah sent for Jeremiah the prophet and received him at the third entrance of the temple of the

---

n Heb obscure   *o* Cn: Heb *to under*

LORD. The king said to Jeremiah, "I will ask you a question; hide nothing from me." 15 Jeremiah said to Zed·e·ki′ah, "If I tell you, will you not be sure to put me to death? And if I give you counsel, you will not listen to me." 16 Then King Zed·e·ki′ah swore secretly to Jeremiah, "As the LORD lives, who made our souls, I will not put you to death or deliver you into the hand of these men who seek your life."

17 Then Jeremiah said to Zed·e·ki′ah, "Thus says the LORD, the God of hosts, the God of Israel, If you will surrender to the princes of the king of Babylon, then your life shall be spared, and this city shall not be burned with fire, and you and your house shall live. 18 But if you do not surrender to the princes of the king of Babylon, then this city shall be given into the hand of the Chal·de′ans, and they shall burn it with fire, and you shall not escape from their hand." 19 King Zed·e·ki′ah said to Jeremiah, "I am afraid of the Jews who have deserted to the Chal·de′ans, lest I be handed over to them and they abuse me." 20 Jeremiah said, "You shall not be given to them. Obey now the voice of the LORD in what I say to you, and it shall be well with you, and your life shall be spared. 21 But if you refuse to surrender, this is the vision which the LORD has shown to me: 22 Behold, all the women left in the house of the king of Judah were being led out to the princes of the king of Babylon and were saying,

'Your trusted friends have deceived you
　and prevailed against you;
now that your feet are sunk in the mire,
　they turn away from you.'

23 All your wives and your sons shall be led out to the Chal·de′ans, and you yourself shall not escape from their hand, but shall be seized by the king of Babylon; and this city shall be burned with fire."

24 Then Zed·e·ki′ah said to Jeremiah, "Let no one know of these words and you shall not die. 25 If the princes hear that I have spoken with you and come to you and say to you, 'Tell us what you said to the king and what the king said to you; hide nothing from us and we will not put you to death,' 26 then you shall say to them, 'I made a humble plea to the king that he would not send me back to the house of Jonathan to die there.'"

27 Then all the princes came to Jeremiah and asked him, and he answered them as the king had instructed him. So they left off speaking with him, for the conversation had not been overheard. 28 And Jeremiah remained in the court of the guard until the day that Jerusalem was taken.

39

In the ninth year of Zed·e·ki′ah king of Judah, in the tenth month, Ne·bu·chad·rez′zar king of Babylon and all his army came against Jerusalem and besieged it; 2 in the eleventh year of Zed·e·ki′ah, in the fourth month, on the ninth day of the month, a breach was made in the city. 3 When Jerusalem was taken,*p* all the princes of the king of Babylon came and sat in the middle gate: Ner′gal-shä·re′zer, Sam′gär-ne′bo, Sär′se·chim the Rab′sa·ris, Nergal-sharezer the Rab′mag, with all the rest of the officers of the king of Babylon. 4 When Zed·e·ki′ah king of Judah and all the soldiers saw them, they fled, going out of the city at night by way of the king's garden through the gate between the two walls; and they went toward the Ar′a·bah. 5 But the army of the Chal·de′ans pursued them, and overtook Zed·e·ki′ah in the plains of Jericho; and when they had taken him, they brought him up to Ne·bu·chad·rez′zar king of Babylon, at Rib′lah, in the land of Ha′math; and he passed sentence upon him. 6 The king of Babylon slew the sons of Zed·e·ki′ah at Rib′lah before his eyes; and the king of Babylon slew all the nobles of Judah. 7 He put out the eyes of Zed·e·ki′ah, and bound him in fetters to take him to Babylon. 8 The Chal·de′ans burned the king's house and the house of the people, and broke down the walls of Jerusalem. 9 Then Ne·bu′za·rad′an, the captain of the guard, carried into exile to Babylon the rest of the people who were left in the city, those who had deserted to him, and the people who remained. 10 Ne·bu′za·rad′an, the captain of the guard, left in the land of Judah some of the poor people who owned nothing, and gave them vineyards and fields at the same time.

11 Ne·bu·chad·rez′zar king of Babylon gave command concerning Jeremiah through Ne·bu′za·rad′an, the captain of the guard, saying, 12 "Take him, look after him well and do him no harm, but deal with him as he tells you." 13 So Ne·bu′za·rad′an the captain of the guard, Ne·bu·shaz′ban the Rab′sa·ris, Ner′gal-shä·re′zer the Rab′-

p This clause has been transposed from the end of Chapter 38

mag, and all the chief officers of the king of Babylon ¹⁴ sent and took Jeremiah from the court of the guard. They entrusted him to Ged·à·lī′ah the son of Å·hī′kam, son of Shā′phàn, that he should take him home. So he dwelt among the people.

15 The word of the LORD came to Jeremiah while he was shut up in the court of the guard: ¹⁶ "Go, and say to E′bed-mel′ech the Ethiopian, 'Thus says the LORD of hosts, the God of Israel: Behold, I will fulfil my words against this city for evil and not for good, and they shall be accomplished before you on that day. ¹⁷ But I will deliver you on that day, says the LORD, and you shall not be given into the hand of the men of whom you are afraid. ¹⁸ For I will surely save you, and you shall not fall by the sword; but you shall have your life as a prize of war, because you have put your trust in me, says the LORD.' "

40 The word that came to Jeremiah from the LORD after Ne·bū′zà·rad′àn the captain of the guard had let him go from Rā′màh, when he took him bound in chains along with all the captives of Jerusalem and Judah who were being exiled to Babylon. ² The captain of the guard took Jeremiah and said to him, "The LORD your God pronounced this evil against this place; ³ the LORD has brought it about, and has done as he said. Because you sinned against the LORD, and did not obey his voice, this thing has come upon you. ⁴ Now, behold, I release you today from the chains on your hands. If it seems good to you to come with me to Babylon, come, and I will look after you well; but if it seems wrong to you to come with me to Babylon, do not come. See, the whole land is before you; go wherever you think it good and right to go. ⁵ If you remain,ᵃ then return to Ged·à·lī′ah the son of Å·hī′kam, son of Shā′phàn, whom the king of Babylon appointed governor of the cities of Judah, and dwell with him among the people; or go wherever you think it right to go." So the captain of the guard gave him an allowance of food and a present, and let him go. ⁶ Then Jeremiah went to Ged·à·lī′ah the son of Å·hī′kam, at Miz′pàh, and dwelt with him among the people who were left in the land.

7 When all the captains of the forces in the open country and their men heard that the king of Babylon had appointed Ged·à·lī′ah the son of

Å·hī′kam governor in the land, and had committed to him men, women, and children, those of the poorest of the land who had not been taken into exile to Babylon, ⁸ they went to Ged·à·lī′ah at Miz′pàh—Ish′mà·el the son of Neth·à·nī′ah, Jō·hā′nàn the son of Kà·rē′àh, Se·rāi′àh the son of Tan′hü·meth, the sons of E′phäi the Né·toph′à·thīte, Jez·à·nī′ah the son of the Mā·ac′à·thīte, they and their men. ⁹ Ged·à·lī′ah the son of Å·hī′kam, son of Shā′phàn, swore to them and their men, saying, "Do not be afraid to serve the Chal·dē′àns. Dwell in the land, and serve the king of Babylon, and it shall be well with you. ¹⁰ As for me, I will dwell at Miz′pàh, to stand for you before the Chal·dē′àns who will come to us; but as for you, gather wine and summer fruits and oil, and store them in your vessels, and dwell in your cities that you have taken." ¹¹ Likewise, when all the Jews who were in Mō′ab and among the Am′mò·nites and in E′dòm and in other lands heard that the king of Babylon had left a remnant in Judah and had appointed Ged·à·lī′ah the son of Å·hī′kam, son of Shā′phàn, as governor over them, ¹² then all the Jews returned from all the places to which they had been driven and came to the land of Judah, to Ged·à·lī′ah at Miz′pàh; and they gathered wine and summer fruits in great abundance.

13 Now Jō·hā′nàn the son of Kà·rē′àh and all the leaders of the forces in the open country came to Ged·à·lī′ah at Miz′pàh ¹⁴ and said to him, "Do you know that Bā′à·lis the king of the Am′mò·nites has sent Ish′mà·el the son of Neth·à·nī′ah to take your life?" But Ged·à·lī′ah the son of Å·hī′kam would not believe them. ¹⁵ Then Jō·hā′nàn the son of Kà·rē′àh spoke secretly to Ged·à·lī′ah at Miz′pàh, "Let me go and slay Ish′mà·el the son of Neth·à·nī′ah, and no one will know it. Why should he take your life, so that all the Jews who are gathered about you would be scattered, and the remnant of Judah would perish?" ¹⁶ But Ged·à·lī′ah the son of Å·hī′kam said to Jō·hā′nàn the son of Kà·rē′àh, "You shall not do this thing, for you are speaking falsely of Ish′mà·el."

41 In the seventh month, Ish′mà·el the son of Neth·à·nī′ah, son of E·lish′à·mà, of the royal family, one of the chief officers of the king, came with ten men to Ged·à·lī′ah the son of Å·hī′kam, at Miz′pàh. As they ate

─────────
ᵃ Syr: Heb obscure

bread together there at Mizpah, 2 Ish'-mà·el the son of Neth·à·ni'áh and the ten men with him rose up and struck down Ged·à·li'áh the son of Á·hi'kam, son of Shā'phàn, with the sword, and killed him, whom the king of Babylon had appointed governor in the land. 3 Ish'mà·el also slew all the Jews who were with Ged·à·li'áh at Miz'pàh, and the Chal·dē'án soldiers who happened to be there.

4 On the day after the murder of Ged·à·li'áh, before any one knew of it, 5 eighty men arrived from Shē'chem and Shi'lōh and Sà·mâr'i·à, with their beards shaved and their clothes torn, and their bodies gashed, bringing cereal offerings and incense to present at the temple of the LORD. 6And Ish'mà·el the son of Neth·à·ni'áh came out from Miz'pàh to meet them, weeping as he came. As he met them, he said to them, "Come in to Ged·à·li'áh the son of Á·hi'kam." 7 When they came into the city, Ish'mà·el the son of Neth·à·ni'áh and the men with him slew them, and cast them into a cistern. 8 But there were ten men among them who said to Ish'mà·el, "Do not kill us, for we have stores of wheat, barley, oil, and honey hidden in the fields." So he refrained and did not kill them with their companions.

9 Now the cistern into which Ish'-mà·el cast all the bodies of the men whom he had slain was the large cistern[r] which King Asa had made for defense against Bā'à·shà king of Israel; Ishmael the son of Neth·à·ni'áh filled it with the slain. 10 Then Ish'mà·el took captive all the rest of the people who were in Miz'pàh, the king's daughters and all the people who were left at Mizpah, whom Ne·bū'zà·rad'án, the captain of the guard, had committed to Ged·à·li'áh the son of Á·hi'-kam. Ishmael the son of Neth·à·ni'áh took them captive and set out to cross over to the Am'mò·nites.

11 But when Jō·hā'nàn the son of Kà·rē'áh and all the leaders of the forces with him heard of all the evil which Ish'mà·el the son of Neth·à·ni'áh had done, 12 they took all their men and went to fight against Ish'-mà·el the son of Neth·à·ni'áh. They came upon him at the great pool which is in Gib'ē·ón. 13And when all the people who were with Ish'mà·el saw Jō·hā'nàn the son of Kà·rē'áh and all the leaders of the forces with him, they rejoiced. 14 So all the people whom Ish'mà·el had carried away

captive from Miz'páh turned about and came back, and went to Jō·hā'nàn the son of Kà·rē'áh. 15 But Ish'mà·el the son of Neth·à·ni'áh escaped from Jō·hā'nàn with eight men, and went to the Am'mò·nites. 16 Then Jō·hā'nàn the son of Kà·rē'áh and all the leaders of the forces with him took all the rest of the people whom Ish'mà·el the son of Neth·à·ni'áh had carried away cap-tive[s] from Miz'páh after he had slain Ged·à·li'áh the son of Á·hi'kam—soldiers, women, children, and eu-nuchs, whom Jō·hā'nàn brought back from Gib'ē·ón. 17And they went and stayed at Gē'rüth Chim'hàm near Bethlehem, intending to go to Egypt 18 because of the Chal·dē'áns; for they were afraid of them, because Ish'-mà·el the son of Neth·à·ni'áh had slain Ged·à·li'áh the son of Á·hi'kam, whom the king of Babylon had made governor over the land.

42 Then all the commanders of the forces, and Jō·hā'nàn the son of Kà·rē'áh and Az·à·ri'áh[t] the son of Hō·shäi'áh, and all the people from the least to the greatest, came near 2 and said to Jeremiah the prophet, "Let our supplication come before you, and pray to the LORD your God for us, for all this remnant (for we are left but a few of many, as your eyes see us), 3 that the LORD your God may show us the way we should go, and the thing that we should do." 4 Jeremiah the prophet said to them, "I have heard you; behold, I will pray to the LORD your God according to your request, and whatever the LORD answers you I will tell you; I will keep nothing back from you." 5 Then they said to Jeremiah, "May the LORD be a true and faithful witness against us if we do not act according to all the word with which the LORD your God sends you to us. 6 Whether it is good or evil, we will obey the voice of the LORD our God to whom we are sending you, that it may be well with us when we obey the voice of the LORD our God."

7 At the end of ten days the word of the LORD came to Jeremiah. 8 Then he summoned Jō·hā'nàn the son of Kà·rē'áh and all the commanders of the forces who were with him, and all the people from the least to the great-est, 9 and said to them, "Thus says the LORD, the God of Israel, to whom you sent me to present your supplica-tion before him: 10 If you will remain in this land, then I will build you up and not pull you down; I will plant

---

[r] Gk: Heb *he had slain by the hand of Gedaliah*

[s] Cn: Heb *whom he recovered from Ishmael*   [t] Gk: Heb *Jezaniah*

you, and not pluck you up; for I repent of the evil which I did to you. 11 Do not fear the king of Babylon, of whom you are afraid; do not fear him, says the LORD, for I am with you, to save you and to deliver you from his hand. 12 I will grant you mercy, that he may have mercy on you and let you remain in your own land. 13 But if you say, 'We will not remain in this land,' disobeying the voice of the LORD your God 14 and saying, 'No, we will go to the land of Egypt, where we shall not see war, or hear the sound of the trumpet, or be hungry for bread, and we will dwell there,' 15 then hear the word of the LORD, O remnant of Judah. Thus says the LORD of hosts, the God of Israel: If you set your faces to enter Egypt and go to live there, 16 then the sword which you fear shall overtake you there in the land of Egypt; and the famine of which you are afraid shall follow hard after you to Egypt; and there you shall die. 17All the men who set their faces to go to Egypt to live there shall die by the sword, by famine, and by pestilence; they shall have no remnant or survivor from the evil which I will bring upon them.

18 "For thus says the LORD of hosts, the God of Israel: As my anger and my wrath were poured out on the inhabitants of Jerusalem, so my wrath will be poured out on you when you go to Egypt. You shall become an execration, a horror, a curse, and a taunt. You shall see this place no more. 19 The LORD has said to you, O remnant of Judah, 'Do not go to Egypt.' Know for a certainty that I have warned you this day 20 that you have gone astray at the cost of your lives. For you sent me to the LORD your God, saying, 'Pray for us to the LORD our God, and whatever the LORD our God says declare to us and we will do it.' 21And I have this day declared it to you, but you have not obeyed the voice of the LORD your God in anything that he sent me to tell you. 22 Now therefore know for a certainty that you shall die by the sword, by famine, and by pestilence in the place where you desire to go to live."

43 When Jeremiah finished speaking to all the people all these words of the LORD their God with which the LORD their God had sent him to them, 2Az·a·rī'ah the son of Hō·shäi'ah and Jō·hā'nän the son of Kà·rē'ah and all the insolent men said to Jeremiah, "You are telling a lie. The

LORD our God did not send you to say, 'Do not go to Egypt to live there'; 3 but Bâr'uch the son of Ne·rī'ah has set you against us, to deliver us into the hand of the Chal·dē'ans, that they may kill us or take us into exile in Babylon." 4 So Jō·hā'nän the son of Kà·rē'ah and all the commanders of the forces and all the people did not obey the voice of the LORD, to remain in the land of Judah. 5 But Jō·hā'nän the son of Kà·rē'ah and all the commanders of the forces took all the remnant of Judah who had returned to live in the land of Judah from all the nations to which they had been driven—6 the men, the women, the children, the princesses, and every person whom Ne·bū'zà·rad'än the captain of the guard had left with Ged·à·lī'äh the son of À·hī'kam, son of Shā'phän; also Jeremiah the prophet and Bâr'uch the son of Ne·rī'ah. 7And they came into the land of Egypt, for they did not obey the voice of the LORD. And they arrived at Täh'pàn·hĕš.

8 Then the word of the LORD came to Jeremiah in Täh'pàn·hĕš: 9 "Take in your hands large stones, and hide them in the mortar in the pavement which is at the entrance to Pharaoh's palace in Täh'pàn·hĕš, in the sight of the men of Judah, 10 and say to them, 'Thus says the LORD of hosts, the God of Israel: Behold, I will send and take Ne·bù·chàd·rez'zàr the king of Babylon, my servant, and he[u] will set his throne above these stones which I have hid, and he will spread his royal canopy over them. 11 He shall come and smite the land of Egypt, giving to the pestilence those who are doomed to the pestilence, to captivity those who are doomed to captivity, and to the sword those who are doomed to the sword. 12 He[v] shall kindle a fire in the temples of the gods of Egypt; and he shall burn them and carry them away captive; and he shall clean the land of Egypt, as a shepherd cleans his cloak of vermin; and he shall go away from there in peace. 13 He shall break the obelisks of Hē·lĭ·ŏp'ŏ·lis which is in the land of Egypt; and the temples of the gods of Egypt he shall burn with fire.'"

44 The word that came to Jeremiah concerning all the Jews that dwelt in the land of Egypt, at Mig'dōl, at Täh'pàn·hĕš, at Memphis, and in the land of Path'ros, 2 "Thus says the LORD of hosts, the God of Israel: You have seen all the evil that

u Gk Syr: Heb *I*   *v* Gk Syr Vg: Heb *I*

I brought upon Jerusalem and upon all the cities of Judah. Behold, this day they are a desolation, and no one dwells in them, 3 because of the wickedness which they committed, provoking me to anger, in that they went to burn incense and serve other gods that they knew not, neither they, nor you, nor your fathers. 4 Yet I persistently sent to you all my servants the prophets, saying, 'Oh, do not do this abominable thing that I hate!' 5 But they did not listen or incline their ear, to turn from their wickedness and burn no incense to other gods. 6 Therefore my wrath and my anger were poured forth and kindled in the cities of Judah and in the streets of Jerusalem; and they became a waste and a desolation, as at this day. 7And now thus says the LORD God of hosts, the God of Israel: Why do you commit this great evil against yourselves, to cut off from you man and woman, infant and child, from the midst of Judah, leaving you no remnant? 8 Why do you provoke me to anger with the works of your hands, burning incense to other gods in the land of Egypt where you have come to live, that you may be cut off and become a curse and a taunt among all the nations of the earth? 9 Have you forgotten the wickedness of your fathers, the wickedness of the kings of Judah, the wickedness of their*w* wives, your own wickedness, and the wickedness of your wives, which they committed in the land of Judah and in the streets of Jerusalem? 10 They have not humbled themselves even to this day, nor have they feared, nor walked in my law and my statutes which I set before you and before your fathers.

11 "Therefore thus says the LORD of hosts, the God of Israel: Behold, I will set my face against you for evil, to cut off all Judah. 12 I will take the remnant of Judah who have set their faces to come to the land of Egypt to live, and they shall all be consumed; in the land of Egypt they shall fall; by the sword and by famine they shall be consumed; from the least to the greatest, they shall die by the sword and by famine; and they shall become an execration, a horror, a curse, and a taunt. 13 I will punish those who dwell in the land of Egypt, as I have punished Jerusalem, with the sword, with famine, and with pestilence, 14 so that none of the remnant of Judah who have come to live in the land of Egypt shall escape or survive or return to the land of Judah, to which they desire to

return to dwell there; for they shall not return, except some fugitives."

15 Then all the men who knew that their wives had offered incense to other gods, and all the women who stood by, a great assembly, all the people who dwelt in Path'ros in the land of Egypt, answered Jeremiah: 16 "As for the word which you have spoken to us in the name of the LORD, we will not listen to you. 17 But we will do everything that we have vowed, burn incense to the queen of heaven and pour out libations to her, as we did, both we and our fathers, our kings and our princes, in the cities of Judah and in the streets of Jerusalem; for then we had plenty of food, and prospered, and saw no evil. 18 But since we left off burning incense to the queen of heaven and pouring out libations to her, we have lacked everything and have been consumed by the sword and by famine." 19And the women said,*x* "When we burned incense to the queen of heaven and poured out libations to her, was it without our husbands' approval that we made cakes for her bearing her image and poured out libations to her?"

20 Then Jeremiah said to all the people, men and women, all the people who had given him this answer: 21 "As for the incense that you burned in the cities of Judah and in the streets of Jerusalem, you and your fathers, your kings and your princes, and the people of the land, did not the LORD remember it?*y* Did it not come into his mind? 22 The LORD could no longer bear your evil doings and the abominations which you committed; therefore your land has become a desolation and a waste and a curse, without inhabitant, as it is this day. 23 It is because you burned incense, and because you sinned against the LORD and did not obey the voice of the LORD or walk in his law and in his statutes and in his testimonies, that this evil has befallen you, as at this day."

24 Jeremiah said to all the people and all the women, "Hear the word of the LORD, all you of Judah who are in the land of Egypt, 25 Thus says the LORD of hosts, the God of Israel: You and your wives have declared with your mouths, and have fulfilled it with your hands, saying, 'We will surely perform our vows that we have made to burn incense to the queen of heaven and to pour out libations to her.' Then confirm your vows and perform your vows! 26 Therefore hear the word of

w Heb *his*   *x* Compare Syr: Heb lacks *And the women said*   *y* Syr: Heb *them*

the Lord, all you of Judah who dwell in the land of Egypt: Behold, I have sworn by my great name, says the Lord, that my name shall no more be invoked by the mouth of any man of Judah in all the land of Egypt, saying, 'As the Lord God lives.' 27 Behold, I am watching over them for evil and not for good; all the men of Judah who are in the land of Egypt shall be consumed by the sword and by famine, until there is an end of them. 28And those who escape the sword shall return from the land of Egypt to the land of Judah, few in number; and all the remnant of Judah, who came to the land of Egypt to live, shall know whose word will stand, mine or theirs. 29 This shall be the sign to you, says the Lord, that I will punish you in this place, in order that you may know that my words will surely stand against you for evil: 30 Thus says the Lord, Behold, I will give Pharaoh Hoph'ra king of Egypt into the hand of his enemies and into the hand of those who seek his life, as I gave Zed·e·ki'ah king of Judah into the hands of Ne·bu·chad·rez'zar king of Babylon, who was his enemy and sought his life."

45 The word that Jeremiah the prophet spoke to Bâr'uch the son of Ne·ri'ah, when he wrote these words in a book at the dictation of Jeremiah, in the fourth year of Je·hoi'a·kim the son of Jo·si'ah, king of Judah: 2 "Thus says the Lord, the God of Israel, to you, O Bâr'uch: 3 You said, 'Woe is me! for the Lord has added sorrow to my pain; I am weary with my groaning, and I find no rest.' 4 Thus shall you say to him, Thus says the Lord: Behold, what I have built I am breaking down, and what I have planted I am plucking up—that is, the whole land. 5And do you seek great things for yourself? Seek them not; for, behold, I am bringing evil upon all flesh, says the Lord; but I will give you your life as a prize of war in all places to which you may go."

46 The word of the Lord which came to Jeremiah the prophet concerning the nations.

2 About Egypt. Concerning the army of Pharaoh Nē'cō, king of Egypt, which was by the river Eū·phrā'tēs at Cär'chē·mish and which Ne·bu·chad·rez'zar king of Babylon defeated in the fourth year of Je·hoi'a·kim the son of Jo·si'ah, king of Judah:

3 "Prepare buckler and shield,
    and advance for battle!
4 Harness the horses;
    mount, O horsemen!
Take your stations with your helmets,
    polish your spears,
    put on your coats of mail!
5 Why have I seen it?
They are dismayed
    and have turned backward.
Their warriors are beaten down,
    and have fled in haste;
they look not back—
    terror on every side!
              says the Lord.
6 The swift cannot flee away,
    nor the warrior escape;
in the north by the river Eū·phrā'tēs
    they have stumbled and fallen.

7 "Who is this, rising like the Nile,
    like rivers whose waters surge?
8 Egypt rises like the Nile,
    like rivers whose waters surge.
He said, I will rise, I will cover the earth,
    I will destroy cities and their inhabitants.
9 Advance, O horses,
    and rage, O chariots!
Let the warriors go forth:
    men of Ethiopia and Püt who handle the shield,
    men of Lüd, skilled in handling the bow.
10 That day is the day of the Lord God of hosts,
    a day of vengeance,
    to avenge himself on his foes.
The sword shall devour and be sated,
    and drink its fill of their blood.
For the Lord God of hosts holds a sacrifice
    in the north country by the river Eū·phrā'tēs.
11 Go up to Gilead, and take balm,
    O virgin daughter of Egypt!
In vain you have used many medicines;
    there is no healing for you.
12 The nations have heard of your shame,
    and the earth is full of your cry;
for warrior has stumbled against warrior;
    they have both fallen together."

13 The word which the Lord spoke to Jeremiah the prophet about the coming of Ne·bu·chad·rez'zar king of Babylon to smite the land of Egypt:

14 "Declare in Egypt, and proclaim in
    Mig'dōl;
  proclaim in Memphis and Täh'-
    pån·hĕś;
  Say, 'Stand ready and be prepared,
    for the sword shall devour round
    about you.'
15 Why has A'pis fled?*z*
  Why did not your bull stand?
  Because the LORD thrust him
    down.
16 Your multitude stumbled*a* and fell,
    and they said one to another,
  'Arise, and let us go back to our
    own people
  and to the land of our birth,
    because of the sword of the op-
    pressor.'
17 Call the name of Pharaoh, king of
    Egypt,
  'Noisy one who lets the hour go by.'

18 "As I live, says the King,
    whose name is the LORD of hosts,
  like Tā'bôr among the mountains,
    and like Cär'mĕl by the sea, shall
    one come.
19 Prepare yourselves baggage for
    exile,
  O inhabitants of Egypt!
  For Memphis shall become a waste,
    a ruin, without inhabitant.

20 "A beautiful heifer is Egypt,
    but a gadfly from the north has
    come upon her.
21 Even her hired soldiers in her midst
    are like fatted calves;
  yea, they have turned and fled to-
    gether,
    they did not stand;
  for the day of their calamity has
    come upon them,
    the time of their punishment.

22 "She makes a sound like a serpent
    gliding away;
  for her enemies march in force,
  and come against her with axes,
    like those who fell trees.
23 They shall cut down her forest,
              says the LORD,
    though it is impenetrable,
  because they are more numerous
    than locusts;
    they are without number.
24 The daughter of Egypt shall be put
    to shame,
  she shall be delivered into the
    hand of a people from the
    north."

25 The LORD of hosts, the God of

Israel, said: "Behold, I am bringing
punishment upon Ā'mon of Thebes,
and Pharaoh, and Egypt and her gods
and her kings, upon Pharaoh and those
who trust in him. 26 I will deliver them
into the hand of those who seek their
life, into the hand of Ne·bu·chăd·rez'-
zår king of Babylon and his officers.
Afterward Egypt shall be inhabited as
in the days of old, says the LORD.

27 "But fear not, O Jacob my servant,
    nor be dismayed, O Israel;
  for lo, I will save you from afar,
    and your offspring from the land
    of their captivity.
  Jacob shall return and have quiet
    and ease,
    and none shall make him afraid.
28 Fear not, O Jacob my servant,
              says the LORD,
    for I am with you.
  I will make a full end of all the
    nations
    to which I have driven you,
  but of you I will not make a full end.
  I will chasten you in just measure,
    and I will by no means leave you
    unpunished."

47 The word of the LORD that
    came to Jeremiah the prophet
concerning the Philistines, before
Pharaoh smote Gā'zà.
2 "Thus says the LORD:
  Behold, waters are rising out of the
    north,
    and shall become an overflowing
    torrent;
  they shall overflow the land and all
    that fills it,
    the city and those who dwell in it.
  Men shall cry out,
    and every inhabitant of the land
    shall wail.
3 At the noise of the stamping of the
    hoofs of his stallions,
    at the rushing of his chariots, at
    the rumbling of their wheels,
  the fathers look not back to their
    children,
    so feeble are their hands,
4 because of the day that is coming
    to destroy
    all the Philistines,
  to cut off from Tyre and Si'don
    every helper that remains.
  For the LORD is destroying the
    Philistines,
    the remnant of the coastland of
    Caph'tor.
5 Baldness has come upon Gā'zà
    Ash'kĕ·lon has perished.

z Gk: Heb *Why was it swept away*   *a* Gk: Heb *He made many stumble*
47: Is 14.29-31; Ezek 25.15-17; Amos 1.6-8; Zeph 2.4-7; Zech 9.5-7.

O remnant of the An′a·kim,[b]
  how long will you gash your-
    selves?
6 Ah, sword of the LORD!
  How long till you are quiet?
Put yourself into your scabbard,
  rest and be still!
7 How can it[c] be quiet,
  when the LORD has given it a
    charge?
Against Ash′ke·lon and against the
  seashore
  he has appointed it.”

48 Concerning Mō′ab.
    Thus says the LORD of hosts,
the God of Israel:
  “Woe to Ne′bō, for it is laid waste!
  Kir·i·a·thā′im is put to shame, it
    is taken;
  the fortress is put to shame and
    broken down;
2   the renown of Mō′ab is no more.
In Hesh′bon they planned evil
  against her:
  ‘Come, let us cut her off from
    being a nation!’
You also, O Madmen, shall be
  brought to silence;
  the sword shall pursue you.

3 “Hark! a cry from Hor·ō·nā′im,
  ‘Desolation and great destruc-
    tion!’
4 Mō′ab is destroyed;
  a cry is heard as far as Zō′ar.[d]
5 For at the ascent of Lū′hith
  they go up weeping;[e]
for at the descent of Hor·ō·nā′im
  they have heard the cry[f] of de-
    struction.
6 Flee! Save yourselves!
  Be like a wild ass[g] in the desert!
7 For, because you trusted in your
  strongholds[h] and your treasures,
  you also shall be taken;
and Chē′mosh shall go forth into
  exile,
  with his priests and his princes.
8 The destroyer shall come upon every
  city,
  and no city shall escape;
the valley shall perish,
  and the plain shall be destroyed,
  as the LORD has spoken.

9 “Give wings to Mō′ab,
  for she would fly away;
her cities shall become a desolation,
  with no inhabitant in them.

10 “Cursed is he who does the work
of the LORD with slackness; and cursed
is he who keeps back his sword from
bloodshed.

11 “Mō′ab has been at ease from his
  youth
  and has settled on his lees;
he has not been emptied from vessel
  to vessel,
  nor has he gone into exile;
so his taste remains in him,
  and his scent is not changed.

12 “Therefore, behold, the days are
coming, says the LORD, when I shall
send to him tilters who will tilt him,
and empty his vessels, and break his[i]
jars in pieces. 13 Then Mō′ab shall be
ashamed of Chē′mosh, as the house of
Israel was ashamed of Beth′el, their
confidence.

14 “How do you say, ‘We are heroes
  and mighty men of war’?
15 The destroyer of Mō′ab and his
  cities has come up,
  and the choicest of his young men
  have gone down to slaughter,
  says the King, whose name is the
    LORD of hosts.
16 The calamity of Mō′ab is near at
  hand
  and his affliction hastens apace.
17 Bemoan him, all you who are round
  about him,
  and all who know his name;
say, ‘How the mighty scepter is
  broken,
  the glorious staff.’

18 “Come down from your glory,
  and sit on the parched ground,
  O inhabitant of Dī′bon!
For the destroyer of Mō′ab has
  come up against you;
  he has destroyed your strong-
    holds.
19 Stand by the way and watch,
  O inhabitant of A·rō′er!
Ask him who flees and her who
  escapes;
  say, ‘What has happened?’
20 Mō′ab is put to shame, for it is
  broken;
  wail and cry!
Tell it by the Ar′non,
  that Moab is laid waste.

21 “Judgment has come upon the
tableland, upon Hō′lon, and Jäh′zah,

---

b Gk: Heb *their valley*   c Gk Vg: Heb *you*   d Gk: Heb *her little ones*
e Cn: Heb *weeping goes up with weeping*
f Gk Compare Is 15.5: Heb *the distress of the cry*   g Gk Aquila: Heb *like Aroer*
h Gk: Heb *works*   i Gk Aquila: Heb *their*
48: Is 15-16; 25.10-12; Ezek 25.8-11; Amos 2.1-3; Zeph 2.8-11.

and Meph'a-ath, 22 and Dī'bon, and Nē'bō, and Beth-dib·lā·thā'im, 23 and Kīr·i·ā·thā'im, and Beth-gā'mŭl, and Beth-mē'on, 24 and Ker'i·oth, and Boz'rah, and all the cities of the land of Mō'ab, far and near. 25 The horn of Mō'ab is cut off, and his arm is broken, says the LORD.

26 "Make him drunk, because he magnified himself against the LORD; so that Mō'ab shall wallow in his vomit, and he too shall be held in derision. 27 Was not Israel a derision to you? Was he found among thieves, that whenever you spoke of him you wagged your head?

28 "Leave the cities, and dwell in the
　　rock,
　　O inhabitants of Mō'ab!
Be like the dove that nests
　　in the sides of the mouth of a
　　gorge.
29 We have heard of the pride of
　　Mō'ab—
　　he is very proud—
of his loftiness, his pride, and his
　　arrogance,
　　and the haughtiness of his heart.
30 I know his insolence, says the LORD;
　　his boasts are false,
　　his deeds are false.
31 Therefore I wail for Mō'ab;
　　I cry out for all Moab;
　　for the men of Kīr-hē'res I mourn.
32 More than for Jā'zēr I weep for
　　you,
　　O vine of Sib'mah!
Your branches passed over the sea,
　　reached as far as Jazer;[j]
upon your summer fruits and your
　　vintage
　　the destroyer has fallen.
33 Gladness and joy have been taken
　　away
　　from the fruitful land of Mō'ab;
I have made the wine cease from
　　the wine presses;
　　no one treads them with shouts
　　of joy;
　　the shouting is not the shout of
　　joy.

34 "Hesh'bŏn and Ĕ·lĕ·ā'lĕh cry out;[k] as far as Jā'haz they utter their voice, from Zō'ar to Hor-ō·nā'im and Eg'lăth-she·lish'i·yăh. For the waters of Nim'rim also have become desolate. 35 And I will bring to an end in Mō'ab, says the LORD, him who offers sacrifice in the high place and burns incense to his god. 36 Therefore my heart moans

for Mō'ab like a flute, and my heart moans like a flute for the men of Kīr-hē'res; therefore the riches they gained have perished.

37 "For every head is shaved and every beard cut off; upon all the hands are gashes, and on the loins is sackcloth. 38 On all the housetops of Mō'ab and in the squares there is nothing but lamentation; for I have broken Moab like a vessel for which no one cares, says the LORD. 39 How it is broken! How they wail! How Mō'ab has turned his back in shame! So Moab has become a derision and a horror to all that are round about him."

40 For thus says the LORD:
"Behold, one shall fly swiftly like
　　an eagle,
　　and spread his wings against
　　Mō'ab;
41 the cities shall be taken
　　and the strongholds seized.
The heart of the warriors of Mō'ab
　　shall be in that day
　　like the heart of a woman in her
　　pangs;
42 Mō'ab shall be destroyed and be
　　no longer a people,
　　because he magnified himself
　　against the LORD.
43 Terror, pit, and snare
　　are before you, O inhabitant of
　　Mō'ab!
　　　　　　　　　　says the LORD.
44 He who flees from the terror
　　shall fall into the pit,
and he who climbs out of the pit
　　shall be caught in the snare.
For I will bring these things[l] upon
　　Mō'ab
　　in the year of their punishment,
　　　　　　　　　　says the LORD.

45 "In the shadow of Hesh'bŏn
　　fugitives stop without strength;
for a fire has gone forth from
　　Heshbon,
　　a flame from the house of Sī'hon;
it has destroyed the forehead of
　　Mō'ab,
　　the crown of the sons of tumult.
46 Woe to you, O Mō'ab!
　　The people of Chē'mosh is un-
　　done;
for your sons have been taken
　　captive,
　　and your daughters into captivity.
47 Yet I will restore the fortunes of
　　Mō'ab
　　in the latter days, says the LORD."
Thus far is the judgment on Mō'ab.

j Cn: Heb *the sea of Jazer*
k Cn: Heb *From the cry of Heshbon to Elealeh*
l Gk Syr: Heb *to her*

49

Concerning the Am′mo·nites.
Thus says the LORD:

"Has Israel no sons?
    Has he no heir?
Why then has Mil′com dispossessed
        Gad,
    and his people settled in its cities?
2 Therefore, behold, the days are
        coming,
    says the LORD,
when I will cause the battle cry to
        be heard
    against Rab′bah of the Am′mo·
        nites;
it shall become a desolate mound,
    and its villages shall be burned
        with fire;
then Israel shall dispossess those
        who dispossessed him,
    says the LORD.

3 "Wail, O Hesh′bon, for Ai is laid
        waste!
    Cry, O daughters of Rab′bah!
Gird yourselves with sackcloth,
    lament, and run to and fro among
        the hedges!
For Mil′com shall go into exile,
    with his priests and his princes.
4 Why do you boast of your valleys,ᵐ
    O faithless daughter,
who trusted in her treasures, saying,
    'Who will come against me?'
5 Behold, I will bring terror upon you,
    says the Lord GOD of hosts,
from all who are round about you,
    and you shall be driven out, every
        man straight before him,
    with none to gather the fugitives.
6 But afterward I will restore the
fortunes of the Am′mo·nites, says the
LORD."

7 Concerning E′dom.
Thus says the LORD of hosts:

"Is wisdom no more in Te′man?
    Has counsel perished from the
        prudent?
    Has their wisdom vanished?
8 Flee, turn back, dwell in the depths,
    O inhabitants of De′dan!
For I will bring the calamity of Esau
        upon him,
    the time when I punish him.
9 If grape-gatherers came to you,
    would they not leave gleanings?
If thieves came by night,
    would they not destroy only
        enough for themselves?
10 But I have stripped Esau bare,
    I have uncovered his hiding
        places,

and he is not able to conceal
    himself.
His children are destroyed, and his
        brothers,
    and his neighbors; and he is no
        more.
11 Leave your fatherless children, I
        will keep them alive;
    and let your widows trust in me."
12 For thus says the LORD: "If
those who did not deserve to drink the
cup must drink it, will you go unpunished? You shall not go unpunished, but you must drink. 13 For I
have sworn by myself, says the LORD,
that Boz′rah shall become a horror, a
taunt, a waste, and a curse; and all her
cities shall be perpetual wastes."
14 I have heard tidings from the LORD,
    and a messenger has been sent
        among the nations:
"Gather yourselves together and
        come against her,
    and rise up for battle!"
15 For behold, I will make you small
        among the nations,
    despised among men.
16 The horror you inspire has deceived
        you,
    and the pride of your heart,
you who live in the clefts of the
        rock,ⁿ
    who hold the height of the hill.
Though you make your nest as high
        as the eagle's,
    I will bring you down from there,
        says the LORD.

17 "E′dom shall become a horror;
every one who passes by it will be
horrified and will hiss because of all
its disasters. 18As when Sod′om and
Go·mor′rah and their neighbor cities
were overthrown, says the LORD, no
man shall dwell there, no man shall
sojourn in her. 19 Behold, like a lion
coming up from the jungle of the
Jordan against a strong sheepfold, I
will suddenly make themᵒ run away
from her; and I will appoint over her
whomever I choose. For who is like
me? Who will summon me? What
shepherd can stand before me?
20 Therefore hear the plan which the
LORD has made against E′dom and the
purposes which he has formed against
the inhabitants of Te′man: Even the
little ones of the flock shall be dragged
away; surely their fold shall be
appalled at their fate. 21At the sound
of their fall the earth shall tremble; the
sound of their cry shall be heard at the
Red Sea. 22 Behold, one shall mount

ᵐ Heb valleys, your valley flows   ⁿ Or Sela   ᵒ Gk Syr: Heb him
49.1-6: Ezek 21.28-32; 25.1-7; Amos 1.13-15; Zeph 2.8-11.
49.7-22: Is 34; 63.1-6; Ezek 25.12-14; 35; Amos 1.11-12; Obad; Mal 1.2-5.

up and fly swiftly like an eagle, and
spread his wings against Bozʹráh, and
the heart of the warriors of Eʹdŏm shall
be in that day like the heart of a
woman in her pangs.''

23 Concerning Damascus.
"Hăʹmath and Ärʹpad are confounded,
  for they have heard evil tidings;
they melt in fear, they are troubled
  like the sea[p]
  which cannot be quiet.
24 Damascus has become feeble, she
  turned to flee,
  and panic seized her;
anguish and sorrows have taken hold
  of her,
  as of a woman in travail.
25 How the famous city is forsaken,[q]
  the joyful city![r]
26 Therefore her young men shall fall
  in her squares,
  and all her soldiers shall be destroyed in that day,
           says the LORD of hosts.
27 And I will kindle a fire in the wall
  of Damascus,
  and it shall devour the strongholds of Ben-hăʹdad.''

28 Concerning Kĕʹdär and the kingdoms of Hăʹzôr which Ne·bů·chădʹ-
rezʹzăr king of Babylon smote.
Thus says the LORD:
"Rise up, advance against Kedar!
  Destroy the people of the east!
29 Their tents and their flocks shall be
  taken,
  their curtains and all their goods;
their camels shall be borne away
  from them,
  and men shall cry to them:
  'Terror on every side!'
30 Flee, wander far away, dwell in the
  depths,
  O inhabitants of Hăʹzôr!
           says the LORD.
for Ne·bů·chăd·rezʹzăr king of
  Babylon
  has made a plan against you,
  and formed a purpose against you.

31 "Rise up, advance against a nation
  at ease,
  that dwells securely,
           says the LORD,
that has no gates or bars,
  that dwells alone.
32 Their camels shall become booty,
  their herds of cattle a spoil.

I will scatter to every wind
  those who cut the corners of their
  hair,
  and I will bring their calamity
  from every side of them,
           says the LORD.
33 Hăʹzôr shall become a haunt of
  jackals,
  and everlasting waste;
no man shall dwell there,
  no man shall sojourn in her.''

34 The word of the LORD that came
to Jeremiah the prophet concerning
Eʹlăm, in the beginning of the reign
of Zed·ė·kiʹăh king of Judah.
35 Thus says the LORD of hosts:
"Behold, I will break the bow of
Eʹlăm, the mainstay of their might;
36 and I will bring upon Eʹlăm the
four winds from the four quarters of
heaven; and I will scatter them to all
those winds, and there shall be no
nation to which those driven out of
Elam shall not come. 37 I will terrify
Eʹlăm before their enemies, and before
those who seek their life; I will bring
evil upon them, my fierce anger, says
the LORD. I will send the sword after
them, until I have consumed them;
38 and I will set my throne in Eʹlăm,
and destroy their king and princes,
says the LORD.
39 "But in the latter days I will
restore the fortunes of Eʹlăm, says the
LORD.''

50 The word which the LORD
    spoke concerning Babylon, con-
cerning the land of the Chal·dėʹănś, by
Jeremiah the prophet:
2 "Declare among the nations and
  proclaim,
  set up a banner and proclaim,
  conceal it not, and say:
'Babylon is taken,
  Bel is put to shame,
  Merʹô·dach is dismayed.
Her images are put to shame,
  her idols are dismayed.'
3 "For out of the north a nation has
come up against her, which shall make
her land a desolation, and none shall
dwell in it; both man and beast shall
flee away.

4 "In those days and in that time,
says the LORD, the people of Israel and
the people of Judah shall come together, weeping as they come; and
they shall seek the LORD their God.

[p] Cn: Heb *there is trouble in the sea*   [q] Vg: Heb *not forsaken*
[r] Syr Vg Tg: Heb *city of my joy*

49.23-27: Is 17.1-3; Amos 1.3-5; Zech 9.1.   49.29: Ps 31.13; Jer 6.25; 20.3, 10; 46.5.
50-51: Is 13.1-14.23; 47; Hab 1-2.

5 They shall ask the way to Zion, with faces turned toward it, saying, 'Come, let us join ourselves to the LORD in an everlasting covenant which will never be forgotten.'

6 "My people have been lost sheep;
their shepherds have led them astray,
turning them away on the mountains;
from mountain to hill they have gone,
they have forgotten their fold. 7All who found them have devoured them, and their enemies have said, 'We are not guilty, for they have sinned against the LORD, their true habitation, the LORD, the hope of their fathers.'

8 "Flee from the midst of Babylon, and go out of the land of the Chal·dē′-ǎns, and be as he-goats before the flock. 9 For behold, I am stirring up and bringing against Babylon a company of great nations, from the north country; and they shall array themselves against her; from there she shall be taken. Their arrows are like a skilled warrior who does not return empty-handed. 10 Chal·dē′ǎ shall be plundered; all who plunder her shall be sated, says the LORD.

11 "Though you rejoice, though you exult,
O plunderers of my heritage,
though you are wanton as a heifer at grass,
and neigh like stallions,
12 your mother shall be utterly shamed,
and she who bore you shall be disgraced.
Lo, she shall be the last of the nations,
a wilderness dry and desert.
13 Because of the wrath of the LORD she shall not be inhabited,
but shall be an utter desolation;
every one who passes by Babylon shall be appalled,
and hiss because of all her wounds.
14 Set yourselves in array against Babylon round about,
all you that bend the bow;
shoot at her, spare no arrows,
for she has sinned against the LORD.
15 Raise a shout against her round about,
she has surrendered;
her bulwarks have fallen,
her walls are thrown down.
For this is the vengeance of the LORD:

take vengeance on her,
do to her as she has done.
16 Cut off from Babylon the sower,
and the one who handles the sickle in time of harvest;
because of the sword of the oppressor,
every one shall turn to his own people,
and every one shall flee to his own land.

17 "Israel is a hunted sheep driven away by lions. First the king of Assyria devoured him, and now at last Ne·bù·chǎd·rez′zǎr king of Babylon has gnawed his bones. 18 Therefore, thus says the LORD of hosts, the God of Israel: Behold, I am bringing punishment on the king of Babylon and his land, as I punished the king of Assyria. 19 I will restore Israel to his pasture, and he shall feed on Cär′měl and in Bā′shàn, and his desire shall be satisfied on the hills of Ē′phrà·im and in Gilead. 20 In those days and in that time, says the LORD, iniquity shall be sought in Israel, and there shall be none; and sin in Judah, and none shall be found; for I will pardon those whom I leave as a remnant.

21 "Go up against the land of Mer·à-thā′im,*
and against the inhabitants of Pē′kod.†
Slay, and utterly destroy after them,
says the LORD,
and do all that I have commanded you.
22 The noise of battle is in the land, and great destruction!
23 How the hammer of the whole earth
is cut down and broken!
How Babylon has become
a horror among the nations!
24 I set a snare for you and you were taken, O Babylon,
and you did not know it;
you were found and caught,
because you strove against the LORD.
25 The LORD has opened his armory,
and brought out the weapons of his wrath,
for the Lord GOD of hosts has a work to do
in the land of the Chal·dē′ǎns.
26 Come against her from every quarter;
open her granaries;

* Or *Double Rebellion*   † Or *Punishment*
50.8: Jer 51.6, 9, 45; 2 Cor 6.17; Rev 18.4.

pile her up like heaps of grain, and
destroy her utterly;
let nothing be left of her.
27 Slay all her bulls,
let them go down to the slaughter.
Woe to them, for their day has come,
the time of their punishment.

28 "Hark! they flee and escape from
the land of Babylon, to declare in Zion
the vengeance of the LORD our God,
vengeance for his temple.

29 "Summon archers against Babylon, all those who bend the bow. Encamp round about her; let no one
escape. Requite her according to her
deeds, do to her according to all that
she has done; for she has proudly
defied the LORD, the Holy One of
Israel. 30 Therefore her young men
shall fall in her squares, and all her
soldiers shall be destroyed on that day,
says the LORD.

31 "Behold, I am against you, O proud
one,
says the Lord GOD of hosts;
for your day has come,
the time when I will punish you.
32 The proud one shall stumble and fall
with none to raise him up,
and I will kindle a fire in his cities,
and it will devour all that is round
about him.

33 "Thus says the LORD of hosts:
The people of Israel are oppressed,
and the people of Judah with them;
all who took them captive have held
them fast, they refuse to let them go.
34 Their Redeemer is strong; the LORD
of hosts is his name. He will surely
plead their cause, that he may give rest
to the earth, but unrest to the inhabitants of Babylon.

35 "A sword upon the Chal·dē′ǎns,
says the LORD,
and upon the inhabitants of
Babylon,
and upon her princes and her
wise men!
36 A sword upon the diviners,
that they may become fools!
A sword upon her warriors,
that they may be destroyed!
37 A sword upon her horses and upon
her chariots,
and upon all the foreign troops in
her midst,
that they may become women!
A sword upon all her treasures,
that they may be plundered!

u Heb *Leb-qamai*, a cipher for Chaldea

38 A drought upon her waters,
that they may be dried up!
For it is a land of images,
and they are mad over idols.

39 "Therefore wild beasts shall
dwell with hyenas in Babylon, and
ostriches shall dwell in her; she shall
be peopled no more for ever, nor inhabited for all generations. 40 As when
God overthrew Sod′ŏm and Gŏ·môr′-
răh and their neighbor cities, says the
LORD, so no man shall dwell there, and
no son of man shall sojourn in her.

41 "Behold, a people comes from the
north;
a mighty nation and many kings
are stirring from the farthest parts
of the earth.
42 They lay hold of bow and spear;
they are cruel, and have no mercy.
The sound of them is like the roaring of the sea;
they ride upon horses,
arrayed as a man for battle
against you, O daughter of
Babylon!

43 "The king of Babylon heard the
report of them,
and his hands fell helpless;
anguish seized him,
pain as of a woman in travail.

44 "Behold, like a lion coming up
from the jungle of the Jordan against
a strong sheepfold, I will suddenly
make them run away from her; and I
will appoint over her whomever I
choose. For who is like me? Who will
summon me? What shepherd can
stand before me? 45 Therefore hear the
plan which the LORD has made against
Babylon, and the purposes which he
has formed against the land of the
Chal·dē′ǎns: Surely the little ones of
their flock shall be dragged away;
surely their fold shall be appalled at
their fate. 46 At the sound of the capture
of Babylon the earth shall tremble, and
her cry shall be heard among the
nations."

51 Thus says the LORD:
"Behold, I will stir up the spirit
of a destroyer
against Babylon,
against the inhabitants of Chal-
dē′à;ᵘ
2 and I will send to Babylon win-
nowers,
and they shall winnow her,
and they shall empty her land,

when they come against her from
every side
on the day of trouble.
3 Let not the archer bend his bow,
and let him not stand up in his
coat of mail.
Spare not her young men;
utterly destroy all her host.
4 They shall fall down slain in the
land of the Chal·dē′ans,
and wounded in her streets.
5 For Israel and Judah have not been
forsaken
by their God, the LORD of hosts;
but the land of the Chal·dē′ans[v] is
full of guilt
against the Holy One of Israel.

6 "Flee from the midst of Babylon,
let every man save his life!
Be not cut off in her punishment,
for this is the time of the LORD'S
vengeance,
the requital he is rendering her.
7 Babylon was a golden cup in the
LORD'S hand,
making all the earth drunken;
the nations drank of her wine,
therefore the nations went
mad.
8 Suddenly Babylon has fallen and
been broken!
wail for her!
Take balm for her pain;
perhaps she may be healed.
9 We would have healed Babylon,
but she was not healed.
Forsake her, and let us go
each to his own country;
for her judgment has reached up to
heaven
and has been lifted up even to the
skies.
10 The LORD has brought forth our
vindication;
come, let us declare in Zion
the work of the LORD our God.

11 "Sharpen the arrows!
Take up the shields!
The LORD has stirred up the spirit of
the kings of the Medes, because his
purpose concerning Babylon is to destroy it, for that is the vengeance of the
LORD, the vengeance for his temple.
12 Set up a standard against the walls
of Babylon;
make the watch strong;
set up watchmen;
prepare the ambushes;
for the LORD has both planned and
done

what he spoke concerning the
inhabitants of Babylon.
13 O you who dwell by many waters,
rich in treasures,
your end has come,
the thread of your life is cut.
14 The LORD of hosts has sworn by
himself:
Surely I will fill you with men, as
many as locusts,
and they shall raise the shout of
victory over you.

15 "It is he who made the earth by his
power,
who established the world by his
wisdom,
and by his understanding
stretched out the heavens.
16 When he utters his voice there is a
tumult of waters in the heavens,
and he makes the mist rise from
the ends of the earth.
He makes lightnings for the rain,
and he brings forth the wind from
his storehouses.
17 Every man is stupid and without
knowledge;
every goldsmith is put to shame
by his idols;
for his images are false,
and there is no breath in them.
18 They are worthless, a work of delusion;
at the time of their punishment
they shall perish.
19 Not like these is he who is the portion of Jacob,
for he is the one who formed all
things,
and Israel is the tribe of his inheritance;
the LORD of hosts is his name.]

20 "You are my hammer and weapon
of war:
with you I break nations in pieces;
with you I destroy kingdoms;
21 with you I break in pieces the horse
and his rider;
with you I break in pieces the
chariot and the charioteer;
22 with you I break in pieces man and
woman;
with you I break in pieces the
old man and the youth;
with you I break in pieces the
young man and the maiden;
23 with you I break in pieces the
shepherd and his flock;
with you I break in pieces the
farmer and his team;

v Heb *their land*
51.6, 9, 45: Jer 50.8; 2 Cor 6.17; Rev 18.4.
51.7-8: Jer 25.15; Rev 14.8, 10; 16.19; 17.4; 18.3.   **51.13:** Rev 17.1.

with you I break in pieces governors and commanders.

24 "I will requite Babylon and all the inhabitants of Chal·dē'á before your very eyes for all the evil that they have done in Zion, says the LORD.

25 "Behold, I am against you, O destroying mountain,
          says the LORD,
    which destroys the whole earth;
I will stretch out my hand against you,
    and roll you down from the crags,
    and make you a burnt mountain.
26 No stone shall be taken from you for a corner
    and no stone for a foundation,
but you shall be a perpetual waste, says the LORD.

27 "Set up a standard on the earth,
    blow the trumpet among the nations;
prepare the nations for war against her,
    summon against her the kingdoms,
    Ar'á·rat, Min'nī, and Ash'kė·naz;
appoint a marshal against her,
    bring up horses like bristling locusts.
28 Prepare the nations for war against her,
    the kings of the Medes, with their governors and deputies,
    and every land under their dominion.
29 The land trembles and writhes in pain,
    for the LORD'S purposes against Babylon stand,
to make the land of Babylon a desolation,
    without inhabitant.
30 The warriors of Babylon have ceased fighting,
    they remain in their strongholds;
their strength has failed,
    they have become women;
her dwellings are on fire,
    her bars are broken.
31 One runner runs to meet another,
    and one messenger to meet another,
to tell the king of Babylon
    that his city is taken on every side;
32 the fords have been seized,
    the bulwarks are burned with fire,
    and the soldiers are in panic.
33 For thus says the LORD of hosts, the God of Israel:

The daughter of Babylon is like a threshing floor
    at the time when it is trodden;
yet a little while
    and the time of her harvest will come."

34 "Ne·bù·chȧd·rez'zȧr the king of Babylon has devoured me,
    he has crushed me;
he has made me an empty vessel,
    he has swallowed me like a monster;
he has filled his belly with my delicacies,
    he has rinsed me out.
35 The violence done to me and to my kinsmen be upon Babylon,"
    let the inhabitant of Zion say.
"My blood be upon the inhabitants of Chal·dē'á,"
    let Jerusalem say.
36 Therefore thus says the LORD:
"Behold, I will plead your cause
    and take vengeance for you.
I will dry up her sea
    and make her fountain dry;
37 and Babylon shall become a heap of ruins,
    the haunt of jackals,
a horror and a hissing,
    without inhabitant.
38 "They shall roar together like lions;
    they shall growl like lions' whelps.
39 While they are inflamed I will prepare them a feast
    and make them drunk, till they swoon away[w]
and sleep a perpetual sleep
    and not wake, says the LORD.
40 I will bring them down like lambs to the slaughter,
    like rams and he-goats.

41 "How Babylon[x] is taken,
    the praise of the whole earth seized!
How Babylon has become
    a horror among the nations!
42 The sea has come up on Babylon;
    she is covered with its tumultuous waves.
43 Her cities have become a horror,
    a land of drought and a desert,
a land in which no one dwells,
    and through which no son of man passes.
44 And I will punish Bel in Babylon,
    and take out of his mouth what he has swallowed.
The nations shall no longer flow to him;
    the wall of Babylon has fallen.

---

w Gk Vg: Heb *rejoice*   x Heb *Sheshach*, a cipher for Babylon

45 "Go out of the midst of her, my
        people!
    Let every man save his life
        from the fierce anger of the LORD!
46 Let not your heart faint, and be not
        fearful
    at the report heard in the land,
    when a report comes in one year
        and afterward a report in another
            year,
    and violence is in the land,
        and ruler is against ruler.

47 "Therefore, behold, the days are
        coming
    when I will punish the images of
        Babylon;
    her whole land shall be put to shame,
        and all her slain shall fall in the
            midst of her.
48 Then the heavens and the earth,
        and all that is in them,
    shall sing for joy over Babylon;
        for the destroyers shall come
            against them out of the north,
                says the LORD.
49 Babylon must fall for the slain of
        Israel,
    as for Babylon have fallen the
        slain of all the earth.

50 "You that have escaped from the
        sword,
    go, stand not still!
    Remember the LORD from afar,
        and let Jerusalem come into your
            mind:
51 'We are put to shame, for we have
        heard reproach;
    dishonor has covered our face,
    for aliens have come
        into the holy places of the LORD's
            house.'

52 "Therefore, behold, the days are
        coming, says the LORD,
    when I will execute judgment
        upon her images,
    and through all her land
        the wounded shall groan.
53 Though Babylon should mount up
        to heaven,
    and though she should fortify her
        strong height,
    yet destroyers would come from me
        upon her,
            says the LORD.

54 "Hark! a cry from Babylon!
    The noise of great destruction
        from the land of the Chal·dē'-
            ans!
55 For the LORD is laying Babylon
        waste,
    and stilling her mighty voice.
    Their waves roar like many waters,
        the noise of their voice is raised;
56 for a destroyer has come upon her,
        upon Babylon;
    her warriors are taken,
        their bows are broken in pieces;
    for the LORD is a God of recom-
        pense,
    he will surely requite.
57 I will make drunk her princes and
        her wise men,
    her governors, her commanders,
        and her warriors;
    they shall sleep a perpetual sleep
        and not wake,
    says the King, whose name is the
        LORD of hosts.

58 "Thus says the LORD of hosts:
    The broad wall of Babylon
        shall be leveled to the ground
    and her high gates
        shall be burned with fire.
    The peoples labor for nought,
        and the nations weary themselves
            only for fire."

59 The word which Jeremiah the
prophet commanded Se·rāi'ah the son
of Ne·rī'ah, son of Māh·sēi'ah, when
he went with Zed·e·kī'ah king of Judah
to Babylon, in the fourth year of his
reign. Seraiah was the quartermaster.
60 Jeremiah wrote in a book all the
evil that should come upon Babylon,
all these words that are written concerning Babylon. 61 And Jeremiah said
to Se·rāi'ah: "When you come to
Babylon, see that you read all these
words, 62 and say, 'O LORD, thou hast
said concerning this place that thou
wilt cut it off, so that nothing shall
dwell in it, neither man nor beast, and
it shall be desolate for ever.' 63 When
you finish reading this book, bind a
stone to it, and cast it into the midst
of the Eū·phra'tēs, 64 and say, 'Thus
shall Babylon sink, to rise no more,
because of the evil that I am bringing
upon her.' "y
    Thus far are the words of Jere-
miah.

52 Zed·e·kī'ah was twenty-one
    years old when he became king;
and he reigned eleven years in Jerusalem. His mother's name was Hā·mū'-
tal the daughter of Jeremiah of Lib'-
nah. 2 And he did what was evil in the

y Gk: Heb upon her. And they shall weary themselves
51.48: Is 44.23; Rev 12.12; 18.20.   **51.63-64:** Rev 18.21.
52: 2 Kings 24.18-25.30; 2 Chron 36.11-13.

sight of the LORD, according to all that Je·hoi′a·kim had done. 3 Surely because of the anger of the LORD things came to such a pass in Jerusalem and Judah that he cast them out from his presence.

And Zed·e·ki′ah rebelled against the king of Babylon. 4 And in the ninth year of his reign, in the tenth month, on the tenth day of the month, Ne·bu·chad·rez′zar king of Babylon came with all his army against Jerusalem, and they laid siege to it and built siegeworks against it round about. 5 So the city was besieged till the eleventh year of King Zed·e·ki′ah. 6 On the ninth day of the fourth month the famine was so severe in the city, that there was no food for the people of the land. 7 Then a breach was made in the city; and all the men of war fled and went out from the city by night by the way of a gate between the two walls, by the king's garden, while the Chal·de′ans were round about the city. And they went in the direction of the Ar′a·bah. 8 But the army of the Chal·de′ans pursued the king, and overtook Zed·e·ki′ah in the plains of Jericho; and all his army was scattered from him. 9 Then they captured the king, and brought him up to the king of Babylon at Rib′lah in the land of Ha′math, and he passed sentence upon him. 10 The king of Babylon slew the sons of Zed·e·ki′ah before his eyes, and also slew all the princes of Judah at Rib′lah. 11 He put out the eyes of Zed·e·ki′ah, and bound him in fetters, and the king of Babylon took him to Babylon, and put him in prison till the day of his death.

12 In the fifth month, on the tenth day of the month—which was the nineteenth year of King Ne·bu·chad·rez′zar, king of Babylon—Ne·bu′za·rad′an the captain of the bodyguard who served the king of Babylon, entered Jerusalem. 13 And he burned the house of the LORD, and the king's house and all the houses of Jerusalem; every great house he burned down. 14 And all the army of the Chal·de′ans, who were with the captain of the guard, broke down all the walls round about Jerusalem. 15 And Ne·bu′za·rad′an the captain of the guard carried away captive some of the poorest of the people and the rest of the people who were left in the city and the deserters who had deserted to the king of Babylon, together with the rest of the artisans. 16 But Ne·bu′za·rad′an the captain of the guard left some of the poorest of the land to be vine-dressers and plowmen.

17 And the pillars of bronze that were in the house of the LORD, and the stands and the bronze sea that were in the house of the LORD, the Chal·de′ans broke in pieces, and carried all the bronze to Babylon. 18 And they took away the pots, and the shovels, and the snuffers, and the basins, and the dishes for incense, and all the vessels of bronze used in the temple service; 19 also the small bowls, and the fire-pans, and the basins, and the pots, and the lampstands, and the dishes for incense, and the bowls for libation. What was of gold the captain of the guard took away as gold, and what was of silver, as silver. 20 As for the two pillars, the one sea, the twelve bronze bulls which were under the sea,z and the stands, which Solomon the king had made for the house of the LORD, the bronze of all these things was beyond weight. 21 As for the pillars, the height of the one pillar was eighteen cubits, its circumference was twelve cubits, and its thickness was four fingers, and it was hollow. 22 Upon it was a capital of bronze; the height of the one capital was five cubits; a network and pomegranates, all of bronze, were upon the capital round about. And the second pillar had the like, with pomegranates. 23 There were ninety-six pomegranates on the sides; all the pomegranates were a hundred upon the network round about.

24 And the captain of the guard took Se·rai′ah the chief priest, and Zeph·a·ni′ah the second priest, and the three keepers of the threshold; 25 and from the city he took an officer who had been in command of the men of war, and seven men of the king's council, who were found in the city; and the secretary of the commander of the army who mustered the people of the land; and sixty men of the people of the land, who were found in the midst of the city. 26 And Ne·bu′za·rad′an the captain of the guard took them, and brought them to the king of Babylon at Rib′lah. 27 And the king of Babylon smote them, and put them to death at Rib′lah in the land of Ha′math. So Judah was carried captive out of its land.

28 This is the number of the people whom Ne·bu·chad·rez′zar carried away captive: in the seventh year, three thousand and twenty-three Jews; 29 in the eighteenth year of Ne·bu·chad·rez′zar he carried away captive from

z Heb lacks *the sea*

Jerusalem eight hundred and thirty-two persons; 30 in the twenty-third year of Neb·u·chad·rez´zar, Neb·u´za-rad´an the captain of the guard carried away captive of the Jews seven hundred and forty-five persons; all the persons were four thousand and six hundred.

31 And in the thirty-seventh year of the captivity of Je·hoi´a·chin king of Judah, in the twelfth month, on the twenty-fifth day of the month, E´vil-mer´o·dach king of Babylon, in the year that he became king, lifted up the head of Je·hoi´a·chin king of Judah and brought him out of prison; 32 and he spoke kindly to him, and gave him a seat above the seats of the kings who were with him in Babylon. 33 So Je·hoi´a·chin put off his prison garments. And every day of his life he dined regularly at the king's table; 34 as for his allowance, a regular allowance was given him by the king according to his daily need, until the day of his death as long as he lived.

THE LAMENTATIONS

OF JEREMIAH

1   How lonely sits the city
     that was full of people!
How like a widow has she become,
     she that was great among the
       nations!
She that was a princess among the
       cities
     has become a vassal.

2 She weeps bitterly in the night,
     tears on her cheeks;
among all her lovers
     she has none to comfort her;
all her friends have dealt treach-
       erously with her,
     they have become her enemies.

3 Judah has gone into exile because
     of affliction
     and hard servitude;
she dwells now among the nations,
     but finds no resting place;
her pursuers have all overtaken her
     in the midst of her distress.

4 The roads to Zion mourn,
     for none come to the appointed
       feasts;
all her gates are desolate,
     her priests groan;
her maidens have been dragged
       away,[a]
and she herself suffers bitterly.

5 Her foes have become the head,
     her enemies prosper,
because the LORD has made her
       suffer

for the multitude of her trans-
       gressions;
her children have gone away,
     captives before the foe.

6 From the daughter of Zion has de-
       parted
     all her majesty.
Her princes have become like harts
     that find no pasture;
they fled without strength
     before the pursuer.

7 Jerusalem remembers
     in the days of her affliction and
       bitterness[b]
all the precious things
     that were hers from days of old.
When her people fell into the hand
       of the foe,
     and there was none to help her,
the foe gloated over her,
     mocking at her downfall.

8 Jerusalem sinned grievously,
     therefore she became filthy;
all who honored her despise her,
     for they have seen her naked-
       ness;
yea, she herself groans,
     and turns her face away.

9 Her uncleanness was in her skirts;
     she took no thought of her doom;
therefore her fall is terrible,
     she has no comforter.
"O LORD, behold my affliction,
     for the enemy has triumphed!"

a Gk Old Latin: Heb *afflicted*
b Cn: Heb *wandering*

10 The enemy has stretched out his hands
    over all her precious things;
yea, she has seen the nations
    invade her sanctuary,
those whom thou didst forbid
    to enter thy congregation.

11 All her people groan
    as they search for bread;
they trade their treasures for food
    to revive their strength.
"Look, O LORD, and behold,
    for I am despised."

12 "Is it nothing to you,*c* all you who
      pass by?
    Look and see
if there is any sorrow like my sorrow
    which was brought upon me,
which the LORD inflicted
    on the day of his fierce anger.

13 "From on high he sent fire;
    into my bones*d* he made it de-
      scend;
he spread a net for my feet;
    he turned me back;
he has left me stunned,
    faint all the day long.

14 "My transgressions were bound*e* in-
      to a yoke;
    by his hand they were fastened
      together;
they were set upon my neck;
    he caused my strength to fail;
the Lord gave me into the hands
    of those whom I cannot with-
      stand.

15 "The LORD flouted all my mighty
      men
    in the midst of me;
he summoned an assembly against me
    to crush my young men;
the Lord has trodden as in a wine
      press
    the virgin daughter of Judah.

16 "For these things I weep;
    my eyes flow with tears;
for a comforter is far from me,
    one to revive my courage;
my children are desolate,
    for the enemy has prevailed."

17 Zion stretches out her hands,
    but there is none to comfort her;
the LORD has commanded against
      Jacob
    that his neighbors should be his
      foes;
Jerusalem has become
    a filthy thing among them.

18 "The LORD is in the right,
    for I have rebelled against his
      word;
but hear, all you peoples,
    and behold my suffering;
my maidens and my young men
    have gone into captivity.

19 "I called to my lovers
    but they deceived me;
my priests and elders
    perished in the city,
while they sought food
    to revive their strength.

20 "Behold, O LORD, for I am in dis-
      tress,
    my soul is in tumult,
my heart is wrung within me,
    because I have been very rebel-
      lious.
In the street the sword bereaves;
    in the house it is like death.

21 "Hear*f* how I groan;
    there is none to comfort me.
All my enemies have heard of my
      trouble;
    they are glad that thou hast done
      it.
Bring thou*g* the day thou hast an-
      nounced,
    and let them be as I am.

22 "Let all their evil doing come be-
      fore thee;
    and deal with them
as thou hast dealt with me
    because of all my transgressions;
for my groans are many
    and my heart is faint."

2   How the Lord in his anger
    has set the daughter of Zion under
      a cloud!
He has cast down from heaven to
      earth
    the splendor of Israel;
he has not remembered his footstool
    in the day of his anger.

2 The Lord has destroyed without
      mercy
    all the habitations of Jacob;
in his wrath he has broken down
    the strongholds of the daughter of
      Judah;
he has brought down to the ground
      in dishonor
    the kingdom and its rulers.

c Heb uncertain   *d* Gk: Heb *bones and*   *e* Cn: Heb uncertain
f Gk Syr: Heb *they heard*   *g* Syr: Heb *thou hast brought*

3 He has cut down in fierce anger
     all the might of Israel;
  he has withdrawn from them his
     right hand
     in the face of the enemy;
  he has burned like a flaming fire in
     Jacob,
     consuming all around.

4 He has bent his bow like an enemy,
     with his right hand set like a foe;
  and he has slain all the pride of our
     eyes
     in the tent of the daughter of
     Zion;
  he has poured out his fury like fire.

5 The Lord has become like an enemy,
     he has destroyed Israel;
  he has destroyed all its palaces,
     laid in ruins its strongholds;
  and he has multiplied in the daugh-
     ter of Judah
     mourning and lamentation.

6 He has broken down his booth like
     that of a garden,
     laid in ruins the place of his ap-
     pointed feasts;
  the LORD has brought to an end in
     Zion
     appointed feast and sabbath,
  and in his fierce indignation has
     spurned
     king and priest.

7 The Lord has scorned his altar,
     disowned his sanctuary;
  he has delivered into the hand of
     the enemy
     the walls of her palaces;
  a clamor was raised in the house of
     the LORD
     as on the day of an appointed
     feast.

8 The LORD determined to lay in
     ruins
     the wall of the daughter of Zion;
  he marked it off by the line;
     he restrained not his hand from
     destroying;
  he caused rampart and wall to la-
     ment,
     they languish together.

9 Her gates have sunk into the
     ground;
     he has ruined and broken her bars;
  her king and princes are among the
     nations;
     the law is no more,
  and her prophets obtain
     no vision from the LORD.

10 The elders of the daughter of Zion
     sit on the ground in silence;
  they have cast dust on their heads
     and put on sackcloth;
  the maidens of Jerusalem
     have bowed their heads to the
     ground.

11 My eyes are spent with weeping;
     my soul is in tumult;
  my heart is poured out in grief[h]
     because of the destruction of the
     daughter of my people,
  because infants and babes faint
     in the streets of the city.

12 They cry to their mothers,
     "Where is bread and wine?"
  as they faint like wounded men
     in the streets of the city,
  as their life is poured out
     on their mothers' bosom.

13 What can I say for you, to what
     compare you,
     O daughter of Jerusalem?
  What can I liken to you, that I may
     comfort you,
     O virgin daughter of Zion?
  For vast as the sea is your ruin;
     who can restore you?

14 Your prophets have seen for you
     false and deceptive visions;
  they have not exposed your iniquity
     to restore your fortunes,
  but have seen for you oracles
     false and misleading.

15 All who pass along the way
     clap their hands at you;
  they hiss and wag their heads
     at the daughter of Jerusalem;
  "Is this the city which was called
     the perfection of beauty,
     the joy of all the earth?"

16 All your enemies
     rail against you;
  they hiss, they gnash their teeth,
     they cry: "We have destroyed her!
  Ah, this is the day we longed for;
     now we have it; we see it!"

17 The LORD has done what he pur-
     posed,
     has carried out his threat;
  as he ordained long ago,
     he has demolished without pity;
  he has made the enemy rejoice over
     you,
     and exalted the might of your foes.

18 Cry aloud[i] to the Lord!

---

[h] Heb *to the ground*   [i] Cn: Heb *Their heart cried*

O[j] daughter of Zion!
Let tears stream down like a torrent
  day and night!
Give yourself no rest,
  your eyes no respite!

19 Arise, cry out in the night,
  at the beginning of the watches!
Pour out your heart like water
  before the presence of the Lord!
Lift your hands to him
  for the lives of your children,
who faint for hunger
  at the head of every street.

20 Look, O LORD, and see!
  With whom hast thou dealt thus?
Should women eat their offspring,
  the children of their tender care?
Should priest and prophet be slain
  in the sanctuary of the Lord?

21 In the dust of the streets
  lie the young and the old;
my maidens and my young men
  have fallen by the sword;
in the day of thy anger thou hast
  slain them,
slaughtering without mercy.

22 Thou didst invite as to the day of
  an appointed feast
my terrors on every side;
and on the day of the anger of the
  LORD
none escaped or survived;
those whom I dandled and reared
  my enemy destroyed.

3 I am the man who has seen
  affliction
  under the rod of his wrath;
2 he has driven and brought me
  into darkness without any light;
3 surely against me he turns his hand
  again and again the whole day
  long.

4 He has made my flesh and my skin
  waste away,
  and broken my bones;
5 he has besieged and enveloped me
  with bitterness and tribulation;
6 he has made me dwell in darkness
  like the dead of long ago.

7 He has walled me about so that I
  cannot escape;
  he has put heavy chains on me;
8 though I call and cry for help,
  he shuts out my prayer,
9 he has blocked my ways with hewn
  stones,
  he has made my paths crooked.

10 He is to me like a bear lying in wait,
  like a lion in hiding;
11 he led me off my way and tore me
  to pieces;
  he has made me desolate;
12 he bent his bow and set me
  as a mark for his arrow.

13 He drove into my heart
  the arrows of his quiver;
14 I have become the laughingstock of
  all peoples,
  the burden of their songs all day
  long.
15 He has filled me with bitterness,
  he has sated me with wormwood.

16 He has made my teeth grind on
  gravel,
  and made me cower in ashes;
17 my soul is bereft of peace,
  I have forgotten what happiness
  is;
18 so I say, "Gone is my glory,
  and my expectation from the
  LORD."

19 Remember my affliction and my
  bitterness,[k]
  the wormwood and the gall!
20 My soul continually thinks of it
  and is bowed down within me.
21 But this I call to mind,
  and therefore I have hope:

22 The steadfast love of the LORD
  never ceases,[l]
  his mercies never come to an end;
23 they are new every morning;
  great is thy faithfulness.
24 "The LORD is my portion," says my
  soul,
  "therefore I will hope in him."

25 The LORD is good to those who wait
  for him,
  to the soul that seeks him.
26 It is good that one should wait
  quietly
  for the salvation of the LORD.
27 It is good for a man that he bear
  the yoke in his youth.

28 Let him sit alone in silence
  when he has laid it on him;
29 let him put his mouth in the dust—
  there may yet be hope;
30 let him give his cheek to the smiter,
  and be filled with insults.

31 For the Lord will not
  cast off for ever,
32 but, though he cause grief, he will
  have compassion

[j] Cn: Heb *O wall of*   [k] Cn: Heb *wandering*   [l] Syr Tg: Heb *we are not cut off*

according to the abundance of his
    steadfast love;
33 for he does not willingly afflict
    or grieve the sons of men.

34 To crush under foot
    all the prisoners of the earth,
35 to turn aside the right of a man
    in the presence of the Most High,
36 to subvert a man in his cause,
    the Lord does not approve.

37 Who has commanded and it came
    to pass,
    unless the Lord has ordained it?
38 Is it not from the mouth of the Most
    High
    that good and evil come?
39 Why should a living man complain,
    a man, about the punishment of
    his sins?

40 Let us test and examine our ways,
    and return to the LORD!
41 Let us lift up our hearts and hands
    to God in heaven:
42 "We have transgressed and rebelled,
    and thou hast not forgiven.

43 "Thou hast wrapped thyself with
    anger and pursued us,
    slaying without pity;
44 thou hast wrapped thyself with a
    cloud
    so that no prayer can pass through.
45 Thou hast made us offscouring and
    refuse
    among the peoples.

46 "All our enemies
    rail against us;
47 panic and pitfall have come upon us,
    devastation and destruction;
48 my eyes flow with rivers of tears
    because of the destruction of the
    daughter of my people.

49 "My eyes will flow without ceasing,
    without respite,
50 until the LORD from heaven
    looks down and sees;
51 my eyes cause me grief
    at the fate of all the maidens of
    my city.

52 "I have been hunted like a bird
    by those who were my enemies
    without cause;
53 they flung me alive into the pit
    and cast stones on me;
54 water closed over my head;
    I said, 'I am lost.'

55 "I called on thy name, O LORD,

    from the depths of the pit;
56 thou didst hear my plea, 'Do not
    close
    thine ear to my cry for help!'[m]
57 Thou didst come near when I called
    on thee;
    thou didst say, 'Do not fear!'

58 "Thou hast taken up my cause, O
    Lord,
    thou hast redeemed my life.
59 Thou hast seen the wrong done to
    me, O LORD;
    judge thou my cause.
60 Thou hast seen all their vengeance,
    all their devices against me.

61 "Thou hast heard their taunts, O
    LORD,
    all their devices against me.
62 The lips and thoughts of my as-
    sailants
    are against me all the day long.
63 Behold their sitting and their rising;
    I am the burden of their songs.

64 "Thou wilt requite them, O LORD,
    according to the work of their
    hands.
65 Thou wilt give them dullness of
    heart;
    thy curse will be on them.
66 Thou wilt pursue them in anger and
    destroy them
    from under thy heavens, O
    LORD.'"[n]

4 How the gold has grown dim,
    how the pure gold is changed!
The holy stones lie scattered
    at the head of every street.

2 The precious sons of Zion,
    worth their weight in fine gold,
how they are reckoned as earthen
    pots,
    the work of a potter's hands!

3 Even the jackals give the breast
    and suckle their young,
but the daughter of my people has
    become cruel,
    like the ostriches in the wilderness.

4 The tongue of the nursling cleaves
    to the roof of its mouth for thirst;
the children beg for food,
    but no one gives to them.

5 Those who feasted on dainties
    perish in the streets;
those who were brought up in
    purple
    lie on ash heaps.

m Heb uncertain   *n* Syr Compare Gk Vg: Heb *the heavens of the* LORD

6 For the chastisement^o of the daughter of my people has been greater
  than the punishment^p of Sod'óm,
which was overthrown in a moment, no hand being laid on it.^q

7 Her princes were purer than snow, whiter than milk;
  their bodies were more ruddy than coral,
  the beauty of their form^r was like sapphire.^s

8 Now their visage is blacker than soot,
  they are not recognized in the streets;
  their skin has shriveled upon their bones,
  it has become as dry as wood.

9 Happier were the victims of the sword
  than the victims of hunger,
  who pined away, stricken
  by want of the fruits of the field.

10 The hands of compassionate women have boiled their own children;
  they became their food
  in the destruction of the daughter of my people.

11 The LORD gave full vent to his wrath,
  he poured out his hot anger;
and he kindled a fire in Zion,
  which consumed its foundations.

12 The kings of the earth did not believe,
  or any of the inhabitants of the world,
that foe or enemy could enter
  the gates of Jerusalem.

13 This was for the sins of her prophets
  and the iniquities of her priests,
who shed in the midst of her
  the blood of the righteous.

14 They wandered, blind, through the streets,
  so defiled with blood
that none could touch
  their garments.

15 "Away! Unclean!" men cried at them;
  "Away! Away! Touch not!"
So they became fugitives and wanderers;

men said among the nations,
  "They shall stay with us no longer."

16 The LORD himself has scattered them,
  he will regard them no more;
no honor was shown to the priests,
  no favor to the elders.

17 Our eyes failed, ever watching vainly for help;
in our watching^t we watched
  for a nation which could not save.

18 Men dogged our steps
  so that we could not walk in our streets;
our end drew near; our days were numbered;
  for our end had come.

19 Our pursuers were swifter
  than the vultures in the heavens;
they chased us on the mountains,
  they lay in wait for us in the wilderness.

20 The breath of our nostrils, the LORD's anointed,
  was taken in their pits,
he of whom we said, "Under his shadow
  we shall live among the nations."

21 Rejoice and be glad, O daughter of E'dóm,
  dweller in the land of Uz;
but to you also the cup shall pass;
  you shall become drunk and strip yourself bare.

22 The punishment of your iniquity, O daughter of Zion, is accomplished,
  he will keep you in exile no longer;
but your iniquity, O daughter of E'dóm, he will punish,
  he will uncover your sins.

5 Remember, O LORD, what has befallen us;
  behold, and see our disgrace!
2 Our inheritance has been turned over to strangers,
  our homes to aliens.
3 We have become orphans, fatherless;
  our mothers are like widows.
4 We must pay for the water we drink,
  the wood we get must be bought.
5 With a yoke^u on our necks we are hard driven;

^o Or *iniquity*   ^p Or *sin*   ^q Heb uncertain   ^r Heb uncertain   ^s Heb *lapis lazuli*
^t Heb uncertain   ^u Symmachus: Heb lacks *with a yoke*

we are weary, we are given no
    rest.
6 We have given the hand to Egypt,
    and to Assyria, to get bread
    enough.
7 Our fathers sinned, and are no more;
    and we bear their iniquities.
8 Slaves rule over us;
    there is none to deliver us from
    their hand.
9 We get our bread at the peril of our
    lives,
    because of the sword in the wil-
    derness.
10 Our skin is hot as an oven
    with the burning heat of famine.
11 Women are ravished in Zion,
    virgins in the towns of Judah.
12 Princes are hung up by their hands;
    no respect is shown to the elders.
13 Young men are compelled to grind
    at the mill;
    and boys stagger under loads of
    wood.
14 The old men have quit the city gate,
    the young men their music.
15 The joy of our hearts has ceased;
    our dancing has been turned to
    mourning.
16 The crown has fallen from our
    head;
    woe to us, for we have sinned!
17 For this our heart has become sick,
    for these things our eyes have
    grown dim,
18 for Mount Zion which lies desolate;
    jackals prowl over it.

19 But thou, O LORD, dost reign for
    ever;
    thy throne endures to all genera-
    tions.
20 Why dost thou forget us for ever,
    why dost thou so long forsake us?
21 Restore us to thyself, O LORD, that
    we may be restored!
    Renew our days as of old!
22 Or hast thou utterly rejected us?
    Art thou exceedingly angry with
    us?

THE BOOK OF

EZEKIEL

In the thirtieth year, in the fourth
month, on the fifth day of the
month, as I was among the exiles by
the river Chē′bär, the heavens were
opened, and I saw visions of God.
2 On the fifth day of the month (it was
the fifth year of the exile of King
Je·hoi′a·chin), 3 the word of the LORD
came to E·zēk′i·el the priest, the son
of Bū′zī, in the land of the Chal·dē′-
ans by the river Chē′bär; and the hand
of the LORD was upon him there.

4 As I looked, behold, a stormy
wind came out of the north, and a great
cloud, with brightness round about it,
and fire flashing forth continually, and
in the midst of the fire, as it were
gleaming bronze. 5 And from the midst
of it came the likeness of four living
creatures. And this was their appearance: they had the form of men, 6 but
each had four faces, and each of them
had four wings. 7 Their legs were
straight, and the soles of their feet
were like the sole of a calf's foot; and

they sparkled like burnished bronze.
8 Under their wings on their four sides
they had human hands. And the four
had their faces and their wings thus:
9 their wings touched one another;
they went every one straight forward,
without turning as they went. 10 As for
the likeness of their faces, each had
the face of a man in front;*a* the four had
the face of a lion on the right side, the
four had the face of an ox on the left
side, and the four had the face of an
eagle at the back.*b* 11 Such were their
faces. And their wings were spread out
above; each creature had two wings,
each of which touched the wing of
another, while two covered their
bodies. 12 And each went straight forward; wherever the spirit would go,
they went, without turning as they
went. 13 In the midst of*c* the living
creatures there was something that
looked like burning coals of fire, like
torches moving to and fro among the
living creatures; and the fire was bright,

a Cn: Heb lacks *in front*   *b* Cn: Heb lacks *at the back*
c Gk Old Latin: Heb *And the likeness of*
1.1: Rev 19.11.   **1.5, 18:** Rev 4.6.   **1.10:** Rev 4.7.   **1.13:** Rev 4.5.

and out of the fire went forth lightning. [14]And the living creatures darted to and fro, like a flash of lightning.

15 Now as I looked at the living creatures, I saw a wheel upon the earth beside the living creatures, one for each of the four of them.[d] [16]As for the appearance of the wheels and their construction: their appearance was like the gleaming of a chrysolite; and the four had the same likeness, their construction being as it were a wheel within a wheel. [17]When they went, they went in any of their four directions[e] without turning as they went. [18]The four wheels had rims and they had spokes;[f] and their rims were full of eyes round about. [19]And when the living creatures went, the wheels went beside them; and when the living creatures rose from the earth, the wheels rose. [20]Wherever the spirit would go, they went, and the wheels rose along with them; for the spirit of the living creatures was in the wheels. [21]When those went, these went; and when those stood, these stood; and and when those rose from the earth, the wheels rose along with them; for the spirit of the living creatures was in the wheels.

22 Over the heads of the living creatures there was the likeness of a firmament, shining like crystal,[g] spread out above their heads. [23]And under the firmament their wings were stretched out straight, one toward another; and each creature had two wings covering its body. [24]And when they went, I heard the sound of their wings like the sound of many waters, like the thunder of the Almighty, a sound of tumult like the sound of a host; when they stood still, they let down their wings. [25]And there came a voice from above the firmament over their heads; when they stood still, they let down their wings.

26 And above the firmament over their heads there was the likeness of a throne, in appearance like sapphire;[h] and seated above the likeness of a throne was a likeness as it were of a human form. [27]And upward from what had the appearance of his loins I saw as it were gleaming bronze, like the appearance of fire enclosed round about; and downward from what had the appearance of his loins I saw as it were the appearance of fire, and there was brightness round about him.[i]

[28] Like the appearance of the bow that is in the cloud on the day of rain, so was the appearance of the brightness round about.

Such was the appearance of the likeness of the glory of the LORD. And when I saw it, I fell upon my face, and I heard the voice of one speaking.

2 And he said to me, "Son of man, stand upon your feet, and I will speak with you." [2]And when he spoke to me, the Spirit entered into me and set me upon my feet; and I heard him speaking to me. [3]And he said to me, "Son of man, I send you to the people of Israel, to a nation[j] of rebels, who have rebelled against me; they and their fathers have transgressed against me to this very day. [4] The people also are impudent and stubborn: I send you to them; and you shall say to them, 'Thus says the Lord GOD.' [5]And whether they hear or refuse to hear (for they are a rebellious house) they will know that there has been a prophet among them. [6]And you, son of man, be not afraid of them, nor be afraid of their words, though briers and thorns are with you and you sit upon scorpions; be not afraid of their words, nor be dismayed at their looks, for they are a rebellious house. [7]And you shall speak my words to them, whether they hear or refuse to hear; for they are a rebellious house.

8 "But you, son of man, hear what I say to you; be not rebellious like that rebellious house; open your mouth, and eat what I give you." [9]And when I looked, behold, a hand was stretched out to me, and, lo, a written scroll was in it; [10] and he spread it before me; and it had writing on the front and on the back, and there were written on it words of lamentation and mourning and woe.

3 And he said to me, "Son of man, eat what is offered to you; eat this scroll, and go, speak to the house of Israel." [2] So I opened my mouth, and he gave me the scroll to eat. [3]And he said to me, "Son of man, eat this scroll that I give you and fill your stomach with it." Then I ate it; and it was in my mouth as sweet as honey.

4 And he said to me, "Son of man, go, get you to the house of Israel, and speak with my words to them. [5] For you are not sent to a people of foreign speech and a hard language, but to the house of Israel—[6] not to many peo-

---

[d] Heb *of their faces*   [e] Heb *on their four sides*   [f] Cn: Heb uncertain
[g] Gk: Heb *awesome crystal*   [h] Heb *lapis lazuli*   [i] Or *it*   [j] Syr: Heb *nations*
1.18: Ezek 10.12; Rev 4.8.   **1.24:** Ezek 43.2; Rev 1.15; 14.2; 19.6.
1.26: Rev 1.13; 4.2.   **2.8–3.3:** Rev 5.1; 10.8–10.

ples of foreign speech and a hard language, whose words you cannot understand. Surely, if I sent you to such, they would listen to you. 7 But the house of Israel will not listen to you; for they are not willing to listen to me; because all the house of Israel are of a hard forehead and of a stubborn heart. 8 Behold, I have made your face hard against their faces, and your forehead hard against their foreheads. 9 Like adamant harder than flint have I made your forehead; fear them not, nor be dismayed at their looks, for they are a rebellious house." 10 Moreover he said to me, "Son of man, all my words that I shall speak to you receive in your heart, and hear with your ears. 11And go, get you to the exiles, to your people, and say to them, 'Thus says the Lord GOD'; whether they hear or refuse to hear."

12 Then the Spirit lifted me up, and as the glory of the LORD arose^k from its place, I heard behind me the sound of a great earthquake; 13 it was the sound of the wings of the living creatures as they touched one another, and the sound of the wheels beside them, that sounded like a great earthquake. 14 The Spirit lifted me up and took me away, and I went in bitterness in the heat of my spirit, the hand of the LORD being strong upon me; 15 and I came to the exiles at Tel-a´bib, who dwelt by the river Che´bär.^l And I sat there overwhelmed among them seven days.

16 And at the end of seven days, the word of the LORD came to me: 17 "Son of man, I have made you a watchman for the house of Israel; whenever you hear a word from my mouth, you shall give them warning from me. 18 If I say to the wicked, 'You shall surely die,' and you give him no warning, nor speak to warn the wicked from his wicked way, in order to save his life, that wicked man shall die in his iniquity; but his blood I will require at your hand. 19 But if you warn the wicked, and he does not turn from his wickedness, or from his wicked way, he shall die in his iniquity; but you will have saved your life. 20Again, if a righteous man turns from his righteousness and commits iniquity, and I lay a stumbling block before him, he shall die; because you have not warned him, he shall die for his sin, and his righteous deeds which

he has done shall not be remembered; but his blood I will require at your hand. 21 Nevertheless if you warn the righteous man not to sin, and he does not sin, he shall surely live, because he took warning; and you will have saved your life."

22 And the hand of the LORD was there upon me; and he said to me, "Arise, go forth into the plain,^m and there I will speak with you." 23 So I arose and went forth into the plain;^m and, lo, the glory of the LORD stood there, like the glory which I had seen by the river Che´bär; and I fell on my face. 24 But the Spirit entered into me, and set me upon my feet; and he spoke with me and said to me, "Go, shut yourself within your house. 25And you, O son of man, behold, cords will be placed upon you, and you shall be bound with them, so that you cannot go out among the people; 26 and I will make your tongue cleave to the roof of your mouth, so that you shall be dumb and unable to reprove them; for they are a rebellious house. 27 But when I speak with you, I will open your mouth, and you shall say to them, 'Thus says the Lord GOD'; he that will hear, let him hear; and he that will refuse to hear, let him refuse; for they are a rebellious house.

4 "And you, O son of man, take a brick and lay it before you, and portray upon it a city, even Jerusalem; 2 and put siegeworks against it, and build a siege wall against it, and cast up a mound against it; set camps also against it, and plant battering rams against it round about. 3And take an iron plate, and place it as an iron wall between you and the city; and set your face toward it, and let it be a state of siege, and press the siege against it. This is a sign for the house of Israel.

4 "Then lie upon your left side, and I will lay the punishment of the house of Israel upon you;^n for the number of the days that you lie upon it, you shall bear their punishment. 5 For I assign to you a number of days, three hundred and ninety days, equal to the number of the years of their punishment; so long shall you bear the punishment of the house of Israel. 6And when you have completed these, you shall lie down a second time, but on your right side, and bear the punishment of the house of Judah; forty days I assign you, a day for each year. 7And

k Cn: Heb *blessed be the glory of the LORD*
l Heb *Chebar, and to where they dwelt.* Another reading is *Chebar, and I sat where they sat*
m Or *valley*   *n* Cn: Heb *you shall lay . . . upon it*
3.16-21: Ezek 33.1-9.

you shall set your face toward the siege of Jerusalem, with your arm bared; and you shall prophesy against the city. 8And, behold, I will put cords upon you, so that you cannot turn from one side to the other, till you have completed the days of your siege.

9 "And you, take wheat and barley, beans and lentils, millet and spelt, and put them into a single vessel, and make bread of them. During the number of days that you lie upon your side, three hundred and ninety days, you shall eat it. 10And the food which you eat shall be by weight, twenty shekels a day; once a day you shall eat it. 11And water you shall drink by measure, the sixth part of a hin; once a day you shall drink. 12And you shall eat it as a barley cake, baking it in their sight on human dung." 13And the LORD said, "Thus shall the people of Israel eat their bread unclean, among the nations whither I will drive them." 14 Then I said, "Ah Lord GOD! behold, I have never defiled myself; from my youth up till now I have never eaten what died of itself or was torn by beasts, nor has foul flesh come into my mouth." 15 Then he said to me, "See, I will let you have cow's dung instead of human dung, on which you may prepare your bread." 16 Moreover he said to me, "Son of man, behold, I will break the staff of bread in Jerusalem; they shall eat bread by weight and with fearfulness; and they shall drink water by measure and in dismay. 17 I will do this that they may lack bread and water, and look at one another in dismay, and waste away under their punishment.

5 "And you, O son of man, take a sharp sword; use it as a barber's razor and pass it over your head and your beard; then take balances for weighing, and divide the hair. 2A third part you shall burn in the fire in the midst of the city, when the days of the siege are completed; and a third part you shall take and strike with the sword round about the city; and a third part you shall scatter to the wind, and I will unsheathe the sword after them. 3And you shall take from these a small number, and bind them in the skirts of your robe. 4And of these again you shall take some, and cast them into the fire, and burn them in the fire; from there a fire will come forth into all the house of Israel. 5 Thus says the Lord GOD: This is Jerusalem; I have

set her in the center of the nations, with countries round about her. 6And she has wickedly rebelled against my ordinances*o* more than the nations, and against my statutes more than the countries round about her, by rejecting my ordinances and not walking in my statutes. 7 Therefore thus says the Lord GOD: Because you are more turbulent than the nations that are round about you, and have not walked in my statutes or kept my ordinances, but have acted*p* according to the ordinances of the nations that are round about you; 8 therefore thus says the Lord GOD: Behold, I, even I, am against you; and I will execute judgments in the midst of you in the sight of the nations. 9And because of all your abominations I will do with you what I have never yet done, and the like of which I will never do again. 10 Therefore fathers shall eat their sons in the midst of you, and sons shall eat their fathers; and I will execute judgments on you, and any of you who survive I will scatter to all the winds. 11 Wherefore, as I live, says the Lord GOD, surely, because you have defiled my sanctuary with all your detestable things and with all your abominations, therefore I will cut you down;*q* my eye will not spare, and I will have no pity. 12A third part of you shall die of pestilence and be consumed with famine in the midst of you; a third part shall fall by the sword round about you; and a third part I will scatter to all the winds and will unsheathe the sword after them.

13 "Thus shall my anger spend itself, and I will vent my fury upon them and satisfy myself; and they shall know that I, the LORD, have spoken in my jealousy, when I spend my fury upon them. 14 Moreover I will make you a desolation and an object of reproach among the nations round about you and in the sight of all that pass by. 15 You shall be*r* a reproach and a taunt, a warning and a horror, to the nations round about you, when I execute judgments on you in anger and fury, and with furious chastisements—I, the LORD, have spoken—16 when I loose against you*s* my deadly arrows of famine, arrows for destruction, which I will loose to destroy you, and when I bring more and more famine upon you, and break your staff of bread. 17 I will send famine and wild beasts against you, and they will rob you of

o Or *changed my ordinances into wickedness*   *p* Another reading is *and have not acted*
q Another reading is *I will withdraw*   *r* Gk Syr Vg Tg: Heb *And it shall be*
s Heb *them*

your children; pestilence and blood shall pass through you; and I will bring the sword upon you. I, the LORD, have spoken."

6 The word of the LORD came to me: 2 "Son of man, set your face toward the mountains of Israel, and prophesy against them, 3 and say, You mountains of Israel, hear the word of the Lord GOD! Thus says the Lord GOD to the mountains and the hills, to the ravines and the valleys: Behold, I, even I, will bring a sword upon you, and I will destroy your high places. 4 Your altars shall become desolate, and your incense altars shall be broken; and I will cast down your slain before your idols. 5 And I will lay the dead bodies of the people of Israel before their idols; and I will scatter your bones round about your altars. 6 Wherever you dwell your cities shall be waste and your high places ruined, so that your altars will be waste and ruined,*t* your idols broken and destroyed, your incense altars cut down, and your works wiped out. 7 And the slain shall fall in the midst of you, and you shall know that I am the LORD.

8 "Yet I will leave some of you alive. When you have among the nations some who escape the sword, and when you are scattered through the countries, 9 then those of you who escape will remember me among the nations where they are carried captive, when I have broken*u* their wanton heart which has departed from me, and blinded their eyes which turn wantonly after their idols; and they will be loathsome in their own sight for the evils which they have committed, for all their abominations. 10 And they shall know that I am the LORD; I have not said in vain that I would do this evil to them."

11 Thus says the Lord GOD: "Clap your hands, and stamp your foot, and say, Alas! because of all the evil abominations of the house of Israel; for they shall fall by the sword, by famine, and by pestilence. 12 He that is far off shall die of pestilence; and he that is near shall fall by the sword; and he that is left and is preserved shall die of famine. Thus I will spend my fury upon them. 13 And you shall know that I am the LORD, when their slain lie among their idols round about their altars, upon every high hill, on all the

mountain tops, under every green tree, and under every leafy oak, wherever they offered pleasing odor to all their idols. 14 And I will stretch out my hand against them, and make the land desolate and waste, throughout all their habitations, from the wilderness to Rib'lah.*v* Then they will know that I am the LORD."

7 The word of the LORD came to me: 2 "And you, O son of man, thus says the Lord GOD to the land of Israel: An end! The end has come upon the four corners of the land. 3 Now the end is upon you, and I will let loose my anger upon you, and will judge you according to your ways; and I will punish you for all your abominations. 4 And my eye will not spare you, nor will I have pity; but I will punish you for your ways, while your abominations are in your midst. Then you will know that I am the LORD.

5 "Thus says the Lord GOD: Disaster after disaster! Behold, it comes. 6 An end has come, the end has come; it has awakened against you. Behold, it comes. 7 Your doom*w* has come to you, O inhabitant of the land; the time has come, the day is near, a day of tumult, and not of joyful shouting upon the mountains. 8 Now I will soon pour out my wrath upon you, and spend my anger against you, and judge you according to your ways; and I will punish you for all your abominations. 9 And my eye will not spare, nor will I have pity; I will punish you according to your ways, while your abominations are in your midst. Then you will know that I am the LORD, who smite.

10 "Behold, the day! Behold, it comes! Your doom*w* has come, injustice*x* has blossomed, pride has budded. 11 Violence has grown up into a rod of wickedness; none of them shall remain, nor their abundance, nor their wealth; neither shall there be preeminence among them.*y* 12 The time has come, the day draws near. Let not the buyer rejoice, nor the seller mourn, for wrath is upon all their multitude. 13 For the seller shall not return to what he has sold, while they live. For wrath*z* is upon all their multitude; it shall not turn back; and because of his iniquity, none can maintain his life.*a*

14 "They have blown the trumpet and made all ready; but none goes to

---

t Syr Vg Tg: Heb *and be made guilty*   *u* Syr Vg Tg: Heb *I have been broken*
v Another reading is *Diblah*   *w* The meaning of the Hebrew word is uncertain
x Or *the rod*   *y* The Hebrew of verse 11 is uncertain   *z* Cn: Heb *vision*
a Heb obscure

6.9: Ezek 20.43; 36.31.   **7.2:** Rev 7.1; 20.8.

battle, for my wrath is upon all their multitude. [15] The sword is without, pestilence and famine are within; he that is in the field dies by the sword; and him that is in the city famine and pestilence devour. [16]And if any survivors escape, they will be on the mountains, like doves of the valleys, all of them moaning, every one over his iniquity. [17]All hands are feeble, and all knees weak as water. [18] They gird themselves with sackcloth, and horror covers them; shame is upon all faces, and baldness on all their heads. [19] They cast their silver into the streets, and their gold is like an unclean thing; their silver and gold are not able to deliver them in the day of the wrath of the LORD; they cannot satisfy their hunger or fill their stomachs with it. For it was the stumbling block of their iniquity. [20] Their[b] beautiful ornament they used for vainglory, and they made their abominable images and their detestable things of it; therefore I will make it an unclean thing to them. [21]And I will give it into the hands of foreigners for a prey, and to the wicked of the earth for a spoil; and they shall profane it. [22] I will turn my face from them, that they may profane my precious[c] place; robbers shall enter and profane it, [23] and make a desolation.[d]

"Because the land is full of bloody crimes and the city is full of violence, [24] I will bring the worst of the nations to take possession of their houses; I will put an end to their proud might, and their holy places shall be profaned. [25] When anguish comes, they will seek peace, but there shall be none. [26] Disaster comes upon disaster, rumor follows rumor; they seek a vision from the prophet, but the law perishes from the priest, and counsel from the elders. [27] The king mourns, the prince is wrapped in despair, and the hands of the people of the land are palsied by terror. According to their way I will do to them, and according to their own judgments I will judge them; and they shall know that I am the LORD."

8 In the sixth year, in the sixth month, on the fifth day of the month, as I sat in my house, with the elders of Judah sitting before me, the hand of the Lord GOD fell there upon me. [2] Then I beheld, and, lo, a form that had the appearance of a man;[e] below what appeared to be his loins it was fire, and above his loins it was like the appearance of brightness, like

gleaming bronze. [3] He put forth the form of a hand, and took me by a lock of my head; and the Spirit lifted me up between earth and heaven, and brought me in visions of God to Jerusalem, to the entrance of the gateway of the inner court that faces north, where was the seat of the image of jealousy, which provokes to jealousy. [4]And behold, the glory of the God of Israel was there, like the vision that I saw in the plain.

5 Then he said to me, "Son of man, lift up your eyes now in the direction of the north." So I lifted up my eyes toward the north, and behold, north of the altar gate, in the entrance, was this image of jealousy. [6]And he said to me, "Son of man, do you see what they are doing, the great abominations that the house of Israel are committing here, to drive me far from my sanctuary? But you will see still greater abominations."

7 And he brought me to the door of the court; and when I looked, behold, there was a hole in the wall. [8] Then said he to me, "Son of man, dig in the wall"; and when I dug in the wall, lo, there was a door. [9]And he said to me, "Go in, and see the vile abominations that they are committing here." [10] So I went in and saw; and there, portrayed upon the wall round about, were all kinds of creeping things, and loathsome beasts, and all the idols of the house of Israel. [11]And before them stood seventy men of the elders of the house of Israel, with Jā-az-à-nī'àh the son of Shā'phàn standing among them. Each had his censer in his hand, and the smoke of the cloud of incense went up. [12] Then he said to me, "Son of man, have you seen what the elders of the house of Israel are doing in the dark, every man in his room[f] of pictures? For they say, 'The LORD does not see us, the LORD has forsaken the land.'" [13] He said also to me, "You will see still greater abominations which they commit."

14 Then he brought me to the entrance of the north gate of the house of the LORD; and behold, there sat women weeping for Tăm'müz. [15] Then he said to me, "Have you seen this, O son of man? You will see still greater abominations than these."

16 And he brought me into the inner court of the house of the LORD; and behold, at the door of the temple of the LORD, between the porch and the altar, were about twenty-five men,

[b] Syr Symmachus: Heb *Its*   [c] Or *secret*   [d] Cn: Heb *make the chain*   [e] Gk: Heb *fire*
[f] Gk Syr Vg Tg: Heb *rooms*

with their backs to the temple of the LORD, and their faces toward the east, worshiping the sun toward the east. [17] Then he said to me, "Have you seen this, O son of man? Is it too slight a thing for the house of Judah to commit the abominations which they commit here, that they should fill the land with violence, and provoke me further to anger? Lo, they put the branch to their nose. [18] Therefore I will deal in wrath; my eye will not spare, nor will I have pity; and though they cry in my ears with a loud voice, I will not hear them."

9 Then he cried in my ears with a loud voice, saying, "Draw near, you executioners of the city, each with his destroying weapon in his hand." [2] And lo, six men came from the direction of the upper gate, which faces north, every man with his weapon for slaughter in his hand, and with them was a man clothed in linen, with a writing case at his side. And they went in and stood beside the bronze altar.

[3] Now the glory of the God of Israel had gone up from the cherubim on which it rested to the threshold of the house; and he called to the man clothed in linen, who had the writing case at his side. [4] And the LORD said to him, "Go through the city, through Jerusalem, and put a mark upon the foreheads of the men who sigh and groan over all the abominations that are committed in it." [5] And to the others he said in my hearing, "Pass through the city after him, and smite; your eye shall not spare, and you shall show no pity; [6] slay old men outright, young men and maidens, little children and women, but touch no one upon whom is the mark. And begin at my sanctuary." So they began with the elders who were before the house. [7] Then he said to them, "Defile the house, and fill the courts with the slain. Go forth." So they went forth, and smote in the city. [8] And while they were smiting, and I was left alone, I fell upon my face, and cried, "Ah Lord GOD! wilt thou destroy all that remains of Israel in the outpouring of thy wrath upon Jerusalem?"

[9] Then he said to me, "The guilt of the house of Israel and Judah is exceedingly great; the land is full of blood, and the city full of injustice; for they say, 'The LORD has forsaken the land, and the LORD does not see.' [10] As

for me, my eye will not spare, nor will I have pity, but I will requite their deeds upon their heads."

[11] And lo, the man clothed in linen, with the writing case at his side, brought back word, saying, "I have done as thou didst command me."

10 Then I looked, and behold, on the firmament that was over the heads of the cherubim there appeared above them something like a sapphire, in form resembling a throne. [2] And he said to the man clothed in linen, "Go in among the whirling wheels underneath the cherubim; fill your hands with burning coals from between the cherubim, and scatter them over the city." And he went in before my eyes.

[3] Now the cherubim were standing on the south side of the house, when the man went in; and a cloud filled the inner court. [4] And the glory of the LORD went up from the cherubim to the threshold of the house; and the house was filled with the cloud, and the court was full of the brightness of the glory of the LORD. [5] And the sound of the wings of the cherubim was heard as far as the outer court, like the voice of God Almighty when he speaks.

[6] And when he commanded the man clothed in linen, "Take fire from between the whirling wheels, from between the cherubim," he went in and stood beside a wheel. [7] And a cherub stretched forth his hand from between the cherubim to the fire that was between the cherubim and took some of it, and put it into the hands of the man clothed in linen, who took it and went out. [8] The cherubim appeared to have the form of a human hand under their wings.

[9] And I looked, and behold, there were four wheels beside the cherubim, one beside each cherub; and the appearance of the wheels was like sparkling chrysolite. [10] And as for their appearance, the four had the same likeness, as if a wheel were within a wheel. [11] When they went, they went in any of their four directions[g] without turning as they went, but in whatever direction the front wheel faced the others followed without turning as they went. [12] And[h] their rims, and their spokes,[i] and the wheels were full of eyes round about—the wheels that the four of them had. [13] As for the wheels, they were called in my hearing the whirling wheels. [14] And every one had

g Heb *on their four sides*   h Gk: Heb *And their whole body and*
i Heb *spokes and their wings*
9.4, 6: 1 Pet 4.17; Rev 7.3; 9.4; 14.1.   **10.1:** Rev 4.2.   **10.2:** Rev 8.5.
10.12: Ezek 1.18; Rev 4.8.   **10.14:** Ezek 1.10; Rev 4.7.

four faces: the first face was the face of the cherub, and the second face was the face of a man, and the third the face of a lion, and the fourth the face of an eagle.

15 And the cherubim mounted up. These were the living creatures that I saw by the river Chē′bär. 16And when the cherubim went, the wheels went beside them; and when the cherubim lifted up their wings to mount up from the earth, the wheels did not turn from beside them. 17 When they stood still, these stood still, and when they mounted up, these mounted up with them; for the spirit of the living creatures*ʲ* was in them.

18 Then the glory of the LORD went forth from the threshold of the house, and stood over the cherubim. 19And the cherubim lifted up their wings and mounted up from the earth in my sight as they went forth, with the wheels beside them; and they stood at the door of the east gate of the house of the LORD; and the glory of the God of Israel was over them.

20 These were the living creatures that I saw underneath the God of Israel by the river Chē′bär; and I knew that they were cherubim. 21 Each had four faces, and each four wings, and underneath their wings the semblance of human hands. 22And as for the likeness of their faces, they were the very faces whose appearance I had seen by the river Chē′bär. They went every one straight forward.

11 The Spirit lifted me up, and brought me to the east gate of the house of the LORD, which faces east. And behold, at the door of the gateway there were twenty-five men; and I saw among them Jā-az-à-nī′äh the son of Az′zūr, and Pel-à-tī′äh the son of Be-nā′iäh, princes of the people. 2And he said to me, "Son of man, these are the men who devise iniquity and who give wicked counsel in this city; 3 who say, 'The time is not near*ᵏ* to build houses; this city is the caldron, and we are the flesh.' 4 Therefore prophesy against them, prophesy, O son of man."

5 And the Spirit of the LORD fell upon me, and he said to me, "Say, Thus says the LORD: So you think, O house of Israel; for I know the things that come into your mind. 6 You have multiplied your slain in this city, and have filled its streets with the slain. 7 Therefore thus says the Lord GOD:

Your slain whom you have laid in the midst of it, they are the flesh, and this city is the caldron; but you shall be brought forth out of the midst of it. 8 You have feared the sword; and I will bring the sword upon you, says the Lord GOD. 9And I will bring you forth out of the midst of it, and give you into the hands of foreigners, and execute judgments upon you. 10 You shall fall by the sword; I will judge you at the border of Israel; and you shall know that I am the LORD. 11 This city shall not be your caldron, nor shall you be the flesh in the midst of it; I will judge you at the border of Israel; 12 and you shall know that I am the LORD; for you have not walked in my statutes, nor executed my ordinances, but have acted according to the ordinances of the nations that are round about you."

13 And it came to pass, while I was prophesying, that Pel-à-tī′äh the son of Be-nā′iäh died. Then I fell down upon my face, and cried with a loud voice, and said, "Ah Lord GOD! wilt thou make a full end of the remnant of Israel?"

14 And the word of the LORD came to me: 15 "Son of man, your brethren, even your brethren, your fellow exiles,*ˡ* the whole house of Israel, all of them, are those of whom the inhabitants of Jerusalem have said, 'They have gone far from the LORD; to us this land is given for a possession.' 16 Therefore say, 'Thus says the Lord GOD: Though I removed them far off among the nations, and though I scattered them among the countries, yet I have been a sanctuary to them for a while*ᵐ* in the countries where they have gone.' 17 Therefore say, 'Thus says the Lord GOD: I will gather you from the peoples, and assemble you out of the countries where you have been scattered, and I will give you the land of Israel.' 18And when they come there, they will remove from it all its detestable things and all its abominations. 19And I will give them one*ⁿ* heart, and put a new spirit within them; I will take the stony heart out of their flesh and give them a heart of flesh, 20 that they may walk in my statutes and keep my ordinances and obey them; and they shall be my people, and I will be their God. 21 But as for those*ᵒ* whose heart goes after their detestable things and their abominations, I will requite

---

ⁱ Or of life   ᵏ Or Is not the time near . . .?   ˡ Gk Syr: Heb men of your kindred
ᵐ Or in small measure   ⁿ Another reading is a new
ᵒ Cn: Heb To the heart of their detestable things and their abominations their heart goes
11.19: Ezek 18.31; 36.26; 2 Cor 3.3.

their deeds upon their own heads, says the Lord GOD."

22 Then the cherubim lifted up their wings, with the wheels beside them; and the glory of the God of Israel was over them. 23And the glory of the LORD went up from the midst of the city, and stood upon the mountain which is on the east side of the city. 24And the Spirit lifted me up and brought me in the vision by the Spirit of God into Chal·dē′ă, to the exiles. Then the vision that I had seen went up from me. 25And I told the exiles all the things that the LORD had showed me.

12 The word of the LORD came to me: 2 "Son of man, you dwell in the midst of a rebellious house, who have eyes to see, but see not, who have ears to hear, but hear not; 3 for they are a rebellious house. Therefore, son of man, prepare for yourself an exile's baggage, and go into exile by day in their sight; you shall go like an exile from your place to another place in their sight. Perhaps they will understand, though*p* they are a rebellious house. 4 You shall bring out your baggage by day in their sight, as baggage for exile; and you shall go forth yourself at evening in their sight, as men do who must go into exile. 5 Dig through the wall in their sight, and go*q* out through it. 6 In their sight you shall lift the baggage upon your shoulder, and carry it out in the dark; you shall cover your face, that you may not see the land; for I have made you a sign for the house of Israel."

7 And I did as I was commanded. I brought out my baggage by day, as baggage for exile, and in the evening I dug through the wall with my own hands; I went forth in the dark, carrying my outfit upon my shoulder in their sight.

8 In the morning the word of the LORD came to me: 9 "Son of man, has not the house of Israel, the rebellious house, said to you, 'What are you doing?' 10 Say to them, 'Thus says the Lord GOD: This oracle concerns the prince in Jerusalem and all the house of Israel who are in it.'*r* 11 Say, 'I am a sign for you: as I have done, so shall it be done to them; they shall go into exile, into captivity.' 12And the prince who is among them shall lift his baggage upon his shoulder in the dark, and shall go forth; he*s* shall dig through

the wall and go*t* out through it; he shall cover his face, that he may not see the land with his eyes. 13And I will spread my net over him, and he shall be taken in my snare; and I will bring him to Babylon in the land of the Chal·dē′ăns, yet he shall not see it; and he shall die there. 14And I will scatter toward every wind all who are round about him, his helpers*u* and all his troops; and I will unsheathe the sword after them. 15And they shall know that I am the LORD, when I disperse them among the nations and scatter them through the countries. 16 But I will let a few of them escape from the sword, from famine and pestilence, that they may confess all their abominations among the nations where they go, and may know that I am the LORD."

17 Moreover the word of the LORD came to me: 18 "Son of man, eat your bread with quaking, and drink water with trembling and with fearfulness; 19 and say of the people of the land, Thus says the Lord GOD concerning the inhabitants of Jerusalem in the land of Israel: They shall eat their bread with fearfulness, and drink water in dismay, because their land will be stripped of all it contains, on account of the violence of all those who dwell in it. 20And the inhabited cities shall be laid waste, and the land shall become a desolation: and you shall know that I am the LORD."

21 And the word of the LORD came to me: 22 "Son of man, what is this proverb that you have about the land of Israel, saying, 'The days grow long, and every vision comes to nought'? 23 Tell them therefore, 'Thus says the Lord GOD: I will put an end to this proverb, and they shall no more use it as a proverb in Israel.' But say to them, The days are at hand, and the fulfilment*v* of every vision. 24 For there shall be no more any false vision or flattering divination within the house of Israel. 25 But I the LORD will speak the word which I will speak, and it will be performed. It will no longer be delayed, but in your days, O rebellious house, I will speak the word and perform it, says the Lord GOD."

26 Again the word of the LORD came to me: 27 "Son of man, behold, they of the house of Israel say, 'The vision that he sees is for many days hence, and he prophesies of times far off.' 28 Therefore say to them, Thus

p Or *will see that*   *q* Gk Syr Vg Tg: Heb *bring*   *r* Heb *in the midst of them*   *s* Gk Syr: Heb *they*   *t* Gk Syr Tg: Heb *bring*   *u* Gk Syr Tg: Heb *his help*   *v* Heb *word*   **12.2:** Mk 8.18.

says the Lord GOD: None of my words will be delayed any longer, but the word which I speak will be performed, says the Lord GOD."

13 The word of the LORD came to me: 2 "Son of man, prophesy against the prophets of Israel, prophesy[w] and say to those who prophesy out of their own minds: 'Hear the word of the LORD!' 3 Thus says the Lord GOD, Woe to the foolish prophets who follow their own spirit, and have seen nothing! 4 Your prophets have been like foxes among ruins, O Israel. 5 You have not gone up into the breaches, or built up a wall for the house of Israel, that it might stand in battle in the day of the LORD. 6 They have spoken falsehood and divined a lie; they say, 'Says the LORD,' when the LORD has not sent them, and yet they expect him to fulfil their word. 7 Have you not seen a delusive vision, and uttered a lying divination, whenever you have said, 'Says the LORD,' although I have not spoken?"

8 Therefore thus says the Lord GOD: "Because you have uttered delusions and seen lies, therefore behold, I am against you, says the Lord GOD. 9 My hand will be against the prophets who see delusive visions and who give lying divinations; they shall not be in the council of my people, nor be enrolled in the register of the house of Israel, nor shall they enter the land of Israel; and you shall know that I am the Lord GOD. 10 Because, yea, because they have misled my people, saying, 'Peace,' when there is no peace; and because, when the people build a wall, these prophets daub it with whitewash; 11 say to those who daub it with whitewash that it shall fall! There will be a deluge of rain,[x] great hailstones will fall, and a stormy wind break out; 12 and when the wall falls, will it not be said to you, 'Where is the daubing with which you daubed it?' 13 Therefore thus says the Lord GOD: I will make a stormy wind break out in my wrath; and there shall be a deluge of rain in my anger, and great hailstones in wrath to destroy it. 14 And I will break down the wall that you have daubed with whitewash, and bring it down to the ground, so that its foundation will be laid bare; when it falls, you shall perish in the midst of it; and you shall know that I am the LORD. 15 Thus will I spend my wrath upon the wall, and upon those who have daubed it with whitewash; and I will say to you, The wall is no more, nor those who daubed it, 16 the prophets of Israel who prophesied concerning Jerusalem and saw visions of peace for her, when there was no peace, says the Lord GOD.

17 "And you, son of man, set your face against the daughters of your people, who prophesy out of their own minds; prophesy against them 18 and say, Thus says the Lord GOD: Woe to the women who sew magic bands upon all wrists, and make veils for the heads of persons of every stature, in the hunt for souls! Will you hunt down souls belonging to my people, and keep other souls alive for your profit? 19 You have profaned me among my people for handfuls of barley and for pieces of bread, putting to death persons who should not die and keeping alive persons who should not live, by your lies to my people, who listen to lies.

20 "Wherefore thus says the Lord GOD: Behold, I am against your magic bands with which you hunt the souls,[y] and I will tear them from your arms; and I will let the souls that you hunt go free[z] like birds. 21 Your veils also I will tear off, and deliver my people out of your hand, and they shall be no more in your hand as prey; and you shall know that I am the LORD. 22 Because you have disheartened the righteous falsely, although I have not disheartened him, and you have encouraged the wicked, that he should not turn from his wicked way to save his life; 23 therefore you shall no more see delusive visions nor practice divination; I will deliver my people out of your hand. Then you will know that I am the LORD."

14 Then came certain of the elders of Israel to me, and sat before me. 2 And the word of the LORD came to me: 3 "Son of man, these men have taken their idols into their hearts, and set the stumbling block of their iniquity before their faces; should I let myself be inquired of at all by them? 4 Therefore speak to them, and say to them, Thus says the Lord GOD: Any man of the house of Israel who takes his idols into his heart and sets the stumbling block of his iniquity before his face, and yet comes to the prophet, I the LORD will answer him myself[a] because of the multitude of his idols, 5 that I may lay hold of the hearts of the house of Israel, who are all estranged from me through their idols.

6 "Therefore say to the house of

Israel, Thus says the Lord God: Repent and turn away from your idols; and turn away your faces from all your abominations. 7 For any one of the house of Israel, or of the strangers that sojourn in Israel, who separates himself from me, taking his idols into his heart and putting the stumbling block of his iniquity before his face, and yet comes to a prophet to inquire for himself of me, I the Lord will answer him myself; 8 and I will set my face against that man, I will make him a sign and a byword and cut him off from the midst of my people; and you shall know that I am the Lord. 9And if the prophet be deceived and speak a word, I, the Lord, have deceived that prophet, and I will stretch out my hand against him, and will destroy him from the midst of my people Israel. 10And they shall bear their punishment—the punishment of the prophet and the punishment of the inquirer shall be alike—11 that the house of Israel may go no more astray from me, nor defile themselves any more with all their transgressions, but that they may be my people and I may be their God, says the Lord God."

12 And the word of the Lord came to me: 13 "Son of man, when a land sins against me by acting faithlessly, and I stretch out my hand against it, and break its staff of bread and send famine upon it, and cut off from it man and beast, 14 even if these three men, Noah, Daniel, and Job, were in it, they would deliver but their own lives by their righteousness, says the Lord God. 15 If I cause wild beasts to pass through the land, and they ravage it, and it be made desolate, so that no man may pass through because of the beasts; 16 even if these three men were in it, as I live, says the Lord God, they would deliver neither sons nor daughters; they alone would be delivered, but the land would be desolate. 17 Or if I bring a sword upon that land, and say, Let a sword go through the land; and I cut off from it man and beast; 18 though these three men were in it, as I live, says the Lord God, they would deliver neither sons nor daughters, but they alone would be delivered. 19 Or if I send a pestilence into that land, and pour out my wrath upon it with blood, to cut off from it man and beast; 20 even if Noah, Daniel, and Job were in it, as I live, says the Lord God, they would deliver neither son nor daughter; they would deliver but their own lives by their righteousness.

21 "For thus says the Lord God: How much more when I send upon Jerusalem my four sore acts of judgment, sword, famine, evil beasts, and pestilence, to cut off from it man and beast! 22 Yet, if there should be left in it any survivors to lead out sons and daughters, when they come forth to you, and you see their ways and their doings, you will be consoled for the evil that I have brought upon Jerusalem, for all that I have brought upon it. 23 They will console you, when you see their ways and their doings; and you shall know that I have not done without cause all that I have done in it, says the Lord God."

15 And the word of the Lord came to me: 2 "Son of man, how does the wood of the vine branch which is among the trees of the forest? 3 Is wood taken from it to make anything? Do men take a peg from it to hang any vessel on? 4 Lo, it is given to the fire for fuel; when the fire has consumed both ends of it, and the middle of it is charred, is it useful for anything? 5 Behold, when it was whole, it was used for nothing; how much less, when the fire has consumed it and it is charred, can it ever be used for anything! 6 Therefore thus says the Lord God: Like the wood of the vine among the trees of the forest, which I have given to the fire for fuel, so will I give up the inhabitants of Jerusalem. 7And I will set my face against them; though they escape from the fire, the fire shall yet consume them; and you will know that I am the Lord, when I set my face against them. 8And I will make the land desolate, because they have acted faithlessly, says the Lord God."

16 Again the word of the Lord came to me: 2 "Son of man, make known to Jerusalem her abominations, 3 and say, Thus says the Lord God to Jerusalem: Your origin and your birth are of the land of the Canaanites; your father was an Am'ó·rite, and your mother a Hit'tite. 4And as for your birth, on the day you were born your navel string was not cut, nor were you washed with water to cleanse you, nor rubbed with salt, nor swathed with bands. 5 No eye pitied you, to do any of these things to you out of compassion for you; but you were cast out on the open field, for you were abhorred, on the day that you were born.

6 "And when I passed by you, and saw you weltering in your blood, I said to you in your blood, 'Live, 7 and

14.21: Rev 6.8.   **16.3:** Ezek 16.45.

grow up[b] like a plant of the field.' And you grew up and became tall and arrived at full maidenhood;[c] your breasts were formed, and your hair had grown; yet you were naked and bare.

8 "When I passed by you again and looked upon you, behold, you were at the age for love; and I spread my skirt over you, and covered your nakedness: yea, I plighted my troth to you and entered into a covenant with you, says the Lord GOD, and you became mine. 9 Then I bathed you with water and washed off your blood from you, and anointed you with oil. 10 I clothed you also with embroidered cloth and shod you with leather, I swathed you in fine linen and covered you with silk. 11And I decked you with ornaments, and put bracelets on your arms, and a chain on your neck. 12And I put a ring on your nose, and earrings in your ears, and a beautiful crown upon your head. 13 Thus you were decked with gold and silver; and your raiment was of fine linen, and silk, and embroidered cloth; you ate fine flour and honey and oil. You grew exceedingly beautiful, and came to regal estate. 14And your renown went forth among the nations because of your beauty, for it was perfect through the splendor which I had bestowed upon you, says the Lord GOD.

15 "But you trusted in your beauty, and played the harlot because of your renown, and lavished your harlotries on any passer-by. 16 You took some of your garments, and made for yourself gaily decked shrines, and on them played the harlot; the like has never been, nor ever shall be. 17 You also took your fair jewels of my gold and of my silver, which I had given you, and made for yourself images of men, and with them played the harlot; 18 and you took your embroidered garments to cover them, and set my oil and my incense before them. 19Also my bread which I gave you—I fed you with fine flour and oil and honey—you set before them for a pleasing odor, says the Lord GOD.[d] 20And you took your sons and your daughters, whom you had borne to me, and these you sacrificed to them to be devoured. Were your harlotries so small a matter 21 that you slaughtered my children and delivered them up as an offering by fire to them? 22And in all your abominations and your harlotries you did not remember the days of your youth, when you were

naked and bare, weltering in your blood.

23 "And after all your wickedness (woe, woe to you! says the Lord GOD), 24 you built yourself a vaulted chamber, and made yourself a lofty place in every square; 25 at the head of every street you built your lofty place and prostituted your beauty, offering yourself to any passer-by, and multiplying your harlotry. 26 You also played the harlot with the Egyptians, your lustful neighbors, multiplying your harlotry, to provoke me to anger. 27 Behold, therefore, I stretched out my hand against you, and diminished your allotted portion, and delivered you to the greed of your enemies, the daughters of the Philistines, who were ashamed of your lewd behavior. 28 You played the harlot also with the Assyrians, because you were insatiable; yea, you played the harlot with them, and still you were not satisfied. 29 You multiplied your harlotry also with the trading land of Chal-dē′à; and even with this you were not satisfied.

30 "How lovesick is your heart, says the Lord GOD, seeing you did all these things, the deeds of a brazen harlot; 31 building your vaulted chamber at the head of every street, and making your lofty place in every square. Yet you were not like a harlot, because you scorned hire. 32Adulterous wife, who receives strangers instead of her husband! 33 Men give gifts to all harlots; but you gave your gifts to all your lovers, bribing them to come to you from every side for your harlotries. 34 So you were different from other women in your harlotries: none solicited you to play the harlot; and you gave hire, while no hire was given to you; therefore you were different.

35 "Wherefore, O harlot, hear the word of the LORD: 36 Thus says the Lord GOD, Because your shame was laid bare and your nakedness uncovered in your harlotries with your lovers, and because of all your idols, and because of the blood of your children that you gave to them, 37 therefore, behold, I will gather all your lovers, with whom you took pleasure, all those you loved and all those you loathed; I will gather them against you from every side, and will uncover your nakedness to them, that they may see all your nakedness. 38And I will judge you as women who break wedlock and shed blood are judged, and bring upon you the blood of wrath and jealousy.

39And I will give you into the hand of your lovers, and they shall throw down your vaulted chamber and break down your lofty places; they shall strip you of your clothes and take your fair jewels, and leave you naked and bare. 40 They shall bring up a host against you, and they shall stone you and cut you to pieces with their swords. 41And they shall burn your houses and execute judgments upon you in the sight of many women; I will make you stop playing the harlot, and you shall also give hire no more. 42 So will I satisfy my fury on you, and my jealousy shall depart from you; I will be calm, and will no more be angry. 43 Because you have not remembered the days of your youth, but have enraged me with all these things; therefore, behold, I will requite your deeds upon your head, says the Lord GOD.

"Have you not committed lewdness in addition to all your abominations? 44 Behold, every one who uses proverbs will use this proverb about you, 'Like mother, like daughter.' 45 You are the daughter of your mother, who loathed her husband and her children; and you are the sister of your sisters, who loathed their husbands and their children. Your mother was a Hit'tite and your father an Am'o·rite. 46And your elder sister is Sà·mâr'i·à, who lived with her daughters to the north of you; and your younger sister, who lived to the south of you, is Sod'om with her daughters. 47 Yet you were not content to walk in their ways, or do according to their abominations; within a very little time you were more corrupt than they in all your ways. 48As I live, says the Lord GOD, your sister Sod'om and her daughters have not done as you and your daughters have done. 49 Behold, this was the guilt of your sister Sod'om: she and her daughters had pride, surfeit of food, and prosperous ease, but did not aid the poor and needy. 50 They were haughty, and did abominable things before me; therefore I removed them, when I saw it. 51 Sà·mâr'i·à has not committed half your sins; you have committed more abominations than they, and have made your sisters appear righteous by all the abominations which you have committed. 52 Bear your disgrace, you also, for you have made judgment favorable to your sisters; because of your sins in which you acted more abominably than they, they are more in the right than you. So be ashamed,

you also, and bear your disgrace, for you have made your sisters appear righteous.

53 "I will restore their fortunes, both the fortunes of Sod'om and her daughters, and the fortunes of Sà·mâr'i·à and her daughters, and I will restore your own fortunes in the midst of them, 54 that you may bear your disgrace and be ashamed of all that you have done, becoming a consolation to them. 55As for your sisters, Sod'om and her daughters shall return to their former estate, and Sà·mâr'i·à and her daughters shall return to their former estate; and you and your daughters shall return to your former estate. 56 Was not your sister Sod'om a byword in your mouth in the day of your pride, 57 before your wickedness was uncovered? Now you have become like her*e* an object of reproach for the daughters of E'dom*f* and all her neighbors, and for the daughters of the Philistines, those round about who despise you. 58 You bear the penalty of your lewdness and your abominations, says the LORD.

59 "Yea, thus says the Lord GOD: I will deal with you as you have done, who have despised the oath in breaking the covenant, 60 yet I will remember my covenant with you in the days of your youth, and I will establish with you an everlasting covenant. 61 Then you will remember your ways, and be ashamed when I*g* take your sisters, both your elder and your younger, and give them to you as daughters, but not on account of the covenant with you. 62 I will establish my covenant with you, and you shall know that I am the LORD, 63 that you may remember and be confounded, and never open your mouth again because of your shame, when I forgive you all that you have done, says the Lord GOD."

17 The word of the LORD came to me: 2 "Son of man, propound a riddle, and speak an allegory to the house of Israel; 3 say, Thus says the Lord GOD: A great eagle with great wings and long pinions, rich in plumage of many colors, came to Lebanon and took the top of the cedar; 4 he broke off the topmost of its young twigs and carried it to a land of trade, and set it in a city of merchants. 5 Then he took of the seed of the land and planted it in fertile soil; he placed it beside abundant waters. He set it like a willow twig, 6 and it sprouted and became a low spreading vine, and its

e Cn: Heb uncertain   *f* Another reading is *Aram*   *g* Syr: Heb *you*
16.45: Ezek 16.3.

branches turned toward him, and its roots remained where it stood. So it became a vine, and brought forth branches and put forth foliage. 7 "But there was another great eagle with great wings and much plumage; and behold, this vine bent its roots toward him, and shot forth its branches toward him that he might water it. From the bed where it was planted 8 he transplanted it[h] to good soil by abundant waters, that it might bring forth branches, and bear fruit, and become a noble vine. 9 Say, Thus says the Lord GOD: Will it thrive? Will he not pull up its roots and cut off its branches,[i] so that all its fresh sprouting leaves wither? It will not take a strong arm or many people to pull it from its roots. 10 Behold, when it is transplanted, will it thrive? Will it not utterly wither when the east wind strikes it—wither away on the bed where it grew?"

11 Then the word of the LORD came to me: 12 "Say now to the rebellious house. Do you not know what these things mean? Tell them, Behold, the king of Babylon came to Jerusalem, and took her king and her princes and brought them to him to Babylon. 13And he took one of the seed royal and made a covenant with him, putting him under oath. (The chief men of the land he had taken away, 14 that the kingdom might be humble and not lift itself up, and that by keeping his covenant it might stand.) 15 But he rebelled against him by sending ambassadors to Egypt, that they might give him horses and a large army. Will he succeed? Can a man escape who does such things? Can he break the covenant and yet escape? 16As I live, says the Lord GOD, surely in the place where the king dwells who made him king, whose oath he despised, and whose covenant with him he broke, in Babylon he shall die. 17 Pharaoh with his mighty army and great company will not help him in war, when mounds are cast up and siege walls built to cut off many lives. 18 Because he despised the oath and broke the covenant, because he gave his hand and yet did all these things, he shall not escape. 19 Therefore thus says the Lord GOD: As I live, surely my oath which he despised, and my covenant which he broke, I will requite upon his head. 20 I will spread my net over him, and

he shall be taken in my snare, and I will bring him to Babylon and enter into judgment with him there for the treason he has committed against me. 21And all the pick[j] of his troops shall fall by the sword, and the survivors shall be scattered to every wind; and you shall know that I, the LORD, have spoken."

22 Thus says the Lord GOD: "I myself will take a sprig from the lofty top of the cedar, and will set it out; I will break off from the topmost of its young twigs a tender one, and I myself will plant it upon a high and lofty mountain; 23 on the mountain height of Israel will I plant it, that it may bring forth boughs and bear fruit, and become a noble cedar; and under it will dwell all kinds of beasts;[k] in the shade of its branches birds of every sort will nest. 24And all the trees of the field shall know that I the LORD bring low the high tree, and make high the low tree, dry up the green tree, and make the dry tree flourish. I the LORD have spoken, and I will do it."

18 The word of the LORD came to me again: 2 "What do you mean by repeating this proverb concerning the land of Israel, 'The fathers have eaten sour grapes, and the children's teeth are set on edge'? 3As I live, says the Lord GOD, this proverb shall no more be used by you in Israel. 4 Behold, all souls are mine; the soul of the father as well as the soul of the son is mine: the soul that sins shall die.

5 "If a man is righteous and does what is lawful and right—6 if he does not eat upon the mountains or lift up his eyes to the idols of the house of Israel, does not defile his neighbor's wife or approach a woman in her time of impurity, 7 does not oppress any one, but restores to the debtor his pledge, commits no robbery, gives his bread to the hungry and covers the naked with a garment, 8 does not lend at interest or take any increase, withholds his hand from iniquity, executes true justice between man and man, 9 walks in my statutes, and is careful to observe my ordinances[l]—he is righteous, he shall surely live, says the Lord GOD.

10 "If he begets a son who is a robber, a shedder of blood,[m] 11 who does none of these duties, but eats upon the mountains, defiles his neighbor's wife, 12 oppresses the poor

h Cn: Heb *it was transplanted*   i Cn: Heb *fruit*   j Another reading is *fugitives*
k Gk: Heb lacks *all kinds of beasts*   l Gk: Heb *has kept my ordinances, to deal truly*
m Heb *blood, and he does any one of these things*
17.23: Ezek 31.6; Mt 13.32; Mk 4.32; Lk 13.19.   18.2: Jer 31.29.   18.4: Ezek 18.20.

and needy, commits robbery, does not restore the pledge, lifts up his eyes to the idols, commits abomination, [13] lends at interest, and takes increase; shall he then live? He shall not live. He has done all these abominable things; he shall surely die; his blood shall be upon himself.

14 "But if this man begets a son who sees all the sins which his father has done, and fears, and does not do likewise, [15] who does not eat upon the mountains or lift up his eyes to the idols of the house of Israel, does not defile his neighbor's wife, [16] does not wrong any one, exacts no pledge, commits no robbery, but gives his bread to the hungry and covers the naked with a garment, [17] withholds his hand from iniquity,[n] takes no interest or increase, observes my ordinances, and walks in my statutes, he shall not die for his father's iniquity; he shall surely live. [18] As for his father, because he practiced extortion, robbed his brother, and did what is not good among his people, behold, he shall die for his iniquity.

19 "Yet you say, 'Why should not the son suffer for the iniquity of the father?' When the son has done what is lawful and right, and has been careful to observe all my statutes, he shall surely live. [20] The soul that sins shall die. The son shall not suffer for the iniquity of the father, nor the father suffer for the iniquity of the son; the righteousness of the righteous shall be upon himself, and the wickedness of the wicked shall be upon himself.

21 "But if a wicked man turns away from all his sins which he has committed and keeps all my statutes and does what is lawful and right, he shall surely live; he shall not die. [22] None of the transgressions which he has committed shall be remembered against him; for the righteousness which he has done he shall live. [23] Have I any pleasure in the death of the wicked, says the Lord God, and not rather that he should turn from his way and live? [24] But when a righteous man turns away from his righteousness and commits iniquity and does the same abominable things that the wicked man does, shall he live? None of the righteous deeds which he has done shall be remembered; for the treachery of which he

is guilty and the sin he has committed, he shall die.

25 "Yet you say, 'The way of the Lord is not just.' Hear now, O house of Israel: Is my way not just? Is it not your ways that are not just? [26] When a righteous man turns away from his righteousness and commits iniquity, he shall die for it; for the iniquity which he has committed he shall die. [27] Again, when a wicked man turns away from the wickedness he has committed and does what is lawful and right, he shall save his life. [28] Because he considered and turned away from all the transgressions which he had committed, he shall surely live, he shall not die. [29] Yet the house of Israel says, 'The way of the Lord is not just.' O house of Israel, are my ways not just? Is it not your ways that are not just?

30 "Therefore I will judge you, O house of Israel, every one according to his ways, says the Lord God. Repent and turn from all your transgressions, lest iniquity be your ruin.[o] [31] Cast away from you all the transgressions which you have committed against me, and get yourselves a new heart and a new spirit! Why will you die, O house of Israel? [32] For I have no pleasure in the death of any one, says the Lord God; so turn, and live."

19 And you, take up a lamentation for the princes of Israel, [2] and say:

What a lioness was your mother
    among lions!
She couched in the midst of young
    lions,
    rearing her whelps.
3 And she brought up one of her
    whelps;
    he became a young lion,
and he learned to catch prey;
    he devoured men.
4 The nations sounded an alarm
    against him;
    he was taken in their pit;
and they brought him with hooks
    to the land of Egypt.
5 When she saw that she was baffled,[p]
    that her hope was lost,
she took another of her whelps
    and made him a young lion.
6 He prowled among the lions;
    he became a young lion,
and he learned to catch prey;
    he devoured men.
7 And he ravaged their strongholds,[q]

---

[n] Gk: Heb *the poor*   [o] Or *so that they shall not be a stumbling block of iniquity to you*   [p] Heb *had waited*   [q] Tg Compare Theodotion: Heb *knew his widows*

18.20: Ezek 18.4.   **18.23:** Ezek 18.32; 33.11.   **18.31:** Ezek 11.19; 36.26.
18.32: Ezek 18.23; 33.11.

and laid waste their cities;
and the land was appalled and all
who were in it
at the sound of his roaring.
8 Then the nations set against him
snares^r on every side;
they spread their net over him;
he was taken in their pit.
9 With hooks they put him in a cage,
and brought him to the king of
Babylon;
they brought him into custody,
that his voice should no more be
heard
upon the mountains of Israel.

10 Your mother was like a vine in a
vineyard^s
transplanted by the water,
fruitful and full of branches
by reason of abundant water.
11 Its strongest stem became
a ruler's scepter;
it towered aloft
among the thick boughs;
it was seen in its height
with the mass of its branches.
12 But the vine was plucked up in fury,
cast down to the ground;
the east wind dried it up;
its fruit was stripped off,
its strong stem was withered;
the fire consumed it.
13 Now it is transplanted in the
wilderness,
in a dry and thirsty land.
14 And fire has gone out from its stem,
has consumed its branches and
fruit,
so that there remains in it no strong
stem,
no scepter for a ruler.

This is a lamentation, and has become a lamentation.

20 In the seventh year, in the
fifth month, on the tenth day
of the month, certain of the elders of
Israel came to inquire of the LORD,
and sat before me. 2And the word of
the LORD came to me: 3 "Son of man,
speak to the elders of Israel, and say
to them, Thus says the Lord GOD, Is
it to inquire of me that you come? As
I live, says the Lord GOD, I will not
be inquired of by you. 4 Will you
judge them, son of man, will you judge
them? Then let them know the abominations of their fathers, 5 and say to
them, Thus says the Lord GOD: On
the day when I chose Israel, I swore
to the seed of the house of Jacob, making myself known to them in the land

of Egypt, I swore to them, saying, I
am the LORD your God. 6 On that day
I swore to them that I would bring
them out of the land of Egypt into a
land that I had searched out for them,
a land flowing with milk and honey,
the most glorious of all lands. 7And I
said to them, Cast away the detestable
things your eyes feast on, every one of
you, and do not defile yourselves with
the idols of Egypt; I am the LORD your
God. 8 But they rebelled against me
and would not listen to me; they did
not every man cast away the detestable
things their eyes feasted on, nor did
they forsake the idols of Egypt.

"Then I thought I would pour out
my wrath upon them and spend my
anger against them in the midst of
the land of Egypt. 9 But I acted for
the sake of my name, that it should
not be profaned in the sight of the
nations among whom they dwelt, in
whose sight I made myself known to
them in bringing them out of the land
of Egypt. 10 So I led them out of the
land of Egypt and brought them into
the wilderness. 11 I gave them my
statutes and showed them my ordinances, by whose observance man
shall live. 12 Moreover I gave them my
sabbaths, as a sign between me and
them, that they might know that I the
LORD sanctify them. 13 But the house
of Israel rebelled against me in the
wilderness; they did not walk in my
statutes but rejected my ordinances,
by whose observance man shall live;
and my sabbaths they greatly profaned.

"Then I thought I would pour out
my wrath upon them in the wilderness,
to make a full end of them. 14 But I
acted for the sake of my name, that it
should not be profaned in the sight of
the nations, in whose sight I had
brought them out. 15 Moreover I
swore to them in the wilderness that
I would not bring them into the land
which I had given them, a land flowing
with milk and honey, the most glorious
of all lands, 16 because they rejected
my ordinances and did not walk in my
statutes, and profaned my sabbaths;
for their heart went after their idols.
17 Nevertheless my eye spared them,
and I did not destroy them or make a
full end of them in the wilderness.
18 "And I said to their children in
the wilderness, Do not walk in the
statutes of your fathers, nor observe
their ordinances, nor defile yourselves
with their idols. 19 I the LORD am
your God; walk in my statutes, and be
careful to observe my ordinances,

^r Cn: Heb *from the provinces*   ^s Cn: Heb *in your blood*

20 and hallow my sabbaths that they may be a sign between me and you, that you may know that I the LORD am your God. 21 But the children rebelled against me; they did not walk in my statutes, and were not careful to observe my ordinances, by whose observance man shall live; they profaned my sabbaths.

"Then I thought I would pour out my wrath upon them and spend my anger against them in the wilderness. 22 But I withheld my hand, and acted for the sake of my name, that it should not be profaned in the sight of the nations, in whose sight I had brought them out. 23 Moreover I swore to them in the wilderness that I would scatter them among the nations and disperse them through the countries, 24 because they had not executed my ordinances, but had rejected my statutes and profaned my sabbaths, and their eyes were set on their fathers' idols. 25 Moreover I gave them statutes that were not good and ordinances by which they could not have life; 26 and I defiled them through their very gifts in making them offer by fire all their first-born, that I might horrify them; I did it that they might know that I am the LORD.

27 "Therefore, son of man, speak to the house of Israel and say to them, Thus says the Lord GOD: In this again your fathers blasphemed me, by dealing treacherously with me. 28 For when I had brought them into the land which I swore to give them, then wherever they saw any high hill or any leafy tree, there they offered their sacrifices and presented the provocation of their offering; there they sent up their soothing odors, and there they poured out their drink offerings. 29 (I said to them, What is the high place to which you go? So its name is called Bā'māh[t] to this day.) 30 Wherefore say to the house of Israel, Thus says the Lord GOD: Will you defile yourselves after the manner of your fathers and go astray after their detestable things? 31 When you offer your gifts and sacrifice your sons by fire, you defile yourselves with all your idols to this day. And shall I be inquired of by you, O house of Israel? As I live, says the Lord GOD, I will not be inquired of by you.

32 "What is in your mind shall never happen—the thought, 'Let us be like the nations, like the tribes of

the countries, and worship wood and stone.'

33 "As I live, says the Lord GOD, surely with a mighty hand and an outstretched arm, and with wrath poured out, I will be king over you. 34 I will bring you out from the peoples and gather you out of the countries where you are scattered, with a mighty hand and an outstretched arm, and with wrath poured out; 35 and I will bring you into the wilderness of the peoples, and there I will enter into judgment with you face to face. 36 As I entered into judgment with your fathers in the wilderness of the land of Egypt, so I will enter into judgment with you, says the Lord GOD. 37 I will make you pass under the rod, and I will let you go in by number.[u] 38 I will purge out the rebels from among you, and those who transgress against me; I will bring them out of the land where they sojourn, but they shall not enter the land of Israel. Then you will know that I am the LORD.

39 "As for you, O house of Israel, thus says the Lord GOD: Go serve every one of you his idols, now and hereafter, if you will not listen to me; but my holy name you shall no more profane with your gifts and your idols.

40 "For on my holy mountain, the mountain height of Israel, says the Lord GOD, there all the house of Israel, all of them, shall serve me in the land; there I will accept them, and there I will require your contributions and the choicest of your gifts, with all your sacred offerings. 41 As a pleasing odor I will accept you, when I bring you out from the peoples, and gather you out of the countries where you have been scattered; and I will manifest my holiness among you in the sight of the nations. 42 And you shall know that I am the LORD, when I bring you into the land of Israel, the country which I swore to give to your fathers. 43 And there you shall remember your ways and all the doings with which you have polluted yourselves; and you shall loathe yourselves for all the evils that you have committed. 44 And you shall know that I am the LORD, when I deal with you for my name's sake, not according to your evil ways, nor according to your corrupt doings, O house of Israel, says the Lord GOD."

45[v] And the word of the LORD came to me: 46 "Son of man, set your

---

[t] That is High Place   [u] Gk: Heb bring you into the bond of the covenant
[v] Ch 21.1 in Heb

20.41: Eph 5.2; Phil 4.18.   20.43: Ezek 6.9; 36.31.

face toward the south, preach against the south, and prophesy against the forest land in the Negeb; [47] say to the forest of the Negeb, Hear the word of the LORD: Thus says the Lord GOD, Behold, I will kindle a fire in you, and it shall devour every green tree in you and every dry tree; the blazing flame shall not be quenched, and all faces from south to north shall be scorched by it. [48] All flesh shall see that I the LORD have kindled it; it shall not be quenched." [49] Then I said, "Ah Lord GOD! they are saying of me, 'Is he not a maker of allegories?'"

21[w] The word of the LORD came to me: [2] "Son of man, set your face toward Jerusalem and preach against the sanctuaries; prophesy against the land of Israel [3] and say to the land of Israel, Thus says the LORD: Behold, I am against you, and will draw forth my sword out of its sheath, and will cut off from you both righteous and wicked. [4] Because I will cut off from you both righteous and wicked, therefore my sword shall go out of its sheath against all flesh from south to north; [5] and all flesh shall know that I the LORD have drawn my sword out of its sheath; it shall not be sheathed again. [6] Sigh therefore, son of man; sigh with breaking heart and bitter grief before their eyes. [7] And when they say to you, 'Why do you sigh?' you shall say, 'Because of the tidings. When it comes, every heart will melt and all hands will be feeble, every spirit will faint and all knees will be weak as water. Behold, it comes and it will be fulfilled,'" says the Lord GOD.

8 And the word of the LORD came to me; [9] "Son of man, prophesy and say, Thus says the Lord, Say:

A sword, a sword is sharpened
　　and also polished,
[10] sharpened for slaughter,
　　polished to flash like lightning!
Or do we make mirth? You have despised the rod, my son, with everything of wood. [11] So the sword is given to be polished, that it may be handled; it is sharpened and polished to be given into the hand of the slayer. [12] Cry and wail, son of man, for it is against my people; it is against all the princes of Israel; they are delivered over to the sword with my people. Smite therefore upon your thigh. [13] For it will not be a testing—what

could it do if you despise the rod?" says the Lord GOD.

14 "Prophesy therefore, son of man; clap your hands and let the sword come down twice, yea thrice, the sword for those to be slain; it is the sword for the great slaughter, which encompasses them, [15] that their hearts may melt, and many fall at all their gates. I have given the glittering sword; ah! it is made like lightning, it is polished[x] for slaughter. [16] Cut sharply to right[y] and left where your edge is directed. [17] I also will clap my hands, and I will satisfy my fury; I the LORD have spoken."

18 The word of the LORD came to me again: [19] "Son of man, mark two ways for the sword of the king of Babylon to come; both of them shall come forth from the same land. And make a signpost, make it at the head of the way to a city; [20] mark a way for the sword to come to Rab′bah of the Am′mo·nites and to Judah and to[z] Jerusalem the fortified. [21] For the king of Babylon stands at the parting of the way, at the head of the two ways, to use divination; he shakes the arrows, he consults the teraphim, he looks at the liver. [22] Into his right hand comes the lot for Jerusalem,[a] to open the mouth with a cry,[b] to lift up the voice with shouting, to set battering rams against the gates, to cast up mounds, to build siege towers. [23] But to them it will seem like a false divination; they have sworn solemn oaths; but he brings their guilt to remembrance, that they may be captured.

24 "Therefore thus says the Lord GOD: Because you have made your guilt to be remembered, in that your transgressions are uncovered, so that in all your doings your sins appear— because you have come to remembrance, you shall be taken in them.[c] [25] And you, O unhallowed wicked one, prince of Israel, whose day has come, the time of your final punishment, [26] thus says the Lord GOD: Remove the turban, and take off the crown; things shall not remain as they are; exalt that which is low, and abase that which is high. [27] A ruin, ruin, ruin I will make it; there shall not be even a trace[d] of it until he comes whose right it is; and to him I will give it.

28 "And you, son of man, prophesy, and say, Thus says the Lord GOD concerning the Am′mo·nites, and concern-

---

[w] Ch 21.6 in Heb　　[x] Tg: Heb *wrapped up*　　[y] Gk Syr Vg: Heb *right, set*
[z] Gk Syr: Heb *in*　　[a] Heb *Jerusalem, to set battering rams*　　[b] Gk: Heb *with slaughter*
[c] Gk: Heb *with the hand*　　[d] Cn: Heb *not even this*
21.28-32: Ezek 25.1-7; Jer 49.1-6; Amos 1.13-15; Zeph 2.8-11.

ing their reproach; say, A sword, a sword is drawn for the slaughter, it is polished to glitter^e and to flash like lightning—29 while they see for you false visions, while they divine lies for you—to be laid on the necks of the unhallowed wicked, whose day has come, the time of their final punishment. 30 Return it to its sheath. In the place where you were created, in the land of your origin, I will judge you. 31And I will pour out my indignation upon you; I will blow upon you with the fire of my wrath; and I will deliver you into the hands of brutal men, skilful to destroy. 32 You shall be fuel for the fire; your blood shall be in the midst of the land; you shall be no more remembered; for I the LORD have spoken."

22 Moreover the word of the LORD came to me, saying, 2 "And you, son of man, will you judge, will you judge the bloody city? Then declare to her all her abominable deeds. 3 You shall say, Thus says the Lord GOD: A city that sheds blood in the midst of her, that her time may come, and that makes idols to defile herself! 4 You have become guilty by the blood which you have shed, and defiled by the idols which you have made; and you have brought your day near; the appointed time^f of your years has come. Therefore I have made you a reproach to the nations, and a mocking to all the countries. 5 Those who are near and those who are far from you will mock you, you infamous one, full of tumult.

6 "Behold, the princes of Israel in you, every one according to his power, have been bent on shedding blood. 7 Father and mother are treated with contempt in you; the sojourner suffers extortion in your midst; the fatherless and the widow are wronged in you. 8 You have despised my holy things, and profaned my sabbaths. 9 There are men in you who slander to shed blood, and men in you who eat upon the mountains; men commit lewdness in your midst. 10 In you men uncover their fathers' nakedness; in you they humble women who are unclean in their impurity. 11 One commits abomination with his neighbor's wife; another lewdly defiles his daughter-in-law; another in you defiles his sister, his father's daughter. 12 In you men take bribes to shed blood; you take interest and increase and make gain

of your neighbors by extortion; and you have forgotten me, says the Lord GOD.

13 "Behold, therefore, I strike my hands together at the dishonest gain which you have made, and at the blood which has been in the midst of you. 14 Can your courage endure, or can your hands be strong in the days that I shall deal with you? I the LORD have spoken, and I will do it. 15 I will scatter you among the nations and disperse you through the countries, and I will consume your filthiness out of you. 16And I^g shall be profaned through you in the sight of the nations; and you shall know that I am the LORD."

17 And the word of the LORD came to me: 18 "Son of man, the house of Israel has become dross to me; all of them, silver^h and bronze and tin and iron and lead in the furnace, have become dross. 19 Therefore thus says the Lord GOD: Because you have all become dross, therefore, behold, I will gather you into the midst of Jerusalem. 20As men gather silver and bronze and iron and lead and tin into a furnace, to blow the fire upon it in order to melt it; so I will gather you in my anger and in my wrath, and I will put you in and melt you. 21 I will gather you and blow upon you with the fire of my wrath, and you shall be melted in the midst of it. 22As silver is melted in a furnace, so you shall be melted in the midst of it; and you shall know that I the LORD have poured out my wrath upon you."

23 And the word of the LORD came to me: 24 "Son of man, say to her, You are a land that is not cleansed, or rained upon in the day of indignation. 25 Her princes^i in the midst of her are like a roaring lion tearing the prey; they have devoured human lives; they have taken treasure and precious things; they have made many widows in the midst of her. 26 Her priests have done violence to my law and have profaned my holy things; they have made no distinction between the holy and the common, neither have they taught the difference between the unclean and the clean, and they have disregarded my sabbaths, so that I am profaned among them. 27 Her princes in the midst of her are like wolves tearing the prey, shedding blood, destroying lives to get dishonest gain. 28And her prophets have daubed for them with whitewash, seeing false

---

^{e} Cn: Heb *to contain* ^{f} Two Mss Gk Syr Vg Tg: Heb *until*
^{g} Gk Syr Vg: Heb *you* ^{h} Transposed from the end of the verse. Compare verse 20
^{i} Gk: Heb *a conspiracy of her prophets*

visions and divining lies for them, saying, 'Thus says the Lord GOD,' when the LORD has not spoken. ²⁹ The people of the land have practiced extortion and committed robbery; they have oppressed the poor and needy, and have extorted from the sojourner without redress. ³⁰And I sought for a man among them who should build up the wall and stand in the breach before me for the land, that I should not destroy it; but I found none. ³¹ Therefore I have poured out my indignation upon them; I have consumed them with the fire of my wrath; their way have I requited upon their heads, says the Lord GOD."

23 The word of the LORD came to me: ² "Son of man, there were two women, the daughters of one mother; ³ they played the harlot in Egypt; they played the harlot in their youth; there their breasts were pressed and their virgin bosoms handled. ⁴ Ō·hō′lăh was the name of the elder and Ō·hol′i·băh the name of her sister. They became mine, and they bore sons and daughters. As for their names, Ō·hō′lăh is Să·mâr′i·à, and Ō·hol′i·băh is Jerusalem.

⁵ "Ō·hō′lăh played the harlot while she was mine; and she doted on her lovers the Assyrians, ⁶ warriors clothed in purple, governors and commanders, all of them desirable young men, horsemen riding on horses. ⁷ She bestowed her harlotries upon them, the choicest men of Assyria all of them; and she defiled herself with all the idols of every one on whom she doted. ⁸ She did not give up her harlotry which she had practiced since her days in Egypt; for in her youth men had lain with her and handled her virgin bosom and poured out their lust upon her. ⁹ Therefore I delivered her into the hands of her lovers, into the hands of the Assyrians, upon whom she doted. ¹⁰ These uncovered her nakedness; they seized her sons and her daughters; and her they slew with the sword; and she became a byword among women, when judgment had been executed upon her.

¹¹ "Her sister Ō·hol′i·băh saw this, yet she was more corrupt than she in her doting and in her harlotry, which was worse than that of her sister. ¹² She doted upon the Assyrians, governors and commanders, warriors clothed in full armor, horsemen riding

on horses, all of them desirable young men. ¹³And I saw that she was defiled; they both took the same way. ¹⁴ But she carried her harlotry further; she saw men portrayed upon the wall, the images of the Chăl·dē′ăns portrayed in vermilion, ¹⁵ girded with belts on their loins, with flowing turbans on their heads, all of them looking like officers, a picture of Babylonians whose native land was Chăl·dē′à. ¹⁶ When she saw them she doted upon them, and sent messengers to them in Chăl·dē′à. ¹⁷And the Babylonians came to her into the bed of love, and they defiled her with their lust; and after she was polluted by them, she turned from them in disgust. ¹⁸ When she carried on her harlotry so openly and flaunted her nakedness, I turned in disgust from her, as I had turned from her sister. ¹⁹ Yet she increased her harlotry, remembering the days of her youth, when she played the harlot in the land of Egypt²⁰ and doted upon her paramours there, whose members were like those of asses, and whose issue was like that of horses. ²¹ Thus you longed for the lewdness of your youth, when the Egyptiansʲ handled your bosom and pressedᵏ your young breasts."

²² Therefore, O Ō·hol′i·băh, thus says the Lord GOD: "Behold, I will rouse against you your lovers from whom you turned in disgust, and I will bring them against you from every side: ²³ the Babylonians and all the Chăl·dē′ăns, Pē′kod and Shō′à and Kō′à, and all the Assyrians with them, desirable young men, governors and commanders all of them, officers and warriors,ˡ all of them riding on horses. ²⁴And they shall come against you from the northᵐ with chariots and wagons and a host of peoples; they shall set themselves against you on every side with buckler, shield, and helmet, and I will commit the judgment to them, and they shall judge you according to their judgments. ²⁵And I will direct my indignation against you, that they may deal with you in fury. They shall cut off your nose and your ears, and your survivors shall fall by the sword. They shall seize your sons and your daughters, and your survivors shall be devoured by fire. ²⁶ They shall also strip you of your clothes and take away your fine jewels. ²⁷ Thus I will put an end to your lewdness and your harlotry brought from the land of

---

ʲ Two Mss: Heb *from Egypt*   ᵏ Cn: Heb *for the sake of*
ˡ Compare verses 6 and 12: Heb *called*
ᵐ Gk: The meaning of the Hebrew word is unknown

Egypt; so that you shall not lift up your eyes to the Egyptians or remember them any more. 28 For thus says the Lord GOD: Behold, I will deliver you into the hands of those whom you hate, into the hands of those from whom you turned in disgust; 29 and they shall deal with you in hatred, and take away all the fruit of your labor, and leave you naked and bare, and the nakedness of your harlotry shall be uncovered. Your lewdness and your harlotry 30 have brought this upon you, because you played the harlot with the nations, and polluted yourself with their idols. 31 You have gone the way of your sister; therefore I will give her cup into your hand. 32 Thus says the Lord GOD:

"You shall drink your sister's cup
   which is deep and large;
you shall be laughed at and held in
   derision,
   for it contains much;
33 you will be filled with drunkenness
   and sorrow.

A cup of horror and desolation,
   is the cup of your sister Sȧ·mâr'i·ȧ;
34 you shall drink it and drain it out,
   and pluck out your hair,[n]
   and tear your breasts;

for I have spoken, says the Lord GOD. 35 Therefore thus says the Lord GOD: Because you have forgotten me and cast me behind your back, therefore bear the consequences of your lewdness and harlotry."

36 The LORD said to me: "Son of man, will you judge Ȯ·hō'läh and Ȯ·hol'i·bäh? Then declare to them their abominable deeds. 37 For they have commited adultery, and blood is upon their hands; with their idols they have committed adultery; and they have even offered up to them for food the sons whom they had borne to me. 38 Moreover this they have done to me: they have defiled my sanctuary on the same day and profaned my sabbaths. 39 For when they had slaughtered their children in sacrifice to their idols, on the same day they came into my sanctuary to profane it. And lo, this is what they did in my house. 40 They even sent for men to come from far, to whom a messenger was sent, and lo, they came. For them you bathed yourself, painted your eyes, and decked yourself with ornaments; 41 you sat upon a stately couch, with a table spread before it on which you had placed my incense and my oil.

42 The sound of a carefree multitude was with her; and with men of the common sort drunkards[o] were brought from the wilderness; and they put bracelets upon the hands of the women, and beautiful crowns upon their heads.

43 "Then I said, Do not men now commit adultery[p] when they practice harlotry with her? 44 For they have gone in to her, as men go in to a harlot. Thus they went in to Ȯ·hō'läh and to Ȯ·hol'i·bäh to commit lewdness.[q] 45 But righteous men shall pass judgment on them with the sentence of adulteresses, and with the sentence of women that shed blood; because they are adulteresses, and blood is upon their hands."

46 For thus says the Lord GOD: "Bring up a host against them, and make them an object of terror and a spoil. 47 And the host shall stone them and dispatch them with their swords; they shall slay their sons and their daughters, and burn up their houses. 48 Thus will I put an end to lewdness in the land, that all women may take warning and not commit lewdness as you have done. 49 And your lewdness shall be requited upon you, and you shall bear the penalty for your sinful idolatry; and you shall know that I am the Lord GOD."

24 In the ninth year, in the tenth month, on the tenth day of the month, the word of the LORD came to me: 2 "Son of man, write down the name of this day, this very day. The king of Babylon has laid siege to Jerusalem this very day. 3 And utter an allegory to the rebellious house and say to them, Thus says the Lord GOD:

Set on the pot, set it on,
   pour in water also;
4 put in it the pieces of flesh,
   all the good pieces, the thigh and
     the shoulder;
   fill it with choice bones.
5 Take the choicest one of the flock,
   pile the logs[r] under it;
   boil its pieces,[s]
   seethe[t] also its bones in it.

6 "Therefore thus says the Lord GOD: Woe to the bloody city, to the pot whose rust is in it, and whose rust has not gone out of it! Take out of it piece after piece, without making any choice.[u] 7 For the blood she has shed is still in the midst of her; she put it on the bare rock, she did not pour it upon the ground to cover it with dust.

---

[n] Compare Syr: Heb *gnaw its sherds* [o] Heb uncertain [p] Compare Gk: Heb obscure
[q] Gk: Heb *a woman of lewdness* [r] Compare verse 10: Heb *the bones*
[s] Two Mss: Heb *its boilings* [t] Cn: Heb *its bones seethe* [u] Heb *no lot has fallen upon it*

8 To rouse my wrath, to take vengeance, I have set on the bare rock the blood she has shed, that it may not be covered. 9 Therefore thus says the Lord GOD: Woe to the bloody city! I also will make the pile great. 10 Heap on the logs, kindle the fire, boil well the flesh, and empty out the broth,ᵛ and let the bones be burned up. 11 Then set it empty upon the coals, that it may become hot, and its copper may burn, that its filthiness may be melted in it, its rust consumed. 12 In vain I have wearied myself;ʷ its thick rust does not go out of it by fire. 13 Its rust is your filthy lewdness. Because I would have cleansed you and you were not cleansed from your filthiness, you shall not be cleansed any more till I have satisfied my fury upon you. 14 I the LORD have spoken; it shall come to pass, I will do it; I will not go back, I will not spare, I will not repent; according to your ways and your doings I will judge you, says the Lord GOD."

15 Also the word of the LORD came to me: 16 "Son of man, behold, I am about to take the delight of your eyes away from you at a stroke; yet you shall not mourn or weep nor shall your tears run down. 17 Sigh, but not aloud; make no mourning for the dead. Bind on your turban, and put your shoes on your feet; do not cover your lips, nor eat the bread of mourners."ˣ 18 So I spoke to the people in the morning, and at evening my wife died. And on the next morning I did as I was commanded.

19 And the people said to me, "Will you not tell us what these things mean for us, that you are acting thus?" 20 Then I said to them, "The word of the LORD came to me: 21 'Say to the house of Israel, Thus says the Lord GOD: Behold, I will profane my sanctuary, the pride of your power, the delight of your eyes, and the desire of your soul; and your sons and your daughters whom you left behind shall fall by the sword. 22And you shall do as I have done; you shall not cover your lips, nor eat the bread of mourners.ˣ 23 Your turbans shall be on your heads and your shoes on your feet; you shall not mourn or weep, but you shall pine away in your iniquities and groan to one another. 24 Thus shall E·zek′i·el be to you a sign; according to all that

he has done you shall do. When this comes, then you will know that I am the Lord GOD.'

25 "And you, son of man, on the day when I take from them their stronghold, their joy and glory, the delight of their eyes and their heart's desire, and also their sons and daughters, 26 on that day a fugitive will come to you to report to you the news. 27 On that day your mouth will be opened to the fugitive, and you shall speak and be no longer dumb. So you will be a sign to them; and they will know that I am the LORD."

25

The word of the LORD came to me: 2 "Son of man, set your face toward the Am′mo·nites, and prophesy against them. 3 Say to the Am′mo·nites, Hear the word of the Lord GOD: Thus says the Lord GOD, Because you said, 'Aha!' over my sanctuary when it was profaned, and over the land of Israel when it was made desolate, and over the house of Judah when it went into exile; 4 therefore I am handing you over to the people of the East for a possession, and they shall set their encampments among you and make their dwellings in your midst; they shall eat your fruit, and they shall drink your milk. 5 I will make Rab′bah a pasture for camels and the cities of the Am′mo·nitesʸ a fold for flocks. Then you will know that I am the LORD. 6 For thus says the Lord GOD: Because you have clapped your hands and stamped your feet and rejoiced with all the malice within you against the land of Israel, 7 therefore, behold, I have stretched out my hand against you, and will hand you over as spoil to the nations; and I will cut you off from the peoples and will make you perish out of the countries; I will destroy you. Then you will know that I am the LORD.

8 "Thus says the Lord GOD: Because Mo′abᶻ said, Behold, the house of Judah is like all the other nations, 9 therefore I will lay open the flank of Mo′ab from the citiesᵃ on its frontier, the glory of the country, Beth-jesh′i-moth, Ba′al-me′on, and Kir·i·a·tha′im. 10 I will give it along with the Am′mo-nites to the people of the East as a possession, that itᵇ may be remembered no more among the nations, 11 and I will execute judgments upon

---

ᵛ Compare Gk: Heb *mix the spices*　ʷ Cn: Heb uncertain　ˣ Vg Tg: Heb *men*
ʸ Cn: Heb lacks *the cities of*　ᶻ Gk Old Latin: Heb *Moab and Seir*
ᵃ Heb *cities from its cities*　ᵇ Cn: Heb *the Ammonites*

25.1-7: Ezek 21.28-32; Jer 49.1-6; Amos 1.13-15; Zeph 2.8-11.
25.8-11: Is 15-16; 25.10-12; Jer 48; Amos 2.1-3; Zeph 2.8-11.

Mō′ab. Then they will know that I am the LORD.

12 "Thus says the Lord GOD: Because Ē′dŏm acted revengefully against the house of Judah and has grievously offended in taking vengeance upon them, 13 therefore thus says the Lord GOD, I will stretch out my hand against Ē′dŏm, and cut off from it man and beast; and I will make it desolate; from Tē′măn even to Dē′dan they shall fall by the sword. 14And I will lay my vengeance upon Ē′dŏm by the hand of my people Israel; and they shall do in Edom according to my anger and according to my wrath; and they shall know my vengeance, says the Lord GOD.

15 "Thus says the Lord GOD: Because the Philistines acted revengefully and took vengeance with malice of heart to destroy in never-ending enmity; 16 therefore thus says the Lord GOD, Behold, I will stretch out my hand against the Philistines, and I will cut off the Cher′ē·thītes, and destroy the rest of the seacoast. 17 I will execute great vengeance upon them with wrathful chastisements. Then they will know that I am the LORD, when I lay my vengeance upon them."

26 In the eleventh year, on the first day of the month, the word of the LORD came to me: 2 "Son of man, because Tyre said concerning Jerusalem, 'Aha, the gate of the peoples is broken, it has swung open to me; I shall be replenished, now that she is laid waste,' 3 therefore thus says the Lord GOD: Behold, I am against you, O Tyre, and will bring up many nations against you, as the sea brings up its waves. 4 They shall destroy the walls of Tyre, and break down her towers; and I will scrape her soil from her, and make her a bare rock. 5 She shall be in the midst of the sea a place for the spreading of nets; for I have spoken, says the Lord GOD; and she shall become a spoil to the nations; 6 and her daughters on the mainland shall be slain by the sword. Then they will know that I am the LORD.

7 "For thus says the Lord GOD: Behold, I will bring upon Tyre from the north Ne·bù·chăd·rez′zăr king of Babylon, king of kings, with horses and chariots, and with horsemen and a host of many soldiers. 8 He will slay

with the sword your daughters on the mainland; he will set up a siege wall against you, and throw up a mound against you, and raise a roof of shields against you. 9 He will direct the shock of his battering rams against your walls, and with his axes he will break down your towers. 10 His horses will be so many that their dust will cover you; your walls will shake at the noise of the horsemen and wagons and chariots, when he enters your gates as one enters a city which has been breached. 11 With the hoofs of his horses he will trample all your streets; he will slay your people with the sword; and your mighty pillars will fall to the ground. 12 They will make a spoil of your riches and a prey of your merchandise; they will break down your walls and destroy your pleasant houses; your stones and timber and soil they will cast into the midst of the waters. 13And I will stop the music of your songs, and the sound of your lyres shall be heard no more. 14 I will make you a bare rock; you shall be a place for the spreading of nets; you shall never be rebuilt; for I the LORD have spoken, says the Lord GOD.

15 "Thus says the Lord GOD to Tyre: Will not the coastlands shake at the sound of your fall, when the wounded groan, when slaughter is made in the midst of you? 16 Then all the princes of the sea will step down from their thrones, and remove their robes, and strip off their embroidered garments; they will clothe themselves with trembling; they will sit upon the ground and tremble every moment, and be appalled at you. 17And they will raise a lamentation over you, and say to you,

'How you have vanished[c] from the
        seas,
    O city renowned,
that was mighty on the sea,
    you and your inhabitants,
who imposed your terror
    on all the mainland![d]
18 Now the isles tremble
    on the day of your fall;
yea, the isles that are in the sea
    are dismayed at your passing.'

19 "For thus says the Lord GOD: When I make you a city laid waste, like the cities that are not inhabited, when I bring up the deep over you,

c Gk Old Latin Aquila: Heb *vanished, O inhabited one,*   *d* Cn: Heb *her inhabitants*

25.12-14: Ezek 35; Is 34; 63.1-6; Jer 49.7-22; Amos 1.11-12; Obad; Mal 1.2-5.
25.15-17: Is 14.29-31; Jer 47; Amos 1.6-8; Zeph 2.4-7; Zech 9.5-7.
26.1-28.19: Is 23; Joel 3.4-8; Amos 1.9-10; Zech 9.3-4.   26.13: Rev 18.22.
26.16-17: Rev 18.9-10.

and the great waters cover you, [20] then I will thrust you down with those who descend into the Pit, to the people of old, and I will make you to dwell in the nether world, among primeval ruins, with those who go down to the Pit, so that you will not be inhabited or have a place[e] in the land of the living. [21] I will bring you to a dreadful end, and you shall be no more; though you be sought for, you will never be found again, says the Lord God."

27 The word of the LORD came to me: [2] "Now you, son of man, raise a lamentation over Tȳre, [3] and say to Tȳre, who dwells at the entrance to the sea, merchant of the peoples on many coastlands, thus says the Lord God:

"O Tyre, you have said,
    'I am perfect in beauty.'
[4] Your borders are in the heart of the
        seas;
    your builders made perfect your
        beauty.
[5] They made all your planks
    of fir trees from Sē´nir;
    they took a cedar from Lebanon
        to make a mast for you.
[6] Of oaks of Bā´shan
        they made your oars;
    they made your deck of pines
        from the coasts of Cyprus,
        inlaid with ivory.
[7] Of fine embroidered linen from
        Egypt
    was your sail,
        serving as your ensign;
    blue and purple from the coasts of
        E·lī´shāh
    was your awning.
[8] The inhabitants of Sī´don and
        Ar´vad
    were your rowers;
    skilled men of Zē´mer[f] were in
        you,
        they were your pilots.
[9] The elders of Gē´bal and her skilled
        men were in you,
        caulking your seams;
    all the ships of the sea with their
        mariners were in you,
        to barter for your wares.
[10] "Persia and Lüd and Püt were in your army as your men of war; they hung the shield and helmet in you; they gave you splendor. [11] The men of Ar´vad and Hē´lech[g] were upon your walls round about, and men of Gā´mad

were in your towers; they hung their shields upon your walls round about; they made perfect your beauty. [12] "Tär´shish trafficked with you because of your great wealth of every kind; silver, iron, tin, and lead they exchanged for your wares. [13] Jā´van, Tü´bal, and Mē´shech traded with you; they exchanged the persons of men and vessels of bronze for your merchandise. [14] Beth-tō·gär´mah exchanged for your wares horses, war horses, and mules. [15] The men of Rhodes[h] traded with you; many coastlands were your own special markets, they brought you in payment ivory tusks and ebony. [16] E´dom[i] trafficked with you because of your abundant goods; they exchanged for your wares emeralds, purple, embroidered work, fine linen, coral, and agate. [17] Judah and the land of Israel traded with you; they exchanged for your merchandise wheat, olives and early figs,[j] honey, oil, and balm. [18] Damascus trafficked with you for your abundant goods, because of your great wealth of every kind; wine of Hel´bon, and white wool, [19] and wine[k] from Ü´zal they exchanged for your wares; wrought iron, cassia, and calamus were bartered for your merchandise. [20] Dē´dan traded with you in saddlecloths for riding. [21] Arabia and all the princes of Kē´dar were your favored dealers in lambs, rams, and goats; in these they trafficked with you. [22] The traders of Sheba and Rā´a·mah traded with you; they exchanged for your wares the best of all kinds of spices, and all precious stones, and gold. [23] Hār´an, Can´neh, Eden,[l] As´shür, and Chil´mad traded with you. [24] These traded with you in choice garments, in clothes of blue and embroidered work, and in carpets of colored stuff, bound with cords and made secure; in these they traded with you.[m] [25] The ships of Tär´shish traveled for you with your merchandise.[n]

"So you were filled and heavily
        laden
    in the heart of the seas.
[26] Your rowers have brought you out
        into the high seas.
    The east wind has wrecked you
        in the heart of the seas.
[27] Your riches, your wares, your merchandise,
    your mariners and your pilots,

---

[e] Gk: Heb *I will give beauty*   [f] Compare Gen 10.18: Heb *your skilled men, O Tyre*
[g] Or *and your army*   [h] Gk: Heb *Dedan*   [i] Another reading is *Aram*
[j] Cn: Heb *wheat of minnith and pannag*   [k] Gk: Heb *Vedan and Javan*
[l] Cn: Heb *Eden the traders of Sheba*   [m] Cn: Heb *in your market*
[n] Cn: Heb *your travelers your merchandise*
27.13: Rev 18.13.   **27.27-36:** Rev 18.9-19.

your caulkers, your dealers in mer-
        chandise,
    and all your men of war who are
        in you,
    with all your company
        that is in your midst,
    sink into the heart of the seas
        on the day of your ruin.
28 At the sound of the cry of your
        pilots
    the countryside shakes,
29 and down from their ships
    come all that handle the oar.
    The mariners and all the pilots of
        the sea
    stand on the shore
30 and wail aloud over you,
        and cry bitterly.
    They cast dust on their heads
        and wallow in ashes;
31 they make themselves bald for you,
    and gird themselves with sack-
        cloth,
    and they weep over you in bitterness
        of soul,
    with bitter mourning.
32 In their wailing they raise a lam-
        entation for you,
    and lament over you:
    'Who was ever destroyed[o] like Tȳre
        in the midst of the sea?
33 When your wares came from the
        seas,
    you satisfied many peoples;
    with your abundant wealth and
        merchandise
    you enriched the kings of the
        earth.
34 Now you are wrecked by the seas,
        in the depths of the waters;
    your merchandise and all your crew
    have sunk with you.
35 All the inhabitants of the coastlands
        are appalled at you;
    and their kings are horribly afraid,
        their faces are convulsed.
36 The merchants among the peoples
        hiss at you;
    you have come to a dreadul end
        and shall be no more for ever.' "

28 The word of the LORD came
        to me: 2 "Son of man, say to
the prince of Tȳre, Thus says the
Lord GOD:
    "Because your heart is proud,
        and you have said, 'I am a god,
    I sit in the seat of the gods,
        in the heart of the seas,'
    yet you are but a man, and no god,
        though you consider yourself as
        wise as a god—
3 you are indeed wiser than Daniel;

no secret is hidden from you;
4 by your wisdom and your under-
        standing
    you have gotten wealth for your-
        self,
    and have gathered gold and silver
        into your treasuries;
5 by your great wisdom in trade
    you have increased your wealth,
    and your heart has become proud
        in your wealth—
6 therefore thus says the Lord GOD:
    "Because you consider yourself
        as wise as a god,
7 therefore, behold, I will bring
        strangers upon you,
    the most terrible of the nations;
    and they shall draw their swords
        against the beauty of your
        wisdom
    and defile your splendor.
8 They shall thrust you down into the
        Pit,
    and you shall die the death of the
        slain
    in the heart of the seas.
9 Will you still say, 'I am a god,'
    in the presence of those who slay
        you,
    though you are but a man, and no
        god,
    in the hands of those who wound
        you?
10 You shall die the death of the un-
        circumcised
    by the hand of foreigners;
    for I have spoken, says the Lord
        GOD."

11 Moreover the word of the LORD
came to me: 12 "Son of man, raise a
lamentation over the king of Tȳre,
and say to him, Thus says the Lord
GOD:
    "You were the signet of perfection,[p]
        full of wisdom
    and perfect in beauty.
13 You were in Eden, the garden of
        God;
    every precious stone was your
        covering,
    carnelian, topaz, and jasper,
        chrysolite, beryl, and onyx;
    sapphire,[q] carbuncle, and emerald;
    and wrought in gold were your
        settings
    and your engravings.[r]
    On the day that you were created
    they were prepared.
14 With an anointed guardian cherub
        I placed you;[s]
    you were on the holy mountain
        of God;

---

o Tg Vg: Heb *like silence*   *p* Heb obscure
s Heb uncertain
28.2: Dan 11.36; 2 Thess 2.4; Rev 13.5.

q Or *lapis lazuli*   *r* Heb uncertain

in the midst of the stones of fire
you walked.
15 You were blameless in your ways
from the day you were created,
till iniquity was found in you.
16 In the abundance of your trade
you were filled with violence, and
you sinned;
so I cast you as a profane thing from
the mountain of God,
and the guardian cherub drove
you out
from the midst of the stones of
fire.
17 Your heart was proud because of
your beauty;
you corrupted your wisdom for
the sake of your splendor.
I cast you to the ground;
I exposed you before kings,
to feast their eyes on you.
18 By the multitude of your iniquities,
in the unrighteousness of your
trade
you profaned your sanctuaries;
so I brought forth fire from the
midst of you;
it consumed you,
and I turned you to ashes upon the
earth
in the sight of all who saw you.
19 All who know you among the peoples
are appalled at you;
you have come to a dreadful end
and shall be no more for ever."

20 The word of the LORD came to
me: 21 "Son of man, set your face toward Si'don, and prophesy against her
22 and say, Thus says the Lord GOD:
"Behold, I am against you, O
Si'don,
and I will manifest my glory in
the midst of you.
And they shall know that I am the
LORD
when I execute judgments in her,
and manifest my holiness in her;
23 for I will send pestilence into her,
and blood into her streets;
and the slain shall fall in the midst
of her,
by the sword that is against her
on every side.
Then they will know that I am the
LORD.
24 "And for the house of Israel
there shall be no more a brier to prick
or a thorn to hurt them among all
their neighbors who have treated them
with contempt. Then they will know
that I am the Lord GOD.

25 "Thus says the Lord GOD:
When I gather the house of Israel
from the peoples among whom they
are scattered, and manifest my holiness
in them in the sight of the nations,
then they shall dwell in their own land
which I gave to my servant Jacob.
26 And they shall dwell securely in it,
and they shall build houses and plant
vineyards. They shall dwell securely,
when I execute judgments upon all
their neighbors who have treated them
with contempt. Then they will know
that I am the LORD their God."

29 In the tenth year, in the tenth
month, on the twelfth day of
the month, the word of the LORD came
to me: 2 "Son of man, set your face
against Pharaoh king of Egypt, and
prophesy against him and against all
Egypt; 3 speak, and say, Thus says the
Lord GOD:
"Behold, I am against you,
Pharaoh king of Egypt,
the great dragon that lies
in the midst of his streams,
that says, 'My Nile is my own;
I made it.'ᵗ
4 I will put hooks in your jaws,
and make the fish of your streams
stick to your scales;
and I will draw you up out of the
midst of your streams,
with all the fish of your streams
which stick to your scales.
5 And I will cast you forth into the
wilderness,
you and all the fish of your
streams;
you shall fall upon the open field,
and not be gathered and buried.
To the beasts of the earth and to
the birds of the air
I have given you as food.
6 "Then all the inhabitants of Egypt
shall know that I am the LORD. Because youᵘ have been a staff of reed to
the house of Israel; 7 when they
grasped you with the hand, you broke,
and tore all their shoulders; and when
they leaned upon you, you broke, and
made all their loins to shake;ᵛ 8 therefore thus says the Lord GOD: Behold,
I will bring a sword upon you, and
will cut off from you man and beast;
9 and the land of Egypt shall be a
desolation and a waste. Then they will
know that I am the LORD.
"Because youʷ said, 'The Nile is
mine, and I made it,' 10 therefore,
behold, I am against you, and against
your streams, and I will make the land

ᵗ Syr Compare Gk: Heb *I have made myself*   ᵘ Gk Syr Vg: Heb *they*
ᵛ Syr: Heb *stand*   ʷ Gk Syr Vg: Heb *he*
28.20-26: Joel 3.4-8; Zech 9.2.   29-32: Is 19; Jer 46; Zech 14.18-19.

of Egypt an utter waste and desolation, from Mig'dōl to Sȳ·ē'nē, as far as the border of Ethiopia. [11] No foot of man shall pass through it, and no foot of beast shall pass through it; it shall be uninhabited forty years. [12] And I will make the land of Egypt a desolation in the midst of desolated countries; and her cities shall be a desolation forty years among cities that are laid waste. I will scatter the Egyptians among the nations, and disperse them among the countries.

13 "For thus says the Lord GOD: At the end of forty years I will gather the Egyptians from the peoples among whom they were scattered; [14] and I will restore the fortunes of Egypt, and bring them back to the land of Path'-ros, the land of their origin; and there they shall be a lowly kingdom. [15] It shall be the most lowly of the kingdoms, and never again exalt itself above the nations; and I will make them so small that they will never again rule over the nations. [16] And it shall never again be the reliance of the house of Israel, recalling their iniquity, when they turn to them for aid. Then they will know that I am the Lord GOD."

17 In the twenty-seventh year, in the first month, on the first day of the month, the word of the LORD came to me: [18] "Son of man, Ne·bu·chad·rez'-zàr king of Babylon made his army labor hard against Tȳre; every head was made bald and every shoulder was rubbed bare; yet neither he nor his army got anything from Tyre to pay for the labor that he had performed against it. [19] Therefore thus says the Lord GOD: Behold, I will give the land of Egypt to Ne·bu·chad·rez'zàr king of Babylon; and he shall carry off its wealth[x] and despoil it and plunder it; and it shall be the wages for his army. [20] I have given him the land of Egypt as his recompense for which he labored, because they worked for me, says the Lord GOD.

21 "On that day I will cause a horn to spring forth to the house of Israel, and I will open your lips among them. Then they will know that I am the LORD."

30 The word of the LORD came to me: [2] "Son of man, prophesy, and say, Thus says the Lord GOD:

"Wail, 'Alas for the day!'
3 For the day is near,
    the day of the LORD is near;
  it will be a day of clouds,

a time of doom for the nations.
4 A sword shall come upon Egypt,
    and anguish shall be in Ethiopia,
  when the slain fall in Egypt,
    and her wealth is carried away,
    and her foundations are torn
      down.
5 Ethiopia, and Pūt, and Lūd, and all
    Arabia, and Libya,[y] and the people of
    the land that is in league, shall fall
    with them by the sword.

6 "Thus says the LORD:
  Those who support Egypt shall fall,
    and her proud might shall come
      down;
  from Mig'dōl to Sȳ·ē'nē
    they shall fall within her by the
      sword,
  says the Lord GOD.
7 And she[z] shall be desolated in the
    midst of desolated countries
  and her cities shall be in the midst
    of cities that are laid waste.
8 Then they will know that I am the
    LORD,
  when I have set fire to Egypt,
    and all her helpers are broken.
9 "On that day swift[a] messengers
    shall go forth from me to terrify the
    unsuspecting Ethiopians; and anguish
    shall come upon them on the day of
    Egypt's doom; for, lo, it comes!

10 "Thus says the Lord GOD:
  I will put an end to the wealth[b] of
      Egypt,
    by the hand of Ne·bu·chad·rez'-
      zàr king of Babylon.
11 He and his people with him, the
      most terrible of the nations,
    shall be brought in to destroy the
      land;
  and they shall draw their swords
      against Egypt,
    and fill the land with the slain.
12 And I will dry up the Nile,
    and will sell the land into the hand
      of evil men;
  I will bring desolation upon the land
      and everything in it,
    by the hand of foreigners;
  I, the LORD, have spoken.

13 "Thus says the Lord GOD:
  I will destroy the idols,
    and put an end to the images, in
      Memphis;
  there shall no longer be a prince in
      the land of Egypt;
    so I will put fear in the land of
      Egypt.
14 I will make Path'ros a desolation,

---

x Or *multitude* *y* Gk Compare Syr Vg: Heb *Cub* *z* Gk: Heb *they*
a Gk Syr: Heb *in ships* *b* Or *multitude*

and will set fire to Zō′an,
and will execute acts of judgment
upon Thebes.
15 And I will pour my wrath upon
Pe·lü′si·um,
the stronghold of Egypt,
and cut off the multitude of
Thebes.
16 And I will set fire to Egypt;
Pe·lü′si·um shall be in great
agony;
Thebes shall be breached,
and its walls broken down.*c*
17 The young men of On and of Pī-
bē′seth shall fall by the sword;
and the women shall go into captivity.
18 At Te·haph′ne·hēs the day shall be
dark,
when I break there the dominion
of Egypt,
and her proud might shall come to
an end;
she shall be covered by a cloud,
and her daughters shall go into
captivity.
19 Thus I will execute acts of judgment
upon Egypt.
Then they will know that I am
the LORD.''

20 In the eleventh year, in the first
month, on the seventh day of the
month, the word of the LORD came to
me: 21 "Son of man, I have broken the
arm of Pharaoh king of Egypt; and lo,
it has not been bound up, to heal it
by binding it with a bandage, so that
it may become strong to wield the
sword. 22 Therefore thus says the
Lord GOD: Behold, I am against
Pharaoh king of Egypt, and will break
his arms, both the strong arm and the
one that was broken; and I will make
the sword fall from his hand. 23 I will
scatter the Egyptians among the
nations, and disperse them throughout
the lands. 24 And I will strengthen the
arms of the king of Babylon, and put
my sword in his hand: but I will break
the arms of Pharaoh, and he will groan
before him like a man mortally
wounded. 25 I will strengthen the arms
of the king of Babylon, but the arms
of Pharaoh shall fall; and they shall
know that I am the LORD. When I put
my sword into the hand of the king
of Babylon, he shall stretch it out
against the land of Egypt; 26 and I will
scatter the Egyptians among the nations and disperse them throughout
the countries. Then they will know
that I am the LORD.''

31 In the eleventh year, in the third
month, on the first day of the
month, the word of the LORD came to
me: 2 "Son of man, say to Pharaoh
king of Egypt and to his multitude:
"Whom are you like in your greatness?
3 Behold, I will liken you to*d* a
cedar in Lebanon,
with fair branches and forest shade,
and of great height,
its top among the clouds.*e*
4 The waters nourished it,
the deep made it grow tall,
making its river flow*f*
round the place of its planting,
sending forth its streams
to all the trees of the forest.
5 So it towered high
above all the trees of the forest;
its boughs grew large
and its branches long,
from abundant water in its shoots.
6 All the birds of the air
made their nests in its boughs;
under its branches all the beasts of
the field
brought forth their young;
and under its shadow
dwelt all great nations.
7 It was beautiful in its greatness,
in the length of its branches;
for its roots went down
to abundant waters.
8 The cedars in the garden of God
could not rival it,
nor the fir trees equal its boughs;
the plane trees were as nothing
compared with its branches;
no tree in the garden of God
was like it in beauty.
9 I made it beautiful
in the mass of its branches,
and all the trees of Eden envied it,
that were in the garden of God.

10 "Therefore thus says the Lord
GOD: Because it*g* towered high and set
its top among the clouds,*h* and its heart
was proud of its height, 11 I will give
it into the hand of a mighty one of the
nations; he shall surely deal with it as
its wickedness deserves. I have cast it
out. 12 Foreigners, the most terrible of
the nations, will cut it down and leave
it. On the mountains and in all the
valleys its branches will fall, and its
boughs will lie broken in all the watercourses of the land; and all the peoples
of the earth will go from its shadow
and leave it. 13 Upon its ruin will
dwell all the birds of the air, and upon
its branches will be all the beasts of

c Cn: Heb *and Memphis, distresses by day*   *d* Cn: Heb *Behold, Assyria*
e Gk: Heb *thick boughs*   *f* Gk: Heb *going*   *g* Syr Vg: Heb *you*   *h* Gk: Heb *thick boughs*
31.6: Ezek 17.23; Dan 4.12-21; Mt 13.32; Mk 4.32; Lk 13.19.   **31.8 (Gk):** Rev 2.7.

the field. [14]All this is in order that no trees by the waters may grow to lofty height or set their tops among the clouds,[h] and that no trees that drink water may reach up to them in height; for they are all given over to death, to the nether world among mortal men, with those who go down to the Pit.

[15] "Thus says the Lord GOD: When it goes down to Shĕ′ōl I will make the deep mourn for[i] it, and restrain its rivers, and many waters shall be stopped; I will clothe Lebanon in gloom for it, and all the trees of the field shall faint because of it. [16] I will make the nations quake at the sound of its fall, when I cast it down to Shĕ′ōl with those who go down to the Pit; and all the trees of Eden, the choice and best of Lebanon, all that drink water, will be comforted in the nether world. [17] They also shall go down to Shĕ′ōl with it, to those who are slain by the sword; yea, those who dwelt under its shadow among the nations shall perish.[j] [18] Whom are you thus like in glory and in greatness among the trees of Eden? You shall be brought down with the trees of Eden to the nether world; you shall lie among the uncircumcised, with those who are slain by the sword.

"This is Pharaoh and all his multitude, says the Lord GOD."

32 In the twelfth year, in the twelfth month, on the first day of the month, the word of the LORD came to me: [2] "Son of man, raise a lamentation over Pharaoh king of Egypt, and say to him:

"You consider yourself a lion among the nations,
but you are like a dragon in the seas;
you burst forth in your rivers,
trouble the waters with your feet,
and foul their rivers.

[3] Thus says the Lord GOD:
I will throw my net over you
with a host of many peoples;
and I[k] will haul you up in my dragnet.

[4] And I will cast you on the ground,
on the open field I will fling you,
and will cause all the birds of the air to settle on you,
and I will gorge the beasts of the whole earth with you.

[5] I will strew your flesh upon the mountains,

and fill the valleys with your carcass.[l]

[6] I will drench the land even to the mountains
with your flowing blood;
and the watercourses will be full of you.

[7] When I blot you out, I will cover the heavens,
and make their stars dark;
I will cover the sun with a cloud,
and the moon shall not give its light.

[8] All the bright lights of heaven
will I make dark over you,
and put darkness upon your land,
says the Lord GOD.

[9] "I will trouble the hearts of many peoples, when I carry you captive[m] among the nations, into the countries which you have not known. [10] I will make many peoples appalled at you, and their kings shall shudder because of you, when I brandish my sword before them; they shall tremble every moment, every one for his own life, on the day of your downfall. [11] For thus says the Lord GOD: The sword of the king of Babylon shall come upon you. [12] I will cause your multitude to fall by the swords of mighty ones, all of them most terrible among the nations.

"They shall bring to nought the pride of Egypt,
and all its multitudes shall perish.

[13] I will destroy all its beasts
from beside many waters;
and no foot of man shall trouble them any more,
nor shall the hoofs of beasts trouble them.

[14] Then I will make their waters clear,
and cause their rivers to run like oil, says the Lord GOD.

[15] When I make the land of Egypt desolate
and when the land is stripped of all that fills it,

when I smite all who dwell in it,
then they will know that I am the LORD.

[16] This is a lamentation which shall be chanted; the daughters of the nations shall chant it; over Egypt, and over all her multitude, shall they chant it, says the Lord GOD."

[17] In the twelfth year, in the first month,[n] on the fifteenth day of the month, the word of the LORD came to me: [18] "Son of man, wail over the multitude of Egypt, and send them

h Gk: Heb *thick boughs*   i Gk: Heb *mourn for, I have covered*
j Compare Gk: Heb obscure   k Gk Vg: Heb *they*
l Symmachus Syr Vg: Heb *your height*   m Gk: Heb *bring your destruction*
n Gk: Heb lacks *in the first month*

down, her and the daughters of majestic nations, to the nether world, to those who have gone down to the Pit: 19 'Whom do you surpass in beauty? Go down, and be laid with the uncircumcised.'

20 They shall fall amid those who are slain by the sword,*o* and with her shall lie all her multitudes.*p* 21 The mighty chiefs shall speak of them, with their helpers, out of the midst of Shē'ōl: 'They have come down, they lie still, the uncircumcised, slain by the sword.'

22 "Assyria is there, and all her company, their graves round about her, all of them slain, fallen by the sword; 23 whose graves are set in the uttermost parts of the Pit, and her company is round about her grave; all of them slain, fallen by the sword, who spread terror in the land of the living.

24 "Ē'lăm is there, and all her multitude about her grave; all of them slain, fallen by the sword, who went down uncircumcised into the nether world, who spread terror in the land of the living, and they bear their shame with those who go down to the Pit. 25 They have made her a bed among the slain with all her multitude, their graves round about her, all of them uncircumcised, slain by the sword; for terror of them was spread in the land of the living, and they bear their shame with those who go down to the Pit; they are placed among the slain.

26 "Mē'shech and Tü'băl are there, and all their multitude, their graves round about them, all of them uncircumcised, slain by the sword; for they spread terror in the land of the living. 27 And they do not lie with the fallen mighty men of old*q* who went down to Shē'ōl with their weapons of war, whose swords were laid under their heads, and whose shields*r* are upon their bones; for the terror of the mighty men was in the land of the living. 28 So you shall be broken and lie among the uncircumcised, with those who are slain by the sword.

29 "Ē'dŏm is there, her kings and all her princes, who for all their might are laid with those who are slain by the sword; they lie with the uncircumcised, with those who go down to the Pit.

30 "The princes of the north are there, all of them, and all the Sī-dō'ni-ănṣ, who have gone down in shame with the slain, for all the terror which

they caused by their might; they lie uncircumcised with those who are slain by the sword, and bear their shame with those who go down to the Pit.

31 "When Pharaoh sees them, he will comfort himself for all his multitude, Pharaoh and all his army, slain by the sword, says the Lord GOD. 32 For he*s* spread terror in the land of the living; therefore he shall be laid among the uncircumcised, with those who are slain by the sword, Pharaoh and all his multitude, says the Lord GOD."

33 The word of the LORD came to me: 2 "Son of man, speak to your people and say to them, If I bring the sword upon a land, and the people of the land take a man from among them, and make him their watchman; 3 and if he sees the sword coming upon the land and blows the trumpet and warns the people; 4 then if any one who hears the sound of the trumpet does not take warning, and the sword comes and takes him away, his blood shall be upon his own head. 5 He heard the sound of the trumpet, and did not take warning; his blood shall be upon himself. But if he had taken warning, he would have saved his life. 6 But if the watchman sees the sword coming and does not blow the trumpet, so that the people are not warned, and the sword comes, and takes any one of them; that man is taken away in his iniquity, but his blood I will require at the watchman's hand.

7 "So you, son of man, I have made a watchman for the house of Israel; whenever you hear a word from my mouth, you shall give them warning from me. 8 If I say to the wicked, O wicked man, you shall surely die, and you do not speak to warn the wicked to turn from his way, that wicked man shall die in his iniquity, but his blood I will require at your hand. 9 But if you warn the wicked to turn from his way, and he does not turn from his way; he shall die in his iniquity, but you will have saved your life.

10 "And you, son of man, say to the house of Israel, Thus have you said: 'Our transgressions and our sins are upon us, and we waste away because of them; how then can we live?' 11 Say to them, As I live, says the Lord GOD, I have no pleasure in the death of the wicked, but that the

---

o Gk Syr: Heb *sword, the sword is delivered*
p Gk: Heb *they have drawn her away and all her multitudes*
q Gk Old Latin: Heb *of the uncircumcised*   *r* Cn: Heb *iniquities*   *s* Cn: Heb *I*
33.1-9: Ezek 3.16-21.   **33.11:** Ezek 18.23, 32.

wicked turn from his way and live; turn back, turn back from your evil ways; for why will you die, O house of Israel? [12]And you, son of man, say to your people, The righteousness of the righteous shall not deliver him when he transgresses; and as for the wickedness of the wicked, he shall not fall by it when he turns from his wickedness; and the righteous shall not be able to live by his righteousness[f] when he sins. [13] Though I say to the righteous that he shall surely live, yet if he trusts in his righteousness and commits iniquity, none of his righteous deeds shall be remembered; but in the iniquity that he has committed he shall die. [14]Again, though I say to the wicked, 'You shall surely die,' yet if he turns from his sin and does what is lawful and right, [15] if the wicked restores the pledge, gives back what he has taken by robbery, and walks in the statutes of life, committing no iniquity; he shall surely live, he shall not die. [16] None of the sins that he has committed shall be remembered against him; he has done what is lawful and right, he shall surely live.

[17] "Yet your people say, 'The way of the Lord is not just'; when it is their own way that is not just. [18] When the righteous turns from his righteousness, and commits iniquity, he shall die for it. [19]And when the wicked turns from his wickedness, and does what is lawful and right, he shall live by it. [20] Yet you say, 'The way of the Lord is not just.' O house of Israel, I will judge each of you according to his ways."

21 In the twelfth year of our exile, in the tenth month, on the fifth day of the month, a man who had escaped from Jerusalem came to me and said, "The city has fallen." [22] Now the hand of the LORD had been upon me the evening before the fugitive came; and he had opened my mouth by the time the man came to me in the morning; so my mouth was opened, and I was no longer dumb.

23 The word of the LORD came to me: [24] "Son of man, the inhabitants of these waste places in the land of Israel keep saying, 'Abraham was only one man, yet he got possession of the land; but we are many; the land is surely given us to possess.' [25] Therefore say to them, Thus says the Lord GOD: You eat flesh with the blood, and lift up your eyes to your idols, and shed blood; shall you then possess the land? [26] You resort to the sword, you commit abominations and each of you defiles his neighbor's wife; shall you then possess the land? [27] Say this to them, Thus says the Lord GOD: As I live, surely those who are in the waste places shall fall by the sword; and him that is in the open field I will give to the beasts to be devoured; and those who are in strongholds and in caves shall die by pestilence. [28]And I will make the land a desolation and a waste; and her proud might shall come to an end; and the mountains of Israel shall be so desolate that none will pass through. [29] Then they will know that I am the LORD, when I have made the land a desolation and a waste because of all their abominations which they have committed.

30 "As for you, son of man, your people who talk together about you by the walls and at the doors of the houses, say to one another, each to his brother, 'Come, and hear what the word is that comes forth from the LORD.' [31]And they come to you as people come, and they sit before you as my people, and they hear what you say but they will not do it; for with their lips they show much love, but their heart is set on their gain. [32]And, lo, you are to them like one who sings love songs[u] with a beautiful voice and plays well on an instrument, for they hear what you say, but they will not do it. [33] When this comes—and come it will!—then they will know that a prophet has been among them."

34 The word of the LORD came to me: 2 "Son of man, prophesy against the shepherds of Israel, prophesy, and say to them, even to the shepherds, Thus says the Lord GOD: Ho, shepherds of Israel who have been feeding yourselves! Should not shepherds feed the sheep? [3] You eat the fat, you clothe yourselves with the wool, you slaughter the fatlings; but you do not feed the sheep. [4] The weak you have not strengthened, the sick you have not healed, the crippled you have not bound up, the strayed you have not brought back, the lost you have not sought, and with force and harshness you have ruled them. [5] So they were scattered, because there was no shepherd; and they became food for all the wild beasts. [6] My sheep were scattered, they wandered over all the mountains and on every high hill; my sheep were scattered over all the face of the earth, with none to search or seek for them.

[f] Heb by it   [u] Cn: Heb like a love song
34.5: Mt 9.36; Mk 6.34.

7 "Therefore, you shepherds, hear the word of the LORD: 8As I live, says the Lord GOD, because my sheep have become a prey, and my sheep have become food for all the wild beasts, since there was no shepherd; and because my shepherds have not searched for my sheep, but the shepherds have fed themselves, and have not fed my sheep; 9 therefore, you shepherds, hear the word of the LORD: 10 Thus says the Lord GOD, Behold, I am against the shepherds; and I will require my sheep at their hand, and I will put a stop to their feeding the sheep; no longer shall the shepherds feed themselves. I will rescue my sheep from their mouths, that they may not be food for them.

11 "For thus says the Lord GOD: Behold, I, I myself will search for my sheep, and will seek them out. 12As a shepherd seeks out his flock when some of his sheep*v* have been scattered abroad, so will I seek out my sheep; and I will rescue them from all places where they have been scattered on a day of clouds and thick darkness. 13And I will bring them out from the peoples, and gather them from the countries, and will bring them into their own land; and I will feed them on the mountains of Israel, by the fountains, and in all the inhabited places of the country. 14 I will feed them with good pasture, and upon the mountain heights of Israel shall be their pasture; there they shall lie down in good grazing land, and on fat pasture they shall feed on the mountains of Israel. 15 I myself will be the shepherd of my sheep, and I will make them lie down, says the Lord GOD. 16 I will seek the lost, and I will bring back the strayed, and I will bind up the crippled, and I will strengthen the weak, and the fat and the strong I will watch over;*w* I will feed them in justice.

17 "As for you, my flock, thus says the Lord GOD: Behold, I judge between sheep and sheep, rams and he-goats. 18 Is it not enough for you to feed on the good pasture, that you must tread down with your feet the rest of your pasture; and to drink of clear water, that you must foul the rest with your feet? 19And must my sheep eat what you have trodden with your feet, and drink what you have fouled with your feet?

20 "Therefore, thus says the Lord GOD to them: Behold, I, I myself will judge between the fat sheep and the lean sheep. 21 Because you push with side and shoulder, and thrust at all the weak with your horns, till you have scattered them abroad, 22 I will save my flock, they shall no longer be a prey; and I will judge between sheep and sheep. 23And I will set up over them one shepherd, my servant David, and he shall feed them: he shall feed them and be their shepherd. 24And I, the LORD, will be their God, and my servant David shall be prince among them; I, the LORD, have spoken.

25 "I will make with them a covenant of peace and banish wild beasts from the land, so that they may dwell securely in the wilderness and sleep in the woods. 26And I will make them and the places round about my hill a blessing; and I will send down the showers in their season; they shall be showers of blessing. 27And the trees of the field shall yield their fruit, and the earth shall yield its increase, and they shall be secure in their land; and they shall know that I am the LORD, when I break the bars of their yoke, and deliver them from the hand of those who enslaved them. 28 They shall no more be a prey to the nations, nor shall the beasts of the land devour them; they shall dwell securely, and none shall make them afraid. 29And I will provide for them prosperous*x* plantations so that they shall no more be consumed with hunger in the land, and no longer suffer the reproach of the nations. 30And they shall know that I, the LORD their God, am with them, and that they, the house of Israel, are my people, says the Lord GOD. 31And you are my sheep, the sheep of my pasture,*y* and I am your God, says the Lord GOD."

35 The word of the LORD came to me: 2 "Son of man, set your face against Mount Sē'ir, and prophesy against it, 3 and say to it, Thus says the Lord GOD: Behold, I am against you, Mount Sē'ir, and I will stretch out my hand against you, and I will make you a desolation and a waste. 4 I will lay your cities waste, and you shall become a desolation; and you shall know that I am the LORD. 5 Because you cherished perpetual enmity, and gave over the people of Israel to the power of the sword at the time of their calamity, at the time of their final punishment; 6 therefore, as I live, says the Lord GOD, I will prepare you

v Cn: Heb *when he is among his sheep* *w* Gk Syr Vg: Heb *destroy*
x Gk Syr Old Latin: Heb *for renown* *y* Gk Old Latin: Heb *pasture you are men*
34.16: Lk 19.10. 34.23: Ezek 37.24.

for blood, and blood shall pursue you; because you are guilty of blood,[z] therefore blood shall pursue you. [7] I will make Mount Se'ir a waste and a desolation; and I will cut off from it all who come and go. [8]And I will fill your mountains with the slain; on your hills and in your valleys and in all your ravines those slain with the sword shall fall. [9] I will make you a perpetual desolation, and your cities shall not be inhabited. Then you will know that I am the LORD.

[10] "Because you said, 'These two nations and these two countries shall be mine, and we will take possession of them'—although the LORD was there—[11] therefore, as I live, says the Lord GOD, I will deal with you according to the anger and envy which you showed because of your hatred against them; and I will make myself known among you,[a] when I judge you. [12]And you shall know that I, the LORD, have heard all the revilings which you uttered against the mountains of Israel, saying, 'They are laid desolate, they are given us to devour.' [13]And you magnified yourselves against me with your mouth, and multiplied your words against me; I heard it. [14] Thus says the Lord GOD: For the rejoicing of the whole earth I will make you desolate. [15]As you rejoiced over the inheritance of the house of Israel, because it was desolate, so I will deal with you; you shall be desolate, Mount Se'ir, and all E'dom, all of it. Then they will know that I am the LORD.

36 "And you, son of man, prophesy to the mountains of Israel, and say, O mountains of Israel, hear the word of the LORD. [2] Thus says the Lord GOD: Because the enemy said of you, 'Aha!' and, 'The ancient heights have become our possession,' [3] therefore prophesy, and say, Thus says the Lord GOD: Because, yea, because they made you desolate, and crushed you from all sides, so that you became the possession of the rest of the nations, and you became the talk and evil gossip of the people; [4] therefore, O mountains of Israel, hear the word of the Lord GOD: Thus says the Lord GOD to the mountains and the hills, the ravines and the valleys, the desolate wastes and the deserted cities, which have become a prey and derision to the rest of the nations round about; [5] therefore thus says the Lord GOD: I speak in my hot jealousy against the rest of the nations, and

against all E'dom, who gave my land to themselves as a possession with wholehearted joy and utter contempt, that they might possess[b] it and plunder it. [6] Therefore prophesy concerning the land of Israel, and say to the mountains and hills, to the ravines and valleys, Thus says the Lord GOD: Behold, I speak in my jealous wrath, because you have suffered the reproach of the nations; [7] therefore thus says the Lord GOD: I swear that the nations that are round about you shall themselves suffer reproach.

[8] "But you, O mountains of Israel, shall shoot forth your branches, and yield your fruit to my people Israel; for they will soon come home. [9] For, behold, I am for you, and I will turn to you, and you shall be tilled and sown; [10] and I will multiply men upon you, the whole house of Israel, all of it; the cities shall be inhabited and the waste places rebuilt; [11] and I will multiply upon you man and beast; and they shall increase and be fruitful; and I will cause you to be inhabited as in your former times, and will do more good to you than ever before. Then you will know that I am the LORD. [12] Yea, I will let men walk upon you, even my people Israel; and they shall possess you, and you shall be their inheritance, and you shall no longer bereave them of children. [13] Thus says the Lord GOD: Because men say to you, 'You devour men and you bereave your nation of children,' [14] therefore you shall no longer devour men and no longer bereave your nation of children, says the Lord GOD; [15] and I will not let you hear any more the reproach of the nations, and you shall no longer bear the disgrace of the peoples and no longer cause your nation to stumble, says the Lord GOD."

[16] The word of the LORD came to me: [17] "Son of man, when the house of Israel dwelt in their own land, they defiled it by their ways and their doings; their conduct before me was like the uncleanness of a woman in her impurity. [18] So I poured out my wrath upon them for the blood which they had shed in the land, for the idols with which they had defiled it. [19] I scattered them among the nations, and they were dispersed through the countries; in accordance with their conduct and their deeds I judged them. [20] But when they came to the nations, wherever they came, they profaned my holy name, in that men said of them, 'These are the people of the LORD, and yet

---

[z] Gk: Heb *you have hated blood*   [a] Gk: Heb *them*   [b] One Ms: Heb *drive out*

they had to go out of his land.' 21 But I had concern for my holy name, which the house of Israel caused to be profaned among the nations to which they came.

22 "Therefore say to the house of Israel, Thus says the Lord GOD: It is not for your sake, O house of Israel, that I am about to act, but for the sake of my holy name, which you have profaned among the nations to which you came. 23And I will vindicate the holiness of my great name, which has been profaned among the nations, and which you have profaned among them; and the nations will know that I am the LORD, says the Lord GOD, when through you I vindicate my holiness before their eyes. 24 For I will take you from the nations, and gather you from all the countries, and bring you into your own land. 25 I will sprinkle clean water upon you, and you shall be clean from all your uncleannesses, and from all your idols I will cleanse you. 26A new heart I will give you, and a new spirit I will put within you; and I will take out of your flesh the heart of stone and give you a heart of flesh. 27And I will put my spirit within you, and cause you to walk in my statutes and be careful to observe my ordinances. 28 You shall dwell in the land which I gave to your fathers; and you shall be my people, and I will be your God. 29And I will deliver you from all your uncleannesses; and I will summon the grain and make it abundant and lay no famine upon you. 30 I will make the fruit of the tree and the increase of the field abundant, that you may never again suffer the disgrace of famine among the nations. 31 Then you will remember your evil ways, and your deeds that were not good; and you will loathe yourselves for your iniquities and your abominable deeds. 32 It is not for your sake that I will act, says the Lord GOD; let that be known to you. Be ashamed and confounded for your ways, O house of Israel.

33 "Thus says the Lord GOD: On the day that I cleanse you from all your iniquities, I will cause the cities to be inhabited, and the waste places shall be rebuilt. 34And the land that was desolate shall be tilled, instead of being the desolation that it was in the sight of all who passed by. 35And they will say, 'This land that was desolate has become like the garden of Eden; and the waste and desolate and ruined cities are now inhabited and fortified.' 36 Then the nations that are left round about you shall know that I, the LORD, have rebuilt the ruined places, and replanted that which was desolate; I, the LORD, have spoken, and I will do it.

37 "Thus says the Lord GOD: This also I will let the house of Israel ask me to do for them: to increase their men like a flock. 38 Like the flock for sacrifices,c like the flock at Jerusalem during her appointed feasts, so shall the waste cities be filled with flocks of men. Then they will know that I am the LORD."

37 The hand of the LORD was upon me, and he brought me out by the Spirit of the LORD, and set me down in the midst of the valley;d it was full of bones. 2And he led me round among them; and behold, there were very many upon the valley;d and lo, they were very dry. 3And he said to me, "Son of man, can these bones live?" And I answered, "O Lord GOD, thou knowest." 4Again he said to me, "Prophesy to these bones, and say to them, O dry bones, hear the word of the LORD. 5 Thus says the Lord GOD to these bones: Behold, I will cause breathe to enter you, and you shall live. 6And I will lay sinews upon you, and will cause flesh to come upon you, and cover you with skin, and put breathe in you, and you shall live; and you shall know that I am the LORD."

7 So I prophesied as I was commanded; and as I prophesied, there was a noise, and behold, a rattling; and the bones came together, bone to its bone. 8And as I looked, there were sinews on them, and flesh had come upon them, and skin had covered them; but there was no breath in them. 9 Then he said to me, "Prophesy to the breath, prophesy, son of man, and say to the breath,f Thus says the Lord GOD: Come from the four winds, O breath,f and breathe upon these slain, that they may live." 10 So I prophesied as he commanded me, and the breath came into them, and they lived, and stood upon their feet, an exceedingly great host.

11 Then he said to me, "Son of man, these bones are the whole house of Israel. Behold, they say, 'Our bones are dried up, and our hope is lost; we are clean cut off.' 12 Therefore prophesy, and say to them, Thus says the

---

c Heb *flock of holy things*   d Or *plain*   e Or *spirit*   f Or *wind* or *spirit*
36.26: Ezek 11.19; 18.31; 2 Cor 3.3.   36.27: Ezek 37.14; 1 Thess 4.8.
36.31: Ezek 6.9; 20.43.   37.5, 10: Rev 11.11.

Lord GOD: Behold, I will open your graves, and raise you from your graves, O my people; and I will bring you home into the land of Israel. [13]And you shall know that I am the LORD, when I open your graves, and raise you from your graves, O my people. [14]And I will put my Spirit within you, and you shall live, and I will place you in your own land; then you shall know that I, the LORD, have spoken, and I have done it, says the LORD."

[15] The word of the LORD came to me: [16] "Son of man, take a stick and write on it, 'For Judah, and the children of Israel associated with him'; then take another stick and write upon it, 'For Joseph (the stick of É'phra·im) and all the house of Israel associated with him'; [17] and join them together into one stick, that they may become one in your hand. [18]And when your people say to you, 'Will you not show us what you mean by these?' [19] say to them, Thus says the Lord GOD: Behold, I am about to take the stick of Joseph (which is in the hand of É'phra·im) and the tribes of Israel associated with him; and I will join[g] with it the stick of Judah, and make them one stick, that they may be one in my hand. [20] When the sticks on which you write are in your hand before their eyes, [21] then say to them, Thus says the Lord GOD: Behold, I will take the people of Israel from the nations among which they have gone, and will gather them from all sides, and bring them to their own land; [22] and I will make them one nation in the land, upon the mountains of Israel; and one king shall be king over them all; and they shall be no longer two nations, and no longer divided into two kingdoms. [23] They shall not defile themselves any more with their idols and their detestable things, or with any of their transgressions; but I will save them from all the backslidings in which they have sinned, and will cleanse them; and they shall be my people, and I will be their God.

[24] "My servant David shall be king over them; and they shall all have one shepherd. They shall follow my ordinances and be careful to observe my statutes. [25] They shall dwell in the land where your fathers dwelt that I gave to my servant Jacob; and they and their children and their children's children shall dwell there for ever; and

David my servant shall be their prince for ever. [26] I will make a covenant of peace with them; it shall be an everlasting covenant with them; and I will bless[h] them and multiply them, and will set my sanctuary in the midst of them for evermore. [27] My dwelling place shall be with them; and I will be their God, and they shall be my people. [28] Then the nations will know that I the LORD sanctify Israel, when my sanctuary is in the midst of them for evermore."

38 The word of the LORD came to me: [2] "Son of man, set your face toward Gog, of the land of Mā'-gog, the chief prince of Mē'shech and Tu'bal, and prophesy against him [3] and say, Thus says the Lord GOD: Behold, I am against you, O Gog, chief prince of Mē'shech and Tü'bal; [4] and I will turn you about, and put hooks into your jaws, and I will bring you forth, and all your army, horses and horsemen, all of them clothed in full armor, a great company, all of them with buckler and shield, wielding swords; [5] Persia, Cush, and Püt are with them, all of them with shield and helmet; [6] Gō'mer and all his hordes; Beth-tō·gär'mäh from the uttermost parts of the north with all his hordes—many peoples are with you.

[7] "Be ready and keep ready, you and all the hosts that are assembled about you, and be a guard for them. [8]After many days you will be mustered; in the latter years you will go against the land that is restored from war, the land where people were gathered from many nations upon the mountains of Israel, which had been a continual waste; its people were brought out from the nations and now dwell securely, all of them. [9] You will advance, coming on like a storm, you will be like a cloud covering the land, you and all your hordes, and many peoples with you.

[10] "Thus says the Lord GOD: On that day thoughts will come into your mind, and you will devise an evil scheme [11] and say, 'I will go up against the land of unwalled villages; I will fall upon the quiet people who dwell securely, all of them dwelling without walls, and having no bars or gates'; [12] to seize spoil and carry off plunder; to assail the waste places which are now inhabited, and the people who were gathered from the nations, who

g Heb *join them*   *h* Tg: Heb *give*

37.14: Ezek 36.27; 1 Thess 4.8.   37.26: Heb 13.20.
37.27: Ex 25.8; 29.45; Lev 26.12; Jer 31.1; 2 Cor 6.16; Rev 21.3.
38.2, 9, 15: Rev 20.8.

have gotten cattle and goods, who dwell at the center of the earth. [13] Sheba and Dē′dan and the merchants of Tär′shish and all its villages will say to you, 'Have you come to seize spoil? Have you assembled your hosts to carry off plunder, to carry away silver and gold, to take away cattle and goods, to seize great spoil?' [14] "Therefore, son of man, prophesy, and say to Gog, Thus says the Lord GOD: On that day when my people Israel are dwelling securely, you will bestir yourself[i] [15] and come from your place out of the uttermost parts of the north, you and many peoples with you, all of them riding on horses, a great host, a mighty army; [16] you will come up against my people Israel, like a cloud covering the land. In the latter days I will bring you against my land, that the nations may know me, when through you, O Gog, I vindicate my holiness before their eyes.

[17] "Thus says the Lord GOD: Are you he of whom I spoke in former days by my servants the prophets of Israel, who in those days prophesied for years that I would bring you against them? [18] But on that day, when Gog shall come against the land of Israel, says the Lord GOD, my wrath will be roused. [19] For in my jealousy and in my blazing wrath I declare, On that day there shall be a great shaking in the land of Israel; [20] the fish of the sea, and the birds of the air, and the beasts of the field, and all creeping things that creep on the ground, and all the men that are upon the face of the earth, shall quake at my presence, and the mountains shall be thrown down, and the cliffs shall fall, and every wall shall tumble to the ground. [21] I will summon every kind of terror[j] against Gog,[k] says the Lord GOD; every man's sword will be against his brother. [22] With pestilence and bloodshed I will enter into judgment with him; and I will rain upon him and his hordes and the many peoples that are with him, torrential rains and hailstones, fire and brimstone. [23] So I will show my greatness and my holiness and make myself known in the eyes of many nations. Then they will know that I am the LORD.

39 "And you, son of man, prophesy against Gog, and say, Thus says the Lord GOD: Behold, I am against you, O Gog, chief prince of

Mē′shech and Tü′bäl; [2] and I will turn you about and drive you forward, and bring you up from the uttermost parts of the north, and lead you against the mountains of Israel; [3] then I will strike your bow from your left hand, and will make your arrows drop out of your right hand. [4] You shall fall upon the mountains of Israel, you and all your hordes and the peoples that are with you; I will give you to birds of prey of every sort and to the wild beasts to be devoured. [5] You shall fall in the open field; for I have spoken, says the Lord GOD. [6] I will send fire on Mä′gog and on those who dwell securely in the coastlands; and they shall know that I am the LORD.

[7] "And my holy name I will make known in the midst of my people Israel; and I will not let my holy name be profaned any more; and the nations shall know that I am the LORD, the Holy One in Israel. [8] Behold, it is coming and it will be brought about, says the Lord GOD. That is the day of which I have spoken.

[9] "Then those who dwell in the cities of Israel will go forth and make fires of the weapons and burn them, shields and bucklers, bows and arrows, handpikes and spears, and they will make fires of them for seven years; [10] so that they will not need to take wood out of the field or cut down any out of the forests, for they will make their fires of the weapons; they will despoil those who despoiled them, and plunder those who plundered them, says the Lord GOD.

[11] "On that day I will give to Gog a place for burial in Israel, the Valley of the Travelers[l] east of the sea; it will block the travelers, for there Gog and all his multitude will be buried; it will be called the Valley of Hä′mon-gog.[m] [12] For seven months the house of Israel will be burying them, in order to cleanse the land. [13] All the people of the land will bury them; and it will redound to their honor on the day that I show my glory, says the Lord GOD. [14] They will set apart men to pass through the land continually and bury[n] those remaining upon the face of the land, so as to cleanse it; at the end of seven months they will make their search. [15] And when these pass through the land and any one sees a man's bone, then he shall set up a sign by it, till the buriers have buried it in the

---

[i] Gk: Heb *will you not know?*   [j] Gk: Heb *a sword to all my mountains*   [k] Heb *him*
[l] Or *Abarim*   [m] That is *the multitude of Gog*   [n] Gk Syr: Heb *bury the travelers*
38.22: Rev 8.7; 14.10.   **39.4, 17-20:** Rev 19.17, 18, 21.

Valley of Hā′mon-gog. 16 (A city Hȧ·mō′nȧh[o] is there also.) Thus shall they cleanse the land.

17 "As for you, son of man, thus says the Lord GOD: Speak to the birds of every sort and to all beasts of the field, 'Assemble and come, gather from all sides to the sacrificial feast which I am preparing for you, a great sacrificial feast upon the mountains of Israel, and you shall eat flesh and drink blood. 18 You shall eat the flesh of the mighty, and drink the blood of the princes of the earth—of rams, of lambs, and of goats, of bulls, all of them fatlings of Bā′shȧn. 19 And you shall eat fat till you are filled, and drink blood till you are drunk, at the sacrificial feast which I am preparing for you. 20 And you shall be filled at my table with horses and riders, with mighty men and all kinds of warriors,' says the Lord GOD.

21 "And I will set my glory among the nations; and all the nations shall see my judgments which I have executed, and my hand which I have laid on them. 22 The house of Israel shall know that I am the LORD their God, from that day forward. 23 And the nations shall know that the house of Israel went into captivity for their iniquity, because they dealt so treacherously with me that I hid my face from them and gave them into the hand of their adversaries, and they all fell by the sword. 24 I dealt with them according to their uncleanness and their transgressions, and hid my face from them.

25 "Therefore thus says the Lord GOD: Now I will restore the fortunes of Jacob, and have mercy upon the whole house of Israel; and I will be jealous for my holy name. 26 They shall forget their shame, and all the treachery they have practiced against me, when they dwell securely in their land with none to make them afraid, 27 when I have brought them back from the peoples and gathered them from their enemies' lands, and through them have vindicated my holiness in the sight of many nations. 28 Then they shall know that I am the LORD their God because I sent them into exile among the nations, and then gathered them into their own land. I will leave none of them remaining among the nations any more; 29 and I will not hide my face any more from them, when I pour out my Spirit upon the house of Israel, says the Lord GOD."

40

In the twenty-fifth year of our exile, at the beginning of the year, on the tenth day of the month, in the fourteenth year after the city was conquered, on that very day, the hand of the LORD was upon me, 2 and brought me in the visions of God into the land of Israel, and set me down upon a very high mountain, on which was a structure like a city opposite me.[p] 3 When he brought me there, behold, there was a man, whose appearance was like bronze, with a line of flax and a measuring reed in his hand; and he was standing in the gateway. 4 And the man said to me, "Son of man, look with your eyes, and hear with your ears, and set your mind upon all that I shall show you, for you were brought here in order that I might show it to you; declare all that you see to the house of Israel."

5 And behold, there was a wall all around the outside of the temple area, and the length of the measuring reed in the man's hand was six long cubits, each being a cubit and a handbreadth in length; so he measured the thickness of the wall, one reed; and the height, one reed. 6 Then he went into the gateway facing east, going up its steps, and measured the threshold of the gate, one reed deep;[q] 7 and the side rooms, one reed long, and one reed broad; and the space between the side rooms, five cubits; and the threshold of the gate by the vestibule of the gate at the inner end, one reed. 8 Then he measured the vestibule of the gateway, eight cubits; 9 and its jambs, two cubits; and the vestibule of the gate was at the inner end. 10 And there were three side rooms on either side of the east gate; the three were of the same size; and the jambs on either side were of the same size. 11 Then he measured the breadth of the opening of the gateway, ten cubits; and the breadth of the gateway, thirteen cubits. 12 There was a barrier before the side rooms, one cubit on either side; and the side rooms were six cubits on either side. 13 Then he measured the gate from the back[r] of the one side room to the back[r] of the other, a breadth of five and twenty cubits, from door to door. 14 He measured also the vestibule, twenty cubits; and round about the vestibule of the gate-

[o] That is *Multitude* [p] Gk: Heb *on the south*
[q] Heb *deep, and one threshold, one reed deep* [r] Compare Gk: Heb *roof*

40.1-43.17: 1 Kings 6-7; 2 Chron 3-4. **40.2:** Rev 21.10. **40.3, 5:** Rev 21.15.

way was the court.^{s} 15 From the front of the gate at the entrance to the inner of the inner vestibule of the gate was fifty cubits. 16And the gateway had windows round about, narrowing inwards into their jambs in the side rooms, and likewise the vestibule had windows round about inside, and on the jambs were palm trees.

17 Then he brought me into the outer court; and behold, there were chambers and a pavement, round about the court; thirty chambers fronted on the pavement. 18And the pavement ran along the side of the gates, corresponding to the length of the gates; this was the lower pavement. 19 Then he measured the distance from the inner front of^t the lower gate to the outer front of the inner court, a hundred cubits.

Then he went before me to the north, 20 and behold, there was a gate^u which faced toward the north, belonging to the outer court. He measured its length and its breadth. 21 Its side rooms, three on either side, and its jambs and its vestibule were of the same size as those of the first gate; its length was fifty cubits, and its breadth twenty-five cubits. 22And its windows, its vestibule, and its palm trees were of the same size as those of the gate which faced toward the east; and seven steps led up to it; and its vestibule was on the inside. 23And opposite the gate on the north, as on the east, was a gate to the inner court; and he measured from gate to gate, a hundred cubits.

24 And he led me toward the south, and behold, there was a gate on the south; and he measured its jambs and its vestibule; they had the same size as the others. 25And there were windows round about in it and in its vestibule, like the windows of the others; its length was fifty cubits, and its breadth twenty-five cubits. 26And there were seven steps leading up to it, and its vestibule was on the inside; and it had palm trees on its jambs, one on either side. 27And there was a gate on the south of the inner court; and he measured from gate to gate toward the south, a hundred cubits.

28 Then he brought me to the inner court by the south gate, and he measured the south gate; it was of the

same size as the others. 29 Its side rooms, its jambs, and its vestibule were of the same size as the others; and there were windows round about in it and in its vestibule; its length was fifty cubits, and its breadth twenty-five cubits. 30And there were vestibules round about, twenty-five cubits long and five cubits broad. 31 Its vestibule faced the outer court, and palm trees were on its jambs, and its stairway had eight steps.

32 Then he brought me to the inner court on the east side, and he measured the gate; it was of the same size as the others. 33 Its side rooms, its jambs, and its vestibule were of the same size as the others; and there were windows round about in it and in its vestibule; its length was fifty cubits, and its breadth twenty-five cubits. 34 Its vestibule faced the outer court, and it had palm trees on its jambs, one on either side; and its stairway had eight steps.

35 Then he brought me to the north gate, and he measured it; it had the same size as the others. 36 Its side rooms, its jambs, and its vestibule were of the same size as the others;^{v} and it had windows round about; its length was fifty cubits, and its breadth twenty-five cubits. 37 Its vestibule^w faced the outer court, and it had palm trees on its jambs, one on either side; and its stairway had eight steps.

38 There was a chamber with its door in the vestibule of the gate,^{x} where the burnt offering was to be washed. 39And in the vestibule of the gate were two tables on either side, on which the burnt offering and the sin offering and the guilt offering were to be slaughtered. 40And on the outside of the vestibule^y at the entrance of the north gate were two tables; and on the other side of the vestibule of the gate were two tables. 41 Four tables were on the inside, and four tables on the outside of the side of the gate, eight tables, on which the sacrifices were to be slaughtered. 42And there were also four tables of hewn stone for the burnt offering, a cubit and a half long, and a cubit and a half broad, and one cubit high, on which the instruments were to be laid with which the burnt offerings and the sacrifices were slaughtered. 43And hooks, a hand-

---

^{s} Compare Gk: Heb *and he made the jambs sixty cubits, and to the jamb of the court was the gateway round about* ^{t} Compare Gk: Heb *from before*
^{u} Gk: Heb *a hundred cubits on the east and on the north.* 20*And the gate*
^{v} One Ms Compare verses 29 and 33: Heb lacks *were of the same size as the others*
^{w} Gk Vg Compare verses 26, 31, 34: Heb *jambs* ^{x} Cn: Heb *at the jambs of the gates*
^{y} Cn: Heb *to him who goes up*

breadth long, were fastened round about within. And on the tables the flesh of the offering was to be laid.

44 Then he brought me from without into the inner court, and behold, there were two chambers[z] in the inner court, one[a] at the side of the north gate facing south, the other at the side of the south[b] gate facing north. 45 And he said to me, This chamber which faces south is for the priests who have charge of the temple, 46 and the chamber which faces north is for the priests who have charge of the altar; these are the sons of Za'dok, who alone among the sons of Levi may come near to the LORD to minister to him. 47 And he measured the court, a hundred cubits long, and a hundred cubits broad, foursquare; and the altar was in front of the temple.

48 Then he brought me to the vestibule of the temple and measured the jambs of the vestibule, five cubits on either side; and the breadth of the gate was fourteen cubits; and the side-walls of the gate were three cubits[c] on either side. 49 The length of the vestibule was twenty cubits, and the breadth twelve[d] cubits; and ten steps led up to it; and there were pillars beside the jambs on either side.

41 Then he brought me to the nave, and measured the jambs; on each side six cubits was the breadth of the jambs.[f] 2 And the breadth of the entrance was ten cubits; and the side-walls of the entrance were five cubits on either side; and he measured the length of the nave forty cubits, and its breadth, twenty cubits. 3 Then he went into the inner room and measured the jambs of the entrance, two cubits; and the breadth of the entrance, six cubits; and the sidewalls[g] of the entrance, seven cubits. 4 And he measured the length of the room, twenty cubits, and its breadth, twenty cubits, beyond the nave. And he said to me, This is the most holy place.

5 Then he measured the wall of the temple, six cubits thick; and the breadth of the side chambers, four cubits, round about the temple. 6 And the side chambers were in three stories, one

over another, thirty in each story. There were offsets[h] all around the wall of the temple to serve as supports for the side chambers, so that they should not be supported by the wall of the temple. 7 And the side chambers became broader as they rose[i] from story to story, corresponding to the enlargement of the offset[j] from story to story round about the temple; on the side of the temple a stairway led upward, and thus one went up from the lowest story to the top story through the middle story. 8 I saw also that the temple had a raised platform round about; the foundations of the side chambers measured a full reed of six long cubits. 9 The thickness of the outer wall of the side chambers was five cubits; and the part of the platform which was left free was five cubits.[k] Between the platform[l] of the temple and the 10 chambers of the court was a breadth of twenty cubits round about the temple on every side. 11 And the doors of the side chambers opened on the part of the platform that was left free, one door toward the north, and another door toward the south; and the breadth of the part that was left free was five cubits round about.

12 The building that was facing the temple yard on the west side was seventy cubits broad; and the wall of the building was five cubits thick round about, and its length ninety cubits.

13 Then he measured the temple, a hundred cubits long; and the yard and the building with its walls, a hundred cubits long; 14 also the breadth of the east front of the temple and the yard, a hundred cubits.

15 Then he measured the length of the building facing the yard which was at the west and its walls[m] on either side, a hundred cubits.

The nave of the temple and the inner room and the outer[n] vestibule 16 were paneled[o] and round about all three had windows with recessed[p] frames. Over against the threshold of the temple was paneled with wood round about, from the floor up to the windows (now the windows were

z Gk: Heb *and from without to the inner gate were chambers for singers*
a Gk: Heb *which*   b Gk: Heb *east*
c Gk: Heb *and the breadth of the gates was three cubits*   d Gk: Heb *eleven*
e Gk: Heb *and by steps which went up*   f Compare Gk: Heb *tent*   g Gk: Heb *breadth*
Gk Compare 1 Kings 6.6: Heb *they entered*   i Cn: Heb *it was surrounded*
j Gk: Heb *for the encompassing of the temple*   k Syr: Heb lacks *five cubits*
l Cn: Heb *house of the side chambers*
m Cn: The meaning of the Hebrew term is unknown   n Gk: Heb *of the court*
o Gk: Heb *the thresholds*
p Compare Gk 1 Kings 6.4: The meaning of the Hebrew term is unknown

covered), [17] to the space above the door, even to the inner room, and on the outside. And on all the walls round about in the inner room and the nave were carved likenesses[q] [18] of cherubim and palm trees, a palm tree between cherub and cherub. Every cherub had two faces: [19] the face of a man toward the palm tree on the one side, and the face of a young lion toward the palm tree on the other side. They were carved on the whole temple round about; [20] from the floor to above the door cherubim and palm trees were carved on the wall.[r]

[21] The doorposts of the nave were squared; and in front of the holy place was something resembling [22] an altar of wood, three cubits high, two cubits long, and two cubits broad;[s] its corners, its base,[t] and its walls were of wood. He said to me, "This is the table which is before the LORD." [23] The nave and the holy place had each a double door. [24] The doors had two leaves apiece, two swinging leaves for each door. [25] And on the doors of the nave were carved cherubim and palm trees, such as were carved on the walls; and there was a canopy of wood in front of the vestibule outside. [26] And there were recessed windows and palm trees on either side, on the sidewalls of the vestibule.[u]

42 Then he led me out into the inner[v] court, toward the north, and he brought me to the chambers which were opposite the temple yard and opposite the building on the north. [2] The length of the building which was on the north side[w] was[x] a hundred cubits, and the breadth fifty cubits. [3] Adjoining the twenty cubits which belonged to the inner court, and facing the pavement which belonged to the outer court, was gallery[y] against gallery[y] in three stories. [4] And before the chambers was a passage inward, ten cubits wide and a hundred cubits long;[z] and their doors were on the north. [5] Now the upper chambers were narrower, for the galleries[y] took more away from them than from the lower and middle chambers in the building. [6] For they were in three

stories, and they had no pillars like the pillars of the outer[a] court; hence the upper chambers were set back from the ground more than the lower and the middle ones. [7] And there was a wall outside parallel to the chambers, toward the outer court, opposite the chambers, fifty cubits long. [8] For the chambers on the outer court were fifty cubits long, while those opposite the temple were a hundred cubits long. [9] Below these chambers was an entrance on the east side, as one enters them from the outer court, [10] where the outside wall begins.[b]

On the south[c] also, opposite the yard and opposite the building, there were chambers [11] with a passage in front of them; they were similar to the chambers on the north, of the same length and breadth, with the same exits[d] and arrangements and doors. [12] And below the south chambers wa̲ an entrance on the east side, where o̲ enters the passage, and opposite th̲ was a dividing wall.[e]

[13] Then he said to me, "Th̲ chambers and the south c̲ opposite the yard are the hol̲ bers, where the priests who a̲ the LORD shall eat the mos̲ offerings; there they shall put th̲ holy offerings—the cereal offeri̲ sin offering, and the guilt offeri̲ the place is holy. [14] When the̲ enter the holy place, they shall̲ out of it into the outer court w̲ laying there the garments in w̲ they minister, for these are holy; t̲ shall put on other garments befor̲ they go near to that which is for the̲ people."

[15] Now when he had finished measuring the interior of the temple area, he led me out by the gate which faced east, and measured the temple area round about. [16] He measured the east side with the measuring reed, five hundred cubits by the measuring reed. [17] Then he turned and measured[f] the north side, five hundred cubits by the measuring reed. [18] Then he turned and measured[f] the south side, five hundred cubits by the measuring reed. [19] Then he turned to the west side and

q Cn: Heb *measures and carved*   r Cn Compare verse 25: Heb *and the wall*
s Gk: Heb lacks *two cubits broad*   t Gk: Heb *length*
u Cn: Heb *vestibule. And the side chambers of the temple and the canopies*
v Gk: Heb *outer*   w Gk: Heb *door*   x Gk: Heb *before the length*
y The meaning of the Hebrew word is unknown   z Gk Syr: Heb *a way of one cubit*
a Gk: Heb lacks *outer*   b Cn Compare Gk: Heb *in the breadth of the wall of the court*
c Gk: Heb *east*   d Heb *and all their exits*
e Cn: Heb *And according to the entrances of the chambers that were toward the south wa̲ an entrance at the head of the way, the way before the dividing wall toward the east a̲ one enters them*   f Gk: Heb *measuring reed round about. He measured*

measured, five hundred cubits by the measuring reed. [20] He measured it on the four sides. It had a wall around it, five hundred cubits long and five hundred cubits broad, to make a separation between the holy and the common.

43 Afterward he brought me to the gate, the gate facing east. [2] And behold, the glory of the God of Israel came from the east; and the sound of his coming was like the sound of many waters; and the earth shone with his glory. [3] And[g] the vision I saw was like the vision which I had seen when he came to destroy the city, and[h] like the vision which I had seen by the river Che'bar; and I fell upon my face. [4] As the glory of the LORD entered the temple by the gate facing east, [5] the Spirit lifted me up, and brought me into the inner court; and behold, the glory of the LORD filled the temple.

[6] While the man was standing beside me, I heard one speaking to me out of the temple; [7] and he said to me, "Son of man, this is the place of my throne and the place of the soles of my feet, where I will dwell in the midst of the people of Israel for ever. And the house of Israel shall no more defile my holy name, neither they, nor their kings, by their harlotry, and by the dead bodies[i] of their kings, [8] by their setting their threshold by my threshold and their doorposts beside my doorposts, with only a wall between me and them. They have defiled my holy name by their abominations which they have committed, so I have consumed them in my anger. [9] Now let them put away their idolatry and the dead bodies[i] of their kings far from me, and I will dwell in their midst for ever.

[10] "And you, son of man, describe to the house of Israel the temple and its appearance and plan,[j] that they may be ashamed of their iniquities. [11] And if they are ashamed of all that they have done, portray[k] the temple, its arrangement, its exits and its entrances, and its whole form; and make known to them all its ordinances and all its laws; and write it down in their sight, so that they may observe and perform all its laws[l] and all its ordinances. [12] This is the law of the temple: the whole territory round about upon the top of the mountain

shall be most holy. Behold, this is the law of the temple.

[13] "These are the dimensions of the altar by cubits (the cubit being a cubit and a handbreadth): its base shall be one cubit high,[m] and one cubit broad, with a rim of one span around its edge. And this shall be the height[x] of the altar: [14] from the base on the ground to the lower ledge, two cubits, with a breadth of one cubit; and from the smaller ledge to the larger ledge, four cubits, with a breadth of one cubit; [15] and the altar hearth, four cubits; and from the altar hearth projecting upward, four horns, one cubit high.[n] [16] The altar hearth shall be square, twelve cubits long by twelve broad. [17] The ledge also shall be square, fourteen cubits long by fourteen broad, with a rim around it half a cubit broad, and its base one cubit round about. The steps of the altar shall face east."

[18] And he said to me, "Son of man, thus says the Lord G[OD]: the ordinances for the altar on the day when it is erected, that burnt offerings upon it and for sprinkling blood against it, [19] you shall give to the Levitical priests of the family of Za'dok, who draw near to me to minister to me, says the Lord G[OD], a bull for a sin offering. [20] And you shall take some of its blood, and put it on the four horns of the altar, and on the four corners of the ledge, and upon the rim round about; thus you shall cleanse the altar and make atonement for it. [21] You shall also take the bull of the sin offering, and it shall be burnt in the appointed place belonging to the temple, outside the sacred area. [22] And on the second day you shall offer a he-goat without blemish for a sin offering; and the altar shall be cleansed, as it was cleansed with the bull. [23] When you have finished cleansing it, you shall offer a bull without blemish and a ram from the flock without blemish. [24] You shall present them before the LORD, and the priests shall sprinkle salt upon them and offer them up as a burnt offering to the LORD. [25] For seven days you shall provide daily a goat for a sin offering; also a bull and a ram from the flock, without blemish, shall be provided. [26] Seven days shall they make atonement for the altar and purify it, and so consecrate it. [27] And when they

g Gk: Heb *And like the vision*   *h* Syr: Heb *and the visions*   *i* Or *the monuments*
j Gk: Heb *the temple that they may measure the pattern*   *k* Gk: Heb *the form of*
l Compare Gk: Heb *its whole form*   *m* Gk: Heb lacks *high*   *x* Gk: Heb *back*
n Gk: Heb lacks *one cubit high*

43.2: Ezek 1.24; Rev 1.15; 14.2; 19.6.

have completed these days, then from the eighth day onward the priests shall offer upon the altar your burnt offerings and your peace offerings; and I will accept you, says the Lord GOD."

44 Then he brought me back to the outer gate of the sanctuary, which faces east; and it was shut. [2]And he[o] said to me, "This gate shall remain shut; it shall not be opened, and no one shall enter by it; for the LORD, the God of Israel, has entered by it; therefore it shall remain shut. [3] Only the prince may sit in it to eat bread before the LORD; he shall enter by way of the vestibule of the gate, and shall go out by the same way."

[4] Then he brought me by way of the north gate to the front of the temple; and I looked, and behold, the glory of the LORD filled the temple of the LORD; and I fell upon my face. [5]And the LORD said to me, "Son of man, mark well, see with your eyes, and hear with your ears all that I shall tell you concerning all the ordinances of the temple of the LORD and all its laws; and mark well those who may be admitted to[p] the temple and all those who are to be excluded from the sanctuary. [6]And say to the rebellious house,[q] to the house of Israel, Thus says the Lord GOD: O house of Israel, let there be an end to all your abominations, [7] in admitting foreigners, uncircumcised in heart and flesh, to be in my sanctuary, profaning it,[r] when you offer to me my food, the fat and the blood. You[s] have broken my covenant, in addition to all your abominations. [8]And you have not kept charge of my holy things; but you have set foreigners to keep my charge in my sanctuary.

[9] "Therefore[t] thus says the Lord GOD: No foreigners, uncircumcised in heart and flesh, of all the foreigners who are among the people of Israel, shall enter my sanctuary. [10] But the Levites who went far from me, going astray from me after their idols when Israel went astray, shall bear their punishment. [11] They shall be ministers in my sanctuary, having oversight at the gates of the temple, and serving in the temple; they shall slay the burnt offering and the sacrifice for the people, and they shall attend on the people, to serve them. [12] Because they ministered to them before their idols and became a stumbling block of iniquity to the house of Israel, there-

fore I have sworn concerning them, says the Lord GOD, that they shall bear their punishment. [13] They shall not come near to me, to serve me as priest, nor come near any of my sacred things and the things that are most sacred; but they shall bear their shame, because of the abominations which they have committed. [14] Yet I will appoint them to keep charge of the temple, to do all its service and all that is to be done in it.

[15] "But the Levitical priests, the sons of Zā′dok, who kept the charge of my sanctuary when the people of Israel went astray from me, shall come near to me to minister to me; and they shall attend on me to offer me the fat and the blood, says the Lord GOD; [16] they shall enter my sanctuary, and they shall approach my table, to minister to me, and they shall keep my charge. [17] When they enter the gates of the inner court, they shall wear linen garments; they shall have nothing of wool on them, while they minister at the gates of the inner court, and within. [18] They shall have linen turbans upon their heads, and linen breeches upon their loins; they shall not gird themselves with anything that causes sweat. [19]And when they go out into the outer court to the people, they shall put off the garments in which they have been ministering, and lay them in the holy chambers; and they shall put on other garments, lest they communicate holiness to the people with their garments. [20] They shall not shave their heads or let their locks grow long; they shall only trim the hair of their heads. [21] No priest shall drink wine, when he enters the inner court. [22] They shall not marry a widow, or a divorced woman, but only a virgin of the stock of the house of Israel, or a widow who is the widow of a priest. [23] They shall teach my people the difference between the holy and the common, and show them how to distinguish between the unclean and the clean. [24] In a controversy they shall act as judges, and they shall judge it according to my judgments. They shall keep my laws and my statutes in all my appointed feasts, and they shall keep my sabbaths holy. [25] They shall not defile themselves by going near to a dead person; however, for father or mother, for son or daughter, for brother or unmarried sister they may defile themselves. [26]After he is de-

o Cn: Heb *the* LORD　　p Cn: Heb *the entrance of*　　q Gk: Heb lacks *house*
r Gk: Heb *it my temple*　　s Gk Syr Vg: Heb *they*　　t Gk: Heb *for you*
44.4: Rev 15.8.

filed,[u] he shall count for himself seven days, and then he shall be clean.[v] 27And on the day that he goes into the holy place, into the inner court, to minister in the holy place, he shall offer his sin offering, says the Lord God.

28 "They shall have no[w] inheritance; I am their inheritance: and you shall give them no possession in Israel; I am their possession. 29 They shall eat the cereal offering, the sin offering, and the guilt offering; and every devoted thing in Israel shall be theirs. 30And the first of all the first fruits of all kinds, and every offering of all kinds from all your offerings, shall belong to the priests; you shall also give to the priests the first of your coarse meal, that a blessing may rest on your house. 31 The priests shall not eat of anything, whether bird or beast, that has died of itself or is torn.

45 "When you allot the land as a possession, you shall set apart for the Lord a portion of the land as a holy district, twenty-five thousand cubits long and twenty[x] thousand cubits broad; it shall be holy throughout its whole extent. 2 Of this a square plot of five hundred by five hundred cubits shall be for the sanctuary, with fifty cubits for an open space around it. 3And in the holy district you shall measure off a section twenty-five thousand cubits long and ten thousand broad, in which shall be the sanctuary, the most holy place. 4 It shall be the holy portion of the land; it shall be for the priests, who minister in the sanctuary and approach the Lord to minister to him; and it shall be a place for their houses and a holy place for the sanctuary. 5Another section, twenty-five thousand cubits long and ten thousand cubits broad, shall be for the Levites who minister at the temple, as their possession for cities to live in.[y]

6 "Alongside the portion set apart as the holy district you shall assign for the possession of the city an area five thousand cubits broad, and twenty-five thousand cubits long; it shall belong to the whole house of Israel.

7 "And to the prince shall belong the land on both sides of the holy district and the property of the city, alongside the holy district and the property of the city, on the west and on the east, corresponding in length

to one of the tribal portions, and extending from the western to the eastern boundary of the land. 8 It is to be his property in Israel. And my princes shall no more oppress my people; but they shall let the house of Israel have the land according to their tribes.

9 "Thus says the Lord God: Enough, O princes of Israel! Put away violence and oppression, and execute justice and righteousness; cease your evictions of my people, says the Lord God.

10 "You shall have just balances, a just ephah, and a just bath. 11 The ephah and the bath shall be of the same measure, the bath containing one tenth of a homer, and the ephah one tenth of a homer; the homer shall be the standard measure. 12 The shekel shall be twenty gerahs; five shekels shall be five shekels, and ten shekels shall be ten shekels, and your mina shall be fifty shekels.[z]

13 "This is the offering which you shall make: one sixth of an ephah from each homer of wheat, and one sixth of an ephah from each homer of barley, 14 and as the fixed portion of oil,[a] one tenth of a bath from each cor (the cor,[b] like the homer, contains ten baths); 15 and one sheep from every flock of two hundred, from the families[c] of Israel. This is the offering for cereal offerings, burnt offerings, and peace offerings, to make atonement for them, says the Lord God. 16All the people of the land shall give[d] this offering to the prince in Israel. 17 It shall be the prince's duty to furnish the burnt offerings, cereal offerings, and drink offerings, at the feasts, the new moons, and the sabbaths, all the appointed feasts of the house of Israel: he shall provide the sin offerings, cereal offerings, burnt offerings, and peace offerings, to make atonement for the house of Israel.

18 "Thus says the Lord God: In the first month, on the first day of the month, you shall take a young bull without blemish, and cleanse the sanctuary. 19 The priest shall take some of the blood of the sin offering and put it on the doorposts of the temple, the four corners of the ledge of the altar, and the posts of the gate of the inner court. 20 You shall do the same on the seventh day of the month for any one who has sinned through

---

[u] Syr: Heb *cleansed*   [v] Syr: Heb lacks *and then he shall be clean*   [w] Vg: Heb *as an*
[x] Gk: Heb *ten*   [y] Gk: Heb *twenty chambers*
[z] Gk: Heb *twenty shekels, twenty-five shekels, fifteen shekels shall be your mina*
[a] Cn: Heb *oil, the bath the oil*   [b] Vg: Heb *homer*   [c] Gk: Heb *watering places*
[d] Gk Compare Syr: Heb *shall be to*

error or ignorance; so you shall make atonement for the temple.

21 "In the first month, on the fourteenth day of the month, you shall celebrate the feast of the passover, and for seven days unleavened bread shall be eaten. 22 On that day the prince shall provide for himself and all the people of the land a young bull for a sin offering. 23 And on the seven days of the festival he shall provide as a burnt offering to the LORD seven young bulls and seven rams without blemish, on each of the seven days; and a he-goat daily for a sin offering. 24 And he shall provide as a cereal offering an ephah for each bull, an ephah for each ram, and a hin of oil to each ephah. 25 In the seventh month, on the fifteenth day of the month and for the seven days of the feast, he shall make the same provision for sin offerings, burnt offerings, and cereal offerings, and for the oil.

46 "Thus says the Lord GOD: The gate of the inner court that faces east shall be shut on the six working days; but on the sabbath day it shall be opened and on the day of the new moon it shall be opened. 2 The prince shall enter by the vestibule of the gate from without, and shall take his stand by the post of the gate. The priests shall offer his burnt offering and his peace offerings, and he shall worship at the threshold of the gate. Then he shall go out, but the gate shall not be shut until evening. 3 The people of the land shall worship at the entrance of that gate before the LORD on the sabbaths and on the new moons. 4 The burnt offering that the prince offers to the LORD on the sabbath day shall be six lambs without blemish and a ram without blemish; 5 and the cereal offering with the ram shall be an ephah, and the cereal offering with the lambs shall be as much as he is able, together with a hin of oil to each ephah. 6 On the day of the new moon he shall offer a young bull without blemish, and six lambs and a ram, which shall be without blemish; 7 as a cereal offering he shall provide an ephah with the bull and an ephah with the ram, and with the lambs as much as he is able, together with a hin of oil to each ephah. 8 When the prince enters, he shall go in by the vestibule of the gate, and he shall go out by the same way.

9 "When the people of the land come before the LORD at the appointed feasts, he who enters by the north gate to worship shall go out by the south gate; and he who enters by the south gate shall go out by the north gate: no one shall return by way of the gate by which he entered, but each shall go out straight ahead. 10 When they go in, the prince shall go in with them; and when they go out, he shall go out.

11 "At the feasts and the appointed seasons the cereal offering with a young bull shall be an ephah, and with a ram an ephah, and with the lambs as much as one is able to give, together with a hin of oil to an ephah. 12 When the prince provides a freewill offering, either a burnt offering or peace offerings as a freewill offering to the LORD, the gate facing east shall be opened for him; and he shall offer his burnt offering or his peace offerings as he does on the sabbath day. Then he shall go out, and after he has gone out the gate shall be shut.

13 "He shall provide a lamb a year old without blemish for a burnt offering to the LORD daily; morning by morning he shall provide it. 14 And he shall provide a cereal offering with it morning by morning, one sixth of an ephah, and one third of a hin of oil to moisten the flour, as a cereal offering to the LORD; this is the ordinance for the continual burnt offering.*e* 15 Thus the lamb and the meal offering and the oil shall be provided, morning by morning, for a continual burnt offering.

16 "Thus says the Lord GOD: If the prince makes a gift to any of his sons out of *f* his inheritance, it shall belong to his sons, it is their property by inheritance. 17 But if he makes a gift out of his inheritance to one of his servants, it shall be his to the year of liberty; then it shall revert to the prince; only his sons may keep a gift from his inheritance. 18 The prince shall not take any of the inheritance of the people, thrusting them out of their property; he shall give his sons their inheritance out of his own property, so that none of my people shall be dispossessed of his property."

19 Then he brought me through the entrance, which was at the side of the gate, to the north row of the holy chambers for the priests; and there I saw a place at the extreme western end of them. 20 And he said to me, "This is the place where the priests shall boil the guilt offering and the sin offering, and where they shall bake the cereal offering, in order not to bring them out into the outer court and so communicate holiness to the people."

e Cn: Heb *perpetual ordinances continually*   *f* Gk: Heb *it is his inheritance*

21 Then he brought me forth to the outer court, and led me to the four corners of the court; and in each corner of the court there was a court— 22 in the four corners of the court were small[g] courts, forty cubits long and thirty broad; the four were of the same size. 23 On the inside, around each of the four courts was a row of masonry, with hearths made at the bottom of the rows round about. 24 Then he said to me, "These are the kitchens where those who minister at the temple shall boil the sacrifices of the people."

47 Then he brought me back to the door of the temple; and behold, water was issuing from below the threshold of the temple toward the east (for the temple faced east); and the water was flowing down from below the south end of the threshold of the temple, south of the altar. 2 Then he brought me out by way of the north gate, and led me round on the outside to the outer gate, that faces toward the east;[h] and the water was coming out on the south side.

3 Going on eastward with a line in his hand, the man measured a thousand cubits, and then led me through the water; and it was ankle-deep. 4Again he measured a thousand, and led me through the water; and it was knee-deep. Again he measured a thousand, and led me through the water; and it was up to the loins. 5Again he measured a thousand, and it was a river that I could not pass through, for the water had risen; it was deep enough to swim in, a river that could not be passed through. 6And he said to me, "Son of man, have you seen this?"

Then he led me back along the bank of the river. 7As I went back, I saw upon the bank of the river very many trees on the one side and on the other. 8And he said to me, "This water flows toward the eastern region and goes down into the Ar′a·bah; and when it enters the stagnant waters of the sea,[i] the water will become fresh. 9And wherever the river[j] goes every living creature which swarms will live, and there will be very many fish; for this water goes there, that the waters of the sea[k] may become fresh; so everything will live where the river goes. 10 Fishermen will stand beside the sea; from

En-ge′di to En-eg′la·im it will be a place for the spreading of nets; its fish will be of very many kinds, like the fish of the Great Sea. 11 But its swamps and marshes will not become fresh; they are to be left for salt. 12And on the banks, on both sides of the river, there will grow all kinds of trees for food. Their leaves will not wither nor their fruit fail, but they will bear fresh fruit every month, because the water for them flows from the sanctuary. Their fruit will be for food, and their leaves for healing."

13 Thus says the Lord GOD: "These are the boundaries by which you shall divide the land for inheritance among the twelve tribes of Israel. Joseph shall have two portions. 14And you shall divide it equally; I swore to give it to your fathers, and this land shall fall to you as your inheritance.

15 "This shall be the boundary of the land: On the north side, from the Great Sea by way of Heth′lon to the entrance of Ha′math, and on to Ze′dad,[l] 16 Be·ro′thah, Sib′ra·im (which lies on the border between Damascus and of Ha′math), as far as Ha′zer-hat′-ti·con, which is on the border of Hau′ran. 17 So the boundary shall run from the sea to Ha′zar-e′non, which is on the northern border of Damascus, with the border of Ha′math to the north.[m] This shall be the north side.

18 "On the east side, the boundary shall run from Ha′zar-e′non[n] between Hau′ran and Damascus;[m] along the Jordan between Gilead and the land of Israel; to the eastern sea and as far as Ta′mar.[o] This shall be the east side.

19 "On the south side, it shall run from Ta′mar as far as the waters of Mer′i·bath-ka′desh, thence along the Brook of Egypt to the Great Sea. This shall be the south side.

20 "On the west side, the Great Sea shall be the boundary to a point opposite the entrance of Ha′math. This shall be the west side.

21 "So you shall divide this land among you according to the tribes of Israel. 22 You shall allot it as an inheritance for yourselves and for the aliens who reside among you and have begotten children among you. They shall be to you as native-born sons of Israel; with you they shall be allotted an inheritance among the tribes of

g Gk Syr Vg: The meaning of the Hebrew word is uncertain   h Heb obscure
i Compare Syr: Heb into the sea to the sea those that were made to issue forth
j Gk Syr Vg Tg: Heb two rivers   k Compare Syr: Heb lacks the waters of the sea
l Gk: Heb the entrance of Zedad, Hamath   m Heb obscure
n Cn: Heb lacks Hazar-enon   o Compare Syr: Heb you shall measure
47.1-2: Zech 14.8; Rev 22.1-2.

Israel. 23 In whatever tribe the alien resides, there you shall assign him his inheritance, says the Lord GOD.

48 "These are the names of the tribes: Beginning at the northern border, from the sea by way^p of Heth'lon to the entrance of Hā'math, as far as Hā'zär-ē'non (which is on the northern border of Damascus over against Hamath), and^q extending from the east side to the west,^{r} Dan, one portion. 2Adjoining the territory of Dan, from the east side to the west, Ash'ér, one portion. 3Adjoining the territory of Ash'ér, from the east side to the west, Naph'tà·lĭ, one portion. 4Adjoining the territory of Naph'tà·lĭ, from the east side to the west, Mà·nas'sēh, one portion. 5Adjoining the territory of Mà·nas'sēh, from the east side to the west, Ē'phrà·im, one portion. 6Adjoining the territory of Ē'phrà·im, from the east side to the west, Reuben, one portion. 7Adjoining the territory of Reuben, from the east side to the west, Judah, one portion.

8 "Adjoining the territory of Judah, from the east side to the west, shall be the portion which you shall set apart, twenty-five thousand cubits in breadth, and in length equal to one of the tribal portions, from the east side to the west, with the sanctuary in the midst of it. 9 The portion which you shall set apart for the LORD shall be twenty-five thousand cubits in length, and twenty^s thousand in breadth. 10 These shall be the allotments of the holy portion: the priests shall have an allotment measuring twenty-five thousand cubits on the northern side, ten thousand cubits in breadth on the western side, ten thousand in breadth on the eastern side, and twenty-five thousand in length on the southern side, with the sanctuary of the LORD in the midst of it. 11 This shall be for the consecrated priests, the sons^t of Zā'dok, who kept my charge, who did not go astray when the people of Israel went astray, as the Levites did. 12And it shall belong to them as a special portion from the holy portion of the land, a most holy place, adjoining the territory of the Levites. 13And alongside the territory of the priests, the Levites shall have an allotment twenty-five thousand cubits in length and ten thousand in breadth. The whole length shall be twenty-five thou-

sand cubits and the breadth twenty^u thousand. 14 They shall not sell or exchange any of it; they shall not alienate this choice portion of the land, for it is holy to the LORD.

15 "The remainder, five thousand cubits in breadth and twenty-five thousand in length, shall be for ordinary use for the city, for dwellings and for open country. In the midst of it shall be the city; 16 and these shall be its dimensions: the north side four thousand five hundred cubits, the south side four thousand five hundred, the east side four thousand five hundred, and the west side four thousand and five hundred. 17And the city shall have open land: on the north two hundred and fifty cubits, on the south two hundred and fifty, on the east two hundred and fifty, and on the west two hundred and fifty. 18 The remainder of the length alongside the holy portion shall be ten thousand cubits to the east, and ten thousand to the west, and it shall be alongside the holy portion. Its produce shall be food for the workers of the city. 19And the workers of the city, from all the tribes of Israel, shall till it. 20 The whole portion which you shall set apart shall be twenty-five thousand cubits square, that is, the holy portion together with the property of the city.

21 "What remains on both sides of the holy portion and of the property of the city shall belong to the prince. Extending from the twenty-five thousand cubits of the holy portion to the east border, and westward from the twenty-five thousand cubits to the west border, parallel to the tribal portions, it shall belong to the prince. The holy portion with the sanctuary of the temple in its midst, 22 and the property of the Levites and the property of the city,^{y} shall be in the midst of that which belongs to the prince. The portion of the prince shall lie between the territory of Judah and the territory of Benjamin.

23 "As for the rest of the tribes: from the east side to the west, Benjamin, one portion. 24Adjoining the territory of Benjamin, from the east side to the west, Simeon, one portion. 25Adjoining the territory of Simeon, from the east side to the west, Is'sà·chär, one portion. 26Adjoining the territory of Is'sà·chär, from the east

^{p} Compare 47.15: Heb *by the side of the way* ^{q} Cn: Heb *and they shall be his*
^{r} Gk Compare verses 2-8: Heb *the east side the west* ^{s} Compare 45.1: Heb *ten*
^{t} One Ms Gk: Heb *of the sons* ^{u} Gk: Heb *ten*
^{y} Cn: Heb *and from the property of the Levites and from the property of the city*
48.16: Rev 21.16.

side to the west, Zeb′ū·lŭn, one portion. 27Adjoining the territory of Zeb′ū·lŭn, from the east side to the west, Gad, one portion. 28And adjoining the territory of Gad to the south, the boundary shall run from Tā′mär to the waters of Mer′i·bath-kā′desh, thence along the Brook of Egypt to the Great Sea. 29 This is the land which you shall allot as an inheritance among the tribes of Israel, and these are their several portions, says the Lord GOD.

30 "These shall be the exits of the city: On the north side, which is to be four thousand five hundred cubits by measure, 31three gates, the gate of Reuben, the gate of Judah, and the gate of Levi, the gates of the city being named after the tribes of Israel. 32 On the east side, which is to be four thousand five hundred cubits, three gates, the gate of Joseph, the gate of Benjamin, and the gate of Dan. 33 On the south side, which is to be four thousand five hundred cubits by measure, three gates, the gate of Simeon, the gate of Is′sä·chär, and the gate of Zeb′ū·lŭn. 34 On the west side, which is to be four thousand five hundred cubits, three gates,w the gate of Gad, the gate of Ash′ẽr, and the gate of Naph′tá·lï. 35 The circumference of the city shall be eighteen thousand cubits. And the name of the city henceforth shall be, The LORD is there."

THE BOOK OF

DANIEL

1 In the third year of the reign of Je·hoi′á·kim king of Judah, Ne·bŭ·chăd·nez′zär king of Babylon came to Jerusalem and besieged it. 2And the Lord gave Je·hoi′á·kim king of Judah into his hand, with some of the vessels of the house of God; and he brought them to the land of Shi′när, to the house of his god, and placed the vessels in the treasury of his god. 3 Then the king commanded Ash′pĕ·naz, his chief eunuch, to bring some of the people of Israel, both of the royal family and of the nobility, 4 youths without blemish, handsome and skilful in all wisdom, endowed with knowledge, understanding learning, and competent to serve in the king's palace, and to teach them the letters and language of the Chal·dē′ăns. 5 The king assigned them a daily portion of the rich food which the king ate, and of the wine which he drank. They were to be educated for three years, and at the end of that time they were to stand before the king. 6Among these were Daniel, Han·á·nï′äh, Mish′á-el, and Az·á·rï′äh of the tribe of Judah. 7And the chief of the eunuchs gave them names: Daniel he called Bel·tĕ·shaz′zär, Han·á·nï′äh he called Shad′rach, Mish′á-el he called Mē′shach, and Az·á·rï′äh he called Á·bed′ne·gō.

8 But Daniel resolved that he would not defile himself with the king's rich food, or with the wine which he drank; therefore he asked the chief of the eunuchs to allow him not to defile himself. 9And God gave Daniel favor and compassion in the sight of the chief of the eunuchs; 10 and the chief of the eunuchs said to Daniel, "I fear lest my lord the king, who appointed your food and your drink, should see that you were in poorer condition than the youths who are of your own age. So you would endanger my head with the king." 11 Then Daniel said to the steward whom the chief of the eunuchs had appointed over Daniel, Han·á·nï′äh, Mish′á-el, and Az·á·rï′äh; 12 "Test your servants for ten days; let us be given vegetables to eat and water to drink. 13 Then let our appearance and the appearance of the youths who eat the king's rich food be observed by you, and according to what you see deal with your servants." 14 So he hearkened to them in this matter, and tested them for ten days. 15At the end of ten days it was seen that they were better in appearance and fatter in flesh than all the youths who ate the king's rich food. 16 So the steward took away their rich food and the wine they

were to drink, and gave them vegetables.

17 As for these four youths, God gave them learning and skill in all letters and wisdom; and Daniel had understanding in all visions and dreams. 18 At the end of the time, when the king had commanded that they should be brought in, the chief of the eunuchs brought them in before Ne-bu·chad·nez′zar, 19 And the king spoke with them, and among them all none was found like Daniel, Han·a·ni′ah, Mish′a-el, and Az·a·ri′ah; therefore they stood before the king. 20 And in every matter of wisdom and understanding concerning which the king inquired of them, he found them ten times better than all the magicians and enchanters that were in all his kingdom. 21 And Daniel continued until the first year of King Cyrus.

2 In the second year of the reign of Ne·bu·chad·nez′zar, Nebuchadnezzar had dreams; and his spirit was troubled, and his sleep left him. 2 Then the king commanded that the magicians, the enchanters, the sorcerers, and the Chal·de′ans be summoned, to tell the king his dreams. So they came in and stood before the king. 3 And the king said to them, "I had a dream, and my spirit is troubled to know the dream." 4 Then the Chal·de′ans said to the king,ᵃ "O king, live for ever! Tell your servants the dream, and we will show the interpretation." 5 The king answered the Chal·de′ans, "The word from me is sure: if you do not make known to me the dream and its interpretation, you shall be torn limb from limb, and your houses shall be laid in ruins. 6 But if you show the dream and its interpretation, you shall receive from me gifts and rewards and great honor. Therefore show me the dream and its interpretation." 7 They answered a second time, "Let the king tell his servants the dream, and we will show its interpretation." 8 The king answered, "I know with certainty that you are trying to gain time, because you see that the word from me is sure 9 that if you do not make the dream known to me, there is but one sentence for you. You have agreed to speak lying and corrupt words before me till the times change. Therefore tell me the dream, and I shall know that you can show me its interpretation." 10 The Chal·de′ans answered the king, "There is not a man on earth who can meet the king's demand; for

no great and powerful king has asked such a thing of any magician or enchanter or Chaldean. 11 The thing that the king asks is difficult, and none can show it to the king except the gods, whose dwelling is not with flesh."

12 Because of this the king was angry and very furious, and commanded that all the wise men of Babylon be destroyed. 13 So the decree went forth that the wise men were to be slain, and they sought Daniel and his companions, to slay them. 14 Then Daniel replied with prudence and discretion to Ar′i·och, the captain of the king's guard, who had gone out to slay the wise men of Babylon; 15 he said to Ar′i·och, the king's captain, "Why is the decree of the king so severe?" Then Arioch made the matter known to Daniel. 16 And Daniel went in and besought the king to appoint him a time, that he might show to the king the interpretation.

17 Then Daniel went to his house and made the matter known to Han·a·ni′ah, Mish′a-el, and Az·a·ri′ah, his companions, 18 and told them to seek mercy of the God of heaven concerning this mystery, so that Daniel and his companions might not perish with the rest of the wise men of Babylon. 19 Then the mystery was revealed to Daniel in a vision of the night. Then Daniel blessed the God of heaven. 20 Daniel said:

"Blessed be the name of God for
    ever and ever,
  to whom belong wisdom and
    might.
21 He changes times and seasons;
  he removes kings and sets up
    kings;
he gives wisdom to the wise
  and knowledge to those who have
    understanding;
22 he reveals deep and mysterious
    things;
he knows what is in the darkness,
  and the light dwells with him.
23 To thee, O God of my fathers,
  I give thanks and praise,
for thou hast given me wisdom
    and strength,
  and hast now made known to me
    what we asked of thee,
for thou hast made known to us
    the king's matter."

24 Therefore Daniel went in to Ar′i·och, whom the king had appointed to destroy the wise men of Babylon; he went and said thus to him, "Do not destroy the wise men of Babylon;

ᵃ Heb adds *in Aramaic,* indicating that the text from this point to the end of chapter 7 is in Aramaic

bring me in before the king, and I will show the king the interpretation."

25 Then Ar′i·och brought in Daniel before the king in haste, and said thus to him: "I have found among the exiles from Judah a man who can make known to the king the interpretation." 26 The king said to Daniel, whose name was Bel·te·shaz′zar, "Are you able to make known to me the dream that I have seen and its interpretation?" 27 Daniel answered the king, "No wise men, enchanters, magicians, or astrologers can show to the king the mystery which the king has asked, 28 but there is a God in heaven who reveals mysteries, and he has made known to King Ne·bu·chad·nez′zar what will be in the latter days. Your dream and the visions of your head as you lay in bed are these: 29 To you, O king, as you lay in bed came thoughts of what would be hereafter, and he who reveals mysteries made known to you what is to be. 30 But as for me, not because of any wisdom that I have more than all the living has this mystery been revealed to me, but in order that the interpretation may be made known to the king, and that you may know the thoughts of your mind.

31 "You saw, O king, and behold, a great image. This image, mighty and of exceeding brightness, stood before you, and its appearance was frightening. 32 The head of this image was of fine gold, its breast and arms of silver, its belly and thighs of bronze, 33 its legs of iron, its feet partly of iron and partly of clay. 34As you looked, a stone was cut out by no human hand, and it smote the image on its feet of iron and clay, and broke them in pieces; 35 then the iron, the clay, the bronze, the silver, and the gold, all together were broken in pieces, and became like the chaff of the summer threshing floors; and the wind carried them away, so that not a trace of them could be found. But the stone that struck the image became a great mountain and filled the whole earth.

36 "This was the dream; now we will tell the king its interpretation. 37 You, O king, the king of kings, to whom the God of heaven has given the kingdom, the power, and the might, and the glory, 38 and into whose hand he has given, wherever they dwell, the sons of men, the beasts of the field, and the birds of the air, making you rule over them all—you are the head

of gold. 39After you shall arise another kingdom inferior to you, and yet a third kingdom of bronze, which shall rule over all the earth. 40And there shall be a fourth kingdom, strong as iron, because iron breaks to pieces and shatters all things; and like iron which crushes, it shall break and crush all these. 41And as you saw the feet and toes partly of potter's clay and partly of iron, it shall be a divided kingdom; but some of the firmness of iron shall be in it, just as you saw iron mixed with the miry clay. 42And as the toes of the feet were partly iron and partly clay, so the kingdom shall be partly strong and partly brittle. 43As you saw the iron mixed with miry clay, so they will mix with one another in marriage,[b] but they will not hold together, just as iron does not mix with clay. 44And in the days of those kings the God of heaven will set up a kingdom which shall never be destroyed, nor shall its sovereignty be left to another people. It shall break in pieces all these kingdoms and bring them to an end, and it shall stand for ever; 45 just as you saw that a stone was cut from a mountain by no human hand, and that it broke in pieces the iron, the bronze, the clay, the silver, and the gold. A great God has made known to the king what shall be hereafter. The dream is certain, and its interpretation sure."

46 Then King Ne·bu·chad·nez′zar fell upon his face, and did homage to Daniel, and commanded that an offering and incense be offered up to him. 47 The king said to Daniel, "Truly, your God is God of gods and Lord of kings, and a revealer of mysteries, for you have been able to reveal this mystery." 48 Then the king gave Daniel high honors and many great gifts, and made him ruler over the whole province of Babylon, and chief prefect over all the wise men of Babylon. 49 Daniel made request of the king, and he appointed Shad′rach, Me′shach, and A·bed′ne·go over the affairs of the province of Babylon; but Daniel remained at the king's court.

3 King Ne·bu·chad·nez′zar made an image of gold, whose height was sixty cubits and its breadth six cubits. He set it up on the plain of Du′ra, in the province of Babylon. 2 Then King Ne·bu·chad·nez′zar sent to assemble the satraps, the prefects, and the governors, the counselors, the treasurers, the justices, the magistrates,

[b] Aram *by the seed of men*
2.44: Rev 11.15.

and all the officials of the provinces to come to the dedication of the image which King Nebuchadnezzar had set up. 3 Then the satraps, the prefects, and the governors, the counselors, the treasurers, the justices, the magistrates, and all the officials of the provinces, were assembled for the dedication of the image that King Ne·bu·chàd·nez´-zàr had set up; and they stood before the image that Nebuchadnezzar had set up. 4And the herald proclaimed aloud, "You are commanded, O peoples, nations, and languages, 5 that when you hear the sound of the horn, pipe, lyre, trigon, harp, bagpipe, and every kind of music, you are to fall down and worship the golden image that King Ne·bu·chàd·nez´zàr has set up; 6 and whoever does not fall down and worship shall immediately be cast into a burning fiery furnace." 7 Therefore, as soon as all the peoples heard the sound of the horn, pipe, lyre, trigon, harp, bagpipe, and every kind of music, all the peoples, nations, and languages fell down and worshiped the golden image which King Ne·bu·chàd·nez´zàr had set up.

8 Therefore at that time certain Chal·dē´áns came forward and maliciously accused the Jews. 9 They said to King Ne·bu·chàd·nez´zàr, "O king, live for ever! 10 You, O king, have made a decree, that every man who hears the sound of the horn, pipe, lyre, trigon, harp, bagpipe, and every kind of music, shall fall down and worship the golden image; 11 and whoever does not fall down and worship shall be cast into a burning fiery furnace. 12 There are certain Jews whom you have appointed over the affairs of the province of Babylon: Shad´rach, Mē´shach, and A·bed´ne·gō. These men, O king, pay no heed to you; they do not serve your gods or worship the golden image which you have set up."

13 Then Ne·bu·chàd·nez´zàr in furious rage commanded that Shad´rach, Mē´shach, and A·bed´ne·gō be brought. Then they brought these men before the king. 14Ne·bu·chàd·nez´zàr said to them, "Is it true, O Shad´rach, Mē´-shach, and A·bed´ne·gō, that you do not serve my gods or worship the golden image which I have set up? 15 Now if you are ready when you hear the sound of the horn, pipe, lyre, trigon, harp, bagpipe, and every kind

of music, to fall down and worship the image which I have made, well and good; but if you do not worship, you shall immediately be cast into a burning fiery furnace; and who is the god that will deliver you out of my hands?"

16 Shad´rach, Mē´shach, and A·bed´-ne·gō answered the king, "O Ne·bu·chàd·nez´zàr, we have no need to answer you in this matter. 17 If it be so, our God whom we serve is able to deliver us from the burning fiery furnace; and he will deliver us out of your hand, O king.c 18 But if not, be it known to you, O king, that we will not serve your gods or worship the golden image which you have set up."

19 Then Ne·bu·chàd·nez´zàr was full of fury, and the expression of his face was changed against Shad´rach, Mē´shach, and A·bed´ne·gō. He ordered the furnace heated seven times more than it was wont to be heated. 20And he ordered certain mighty men of his army to bind Shad´-rach, Mē´shach, and A·bed´ne·gō, and to cast them into the burning fiery furnace. 21 Then these men were bound in their mantles,d their tunics,d their hats, and their other garments, and they were cast into the burning fiery furnace. 22 Because the king's order was strict and the furnace very hot, the flame of the fire slew those men who took up Shad´rach, Mē´-shach, and A·bed´ne·gō. 23And these three men, Shad´rach, Mē´shach, and A·bed´ne·gō, fell bound into the burning fiery furnace.

24 Then King Ne·bu·chàd·nez´zàr was astonished and rose up in haste. He said to his counselors, "Did we not cast three men bound into the fire?" They answered the king, "True, O king." 25 He answered, "But I see four men loose, walking in the midst of the fire, and they are not hurt; and the appearance of the fourth is like a son of the gods."

26 Then Ne·bu·chàd·nez´zàr came near to the door of the burning fiery furnace and said, "Shad´rach, Mē´-shach, and A·bed´ne·gō, servants of the Most High God, come forth, and come here!" Then Shadrach, Meshach, and Abednego came out from the fire. 27And the satraps, the prefects, the governors, and the king's counselors gathered together and saw that the fire had not had any power over the bodies of those men; the hair of

c Or *Behold, our God . . . king.* Or *If our God is able to deliver us, he will deliver us from*
　the burning fiery furnace and out of your hand, O king
d The meaning of the Aramaic word is uncertain
3.5-6: Rev 13.15.

their heads was not singed, their mantles[d] were not harmed, and no smell of fire had come upon them. [28] Ne·bu·chad·nez′zar said, "Blessed be the God of Shad′rach, Me′shach, and A·bed′ne·go, who has sent his angel and delivered his servants, who trusted in him, and set at nought the king's command, and yielded up their bodies rather than serve and worship any god except their own God. [29] Therefore I make a decree: Any people, nation, or language that speaks anything against the God of Shad′rach, Me′shach, and A·bed′ne·go shall be torn limb from limb, and their houses laid in ruins; for there is no other god who is able to deliver in this way." [30] Then the king promoted Shad′rach, Me′shach, and A·bed′ne·go in the province of Babylon.

[4][e] King Ne·bu·chad·nez′zar to all peoples, nations, and languages, that dwell in all the earth: Peace be multiplied to you! [2] It has seemed good to me to show the signs and wonders that the Most High God has wrought toward me.

[3] How great are his signs,
      how mighty his wonders!
   His kingdom is an everlasting
      kingdom,
   and his dominion is from genera-
      tion to generation.

[4][f] I, Ne·bu·chad·nez′zar, was at ease in my house and prospering in my palace. [5] I had a dream which made me afraid; as I lay in bed the fancies and the visions of my head alarmed me. [6] Therefore I made a decree that all the wise men of Babylon should be brought before me, that they might make known to me the interpretation of the dream. [7] Then the magicians, the enchanters, the Chal·de′ans, and the astrologers came in; and I told them the dream, but they could not make known to me its interpretation. [8] At last Daniel came in before me—he who was named Bel·te·shaz′zar after the name of my god, and in whom is the spirit of the holy gods[g]—and I told him the dream, saying, [9] "O Bel·te·shaz′zar, chief of the magicians, because I know that the spirit of the holy gods[g] is in you and that no mystery is difficult for you, here is[h] the dream which I saw; tell me its interpretation. [10] The visions of my head as I lay in bed were these: I saw, and behold, a tree in the midst of the earth; and its height was great. [11] The

tree grew and became strong, and its top reached to heaven, and it was visible to the end of the whole earth. [12] Its leaves were fair and its fruit abundant, and in it was food for all. The beasts of the field found shade under it, and the birds of the air dwelt in its branches, and all flesh was fed from it.

[13] "I saw in the visions of my head as I lay in bed, and behold, a watcher, a holy one, came down from heaven. [14] He cried aloud and said thus, 'Hew down the tree and cut off its branches, strip off its leaves and scatter its fruit; let the beasts flee from under it and the birds from its branches. [15] But leave the stump of its roots in the earth, bound with a band of iron and bronze, amid the tender grass of the field. Let him be wet with the dew of heaven; let his lot be with the beasts in the grass of the earth; [16] let his mind be changed from a man's, and let a beast's mind be given to him; and let seven times pass over him. [17] The sentence is by the decree of the watchers, the decision by the word of the holy ones, to the end that the living may know that the Most High rules the kingdom of men, and gives it to whom he will, and sets over it the lowliest of men.' [18] This dream I, King Ne·bu·chad·nez′zar, saw. And you, O Bel·te·shaz′zar, declare the interpretation, because all the wise men of my kingdom are not able to make known to me the interpretation, but you are able, for the spirit of the holy gods[i] is in you."

[19] Then Daniel, whose name was Bel·te·shaz′zar, was dismayed for a moment, and his thoughts alarmed him. The king said, "Belteshazzar, let not the dream or the interpretation alarm you." Belteshazzar answered, "My lord, may the dream be for those who hate you and its interpretation for your enemies! [20] The tree you saw, which grew and became strong, so that its top reached to heaven, and it was visible to the end of the whole earth; [21] whose leaves were fair and its fruit abundant, and in which was food for all; under which beasts of the field found shade, and in whose branches the birds of the air dwelt—[22] it is you, O king, who have grown and become strong. Your greatness has grown and reaches to heaven, and your dominion to the ends of the earth. [23] And whereas the king saw a watcher, a holy one,

The meaning of the Aramaic word is uncertain   [e] Ch 3.31 in Aram   [f] Ch 4.1 in Aram   Or *Spirit of the holy God*   [h] Cn: Aram *visions of*   [i] Or *Spirit of the holy God*
[12, 21]: Ezek 17.23; 31.6; Mt 13.32; Mk 4.32; Lk 13.19.

coming down from heaven and saying, 'Hew down the tree and destroy it, but leave the stump of its roots in the earth, bound with a band of iron and bronze, in the tender grass of the field; and let him be wet with the dew of heaven; and let his lot be with the beasts of the field, till seven times pass over him;' 24 this is the interpretation, O king: It is a decree of the Most High, which has come upon my lord the king, 25 that you shall be driven from among men, and your dwelling shall be with the beasts of the field; you shall be made to eat grass like an ox, and you shall be wet with the dew of heaven, and seven times shall pass over you, till you know that the Most High rules the kingdom of men, and gives it to whom he will. 26And as it was commanded to leave the stump of the roots of the tree, your kingdom shall be sure for you from the time that you know that Heaven rules. 27 Therefore, O king, let my counsel be acceptable to you; break off your sins by practicing righteousness, and your iniquities by showing mercy to the oppressed, that there may perhaps be a lengthening of your tranquility."

28 All this came upon King Ne·bu·chad·nez′zar. 29At the end of twelve months he was walking on the roof of the royal palace of Babylon, 30 and the king said, "Is not this great Babylon, which I have built by my mighty power as a royal residence and for the glory of my majesty?" 31 While the words were still in the king's mouth, there fell a voice from heaven, "O King Ne·bu·chad·nez′zar, to you it is spoken: The kingdom has departed from you, 32 and you shall be driven from among men, and your dwelling shall be with the beasts of the field; and you shall be made to eat grass like an ox, and seven times shall pass over you, until you have learned that the Most High rules the kingdom of men and gives it to whom he will." 33 Immediately the word was fulfilled upon Ne·bu·chad·nez′zar. He was driven from among men, and ate grass like an ox, and his body was wet with the dew of heaven till his hair grew as long as eagles' feathers, and his nails were like birds' claws.

34 At the end of the days I, Ne·bu·chad·nez′zar, lifted my eyes to heaven, and my reason returned to me, and I blessed the Most High, and praised and honored him who lives for ever;

for his dominion is an everlasting dominion,

and his kingdom endures from generation to generation;
35 all the inhabitants of the earth are accounted as nothing;
and he does according to his will in the host of heaven
and among the inhabitants of the earth;
and none can stay his hand or say to him, "What doest thou?"

36 At the same time my reason returned to me; and for the glory of my kingdom, my majesty and splendor returned to me. My counselors and my lords sought me, and I was established in my kingdom, and still more greatness was added to me. 37 Now I, Ne·bu·chad·nez′zar, praise and extol and honor the King of heaven; for all his works are right and his ways are just; and those who walk in pride he is able to abase.

5 King Bel·shaz′zar made a great feast for a thousand of his lords, and drank wine in front of the thousand.

2 Bel·shaz′zar, when he tasted the wine, commanded that the vessels of gold and of silver which Ne·bu·chad·nez′zar his father had taken out of the temple in Jerusalem be brought, that the king and his lords, his wives, and his concubines might drink from them. 3 Then they brought in the golden and silver vessels/ which had been taken out of the temple, the house of God in Jerusalem; and the king and his lords, his wives, and his concubines drank from them. 4 They drank wine, and praised the gods of gold and silver, bronze, iron, wood, and stone.

5 Immediately the fingers of a man's hand appeared and wrote on the plaster of the wall of the king's palace, opposite the lampstand; and the king saw the hand as it wrote. 6 Then the king's color changed, and his thoughts alarmed him; his limbs gave way, and his knees knocked together. 7 The king cried aloud to bring in the enchanters, the Chal·de′ans, and the astrologers. The king said to the wise men of Babylon, "Whoever reads this writing, and shows me its interpretation, shall be clothed with purple, and have a chain of gold about his neck, and shall be the third ruler in the kingdom." 8 Then all the king's wise men came in, but they could not read the writing or make known to the king the interpretation. 9 Then King Bel·shaz′zar was greatly alarmed, and his color changed; and his lords were perplexed.

10 The queen, because of the words

/ Theodotion Vg: Aram *golden vessels*

of the king and his lords, came into the banqueting hall; and the queen said, "O king, live for ever! Let not your thoughts alarm you or your color change. ¹¹ There is in your kingdom a man in whom is the spirit of the holy gods.*ᵏ* In the days of your father light and understanding and wisdom, like the wisdom of the gods, were found in him, and King Ne·bù·chàd·nez′zàr, your father, made him chief of the magicians, enchanters, Chal·dē′ảnš, and astrologers,*ˡ* ¹² because an excellent spirit, knowledge, and understanding to interpret dreams, explain riddles, and solve problems were found in this Daniel, whom the king named Bel·te·shaz′zàr. Now let Daniel be called, and he will show the interpretation."

13 Then Daniel was brought in before the king. The king said to Daniel, "You are that Daniel, one of the exiles of Judah, whom the king my father brought from Judah. ¹⁴ I have heard of you that the spirit of the holy gods*ᵏ* is in you, and that light and understanding and excellent wisdom are found in you. ¹⁵ Now the wise men, the enchanters, have been brought in before me to read this writing and make known to me its interpretation; but they could not show the interpretation of the matter. ¹⁶ But I have heard that you can give interpretations and solve problems. Now if you can read the writing and make known to me its interpretation, you shall be clothed with purple, and have a chain of gold about your neck, and shall be the third ruler in the kingdom."

17 Then Daniel answered before the king, "Let your gifts be for yourself, and give your rewards to another; nevertheless I will read the writing to the king and make known to him the interpretation. ¹⁸ O king, the Most High God gave Ne·bù·chàd·nez′zàr your father kingship and greatness and glory and majesty; ¹⁹ and because of the greatness that he gave him, all peoples, nations, and languages trembled and feared before him; whom he would he slew, and whom he would he kept alive; whom he would he raised up, and whom he would he put down. ²⁰ But when his heart was lifted up and his spirit was hardened so that he dealt proudly, he was deposed from his kingly throne, and his glory was taken from him; ²¹ he was driven from among men, and his mind was made like that of a beast, and his dwelling was with the wild asses; he was fed

grass like an ox, and his body was wet with the dew of heaven, until he knew that the Most High God rules the kingdom of men, and sets over it whom he will. ²²And you his son, Bel·shaz′zàr, have not humbled your heart, though you knew all this, ²³ but you have lifted up yourself against the Lord of heaven; and the vessels of his house have been brought in before you, and you and your lords, your wives, and your concubines have drunk wine from them; and you have praised the gods of silver and gold, of bronze, iron, wood, and stone, which do not see or hear or know, but the God in whose hand is your breath, and whose are all your ways, you have not honored.

24 "Then from his presence the hand was sent, and this writing was inscribed. ²⁵And this is the writing that was inscribed: MĚ′NĒ, MĚ′NĒ, TEK′ĚL, and PÄR′SIN. ²⁶ This is the interpretation of the matter: MĚ′NĒ, God has numbered the days of your kingdom and brought it to an end; ²⁷ TEK′-ĚL, you have been weighed in the balances and found wanting; ²⁸ PĒ′RES, your kingdom is divided and given to the Medes and Persians."

29 Then Bel·shaz′zàr commanded, and Daniel was clothed with purple, a chain of gold was put about his neck, and proclamation was made concerning him, that he should be the third ruler in the kingdom.

30 That very night Bel·shaz′zàr the Chal·dē′ản king was slain. ³¹And Dà·rī′ûs the Mede received the kingdom, being about sixty-two years old.

6 It pleased Dà·rī′ûs to set over the kingdom a hundred and twenty satraps, to be throughout the whole kingdom, ² and over them three presidents, of whom Daniel was one, to whom these satraps should give account, so that the king might suffer no loss. ³ Then this Daniel became distinguished above all the other presidents and satraps, because an excellent spirit was in him; and the king planned to set him over the whole kingdom. ⁴ Then the presidents and the satraps sought to find a ground for complaint against Daniel with regard to the kingdom; but they could find no ground for complaint or any fault, because he was faithful, and no error or fault was found in him. ⁵ Then these men said, "We shall not find any ground for complaint against this Daniel unless we find it in connection with the law of his God."

ᵏ Or *Spirit of the holy God*　*ˡ* Aram repeats *the king your father*

6 Then these presidents and satraps came by agreement[m] to the king and said to him, "O King Dà·rī′us, live for ever! 7All the presidents of the kingdom, the prefects and the satraps, the counselors and the governors are agreed that the king should establish an ordinance and enforce an interdict, that whoever makes petition to any god or man for thirty days, except to you, O king, shall be cast into the den of lions. 8 Now, O king, establish the interdict, and sign the document, so that it cannot be changed, according to the law of the Medes and the Persians, which cannot be revoked." 9 Therefore King Dà·rī′us signed the document and interdict.

10 When Daniel knew that the document had been signed, he went to his house where he had windows in his upper chamber open toward Jerusalem; and he got down upon his knees three times a day and prayed and gave thanks before his God, as he had done previously. 11 Then these men came by agreement[m] and found Daniel making petition and supplication before his God. 12 Then they came near and said before the king, concerning the interdict, "O king! Did you not sign an interdict, that any man who makes petition to any god or man within thirty days except to you, O king, shall be cast into the den of lions?" The king answered, "The thing stands fast, according to the law of the Medes and Persians, which cannot be revoked." 13 Then they answered before the king, "That Daniel, who is one of the exiles from Judah, pays no heed to you, O king, or the interdict you have signed, but makes his petition three times a day."

14 Then the king, when he heard these words, was much distressed, and set his mind to deliver Daniel; and he labored till the sun went down to rescue him. 15 Then these men came by agreement[m] to the king, and said to the king, "Know, O king, that it is a law of the Medes and Persians that no interdict or ordinance which the king establishes can be changed."

16 Then the king commanded, and Daniel was brought and cast into the den of lions. The king said to Daniel, "May your God, whom you serve continually, deliver you!" 17And a stone was brought and laid upon the mouth of the den, and the king sealed it with his own signet and with the signet of his lords, that nothing might be

changed concerning Daniel. 18 Then the king went to his palace, and spent the night fasting; no diversions were brought to him, and sleep fled from him.

19 Then, at break of day, the king arose and went in haste to the den of lions. 20 When he came near to the den where Daniel was, he cried out in a tone of anguish and said to Daniel, "O Daniel, servant of the living God, has your God, whom you serve continually, been able to deliver you from the lions?" 21 Then Daniel said to the king, "O king, live for ever! 22 My God sent his angel and shut the lions' mouths, and they have not hurt me, because I was found blameless before him; and also before you, O king, I have done no wrong." 23 Then the king was exceedingly glad, and commanded that Daniel be taken up out of the den. So Daniel was taken up out of the den, and no kind of hurt was found upon him, because he had trusted in his God. 24And the king commanded, and those men who had accused Daniel were brought and cast into the den of lions—they, their children, and their wives; and before they reached the bottom of the den the lions overpowered them and broke all their bones in pieces.

25 Then King Dà·rī′us wrote to all the peoples, nations, and languages that dwell in all the earth: "Peace be multiplied to you. 26 I make a decree, that in all my royal dominion men tremble and fear before the God of Daniel,

> for he is the living God,
>   enduring for ever;
> his kingdom shall never be destroyed,
>   and his dominion shall be to the end.

27 He delivers and rescues,
> he works signs and wonders
>   in heaven and on earth,
> he who has saved Daniel
>   from the power of the lions."

28 So this Daniel prospered during the reign of Dà·rī′us and the reign of Cyrus the Persian.

7 In the first year of Bel·shaz′zar king of Babylon, Daniel had a dream and visions of his head as he lay in his bed. Then he wrote down the dream, and told the sum of the matter. 2 Daniel said, "I saw in my vision by night, and behold, the four winds of heaven were stirring up the great sea.

m Or *thronging*
6.22: 2 Tim 4.17.

³And four great beasts came up out of the sea, different from one another. ⁴ The first was like a lion and had eagles' wings. Then as I looked its wings were plucked off, and it was lifted up from the ground and made to stand upon two feet like a man; and the mind of a man was given to it. ⁵And behold, another beast, a second one, like a bear. It was raised up on one side; it had three ribs in its mouth between its teeth; and it was told, 'Arise, devour much flesh.' ⁶After this I looked, and lo, another, like a leopard, with four wings of a bird on its back; and the beast had four heads; and dominion was given to it. ⁷After this I saw in the night visions, and behold, a fourth beast, terrible and dreadful and exceedingly strong; and it had great iron teeth; it devoured and broke in pieces, and stamped the residue with its feet. It was different from all the beasts that were before it; and it had ten horns. ⁸ I considered the horns, and behold, there came up among them another horn, a little one, before which three of the first horns were plucked up by the roots; and behold, in this horn were eyes like the eyes of a man, and a mouth speaking great things. ⁹As I looked,

thrones were placed
   and one that was ancient of days
       took his seat;
his raiment was white as snow,
   and the hair of his head like pure
       wool;
his throne was fiery flames,
   its wheels were burning fire.
¹⁰ A stream of fire issued
   and came forth from before
       him;
a thousand thousands served him,
   and ten thousand times ten thou-
       sand stood before him;
the court sat in judgment,
   and the books were opened.

¹¹ I looked then because of the sound of the great words which the horn was speaking. And as I looked, the beast was slain, and its body destroyed and given over to be burned with fire. ¹²As for the rest of the beasts, their dominion was taken away, but their lives were prolonged for a season and a time. ¹³ I saw in the night visions,

and behold, with the clouds of
       heaven
   there came one like a son of man,
and he came to the Ancient of Days

and was presented before him.
¹⁴ And to him was given dominion
   and glory and kingdom,
that all peoples, nations, and lan-
       guages
   should serve him;
his dominion is an everlasting do-
       minion,
   which shall not pass away,
and his kingdom one
   that shall not be destroyed.

15 "As for me, Daniel, my spirit within me was anxious and the visions of my head alarmed me. ¹⁶ I approached one of those who stood there and asked him the truth concerning all this. So he told me, and made known to me the interpretation of the things. ¹⁷ 'These four great beasts are four kings who shall arise out of the earth. ¹⁸ But the saints of the Most High shall receive the kingdom, and possess the kingdom for ever, for ever and ever.'

19 "Then I desired to know the truth concerning the fourth beast, which was different from all the rest, exceedingly terrible, with its teeth of iron and claws of bronze; and which devoured and broke in pieces, and stamped the residue with its feet; ²⁰ and concerning the ten horns that were on its head, and the other horn which came up and before which three of them fell, the horn which had eyes and a mouth that spoke great things, and which seemed greater than its fellows. ²¹As I looked, this horn made war with the saints, and prevailed over them, ²² until the Ancient of Days came, and judgment was given for the saints of the Most High, and the time came when the saints received the kingdom.

23 "Thus he said: 'As for the fourth beast,

there shall be a fourth kingdom on
       earth,
   which shall be different from all
       the kingdoms,
and it shall devour the whole earth,
   and trample it down, and break
       it to pieces.
24 As for the ten horns,
   out of this kingdom
       ten kings shall arise,
   and another shall arise after
       them;
he shall be different from the
       former ones,
   and shall put down three kings.

7.3: Rev 13.1.   7.3, 7, 21: Rev 11.7.   7.4-6: Rev 13.2.   7.7: Rev 12.3; 13.1; 17.3.
7.8, 11: Rev 13.5.   7.9: Rev 1.14; 20.4, 11.   7.10: Rev 5.11; 20.12.
7.13-14: Mt 24.30; 26.64; Mk 13.26; 14.62; Lk 21.27; 22.69; Rev 1.7, 13; 14.14.
7.14, 18, 22, 27: Rev 11.15.   7.20, 24: Rev 17.12.   7.21: Rev 13.7.

25 He shall speak words against the Most High,
and shall wear out the saints of the Most High,
and shall think to change the times and the law;
and they shall be given into his hand
for a time, two times, and half a time.
26 But the court shall sit in judgment,
and his dominion shall be taken away,
to be consumed and destroyed to the end.
27 And the kingdom and the dominion
and the greatness of the kingdoms under the whole heaven
shall be given to the people of the saints of the Most High;
their kingdom shall be an everlasting kingdom,
and all dominions shall serve and obey them.'

28 "Here is the end of the matter.
As for me, Daniel, my thoughts
greatly alarmed me, and my color
changed; but I kept the matter in my
mind."

8 In the third year of the reign of
King Bel·shaz′zar a vision appeared to me, Daniel, after that which
appeared to me at the first. 2 And I
saw in the vision; and when I saw, I
was in Su′sa the capital, which is in
the province of E′lam; and I saw in
the vision, and I was at the river
U′lai. 3 I raised my eyes and saw, and
behold, a ram standing on the bank of
the river. It had two horns; and both
horns were high, but one was higher
than the other, and the higher one
came up last. 4 I saw the ram charging
westward and northward and southward; no beast could stand before him,
and there was no one who could rescue
from his power; he did as he pleased
and magnified himself.

5 As I was considering, behold, a
he-goat came from the west across the
face of the whole earth, without
touching the ground; and the goat had
a conspicuous horn between his eyes.
6 He came to the ram with the two
horns, which I had seen standing on
the bank of the river, and he ran at
him in his mighty wrath. 7 I saw him
come close to the ram, and he was
enraged against him and struck the
ram and broke his two horns; and the
ram had no power to stand before him,
but he cast him down to the ground
and trampled upon him; and there was
no one who could rescue the ram from
his power. 8 Then the he-goat magnified himself exceedingly; but when he
was strong, the great horn was broken,
and instead of it there came up four
conspicuous horns toward the four
winds of heaven.

9 Out of one of them came forth a
little horn, which grew exceedingly
great toward the south, toward the
east, and toward the glorious land.
10 It grew great, even to the host of
heaven; and some of the host of the
stars it cast down to the ground, and
trampled upon them. 11 It magnified
itself, even up to the Prince of the
host; and the continual burnt offering
was taken away from him, and the
place of his sanctuary was overthrown.
12 And the host was given over to it together with the continual burnt offering through transgression;[n] and truth
was cast down to the ground, and the
horn acted and prospered. 13 Then I
heard a holy one speaking; and another
holy one said to the one that spoke,
"For how long is the vision concerning
the continual burnt offering, the transgression that makes desolate, and the
giving over of the sanctuary and host
to be trampled under foot?"[o] 14 And he
said to him,[p] "For two thousand and
three hundred evenings and mornings;
then the sanctuary shall be restored to
its rightful state."

15 When I, Daniel, had seen the
vision, I sought to understand it; and
behold, there stood before me one
having the appearance of a man. 16 And
I heard a man's voice between the
banks of the U′lai, and it called,
"Gabriel, make this man understand
the vision." 17 So he came near where
I stood; and when he came, I was
frightened and fell upon my face. But
he said to me, "Understand, O son of
man, that the vision is for the time of
the end."

18 As he was speaking to me, I fell
into a deep sleep with my face to the
ground; but he touched me and set me
on my feet. 19 He said, "Behold, I will
make known to you what shall be at
the latter end of the indignation; for it
pertains to the appointed time of the
end. 20 As for the ram which you saw
with the two horns, these are the kings
of Media and Persia. 21 And the he-goat[q] is the king of Greece; and the
great horn between his eyes is the first
king. 22 As for the horn that was broken,

[n] Heb obscure [o] Heb obscure [p] Theodotion Gk Syr Vg: Heb *me*
[q] Or *shaggy he-goat*

7.25: Rev 12.14. **8.10:** Rev 12.4. **8.13:** Lk 21.24.

in place of which four others arose, four kingdoms shall arise from his[r] nation, but not with his power. 23 And at the latter end of their rule, when the transgressors have reached their full measure, a king of bold countenance, one who understands riddles, shall arise. 24 His power shall be great,[s] and he shall cause fearful destruction, and shall succeed in what he does, and destroy mighty men and the people of the saints. 25 By his cunning he shall make deceit prosper under his hand, and in his own mind he shall magnify himself. Without warning he shall destroy many; and he shall even rise up against the Prince of princes; but, by no human hand, he shall be broken. 26 The vision of the evenings and the mornings which has been told is true; but seal up the vision, for it pertains to many days hence."

27 And I, Daniel, was overcome and lay sick for some days; then I rose and went about the king's business; but I was appalled by the vision and did not understand it.

9 In the first year of Dà·rī′us the son of A·haś′u-ē′rus, by birth a Mede, who became king over the realm of the Chal·dē′ans—[2] in the first year of his reign, I, Daniel, perceived in the books the number of years which, according to the word of the LORD to Jeremiah the prophet, must pass before the end of the desolations of Jerusalem, namely, seventy years.

3 Then I turned my face to the Lord God, seeking him by prayer and supplications with fasting and sackcloth and ashes. 4 I prayed to the LORD my God and made confession, saying, "O Lord, the great and terrible God, who keepest covenant and steadfast love with those who love him and keep his commandments, 5 we have sinned and done wrong and acted wickedly and rebelled, turning aside from thy commandments and ordinances; 6 we have not listened to thy servants the prophets, who spoke in thy name to our kings, our princes, and our fathers, and to all the people of the land. 7 To thee, O Lord, belongs righteousness, but to us confusion of face, as at this day, to the men of Judah, to the inhabitants of Jerusalem, and to all Israel, those that are near and those that are far away, in all the lands to which thou hast driven them, because of the treachery which they have committed against thee. 8 To us,

O Lord, belongs confusion of face, to our kings, to our princes, and to our fathers, because we have sinned against thee. 9 To the Lord our God belong mercy and forgiveness; because we have rebelled against him, 10 and have not obeyed the voice of the LORD our God by following his laws, which he set before us by his servants the prophets. 11 All Israel has transgressed thy law and turned aside, refusing to obey thy voice. And the curse and oath which are written in the law of Moses the servant of God have been poured out upon us, because we have sinned against him. 12 He has confirmed his words, which he spoke against us and against our rulers who ruled us, by bringing upon us a great calamity; for under the whole heaven there has not been done the like of what has been done against Jerusalem. 13 As it is written in the law of Moses, all this calamity has come upon us, yet we have not entreated the favor of the LORD our God, turning from our iniquities and giving heed to thy truth. 14 Therefore the LORD has kept ready the calamity and has brought it upon us; for the LORD our God is righteous in all the works which he has done, and we have not obeyed his voice. 15 And now, O Lord our God, who didst bring thy people out of the land of Egypt with a mighty hand, and hast made thee a name, as at this day, we have sinned, we have done wickedly. 16 O Lord, according to all thy righteous acts, let thy anger and thy wrath turn away from thy city Jerusalem, thy holy hill; because for our sins, and for the iniquities of our fathers, Jerusalem and thy people have become a byword among all who are round about us. 17 Now therefore, O our God, hearken to the prayer of thy servant and to his supplications, and for thy own sake, O Lord,[t] cause thy face to shine upon thy sanctuary, which is desolate. 18 O my God, incline thy ear and hear; open thy eyes and behold our desolations, and the city which is called by thy name; for we do not present our supplications before thee on the ground of our righteousness, but on the ground of thy great mercy. 19 O LORD, hear; O LORD, forgive; O LORD, give heed and act; delay not, for thy own sake, O my God, because thy city and thy people are called by thy name."

20 While I was speaking and praying, confessing my sin and the sin of my people Israel, and presenting my supplication before the LORD my God for the holy hill of my God; 21 while I was speaking in prayer, the man Gabriel, whom I had seen in the vision at the first, came to me in swift flight at the time of the evening sacrifice. 22 He came*u* and he said to me, "O Daniel, I have now come out to give you wisdom and understanding. 23 At the beginning of your supplications a word went forth, and I have come to tell it to you, for you are greatly beloved; therefore consider the word and understand the vision.

24 "Seventy weeks of years are decreed concerning your people and your holy city, to finish the transgression, to put an end to sin, and to atone for iniquity, to bring in everlasting righteousness, to seal both vision and prophet, and to anoint a most holy place.*v* 25 Know therefore and understand that from the going forth of the word to restore and build Jerusalem to the coming of an anointed one, a prince, there shall be seven weeks. Then for sixty-two weeks it shall be built again with squares and moat, but in a troubled time. 26 And after the sixty-two weeks, an anointed one shall be cut off, and shall have nothing; and the people of the prince who is to come shall destroy the city and the sanctuary. Its*w* end shall come with a flood, and to the end there shall be war; desolations are decreed. 27 And he shall make a strong covenant with many for one week; and for half of the week he shall cause sacrifice and offering to cease; and upon the wing of abominations shall come one who makes desolate, until the decreed end is poured out on the desolator."

10 In the third year of Cyrus king of Persia a word was revealed to Daniel, who was named Bel·tĕ·shaz′-zăr. And the word was true, and it was a great conflict. And he understood the word and had understanding of the vision.

2 In those days I, Daniel, was mourning for three weeks. 3 I ate no delicacies, no meat or wine entered my mouth, nor did I anoint myself at all, for the full three weeks. 4 On the twenty-fourth day of the first month, as I was standing on the bank of the great river, that is, the Ti′gris, 5 I

lifted up my eyes and looked, and behold, a man clothed in linen, whose loins were girded with gold of U′phaz. 6 His body was like beryl, his face like the appearance of lightning, his eyes like flaming torches, his arms and legs like the gleam of burnished bronze, and the sound of his words like the noise of a multitude. 7 And I, Daniel, alone saw the vision, for the men who were with me did not see the vision, but a great trembling fell upon them, and they fled to hide themselves. 8 So I was left alone and saw this great vision, and no strength was left in me; my radiant appearance was fearfully changed, and I retained no strength. 9 Then I heard the sound of his words; and when I heard the sound of his words, I fell on my face in a deep sleep with my face to the ground.

10 And behold, a hand touched me and set me trembling on my hands and knees. 11 And he said to me, "O Daniel, man greatly beloved, give heed to the words that I speak to you, and stand upright, for now I have been sent to you." While he was speaking this word to me, I stood up trembling. 12 Then he said to me, "Fear not, Daniel, for from the first day that you set your mind to understand and humbled yourself before your God, your words have been heard, and I have come because of your words. 13 The prince of the kingdom of Persia withstood me twenty-one days; but Michael, one of the chief princes, came to help me, so I left him there with the prince of the kingdom of Persia*x* 14 and came to make you understand what is to befall your people in the latter days. For the vision is for days yet to come."

15 When he had spoken to me according to these words, I turned my face toward the ground and was dumb. 16 And behold, one in the likeness of the sons of men touched my lips; then I opened my mouth and spoke. I said to him who stood before me, "O my lord, by reason of the vision pains have come upon me, and I retain no strength. 17 How can my lord's servant talk with my lord? For now no strength remains in me, and no breath is left in me."

18 Again one having the appearance of a man touched me and strengthened me. 19 And he said, "O man greatly beloved, fear not, peace be with you;

u Gk Syr: Heb *made to understand*   *v* Or *thing* or *one*   *w* Or *his*
x Theodotion Compare Gk: Heb *I was left there with the kings of Persia*
9.27: Dan 11.31; 12.11; Mt 24.15; Mk 13.14.   **10.5-6:** Rev 1.13-14; 2.18.
10.13, 21: Rev 12.7.

be strong and of good courage." And when he spoke to me, I was strengthened and said, "Let my lord speak, for you have strengthened me." 20 Then he said, "Do you know why I have come to you? But now I will return to fight against the prince of Persia; and when I am through with him, lo, the prince of Greece will come. 21 But I will tell you what is inscribed in the book of truth: there is none who contends by my side against these except Michael, your prince.

11 1And as for me, in the first year of Dā·rī'us the Mede, I stood up to confirm and strengthen him.

2 "And now I will show you the truth. Behold, three more kings shall arise in Persia; and a fourth shall be far richer than all of them; and when he has become strong through his riches, he shall stir up all against the kingdom of Greece. 3 Then a mighty king shall arise, who shall rule with great dominion and do according to his will. 4And when he has arisen, his kingdom shall be broken and divided toward the four winds of heaven, but not to his posterity, nor according to the dominion with which he ruled; for his kingdom shall be plucked up and go to others besides these.

5 "Then the king of the south shall be strong, but one of his princes shall be stronger than he and his dominion shall be a great dominion. 6After some years they shall make an alliance, and the daughter of the king of the south shall come to the king of the north to make peace; but she shall not retain the strength of her arm, and he and his offspring shall not endure; but she shall be given up, and her attendants, her child, and he who got possession of*y* her.

7 "In those times a branch*z* from her roots shall arise in his place; he shall come against the army and enter the fortress of the king of the north, and he shall deal with them and shall prevail. 8 He shall also carry off to Egypt their gods with their molten images and with their precious vessels of silver and of gold; and for some years he shall refrain from attacking the king of the north. 9 Then the latter shall come into the realm of the king of the south but shall return into his own land.

10 "His sons shall wage war and assemble a multitude of great forces, which shall come on and overflow and pass through, and again shall carry the war as far as his fortress. 11 Then the king of the south, moved with anger, shall come out and fight with the king of the north; and he shall raise a great multitude, but it shall be given into his hand. 12And when the multitude is taken, his heart shall be exalted, and he shall cast down tens of thousands, but he shall not prevail. 13 For the king of the north shall again raise a multitude, greater than the former; and after some years*a* he shall come on with a great army and abundant supplies.

14 "In those times many shall rise against the king of the south; and the men of violence among your own people shall lift themselves up in order to fulfil the vision; but they shall fail. 15 Then the king of the north shall come and throw up siegeworks, and take a well-fortified city. And the forces of the south shall not stand, or even his picked troops, for there shall be no strength to stand. 16 But he who comes against him shall do according to his own will, and none shall stand before him; and he shall stand in the glorious land, and all of it shall be in his power. 17 He shall set his face to come with the strength of his whole kingdom, and he shall bring terms of peace*b* and perform them. He shall give him the daughter of women to destroy the kingdom;*c* but it shall not stand or be to his advantage. 18Afterward he shall turn his face to the coastlands, and shall take many of them; but a commander shall put an end to his insolence; indeed*d* he shall turn his insolence back upon him. 19 Then he shall turn his face back toward the fortresses of his own land; but he shall stumble and fall, and shall not be found.

20 "Then shall arise in his place one who shall send an exactor of tribute through the glory of the kingdom; but within a few days he shall be broken, neither in anger nor in battle. 21 In his place shall arise a contemptible person to whom royal majesty has not been given; he shall come in without warning and obtain the kingdom by flatteries. 22Armies shall be utterly swept away before him and broken, and the prince of the covenant also. 23And from the time that an alliance is made with him he shall act deceitfully; and he shall become strong with a small people. 24 Without warning he shall come into the richest parts*e* of the province; and he shall do what neither his fathers nor his fathers' fathers have

y Or supported *z* Gk: Heb from a branch *a* Heb at the end of the times years *b* Gk: Heb upright ones *c* Heb her or it *d* Heb obscure *e* Or among the richest men

done, scattering among them plunder, spoil, and goods. He shall devise plans against strongholds, but only for a time. 25And he shall stir up his power and his courage against the king of the south with a great army; and the king of the south shall wage war with an exceedingly great and mighty army; but he shall not stand, for plots shall be devised against him. 26 Even those who eat his rich food shall be his undoing; his army shall be swept away, and many shall fall down slain. 27And as for the two kings, their minds shall be bent on mischief; they shall speak lies at the same table, but to no avail; for the end is yet to be at the time appointed. 28And he shall return to his land with great substance, but his heart shall be set against the holy covenant. And he shall work his will, and return to his own land.

29 "At the time appointed he shall return and come into the south; but it shall not be this time as it was before. 30 For ships of Kit'tim shall come against him, and he shall be afraid and withdraw, and shall turn back and be enraged and take action against the holy covenant. He shall turn back and give heed to those who forsake the holy covenant. 31 Forces from him shall appear and profane the temple and fortress, and shall take away the continual burnt offering. And they shall set up the abomination that makes desolate. 32 He shall seduce with flattery those who violate the covenant; but the people who know their God shall stand firm and take action. 33And those among the people who are wise shall make many understand, though they shall fall by sword and flame, by captivity and plunder, for some days. 34 When they fall, they shall receive a little help. And many shall join themselves to them with flattery; 35 and some of those who are wise shall fall, to refine and to cleanse them*f* and to make them white, until the time of the end, for it is yet for the time appointed.

36 "And the king shall do according to his will; he shall exalt himself and magnify himself above every god, and shall speak astonishing things against the God of gods. He shall prosper till the indignation is accomplished; for what is determined shall be done. 37 He shall give no heed to the gods of his fathers, or to the one beloved by

women; he shall not give heed to any other god, for he shall magnify himself above all. 38 He shall honor the god of fortresses instead of these; a god whom his fathers did not know he shall honor with gold and silver, with precious stones and costly gifts. 39 He shall deal with the strongest fortresses by the help of a foreign god; those who acknowledge him he shall magnify with honor. He shall make them rulers over many and shall divide the land for a price.

40 "At the time of the end the king of the south shall attack*g* him; but the king of the north shall rush upon him like a whirlwind, with chariots and horsemen, and with many ships; and he shall come into countries and shall overflow and pass through. 41 He shall come into the glorious land. And tens of thousands shall fall, but these shall be delivered out of his hand: E'dom and Mo'ab and the main part of the Am'mo-nites. 42 He shall stretch out his hand against the countries, and the land of Egypt shall not escape. 43 He shall become ruler of the treasures of gold and of silver, and all the precious things of Egypt; and the Libyans and the Ethiopians shall follow in his train. 44 But tidings from the east and the north shall alarm him, and he shall go forth with great fury to exterminate and utterly destroy many. 45And he shall pitch his palatial tents between the sea and the glorious holy mountain; yet he shall come to his end, with none to help him.

12 "At that time shall arise Michael, the great prince who has charge of your people. And there shall be a time of trouble, such as never has been since there was a nation till that time; but at that time your people shall be delivered, every one whose name shall be found written in the book. 2And many of those who sleep in the dust of the earth shall awake, some to everlasting life, and some to shame and everlasting contempt. 3And those who are wise shall shine like the brightness of the firmament; and those who turn many to righteousness, like the stars for ever and ever. 4 But you, Daniel, shut up the words, and seal the book, until the time of the end. Many shall run to and fro, and knowledge shall increase."

5 Then I Daniel looked, and behold, two others stood, one on this

f Gk: Heb *among them*   *g* Heb *thrust at*

11.31: Dan 9.27; 12.11; Mt 24.15; Mk 13.14.
11.36: Ezek 28.2; 2 Thess 2.4; Rev 13.5.   12.1: Mt 24.21; Mk 13.19; Rev 12.7; 16.18.
12.2: Mt 25.46.   12.3: Mt 13.43.   12.4: Rev 22.10.

bank of the stream and one on that bank of the stream. [6]And I[h] said to the man clothed in linen, who was above the waters of the stream, "How long shall it be till the end of these wonders?" [7] The man clothed in linen, who was above the waters of the stream, raised his right hand and his left hand toward heaven; and I heard him swear by him who lives for ever that it would be for a time, two times, and half a time; and that when the shattering of the power of the holy people comes to an end all these things would be accomplished. [8] I heard, but I did not understand. Then I said, "O my lord, what shall be the issue of these things?" [9] He said, "Go your way, Daniel, for the words are shut up and sealed until the time of the end. [10] Many shall purify themselves, and make themselves white, and be refined; but the wicked shall do wickedly; and none of the wicked shall understand; but those who are wise shall understand. [11]And from the time that the continual burnt offering is taken away, and the abomination that makes desolate is set up, there shall be a thousand two hundred and ninety days. [12] Blessed is he who waits and comes to the thousand three hundred and thirty-five days. [13] But go your way till the end; and you shall rest, and shall stand in your allotted place at the end of the days."

THE BOOK OF

HOSEA

1 The word of the LORD that came to Hō·sē′á the son of Be·ē′rī, in the days of Uz·zī′ah, Jō′tham, Ā′haz, and Hez·e·kī′ah, kings of Judah, and in the days of Jer·o·bō′am the son of Jō′ash, king of Israel.

2 When the LORD first spoke through Hō·sē′á, the LORD said to Hosea, "Go, take to yourself a wife of harlotry and have children of harlotry, for the land commits great harlotry by forsaking the LORD." [3] So he went and took Gō′mer the daughter of Dib·lā′im, and she conceived and bore him a son.

4 And the LORD said to him, "Call his name Jez′re·el; for yet a little while, and I will punish the house of Jē′hū for the blood of Jezreel, and I will put an end to the kingdom of the house of Israel. [5]And on that day, I will break the bow of Israel in the valley of Jez′re·el."

6 She conceived again and bore a daughter. And the LORD said to him, "Call her name Not pitied, for I will no more have pity on the house of Israel, to forgive them at all. [7] But I will have pity on the house of Judah, and I will deliver them by the LORD their God; I will not deliver them by bow, nor by sword, nor by war, nor by horses, nor by horsemen."

8 When she had weaned Not pitied, she conceived and bore a son. [9]And the LORD said, "Call his name Not my people, for you are not my people and I am not your God."[a]

10[b] Yet the number of the people of Israel shall be like the sand of the sea, which can be neither measured nor numbered; and in the place where it was said to them, "You are not my people," it shall be said to them, "Sons of the living God." [11]And the people of Judah and the people of Israel shall be gathered together, and they shall appoint for themselves one head; and they shall go up from the land, for great shall be the day of Jez′re·el.

2[c] Say to your brother,[d] "My people," and to your sister,[e] "She has obtained pity."

2 "Plead with your mother, plead—
     for she is not my wife,
     and I am not her husband—
that she put away her harlotry from
     her face,
     and her adultery from between
     her breasts;
3 lest I strip her naked

---

h Gk Vg: Heb *he*   *a* Heb *I am not yours*   *b* Ch 2.1 in Heb   *c* Ch 2.3 in Heb
d Gk: Heb *brothers*   *e* Gk Vg: Heb *sisters*

12.7: Rev 4.9; 10.5; 12.14.   **12.11:** Dan 9.27; 11.31; Mt 24.15; Mk 13.14.
1.6, 9: Hos 2.23; 1 Pet 2.10.   **1.10:** Rom 9.26.   **2.1, 23:** Rom 9.25; 1 Pet 2.10.

and make her as in the day she
    was born,
and make her like a wilderness,
  and set her like a parched land,
  and slay her with thirst.
4 Upon her children also I will have
    no pity,
  because they are children of
    harlotry.
5 For their mother has played the
    harlot;
  she that conceived them has acted
    shamefully.
For she said, 'I will go after my
    lovers,
  who give me my bread and my
    water,
  my wool and my flax, my oil and
    my drink.'
6 Therefore I will hedge up her^f way
    with thorns;
  and I will build a wall against her,
  so that she cannot find her paths.
7 She shall pursue her lovers,
  but not overtake them;
  and she shall seek them,
  but shall not find them.
Then she shall say, 'I will go
  and return to my first husband,
  for it was better with me then
    than now.'
8 And she did not know
  that it was I who gave her
  the grain, the wine, and the oil,
  and who lavished upon her silver
    and gold which they used for
    Ba'al.
Therefore I will take back
  my grain in its time,
  and my wine in its season;
  and I will take away my wool and
    my flax,
  which were to cover her naked-
    ness.
10 Now I will uncover her lewdness
  in the sight of her lovers,
  and no one shall rescue her out of
    my hand.
11 And I will put an end to all her
    mirth,
  her feasts, her new moons, her
    sabbaths,
  and all her appointed feasts.
12 And I will lay waste her vines and
    her fig trees,
  of which she said,
'These are my hire,
  which my lovers have given me.'
I will make them a forest,
  and the beasts of the field shall
    devour them.
13 And I will punish her for the feast
    days of the Ba'als
  when she burned incense to them

and decked herself with her ring and
    jewelry,
  and went after her lovers,
  and forgot me, says the LORD.
14 "Therefore, behold, I will allure
    her,
  and bring her into the wilderness,
  and speak tenderly to her.
15 And there I will give her her vine-
    yards,
  and make the Valley of A'chor a
    door of hope.
And there she shall answer as in the
    days of her youth,
  as at the time when she came out
    of the land of Egypt.
16 "And in that day, says the LORD,
you will call me, 'My husband,' and no
longer will you call me, 'My Ba'al.'
17 For I will remove the names of the
Ba'als from her mouth, and they shall
be mentioned by name no more. 18And
I will make for you^g a covenant on that
day with the beasts of the field, the
birds of the air, and the creeping things
of the ground; and I will abolish^h the
bow, the sword, and war from the
land; and I will make you lie down in
safety. 19And I will betroth you to me
for ever; I will betroth you to me in
righteousness and in justice, in steadfast love, and in mercy. 20 I will betroth you to me in faithfulness; and
you shall know the LORD.
21 "And in that day, says the LORD,
  I will answer the heavens
  and they shall answer the earth;
22 and the earth shall answer the grain,
    the wine, and the oil,
  and they shall answer Jez're-el;^{i}
23   and I will sow him^j for myself in
    the land.
And I will have pity on Not pitied,
  and I will say to Not my people,
    'You are my people';
  and he shall say, 'Thou art my
    God.'"

3 And the LORD said to me, "Go
again, love a woman who is beloved of a paramour and is an adulteress; even as the LORD loves the people of Israel, though they turn to other
gods and love cakes of raisins." 2 So I
bought her for fifteen shekels of silver
and a homer and a lethech of barley.
3And I said to her, "You must dwell
as mine for many days; you shall not
play the harlot, or belong to another
man; so will I also be to you." 4 For
the children of Israel shall dwell many
days without king or prince, without
sacrifice or pillar, without ephod or
teraphim. 5Afterward the children of

^{f} Gk Syr: Heb *your* ^{g} Heb *them* ^{h} Heb *break* ^{i} That is *God sows* ^{j} Cn: Heb *her*

Israel shall return and seek the LORD their God, and David their king; and they shall come in fear to the LORD and to his goodness in the latter days.

4 Hear the word of the LORD, O people of Israel;
  for the LORD has a controversy with the inhabitants of the land.
There is no faithfulness or kindness, and no knowledge of God in the land;
2 there is swearing, lying, killing, stealing, and committing adultery;
  they break all bounds and murder follows murder.
3 Therefore the land mourns,
  and all who dwell in it languish,
and also the beasts of the field,
  and the birds of the air;
  and even the fish of the sea are taken away.

4 Yet let no one contend,
  and let none accuse,
  for with you is my contention, O priest.[k]
5 You shall stumble by day,
  the prophet also shall stumble with you by night;
  and I will destroy your mother.
6 My people are destroyed for lack of knowledge;
  because you have rejected knowledge,
  I reject you from being a priest to me.
And since you have forgotten the law of your God,
  I also will forget your children.

7 The more they increased,
  the more they sinned against me;
  I will change their glory into shame.
8 They feed on the sin of my people;
  they are greedy for their iniquity.
9 And it shall be like people, like priest;
  I will punish them for their ways,
  and requite them for their deeds.
10 They shall eat, but not be satisfied;
  they shall play the harlot, but not multiply;
because they have forsaken the LORD to cherish harlotry.

11 Wine and new wine
  take away the understanding.
12 My people inquire of a thing of wood,
  and their staff gives them oracles.

For a spirit of harlotry has led them astray,
  and they have left their God to play the harlot.
13 They sacrifice on the tops of the mountains,
  and make offerings upon the hills,
under oak, poplar, and terebinth,
  because their shade is good.

Therefore your daughters play the harlot,
  and your brides commit adultery.
14 I will not punish your daughters when they play the harlot,
  nor your brides when they commit adultery;
for the men themselves go aside with harlots,
  and sacrifice with cult prostitutes,
and a people without understanding shall come to ruin.

15 Though you play the harlot, O Israel,
  let not Judah become guilty.
Enter not into Gil′gàl,
  nor go up to Beth-a′ven,
  and swear not, "As the LORD lives."
16 Like a stubborn heifer,
  Israel is stubborn;
can the LORD now feed them
  like a lamb in a broad pasture?

17 E′phra·im is joined to idols,
  let him alone.
18 A band[l] of drunkards, they give themselves to harlotry;
  they love shame more than their glory.[m]
19 A wind has wrapped them[n] in its wings,
  and they shall be ashamed because of their altars.[o]

5 Hear this, O priests!
  Give heed, O house of Israel!
Hearken, O house of the king!
  For the judgment pertains to you;
for you have been a snare at Miz′pàh,
  and a net spread upon Tā′bôr.
2 And they have made deep the pit of Shit′tim[p];
  but I will chastise all of them.

3 I know E′phra·im,
  and Israel is not hid from me;
for now, O Ephraim, you have played the harlot,
  Israel is defiled.
4 Their deeds do not permit them to return to their God.

k Cn: Heb uncertain   l Cn: Heb uncertain
m Cn Compare Gk: Heb of this line uncertain   n Heb *her*   o Gk Syr: Heb *sacrifices*
p Cn: Heb uncertain

For the spirit of harlotry is within
    them,
   and they know not the LORD.

5 The pride of Israel testifies to his
    face;
  E′phrà·im*a* shall stumble in his
    guilt;
  Judah also shall stumble with
    them.
6 With their flocks and herds they
    shall go
  to seek the LORD,
but they will not find him;
  he has withdrawn from them.
7 They have dealt faithlessly with the
    LORD;
  for they have borne alien children.
  Now the new moon shall devour
    them with their fields.

8 Blow the horn in Gib′ē·àh,
  the trumpet in Rā′màh.
  Sound the alarm at Beth-ā′vèn;
    tremble,*r* O Benjamin!
9 E′phrà·im shall become a desolation
  in the day of punishment;
  among the tribes of Israel
  I declare what is sure.
10 The princes of Judah have become
  like those who remove the land-
    mark;
  upon them I will pour out
    my wrath like water.
11 E′phrà·im is oppressed, crushed in
    judgment,
  because he was determined to go
    after vanity.*s*
12 Therefore I am like a moth to
    E′phrà·im,
  and like dry rot to the house of
    Judah.

13 When E′phrà·im saw his sickness,
  and Judah his wound,
  then Ephraim went to Assyria,
  and sent to the great king.*t*
  But he is not able to cure you
    or heal your wound.
14 For I will be like a lion to E′phrà·im,
  and like a young lion to the house
    of Judah.
  I, even I, will rend and go away,
    I will carry off, and none shall
    rescue.

15 I will return again to my place,
  until they acknowledge their guilt
    and seek my face,
  and in their distress they seek me,
    saying,

6 "Come, let us return to the LORD;
  for he has torn, that he may heal us;
  he has stricken, and he will bind
    us up.
2 After two days he will revive us;
  on the third day he will raise us
    up,
  that we may live before him.
3 Let us know, let us press on to know
    the LORD;
  his going forth is sure as the dawn;
  he will come to us as the showers,
  as the spring rains that water the
    earth.''

4 What shall I do with you, O
    E′phrà·im?
  What shall I do with you, O
    Judah?
  Your love is like a morning cloud,
    like the dew that goes early away.
5 Therefore I have hewn them by the
    prophets,
  I have slain them by the words
    of my mouth,
  and my judgment goes forth as
    the light.*u*
6 For I desire steadfast love and not
    sacrifice,
  the knowledge of God, rather than
    burnt offerings.

7 But at*v* Adam they transgressed the
    covenant;
  there they dealt faithlessly with
    me.
8 Gilead is a city of evildoers,
  tracked with blood.
9 As robbers lie in wait*w* for a man,
  so the priests are banded to-
    gether;*x*
  they murder on the way to Shē′chem,
  yea, they commit villainy.
10 In the house of Israel I have seen a
    horrible thing;
  E′phrà·im′s harlotry is there, Is-
    rael is defiled.

11 For you also, O Judah, a harvest is
    appointed.

When I would restore the fortunes
    of my people,
7 1 when I would heal Israel,
  the corruption of E′phrà·im is re-
    vealed,
  and the wicked deeds of Sà-
    mâr′i·à;
  for they deal falsely,
  the thief breaks in,
  and the bandits raid without.

a Heb *Israel and Ephraim*   *r* Cn Compare Gk: Heb *after you*   *s* Gk: Heb *a command*
t Cn: Heb *a king that will contend*   *u* Gk Syr: Heb *thy judgment goes forth*
v Cn: Heb *like*   *w* Cn: Heb uncertain   *x* Syr: Heb *a company*
6.6: Mt 9.13; 12.7.

2 But they do not consider
     that I remember all their evil
        works.
   Now their deeds encompass them,
     they are before my face.
3 By their wickedness they make the
        king glad,
     and the princes by their treachery.
4 They are all adulterers;
     they are like a heated oven,
   whose baker ceases to stir the fire,
     from the kneading of the dough
        until it is leavened.
5 On the day of our king the princes
        became sick with the heat of wine;
   he stretched out his hand with
        mockers.
6 For like an oven their hearts
        burn[y] with intrigue;
     all night their anger smolders;
     in the morning it blazes like a
        flaming fire.
7 All of them are hot as an oven,
     and they devour their rulers.
   All their kings have fallen;
     and none of them calls upon me.

8 E'phra·im mixes himself with the
        peoples;
     Ephraim is a cake not turned.
9 Aliens devour his strength,
     and he knows it not;
   gray hairs are sprinkled upon him,
     and he knows it not.
10 The pride of Israel witnesses against
        him;
     yet they do not return to the LORD
        their God,
     nor seek him, for all this.

11 E'phra·im is like a dove,
     silly and without sense,
     calling to Egypt, going to Assyria.
12 As they go, I will spread over them
        my net;
   I will bring them down like birds
        of the air;
   I will chastise them for their
        wicked deeds.[z]
13 Woe to them, for they have strayed
        from me!
   Destruction to them, for they
        have rebelled against me!
   I would redeem them,
     but they speak lies against me.

14 They do not cry to me from the
        heart,
     but they wail upon their beds;
   for grain and wine they gash them-
        selves,
     they rebel against me.

15 Although I trained and strengthened
        their arms,
     yet they devise evil against me.
16 They turn to Bā'ȧl;[a]
     they are like a treacherous bow,
   their princes shall fall by the sword
     because of the insolence of their
        tongue.
   This shall be their derision in the
     land of Egypt.

8   Set the trumpet to your lips,
        for[b] a vulture is over the house
        of the LORD,
   because they have broken my cove-
        nant,
     and transgressed my law.
2 To me they cry,
     My God, we Israel know thee.
3 Israel has spurned the good;
     the enemy shall pursue him.

4 They made kings, but not through
        me.
   They set up princes, but without
        my knowledge.
   With their silver and gold they made
        idols
     for their own destruction.
5 I have[c] spurned your calf, O Sȧ-
        mâr'i·à.
   My anger burns against them.
   How long will it be
     till they are pure 6 in Israel?[d]

   A workman made it;
     it is not God.
   The calf of Sȧ·mâr'i·à
     shall be broken to pieces.[e]

7 For they sow the wind,
     and they shall reap the whirl-
        wind.
   The standing grain has no heads,
     it shall yield no meal;
   if it were to yield,
     aliens would devour it.
8 Israel is swallowed up;
     already they are among the nations
        as a useless vessel.
9 For they have gone up to Assyria,
     a wild ass wandering alone;
   E'phra·im has hired lovers.
10 Though they hire allies among the
        nations,
   I will soon gather them up.
   And they shall cease[f] for a little
        while
     from anointing[g] king and princes.

11 Because E'phra·im has multiplied
        altars for sinning,

[y] Gk Syr: Heb *brought near*   [z] Cn: Heb *according to the report to their congregation*
[a] Cn: Heb *uncertain*   [b] Cn: Heb *as*   [c] Heb *He has*   [d] Gk: Heb *for from Israel*
[e] Or *shall go up in flames*   [f] Gk: Heb *begin*   [g] Gk: Heb *burden*

they have become to him altars
for sinning.

12 Were I to write for him my laws by
ten thousands,
they would be regarded as a
strange thing.

13 They love sacrifice;[h]
they sacrifice flesh and eat it;
but the LORD has no delight in
them.
Now he will remember their iniquity,
and punish their sins;
they shall return to Egypt.

14 For Israel has forgotten his Maker,
and built palaces;
and Judah has multiplied fortified
cities;
but I will send a fire upon his
cities,
and it shall devour his strongholds.

9 Rejoice not, O Israel!
Exult not[i] like the peoples;
for you have played the harlot, forsaking your God.
You have loved a harlot's hire
upon all threshing floors.

2 Threshing floor and winevat shall
not feed them,
and the new wine shall fail
them.

3 They shall not remain in the land of
the LORD;
but E'phra·im shall return to
Egypt,
and they shall eat unclean food in
Assyria.

4 They shall not pour libations of
wine to the LORD;
and they shall not please him with
their sacrifices.
Their bread[j] shall be like mourners'
bread;
all who eat of it shall be defiled;
for their bread shall be for their
hunger only;
it shall not come to the house of the
LORD.

5 What will you do on the day of
appointed festival,
and on the day of the feast of the
LORD?

6 For behold, they are going to Assyria;[k]
Egypt shall gather them,
Memphis shall bury them.
Nettles shall possess their precious
things of silver;
thorns shall be in their tents.

7 The days of punishment have come,
the days of recompense have come;
Israel shall know it.
The prophet is a fool,
the man of the spirit is mad,
because of your great iniquity
and great hatred.

8 The prophet is the watchman of
E'phra·im,
the people of my God,
yet a fowler's snare is on all his
ways,
and hatred in the house of his
God.

9 They have deeply corrupted themselves
as in the days of Gib'ē·àh:
he will remember their iniquity,
he will punish their sins.

10 Like grapes in the wilderness,
I found Israel.
Like the first fruit on the fig tree,
in its first season,
I saw your fathers.
But they came to Bā'al-pē'ôr,
and consecrated themselves to
Bā'al[l],
and became detestable like the
thing they loved.

11 E'phra·im's glory shall fly away like
a bird—
no birth, no pregnancy, no conception!

12 Even if they bring up children,
I will bereave them till none is
left.
Woe to them
when I depart from them!

13 E'phra·im's sons, as I have seen, are
destined for a prey;[m]
Ephraim must lead forth his sons
to slaughter.

14 Give them, O LORD—
what wilt thou give?
Give them a miscarrying womb
and dry breasts.

15 Every evil of theirs is in Gil'gàl;
there I began to hate them.
Because of the wickedness of their
deeds
I will drive them out of my house.
I will love them no more;
all their princes are rebels.

16 E'phra·im is stricken,
their root is dried up,
they shall bear no fruit.
Even though they bring forth,
I will slay their beloved children.

17 My God will cast them off,

h Cn: Heb uncertain   *i* Gk: Heb *to exultation*   *j* Cn: Heb *to them*
k Cn: Heb *from destruction*   *l* Heb *shame*   *m* Cn Compare Gk: Heb uncertain
8.14: Amos 1.4, 7, 10, 12, 14; 2.2, 5.   **9.7:** Lk 21.22.

because they have not hearkened
to him;
they shall be wanderers among
the nations.

10

Israel is a luxuriant vine
that yields its fruit.
The more his fruit increased
the more altars he built;
as his country improved
he improved his pillars.
2 Their heart is false;
now they must bear their guilt.
The Lord[n] will break down their
altars,
and destroy their pillars.

3 For now they will say:
"We have no king,
for we fear not the Lord,
and a king, what could he do for
us?"
4 They utter mere words;
with empty oaths they make
covenants;
so judgment springs up like poisonous weeds
in the furrows of the field.
5 The inhabitants of Sà·mâr′i·à tremble
for the calf[o] of Beth-ā′ven.
Its people shall mourn for it,
and its idolatrous priests shall
wail[p] over it,
over its glory which has departed
from it.
6 Yea, the thing itself shall be carried
to Assyria,
as tribute to the great king.[q]
Ē′phrà·im shall be put to shame,
and Israel shall be ashamed of his
idol.[r]

7 Sà·mâr′i·à′s king shall perish,
like a chip on the face of the
waters.
8 The high places of A′ven, the sin of
Israel,
shall be destroyed.
Thorn and thistle shall grow up
on their altars;
and they shall say to the mountains,
Cover us,
and to the hills, Fall upon us.

9 From the days of Gib′ē·àh, you
have sinned, O Israel;
there they have continued.
Shall not war overtake them in
Gibe-ah?

10 I will come[s] against the wayward
people to chastise them;
and nations shall be gathered
against them
when they are chastised[t] for their
double iniquity.

11 Ē′phrà·im was a trained heifer
that loved to thresh,
and I spared her fair neck;
but I will put Ephraim to the yoke,
Judah must plow,
Jacob must harrow for himself.
12 Sow for yourselves righteousness,
reap the fruit[u] of steadfast love;
break up your fallow ground,
for it is the time to seek the Lord,
that he may come and rain salvation upon you.

13 You have plowed iniquity,
you have reaped injustice,
you have eaten the fruit of lies.
Because you have trusted in your
chariots[v]
and in the multitude of your
warriors,
14 therefore the tumult of war shall
arise among your people,
and all your fortresses shall be
destroyed,
as Shal′man destroyed Beth-är′bel
on the day of battle;
mothers were dashed in pieces
with their children.
15 Thus it shall be done to you, O
house of Israel,[w]
because of your great wickedness.
In the storm[x] the king of Israel
shall be utterly cut off.

11

When Israel was a child, I loved
him,
and out of Egypt I called my son.
2 The more I[y] called them,
the more they went from me;[z]
they kept sacrificing to the Bā′als,
and burning incense to idols.

3 Yet it was I who taught Ē′phrà·im
to walk,
I took them up in my[a] arms;
but they did not know that I
healed them.
4 I led them with cords of compassion,[b]
with the bands of love,
and I became to them as one
who eases the yoke on their jaws,

---

n Heb he o Gk Syr: Heb calves p Cn: Heb exult q Cn: Heb a king that will contend
r Cn: Heb counsel s Cn Compare Gk: Heb in my desire t Gk: Heb bound
u Gk: Heb according to v Gk: Heb way w Gk: Heb O Bethel x Cn: Heb dawn
y Gk: Heb they z Gk: Heb them a Gk Syr Vg: Heb his
b Heb man
10.8: Lk 23.30; Rev 6.16. **10.12:** 2 Cor 9.10. **11.1:** Mt 2.15.

and I bent down to them and fed
them.

5 They shall return to the land of
Egypt,
and Assyria shall be their king,
because they have refused to
return to me.
6 The sword shall rage against their
cities,
consume the bars of their gates,
and devour them in their fortresses.[c]
7 My people are bent on turning away
from me;[d]
so they are appointed to the
yoke,
and none shall remove it.

8 How can I give you up, O Ē′phrā·im!
How can I hand you over, O
Israel!
How can I make you like Ad′mah!
How can I treat you like Ze·boi′im!
My heart recoils within me,
my compassion grows warm and
tender.
9 I will not execute my fierce anger,
I will not again destroy Ē′phrā·im;
for I am God and not man,
the Holy One in your midst,
and I will not come to destroy.[e]

10 They shall go after the LORD,
he will roar like a lion;
yea, he will roar,
and his sons shall come trembling
from the west;
11 they shall come trembling like birds
from Egypt,
and like doves from the land of
Assyria;
and I will return them to their
homes, says the LORD.
12[f] Ē′phrā·im has encompassed me
with lies,
and the house of Israel with deceit;
but Judah is still known by[g] God,
and is faithful to the Holy One.

12 Ē′phrā·im herds the wind,
and pursues the east wind all day
long;
they multiply falsehood and violence;
they make a bargain with Assyria,
and oil is carried to Egypt.

2 The LORD has an indictment against
Judah,

and will punish Jacob according
to his ways,
and requite him according to his
deeds.
3 In the womb he took his brother by
the heel,
and in his manhood he strove
with God.
4 He strove with the angel and prevailed,
he wept and sought his favor.
He met God at Beth′el,
and there God spoke with him[h]—
5 the LORD the God of hosts,
the LORD is his name:
6 "So you, by the help of your God,
return,
hold fast to love and justice,
and wait continually for your
God."

7 A trader, in whose hands are false
balances,
he loves to oppress.
8 Ē′phrā·im has said, "Ah, but I am
rich,
I have gained wealth for myself";
but all his riches can never offset[i]
the guilt he has incurred.
9 I am the LORD your God
from the land of Egypt;
I will again make you dwell in tents,
as in the days of the appointed
feast.

10 I spoke to the prophets;
it was I who multiplied visions,
and through the prophets gave
parables.
11 If there is iniquity in Gilead
they shall surely come to nought;
if in Gil′gal they sacrifice bulls,
their altars also shall be like stone
heaps
on the furrows of the field.
12 (Jacob fled to the land of Ar′am,
there Israel did service for a wife,
and for a wife he herded sheep.)
13 By a prophet the LORD brought
Israel up from Egypt,
and by a prophet he was preserved.
14 Ē′phrā·im has given bitter provocation;
so his LORD will leave his bloodguilt upon him,
and will turn back upon him his
reproaches.

13 When Ē′phrā·im spoke, men
trembled;
he was exalted in Israel;

---

c Cn: Heb *counsels*   *d* The meaning of the Hebrew is uncertain
e Cn: Heb *into the city*   *f* Ch 12.1 in Heb   *g* Cn Compare Gk: Heb *roams with*
h Gk Syr: Heb *us*   *i* Cn Compare Gk: Heb obscure
12.8: Rev 3.17.

but he incurred guilt through
   Bā′al and died.
2 And now they sin more and more,
   and make for themselves molten
    images,
idols skilfully made of their silver,
   all of them the work of craftsmen.
Sacrifice to these, they say.*j*
Men kiss calves!
3 Therefore they shall be like the
   morning mist
   or like the dew that goes early
    away,
like the chaff that swirls from the
   threshing floor
   or like smoke from a window.

4 I am the LORD your God
   from the land of Egypt;
you know no God but me,
   and besides me there is no savior.
5 It was I who knew you in the wilderness,
   in the land of drought;
6 but when they had fed*k* to the full,
   they were filled, and their heart
    was lifted up;
   therefore they forgot me.
7 So I will be to them like a lion,
   like a leopard I will lurk beside
    the way.
8 I will fall upon them like a bear
   robbed of her cubs,
   I will tear open their breast,
and there I will devour them like a
   lion,
   as a wild beast would rend them.

9 I will destroy you, O Israel;
   who*l* can help you?
10 Where*m* now is your king, to save
   you;
   where are all*n* your princes,*o* to
    defend you*p*—
those of whom you said,
   "Give me a king and princes"?
11 I have given you kings in my anger,
   and I have taken them away in
    my wrath.

12 The iniquity of E′phrá·im is bound
   up,
   his sin is kept in store.
13 The pangs of childbirth come for
   him,
   but he is an unwise son;
for now he does not present himself
   at the mouth of the womb.

14 Shall I ransom them from the power
   of Shē′ol?
Shall I redeem them from Death?
O Death, where*q* are your plagues?
O Sheol, where*q* is your de-
   struction?
Compassion is hid from my eyes.

15 Though he may flourish as the reed
   plant,*r*
   the east wind, the wind of the
    LORD, shall come,
   rising from the wilderness;
and his fountain shall dry up,
   his spring shall be parched;
it shall strip his treasury
   of every precious thing.
16*s* Sà·mâr′i·à shall bear her guilt,
   because she has rebelled against
    her God;
they shall fall by the sword,
   their little ones shall be dashed in
    pieces,
   and their pregnant women ripped
    open.

14 Return, O Israel, to the LORD
   your God,
for you have stumbled because of
   your iniquity.
2 Take with you words
   and return to the LORD;
say to him,
   "Take away all iniquity;
accept that which is good
and we will render
   the fruit*t* of our lips.
3 Assyria shall not save us,
   we will not ride upon horses;
and we will say no more, 'Our
   God', to the work of our
    hands.
In thee the orphan finds mercy."

4 I will heal their faithlessness;
   I will love them freely,
   for my anger has turned from
    them.
5 I will be as the dew to Israel;
   he shall blossom as the lily,
   he shall strike root as the poplar;*u*
6 his shoots shall spread out;
   his beauty shall be like the olive,
   and his fragrance like Lebanon.
7 They shall return and dwell beneath
   my*v* shadow,
   they shall flourish as a garden;*w*
   they shall blossom as the vine,

---

j Gk: Heb *to these they say sacrifices of*   *k* Heb *according to their pasture*
l Gk Syr: Heb *for in me*   *m* Gk Syr Vg: Heb *I will be*   *n* Cn: Heb *in all*
o Cn: Heb *cities*   *p* Cn Compare Gk: Heb *and your judges*
q Gk Syr: Heb *I will be*
r Cn: Heb *among brothers*   *s* Ch 14.1 in Heb   *t* Gk Syr: Heb *bulls*
u Cn: Heb *Lebanon*   *v* Heb *his*   *w* Cn: Heb *they shall grow grain*
13.14: 1 Cor 15.55.   **14.2:** Heb 13.15.

their fragrance shall be like the
wine of Lebanon.

8 O E´phrà·im, what have I to do with
    idols?
It is I who answer and look after
    you.[x]
I am like an evergreen cypress,
from me comes your fruit.

9 Whoever is wise, let him under-
    stand these things;
    whoever is discerning, let him
    know them;
for the ways of the LORD are right,
    and the upright walk in them,
    but transgressors stumble in them.

THE BOOK OF

JOEL

1 The word of the LORD that came
to Jō´el, the son of Pe·thū´el:

2 Hear this, you aged men,
    give ear, all inhabitants of the land!
Has such a thing happened in your
    days,
    or in the days of your fathers?
3 Tell your children of it,
    and let your children tell their
    children,
    and their children another gen-
    eration.

4 What the cutting locust left,
    the swarming locust has eaten.
What the swarming locust left,
    the hopping locust has eaten,
and what the hopping locust left,
    the destroying locust has eaten.

5 Awake, you drunkards, and weep;
    and wail, all you drinkers of wine,
because of the sweet wine,
    for it is cut off from your mouth.

6 For a nation has come up against my
    land,
    powerful and without number;
its teeth are lions' teeth,
    and it has the fangs of a lioness.
7 It has laid waste my vines,
    and splintered my fig trees;
it has stripped off their bark and
    thrown it down;
    their branches are made white.

8 Lament like a virgin girded with
    sackcloth
    for the bridegroom of her youth.
9 The cereal offering and the drink
    offering are cut off
    from the house of the LORD.
The priests mourn,
the ministers of the LORD.
10 The fields are laid waste,
    the ground mourns;
because the grain is destroyed,
    the wine fails,
    the oil languishes.

11 Be confounded, O tillers of the soil,
    wail, O vinedressers,
for the wheat and the barley;
    because the harvest of the field
    has perished.
12 The vine withers,
    the fig tree languishes.
Pomegranate, palm, and apple,
    all the trees of the field are
    withered;
and gladness fails
    from the sons of men.

13 Gird on sackcloth and lament, O
    priests,
    wail, O ministers of the altar.
Go in, pass the night in sackcloth,
    O ministers of my God!
Because cereal offering and drink
    offering
    are withheld from the house of
    your God.

14 Sanctify a fast,
    call a solemn assembly.
Gather the elders
    and all the inhabitants of the land
to the house of the LORD your God;
    and cry to the LORD.

15 Alas for the day!
For the day of the LORD is near,
    and as destruction from the Al-
    mighty it comes.
16 Is not the food cut off
    before our eyes,
    joy and gladness

[x] Heb *him*
14.9: Acts 13.10.   **1.6:** Rev 9.8.

from the house of our God?

17 The seed shrivels under the clods,[a]
   the storehouses are desolate;
the granaries are ruined
   because the grain has failed.
18 How the beasts groan!
   The herds of cattle are perplexed
because there is no pasture for them;
   even the flocks of sheep are dismayed.

19 Unto thee, O LORD, I cry.
   For fire has devoured
   the pastures of the wilderness,
and flame has burned
   all the trees of the field.
20 Even the wild beasts cry to thee
because the water brooks are dried up,
and fire has devoured
   the pastures of the wilderness.

2 Blow the trumpet in Zion;
   sound the alarm on my holy mountain!
Let all the inhabitants of the land tremble,
   for the day of the LORD is coming,
   it is near,
2 a day of darkness and gloom,
   a day of clouds and thick darkness!
Like blackness there is spread upon the mountains
   a great and powerful people;
their like has never been from of old,
   nor will be again after them
through the years of all generations.

3 Fire devours before them,
   and behind them a flame burns.
The land is like the garden of Eden before them,
   but after them a desolate wilderness,
and nothing escapes them.

4 Their appearance is like the appearance of horses,
   and like war horses they run.
5 As with the rumbling of chariots,
   they leap on the tops of the mountains,
like the crackling of a flame of fire
   devouring the stubble,
like a powerful army
   drawn up for battle.

6 Before them peoples are in anguish,
   all faces grow pale.
7 Like warriors they charge,
   like soldiers they scale the wall.

They march each on his way,
   they do not swerve[b] from their paths.
8 They do not jostle one another,
   each marches in his path;
they burst through the weapons
   and are not halted.
9 They leap upon the city,
   they run upon the walls;
they climb up into the houses,
   they enter through the windows
   like a thief.

10 The earth quakes before them,
   the heavens tremble.
The sun and the moon are darkened,
   and the stars withdraw their shining.
11 The LORD utters his voice
   before his army,
for his host is exceedingly great;
   he that executes his word is powerful.
For the day of the LORD is great and very terrible;
   who can endure it?

12 "Yet even now," says the LORD,
   "return to me with all your heart,
with fasting, with weeping, and with mourning;
13   and rend your hearts and not your garments."
Return to the LORD, your God,
   for he is gracious and merciful,
slow to anger, and abounding in steadfast love,
   and repents of evil.
14 Who knows whether he will not turn and repent,
   and leave a blessing behind him,
a cereal offering and a drink offering
   for the LORD, your God?

15 Blow the trumpet in Zion;
   sanctify a fast;
call a solemn assembly;
16   gather the people.
Sanctify the congregation;
   assemble the elders;
gather the children,
   even nursing infants.
Let the bridegroom leave his room,
   and the bride her chamber.

17 Between the vestibule and the altar
   let the priests, the ministers of the LORD, weep
and say, "Spare thy people, O LORD,
   and make not thy heritage a reproach,
a byword among the nations.

---

a Heb uncertain   *b* Gk Syr Vg: Heb *take a pledge*
2.4–5: Rev 9.7,9.   2.10: Rev 9.2.   2.11: Rev 6.17.

Why should they say among the
peoples,
'Where is their God?' "

18 Then the LORD became jealous for
his land,
and had pity on his people.
19 The LORD answered and said to his
people,
"Behold, I am sending to you
grain, wine, and oil,
and you will be satisfied;
and I will no more make you
a reproach among the nations.

20 "I will remove the northerner far
from you,
and drive him into a parched and
desolate land,
his front into the eastern sea,
and his rear into the western
sea;
the stench and foul smell of him
will rise,
for he has done great things.

21 "Fear not, O land;
be glad and rejoice,
for the LORD has done great
things!
22 Fear not, you beasts of the field,
for the pastures of the wilderness
are green;
the tree bears its fruit,
the fig tree and vine give their full
yield.

23 "Be glad, O sons of Zion,
and rejoice in the LORD, your
God;
for he has given the early rain for
your vindication,
he has poured down for you
abundant rain,
the early and the latter rain, as
before.

24 "The threshing floors shall be full
of grain,
the vats shall overflow with wine
and oil.
25 I will restore to you the years
which the swarming locust has
eaten,
the hopper, the destroyer, and the
cutter,
my great army, which I sent
among you.

26 "You shall eat in plenty and be
satisfied,

and praise the name of the LORD
your God,
who has dealt wondrously with
you.
And my people shall never again be
put to shame.
27 You shall know that I am in the
midst of Israel,
and that I, the LORD, am your
God and there is none else.
And my people shall never again
be put to shame.

28c "And it shall come to pass afterward,
that I will pour out my spirit on
all flesh;
your sons and your daughters shall
prophesy,
your old men shall dream dreams,
and your young men shall see
visions.
29 Even upon the menservants and
maidservants
in those days, I will pour out my
spirit.

30 "And I will give portents in the
heavens and on the earth, blood and
fire and columns of smoke. 31 The sun
shall be turned to darkness, and the
moon to blood, before the great and
terrible day of the LORD comes. 32And
it shall come to pass that all who call
upon the name of the LORD shall be
delivered; for in Mount Zion and in
Jerusalem there shall be those who
escape, as the LORD has said, and
among the survivors shall be those
whom the LORD calls.

3d "For behold, in those days and
at that time, when I restore the
fortunes of Judah and Jerusalem, 2 I
will gather all the nations and bring
them down to the valley of Je·hosh′à-
phat, and I will enter into judgment
with them there, on account of my
people and my heritage Israel, because
they have scattered them among the
nations, and have divided up my land,
3 and have cast lots for my people, and
have given a boy for a harlot, and have
sold a girl for wine, and have drunk it.

4 "What are you to me, O Tȳre and
Si′don, and all the regions of Phi·lis′-
ti·à? Are you paying me back for something? If you are paying me back, I
will requite your deed upon your own
head swiftly and speedily. 5 For you
have taken my silver and my gold, and
have carried my rich treasures into

c Ch 3.1 in Heb　　d Ch 4.1 in Heb
2.28-32: Acts 2.17-21.　2.31: Rev 6.12.　2.32: Rom 10.13.
3.4-8: Is 23; Ezek 26.1-28.19; Amos 1.9-10; Zech 9.3-4; Ezek 28.20-26; Zech 9.2; Is
14.29-31; Jer 47; Ezek 25.15-17; Amos 1.6-8; Zeph 2.4-7; Zech 9.5-7.

your temples.*e* 6 You have sold the people of Judah and Jerusalem to the Greeks, removing them far from their own border. 7 But now I will stir them up from the place to which you have sold them, and I will requite your deed upon your own head. 8 I will sell your sons and your daughters into the hand of the sons of Judah, and they will sell them to the Sǎ·bē′ǎns, to a nation far off; for the LORD has spoken."

9 Proclaim this among the nations:
Prepare war,
   stir up the mighty men.
Let all the men of war draw near,
   let them come up.
10 Beat your plowshares into swords,
   and your pruning hooks into spears;
   let the weak say, "I am a warrior."

11 Hasten and come,
   all you nations round about,
   gather yourselves there.
Bring down thy warriors, O LORD.
12 Let the nations bestir themselves,
   and come up to the valley of Je·hosh′a·phat;
for there I will sit to judge
   all the nations round about.

13 Put in the sickle,
   for the harvest is ripe.
Go in, tread,
   for the wine press is full.
The vats overflow,
   for their wickedness is great.

14 Multitudes, multitudes,
   in the valley of decision!
For the day of the LORD is near
   in the valley of decision.

15 The sun and the moon are darkened,
   and the stars withdraw their shining.

16 And the LORD roars from Zion,
   and utters his voice from Jerusalem,
   and the heavens and the earth shake.
But the LORD is a refuge to his people,
   a stronghold to the people of Israel.

17 "So you shall know that I am the LORD your God,
   who dwell in Zion, my holy mountain.
And Jerusalem shall be holy
   and strangers shall never again pass through it.

18 "And in that day
the mountains shall drip sweet wine,
   and the hills shall flow with milk,
and all the stream beds of Judah
   shall flow with water;
and a fountain shall come forth
   from the house of the LORD
   and water the valley of Shit′tim.

19 "Egypt shall become a desolation
   and Ē′dom a desolate wilderness,
for the violence done to the people of Judah,
   because they have shed innocent blood in their land.
20 But Judah shall be inhabited for ever,
   and Jerusalem to all generations.
21 I will avenge their blood, and I will not clear the guilty,*g*
   for the LORD dwells in Zion."

e Or *palaces*
g Gk Syr: Heb *I will hold innocent their blood which I have not held innocent*
3.10: Is 2.4; Mic 4.3.   **3.13:** Mk 4.29; Rev 14.15, 18-19.   **3.16:** Amos 1.2.
3.18: Ezek 47.1-12; Amos 9.13; Zech 14.8; Rev 22.1.

THE BOOK OF

AMOS

The words of Amos, who was
among the shepherds of Te·kō´à,
which he saw concerning Israel in the
days of Uz·zi´ah king of Judah and in
the days of Jer·o·bō´am the son of
Jō´ash, king of Israel, two years[a] before the earthquake. 2And he said:
"The LORD roars from Zion,
    and utters his voice from Jeru-
        salem;
the pastures of the shepherds mourn,
    and the top of Cär´mĕl withers."

3 Thus says the LORD:
"For three transgressions of Da-
    mascus,
    and for four, I will not revoke the
        punishment;[b]
because they have threshed Gilead
    with threshing sledges of iron.
4 So I will send a fire upon the house
        of Haz´à·el,
    and it shall devour the strongholds
        of Ben-hā´dad.
5 I will break the bar of Damascus,
    and cut off the inhabitants from
        the Valley of A´vĕn,[c]
and him that holds the scepter from
        Beth-ē´dĕn;
    and the people of Syria shall go
        into exile to Kĭr,"
            says the LORD.

6 Thus says the LORD:
"For three transgressions of Gä´zà,
    and for four, I will not revoke the
        punishment;[b]
because they carried into exile a
        whole people
    to deliver them up to É´dòm.
7 So I will send a fire upon the wall of
        Gä´zà,
    and it shall devour her strong-
        holds.
8 I will cut off the inhabitants from
        Ash´dod,
    and him that holds the scepter
        from Ash´kĕ·lon;
I will turn my hand against Ek´ròn,

and the remnant of the Philistines
    shall perish,"
            says the Lord GOD.

9 Thus says the LORD:
"For three transgressions of Tȳre,
    and for four, I will not revoke the
        punishment;[b]
because they delivered up a whole
        people to É´dòm,
    and did not remember the cove-
        nant of brotherhood.
10 So I will send a fire upon the wall
        of Tȳre,
    and it shall devour her strong-
        holds."

11 Thus says the LORD:
"For three transgressions of É´dòm,
    and for four, I will not revoke the
        punishment;[b]
because he pursued his brother with
        the sword,
    and cast off all pity,
and his anger tore perpetually,
    and he kept his wrath[d] for ever.
12 So I will send a fire upon Tē´màn,
    and it shall devour the strong-
        holds of Boz´ràh."

13 Thus says the LORD:
"For three transgressions of the
        Am´mò·nites,
    and for four, I will not revoke the
        punishment;[b]
because they have ripped up women
        with child in Gilead,
    that they might enlarge their
        border.
14 So I will kindle a fire in the wall of
        Rab´bàh,
    and it shall devour her strong-
        holds,
with shouting in the day of battle,
    with a tempest in the day of the
        whirlwind;
15 and their king shall go into exile,
    he and his princes together,"
            says the LORD.

a Or *during two years*   b Heb *cause it to return*   c Or *On*
d Gk Syr Vg: Heb *his wrath kept*
1.2: Joel 3.16.   **1.3-5:** Is 17.1-3; Jer 49.23-27; Zech 9.1.
1.6-8: Is 14.29-31; Jer 47; Ezek 25.15-17; Joel 3.4-8; Zeph 2.4-7; Zech 9.5-7.
1.9-10: Is 23; Ezek 26.1-28.19; Joel 3.4-8; Zech 9.3-4.
1.11-12: Is 34; 63.1-6; Jer 49.7-22; Ezek 25.12-14; 35; Obad; Mal 1.2-5.
1.13-15: Jer 49.1-6; Ezek 21.28-32; 25.1-7; Zeph 2.8-11.

2 Thus says the LORD:
"For three transgressions of Mō′ab,
   and for four, I will not revoke the
     punishment;[e]
because he burned to lime
   the bones of the king of E′dŏm.
2 So I will send a fire upon Mō′ab,
   and it shall devour the strong-
     holds of Ker′i·oth,
and Moab shall die amid uproar,
   amid shouting and the sound of
     the trumpet;
3 I will cut off the ruler from its midst,
   and will slay all its princes with
     him,"

                says the LORD.

4 Thus says the LORD:
"For three transgressions of Judah,
   and for four, I will not revoke the
     punishment;[e]
because they have rejected the law
   of the LORD,
and have not kept his statutes,
but their lies have led them astray,
   after which their fathers walked.
5 So I will send a fire upon Judah,
   and it shall devour the strong-
     holds of Jerusalem."

6 Thus says the LORD:
"For three transgressions of Israel,
   and for four, I will not revoke
     the punishment;[e]
because they sell the righteous for
     silver,
   and the needy for a pair of shoes—
7 they that trample the head of the
   poor into the dust of the earth,
   and turn aside the way of the
     afflicted;
a man and his father go in to the
   same maiden,
so that my holy name is profaned;
8 they lay themselves down beside
   every altar
upon garments taken in pledge;
and in the house of their God they
   drink
the wine of those who have been
   fined.

9 "Yet I destroyed the Am′ŏ·rite before them,
whose height was like the height
   of the cedars,
and who was as strong as the oaks;
I destroyed his fruit above,
   and his roots beneath.
10 Also I brought you up out of the
   land of Egypt,
and led you forty years in the
   wilderness,

to possess the land of the Am′ŏ-
   rite.
11 And I raised up some of your sons
   for prophets,
and some of your young men for
   Naz′i·rites.
Is it not indeed so, O people of
   Israel?"

                says the LORD.

12 "But you made the Naz′i·rites drink
   wine,
and commanded the prophets,
   saying, 'You shall not prophesy.'

13 "Behold, I will press you down in
   your place,
as a cart full of sheaves presses
   down.
14 Flight shall perish from the swift,
   and the strong shall not retain
     his strength,
   nor shall the mighty save his life;
15 he who handles the bow shall not
     stand,
   and he who is swift of foot shall
     not save himself,
   nor shall he who rides the horse
     save his life;
16 and he who is stout of heart among
   the mighty
shall flee away naked in that day,"
                says the LORD.

3 Hear this word that the LORD has
   spoken against you, O people of
Israel, against the whole family which
I brought up out of the land of Egypt:
2 "You only have I known
   of all the families of the earth;
therefore I will punish you
   for all your iniquities.

3 "Do two walk together,
   unless they have made an ap-
     pointment?
4 Does a lion roar in the forest,
   when he has no prey?
Does a young lion cry out from his
   den,
   if he has taken nothing?
5 Does a bird fall in a snare on the
   earth,
   when there is no trap for it?
Does a snare spring up from the
   ground,
   when it has taken nothing?
6 Is a trumpet blown in a city,
   and the people are not afraid?
Does evil befall a city,
   unless the LORD has done it?
7 Surely the Lord GOD does nothing,
   without revealing his secret

e Heb *cause it to return*
2.1-3: Is 15-16; 25.10-12; Jer 48; Ezek 25.8-11; Zeph 2.8-11.   **3.7:** Rev 10.7.

to his servants the prophets.

8 The lion has roared;
  who will not fear?
The Lord God has spoken;
  who can but prophesy?"

9 Proclaim to the strongholds in As-
    syria,*f*
  and to the strongholds in the land
    of Egypt,
and say, "Assemble yourselves upon
  the mountains of Sȧ·mâr′i·ȧ,
and see the great tumults within her,
  and the oppressions in her midst."
10 "They do not know how to do
    right," says the Lord,
  "those who store up violence and
    robbery in their strongholds."
11 Therefore thus says the Lord God:
"An adversary shall surround the
    land,
  and bring down your defenses
    from you,
  and your strongholds shall be
    plundered."

12 Thus says the Lord: "As the
shepherd rescues from the mouth of
the lion two legs, or a piece of an ear,
so shall the people of Israel who dwell
in Sȧ·mâr′i·ȧ be rescued, with the
corner of a couch and part*g* of a bed."

13 "Hear, and testify against the house
    of Jacob,"
  says the Lord God, the God of
    hosts,
14 "that on the day I punish Israel for
    his transgressions,
  I will punish the altars of Beth′él,
and the horns of the altar shall be
    cut off
  and fall to the ground.
15 I will smite the winter house with
    the summer house;
  and the houses of ivory shall
    perish,
and the great houses*h* shall come to
    an end,"
        says the Lord.

4 "Hear this word, you cows of
    Bā′shȧn,
  who are in the mountain of
    Sȧ·mâr′i·ȧ,
who oppress the poor, who crush
    the needy,
who say to their husbands,
  'Bring, that we may drink!'
2 The Lord God has sworn by his
    holiness
  that, behold, the days are coming
    upon you,

when they shall take you away with
    hooks,
  even the last of you with fish-
    hooks.
3 And you shall go out through the
    breaches,
  every one straight before her;
  and you shall be cast forth into
    Här′mòn,"
        says the Lord.

4 "Come to Beth′él, and transgress;
  to Gil′gȧl, and multiply trans-
    gression;
bring your sacrifices every morning,
  your tithes every three days;
5 offer a sacrifice of thanksgiving of
    that which is leavened,
  and proclaim freewill offerings,
    publish them;
for so you love to do, O people of
    Israel!"
        says the Lord God.

6 "I gave you cleanness of teeth in all
    your cities,
  and lack of bread in all your places,
yet you did not return to me,"
        says the Lord.

7 "And I also withheld the rain from
    you
  when there were yet three months
    to the harvest;
I would send rain upon one city,
  and send no rain upon another
    city;
one field would be rained upon,
  and the field on which it did not
    rain withered;
8 so two or three cities wandered to
    one city
  to drink water, and were not
    satisfied;
yet you did not return to me,"
        says the Lord.

9 "I smote you with blight and mil-
    dew;
  I laid waste*i* your gardens and
    your vineyards;
your fig trees and your olive trees
    the locust devoured;
yet you did not return to me,"
        says the Lord.

10 "I sent among you a pestilence after
    the manner of Egypt;
  I slew your young men with the
    sword;
I carried away your horses;*j*
  and I made the stench of your
    camp go up into your nostrils;

f Gk: Heb *Ashdod*   *g* The meaning of the Hebrew word is uncertain
h Or *many houses*   *i* Cn: Heb *the multitude of*   *j* Heb *with the captivity of your horses*

yet you did not return to me,"
     says the LORD.

11 "I overthrew some of you,
   as when God overthrew Sod'óm
     and Gò·môr'ràh,
   and you were as a brand plucked
     out of the burning;
yet you did not return to me,"
     says the LORD.

12 "Therefore thus I will do to you,
     O Israel;
because I will do this to you,
   prepare to meet your God, O
     Israel!"

13 For lo, he who forms the mountains,
     and creates the wind,
   and declares to man what is his
     thought;
who makes the morning darkness,
   and treads on the heights of the
     earth—
the LORD, the God of hosts, is his
     name!

5   Hear this word which I take up
   over you in lamentation, O house
of Israel:
2 "Fallen, no more to rise,
   is the virgin Israel;
forsaken on her land,
   with none to raise her up."

3 For thus says the Lord GOD:
"The city that went forth a thou-
     sand
   shall have a hundred left,
and that which went forth a hundred
   shall have ten left
     to the house of Israel."

4 For thus says the LORD to the house
     of Israel:
"Seek me and live;
5   but do not seek Beth'él,
   and do not enter into Gil'gàl
   or cross over to Beer-sheba;
for Gilgal shall surely go
     into exile;
   and Bethel shall come to nought."

6 Seek the LORD and live,
   lest he break out like fire in the
     house of Joseph,
   and it devour, with none to
     quench it for Beth'él,
7 O you who turn justice to worm-
     wood,
   and cast down righteousness to
     the earth!

8 He who made the Plëi'á·dës and
     Ö·rï'ón,

and turns deep darkness into the
     morning,
   and darkens the day into night,
who calls for the waters
     of the sea,
   and pours them out upon the
     surface of the earth,
the LORD is his name,
9 who makes destruction flash forth
     against the strong,
   so that destruction comes upon
     the fortress.

10 They hate him who reproves in the
     gate,
   and they abhor him who speaks
     the truth.
11 Therefore because you trample
     upon the poor
   and take from him exactions of
     wheat,
you have built houses of hewn stone,
   but you shall not dwell in them;
you have planted pleasant vineyards,
   but you shall not drink their wine.
12 For I know how many are your
     transgressions,
   and how great are your sins—
you who afflict the righteous, who
     take a bribe,
   and turn aside the needy in the gate.
13 Therefore he who is prudent will
     keep silent in such a time;
   for it is an evil time.

14 Seek good, and not evil,
     that you may live;
and so the LORD, the God of hosts,
     will be with you,
     as you have said.
15 Hate evil, and love good,
   and establish justice in the gate;
it may be that the LORD, the God
     of hosts,
   will be gracious to the remnant of
     Joseph.

16 Therefore thus says the LORD, the
     God of hosts, the Lord:
"In all the squares there shall be
     wailing;
   and in all the streets they shall
     say, 'Alas! alas!'
They shall call the farmers to
     mourning
   and to wailing those who are
     skilled in lamentation,
17 and in all vineyards there shall be
     wailing,
   for I will pass through the midst
     of you,"
     says the LORD.

18 Woe to you who desire the day of
     the LORD!

Why would you have the day of
the LORD?
It is darkness, and not light;
19 as if a man fled from a lion,
and a bear met him;
or went into the house and leaned
with his hand against the wall,
and a serpent bit him.
20 Is not the day of the LORD darkness,
and not light,
and gloom with no brightness in
it?

21 "I hate, I despise your feasts,
and I take no delight in your
solemn assemblies.
22 Even though you offer me your
burnt offerings and cereal offerings,
I will not accept them,
and the peace offerings of your
fatted beasts
I will not look upon.
23 Take away from me the noise of
your songs;
to the melody of your harps I will
not listen.
24 But let justice roll down like waters,
and righteousness like an ever-
flowing stream.

25 "Did you bring to me sacrifices
and offerings the forty years in the
wilderness, O house of Israel? 26 You
shall take up Sak'kŭth your king, and
Käi'wän your star-god, your images,[k]
which you made for yourselves;
27 therefore I will take you into exile
beyond Damascus," says the LORD,
whose name is the God of hosts.

6 "Woe to those who are at ease in
Zion,
and to those who feel secure on
the mountain of Să·măr'i·à,
the notable men of the first of the
nations,
to whom the house of Israel come!
2 Pass over to Cal'něh, and see;
and thence go to Hā'math the
great;
then go down to Gath of the
Philistines.
Are they better than these kingdoms?
Or is their territory greater than
your territory,
3 O you who put far away the evil
day,
and bring near the seat of violence?

4 "Woe to those who lie upon beds
of ivory,

and stretch themselves upon their
couches,
and eat lambs from the flock,
and calves from the midst of the
stall;
5 who sing idle songs to the sound of
the harp,
and like David invent for themselves instruments of music;
6 who drink wine in bowls, and anoint
themselves with the finest oils,
but are not grieved over the ruin
of Joseph!
7 Therefore they shall now be the first
of those to go into exile,
and the revelry of those who
stretch themselves shall pass
away."

8 The Lord GOD has sworn by himself
(says the LORD, the God of hosts):
"I abhor the pride of Jacob,
and hate his strongholds;
and I will deliver up the city and
all that is in it."

9 And if ten men remain in one
house, they shall die. 10 And when a
man's kinsman, he who burns him,[l]
shall take him up to bring the bones
out of the house, and shall say to him
who is in the innermost parts of the
house, "Is there still any one with
you?" he shall say, "No"; and he shall
say, "Hush! We must not mention the
name of the LORD."

11 For behold, the LORD commands,
and the great house shall be
smitten into fragments,
and the little house into bits.
12 Do horses run upon rocks?
Does one plow the sea with oxen?
But you have turned justice into
poison
and the fruit of righteousness into
wormwood—
13 you who rejoice in Lō-dē'bär,[n]
who say, "Have we not by our
own strength
taken Kär·nā'im[o] for ourselves?"
14 "For behold, I will raise up against
you a nation,
O house of Israel," says the LORD,
the God of hosts;
"and they shall oppress you from
the entrance of Hā'math
to the brook of the Ar·à·băh."

7 Thus the Lord GOD showed me:
behold, he was forming locusts in

k Heb *your images, your star-god*   l Or *who makes a burning for him*
n Or *a thing of nought*   o Or *horns*
5.25-27: Acts 7.42-43.

the beginning of the shooting up of the
latter growth; and lo, it was the latter
growth after the king's mowings.
2 When they had finished eating the
grass of the land, I said,
"O Lord GOD, forgive, I beseech
thee!
How can Jacob stand?
He is so small!"
3 The LORD repented concerning
this;
"It shall not be," said the LORD.

4 Thus the Lord GOD showed me:
behold, the Lord GOD was calling for
a judgment by fire, and it devoured the
great deep and was eating up the land.
5 Then I said,
"O Lord GOD, cease, I beseech thee!
How can Jacob stand?
He is so small!"
6 The LORD repented concerning this;
"This also shall not be," said the
Lord GOD.

7 He showed me: behold, the Lord
was standing beside a wall built with
a plumb line, with a plumb line in his
hand. 8And the LORD said to me,
"Amos, what do you see?" And I said,
"A plumb line." Then the Lord said,
"Behold, I am setting a plumb line
in the midst of my people Israel;
I will never again pass by them;
9 the high places of Isaac shall be
made desolate,
and the sanctuaries of Israel shall
be laid waste,
and I will rise against the house
of Jer·ŏ·bō'ăm with the sword."

10 Then Am·ȧ·zī'ăh the priest of
Beth'ĕl sent to Jer·ŏ·bō'ăm king of Israel, saying, "Amos has conspired
against you in the midst of the house
of Israel; the land is not able to bear
all his words. 11 For thus Amos has
said,
'Jer·ŏ·bō'ăm shall die by the sword,
and Israel must go into exile
away from his land.'"
12And Am·ȧ·zī'ăh said to Amos, "O
seer, go, flee away to the land of Judah,
and eat bread there, and prophesy there;
13 but never again prophesy at Beth'ĕl,
for it is the king's sanctuary, and it is a
temple of the kingdom."
14 Then Amos answered Am·ȧ-
zī'ăh, "I am no prophet, nor a prophet's son;[p] but I am a herdsman, and a
dresser of sycamore trees, 15 and the
LORD took me from following the
flock, and the LORD said to me, 'Go,
prophesy to my people Israel.'
16 "Now therefore hear the word of
the LORD.
You say, 'Do not prophesy against
Israel,
and do not preach against the
house of Isaac.'
17 Therefore thus says the LORD:
'Your wife shall be a harlot in the
city,
and your sons and your daughters
shall fall by the sword,
and your land shall be parceled
out by line;
you yourself shall die in an unclean
land,
and Israel shall surely go into
exile away from its land.'"

8 Thus the Lord GOD showed me:
behold, a basket of summer fruit.[q]
2And he said, "Amos, what do you
see?" And I said, "A basket of summer
fruit."[q] Then the LORD said to me,
"The end[r] has come upon my people Israel;
I will never again pass by them.
3 The songs of the temple[s] shall become wailings in that day,"
says the Lord GOD;
"the dead bodies shall be many;
in every place they shall be cast
out in silence."[t]

4 Hear this, you who trample upon
the needy,
and bring the poor of the land to
an end,
5 saying, "When will the new moon
be over,
that we may sell grain?
And the sabbath,
that we may offer wheat for sale,
that we may make the ephah small
and the shekel great,
and deal deceitfully with false
balances,
6 that we may buy the poor for silver
and the needy for a pair of sandals,
and sell the refuse of the wheat?"

7 The LORD has sworn by the pride
of Jacob:
"Surely I will never forget any of
their deeds.
8 Shall not the land tremble on this
account,
and every one mourn who dwells
in it,
and all of it rise like the Nile,
and be tossed about and sink
again, like the Nile of Egypt?"

9 "And on that day," says the Lord
GOD,

[p] Or *one of the sons of the prophets* [q] *qayits* [r] *qets* [s] Or *palace* [t] Or *be silent!*

" I will make the sun go down at
  noon,
  and darken the earth in broad
  daylight.
10 I will turn your feasts into mourning,
   and all your songs into lamentation;
  I will bring sackcloth upon all loins,
   and baldness on every head;
  I will make it like the mourning for
   an only son,
   and the end of it like a bitter day.

11 "Behold, the days are coming," says
   the Lord GOD,
   "when I will send a famine on
    the land;
  not a famine of bread, nor a thirst
   for water,
   but of hearing the words of the
    LORD.
12 They shall wander from sea to sea,
   and from north to east;
  they shall run to and fro, to seek the
   word of the LORD,
   but they shall not find it.

13 "In that day the fair virgins and the
   young men
   shall faint for thirst.
14 Those who swear by Ash'i·màh of
   Sà·mâr'i·à,
  and say, 'As thy god lives, O Dan,'
  and, 'As the way of Beer-sheba lives,'
   they shall fall, and never rise
    again."

9 I saw the LORD standing beside[u]
   the altar, and he said:
  "Smite the capitals until the thresholds shake,
   and shatter them on the heads of
    all the people;[v]
  and what are left of them I will slay
   with the sword;
   not one of them shall flee away,
   not one of them shall escape.

2 "Though they dig into Shē'ōl,
   from there shall my hand take
    them;
  though they climb up to heaven,
   from there I will bring them down.
3 Though they hide themselves on the
   top of Cär'mĕl,
   from there I will search out and
    take them;
  and though they hide from my sight
   at the bottom of the sea,
   there I will command the serpent,
   and it shall bite them.

u Or *upon*   v Heb *all of them*
9.11-12: Acts 15.16-17.
9.13: Joel 3.18.

4 And though they go into captivity
   before their enemies,
  there I will command the sword,
   and it shall slay them;
  and I will set my eyes upon them
   for evil and not for good."

5 The Lord, GOD of hosts,
  he who touches the earth and it
   melts,
   and all who dwell in it mourn,
  and all of it rises like the Nile,
   and sinks again, like the Nile of
    Egypt;
6 who builds his upper chambers in
   the heavens,
   and founds his vault upon the
    earth;
  who calls for the waters of the sea,
   and pours them out upon the
    surface of the earth—
  the LORD is his name.

7 "Are you not like the Ethiopians to
   me,
   O people of Israel?" says the
    LORD.
  "Did I not bring up Israel from the
   land of Egypt,
   and the Philistines from Caph'tor
    and the Syrians from Kir?
8 Behold, the eyes of the Lord GOD
   are upon the sinful kingdom,
   and I will destroy it from the
    surface of the ground;
  except that I will not utterly destroy the house of Jacob,"
               says the LORD.
9 "For lo, I will command,
   and shake the house of Israel
    among all the nations
  as one shakes with a sieve,
   but no pebble shall fall upon the
    earth.
10 All the sinners of my people shall
   die by the sword,
  who say, 'Evil shall not overtake
   or meet us.'

11 "In that day I will raise up
   the booth of David that is fallen
  and repair its breaches,
   and raise up its ruins,
   and rebuild it as in the days of old;
12 that they may possess the remnant
   of E'dòm
  and all the nations who are called
   by my name,"
   says the LORD who does this.

13 "Behold, the days are coming," says
   the LORD,

"when the plowman shall overtake the reaper
and the treader of grapes him who
sows the seed;
the mountains shall drip sweet wine,
and all the hills shall flow with it.
14 I will restore the fortunes of my
people Israel,
and they shall rebuild the ruined
cities and inhabit them;

they shall plant vineyards and drink
their wine,
and they shall make gardens and
eat their fruit.
15 I will plant them upon their land,
and they shall never again be
plucked up
out of the land which I have given
them,"
says the LORD your God.

THE BOOK OF

OBADIAH

1 The vision of Ō·ba·dī′ah.

Thus says the Lord GOD concerning
Ē′dom:
We have heard tidings from the
LORD,
and a messenger has been sent
among the nations:
"Rise up! let us rise against her for
battle!"
2 Behold, I will make you small among
the nations,
you shall be utterly despised.
3 The pride of your heart has deceived
you,
you who live in the clefts of the
rock,[a]
whose dwelling is high,
who say in your heart,
"Who will bring me down to the
ground?"
4 Though you soar aloft like the eagle,
though your nest is set among the
stars,
thence I will bring you down,
says the LORD.

5 If thieves came to you,
if plunderers by night—
how you have been destroyed!—
would they not steal only enough
for themselves?
If grape gatherers came to you,
would they not leave gleanings?
6 How Esau has been pillaged,
his treasures sought out!
7 All your allies have deceived you,
they have driven you to the
border;
your confederates have prevailed
against you;

your trusted friends have set a
trap under you—
there is no understanding of it.
8 Will I not on that day, says the
LORD,
destroy the wise men out of
Ē′dom,
and understanding out of Mount
Esau?
9 And your mighty men shall be dismayed, O Tē′man,
so that every man from Mount
Esau will be cut off by slaughter.
10 For the violence done to your
brother Jacob,
shame shall cover you,
and you shall be cut off for ever.
11 On the day that you stood aloof,
on the day that strangers carried
off his wealth,
and foreigners entered his gates
and cast lots for Jerusalem,
you were like one of them.
12 But you should not have gloated
over the day of your brother
in the day of his misfortune;
you should not have rejoiced over
the people of Judah
in the day of their ruin;
you should not have boasted
in the day of distress.
13 You should not have entered the
gate of my people
in the day of his calamity;
you should not have gloated over
his disaster
in the day of his calamity;
you should not have looted his goods
in the day of his calamity.
14 You should not have stood at the
parting of the ways

a Or *Sela*
1-21: Is 34; 63.1-6; Jer 49.7-22; Ezek 25.12-14; 35; Amos 1.11-12; Mal 1.2-5.

to cut off his fugitives;
you should not have delivered up
his survivors
in the day of distress.

15 For the day of the LORD is near
upon all the nations.
As you have done, it shall be done
to you,
your deeds shall return on your
own head.
16 For as you have drunk upon my
holy mountain,
all the nations round about shall
drink;
they shall drink, and stagger,[b]
and shall be as though they had
not been.
17 But in Mount Zion there shall be
those that escape,
and it shall be holy;
and the house of Jacob shall possess
their own possessions.
18 The house of Jacob shall be a fire,
and the house of Joseph a flame,
and the house of Esau stubble;

they shall burn them and consume
them,
and there shall be no survivor to
the house of Esau;
for the LORD has spoken.
19 Those of the Negeb shall possess
Mount Esau,
and those of the She·phē′làh the
land of the Philistines;
they shall possess the land of
E′phrà·im and the land of
Sà·mâr′i·à
and Benjamin shall possess Gilead.
20 The exiles in Hā′làh[c] who are of the
people of Israel
shall possess[d] Phoê·ni′ci·à as far as
Zar′ê·phath;
and the exiles of Jerusalem who are
in Se·phär′ad
shall possess the cities of the
Negeb.
21 Saviors shall go up to Mount Zion
to rule Mount Esau;
and the kingdom shall be the
LORD'S.

THE BOOK OF

JONAH

I Now the word of the LORD came
to Jō′nàh the son of A·mit′tāi, saying, 2 "Arise, go to Nin′ê·vêh, that
great city, and cry against it; for their
wickedness has come up before me."
3 But Jō′nàh rose to flee to Tär′shish
from the presence of the LORD. He
went down to Jop′pà and found a ship
going to Tarshish; so he paid the fare,
and went on board, to go with them
to Tarshish, away from the presence
of the LORD.

4 But the LORD hurled a great wind
upon the sea, and there was a mighty
tempest on the sea, so that the ship
threatened to break up. 5 Then the
mariners were afraid, and each cried
to his god; and they threw the wares
that were in the ship into the sea, to
lighten it for them. But Jō′nàh had
gone down into the inner part of the
ship and had lain down, and was fast
asleep. 6 So the captain came and said
to him, "What do you mean, you
sleeper? Arise, call upon your god!

Perhaps the god will give a thought to
us, that we do not perish."

7 And they said to one another,
"Come, let us cast lots, that we may
know on whose account this evil has
come upon us." So they cast lots, and
the lot fell upon Jō′nàh. 8 Then they
said to him, "Tell us, on whose
account this evil has come upon us?
What is your occupation? And whence
do you come? What is your country?
And of what people are you?" 9 And he
said to them, "I am a Hebrew; and I
fear the LORD, the God of heaven,
who made the sea and the dry land."
10 Then the men were exceedingly
afraid, and said to him, "What is this
that you have done!" For the men
knew that he was fleeing from the
presence of the LORD, because he had
told them.

11 Then they said to him, "What
shall we do to you, that the sea may
quiet down for us?" For the sea grew
more and more tempestuous. 12 He

b Cn: Heb *swallow*   c Cn: Heb *this army*   d Cn: Heb *which* said to them, "Take me up and throw me into the sea; then the sea will quiet down for you; for I know it is because of me that this great tempest has come upon you." 13 Nevertheless the men rowed hard to bring the ship back to land, but they could not, for the sea grew more and more tempestuous against them. 14 Therefore they cried to the LORD, "We beseech thee, O LORD, let us not perish for this man's life, and lay not on us innocent blood; for thou, O LORD, hast done as it pleased thee." 15 So they took up Jō'nàh and threw him into the sea; and the sea ceased from its raging. 16 Then the men feared the LORD exceedingly, and they offered a sacrifice to the LORD and made vows.

17ᵃ And the LORD appointed a great fish to swallow up Jō'nàh; and Jonah was in the belly of the fish three days and three nights.

2 Then Jō'nàh prayed to the LORD his God from the belly of the fish, 2 saying,

"I called to the LORD, out of my distress,
    and he answered me;
out of the belly of Shē'ōl I cried,
    and thou didst hear my voice.
3 For thou didst cast me into the deep,
    into the heart of the seas,
    and the flood was round about me;
all thy waves and thy billows
    passed over me.
4 Then I said, 'I am cast out
    from thy presence;
how shall I again look
    upon thy holy temple?'
5 The waters closed in over me,
    the deep was round about me;
weeds were wrapped about my head
6   at the roots of the mountains.
I went down to the land
    whose bars closed upon me for ever;
yet thou didst bring up my life from
    the Pit,
    O LORD my God.
7 When my soul fainted within me,
    I remembered the LORD;
and my prayer came to thee,
    into thy holy temple.
8 Those who pay regard to vain idols
    forsake their true loyalty.
9 But I with the voice of thanksgiving
    will sacrifice to thee;
what I have vowed I will pay.
Deliverance belongs to the LORD!"
10 And the LORD spoke to the fish, and it vomited out Jō'nàh upon the dry land.

3 Then the word of the LORD came to Jō'nàh the second time, saying, 2 "Arise, go to Nin'ê·vêh, that great city, and proclaim to it the message that I tell you." 3 So Jō'nàh arose and went to Nin'ê·vêh, according to the word of the LORD. Now Nineveh was an exceedingly great city, three days' journey in breadth. 4 Jō'nàh began to go into the city, going a day's journey. And he cried, "Yet forty days, and Nin'ê·vêh shall be overthrown!" 5 And the people of Nin'ê·vêh believed God; they proclaimed a fast, and put on sackcloth, from the greatest of them to the least of them.

6 Then tidings reached the king of Nin'ê·vêh, and he arose from his throne, removed his robe, and covered himself with sackcloth, and sat in ashes. 7 And he made proclamation and published through Nin'ê·vêh, "By the decree of the king and his nobles: Let neither man nor beast, herd nor flock, taste anything; let them not feed, or drink water, 8 but let man and beast be covered with sackcloth, and let them cry mightily to God; yea, let everyone turn from his evil way and from the violence which is in his hands. 9 Who knows, God may yet repent and turn from his fierce anger, so that we perish not?"

10 When God saw what they did, how they turned from their evil way, God repented of the evil which he had said he would do to them; and he did not do it.

4 But it displeased Jō'nàh exceedingly, and he was angry. 2 And he prayed to the LORD and said, "I pray thee, LORD, is not this what I said when I was yet in my country? That is why I made haste to flee to Tär'-shish; for I knew that thou art a gracious God and merciful, slow to anger, and abounding in steadfast love, and repentest of evil. 3 Therefore now, O LORD, take my life from me, I beseech thee, for it is better for me to die than to live." 4 And the LORD said, "Do you do well to be angry?" 5 Then Jō'nàh went out of the city and sat to the east of the city, and made a booth for himself there. He sat under it in the shade, till he should see what would become of the city.

6 And the LORD God appointed a plant,ᵇ and made it come up over Jō'nàh, that it might be a shade over his head, to save him from his discomfort. So Jonah was exceedingly glad because of the plant.ᵇ 7 But when

---

ᵃ Ch 2.1 in Heb   ᵇ Heb *qiqayon*, probably *the castor oil plant*
1.17: Mt 12.40.   **3.9:** Joel 2.14.   **4.2:** Ex 34.6.

dawn came up the next day, God appointed a worm which attacked the plant,[b] so that it withered. 8 When the sun rose, God appointed a sultry east wind, and the sun beat upon the head of Jō′nàh so that he was faint; and he asked that he might die, and said, "It is better for me to die than to live." 9 But God said to Jō′nàh, "Do you do well to be angry for the plant?"[b] And he said, "I do well to be angry, angry enough to die." 10 And the LORD said, "You pity the plant,[b] for which you did not labor, nor did you make it grow, which came into being in a night, and perished in a night. 11 And should not I pity Nin′ė·vėh, that great city, in which there are more than a hundred and twenty thousand persons who do not know their right hand from their left, and also much cattle?"

THE BOOK OF

MICAH

1 The word of the LORD that came to Mī′càh of Mō′rė·sheth in the days of Jō′thàm, Ä′haz, and Hez·ė·kī′àh, kings of Judah, which he saw concerning Sà·mâr′i·à and Jerusalem.

2 Hear, you peoples, all of you;
  hearken, O earth, and all that is in it;
and let the Lord GOD be a witness against you,
  the Lord from his holy temple.
3 For behold, the LORD is coming forth out of his place,
  and will come down and tread upon the high places of the earth.
4 And the mountains will melt under him
  and the valleys will be cleft,
like wax before the fire,
  like waters poured down a steep place.
5 All this is for the transgression of Jacob
  and for the sins of the house of Israel.
What is the transgression of Jacob?
  Is it not Sà·mâr′i·à?
And what is the sin of the house[a] of Judah?
  Is it not Jerusalem?
6 Therefore I will make Sà·mâr′i·à a heap in the open country,
  a place for planting vineyards;
and I will pour down her stones into the valley,
  and uncover her foundations.

7 All her images shall be beaten to pieces,
  all her hires shall be burned with fire,
and all her idols I will lay waste;
for from the hire of a harlot she gathered them,
  and to the hire of a harlot they shall return.

8 For this I will lament and wail;
  I will go stripped and naked;
I will make lamentation like the jackals,
  and mourning like the ostriches.
9 For her wound[b] is incurable;
  and it has come to Judah,
it has reached to the gate of my people,
  to Jerusalem.

10 Tell it not in Gath,
  weep not at all;
in Beth-le-aph′ràh
  roll yourselves in the dust.
11 Pass on your way,
  inhabitants of Shä′phir,
  in nakedness and shame;
the inhabitants of Zä′à·nan
  do not come forth;
the wailing of Beth-ē′zel
  shall take away from you its standing place.
12 For the inhabitants of Mä′roth
  wait anxiously for good,
because evil has come down from the LORD
  to the gate of Jerusalem.

b Heb *qiqayon*, probably *the castor oil plant*
a Gk Tg Compare Syr: Heb *what are the high places*   b Gk Syr Vg: Heb *wounds*
1.2: 1 Kings 22.28.

13 Harness the steeds to the chariots,
   inhabitants of Lā′chish;
   you were[c] the beginning of sin
      to the daughter of Zion,
   for in you were found
      the transgressions of Israel.
14 Therefore you shall give parting
      gifts
      to Mō′rĕ-sheth-gath;
   the houses of Ach′zib shall be a
      deceitful thing
      to the kings of Israel.
15 I will again bring a conqueror upon
      you,
      inhabitants of Mâ-rē′shăh;
   the glory of Israel
      shall come to Ă-dul′lăm.
16 Make yourselves bald and cut off
      your hair,
      for the children of your delight;
   make yourselves as bald as the eagle,
      for they shall go from you into
      exile.

2 Woe to those who devise wicked-
      ness
      and work evil upon their beds!
   When the morning dawns, they
      perform it,
   because it is in the power of their
      hand.
2 They covet fields, and seize them;
      and houses, and take them
      away;
   they oppress a man and his house,
      a man and his inheritance.
3 Therefore thus says the LORD:
   Behold, against this family I am
      devising evil,
   from which you cannot remove
      your necks;
   and you shall not walk haughtily,
      for it will be an evil time.
4 In that day they shall take up a
      taunt song against you,
   and wail with bitter lamentation,
      and say, "We are utterly ruined;
   he changes the portion of my
      people;
   how he removes it from me!
      Among our captors[d] he divides
      our fields."
5 Therefore you will have none to cast
      the line by lot
      in the assembly of the LORD.

6 "Do not preach"—thus they
      preach—
   "one should not preach of such
      things;
      disgrace will not overtake us."
7 Should this be said, O house of
      Jacob?

Is the Spirit of the LORD im-
      patient?
   Are these his doings?
Do not my words do good
      to him who walks uprightly?
8 But you rise against my people[e] as
      an enemy;
   you strip the robe from the
      peaceful,[f]
   from those who pass by trustingly
      with no thought of war.
9 The women of my people you drive
      out
      from their pleasant houses;
   from their young children you take
      away
      my glory for ever.
10 Arise and go,
      for this is no place to rest;
   because of uncleanness that destroys
      with a grievous destruction.
11 If a man should go about and utter
      wind and lies,
   saying, "I will preach to you of
      wine and strong drink,"
   he would be the preacher for this
      people!

12 I will surely gather all of you, O
      Jacob,
   I will gather the remnant of Israel;
   I will set them together
      like sheep in a fold,
   like a flock in its pasture,
      a noisy multitude of men.
13 He who opens the breach will go
      up before them;
   they will break through and pass
      the gate,
      going out by it.
   Their king will pass on before them,
      the LORD at their head.

3 And I said:
   Hear, you heads of Jacob
      and rulers of the house of Israel!
   Is it not for you to know justice?—
2   you who hate the good and love
      the evil,
   who tear the skin from off my people,
      and their flesh from off their
      bones;
3 who eat the flesh of my people,
      and flay their skin from off them,
   and break their bones in pieces,
      and chop them up like meat[g] in a
      kettle,
      like flesh in a caldron.

4 Then they will cry to the LORD,
      but he will not answer them;
   he will hide his face from them at
      that time,

c Cn: Heb *it was*   d Cn: Heb *the rebellious*   e Cn: Heb *yesterday my people rose*
f Cn: Heb *from before a garment*   g Gk: Heb *as*

because they have made their
deeds evil.

5 Thus says the LORD concerning the
prophets
who lead my people astray,
who cry "Peace"
when they have something to eat,
but declare war against him
who puts nothing into their
mouths.
6 Therefore it shall be night to you,
without vision,
and darkness to you, without
divination.
The sun shall go down upon the
prophets,
and the day shall be black over
them;
7 the seers shall be disgraced,
and the diviners put to shame;
they shall all cover their lips,
for there is no answer from God.
8 But as for me, I am filled with
power,
with the Spirit of the LORD,
and with justice and might,
to declare to Jacob his transgression
and to Israel his sin.

9 Hear this, you heads of the house
of Jacob
and rulers of the house of Israel,
who abhor justice
and pervert all equity,
10 who build Zion with blood
and Jerusalem with wrong.
11 Its heads give judgment for a bribe,
its priests teach for hire,
its prophets divine for money;
yet they lean upon the LORD and
say,
"Is not the LORD in the midst of
us?
No evil shall come upon us."
12 Therefore because of you
Zion shall be plowed as a field;
Jerusalem shall become a heap of
ruins,
and the mountain of the house a
wooden height.

4 It shall come to pass in the latter
days
that the mountain of the house
of the LORD
shall be established as the highest
of the mountains,
and shall be raised up above the
hills;
and peoples shall flow to it,
2 and many nations shall come, and
say:

"Come, let us go up to the mountain
of the LORD,
to the house of the God of Jacob;
that he may teach us his ways
and we may walk in his paths."
For out of Zion shall go forth the
law,
and the word of the LORD from
Jerusalem.
3 He shall judge between many peoples,
and shall decide for strong nations
afar off;
and they shall beat their swords into
plowshares,
and their spears into pruning
hooks;
nation shall not lift up sword against
nation,
neither shall they learn war any
more;
4 but they shall sit every man under
his vine and under his fig
tree,
and none shall make them afraid;
for the mouth of the LORD of
hosts has spoken.

5 For all the peoples walk
each in the name of its god,
but we will walk in the name of the
LORD our God
for ever and ever.

6 In that day, says the LORD,
I will assemble the lame
and gather those who have been
driven away,
and those whom I have afflicted;
7 and the lame I will make the remnant;
and those who were cast off, a
strong nation;
and the LORD will reign over them
in Mount Zion
from this time forth and for evermore.

8 And you, O tower of the flock,
hill of the daughter of Zion,
to you shall it come,
the former dominion shall come,
the kingdom of the daughter of
Jerusalem.

9 Now why do you cry aloud?
Is there no king in you?
Has your counselor perished,
that pangs have seized you like
a woman in travail?
10 Writhe and groan,h O daughter of
Zion,
like a woman in travail;

h Heb uncertain
4.1-3: Is 2.2-4.   4.4: Zech 3.10.

for now you shall go forth from the
   city
   and dwell in the open country;
you shall go to Babylon.
There you shall be rescued,
   there the LORD will redeem you
   from the hand of your enemies.

11 Now many nations
   are assembled against you,
saying, "Let her be profaned,
   and let our eyes gaze upon Zion."
12 But they do not know
   the thoughts of the LORD,
they do not understand his plan,
   that he has gathered them as
     sheaves to the threshing floor.
13 Arise and thresh,
   O daughter of Zion,
for I will make your horn iron
   and your hoofs bronze;
you shall beat in pieces many peo-
     ples,
   and shall*i* devote their gain to the
     LORD,
   their wealth to the Lord of the
     whole earth.

5*j* Now you are walled about with
   a wall;*k*
   siege is laid against us;
with a rod they strike upon the
     cheek
   the ruler of Israel.

2*l* But you, O Bethlehem Eph′ra·thah,
   who are little to be among the
     clans of Judah,
from you shall come forth for me
   one who is to be ruler in Israel,
whose origin is from of old,
   from ancient days.
3 Therefore he shall give them up
   until the time
   when she who is in travail has
     brought forth;
then the rest of his brethren shall
     return
   to the people of Israel.
4 And he shall stand and feed his
   flock in the strength of the
     LORD,
   in the majesty of the name of the
     LORD his God.
And they shall dwell secure, for
     now he shall be great
   to the ends of the earth.

5 And this shall be peace,
   when the Assyrian comes into our
     land
   and treads upon our soil,*m*

that we will raise against him seven
     shepherds
   and eight princes of men;
6 they shall rule the land of Assyria
   with the sword,
   and the land of Nim′rod with the
     drawn sword;*n*
and they*o* shall deliver us from the
     Assyrian
   when he comes into our land
   and treads within our border.

7 Then the remnant of Jacob shall be
   in the midst of many peoples
like dew from the LORD,
   like showers upon the grass,
which tarry not for men
   nor wait for the sons of men.
8 And the remnant of Jacob shall be
   among the nations,
   in the midst of many peoples,
like a lion among the beasts of the
     forest,
like a young lion among the flocks
     of sheep,
which, when it goes through, treads
     down
   and tears in pieces, and there is
     none to deliver.
9 Your hand shall be lifted up over
   your adversaries,
   and all your enemies shall be cut
     off.

10 And in that day, says the LORD,
   I will cut off your horses from
     among you
   and will destroy your chariots;
11 and I will cut off the cities of your
   land
   and throw down all your strong-
     holds;
12 and I will cut off sorceries from your
   hand,
   and you shall have no more sooth-
     sayers;
13 and I will cut off your images
   and your pillars from among
     you,
and you shall bow down no more
   to the work of your hands;
14 and I will root out your A·she′rim
   from among you
   and destroy your cities.
15 And in anger and wrath I will ex-
     ecute vengeance
   upon the nations that did not
     obey.

6 Hear what the LORD says:
   Arise, plead your case before the
     mountains,

i Gk Syr Tg: Heb *I will*   *j* Ch 4.14 in Heb
l Ch 5.1 in Heb   *m* Gk: Heb *in our palaces*
5.2: Mt 2.6; Jn 7.42.
k Cn Compare Gk: Heb obscure
n Cn: Heb *in its entrances*   *o* Heb *he*

and let the hills hear your voice.
2 Hear, you mountains, the controversy of the LORD,
and you enduring foundations of the earth;
for the LORD has a controversy with his people,
and he will contend with Israel.

3 "O my people, what have I done to you?
In what have I wearied you?
Answer me!
4 For I brought you up from the land of Egypt,
and redeemed you from the house of bondage;
and I sent before you Moses, Aaron, and Miriam.
5 O my people, remember what Bā'lak king of Mō'ab devised,
and what Balaam the son of Bē'ôr answered him,
and what happened from Shit'tim to Gil'gàl,
that you may know the saving acts of the LORD."

6 "With what shall I come before the LORD,
and bow myself before God on high?
Shall I come before him with burnt offerings,
with calves a year old?
7 Will the LORD be pleased with thousands of rams,
with ten thousands of rivers of oil?
Shall I give my first-born for my transgression,
the fruit of my body for the sin of my soul?"
8 He has showed you, O man, what is good;
and what does the LORD require of you
but to do justice, and to love kindness,[p]
and to walk humbly with your God?

9 The voice of the LORD cries to the city—
and it is sound wisdom to fear thy name:
"Hear, O tribe and assembly of the city![q]
10   Can I forget[r] the treasures of wickedness in the house of the wicked,

and the scant measure that is accursed?
11 Shall I acquit the man with wicked scales
and with a bag of deceitful weights?
12 Your[s] rich men are full of violence;
your[s] inhabitants speak lies,
and their tongue is deceitful in their mouth.
13 Therefore I have begun[t] to smite you,
making you desolate because of your sins.
14 You shall eat, but not be satisfied,
and there shall be hunger in your inward parts;
you shall put away, but not save,
and what you save I will give to the sword.
15 You shall sow, but not reap;
you shall tread olives, but not anoint yourselves with oil;
you shall tread grapes, but not drink wine.
16 For you have kept the statutes of Om'ri,[u]
and all the works of the house of Ā'hab;
and you have walked in their counsels;
that I may make you a desolation,
and your[v] inhabitants a hissing;
so you shall bear the scorn of the peoples."[w]

7 Woe is me! For I have become as when the summer fruit has been gathered,
as when the vintage has been gleaned:
there is no cluster to eat,
no first-ripe fig which my soul desires.
2 The godly man has perished from the earth,
and there is none upright among men;
they all lie in wait for blood,
and each hunts his brother with a net.
3 Their hands are upon what is evil, to do it diligently;
the prince and the judge ask for a bribe,
and the great man utters the evil desire of his soul;
thus they weave it together.
4 The best of them is like a brier,
the most upright of them a thorn hedge.

[p] Or *steadfast love*   [q] Cn Compare Gk: Heb *and who has appointed it yet*
[r] Cn: Heb *uncertain*   [s] Heb *whose*   [t] Gk Syr Vg: Heb *have made sick*
[u] Gk Syr Vg Tg: Heb *the statutes of Omri are kept*   [v] Heb *its*
[w] Gk: Heb *my people*

The day of their[x] watchmen, of
   their[x] punishment, has come;
now their confusion is at hand.

5 Put no trust in a neighbor,
   have no confidence in a friend;
guard the doors of your mouth
   from her who lies in your bosom;
6 for the son treats the father with
   contempt,
the daughter rises up against her
   mother,
the daughter-in-law against her
   mother-in-law;
a man's enemies are the men of
   his own house.

7 But as for me, I will look to the
   LORD,
I will wait for the God of my
   salvation;
   my God will hear me.

8 Rejoice not over me, O my enemy;
   when I fall, I shall rise;
when I sit in darkness,
   the LORD will be a light to me.
9 I will bear the indignation of the
   LORD
because I have sinned against him,
until he pleads my cause
   and executes judgment for me.
He will bring me forth to the light;
   I shall behold his deliverance.
10 Then my enemy will see,
   and shame will cover her who said
   to me,
"Where is the LORD your God?"
My eyes will gloat over her;
   now she will be trodden down
   like the mire of the streets.

11 A day for the building of your walls!
   In that day the boundary shall be
   far extended.
12 In that day they will come to you,
   from Assyria to[y] Egypt,
and from Egypt to the River,
   from sea to sea and from mountain to mountain.
13 But the earth will be desolate

because of its inhabitants,
   for the fruit of their doings.

14 Shepherd thy people with thy staff,
   the flock of thy inheritance,
who dwell alone in a forest
   in the midst of a garden land;
let them feed in Bā'shàn and Gilead
   as in the days of old.

15 As in the days when you came out
   of the land of Egypt
I will show them[z] marvelous
   things.

16 The nations shall see and be
   ashamed
of all their might;
they shall lay their hands on their
   mouths;
   their ears shall be deaf;
17 they shall lick the dust like a serpent,
like the crawling things of the
   earth;
they shall come trembling out of
   their strongholds,
they shall turn in dread to the
   LORD our God,
and they shall fear because of thee.

18 Who is a God like thee, pardoning
   iniquity
and passing over transgression
   for the remnant of his inheritance?
He does not retain his anger for ever
   because he delights in steadfast
   love.
19 He will again have compassion upon
   us,
he will tread our iniquities under
   foot.
Thou wilt cast all our[a] sins
   into the depths of the sea.
20 Thou wilt show faithfulness to
   Jacob
and steadfast love to Abraham,
   as thou hast sworn to our fathers
   from the days of old.

x Heb *your*   y Cn: Heb *and cities of*   z Heb *him*
a Gk Syr Vg Tg: Heb *their*
7.6: Mt 10.21, 35-36; Mk 13.12; Lk 12.53.   7.20: Lk 1.55.

THE BOOK OF

NAHUM

1 An oracle concerning Nin′e·veh.
The book of the vision of Nā′hum
of El′kosh.
2 The LORD is a jealous God and
avenging,
 the LORD is avenging and wrathful;
 the LORD takes vengeance on his
adversaries
 and keeps wrath for his enemies.
3 The LORD is slow to anger and of
great might,
 and the LORD will by no means
clear the guilty.

His way is in whirlwind and storm,
 and the clouds are the dust of his
feet.
4 He rebukes the sea and makes it dry,
 he dries up all the rivers;
Bā′shan and Cär′mel wither,
 the bloom of Lebanon fades.
5 The mountains quake before him,
 the hills melt;
 the earth is laid waste before him,
 the world and all that dwell
therein.

6 Who can stand before his indignation?
 Who can endure the heat of his
anger?
His wrath is poured out like fire,
 and the rocks are broken asunder
by him.
7 The LORD is good,
 a stronghold in the day of trouble;
 he knows those who take refuge
in him.
8 But with an overflowing flood
 he will make a full end of his
adversaries,[a]
 and will pursue his enemies into
darkness.
9 What do you plot against the LORD?
 He will make a full end;
 he will not take vengeance[b] twice
on his foes.[c]
10 Like entangled thorns they are
consumed,[d]
 like dry stubble.
11 Did one not[e] come out from you,

who plotted evil against the
LORD,
 and counseled villainy?

12 Thus says the LORD,
"Though they be strong and many,[f]
 they will be cut off and pass away.
Though I have afflicted you,
 I will afflict you no more.
13 And now I will break his yoke from
off you
 and will burst your bonds
asunder."

14 The LORD has given commandment
about you:
 "No more shall your name be
perpetuated;
from the house of your gods I will
cut off
 the graven image and the molten
image.
I will make your grave, for you are
vile."

15[g] Behold, on the mountains the feet
of him
 who brings good tidings,
 who proclaims peace!
Keep your feasts, O Judah,
 fulfil your vows,
for never again shall the wicked
 come against you,
 he is utterly cut off.

2 The shatterer has come up against
you.
 Man the ramparts;
 watch the road;
gird your loins;
 collect all your strength.

2 (For the LORD is restoring the
majesty of Jacob
 as the majesty of Israel,
for plunderers have stripped them
 and ruined their branches.)

3 The shield of his mighty men is red,
 his soldiers are clothed in scarlet.
The chariots flash like flame[h]
 when mustered in array;

---

a Gk: Heb *her place* b Gk: Heb *rise up* c Cn: Heb *distress*
d Heb *are consumed, drunken as with their drink* e Cn: Heb *fully* f Heb uncertain
g Ch 2.1 in Heb h Cn: The meaning of the Hebrew word is uncertain
1.3: Is 10.5-34; Zeph 2.12-15. **1.15:** Is 40.9; 52.7; Acts 10.36; Rom 10.15.

the chargers[i] prance.

4 The chariots rage in the streets,
    they rush to and fro through the
      squares;
they gleam like torches,
    they dart like lightning.
5 The officers are summoned,
    they stumble as they go,
they hasten to the wall,
    the mantelet is set up.
6 The river gates are opened,
    the palace is in dismay;
7 its mistress[j] is stripped, she is
      carried off,
    her maidens lamenting,
moaning like doves,
    and beating their breasts.
8 Nin′e·veh is like a pool
    whose waters[k] run away.
"Halt! Halt!" they cry;
    but none turns back.
9 Plunder the silver,
    plunder the gold!
There is no end of treasure,
    or wealth of every precious thing.

10 Desolate! Desolation and ruin!
    Hearts faint and knees tremble,
anguish is on all loins,
    all faces grow pale!
11 Where is the lions' den,
    the cave[l] of the young lions,
where the lion brought his prey,
    where his cubs were, with none to
      disturb?
12 The lion tore enough for his whelps
    and strangled prey for his lion-
      esses;
he filled his caves with prey
    and his dens with torn flesh.

13 Behold, I am against you, says
the LORD of hosts, and I will burn
your[m] chariots in smoke, and the sword
shall devour your young lions; I will
cut off your prey from the earth, and
the voice of your messengers shall no
more be heard.

3 Woe to the bloody city,
    all full of lies and booty—
    no end to the plunder!
2 The crack of whip, and rumble of
      wheel,
    galloping horse and bounding
      chariot!
3 Horsemen charging,
    flashing sword and glittering spear,
hosts of slain,
    heaps of corpses,
dead bodies without end—
    they stumble over the bodies!

4 And all for the countless harlotries
    of the harlot,
graceful and of deadly charms,
who betrays nations with her har-
      lotries,
    and peoples with her charms.

5 Behold, I am against you,
    says the LORD of hosts,
and will lift up your skirts over
    your face;
and I will let nations look on your
    nakedness
    and kingdoms on your shame.
6 I will throw filth at you
    and treat you with contempt,
    and make you a gazingstock.
7 And all who look on you will shrink
    from you and say,
Wasted is Nin′e·veh; who will be-
      moan her?
    whence shall I seek comforters
    for her?[n]

8 Are you better than Thebes[o]
    that sat by the Nile,
with water around her,
    her rampart a sea,
    and water her wall?
9 Ethiopia was her strength,
    Egypt too, and that without
      limit;
Put and the Libyans were her[p]
    helpers.

10 Yet she was carried away,
    she went into captivity;
her little ones were dashed in pieces
    at the head of every street;
for her honored men lots were cast,
    and all her great men were bound
      in chains.
11 You also will be drunken,
    you will be dazed;
you will seek
    a refuge from the enemy.
12 All your fortresses are like fig trees
    with first-ripe figs—
if shaken they fall
    into the mouth of the eater.
13 Behold, your troops
    are women in your midst.
The gates of your land
    are wide open to your foes;
    fire has devoured your bars.

14 Draw water for the siege,
    strengthen your forts;
go into the clay,
    tread the mortar,
    take hold of the brick mold!

i Cn Compare Gk Syr: Heb *cypresses* j The meaning of the Hebrew is uncertain
k Cn Compare Gk: Heb *from the days that she has become, and they*
l Cn: Heb *pasture* m Heb *her* n Gk: Heb *you* o Heb *No-amon*
p Gk: Heb *your*

15 There will the fire devour you,
   the sword will cut you off.
   It will devour you like the locust.

Multiply yourselves like the locust,
   multiply like the grasshopper!
16 You increased your merchants
   more than the stars of the heavens.
   The locust spreads its wings and
   flies away.
17 Your princes are like grasshoppers,
   your scribes^a like clouds of
   locusts
settling on the fences
   in a day of cold—

when the sun rises, they fly away;
   no one knows where they are.

18 Your shepherds are asleep,
   O king of Assyria;
   your nobles slumber.
Your people are scattered on the
   mountains
   with none to gather them.
19 There is no assuaging your hurt,
   your wound is grievous.
All who hear the news of you
   clap their hands over you.
For upon whom has not come
   your unceasing evil?

THE BOOK OF

HABAKKUK

1 The oracle of God which Há·bak'-
   kŭk the prophet saw.
2 O LORD, how long shall I cry for
   help,
   and thou wilt not hear?
Or cry to thee "Violence!"
   and thou wilt not save?
3 Why dost thou make me see wrongs
   and look upon trouble?
Destruction and violence are before
   me;
   strife and contention arise.
4 So the law is slacked
   and justice never goes forth.
For the wicked surround the righteous,
   so justice goes forth perverted.

5 Look among the nations, and see;
   wonder and be astounded.
For I am doing a work in your days
   that you would not believe if told.
6 For lo, I am rousing the Chal·dē'áns,
   that bitter and hasty nation,
who march through the breadth of
   the earth,
   to seize habitations not their own.
7 Dread and terrible are they;
   their justice and dignity proceed
   from themselves.
8 Their horses are swifter than
   leopards,
   more fierce than the evening
   wolves;
their horsemen press proudly on.
Yea, their horsemen come from afar;

they fly like an eagle swift to
   devour.
9 They all come for violence;
   terror^a of them goes before them.
   They gather captives like sand.
10 At kings they scoff,
   and of rulers they make sport.
They laugh at every fortress,
   for they heap up earth and take it.
11 Then they sweep by like the wind
   and go on,
   guilty men, whose own might is
   their god!

12 Art thou not from everlasting,
   O LORD my God, my Holy One?
   We shall not die.
O LORD, thou hast ordained them
   as a judgment;
   and thou, O Rock, hast established them for chastisement.
13 Thou who art of purer eyes than to
   behold evil
   and canst not look on wrong,
why dost thou look on faithless men,
   and art silent when the wicked
   swallows up
   the man more righteous than he?
14 For thou makest men like the fish
   of the sea,
   like crawling things that have no
   ruler.
15 He brings all of them up with a
   hook,
   he drags them out with his net,
   he gathers them in his seine;

^a Or marshals   ^a Cn: Heb uncertain
1-2: Is 13.1-14.23; 47; Jer 50-51.   **1.5:** Acts 13.41.   **1.6:** Rev 20.9.

so he rejoices and exults.

16 Therefore he sacrifices to his net
    and burns incense to his seine;
for by them he lives in luxury,[b]
    and his food is rich.

17 Is he then to keep on emptying his
    net,
    and mercilessly slaying nations
      for ever?

2 I will take my stand to watch,
  and station myself on the tower,
and look forth to see what he will
    say to me,
and what I will answer concerning
    my complaint.

2 And the LORD answered me:
  "Write the vision;
    make it plain upon tablets,
  so he may run who reads it.

3 For still the vision awaits its time;
  it hastens to the end—it will not lie.
If it seem slow, wait for it;
  it will surely come, it will not
    delay.

4 Behold, he whose soul is not upright
    in him shall fail,[c]
  but the righteous shall live by his
    faith.[d]

5 Moreover, wine is treacherous;
  the arrogant man shall not abide.[e]
His greed is as wide as She'ōl;
  like death he has never enough.
He gathers for himself all nations,
  and collects as his own all peo-
    ples."

6 Shall not all these take up their taunt
against him, in scoffing derision of
him, and say,
  "Woe to him who heaps up what
    is not his own—
    for how long?—
  and loads himself with pledges!"

7 Will not your debtors suddenly
    arise,
  and those awake who will make
    you tremble?
Then you will be booty for them.

8 Because you have plundered many
    nations,
  all the remnant of the peoples
    shall plunder you,
for the blood of men and violence
    to the earth,
  to cities and all who dwell therein.

9 Woe to him who gets evil gain for
    his house,
  to set his nest on high,

to be safe from the reach of harm!

10 You have devised shame to your
    house
  by cutting off many peoples;
  you have forfeited your life.

11 For the stone will cry out from the
    wall,
  and the beam from the woodwork
    respond.

12 Woe to him who builds a town with
    blood,
  and founds a city on iniquity!

13 Behold, is it not from the LORD of
    hosts
  that peoples labor only for fire,
  and nations weary themselves for
    nought?

14 For the earth will be filled
  with the knowledge of the glory
    of the LORD,
  as the waters cover the sea.

15 Woe to him who makes his neigh-
    bors drink
  of the cup of his wrath,[f] and
    makes them drunk,
  to gaze on their shame!

16 You will be sated with contempt
    instead of glory.
  Drink, yourself, and stagger![g]
The cup in the LORD'S right hand
  will come around to you,
  and shame will come upon your
    glory!

17 The violence done to Lebanon will
    overwhelm you;
  the destruction of the beasts will
    terrify you,[h]
for the blood of men and violence
    to the earth,
  to cities and all who dwell therein.

18 What profit is an idol
  when its maker has shaped it,
  a metal image, a teacher of lies?
For the workman trusts in his own
    creation
  when he makes dumb idols!

19 Woe to him who says to a wooden
    thing, Awake;
  to a dumb stone, Arise!
Can this give revelation?
Behold, it is overlaid with gold and
    silver,
  and there is no breath at all in it.

20 But the LORD is in his holy temple;
  let all the earth keep silence be-
    fore him.

---

b Heb *his portion is fat*   *c* Cn: Heb *is puffed up*   *d* Or *faithfulness*
e The Hebrew of these two lines is obscure   *f* Cn: Heb *joining to your wrath*
g Cn Compare Gk Syr: Heb *be uncircumcised*   *h* Gk Syr: Heb *them*

2.1: Is 21.8.   **2.3**: Heb 10.37.   **2.4**: Rom 1.17; Gal 3.11; Heb 10.38-39.
2.14: Is 11.9.   **2.20**: Zeph 1.7; Zech 2.13.

3 A prayer of Hȧ·bak′kŭk the prophet, according to Shig·i·ōn′-oth.

2 O LORD, I have heard the report of thee,
   and thy work, O LORD, do I fear.
In the midst of the years renew it;
   in the midst of the years make it known;
   in wrath remember mercy.
3 God came from Tē′mȧn,
   and the Holy One from Mount Pâr′an.
His glory covered the heavens,
   and the earth was full of his praise.   *Selah*
4 His brightness was like the light,
   rays flashed from his hand;
   and there he veiled his power.
5 Before him went pestilence,
   and plague followed close behind.
6 He stood and measured the earth;
   he looked and shook the nations;
   then the eternal mountains were scattered,
   the everlasting hills sank low.
   His ways were as of old.
7 I saw the tents of Cü′shan in affliction;
   the curtains of the land of Mid′i-ȧn did tremble.
8 Was thy wrath against the rivers, O LORD?
Was thy anger against the rivers,
   or thy indignation against the sea,
when thou didst ride upon thy horses,
   upon thy chariot of victory?
9 Thou didst strip the sheath from thy bow,
   and put the arrows to the string.[i]   *Selah*
   Thou didst cleave the earth with rivers.
10 The mountains saw thee, and writhed;
   the raging waters swept on;
   the deep gave forth its voice,
   it lifted its hands on high.

11 The sun and moon stood still in their habitation[j]
   at the light of thine arrows as they sped,
   at the flash of thy glittering spear.
12 Thou didst bestride the earth in fury,
   thou didst trample the nations in anger.
13 Thou wentest forth for the salvation of thy people,
   for the salvation of thy anointed.
Thou didst crush the head of the wicked,[k]
   laying him bare from thigh to neck.[l]   *Selah*
14 Thou didst pierce with thy[m] shafts the head of his warriors,[n]
   who came like a whirlwind to scatter me,
   rejoicing as if to devour the poor in secret.
15 Thou didst trample the sea with thy horses,
   the surging of mighty waters.

16 I hear, and my body trembles,
   my lips quiver at the sound;
rottenness enters into my bones,
   my steps totter[o] beneath me.
I will quietly wait for the day of trouble
   to come upon people who invade us.

17 Though the fig tree do not blossom,
   nor fruit be on the vines,
the produce of the olive fail
   and the fields yield no food,
the flock be cut off from the fold
   and there be no herd in the stalls,
18 yet I will rejoice in the LORD,
   I will joy in the God of my salvation.
19 GOD, the Lord, is my strength;
   he makes my feet like hinds' feet,
   he makes me tread upon my high places.

To the choirmaster: with stringed[p] instruments.

i Cn: Heb obscure   *j* Heb uncertain   *k* Cn: Heb *head from the house of the wicked*
l Heb obscure   *m* Heb *his*   *n* Vg Compare Gk Syr: Heb uncertain
o Cn Compare Gk: Heb *I tremble because*   *p* Heb *my stringed*

THE BOOK OF

ZEPHANIAH

1 The word of the LORD which came
to Zeph·a·nī′ah the son of Cū′shī,
son of Gĕd·a·lī′ah, son of Am·a·rī′ah,
son of Hĕz·ė·kī′ah, in the days of
Jō·sī′ah the son of A′mon, king of
Judah.

2 "I will utterly sweep away everything
from the face of the earth," says
the LORD.
3 "I will sweep away man and beast;
I will sweep away the birds of the
air
and the fish of the sea.
I will overthrow[a] the wicked;
I will cut off mankind
from the face of the earth," says
the LORD.
4 "I will stretch out my hand against
Judah,
and against all the inhabitants of
Jerusalem;
and I will cut off from this place
the remnant of Bā′al
and the name of the idolatrous
priests;[b]
5 those who bow down on the roofs
to the host of the heavens;
those who bow down and swear to
the LORD
and yet swear by Mil′com;
6 those who have turned back from
following the LORD,
who do not seek the LORD or
inquire of him."

7 Be silent before the Lord GOD!
For the day of the LORD is at
hand;
the LORD has prepared a sacrifice
and consecrated his guests.
8 And on the day of the LORD's
sacrifice—
"I will punish the officials and the
king's sons
and all who array themselves in
foreign attire.
9 On that day I will punish
every one who leaps over the
threshold,
and those who fill their master's
house
with violence and fraud."

10 "On that day," says the LORD,
"a cry will be heard from the
Fish Gate,
a wail from the Second Quarter,
a loud crash from the hills.
11 Wail, O inhabitants of the Mortar!
For all the traders are no more;
all who weigh out silver are cut
off.
12 At that time I will search Jerusalem
with lamps,
and I will punish the men
who are thickening upon their lees,
those who say in their hearts,
'The LORD will not do good,
nor will he do ill.'
13 Their goods shall be plundered,
and their houses laid waste.
Though they build houses,
they shall not inhabit them;
though they plant vineyards,
they shall not drink wine from
them."

14 The great day of the LORD is near,
near and hastening fast;
the sound of the day of the LORD
is bitter,
the mighty man cries aloud there.
15 A day of wrath is that day,
a day of distress and anguish,
a day of ruin and devastation,
a day of darkness and gloom,
a day of clouds and thick darkness,
16 a day of trumpet blast and battle
cry
against the fortified cities
and against the lofty battlements.

17 I will bring distress on men,
so that they shall walk like the
blind,
because they have sinned against
the LORD;
their blood shall be poured out like
dust,
and their flesh like dung.
18 Neither their silver nor their gold
shall be able to deliver them
on the day of the wrath of the
LORD.
In the fire of his jealous wrath,
all the earth shall be consumed;
for a full, yea, sudden end

a Cn: Heb the stumbling blocks   b Compare Gk: Heb idolatrous priests with the priests
1.7: Hab 2.20; Zech 2.13.

779

he will make of all the inhabitants
of the earth.

2 Come together and hold assembly,
O shameless nation,

2 before you are driven away
like the drifting chaff,[c]
before there comes upon you
the fierce anger of the LORD,
before there comes upon you
the day of the wrath of the LORD.

3 Seek the LORD, all you humble of
the land,
who do his commands;
seek righteousness, seek humility;
perhaps you may be hidden
on the day of the wrath of the
LORD.

4 For Gā′zà shall be deserted,
and Ash′kè·lon shall become a
desolation;
Ash′dod′s̆ people shall be driven
out at noon,
and Ek′ron shall be uprooted.

5 Woe to you inhabitants of the seacoast,
you nation of the Cher′é·thites!
The word of the LORD is against you,
O Canaan, land of the Philistines;
and I will destroy you till no
inhabitant is left.

6 And you, O seacoast, shall be pastures,
meadows for shepherds
and folds for flocks.

7 The seacoast shall become the
possession
of the remnant of the house of
Judah,
on which they shall pasture,
and in the houses of Ash′kè·lon
they shall lie down at evening.
For the LORD their God will be
mindful of them
and restore their fortunes.

8 "I have heard the taunts of Mō′ab
and the revilings of the Am′mò-
nites,
how they have taunted my people
and made boasts against their
territory.

9 Therefore, as I live," says the LORD
of hosts,
the God of Israel,
"Mō′ab shall become like Sod′òm,
and the Am′mò·nites like Gò-
môr′rah,

a land possessed by nettles and salt
pits,
and a waste for ever.
The remnant of my people shall
plunder them,
and the survivors of my nation
shall possess them."

10 This shall be their lot in return for
their pride,
because they scoffed and boasted
against the people of the LORD of
hosts.

11 The LORD will be terrible against
them;
yea, he will famish all the gods
of the earth,
and to him shall bow down,
each in its place,
all the lands of the nations.

12 You also, O Ethiopians,
shall be slain by my sword.

13 And he will stretch out his hand
against the north,
and destroy Assyria;
and he will make Nin′é·véh a desolation,
a dry waste like the desert.

14 Herds shall lie down in the midst
of her,
all the beasts of the field;[d]
the vulture[e] and the hedgehog
shall lodge in her capitals;
the owl[f] shall hoot in the
window,
the raven[g] croak on the threshold;
for her cedar work will be laid
bare.

15 This is the exultant city
that dwelt secure,
that said to herself,
"I am and there is none else."
What a desolation she has become,
a lair for wild beasts!
Every one who passes by her
hisses and shakes his fist.

3 Woe to her that is rebellious and
defiled,
the oppressing city!

2 She listens to no voice,
she accepts no correction.
She does not trust in the LORD,
she does not draw near to her
God.

3 Her officials within her
are roaring lions;
her judges are evening wolves

---

c Cn Compare Gk Syr: Heb *before a decree is born; like chaff a day has passed away*
d Tg Compare Gk: Heb *nation*   e The meaning of the Hebrew word is uncertain
f Cn: Heb *a voice*   g Gk Vg: Heb *desolation*

2.4-7: Is 14.29-31; Jer 47; Ezek 25.15-17; Joel 3.4-8; Amos 1.6-8; Zech 9.5-7.
2.8-11: Is 15-16; 25.10-12; Jer 48; Ezek 25.8-11; Amos 2.1-3.   2.12: Is 18.
2.13-15: Is 10.5-34; Nahum.

that leave nothing till the morning.

4 Her prophets are wanton,
    faithless men;
her priests profane what is sacred,
    they do violence to the law.
5 The LORD within her is righteous,
    he does no wrong;
every morning he shows forth his
    justice,
    each dawn he does not fail;
but the unjust knows no shame.

6 "I have cut off nations;
    their battlements are in ruins;
I have laid waste their streets
    so that none walks in them;
their cities have been made desolate,
    without a man, without an in-
    habitant.
7 I said, 'Surely she will fear me,
    she will accept correction;
    she will not lose sight[h]
of all that I have enjoined upon
    her.'
But all the more they were eager
    to make all their deeds corrupt."

8 "Therefore wait for me," says the
    LORD,
    "for the day when I arise as a
    witness.
For my decision is to gather nations,
    to assemble kingdoms,
to pour out upon them my indig-
    nation,
    all the heat of my anger;
for in the fire of my jealous wrath
    all the earth shall be consumed.

9 "Yea, at that time I will change the
    speech of the peoples
to a pure speech,
that all of them may call on the
    name of the LORD
    and serve him with one accord.
10 From beyond the rivers of Ethiopia
    my suppliants, the daughter of
    my dispersed ones,
    shall bring my offering.

11 "On that day you shall not be put
    to shame
    because of the deeds by which
    you have rebelled against me;
for then I will remove from your
    midst
    your proudly exultant ones,

and you shall no longer be haughty
    in my holy mountain.
12 For I will leave in the midst of you
    a people humble and lowly.
They shall seek refuge in the name
    of the LORD,
13 those who are left in Israel;
they shall do no wrong
    and utter no lies,
nor shall there be found in their
    mouth
    a deceitful tongue.
For they shall pasture and lie down,
    and none shall make them afraid."

14 Sing aloud, O daughter of Zion;
    shout, O Israel!
Rejoice and exult with all your
    heart,
    O daughter of Jerusalem!
15 The LORD has taken away the judg-
    ments against you,
    he has cast out your enemies.
The King of Israel, the LORD, is in
    your midst;
    you shall fear evil no more.
16 On that day it shall be said to
    Jerusalem:
    "Do not fear, O Zion;
    let not your hands grow weak.
17 The LORD, your God, is in your
    midst,
    a warrior who gives victory;
he will rejoice over you with glad-
    ness,
    he will renew you[i] in his love;
he will exult over you with loud
    singing
18   as on a day of festival.[j]
"I will remove disaster[k] from you,
    so that you will not bear reproach
    for it.
19 Behold, at that time I will deal
    with all your oppressors.
And I will save the lame
    and gather the outcast,
and I will change their shame into
    praise
    and renown in all the earth.
20 At that time I will bring you home,
    at the time when I gather you
    together;
yea, I will make you renowned and
    praised
    among all the peoples of the
    earth,
when I restore your fortunes
    before your eyes," says the LORD.

h Gk Syr: Heb *and her dwelling will not be cut off*   i Gk Syr: Heb *he will be silent*
j Gk Syr: Heb obscure   k Cn: Heb *they were*
3.13: Rev 14.5.

THE BOOK OF

HAGGAI

1 In the second year of Dà·rī′ús the king, in the sixth month, on the first day of the month, the word of the LORD came by Hag′gäi the prophet to Ze·rub′bà·bel the son of She-al′ti-el, governor of Judah, and to Joshua the son of Je·hoz′á·dak, the high priest, 2 "Thus says the LORD of hosts: This people say the time has not yet come to rebuild the house of the LORD." 3 Then the word of the LORD came by Hag′gäi the prophet, 4 "Is it a time for you yourselves to dwell in your paneled houses, while this house lies in ruins? 5 Now therefore thus says the LORD of hosts: Consider how you have fared. 6 You have sown much, and harvested little; you eat, but you never have enough; you drink, but you never have your fill; you clothe yourselves, but no one is warm; and he who earns wages earns wages to put them into a bag with holes.

7 "Thus says the LORD of hosts: Consider how you have fared. 8 Go up to the hills and bring wood and build the house, that I may take pleasure in it and that I may appear in my glory, says the LORD. 9 You have looked for much, and, lo, it came to little; and when you brought it home, I blew it away. Why? says the LORD of hosts. Because of my house that lies in ruins, while you busy yourselves each with his own house. 10 Therefore the heavens above you have withheld the dew, and the earth has withheld its produce. 11 And I have called for a drought upon the land and the hills, upon the grain, the new wine, the oil, upon what the ground brings forth, upon men and cattle, and upon all their labors."

12 Then Ze·rub′bà·bel the son of She-al′ti-el, and Joshua the son of Je·hoz′á·dak, the high priest, with all the remnant of the people, obeyed the voice of the LORD their God, and the words of Hag′gäi the prophet, as the LORD their God had sent him; and the people feared before the LORD. 13 Then Hag′gäi, the messenger of the LORD, spoke to the people with the LORD's message, "I am with you, says the LORD." 14 And the LORD stirred up

2.6: Heb 12.26.

the spirit of Ze·rub′bà·bel the son of She-al′ti-el, governor of Judah, and the spirit of Joshua the son of Je·hoz′á·dak, the high priest, and the spirit of all the remnant of the people; and they came and worked on the house of the LORD of hosts, their God, 15 on the twenty-fourth day of the month, in the sixth month.

2 In the second year of Dà·rī′ús the king, 1 in the seventh month, on the twenty-first day of the month, the word of the LORD came by Hag′gäi the prophet, 2 "Speak now to Ze·rub′-bà·bel the son of She-al′ti-el, governor of Judah, and to Joshua the son of Je·hoz′á·dak, the high priest, and to all the remnant of the people, and say, 3 'Who is left among you that saw this house in its former glory? How do you see it now? Is it not in your sight as nothing? 4 Yet now take courage, O Ze·rub′bà·bel, says the LORD; take courage, O Joshua, son of Je·hoz′á·dak, the high priest; take courage, all you people of the land, says the LORD; work, for I am with you, says the LORD of hosts, 5 according to the promise that I made you when you came out of Egypt. My Spirit abides among you; fear not. 6 For thus says the LORD of hosts: Once again, in a little while, I will shake the heavens and the earth and the sea and the dry land; 7 and I will shake all nations, so that the treasures of all nations shall come in, and I will fill this house with splendor, says the LORD of hosts. 8 The silver is mine, and the gold is mine, says the LORD of hosts. 9 The latter splendor of this house shall be greater than the former, says the LORD of hosts; and in this place I will give prosperity, says the LORD of hosts.' "

10 On the twenty-fourth day of the ninth month, in the second year of Dà·rī′ús, the word of the LORD came by Hag′gäi the prophet, 11 "Thus says the LORD of hosts: Ask the priests to decide this question, 12 'If one carries holy flesh in the skirt of his garment, and touches with his skirt bread, or pottage, or wine, or oil, or any kind of food, does it become holy?' " The priests answered, "No." 13 Then said

Hag′gäi, "If one who is unclean by contact with a dead body touches any of these, does it become unclean?"'The priests answered, "It does become unclean." 14 Then Hag′gäi said, "So is it with this people, and with this nation before me, says the LORD; and so with every work of their hands; and what they offer there is unclean. 15 Pray now, consider what will come to pass from this day onward. Before a stone was placed upon a stone in the temple of the LORD, 16 how did you fare?*a* When one came to a heap of twenty measures, there were but ten; when one came to the winevat to draw fifty measures, there were but twenty. 17 I smote you and all the products of your toil with blight and mildew and hail; yet you did not return to me, says the LORD. 18 Consider from this day onward, from the twenty-fourth day of the ninth month. Since the day that the foundation

of the LORD's temple was laid, consider: 19 Is the seed yet in the barn? Do the vine, the fig tree, the pomegranate, and the olive tree still yield nothing? From this day on I will bless you."

20 The word of the LORD came a second time to Hag′gäi on the twenty-fourth day of the month, 21 "Speak to Ze·rub′ba·bel, governor of Judah, saying, I am about to shake the heavens and the earth, 22 and to overthrow the throne of kingdoms; I am about to destroy the strength of the kingdoms of the nations, and overthrow the chariots and their riders; and the horses and their riders shall go down, every one by the sword of his fellow. 23 On that day, says the LORD of hosts, I will take you, O Ze·rub′ba·bel my servant, the son of She·al′ti·el, says the LORD, and make you like a signet ring; for I have chosen you, says the LORD of hosts."

THE BOOK OF

ZECHARIAH

In the eighth month, in the second year of Da·ri′us, the word of the LORD came to Zech·a·ri′ah the son of Ber·e·chi′ah, son of Id′do, the prophet, saying, 2 "The LORD was very angry with your fathers. 3 Therefore say to them, Thus says the LORD of hosts: Return to me, says the LORD of hosts, and I will return to you, says the LORD of hosts. 4 Be not like your fathers, to whom the former prophets cried out, 'Thus says the LORD of hosts, Return from your evil ways and from your evil deeds.' But they did not hear or heed me, says the LORD. 5 Your fathers, where are they? And the prophets, do they live for ever? 6 But my words and my statutes, which I commanded my servants the prophets, did they not overtake your fathers? So they repented and said, As the LORD of hosts purposed to deal with us for our ways and deeds, so has he dealt with us."

7 On the twenty-fourth day of the eleventh month which is the month of Shĕ·bät′, in the second year of Da·ri′us, the word of the LORD came to Zech·a·ri′ah the son of Ber·e·chi′ah,

son of Id′do, the prophet; and Zechariah said, 8 "I saw in the night, and behold, a man riding upon a red horse! He was standing among the myrtle trees in the glen; and behind him were red, sorrel, and white horses. 9 Then I said, 'What are these, my lord?' The angel who talked with me said to me, 'I will show you what they are.' 10 So the man who was standing among the myrtle trees answered, 'These are they whom the LORD has sent to patrol the earth.' 11And they answered the angel of the LORD who was standing among the myrtle trees, 'We have patrolled the earth, and behold, all the earth remains at rest.' 12 Then the angel of the LORD said, 'O LORD of hosts, how long wilt thou have no mercy on Jerusalem and the cities of Judah, against which thou hast had indignation these seventy years?' 13And the LORD answered gracious and comforting words to the angel who talked with me. 14 So the angel who talked with me said to me, 'Cry out, Thus says the LORD of hosts: I am exceedingly jealous for Jerusalem and for Zion. 15And I am

a Gk: Heb since they were

very angry with the nations that are at ease; for while I was angry but a little they furthered the disaster. 16 Therefore, thus says the LORD, I have returned to Jerusalem with compassion; my house shall be built in it, says the LORD of hosts, and the measuring line shall be stretched out over Jerusalem. 17 Cry again, Thus says the LORD of hosts: My cities shall again overflow with prosperity, and the LORD will again comfort Zion and again choose Jerusalem.' "

18ª And I lifted my eyes and saw, and behold, four horns! 19And I said to the angel who talked with me, "What are these?" And he answered me, "These are the horns which have scattered Judah, Israel, and Jerusalem." 20 Then the LORD showed me four smiths. 21And I said, "What are these coming to do?" He answered, "These are the horns which scattered Judah, so that no man raised his head; and these have come to terrify them, to cast down the horns of the nations who lifted up their horns against the land of Judah to scatter it."

2ᵇ And I lifted my eyes and saw, and behold, a man with a measuring line in his hand! 2 Then I said, "Where are you going?" And he said to me, "To measure Jerusalem, to see what is its breadth and what is its length." 3And behold, the angel who talked with me came forward, and another angel came forward to meet him, 4 and said to him, "Run, say to that young man, 'Jerusalem shall be inhabited as villages without walls, because of the multitude of men and cattle in it. 5 For I will be to her a wall of fire round about, says the LORD, and I will be the glory within her.' "

6 Ho! ho! Flee from the land of the north, says the LORD; for I have spread you abroad as the four winds of the heavens, says the LORD. 7 Ho! Escape to Zion, you who dwell with the daughter of Babylon. 8 For thus said the LORD of hosts, after his glory sent me to the nations who plundered you, for he who touches you touches the apple of his eye: 9 "Behold, I will shake my hand over them, and they shall become plunder for those who served them. Then you will know that the LORD of hosts has sent me. 10 Sing and rejoice, O daughter of Zion; for lo, I come and I will dwell in the midst of you, says the LORD. 11And many nations shall join themselves to the LORD

in that day, and shall be my people; and I will dwell in the midst of you, and you shall know that the LORD of hosts has sent me to you. 12And the LORD will inherit Judah as his portion in the holy land, and will again choose Jerusalem."

13 Be silent, all flesh, before the LORD; for he has roused himself from his holy dwelling.

3 Then he showed me Joshua the high priest standing before the angel of the LORD, and Satan standing at his right hand to accuse him. 2And the LORD said to Satan, "The LORD rebuke you, O Satan! The LORD who has chosen Jerusalem rebuke you! Is not this a brand plucked from the fire?" 3 Now Joshua was standing before the angel, clothed with filthy garments. 4And the angel said to those who were standing before him, "Remove the filthy garments from him." And to him he said, "Behold, I have taken your iniquity away from you, and I will clothe you with rich apparel." 5And I said, "Let them put a clean turban on his head." So they put a clean turban on his head and clothed him with garments; and the angel of the LORD was standing by.

6 And the angel of the LORD enjoined Joshua, 7 "Thus says the LORD of hosts: If you will walk in my ways and keep my charge, then you shall rule my house and have charge of my courts, and I will give you the right of access among those who are standing here. 8 Hear now, O Joshua the high priest, you and your friends who sit before you, for they are men of good omen: behold, I will bring my servant the Branch. 9 For behold, upon the stone which I have set before Joshua, upon a single stone with seven facets, I will engrave its inscription, says the LORD of hosts, and I will remove the guilt of this land in a single day. 10 In that day, says the LORD of hosts, every one of you will invite his neighbor under his vine and under his fig tree."

4 And the angel who talked with me came again, and waked me, like a man that is wakened out of his sleep. 2And he said to me, "What do you see?" I said, "I see, and behold, a lampstand all of gold, with a bowl on the top of it, and seven lamps on it, with seven lips on each of the lamps which are on the top of it. 3And there are two olive trees by it, one on the right of the bowl and the other on its

---

ª Ch 2.1 in Heb   ᵇ Ch 2.5 in Heb

2.13: Hab 2.20; Zeph 1.7.   **3.2:** Jude 9.   **3.8:** Is 4.2; Jer 23.5; 33.15; Zech 6.12.
3.10: Mic 4.4.   **4.3, 11–14:** Rev 11.4.

left." ⁴And I said to the angel who talked with me, "What are these, my lord?" ⁵ Then the angel who talked with me answered me, "Do you not know what these are?" I said, "No, my lord." ⁶ Then he said to me, "This is the word of the LORD to Ze·rub′ba·bel: Not by might, nor by power, but by my Spirit, says the LORD of hosts. ⁷ What are you, O great mountain? Before Ze·rub′ba·bel you shall become a plain; and he shall bring forward the top stone amid shouts of 'Grace, grace to it!' " ⁸ Moreover the word of the LORD came to me, saying, ⁹ "The hands of Ze·rub′ba·bel have laid the foundation of this house; his hands shall also complete it. Then you will know that the LORD of hosts has sent me to you. ¹⁰ For whoever has despised the day of small things shall rejoice, and shall see the plummet in the hand of Ze·rub′ba·bel.

"These seven are the eyes of the LORD, which range through the whole earth." ¹¹ Then I said to him, "What are these two olive trees on the right and the left of the lampstand?" ¹²And a second time I said to him, "What are these two branches of the olive trees, which are beside the two golden pipes from which the oil*c* is poured out?" ¹³ He said to me, "Do you not know what these are?" I said, "No, my lord." ¹⁴ Then he said, "These are the two anointed who stand by the Lord of the whole earth."

5 Again I lifted my eyes and saw, and behold, a flying scroll! ²And he said to me, "What do you see?" I answered, "I see a flying scroll; its length is twenty cubits, and its breadth ten cubits." ³ Then he said to me, "This is the curse that goes out over the face of the whole land; for every one who steals shall be cut off henceforth according to it, and every one who swears falsely shall be cut off henceforth according to it. ⁴ I will send it forth, says the LORD of hosts, and it shall enter the house of the thief, and the house of him who swears falsely by my name; and it shall abide in his house and consume it, both timber and stones."

⁵ Then the angel who talked with me came forward and said to me, "Lift your eyes, and see what this is that goes forth." ⁶And I said, "What is it?" He said, "This is the ephah that

goes forth." And he said, "This is their iniquity*d* in all the land." ⁷And behold, the leaden cover was lifted, and there was a woman sitting in the ephah! ⁸And he said, "This is Wickedness." And he thrust her back into the ephah, and thrust down the leaden weight upon its mouth. ⁹ Then I lifted my eyes and saw, and behold, two women coming forward! The wind was in their wings; they had wings like the wings of a stork, and they lifted up the ephah between earth and heaven. ¹⁰ Then I said to the angel who talked with me, "Where are they taking the ephah?" ¹¹ He said to me, "To the land of Shi′när, to build a house for it; and when this is prepared, they will set the ephah down there on its base."

6 And again I lifted my eyes and saw, and behold, four chariots came out from between two mountains; and the mountains were mountains of bronze. ² The first chariot had red horses, the second black horses, ³ the third white horses, and the fourth chariot dappled gray*e* horses. ⁴ Then I said to the angel who talked with me, "What are these, my lord?" ⁵And the angel answered me, "These are going forth to the four winds of heaven, after presenting themselves before the LORD of all the earth. ⁶ The chariot with the black horses goes toward the north country, the white ones go toward the west country,*f* and the dappled ones go toward the south country." ⁷ When the steeds came out, they were impatient to get off and patrol the earth. And he said, "Go, patrol the earth." So they patrolled the earth. ⁸ Then he cried to me, "Behold, those who go toward the north country have set my Spirit at rest in the north country."

⁹ And the word of the LORD came to me: ¹⁰ "Take from the exiles Hel′däi, Tō·bi′jäh, and Je·däi′äh, who have arrived from Babylon; and go the same day to the house of Jō·si′äh, the son of Zeph·a·ni′äh. ¹¹ Take from them silver and gold, and make a crown,*g* and set it upon the head of Joshua, the son of Je·hoz′a·dak, the high priest; ¹² and say to him, 'Thus says the LORD of hosts, "Behold, the man whose name is the Branch: for he shall grow up in his place, and he shall build the temple of the LORD. ¹³ It is he who shall build the temple of the LORD, and shall bear royal honor, and shall sit and rule upon

c Cn: Heb *gold*   *d* Gk Compare Syr: Heb *eye*
e Compare Gk: The meaning of the Hebrew word is uncertain   *f* Cn: Heb *after them*
g Gk Mss: Heb *crowns*

4.10: Rev 5.6.   **6.1-3:** Rev 6.2-8.   **6.5:** Rev 7.1.
6.12: Zech 3.8; Is 4.2; Jer 23.5; 33.15.

his throne. And there shall be a priest by his throne, and peaceful understanding shall be between them both." ' 14And the crown[h] shall be in the temple of the LORD as a reminder to Hel'däi[i], Tō·bi'jàh, Je·däi'àh, and Jō·si'àh[j] the son of Zeph·à·ni'àh.

15 "And those who are far off shall come and help to build the temple of the LORD; and you shall know that the LORD of hosts has sent me to you. And this shall come to pass, if you will diligently obey the voice of the LORD your God."

7 In the fourth year of King Dà·rī'-ùs, the word of the LORD came to Zech·à·ri'àh in the fourth day of the ninth month, which is Chis'lev. 2 Now the people of Beth'él had sent Shà·rē'-zèr and Reg'em-mel'ech and their men, to entreat the favor of the LORD, 3 and to ask the priests of the house of the LORD of hosts and the prophets, "Should I mourn and fast in the fifth month, as I have done for so many years?" 4 Then the word of the LORD of hosts came to me; 5 "Say to all the people of the land and the priests, When you fasted and mourned in the fifth month and in the seventh, for these seventy years, was it for me that you fasted? 6And when you eat and when you drink, do you not eat for yourselves and drink for yourselves? 7 When Jerusalem was inhabited and in prosperity, with her cities round about her, and the South and the lowland were inhabited, were not these the words which the LORD proclaimed by the former prophets?"

8 And the word of the LORD came to Zech·à·ri'àh, saying, 9 "Thus says the LORD of hosts, Render true judgments, show kindness and mercy each to his brother, 10 do not oppress the widow, the fatherless, the sojourner, or the poor; and let none of you devise evil against his brother in your heart." 11 But they refused to hearken, and turned a stubborn shoulder, and stopped their ears that they might not hear. 12 They made their hearts like adamant lest they should hear the law and the words which the LORD of hosts had sent by his Spirit through the former prophets. Therefore great wrath came from the LORD of hosts. 13 "As I called, and they would not hear, so they called, and I would not hear," says the LORD of hosts, 14 "and I scattered them with a whirlwind among all the nations which they had not known. Thus the land they left was desolate, so that no one went to and

fro, and the pleasant land was made desolate."

8 And the word of the LORD of hosts came to me, saying, 2 "Thus says the LORD of hosts: I am jealous for Zion with great jealousy, and I am jealous for her with great wrath. 3 Thus says the LORD: I will return to Zion, and will dwell in the midst of Jerusalem, and Jerusalem shall be called the faithful city, and the mountain of the LORD of hosts, the holy mountain. 4 Thus says the LORD of hosts: Old men and old women shall again sit in the streets of Jerusalem, each with staff in hand for very age. 5And the streets of the city shall be full of boys and girls playing in its streets. 6 Thus says the LORD of hosts: If it is marvelous in the sight of the remnant of this people in these days, should it also be marvelous in my sight, says the LORD of hosts? 7 Thus says the LORD of hosts: Behold, I will save my people from the east country and from the west country; 8 and I will bring them to dwell in the midst of Jerusalem; and they shall be my people and I will be their God, in faithfulness and in righteousness."

9 Thus says the LORD of hosts: "Let your hands be strong, you who in these days have been hearing these words from the mouth of the prophets, since the day that the foundation of the house of the LORD of hosts was laid, that the temple might be built. 10 For before those days there was no wage for man or any wage for beast, neither was there any safety from the foe for him who went out or came in; for I set every man against his fellow. 11 But now I will not deal with the remnant of this people as in the former days, says the LORD of hosts. 12 For there shall be a sowing of peace; the vine shall yield its fruit, and the ground shall give its increase, and the heavens shall give their dew; and I will cause the remnant of this people to possess all these things. 13And as you have been a byword of cursing among the nations, O house of Judah and house of Israel, so will I save you and you shall be a blessing. Fear not, but let your hands be strong."

14 For thus says the LORD of hosts: "As I purposed to do evil to you, when your fathers provoked me to wrath, and I did not relent, says the LORD of hosts, 15 so again have I purposed in these days to do good to Jerusalem and to the house of Judah; fear not. 16 These are the things that you shall do: Speak

[h] Gk: Heb *crowns*   [i] With verse 10: Heb *Helem*   [j] With verse 10: Heb *Hen*   **8.16:** Eph 4.25.

the truth to one another, render in your gates judgments that are true and make for peace, 17 do not devise evil in your hearts against one another, and love no false oath, for all these things I hate, says the LORD."

18 And the word of the LORD of hosts came to me, saying, 19 "Thus says the LORD of hosts: The fast of the fourth month, and the fast of the fifth, and the fast of the seventh, and the fast of the tenth, shall be to the house of Judah seasons of joy and gladness, and cheerful feasts; therefore love truth and peace.

20 "Thus says the LORD of hosts: Peoples shall yet come, even the inhabitants of many cities; 21 the inhabitants of one city shall go to another, saying, 'Let us go at once to entreat the favor of the LORD, and to seek the LORD of hosts; I am going.' 22 Many peoples and strong nations shall come to seek the LORD of hosts in Jerusalem, and to entreat the favor of the LORD. 23 Thus says the LORD of hosts: In those days ten men from the nations of every tongue shall take hold of the robe of a Jew, saying, 'Let us go with you, for we have heard that God is with you.' "

9   An Oracle

The word of the LORD is against
   the land of Had′rach
and will rest upon Damascus.
For to the LORD belong the cities of
   Ar′am,[k]
   even as all the tribes of Israel;
2 Hā′math also, which borders thereon,
   Tyre and Si′don, though they are
     very wise.
3 Tyre has built herself a rampart,
   and heaped up silver like dust,
   and gold like the dirt of the
     streets.
4 But lo, the Lord will strip her of her
   possessions
   and hurl her wealth into the
     sea,
and she shall be devoured by fire.

5 Ash′kė·lon shall see it, and be afraid;
   Gā′za too, and shall writhe in
     anguish;
   Ek′ron also, because its hopes are
     confounded.
The king shall perish from Gaza;
   Ashkelon shall be uninhabited;
6 a mongrel people shall dwell in
   Ash′dod;

and I will make an end of the
   pride of Phi·lis′ti·à.
7 I will take away its blood from its
   mouth,
   and its abominations from be-
     tween its teeth;
it too shall be a remnant for our God;
   it shall be like a clan in Judah,
   and Ek′ron shall be like the
     Jeb′u·sites.
8 Then I will encamp at my house as
   a guard,
   so that none shall march to and
     fro;
no oppressor shall again overrun
   them,
   for now I see with my own eyes.

9 Rejoice greatly, O daughter of Zion!
   Shout aloud, O daughter of Je-
     rusalem!
Lo, your king comes to you;
   triumphant and victorious is he,
humble and riding on an ass,
   on a colt the foal of an ass.
10 I will cut off the chariot from
   E′phra·im
   and the war horse from Jeru-
     salem;
and the battle bow shall be cut off,
   and he shall command peace to
     the nations;
his dominion shall be from sea to
   sea,
   and from the River to the ends of
     the earth.

11 As for you also, because of the blood
   of my covenant with you,
   I will set your captives free from
     the waterless pit.
12 Return to your stronghold, O
   prisoners of hope;
today I declare that I will restore
   to you double.
13 For I have bent Judah as my bow;
   I have made E′phra·im its arrow.
I will brandish your sons, O Zion,
   over your sons, O Greece,
   and wield you like a warrior's
     sword.

14 Then the LORD will appear over
   them,
   and his arrow go forth like
     lightning;
the Lord GOD will sound the
   trumpet,
   and march forth in the whirlwinds
     of the south.
15 The LORD of hosts will protect them,
   and they shall devour and tread
     down the slingers;[l]

k Cn: Heb *the eye of Adam* (or *man*)   *l* Cn: Heb *the slingstones*
9.9: Mt 21.5; Jn 12.15.

and they shall drink their blood[m]
   like wine,
and be full like a bowl,
   drenched like the corners of the
     altar.

16 On that day the LORD their God
   will save them
   for they are the flock of his
     people;
for like the jewels of a crown
   they shall shine on his land.
17 Yea, how good and how fair it shall
   be!
Grain shall make the young men
   flourish,
and new wine the maidens.

10 Ask rain from the LORD
   in the season of the spring
     rain,
from the LORD who makes the storm
   clouds,
who gives men showers of rain,
   to every one the vegetation in the
     field.
2 For the teraphim utter nonsense,
   and the diviners see lies;
the dreamers tell false dreams,
   and give empty consolation.
Therefore the people wander like
   sheep;
they are afflicted for want of a
   shepherd.

3 "My anger is hot against the shepherds,
and I will punish the leaders;[n]
for the LORD of hosts cares for his
   flock, the house of Judah,
and will make them like his proud
   steed in battle.
4 Out of them shall come the cornerstone,
out of them the tent peg,
out of them the battle bow,
   out of them every ruler.
5 Together they shall be like mighty
   men in battle,
trampling the foe in the mud of
   the streets;
they shall fight because the LORD is
   with them,
and they shall confound the riders
   on horses.

6 "I will strengthen the house of
   Judah,
and I will save the house of
   Joseph.
I will bring them back because I
   have compassion on them,
and they shall be as though I had
   not rejected them;

for I am the LORD their God and
   I will answer them.
7 Then E'phra-im shall become like a
   mighty warrior,
and their hearts shall be glad as
   with wine.
Their children shall see it and rejoice,
their hearts shall exult in the
   LORD.

8 "I will signal for them and gather
   them in,
for I have redeemed them,
   and they shall be as many as of
     old.
9 Though I scattered them among the
   nations,
yet in far countries they shall
   remember me,
and with their children they shall
   live and return.
10 I will bring them home from the
   land of Egypt,
and gather them from Assyria;
and I will bring them to the land of
   Gilead and to Lebanon,
till there is no room for them.
11 They shall pass through the sea of
   Egypt,[o]
and the waves of the sea shall be
   smitten,
and all the depths of the Nile
   dried up.
The pride of Assyria shall be laid
   low,
and the scepter of Egypt shall
   depart.
12 I will make them strong in the
   LORD
and they shall glory[p] in his name,"
   says the LORD.

11 Open your doors, O Lebanon,
   that the fire may devour your
     cedars!
2 Wail, O cypress, for the cedar has
   fallen,
for the glorious trees are ruined!
Wail, oaks of Ba'shan,
   for the thick forest has been
     felled!
3 Hark, the wail of the shepherds,
   for their glory is despoiled!
Hark, the roar of the lions,
   for the jungle of the Jordan is
     laid waste!

4 Thus said the LORD my God:
"Become shepherd of the flock doomed
to slaughter. 5 Those who buy them
slay them and go unpunished; and
those who sell them say, 'Blessed be
the LORD, I have become rich'; and

their own shepherds have no pity on them. 6 For I will no longer have pity on the inhabitants of this land, says the LORD. Lo, I will cause men to fall each into the hand of his shepherd, and each into the hand of his king; and they shall crush the earth, and I will deliver none from their hand."

7 So I became the shepherd of the flock doomed to be slain for those who trafficked in the sheep. And I took two staffs; one I named Grace, the other I named Union. And I tended the sheep. 8 In one month I destroyed the three shepherds. But I became impatient with them, and they also detested me. 9 So I said, "I will not be your shepherd. What is to die, let it die; what is to be destroyed, let it be destroyed; and let those that are left devour the flesh of one another." 10And I took my staff Grace, and I broke it, annulling the covenant which I had made with all the peoples. 11 So it was annulled on that day, and the traffickers in the sheep, who were watching me, knew that it was the word of the LORD. 12 Then I said to them, "If it seems right to you, give me my wages; but if not, keep them." And they weighed out as my wages thirty shekels of silver. 13 Then the LORD said to me, "Cast it into the treasury"*q*—the lordly price at which I was paid off by them. So I took the thirty shekels of silver and cast them into the treasury*q* in the house of the LORD. 14 Then I broke my second staff Union, annulling the brotherhood between Judah and Israel.

15 Then the LORD said to me, "Take once more the implements of a worthless shepherd. 16 For lo, I am raising up in the land a shepherd who does not care for the perishing, or seek the wandering,*r* or heal the maimed, or nourish the sound, but devours the flesh of the fat ones, tearing off even their hoofs.

17 Woe to my worthless shepherd,
who deserts the flock!
May the sword smite his arm
and his right eye!
Let his arm be wholly withered,
his right eye utterly blinded!"

12 An Oracle

The word of the LORD concerning Israel: Thus says the LORD, who stretched out the heavens and founded the earth and formed the spirit of man within him: 2 "Lo, I am about to make Jerusalem a cup of reeling to all the

peoples round about; it will be against Judah also in the siege against Jerusalem. 3 On that day I will make Jerusalem a heavy stone for all the peoples; all who lift it shall grievously hurt themselves. And all the nations of the earth will come together against it. 4 On that day, says the LORD, I will strike every horse with panic, and its rider with madness. But upon the house of Judah I will open my eyes, when I strike every horse of the peoples with blindness. 5 Then the clans of Judah shall say to themselves, 'The inhabitants of Jerusalem have strength through the LORD of hosts, their God.'

6 "On that day I will make the clans of Judah like a blazing pot in the midst of wood, like a flaming torch among sheaves; and they shall devour to the right and to the left all the peoples round about, while Jerusalem shall still be inhabited in its place, in Jerusalem.

7 "And the LORD will give victory to the tents of Judah first, that the glory of the house of David and the glory of the inhabitants of Jerusalem may not be exalted over that of Judah. 8 On that day the LORD will put a shield about the inhabitants of Jerusalem so that the feeblest among them on that day shall be like David, and the house of David shall be like God, like the angel of the LORD, at their head. 9And on that day I will seek to destroy all the nations that come against Jerusalem.

10 "And I will pour out on the house of David and the inhabitants of Jerusalem a spirit of compassion and supplication, so that, when they look on him whom they have pierced, they shall mourn for him, as one mourns for an only child, and weep bitterly over him, as one weeps over a firstborn. 11 On that day the mourning in Jerusalem will be as great as the mourning for Hā'dad-rim'mon in the plain of Mĕ.gid'dō. 12 The land shall mourn, each family by itself; the family of the house of David by itself, and their wives by themselves; the family of the house of Nathan by itself, and their wives by themselves; 13 the family of the house of Levi by itself, and their wives by themselves; the family of the Shim'ē-ites by itself, and their wives by themselves; 14 and all the families that are left, each by itself, and their wives by themselves.

13

"On that day there shall be a fountain opened for the house of

q Syr: Heb *to the potter* *r* Syr Compare Gk Vg: Heb *the youth*
11.12-13: Mt 26.15; 27.9. 12.10: Jn 19.37.

David and the inhabitants of Jerusalem to cleanse them from sin and uncleanness.

2 "And on that day, says the LORD of hosts, I will cut off the names of the idols from the land, so that they shall be remembered no more; and also I will remove from the land the prophets and the unclean spirit. 3And if any one again appears as a prophet, his father and mother who bore him will say to him, 'You shall not live, for you speak lies in the name of the LORD'; and his father and mother who bore him shall pierce him through when he prophesies. 4 On that day every prophet will be ashamed of his vision when he prophesies; he will not put on a hairy mantle in order to deceive, 5 but he will say, 'I am no prophet, I am a tiller of the soil; for the land has been my possession[t] since my youth.' 6And if one asks him, 'What are these wounds on your back?' he will say, 'The wounds I received in the house of my friends.'"

7 "Awake, O sword, against my shepherd,
    against the man who stands next to me,"
            says the LORD of hosts.
"Strike the shepherd, that the sheep may be scattered;
    I will turn my hand against the little ones.
8 In the whole land, says the LORD, two thirds shall be cut off and perish,
    and one third shall be left alive.
9 And I will put this third into the fire,
    and refine them as one refines silver,
    and test them as gold is tested.
They will call on my name,
    and I will answer them.
I will say, 'They are my people';
    and they will say, 'The LORD is my God.'"

14 Behold, a day of the LORD is coming, when the spoil taken from you will be divided in the midst of you. 2 For I will gather all the nations against Jerusalem to battle, and the city shall be taken and the houses plundered and the women ravished; half of the city shall go into exile, but the rest of the people shall not be cut off from the city. 3 Then the LORD will go forth and fight against those nations as when he fights on a day of battle. 4 On that day his feet shall stand on the Mount of Olives which lies before Jerusalem on the east; and the Mount of Olives shall be split in two from east to west by a very wide valley; so that one half of the Mount shall withdraw northward, and the other half southward. 5And the valley of my mountains shall be stopped up, for the valley of the mountains shall touch the side of it; and you shall flee as you fled from the earthquake in the days of Uz·zi'ah king of Judah. Then the LORD your[u] God will come, and all the holy ones with him.[v]

6 On that day there shall be neither cold nor frost.[w] 7And there shall be continuous day (it is known to the LORD), not day and not night, for at evening time there shall be light.

8 On that day living waters shall flow out from Jerusalem, half of them to the eastern sea and half of them to the western sea; it shall continue in summer as in winter.

9 And the LORD will become king over all the earth; on that day the LORD will be one and his name one.

10 The whole land shall be turned into a plain from Gē'bā to Rim'mon south of Jerusalem. But Jerusalem shall remain aloft upon its site from the Gate of Benjamin to the place of the former gate, to the Corner Gate, and from the Tower of Hā·nan'el to the king's wine presses. 11And it shall be inhabited, for there shall be no more curse;[x] Jerusalem shall dwell in security.

12 And this shall be the plague with which the LORD will smite all the peoples that wage war against Jerusalem: their flesh shall rot while they are still on their feet, their eyes shall rot in their sockets, and their tongues shall rot in their mouths. 13And on that day a great panic from the LORD shall fall on them, so that each will lay hold on the hand of his fellow, and the hand of the one will be raised against the hand of the other; 14 even Judah will fight against Jerusalem. And the wealth of all the nations round about shall be collected, gold, silver, and garments in great abundance. 15And a plague like this plague shall fall on the horses, the mules, the camels, the asses, and whatever beasts may be in those camps.

16 Then every one that survives of all the nations that have come against

t Cn: Heb *for man has caused me to possess*   u Heb *my*   v Gk Syr Vg Tg: Heb *you*
w Compare Gk Syr Vg Tg: Heb uncertain   x Or *ban of utter destruction*
13.7: Mt 26.31; Mk 14.27.   **14.8:** Ezek 47.1-12; Rev 22.1-2.   **14.11:** Rev 22.3.

Jerusalem shall go up year after year to worship the King, the LORD of hosts, and to keep the feast of booths. [17]And if any of the families of the earth do not go up to Jerusalem to worship the King, the LORD of hosts, there will be no rain upon them. [18]And if the family of Egypt do not go up and present themselves, then upon them shall[y] come the plague with which the LORD afflicts the nations that do not go up to keep the feast of booths. [19] This shall be the punishment to Egypt and the punishment to all the nations that do not go up to keep the feast of booths.

[20] And on that day there shall be inscribed on the bells of the horses, "Holy to the LORD." And the pots in the house of the LORD shall be as the bowls before the altar; [21] and every pot in Jerusalem and Judah shall be sacred to the LORD of hosts, so that all who sacrifice may come and take of them and boil the flesh of the sacrifice in them. And there shall no longer be a trader in the house of the LORD of hosts on that day.

THE BOOK OF

MALACHI

1 The oracle of the word of the LORD to Israel by Mal′a·chi.[a]
[2] "I have loved you," says the LORD. But you say, "How hast thou loved us?" "Is not Esau Jacob's brother?" says the LORD. "Yet I have loved Jacob [3] but I have hated Esau; I have laid waste his hill country and left his heritage to jackals of the desert." [4] If E′dom says, "We are shattered but we will rebuild the ruins," the LORD of hosts says, "They may build, but I will tear down, till they are called the wicked country, the people with whom the LORD is angry for ever." [5] Your own eyes shall see this, and you shall say, "Great is the LORD, beyond the border of Israel!"

[6] "A son honors his father, and a servant his master. If then I am a father, where is my honor? And if I am a master, where is my fear? says the LORD of hosts to you, O priests, who despise my name. You say, 'How have we despised thy name?' [7] By offering polluted food upon my altar. And you say, 'How have we polluted it?'[b] By thinking that the LORD's table may be despised. [8] When you offer blind animals in sacrifice, is that no evil? And when you offer those that are lame or sick, is that no evil? Present that to your governor; will he be pleased with you or show you favor? says the LORD of hosts. [9]And now

entreat the favor of God, that he may be gracious to us. With such a gift from your hand, will he show favor to any of you? says the LORD of hosts. [10] Oh, that there were one among you who would shut the doors, that you might not kindle fire upon my altar in vain! I have no pleasure in you, says the LORD of hosts, and I will not accept an offering from your hand. [11] For from the rising of the sun to its setting my name is great among the nations, and in every place incense is offered to my name, and a pure offering; for my name is great among the nations, says the LORD of hosts. [12] But you profane it when you say that the LORD's table is polluted, and the food for it[c] may be despised. [13] 'What a weariness this is,' you say, and you sniff at me,[d] says the LORD of hosts. You bring what has been taken by violence or is lame or sick, and this you bring as your offering! Shall I accept that from your hand? says the LORD. [14] Cursed be the cheat who has a male in his flock, and vows it, and yet sacrifices to the Lord what is blemished; for I am a great King, says the LORD of hosts, and my name is feared among the nations.

2 "And now, O priests, this command is for you. [2] If you will not listen, if you will not lay it to heart to give glory to my name, says the LORD of hosts, then I will send the curse

[y] Gk Syr: Heb *shall not*
[a] Or *my messenger*   [b] Gk: Heb *thee*   [c] Heb *its fruit, its food*   [d] Another reading is *it*
14.18-19: Is 19; Jer 46; Ezek 29-32.   **1.2-3:** Rom 9.13.
1.2-5: Is 34; 63.1-6; Jer 49.7-22; Ezek 25.12-14; 35; Amos 1.11-12; Obad.

upon you and I will curse your blessings; indeed I have already cursed them, because you do not lay it to heart. ³ Behold, I will rebuke your offspring, and spread dung upon your faces, the dung of your offerings, and I will put you out of my presence.ᵉ ⁴ So shall you know that I have sent this command to you, that my covenant with Levi may hold, says the LORD of hosts. ⁵ My covenant with him was a covenant of life and peace, and I gave them to him, that he might fear; and he feared me, he stood in awe of my name. ⁶ True instructionᶠ was in his mouth, and no wrong was found on his lips. He walked with me in peace and uprightness, and he turned many from iniquity. ⁷ For the lips of a priest should guard knowledge, and men should seek instructionᶠ from his mouth, for he is the messenger of the LORD of hosts. ⁸ But you have turned aside from the way; you have caused many to stumble by your instruction;ᶠ you have corrupted the covenant of Levi, says the LORD of hosts, ⁹ and so I make you despised and abased before all the people, inasmuch as you have not kept my ways but have shown partiality in your instruction."ᶠ

¹⁰ Have we not all one father? Has not one God created us? Why then are we faithless to one another, profaning the covenant of our fathers? ¹¹ Judah has been faithless, and abomination has been committed in Israel and in Jerusalem; for Judah has profaned the sanctuary of the LORD, which he loves, and has married the daughter of a foreign god. ¹² May the LORD cut off from the tents of Jacob, for the man who does this, any to witnessᵍ or answer, or to bring an offering to the LORD of hosts!

¹³ And this again you do. You cover the LORD's altar with tears, with weeping and groaning because he no longer regards the offering or accepts it with favor at your hand. ¹⁴ You ask, "Why does he not?" Because the LORD was witness to the covenant between you and the wife of your youth, to whom you have been faithless, though she is your companion and your wife by covenant. ¹⁵ Has not the one God madeʰ and sustained for us the spirit of life?ⁱ And what does he desire? Godly offspring. So take heed to yourselves, and let none be faithless to the wife of his youth. ¹⁶ "For I hateⁱ

divorce, says the LORD the God of Israel, and covering one's garment with violence, says the LORD of hosts. So take heed to yourselves and do not be faithless."

¹⁷ You have wearied the LORD with your words. Yet you say, "How have we wearied him?" By saying, "Every one who does evil is good in the sight of the LORD, and he delights in them." Or by asking, "Where is the God of justice?"

3 "Behold, I send my messenger to prepare the way before me, and the Lord whom you seek will suddenly come to his temple; the messenger of the covenant in whom you delight, behold, he is coming, says the LORD of hosts. ² But who can endure the day of his coming, and who can stand when he appears?

"For he is like a refiner's fire and like fullers' soap; ³ he will sit as a refiner and purifier of silver, and he will purify the sons of Levi and refine them like gold and silver, till they present right offerings to the LORD. ⁴ Then the offering of Judah and Jerusalem will be pleasing to the LORD as in the days of old and as in former years.

⁵ "Then I will draw near to you for judgment; I will be a swift witness against the sorcerers, against the adulterers, against those who swear falsely, against those who oppress the hireling in his wages, the widow and the orphan, against those who thrust aside the sojourner, and do not fear me, says the LORD of hosts.

⁶ "For I the LORD do not change; therefore you, O sons of Jacob, are not consumed. ⁷ From the days of your fathers you have turned aside from my statutes and have not kept them. Return to me, and I will return to you, says the LORD of hosts. But you say, 'How shall we return?' ⁸ Will man rob God? Yet you are robbing me. But you say, 'How are we robbing thee?' In your tithes and offerings. ⁹ You are cursed with a curse, for you are robbing me; the whole nation of you. ¹⁰ Bring the full tithes into the storehouse, that there may be food in my house; and thereby put me to the test, says the LORD of hosts, if I will not open the windows of heaven for you and pour down for you an overflowing blessing. ¹¹ I will rebuke the devourerᵏ for you, so that it will not destroy the fruits of your soil; and your vine in the

---

ᵉ Cn Compare Gk Syr: Heb *and he shall bear you to it*   ᶠ Or *law*
ᵍ Cn Compare Gk: Heb *arouse*   ʰ Or *has he not made one?*
ⁱ Cn: Heb *and a remnant of spirit was his*   ⁱ Cn: Heb *he hates*   ᵏ Or *devouring locust*
3.1: Mt 11.10; Mk 1.2; Lk 1.17, 76; 7.27.   **3.2:** Rev 6.17.

field shall not fail to bear, says the LORD of hosts. 12 Then all nations will call you blessed, for you will be a land of delight, says the LORD of hosts.

13 "Your words have been stout against me, says the LORD. Yet you say, 'How have we spoken against thee?' 14 You have said, 'It is vain to serve God. What is the good of our keeping his charge or of walking as in mourning before the LORD of hosts? 15 Henceforth we deem the arrogant blessed; evildoers not only prosper but when they put God to the test they escape.'"

16 Then those who feared the LORD spoke with one another; the LORD heeded and heard them, and a book of remembrance was written before him of those who feared the LORD and thought on his name. 17 "They shall be mine, says the LORD of hosts, my special possession on the day when I act, and I will spare them as a man spares his son who serves him. 18 Then once more you shall distinguish between the righteous and the wicked,

between one who serves God and one who does not serve him.

4 "For behold, the day comes, burning like an oven, when all the arrogant and all evildoers will be stubble; the day that comes shall burn them up, says the LORD of hosts, so that it will leave them neither root nor branch. 2 But for you who fear my name the sun of righteousness shall rise, with healing in its wings. You shall go forth leaping like calves from the stall. 3 And you shall tread down the wicked, for they will be ashes under the soles of your feet, on the day when I act, says the LORD of hosts.

4 "Remember the law of my servant Moses, the statutes and ordinances that I commanded him at Hō'reb for all Israel.

5 "Behold, I will send you E·li'jah the prophet before the great and terrible day of the LORD comes. 6 And he will turn the hearts of fathers to their children and the hearts of children to their fathers, lest I come and smite the land with a curse."*m*

---

l Ch 4.1-6 are Ch 3.19-24 in the Hebrew   *m* Or *ban of utter destruction*
4.5: Mt 17.11; Mk 9.12.   **4.6:** Lk 1.17.

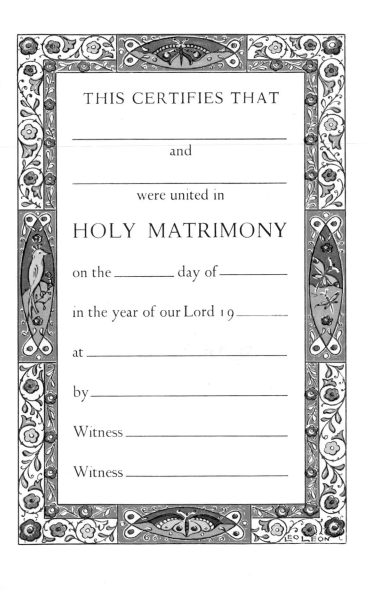

THIS CERTIFIES THAT

_____

and

_____

were united in

HOLY MATRIMONY

on the _____ day of _____

in the year of our Lord 19_____

at _____

by_____

Witness _____

Witness _____

BIRTHS

MARRIAGES

DEATHS

_____

_____

_____

_____

_____

_____

_____

_____

_____

_____

_____

THE
New Testament

OF OUR LORD AND SAVIOR

JESUS CHRIST

REVISED STANDARD VERSION

Red Letter Edition

THE

New Testament

OF OUR LORD AND SAVIOR

JESUS CHRIST

REVISED STANDARD VERSION

Red Letter Edition

THE GOSPEL ACCORDING TO

MATTHEW

The book of the genealogy of Jesus Christ, the son of David, the son of Abraham.

2 Abraham was the father of Isaac, and Isaac the father of Jacob, and Jacob the father of Judah and his brothers, 3 and Judah the father of Per′ez and Ze′rah by Ta′mar, and Perez the father of Hez′ron, and Hezron the father of Ram,ᵃ 4 and Ramᵃ the father of Am·min′a·dab, and Amminadab the father of Nah′shon, and Nahshon the father of Sal′mon, 5 and Sal′mon the father of Bo′az by Ra′hab, and Boaz the father of O′bed by Ruth, and Obed the father of Jesse, 6 Jesse the father of David the king.

And David was the father of Solomon by the wife of U·ri′ah, 7 and Solomon the father of Re·ho·bo′am, and Rehoboam the father of A·bi′jah, and Abijah the father of Asa,ᵇ 8 and Asaᵇ the father of Je·hosh′a·phat, and Jehoshaphat the father of Jo′ram, and Joram the father of Uz·zi′ah, 9 and Uzzi′ah the father of Jo′tham, and Jotham the father of A′haz, and Ahaz the father of Hez·e·ki′ah, 10 and Hez·e·ki′ah the father of Ma·nas′seh, and Manasseh the father of Amos,ᶜ and Amosᶜ the father of Jo·si′ah, 11 and Jo·si′ah the father of Jech·o·ni′ah and his brothers, at the time of the deportation to Babylon.

12 And after the deportation to Babylon: Jech·o·ni′ah was the father of She·al′ti·el,ᵈ and She-alti-elᵈ the father of Ze·rub′ba·bel, 13 and Ze·rub′ba·bel the father of A·bi′ud, and Abiud the father of E·li′a·kim, and Eliakim the father of A′zor, 14 and A′zor the father of Za′dok, and Zadok the father of A′chim, and Achim the father of E·li′ud, 15 and E·li′ud the father of El·e·a′zar, and Eleazar the father of Mat′than, and Matthan the father of Jacob, 16 and Jacob the father of Joseph the husband of Mary, of whom Jesus was born, who is called Christ.

17 So all the generations from Abraham to David were fourteen generations, and from David to the deportation to Babylon fourteen generations, and from the deportation to Babylon to the Christ fourteen generations.

18 Now the birth of Jesus Christᶠ took place in this way. When his mother Mary had been betrothed to Joseph, before they came together she was found to be with child of the Holy Spirit; 19 and her husband Joseph, being a just man and unwilling to put her to shame, resolved to divorce her quietly. 20 But as he considered this, behold, an angel of the Lord appeared to him in a dream, saying, "Joseph, son of David, do not fear to take Mary your wife, for that which is conceived in her is of the Holy Spirit; 21 she will bear a son, and you shall call his name Jesus, for he will save his people from their sins." 22 All this took place to fulfil what the Lord had spoken by the prophet:

23 "Behold, a virgin shall conceive and bear a son,
and his name shall be called Em·man′u·el"

(which means, God with us). 24 When Joseph woke from sleep, he did as the angel of the Lord commanded him; he took his wife, 25 but knew her not until she had borne a son; and he called his name Jesus.

2 Now when Jesus was born in Bethlehem of Judea in the days of Her′od the king, behold, wise men from the East came to Jerusalem, saying, 2 "Where is he who has been born king of the Jews? For we have seen his star in the East, and have come to worship him." 3 When Her′od the king heard this, he was troubled, and all Jerusalem with him; 4 and assembling all the chief priests and scribes of the people, he inquired of them where the Christ was to be born. 5 They told him, "In Bethlehem of

ᵃ Greek Aram ᵇ Greek Asaph ᶜ Other authorities read Amon ᵈ Greek Salathiel
ᶠ Other ancient authorities read of the Christ
1.1-17: Lk 3.23-38. 1.3-6: Ruth 4.18-22; 1 Chron 2.1-15.
1.11: 2 Kings 24.14; Jer 27.20. 1.18: Lk 1.26-38. 1.21: Lk 2.21; Jn 1.29; Acts 13.23.
1.23: Is 7.14. 2.1: Lk 2.4-7; 1.5.
2.2: Jer 23.5; Zech 9.9; Mk 15.2; Jn 1.49; Num 24.17. 2.5: Jn 7.42.

Judea; for so it is written by the prophet:

6 'And you, O Bethlehem, in the land of Judah,
are by no means least among the rulers of Judah;
for from you shall come a ruler
who will govern my people Israel.'"

7 Then Her′ŏd summoned the wise men secretly and ascertained from them what time the star appeared; 8 and he sent them to Bethlehem, saying, "Go and search diligently for the child, and when you have found him bring me word, that I too may come and worship him." 9 When they had heard the king they went their way; and lo, the star which they had seen in the East went before them, till it came to rest over the place where the child was. 10 When they saw the star, they rejoiced exceedingly with great joy; 11 and going into the house they saw the child with Mary his mother, and they fell down and worshiped him. Then, opening their treasures, they offered him gifts, gold and frankincense and myrrh. 12And being warned in a dream not to return to Her′ŏd, they departed to their own country by another way.

13 Now when they had departed, behold, an angel of the Lord appeared to Joseph in a dream and said, "Rise, take the child and his mother, and flee to Egypt, and remain there till I tell you; for Her′ŏd is about to search for the child, to destroy him." 14And he rose and took the child and his mother by night, and departed to Egypt, 15 and remained there until the death of Her′ŏd. This was to fulfil what the Lord had spoken by the prophet, "Out of Egypt have I called my son."

16 Then Her′ŏd, when he saw that he had been tricked by the wise men, was in a furious rage, and he sent and killed all the male children in Bethlehem and in all that region who were two years old or under, according to the time which he had ascertained from the wise men. 17 Then was fulfilled what was spoken by the prophet Jeremiah:

18 "A voice was heard in Rā′màh,
wailing and loud lamentation,
Rachel weeping for her children;

she refused to be consoled,
because they were no more."

19 But when Her′ŏd died, behold, an angel of the Lord appeared in a dream to Joseph in Egypt, saying, 20 "Rise, take the child and his mother, and go to the land of Israel, for those who sought the child's life are dead." 21And he rose and took the child and his mother, and went to the land of Israel. 22 But when he heard that Ăr·chĕ·lā′ŭs reigned over Judea in place of his father Her′ŏd, he was afraid to go there, and being warned in a dream he withdrew to the district of Galilee. 23And he went and dwelt in a city called Nazareth, that what was spoken by the prophets might be fulfilled, "He shall be called a Nazarene."

3 In those days came John the Baptist, preaching in the wilderness of Judea, 2 "Repent, for the kingdom of heaven is at hand." 3 For this is he who was spoken of by the prophet I·śāi′áh when he said,
"The voice of one crying in the wilderness:
Prepare the way of the Lord,
make his paths straight."

4 Now John wore a garment of camel's hair, and a leather girdle around his waist; and his food was locusts and wild honey. 5 Then went out to him Jerusalem and all Judea and all the region about the Jordan, 6 and they were baptized by him in the river Jordan, confessing their sins.

7 But when he saw many of the Pharisees and Sad′dū·ćeeś coming for baptism, he said to them, "You brood of vipers! Who warned you to flee from the wrath to come? 8 Bear fruit that befits repentance, 9 and do not presume to say to yourselves, 'We have Abraham as our father'; for I tell you, God is able from these stones to raise up children to Abraham. 10 Even now the axe is laid to the root of the trees; every tree therefore that does not bear good fruit is cut down and thrown into the fire.

11 "I baptize you with water for repentance, but he who is coming after me is mightier than I, whose sandals I am not worthy to carry; he will baptize you with the Holy Spirit and with fire. 12 His winnowing fork is in his hand, and he will clear his

2.6: Mic 5.2; Jn 21.16. **2.11:** Mt 1.18; 12.46. **2.12:** Mt 2.22; Acts 10.22; Heb 11.7. **2.15:** Hos 11.1; Ex 4.22. **2.18:** Jer 31.15. **2.19:** Mt 1.20; 2.13. **2.23:** Lk 1.26; Is 11.1; Mk 1.24. **3.1-12:** Mk 1.3-8; Lk 3.2-17; Jn 1.6-8, 19-28. **3.2:** Mt 4.17; Dan 2.44; 4.17; Mt 10.7. **3.3:** Is 40.3. **3.4:** 2 Kings 1.8; Zech 13.4; Lev 11.22. **3.7:** Mt 12.34; 23.33; 1 Thess 1.10. **3.9:** Jn 8.33; Rom 4.16. **3.10:** Mt 7.19. **3.12:** Mt 13.30.

threshing floor and gather his wheat into the granary, but the chaff he will burn with unquenchable fire."

13 Then Jesus came from Galilee to the Jordan to John, to be baptized by him. 14 John would have prevented him, saying, "I need to be baptized by you, and do you come to me?" 15 But Jesus answered him, "Let it be so now; for thus it is fitting for us to fulfil all righteousness." Then he consented. 16And when Jesus was baptized, he went up immediately from the water, and behold, the heavens were opened*g* and he saw the Spirit of God descending like a dove, and alighting on him; 17 and lo, a voice from heaven, saying, "This is my beloved Son,*h* with whom I am well pleased."

4 Then Jesus was led up by the Spirit into the wilderness to be tempted by the devil. 2And he fasted forty days and forty nights, and afterward he was hungry. 3And the tempter came and said to him, "If you are the Son of God, command these stones to become loaves of bread." 4 But he answered, "It is written,

'Man shall not live by bread alone, but by every word that proceeds from the mouth of God.'"

5 Then the devil took him to the holy city, and set him on the pinnacle of the temple, 6 and said to him, "If you are the Son of God, throw yourself down; for it is written,

'He will give his angels charge of you,'

and

'On their hands they will bear you up, lest you strike your foot against a stone.'"

7 Jesus said to him, "Again it is written, 'You shall not tempt the Lord your God.'" 8Again, the devil took him to a very high mountain, and showed him all the kingdoms of the world and the glory of them; 9 and he said to him, "All these I will give you, if you will fall down and worship me." 10 Then Jesus said to him, "Begone, Satan! for it is written,

'You shall worship the Lord your God

and him only shall you serve.'"
11 Then the devil left him, and behold, angels came and ministered to him.

12 Now when he heard that John had been arrested, he withdrew into Galilee; 13 and leaving Nazareth he went and dwelt in Ca·pēr'na·um by the sea, in the territory of Zeb'ū·lun and Naph'ta·lī, 14 that what was spoken by the prophet I·sāi'ah might be fulfilled:

15 "The land of Zeb'ū·lun and the land of Naph'ta·lī,

toward the sea, across the Jordan,

Galilee of the Gentiles—
16 the people who sat in darkness have seen a great light,

and for those who sat in the region and shadow of death light has dawned."

17 From that time Jesus began to preach, saying, "Repent, for the kingdom of heaven is at hand."

18 As he walked by the Sea of Galilee, he saw two brothers, Simon who is called Peter and Andrew his brother, casting a net into the sea; for they were fishermen. 19And he said to them, "Follow me, and I will make you fishers of men." 20 Immediately they left their nets and followed him. 21And going on from there he saw two other brothers, James the son of Zeb'e·dee and John his brother, in the boat with Zebedee their father, mending their nets, and he called them. 22 Immediately they left the boat and their father, and followed him.

23 And he went about all Galilee, teaching in their synagogues and preaching the gospel of the kingdom and healing every disease and every infirmity among the people. 24 So his fame spread throughout all Syria, and they brought him all the sick, those afflicted with various diseases and pains, demoniacs, epileptics, and paralytics, and he healed them. 25And great crowds followed him from Galilee and the De·cap'ó·lis and Jerusalem and Judea and from beyond the Jordan.

---

g Other ancient authorities add *to him* *h* Or *my Son, my* (or *the*) *Beloved*

3.13-17: Mk 1.9-11; Lk 3.21-22; Jn 1.31-34.
3.17: Mt 12.18; 17.5; Mk 9.7; Lk 9.35; Ps 2.7; Is 42.1.
4.1-11: Mk 1.12-13; Lk 4.1-13; Heb 2.18; 4.15. **4.2:** Ex 34.28; 1 Kings 19.8.
4.4: Deut 8.3. **4.5:** Mt 27.53; Neh 11.1; Dan 9.24; Rev 21.10. **4.6:** Ps 91.11-12.
4.7: Deut 6.16. **4.10:** Deut 6.13; Mk 8.33. **4.11:** Mt 26.53; Lk 22.43.
4.12: Mk 1.14; Lk 4.14; Mt 14.3; Jn 1.43. **4.13:** Jn 2.12; Mk 1.21; Lk 4.23.
4.15: Is 9.1-2. **4.17:** Mk 1.15; Mt 3.2; 10.7.
4.18-22: Mk 1.16-20; Lk 5.1-11; Jn 1.35-42.
4.23-25: Mk 1.39; Lk 4.15, 44; Mt 9.35; Mk 3.7-8; Lk 6.17.

5 Seeing the crowds, he went up on the mountain, and when he sat down his disciples came to him. 2And he opened his mouth and taught them, saying:

3 "Blessed are the poor in spirit, for theirs is the kingdom of heaven.

4 "Blessed are those who mourn, for they shall be comforted.

5 "Blessed are the meek, for they shall inherit the earth.

6 "Blessed are those who hunger and thirst for righteousness, for they shall be satisfied.

7 "Blessed are the merciful, for they shall obtain mercy.

8 "Blessed are the pure in heart, for they shall see God.

9 "Blessed are the peacemakers, for they shall be called sons of God.

10 "Blessed are those who are persecuted for righteousness' sake, for theirs is the kingdom of heaven.

11 "Blessed are you when men revile you and persecute you and utter all kinds of evil against you falsely on my account. 12 Rejoice and be glad, for your reward is great in heaven, for so men persecuted the prophets who were before you.

13 "You are the salt of the earth; but if salt has lost its taste, how shall its saltness be restored? It is no longer good for anything except to be thrown out and trodden under foot by men.

14 "You are the light of the world. A city set on a hill cannot be hid. 15 Nor do men light a lamp and put it under a bushel, but on a stand, and it gives light to all in the house. 16 Let your light so shine before men, that they may see your good works and give glory to your Father who is in heaven.

17 "Think not that I have come to abolish the law and the prophets; I have come not to abolish them but to fulfil them. 18 For truly, I say to you, till heaven and earth pass away, not an iota, not a dot, will pass from the law until all is accomplished. 19 Whoever then relaxes one of the least of these commandments and teaches men

so, shall be called least in the kingdom of heaven; but he who does them and teaches them shall be called great in the kingdom of heaven. 20 For I tell you, unless your righteousness exceeds that of the scribes and Pharisees, you will never enter the kingdom of heaven.

21 "You have heard that it was said to the men of old, 'You shall not kill; and whoever kills shall be liable to judgment.' 22 But I say to you that every one who is angry with his brother*i* shall be liable to judgment; whoever insults*j* his brother shall be liable to the council, and whoever says, 'You fool!' shall be liable to the hell*k* of fire. 23 So if you are offering your gift at the altar, and there remember that your brother has something against you, 24 leave your gift there before the altar and go; first be reconciled to your brother, and then come and offer your gift. 25 Make friends quickly with your accuser, while you are going with him to court, lest your accuser hand you over to the judge, and the judge to the guard, and you be put in prison; 26 truly, I say to you, you will never get out till you have paid the last penny.

27 "You have heard that it was said, 'You shall not commit adultery.' 28 But I say to you that every one who looks at a woman lustfully has already committed adultery with her in his heart. 29 If your right eye causes you to sin, pluck it out and throw it away; it is better that you lose one of your members than that your whole body be thrown into hell.*k* 30And if your right hand causes you to sin, cut it off and throw it away; it is better that you lose one of your members than that your whole body go into hell.*k*

31 "It was also said, 'Whoever divorces his wife, let him give her a certificate of divorce.' 32 But I say to you that every one who divorces his wife, except on the ground of unchastity, makes her an adulteress; and whoever marries a divorced woman commits adultery.

---

i Other ancient authorities insert *without cause*
j Greek *says Raca to* (an obscure term of abuse)   *k* Greek *Gehenna*

5.1-12: Lk 6.17, 20-23; Mk 3.13; Jn 6.3.   5.3: Mk 10.14; Lk 22.29.
5.4: Is 61.2; Jn 16.20; Rev 7.17.   5.5: Ps 37.11.
5.6: Is 55.1-2; Jn 4.14; 6.48-51.   5.8: Ps 24.4; Heb 12.14; 1 Jn 3.2; Rev 22.4.
5.10: 1 Pet 3.14; 4.14.
5.12: 2 Chron 36.16; Mt 23.37; Acts 7.52; 1 Thess 2.15; Jas 5.10.
5.13: Mk 9.49-50; Lk 14.34-35.   5.14: Eph 5.8; Phil 2.15; Jn 8.12.
5.15-16: Lk 11.33; Mk 4.21; 1 Pet 2.12.   5.18: Lk 16.17; Mk 13.31.
5.19: Jas 2.10.   5.21: Ex 20.13; Deut 5.17; 16.18.
5.25-26: Lk 12.57-59.   5.27: Ex 20.14; Deut 5.18.   5.29-30: Mk 9.43-48; Mt 18.8-9.
5.31-32: Lk 16.18; Mk 10.11-12; Mt 19.9; 1 Cor 7.10-11; Deut 24.1-4.

33 "Again you have heard that it was said to the men of old, 'You shall not swear falsely, but shall perform to the Lord what you have sworn.' 34 But I say to you, Do not swear at all, either by heaven, for it is the throne of God, 35 or by the earth, for it is his footstool, or by Jerusalem, for it is the city of the great King. 36 And do not swear by your head, for you cannot make one hair white or black. 37 Let what you say be simply 'Yes' or 'No'; anything more than this comes from evil.*l*

38 "You have heard that it was said, 'An eye for an eye and a tooth for a tooth.' 39 But I say to you, Do not resist one who is evil. But if any one strikes you on the right cheek, turn to him the other also, 40 and if any one would sue you and take your coat, let him have your cloak as well; 41 and if any one forces you to go one mile, go with him two miles. 42 Give to him who begs from you, and do not refuse him who would borrow from you.

43 "You have heard that it was said, 'You shall love your neighbor and hate your enemy.' 44 But I say to you, Love your enemies and pray for those who persecute you, 45 so that you may be sons of your Father who is in heaven; for he makes his sun rise on the evil and on the good, and sends rain on the just and on the unjust. 46 For if you love those who love you, what reward have you? Do not even the tax collectors do the same? 47 And if you salute only your brethren, what more are you doing than others? Do not even the Gentiles do the same? 48 You, therefore, must be perfect, as your heavenly Father is perfect.

6 "Beware of practicing your piety before men in order to be seen by them; for then you will have no reward from your Father who is in heaven.

2 "Thus, when you give alms, sound no trumpet before you, as the hypocrites do in the synagogues and in the streets, that they may be praised by men. Truly, I say to you, they have their reward. 3 But when you give alms, do not let your left hand know what your right hand is doing, 4 so that your alms may be in secret; and your Father who sees in secret will reward you.

5 "And when you pray, you must not be like the hypocrites; for they love to stand and pray in the synagogues and at the street corners, that they may be seen by men. Truly, I say to you, they have their reward. 6 But when you pray, go into your room and shut the door and pray to your Father who is in secret; and your Father who sees in secret will reward you.

7 "And in praying do not heap up empty phrases as the Gentiles do; for they think that they will be heard for their many words. 8 Do not be like them, for your Father knows what you need before you ask him. 9 Pray then like this:

Our Father who art in heaven,
Hallowed be thy name.
10 Thy kingdom come,
Thy will be done,
On earth as it is in heaven.
11 Give us this day our daily bread;*m*
12 And forgive us our debts,
As we also have forgiven our debtors;
13 And lead us not into temptation,
But deliver us from evil.*n*

14 For if you forgive men their trespasses, your heavenly Father also will forgive you; 15 but if you do not forgive men their trespasses, neither will your Father forgive your trespasses.

16 "And when you fast, do not look dismal, like the hypocrites, for they disfigure their faces that their fasting may be seen by men. Truly, I say to you, they have their reward. 17 But when you fast, anoint your head and wash your face, 18 that your fasting may not be seen by men but by your Father who is in secret; and your Father who sees in secret will reward you.

19 "Do not lay up for yourselves treasures on earth, where moth and rust*o* consume and where thieves break in and steal, 20 but lay up for yourselves treasures in heaven, where neither moth nor rust*o* consumes and where thieves do not break in and

---

l Or *the evil one*   *m* Or *our bread for the morrow*
n Or *the evil one.* Other authorities, some ancient, add, in some form, *For thine is the kingdom and the power and the glory, for ever. Amen.*   *o* Or *worm*

5.33-37: Mt 23.16-22; Jas 5.12; Lev 19.12; Num 30.2; Deut 23.21.
5.35: Is 66.1; Acts 7.49; Ps 48.2.   **5.38:** Ex 21.24; Lev 24.20; Deut 19.21.
5.39-42: Lk 6.29-30; 1 Cor 6.7; Rom 12.17; 1 Pet 2.19; 3.9; Prov 24.29.
5.43-48: Lk 6.27-28, 32-36; Lev 19.18; Prov 25.21-22.   **5.48:** Lev 19.2.   **6.1:** Mt 23.5.
6.4: Col 3.23-24.   **6.5:** Mk 11.25; Lk 18.10-14.   **6.7:** 1 Kings 18.25-29.
6.8: Mt 6.32; Lk 12.30.   **6.9-13:** Lk 11.2-4.   **6.13:** 2 Thess 3.3; Jn 17.15; Jas 1.13.
6.14-15: Mt 18.35; Mk 11.25; Eph 4.32; Col 3.13.   **6.16:** Is 58.5.   **6.18:** Mt 6.4, 6.
6.19-21: Lk 12.33-34; Mk 10.21; 1 Tim 6.17-19; Jas 5.1-3.

steal.[21] For where your treasure is, there will your heart be also.

22 "The eye is the lamp of the body. So, if your eye is sound, your whole body will be full of light;[23] but if your eye is not sound, your whole body will be full of darkness. If then the light in you is darkness, how great is the darkness!

24 "No one can serve two masters; for either he will hate the one and love the other, or he will be devoted to the one and despise the other. You cannot serve God and mammon.

25 "Therefore I tell you, do not be anxious about your life, what you shall eat or what you shall drink, nor about your body, what you shall put on. Is not life more than food, and the body more than clothing? [26] Look at the birds of the air: they neither sow nor reap nor gather into barns, and yet your heavenly Father feeds them. Are you not of more value than they?[27] And which of you by being anxious can add one cubit to his span of life? [28] And why are you anxious about clothing? Consider the lilies of the field, how they grow; they neither toil nor spin; [29] yet I tell you, even Solomon in all his glory was not arrayed like one of these. [30] But if God so clothes the grass of the field, which today is alive and tomorrow is thrown into the oven, will he not much more clothe you, O men of little faith?[31] Therefore do not be anxious, saying, 'What shall we eat?' or 'What shall we drink?' or 'What shall we wear?' [32] For the Gentiles seek all these things; and your heavenly Father knows that you need them all. [33] But seek first his kingdom and his righteousness, and all these things shall be yours as well.

34 "Therefore do not be anxious about tomorrow, for tomorrow will be anxious for itself. Let the day's own trouble be sufficient for the day.

7 "Judge not, that you be not judged.[2] For with the judgment you pronounce you will be judged, and the measure you give will be the measure you get.[3] Why do you see the speck that is in your brother's eye, but

do not notice the log that is in your own eye?[4] Or how can you say to your brother, 'Let me take the speck out of your eye,' when there is the log in your own eye?[5] You hypocrite, first take the log out of your own eye, and then you will see clearly to take the speck out of your brother's eye.

6 "Do not give dogs what is holy; and do not throw your pearls before swine, lest they trample them under foot and turn to attack you.

7 "Ask, and it will be given you; seek, and you will find; knock, and it will be opened to you.[8] For every one who asks receives, and he who seeks finds, and to him who knocks it will be opened.[9] Or what man of you, if his son asks him for bread, will give him a stone?[10] Or if he asks for a fish, will give him a serpent?[11] If you then, who are evil, know how to give good gifts to your children, how much more will your Father who is in heaven give good things to those who ask him! [12] So whatever you wish that men would do to you, do so to them; for this is the law and the prophets.

13 "Enter by the narrow gate; for the gate is wide and the way is easy,[q] that leads to destruction, and those who enter by it are many.[14] For the gate is narrow and the way is hard, that leads to life, and those who find it are few.

15 "Beware of false prophets, who come to you in sheep's clothing but inwardly are ravenous wolves.[16] You will know them by their fruits. Are grapes gathered from thorns, or figs from thistles?[17] So, every sound tree bears good fruit, but the bad tree bears evil fruit.[18] A sound tree cannot bear evil fruit, nor can a bad tree bear good fruit.[19] Every tree that does not bear good fruit is cut down and thrown into the fire.[20] Thus you will know them by their fruits.

21 "Not every one who says to me, 'Lord, Lord,' shall enter the kingdom of heaven, but he who does the will of my Father who is in heaven.[22] On that day many will say to me, 'Lord, Lord, did we not prophesy in your

p Or *to his stature*   q Other ancient authorities read *for the way is wide and easy*

6.22-23: Lk 11.34-36; Mt 20.15; Mk 7.22.   6.24: Lk 16.13.
6.25-33: Lk 12.22-31; 10.41; 12.11; Phil 4.6; 1 Pet 5.7.   6.26: Mt 10.29.
6.27: Ps 39.5.   6.29: 1 Kings 10.4-7.   6.30: Mt 8.26; 14.31; 16.8.
6.33: Mt 19.28; Mk 10.29-30; Lk 18.29-30.
7.1-2: Lk 6.37-38; Mk 4.24; Rom 2.1; 14.10.   7.3-5: Lk 6.41-42.
7.7-11: Lk 11.9-13; Mk 11.24; Jn 15.7; 16.23-24; Jas 4.3; 1 Jn 3.22; 5.14.
7.12: Lk 6.31.   7.13-14: Lk 13.23-24; Jer 21.8; Deut 30.19; Jn 14.6; 10.7.
7.15: Mt 24.11, 24; Ezek 22.27; 1 Jn 4.1; Jn 10.12.
7.16-20: Lk 6.43-44; Mt 12.33-35; Mt 3.10; Jas 3.12; Lk 13.7.   7.21: Lk 6.46.
7.22-23: Lk 13.26-27; Mt 25.12; Ps 6.8.

name, and cast out demons in your name, and do many mighty works in your name?' [23]And then will I declare to them, 'I never knew you; depart from me, you evildoers.'

24 "Every one then who hears these words of mine and does them will be like a wise man who built his house upon the rock; [25] and the rain fell, and the floods came, and the winds blew and beat upon that house, but it did not fall, because it had been founded on the rock. [26]And every one who hears these words of mine and does not do them will be like a foolish man who built his house upon the sand; [27] and the rain fell, and the floods came, and the winds blew and beat against that house, and it fell; and great was the fall of it."

28 And when Jesus finished these sayings, the crowds were astonished at his teaching, [29] for he taught them as one who had authority, and not as their scribes.

8 When he came down from the mountain, great crowds followed him; [2] and behold, a leper came to him and knelt before him, saying, "Lord, if you will, you can make me clean." [3]And he stretched out his hand and touched him, saying, "I will; be clean." And immediately his leprosy was cleansed. [4]And Jesus said to him, "See that you say nothing to any one; but go, show yourself to the priest, and offer the gift that Moses commanded, for a proof to the people."

5 As he entered Ca·pēr′nȧ-ùm, a centurion came forward to him, beseeching him [6] and saying, "Lord, my servant is lying paralyzed at home, in terrible distress." [7]And he said to him, "I will come and heal him." [8] But the centurion answered him, "Lord, I am not worthy to have you come under my roof; but only say the word, and my servant will be healed. [9] For I am a man under authority, with soldiers under me; and I say to one, 'Go,' and he goes, and to another, 'Come,' and he comes, and to my slave, 'Do this,' and he does it." [10] When Jesus heard

him, he marveled, and said to those who followed him, "Truly, I say to you, not even[r] in Israel have I found such faith. [11] I tell you, many will come from east and west and sit at table with Abraham, Isaac, and Jacob in the kingdom of heaven, [12]while the sons of the kingdom will be thrown into the outer darkness; there men will weep and gnash their teeth." [13]And to the centurion Jesus said, "Go; be it done for you as you have believed." And the servant was healed at that very moment.

14 And when Jesus entered Peter's house, he saw his mother-in-law lying sick with a fever; [15] he touched her hand, and the fever left her, and she rose and served him. [16] That evening they brought to him many who were possessed with demons; and he cast out the spirits with a word, and healed all who were sick. [17] This was to fulfil what was spoken by the prophet I·śāi′āh, "He took our infirmities and bore our diseases."

18 Now when Jesus saw great crowds around him, he gave orders to go over to the other side. [19]And a scribe came up and said to him, "Teacher, I will follow you wherever you go." [20]And Jesus said to him, "Foxes have holes, and birds of the air have nests; but the Son of man has nowhere to lay his head." [21]Another of the disciples said to him, "Lord, let me first go and bury my father." [22] But Jesus said to him, "Follow me, and leave the dead to bury their own dead."

23 And when he got into the boat, his disciples followed him. [24]And behold, there arose a great storm on the sea, so that the boat was being swamped by the waves; but he was asleep. [25]And they went and woke him, saying, "Save, Lord; we are perishing." [26]And he said to them, "Why are you afraid, O men of little faith?" Then he rose and rebuked the winds and the sea; and there was a great calm. [27]And the men marveled, saying, "What sort of man is this, that even winds and sea obey him?"

28 And when he came to the other side, to the country of the Gad′ȧ-

r Greek *to them*   *s* Other ancient authorities read *with no one*

7.24-27: Lk 6.47-49; Jas 1.22-25.
7.28-29: Mk 1.22; Lk 4.32; Mt 11.1; 13.53; 19.1; 26.1.
8.2-4: Mk 1.40-44; Lk 5.12-14.   **8.2:** Mt 9.18; 15.25; 18.26; 20.20; Jn 9.38.
8.4: Mk 3.12; 5.43; 7.36; 8.30; 9.9; Lev 14.2.   **8.5-13:** Lk 7.1-10; Jn 4.46-53.
8.11-12: Lk 13.28-29; Is 49.12; 59.19; Mal 1.11; Ps 107.3.
8.12: Mt 13.42, 50; 22.13; 24.51; 25.30; Lk 13.28.
8.14-16: Mk 1.29-34; Lk 4.38-41; Mt 4.23-24.   **8.17:** Is 53.4.
8.18-22: Lk 9.57-60; Mk 4.35; Lk 8.22.   **8.22:** Mt 9.9; Jn 1.43; 21.19.
8.23-27: Mk 4.36-41; Lk 8.22-25.   **8.26:** Mt 6.30; 14.31; 16.8.
8.28-34: Mk 5.1-17; Lk 8.26-37.

rēnes,[t] two demoniacs met him, coming out of the tombs, so fierce that no one could pass that way. [29]And behold, they cried out, "What have you to do with us, O Son of God? Have you come here to torment us before the time?" [30] Now a herd of many swine was feeding at some distance from them. [31]And the demons begged him, "If you cast us out, send us away into the herd of swine." [32]And he said to them, "Go." So they came out and went into the swine; and behold, the whole herd rushed down the steep bank into the sea, and perished in the waters. [33] The herdsmen fled, and going into the city they told everything, and what had happened to the demoniacs. [34]And behold, all the city came out to meet Jesus; and when they saw him, they begged him to leave their neighborhood.

9 And getting into a boat he crossed over and came to his own city. [2]And behold, they brought to him a paralytic, lying on his bed; and when Jesus saw their faith he said to the paralytic, "Take heart, my son; your sins are forgiven." [3]And behold, some of the scribes said to themselves, "This man is blaspheming." [4] But Jesus, knowing[u] their thoughts, said, "Why do you think evil in your hearts? [5]For which is easier, to say, 'Your sins are forgiven,' or to say, 'Rise and walk'? [6]But that you may know that the Son of man has authority on earth to forgive sins" —he then said to the paralytic—"Rise, take up your bed and go home." [7]And he rose and went home. [8] When the crowds saw it, they were afraid, and they glorified God, who had given such authority to men.

[9] As Jesus passed on from there, he saw a man called Matthew sitting at the tax office; and he said to him, "Follow me." And he rose and followed him.

[10] And as he sat at table[v] in the house, behold, many tax collectors and sinners came and sat down with Jesus and his disciples. [11]And when the Pharisees saw this, they said to his disciples, "Why does your teacher eat with tax collectors and sinners?" [12] But when he heard it, he said, "Those who are well have no need of a physician, but those who are sick. [13]Go and learn what this means, 'I desire mercy, and not sacrifice.' For I came not to call the righteous, but sinners."

[14] Then the disciples of John came to him, saying, "Why do we and the Pharisees fast,[w] but your disciples do not fast?" [15]And Jesus said to them, "Can the wedding guests mourn as long as the bridegroom is with them? The days will come, when the bridegroom is taken away from them, and then they will fast. [16]And no one puts a piece of unshrunk cloth on an old garment, for the patch tears away from the garment, and a worse tear is made. [17]Neither is new wine put into old wineskins; if it is, the skins burst, and the wine is spilled, and the skins are destroyed; but new wine is put into fresh wineskins, and so both are preserved."

[18] While he was thus speaking to them, behold, a ruler came in and knelt before him, saying, "My daughter has just died; but come and lay your hand on her, and she will live." [19]And Jesus rose and followed him, with his disciples. [20]And behold, a woman who had suffered from a hemorrhage for twelve years came up behind him and touched the fringe of his garment; [21] for she said to herself, "If I only touch his garment, I shall be made well." [22] Jesus turned, and seeing her he said, "Take heart, daughter; your faith has made you well." And instantly the woman was made well. [23]And when Jesus came to the ruler's house, and saw the flute players, and the crowd making a tumult, [24] he said, "Depart; for the girl is not dead but sleeping." And they laughed at him. [25] But when the crowd had been put outside, he went in and took her by the hand, and the girl arose. [26]And the report of this went through all that district.

[27] And as Jesus passed on from there, two blind men followed him, crying aloud, "Have mercy on us, Son of David." [28] When he entered the house, the blind men came to him;

t Other ancient authorities read *Gergesenes;* some, *Gerasenes*
u Other ancient authorities read *seeing* *v* Greek *reclined*
w Other ancient authorities add *much* or *often*

8.29: Judg 11.12; 2 Sam 16.10; Mk 1.24; Jn 2.4.   **9.1-8:** Mk 2.1-12; Lk 5.17-26.
9.2: Mt 9.22; Mk 6.50; 10.49; Jn 16.33; Acts 23.11; Lk 7.48.
9.9-13: Mk 2.13-17; Lk 5.27-32; 15.1-2; 7.34.   **9.13:** Hos 6.6; Mt 12.7; 1 Tim 1.15.
9.14-17: Mk 2.18-22; Lk 5.33-39; 18.12.   **9.18-26:** Mk 5.21-43; Lk 8.40-56.
9.18: Mt 8.2; 15.25; 18.26; 20.20; Jn 9.38.
9.20: Num 15.38; Deut 22.12; Mt 14.36; Mk 3.10.
9.22: Mk 10.52; Lk 7.50; 17.19; Mt 15.28; 9.29.   **9.27-31:** Mt 20.29-34.

and Jesus said to them, "Do you believe that I am able to do this?" They said to him, "Yes, Lord." [29] Then he touched their eyes, saying, "According to your faith be it done to you." [30] And their eyes were opened. And Jesus sternly charged them, "See that no one knows it." [31] But they went away and spread his fame through all that district.

[32] As they were going away, behold, a dumb demoniac was brought to him. [33] And when the demon had been cast out, the dumb man spoke; and the crowds marveled, saying, "Never was anything like this seen in Israel." [34] But the Pharisees said, "He casts out demons by the prince of demons."

[35] And Jesus went about all the cities and villages, teaching in their synagogues and preaching the gospel of the kingdom, and healing every disease and every infirmity. [36] When he saw the crowds, he had compassion for them, because they were harassed and helpless, like sheep without a shepherd. [37] Then he said to his disciples, "The harvest is plentiful, but the laborers are few; [38] pray therefore the Lord of the harvest to send out laborers into his harvest."

10 And he called to him his twelve disciples and gave them authority over unclean spirits, to cast them out, and to heal every disease and every infirmity. [2] The names of the twelve apostles are these: first, Simon, who is called Peter, and Andrew his brother; James the son of Zeb'e·dee, and John his brother; [3] Philip and Bartholomew; Thomas and Matthew the tax collector; James the son of Al·phae'us, and Thad·dae'us;[x] [4] Simon the Ca·nä·nae'an, and Judas Is·car'i·ot, who betrayed him.

[5] These twelve Jesus sent out, charging them, "Go nowhere among the Gentiles, and enter no town of the Samaritans, [6] but go rather to the lost sheep of the house of Israel. [7] And preach as you go, saying, 'The kingdom of heaven is at hand.' [8] Heal the

sick, raise the dead, cleanse lepers, cast out demons. You received without pay, give without pay. [9] Take no gold, nor silver, nor copper in your belts, [10] no bag for your journey, nor two tunics, nor sandals, nor a staff; for the laborer deserves his food. [11] And whatever town or village you enter, find out who is worthy in it, and stay with him until you depart. [12] As you enter the house, salute it. [13] And if the house is worthy, let your peace come upon it; but if it is not worthy, let your peace return to you. [14] And if any one will not receive you or listen to your words, shake off the dust from your feet as you leave that house or town. [15] Truly, I say to you, it shall be more tolerable on the day of judgment for the land of Sod'om and Go·mor'rah than for that town.

[16] "Behold, I send you out as sheep in the midst of wolves; so be wise as serpents and innocent as doves. [17] Beware of men; for they will deliver you up to councils, and flog you in their synagogues, [18] and you will be dragged before governors and kings for my sake, to bear testimony before them and the Gentiles. [19] When they deliver you up, do not be anxious how you are to speak or what you are to say; for what you are to say will be given to you in that hour; [20] for it is not you who speak, but the Spirit of your Father speaking through you. [21] Brother will deliver up brother to death, and the father his child, and children will rise against parents and have them put to death; [22] and you will be hated by all for my name's sake. But he who endures to the end will be saved. [23] When they persecute you in one town, flee to the next; for truly, I say to you, you will not have gone through all the towns of Israel, before the Son of man comes.

[24] "A disciple is not above his teacher, nor a servant[y] above his master; [25] it is enough for the disciple to be like his teacher, and the servant[y] like his master. If they have called the master of the house Be·el'ze·bul, how

x Other ancient authorities read Lebbaeus or Lebbaeus called Thaddaeus   y Or slave

9.32-34: Lk 11.14-15; Mt 12.22-24; Mk 3.22; Jn 7.20.   9.35: Mt 4.23; Mk 6.6.
9.36: Mk 6.34; Mt 14.14; 15.32; Num 27.17; Zech 10.2.   9.37-38: Lk 10.2; Jn 4.35.
10.1-4: Mk 6.7; 3.16-19; Lk 9.1; 6.14-16; Acts 1.13.
10.5: Lk 9.52; Jn 4.9; Acts 8.5, 25.   10.6: Mt 15.24; 10.23.
10.7-8: Mk 9.2; 10.9-11; Mt 4.17.   10.9-14: Mk 6.8-11; Lk 9.3-5; 10.4-12; 22.35-36.
10.10: 1 Cor 9.14; 1 Tim 5.18.   10.14: Acts 13.51.
10.15: Mt 11.24; Lk 10.12; Jude 7; 2 Pet 2.6.   10.16: Lk 10.3; Gen 3.1; Rom 16.19.
10.17-22: Mk 13.9-13; Lk 12.11-12; 21.12-19; Jn 16.2.   10.18: Acts 25.24-26.
10.20: Jn 16.7-11.   10.21: Mt 10.35-36; Lk 12.52-53.   10.22: Jn 15.18; Mt 24.9.
10.23: Mt 16.27; 1 Thess 4.17.   10.24: Lk 6.40; Jn 13.16; 15.20.
10.25: Mt 9.34; 12.24; Mk 3.22; Lk 11.15; 2 Kings 1.2.

much more will they malign those of his household.

26 "So have no fear of them; for nothing is covered that will not be revealed, or hidden that will not be known. 27 What I tell you in the dark, utter in the light; and what you hear whispered, proclaim upon the house-tops.28 And do not fear those who kill the body but cannot kill the soul; rather fear him who can destroy both soul and body in hell. 29 Are not two sparrows sold for a penny? And not one of them will fall to the ground without your Father's will.30 But even the hairs of your head are all numbered. 31 Fear not, therefore; you are of more value than many sparrows. 32 So every one who acknowledges me before men, I also will acknowledge before my Father who is in heaven;33 but whoever denies me before men, I also will deny before my Father who is in heaven.

34 "Do not think that I have come to bring peace on earth; I have not come to bring peace, but a sword. 35 For I have come to set a man against his father, and a daughter against her mother, and a daughter-in-law against her mother-in-law;36 and a man's foes will be those of his own household. 37 He who loves father or mother more than me is not worthy of me; and he who loves son or daughter more than me is not worthy of me;38 and he who does not take his cross and follow me is not worthy of me. 39 He who finds his life will lose it, and he who loses his life for my sake will find it.

40 "He who receives you receives me, and he who receives me receives him who sent me.41 He who receives a prophet because he is a prophet shall receive a prophet's reward, and he who receives a righteous man because he is a righteous man shall receive a righteous man's reward. 42 And whoever gives to one of these little ones even a cup of cold water because he is a disciple, truly, I say to you, he shall not lose his reward."

11 And when Jesus had finished instructing his twelve disciples, he went on from there to teach and preach in their cities.

2 Now when John heard in prison about the deeds of the Christ, he sent word by his disciples 3 and said to him, "Are you he who is to come, or shall we look for another?" 4And Jesus answered them, "Go and tell John what you hear and see: 5 the blind receive their sight and the lame walk, lepers are cleansed and the deaf hear, and the dead are raised up, and the poor have good news preached to them. 6 And blessed is he who takes no offense at me."

7 As they went away, Jesus began to speak to the crowds concerning John: "What did you go out into the wilderness to behold? A reed shaken by the wind? 8 Why then did you go out? To see a man clothed in soft raiment? Behold, those who wear soft raiment are in kings' houses. 9 Why then did you go out? To see a prophet? Yes, I tell you, and more than a prophet.10 This is he of whom it is written,

'Behold, I send my messenger before thy face,
who shall prepare thy way before thee.'

11 Truly, I say to you, among those born of women there has risen no one greater than John the Baptist; yet he who is least in the kingdom of heaven is greater than he.12 From the days of John the Baptist until now the kingdom of heaven has suffered violence, and men of violence take it by force. 13 For all the prophets and the law prophesied until John; 14 and if you are willing to accept it, he is E·li′jah who is to come.15 He who has ears to hear, let him hear.

16 "But to what shall I compare this generation? It is like children sitting in the market places and calling to their playmates,

17 'We piped to you, and you did not dance;
we wailed, and you did not mourn.'

z Greek *Gehenna*   a Or *What then did you go out to see? A man . . .*
b Other ancient authorities read *What then did you go out to see? A prophet?*
c Or *has been coming violently*   d Other ancient authorities omit *to hear*
10.26-33: Lk 12.2-9.   10.26: Mk 4.22; Lk 8.17; Eph 5.13.   10.28: Heb 10.31.
10.31: Mt 12.12.   10.32: Mk 8.38; Lk 9.26; Rev 3.5; 2 Tim 2.12.
10.34-36: Lk 12.51-53; Mt 10.21; Mk 13.12; Mic 7.6.
10.37-39: Lk 14.25-27; 17.33; 9.23-24; Mt 16.24-25; Mk 8.34-35; Jn 12.25.
10.40: Lk 10.16; Jn 13.20; Gal 4.14; Mk 9.37; Mt 18.5; Lk 9.48.
10.42: Mk 9.41; Mt 25.40.   11.1: Mt 7.28; 13.53; 19.1; 26.1.   11.2-19: Lk 7.18-35.
11.3: Mk 1.7-8; Hab 2.3; Jn 11.27.   11.5: Is 35.5-6; 61.1; Lk 4.18-19.
11.9: Mt 14.5; 21.26; Lk 1.76.   11.10: Mal 3.1; Mk 1.2.   11.12-13: Lk 16.16.
11.14: Mal 4.5; Mt 17.10-13; Jn 1.21; Lk 1.17.
11.15: Mt 13.9, 43; Mk 4.23; Rev 13.9; 2.7.   11.16-19: Lk 7.31-35.

18 For John came neither eating nor drinking, and they say, 'He has a demon'; 19 the Son of man came eating and drinking, and they say, 'Behold, a glutton and a drunkard, a friend of tax collectors and sinners!' Yet wisdom is justified by her deeds."*e*

20 Then he began to upbraid the cities where most of his mighty works had been done, because they did not repent. 21 "Woe to you, Chŏ-rā′zin! woe to you, Beth-sā′i-dả! for if the mighty works done in you had been done in Tÿre and Si′don, they would have repented long ago in sackcloth and ashes. 22 But I tell you, it shall be more tolerable on the day of judgment for Tÿre and Si′don than for you. 23And you, Cả-pẽr′nả-ủm, will you be exalted to heaven? You shall be brought down to Hades. For if the mighty works done in you had been done in Sod′ŏm, it would have remained until this day. 24 But I tell you that it shall be more tolerable on the day of judgment for the land of Sod′ŏm than for you."

25 At that time Jesus declared, "I thank thee, Father, Lord of heaven and earth, that thou hast hidden these things from the wise and understanding and revealed them to babes; 26yea, Father, for such was thy gracious will.*f* 27All things have been delivered to me by my Father; and no one knows the Son except the Father, and no one knows the Father except the Son and any one to whom the Son chooses to reveal him. 28Come to me, all who labor and are heavy laden, and I will give you rest. 29Take my yoke upon you, and learn from me; for I am gentle and lowly in heart, and you will find rest for your souls. 30For my yoke is easy, and my burden is light."

12 At that time Jesus went through the grainfields on the sabbath; his disciples were hungry, and they began to pluck ears of grain and to eat. 2 But when the Pharisees saw it, they said to him, "Look, your disciples are doing what is not lawful to do on the sabbath." 3 He said to them, "Have you not read what David did, when he

was hungry, and those who were with him: 4 how he entered the house of God and ate the bread of the Presence, which it was not lawful for him to eat nor for those who were with him, but only for the priests? 5 Or have you not read in the law how on the sabbath the priests in the temple profane the sabbath, and are guiltless? 6 I tell you, something greater than the temple is here. 7And if you had known what this means, 'I desire mercy, and not sacrifice,' you would not have condemned the guiltless. 8 For the Son of man is lord of the sabbath."

9 And he went on from there, and entered their synagogue. 10And behold, there was a man with a withered hand. And they asked him, "Is it lawful to heal on the sabbath?" so that they might accuse him. 11 He said to them, "What man of you, if he has one sheep and it falls into a pit on the sabbath, will not lay hold of it and lift it out? 12Of how much more value is a man than a sheep! So it is lawful to do good on the sabbath." 13 Then he said to the man, "Stretch out your hand." And the man stretched it out, and it was restored, whole like the other. 14 But the Pharisees went out and took counsel against him, how to destroy him.

15 Jesus, aware of this, withdrew from there. And many followed him, and he healed them all, 16 and ordered them not to make him known. 17 This was to fulfil what was spoken by the prophet I·şāi′ảh:

18 "Behold, my servant whom I have chosen,
> my beloved with whom my soul
>   is well pleased.
I will put my Spirit upon him,
> and he shall proclaim justice to
>   the Gentiles.
19 He will not wrangle or cry aloud,
> nor will any one hear his voice in
>   the streets;
20 he will not break a bruised reed
> or quench a smoldering wick,
> till he brings justice to victory;
21   and in his name will the Gentiles
>   hope."

22 Then a blind and dumb de-

---

e Other ancient authorities read *children* (Luke 7.35)
f Or *so it was well-pleasing before thee*

11.20-24: Lk 10.13-15.   **11.24:** Mt 10.15; Lk 10.12.   **11.25-27:** Lk 10.21-22.
11.25: 1 Cor 1.26-29.   **11.27:** Jn 3.35; 5.20; 13.3; 7.29; 10.15; 17.25; Mt 28.18.
11.29: Jn 13.15; Phil 2.5; 1 Pet 2.21; Jer 6.16.   **12.1-8:** Mk 2.23-28; Lk 6.1-5.
12.1: Deut 23.25.   **12.3:** 1 Sam 21.1-6; Lev 24.9.   **12.5:** Num 28.9-10.
12.6: Mt 12.41-42; Lk 11.31-32.   **12.7:** Hos 6.6; Mt 9.13.
12.8: Jn 5.1-18; 7.19-24; 9.1-41.   **12.9-14:** Mk 3.1-6; Lk 6.6-11.   **12.11:** Lk 14.5.
12.12: Mt 10.31.   **12.14:** Mk 14.1; Jn 7.30; 8.59; 10.39; 11.53.
12.15-16: Mk 3.7-12; Lk 6.17-19.   **12.18-21:** Is 42.1-4.
12.22-29: Mk 3.22-27; Lk 11.14-22.   **12.22:** Mt 9.32-33.

moniac was brought to him, and he healed him, so that the dumb man spoke and saw. 23And all the people were amazed, and said, "Can this be the Son of David?" 24 But when the Pharisees heard it they said, "It is only by Bē-elʹzė-bul, the prince of demons, that this man casts out demons." 25 Knowing their thoughts, he said to them, "Every kingdom divided against itself is laid waste, and no city or house divided against itself will stand; 26 and if Satan casts out Satan, he is divided against himself; how then will his kingdom stand? 27And if I cast out demons by Bē-elʹzė-bul, by whom do your sons cast them out? Therefore they shall be your judges. 28 But if it is by the Spirit of God that I cast out demons, then the kingdom of God has come upon you. 29 Or how can one enter a strong man's house and plunder his goods, unless he first binds the strong man? Then indeed he may plunder his house. 30 He who is not with me is against me, and he who does not gather with me scatters. 31 Therefore I tell you, every sin and blasphemy will be forgiven men, but the blasphemy against the Spirit will not be forgiven. 32And whoever says a word against the Son of man will be forgiven; but whoever speaks against the Holy Spirit will not be forgiven, either in this age or in the age to come.

33 "Either make the tree good, and its fruit good; or make the tree bad, and its fruit bad; for the tree is known by its fruit. 34 You brood of vipers! how can you speak good, when you are evil? For out of the abundance of the heart the mouth speaks. 35 The good man out of his good treasure brings forth good, and the evil man out of his evil treasure brings forth evil. 36 I tell you, on the day of judgment men will render account for every careless word they utter; 37 for by your words you will be justified, and by your words you will be condemned."

38 Then some of the scribes and Pharisees said to him, "Teacher, we wish to see a sign from you." 39 But he answered them, "An evil and adulterous generation seeks for a sign; but no

sign shall be given to it except the sign of the prophet Jōʹnäh. 40 For as Jōʹnäh was three days and three nights in the belly of the whale, so will the Son of man be three days and three nights in the heart of the earth. 41 The men of Ninʹė-vêh will arise at the judgment with this generation and condemn it; for they repented at the preaching of Jōʹnäh, and behold, something greater than Jonah is here. 42 The queen of the South will arise at the judgment with this generation and condemn it; for she came from the ends of the earth to hear the wisdom of Solomon, and behold, something greater than Solomon is here.

43 "When the unclean spirit has gone out of a man, he passes through waterless places seeking rest, but he finds none. 44 Then he says, 'I will return to my house from which I came.' And when he comes he finds it empty, swept, and put in order. 45 Then he goes and brings with him seven other spirits more evil than himself, and they enter and dwell there; and the last state of that man becomes worse than the first. So shall it be also with this evil generation."

46 While he was still speaking to the people, behold, his mother and his brothers stood outside, asking to speak to him.g 48 But he replied to the man who told him, "Who is my mother, and who are my brothers?" 49And stretching out his hand toward his disciples, he said, "Here are my mother and my brothers! 50 For whoever does the will of my Father in heaven is my brother, and sister, and mother."

13 That same day Jesus went out of the house and sat beside the sea. 2And great crowds gathered about him, so that he got into a boat and sat there; and the whole crowd stood on the beach. 3And he told them many things in parables, saying: "A sower went out to sow. 4And as he sowed, some seeds fell along the path, and the birds came and devoured them. 5 Other seeds fell on rocky ground, where they had not much soil, and immediately they sprang up, since they had no

g Other ancient authorities insert verse 47, *Some one told him, "Your mother and your brothers are standing outside, asking to speak to you"*

12.24: Mt 9.34; 10.25; Jn 7.20; 8.52; 10.20.   12.30: Lk 11.23; Mk 9.40.
12.31-32: Mk 3.28-30; Lk 12.10.
12.33-35: Lk 6.43-45; Mt 7.16-20; Jas 3.11-12; Mt 15.18.
12.38-42: Lk 11.16, 29-32; Mk 8.11-12; Mt 16.1-4; Jn 2.18; 6.30; 1 Cor 1.22.
12.40: Jon 1.17.   12.41: Jon 3.5.   12.42: 1 Kings 10.1-10; 2 Chron 9.1-12.
12.43-45: Lk 11.24-26; 2 Pet 2.20.   12.46-50: Mk 3.31-35; Lk 8.19-21.
12.46: Jn 2.1-12; 19.25-27; 7.1-10; Mk 6.3; 1 Cor 9.5.   12.50: Jn 15.14.
13.1-9: Mk 4.1-9; Lk 8.4-8; 5.1-3.

depth of soil, 6 but when the sun rose they were scorched; and since they had no root they withered away. 7 Other seeds fell upon thorns, and the thorns grew up and choked them. 8 Other seeds fell on good soil and brought forth grain, some a hundredfold, some sixty, some thirty. 9 He who has ears,*h* let him hear."

10 Then the disciples came and said to him, "Why do you speak to them in parables?" 11And he answered them, "To you it has been given to know the secrets of the kingdom of heaven, but to them it has not been given. 12 For to him who has will more be given, and he will have abundance; but from him who has not, even what he has will be taken away. 13 This is why I speak to them in parables, because seeing they do not see, and hearing they do not hear, nor do they understand. 14 With them indeed is fulfilled the prophecy of I·sā̇i′ah which says:

'You shall indeed hear but never understand,
　and you shall indeed see but never perceive.
15 For this people's heart has grown dull,
　and their ears are heavy of hearing,
　and their eyes they have closed,
　lest they should perceive with their eyes,
　and hear with their ears,
　and understand with their heart,
　and turn for me to heal them.'
16 But blessed are your eyes, for they see, and your ears, for they hear. 17 Truly, I say to you, many prophets and righteous men longed to see what you see, and did not see it, and to hear what you hear, and did not hear it.

18 "Hear then the parable of the sower. 19 When any one hears the word of the kingdom and does not understand it, the evil one comes and snatches away what is sown in his heart; this is what was sown along the path. 20 As for what was sown on rocky ground, this is he who hears the word and immediately receives it with joy; 21 yet he has no root in himself, but endures for a while, and when tribulation or persecution arises on account

of the word, immediately he falls away.*i* 22As for what was sown among thorns, this is he who hears the word, but the cares of the world and the delight in riches choke the word, and it proves unfruitful. 23As for what was sown on good soil, this is he who hears the word and understands it; he indeed bears fruit, and yields, in one case a hundredfold, in another sixty, and in another thirty."

24 Another parable he put before them, saying, "The kingdom of heaven may be compared to a man who sowed good seed in his field; 25 but while men were sleeping, his enemy came and sowed weeds among the wheat, and went away. 26 So when the plants came up and bore grain, then the weeds appeared also. 27And the servants*j* of the householder came and said to him, 'Sir, did you not sow good seed in your field? How then has it weeds?' 28 He said to them, 'An enemy has done this.' The servants said to him, 'Then do you want us to go and gather them?' 29 But he said, 'No; lest in gathering the weeds you root up the wheat along with them. 30 Let both grow together until the harvest; and at harvest time I will tell the reapers, Gather the weeds first and bind them in bundles to be burned, but gather the wheat into my barn.'"

31 Another parable he put before them, saying, "The kingdom of heaven is like a grain of mustard seed which a man took and sowed in his field; 32 it is the smallest of all seeds, but when it has grown it is the greatest of shrubs and becomes a tree, so that the birds of the air come and make nests in its branches."

33 He told them another parable. "The kingdom of heaven is like leaven which a woman took and hid in three measures of meal, till it was all leavened."

34 All this Jesus said to the crowds in parables; indeed he said nothing to them without a parable. 35 This was to fulfil what was spoken by the prophet:*k*
"I will open my mouth in parables,
I will utter what has been hidden since the foundation of the world."

h Other ancient authorities add here and in verse 43 *to hear* *i* Or *stumbles* *j* Or *slaves*
k Other ancient authorities read *the prophet Isaiah*

13.10-13: Mk 4.10-12; Lk 8.9-10.　**13.12:** Mk 4.25; Lk 8.18; Mt 25.29; Lk 19.26.
13.14-15: Is 6.9-10; Mk 8.18; Jn 12.39-41; Acts 28.26-27.
13.16-17: Lk 10.23-24; Jn 8.56; Heb 11.13; 1 Pet 1.10-12.
13.18-23: Mk 4.13-20; Lk 8.11-15.　**13.22:** Mt 19.23; 1 Tim 6.9-10, 17.
13.24-30: Mk 4.26-29.　**13.31-32:** Mk 4.30-32; Lk 13.18-19; Mt 17.20.
13.33: Lk 13.20-21; Gal 5.9; Gen 18.6.　**13.34:** Mk 4.33-34; Jn 10.6; 16.25.
13.35: Ps 78.2.

36 Then he left the crowds and went into the house. And his disciples came to him, saying, "Explain to us the parable of the weeds of the field." 37 He answered, "He who sows the good seed is the Son of man; 38 the field is the world, and the good seed means the sons of the kingdom; the weeds are the sons of the evil one, 39 and the enemy who sowed them is the devil; the harvest is the close of the age, and the reapers are angels. 40 Just as the weeds are gathered and burned with fire, so will it be at the close of the age. 41 The Son of man will send his angels, and they will gather out of his kingdom all causes of sin and all evildoers, 42 and throw them into the furnace of fire; there men will weep and gnash their teeth. 43 Then the righteous will shine like the sun in the kingdom of their Father. He who has ears, let him hear.

44 "The kingdom of heaven is like treasure hidden in a field, which a man found and covered up; then in his joy he goes and sells all that he has and buys that field.

45 "Again, the kingdom of heaven is like a merchant in search of fine pearls, 46 who, on finding one pearl of great value, went and sold all that he had and bought it.

47 "Again, the kingdom of heaven is like a net which was thrown into the sea and gathered fish of every kind; 48 when it was full, men drew it ashore and sat down and sorted the good into vessels but threw away the bad. 49 So it will be at the close of the age. The angels will come out and separate the evil from the righteous, 50 and throw them into the furnace of fire; there men will weep and gnash their teeth.

51 "Have you understood all this?" They said to him, "Yes." 52 And he said to them, "Therefore every scribe who has been trained for the kingdom of heaven is like a householder who brings out of his treasure what is new and what is old."

53 And when Jesus had finished these parables, he went away from there, 54 and coming to his own country he taught them in their synagogue, so that they were astonished, and said, "Where did this man

get this wisdom and these mighty works? 55 Is not this the carpenter's son? Is not his mother called Mary? And are not his brothers James and Joseph and Simon and Judas? 56 And are not all his sisters with us? Where then did this man get all this?" 57 And they took offense at him. But Jesus said to them, "A prophet is not without honor except in his own country and in his own house." 58 And he did not do many mighty works there, because of their unbelief.

14 At that time Her′od the tetrarch heard about the fame of Jesus; 2 and he said to his servants, "This is John the Baptist, he has been raised from the dead; that is why these powers are at work in him." 3 For Her′od had seized John and bound him and put him in prison, for the sake of He·rō′di·as, his brother Philip's wife; *l* 4 because John said to him, "It is not lawful for you to have her." 5 And though he wanted to put him to death, he feared the people, because they held him to be a prophet. 6 But when Her′od's birthday came, the daughter of He·rō′di·as danced before the company, and pleased Herod, 7 so that he promised with an oath to give her whatever she might ask. 8 Prompted by her mother, she said, "Give me the head of John the Baptist here on a platter." 9 And the king was sorry; but because of his oaths and his guests he commanded it to be given; 10 he sent and had John beheaded in the prison, 11 and his head was brought on a platter and given to the girl, and she brought it to her mother. 12 And his disciples came and took the body and buried it; and they went and told Jesus.

13 Now when Jesus heard this, he withdrew from there in a boat to a lonely place apart. But when the crowds heard it, they followed him on foot from the towns. 14 As he went ashore he saw a great throng; and he had compassion on them, and healed their sick. 15 When it was evening, the disciples came to him and said, "This is a lonely place, and the day is now over; send the crowds away to go into the villages and buy food for themselves." 16 Jesus said, "They need not go away; you give them something to

l Other ancient authorities read *his brother's wife*

13.38: Jn 8.44; 1 Jn 3.10.　13.41: Mt 24.31.
13.42: Mt 13.50; 8.12; 22.13; 24.51; 25.30; Lk 13.28.　13.47-50: Mt 13.40-42.
13.53: Mt 7.28; 11.1; 19.1; 26.1.　13.54-58: Mk 6.1-6; Lk 4.16-30.
14.1-2: Mk 6.14-16; Lk 9.7-9; Mk 8.28.
14.3-4: Mk 6.17-18; Lk 3.19-20; Lev 18.16; 20.21.　14.5-12: Mk 6.19-29.
14.13-21: Mk 6.32-44; Lk 9.10-17; Jn 6.1-13; Mt 15.32-38.

eat." 17 They said to him, "We have only five loaves here and two fish." 18And he said, "Bring them here to me." 19 Then he ordered the crowds to sit down on the grass; and taking the five loaves and the two fish he looked up to heaven, and blessed, and broke and gave the loaves to the disciples, and the disciples gave them to the crowds. 20And they all ate and were satisfied. And they took up twelve baskets full of the broken pieces left over. 21And those who ate were about five thousand men, besides women and children.

22 Then he made the disciples get into the boat and go before him to the other side, while he dismissed the crowds. 23And after he had dismissed the crowds, he went up into the hills by himself to pray. When evening came, he was there alone, 24 but the boat by this time was many furlongs distant from the land,*m* beaten by the waves; for the wind was against them. 25And in the fourth watch of the night he came to them, walking on the sea. 26 But when the disciples saw him walking on the sea, they were terrified, saying, "It is a ghost!" And they cried out for fear. 27 But immediately he spoke to them, saying, "Take heart, it is I; have no fear."

28 And Peter answered him, "Lord, if it is you, bid me come to you on the water." 29 He said, "Come." So Peter got out of the boat and walked on the water and came to Jesus; 30 but when he saw the wind,*n* he was afraid, and beginning to sink he cried out, "Lord, save me." 31 Jesus immediately reached out his hand and caught him, saying to him, "O man of little faith, why did you doubt?" 32And when they got into the boat, the wind ceased. 33And those in the boat worshiped him, saying, "Truly you are the Son of God."

34 And when they had crossed over, they came to land at Gen·nes'a·ret. 35And when the men of that place recognized him, they sent round to all that region and brought to him all that were sick, 36 and besought him that they might only touch the fringe of his

garment; and as many as touched it were made well.

15 Then Pharisees and scribes came to Jesus from Jerusalem and said, 2 "Why do your disciples transgress the tradition of the elders? For they do not wash their hands when they eat." 3 He answered them, "And why do you transgress the commandment of God for the sake of your tradition? 4 For God commanded, 'Honor your father and your mother,' and, 'He who speaks evil of father or mother, let him surely die.' 5 But you say, 'If any one tells his father or his mother, What you would have gained from me is given to God,*o* he need not honor his father.' 6 So for the sake of your tradition, you have made void the word*p* of God. 7 You hypocrites! Well did I·sāi'ah prophesy of you, when he said:

8 'This people honors me with their lips,

but their heart is far from me;

9 in vain do they worship me,

teaching as doctrines the precepts of men.' "

10 And he called the people to him and said to them, "Hear and understand: 11 not what goes into the mouth defiles a man, but what comes out of the mouth, this defiles a man." 12 Then the disciples came and said to him, "Do you know that the Pharisees were offended when they heard this saying?" 13 He answered, "Every plant which my heavenly Father has not planted will be rooted up. 14 Let them alone; they are blind guides. And if a blind man leads a blind man, both will fall into a pit." 15 But Peter said to him, "Explain the parable to us." 16And he said, "Are you also still without understanding? 17 Do you not see that whatever goes into the mouth passes into the stomach, and so passes on?*q* 18 But what comes out of the mouth proceeds from the heart, and this defiles a man. 19 For out of the heart come evil thoughts, murder, adultery, fornication, theft, false witness, slander. 20 These are what defile

m Other ancient authorities read *was out on the sea*
n Other ancient authorities read *strong wind*   *o* Or *an offering*
p Other ancient authorities read *law*   *q* Or *is evacuated*

14.19: Mk 14.22; Lk 24.30.   14.22-23: Mk 6.45-46; Jn 6.15-17.
14.24-33: Mk 6.47-52; Jn 6.16-21.   14.26: Lk 24.37.   14.29: Jn 21.7.
14.31: Mt 6.30; 8.26; 16.8.   14.33: Mt 28.9, 17.   14.34-36: Mk 6.53-56; Jn 6.22-26.
14.36: Mk 3.10; Num 15.38; Mt 9.20.   15.1-20: Mk 7.1-23.
15.4: Ex 20.12; Deut 5.16; Ex 21.17; Lev 20.9.   15.8-9: Is 29.13.
15.11: Acts 10.14-15; 1 Tim 4.3.   15.13: Is 60.21; Jn 15.2.
15.14: Lk 6.39; Mt 23.16, 24; Rom 2.19.
15.19: Gal 5.19-21; 1 Cor 6.9-10; Rom 14.14.

a man; but to eat with unwashed hands does not defile a man."

21 And Jesus went away from there and withdrew to the district of Tyre and Si'don. 22And behold, a Canaanite woman from that region came out and cried, "Have mercy on me, O Lord, Son of David; my daughter is severely possessed by a demon." 23 But he did not answer her a word. And his disciples came and begged him, saying, "Send her away, for she is crying after us." 24 He answered, "I was sent only to the lost sheep of the house of Israel." 25 But she came and knelt before him, saying, "Lord, help me." 26And he answered, "It is not fair to take the children's bread and throw it to the dogs." 27 She said, "Yes, Lord, yet even the dogs eat the crumbs that fall from their master's table." 28 Then Jesus answered her, "O woman, great is your faith! Be it done for you as you desire." And her daughter was healed instantly.

29 And Jesus went on from there and passed along the Sea of Galilee. And he went up into the hills, and sat down there. 30And great crowds came to him, bringing with them the lame, the maimed, the blind, the dumb, and many others, and they put them at his feet, and he healed them, 31 so that the throng wondered, when they saw the dumb speaking, the maimed whole, the lame walking, and the blind seeing; and they glorified the God of Israel.

32 Then Jesus called his disciples to him and said, "I have compassion on the crowd, because they have been with me now three days, and have nothing to eat; and I am unwilling to send them away hungry, lest they faint on the way." 33And the disciples said to him, "Where are we to get bread enough in the desert to feed so great a crowd?" 34And Jesus said to them, "How many loaves have you?" They said, "Seven, and a few small fish." 35And commanding the crowd to sit down on the ground, 36 he took the seven loaves and the fish, and having given thanks he broke them and gave them to the disciples, and the disciples gave them to the crowds. 37And they all ate and were satisfied; and they

took up seven baskets full of the broken pieces left over. 38 Those who ate were four thousand men, besides women and children. 39And sending away the crowds, he got into the boat and went to the region of Mag'a-dan.

16 And the Pharisees and Sad'du-cees came, and to test him they asked him to show them a sign from heaven. 2 He answered them, "When it is evening, you say, 'It will be fair weather; for the sky is red.' 3And in the morning, 'It will be stormy today, for the sky is red and threatening.' You know how to interpret the appearance of the sky, but you cannot interpret the signs of the times. 4An evil and adulterous generation seeks for a sign, but no sign shall be given to it except the sign of Jo'nah." So he left them and departed.

5 When the disciples reached the other side, they had forgotten to bring any bread. 6 Jesus said to them, "Take heed and beware of the leaven of the Pharisees and Sad'du-cees." 7And they discussed it among themselves, saying, "We brought no bread." 8 But Jesus, aware of this, said, "O men of little faith, why do you discuss among yourselves the fact that you have no bread? 9 Do you not yet perceive? Do you not remember the five loaves of the five thousand, and how many baskets you gathered? 10 Or the seven loaves of the four thousand, and how many baskets you gathered? 11 How is it that you fail to perceive that I did not speak about bread? Beware of the leaven of the Pharisees and Sad'du-cees." 12 Then they understood that he did not tell them to beware of the leaven of bread, but of the teaching of the Pharisees and Sad'du-cees.

13 Now when Jesus came into the district of Caes-a-re'a Phi-lip'pi, he asked his disciples, "Who do men say that the Son of man is?" 14And they said, "Some say John the Baptist, others say E-li'jah, and others Jeremiah or one of the prophets." 15 He said to them, "But who do you say that I am?" 16 Simon Peter replied, "You are the Christ, the Son of the living God." 17And Jesus answered him, "Blessed are you, Simon Bar-Jo'na! For flesh

r Other ancient authorities omit the following words to the end of verse 3

15.21-28: Mk 7.24-30.   15.24: Mt 10.6, 23.   15.25: Mt 8.2; 18.26; 20.20; Jn 9.38. 15.28: Mt 9.22, 28; Mk 10.52; Lk 7.50; 17.19.   15.29-31: Mk 7.31-37. 15.32-39: Mk 8.1-10; Mt 14.13-21.   15.32: Mt 9.36.
16.1-4: Mk 8.11-12; Lk 11.16, 29; 12.54-56; Mt 12.38-39; Jn 2.18; 6.30. 16.4: Jon 3.4-5.   16.5-12: Mk 8.13-21.   16.6: Lk 12.1.   16.8: Mt 6.30; 8.26; 14.31. 16.9: Mt 14.17-21.   16.10: Mt 15.34-38.   16.13-16: Mk 8.27-30; Lk 9.18-21. 16.14: Mt 14.2; Mk 6.15; Lk 9.7-8; Jn 1.21.   16.16: Mt 1.16; Jn 11.27; 1.49. 16.17: 1 Cor 15.50; Gal 1.16; Eph 6.12; Heb 2.14.

and blood has not revealed this to you, but my Father who is in heaven. 18And I tell you, you are Peter,ˢ and on this rockᵗ I will build my church, and the powers of deathᵘ shall not prevail against it. 19 I will give you the keys of the kingdom of heaven, and whatever you bind on earth shall be bound in heaven, and whatever you loose on earth shall be loosed in heaven." 20 Then he strictly charged the disciples to tell no one that he was the Christ.

21 From that time Jesus began to show his disciples that he must go to Jerusalem and suffer many things from the elders and chief priests and scribes, and be killed, and on the third day be raised. 22And Peter took him and began to rebuke him, saying, "God forbid, Lord! This shall never happen to you." 23 But he turned and said to Peter, "Get behind me, Satan! You are a hindranceᵛ to me; for you are not on the side of God, but of men."

24 Then Jesus told his disciples, "If any man would come after me, let him deny himself and take up his cross and follow me. 25 For whoever would save his life will lose it, and whoever loses his life for my sake will find it. 26 For what will it profit a man, if he gains the whole world and forfeits his life? Or what shall a man give in return for his life? 27 For the Son of man is to come with his angels in the glory of his Father, and then he will repay every man for what he has done. 28 Truly, I say to you, there are some standing here who will not taste death before they see the Son of man coming in his kingdom."

17 And after six days Jesus took with him Peter and James and John his brother, and led them up a high mountain apart. 2And he was transfigured before them, and his face shone like the sun, and his garments became white as light. 3And behold, there appeared to them Moses and E-liʹjah, talking with him. 4And Peter

said to Jesus, "Lord, it is well that we are here; if you wish, I will make three booths here, one for you and one for Moses and one for E-liʹjah." 5 He was still speaking, when lo, a bright cloud overshadowed them, and a voice from the cloud said, "This is my beloved Son,ʷ with whom I am well pleased; listen to him." 6 When the disciples heard this, they fell on their faces, and were filled with awe. 7 But Jesus came and touched them, saying, "Rise, and have no fear." 8And when they lifted up their eyes, they saw no one but Jesus only.

9 And as they were coming down the mountain, Jesus commanded them, "Tell no one the vision, until the Son of man is raised from the dead." 10And the disciples asked him, "Then why do the scribes say that first E-liʹjah must come?" 11 He replied, "E-liʹjah does come, and he is to restore all things; 12 but I tell you that E-liʹjah has already come, and they did not know him, but did to him whatever they pleased. So also the Son of man will suffer at their hands." 13 Then the disciples understood that he was speaking to them of John the Baptist.

14 And when they came to the crowd, a man came up to him and kneeling before him said, 15 "Lord, have mercy on my son, for he is an epileptic and he suffers terribly; for often he falls into the fire, and often into the water. 16And I brought him to your disciples, and they could not heal him." 17And Jesus answered, "O faithless and perverse generation, how long am I to be with you? How long am I to bear with you? Bring him here to me." 18And Jesus rebuked him, and the demon came out of him, and the boy was cured instantly. 19 Then the disciples came to Jesus privately and said, "Why could we not cast it out?" 20 He said to them, "Because of your little faith. For truly, I say to you, if you have faith as a grain of mustard seed, you will say to this mountain,

ˢ Greek *Petros*   ᵗ Greek *petra*   ᵘ Greek *the gates of Hades*   ᵛ Greek *stumbling block*
ʷ Or *my Son, my* (or *the*) *Beloved*

16.18: Jn 1.40-42; 21.15-17; 1 Cor 15.5.
16.19: Is 22.22; Rev 1.18; Mt 18.18; Jn 20.23.
16.20: Mt 8.4; Mk 3.12; 5.43; 7.36; 9.9.   16.21-28: Mk 8.31-9.1; Lk 9.22-27.
16.21: Mt 17.22-23; 20.17-19; Lk 17.25; Mt 17.12; 26.2.   16.23: Mt 4.10.
16.24-26: Mt 10.38-39; Lk 14.27; 17.33; Jn 12.25.
16.27: Mt 10.33; Lk 12.9; 1 Jn 2.28; Rom 2.6; Rev 22.12.
16.28: Mt 10.23; 1 Cor 16.22; 1 Thess 4.15-18; Rev 1.7; Jas 5.7.
17.1-9: Mk 9.2-10; Lk 9.28-36; 2 Pet 1.17-18.
17.1: Mt 26.37; Mk 5.37; 13.3.   17.5: Mt 3.17; Is 42.1; Ps 2.7; Jn 12.28.
17.9: Mt 8.4; 16.20; Mk 3.12; 5.43; 7.36.   17.10-13: Mk 9.11-13; Mt 11.14; Mal 4.5.
17.12: Mk 16.21; 17.22; 20.17; 26.2; Lk 17.25.   17.14-18: Mk 9.14-27; Lk 9.37-43.
17.19-21: Mk 9.28-29.   17.20: Lk 17.6; Mt 21.21; Mk 11.22-23; 1 Cor 13.2; Mk 9.23.

'Move hence to yonder place,' and it will move; and nothing will be impossible to you."ˣ

22 As they were gatheringʸ in Galilee, Jesus said to them, "The Son of man is to be delivered into the hands of men, ²³ and they will kill him, and he will be raised on the third day." And they were greatly distressed.

24 When they came to Cả-pẽr'nả-ům, the collectors of the half-shekel tax went up to Peter and said, "Does not your teacher pay the tax?" ²⁵ He said, "Yes." And when he came home, Jesus spoke to him first, saying, "What do you think, Simon? From whom do kings of the earth take toll or tribute? From their sons or from others?" ²⁶ And when he said, "From others," Jesus said to him, "Then the sons are free. ²⁷ However, not to give offense to them, go to the sea and cast a hook, and take the first fish that comes up, and when you open its mouth you will find a shekel; take that and give it to them for me and for yourself."

18 At that time the disciples came to Jesus, saying, "Who is the greatest in the kingdom of heaven?" ²And calling to him a child, he put him in the midst of them, ³ and said, "Truly, I say to you, unless you turn and become like children, you will never enter the kingdom of heaven. ⁴ Whoever humbles himself like this child, he is the greatest in the kingdom of heaven.

5 "Whoever receives one such child in my name receives me; ⁶ but whoever causes one of these little ones who believe in me to sin,ᶻ it would be better for him to have a great millstone fastened round his neck and to be drowned in the depth of the sea.

7 "Woe to the world for temptations to sin!ᵃ For it is necessary that temptations come, but woe to the man by whom the temptation comes! ⁸ And if your hand or your foot causes you to sin,ᶻ cut it off and throw it from you; it is better for you to enter life maimed

or lame than with two hands or two feet to be thrown into the eternal fire. ⁹And if your eye causes you to sin,ᶻ pluck it out and throw it from you; it is better for you to enter life with one eye than with two eyes to be thrown into the hellᵇ of fire.

10 "See that you do not despise one of these little ones; for I tell you that in heaven their angels always behold the face of my Father who is in heaven.ᶜ ¹²What do you think? If a man has a hundred sheep, and one of them has gone astray, does he not leave the ninety-nine on the hills and go in search of the one that went astray? ¹³And if he finds it, truly, I say to you, he rejoices over it more than over the ninety-nine that never went astray. ¹⁴ So it is not the will of myᵈ Father who is in heaven that one of these little ones should perish.

15 "If your brother sins against you, go and tell him his fault, between you and him alone. If he listens to you, you have gained your brother. ¹⁶ But if he does not listen, take one or two others along with you, that every word may be confirmed by the evidence of two or three witnesses. 17 If he refuses to listen to them, tell it to the church; and if he refuses to listen even to the church, let him be to you as a Gentile and a tax collector. ¹⁸ Truly, I say to you, whatever you bind on earth shall be bound in heaven, and whatever you loose on earth shall be loosed in heaven. ¹⁹Again I say to you, if two of you agree on earth about anything they ask, it will be done for them by my Father in heaven. ²⁰ For where two or three are gathered in my name, there am I in the midst of them."

21 Then Peter came up and said to him, "Lord, how often shall my brother sin against me, and I forgive him? As many as seven times?" ²² Jesus said to him, "I do not say to you seven times, but seventy times seven.ᵉ

23 "Therefore the kingdom of heaven may be compared to a king who wished to settle accounts with his

ˣ Other ancient authorities insert verse 21, "*But this kind never comes out except by prayer and fasting*"   ʸ Other ancient authorities read *abode*
ᶻ Greek *causes . . . to stumble*   ᵃ Greek *stumbling blocks*   ᵇ Greek *Gehenna*
ᶜ Other ancient authorities add verse 11, *For the Son of man came to save the lost*
ᵈ Other ancient authorities read *your*   ᵉ Or *seventy-seven times*

17.22-23: Mk 9.30-32; Lk 9.43-45; Mt 16.21; 20.17-19; 26.2.   **17.24**: Ex 30.13; 38.26.
17.25: Rom 13.7; Mt 22.17-21.   **17.27**: Mt 5.29; 18.6-9; Jn 6.61; 1 Cor 8.13.
18.1-5: Mk 9.33-37; Lk 9.46-48.   **18.3**: Mk 10.15; Lk 18.17; 1 Pet 2.2.
18.5: Mt 10.40; Lk 10.16; Jn 13.20.   **18.6-9**: Mk 9.42-48; Lk 17.1-2.
18.8-9: Mt 5.29-30; 17.27.   **18.10**: Acts 12.11.   **18.11**: Lk 19.10.   **18.12-14**: Lk 15.3-7.
18.15-17: Lk 17.3; 1 Cor 6.1-6; Gal 6.1; Jas 5.19-20; Lev 19.17; Deut 19.15.
18.18: Mt 16.19; Jn 20.23.   **18.19-20**: Mt 7.7; 21.22; Jas 1.5-7; 1 Jn 5.14; Jn 14.13.
18.21-22: Lk 17.4; Gen 4.24.   **18.23**: Mt 25.19.

servants. ²⁴ When he began the reckoning, one was brought to him who owed him ten thousand talents;ᶠ ²⁵ and as he could not pay, his lord ordered him to be sold, with his wife and children and all that he had, and payment to be made. ²⁶ So the servant fell on his knees, imploring him, 'Lord, have patience with me, and I will pay you everything.' ²⁷ And out of pity for him the lord of that servant released him and forgave him the debt. ²⁸ But that same servant, as he went out, came upon one of his fellow servants who owed him a hundred denarii;ᵍ and seizing him by the throat he said, 'Pay what you owe.' ²⁹ So his fellow servant fell down and besought him, 'Have patience with me, and I will pay you.' ³⁰ He refused and went and put him in prison till he should pay the debt. ³¹ When his fellow servants saw what had taken place, they were greatly distressed, and they went and reported to their lord all that had taken place. ³² Then his lord summoned him and said to him, 'You wicked servant! I forgave you all that debt because you besought me; ³³ and should not you have had mercy on your fellow servant, as I had mercy on you?' ³⁴ And in anger his lord delivered him to the jailers,ʰ till he should pay all his debt. ³⁵ So also my heavenly Father will do to every one of you, if you do not forgive your brother from your heart."

19 Now when Jesus had finished these sayings, he went away from Galilee and entered the region of Judea beyond the Jordan; ² and large crowds followed him, and he healed them there.

3 And Pharisees came up to him and tested him by asking, "Is it lawful to divorce one's wife for any cause?" ⁴ He answered, "Have you not read that he who made them from the beginning made them male and female, ⁵ and said, 'For this reason a man shall leave his father and mother and be joined to his wife, and the two shall become one'?ⁱ ⁶ So they are no longer two but one.ⁱ What therefore God has joined together, let no man put asunder." ⁷ They said to him, "Why then did Moses command one to give a certificate of divorce, and to put her away?" ⁸ He said to them, "For your hardness of heart Moses allowed you to divorce your wives, but from the beginning it was not so. ⁹ And I say to you: whoever divorces his wife, except for unchastity,ʲ and marries another, commits adultery."ᵏ

10 The disciples said to him, "If such is the case of a man with his wife, it is not expedient to marry." ¹¹ But he said to them, "Not all men can receive this precept, but only those to whom it is given. ¹² For there are eunuchs who have been so from birth, and there are eunuchs who have been made eunuchs by men, and there are eunuchs who have made themselves eunuchs for the sake of the kingdom of heaven. He who is able to receive this, let him receive it."

13 Then children were brought to him that he might lay his hands on them and pray. The disciples rebuked the people; ¹⁴ but Jesus said, "Let the children come to me, and do not hinder them; for to such belongs the kingdom of heaven." ¹⁵ And he laid his hands on them and went away.

16 And behold, one came up to him, saying, "Teacher, what good deed must I do, to have eternal life?" ¹⁷ And he said to him, "Why do you ask me about what is good? One there is who is good. If you would enter life, keep the commandments." ¹⁸ He said to him, "Which?" And Jesus said, "You shall not kill, You shall not commit adultery, You shall not steal, You shall not bear false witness, ¹⁹ Honor your father and mother, and, You shall love your neighbor as yourself." ²⁰ The young man said to him, "All these I have observed; what do I still lack?" ²¹ Jesus said to him, "If you would be perfect, go, sell what you possess and give to the poor, and you will have treasure in heaven; and come, follow me." ²² When the young man heard this he went away sorrowful; for he had great possessions.

ᶠ This talent was probably worth about a thousand dollars
ᵍ The denarius was worth about twenty cents   ʰ Greek *torturers*   ⁱ Greek *one flesh*
ʲ Other ancient authorities, after *unchastity*, read *makes her commit adultery*
ᵏ Other ancient authorities insert *and he who marries a divorced woman commits adultery*
18.25: Lk 7.42.   **18.26:** Mt 8.2.   **18.35:** Mt 6.14.   **19.1:** Mt 7.28; 11.1; 13.53; 26.1.
19.1-9: Mk 10.1-12.   **19.5:** Gen 1.27; 2.24; Eph 5.31; 1 Cor 6.16.   **19.7:** Deut 24.1-4.
19.9: Mt 5.32; Lk 16.18; 1 Cor 7.10-13.   **19.11:** 1 Cor 7.7-9.
19.13-15: Mk 10.13-16; Lk 18.15-17; Mt 18.2-3; 1 Cor 14.20.
19.16-22: Mk 10.17-22; Lk 18.18-23.   **19.16:** Lk 10.25; Lev 18.5.
19.18: Ex 20.12-16; Deut 5.16-20; Rom 13.9; Jas 2.11.   **19.19:** Lev 19.18; Mt 22.39.
19.21: Lk 12.33; Acts 2.45; 4.34; Mt 6.20.

23 And Jesus said to his disciples, "Truly, I say to you, it will be hard for a rich man to enter the kingdom of heaven. 24 Again I tell you, it is easier for a camel to go through the eye of a needle than for a rich man to enter the kingdom of God." 25 When the disciples heard this they were greatly astonished, saying, "Who then can be saved?" 26 But Jesus looked at them and said to them, "With men this is impossible, but with God all things are possible." 27 Then Peter said in reply, "Lo, we have left everything and followed you. What then shall we have?" 28 Jesus said to them, "Truly, I say to you, in the new world, when the Son of man shall sit on his glorious throne, you who have followed me will also sit on twelve thrones, judging the twelve tribes of Israel. 29 And every one who has left houses or brothers or sisters or father or mother or children or lands, for my name's sake, will receive a hundredfold,*l* and inherit eternal life. 30 But many that are first will be last, and the last first.

20 "For the kingdom of heaven is like a householder who went out early in the morning to hire laborers for his vineyard. 2 After agreeing with the laborers for a denarius*m* a day, he sent them into his vineyard. 3 And going out about the third hour he saw others standing idle in the market place; 4 and to them he said, 'You go into the vineyard too, and whatever is right I will give you.' So they went. 5 Going out again about the sixth hour and the ninth hour, he did the same. 6 And about the eleventh hour he went out and found others standing; and he said to them, 'Why do you stand here idle all day?' 7 They said to him, 'Because no one has hired us.' He said to them, 'You go into the vineyard too.' 8 And when evening came, the owner of the vineyard said to his steward, 'Call the laborers and pay them their wages, beginning with the last, up to the first.' 9 And when those hired about the eleventh hour came, each of them received a denarius. 10 Now when the first came, they

thought they would receive more; but each of them also received a denarius. 11 And on receiving it they grumbled at the householder, 12 saying, 'These last worked only one hour, and you have made them equal to us who have borne the burden of the day and the scorching heat.' 13 But he replied to one of them, 'Friend, I am doing you no wrong; did you not agree with me for a denarius? 14 Take what belongs to you, and go; I choose to give to this last as I give to you. 15 Am I not allowed to do what I choose with what belongs to me? Or do you begrudge my generosity?'*n* 16 So the last will be first, and the first last."

17 And as Jesus was going up to Jerusalem, he took the twelve disciples aside, and on the way he said to them, 18 "Behold, we are going up to Jerusalem; and the Son of man will be delivered to the chief priests and scribes, and they will condemn him to death, 19 and deliver him to the Gentiles to be mocked and scourged and crucified, and he will be raised on the third day."

20 Then the mother of the sons of Zeb'e·dee came up to him with her sons, and kneeling before him she asked him for something. 21 And he said to her, "What do you want?" She said to him, "Command that these two sons of mine may sit, one at your right hand and one at your left, in your kingdom." 22 But Jesus answered, "You do not know what you are asking. Are you able to drink the cup that I am to drink?" They said to him, "We are able." 23 He said to them, "You will drink my cup, but to sit at my right hand and at my left is not mine to grant, but it is for those for whom it has been prepared by my Father." 24 And when the ten heard it, they were indignant at the two brothers. 25 But Jesus called them to him and said, "You know that the rulers of the Gentiles lord it over them, and their great men exercise authority over them. 26 It shall not be so among you; but whoever would be great among you must be your servant, 27 and who-

l Other ancient authorities read *manifold*
m The denarius was worth about twenty cents   *n* Or *is your eye evil because I am good?*

19.23-26: Mk 10.23-27; Lk 18.24-27.   19.26: Gen 18.14; Job 42.2.
19.27-30: Mk 10.28-31; Lk 18.28-30; Mt 4.18-22.
19.28: Lk 22.30; Mt 20.21; Rev 3.21.   19.30: Mt 20.16; Lk 13.30.   20.1: Mt 21.28,33.
20.8: Lev 19.13; Deut 24.15.   20.13: Mt 22.12; 26.50.
20.15: Mt 6.23; Mk 7.22; Deut 15.9.   20.16: Lk 13.30; Mt 19.30; Mk 10.31.
20.17-19: Mk 10.32-34; Lk 18.31-34; Mt 16.21; 17.12, 22-23; 26.2.
20.20-24: Mk 10.35-41.   20.20: Mt 8.2; 9.18; 15.25; 18.26; Jn 9.38.   20.21: Mt 19.28.
20.22: Mt 26.39; Jn 18.11.   20.23: Acts 12.2; Rev 1.9; Mt 13.11.
20.25-28: Mk 10.42-45; Lk 22.25-27.   20.26: Mt 23.11; Mk 9.35; Lk 9.48.

ever would be first among you must be your slave; 28 even as the Son of man came not to be served but to serve, and to give his life as a ransom for many."

29 And as they went out of Jericho, a great crowd followed him. 30And behold, two blind men sitting by the roadside, when they heard that Jesus was passing by, cried out,*o* "Have mercy on us, Son of David!" 31 The crowd rebuked them, telling them to be silent; but they cried out the more, "Lord, have mercy on us, Son of David!" 32And Jesus stopped and called them, saying, "What do you want me to do for you?" 33 They said to him, "Lord, let our eyes be opened." 34And Jesus in pity touched their eyes, and immediately they received their sight and followed him.

21 And when they drew near to Jerusalem and came to Beth'-phă·gē, to the Mount of Olives, then Jesus sent two disciples, 2 saying to them, "Go into the village opposite you, and immediately you will find an ass tied, and a colt with her; untie them and bring them to me. 3 If any one says anything to you, you shall say, 'The Lord has need of them,' and he will send them immediately." 4 This took place to fulfil what was spoken by the prophet, saying,

5 "Tell the daughter of Zion,
    Behold, your king is coming to you,
    humble, and mounted on an ass,
    and on a colt, the foal of an ass."

6 The disciples went and did as Jesus had directed them; 7 they brought the ass and the colt, and put their garments on them, and he sat thereon. 8 Most of the crowd spread their garments on the road, and others cut branches from the trees and spread them on the road. 9And the crowds that went before him and that followed him shouted, "Hosanna to the Son of David! Blessed is he who comes in the name of the Lord! Hosanna in the highest!" 10And when he entered Jerusalem, all the city was stirred, saying, "Who is this?" 11And the crowds said, "This is the prophet Jesus from Nazareth of Galilee."

12 And Jesus entered the temple of God*p* and drove out all who sold and bought in the temple, and he overturned the tables of the money-changers and the seats of those who sold pigeons. 13 He said to them, "It is written, 'My house shall be called a house of prayer'; but you make it a den of robbers."

14 And the blind and the lame came to him in the temple, and he healed them. 15 But when the chief priests and the scribes saw the wonderful things that he did, and the children crying out in the temple, "Hosanna to the Son of David!" they were indignant; 16 and they said to him, "Do you hear what these are saying?" And Jesus said to them, "Yes; have you never read,

'Out of the mouth of babes and
    sucklings
    thou hast brought perfect praise'?"

17And leaving them, he went out of the city to Beth'a·ny and lodged there.

18 In the morning, as he was returning to the city, he was hungry. 19And seeing a fig tree by the wayside he went to it, and found nothing on it but leaves only. And he said to it, "May no fruit ever come from you again!" And the fig tree withered at once. 20 When the disciples saw it they marveled, saying, "How did the fig tree wither at once?" 21And Jesus answered them, "Truly, I say to you, if you have faith and never doubt, you will not only do what has been done to the fig tree, but even if you say to this mountain, 'Be taken up and cast into the sea,' it will be done. 22And whatever you ask in prayer, you will receive, if you have faith."

23 And when he entered the temple, the chief priests and the elders of the people came up to him as he was teaching, and said, "By what authority are you doing these things, and who gave you this authority?" 24 Jesus answered them, "I also will ask you a question; and if you tell me the answer, then I also will tell you by what authority I do these things. 25 The baptism of John, whence was it? From

o Other ancient authorities insert *Lord*   *p* Other ancient authorities omit *of God*

20.28: Mt 26.28; 1 Tim 2.5-6; Jn 13.15-16; Tit 2.14; 1 Pet 1.18.
20.29-34: Mk 10.46-52; Lk 18.35-43; Mt 9.27-31.
21.1-9: Mk 11.1-10; Lk 19.29-38; Jn 12.12-18.   21.5: Is 62.11; Zech 9.9.
21.8: 2 Kings 9.13.   21.9: Ps 118.26; Lk 2.14; Mt 21.15; 23.39.
21.11: Jn 6.14; 7.40; Acts 3.22; Mk 6.15; Lk 13.33.
21.12-13: Mk 11.15-17; Lk 19.45-46; Jn 2.13-17; Ex 30.13; Lev 1.14.
21.13: Is 56.7; Jer 7.11.   21.15: Lk 19.39; Mt 21.9.   21.16: Ps 8.2.
21.17-19: Mk 11.11-14; Lk 13.6-9.   21.20-22: Mk 11.20-24.
21.21: Mt 17.20; Lk 17.6; 1 Cor 13.2; Jas 1.6.   21.22: Jn 14.13-14; 16.23.
21.23-27: Mk 11.27-33; Lk 20.1-8; Jn 2.18-22.

heaven or from men?" And they argued with one another, "If we say, 'From heaven,' he will say to us, 'Why then did you not believe him?' [26] But if we say, 'From men,' we are afraid of the multitude; for all hold that John was a prophet." [27] So they answered Jesus, "We do not know." And he said to them, "Neither will I tell you by what authority I do these things.

[28] "What do you think? A man had two sons; and he went to the first and said, 'Son, go and work in the vineyard today.' [29] And he answered, 'I will not'; but afterward he repented and went. [30] And he went to the second and said the same; and he answered, 'I go, sir,' but did not go. [31] Which of the two did the will of his father?" They said, "The first." Jesus said to them, "Truly, I say to you, the tax collectors and the harlots go into the kingdom of God before you. [32] For John came to you in the way of righteousness, and you did not believe him, but the tax collectors and the harlots believed him; and even when you saw it, you did not afterward repent and believe him.

[33] "Hear another parable. There was a householder who planted a vineyard, and set a hedge around it, and dug a wine press in it, and built a tower, and let it out to tenants, and went into another country. [34] When the season of fruit drew near, he sent his servants to the tenants, to get his fruit; [35] and the tenants took his servants and beat one, killed another, and stoned another. [36] Again he sent other servants, more than the first; and they did the same to them. [37] Afterward he sent his son to them, saying, 'They will respect my son.' [38] But when the tenants saw the son, they said to themselves, 'This is the heir; come, let us kill him and have his inheritance.' [39] And they took him and cast him out of the vineyard, and killed him. [40] When therefore the owner of the vineyard comes, what will he do to those tenants?" [41] They said to him, "He will put those wretches to a miserable death, and let out the vineyard to other tenants who will give him the fruits in their seasons."

[42] Jesus said to them, "Have you never read in the scriptures:

'The very stone which the builders rejected
has become the head of the corner;
this was the Lord's doing,
and it is marvelous in our eyes'?

[43] Therefore I tell you, the kingdom of God will be taken away from you and given to a nation producing the fruits of it."[a]

[45] When the chief priests and the Pharisees heard his parables, they perceived that he was speaking about them. [46] But when they tried to arrest him, they feared the multitudes, because they held him to be a prophet.

22 And again Jesus spoke to them in parables, saying, [2] "The kingdom of heaven may be compared to a king who gave a marriage feast for his son, [3] and sent his servants to call those who were invited to the marriage feast; but they would not come. [4] Again he sent other servants, saying, 'Tell those who are invited, Behold, I have made ready my dinner, my oxen and my fat calves are killed, and everything is ready; come to the marriage feast.' [5] But they made light of it and went off, one to his farm, another to his business, [6] while the rest seized his servants, treated them shamefully, and killed them. [7] The king was angry, and he sent his troops and destroyed those murderers and burned their city. [8] Then he said to his servants, 'The wedding is ready, but those invited were not worthy. [9] Go therefore to the thoroughfares, and invite to the marriage feast as many as you find.' [10] And those servants went out into the streets and gathered all whom they found, both bad and good; so the wedding hall was filled with guests.

[11] "But when the king came in to look at the guests, he saw there a man who had no wedding garment; [12] and he said to him, 'Friend, how did you get in here without a wedding garment?' And he was speechless. [13] Then the king said to the attendants, 'Bind him hand and foot, and cast him into the outer darkness; there men will weep and gnash their teeth.' [14] For many are called, but few are chosen."

[15] Then the Pharisees went and took counsel how to entangle him in his talk. [16] And they sent their disciples

---

[a] Other ancient authorities add verse 44, "*And he who falls on this stone will be broken to pieces; but when it falls on any one, it will crush him*"

21.26: Mt 11.9; 14.5; Lk 1.76.   21.28: Mt 20.1; 21.33.   21.32: Lk 7.29-30.
21.33-46: Mk 12.1-12; Lk 20.9-19; Is 5.1-7.   21.34: Mt 22.3.
21.41: Mt 8.11; Acts 13.46; 18.6; 28.28.   21.42: Ps 118.22-23; Acts 4.11; 1 Pet 2.7.
22.1-10: Lk 14.16-24.   22.3: Mt 21.34.   22.10: Mt 13.47.   22.12: Mt 20.13; 26.50.
22.13: Mt 8.12; 13.42, 50; 24.51; 25.30; Lk 13.28.
22.15-22: Mk 12.13-17; Lk 20.20-26.   22.15: Mk 3.6; 8.15.

to him, along with the He·rō'di·anś, saying, "Teacher, we know that you are true, and teach the way of God truthfully, and care for no man; for you do not regard the position of men. 17 Tell us, then, what you think. Is it lawful to pay taxes to Caesar, or not?" 18 But Jesus, aware of their malice, said, "Why put me to the test, you hypocrites? 19 Show me the money for the tax." And they brought him a coin.ʳ 20And Jesus said to them, "Whose likeness and inscription is this?"21 They said, "Caesar's." Then he said to them, "Render therefore to Caesar the things that are Caesar's, and to God the things that are God's." 22 When they heard it, they marveled; and they left him and went away.

23 The same day Sad'dū·ceeś came to him, who say that there is no resurrection; and they asked him a question, 24 saying, "Teacher, Moses said, 'If a man dies, having no children, his brother must marry the widow, and raise up children for his brother.' 25 Now there were seven brothers among us; the first married, and died, and having no children left his wife to his brother. 26 So too the second and third, down to the seventh. 27After them all, the woman died. 28 In the resurrection, therefore, to which of the seven will she be wife? For they all had her."

29 But Jesus answered them, "You are wrong, because you know neither the scriptures nor the power of God. 30 For in the resurrection they neither marry nor are given in marriage, but are like angelsˢ in heaven. 31And as for the resurrection of the dead, have you not read what was said to you by God, 32 'I am the God of Abraham, and the God of Isaac, and the God of Jacob'? He is not God of the dead, but of the living." 33And when the crowd heard it, they were astonished at his teaching.

34 But when the Pharisees heard that he had silenced the Sad'dū·ceeś, they came together. 35And one of them, a lawyer, asked him a question, to test him. 36 "Teacher, which is the great commandment in the law?" 37And he said to him, "You shall love the Lord your God with all your heart, and with all your soul, and with all your mind. 38 This is the great and first commandment. 39And a second is like it, You shall love your neighbor as yourself. 40On these two commandments depend all the law and the prophets."

41 Now while the Pharisees were gathered together, Jesus asked them a question, 42 saying, "What do you think of the Christ? Whose son is he?" They said to him, "The son of David." 43 He said to them, "How is it then, that David, inspired by the Spirit,ᵗ calls him Lord, saying,

44'The Lord said to my Lord,
  Sit at my right hand,
till I put thy enemies under thy feet'?

45 If David thus calls him Lord, how is he his son?" 46And no one was able to answer him a word, nor from that day did any one dare to ask him any more questions.

23 Then said Jesus to the crowds and to his disciples, 2 "The scribes and the Pharisees sit on Moses' seat; 3 so practice and observe whatever they tell you, but not what they do; for they preach, but do not practice. 4 They bind heavy burdens, hard to bear,ᵘ and lay them on men's shoulders; but they themselves will not move them with their finger. 5 They do all their deeds to be seen by men; for they make their phylacteries broad and their fringes long, 6 and they love the place of honor at feasts and the best seats in the synagogues, 7 and salutations in the market places, and being called rabbi by men. 8 But you are not to be called rabbi, for you have one teacher, and you are all brethren. 9And call no man your father on earth, for you have one Father, who is in heaven. 10 Neither be called masters, for you have one master, the Christ. 11 He who is greatest among you shall be your servant; 12 whoever exalts himself will be humbled, and whoever humbles himself will be exalted.

ʳ Greek *a denarius*   ˢ Other ancient authorities add *of God*   ᵗ Or *David in the Spirit*
ᵘ Other ancient authorities omit *hard to bear*
22.21: Rom 13.7.   **22.23-33:** Mk 12.18-27; Lk 20.27-38.   **22.23:** Acts 4.1-2; 23.6-10.
22.24: Deut 25.5.   **22.32:** Ex 3.6.   **22.33:** Mt 7.28.
22.34-40: Mk 12.28-34; Lk 20.39-40; 10.25-28.   **22.35:** Lk 7.30; 11.45; 14.3.
22.37: Deut 6.5.   **22.39:** Lev 19.18; Mt 19.19; Gal 5.14; Rom 13.9; Jas 2.8.
22.41-46: Mk 12.35-37; Lk 20.41-44.   **22.44:** Ps 110.1; Acts 2.34-35; Heb 1.13; 10.13.
22.46: Mt 12.34; Lk 20.40.   **23.4:** Lk 11.46; Acts 15.10.
23.5: Mt 6.1, 5, 16; Ex 13.9; Deut 6.8; Mt 9.20.
23.6-7: Mk 12.38-39; Lk 20.46; 14.7-11; 11.43.   **23.8:** Jas 3.1.
23.11: Mt 20.26; Mk 9.35; 10.43; Lk 9.48; 22.26.
23.12: Lk 14.11; 18.14; Mt 18.4; 1 Pet 5.6.

13 "But woe to you, scribes and Pharisees, hypocrites! because you shut the kingdom of heaven against men; for you neither enter yourselves, nor allow those who would enter to go in.ᵛ 15 Woe to you, scribes and Pharisees, hypocrites! for you traverse sea and land to make a single proselyte, and when he becomes a proselyte, you make him twice as much a child of hellʷ as yourselves.

16 "Woe to you, blind guides, who say, 'If any one swears by the temple, it is nothing; but if any one swears by the gold of the temple, he is bound by his oath.' 17 You blind fools! For which is greater, the gold or the temple that has made the gold sacred? 18 And you say, 'If any one swears by the altar, it is nothing; but if any one swears by the gift that is on the altar, he is bound by his oath. 19 You blind men! For which is greater, the gift or the altar that makes the gift sacred? 20 So he who swears by the altar, swears by it and by everything on it; 21 and he who swears by the temple, swears by it and by him who dwells in it; 22 and he who swears by heaven, swears by the throne of God and by him who sits upon it.

23 "Woe to you, scribes and Pharisees, hypocrites! for you tithe mint and dill and cummin, and have neglected the weightier matters of the law, justice and mercy and faith; these you ought to have done, without neglecting the others. 24 You blind guides, straining out a gnat and swallowing a camel!

25 "Woe to you, scribes and Pharisees, hypocrites! for you cleanse the outside of the cup and of the plate, but inside they are full of extortion and rapacity. 26 You blind Pharisee! first cleanse the inside of the cup and of the plate, that the outside also may be clean.

27 "Woe to you, scribes and Pharisees, hypocrites! for you are like whitewashed tombs, which outwardly appear beautiful, but within they are full of dead men's bones and all uncleanness. 28 So you also outwardly appear righteous to men, but within you are full of hypocrisy and iniquity.

29 "Woe to you, scribes and Pharisees, hypocrites! for you build the tombs of the prophets and adorn the monuments of the righteous, 30 saying, 'If we had lived in the days of our fathers, we would not have taken part with them in shedding the blood of the prophets.' 31 Thus you witness against yourselves, that you are sons of those who murdered the prophets. 32 Fill up, then, the measure of your fathers. 33 You serpents, you brood of vipers, how are you to escape being sentenced to hell?ʷ 34 Therefore I send you prophets and wise men and scribes, some of whom you will kill and crucify, and some you will scourge in your synagogues and persecute from town to town, 35 that upon you may come all the righteous blood shed on earth, from the blood of innocent Abel to the blood of Zech·a·ri′ah the son of Bar·a·chi′ah, whom you murdered between the sanctuary and the altar. 36 Truly, I say to you, all this will come upon this generation.

37 "O Jerusalem, Jerusalem, killing the prophets and stoning those who are sent to you! How often would I have gathered your children together as a hen gathers her brood under her wings, and you would not! 38 Behold, your house is forsaken and desolate.ˣ 39 For I tell you, you will not see me again, until you say, 'Blessed is he who comes in the name of the Lord.'"

24 Jesus left the temple and was going away, when his disciples came to point out to him the buildings of the temple. 2 But he answered them, "You see all these, do you not? Truly, I say to you, there will not be left here one stone upon another, that will not be thrown down."

3 As he sat on the Mount of Olives, the disciples came to him privately,

ᵛ Other authorities add here (or after verse 12) verse 14, *Woe to you, scribes and Pharisees, hypocrites! for you devour widows' houses and for a pretense you make long prayers; therefore you will receive the greater condemnation*
ʷ Greek *Gehenna*
ˣ Other ancient authorities omit *and desolate*

23.13: Lk 11.52.   23.15: Acts 2.10; 6.5; 13.43.   23.16-22: Mt 5.33-37; 15.14.
23.17: Ex 30.29.   23.21: 1 Kings 8.13; Ps 26.8.
23.23-24: Lk 11.42; Lev 27.30; Mic 6.8.   23.25-26: Lk 11.39-41; Mk 7.4.
23.27-28: Lk 11.44; Acts 23.3; Ps 5.9.   23.29-32: Lk 11.47-48; Acts 7.51-53.
23.33: Mt 3.7; Lk 3.7.   23.34-36: Lk 11.49-51; 2 Chron 36.15-16.
23.34: Mt 10.17, 23.   23.35: Gen 4.8; Heb 11.4; Zech 1.1; 2 Chron 24.21.
23.36: Mt 10.23; 16.28; 24.34.   23.37-39: Lk 13.34-35.   23.38: 1 Kings 9.7; Jer 22.5.
23.39: Mt 21.9; Ps 118.26.   24.1-25: Mk 13.1-31; Lk 21.1-33.
24.2: Mt 26.61; 27.39-40; Lk 19.44; Jn 2.19.
24.3: Lk 17.20; Mt 13.39, 40, 49; 28.20; 16.27.

saying, "Tell us, when will this be, and what will be the sign of your coming and of the close of the age?" 4And Jesus answered them, "Take heed that no one leads you astray. 5For many will come in my name, saying, 'I am the Christ,' and they will lead many astray. 6And you will hear of wars and rumors of wars; see that you are not alarmed; for this must take place, but the end is not yet. 7For nation will rise against nation, and kingdom against kingdom, and there will be famines and earthquakes in various places: 8all this is but the beginning of the sufferings.

9"Then they will deliver you up to tribulation, and put you to death; and you will be hated by all nations for my name's sake. 10And then many will fall away,y and betray one another, and hate one another. 11And many false prophets will arise and lead many astray. 12And because wickedness is multiplied, most men's love will grow cold. 13 But he who endures to the end will be saved. 14And this gospel of the kingdom will be preached throughout the whole world, as a testimony to all nations; and then the end will come.

15 "So when you see the desolating sacrilege spoken of by the prophet Daniel, standing in the holy place (let the reader understand), 16 then let those who are in Judea flee to the mountains; 17 let him who is on the housetop not go down to take what is in his house; 18 and let him who is in the field not turn back to take his mantle. 19And alas for those who are with child and for those who give suck in those days! 20 Pray that your flight may not be in winter or on a sabbath. 21 For then there will be great tribulation, such as has not been from the beginning of the world until now, no, and never will be. 22And if those days had not been shortened, no human being would be saved; but for the sake of the elect those days will be shortened. 23 Then if any one says to you, 'Lo, here is the Christ!' or 'There he is!' do not believe it. 24 For false Christs and false prophets will arise

and show great signs and wonders, so as to lead astray, if possible, even the elect. 25 Lo, I have told you beforehand. 26 So, if they say to you, 'Lo, he is in the wilderness,' do not go out; if they say, 'Lo, he is in the inner rooms,' do not believe it. 27 For as the lightning comes from the east and shines as far as the west, so will be the coming of the Son of man. 28 Wherever the body is, there the eaglesz will be gathered together.

29 "Immediately after the tribulation of those days the sun will be darkened, and the moon will not give its light, and the stars will fall from heaven, and the powers of the heavens will be shaken; 30 then will appear the sign of the Son of man in heaven, and then all the tribes of the earth will mourn, and they will see the Son of man coming on the clouds of heaven with power and great glory; 31and he will send out his angels with a loud trumpet call, and they will gather his elect from the four winds, from one end of heaven to the other.

32 "From the fig tree learn its lesson: as soon as its branch becomes tender and puts forth its leaves, you know that summer is near. 33 So also, when you see all these things, you know that he is near, at the very gates. 34 Truly, I say to you, this generation will not pass away till all these things take place. 35 Heaven and earth will pass away, but my words will not pass away.

36 "But of that day and hour no one knows, not even the angels of heaven, nor the Son,a but the Father only. 37As were the days of Noah, so will be the coming of the Son of man. 38 For as in those days before the flood they were eating and drinking, marrying and giving in marriage, until the day when Noah entered the ark, 39 and they did not know until the flood came and swept them all away, so will be the coming of the Son of man. 40 Then two men will be in the field; one is taken and one is left. 41 Two women will be grinding at the mill; one is taken and one is left. 42 Watch there-

y Or *stumble*   z Or *vultures*   a Other ancient authorities omit *nor the Son*

24.5: Mt 24.11, 23-24; 1 Jn 2.18.   **24.6-7:** Rev 6.3-8, 12-17; Is 19.2.
24.9: Mt 10.17-18, 22; Jn 15.18; 16.2.   **24.13:** Mt 10.22; Rev 2.7.
24.14: Mt 28.19; Rom 10.18.   **24.15:** Dan 9.27; 11.31; 12.11.   **24.17-18:** Lk 17.31.
24.19: Lk 23.29.   **24.21:** Dan 12.1; Joel 2.2.   **24.26-27:** Lk 17.22-24; Rev 1.7.
24.28: Lk 17.37; Job 39.30.
24.29: Rev 8.12; Is 13.10; Ezek 32.7; Joel 2.10-11; Zeph 1.15.
24.30: Mt 16.27; Dan 7.13; Rev 1.7.
24.31: 1 Cor 15.52; 1 Thess 4.16; Is 27.13; Zech 9.14.   **24.34:** Mt 16.28.
24.35: Mt 5.18; Lk 16.17.   **24.36:** Acts 1.6-7.   **24.37-39:** Lk 17.26-27; Gen 6.5-8; 7.6-24.
24.40-41: Lk 17.34-35.   **24.42:** Mk 13.35; Lk 12.40; Mt 25.13.

fore, for you do not know on what day your Lord is coming. 43But know this, that if the householder had known in what part of the night the thief was coming, he would have watched and would not have let his house be broken into. 44Therefore you also must be ready; for the Son of man is coming at an hour you do not expect.

45 "Who then is the faithful and wise servant, whom his master has set over his household, to give them their food at the proper time? 46Blessed is that servant whom his master when he comes will find so doing. 47Truly, I say to you, he will set him over all his possessions. 48But if that wicked servant says to himself, 'My master is delayed,' 49and begins to beat his fellow servants, and eats and drinks with the drunken, 50the master of that servant will come on a day when he does not expect him and at an hour he does not know, 51and will punish *b*him, and put him with the hypocrites; there men will weep and gnash their teeth.

25 "Then the kingdom of heaven shall be compared to ten maidens who took their lamps and went to meet the bridegroom.*c* 2Five of them were foolish, and five were wise. 3For when the foolish took their lamps, they took no oil with them; 4but the wise took flasks of oil with their lamps. 5As the bridegroom was delayed, they all slumbered and slept. 6But at midnight there was a cry, 'Behold, the bridegroom! Come out to meet him.' 7Then all those maidens rose and trimmed their lamps. 8And the foolish said to the wise, 'Give us some of your oil, for our lamps are going out.' 9But the wise replied, 'Perhaps there will not be enough for us and for you; go rather to the dealers and buy for yourselves.' 10And while they went to buy, the bridegroom came, and those who were ready went in with him to the marriage feast; and the door was shut. 11Afterward the other maidens came also, saying, 'Lord, lord, open to us.' 12But he replied, 'Truly, I say to you, I do not know you.' 13Watch therefore, for you know neither the day nor the hour.

14 "For it will be as when a man going on a journey called his servants and entrusted to them his property; 15to one he gave five talents,*d* to another two, to another one, to each according to his ability. Then he went away. 16He who had received the five talents went at once and traded with them; and he made five talents more. 17So also, he who had the two talents made two talents more. 18But he who had received the one talent went and dug in the ground and hid his master's money. 19Now after a long time the master of those servants came and settled accounts with them. 20And he who had received the five talents came forward, bringing five talents more, saying, 'Master, you delivered to me five talents; here I have made five talents more.' 21His master said to him, 'Well done, good and faithful servant; you have been faithful over a little, I will set you over much; enter into the joy of your master.' 22And he also who had the two talents came forward, saying, 'Master, you delivered to me two talents; here I have made two talents more.' 23His master said to him, 'Well done, good and faithful servant; you have been faithful over a little, I will set you over much; enter into the joy of your master.' 24He also who had received the one talent came forward, saying, 'Master, I knew you to be a hard man, reaping where you did not sow, and gathering where you did not winnow; 25so I was afraid, and I went and hid your talent in the ground. Here you have what is yours.' 26But his master answered him, 'You wicked and slothful servant! You knew that I reap where I have not sowed, and gather where I have not winnowed? 27Then you ought to have invested my money with the bankers, and at my coming I should have received what was my own with interest. 28So take the talent from him, and give it to him who has the ten talents. 29For to every one who has will more be given, and he will have abundance; but from him who has not, even what he has will be taken away. 30And cast the worthless servant into the outer darkness; there men will weep and gnash their teeth.'

b Or *cut him in pieces*   *c* Other ancient authorities add *and the bride*
d This talent was probably worth about a thousand dollars

24.43-51: Lk 12.39-46.   24.43: 1 Thess 5.2; Rev 3.3; 16.15; 2 Pet 3.10.
24.45: Mt 25.21, 23.   24.49: Lk 21.34.   24.51: Mt 8.12; 13.42, 50; 22.13; 25.30; Lk 13.28.
25.1: Lk 12.35-38; Mk 13.34.   25.2: Mt 7.24-27.   25.10: Rev 19.9.
25.11-12: Lk 13.25; Mt 7.21-23.   25.13: Mt 24.42; Mk 13.35; Lk 12.40.
25.14-30: Lk 19.12-28.   25.19: Mt 18.23.   25.21: Lk 16.10; Mt 24.45.
25.29: Mt 13.12; Mk 4.25; Lk 8.18.   25.30: Mt 8.12; 13.42, 50; 22.13; Lk 13.28.

31 "When the Son of man comes in his glory, and all the angels with him, then he will sit on his glorious throne. 32 Before him will be gathered all the nations, and he will separate them one from another as a shepherd separates the sheep from the goats, 33 and he will place the sheep at his right hand, but the goats at the left. 34 Then the King will say to those at his right hand, 'Come, O blessed of my Father, inherit the kingdom prepared for you from the foundation of the world; 35 for I was hungry and you gave me food, I was thirsty and you gave me drink, I was a stranger and you welcomed me, 36 I was naked and you clothed me, I was sick and you visited me, I was in prison and you came to me.' 37 Then the righteous will answer him, "Lord, when did we see thee hungry and feed thee, or thirsty and give thee drink? 38 And when did we see thee a stranger and welcome thee, or naked and clothe thee? 39 And when did we see thee sick or in prison and visit thee?' 40 And the King will answer them, 'Truly, I say to you, as you did it to one of the least of these my brethren, you did it to me.' 41 Then he will say to those at his left hand, 'Depart from me, you cursed, into the eternal fire prepared for the devil and his angels; 42 for I was hungry and you gave me no food, I was thirsty and you gave me no drink, 43 I was a stranger and you did not welcome me, naked and you did not clothe me, sick and in prison and you did not visit me.' 44 Then they also will answer, 'Lord, when did we see thee hungry or thirsty or a stranger or naked or sick or in prison, and did not minister to thee?' 45 Then he will answer them, 'Truly, I say to you, as you did it not to one of the least of these, you did it not to me.' 46 And they will go away into eternal punishment, but the righteous into eternal life."

26 When Jesus had finished all these sayings, he said to his disciples, 2 "You know that after two days the Passover is coming, and the Son of man will be delivered up to be crucified."

3 Then the chief priests and the elders of the people gathered in the palace of the high priest, who was called Cā′iā·phàs, 4 and took counsel together in order to arrest Jesus by stealth and kill him. 5 But they said, "Not during the feast, lest there be a tumult among the people."

6 Now when Jesus was at Beth′ȧ·ny in the house of Simon the leper, 7 a woman came up to him with an alabaster jar of very expensive ointment, and she poured it on his head, as he sat at table. 8 But when the disciples saw it, they were indignant, saying, "Why this waste? 9 For this ointment might have been sold for a large sum, and given to the poor." 10 But Jesus, aware of this, said to them, "Why do you trouble the woman? For she has done a beautiful thing to me. 11 For you always have the poor with you, but you will not always have me. 12 In pouring this ointment on my body she has done it to prepare me for burial. 13 Truly, I say to you, wherever this gospel is preached in the whole world, what she has done will be told in memory of her."

14 Then one of the twelve, who was called Judas Is·car′i·ŏt, went to the chief priests 15 and said, "What will you give me if I deliver him to you?" And they paid him thirty pieces of silver. 16 And from that moment he sought an opportunity to betray him.

17 Now on the first day of Unleavened Bread the disciples came to Jesus, saying, "Where will you have us prepare for you to eat the passover?" 18 He said, "Go into the city to such a one, and say to him, 'The Teacher says, My time is at hand; I will keep the passover at your house with my disciples.'" 19 And the disciples did as Jesus had directed them, and they prepared the passover.

20 When it was evening, he sat at table with the twelve disciples;*e* 21 and as they were eating, he said, "Truly, I say to you, one of you will betray me." 22 And they were very sorrowful, and

e Other authorities omit *disciples*

25:31: Mt 16.27; 19.28.   25.32: Ezek 34.17.   25.34: Lk 12.32; Mt 5.3; Rev 13.8; 17.8.
25.35-36: Is 58.7; Jas 1.27; 2.15-16; Heb 13.2; 2 Tim 1.16.
25.40: Mt 10.42; Mk 9.41; Heb 6.10; Prov 19.17.
25.41: Mk 9.48; Lk 16.23; Rev 20.10.   25.46: Dan 12.2; Jn 5.29.
26.1: Mt 7.28; 11.1; 13.53; 19.1.   26.2-5: Mk 14.1-2; Lk 22.1-2; Jn 11.47-53.
26.6-13: Mk 14.3-9; Jn 12.1-8; Lk 7.36-38.   26.11: Deut 15.11.   26.12: Jn 19.40.
26.14-16: Mk 14.10-11; Lk 22.3-6.   26.15: Ex 21.32; Zech 11.12.
26.17-19: Mk 14.12-16; Lk 22.7-13.   26.18: Mt 26.45; Jn 7.6; 12.23; 13.1; 17.1.
26.19: Mt 21.6; Deut 16.5-8.
26.20-24: Mk 14.17-21; Lk 22.14, 21-23; Jn 13.21-30.

MATTHEW 26 28 *The Last Supper*

began to say to him one after another, "Is it I, Lord?" 23 He answered, "He who has dipped his hand in the dish with me, will betray me. 24 The Son of man goes as it is written of him, but woe to that man by whom the Son of man is betrayed! It would have been better for that man if he had not been born." 25 Judas, who betrayed him, said, "Is it I, Master?"[f] He said to him, "You have said so."

26 Now as they were eating, Jesus took bread, and blessed, and broke it, and gave it to the disciples and said, "Take, eat; this is my body." 27And he took a cup, and when he had given thanks he gave it to them, saying, "Drink of it, all of you; 28 for this is my blood of the[g] covenant, which is poured out for many for the forgiveness of sins. 29 I tell you I shall not drink again of this fruit of the vine until that day when I drink it new with you in my Father's kingdom."

30 And when they had sung a hymn, they went out to the Mount of Olives. 31 Then Jesus said to them, "You will all fall away because of me this night; for it is written, 'I will strike the shepherd, and the sheep of the flock will be scattered.' 32 But after I am raised up, I will go before you to Galilee." 33 Peter declared to him, "Though they all fall away because of you, I will never fall away." 34 Jesus said to him, "Truly, I say to you, this very night, before the cock crows, you will deny me three times." 35 Peter said to him, "Even if I must die with you, I will not deny you." And so said all the disciples.

36 Then Jesus went with them to a place called Geth·sem´a·nē, and he said to his disciples, "Sit here, while I go yonder and pray." 37And taking with him Peter and the two sons of Zeb´e·dee, he began to be sorrowful and troubled. 38 Then he said to them, "My soul is very sorrowful, even to death; remain here, and watch[h] with me." 39And going a little farther he fell on his face and prayed, "My Father, if it be possible, let this cup

pass from me; nevertheless, not as I will, but as thou wilt." 40And he came to the disciples and found them sleeping; and he said to Peter, "So, could you not watch[h] with me one hour? 41 Watch[h] and pray that you may not enter into temptation; the spirit indeed is willing, but the flesh is weak." 42Again, for the second time, he went away and prayed, "My Father, if this cannot pass unless I drink it, thy will be done." 43And again he came and found them sleeping, for their eyes were heavy. 44 So, leaving them again, he went away and prayed for the third time, saying the same words. 45 Then he came to the disciples and said to them, "Are you still sleeping and taking your rest? Behold, the hour is at hand, and the Son of man is betrayed into the hands of sinners. 46 Rise, let us be going; see, my betrayer is at hand."

47 While he was still speaking, Judas came, one of the twelve, and with him a great crowd with swords and clubs, from the chief priests and the elders of the people. 48 Now the betrayer had given them a sign, saying, "The one I shall kiss is the man; seize him." 49And he came up to Jesus at once and said, "Hail, Master!"[i] And he kissed him. 50 Jesus said to him, "Friend, why are you here?"[j] Then they came up and laid hands on Jesus and seized him. 51And behold, one of those who were with Jesus stretched out his hand and drew his sword, and struck the slave of the high priest, and cut off his ear. 52 Then Jesus said to him, "Put your sword back into its place; for all who take the sword will perish by the sword. 53 Do you think that I cannot appeal to my Father, and he will at once send me more than twelve legions of angels? 54 But how then should the scriptures be fulfilled, that it must be so?" 55At that hour Jesus said to the crowds, "Have you come out as against a robber, with swords and clubs to capture me? Day after day I sat in the temple teaching, and you did not seize me. 56 But all

f Or *Rabbi*   *g* Other ancient authorities insert *new*   *h* Or *keep awake*   *i* Or *Rabbi*
j Or *do that for which you have come*

26.24: Ps 41.9; Lk 24.25; 1 Cor 15.3; Acts 17.2-3; Mt 18.7.
26.26-29: Mk 14.22-25; Lk 22.17-19; 1 Cor 10.16; 11.23-26; Mt **14.19**; **15.36**.
26.28: Heb 9.20; Mt 20.28; Mk 1.4; Ex 24.6-8.
26.30-35: Mk 14.26-31; Lk 22.33-34, 39; Jn 14.31; 18.1; 13.36-38.
26.31: Zech 13.7; Jn 16.32.   26.32: Mt 28.7, 10, 16.
26.36-46: Mk 14.32-42; Lk 22.40-46.   26.38: Jn 12.27; Heb 5.7-8.
26.39: Jn 18.11; Mt 20.22.   26.41: Mt 6.13; Lk 11.4.   26.42: Jn 4.34; 5.30; 6.38.
26.45: Mt 26.18; Jn 12.23; 13.1; 17.1.
26.47-56: Mk 14.43-50; Lk 22.47-53; Jn 18.2-11.   26.50: Mt 20.13; 22.12.
26.52: Gen 9.6; Rev 13.10.   26.55: Lk 19.47; Jn 18.19-21.

this has taken place, that the scriptures of the prophets might be fulfilled." Then all the disciples forsook him and fled.

57 Then those who had seized Jesus led him to Cā́i·a·phàs the high priest, where the scribes and the elders had gathered. 58 But Peter followed him at a distance, as far as the courtyard of the high priest, and going inside he sat with the guards to see the end. 59 Now the chief priests and the whole council sought false testimony against Jesus that they might put him to death, 60 but they found none, though many false witnesses came forward. At last two came forward 61 and said, "This fellow said, 'I am able to destroy the temple of God, and to build it in three days.' " 62And the high priest stood up and said, "Have you no answer to make? What is it that these men testify against you?" 63 But Jesus was silent. And the high priest said to him, "I adjure you by the living God, tell us if you are the Christ, the Son of God." 64 Jesus said to him, "You have said so. But I tell you, hereafter you will see the Son of man seated at the right hand of Power, and coming on the clouds of heaven." 65 Then the high priest tore his robes, and said, "He has uttered blasphemy. Why do we still need witnesses? You have now heard his blasphemy. 66 What is your judgment?" They answered, "He deserves death." 67 Then they spat in his face, and struck him; and some slapped him, 68 saying, "Prophesy to us, you Christ! Who is it that struck you?"

69 Now Peter was sitting outside in the courtyard. And a maid came up to him, and said, "You also were with Jesus the Galilean." 70 But he denied it before them all, saying, "I do not know what you mean." 71And when he went out to the porch, another maid saw him, and she said to the bystanders, "This man was with Jesus of Nazareth." 72And again he denied it with an oath, "I do not know the man." 73After a little while the bystanders came up and said to Peter, "Certainly you are also one of them, for your accent betrays you." 74 Then he began to invoke a curse on himself

and to swear, "I do not know the man." And immediately the cock crowed. 75And Peter remembered the saying of Jesus, "Before the cock crows, you will deny me three times." And he went out and wept bitterly.

27 When morning came, all the chief priests and the elders of the people took counsel against Jesus to put him to death; 2 and they bound him and led him away and delivered him to Pilate the governor.

3 When Judas, his betrayer, saw that he was condemned, he repented and brought back the thirty pieces of silver to the chief priests and the elders, 4 saying, "I have sinned in betraying innocent blood." They said, "What is that to us? See to it yourself." 5And throwing down the pieces of silver in the temple, he departed; and he went and hanged himself. 6 But the chief priests, taking the pieces of silver, said, "It is not lawful to put them into the treasury, since they are blood money." 7 So they took counsel, and bought with them the potter's field, to bury strangers in. 8 Therefore that field has been called the Field of Blood to this day. 9 Then was fulfilled what had been spoken by the prophet Jeremiah, saying, "And they took the thirty pieces of silver, the price of him on whom a price had been set by some of the sons of Israel, 10 and they gave them for the potter's field, as the Lord directed me."

11 Now Jesus stood before the governor; and the governor asked him, "Are you the King of the Jews?" Jesus said to him, "You have said so." 12 But when he was accused by the chief priests and elders, he made no answer. 13 Then Pilate said to him, "Do you not hear how many things they testify against you?" 14 But he gave him no answer, not even to a single charge; so that the governor wondered greatly.

15 Now at the feast the governor was accustomed to release for the crowd any one prisoner whom they wanted. 16And they had then a notorious prisoner, called Bà·rab́·bàs.[k] 17 So when they had gathered, Pilate said to them, "Whom do you want me to release for you, Bà·rab́·bàs[k] or Jesus

k Other ancient authorities read *Jesus Barabbas*

26.57-75: Mk 14.53-72; Lk 22.54-71; Jn 18.12-27.
26.61: Mt 24.2; 27.40; Acts 6.14; Jn 2.19.   26.63: Mt 27.11; Jn 18.33.
26.64: Mt 16.28; Dan 7.13; Ps 110.1.   26.65: Num 14.6; Acts 14.14; Lev 24.16.
26.75: Mt 26.34.   27.1-2: Mk 15.1; Lk 23.1; Jn 18.28.   27.3-10: Acts 1.16-20.
27.3: Mt 26.15; Ex 21.32.   27.6: Deut 23.18.   27.9: Zech 11.12-13; Jer 32.6-15; 18.2-3.
27.11-26: Mk 15.2-15; Lk 23.3, 18-25; Jn 18.29-19.16.
27.14: Lk 23.9; Mt 26.62; Mk 14.60; 1 Tim 6.13.

who is called Christ?" 18 For he knew that it was out of envy that they had delivered him up. 19 Besides, while he was sitting on the judgment seat, his wife sent word to him, "Have nothing to do with that righteous man, for I have suffered much over him today in a dream." 20 Now the chief priests and the elders persuaded the people to ask for Bȧ·rab′bȧs and destroy Jesus. 21 The governor again said to them, "Which of the two do you want me to release for you?" And they said, "Bȧ·rab′bȧs." 22 Pilate said to them, "Then what shall I do with Jesus who is called Christ?" They all said, "Let him be crucified." 23And he said, "Why, what evil has he done?" But they shouted all the more, "Let him be crucified."

24 So when Pilate saw that he was gaining nothing, but rather that a riot was beginning, he took water and washed his hands before the crowd, saying, "I am innocent of this man's blood;¹ see to it yourselves." 25And all the people answered, "His blood be on us and on our children!" 26 Then he released for them Bȧ·rab′bȧs, and having scourged Jesus, delivered him to be crucified.

27 Then the soldiers of the governor took Jesus into the praetorium, and they gathered the whole battalion before him. 28And they stripped him and put a scarlet robe upon him, 29 and plaiting a crown of thorns they put it on his head, and put a reed in his right hand. And kneeling before him they mocked him, saying, "Hail, King of the Jews!" 30And they spat upon him, and took the reed and struck him on the head. 31And when they had mocked him, they stripped him of the robe, and put his own clothes on him, and led him away to crucify him.

32 As they were marching out, they came upon a man of Cȳ·rē′nē, Simon by name; this man they compelled to carry his cross. 33And when they came to a place called Gol′gȯ·thȧ (which means the place of a skull), 34 they offered him wine to drink, mingled with gall; but when he tasted it, he would not drink it. 35And when they had crucified him, they divided his garments among them by casting lots; 36 then they sat down and kept watch over him there. 37And over his head they put the charge against him, which read, "This is Jesus the King of the Jews." 38 Then two robbers were crucified with him, one on the right and one on the left. 39And those who passed by derided him, wagging their heads 40 and saying, "You who would destroy the temple and build it in three days, save yourself! If you are the Son of God, come down from the cross." 41 So also the chief priests, with the scribes and elders, mocked him, saying, 42 "He saved others; he cannot save himself. He is the King of Israel; let him come down now from the cross, and we will believe in him. 43 He trusts in God; let God deliver him now, if he desires him; for he said, 'I am the Son of God.'" 44And the robbers who were crucified with him also reviled him in the same way.

45 Now from the sixth hour there was darkness over all the landᵐ until the ninth hour. 46And about the ninth hour Jesus cried with a loud voice, "E′li, E′li, lä′mȧ sȧ·bach′-thä′ni?" that is, "My God, my God, why hast thou forsaken me?" 47And some of the bystanders hearing it said, "This man is calling E·li′jȧh." 48And one of them at once ran and took a sponge, filled it with vinegar, and put it on a reed, and gave it to him to drink. 49 But the others said, "Wait, let us see whether E·li′jȧh will come to save him."ⁿ 50And Jesus cried again with a loud voice and yielded up his spirit.

51 And behold, the curtain of the temple was torn in two, from top to bottom; and the earth shook, and the rocks were split; 52 the tombs also were opened, and many bodies of the saints who had fallen asleep were raised, 53 and coming out of the tombs after his resurrection they went into the holy city and appeared to many. 54 When the centurion and those who were with him, keeping watch over Jesus, saw the earthquake and what

l Other authorities read *this righteous blood* or *this righteous man's blood*   *m* Or *earth*
n Other ancient authorities insert *And another took a spear and pierced his side, and out came water and blood*

27.19: Lk 23.4.   **27.21:** Acts 3.13-14.   **27.24:** Deut 21.6-9; Ps 26.6.
27.25: Acts 5.28; Josh 2.19.   **27.27-31:** Mk 15.16-20; Lk 23.11; Jn 19.2-3.
27.32: Mk 15.21; Lk 23.26; Jn 19.17; Heb 13.12.
27.33-44: Mk 15.22-32; Lk 23.33-39; Jn 19.17-24.   **27.35:** Ps 22.18.
27.39: Ps 22.7-8; 109.25.   **27.40:** Mt 26.61; Acts 6.14; Jn 2.19.
27.45-56: Mk 15.33-41; Lk 23.44-54; Jn 19.28-30.   **27.46:** Ps 22.1.   **27.48:** Ps 69.21.
27.51: Heb 9.8; 10.19; Ex 26.31-35; Mt 28.2.   **27.54:** Mt 3.17; 17.5.

took place, they were filled with awe, and said, "Truly this was the Son[x] of God!"

55 There were also many women there, looking on from afar, who had followed Jesus from Galilee, ministering to him; 56 among whom were Mary Mag'dà·lēne, and Mary the mother of James and Joseph, and the mother of the sons of Zeb'ė·dee.

57 When it was evening, there came a rich man from Ar·i·mà·thē'à, named Joseph, who also was a disciple of Jesus. 58 He went to Pilate and asked for the body of Jesus. Then Pilate ordered it to be given to him. 59 And Joseph took the body, and wrapped it in a clean linen shroud, 60 and laid it in his own new tomb, which he had hewn in the rock; and he rolled a great stone to the door of the tomb, and departed. 61 Mary Mag'dà·lēne and the other Mary were there, sitting opposite the sepulchre.

62 Next day, that is, after the day of Preparation, the chief priests and the Pharisees gathered before Pilate 63 and said, "Sir, we remember how that impostor said, while he was still alive, 'After three days I will rise again.' 64 Therefore order the sepulchre to be made secure until the third day, lest his disciples go and steal him away, and tell the people, 'He is risen from the dead,' and the last fraud will be worse than the first." 65 Pilate said to them, "You have a guard[o] of soldiers; go, make it as secure as you can."[p] 66 So they went and made the sepulchre secure by sealing the stone and setting a guard.

28 Now after the sabbath, toward the dawn of the first day of the week, Mary Mag'dà·lēne and the other Mary went to see the sepulchre. 2 And behold, there was a great earthquake; for an angel of the Lord descended from heaven and came and rolled back the stone, and sat upon it. 3 His appearance was like lightning, and his raiment white as snow. 4 And for fear of him the guards trembled and became like dead men. 5 But the angel said to the women, "Do not be afraid; for I know that you seek Jesus who was crucified. 6 He is not here; for he has risen, as he said. Come, see the place where he[q] lay. 7 Then go quickly and tell his disciples that he has risen from the dead, and behold, he is going before you to Galilee; there you will see him. Lo, I have told you." 8 So they departed quickly from the tomb with fear and great joy, and ran to tell his disciples. 9 And behold, Jesus met them and said, "Hail!" And they came up and took hold of his feet and worshiped him. 10 Then Jesus said to them, "Do not be afraid; go and tell my brethren to go to Galilee, and there they will see me."

11 While they were going, behold, some of the guard went into the city and told the chief priests all that had taken place. 12 And when they had assembled with the elders and taken counsel, they gave a sum of money to the soldiers 13 and said, "Tell people, 'His disciples came by night and stole him away while we were asleep.' 14 And if this comes to the governor's ears, we will satisfy him and keep you out of trouble." 15 So they took the money and did as they were directed; and this story has been spread among the Jews to this day.

16 Now the eleven disciples went to Galilee, to the mountain to which Jesus had directed them. 17 And when they saw him they worshiped him; but some doubted. 18 And Jesus came and said to them, "All authority in heaven and on earth has been given to me. 19 Go therefore and make disciples of all nations, baptizing them in the name of the Father and of the Son and of the Holy Spirit, 20 teaching them to observe all that I have commanded you; and lo, I am with you always, to the close of the age."

---

x Or *a son*   *o* Or *Take a guard*   *p* Greek *know*
q Other ancient authorities read *the Lord*

27.56: Lk 24.10. **27.57-61:** Mk 15.42-47; Lk 23.50-56; Jn 19.38-42; Acts 13.29. **27.63:** Mt 16.21; 17.23; 20.19. **27.66:** Mt 27.60; 28.11-15.
28.1-8: Mk 16.1-8; Lk 24.1-9; Jn 20.1-2.   **28.1:** Lk 8.2; Mt 27.56.
28.2: Mt 27.51, 60.   **28.4:** Mt 27.62-66.   **28.7:** Mt 26.32; 28.16; Jn 21.1-23.
28.9: Jn 20.14-18.   **28.11:** Mt 27.62-66.   **28.16-17:** 1 Cor 15.5; Jn 21.1-23.
28.18: Mt 11.27; Lk 10.22; Phil 2.9; Eph 1.20-22.   **28.19:** Lk 24.47; Acts 1.8.
28.20: Mt 13.39, 49; 24.3; 18.20; Acts 18.10.

THE GOSPEL ACCORDING TO

MARK

1 The beginning of the gospel of Jesus Christ, the Son of God.*a*

2 As it is written in I·sāi'ah the prophet,*b*

"Behold, I send my messenger before thy face,
who shall prepare thy way;

3 the voice of one crying in the wilderness:

Prepare the way of the Lord,
make his paths straight—"

4 John the baptizer appeared*c* in the wilderness, preaching a baptism of repentance for the forgiveness of sins. 5 And there went out to him all the country of Judea, and all the people of Jerusalem; and they were baptized by him in the river Jordan, confessing their sins. 6 Now John was clothed with camel's hair, and had a leather girdle around his waist, and ate locusts and wild honey. 7 And he preached, saying, "After me comes he who is mightier than I, the thong of whose sandals I am not worthy to stoop down and untie. 8 I have baptized you with water; but he will baptize you with the Holy Spirit."

9 In those days Jesus came from Nazareth of Galilee and was baptized by John in the Jordan. 10 And when he came up out of the water, immediately he saw the heavens opened and the Spirit descending upon him like a dove; 11 and a voice came from heaven, "Thou art my beloved Son;*d* with thee I am well pleased."

12 The Spirit immediately drove him out into the wilderness. 13 And he was in the wilderness forty days, tempted by Satan; and he was with the wild beasts; and the angels ministered to him.

14 Now after John was arrested, Jesus came into Galilee, preaching the gospel of God, 15 and saying, "The time is fulfilled, and the kingdom of God is at hand; repent, and believe in the gospel."

16 And passing along by the Sea of Galilee, he saw Simon and Andrew the brother of Simon casting a net in the sea; for they were fishermen. 17 And Jesus said to them, "Follow me and I will make you become fishers of men." 18 And immediately they left their nets and followed him. 19 And going on a little farther, he saw James the son of Zeb'ē·dee and John his brother, who were in their boat mending the nets. 20 And immediately he called them; and they left their father Zeb'ē·dee in the boat with the hired servants, and followed him.

21 And they went into Cà·pēr'nà·um; and immediately on the sabbath he entered the synagogue and taught. 22 And they were astonished at his teaching, for he taught them as one who had authority, and not as the scribes. 23 And immediately there was in their synagogue a man with an unclean spirit; 24 and he cried out, "What have you to do with us, Jesus of Nazareth? Have you come to destroy us? I know who you are, the Holy One of God." 25 But Jesus rebuked him, saying, "Be silent, and come out of him!" 26 And the unclean spirit, convulsing him and crying with a loud voice, came out of him. 27 And they were all amazed, so that they questioned among themselves, saying, "What is this? A new teaching! With authority he commands even the unclean spirits, and they obey him." 28 And at once his fame spread everywhere throughout all the surrounding region of Galilee.

29 And immediately he*e* left the synagogue, and entered the house of Simon and Andrew, with James and

a Other ancient authorities omit the Son of God
b Other ancient authorities read in the prophets
c Other ancient authorities read John was baptizing
d Or my Son, my (or the) Beloved
e Other ancient authorities read they

1.2-8: Mt 3.1-12; Lk 3.2-16; Jn 1.6, 15, 19-28.   **1.2:** Mal 3.1; Mt 11.10; Lk 7.27.
1.3: Is 40.3.   **1.4:** Acts 13.24.   **1.9-11:** Mt 3.13-17; Lk 3.21-22; Jn 1.29-34.
1.11: Ps 2.7; Is 42.1.   **1.12-13:** Mt 4.1-11; Lk 4.1-13.
1.14-15: Mt 4.12-17; Lk 4.14-15.   **1.16-20:** Mt 4.18-22; Lk 5.1-11; Jn 1.40-42.
1.21-22: Mt 7.28-29; Lk 4.31-32.   **1.23-28:** Lk 4.33-37.   **1.24:** Jn 6.69.
1.29-31: Mt 8.14-15; Lk 4.38-39.

John. 30 Now Simon's mother-in-law lay sick with a fever, and immediately they told him of her. 31And he came and took her by the hand and lifted her up, and the fever left her; and she served them.

32 That evening, at sundown, they brought to him all who were sick or possessed with demons. 33And the whole city was gathered together about the door. 34And he healed many who were sick with various diseases, and cast out many demons; and he would not permit the demons to speak, because they knew him.

35 And in the morning, a great while before day, he rose and went out to a lonely place, and there he prayed. 36And Simon and those who were with him followed him, 37 and they found him and said to him, "Every one is searching for you." 38And he said to them, "Let us go on to the next towns, that I may preach there also; for that is why I came out." 39And he went throughout all Galilee, preaching in their synagogues and casting out demons.

40 And a leper came to him beseeching him, and kneeling said to him, "If you will, you can make me clean." 41 Moved with pity, he stretched out his hand and touched him, and said to him, "I will; be clean." 42And immediately the leprosy left him, and he was made clean. 43And he sternly charged him, and sent him away at once, 44 and said to him, "See that you say nothing to any one; but go, show yourself to the priest, and offer for your cleansing what Moses commanded, for a proof to the people." f 45 But he went out and began to talk freely about it, and to spread the news, so that Jesusg could no longer openly enter a town, but was out in the country; and people came to him from every quarter.

2 And when he returned to Cà-pĕr′nà-ŭm after some days, it was reported that he was at home. 2And many were gathered together, so that there was no longer room for them, not even about the door; and he was preaching the word to them. 3And they came, bringing to him a paralytic carried by four men. 4And when they could not get near him because of the crowd, they removed the roof above

him; and when they had made an opening, they let down the pallet on which the paralytic lay. 5And when Jesus saw their faith, he said to the paralytic, "My son, your sins are forgiven." 6 Now some of the scribes were sitting there, questioning in their hearts, 7 "Why does this man speak thus? It is blasphemy! Who can forgive sins but God alone?" 8And immediately Jesus, perceiving in his spirit that they thus questioned within themselves, said to them, "Why do you question thus in your hearts? 9 Which is easier, to say to the paralytic, 'Your sins are forgiven,' or to say, 'Rise, take up your pallet and walk'? 10 But that you may know that the Son of man has authority on earth to forgive sins"—he said to the paralytic—11 "I say to you, rise, take up your pallet and go home." 12And he rose, and immediately took up the pallet and went out before them all; so that they were all amazed and glorified God, saying, "We never saw anything like this!"

13 He went out again beside the sea; and all the crowd gathered about him, and he taught them. 14And as he passed on, he saw Levi the son of Al·phæ′ús sitting at the tax office, and he said to him, "Follow me." And he rose and followed him.

15 And as he sat at table in his house, many tax collectors and sinners were sitting with Jesus and his disciples; for there were many who followed him. 16And the scribes ofh the Pharisees, when they saw that he was eating with sinners and tax collectors, said to his disciples, "Why does he eati with tax collectors and sinners?" 17And when Jesus heard it, he said to them, "Those who are well have no need of a physician, but those who are sick; I came not to call the righteous, but sinners."

18 Now John's disciples and the Pharisees were fasting; and people came and said to him, "Why do John's disciples and the disciples of the Pharisees fast, but your disciples do not fast?" 19And Jesus said to them, "Can the wedding guests fast while the bridegroom is with them? As long as they have the bridegroom with them, they cannot fast. 20The days will come, when the bridegroom

f Greek *to them*   g Greek *he*   h Other ancient authorities read *and*
i Other ancient authorities add *and drink*
1.32-34: Mt 8.16-17; Lk 4.40-41.   **1.35-38:** Lk 4.42-43.   **1.39:** Mt 4.23-25; Lk 4.44.
1.44: Lev 13.49; 14.2-32.   **1.40-45:** Mt 8.2-4; Lk 5.12-16.
2.3-12: Mt 9.2-8; Lk 5.18-26.   **2.12:** Mt 9.33.   **2.14-17:** Mt 9.9-13; Lk 5.27-32.
2.16: Acts 23.9.   **2.18-22:** Mt 9.14-17; Lk 5.33-38.   **2.20:** Lk 17.22.

is taken away from them, and then they will fast in that day. 21 No one sews a piece of unshrunk cloth on an old garment; if he does, the patch tears away from it, the new from the old, and a worse tear is made. 22And no one puts new wine into old wine-skins; if he does, the wine will burst the skins, and the wine is lost, and so are the skins; but new wine is for fresh skins."*i*

23 One sabbath he was going through the grainfields; and as they made their way his disciples began to pluck ears of grain. 24And the Pharisees said to him, "Look, why are they doing what is not lawful on the sabbath?" 25And he said to them, "Have you never read what David did, when he was in need and was hungry, he and those who were with him: 26 how he entered the house of God, when A·bī'a·thär was high priest, and ate the bread of the Presence, which is not lawful for any but the priests to eat, and also gave it to those who were with him?" 27And he said to them, "The sabbath was made for man, not man for the sabbath; 28 so the Son of man is lord even of the sabbath."

3 Again he entered the synagogue, and a man was there who had a withered hand. 2And they watched him, to see whether he would heal him on the sabbath, so that they might accuse him. 3And he said to the man who had the withered hand, "Come here." 4And he said to them, "Is it lawful on the sabbath to do good or to do harm, to save life or to kill?" But they were silent. 5And he looked around at them with anger, grieved at their hardness of heart, and said to the man, "Stretch out your hand." He stretched it out, and his hand was restored. 6 The Pharisees went out, and immediately held counsel with the He·rō'di·ans against him, how to destroy him.

7 Jesus withdrew with his disciples to the sea, and a great multitude from Galilee followed; also from Judea 8 and Jerusalem and Id·ū·mē'a and from beyond the Jordan and from about Tyre and Sī'don a great multi-

tude, hearing all that he did, came to him. 9And he told his disciples to have a boat ready for him because of the crowd, lest they should crush him; 10 for he had healed many, so that all who had diseases pressed upon him to touch him. 11And whenever the unclean spirits beheld him, they fell down before him and cried out, "You are the Son of God." 12And he strictly ordered them not to make him known.

13 And he went up into the hills, and called to him those whom he desired; and they came to him. 14And he appointed twelve,*k* to be with him, and to be sent out to preach 15 and have authority to cast out demons: 16 Simon whom he surnamed Peter; 17 James the son of Zeb'e·dee and John the brother of James, whom he surnamed Bō·a·nēr'gēs, that is, sons of thunder; 18Andrew, and Philip, and Bartholomew, and Matthew, and Thomas, and James the son of Al-phaē'us, and Thad·daē'us, and Simon the Cā·na·naē'an, 19 and Judas Is·car'-i·ot, who betrayed him.

Then he went home; 20 and the crowd came together again, so that they could not even eat. 21And when his friends heard it, they went out to seize him, for they said, "He is beside himself." 22And the scribes who came down from Jerusalem said, "He is possessed by Bē·el'zē·bul, and by the prince of demons he casts out the demons." 23And he called them to him, and said to them in parables, "How can Satan cast out Satan? 24 If a kingdom is divided against itself, that kingdom cannot stand. 25And if a house is divided against itself, that house will not be able to stand. 26And if Satan has risen up against himself and is divided, he cannot stand, but is coming to an end. 27 But no one can enter a strong man's house and plunder his goods, unless he first binds the strong man; then indeed he may plunder his house.

28 "Truly, I say to you, all sins will be forgiven the sons of men, and whatever blasphemies they utter; 29 but whoever blasphemes against the Holy Spirit never has forgiveness, but is

i Other ancient authorities omit *but new wine is for fresh skins*
k Other ancient authorities add *whom also he named apostles*

2.23-28: Mt 12.1-8; Lk 6.1-5.   **2.23:** Deut 23.25.   **2.26:** 1 Sam 21.1-6; 2 Sam 8.17.
2.27: Ex 23.12; Deut 5.14.   **3.1-6:** Mt 12.9-14; Lk 6.6-11.   **3.2:** Lk 11.54.
3.6: Mk 12.13.   **3.7-12:** Mt 4.24-25; 12.15-16; Lk 6.17-19.   **3.8:** Mt 11.21.
3.10: Mk 5.29, 34; 6.56.   **3.12:** Mk 1.45.   **3.13:** Mt 5.1; Lk 6.12.   **3.14-15:** Mt 10.1.
3.16-19: Mt 10.2-4; Lk 6.14-16; Acts 1.13.   **3.19:** Mt 2.1; 7.17.   **3.20:** Mk 6.31.
3.21: Mk 3.31-35; Jn 10.20.   **3.22-27:** Mt 12.24-29; Lk 11.15-22.
3.22: Mt 9.34; 10.25.   **3.27:** Is 49.24-25.   **3.28-30:** Mt 12.31-32; Lk 12.10.

guilty of an eternal sin"—30 for they had said, "He has an unclean spirit."

31 And his mother and his brothers came; and standing outside they sent to him and called him. 32And a crowd was sitting about him; and they said to him, "Your mother and your brothers*l* are outside, asking for you." 33And he replied, "Who are my mother and my brothers?" 34And looking around on those who sat about him, he said, "Here are my mother and my brother! 35 Whoever does the will of God is my brother, and sister, and mother."

4 Again he began to teach beside the sea. And a very large crowd gathered about him, so that he got into a boat and sat in it on the sea; and the whole crowd was beside the sea on the land. 2And he taught them many things in parables, and in his teaching he said to them: 3 "Listen! A sower went out to sow. 4And as he sowed, some seed fell along the path, and the birds came and devoured it. 5 Other seed fell on rocky ground, where it had not much soil, and immediately it sprang up, since it had no depth of soil; 6 and when the sun rose it was scorched, and since it had no root it withered away. 7 Other seed fell among thorns and the thorns grew up and choked it, and it yielded no grain. 8And other seeds fell into good soil and brought forth grain, growing up and increasing and yielding thirtyfold and sixtyfold and a hundredfold." 9And he said, "He who has ears to hear, let him hear."

10 And when he was alone, those who were about him with the twelve asked him concerning the parables. 11And he said to them, "To you has been given the secret of the kingdom of God, but for those outside everything is in parables; 12 so that they may indeed see but not perceive, and may indeed hear but not understand; lest they should turn again, and be forgiven." 13And he said to them, "Do you not understand this parable? How then will you understand all the parables? 14 The sower sows the word. 15And these are the ones along the path, where the word is sown; when they hear, Satan immediately comes

and takes away the word which is sown in them. 16And these in like manner are the ones sown upon rocky ground, who, when they hear the word, immediately receive it with joy; 17 and they have no root in themselves, but endure for a while; then, when tribulation or persecution arises on account of the word, immediately they fall away.*m* 18And others are the ones sown among thorns; they are those who hear the word, 19 but the cares of the world, and the delight in riches, and the desire for other things, enter in and choke the word, and it proves unfruitful. 20 But those that were sown upon the good soil are the ones who hear the word and accept it and bear fruit, thirtyfold and sixtyfold and a hundredfold."

21 And he said to them, "Is a lamp brought in to be put under a bushel, or under a bed, and not on a stand? 22 For there is nothing hid, except to be made manifest; nor is anything secret, except to come to light. 23 If any man has ears to hear, let him hear." 24And he said to them, "Take heed what you hear; the measure you give will be the measure you get, and still more will be given you. 25 For to him who has will more be given; and from him who has not, even what he has will be taken away."

26 And he said, "The kingdom of God is as if a man should scatter seed upon the ground, 27 and should sleep and rise night and day, and the seed should sprout and grow, he knows not how. 28 The earth produces of itself, first the blade, then the ear, then the full grain in the ear. 29 But when the grain is ripe, at once he puts in the sickle, because the harvest has come."

30 And he said, "With what can we compare the kingdom of God, or what parable shall we use for it? 31 It is like a grain of mustard seed, which, when sown upon the ground, is the smallest of all the seeds on earth; 32 yet when it is sown it grows up and becomes the greatest of all shrubs, and puts forth large branches, so that the birds of the air can make nests in its shade."

33 With many such parables he spoke the word to them, as they were

l Other early authorities add *and your sisters*   *m* Or *stumble*

3.31-35: Mt 12.46-50; Lk 8.19-21.   4.1-9: Mt 13.1-9; Lk 8.4-8.
4.10-12: Mt 13.10-15; Lk 8.9-10.
4.11: 1 Cor 5.12-13; Col 4.5; 1 Thess 4.12; 1 Tim 3.7.   4.12: Is 6.9-10.
4.13-20: Mt 13.18-23; Lk 8.11-15.   4.21: Mt 5.15; Lk 8.16; 11.33.
4.22: Mt 10.26; Lk 8.17; 12.2.   4.23: Mt 11.15; Mk 4.9.   4.24: Mt 7.2; Lk 6.38.
4.25: Mt 13.12; 25.29; Lk 8.18; 19.26.   4.26-29: Mt 13.24-30.
4.30-32: Mt 13.31-32; Lk 13.18-19.

able to hear it; [34] he did not speak to them without a parable, but privately to his own disciples he explained everything.

35 On that day, when evening had come, he said to them, "Let us go across to the other side." [36]And leaving the crowd, they took him with them, just as he was, in the boat. And other boats were with him. [37]And a great storm of wind arose, and the waves beat into the boat, so that the boat was already filling. [38] But he was in the stern, asleep on the cushion; and they woke him and said to him, "Teacher, do you not care if we perish?" [39]And he awoke and rebuked the wind, and said to the sea, "Peace! Be still!" And the wind ceased, and there was a great calm. [40] He said to them, "Why are you afraid? Have you no faith?" [41]And they were filled with awe, and said to one another, "Who then is this, that even wind and sea obey him?"

5 They came to the other side of the sea, to the country of the Ger'a·senes.[n] [2]And when he had come out of the boat, there met him out of the tombs a man with an unclean spirit, [3] who lived among the tombs; and no one could bind him any more, even with a chain; [4] for he had often been bound with fetters and chains, but the chains he wrenched apart, and the fetters he broke in pieces; and no one had the strength to subdue him. [5] Night and day among the tombs and on the mountains he was always crying out, and bruising himself with stones. [6]And when he saw Jesus from afar, he ran and worshiped him; [7] and crying out with a loud voice, he said, "What have you to do with me, Jesus, Son of the Most High God? I adjure you by God, do not torment me." [8] For he had said to him, "Come out of the man, you unclean spirit!" [9]And Jesus[o] asked him, "What is your name?" He replied, "My name is Legion; for we are many." [10]And he begged him eagerly not to send them out of the country. [11] Now a great herd of swine was feeding there on the hillside; [12] and they begged him, "Send us to the swine, let us enter them." [13] So he gave them leave. And the unclean spirits came out, and entered the swine; and the herd, numbering about two thousand, rushed down the steep

bank into the sea, and were drowned in the sea.

14 The herdsmen fled, and told it in the city and in the country. And people came to see what it was that had happened. [15]And they came to Jesus, and saw the demoniac sitting there, clothed and in his right mind, the man who had had the legion; and they were afraid. [16]And those who had seen it told what had happened to the demoniac and to the swine. [17]And they began to beg Jesus[p] to depart from their neighborhood. [18]And as he was getting into the boat, the man who had been possessed with demons begged him that he might be with him. [19] But he refused, and said to him, "Go home to your friends, and tell them how much the Lord has done for you, and how he has had mercy on you." [20]And he went away and began to proclaim in the De·cap'o·lis how much Jesus had done for him; and all men marveled.

21 And when Jesus had crossed again in the boat to the other side, a great crowd gathered about him; and he was beside the sea. [22] Then came one of the rulers of the synagogue, Ja'i·rus by name; and seeing him, he fell at his feet, [23] and besought him, saying, "My little daughter is at the point of death. Come and lay your hands on her, so that she may be made well, and live." [24]And he went with him.

And a great crowd followed him and thronged about him. [25]And there was a woman who had had a flow of blood for twelve years, [26] and who had suffered much under many physicians, and had spent all that she had, and was no better but rather grew worse. [27] She had heard the reports about Jesus, and came up behind him in the crowd and touched his garment. [28] For she said, "If I touch even his garments, I shall be made well." [29]And immediately the hemorrhage ceased; and she felt in her body that she was healed of her disease. [30]And Jesus, perceiving in himself that power had gone forth from him, immediately turned about in the crowd, and said, "Who touched my garments?" [31]And his disciples said to him, "You see the crowd pressing around you, and yet you say, 'Who touched me?'" [32]And he looked around to see who had done

n Other ancient authorities read *Gergesenes*, some *Gadarenes*   o Greek *he*   p Greek *him*
4.34: Mt 13.34; Jn 16.25.   4.35-41: Mt 8.18, 23-27; Lk 8.22-25.
5.1-20: Mt 8.28-34; Lk 8.26-39.   5.7: Acts 16.17; Heb 7.1; Mk 1.24.   5.20: Mk 7.31.
5.21-43: Mt 9.18-26; 8.40-56. Lk   5.22: Lk 13.14; Acts 13.15; 18.8, 17.
5.23: Mk 6.5; 7.32; 8.23; Acts 9.17; 28.8.   5.30: Lk 5.17.

it. 33 But the woman, knowing what had been done to her, came in fear and trembling and fell down before him, and told him the whole truth. 34And he said to her, "Daughter, your faith has made you well; go in peace, and be healed of your disease."

35 While he was still speaking, there came from the ruler's house some who said, "Your daughter is dead. Why trouble the Teacher any further?" 36 But ignoring^q what they said, Jesus said to the ruler of the synagogue, "Do not fear, only believe." 37And he allowed no one to follow him except Peter and James and John the brother of James. 38 When they came to the house of the ruler of the synagogue, he saw a tumult, and people weeping and wailing loudly. 39And when he had entered, he said to them, "Why do you make a tumult and weep? The child is not dead but sleeping." 40And they laughed at him. But he put them all outside, and took the child's father and mother and those who were with him, and went in where the child was. 41 Taking her by the hand he said to her, "Tal'i·tha cu'mi"; which means, "Little girl, I say to you, arise." 42And immediately the girl got up and walked; for she was twelve years old. And immediately they were overcome with amazement. 43And he strictly charged them that no one should know this, and told them to give her something to eat.

6 He went away from there and came to his own country; and his disciples followed him. 2And on the sabbath he began to teach in the synagogue; and many who heard him were astonished, saying, "Where did this man get all this? What is the wisdom given to him? What mighty works are wrought by his hands! 3 Is not this the carpenter, the son of Mary and brother of James and Jō'sēs and Judas and Simon, and are not his sisters here with us?" And they took offense^r at him. 4And Jesus said to them, "A prophet is not without honor, except in his own country, and among his own kin, and in his own house." 5And he could do no mighty work there, except that he laid his

hands upon a few sick people and healed them. 6And he marveled because of their unbelief.

And he went about among the villages teaching.

7 And he called to him the twelve, and began to send them out two by two, and gave them authority over the unclean spirits. 8 He charged them to take nothing for their journey except a staff; no bread, no bag, no money in their belts; 9 but to wear sandals and not put on two tunics. 10And he said to them, "Where you enter a house, stay there until you leave the place. 11And if any place will not receive you and you they refuse to hear you, when you leave, shake off the dust that is on your feet for a testimony against them." 12 So they went out and preached that men should repent. 13And they cast out many demons, and anointed with oil many that were sick and healed them.

14 King Her'od heard of it; for Jesus'^s name had become known. Some^t said, "John the baptizer has been raised from the dead; that is why these powers are at work in him." 15 But others said, "It is E·li'jah." And others said, "It is a prophet, like one of the prophets of old." 16 But when Her'od heard of it he said, "John, whom I beheaded, has been raised." 17 For Her'od had sent and seized John, and bound him in prison for the sake of He·rō'di·as, his brother Philip's wife; because he had married her. 18 For John said to Her'od, "It is not lawful for you to have your brother's wife." 19And He·rō'di·as had a grudge against him, and wanted to kill him. But she could not, 20 for Her'od feared John, knowing that he was a righteous and holy man, and kept him safe. When he heard him, he was much perplexed; and yet he heard him gladly. 21 But an opportunity came when Her'od on his birthday gave a banquet for his courtiers and officers and the leading men of Galilee. 22 For when He·rō'di·as' daughter came in and danced, she pleased Her'od and his guests; and the king said to the girl, "Ask me for whatever you wish, and I will grant it." 23And he vowed to her,

q Or overhearing. Other ancient authorities read hearing   r Or stumbled   s Greek his
t Other ancient authorities read he
5.34: Lk 7.50; Mk 10.52   5.37: Mk 9.2; 13.3.   5.41: Lk 7.14; Acts 9.40.
5.43: Mk 1.43-44; 7.36.   6.1-6: Mt 13.53-58; Lk 4.16-30.   6.2: Mk 1.21; Mt 7.28.
6.3: Mt 11.6.   6.5: Mk 5.23; 7.32; 8.23.   6.6: Mt 9.35.
6.7-11: Mt 10.1, 5, 7-11; Lk 9.1-5   6.7: Lk 10.1.   6.11: Mt 10.14.
6.12-13: Mt 11.1; Lk 9.6.   6.13: Jas 5.14.
6.14-16: Mt 14.1-2; Lk 9.7-9; 9.19; Mt 21.11.   6.17-18: Mt 14.3-4; Lk 3.19-20.
6.19-29: Mt 14.5-12.   6.20: Mt 21.26.   6.23: Esther 5.3, 6.

"Whatever you ask me, I will give you, even half of my kingdom." 24And she went out, and said to her mother, "What shall I ask?" And she said, "The head of John the baptizer." 25And she came in immediately with haste to the king, and asked, saying, "I want you to give me at once the head of John the Baptist on a platter." 26And the king was exceedingly sorry; but because of his oaths and his guests he did not want to break his word to her. 27And immediately the king sent a soldier of the guard and gave orders to bring his head. He went and beheaded him in the prison, 28 and brought his head on a platter, and gave it to the girl; and the girl gave it to her mother. 29 When his disciples heard of it, they came and took his body, and laid it in a tomb.

30 The apostles returned to Jesus, and told him all that they had done and taught. 31And he said to them, "Come away by yourselves to a lonely place, and rest a while." For many were coming and going, and they had no leisure even to eat. 32And they went away in the boat to a lonely place by themselves. 33 Now many saw them going, and knew them, and they ran there on foot from all the towns, and got there ahead of them. 34As he landed he saw a great throng, and he had compassion on them, because they were like sheep without a shepherd; and he began to teach them many things. 35And when it grew late, his disciples came to him and said, "This is a lonely place, and the hour is now late; 36 send them away, to go into the country and villages round about and buy themselves something to eat." 37 But he answered them, "You give them something to eat." And they said to him, "Shall we go and buy two hundred denarii*u* worth of bread, and give it to them to eat? 38And he said to them, "How many loaves have you? Go and see." And when they had found out, they said, "Five, and two fish." 39 Then he commanded them all to sit down by companies upon the green grass. 40 So they sat down in groups, by hundreds and by fifties. 41And taking the five loaves and the two fish he looked up to heaven, and

blessed, and broke the loaves, and gave them to the disciples to set before the people; and he divided the two fish among them all. 42And they all ate and were satisfied. 43And they took up twelve baskets full of broken pieces and of the fish. 44And those who ate the loaves were five thousand men.

45 Immediately he made his disciples get into the boat and go before him to the other side, to Beth-sā´i·dà, while he dismissed the crowd. 46And after he had taken leave of them, he went into the hills to pray. 47And when evening came, the boat was out on the sea, and he was alone on the land. 48And he saw that they were distressed in rowing, for the wind was against them. And about the fourth watch of the night he came to them, walking on the sea. He meant to pass by them, 49 but when they saw him walking on the sea they thought it was a ghost, and cried out; 50 for they all saw him, and were terrified. But immediately he spoke to them and said, "Take heart, it is I; have no fear." 51And he got into the boat with them and the wind ceased. And they were utterly astounded, 52 for they did not understand about the loaves, but their hearts were hardened.

53 And when they had crossed over, they came to land at Gen·nes´a·ret, and moored to the shore. 54And when the got out of the boat, immediately the people recognized him, 55 and ran about the whole neighborhood and began to bring sick people on their pallets to any place where they heard he was. 56And wherever he came, in villages, cities, or country, they laid the sick in the market places, and besought him that they might touch even the fringe of his garment; and as many as touched it were made well.

7 Now when the Pharisees gathered together to him, with some of the scribes, who had come from Jerusalem, 2 they saw that some of his disciples ate with hands defiled, that is, unwashed. 3 (For the Pharisees, and all the Jews, do not eat unless they wash their hands,*v* observing the tradition of the elders; 4 and when they come from the market place, they do not eat unless they purify*w* themselves;

u The denarius was worth about twenty cents
v One Greek word is of uncertain meaning and is not translated
w Other ancient authorities read *baptize*

6.30-31: Lk 9.10; Mk 3.20.
6.32-44: Mt 14.13-21; Lk 9.11-17; Jn 6.5-13; Mk 8.1-10; Mt 15.32-39.　**6.34:** Mt 9.36.
6.37: 2 Kings 4.42-44.　**6.41:** Mk 14.22; Lk 24.30-31.　**6.45-52:** Mt 14.22-33; Jn 6.15-21.
6.48: Mk 13.35.　**6.50:** Mt 9.2.　**6.52:** Mk 8.17.　**6.53-56:** Mt 14.34-36.
6.56: Mk 3.10; Mt 9.20.　**7.1-15:** Mt 15.1-11; Lk 11.38.　**7.4:** Mt 23.25; Lk 11.39.

and there are many other traditions which they observe, the washing of cups and pots and vessels of bronze.[x]) [5]And the Pharisees and the scribes asked him, "Why do your disciples not live[y] according to the tradition of the elders, but eat with hands defiled?" [6]And he said to them, "Well did I·ṣāi'āh prophesy of you hypocrites, as it is written,

'This people honors me with their lips,
but their heart is far from me;
[7] in vain do they worship me,
teaching as doctrines the precepts of men.'

[8] You leave the commandment of God, and hold fast the tradition of men."

[9] And he said to them, "You have a fine way of rejecting the commandment of God, in order to keep your tradition! [10] For Moses said, 'Honor your father and your mother'; and, 'He who speaks evil of father or mother, let him surely die'; [11] but you say, 'If a man tell his father or his mother, What you would have gained from me is Côr'bàn' (that is, given to God)—[12] then you no longer permit him to do anything for his father or mother, [13] thus making void the word of God through your tradition which you hand on. And many such things you do."

[14] And he called the people to him again, and said to them, "Hear me, all of you, and understand; [15] there is nothing outside a man which by going into him can defile him; but the things which come out of a man are what defile him."[a] [17]And when he had entered the house, and left the people, his disciples asked him about the parable. [18]And he said to them, "Then are you also without understanding? Do you not see that whatever goes into a man from outside cannot defile him, [19] since it enters, not his heart but his stomach, and so passes on?" (Thus he declared all foods clean.) [20]And he said, "What comes out of a man is what defiles a man. [21] For from within, out of the heart of man, come evil thoughts, fornication, theft, murder, adultery,[z] coveting, wickedness, deceit, licentiousness, envy, slander,

pride, foolishness. [23]All these evil things come from within, and they defile a man."

[24] And from there he arose and went away to the region of Tŷre and Si'don.[c] And he entered a house, and would not have any one know it; yet he could not be hid. [25] But immediately a woman, whose little daughter was possessed by an unclean spirit, heard of him, and came and fell down at his feet. [26] Now the woman was a Greek, a Sŷ·rō·phòe·ni'ciăn by birth. And she begged him to cast the demon out of her daughter. [27]And he said to her, "Let the children first be fed, for it is not right to take the children's bread and throw it to the dogs." [28] But she answered him, "Yes, Lord; yet even the dogs under the table eat the children's crumbs." [29]And he said to her, "For this saying you may go your way; the demon has left your daughter." [30]And she went home, and found the child lying in bed, and the demon gone.

[31] Then he returned from the region of Tŷre, and went through Si'don to the Sea of Galilee, through the region of the De·cap'ó·lis. [32]And they brought to him a man who was deaf and had an impediment in his speech; and they besought him to lay his hand upon him. [33]And taking him aside from the multitude privately, he put his fingers into his ears, and he spat and touched his tongue; [34] and looking up to heaven, he sighed, and said to him, "Eph'phà·thà," that is, "Be opened." [35]And his ears were opened, his tongue was released, and he spoke plainly. [36]And he charged them to tell no one; but the more he charged them, the more zealously they proclaimed it. [37]And they were astonished beyond measure, saying, "He has done all things well; he even makes the deaf hear and the dumb speak."

8 In those days, when again a great crowd had gathered, and they had nothing to eat, he called his disciples to him, and said to them, [2] "I have compassion on the crowd, because they have been with me now three days, and have nothing to eat; [3] and if I send them away hungry to their

---

[x] Other ancient authorities add *and beds*   [y] Greek *walk*   [z] Or *an offering*
[a] Other ancient authorities add verse 16, *"If any man has ears to hear, let him hear"*
[b] Or *is evacuated*   [c] Other ancient authorities omit *and Sidon*

7.5: Gal 1.14.   **7.6-7:** Is 29.13.   **7.10:** Ex 20.12; Deut 5.16; Ex 21.17; Lev 20.9.
7.17-23: Mt 15.15-20; Mk 4.10.
7.18-19: 1 Cor 10.25-27; Rom 14.14; Tit 1.15; Acts 10.15.
7.20-23: Rom 1.28-31; Gal 5.19-21.   **7.22:** Mt 6.23; 20.15.   **7.24-30:** Mt 15.21-28.
7.31-37: Mt 15.29-31.   **7.32:** Mk 5.23.   **7.33:** Mk 8.23.   **7.36:** Mk 1.44; 5.43.
8.1-10: Mt 15.32-39; Mk 6.32-44; Mt 14.13-21; Lk 9.11-17; Jn 6.5-13.

homes, they will faint on the way; and some of them have come a long way." ⁴And his disciples answered him, "How can one feed these men with bread here in the desert?" ⁵And he asked them, "How many loaves have you?" They said, "Seven." ⁶And he commanded the crowd to sit down on the ground; and he took the seven loaves, and having given thanks he broke them and gave them to his disciples to set before the people; and they set them before the crowd. ⁷And they had a few small fish; and having blessed them, he commanded that these also should be set before them. ⁸And they ate, and were satisfied; and they took up the broken pieces left over, seven baskets full. ⁹And there were about four thousand people. ¹⁰And he sent them away and immediately he got into the boat with his disciples, and went to the district of Dal·ma·nuʹtha.ᵈ

11 The Pharisees came and began to argue with him, seeking from him a sign from heaven, to test him. ¹²And he sighed deeply in his spirit, and said, "Why does this generation seek a sign? Truly, I say to you, no sign shall be given to this generation." ¹³And he left them, and getting into the boat again he departed to the other side.

14 Now they had forgotten to bring bread; and they had only one loaf with them in the boat. ¹⁵And he cautioned them, saying, "Take heed, beware of the leaven of the Pharisees and the leaven of Herʹod."ᵉ ¹⁶And they discussed it with one another, saying, "We have no bread." ¹⁷And being aware of it, Jesus said to them, "Why do you discuss the fact that you have no bread? Do you not yet perceive or understand? Are your hearts hardened? ¹⁸Having eyes do you not see, and having ears do you not hear? And do you not remember? ¹⁹When I broke the five loaves for the five thousand, how many baskets full of broken pieces did you take up?" They said to him, "Twelve." ²⁰"And the seven for the four thousand, how many baskets full of broken pieces did you take up?" And they said to him, "Seven." ²¹And

he said to them, "Do you not yet understand?"

22 And they came to Beth-saʹi·da. And some people brought to him a blind man, and begged him to touch him. ²³And he took the blind man by the hand, and led him out of the village; and when he had spit on his eyes and laid his hands upon him, he asked him, "Do you see anything?" ²⁴And he looked up and said, "I see men; but they look like trees, walking." ²⁵Then again he laid his hands upon his eyes; and he looked intently and was restored, and saw everything clearly. ²⁶And he sent him away to his home, saying, "Do not even enter the village."

27 And Jesus went on with his disciples, to the villages of Caes·a·reʹa Phi·lipʹpi; and on the way he asked his disciples, "Who do men say that I am?" ²⁸And they told him, "John the Baptist; and others say, E·liʹjah; and others one of the prophets." ²⁹And he asked them, "But who do you say that I am?" Peter answered him, "You are the Christ." ³⁰And he charged them to tell no one about him.

31 And he began to teach them that the Son of man must suffer many things, and be rejected by the elders and the chief priests and the scribes, and be killed, and after three days rise again. ³²And he said this plainly. And Peter took him, and began to rebuke him. ³³But turning and seeing his disciples, he rebuked Peter, and said, "Get behind me, Satan! For you are not on the side of God, but of men."

34 And he called to him the multitude with his disciples, and said to them, "If any man would come after me, let him deny himself and take up his cross and follow me. ³⁵For whoever would save his life will lose it; and whoever loses his life for my sake and the gospel's will save it. ³⁶For what does it profit a man, to gain the whole world and forfeit his life? ³⁷For what can a man give in return for his life? ³⁸For whoever is ashamed of me and of my words in this adulterous and sinful generation, of him will the Son of man also be ashamed, when he comes in the glory of his Father with

ᵈ Other ancient authorities read *Magadan* or *Magdala*
ᵉ Other ancient authorities read *the Herodians*
8.11-12: Mt 16.1-4; 12.38-39; Lk 11.29.   8.13-21: Mt 16.4-12.
8.15: Lk 12.1; Mk 6.14; 12.13.   8.17: Mk 6.52; Jer 5.21; Is 6.9-10; Mt 13.10-15.
8.19: Mk 6.41-44.   8 20: Mk 8.1-10.   8.22-26: Mk 10.46-52; Jn 9.1-7.
8.22: Mk 6 45; Lk 9.10.   8 23: Mk 7.33; 5.23.
8.27-30: Mt 16.13-20; Lk 9.18-21; Jn 6.66-69   8.28: Mk 6.14.   8 30: Mk 9.9; 1.34.
8.31-9 1: Mt 16.21-28; Lk 9.22-27.   8.33: Mt 4.10.   8.34: Mt 10.38; Lk 14.27.
8.35: Mk 10.39; Lk 17.33; Jn 12.25.   8.38: Mt 10.33; Lk 12.9.

9 the holy angels." [1]And he said to them, "Truly, I say to you, there are some standing here who will not taste death before they see the kingdom of God come with power."

2 And after six days Jesus took with him Peter and James and John, and led them up a high mountain apart by themselves; and he was transfigured before them, [3] and his garments became glistening, intensely white, as no fuller on earth could bleach them. [4]And there appeared to them E·lī'jah with Moses; and they were talking to Jesus. [5]And Peter said to Jesus, "Master,[f] it is well that we are here; let us make three booths, one for you and one for Moses and one for E·lī'jah." [6] For he did not know what to say, for they were exceedingly afraid. [7]And a cloud overshadowed them, and a voice came out of the cloud, "This is my beloved Son;[g] listen to him." [8]And suddenly looking around they no longer saw any one with them but Jesus only.

9 And as they were coming down the mountain, he charged them to tell no one what they had seen, until the Son of man should have risen from the dead. [10] So they kept the matter to themselves, questioning what the rising from the dead meant. [11]And they asked him, "Why do the scribes say that first E·lī'jah must come?" [12]And he said to them, "E·lī'jah does come first to restore all things; and how is it written of the Son of man, that he should suffer many things and be treated with contempt? [13]But I tell you that E·lī'jah has come, and they did to him whatever they pleased, as it is written of him."

14 And when they came to the disciples, they saw a great crowd about them, and scribes arguing with them. [15]And immediately all the crowd, when they saw him, were greatly amazed, and ran up to him and greeted him. [16]And he asked them, "What are you discussing with them?" [17]And one of the crowd answered him, "Teacher, I brought my son to you, for he has a dumb spirit; [18] and wherever it seizes him, it dashes him down; and he foams and grinds his teeth and

becomes rigid; and I asked your disciples to cast it out, and they were not able." [19]And he answered them, "O faithless generation, how long am I to be with you? How long am I to bear with you? Bring him to me." [20]And they brought the boy to him; and when the spirit saw him, immediately it convulsed the boy, and he fell on the ground and rolled about, foaming at the mouth. [21]And Jesus[h] asked his father, "How long has he had this?" And he said, "From childhood. [22]And it has often cast him into the fire and into the water, to destroy him; but if you can do anything, have pity on us and help us." [23]And Jesus said to him, "If you can! All things are possible to him who believes." [24] Immediately the father of the child cried out[i] and said, "I believe; help my unbelief!" [25]And when Jesus saw that a crowd came running together, he rebuked the unclean spirit, saying to it, "You dumb and deaf spirit, I command you, come out of him, and never enter him again." [26]And after crying out and convulsing him terribly, it came out, and the boy was like a corpse; so that most of them said, "He is dead." [27] But Jesus took him by the hand and lifted him up, and he arose. [28]And when he had entered the house, his disciples asked him privately, "Why could we not cast it out?" [29]And he said to them, "This kind cannot be driven out by anything but prayer."[j]

30 They went on from there and passed through Galilee. And he would not have any one know it; [31] for he was teaching his disciples, saying to them, "The Son of man will be delivered into the hands of men, and they will kill him; and when he is killed, after three days he will rise." [32] But they did not understand the saying, and they were afraid to ask him.

33 And they came to Ca·pẽr'na-ŭm; and when he was in the house he asked them, "What were you discussing on the way?" [34] But they were silent; for on the way they had discussed with one another who was the greatest. [35]And he sat down and called the twelve; and he said to them, "If any one would be first, he must be

---

f Or *Rabbi* *g* Or *my Son, my* (or *the*) *Beloved* *h* Greek *he*
i Other ancient authorities add *with tears* *j* Other ancient authorities add *and fasting*
9.1: Mk 13.30; Mt 10.23; Lk 22.18. **9.2-8:** Mt 17.1-8; Lk 9.28-36.
9.2: Mk 5.37; 13.3. **9.3:** Mt 28.3. **9.7:** 2 Pet 1.17-18; Mt 3.17; Jn 12.28-29.
9.9-13: Mt 17.9-13; Lk 9.36. **9.9:** Mk 8.30; 5.43; 7.36. **9.11:** Mt 11.14.
9.12: Mk 8.31; 9.31; 10.33. **9.14-27:** Mt 17.14-18; Lk 9.37-43.
9.23: Mt 17.20; Lk 17.6; Mk 11.22-24. **9.30-32:** Mt 17.22-23; Lk 9.43-45.
9.31: Mk 8.31; 10.33. **9.32:** Jn 12.16. **9.33-37:** Mt 18.1-5; Lk 9.46-48.
9.34: Lk 22.24. **9.35:** Mk 10.43-44; Mt 20.26-27; 23.11; Lk 22.26.

last of all, and servant of all."³⁶And he took a child, and put him in the midst of them; and taking him in his arms, he said to them, ³⁷ "Whoever receives one such child in my name receives me; and whoever receives me, receives not me but him who sent me."

³⁸ John said to him, "Teacher, we saw a man casting out demons in your name,ᵏ and we forbade him, because he was not following us." ³⁹ But Jesus said, "Do not forbid him; for no one who does a mighty work in my name will be able soon after to speak evil of me.⁴⁰ For he that is not against us is for us.⁴¹ For truly, I say to you, whoever gives you a cup of water to drink because you bear the name of Christ, will by no means lose his reward.

⁴² "Whoever causes one of these little ones who believe in me to sin, it would be better for him if a great millstone were hung round his neck and he were thrown into the sea.⁴³ And if your hand causes you to sin, cut it off; it is better for you to enter life maimed than with two hands to go to hellᵐ to the unquenchable fire.⁴⁵ And if your foot causes you to sin, cut it off; it is better for you to enter life lame than with two feet to be thrown into hell.ᵐ, ⁿ ⁴⁷ And if your eye causes you to sin, pluck it out; it is better for you to enter the kingdom of God with one eye than with two eyes to be thrown into hell.ᵐ ⁴⁸ where their worm does not die, and the fire is not quenched. ⁴⁹ For every one will be salted with fire.⁵⁰ Salt is good; but if the salt has lost its saltness, how will you season it? Have salt in yourselves, and be at peace with one another."

10 And he left there and went to the region of Judea and beyond the Jordan, and crowds gathered to him again; and again, as his custom was, he taught them.

² And Pharisees came up and in order to test him asked, "Is it lawful for a man to divorce his wife?" ³ He answered them, "What did Moses command you?"⁴ They said, "Moses allowed a man to write a certificate of divorce, and to put her away." ⁵ But Jesus said to them, "For your hardness of heart he wrote you this commandment. ⁶ But from the beginning of creation, 'God made them male and female.' ⁷ 'For this reason a man shall leave his father and mother and be joined to his wife,' ⁸ and the two shall become one. ⁹ So they are no longer two but one. ⁹ What therefore God has joined together, let not man put asunder."

¹⁰ And in the house the disciples asked him again about this matter. ¹¹And he said to them, "Whoever divorces his wife and marries another, commits adultery against her; ¹² and if she divorces her husband and marries another, she commits adultery."

¹³ And they were bringing children to him, that he might touch them; and the disciples rebuked them. ¹⁴ But when Jesus saw it he was indignant, and said to them, "Let the children come to me, do not hinder them; for to such belongs the kingdom of God. ¹⁵ Truly, I say to you, whoever does not receive the kingdom of God like a child shall not enter it."¹⁶And he took them in his arms and blessed them, laying his hands upon them.

¹⁷ And as he was setting out on his journey, a man ran up and knelt before him, and asked him, "Good Teacher, what must I do to inherit eternal life?" ¹⁸And Jesus said to him, "Why do you call me good? No one is good but God alone. ¹⁹ You know the commandments: 'Do not kill, Do not commit adultery, Do not steal, Do not bear false witness, Do not defraud, Honor your father and mother.'" ²⁰And he said to him, "Teacher, all these I have observed from my youth." ²¹And Jesus looking upon him

ᵏ Other ancient authorities add *who does not follow us*   ˡ Greek *stumble*
ᵐ Greek *Gehenna*
ⁿ Verses 44 and 46 (which are identical with verse 48) are omitted by the best ancient authorities
ᵒ Other ancient authorities add *and every sacrifice will be salted with salt*
ᵖ Other ancient authorities omit *and be joined to his wife*   ᑫ Greek *one flesh*

9.36: Mk 10.16.   **9.37:** Mt 10.40; Lk 10.16; Jn 12.44; 13.20.
9.38-40: Lk 9.49-50; 11.23; Mt 12.30; Num 11.27-29.   **9.41:** Mt 10.42.
9.42-48: Mt 18.6-9; 5.29-30; Lk 17.1-2.   **9.48:** Is 66.24.
9.49-50: Mt 5.13; Lk 14.34-35.   **9.50:** Col 4.6;1Thess 5.13.   **10.1-12:** Mt 19.1-9.
10.1: Lk 9.51; Jn 10.40; 11.7.   **10.4:** Deut 24.1-4.   **10.6:** Gen 1.27; 5.2.
10.7-8: Gen 2.24.   **10.11:** Mt 5.32; Lk 16.18; I Cor 7.10-11; Rom 7.2-3.
10.13-16: Mt 19.13-15; 18.3; Lk 18.15-17.   **10.16:** Mk 9.36.
10.17-31: Mt 19.16-30; Lk 18.30-30.   **10.17:** Lk 10.25; Mk 1.40.
10.19: Ex 20.12-16; Deut 5.16-20.   **10.21:** Mt 6.20; Lk 12.33; Acts 2.45; 4.34-35.

loved him, and said to him, "You lack one thing; go, sell what you have, and give to the poor, and you will have treasure in heaven; and come, follow me." [22]At that saying his countenance fell, and he went away sorrowful; for he had great possessions.

23 And Jesus looked around and said to his disciples, "How hard it will be for those who have riches to enter the kingdom of God!" [24]And the disciples were amazed at his words. But Jesus said to them again, "Children, how hard it is [r] to enter the kingdom of God! [25]It is easier for a camel to go through the eye of a needle than for a rich man to enter the kingdom of God." [26]And they were exceedingly astonished, and said to him,[s] "Then who can be saved?" [27] Jesus looked at them and said, "With men it is impossible, but not with God; for all things are possible with God." [28] Peter began to say to him, "Lo, we have left everything and followed you." [29] Jesus said, "Truly, I say to you, there is no one who has left house or brothers or sisters or mother or father or children or lands, for my sake and for the gospel, [30]who will not receive a hundredfold now in this time, houses and brothers and sisters and mothers and children and lands, with persecutions, and in the age to come eternal life. [31]But many that are first will be last, and the last first."

32 And they were on the road, going up to Jerusalem, and Jesus was walking ahead of them; and they were amazed, and those who followed were afraid. And taking the twelve again, he began to tell them what was to happen to him, [33] saying, "Behold, we are going up to Jerusalem; and the Son of man will be delivered to the chief priests and the scribes, and they will condemn him to death, and deliver him to the Gentiles; [34]and they will mock him, and spit upon him, and scourge him, and kill him; and after three days he will arise."

35 And James and John, the sons of Zeb'e·dee, came forward to him, and said to him, "Teacher, we want you to do for us whatever we ask of you." [36]And he said to them, "What do you want me to do for you?" [37]And they said to him, "Grant us to sit, one at your right hand and one at your left, in your glory." [38] But Jesus said to them, "You do not know what you are asking. Are you able to drink the cup that I drink, or to be baptized with the baptism with which I am baptized?" [39]And they said to him, "We are able." And Jesus said to them, "The cup that I drink you will drink; and with the baptism with which I am baptized, you will be baptized; [40]but to sit at my right hand or at my left is not mine to grant, but it is for those for whom it has been prepared." [41]And when the ten heard it, they began to be indignant at James and John. [42]And Jesus called them to him and said to them, "You know that those who are supposed to rule over the Gentiles lord it over them, and their great men exercise authority over them. [43]But it shall not be so among you; but whoever would be great among you must be your servant, [44]and whoever would be first among you must be slave of all. [45]For the Son of man also came not to be served but to serve, and to give his life as a ransom for many."

46 And they came to Jericho; and as he was leaving Jericho with his disciples and a great multitude, Bär-ti·mae'us, a blind beggar, the son of Ti·mae'us, was sitting by the roadside. [47]And when he heard that it was Jesus of Nazareth, he began to cry out and say, "Jesus, Son of David, have mercy on me!" [48]And many rebuked him, telling him to be silent; but he cried out all the more, "Son of David, have mercy on me!" [49]And Jesus stopped and said, "Call him." And they called the blind man, saying to him, "Take heart; rise, he is calling you." [50]And throwing off his mantle he sprang up and came to Jesus. [51]And Jesus said to him, "What do you want me to do for you?" And the blind man said to him, "Master,[t] let me receive my sight." [52]And Jesus said to him, "Go your way; your faith has made you well." And immediately he received his sight and followed him on the way.

11 And when they drew near to Jerusalem, to Beth'pha·ge and

---

[r] Other ancient authorities add *for those who trust in riches*
[s] Other ancient authorities read *to one another*   [t] Or *Rabbi*

10.28: Mk 1.16-20.
10.30: Mt 6.33.   **10.31**: Mt 20.16; Lk 13.30.   **10.32-34**: Mt 20.17-19; Lk 18.31-34.
10.33: Mk 8.31; 9.12, 33.   **10.34**: Mk 14.65; 15.19, 26-32.   **10.35-45**: Mt 20.20-28.
10.37: Mt 19.28; Lk 22.30.   **10.38**: Lk 12.50; Jn 18.11.   **10.39**: Acts 12.2; Rev 1.9.
10.42-45: Lk 22.25-27.   **10.43**: Mk 9.35.   **10.45**: 1 Tim 2.5-6.
10.46-52: Mt 20.29-34; Lk 18.35-43; Mk 8.22-26.   **10.47**: Mt 9.27.
10.52: Mt 9.22; Mk 5.34; Lk 7.50; 8.48; 17.19.   **11.1-10**: Mt 21.1-9; Lk 19.29-38.

Beth'a·ny, at the Mount of Olives, he sent two of his disciples, [2] and said to them, "Go into the village opposite you, and immediately as you enter it you will find a colt tied, on which no one has ever sat; untie it and bring it. [3] If any one says to you, 'Why are you doing this?' say, 'The Lord has need of it and will send it back here immediately.'" [4] And they went away, and found a colt tied at the door out in the open street; and they untied it. [5] And those who stood there said to them, "What are you doing, untying the colt?" [6] And they told them what Jesus had said; and they let them go. [7] And they brought the colt to Jesus, and threw their garments on it; and he sat upon it. [8] And many spread their garments on the road, and others spread leafy branches which they had cut from the fields. [9] And those who went before and those who followed cried out, "Hosanna! Blessed is he who comes in the name of the Lord! [10] Blessed is the kingdom of our father David that is coming! Hosanna in the highest!"

[11] And he entered Jerusalem, and went into the temple; and when he had looked round at everything, as it was already late, he went out to Beth'a·ny with the twelve.

[12] On the following day, when they came from Beth'a·ny, he was hungry. [13] And seeing in the distance a fig tree in leaf, he went to see if he could find anything on it. When he came to it, he found nothing but leaves, for it was not the season for figs. [14] And he said to it, "May no one ever eat fruit from you again." And his disciples heard it.

[15] And they came to Jerusalem. And he entered the temple and began to drive out those who sold and those who bought in the temple, and he overturned the tables of the money-changers and the seats of those who sold pigeons; [16] and he would not allow any one to carry anything through the temple. [17] And he taught, and said to them, "Is it not written, 'My house shall be called a house of prayer for all the nations'? But you have made it a den of robbers." [18] And the chief priests and the scribes heard

it and sought a way to destroy him; for they feared him, because all the multitude was astonished at his teaching. [19] And when evening came they[u] went out of the city.

[20] As they passed by in the morning, they saw the fig tree withered away to its roots. [21] And Peter remembered and said to him, "Master,[v] look! The fig tree which you cursed has withered." [22] And Jesus answered them, "Have faith in God. [23] Truly, I say to you, whoever says to this mountain, 'Be taken up and cast into the sea,' and does not doubt in his heart, but believes that what he says will come to pass, it will be done for him. [24] Therefore I tell you, whatever you ask in prayer, believe that you receive it, and you will. [25] And whenever you stand praying, forgive, if you have anything against any one; so that your Father also who is in heaven may forgive you your trespasses."[w]

[27] And they came again to Jerusalem. And as he was walking in the temple, the chief priests and the scribes and the elders came to him, [28] and they said to him, "By what authority are you doing these things, or who gave you this authority to do them?" [29] Jesus said to them, "I will ask you a question; answer me, and I will tell you by what authority I do these things. [30] Was the baptism of John from heaven or from men? Answer me." [31] And they argued with one another, "If we say, 'From heaven,' he will say, 'Why then did you not believe him?' [32] But shall we say, 'From men'?"—they were afraid of the people, for all held that John was a real prophet. [33] So they answered Jesus, "We do not know." And Jesus said to them, "Neither will I tell you by what authority I do these things."

12 And he began to speak to them in parables. "A man planted a vineyard, and set a hedge around it, and dug a pit for the wine press, and built a tower, and let it out to tenants, and went into another country. [2] When the time came, he sent a servant to the tenants, to get from them some of the fruit of the vineyard. [3] And they took him and beat him, and sent him away

[u] Other ancient authorities read *he*   [v] Or *Rabbi*
[w] Other ancient authorities add verse 26, "*But if you do not forgive, neither will your Father who is in heaven forgive your trespasses*"

11.4: Mk 14.16.   11.7-10: Jn 12.12-15.   11.9: Ps 118.26; Mt 21.15; 23.39.
11.11: Mt 21.10-11, 17.   11.12-14: Mt 21.18-19; Lk 13.6-9.
11.15-18: Mt 21.12-16; Lk 19.45-48; Jn 2.13-16.   11.17: Is 56.7; Jer 7.11.
11.19: Lk 21.37.   11.20-25: Mt 21.20-22; Mt 17.20; Lk 17.6.
11.24: Jn 14.13-14; 16.23; Mt 7.7-11.   11.25: Mt 6.14-15; 18.35.
11.27-33: Mt 21.23-27; Lk 20.1-8; Jn 2.18.   12.1-12: Mt 21.33-46; Lk 20.9-19; Is 5.1-7.

empty-handed. 4 Again he sent to them another servant, and they wounded him in the head, and treated him shamefully. 5 And he sent another, and him they killed; and so with many others, some they beat and some they killed. 6 He had still one other, a beloved son; finally he sent him to them, saying, 'They will respect my son.' 7 But those tenants said to one another, 'This is the heir; come, let us kill him, and the inheritance will be ours.' 8 And they took him and killed him, and cast him out of the vineyard. 9 What will the owner of the vineyard do? He will come and destroy the tenants, and give the vineyard to others. 10 Have you not read this scripture:

'The very stone which the builders rejected

has become the head of the corner;
11 this was the Lord's doing,

and it is marvelous in our eyes'?"

12 And they tried to arrest him, but feared the multitude, for they perceived that he had told the parable against them; so they left him and went away.

13 And they sent to him some of the Pharisees and some of the He·rō′-di-ăns, to entrap him in his talk. 14 And they came and said to him, "Teacher, we know that you are true, and care for no man: for you do not regard the position of men, but truly teach the way of God. Is it lawful to pay taxes to Caesar, or not? 15 Should we pay them, or should we not?" But knowing their hypocrisy, he said to them, "Why put me to the test? Bring me a coin,x and let me look at it." 16 And they brought one. And he said to them, "Whose likeness and inscription is this?" They said to him, "Caesar's." 17 Jesus said to them, "Render to Caesar the things that are Caesar's, and to God the things that are God's." And they were amazed at him.

18 And Sad′dū·cees came to him, who say that there is no resurrection; and they asked him a question, saying, 19 "Teacher, Moses wrote for us that if a man's brother dies and leaves a wife, but leaves no child, the many must take the wife, and raise up children for his brother. 20 There

were seven brothers; the first took a wife, and when he died left no children; 21 and the second took her, and died, leaving no children; and the third likewise; 22 and the seven left no children. Last of all the woman also died. 23 In the resurrection whose wife will she be? For the seven had her as wife."

24 Jesus said to them, "Is not this why you are wrong, that you know neither the scriptures nor the power of God? 25 For when they rise from the dead, they neither marry nor are given in marriage, but are like angels in heaven. 26 And as for the dead being raised, have you not read in the book of Moses, in the passage about the bush, how God said to him, 'I am the God of Abraham, and the God of Isaac, and the God of Jacob'? 27 He is not God of the dead, but of the living; you are quite wrong."

28 And one of the scribes came up and heard them disputing with one another, and seeing that he answered them well, asked him, "Which commandment is the first of all?" 29 Jesus answered, "The first is, 'Hear, O Israel: The Lord our God, the Lord is one; 30 and you shall love the Lord your God with all your heart, and with all your soul, and with all your mind, and with all your strength.' 31 The second is this, 'You shall love your neighbor as yourself.' There is no other commandment greater than these." 32 And the scribe said to him, "You are right, Teacher; you have truly said that he is one, and there is no other but he; 33 and to love him with all the heart, and with all the understanding, and with all the strength, and to love one's neighbor as oneself, is much more than all whole burnt offerings and sacrifices." 34 And when Jesus saw that he answered wisely, he said to him, "You are not far from the kingdom of God." And after that no one dared to ask him any question.

35 And as Jesus taught in the temple, he said, "How can the scribes say that the Christ is the son of David? 36 David himself, inspired byz the Holy Spirit, declared,

'The Lord said to my Lord,

x Greek a denarius   y Greek his brother   z Or himself, in

12.10-11: Ps 118.22-23; Acts 4.11; 1 Pet 2.7.   **12.12:** Mk 11.18.
12.13-17: Mt 22.15-22; Lk 20.20-26.   **12.13:** Mk 3.6; Lk 11.54.   **12.17:** Rom 13.7.
12.18-27: Mt 22.23-33; Lk 20.27-38.   **12.19:** Deut 25.5.   **12.26:** Ex 3.6.
12.28-34: Mt 22.34-40; Lk 20.39-40; 10.25-28.   **12.29:** Deut 6.4.
12.31: Lev 18.18; Rom 13.9; Gal 5.14; Jas 2.8.
12.33: 1 Sam 15.22; Hos 6.6; Mic 6.6-8; Mt 9.13.   **12.35-37:** Mt 22.41-46; Lk 20.41-44.
12.36: Ps 110.1; Acts 2.34-35; Heb 1.13.

Sit at my right hand,
till I put thy enemies under thy
feet.'
37 David himself calls him Lord; so
how is he his son?" And the great
throng heard him gladly.

38 And in his teaching he said,
"Beware of the scribes, who like to go
about in long robes, and to have salutations in the market places 39 and the
best seats in the synagogues and the
places of honor at feasts, 40 who devour
widows' houses and for a pretense
make long prayers. They will receive
the greater condemnation."

41 And he sat down opposite the
treasury, and watched the multitude
putting money into the treasury.
Many rich people put in large sums.
42And a poor widow came, and put
in two copper coins, which make a
penny. 43And he called his disciples
to him, and said to them, "Truly, I
say to you, this poor widow has put in
more than all those who are contribut-
ing to the treasury. 44 For they all
contributed out of their abundance;
but she out of her poverty has put in
everything she had, her whole living."

13 And as he came out of the temple, one of his disciples said to
him, "Look, Teacher, what wonderful
stones and what wonderful buildings!"
2And Jesus said to him, "Do you see
these great buildings? There will not
be left here one stone upon another,
that will not be thrown down."

3 And as he sat on the Mount of
Olives opposite the temple, Peter and
James and John and Andrew asked him
privately, 4 "Tell us, when will this
be, and what will be the sign when
these things are all to be accomplished?" 5And Jesus began to say to
them, "Take heed that no one leads
you astray. 6 Many will come in my
name, saying, 'I am he!' and they will
lead many astray. 7 And when you hear
of wars and rumors of wars, do not be
alarmed; this must take place, but the
end is not yet. 8 For nation will rise
against nation, and kingdom against
kingdom; there will be earthquakes in
various places, there will be famines;
this is but the beginning of the sufferings.

9 "But take heed to yourselves; for
they will deliver you up to councils;
and you will be beaten in synagogues;
and you will stand before governors
and kings for my sake, to bear testimony before them. 10And the gospel
must first be preached to all nations.
11And when they bring you to trial
and deliver you up, do not be anxious
beforehand what you are to say; but
say whatever is given you in that hour,
for it is not you who speak, but the
Holy Spirit. 12And brother will deliver
up brother to death, and the father his
child, and children will rise against
parents and have them put to death;
13 and you will be hated by all for my
name's sake. But he who endures to
the end will be saved.

14 "But when you see the desolating sacrilege set up where it ought not
to be (let the reader understand), then
let those who are in Judea flee to the
mountains; 15 let him who is on the
housetop not go down, nor enter his
house, to take anything away; 16 and
let him who is in the field not turn
back to take his mantle. 17And alas for
those who are with child and for those
who give suck in those days! 18 Pray
that it may not happen in winter.
19 For in those days there will be such
tribulation as has not been from the
beginning of the creation which God
created until now, and never will be.
20And if the Lord had not shortened
the days, no human being would be
saved; but for the sake of the elect,
whom he chose, he shortened the
days. 21And then if any one says to
you, 'Look, here is the Christ!' or
'Look, there he is!' do not believe it.
22 False Christs and false prophets
will arise and show signs and wonders,
to lead astray, if possible, the elect.
23 But take heed; I have told you all
things beforehand.

24 "But in those days, after that
tribulation, the sun will be darkened,
and the moon will not give its light,
25 and the stars will be falling from
heaven, and the powers in the heavens
will be shaken. 26And then they will
see the Son of man coming in clouds
with great power and glory. 27And then
he will send out the angels, and gather
his elect from the four winds, from the
ends of the earth to the ends of
heaven.

28 "From the fig tree learn its lesson: as soon as its branch becomes
tender and puts forth its leaves, you
know that summer is near. 29 So also,

12.38-40: Mt 23.5-7; Lk 20.46-47; 11.43.   12.41-44: Lk 21.1-4; Jn 8.20.
13.1-37: Mt 24; Lk 21.5-36.   13.2: Lk 19.43-44; Mk 14.58; 15.29; Jn 2.19; Acts 6.14.
13.3: Mk 5.37; 9.2.   13.4: Lk 17.20.   13.6: Jn 8.24; 1 Jn 2.18.   13.9-13: Mt 10.17-22.
13.11: Jn 14.26; 16.7-11; Lk 12.11-12.   13.13: Jn 15.21.   13.14: Dan 9.27; 11.31; 12.11.
13.17: Lk 23.29.   13.22: Mt 7.15; Jn 4.48.   13.26: Mk 8.38; Mt 10.23; Dan 7.13.

when you see these things taking place, you know that he is near, at the very gates. 30 Truly, I say to you, this generation will not pass away before all these things take place. 31 Heaven and earth will pass away, but my words will not pass away.

32 "But of that day or that hour no one knows, not even the angels in heaven, nor the Son, but only the Father. 33 Take heed, watch;* for you do not know when the time will come. 34 It is like a man going on a journey, when he leaves home and puts his servants in charge, each with his work, and commands the doorkeeper to be on the watch. 35 Watch therefore—for you do not know when the master of the house will come, in the evening, or at midnight, or at cockcrow, or in the morning—36 lest he come suddenly and find you asleep. 37 And what I say to you I say to all: Watch."

14 It was now two days before the Passover and the feast of Unleavened Bread. And the chief priests and the scribes were seeking how to arrest him by stealth, and kill him; 2 for they said, "Not during the feast, lest there be a tumult of the people."

3 And while he was at Beth′a·ny in the house of Simon the leper, as he sat at table, a woman came with an alabaster jar of ointment of pure nard, very costly, and she broke the jar and poured it over his head. 4 But there were some who said to themselves indignantly, "Why was the ointment thus wasted? 5 For this ointment might have been sold for more than three hundred denarii,*b* and given to the poor." And they reproached her. 6 But Jesus said, "Let her alone; why do you trouble her? She has done a beautiful thing to me.7 For you always have the poor with you, and whenever you will, you can do good to them; but you will not always have me.8 She has done what she could; she has anointed my body beforehand for burying. 9 And truly, I say to you, wherever the gospel is preached in the whole world, what she has done will be told in memory of her."

10 Then Judas Is·car′i·ot, who was one of the twelve, went to the chief priests in order to betray him to them. 11 And when they heard it they were glad, and promised to give him money. And he sought an opportunity to betray him.

12 And on the first day of Unleavened Bread, when they sacrificed the passover lamb, his disciples said to him, "Where will you have us go and prepare for you to eat the passover?" 13 And he sent two of his disciples, and said to them, "Go into the city, and a man carrying a jar of water will meet you; follow him, 14 and wherever he enters, say to the householder, 'The Teacher says, Where is my guest room, where I am to eat the passover with my disciples? 15 And he will show you a large upper room furnished and ready; there prepare for us." 16 And the disciples set out and went to the city, and found it as he had told them; and they prepared the passover.

17 And when it was evening he came with the twelve. 18 And as they were at table eating, Jesus said, "Truly, I say to you, one of you will betray me, one who is eating with me." 19 They began to be sorrowful, and to say to him one after another, "Is it I?" 20 He said to them, "It is one of the twelve, one who is dipping bread in the same dish with me. 21 For the Son of man goes as it is written of him, but woe to that man by whom the Son of man is betrayed! It would have been better for that man if he had not been born."

22 And as they were eating, he took bread, and blessed, and broke it, and gave it to them, and said, "Take; this is my body." 23 And he took a cup, and when he had given thanks he gave it to them, and they all drank of it. 24 And he said to them, "This is my blood of the*c* covenant, which is poured out for many. 25 Truly, I say to you, I shall not drink again of the fruit of the vine until that day when I drink it new in the kingdom of God."

26 And when they had sung a hymn, they went out to the Mount of Olives. 27 And Jesus said to them, "You will all fall away; for it is written,

a Other ancient authorities add *and pray*
b The denarius was worth about twenty cents　*c* Other ancient authorities insert *new*

13.30: Mk 9.1.　13.31: Mt 5.18; Lk 16.17.　13.32: Acts 1.7.　13.33: Eph 6.18; Col 4.2.
13.34: Mt 25.14.　13.35: Lk 12.35-40.　14.1-2: Mt 26.1-5; Lk 22.1-2; Jn 11.47-53.
14.3-9: Mt 26.6-13; Lk 7.36-38; Jn 12.1-8.　14.7: Deut 15.11.　14.8: Jn 19.40.
14.10-11: Mt 26.14-16; Lk 22.3-6.　14.12-16: Mt 26.17-19; Lk 22.7-13.
14.17-21: Mt 26.20-25; Lk 22.14, 21-23; Jn 13.21-30; Ps 41.9.
14.22-25: Mt 26.26-29; Lk 22.17-19; 1 Cor 11.23-26.　14.22: Mk 6.41; 8.6; Lk 24.30.
14.23: 1 Cor 10.16.　14.24: Ex 24.8; Heb 9.20.
14.26-31: Mt 26.30-35; Lk 22.39, 33-34.　14.27: Zech 13.7; Jn 16.32.

'I will strike the shepherd, and the sheep will be scattered.' 28But after I am raised up, I will go before you to Galilee." 29 Peter said to him, "Even though they all fall away, I will not." 30And Jesus said to him, "Truly, I say to you, this very night, before the cock crows twice, you will deny me three times." 31 But he said vehemently, "If I must die with you, I will not deny you." And they all said the same.

32 And they went to a place which was called Geth·sem′a·nē; and he said to his disciples, "Sit here, while I pray." 33And he took with him Peter and James and John, and began to be greatly distressed and troubled. 34And he said to them, "My soul is very sorrowful, even to death; remain here, and watch." d 35And going a little farther, he fell on the ground and prayed that, if it were possible, the hour might pass from him. 36And he said, "Ab′ba, Father, all things are possible to thee; remove this cup from me; yet not what I will, but what thou wilt." 37And he came and found them sleeping, and he said to Peter, "Simon, are you asleep? Could you not watch one hour? 38 Watch d and pray that you may not enter into temptation; the spirit indeed is willing, but the flesh is weak." 39And again he went away and prayed, saying the same words. 40And again he came and found them sleeping, for their eyes were very heavy; and they did not know what to answer him. 41And he came the third time, and said to them, "Are you still sleeping and taking your rest? It is enough; the hour has come; the Son of man is betrayed into the hands of sinners. 42 Rise, let us be going; see, my betrayer is at hand."

43 And immediately, while he was still speaking, Judas came, one of the twelve, and with him a crowd with swords and clubs, from the chief priests and the scribes and the elders. 44 Now the betrayer had given them a sign, saying, "The one I shall kiss is the man; seize him and lead him away safely." 45And when he came, he went up to him at once, and said, "Master!"e And he kissed him. 46And they laid

hands on him and seized him. 47 But one of those who stood by drew his sword, and struck the slave of the high priest and cut off his ear. 48And Jesus said to them, "Have you come out as against a robber, with swords and clubs to capture me? 49Day after day I was with you in the temple teaching, and you did not seize me. But let the scriptures be fulfilled." 50And they all forsook him and fled.

51 And a young man followed him, with nothing but a linen cloth about his body; and they seized him. 52 but he left the linen cloth and ran away naked.

53 And they led Jesus to the high priest; and all the chief priests and the elders and the scribes were assembled. 54And Peter had followed him at a distance, right into the courtyard of the high priest; and he was sitting with the guards, and warming himself at the fire. 55 Now the chief priests and the whole council sought testimony against Jesus to put him to death; but they found none. 56 For many bore false witness against him, and their witness did not agree. 57And some stood up and bore false witness against him, saying, 58 "We heard him say, 'I will destroy this temple that is made with hands, and in three days I will build another, not made with hands.'" 59 Yet not even so did their testimony agree. 60And the high priest stood up in the midst, and asked Jesus, "Have you no answer to make? What is it that these men testify against you?" 61 But he was silent and made no answer. Again the high priest asked him, "Are you the Christ, the Son of the Blessed?" 62And Jesus said, "I am; and you will see the Son of man sitting at the right hand of Power, and coming with the clouds of heaven." 63And the high priest tore his mantle, and said, "Why do we still need witnesses? 64 You have heard his blasphemy. What is your decision?" And they all condemned him as deserving death. 65And some began to spit on him, and to cover his face, and to strike him, saying to him, "Prophesy!" And the guards received him with blows.

66 And as Peter was below in the

d Or *keep awake*   e Or *Rabbi*

14.28: Mk 16.7.   14.30: Mk 14.66-72; Jn 13.36-38; 18.17-18, 25-27.
14.32-42: Mt 26.36-46; Lk 22.40-46; Heb 5.7-8.   14.34: Jn 12.27.
14.36: Rom 8.15; Gal 4.6; Mk 10.38; Jn 18.11.   14.38: Mt 6.13; Lk 11.4.
14.43-50: Mt 26.47-56; Lk 22.47-53; Jn 18.2-11.   14.49: Lk 19.47; Jn 18.19-21.
14.53-65: Mt 26.57-68; Lk 22.54-55, 63-71; Jn 18.12-24.
14.58: Mk 13.2; 15.29; Acts 6.14; Jn 2.19.   14.62: Dan 7.13; Mk 9.1; 13.26.
14.63: Acts 14.14; Num 14.6.   14.64: Lev 24.16.
14.66-72: Mt 26.69-75; Lk 22.56-62; Jn 18.16-18, 25-27; Mk 14.30.

courtyard, one of the maids of the high priest came; 67 and seeing Peter warming himself, she looked at him, and said, "You also were with the Nazarene, Jesus." 68 But he denied it, saying, "I neither know nor understand what you mean." And he went out into the gateway.*f* 69 And the maid saw him, and began again to say to the bystanders, "This man is one of them." 70 But again he denied it. And after a little while again the bystanders said to Peter, "Certainly you are one of them; for you are a Galilean." 71 But he began to invoke a curse on himself and to swear, "I do not know this man of whom you speak." 72 And immediately the cock crowed a second time. And Peter remembered how Jesus had said to him, "Before the cock crows twice, you will deny me three times." And he broke down and wept.

15 And as soon as it was morning the chief priests, with the elders and scribes, and the whole council held a consultation; and they bound Jesus and led him away and delivered him to Pilate. 2 And Pilate asked him, "Are you the King of the Jews?" And he answered him, **"You have said so."** 3 And the chief priests accused him of many things. 4 And Pilate again asked him, "Have you no answer to make? See how many charges they bring against you." 5 But Jesus made no further answer, so that Pilate wondered.

6 Now at the feast he used to release for them one prisoner whom they asked. 7 And among the rebels in prison, who had committed murder in the insurrection, there was a man called Bà·rab′bàs. 8 And the crowd came up and began to ask Pilate to do as he was wont to do for them. 9 And he answered them, "Do you want me to release for you the King of the Jews?" 10 For he perceived that it was out of envy that the chief priests had delivered him up. 11 But the chief priests stirred up the crowd to have him release for them Bà·rab′bàs instead. 12 And Pilate again said to them, "Then what shall I do with the man whom you call the King of the Jews?"

13 And they cried out again, "Crucify him." 14 And Pilate said to them, "Why, what evil has he done?" But they shouted all the more, "Crucify him." 15 So Pilate, wishing to satisfy the crowd, released for them Bà·rab′bàs; and having scourged Jesus, he delivered him to be crucified.

16 And the soldiers led him away inside the palace (that is, the praetorium); and they called together the whole battalion. 17 And they clothed him in a purple cloak, and plaiting a crown of thorns they put it on him. 18 And they began to salute him, "Hail, King of the Jews!" 19 And they struck his head with a reed, and spat upon him, and they knelt down in homage to him. 20 And when they had mocked him, they stripped him of the purple cloak, and put his own clothes on him. And they led him out to crucify him.

21 And they compelled a passerby, Simon of Cy·re′ne, who was coming in from the country, the father of Alexander and Rufus, to carry his cross. 22 And they brought him to the place called Gol′go·tha (which means the place of a skull). 23 And they offered him wine mingled with myrrh; but he did not take it. 24 And they crucified him, and divided his garments among them, casting lots for them, to decide what each should take. 25 And it was the third hour, when they crucified him. 26 And the inscription of the charge against him read, "The King of the Jews." 27 And with him they crucified two robbers, one on his right and one on his left.*g* 29 And those who passed by derided him, wagging their heads, and saying, "Aha! You who would destroy the temple and build it in three days, 30 save yourself, and come down from the cross!" 31 So also the chief priests mocked him to one another with the scribes, saying, "He saved others; he cannot save himself. 32 Let the Christ, the King of Israel, come down now from the cross, that we may see and believe." Those who were crucified with him also reviled him.

33 And when the sixth hour had come, there was darkness over the whole land*h* until the ninth hour.

f Or *fore-court*. Other ancient authorities add *and the cock crowed*
g Other ancient authorities insert verse 28, *And the scripture was fulfilled which says,* "He was reckoned with the transgressors"   *h* Or *earth*

15.1: Mt 27.1-2; Lk 23.1; Jn 18.28.
15.2-15: Mt 27.11-26; Lk 23.2-3, 18-25; Jn 18.29-19.16.   15.11: Acts 3.14.
15.16-20: Mt 27.27-31; Lk 23.11; Jn 19.2-3.   15.21: Mt 27.32; Lk 23.26; Rom 16.13.
15.22-32: Mt 27.33-44; Lk 23.33-39; Jn 19.17-24.   15.24: Ps 22.18.
15.29: Mk 13.2; 14.58; Jn 2.19.   15.31: Ps 22.7-8.
15.33-41: Mt 27.45-56; Lk 23.44-49; Jn 19.28-30.

34And at the ninth hour Jesus cried with a loud voice, "E'lo-i, E'lo-i, la'mà sà·bach'-thä'ni?" which means, "My God, my God, why hast thou forsaken me?" 35And some of the bystanders hearing it said, "Behold, he is calling E·li'jäh." 36And one ran and, filling a sponge full of vinegar, put it on a reed and gave it to him to drink, saying, "Wait, let us see whether E·li'jäh will come to take him down." 37And Jesus uttered a loud cry, and breathed his last. 38And the curtain of the temple was torn in two, from top to bottom. 39And when the centurion, who stood facing him, saw that he thusⁱ breathed his last, he said, "Truly this man was the Sonˣ of God!"

40 There were also women looking on from afar, among whom were Mary Mag'dà·lēne, and Mary the mother of James the younger and of Jō'sēs, and Sà·lō'mē, 41who, when he was in Galilee, followed him, and ministered to him; and also many other women who came up with him to Jerusalem.

42 And when evening had come, since it was the day of Preparation, that is, the day before the sabbath, 43Joseph of Ar·i·mà·thē'à, a respected member of the council, who was also himself looking for the kingdom of God, took courage and went to Pilate, and asked for the body of Jesus. 44And Pilate wondered if he were already dead; and summoning the centurion, he asked him whether he was already dead.ʲ 45And when he learned from the centurion that he was dead, he granted the body to Joseph. 46And he bought a linen shroud, and taking him down, wrapped him in the linen shroud, and laid him in a tomb which had been hewn out of the rock; and he rolled a stone against the door of the tomb. 47Mary Mag'dà·lēne and Mary the mother of Jō'sēs saw where he was laid.

16 And when the sabbath was past, Mary Mag'dà·lēne, and Mary the mother of James, and Sà·lō'mē, bought spices, so that they might go and anoint him. 2And very early on the first day of the week they went to the tomb when the sun had risen. 3And they were saying to one another, "Who will roll away the stone for us from the door of the tomb?" 4And looking up, they saw that the stone was rolled back; for it was very large. 5And entering the tomb, they saw a young man sitting on the right side, dressed in a white robe; and they were amazed. 6And he said to them, "Do not be amazed; you seek Jesus of Nazareth, who was crucified. He has risen, he is not here; see the place where they laid him. 7But go, tell his disciples and Peter that he is going before you to Galilee; there you will see him, as he told you." 8And they went out and fled from the tomb; for trembling and astonishment had come upon them; and they said nothing to any one, for they were afraid.ᵏ

i Other ancient authorities insert cried out and   x Or a son
l Other ancient authorities read whether he had been some time dead
k Other texts and versions add as 16.9-20 the following passage:

9 Now when he rose early on the first day of the week, he appeared first to Mary Magdalene, from whom he had cast out seven demons. 10 She went and told those who had been with him, as they mourned and wept. 11 But when they heard that he was alive and had been seen by her, they would not believe it.

12 After this he appeared in another form to two of them, as they were walking into the country. 13 And they went back and told the rest, but they did not believe them.

14 Afterward he appeared to the eleven themselves as they sat at table; and he upbraided them for their unbelief and hardness of heart, because they had not believed those who saw him after he had risen. 15And he said to them, "Go into all the world and preach the gospel to the whole creation. 16 He who believes and is baptized will be saved; but he who does not believe will be condemned. 17 And these signs will accompany those who believe: in my name they will cast out demons; they will speak in new tongues; 18 they will pick up serpents, and if they drink any deadly thing, it will not hurt them; they will lay their hands on the sick, and they will recover."

19 So then the Lord Jesus, after he had spoken to them, was taken up into heaven, and sat down at the right hand of God. 20And they went forth and preached everywhere, while the Lord worked with them and confirmed the message by the signs that attended it. Amen.

Other ancient authorities add after verse 8 the following: But they reported briefly to Peter and those with him all that they had been told. And after this, Jesus himself sent out by means of them, from east to west, the sacred and imperishable proclamation of eternal salvation.

15.34: Ps 22.1.   15.36: Ps 69.21.   15.38: Heb 10.19-20.   15.39: Mk 1.11; 9.7.
15.40: Jn 19.25.   15.41: Lk 8.1-3.   15.42-47: Mt 27.57-61; Lk 23.50-56; Jn 19.38-42; Acts 13.29.   15.42: Deut 21.22-23.   16.1-8: Mt 28.1-8; Lk 24.1-10; Jn 20.1-2.
16.1: Lk 23.56; Jn 19.39.   16.7: Mk 14.28; Jn 21.1-23; Mt 28.7.

THE GOSPEL ACCORDING TO

LUKE

Inasmuch as many have undertaken to compile a narrative of the things which have been accomplished among us, 2 just as they were delivered to us by those who from the beginning were eyewitnesses and ministers of the word, 3 it seemed good to me also, having followed all things closely*a* for some time past, to write an orderly account for you, most excellent Thē-oph'i·lùs, 4 that you may know the truth concerning the things of which you have been informed.

5 In the days of Her'ŏd, king of Judea, there was a priest named Zech-a·rī'ah,*b* of the division of A·bī'jah; and he had a wife of the daughters of Aaron, and her name was Elizabeth. 6 And they were both righteous before God, walking in all the commandments and ordinances of the Lord blameless. 7 But they had no child, because Elizabeth was barren, and both were advanced in years.

8 Now while he was serving as priest before God when his division was on duty, 9 according to the custom of the priesthood, it fell to him by lot to enter the temple of the Lord and burn incense. 10 And the whole multitude of the people were praying outside at the hour of incense. 11 And there appeared to him an angel of the Lord standing on the right side of the altar of incense. 12 And Zech·a·rī'ah was troubled when he saw him, and fear fell upon him. 13 But the angel said to him, "Do not be afraid, Zech-a·rī'ah, for your prayer is heard, and your wife Elizabeth will bear you a son, and you shall call his name John. 14 And you will have joy and gladness, and many will rejoice at his birth;
15 for he will be great before the Lord,
    and he shall drink no wine nor
        strong drink,
    and he will be filled with the Holy
        Spirit,

even from his mother's womb.
16 And he will turn many of the sons
        of Israel to the Lord their God,
17 and he will go before him in the
        spirit and power of E·lī'jah,
    to turn the hearts of the fathers to
        the children,
    and the disobedient to the wisdom
        of the just,
    to make ready for the Lord a people
        prepared."
18 And Zech·a·rī'ah said to the angel, "How shall I know this? For I am an old man, and my wife is advanced in years." 19 And the angel answered him, "I am Gabriel, who stand in the presence of God; and I was sent to speak to you, and to bring you this good news. 20 And behold, you will be silent and unable to speak until the day that these things come to pass, because you did not believe my words, which will be fulfilled in their time." 21 And the people were waiting for Zech·a·rī'ah, and they wondered at his delay in the temple. 22 And when he came out, he could not speak to them, and they perceived that he had seen a vision in the temple; and he made signs to them and remained dumb. 23 And when his time of service was ended, he went to his home.

24 After these days his wife Elizabeth conceived, and for five months she hid herself, saying, 25 "Thus the Lord has done to me in the days when he looked on me, to take away my reproach among men."

26 In the sixth month the angel Gabriel was sent from God to a city of Galilee named Nazareth, 27 to a virgin betrothed to a man whose name was Joseph, of the house of David; and the virgin's name was Mary. 28 And he came to her and said, "Hail, O favored one, the Lord is with you!"*c* 29 But she was greatly troubled at the saying, and considered in her mind what sort of greeting this might be. 30 And the

a Or *accurately*   *b* Greek *Zacharias*
c Other ancient authorities add "*Blessed are you among women!*"
1.2: 1 Jn 1.1; Acts 1.21; Heb 2.3.   **1.3:** Acts 1.1.   **1.4:** Jn 20.31.
1.5: Mt 2.1; 1 Chron 24.10; 2 Chron 31.2.   **1.9:** Ex 30.7.   **1.11:** Lk 2.9; Acts 5.19.
1.13: Lk 1.30, 60.   **1.15:** Num 6.3; Lk 7.33.   **1.17:** Mt 11.14; 17.13; Mal 4.5.
1.18: Lk 1.34.   **1.19:** Dan 8.16; 9.21; Mt 18.10.   **1.25:** Gen 30.23; Is 4.1.
1.30: Lk 1.13.

angel said to her, "Do not be afraid, Mary, for you have found favor with God. 31And behold, you will conceive in your womb and bear a son, and you shall call his name Jesus.

32 He will be great, and will be called the Son of the Most High;
and the Lord God will give to him the throne of his father David,

33 and he will reign over the house of Jacob for ever;
and of his kingdom there will be no end."

34 And Mary said to the angel, "How can this be, since I have no husband?"

35 And the angel said to her,

"The Holy Spirit will come upon you, and the power of the Most High will overshadow you;
therefore the child to be born*d* will be called holy,
the Son of God.

36And behold, your kinswoman Elizabeth in her old age has also conceived a son; and this is the sixth month with her who was called barren. 37 For with God nothing will be impossible." 38And Mary said, "Behold, I am the handmaid of the Lord; let it be to me according to your word." And the angel departed from her.

39 In those days Mary arose and went with haste into the hill country, to a city of Judah, 40 and she entered the house of Zech·a·ri'ah and greeted Elizabeth. 41And when Elizabeth heard the greeting of Mary, the babe leaped in her womb; and Elizabeth was filled with the Holy Spirit 42 and she exclaimed with a loud cry, "Blessed are you among women, and blessed is the fruit of your womb! 43And why is this granted me, that the mother of my Lord should come to me? 44 For behold, when the voice of your greeting came to my ears, the babe in my womb leaped for joy. 45And blessed is she who believed that there would be*e* fulfilment of what was spoken to her from the Lord."

46 And Mary said,

"My soul magnifies the Lord,

47 and my spirit rejoices in God my Savior,

48 for he has regarded the low estate of his handmaiden.
For behold, henceforth all generations will call me blessed;

49 for he who is mighty has done great things for me,
and holy is his name.

50 And his mercy is on those who fear him
from generation to generation.

51 He has shown strength with his arm,
he has scattered the proud in the imagination of their hearts,

52 he has put down the mighty from their thrones,
and exalted those of low degree;

53 he has filled the hungry with good things,
and the rich he has sent empty away.

54 He has helped his servant Israel,
in remembrance of his mercy,

55 as he spoke to our fathers,
to Abraham and to his posterity for ever."

56And Mary remained with her about three months, and returned to her home.

57 Now the time came for Elizabeth to be delivered, and she gave birth to a son. 58And her neighbors and kinsfolk heard that the Lord had shown great mercy to her, and they rejoiced with her. 59And on the eighth day they came to circumcise the child; and they would have named him Zech·a·ri'ah after his father, 60 but his mother said, "Not so; he shall be called John." 61And they said to her, "None of your kindred is called by this name." 62And they made signs to his father, inquiring what he would have him called. 63And he asked for a writing tablet, and wrote, "His name is John." And they all marveled. 64And immediately his mouth was opened and his tongue loosed, and he spoke, blessing God. 65And fear came on all their neighbors. And all these things were talked about through all the hill country of Judea; 66 and all who heard them laid them up in their hearts, saying, "What then will this child be?" For the hand of the Lord was with him.

67 And his father Zech·a·ri'ah was filled with the Holy Spirit, and prophesied, saying,

68 "Blessed be the Lord God of Israel,
for he has visited and redeemed his people,

69 and has raised up a horn of salvation for us
in the house of his servant David,

70 as he spoke by the mouth of his holy prophets from of old,

71 that we should be saved from our enemies,

d Other ancient authorities add *of you*   *e* Or *believed, for there will be*
1.31: Lk 2.21; Mt 1.21.   1.33: Mt 28.18; Dan 2.44.   1.34: Lk 1.18.   1.35: Mt 1.20.
1.37: Gen 18.14.   1.42: Lk 11.27-28.   1.46-55: 1 Sam 2.1-10.
1.47: 1 Tim 2.3; Tit 2.10; Jude 25.   1.55: Mic 7.20; Gen 17.7; 18.18; 22.17.
1.59: Lev 12.3; Gen 17.12.   1.63: Lk 1.13.

and from the hand of all who hate
us;

72 to perform the mercy promised to
our fathers,
and to remember his holy covenant,

73 the oath which he swore to our
father Abraham, 74 to grant us
that we, being delivered from the
hand of our enemies,
might serve him without fear,

75 in holiness and righteousness before
him all the days of our life.

76 And you, child, will be called the
prophet of the Most High;
for you will go before the Lord to
prepare his ways,

77 to give knowledge of salvation to his
people
in the forgiveness of their sins,

78 through the tender mercy of our
God,
when the day shall dawn upon⸍ us
from on high

79 to give light to those who sit in
darkness and in the shadow of
death,
to guide our feet into the way of
peace."

80 And the child grew and became
strong in spirit, and he was in the
wilderness till the day of his manifestation to Israel.

2 In those days a decree went out
from Caesar Augustus that all the
world should be enrolled. 2 This was
the first enrollment, when Qui·rin′i-us
was governor of Syria. 3 And all went
to be enrolled, each to his own city.
4 And Joseph also went up from
Galilee, from the city of Nazareth, to
Judea, to the city of David, which is
called Bethlehem, because he was of
the house and lineage of David, 5 to be
enrolled with Mary his betrothed, who
was with child. 6 And while they were
there, the time came for her to be
delivered. 7 And she gave birth to her
first-born son and wrapped him in
swaddling cloths, and laid him in a
manger, because there was no place for
them in the inn.

8 And in that region there were
shepherds out in the field, keeping
watch over their flock by night. 9 And
an angel of the Lord appeared to them,
and the glory of the Lord shone
around them, and they were filled

with fear. 10 And the angel said to them,
"Be not afraid; for behold, I bring you
good news of a great joy which will
come to all the people; 11 for to you is
born this day in the city of David a
Savior, who is Christ the Lord. 12 And
this will be a sign for you: you will
find a babe wrapped in swaddling
cloths and lying in a manger." 13 And
suddenly there was with the angel a
multitude of the heavenly host praising
God and saying,

14 "Glory to God in the highest,
and on earth peace among men
with whom he is pleased!"ᵍ

15 When the angels went away
from them into heaven, the shepherds
said to one another, "Let us go over
to Bethlehem and see this thing that
has happened, which the Lord has
made known to us." 16 And they went
with haste, and found Mary and
Joseph, and the babe lying in a manger. 17 And when they saw it they made
known the saying which had been told
them concerning this child; 18 and all
who heard it wondered at what the
shepherds told them. 19 But Mary kept
all these things, pondering them in her
heart. 20 And the shepherds returned,
glorifying and praising God for all
they had heard and seen, as it had been
told them.

21 And at the end of eight days,
when he was circumcised, he was
called Jesus, the name given by the
angel before he was conceived in the
womb.

22 And when the time came for
their purification according to the law
of Moses, they brought him up to
Jerusalem to present him to the Lord
23 (as it is written in the law of the
Lord, "Every male that opens the
womb shall be called holy to the
Lord") 24 and to offer a sacrifice according to what is said in the law of
the Lord, "a pair of turtledoves, or
two young pigeons." 25 Now there was
a man in Jerusalem, whose name was
Simeon, and this man was righteous
and devout, looking for the consolation
of Israel, and the Holy Spirit was upon
him. 26 And it had been revealed to
him by the Holy Spirit that he should
not see death before he had seen the
Lord's Christ. 27 And inspired by the

⸍ Or whereby the dayspring will visit. Other ancient authorities read since the dayspring
has visited   ᵍ Other ancient authorities read peace, good will among men

1.76: Lk 7.26; Mal 4.5.   1.77: Mk 1.4.   1.78: Mal 4.2; Eph 5.14.   1.79: Is 9.2; Mt 4.16.
1.80: Lk 2.40; 2.52.   2.1: Lk 3.1.   2.4: Lk 1.27.   2.9: Lk 1.11; Acts 5.19.
2.11: Jn 4.42; Acts 5.31; Mt 16.16; Acts 2.36.
2.12: 1 Sam 2.34; 2 Kings 19.29; Is 7.14.   2.14: Lk 19.38; 3.22.   2.19: Lk 2.51.
2.21: Lk 1.59, 31; Mt 1.25.   2.22-24: Lev 12.2-8.   2.23: Ex 13.2, 12.
2.25: Lk 2.38; 23.51.

Spirit[h] he came into the temple; and when the parents brought in the child Jesus, to do for him according to the custom of the law, 28 he took him up in his arms and blessed God and said, 29 "Lord, now lettest thou thy servant depart in peace,

according to thy word;
30 for mine eyes have seen thy salvation
31 which thou hast prepared in the presence of all peoples,
32 a light for revelation to the Gentiles, and for glory to thy people Israel."

33 And his father and his mother marveled at what was said about him; 34 and Simeon blessed them and said to Mary his mother,

"Behold, this child is set for the fall and rising of many in Israel, and for a sign that is spoken against
35 (and a sword will pierce through your own soul also), that thoughts out of many hearts may be revealed."

36 And there was a prophetess, Anna, the daughter of Phan'u-el, of the tribe of Ash'er; she was of a great age, having lived with her husband seven years from her virginity, 37 and as a widow till she was eighty-four. She did not depart from the temple, worshiping with fasting and prayer night and day. 38 And coming up at that very hour she gave thanks to God, and spoke of him to all who were looking for the redemption of Jerusalem.

39 And when they had performed everything according to the law of the Lord, they returned into Galilee, to their own city, Nazareth. 40 And the child grew and became strong, filled with wisdom; and the favor of God was upon him.

41 Now his parents went to Jerusalem every year at the feast of the Passover. 42 And when he was twelve years old, they went up according to custom; 43 and when the feast was ended, as they were returning, the boy Jesus stayed behind in Jerusalem. His parents did not know it, 44 but supposing him to be in the company they went a day's journey, and they sought him among their kinsfolk and acquaintances; 45 and when they did not find him, they returned to Jerusalem, seeking him. 46 After three days they found him in the temple, sitting among the teachers, listening to them and asking them questions; 47 and all who heard him were amazed at his understanding and his answers. 48 And when they saw him they were astonished; and his mother said to him, "Son, why have you treated us so? Behold, your father and I have been looking for you anxiously." 49 And he said to them, "How is it that you sought me? Did you not know that I must be in my Father's house?" 50 And they did not understand the saying which he spoke to them. 51 And he went down with them and came to Nazareth, and was obedient to them: and his mother kept all these things in her heart.

52 And Jesus increased in wisdom and in stature,[i] and in favor with God and man.

3 In the fifteenth year of the reign of Ti-be'ri-us Caesar, Pontius Pilate being governor of Judea, and Her'od being tetrarch of Galilee, and his brother Philip tetrarch of the region of I-tu-rae'a and Trach-o-ni'tis, and Ly-sa'ni-as tetrarch of Ab-i-le'ne, 2 in the high-priesthood of An'nas and Ca'ia-phas, the word of God came to John the son of Zech-a-ri'ah in the wilderness; 3 and he went into all the region about the Jordan, preaching a baptism of repentance for the forgiveness of sins. 4 As it is written in the book of the words of I-sai'ah the prophet,

"The voice of one crying in the wilderness:
Prepare the way of the Lord, make his paths straight.
5 Every valley shall be filled, and every mountain and hill shall be brought low, and the crooked shall be made straight, and the rough ways shall be made smooth;
6 and all flesh shall see the salvation of God."

7 He said therefore to the multitudes that came out to be baptized by him, "You brood of vipers! Who warned you to flee from the wrath to come? 8 Bear fruits that befit repentance, and do not begin to say to yourselves, 'We have Abraham as our father'; for I tell you, God is able from

h Or *in the Spirit*   i Or *years*
2.30: Is 52.10; Lk 3.6.   2.32: Is 42.6; 49.6; Acts 13.47; 26.23.
2.36: Acts 21.9; Josh 19.24; 1 Tim 5.9.   2.40: Judg 13.24; 1 Sam 2.26.
2.41: Deut 16.1-8; Ex 23.15.   2.48: Mk 3.31-35.   2.51: Lk 2.19.   2.52: Lk 1.80; 2.40.
3.1: Lk 23.1; 9.7; 13.31; 23.7.   3.2: Jn 18.13; Acts 4.6; Mt 26.3; Jn 11.49.
3.3-9: Mt 3.1-10; Mk 1.1-5; Jn 1.6, 23.   3.4-6: Is 40.3-5.   3.6: Lk 2.30.
3.7: Mt 12.34; 23.33.   3.8: Jn 8.33, 39.

WISE MEN WORSHIP JESUS   *Matt. 2:11*

THE SERMON ON THE MOUNT   *Matt. 5:1*

these stones to raise up children to Abraham. 9 Even now the axe is laid to the root of the trees; every tree therefore that does not bear good fruit is cut down and thrown into the fire."

10 And the multitudes asked him, "What then shall we do?" 11And he answered them, "He who has two coats, let him share with him who has none; and he who has food, let him do likewise." 12 Tax collectors also came to be baptized, and said to him, "Teacher, what shall we do?" 13And he said to them, "Collect no more than is appointed you." 14 Soldiers also asked him, "And we, what shall we do?" And he said to them, "Rob no one by violence or by false accusation, and be content with your wages."

15 As the people were in expectation, and all men questioned in their hearts concerning John, whether perhaps he were the Christ, 16 John answered them all, "I baptize you with water; but he who is mightier than I is coming, the thong of whose sandals I am not worthy to untie; he will baptize you with the Holy Spirit and with fire. 17 His winnowing fork is in his hand, to clear his threshing floor, and to gather the wheat into his granary, but the chaff he will burn with unquenchable fire."

18 So, with many other exhortations, he preached good news to the people. 19 But Her'od the tetrarch, who had been reproved by him for He·rō'di·as, his brother's wife, and for all the evil things that Herod had done, 20 added this to them all, that he shut up John in prison.

21 Now when all the people were baptized, and when Jesus also had been baptized and was praying, the heaven was opened, 22 and the Holy Spirit descended upon him in bodily form, as a dove, and a voice came from heaven, "Thou art my beloved Son;*k* with thee I am well pleased."*k*

23 Jesus, when he began his ministry, was about thirty years of age, being the son (as was supposed) of Joseph, the son of Hē'li, 24 the son of Mat'that, the son of Levi, the son of

Mel'chi, the son of Jan'na-i, the son of Joseph, 25 the son of Mat·ta·thī'as, the son of Amos, the son of Nā'hum, the son of Es'li, the son of Nag'ga-i, 26 the son of Mā'ath, the son of Mat·ta·thī'as, the son of Sem'e-in, the son of Jō'sech, the son of Jō'dà, 27 the son of Jō-an'an, the son of Rhē'sà, the son of Ze·rub'bà·bel, the son of She·al'ti-el,*l* the son of Nē'ri, 28 the son of Mel'chi, the son of Ad'di, the son of Cō'sàm, the son of El·ma'dàm, the son of Ēr, 29 the son of Joshua, the son of E·li·ē'zēr, the son of Jō'rim, the son of Mat'thàt, the son of Levi, 30 the son of Simeon, the son of Judah, the son of Joseph, the son of Jō'nàm, the son of E·li'à·kim, 31 the son of Mē'le-ä, the son of Men'nà, the son of Mat'tà·thà, the son of Nathan, the son of David, 32 the son of Jesse, the son of Ō'bed, the son of Bō'az, the son of Sā'là, the son of Näh'shōn, 33 the son of Am·min'à·dab, the son of Ad'min, the son of Ar'ni, the son of Hez'ron, the son of Per'ez, the son of Judah, 34 the son of Jacob, the son of Isaac, the son of Abraham, the son of Tē'ràh, the son of Nā'hôr, 35 the son of Sē'rug, the son of Rē'ü, the son of Pē'leg, the son of E'bēr, the son of Shē'làh, 36 the son of Cā-i'nàn, the son of Ar·phà'xàd, the son of Shem, the son of Noah, the son of Lā'mech, 37 the son of Mē·thū'sè·làh, the son of E'nôch, the son of Jàr'ēd, the son of Ma·ha'là·lē-el, the son of Cā-i'nàn, 38 the son of E'nôs, the son of Seth, the son of Adam, the son of God.

4 And Jesus, full of the Holy Spirit, returned from the Jordan, and was led by the Spirit 2 for forty days in the wilderness, tempted by the devil. And he ate nothing in those days; and when they were ended, he was hungry. 3 The devil said to him, "If you are the Son of God, command this stone to become bread." 4And Jesus answered him, "It is written, 'Man shall not live by bread alone.'" 5And the devil took him up, and showed him all the kingdoms of the world in a moment of time, 6 and said to him,

l Or *my Son, my* (or *the*) *Beloved*
k Other ancient authorities read *today I have begotten thee*   *l* Greek *Salathiel*

3.9: Mt 7.19; Heb 6.7-8.   **3.11:** Lk 6.29.   **3.15:** Acts 13.25; Jn 1.19-22.
3.16-18: Mt 3.11-12; Mk 1.7-8; Jn 1.26-27, 33; Acts 1.5; 11.16; 19.4.
3.19-20: Mt 14.3-4; Mk 6.17-18.   **3.21-22:** Mt 3.13-17; Mk 1.9-11; Jn 1.29-34.
3.21: Lk 5.16; 6.12; 9.18; 9.28; 11.1; Mk 1.35.
3.22: Ps 2.7; Is 42.1; Lk 9.35; Acts 10.38; 2 Pet 1.17.
3.23-38: Mt 1.1-17; Gen 5.3-32; 11.10-26; Ruth 4.18-22; 1 Chron 1.1-4, 24-28; 2.1-15.
3.23: Jn 8.57; Lk 1.27.   **4.1-13:** Mt 4.1-11; Mk 1.12-13.   **4.2:** Deut 9.9; 1 Kings 19.8.
4.4: Deut 8.3.   **4.6:** 1 Jn 5.19.

"To you I will give all this authority and their glory; for it has been delivered to me, and I give it to whom I will. 7 If you, then, will worship me, it shall all be yours." 8And Jesus answered him, "It is written,

'You shall worship the Lord your God,
   and him only shall you serve.'"

9And he took him to Jerusalem, and set him on the pinnacle of the temple, and said to him, "If you are the Son of God, throw yourself down from here; 10 for it is written,

'He will give his angels charge of you, to guard you,'

11 and

'On their hands they will bear you up,
   lest you strike your foot against a stone.'"

12And Jesus answered him, "It is said, 'You shall not tempt the Lord your God.'" 13And when the devil had ended every temptation, he departed from him until an opportune time.

14 And Jesus returned in the power of the Spirit into Galilee, and a report concerning him went out through all the surrounding country. 15And he taught in their synagogues, being glorified by all.

16 And he came to Nazareth, where he had been brought up; and he went to the synagogue, as his custom was, on the sabbath day. And he stood up to read; 17 and there was given to him the book of the prophet I·sāi′ah. He opened the book and found the place where it was written,

18 "The Spirit of the Lord is upon me, because he has anointed me to preach good news to the poor.
   He has sent me to proclaim release to the captives
   and recovering of sight to the blind, to set at liberty those who are oppressed,
19 to proclaim the acceptable year of the Lord."

20And he closed the book, and gave it back to the attendant, and sat down; and the eyes of all in the synagogue were fixed on him. 21And he began to say to them, "Today this scripture has been fulfilled in your hearing."22And all spoke well of him, and wondered at the gracious words which proceeded out of his mouth; and they said, "Is not this Joseph's son?" 23And he said to them, "Doubtless you will quote to me this proverb, 'Physician, heal yourself; what we have heard you did at Cà·pēr′nà·ùm, do here also in your own country.'"24And he said, "Truly, I say to you, no prophet is acceptable in his own country. 25 But in truth, I tell you, there were many widows in Israel in the days of E·lī′jàh, when the heaven was shut up three years and six months, when there came a great famine over all the land;26 and E·lī′jàh was sent to none of them but only to Zar′é·phath, in the land of Sī′don, to a woman who was a widow. 27 And there were many lepers in Israel in the time of the prophet E·lī′shà; and none of them was cleansed, but only Nā′à·man the Syrian."28 When they heard this, all in the synagogue were filled with wrath. 29And they rose up and put him out of the city, and led him to the brow of the hill on which their city was built, that they might throw him down headlong. 30 But passing through the midst of them he went away.

31 And he went down to Cà·pēr′nà·ùm, a city of Galilee. And he was teaching them on the sabbath; 32 and they were astonished at his teaching, for his word was with authority. 33And in the synagogue there was a man who had the spirit of an unclean demon; and he cried out with a loud voice, 34 "Ah!*m* What have you to do with us, Jesus of Nazareth? Have you come to destroy us? I know who you are, the Holy One of God." 35 But Jesus rebuked him, saying, "Be silent, and come out of him!" And when the demon had thrown him down in the midst, he came out of him, having done him no harm. 36And they were all amazed and said to one another, "What is this word? For with authority and power he commands the unclean spirits, and they come out." 37And reports of him went out into every place in the surrounding region.

38 And he arose and left the synagogue, and entered Simon's house. Now Simon's mother-in-law was ill

m Or *Let us alone*

4.8: Deut 6.13.   4.10-11: Ps 91.11-12.   4.12: Deut 6.16.   4.13: Lk 22.28.
4.14: Mt 4.12; Mk 1.14; Mt 9.26; Lk 4.37.   4.15: Mt 4.23; 9.35; 11.1.
4.16-30: Mt 13.53-58; Mk 6.1-6; Acts 13.14-16.   4.18-19: Is 61.1-2.
4.22: Jn 6.42; 7.15.   4.23: Mk 1.21, 2.1; Jn 4.46.   4.24: Jn 4.44.
4.25: 1 Kings 17.1, 8-16; 18.1; Jas 5.17-18.   4.27: 2 Kings 5.1-14.
4.29: Acts 7.58; Num 15.35.   4.30: Jn 8.59; 10.39.   4.31-37: Mk 1.21-28.
4.32: Mt 7.28; 13.54; 22.33; Mk 11.18; Jn 7.46.   4.37: Lk 4.14; 5.15; Mt 9.26.
4.38-41: Mt 8.14-17; Mk 1.29-34.

with a high fever, and they besought him for her. 39 And he stood over her and rebuked the fever, and it left her; and immediately she rose and served them.

40 Now when the sun was setting, all those who had any that were sick with various diseases brought them to him; and he laid his hands on every one of them and healed them. 41 And demons also came out of many, crying, "You are the Son of God!" But he rebuked them, and would not allow them to speak, because they knew that he was the Christ.

42 And when it was day he departed and went into a lonely place. And the people sought him and came to him, and would have kept him from leaving them; 43 but he said to them, "I must preach the good news of the kingdom of God to the other cities also; for I was sent for this purpose." 44 And he was preaching in the synagogues of Judea.[n]

5 While the people pressed upon him to hear the word of God, he was standing by the lake of Gen·nes´a-ret. 2 And he saw two boats by the lake; but the fishermen had gone out of them and were washing their nets. 3 Getting into one of the boats, which was Simon's, he asked him to put out a little from the land. And he sat down and taught the people from the boat. 4 And when he had ceased speaking, he said to Simon, "Put out into the deep and let down your nets for a catch." 5 And Simon answered, "Master, we toiled all night and took nothing! But at your word I will let down the nets." 6 And when they had done this, they enclosed a great shoal of fish; and as their nets were breaking, 7 they beckoned to their partners in the other boat to come and help them. And they came and filled both the boats, so that they began to sink. 8 But when Simon Peter saw it, he fell down at Jesus' knees, saying, "Depart from me, for I am a sinful man, O Lord." 9 For he was astonished, and all that were with him, at the catch of fish which they had taken; 10 and so also were James and John, sons of Zeb´e-dee, who were partners with Simon. And Jesus said to Simon, "Do not be afraid; henceforth you will be catching

men." 11 And when they had brought their boats to land, they left everything and followed him.

12 While he was in one of the cities, there came a man full of leprosy; and when he saw Jesus, he fell on his face and besought him, "Lord, if you will, you can make me clean." 13 And he stretched out his hand, and touched him, saying, "I will; be clean." And immediately the leprosy left him. 14 And he charged him to tell no one; but "go and show yourself to the priest, and make an offering for your cleansing, as Moses commanded, for a proof to the people."[o] 15 But so much the more the report went abroad concerning him; and great multitudes gathered to hear and to be healed of their infirmities. 16 But he withdrew to the wilderness and prayed.

17 On one of those days, as he was teaching, there were Pharisees and teachers of the law sitting by, who had come from every village of Galilee and Judea and from Jerusalem; and the power of the Lord was with him to heal.[p] 18 And behold, men were bringing on a bed a man who was paralyzed, and they sought to bring him in and lay him before Jesus;[q] 19 but finding no way to bring him in, because of the crowd, they went up on the roof and let him down with his bed through the tiles into the midst before Jesus. 20 And when he saw their faith he said, "Man, your sins are forgiven you." 21 And the scribes and the Pharisees began to question, saying, "Who is this that speaks blasphemies? Who can forgive sins but God only?" 22 When Jesus perceived their questionings, he answered them, "Why do you question in your hearts? 23 Which is easier, to say, 'Your sins are forgiven you,' or to say, 'Rise and walk'? 24 But that you may know that the Son of man has authority on earth to forgive sins"— he said to the man who was paralyzed—"I say to you, rise, take up your bed and go home." 25 And immediately he rose before them, and took up that on which he lay, and went home, glorifying God. 26 And amazement seized them all, and they glorified God and were filled with awe, saying, "We have seen strange things today."

n Other ancient authorities read Galilee　o Greek to them
p Other ancient authorities read was present to heal them　q Greek him
4.42-43: Mk 1.35-38.　4.44: Mt 4.23; Mk 1.39; Mt 9.35.
5.1-11: Mt 4.18-22; Mk 1.16-20; Jn 1.40-42; 21.1-19.　5.3: Mt 13.1-2; Mk 4.1.
5.5: Lk 8.24, 45; 9.33, 49; 17.13.　5.12-16: Mt 8.1-4; Mk 1.40-45; Lk 17.11-19.
5.14: Lev 13.49; 14.2-32.　5.15: Lk 4.14, 37; Mk 9.26.
5.16: Lk 3.21; 6.12; 9.18, 28; 11.1.　5.17-26: Mt 9.1-8; Mk 2.1-12; Jn 5.1-9
5.17: Mt 15.1; Mk 5.30; Lk 6.19.　5.20: Lk 7.48-49.

27 After this he went out, and saw a tax collector, named Levi, sitting at the tax office; and he said to him, "Follow me." 28And he left everything, and rose and followed him.

29 And Levi made him a great feast in his house; and there was a large company of tax collectors and others sitting at table* with them. 30And the Pharisees and their scribes murmured against his disciples, saying, "Why do you eat and drink with tax collectors and sinners?" 31And Jesus answered them, "Those who are well have no need of a physician, but those who are sick; 32 I have not come to call the righteous, but sinners to repentance."

33 And they said to him, "The disciples of John fast often and offer prayers, and so do the disciples of the Pharisees, but yours eat and drink." 34And Jesus said to them, "Can you make wedding guests fast while the bridegroom is with them? 35The days will come, when the bridegroom is taken away from them, and then they will fast in those days." 36 He told them a parable also: "No one tears a piece from a new garment and puts it upon an old garment; if he does, he will tear the new, and the piece from the new will not match the old. 37And no one puts new wine into old wineskins; if he does, the new wine will burst the skins and it will be spilled, and the skins will be destroyed. 38 But new wine must be put into fresh wineskins. 39And no one after drinking old wine desires new; for he says, 'The old is good.' "*s*

6 On a sabbath,* while he was going through the grainfields, his disciples plucked and ate some ears of grain, rubbing them in their hands. 2 But some of the Pharisees said, "Why are you doing what is not lawful to do on the sabbath?" 3And Jesus answered, "Have you not read what David did when he was hungry, he and those who were with him: 4how he entered the house of God, and took and ate the bread of the Presence, which it is not lawful for any but the priests to eat, and also gave it to those

with him?" 5And he said to them, "The Son of man is lord of the sabbath."

6 On another sabbath, when he entered the synagogue and taught, a man was there whose right hand was withered. 7And the scribes and the Pharisees watched him, to see whether he would heal on the sabbath, so that they might find an accusation against him. 8 But he knew their thoughts, and he said to the man who had the withered hand, "Come and stand here." And he rose and stood there. 9And Jesus said to them, "I ask you, is it lawful on the sabbath to do good or to do harm, to save life or to destroy it?" 10And he looked around on them all, and said to him, "Stretch out your hand." And he did so, and his hand was restored. 11 But they were filled with fury and discussed with one another what they might do to Jesus.

12 In these days he went out into the hills to pray; and all night he continued in prayer to God. 13And when it was day, he called his disciples, and chose from them twelve, whom he named apostles; 14 Simon, whom he named Peter, and Andrew his brother, and James and John, and Philip, and Bartholomew, 15 and Matthew, and Thomas, and James the son of Alphaē'us, and Simon who was called the Zealot, 16 and Judas the son of James, and Judas Is·car'i·ot, who became a traitor.

17 And he came down with them and stood on a level place, with a great crowd of his disciples and a great multitude of people from all Judea and Jerusalem and the seacoast of Tyre and Si'don, who came to hear him and to be healed of their diseases; 18 and those who were troubled with unclean spirits were cured. 19And all the crowd sought to touch him, for power came forth from him and healed them all.

20 And he lifted up his eyes on his disciples, and said:

"Blessed are you poor, for yours is the kingdom of God.

21 "Blessed are you that hunger now, for you shall be satisfied.

r Greek *reclining*   *s* Other ancient authorities read *better*
t Other ancient authorities read *On the second first sabbath* (on the second sabbath after the first)

5.27-32: Mt 9.9-13; Mk 2.13-17.   **5.30:** Lk 15.1-2.   **5.32:** 1 Tim 1.15.
5.33-38: Mt 9.14-17; Mk 2.18-22.   **5.33:** Lk 7.18; 11.1; Jn 3.25-26.
5.35: Lk 9.22; 17.22.   **6.1-5:** Mt 12.1-8; Mk 2.23-28.   **6.1:** Deut 23.25.
6.2: Ex 20.10; 23.12; Deut 5.14.   **6.3:** 1 Sam 21.1-6.   **6.4:** Lev 24.9.
6.6-11: Mt 12.9-14; Mk 3.1-6.   **6.12-16:** Mk 3.13-19; Mt 10.2-4; Acts 1.13.
6.12: Lk 3.21; 5.16; 9.18, 28; 11.1.   **6.17-19:** Mt 5.1-2; 4.24-25; Mk 3.7-12.
6.19: Mk 3.10; Mt 9.21; 14.36; Lk 5.17.   **6.20-23:** Mt 5.3-12.

"Blessed are you that weep now, for you shall laugh.

22 "Blessed are you when men hate you, and when they exclude you and revile you, and cast out your name as evil, on account of the Son of man! 23 Rejoice in that day, and leap for joy, for behold, your reward is great in heaven; for so their fathers did to the prophets.

24 "But woe to you that are rich, for you have received your consolation.

25 "Woe to you that are full now, for you shall hunger.

"Woe to you that laugh now, for you shall mourn and weep.

26 "Woe to you, when all men speak well of you, for so their fathers did to the false prophets.

27 "But I say to you that hear, Love your enemies, do good to those who hate you, 28 bless those who curse you, pray for those who abuse you. 29 To him who strikes you on the cheek, offer the other also; and from him who takes away your cloak do not withhold your coat as well. 30 Give to every one who begs from you; and of him who takes away your goods do not ask them again. 31 And as you wish that men would do to you, do so to them.

32 "If you love those who love you, what credit is that to you? For even sinners love those who love them. 33 And if you do good to those who do good to you, what credit is that to you? For even sinners do the same. 34 And if you lend to those from whom you hope to receive, what credit is that to you? Even sinners lend to sinners, to receive as much again. 35 But love your enemies, and do good, and lend, expecting nothing in return;*y* and your reward will be great, and you will be sons of the Most High; for he is kind to the ungrateful and the selfish. 36 Be merciful, even as your Father is merciful.

37 "Judge not, and you will not be judged; condemn not, and you will not be condemned; forgive, and you will be forgiven; 38 give, and it will be given to you; good measure, pressed down, shaken together, running over, will be put into your lap. For the measure you give will be the measure you get back."

39 He also told them a parable: "Can a blind man lead a blind man? Will they not both fall into a pit? 40 A disciple is not above his teacher, but every one when he is fully taught will be like his teacher. 41 Why do you see the speck that is in your brother's eye, but do not notice the log that is in your own eye? 42 Or how can you say to your brother, 'Brother, let me take out the speck that is in your eye,' when you yourself do not see the log that is in your own eye? You hypocrite, first take the log out of your own eye, and then you will see clearly to take out the speck that is in your brother's eye.

43 "For no good tree bears bad fruit, nor again does a bad tree bear good fruit; 44 for each tree is known by its own fruit. For figs are not gathered from thorns, nor are grapes picked from a bramble bush. 45 The good man out of the good treasure of his heart produces good, and the evil man out of his evil treasure produces evil; for out of the abundance of the heart his mouth speaks.

46 "Why do you call me 'Lord, Lord,' and not do what I tell you? 47 Every one who comes to me and hears my words and does them, I will show you what he is like: 48 he is like a man building a house, who dug deep, and laid the foundation upon rock; and when a flood arose, the stream broke against that house and could not shake it, because it had been well built.*w* 49 But he who hears and does not do them is like a man who built a house on the ground without a foundation; against which the stream broke, and immediately it fell, and the ruin of that house was great."

7 After he had ended all his sayings in the hearing of the people he entered Ca·pēr′na·um. 2 Now a centurion had a slave who was dear*x* to him, who was sick and at the point of death. 3 When he heard of Jesus, he sent to him elders of the Jews, asking him to come and heal his slave. 4 And when they came to Jesus, they besought him earnestly, saying, "He is

v Other ancient authorities read *despairing of no man*
w Other ancient authorities read *founded upon the rock*   *x* Or *valuable*

6.22: 1 Pet 4.14; Jn 9.22; 16.2.   **6.24-26:** Lk 10.13-15; 11.38-52; 17.1; 21.23; 22.22.
6.24: Lk 16.25; Jas 5.1-5; Mt 6.2.   **6.27-30:** Mt 5.39-44; Rom 12.17; 1 Cor 6.7.
6.31: Mt 7.12.   **6.32-36:** Mt 5.44-48.   **6.35:** Mt 5.9.   **6.37-38:** Mt 7.1-2; Rom 2.1.
6.38: Mk 4.24; Acts 20.35.   **6.39:** Mt 15.14.   **6.40:** Mt 10.24-25; Jn 13.16; 15.20.
6.41-42: Mt 7.3-5.   **6.43-45:** Mt 7.18-19; 12.33-35; Jas 3.11-12.   **6.45:** Mk 7.20.
6.46: Mt 7.21.   **6.47-49:** Mt 7.24-27; Jas 1.22-25.
7.1-10: Mt 8.5-10, 13; Jn 4.46-53.

worthy to have you do this for him, 5 for he loves our nation, and he built us our synagogue." 6And Jesus went with them. When he was not far from the house, the centurion sent friends to him, saying to him, "Lord, do not trouble yourself, for I am not worthy to have you come under my roof; 7 therefore I did not presume to come to you. But say the word, and let my servant be healed. 8 For I am a man set under authority, with soldiers under me: and I say to one, 'Go,' and he goes; and to another, 'Come,' and he comes; and to my slave, 'Do this,' and he does it." 9 When Jesus heard this he marveled at him, and turned and said to the multitude that followed him, "I tell you, not even in Israel have I found such faith." 10And when those who had been sent returned to the house, they found the slave well.

11 Soon afterward*y* he went to a city called Nāʹin, and his disciples and a great crowd went with him. 12As he drew near to the gate of the city, behold, a man who had died was being carried out, the only son of his mother, and she was a widow; and a large crowd from the city was with her. 13And when the Lord saw her, he had compassion on her and said to her, "Do not weep." 14And he came and touched the bier, and the bearers stood still. And he said, "Young man, I say to you, arise." 15And the dead man sat up, and began to speak. And he gave him to his mother. 16 Fear seized them all; and they glorified God, saying, "A great prophet has arisen among us!" and "God has visited his people!" 17And this report concerning him spread through the whole of Judea and all the surrounding country.

18 The disciples of John told him of all these things. 19And John, calling to him two of his disciples, sent them to the Lord, saying, "Are you he who is to come, or shall we look for another?" 20And when the men had come to him, they said, "John the Baptist has sent us to you, saying, 'Are you he who is to come, or shall we look for another?'" 21 In that hour he cured many of diseases and plagues and evil spirits, and on many that were

blind he bestowed sight. 22And he answered them, "Go and tell John what you have seen and heard: the blind receive their sight, the lame walk, lepers are cleansed, and the deaf hear, the dead are raised up, the poor have good news preached to them. 23And blessed is he who takes no offense at me."

24 When the messengers of John had gone, he began to speak to the crowds concerning John: "What did you go out into the wilderness to behold? A reed shaken by the wind? 25What then did you go out to see? A man clothed in soft raiment? Behold, those who are gorgeously appareled and live in luxury are in kings' courts. 26What then did you go out to see? A prophet? Yes, I tell you, and more than a prophet. 27This is he of whom it is written,

'Behold, I send my messenger before thy face,
who shall prepare thy way before thee.'

28I tell you, among those born of women none is greater than John; yet he who is least in the kingdom of God is greater than he." 29 (When they heard this all the people and the tax collectors justified God, having been baptized with the baptism of John; 30 but the Pharisees and the lawyers rejected the purpose of God for themselves, not having been baptized by him.)

31 "To what then shall I compare the men of this generation, and what are they like? 32They are like children sitting in the market place and calling to one another,

'We piped to you, and you did not dance;
we wailed, and you did not weep.'

33For John the Baptist has come eating no bread and drinking no wine; and you say, 'He has a demon.' 34The Son of man has come eating and drinking; and you say, 'Behold, a glutton and a drunkard, a friend of tax collectors and sinners!' 35Yet wisdom is justified by all her children."

36 One of the Pharisees asked him to eat with him, and he went into the Pharisee's house, and sat at table.

y Other ancient authorities read *Next day*

7.5: Acts 10.2.
7.11-17: Mk 5.21-24, 35-43; Jn 11.1-44; 1 Kings 17.17-24; 2 Kings 4.32-37.
7.13: Lk 7.19; 10.1; 11.39; 12.42; 13.15; 17.5-6; 18.6; 19.8; 22.61; 24.3.
7.16: Lk 7.39; 24.19; Mt 21.11; Jn 6.14.   7.18-35: Mt 11.2-19.
7.21: Mt 4.23; Mk 3.10.   7.22: Is 29.18-19; 35.5-6; 61.1; Lk 4.18-19.
7.27: Mal 3.1; Mk 1.2.   7.29-30: Mt 21.32; Lk 3.12.   7.33: Lk 1.15.
7.34: Lk 5.29; 15.1-2; 7.36-50.   7.36-50: Mt 26.6-13; Mk 14.3-9; Jn 12.1-8.
7.36: Lk 11.37; 14.1.

37And behold, a woman of the city, who was a sinner, when she learned that he was sitting at table in the Pharisee's house, brought an alabaster flask of ointment, 38 and standing behind him at his feet, weeping, she began to wet his feet with her tears, and wiped them with the hair of her head, and kissed his feet, and anointed them with the ointment. 39 Now when the Pharisee who had invited him saw it, he said to himself, "If this man were a prophet, he would have known who and what sort of woman this is who is touching him, for she is a sinner." 40And Jesus answering said to him, "Simon, I have something to say to you." And he answered, "What is it, Teacher?" 41"A certain creditor had two debtors; one owed five hundred denarii, and the other fifty. 42When they could not pay, he forgave them both. Now which of them will love him more?" 43 Simon answered, "The one, I suppose, to whom he forgave more." And he said to him, "You have judged rightly." 44 Then turning toward the woman he said to Simon, "Do you see this woman? I entered your house, you gave me no water for my feet, but she has wet my feet with her tears and wiped them with her hair. 45 You gave me no kiss, but from the time I came in she has not ceased to kiss my feet. 46 You did not anoint my head with oil, but she has anointed my feet with ointment. 47Therefore I tell you, her sins, which are many, are forgiven, for she loved much; but he who is forgiven little, loves little." 48And he said to her, "Your sins are forgiven." 49 Then those who were at table with him began to say among themselves, "Who is this, who even forgives sins?" 50And he said to the woman, "Your faith has saved you; go in peace."

8 Soon afterward he went on through cities and villages, preaching and bringing the good news of the kingdom of God. And the twelve were with him, 2 and also some women who had been healed of evil spirits and infirmities: Mary, called Mag′da·lēne, from whom seven demons had gone out, 3 and Jō-an′nà, the wife of

Chü′zà, Her′ŏd's steward, and Susanna, and many others, who provided for them[z] out of their means.

4 And when a great crowd came together and people from town after town came to him, he said in a parable: 5"A sower went out to sow his seed; and as he sowed, some fell along the path, and was trodden under foot, and the birds of the air devoured it. 6And some fell on the rock; and as it grew up, it withered away, because it had no moisture. 7And some fell among thorns; and the thorns grew with it and choked it. 8And some fell into good soil and grew, and yielded a hundredfold." As he said this, he called out, "He who has ears to hear, let him hear."

9 And when his disciples asked him what this parable meant, 10 he said, "To you it has been given to know the secrets of the kingdom of God; but for others they are in parables, so that seeing they may not see, and hearing they may not understand. 11Now the parable is this: The seed is the word of God. 12The ones along the path are those who have heard; then the devil comes and takes away the word from their hearts, that they may not believe and be saved. 13And the ones on the rock are those who, when they hear the word, receive it with joy; but these have no root, they believe for a while and in time of temptation fall away. 14And as for what fell among the thorns, they are those who hear, but as they go on their way they are choked by the cares and riches and pleasures of life, and their fruit does not mature. 15And as for that in the good soil, they are those who, hearing the word, hold it fast in an honest and good heart, and bring forth fruit with patience.

16 "No one after lighting a lamp covers it with a vessel, or puts it under a bed, but puts it on a stand, that those who enter may see the light. 17For nothing is hid that shall not be made manifest, nor anything secret that shall not be known and come to light. 18 Take heed then how you hear; for to him who has will more be given, and from him who has not, even what

z Other ancient authorities read *him*
7.39: Lk 7.16; 24.19; Mt 21.11; Jn 6.14.　**7.42:** Mt 18.25.　**7.43:** Lk 10.28.
7.48: Mt 9.2; Mk 2.5; Lk 5.20.　**7.50:** Mt 9.22; Mk 5.34; Lk 8.48.
8.1-3: Lk 4.15; Mk 15.40-41; Mt 27.55-56; Lk 23.49.　**8.4-8:** Mt 13.1-9; Mk 4.1-9.
8.8: Mt 11.15.　**8.9-10:** Mt 13.10-13; Mk 4.10-12; Is 6.9-10; Jer 5.21; Ezek 12.2.
8.11-15: Mt 13.18-23; Mk 4.13-20.　**8.11:** 1 Thess 2.13; 1 Pet 1.23.
8.16: Mk 4.21; Mt 5.15; Lk 11.33.
8.17: Mk 4.22-23; Mt 10.26-27; Lk 12.2-3; Eph 5.13.
8.18: Mk 4.24-25; Mt 13.12; 25.29; Lk 19.26.

he thinks that he has will be taken away."

19 Then his mother and his brothers came to him, but they could not reach him for the crowd. 20 And he was told, "Your mother and your brothers are standing outside, desiring to see you." 21 But he said to them, "My mother and my brothers are those who hear the word of God and do it."

22 One day he got into a boat with his disciples, and he said to them, "Let us go across to the other side of the lake." So they set out, 23 and as they sailed he fell asleep. And a storm of wind came down on the lake, and they were filling with water, and were in danger. 24 And they went and woke him saying, "Master, Master, we are perishing!" And he awoke and rebuked the wind and the raging waves; and they ceased, and there was a calm. 25 He said to them, "Where is your faith?" And they were afraid, and they marveled, saying to one another, "Who then is this, that he commands even wind and water, and they obey him?"

26 Then they arrived at the country of the Ger'a·senes,[a] which is opposite Galilee. 27 And as he stepped out on land there met him a man from the city who had demons; for a long time he had worn no clothes, and he lived not in a house but among the tombs. 28 When he saw Jesus, he cried out and fell down before him, and said with a loud voice, "What have you to do with me, Jesus, Son of the Most High God? I beseech you, do not torment me." 29 For he had commanded the unclean spirit to come out of the man. (For many a time it had seized him; he was kept under guard, and bound with chains and fetters, but he broke the bonds and was driven by the demon into the desert.) 30 Jesus then asked him, "What is your name?" And he said, "Legion"; for many demons had entered him. 31 And they begged him not to command them to depart into the abyss. 32 Now a large herd of swine was feeding there on the hillside; and they begged him to let them enter these. So he gave them leave. 33 Then the demons came out of the man and entered the swine, and

the herd rushed down the steep bank into the lake and were drowned.

34 When the herdsmen saw what had happened, they fled, and told it in the city and in the country. 35 Then people went out to see what had happened, and they came to Jesus, and found the man from whom the demons had gone, sitting at the feet of Jesus, clothed and in his right mind; and they were afraid. 36 And those who had seen it told them how he who had been possessed with demons was healed. 37 Then all the people of the surrounding country of the Ger'a·senes[a] asked him to depart from them; for they were seized with great fear; so he got into the boat and returned. 38 The man from whom the demons had gone begged that he might be with him; but he sent him away, saying, 39 "Return to your home, and declare how much God has done for you." And he went away, proclaiming throughout the whole city how much Jesus had done for him.

40 Now when Jesus returned, the crowd welcomed him, for they were all waiting for him. 41 And there came a man named Jā'i·rus, who was a ruler of the synagogue; and falling at Jesus' feet he besought him to come to his house, 42 for he had an only daughter, about twelve years of age, and she was dying.

As he went, the people pressed round him. 43 And a woman who had had a flow of blood for twelve years[b] and could not be healed by any one, 44 came up behind him, and touched the fringe of his garment; and immediately her flow of blood ceased. 45 And Jesus said, "Who was it that touched me?" When all denied it, Peter[c] said, "Master, the multitudes surround you and press upon you!" 46 But Jesus said, "Some one touched me; for I perceive that power has gone forth from me." 47 And when the woman saw that she was not hidden, she came trembling, and falling down before him declared in the presence of all the people why she had touched him, and how she had been immediately healed. 48 And he said to her, "Daughter, your faith has made you well; go in peace."

a Other ancient authorities read *Gadarenes,* others *Gergesenes*
b Other ancient authorities add *and had spent all her living upon physicians*
c Other ancient authorities add *and those who were with him*

8.19-21: Mt 12.46-50; Mk 3.31-35.   8.21: Lk 11.28; Jn 15.14.
8.22-25: Mt 8.23-27; Mk 4.35-41; 6.47-52; Jn 6.16-21.
8.24: Lk 5.5; 8.45; 9.33, 49; 17.13.   8.26-39: Mt 8.28-34; Mk 5.1-20.
8.28: Mk 1.24; Jn 2.4.   8.40-56: Mt 9.18-26; Mk 5.21-43.   8.45: Lk 8.24.
8.46: Lk 5.17; 6.19.   8.48: Mt 9.22; Lk 7.50; 17.19; 18.42.

49 While he was still speaking, a man from the ruler's house came and said, "Your daughter is dead; do not trouble the Teacher any more." 50 But Jesus on hearing this answered him, "Do not fear; only believe, and she shall be well." 51And when he came to the house, he permitted no one to enter with him, except Peter and John and James, and the father and mother of the child. 52And all were weeping and bewailing her; but he said, "Do not weep; for she is not dead but sleeping." 53And they laughed at him, knowing that she was dead. 54 But taking her by the hand he called, saying, "Child, arise." 55And her spirit returned, and she got up at once; and he directed that something should be given her to eat. 56And her parents were amazed; but he charged them to tell no one what had happened.

9 And he called the twelve together and gave them power and authority over all demons and to cure diseases, 2 and he sent them out to preach the kingdom of God and to heal. 3And he said to them, "Take nothing for your journey, no staff, nor bag, nor bread, nor money; and do not have two tunics. 4And whatever house you enter, stay there, and from there depart. 5And wherever they do not receive you, when you leave that town shake off the dust from your feet as a testimony against them." 6And they departed and went through the villages, preaching the gospel and healing everywhere.

7 Now Her'od the tetrarch heard of all that was done, and he was perplexed, because it was said by some that John had been raised from the dead, 8 by some that E·li'jah had appeared, and by others that one of the old prophets had risen. 9 Her'od said, "John I beheaded; but who is this about whom I hear such things?" And he sought to see him.

10 On their return the apostles told him what they had done. And he took them and withdrew apart to a city called Beth-sa'i·da. 11 When the crowds learned it, they followed him; and he welcomed them and spoke to them of the kingdom of God, and cured those who had need of healing. 12 Now the day began to wear away; and the twelve came and said to him, "Send the crowd away, to go into the villages and country round about, to lodge and get provisions; for we are here in a lonely place." 13 But he said to them, "You give them something to eat." They said, "We have no more than five loaves and two fish—unless we are to go and buy food for all these people." 14 For there were about five thousand men. And he said to his disciples, "Make them sit down in companies, about fifty each." 15And they did so, and made them all sit down. 16And taking the five loaves and the two fish he looked up to heaven, and blessed and broke them, and gave them to the disciples to set before the crowd, 17And all ate and were satisfied. And they took up what was left over, twelve baskets of broken pieces.

18 Now it happened that as he was praying alone the disciples were with him; and he asked them, "Who do the people say that I am?" 19And they answered, "John the Baptist; but others say, E·li'jah; and others, that one of the old prophets has risen." 20And he said to them, "But who do you say that I am?" And Peter answered, "The Christ of God." 21 But he charged and commanded them to tell this to no one, 22 saying, "The Son of man must suffer many things, and be rejected by the elders and chief priests and scribes, and be killed, and on the third day be raised."

23 And he said to all, "If any man would come after me, let him deny himself and take up his cross daily and follow me. 24For whoever would save his life will lose it; and whoever loses his life for my sake, he will save it. 25For what does it profit a man if he gains the whole world and loses or forfeits himself? 26For whoever is ashamed of me and of my words, of him will the Son of man be ashamed when he comes in his glory and the glory of the Father and of the holy

8.56: Mt 8.4; Mk 3.12; 7.36; Lk 9.21.
9.1-6: Mt 10.1, 5, 7-11, 14; Mk 6.7-12; Lk 10.4-11.   **9.5:** Acts 13.51.
9.7-9: Mt 14.1-2; Mk 6.14-16; Lk 9.19.   **9.9:** Lk 23.8.
9.10: Mk 6.30-31; Lk 10.17; Jn 1.44.
9.11-17: Mt 14.13-21; Mk 6.32-44; Jn 6.1-14; Mk 8.4-10.   **9.13:** 2 Kings 4.42-44.
9.16: Lk 22.19; 24.30-31; Acts 2.42; 20.11; 27.35.
9.18-21: Mt 16.13-20; Mk 8.27-30; Jn 1.49; 11.27; 6.66-69.
9.18: Lk 3.21; 5.16; 6.12; 9.28; 11.1.   **9.19:** Lk 9.9; Mk 9.11-13.
9.22: Mt 16.21; Mk 8.31; Lk 9.43-45; 18.31-34; 17.25.
9.23-27: Mt 16.24-28; Mk 8.34-9.1.
9.24-25: Mt 10.38-39; Lk 14.27; 17.33; Jn 12.25.   **9.26:** Mt 10.33; Lk 12.9; 1 Jn 2.28.

angels. 27 But I tell you truly, there are some standing here who will not taste death before they see the kingdom of God."

28 Now about eight days after these sayings he took with him Peter and John and James, and went up on the mountain to pray. 29And as he was praying, the appearance of his countenance was altered, and his raiment became dazzling white. 30And behold, two men talked with him, Moses and E.li'jáh, 31 who appeared in glory and spoke of his departure, which he was to accomplish at Jerusalem. 32 Now Peter and those who were with him were heavy with sleep but kept awake, and they saw his glory and the two men who stood with him. 33And as the men were parting from him, Peter said to Jesus, "Master, it is well that we are here; let us make three booths, one for you and one for Moses and one for E.li'jáh"—not knowing what he said. 34As he said this, a cloud came and overshadowed them; and they were afraid as they entered the cloud. 35And a voice came out of the cloud, saying, "This is my Son, my Chosen;*d* listen to him!" 36And when the voice had spoken, Jesus was found alone. And they kept silence and told no one in those days anything of what they had seen.

37 On the next day, when they had come down from the mountain, a great crowd met him. 38And behold, a man from the crowd cried, "Teacher, I beg you to look upon my son, for he is my only child; 39 and behold, a spirit seizes him, and he suddenly cries out; it convulses him till he foams, and shatters him, and will hardly leave him. 40And I begged your disciples to cast it out, but they could not." 41 Jesus answered, "O faithless and perverse generation, how long am I to be with you and bear with you? Bring your son here." 42 While he was coming, the demon tore him and convulsed him. But Jesus rebuked the un-

clean spirit, and healed the boy, and gave him back to his father. 43And all were astonished at the majesty of God.

But while they were all marveling at everything he did, he said to his disciples, 44 "Let these words sink into your ears; for the Son of man is to be delivered into the hands of men." 45 But they did not understand this saying, and it was concealed from them, that they should not perceive it; and they were afraid to ask him about this saying.

46 And an argument arose among them as to which of them was the greatest. 47 But when Jesus perceived the thought of their hearts, he took a child and put him by his side, 48 and said to them, "Whoever receives this child in my name receives me, and whoever receives me receives him who sent me; for he who is least among you all is the one who is great."

49 John answered, "Master, we saw a man casting out demons in your name, and we forbade him, because he does not follow with us." 50 But Jesus said to him, "Do not forbid him; for he that is not against you is for you."

51 When the days drew near for him to be received up, he set his face to go to Jerusalem. 52And he sent messengers ahead of him, who went and entered a village of the Samaritans, to make ready for him; 53 but the people would not receive him, because his face was set toward Jerusalem. 54And when his disciples James and John saw it, they said, "Lord, do you want us to bid fire come down from heaven and consume them?"*e* 55 But he turned and rebuked them.*f* 56And they went on to another village.

57 As they were going along the road, a man said to him, "I will follow you wherever you go." 58And Jesus said to him, "Foxes have holes, and birds of the air have nests; but the Son of man has nowhere to lay his head." 59 To another he said, "Follow

d Other ancient authorities read *my Beloved*
e Other ancient authorities add *as Elijah did*
f Other ancient authorities add *and he said, "You do not know what manner of spirit you are of; for the Son of man came not to destroy men's lives but to save them"*

9.27: Lk 22.18; Mt 10.23; 1 Thess 4.15-18; Jn 21.22.
9.28-36: Mt 17.1-8; Mk 9.2-8; 2 Pet 1.17-18.
9.28: Lk 8.51; 3.21; 5.16; 6.12; 9.18; 11.1. 9.30: Acts 1.9-11. 9.32: Jn 1.14.
9.33: Lk 5.5; 8.24, 45; 9.49; 17.13. 9.35: Lk 3.22; Jn 12.28-30.
9.36: Mt 17.9; Mk 9.9-10. 9.37-43: Mt 17.14-18; Mk 9.14-27.
9.43-45: Mt 17.22-23; Mk 9.30-32; Lk 9.22; 18.31-34; 17.25.
9.46-48: Mt 18.1-5; Mk 9.33-37. 9.48: Lk 10.16; Mt 10.40.
9.49-50: Mk 9.38-40; Lk 11.23. 9.49: Lk 5.5; 8.24, 45; 9.33; 17.13.
9.51-56: Mk 10.1; Lk 17.11; Jn 4.40-42. 9.52: Mt 10.5; Jn 4.4.
9.54: Mk 3.17; 2 Kings 1.9-16. 9.57-60: Mt 8.19-22.

me." But he said, "Lord, let me first go and bury my father." 60 But he said to him, "Leave the dead to bury their own dead; but as for you, go and proclaim the kingdom of God." 61 Another said, "I will follow you, Lord; but let me first say farewell to those at my home." 62 Jesus said to him, "No one who puts his hand to the plow and looks back is fit for the kingdom of God."

10 After this the Lord appointed seventy*g* others, and sent them on ahead of him, two by two, into every town and place where he himself was about to come. 2 And he said to them, "The harvest is plentiful, but the laborers are few; pray therefore the Lord of the harvest to send out laborers into his harvest. 3 Go your way; behold, I send you out as lambs in the midst of wolves. 4 Carry no purse, no bag, no sandals; and salute no one on the road. 5 Whatever house you enter, first say, 'Peace be to this house!' 6 And if a son of peace is there, your peace shall rest upon him; but if not, it shall return to you. 7 And remain in the same house, eating and drinking what they provide, for the laborer deserves his wages; do not go from house to house. 8 Whenever you enter a town and they receive you, eat what is set before you; 9 heal the sick in it and say to them, 'The kingdom of God has come near to you.' 10 But whenever you enter a town and they do not receive you, go into its streets and say, 11 'Even the dust of your town that clings to our feet, we wipe off against you; nevertheless know this, that the kingdom of God has come near.' 12 I tell you, it shall be more tolerable on that day for Sod'óm than for that town.

13 "Woe to you, Chō-rā'zin! woe to you, Beth-sā'i-dà! for if the mighty works done in you had been done in Tỹre and Sī'don, they would have repented long ago, sitting in sackcloth and ashes. 14 But it shall be more tolerable in the judgment for Tỹre and Sī'don than for you. 15 And you,

Cà·pēr'nà-ùm, will you be exalted to heaven? You shall be brought down to Hades.

16 "He who hears you hears me, and he who rejects you rejects me, and he who rejects me rejects him who sent me."

17 The seventy*g* returned with joy, saying, "Lord, even the demons are subject to us in your name!" 18 And he said to them, "I saw Satan fall like lightning from heaven. 19 Behold, I have given you authority to tread upon serpents and scorpions, and over all the power of the enemy; and nothing shall hurt you. 20 Nevertheless do not rejoice in this, that the spirits are subject to you; but rejoice that your names are written in heaven."

21 In that same hour he rejoiced in the Holy Spirit and said, "I thank thee, Father, Lord of heaven and earth, that thou hast hidden these things from the wise and understanding and revealed them to babes; yea, Father, for such was thy gracious will.*h* 22 All things have been delivered to me by my Father; and no one knows who the Son is except the Father, or who the Father is except the Son and any one to whom the Son chooses to reveal him."

23 Then turning to the disciples he said privately, "Blessed are the eyes which see what you see! 24 For I tell you that many prophets and kings desired to see what you see, and did not see it, and to hear what you hear, and did not hear it."

25 And behold, a lawyer stood up to put him to the test, saying, "Teacher, what shall I do to inherit eternal life?" 26 He said to him, "What is written in the law? How do you read?" 27 And he answered, "You shall love the Lord your God with all your heart, and with all your soul, and with all your strength, and with all your mind; and your neighbor as yourself." 28 And he said to him, "You have answered right; do this, and you will live."

29 But he, desiring to justify himself, said to Jesus, "And who is my

9.61: 1 Kings 19.20; Phil 3.13.   10.2: Lk 9.1-2, 51-52; 7.13.   10.2: Mt 9.37-38; Jn 4.35.
10.3-12: Mt 10.7-16; Mk 6.8-11; Lk 9.2-5; 22.35-36.   10.5: 1 Sam 25.6.
10.7: 1 Cor 10.27; 9.14; 1 Tim 5.18; Deut 24.15.   10.11: Acts 13.51.
10.12: Mt 11.24; Gen 19.24-28; Jude 7.   10.13-15: Mt 11.21-23; Lk 6.24-26.
10.16: Mt 10.40; 18.5; Mk 9.37; Lk 9.48; Jn 13.20; 12.48.   10.18: Rev 12.9; Jn 12.31.
10.20: Ex 32.32; Ps 69.28; Dan 12.1; Phil 4.3; Heb 12.23; Rev 3.5; 13.8; 21.27.
10.21-22: Mt 11.25-27.   10.21: 1 Cor 1.26-29.
10.22: Mt 28.18; Jn 3.35; 13.3; 10.15; 17.25.
10.23-24: Mt 13.16-17; Jn 8.56; Heb 11.13; 1 Pet 1.10-12.
10.25-28: Mt 22.34-39; Mk 12.28-31.   10.25: Mk 10.17; Mt 19.16; Lk 18.18.
10.27: Deut 6.5; Lev 19.18; Rom 13.9; Gal 5.14; Jas 2.8.   10.28: Lk 20.39; Lev 18.5.

neighbor?" 30 Jesus replied, "A man was going down from Jerusalem to Jericho, and he fell among robbers, who stripped him and beat him, and departed, leaving him half dead. 31 Now by chance a priest was going down that road; and when he saw him he passed by on the other side. 32 So likewise a Levite, when he came to the place and saw him, passed by on the other side. 33 But a Samaritan, as he journeyed, came to where he was; and when he saw him, he had compassion, 34 and went to him and bound up his wounds, pouring on oil and wine; then he set him on his own beast and brought him to an inn, and took care of him. 35 And the next day he took out two denarii*i* and gave them to the innkeeper, saying, 'Take care of him; and whatever more you spend, I will repay you when I come back.' 36 Which of these three, do you think, proved neighbor to the man who fell among the robbers?" 37 He said, "The one who showed mercy on him." And Jesus said to him, "Go and do likewise."

38 Now as they went on their way, he entered a village; and a woman named Martha received him into her house. 39 And she had a sister called Mary, who sat at the Lord's feet and listened to his teaching. 40 But Martha was distracted with much serving; and she went to him and said, "Lord, do you not care that my sister has left me to serve alone? Tell her then to help me." 41 But the Lord answered her, "Martha, Martha, you are anxious and troubled about many things; 42 one thing is needful.*j* Mary has chosen the good portion, which shall not be taken away from her."

|| He was praying in a certain place, and when he ceased, one of his disciples said to him, "Lord, teach us to pray, as John taught his disciples." 2 And he said to them, "When you pray, say:
    "Father, hallowed be thy name. Thy kingdom come. 3 Give us each day our daily bread;*k* 4 and forgive us our sins, for we ourselves forgive every one who is indebted to us; and lead us not into temptation."

5 And he said to them, "Which of you who has a friend will go to him at midnight and say to him, 'Friend, lend me three loaves; 6 for a friend of mine has arrived on a journey, and I have nothing to set before him'; 7 and he will answer from within, 'Do not bother me; the door is now shut, and my children are with me in bed; I cannot get up and give you anything'? 8 I tell you, though he will not get up and give him anything because he is his friend, yet because of his importunity he will rise and give him whatever he needs. 9 And I tell you, Ask, and it will be given you; seek, and you will find; knock, and it will be opened to you. 10 For every one who asks receives, and he who seeks finds, and to him who knocks it will be opened. 11 What father among you, if his son asks for*l* a fish, will instead of a fish give him a serpent; 12 or if he asks for an egg, will give him a scorpion? 13 If you then, who are evil, know how to give good gifts to your children, how much more will the heavenly Father give the Holy Spirit to those who ask him!"

14 Now he was casting out a demon that was dumb; when the demon had gone out, the dumb man spoke, and the people marveled. 15 But some of them said, "He casts out demons by Bē-el′zĕ-bul, the prince of demons"; 16 while others, to test him, sought from him a sign from heaven. 17 But he, knowing their thoughts, said to them, "Every kingdom divided against itself is laid waste, and house falls upon house. 18 And if Satan also is divided against himself, how will his kingdom stand? For you say that I cast out demons by Bē-el′zĕ-bul. 19 And if I cast out demons by Bē-el′zĕ-bul, by whom do your sons cast them out? Therefore they shall be your judges. 20 But if it is by the finger of God that I cast out demons, then the kingdom of God has come upon you. 21 When a strong man, fully armed, guards his own palace, his goods are in peace; 22 but when one stronger than he assails him and overcomes him, he takes away his armor in which he trusted, and divides his spoil. 23 He

---

i The denarius was worth about twenty cents
j Other ancient authorities read *few things are needful, or only one*
k Or *our bread for the morrow*
l Other ancient authorities insert *bread, will give him a stone; or if he asks for*

10.33: Lk 9.51-56; 17.11-19; Jn 4.4-42.   **10.38-42:** Jn 12.1-3; 11.1-45.   **10.41:** Lk 7.13.
11.1: Mk 1.35; Lk 3.21; 5.16; 6.12; 9.18, 28; 5.33; 7.18.   **11.2-4:** Mt 6.9-13.
11.4: Mk 11.25; Mt 18.35.   **11.5-8:** Lk 18.1-8.   **11.9-13:** Mt 7.7-11.
11.9: Mt 18.19; 21.22; Mk 11.24; Jas 1.5-8; 1 Jn 5.14-15; Jn 15.7; 16.23-24.
11.14-23: Mt 12.22-30; 10.25; Mk 3.23-27.   **11.14-15:** Mt 9.32-34.
11.16: Mt 12.38; 16.1; Mk 8.11; Jn 2.18; 6.30.   **11.23:** Lk 9.50.

who is not with me is against me, and he who does not gather with me scatters.

24 "When the unclean spirit has gone out of a man, he passes through waterless places seeking rest; and finding none he says, 'I will return to my house from which I came.'²⁵ And when he comes he finds it swept and put in order.²⁶ Then he goes and brings seven other spirits more evil than himself, and they enter and dwell there; and the last state of that man becomes worse than the first."

27 As he said this, a woman in the crowd raised her voice and said to him, "Blessed is the womb that bore you, and the breasts that you sucked!" ²⁸ But he said, "Blessed rather are those who hear the word of God and keep it!"

29 When the crowds were increasing, he began to say, "This generation is an evil generation; it seeks a sign, but no sign shall be given to it except the sign of Jō'nah.³⁰ For as Jō'nah became a sign to the men of Nin'é·vēh, so will the Son of man be to this generation.³¹ The queen of the South will arise at the judgment with the men of this generation and condemn them; for she came from the ends of the earth to hear the wisdom of Solomon, and behold, something greater than Solomon is here.³² The men of Nin'-é·vēh will arise at the judgment with this generation and condemn it; for they repented at the preaching of Jō'nah, and behold, something greater than Jonah is here.

33 "No one after lighting a lamp puts it in a cellar or under a bushel, but on a stand, that those who enter may see the light. ³⁴ Your eye is the lamp of your body; when your eye is sound, your whole body is full of light; but when it is not sound, your body is full of darkness. ³⁵ Therefore be careful lest the light in you be darkness.³⁶ If then your whole body is full of light, having no part dark, it will be wholly bright, as when a lamp with its rays gives you light."

37 While he was speaking, a Pharisee asked him to dine with him; so he went in and sat at table. ³⁸ The Pharisee was astonished to see that he did not first wash before dinner. ³⁹ And the Lord said to him, "Now you Pharisees cleanse the outside of the cup and of the dish, but inside you are full of extortion and wickedness.⁴⁰ You fools! Did not he who made the outside make the inside also?⁴¹ But give for alms those things which are within; and behold, everything is clean for you.

42 "But woe to you Pharisees! for you tithe the mint and rue and every herb, and neglect justice and the love of God; these you ought to have done, without neglecting the others.⁴³ Woe to you Pharisees! for you love the best seat in the synagogues and salutations in the market places.⁴⁴ Woe to you; for you are like graves which are not seen, and men walk over them without knowing it."

45 One of the lawyers answered him, "Teacher, in saying this you reproach us also." ⁴⁶ And he said, "Woe to you lawyers also! for you load men with burdens hard to bear, and you yourselves do not touch the burdens with one of your fingers. ⁴⁷ Woe to you! for you build the tombs of the prophets whom your fathers killed. ⁴⁸ So you are witnesses and consent to the deeds of your fathers; for they killed them, and you build their tombs.⁴⁹ Therefore also the Wisdom of God said, 'I will send them prophets and apostles, some of whom they will kill and persecute,'⁵⁰ that the blood of all the prophets, shed from the foundation of the world, may be required of this generation,⁵¹ from the blood of A'bel to the blood of Zech·à·rī'ah, who perished between the altar and the sanctuary. Yes, I tell you, it shall be required of this generation. ⁵² Woe to you lawyers! for you have taken away the key of knowledge; you did not enter yourselves, and you hindered those who were entering."

53 As he went away from there, the scribes and the Pharisees began to press him hard, and to provoke him to speak of many things, ⁵⁴ lying in wait for him, to catch at something he might say.

11.24-26: Mt 12.43-45.   11.27: Lk 1.42; 23.29.   11.28: Lk 8.21; Jn 15.14.
11.29-32: Mt 12.39-42.   11.29: Mt 16.4; Mk 8.12; Lk 11.16; Jon 3.4-5.
11.31: 1 Kings 10.1-10; 2 Chron 9.1-12.   11.32: Mt 12.6.
11.33: Mt 5.15; Mk 4.21; Lk 8.16.
11.34-35: Mt 6.22-23.   11.37: Lk 7.36; 14.1.   11.38: Mk 7.1-5.
11.39-41: Mt 23.25-26.   11.39: Lk 7.13.   11.41: Tit 1.15; Mk 7.19.
11.42: Mt 23.23-24; Lev 27.30; Mic 6.8.   11.43: Mt 23.6-7; Mk 12.38-39; Lk 20.46.
11.44: Mt 23.27.   11.46: Mt 23.4.   11.47-48: Mt 23.29-32; Acts 7.51-53.
11.49-51: Mt 23.34-36.   11.49: 1 Cor 1.24; Col 2.3.
11.51: Gen 4.8; 2 Chron 24.20-21; Zech 1.1.   11.52: Mt 23.13.   11.53-54: Mk 12.13.

12 In the meantime, when so many thousands of the multitude had gathered together that they trod upon one another, he began to say to his disciples first, "Beware of the leaven of the Pharisees, which is hypocrisy. 2 Nothing is covered up that will not be revealed, or hidden that will not be known. 3 Whatever you have said in the dark shall be heard in the light, and what you have whispered in private rooms shall be proclaimed upon the housetops.

4 "I tell you, my friends, do not fear those who kill the body, and after that have no more that they can do. 5 But I will warn you whom to fear: fear him who, after he has killed, has power to cast into hell[m] yes, I tell you, fear him! 6 Are not five sparrows sold for two pennies? And not one of them is forgotten before God. 7 Why, even the hairs of your head are all numbered. Fear not; you are of more value than many sparrows.

8 "And I tell you, every one who acknowledges me before men, the Son of man also will acknowledge before the angels of God; 9 but he who denies me before men will be denied before the angels of God. 10 And every one who speaks a word against the Son of man will be forgiven; but he who blasphemes against the Holy Spirit will not be forgiven. 11 And when they bring you before the synagogues and the rulers and the authorities, do not be anxious how or what you are to answer or what you are to say; 12 for the Holy Spirit will teach you in that very hour what you ought to say."

13 One of the multitude said to him, "Teacher, bid my brother divide the inheritance with me." 14 But he said to him, "Man, who made me a judge or divider over you?" 15 And he said to them, "Take heed, and beware of all covetousness; for a man's life does not consist in the abundance of his possessions." 16 And he told them a parable, saying, "The land of a rich man brought forth plentifully; 17 and he thought to himself, 'What shall I do, for I have nowhere to store my crops?' 18 And he said, 'I will do this; I will pull down my barns, and build larger ones; and there I will store all my grain and my goods. 19 And I will say to my soul, Soul, you have ample goods laid up for many years; take your ease, eat, drink, be merry.' 20 But God said to him, 'Fool! This night your soul is required of you; and the things you have prepared, whose will they be?' 21 So is he who lays up treasure for himself, and is not rich toward God."

22 **And he said to his disciples,** "Therefore I tell you, do not be anxious about your life, what you shall eat, nor about your body, what you shall put on. 23 For life is more than food, and the body more than clothing. 24 Consider the ravens: they neither sow nor reap, they have neither storehouse nor barn, and yet God feeds them. Of how much more value are you than the birds! 25 And which of you by being anxious can add a cubit to his span of life?[n] 26 If then you are not able to do as small a thing as that, why are you anxious about the rest? 27 Consider the lilies, how they grow; they neither toil nor spin;[o] yet I tell you, even Solomon in all his glory was not arrayed like one of these. 28 But if God so clothes the grass which is alive in the field today and tomorrow is thrown into the oven, how much more will he clothe you, O men of little faith! 29 And do not seek what you are to eat and what you are to drink, nor be of anxious mind. 30 For all the nations of the world seek these things; and your Father knows that you need them. 31 Instead, seek his[p] kingdom, and these things shall be yours as well.

32 "Fear not, little flock, for it is your Father's good pleasure to give you the kingdom. 33 Sell your possessions, and give alms; provide yourselves with purses that do not grow old, with a treasure in the heavens that does not fail, where no thief approaches and no moth destroys. 34 For where your treasure is, there will your heart also be.

35 "Let your loins be girded and

---

[m] Greek *Gehenna*   [n] Or *to his stature*
[o] Other ancient authorities read *Consider the lilies; they neither spin nor weave*
[p] Other ancient authorities read *God's*

12.1: Mt 16.6; Mk 8.15.   12.2-3: Mt 10.26-27; Mk 4.22; Lk 8.17; Eph 5.13.
12.4: Jn 15.14-15.   12.4-9: Mt 10.28-33.   12.5: Heb 10.31.
12.7: Lk 21.18; Acts 27.34; Mt 12.12.   12.9: Mk 8.38; Lk 9.26; 2 Tim 2.12.
12.10: Mt 12.31-32; Mk 3.28-29.   12.11-12: Mt 10.19-20; Mk 13.11; Lk 21.14-15.
12.15: 1 Tim 6.6-10.   12.20: Jer 17.11; Job 27.8; Ps 39.6; Lk 12.33-34.
12.22-31: Mt 6.25-33.   12.24: Lk 12.6-7.   12.27: 1 Kings 10.1-10.   12.30: Mt 6.8.
12.32: Jn 21.15-17.   12.33-34: Mt 6.19-21; Lk 18.22.   12.35: Eph 6.14; Mt 25.1-13; Mk 13.33-37.

your lamps burning, 36and be like men who are waiting for their master to come home from the marriage feast, so that they may open to him at once when he comes and knocks. 37Blessed are those servants whom the master finds awake when he comes; truly, I say to you, he will gird himself and have them sit at table, and he will come and serve them. 38If he comes in the second watch, or in the third, and finds them so, blessed are those servants! 39But know this, that if the householder had known at what hour the thief was coming, he would have been awake and *q*would not have left his house to be broken into. 40You also must be ready; for the Son of man is coming at an hour you do not expect."

41 Peter said, "Lord, are you telling this parable for us or for all?" 42And the Lord said, "Who then is the faithful and wise steward, whom his master will set over his household, to give them their portion of food at the proper time? 43Blessed is that servant whom his master when he comes will find so doing. 44Truly I tell you, he will set him over all his possessions. 45But if that servant says to himself, 'My master is delayed in coming,' and begins to beat the menservants and the maidservants, and to eat and drink and get drunk, 46the master of that servant will come on a day when he does not expect him and at an hour he does not know, and will punish*r* him, and put him with the unfaithful. 47And that servant who knew his master's will, but did not make ready or act according to his will, shall receive a severe beating. 48But he who did not know, and did what deserved a beating, shall receive a light beating. Every one to whom much is given, of him will much be required; and of him to whom men commit much they will demand the more.

49 "I came to cast fire upon the earth; and would that it were already kindled! 50I have a baptism to be baptized with; and how I am constrained until it is accomplished! 51Do you think that I have come to give peace on earth? No, I tell you, but rather division; 52for henceforth in

one house there will be five divided, three against two and two against three; 53they will be divided, father against son and son against father, mother against daughter and daughter against her mother, mother-in-law against her daughter-in-law and daughter-in-law against her mother-in-law."

54 He also said to the multitudes, "When you see a cloud rising in the west, you say at once, 'A shower is coming'; and so it happens. 55And when you see the south wind blowing, you say, 'There will be scorching heat'; and it happens. 56You hypocrites! You know how to interpret the appearance of earth and sky; but why do you not know how to interpret the present time?

57 "And why do you not judge for yourselves what is right? 58As you go with your accuser before the magistrate, make an effort to settle with him on the way, lest he drag you to the judge, and the judge hand you over to the officer, and the officer put you in prison. 59I tell you, you will never get out till you have paid the very last copper."

13 There were some present at that very time who told him of the Galileans whose blood Pilate had mingled with their sacrifices. 2And he answered them, "Do you think that these Galileans were worse sinners than all the other Galileans, because they suffered thus? 3I tell you, No; but unless you repent you will all likewise perish. 4Or those eighteen upon whom the tower in Si·lo′am fell and killed them, do you think that they were worse offenders than all the others who dwelt in Jerusalem? 5I tell you, No; but unless you repent you will all likewise perish."

6 And he told this parable: "A man had a fig tree planted in his vineyard; and he came seeking fruit on it and found none. 7And he said to the vinedresser, 'Lo, these three years I have come seeking fruit on this fig tree, and I find none. Cut it down; why should it use up the ground?' 8And he answered him, 'Let it alone, sir, this year also, till I dig about it and put on manure. 9And if it bears fruit next

q Other ancient authorities omit *would have been awake and*   *r* Or *cut him in pieces*

12.37: Jn 13.3-5; Mt 24.42; Lk 21.36.
12.39-40: Mt 24.43-44; 1 Thess 5.2; Rev 3.3; 16.15; 2 Pet 3.10.
12.42-46: Mt 24.45-51.   **12.42:** Lk 7.13.
12.47-48: Deut 25.2-3; Num 15.29-30; Lk 8.18; 19.26.   **12.49:** Lk 22.15.
12.50: Mk 10.38-39; Jn 12.27.   **12.51-53:** Mt 10.34-36; Lk 21.16; Mic 7.6.
12.54-56: Mt 16.2-3.   **12.57-59:** Mt 5.25-26.   **13.2:** Jn 9.1-3.
13.6-9: Mt 21.18-20; Mk 11.12-14, 20-21.   **13.7:** Mt 3.10; 7.19; Lk 3.9.

year, well and good; but if not, you can cut it down.'"

10 Now he was teaching in one of the synagogues on the sabbath. 11And there was a woman who had had a spirit of infirmity for eighteen years; she was bent over and could not fully straighten herself. 12And when Jesus saw her, he called her and said to her, "Woman, you are freed from your infirmity." 13And he laid his hands upon her, and immediately she was made straight, and she praised God. 14 But the ruler of the synagogue, indignant because Jesus had healed on the sabbath, said to the people, "There are six days on which work ought to be done; come on those days and be healed, and not on the sabbath day." 15 Then the Lord answered him, "You hypocrites! Does not each of you on the sabbath untie his ox or his ass from the manger, and lead it away to water it? 16 And ought not this woman, a daughter of Abraham whom Satan bound for eighteen years, be loosed from this bond on the sabbath day?" 17As he said this, all his adversaries were put to shame; and all the people rejoiced at all the glorious things that were done by him.

18 He said therefore, "What is the kingdom of God like? And to what shall I compare it? 19 It is like a grain of mustard seed which a man took and sowed in his garden; and it grew and became a tree, and the birds of the air made nests in its branches."

20 And again he said, "To what shall I compare the kingdom of God? 21 It is like leaven which a woman took and hid in three measures of meal, till it was all leavened."

22 He went on his way through towns and villages, teaching, and journeying toward Jerusalem. 23And some one said to him, "Lord, will those who are saved be few?" And he said to them, 24 "Strive to enter by the narrow door; for many, I tell you, will seek to enter and will not be able. 25 When once the householder has risen up and shut the door, you will begin to stand outside and to knock at the door, saying, 'Lord, open to us.' He will answer you, 'I do not know

where you come from.' 26 Then you will begin to say, 'We ate and drank in your presence, and you taught in our streets.' 27 But he will say, 'I tell you, I do not know where you come from; depart from me, all you workers of iniquity!' 28 There you will weep and gnash your teeth, when you see Abraham and Isaac and Jacob and all the prophets in the kingdom of God and you yourselves thrust out. 29 And men will come from east and west, and from north and south, and sit at table in the kingdom of God. 30 And behold, some are last who will be first, and some are first who will be last."

31 At that very hour some Pharisees came, and said to him, "Get away from here, for Her'od wants to kill you." 32And he said to them, "Go and tell that fox, 'Behold, I cast out demons and perform cures today and tomorrow, and the third day I finish my course. 33 Nevertheless I must go on my way today and tomorrow and the day following; for it cannot be that a prophet should perish away from Jerusalem.' 34 O Jerusalem, Jerusalem, killing the prophets and stoning those who are sent to you! How often would I have gathered your children together as a hen gathers her brood under her wings, and you would not! 35 Behold, your house is forsaken. And I tell you, you will not see me until you say, 'Blessed is he who comes in the name of the Lord!' "

14 One sabbath when he went to dine at the house of a ruler who belonged to the Pharisees, they were watching him. 2And behold, there was a man before him who had dropsy. 3And Jesus spoke to the lawyers and Pharisees, saying, "Is it lawful to heal on the sabbath, or not?" 4 But they were silent. Then he took him and healed him, and let him go. 5And he said to them, "Which of you, having an ass*s* or an ox that has fallen into a well, will not immediately pull him out on a sabbath day?" 6And they could not reply to this.

7 Now he told a parable to those who were invited, when he marked how they chose the places of honor, saying to them, 8 "When you are in-

s Other ancient authorities read *a son*
13.14: Ex 20.9-10; Lk 6.6-11; 14.1-6; Jn 5.1-18.　13.15: Lk 7.13; 14.5; Mt 12.11.
13.16: Lk 19.9.　13.18-19: Mt 13.31-32; Mk 4.30-32.　13.20-21: Mt 13.33.
13.22: Lk 9.51; 17.11; 18.31; 19.11.　13.23-24: Mt 7.13-14; Jn 10.7.
13.25: Mt 25.10-12.　13.26-27: Mt 7.21-23, 25.41; Lk 6.46.　13.28-29: Mt 8.11-12.
13.30: Mt 19.30; Mk 10.31.　13.32: Heb 2.10; 7.28.　13.34-35: Mt 23.37-39; Lk 19.41.
13.35: Jer 22.5; Ps 118.26; Lk 19.38.　14.1: Lk 7.36; 11.37; Mk 3.2.
14.3: Mt 12.10; Mk 3.4; Lk 6.9.　14.5: Mt 12.11; Lk 13.15.
14.8: Prov 25.6-7; Lk 11.43; 20.46.

vited by any one to a marriage feast, do not sit down in a place of honor, lest a more eminent man than you be invited by him;[9] and he who invited you both will come and say to you, 'Give place to this man,' and then you will begin with shame to take the lowest place. [10] But when you are invited, go and sit in the lowest place, so that when your host comes he may say to you, 'Friend, go up higher'; then you will be honored in the presence of all who sit at table with you.[11] For every one who exalts himself will be humbled, and he who humbles himself will be exalted."

12 He said also to the man who had invited him, "When you give a dinner or a banquet, do not invite your friends or your brothers or your kinsmen or rich neighbors, lest they also invite you in return, and you be repaid. [13] But when you give a feast, invite the poor, the maimed, the lame, the blind, [14] and you will be blessed, because they cannot repay you. You will be repaid at the resurrection of the just."

15 When one of those who sat at table with him heard this, he said to him, "Blessed is he who shall eat bread in the kingdom of God!" [16] But he said to him, "A man once gave a great banquet, and invited many;[17] and at the time for the banquet he sent his servant to say to those who had been invited, 'Come; for all is now ready.' [18] But they all alike began to make excuses. The first said to him, 'I have bought a field, and I must go out and see it; I pray you, have me excused.' [19] And another said, 'I have bought five yoke of oxen, and I go to examine them; I pray you, have me excused.' [20] And another said, 'I have married a wife, and therefore I cannot come.' [21] So the servant came and reported this to his master. Then the householder in anger said to his servant, 'Go out quickly to the streets and lanes of the city, and bring in the poor and maimed and blind and lame.' [22] And the servant said, 'Sir, what you commanded has been done, and still there is room.' [23] And the master said to the servant, 'Go out to the highways and hedges, and compel people to come in, that my house may be filled. [24] For I tell you, none of those men who were invited shall taste my banquet.' "

25 Now great multitudes accompanied him; and he turned and said to them, [26] "If any one comes to me and does not hate his own father and mother and wife and children and brothers and sisters, yes, and even his own life, he cannot be my disciple. [27] Whoever does not bear his own cross and come after me, cannot be my disciple. [28] For which of you, desiring to build a tower, does not first sit down and count the cost, whether he has enough to complete it? [29] Otherwise, when he has laid a foundation, and is not able to finish, all who see it begin to mock him, [30] saying, 'This man began to build, and was not able to finish.' [31] Or what king, going to encounter another king in war, will not sit down first and take counsel whether he is able with ten thousand to meet him who comes against him with twenty thousand? [32] And if not, while the other is yet a great way off, he sends an embassy and asks terms of peace. [33] So therefore, whoever of you does not renounce all that he has cannot be my disciple.

34 "Salt is good; but if salt has lost its taste, how shall it be restored? [35] It is fit neither for the land nor for the dunghill; men throw it away. He who has ears to hear, let him hear."

15 Now the tax collectors and sinners were all drawing near to hear him. [2] And the Pharisees and the scribes murmured, saying, "This man receives sinners and eats with them."

3 So he told them this parable: [4] "What man of you, having a hundred sheep, if he has lost one of them, does not leave the ninety-nine in the wilderness, and go after the one which is lost, until he finds it? [5] And when he has found it, he lays it on his shoulders, rejoicing. [6] And when he comes home, he calls together his friends and his neighbors, saying to them, 'Rejoice with me, for I have found my sheep which was lost.' [7] Just so, I tell you, there will be more joy in heaven over one sinner who repents than over ninety-nine righteous persons who need no repentance.

8 "Or what woman, having ten silver coins,[t] if she loses one coin, does not light a lamp and sweep the house and seek diligently until she finds it?

[t] The drachma, rendered here by *silver coin*, was about sixteen cents

14.11: Mt 23.12; Lk 18.14; Mt 18.4; 1 Pet 5.6.   **14.12:** Jas 2.2-4.   **14.13:** Lk 14.21.
14.15: Rev 19.9.   **14.16-24:** Mt 22.1-10.   **14.20:** Deut 24.5; 1 Cor 7.33.
14.21: Lk 14.13.   **14.26-27:** Mt 10.37-38.   **14.27:** Mt 16.24; Mk 8.34; Lk 9.23.
14.33: Lk 18.29-30; Phil 3.7.   **14.34-35:** Mt 5.13; Mk 9.49-50; Mt 11.15.
15.1-2: Lk 5.29-30; 19.7.   **15.4-7:** Mt 18.10-14.   **15.7:** Jas 5.20; Lk 19.10; 15.10.

9 And when she has found it, she calls together her friends and neighbors, saying, 'Rejoice with me, for I have found the coin which I had lost.' 10 Just so, I tell you, there is joy before the angels of God over one sinner who repents."

11 **And he said,** "There was a man who had two sons; 12 and the younger of them said to his father, 'Father, give me the share of property that falls to me.' And he divided his living between them. 13 Not many days later, the younger son gathered all he had and took his journey into a far country, and there he squandered his property in loose living. 14 And when he had spent everything, a great famine arose in that country, and he began to be in want. 15 So he went and joined himself to one of the citizens of that country, who sent him into his fields to feed swine. 16 And he would gladly have fed on*u* the pods that the swine ate; and no one gave him anything. 17 But when he came to himself he said, 'How many of my father's hired servants have bread enough and to spare, but I perish here with hunger! 18 I will arise and go to my father, and I will say to him, "Father, I have sinned against heaven and before you; 19 I am no longer worthy to be called your son; treat me as one of your hired servants."' 20 And he arose and came to his father. But while he was yet at a distance, his father saw him and had compassion, and ran and embraced him and kissed him. 21 And the son said to him, 'Father, I have sinned against heaven and before you; I am no longer worthy to be called your son.'*v* 22 But the father said to his servants, 'Bring quickly the best robe, and put it on him; and put a ring on his hand, and shoes on his feet; 23 and bring the fatted calf and kill it, and let us eat and make merry; 24 for this my son was dead, and is alive again; he was lost, and is found.' And they began to make merry.

25 "Now his elder son was in the field; and as he came and drew near to the house, he heard music and dancing. 26 And he called one of the servants and asked what this meant. 27 And he said to him, 'Your brother has come, and your father has killed the fatted calf, because he has received him safe and sound.' 28 But he was angry and

refused to go in. His father came out and entreated him, 29 but he answered his father, 'Lo, these many years I have served you, and I never disobeyed your command; yet you never gave me a kid, that I might make merry with my friends. 30 But when this son of yours came, who has devoured your living with harlots, you killed for him the fatted calf! 31 And he said to him, 'Son, you are always with me, and all that is mine is yours. 32 It was fitting to make merry and be glad, for this your brother was dead, and is alive; he was lost and is found.'"

16 **He also said to the disciples,** "There was a rich man who had a steward, and charges were brought to him that this man was wasting his goods. 2 And he called him and said to him, 'What is this that I hear about you? Turn in the account of your stewardship, for you can no longer be steward.' 3 And the steward said to himself, 'What shall I do, since my master is taking the stewardship away from me? I am not strong enough to dig, and I am ashamed to beg. 4 I have decided what to do, so that people may receive me into their houses when I am put out of the stewardship.' 5 So, summoning his master's debtors one by one, he said to the first, 'How much do you owe my master?' 6 He said, 'A hundred measures of oil.' And he said to him, 'Take your bill, and sit down quickly and write fifty.' 7 Then he said to another, 'And how much do you owe?' He said, 'A hundred measures of wheat.' He said to him, 'Take your bill, and write eighty.' 8 The master commended the dishonest steward for his prudence; for the sons of this world*w* are wiser in their own generation than the sons of light. 9 And I tell you, make friends for yourselves by means of unrighteous mammon, so that when it fails they may receive you into the eternal habitations.

10 "He who is faithful in a very little is faithful also in much; and he who is dishonest in a very little is dishonest also in much. 11 If then you have not been faithful in the unrighteous mammon, who will entrust to you the true riches? 12 And if you have not been faithful in that which is another's, who will give you that which is your own? 13 No servant can serve two masters; for either he will hate the

u Other ancient authorities read *filled his belly with*
v Other ancient authorities add *treat me as one of your hired servants*   *w* Greek *age*
15.11: Mt 21.28.   **15.12:** Deut 21.15-17.   **15.22:** Gen 41.42; Zech 3.4.
15.24: 1 Tim 5.6; Eph 2.1; Lk 9.60.   **16.8:** 1 Thess 5.5; Eph 5.8; Lk 20.34; Jn 12.36.
16.9: Lk 12.33; 18.22.   **16.10:** Mt 25.21; Lk 19.17.   **16.13:** Mt 6.24.

one and love the other, or he will be devoted to the one and despise the other. You cannot serve God and mammon."

14 The Pharisees, who were lovers of money, heard all this, and they scoffed at him. **15** But he said to them, "You are those who justify yourselves before men, but God knows your hearts; for what is exalted among men is an abomination in the sight of God.

16 "The law and the prophets were until John; since then the good news of the kingdom of God is preached, and every one enters it violently. **17** But it is easier for heaven and earth to pass away, than for one dot of the law to become void.

18 "Every one who divorces his wife and marries another commits adultery, and he who marries a woman divorced from her husband commits adultery.

19 "There was a rich man, who was clothed in purple and fine linen and who feasted sumptuously every day. **20** And at his gate lay a poor man named Lazʹa·rus, full of sores, **21** who desired to be fed with what fell from the rich man's table; moreover the dogs came and licked his sores. **22** The poor man died and was carried by the angels to Abraham's bosom. The rich man also died and was buried; **23** and in Hades, being in torment, he lifted up his eyes, and saw Abraham far off and Lazʹa·rus in his bosom. **24** And he called out, 'Father Abraham, have mercy upon me, and send Lazʹa·rus to dip the end of his finger in water and cool my tongue; for I am in anguish in this flame.' **25** But Abraham said, 'Son, remember that you in your lifetime received your good things, and Lazʹa·rus in like manner evil things; but now he is comforted here, and you are in anguish. **26** And besides all this, between us and you a great chasm has been fixed, in order that those who would pass from here to you may not be able, and none may cross from there to us.' **27** And he said, 'Then I beg you, father, to send him to my father's house, **28** for I have five brothers, so that he may warn them, lest they also come into this place of

torment.' **29** But Abraham said, 'They have Moses and the prophets; let them hear them.' **30** And he said, 'No, father Abraham; but if some one goes to them from the dead, they will repent.' **31** He said to him, 'If they do not hear Moses and the prophets, neither will they be convinced if some one should rise from the dead.'"

17 And he said to his disciples, "Temptations to sin*x* are sure to come; but woe to him by whom they come! **2** It would be better for him if a millstone were hung round his neck and he were cast into the sea, than that he should cause one of these little ones to sin.*y* **3** Take heed to yourselves; if your brother sins, rebuke him, and if he repents, forgive him; **4** and if he sins against you seven times in the day, and turns to you seven times, and says, 'I repent,' you must forgive him."

5 The apostles said to the Lord, "Increase our faith!" **6** And the Lord said, "If you had faith as a grain of mustard seed, you could say to this sycamine tree, 'Be rooted up, and be planted in the sea,' and it would obey you.

7 "Will any one of you, who has a servant plowing or keeping sheep, say to him when he has come in from the field, 'Come at once and sit down at table'? **8** Will he not rather say to him, 'Prepare supper for me, and gird yourself and serve me, till I eat and drink; and afterward you shall eat and drink'? **9** Does he thank the servant because he did what was commanded? **10** So you also, when you have done all that is commanded you, say, 'We are unworthy servants; we have only done what was our duty.'"

11 On the way to Jerusalem he was passing along between Sa·marʹi·a and Galilee. **12** And as he entered a village, he was met by ten lepers, who stood at a distance **13** and lifted up their voices and said, "Jesus, Master, have mercy on us." **14** When he saw them he said to them, "Go and show yourselves to the priests." And as they went they were cleansed. **15** Then one of them, when he saw that he was healed, turned back, praising God with a loud voice; **16** and he fell on his face at Jesus' feet,

x Greek *stumbling blocks*   *y* Greek *stumble*

16.15: 1 Sam 16.7; Prov 21.2; Acts 1.24; Lk 10.29.   **16.16:** Mt 11.12-13.
16.17: Mt 5.17-18; Lk 21.33.   **16.18:** Mt 5.31-32; 19.9; Mk 10.11-12; 1 Cor 7.10-11.
16.20: Jn 11.1-44; 12.1, 9.   **16.22:** Jn 13.23.   **16.25:** Lk 6.24.
16.29: Jn 5.45-47; Acts 15.21; Lk 4.17.   **16.30:** Lk 3.8; 19.9.
17.1-2: Mt 18.6-7; Mk 9.42; 1 Cor 8.12.   **17.3-4:** Mt 18.15, 21-22.
17.5-6: Mt 17.20; 21.21; Mk 11.22-23.   **17.5:** Lk 7.13.   **17.8:** Lk 12.37; Jn 13.3-5.
17.11: Lk 9.51; 13.22; 19.11.   **17.12:** Lev 13.45-46.   **17.13:** Lk 5.5; 8.24, 45; 9.33, 49.
17.14: Lk 5.14; Mt 8.4; Mk 1.44; Lev 14.2-32.

giving him thanks. Now he was a Samaritan. [17] Then said Jesus, "Were not ten cleansed? Where are the nine? [18] Was no one found to return and give praise to God except this foreigner?" [19] And he said to him, "Rise and go your way; your faith has made you well."

20 Being asked by the Pharisees when the kingdom of God was coming, he answered them, "The kingdom of God is not coming with signs to be observed; [21] nor will they say, 'Lo, here it is!' or 'There!' for behold, the kingdom of God is in the midst of you."[z]

22 And he said to the disciples, "The days are coming when you will desire to see one of the days of the Son of man, and you will not see it. [23] And they will say to you, 'Lo, there!' or 'Lo, here!' Do not go, do not follow them. [24] For as the lightning flashes and lights up the sky from one side to the other, so will the Son of man be in his day.[a] [25] But first he must suffer many things and be rejected by this generation. [26] As it was in the days of Noah, so will it be in the days of the Son of man. [27] They ate, they drank, they married, they were given in marriage, until the day when Noah entered the ark, and the flood came and destroyed them all. [28] Likewise as it was in the days of Lot—they ate, they drank, they bought, they sold, they planted, they built, [29] but on the day when Lot went out from Sod′om fire and brimstone rained from heaven and destroyed them all—[30] so will it be on the day when the Son of man is revealed. [31] On that day, let him who is on the housetop, with his goods in the house, not come down to take them away; and likewise let him who is in the field not turn back. [32] Remember Lot's wife. [33] Whoever seeks to gain his life will lose it, but whoever loses his life will preserve it. [34] I tell you, in that night there will be two men in one bed; one will be taken and the other left. [35] There will be two women grinding together; one will be

taken and the other left."[b] [37] And they said to him, "Where, Lord?" He said to them, "Where the body is, there the eagles[c] will be gathered together."

18 And he told them a parable, to the effect that they ought always to pray and not lose heart. [2] He said, "In a certain city there was a judge who neither feared God nor regarded man; [3] and there was a widow in that city who kept coming to him and saying, 'Vindicate me against my adversary.' [4] For a while he refused; but afterward he said to himself, 'Though I neither fear God nor regard man, [5] yet because this widow bothers me, I will vindicate her, or she will wear me out by her continual coming.'" [6] And the Lord said, "Hear what the unrighteous judge says. [7] And will not God vindicate his elect, who cry to him day and night? Will he delay long over them? [8] I tell you, he will vindicate them speedily. Nevertheless, when the Son of man comes, will he find faith on earth?"

9 He also told this parable to some who trusted in themselves that they were righteous and despised others: [10] "Two men went up into the temple to pray, one a Pharisee and the other a tax collector. [11] The Pharisee stood and prayed thus with himself, 'God, I thank thee that I am not like other men, extortioners, unjust, adulterers, or even like this tax collector. [12] I fast twice a week, I give tithes of all that I get.' [13] But the tax collector, standing far off, would not even lift up his eyes to heaven, but beat his breast, saying, 'God, be merciful to me a sinner!' [14] I tell you, this man went down to his house justified rather than the other; for every one who exalts himself will be humbled, but he who humbles himself will be exalted."

15 Now they were bringing even infants to him that he might touch them; and when the disciples saw it, they rebuked them. [16] But Jesus called them to him, saying, "Let the children come to me, and do not hinder them; for to such belongs the kingdom of

z Or *within you* a Other ancient authorities omit *in his day*
b Other ancient authorities add verse 36, "*Two men will be in the field; one will be taken and the other left*" c Or *vultures*

17.19: Mt 9.22; Mk 5.34; Lk 8.48; 18.42.   17.20: Lk 19.11; 21.7; Acts 1.6.
17.22: Mt 9.15; Mk 2.20; Lk 5.35.   17.23: Mt 24.23; Mk 13.21.
17.24: Mt 24.27; Rev 1.7.   17.25: Lk 9.22.   17.26-27: Mt 24.37-39; Gen 6.5-8; 7.6-24.
17.28-30: Gen 18.20-33; 19.24-25.   17.31: Mt 24.17-18; Mk 13.15-16; Lk 21.21.
17.32: Gen 19.26.   17.33: Mt 10.39; 16.25; Mk 8.35; Lk 9.24; Jn 12.25.
17.34-35: Mt 24.40-41.   17.37: Mt 24.28.   18.1-8: Mt 11.5-8.   18.6: Lk 7.13.
18.7: Rev 6.10; Mt 24.22; Rom 8.33; Col 3.12; 2 Tim 2.10.   18.11: Mt 6.5; Mk 11.25.
18.12: Lk 5.33; 11.42.   18.14: Mt 18.4; 23.12; Lk 14.11; 1 Pet 5.6.
18.15-17: Mt 19.13-15; 18.3; Mk 10.13-16.

God. ¹⁷ Truly, I say to you, whoever does not receive the kingdom of God like a child shall not enter it."

18 And a ruler asked him, "Good Teacher, what shall I do to inherit eternal life?" ¹⁹And Jesus said to him, "Why do you call me good? No one is good but God alone. ²⁰ You know the commandments: 'Do not commit adultery, Do not kill, Do not steal, Do not bear false witness, Honor your father and mother.'" ²¹And he said, "All these I have observed from my youth." ²²And when Jesus heard it, he said to him, "One thing you still lack. Sell all that you have and distribute to the poor, and you will have treasure in heaven; and come, follow me." ²³ But when he heard this he became sad, for he was very rich. ²⁴ Jesus looking at him said, "How hard it is for those who have riches to enter the kingdom of God! ²⁵ For it is easier for a camel to go through the eye of a needle than for a rich man to enter the kingdom of God." ²⁶ Those who heard it said, "Then who can be saved?" ²⁷ But he said, "What is impossible with men is possible with God." ²⁸And Peter said, "Lo, we have left our homes and followed you." ²⁹And he said to them, "Truly, I say to you, there is no man who has left house or wife or brothers or parents or children, for the sake of the kingdom of God, ³⁰ who will not receive manifold more in this time, and in the age to come eternal life."

31 And taking the twelve, he said to them, "Behold, we are going up to Jerusalem, and everything that is written of the Son of man by the prophets will be accomplished. ³² For he will be delivered to the Gentiles, and will be mocked and shamefully treated and spit upon, ³³ they will scourge him and kill him, and on the third day he will rise." ³⁴ But they understood none of these things; this saying was hid from them, and they did not grasp what was said.

35 As he drew near to Jericho, a blind man was sitting by the roadside begging; ³⁶ and hearing a multitude going by, he inquired what this meant. ³⁷ They told him, "Jesus of Nazareth is passing by." ³⁸And he cried, "Jesus, Son of David, have mercy on me!" ³⁹And those who were in front rebuked him, telling him to be silent; but he cried out all the more, "Son of David, have mercy on me!" ⁴⁰And Jesus stopped, and commanded him to be brought to him; and when he came near, he asked him, ⁴¹ "What do you want me to do for you?" He said, "Lord, let me receive my sight." ⁴²And Jesus said to him, "Receive your sight; your faith has made you well." ⁴³And immediately he received his sight and followed him, glorifying God; and all the people, when they saw it, gave praise to God.

19 He entered Jericho and was passing through. ²And there was a man named Zac·chae´us; he was a chief tax collector, and rich. ³And he sought to see who Jesus was, but could not, on account of the crowd, because he was small of stature. ⁴ So he ran on ahead and climbed up into a sycamore tree to see him, for he was to pass that way. ⁵And when Jesus came to the place, he looked up and said to him, "Zac·chae´us, make haste and come down; for I must stay at your house today." ⁶ So he made haste and came down, and received him joyfully. ⁷And when they saw it they all murmured, "He has gone in to be the guest of a man who is a sinner." ⁸And Zac·chae´us stood and said to the Lord, "Behold, Lord, the half of my goods I give to the poor; and if I have defrauded any one of anything, I restore it fourfold." ⁹And Jesus said to him, "Today salvation has come to this house, since he also is a son of Abraham. ¹⁰ For the Son of man came to seek and to save the lost."

11 As they heard these things, he proceeded to tell a parable, because he was near to Jerusalem, and because they supposed that the kingdom of God was to appear immediately. ¹² He said therefore, "A nobleman went into a far country to receive kingly power *d* and then return. ¹³ Calling ten of his

d Greek *a kingdom*.

18.18-23: Mt 19.16-22; Mk 10.17-22.   **18.18:** Lk 10.25.
18.20: Ex 20.12-16; Deut 5.16-20; Rom 13.9; Jas 2.11.
18.22: Lk 12.33; Acts 2.45; 4.32.   **18.24-27:** Mt 19.23-26; Mk 10.23-27.
18.27: Gen 18.14; Job 42.2; Jer 32.17; Lk 1.37.   **18.28-30:** Mt 19.27-30; Mk 10.28-31;
Lk 5.1-11.   **18.31-34:** Mt 20.17-19; Mk 10.32-34; Lk 9.22, 44-45; 17.25.
18.35-43: Mt 20.29-34; Mk 10.46-52; Mt 9.27-31; Mk 8.22; Jn 9.1-7.
18.42: Mt 9.22; Mk 5.34; 10.52; Lk 7.50; 8.48; 17.19.   **19.1:** Mk 10.46.
19.7: Lk 5.29-30; 15.1-2.   **19.8:** Lk 7.13; 3.14; Ex 22.1; Lev 6.5; Num 5.6-7.
19.9: Lk 3.8; 13.16; Rom 4.16.   **19.11:** Lk 9.51; 13.22; 17.11; 18.31; 9.27.
19.12-28: Mt 25.14-30.   **19.12:** Mk 13.34.

servants, he gave them ten pounds,d and said to them, 'Trade with these till I come.' 14 But his citizens hated him and sent an embassy after him, saying, 'We do not want this man to reign over us.' 15 When he returned, having received the kingly power,d he commanded these servants, to whom he had given the money, to be called to him, that he might know what they had gained by trading. 16 The first came before him, saying, 'Lord, your pound has made ten pounds more.' 17And he said to him, 'Well done, good servant! Because you have been faithful in a very little, you shall have authority over ten cities.' 18And the second came, saying, 'Lord, your pound has made five pounds.' 19And he said to him, 'And you are to be over five cities.' 20 Then another came, saying, 'Lord, here is your pound, which I kept laid away in a napkin; 21 for I was afraid of you, because you are a severe man; you take up what you did not lay down, and reap what you did not sow.' 22 He said to him, 'I will condemn you out of your own mouth, you wicked servant! You knew that I was a severe man, taking up what I did not lay down and reaping what I did not sow? 23 Why then did you not put my money into the bank, and at my coming I should have collected it with interest?' 24And he said to those who stood by, 'Take the pound from him, and give it to him who has the ten pounds.' 25 (And they said to him, 'Lord, he has ten pounds!') 26 'I tell you, that to every one who has will more be given; but from him who has not, even what he has will be taken away. 27 But as for these enemies of mine, who did not want me to reign over them, bring them here and slay them before me.'"

28 And when he had said this, he went on ahead, going up to Jerusalem. 29 When he drew near to Beth'pha·gē and Beth'a·ny, at the mount that is called Ol'i·vet, he sent two of the disciples, 30 saying, "Go into the village opposite, where on entering you will find a colt tied, on which no one has ever yet sat; untie it and bring it here. 31 If any one asks you, 'Why are you

untying it?' you shall say this, 'The Lord has need of it.'" 32 So those who were sent went away and found it as he had told them. 33And as they were untying the colt, its owners said to them, "Why are you untying the colt?" 34And they said, "The Lord has need of it." 35And they brought it to Jesus, and throwing their garments on the colt they set Jesus upon it. 36And as he rode along, they spread their garments on the road. 37As he was now drawing near, at the descent of the Mount of Olives, the whole multitude of the disciples began to rejoice and praise God with a loud voice for all the mighty works that they had seen, 38 saying, "Blessed is the King who comes in the name of the Lord! Peace in heaven and glory in the highest!" 39And some of the Pharisees in the multitude said to him, "Teacher, rebuke your disciples." 40 He answered, "I tell you, if these were silent, the very stones would cry out."

41 And when he drew near and saw the city he wept over it, 42 saying, "Would that even today you knew the things that make for peace! But now they are hid from your eyes. 43 For the days shall come upon you, when your enemies will cast up a bank about you and surround you, and hem you in on every side, 44 and dash you to the ground, you and your children within you, and they will not leave one stone upon another in you; because you did not know the time of your visitation."

45 And he entered the temple and began to drive out those who sold, 46 saying to them, "It is written, 'My house shall be a house of prayer'; but you have made it a den of robbers."

47 And he was teaching daily in the temple. The chief priests and the scribes and the principal men of the people sought to destroy him; 48 but they did not find anything they could do, for all the people hung upon his words.

20 One day, as he was teaching the people in the temple and preaching the gospel, the chief priests and the scribes with the elders came up 2 and said to him, "Tell us by what

---

d Greek *a kingdom*
e The mina, rendered here by *pound*, was equal to about twenty dollars

19.17: Lk 16.10.   19.26: Mt 13.12; Mk 4.25; Lk 8.18.   19.28: Mk 10.32.
19.29-38: Mt 21.1-9; Mk 11.1-10; Jn 12.12-18.   19.32: Lk 22.13.   19.34: Lk 7.13.
19.36: 2 Kings 9.13.   19.38: Ps 118.26; Lk 13.35; 2.14.
19.39-40: Mt 21.15-16; Hab 2.11.   19.41: Lk 13.33-34.
19.43: Lk 21.21-24; 21.6; Is 29.3; Jer 6.6; Ezek 4.2.   19.44: 1 Pet 2.12.
19.45-46: Mt 21.12-13; Mk 11.15-17; Jn 2.13-17.   19.47-48: Mk 11.18; Lk 21.37; 22.53.
20.1-8: Mt 21.23-27; Mk 11.27-33.   20.2: Jn 2.18.

authority you do these things, or who it is that gave you this authority." [3] He answered them, "I also will ask you a question; now tell me, [4] Was the baptism of John from heaven or from men?" [5]And they discussed it with one another, saying, "If we say, 'From heaven,' he will say, 'Why did you not believe him?' [6] But if we say, 'From men,' all the people will stone us; for they are convinced that John was a prophet." [7] So they answered that they did not know whence it was. [8]And Jesus said to them, "Neither will I tell you by what authority I do these things."

[9] And he began to tell the people this parable: "A man planted a vineyard, and let it out to tenants, and went into another country for a long while. [10] When the time came, he sent a servant to the tenants, that they should give him some of the fruit of the vineyard; but the tenants beat him, and sent him away empty-handed. [11]And he sent another servant; him also they beat and treated shamefully, and sent him away empty-handed. [12]And he sent yet a third; this one they wounded and cast out. [13] Then the owner of the vineyard said, 'What shall I do? I will send my beloved son; it may be they will respect him.' [14] But when the tenants saw him, they said to themselves, 'This is the heir; let us kill him, that the inheritance may be ours.' [15]And they cast him out of the vineyard and killed him. What then will the owner of the vineyard do to them? [16] He will come and destroy those tenants, and give the vineyard to others." When they heard this, they said, "God forbid!" [17] But he looked at them and said, "What then is this that is written:

'The very stone which the builders rejected

has become the head of the corner'? [18] Every one who falls on that stone will be broken to pieces; but when it falls on any one it will crush him."

[19] The scribes and the chief priests tried to lay hands on him at that very hour, but they feared the people; for they perceived that he had told this parable against them. [20] So they watched him, and sent spies, who pretended to be sincere, that they

might take hold of what he said, so as to deliver him up to the authority and jurisdiction of the governor. [21] They asked him, "Teacher, we know that you speak and teach rightly, and show no partiality, but truly teach the way of God. [22] Is it lawful for us to give tribute to Caesar, or not?" [23] But he perceived their craftiness, and said to them, [24] "Show me a coin.*f* Whose likeness and inscription has it?" They said, "Caesar's." [25] He said to them, "Then render to Caesar the things that are Caesar's, and to God the things that are God's." [26]And they were not able in the presence of the people to catch him by what he said; but marveling at his answer they were silent.

[27] There came to him some Sad'-du-cees, those who say that there is no resurrection, [28] and they asked him a question, saying, "Teacher, Moses wrote for us that if a man's brother dies, having a wife but no children, the man*g* must take the wife and raise up children for his brother. [29] Now there were seven brothers; the first took a wife, and died without children; [30] and the second [31] and the third took her, and likewise all seven left no children and died. [32]Afterward the woman also died. [33] In the resurrection, therefore, whose wife will the woman be? For the seven had her as wife."

[34] And Jesus said to them, "The sons of this age marry and are given in marriage; [35] but those who are accounted worthy to attain to that age and to the resurrection from the dead neither marry nor are given in marriage, [36] for they cannot die any more, because they are equal to angels and are sons of God, being sons of the resurrection. [37] But that the dead are raised, even Moses showed, in the passage about the bush, where he calls the Lord the God of Abraham and the God of Isaac and the God of Jacob. [38] Now he is not God of the dead, but of the living; for all live to him." [39]And some of the scribes answered, "Teacher, you have spoken well." [40] For they no longer dared to ask him any question.

[41] But he said to them, "How can they say that the Christ is David's son? [42] For David himself says in the Book of Psalms,

f Greek *denarius*   *g* Greek *his brother*

20.6: Mt 14.5; Lk 7.29.   **20.9-19:** Mt 21.33-46; Mk 12.1-12.   **20.9:** Is 5.1-7; Mt 25.14.
20.16: Acts 13.46; 18.6; 28.28.   **20.17:** Ps 118.22-23; Acts 4.11; 1 Pet 2.6-7.
20.18: Is 8.14-15.   **20.19:** Lk 19.47.   **20.20-26:** Mt 22.15-22; Mk 12.13-17.
20.21: Jn 3.2.   **20.25:** Rom 13.7; Lk 23.2.   **20.27-38:** Mt 22.23-33; Mk 12.18-27.
20.27: Acts 4.1-2; 23.6-10.   **20.28:** Deut 25.5.   **20.37:** Ex 3.6.   **20.39:** Mk 12.28.
20.40: Mk 12.34; Mt 22.46.   **20.41-44:** Mt 22.41-45; Mk 12.35-37; Ps 110.1.

'The Lord said to my Lord,
Sit at my right hand,
43 till I make thy enemies a stool for thy feet.'
44 David thus calls him Lord; so how is he his son?''

45 And in the hearing of all the people he said to his disciples, 46 ''Beware of the scribes, who like to go about in long robes, and love salutations in the market places and the best seats in the synagogues and the places of honor at feasts, 47 who devour widows' houses and for a pretense make long prayers. They will receive the greater condemnation.''

21 He looked up and saw the rich putting their gifts into the treasury; 2 and he saw a poor widow put in two copper coins. 3 And he said, ''Truly I tell you, this poor widow has put in more than all of them; 4 for they all contributed out of their abundance, but she out of her poverty put in all the living that she had.''

5 And as some spoke of the temple, how it was adorned with noble stones and offerings, he said, 6 ''As for these things which you see, the days will come when there shall not be left here one stone upon another that will not be thrown down.'' 7 And they asked him, ''Teacher, when will this be, and what will be the sign when this is about to take place?'' 8 And he said, ''Take heed that you are not led astray; for many will come in my name, saying, 'I am he!' and, 'The time is at hand!' Do not go after them. 9 And when you hear of wars and tumults, do not be terrified; for this must first take place, but the end will not be at once.''

10 Then he said to them, ''Nation will rise against nation, and kingdom against kingdom; 11 there will be great earthquakes, and in various places famines and pestilences; and there will be terrors and great signs from heaven. 12 But before all this they will lay their hands on you and persecute you, delivering you up to the synagogues and prisons, and you will be brought before kings and governors for my name's sake. 13 This will be a

time for you to bear testimony. 14 Settle it therefore in your minds, not to meditate beforehand how to answer; 15 for I will give you a mouth and wisdom, which none of your adversaries will be able to withstand or contradict. 16 You will be delivered up even by parents and brothers and kinsmen and friends, and some of you they will put to death; 17 you will be hated by all for my name's sake. 18 But not a hair of your head will perish. 19 By your endurance you will gain your lives.

20 ''But when you see Jerusalem surrounded by armies, then know that its desolation has come near. 21 Then let those who are in Judea flee to the mountains, and let those who are inside the city depart, and let not those who are out in the country enter it; 22 for these are days of vengeance, to fulfil all that is written. 23 Alas for those who are with child and for those who give suck in those days! For great distress shall be upon the earth and wrath upon this people; 24 they will fall by the edge of the sword, and be led captive among all nations; and Jerusalem will be trodden down by the Gentiles, until the times of the Gentiles are fulfilled.

25 ''And there will be signs in sun and moon and stars, and upon the earth distress of nations in perplexity at the roaring of the sea and the waves, 26 men fainting with fear and with foreboding of what is coming on the world; for the powers of the heavens will be shaken. 27 And then they will see the Son of man coming in a cloud with power and great glory. 28 Now when these things begin to take place, look up and raise your heads, because your redemption is drawing near.''

29 And he told them a parable: ''Look at the fig tree, and all the trees; 30 as soon as they come out in leaf, you see for yourselves and know that the summer is already near. 31 So also, when you see these things taking place, you know that the kingdom of God is near. 32 Truly, I say to you, this generation will not pass away till

20.45-47: Mk 12.38-40; Mt 23.6-7; Lk 11.43; 14.7-11.　21.1-4: Mk 12.41-44.
21.5-23: Mt 24.1-19; Mk 13.1-17.　21.6: Lk 19.43-44; Mk 14.58; 15.29; Acts 6.14.
21.7: Lk 17.20; Acts 1.6.　21.8: Lk 17.23; Mk 13.21; 1 Jn 2.18.
21.10: 2 Chron 15.6; Is 19.2.　21.12-17: Mt 10.17-21.　21.12: Acts 25.24; Jn 16.2.
21.13: Phil 1.12.　21.14-15: Lk 12.11-12.　21.16: Lk 12.52-53.
21.17: Mt 10.22; Jn 15.18-25.　21.18: Lk 12.7; Mt 10.30; Acts 27.34; 1 Sam 14.45.
21.19: Mt 10.22; Rev 2.7.　21.20-22: Lk 19.41-44; 23.28-31; 17.31.
21.23: Lk 23.29.　21.24: Rom 11.25; Is 63.18; Dan 8.13; Rev 11.2.
21.25-27: Mt 24.29-30; Mk 13.24-26.
21.25: Rev 6.12-13; Is 13.10; Joel 2.10; Zeph 1.15.　21.27: Lk 9.27; Dan 7.13-14.
21.28: Lk 18.7-8.　21.29-33: Mt 24.32-35; Mk 13.28-31.　21.32: Lk 9.27.

all has taken place. 33 Heaven and earth will pass away, but my words will not pass away.

34 "But take heed to yourselves lest your hearts be weighed down with dissipation and drunkenness and cares of this life, and that day come upon you suddenly like a snare; 35 for it will come upon all who dwell upon the face of the whole earth. 36 But watch at all times, praying that you may have strength to escape all these things that will take place, and to stand before the Son of man."

37 And every day he was teaching in the temple, but at night he went out and lodged on the mount called Ol´i-vet. 38 And early in the morning all the people came to him in the temple to hear him.

22 Now the feast of Unleavened Bread drew near, which is called the Passover. 2 And the chief priests and the scribes were seeking how to put him to death; for they feared the people.

3 Then Satan entered into Judas called Is-car´i-ot, who was of the number of the twelve; 4 he went away and conferred with the chief priests and captains how he might betray him to them. 5 And they were glad, and engaged to give him money. 6 So he agreed, and sought an opportunity to betray him to them in the absence of the multitude.

7 Then came the day of Unleavened Bread, on which the passover lamb had to be sacrificed. 8 So Jesus^h sent Peter and John, saying, "Go and prepare the passover for us, that we may eat it." 9 They said to him, "Where will you have us prepare it?" 10 He said to them, "Behold, when you have entered the city, a man carrying a jar of water will meet you; follow him into the house which he enters, 11 and tell the householder, 'The Teacher says to you, Where is the guest room, where

I am to eat the passover with my disciples?' 12 And he will show you a large upper room furnished; there make ready." 13 And they went, and found it as he had told them; and they prepared the passover.

14 And when the hour came, he sat at table, and the apostles with him. 15 And he said to them, "I have earnestly desired to eat this passover with you before I suffer; 16 for I tell you I shall not eat it. until it is fulfilled in the kingdom of God." 17 And he took a cup, and when he had given thanks he said, "Take this, and divide it among yourselves; 18 for I tell you that from now on I shall not drink of the fruit of the vine until the kingdom of God comes." 19 And he took bread, and when he had given thanks he broke it and gave it to them, saying, "This is my body.^i 21 But behold the hand of him who betrays me is with me on the table. 22 For the Son of man goes as it has been determined; but woe to that man by whom he is betrayed!" 23 And they began to question one another, which of them it was that would do this.

24 A dispute also arose among them, which of them was to be regarded as the greatest. 25 And he said to them, "The kings of the Gentiles exercise lordship over them; and those in authority over them are called benefactors. 26 But not so with you; rather let the greatest among you become as the youngest, and the leader as one who serves. 27 For which is the greater, one who sits at table, or one who serves? Is it not the one who sits at table? But I am among you as one who serves.

28 "You are those who have continued with me in my trials; 29 as my Father appointed a kingdom for me, so do I appoint for you 30 that you may eat and drink at my table in my kingdom, and sit on thrones judging the twelve tribes of Israel.

31 "Simon, Simon, behold, Satan

---

h Greek *he*   *i* Other ancient authorities read *never eat it again*
i Other ancient authorities add *which is given for you. Do this in remembrance of me."* 20 *And likewise the cup after supper, saying, "This cup which is poured out for you is the new covenant in my blood."*

21.33: Lk 16.17.   **21.34:** Lk 12.45; Mk 4.19; 1 Thess 5.6-7.   **21.36:** Mk 13.33.
21.37: Lk 19.47; Mk 11.19.   **22.1-2:** Mt 26.2-5; Mk 14.1-2; Jn 11.47-53.
22.3-6: Mt 26.14-16; Mk 14.10-11; Jn 13.2.   **22.7-13:** Mt 26.17-19; Mk 14.12-16.
22.7: Ex 12.18-20; Deut 16.5-8.   **22.8:** Acts 3.1; Lk 19.29.
22.14: Mt 26.20; Mk 14.17; Jn 13.17.   **22.15:** Lk 12.49-50.   **22.16:** Lk 14.15.
22.17: Mt 26.27; Mk 14.23; 1 Cor 10.16.   **22.18:** Mt 26.29; Mk 14.25.
22.19: Mt 26.26; Mk 14.22; 1 Cor 10.16; 11.23-26; Lk 9.16.
22.21-23: Mt 26.21-24; Mk 14.18-21; Ps 41.9; Jn 13.21-30.   **22.24:** Lk 9.46; Mk 9.34.
22.25-27: Mt 20.25-28; Mk 10.42-45; Jn 13.3-16.   **22.26:** Lk 9.48.
22.28-30: Mt 19.28.   **22.28:** Lk 4.13; Heb 2.18; 4.15.   **22.29:** Mk 14.24; Heb 9.20.
22.30: Mk 10.37; Rev 3.21; 20.4.   **22.31:** Job 1.6-12; Amos 9.9.

demanded to have you, *k*that he might sift you *k* like wheat, 32but I have prayed for you that your faith may not fail; and when you have turned again, strengthen your brethren." 33And he said to him, "Lord, I am ready to go with you to prison and to death." 34 He said, "I tell you, Peter, the cock will not crow this day, until you three times deny that you know me."

35 And he said to them, "When I sent you out with no purse or bag or sandals, did you lack anything?" They said, "Nothing." 36 He said to them, "But now, let him who has a purse take it, and likewise a bag. And let him who has no sword sell his mantle and buy one. 37For I tell you that this scripture must be fulfilled in me, 'And he was reckoned with transgressors'; for what is written about me has its fulfilment." 38And they said, "Look, Lord, here are two swords." And he said to them, "It is enough."

39 And he came out, and went, as was his custom, to the Mount of Olives; and the disciples followed him. 40And when he came to the place he said to them, "Pray that you may not enter into temptation." 41And he withdrew from them about a stone's throw, and knelt down and prayed, 42"Father, if thou art willing, remove this cup from me; nevertheless not my will, but thine, be done." 43And there appeared to him an angel from heaven, strengthening him. 44And being in an agony he prayed more earnestly; and his sweat became like great drops of blood falling down upon the ground.*l* 45And when he rose from prayer, he came to the disciples and found them sleeping for sorrow, 46 and he said to them, "Why do you sleep? Rise and pray that you may not enter into temptation."

47 While he was still speaking, there came a crowd, and the man called Judas, one of the twelve, was leading them. He drew near to Jesus to kiss him; 48 but Jesus said to him, "Judas, would you betray the Son of man with a kiss?" 49And when those who were about him saw what would

follow, they said, "Lord, shall we strike with the sword?" 50And one of them struck the slave of the high priest and cut off his right ear, 51 But Jesus said, "No more of this!" And he touched his ear and healed him. 52 Then Jesus said to the chief priests and captains of the temple and elders, who had come out against him, "Have you come out as against a robber, with swords and clubs? 53When I was with you day after day in the temple, you did not lay hands on me. But this is your hour, and the power of darkness."

54 Then they seized him and led him away, bringing him into the high priest's house. Peter followed at a distance; 55 and when they had kindled a fire in the middle of the courtyard and sat down together, Peter sat among them. 56 Then a maid, seeing him as he sat in the light and gazing at him, said, "This man also was with him." 57 But he denied it, saying, "Woman, I do not know him." 58And a little later some one else saw him and said, "You also are one of them." But Peter said, "Man, I am not." 59And after an interval of about an hour still another insisted, saying, "Certainly this man also was with him; for he is a Galilean." 60 But Peter said, "Man, I do not know what you are saying." And immediately, while he was still speaking, the cock crowed. 61And the Lord turned and looked at Peter. And Peter remembered the word of the Lord, how he had said to him, "Before the cock crows today, you will deny me three times." 62And he went out and wept bitterly.

63 Now the men who were holding Jesus mocked him and beat him; 64 they also blindfolded him and asked him, "Prophesy! Who is it that struck you?" 65And they spoke many other words against him, reviling him.

66 When day came, the assembly of the elders of the people gathered together, both chief priests and scribes; and they led him away to their council, and they said, 67 "If you are the Christ, tell us." But he said to them, "If I tell

k The Greek word for *you* here is plural; in verse 32 it is singular
l Other ancient authorities omit verses 43 and 44

22.32: Jn 17.15; 21.15-17.   **22.33-34:** Mt 26.33-35; Mk 14.29-31; Jn 13.37-38.
22.35: Lk 10.4; Mt 10.9.   **22.36:** Lk 22.49-50.   **22.37:** Is 53.12.
22.39: Mt 26.30; Mk 14.26; Jn 18.1.   **22.40-46:** Mt 26.36-46; Mk 14.32-42; Heb 5.7-8.
22.40: Lk 11.4.   **22.42:** Mk 10.38; Jn 18.11; 5.30.
22.47-53: Mt 26.47-56; Mk 14.43-49; Jn 18.3-11.   **22.49:** Lk 22.38.
22.53: Lk 19.47.   **22.54-55:** Mt 26.57-58; Mk 14.53-54; Jn 18.12-16.
22.56-62: Mt 26.69-75; Mk 14.66-72; Jn 18.16-18, 25-27.
22.61: Lk 7.13; 22.34.
22.63-65: Mt 26.67-68; Mk 14.65; Jn 18.22-24.   **22.66:** Mt 26.57; Mk 14.53; Lk 22.54.
22.67-71: Mt 26.63-66; Mk 14.61-64; Jn 18.19-21.

you, you will not believe; 68and if I ask you, you will not answer. 69But from now on the Son of man shall be seated at the right hand of the power of God." 70And they all said, "Are you the Son of God, then?" And he said to them, "You say that I am." 71And they said, "What further testimony do we need? We have heard it ourselves from his own lips."

23 Then the whole company of them arose, and brought him before Pilate. 2And they began to accuse him, saying, "We found this man perverting our nation, and forbidding us to give tribute to Caesar, and saying that he himself is Christ a king." 3And Pilate asked him, "Are you the King of the Jews?" And he answered him, "You have said so." 4And Pilate said to the chief priests and the multitudes, "I find no crime in this man." 5 But they were urgent, saying, "He stirs up the people, teaching throughout all Judea, from Galilee even to this place."

6 When Pilate heard this, he asked whether the man was a Galilean. 7And when he learned that he belonged to Her'od's jurisdiction, he sent him over to Herod, who was himself in Jerusalem at that time. 8 When Her'od saw Jesus, he was very glad, for he had long desired to see him, because he had heard about him, and he was hoping to see some sign done by him. 9 So he questioned him at some length; but he made no answer. 10 The chief priests and the scribes stood by, vehemently accusing him. 11And Her'od with his soldiers treated him with contempt and mocked him; then, arraying him in gorgeous apparel, he sent him back to Pilate. 12And Her'od and Pilate became friends with each other that very day, for before this they had been at enmity with each other.

13 Pilate then called together the chief priests and the rulers and the people, 14 and said to them, "You brought me this man as one who was perverting the people; and after examining him before you, behold, I did not find this man guilty of any of your

charges against him; 15 neither did Her'od, for he sent him back to us. Behold, nothing deserving death has been done by him; 16 I will therefore chastise him and release him."*m*

18 But they all cried out together, "Away with this man, and release to us Ba·rab'bas"—19 a man who had been thrown into prison for an insurrection started in the city, and for murder. 20 Pilate addressed them once more, desiring to release Jesus; 21 but they shouted out, "Crucify, crucify him!" 22A third time he said to them, "Why, what evil has he done? I have found in him no crime deserving death; I will therefore chastise him and release him." 23 But they were urgent, demanding with loud cries that he should be crucified. And their voices prevailed. 24 So Pilate gave sentence that their demand should be granted. 25 He released the man who had been thrown into prison for insurrection and murder, whom they asked for; but Jesus he delivered up to their will.

26 And as they led him away, they seized one Simon of Cy·re'ne, who was coming in from the country, and laid on him the cross, to carry it behind Jesus. 27And there followed him a great multitude of the people, and of women who bewailed and lamented him. 28 But Jesus turning to them said, "Daughters of Jerusalem, do not weep for me, but weep for yourselves and for your children. 29For behold, the days are coming when they will say, 'Blessed are the barren, and the wombs that never bore, and the breasts that never gave suck!' 30Then they will begin to say to the mountains, 'Fall on us'; and to the hills, 'Cover us.' 31For if they do this when the wood is green, what will happen when it is dry?"

32 Two others also, who were criminals, were led away to be put to death with him. 33And when they came to the place which is called The Skull, there they crucified him, and the criminals, one on the right and one on the left. 34And Jesus said, "Father, forgive them; for they know not what they do." *n* And they cast lots to divide

m Here, or after verse 19, other ancient authorities omit the sentence *And Jesus . . . what they do."*

n Other ancient authorities add verse 17, *Now he was obliged to release one man to them at the festival*

22.70: Lk 23.3; Mt 27.11.   23.1: Mt 27.1-2; Mk 15.1; Jn 18.28.   23.2: Lk 20.25.
23.3: Mt 27.11-12; Mk 15.2-3; Jn 18.29-38; Lk 22.70.
23.4: Lk 23.14, 22, 41; Mt 27.24; Jn 19.4, 6; Acts 13.28.   23.8: Lk 9.9; Acts 4.27-28.
23.9: Mk 15.5.   23.11: Mk 15.17-19; Jn 19.2-3.   23.14: Lk 23.4, 22, 41.
23.16: Lk 23.22; Jn 19.12-14.   23.18-23: Mt 27.20-23; Mk 15.11-14; Acts 3.13-14;
Jn 18.38-40; 19.14-15.   23.23-25: Mt 27.26; Mk15.15.   23.26: Mt 27.32; Mk 15.21;
Jn 19.17.   23.28-31: Lk 21.23-24; 19.41-44.
23.33-39: Mt 27.33-44; Mk 15.22-32; Jn 19.17-24.   23.34: Acts 7.60; Ps 22.18.

his garments. 35And the people stood by, watching; but the rulers scoffed at him, saying, "He saved others; let him save himself, if he is the Christ of God, his Chosen One!" 36 The soldiers also mocked him, coming up and offering him vinegar, 37 and saying, "If you are the King of the Jews, save yourself!" 38 There was also an inscription over him,*o* "This is the King of the Jews."

39 One of the criminals who were hanged railed at him, saying, "Are you not the Christ? Save yourself and us!" 40 But the other rebuked him, saying, "Do you not fear God, since you are under the same sentence of condemnation? 41And we indeed justly; for we are receiving the due reward of our deeds; but this man has done nothing wrong." 42And he said, "Jesus, remember me when you come in your kingly power."*p* 43And he said to him, "Truly, I say to you, today you will be with me in Paradise."

44 It was now about the sixth hour, and there was darkness over the whole land*q* until the ninth hour, 45 while the sun's light failed;*r* and the curtain of the temple was torn in two. 46 Then Jesus, crying with a loud voice, said, "Father, into thy hands I commit my spirit!" And having said this he breathed his last. 47 Now when the centurion saw what had taken place, he praised God, and said, "Certainly this man was innocent!" 48And all the multitudes who assembled to see the sight, when they saw what had taken place, returned home beating their breasts. 49And all his acquaintances and the women who had followed him from Galilee stood at a distance and saw these things.

50 Now there was a man named Joseph from the Jewish town of A·ri·ma·thē′a. He was a member of the council, a good and righteous man, 51 who had not consented to their purpose and deed, and he was looking for the kingdom of God. 52 This man went to Pilate and asked for the body of Jesus. 53 Then he took it down and wrapped it in a linen shroud, and laid him in a rock-hewn tomb, where no one had ever yet been laid. 54 It was the day of Preparation, and the sabbath was beginning.*s* 55 The women who had come with him from Galilee followed, and saw the tomb, and how his body was laid; 56 then they returned, and prepared spices and ointments.

On the sabbath they rested according to the commandment.

24 But on the first day of the week, at early dawn, they went to the tomb, taking the spices which they had prepared. 2And they found the stone rolled away from the tomb, 3 but when they went in they did not find the body.*t* 4 While they were perplexed about this, behold, two men stood by them in dazzling apparel; 5 and as they were frightened and bowed their faces to the ground, the men said to them, "Why do you seek the living among the dead?*u* 6 Remember how he told you, while he was still in Galilee, 7 that the Son of man must be delivered into the hands of sinful men, and be crucified, and on the third day rise." 8And they remembered his words, 9 and returning from the tomb they told all this to the eleven and to all the rest. 10 Now it was Mary Mag′da·lēne and Jō·an′na and Mary the mother of James and the other women with them who told this to the apostles; 11 but these words seemed to them an idle tale, and they did not believe them.*v*

13 That very day two of them were going to a village named Em·mā′us, about seven miles*w* from Jerusalem, 14 and talking with each other about all these things that had happened. 15 While they were talking and discussing together, Jesus himself drew near and went with them. 16 But their eyes were kept from recognizing him.

o Other ancient authorities add *in letters of Greek and Latin and Hebrew*
p Greek *kingdom*　*q* Or *earth*
r Or *the sun was eclipsed.* Other ancient authorities read *the sun was darkened*
s Greek *was dawning*　*t* Other ancient authorities add *of the Lord Jesus*
u Other ancient authorities add *He is not here, but has risen*
v Other ancient authorities add verse 12, *But Peter rose and ran to the tomb; stooping and looking in, he saw the linen cloths by themselves; and he went home wondering at what had happened*
w Greek *sixty stadia;* some ancient authorities read *a hundred and sixty stadia*
23.35: Lk 4.23.　**23.36:** Mk 15.23; Ps 69.21.　**23.41:** Lk 23.4, 14, 22.
23.43: 2 Cor 12.3; Rev 2.7.　**23.44-49:** Mt 27.45-56; Mk 15.33-41; Jn 19.25-30.
23.45: Ex 26.31-35; Heb 9.8; 10.19.　**23.46:** Ps 31.5.　**23.49:** Lk 8.1-3; 23.55-56; 24.10.
23.50-56: Mt 27.57-61; Mk 15.42-47; Jn 19.38-42; Acts 13.29.
23.56: Mk 16.1; Ex 12.16; 20.10.　**24.1-9:** Mt 28.1-8; Mk 16.1-7; Jn 20.1, 11-13.
24.6: Lk 9.22; 13.32-33.　**24.10:** Mk 16.1 ;Lk 8.1-3; Jn 20.2.　**24.16:** Jn 20.14; 21.4.

17And he said to them, "What is this conversation which you are holding with each other as you walk?" And they stood still, looking sad. 18 Then one of them, named Clē'ó·pàs, answered him, "Are you the only visitor to Jerusalem who does not know the things that have happened there in these days?" 19And he said to them, "What things?" And they said to him, "Concerning Jesus of Nazareth, who was a prophet mighty in deed and word before God and all the people, 20 and how our chief priests and rulers delivered him up to be condemned to death, and crucified him. 21 But we had hoped that he was the one to redeem Israel. Yes, and besides all this, it is now the third day since this happened. 22 Moreover, some women of our company amazed us. They were at the tomb early in the morning 23 and did not find his body; and they came back saying that they had even seen a vision of angels, who said that he was alive. 24 Some of those who were with us went to the tomb, and found it just as the women had said; but him they did not see." 25And he said to them, "O foolish men, and slow of heart to believe all that the prophets have spoken! 26 Was it not necessary that the Christ should suffer these things and enter into his glory?" 27And beginning with Moses and all the prophets, he interpreted to them in all the scriptures the things concerning himself.

28 So they drew near to the village to which they were going. He appeared to be going further, 29 but they constrained him, saying, "Stay with us, for it is toward evening and the day is now far spent." So he went in to stay with them. 30 When he was at table with them, he took the bread and blessed, and broke it, and gave it to them. 31And their eyes were opened and they recognized him; and he vanished out of their sight. 32 They said to each other, "Did not our hearts burn within us while he talked to us on the road, while he opened to us the scriptures?" 33And they rose that same hour and returned to Jerusalem; and they found the eleven gathered together and those who were with them, 34 who said, "The Lord has risen indeed, and has appeared to Simon!" 35 Then they told what had happened on the road, and how he was known to them in the breaking of the bread.

36 As they were saying this, Jesus himself stood among them.^{x} 37 But they were startled and frightened, and supposed that they saw a spirit. 38And he said to them, "Why are you troubled, and why do questionings rise in your hearts? 39 See my hands and my feet, that it is I myself; handle me, and see; for a spirit has not flesh and bones as you see that I have."^{y} 41And while they still disbelieved for joy, and wondered, he said to them, "Have you anything here to eat?" 42 They gave him a piece of broiled fish, 43 and he took it and ate before them.

44 Then he said to them, "These are my words which I spoke to you, while I was still with you, that everything written about me in the law of Moses and the prophets and the psalms must be fulfilled." 45 Then he opened their minds to understand the scriptures, 46 and said to them, "Thus it is written, that the Christ should suffer and on the third day rise from the dead, 47 and that repentance and forgiveness of sins should be preached in his name to all nations,^{z} beginning from Jerusalem. 48 You are witnesses of these things. 49And behold, I send the promise of my Father upon you; but stay in the city, until you are clothed with power from on high."

50 Then he led them out as far as Beth'á·ny, and lifting up his hands he blessed them. 51 While he blessed them, he parted from them.^{a} 52And they^b returned to Jerusalem with great joy, 53 and were continually in the temple blessing God.

x Other ancient authorities add and said to them, "Peace to you!"
y Other ancient authorities add verse 40, And when he had said this, he showed them his hands and his feet
z Or nations. Beginning from Jerusalem you are witnesses
a Other ancient authorities add and was carried up into heaven
b Other ancient authorities add worshiped him, and
24.19: Mt 21.11; Lk 7.16; 13.33; Acts 3.22.　24.24: Jn 20.3-10.
24.27: Lk 24.44-45; Acts 28.23; 1 Pet 1.11.　24.28: Mk 6.48.　24.30: Lk 9.16; 22.19.
24.34: 1 Cor 15.5.　24.36-43: Jn 20.19-20, 27; Jn 21.5, 9-13; 1 Cor 15.5; Acts 10.40-41.
24.39: 1 Jn 1.1.　24.44: Lk 24.26-27; Acts 28.23.　24.46: Hos 6.2; 1 Cor 15.3-4.
24.47: Acts 1.4-8; Mt 28.19.　24.49: Acts 2.1-4; Jn 14.26; 20.21-23.
24.51: Acts 1.9-11.　24.52-53: Acts 1.12-14.

THE GOSPEL ACCORDING TO

JOHN

In the beginning was the Word, and the Word was with God, and the Word was God. 2 He was in the beginning with God; 3 all things were made through him, and without him was not anything made that was made. 4 In him was life,*a* and the life was the light of men. 5 The light shines in the darkness, and the darkness has not overcome it.

6 There was a man sent from God, whose name was John. 7 He came for testimony, to bear witness to the light, that all might believe through him. 8 He was not the light, but came to bear witness to the light.

9 The true light that enlightens every man was coming into the world. 10 He was in the world, and the world was made through him, yet the world knew him not. 11 He came to his own home, and his own people received him not. 12 But to all who received him, who believed in his name, he gave power to become children of God; 13 who were born, not of blood nor of the will of the flesh nor of the will of man, but of God.

14 And the Word became flesh and dwelt among us, full of grace and truth; we have beheld his glory, glory as of the only Son from the Father. 15 (John bore witness to him, and cried, "This was he of whom I said, 'He who comes after me ranks before me, for he was before me.'") 16And from his fulness have we all received, grace upon grace. 17 For the law was given through Moses; grace and truth came through Jesus Christ. 18 No one has ever seen God; the only Son,*b* who is in the bosom of the Father, he has made him known.

19 And this is the testimony of John, when the Jews sent priests and Levites from Jerusalem to ask him, "Who are you?" 20 He confessed, he did not deny, but confessed, "I am not the Christ." 21And they asked him, "What then? Are you E·li′jah?" He said, "I am not." "Are you the prophet?" And he answered, "No." 22 They said to him then, "Who are you? Let us have an answer for those who sent us. What do you say about yourself?" 23 He said, "I am the voice of one crying in the wilderness, 'Make straight the way of the Lord,' as the prophet I·sai′ah said."

24 Now they had been sent from the Pharisees. 25 They asked him, "Then why are you baptizing, if you are neither the Christ, nor E·li′jah, nor the prophet?" 26 John answered them, "I baptize with water; but among you stands one whom you do not know, 27 even he who comes after me, the thong of whose sandal I am not worthy to untie." 28 This took place in Beth′a·ny beyond the Jordan, where John was baptizing.

29 The next day he saw Jesus coming toward him, and said, "Behold, the Lamb of God, who takes away the sin of the world! 30 This is he of whom I said, 'After me comes a man who ranks before me, for he was before me.' 31 I myself did not know him; but for this I came baptizing with water, that he might be revealed to Israel." 32And John bore witness, "I saw the Spirit descend as a dove from heaven, and it remained on him. 33 I myself did not know him; but he who sent me to baptize with water said to me, 'He on whom you see the Spirit descend and remain, this is he who baptizes with the Holy Spirit.' 34And

a Or *was not anything made. That which has been made was life in him*
b Other ancient authorities read *God*

1.1: Gen 1.1; 1 Jn 1.1; Rev 19.13; Jn 17.5.   **1.3:** Col 1.16; 1 Cor 8.6; Heb 1.2.
1.4: Jn 5.26; 11.25; 14.6.   **1.5:** Jn 9.5; 12.46.   **1.6:** Mk 1.4; Mt 3.1; Lk 3.3; Jn 1.19-23.
1.9: 1 Jn 2.8.   **1.12:** Gal 3.26; Jn 3.18; 1 Jn 5.13.
1.13: Jn 3.5; 1 Pet 1.23; Jas 1.18; 1 Jn 3.9.
1.14: Rom 1.3; Gal 4.4; Phil 2.7; 1 Tim 3.16; Heb 2.14; 1 Jn 4.2.   **1.15:** Jn 1.30.
1.16: Col 1.19; 2.9; Eph 1.23; Rom 5.21.   **1.17:** Jn 7.19.
1.18: Ex 33.20; Jn 6.26; 1 Jn 4.12; Jn 3.11.   **1.19:** Jn 1.6.   **1.20:** Jn 3.28.
1.21: Mt 11.14; 16.14; Mk 9.13; Mt 17.13; Deut 18.15, 18.
1.23: Is 40.3; Mk 1.3; Mt 3.3; Lk 3.4.   **1.26-27:** Mk 1.7-8; Mt 3.11; Lk 3.16.
1.28: Jn 3.26; 10.40.   **1.29:** Jn 1.36; Is 53.7; Acts 8.32; 1 Pet 1.19; Rev 5.6; 1 Jn 3.5.
1.30: Jn 1.15.   **1.32:** Mk 1.10; Mt 3.16; Lk 3.22.

I have seen and have borne witness that this is the Son of God."

35 The next day again John was standing with two of his disciples; 36 and he looked at Jesus as he walked, and said, "Behold, the Lamb of God!" 37 The two disciples heard him say this, and they followed Jesus. 38 Jesus turned, and saw them following, and said to them, "What do you seek?" And they said to him, "Rabbi" (which means Teacher), "where are you staying?" 39 He said to them, "Come and see." They came and saw where he was staying; and they stayed with him that day, for it was about the tenth hour. 40 One of the two who heard John speak, and followed him, was Andrew, Simon Peter's brother. 41 He first found his brother Simon, and said to him, "We have found the Messiah" (which means Christ). 42 He brought him to Jesus. Jesus looked at him, and said, "So you are Simon the son of John? You shall be called Cē′phàs" (which means Peter c).

43 The next day Jesus decided to go to Galilee. And he found Philip and said to him, "Follow me." 44 Now Philip was from Beth-sā′i-dà, the city of Andrew and Peter. 45 Philip found Nà·than′à-el, and said to him, "We have found him of whom Moses in the law and also the prophets wrote, Jesus of Nazareth, the son of Joseph." 46 Nà·than′à-el said to him, "Can anything good come out of Nazareth?" Philip said to him, "Come and see." 47 Jesus saw Nà·than′à-el coming to him, and said of him, "Behold, an Israelite indeed, in whom is no guile!" 48 Nà·than′à-el said to him, "How do you know me?" Jesus answered him, "Before Philip called you, when you were under the fig tree, I saw you." 49 Nà·than′à-el answered him, "Rabbi, you are the Son of God! You are the King of Israel!" 50 Jesus answered him, "Because I said to you, I saw you under the fig tree, do you believe? You shall see greater things than these." 51 And he said to him, "Truly, truly, I say to you, you will see heaven opened, and the angels of God ascending and descending upon the Son of man."

2 On the third day there was a marriage at Cā′nà in Galilee, and the mother of Jesus was there; 2 Jesus also was invited to the marriage, with his disciples. 3 When the wine failed, the mother of Jesus said to him, "They have no wine." 4 And Jesus said to her, "O woman, what have you to do with me? My hour has not yet come." 5 His mother said to the servants, "Do whatever he tells you." 6 Now six stone jars were standing there, for the Jewish rites of purification, each holding twenty or thirty gallons. 7 Jesus said to them, "Fill the jars with water." And they filled them up to the brim. 8 He said to them, "Now draw some out, and take it to the steward of the feast." So they took it. 9 When the steward of the feast tasted the water now become wine, and did not know where it came from (though the servants who had drawn the water knew), the steward of the feast called the bridegroom 10 and said to him, "Every man serves the good wine first; and when men have drunk freely, then the poor wine; but you have kept the good wine until now." 11 This, the first of his signs, Jesus did at Cā′nà in Galilee, and manifested his glory; and his disciples believed in him.

12 After this he went down to Cà·pēr′nà·ùm, with his mother and his brothers and his disciples; and there they stayed for a few days.

13 The Passover of the Jews was at hand, and Jesus went up to Jerusalem. 14 In the temple he found those who were selling oxen and sheep and pigeons, and the money-changers at their business. 15 And making a whip of cords, he drove them all, with the sheep and oxen, out of the temple; and he poured out the coins of the money-changers and overturned their tables. 16 And he told those who sold the pigeons, "Take these things away; you shall not make my Father's house a house of trade." 17 His disciples remembered that it was written, "Zeal for thy house will consume me." 18 The Jews then said to him, "What sign have you to show us for doing this?" 19 Jesus answered them, "Destroy this temple, and in three days I

c From the word for *rock* in Aramaic and Greek respectively

1.35: Lk 7.18.   **1.40-42:** Mt 4.18-22; Mk 1.16-20; Lk 5.2-11.   **1.41:** Dan 9.25; Jn 4.25.   **1.42:** Jn 21.15-17; 1 Cor 15.5; Mt 16.18.   **1.43:** Mt 10.3; Jn 6.5; 12.21; 14.8.   **1.45:** Lk 24.27.   **1.46:** Jn 7.41; Mk 6.2.   **1.49:** Ps 2.7; Mk 15.32; Jn 12.13.   **1.51:** Lk 3.21; Gen 28.12.   **2.1:** Jn 4.46; 21.2.   **2.3:** Jn 19.26; Mk 3.31.   **2.4:** Mk 1.24; 5.7; Jn 7.6, 30; 8.20.   **2.6:** Mk 7.3; Jn 3.25.   **2.11:** Jn 2.23; 3.2; 4.54; 6.2.   **2.12:** Mt 4.13; Jn 7.3; Mk 3.31.   **2.13:** Jn 6.4; 11.55; Deut 16.1-6; Jn 2.41.   **2.14-16:** Mt 21.12-13; Mk 11.15-17; Lk 19.45-46.   **2.16:** Lk 2.49.   **2.17:** Ps 69.9.   **2.18:** Mk 11.28; Mt 21.23; Lk 20.2.   **2.19:** Mk 14.58; Acts 6.14.

will raise it up." 20 The Jews then said, "It has taken forty-six years to build this temple, and will you raise it up in three days?" 21 But he spoke of the temple of his body. 22 When therefore he was raised from the dead, his disciples remembered that he had said this; and they believed the scripture and the word which Jesus had spoken.

23 Now when he was in Jerusalem at the Passover feast, many believed in his name when they saw the signs which he did; 24 but Jesus did not trust himself to them, 25 because he knew all men and needed no one to bear witness of man; for he himself knew what was in man.

3 Now there was a man of the Pharisees, named Nic·o·dē'mŭs, a ruler of the Jews. 2 This man came to Jesus[d] by night and said to him, "Rabbi, we know that you are a teacher come from God; for no one can do these signs that you do, unless God is with him." 3 Jesus answered him, "Truly, truly, I say to you, unless one is born anew,[e] he cannot see the kingdom of God." 4 Nic·o·dē'mŭs said to him, "How can a man be born when he is old? Can he enter a second time into his mother's womb and be born?" 5 Jesus answered, "Truly, truly, I say to you, unless one is born of water and the Spirit, he cannot enter the kingdom of God. 6 That which is born of the flesh is flesh, and that which is born of the Spirit is spirit. [f] 7 Do not marvel that I said to you, 'You must be born anew.'[e] 8 The wind[f] blows where it wills, and you hear the sound of it, but you do not know whence it comes or whither it goes; so it is with every one who is born of the Spirit." 9 Nic·o·dē'mŭs said to him, "How can this be?" 10 Jesus answered him, "Are you a teacher of Israel, and yet you do not understand this? 11 Truly, truly, I say to you, we speak of what we know, and bear witness to what we have seen; but you do not receive our testimony. 12 If I have told you earthly things and you do not believe, how can you believe if I tell you heavenly things?

13 No one has ascended into heaven but he who descended from heaven, the Son of man.[g] 14 And as Moses lifted up the serpent in the wilderness, so must the Son of man be lifted up, 15 that whoever believes in him may have eternal life."[h]

16 For God so loved the world that he gave his only Son, that whoever believes in him should not perish but have eternal life. 17 For God sent the Son into the world, not to condemn the world, but that the world might be saved through him. 18 He who believes in him is not condemned; he who does not believe is condemned already, because he has not believed in the name of the only Son of God. 19 And this is the judgment, that the light has come into the world, and men loved darkness rather than light, because their deeds were evil. 20 For every one who does evil hates the light, and does not come to the light, lest his deeds should be exposed. 21 But he who does what is true comes to the light, that it may be clearly seen that his deeds have been wrought in God.

22 After this Jesus and his disciples went into the land of Judea; there he remained with them and baptized. 23 John also was baptizing at Aē'non near Sā'lim, because there was much water there; and people came and were baptized. 24 For John had not yet been put in prison.

25 Now a discussion arose between John's disciples and a Jew over purifying. 26 And they came to John, and said to him, "Rabbi, he who was with you beyond the Jordan, to whom you bore witness, here he is, baptizing, and all are going to him." 27 John answered, "No one can receive anything except what is given him from heaven. 28 You yourselves bear me witness, that I said, I am not the Christ, but I have been sent before him. 29 He who has the bride is the bridegroom; the friend of the bridegroom, who stands and hears him, rejoices greatly at the bridegroom's voice; therefore this joy

d Greek him   e Or from above   f The same Greek word means both wind and spirit
g Other ancient authorities add who is in heaven
h Some interpreters hold that the quotation continues through verse 21

2.21: 1 Cor 6.19; Jn 8.57.   **2.22:** Jn 12.16; 14.26.   **2.25:** Jn 1.47; 6.61; 13.11; Mk 2.8.
3.1: Jn 7.50; 19.39; Lk 23.13; Jn 7.26.   **3.2:** Jn 2.11; 7.31; 9.16; Acts 10.38.
3.3: Jn 1.13; 1 Pet 1.23; Jas 1.18; 1 Jn 3.9.   **3.5:** Ezek 36.25-27; Eph 5.26; Tit 3.5.
3.6: 1 Cor 15.50.   **3.8:** Ezek 37.9.   **3.11:** Jn 8.26; 1.18; 3.32.   **3.13:** Rom 10.6; Eph 4.9.
3.14: Num 21.9; Jn 8.28; 12.34.   **3.16:** Rom 5.8; 8.32; Eph 2.4; 1 Jn 4.9-10.
3.17: Jn 8.15; 12.47; Lk 19.10; 1 Jn 4.14.   **3.19:** Jn 1.4; 8.12; Eph 5.11, 13.
3.21: 1 Jn 1.6.   **3.22:** Jn 4.2.   **3.24:** Mk 1.14; 6.17-18.   **3.26:** Jn 1.7, 28.
3.27: 1 Cor 4.7.   **3.28:** Jn 1.20, 23.   **3.29:** Mk 2.19-20; Mt 25.1; Jn 15.11.

of mine is now full. 30 He must increase, but I must decrease."*i*

31 He who comes from above is above all; he who is of the earth belongs to the earth, and of the earth he speaks; he who comes from heaven is above all. 32 He bears witness to what he has seen and heard, yet no one receives his testimony; 33 he who receives his testimony sets his seal to this, that God is true. 34 For he whom God has sent utters the words of God, for it is not by measure that he gives the Spirit; 35 the Father loves the Son, and has given all things into his hand. 36 He who believes in the Son has eternal life; he who does not obey the Son shall not see life, but the wrath of God rests upon him.

4 Now when the Lord knew that the Pharisees had heard that Jesus was making and baptizing more disciples than John 2 (although Jesus himself did not baptize, but only his disciples), 3 he left Judea and departed again to Galilee. 4 He had to pass through Sà·mâr′i·à. 5 So he came to a city of Sà·mâr′i·à, called Sӯ′chär, near the field that Jacob gave to his son Joseph. 6 Jacob's well was there, and so Jesus, wearied as he was with his journey, sat down beside the well. It was about the sixth hour.

7 There came a woman of Sà·mâr′i·à to draw water. Jesus said to her, "Give me a drink." 8 For his disciples had gone away into the city to buy food. 9 The Samaritan woman said to him, "How is it that you, a Jew, ask a drink of me, a woman of Sà·mâr′i·à?" For Jews have no dealings with Samaritans. 10 Jesus answered her, "If you knew the gift of God, and who it is that is saying to you, 'Give me a drink,' you would have asked him and he would have given you living water." 11 The woman said to him, "Sir, you have nothing to draw with, and the well is deep; where do you get that living water? 12 Are you greater than our father Jacob, who gave us the well, and drank from it himself, and his sons, and his cattle?" 13 Jesus said to her, "Every one who drinks of this water will thirst again, 14 but whoever drinks of the water that I shall give him will never thirst; the water that I

shall give him will become in him a spring of water welling up to eternal life." 15 The woman said to him, "Sir, give me this water, that I may not thirst, nor come here to draw."

16 Jesus said to her, "Go, call your husband, and come here." 17 The woman answered him, "I have no husband." Jesus said to her, "You are right in saying, 'I have no husband'; 18 for you have had five husbands, and he whom you now have is not your husband; this you said truly." 19 The woman said to him, "Sir, I perceive that you are a prophet. 20 Our fathers worshiped on this mountain; and you say that in Jerusalem is the place where men ought to worship." 21 Jesus said to her, "Woman, believe me, the hour is coming when neither on this mountain nor in Jerusalem will you worship the Father. 22 You worship what you do not know; we worship what we know, for salvation is from the Jews. 23 But the hour is coming, and now is, when the true worshipers will worship the Father in spirit and truth, for such the Father seeks to worship him. 24 God is spirit, and those who worship him must worship in spirit and truth." 25 The woman said to him, "I know that Messiah is coming (he who is called Christ); when he comes, he will show us all things." 26 Jesus said to her, "I who speak to you am he."

27 Just then his disciples came. They marveled that he was talking with a woman, but none said, "What do you wish?" or, "Why are you talking with her?" 28 So the woman left her water jar, and went away into the city, and said to the people, 29 "Come, see a man who told me all that I ever did. Can this be the Christ?" 30 They went out of the city and were coming to him.

31 Meanwhile the disciples besought him, saying, "Rabbi, eat." 32 But he said to them, "I have food to eat of which you do not know." 33 So the disciples said to one another, "Has any one brought him food?" 34 Jesus said to them, "My food is to do the will of him who sent me, and to accomplish his work. 35 Do you not say, 'There are yet four months, then

i Some interpreters hold that the quotation continues through verse 36

3.31: Jn 3.13; 8.23; 1 Jn 4.5.   3.32: Jn 3.11.   3.36: Jn 3.16; 5.24.   4.1: Jn 3.22.
4.4: Lk 9.52; 17.11.   4.5: Gen 33.19; 48.22; Josh 24.32.
4.9: Mt 10.5; Jn 8.48; Ezra 4.3-6.   4.10: Jn 7.37; Rev 21.6; 22.17.   4.14: Jn 6.35; 7.38.
4.15: Jn 6.34.   4.18: 2 Kings 17.24; Hos 2.7.   4.20: Deut 11.29; Josh 8.33; Lk 9.53.
4.21: Jn 5.25; 16.2, 32; Mal 1.11.   4.22: 2 Kings 17.28-41; Is 2.3; Rom 9.4.
4.24: Phil 3.3.   4.26: Jn 8.24.   4.29: Jn 7.26; Mt 12.23.   4.32: Mt 4.4.
4.34: Jn 5.30; 6.38; 17.4.   4.35: Lk 10.2; Mt 9.37.

comes the harvest'? I tell you, lift up your eyes, and see how the fields are already white for harvest. 36 He who reaps receives wages, and gathers fruit for eternal life, so that sower and reaper may rejoice together. 37 For here the saying holds true, 'One sows and another reaps.' 38 I sent you to reap that for which you did not labor; others have labored, and you have entered into their labor."

39 Many Samaritans from that city believed in him because of the woman's testimony, "He told me all that I ever did." 40 So when the Samaritans came to him, they asked him to stay with them; and he stayed there two days. 41 And many more believed because of his word. 42 They said to the woman, "It is no longer because of your words that we believe, for we have heard for ourselves, and we know that this is indeed the Savior of the world."

43 After the two days he departed to Galilee. 44 For Jesus himself testified that a prophet has no honor in his own country. 45 So when he came to Galilee, the Galileans welcomed him, having seen all that he had done in Jerusalem at the feast, for they too had gone to the feast.

46 So he came again to Cāʹnà in Galilee, where he had made the water wine. And at Cà·pērʹnà-ùm there was an official whose son was ill. 47 When he heard that Jesus had come from Judea to Galilee, he went and begged him to come down and heal his son, for he was at the point of death. 48 Jesus therefore said to him, "Unless you see signs and wonders you will not believe." 49 The official said to him, "Sir, come down before my child dies." 50 Jesus said to him, "Go; your son will live." The man believed the word that Jesus spoke to him and went his way. 51 As he was going down, his servants met him and told him that his son was living. 52 So he asked them the hour when he began to mend, and they said to him, "Yesterday at the seventh hour the fever left him." 53 The father knew that was the hour

when Jesus had said to him, "Your son will live"; and he himself believed, and all his household. 54 This was now the second sign that Jesus did when he had come from Judea to Galilee.

5 After this there was a feast of the Jews, and Jesus went up to Jerusalem.

2 Now there is in Jerusalem by the Sheep Gate a pool, in Hebrew called Beth-zāʹthà,*j* which has five porticoes. 3 In these lay a multitude of invalids, blind, lame, paralyzed.*k* 5 One man was there, who had been ill for thirty-eight years. 6 When Jesus saw him and knew that he had been lying there a long time, he said to him, "Do you want to be healed?" 7 The sick man answered him, "Sir, I have no man to put me into the pool when the water is troubled, and while I am going another steps down before me." 8 Jesus said to him, "Rise, take up your pallet, and walk." 9 And at once the man was healed, and he took up his pallet and walked.

Now that day was the sabbath. 10 So the Jews said to the man who was cured, "It is the sabbath, it is not lawful for you to carry your pallet." 11 But he answered them, "The man who healed me said to me, 'Take up your pallet, and walk.'" 12 They asked him, "Who is the man who said to you, 'Take up your pallet, and walk'?" 13 Now the man who had been healed did not know who it was, for Jesus had withdrawn, as there was a crowd in the place. 14 Afterward, Jesus found him in the temple, and said to him, "See, you are well! Sin no more, that nothing worse befall you." 15 The man went away and told the Jews that it was Jesus who had healed him. 16 And this was why the Jews persecuted Jesus, because he did this on the sabbath. 17 But Jesus answered them, "My Father is working still, and I am working." 18 This was why the Jews sought all the more to kill him, because he not only broke the sabbath but also called God his Father, making himself equal with God.

---

j Other ancient authorities read *Bethesda*, others *Bethsaida*

k Other ancient authorities insert, wholly or in part, *waiting for the moving of the water;* 4 *for an angel of the Lord went down at certain seasons into the pool, and troubled the water: whoever stepped in first after the troubling of the water was healed of whatever disease he had*

4.37: Job 31.8; Mic 6.15.   **4.42:** 1 Jn 4.14; 2 Tim 1.10.   **4.44:** Mk 6.4; Mt 13.57.
4.46: Jn 2.1-11; Mt 8.5-10; Lk 7.2-10.
4.48: Dan 4.2; Mt 13.22; Acts 2.19; 4.30; Rom 15.19; Heb 2.4.   **4.53:** Acts 11.14.
4.54: Jn 2.11.   **5.2:** Neh 3.1; 12.39.   **5.8:** Mk 2.11; Mt 9.6; Lk 5.24.
5.10: Neh 13.19; Jer 17.21; Jn 7.23; 9.16; Mk 2.24.   **5.14:** Mk 2.5.   **5.17:** Gen 2.3.
5.18: Jn 7.1; 10.33.

19 Jesus said to them, "Truly, truly, I say to you, the Son can do nothing of his own accord, but only what he sees the Father doing; for whatever he does, that the Son does likewise. 20 For the Father loves the Son, and shows him all that he himself is doing; and greater works than these will he show him, that you may marvel. 21 For as the Father raises the dead and gives them life, so also the Son gives life to whom he will. 22 The Father judges no one, but has given all judgment to the Son, 23 that all may honor the Son, even as they honor the Father. He who does not honor the Son does not honor the Father who sent him. 24 Truly, truly, I say to you, he who hears my word and believes him who sent me, has eternal life; he does not come into judgment, but has passed from death to life.

25 "Truly, truly, I say to you, the hour is coming, and now is, when the dead will hear the voice of the Son of God, and those who hear will live. 26 For as the Father has life in himself, so he has granted the Son also to have life in himself, 27 and has given him authority to execute judgment, because he is the Son of man. 28 Do not marvel at this; for the hour is coming when all who are in the tombs will hear his voice 29 and come forth, those who have done good, to the resurrection of life, and those who have done evil, to the resurrection of judgment.

30 "I can do nothing on my own authority; as I hear, I judge; and my judgment is just, because I seek not my own will but the will of him who sent me. 31 If I bear witness to myself, my testimony is not true; 32 there is another who bears witness to me, and I know that the testimony which he bears to me is true. 33 You sent to John, and he has borne witness to the truth. 34 Not that the testimony which I receive is from man; but I say this that you may be saved. 35 He was a burning and shining lamp, and you were willing to rejoice for a while in his light. 36 But the testimony which I have is greater than that of John; for the works which the Father has granted me to accomplish, these very

works which I am doing, bear me witness that the Father has sent me. 37 And the Father who sent me has himself borne witness to me. His voice you have never heard, his form you have never seen; 38 and you do not have his word abiding in you, for you do not believe him whom he has sent. 39 You search the scriptures, because you think that in them you have eternal life; and it is they that bear witness to me; 40 yet you refuse to come to me that you may have life. 41 I do not receive glory from men. 42 But I know that you have not the love of God within you. 43 I have come in my Father's name, and you do not receive me; if another comes in his own name, him you will receive. 44 How can you believe, who receive glory from one another and do not seek the glory that comes from the only God? 45 Do not think that I shall accuse you to the Father; it is Moses who accuses you, on whom you set your hope. 46 If you believed Moses, you would believe me, for he wrote of me. 47 But if you do not believe his writings, how will you believe my words?"

6 After this Jesus went to the other side of the Sea of Galilee, which is the Sea of Ti-bē'ri-às. 2 And a multitude followed him, because they saw the signs which he did on those who were diseased. 3 Jesus went up into the hills, and there sat down with his disciples. 4 Now the Passover, the feast of the Jews, was at hand. 5 Lifting up his eyes, then, and seeing that a multitude was coming to him, Jesus said to Philip, "How are we to buy bread, so that these people may eat?" 6 This he said to test him, for he himself knew what he would do. 7 Philip answered him, "Two hundred denarii[l] would not buy enough bread for each of them to get a little." 8 One of his disciples, Andrew, Simon Peter's brother, said to him, 9 "There is a lad here who has five barley loaves and two fish; but what are they among so many?" 10 Jesus said, "Make the people sit down." Now there was much grass in the place; so the men sat down, in number about five thousand. 11 Jesus

---

5.19: Jn 5.30; 8.28; 14.10. **5.20:** Jn 14.12. **5.21:** Rom 4.17; 8.11; Jn 11.25.
5.23: Lk 10.16; 1 Jn 2.23. **5.24:** Jn 3.18. **5.25:** Jn 4.21; 16.2, 32.
5.29: Dan 12.2; Acts 24.15; Jn 11.24; Mt 25.46; 1 Cor 15.52. **5.30:** Jn 5.19; 8.16; 6.38.
5.31-37: Jn 8.14-18. **5.33:** Jn 1.7, 19. **5.34:** 1 Jn 5.9.
5.36: Jn 10.25; 14.11; 15.24; Mt 11.4. **5.39:** Lk 24.27; Acts 13.27. **5.43:** Mt 24.5.
5.45: Jn 9.28; Rom 2.17. **5.47:** Lk 16.29, 31.
6.1-13: Mt 14.13-21; Mk 6.32-44; Lk 9.10-17. **6.5:** Jn 1.43; 12.21.
6.8: Jn 1.40; 12.22. **6.9:** Jn 21.9-13.

then took the loaves, and when he had given thanks, he distributed them to those who were seated; so also the fish, as much as they wanted. 12And when they had eaten their fill, he told his disciples, "Gather up the fragments left over, that nothing may be lost." 13 So they gathered them up and filled twelve baskets with fragments from the five barley loaves, left by those who had eaten. 14 When the people saw the sign which he had done, they said, "This is indeed the prophet who is to come into the world!"

15 Perceiving then that they were about to come and take him by force to make him king, Jesus withdrew again to the hills by himself.

16 When evening came, his disciples went down to the sea, 17 got into a boat, and started across the sea to Cȧ·pẽr'nȧ-ŭm. It was now dark, and Jesus had not yet come to them. 18 The sea rose because a strong wind was blowing. 19 When they had rowed about three or four miles,*m* they saw Jesus walking on the sea and drawing near to the boat. They were frightened, 20 but he said to them, "It is I; do not be afraid." 21 Then they were glad to take him into the boat, and immediately the boat was at the land to which they were going.

22 On the next day the people who remained on the other side of the sea saw that there had been only one boat there, and that Jesus had not entered the boat with his disciples, but that his disciples had gone away alone. 23 However, boats from Ti·bē'ri-ȧs came near the place where they ate the bread after the Lord had given thanks. 24 So when the people saw that Jesus was not there, nor his disciples, they themselves got into the boats and went to Cȧ·pẽr'nȧ-ŭm, seeking Jesus.

25 When they found him on the other side of the sea, they said to him, "Rabbi, when did you come here?" 26 Jesus answered them, "Truly, truly, I say to you, you seek me, not because you saw signs, but because you ate your fill of the loaves. 27 Do not labor for the food which perishes, but for the food which endures to eternal life, which the Son of man will give to you; for on him has God the Father set his seal." 28 Then they said to him, "What must we do, to be doing the works of God?" 29 Jesus answered them, "This is the work of God, that you believe in him whom he has sent." 30 So they said to him, "Then what sign do you do, that we may see, and believe you? What work do you perform? 31 Our fathers ate the manna in the wilderness; as it is written, 'He gave them bread from heaven to eat.'" 32 Jesus then said to them, "Truly, truly, I say to you, it was not Moses who gave you the bread from heaven; my Father gives you the true bread from heaven. 33 For the bread of God is that which comes down from heaven, and gives life to the world." 34 They said to him, "Lord, give us this bread always."

35 Jesus said to them, "I am the bread of life; he who comes to me shall not hunger, and he who believes in me shall never thirst. 36 But I said to you that you have seen me and yet do not believe. 37 All that the Father gives me will come to me; and him who comes to me I will not cast out. 38 For I have come down from heaven, not to do my own will, but the will of him who sent me; 39 and this is the will of him who sent me, that I should lose none of all that he has given me, but raise it up at the last day. 40 For this is the will of my Father, that every one who sees the Son and believes in him should have eternal life; and I will raise him up at the last day."

41 The Jews then murmured at him, because he said, "I am the bread which came down from heaven." 42 They said, "Is not this Jesus, the son of Joseph, whose father and mother we know? How does he now say, 'I have come down from heaven'?" 43 Jesus answered them, "Do not murmur among yourselves. 44 No one can come to me unless the Father who sent me draws him; and I will raise him up at the last day. 45 It is written in the prophets, 'And they shall all be taught by God.' Every one who has heard and learned from the Father comes to me. 46 Not that any one has seen the Father except him who is from God; he has seen the Father. 47 Truly, truly, I say to you, he who believes has

m Greek *twenty-five or thirty stadia*

6.14: Mt 21.11.　**6.15:** Jn 6.3; 18.36.　**6.16-21:** Mt 14.22-27; Mk 6.45-51.
6.27: Is 55.2.　**6.29:** 1 Thess 1.3; 1 Jn 3.23.　**6.30:** Mt 12.38; Mk 8.11.
6.31: Ex 16.4, 15; Num 11.8; Neh 9.15; Ps 78.24; 105.40.　**6.34:** Jn 4.15; Mt 6.11.
6.35: Jn 6.48-50; 4.14.　**6.37:** Jn 17.2.　**6.38:** Jn 4.34; 5.30.　**6.39:** Jn 17.12; 18.9.
6.40: Jn 5.29; 11.24; 6.54.　**6.42:** Lk 4.22; Jn 7.27.
6.44: Jer 31.3; Hos 11.4; Jn 12.32; 6.65.　**6.45:** 1 Thess 4.9; 1 Jn 2.27; Is 54.13.
6.46: Jn 1.18.

eternal life. 48 I am the bread of life. 49 Your fathers ate the manna in the wilderness, and they died. 50 This is the bread which comes down from heaven, that a man may eat of it and not die. 51 I am the living bread which came down from heaven; if any one eats of this bread, he will live for ever; and the bread which I shall give for the life of the world is my flesh."

52 The Jews then disputed among themselves, saying, "How can this man give us his flesh to eat?" 53 So Jesus said to them, "Truly, truly, I say to you, unless you eat the flesh of the Son of man and drink his blood, you have no life in you; 54 he who eats my flesh and drinks my blood has eternal life, and I will raise him up at the last day. 55 For my flesh is food indeed, and my blood is drink indeed. 56 He who eats my flesh and drinks my blood abides in me, and I in him. 57 As the living Father sent me, and I live because of the Father, so he who eats me will live because of me. 58 This is the bread which came down from heaven, not such as the fathers ate and died; he who eats this bread will live for ever." 59 This he said in the synagogue, as he taught at Cà·pẽr′nà·ùm.

60 Many of his disciples, when they heard it, said, "This is a hard saying; who can listen to it?" 61 But Jesus, knowing in himself that his disciples murmured at it, said to them, "Do you take offense at this? 62 Then what if you were to see the Son of man ascending where he was before? 63 It is the spirit that gives life, the flesh is of no avail; the words that I have spoken to you are spirit and life. 64 But there are some of you that do not believe." For Jesus knew from the first who those were that did not believe, and who it was that should betray him. 65 And he said, "This is why I told you that no one can come to me unless it is granted him by the Father."

66 After this many of his disciples drew back and no longer went about with him. 67 Jesus said to the twelve, "Will you also go away?" 68 Simon Peter answered him, "Lord, to whom shall we go? You have the words of eternal life; 69 and we have believed, and have come to know, that you are the Holy One of God." 70 Jesus an-

swered them, "Did I not choose you, the twelve, and one of you is a devil?" 71 He spoke of Judas the son of Simon Is·car′i·ŏt, for he, one of the twelve, was to betray him.

7 After this Jesus went about in Galilee; he would not go about in Judea, because the Jews*n* sought to kill him. 2 Now the Jews' feast of Tabernacles was at hand. 3 So his brothers said to him, "Leave here and go to Judea, that your disciples may see the works you are doing. 4 For no man works in secret if he seeks to be known openly. If you do these things, show yourself to the world." 5 For even his brothers did not believe in him. 6 Jesus said to them, "My time has not yet come, but your time is always here. 7 The world cannot hate you, but it hates me because I testify of it that its works are evil. 8 Go to the feast yourselves; I am not*o* going up to this feast, for my time has not yet fully come." 9 So saying, he remained in Galilee.

10 But after his brothers had gone up to the feast, then he also went up, not publicly, but in private. 11 The Jews were looking for him at the feast, and saying, "Where is he?" 12 And there was much muttering about him among the people. While some said, "He is a good man," others said, "No, he is leading the people astray." 13 Yet for fear of the Jews no one spoke openly of him.

14 About the middle of the feast Jesus went up into the temple and taught. 15 The Jews marveled at it, saying, "How is it that this man has learning,*p* when he has never studied?" 16 So Jesus answered them, "My teaching is not mine, but his who sent me; 17 if any man's will is to do his will, he shall know whether the teaching is from God or whether I am speaking on my own authority. 18 He who speaks on his own authority seeks his own glory; but he who seeks the glory of him who sent him is true, and in him there is no falsehood. 19 Did not Moses give you the law? Yet none of you keeps the law. Why do you seek to kill me?" 20 The people answered, "You have a demon! Who is seeking to kill you?" 21 Jesus answered them,

n Or *Judeans*   *o* Other ancient authorities add *yet*   *p* Or *this man knows his letters*
6.52: Jn 3.4; 4.9.   **6.56:** Jn 15.4; 1 Jn 3.24; 4.15.   **6.58:** Jn 6.41, 51.   **6.59:** Jn 6.25.
6.61: Mt 11.6.   **6.62:** Jn 3.13; 17.5.   **6.63:** 2 Cor 3.6; Jn 6.68.   **6.64:** Jn 2.25.
6.65: Jn 6.44; 3.27.   **6.68-69:** Mk 8.27-30.   **6.70:** Jn 15.16, 19.
6.71: Jn 13.2, 27; 17.12.   **7.2:** Lev 23.34; Deut 16.16.   **7.3:** Mk 3.21, 31; Mt 12.46.
7.6: Mt 26.18; Jn 2.4; 7.30.   **7.7:** Jn 15.18-21.   **7.12:** Jn 7.40-43.   **7.13:** Jn 19.38; 20.19.
7.19: Jn 1.17.   **7.20:** Jn 8.48; 10.20; Mt 11.18; Mk 3.22.   **7.21:** Jn 5.2-9.

"I did one deed, and you all marvel at it. 22Moses gave you circumcision (not that it is from Moses, but from the fathers), and you circumcise a man upon the sabbath. 23If on the sabbath a man receives circumcision, so that the law of Moses may not be broken, are you angry with me because on the sabbath I made a man's whole body well? 24Do not judge by appearances, but judge with right judgment."

25 Some of the people of Jerusalem therefore said, "Is not this the man whom they seek to kill? 26And here he is, speaking openly, and they say nothing to him! Can it be that the authorities really know that this is the Christ? 27 Yet we know where this man comes from; and when the Christ appears, no one will know where he comes from." 28 So Jesus proclaimed, as he taught in the temple, "You know me, and you know where I come from? But I have not come of my own accord; he who sent me is true, and him you do not know. 29I know him, for I come from him, and he sent me." 30 So they sought to arrest him; but no one laid hands on him, because his hour had not yet come. 31 Yet many of the people believed in him; they said, "When the Christ appears, will he do more signs than this man has done?"

32 The Pharisees heard the crowd thus muttering about him, and the chief priests and Pharisees sent officers to arrest him. 33 Jesus then said, "I shall be with you a little longer, and then I go to him who sent me; 34you will seek me and you will not find me; where I am you cannot come." 35 The Jews said to one another, "Where does this man intend to go that we shall not find him? Does he intend to go to the Dispersion among the Greeks and teach the Greeks? 36 What does he mean by saying, 'You will seek me and you will not find me,' and, 'Where I am you cannot come'?"

37 On the last day of the feast, the great day, Jesus stood up and proclaimed, "If any one thirst, let him come to me and drink. 38He who believes in me, as *q* the scripture has said, 'Out of his heart shall flow rivers of living water.'" 39 Now this he said about the Spirit, which those who believed in him were to receive; for as yet the Spirit had not been given, because Jesus was not yet glorified.

40 When they heard these words, some of the people said, "This is really the prophet." 41 Others said, "This is the Christ." But some said, "Is the Christ to come from Galilee? 42 Has not the scripture said that the Christ is descended from David, and comes from Bethlehem, the village where David was?" 43 So there was a division among the people over him. 44 Some of them wanted to arrest him, but no one laid hands on him.

45 The officers then went back to the chief priests and Pharisees, who said to them, "Why did you not bring him?" 46 The officers answered, "No man ever spoke like this man!" 47 The Pharisees answered them, "Are you led astray, you also? 48 Have any of the authorities or of the Pharisees believed in him? 49 But this crowd, who do not know the law, are accursed." 50 Nic-ŏ-dē'mŭs, who had gone to him before, and who was one of them, said to them, 51 "Does our law judge a man without first giving him a hearing and learning what he does?" 52 They replied, "Are you from Galilee too? Search and you will see that no prophet is to rise from Galilee."*r*

q Or *let him come to me, and let him who believes in me drink. As*
r Other ancient authorities add 7.53-8.11 either here or at the end of this gospel or after
     Luke 21.38, with variations of the text:

8 53 *They went each to his own house,* 1 *but Jesus went to the Mount of Olives.* 2 *Early in the morning he came again to the temple; all the people came to him, and he sat down and taught them.* 3 *The scribes and the Pharisees brought a woman who had been caught in adultery, and placing her in the midst* 4 *they said to him, "Teacher, this woman has been caught in the act of adultery.* 5 *Now in the law Moses commanded us to stone such. What do you say about her?"* 6 *This they said to test him, that they might have some charge to bring against him. Jesus bent down and wrote with his finger on the ground.* 7 *And as they continued to ask him, he stood up and said to them, "Let him who is without sin among*

7.22: Lev 12.3; Gen 17.10; 21.4.   7.23: Mk 3.5; Lk 13.12; 14.4.
7.24: Jn 8.15; Is 11.3; Zech 7.9.   7.27: Jn 6.42; 7.41; 9.29.   7.28: Jn 8.42.
7.29: Jn 8.55; 17.25; Mt 11.27.   7.30: Jn 7.44; 10.39; Mk 12.12; Jn 8.20.
7.31: Jn 8.30; 10.42; 11.45.   7.33: Jn 8.21; 12.35; 13.33; 14.19; 16.16-19.
7.35: Jas 1.1; 1 Pet 1.1; Jn 12.20; Acts 11.20.   7.37: Lev 23.36; Jn 4.10, 14.
7.38: Is 44.3; 55.1; 58.11.   7.39: Jn 20.22; 12.23.   7.40: Jn 1.21; Mt 21.11.
7.42: Mic 5.2; Mt 1.1; Lk 2.4.   7.44: Jn 7.30; 10.39.   7.46: Mt 7.28.
7.50: Jn 3.1; 19.39.   7.51: Deut 17.6; Ex 23.1.   7.52: 2 Kings 14.25.

8 [12]Again Jesus spoke to them saying, "I am the light of the world; he who follows me will not walk in darkness, but will have the light of life." [13] The Pharisees then said to him, "You are bearing witness to yourself; your testimony is not true." [14] Jesus answered, "Even if I do bear witness to myself, my testimony is true, for I know whence I have come and whither I am going, but you do not know whence I come or whither I am going. [15] You judge according to the flesh, I judge no one. [16] Yet even if I do judge, my judgment is true, for it is not I alone that judge, but I and he[s] who sent me. [17] In your law it is written that the testimony of two men is true; [18] I bear witness to myself, and the Father who sent me bears witness to me." [19] They said to him therefore, "Where is your Father?" Jesus answered, "You know neither me nor my Father; if you knew me, you would know my Father also." [20] These words he spoke in the treasury, as he taught in the temple; but no one arrested him, because his hour had not yet come.

[21] Again he said to them, "I go away, and you will seek me and die in your sin; where I am going, you cannot come." [22] Then said the Jews, "Will he kill himself, since he says, 'Where I am going, you cannot come'?" [23] He said to them, "You are from below, I am from above; you are of this world, I am not of this world. [24] I told you that you would die in your sins, for you will die in your sins unless you believe that I am he." [25] They said to him, "Who are you?" Jesus said to them, "Even what I have told you from the beginning.[t] [26] I have much to say about you and much to judge; but he who sent me is true, and I declare to the world what I have heard from him." [27] They did not understand that he spoke to them of the Father. [28] So Jesus said, "When you have lifted up the Son of man, then you will know that I am he, and that

I do nothing on my own authority but speak thus as the Father taught me. [29]And he who sent me is with me; he has not left me alone, for I always do what is pleasing to him." [30]As he spoke thus, many believed in him.

[31] Jesus then said to the Jews who had believed in him, "If you continue in my word, you are truly my disciples, [32] and you will know the truth, and the truth will make you free." [33] They answered him, "We are descendants of Abraham, and have never been in bondage to any one. How is it that you say, 'You will be made free'?"

[34] Jesus answered them, "Truly, truly, I say to you, every one who commits sin is a slave to sin. [35] The slave does not continue in the house for ever; the son continues for ever. [36] So if the Son makes you free, you will be free indeed. [37] I know that you are descendants of Abraham; yet you seek to kill me, because my word finds no place in you. [38] I speak of what I have seen with my Father, and you do what you have heard from your father."

[39] They answered him, "Abraham is our father." Jesus said to them, "If you were Abraham's children, you would do what Abraham did, [40] but now you seek to kill me, a man who has told you the truth which I heard from God; this is not what Abraham did. [41] You do what your father did." They said to him, "We were not born of fornication; we have one Father, even God." [42] Jesus said to them, "If God were your Father, you would love me, for I proceeded and came forth from God; I came not of my own accord, but he sent me. [43] Why do you not understand what I say? It is because you cannot bear to hear my word. [44] You are of your father the devil, and your will is to do your father's desires. He was a murderer from the beginning, and has nothing to do with the truth, because there is no truth in him. When he lies, he

you be the first to throw a stone at her." [8]*And once more he bent down and wrote with his finger on the ground.* [9] *But when they heard it, they went away, one by one, beginning with the eldest, and Jesus was left alone with the woman standing before him.* [10] *Jesus looked up and said to her, "Woman, where are they? Has no one condemned you?"* [11] *She said, "No one, Lord." And Jesus said, "Neither do I condemn you; go, and do not sin again."*

[s] Other ancient authorities read *the Father*   [t] Or *Why do I talk to you at all?*

8.12: Jn 9.5; 12.35; 1.4.   **8.13-18:** Jn 5.31-39.   **8.15:** Jn 7.24; 3.17.   **8.16:** Jn 5.30.
8.17: Deut 19.15; Mt 18.16.   **8.19:** Jn 14.7.   **8.20:** Mk 12.41; Jn 7.30.
8.21-22: Jn 7.33-36.   **8.23:** Jn 3.31; 17.14; 1 Jn 4.5.
8.24: Jn 8.28; 4.26; 13.19; Mk 13.6.   **8.28:** Jn 3.14; 12.32.   **8.30:** Jn 7.31; 10.42; 11.45.
8.31: Jn 15.7; Jn 9.   **8.32:** 2 Cor 3.17; Gal 5.1.   **8.33:** Mt 3.9; Gal 3.7.
8.34: Rom 6.16; 2 Pet 2.19.   **8.35:** Gen 21.10; Gal 4.30.
8.41: Deut 32.6; Is 63.16; 64.8.   **8.42:** Jn 13.3; 16.28.
8.44: 1 Jn 3.8, 15; Gen 3.4; 1 Jn 2.4; Mt 12.34.

speaks according to his own nature, for he is a liar and the father of lies. 45 But, because I tell the truth, you do not believe me. 46 Which of you convicts me of sin? If I tell the truth, why do you not believe me? 47 He who is of God hears the words of God; the reason why you do not hear them is that you are not of God."

48 The Jews answered him, "Are we not right in saying that you are a Samaritan and have a demon?" 49 Jesus answered, "I have not a demon; but I honor my Father, and you dishonor me. 50 Yet I do not seek my own glory; there is One who seeks it and he will be the judge. 51 Truly, truly, I say to you, if any one keeps my word, he will never see death." 52 The Jews said to him, "Now we know that you have a demon. Abraham died, as did the prophets; and you say, 'If any one keeps my word, he will never taste death.' 53 Are you greater than our father Abraham, who died? And the prophets died! Who do you claim to be?" 54 Jesus answered, "If I glorify myself, my glory is nothing; it is my Father who glorifies me, of whom you say that he is your God. 55 But you have not known him; I know him. If I said, I do not know him, I should be a liar like you; but I do know him and I keep his word. 56 Your father Abraham rejoiced that he was to see my day; he saw it and was glad." 57 The Jews then said to him, "You are not yet fifty years old, and have you seen Abraham?"[u] 58 Jesus said to them, "Truly, truly, I say to you, before Abraham was, I am." 59 So they took up stones to throw at him; but Jesus hid himself, and went out of the temple.

9 As he passed by, he saw a man blind from his birth. 2 And his disciples asked him, "Rabbi, who sinned, this man or his parents, that he was born blind?" 3 Jesus answered, "It was not that this man sinned, or his parents, but that the works of God might be made manifest in him. 4 We must work the works of him who sent me, while it is day; night comes, when no one can work. 5 As long as I am in the world, I am the light of the world." 6 As he said this, he spat on the ground and made clay of the spittle and anointed the man's eyes with the clay,

7 saying to him, "Go, wash in the pool of Si-lō′am" (which means Sent). So he went and washed and came back seeing. 8 The neighbors and those who had seen him before as a beggar, said, "Is not this the man who used to sit and beg?" 9 Some said, "It is he"; others said, "No, but he is like him." He said, "I am the man." 10 They said to him, "Then how were your eyes opened?" 11 He answered, "The man called Jesus made clay and anointed my eyes and said to me, 'Go to Si-lō′am and wash'; so I went and washed and received my sight." 12 They said to him, "Where is he?" He said, "I do not know."

13 They brought to the Pharisees the man who had formerly been blind. 14 Now it was a sabbath day when Jesus made the clay and opened his eyes. 15 The Pharisees again asked him how he had received his sight. And he said to them, "He put clay on my eyes, and I washed, and I see." 16 Some of the Pharisees said, "This man is not from God, for he does not keep the sabbath." But others said, "How can a man who is a sinner do such signs?" There was a division among them. 17 So they again said to the blind man, "What do you say about him, since he has opened your eyes?" He said, "He is a prophet."

18 The Jews did not believe that he had been blind and had received his sight, until they called the parents of the man who had received his sight, 19 and asked them, "Is this your son, who you say was born blind? How then does he now see?" 20 His parents answered, "We know that this is our son, and that he was born blind; 21 but how he now sees we do not know, nor do we know who opened his eyes. Ask him; he is of age, he will speak for himself." 22 His parents said this because they feared the Jews, for the Jews had already agreed that if any one should confess him to be Christ, he was to be put out of the synagogue. 23 Therefore his parents said, "He is of age, ask him."

24 So for the second time they called the man who had been blind, and said to him, "Give God the praise; we know that this man is a sinner." 25 He answered, "Whether he is a sinner, I do not know; one thing I

8.46: 1 Jn 3.5; Jn 18.37.   **8.48:** Jn 7.20; 10.20; 4.9.   **8.53:** Jn 4.12.
8.56: Mt 13.17; Heb 11.13.   **8.57:** Jn 2.20.   **8.58:** Jn 1.1; 17.5, 24.
8.59: Jn 10.31; 11.8.   **9.2:** Lk 13.2; Acts 28.4; Ezek 18.20; Ex 20.5.   **9.3:** Jn 11.4.
9.4: Jn 11.9; 12.35.   **9.5:** Jn 1.4; 8.12; 12.46.   **9.6:** Mk 7.33; 8.23.   **9.7:** Lk 13.4.
9.16: Mt 12.2; Jn 5.9; 7.43; 10.19.   **9.22:** Jn 7.13; 12.42; Lk 6.22.

know, that though I was blind, now I see." 26 They said to him, "What did he do to you? How did he open your eyes?" 27 He answered them, "I have told you already, and you would not listen. Why do you want to hear it again? Do you too want to become his disciples?" 28And they reviled him, saying, "You are his disciple, but we are disciples of Moses. 29 We know that God has spoken to Moses, but as for this man, we do not know where he comes from." 30 The man answered, "Why, this is a marvel! You do not know where he comes from, and yet he opened my eyes. 31 We know that God does not listen to sinners, but if any one is a worshiper of God and does his will, God listens to him. 32 Never since the world began has it been heard that any one opened the eyes of a man born blind. 33 If this man were not from God, he could do nothing." 34 They answered him, "You were born in utter sin, and would you teach us?" And they cast him out.

35 Jesus heard that they had cast him out, and having found him he said, "Do you believe in the Son of man?"*v* 36 He answered, "And who is he, sir, that I may believe in him?" 37 Jesus said to him, "You have seen him, and it is he who speaks to you." 38 He said, "Lord, I believe"; and he worshiped him. 39 Jesus said, "For judgment I came into this world, that those who do not see may see, and that those who see may become blind." 40 Some of the Pharisees near him heard this, and they said to him, "Are we also blind?" 41 Jesus said to them, "If you were blind, you would have no guilt; but now that you say, 'We see,' your guilt remains.

10 "Truly, truly, I say to you, he who does not enter the sheepfold by the door but climbs in by another way, that man is a thief and a robber; 2 but he who enters by the door is the shepherd of the sheep. 3 To him the gatekeeper opens; the sheep hear his voice, and he calls his own sheep by name and leads them out. 4 When he has brought out all his own, he goes before them, and the sheep follow him, for they know his voice. 5A stranger they will not follow, but they will flee

from him, for they do not know the voice of strangers." 6 This figure Jesus used with them, but they did not understand what he was saying to them.

7 So Jesus again said to them, "Truly, truly, I say to you, I am the door of the sheep. 8All who came before me are thieves and robbers; but the sheep did not heed them. 9 I am the door; if any one enters by me, he will be saved, and will go in and out and find pasture. 10 The thief comes only to steal and kill and destroy; I came that they may have life, and have it abundantly. 11 I am the good shepherd. The good shepherd lays down his life for the sheep. 12 He who is a hireling and not a shepherd, whose own the sheep are not, sees the wolf coming and leaves the sheep and flees; and the wolf snatches them and scatters them. 13 He flees because he is a hireling and cares nothing for the sheep. 14 I am the good shepherd; I know my own and my own know me, 15 as the Father knows me and I know the Father; and I lay down my life for the sheep. 16And I have other sheep, that are not of this fold; I must bring them also, and they will heed my voice. So there shall be one flock, one shepherd. 17 For this reason the Father loves me, because I lay down my life, that I may take it again. 18 No one takes it from me, but I lay it down of my own accord. I have power to lay it down, and I have power to take it again; this charge I have received from my Father."

19 There was again a division among the Jews because of these words. 20 Many of them said, "He has a demon, and he is mad; why listen to him?" 21 Others said, "These are not the sayings of one who has a demon. Can a demon open the eyes of the blind?"

22 It was the feast of the Dedication at Jerusalem; 23 it was winter, and Jesus was walking in the temple, in the portico of Solomon. 24 So the Jews gathered round him and said to him, "How long will you keep us in suspense? If you are the Christ, tell us plainly." 25 Jesus answered them, "I told you, and you do not believe. The works that I do in my Father's name,

v Other ancient authorities read *the Son of God*
9.28: Jn 5.45. **9.38:** Mt 28.9. **9.39:** Jn 5.27; 3.19; Mt 15.14. **9.41:** Jn 15.22.
10.2: Mk 6.34. **10.6:** Jn 16.25. **10.8:** Jer 23.1; Ezek 34.2.
10.11: Is 40.11; Ezek 34.11-16; Heb 13.20; 1 Pet 5.4; Rev 7.17; 1 Jn 3.16; Jn 15.13.
10.15: Mt 11.27. **10.16:** Is 56.8; Jn 11.52; 17.20; Eph 2.13-18; 1 Pet 2.25.
10.18: Jn 14.31; 15.10; Phil 2.8; Heb 5.8. **10.19:** Jn 7.43; 9.16.
10.20: Jn 7.20; 8.48; Mt 11.18. **10.21:** Jn 9.32; Ex 4.11. **10.23:** Acts 3.11; 5.12.
10.25: Jn 5.36; 10.38.

they bear witness to me; 26 but you do not believe, because you do not belong to my sheep. 27 My sheep hear my voice, and I know them, and they follow me; 28 and I give them eternal life, and they shall never perish, and no one shall snatch them out of my hand. 29 My Father, who has given them to me,*w* is greater than all, and no one is able to snatch them out of the Father's hand. 30 I and the Father are one."

31 The Jews took up stones again to stone him. 32 Jesus answered them, "I have shown you many good works from the Father; for which of these do you stone me?" 33 The Jews answered him, "We stone you for no good work but for blasphemy; because you, being a man, make yourself God." 34 Jesus answered them, "Is it not written in your law, 'I said, you are gods'? 35 If he called them gods to whom the word of God came (and scripture cannot be broken), 36 do you say of him whom the Father consecrated and sent into the world, 'You are blaspheming,' because I said, I am the Son of God'? 37 If I am not doing the works of my Father, then do not believe me; 38 but if I do them, even though you do not believe me, believe the works, that you may know and understand that the Father is in me and I am in the Father." 39 Again they tried to arrest him, but he escaped from their hands.

40 He went away again across the Jordan to the place where John at first baptized, and there he remained. 41 And many came to him; and they said, "John did no sign, but everything that John said about this man was true." 42 And many believed in him there.

11 Now a certain man was ill, Laz′a·rus of Beth′a·ny, the village of Mary and her sister Martha. 2 It was Mary who anointed the Lord with ointment and wiped his feet with her hair, whose brother Laz′a·rus was ill. 3 So the sisters sent to him, saying, "Lord, he whom you love is ill." 4 But when Jesus heard it he said, "This illness is not unto death; it is for the glory of God, so that the Son of God may be glorified by means of it."

5 Now Jesus loved Martha and her sister and Laz′a·rus. 6 So when he heard that he was ill, he stayed two days longer in the place where he was. 7 Then after this he said to the disciples, "Let us go into Judea again." 8 The disciples said to him, "Rabbi, the Jews were but now seeking to stone you, and are you going there again?" 9 Jesus answered, "Are there not twelve hours in the day? If any one walks in the day, he does not stumble, because he sees the light of this world. 10 But if any one walks in the night, he stumbles, because the light is not in him." 11 Thus he spoke, and then he said to them, "Our friend Laz′a·rus has fallen asleep, but I go to awake him out of sleep." 12 The disciples said to him, "Lord, if he has fallen asleep, he will recover." 13 Now Jesus had spoken of his death, but they thought that he meant taking rest in sleep. 14 Then Jesus told them plainly, "Laz′a·rus is dead; 15 and for your sake I am glad that I was not there, so that you may believe. But let us go to him." 16 Thomas, called the Twin, said to his fellow disciples, "Let us also go, that we may die with him."

17 Now when Jesus came, he found that Laz′a·rus*x* had already been in the tomb four days. 18 Beth′a·ny was near Jerusalem, about two miles*y* off, 19 and many of the Jews had come to Martha and Mary to console them concerning their brother. 20 When Martha heard that Jesus was coming, she went and met him, while Mary sat in the house. 21 Martha said to Jesus, "Lord, if you had been here, my brother would not have died. 22 And even now I know that whatever you ask from God, God will give you." 23 Jesus said to her, "Your brother will rise again." 24 Martha said to him, "I know that he will rise again in the resurrection at the last day." 25 Jesus said to her, "I am the resurrection and the life;*z* he who believes in me, though he die, yet shall he live, 26 and whoever lives and believes in me shall never die. Do you believe this?" 27 She said to him, "Yes, Lord; I believe that you are the Christ, the Son of God, he who is coming into the world."

w Other ancient authorities read *What my Father has given to me*   *x* Greek *he*   *y* Greek *fifteen stadia*   *z* Other ancient authorities omit *and the life*
10.26: Jn 8.47.   10.28: Jn 17.2; 1 Jn 2.25.   10.30: Jn 17.21.   10.31: Jn 8.59; 11.8.
10.33: Lev 24.16; Mk 14.64.   10.34: Jn 8.17; Ps 82.6.   10.39: Jn 7.30; 8.59; Lk 4.30.
10.40: Jn 1.28.   10.42: Jn 7.31; 11.45.   11.1: Mk 11.1; Lk 10.38.
11.2: Jn 12.3; Lk 7.38; Mk 14.3.   11.4: Jn 9.3.   11.8: Jn 8.59; 10.31.
11.9: Jn 9.4; 12.35; Lk 13.33.   11.11: Mk 5.39; Acts 7.60.   11.16: Mt 10.3; Jn 20.24-28.
11.19: Job 2.11.   11.24: Dan 12.2; Jn 5.28; Acts 24.15.   11.25: Jn 1.4; 5.26; Rev 1.18.
11.26: Jn 6.47; 8.51.   11.27: Mt 16.16.

28 When she had said this, she went and called her sister Mary, saying quietly, "The Teacher is here and is calling for you." 29And when she heard it, she rose quickly and went to him. 30 Now Jesus had not yet come to the village, but was still in the place where Martha had met him. 31 When the Jews who were with her in the house, consoling her, saw Mary rise quickly and go out, they followed her, supposing that she was going to the tomb to weep there. 32 Then Mary, when she came where Jesus was and saw him, fell at his feet, saying to him, "Lord, if you had been here, my brother would not have died." 33 When Jesus saw her weeping, and the Jews who came with her also weeping, he was deeply moved in spirit and troubled; 34 and he said, "Where have you laid him?" They said to him, "Lord, come and see." 35 Jesus wept. 36 So the Jews said, "See how he loved him!" 37 But some of them said, "Could not he who opened the eyes of the blind man have kept this man from dying?"

38 Then Jesus, deeply moved again, came to the tomb; it was a cave, and a stone lay upon it. 39 Jesus said, "Take away the stone." Martha, the sister of the dead man, said to him, "Lord, by this time there will be an odor, for he has been dead four days." 40 Jesus said to her, "Did I not tell you that if you would believe you would see the glory of God?" 41 So they took away the stone. And Jesus lifted up his eyes and said, "Father, I thank thee that thou hast heard me. 42 I knew that thou hearest me always, but I have said this on account of the people standing by, that they may believe that thou didst send me." 43 When he had said this, he cried with a loud voice, "Laz'a·rus, come out." 44 The dead man came out, his hands and feet bound with bandages, and his face wrapped with a cloth. Jesus said to them, "Unbind him, and let him go."

45 Many of the Jews therefore, who had come with Mary and had seen what he did, believed in him; 46 but some of them went to the Pharisees and told them what Jesus had done. 47 So the chief priests and the Pharisees gathered the council, and said, "What are we to do? For this man performs many signs. 48 If we let him go on thus, every one will believe in him, and the Romans will come and destroy both our holy place*a* and our nation." 49 But one of them, Cā'ià·phàs, who was high priest that year, said to them, "You know nothing at all; 50 you do not understand that it is expedient for you that one man should die for the people, and that the whole nation should not perish." 51 He did not say this of his own accord, but being high priest that year he prophesied that Jesus should die for the nation, 52 and not for the nation only, but to gather into one the children of God who are scattered abroad. 53 So from that day on they took counsel how to put him to death.

54 Jesus therefore no longer went about openly among the Jews, but went from there to the country near the wilderness, to a town called E'phra·im; and there he stayed with the disciples. 55 Now the Passover of the Jews was at hand, and many went up from the country to Jerusalem before the Passover, to purify themselves. 56 They were looking for Jesus and saying to one another as they stood in the temple, "What do you think? That he will not come to the feast?" 57 Now the chief priests and the Pharisees had given orders that if any one knew where he was, he should let them know, so that they might arrest him.

12 Six days before the Passover, Jesus came to Beth'a·ny, where Laz'a·rus was, whom Jesus had raised from the dead. 2 There they made him a supper; Martha served, and Laz'a·rus was one of those at table with him. 3 Mary took a pound of costly ointment of pure nard and anointed the feet of Jesus and wiped his feet with her hair; and the house was filled with the fragrance of the ointment. 4 But Judas Is·car'i·ŏt, one of his disciples (he who was to betray him), said, 5 "Why was this ointment not sold for three hundred denarii*b* and given to the poor?" 6 This he said, not that he cared for the poor but because he was a thief, and as he had the money box he used to take what was put into it. 7 Jesus said, "Let her alone, let her keep it for the day of my burial. 8 The

a Greek our place   b The denarius was worth about twenty cents

11.32: Jn 11.22.   11.35: Lk 19.41.   11.37: Jn 9.7.
11.38: Mt 27.60; Mk 15.46; Lk 24.2; Jn 20.1.   11.41: Jn 17.1;Mt 11.25.
11.42: Jn 12.30.   11.44: Jn 19.40; 20.7.   11.49: Mt 26.3.   11.52: Jn 10.16; 17.21.
11.55: Mt 26.1; Mk 14.1; Lk 22.1; Jn 13.1.   11.56: Jn 7.11.
12.1–8: Mt 26.6–13; Mk 14.3–9; Lk 7.37–38.   12.4: Jn 6.71; 13.26.   12.6: Lk 8.3.
12.7: Jn 19.40.

poor you always have with you, but you do not always have me."

9 When the great crowd of the Jews learned that he was there, they came, not only on account of Jesus but also to see Laz′a·rus, whom he had raised from the dead. 10 So the chief priests planned to put Laz′a·rus also to death, 11 because on account of him many of the Jews were going away and believing in Jesus.

12 The next day a great crowd who had come to the feast heard that Jesus was coming to Jerusalem. 13 So they took branches of palm trees and went out to meet him, crying, "Hosanna! Blessed is he who comes in the name of the Lord, even the King of Israel!" 14 And Jesus found a young ass and sat upon it; as it is written,

15 "Fear not, daughter of Zion;
  behold, your king is coming,
    sitting on an ass's colt!"

16 His disciples did not understand this at first; but when Jesus was glorified, then they remembered that this had been written of him and had been done to him. 17 The crowd that had been with him when he called Laz′a·rus out of the tomb and raised him from the dead bore witness. 18 The reason why the crowd went to meet him was that they heard he had done this sign. 19 The Pharisees then said to one another, "You see that you can do nothing; look, the world has gone after him."

20 Now among those who went up to worship at the feast were some Greeks. 21 So these came to Philip, who was from Beth·sa′i·da in Galilee, and said to him, "Sir, we wish to see Jesus." 22 Philip went and told Andrew; Andrew went with Philip and they told Jesus. 23 And Jesus answered them, "The hour has come for the Son of man to be glorified. 24 Truly, truly, I say to you, unless a grain of wheat falls into the earth and dies, it remains alone; but if it dies, it bears much fruit. 25 He who loves his life loses it, and he who hates his life in this world will keep it for eternal life. 26 If any one serves me, he must follow me; and where I am, there shall my servant be also; if any one serves me, the Father will honor him.

27 "Now is my soul troubled. And what shall I say? 'Father, save me from this hour'? No, for this purpose I have come to this hour. 28 Father, glorify thy name." Then a voice came from heaven, "I have glorified it, and I will glorify it again." 29 The crowd standing by heard it and said that it had thundered. Others said, "An angel has spoken to him." 30 Jesus answered, "This voice has come for your sake, not for mine. 31 Now is the judgment of this world, now shall the ruler of this world be cast out; 32 and I, when I am lifted up from the earth, will draw all men to myself." 33 He said this to show by what death he was to die. 34 The crowd answered him, "We have heard from the law that the Christ remains for ever. How can you say that the Son of man must be lifted up? Who is this Son of man?" 35 Jesus said to them, "The light is with you for a little longer. Walk while you have the light, lest the darkness overtake you; he who walks in the darkness does not know where he goes. 36 While you have the light, believe in the light, that you may become sons of light."

When Jesus had said this, he departed and hid himself from them. 37 Though he had done so many signs before them, yet they did not believe in him; 38 it was that the word spoken by the prophet I·sa′iah might be fulfilled:

"Lord, who has believed our report,
  and to whom has the arm of the
    Lord been revealed?"

39 Therefore they could not believe. For I·sa′iah again said,

40 "He has blinded their eyes and
    hardened their heart,
  lest they should see with their eyes
    and perceive with their heart,
  and turn for me to heal them."

41 I·sa′iah said this because he saw his glory and spoke of him. 42 Nevertheless many even of the authorities believed in him, but for fear of the Pharisees they did not confess it, lest they should be put out of the synagogue: 43 for they loved the praise of men more than the praise of God.

44 And Jesus cried out and said, "He who believes in me, believes not

12:10: Mk 14.1.   12.12-15: Mt 21.4-9; Mk 11.7-10; Lk 19.35-38.
12.13: Ps 118.25; Jn 1.49.   12.15: Zech 9.9.   12.16: Mk 9.32; Jn 2.22.
12.20: Jn 7.35; Acts 11.20.   12.21: Jn 1.44; 6.5.   12.23: Jn 13.1; 17.1; Mk 14.35, 41.
12.24: 1 Cor 15.36.   12.25: Mt 10.39; Mk 8.35; Lk 9.24; 14.26.
12.27: Jn 11.33; Mt 26.38; Mk 14.34.   12.28: Mk 1.11; 9.7.
12.31: Jn 16.11; 2 Cor 4.4; Eph 2.2.   12.32: Jn 3.14; 8.28.
12.34: Ps 110.4; Is 9.7; Ezek 37.25; Dan 7.14.   12.35: Jn 7.33; 9.4; Eph 5.8; 1 Jn 2.11.
12.36: Lk 16.8; Jn 8.59.   12.38: Is 53.1; Rom 10.16.   12.40: Is 6.10; Mt 13.14.
12.41: Is 6.1; Lk 24.27.   12.42: Jn 9.22; Lk 6.22.   12.44: Mt 10.40; Jn 5.24.

in me but in him who sent me. 45And he who sees me sees him who sent me. 46 I have come as light into the world, that whoever believes in me may not remain in darkness. 47 If any one hears my sayings and does not keep them, I do not judge him; for I did not come to judge the world but to save the world. 48 He who rejects me and does not receive my sayings has a judge; the word that I have spoken will be his judge on the last day. 49 For I have not spoken on my own authority; the Father who sent me has himself given me commandment what to say and what to speak. 50And I know that his commandment is eternal life. What I say, therefore, I say as the Father has bidden me.''

13 Now before the feast of the Passover, when Jesus knew that his hour had come to depart out of this world to the Father, having loved his own who were in the world, he loved them to the end. 2And during supper, when the devil had already put it into the heart of Judas Is·car′i·ot, Simon's son, to betray him, 3 Jesus, knowing that the Father had given all things into his hands, and that he had come from God and was going to God, 4 rose from supper, laid aside his garments, and girded himself with a towel. 5 Then he poured water into a basin, and began to wash the disciples' feet, and to wipe them with the towel with which he was girded. 6 He came to Simon Peter; and Peter said to him, "Lord, do you wash my feet?" 7 Jesus answered him, "What I am doing you do not know now, but afterward you will understand." 8 Peter said to him, "You shall never wash my feet." Jesus answered him, "If I do not wash you, you have no part in me." 9 Simon Peter said to him, "Lord, not my feet only but also my hands and my head!" 10 Jesus said to him, "He who has bathed does not need to wash, except for his feet,*c* but he is clean all over; and you are clean, but not all of you." 11 For he knew who was to betray him; that was why he said, "You are not all clean."

12 When he had washed their feet, and taken his garments, and resumed

his place, he said to them, "Do you know what I have done to you? 13 You call me Teacher and Lord; and you are right, for so I am. 14 If I then, your Lord and Teacher, have washed your feet, you also ought to wash one another's feet. 15 For I have given you an example, that you also should do as I have done to you. 16 Truly, truly, I say to you, a servant*d* is not greater than his master; nor is he who is sent greater than he who sent him. 17 If you know these things, blessed are you if you do them. 18 I am not speaking of you all; I know whom I have chosen; it is that the scripture may be fulfilled, 'He who ate my bread has lifted his heel against me.' 19 I tell you this now, before it takes place, that when it does take place you may believe that I am he. 20 Truly, truly, I say to you, he who receives any one whom I send receives me; and he who receives me receives him who sent me.''

21 When Jesus had thus spoken, he was troubled in spirit, and testified, "Truly, truly, I say to you, one of you will betray me." 22 The disciples looked at one another, uncertain of whom he spoke. 23 One of his disciples, whom Jesus loved, was lying close to the breast of Jesus; 24 so Simon Peter beckoned to him and said, "Tell us who it is of whom he speaks." 25 So lying thus, close to the breast of Jesus, he said to him, "Lord, who is it?" 26 Jesus answered, "It is he to whom I shall give this morsel when I have dipped it." So when he had dipped the morsel, he gave it to Judas, the son of Simon Is·car′i·ot. 27 Then after the morsel, Satan entered into him. Jesus said to him, "What you are going to do, do quickly." 28 Now no one at the table knew why he said this to him. 29 Some thought that, because Judas had the money box, Jesus was telling him, "Buy what we need for the feast"; or, that he should give something to the poor. 30 So, after receiving the morsel, he immediately went out; and it was night.

31 When he had gone out, Jesus said, "Now is the Son of man glorified, and in him God is glorified; 32 if God is glorified in him, God will also glorify him in himself, and glorify him

---

c Other ancient authorities omit *except for his feet*   *d* Or *slave*

12.45: Jn 14.9.   12.46: Jn 1.4; 8.12; 9.5.   12.47: Jn 3.17.   12.48: Mt 10.14-15.
13.1: Jn 11.55; 12.23; 16.28.   13.2: Jn 6.71; Mk 14.10.   13.5: Lk 7.44; 22.27.
13.8: Deut 12.12; Jn 3.5; 9.7.   13.11: Jn 13.2.   13.15: 1 Pet 2.21.
13.16: Mt 10.24; Lk 6.40.   13.17: Lk 11.28; Jas 1.25.   13.18: Ps 41.9.
13.19: Jn 14.29; 8.28.   13.20: Mt 10.40; Lk 10.16.
13.21-26: Mt 26.21-25; Mk 14.18-21; Lk 22.21-23.   13.23: Jn 19.26; 20.2; 21.7, 20.
13.26: Jn 6.71.   13.29: Jn 12.6.   13.30: Lk 22.53.   13.31-32: Jn 17.1.

at once. ³³ Little children, yet a little while I am with you. You will seek me; and as I said to the Jews so now I say to you, 'Where I am going you cannot come.' ³⁴A new commandment I give to you, that you love one another; even as I have loved you, that you also love one another. ³⁵ By this all men will know that you are my disciples, if you have love for one another."

³⁶ **Simon Peter said to him, "Lord, where are you going?" Jesus answered,** "Where I am going you cannot follow me now; but you shall follow afterward." ³⁷ **Peter said to him, "Lord, why cannot I follow you now? I will lay down my life for you."** ³⁸ Jesus answered, "Will you lay down your life for me? Truly, truly, I say to you, the cock will not crow, till you have denied me three times.

14 "Let not your hearts be troubled; believe*e* in God, believe also in me. ² In my Father's house are many rooms; if it were not so, would I have told you that I go to prepare a place for you? ³And when I go and prepare a place for you, I will come again and will take you to myself, that where I am you may be also. ⁴And you know the way where I am going."*f* ⁵ **Thomas said to him, "Lord, we do not know where you are going; how can we know the way?"** ⁶ Jesus said to him, "I am the way, and the truth, and the life; no one comes to the Father, but by me. ⁷ If you had known me, you would have known my Father also; henceforth you know him and have seen him."

⁸ **Philip said to him, "Lord, show us the Father, and we shall be satisfied."** ⁹ Jesus said to him, "Have I been with you so long, and yet you do not know me, Philip? He who has seen me has seen the Father; how can you say, 'Show us the Father'? ¹⁰ Do you not believe that I am in the Father and the Father in me? The words that I say to you I do not speak on my own authority; but the Father who dwells in me does his works. ¹¹ Believe me that I am in the Father and the Father in me; or else believe me for the sake of the works themselves.

¹² "Truly, truly, I say to you, he who believes in me will also do the works that I do; and greater works than these will he do, because I go to the Father. ¹³Whatever you ask in my name, I will do it, that the Father may be glorified in the Son; ¹⁴if you ask*g* anything in my name, I will do it.

¹⁵ "If you love me, you will keep my commandments. ¹⁶And I will pray the Father, and he will give you another Counselor, to be with you for ever, ¹⁷ even the Spirit of truth, whom the world cannot receive, because it neither sees him nor knows him; you know him, for he dwells with you, and will be in you.

¹⁸ "I will not leave you desolate; I will come to you. ¹⁹ Yet a little while, and the world will see me no more, but you will see me; because I live, you will live also. ²⁰ In that day you will know that I am in my Father, and you in me, and I in you. ²¹ He who has my commandments and keeps them, he it is who loves me; and he who loves me will be loved by my Father, and I will love him and manifest myself to him." ²² **Judas (not Is·car'i·ot) said to him, "Lord, how is it that you will manifest yourself to us, and not to the world?"** ²³ Jesus answered him, "If a man loves me, he will keep my word, and my Father will love him, and we will come to him and make our home with him. ²⁴ He who does not love me does not keep my words; and the word which you hear is not mine but the Father's who sent me.

²⁵ "These things I have spoken to you, while I am still with you. ²⁶ But the Counselor, the Holy Spirit, whom the Father will send in my name, he will teach you all things, and bring to your remembrance all that I have said to you. ²⁷ Peace I leave with you; my peace I give to you; not as the world gives do I give to you. Let not your hearts be troubled, neither let them be afraid. ²⁸ You heard me say to you, 'I go away, and I will come to you.' If you loved me, you would have rejoiced, because I go to the Father; for the Father is greater than I. ²⁹And now I have told you before it takes

e Or *you believe*
f Other ancient authorities read *where I am going you know, and the way you know*
g Other ancient authorities add *me*   **13.33:** 1 Jn 2.1; Jn 7.33.
13.34: Jn 15.12, 17; 1 Jn 3.23; 2 Jn 5; Lev 19.18; 1 Thess 4.9; 1 Pet 1.22; Heb 13.1; Eph 5.2; 1 Jn 4.10.   **13.36:** Jn 21.18; 2 Pet 1.14.
13.37-38: Mt 26.33-35; Mk 14.29-31; Lk 22.33-34.   **14.2:** Jn 13.33.   **14.5:** Jn 11.16.
14.6: Jn 10.9; 1.4, 14.   **14.9:** Jn 12.45.   **14.11:** Jn 10.38.
14.13: Mt 7.7; Jn 15.7, 16; 16.23; Jas 1.5.   **14.15:** Jn 15.10; 1 Jn 5.3; 2 Jn 6.
14.16: Jn 14.26; 15.26; 16.7; 1 Jn 2.1.   **14.19:** Jn 7.33.   **14.22:** Acts 1.13; 10.40-41.
14.23: 1 Jn 2.24; Rev 21.3.   **14.27:** Jn 16.33; Phil 4.7; Col 3.15; Jn 20.19.   **14.29:** Jn 13.19.

place, so that when it does take place, you may believe. 30 I will no longer talk much with you, for the ruler of this world is coming. He has no power over me; 31 but I do as the Father has commanded me, so that the world may know that I love the Father. Rise, let us go hence.

15 "I am the true vine, and my Father is the vinedresser. 2 Every branch of mine that bears no fruit, takes away, and every branch that does bear fruit he prunes, that it may bear more fruit. 3 You are already made clean by the word which I have spoken to you. 4 Abide in me, and I in you. As the branch cannot bear fruit by itself, unless it abides in the vine, neither can you, unless you abide in me. 5 I am the vine, you are the branches. He who abides in me, and I in him, he it is that bears much fruit, for apart from me you can do nothing. 6 If a man does not abide in me, he is cast forth as a branch and withers; and the branches are gathered, thrown into the fire and burned. 7 If you abide in me, and my words abide in you, ask whatever you will, and it shall be done for you. 8 By this my Father is glorified, that you bear much fruit, and so prove to be my disciples. 9 As the Father has loved me, so have I loved you; abide in my love. 10 If you keep my commandments, you will abide in my love, just as I have kept my Father's commandments and abide in his love. 11 These things I have spoken to you, that my joy may be in you, and that your joy may be full.

12 "This is my commandment, that you love one another as I have loved you. 13 Greater love has no man than this, that a man lay down his life for his friends. 14 You are my friends if you do what I command you. 15 No longer do I call you servants,*h* for the servant*i* does not know what his master is doing; but I have called you friends, for all that I have heard from my Father I have made known to you. 16 You did not choose me, but I chose you and appointed you that you should go and bear fruit and that your fruit should abide; so that whatever you ask

the Father in my name, he may give it to you. 17 This I command you, to love one another.

18 "If the world hates you, know that it has hated me before it hated you. 19 If you were of the world, the world would love its own; but because you are not of the world, but I chose you out of the world, therefore the world hates you. 20 Remember the word that I said to you, 'A servant *i* is not greater than his master.' If they persecuted me, they will persecute you; if they kept my word, they will keep yours also. 21 But all this they will do to you on my account, because they do not know him who sent me. 22 If I had not come and spoken to them, they would not have sin; but now they have no excuse for their sin. 23 He who hates me hates my Father also. 24 If I had not done among them the works which no one else did, they would not have sin; but now they have seen and hated both me and my Father. 25 It is to fulfil the word that is written in their law, 'They hated me without a cause.' 26 But when the Counselor comes, whom I shall send to you from the Father, even the Spirit of truth, who proceeds from the Father, he will bear witness to me; 27 and you also are witnesses, because you have been with me from the beginning.

16 "I have said all this to you to keep you from falling away. 2 They will put you out of the synagogues; indeed, the hour is coming when whoever kills you will think he is offering service to God. 3 And they will do this because they have not known the Father, nor me. 4 But I have said these things to you, that when their hour comes you may remember that I told you of them.

"I did not say these things to you from the beginning, because I was with you. 5 But now I am going to him who sent me, yet none of you asks me, 'Where are you going?' 6 But because I have said these things to you, sorrow has filled your hearts. 7 Nevertheless I tell you the truth: it is to your advantage that I go away, for if I do not go away, the Counselor will not

h Or *slaves*   *i* Or *slave*

14.30: Jn 12.31.   **14.31:** Mk 14.42; Jn 18.1.
15.1: Is 5.1-7; Ezek 19.10; Mk 12.1-9; Mt 15.13; Rom 11.17.   **15.3:** Jn 13.10.
15.4: Jn 6.56; 1 Jn 2.6.   **15.7:** Jn 14.13; 16.23; Mt 7.7; Jas 1.5.   **15.8:** Mt 5.16.
15.10: Jn 14.15; 1 Jn 5.3.   **15.12:** Jn 13.34.   **15.13:** Rom 5.7; Jn 10.11.   **15.14:** Lk 12.4.
15.16: Jn 6.70; 13.18; 14.13; 16.23.   **15.18:** Jn 7.7; 1 Jn 3.13; Mt 10.22; 24.9.
15.20: Jn 13.16; Mt 10.24; 1 Cor 4.12; Acts 4.17; 1 Pet 4.14; Rev 2.3.   **15.22:** Jn 9.41.
15.25: Ps 35.19; 69.4.   **15.26:** Jn 14.16, 26; 16.7; Jn 2.1; 5.7.
15.27: Jn 19.35; 21.24; 1 Jn 4.14.   **16.2:** Jn 9.22; Acts 26.9-11; Is 66.5.
16.5: Jn 7.33; 14.5.   **16.7:** Jn 14.16, 26; 15.26.

come to you; but if I go, I will send him to you. 8 And when he comes, he will convince the world of sin and of righteousness and of judgment: 9 of sin, because they do not believe in me; 10 of righteousness, because I go to the Father, and you will see me no more; 11 of judgment, because the ruler of this world is judged.

12 "I have yet many things to say to you, but you cannot bear them now. 13 When the Spirit of truth comes, he will guide you into all the truth; for he will not speak on his own authority, but whatever he hears he will speak, and he will declare to you the things that are to come. 14 He will glorify me, for he will take what is mine and declare it to you. 15 All that the Father has is mine; therefore I said that he will take what is mine and declare it to you.

16 "A little while, and you will see me no more; again a little while, and you will see me." 17 Some of his disciples said to one another, "What is this that he says to us, 'A little while, and you will not see me, and again a little while, and you will see me'; and, 'because I go to the Father'? 18 They said, "What does he mean by 'a little while'? We do not know what he means." 19 Jesus knew that they wanted to ask him; so he said to them, "Is this what you are asking yourselves, what I meant by saying, 'A little while, and you will not see me, and again a little while, and you will see me'? 20 Truly, truly, I say to you, you will weep and lament, but the world will rejoice; you will be sorrowful, but your sorrow will turn into joy. 21 When a woman is in travail she has sorrow, because her hour has come; but when she is delivered of the child, she no longer remembers the anguish, for joy that a childᶠ is born into the world. 22 So you have sorrow now, but I will see you again and your hearts will rejoice, and no one will take your joy from you. 23 In that day you will ask nothing of me. Truly, truly, I say to you, if you ask anything of the Father, he will give it to you in my name. 24 Hitherto you have asked nothing in my name; ask, and you will receive, that your joy may be full.

25 "I have said this to you in fig-ures; the hour is coming when I shall no longer speak to you in figures but tell you plainly of the Father. 26 In that day you will ask in my name; and I do not say to you that I shall pray the Father for you; 27 for the Father himself loves you, because you have loved me and have believed that I came from the Father. 28 I came from the Father and have come into the world; again, I am leaving the world and going to the Father."

29 His disciples said, "Ah, now you are speaking plainly, not in any figure! 30 Now we know that you know all things, and need none to question you; by this we believe that you came from God." 31 Jesus answered them, "Do you now believe? 32 The hour is coming, indeed it has come, when you will be scattered, every man to his home, and will leave me alone; yet I am not alone, for the Father is with me. 33 I have said this to you, that in me you may have peace. In the world you have tribulation; but be of good cheer, I have overcome the world."

17 When Jesus had spoken these words, he lifted up his eyes to heaven and said, "Father, the hour has come; glorify thy Son that the Son may glorify thee, 2 since thou hast given him power over all flesh, to give eternal life to all whom thou hast given him. 3 And this is eternal life, that they know thee the only true God, and Jesus Christ whom thou hast sent. 4 I glorified thee on earth, having accomplished the work which thou gavest me to do; 5 and now, Father, glorify thou me in thy own presence with the glory which I had with thee before the world was made.

6 "I have manifested thy name to the men whom thou gavest me out of the world; thine they were, and thou gavest them to me, and they have kept thy word. 7 Now they know that everything that thou hast given me is from thee; 8 for I have given them the words which thou gavest me, and they have received them and know in truth that I came from thee; and they have believed that thou didst send me. 9 I am praying for them; I am not praying for the world but for those whom thou hast given me, for they are thine; 10 all

ᶠ Greek *a human being*

16.9: Jn 15.22.   16.10: Acts 3.14; 7.52; 1 Pet 3.18.   16.11: Jn 12.31.
16.14: Jn 7.39.   16.16-24: Jn 14.18-24.   16.20: Jn 20.20.
16.21: Is 13.8; Hos 13.13; Mic 4.9; 1 Thess 5.3.   16.24: Jn 14.14; 15.11.
16.25: Jn 10.6; Mt 13.34.   16.32: Jn 4.23; Mk 14.27; Zech 13.7.
16.33: Jn 14.27; 15.18; Rom 8.37; 2 Cor 2.14; Rev 3.21.   17.1: Jn 11.41; 13.31.
17.5: Jn 1.1; 8.58; Phil 2.6.   17.9: Lk 22.32; Jn 14.16.

mine are thine, and thine are mine, and I am glorified in them. 11 And now I am no more in the world, but they are in the world, and I am coming to thee. Holy Father, keep them in thy name, which thou hast given me, that they may be one, even as we are one. 12 While I was with them, I kept them in thy name, which thou hast given me; I have guarded them, and none of them is lost but the son of perdition, that the scripture might be fulfilled. 13 But now I am coming to thee; and these things I speak in the world, that they may have my joy fulfilled in themselves. 14 I have given them thy word; and the world has hated them because they are not of the world, even as I am not of the world. 15 I do not pray that thou shouldst take them out of the world, but that thou shouldst keep them from the evil one.*k* 16 They are not of the world, even as I am not of the world. 17 Sanctify them in the truth; thy word is truth. 18 As thou didst send me into the world, so I have sent them into the world. 19 And for their sake I consecrate myself, that they also may be consecrated in truth.

20 "I do not pray for these only, but also for those who believe in me through their word, 21 that they may all be one; even as thou, Father, art in me, and I in thee, that they also may be in us, so that the world may believe that thou hast sent me. 22 The glory which thou hast given me I have given to them, that they may be one even as we are one, 23 I in them and thou in me, that they may become perfectly one, so that the world may know that thou hast sent me and hast loved them even as thou hast loved me. 24 Father, I desire that they also, whom thou hast given me, may be with me where I am, to behold my glory which thou hast given me in thy love for me before the foundation of the world. 25 O righteous Father, the world has not known thee, but I have known thee; and these know that thou hast sent me. 26 I made known to them thy name, and I will make it known, that the love with which thou hast loved me may be in them, and I in them."

18 When Jesus had spoken these words, he went forth with his disciples across the Kid'ron valley, where there was a garden, which he and his disciples entered. 2 Now Judas, who betrayed him, also knew the place; for Jesus often met there with his disciples. 3 So Judas, procuring a band of soldiers and some officers from the chief priests and the Pharisees, went there with lanterns and torches and weapons. 4 Then Jesus, knowing all that was to befall him, came forward and said to them, "Whom do you seek?" 5 They answered him, "Jesus of Nazareth." Jesus said to them, "I am he." Judas, who betrayed him, was standing with them. 6 When he said to them, "I am he," they drew back and fell to the ground. 7 Again he asked them, "Whom do you seek?" And they said, "Jesus of Nazareth." 8 Jesus answered, "I told you that I am he; so, if you seek me, let these men go." 9 This was to fulfil the word which he had spoken, "Of those whom thou gavest me I lost not one." 10 Then Simon Peter, having a sword, drew it and struck the high priest's slave and cut off his right ear. The slave's name was Mal'chus. 11 Jesus said to Peter, "Put your sword into its sheath; shall I not drink the cup which the Father has given me?"

12 So the band of soldiers and their captain and the officers of the Jews seized Jesus and bound him. 13 First they led him to An'nas; for he was the father-in-law of Ca'ia-phas, who was high priest that year. 14 It was Ca'ia-phas who had given counsel to the Jews that it was expedient that one man should die for the people.

15 Simon Peter followed Jesus, and so did another disciple. As this disciple was known to the high priest, he entered the court of the high priest along with Jesus, 16 while Peter stood outside at the door. So the other disciple, who was known to the high priest, went out and spoke to the maid who kept the door, and brought Peter in. 17 The maid who kept the door said to Peter, "Are not you also one of this man's disciples?" He said, "I am

k Or from evil

17.11: Phil 2.9; Rev 19.12; Rom 12.5; Gal 3.28; Jn 17.21.
17.12: Ps 41.9; Jn 6.70; 18.9.   17.14: Jn 15.19; 8.23.   17.21: Jn 10.38; 17.11.
17.24: Jn 1.14; 17.5; Mt 25.34.
18.1: Mt 26.30, 36; Mk 14.26, 32; Lk 22.39; 2 Sam 15.23.
18.3-11: Mt 26.47-56; Mk 14.43-50; Lk 22.47-53.   18.4: Jn 6.64; 13.1.
18.9: Jn 17.12; 6.39.   18.11: Mk 10.38; 14.36.
18.12-13: Mt 26.57; Mk 14.53; Lk 22.54; 3.2.   18.14: Jn 11.49-51.
18.15-16: Mt 26.58; Mk 14.54; Lk 22.54.
18.17-18: Mt 26.69-72; Mk 14.66-69; Lk 22.56-58.

not." 18 Now the servants[l] and officers had made a charcoal fire, because it was cold, and they were standing and warming themselves; Peter also was with them, standing and warming himself.

19 The high priest then questioned Jesus about his disciples and his teaching. 20 Jesus answered him, "I have spoken openly to the world; I have always taught in synagogues and in the temple, where all Jews come together; I have said nothing secretly. 21 Why do you ask me? Ask those who have heard me, what I said to them; they know what I said." 22 When he had said this, one of the officers standing by struck Jesus with his hand, saying, "Is that how you answer the high priest?" 23 Jesus answered him, "If I have spoken wrongly, bear witness to the wrong; but if I have spoken rightly, why do you strike me?" 24 An'nas then sent him bound to Cā'iȧ·phȧs the high priest.

25 Now Simon Peter was standing and warming himself. They said to him, "Are not you also one of his disciples?" He denied it and said, "I am not." 26 One of the servants[l] of the high priest, a kinsman of the man whose ear Peter had cut off, asked, "Did I not see you in the garden with him?" 27 Peter again denied it; and at once the cock crowed.

28 Then they led Jesus from the house of Cā'iȧ·phȧs to the praetorium. It was early. They themselves did not enter the praetorium, so that they might not be defiled, but might eat the passover. 29 So Pilate went out to them and said, "What accusation do you bring against this man?" 30 They answered him, "If this man were not an evildoer, we would not have handed him over." 31 Pilate said to them, "Take him yourselves and judge him by your own law." The Jews said to him, "It is not lawful for us to put any man to death." 32 This was to fulfil the word which Jesus had spoken to show by what death he was to die.

33 Pilate entered the praetorium again and called Jesus, and said to him, "Are you the King of the Jews?" 34 Jesus answered, "Do you say this of your own accord, or did others say it to you about me?" 35 Pilate answered, "Am I a Jew? Your own nation and the chief priests have handed you over to me; what have you done?" 36 Jesus answered, "My kingship is not of this world; if my kingship were of this world, my servants would fight, that I might not be handed over to the Jews; but my kingship is not from the world." 37 Pilate said to him, "So you are a king?" Jesus answered, "You say that I am a king. For this I was born, and for this I have come into the world, to bear witness to the truth. Every one who is of the truth hears my voice." 38 Pilate said to him, "What is truth?"

After he had said this, he went out to the Jews again, and told them, "I find no crime in him. 39 But you have a custom that I should release one man for you at the Passover; will you have me release for you the King of the Jews?" 40 They cried out again, "Not this man, but Bȧ·rab'bȧs!" Now Barabbas was a robber.

19 Then Pilate took Jesus and scourged him. 2 And the soldiers plaited a crown of thorns, and put it on his head, and arrayed him in a purple robe; 3 they came up to him, saying, "Hail, King of the Jews!" and struck him with their hands. 4 Pilate went out again, and said to them, "Behold, I am bringing him out to you, that you may know that I find no crime in him." 5 So Jesus came out, wearing the crown of thorns and the purple robe. Pilate said to them, "Here is the man!" 6 When the chief priests and the officers saw him, they cried out, "Crucify him, crucify him!" Pilate said to them, "Take him yourselves and crucify him, for I find no crime in him." 7 The Jews answered him, "We have a law, and by that law he ought to die, because he has made himself the Son of God." 8 When Pilate heard these words, he was the more afraid; 9 he entered the praetorium again and said to Jesus, "Where are you from?" But Jesus gave no answer. 10 Pilate therefore said to him, "You will not speak to me? Do you not know that I have power to release

l Or *slaves*
18.19-23: Mt 26.59-66; Mk 14.55-64; Lk 22.67-71.   **18.23:** Mt 5.39; Acts 23.2-5.
18.24: Jn 18.13; Lk 3.2.   **18.25-27:** Mt 26.73-75; Mk 14.70-72; Lk 22.59-62.
18.28: Jn 11.55; Mt 27.1-2; Mk 15.1; Lk 23.1.
18.29-38: Mt 27.11-14; Mk 15.2-5; Lk 23.2-3.   **18.32:** Jn 3.14; 12.32.
18.36: Jn 6.15; Mt 26.53.   **18.37:** Jn 3.32; 8.14, 47; 1 Jn 4.6.
18.38-40: Mt 27.15-26; Mk 15.6-15; Lk 23.18-19; Acts 3.14.
19.2-3: Mt 27.27-31; Mk 15.16-20; Lk 22.63-65; 23.11.   **19.4:** Jn 18.38; 19.6; Lk 23.4.
19.7: Lev 24.16; Mk 14.61-64; Jn 5.18; 10.33.

you, and power to crucify you?" 11 Jesus answered him, "You would have no power over me unless it had been given you from above; therefore he who delivered me to you has the greater sin."

12 Upon this Pilate sought to release him, but the Jews cried out, "If you release this man, you are not Caesar's friend; every one who makes himself a king sets himself against Caesar." 13 When Pilate heard these words, he brought Jesus out and sat down on the judgment seat at a place called The Pavement, and in Hebrew, Gab′ba·tha. 14 Now it was the day of Preparation of the Passover; it was about the sixth hour. He said to the Jews, "Here is your King!" 15 They cried out, "Away with him, away with him, crucify him!" Pilate said to them, "Shall I crucify your King?" The chief priests answered, "We have no king but Caesar." 16 Then he handed him over to them to be crucified.

17 So they took Jesus, and he went out, bearing his own cross, to the place called the place of a skull, which is called in Hebrew Gol′go·tha. 18 There they crucified him, and with him two others, one on either side, and Jesus between them. 19 Pilate also wrote a title and put it on the cross; it read, "Jesus of Nazareth, the King of the Jews." 20 Many of the Jews read this title, for the place where Jesus was crucified was near the city; and it was written in Hebrew, in Latin, and in Greek. 21 The chief priests of the Jews then said to Pilate, "Do not write, 'The King of the Jews,' but, 'This man said, I am King of the Jews.'" 22 Pilate answered, "What I have written I have written."

23 When the soldiers had crucified Jesus they took his garments and made four parts, one for each soldier; also his tunic. But the tunic was without seam, woven from top to bottom; 24 so they said to one another, "Let us not tear it, but cast lots for it to see whose it shall be." This was to fulfil the scripture,

"They parted my garments among them,
and for my clothing they cast lots."

25 So the soldiers did this. But standing by the cross of Jesus were his mother, and his mother's sister, Mary the wife of Clo′pas, and Mary Mag′da·lene. 26 When Jesus saw his mother, and the disciple whom he loved standing near, he said to his mother, "Woman, behold, your son!" 27 Then he said to the disciple, "Behold, your mother!" And from that hour the disciple took her to his own home.

28 After this Jesus, knowing that all was now finished, said (to fulfil the scripture), "I thirst." 29 A bowl full of vinegar stood there; so they put a sponge full of the vinegar on hyssop and held it to his mouth. 30 When Jesus had received the vinegar, he said, "It is finished"; and he bowed his head and gave up his spirit.

31 Since it was the day of Preparation, in order to prevent the bodies from remaining on the cross on the sabbath (for that sabbath was a high day), the Jews asked Pilate that their legs might be broken, and that they might be taken away. 32 So the soldiers came and broke the legs of the first, and of the other who had been crucified with him; 33 but when they came to Jesus and saw that he was already dead, they did not break his legs. 34 But one of the soldiers pierced his side with a spear, and at once there came out blood and water. 35 He who saw it has borne witness—his testimony is true, and he knows that he tells the truth—that you also may believe. 36 For these things took place that the scripture might be fulfilled, "Not a bone of him shall be broken." 37 And again another scripture says, "They shall look on him whom they have pierced."

38 After this Joseph of Ar·i·ma·the′a, who was a disciple of Jesus, but secretly, for fear of the Jews, asked Pilate that he might take away the body of Jesus, and Pilate gave him leave. So he came and took away his body. 39 Nic·o·de′mus also, who had at first come to him by night, came bringing a mixture of myrrh and aloes, about a hundred pounds' weight. 40 They took the body of Jesus, and bound it in linen cloths with the

19.11: Rom 13.1; Jn 18.28.   **19.12:** Lk 23.2.
19.14: Mk 15.42; Jn 19.31, 42; Mk 15.25, 33.
19.17-24: Mt 27.33-44; Mk 15.22-32; Lk 23.33-43.   **19.24:** Ex 28.32; Ps 22.18.
19.25: Mt 27.55-56; Mk 15.40-41; Lk 23.49; Jn 2.3; Mk 3.31; Lk 24.18; Jn 20.1, 18.
19.26: Jn 13.23; 20.2; 21.20.
19.28-30: Ps 69.21; Mt 27.45-50; Mk 15.33-37; Lk 23.44-46; Jn 17.4.
19.31: Deut 21.23; Ex 12.16.   **19.34:** 1 Jn 5.6-8.   **19.35:** Jn 15.27; 21.24.
19.36: Ex 12.46; Num 9.12; Ps 34.20.   **19.37:** Zech 12.10.   **19.38-42:** Mt 27.57-61;
Mk 15.42-47; Lk 23.50-56.   **19.39:** Jn 3.1; 7.50.   **19.40:** Mk 16.1; 14.8.

spices, as is the burial custom of the Jews. 41 Now in the place where he was crucified there was a garden, and in the garden a new tomb where no one had ever been laid. 42 So because of the Jewish day of Preparation, as the tomb was close at hand, they laid Jesus there.

20 Now on the first day of the week Mary Mag′dà·lēne came to the tomb early, while it was still dark, and saw that the stone had been taken away from the tomb. 2 So she ran, and went to Simon Peter and the other disciple, the one whom Jesus loved, and said to them, "They have taken the Lord out of the tomb, and we do not know where they have laid him." 3 Peter then came out with the other disciple, and they went toward the tomb. 4 They both ran, but the other disciple outran Peter and reached the tomb first; 5 and stooping to look in, he saw the linen cloths lying there, but he did not go in. 6 Then Simon Peter came, following him, and went into the tomb; he saw the linen cloths lying, 7 and the napkin, which had been on his head, not lying with the linen cloths but rolled up in a place by itself. 8 Then the other disciple, who reached the tomb first, also went in, and he saw and believed; 9 for as yet they did not know the scripture, that he must rise from the dead. 10 Then the disciples went back to their homes.

11 But Mary stood weeping outside the tomb, and as she wept she stooped to look into the tomb; 12 and she saw two angels in white, sitting where the body of Jesus had lain, one at the head and one at the feet. 13 They said to her, "Woman, why are you weeping?" She said to them, "Because they have taken away my Lord, and I do not know where they have laid him." 14 Saying this, she turned round and saw Jesus standing, but she did not know that it was Jesus. 15 Jesus said to her, "Woman, why are you weeping? Whom do you seek?" Supposing him to be the gardener, she said to him, "Sir, if you have carried him away, tell me where you have laid him, and I will take him away." 16 Jesus said to her, "Mary." She turned and said to him in Hebrew, "Ràb-bō′ni!" (which means Teacher). 17 Jesus said to her, "Do not hold me, for I have

not yet ascended to the Father; but go to my brethren and say to them, I am ascending to my Father and your Father, to my God and your God." 18 Mary Mag′dà·lēne went and said to the disciples, "I have seen the Lord"; and she told them that he had said these things to her.

19 On the evening of that day, the first day of the week, the doors being shut where the disciples were, for fear of the Jews, Jesus came and stood among them and said to them, "Peace be with you." 20 When he had said this, he showed them his hands and his side. Then the disciples were glad when they saw the Lord. 21 Jesus said to them again, "Peace be with you. As the Father has sent me, even so I send you." 22 And when he had said this, he breathed on them, and said to them, "Receive the Holy Spirit. 23 If you forgive the sins of any, they are forgiven; if you retain the sins of any, they are retained."

24 Now Thomas, one of the twelve, called the Twin, was not with them when Jesus came. 25 So the other disciples told him, "We have seen the Lord." But he said to them, "Unless I see in his hands the print of the nails, and place my finger in the mark of the nails, and place my hand in his side, I will not believe."

26 Eight days later, his disciples were again in the house, and Thomas was with them. The doors were shut, but Jesus came and stood among them, and said, "Peace be with you." 27 Then he said to Thomas, "Put your finger here, and see my hands; and put out your hand, and place it in my side; do not be faithless, but believing." 28 Thomas answered him, "My Lord and my God!" 29 Jesus said to him, "Have you believed because you have seen me? Blessed are those who have not seen and yet believe."

30 Now Jesus did many other signs in the presence of the disciples, which are not written in this book; 31 but these are written that you may believe that Jesus is the Christ, the Son of God, and that believing you may have life in his name.

21 After this Jesus revealed himself again to the disciples by the Sea of Tĭ·bē′ri·às; and he revealed himself

20.1-10: Mt 28.1-8; Mk 16.1-8; Lk 24.1-10.　20.3-10: Lk 24.11-12.
20.9: Lk 24.26, 46.　20.12: Lk 24.4; Mt 28.5; Mk 16.5.　20.13: Jn 20.2.
20.14: Mt 28.9; Jn 21.4.　20.17: Jn 20.27; Mt 28.10; Jn 7.33.　20.18: Lk 24.10, 23.
20.19-20: Lk 24.36-39.　20.21: Jn 17.18; Mt 28.19.　20.22: Acts 2.4, 33.
20.23: Mt 16.19; 18.18.　20.24: Jn 11.16.　20.27: Lk 24.40.　20.29: 1 Pet 1.8.
20.30: Jn 21.25.　20.31: Jn 3.15.

in this way. 2 Simon Peter, Thomas called the Twin, Nā·than′a·el of Cā′nà in Galilee, the sons of Zeb′e·dee, and two others of his disciples were together. 3 Simon Peter said to them, "I am going fishing." They said to him, "We will go with you." They went out and got into the boat; but that night they caught nothing.

4 Just as day was breaking, Jesus stood on the beach; yet the disciples did not know that it was Jesus. 5 Jesus said to them, "Children, have you any fish?" They answered him, "No." 6 He said to them, "Cast the net on the right side of the boat, and you will find some." So they cast it, and now they were not able to haul it in, for the quantity of fish. 7 That disciple whom Jesus loved said to Peter, "It is the Lord!" When Simon Peter heard that it was the Lord, he put on his clothes, for he was stripped for work, and sprang into the sea. 8 But the other disciples came in the boat, dragging the net full of fish, for they were not far from the land, but about a hundred yards[m] off.

9 When they got out on land, they saw a charcoal fire there, with fish lying on it, and bread. 10 Jesus said to them, "Bring some of the fish that you have just caught." 11 So Simon Peter went aboard and hauled the net ashore, full of large fish, a hundred and fifty-three of them; and although there were so many, the net was not torn. 12 Jesus said to them, "Come and have breakfast." Now none of the disciples dared ask him, "Who are you?" They knew it was the Lord. 13 Jesus came and took the bread and gave it to them, and so with the fish. 14 This was now the third time that Jesus was revealed to the disciples after he was raised from the dead.

15 When they had finished breakfast, Jesus said to Simon Peter, "Simon, son of John, do you love me more than these?" He said to him, "Yes, Lord; you know that I love you." He said to him, "Feed my lambs." 16 A second time he said to him, "Simon, son of John, do you love me?" He said to him, "Yes, Lord; you know that I love you." He said to him, "Tend my sheep." 17 He said to him the third time, "Simon, son of John, do you love me?" Peter was grieved because he said to him the third time, "Do you love me?" And he said to him, "Lord, you know everything; you know that I love you." Jesus said to him, "Feed my sheep. 18 Truly, truly, I say to you, when you were young, you girded yourself and walked where you would; but when you are old, you will stretch out your hands, and another will gird you and carry you where you do not wish to go." 19 (This he said to show by what death he was to glorify God.) And after this he said to him, "Follow me."

20 Peter turned and saw following them the disciple whom Jesus loved, who had lain close to his breast at the supper and had said, "Lord, who is it that is going to betray you?" 21 When Peter saw him, he said to Jesus, "Lord, what about this man?" 22 Jesus said to him, "If it is my will that he remain until I come, what is that to you? Follow me!" 23 The saying spread abroad among the brethren that this disciple was not to die; yet Jesus did not say to him that he was not to die, but, "If it is my will that he remain until I come, what is that to you?"

24 This is the disciple who is bearing witness to these things, and who has written these things; and we know that his testimony is true.

25 But there are also many other things which Jesus did; were every one of them to be written, I suppose that the world itself could not contain the books that would be written.

---

m Greek *two hundred cubits*

21.2: Jn 11.16; 1.45; Lk 5.10.   **21.3-6:** Lk 5.3-7.   **21.4:** Jn 20.14; Lk 24.16.
21.5: Lk 24.41.   **21.7:** Jn 13.23; 19.26; 20.2; 21.20.   **21.14:** Jn 20.19, 26.
21.15: Jn 1.42; 13.37; Mk 14.29-31; Lk 12.32.
21.16: Mt 2.6; Acts 20.28; 1 Pet 5.2; Rev 7.17.   **21.19:** 2 Pet 1.14; Mk 1.17.
21.20: Jn 13.25.   **21.22:** 1 Cor 4.5; Jas 5.7; Rev 2.25; Mt 16.28.
21.24: Jn 15.27; 19.35.   **21.25:** Jn 20.30.

THE
ACTS OF THE APOSTLES

1 In the first book, O Thē·oph′i·lùs, I have dealt with all that Jesus began to do and teach, 2 until the day when he was taken up, after he had given commandment through the Holy Spirit to the apostles whom he had chosen. 3 To them he presented himself alive after his passion by many proofs, appearing to them during forty days, and speaking of the kingdom of God. 4 And while staying*a* with them he charged them not to depart from Jerusalem, but to wait for the promise of the Father, which, he said, "you heard from me, 5 for John baptized with water, but before many days you shall be baptized with the Holy Spirit."

6 So when they had come together, they asked him, "Lord, will you at this time restore the kingdom to Israel?" 7 He said to them, "It is not for you to know times or seasons which the Father has fixed by his own authority. 8 But you shall receive power when the Holy Spirit has come upon you; and you shall be my witnesses in Jerusalem and in all Judea and Sā·mār′i·à and to the end of the earth." 9 And when he had said this, as they were looking on, he was lifted up, and a cloud took him out of their sight. 10 And while they were gazing into heaven as he went, behold, two men stood by them in white robes, 11 and said, "Men of Galilee, why do you stand looking into heaven? This Jesus, who was taken up from you into heaven, will come in the same way as you saw him go into heaven."

12 Then they returned to Jerusalem from the mount called Ol′i·vet, which is near Jerusalem, a sabbath day's journey away; 13 and when they had entered, they went up to the upper room, where they were staying, Peter and John and James and Andrew, Philip and Thomas, Bartholomew and Matthew, James the son of Al·phaē′ùs and Simon the Zealot and Judas the son of James. 14 All these with one accord devoted themselves to prayer, together with the women and Mary the mother of Jesus, and with his brothers.

15 In those days Peter stood up among the brethren (the company of persons was in all about a hundred and twenty), and said, 16 "Brethren, the scripture had to be fulfilled, which the Holy Spirit spoke beforehand by the mouth of David, concerning Judas who was guide to those who arrested Jesus. 17 For he was numbered among us, and was allotted his share in this ministry. 18 (Now this man bought a field with the reward of his wickedness; and falling headlong*b* he burst open in the middle and all his bowels gushed out. 19 And it became known to all the inhabitants of Jerusalem, so that the field was called in their language À·kel′dà·mà, that is, Field of Blood.) 20 For it is written in the book of Psalms,

'Let his habitation become desolate,
 and let there be no one to live in it';
and

'His office let another take.'

21 So one of the men who have accompanied us during all the time that the Lord Jesus went in and out among us, 22 beginning from the baptism of John until the day when he was taken up from us—one of these men must become with us a witness to his resurrection." 23 And they put forward two, Joseph called Bär′sab·bàs, who was surnamed Justus, and Mat·thi′às. 24 And they prayed and said, "Lord, who knowest the hearts of all men, show which one of these two thou hast chosen 25 to take the place in this ministry and apostleship from which Judas turned aside, to go to his own place." 26 And they cast lots for them, and the lot fell on Mat·thi′às; and he was enrolled with the eleven apostles.

2 When the day of Pentecost had come, they were all together in one place, 2 And suddenly a sound came from heaven like the rush of a mighty wind, and it filled all the house where they were sitting. 3 And there appeared to them tongues as of fire, distributed and resting on each one of them. 4 And they were all filled with the Holy Spirit and began to speak in other tongues, as the Spirit gave them utterance.

5 Now there were dwelling in Jeru-

a Or *eating*   *b* Or *swelling up*
1.1: Lk 1.1-4.   **1.4:** Lk 24.49.   **1.8:** Lk 24.48-49.   **1.9-12:** Lk 24.50-53.
1.13: Mt 10.2-4; Mk 3.16-19; Lk 6.14-16.   **1.16-19:** Mt 27.3-10.   **1.20:** Ps 69.25; 109.8.

salem Jews, devout men from every nation under heaven. 6And at this sound the multitude came together, and they were bewildered, because each one heard them speaking in his own language. 7And they were amazed and wondered, saying, "Are not all these who are speaking Galileans? 8And how is it that we hear, each of us in his own native language? 9 Pär'thi·ăns and Medes and E'lā·mites and residents of Měs·ŏ·pŏ·tā'mi·à, Judea and Cap·pā·dō'çi·à, Pon'tŭs and Asia, 10 Phryg'i·à and Pam·phyl'i·à, Egypt and the parts of Libya belonging to Cȳ·rē'nē, and visitors from Rome, both Jews and proselytes, 11 Cretans and Arabians, we hear them telling in our own tongues the mighty works of God." 12And all were amazed and perplexed, saying to one another, "What does this mean?" 13 But others mocking said, "They are filled with new wine."

14 But Peter, standing with the eleven, lifted up his voice and addressed them, "Men of Judea and all who dwell in Jerusalem, let this be known to you, and give ear to my words. 15 For these men are not drunk, as you suppose, since it is only the third hour of the day; 16 but this is what was spoken by the prophet Jō'ĕl:
17 'And in the last days it shall be, God declares,
that I will pour out my Spirit upon all flesh,
and your sons and your daughters shall prophesy,
and your young men shall see visions,
and your old men shall dream dreams;
18 yea, and on my menservants and my maidservants in those days I will pour out my Spirit; and they shall prophesy.
19 And I will show wonders in the heaven above
and signs on the earth beneath,
blood, and fire, and vapor of smoke;
20 the sun shall be turned into darkness and the moon into blood,
before the day of the Lord comes, the great and manifest day.
21 And it shall be that whoever calls on the name of the Lord shall be saved."

22 "Men of Israel, hear these words: Jesus of Nazareth, a man attested to you by God with mighty works and wonders and signs which God did through him in your midst, as you yourselves know—23 this Jesus, de-

livered up according to the definite plan and foreknowledge of God, you crucified and killed by the hands of lawless men. 24 But God raised him up, having loosed the pangs of death, because it was not possible for him to be held by it. 25 For David says concerning him,
'I saw the Lord always before me, for he is at my right hand that I may not be shaken;
26 therefore my heart was glad, and my tongue rejoiced;
moreover my flesh will dwell in hope.
27 For thou wilt not abandon my soul to Hades,
nor let thy Holy One see corruption.
28 Thou hast made known to me the ways of life;
thou wilt make me full of gladness with thy presence.'

29 "Brethren, I may say to you confidently of the patriarch David that he both died and was buried, and his tomb is with us to this day. 30 Being therefore a prophet, and knowing that God had sworn with an oath to him that he would set one of his descendants upon his throne, 31 he foresaw and spoke of the resurrection of the Christ, that he was not abandoned to Hades, nor did his flesh see corruption. 32 This Jesus God raised up, and of that we all are witnesses. 33 Being therefore exalted at the right hand of God, and having received from the Father the promise of the Holy Spirit, he has poured out this which you see and hear. 34 For David did not ascend into the heavens; but he himself says,
'The Lord said to my Lord, Sit at my right hand,
35 till I make thy enemies a stool for thy feet.'
36 Let all the house of Israel therefore know assuredly that God has made him both Lord and Christ, this Jesus whom you crucified."

37 Now when they heard this they were cut to the heart, and said to Peter and the rest of the apostles, "Brethren, what shall we do?" 38And Peter said to them, "Repent, and be baptized every one of you in the name of Jesus Christ for the forgiveness of your sins; and you shall receive the gift of the Holy Spirit. 39 For the promise is to you and to your children and to all that are far off, every one whom the Lord our God calls to him." 40And he testified with many other words and exhorted them, saying, "Save your-

2.17-21: Joel 2.28-32.   2.25-28: Ps 16.8-11.   2.30: Ps 132.11.   2.31: Ps 16.10.
2.34-35: Ps 110.1.   2.39: Is 57.19; Joel 2.32.

selves from this crooked generation." 41 So those who received his word were baptized, and there were added that day about three thousand souls. 42And they devoted themselves to the apostles' teaching and fellowship, to the breaking of bread and the prayers.

43 And fear came upon every soul; and many wonders and signs were done through the apostles. 44And all who believed were together and had all things in common; 45 and they sold their possessions and goods and distributed them to all, as any had need. 46And day by day, attending the temple together and breaking bread in their homes, they partook of food with glad and generous hearts, 47 praising God and having favor with all the people. And the Lord added to their number day by day those who were being saved.

3 Now Peter and John were going up to the temple at the hour of prayer, the ninth hour. 2And a man lame from birth was being carried, whom they laid daily at that gate of the temple which is called Beautiful to ask alms of those who entered the temple. 3 Seeing Peter and John about to go into the temple, he asked for alms. 4And Peter directed his gaze at him, with John, and said, "Look at us." 5And he fixed his attention upon them, expecting to receive something from them. 6 But Peter said, "I have no silver and gold, but I give you what I have; in the name of Jesus Christ of Nazareth, walk." 7And he took him by the right hand and raised him up; and immediately his feet and ankles were made strong. 8And leaping up he stood and walked and entered the temple with them, walking and leaping and praising God. 9And all the people saw him walking and praising God, 10 and recognized him as the one who sat for alms at the Beautiful Gate of the temple; and they were filled with wonder and amazement at what had happened to him.

11 While he clung to Peter and John, all the people ran together to them in the portico called Solomon's, astounded. 12And when Peter saw it he addressed the people, "Men of Israel, why do you wonder at this, or why do you stare at us, as though by our own power or piety we had made him walk? 13 The God of Abraham and of Isaac and of Jacob, the God of our fathers, glorified his servant^c

Jesus, whom you delivered up and denied in the presence of Pilate, when he had decided to release him. 14 But you denied the Holy and Righteous One, and asked for a murderer to be granted to you, 15 and killed the Author of life, whom God raised from the dead. To this we are witnesses. 16And his name, by faith in his name, has made this man strong whom you see and know; and the faith which is through Jesus^d has given the man this perfect health in the presence of you all.

17 "And now, brethren, I know that you acted in ignorance, as did also your rulers. 18 But what God foretold by the mouth of all the prophets, that his Christ should suffer, he thus fulfilled. 19 Repent therefore, and turn again, that your sins may be blotted out, that times of refreshing may come from the presence of the Lord, 20 and that he may send the Christ appointed for you, Jesus, 21 whom heaven must receive until the time for establishing all that God spoke by the mouth of his holy prophets from of old. 22 Moses said, 'The Lord God will raise up for you a prophet from your brethren as he raised me up. You shall listen to him in whatever he tells you. 23And it shall be that every soul that does not listen to that prophet shall be destroyed from the people.' 24And all the prophets who have spoken, from Samuel and those who came afterwards, also proclaimed these days. 25 You are the sons of the prophets and of the covenant which God gave to your fathers, saying to Abraham, 'And in your posterity shall all the families of the earth be blessed.' 26 God, having raised up his servant,^c sent him to you first, to bless you in turning every one of you from your wickedness."

4 And as they were speaking to the people, the priests and the captain of the temple and the Sad'du·cees came upon them, 2 annoyed because they were teaching the people and proclaiming in Jesus the resurrection from the dead. 3And they arrested them and put them in custody until the morrow, for it was already evening. 4 But many of those who heard the word believed; and the number of the men came to about five thousand.

5 On the morrow their rulers and elders and scribes were gathered together in Jerusalem, 6 with An'nas the

^c Or *child*   ^d Greek *him*

2.44-45: Acts 4.32-35.   3.13: Ex 3.6; Is 52.13.   3.22: Deut 18.15-16.
3.23: Deut 18.19; Lev 23.29.   3.25: Gen 22.18.

high priest and Cā′iȧ·phás and John and Alexander, and all who were of the high-priestly family. 7And when they had set them in the midst, they inquired, "By what power or by what name did you do this?" 8 Then Peter, filled with the Holy Spirit, said to them, "Rulers of the people and elders, 9 if we are being examined today concerning a good deed done to a cripple, by what means this man has been healed, 10 be it known to you all, and to all the people of Israel, that by the name of Jesus Christ of Nazareth, whom you crucified, whom God raised from the dead, by him this man is standing before you well. 11 This is the stone which was rejected by you builders, but which has become the head of the corner. 12And there is salvation in no one else, for there is no other name under heaven given among men by which we must be saved."

13 Now when they saw the boldness of Peter and John, and perceived that they were uneducated, common men, they wondered; and they recognized that they had been with Jesus. 14 But seeing the man that had been healed standing beside them, they had nothing to say in opposition. 15 But when they had commanded them to go aside out of the council, they conferred with one another, 16 saying, "What shall we do with these men? For that a notable sign has been performed through them is manifest to all the inhabitants of Jerusalem, and we cannot deny it. 17 But in order that it may spread no further among the people, let us warn them to speak no more to any one in this name." 18 So they called them and charged them not to speak or teach at all in the name of Jesus. 19 But Peter and John answered them, "Whether it is right in the sight of God to listen to you rather than to God, you must judge; 20 for we cannot but speak of what we have seen and heard." 21And when they had further threatened them, they let them go, finding no way to punish them, because of the people; for all men praised God for what had happened. 22 For the man on whom this sign of healing was performed was more than forty years old.

23 When they were released they went to their friends and reported what the chief priests and the elders had said to them. 24And when they heard it, they lifted their voices to-

gether to God and said, "Sovereign Lord, who didst make the heaven and the earth and the sea and everything in them, 25 who by the mouth of our father David, thy servant,ᶜ didst say by the Holy Spirit,

  'Why did the Gentiles rage,
    and the peoples imagine vain things?
26 The kings of the earth set themselves in array,
    and the rulers were gathered together,
    against the Lord and against his Anointed'—ᵉ

27 for truly in this city there were gathered together against thy holy servantᶜ Jesus, whom thou didst anoint, both Her′ód and Pontius Pilate, with the Gentiles and the peoples of Israel, 28 to do whatever thy hand and thy plan had predestined to take place. 29And now, Lord, look upon their threats, and grant to thy servantsᶠ to speak thy word with all boldness, 30 while thou stretchest out thy hand to heal, and signs and wonders are performed through the name of thy holy servantᶜ Jesus." 31And when they had prayed, the place in which they were gathered together was shaken; and they were all filled with the Holy Spirit and spoke the word of God with boldness.

32 Now the company of those who believed were of one heart and soul, and no one said that any of the things which he possessed was his own, but they had everything in common. 33And with great power the apostles gave their testimony to the resurrection of the Lord Jesus, and great grace was upon them all. 34 There was not a needy person among them, for as many as were possessors of lands or houses sold them, and brought the proceeds of what was sold 35 and laid it at the apostles' feet; and distribution was made to each as any had need. 36 Thus Joseph who was surnamed by the apostles Bär′nȧ·bás (which means, Son of encouragement), a Levite, a native of Cyprus, 37 sold a field which belonged to him, and brought the money and laid it at the apostles' feet.

5 But a man named An·a·ni′ás with his wife Sap·phi′rȧ sold a piece of property, 2 and with his wife's knowledge he kept back some of the proceeds, and brought only a part and laid it at the apostles' feet. 3 But Peter said, "An·a·ni′ás, why has Satan filled your heart to lie to the Holy Spirit and to keep back part of the proceeds of

ᶜ Or *child* ᵉ Or *Christ* ᶠ Or *slaves*
4.11: Ps 118.22. **4.24:** Ex 20.11; Ps 146.6. **4.25-26:** Ps 2.1-2. **4.27:** Ps 2.2; 2.1.
4.32-35: Acts 2.44-45.

the land? 4 While it remained unsold, did it not remain your own? And after it was sold, was it not at your disposal? How is it that you have contrived this deed in your heart? You have not lied to men but to God." 5 When An·à·ni'ás heard these words, he fell down and died. And great fear came upon all who heard of it. 6 The young men rose and wrapped him up and carried him out and buried him.

7 After an interval of about three hours his wife came in, not knowing what had happened. 8And Peter said to her, "Tell me whether you sold the land for so much." And she said, "Yes, for so much." 9 But Peter said to her, "How is it that you have agreed together to tempt the Spirit of the Lord? Hark, the feet of those that have buried your husband are at the door, and they will carry you out." 10 Immediately she fell down at his feet and died. When the young men came in they found her dead, and they carried her out and buried her beside her husband. 11And great fear came upon the whole church, and upon all who heard of these things.

12 Now many signs and wonders were done among the people by the hands of the apostles. And they were all together in Solomon's Portico. 13 None of the rest dared join them, but the people held them in high honor. 14And more than ever believers were added to the Lord, multitudes both of men and women, 15 so that they even carried out the sick into the streets, and laid them on beds and pallets, that as Peter came by at least his shadow might fall on some of them. 16 The people also gathered from the towns around Jerusalem, bringing the sick and those afflicted with unclean spirits, and they were all healed.

17 But the high priest rose up and all who were with him, that is, the party of the Sad'du·cees, and filled with jealousy 18 they arrested the apostles and put them in the common prison. 19 But at night an angel of the Lord opened the prison doors and brought them out and said, 20 "Go and stand in the temple and speak to the people all the words of this Life." 21And when they heard this, they entered the temple at daybreak and taught.

Now the high priest came and those who were with him and called together the council and all the senate of Israel, and sent to the prison to have them brought. 22 But when the officers came,

they did not find them in the prison, and they returned and reported, 23 "We found the prison securely locked and the sentries standing at the doors, but when we opened it we found no one inside." 24 Now when the captain of the temple and the chief priests heard these words, they were much perplexed about them, wondering what this would come to. 25And some one came and told them, "The men whom you put in prison are standing in the temple and teaching the people." 26 Then the captain with the officers went and brought them, but without violence, for they were afraid of being stoned by the people.

27 And when they had brought them, they set them before the council. And the high priest questioned them, 28 saying, "We strictly charged you not to teach in this name, yet here you have filled Jerusalem with your teaching and you intend to bring this man's blood upon us." 29 But Peter and the apostles answered, "We must obey God rather than men. 30 The God of our fathers raised Jesus whom you killed by hanging him on a tree. 31 God exalted him at his right hand as Leader and Savior, to give repentance to Israel and forgiveness of sins. 32And we are witnesses to these things, and so is the Holy Spirit whom God has given to those who obey him."

33 When they heard this they were enraged and wanted to kill them. 34 But a Pharisee in the council named Gà·mā'li·èl, a teacher of the law, held in honor by all the people, stood up and ordered the men to be put outside for a while. 35And he said to them, "Men of Israel, take care what you do with these men. 36 For before these days Theū'dàs arose, giving himself out to be somebody, and a number of men, about four hundred, joined him; but he was slain and all who followed him were dispersed and came to nothing. 37After him Judas the Galilean arose in the days of the census and drew away some of the people after him; he also perished, and all who followed him were scattered. 38 So in the present case I tell you, keep away from these men and let them alone; for if this plan or this undertaking is of men, it will fail; 39 but if it is of God, you will not be able to overthrow them. You might even be found opposing God!"

40 So they took his advice, and when they had called in the apostles, they beat them and charged them not

5.30: Deut 21.22-23.

to speak in the name of Jesus, and let them go. [41] Then they left the presence of the council, rejoicing that they were counted worthy to suffer dishonor for the name. [42] And every day in the temple and at home they did not cease teaching and preaching Jesus as the Christ.

6 Now in these days when the disciples were increasing in number, the Hellenists murmured against the Hebrews because their widows were neglected in the daily distribution. [2] And the twelve summoned the body of the disciples and said, "It is not right that we should give up preaching the word of God to serve tables. [3] Therefore, brethren, pick out from among you seven men of good repute, full of the Spirit and of wisdom, whom we may appoint to this duty. [4] But we will devote ourselves to prayer and to the ministry of the word." [5] And what they said pleased the whole multitude, and they chose Stephen, a man full of faith and of the Holy Spirit, and Philip, and Proch′o·rús, and Ni·cā′nór, and Ti′món, and Pắr′mė·nas, and Nic·ỏ·lā′ús, a proselyte of An′ti·och. [6] These they set before the apostles, and they prayed and laid their hands upon them.

[7] And the word of God increased; and the number of the disciples multiplied greatly in Jerusalem, and a great many of the priests were obedient to the faith.

[8] And Stephen, full of grace and power, did great wonders and signs among the people. [9] Then some of those who belonged to the synagogue of the Freedmen (as it was called), and of the Cȳ·rē′ni·áns, and of the Alexandrians, and of those from Ci·li′ci·à and Asia, arose and disputed with Stephen. [10] But they could not withstand the wisdom and the Spirit with which he spoke. [11] Then they secretly instigated men, who said, "We have heard him speak blasphemous words against Moses and God." [12] And they stirred up the people and the elders and the scribes, and they came upon him and seized him and brought him before the council, [13] and set up false witnesses who said, "This man never ceases to speak words against this holy place and the law; [14] for we have heard him say

that this Jesus of Nazareth will destroy this place, and will change the customs which Moses delivered to us." [15] And gazing at him, all who sat in the council saw that his face was like the face of an angel.

7 And the high priest said, "Is this so?" [2] And Stephen said:

"Brethren and fathers, hear me. The God of glory appeared to our father Abraham, when he was in Mes·ỏ·pỏ·tā′mi·à, before he lived in Hâr′án, [3] and said to him, 'Depart from your land and from your kindred and go into the land which I will show you.' [4] Then he departed from the land of the Chal·dĕ′áns, and lived in Hâr′án. And after his father died, God removed him from there into this land in which you are now living; [5] yet he gave him no inheritance in it, not even a foot's length, but promised to give it to him in possession and to his posterity after him, though he had no child. [6] And God spoke to this effect, that his posterity would be aliens in a land belonging to others, who would enslave them and ill-treat them four hundred years. [7] 'But I will judge the nation which they serve,' said God, 'and after that they shall come out and worship me in this place.' [8] And he gave him the covenant of circumcision. And so Abraham became the father of Isaac, and circumcised him on the eighth day; and Isaac became the father of Jacob, and Jacob of the twelve patriarchs.

[9] "And the patriarchs, jealous of Joseph, sold him into Egypt; but God was with him, [10] and rescued him out of all his afflictions, and gave him favor and wisdom before Pharaoh, king of Egypt, who made him governor over Egypt and over all his household. [11] Now there came a famine throughout all Egypt and Canaan, and great affliction, and our fathers could find no food. [12] But when Jacob heard that there was grain in Egypt, he sent forth our fathers the first time. [13] And at the second visit Joseph made himself known to his brothers, and Joseph's family became known to Pharaoh. [14] And Joseph sent and called to him Jacob his father and all his kindred, seventy-five souls; [15] and Jacob went down into Egypt. And he died, himself and our fathers, [16] and they were

7.2: Ps 29.3; Gen 11.31; 15.7.   **7.3:** Gen 12.1.   **7.4:** Gen 11.31; 15.7; 12.5.
7.5: Deut 2.5; Gen 12.7; 17.8.   **7.6-7:** Gen 15.13-14.   **7.7:** Ex 3.12.
7.8: Gen 17.10-14; 21.2-4; 25.26; 29.31-35; 30.1-24; 35.16-18, 23-26.
7.9: Gen 37.11, 28; 45.4.   **7.9-10:** Gen 39.2-3, 21.   **7.10:** Gen 41.40-46; Ps 105.21.
7.11: Gen 41.54-55; 42.5.   **7.12:** Gen 42.2.   **7.13:** Gen 45.1-4.   **7.14:** Gen 45.9-10.
7.14-15: Deut 10.22.   **7.16:** Josh 24.32; Gen 50.13.

carried back to Shĕ'chem and laid in the tomb that Abraham had bought for a sum of silver from the sons of Hā'mor in Shechem.

17 "But as the time of the promise drew near, which God had granted to Abraham, the people grew and multiplied in Egypt [18] till there arose over Egypt another king who had not known Joseph. [19] He dealt craftily with our race and forced our fathers to expose their infants, that they might not be kept alive. [20]At this time Moses was born, and was beautiful before God. And he was brought up for three months in his father's house; [21] and when he was exposed, Pharaoh's daughter adopted him and brought him up as her own son. [22]And Moses was instructed in all the wisdom of the Egyptians, and he was mighty in his words and deeds.

23 "When he was forty years old, it came into his heart to visit his brethren, the sons of Israel. [24]And seeing one of them being wronged, he defended the oppressed man and avenged him by striking the Egyptian. [25] He supposed that his brethren understood that God was giving them deliverance by his hand, but they did not understand. [26]And on the following day he appeared to them as they were quarreling and would have reconciled them, saying, 'Men, you are brethren, why do you wrong each other?' [27] But the man who was wronging his neighbor thrust him aside, saying, 'Who made you a ruler and a judge over us? [28] Do you want to kill me as you killed the Egyptian yesterday?' [29]At this retort Moses fled, and became an exile in the land of Mid'i·àn, where he became the father of two sons.

30 "Now when forty years had passed, an angel appeared to him in the wilderness of Mount Sinai, in a flame of fire in a bush. [31] When Moses saw it he wondered at the sight; and as he drew near to look, the voice of the Lord came, [32] 'I am the God of your fathers, the God of Abraham and of Isaac and of Jacob.' And Moses trembled and did not dare to look. [33]And the Lord said to him, 'Take off the shoes from your feet, for the place where you are standing is holy ground. [34] I have surely seen the ill-treatment of my people that are in Egypt and heard their groaning, and I have come down to deliver them. And now come, I will send you to Egypt.'

35 "This Moses whom they refused, saying, 'Who made you a ruler and a judge?' God sent as both ruler and deliverer by the hand of the angel that appeared to him in the bush. [36] He led them out, having performed wonders and signs in Egypt and at the Red Sea, and in the wilderness for forty years. [37] This is the Moses who said to the Israelites, 'God will raise up for you a prophet from your brethren as he raised me up.' [38] This is he who was in the congregation in the wilderness with the angel who spoke to him at Mount Sinai, and with our fathers; and he received living oracles to give to us. [39] Our fathers refused to obey him, but they thrust him aside, and in their hearts they turned to Egypt, [40] saying to Aaron, 'Make for us gods to go before us; as for this Moses who led us out from the land of Egypt, we do not know what has become of him.' [41]And they made a calf in those days, and offered a sacrifice to the idol and rejoiced in the works of their hands. [42] But God turned and gave them over to worship the host of heaven, as it is written in the book of the prophets:

'Did you offer to me slain beasts
    and sacrifices,
forty years in the wilderness, O
    house of Israel?
[43] And you took up the tent of Mō'loch,
    and the star of the god Rĕ'phàn,
    the figures which you made to
    worship;
and I will remove you beyond
    Babylon.'

44 "Our fathers had the tent of witness in the wilderness, even as he who spoke to Moses directed him to make it, according to the pattern that he had seen. [45] Our fathers in turn brought it in with Joshua when they dispossessed the nations which God thrust out before our fathers. So it was until the days of David, [46] who found favor in the sight of God and asked leave to find a habitation for the God of Jacob. [47] But it was Solomon who built a house for him. [48] Yet the Most High does not dwell in houses made with hands; as the prophet says,

7.17-18: Ex 1.7-8.   7.19: Ex 1.10-11, 15-22.   7.20: Ex 2.2.   7.21: Ex 2.5-6, 10.
7.23-29: Ex 2.11-15.   7.29: Ex 2.22; 18.3-4.   7.30-34: Ex 3.1-10.   7.35: Ex 2.14.
7.36: Ex 7.3; 14.21; Num 14.33.   7.37: Deut 18.15, 18.   7.38: Ex 19.   7.39: Num 14.3-4.
7.40: Ex 32.1, 23.   7.41: Ex 32.4, 6.   7.42: Jer 19.13.   7.42-43: Amos 5.25-27.
7.44: Ex 25.9, 40.   7.45: Josh 3.14-17; Deut 32.49.   7.46: 2 Sam 7.8-16; Ps 132.1-5.
7.47: 1 Kings 6.

49 'Heaven is my throne,
and earth my footstool.
What house will you build for me,
says the Lord,
or what is the place of my rest?
50 Did not my hand make all these things?'

51 "You stiff-necked people, uncircumcised in heart and ears, you always resist the Holy Spirit. As your fathers did, so do you. 52 Which of the prophets did not your fathers persecute? And they killed those who announced beforehand the coming of the Righteous One, whom you have now betrayed and murdered, 53 you who received the law as delivered by angels and did not keep it."

54 Now when they heard these things they were enraged, and they ground their teeth against him. 55 But he, full of the Holy Spirit, gazed into heaven and saw the glory of God, and Jesus standing at the right hand of God; 56 and he said, "Behold, I see the heavens opened, and the Son of man standing at the right hand of God." 57 But they cried out with a loud voice and stopped their ears and rushed together upon him. 58 Then they cast him out of the city and stoned him; and the witnesses laid down their garments at the feet of a young man named Saul. 59 And as they were stoning Stephen, he prayed, "Lord Jesus, receive my spirit." 60 And he knelt down and cried with a loud voice, "Lord, do not hold this sin against them." And when he had said this, he fell asleep. 1 And Saul was consenting to his death.

8 And on that day a great persecution arose against the church in Jerusalem; and they were all scattered throughout the region of Judea and Sà·mâr′i·à, except the apostles. 2 Devout men buried Stephen, and made great lamentation over him. 3 But Saul laid waste the church, and entering house after house, he dragged off men and women and committed them to prison.

4 Now those who were scattered went about preaching the word. 5 Philip went down to a city of Sà·mâr′i·à, and proclaimed to them the Christ. 6 And the multitudes with one accord gave heed to what was said by Philip, when they heard him and saw the signs which he did. 7 For unclean spirits came out of many who were possessed, crying with a loud voice; and many who were paralyzed or lame

were healed. 8 So there was much joy in that city.

9 But there was a man named Simon who had previously practiced magic in the city and amazed the nation of Sà·mâr′i·à, saying that he himself was somebody great. 10 They all gave heed to him, from the least to the greatest, saying, "This man is that power of God which is called Great." 11 And they gave heed to him, because for a long time he had amazed them with his magic. 12 But when they believed Philip as he preached good news about the kingdom of God and the name of Jesus Christ, they were baptized, both men and women. 13 Even Simon himself believed, and after being baptized he continued with Philip. And seeing signs and great miracles performed, he was amazed.

14 Now when the apostles at Jerusalem heard that Sà·mâr′i·à had received the word of God, they sent to them Peter and John, 15 who came down and prayed for them that they might receive the Holy Spirit; 16 for it had not yet fallen on any of them, but they had only been baptized in the name of the Lord Jesus. 17 Then they laid their hands on them and they received the Holy Spirit. 18 Now when Simon saw that the Spirit was given through the laying on of the apostles' hands, he offered them money, 19 saying, "Give me also this power, that any one on whom I lay my hands may receive the Holy Spirit." 20 But Peter said to him, "Your silver perish with you, because you thought you could obtain the gift of God with money! 21 You have neither part nor lot in this matter, for your heart is not right before God. 22 Repent therefore of this wickedness of yours, and pray to the Lord that, if possible, the intent of your heart may be forgiven you. 23 For I see that you are in the gall of bitterness and in the bond of iniquity." 24 And Simon answered, "Pray for me to the Lord, that nothing of what you have said may come upon me."

25 Now when they had testified and spoken the word of the Lord, they returned to Jerusalem, preaching the gospel to many villages of the Samaritans.

26 But an angel of the Lord said to Philip, "Rise and go toward the south[g] to the road that goes down from Jerusalem to Gā′zà." This is a desert road. 27 And he rose and went. And behold,

g Or at noon

7.49-50: Is 66.1-2.   7.51: Ex 33.3, 5; Jer 9.26; 6.10; Num 27.14; Is 63.10.
8.1: Acts 11.19.   8.21: Ps 78.37.   8.23: Is 58.6.

an Ethiopian, a eunuch, a minister of Can·dā´çē the queen of the Ethiopians, in charge of all her treasure, had come to Jerusalem to worship 28 and was returning; seated in his chariot, he was reading the prophet I·ṣāi´áh. 29And the Spirit said to Philip, "Go up and join this chariot." 30 So Philip ran to him, and heard him reading I·ṣāi´áh the prophet, and asked, "Do you understand what you are reading?" 31And he said, "How can I, unless some one guides me?" And he invited Philip to come up and sit with him. 32 Now the passage of the scripture which he was reading was this:

"As a sheep led to the slaughter
or a lamb before its shearer is dumb,
so he opens not his mouth.
33 In his humiliation justice was denied him.
Who can describe his generation?
For his life is taken up from the earth."

34And the eunuch said to Philip, "About whom, pray, does the prophet say this, about himself or about some one else?" 35 Then Philip opened his mouth, and beginning with this scripture he told him the good news of Jesus. 36And as they went along the road they came to some water, and the eunuch said, "See, here is water! What is to prevent my being baptized?"ʰ 38And he commanded the chariot to stop, and they both went down into the water, Philip and the eunuch, and he baptized him. 39And when they came up out of the water, the Spirit of the Lord caught up Philip; and the eunuch saw him no more, and went on his way rejoicing. 40 But Philip was found at A·zō´tŭs, and passing on he preached the gospel to all the towns till he came to Caes·a·rē´á.

9 But Saul, still breathing threats and murder against the disciples of the Lord, went to the high priest 2 and asked him for letters to the synagogues at Damascus, so that if he found any belonging to the Way, men or women, he might bring them bound to Jerusalem. 3 Now as he journeyed he approached Damascus, and suddenly a light from heaven flashed about him. 4And he fell to the ground and heard a voice saying to him, "Saul, Saul, why do you persecute me?" 5And he said, "Who are you, Lord?" And he said, "I am Jesus, whom you are persecuting; 6 but rise and enter the

city, and you will be told what you are to do."7 The men who were traveling with him stood speechless, hearing the voice but seeing no one. 8 Saul arose from the ground; and when his eyes were opened, he could see nothing; so they led him by the hand and brought him into Damascus. 9And for three days he was without sight, and neither ate nor drank.

10 Now there was a disciple at Damascus named An·à·nī´ás. The Lord said to him in a vision, "Ananias."And he said, "Here I am, Lord." 11And the Lord said to him, "Rise and go to the street called Straight, and inquire in the house of Judas for a man of Tär´sŭs named Saul; for behold, he is praying,12 and he has seen a man named An·à·nī´ás come in and lay his hands on him so that he might regain his sight." 13 But An·à·nī´ás answered, "Lord, I have heard from many about this man, how much evil he has done to thy saints at Jerusalem; 14 and here he has authority from the chief priests to bind all who call upon thy name." 15 But the Lord said to him, "Go, for he is a chosen instrument of mine to carry my name before the Gentiles and kings and the sons of Israel; 16 for I will show him how much he must suffer for the sake of my name." 17 So An·à·nī´ás departed and entered the house. And laying his hands on him he said, "Brother Saul, the Lord Jesus who appeared to you on the road by which you came, has sent me that you may regain your sight and be filled with the Holy Spirit." 18And immediately something like scales fell from his eyes and he regained his sight. Then he rose and was baptized, 19 and took food and was strengthened.

For several days he was with the disciples at Damascus. 20And in the synagogues immediately he proclaimed Jesus, saying, "He is the Son of God." 21And all who heard him were amazed, and said, "Is not this the man who made havoc in Jerusalem of those who called on this name? And he has come here for this purpose, to bring them bound before the chief priests." 22 But Saul increased all the more in strength, and confounded the Jews who lived in Damascus by proving that Jesus was the Christ.

23 When many days had passed, the Jews plotted to kill him, 24 but

ʰ Other ancient authorities add all or most of verse 37, *And Philip said, "If you believe with all your heart, you may." And he replied, "I believe that Jesus Christ is the Son of God."*

8.32-33: Is 53.7-8.   **9.1-19:** Acts 22.4-16; 26.9-18.   **9.24-25:** 2 Cor 11.32-33.

their plot became known to Saul. They were watching the gates day and night, to kill him; [25] but his disciples took him by night and let him down over the wall, lowering him in a basket.

26 And when he had come to Jerusalem he attempted to join the disciples; and they were all afraid of him, for they did not believe that he was a disciple. 27 But Bär′nȧ·bȧs took him, and brought him to the apostles, and declared to them how on the road he had seen the Lord, who spoke to him, and how at Damascus he had preached boldly in the name of Jesus. 28 So he went in and out among them at Jerusalem, 29 preaching boldly in the name of the Lord. And he spoke and disputed against the Hellenists; but they were seeking to kill him. 30And when the brethren knew it, they brought him down to Çaes·ȧ·rē′ȧ, and sent him off to Tär′sŭs.

31 So the church throughout all Judea and Galilee and Sȧ·mâr′i·ȧ had peace and was built up; and walking in the fear of the Lord and in the comfort of the Holy Spirit it was multiplied.

32 Now as Peter went here and there among them all, he came down also to the saints that lived at Lyd′dȧ. 33 There he found a man named Aē-nē′ȧs, who had been bedridden for eight years and was paralyzed. 34And Peter said to him, "Aē·nē′ȧs, Jesus Christ heals you; rise and make your bed." And immediately he rose. 35And all the residents of Lyd′dȧ and Sharon saw him, and they turned to the Lord.

36 Now there was at Jop′pȧ a disciple named Tab′i·thȧ, which means Dôr′cȧs or Gȧ·zelle′. She was full of good works and acts of charity. 37 In those days she fell sick and died; and when they had washed her, they laid her in an upper room. 38 Since Lyd′dȧ was near Jop′pȧ, the disciples, hearing that Peter was there, sent two men to him entreating him, "Please come to us without delay." 39 So Peter rose and went with them. And when he had come, they took him to the upper room. All the widows stood beside him weeping, and showing coats and garments which Dôr′cȧs made while she was with them. 40 But Peter put them all outside and knelt down and prayed; then turning to the body he said, "Tab′i·thȧ, rise." And she opened her eyes, and when she saw Peter she sat up. 41And he gave her his hand and lifted her up. Then calling the saints and widows he presented her alive.

10.1-48: Acts 11.4-17.

42And it became known throughout all Jop′pȧ, and many believed in the Lord. 43And he stayed in Jop′pȧ for many days with one Simon, a tanner.

10 At Çaes·ȧ·rē′ȧ there was a man named Cornelius, a centurion of what was known as the Italian Cohort, 2 a devout man who feared God with all his household, gave alms liberally to the people, and prayed constantly to God. 3About the ninth hour of the day he saw clearly in a vision an angel of God coming in and saying to him, "Cornelius." 4And he stared at him in terror, and said, "What is it, Lord?" And he said to him, "Your prayers and your alms have ascended as a memorial before God. 5And now send men to Jop′pȧ, and bring one Simon who is called Peter; 6 he is lodging with Simon, a tanner, whose house is by the seaside." 7 When the angel who spoke to him had departed, he called two of his servants and a devout soldier from among those that waited on him, 8 and having related everything to them, he sent them to Jop′pȧ.

9 The next day, as they were on their journey and coming near the city, Peter went up on the housetop to pray, about the sixth hour. 10And he became hungry and desired something to eat; but while they were preparing it, he fell into a trance 11 and saw the heaven opened, and something descending, like a great sheet, let down by four corners upon the earth. 12 In it were all kinds of animals and reptiles and birds of the air. 13And there came a voice to him, "Rise, Peter; kill and eat." 14 But Peter said, "No, Lord; for I have never eaten anything that is common or unclean." 15And the voice came to him again a second time, "What God has cleansed, you must not call common." 16 This happened three times, and the thing was taken up at once to heaven.

17 Now while Peter was inwardly perplexed as to what the vision which he had seen might mean, behold, the men that were sent by Cornelius, having made inquiry for Simon's house, stood before the gate 18 and called out to ask whether Simon who was called Peter was lodging there. 19And while Peter was pondering the vision, the Spirit said to him, "Behold, three men are looking for you. 20 Rise and go down, and accompany them without hesitation; for I have sent them." 21And Peter went down to the men and said, "I am the one you are looking for; what is the reason for

your coming?" ²²And they said, "Cornelius, a centurion, an upright and God-fearing man, who is well spoken of by the whole Jewish nation, was directed by a holy angel to send for you to come to his house, and to hear what you have to say." ²³ So he called them in to be his guests.

The next day he rose and went off with them, and some of the brethren from Jop'pà accompanied him. ²⁴And on the following day they entered Caes·à·rē'á. Cornelius was expecting them and had called together his kinsmen and close friends. ²⁵ When Peter entered, Cornelius met him and fell down at his feet and worshiped him. ²⁶ But Peter lifted him up, saying, "Stand up; I too am a man." ²⁷And as he talked with him, he went in and found many persons gathered; ²⁸ and he said to them, "You yourselves know how unlawful it is for a Jew to associate with or to visit any one of another nation, but God has shown me that I should not call any man common or unclean. ²⁹ So when I was sent for, I came without objection. I ask then why you sent for me."

30 And Cornelius said, "Four days ago, about this hour, I was keeping the ninth hour of prayer in my house; and behold, a man stood before me in bright apparel, ³¹ saying, 'Cornelius, your prayer has been heard and your alms have been remembered before God. ³² Send therefore to Jop'pà and ask for Simon who is called Peter; he is lodging in the house of Simon, a tanner, by the seaside.' ³³ So I sent to you at once, and you have been kind enough to come. Now therefore we are all here present in the sight of God, to hear all that you have been commanded by the Lord."

34 And Peter opened his mouth and said: "Truly I perceive that God shows no partiality, ³⁵ but in every nation any one who fears him and does what is right is acceptable to him. ³⁶ You know the word which he sent to Israel, preaching good news of peace by Jesus Christ (he is Lord of all), ³⁷ the word which was proclaimed throughout all Judea, beginning from Galilee after the baptism which John preached: ³⁸ how God anointed Jesus of Nazareth with the Holy Spirit and with power; how he went about doing good and healing all that were oppressed by the devil, for God was with him. ³⁹And we are witnesses to all that he did both in the country of the Jews and in Jerusalem. They put him to

11.4-17: Acts 10.1-48.

death by hanging him on a tree; ⁴⁰ but God raised him on the third day and made him manifest; ⁴¹ not to all the people but to us who were chosen by God as witnesses, who ate and drank with him after he rose from the dead. ⁴²And he commanded us to preach to the people, and to testify that he is the one ordained by God to be judge of the living and the dead. ⁴³ To him all the prophets bear witness that every one who believes in him receives forgiveness of sins through his name."

44 While Peter was still saying this, the Holy Spirit fell on all who heard the word. ⁴⁵And the believers from among the circumcised who came with Peter were amazed, because the gift of the Holy Spirit had been poured out even on the Gentiles. ⁴⁶ For they heard them speaking in tongues and extolling God. Then Peter declared, ⁴⁷ "Can any one forbid water for baptizing these people who have received the Holy Spirit just as we have?" ⁴⁸And he commanded them to be baptized in the name of Jesus Christ. Then they asked him to remain for some days.

11 Now the apostles and the brethren who were in Judea heard that the Gentiles also had received the word of God. ² So when Peter went up to Jerusalem, the circumcision party criticized him, ³ saying, "Why did you go to uncircumcised men and eat with them?" ⁴ But Peter began and explained to them in order: ⁵ "I was in the city of Jop'pà praying; and in a trance I saw a vision, something descending, like a great sheet, let down from heaven by four corners; and it came down to me. ⁶ Looking at it closely I observed animals and beasts of prey and reptiles and birds of the air. ⁷And I heard a voice saying to me, 'Rise, Peter; kill and eat.' ⁸ But I said, 'No, Lord; for nothing common or unclean has ever entered my mouth.' ⁹ But the voice answered a second time from heaven, 'What God has cleansed you must not call common.' ¹⁰ This happened three times, and all was drawn up again into heaven. ¹¹At that very moment three men arrived at the house in which we were, sent to me from Caes·à·rē'á. ¹²And the Spirit told me to go with them, making no distinction. These six brethren also accompanied me, and we entered the man's house. ¹³And he told us how he had seen the angel standing in his house and saying, 'Send to Jop'pà and bring Simon called Peter; ¹⁴ he will declare to you a message by which you will be

JESUS TEACHING HIS DISCIPLES TO PRAY   *Matt. 11:1*

JESUS AND THE CHILDREN   *Matt. 19:13*

saved, you and all your household.'
¹⁵As I began to speak, the Holy Spirit
fell on them just as on us at the beginning. ¹⁶And I remembered the word
of the Lord, how he said, 'John baptized with water, but you shall be
baptized with the Holy Spirit.' ¹⁷ If
then God gave the same gift to them
as he gave to us when we believed in
the Lord Jesus Christ, who was I that
I could withstand God?" ¹⁸ When they
heard this they were silenced. And
they glorified God, saying, "Then to
the Gentiles also God has granted
repentance unto life."

19 Now those who were scattered
because of the persecution that arose
over Stephen traveled as far as Phoe-
ni'ci-a and Cyprus and An'ti-och,
speaking the word to none except
Jews. ²⁰ But there were some of them,
men of Cyprus and Cȳ-rē'nē, who on
coming to An'ti-och spoke to the
Greeksⁱ also, preaching the Lord
Jesus. ²¹And the hand of the Lord was
with them, and a great number that
believed turned to the Lord. ²² News
of this came to the ears of the church
in Jerusalem, and they sent Bär'na-bas
to An'ti-och. ²³ When he came and
saw the grace of God, he was glad; and
he exhorted them all to remain faithful
to the Lord with steadfast purpose;
²⁴ for he was a good man, full of the
Holy Spirit and of faith. And a large
company was added to the Lord. ²⁵ So
Bär'na-bas went to Tär'sus to look for
Saul; ²⁶ and when he had found him,
he brought him to An'ti-och. For a
whole year they met withⁱ the church,
and taught a large company of people;
and in Antioch the disciples were for
the first time called Christians.

27 Now in these days prophets
came down from Jerusalem to An'ti-
och. ²⁸And one of them named Ag'a-
bus stood up and foretold by the Spirit
that there would be a great famine over
all the world; and this took place in the
days of Claudius. ²⁹And the disciples
determined, every one according to his
ability, to send relief to the brethren
who lived in Judea; ³⁰ and they did so,
sending it to the elders by the hand of
Bär'na-bas and Saul.

12 About that time Her'od the king
laid violent hands upon some who
belonged to the church. ² He killed
James the brother of John with the
sword; ³ and when he saw that it
pleased the Jews, he proceeded to
arrest Peter also. This was during the
days of Unleavened Bread. ⁴And when

he had seized him, he put him in
prison, and delivered him to four
squads of soldiers to guard him,
intending after the Passover to bring
him out to the people. ⁵ So Peter was
kept in prison; but earnest prayer for
him was made to God by the church.

6 The very night when Her'od was
about to bring him out, Peter was
sleeping between two soldiers, bound
with two chains, and sentries before
the door were guarding the prison;
⁷ and behold, an angel of the Lord
appeared, and a light shone in the
cell; and he struck Peter on the side
and woke him, saying, "Get up
quickly." And the chains fell off his
hands. ⁸And the angel said to him,
"Dress yourself and put on your
sandals." And he did so. And he said
to him, "Wrap your mantle around
you and follow me." ⁹And he went out
and followed him; he did not know
that what was done by the angel was
real, but thought he was seeing a
vision. ¹⁰ When they had passed the
first and the second guard, they came
to the iron gate leading into the city.
It opened to them of its own accord,
and they went out and passed on
through one street; and immediately
the angel left him. ¹¹And Peter came
to himself, and said, "Now I am sure
that the Lord has sent his angel and
rescued me from the hand of Her'od
and from all that the Jewish people
were expecting."

12 When he realized this, he went
to the house of Mary, the mother of
John whose other name was Mark,
where many were gathered together
and were praying. ¹³And when he
knocked at the door of the gateway, a
maid named Rhō'da came to answer.
¹⁴ Recognizing Peter's voice, in her
joy she did not open the gate but ran
in and told that Peter was standing at
the gate. ¹⁵ They said to her, "You are
mad." But she insisted that it was so.
They said, "It is his angel!" ¹⁶ But
Peter continued knocking; and when
they opened, they saw him and were
amazed. ¹⁷ But motioning to them
with his hand to be silent, he described
to them how the Lord had brought
him out of the prison. And he said,
"Tell this to James and to the brethren." Then he departed and went to
another place.

18 Now when day came, there was
no small stir among the soldiers over
what had become of Peter. ¹⁹And
when Her'od had sought for him and

ⁱ Other ancient authorities read *Hellenists* ⁱ Or *were guests of*
11.16: Acts 1.5. **11.19:** Acts 8.4.

could not find him, he examined the sentries and ordered that they should be put to death. Then he went down from Judea to Caes·à·rē′à, and remained there.

20 Now Her′ód was angry with the people of Tȳre and Sī′don; and they came to him in a body, and having persuaded Blas′tús, the king's chamberlain, they asked for peace, because their country depended on the king's country for food. 21 On an appointed day Her′ód put on his royal robes, took his seat upon the throne, and made an oration to them. 22And the people shouted, "The voice of a god, and not of man!" 23 Immediately an angel of the Lord smote him, because he did not give God the glory; and he was eaten by worms and died.

24 But the word of God grew and multiplied.

25 And Bär′nà·bàs and Saul returned from^k Jerusalem when they had fulfilled their mission, bringing with them John whose other name was Mark.

13 Now in the church at An′ti·och there were prophets and teachers, Bär′nà·bàs, Sym′ē·ón who was called Nī′gẽr, Lucius of Cȳ·rē′nē, Man′à·en a member of the court of Her′ód the tetrarch, and Saul. 2 While they were worshiping the Lord and fasting, the Holy Spirit said, "Set apart for me Bär′nà·bàs and Saul for the work to which I have called them." 3 Then after fasting and praying they laid their hands on them and sent them off.

4 So, being sent out by the Holy Spirit, they went down to Sè·leü′cí·à; and from there they sailed to Cyprus. 5 When they arrived at Sal′à·mis, they proclaimed the word of God in the synagogues of the Jews. And they had John to assist them. 6 When they had gone through the whole island as far as Pā′phos, they came upon a certain magician, a Jewish false prophet, named Bär-Jē′sús. 7 He was with the proconsul, Sēr′gí·ús Pāul′ús, a man of intelligence, who summoned Bär′nà·bàs and Saul and sought to hear the word of God. 8 But El′y·màs the magician (for that is the meaning of his name) withstood them, seeking to turn away the proconsul from the faith. 9 But Saul, who is also called Paul, filled with the Holy Spirit,

looked intently at him 10 and said, "You son of the devil, you enemy of all righteousness, full of all deceit and villainy, will you not stop making crooked the straight paths of the Lord? 11And now, behold, the hand of the Lord is upon you, and you shall be blind and unable to see the sun for a time." Immediately mist and darkness fell upon him and he went about seeking people to lead him by the hand. 12 Then the proconsul believed, when he saw what had occurred, for he was astonished at the teaching of the Lord.

13 Now Paul and his company set sail from Pā′phos, and came to Pēr′gà in Pam·phyl′i·à. And John left them and returned to Jerusalem; 14 but they passed on from Pēr′gà and came to An′ti·och of Pi·sid′i·à. And on the sabbath day they went into the synagogue and sat down. 15After the reading of the law and the prophets, the rulers of the synagogue sent to them, saying, "Brethren, if you have any word of exhortation for the people, say it." 16 So Paul stood up, and motioning with his hand said:

"Men of Israel, and you that fear God, listen. 17 The God of this people Israel chose our fathers and made the people great during their stay in the land of Egypt, and with uplifted arm he led them out of it. 18And for about forty years he bore with^m them in the wilderness. 19And when he had destroyed seven nations in the land of Canaan, he gave them their land as an inheritance, for about four hundred and fifty years. 20And after that he gave them judges until Samuel the prophet. 21 Then they asked for a king; and God gave them Saul the son of Kish, a man of the tribe of Benjamin, for forty years. 22And when he had removed him, he raised up David to be their king; of whom he testified and said, 'I have found in David the son of Jesse a man after my heart, who will do all my will.' 23 Of this man's posterity God has brought to Israel a Savior, Jesus, as he promised. 24 Before his coming John had preached the baptism of repentance to all the people of Israel. 25And as John was finishing his course, he said, 'What do you suppose that I am? I am not he. No, but after me one is coming, the sandals of whose feet I am not worthy to untie.' 26 "Brethren, sons of the family of

^{k} Other ancient authorities read *to*
^{m} Other ancient authorities read *cared for* (Deut 1.31)

13.10: Hos 14.9.   **13.17:** Ex 6.1, 6.   **13.18:** Deut 1.31.   **13.19:** Deut 7.1; Josh 14.1.
13.22: Ps 89.20; 1 Sam 13.14; Is 44.28.   **13.24:** Mk 1.1-4.
13.25: Jn 1.20; Mt 3.11; Mk 1.7; Lk 3.16.   **13.26:** Ps 107.20.

Abraham, and those among you that fear God, to us has been sent the message of this salvation. 27 For those who live in Jerusalem and their rulers, because they did not recognize him nor understand the utterances of the prophets which are read every sabbath, fulfilled these by condemning him. 28 Though they could charge him with nothing deserving death, yet they asked Pilate to have him killed. 29And when they had fulfilled all that was written of him, they took him down from the tree, and laid him in a tomb. 30 But God raised him from the dead; 31 and for many days he appeared to those who came up with him from Galilee to Jerusalem, who are now his witnesses to the people. 32And we bring you the good news that what God promised to the fathers, 33 this he has fulfilled to us their children by raising Jesus; as also it is written in the second psalm,

'Thou art my Son,
    today I have begotten thee.'

34And as for the fact that he raised him from the dead, no more to return to corruption, he spoke in this way,

'I will give you the holy and sure
    blessings of David.'

35 Therefore he says also in another psalm,

'Thou wilt not let thy Holy One see
    corruption.'

36 For David, after he had served the counsel of God in his own generation, fell asleep, and was laid with his fathers, and saw corruption; 37 but he whom God raised up saw no corruption. 38 Let it be known to you therefore, brethren, that through this man forgiveness of sins is proclaimed to you, 39 and by him every one that believes is freed from everything from which you could not be freed by the law of Moses. 40 Beware, therefore, lest there come upon you what is said in the prophets:

41 'Behold, you scoffers, and wonder,
    and perish;
for I do a deed in your days,
    a deed you will never believe, if one
        declares it to you.'"

42 As they went out, the people begged that these things might be told them the next sabbath. 43And when the meeting of the synagogue broke up, many Jews and devout converts to Judaism followed Paul and Bär´nȧ-bȧs, who spoke to them and urged them to continue in the grace of God.

44 The next sabbath almost the whole city gathered together to hear the word of God. 45 But when the Jews saw the multitudes, they were filled with jealousy, and contradicted what was spoken by Paul, and reviled him. 46And Paul and Bär´nȧ-bȧs spoke out boldly, saying, "It was necessary that the word of God should be spoken first to you. Since you thrust it from you, and judge yourselves unworthy of eternal life, behold, we turn to the Gentiles. 47 For so the Lord has commanded us, saying,

'I have set you to be a light for the
    Gentiles,
that you may bring salvation to the
    uttermost parts of the earth.'"

48 And when the Gentiles heard this, they were glad and glorified the word of God; and as many as were ordained to eternal life believed. 49And the word of the Lord spread throughout all the region. 50 But the Jews incited the devout women of high standing and the leading men of the city, and stirred up persecution against Paul and Bär´nȧ-bȧs, and drove them out of their district. 51 But they shook off the dust from their feet against them, and went to I-cō´ni-ŭm. 52And the disciples were filled with joy and with the Holy Spirit.

14 Now at I-cō´ni-ŭm they entered together into the Jewish synagogue, and so spoke that a great company believed, both of Jews and of Greeks. 2 But the unbelieving Jews stirred up the Gentiles and poisoned their minds against the brethren. 3 So they remained for a long time, speaking boldly for the Lord, who bore witness to the word of his grace, granting signs and wonders to be done by their hands. 4 But the people of the city were divided; some sided with the Jews, and some with the apostles. 5 When an attempt was made by both Gentiles and Jews, with their rulers, to molest them and to stone them, 6 they learned of it and fled to Lys´trȧ and Dēr´bē, cities of Lyc-ā-ō´ni-ȧ, and to the surrounding country; 7 and there they preached the gospel.

8 Now at Lys´trȧ there was a man sitting, who could not use his feet; he was a cripple from birth, who had never walked. 9 He listened to Paul speaking; and Paul, looking intently at him and seeing that he had faith to be made well, 10 said in a loud voice, "Stand upright on your feet." And he sprang up and walked. 11And when the crowds saw what Paul had done, they lifted up their voices, saying in Lyc-ā-ō´ni-ȧn, "The gods have come

13.33: Ps 2.7.   13.34: Is 55.3.   13.35: Ps 16.10.   13.41: Hab 1.5.   13.47: Is 49.6.

down to us in the likeness of men!" 12 Bär'nȧ·bȧs they called Zeus, and Paul, because he was the chief speaker, they called Hẽr'mēš. 13 And the priest of Zeus, whose temple was in front of the city, brought oxen and garlands to the gates and wanted to offer sacrifice with the people. 14 But when the apostles Bär'nȧ·bȧs and Paul heard of it, they tore their garments and rushed out among the multitude, crying, 15 "Men, why are you doing this? We also are men, of like nature with you, and bring you good news, that you should turn from these vain things to a living God who made the heaven and the earth and the sea and all that is in them. 16 In past generations he allowed all the nations to walk in their own ways; 17 yet he did not leave himself without witness, for he did good and gave you from heaven rains and fruitful seasons, satisfying your hearts with food and gladness." 18 With these words they scarcely restrained the people from offering sacrifice to them.

19 But Jews came there from An'ti·och and I·cō'ni·ùm; and having persuaded the people, they stoned Paul and dragged him out of the city, supposing that he was dead. 20 But when the disciples gathered about him, he rose up and entered the city; and on the next day he went on with Bär'nȧ·bȧs to Dẽr'bē. 21 When they had preached the gospel to that city and had made many disciples, they returned to Lys'trȧ and to I·cō'ni·ùm and to An'ti·och, 22 strengthening the souls of the disciples, exhorting them to continue in the faith, and saying that through many tribulations we must enter the kingdom of God. 23 And when they had appointed elders for them in every church, with prayer and fasting, they committed them to the Lord in whom they believed.

24 Then they passed through Pi·sid'i·ȧ, and came to Pam·phyl'i·ȧ. 25 And when they had spoken the word in Pẽr'gȧ, they went down to At·tȧ·li'ȧ; 26 and from there they sailed to An'ti·och, where they had been commended to the grace of God for the work which they had fulfilled. 27 And when they arrived, they gathered the church together and declared all that God had done with them, and how he had opened a door of faith to the Gentiles. 28 And they remained no little time with the disciples.

15 But some men came down from Judea and were teaching the

brethren, "Unless you are circumcised according to the custom of Moses, you cannot be saved." 2 And when Paul and Bär'nȧ·bȧs had no small dissension and debate with them, Paul and Barnabas and some of the others were appointed to go up to Jerusalem to the apostles and the elders about this question. 3 So, being sent on their way by the church, they passed through both Phoè·ni'ci·ȧ and Sȧ·mâr'i·ȧ, reporting the conversion of the Gentiles, and they gave great joy to all the brethren. 4 When they came to Jerusalem, they were welcomed by the church and the apostles and the elders, and they declared all that God had done with them. 5 But some believers who belonged to the party of the Pharisees rose up, and said, "It is necessary to circumcise them, and to charge them to keep the law of Moses."

6 The apostles and the elders were gathered together to consider this matter. 7 And after there had been much debate, Peter rose and said to them, "Brethren, you know that in the early days God made choice among you, that by my mouth the Gentiles should hear the word of the gospel and believe. 8 And God who knows the heart bore witness to them, giving them the Holy Spirit just as he did to us; 9 and he made no distinction between us and them, but cleansed their hearts by faith. 10 Now therefore why do you make trial of God by putting a yoke upon the neck of the disciples which neither our fathers nor we have been able to bear? 11 But we believe that we shall be saved through the grace of the Lord Jesus, just as they will."

12 And all the assembly kept silence; and they listened to Bär'nȧ·bȧs and Paul as they related what signs and wonders God had done through them among the Gentiles. 13 After they finished speaking, James replied, "Brethren, listen to me. 14 Sym'ē·òn has related how God first visited the Gentiles, to take out of them a people for his name. 15 And with this the words of the prophets agree, as it is written,

16 'After this I will return,
    and I will rebuild the dwelling of
        David, which has fallen;
I will rebuild its ruins,
    and I will set it up,
17 that the rest of men may seek the
      Lord,
    and all the Gentiles who are called
      by my name,

14.15: Ex 20.11; Ps 146.6.   **14.19:** 2 Cor 11.25.   **15.1-30:** Gal 2.1-10. **15.16-18:** Amos 9.11-12; Jer 12.15; Is 45.21.

18 says the Lord, who has made these things known from of old.'
19 Therefore my judgment is that we should not trouble those of the Gentiles who turn to God, 20 but should write to them to abstain from the pollutions of idols and from unchastity and from what is strangled[n] and from blood. 21 For from early generations Moses has had in every city those who preach him, for he is read every sabbath in the synagogues."

22 Then it seemed good to the apostles and the elders, with the whole church, to choose men from among them and send them to An'ti·och with Paul and Bär'na·bas. They sent Judas called Bär'sab·bas, and Silas, leading men among the brethren, 23 with the following letter: "The brethren, both the apostles and the elders, to the brethren who are of the Gentiles in An'ti·och and Syria and Ci·li'ci·a, greeting. 24 Since we have heard that some perons from us have troubled you with words, unsettling your minds, although we gave them no instructions, 25 it has seemed good to us in assembly to choose men and send them to you with our beloved Bär'na·bas and Paul, 26 men who have risked their lives for the sake of our Lord Jesus Christ. 27 We have therefore sent Judas and Silas, who themselves will tell you the same things by word of mouth. 28 For it has seemed good to the Holy Spirit and to us to lay upon you no greater burden than these necessary things: 29 that you abstain from what has been sacrificed to idols and from blood and from what is strangled[n] and from unchastity. If you keep yourselves from these, you will do well. Farewell."

30 So when they were sent off, they went down to An'ti·och; and having gathered the congregation together, they delivered the letter. 31 And when they read it, they rejoiced at the exhortation. 32 And Judas and Silas, who were themselves prophets, exhorted the brethren with many words and strengthened them. 33 And after they had spent some time, they were sent off in peace by the brethren to those who had sent them.[o] 35 But Paul and Bär'na·bas remained in An'ti·och, teaching and preaching the word of the Lord, with many others also.

36 And after some days Paul said to Bär'na·bas, "Come, let us return and visit the brethren in every city where we proclaimed the word of the Lord, and see how they are." 37 And Bär'na·bas wanted to take with them John called Mark. 38 But Paul thought best not to take with them one who had withdrawn from them in Pam·phyl'i·a, and had not gone with them to the work. 39 And there arose a sharp contention, so that they separated from each other; Bär'na·bas took Mark with him and sailed away to Cyprus, 40 but Paul chose Silas and departed, being commended by the brethren to the grace of the Lord. 41 And he went through Syria and Ci·li'ci·a, strengthening the churches.

16 And he came also to Dēr'bē and to Lys'trà. A disciple was there, named Timothy, the son of a Jewish woman who was a believer; but his father was a Greek. 2 He was well spoken of by the brethren at Lys'trà and I·cō'ni·ùm. 3 Paul wanted Timothy to accompany him; and he took him and circumcised him because of the Jews that were in those places, for they all knew that his father was a Greek. 4 As they went on their way through the cities, they delivered to them for observance the decisions which had been reached by the apostles and elders who were at Jerusalem. 5 So the churches were strengthened in the faith, and they increased in numbers daily.

6 And they went through the region of Phryg'i·a and Galatia, having been forbidden by the Holy Spirit to speak the word in Asia. 7 And when they had come opposite My'si·à, they attempted to go into Bi·thyn'i·à, but the Spirit of Jesus did not allow them; 8 so, passing by My'si·à, they went down to Trō'as. 9 And a vision appeared to Paul in the night: a man of Mac·e·dō'ni·à was standing beseeching him and saying, "Come over to Macedonia and help us." 10 And when he had seen the vision, immediately we sought to go on into Mac·e·dō'ni·à, concluding that God had called us to preach the gospel to them.

11 Setting sail therefore from Trō'as, we made a direct voyage to Sam'ò·thràce, and the following day to Nē·ap'ò·lis, 12 and from there to Phi·lip'pi, which is the leading city of the district[x] of Mac·e·dō'ni·à, and a Roman colony. We remained in this city some days; 13 and on the sabbath day we went outside the gate to the riverside, where

[n] Other early authorities omit *and from what is strangled*
[o] Other ancient authorities insert verse 34, *But it seemed good to Silas to remain there*
[x] The Greek text is uncertain

we supposed there was a place of prayer; and we sat down and spoke to the women who had come together. 14 One who heard us was a woman named Lyd´i·à, from the city of Thy·à·ti´rà, a seller of purple goods, who was a worshiper of God. The Lord opened her heart to give heed to what was said by Paul. 15 And when she was baptized, with her household, she besought us, saying, "If you have judged me to be faithful to the Lord, come to my house and stay." And she prevailed upon us.

16 As we were going to the place of prayer, we were met by a slave girl who had a spirit of divination and brought her owners much gain by soothsaying. 17 She followed Paul and us, crying, "These men are servants of the Most High God, who proclaim to you the way of salvation." 18 And this she did for many days. But Paul was annoyed, and turned and said to the spirit, "I charge you in the name of Jesus Christ to come out of her." And it came out that very hour.

19 But when her owners saw that their hope of gain was gone, they seized Paul and Silas and dragged them into the market place before the rulers; 20 and when they had brought them to the magistrates they said, "These men are Jews and they are disturbing our city. 21 They advocate customs which it is not lawful for us Romans to accept or practice." 22 The crowd joined in attacking them; and the magistrates tore the garments off them and gave orders to beat them with rods. 23 And when they had inflicted many blows upon them, they threw them into prison, charging the jailer to keep them safely. 24 Having received this charge, he put them into the inner prison and fastened their feet in the stocks.

25 But about midnight Paul and Silas were praying and singing hymns to God, and the prisoners were listening to them, 26 and suddenly there was a great earthquake, so that the foundations of the prison were shaken; and immediately all the doors were opened and every one's fetters were unfastened. 27 When the jailer woke and saw that the prison doors were open, he drew his sword and was about to kill himself, supposing that the prisoners had escaped. 28 But Paul cried with a loud voice, "Do not harm yourself, for we are all here." 29 And he called for lights and rushed in, and trembling with fear he fell down before Paul and

Silas, 30 and brought them out and said, "Men, what must I do to be saved?" 31 And they said, "Believe in the Lord Jesus, and you will be saved, you and your household." 32 And they spoke the word of the Lord to him and to all that were in his house. 33 And he took them the same hour of the night, and washed their wounds, and he was baptized at once, with all his family. 34 Then he brought them up into his house, and set food before them; and he rejoiced with all his household that he had believed in God.

35 But when it was day, the magistrates sent the police, saying, "Let those men go." 36 And the jailer reported the words to Paul, saying, "The magistrates have sent to let you go; now therefore come out and go in peace." 37 But Paul said to them, "They have beaten us publicly, uncondemned, men who are Roman citizens, and have thrown us into prison; and do they now cast us out secretly? No! let them come themselves and take us out." 38 The police reported these words to the magistrates, and they were afraid when they heard that they were Roman citizens; 39 so they came and apologized to them. And they took them out and asked them to leave the city. 40 So they went out of the prison, and visited Lyd´i·à; and when they had seen the brethren they exhorted them and departed.

17 Now when they had passed through Am·phip´o·lis and Ap·ol·lo´ni·à, they came to Thes·sà·lo´ni´cà, where there was a synagogue of the Jews. 2 And Paul went in, as was his custom, and for three weeks*ᵖ* he argued with them from the scriptures, 3 explaining and proving that it was necessary for the Christ to suffer and to rise from the dead, and saying, "This Jesus, whom I proclaim to you, is the Christ." 4 And some of them were persuaded, and joined Paul and Silas; as did a great many of the devout Greeks and not a few of the leading women. 5 But the Jews were jealous, and taking some wicked fellows of the rabble, they gathered a crowd, set the city in an uproar, and attacked the house of Jason, seeking to bring them out to the people. 6 And when they could not find them, they dragged Jason and some of the brethren before the city authorities, crying, "These men who have turned the world upside down have come here also, 7 and Jason has received them; and they are all

ᵖ Or *sabbaths*   16.22-23: 2 Cor 11.25.

acting against the decrees of Caesar, saying that there is another king, Jesus." [8]And the people and the city authorities were disturbed when they heard this. [9]And when they had taken security from Jason and the rest, they let them go.

10 The brethren immediately sent Paul and Silas away by night to Be·roē′á; and when they arrived they went into the Jewish synagogue. [11]Now these Jews were more noble than those in Thes·sa·lo·ní′ca, for they received the word with all eagerness, examining the scriptures daily to see if these things were so. [12]Many of them therefore believed, with not a few Greek women of high standing as well as men. [13]But when the Jews of Thes·sa·lo·ní′ca learned that the word of God was proclaimed by Paul at Be·roē′á also, they came there too, stirring up and inciting the crowds. [14]Then the brethren immediately sent Paul off on his way to the sea, but Silas and Timothy remained there. [15]Those who conducted Paul brought him as far as Athens; and receiving a command for Silas and Timothy to come to him as soon as possible, they departed.

16 Now while Paul was waiting for them at Athens, his spirit was provoked within him as he saw that the city was full of idols. [17]So he argued in the synagogue with the Jews and the devout persons, and in the market place every day with those who chanced to be there. [18]Some also of the Epicurean and Stoic philosophers met him. And some said, "What would this babbler say?" Others said, "He seems to be a preacher of foreign divinities"—because he preached Jesus and the resurrection. [19]And they took hold of him and brought him to the Ar′ē·op′a·gus, saying, "May we know what this new teaching is which you present? [20]For you bring some strange things to our ears; we wish to know therefore what these things mean." [21]Now all the Athenians and the foreigners who lived there spent their time in nothing except telling or hearing something new.

22 So Paul, standing in the middle of the Ar′ē·op′a·gus, said: "Men of Athens, I perceive that in every way you are very religious. [23]For as I passed along, and observed the objects of your worship, I found also an altar with this inscription, 'To an unknown god.' What therefore you worship as unknown, this I proclaim to you.

[24]The God who made the world and everything in it, being Lord of heaven and earth, does not live in shrines made by man, [25]nor is he served by human hands, as though he needed anything, since he himself gives to all men life and breath and everything. [26]And he made from one every nation of men to live on all the face of the earth, having determined allotted periods and the boundaries of their habitation, [27]that they should seek God, in the hope that they might feel after him and find him. Yet he is not far from each one of us, [28]for

'In him we live and move and have our being';

as even some of your poets have said,

'For we are indeed his offspring.'

[29]Being then God's offspring, we ought not to think that the Deity is like gold, or silver, or stone, a representation by the art and imagination of man. [30]The times of ignorance God overlooked, but now he commands all men everywhere to repent, [31]because he has fixed a day on which he will judge the world in righteousness by a man whom he has appointed, and of this he has given assurance to all men by raising him from the dead."

32 Now when they heard of the resurrection of the dead, some mocked; but others said, "We will hear you again about this." [33]So Paul went out from among them. [34]But some men joined him and believed, among them Di·ó·nys′i·us the Ar′ē·op′a·gite and a woman named Dam′a·ris and others with them.

18 After this he left Athens and went to Corinth. [2]And he found a Jew named Aq′ui·la, a native of Pon′tus, lately come from Italy with his wife Priscilla, because Claudius had commanded all the Jews to leave Rome. And he went to see them; [3]and because he was of the same trade he stayed with them, and they worked, for by trade they were tentmakers. [4]And he argued in the synagogue every sabbath, and persuaded Jews and Greeks.

5 When Silas and Timothy arrived from Mac·e·dō′ni·a, Paul was occupied with preaching, testifying to the Jews that the Christ was Jesus. [6]And when they opposed and reviled him, he shook out his garments and said to them, "Your blood be upon your heads! I am innocent. From now on I will go to the Gentiles." [7]And he left there and went to the house of a man named Tit′i·us[q] Justus, a worshiper of

[q] Other early authorities read *Titus*   17.24-25: Is 42.5.
17.28: Epimenides; Aratus, *Phaenomena*, 5.   17.31: Ps 9.8; 96.13; 98.9.

God; his house was next door to the synagogue. 8 Cris'pus, the ruler of the synagogue, believed in the Lord, together with all his household; and many of the Corinthians hearing Paul believed and were baptized. 9And the Lord said to Paul one night in a vision, "Do not be afraid, but speak and do not be silent; 10 for I am with you, and no man shall attack you to harm you; for I have many people in this city." 11And he stayed a year and six months, teaching the word of God among them.

12 But when Gal'li·ō was proconsul of A·chā'iä, the Jews made a united attack upon Paul and brought him before the tribunal, 13 saying, "This man is persuading men to worship God contrary to the law." 14 But when Paul was about to open his mouth, Gal'li·ō said to the Jews, "If it were a matter of wrongdoing or vicious crime, I should have reason to bear with you, O Jews; 15 but since it is a matter of questions about words and names and your own law, see to it yourselves; I refuse to be a judge of these things." 16And he drove them from the tribunal. 17And they all seized Sos'thė·nēs, the ruler of the synagogue, and beat him in front of the tribunal. But Gal'li·ō paid no attention to this.

18 After this Paul stayed many days longer, and then took leave of the brethren and sailed for Syria, and with him Priscilla and Aq'ui·là. At Cen'chrē·áe he cut his hair, for he had a vow. 19And they came to Eph'é·sùs, and he left them there; but he himself went into the synagogue and argued with the Jews. 20 When they asked him to stay for a longer period, he declined; 21 but on taking leave of them he said, "I will return to you if God wills," and he set sail from Eph'é·sùs.

22 When he had landed at Caes·à·rē'á, he went up and greeted the church, and then went down to An'ti·och. 23After spending some time there he departed and went from place to place through the region of Galatia and Phryğ'i·à, strengthening all the disciples.

24 Now a Jew named A·pol'los, a native of Alexandria, came to Eph'é·sùs. He was an eloquent man, well versed in the scriptures. 25 He had been instructed in the way of the Lord; and being fervent in spirit, he spoke and taught accurately the things concerning Jesus, though he knew only the baptism of John. 26 He began to speak boldly in the synagogue; but

when Priscilla and Aq'ui·là heard him, they took him and expounded to him the way of God more accurately. 27And when he wished to cross to A·chā'iä, the brethren encouraged him, and wrote to the disciples to receive him. When he arrived, he greatly helped those who through grace had believed, 28 for he powerfully confuted the Jews in public, showing by the scriptures that the Christ was Jesus.

19 While A·pol'los was at Corinth, Paul passed through the upper country and came to Eph'é·sùs. There he found some disciples. 2And he said to them, "Did you receive the Holy Spirit when you believed?" And they said, "No, we have never even heard that there is a Holy Spirit." 3And he said, "Into what then were you baptized?" They said, "Into John's baptism." 4And Paul said, "John baptized with the baptism of repentance, telling the people to believe in the one who was to come after him, that is, Jesus." 5 On hearing this, they were baptized in the name of the Lord Jesus. 6And when Paul had laid his hands upon them, the Holy Spirit came on them; and they spoke with tongues and prophesied. 7 There were about twelve of them in all.

8 And he entered the synagogue and for three months spoke boldly, arguing and pleading about the kingdom of God; 9 but when some were stubborn and disbelieved, speaking evil of the Way before the congregation, he withdrew from them, taking the disciples with him, and argued daily in the hall of Ty·ran'nùs.r 10 This continued for two years, so that all the residents of Asia heard the word of the Lord, both Jews and Greeks.

11 And God did extraordinary miracles by the hands of Paul, 12 so that handkerchiefs or aprons were carried away from his body to the sick, and diseases left them and the evil spirits came out of them. 13 Then some of the itinerant Jewish exorcists undertook to pronounce the name of the Lord Jesus over those who had evil spirits, saying, "I adjure you by the Jesus whom Paul preaches." 14 Seven sons of a Jewish high priest named Scē'và were doing this. 15 But the evil spirit answered them, "Jesus I know, and Paul I know; but who are you?" 16And the man in whom the evil spirit was leaped on them, mastered all of them, and overpowered them, so that they fled out of that house naked and

r Other ancient authorities add *from the fifth hour to the tenth*
18.9-10: Is 43.5; Jer 1.8.

wounded. 17And this became known to all residents of Eph′ė·sŭs, both Jews and Greeks; and fear fell upon them all; and the name of the Lord Jesus was extolled. 18 Many also of those who were now believers came, confessing and divulging their practices. 19And a number of those who practiced magic arts brought their books together and burned them in the sight of all; and they counted the value of them and found it came to fifty thousand pieces of silver. 20 So the word of the Lord grew and prevailed mightily.

21 Now after these events Paul resolved in the Spirit to pass through Măc·ė·dō′ni·à and A·chā′ià and go to Jerusalem, saying, "After I have been there, I must also see Rome." 22And having sent into Măc·ė·dō′ni·à two of his helpers, Timothy and E·răs′tŭs, he himself stayed in Asia for a while.

23 About that time there arose no little stir concerning the Way. 24 For a man named De·mē′tri·ŭs, a silversmith, who made silver shrines of Är′tė·mis, brought no little business to the craftsmen. 25 These he gathered together, with the workmen of like occupation, and said, "Men, you know that from this business we have our wealth. 26And you see and hear that not only at Eph′ė·sŭs but almost throughout all Asia this Paul has persuaded and turned away a considerable company of people, saying that gods made with hands are not gods. 27And there is danger not only that this trade of ours may come into disrepute but also that the temple of the great goddess Är′tė·mis may count for nothing, and that she may even be deposed from her magnificence, she whom all Asia and the world worship."

28 When they heard this they were enraged, and cried out, "Great is Är′tė·mis of the E·phē′siàns!" 29 So the city was filled with the confusion; and they rushed together into the theater, dragging with them Gā′iŭs and Ar·is·tär′chŭs, Măc·ė·dō′ni·àns who were Paul's companions in travel. 30 Paul wished to go in among the crowd, but the disciples would not let him; 31 some of the Ā′si·ärchs also, who were friends of his, sent to him and begged him not to venture into the theater. 32 Now some cried one thing, some another; for the assembly was in confusion, and most of them did not know why they had come together. 33 Some of the crowd prompted Alexander, whom the Jews had put forward. And Alexander motioned with his hand, wishing to make a defense to the people. 34 But when they recognized that he was a Jew, for about two hours they all with one voice cried out, "Great is Är′tė·mis of the E·phē′siàns!" 35And when the town clerk had quieted the crowd, he said, "Men of Eph′ė·sŭs, what man is there who does not know that the city of the Ephesians is temple keeper of the great Är′tė·mis, and of the sacred stone that fell from the sky?s 36 Seeing then that these things cannot be contradicted, you ought to be quiet and do nothing rash. 37 For you have brought these men here who are neither sacrilegious nor blasphemers of our goddess. 38 If therefore De·mē′tri·ŭs and the craftsmen with him have a complaint against any one, the courts are open, and there are proconsuls; let them bring charges against one another. 39 But if you seek anything further,t it shall be settled in the regular assembly. 40 For we are in danger of being charged with rioting today, there being no cause that we can give to justify this commotion." 41And when he had said this, he dismissed the assembly.

20 After the uproar ceased, Paul sent for the disciples and having exhorted them took leave of them and departed for Măc·ė·dō′ni·à. 2 When he had gone through these parts and had given them much encouragement, he came to Greece. 3 There he spent three months, and when a plot was made against him by the Jews as he was about to set sail for Syria, he determined to return through Măc·ė·dō′ni·à. 4 Sŏp′à·tėr of Bė·roē′à, the son of Pyr′rhŭs, accompanied him; and of the Thes·sà·lō′ni·àns, Ar·is·tär′chŭs and Se·cun′dŭs; and Gā′iŭs of Dēr′bē, and Timothy; and the Asians, Tych′i·cŭs and Troph′i·mŭs. 5 These went on and were waiting for us at Trō′as, 6 but we sailed away from Phi·lip′pī after the days of Unleavened Bread, and in five days we came to them at Trō′as, where we stayed for seven days.

7 On the first day of the week, when we were gathered together to break bread, Paul talked with them, intending to depart on the morrow; and he prolonged his speech until midnight. 8 There were many lights in the upper chamber where we were gathered. 9And a young man named Eū′ty·chŭs

---

s The meaning of the Greek is uncertain
t Other ancient authorities read *about other matters*

was sitting in the window. He sank into a deep sleep as Paul talked still longer; and being overcome by sleep, he fell down from the third story and was taken up dead. 10 But Paul went down and bent over him, and embracing him said, "Do not be alarmed, for his life is in him." 11And when Paul had gone up and had broken bread and eaten, he conversed with them a long while, until daybreak, and so departed. 12And they took the lad away alive, and were not a little comforted.

13 But going ahead to the ship, we set sail for As'sos, intending to take Paul aboard there; for so he had arranged, intending himself to go by land. 14And when he met us at As'sos, we took him on board and came to Mit·y·lē'nē. 15And sailing from there we came the following day opposite Chi'os; the next day we touched at Sā'mos; and*u* the day after that we came to Mi·lē'tùs. 16 For Paul had decided to sail past Eph'é·sús, so that he might not have to spend time in Asia; for he was hastening to be at Jerusalem, if possible, on the day of Pentecost.

17 And from Mi·lē'tùs he sent to Eph'é·sùs and called to him the elders of the church. 18And when they came to him, he said to them:

"You yourselves know how I lived among you all the time from the first day that I set foot in Asia, 19 serving the Lord with all humility and with tears and with trials which befell me through the plots of the Jews; 20 how I did not shrink from declaring to you anything that was profitable, and teaching you in public and from house to house, 21 testifying both to Jews and to Greeks of repentance to God and of faith in our Lord Jesus Christ. 22And now, behold, I am going to Jerusalem, bound in the Spirit, not knowing what shall befall me there; 23 except that the Holy Spirit testifies to me in every city that imprisonment and afflictions await me. 24 But I do not account my life of any value nor as precious to myself, if only I may accomplish my course and the ministry which I received from the Lord Jesus, to testify to the gospel of the grace of God. 25And now, behold, I know that all you among whom I have gone about preaching the kingdom will see my face no more. 26 Therefore I testify to you this day that I am innocent of the blood of all of you, 27 for I did not

shrink from declaring to you the whole counsel of God. 28 Take heed to yourselves and to all the flock, in which the Holy Spirit has made you guardians, to feed the church of the Lord*y* which he obtained with his own blood.*w* 29 I know that after my departure fierce wolves will come in among you, not sparing the flock; 30 and from among your own selves will arise men speaking perverse things, to draw away the disciples after them. 31 Therefore be alert, remembering that for three years I did not cease night or day to admonish every one with tears. 32And now I commend you to God and to the word of his grace, which is able to build you up and to give you the inheritance among all those who are sanctified. 33 I coveted no one's silver or gold or apparel. 34 You yourselves know that these hands ministered to my necessities, and to those who were with me. 35 In all things I have shown you that by so toiling one must help the weak, remembering the words of the Lord Jesus, how he said, 'It is more blessed to give than to receive.'"

36 And when he had spoken thus, he knelt down and prayed with them all. 37And they all wept and embraced Paul and kissed him, 38 sorrowing most of all because of the word he had spoken, that they should see his face no more. And they brought him to the ship.

21 And when we had parted from them and set sail, we came by a straight course to Cos, and the next day to Rhodes, and from there to Pat'á·rá.*x* 2And having found a ship crossing to Phoenicia, we went aboard, and set sail. 3 When we had come in sight of Cyprus, leaving it on the left we sailed to Syria, and landed at Tȳre; for there the ship was to unload its cargo. 4And having sought out the disciples, we stayed there for seven days. Through the Spirit they told Paul not to go on to Jerusalem. 5And when our days there were ended, we departed and went on our journey; and they all, with wives and children, brought us on our way till we were outside the city; and kneeling down on the beach we prayed and bade one another farewell. 6 Then we went on board the ship, and they returned home.

7 When we had finished the voyage from Tȳre, we arrived at Ptol·é·mā'is; and we greeted the brethren and stayed with them for one day. 8 On the

u Other ancient authorities add *after remaining at Trogyllium*
v Other ancient authorities read *of God*   *w* Or *with the blood of his Own*
x Other ancient authorities add *and Myra*

morrow we departed and came to Caes·a·rē'ȧ; and we entered the house of Philip the evangelist, who was one of the seven, and stayed with him. [9]And he had four unmarried daughters, who prophesied. [10] While we were staying for some days, a prophet named Ag'a·bùs came down from Judea. [11]And coming to us he took Paul's girdle and bound his own feet and hands, and said, "Thus says the Holy Spirit, 'So shall the Jews at Jerusalem bind the man who owns this girdle and deliver him into the hands of the Gentiles.' " [12] When we heard this, we and the people there begged him not to go up to Jerusalem. [13] Then Paul answered, "What are you doing, weeping and breaking my heart? For I am ready not only to be imprisoned but even to die at Jerusalem for the name of the Lord Jesus." [14]And when he would not be persuaded, we ceased and said, "The will of the Lord be done."

[15] After these days we made ready and went up to Jerusalem. [16]And some of the disciples from Caes·a·rē'ȧ went with us, bringing us to the house of Mnā'sòn of Cyprus, an early disciple, with whom we should lodge.

[17] When we had come to Jerusalem, the brethren received us gladly. [18] On the following day Paul went in with us to James; and all the elders were present. [19]After greeting them, he related one by one the things that God had done among the Gentiles through his ministry. [20]And when they heard it, they glorified God. And they said to him, "You see, brother, how many thousands there are among the Jews of those who have believed; they are all zealous for the law, [21] and they have been told about you that you teach all the Jews who are among the Gentiles to forsake Moses, telling them not to circumcise their children or observe the customs. [22] What then is to be done? They will certainly hear that you have come. [23] Do therefore what we tell you. We have four men who are under a vow; [24] take these men and purify yourself along with them and pay their expenses, so that they may shave their heads. Thus all will know that there is nothing in what they have been told about you but that you yourself live in observance of the law. [25] But as for the Gentiles who have believed, we have sent a letter with our judgment that they should abstain from what has been sacrificed to idols and from blood and from what is

strangled[y] and from unchastity." [26] Then Paul took the men, and the next day he purified himself with them and went into the temple, to give notice when the days of purification would be fulfilled and the offering presented for every one of them.

[27] When the seven days were almost completed, the Jews from Asia, who had seen him in the temple, stirred up all the crowd, and laid hands on him, [28] crying out, "Men of Israel, help! This is the man who is teaching men everywhere against the people and the law and this place; moreover he also brought Greeks into the temple, and he has defiled this holy place." [29] For they had previously seen Troph'i·mùs the E·phē'sian with him in the city, and they supposed that Paul had brought him into the temple. [30] Then all the city was aroused, and the people ran together; they seized Paul and dragged him out of the temple, and at once the gates were shut. [31]And as they were trying to kill him, word came to the tribune of the cohort that all Jerusalem was in confusion. [32] He at once took soldiers and centurions, and ran down to them; and when they saw the tribune and the soldiers, they stopped beating Paul. [33] Then the tribune came up and arrested him, and ordered him to be bound with two chains. He inquired who he was and what he had done. [34] Some in the crowd shouted one thing, some another; and as he could not learn the facts because of the uproar, he ordered him to be brought into the barracks. [35]And when he came to the steps, he was actually carried by the soldiers, because of the violence of the crowd; [36] for the mob of the people followed, crying, "Away with him!"

[37] As Paul was about to be brought into the barracks, he said to the tribune, "May I say something to you?" And he said, "Do you know Greek? [38]Are you not the Egyptian, then, who recently stirred up a revolt and led the four thousand men of the Assassins out into the wilderness?" [39] Paul replied, "I am a Jew, from Tär'sús in Ci·li'ci·à, a citizen of no mean city; I beg you, let me speak to the people." [40]And when he had given him leave, Paul, standing on the steps, motioned with his hand to the people; and when there was a great hush, he spoke to them in the Hebrew language, saying:

22 "Brethren and fathers, hear the defense which I now make before you."

[y] Other early authorities omit *and from what is strangled*

2 And when they heard that he addressed them in the Hebrew language, they were the more quiet. And he said:

3 "I am a Jew, born at Tär′sùs in Ci·li′ci·à, but brought up in this city at the feet of Gà·mā′li·él, educated according to the strict manner of the law of our fathers, being zealous for God as you all are this day. 4 I persecuted this Way to the death, binding and delivering to prison both men and women, 5 as the high priest and the whole council of elders bear me witness. From them I received letters to the brethren, and I journeyed to Damascus to take those also who were there and bring them in bonds to Jerusalem to be punished.

6 "As I made my journey and drew near to Damascus, about noon a great light from heaven suddenly shone about me. 7And I fell to the ground and heard a voice saying to me, 'Saul, Saul, why do you persecute me?' 8And I answered, 'Who are you, Lord?' And he said to me, 'I am Jesus of Nazareth whom you are persecuting.' 9 Now those who were with me saw the light but did not hear the voice of the one who was speaking to me. 10And I said, 'What shall I do, Lord?' And the Lord said to me, 'Rise, and go into Damascus, and there you will be told all that is appointed for you to do.' 11And when I could not see because of the brightness of that light, I was led by the hand by those who were with me, and came into Damascus.

12 "And one An·à·ni′às, a devout man according to the law, well spoken of by all the Jews who lived there, 13 came to me, and standing by me said to me, 'Brother Saul, receive your sight.' And in that very hour I received my sight and saw him. 14And he said, 'The God of our fathers appointed you to know his will, to see the Just One and to hear a voice from his mouth; 15 for you will be a witness for him to all men of what you have seen and heard. 16And now why do you wait? Rise and be baptized, and wash away your sins, calling on his name.'

17 "When I had returned to Jerusalem and was praying in the temple, I fell into a trance 18 and saw him saying to me, 'Make haste and get quickly out of Jerusalem, because they will not accept your testimony about me.' 19And I said, 'Lord, they themselves know that in every synagogue I imprisoned and beat those who believed in thee. 20And when the blood of

Stephen thy witness was shed, I also was standing by and approving, and keeping the garments of those who killed him.' 21And he said to me, 'Depart; for I will send you far away to the Gentiles.' "

22 Up to this word they listened to him; then they lifted up their voices and said, "Away with such a fellow from the earth! For he ought not to live." 23And as they cried out and waved their garments and threw dust into the air, 24 the tribune commanded him to be brought into the barracks, and ordered him to be examined by scourging, to find out why they shouted thus against him. 25 But when they had tied him up with the thongs, Paul said to the centurion who was standing by, "Is it lawful for you to scourge a man who is a Roman citizen, and uncondemned?" 26 When the centurion heard that, he went to the tribune and said to him, "What are you about to do? For this man is a Roman citizen." 27 So the tribune came and said to him, "Tell me, are you a Roman citizen?" And he said, "Yes." 28 The tribune answered, "I bought this citizenship for a large sum." Paul said, "But I was born a citizen." 29 So those who were about to examine him withdrew from him instantly; and the tribune also was afraid, for he realized that Paul was a Roman citizen and that he had bound him.

30 But on the morrow, desiring to know the real reason why the Jews accused him, he unbound him, and commanded the chief priests and all the council to meet, and he brought Paul down and set him before them.

23 And Paul, looking intently at the council, said, "Brethren, I have lived before God in all good conscience up to this day." 2And the high priest An·à·ni′às commanded those who stood by him to strike him on the mouth. 3 Then Paul said to him, "God shall strike you, you whitewashed wall! Are you sitting to judge me according to the law, and yet contrary to the law you order me to be struck?" 4 Those who stood by said, "Would you revile God's high priest?" 5And Paul said, "I did not know, brethren, that he was the high priest; for it is written, 'You shall not speak evil of a ruler of your people.' "

6 But when Paul perceived that one part were Sad′dū·ceēs and the other Pharisees, he cried out in the council, "Brethren, I am a Pharisee, a son of

22.4-16: Acts 9.1-19; 26.9-18; Gal 1.14.　　23.5: Ex 22.28.

Pharisees; with respect to the hope and the resurrection of the dead I am on trial." [7]And when he had said this, a dissension arose between the Pharisees and the Sad'dū·ceeś; and the assembly was divided. [8] For the Sad'dū·ceeś say that there is no resurrection, nor angel, nor spirit; but the Pharisees acknowledge them all. [9] Then a great clamor arose; and some of the scribes of the Pharisees' party stood up and contended, "We find nothing wrong in this man. What if a spirit or an angel spoke to him?" [10]And when the dissension became violent, the tribune, afraid that Paul would be torn in pieces by them, commanded the soldiers to go down and take him by force from among them and bring him into the barracks.

11 The following night the Lord stood by him and said, "Take courage, for as you have testified about me at Jerusalem, so you must bear witness also at Rome."

12 When it was day, the Jews made a plot and bound themselves by an oath neither to eat nor drink till they had killed Paul. [13] There were more than forty who made this conspiracy. [14]And they went to the chief priests and elders, and said, "We have strictly bound ourselves by an oath to taste no food till we have killed Paul. [15] You therefore, along with the council, give notice now to the tribune to bring him down to you, as though you were going to determine his case more exactly. And we are ready to kill him before he comes near."

16 Now the son of Paul's sister heard of their ambush; so he went and entered the barracks and told Paul. [17]And Paul called one of the centurions and said, "Bring this young man to the tribune; for he has something to tell him." [18] So he took him and brought him to the tribune and said, "Paul the prisoner called me and asked me to bring this young man to you, as he has something to say to you." [19] The tribune took him by the hand, and going aside asked him privately, "What is it that you have to tell me?" [20]And he said, "The Jews have agreed to ask you to bring Paul down to the council tomorrow, as though they were going to inquire somewhat more closely about him. [21] But do not yield to them; for more than forty of their men lie in ambush for him, having bound themselves by an oath neither to eat nor drink till they have killed him; and now they are ready, waiting for the promise from you." [22] So the tribune

dismissed the young man, charging him, "Tell no one that you have informed me of this."

23 Then he called two of the centurions and said, "At the third hour of the night get ready two hundred soldiers with seventy horsemen and two hundred spearmen to go as far as Caes·a·rē'á. [24]Also provide mounts for Paul to ride, and bring him safely to Felix the governor." [25]And he wrote a letter to this effect:

26 "Claudius Lys'i·às to his Excellency the governor Felix, greeting. [27] This man was seized by the Jews, and was about to be killed by them, when I came upon them with the soldiers and rescued him, having learned that he was a Roman citizen. [28]And desiring to know the charge on which they accused him, I brought him down to their council. [29] I found that he was accused about questions of their law, but charged with nothing deserving death or imprisonment. [30]And when it was disclosed to me that there would be a plot against the man, I sent him to you at once, ordering his accusers also to state before you what they have against him."

31 So the soldiers, according to their instructions, took Paul and brought him by night to An·tip'à·tris. [32]And on the morrow they returned to the barracks, leaving the horsemen to go on with him. [33] When they came to Caes·a·rē'á and delivered the letter to the governor, they presented Paul also before him. [34] On reading the letter, he asked to what province he belonged. When he learned that he was from Ci·li'ci·à [35] he said, "I will hear you when your accusers arrive." And he commanded him to be guarded in Her'ŏd's praetorium.

24 And after five days the high priest An·à·ni'ás came down with some elders and a spokesman, one Tèr·tul'lùs. They laid before the governor their case against Paul; [2] and when he was called, Tèr·tul'lùs began to accuse him, saying:

"Since through you we enjoy much peace, and since by your provision, most excellent Felix, reforms are introduced on behalf of this nation, [3] in every way and everywhere we accept this with all gratitude. [4] But, to detain you no further, I beg you in your kindness to hear us briefly. [5] For we have found this man a pestilent fellow, an agitator among all the Jews throughout the world, and a ringleader of the sect of the Nazarenes. [6] He even tried to profane the temple, but we seized him.ᶻ 8 By examining him yourself you will be able to learn from him about everything of which we accuse him."

9 The Jews also joined in the charge, affirming that all this was so.

10 And when the governor had motioned to him to speak, Paul replied: "Realizing that for many years you have been judge over this nation, I cheerfully make my defense. 11As you may ascertain, it is not more than twelve days since I went up to worship at Jerusalem; 12 and they did not find me disputing with any one or stirring up a crowd, either in the temple or in the synagogues, or in the city. 13 Neither can they prove to you what they now bring up against me. 14 But this I admit to you, that according to the Way, which they call a sect, I worship the God of our fathers, believing everything laid down by the law or written in the prophets, 15 having a hope in God which these themselves accept, that there will be a resurrection of both the just and the unjust. 16 So I always take pains to have a clear conscience toward God and toward men. 17 Now after some years I came to bring to my nation alms and offerings. 18As I was doing this, they found me purified in the temple, without any crowd or tumult. But some Jews from Asia—19 they ought to be here before you and to make an accusation, if they have anything against me. 20 Or else let these men themselves say what wrongdoing they found when I stood before the council, 21 except this one thing which I cried out while standing among them, 'With respect to the resurrection of the dead I am on trial before you this day.'"

22 But Felix, having a rather accurate knowledge of the Way, put them off, saying, "When Lysʹi·as the tribune comes down, I will decide your case." 23 Then he gave orders to the centurion that he should be kept in custody but should have some liberty, and that none of his friends should be prevented from attending to his needs.

24 After some days Felix came with his wife Drü·silʹlà, who was a Jewess; and he sent for Paul and heard him speak upon faith in Christ Jesus. 25And as he argued about justice and self-control and future judgment, Felix was alarmed and said, "Go away for the present; when I have an opportunity I will summon you." 26At the same time he hoped that money would be given

him by Paul. So he sent for him often and conversed with him. 27 But when two years had elapsed, Felix was succeeded by Pôrʹci·ús Fesʹtús; and desiring to do the Jews a favor, Felix left Paul in prison.

25 Now when Fesʹtús had come into his province, after three days he went up to Jerusalem from Caes·à·rēʹà. 2And the chief priests and the principal men of the Jews informed him against Paul; and they urged him, 3 asking as a favor to have the man sent to Jerusalem, planning an ambush to kill him on the way. 4 Fesʹtús replied that Paul was being kept at Caes·à·rēʹà, and that he himself intended to go there shortly. 5 "So," said he, "let the men of authority among you go down with me, and if there is anything wrong about the man, let them accuse him."

6 When he had stayed among them not more than eight or ten days, he went down to Caes·à·rēʹà; and the next day he took his seat on the tribunal and ordered Paul to be brought. 7And when he had come, the Jews who had gone down from Jerusalem stood about him, bringing against him many serious charges which they could not prove. 8 Paul said in his defense, "Neither against the law of the Jews, nor against the temple, nor against Caesar have I offended at all." 9 But Fesʹtús, wishing to do the Jews a favor, said to Paul, "Do you wish to go up to Jerusalem, and there be tried on these charges before me?" 10 But Paul said, "I am standing before Caesar's tribunal, where I ought to be tried; to the Jews I have done no wrong, as you know very well. 11 If then I am a wrongdoer, and have committed anything for which I deserve to die, I do not seek to escape death; but if there is nothing in their charges against me, no one can give me up to them. I appeal to Caesar." 12 Then Fesʹtús, when he had conferred with his council, answered, "You have appealed to Caesar; to Caesar you shall go."

13 Now when some days had passed, À·gripʹpà the king and Bẽr·niʹcē arrived at Caes·à·rēʹà to welcome Fesʹtús. 14And as they stayed there many days, Fesʹtús laid Paul's case before the king, saying, "There is a man left prisoner by Felix; 15 and when I was at Jerusalem, the chief priests and the elders of the Jews gave information about him, asking for sentence against him. 16 I answered them that it was

ᶻ Other ancient authorities add *and we would have judged him according to our law.* 7 *But the chief captain Lysias came and with great violence took him out of our hands,* 8 *commanding his accusers to come before you.*

not the custom of the Romans to give up any one before the accused met the accusers face to face, and had opportunity to make his defense concerning the charge laid against him. [17] When therefore they came together here, I made no delay, but on the next day took my seat on the tribunal and ordered the man to be brought in. [18] When the accusers stood up, they brought no charge in his case of such evils as I supposed; [19] but they had certain points of dispute with him about their own superstition and about one Jesus, who was dead, but whom Paul asserted to be alive. [20] Being at a loss how to investigate these questions, I asked whether he wished to go to Jerusalem and be tried there regarding them. [21] But when Paul had appealed to be kept in custody for the decision of the emperor, I commanded him to be held until I could send him to Caesar." [22] And A·grip′pa said to Fes′tus, "I should like to hear the man myself." "Tomorrow," said he, "you shall hear him."

[23] So on the morrow A·grip′pa and Ber·ni′cē came with great pomp, and they entered the audience hall with the military tribunes and the prominent men of the city. Then by command of Fes′tus Paul was brought in. [24] And Fes′tus said, "King A·grip′pa and all who are present with us, you see this man about whom the whole Jewish people petitioned me, both at Jerusalem and here, shouting that he ought not to live any longer. [25] But I found that he had done nothing deserving death; and as he himself appealed to the emperor, I decided to send him. [26] But I have nothing definite to write to my lord about him. Therefore I have brought him before you, and, especially before you, King A·grip′pa, that, after we have examined him, I may have something to write. [27] For it seems to me unreasonable, in sending a prisoner, not to indicate the charges against him."

26 A·grip′pa said to Paul, "You have permission to speak for yourself." Then Paul stretched out his hand and made his defense:

[2] "I think myself fortunate that it is before you, King A·grip′pa, I am to make my defense today against all the accusations of the Jews, [3] because you are especially familiar with all customs and controversies of the Jews; therefore I beg you to listen to me patiently.

[4] "My manner of life from my youth, spent from the beginning

among my own nation and at Jerusalem, is known by all the Jews. [5] They have known for a long time, if they are willing to testify, that according to the strictest party of our religion I have lived as a Pharisee. [6] And now I stand here on trial for hope in the promise made by God to our fathers, [7] to which our twelve tribes hope to attain, as they earnestly worship night and day. And for this hope I am accused by Jews, O king! [8] Why is it thought incredible by any of you that God raises the dead?

[9] "I myself was convinced that I ought to do many things in opposing the name of Jesus of Nazareth. [10] And I did so in Jerusalem; I not only shut up many of the saints in prison, by authority from the chief priests, but when they were put to death I cast my vote against them. [11] And I punished them often in all the synagogues and tried to make them blaspheme; and in raging fury against them, I persecuted them even to foreign cities.

[12] "Thus I journeyed to Damascus with the authority and commission of the chief priests. [13] At midday, O king, I saw on the way a light from heaven, brighter than the sun, shining round me and those who journeyed with me. [14] And when we had all fallen to the ground, I heard a voice saying to me in the Hebrew language, 'Saul, Saul, why do you persecute me? It hurts you to kick against the goads.' [15] And I said, 'Who are you, Lord?' And the Lord said, 'I am Jesus whom you are persecuting. [16] But rise and stand upon your feet; for I have appeared to you for this purpose, to appoint you to serve and bear witness to the things in which you have seen me and to those in which I will appear to you, [17] delivering you from the people and from the Gentiles—to whom I send you [18] to open their eyes, that they may turn from darkness to light and from the power of Satan to God, that they may receive forgiveness of sins and a place among those who are sanctified by faith in me.'

[19] "Wherefore, O King A·grip′pa, I was not disobedient to the heavenly vision, [20] but declared first to those at Damascus, then at Jerusalem and throughout all the country of Judea, and also to the Gentiles, that they should repent and turn to God and perform deeds worthy of their repentance. [21] For this reason the Jews seized me in the temple and tried to kill me. [22] To this day I have had the help that

26.9-18: Acts 9.1-8; 22.4-16.   **26.16-17:** Ezek 2.1, 3.   **26.18:** Is 42.7, 16.

comes from God, and so I stand here testifying both to small and great, saying nothing but what the prophets and Moses said would come to pass: 23 that the Christ must suffer, and that, by being the first to rise from the dead, he would proclaim light both to the people and to the Gentiles."

24 And as he thus made his defense, Fes′tŭs said with a loud voice, "Paul, you are mad; your great learning is turning you mad." 25 But Paul said, "I am not mad, most excellent Fes′tŭs, but I am speaking the sober truth. 26 For the king knows about these things, and to him I speak freely; for I am persuaded that none of these things has escaped his notice, for this was not done in a corner. 27 King A·grip′pă, do you believe the prophets? I know that you believe." 28 And A·grip′pă said to Paul, "In a short time you think to make me a Christian!" 29 And Paul said, "Whether short or long, I would to God that not only you but also all who hear me this day might become such as I am—except for these chains."

30 Then the king rose, and the governor and Bĕr·ni′cē and those who were sitting with them; 31 and when they had withdrawn, they said to one another, "This man is doing nothing to deserve death or imprisonment." 32 And A·grip′pă said to Fes′tŭs, "This man could have been set free if he had not appealed to Caesar."

27 And when it was decided that we should sail for Italy, they delivered Paul and some other prisoners to a centurion of the Augustan Cohort, named Julius. 2 And embarking in a ship of Ad·ra·myt′ti·ŭm, which was about to sail to the ports along the coast of Asia, we put to sea, accompanied by Ar·is·tär′chŭs, a Măc·ĕ·dō′ni·ăn from Thes·sa·lŏ·ni′ca. 3 The next day we put in at Si′don; and Julius treated Paul kindly, and gave him leave to go to his friends and be cared for. 4 And putting to sea from there we sailed under the lee of Cyprus, because the winds were against us. 5 And when we had sailed across the sea which is off Ci·li′ci·ă and Pamphyl′i·ă, we came to Myra in Ly′ci·ă. 6 There the centurion found a ship of Alexandria sailing for Italy, and put us on board. 7 We sailed slowly for a number of days, and arrived with difficulty off Cni′dŭs, and as the wind did not allow us to go on, we sailed under the lee of Crete off Sal·mō′nē. 8 Coasting along it with difficulty, we

came to a place called Fair Havens, near which was the city of Lā·sē′ă.

9 As much time had been lost, and the voyage was already dangerous because the fast had already gone by, Paul advised them, 10 saying, "Sirs, I perceive that the voyage will be with injury and much loss, not only of the cargo and the ship, but also of our lives." 11 But the centurion paid more attention to the captain and to the owner of the ship than to what Paul said. 12 And because the harbor was not suitable to winter in, the majority advised to put to sea from there, on the chance that somehow they could reach Phoenix, a harbor of Crete, looking northeast and southeast,ᵃ and winter there.

13 And when the south wind blew gently, supposing that they had obtained their purpose, they weighed anchor and sailed along Crete, close inshore. 14 But soon a tempestuous wind, called the northeaster, struck down from the land; 15 and when the ship was caught and could not face the wind, we gave way to it and were driven. 16 And running under the lee of a small island called Cäu′dă,ᵇ we managed with difficulty to secure the boat; 17 after hoisting it up, they took measuresᶜ to undergird the ship; then, fearing that they should run on the Syr′tis, they lowered the gear, and so were driven. 18 As we were violently storm-tossed, they began next day to throw the cargo overboard; 19 and the third day they cast out with their own hands the tackle of the ship. 20 And when neither sun or stars appeared for many a day, and no small tempest lay on us, all hope of our being saved was at last abandoned.

21 As they had been long without food, Paul then came forward among them and said, "Men, you should have listened to me, and should not have set sail from Crete and incurred this injury and loss. 22 I now bid you take heart; for there will be no loss of life among you, but only of the ship. 23 For this very night there stood by me an angel of the God to whom I belong and whom I worship, 24 and he said, 'Do not be afraid, Paul; you must stand before Caesar; and lo, God has granted you all those who sail with you." 25 So take heart, men, for I have faith in God that it will be exactly as I have been told. 26 But we shall have to run on some island."

27 When the fourteenth night had come, as we were drifting across the

ᵃ Or *southwest and northwest*   ᵇ Other ancient authorities read *Clauda*   ᶜ Greek *helps*

JESUS AND THE TEACHERS IN THE TEMPLE   *Luke 2:46*

PAUL ON THE ROAD TO DAMASCUS   *Acts 9:3*

sea of A′dri·à, about midnight the sailors suspected that they were nearing land. 28 So they sounded and found twenty fathoms; a little farther on they sounded again and found fifteen fathoms. 29And fearing that we might run on the rocks, they let out four anchors from the stern, and prayed for day to come. 30And as the sailors were seeking to escape from the ship, and had lowered the boat into the sea, under pretense of laying out anchors from the bow, 31 Paul said to the centurion and the soldiers, "Unless these men stay in the ship, you cannot be saved." 32 Then the soldiers cut away the ropes of the boat, and let it go.

33 As day was about to dawn, Paul urged them all to take some food, saying, "Today is the fourteenth day that you have continued in suspense and without food, having taken nothing. 34 Therefore I urge you to take some food; it will give you strength, since not a hair is to perish from the head of any of you." 35And when he had said this, he took bread, and giving thanks to God in the presence of all he broke it and began to eat. 36 Then they all were encouraged and ate some food themselves. 37 (We were in all two hundred and seventy-six*d* persons in the ship.) 38And when they had eaten enough, they lightened the ship, throwing out the wheat into the sea.

39 Now when it was day, they did not recognize the land, but they noticed a bay with a beach, on which they planned if possible to bring the ship ashore. 40 So they cast off the anchors and left them in the sea, at the same time loosening the ropes that tied the rudders; then hoisting the foresail to the wind they made for the beach. 41 But striking a shoal*e* they ran the vessel aground; the bow stuck and remained immovable, and the stern was broken up by the surf. 42 The soldiers' plan was to kill the prisoners, lest any should swim away and escape; 43 but the centurion, wishing to save Paul, kept them from carrying out their purpose. He ordered those who could swim to throw themselves overboard first and make for the land, 44 and the rest on planks or on pieces of the ship. And so it was that all escaped to land.

28 After we had escaped, we then learned that the island was called Malta. 2And the natives showed us unusual kindness, for they kindled

a fire and welcomed us all, because it had begun to rain and was cold. 3 Paul had gathered a bundle of sticks and put them on the fire, when a viper came out because of the heat and fastened on his hand. 4 When the natives saw the creature hanging from his hand, they said to one another, "No doubt this man is a murderer. Though he has escaped from the sea, justice has not allowed him to live." 5 He, however, shook off the creature into the fire and suffered no harm. 6 They waited, expecting him to swell up or suddenly fall down dead; but when they had waited a long time and saw no misfortune come to him, they changed their minds and said that he was a god.

7 Now in the neighborhood of that place were lands belonging to the chief man of the island, named Pub′li·ùs, who received us and entertained us hospitably for three days. 8 It happened that the father of Pub′li·ùs lay sick with fever and dysentery; and Paul visited him and prayed, and putting his hands on him healed him. 9And when this had taken place, the rest of the people on the island who had diseases also came and were cured. 10 They presented many gifts to us;*f* and when we sailed, they put on board whatever we needed.

11 After three months we set sail in a ship which had wintered in the island, a ship of Alexandria, with the Twin Brothers as figurehead. 12 Putting in at Syracuse, we stayed there for three days. 13And from there we made a circuit and arrived at Rhē′gi·ùm; and after one day a south wind sprang up, and on the second day we came to Pū·tē′ò·li. 14 There we found brethren, and were invited to stay with them for seven days. And so we came to Rome. 15And the brethren there, when they heard of us, came as far as the Forum of Ap′pi·ùs and Three Taverns to meet us. On seeing them Paul thanked God and took courage. 16And when we came into Rome, Paul was allowed to stay by himself, with the soldier that guarded him.

17 After three days he called together the local leaders of the Jews; and when they had gathered, he said to them, "Brethren, though I had done nothing against the people or the customs of our fathers, yet I was delivered prisoner from Jerusalem into the hands of the Romans. 18 When they had examined me, they wished

d Other ancient authorities read *seventy-six* or *about seventy-six*
e Greek *place of two seas*   *f* Or *honored us with many honors*

to set me at liberty, because there was no reason for the death penalty in my case. [19] But when the Jews objected, I was compelled to appeal to Caesar—though I had no charge to bring against my nation. [20] For this reason therefore I have asked to see you and speak with you, since it is because of the hope of Israel that I am bound with this chain." [21]And they said to him, "We have received no letters from Judea about you, and none of the brethren coming here has reported or spoken any evil about you. [22] But we desire to hear from you what your views are; for with regard to this sect we know that everywhere it is spoken against."

[23] When they had appointed a day for him, they came to him at his lodging in great numbers. And he expounded the matter to them from morning till evening, testifying to the kingdom of God and trying to convince them about Jesus both from the law of Moses and from the prophets. [24]And some were convinced by what he said, while others disbelieved. [25] So, as they disagreed among themselves,

they departed, after Paul had made one statement: "The Holy Spirit was right in saying to your fathers through I·śāi′ah the prophet:
[26] 'Go to this people, and say,
    You shall indeed hear but never
        understand,
    and you shall indeed see but never
        perceive.
[27] For this people's heart has grown
        dull,
    and their ears are heavy of hear-
        ing,
    and their eyes they have closed;
    lest they should perceive with their
        eyes,
    and hear with their ears,
    and understand with their heart,
    and turn for me to heal them.'
[28] Let it be known to you then that this salvation of God has been sent to the Gentiles; they will listen."[g]

[30] And he lived there two whole years at his own expense,[h] and welcomed all who came to him, [31] preaching the kingdom of God and teaching about the Lord Jesus Christ quite openly and unhindered.

THE LETTER OF PAUL TO THE

ROMANS

Paul, a servant[a] of Jesus Christ, called to be an apostle, set apart for the gospel of God [2] which he promised beforehand through his prophets in the holy scriptures, [3] the gospel concerning his Son, who was descended from David according to the flesh [4] and designated Son of God in power according to the Spirit of holiness by his resurrection from the dead, Jesus Christ our Lord, [5] through whom we have received grace and apostleship to bring about the obedience of faith for the sake of his name among all the nations, [6] including yourselves who are called to belong to Jesus Christ;

[7] To all God's beloved in Rome, who are called to be saints:

Grace to you and peace from God our Father and the Lord Jesus Christ.

[8] First, I thank my God through Jesus Christ for all of you, because your faith is proclaimed in all the world. [9] For God is my witness, whom I serve with my spirit in the gospel of his Son, that without ceasing I mention you always in my prayers, [10] asking that somehow by God's will I may now at last succeed in coming to you. [11] For I long to see you, that I may impart to you some spiritual gift to strengthen you, [12] that is, that we may be mutually encouraged by each other's faith, both yours and mine. [13] I want you to know, brethren, that I have

g Other ancient authorities add verse 29, *And when he had said these words, the Jews departed, holding much dispute among themselves*   h Or *in his own hired dwelling*
a Or *slave*   **28.26-27:** Is 6.9-10.   **28.28:** Ps 67.2.
1.1: Acts 9.15; 13.2; 1 Cor 1.1; 2 Cor 1.1; Gal 1.15.
1.5: Acts 26.16-18; Rom 15.18; Gal 2.7, 9.
1.7: 1 Cor 1.3; 2 Cor 1.2; Gal 1.3; Eph 1.2; Phil 1.2; Col 1.2; 1 Thess 1.2; 2 Thess 1.2;
    1 Tim 1.2; 2 Tim 1.2; Tit 1.4; Philem 3; 2 Jn 3.   **1.8:** Rom 16.19.
1.10: Rom 15.23, 32; Acts 19.21.   **1.13:** Rom 15.22.

often intended to come to you (but thus far have been prevented), in order that I may reap some harvest among you as well as among the rest of the Gentiles. 14 I am under obligation both to Greeks and to barbarians, both to the wise and to the foolish: 15 so I am eager to preach the gospel to you also who are in Rome.

16 For I am not ashamed of the gospel: it is the power of God for salvation to every one who has faith, to the Jew first and also to the Greek. 17 For in it the righteousness of God is revealed through faith for faith; as it is written, "He who through faith is righteous shall live."*b*

18 For the wrath of God is revealed from heaven against all ungodliness and wickedness of men who by their wickedness suppress the truth. 19 For what can be known about God is plain to them, because God has shown it to them. 20 Ever since the creation of the world his invisible nature, namely, his eternal power and deity, has been clearly perceived in the things that have been made. So they are without excuse; 21 for although they knew God they did not honor him as God or give thanks to him, but they became futile in their thinking and their senseless minds were darkened. 22 Claiming to be wise, they became fools, 23 and exchanged the glory of the immortal God for images resembling mortal man or birds or animals or reptiles.

24 Therefore God gave them up in the lusts of their hearts to impurity, to the dishonoring of their bodies among themselves, 25 because they exchanged the truth about God for a lie and worshiped and served the creature rather than the Creator, who is blessed for ever! Amen.

26 For this reason God gave them up to dishonorable passions. Their women exchanged natural relations for unnatural, 27 and the men likewise gave up natural relations with women and were consumed with passion for one another, men committing shameless acts with men and receiving in their own persons the due penalty for their error.

28 And since they did not see fit to acknowledge God, God gave them up to a base mind and to im-

proper conduct. 29 They were filled with all manner of wickedness, evil, covetousness, malice. Full of envy, murder, strife, deceit, malignity, they are gossips, 30 slanderers, haters of God, insolent, haughty, boastful, inventors of evil, disobedient to parents, 31 foolish, faithless, heartless, ruthless. 32 Though they know God's decree that those who do such things deserve to die, they not only do them but approve those who practice them.

2 Therefore you have no excuse, O man, whoever you are, when you judge another; for in passing judgment upon him you condemn yourself, because you, the judge, are doing the very same things. 2 We know that the judgment of God rightly falls upon those who do such things. 3 Do you suppose, O man, that when you judge those who do such things and yet do them yourself, you will escape the judgment of God? 4 Or do you presume upon the riches of his kindness and forbearance and patience? Do you not know that God's kindness is meant to lead you to repentance? 5 But by your hard and impenitent heart you are storing up wrath for yourself on the day of wrath when God's righteous judgment will be revealed. 6 For he will render to every man according to his works: 7 to those who by patience in well-doing seek for glory and honor and immortality, he will give eternal life; 8 but for those who are factious and do not obey the truth, but obey wickedness, there will be wrath and fury. 9 There will be tribulation and distress for every human being who does evil, the Jew first and also the Greek, 10 but glory and honor and peace for every one who does good, the Jew first and also the Greek. 11 For God shows no partiality.

12 All who have sinned without the law will also perish without the law, and all who have sinned under the law will be judged by the law. 13 For it is not the hearers of the law who are righteous before God, but the doers of the law who will be justified. 14 When Gentiles who have not the law do by nature what the law requires, they are a law to themselves, even though they do not have the law. 15 They show

b Or *The righteous shall live by faith*

1.14: 1 Cor 9.16. 1.16: 1 Cor 1.18, 24.
1.17: Rom 3.21; Gal 3.11; Phil 3.9; Heb 10.38; Hab 2.4. 1.18: Eph 5.6; Col 3.6.
1.20: Ps 19.1-4. 1.21: Eph 4.17-18. 1.23: Acts 17.29. 2.1: Rom 14.22.
2.4: Eph 1.7; 2.7; Phil 4.19; Col 1.27. 2.6: Mt 16.27; 1Cor 3.8; 2 Cor 5.10; Rev 22.12.
2.11: Deut 10.17; 2 Chron 19.7; Gal 2.6; Eph 6.9; Col 3.25; 1 Pet 1.17.
2.12: Rom 3.19; 1 Cor 9.21. 2.13: Jas 1.22-23, 25.

that what the law requires is written on their hearts, while their conscience also bears witness and their conflicting thoughts accuse or perhaps excuse them [16] on that day when, according to my gospel, God judges the secrets of men by Christ Jesus.

[17] But if you call yourself a Jew and rely upon the law and boast of your relation to God [18] and know his will and approve what is excellent, because you are instructed in the law, [19] and if you are sure that you are a guide to the blind, a light to those who are in darkness, [20] a corrector of the foolish, a teacher of children, having in the law the embodiment of knowledge and truth—[21] you then who teach others, will you not teach yourself? While you preach against stealing, do you steal? [22] You who say that one must not commit adultery, do you commit adultery? You who abhor idols, do you rob temples? [23] You who boast in the law, do you dishonor God by breaking the law? [24] For, as it is written, "The name of God is blasphemed among the Gentiles because of you."

[25] Circumcision indeed is of value if you obey the law; but if you break the law, your circumcision becomes uncircumcision. [26] So, if a man who is uncircumcised keeps the precepts of the law, will not his uncircumcision be regarded as circumcision? [27] Then those who are physically uncircumcised but keep the law will condemn you who have the written code and circumcision but break the law. [28] For he is not a real Jew who is one outwardly, nor is true circumcision something external and physical. [29] He is a Jew who is one inwardly, and real circumcision is a matter of the heart, spiritual and not literal. His praise is not from men but from God.

3 Then what advantage has the Jew? Or what is the value of circumcision? [2] Much in every way. To begin with, the Jews are entrusted with the oracles of God. [3] What if some were unfaithful? Does their faithlessness nullify the faithfulness of God? [4] By no means! Let God be true

though every man be false, as it is written,

"That thou mayest be justified in thy words,

and prevail when thou art judged."

[5] But if our wickedness serves to show the justice of God, what shall we say? That God is unjust to inflict wrath on us? (I speak in a human way.) [6] By no means! For then how could God judge the world? [7] But if through my falsehood God's truthfulness abounds to his glory, why am I still being condemned as a sinner? [8] And why not do evil that good may come?—as some people slanderously charge us with saying. Their condemnation is just.

[9] What then? Are we Jews any better off?[c] No, not at all; for I[d] have already charged that all men, both Jews and Greeks, are under the power of sin, [10] as it is written:

"None is righteous, no, not one;

[11] no one understands, no one seeks for God.

[12] All have turned aside, together they have gone wrong;

no one does good, not even one."

[13] "Their throat is an open grave,

they use their tongues to deceive."

"The venom of asps is under their lips."

[14] "Their mouth is full of curses and bitterness."

[15] "Their feet are swift to shed blood,

[16] in their paths are ruin and misery,

[17] and the way of peace they do not know."

[18] "There is no fear of God before their eyes."

[19] Now we know that whatever the law says it speaks to those who are under the law, so that every mouth may be stopped, and the whole world may be held accountable to God. [20] For no human being will be justified in his sight by works of the law, since through the law comes knowledge of sin.

[21] But now the righteousness of God has been manifested apart from law, although the law and the prophets bear witness to it, [22] the righteousness of God through faith in Jesus Christ for all who believe. For there is no

---

c Or *at any disadvantage?* *d* Greek *we*

2.16: Eccles 12.14; Rom 16.25; 1 Cor 4.5. **2.18:** Phil 1.10. **2.20:** Rom 6.17; 2 Tim 1.13.
2.21: Mt 23.3-4. **2.24:** Is 52.5. **2.25:** Jer 9.25. **2.26:** 1 Cor 7.19; Acts 10.35.
2.27: Mt 12.41. **2.28:** Mt 3.9; Jn 8.39; Rom 9.6-7; Gal 6.15.
2.29: 2 Cor 3.6; Phil 3.3; Col 2.11; 1 Pet 3.4. **3.2:** Ps 147.19; Rom 9.4. **3.4:** Ps 51.4.
3.5: Rom 5.9; 6.19; 1 Cor 9.8; Gal 3.15. **3.8:** Rom 6.1, 15.
3.9: Rom 1.18-32; 2.1-29; 11.32; 3.23. **3.10-12:** Ps 14.1-2; 53. 1-2. **3.13:** Ps 5.9; 140.3.
3.14: Ps 10.7. **3.15-17:** Is 59.7-8. **3.18:** Ps 36.1. **3.19:** Rom 2.12.
3.20: Ps 143.2; Acts 13.39; Gal 2.16; 3.11; Rom 7.7.
3.21: Rom 1.17; Phil 3.9; 2 Pet 1.1. **3.22:** Rom 4.5; 9.30; 10.12; Gal 2.16.

distinction; 23 since all have sinned and fall short of the glory of God, 24 they are justified by his grace as a gift, through the redemption which is in Christ Jesus, 25 whom God put forward as an expiation by his blood, to be received by faith. This was to show God's righteousness, because in his divine forbearance he had passed over former sins; 26 it was to prove at the present time that he himself is righteous and that he justifies him who has faith in Jesus.

27 Then what becomes of our boasting? It is excluded. On what principle? On the principle of works? No, but on the principle of faith. 28 For we hold that a man is justified by faith apart from works of law. 29 Or is God the God of Jews only? Is he not the God of Gentiles also? Yes, of Gentiles also, 30 since God is one; and he will justify the circumcised on the ground of their faith and the uncircumcised through their faith. 31 Do we then overthrow the law by this faith? By no means! On the contrary, we uphold the law.

4 What then shall we say about Abraham, our forefather according to the flesh? 2 For if Abraham was justified by works, he has something to boast about, but not before God. 3 For what does the scripture say? "Abraham believed God, and it was reckoned to him as righteousness." 4 Now to one who works, his wages are not reckoned as a gift but as his due. 5 And to one who does not work but trusts him who justifies the ungodly, his faith is reckoned as righteousness. 6 So also David pronounces a blessing upon the man to whom God reckons righteousness apart from works:

7 "Blessed are those whose iniquities are forgiven, and whose sins are covered;

8 blessed is the man against whom the Lord will not reckon his sin."

9 Is this blessing pronounced only upon the circumcised, or also upon the uncircumcised? We say that faith was reckoned to Abraham as righteousness. 10 How then was it reckoned to him? Was it before or after he had been circumcised? It was not after, but before he was circumcised. 11 He received circumcision as a sign or seal of the righteousness which he had by faith while he was still uncircumcised. The purpose was to make him the father of all who believe without being circumcised and who thus have righteousness reckoned to them, 12 and likewise the father of the circumcised who are not merely circumcised but also follow the example of the faith which our father Abraham had before he was circumcised.

13 The promise to Abraham and his descendants, that they should inherit the world, did not come through the law but through the righteousness of faith. 14 If it is the adherents of the law who are to be the heirs, faith is null and the promise is void. 15 For the law brings wrath, but where there is no law there is no transgression.

16 That is why it depends on faith, in order that the promise may rest on grace and be guaranteed to all his descendants—not only to the adherents of the law but also to those who share the faith of Abraham, for he is the father of us all, 17 as it is written, "I have made you the father of many nations"—in the presence of the God in whom he believed, who gives life to the dead and calls into existence the things that do not exist. 18 In hope he believed against hope, that he should become the father of many nations; as he had been told, "So shall your descendants be." 19 He did not weaken in faith when he considered his own body, which was as good as dead because he was about a hundred years old, or when he considered the barrenness of Sarah's womb. 20 No distrust made him waver concerning the promise of God, but he grew strong in his faith as he gave glory to God, 21 fully convinced that God was able to do what he had promised. 22 That is why his faith was "reckoned to him as righteousness." 23 But the words, "it was reckoned to him," were written not for his sake alone, 24 but for ours also. It will be reckoned to us who believe in him that raised from the dead Jesus our Lord, 25 who was put to death for

e Other ancient authorities read *was gained by*

3.23: Rom 3.9.   3.24: Rom 4.16; 5.9; Eph 2.8; Tit 3.7; Eph 1.7; Col 1.14; Heb 9.15.
3.26: 1 Jn 2.2; Col 1.20.   3.28: Acts 13.39; Rom 5.1; Eph 2.9.
3.29: Rom 9.24; Acts 10.34-35.   3.30: Rom 4.11-12, 16.   3.31: Rom 8.4; Mt 5.17.
4.2: 1 Cor 1.31.   4.3: Gen 15.6; Rom 4.9, 22; Gal 3.6; Jas 2.23.   4.4: Rom 11.6.
4.5: Rom 3.22.   4.7: Ps 32.1-2.   4.11: Gen 17.10; Rom 3.22, 30.
4.13: Gen 17.4-6; 22.17-18; Gal 3.29.   4.14: Gal 3.18.   4.15: Gal 3.10.
4.17: Gen 17.5; Jn 5.21.   4.18: Gen 15.5.   4.19: Heb 11.12; Gen 17.17; 18.11.
4.22: Rom 4.3.   4.23-24: Rom 15.4; 1 Cor 9.10; 10.11.   4.25: Rom 8.32.

our trespasses and raised for our justification.

5 Therefore, since we are justified by faith, we[f] have peace with God through our Lord Jesus Christ. [2] Through him we have obtained access[g] to this grace in which we stand, and we[h] rejoice in our hope of sharing the glory of God. [3] More than that, we[h] rejoice in our sufferings, knowing that suffering produces endurance, [4] and endurance produces character, and character produces hope, [5] and hope does not disappoint us, because God's love has been poured into our hearts through the Holy Spirit which has been given to us.

[6] While we were yet helpless, at the right time Christ died for the ungodly. [7] Why, one will hardly die for a righteous man—though perhaps for a good man one will dare even to die. [8] But God shows his love for us in that while we were yet sinners Christ died for us. [9] Since, therefore, we are now justified by his blood, much more shall we be saved by him from the wrath of God. [10] For if while we were enemies we were reconciled to God by the death of his Son, much more, now that we are reconciled, shall we be saved by his life. [11] Not only so, but we also rejoice in God through our Lord Jesus Christ, through whom we have now received our reconciliation.

[12] Therefore as sin came into the world through one man and death through sin, and so death spread to all men because all men sinned——[13] sin indeed was in the world before the law was given, but sin is not counted where there is no law. [14] Yet death reigned from Adam to Moses, even over those whose sins were not like the transgression of Adam, who was a type of the one who was to come.

[15] But the free gift is not like the trespass. For if many died through one man's trespass, much more have the grace of God and the free gift in the grace of that one man Jesus Christ abounded for many. [16] And the free gift is not like the effect of that one man's sin. For the judgment following one trespass brought condemnation, but the free gift following many trespasses brings justification. [17] If, because of one man's trespass, death reigned through that one man, much more will those who receive the abundance of grace and the free gift of righteousness reign in life through the one man Jesus Christ.

[18] Then as one man's trespass led to condemnation for all men, so one man's act of righteousness leads to acquittal and life for all men. [19] For as by one man's disobedience many were made sinners, so by one man's obedience many will be made righteous. [20] Law came in, to increase the trespass; but where sin increased, grace abounded all the more, [21] so that, as sin reigned in death, grace also might reign through righteousness to eternal life through Jesus Christ our Lord.

6 What shall we say then? Are we to continue in sin that grace may abound? [2] By no means! How can we who died to sin still live in it? [3] Do you not know that all of us who have been baptized into Christ Jesus were baptized into his death? [4] We were buried therefore with him by baptism into death, so that as Christ was raised from the dead by the glory of the Father, we too might walk in newness of life.

[5] For if we have been united with him in a death like his, we shall certainly be united with him in a resurrection like his. [6] We know that our old self was crucified with him so that the sinful body might be destroyed, and we might no longer be enslaved to sin. [7] For he who has died is freed from sin. [8] But if we have died with Christ, we believe that we shall also live with him. [9] For we know that Christ being raised from the dead will never die again; death no longer has dominion over him. [10] The death he died he died to sin, once for all, but the life he lives he lives to God. [11] So

---

f Other ancient authorities read *let us*   g Other ancient authorities add *by faith*
h Or *let us*

5.1: Rom 3.28.   **5.2:** Eph 2.18; 3.12; Heb 10.19-20.
5.3: Rom 5.11; 2 Cor 12.10; Jas 1.3.   **5.5:** Ps 119.116; Acts 2.33; Phil 1.20.
5.8: Jn 15.13; Rom 8.32; 1 Pet 3.18; 1 Jn 3.16; 4.10.
5.9: Rom 3.5, 24-25; Eph 1.7; 1 Thess 1.10.   **5.10:** Col 1.21.   **5.11:** Rom 5.3.
5.12: 1 Cor 15.21-22; Rom 6.23; Jas 1.15.   **5.14:** 1 Cor 15.22, 45.   **5.15:** Acts 15.11.
5.16: Rom 8.1.   **5.19:** Phil 2.8.   **5.20:** Rom 7.7-8; Gal 3.19; 1 Tim 1.14.
5.21: Rom 6.23.   **6.1:** Rom 3.8; 6.15.   **6.2:** Rom 7.4, 6; Gal 2.19; 1 Pet 2.24.
6.3: Acts 2.38; 8.16; 19.5.   **6.4:** Col 2.12.   **6.5:** 2 Cor 4.10; Col 2.12.
6.6: Rom 7.24; Col 2.13.   **6.7:** 1 Pet 4.1.   **6.8:** 2 Tim 2.11.   **6.9:** Acts 2.24; Rev 1.18.
6.11: Rom 7.4, 6; Gal 2.19; 1 Pet 2.24.

you also must consider yourselves dead to sin and alive to God in Christ Jesus.

12 Let not sin therefore reign in your mortal bodies, to make you obey their passions. 13 Do not yield your members to sin as instruments of wickedness, but yield yourselves to God as men who have been brought from death to life, and your members to God as instruments of righteousness. 14 For sin will have no dominion over you, since you are not under law but under grace.

15 What then? Are we to sin because we are not under law but under grace? By no means! 16 Do you not know that if you yield yourselves to any one as obedient slaves, you are slaves of the one whom you obey, either of sin, which leads to death, or of obedience, which leads to righteousness? 17 But thanks be to God, that you who were once slaves of sin have become obedient from the heart to the standard of teaching to which you were committed, 18 and, having been set free from sin, have become slaves of righteousness. 19 I am speaking in human terms, because of your natural limitations. For just as you once yielded your members to impurity and to greater and greater iniquity, so now yield your members to righteousness for sanctification.

20 When you were slaves of sin, you were free in regard to righteousness. 21 But then what return did you get from the things of which you are now ashamed? The end of those things is death. 22 But now that you have been set free from sin and have become slaves of God, the return you get is sanctification and its end, eternal life. 23 For the wages of sin is death, but the free gift of God is eternal life in Christ Jesus our Lord.

7 Do you not know, brethren—for I am speaking to those who know the law—that the law is binding on a person only during his life? 2 Thus a married woman is bound by law to her husband as long as he lives; but if her husband dies she is discharged from the law concerning the husband. 3Accordingly, she will be called an adulteress if she lives with another man while her husband is alive. But if her husband dies she is free from that law, and if she marries another man she is not an adulteress.

4 Likewise, my brethren, you have died to the law through the body of Christ, so that you may belong to another, to him who has been raised from the dead in order that we may bear fruit for God. 5 While we were living in the flesh, our sinful passions, aroused by the law, were at work in our members to bear fruit for death. 6 But now we are discharged from the law, dead to that which held us captive, so that we serve not under the old written code but in the new life of the Spirit.

7 What then shall we say? That the law is sin? By no means! Yet, if it had not been for the law, I should not have known sin. I should not have known what it is to covet if the law had not said, "You shall not covet." 8 But sin, finding opportunity in the commandment, wrought in me all kinds of covetousness. Apart from the law sin lies dead. 9 I was once alive apart from the law, but when the commandment came, sin revived and I died; 10 the very commandment which promised life proved to be death to me. 11 For sin, finding opportunity in the commandment, deceived me and by it killed me. 12 So the law is holy, and the commandment is holy and just and good.

13 Did that which is good, then, bring death to me? By no means! It was sin, working death in me through what is good, in order that sin might be shown to be sin, and through the commandment might become sinful beyond measure. 14 We know that the law is spiritual; but I am carnal, sold under sin. 15 I do not understand my own actions. For I do not do what I want, but I do the very thing I hate. 16 Now if I do what I do not want, I agree that the law is good. 17 So then it is no longer I that do it, but sin which dwells within me. 18 For I know that nothing good dwells within me, that is, in my flesh. I can will what is right, but I cannot do it. 19 For I do not do the good I want, but the evil I do not want is what I do. 20 Now if I do what I do not want, it is no longer I that do it, but sin which dwells within me.

6.13: Rom 6.19; 7.5; 12.1.   **6.14:** Rom 8.2.   **6.15:** Rom 3.8; 6.1.
6.16: Mt 6.24; Jn 8.34; Rom 12.1.   **6.18:** Rom 8.2.   **6.19:** Rom 3.5; 6.13; 12.1.
6.20: Mt 6.24; Jn 8.34.   **6.21:** Rom 7.5; 8.6, 13, 21.   **6.23:** Rom 5.12, 21; Gal 6.7, 8.
7.2: 1 Cor 7.39.   **7.4:** Rom 6.2, 11; Gal 2.19; Col 1.22.
7.5: Rom 6.13, 21; 8.8; Jas 1.15.   **7.7:** Rom 3.20; 5.20; Ex 20.17; Deut 5.21.
7.8: 1 Cor 15.56.   **7.10:** Lev 18.5; Rom 10.5.   **7.12:** 1 Tim 1.8.   **7.14:** 1 Cor 3.1.
7.15: Gal 5.17.

21 So I find it to be a law that when I want to do right, evil lies close at hand. 22 For I delight in the law of God, in my inmost self, 23 but I see in my members another law at war with the law of my mind and making me captive to the law of sin which dwells in my members. 24 Wretched man that I am! Who will deliver me from this body of death? 25 Thanks be to God through Jesus Christ our Lord! So then, I of myself serve the law of God with my mind, but with my flesh I serve the law of sin.

8 There is therefore now no condemnation for those who are in Christ Jesus. 2 For the law of the Spirit of life in Christ Jesus has set me free from the law of sin and death. 3 For God has done what the law, weakened by the flesh, could not do: sending his own Son in the likeness of sinful flesh and for sin,*i* he condemned sin in the flesh, 4 in order that the just requirement of the law might be fulfilled in us, who walk not according to the flesh but according to the Spirit. 5 For those who live according to the flesh set their minds on the things of the flesh, but those who live according to the Spirit set their minds on the things of the Spirit. 6 To set the mind on the flesh is death, but to set the mind on the Spirit is life and peace. 7 For the mind that is set on the flesh is hostile to God; it does not submit to God's law, indeed it cannot; 8 and those who are in the flesh cannot please God.

9 But you are not in the flesh, you are in the Spirit, if the Spirit of God really dwells in you. Any one who does not have the Spirit of Christ does not belong to him. 10 But if Christ is in you, although your bodies are dead because of sin, your spirits are alive because of righteousness. 11 If the Spirit of him who raised Jesus from the dead dwells in you, he who raised Christ Jesus from the dead will give life to your mortal bodies also through his Spirit which dwells in you.

12 So then, brethren, we are debt-ors, not to the flesh, to live according to the flesh—13 for if you live according to the flesh you will die, but if by the Spirit you put to death the deeds of the body you will live. 14 For all who are led by the Spirit of God are sons of God. 15 For you did not receive the spirit of slavery to fall back into fear, but you have received the spirit of sonship. When we cry, "Ab'ba! Father!" 16 it is the Spirit himself bearing witness with our spirit that we are children of God, 17 and if children, then heirs, heirs of God and fellow heirs with Christ, provided we suffer with him in order that we may also be glorified with him.

18 I consider that the sufferings of this present time are not worth comparing with the glory that is to be revealed to us. 19 For the creation waits with eager longing for the revealing of the sons of God; 20 for the creation was subjected to futility, not of its own will but by the will of him who subjected it in hope; 21 because the creation itself will be set free from its bondage to decay and obtain the glorious liberty of the children of God. 22 We know that the whole creation has been groaning in travail together until now; 23 and not only the creation, but we ourselves, who have the first fruits of the Spirit, groan inwardly as we wait for adoption as sons, the redemption of our bodies. 24 For in this hope we were saved. Now hope that is seen is not hope. For who hopes for what he sees? 25 But if we hope for what we do not see, we wait for it with patience.

26 Likewise the Spirit helps us in our weakness; for we do not know how to pray as we ought, but the Spirit himself intercedes for us with sighs too deep for words. 27 And he who searches the hearts of men knows what is the mind of the Spirit, because*j* the Spirit intercedes for the saints according to the will of God.

28 We know that in everything God works for good*k* with those who love

i Or *and as a sin offering*   *j* Or *that*

k Other ancient authorities read *in everything he works for good*, or *everything works for good*

7.22: Ps 1.2.   7.23: Gal 5.17.   7.24: Rom 6.6; Col 2.11.   8.1: Rom 5.16.
8.2: 1 Cor 15.45; Rom 6.14, 18.   8.3: Acts 13.39; Heb 7.18; 10.1-2; Phil 2.7; Heb 2.14.
8.4: Rom 3.31; Gal 5.16, 25.   8.5: Gal 5.19-25.   8.6: Rom 6.21; 8.13, 27; Gal 6.8.
8.8: Rom 7.5.   8.9: 1 Cor 3.16; 6.19; 2 Cor 6.16; 2 Tim 1.14.
8.10: Gal 2.20; Eph 3.17.   8.11: Jn 5.21.   8.13: Rom 8.6; Col 3.5.   8.14: Gal 5.18.
8.15: Rom 9.4; Gal 4.5-7; Mk 14.36.   8.16: Acts 5.32.
8.17: Gal 3.29; 4.7; 2 Cor 1.5, 7; 2 Tim 2.12; 1 Pet 4.13.
8.18: 2 Cor 4.17; Col 3.4; 1 Pet 5.1.   8.19: 1 Pet 1.7, 13; 1 Jn 3.2.   8.20: Eccles 1.2.
8.21: Acts 3.21; Rom 6.21; 2 Pet 3.13; Rev 21.1.   8.22: Jer 12.4, 11.
8.23: 2 Cor 1.22; 5.2, 4; Gal 5.5.   8.24: 2 Cor 5.7; Heb 11.1.
8.27: Ps 139.1-2; Lk 16.15; Rev 2.23; Rom 8.6, 34.

him,[l] who are called according to his purpose. 29 For those whom he foreknew he also predestined to be conformed to the image of his Son, in order that he might be the first-born among many brethren. 30And those whom he predestined he also called; and those whom he called he also justified; and those whom he justified he also glorified.

31 What then shall we say to this? If God is for us, who is against us? 32 He who did not spare his own Son but gave him up for us all, will he not also give us all things with him? 33 Who shall bring any charge against God's elect? It is God who justifies; 34 who is to condemn? Is it Christ Jesus, who died, yes, who was raised from the dead, who is at the right hand of God, who indeed intercedes for us?[m] 35 Who shall separate us from the love of Christ? Shall tribulation, or distress, or persecution, or famine, or nakedness, or peril, or sword? 36As it is written,

"For thy sake we are being killed all the day long;
we are regarded as sheep to be slaughtered."

37 No, in all these things we are more than conquerors through him who loved us. 38 For I am sure that neither death, nor life, nor angels, nor principalities, nor things present, nor things to come, nor powers, 39 nor height, nor depth, nor anything else in all creation, will be able to separate us from the love of God in Christ Jesus our Lord.

9 I am speaking the truth in Christ, I am not lying; my conscience bears me witness in the Holy Spirit, 2 that I have great sorrow and unceasing anguish in my heart. 3 For I could wish that I myself were accursed and cut off from Christ for the sake of my brethren, my kinsmen by race. 4 They are Israelites, and to them belong the sonship, the glory, the covenants, the giving of the law, the worship, and the promises; 5 to them belong the patriarchs, and of their race, according to the flesh, is the Christ. God who is over all be blessed for ever.[n] Amen.

6 But it is not as though the word of God had failed. For not all who are descended from Israel belong to Israel, 7 and not all are children of Abraham because they are his descendants; but "Through Isaac shall your descendants be named." 8 This means that it is not the children of the flesh who are the children of God, but the children of the promise are reckoned as descendants. 9 For this is what the promise said, "About this time I will return and Sarah shall have a son." 10And not only so, but also when Rebecca had conceived children by one man, our forefather Isaac, 11 though they were not yet born and had done nothing either good or bad, in order that God's purpose of election might continue, not because of works but because of his call, 12 she was told, "The elder will serve the younger." 13As it is written, "Jacob I loved, but Esau I hated."

14 What shall we say then? Is there injustice on God's part? By no means! 15 For he says to Moses, "I will have mercy on whom I have mercy, and I will have compassion on whom I have compassion." 16 So it depends not upon man's will or exertion, but upon God's mercy. 17 For the scripture says to Pharaoh, "I have raised you up for the very purpose of showing my power in you, so that my name may be proclaimed in all the earth." 18 So then he has mercy upon whomever he wills, and he hardens the heart of whomever he wills.

19 You will say to me then, "Why does he still find fault? For who can resist his will?" 20 But who are you, a man, to answer back to God? Will what is molded say to its molder, "Why have you made me thus?" 21 Has the potter no right over the clay, to make out of the same lump one vessel for beauty and another for menial use? 22 What if God, desiring to show his wrath and to make known his power, has endured with much patience the vessels of wrath made for destruction, 23 in order to make known the riches of his glory for the vessels of mercy, which he has prepared beforehand for glory, 24 even us whom he has called, not from the

l Greek God   m Or It is Christ Jesus . . . for us
n Or Christ, who is God over all, blessed for ever

8.29: Rom 9.23; 11.2; 1 Pet 1.2, 20; Eph 1.5, 11.   8.31: Ps 118.6.
8.32: Jn 3.16; Rom 4.25; 5.8.   8.33: Lk 18.7; Is 50.8-9.   8.34: Rom 8.27.
8.36: Ps 44.22.   8.37: 1 Cor 15.57.   9.3: Ex 32.32.   9.4: Rom 3.2; 8.15.
9.6: Rom 2.28-29.   9.7: Gen 21.12; Heb 11.18.   9.8: Gal 3.29; 4.28.   9.9: Gen 18.10.
9.10: Gen 25.21.   9.12: Gen 25.23.   9.13: Mal 1.2-3.   9.14: 2 Chron 19.7.
9.15: Ex 33.19.   9.17: Ex 9.16.   9.18: Rom 11.7.   9.20: Is 29.16; 45.9.
9.21: 2 Tim 2.20.   9.22: Prov 16.4.   9.23: Rom 8.29.   9.24: Rom 3.29.

Jews only but also from the Gentiles? 25 As indeed he says in Hō·sē′à, "Those who were not my people I will call 'my people,' and her who was not beloved I will call 'my beloved.' " 26 "And in the very place where it was said to them, 'You are not my people,' they will be called 'sons of the living God.' "

27 And I·śāi′àh cries out concerning Israel: "Though the number of the sons of Israel be as the sand of the sea, only a remnant of them will be saved; 28 for the Lord will execute his sentence upon the earth with rigor and dispatch." 29And as I·śāi′àh predicted,

"If the Lord of hosts had not left us children,
we would have fared like Sod′òm and been made like Gò·môr′ràh."

30 What shall we say, then? That Gentiles who did not pursue righteousness have attained it, that is, righteousness through faith; 31 but that Israel who pursued the righteousness which is based on law did not succeed in fulfilling that law. 32 Why? Because they did not pursue it through faith, but as if it were based on works. They have stumbled over the stumbling stone, 33 as it is written,

"Behold, I am laying in Zion a stone that will make men stumble,
a rock that will make them fall;
and he who believes in him will not be put to shame."

10 Brethren, my heart's desire and prayer to God for them is that they may be saved. 2 I bear them witness that they have a zeal for God, but it is not enlightened. 3 For, being ignorant of the righteousness that comes from God, and seeking to establish their own, they did not submit to God's righteousness. 4 For Christ is the end of the law, that every one who has faith may be justified.

5 Moses writes that the man who practices the righteousness which is based on the law shall live by it. 6 But the righteousness based on faith says,

Do not say in your heart, "Who will ascend into heaven?" (that is, to bring Christ down) 7 or "Who will descend into the abyss?" (that is, to bring Christ up from the dead). 8 But what does it say? The word is near you, on your lips and in your heart (that is, the word of faith which we preach); 9 because, if you confess with your lips that Jesus is Lord and believe in your heart that God raised him from the dead, you will be saved. 10 For man believes with his heart and so is justified, and he confesses with his lips and so is saved. 11 The scripture says, "No one who believes in him will be put to shame." 12 For there is no distinction between Jew and Greek; the same Lord is Lord of all and bestows his riches upon all who call upon him. 13 For, "every one who calls upon the name of the Lord will be saved."

14 But how are men to call upon him in whom they have not believed? And how are they to believe in him of whom they have never heard? And how are they to hear without a preacher? 15And how can men preach unless they are sent? As it is written, "How beautiful are the feet of those who preach good news!" 16 But they have not all heeded the gospel; for I·śāi′àh says, "Lord, who has believed what he has heard from us?" 17 So faith comes from what is heard, and what is heard comes by the preaching of Christ.

18 But I ask, have they not heard? Indeed they have; for

"Their voice has gone out to all the earth,
and their words to the ends of the world."

19Again I ask, did Israel not understand? First Moses says,

"I will make you jealous of those who are not a nation;
with a foolish nation I will make you angry."

20 Then I·śāi′àh is so bold as to say;

"I have been found by those who did not seek me;
I have shown myself to those who did not ask for me."

9.25: Hos 2.23; 1 Pet 2.10.　9.26: Hos 1.10.
9.27: Is 10.22-23; Gen 22.17; Hos 1.10; Rom 11.5; 2 Kings 19.4; Is 11.11.
9.29: Is 1.9.　9.30: Rom 3.22; 10.6, 20; Gal 2.16; 3.24; Phil 3.9; Heb 11.7.
9.31: Is 51.1; Rom 10.2-3; 11.7.　9.32: 1 Pet 2.8.　9.33: Is 28.16; Rom 10.11.
10.2-4: Rom 9.31.　10.3: Rom 1.17.　10.4: Gal 3.24; Rom 3.22; 7.1-4.
10.5: Lev 18.5; Neh 9.29; Ezek 20.11, 13, 21; Rom 7.10.
10.6: Deut 30.12-13; Rom 9.30.　10.8: Deut 30.14.　10.9: Mt 10.32; Lk 12.8; Acts 16.31.
10.11: Is 28.16; Rom 9.33.　10.12: Rom 3.22, 29; Gal 3.28; Col 3.11; Acts 10.36.
10.13: Joel 2.32; Acts 2.21.　10.15: Is 52.7.　10.16: Is 53.1; Jn 12.38.
10.18: Ps 19.4; Col 1.6, 23.　10.19: Deut 32.21; Rom 11.11, 14.
10.20: Is 65.1; Rom 9.30.

21 But of Israel he says, "All day long I have held out my hands to a disobedient and contrary people."

11 I ask, then, has God rejected his people? By no means! I myself am an Israelite, a descendant of Abraham, a member of the tribe of Benjamin. 2 God has not rejected his people whom he foreknew. Do you not know what the scripture says of E·li′jah, how he pleads with God against Israel? 3 "Lord, they have killed thy prophets, they have demolished thy altars, and I alone am left, and they seek my life." 4 But what is God's reply to him? "I have kept for myself seven thousand men who have not bowed the knee to Ba′al." 5 So too at the present time there is a remnant, chosen by grace. 6 But if it is by grace, it is no longer on the basis of works; otherwise grace would no longer be grace.

7 What then? Israel failed to obtain what it sought. The elect obtained it, but the rest were hardened, 8 as it is written,

"God gave them a spirit of stupor,
eyes that should not see and ears that should not hear,
down to this very day."

9 And David says,
"Let their feast become a snare and a trap,
a pitfall and a retribution for them;
10 let their eyes be darkened so that they cannot see,
and bend their backs for ever."

11 So I ask, have they stumbled so as to fall? By no means! But through their trespass salvation has come to the Gentiles, so as to make Israel jealous. 12 Now if their trespass means riches for the world, and if their failure means riches for the Gentiles, how much more will their full inclusion mean!

13 Now I am speaking to you Gentiles. Inasmuch then as I am an apostle to the Gentiles, I magnify my ministry 14 in order to make my fellow Jews jealous, and thus save some of them. 15 For if their rejection means the reconciliation of the world, what will their acceptance mean but life from the dead? 16 If the dough offered as

first fruits is holy, so is the whole lump; and if the root is holy, so are the branches.

17 But if some of the branches were broken off, and you, a wild olive shoot, were grafted in their place to share the richness*o* of the olive tree, 18 do not boast over the branches. If you do boast, remember it is not you that support the root, but the root that supports you. 19 You will say, "Branches were broken off so that I might be grafted in." 20 That is true. They were broken off because of their unbelief, but you stand fast only through faith. So do not become proud, but stand in awe. 21 For if God did not spare the natural branches, neither will he spare you. 22 Note then the kindness and the severity of God: severity toward those who have fallen, but God's kindness to you, provided you continue in his kindness; otherwise you too will be cut off. 23 And even the others, if they do not persist in their unbelief, will be grafted in, for God has the power to graft them in again. 24 For if you have been cut from what is by nature a wild olive tree, and grafted, contrary to nature, into a cultivated olive tree, how much more will these natural branches be grafted back into their own olive tree.

25 Lest you be wise in your own conceits, I want you to understand this mystery, brethren: a hardening has come upon part of Israel, until the full number of the Gentiles come in, 26 so all Israel will be saved; as it is written,

"The Deliverer will come from Zion,
he will banish ungodliness from Jacob";
27 "and this will be my covenant with them
when I take away their sins."

28 As regards the gospel they are enemies of God, for your sake; but as regards election they are beloved for the sake of their forefathers. 29 For the gifts and the call of God are irrevocable. 30 Just as you were once disobedient to God but now have received mercy because of their disobedience, 31 so they have now been disobedient in order that by the mercy

o Other ancient authorities read *rich root*

10.21: Is 65.2.   **11.1:** 1 Sam 12.22; Jer 31.37; 33.24-26; 2 Cor 11.22; Phil 3.5.
11.2: Ps 94.14; 1 Kings 19.10.   **11.4:** 1 Kings 19.18.
11.5: 2 Kings 19.4; Is 11.11; Rom 9.27.   **11.6:** Rom 4.4.   **11.7:** Rom 9.18, 31; 11.25.
11.8: Is 29.10; Deut 29.4; Mt 13.13-14.   **11.9:** Ps 69.22-23.   **11.11:** Rom 10.19; 11.14.
11.13: Acts 9.15.   **11.14:** Rom 10.19; 11.11; 1 Cor 9.22.   **11.15:** Lk 15.24, 32.
11.20: 2 Cor 1.24.   **11.25:** 1 Cor 2.7-10; Eph 3.3-5, 9; Rom 9.18; 11.7; Lk 21.24.
11.26: Is 59.20-21.   **11.27:** Jer 31.33; Is 27.9.

shown to you they also may*p* receive mercy. 32 For God has consigned all men to disobedience, that he may have mercy upon all.

33 O the depth of the riches and wisdom and knowledge of God! How unsearchable are his judgments and how inscrutable his ways!

34 "For who has known the mind of the Lord,
or who has been his counselor?"

35 "Or who has given a gift to him that he might be repaid?"

36 For from him and through him and to him are all things. To him be glory for ever. Amen.

12 I appeal to you therefore, brethren, by the mercies of God, to present your bodies as a living sacrifice, holy and acceptable to God, which is your spiritual worship. 2 Do not be conformed to this world*q* but be transformed by the renewal of your mind, that you may prove what is the will of God, what is good and acceptable and perfect.*r*

3 For by the grace given to me I bid every one among you not to think of himself more highly than he ought to think, but to think with sober judgment, each according to the measure of faith which God has assigned him. 4 For as in one body we have many members, and all the members do not have the same function, 5 so we, though many, are one body in Christ, and individually members one of another. 6 Having gifts that differ according to the grace given to us, let us use them: if prophecy, in proportion to our faith; 7 if service, in our serving; he who teaches, in his teaching; 8 he who exhorts, in his exhortation; he who contributes, in liberality; he who gives aid, with zeal; he who does acts of mercy, with cheerfulness.

9 Let love be genuine; hate what is evil, hold fast to what is good; 10 love one another with brotherly affection; outdo one another in showing honor. 11 Never flag in zeal, be aglow with the

Spirit, serve the Lord. 12 Rejoice in your hope, be patient in tribulation, be constant in prayer. 13 Contribute to the needs of the saints, practice hospitality.

14 Bless those who persecute you; bless and do not curse them. 15 Rejoice with those who rejoice, weep with those who weep. 16 Live in harmony with one another; do not be haughty, but associate with the lowly;*s* never be conceited. 17 Repay no one evil for evil, but take thought for what is noble in the sight of all. 18 If possible, so far as it depends upon you, live peaceably with all. 19 Beloved, never avenge yourselves, but leave it*t* to the wrath of God; for it is written, "Vengeance is mine, I will repay, says the Lord." 20 No, "if your enemy is hungry, feed him; if he is thirsty, give him drink; for by so doing you will heap burning coals upon his head." 21 Do not be overcome by evil, but overcome evil with good.

13 Let every person be subject to the governing authorities. For there is no authority except from God, and those that exist have been instituted by God. 2 Therefore he who resists the authorities resists what God has appointed, and those who resist will incur judgment. 3 For rulers are not a terror to good conduct, but to bad. Would you have no fear of him who is in authority? Then do what is good, and you will receive his approval, 4 for he is God's servant for your good. But if you do wrong, be afraid, for he does not bear the sword in vain; he is the servant of God to execute his wrath on the wrongdoer. 5 Therefore one must be subject, not only to avoid God's wrath but also for the sake of conscience. 6 For the same reason you also pay taxes, for the authorities are ministers of God, attending to this very thing. 7 Pay all of them their dues, taxes to whom taxes are due, revenue to whom revenue is due, respect to whom respect is due, honor to whom honor is due.

p Other ancient authorities add *now*   *q* Greek *age*   *r* Or *what is the good and acceptable and perfect will of God*   *s* Or *give yourselves to humble tasks*   *t* Greek *give place*

11.32: Rom 3.9; Gal 3.22-29.   **11.33:** Col 2.3.   **11.34:** Is 40.13-14; 1 Cor 2.16.
11.35: Job 35.7; 41.11.   **11.36:** 1 Cor 8.6; 11.12; Col 1.16; Heb 2.10.
12.1: Rom 6.13, 16, 19; 1 Pet 2.5.   **12.2:** 1 Jn 2.15; Eph 4.23; 5.10.
12.4: 1 Cor 12.12-14; Eph 4.4,16.   **12.5:** 1 Cor 10.17; 12.20, 27; Eph 4.25.
12.6-8: 1 Cor 7.7; 12.4-11; 1 Pet 4.10-11.   **12.12:** Acts 1.14; Rom 5.2; 1 Thess 5.17.
12.14: Mt 5.44; Lk 6.28.
12.16: Rom 11.25; 15.5; 1 Cor 1.10; 2 Cor 13.11; Phil 2.2; 4.2; Prov 3.7; 26.12.
12.17: Prov 20.22; 2 Cor 8.21; 1 Thess 5.15.   **12.18:** Mk 9.50; Rom 14.19.
12.19: Lev 19.18; Deut 32.35; Heb 10.30.   **12.20:** Prov 25.21-22; Mt 5.44; Lk 6.27.
13.1: Tit 3.1; 1 Pet 2.13-14; Prov 8.15; Jn 19.11.   **13.3:** 1 Pet 2.14.   **13.4:** 1 Thess 4.6.
13.7: Mt 22.21; Mk 12.17; Lk 20.25.

8 Owe no one anything, except to love one another; for he who loves his neighbor has fulfilled the law. 9 The commandments, "You shall not commit adultery, You shall not kill, You shall not steal, You shall not covet," and any other commandment, are summed up in this sentence, "You shall love your neighbor as yourself." 10 Love does no wrong to a neighbor; therefore love is the fulfilling of the law.

11 Besides this you know what hour it is, how it is full time now for you to wake from sleep. For salvation is nearer to us now than when we first believed; 12 the night is far gone, the day is at hand. Let us then cast off the works of darkness and put on the armor of light; 13 let us conduct ourselves becomingly as in the day, not in reveling and drunkenness, not in debauchery and licentiousness, not in quarreling and jealousy. 14 But put on the Lord Jesus Christ, and make no provision for the flesh, to gratify its desires.

14 As for the man who is weak in faith, welcome him, but not for disputes over opinions. 2 One believes he may eat anything, while the weak man eats only vegetables. 3 Let not him who eats despise him who abstains, and let not him who abstains pass judgment on him who eats; for God has welcomed him. 4 Who are you to pass judgment on the servant of another? It is before his own master that he stands or falls. And he will be upheld, for the Master is able to make him stand.

5 One man esteems one day as better than another, while another man esteems all days alike. Let every one be fully convinced in his own mind. 6 He who observes the day, observes it in honor of the Lord. He also who eats, eats in honor of the Lord, since he gives thanks to God; while he who abstains, abstains in honor of the Lord and gives thanks to God. 7 None of us lives to himself, and none of us dies to himself. 8 If we live, we live to the Lord, and if we die, we die to the Lord; so then, whether we live or whether

we die, we are the Lord's. 9 For to this end Christ died and lived again, that he might be Lord both of the dead and of the living.

10 Why do you pass judgment on your brother? Or you, why do you despise your brother? For we shall all stand before the judgment seat of God; 11 for it is written,

"As I live, says the Lord, every knee
    shall bow to me,
and every tongue shall give praise[u]
    to God."

12 So each of us shall give account of himself to God.

13 Then let us no more pass judgment on one another, but rather decide never to put a stumbling block or hindrance in the way of a brother. 14 I know and am persuaded in the Lord Jesus that nothing is unclean in itself; but it is unclean for any one who thinks it unclean. 15 If your brother is being injured by what you eat, you are no longer walking in love. Do not let what you eat cause the ruin of one for whom Christ died. 16 So do not let what is good to you be spoken of as evil. 17 For the kingdom of God does not mean food and drink but righteousness and peace and joy in the Holy Spirit; 18 he who thus serves Christ is acceptable to God and approved by men. 19 Let us then pursue what makes for peace and for mutual upbuilding. 20 Do not, for the sake of food, destroy the work of God. Everything is indeed clean, but it is wrong for any one to make others fall by what he eats; 21 it is right not to eat meat or drink wine or do anything that makes your brother stumble.[v] 22 The faith that you have, keep between yourself and God; happy is he who has no reason to judge himself for what he approves. 23 But he who has doubts is condemned, if he eats, because he does not act from faith; for whatever does not proceed from faith is sin.[w]

15 We who are strong ought to bear with the failings of the weak, and not to please ourselves; 2 let each of us please his neighbor for his good, to edify him. 3 For Christ did not please himself; but, as it is written, "The reproaches of those who reproached

u Or *confess*   v Other ancient authorities add *or be upset or be weakened*
w Other authorities, some ancient, insert here Ch 16.25-27
13.8: Mt 22.39-40; Rom 13.10; Gal 5.14; Col 3.14; Jas 2.8.   **13.9:** Ex 20.13-14; Deut 5.17-18; Lev 19.18; Mt 19.19.   **13.10:** Mt 22.39-40; Rom 13.8; Gal 5.14; Jas 2.8.   **13.11:** Eph 5.14; 1 Thess 5.6.   **13.12:** 1 Jn 2.8; Eph 5.11; 1 Thess 5.8.   **13.13:** 1 Thess 4.12; Gal 5.19-21.   **13.14:** Gal 3.27; 5.16.   **14.3:** Col 2.16.   **14.5:** Gal 4.10.   **14.7:** Gal 2.20; 2 Cor 5.15.   **14.8:** Phil 1.20.   **14.10:** 2 Cor 5.10.   **14.11:** Is 45.23; Phil 2.10-11.   **14.13:** Mt 7.1; 1 Cor 8.13.   **14.15:** Rom 14.20; 1 Cor 8.11.   **14.16:** 1 Cor 10.30.   **14.19:** Mk 9.50; Rom 12.18; 1 Thess 5.11.   **14.20:** Rom 14.15; 1 Cor 8.9-12.   **14.21:** 1 Cor 8.13.   **14.22:** Rom 2.1.   **15.3:** Ps 69.9.

thee fell on me." 4 For whatever was written in former days was written for our instruction, that by steadfastness and by the encouragement of the scriptures we might have hope. 5 May the God of steadfastness and encouragement grant you to live in such harmony with one another, in accord with Christ Jesus, 6 that together you may with one voice glorify the God and Father of our Lord Jesus Christ.

7 Welcome one another, therefore, as Christ has welcomed you, for the glory of God. 8 For I tell you that Christ became a servant to the circumcised to show God's truthfulness, in order to confirm the promises given to the patriarchs, 9 and in order that the Gentiles might glorify God for his mercy. As it is written,

"Therefore I will praise thee among the Gentiles,
and sing to thy name";

10 and again it is said,

"Rejoice, O Gentiles, with his people";

11 and again,

"Praise the Lord, all Gentiles,
and let all the peoples praise him";

12 and further I·śai′ah says,

"The root of Jesse shall come,
he who rises to rule the Gentiles;
in him shall the Gentiles hope."

13 May the God of hope fill you with all joy and peace in believing, so that by the power of the Holy Spirit you may abound in hope.

14 I myself am satisfied about you, my brethren, that you yourselves are full of goodness, filled with all knowledge, and able to instruct one another. 15 But on some points I have written to you very boldly by way of reminder, because of the grace given me by God 16 to be a minister of Christ Jesus to the Gentiles in the priestly service of the gospel of God, so that the offering of the Gentiles may be acceptable, sanctified by the Holy Spirit. 17 In Christ Jesus, then, I have reason to be proud of my work for God. 18 For I will not venture to speak of anything except what Christ has wrought through me to win obedience from the

Gentiles, by word and deed, 19 by the power of signs and wonders, by the power of the Holy Spirit, so that from Jerusalem and as far round as Il·lyr′i·cùm I have fully preached the gospel of Christ, 20 thus making it my ambition to preach the gospel, not where Christ has already been named, lest I build on another man's foundation, 21 but as it is written,

"They shall see who have never been told of him,
and they shall understand who have never heard of him."

22 This is the reason why I have so often been hindered from coming to you. 23 But now, since I no longer have any room for work in these regions, and since I have longed for many years to come to you, 24 I hope to see you in passing as I go to Spain, and to be sped on my journey there by you, once I have enjoyed your company for a little. 25 At present, however, I am going to Jerusalem with aid for the saints. 26 For Mac·e·do′ni·a and A·cha′ia have been pleased to make some contribution for the poor among the saints at Jerusalem; 27 they were pleased to do it, and indeed they are in debt to them, for if the Gentiles have come to share in their spiritual blessings, they ought also to be of service to them in material blessings. 28 When therefore I have completed this, and have delivered to them what has been raised,ˣ I shall go on by way of you to Spain; 29 and I know that when I come to you I shall come in the fulness of the blessingʸ of Christ.

30 I appeal to you, brethren, by our Lord Jesus Christ and by the love of the Spirit, to strive together with me in your prayers to God on my behalf, 31 that I may be delivered from the unbelievers in Judea, and that my service for Jerusalem may be acceptable to the saints, 32 so that by God's will I may come to you with joy and be refreshed in your company. 33 The God of peace be with you all. Amen.

16 I commend to you our sister Phoebe, a deaconess of the church

---

ˣ Greek *sealed to them this fruit*   ʸ Other ancient authorities insert *of the gospel*

15.4: Rom 4.23-24; 1 Cor 9.10; 2 Tim 3.16.
15.5: Rom 12.16; 1 Cor 1.10; 2 Cor 13.11; Phil 2.2; 4.2.   **15.9:** Ps 18.49; 2 Sam 22.50.
15.10: Deut 32.43.   **15.11:** Ps 117.1.   **15.12:** Is 11.10; Mt 12.21.   **15.16:** Acts 9.15.
15.18: Rom 1.5; Acts 15.12; 21.19.   **15.19:** Acts 19.11; 2 Cor 12.12.
15.20: 2 Cor 10.15-16.   **15.21:** Is 52.15.   **15.22:** Rom 1.13.
15.23: Acts 19.21; Rom 1.10-11; 15.32.   **15.24:** Rom 15.28.
15.25: Acts 19.21; 24.17; 15.31.   **15.26:** 2 Cor 8.1-5; 9.2; 1 Thess 1.7-8.
15.27: 1 Cor 9.11.   **15.28:** Rom 15.24.   **15.29:** Acts 19.21.
15.31: 2 Thess 3.2; Rom 15.25-26; 2 Cor 8.4; 9.1.   **15.32:** Rom 1.10; Acts 19.21.
15.33: 2 Cor 13.11; Phil 4.9.

at Cen'chrē-ae, 2 that you may receive her in the Lord as befits the saints, and help her in whatever she may require from you, for she has been a helper of many and of myself as well.

3 Greet Pris'cà and Aq'ui·là, my fellow workers in Christ Jesus, 4 who risked their necks for my life, to whom not only I but also all the churches of the Gentiles give thanks; 5 greet also the church in their house. Greet my beloved E·pae'nē·tùs, who was the first convert in Asia for Christ. 6 Greet Mary, who has worked hard among you. 7 Greet An·dron'i·cùs and Jū'ni·às, my kinsmen and my fellow prisoners; they are men of note among the apostles, and they were in Christ before me. 8 Greet Am·pli·a'tùs, my beloved in the Lord. 9 Greet Ūr·bā'nùs, our fellow worker in Christ, and my beloved Stā'chys. 10 Greet À·pel'lēs, who is approved in Christ. Greet those who belong to the family of Ar·is·tob'ū·lùs. 11 Greet my kinsman He·rō'di·òn. Greet those in the Lord who belong to the family of När·cis'sùs. 12 Greet those workers in the Lord, Trÿ·phae'nà and Trÿ·phō'sà. Greet the beloved Per'sis, who has worked hard in the Lord. 13 Greet Rufus, eminent in the Lord; also his mother and mine. 14 Greet À·syn'cri·tùs, Phlē'gon, Hēr'mēs, Pat'rō·bàs, Hēr'màs, and the brethren who are with them. 15 Greet Phi·lol'ò·gùs, Julia, Nē'rè·us and his sister, and Ò·lym'pàs, and all the saints who are with them. 16 Greet one another with a holy kiss. All the churches of Christ greet you.

17 I appeal to you, brethren, to take note of those who create dissensions and difficulties, in opposition to the doctrine which you have been taught; avoid them. 18 For such persons do not serve our Lord Christ, but their own appetites,[z] and by fair and flattering words they deceive the hearts of the simple-minded. 19 For while your obedience is known to all, so that I rejoice over you, I would have you wise as to what is good and guileless as to what is evil; 20 then the God of peace will soon crush Satan under your feet. The grace of our Lord Jesus Christ be with you.[a]

21 Timothy, my fellow worker, greets you; so do Lucius and Jason and Sō·sip'à·tèr, my kinsmen.

22 I Tertius, the writer of this letter, greet you in the Lord.

23 Gā'iùs, who is host to me and to the whole church, greets you. E·ras'tùs, the city treasurer, and our brother Quär'tùs, greet you.[b]

25 Now to him who is able to strengthen you according to my gospel and the preaching of Jesus Christ, according to the revelation of the mystery which was kept secret for long ages 26 but is now disclosed and through the prophetic writings is made known to all nations, according to the command of the eternal God, to bring about the obedience of faith—27 to the only wise God be glory for evermore through Jesus Christ! Amen.

THE FIRST LETTER OF PAUL TO THE

CORINTHIANS

1 Paul, called by the will of God to be an apostle of Christ Jesus, and our brother Sos'thē·nēs,

2 To the church of God which is at Corinth, to those sanctified in Christ Jesus, called to be saints together with all those who in every place call on the name of our Lord Jesus Christ, both their Lord and ours:

3 Grace to you and peace from God our Father and the Lord Jesus Christ.

z Greek *their own belly* (Phil 3.19)   *a* Other ancient authorities omit this sentence
b Other ancient authorities insert verse 24, *The grace of our Lord Jesus Christ be with you all. Amen.*

16.3: Acts 18.2.   **16.5:** 1 Cor 16.19.   **16.16:** 2 Cor 13.12; 1 Thess 5.26; 1 Pet 5.14.
16.17: Gal 1.8-9; 2 Thess 3.6, 14; 2 Jn 10.   **16.19:** Rom 1.8; 1 Cor 14.20.
16.20: 1 Cor 16.23; 2 Cor 13.14; Gal 6.18; Phil 4.23; 1 Thess 5.28; 2 Thess 3.18; Rev 22.21.
16.21: Acts 16.1.   **16.23:** 1 Cor 1.14.   **1.1:** Rom 1.1; Acts 18.17.
1.2: Acts 18.1.   **1.3:** Rom 1.7.

4 I give thanks to God[a] always for you because of the grace of God which was given you in Christ Jesus, 5 that in every way you were enriched in him with all speech and all knowledge— 6 even as the testimony to Christ was confirmed among you—7 so that you are not lacking in any spiritual gift, as you wait for the revealing of our Lord Jesus Christ; 8 who will sustain you to the end, guiltless in the day of our Lord Jesus Christ. 9 God is faithful, by whom you were called into the fellowship of his Son, Jesus Christ our Lord.

10 I appeal to you, brethren, by the name of our Lord Jesus Christ, that all of you agree and that there be no dissensions among you, but that you be united in the same mind and the same judgment. 11 For it has been reported to me by Chlō′e′s̄ people that there is quarreling among you, my brethren. 12 What I mean is that each one of you says, "I belong to Paul," or "I belong to A·pol′los," or "I belong to Cē′phas," or "I belong to Christ." 13 Is Christ divided? Was Paul crucified for you? Or were you baptized in the name of Paul? 14 I am thankful[b] that I baptized none of you except Cris′pus and Gā′iŭs; 15 lest any one should say that you were baptized in my name, 16 (I did baptize also the household of Steph′a·nås. Beyond that, I do not know whether I baptized any one else.) 17 For Christ did not send me to baptize but to preach the gospel, and not with eloquent wisdom, lest the cross of Christ be emptied of its power.

18 For the word of the cross is folly to those who are perishing, but to us who are being saved it is the power of God. 19 For it is written,

"I will destroy the wisdom of the wise,
and the cleverness of the clever I will thwart."

20 Where is the wise man? Where is the scribe? Where is the debater of this age? Has not God made foolish the wisdom of the world? 21 For since,

in the wisdom of God, the world did not know God through wisdom, it pleased God through the folly of what we preach to save those who believe. 22 For Jews demand signs and Greeks seek wisdom, 23 but we preach Christ crucified, a stumbling block to Jews and folly to Gentiles, 24 but to those who are called, both Jews and Greeks, Christ the power of God and the wisdom of God. 25 For the foolishness of God is wiser than men, and the weakness of God is stronger than men.

26 For consider your call, brethren; not many of you were wise according to worldly standards, not many were powerful, not many were of noble birth; 27 but God chose what is foolish in the world to shame the wise, God chose what is weak in the world to shame the strong, 28 God chose what is low and despised in the world, even things that are not, to bring to nothing things that are, 29 so that no human being might boast in the presence of God. 30 He is the source of your life in Christ Jesus, whom God made our wisdom, our righteousness and sanctification and redemption; 31 therefore, as it is written, "Let him who boasts, boast of the Lord."

2 When I came to you, brethren, I did not come proclaiming to you the testimony[c] of God in lofty words or wisdom. 2 For I decided to know nothing among you except Jesus Christ and him crucified. 3 And I was with you in weakness and in much fear and trembling; 4 and my speech and my message were not in plausible words of wisdom, but in demonstration of the Spirit and power, 5 that your faith might not rest in the wisdom of men but in the power of God.

6 Yet among the mature we do impart wisdom, although it is not a wisdom of this age or of the rulers of this age, who are doomed to pass away. 7 But we impart a secret and hidden wisdom of God, which God decreed before the ages for our glorification. 8 None of the rulers of this age understood this; for if they had, they would

---

[a] Other ancient authorities read *my God*   [b] Other ancient authorities read *I thank God*
[c] Other ancient authorities read *mystery* (or *secret*)

1.4: Rom 1.8.   **1.8:** 1 Cor 5.5; 2 Cor 1.14.   **1.9:** Rom 8.28; 1 Jn 1.3.
1.12: 1 Cor 3.4; Acts 18.24; 1 Cor 3.22; Jn 1.42; 1 Cor 9.5; 15.5.
1.13: Mt 28.19; Acts 2.38.   **1.14:** Acts 18.8; Rom 16.23.   **1.16:** 1 Cor 16.15.
1.17: Jn 4.2; Acts 10.48; 1 Cor 2.1, 4, 13.   **1.19:** Is 29.14.   **1.22:** Mt 12.38.
1.23: 1 Cor 2.2; Gal 3.1; 5.11.   **1.27:** Jas 2.5.   **1.28:** Rom 4.17.   **1.29:** Eph 2.9.
1.30: 1 Cor 4.15; Rom 8.1; 2 Cor 5.21; 1 Cor 6.11; 1 Thess 5.23; Eph 1.7, 14; Col 1.14; Rom 3.24.   **1.31:** Jer 9.24; 2 Cor 10.17.   **2.1:** 1 Cor 1.17.
2.2: Gal 6.14; 1 Cor 1.23.   **2.3:** Acts 18.1, 6, 12; 1 Cor 4.10; 2 Cor 11.30.
2.4: Rom 15.19; 1 Cor 4.20.   **2.5:** 2 Cor 4.7; 6.7; 1 Cor 12.9.   **2.6:** Eph 4.13.
2.7: Rom 8.29-30.   **2.8:** Acts 7.2; Jas 2.1.

not have crucified the Lord of glory. 9 But, as it is written,

"What no eye has seen, nor ear heard,

nor the heart of man conceived,

what God has prepared for those who love him,"

10 God has revealed to us through the Spirit. For the Spirit searches everything, even the depths of God. 11 For what person knows a man's thoughts except the spirit of the man which is in him? So also no one comprehends the thoughts of God except the Spirit of God. 12 Now we have received not the spirit of the world, but the Spirit which is from God, that we might understand the gifts bestowed on us by God. 13And we impart this in words not taught by human wisdom but taught by the Spirit, interpreting spiritual truths to those who possess the Spirit.*d*

14 The unspiritual*e* man does not receive the gifts of the Spirit of God, for they are folly to him, and he is not able to understand them because they are spiritually discerned. 15 The spiritual man judges all things, but is himself to be judged by no one. 16 "For who has known the mind of the Lord so as to instruct him?" But we have the mind of Christ.

3 But I, brethren, could not address you as spiritual men, but as men of the flesh, as babes in Christ. 2 I fed you with milk, not solid food; for you were not ready for it; and even yet you are not ready, 3 for you are still of the flesh. For while there is jealousy and strife among you, are you not of the flesh, and behaving like ordinary men? 4 For when one says, "I belong to Paul," and another, "I belong to Á·pol'los," are you not merely men?

5 What then is Á·pol'los? What is Paul? Servants through whom you believed, as the Lord assigned to each. 6 I planted, Á·pol'los watered, but God gave the growth. 7 So neither he who plants nor he who waters is anything, but only God who gives the growth. 8 He who plants and he who waters are equal, and each shall receive his wages

according to his labor. 9 For we are fellow workers for God;*f* you are God's field, God's building.

10 According to the commission of God given to me, like a skilled master builder I laid a foundation, and another man is building upon it. Let each man take care how he builds upon it. 11 For no other foundation can any one lay than that which is laid, which is Jesus Christ. 12 Now if any one builds on the foundation with gold, silver, precious stones, wood, hay, stubble—13 each man's work will become manifest; for the Day will disclose it, because it will be revealed with fire, and the fire will test what sort of work each one has done. 14 If the work which any man has built on the foundation survives, he will receive a reward. 15 If any man's work is burned up, he will suffer loss, though he himself will be saved, but only as through fire.

16 Do you not know that you are God's temple and that God's Spirit dwells in you? 17 If any one destroys God's temple, God will destroy him. For God's temple is holy, and that temple you are.

18 Let no one deceive himself. If any one among you thinks that he is wise in this age, let him become a fool that he may become wise. 19 For the wisdom of this world is folly with God. For it is written, "He catches the wise in their craftiness," 20 and again, "The Lord knows that the thoughts of the wise are futile." 21 So let no one boast of men. For all things are yours, 22 whether Paul or Á·pol'los or Cē'phàs or the world or life or death or the present or the future, all are yours; 23 and you are Christ's; and Christ is God's.

4 This is how one should regard us, as servants of Christ and stewards of the mysteries of God. 2 Moreover it is required of stewards that they be found trustworthy. 3 But with me it is a very small thing that I should be judged by you or by any human court. I do not even judge myself. 4 I am not aware of anything against myself, but

d Or *interpreting spiritual truths in spiritual language;* or *comparing spiritual things with spiritual*   *e* or *natural*   *f* Greek *God's fellow workers*

2.9: Is 64.4; 65.17.   **2.10:** Mt 11.25; 13.11; 16.17; Eph 3.3, 5.   **2.12:** Rom 8.15.
2.13: 1 Cor 1.17.   **2.14:** 1 Cor 1.18; Jas 3.15.   **2.15:** 1 Cor 3.1; 14.37; Gal 6.1.
2.16: Is 40.13; Rom 11.34.   **3.1:** Rom 7.14; Heb 5.13.   **3.2:** Heb 5.12-13; 1 Pet 2.2.
3.4: 1 Cor 1.12.   **3.5:** 2 Cor 6.4; Eph 3.7; Col 1.25.
3.6: Acts 18.4-11, 24-27; 1 Cor 1.12.   **3.9:** Is 61.3; Eph 2.20-22; 1 Pet 2.5.
3.10: Rom 12.3; 1 Cor 15.10.   **3.11:** Eph 2.20.   **3.13:** 2 Thess 1.7-10.   **3.15:** Job 23.10.
3.16: 1 Cor 6.19; 2 Cor 6.16.   **3.18:** Is 5.21; 1 Cor 8.2; Gal 6.3.
3.19: Job 5.13; 1 Cor 1.20.   **3.20:** Ps 94.11.   **3.21:** 1 Cor 4.6; Rom 8.32.
3.22: 1 Cor 1.12; Rom 8.38.   **4.1:** 1 Cor 9.17; Rom 11.25; 16.25.   **4.4:** 2 Cor 1.12.

I am not thereby acquitted. It is the Lord who judges me. 5 Therefore do not pronounce judgment before the time, before the Lord comes, who will bring to light the things now hidden in darkness and will disclose the purposes of the heart. Then every man will receive his commendation from God.

6 I have applied all this to myself and Ạ·pol'los for your benefit, brethren, that you may learn by us to live according to scripture, that none of you may be puffed up in favor of one against another. 7 For who sees anything different in you? What have you that you did not receive? If then you received it, why do you boast as if it were not a gift?

8 Already you are filled! Already you have become rich! Without us you have become kings! And would that you did reign, so that we might share the rule with you! 9 For I think that God has exhibited us apostles as last of all, like men sentenced to death; because we have become a spectacle to the world, to angels and to men. 10 We are fools for Christ's sake, but you are wise in Christ. We are weak, but you are strong. You are held in honor, but we are in disrepute. 11 To the present hour we hunger and thirst, we are ill-clad and buffeted and homeless, 12 and we labor, working with our own hands. When reviled, we bless; when persecuted, we endure; 13 when slandered, we try to conciliate; we have become, and are now, as the refuse of the world, the offscouring of all things.

14 I do not write this to make you ashamed, but to admonish you as my beloved children. 15 For though you have countless guides in Christ, you do not have many fathers. For I became your father in Christ Jesus through the gospel. 16 I urge you, then, be imitators of me. 17 Therefore I sent^g to you Timothy, my beloved and faithful child in the Lord, to remind you of my ways in Christ, as I teach them everywhere in every church. 18 Some are arrogant, as though I were not coming to you. 19 But I will come to you soon,

if the Lord wills, and I will find out not the talk of these arrogant people but their power. 20 For the kingdom of God does not consist in talk but in power. 21 What do you wish? Shall I come to you with a rod, or with love in a spirit of gentleness?

5 It is actually reported that there is immorality among you, and of a kind that is not found even among pagans; for a man is living with his father's wife. 2 And you are arrogant! Ought you not rather to mourn? Let him who has done this be removed from among you.

3 For though absent in body I am present in spirit, and as if present, I have already pronounced judgment 4 in the name of the Lord Jesus on the man who has done such a thing. When you are assembled, and my spirit is present, with the power of our Lord Jesus, 5 you are to deliver this man to Satan for the destruction of the flesh, that his spirit may be saved in the day of the Lord Jesus.^{h}

6 Your boasting is not good. Do you not know that a little leaven leavens the whole lump? 7 Cleanse out the old leaven that you may be a new lump, as you really are unleavened. For Christ, our paschal lamb, has been sacrificed. 8 Let us, therefore, celebrate the festival, not with the old leaven, the leaven of malice and evil, but with the unleavened bread of sincerity and truth.

9 I wrote to you in my letter not to associate with immoral men; 10 not at all meaning the immoral of this world, or the greedy and robbers, or idolaters, since then you would need to go out of the world. 11 But rather I wrote^i to you not to associate with any one who bears the name of brother if he is guilty of immorality or greed, or is an idolater, reviler, drunkard, or robber—not even to eat with such a one. 12 For what have I to do with judging outsiders? Is it not those inside the church whom you are to judge? 13 God judges those outside. "Drive out the wicked person from among you."

g Or *am sending*   h Other ancient authorities omit *Jesus*   i Or *now I write*

4.5: Rom 2.16; 1 Cor 3.13; 2 Cor 10.18; Rom 2.29.
4.6: 1 Cor 1.19, 31; 3.19-20; 1.12; 3.4.
4.9: 1 Cor 15.31; 2 Cor 11.23; Rom 8.36; Heb 10.33.
4.10: 1 Cor 1.18; 2 Cor 11.19; 1 Cor 3.18; 2 Cor 13.9; 1 Cor 2.3.
4.11: Rom 8.35; 2 Cor 11.23-27.   **4.12:** Acts 18.3; 1 Pet 3.9.
4.15: 1 Cor 1.30; Philem 10.   **4.17:** 1 Cor 16.10; Acts 16.1; 1 Cor 7.17.
4.21: 2 Cor 1.23.   **5.1:** Deut 22.30; 27.20.   **5.3:** Col 2.5.   **5.4:** 2 Thess 3.6.
5.5: Mt 4.10; 1 Cor 1.8.   **5.6:** Gal 5.9.   **5.8:** Ex 12.19; 13.7; Deut 16.3.
5.9: 2 Cor 6.14.   **5.10:** 1 Cor 10.27.   **5.11:** 2 Thess 3.6; 1 Cor 10.7, 14, 20-21.
5.12: Mk 4.11.   **5.13:** Deut 17.7; 1 Cor 5.2.

6 When one of you has a grievance against a brother, does he dare go to law before the unrighteous instead of the saints? [2] Do you not know that the saints will judge the world? And if the world is to be judged by you, are you incompetent to try trivial cases? [3] Do you not know that we are to judge angels? How much more, matters pertaining to this life! [4] If then you have such cases, why do you lay them before those who are least esteemed by the church? [5] I say this to your shame. Can it be that there is no man among you wise enough to decide between members of the brotherhood, [6] but brother goes to law against brother, and that before unbelievers?

7 To have lawsuits at all with one another is defeat for you. Why not rather suffer wrong? Why not rather be defrauded? [8] But you yourselves wrong and defraud, and that even your own brethren.

9 Do you not know that the unrighteous will not inherit the kingdom of God? Do not be deceived; neither the immoral, nor idolaters, nor adulterers, nor homosexuals,*j* [10] nor thieves, nor the greedy, nor drunkards, nor revilers, nor robbers will inherit the kingdom of God. [11] And such were some of you. But you were washed, you were sanctified, you were justified in the name of the Lord Jesus Christ and in the Spirit of our God.

12 "All things are lawful for me," but not all things are helpful. "All things are lawful for me," but I will not be enslaved by anything. [13] "Food is meant for the stomach and the stomach for food"—and God will destroy both one and the other. The body is not meant for immorality, but for the Lord, and the Lord for the body. [14] And God raised the Lord and will also raise us up by his power. [15] Do you not know that your bodies are members of Christ? Shall I therefore take the members of Christ and make them members of a prostitute? Never! [16] Do you not know that he who joins himself to a prostitute becomes one body with her? For, as it is written, "The two shall become one."*k* [17] But he who is united to the Lord becomes one spirit with him. [18] Shun immorality. Every other sin which a man commits is outside the body; but

the immoral man sins against his own body. [19] Do you not know that your body is a temple of the Holy Spirit within you, which you have from God? You are not your own; [20] you were bought with a price. So glorify God in your body.

7 Now concerning the matters about which you wrote. It is well for a man not to touch a woman. [2] But because of the temptation to immorality, each man should have his own wife and each woman her own husband. [3] The husband should give to his wife her conjugal rights, and likewise the wife to her husband. [4] For the wife does not rule over her own body, but the husband does; likewise the husband does not rule over his own body, but the wife does. [5] Do not refuse one another except perhaps by agreement for a season, that you may devote yourselves to prayer; but then come together again, lest Satan tempt you through lack of self-control. [6] I say this by way of concession, not of command. [7] I wish that all were as I myself am. But each has his own special gift from God, one of one kind and one of another.

8 To the unmarried and the widows I say that it is well for them to remain single as I do. [9] But if they cannot exercise self-control, they should marry. For it is better to marry than to be aflame with passion.

10 To the married I give charge, not I but the Lord, that the wife should not separate from her husband [11] (but if she does, let her remain single or else be reconciled to her husband)— and that the husband should not divorce his wife.

12 To the rest I say, not the Lord, that if any brother has a wife who is an unbeliever, and she consents to live with him, he should not divorce her. [13] If any woman has a husband who is an unbeliever, and he consents to live with her, she should not divorce him. [14] For the unbelieving husband is consecrated through his wife, and the unbelieving wife is consecrated through her husband. Otherwise, your children would be unclean, but as it is they are holy. [15] But if the unbelieving partner desires to separate, let it be so; in such a case the brother or sister is not

j Two Greek words are rendered by this expression   *k* Greek *one flesh*

6.1: Mt 18.17.   **6.7:** Mt 5.39-40.   **6.9:** 1 Cor 15.50.   **6.11:** Acts 22.16; Rom 8.30.
6.12: 1 Cor 10.23.   **6.15:** Rom 12.5; 1 Cor 12.27.
6.16: Gen 2.24; Mt 19.5; Mk 10.8; Eph 5.31.   **6.17:** Jn 17.21-23; Rom 8.9; Gal 2.20.
6.19: 1 Cor 3.16; Jn 2.21.   **6.20:** 1 Cor 7.23; Acts 20.28; Rom 12.1.   **7.5:** Ex 19.15.
7.7: 1 Cor 7.8; 9.5.   **7.9:** 1 Tim 5.14.   **7.12:** 2 Cor 11.17.

bound. For God has called us[l] to peace. 16 Wife, how do you know whether you will save your husband? Husband, how do you know whether you will save your wife?

17 Only, let every one lead the life which the Lord has assigned to him, and in which God has called him. This is my rule in all the churches. 18 Was any one at the time of his call already circumcised? Let him not seek to remove the marks of circumcision. Was any one at the time of his call uncircumcised? Let him not seek circumcision. 19 For neither circumcision counts for anything nor uncircumcision, but keeping the commandments of God. 20 Every one should remain in the state in which he was called. 21 Were you a slave when called? Never mind. But if you can gain your freedom, avail yourself of the opportunity.[x] 22 For he who was called in the Lord as a slave is a freedman of the Lord. Likewise he who was free when called is a slave of Christ. 23 You were bought with a price; do not become slaves of men. 24 So, brethren, in whatever state each was called, there let him remain with God.

25 Now concerning the unmarried, I have no command of the Lord, but I give my opinion as one who by the Lord's mercy is trustworthy. 26 I think that in view of the impending[m] distress it is well for a person to remain as he is. 27 Are you bound to a wife? Do not seek to be free. Are you free from a wife? Do not seek marriage. 28 But if you marry, you do not sin, and if a girl marries she does not sin. Yet those who marry will have worldly troubles, and I would spare you that. 29 I mean, brethren, the appointed time has grown very short; from now on, let those who have wives live as though they had none, 30 and those who mourn as though they were not mourning, and those who rejoice as though they were not rejoicing, and those who buy as though they had no goods, 31 and those who deal with the world as though they had no dealings with it. For the form of this world is passing away.

32 I want you to be free from anxieties. The unmarried man is anxious about the affairs of the Lord, how to please the Lord; 33 but the married man is anxious about worldly affairs, how to please his wife, 34 and his interests are divided. And the unmarried woman or girl is anxious about the affairs of the Lord, how to be holy in body and spirit; but the married woman is anxious about worldly affairs, how to please her husband. 35 I say this for your own benefit, not to lay any restraint upon you, but to promote good order and to secure your undivided devotion to the Lord.

36 If any one thinks that he is not behaving properly toward his betrothed, if his passions are strong, and it has to be, let him do as he wishes; let them marry—it is no sin. 37 But whoever is firmly established in his heart, being under no necessity but having his desire under control, and has determined this in his heart, to keep her as his betrothed, he will do well. 38 So that he who marries his betrothed does well; and he who refrains from marriage will do better.

39 A wife is bound to her husband as long as he lives. If the husband dies, she is free to be married to whom she wishes, only in the Lord. 40 But in my judgment she is happier if she remains as she is. And I think that I have the Spirit of God.

8 Now concerning food offered to idols: we know that "all of us possess knowledge." "Knowledge" puffs up, but love builds up. 2 If any one imagines that he knows something, he does not yet know as he ought to know. 3 But if one loves God, one is known by him.

4 Hence, as to the eating of food offered to idols, we know that "an idol has no real existence," and that "there is no God but one." 5 For although there may be so-called gods in heaven or on earth—as indeed there are many "gods" and many "lords"—6 yet for us there is one God, the Father, from whom are all things and for whom we exist, and one Lord, Jesus Christ, through whom are all things and through whom we exist.

7 However, not all possess this knowledge. But some, through being

l Other ancient authorities read you   x Or make use of your present condition instead
m Or present   7.16: 1 Pet 3.1.   7.17: Rom 12.3; 1 Cor 14.33; 2 Cor 8.18; 11.28.
7.18: 1 Maccabees 1.15; Acts 15.1-2.   7.19: Gal 5.6; 6.15; Rom 2.25.   7.22: Jn 8.32, 36.
7.23: 1 Cor 6.20.   7.29: Rom 13.11-12; 1 Cor 7.31.   7.32: 1 Tim 5.5.   7.39: Rom 7.2.
7.40: 1 Cor 7.25.   8.1: Rom 15.14.   8.2: 1 Cor 3.18; 13.8, 9, 12.
8.3: Gal 4.9; Rom 8.29.   8.4: 1 Cor 10.19; Deut 6.4.
8.6: Mal 2.10; Eph 4.6; Rom 11.36; 1 Cor 1.2; Eph 4.5; Jn 1.3; Col 1.16.
8.7: 1 Cor 8.4-5.

hitherto accustomed to idols, eat food as really offered to an idol; and their conscience, being weak, is defiled. [8] Food will not commend us to God. We are no worse off if we do not eat, and no better off if we do. [9] Only take care lest this liberty of yours somehow become a stumbling block to the weak. [10] For if any one sees you, a man of knowledge, at table in an idol's temple, might he not be encouraged, if his conscience is weak, to eat food offered to idols? [11]And so by your knowledge this weak man is destroyed, the brother for whom Christ died. [12] Thus, sinning against your brethren and wounding their conscience when it is weak, you sin against Christ. [13] Therefore, if food is a cause of my brother's falling, I will never eat meat, lest I cause my brother to fall.

9 Am I not free? Am I not an apostle? Have I not seen Jesus our Lord? Are not you my workmanship in the Lord? [2] If to others I am not an apostle, at least I am to you; for you are the seal of my apostleship in the Lord.

[3] This is my defense to those who would examine me. [4] Do we not have the right to our food and drink? [5] Do we not have the right to be accompanied by a wife,[n] as the other apostles and the brothers of the Lord and Cĕ'phàs? [6] Or is it only Bär'nå·bàs and I who have no right to refrain from working for a living? [7] Who serves as a soldier at his own expense? Who plants a vineyard without eating any of its fruit? Who tends a flock without getting some of the milk?

[8] Do I say this on human authority? Does not the law say the same? [9] For it is written in the law of Moses, "You shall not muzzle an ox when it is treading out the grain." Is it for oxen that God is concerned? [10] Does he not speak entirely for our sake? It was written for our sake, because the plowman should plow in hope and the thresher thresh in hope of a share in the crop. [11] If we have sown spiritual good among you, is it too much if we reap your material benefits? [12] If

others share this rightful claim upon you, do not we still more?

Nevertheless, we have not made use of this right, but we endure anything rather than put an obstacle in the way of the gospel of Christ. [13] Do you not know that those who are employed in the temple service get their food from the temple, and those who serve at the altar share in the sacrificial offerings? [14] In the same way, the Lord commanded that those who proclaim the gospel should get their living by the gospel.

[15] But I have made no use of any of these rights, nor am I writing this to secure any such provision. For I would rather die than have any one deprive me of my ground for boasting. [16] For if I preach the gospel, that gives me no ground for boasting. For necessity is laid upon me. Woe to me if I do not preach the gospel! [17] For if I do this of my own will, I have a reward; but if not of my own will, I am entrusted with a commission. [18] What then is my reward? Just this: that in my preaching I may make the gospel free of charge, not making full use of my right in the gospel.

[19] For though I am free from all men, I have made myself a slave to all, that I might win the more. [20] To the Jews I became as a Jew, in order to win Jews; to those under the law I became as one under the law—though not being myself under the law—that I might win those under the law. [21] To those outside the law I became as one outside the law—not being without law toward God but under the law of Christ—that I might win those outside the law. [22] To the weak I became weak, that I might win the weak. I have become all things to all men, that I might by all means save some. [23] I do it all for the sake of the gospel, that I may share in its blessings.

[24] Do you not know that in a race all the runners compete, but only one receives the prize? So run that you may obtain it. [25] Every athlete exercises self-control in all things. They do it to receive a perishable wreath, but we an imperishable. [26] Well, I do not run

[n] Greek *a sister as wife*

8.8: Rom 14.17.   **8.9:** 1 Cor 8.10-11; Rom 14.1.   **8.11:** Rom 14.15, 20.
8.12: Mt 18.6; Rom 14.20.   **8.13:** Rom 14.21.
9.1: 1 Cor 9.19; 2 Cor 12.12; 1 Thess 2.6; Acts 9.3, 17; 1 Cor 15.8.   **9.4:** 1 Cor 9.14.
9.5: 1 Cor 7.7-8; Mt 12.46; 8.14; Jn 1.42.   **9.6:** Acts 4.36.   **9.9:** Deut 25.4; 1 Tim 5.18.
9.10: 2 Tim 2.6.   **9.11:** Rom 15.27.   **9.12:** Cor 6.3.   **9.13:** Deut 18.1.
9.14: Mt 10.10; Lk 10.7-8.   **9.15:** 2 Cor 11.10.   **9.17:** 1 Cor 4.1; Gal 2.7.
9.18: 2 Cor 11.7.   **9.20:** Rom 11.14.   Rom 2.12, 14.
9.22: 2 Cor 11.29; Rom 15.1; 1 Cor 10.33; Rom 11.14.   **9.24:** Heb 12.1.
9.25: 2 Tim 2.5; 4.8; Jas 1.12; 1 Pet 5.4.

aimlessly, I do not box as one beating the air; 27 but I pommel my body and subdue it, lest after preaching to others I myself should be disqualified.

10 I want you to know, brethren, that our fathers were all under the cloud, and all passed through the sea, 2 and all were baptized into Moses in the cloud and in the sea, 3 and all ate the same supernatural*o* food 4 and all drank the same supernatural*o* drink. For they drank from the supernatural*o* Rock which followed them, and the Rock was Christ. 5 Nevertheless with most of them God was not pleased; for they were overthrown in the wilderness.

6 Now these things are warnings for us, not to desire evil as they did. 7 Do not be idolaters as some of them were; as it is written, "The people sat down to eat and drink and rose up to dance." 8 We must not indulge in immorality as some of them did, and twenty-three thousand fell in a single day. 9 We must not put the Lord*p* to the test, as some of them did and were destroyed by serpents; 10 nor grumble, as some of them did and were destroyed by the Destroyer. 11 Now these things happened to them as a warning, but they were written down for our instruction, upon whom the end of the ages has come. 12 Therefore let any one who thinks that he stands take heed lest he fall. 13 No temptation has overtaken you that is not common to man. God is faithful, and he will not let you be tempted beyond your strength, but with the temptation will also provide the way of escape, that you may be able to endure it.

14 Therefore, my beloved, shun the worship of idols. 15 I speak as to sensible men; judge for yourselves what I say. 16 The cup of blessing which we bless, is it not a participation*q* in the blood of Christ? The bread which we break, is it not a participation*q* in the body of Christ? 17 Because there is one bread, we who are many are one body, for we all partake of the one bread. 18 Consider the practice of Israel; are not those who eat the sacri-

fices partners in the altar? 19 What do I imply then? That food offered to idols is anything, or that an idol is anything? 20 No, I imply that what pagans sacrifice they offer to demons and not to God. I do not want you to be partners with demons. 21 You cannot drink the cup of the Lord and the cup of demons. You cannot partake of the table of the Lord and the table of demons. 22 Shall we provoke the Lord to jealousy? Are we stronger than he?

23 "All things are lawful," but not all things are helpful. "All things are lawful," but not all things build up. 24 Let no one seek his own good, but the good of his neighbor. 25 Eat whatever is sold in the meat market without raising any question on the ground of conscience. 26 For "the earth is the Lord's, and everything in it." 27 If one of the unbelievers invites you to dinner and you are disposed to go, eat whatever is set before you without raising any question on the ground of conscience. 28 (But if some one says to you, "This has been offered in sacrifice," then out of consideration for the man who informed you, and for conscience' sake—29 I mean his conscience, not yours—do not eat it.) For why should my liberty be determined by another man's scruples? 30 If I partake with thankfulness, why am I denounced because of that for which I give thanks?

31 So, whether you eat or drink, or whatever you do, do all to the glory of God. 32 Give no offense to Jews or to Greeks or to the church of God, 33 just as I try to please all men in everything I do, not seeking my own advantage, but that of many, that they may be saved. 11 1 Be imitators of me, as I am of Christ.

2 I commend you because you remember me in everything and maintain the traditions even as I have delivered them to you. 3 But I want you to understand that the head of every man is Christ, the head of a woman is her husband, and the head of Christ is God. 4 Any man who prays or prophesies with his head covered dishonors

o Greek *spiritual*   *p* Other ancient authorities read *Christ*   *q* Or *communion*

10.1: Rom 1.13; Ex 13.21; 14.22, 29.   **10.2:** Rom 6.3; Gal 3.27.   **10.3:** Ex 16.4, 35.
10.4: Ex 17.6; Num 20.11.   **10.5:** Num 14.29-30.   **10.6:** Num 11.4, 34.
10.7: Ex 32.4, 6.   **10.8:** Num 25.1-18.   **10.9:** Num 21.5-6.   **10.10:** Num 16.41, 49.
10.13: 1 Cor 1.9.   **10.14:** 1 Jn 5.21.   **10.16:** Mt 26.27-28; Acts 2.42.   **10.17:** Rom 12.5.
10.18: Lev 7.6.   **10.20:** Deut 32.17.   **10.21:** 2 Cor 6.16.
10.22: Deut 32.21; Eccles 6.10; Is 45.9.   **10.23:** 1 Cor 6.12; Phil 2.21.
10.26: Ps 24.1; 50.12.   **10.28:** 1 Cor 8.7, 10-12.   **10.32:** 1 Cor 8.13.
10.33: 1 Cor 9.22; Rom 15.2; 1 Cor 13.5.   **11.1:** 1 Cor 4.16.   **11.2:** 2 Thess 2.15.
11.3: Eph 1.22; 4.15; 5.23; Col 1,8; 2.19.

his head, 5 but any woman who prays or prophesies with her head unveiled dishonors her head—it is the same as if her head were shaven. 6 For if a woman will not veil herself, then she should cut off her hair; but if it is disgraceful for a woman to be shorn or shaven, let her wear a veil. 7 For a man ought not to cover his head, since he is the image and glory of God; but woman is the glory of man. 8 (For man was not made from woman, but woman from man. 9 Neither was man created for woman, but woman for man.) 10 That is why a woman ought to have a veil[r] on her head, because of the angels. 11 (Nevertheless, in the Lord woman is not independent of man nor man of woman; 12 for as woman was made from man, so man is now born of woman. And all things are from God.) 13 Judge for yourselves; is it proper for a woman to pray to God with her head uncovered? 14 Does not nature itself teach you that for a man to wear long hair is degrading to him, 15 but if a woman has long hair, it is her pride? For her hair is given to her for a covering. 16 If any one is disposed to be contentious, we recognize no other practice, nor do the churches of God.

17 But in the following instructions I do not commend you, because when you come together it is not for the better but for the worse. 18 For, in the first place, when you assemble as a church, I hear that there are divisions among you; and I partly believe it, 19 for there must be factions among you in order that those who are genuine among you may be recognized. 20 When you meet together, it is not the Lord's supper that you eat. 21 For in eating, each one goes ahead with his own meal, and one is hungry and another is drunk. 22 What! Do you not have houses to eat and drink in? Or do you despise the church of God and humiliate those who have nothing? What shall I say to you? Shall I commend you in this? No, I will not.

23 For I received from the Lord what I also delivered to you, that the Lord Jesus on the night when he was betrayed took bread, 24 and when he had given thanks, he broke it, and said, "This is my body which is for[s] you.

Do this in remembrance of me." 25 In the same way also the cup, after supper, saying, "This cup is the new covenant in my blood. Do this, as often as you drink it, in remembrance of me." 26 For as often as you eat this bread and drink the cup, you proclaim the Lord's death until he comes.

27 Whoever, therefore, eats the bread or drinks the cup of the Lord in an unworthy manner will be guilty of profaning the body and blood of the Lord. 28 Let a man examine himself, and so eat of the bread and drink of the cup. 29 For any one who eats and drinks without discerning the body eats and drinks judgment upon himself. 30 That is why many of you are weak and ill, and some have died.[t] 31 But if we judged ourselves truly, we should not be judged. 32 But when we are judged by the Lord, we are chastened[u] so that we may not be condemned along with the world.

33 So then, my brethren, when you come together to eat, wait for one another—34 if any one is hungry, let him eat at home—lest you come together to be condemned. About the other things I will give directions when I come.

12 Now concerning spiritual gifts, brethren, I do not want you to be uninformed. 2 You know that when you were heathen, you were led astray to dumb idols, however you may have been moved. 3 Therefore I want you to understand that no one speaking by the Spirit of God ever says "Jesus be cursed!" and no one can say "Jesus is Lord" except by the Holy Spirit.

4 Now there are varieties of gifts, but the same Spirit; 5 and there are varieties of service, but the same Lord; 6 and there are varieties of working, but it is the same God who inspires them all in every one. 7 To each is given the manifestation of the Spirit for the common good. 8 To one is given through the Spirit the utterance of wisdom, and to another the utterance of knowledge according to the same Spirit, 9 to another faith by the same Spirit, to another gifts of healing by the one Spirit, 10 to another the working of miracles, to another proph-

r Greek authority (the veil being a symbol of this)
s Other ancient authorities read broken for   t Greek have fallen asleep (as in 15.6, 20)
u Or when we are judged we are being chastened by the Lord
11.5: Lk 2.36; Acts 21.9; 1 Cor 14.34.   11.7: Gen 1.26.   11.8: Gen 2.21-23.
11.9: Gen 2.18.   11.12: 2 Cor 5.18; Rom 11.36.   11.16: 1 Cor 7.17.   11.18: 1 Cor 1.10.
11.23: 1 Cor 15.3.   11.23-25: Mt 26.26-28; Mk 14.22-24; Lk 22.17-19; 1 Cor 10.16.
11.25: 2 Cor 3.6; Lk 22.20.   11.26: 1 Cor 4.5.   11.32: 1 Cor 1.20.   11.34: 1 Cor 4.19.
12.2: Eph 2.11-12.   12.3: Rom 10.9.   12.10: 1 Cor 14.26.

ecy, to another the ability to distinguish between spirits, to another various kinds of tongues, to another the interpretation of tongues. ¹¹All these are inspired by one and the same Spirit who apportions to each one individually as he wills.

12 For just as the body is one and has many members, and all the members of the body, though many, are one body, so it is with Christ. ¹³ For by one Spirit we were all baptized into one body—Jews or Greeks, slaves or free—and all were made to drink of one Spirit.

14 For the body does not consist of one member but of many. ¹⁵ If the foot should say, "Because I am not a hand, I do not belong to the body," that would not make it any less a part of the body. ¹⁶And if the ear should say, "Because I am not an eye, I do not belong to the body," that would not make it any less a part of the body. ¹⁷ If the whole body were an eye, where would be the hearing? If the whole body were an ear, where would be the sense of smell? ¹⁸ But as it is, God arranged the organs in the body, each one of them, as he chose. ¹⁹ If all were a single organ, where would the body be? ²⁰As it is, there are many parts, yet one body. ²¹ The eye cannot say to the hand, "I have no need of you," nor again the head to the feet, "I have no need of you." ²² On the contrary, the parts of the body which seem to be weaker are indispensable, ²³ and those parts of the body which we think less honorable we invest with the greater honor, and our unpresentable parts are treated with greater modesty, ²⁴ which our more presentable parts do not require. But God has so adjusted the body, giving the greater honor to the inferior part, ²⁵ that there may be no discord in the body, but that the members may have the same care for one another. ²⁶ If one member suffers, all suffer together; if one member is honored, all rejoice together.

27 Now you are the body of Christ and individually members of it. ²⁸And God has appointed in the church first apostles, second prophets, third teachers, then workers of miracles, then healers, helpers, administrators, speakers in various kinds of tongues. ²⁹Are all apostles? Are all prophets? Are all teachers? Do all work miracles?

30 Do all possess gifts of healing? Do all speak with tongues? Do all interpret? ³¹ But earnestly desire the higher gifts.

And I will show you a still more excellent way.

13 If I speak in the tongues of men and of angels, but have not love, I am a noisy gong or a clanging cymbal. ²And if I have prophetic powers, and understand all mysteries and all knowledge, and if I have all faith, so as to remove mountains, but have not love, I am nothing. ³ If I give away all I have, and if I deliver my body to be burned,ᵛ but have not love, I gain nothing.

4 Love is patient and kind; love is not jealous or boastful; ⁵ it is not arrogant or rude. Love does not insist on its own way; it is not irritable or resentful; ⁶ it does not rejoice at wrong, but rejoices in the right. ⁷ Love bears all things, believes all things, hopes all things, endures all things.

8 Love never ends; as for prophecies, they will pass away; as for tongues, they will cease; as for knowledge, it will pass away. ⁹ For our knowledge is imperfect and our prophecy is imperfect; ¹⁰ but when the perfect comes, the imperfect will pass away. ¹¹ When I was a child, I spoke like a child, I thought like a child, I reasoned like a child; when I became a man, I gave up childish ways. ¹² For now we see in a mirror dimly, but then face to face. Now I know in part; then I shall understand fully, even as I have been fully understood. ¹³ So faith, hope, love abide, these three; but the greatest of these is love.

14 Make love your aim, and earnestly desire the spiritual gifts, especially that you may prophesy. ² For one who speaks in a tongue speaks not to men but to God; for no one understands him, but he utters mysteries in the Spirit. ³ On the other hand, he who prophesies speaks to men for their upbuilding and encouragement and consolation. ⁴ He who speaks in a tongue edifies himself, but he who prophesies edifies the church. ⁵ Now I want you all to speak in tongues, but even more to prophesy. He who prophesies is greater than he who speaks in tongues, unless some one interprets, so that the church may be edified.

ᵛ Other ancient authorities read *body that I may glory*
12.12: Rom 12.4. **12.13:** Gal 3.28; Col 3.11; Eph 2.13-18; Jn 7.37-39.
12.27: Eph 1.23; 4.12; Col 1.18, 24; Eph 5.30; Rom 12.5. **12.28:** Eph 4.11; 2.20; 3.5.
13.1: Ps 150.5. **13.2:** 1 Cor 14.2; Mt 17.20; 21.21. **13.5:** 1 Cor 10.24.
13.7: 1 Cor 9.12.

6 Now, brethren, if I come to you speaking in tongues, how shall I benefit you unless I bring you some revelation or knowledge or prophecy or teaching? 7 If even lifeless instruments, such as the flute or the harp, do not give distinct notes, how will any one know what is played? 8 And if the bugle gives an indistinct sound, who will get ready for battle? 9 So with yourselves; if you in a tongue utter speech that is not intelligible, how will any one know what is said? For you will be speaking into the air. 10 There are doubtless many different languages in the world, and none is without meaning; 11 but if I do not know the meaning of the language, I shall be a foreigner to the speaker and the speaker a foreigner to me. 12 So with yourselves; since you are eager for manifestations of the Spirit, strive to excel in building up the church.

13 Therefore, he who speaks in a tongue should pray for the power to interpret. 14 For if I pray in a tongue, my spirit prays but my mind is unfruitful. 15 What am I to do? I will pray with the spirit and I will pray with the mind also; I will sing with the spirit and I will sing with the mind also. 16 Otherwise, if you bless*w* with the spirit, how can any one in the position of an outsider*x* say the "Amen" to your thanksgiving when he does not know what you are saying? 17 For you may give thanks well enough, but the other man is not edified. 18 I thank God that I speak in tongues more than you all; 19 nevertheless, in church I would rather speak five words with my mind, in order to instruct others, than ten thousand words in a tongue.

20 Brethren, do not be children in your thinking; be babes in evil, but in thinking be mature. 21 In the law it is written, "By men of strange tongues and by the lips of foreigners will I speak to this people, and even then they will not listen to me, says the Lord." 22 Thus, tongues are a sign not for believers but for unbelievers, while prophecy is not for unbelievers but for believers. 23 If, therefore, the whole church assembles and all speak in tongues, and outsiders or unbelievers enter, will they not say that you are mad? 24 But if all prophesy, and an unbeliever or outsider enters, he is convicted by all, he is called to account by all, 25 the secrets of his heart are disclosed; and so, falling on his face, he will worship God and declare that God is really among you.

26 What then, brethren? When you come together, each one has a hymn, a lesson, a revelation, a tongue, or an interpretation. Let all things be done for edification. 27 If any speak in a tongue, let there be only two or at most three, and each in turn; and let one interpret. 28 But if there is no one to interpret, let each of them keep silence in church and speak to himself and to God. 29 Let two or three prophets speak, and let the others weigh what is said. 30 If a revelation is made to another sitting by, let the first be silent. 31 For you can all prophesy one by one, so that all may learn and all be encouraged; 32 and the spirits of prophets are subject to prophets. 33 For God is not a God of confusion but of peace.

As in all the churches of the saints, 34 the women should keep silence in the churches. For they are not permitted to speak, but should be subordinate, as even the law says. 35 If there is anything they desire to know, let them ask their husbands at home. For it is shameful for a woman to speak in church. 36 What! Did the word of God originate with you, or are you the only ones it has reached?

37 If any one thinks that he is a prophet, or spiritual, he should acknowledge that what I am writing to you is a command of the Lord. 38 If any one does not recognize this, he is not recognized. 39 So, my brethren, earnestly desire to prophesy, and do not forbid speaking in tongues; 40 but all things should be done decently and in order.

15 Now I would remind you, brethren, in what terms I preached to you the gospel, which you received, in which you stand, 2 by which you are saved, if you hold it fast—unless you believed in vain.

3 For I delivered to you as of first importance what I also received, that Christ died for our sins in accordance with the scriptures, 4 that he was buried, that he was raised on the third day in accordance with the scriptures, 5 and that he appeared to Cē′phas, then to the twelve. 6 Then he appeared to more than five hundred brethren at

w That is, *give thanks to God*   *x* Or *him that is without gifts*   **14.15:** Eph 5.19; Col 3.16. **14.16:** 1 Chron 16.36; Ps 106.48; Mt 15.36. **14.20:** Eph 4.14. **14.21:** Is 28.11-12. **14.26:** Eph 5.19. **14.34:** 1 Tim 2.11-12; 1 Pet 3.1. **15.3:** 1 Cor 11.23; 1 Pet 2.24; Is 53.5-12. **15.4:** Mt 16.21; Ps 16.8-9. **15.5:** Lk 24.34; Mt 28.17.

one time, most of whom are still alive, though some have fallen asleep. 7 Then he appeared to James, then to all the apostles. 8 Last of all, as to one untimely born, he appeared also to me. 9 For I am the least of the apostles, unfit to be called an apostle, because I persecuted the church of God. 10 But by the grace of God I am what I am, and his grace toward me was not in vain. On the contrary, I worked harder than any of them, though it was not I, but the grace of God which is with me. 11 Whether then it was I or they, so we preach and so you believed.

12 Now if Christ is preached as raised from the dead, how can some of you say that there is no resurrection of the dead? 13 But if there is no resurrection of the dead, then Christ has not been raised; 14 if Christ has not been raised, then our preaching is in vain and your faith is in vain. 15 We are even found to be misrepresenting God, because we testified of God that he raised Christ, whom he did not raise if it is true that the dead are not raised. 16 For if the dead are not raised, then Christ has not been raised. 17 If Christ has not been raised, your faith is futile and you are still in your sins. 18 Then those also who have fallen asleep in Christ have perished. 19 If for this life only we have hoped in Christ, we are of all men most to be pitied.

20 But in fact Christ has been raised from the dead, the first fruits of those who have fallen asleep. 21 For as by a man came death, by a man has come also the resurrection of the dead. 22 For as in Adam all die, so also in Christ shall all be made alive. 23 But each in his own order: Christ the first fruits, then at his coming those who belong to Christ. 24 Then comes the end, when he delivers the kingdom to God the Father after destroying every rule and every authority and power. 25 For he must reign until he has put all his enemies under his feet. 26 The last enemy to be destroyed is death. 27 "For God[z] has put all things in subjection under his feet." But when it says, "All things are put in subjection under him," it is plain that he is excepted who put all things under him. 28 When all things are subjected to him, then the Son himself will also

be subjected to him who put all things under him, that God may be everything to every one.

29 Otherwise, what do people mean by being baptized on behalf of the dead? If the dead are not raised at all, why are people baptized on their behalf? 30 Why am I in peril every hour? 31 I protest, brethren, by my pride in you which I have in Christ Jesus our Lord, I die every day! 32 What do I gain if, humanly speaking, I fought with beasts at Eph′e·sus? If the dead are not raised, "Let us eat and drink, for tomorrow we die." 33 Do not be deceived: "Bad company ruins good morals." 34 Come to your right mind, and sin no more. For some have no knowledge of God. I say this to your shame.

35 But some one will ask, "How are the dead raised? With what kind of body do they come?" 36 You foolish man! What you sow does not come to life unless it dies. 37And what you sow is not the body which is to be, but a bare kernel, perhaps of wheat or of some other grain. 38 But God gives it a body as he has chosen, and to each kind of seed its own body. 39 For not all flesh is alike, but there is one kind for men, another for animals, another for birds, and another for fish. 40 There are celestial bodies and there are terrestrial bodies; but the glory of the celestial is one, and the glory of the terrestrial is another. 41 There is one glory of the sun, and another glory of the moon, and another glory of the stars; for star differs from star in glory.

42 So is it with the resurrection of the dead. What is sown is perishable, what is raised is imperishable. 43 It is sown in dishonor, it is raised in glory. It is sown in weakness, it is raised in power. 44 It is sown a physical body, it is raised a spiritual body. If there is a physical body, there is also a spiritual body. 45 Thus it is written, "The first man Adam became a living being"; the last Adam became a life-giving spirit. 46 But it is not the spiritual which is first but the physical, and then the spiritual. 47 The first man was from the earth, a man of dust; the second man is from heaven. 48As was the man of dust, so are those who are of the dust; and as is the man of heaven, so are those who are of heaven.

z Greek *he*

15.8: 1 Cor 9.1; Gal 1.16; Acts 9.3-6. **15.9:** Acts 8.3. **15.14:** 1 Thess 4.14.
15.18: 1 Thess 4.16. **15.21:** Rom 5.12. **15.22:** Rom 5.14-18. **15.23:** 1 Thess 2.19.
15.25: Ps 110.1. **15.27:** Ps 8.6; Eph 1.22. **15.28:** Phil 3.21. **15.30:** 2 Esdr 7.89.
15.31: Rom 8.36. **15.32:** 2 Cor 1.8, 9; Is 22.13. **15.33:** Menander, *Thais*.
15.34: Rom 13.11. **15.36:** Jn 12.24. **15.38:** Gen 1.11. **15.42:** Dan 12.3. **15.45:** Gen 2.7.

49 Just as we have borne the image of the man of dust, we shall[a] also bear the image of the man of heaven. 50 I tell you this, brethren: flesh and blood cannot inherit the kingdom of God, nor does the perishable inherit the imperishable.

51 Lo! I tell you a mystery. We shall not all sleep, but we shall all be changed, 52 in a moment, in the twinkling of an eye, at the last trumpet. For the trumpet will sound, and the dead will be raised imperishable, and we shall be changed. 53 For this perishable nature must put on the imperishable, and this mortal nature must put on immortality. 54 When the perishable puts on the imperishable, and the mortal puts on immortality, then shall come to pass the saying that is written:

"Death is swallowed up in victory."
55 "O death, where is thy victory?
O death, where is thy sting?"

56 The sting of death is sin, and the power of sin is the law. 57 But thanks be to God, who gives us the victory through our Lord Jesus Christ.

58 Therefore, my beloved brethren, be steadfast, immovable, always abounding in the work of the Lord, knowing that in the Lord your labor is not in vain.

16 Now concerning the contribution for the saints: as I directed the churches of Galatia, so you also are to do. 2 On the first day of every week, each of you is to put something aside and store it up, as he may prosper, so that contributions need not be made when I come. 3 And when I arrive, I will send those whom you accredit by letter to carry your gift to Jerusalem. 4 If it seems advisable that I should go also, they will accompany me.

5 I will visit you after passing through Maç·ė·dō'ni·à, for I intend to pass through Macedonia, 6 and perhaps I will stay with you or even spend the winter, so that you may speed me on my journey, wherever I go. 7 For I do not want to see you now just in passing; I hope to spend some time with you, if the Lord permits. 8 But I will stay in Eph'ė·sùs until Pentecost, 9 for a wide door for effective work has opened to me, and there are many adversaries.

10 When Timothy comes, see that you put him at ease among you, for he is doing the work of the Lord, as I am. 11 So let no one despise him. Speed him on his way in peace, that he may return to me; for I am expecting him with the brethren.

12 As for our brother Å·pol'los, I strongly urged him to visit you with the other brethren, but it was not at all his will[b] to come now. He will come when he has opportunity.

13 Be watchful, stand firm in your faith, be courageous, be strong. 14 Let all that you do be done in love.

15 Now, brethren, you know that the household of Steph'à·nàs were the first converts in Å·chā'ià, and they have devoted themselves to the service of the saints; 16 I urge you to be subject to such men and to every fellow worker and laborer. 17 I rejoice at the coming of Steph'á·nàs and Fôr·tū·nā'tùs and Å·chā'i·cùs, because they have made up for your absence; 18 for they refreshed my spirit as well as yours. Give recognition to such men.

19 The churches of Asia send greetings. Aq'ui·là and Pris'cà, together with the church in their house, send you hearty greetings in the Lord. 20 All the brethren send greetings. Greet one another with a holy kiss.

21 I, Paul, write this greeting with my own hand. 22 If any one has no love for the Lord, let him be accursed. Our Lord, come![c] 23 The grace of the Lord Jesus be with you. 24 My love be with you all in Christ Jesus. Amen.

a Other ancient authorities read let us   b Or God's will for him   c Greek Maranatha
15.51-52: 1 Thess 4.15-17.   15.54: Is 25.8.   15.55: Hos 13.14.   16.1: Acts 24.17.
16.2: Acts 20.7; 2 Cor 9.4-5.   16.3: 2 Cor 8.18-19.   16.5: Rom 15.26; Acts 19.21.
16.7: Acts 18.21.   16.8: Acts 18.19.   16.9: Acts 19.9.   16.10: Acts 16.1.
16.12: Acts 18.24.   16.13: Ps 31.24; Eph 6.10.   16.19: Acts 18.2; Rom 16.5.
16.20: Rom 16.16.   16.21: Col 4.18; Gal 6.11; 2 Thess 3.17.   16.22: Rom 9.3.
16.23: Rom 16.20.

THE SECOND LETTER OF PAUL TO THE
CORINTHIANS

1 Paul, an apostle of Christ Jesus by the will of God, and Timothy our brother.

To the church of God which is at Corinth, with all the saints who are in the whole of A·chā′ia:

2 Grace to you and peace from God our Father and the Lord Jesus Christ.

3 Blessed be the God and Father of our Lord Jesus Christ, the Father of mercies and God of all comfort, 4 who comforts us in all our affliction, so that we may be able to comfort those who are in any affliction, with the comfort with which we ourselves are comforted by God. 5 For as we share abundantly in Christ's sufferings, so through Christ we share abundantly in comfort too.ᵃ 6 If we are afflicted, it is for your comfort and salvation; and if we are comforted, it is for your comfort, which you experience when you patiently endure the same sufferings that we suffer. 7 Our hope for you is unshaken; for we know that as you share in our sufferings, you will also share in our comfort.

8 For we do not want you to be ignorant, brethren, of the affliction we experienced in Asia; for we were so utterly, unbearably crushed that we despaired of life itself. 9 Why, we felt that we had received the sentence of death; but that was to make us rely not on ourselves but on God who raises the dead; 10 he delivered us from so deadly a peril, and he will deliver us; on him we have set our hope that he will deliver us again. 11 You also must help us by prayer, so that many will give thanks on our behalf for the blessing granted us in answer to many prayers.

12 For our boast is this, the testimony of our conscience that we have behaved in the world, and still more toward you, with holiness and godly sincerity, not by earthly wisdom but by the grace of God. 13 For we write you nothing but what you can read and

understand; I hope you will understand fully, 14 as you have understood in part, that you can be proud of us as we can be of you, on the day of the Lord Jesus.

15 Because I was sure of this, I wanted to come to you first, so that you might have a double pleasure;ᵇ 16 I wanted to visit you on my way to Măc·ẹ·dō′ni·â, and to come back to you from Macedonia and have you send me on my way to Judea. 17 Was I vacillating when I wanted to do this? Do I make my plans like a worldly man, ready to say Yes and No at once? 18 As surely as God is faithful, our word to you has not been Yes and No. 19 For the Son of God, Jesus Christ, whom we preached among you, Sil·vā′nŭs and Timothy and I, was not Yes and No; but in him it is always Yes. 20 For all the promises of God find their Yes in him. That is why we utter the Amen through him, to the glory of God. 21 But it is God who establishes us with you in Christ, and has commissioned us; 22 he has put his seal upon us and given us his Spirit in our hearts as a guarantee.

23 But I call God to witness against me—it was to spare you that I refrained from coming to Corinth. 24 Not that we lord it over your faith; we work with you for your joy, for you stand firm in your faith. 2 1 For I made up my mind not to make you another painful visit. 2 For if I cause you pain, who is there to make me glad but the one whom I have pained? 3 And I wrote as I did, so that when I came I might not be pained by those who should have made me rejoice, for I felt sure of all of you, that my joy would be the joy of you all. 4 For I wrote you out of much affliction and anguish of heart and with many tears, not to cause you pain but to let you know the abundant love that I have for you.

5 But if any one has caused pain, he has caused it not to me, but in some measure—not to put it too severely—

ᵃ Or, For as the sufferings of Christ abound for us, so also our comfort abounds through Christ ᵇ Other ancient authorities read favor

1.1: Eph 1.1; Col 1.1; 2 Cor 1.19; Acts 16.1; 18.1. **1.2:** Rom 1.7.
1.3: Eph 1.3; 1 Pet 1.3; Rom 15.5. **1.4:** 2 Cor 7.6-7, 13. **1.16:** Acts 19.21.
1.19: 1 Thess 1.1; Acts 15.22. **1.20:** 1 Cor 14.16; Rev 3.14.

to you all. ⁶ For such a one this punishment by the majority is enough; ⁷ so you should rather turn to forgive and comfort him, or he may be overwhelmed by excessive sorrow. ⁸ So I beg you to reaffirm your love for him. ⁹ For this is why I wrote, that I might test you and know whether you are obedient in everything. ¹⁰ Any one whom you forgive, I also forgive. What I have forgiven, if I have forgiven anything, has been for your sake in the presence of Christ, ¹¹ to keep Satan from gaining the advantage over us; for we are not ignorant of his designs.

¹² When I came to Trō′as to preach the gospel of Christ, a door was opened for me in the Lord; ¹³ but my mind could not rest because I did not find my brother Titus there. So I took leave of them and went on to Măc̄·ĕ·dō′ni·à.

¹⁴ But thanks be to God, who in Christ always leads us in triumph, and through us spreads the fragrance of the knowledge of him everywhere. ¹⁵ For we are the aroma of Christ to God among those who are being saved and among those who are perishing, ¹⁶ to one a fragrance from death to death, to the other a fragrance from life to life. Who is sufficient for these things? ¹⁷ For we are not, like so many, peddlers of God's word; but as men of sincerity, as commissioned by God, in the sight of God we speak in Christ.

3 Are we beginning to commend ourselves again? Or do we need, as some do, letters of recommendation to you, or from you? ² You yourselves are our letter of recommendation, written on your* hearts, to be known and read by all men; ³ and you show that you are a letter from Christ delivered by us, written not with ink but with the Spirit of the living God, not on tablets of stone but on tablets of human hearts.

⁴ Such is the confidence that we have through Christ toward God. ⁵ Not that we are sufficient of ourselves to claim anything as coming from us; our sufficiency is from God, ⁶ who has qualified us to be ministers of a new covenant, not in a written code but in the Spirit; for the written code kills, but the Spirit gives life.

⁷ Now if the dispensation of death, carved in letters on stone, came with such splendor that the Israelites could

not look at Moses' face because of its brightness, fading as this was, ⁸ will not the dispensation of the Spirit be attended with greater splendor? ⁹ For if there was splendor in the dispensation of condemnation, the dispensation of righteousness must far exceed it in splendor. ¹⁰ Indeed, in this case, what once had spendor has come to have no splendor at all, because of the splendor that surpasses it. ¹¹ For if what faded away came with splendor, what is permanent must have much more splendor.

¹² Since we have such a hope, we are very bold, ¹³ not like Moses, who put a veil over his face so that the Israelites might not see the end of the fading splendor. ¹⁴ But their minds were hardened; for to this day, when they read the old covenant, that same veil remains unlifted, because only through Christ is it taken away. ¹⁵ Yes, to this day whenever Moses is read a veil lies over their minds; ¹⁶ but when a man turns to the Lord the veil is removed. ¹⁷ Now the Lord is the Spirit, and where the Spirit of the Lord is, there is freedom. ¹⁸ And we all, with unveiled face, beholding*d* the glory of the Lord, are being changed into his likeness from one degree of glory to another; for this comes from the Lord who is the Spirit.

4 Therefore, having this ministry by the mercy of God,*e* we do not lose heart. ² We have renounced disgraceful, underhanded ways; we refuse to practice cunning or to tamper with God's word, but by the open statement of the truth we would commend ourselves to every man's conscience in the sight of God. ³ And even if our gospel is veiled, it is veiled only to those who are perishing. ⁴ In their case the god of this world has blinded the minds of the unbelievers, to keep them from seeing the light of the gospel of the glory of Christ, who is the likeness of God. ⁵ For what we preach is not ourselves, but Jesus Christ as Lord, with ourselves as your servants*f* for Jesus' sake. ⁶ For it is the God who said, "Let light shine out of darkness," who has shone in our hearts to give the light of the knowledge of the glory of God in the face of Christ.

⁷ But we have this treasure in earthen vessels, to show that the transcendent power belongs to God and

c Other ancient authorities read *our*   *d* Or *reflecting*
e Greek *as we have received mercy*   *f* Or *slaves*

2.12: Acts 16.8.   **3.1:** Acts 18.27; Rom 16.1; 1 Cor 16.3.
3.3: Ex 24.12; 31.18; 32.15-16; Jer 31.33.   **3.6:** Jer 31.31.   **3.7:** Ex 34.29-35.
3.17: Is 61.1-2.   **4.4:** Jn 12.31; Col 1.15.   **4.6:** Gen 1.3.

not to us. 8 We are afflicted in every way, but not crushed; perplexed, but not driven to despair; 9 persecuted, but not forsaken; struck down, but not destroyed; 10 always carrying in the body the death of Jesus, so that the life of Jesus may also be manifested in our bodies. 11 For while we live we are always being given up to death for Jesus' sake, so that the life of Jesus may be manifested in our mortal flesh. 12 So death is at work in us, but life in you.

13 Since we have the same spirit of faith as he had who wrote, "I believed, and so I spoke," we too believe, and so we speak, 14 knowing that he who raised the Lord Jesus will raise us also with Jesus and bring us with you into his presence. 15 For it is all for your sake, so that as grace extends to more and more people it may increase thanksgiving, to the glory of God.

16 So we do not lose heart. Though our outer nature is wasting away, our inner nature is being renewed every day. 17 For this slight momentary affliction is preparing for us an eternal weight of glory beyond all comparison, 18 because we look not to the things that are seen but to the things that are unseen; for the things that are seen are transient, but the things that are unseen are eternal.

5 For we know that if the earthly tent we live in is destroyed, we have a building from God, a house not made with hands, eternal in the heavens. 2 Here indeed we groan, and long to put on our heavenly dwelling, 3 so that by putting it on we may not be found naked. 4 For while we are still in this tent, we sigh with anxiety; not that we would be unclothed, but that we would be further clothed, so that what is mortal may be swallowed up by life. 5 He who has prepared us for this very thing is God, who has given us the Spirit as a guarantee.

6 So we are always of good courage; we know that while we are at home in the body we are away from the Lord, 7 for we walk by faith, not by sight. 8 We are of good courage, and we would rather be away from the body and at home with the Lord. 9 So whether we are at home or away, we make it our aim to please him. 10 For we must all appear before the judg-

ment seat of Christ, so that each one may receive good or evil, according to what he has done in the body.

11 Therefore, knowing the fear of the Lord, we persuade men; but what we are is known to God, and I hope it is known also to your conscience. 12 We are not commending ourselves to you again but giving you cause to be proud of us, so that you may be able to answer those who pride themselves on a man's position and not on his heart. 13 For if we are beside ourselves, it is for God; if we are in our right mind, it is for you. 14 For the love of Christ controls us, because we are convinced that one has died for all; therefore all have died. 15 And he died for all, that those who live might live no longer for themselves but for him who for their sake died and was raised.

16 From now on, therefore, we regard no one from a human point of view; even though we once regarded Christ from a human point of view, we regard him thus no longer. 17 Therefore, if any one is in Christ, he is a new creation;g the old has passed away, behold, the new has come. 18 All this is from God, who through Christ reconciled us to himself and gave us the ministry of reconciliation; 19 that is, God was in Christ reconcilingh the world to himself, not counting their trespasses against them, and entrusting to us the message of reconciliation. 20 So we are ambassadors for Christ, God making his appeal through us. We beseech you on behalf of Christ, be reconciled to God. 21 For our sake he made him to be sin who knew no sin, so that in him we might become the righteousness of God.

6 Working together with him, then, we entreat you not to accept the grace of God in vain. 2 For he says,

> "At the acceptable time I have listened to you,
> and helped you on the day of salvation."

Behold, now is the acceptable time; behold, now is the day of salvation. 3 We put no obstacle in any one's way, so that no fault may be found with our ministry, 4 but as servants of God we commend ourselves in every way: through great endurance, in afflictions, hardships, calamities, 5 beatings, imprisonments, tumults, labors, watch-

g Or *creature*   h Or *in Christ God was reconciling*
4.13: Ps 116.10.   **4.14:** 1 Thess 4.14.   **5.10:** Mt 16.27.   **5.12:** 2 Cor 3.1.
5.14: Rom 5.15; 6.6-7.   **5.17:** Rom 16.7; Gal 6.15.
5.18: 1 Cor 11.12; Col 1.20; Rom 5.10.   **5.20:** Eph 6.20.
5.21: Heb 4.15; 7.25; 1 Pet 2.22; 1 Jn 3.5; Acts 3.14.   **6.2:** Is 49.8.
6.4: 2 Cor 4.8-11; 11.23-27.   **6.5:** Acts 16.23.

ing, hunger; 6 by purity, knowledge, forbearance, kindness, the Holy Spirit, genuine love, 7 truthful speech, and the power of God; with the weapons of righteousness for the right hand and for the left; 8 in honor and dishonor, in ill repute and good repute. We are treated as impostors, and yet are true; 9 as unknown, and yet well known; as dying, and behold we live; as punished, and yet not killed; 10 as sorrowful, yet always rejoicing; as poor, yet making many rich; as having nothing, and yet possessing everything.

11 Our mouth is open to you, Corinthians; our heart is wide. 12 You are not restricted by us, but you are restricted in your own affections. 13 In return—I speak as to children—widen your hearts also.

14 Do not be mismated with unbelievers. For what partnership have righteousness and iniquity? Or what fellowship has light with darkness? 15 What accord has Christ with Bē′li-ȧl?*i* Or what has a believer in common with an unbeliever? 16 What agreement has the temple of God with idols? For we are the temple of the living God; as God said,

"I will live in them and move among them,
and I will be their God,
and they shall be my people.
17 Therefore come out from them,
and be separate from them, says the Lord,
and touch nothing unclean;
then I will welcome you,
18 and I will be a father to you,
and you shall be my sons and daughters,
says the Lord Almighty."

7 Since we have these promises, beloved, let us cleanse ourselves from every defilement of body and spirit, and make holiness perfect in the fear of God.

2 Open your hearts to us; we have wronged no one, we have corrupted no one, we have taken advantage of no one. 3 I do not say this to condemn you, for I said before that you are in our hearts, to die together and to live together. 4 I have great confidence in you; I have great pride in you; I am

i Greek *Beliar*

filled with comfort. With all our affliction, I am overjoyed.

5 For even when we came into Măc̣·ė·dō′ni·à, our bodies had no rest but we were afflicted at every turn—fighting without and fear within. 6 But God, who comforts the downcast, comforted us by the coming of Titus, 7 and not only by his coming but also by the comfort with which he was comforted in you, as he told us of your longing, your mourning, your zeal for me, so that I rejoiced still more. 8 For even if I made you sorry with my letter, I do not regret it (though I did regret it), for I see that that letter grieved you, though only for a while. 9 As it is, I rejoice, not because you were grieved, but because you were grieved into repenting; for you felt a godly grief, so that you suffered no loss through us. 10 For godly grief produces a repentance that leads to salvation and brings no regret, but worldly grief produces death. 11 For see what earnestness this godly grief has produced in you, what eagerness to clear yourselves, what indignation, what alarm, what longing, what zeal, what punishment! At every point you have proved yourselves guiltless in the matter. 12 So although I wrote to you, it was not on account of the one who did the wrong, nor on account of the one who suffered the wrong, but in order that your zeal for us might be revealed to you in the sight of God. 13 Therefore we are comforted.

And besides our own comfort we rejoiced still more at the joy of Titus, because his mind has been set at rest by you all. 14 For if I have expressed to him some pride in you, I was not put to shame; but just as everything we said to you was true, so our boasting before Titus has proved true. 15 And his heart goes out all the more to you, as he remembers the obedience of you all, and the fear and trembling with which you received him. 16 I rejoice, because I have perfect confidence in you.

8 We want you to know, brethren, about the grace of God which has been shown in the churches of Măc̣·ė·dō′ni·à, 2 for in a severe test of affliction, their abundance of joy and their

6.7: 2 Cor 10.4; 13.12; Eph 6.11-12.   **6.9:** Rom 8.36.
6.10: Rom 8.32; 1 Cor 3.21.   **6.11:** Ezek 33.22; Is 60.5.
6.16: 1 Cor 10.21; 3.16; Ex 25.8; 29.45; Lev 26.12; Ezek 37.27; Jer 31.1.
6.17: Is 52.11.   **6.18:** Hos 1.10; Is 43.6.   **7.2:** 2 Cor 6.12-13.   **7.3:** 2 Cor 6.11-12.
7.5: 2 Cor 2.13; 4.8.   **7.6:** 2 Cor 2.13; 7.13-14.
7.8: 2 Cor 2.2.   **7.12:** 2 Cor 7.8; 2.3, 9.

extreme poverty have overflowed in a wealth of liberality on their part. 3 For they gave according to their means, as I can testify, and beyond their means, of their own free will, 4 begging us earnestly for the favor of taking part in the relief of the saints— 5 and this, not as we expected, but first they gave themselves to the Lord and to us by the will of God. 6Accordingly we have urged Titus that as he had already made a beginning, he should also complete among you this gracious work. 7 Now as you excel in everything—in faith, in utterance, in knowledge, in all earnestness, and in your love for us— see that you excel in this gracious work also.

8 I say this not as a command, but to prove by the earnestness of others that your love also is genuine. 9 For you know the grace of our Lord Jesus Christ, that though he was rich, yet for your sake he became poor, so that by his poverty you might become rich. 10And in this matter I give my advice: it is best for you now to complete what a year ago you began not only to do but to desire, 11 so that your readiness in desiring it may be matched by your completing it out of what you have. 12 For if the readiness is there, it is acceptable according to what a man has, not according to what he has not. 13 I do not mean that others should be eased and you burdened, 14 but that as a matter of equality your abundance at the present time should supply their want, so that their abundance may supply your want, that there may be equality. 15As it is written, "He who gathered much had nothing over, and he who gathered little had no lack."

16 But thanks be to God who puts the same earnest care for you into the heart of Titus. 17 For he not only accepted our appeal, but being himself very earnest he is going to you of his own accord. 18 With him we are sending the brother who is famous among all the churches for his preaching of the gospel; 19 and not only that, but he has been appointed by the churches to travel with us in this gracious work which we are carrying on, for the glory of the Lord and to show our good will. 20 We intend that no one should blame us about this liberal gift which we are administering, 21 for we aim at what is honorable not only in

the Lord's sight but also in the sight of men. 22And with them we are sending our brother whom we have often tested and found earnest in many matters, but who is now more earnest than ever because of his great confidence in you. 23As for Titus, he is my partner and fellow worker in your service; and as for our brethren, they are messengers*j* of the churches, the glory of Christ. 24 So give proof, before the churches, of your love and of our boasting about you to these men.

9 Now it is superfluous for me to write to you about the offering for the saints, 2 for I know your readiness, of which I boast about you to the people of Măc·ė·dōʹni·ȧ, saying that Ȧ·chāʹiȧ has been ready since last year; and your zeal has stirred up most of them. 3 But I am sending the brethren so that our boasting about you may not prove vain in this case, so that you may be ready, as I said you would be; 4 lest if some Măc·ė·dōʹni·ȧnš come with me and find that you are not ready, we be humiliated—to say nothing of you—for being so confident. 5 So I thought it necessary to urge the brethren to go on to you before me, and arrange in advance for this gift you have promised, so that it may be ready not as an exaction but as a willing gift.

6 The point is this: he who sows sparingly will also reap sparingly, and he who sows bountifully will also reap bountifully. 7 Each one must do as he has made up his mind, not reluctantly or under compulsion, for God loves a cheerful giver. 8And God is able to provide you with every blessing in abundance, so that you may always have enough of everything and may provide in abundance for every good work. 9As it is written,

"He scatters abroad, he gives to the poor;
his righteousness*k* endures for ever."

10 He who supplies seed to the sower and bread for food will supply and multiply your resources*l* and increase the harvest of your righteousness.*k* 11 You will be enriched in every way for great generosity, which through us will produce thanksgiving to God; 12 for the rendering of this service not only supplies the wants of the saints but also overflows in many thanksgiv-

j Greek *apostles*   *k* Or *benevolence*   *l* Greek *sowing*

8.3: 1 Cor 16.2.   **8.4:** Acts 24.17; Rom 15.31.   **8.6:** 2 Cor 8.16, 23; 2.13.
8.9: 2 Cor 6.10.   **8.10:** 2 Cor 9.2; 1 Cor 16.2-3.   **8.15:** Ex 16.18.   **8.18:** 2 Cor 12.18.
8.19: 1 Cor 16.3-4.   **9.1:** 2 Cor 8.4.   **9.2:** Rom 15.26; 2 Cor 8.10.   **9.3:** 1 Cor 16.2.
9.7: Prov 22.8 (Gk.).   **9.8:** Eph 3.20.   **9.9:** Ps 112.9.   **9.10:** Is 55.10; Hos 10.12.

PAUL IN AREOPAGUS   *Acts 17:22*

PAUL WRITES FROM PRISON   *Col. 4:18*

ings to God. [13] Under the test of this service, you[m] will glorify God by your obedience in acknowledging the gospel of Christ, and by the generosity of your contribution for them and for all others; [14] while they long for you and pray for you, because of the surpassing grace of God in you. [15] Thanks be to God for his inexpressible gift!

[10] I, Paul, myself entreat you, by the meekness and gentleness of Christ—I who am humble when face to face with you, but bold to you when I am away!— [2] I beg of you that when I am present I may not have to show boldness with such confidence as I count on showing against some who suspect us of acting in worldly fashion. [3] For though we live in the world we are not carrying on a worldly war, [4] for the weapons of our warfare are not worldly but have divine power to destroy strongholds. [5] We destroy arguments and every proud obstacle to the knowledge of God, and take every thought captive to obey Christ, [6] being ready to punish every disobedience, when your obedience is complete.

[7] Look at what is before your eyes. If any one is confident that he is Christ's, let him remind himself that as he is Christ's, so are we. [8] For even if I boast a little too much of our authority, which the Lord gave for building you up and not for destroying you, I shall not be put to shame. [9] I would not seem to be frightening you with letters. [10] For they say, "His letters are weighty and strong, but his bodily presence is weak, and his speech is of no account." [11] Let such people understand that what we say by letter when absent, we do when present. [12] Not that we venture to class or compare ourselves with some of those who commend themselves. But when they measure themselves by one another, and compare themselves with one another, they are without understanding. [13] But we will not boast beyond limit, but will keep to the limits God has apportioned us, to reach even to you. [14] For we are not overextending ourselves, as though we did not reach you; we were the first to come all the way to you with the gospel of Christ. [15] We do not boast beyond limit, in

other men's labors; but our hope is that as your faith increases, our field among you may be greatly enlarged, [16] so that we may preach the gospel in lands beyond you, without boasting of work already done in another's field. [17] "Let him who boasts, boast of the Lord." [18] For it is not the man who commends himself that is accepted, but the man whom the Lord commends.

[11] I wish you would bear with me in a little foolishness. Do bear with me! [2] I feel a divine jealousy for you, for I betrothed you to Christ to present you as a pure bride to her one husband. [3] But I am afraid that as the serpent deceived Eve by his cunning, your thoughts will be led astray from a sincere and pure devotion to Christ. [4] For if some one comes and preaches another Jesus than the one we preached, or if you receive a different spirit from the one you received, or if you accept a different gospel from the one you accepted, you submit to it readily enough. [5] I think that I am not in the least inferior to these superlative apostles. [6] Even if I am unskilled in speaking, I am not in knowledge; in every way we have made this plain to you in all things.

[7] Did I commit a sin in abasing myself so that you might be exalted, because I preached God's gospel without cost to you? [8] I robbed other churches by accepting support from them in order to serve you. [9] And when I was with you and was in want, I did not burden any one, for my needs were supplied by the brethren who came from Măc·ē·dō′ni·à. So I refrained and will refrain from burdening you in any way. [10] As the truth of Christ is in me, this boast of mine shall not be silenced in the regions of A·chā′ia. [11] And why? Because I do not love you? God knows I do!

[12] And what I do I will continue to do, in order to undermine the claim of those who would like to claim that in their boasted mission they work on the same terms as we do. [13] For such men are false apostles, deceitful workmen, disguising themselves as apostles of Christ. [14] And no wonder, for even Satan disguises himself as an angel of light. [15] So it is not strange if his ser-

[m] Or *they*

9.13: 2 Cor 8.4; Rom 15.31.   **9.15:** Rom 5.15-16.   **10.1:** 2 Cor 10.10.
10.2: 2 Cor 13.2, 10; 1 Cor 4.21.   **10.6:** 2 Cor 2.9.   **10.7:** 1 Cor 1.12.   **10.10:** 1 Cor 2.3.
10.15: Rom 15.20.   **10.17:** Jer 9.24.   **11.1:** 2 Cor 11.21.
11.2: Hos 2.19-20; Eph 5.26-27.   **11.3:** Gen 3.4.   **11.4:** Gal 1.6.
11.5: 2 Cor 12.11; Gal 2.6.   **11.6:** 1 Cor 1.17.   **11.7:** 2 Cor 12.13; 1 Cor 9.18.
11.8: Phil 4.15, 18.   **11.10:** 1 Cor 9.15.   **11.11:** 2 Cor 12.15.   **11.12:** 1 Cor 9.12.

vants also disguise themselves as servants of righteousness. Their end will correspond to their deeds.

16 I repeat, let no one think me foolish; but even if you do, accept me as a fool, so that I too may boast a little. 17 (What I am saying I say not with the Lord's authority but as a fool, in this boastful confidence; 18 since many boast of worldly things, I too will boast.) 19 For you gladly bear with fools, being wise yourselves! 20 For you bear it if a man makes slaves of you, or preys upon you, or takes advantage of you, or puts on airs, or strikes you in the face. 21 To my shame, I must say, we were too weak for that!

But whatever any one dares to boast of—I am speaking as a fool—I also dare to boast of that. 22 Are they Hebrews? So am I. Are they Israelites? So am I. Are they descendants of Abraham? So am I. 23 Are they servants of Christ? I am a better one—I am talking like a madman—with far greater labors, far more imprisonments, with countless beatings, and often near death. 24 Five times I have received at the hands of the Jews the forty lashes less one. 25 Three times I have been beaten with rods; once I was stoned. Three times I have been shipwrecked; a night and a day I have been adrift at sea; 26 on frequent journeys, in danger from rivers, danger from robbers, danger from my own people, danger from Gentiles, danger in the city, danger in the wilderness, danger at sea, danger from false brethren; 27 in toil and hardship, through many a sleepless night, in hunger and thirst, often without food, in cold and exposure, 28 And, apart from other things, there is the daily pressure upon me of my anxiety for all the churches. 29 Who is weak, and I am not weak? Who is made to fall, and I am not indignant?

30 If I must boast, I will boast of the things that show my weakness. 31 The God and Father of the Lord Jesus, he who is blessed for ever, knows that I do not lie. 32 At Damascus, the governor under King Ar'e·tas guarded the city of Damascus in order to seize me, 33 but I was let down in a basket through a window in the wall, and escaped his hands.

12 I must boast; there is nothing to be gained by it, but I will go on to visions and revelations of the Lord.

2 I know a man in Christ who fourteen years ago was caught up to the third heaven—whether in the body or out of the body I do not know, God knows. 3 And I know that this man was caught up into Paradise—whether in the body or out of the body I do not know, God knows— 4 and he heard things that cannot be told, which man may not utter. 5 On behalf of this man I will boast, but on my own behalf I will not boast, except of my weaknesses. 6 Though if I wish to boast, I shall not be a fool, for I shall be speaking the truth. But I refrain from it, so that no one may think more of me than he sees in me or hears from me. 7 And to keep me from being too elated by the abundance of revelations, a thorn was given me in the flesh, a messenger of Satan, to harass me, to keep me from being too elated. 8 Three times I besought the Lord about this, that it should leave me; 9 but he said to me, "My grace is sufficient for you, for my power is made perfect in weakness." I will all the more gladly boast of my weaknesses, that the power of Christ may rest upon me. 10 For the sake of Christ, then, I am content with weaknesses, insults, hardships, persecutions, and calamities; for when I am weak, then I am strong.

11 I have been a fool! You forced me to it, for I ought to have been commended by you. For I am not at all inferior to these superlative apostles, even though I am nothing. 12 The signs of a true apostle were performed among you in all patience, with signs and wonders and mighty works. 13 For in what were you less favored than the rest of the churches, except that I myself did not burden you? Forgive me this wrong!

14 Here for the third time I am ready to come to you. And I will not be a burden, for I seek not what is yours but you; for children ought not to lay up for their parents, but parents for their children. 15 I will most gladly spend and be spent for your souls. If I love you the more, am I to be loved the less? 16 But granting that I myself did not burden you, I was crafty, you say, and got the better of you by guile. 17 Did I take advantage of you through any of those whom I sent to you? 18 I urged Titus to go, and sent the brother with him. Did Titus take advantage of

11.17: 1 Cor 7.12, 25.   **11.19:** 1 Cor 4.10.   **11.23:** Acts 16.23; 2 Cor 6.5.
11.24: Deut 25.3.   **11.25:** Acts 16.22; 14.19.   **11.26:** Acts 9.23; 14.5.
11.27: 1 Cor 4.11.   **11.29:** 1 Cor 9.22.   **11.32-33:** Acts 9.24-25.   **12.4:** Lk 23.43.
12.7: Job 2.6.   **12.10:** Rom 5.3; 2 Cor 6.4-5.   **12.11:** 2 Cor 11.5.   **12.13:** 2 Cor 11.7.
12.16: 2 Cor 11.9.   **12.18:** 2 Cor 2.13; 8.18.

you? Did we not act in the same spirit? Did we not take the same steps?

19 Have you been thinking all along that we have been defending ourselves before you? It is in the sight of God that we have been speaking in Christ, and all for your upbuilding, beloved. 20 For I fear that perhaps I may come and find you not what I wish, and that you may find me not what you wish; that perhaps there may be quarreling, jealousy, anger, selfishness, slander, gossip, conceit, and disorder. 21 I fear that when I come again my God may humble me before you, and I may have to mourn over many of those who sinned before and have not repented of the impurity, immorality, and licentiousness which they have practiced.

13 This is the third time I am coming to you. Any charge must be sustained by the evidence of two or three witnesses. 2 I warned those who sinned before and all the others, and I warn them now while absent, as I did when present on my second visit, that if I come again I will not spare them— 3 since you desire proof that Christ is speaking in me. He is not weak in dealing with you, but is powerful in you. 4 For he was crucified in weakness, but lives by the power of God. For we are weak in him, but in dealing with you

we shall live with him by the power of God.

5 Examine yourselves, to see whether you are holding to your faith. Test yourselves. Do you not realize that Jesus Christ is in you?—unless indeed you fail to meet the test! 6 I hope you will find out that we have not failed. 7 But we pray God that you may not do wrong—not that we may appear to have met the test, but that you may do what is right, though we may seem to have failed. 8 For we cannot do anything against the truth, but only for the truth. 9 For we are glad when we are weak and you are strong. What we pray for is your improvement. 10 I write this while I am away from you, in order that when I come I may not have to be severe in my use of the authority which the Lord has given me for building up and not for tearing down.

11 Finally, brethren, farewell. Mend your ways, heed my appeal, agree with one another, live in peace, and the God of love and peace will be with you. 12 Greet one another with a holy kiss. 13All the saints greet you.

14 The grace of the Lord Jesus Christ and the love of God and the fellowship of[n] the Holy Spirit be with you all.

THE LETTER OF PAUL TO THE

GALATIANS

1 Paul an apostle—not from men nor through man, but through Jesus Christ and God the Father, who raised him from the dead—2 and all the brethren who are with me,

To the churches of Galatia:

3 Grace to you and peace from God the Father and our Lord Jesus Christ, 4 who gave himself for our sins to deliver us from the present evil age, according to the will of our God and Father; 5 to whom be the glory for ever and ever. Amen.

6 I am astonished that you are so

quickly deserting him who called you in the grace of Christ and turning to a different gospel— 7 not that there is another gospel, but there are some who trouble you and want to pervert the gospel of Christ. 8 But even if we, or an angel from heaven, should preach to you a gospel contrary to that which we preached to you, let him be accursed. 9As we have said before, so now I say again, If any one is preaching to you a gospel contrary to that which you received, let him be accursed.

10 Am I now seeking the favor of men, or of God? Or am I trying to

n Or *and participation in*

12.20: 2 Cor 2.1-4; 1 Cor 1.11; 3.3. **13.1:** 2 Cor 12.14; Deut 19.15.
13.4: Phil 2.7-8; Rom 6.8. **13.10:** 2 Cor 2.3. **13.12:** Rom 16.16. **13.13:** Phil 4.22.
13.14: Rom 16.20. **1.3:** Rom 1.7. **1.4:** Gal 2.20; 1 Tim 2.6. **1.5:** Rom 16.27.
1.8: 2 Cor 11.4. **1.10:** 1 Thess 2.4.

please men? If I were still pleasing men, I should not be a servant*a* of Christ.

11 For I would have you know, brethren, that the gospel which was preached by me is not man's*b* gospel. 12 For I did not receive it from man, nor was I taught it, but it came through a revelation of Jesus Christ. 13 For you have heard of my former life in Judaism, how I persecuted the church of God violently and tried to destroy it; 14 and I advanced in Judaism beyond many of my own age among my people, so extremely zealous was I for the traditions of my fathers. 15 But when he who had set me apart before I was born, and had called me through his grace, 16 was pleased to reveal his Son to*c* me, in order that I might preach him among the Gentiles, I did not confer with flesh and blood, 17 nor did I go up to Jerusalem to those who were apostles before me, but I went away into Arabia; and again I returned to Damascus.

18 Then after three years I went up to Jerusalem to visit Cĕ′phȧs, and remained with him fifteen days. 19 But I saw none of the other apostles except James the Lord's brother. 20 (In what I am writing to you, before God, I do not lie!) 21 Then I went into the regions of Syria and Ci·li′ci·a. 22 And I was still not known by sight to the churches of Christ in Judea; 23 they only heard it said, "He who once persecuted us is now preaching the faith he once tried to destroy." 24 And they glorified God because of me.

2 Then after fourteen years I went up again to Jerusalem with Bär′nȧ·bȧs, taking Titus along with me. 2 I went up by revelation; and I laid before them (but privately before those who were of repute) the gospel which I preach among the Gentiles, lest somehow I should be running or had run in vain. 3 But even Titus, who was with me, was not compelled to be circumcised, though he was a Greek. 4 But because of false brethren secretly brought in, who slipped in to spy out our freedom which we have in Christ Jesus, that they might bring us into bondage— 5 to them we did not yield submission even for a moment, that the truth of the gospel might be preserved for you. 6 And from those who

were reputed to be something (what they were makes no difference to me; God shows no partiality)—those, I say, who were of repute added nothing to me; 7 but on the contrary, when they saw that I had been entrusted with the gospel to the uncircumcised, just as Peter had been entrusted with the gospel to the circumcised 8 (for he who worked through Peter for the mission to the circumcised worked through me also for the Gentiles), 9 and when they perceived the grace that was given to me, James and Cĕ′phȧs and John, who were reputed to be pillars, gave to me and Bär′nȧ·bȧs the right hand of fellowship, that we should go to the Gentiles and they to the circumcised; 10 only they would have us remember the poor, which very thing I was eager to do.

11 But when Cĕ′phȧs came to An′ti·och I opposed him to his face, because he stood condemned. 12 For before certain men came from James, he ate with the Gentiles; but when they came he drew back and separated himself, fearing the circumcision party. 13 And with him the rest of the Jews acted insincerely, so that even Bär′nȧ·bȧs was carried away by their insincerity. 14 But when I saw that they were not straightforward about the truth of the gospel, I said to Cĕ′phȧs before them all, "If you, though a Jew, live like a Gentile and not like a Jew, how can you compel the Gentiles to live like Jews?" 15 We ourselves, who are Jews by birth and not Gentile sinners, 16 yet who know that a man is not justified*d* by works of the law but through faith in Jesus Christ, even we have believed in Christ Jesus, in order to be justified by faith in Christ, and not by works of the law, because by works of the law shall no one be justified. 17 But if, in our endeavor to be justified in Christ, we ourselves were found to be sinners, is Christ then an agent of sin? Certainly not! 18 But if I build up again those things which I tore down, then I prove myself a transgressor. 19 For I through the law died to the law, that I might live to God. 20 I have been crucified with Christ; it is no longer I who live, but Christ who lives in me; and the life I now live in the flesh I live by faith in the Son of God, who loved me and

---

a Or *slave*   *b* Greek *according to man*   *c* Greek *in*
d Or *reckoned righteous;* and so elsewhere

1.11: Rom 1.16-17.   **1.13:** Acts 8.3.   **1.14:** Acts 22.3.
1.15: Acts 9.1-19; Is 49.1; Jer 1.5.   **1.18:** Acts 9.26-30; 11.30.   **2.1:** Acts 15.2.
2.5: Acts 15.23-29.   **2.6:** Deut 10.17.   **2.11:** Acts 11.19-26.   **2.16:** Ps 143.2; Rom 3.20,
2.20: Gal 1.4.

gave himself for me. 21 I do not nullify the grace of God; for if justification*e* were through the law, then Christ died to no purpose.

3 O foolish Galatians! Who has bewitched you, before whose eyes Jesus Christ was publicly portrayed as crucified? 2 Let me ask you only this: Did you receive the Spirit by works of the law, or by hearing with faith? 3Are you so foolish? Having begun with the Spirit, are you now ending with the flesh? 4 Did you experience so many things in vain?—if it really is in vain. 5Does he who supplies the Spirit to you and works miracles among you do so by works of the law, or by hearing with faith?

6 Thus Abraham "believed God, and it was reckoned to him as righteousness." 7 So you see that it is men of faith who are the sons of Abraham. 8And the scripture, foreseeing that God would justify the Gentiles by faith, preached the gospel beforehand to Abraham, saying, "In you shall all the nations be blessed." 9 So then, those who are men of faith are blessed with Abraham who had faith.

10 For all who rely on works of the law are under a curse; for it is written, "Cursed be every one who does not abide by all things written in the book of the law, and do them." 11 Now it is evident that no man is justified before God by the law; for "He who through faith is righteous shall live";*f* 12 but the law does not rest on faith, for "He who does them shall live by them." 13 Christ redeemed us from the curse of the law, having become a curse for us—for it is written, "Cursed be every one who hangs on a tree"—14 that in Christ Jesus the blessing of Abraham might come upon the Gentiles, that we might receive the promise of the Spirit through faith.

15 To give a human example, brethren: no one annuls even a man's will,*g* or adds to it, once it has been ratified. 16 Now the promises were made to Abraham and to his offspring. It does not say, "And to offsprings," referring to many; but, referring to one, "And to your offspring," which is Christ. 17 This is what I mean: the law, which came four hundred and thirty years afterward, does not annul

a covenant previously ratified by God, so as to make the promise void. 18 For if the inheritance is by the law, it is no longer by promise; but God gave it to Abraham by a promise.

19 Why then the law? It was added because of transgressions, till the offspring should come to whom the promise had been made; and it was ordained by angels through an intermediary. 20 Now an intermediary implies more than one; but God is one. 21 Is the law then against the promises of God? Certainly not; for if a law had been given which could make alive, then righteousness would indeed be by the law. 22 But the scripture consigned all things to sin, that what was promised to faith in Jesus Christ might be given to those who believe.

23 Now before faith came, we were confined under the law, kept under restraint until faith should be revealed. 24 So that the law was our custodian until Christ came, that we might be justified by faith. 25 But now that faith has come, we are no longer under a custodian; 26 for in Christ Jesus you are all sons of God, through faith. 27 For as many of you as were baptized into Christ have put on Christ. 28 There is neither Jew nor Greek, there is neither slave nor free, there is neither male nor female; for you are all one in Christ Jesus. 29And if you are Christ's, then you are Abraham's offspring, heirs according to promise.

4 I mean that the heir, as long as he is a child, is no better than a slave, though he is the owner of all the estate; 2 but he is under guardians and trustees until the date set by the father. 3 So with us; when we were children, we were slaves to the elemental spirits of the universe. 4 But when the time had fully come, God sent forth his Son, born of woman, born under the law, 5 to redeem those who were under the law, so that we might receive adoption as sons. 6And because you are sons, God has sent the Spirit of his Son into our hearts, crying, "Ab'bà! Father!" 7 So through God you are no longer a slave but a son, and if a son then an heir.

8 Formerly, when you did not know God, you were in bondage to beings that by nature are no gods; 9 but now

e Or righteousness f Or the righteous shall live by faith g Or covenant (as in verse 17)
3.6: Gen 15.6; Rom 4.3. **3.8:** Gen 12.3; 18.18; Acts 3.25. **3.9:** Rom 4.16.
3.10: Deut 27.26. **3.11:** Hab 2.4; Rom 1.17; Heb 10.38. **3.12:** Lev 18.5; Rom 10.5.
3.13: Deut 21.23. **3.16:** Gen 12.7. **3.17:** Ex 12.40. **3.18:** Rom 11.6.
3.19: Rom 5.20. **3.21:** Rom 8.2-4. **3.22:** Rom 3.9-19; 11.32. **3.28:** Rom 10.12.
4.3: Col 2.20. **4.6:** Rom 8.15.

that you have come to know God, or rather to be known by God, how can you turn back again to the weak and beggarly elemental spirits, whose slaves you want to be once more? 10 You observe days, and months, and seasons, and years! 11 I am afraid I have labored over you in vain.

12 Brethren, I beseech you, become as I am, for I also have become as you are. You did me no wrong; 13 you know it was because of a bodily ailment that I preached the gospel to you at first; 14 and though my condition was a trial to you, you did not scorn or despise me, but received me as an angel of God, as Christ Jesus. 15 What has become of the satisfaction you felt? For I bear you witness that, if possible, you would have plucked out your eyes and given them to me. 16 Have I then become your enemy by telling you the truth?*h* 17 They make much of you, but for no good purpose; they want to shut you out, that you may make much of them. 18 For a good purpose it is always good to be made much of, and not only when I am present with you. 19 My little children, with whom I am again in travail until Christ be formed in you! 20 I could wish to be present with you now and to change my tone, for I am perplexed about you.

21 Tell me, you who desire to be under law, do you not hear the law? 22 For it is written that Abraham had two sons, one by a slave and one by a free woman. 23 But the son of the slave was born according to the flesh, the son of the free woman through promise. 24 Now this is an allegory: these women are two covenants. One is from Mount Sinai, bearing children for slavery; she is Hā′gàr. 25 Now Hā′-gàr is Mount Sinai in Arabia;*i* she corresponds to the present Jerusalem, for she is in slavery with her children. 26 But the Jerusalem above is free, and she is our mother. 27 For it is written,

"Rejoice, O barren one that dost not bear;
break forth and shout, thou who art not in travail;
for the desolate hath more children than she who hath a husband."

28 Now we,*j* brethren, like Isaac, are children of promise. 29 But as at that time he who was born according to the flesh persecuted him who was born according to the Spirit, so it is now. 30 But what does the scripture say? "Cast out the slave and her son; for the son of the slave shall not inherit with the son of the free woman." 31 So, brethren, we are not children of the slave but of the free woman.

5 For freedom Christ has set us free; stand fast therefore, and do not submit again to a yoke of slavery.

2 Now I, Paul, say to you that if you receive circumcision, Christ will be of no advantage to you. 3 I testify again to every man who receives circumcision that he is bound to keep the whole law. 4 You are severed from Christ, you who would be justified by the law; you have fallen away from grace. 5 For through the Spirit, by faith, we wait for the hope of righteousness. 6 For in Christ Jesus neither circumcision nor uncircumcision is of any avail, but faith working through love. 7 You were running well; who hindered you from obeying the truth? 8 This persuasion is not from him who called you. 9A little leaven leavens the whole lump. 10 I have confidence in the Lord that you will take no other view than mine; and he who is troubling you will bear his judgment, whoever he is. 11 But if I, brethren, still preach circumcision, why am I still persecuted? In that case the stumbling block of the cross has been removed. 12 I wish those who unsettle you would mutilate themselves!

13 For you were called to freedom, brethren; only do not use your freedom as an opportunity for the flesh, but through love be servants of one another. 14 For the whole law is fulfilled in one word, "You shall love your neighbor as yourself." 15 But if you bite and devour one another take heed that you are not consumed by one another.

16 But I say, walk by the Spirit, and do not gratify the desires of the flesh. 17 For the desires of the flesh are against the Spirit, and the desires of the Spirit are against the flesh; for these are opposed to each other, to prevent you from doing what you would. 18 But if you are led by the Spirit you are not under the law. 19 Now the works of the flesh are plain:

---

h Or *by dealing truly with you*
i Other ancient authorities read *For Sinai is a mountain in Arabia*
j Other ancient authorities read *you*
4.13: Acts 16.6.   **4.19:** 1 Cor 4.15.   **4.22:** Gen 16.15; 21.2, 9.   **4.23:** Rom 9.7-9.
4.27: Is 54.1.   **4.29:** Gen 21.9.   **4.30:** Gen 21.10-12.   **5.6:** 1 Cor 7.19; Gal 6.15.
5.9: 1 Cor 5.6.   **5.14:** Lev 19.18; Rom 13.8-10.   **5.17:** Rom 7.15-23.   **5.19:** Rom 1.28.

immorality, impurity, licentiousness, [20] idolatry, sorcery, enmity, strife, jealousy, anger, selfishness, dissension, party spirit, [21] envy,[k] drunkenness, carousing, and the like. I warn you, as I warned you before, that those who do such things shall not inherit the kingdom of God. [22] But the fruit of the Spirit is love, joy, peace, patience, kindness, goodness, faithfulness, [23] gentleness, self-control; against such there is no law. [24] And those who belong to Christ Jesus have crucified the flesh with its passions and desires.

[25] If we live by the Spirit, let us also walk by the Spirit. [26] Let us have no self-conceit, no provoking of one another, no envy of one another.

6 Brethren, if a man is overtaken in any trespass, you who are spiritual should restore him in a spirit of gentleness. Look to yourself, lest you too be tempted. [2] Bear one another's burdens, and so fulfil the law of Christ. [3] For if any one thinks he is something, when he is nothing, he deceives himself. [4] But let each one test his own work, and then his reason to boast will be in himself alone and not in his neighbor. [5] For each man will have to bear his own load.

[6] Let him who is taught the word share all good things with him who teaches.

[7] Do not be deceived; God is not mocked, for whatever a man sows, that he will also reap. [8] For he who

sows to his own flesh will from the flesh reap corruption; but he who sows to the Spirit will from the Spirit reap eternal life. [9] And let us not grow weary in well-doing, for in due season we shall reap, if we do not lose heart. [10] So then, as we have opportunity, let us do good to all men, and especially to those who are of the household of faith.

[11] See with what large letters I am writing to you with my own hand. [12] It is those who want to make a good showing in the flesh that would compel you to be circumcised, and only in order that they may not be persecuted for the cross of Christ. [13] For even those who receive circumcision do not themselves keep the law, but they desire to have you circumcised that they may glory in your flesh. [14] But far be it from me to glory except in the cross of our Lord Jesus Christ, by which[l] the world has been crucified to me, and I to the world. [15] For neither circumcision counts for anything, nor uncircumcision, but a new creation. [16] Peace and mercy be upon all who walk by this rule, upon the Israel of God.

[17] Henceforth let no man trouble me; for I bear on my body the marks of Jesus.

[18] The grace of our Lord Jesus Christ be with your spirit, brethren. Amen.

THE LETTER OF PAUL TO THE

EPHESIANS

1 Paul, an apostle of Christ Jesus by the will of God,

To the saints who are also faithful[a] in Christ Jesus:

[2] Grace to you and peace from God our Father and the Lord Jesus Christ.

[3] Blessed be the God and Father of our Lord Jesus Christ, who has blessed us in Christ with every spiritual blessing in the heavenly places, [4] even as he chose us in him before the founda-

tion of the world, that we should be holy and blameless before him. [5] He destined us in love[b] to be his sons through Jesus Christ, according to the purpose of his will, [6] to the praise of his glorious grace which he freely bestowed on us in the Beloved. [7] In him we have redemption through his blood, the forgiveness of our trespasses, according to the riches of his grace [8] which he lavished upon us. [9] For he has made known to us in all wisdom

k Other ancient authorities add *murder*   l Or *through whom*
a Other ancient authorities read *who are at Ephesus and faithful*
b Or *before him in love, having destined us*
6.11: 1 Cor 16.21.   **6.16:** Ps 125.5.   **1.3:** 2 Cor 1.3.   **1.6:** Col 1.13.   **1.7:** Col 1.14.

and insight the mystery of his will, according to his purpose which he set forth in Christ [10] as a plan for the fulness of time, to unite all things in him, things in heaven and things on earth.

11 In him, according to the purpose of him who accomplishes all things according to the counsel of his will, [12] we who first hoped in Christ have been destined and appointed to live for the praise of his glory. [13] In him you also, who have heard the word of truth, the gospel of your salvation, and have believed in him, were sealed with the promised Holy Spirit, [14] which is the guarantee of our inheritance until we acquire possession of it, to the praise of his glory.

15 For this reason, because I have heard of your faith in the Lord Jesus and your love[c] toward all the saints, [16] I do not cease to give thanks for you, remembering you in my prayers, [17] that the God of our Lord Jesus Christ, the Father of glory, may give you a spirit of wisdom and of revelation in the knowledge of him, [18] having the eyes of your hearts enlightened, that you may know what is the hope to which he has called you, what are the riches of his glorious inheritance in the saints, [19] and what is the immeasurable greatness of his power in us who believe, according to the working of his great might [20] which he accomplished in Christ when he raised him from the dead and made him sit at his right hand in the heavenly places, [21] far above all rule and authority and power and dominion, and above every name that is named, not only in this age but also in that which is to come; [22] and he has put all things under his feet and has made him the head over all things for the church, [23] which is his body, the fulness of him who fills all in all.

2 And you he made alive, when you were dead through the trespasses and sins [2] in which you once walked, following the course of this world, following the prince of the power of the air, the spirit that is now at work in the sons of disobedience. [3] Among these we all once lived in the passions of our flesh, following the desires of body and mind, and so we were by nature children of wrath, like the rest of mankind. [4] But God, who is rich in mercy, out of the great love with which he loved us, [5] even when we were dead

through our trespasses, made us alive together with Christ (by grace you have been saved), [6] and raised us up with him, and made us sit with him in the heavenly places in Christ Jesus, [7] that in the coming ages he might show the immeasurable riches of his grace in kindness toward us in Christ Jesus. [8] For by grace you have been saved through faith; and this is not your own doing, it is the gift of God— [9] not because of works, lest any man should boast. [10] For we are his workmanship, created in Christ Jesus for good works, which God prepared beforehand, that we should walk in them.

11 Therefore remember that at one time you Gentiles in the flesh, called the uncircumcision by what is called the circumcision, which is made in the flesh by hands— [12] remember that you were at that time separated from Christ, alienated from the commonwealth of Israel, and strangers to the covenants of promise, having no hope and without God in the world. [13] But now in Christ Jesus you who once were far off have been brought near in the blood of Christ. [14] For he is our peace, who has made us both one, and has broken down the dividing wall of hostility, [15] by abolishing in his flesh the law of commandments and ordinances, that he might create in himself one new man in place of the two, so making peace, [16] and might reconcile us both to God in one body through the cross, thereby bringing the hostility to an end. [17]And he came and preached peace to you who were far off and peace to those who were near; [18] for through him we both have access in one Spirit to the Father. [19] So then you are no longer strangers and sojourners, but you are fellow citizens with the saints and members of the household of God, [20] built upon the foundation of the apostles and prophets, Christ Jesus himself being the cornerstone, [21] in whom the whole structure is joined together and grows into a holy temple in the Lord; [22] in whom you also are built into it for a dwelling place for God in the Spirit.

3 For this reason I, Paul, a prisoner for Christ Jesus on behalf of you Gentiles— [2] assuming that you have heard of the stewardship of God's grace that was given to me for you, [3] how the mystery was made known to

[c] Other ancient authorities omit *your love*

1.10: Gal 4.4. **1.14:** 2 Cor 1.22. **1.15:** Col 1.9. **1.16:** Col 1.3. **1.18:** Deut 33.3.
1.20: Ps 110.1. **1.21:** Col 1.6; 2.10, 15. **1.22:** Ps 8.6; Col 1.19.
1.23: Rom 12.5; Col 2.17. **2.2:** Col 1.13. **2.8:** Gal 2.16. **2.12:** Is 57.19.
2.17: Is 57.19. **3.2:** Col 1.25.

me by revelation, as I have written briefly. 4 When you read this you can perceive my insight into the mystery of Christ, 5 which was not made known to the sons of men in other generations as it has now been revealed to his holy apostles and prophets by the Spirit; 6 that is, how the Gentiles are fellow heirs, members of the same body, and partakers of the promise in Christ Jesus through the gospel.

7 Of this gospel I was made a minister according to the gift of God's grace which was given me by the working of his power. 8 To me, though I am the very least of all the saints, this grace was given, to preach to the Gentiles the unsearchable riches of Christ, 9 and to make all men see what is the plan of the mystery hidden for ages in[d] God who created all things; 10 that through the church the manifold wisdom of God might now be made known to the principalities and powers in the heavenly places. 11 This was according to the eternal purpose which he has realized in Christ Jesus our Lord, 12 in whom we have boldness and confidence of access through our faith in him. 13 So I ask you not to[e] lose heart over what I am suffering for you, which is your glory.

14 For this reason I bow my knees before the Father, 15 from whom every family in heaven and on earth is named, 16 that according to the riches of his glory he may grant you to be strengthened with might through his Spirit in the inner man, 17 and that Christ may dwell in your hearts through faith; that you, being rooted and grounded in love, 18 may have power to comprehend with all the saints what is the breadth and length and height and depth, 19 and to know the love of Christ which surpasses knowledge, that you may be filled with all the fulness of God.

20 Now to him who by the power at work within us is able to do far more abundantly than all that we ask or think, 21 to him be glory in the church and in Christ Jesus to all generations, for ever and ever. Amen.

4 I therefore, a prisoner for the Lord, beg you to lead a life worthy of the calling to which you have been called, 2 with all lowliness and meekness, with patience, forbearing one another in love, 3 eager to maintain the unity of the Spirit in the bond of peace.

4 There is one body and one Spirit, just as you were called to the one hope that belongs to your call, 5 one Lord, one faith, one baptism, 6 one God and Father of us all, who is above all and through all and in all. 7 But grace was given to each of us according to the measure of Christ's gift. 8 Therefore it is said,

"When he ascended on high he led a host of captives,
and he gave gifts to men."

9 (In saying, "He ascended," what does it mean but that he had also descended into the lower parts of the earth? 10 He who descended is he who also ascended far above all the heavens, that he might fill all things.) 11 And his gifts were that some should be apostles, some prophets, some evangelists, some pastors and teachers, 12 for the equipment of the saints, for the work of ministry, for building up the body of Christ, 13 until we all attain to the unity of the faith and of the knowledge of the Son of God, to mature manhood, to the measure of the stature of the fulness of Christ; 14 so that we may no longer be children, tossed to and fro and carried about with every wind of doctrine, by the cunning of men, by their craftiness in deceitful wiles. 15 Rather, speaking the truth in love, we are to grow up in every way into him who is the head, into Christ, 16 from whom the whole body, joined and knit together by every joint with which it is supplied, when each part is working properly, makes bodily growth and upbuilds itself in love.

17 Now this I affirm and testify in the Lord, that you must no longer live as the Gentiles do, in the futility of their minds; 18 they are darkened in their understanding, alienated from the life of God because of the ignorance that is in them, due to their hardness of heart; 19 they have become callous and have given themselves up to licentiousness, greedy to practice every kind of uncleanness. 20 You did not so learn Christ!— 21 assuming that you have heard about him and were taught in him, as the truth is in Jesus. 22 Put off your old nature which belongs to your former manner of life and is corrupt through deceitful lusts, 23 and be renewed in the spirit of your minds, 24 and put on the new nature, created after the likeness of God in true righteousness and holiness.

25 Therefore, putting away false-

d Or by   e Or I ask that I may not
3.6: Col 1.27.   3.9: Col 1.26.   4.2: Col 3.12-13.   4.8: Ps 68.18.   4.15: Col 1.18.
4.16: Col 2.19.   4.25: Zech 8.16; Rom 12.5.

hood, let every one speak the truth with his neighbor, for we are members one of another. 26 Be angry but do not sin; do not let the sun go down on your anger, 27 and give no opportunity to the devil. 28 Let the thief no longer steal, but rather let him labor, doing honest work with his hands, so that he may be able to give to those in need. 29 Let no evil talk come out of your mouths, but only such as is good for edifying, as fits the occasion, that it may impart grace to those who hear. 30And do not grieve the Holy Spirit of God, in whom you were sealed for the day of redemption. 31 Let all bitterness and wrath and anger and clamor and slander be put away from you, with all malice, 32 and be kind to one another, tenderhearted, forgiving one another, as God in Christ forgave you.

5 Therefore be imitators of God, as beloved children. 2And walk in love, as Christ loved us and gave himself up for us, a fragrant offering and sacrifice to God.

3 But immorality and all impurity or covetousness must not even be named among you, as is fitting among saints. 4 Let there be no filthiness, nor silly talk, nor levity, which are not fitting; but instead let there be thanksgiving. 5 Be sure of this, that no immoral or impure man, or one who is covetous (that is an idolater), has any inheritance in the kingdom of Christ and of God. 6 Let no one deceive you with empty words, for it is because of these things that the wrath of God comes upon the sons of disobedience. 7 Therefore do not associate with them, 8 for once you were darkness, but now you are light in the Lord; walk as children of light 9 (for the fruit of light is found in all that is good and right and true), 10 and try to learn what is pleasing to the Lord. 11 Take no part in the unfruitful works of darkness, but instead expose them. 12 For it is a shame even to speak of the things that they do in secret; 13 but when anything is exposed by the light it becomes visible, for anything that becomes visible is light. 14 Therefore it is said,

"Awake, O sleeper, and arise from the dead,
 and Christ shall give you light."

15 Look carefully then how you walk, not as unwise men but as wise, 16 making the most of the time, because the days are evil. 17 Therefore do not befoolish, but understand what

the will of the Lord is. 18And do not get drunk with wine, for that is debauchery; but be filled with the Spirit, 19 addressing one another in psalms and hymns and spiritual songs, singing and making melody to the Lord with all your heart, 20 always and for everything giving thanks in the name of our Lord Jesus Christ to God the Father.

21 Be subject to one another out of reverence for Christ. 22 Wives, be subject to your husbands, as to the Lord. 23 For the husband is the head of the wife as Christ is the head of the church, his body, and is himself its Savior. 24As the church is subject to Christ, so let wives also be subject in everything to their husbands. 25 Husbands, love your wives, as Christ loved the church and gave himself up for her, 26 that he might sanctify her, having cleansed her by the washing of water with the word, 27 that he might present the church to himself in splendor, without spot or wrinkle or any such thing, that she might be holy and without blemish. 28 Even so husbands should love their wives as their own bodies. He who loves his wife loves himself. 29 For no man ever hates his own flesh, but nourishes and cherishes it, as Christ does the church. 30 because we are members of his body. 31 "For this reason a man shall leave his father and mother and be joined to his wife, and the two shall become one." 32 This is a great mystery, and I take it to mean Christ and the church; 33 however, let each one of you love his wife as himself, and let the wife see that she respects her husband.

6 Children, obey your parents in the Lord, for this is right. 2 "Honor your father and mother" (this is the first commandment with a promise), 3 "that it may be well with you and that you may live long on the earth." 4 Fathers, do not provoke your children to anger, but bring them up in the discipline and instruction of the Lord.

5 Slaves, be obedient to those who are your earthly masters, with fear and trembling, in singleness of heart, as to Christ; 6 not in the way of eyeservice, as men-pleasers, but as servants*f* of Christ, doing the will of God from the heart, 7 rendering service with a good will as to the Lord and not to men, 8 knowing that whatever good any one does, he will receive the same again from the Lord, whether he is a slave or free. 9 Masters, do the same to them,

f Or *slaves*

5.2: Ex 29.18; Ezek 20.41. **5.16:** Col 4.5. **5.19:** Col 3.16-17. **5.22-6.9:** Col 3.18-4.1.
5.31: Gen 2.24. **6.2:** Ex 20.12. **6.3:** Deut 5.16.

and forbear threatening, knowing that he who is both their Master and yours is in heaven, and that there is no partiality with him.

10 Finally, be strong in the Lord and in the strength of his might. 11 Put on the whole armor of God, that you may be able to stand against the wiles of the devil. 12 For we are not contending against flesh and blood, but against the principalities, against the powers, against the world rulers of this present darkness, against the spiritual hosts of wickedness in the heavenly places. 13 Therefore take the whole armor of God, that you may be able to withstand in the evil day, and having done all, to stand. 14 Stand therefore, having girded your loins with truth, and having put on the breastplate of righteousness, 15 and having shod your feet with the equipment of the gospel of peace; 16 above all taking the shield of faith, with which you can quench all the flaming darts of the evil one. 17And take the helmet of salvation, and the sword of the Spirit, which is the word of God. 18 Pray at all times in the Spirit, with all prayer and supplication. To that end keep alert with all perseverance, making supplication for all the saints, 19 and also for me, that utterance may be given me in opening my mouth boldly to proclaim the mystery of the gospel, 20 for which I am an ambassador in chains; that I may declare it boldly, as I ought to speak.

21 Now that you also may know how I am and what I am doing, Tych'-i-cús the beloved brother and faithful minister in the Lord will tell you everything. 22 I have sent him to you for this very purpose, that you may know how we are, and that he may encourage your hearts.

23 Peace be to the brethren, and love with faith, from God the Father and the Lord Jesus Christ. 24 Grace be with all who love our Lord Jesus Christ with love undying.

THE LETTER OF PAUL TO THE

PHILIPPIANS

1 Paul and Timothy, servants*a* of Christ Jesus,
To all the saints in Christ Jesus who are at Phi·lip'pi, with the bishops*b* and deacons:
2 Grace to you and peace from God our Father and the Lord Jesus Christ.

3 I thank my God in all my remembrance of you, 4 always in every prayer of mine for you all making my prayer with joy, 5 thankful for your partnership in the gospel from the first day until now. 6And I am sure that he who began a good work in you will bring it to completion at the day of Jesus Christ. 7 It is right for me to feel thus about you all, because I hold you in my heart, for you are all partakers with me of grace, both in my imprisonment and in the defense and confirmation of the gospel. 8 For God is my witness, how I yearn for you all with the affection of Christ Jesus. 9And it is my prayer that your love may abound more and more, with knowledge and all discernment, 10 so that you may approve what is excellent, and may be pure and blameless for the day of Christ, 11 filled with the fruits of righteousness which come through Jesus Christ, to the glory and praise of God.

12 I want you to know, brethren, that what has happened to me has really served to advance the gospel, 13 so that it has become known through out the whole praetorian guard*c* and to all the rest that my imprisonment is for Christ; 14 and most of the brethren have been made confident in the Lord because of my imprisonment, and are much more bold to speak the word of God without fear.

a Or *slaves*   *b* Or *overseers*   *c* Greek *in the whole praetorium*

6.14: Is 11.5; 59.17; 1 Thess 5.8.   **6.15:** Is 52.7.   **6.21-22:** Col 4.7-8.
1.1: Acts 16.1, 12-40; Rom 1.1; 2 Cor 1.1; Gal 1.10; Col 1.1; 1 Thess 1.1; 2 Thess 1.1; Philem 1.   **1.2:** Rom 1.7.   **1.6, 10:** 1 Cor 1.8.
1.7: Acts 21.33; 2 Cor 7.3; Eph 6.20.   **1.12:** Lk 21.13.   **1.13:** Acts 28.30; 2 Tim 2.9.

15 Some indeed preach Christ from envy and rivalry, but others from good will. 16 The latter do it out of love, knowing that I am put here for the defense of the gospel; 17 the former proclaim Christ out of partisanship, not sincerely but thinking to afflict me in my imprisonment. 18 What then? Only that in every way, whether in pretense or in truth, Christ is proclaimed; and in that I rejoice.

19 Yes, and I shall rejoice. For I know that through your prayers and the help of the Spirit of Jesus Christ this will turn out for my deliverance, 20 as it is my eager expectation and hope that I shall not be at all ashamed, but that with full courage now as always Christ will be honored in my body, whether by life or by death. 21 For to me to live is Christ, and to die is gain. 22 If it is to be life in the flesh, that means fruitful labor for me. Yet which I shall choose I cannot tell. 23 I am hard pressed between the two. My desire is to depart and be with Christ, for that is far better. 24 But to remain in the flesh is more necessary on your account. 25 Convinced of this, I know that I shall remain and continue with you all, for your progress and joy in the faith, 26 so that in me you may have ample cause to glory in Christ Jesus, because of my coming to you again.

27 Only let your manner of life be worthy of the gospel of Christ, so that whether I come and see you or am absent, I may hear of you that you stand firm in one spirit, with one mind striving side by side for the faith of the gospel, 28 and not frightened in anything by your opponents. This is a clear omen to them of their destruction, but of your salvation, and that from God. 29 For it has been granted to you that for the sake of Christ you should not only believe in him but also suffer for his sake, 30 engaged in the same conflict which you saw and now hear to be mine.

2 So if there is any encouragement in Christ, any incentive of love, any participation in the Spirit, any affection and sympathy, 2 complete my joy by being of the same mind, having the same love, being in full accord and of one mind. 3 Do nothing from selfishness or conceit, but in humility count others better than yourselves. 4 Let each of you look not only to his own interests, but also to the interests of others. 5 Have this mind among yourselves, which you have in Christ Jesus, 6 who, though he was in the form of God, did not count equality with God a thing to be grasped, 7 but emptied himself, taking the form of a servant,*d* being born in the likeness of men. 8 And being found in human form he humbled himself and became obedient unto death, even death on a cross. 9 Therefore God has highly exalted him and bestowed on him the name which is above every name, 10 that at the name of Jesus every knee should bow, in heaven and on earth and under the earth, 11 and every tongue confess that Jesus Christ is Lord, to the glory of God the Father.

12 Therefore, my beloved, as you have always obeyed, so now, not only as in my presence but much more in my absence, work out your own salvation with fear and trembling; 13 for God is at work in you, both to will and to work for his good pleasure.

14 Do all things without grumbling or questioning, 15 that you may be blameless and innocent, children of God without blemish in the midst of a crooked and perverse generation, among whom you shine as lights in the world, 16 holding fast the word of life, so that in the day of Christ I may be proud that I did not run in vain or labor in vain. 17 Even if I am to be poured as a libation upon the sacrificial offering of your faith, I am glad and rejoice with you all. 18 Likewise you also should be glad and rejoice with me.

19 I hope in the Lord Jesus to send Timothy to you soon, so that I may be cheered by news of you. 20 I have no one like him, who will be genuinely anxious for your welfare. 21 They all look after their own interests, not those of Jesus Christ. 22 But Timothy's worth you know, how as a son with a father he has served with me in the gospel. 23 I hope therefore to send him just as soon as I see how it will go with me; 24 and I trust in the Lord that shortly I myself shall come also.

25 I have thought it necessary to send to you Ep·aph·rō·dī′tŭs my brother and fellow worker and fellow soldier, and your messenger and minister to my need, 26 for he has been

d Or *slave*

1.19: Acts 16.7; 2 Cor 1.11. **1.20:** Rom 14.8. **1.21:** Gal 2.20. **1.28:** 2 Thess 1.5.
1.30: Acts 16.19-40; 1 Thess 2.2. **2.1:** 2 Cor 13.14. **2.3-4:** Rom 12.10; 15.1-2.
2.5-8: Mt 11.29; 20.28; Jn 1.1; 2 Cor 8.9; Heb 5.8.
2.9-11: Rom 10.9; 14.9; Eph 1.20-21. **2.13:** 1 Cor 15.10. **2.15:** Mt 5.45, 48.

longing for you all, and has been distressed because you heard that he was ill. 27 Indeed he was ill, near to death. But God had mercy on him, and not only on him but on me also, lest I should have sorrow upon sorrow. 28 I am the more eager to send him, therefore, that you may rejoice at seeing him again, and that I may be less anxious. 29 So receive him in the Lord with all joy; and honor such men, 30 for he nearly died for the work of Christ, risking his life to complete your service to me.

3 Finally, my brethren, rejoice in the Lord. To write the same things to you is not irksome to me, and is safe for you.

2 Look out for the dogs, look out for the evil-workers, look out for those who mutilate the flesh. 3 For we are the true circumcision, who worship God in spirit,*e* and glory in Christ Jesus, and put no confidence in the flesh. 4 Though I myself have reason for confidence in the flesh also. If any other man thinks he has reason for confidence in the flesh, I have more: 5 circumcised on the eighth day, of the people of Israel, of the tribe of Benjamin, a Hebrew born of Hebrews; as to the law a Pharisee, 6 as to zeal a persecutor of the church, as to righteousness under the law blameless. 7 But whatever gain I had, I counted as loss for the sake of Christ. 8 Indeed I count everything as loss because of the surpassing worth of knowing Christ Jesus my Lord. For his sake I have suffered the loss of all things, and count them as refuse, in order that I may gain Christ 9 and be found in him, not having a righteousness of my own, based on law, but that which is through faith in Christ, the righteousness from God that depends on faith; 10 that I may know him and the power of his resurrection, and may share his sufferings, becoming like him in his death, 11 that if possible I may attain the resurrection from the dead.

12 Not that I have already obtained this or am already perfect; but I press on to make it my own, because Christ Jesus has made me his own. 13 Brethren, I do not consider that I have made it my own; but one thing I do, forgetting what lies behind and straining forward to what lies ahead, 14 I press

on toward the goal for the prize of the upward call of God in Christ Jesus. 15 Let those of us who are mature be thus minded; and if in anything you are otherwise minded, God will reveal that also to you. 16 Only let us hold true to what we have attained.

17 Brethren, join in imitating me, and mark those who so live as you have an example in us. 18 For many, of whom I have often told you and now tell you even with tears, live as enemies of the cross of Christ. 19 Their end is destruction, their god is the belly, and they glory in their shame, with minds set on earthly things. 20 But our commonwealth is in heaven, and from it we await a Savior, the Lord Jesus Christ, 21 who will change our lowly body to be like his glorious body, by the power which enables him even to subject all things to himself.

4 Therefore, my brethren, whom I love and long for, my joy and crown, stand firm thus in the Lord, my beloved.

2 I entreat Eū-ō′di·à and I entreat Syn′ty·chē to agree in the Lord. 3 And I ask you also, true yokefellow, help these women, for they have labored side by side with me in the gospel together with Clement and the rest of my fellow workers, whose names are in the book of life.

4 Rejoice in the Lord always; again I will say, Rejoice. 5 Let all men know your forbearance. The Lord is at hand. 6 Have no anxiety about anything, but in everything by prayer and supplication with thanksgiving let your requests be made known to God. 7 And the peace of God, which passes all understanding, will keep your hearts and your minds in Christ Jesus.

8 Finally, brethren, whatever is true, whatever is honorable, whatever is just, whatever is pure, whatever is lovely, whatever is gracious, if there is any excellence, if there is anything worthy of praise, think about these things. 9 What you have learned and received and heard and seen in me, do; and the God of peace will be with you.

10 I rejoice in the Lord greatly that now at length you have revived your concern for me; you were indeed concerned for me, but you had no opportunity. 11 Not that I complain of want; for I have learned, in whatever state I

e Other ancient authorities read worship by the Spirit of God
3.3: Rom 2.28-29; Gal 6.14-15.
3.4-7: Acts 8.3; 22.3-21; 23.6; 26.4-23; Rom 11.1; 2 Cor 11.18-31.
3.17: 1 Cor 4.15-17. **3.21:** 1 Cor 15.35-58; Col 3.4. **4.3:** Lk 10.20. **4.6:** Mt 6.25-34.
4.9: Rom 15.33. **4.10:** 2 Cor 11.9.

am, to be content. [12] I know how to be abased, and I know how to abound; in any and all circumstances I have learned the secret of facing plenty and hunger, abundance and want. [13] I can do all things in him who strengthens me.

[14] Yet it was kind of you to share my trouble. [15] And you Phi·lip'pi·ans yourselves know that in the beginning of the gospel, when I left Maċ·ė·dō'ni·à, no church entered into partnership with me in giving and receiving except you only; [16] for even in Thes·sà·lò·nī'cà you sent me help[f] once and again. [17] Not that I seek the gift; but I seek the fruit which increases to your

credit. [18] I have received full payment, and more; I am filled, having received from Ep·aph·rō·dī'tŭs the gifts you sent, a fragrant offering, a sacrifice acceptable and pleasing to God. [19] And my God will supply every need of yours according to his riches in glory in Christ Jesus. [20] To our God and Father be glory for ever and ever. Amen.

[21] Greet every saint in Christ Jesus. The brethren who are with me greet you. [22] All the saints greet you, especially those of Caesar's household.

[23] The grace of the Lord Jesus Christ be with your spirit.

THE LETTER OF PAUL TO THE

COLOSSIANS

[1] Paul, an apostle of Christ Jesus by the will of God, and Timothy our brother,

[2] To the saints and faithful brethren in Christ at Cȯ·los'sae:
Grace to you and peace from God our Father.

[3] We always thank God, the Father of our Lord Jesus Christ, when we pray for you, [4] because we have heard of your faith in Christ Jesus and of the love which you have for all the saints, [5] because of the hope laid up for you in heaven. Of this you have heard before in the word of the truth, the gospel [6] which has come to you, as indeed in the whole world it is bearing fruit and growing—so among yourselves, from the day you heard and understood the grace of God in truth, [7] as you learned it from Ep'à·phras our beloved fellow servant. He is a faithful minister of Christ on our[a] behalf [8] and has made known to us your love in the Spirit.

[9] And so, from the day we heard of it, we have not ceased to pray for you, asking that you may be filled with the knowledge of his will in all spiritual wisdom and understanding, [10] to lead a life worthy of the Lord, fully pleasing

to him, bearing fruit in every good work and increasing in the knowledge of God. [11] May you be strengthened with all power, according to his glorious might, for all endurance and patience with joy, [12] giving thanks to the Father, who has qualified us[b] to share in the inheritance of the saints in light. [13] He has delivered us from the dominion of darkness and transferred us to the kingdom of his beloved Son, [14] in whom we have redemption, the forgiveness of sins.

[15] He is the image of the invisible God, the first-born of all creation; [16] for in him all things were created, in heaven and on earth, visible and invisible, whether thrones or dominions or principalities or authorities—all things were created through him and for him. [17] He is before all things, and in him all things hold together. [18] He is the head of the body, the church; he is the beginning, the first-born from the dead, that in everything he might be pre-eminent. [19] For in him all the fulness of God was pleased to dwell, [20] and through him to reconcile to himself all things, whether on earth or in heaven, making peace by the blood of his cross.

[21] And you, who once were es-

f Other ancient authorities read *money for my needs*
a Other ancient authorities read *your*   b Other ancient authorities read *you*
4.13: 2 Cor 12.9.   **4.16:** Acts 17.1-9; 1 Thess 2.9.   **4.23:** Gal 6.18; Philem 25.
1.2: Rom 1.7.   **1.3:** Eph 1.16.   **1.7:** Col 4.12; Philem 23.   **1.9:** Eph 1.15-17.
1.13: Eph 1.21; 2.2.   **1.15:** 2 Cor 4.4.   **1.17:** Prov 8.22-31.   **1.18:** Eph 4.15.

tranged and hostile in mind, doing evil deeds, 22 he has now reconciled in his body of flesh by his death, in order to present you holy and blameless and irreproachable before him, 23 provided that you continue in the faith, stable and steadfast, not shifting from the hope of the gospel which you heard, which has been preached to every creature under heaven, and of which I, Paul, became a minister.

24 Now I rejoice in my sufferings for your sake, and in my flesh I complete what is lacking in Christ's afflictions for the sake of his body, that is, the church, 25 of which I became a minister according to the divine office which was given to me for you, to make the word of God fully known, 26 the mystery hidden for ages and generations*c* but now made manifest to his saints. 27 To them God chose to make known how great among the Gentiles are the riches of the glory of this mystery, which is Christ in you, the hope of glory. 28 Him we proclaim, warning every man and teaching every man in all wisdom, that we may present every man mature in Christ. 29 For this I toil, striving with all the energy which he mightily inspires within me.

2 For I want you to know how greatly I strive for you, and for those at La-od-i-ce'a, and for all who have not seen my face, 2 that their hearts may be encouraged as they are knit together in love, to have all the riches of assured understanding and the knowledge of God's mystery, of Christ, 3 in whom are hid all the treasures of wisdom and knowledge. 4 I say this in order that no one may delude you with beguiling speech. 5 For though I am absent in body, yet I am with you in spirit, rejoicing to see your good order and the firmness of your faith in Christ.

6 As therefore you received Christ Jesus the Lord, so live in him, 7 rooted and built up in him and established in the faith, just as you were taught, abounding in thanksgiving.

8 See to it that no one makes a prey of you by philosophy and empty deceit, according to human tradition, according to the elemental spirits of the universe, and not according to Christ. 9 For in him the whole fulness of deity

dwells bodily, 10 and you have come to fulness of life in him, who is the head of all rule and authority. 11 In him also you were circumcised with a circumcision made without hands, by putting off the body of flesh in the circumcision of Christ; 12 and you were buried with him in baptism, in which you were also raised with him through faith in the working of God, who raised him from the dead. 13And you, who were dead in trespasses and the uncircumcision of your flesh, God made alive together with him, having forgiven us all our trespasses, 14 having canceled the bond which stood against us with its legal demands; this he set aside, nailing it to the cross. 15 He disarmed the principalities and powers and made a public example of them, triumphing over them in him.*d*

16 Therefore let no one pass judgment on you in questions of food and drink or with regard to a festival or a new moon or a sabbath. 17 These are only a shadow of what is to come; but the substance belongs to Christ. 18 Let no one disqualify you, insisting on self-abasement and worship of angels, taking his stand on visions, puffed up without reason by his sensuous mind, 19 and not holding fast to the Head, from whom the whole body, nourished and knit together through its joints and ligaments, grows with a growth that is from God.

20 If with Christ you died to the elemental spirits of the universe, why do you live as if you still belonged to the world? Why do you submit to regulations, 21 "Do not handle, Do not taste, Do not touch" 22 (referring to things which all perish as they are used), according to human precepts and doctrines? 23 These have indeed an appearance of wisdom in promoting rigor of devotion and self-abasement and severity to the body, but they are of no value in checking the indulgence of the flesh.*e*

3 If then you have been raised with Christ, seek the things that are above, where Christ is, seated at the right hand of God. 2 Set your minds on things that are above, not on things that are on earth. 3 For you have died, and your life is hid with Christ in God. 4 When Christ who is our life appears, then you also will appear with him in glory.

c Or *from angels and men*   *d* Or *in it* (that is, the cross)
e Or *are of no value, serving only to indulge the flesh*
1.25: Eph 3.2.   **1.26:** Eph 3.9.   **2.3:** Is 45.3.   **2.10:** Eph 1.21-22.   **2.15:** Eph 1.21.
2.16: Rom 14.1-12.   **2.17:** Eph 1.23.   **2.19:** Eph 1.22; 4.16.   **2.20:** Gal 4.3.
2.22: Is 29.13; Mk 7.7.   **3.1:** Ps 110.1.

5 Put to death therefore what is earthly in you: immorality, impurity, passion, evil desire, and covetousness, which is idolatry. 6 On account of these the wrath of God is coming.*f* 7 In these you once walked, when you lived in them. 8 But now put them all away: anger, wrath, malice, slander, and foul talk from your mouth. 9 Do not lie to one another, seeing that you have put off the old nature with its practices 10 and have put on the new nature, which is being renewed in knowledge after the image of its creator. 11 Here there cannot be Greek and Jew, circumcised and uncircumcised, barbarian, Scýth'i·àn, slave, free man, but Christ is all, and in all.

12 Put on then, as God's chosen ones, holy and beloved, compassion, kindness, lowliness, meekness, and patience, 13 forbearing one another and, if one has a complaint against another, forgiving each other; as the Lord has forgiven you, so you also must forgive. 14 And above all these put on love, which binds everything together in perfect harmony. 15 And let the peace of Christ rule in your hearts, to which indeed you were called in the one body. And be thankful. 16 Let the word of Christ dwell in you richly, as you teach and admonish one another in all wisdom, and as you sing psalms and hymns and spiritual songs with thankfulness in your hearts to God. 17 And whatever you do, in word or deed, do everything in the name of the Lord Jesus, giving thanks to God the Father through him.

18 Wives, be subject to your husbands, as is fitting in the Lord. 19 Husbands, love your wives, and do not be harsh with them. 20 Children, obey your parents in everything, for this pleases the Lord. 21 Fathers, do not provoke your children, lest they become discouraged. 22 Slaves, obey in everything those who are your earthly masters, not with eyeservice, as menpleasers, but in singleness of heart, fearing the Lord. 23 Whatever your task, work heartily, as serving the Lord and not men, 24 knowing that from the Lord you will receive the inheritance as your reward; you are serving the Lord Christ. 25 For the wrongdoer will be paid back for the wrong he has done, and there is no partiality.

4 Masters, treat your slaves justly and fairly, knowing that you also have a Master in heaven.

2 Continue steadfastly in prayer, being watchful in it with thanksgiving; 3 and pray for us also, that God may open to us a door for the word, to declare the mystery of Christ, on account of which I am in prison, 4 that I may make it clear, as I ought to speak.

5 Conduct yourselves wisely toward outsiders, making the most of the time. 6 Let your speech always be gracious, seasoned with salt, so that you may know how you ought to answer every one.

7 Tych'i·cùs will tell you all about my affairs; he is a beloved brother and faithful minister and fellow servant in the Lord. 8 I have sent him to you for this very purpose, that you may know how we are and that he may encourage your hearts, 9 and with him O·nes'i·mùs, the faithful and beloved brother, who is one of yourselves. They will tell you of everything that has taken place here.

10 Ar·is·tär'chùs my fellow prisoner greets you, and Mark the cousin of Bär'nà·bàs (concerning whom you have received instructions—if he comes to you, receive him), 11 and Jesus who is called Justus. These are the only men of the circumcision among my fellow workers for the kingdom of God, and they have been a comfort to me. 12 Ep'à·phras, who is one of yourselves, a servant*g* of Christ Jesus, greets you, always remembering you earnestly in his prayers, that you may stand mature and fully assured in all the will of God. 13 For I bear him witness that he has worked hard for you and for those in Lā·ò·di·cē'à and in Hi·ēr·ap'ó·lis. 14 Luke the beloved physician and Dē'màs greet you. 15 Give my greetings to the brethren at Lā·ò·di·cē'à, and to Nym'phà and the church in her house. 16 And when this letter has been read among you, have it read also in the church of the Lā·ò·di·cē'àns; and see that you read also the letter from Lā·ò·di·cē'à. 17 And say to Är·chip'pùs, "See that you fulfil the ministry which you have received in the Lord."

18 I, Paul, write this greeting with my own hand. Remember my fetters. Grace be with you.

---

f Other ancient authorities add *upon the sons of disobedience*   *g* Or *slave*
3.10: Gen 1.26.   **3.12-13:** Eph 4.2.   **3.16-17:** Eph 5.19.   **3.18-4.1:** Eph 5.22-6.9.
3.23: Rom 12.11.   **4.1:** Lev 25.43, 53.   **4.2:** Rom 12.12.   **4.5:** Eph 5.16.
4.7-8: Eph 6.21-22.   **4.9:** Philem 10.   **4.10-11:** Acts 19.29; 27.2; Philem 24.
4.12: Col 1.7; Philem 23.   **4.14:** 2 Tim 4.10-11; Philem 24.   **4.18:** 1 Cor 16.21.

THE FIRST LETTER OF PAUL TO THE

THESSALONIANS

1 Paul, Sil·va′nus, and Timothy, To the church of the Thes·sa·lō′-ni·ans in God the Father and the Lord Jesus Christ:

Grace to you and peace.

2 We give thanks to God always for you all, constantly mentioning you in our prayers, 3 remembering before our God and Father your work of faith and labor of love and steadfastness of hope in our Lord Jesus Christ. 4 For we know, brethren beloved by God, that he has chosen you; 5 for our gospel came to you not only in word, but also in power and in the Holy Spirit and with full conviction. You know what kind of men we proved to be among you for your sake. 6And you became imitators of us and of the Lord, for you received the word in much affliction, with joy inspired by the Holy Spirit; 7 so that you became an example to all the believers in Mac·e·dō′ni·a and in A·cha′ia. 8 For not only has the word of the Lord sounded forth from you in Mac·e·dō′-ni·a and A·cha′ia, but your faith in God has gone forth everywhere, so that we need not say anything. 9 For they themselves report concerning us what a welcome we had among you, and how you turned to God from idols, to serve a living and true God, 10 and to wait for his Son from heaven, whom he raised from the dead, Jesus who delivers us from the wrath to come.

2 For you yourselves know, brethren, that our visit to you was not in vain; 2 but though we had already suffered and been shamefully treated at Phi·lip′pi, as you know, we had courage in our God to declare to you the gospel of God in the face of great opposition. 3 For our appeal does not spring from error or uncleanness, nor is it made with guile; 4 but just as we have been approved by God to be entrusted with the gospel, so we speak, not to please men, but to please God who tests our hearts. 5 For we never used either words of flattery, as you know, or a cloak for greed, as God is witness; 6 nor did we seek glory from men, whether from you or from others, though we might have made demands as apostles of Christ. 7 But we were gentle[a] among you, like a nurse taking care of her children. 8 So, being affectionately desirous of you, we were ready to share with you not only the gospel of God but also our own selves, because you had become very dear to us.

9 For you remember our labor and toil, brethren; we worked night and day, that we might not burden any of you, while we preached to you the gospel of God. 10 You are witnesses, and God also, how holy and righteous and blameless was our behavior to you believers; 11 for you know how, like a father with his children, we exhorted each one of you and encouraged you and charged you 12 to lead a life worthy of God, who calls you into his own kingdom and glory.

13 And we also thank God constantly for this, that when you received the word of God which you heard from us, you accepted it not as the word of men but as what it really is, the word of God, which is at work in you believers. 14 For you, brethren, became imitators of the churches of God in Christ Jesus which are in Judea; for you suffered the same things from your own countrymen as they did from the Jews, 15 who killed both the Lord Jesus and the prophets, and

<hr/>

a Other ancient authorities read babes

1.1: 2 Thess 1.1; 2 Cor 1.19; Acts 16.1; Acts 17.1; Rom 1.7.
1.2: 2 Thess 1.3; 2.13; Rom 1.9. 1.3: 2 Thess 1.11; 1.3; Rom 8.25; 15.4; Gal 1.4.
1.4: 2 Thess 2.13; Rom 1.7; 2 Pet 1.10. 1.5: 2 Thess 2.14; Rom 15.19.
1.6: Col 2.2; 1 Thess 2.10; 1 Cor 4.16; 11.1; Acts 17.5-10; 13.52.
1.7: Rom 15.26; Acts 18.12. 1.8: 2 Thess 3.1; Rom 1.8. 1.10: Mt 3.7.
2.2: Acts 16.19-24; 17.1-9; Rom 1.1. 2.5: Acts 20.33. 2.6: 1 Cor 9.1.
2.7: 1 Thess 2.11; Gal 4.19. 2.8: 2 Cor 12.15; 1 Jn 3.16. 2.11: 1 Cor 4.14.
2.12: 1 Pet 5.10. 2.13: 1 Thess 1.2.
2.14: 1 Thess 1.6; 1 Cor 7.17; Gal 1.22; Acts 17.5; 2 Thess 1.4.
2.15: Lk 24.20; Acts 2.23; 7.52.

drove us out, and displease God and oppose all men [16] by hindering us from speaking to the Gentiles that they may be saved—so as always to fill up the measure of their sins. But God's wrath has come upon them at last![b]

[17] But since we were bereft of you, brethren, for a short time, in person not in heart, we endeavored the more eagerly and with great desire to see you face to face; [18] because we wanted to come to you—I, Paul, again and again—but Satan hindered us. [19] For what is our hope or joy or crown of boasting before our Lord Jesus at his coming? Is it not you? [20] For you are our glory and joy.

3 Therefore when we could bear it no longer, we were willing to be left behind at Athens alone, [2] and we sent Timothy, our brother and God's servant in the gospel of Christ, to establish you in your faith and to exhort you, [3] that no one be moved by these afflictions. You yourselves know that this is to be our lot. [4] For when we were with you, we told you beforehand that we were to suffer affliction; just as it has come to pass, and as you know. [5] For this reason, when I could bear it no longer, I sent that I might know your faith, for fear that somehow the tempter had tempted you and that our labor would be in vain.

[6] But now that Timothy has come to us from you, and has brought us the good news of your faith and love and reported that you always remember us kindly and long to see us, as we long to see you— [7] for this reason, brethren, in all our distress and affliction we have been comforted about you through your faith; [8] for now we live, if you stand fast in the Lord. [9] For what thanksgiving can we render to God for you, for all the joy which we feel for your sake before our God, [10] praying earnestly night and day that we may see you face to face and supply what is lacking in your faith?

[11] Now may our God and Father himself, and our Lord Jesus, direct our way to you; [12] and may the Lord make you increase and abound in love to one another and to all men, as we do to you, [13] so that he may establish

your hearts unblamable in holiness before our God and Father, at the coming of our Lord Jesus with all his saints.

4 Finally, brethren, we beseech and exhort you in the Lord Jesus, that as you learned from us how you ought to live and to please God, just as you are doing, you do so more and more. [2] For you know what instructions we gave you through the Lord Jesus. [3] For this is the will of God, your sanctification: that you abstain from immorality; [4] that each one of you know how to take a wife for himself in holiness and honor, [5] not in the passion of lust like heathen who do not know God; [6] that no man transgress, and wrong his brother in this matter,[c] because the Lord is an avenger in all these things, as we solemnly forewarned you. [7] For God has not called us for uncleanness, but in holiness. [8] Therefore whoever disregards this, disregards not man but God, who gives his Holy Spirit to you.

[9] But concerning love of the brethren you have no need to have any one write to you, for you yourselves have been taught by God to love one another; [10] and indeed you do love all the brethren throughout Maç-ė-dō′ni-à. But we exhort you, brethren, to do so more and more, [11] to aspire to live quietly, to mind your own affairs, and to work with your hands, as we charged you; [12] so that you may command the respect of outsiders, and be dependent on nobody.

[13] But we would not have you ignorant, brethren, concerning those who are asleep, that you may not grieve as others do who have no hope. [14] For since we believe that Jesus died and rose again, even so, through Jesus, God will bring with him those who have fallen asleep. [15] For this we declare to you by the word of the Lord, that we who are alive, who are left until the coming of the Lord, shall not precede those who have fallen asleep. [16] For the Lord himself will descend from heaven with a cry of command, with the archangel's call, and with the sound of the trumpet of God. And the dead in Christ will rise first; [17] then we

b Or *completely*, or *for ever*   *c* Or *defraud his brother in business*

2.16: Acts 9.23; 13.45, 50; 14.2, 5, 19; 17.5, 13; 18.12; 21.21, 27; 25.2, 7; 1 Cor 10.33; Gen 15.16; 1 Thess 1.10.   **2.17:** 1 Cor 5.3.
2.19: Phil 4.1; 1 Thess 3.13; 4.15; 5.23; Mt 16.27; Mk 8.38.   **2.20:** 2 Cor 1.14.
3.1: Phil 2.19; Acts 17.15.   **3.2:** 2 Cor 1.1; Col 1.1.   **3.3:** Acts 14.22.
3.4: 1 Thess 2.14.   **3.5:** Mt 4.3; Phil 2.16.   **3.6:** Acts 18.5.
3.13: 1 Cor 1.8; 1 Thess 2.19; 4.17.   **4.3:** 1 Cor 6.18.   **4.4:** 1 Cor 7.2; 1 Pet 3.7.
4.11: 2 Thess 3.12; Eph 4.28; 2 Thess 3.10-12.   **4.13:** Eph 2.12.   **4.14:** 2 Cor 4.14.
4.16: Mt 24.31; 1 Cor 15.23; 2 Thess 2.1.

who are alive, who are left, shall be caught up together with them in the clouds to meet the Lord in the air; and so we shall always be with the Lord. [18] Therefore comfort one another with these words.

5 But as to the times and the seasons, brethren, you have no need to have anything written to you. [2] For you yourselves know well that the day of the Lord will come like a thief in the night. [3] When people say, "There is peace and security," then sudden destruction will come upon them as travail comes upon a woman with child, and there will be no escape. [4] But you are not in darkness, brethren, for that day to surprise you like a thief. [5] For you are all sons of light and sons of the day; we are not of the night or of darkness. [6] So then let us not sleep, as others do, but let us keep awake and be sober. [7] For those who sleep sleep at night, and those who get drunk are drunk at night. [8] But, since we belong to the day, let us be sober, and put on the breastplate of faith and love, and for a helmet the hope of salvation. [9] For God has not destined us for wrath, but to obtain salvation through our Lord Jesus Christ, [10] who died for us so that whether we wake or sleep we might live with him. [11] Therefore encourage one another

and build one another up, just as you are doing.

[12] But we beseech you, brethren, to respect those who labor among you and are over you in the Lord and admonish you, [13] and to esteem them very highly in love because of their work. Be at peace among yourselves. [14] And we exhort you, brethren, admonish the idle, encourage the fainthearted, help the weak, be patient with them all. [15] See that none of you repays evil for evil, but always seek to do good to one another and to all. [16] Rejoice always, [17] pray constantly, [18] give thanks in all circumstances; for this is the will of God in Christ Jesus for you. [19] Do not quench the Spirit, [20] do not despise prophesying, [21] but test everything; hold fast what is good, [22] abstain from every form of evil.

[23] May the God of peace himself sanctify you wholly; and may your spirit and soul and body be kept sound and blameless at the coming of our Lord Jesus Christ. [24] He who calls you is faithful, and he will do it.

[25] Brethren, pray for us.

[26] Greet all the brethren with a holy kiss.

[27] I adjure you by the Lord that this letter be read to all the brethren.

[28] The grace of our Lord Jesus Christ be with you.

THE SECOND LETTER OF PAUL TO THE

THESSALONIANS

1 Paul, Sil·vā′nŭs, and Timothy,
To the church of the Thes·sa·lō′-
ni·anṣ in God our Father and the Lord
Jesus Christ:
2 Grace to you and peace from God
the Father and the Lord Jesus Christ.

3 We are bound to give thanks to God always for you, brethren, as is fitting, because your faith is growing

abundantly, and the love of every one of you for one another is increasing. [4] Therefore we ourselves boast of you in the churches of God for your steadfastness and faith in all your persecutions and in the afflictions which you are enduring.

5 This is evidence of the righteous judgment of God, that you may be made worthy of the kingdom of God,

5.1: Acts 1.7.   **5.2:** 1 Cor 1.8.   **5.3:** 2 Thess 1.9.   **5.4:** 1 Jn 2.8; Acts 26.18.
5.5: Lk 16.8.   **5.6:** Rom 13.11; 1 Pet 1.13.   **5.7:** Acts 2.15; 2 Pet 2.13.
5.8: Eph 6.14, 23, 17; Rom 8.24.   **5.9:** 1 Thess 1.10; 2 Thess 2.13; Rom 14.9.
5.12: 1 Cor 16.18; 1 Tim 5.17; 1 Cor 16.16; Rom 16.6, 12; 1 Cor 15.10; Heb 13.17.
5.13: Mk 9.50.   **5.14:** Is 35.4; Rom 14.1; 1 Cor 8.7; 2 Thess 3.6, 7, 11.
5.15: Rom 12.17; 1 Pet 3.9.   **5.16:** Phil 4.4.   **5.17:** Eph 6.18.   **5.18:** Eph 5.20.
5.19: Eph 4.30.   **5.20:** 1 Cor 14.31.   **5.21:** 1 Cor 14.29; 1 Jn 4.1.   **5.23:** Rom 15.33.
5.26: Rom 16.16.   **5.27:** Col 4.16.   **5.28:** Rom 16.20; 2 Thess 3.18.
1.1: 1 Thess 1.1; 2 Cor 1.19; Acts 16.1.   **1.2:** Rom 1.7.   **1.3:** 1 Thess 1.2.

for which you are suffering— 6 since indeed God deems it just to repay with affliction those who afflict you, 7 and to grant rest with us to you who are afflicted, when the Lord Jesus is revealed from heaven with his mighty angels in flaming fire, 8 inflicting vengeance upon those who do not know God and upon those who do not obey the gospel of our Lord Jesus. 9 They shall suffer the punishment of eternal destruction and exclusion from the presence of the Lord and from the glory of his might, 10 when he comes on that day to be glorified in his saints, and to be marveled at in all who have believed, because our testimony to you was believed. 11 To this end we always pray for you, that our God may make you worthy of his call, and may fulfil every good resolve and work of faith by his power, 12 so that the name of our Lord Jesus may be glorified in you, and you in him, according to the grace of our God and the Lord Jesus Christ.

2 Now concerning the coming of our Lord Jesus Christ and our assembling to meet him, we beg you, brethren, 2 not to be quickly shaken in mind or excited, either by spirit or by word, or by letter purporting to be from us, to the effect that the day of the Lord has come. 3 Let no one deceive you in any way; for that day will not come, unless the rebellion comes first, and the man of lawlessness*a* is revealed, the son of perdition, 4 who opposes and exalts himself against every so-called god or object of worship, so that he takes his seat in the temple of God, proclaiming himself to be God. 5 Do you not remember that when I was still with you I told you this? 6And you know what is restraining him now so that he may be revealed in his time. 7 For the mystery of lawlessness is already at work; only he who now restrains it will do so until he is out of the way. 8And then the lawless one will be revealed, and the Lord Jesus will slay him with the breath of his mouth and destroy him by his appearing and his coming. 9 The coming of the lawless one by the activity of Satan will be with all power

and with pretended signs and wonders, 10 and with all wicked deception for those who are to perish, because they refused to love the truth and so be saved. 11 Therefore God sends upon them a strong delusion, to make them believe what is false, 12 so that all may be condemned who did not believe the truth but had pleasure in unrighteousness.

13 But we are bound to give thanks to God always for you, brethren beloved by the Lord, because God chose you from the beginning*b* to be saved through sanctification by the Spirit*c* and belief in the truth. 14 To this he called you through our gospel, so that you may obtain the glory of our Lord Jesus Christ. 15 So then, brethren, stand firm and hold to the traditions which you were taught by us, either by word of mouth or by letter.

16 Now may our Lord Jesus Christ himself, and God our Father, who loved us and gave us eternal comfort and good hope through grace, 17 comfort your hearts and establish them in every good work and word.

3 Finally, brethren, pray for us, that the word of the Lord may speed on and triumph, as it did among you, 2 and that we may be delivered from wicked and evil men; for not all have faith. 3 But the Lord is faithful; he will strengthen you and guard you from evil.*d* 4And we have confidence in the Lord about you, that you are doing and will do the things which we command. 5 May the Lord direct your hearts to the love of God and to the steadfastness of Christ.

6 Now we command you, brethren, in the name of our Lord Jesus Christ, that you keep away from any brother who is living in idleness and not in accord with the tradition that you received from us. 7 For you yourselves know how you ought to imitate us; we were not idle when we were with you, 8 we did not eat any one's bread without paying, but with toil and labor we worked night and day, that we might not burden any of you. 9 It was not because we have not that right, but to give you in our conduct an example to

a Other ancient authorities read *sin*
b Other ancient authorities read *as the first converts*   *c* Or *of spirit*   *d* Or *the evil one*
1.8: Gal 4.8.   **1.11:** 1 Thess 1.3.   **2.1:** 1 Thess 4.15-17.   **2.2:** 2 Thess 3.17.
2.3: Eph 5.6-8; Dan 7.25; 8.25; 11.36; Rev 13.5; Jn 17.12.   **2.4:** Ezek 28.2.
2.5: 1 Thess 3.4.   **2.8:** Is 11.4.   **2.9:** Mt 24.24; Jn 4.48.   **2.11:** Rom 1.28.
2.13: 2 Thess 1.3; Eph 1.4; 1 Pet 1.2.   **2.15:** 1 Cor 16.13; 11.2.
2.16: 1 Thess 3.11; 1 Pet 1.3.   **3.1:** 1 Thess 5.25; 1.8.   **3.2:** Rom 15.31.
3.3: 1 Cor 1.9; 1 Thess 5.24.   **3.6:** 1 Cor 5.4, 5, 11; 1 Thess 5.14.   **3.7:** 1 Thess 1.6, 9.
3.8: 1 Thess 2.9; Acts 18.3; Eph 4.28.   **3.9:** 2 Thess 3.7.

imitate. 10 For even when we were with you, we gave you this command: If any one will not work, let him not eat. 11 For we hear that some of you are living in idleness, mere busybodies, not doing any work. 12 Now such persons we command and exhort in the Lord Jesus Christ to do their work in quietness and to earn their own living. 13 Brethren, do not be weary in well-doing.

14 If any one refuses to obey what we say in this letter, note that man, and have nothing to do with him, that he may be ashamed. 15 Do not look on him as an enemy, but warn him as a brother.

16 Now may the Lord of peace himself give you peace at all times in all ways. The Lord be with you all.

17 I, Paul, write this greeting with my own hand. This is the mark in every letter of mine; it is the way I write. 18 The grace of our Lord Jesus Christ be with you all.

THE FIRST LETTER OF PAUL TO

TIMOTHY

Paul, an apostle of Christ Jesus by command of God our Savior and of Christ Jesus our hope,

2 To Timothy, my true child in the faith:

Grace, mercy, and peace from God the Father and Christ Jesus our Lord.

3 As I urged you when I was going to Maċ·é·dō'ni·à, remain at Eph'é·sùs that you may charge certain persons not to teach any different doctrine, 4 nor to occupy themselves with myths and endless genealogies which promote speculations rather than the divine training[a] that is in faith; 5 whereas the aim of our charge is love that issues from a pure heart and a good conscience and sincere faith. 6 Certain persons by swerving from these have wandered away into vain discussion, 7 desiring to be teachers of the law, without understanding either what they are saying or the things about which they make assertions.

8 Now we know that the law is good, if any one uses it lawfully, 9 understanding this, that the law is not laid down for the just but for the lawless and disobedient, for the ungodly and sinners, for the unholy and profane, for murderers of fathers and murderers of mothers, for manslayers, 10 immoral persons, sodomites, kidnapers, liars, perjurers, and whatever else is contrary to sound doctrine, 11 in accordance with the glorious gospel of the blessed God with which I have been entrusted.

12 I thank him who has given me strength for this, Christ Jesus our Lord, because he judged me faithful by appointing me to his service, 13 though I formerly blasphemed and persecuted and insulted him; but I received mercy because I had acted ignorantly in unbelief, 14 and the grace of our Lord overflowed for me with the faith and love that are in Christ Jesus. 15 The saying is sure and worthy of full acceptance, that Christ Jesus came into the world to save sinners. And I am the foremost of sinners; 16 but I received mercy for this reason, that in me, as the foremost, Jesus Christ might display his perfect patience for an example to those who were to believe in him for eternal life. 17 To the King of ages, immortal, invisible, the only God, be honor and glory for ever and ever.[b] Amen.

18 This charge I commit to you, Timothy, my son, in accordance with the prophetic utterances which pointed to you, that inspired by them you may wage the good warfare, 19 holding faith and a good conscience. By rejecting conscience, certain persons have made shipwreck of their faith, 20 among them Hy̆·mè·naē'ùs and Alexander, whom I have delivered to Satan that they may learn not to blaspheme.

2 First of all, then, I urge that supplications, prayers, intercessions,

a Or stewardship, or order   b Greek to the ages of ages
3.10: 1 Thess 4.11.   3.11: 2 Thess 3.6.   3.12: 1 Thess 4.1, 11.   3.13: Gal 6.9.
3.16: Ruth 2.4.   3.17: 1 Cor 16.21.   3.18: Rom 16.20; 1 Thess 5.28.

and thanksgivings be made for all men, 2 for kings and all who are in high positions, that we may lead a quiet and peaceable life, godly and respectful in every way. 3 This is good, and it is acceptable in the sight of God our Savior, 4 who desires all men to be saved and to come to the knowledge of the truth. 5 For there is one God, and there is one mediator between God and men, the man Christ Jesus, 6 who gave himself as a ransom for all, the testimony to which was borne at the proper time. 7 For this I was appointed a preacher and apostle (I am telling the truth, I am not lying), a teacher of the Gentiles in faith and truth.

8 I desire then that in every place the men should pray, lifting holy hands without anger or quarreling; 9 also that women should adorn themselves modestly and sensibly in seemly apparel, not with braided hair or gold or pearls or costly attire 10 but by good deeds, as befits women who profess religion. 11 Let a woman learn in silence with all submissiveness. 12 I permit no woman to teach or to have authority over men; she is to keep silent. 13 For Adam was formed first, then Eve; 14 and Adam was not deceived, but the woman was deceived and became a transgressor. 15 Yet woman will be saved through bearing children,*c* if she continues*d* in faith and love and holiness, with modesty.

3 The saying is sure: If any one aspires to the office of bishop, he desires a noble task. 2 Now a bishop must be above reproach, the husband of one wife, temperate, sensible, dignified, hospitable, an apt teacher, 3 no drunkard, not violent but gentle, not quarrelsome, and no lover of money. 4 He must manage his own household well, keeping his children submissive and respectful in every way; 5 for if a man does not know how to manage his own household, how can he care for God's church? 6 He must not be a recent convert, or he may be puffed up with conceit and fall into the condemnation of the devil;*f* 7 moreover he must be well thought of by outsiders, or he may fall into reproach and the snare of the devil.*f*

8 Deacons likewise must be serious, not double-tongued, not addicted to much wine, not greedy for gain; 9 they must hold the mystery of the faith with a clear conscience. 10 And let them

also be tested first; then if they prove themselves blameless let them serve as deacons. 11 The women likewise must be serious, no slanderers, but temperate, faithful in all things. 12 Let deacons be the husband of one wife, and let them manage their children and their households well; 13 for those who serve well as deacons gain a good standing for themselves and also great confidence in the faith which is in Christ Jesus.

14 I hope to come to you soon, but I am writing these instructions to you so that, 15 if I am delayed, you may know how one ought to behave in the household of God, which is the church of the living God, the pillar and bulwark of the truth. 16 Great indeed, we confess, is the mystery of our religion:

He*h* was manifested in the flesh,
  vindicated*i* in the Spirit,
    seen by angels,
  preached among the nations,
  believed on in the world,
    taken up in glory.

4 Now the Spirit expressly says that in later times some will depart from the faith by giving heed to deceitful spirits and doctrines of demons, 2 through the pretensions of liars whose consciences are seared, 3 who forbid marriage and enjoin abstinence from foods which God created to be received with thanksgiving by those who believe and know the truth. 4 For everything created by God is good, and nothing is to be rejected if it is received with thanksgiving; 5 for then it is consecrated by the word of God and prayer.

6 If you put these instructions before the brethren, you will be a good minister of Christ Jesus, nourished on the words of the faith and of the good doctrine which you have followed. 7 Have nothing to do with godless and silly myths. Train yourself in godliness; 8 for while bodily training is of some value, godliness is of value in every way, as it holds promise for the present life and also for the life to come. 9 The saying is sure and worthy of full acceptance. 10 For to this end we toil and strive,*j* because we have our hope set on the living God, who is the Savior of all men, especially of those who believe.

11 Command and teach these things. 12 Let no one despise your youth, but set the believers an example

c Or *by the birth of the child*   *d* Greek *they continue*   *f* Or *slanderer*
h Greek *Who;* other ancient authorities read *God;* others, *Which*   *i* Or *justified*
j Other ancient authorities read *suffer reproach*
2.13: Gen 2.7, 21-22.   **2.14:** Gen 3.1-6.

in speech and conduct, in love, in faith, in purity. 13 Till I come, attend to the public reading of scripture, to preaching, to teaching. 14 Do not neglect the gift you have, which was given you by prophetic utterance when the elders laid their hands upon you. 15 Practice these duties, devote yourself to them, so that all may see your progress. 16 Take heed to yourself and to your teaching; hold to that, for by so doing you will save both yourself and your hearers.

5 Do not rebuke an older man but exhort him as you would a father; treat younger men like brothers, 2 older women like mothers, younger women like sisters, in all purity.

3 Honor widows who are real widows. 4 If a widow has children or grandchildren, let them first learn their religious duty to their own family and make some return to their parents; for this is acceptable in the sight of God. 5 She who is a real widow, and is left all alone, has set her hope on God and continues in supplications and prayers night and day; 6 whereas she who is self-indulgent is dead even while she lives. 7 Command this, so that they may be without reproach. 8 If any one does not provide for his relatives, and especially for his own family, he has disowned the faith and is worse than an unbeliever.

9 Let a widow be enrolled if she is not less than sixty years of age, having been the wife of one husband; 10 and she must be well attested for her good deeds, as one who has brought up children, shown hospitality, washed the feet of the saints, relieved the afflicted, and devoted herself to doing good in every way. 11 But refuse to enrol younger widows; for when they grow wanton against Christ they desire to marry, 12 and so they incur condemnation for having violated their first pledge. 13 Besides that, they learn to be idlers, gadding about from house to house, and not only idlers but gossips and busybodies, saying what they should not. 14 So I would have younger widows marry, bear children, rule their households, and give the enemy no occasion to revile us. 15 For some have already strayed after Satan. 16 If any believing woman[l] has relatives who are widows, let her assist them; let the church not be burdened, so that it may assist those who are real widows.

17 Let the elders who rule well be

considered worthy of double honor, especially those who labor in preaching and teaching; 18 for the scripture says, "You shall not muzzle an ox when it is treading out the grain," and, "The laborer deserves his wages." 19 Never admit any charge against an elder except on the evidence of two or three witnesses. 20 As for those who persist in sin, rebuke them in the presence of all, so that the rest may stand in fear. 21 In the presence of God and of Christ Jesus and of the elect angels I charge you to keep these rules without favor, doing nothing from partiality. 22 Do not be hasty in the laying on of hands, nor participate in another man's sins; keep yourself pure.

23 No longer drink only water, but use a little wine for the sake of your stomach and your frequent ailments.

24 The sins of some men are conspicuous, pointing to judgment, but the sins of others appear later. 25 So also good deeds are conspicuous; and even when they are not, they cannot remain hidden.

6 Let all who are under the yoke of slavery regard their masters as worthy of all honor, so that the name of God and the teaching may not be defamed. 2 Those who have believing masters must not be disrespectful on the ground that they are brethren; rather they must serve all the better since those who benefit by their service are believers and beloved.

Teach and urge these duties. 3 If any one teaches otherwise and does not agree with the sound words of our Lord Jesus Christ and the teaching which accords with godliness, 4 he is puffed up with conceit, he knows nothing; he has a morbid craving for controversy and for disputes about words, which produce envy, dissension, slander, base suspicions, 5 and wrangling among men who are depraved in mind and bereft of the truth, imagining that godliness is a means of gain. 6 There is great gain in godliness with contentment; 7 for we brought nothing into the world, and[m] we cannot take anything out of the world; 8 but if we have food and clothing, with these we shall be content. 9 But those who desire to be rich fall into temptation, into a snare, into many senseless and hurtful desires that plunge men into ruin and destruction. 10 For the love of money is the root of all evils; it is through this craving that some have wandered away

l Other ancient authorities read man or woman; others, simply man
m Other ancient authorities insert it is certain that
5.18: Deut 25.4; 1 Cor 9.9; Mt 10.10; Lk 10.7; 1 Cor 9.14.   5.19: Deut 19.15.

from the faith and pierced their hearts with many pangs.

11 But as for you, man of God, shun all this; aim at righteousness, godliness, faith, love, steadfastness, gentleness. 12 Fight the good fight of the faith; take hold of the eternal life to which you were called when you made the good confession in the presence of many witnesses. 13 In the presence of God who gives life to all things, and of Christ Jesus who in his testimony before Pontius Pilate made the good confession, 14 I charge you to keep the commandment unstained and free from reproach until the appearing of our Lord Jesus Christ; 15 and this will be made manifest at the proper time by the blessed and only Sovereign, the King of kings and Lord of lords, 16 who alone has immortality and dwells in unapproachable light, whom no man has ever seen or can see. To him be honor and eternal dominion. Amen.

17 As for the rich in this world, charge them not to be haughty, nor to set their hopes on uncertain riches but on God who richly furnishes us with everything to enjoy. 18 They are to do good, to be rich in good deeds, liberal and generous, 19 thus laying up for themselves a good foundation for the future, so that they may take hold of the life which is life indeed.

20 O Timothy, guard what has been entrusted to you. Avoid the godless chatter and contradictions of what is falsely called knowledge, 21 for by professing it some have missed the mark as regards the faith.

Grace be with you.

THE SECOND LETTER OF PAUL TO

TIMOTHY

Paul, an apostle of Christ Jesus by the will of God according to the promise of the life which is in Christ Jesus.

2 To Timothy, my beloved child:

Grace, mercy, and peace from God the Father and Christ Jesus our Lord.

3 I thank God whom I serve with a clear conscience, as did my fathers, when I remember you constantly in my prayers. 4As I remember your tears, I long night and day to see you, that I may be filled with joy. 5 I am reminded of your sincere faith, a faith that dwelt first in your grandmother Lō′ĭs and your mother Eunice and now, I am sure, dwells in you. 6 Hence I remind you to rekindle the gift of God that is within you through the laying on of my hands; 7 for God did not give us a spirit of timidity but a spirit of power and love and self-control.

8 Do not be ashamed then of testifying to our Lord, nor of me his prisoner, but take your share of suffering for the gospel in the power of God, 9 who saved us and called us with a

holy calling, not in virtue of our works but in virtue of his own purpose and the grace which he gave us in Christ Jesus ages ago, 10 and now has manifested through the appearing of our Savior Christ Jesus, who abolished death and brought life and immortality to light through the gospel. 11 For this gospel I was appointed a preacher and apostle and teacher, 12 and therefore I suffer as I do. But I am not ashamed, for I know whom I have believed, and I am sure that he is able to guard until that Day what has been entrusted to me.*a* 13 Follow the pattern of the sound words which you have heard from me, in the faith and love which are in Christ Jesus; 14 guard the truth that has been entrusted to you by the Holy Spirit who dwells within us.

15 You are aware that all who are in Asia turned away from me, and among them Phy̆′gĕ·lus and Hĕr·mŏg′-ė·nĕs. 16 May the Lord grant mercy to the household of Ŏn·ė·siph′ō·rŭs, for he often refreshed me; he was not ashamed of my chains, 17 but when he arrived in Rome he searched for me eagerly and found me— 18 may the

a Or what I have entrusted to him
6.13: Jn 18.37.   **1.5:** Acts 16.1.

Lord grant him to find mercy from the Lord on that Day—and you well know all the service he rendered at Eph′e·sus.

2 You then, my son, be strong in the grace that is in Christ Jesus, ² and what you have heard from me before many witnesses entrust to faithful men who will be able to teach others also. ³ Take your share of suffering as a good soldier of Christ Jesus. ⁴ No soldier on service gets entangled in civilian pursuits, since his aim is to satisfy the one who enlisted him. ⁵An athlete is not crowned unless he competes according to the rules. ⁶ It is the hard-working farmer who ought to have the first share of the crops. ⁷ Think over what I say, for the Lord will grant you understanding in everything.

8 Remember Jesus Christ, risen from the dead, descended from David, as preached in my gospel, ⁹ the gospel for which I am suffering and wearing fetters like a criminal. But the word of God is not fettered. ¹⁰ Therefore I endure everything for the sake of the elect, that they also may obtain the salvation which in Christ Jesus goes with eternal glory. ¹¹ The saying is sure:

If we have died with him, we shall
    also live with him;
¹² if we endure, we shall also reign
    with him;
if we deny him, he also will deny us,
¹³ if we are faithless, he remains
    faithful—
for he cannot deny himself.

14 Remind them of this, and charge them before the Lord[b] to avoid disputing about words, which does no good, but only ruins the hearers. ¹⁵ Do your best to present yourself to God as one approved, a workman who has no need to be ashamed, rightly handling the word of truth. ¹⁶Avoid such godless chatter, for it will lead people into more and more ungodliness, ¹⁷ and their talk will eat its way like gangrene. Among them are Hy·me·nae′us and Phi·le′tus, ¹⁸ who have swerved from the truth by holding that the resurrection is past already. They are upsetting the faith of some. ¹⁹ But God's firm foundation stands, bearing this seal: "The Lord knows those who are his," and, "Let every one who names the name of the Lord depart from iniquity."

20 In a great house there are not only vessels of gold and silver but also of wood and earthenware, and some for noble use, some for ignoble. ²¹ If any

one purifies himself from what is ignoble, then he will be a vessel for noble use, consecrated and useful to the master of the house, ready for any good work. ²² So shun youthful passions and aim at righteousness, faith, love, and peace, along with those who call upon the Lord from a pure heart. ²³ Have nothing to do with stupid, senseless controversies; you know that they breed quarrels. ²⁴And the Lord's servant must not be quarrelsome but kindly to every one, an apt teacher, forbearing, ²⁵ correcting his opponents with gentleness. God may perhaps grant that they will repent and come to know the truth, ²⁶ and they may escape from the snare of the devil, after being captured by him to do his will.[c]

3 But understand this, that in the last days there will come times of stress. ² For men will be lovers of self, lovers of money, proud, arrogant, abusive, disobedient to their parents, ungrateful, unholy, ³ inhuman, implacable, slanderers, profligates, fierce, haters of good, ⁴ treacherous, reckless, swollen with conceit, lovers of pleasure rather than lovers of God, ⁵ holding the form of religion but denying the power of it. Avoid such people. ⁶ For among them are those who make their way into households and capture weak women, burdened with sins and swayed by various impulses, ⁷ who will listen to anybody and can never arrive at a knowledge of the truth. ⁸As Jan′nes and Jam′bres opposed Moses, so these men also oppose the truth, men of corrupt mind and counterfeit faith; ⁹ but they will not get very far, for their folly will be plain to all, as was that of those two men.

10 Now you have observed my teaching, my conduct, my aim in life, my faith, my patience, my love, my steadfastness, ¹¹ my persecutions, my sufferings, what befell me at An′ti·och, at I·co′ni·um, and at Lys′tra, what persecutions I endured; yet from them all the Lord rescued me. ¹² Indeed all who desire to live a godly life in Christ Jesus will be persecuted, ¹³ while evil men and impostors will go on from bad to worse, deceivers and deceived. ¹⁴ But as for you, continue in what you have learned and have firmly believed, knowing from whom you learned it ¹⁵ and how from childhood you have been acquainted with the sacred writings which are able to instruct you for salvation through faith in Christ Jesus.

---

b Other ancient authorities read *God*   *c* Or *by him, to do his* (that is, God's) *will*
2.19: Num 16.5; Is 26.13.   **3.8:** Ex 7.11.   **3.11:** Acts 13.14-52; 14.1-20; 16.1-5.

16 All scripture is inspired by God and[d] profitable for teaching, for reproof, for correction, and for training in righteousness, 17 that the man of God may be complete, equipped for every good work.

4 I charge you in the presence of God and of Christ Jesus who is to judge the living and the dead, and by his appearing and his kingdom: 2 preach the word, be urgent in season and out of season, convince, rebuke, and exhort, be unfailing in patience and in teaching. 3 For the time is coming when people will not endure sound teaching, but having itching ears they will accumulate for themselves teachers to suit their own likings, 4 and will turn away from listening to the truth and wander into myths. 5 As for you, always be steady, endure suffering, do the work of an evangelist, fulfil your ministry.

6 For I am already on the point of being sacrificed; the time of my departure has come. 7 I have fought the good fight, I have finished the race, I have kept the faith. 8 Henceforth there is laid up for me the crown of righteousness, which the Lord, the righteous judge, will award to me on that Day, and not only to me but also to all who have loved his appearing.

9 Do your best to come to me soon. 10 For Dē'mas, in love with this present world, has deserted me and gone to Thes·sà·lò·ni'cà; Cres'cens has gone to Galatia,[e] Titus to Dalmatia. 11 Luke alone is with me. Get Mark and bring him with you; for he is very useful in serving me. 12 Tych'i·cùs I have sent to Eph'é·sùs. 13 When you come, bring the cloak that I left with Cär'pùs at Trō'as, also the books, and above all the parchments. 14 Alexander the coppersmith did me great harm; the Lord will requite him for his deeds. 15 Beware of him yourself, for he strongly opposed our message. 16 At my first defense no one took my part; all deserted me. May it not be charged against them! 17 But the Lord stood by me and gave me strength to proclaim the word fully, that all the Gentiles might hear it. So I was rescued from the lion's mouth. 18 The Lord will rescue me from every evil and save me for his heavenly kingdom. To him be the glory for ever and ever. Amen.

19 Greet Pris'cà and Aq'ui·là, and the household of On·é·siph'ō·rùs. 20 E·ras'tùs remained at Corinth; Troph'i·mùs I left ill at Mī·lē'tùs. 21 Do your best to come before winter. Eu·bū'lùs sends greetings to you, as do Pū'dens and Lī'nùs and Claudia and all the brethren.

22 The Lord be with your spirit. Grace be with you.

THE LETTER OF PAUL TO

TITUS

1 Paul, a servant[a] of God and an apostle of Jesus Christ, to further the faith of God's elect and their knowledge of the truth which accords with godliness, 2 in hope of eternal life which God, who never lies, promised ages ago 3 and at the proper time manifested in his word through the preaching with which I have been entrusted by command of God our Savior;

4 To Titus, my true child in a common faith:

Grace and peace from God the Father and Christ Jesus our Savior.

5 This is why I left you in Crete, that you might amend what was defective, and appoint elders in every town as I directed you, 6 if any man is blameless, the husband of one wife, and his children are believers and not open to the charge of being profligate or insubordinate. 7 For a bishop, as God's steward, must be blameless; he must not be arrogant or quick-tempered or a drunkard or violent or greedy for gain, 8 but hospitable, a lover of goodness, master of himself, upright, holy, and self-controlled; 9 he must hold firm to the sure word as taught, so that he may be able to give instruction in sound doctrine and also

[d] Or *Every scripture inspired by God is also*
[a] Or *slave*
[e] Other ancient authorities read *Gaul*

to confute those who contradict it. [10] For there are many insubordinate men, empty talkers and deceivers, especially the circumcision party; [11] they must be silenced, since they are upsetting whole families by teaching for base gain what they have no right to teach. [12] One of themselves, a prophet of their own, said, "Cretans are always liars, evil beasts, lazy gluttons." [13] This testimony is true. Therefore rebuke them sharply, that they may be sound in the faith, [14] instead of giving heed to Jewish myths or to commands of men who reject the truth. [15] To the pure all things are pure, but to the corrupt and unbelieving nothing is pure; their very minds and consciences are corrupted. [16] They profess to know God, but they deny him by their deeds; they are detestable, disobedient, unfit for any good deed.

2 But as for you, teach what befits sound doctrine. [2] Bid the older men be temperate, serious, sensible, sound in faith, in love, and in steadfastness. [3] Bid the older women likewise to be reverent in behavior, not to be slanderers or slaves to drink; they are to teach what is good, [4] and so train the young women to love their husbands and children, [5] to be sensible, chaste, domestic, kind, and submissive to their husbands, that the word of God may not be discredited. [6] Likewise urge the younger men to control themselves. [7] Show yourself in all respects a model of good deeds, and in your teaching show integrity, gravity, [8] and sound speech that cannot be censured, so that an opponent may be put to shame, having nothing evil to say of us. [9] Bid slaves to be submissive to their masters and to give satisfaction in every respect; they are not to be refractory, [10] nor to pilfer, but to show entire and true fidelity, so that in everything they may adorn the doctrine of God our Savior.

[11] For the grace of God has appeared for the salvation of all men, [12] training us to renounce irreligion and worldly passions, and to live sober, upright, and godly lives in this world, [13] awaiting our blessed hope, the appearing of the glory of our great God and Savior[c] Jesus Christ, [14] who gave

himself for us to redeem us from all iniquity and to purify for himself a people of his own who are zealous for good deeds.

[15] Declare these things; exhort and reprove with all authority. Let no one disregard you.

3 Remind them to be submissive to rulers and authorities, to be obedient, to be ready for any honest work, [2] to speak evil of no one, to avoid quarreling, to be gentle, and to show perfect courtesy toward all men. [3] For we ourselves were once foolish, disobedient, led astray, slaves to various passions and pleasures, passing our days in malice and envy, hated by men and hating one another; [4] but when the goodness and loving kindness of God our Savior appeared, [5] he saved us, not because of deeds done by us in righteousness, but in virtue of his own mercy, by the washing of regeneration and renewal in the Holy Spirit, [6] which he poured out upon us richly through Jesus Christ our Savior, [7] so that we might be justified by his grace and become heirs in hope of eternal life. [8] The saying is sure.

I desire you to insist on these things, so that those who have believed in God may be careful to apply themselves to good deeds;[d] these are excellent and profitable to men. [9] But avoid stupid controversies, genealogies, dissensions, and quarrels over the law, for they are unprofitable and futile. [10] As for a man who is factious, after admonishing him once or twice, have nothing more to do with him, [11] knowing that such a person is perverted and sinful; he is self-condemned.

[12] When I send Ar′te·mas or Tych′i·cus to you, do your best to come to me at Ni·cop′o·lis, for I have decided to spend the winter there. [13] Do your best to speed Ze′nas the lawyer and A·pol′los on their way; see that they lack nothing. [14] And let our people learn to apply themselves to good deeds,[d] so as to help cases of urgent need, and not to be unfruitful.

[15] All who are with me send greetings to you. Greet those who love us in the faith.

Grace be with you all.

---

c Or *of the great God and our Savior*   *d* Or *enter honorable occupations*
1.12: Epimenides   **2.14:** Ps 130.8; Ezek 37.23; Deut 14.2.

THE LETTER OF PAUL TO

PHILEMON

1 Paul, a prisoner for Christ Jesus, and Timothy our brother,

To Phi·lē'mŏn our beloved fellow worker 2 and Ap'phi·à our sister and Är·chip'pŭs our fellow soldier, and the church in your house:

3 Grace to you and peace from God our Father and the Lord Jesus Christ.

4 I thank my God always when I remember you in my prayers, 5 because I hear of your love and of the faith which you have toward the Lord Jesus and all the saints, 6 and I pray that the sharing of your faith may promote the knowledge of all the good that is ours in Christ. 7 For I have derived much joy and comfort from your love, my brother, because the hearts of the saints have been refreshed through you.

8 Accordingly, though I am bold enough in Christ to command you to do what is required, 9 yet for love's sake I prefer to appeal to you—I, Paul, an ambassador*a* and now a prisoner also for Christ Jesus— 10 I appeal to you for my child, Ō·nes'ĭ·mŭs, whose father I have become in my imprisonment. 11 (Formerly he was useless to you, but now he is indeed useful*b* to you and to me.) 12 I am sending him back to you, sending my very heart. 13 I would have been glad to keep him with me, in order that he might serve me on your behalf during my imprisonment for the gospel; 14 but I preferred to do nothing without your consent in order that your goodness might not be by compulsion but of your own free will.

15 Perhaps this is why he was parted from you for a while, that you might have him back for ever, 16 no longer as a slave but more than a slave, as a beloved brother, especially to me but how much more to you, both in the flesh and in the Lord. 17 So if you consider me your partner, receive him as you would receive me. 18 If he has wronged you at all, or owes you anything, charge that to my account. 19 I, Paul, write this with my own hand, I will repay it—to say nothing of your owing me even your own self. 20 Yes, brother, I want some benefit from you in the Lord. Refresh my heart in Christ.

21 Confident of your obedience, I write to you, knowing that you will do even more than I say. 22 At the same time, prepare a guest room for me, for I am hoping through your prayers to be granted to you.

23 Ep'à·phras, my fellow prisoner in Christ Jesus, sends greetings to you, 24 and so do Mark, Ar·ĭs·tär'chŭs, Dē'màs, and Luke, my fellow workers.

25 The grace of the Lord Jesus Christ be with your spirit.

THE LETTER TO THE

HEBREWS

In many and various ways God spoke of old to our fathers by the prophets; 2 but in these last days he has spoken to us by a Son, whom he appointed the heir of all things, through whom also he created the world. 3 He reflects the glory of God and bears the very stamp of his nature, upholding the universe by his word of power. When he had made purification for sins, he sat down at the right hand of the Majesty on high, 4 having be-

a Or *an old man* *b* The name Onesimus means *useful* or (compare verse 20) *beneficial*
3: Rom 1.7. 4: Rom 1.8. 10: Col 4.9. 23: Col 1.7; 4.12.
24: Col 4.10, 14.

come as much superior to angels as the name he has obtained is more excellent than theirs.

5 For to what angel did God ever say,

"Thou art my Son,
today I have begotten thee"?

Or again,

"I will be to him a father,
and he shall be to me a son"?

6 And again, when he brings the first-born into the world, he says,

"Let all God's angels worship him."

7 Of the angels he says,

"Who makes his angels winds,
and his servants flames of fire."

8 But of the Son he says,

"Thy throne, O God,[a] is for ever and ever,
the righteous scepter is the scepter of thy[b] kingdom.

9 Thou hast loved righteousness and hated lawlessness;
therefore God, thy God, has anointed thee
with the oil of gladness beyond thy comrades."

10 And,

"Thou, Lord, didst found the earth in the beginning,
and the heavens are the work of thy hands;

11 they will perish, but thou remainest;
they will all grow old like a garment,

12 like a mantle thou wilt roll them up,
and they will be changed.[c]
But thou art the same,
and thy years will never end."

13 But to what angel has he ever said,

"Sit at my right hand,
till I make thy enemies
a stool for thy feet"?

14 Are they not all ministering spirits sent forth to serve, for the sake of those who are to obtain salvation?

2 Therefore we must pay the closer attention to what we have heard, lest we drift away from it. 2 For if the message declared by angels was valid and every transgression or disobedience received a just retribution, 3 how shall we escape if we neglect such a great salvation? It was declared at first by the Lord, and it was attested to us by those who heard him, 4 while God also bore witness by signs and wonders and various miracles and by gifts of the Holy Spirit distributed according to his own will.

5 For it was not to angels that God subjected the world to come, of which we are speaking. 6 It has been testified somewhere,

"What is man that thou art mindful of him,
or the son of man, that thou carest for him?

7 Thou didst make him for a little while lower than the angels,
thou hast crowned him with glory and honor,[d]

8 putting everything in subjection under his feet."

Now in putting everything in subjection to him, he left nothing outside his control. As it is, we do not yet see everything in subjection to him. 9 But we see Jesus, who for a little while was made lower than the angels, crowned with glory and honor because of the suffering of death, so that by the grace of God he might taste death for every one.

10 For it was fitting that he, for whom and by whom all things exist, in bringing many sons to glory, should make the pioneer of their salvation perfect through suffering. 11 For he who sanctifies and those who are sanctified have all one origin. That is why he is not ashamed to call them brethren, 12 saying,

"I will proclaim thy name to my brethren,
in the midst of the congregation I will praise thee."

13 And again,

"I will put my trust in him."

And again,

"Here am I, and the children God has given me."

14 Since therefore the children share in flesh and blood, he himself likewise partook of the same nature, that through death he might destroy him who has the power of death, that is, the devil, 15 and deliver all those who through fear of death were subject to lifelong bondage. 16 For surely it is not with angels that he is concerned but with the descendants of Abraham. 17 Therefore he had to be made like his brethren in every respect, so that he might become a merciful and faithful high priest in the service of God, to make expiation for the sins of the people. 18 For because he himself has suffered and been tempted, he is able to help those who are tempted.

a Or God is thy throne   b Other ancient authorities read his
c Other ancient authorities add like a garment
d Other ancient authorities insert and didst set him over the works of thy hands
1.5: Ps 2.7; 2 Sam 7.14.   1.6: Deut 32.43 (Gk.); Ps 97.7.   1.7: Ps 104.4.
1.8-9: Ps 45.6-7.   1.10-12: Ps 102.25-27.   1.13: Ps 110.1.   2.6-9: Ps 8.4-6.
2.12: Ps 22.22.   2.13: Is 8.17-18.   2.16: Is 41.8-9.

3 Therefore, holy brethren, who share in a heavenly call, consider Jesus, the apostle and high priest of our confession. ² He was faithful to him who appointed him, just as Moses also was faithful in*ᵉ* God's house. ³ Yet Jesus has been counted worthy of as much more glory than Moses as the builder of a house has more honor than the house. ⁴ (For every house is built by some one, but the builder of all things is God.) ⁵ Now Moses was faithful in all God's house as a servant, to testify to the things that were to be spoken later, ⁶ but Christ was faithful over God's*ᶠ* house as a son. And we are his house if we hold fast our confidence and pride in our hope.*ᵍ*

7 Therefore, as the Holy Spirit says,
"Today, when you hear his voice,
8 do not harden your hearts as in the
　rebellion,
　on the day of testing in the wilder-
　ness,
9 where your fathers put me to the
　test
　and saw my works for forty years.
10 Therefore I was provoked with that
　generation,
　and said, 'They always go astray in
　their hearts;
　they have not known my ways.'
11 As I swore in my wrath,
　'They shall never enter my rest.'"

¹² Take care, brethren, lest there be in any of you an evil, unbelieving heart, leading you to fall away from the living God. ¹³ But exhort one another every day, as long as it is called "today," that none of you may be hardened by the deceitfulness of sin. ¹⁴ For we share in Christ, if only we hold our first confidence firm to the end, ¹⁵ while it is said,

"Today, when you hear his voice,
　do not harden your hearts
　as in the rebellion."

¹⁶ Who were they that heard and yet were rebellious? Was it not all those who left Egypt under the leadership of Moses? ¹⁷And with whom was he provoked forty years? Was it not with those who sinned, whose bodies fell in the wilderness? ¹⁸And to whom did he swear that they should never enter his rest, but to those who were disobedient? ¹⁹ So we see that they were unable to enter because of unbelief.

4 Therefore, while the promise of entering his rest remains, let us fear lest any of you be judged to have failed to reach it. ² For good news came to us just as to them; but the message which they heard did not benefit them, because it did not meet with faith in the hearers.*ʰ* ³ For we who have believed enter that rest, as he has said,

"As I swore in my wrath,
'They shall never enter my rest,'"

although his works were finished from the foundation of the world. ⁴ For he has somewhere spoken of the seventh day in this way, "And God rested on the seventh day from all his works." ⁵And again in this place he said,

"They shall never enter my rest."

⁶ Since therefore it remains for some to enter it, and those who formerly received the good news failed to enter because of disobedience, ⁷ again he sets a certain day, "Today," saying through David so long afterward, in the words already quoted,

"Today, when you hear his voice,
　do not harden your hearts."

⁸ For if Joshua had given them rest, God*ⁱ* would not speak later of another day. ⁹ So then, there remains a sabbath rest for the people of God; ¹⁰ for whoever enters God's rest also ceases from his labors as God did from his.

11 Let us therefore strive to enter that rest, that no one fall by the same sort of disobedience. ¹² For the word of God is living and active, sharper than any two-edged sword, piercing to the division of soul and spirit, of joints and marrow, and discerning the thoughts and intentions of the heart. ¹³And before him no creature is hidden, but all are open and laid bare to the eyes of him with whom we have to do.

14 Since then we have a great high priest who has passed through the heavens, Jesus, the Son of God, let us hold fast our confession. ¹⁵ For we have not a high priest who is unable to sympathize with our weaknesses, but one who in every respect has been tempted as we are, yet without sinning. ¹⁶ Let us then with confidence draw near to the throne of grace, that we may receive mercy and find grace to help in time of need.

5 For every high priest chosen from among men is appointed to act on behalf of men in relation to God, to

---

ᵉ Other ancient authorities insert *all*　*ᶠ* Greek *his*
ᵍ Other ancient authorities insert *firm to the end*
ʰ Other manuscripts read *they were not united in faith with the hearers*　*ⁱ* Greek *he*
3.2: Num 12.7.　**3.5:** Num 12.7.　**3.7-11:** Ps 95.7-11.　**3.15:** Ps 95.7-8.
3.16-19: Num 14.1-35.　**3.17:** Num 14.29.　**4.3:** Ps 95.11.　**4.4:** Gen 2.2.
4.5: Ps 95.11.　**4.7:** Ps 95.7-8.　**4.10:** Gen 2.2.

offer gifts and sacrifices for sins. 2 He can deal gently with the ignorant and wayward, since he himself is beset with weakness. 3 Because of this he is bound to offer sacrifice for his own sins as well as for those of the people. 4And one does not take the honor upon himself, but he is called by God, just as Aaron was.

5 So also Christ did not exalt himself to be made a high priest, but was appointed by him who said to him,

"Thou art my Son,
today I have begotten thee";

6 as he says also in another place,

"Thou art a priest for ever,
after the order of Mel·chiz′e·dek."

7 In the days of his flesh, Jesus[i] offered up prayers and supplications, with loud cries and tears, to him who was able to save him from death, and he was heard for his godly fear. 8Although he was a Son, he learned obedience through what he suffered; 9 and being made perfect he became the source of eternal salvation to all who obey him, 10 being designated by God a high priest after the order of Mel·chiz′e·dek.

11 About this we have much to say which is hard to explain, since you have become dull of hearing. 12 For though by this time you ought to be teachers, you need some one to teach you again the first principles of God's word. You need milk, not solid food; 13 for every one who lives on milk is unskilled in the word of righteousness, for he is a child. 14 But solid food is for the mature, for those who have their faculties trained by practice to distinguish good from evil.

6 Therefore let us leave the elementary doctrines of Christ and go on to maturity, not laying again a foundation of repentance from dead works and of faith toward God, 2 with instruction[k] about ablutions, the laying on of hands, the resurrection of the dead, and eternal judgment. 3And this we will do if God permits.[l] 4 For it is impossible to restore again to repentance those who have once been enlightened, who have tasted the heavenly gift, and have become partakers of the Holy Spirit, 5 and have tasted the goodness of the word of God and the powers of the age to come, 6 if they then commit apostasy, since

they crucify the Son of God on their own account and hold him up to contempt. 7 For land which has drunk the rain that often falls upon it, and brings forth vegetation useful to those for whose sake it is cultivated, receives a blessing from God. 8 But if it bears thorns and thistles, it is worthless and near to being cursed; its end is to be burned.

9 Though we speak thus, yet in your case, beloved, we feel sure of better things that belong to salvation. 10 For God is not so unjust as to overlook your work and the love which you showed for his sake in serving the saints, as you still do. 11And we desire each one of you to show the same earnestness in realizing the full assurance of hope until the end, 12 so that you may not be sluggish, but imitators of those who through faith and patience inherit the promises.

13 For when God made a promise to Abraham, since he had no one greater by whom to swear, he swore by himself, 14 saying, "Surely I will bless you and multiply you." 15And thus Abraham,[m] having patiently endured, obtained the promise. 16 Men indeed swear by a greater than themselves, and in all their disputes an oath is final for confirmation. 17 So when God desired to show more convincingly to the heirs of the promise the unchangeable character of his purpose, he interposed with an oath, 18 so that through two unchangeable things, in which it is impossible that God should prove false, we who have fled for refuge might have strong encouragement to seize the hope set before us. 19 We have this as a sure and steadfast anchor of the soul, a hope that enters into the inner shrine behind the curtain, 20 where Jesus has gone as a forerunner on our behalf, having become a high priest for ever after the order of Mel·chiz′e·dek.

7 For this Mel·chiz′e·dek, king of Salem, priest of the Most High God, met Abraham returning from the slaughter of the kings and blessed him; 2 and to him Abraham apportioned a tenth part of everything. He is first, by translation of his name, king of righteousness, and then he is also king of Salem, that is, king of peace. 3 He is without father or mother or genealogy, and has neither beginning

i Greek he k Other ancient manuscripts read of instruction
l Other ancient manuscripts read let us do this if God permits m Greek he
5.5: Ps 2.7. 5.6: Ps 110.4. 5.7: Mt 26.36-46; Mk 14.32-42; Lk 22.40-46.
5.9: Is 45.17. 5.10: Ps 110.4. 6.8: Gen 3.17-18. 6.13-14: Gen 22.16-17.
6.19: Lev 16.2. 6.20: Ps 110.4. 7.1-10: Gen 14.17-20.

of days nor end of life, but resembling the Son of God he continues a priest for ever.

4 See how great he is! Abraham the patriarch gave him a tithe of the spoils. 5And those descendants of Levi who receive the priestly office have a commandment in the law to take tithes from the people, that is, from their brethren, though these also are descended from Abraham. 6 But this man who has not their genealogy received tithes from Abraham and blessed him who had the promises. 7 It is beyond dispute that the inferior is blessed by the superior. 8 Here tithes are received by mortal men; there, by one of whom it is testified that he lives. 9 One might even say that Levi himself, who receives tithes, paid tithes through Abraham, 10 for he was still in the loins of his ancestor when Mel·chiz′e·dek met him.

11 Now if perfection had been attainable through the Le·vit′i·cal priesthood (for under it the people received the law), what further need would there have been for another priest to arise after the order of Mel·chiz′e·dek, rather than one named after the order of Aaron? 12 For when there is a change in the priesthood, there is necessarily a change in the law as well. 13 For the one of whom these things are spoken belonged to another tribe, from which no one has ever served at the altar. 14 For it is evident that our Lord was descended from Judah, and in connection with that tribe Moses said nothing about priests.

15 This becomes even more evident when another priest arises in the likeness of Mel·chiz′e·dek, 16 who has become a priest, not according to a legal requirement concerning bodily descent but by the power of an indestructible life. 17 For it is witnessed of him,

"Thou art a priest for ever,
  after the order of Mel·chiz′e·dek."

18 On the one hand, a former commandment is set aside because of its weakness and uselessness 19 (for the law made nothing perfect); on the other hand, a better hope is introduced, through which we draw near to God.

20 And it was not without an oath. 21 Those who formerly became priests took their office without an oath, but this one was addressed with an oath,

"The Lord has sworn
  and will not change his mind,
'Thou art a priest for ever.'"

22 This makes Jesus the surety of a better covenant.

23 The former priests were many in number, because they were prevented by death from continuing in office; 24 but he holds his priesthood permanently, because he continues for ever. 25 Consequently he is able for all time to save those who draw near to God through him, since he always lives to make intercession for them.

26 For it was fitting that we should have such a high priest, holy, blameless, unstained, separated from sinners, exalted above the heavens. 27 He has no need, like those high priests, to offer sacrifices daily, first for his own sins and then for those of the people; he did this once for all when he offered up himself. 28 Indeed, the law appoints men in their weakness as high priests, but the word of the oath, which came later than the law, appoints a Son who has been made perfect for ever.

8 Now the point in what we are saying is this: we have such a high priest, one who is seated at the right hand of the throne of the Majesty in heaven, 2 a minister in the sanctuary and the true tent[n] which is set up not by man but by the Lord. 3 For every high priest is appointed to offer gifts and sacrifices; hence it is necessary for this priest also to have something to offer. 4 Now if he were on earth, he would not be a priest at all, since there are priests who offer gifts according to the law. 5 They serve a copy and shadow of the heavenly sanctuary; for when Moses was about to erect the tent,[n] he was instructed by God, saying, "See that you make everything according to the pattern which was shown you on the mountain." 6 But as it is, Christ[o] has obtained a ministry which is as much more excellent than the old as the covenant he mediates is better, since it is enacted on better promises. 7 For if that first covenant had been faultless, there would have been no occasion for a second.

8 For he finds fault with them when he says:
"The days will come, says the
      Lord,
  when I will establish a new covenant
        with the house of Israel
  and with the house of Judah;
9 not like the covenant that I made
        with their fathers
  on the day when I took them by the
        hand

---

[n] Or *tabernacle*   [o] Greek *he*

7.11, 15, 17, 21, 28: Ps 110.4.   8.1: Ps 110.1.   8.5: Ex 25.40.   8.8-12: Jer 31.31-34.

to lead them out of the land of
Egypt;
for they did not continue in my
covenant,
and so I paid no heed to them, says
the Lord.
10 This is the covenant that I will make
with the house of Israel
after those days, says the Lord:
I will put my laws into their minds,
and write them on their hearts,
and I will be their God,
and they shall be my people.
11 And they shall not teach every one
his fellow
or every one his brother, saying,
'Know the Lord,'
for all shall know me,
from the least of them to the greatest.
12 For I will be merciful toward their
iniquities,
and I will remember their sins no
more."
13 In speaking of a new covenant he
treats the first as obsolete. And what
is becoming obsolete and growing old
is ready to vanish away.

9 Now even the first covenant had
regulations for worship and an
earthly sanctuary. 2 For a tent^p was
prepared, the outer one, in which were
the lampstand and the table and the
bread of the Presence;^{q} it is called the
Holy Place. 3 Behind the second curtain stood a tent^p called the Holy of
Holies, 4 having the golden altar of
incense and the ark of the covenant
covered on all sides with gold, which
contained a golden urn holding the
manna, and Aaron's rod that budded,
and the tables of the covenant; 5 above
it were the cherubim of glory overshadowing the mercy seat. Of these
things we cannot now speak in detail.

6 These preparations having thus
been made, the priests go continually
into the outer tent,^{p} performing their
ritual duties; 7 but into the second only
the high priest goes, and he but once
a year, and not without taking blood
which he offers for himself and for the
errors of the people. 8 By this the Holy
Spirit indicates that the way into the
sanctuary is not yet opened as long
as the outer tent^p is still standing
9 (which is symbolic for the present

age). According to this arrangement,
gifts and sacrifices are offered which
cannot perfect the conscience of the
worshiper, 10 but deal only with food
and drink and various ablutions, regulations for the body imposed until the
time of reformation.

11 But when Christ appeared as a
high priest of the good things that have
come,^{r} then through the greater and
more perfect tent^p (not made with
hands, that is, not of this creation)
12 he entered once for all into the Holy
Place, taking^s not the blood of goats
and calves but his own blood, thus
securing an eternal redemption. 13 For
if the sprinkling of defiled persons with
the blood of goats and bulls and with
the ashes of a heifer sanctifies for the
purification of the flesh, 14 how much
more shall the blood of Christ, who
through the eternal Spirit offered himself without blemish to God, purify
your^t conscience from dead works to
serve the living God.

15 Therefore he is the mediator of
a new covenant, so that those who are
called may receive the promised
eternal inheritance, since a death has
occurred which redeems them from
the transgressions under the first covenant.^{u} 16 For where a will^u is involved,
the death of the one who made it must
be established. 17 For a will^u takes
effect only at death, since it is not in
force as long as the one who made it
is alive. 18 Hence even the first covenant was not ratified without blood.
19 For when every commandment of
the law had been declared by Moses
to all the people, he took the blood of
calves and goats, with water and scarlet
wool and hyssop, and sprinkled both
the book itself and all the people,
20 saying, "This is the blood of the
covenant which God commanded
you." 21 And in the same way he
sprinkled with the blood both the tent^p
and all the vessels used in worship.
22 Indeed, under the law almost everything is purified with blood, and without the shedding of blood there is no
forgiveness of sins.

23 Thus it was necessary for the
copies of the heavenly things to be
purified with these rites, but the

^{p} Or *tabernacle*
^{q} Greek *the presentation of the loaves*
^{r} Other manuscripts read *good things to come*
^{s} Greek *through*
^{t} Other manuscripts read *our*
^{u} The Greek word here used means both *covenant* and *will*

9.1-10: Ex 25.10-40.   **9.2:** Lev 24.5.   **9.3:** Ex 26.31-33.
9.4: Ex 30.1-5; 16.32-33; Num 17.8-10.   **9.7:** Lev 16.
9.13: Lev 16.6, 16; Num 19.9, 17-18.   **9.19-20:** Ex 24.6-8.

heavenly things themselves with better sacrifices than these. 24 For Christ has entered, not into a sanctuary made with hands, a copy of the true one, but into heaven itself, now to appear in the presence of God on our behalf. 25 Nor was it to offer himself repeatedly, as the high priest enters the Holy Place yearly with blood not his own; 26 for then he would have had to suffer repeatedly since the foundation of the world. But as it is, he has appeared once for all at the end of the age to put away sin by the sacrifice of himself. 27And just as it is appointed for men to die once, and after that comes judgment, 28 so Christ, having been offered once to bear the sins of many, will appear a second time, not to deal with sin but to save those who are eagerly waiting for him.

10 For since the law has but a shadow of the good things to come instead of the true form of these realities, it can never, by the same sacrifices which are continually offered year after year, make perfect those who draw near. 2 Otherwise, would they not have ceased to be offered? If the worshipers had once been cleansed, they would no longer have any consciousness of sin. 3 But in these sacrifices there is a reminder of sin year after year. 4 For it is impossible that the blood of bulls and goats should take away sins.

5 Consequently, when Christ*y* came into the world, he said,

"Sacrifices and offerings thou hast not desired,
but a body hast thou prepared for me;
6 in burnt offerings and sin offerings thou hast taken no pleasure.
7 Then I said, 'Lo, I have come to do thy will, O God,'
as it is written of me in the roll of the book."

8 When he said above, "Thou hast neither desired nor taken pleasure in sacrifices and offerings and burnt offerings and sin offerings" (these are offered according to the law), 9 then he added, "Lo, I have come to do thy will." He abolishes the first in order to establish the second. 10And by that will we have been sanctified through the offering of the body of Jesus Christ once for all.

11 And every priest stands daily at his service, offering repeatedly the same sacrifices, which can never take

away sins. 12 But when Christ*w* had offered for all time a single sacrifice for sins, he sat down at the right hand of God, 13 then to wait until his enemies should be made a stool for his feet. 14 For by a single offering he has perfected for all time those who are sanctified. 15And the Holy Spirit also bears witness to us; for after saying,

16 "This is the covenant that I will make with them
after those days, says the Lord:
I will put my laws on their hearts, and write them on their minds,"
17 then he adds,
"I will remember their sins and their misdeeds no more."

18 Where there is forgiveness of these, there is no longer any offering for sin.

19 Therefore, brethren, since we have confidence to enter the sanctuary by the blood of Jesus, 20 by the new and living way which he opened for us through the curtain, that is, through his flesh, 21 and since we have a great priest over the house of God, 22 let us draw near with a true heart in full assurance of faith, with our hearts sprinkled clean from an evil conscience and our bodies washed with pure water. 23 Let us hold fast the confession of our hope without wavering, for he who promised is faithful; 24 and let us consider how to stir up one another to love and good works, 25 not neglecting to meet together, as is the habit of some, but encouraging one another, and all the more as you see the Day drawing near.

26 For if we sin deliberately after receiving the knowledge of the truth, there no longer remains a sacrifice for sins, 27 but a fearful prospect of judgment, and a fury of fire which will consume the adversaries. 28A man who has violated the law of Moses dies without mercy at the testimony of two or three witnesses. 29 How much worse punishment do you think will be deserved by the man who has spurned the Son of God, and profaned the blood of the covenant by which he was sanctified, and outraged the Spirit of grace? 30 For we know him who said, "Vengeance is mine, I will repay." And again, "The Lord will judge his people." 31 It is a fearful thing to fall into the hands of the living God.

32 But recall the former days when, after you were enlightened, you endured a hard struggle with sufferings, 33 sometimes being publicly exposed

y Greek *he*   *w* Greek *this one*
10.5-9: Ps 40.6-8.   10.12-13: Ps 110.1.   10.16-17: Jer 31.33-34.
10.27: Is 26.11.   10.28: Deut 17.2-6.   10.29: Ex 24.8.   10.30: Deut 32.35-36.

to abuse and affliction, and sometimes being partners with those so treated. 34 For you had compassion on the prisoners, and you joyfully accepted the plundering of your property, since you knew that you yourselves had a better possession and an abiding one. 35 Therefore do not throw away your confidence, which has a great reward. 36 For you have need of endurance, so that you may do the will of God and receive what is promised. 37 "For yet a little while,

and the coming one shall come and shall not tarry;
38 but my righteous one shall live by faith,

and if he shrinks back,
my soul has no pleasure in him."
39 But we are not of those who shrink back and are destroyed, but of those who have faith and keep their souls.

II Now faith is the assurance of things hoped for, the conviction of things not seen. 2 For by it the men of old received divine approval. 3 By faith we understand that the world was created by the word of God, so that what is seen was made out of things which do not appear.

4 By faith Abel offered to God a more acceptable sacrifice than Cain, through which he received approval as righteous, God bearing witness by accepting his gifts; he died, but through his faith he is still speaking. 5 By faith E'noch was taken up so that he should not see death; and he was not found, because God had taken him. Now before he was taken he was attested as having pleased God. 6And without faith it is impossible to please him. For whoever would draw near to God must believe that he exists and that he rewards those who seek him. 7 By faith Noah, being warned by God concerning events as yet unseen, took heed and constructed an ark for the saving of his household; by this he condemned the world and became an heir of the righteousness which comes by faith.

8 By faith Abraham obeyed when he was called to go out to a place which he was to receive as an inheritance; and he went out, not knowing where he was to go. 9 By faith he sojourned in the land of promise, as in a foreign land, living in tents with Isaac and Jacob, heirs with him of the same promise. 10 For he looked forward to the city which has foundations, whose builder and maker is God. 11 By faith Sarah herself received power to conceive, even when she was past the age, since she considered him faithful who had promised. 12 Therefore from one man, and him as good as dead, were born descendants as many as the stars of heaven and as the innumerable grains of sand by the seashore.

13 These all died in faith, not having received what was promised, but having seen it and greeted it from afar, and having acknowledged that they were strangers and exiles on the earth. 14 For people who speak thus make it clear that they are seeking a homeland. 15 If they had been thinking of that land from which they had gone out, they would have had opportunity to return. 16 But as it is, they desire a better country, that is, a heavenly one. Therefore God is not ashamed to be called their God, for he has prepared for them a city.

17 By faith Abraham, when he was tested, offered up Isaac, and he who had received the promises was ready to offer up his only son, 18 of whom it was said, "Through Isaac shall your descendants be named." 19 He considered that God was able to raise men even from the dead; hence, figuratively speaking, he did receive him back. 20 By faith Isaac invoked future blessings on Jacob and Esau. 21 By faith Jacob, when dying, blessed each of the sons of Joseph, bowing in worship over the head of his staff. 22 By faith Joseph, at the end of his life, made mention of the exodus of the Israelites and gave directions concerning his burial.x

23 By faith Moses, when he was born, was hid for three months by his parents, because they saw that the child was beautiful; and they were not afraid of the king's edict. 24 By faith Moses, when he was grown up, refused to be called the son of Pharaoh's daughter, 25 choosing rather to share ill-treatment with the people of God than to enjoy the fleeting pleasures of sin. 26 He considered abuse suffered

x Greek bones
10.37: Is 26.20 (Gk.).   10.37-38: Hab 2.3-4.   11.4: Gen 4.3-10.   11.5: Gen 5.21-24.
11.7: Gen 6.13-22.   11.8-9: Gen 12.1-8.   11.11: Gen 17.19; 18.11-14; 21.2.
11.12: Gen 15.5-6; 22.17; 32.12.   11.13: Ps 39.12; Gen 23.4.   11.16: Ex 3.6, 15; 4.5.
11.17: Gen 22.1-10.   11.18: Gen 21.12.   11.20: Gen 27.27-29, 39-40.
11.21: Gen 48; 47.31 (Gk.).   11.22: Gen 50.24-25; Ex 13.19.   11.23: Ex 2.2; 1.22.
11.24: Ex 2.10, 11-15.

for the Christ greater wealth than the treasures of Egypt, for he looked to the reward. 27 By faith he left Egypt, not being afraid of the anger of the king; for he endured as seeing him who is invisible. 28 By faith he kept the Passover and sprinkled the blood, so that the Destroyer of the first-born might not touch them.

29 By faith the people crossed the Red Sea as if on dry land; but the Egyptians, when they attempted to do the same, were drowned. 30 By faith the walls of Jericho fell down after they had been encircled for seven days. 31 By faith Rā′hab the harlot did not perish with those who were disobedient, because she had given friendly welcome to the spies.

32 And what more shall I say? For time would fail me to tell of Gideon, Bâr′ák, Samson, Jeph′thàh, of David and Samuel and the prophets— 33 who through faith conquered kingdoms, enforced justice, received promises, stopped the mouths of lions, 34 quenched raging fire, escaped the edge of the sword, won strength out of weakness, became mighty in war, put foreign armies to flight. 35 Women received their dead by resurrection. Some were tortured, refusing to accept release, that they might rise again to a better life. 36 Others suffered mocking and scourging, and even chains and imprisonment. 37 They were stoned, they were sawn in two,y they were killed with the sword; they went about in skins of sheep and goats, destitute, afflicted, ill-treated— 38 of whom the world was not worthy—wandering over deserts and mountains, and in dens and caves of the earth.

39 And all these, though well attested by their faith, did not receive what was promised, 40 since God had foreseen something better for us, that apart from us they should not be made perfect.

12 Therefore, since we are surrounded by so great a cloud of witnesses, let us also lay aside every weight, and sin which clings so closely, and let us run with perseverance the race that is set before us, 2 looking to Jesus the pioneer and perfecter of our faith, who for the joy that was set before him endured the cross, despising the shame, and is seated at the right hand of the throne of God.

3 Consider him who endured from sinners such hostility against himself, so that you may not grow weary or fainthearted. 4 In your struggle against sin you have not yet resisted to the point of shedding your blood. 5And have you forgotten the exhortation which addresses you as sons?—

"My son, do not regard lightly the
   discipline of the Lord,
nor lose courage when you are
   punished by him.
6 For the Lord disciplines him whom
   he loves,
and chastises every son whom he
   receives."

7 It is for discipline that you have to endure. God is treating you as sons; for what son is there whom his father does not discipline? 8 If you are left without discipline, in which all have participated, then you are illegitimate children and not sons. 9 Besides this, we have had earthly fathers to discipline us and we respected them. Shall we not much more be subject to the Father of spirits and live? 10 For they disciplined us for a short time at their pleasure, but he disciplines us for our good, that we may share his holiness. 11 For the moment all discipline seems painful rather than pleasant; later it yields the peaceful fruit of righteousness to those who have been trained by it.

12 Therefore lift your drooping hands and strengthen your weak knees, 13 and make straight paths for your feet, so that what is lame may not be put out of joint but rather be healed. 14 Strive for peace with all men, and for the holiness without which no one will see the Lord. 15 See to it that no one fail to obtain the grace of God; that no "root of bitterness" spring up and cause trouble, and by it the many become defiled; 16 that no one be immoral or irreligious like Esau, who sold his birthright for a single meal. 17 For you know that afterward, when he desired to inherit the blessing, he was rejected, for he found no chance to repent, though he sought it with tears.

y Other manuscripts add *they were tempted*

11.27: Ex 2.15. 11.28: Ex 12.21-28, 29-30. 11.29: Ex 14.21-31.
11.30: Josh 6.12-21. 11.31: Josh 2.1-21; 6.22-25.
11.32: Judg 6-8; 4-5; 13-16; 11-12; 1 Sam 16-30; 2 Sam 1-24; 1 Kings 1-2.11; 1 Sam 1-12; 15; 16.1-13. 11.33: Dan 6. 11.34: Dan 3.
11.35: 1 Kings 17.17-24; 2 Kings 4.25-37. 12.2: Ps 110.1. 12.5-8: Prov 3.11-12.
12.12: Is 35.3. 12.13: Prov 4.26 (Gk.). 12.15: Deut 29.18 (Gk.).
12.16: Gen 25.29-34. 12.17: Gen 27.30-40.

18 For you have not come to what may be touched, a blazing fire, and darkness, and gloom, and a tempest, 19 and the sound of a trumpet, and a voice whose words made the hearers entreat that no further messages be spoken to them. 20 For they could not endure the order that was given, "If even a beast touches the mountain, it shall be stoned." 21 Indeed, so terrifying was the sight that Moses said, "I tremble with fear." 22 But you have come to Mount Zion and to the city of the living God, the heavenly Jerusalem, and to innumerable angels in festal gathering, 23 and to the assembly^z of the first-born who are enrolled in heaven, and to a judge who is God of all, and to the spirits of just men made perfect, 24 and to Jesus, the mediator of a new covenant, and to the sprinkled blood that speaks more graciously than the blood of Abel.

25 See that you do not refuse him who is speaking. For if they did not escape when they refused him who warned them on earth, much less shall we escape if we reject him who warns from heaven. 26 His voice then shook the earth; but now he has promised, "Yet once more I will shake not only the earth but also the heaven." 27 This phrase, "Yet once more," indicates the removal of what is shaken, as of what has been made, in order that what cannot be shaken may remain. 28 Therefore let us be grateful for receiving a kingdom that cannot be shaken, and thus let us offer to God acceptable worship, with reverence and awe; 29 for our God is a consuming fire.

13 Let brotherly love continue. 2 Do not neglect to show hospitality to strangers, for thereby some have entertained angels unawares. 3 Remember those who are in prison, as though in prison with them; and those who are ill-treated, since you also are in the body. 4 Let marriage be held in honor among all, and let the marriage bed be undefiled; for God will judge the immoral and adulterous. 5 Keep your life free from love of money, and be content with what you have; for he has said, "I will never fail you nor forsake you." 6 Hence we can confidently say,

"The Lord is my helper,
I will not be afraid;
what can man do to me?"

7 Remember your leaders, those who spoke to you the word of God; consider the outcome of their life, and imitate their faith. 8 Jesus Christ is the same yesterday and today and for ever. 9 Do not be led away by diverse and strange teachings; for it is well that the heart be strengthened by grace, not by foods, which have not benefited their adherents. 10 We have an altar from which those who serve the tent^a have no right to eat. 11 For the bodies of those animals whose blood is brought into the sanctuary by the high priest as a sacrifice for sin are burned outside the camp. 12 So Jesus also suffered outside the gate in order to sanctify the people through his own blood. 13 Therefore let us go forth to him outside the camp, bearing abuse for him. 14 For here we have no lasting city, but we seek the city which is to come. 15 Through him then let us continually offer up a sacrifice of praise to God, that is, the fruit of lips that acknowledge his name. 16 Do not neglect to do good and to share what you have, for such sacrifices are pleasing to God.

17 Obey your leaders and submit to them; for they are keeping watch over your souls, as men who will have to give account. Let them do this joyfully, and not sadly, for that would be of no advantage to you.

18 Pray for us, for we are sure that we have a clear conscience, desiring to act honorably in all things. 19 I urge you the more earnestly to do this in order that I may be restored to you the sooner.

20 Now may the God of peace who brought again from the dead our Lord Jesus, the great shepherd of the sheep, by the blood of the eternal covenant, 21 equip you with everything good that you may do his will, working in you^b that which is pleasing in his sight, through Jesus Christ; to whom be glory for ever and ever. Amen.

22 I appeal to you, brethren, bear with my word of exhortation, for I have written to you briefly. 23 You should understand that our brother

z Or *angels, and to the festal gathering and assembly*   a Or *tabernacle*
b Other ancient authorities read *us*

12.18-19: Ex 19.12-22; 20.18-21; Deut 4.11-12; 5.22-27. **12.20:** Ex 19.12-13.
12.21: Deut 9.19. **12.24:** Gen 4.10. **12.25:** Ex 20.19. **12.26:** Hag 2.6.
12.29: Deut 4.24. **13.2:** Gen 18.1-8; 19.1-3. **13.5:** Deut 31.6, 8; Josh 1.5.
13.6: Ps 118.6. **13.11, 13:** Lev 16.27. **13.15:** Lev 7.12; Is 57.19; Hos 14.2.
13.20: Is 63.11; Zech 9.11; Is 55.3; Ezek 37.26.

Timothy has been released, with whom I shall see you if he comes soon. [24] Greet all your leaders and all the saints. Those who come from Italy send you greetings. [25] Grace be with all of you. Amen.

THE LETTER OF

JAMES

[1] James, a servant of God and of the Lord Jesus Christ,

To the twelve tribes in the Dispersion:

Greeting.

[2] Count it all joy, my brethren, when you meet various trials, [3] for you know that the testing of your faith produces steadfastness. [4] And let steadfastness have its full effect, that you may be perfect and complete, lacking in nothing.

[5] If any of you lacks wisdom, let him ask God who gives to all men generously and without reproaching, and it will be given him. [6] But let him ask in faith, with no doubting, for he who doubts is like a wave of the sea that is driven and tossed by the wind. [7,8] For that person must not suppose that a double-minded man, unstable in all his ways, will receive anything from the Lord.

[9] Let the lowly brother boast in his exaltation, [10] and the rich in his humiliation, because like the flower of the grass he will pass away. [11] For the sun rises with its scorching heat and withers the grass; its flower falls, and its beauty perishes. So will the rich man fade away in the midst of his pursuits.

[12] Blessed is the man who endures trial, for when he has stood the test he will receive the crown of life which God has promised to those who love him. [13] Let no one say when he is tempted, "I am tempted by God"; for God cannot be tempted with evil and he himself tempts no one; [14] but each person is tempted when he is lured and enticed by his own desire. [15] Then desire when it has conceived gives birth to sin; and sin when it is full-grown brings forth death.

[16] Do not be deceived, my beloved brethren. [17] Every good endowment and every perfect gift is from above, coming down from the Father of lights with whom there is no variation or shadow due to change.*a* [18] Of his own will he brought us forth by the word of truth that we should be a kind of first fruits of his creatures.

[19] Know this, my beloved brethren. Let every man be quick to hear, slow to speak, slow to anger, [20] for the anger of man does not work the righteousness of God. [21] Therefore put away all filthiness and rank growth of wickedness and receive with meekness the implanted word, which is able to save your souls.

[22] But be doers of the word, and not hearers only, deceiving yourselves. [23] For if any one is a hearer of the word and not a doer, he is like a man who observes his natural face in a mirror; [24] for he observes himself and goes away and at once forgets what he was like. [25] But he who looks into the perfect law, the law of liberty, and perseveres, being no hearer that forgets but a doer that acts, he shall be blessed in his doing.

[26] If any one thinks he is religious, and does not bridle his tongue but deceives his heart, this man's religion is vain. [27] Religion that is pure and undefiled before God and the Father is this: to visit orphans and widows in their affliction, and to keep oneself unstained from the world.

[2] My brethren, show no partiality as you hold the faith of our Lord Jesus Christ, the Lord of glory. [2] For if a man with gold rings and in fine clothing comes into your assembly, and a poor man in shabby clothing also comes in, [3] and you pay attention to the one who wears the fine clothing and say, "Have a seat here, please," while you say to the poor man, "Stand there," or, "Sit at my feet," [4] have you not made distinctions among your-

a Other ancient authorities read *variation due to a shadow of turning*
1.10-11: Is 40.6-7.

selves, and become judges with evil thoughts? [5] Listen, my beloved brethren. Has not God chosen those who are poor in the world to be rich in faith and heirs of the kingdom which he has promised to those who love him? [6] But you have dishonored the poor man. Is it not the rich who oppress you, is it not they who drag you into court? [7] Is it not they who blaspheme that honorable name by which you are called?

[8] If you really fulfil the royal law, according to the scripture, "You shall love your neighbor as yourself," you do well. [9] But if you show partiality, you commit sin, and are convicted by the law as transgressors. [10] For whoever keeps the whole law but fails in one point has become guilty of all of it. [11] For he who said, "Do not commit adultery," said also, "Do not kill." If you do not commit adultery but do kill, you have become a transgressor of the law. [12] So speak and so act as those who are to be judged under the law of liberty. [13] For judgment is without mercy to one who has shown no mercy; yet mercy triumphs over judgment.

[14] What does it profit, my brethren, if a man says he has faith but has not works? Can his faith save him? [15] If a brother or sister is ill-clad and in lack of daily food, [16] and one of you says to them, "Go in peace, be warmed and filled," without giving them the things needed for the body, what does it profit? [17] So faith by itself, if it has no works, is dead.

[18] But some one will say, "You have faith and I have works." Show me your faith apart from your works, and I by my works will show you my faith. [19] You believe that God is one; you do well. Even the demons believe —and shudder. [20] Do you want to be shown, you foolish fellow, that faith apart from works is barren? [21] Was not Abraham our father justified by works, when he offered his son Isaac upon the altar? [22] You see that faith was active along with his works, and faith was completed by works, [23] and the scripture was fulfilled which says, "Abraham believed God, and it was reckoned to him as righteousness"; and he was called the friend of God. [24] You see that a man is justified by works and not by faith alone. [25] And in the same way was not also Rāʾhab the harlot justified by works when she received the messengers and sent them out another way? [26] For as the body apart from the spirit is dead, so faith apart from works is dead.

3 Let not many of you become teachers, my brethren, for you know that we who teach shall be judged with greater strictness. [2] For we all make many mistakes, and if any one makes no mistakes in what he says he is a perfect man, able to bridle the whole body also. [3] If we put bits into the mouths of horses that they may obey us, we guide their whole bodies. [4] Look at the ships also; though they are so great and are driven by strong winds, they are guided by a very small rudder wherever the will of the pilot directs. [5] So the tongue is a little member and boasts of great things. How great a forest is set ablaze by a small fire!

[6] And the tongue is a fire. The tongue is an unrighteous world among our members, staining the whole body, setting on fire the cycle of nature,[b] and set on fire by hell.[c] [7] For every kind of beast and bird, of reptile and sea creature, can be tamed and has been tamed by humankind, [8] but no human being can tame the tongue—a restless evil, full of deadly poison. [9] With it we bless the Lord and Father, and with it we curse men, who are made in the likeness of God. [10] From the same mouth come blessing and cursing. My brethren, this ought not to be so. [11] Does a spring pour forth from the same opening fresh water and brackish? [12] Can a fig tree, my brethren, yield olives, or a grapevine figs? No more can salt water yield fresh.

[13] Who is wise and understanding among you? By his good life let him show his works in the meekness of wisdom. [14] But if you have bitter jealousy and selfish ambition in your hearts, do not boast and be false to the truth. [15] This wisdom is not such as comes down from above, but is earthly, unspiritual, devilish. [16] For where jealousy and selfish ambition exist, there will be disorder and every vile practice. [17] But the wisdom from above is first pure, then peaceable, gentle, open to reason, full of mercy and good fruits, without uncertainty or insincerity. [18] And the harvest of righteousness is sown in peace by those who make peace.

4 What causes wars, and what causes fightings among you? Is it

b Or *wheel of birth*   c Greek *Gehenna*

2.8: Lev 19.18.   **2.11:** Ex 20.13-14; Deut 5.17-18.   **2.21:** Gen 22.1-14.
2.23: Gen 15.6; Is 41.8; 2 Chron 20.7.   **2.25:** Josh 2.1-21.

not your passions that are at war in your members? ² You desire and do not have; so you kill. And you covet*d* and cannot obtain; so you fight and wage war. You do not have, because you do not ask. ³ You ask and do not receive, because you ask wrongly, to spend it on your passions. ⁴ Unfaithful creatures! Do you not know that friendship with the world is enmity with God? Therefore whoever wishes to be a friend of the world makes himself an enemy of God. ⁵ Or do you suppose it is in vain that the scripture says, "He yearns jealously over the spirit which he has made to dwell in us"? ⁶ But he gives more grace; therefore it says, "God opposes the proud, but gives grace to the humble." ⁷ Submit yourselves therefore to God. Resist the devil and he will flee from you. ⁸ Draw near to God and he will draw near to you. Cleanse your hands, you sinners, and purify your hearts, you men of double mind. ⁹ Be wretched and mourn and weep. Let your laughter be turned to mourning and your joy to dejection. ¹⁰ Humble yourselves before the Lord and he will exalt you.

¹¹ Do not speak evil against one another, brethren. He that speaks evil against a brother or judges his brother, speaks evil against the law and judges the law. But if you judge the law, you are not a doer of the law but a judge. ¹² There is one lawgiver and judge, he who is able to save and to destroy. But who are you that you judge your neighbor?

¹³ Come now, you who say, "Today or tomorrow we will go into such and such a town and spend a year there and trade and get gain"; ¹⁴ whereas you do not know about tomorrow. What is your life? For you are a mist that appears for a little time and then vanishes. ¹⁵ Instead you ought to say, "If the Lord wills, we shall live and we shall do this or that." ¹⁶ As it is, you boast in your arrogance. All such boasting is evil. ¹⁷ Whoever knows what is right to do and fails to do it, for him it is sin.

5 Come now, you rich, weep and howl for the miseries that are coming upon you. ² Your riches have rotted and your garments are motheaten. ³ Your gold and silver have rusted, and their rust will be evidence against you and will eat your flesh like fire. You have laid up treasure*e* for the

last days. ⁴ Behold, the wages of the laborers who mowed your fields, which you kept back by fraud, cry out; and the cries of the harvesters have reached the ears of the Lord of hosts. ⁵ You have lived on the earth in luxury and in pleasure; you have fattened your hearts in a day of slaughter. ⁶ You have condemned, you have killed the righteous man; he does not resist you.

⁷ Be patient, therefore, brethren, until the coming of the Lord. Behold, the farmer waits for the precious fruit of the earth, being patient over it until it receives the early and the late rain. ⁸ You also be patient. Establish your hearts, for the coming of the Lord is at hand. ⁹ Do not grumble, brethren, against one another, that you may not be judged; behold, the Judge is standing at the doors. ¹⁰ As an example of suffering and patience, brethren, take the prophets who spoke in the name of the Lord. ¹¹ Behold, we call those happy who were steadfast. You have heard of the steadfastness of Job, and you have seen the purpose of the Lord, how the Lord is compassionate and merciful.

¹² But above all, my brethren, do not swear, either by heaven or by earth or with any other oath, but let your yes be yes and your no be no, that you may not fall under condemnation.

¹³ Is any one among you suffering? Let him pray. Is any cheerful? Let him sing praise. ¹⁴ Is any among you sick? Let him call for the elders of the church, and let them pray over him, anointing him with oil in the name of the Lord; ¹⁵ and the prayer of faith will save the sick man, and the Lord will raise him up; and if he has committed sins, he will be forgiven. ¹⁶ Therefore confess your sins to one another, and pray for one another, that you may be healed. The prayer of a righteous man has great power in its effects. ¹⁷ E·li′jah was a man of like nature with ourselves and he prayed fervently that it might not rain, and for three years and six months it did not rain on the earth. ¹⁸ Then he prayed again and the heaven gave rain, and the earth brought forth its fruit.

¹⁹ My brethren, if any one among you wanders from the truth and some one brings him back, ²⁰ let him know that whoever brings back a sinner from the error of his way will save his soul from death and will cover a multitude of sins.

---

d Or *you kill and you covet*   *e* Or *will eat your flesh, since you have stored up fire*
4.6: Prov 3.34.   **5.11:** Job 1.21-22; 2.10; Ps 103.8; 111.4.   **5.12:** Mt 5.37.
5.17: 1 Kings 17.1; 18.1; Lk 4.25.   **5.18:** 1 Kings 18.42.

THE FIRST LETTER OF

PETER

I Peter, an apostle of Jesus Christ, To the exiles of the Dispersion in Pon'tŭs, Galatia, Cap·pà·dō'ci·à, Asia, and Bĭ·thyn'ĭ·à, 2 chosen and destined by God the Father and sanctified by the Spirit for obedience to Jesus Christ and for sprinkling with his blood:

May grace and peace be multiplied to you.

3 Blessed be the God and Father of our Lord Jesus Christ! By his great mercy we have been born anew to a living hope through the resurrection of Jesus Christ from the dead, 4 and to an inheritance which is imperishable, undefiled, and unfading, kept in heaven for you, 5 who by God's power are guarded through faith for a salvation ready to be revealed in the last time. 6 In this you rejoice,ᵃ though now for a little while you may have to suffer various trials, 7 so that the genuineness of your faith, more precious than gold which though perishable is tested by fire, may redound to praise and glory and honor at the revelation of Jesus Christ. 8 Without having seenᵇ him youᶜ love him; though you do not now see him youᶜ believe in him and rejoice with unutterable and exalted joy. 9As the outcome of your faith you obtain the salvation of your souls.

10 The prophets who prophesied of the grace that was to be yours searched and inquired about this salvation; 11 they inquired what person or time was indicated by the Spirit of Christ within them when predicting the sufferings of Christ and the subsequent glory. 12 It was revealed to them that they were serving not themselves but you, in the things which have now been announced to you by those who preached the good news to you through the Holy Spirit sent from heaven, things into which angels long to look.

13 Therefore gird up your minds, be sober, set your hope fully upon the grace that is coming to you at the revelation of Jesus Christ. 14As obedi-

ent children, do not be conformed to the passions of your former ignorance, 15 but as he who called you is holy, be holy yourselves in all your conduct; 16 since it is written, "You shall be holy, for I am holy." 17And if you invoke as Father him who judges each one impartially according to his deeds, conduct yourselves with fear throughout the time of your exile. 18 You know that you were ransomed from the futile ways inherited from your fathers, not with perishable things such as silver or gold, 19 but with the precious blood of Christ, like that of a lamb without blemish or spot. 20 He was destined before the foundation of the world but was made manifest at the end of the times for your sake. 21 Through him you have confidence in God, who raised him from the dead and gave him glory, so that your faith and hope are in God.ᵈ

22 Having purified your souls by your obedience to the truth for a sincere love of the brethren, love one another earnestly from the heart. 23 You have been born anew, not of perishable seed but of imperishable, through the living and abiding word of God; 24 for

"All flesh is like grass
    and all its glory like the flower of
        grass.
The grass withers, and the flower
        falls,
25 but the word of the Lord abides for
        ever."

That word is the good news which was preached to you.

2 So put away all malice and all guile and insincerity and envy and all slander. 2 Like newborn babes, long for the pure spiritual milk, that by it you may grow up to salvation; 3 for you have tasted the kindness of the Lord.

4 Come to him, to that living stone, rejected by men but in God's sight chosen and precious; 5 and like living stones be yourselves built into a spiritual house, to be a holy priesthood, to offer spiritual sacrifices acceptable

ᵃ Or *Rejoice in this*   ᵇ Other ancient authorities read *known*   ᶜ Or omit *you*
ᵈ Or *so that your faith is hope in God*
1.16: Lev 11.44-45.   1.24-25: Is 40.6-9.   2.3: Ps 34.8.   2.4: Ps 118.22; Is 28.16.

to God through Jesus Christ. 6 For it stands in scripture:

"Behold, I am laying in Zion a stone,
     a cornerstone chosen and
     precious,
and he who believes in him will not
     be put to shame."

7 To you therefore who believe, he is precious, but for those who do not believe,

"The very stone which the builders
     rejected
has become the head of the corner,"

8 and

"A stone that will make men
     stumble,
a rock that will make them fall";

for they stumble because they disobey the word, as they were destined to do.

9 But you are a chosen race, a royal priesthood, a holy nation, God's own people,*e* that you may declare the wonderful deeds of him who called you out of darkness into his marvelous light. 10 Once you were no people but now you are God's people; once you had not received mercy but now you have received mercy.

11 Beloved, I beseech you as aliens and exiles to abstain from the passions of the flesh that wage war against your soul. 12 Maintain good conduct among the Gentiles, so that in case they speak against you as wrongdoers, they may see your good deeds and glorify God on the day of visitation.

13 Be subject for the Lord's sake to every human institution,*f* whether it be to the emperor as supreme, 14 or to governors as sent by him to punish those who do wrong and to praise those who do right. 15 For it is God's will that by doing right you should put to silence the ignorance of foolish men. 16 Live as free men, yet without using your freedom as a pretext for evil; but live as servants of God. 17 Honor all men. Love the brotherhood. Fear God. Honor the emperor.

18 Servants, be submissive to your masters with all respect, not only to the kind and gentle but also to the overbearing. 19 For one is approved if, mindful of God, he endures pain while suffering unjustly. 20 For what credit is it, if when you do wrong and are beaten for it you take it patiently? But if when you do right and suffer for it you take it patiently, you have God's approval. 21 For to this you have been

called, because Christ also suffered for you, leaving you an example, that you should follow in his steps. 22 He committed no sin; no guile was found on his lips. 23 When he was reviled he did not revile in return; when he suffered, he did not threaten; but he trusted to him who judges justly. 24 He himself bore our sins in his body on the tree,*g* that we might die to sin and live to righteousness. By his wounds you have been healed. 25 For you were straying like sheep, but have now returned to the Shepherd and Guardian of your souls.

3 Likewise you wives, be submissive to your husbands, so that some, though they do not obey the word, may be won without a word by the behavior of their wives, 2 when they see your reverent and chaste behavior. 3 Let not yours be the outward adorning with braiding of hair, decoration of gold, and wearing of robes, 4 but let it be the hidden person of the heart with the imperishable jewel of a gentle and quiet spirit, which in God's sight is very precious. 5 So once the holy women who hoped in God used to adorn themselves and were submissive to their husbands, 6 as Sarah obeyed Abraham, calling him lord. And you are now her children if you do right and let nothing terrify you.

7 Likewise you husbands, live considerately with your wives, bestowing honor on the woman as the weaker sex, since you are joint heirs of the grace of life, in order that your prayers may not be hindered.

8 Finally, all of you, have unity of spirit, sympathy, love of the brethren, a tender heart and a humble mind. 9 Do not return evil for evil or reviling for reviling; but on the contrary bless, for to this you have been called, that you may obtain a blessing. 10 For

"He that would love life
     and see good days,
let him keep his tongue from evil
     and his lips from speaking guile;
11 let him turn away from evil and do
     right;
let him seek peace and pursue it.
12 For the eyes of the Lord are upon
     the righteous,
and his ears are open to their prayer.
But the face of the Lord is against
     those that do evil."

13 Now who is there to harm you if you are zealous for what is right?

---

e Greek *a people for his possession*   *f* Or *every institution ordained for men*
g Or *carried up . . . to the tree*
2.6: Is 28.16.   **2.7:** Ps 118.22.   **2.8:** Is 8.14-15.   **2.9:** Ex 19.5-6.   **2.10:** Hos 2.23.   **2.22:** Is 53.9.   **2.24:** Is 53.12 (Gk.).   **2.24-25:** Is 53.5-6.   **3.6:** Gen 18.12.   **3.10-12:** Ps 34.12-16.

14 But even if you do suffer for right-eousness' sake, you will be blessed. Have no fear of them, nor be troubled, 15 but in your hearts reverence Christ as Lord. Always be prepared to make a defense to any one who calls you to account for the hope that is in you, yet do it with gentleness and reverence; 16 and keep your conscience clear, so that, when you are abused, those who revile your good behavior in Christ may be put to shame. 17 For it is better to suffer for doing right, if that should be God's will, than for doing wrong. 18 For Christ also died[h] for sins once for all, the righteous for the unright-eous, that he might bring us to God, being put to death in the flesh but made alive in the spirit; 19 in which he went and preached to the spirits in prison, 20 who formerly did not obey, when God's patience waited in the days of Noah, during the building of the ark, in which a few, that is, eight persons, were saved through water. 21 Baptism, which corresponds to this, now saves you, not as a removal of dirt from the body but as an appeal to God for a clear conscience, through the resurrection of Jesus Christ, 22 who has gone into heaven and is at the right hand of God, with angels, authorities, and powers subject to him.

4 Since therefore Christ suffered in the flesh,[i] arm yourselves with the same thought, for whoever has suffered in the flesh has ceased from sin, 2 so as to live for the rest of the time in the flesh no longer by human passions but by the will of God. 3 Let the time that is past suffice for doing what the Gentiles like to do, living in licentiousness, passions, drunkenness, revels, carousing, and lawless idolatry. 4 They are surprised that you do not now join them in the same wild profligacy, and they abuse you; 5 but they will give account to him who is ready to judge the living and the dead. 6 For this is why the gospel was preached even to the dead, that though judged in the flesh like men, they might live in the spirit like God.

7 The end of all things is at hand; therefore keep sane and sober for your prayers. 8 Above all hold unfailing your love for one another, since love covers a multitude of sins. 9 Practice hospitality ungrudgingly to one another.

10 As each has received a gift, employ it for one another, as good stewards of God's varied grace: 11 whoever speaks, as one who utters oracles of God; who-ever renders service, as one who renders it by the strength which God supplies; in order that in everything God may be glorified through Jesus Christ. To him belong glory and dominion for ever and ever. Amen.

12 Beloved, do not be surprised at the fiery ordeal which comes upon you to prove you, as though something strange were happening to you. 13 But rejoice in so far as you share Christ's sufferings, that you may also rejoice and be glad when his glory is revealed. 14 If you are reproached for the name of Christ, you are blessed, because the spirit of glory[j] and of God rests upon you. 15 But let none of you suffer as a murderer, or a thief, or a wrongdoer, or a mischief-maker; 16 yet if one suffers as a Christian, let him not be ashamed, but under that name let him glorify God. 17 For the time has come for judgment to begin with the house-hold of God; and if it begins with us, what will be the end of those who do not obey the gospel of God? 18 And

"If the righteous man is scarcely saved,
where will the impious and sinner appear?"

19 Therefore let those who suffer according to God's will do right and entrust their souls to a faithful Creator.

5 So I exhort the elders among you, as a fellow elder and a witness of the sufferings of Christ as well as a partaker in the glory that is to be revealed. 2 Tend the flock of God that is your charge,[k] not by constraint but willingly,[l] not for shameful gain but eagerly, 3 not as domineering over those in your charge but being ex-amples to the flock. 4 And when the chief Shepherd is manifested you will obtain the unfading crown of glory. 5 Likewise you that are younger be subject to the elders. Clothe yourselves, all of you, with humility toward one another, for "God opposes the proud, but gives grace to the humble."

6 Humble yourselves therefore un-der the mighty hand of God, that in due time he may exalt you. 7 Cast all

h Other ancient authorities read suffered
i Other ancient authorities add for us; some for you
j Other ancient authorities insert and of power   k Other ancient authorities add
    exercising the oversight   l Other ancient authorities add as God would have you
3.14-15: Is 8.12-13.   3.20: Gen 6-8.   4.14: Is 11.2.   4.18: Prov 11.31 (Gk.).
5.5: Prov 3.34.   5.7: Ps 55.22.

your anxieties on him, for he cares about you. 8 Be sober, be watchful. Your adversary the devil prowls around like a roaring lion, seeking some one to devour. 9 Resist him, firm in your faith, knowing that the same experience of suffering is required of your brotherhood throughout the world. 10And after you have suffered a little while, the God of all grace, who has called you to his eternal glory in Christ, will himself restore, establish,

and strengthen*m* you. 11 To him be the dominion for ever and ever. Amen.

12 By Sil·vā′nŭs, a faithful brother as I regard him, I have written briefly to you, exhorting and declaring that this is the true grace of God; stand fast in it. 13 She who is at Babylon, who is likewise chosen, sends you greetings; and so does my son Mark. 14 Greet one another with the kiss of love.

Peace to all of you that are in Christ.

THE SECOND LETTER OF

PETER

I Simon Peter, a servant and apostle of Jesus Christ,
To those who have obtained a faith of equal standing with ours in the righteousness of our God and Savior Jesus Christ:*a*
2 May grace and peace be multiplied to you in the knowledge of God and of Jesus our Lord.

3 His divine power has granted to us all things that pertain to life and godliness, through the knowledge of him who called us to*b* his own glory and excellence, 4 by which he has granted to us his precious and very great promises, that through these you may escape from the corruption that is in the world because of passion, and become partakers of the divine nature. 5 For this very reason make every effort to supplement your faith with virtue, and virtue with knowledge, 6 and knowledge with self-control, and self-control with steadfastness, and steadfastness with godliness, 7 and godliness with brotherly affection, and brotherly affection with love. 8 For if these things are yours and abound, they keep you from being ineffective or unfruitful in the knowledge of our Lord Jesus Christ. 9 For whoever lacks these things is blind and shortsighted and has forgotten that he was cleansed from his old sins. 10 Therefore, brethren, be the more zealous to confirm your call and election, for if you do

this you will never fall; 11 so there will be richly provided for you an entrance into the eternal kingdom of our Lord and Savior Jesus Christ.
12 Therefore I intend always to remind you of these things, though you know them and are established in the truth that you have. 13 I think it right, as long as I am in this body,*c* to arouse you by way of reminder, 14 since I know that the putting off of my body*c* will be soon, as our Lord Jesus Christ showed me. 15And I will see to it that after my departure you may be able at any time to recall these things.
16 For we did not follow cleverly devised myths when we made known to you the power and coming of our Lord Jesus Christ, but we were eyewitnesses of his majesty. 17 For when he received honor and glory from God the Father and the voice was borne to him by the Majestic Glory, "This is my beloved Son,*d* with whom I am well pleased," 18 we heard this voice borne from heaven, for we were with him on the holy mountain. 19And we have the prophetic word made more sure. You will do well to pay attention to this as to a lamp shining in a dark place, until the day dawns and the morning star rises in your hearts. 20 First of all you must understand this, that no prophecy of scripture is a matter of one's own interpretation, 21 because no prophecy ever came by the impulse of man, but men moved

m Other ancient authorities read *restore, establish, strengthen and settle*
a Or *of our God and the Savior Jesus Christ*   *b* Or *by*   *c* Greek *tent*
d Or *my Son, my* (or *the*) *Beloved*
1.17-18: Mt 17.1-8; Mk 9.2-8; Lk 9.28-36.

by the Holy Spirit spoke from God.*e*

2 But false prophets also arose among the people, just as there will be false teachers among you, who will secretly bring in destructive heresies, even denying the Master who bought them, bringing upon themselves swift destruction. 2And many will follow their licentiousness, and because of them the way of truth will be reviled. 3And in their greed they will exploit you with false words; from of old their condemnation has not been idle, and their destruction has not been asleep.

4 For if God did not spare the angels when they sinned, but cast them into hell*f* and committed them to pits of nether gloom to be kept until the judgment; 5 if he did not spare the ancient world, but preserved Noah, a herald of righteousness, with seven other persons, when he brought a flood upon the world of the ungodly; 6 if by turning the cities of Sod′ŏm and Gŏ-môr′răh to ashes he condemned them to extinction and made them an example to those who were to be ungodly; 7 and if he rescued righteous Lot, greatly distressed by the licentiousness of the wicked 8 (for by what that righteous man saw and heard as he lived among them, he was vexed in his righteous soul day after day with their lawless deeds), 9 then the Lord knows how to rescue the godly from trial, and to keep the unrighteous under punishment until the day of judgment, 10 and especially those who indulge in the lust of defiling passion and despise authority.

Bold and wilful, they are not afraid to revile the glorious ones, 11 whereas angels, though greater in might and power, do not pronounce a reviling judgment upon them before the Lord. 12 But these, like irrational animals, creatures of instinct, born to be caught and killed, reviling in matters of which they are ignorant, will be destroyed in the same destruction with them, 13 suffering wrong for their wrongdoing. They count it pleasure to revel in the daytime. They are blots and blemishes, reveling in their dissipation,*g* carousing with you. 14 They have eyes full of adultery, insatiable for sin. They entice unsteady souls. They have hearts trained in greed. Accursed children!

15 Forsaking the right way they have gone astray; they have followed the way of Balaam, the son of Bĕ′ôr, who loved gain from wrongdoing, 16 but was rebuked for his own transgression; a dumb ass spoke with human voice and restrained the prophet's madness.

17 These are waterless springs and mists driven by a storm; for them the nether gloom of darkness has been reserved. 18 For, uttering loud boasts of folly, they entice with licentious passions of the flesh men who have barely escaped from those who live in error. 19 They promise them freedom, but they themselves are slaves of corruption; for whatever overcomes a man, to that he is enslaved. 20 For if, after they have escaped the defilements of the world through the knowledge of our Lord and Savior Jesus Christ, they are again entangled in them and overpowered, the last state has become worse for them than the first. 21 For it would have been better for them never to have known the way of righteousness than after knowing it to turn back from the holy commandment delivered to them. 22 It has happened to them according to the true proverb, The dog turns back to his own vomit, and the sow is washed only to wallow in the mire.

3 This is now the second letter that I have written to you, beloved, and in both of them I have aroused your sincere mind by way of reminder; 2 that you should remember the predictions of the holy prophets and the commandment of the Lord and Savior through your apostles. 3 First of all you must understand this, that scoffers will come in the last days with scoffing, following their own passions 4 and saying, "Where is the promise of his coming? For ever since the fathers fell asleep, all things have continued as they were from the beginning of creation." 5 They deliberately ignore this fact, that by the word of God heavens existed long ago, and an earth formed out of water and by means of water, 6 through which the world that then existed was deluged with water and perished. 7 But by the same word the heavens and earth that now exist have been stored up for fire, being kept until the day of judgment and destruction of ungodly men.

---

e Other authorities read *moved by the Holy Spirit holy men of God spoke*
f Greek *Tartarus*   *g* Other ancient authorities read *love feasts*
2.1-18: Jude 4-16.   **2.5:** Gen 8.18; 6.6-8.   **2.6:** Gen 19.24.   **2.7:** Gen 19.16, 29
2.15: Num 22.5, 7.   **2.16:** Num 22.21, 23, 28, 30-31.   **2.22:** Prov 26.11.
3.5-6: Gen 1.6-8; 7.11.

8 But do not ignore this one fact, beloved, that with the Lord one day is as a thousand years, and a thousand years as one day. 9 The Lord is not slow about his promise as some count slowness, but is forbearing toward you,*h* not wishing that any should perish, but that all should reach repentance. 10 But the day of the Lord will come like a thief, and then the heavens will pass away with a loud noise, and the elements will be dissolved with fire, and the earth and the works that are upon it will be burned up.

11 Since all these things are thus to be dissolved, what sort of persons ought you to be in lives of holiness and godliness, 12 waiting for and hastening*i* the coming of the day of God, because of which the heavens will be kindled and dissolved, and the elements will melt with fire! 13 But according to his promise we wait for new heavens and a new earth in which righteousness dwells.

14 Therefore, beloved, since you wait for these, be zealous to be found by him without spot or blemish, and at peace. 15And count the forbearance of our Lord as salvation. So also our beloved brother Paul wrote to you according to the wisdom given him, 16 speaking of this as he does in all his letters. There are some things in them hard to understand, which the ignorant and unstable twist to their own destruction, as they do the other scriptures. 17 You therefore, beloved, knowing this beforehand, beware lest you be carried away with the error of lawless men and lose your own stability. 18 But grow in the grace and knowledge of our Lord and Savior Jesus Christ. To him be the glory both now and to the day of eternity. Amen.

THE FIRST LETTER OF

JOHN

That which was from the beginning, which we have heard, which we have seen with our eyes, which we have looked upon and touched with our hands, concerning the word of life—2 the life was made manifest, and we saw it, and testify to it, and proclaim to you the eternal life which was with the Father and was made manifest to us—3 that which we have seen and heard we proclaim also to you, so that you may have fellowship with us; and our fellowship is with the Father and with his Son Jesus Christ. 4And we are writing this that our*a* joy may be complete.

5 This is the message we have heard from him and proclaim to you, that God is light and in him is no darkness at all. 6 If we say we have fellowship with him while we walk in darkness, we lie and do not live according to the truth; 7 but if we walk in the light, as he is in the light, we have fellowship with one another, and the blood of Jesus his Son cleanses us from all sin. 8 If we say we have no sin, we deceive ourselves, and the truth is not in us. 9 If we confess our sins, he is faithful and just, and will forgive our sins and cleanse us from all unrighteousness. 10 If we say we have not sinned, we make him a liar, and his word is not in us.

2 My little children, I am writing this to you so that you may not sin; but if any one does sin, we have an advocate with the Father, Jesus Christ the righteous; 2 and he is the expiation for our sins, and not for ours only but also for the sins of the whole world. 3And by this we may be sure that we know him, if we keep his commandments. 4 He who says "I know him" but disobeys his commandments is a

---

h Other ancient authorities read *on your account*   *i* Or *earnestly desiring*
a Other ancient authorities read *your*

3.8: Ps 90.4.   3.12: Is 34.4.   3.13: Is 65.17; 66.22.
1.1-2: Lk 24.39; Jn 1.1; 4.14; 15.27; 20.20, 25; Acts 4.20; 1 Jn 2.13.
1.4: Jn 15.11; 2 Jn 12.   1.5: 1 Jn 3.11.   1.6-8: Jn 3.21; 1 Jn 2.4, 11.   1.7: Rev 1.5.
1.10: 1 Jn 5.10.   2.1: Jn 14.16.   2.2: Jn 1.29; 3.14-16; 11.51-52; 1 Jn 4.10.
2.3: Jn 15.10.   2.4: 1 Jn 1.6-8; 4.20.

liar, and the truth is not in him; 5 but whoever keeps his word, in him truly love for God is perfected. By this we may be sure that we are in him: 6 he who says he abides in him ought to walk in the same way in which he walked.

7 Beloved, I am writing you no new commandment, but an old commandment which you had from the beginning; the old commandment is the word which you have heard. 8 Yet I am writing you a new commandment, which is true in him and in you, because[b] the darkness is passing away and the true light is already shining. 9 He who says he is in the light and hates his brother is in the darkness still. 10 He who loves his brother abides in the light, and in it[c] there is no cause for stumbling. 11 But he who hates his brother is in the darkness and walks in the darkness, and does not know where he is going, because the darkness has blinded his eyes.

12 I am writing to you, little children, because your sins are forgiven for his sake. 13 I am writing to you, fathers, because you know him who is from the beginning. I am writing to you, young men, because you have overcome the evil one. I write to you, children, because you know the Father. 14 I write to you, fathers, because you know him who is from the beginning. I write to you, young men, because you are strong, and the word of God abides in you, and you have overcome the evil one.

15 Do not love the world or the things in the world. If any one loves the world, love for the Father is not in him. 16 For all that is in the world, the lust of the flesh and the lust of the eyes and the pride of life, is not of the Father but is of the world. 17 And the world passes away, and the lust of it; but he who does the will of God abides for ever.

18 Children, it is the last hour; and as you have heard that antichrist is coming, so now many antichrists have come; therefore we know that it is the last hour. 19 They went out from us, but they were not of us; for if they had been of us, they would have continued with us; but they went out, that it might be plain that they all are not of

us. 20 But you have been anointed by the Holy One, and you all know.[d] 21 I write to you, not because you do not know the truth, but because you know it, and know that no lie is of the truth. 22 Who is the liar but he who denies that Jesus is the Christ? This is the antichrist, he who denies the Father and the Son. 23 No one who denies the Son has the Father. He who confesses the Son has the Father also. 24 Let what you heard from the beginning abide in you. If what you heard from the beginning abides in you, then you will abide in the Son and in the Father. 25 And this is what he has promised us,[e] eternal life.

26 I write this to you about those who would deceive you; 27 but the anointing which you received from him abides in you, and you have no need that any one should teach you; as his anointing teaches you about everything, and is true, and is no lie, just as it has taught you, abide in him. 28 And now, little children, abide in him, so that when he appears we may have confidence and not shrink from him in shame at his coming. 29 If you know that he is righteous, you may be sure that every one who does right is born of him.

3 See what love the Father has given us, that we should be called children of God; and so we are. The reason why the world does not know us is that it did not know him. 2 Beloved, we are God's children now; it does not yet appear what we shall be, but we know that when he appears we shall be like him, for we shall see him as he is. 3 And every one who thus hopes in him purifies himself as he is pure.

4 Every one who commits sin is guilty of lawlessness; sin is lawlessness. 5 You know that he appeared to take away sins, and in him there is no sin. 6 No one who abides in him sins; no one who sins has either seen him or known him. 7 Little children, let no one deceive you. He who does right is righteous, as he is righteous. 8 He who commits sin is of the devil; for the devil has sinned from the beginning. The reason the Son of God appeared was to destroy the works of the devil. 9 No one born of God commits sin; for God's[f] nature abides in him, and he

b Or that　c Or him　d Other ancient authorities read you know everything
e Other ancient authorities read you　f Greek his
2.5: Jn 14.21, 23; 1 Jn 5.3.　**2.6:** Jn 13.15.　**2.7:** Jn 13.34.　**2.8:** Jn 8.12.
2.10-11: Jn 11.9-10; 1 Jn 1.6.　**2.13:** Jn 1.1; 1 Jn 1.1.　**2.18:** 1 Jn 4.3.　**2.22:** 2 Jn 7.
2.23: 1 Jn 4.15; 2 Jn 9.　**2.27:** Jn 14.26.　**2.28:** 1 Jn 4.17.　**2.29:** 1 Jn 3.7-10; 4.7.
3.1: Jn 1.12; 16.3.　**3.5:** Jn 1.29.　**3.8:** Jn 8.34, 44.　**3.9:** 1 Jn 5.18.

cannot sin because he is[g] born of God. 10 By this it may be seen who are the children of God, and who are the children of the devil: whoever does not do right is not of God, nor he who does not love his brother.

11 For this is the message which you have heard from the beginning, that we should love one another, 12 and not be like Cain who was of the evil one and murdered his brother. And why did he murder him? Because his own deeds were evil and his brother's righteous. 13 Do not wonder, brethren, that the world hates you. 14 We know that we have passed out of death into life, because we love the brethren. He who does not love remains in death. 15 Any one who hates his brother is a murderer, and you know that no murderer has eternal life abiding in him. 16 By this we know love, that he laid down his life for us; and we ought to lay down our lives for the brethren. 17 But if any one has the world's goods and sees his brother in need, yet closes his heart against him, how does God's love abide in him? 18 Little children, let us not love in word or speech but in deed and in truth.

19 By this we shall know that we are of the truth, and reassure our hearts before him 20 whenever our hearts condemn us, for God is greater than our hearts, and he knows everything. 21 Beloved, if our hearts do not condemn us, we have confidence before God; 22 and we receive from him whatever we ask, because we keep his commandments and do what pleases him. 23 And this is his commandment, that we should believe in the name of his Son Jesus Christ and love one another, just as he has commanded us. 24 All who keep his commandments abide in him, and he in them. And by this we know that he abides in us, by the Spirit which he has given us.

4 Beloved, do not believe every spirit, but test the spirits to see whether they are of God; for many false prophets have gone out into the world. 2 By this you know the Spirit of God: every spirit which confesses that Jesus Christ has come in the flesh is of God, 3 and every spirit which does not confess Jesus is not of God.

This is the spirit of antichrist, of which you heard that it was coming, and now it is in the world already. 4 Little children, you are of God, and have overcome them; for he who is in you is greater than he who is in the world. 5 They are of the world, therefore what they say is of the world, and the world listens to them. 6 We are of God. Whoever knows God listens to us, and he who is not of God does not listen to us. By this we know the spirit of truth and the spirit of error.

7 Beloved, let us love one another; for love is of God, and he who loves is born of God and knows God. 8 He who does not love does not know God; for God is love. 9 In this the love of God was made manifest among us, that God sent his only Son into the world, so that we might live through him. 10 In this is love, not that we loved God but that he loved us and sent his Son to be the expiation for our sins. 11 Beloved, if God so loved us, we also ought to love one another. 12 No man has ever seen God; if we love one another, God abides in us and his love is perfected in us.

13 By this we know that we abide in him and he in us, because he has given us of his own Spirit. 14 And we have seen and testify that the Father has sent his Son as the Savior of the world. 15 Whoever confesses that Jesus is the Son of God, God abides in him, and he in God. 16 So we know and believe the love God has for us. God is love, and he who abides in love abides in God, and God abides in him. 17 In this is love perfected with us, that we may have confidence for the day of judgment, because as he is so are we in this world. 18 There is no fear in love, but perfect love casts out fear. For fear has to do with punishment, and he who fears is not perfected in love. 19 We love, because he first loved us. 20 If any one says, "I love God," and hates his brother, he is a liar; for he who does not love his brother whom he has seen, cannot^h love God whom he has not seen. 21 And this commandment we have from him, that he who loves God should love his brother also.

5 Every one who believes that Jesus is the Christ is a child of

g Or *for the offspring of God abide in him, and they cannot sin because they are*
h Other ancient authorities read *how can he*

3.11: 1 Jn 1.5.   3.13: Jn 15.18-19.   3.14: Jn 5.24.   3.15: Jn 8.44.   3.16: Jn 13.1; 15.13.
3.18: Jas 1.22.   3.21: 1 Jn 5.14.   3.23: Jn 6.29; 13.34; 15.17.   3.24: 1 Jn 4.13.
4.3: 1 Jn 2.18.   4.5: Jn 15.19.   4.6: Jn 8.47.   4.7: 1 Jn 2.29.   4.9: Jn 3.16.
4.10: Jn 15.12; 1 Jn 4.19; 2.2.   4.12: Jn 1.18.   4.13: 1 Jn 3.24.   4.14: Jn 4.42; 3.17.
4.17: 1 Jn 2.28.   4.19: 1 Jn 4.10.   4.20: 1 Jn 2.4.   5.1: Jn 8.42.

God, and every one who loves the parent loves the child. 2 By this we know that we love the children of God, when we love God and obey his commandments. 3 For this is the love of God, that we keep his commandments. And his commandments are not burdensome. 4 For whatever is born of God overcomes the world; and this is the victory that overcomes the world, our faith. 5 Who is it that overcomes the world but he who believes that Jesus is the Son of God?

6 This is he who came by water and blood, Jesus Christ, not with the water only but with the water and the blood. 7And the Spirit is the witness, because the Spirit is the truth. 8 There are three witnesses, the Spirit, the water, and the blood; and these three agree. 9 If we receive the testimony of men, the testimony of God is greater; for this is the testimony of God that he has borne witness to his Son. 10 He who believes in the Son of God has the testimony in himself. He who does not believe God has made him a liar, because he has not believed in the testimony that God has borne to his Son. 11And this is the testimony, that God gave us eternal life, and this life is in his Son. 12 He who has the Son has life; he who has not the Son of God has not life.

13 I write this to you who believe in the name of the Son of God, that you may know that you have eternal life. 14And this is the confidence which we have in him, that if we ask anything according to his will he hears us. 15And if we know that he hears us in whatever we ask, we know that we have obtained the requests made of him. 16 If any one sees his brother committing what is not a mortal sin, he will ask, and God*i* will give him life for those whose sin is not mortal. There is sin which is mortal; I do not say that one is to pray for that. 17All wrongdoing is sin, but there is sin which is not mortal.

18 We know that any one born of God does not sin, but He who was born of God keeps him, and the evil one does not touch him.

19 We know that we are of God, and the whole world is in the power of the evil one.

20 And we know that the Son of God has come and has given us understanding, to know him who is true; and we are in him who is true, in his Son Jesus Christ. This is the true God and eternal life. 21 Little children, keep yourselves from idols.

THE SECOND LETTER OF

JOHN

1 The elder to the elect lady and her children, whom I love in the truth, and not only I but also all who know the truth, 2 because of the truth which abides in us and will be with us for ever:

3 Grace, mercy, and peace will be with us, from God the Father and from Jesus Christ the Father's Son, in truth and love.

4 I rejoiced greatly to find some of your children following the truth, just as we have been commanded by the Father. 5And now I beg you, lady, not as though I were writing you a new

commandment, but the one we have had from the beginning, that we love one another. 6And this is love, that we follow his commandments; this is the commandment, as you have heard from the beginning, that you follow love. 7 For many deceivers have gone out into the world, men who will not acknowledge the coming of Jesus Christ in the flesh; such a one is the deceiver and the antichrist. 8 Look to yourselves, that you may not lose what you*a* have worked for, but may win a full reward. 9Any one who goes ahead and does not abide in the doctrine of Christ does not have God; he who

i Greek *he*   *a* Other ancient authorities read *we*
5.3: Jn 14.15; 1 Jn 2.5; 2 Jn 6.   **5.4:** Jn 16.33.   **5.6-8:** Jn 19.34; 4.23; 15.26.
5.9: Jn 5.32, 36; 8.18.   **5.10:** 1 Jn 1.10.   **5.12:** Jn 3.36.   **5.13:** Jn 20.31.
5.14: Mt 7.7; 1 Jn 3.21.   **5.18:** Jn 17.15; 1 Jn 3.9.   **5.20-21:** Jn 17.3; Rev **3.7.**
1: 3 Jn 1.   **5:** Jn 13.34.   **6:** 1 Jn 5.3.   **7:** 1 Jn 2.22.

abides in the doctrine has both the Father and the Son. 10 If any one comes to you and does not bring this doctrine, do not receive him into the house or give him any greeting; 11 for he who greets him shares his wicked work.

12 Though I have much to write to you, I would rather not use paper and ink, but I hope to come to see you and talk with you face to face, so that our joy may be complete.

13 The children of your elect sister greet you.

THE THIRD LETTER OF

JOHN

1 The elder to the beloved Gā′ius, whom I love in the truth.

2 Beloved, I pray that all may go well with you and that you may be in health; I know that is is well with your soul. 3 For I greatly rejoiced when some of the brethren arrived and testified to the truth of your life, as indeed you do follow the truth. 4 No greater joy can I have than this, to hear that my children follow the truth.

5 Beloved, it is a loyal thing you do when you render any service to the brethren, especially to strangers, 6 who have testified to your love before the church. You will do well to send them on their journey as befits God's service. 7 For they have set out for his sake and have accepted nothing from the heathen. 8 So we ought to support such men, that we may be fellow workers in the truth

9 I have written something to the church; but Dī·ot′rė·phēš, who likes

to put himself first, does not acknowledge my authority. 10 So if I come, I will bring up what he is doing, prating against me with evil words. And not content with that, he refuses himself to welcome the brethren, and also stops those who want to welcome them and puts them out of the church.

11 Beloved, do not imitate evil but imitate good. He who does good is of God; he who does evil has not seen God. 12 Dė·mē′tri·us has testimony from every one, and from the truth itself; I testify to him too, and you know my testimony is true.

13 I had much to write to you, but I would rather not write with pen and ink; 14 I hope to see you soon, and we will talk together face to face.

15 Peace be to you. The friends greet you. Greet the friends, every one of them.

THE LETTER OF

JUDE

1 Jude, a servant of Jesus Christ and brother of James,

To those who are called, beloved in God the Father and kept for Jesus Christ:

2 May mercy, peace, and love be multiplied to you.

3 Beloved, being very eager to write to you of our common salvation, I found it necessary to write appealing to you to contend for the faith which was once for all delivered to the saints. 4 For admission has been secretly gained by some who long ago were

12 (2 John): 1 Jn 1.4; 3 Jn 13.
1 (3 John): Acts 19.29; 2 Jn 1.   **12** (3 John): Jn 21.24.   **13** (3 John): 2 Jn 12.
4-16 (Jude): 2 Pet 2.1-18.

designated for this condemnation, ungodly persons who pervert the grace of our God into licentiousness and deny our only Master and Lord, Jesus Christ.[a]

5 Now I desire to remind you, though you were once for all fully informed, that he[b] who saved a people out of the land of Egypt, afterward destroyed those who did not believe. 6And the angels that did not keep their own position but left their proper dwelling have been kept by him in eternal chains in the nether gloom until the judgment of the great day; 7 just as Sod'om and Gŏ·môr'răh and the surrounding cities, which likewise acted immorally and indulged in unnatural lust, serve as an example by undergoing a punishment of eternal fire.

8 Yet in like manner these men in their dreamings defile the flesh, reject authority, and revile the glorious ones.[c] 9 But when the archangel Michael, contending with the devil, disputed about the body of Moses, he did not presume to pronounce a reviling judgment upon him, but said, "The Lord rebuke you." 10 But these men revile whatever they do not understand, and by those things that they know by instinct as irrational animals do, they are destroyed. 11 Woe to them! For they walk in the way of Cain, and abandon themselves for the sake of gain to Balaam's error, and perish in Kō'răh's rebellion. 12 These are blemishes[d] on your love feasts, as they boldly carouse together, looking after themselves; waterless clouds, carried along by winds; fruitless trees in late autumn, twice dead, uprooted; 13 wild waves of the sea, casting up the foam of their own shame; wandering stars for whom the nether gloom of darkness has been reserved for ever.

14 It was of these also that Ē'nŏch in the seventh generation from Adam prophesied, saying, "Behold, the Lord came with his holy myriads, 15 to execute judgment on all, and to convict all the ungodly of all their deeds of ungodliness which they have committed in such an ungodly way, and of all the harsh things which ungodly sinners have spoken against him." 16 These are grumblers, malcontents, following their own passions, loud-mouthed boasters, flattering people to gain advantage.

17 But you must remember, beloved, the predictions of the apostles of our Lord Jesus Christ; 18 they said to you, "In the last time there will be scoffers, following their own ungodly passions." 19 It is these who set up divisions, worldly people, devoid of the Spirit. 20 But you, beloved, build yourselves up on your most holy faith; pray in the Holy Spirit; 21 keep yourselves in the love of God; wait for the mercy of our Lord Jesus Christ unto eternal life. 22And convince some, who doubt; 23 save some, by snatching them out of the fire; on some have mercy with fear, hating even the garment spotted by the flesh.[e]

24 Now to him who is able to keep you from falling and to present you without blemish before the presence of his glory with rejoicing, 25 to the only God, our Savior through Jesus Christ our Lord, be glory, majesty, dominion, and authority, before all time and now and for ever. Amen.

THE

REVELATION TO JOHN

I The revelation of Jesus Christ, which God gave him to show to his servants what must soon take place; and he made it known by sending his angel to his servant John, 2 who bore witness to the word of God and to the testimony of Jesus Christ, even to all that he saw. 3 Blessed is he who reads aloud the words of the prophecy, and blessed are those who hear, and who keep what is written therein; for the time is near.

a Or *the only Master and our Lord Jesus Christ*
b Ancient authorities read *Jesus* or *the Lord* or *God*   *c* Greek *glories*   *d* Or *reefs*
e The Greek text in this sentence is uncertain at several points
7: Gen 19.   9: Zech 3.2.   11: Gen 4.3-8; Num 22-24; 16.   14-15: Enoch 1.9.
23: Zech 3.3-4.

4 John to the seven churches that are in Asia:

Grace to you and peace from him who is and who was and who is to come, and from the seven spirits who are before his throne, 5 and from Jesus Christ the faithful witness, the first-born of the dead, and the ruler of kings on earth.

To him who loves us and has freed us from our sins by his blood 6 and made us a kingdom, priests to his God and Father, to him be glory and dominion for ever and ever. Amen. 7 Behold, he is coming with the clouds, and every eye will see him, every one who pierced him; and all tribes of the earth will wail on account of him. Even so. Amen.

8 "I am the Alpha and the Omega," says the Lord God, who is and who was and who is to come, the Almighty.

9 I John, your brother, who share with you in Jesus the tribulation and the kingdom and the patient endurance, was on the island called Pat'mŏs on account of the word of God and the testimony of Jesus. 10 I was in the Spirit on the Lord's day, and I heard behind me a loud voice like a trumpet 11 saying, "Write what you see in a book and send it to the seven churches, to Eph'ĕ·sùs and to Smyr'nà and to Pĕr'gà·mùm and to Thy'à·tī'rà and to Sär'dis and to Philadelphia and to Lā·ŏ·di·cē'à."

12 Then I turned to see the voice that was speaking to me, and on turning I saw seven golden lampstands, 13 and in the midst of the lampstands one like a son of man, clothed with a long robe and with a golden girdle round his breast; 14 his head and his hair were white as white wool, white as snow; his eyes were like a flame of fire, 15 his feet were like burnished bronze, refined as in a furnace, and his voice was like the sound of many waters; 16 in his right hand he held seven stars, from his mouth issued a sharp two-edged sword, and his face was like the sun shining in full strength.

17 When I saw him, I fell at his feet as though dead. But he laid his right hand upon me, saying, "Fear not, I am the first and the last,18 and the living one; I died, and behold I am alive for evermore, and I have the keys of Death and Hades.19 Now write what you see, what is and what is to take place hereafter.20 As for the mystery

of the seven stars which you saw in my right hand, and the seven golden lamp-stands, the seven stars are the angels of the seven churches and the seven lampstands are the seven churches.

2 "To the angel of the church in Eph'ĕ·sùs write: 'The words of him who holds the seven stars in his right hand, who walks among the seven golden lampstands.

2 "'I know your works, your toil and your patient endurance, and how you cannot bear evil men but have tested those who call themselves apostles but are not, and found them to be false; 3 I know you are enduring patiently and bearing up for my name's sake, and you have not grown weary. 4 But I have this against you, that you have abandoned the love you had at first. 5 Remember then from what you have fallen, repent and do the works you did at first. If not, I will come to you and remove your lampstand from its place, unless you repent. 6 Yet this you have, you hate the works of the Nic·ō·lā'i·tàns, which I also hate. 7 He who has an ear, let him hear what the Spirit says to the churches. To him who conquers I will grant to eat of the tree of life, which is in the paradise of God.'

8 "And to the angel of the church in Smyr'nà write: 'The words of the first and the last, who died and came to life.

9 "'I know your tribulation and your poverty (but you are rich) and the slander of those who say that they are Jews and are not, but are a synagogue of Satan. 10 Do not fear what you are about to suffer. Behold, the devil is about to throw some of you into prison, that you may be tested, and for ten days you will have tribulation. Be faithful unto death, and I will give you the crown of life. 11 He who has an ear, let him hear what the Spirit says to the churches. He who conquers shall not be hurt by the second death.'

12 "And to the angel of the church in Pĕr'gà·mùm write: 'The words of him who has the sharp two-edged sword.

13 "'I know where you dwell, where Satan's throne is; you hold fast my name and you did not deny my faith even in the days of An'ti·pas my witness, my faithful one, who was killed among you, where Satan dwells. 14 But I have a few things against you:

you have some there who hold the teaching of Balaam, who taught Bā'lak to put a stumbling block before the sons of Israel, that they might eat food sacrificed to idols and practice immorality. 15 So you also have some who hold the teaching of the Nic·ō·lā'i·tāns. 16 Repent then. If not, I will come to you soon and war against them with the sword of my mouth. 17 He who has an ear, let him hear what the Spirit says to the churches. To him who conquers I will give some of the hidden manna, and I will give him a white stone, with a new name written on the stone which no one knows except him who receives it.'

18 "And to the angel of the church in Thў·à·tī'rà write: 'The words of the Son of God, who has eyes like a flame of fire, and whose feet are like burnished bronze.

19 "'I know your works, your love and faith and service and patient endurance, and that your latter works exceed the first. 20 But I have this against you, that you tolerate the woman Jez'é·bĕl, who calls herself a prophetess and is teaching and beguiling my servants to practice immorality and to eat food sacrificed to idols. 21 I gave her time to repent, but she refuses to repent of her immorality. 22 Behold, I will throw her on a sickbed, and those who commit adultery with her I will throw into great tribulation, unless they repent of her doings; 23 and I will strike her children dead. And all the churches shall know that I am he who searches mind and heart, and I will give to each of you as your works deserve. 24 But to the rest of you in Thў·à·tī'rà, who do not hold this teaching, who have not learned what some call the deep things of Satan, to you I say, I do not lay upon you any other burden; 25 only hold fast what you have, until I come. 26 He who conquers and who keeps my works until the end, I will give him power over the nations, 27 and he shall rule them with a rod of iron, as when earthen pots are broken in pieces, even as I myself have received power from my Father; 28 and I will give him the morning star. 29 He who has an ear, let him hear what the Spirit says to the churches.

3 "And to the angel of the church in Sär'dis write: 'The words of

him who has the seven spirits of God and the seven stars.

"'I know your works; you have the name of being alive, and you are dead. 2 Awake, and strengthen what remains and is on the point of death, for I have not found your works perfect in the sight of my God. 3 Remember then what you received and heard; keep that, and repent. If you will not awake, I will come like a thief, and you will not know at what hour I will come upon you. 4 Yet you have still a few names in Sär'dis, people who have not soiled their garments; and they shall walk with me in white, for they are worthy. 5 He who conquers shall be clad thus in white garments, and I will not blot his name out of the book of life; I will confess his name before my Father and before his angels. 6 He who has an ear, let him hear what the Spirit says to the churches.'

7 "And to the angel of the church in Philadelphia write: 'The words of the holy one, the true one, who has the key of David, who opens and no one shall shut, who shuts and no one opens.

8 "'I know your works. Behold, I have set before you an open door, which no one is able to shut; I know that you have but little power, and yet you have kept my word and have not denied my name. 9 Behold, I will make those of the synagogue of Satan who say that they are Jews and are not, but lie—behold, I will make them come and bow down before your feet, and learn that I have loved you. 10 Because you have kept my word of patient endurance, I will keep you from the hour of trial which is coming on the whole world, to try those who dwell upon the earth. 11 I am coming soon; hold fast what you have, so that no one may seize your crown. 12 He who conquers, I will make him a pillar in the temple of my God; never shall he go out of it, and I will write on him the name of my God, and the name of the city of my God, the new Jerusalem which comes down from my God out of heaven, and my own new name. 13 He who has an ear, let him hear what the Spirit says to the churches.'

14 "And to the angel of the church in Lā·ŏ·di·cē'à write: 'The words of the Amen, the faithful and true witness, the beginning of God's creation.

2.17: Ps 78.24; Is 62.2.   2.18: Dan 10.6.
2.20: 1 Kings 16.31; 2 Kings 9.22, 30; Num 25.1.   2.23: Jer 17.10; Ps 62.12.
2.26: Ps 2.8-9.   3.5: Ex 32.32; Ps 69.28; Dan 12.1; Mt 10.32.   3.7: Is 22.22.
3.9: Is 60.14; 49.23; 43.4.   3.12: Is 62.2; Ezek 48.35; Rev 21.2.
3.14: Ps 89.28; Prov 8.22; Jn 1.1-3.

15 " 'I know your works: you are neither cold nor hot. Would that you were cold or hot! 16 So, because you are lukewarm, and neither cold nor hot, I will spew you out of my mouth. 17 For you say, I am rich, I have prospered, and I need nothing; not knowing that you are wretched, pitiable, poor, blind, and naked. 18 Therefore I counsel you to buy from me gold refined by fire, that you may be rich, and white garments to clothe you and to keep the shame of your nakedness from being seen, and salve to anoint your eyes, that you may see. 19 Those whom I love, I reprove and chasten; so be zealous and repent. 20 Behold, I stand at the door and knock; if any one hears my voice and opens the door, I will come in to him and eat with him, and he with me. 21 He who conquers, I will grant him to sit with me on my throne, as I myself conquered and sat down with my Father on his throne. 22 He who has an ear, let him hear what the Spirit says to the churches.' "

4 After this I looked, and lo, in heaven an open door! And the first voice, which I had heard speaking to me like a trumpet, said, "Come up hither, and I will show you what must take place after this." 2 At once I was in the Spirit, and lo, a throne stood in heaven, with one seated on the throne! 3 And he who sat there appeared like jasper and carnelian, and round the throne was a rainbow that looked like an emerald. 4 Round the throne were twenty-four thrones, and seated on the thrones were twenty-four elders, clad in white garments, with golden crowns upon their heads. 5 From the throne issue flashes of lightning, and voices and peals of thunder, and before the throne burn seven torches of fire, which are the seven spirits of God; 6 and before the throne there is as it were a sea of glass, like crystal.

And round the throne, on each side of the throne, are four living creatures, full of eyes in front and behind: 7 the first living creature like a lion, the second living creature like an ox, the third living creature with the face of a man, and the fourth living creature like a flying eagle. 8 And the four living creatures, each of them with six wings, are full of eyes all round and within, and day and night they never cease to sing,

"Holy, holy, holy, is the Lord God Almighty,
    who was and is and is to come!"
9 And whenever the living creatures give glory and honor and thanks to him who is seated on the throne, who lives for ever and ever, 10 the twenty-four elders fall down before him who is seated on the throne and worship him who lives for ever and ever; they cast their crowns before the throne, singing,
11 "Worthy art thou, our Lord and God,
    to receive glory and honor and power,
for thou didst create all things,
    and by thy will they existed and were created."

5 And I saw in the right hand of him who was seated on the throne a scroll written within and on the back, sealed with seven seals; 2 and I saw a strong angel proclaiming with a loud voice, "Who is worthy to open the scroll and break its seals?" 3 And no one in heaven or on earth or under the earth was able to open the scroll or to look into it, 4 and I wept much that no one was found worthy to open the scroll or to look into it. 5 Then one of the elders said to me, "Weep not; lo, the Lion of the tribe of Judah, the Root of David, has conquered, so that he can open the scroll and its seven seals."

6 And between the throne and the four living creatures and among the elders, I saw a Lamb standing, as though it had been slain, with seven horns and with seven eyes, which are the seven spirits of God sent out into all the earth; 7 and he went and took the scroll from the right hand of him who was seated on the throne. 8 And when he had taken the scroll, the four living creatures and the twenty-four elders fell down before the Lamb, each holding a harp, and with golden bowls full of incense, which are the prayers of the saints; 9 and they sang a new song, saying,

"Worthy art thou to take the scroll
    and to open its seals,
for thou wast slain and by thy blood
    didst ransom men for God
from every tribe and tongue and people and nation,
10 and hast made them a kingdom and priests to our God,
    and they shall reign on earth."
11 Then I looked, and I heard around the throne and the living creatures and

3.17: Hos 12.8.   3.19: Prov 3.12.   4.1: Ex 19.16, 24.   4.2: Ezek 1.26-28.
4.5: Ex 19.16; Zech 4.2.   4.6: Ezek 1.5, 18.   4.7: Ezek 1.10.   4.8: Is 6.2-3.   4.9: Ps 47.8.
5.1: Ezek 2.9; Is 29.11.   5.5: Gen 49.9.   5.6: Is 53.7; Zech 4.10.   5.8: Ps 141.2.
5.9: Ps 33.3.   5.10: Ex 19.6; Is 61.6.   5.11: Dan 7.10.

the elders the voice of many angels, numbering myriads of myriads and thousands of thousands, 12 saying with a loud voice, "Worthy is the Lamb who was slain, to receive power and wealth and wisdom and might and honor and glory and blessing!" 13And I heard every creature in heaven and on earth and under the earth and in the sea, and all therein, saying, "To him who sits upon the throne and to the Lamb be blessing and honor and glory and might for ever and ever!" 14And the four living creatures said, "Amen!" and the elders fell down and worshiped.

6 Now I saw when the Lamb opened one of the seven seals, and I heard one of the four living creatures say, as with a voice of thunder, "Come!" 2And I saw, and behold, a white horse, and its rider had a bow; and a crown was given to him, and he went out conquering and to conquer.

3 When he opened the second seal, I heard the second living creature say, "Come!" 4And out came another horse, bright red; its rider was permitted to take peace from the earth, so that men should slay one another; and he was given a great sword.

5 When he opened the third seal, I heard the third living creature say, "Come!" And I saw, and behold, a black horse, and its rider had a balance in his hand; 6 and I heard what seemed to be a voice in the midst of the four living creatures saying, "A quart of wheat for a denarius,*a* and three quarts of barley for a denarius;*a* but do not harm oil and wine!"

7 When he opened the fourth seal, I heard the voice of the fourth living creature say, "Come!" 8And I saw, and behold, a pale horse, and its rider's name was Death, and Hades followed him; and they were given power over a fourth of the earth, to kill with sword and with famine and with pestilence and by wild beasts of the earth.

9 When he opened the fifth seal, I saw under the altar the souls of those who had been slain for the word of God and for the witness they had borne; 10 they cried out with a loud voice, "O Sovereign Lord, holy and true, how long before thou wilt judge and avenge our blood on those who dwell upon the earth?" 11 Then they were each given a white robe and told

to rest a little longer, until the number of their fellow servants and their brethren should be complete, who were to be killed as they themselves had been.

12 When he opened the sixth seal, I looked, and behold, there was a great earthquake; and the sun became black as sackcloth, the full moon became like blood, 13 and the stars of the sky fell to the earth as the fig tree sheds its winter fruit when shaken by a gale; 14 the sky vanished like a scroll that is rolled up, and every mountain and island was removed from its place. 15 Then the kings of the earth and the great men and the generals and the rich and the strong, and every one, slave and free, hid in the caves and among the rocks of the mountains, 16 calling to the mountains and rocks, "Fall on us and hide us from the face of him who is seated on the throne, and from the wrath of the Lamb; 17 for the great day of their wrath has come, and who can stand before it?"

7 After this I saw four angels standing at the four corners of the earth, holding back the four winds of the earth, that no wind might blow on earth or sea or against any tree. 2 Then I saw another angel ascend from the rising of the sun, with the seal of the living God, and he called with a loud voice to the four angels who had been given power to harm earth and sea, 3 saying, "Do not harm the earth or the sea or the trees, till we have sealed the servants of our God upon their foreheads." 4And I heard the number of the sealed, a hundred and forty-four thousand sealed, out of every tribe of the sons of Israel, 5 twelve thousand sealed out of the tribe of Judah, twelve thousand of the tribe of Reuben, twelve thousand of the tribe of Gad, 6 twelve thousand of the tribe of Ash'-ĕr, twelve thousand of the tribe of Naph'tá·lī, twelve thousand of the tribe of Má·nas'sĕh, 7 twelve thousand of the tribe of Simeon, twelve thousand of the tribe of Levi, twelve thousand of the tribe of Is'sà·chär, 8 twelve thousand of the tribe of Zeb'-ū·lŭn, twelve thousand of the tribe of Joseph, twelve thousand sealed out of the tribe of Benjamin.

9 After this I looked, and behold, a great multitude which no man could number, from every nation, from all tribes and peoples and tongues, standing before the throne and before the

a The denarius was worth about twenty cents

6.2: Zech 1.8; 6.1-3. **6.6:** 2 Kings 6.25. **6.8:** Hos 13.14; Ezek 5.12. **6.10:** Zech 1.12; Ps 79.5; Gen 4.10. **6.12:** Joel 2.31; Acts 2.20. **6.13:** Is 34.4. **6.15:** Is 2.10. **6.16:** Hos 10.8. **6.17:** Joel 2.11; Mal 3.2. **7.1:** Zech 6.5. **7.3:** Ezek 9.4.

Lamb, clothed in white robes, with palm branches in their hands, 10 and crying out with a loud voice, "Salvation belongs to our God who sits upon the throne, and to the Lamb!" 11And all the angels stood round the throne and round the elders and the four living creatures, and they fell on their faces before the throne and worshiped God, 12 saying, "Amen! Blessing and glory and wisdom and thanksgiving and honor and power and might be to our God for ever and ever! Amen."

13 Then one of the elders addressed me, saying, "Who are these, clothed in white robes, and whence have they come?" 14 I said to him, "Sir, you know." And he said to me, "These are they who have come out of the great tribulation; they have washed their robes and made them white in the blood of the Lamb.
15 Therefore are they before the throne of God,
and serve him day and night within his temple;
and he who sits upon the throne will shelter them with his presence.
16 They shall hunger no more, neither thirst any more;
the sun shall not strike them, nor any scorching heat.
17 For the Lamb in the midst of the throne will be their shepherd,
and he will guide them to springs of living water;
and God will wipe away every tear from their eyes."

8 When the Lamb opened the seventh seal, there was silence in heaven for about half an hour. 2 Then I saw the seven angels who stand before God, and seven trumpets were given to them. 3And another angel came and stood at the altar with a golden censer; and he was given much incense to mingle with the prayers of all the saints upon the golden altar before the throne; 4 and the smoke of the incense rose with the prayers of the saints from the hand of the angel before God. 5 Then the angel took the censer and filled it with fire from the altar and threw it on the earth; and there were peals of thunder, loud noises, flashes of lightning, and an earthquake.
6 Now the seven angels who had the seven trumpets made ready to blow them.

7 The first angel blew his trumpet, and there followed hail and fire, mixed with blood, which fell on the earth; and a third of the earth was burnt up, and a third of the trees were burnt up, and all green grass was burnt up.
8 The second angel blew his trumpet, and something like a great mountain, burning with fire, was thrown into the sea; 9 and a third of the sea became blood, a third of the living creatures in the sea died, and a third of the ships were destroyed.
10 The third angel blew his trumpet, and a great star fell from heaven, blazing like a torch, and it fell on a third of the rivers and on the fountains of water. 11 The name of the star is Wormwood. A third of the waters became wormwood, and many men died of the water, because it was made bitter.
12 The fourth angel blew his trumpet, and a third of the sun was struck, and a third of the moon and a third of the stars, so that a third of their light was darkened; a third of the day was kept from shining, and likewise a third of the night.
13 Then I looked, and I heard an eagle crying with a loud voice, as it flew in midheaven, "Woe, woe, woe to those who dwell on the earth, at the blasts of the other trumpets which the three angels are about to blow!"

9 And the fifth angel blew his trumpet, and I saw a star fallen from heaven to earth, and he was given the key of the shaft of the bottomless pit; 2 he opened the shaft of the bottomless pit, and from the shaft rose smoke like the smoke of a great furnace, and the sun and the air were darkened with the smoke from the shaft. 3 Then from the smoke came locusts on the earth, and they were given power like the power of scorpions of the earth; 4 they were told not to harm the grass of the earth or any green growth or any tree, but only those of mankind who have not the seal of God upon their foreheads; 5 they were allowed to torture them for five months, but not to kill them, and their torture was like the torture of a scorpion, when it stings a man. 6And in those days men will seek death and will not find it; they will long to die, and death will fly from them.
7 In appearance the locusts were like horses arrayed for battle; on their

7.14: Dan 12.1; Gen 49.11.   7.16: Is 49.10; Ps 121.6.   7.17: Ezek 34.23; Ps 23.2; Is 25.8.
8.3: Amos 9.1; Ps 141.2.   8.5: Lev 16.12; Ezek 10.2.   8.7: Ex 9.23-25.   8.8: Jer 51.25.
8.10: Is 14.12.   9.2: Gen 19.28; Ex 19.18; Joel 2.10.   9.3: Ex 10.12-15.
9.4: Ezek 9.4.   9.6: Job 3.21.   9.7: Joel 2.4.

heads were what looked like crowns of gold; their faces were like human faces, [8] their hair like women's hair, and their teeth like lions' teeth; [9] they had scales like iron breastplates, and the noise of their wings was like the noise of many chariots with horses rushing into battle. [10] They have tails like scorpions, and stings, and their power of hurting men for five months lies in their tails. [11] They have as king over them the angel of the bottomless pit; his name in Hebrew is A·bad′don, and in Greek he is called A·pol′lyon.[b]

[12] The first woe has passed; behold, two woes are still to come.

[13] Then the sixth angel blew his trumpet, and I heard a voice from the four horns of the golden altar before God, [14] saying to the sixth angel who had the trumpet, "Release the four angels who are bound at the great river Eū·phrā′tēs." [15] So the four angels were released, who had been held ready for the hour, the day, the month, and the year, to kill a third of mankind. [16] The number of the troops of cavalry was twice ten thousand times ten thousand; I heard their number. [17] And this was how I saw the horses in my vision: the riders wore breastplates the color of fire and of sapphire[c] and of sulphur, and the heads of the horses were like lions' heads, and fire and smoke and sulphur issued from their mouths. [18] By these three plagues a third of mankind was killed, by the fire and smoke and sulphur issuing from their mouths. [19] For the power of the horses is in their mouths and in their tails; their tails are like serpents, with heads, and by means of them they wound.

[20] The rest of mankind, who were not killed by these plagues, did not repent of the works of their hands nor give up worshiping demons and idols of gold and silver and bronze and stone and wood, which cannot either see or hear or walk; [21] nor did they repent of their murders or their sorceries or their immorality or their thefts.

10 Then I saw another mighty angel coming down from heaven, wrapped in a cloud, with a rainbow over his head, and his face was like the sun, and his legs like pillars of fire. [2] He had a little scroll open in his hand. And he set his right foot on the sea, and his left foot on the land, [3] and

called out with a loud voice, like a lion roaring; when he called out, the seven thunders sounded. [4] And when the seven thunders had sounded, I was about to write, but I heard a voice from heaven saying, "Seal up what the seven thunders have said, and do not write it down." [5] And the angel whom I saw standing on sea and land lifted up his right hand to heaven [6] and swore by him who lives for ever and ever, who created heaven and what is in it, the earth and what is in it, and the sea and what is in it, that there should be no more delay, [7] but that in the days of the trumpet call to be sounded by the seventh angel, the mystery of God, as he announced to his servants the prophets, should be fulfilled.

[8] Then the voice which I had heard from heaven spoke to me again, saying, "Go, take the scroll which is open in the hand of the angel who is standing on the sea and on the land." [9] So I went to the angel and told him to give me the little scroll; and he said to me, "Take it and eat; it will be bitter to your stomach, but sweet as honey in your mouth." [10] And I took the little scroll from the hand of the angel and ate it; it was sweet as honey in my mouth, but when I had eaten it my stomach was made bitter. [11] And I was told, "You must again prophesy about many peoples and nations and tongues and kings."

11 Then I was given a measuring rod like a staff, and I was told: "Rise and measure the temple of God and the altar and those who worship there, [2] but do not measure the court outside the temple; leave that out, for it is given over to the nations, and they will trample over the holy city for forty-two months. [3] And I will grant my two witnesses power to prophesy for one thousand two hundred and sixty days, clothed in sackcloth."

[4] These are the two olive trees and the two lampstands which stand before the Lord of the earth. [5] And if any one would harm them, fire pours from their mouth and consumes their foes; if any one would harm them, thus he is doomed to be killed. [6] They have power to shut the sky, that no rain may fall during the days of their prophesying, and they have power over the

b Or *Destroyer*   c Greek *hyacinth*
9.8: Joel 1.6.   9.9: Joel 2.5.   9.13: Ex 30.1-3.   9.20: Is 17.8; Ps 115.4-7; 135.15-17.
10.5: Deut 32.40; Dan 12.7.   10.9: Ezek 2.8; 3.1-3.   10.11: Jer 1.10.   11.1: Ezek 40.3.
11.2: Zech 12.3; Is 63.18; Lk 21.24.   11.4: Zech 4.3, 11-14.
11.5: 2 Kings 1.10; Jer 5.14.   11.6: 1 Kings 17.1; Ex 7.17, 19.

waters to turn them into blood, and to smite the earth with every plague, as often as they desire. 7And when they have finished their testimony, the beast that ascends from the bottomless pit will make war upon them and conquer them and kill them, 8 and their dead bodies will lie in the street of the great city which is allegorically*d* called Sod'ôm and Egypt, where their Lord was crucified. 9 For three days and a half men from the peoples and tribes and tongues and nations gaze at their dead bodies and refuse to let them be placed in a tomb, 10 and those who dwell on the earth will rejoice over them and make merry and exchange presents, because these two prophets had been a torment to those who dwell on the earth. 11 But after the three and a half days a breath of life from God entered them, and they stood up on their feet, and great fear fell on those who saw them. 12 Then they heard a loud voice from heaven saying to them, "Come up hither!" And in the sight of their foes they went up to heaven in a cloud. 13And at that hour there was a great earthquake, and a tenth of the city fell; seven thousand people were killed in the earthquake, and the rest were terrified and gave glory to the God of heaven.

14 The second woe has passed; behold, the third woe is soon to come.

15 Then the seventh angel blew his trumpet, and there were loud voices in heaven, saying, "The kingdom of the world has become the kingdom of our Lord and of his Christ, and he shall reign for ever and ever." 16And the twenty-four elders who sit on their thrones before God fell on their faces and worshiped God, 17 saying,

"We give thanks to thee, Lord God
   Almighty, who art and who
   wast,
that thou hast taken thy great
   power and begun to reign.
18 The nations raged, but thy wrath
   came,
and the time for the dead to be
   judged,
for rewarding thy servants, the
   prophets and saints,
and those who fear thy name,
   both small and great,
and for destroying the destroyers of
   the earth."

19 Then God's temple in heaven was opened, and the ark of his covenant was seen within his temple; and there were flashes of lightning, loud noises, peals of thunder, an earthquake, and heavy hail.

12 And a great portent appeared in heaven, a woman clothed with the sun, with the moon under her feet, and on her head a crown of twelve stars; 2 she was with child and she cried out in her pangs of birth, in anguish for delivery. 3And another portent appeared in heaven; behold, a great red dragon, with seven heads and ten horns, and seven diadems upon his heads. 4 His tail swept down a third of the stars of heaven, and cast them to the earth. And the dragon stood before the woman who was about to bear a child, that he might devour her child when she brought it forth; 5 she brought forth a male child, one who is to rule all the nations with a rod of iron, but her child was caught up to God and to his throne, 6 and the woman fled into the wilderness, where she has a place prepared by God, in which to be nourished for one thousand two hundred and sixty days.

7 Now war arose in heaven, Michael and his angels fighting against the dragon; and the dragon and his angels fought, 8 but they were defeated and there was no longer any place for them in heaven. 9And the great dragon was thrown down, that ancient serpent, who is called the Devil and Satan, the deceiver of the whole world—he was thrown down to the earth, and his angels were thrown down with him. 10And I heard a loud voice in heaven, saying, "Now the salvation and the power and the kingdom of our God and the authority of his Christ have come, for the accuser of our brethren has been thrown down, who accuses them day and night before our God. 11And they have conquered him by the blood of the Lamb and by the word of their testimony, for they loved not their lives even unto death. 12 Rejoice then, O heaven and you that dwell therein! But woe to you, O earth and sea, for the devil has come down to you in great wrath, because he knows that his time is short!"

13 And when the dragon saw that he had been thrown down to the earth, he pursued the woman who had borne

d Greek *spiritually*   **11.7:** Dan 7.3, 7, 21.   **11.8:** Is 1.9.   **11.11:** Ezek 37.5, 10.
11.12: 2 Kings 2.11.   **11.15:** Ps 22.28; Dan 7.14, 27.   **11.18:** Ps 2.1.
11.19: 1 Kings 8.1-6; 2 Maccabees 2.4-8.   **12.2:** Mic 4.10.   **12.3:** Dan 7.7.
12.4: Dan 8.10.   **12.5:** Is 66.7; Ps 2.9.   **12.7:** Dan 10.13.   **12.9:** Gen 3.1, 14-15; Zech 3.1.
12.10: Job 1.9-11.   **12.12:** Is 44.23; 49.13.

the male child. 14 But the woman was given the two wings of the great eagle that she might fly from the serpent into the wilderness, to the place where she is to be nourished for a time, and times, and half a time. 15 The serpent poured water like a river out of his mouth after the woman, to sweep her away with the flood. 16 But the earth came to the help of the woman, and the earth opened its mouth and swallowed the river which the dragon had poured from his mouth. 17 Then the dragon was angry with the woman, and went off to make war on the rest of her offspring, on those who keep the commandments of God and bear testimony to Jesus. And he stood*e* on the sand of the sea.

13 And I saw a beast rising out of the sea, with ten horns and seven heads, with ten diadems upon its horns and a blasphemous name upon its heads. 2 And the beast that I saw was like a leopard, its feet were like a bear's, and its mouth was like a lion's mouth. And to it the dragon gave his power and his throne and great authority. 3 One of its heads seemed to have a mortal wound, but its mortal wound was healed, and the whole earth followed the beast with wonder. 4 Men worshiped the dragon, for he had given his authority to the beast, and they worshiped the beast, saying, "Who is like the beast, and who can fight against it?"

5 And the beast was given a mouth uttering haughty and blasphemous words, and it was allowed to exercise authority for forty-two months; 6 it opened its mouth to utter blasphemies against God, blaspheming his name and his dwelling, that is, those who dwell in heaven. 7 Also it was allowed to make war on the saints and to conquer them.*f* And authority was given it over every tribe and people and tongue and nation, 8 and all who dwell on earth will worship it, every one whose name has not been written before the foundation of the world in the book of life of the Lamb that was slain. 9 If any one has an ear, let him hear: 10 If any one is to be taken captive,
to captivity he goes;
if any one slays with the sword,
with the sword must he be slain.
Here is a call for the endurance and faith of the saints.

11 Then I saw another beast which rose out of the earth; it had two horns like a lamb and it spoke like a dragon. 12 It exercises all the authority of the first beast in its presence, and makes the earth and its inhabitants worship the first beast, whose mortal wound was healed. 13 It works great signs, even making fire come down from heaven to earth in the sight of men; 14 and by the signs which it is allowed to work in the presence of the beast, it deceives those who dwell on earth, bidding them make an image for the beast which was wounded by the sword and yet lived; 15 and it was allowed to give breath to the image of the beast so that the image of the beast should even speak, and to cause those who would not worship the image of the beast to be slain. 16 Also it causes all, both small and great, both rich and poor, both free and slave, to be marked on the right hand or the forehead, 17 so that no one can buy or sell unless he has the mark, that is, the name of the beast or the number of its name. 18 This calls for wisdom: let him who has understanding reckon the number of the beast, for it is a human number, its number is six hundred and sixty-six.*g*

14 Then I looked, and lo, on Mount Zion stood the Lamb, and with him a hundred and forty-four thousand who had his name and his Father's name written on their foreheads. 2 And I heard a voice from heaven like the sound of many waters and like the sound of loud thunder; the voice I heard was like the sound of harpers playing on their harps, 3 and they sing a new song before the throne and before the four living creatures and before the elders. No one could learn that song except the hundred and forty-four thousand who had been redeemed from the earth. 4 It is these who have not defiled themselves with women, for they are chaste;*h* it is these who follow the Lamb wherever he goes; these have been redeemed from mankind as first fruits for God and the Lamb, 5 and in their mouth no lie was found, for they are spotless.

6 Then I saw another angel flying in midheaven, with an eternal gospel to proclaim to those who dwell on earth, to every nation and tribe and tongue and people; 7 and he said with

e Other ancient authorities read *And I stood*, connecting the sentence with 13.1
f Other ancient authorities omit this sentence *g* Other ancient authorities read *six hundred and sixteen* *h* Greek *virgins*

12.14: Dan 7.25; 12.7. **13.1:** Dan 7.1-6. **13.5:** Dan 7.8. **13.7:** Dan 7.21.
13.9: Mk 4.23. **13.10:** Jer 15.2. **13.14:** Deut 13.1-5. **13.15:** Dan 3.5. **14.1:** Ezek 9.4.

a loud voice, "Fear God and give him glory, for the hour of his judgment has come; and worship him who made heaven and earth, the sea and the fountains of water."

8 Another angel, a second, followed, saying, "Fallen, fallen is Babylon the great, she who made all nations drink the wine of her impure passion."

9 And another angel, a third, followed them, saying with a loud voice, "If any one worships the beast and its image, and receives a mark on his forehead or on his hand, 10 he also shall drink the wine of God's wrath, poured unmixed into the cup of his anger, and he shall be tormented with fire and brimstone in the presence of the holy angels and in the presence of the Lamb. 11And the smoke of their torment goes up for ever and ever; and they have no rest, day or night, these worshipers of the beast and its image, and whoever receives the mark of its name."

12 Here is a call for the endurance of the saints, those who keep the commandments of God and the faith of Jesus.

13 And I heard a voice from heaven saying, "Write this: Blessed are the dead who die in the Lord henceforth." "Blessed indeed," says the Spirit, "that they may rest from their labors, for their deeds follow them!"

14 Then I looked, and lo, a white cloud, and seated on the cloud one like a son of man, with a golden crown on his head, and a sharp sickle in his hand. 15And another angel came out of the temple, calling with a loud voice to him who sat upon the cloud, "Put in your sickle, and reap, for the hour to reap has come, for the harvest of the earth is fully ripe." 16 So he who sat upon the cloud swung his sickle on the earth, and the earth was reaped.

17 And another angel came out of the temple in heaven, and he too had a sharp sickle. 18 Then another angel came out from the altar, the angel who has power over fire, and he called with a loud voice to him who had the sharp sickle, "Put in your sickle, and gather the clusters of the vine of the earth, for its grapes are ripe." 19 So the angel swung his sickle on the earth and gathered the vintage of the earth, and threw it into the great wine press of the

wrath of God; 20 and the wine press was trodden outside the city, and blood flowed from the wine press, as high as a horse's bridle, for one thousand six hundred stadia.*i*

15 Then I saw another portent in heaven, great and wonderful, seven angels with seven plagues, which are the last, for with them the wrath of God is ended.

2 And I saw what appeared to be a sea of glass mingled with fire, and those who had conquered the beast and its image and the number of its name, standing beside the sea of glass with harps of God in their hands. 3And they sing the song of Moses, the servant of God, and the song of the Lamb, saying,

"Great and wonderful are thy deeds,
　O Lord God the Almighty!
Just and true are thy ways,
　O King of the ages!*j*
4 Who shall not fear and glorify thy
　　name, O Lord?
For thou alone art holy.
All nations shall come and worship
　　thee,
for thy judgments have been revealed."

5 After this I looked, and the temple of the tent of witness in heaven was opened, 6 and out of the temple came the seven angels with the seven plagues, robed in pure bright linen, and their breasts girded with golden girdles. 7And one of the four living creatures gave the seven angels seven golden bowls full of the wrath of God who lives for ever and ever; 8 and the temple was filled with smoke from the glory of God and from his power, and no one could enter the temple until the seven plagues of the seven angels were ended.

16 Then I heard a loud voice from the temple telling the seven angels, "Go and pour out on the earth the seven bowls of the wrath of God."

2 So the first angel went and poured his bowl on the earth, and foul and evil sores came upon the men who bore the mark of the beast and worshiped its image.

3 The second angel poured his bowl into the sea, and it became like the blood of a dead man, and every living thing died that was in the sea.

i About two hundred miles　*j* Other ancient authorities read *the nations*
14.8: Is 21.9.　14.10: Jer 51.7; Gen 19.24.　14.11: Is 34.10.　14.14: Dan 7.13.
14.15: Joel 3.13; Mt 13.30.　14.20: Joel 3.13.　15.1: Lev 26.21.
15.3: Ex 15.1; Ps 145.17.　15.4: Jer 10.7; Ps 86.9-10.　15.5: Ex 40.34.
15.8: 1 Kings 8.10; Is 6.4; Ezek 44.4.　16.1: Is 66.6; Ps 69.24.
16.2: Ex 9.10-11; Deut 28.35.　16.3-4: Ex 7.17-21.

4 The third angel poured his bowl into the rivers and the fountains of water, and they became blood. 5And I heard the angel of water say,

"Just art thou in these thy judgments,
thou who art and wast, O Holy One.
6 For men have shed the blood of
saints and prophets,
and thou hast given them blood to
drink.
It is their due!"

7 And I heard the altar cry,

"Yea, Lord God the Almighty,
true and just are thy judgments!"

8 The fourth angel poured his bowl on the sun, and it was allowed to scorch men with fire; 9 men were scorched by the fierce heat, and they cursed the name of God who had power over these plagues, and they did not repent and give him glory.

10 The fifth angel poured his bowl on the throne of the beast, and its kingdom was in darkness; men gnawed their tongues in anguish 11 and cursed the God of heaven for their pain and sores, and did not repent of their deeds.

12 The sixth angel poured his bowl on the great river Eū·phrā′tēs, and its water was dried up, to prepare the way for the kings from the east. 13And I saw, issuing from the mouth of the dragon and from the mouth of the beast and from the mouth of the false prophet, three foul spirits like frogs; 14 for they are demonic spirits, performing signs, who go abroad to the kings of the whole world, to assemble them for battle on the great day of God the Almighty. 15 ("Lo, I am coming like a thief! Blessed is he who is awake, keeping his garments that he may not go naked and be seen exposed!") 16And they assembled them at the place which is called in Hebrew Ăr·mà·ged′dŏn.

17 The seventh angel poured his bowl into the air, and a great voice came out of the temple, from the throne, saying, "It is done!" 18And there were flashes of lightning, loud noises, peals of thunder, and a great earthquake such as had never been since men were on the earth, so great was that earthquake. 19 The great city was split into three parts, and the cities of the nations fell, and God remembered great Babylon, to make her drain the cup of the fury of his wrath. 20And every island fled away, and no moun-

tains were to be found; 21 and great hailstones, heavy as a hundredweight, dropped on men from heaven, till men cursed God for the plague of the hail, so fearful was that plague.

17 Then one of the seven angels who had the seven bowls came and said to me, "Come, I will show you the judgment of the great harlot who is seated upon many waters, 2 with whom the kings of the earth have committed fornication, and with the wine of whose fornication the dwellers on earth have become drunk." 3And he carried me away in the Spirit into a wilderness, and I saw a woman sitting on a scarlet beast which was full of blasphemous names, and it had seven heads and ten horns. 4 The woman was arrayed in purple and scarlet, and bedecked with gold and jewels and pearls, holding in her hand a golden cup full of abominations and the impurities of her fornication; 5 and on her forehead was written a name of mystery: "Babylon the great, mother of harlots and of earth's abominations." 6And I saw the woman, drunk with the blood of the saints and the blood of the martyrs of Jesus.

When I saw her I marveled greatly. 7 But the angel said to me, "Why marvel? I will tell you the mystery of the woman, and of the beast with seven heads and ten horns that carries her. 8 The beast that you saw was, and is not, and is to ascend from the bottomless pit and go to perdition; and the dwellers on earth whose names have not been written in the book of life from the foundation of the world, will marvel to behold the beast, because it was and is not and is to come. 9 This calls for a mind with wisdom: the seven heads are seven hills on which the woman is seated; 10 they are also seven kings five of whom have fallen, one is, the other has not yet come, and when he comes he must remain only a little while. 11As for the beast that was and is not, it is an eighth but it belongs to the seven, and it goes to perdition. 12And the ten horns that you saw are ten kings who have not yet received royal power, but they are to receive authority as kings for one hour, together with the beast. 13 These are of one mind and give over their power and authority to the beast;

16.6: Ps 79.3. 16.7: Ps 119.137. 16.10: Ex 10.21. 16.12: Is 11.15-16.
16.13: 1 Kings 22.21-23; Ex 8.3. 16.15: 1 Thess 5.2. 16.16: 2 Kings 9.27.
16.17: Is 66.6. 16.18: Ex 19.16; Dan 12.1. 16.21: Ex 9.23. 17.1: Jer 51.13.
17.2: Is 23.17; Jer 25.15-16. 17.4: Jer 51.7. 17.8: Dan 7.3; Rev 3.5.
17.12: Dan 7.20-24.

14 they will make war on the Lamb, and the Lamb will conquer them, for he is Lord of lords and King of kings, and those with him are called and chosen and faithful."

15 And he said to me, "The waters that you saw, where the harlot is seated, are peoples and multitudes and nations and tongues. 16 And the ten horns that you saw, they and the beast will hate the harlot; they will make her desolate and naked, and devour her flesh and burn her up with fire, 17 for God has put it into their hearts to carry out his purpose by being of one mind and giving over their royal power to the beast, until the words of God shall be fulfilled. 18 And the woman that you saw is the great city which has dominion over the kings of the earth."

18 After this I saw another angel coming down from heaven, having great authority; and the earth was made bright with his splendor. 2 And he called out with a mighty voice,

"Fallen, fallen is Babylon the great!
It has become a dwelling place of
　demons,
a haunt of every foul spirit,
a haunt of every foul and hateful
　bird;
3 for all nations have drunk*k* the wine
　of her impure passion,
and the kings of the earth have com-
　mitted fornication with her,
and the merchants of the earth have
　grown rich with the wealth of
　her wantonness."

4 Then I heard another voice from heaven saying,

"Come out of her, my people,
lest you take part in her sins,
lest you share in her plagues;
5 for her sins are heaped high as
　heaven,
and God has remembered her in-
　iquities.
6 Render to her as she herself has
　rendered,
and repay her double for her deeds;
mix a double draught for her in the
　cup she mixed.
7 As she glorified herself and played
　the wanton,
so give her a like measure of torment
　and mourning.
Since in her heart she says, 'A queen
　I sit,
I am no widow, mourning I shall
　never see,'

8 so shall her plagues come in a single
　day,
pestilence and mourning and famine,
　and she shall be burned with fire;
for mighty is the Lord God who
　judges her."

9 And the kings of the earth, who committed fornication and were wanton with her, will weep and wail over her when they see the smoke of her burning; 10 they will stand far off, in fear of her torment, and say,

"Alas! alas! thou great city,
thou mighty city, Babylon!
In one hour has thy judgment
　come."

11 And the merchants of the earth weep and mourn for her, since no one buys their cargo any more, 12 cargo of gold, silver, jewels and pearls, fine linen, purple, silk and scarlet, all kinds of scented wood, all articles of ivory, all articles of costly wood, bronze, iron and marble, 13 cinnamon, spice, incense, myrrh, frankincense, wine, oil, fine flour and wheat, cattle and sheep, horses and chariots, and slaves, that is, human souls.

14 "The fruit for which thy soul longed
　has gone from thee,
and all thy dainties and thy splendor
　are lost to thee, never to be
　found again!"

15 The merchants of these wares, who gained wealth from her, will stand far off, in fear of her torment, weeping and mourning aloud,

16 "Alas, alas, for the great city
that was clothed in fine linen, in
　purple and scarlet,
bedecked with gold, with jewels, and
　with pearls!
17 In one hour all this wealth has been
　laid waste."

And all shipmasters and seafaring men, sailors and all whose trade is on the sea, stood far off 18 and cried out as they saw the smoke of her burning, "What city was like the great city?" 19 And they threw dust on their heads, as they wept and mourned, crying out,

"Alas, alas, for the great city
where all who had ships at sea grew
　rich by her wealth!
In one hour she has been laid waste.
20 Rejoice over her, O heaven,
O saints and apostles and prophets,
for God has given judgment for you
　against her!"

21 Then a mighty angel took up a

---

k Other ancient authorities read *fallen by*

17.14: Dan 2.47. 18.2: Is 21.9; Jer 50.39. 18.3: Jer 25.15, 27. 18.4: Is 48.20; Jer 50.8. 18.5: Jer 51.9. 18.6: Ps 137.8. 18.7: Is 47.8-9. 18.9: Ezek 26.16-17. 18.11: Ezek 27.36. 18.12: Ezek 27.12-13, 22. 18.15: Ezek 27.36, 31. 18.17: Is 23.14; Ezek 27.26-30. 18.19: Ezek 27.30-34. 18.20: Is 44.23; Jer 51.48. 18.21: Jer 51.63; Ezek 26.21.

stone like a great millstone and threw it into the sea, saying,

"So shall Babylon the great city be
thrown down with violence,
and shall be found no more;
22 and the sound of harpers and minstrels, of flute players and
trumpeters,
shall be heard in thee no more;
and a craftsman of any craft
shall be found in thee no more;
and the sound of the millstone
shall be heard in thee no more;
23 and the light of a lamp
shall shine in thee no more;
and the voice of bridegroom and
bride
shall be heard in thee no more;
for thy merchants were the great
men of the earth,
and all nations were deceived by
thy sorcery.
24 And in her was found the blood of
prophets and of saints,
and of all who have been slain on
earth."

19 After this I heard what seemed to be the mighty voice of a great multitude in heaven, crying,

"Hallelujah! Salvation and glory and
power belong to our God,
2 for his judgments are true and
just;
he has judged the great harlot who
corrupted the earth with her
fornication,
and he has avenged on her the blood
of his servants."
3 Once more they cried,
"Hallelujah! The smoke from her
goes up for ever and ever."
4 And the twenty-four elders and the four living creatures fell down and worshiped God who is seated on the throne, saying, "Amen. Hallelujah!"
5 And from the throne came a voice crying,
"Praise our God, all you his servants,
you who fear him, small and great."
6 Then I heard what seemed to be the voice of a great multitude, like the sound of many waters and like the sound of mighty thunderpeals, crying,
"Hallelujah! For the Lord our God
the Almighty reigns.
7 Let us rejoice and exult and give
him the glory,
for the marriage of the Lamb has
come,
and his Bride has made herself
ready;

8 it was granted her to be clothed with
fine linen, bright and pure"—
for the fine linen is the righteous deeds of the saints.

9 And the angel said[l] to me, "Write this: Blessed are those who are invited to the marriage supper of the Lamb." And he said to me, "These are true words of God." 10 Then I fell down at his feet to worship him, but he said to me, "You must not do that! I am a fellow servant with you and your brethren who hold the testimony of Jesus. Worship God." For the testimony of Jesus is the spirit of prophecy.

11 Then I saw heaven opened, and behold, a white horse! He who sat upon it is called Faithful and True, and in righteousness he judges and makes war. 12 His eyes are like a flame of fire, and on his head are many diadems; and he has a name inscribed which no one knows but himself. 13 He is clad in a robe dipped in[m] blood, and the name by which he is called is The Word of God. 14 And the armies of heaven, arrayed in fine linen, white and pure, followed him on white horses. 15 From his mouth issues a sharp sword with which to smite the nations, and he will rule them with a rod of iron; he will tread the wine press of the fury of the wrath of God the Almighty. 16 On his robe and on his thigh he has a name inscribed, King of kings and Lord of lords.

17 Then I saw an angel standing in the sun, and with a loud voice he called to all the birds that fly in midheaven, "Come, gather for the great supper of God, 18 to eat the flesh of kings, the flesh of captains, the flesh of mighty men, the flesh of horses and their riders, and the flesh of all men, both free and slave, both small and great." 19 And I saw the beast and the kings of the earth with their armies gathered to make war against him who sits upon the horse and against his army. 20 And the beast was captured, and with it the false prophet who in its presence had worked the signs by which he deceived those who had received the mark of the beast and those who worshiped its image. These two were thrown alive into the lake of fire that burns with brimstone. 21 And the rest were slain by the sword of him who sits upon the horse, the sword that issues from his mouth; and all the birds were gorged with their flesh.

l Greek *he said*   *m* Other ancient authorities read *sprinkled with*
18.22: Is 24.8; Ezek 26.13.   **18.23:** Jer 25.10.   **18.24:** Jer 51.49.   **19.2:** Deut 32.43.
19.3: Is 34.10.   **19.5:** Ps 115.13.   **19.7:** Ps 118.24.   **19.11:** Ezek 1.1.   **19.12:** Dan 10.6.
19.15: Ps 2.9.   **19.16:** Deut 10.17; Dan 2.47.   **19.17:** Ezek 39.4, 17-20.

20 Then I saw an angel coming down from heaven, holding in his hand the key of the bottomless pit and a great chain. ² And he seized the dragon, that ancient serpent, who is the Devil and Satan, and bound him for a thousand years, ³ and threw him into the pit, and shut it and sealed it over him, that he should deceive the nations no more, till the thousand years were ended. After that he must be loosed for a little while.

4 Then I saw thrones, and seated on them were those to whom judgment was committed. Also I saw the souls of those who had been beheaded for their testimony to Jesus and for the word of God, and who had not worshiped the beast or its image and had not received its mark on their foreheads or their hands. They came to life, and reigned with Christ a thousand years. ⁵ The rest of the dead did not come to life until the thousand years were ended. This is the first resurrection. ⁶ Blessed and holy is he who shares in the first resurrection! Over such the second death has no power, but they shall be priests of God and of Christ, and they shall reign with him a thousand years.

7 And when the thousand years are ended, Satan will be loosed from his prison ⁸ and will come out to deceive the nations which are at the four corners of the earth, that is, Gog and Mā′gog, to gather them for battle; their number is like the sand of the sea. ⁹ And they marched up over the broad earth and surrounded the camp of the saints and the beloved city; but fire came down from heaven*ⁿ* and consumed them, ¹⁰ and the devil who had deceived them was thrown into the lake of fire and brimstone where the beast and the false prophet were, and they will be tormented day and night for ever and ever.

11 Then I saw a great white throne and him who sat upon it; from his presence earth and sky fled away, and no place was found for them. ¹² And I saw the dead, great and small, standing before the throne, and books were opened. Also another book was opened, which is the book of life. And the dead were judged by what was written in the books, by what they had done.

¹³ And the sea gave up the dead in it, Death and Hades gave up the dead in them, and all were judged by what they had done. ¹⁴ Then Death and Hades were thrown into the lake of fire. This is the second death, the lake of fire; ¹⁵ and if any one's name was not found written in the book of life, he was thrown into the lake of fire.

21 Then I saw a new heaven and a new earth; for the first heaven and the first earth had passed away, and the sea was no more. ² And I saw the holy city, new Jerusalem, coming down out of heaven from God, prepared as a bride adorned for her husband; ³ and I heard a great voice from the throne saying, "Behold, the dwelling of God is with men. He will dwell with them, and they shall be his people,*ᵒ* and God himself will be with them;*ᵖ* ⁴ he will wipe away every tear from their eyes, and death shall be no more, neither shall there be mourning nor crying nor pain any more, for the former things have passed away."

5 And he who sat upon the throne said, "Behold, I make all things new." Also he said, "Write this, for these words are trustworthy and true." ⁶ And he said to me, "It is done! I am the Alpha and the Omega, the beginning and the end. To the thirsty I will give water without price from the fountain of the water of life. ⁷ He who conquers shall have this heritage, and I will be his God and he shall be my son. ⁸ But as for the cowardly, the faithless, the polluted, as for murderers, fornicators, sorcerers, idolaters, and all liars, their lot shall be in the lake that burns with fire and brimstone, which is the second death."

9 Then came one of the seven angels who had the seven bowls full of the seven last plagues, and spoke to me, saying, "Come, I will show you the Bride, the wife of the Lamb." ¹⁰ And in the Spirit he carried me away to a great, high mountain, and showed me the holy city Jerusalem coming down out of heaven from God, ¹¹ having the glory of God, its radiance like a most rare jewel, like a jasper, clear as crystal. ¹² It had a great, high wall, with twelve gates, and at the gates twelve angels, and on the gates the names of the

ⁿ Other ancient authorities read *from God, out of heaven,* or *out of heaven from God*
ᵒ Other ancient authorities read *peoples*
ᵖ Other ancient authorities add *and be their God*

20.4: Dan 7.9, 22, 27.   20.8: Ezek 38.2, 9, 15.   20.9: 2 Kings 1.10-12.
20.11-12: Dan 7.9-10.   20.15: Rev 3.5.   21.1: Is 66.22.   21.2: Rev 3.12.
21.3: Ezek 37.27.   21.4: Is 25.8; 35.10.   21.5: Is 43.19.   21.6: Is 55.1.
21.7: Ps 89.27-28.   21.8: Is 30.33.   21.10: Ezek 40.2.   21.12: Ezek 48.30-35; Ex 28.21.

twelve tribes of the sons of Israel were inscribed; [13] on the east three gates, on the north three gates, on the south three gates, and on the west three gates. [14] And the wall of the city had twelve foundations, and on them the twelve names of the twelve apostles of the Lamb.

15 And he who talked to me had a measuring rod of gold to measure the city and its gates and walls. [16] The city lies foursquare, its length the same as its breadth; and he measured the city with his rod, twelve thousand stadia;[q] its length and breadth and height are equal. [17] He also measured its wall, a hundred and forty-four cubits by a man's measure, that is, an angel's. [18] The wall was built of jasper, while the city was pure gold, clear as glass. [19] The foundations of the wall of the city were adorned with every jewel; the first was jasper, the second sapphire, the third agate, the fourth emerald, [20] the fifth onyx, the sixth carnelian, the seventh chrysolite, the eighth beryl, the ninth topaz, the tenth chrysoprase, the eleventh jacinth, the twelfth amethyst. [21] And the twelve gates were twelve pearls, each of the gates made of a single pearl, and the street of the city was pure gold, transparent as glass.

22 And I saw no temple in the city, for its temple is the Lord God the Almighty and the Lamb. [23] And the city has no need of sun or moon to shine upon it, for the glory of God is its light, and its lamp is the Lamb. [24] By its light shall the nations walk; and the kings of the earth shall bring their glory into it, [25] and its gates shall never be shut by day—and there shall be no night there; [26] they shall bring into it the glory and the honor of the nations. [27] But nothing unclean shall enter it, nor any one who practices abomination or falsehood, but only those who are written in the Lamb's book of life.

22 Then he showed me the river of the water of life, bright as crystal, flowing from the throne of God and of the Lamb [2] through the middle of the street of the city; also, on either side of the river, the tree of life[r] with its twelve kinds of fruit, yielding its fruit each month; and the

leaves of the tree were for the healing of the nations. [3] There shall be no more be anything accursed, but the throne of God and of the Lamb shall be in it, and his servants shall worship him; [4] they shall see his face, and his name shall be on their foreheads. [5] And night shall be no more; they need no light of lamp or sun, for the Lord God will be their light, and they shall reign for ever and ever.

6 And he said to me, "These words are trustworthy and true. And the Lord, the God of the spirits of the prophets, has sent his angel to show his servants what must soon take place. [7] And behold, I am coming soon."

Blessed is he who keeps the words of the prophecy of this book.

8 I John am he who heard and saw these things. And when I heard and saw them, I fell down to worship at the feet of the angel who showed them to me; [9] but he said to me, "You must not do that! I am a fellow servant with you and your brethren the prophets, and with those who keep the words of this book. Worship God."

10 And he said to me, "Do not seal up the words of the prophecy of this book, for the time is near. [11] Let the evildoer still do evil, and the filthy still be filthy, and the righteous still do right, and the holy still be holy."

12 "Behold, I am coming soon, bringing my recompense, to repay every one for what he has done. [13] I am the Alpha and the Omega, the first and the last, the beginning and the end."

14 Blessed are those who wash their robes,[s] that they may have the right to the tree of life and that they may enter the city by the gates. [15] Outside are the dogs and sorcerers and fornicators and murderers and idolaters, and every one who loves and practices falsehood.

16 "I Jesus have sent my angel to you with this testimony for the churches. I am the root and the offspring of David, the bright morning star."

17 The Spirit and the Bride say, "Come." And let him who hears say, "Come." And let him who is thirsty come, let him who desires take the water of life without price.

---

[q] About fifteen hundred miles
[r] Or *the Lamb. In the midst of the street of the city, and on either side of the river, was the tree of life,* etc.   [s] Other ancient authorities read *do his commandments*

21.15: Ezek 40.5.   **21.19:** Is 54.11-12.   **21.23:** Is 24.23; 60.1, 19.   **21.25:** Is 60.11.
21.27: Is 52.1; Rev 3.5.   **22.2:** Gen 2.9.   **22.3:** Zech 14.11.   **22.4:** Ps 17.15.
22.11: Dan 12.10.   **22.12:** Is 40.10; Jer 17.10.   **22.13:** Is 44.6; 48.12.
22.14: Gen 2.9; 3.22.   **22.16:** Is 11.1, 10.   **22.17:** Is 55.1.

18 I warn every one who hears the words of the prophecy of this book: if any one adds to them, God will add to him the plagues described in this book, 19 and if any one takes away from the words of the book of this prophecy, God will take away his share in the tree of life and in the holy city, which are described in this book.

20 He who testifies to these things says, "Surely I am coming soon." Amen. Come, Lord Jesus!

21 The grace of the Lord Jesus be with all the saints.ᶦ Amen.

ᶦ Other ancient authorities omit all; others omit the saints
22.21: 2 Thess 3.18.

THE OLD TESTAMENT

THE BOOK OF GENESIS

The word *genesis* means "a beginning or origin," and it is the title given to the first Book of the Bible because this Book tells of the creation of the earth and of mankind. The early history of Israel is told here, including full accounts of Abraham and his descendants, who were the ancestors of the Hebrews; of Noah and his descendants, who spread over the world; and of Joseph, the son of Jacob, who was responsible for the people of Israel going down into Egypt, where they were made welcome and raised their families.

THE BOOK OF EXODUS

Exodus means "departure or a going out." The Book of Exodus tells how the descendants of Jacob, the Israelites, were mistreated by the kings of Egypt, and how they were led to freedom. The story of Moses is begun here, including the story of the pity he felt for his people in their suffering and how he led them out of Egypt, across the Red Sea toward Palestine, the "Promised Land." This Book also tells of how the Israelites camping at Mount Sinai received the Ten Commandments from Moses, who had been given them by God.

THE BOOK OF LEVITICUS

This is the book of the Levites, the members of the tribe of Levi who were chosen to assist the Jewish priests. The laws and rules of worship are set forth in this Book. The Book also contains rules governing such everyday matters as how people should treat one another, how disease should be treated and prevented, and how and what punishments should be administered.

THE BOOK OF NUMBERS

The title *Numbers* is a translation of the name of the Greek version of the Book. It is so called because it gives an account of the two censuses (or numberings) of the Hebrews, taken after their departure from Egypt. The story of the peoples' escape, which was begun in the Book of Exodus, is continued in the Book of Numbers. This Book also tells of the appointment of Joshua as Moses' successor.

THE BOOK OF DEUTERONOMY

Deuteronomy means "the second law"; in this Book the law of Moses is set down for the second time. It was set down the first time in Leviticus. In that Book it was written for the priests; here, in Deuteronomy, it is intended for the instruction of the ordinary people. The Book of Deuteronomy continues the history told in the closing chapters of Numbers. This Book is made up mostly, however, of addresses given by Moses to his people. It includes Moses' farewell speech and his warning to the people.

THE BOOK OF JOSHUA

This Book tells how Joshua, Moses' successor, led the Israelites into the Promised Land. Their journey out of Egypt was described in the Books of Exodus and Numbers, and the history of that journey is continued here. This Book tells how Joshua led the people across the river Jordan, and how they captured the city of Jericho and went on to conquer the rest of the Promised Land. A description of the division of this land among the Israelites is also given.

THE BOOK OF JUDGES

After the death of Joshua, Israel was under the control of a series of leaders who, because they settled disputes, were called Judges. This Book tells the story of those leaders. Some of them were not very important. Others were great men of supreme courage and wisdom, who in times of crisis came forward to deliver the people from evil and suffering.

The Book of Judges covers the history of Israel from the time of Joshua's death until the death of Samson.

THE BOOK OF RUTH

This is an episode concerning the ancestors of David, Israel's greatest king. It is the story of Ruth, a widow of Moab who left her own people to accompany Naomi, her mother-in-law, back to her homeland of Israel. There Ruth met, fell in love with, and married Boaz. They had a son, Obed, who, when he grew up, had a son named Jesse. And the son of Jesse was David. It is thought that the author of this Book tried to show that good could come from lands other than Israel. For if it had not been for Ruth's devotion to Naomi, there never would have been a King David.

THE BOOKS OF SAMUEL

These two Books continue the history of Israel from the times written of in the Book of Judges until the death of King David. The Books were originally one book and are named after Samuel because he is the one who is described in the opening chapters.

The histories of Samuel and Saul and David are told here. Samuel, a spokesman of God, anointed Saul and, later, David as kings of Israel.

The second Book of Samuel is concerned mostly with the hero David, his being made king, and the many good and brave things he did for his people. This Book also tells of David's sins, his confession of them, and his repentance. David was a man who loved God and tried always to do what he thought was right.

THE BOOKS OF KINGS

The history begun in the first Book of Samuel and continued in the second Book of Samuel is carried on in the first and second Books of Kings. The first Book begins when David is old and about to die. Then comes the history of Solomon, David's son, who made the kingdom stronger and wealthier and who built the first Temple. The remainder of the first Book and the opening portions of the second Book are given over to accounts of a long list of kings, some good, but many wicked, and almost all unimportant. The second Book also describes the great religious reformation brought about by the finding of the Book of the Law (the Book of Deuteronomy). However, the closing chapters provide a bleak account of the destruction of Israel by invading Babylonian armies.

Perhaps the best-known chapters in these two Books tell of the prophet Elijah and his disciple, Elisha, and their insistence on right-eousness and their triumph over evil.

THE BOOKS OF CHRONICLES

These two Books deal with the same period of history dealt with in the two Books of Samuel and the two Books of Kings. According to Jewish tradition, Ezra was the author of the Books of Chronicles. It seems clear that his purpose was to glorify King David as the servant of God and the designer of the Temple. Many long family histories are given in these Books for the apparent purpose of showing that from the time of Adam it was God's purpose to create David.

THE BOOK OF EZRA

This Book, as well as the Book of Nehemiah that follows, tells the story of the Jews' return to Jerusalem after the Babylonian exile. These Books tell of the dangers and difficulties that confronted these people after their release by Cyrus, their Babylonian conqueror. The Book of Ezra, in particular, is concerned with the rebuilding of the Temple. It tells Ezra's own story of his return to Jerusalem and how he encouraged the people. Ezra was the priest and scribe who would teach and train the people how to worship and how to follow the law of God after the Temple was rebuilt. It was thought that only in the Temple could worship be celebrated properly.

THE BOOK OF NEHEMIAH

Nehemiah was one of the Jewish exiles under Persian rule after the Persians had conquered Babylon. This Book tells of his return to Jeru-salem and his rallying of the people to rebuild the city's walls. In spite of danger, discouragements, and rivalries among the people themselves, the walls were rebuilt and the people once again made safe from invading armies. After Nehemiah's return to the Persian court, the people fell into wicked ways. Nehemiah came to Jerusalem once again, severely disciplined the people, and taught them that only by following their religion strictly could they endure.

THE BOOK OF ESTHER

This Book is the story of Esther, the beautiful Jewish maiden who became the wife and queen of Ahasuerus, a Persian king. It tells how she risked her life in a successful attempt to foil the king's minister, Haman, in his plot to destroy all the Jews throughout the Persian Empire.

THE BOOK OF JOB

This Book, in the form of a long poem, tells the story of Job. When the story begins he is a rich and happy man, but he soon loses his wealth and his children, and is set upon by a dreadful sickness. The bulk of the Book is a discussion between him and his friends about why he has been made to suffer so many misfortunes. The voice of God finally speaks to Job and rebukes him for questioning the ways of God, which are beyond the power of man to understand. Job then repents and his wealth is restored twofold.

THE BOOK OF PSALMS

The Hebrew word for Psalms means "praise" or "songs of praise." However, this term can be appropriately applied to only some of the 150 religious poems contained in this Book—namely, to those which were set to music and meant to be sung in the Temple as part of the religious ceremony. The other Psalms may be divided into four additional groups: (1) pleas for God's help in times of national disaster; (2) songs of praise to a reigning Hebrew king; (3) pleas or laments of an individual for God's help in trying circumstances; and (4) songs of thanks or gratitude to God for help he had given an individual.

THE BOOK OF PROVERBS

The Book of Proverbs is a collection of wise thoughts and sayings about life and behavior. They were intended for the guidance of the people of Israel. Some authorities say that Solomon, the son of David, was the author of the Proverbs. Others say, however, that Solomon only collected them or supervised their collection.

THE BOOK OF ECCLESIASTES

This Book begins with a statement that it is written by "the Preacher, the son of David, king in Jerusalem." This is commonly thought to mean Solomon.

The words of the author are, generally, of a discouraging nature. He laments over the impossibility of achieving real happiness by material means and, as a result, thinks of life in general as having no meaning. He speaks of, and demonstrates again and again, the vanity of all things, particularly all actions of men. The Book ends with the message that man must fear God and keep his commandments for that is his "whole duty."

THE SONG OF SOLOMON

This Book is a series of poems about two lovers. Opinions differ widely as to how this Book should be interpreted. Some consider the lover to represent God and the maiden to represent the people of Israel. Others see the lover as symbolic of Christ and the maiden as the Church. There are other interpretations, but these two are the most popular. The Song is traditionally supposed to have been composed by Solomon.

THE BOOK OF ISAIAH

This Book deals with the life and times of Isaiah, the greatest of the Hebrew prophets, and his prophecies concerning those times. The Book really falls into two main divisions: the first describes Assyria and its terrible armies, and the second deals with the Jewish people who have been conquered and carried as captives into Babylon.

Isaiah prophesied (in the first part) that Assyrian armies would not capture Jerusalem, and they did not. Later he prophesied, accurately, the return to Israel of the exiles after their Babylonian captivity. He also made a prophecy which Matthew later interpreted as foretelling the virgin birth of Jesus.

THE BOOK OF JEREMIAH

Jeremiah of Jerusalem was called upon to be a prophet. The word of God came to him while he was praying, telling him that the Babylonians would conquer his people. This Book is chiefly a collection of the messages and warnings which he carried from God to the people of Israel, predicting the ruin of their country. The Book tells how Jeremiah, who loved his people, was saddened by their great sinning and was discouraged because they would not heed his warnings of impending doom. Because there was a long delay in the fulfillment of his predictions, he felt forsaken even by the Lord. The prophet does express hope, however, for the renewal of God's covenant with the Jews and for their restoration as God's chosen people.

THE LAMENTATIONS OF JEREMIAH

This Book of five poems concerns the destruction of Jerusalem and the great suffering of the people following that event. The Book is a confession of the sins of the people—a confession based on the sorrowful realization that disaster had come upon them because they had forgotten God. Trust is expressed that God will forgive the people.

THE BOOK OF EZEKIEL

Like Jeremiah, the prophet Ezekiel prophesied both before and after the destruction of Jerusalem. He was one of the captives carried off to Babylon.

Included in this Book are prophecies concerning the exiles in Babylon and others dealing with the people left behind in Jerusalem. His messages are delivered in the form of threats, arguments, and prophecies, but the best-known parts of the Book describe visions which have come to him.

Ezekiel foretells that the land of Israel will again be filled with people of the house of David and that the ruins of Israel will be rebuilt.

Authorities seem certain that Ezekiel himself is the author of this Book.

THE BOOK OF DANIEL

The prophet Daniel lived during the time of the Babylonian conquest. Written under his name by an unknown author, this Book seems to be intended to encourage the people to keep their faith in the restoration of their kingdom. By giving examples in story form of the deliverance of the faithful from certain destruction, the author apparently hoped that the people would gather the courage to overthrow their conquerors. The stories include those of Daniel himself and how he was thrown into the den of lions, of Nebuchadnezzar's dream which was interpreted by Daniel, of Daniel's three friends who were thrown into the fiery furnace, and of King Belshazzar's seeing the handwriting on the wall.

The last part of this Book contains descriptions of visions which came to Daniel—visions of promise and encouragement for the Jewish people.

THE BOOK OF HOSEA

This is the first of twelve Books containing the writings of those who are often called the minor prophets. Hosea lived and preached in Israel at about the same time as Amos; these were prosperous days for Israel, although it was prosperity gained in wicked ways.

Hosea rebuked the people for their unfaithfulness to God and for their sins, and threatened them with punishment if they did not turn from their wicked ways. He also wrote of God's judgment and of His willingness to forgive those who wanted to be forgiven.

THE BOOK OF JOEL

This Book deals with a community of Jews who returned to Jerusalem from exile. When the community was set upon by a plague of locusts and then a drought, the prophet Joel came to them and told them that they were being punished for their sins. He told them to repent and turn to God, who would show them His goodness. Joel also prophesied Israel's eventual triumph over her enemies.

THE BOOK OF AMOS

Although he had never been a prophet, Amos was called upon by God to prophesy and rebuke the people of Israel for their wicked ways. He prophesied that God's judgment would fall on Damascus, Tyre, Edom, Ammon, and Judah, but would fall most heavily on Israel, to which God had given so much and which, in spite of that, had still done evil. The Book ends with Amos' promise that the kingdom of God would again be restored.

THE BOOK OF OBADIAH

Very little is known about the prophet Obadiah. His "vision" makes up this Book, the shortest of the Old Testament prophecies. The Book concerns the Edomites, long the enemies and tormentors of Israel. When Edom is destroyed, Obadiah looks upon the destruction as no accident but, rather, the judgment of God upon a proud and cruel people.

THE BOOK OF JONAH

This Book was written by an unknown author. It is the story of the prophet Jonah, who was commanded by God to preach to the heathen city of Nineveh, disobeyed this command, and was swallowed by a great fish as punishment. After the fish vomited out Jonah, he did preach at Nineveh and the people of Nineveh repented. The story seems to be an attempt to bring home the following message to the Jewish people: the love of God reaches out to all peoples, and he is willing to spare and forgive even the most wicked when they are willing to repent and obey his commands.

THE BOOK OF MICAH

The prophet Micah lived and prophesied in the days of the prophet Isaiah. This Book is full of his sermons urging the people of Israel to repent and give up their ways of sin and unfaithfulness, threatening them with punishment if they do not, and, finally, telling them that, because of their wickedness, they do not deserve to be saved from destruction. The Book also contains many prophecies, including one in which Micah foretells that "one who is to be ruler in Israel" shall come forth from Bethlehem.

THE BOOK OF NAHUM

Little is known of Nahum, but this Book, a "vision," deals with the destruction of Nineveh, the wicked city of the Assyrians. The prophet Nahum writes that no evil nation such as Nineveh can stand up to the final judgment of God.

THE BOOK OF HABAKKUK

All that is known about the prophet Habakkuk is what can be found in his Book. The Book is in the form of a dialogue between Habakkuk and God. The prophet complains that, although his people of Judah have been evil and deserve to be punished, he cannot understand why that punishment should come from the even-more-evil Chaldeans. God replies that His judgment will come to all the wicked of the earth and that only the righteous and the obedient will survive.

THE BOOK OF ZEPHANIAH

Zephaniah, the great-grandson of Hezekiah, lived under Josiah. Josiah's reign followed the wicked reigns of Manasseh and Ammon and, thus, the prophet Zephaniah was certain that God's judgment would fall upon Judah and Jerusalem unless there was a sincere turning to the Lord. The prophet describes the great day of wrath that is to come upon the nations of the earth unless they repent.

THE BOOK OF HAGGAI

This Book of four sermons by the prophet Haggai urges the Jews to complete their rebuilding of the Temple. Haggai came from exile in Babylon to find that work on the Temple was not progressing because of a lack of food and shelter and the opposition of neighboring people. He roused the Jews by describing the glory of the new Temple and by promising them that God would again bless them if they continued their work.

THE BOOK OF ZECHARIAH

The prophet Zechariah lived at the same time as Haggai, and he, with

Haggai, encouraged the people to rebuild the Temple. Whereas Haggai had rebuked the people, Zechariah inspired them with messages that had come to him in the form of visions. Zechariah speaks of the peace and prosperity that will come to Jerusalem and of the destruction of the enemies of the Jews if they will rebuild God's Temple. He also prophesies the coming of "your king . . . humble and riding on an ass."

THE BOOK OF MALACHI

This Book, the last Book of the Old Testament, was written after the Jewish people had returned from captivity in Babylon and had rebuilt the Temple in Jerusalem. The prophet Malachi attacks the wickedness of the people, who had fallen into sinning ways even though they could once again worship God as their fathers had before the Exile. Malachi, about whom nothing is known, encourages the people to be more sincere and to obey the laws of Moses. The Book ends with the prediction that God will send a messenger to prepare His way.

THE NEW TESTAMENT

The first four Books of the New Testament are called the Gospels. *Gospel* is a translation of a Greek word meaning "good tidings" or "good news." The good news in these Books is the story of Jesus, His life, His teachings, His death, and His resurrection. Although there are four Books, there is but one story, a story that four of Jesus' disciples wanted to be carried to as many people as possible. The story was written as the disciples remembered or learned from others the events of the life of Jesus. Thus, each of the Books is somewhat different from the others because each author remembered or learned different things and thought of the life of Jesus in a slightly different way. It is not certain (nor is it regarded as important) that the name of the disciple attached to each of these Books is necessarily the author of that Book.

THE GOSPEL ACCORDING TO MATTHEW

Although it seems quite certain that this Gospel was written after the Gospel of Mark, it is placed first in the New Testament because it was hoped that this Book would convince the Jews that Jesus was their long-awaited Savior. By means of frequent quotations from the Old Testament, Matthew tried to show that the coming of Jesus was the fulfillment of Old Testament prophecy. For example, Matthew says that, on one occasion, Jesus went from Nazareth into Galilee so "that what was spoken by the prophet Isaiah might be fulfilled," and then quotes a passage (Mt 4.15) that is an almost exact equivalent of Isaiah 9.1.

Again and again, Matthew points out such connections between the Old Testament and Jesus' life. He emphasizes that part of Jesus' life and teachings which is summed up in Jesus' own statement: "Think not that I have come to abolish the law and the prophets; I have not come to abolish them but to fulfill them."

The Sermon on the Mount appears only in the Gospel of Matthew, as do several of Jesus' parables and the most familiar accounts of Jesus' last days in Jerusalem and His crucifixion.

THE GOSPEL ACCORDING TO MARK

This is the earliest of the Gospels. According to tradition, Mark listened to Peter, one of the original disciples of Jesus, as he preached the story of Jesus in the churches of Rome, and he wrote down Peter's accounts so that others would have them. To the facts of Jesus' life first set down in this Book, Matthew and Luke later added quotations and details to make their own versions of the story more convincing.

The Gospel of Mark gives little information about Jesus' teachings, and reports nothing of his birth or boyhood. Mark talks mostly about what Jesus did, stressing His Divine power and showing how He used this power, as in overcoming the powers of evil by healing those "of unclean spirit."

THE GOSPEL ACCORDING TO LUKE

Luke was not one of the personal disciples of Jesus. He seems to have worked from and added to the Gospel of Mark in compiling his Book, which was written for his own people, the Greeks. Because he set about to compile a clear, full account of Jesus' life, we find details and stories in his Gospel that we find in none of the others: for instance, the account of the birth of John the Baptist, the record of Mary's song of thankfulness (*The Magnificat*), the story of the shepherds and the song of the angels when Jesus was born, the tale of Jesus at the Temple questioning the learned men, and the account of His visit to the house of the hated tax collector. Furthermore, the story of Jesus' birth and early boyhood is given in much greater detail here than in the other Gospels.

Throughout this Book, Luke shows that he looks upon Jesus as the Savior of all men and not just the fulfillment of Old Testament prophecy.

THE GOSPEL ACCORDING TO JOHN

John, traditionally called one of Jesus' most beloved disciples, may well have been the author of this Book, for it was almost certainly written by one who had known Jesus and understood him in a special way.

The Gospel of John is not so much concerned with telling the story of Jesus' life as with presenting Jesus as the Son of God and explaining how belief in Jesus will benefit all men. By telling who Jesus was, what He stood for, and what He had meant to John personally, John hoped to show all men how to live.

It is thought that no other Book has done more than the Gospel of John to establish the teachings of Jesus as a religion for everyone; for, as John says of Jesus "to all who received him, who believed in his name, he gave power to become children of God."

THE ACTS OF THE APOSTLES

This Book was written by the same person who wrote the Gospel of Luke.

The Book of Acts tells of what the disciples did after the death and resurrection of Jesus and of their early teachings. It tells how they preached in Jerusalem and many other cities. In many cases, their efforts were met with threats and cruel treatment. In fact, Stephen was stoned to death, and Peter and John were arrested as they were spreading the Gospel.

In this Book, the story of Paul (originally Saul) is told—Paul, who had more to do with spreading Christianity than any other person. His story is told from the moment he began to preach the gospel. An account is given of the dangerous journeys he took, of the churches he established, and of the lessons he taught in the name of Christ.

THE LETTER TO THE ROMANS

While Paul was in Corinth, he wrote a letter to the Christians in Rome, whom he planned to visit. In this letter he talks of Christianity as God's plan for bringing about righteousness in man.

Paul shows that all men had sinned so much they could not help themselves, and that then Christ came and died for them while they were still sinners. Now, Paul says, both Jews and Gentiles can look to Christ as their Savior. Paul then explains to the Christians how they should behave toward one another in this new life that Christ has brought to them.

In this letter as well as the others he wrote, he tells things he wanted everyone to know about Jesus.

THE LETTERS TO THE CORINTHIANS

Paul had been to Corinth and had worked and preached there. Afterwards, when he had gone on to Ephesus, he wrote these two letters to the Christians in Corinth. He had heard that they were sinning and living wicked lives; therefore, in his first letter, he rebukes them for their evil ways and points out what they have done wrong. He also answers the many questions they have asked. He encourages them to live up to the standards of unselfishness and freedom from sin taught by Christ.

In his second letter Paul thanks the Christians in Corinth for listening to his messages and for trying to live the life Jesus had expected his followers to live. Answering an earlier complaint about the difficulties of leading a Christian life, Paul tells how he himself had suffered as he traveled about preaching the gospel of Christ. He shows them how richness of the soul can come from following and teaching others to follow Jesus.

THE LETTER TO THE GALATIANS

This letter was written to the Christians of Galatia. Paul had been there and had converted many of the people to Christianity. He wrote this letter because he was troubled by news he had received that the Christians of Galatia had been listening to false teachers—teachers preaching a gospel contrary to the gospel of Christ. These teachers tried to make the people believe that it would be safer to live by the Mosaic law (the ancient Jewish law set down in the first five Books of the Old Testament) than to trust in the love and forgiveness of God as Jesus had taught. But Paul points out that, although the Mosaic law had been handed down by God, it is not to be strictly followed by Christians because faith in Jesus had taken its place.

THE LETTER TO THE EPHESIANS

Paul had founded a church in the city of Ephesus. He later wrote this letter to the Christians of that church, telling them what he thinks the ideal church should be and what it should accomplish. Paul emphasizes the importance of being a Christian and shows what difference being a Christian makes in the way one thinks and acts. He talks about the importance of unity among Christians, not only in the community and the world but among the members of a household. He says that if everyone does his duty and works with others through the unity of a Christian family, the dream of the ideal church will be realized.

Paul concludes by urging the Ephesians to "put on the whole armor of God" so that they will be able to stand against the wickedness that will confront them everywhere.

THE LETTER TO THE PHILIPPIANS

Among the places Paul visited in his travels, according to the *Book of Acts*, was the city of Philippi. In this letter, Paul expresses love and gratitude to the Philippians who had shown him so much kindness when he had been at Philippi many years before.

Although Paul was a prisoner and may have been approaching death, there is no sadness in this Book. Instead, his attitude is cheerful and his outlook far from gloomy as he says "For me . . . to die is gain."

Paul finishes this letter by cautioning the Philippians against those who are enemies of Christ, and by expressing the hope that they would continue to follow Christ.

THE LETTER TO THE COLOSSIANS

It seems that Paul had never been to the city of Colossae, but a companion of his had preached there and established a church.

Paul had heard that there were people in Colossae who were trying to confuse the Christians there and shake their faith in Jesus. Paul wrote to warn the Christians against faulty doctrines and philosophies and against the danger of believing that salvation could be gained in ways other than through God. He tells them that Christ is the only mediator between God and man and that only by turning to Christ can they be saved.

Paul also points out that "Christ is all, and in all" and that, therefore, Christians should live in unity and fellowship and abandon sinful ways.

If they do, it will seem to them that they have been given a new life, a life with Christ.

THE LETTERS TO THE THESSALONIANS

Paul had preached in the city of Thessalonica and had converted many people there to a belief in Christ. While in Corinth he wrote the first of two letters to the Thessalonians, thanking them for the many kindnesses they had shown him. He reminds them how wonderful their new life is now that they are followers of Jesus, and goes on to tell them what sort of people they must be if they are to continue in this new life. He tells them that they should "show love to one another and to all men" and should continue "to mind [their] own affairs."

Paul had learned that the Christians of Thessalonica believed in the early return of the risen Christ to earth. They felt that they could stop working and just wait for His coming. In his second letter to them, Paul warns of troubled times before the coming of Jesus, which may be a long way off. He tells them that nothing is to be gained from idleness and that the way to be ready for the Lord is "to do [your] work in quietness and to earn [your] own living" no matter what the day may bring.

THE LETTERS TO TIMOTHY

Timothy was Paul's friend and helper; he had traveled with Paul on several of his journeys. These two letters are personal letters from Paul to him.

In the first letter Paul tells Timothy about the false beliefs that were being taught in the churches. In order to stop this trend, he points out how the ministers and other church officers should be chosen and what they ought to teach. Paul goes on to discuss a variety of matters, most of them having to do with personal relationships between people.

The second letter contains instructions as to the way in which Timothy, as a minister, should preach the word of God. Paul sees his own end drawing near, and he tells Timothy that he is relying on him to carry on the work that he, Paul, had started. But Paul warns Timothy that he will have to "be strong in the grace that is Christ Jesus" if his teachings are to be successful and if he is to lead the people to salvation.

THE LETTER TO TITUS

Titus was another friend of Paul's and, like Timothy, had done some traveling with Paul. This letter was written to Titus at Crete, where Paul had left him.

Paul tells Titus how to organize the church there. He outlines the needs of the church and explains to Titus that he should fulfill those needs in spite of the opposition he is certain to encounter.

This letter also contains personal advice to Titus, who Paul hopes will carry on his, Paul's, work. Paul puts particular stress on the conduct that is expected of all men, saying that they are "to renounce irreligion and worldly passions, and to live sober, upright, and godly lives."

THE LETTER TO PHILEMON

This letter from Paul to Philemon concerns Philemon's slave, Onesimus, who had run away. Onesimus had met Paul and, apparently, been a help to him. Paul sent Onesimus back, asking Philemon to receive him "no longer as a slave but more than a slave, as a beloved brother."

THE LETTER TO THE HEBREWS

The author of this Book is not known. It is believed that the Book, or Letter, was written not only for the Hebrews, but for all those whose religion was based on the Old Testament.

The author points out that in earlier times God had spoken through the prophets, had handed down his law through Moses, and had given the people a high priest to worship. But now, the author says, in Jesus, God is speaking to them in a new way, for Jesus is superior to the prophets, to Moses, even to the angels, and is Himself the "great high priest." Jesus makes it possible for everyone to become closer to God. By believing in Jesus and following His ways, Christians can live with the confidence that God will forgive their sins and can face life with courage and gladness. Now, the author continues, that life can be approached with new confidence, everyone must approach God with a greater faith.

Finally, the author sets down a list of duties for all Christians to follow in order to offer God "acceptable worship" for having received "a kingdom that cannot be shaken."

THE LETTER OF JAMES

The author of this letter is not definitely known, but according to an old tradition it is James, the brother of Jesus. It does not seem to have been written to any particular church or people, as the letters of Paul were, but rather to Christians in general.

In this letter, James is concerned with giving advice on Christian behavior. He advises against faultfinding, swearing, impatience, jealousy, selfish ambition, and saying unkind things about others.

He encourages Christians to act and "be doers of the word" because only through actions can one prove his faith in God.

THE LETTERS OF PETER

Peter was one of the original disciples of Jesus. The first of his two letters was written to a group of exiles who were being treated cruelly. He reminds them that Jesus, too, had suffered and that, later, glory had come to Him from God. Peter tells them that they also can place their trust in God. They must endure trouble and danger, love and help one another, and remember Jesus. If they do these things and pray, the strength of God will come to them.

Peter's second letter is concerned with conditions in the church when the people began to feel disappointed over the failure of Jesus to return to earth after His death and resurrection. False teachers had been encouraging them to believe that Jesus would not come back and telling them that, therefore, it was useless to hope for better things. But Peter tells the Christians to ignore these teachers and be patient and brave, for God will bring "new heavens and a new earth" according to his promise. He tells them that while they wait they must take care to behave as Christians should so as "to be found by [God] without spot or blemish, and at peace."

THE LETTERS OF JOHN

Most authorities agree that these three short letters were written by John, the author of the fourth Gospel. The general message that John seems to be giving in these letters is that people ought to love one another as God loves them. In the first letter John tells about fellowship and brotherly love and describes the benefit Christians can expect to gain from them.

Although the second letter is addressed to "the elect lady," authorities are not certain whether this means a real lady or, instead, is a metaphor for a church. In either case, it is a warning against taking in anyone who does not believe in Christ.

The third letter is written to a man called Gaius, whom John praises for his hospitality to his fellow Christians. John tells him to continue to do good, for "He who does good is of God."

THE LETTER OF JUDE

This is the last of the letters, and is written by Jude, thought by some authorities to have been the brother of Jesus. This letter seems to be addressed to all Christians. It urges them to be steadfast in defending the truth, warns them against wicked behavior and wrong ideas, and asks them to use sympathy and kindness in helping those who have not been careful to avoid wickedness.

THE REVELATION TO JOHN

This is the only Book in the New Testament that contains prophecies, and it is sometimes called the *Apocalypse*, which means "revelation" or "a sudden disclosure that contains a prophecy." Many authorities believe that this Book, like the three letters of John, was written by the author of the fourth Gospel.

The Book seems to be a collection of earlier prophecies which had to do with the coming of a Savior and the setting up of the kingdom of God on earth, after which all men would exist in perfect peace and justice. The author appears to take these prophecies and use them to foretell the second coming of Jesus, under whom the world will be made perfect.

Between the opening and closing passages of the Book, seven visions are described—visions that are full of symbols and parables, or moral lessons, many of which are very difficult to understand.

The main message that John seems to want to give is that Jesus, who had died and risen, will always be alive and will always be stronger than all the power of evil in the world. The Book ends as it began, with the assurance that Jesus will come again and be victorious over His enemies.

BIBLE READING HELPS

No one ever really finishes reading the Bible. Many persons who began reading it as youngsters continue to read it through old age, still enjoying its stories, still delighting in its noble passages, still finding comfort in the wisdom of God. There is so much in the Bible, so much depth in its teachings, that the reader continues to make new discoveries. The purpose of the Reading Helps in the following pages is to aid the reader in exploring the Bible, to give him useful information about the Bible itself and about Bible times and people.

"Discovering the Bible," the first of these helps, tells briefly about the writing of the Bible, what it contains, and how its sixty-six books were selected. (In the pages preceding this one you will find a summary of the books of the Bible.) "Daily Life and Customs in Biblical Times" will help you picture the way people in the Bible lived. "Plants and Animals of the Bible" and "Money, Weights, and Measures" answer many of the questions about these things that arise as you read the Bible.

This Bible also contains a combination dictionary-concordance, which defines the special meanings many words have in the Bible and in which the reader can locate important passages by looking up the key word. You will not only find the dictionary-concordance helpful in your Bible reading, but you will also learn much of interest by browsing through it and following up the references. Instructions for its use are printed at the front of the dictionary-concordance.

In all matters involving Christine doctrine the most generally held view is given in these Reading Helps. Important alternative views are also included where possible.

Contributors

Robert J. Hastings, Th.D., Editor, *The Illinois Baptist*

Merrill T. Gilbertson, D.D., Pastor, First Lutheran Church, Columbia Heights, Minnesota

Earl L. Core, Ph.D., Chairman of the Biology Department, The University of West Virginia

E. Leslie Carlson, Th.D., late Professor of Biblical Backgrounds and Archaeology, The Southwestern Baptist Theological Seminary

Martha Pounds Weaver, B.Sc. in Education, member Christian Education Commission, First Congregational Church, Twinsburg, Ohio

Consultants on dictionary-concordance

Iris V. Cully, Ph.D., Associate Professor of Christian Education, The Divinity School, Yale University

Kendig Brubaker Cully, Ph.D., Dean and Professor of Christian Education, New York Theological Seminary

DISCOVERING THE BIBLE

by

Robert J. Hastings

The writers of the Bible were scattered over a wide area stretching from Babylon to Rome. They were scattered even farther in time, many of them separated by centuries. They came from many different occupations—king, fisherman, farmer, priest, physician, philosopher, missionary, apostle, tax collector, prophet, shepherd. None of them could have known or imagined that his writings would some day be combined with the others as we have them in the Holy Bible, the most important book in the history of civilization.

And what writing they did! The pages of the Bible resound with the adventures of mankind—"the stories of nations, the fall of empires, the rise of kingdoms, the decline of dynasties, the tramp of armies, the crash and crack of civilizations" and the coming of Christ, "the bright and morning star."* History and prophecy, poetry and drama, humor and tragedy, stories and songs, prayers and theology all join in its mighty theme: man's relationship with God.

The Bible is a challenge to a lifetime of discovery. There are many simply told and dramatic stories, many passages of beautiful poetry, that can be easily read and understood, even by a child. But there are also many passages reflecting deep thought on problems of right and wrong, of religious faith, passages of great depth that tax the abilities of the mind. The Bible brings you the pleasure and excitement of the noblest literature. But what is far more important, it helps you see and understand the nature of God—in the experiences of its people, the words of its prophets, the songs of its psalmists, the sayings of its philosophers, finally in the teachings of Christ and the writings of His early followers.

The Bible got its name from the Greek word, *biblia*, "little books." And it is, indeed, a collection of "little books"—sixty-six of them in all. Some editions of the Bible include other sacred books of the Hebrews we call the Apocrypha. The Apocrypha are counted as Scripture by the Roman Catholic Church and as near Scripture by many other Christians. The Jewish sacred books, which include the 39 books of the Old Testament, were written in Hebrew. The 27 books of the Christian New Testament were written in Greek. The books do not appear in the Bible in the order in which they were written.

* *The Bible in Our Day*, Oxford University Press, New York, 1936

It was a long time, centuries after the first of them was written, before the books of the Bible were put together as one body of sacred writings. There were many such writings known to the Hebrews in Old Testament times and to the Christians in New Testament times. The selection of the books included in our Bible came only after they had first proven their spiritual value through the long experience of God's people. Church leaders simply confirmed what experience had taught in arriving at the Christian "canon" (= "rule"), the list of books officially recognized as sacred Scripture.

The sacred books of the Jews, the Old Testament, considered Scripture by authoritative bodies of rabbis, were known and referred to by the early Christians. These passed over naturally into the Christian Church and were from the beginning regarded as Christian canonical Scripture. Most of the books of the New Testament were accepted as part of the Christian canon within two hundred years of the birth of Christ. The great Christian leader, St. Athanasius, gave a list of New Testament books in 367 A.D. as we now have them in the Bible. This list was accepted in church councils of Hippo Regius in 393 A.D. and Carthage in 397 A.D. and 419 A.D.

Although a single great theme sweeps through the Scriptures, reaching its climax in the life, death, and resurrection of Christ, the Bible is not a continuous story like a novel, unfolding chapter by chapter. Reading it straight through is not the best way to discover the Bible, for there are some passages that have little to say to us today, some that are hard to understand without special training. You will find exploration of the Bible more exciting and more meaningful if you begin with the basic reading list, below. After completing this you will find it even more interesting to explore the entire Bible. As you discover more and more of the Bible, you will appreciate the simple truth in these words from Psalm 119, Verse 105:

"Thy word is a lamp to my feet,
and a light to my path."

Basic Bible Readings

All of Genesis

All of Exodus

Deuteronomy, Chapters 31 to 34

The first 11 chapters of Joshua

All of I and II Samuel

All of Ruth

The first 8 chapters of Esther

The first three chapters and the last chapter of Job

Psalms of your own selection (In all, there are 150)

Proverbs of your own selection

The first four and last two chapters of Ecclesiastes

The first six and the 40th, 53rd, and 55th chapters of Isaiah

The first chapter of Lamentations

The first six chapters of Ezekial

The first six chapters of Daniel

All of Hosea

The 8th chapter of Amos

All of Jonah

The 5th chapter of Micah

The 3rd chapter of Malachi

All of Mark (At the same time, you may wish to read the other Synoptic Gospels, which are Matthew and Luke. Or, you might come back to them after completing the rest of these readings.)

At least the first 11 chapters of John

All of Acts

The first three and 6th, 8th, and 12th chapters of Romans.

Chapters 7, 8, 12, 13, and 16 of I Corinthians

II Corinthians, chapters 5 and 8

The 6th chapter of Galatians

The 4th chapter of Ephesians

All of Philippians

I Thessalonians, chapters 4 and 5

The 3rd chapter of I Timothy

The 2nd chapter of II Timothy

All of Philemon

Hebrews, chapters 1, 2, 6, 11, and 12

All of James

The 3rd chapter of II Peter

All of I John

The first four and last three chapters of Revelation

DAILY LIFE AND CUSTOMS IN BIBLE TIMES

Merrill T. Gilbertson

The Scriptures were written over nineteen centuries ago by Hebrew authors in a land whose culture and way of life were very different from ours. They wore tunics, girded their loins, slept on pallets, lived in tents, and observed what seem to us strange laws of hospitality. Their patriarchal system made them a compact, closely knit people. If we are to understand the purpose and meaning of the Scriptures, it will be helpful to understand their customs.

CUSTOMS

The Patriarchal System

In a Hebrew home the father was the absolute ruler of his household (Gen. 35:2–4). His wife, children, and servants were subject to him in every way, even to the right of life and death. If the father should die, his oldest son automatically took his place. Thus the first-born normally inherited the birthright (Gen. 25:25, 31–34), and was trained to take over the leadership of the family. The early Hebrews had no other form of government until the period of Moses.

The Children in the Home

When a son married, he brought his wife to his father's home to live (Gen. 24:48–54). She was expected to help with the duties of her father-in-law's household. Because of this, the birth of a son was a welcome event. Not to have a son was grounds for divorce. Sons increased the earning power, the military might, and the size of the clan (Ps. 127:4–5). To have a daughter was often considered a cause for sympathy or an occasion for sorrow, since at her marriage she went to the home of her father-in-law, increasing his staff of workers.

When a child was born, it was wrapped snugly in bands of linen or cotton, five or six yards long and four or five inches wide. It was in swaddling cloths like these that Jesus was wrapped by His mother, Mary (Luke 2:7).

The parents were very careful in the selection of a name for their child. Each name was to indicate something connected with the child's birth or the hopes, ideals, and ambitions of its parents. Jewish girls were often named after something beautiful or virtuous. Rachel meant "lamb," Salome meant "peace," and Dorcas meant "gazelle." Boys' names often had something to do with God: Daniel, "God is my judge"; Obadiah, "servant of Jehovah"; Ezekiel, "God will strengthen." Often the son added his father's name after his own to indicate the family he came from.

Arrangements for Marriage

The parents as a rule selected a wife for their son, since she would become a part of the family tribe. Marriage demanded a dowry or bride-price, which the groom's family was required to give to the bride's father (Gen. 34:12; Ex. 22:16–17). After all, when a daughter was given in marriage she left her family and was actually diminishing the clan's efficiency. An unmarried daughter helped take care of her father's flocks, fields, and household (Ex. 2:16). Therefore, the young man who expected to gain possession of someone's daughter was required to provide a "gift" from his father's herds or flocks. Sometimes a gift might be given to the daughter by her father when she left him. Rebekah's father gave her a nurse and maidservants when she left to become the bride of Isaac (Gen. 24:59–61). Usually the prospective groom or his father gave a present directly to the bride (Gen. 24:53; 34:12). By Jesus' time this gift could be in the form of coins which she sewed to her headgear (Luke 15:8–9).

The Betrothal

Among the Hebrews the betrothal was a spoken covenant as binding as the marriage itself. At the betrothal the families of both the bride and groom met with each other to make the necessary arrangements for the marriage. Several people not related to the family were present in case some disagreement arose and to serve as witnesses. The bride received a ring of gold or some article of value from the groom. Then the groom would say, "See by this ring (or token) thou art set aside for me according to the Law of Moses and of Israel." Usually a whole year passed between the betrothal and the man's taking his wife unto himself at the actual wedding (Deut. 20:7).

The Wedding

The wedding consisted only in the ceremony of the groom coming to take the bride to his father's house to live. There was no religious service connected with the wedding. Instead, the benediction of relatives and friends (Ruth 4:11–12) gave the spiritual note. The wedding was a gala affair which consisted chiefly of two features, the procession and the marriage supper. The groom was dressed in his very best for the occasion, looking as much like a king as possible (Is. 61:10). In all this finery, the groom went with his friends to the bride's parental home to bring her through the city streets to the new home (Jer. 7:34). When the wedding procession arrived at the bridegroom's house (Ps. 45:14–15), there was feasting and celebrating (John 2:1–11) which could last for a week (Judg. 14:17). Friends, relatives, and neighbors stayed in the groom's home during this week of festivities. Every guest at the marriage banquet was required to wear the wedding garment supplied by the host (Mat. 22:12).

The adornment of the bride was a costly affair. Everything possible was done to prepare her to receive her husband (Jer. 2:32; Ezek. 16:11–12; Rev. 21:2). Her hair was braided and interwoven with jewels. If the family was poor, jewels were borrowed from friends for the occasion. The bride welcomed the groom and then left her father's house in all of her finery and perfume, with a crown on her head. The bride in the home of her husband's family was now legally a part of the clan. She was assigned a share in the duties of the household.

Divorce

The stability of the family depended upon the absolute authority of the husband. In the neighboring Arab lands he could divorce his wife without giving any explanation and without assuming any responsibility for her care or support. Just a spoken word to this effect was the only requirement for a divorce. The wife could not divorce her husband, because she was his personal property. However she could be sent away at a moment's notice if she burned the food, gave her husband no son, or if she was disobedient. Should the husband find a more desirable wife, he might demand a divorce. When the order for divorce was given to the wife, she was permitted to take with her the clothes which she was wearing. For this reason the coins on her headgear, rings, bracelets, armlets, anklets, and necklaces were very important. She lived in constant fear of becoming a substitute to a second wife whom her husband might prefer and acquire. For the Israelites, however, the Law of Moses limited the power of the husband to divorce his wife by requiring that he must hand her a *written* bill of divorce stating the grounds (Deut. 24:1); but the practice of having more than one wife was still permitted under the Mosaic code (Deut. 21:15–17; witness the grief it brought to Hannah, I Sam. 1: 1–8). Furthermore, God clearly said that He hates "putting away" or divorce (Mal. 2:14–16), long before the Lord Jesus taught clearly on the subject (Mat. 5:31–32; 19:3–12).

Death in the Home

Death was a deep tragedy for the Hebrews. Those watching by the bedside raised a shrieking wail as soon as life departed. This was the signal for loud mourning (Jer. 9:17–21). Friends and relatives crowded into the house (Acts 9:39) and practiced all of the customary signs of mourning: tearing their hair, beating their breasts (Luke 23:48), and crying out loudly until sheer physical exhaustion brought on dullness and depression. Hired mourners were often employed for the occasion (Mark 5:38–39). When an unmarried person died, the event was made all the more pathetic by going through some sort of wedding ceremony.

The art of embalming was not practiced in Palestine, and so the burial occurred on the day of death if at all possible. The body was usually dressed in a cloak or wrapped in a sheet. It was then placed on a bier and carried out to the place of burial (Luke 7:12–15). Friends vied with each other for the privilege of serving as pallbearers.

The body was placed in a tomb cut from rock. The poor often used caves. In the first century A.D. large, round, wheel-like stones were rolled into place to seal the entrance. These tombs were used by the family for generations.

HOMES

Home to the early Israelite was where his tent was pitched. The patriarchs did not settle down in communities but moved from place to place to meet the forage and water requirements of their flocks. What an imposing array the tents of Abraham must have made as they were pitched on the fields of Canaan.

The women of the household wove all of the materials for the "houses of hair" on the family loom. Coarse black goats' hair was woven into strips of varying widths, depending on the size of the family loom. These strips were in turn sewed together to make a tent of the desired proportions. During the first heavy rain the goats' hair shrank, making the material almost waterproof. A curtain hung from the middle of the roof to separate the women's quarters from those of the men. In many families the men and the women had separate tents (cf. Gen. 31:33).

The Israelites loved the out-of-doors and actually preferred the tent to a house of wood and stone.

The Furnishings of the Tent

Everything in the tent was very simple. The floor was the hard packed earth. Along the side of the tent were piled the pallets or bedrolls. A collection of pots, pans, kettles, and the caldron hung from a peg on a wooden pole (cf. Is. 22:23–25; Ezek. 15:3). The family pestle and mortar stood near the door. Every home had a kneading trough. No habitation was complete without the upper and lower millstone. The tent lamp stood on a stand. Over in one corner lay the goatskin bags.

The House of Brick and Stone

During the period of the Judges, the people gradually changed from their nomadic ways and began to settle down to carry on farming. This necessitated constructing a more permanent type of home. The tent gave way to homes of mud, brick, and stone. The Hebrews were still an outdoor people, so they did not build very large homes at first. The house served chiefly as a place of shelter for eating and sleeping, since even the women were usually out in the fields weeding or harvesting (Judg. 13:9; Ruth 2:8).

The average home in the plains or broad valleys was built with walls of mud and clay bricks, which were baked in the sun. Sometimes the corners were constructed of stone so as to support the roof beams. When the art of stonecutting and masonry was introduced, the Hebrews began to build a more permanent style home. Limestone was readily available in the hill country of Palestine for the construction of this new type of house. Mortar made of mud held the stones together.

As the cities grew in size, the people built bigger and better homes. Here they preferred to have more than one room. However, they did not build the rooms side by side as we think of a home today. A two-room house was divided by an open court. If the home consisted of three or four rooms, they were built around a central court. The court-yard was open to the sky and had space for a cistern and often a bread oven. The front of each room faced the court so that the family could remain a closely knit unit even if they did not all sleep, eat, and live in one room.

The Floors

Even in larger homes with several rooms there was usually no floor except the dirt upon which the house was built. The ground was made smooth and packed firm. Sometimes lime was mixed with mud and spread over the floor until it hardened. This kind of floor could be swept with a broom. In some homes cobblestones and shale were mixed with lime and packed into the floor. The wealthiest homes had floors covered with large square slabs of limestone or marble, laid end to end. These floors were permanent and could be scrubbed clean. During the time of Jesus, the Romans introduced mosaic floors, which were made by embedding small, smoothly cut squares of stone into the wet dirt.

The Roof

The roof of the house was supported by several large, roughly dressed logs, which were laid across the walls. Smaller beams were laid at right angles to these big timbers (S. of S. 1:17). On top of these beams was laid a layer of branches. This in turn was covered with reeds, grass, thorns, or mats of straw. Over this surface was spread about ten inches of wet mud and clay, which was packed smooth and tight. Finally a layer of sand and pebbles was scattered over the entire surface. The homes of the wealthy in New Testament times were covered with tiles of baked clay, which could be removed and repaired (Luke 5:19).

Every home had an outside stairway, made of stone, which led to the flat roof. Much of the family living took place upon the housetop in the cool of the evening. In the summer people slept on the roof (I Sam. 9:25, RSV) or chatted with their neighbors on the next roof (Luke 12:3). The streets were dusty and noisy, while up on the roof it was peaceful and quiet (Acts 10:9). Grain, fruits, flax, and fuel were spread on the roof to dry in the heat of the sun (Josh. 2:6).

The Upper Room

Every family longed for an upper room on the housetop. The more prominent people constructed this upper room of wood or stone. Those who could not afford this luxury had to satisfy themselves with a shelter or booth of straw, palm leaves, or reeds so that they too might have, in a small way, an upper room (Neh. 8:15–16). The upper room served as a place of hospitality when guests came to the home, as the one which the Shunammite woman had her husband build for Elisha (II Ki. 4:8–11).

Windows

The Palestinian home had few windows. The small openings which faced the street were located high in the wall as a protection against bandits and thieves. Glass was unknown, so the openings were covered with a frame of lattice work (S. of S. 2:9). At night the windows were closed with shutters for privacy and safety.

The Door

The doorway in these homes was a place of peculiar sanctity and importance. The inside was a haven of shelter, where noise, confusion, and intrusion were shut out. The outside was an impersonal place, where strangers, thieves, and enemies tarried. The doorway was so important that it was always reserved as the father's seat. In wealthier homes a doorkeeper was hired to guard the privacy of the home and to admit the guests. The door was left open all day as symbol of hospitality. A closed door signified that the family had some shame to cover. At sunset the door was closed and remained so until the sun rose in the morning (Luke 11:7). The clumsy locks of the doors were made of wood, as were the big keys which locked them (Judg. 3:24–25).

The Furnishing of the Permanent Home

The furnishings of a one-room home were little different from those of the tent. However, in larger homes the furniture and equipment were much more elaborate. Around three sides of the room were divans or couches covered with goat hair, wool, cotton, or silk cloths. It was the custom for the host and the guests of the home to sit cross-legged on the divan. At night these couches became beds. Piles of bedding and pallets were stored in a recess of the wall. Shelves along the wall served as a place to store the cooking utensils and kitchenware. A large brazier in the center of the room gave warmth and a cheerful glow. The dining table in the average home was a wicker mat laid upon the floor. However the wealthy used large brass trays, which were set upon a carved stand. Rugs and carpets of every color covered the floors of the wealthy, but the poor yearned for mats of straw to adorn their floors.

The lamp which lighted the home was made of clay. The earliest type of lamp was little more than a saucer, with a lip at one end where the wick rested. Later on by Jesus' time the lamps were closed at the top and had a spout at one end from which the wick emerged, and a hole in the middle of the top into which the oil was poured. The more elaborate lamps were ornamented with a handle. The lamp was kept burning all night through fear of darkness; for the lamp to go out or be put out signified the tragedy of death (II Sam. 21:17; Job 18:5–6; Prov. 13:9; 20:20; 24:20).

The Inn

The Hebrews had rigid laws of hospitality, which required them to welcome any stranger or traveler. Travelers were entirely dependent upon this kind of hospitality for their food and lodging. Inns were few and far between and were located close to watering places. In such hostels the traveler provided his own food, cooking utensils, and provisions for sleeping. If the inn was located on an important caravan route, provisions might be made to buy food. The inn was actually a large empty room where men and beasts were housed together. The "inn" of Luke 2:7 may well refer to the guestchamber of one of Mary or Joseph's relatives, for the word is the same as for "guest room" in Luke 22:11, the large upper room furnished with carpets and low couches where Jesus and His disciples ate the Last Supper together.

Foods

In the arid lands of the Near East a fresh and sufficient supply of water and bread was a constant concern (Is. 3:1). The greatest fear was of a crop failure, which would mean no bread (Amos 4:6). Plenty of bread and pure water were symbols of prosperity and abundance to the Hebrews (Prov. 20:13; Deut. 8:7–10).

Bread

Bread was considered so essential that these people had an interesting attitude of reverence toward it. Since bread was the staff of life, they never cut it with a knife, for this would be to cut life itself. Therefore, bread was always broken in tiny bite sizes by those partaking of the meal. The expression "breaking bread" was also used to describe the eating of an entire meal, including whatever food might be served with the bread.

Much of the housewife's time was spent in preparing the flour and baking the bread. Wheat, brought from the threshing floor, had to be cleaned of weed seeds, bits of stones, straw, and dust. To make flour, the grain was pounded with a pestle in a stone mortar or ground in a hand mill (Num. 11:8; Deut. 24:6). During Old Testament times the mill was made of two flat-surfaced, rectangular stones, placed one on top of the other. The upper stone was rubbed back and forth by hand over the lower stone, with the kernels of grain between.

By New Testament days the mill consisted of two circular stones. In the center of the lower stone was a pivot which projected through a hole in the middle of the upper stone. The hole was larger than the pivot, permitting the housewife to pour the grain, a handful at a time, through it into the mill. From the upper stone extended a wooden peg which the housewife could grasp to turn the mill. The larger mills were elevated so that a donkey could be used to turn the stone. The size and weight of this type of stone was illustrated very forcibly by Jesus in the illustration of the millstone (Mark 9:42).

For unleavened bread the flour was mixed with water and salt in a kneading bowl. The dough was made into flat cakes. The Jewish people ate unleavened bread in connection with their feasts or in time of dire need. Leavened bread was made by adding to the dough a lump of leavened dough saved from the previous baking. The batter was left overnight so that the entire mass could be leavened. Early in the morning this dough was mixed with more flour, water, and salt and again set aside until the dough was raised.

To bake the bread, a fire was built on a flat stone. When the stone was thoroughly heated, the burning coals were raked off and the dough laid on this heated rock. To bake the other side, the cake was turned over. Later, bread was baked on a convex sheet of pottery or iron, supported by stones. A fire of wood burned beneath this iron to heat it. In the city, bread dough was taken to a public oven to be baked (Hos. 7:4–7).

Water

The soil of Palestine was always thirsty. All summer it lay parched beneath the scorching sun until the early and latter rains—from late October to early April—would soften the fields. The lowlands in the Jordan Valley, where rain seldom falls, had to wait for irrigation each year until the melting snows of the Lebanon Mountains and Mount Hermon rushed into the Jordan River. The melting snows raised the water table and filled the springs, wells, and rivers. Cisterns were hollowed out in the native rock everywhere to catch the rain water, while wells were dug deep to reach underground water. Jacob's well near Shechem was a good example of this (John 4:6).

The water was carried to the homes in large clay pots, supported and balanced on the heads of the women, in each household. Men almost never carried water; if one did, his doing so could serve as a sign (Mark 14:12–16). These pitchers or water pots were gracefully formed in long cylindrical shapes. The day's supply of water was usually carried late in the afternoon, in the "cool of the evening." The women brought with them to the well a long rope and a leather bucket to reach the water in the bottom of the well.

Oil

Oil played an important role in the diet of the Hebrews; it was essential in the preparation of most of their food. The widow of Zarephath complained to Elijah that she had only a little oil in the cruse and therefore could not prepare a proper meal (I Ki. 17:12). The oil was obtained by crushing olives in a large stone mill and was stored in clay pots. Olive oil was the chief agricultural product for export to other countries.

Milk

Milk came from goats (Prov. 27:27), cows, and camels (Gen. 32:15). Because of the intense heat of Palestine, the milk had to be used at once. The most common food made of milk was "leben" or curds (translated "butter" in the King James Version). To make curds, milk was poured into a goatskin bag suspended from a tripod. This bag was kneaded and squeezed and swung back and forth by the housewife until the clots were formed (Prov. 30:33). This was probably what Jael served to Sisera (Judg. 4:19; 5:25) and Abraham to his three visitors (Gen. 18:8). Cheese, which was also a popular food (I Sam. 17:18; II Sam. 17:29), was prepared by salting the strained curds, condensing them into disks, and drying them.

Honey

God promised the Israelites that He would lead them into a land "flowing with milk and honey" (Ex. 3:8). This was a wonderful promise for the hungry and thirsty wanderers in the wilderness. Wild honey was very common in Bible times. The bees built their hives in the hollows of trees. John the Baptist lived on locusts and wild honey (Mat. 3:4). Honey was also found in the cleft of rocks (Ps. 81:16).

Meat

Meat was not the usual fare for the Israelites. It was expensive, and few people could afford to eat it. Only for very special guests, or if a sacrifice was to be made to God (Amos 5:22), was the "fatted calf" killed. This calf was kept in a stall or pen and was given all the food it could eat so as always to be ready for butchering. It was never killed until the special guest arrived. Abraham hastily prepared a calf for the three men who came to his tent to foretell the birth of Isaac (Gen. 18:7–8). When the father welcomed home the prodigal son, he said to his servants, "Bring hither the fatted calf, and kill it; and let us eat, and be merry" (Luke 15:22). The flesh of ducks, geese, partridges, gazelles, and roebucks was also eaten by the Palestinian people. Fish was abundant and cheap near the Mediterranean Sea and the Sea of Galilee.

Meat was boiled or roasted on hot stones. Often it was cooked with herbs and vegetables into a type of stew. Meat was regularly served in the container in which it was prepared.

God's people were forbidden to eat the flesh of animals that chew the cud and do not have a split hoof. This meant that camels, rabbits, and pigs could not be used as food. The eagle, falcon, raven, ostrich, sea gull, vulture, and heron could not be eaten either. Nor was any creature of the water to be consumed that did not have fins and scales (Lev. 11:1–47).

The locust is mentioned as a part of the diet of John the Baptist. In some cases the legs were roasted and eaten, and at other times the body of the locust was roasted, dried, salted, or ground up with flour and baked. Domestic fowl and eggs were introduced to the Hebrews before the birth of Jesus. Jesus spoke of a son asking his father for an egg (Luke 11:12).

Agricultural Foods

The Hebrews were dependent upon the products of the earth, wherever they could be found. In the oasis, moisture and heat produced dates. Figs and grapes were cultivated. Olives were cured in a strong brine. Raisins were in common use (I Sam. 25:18); pomegranates were also eaten (Deut. 8:8). Anise and mint were used as seasonings. The Hebrews seemed to enjoy strong flavors. They used coriander and cummin (like caraway seeds) to take the place of pepper. Other spices such as cinnamon were imported from India via South Arabia (I Ki. 10:2, 10). Melons, leeks (similar to chives), garlic, and onions were a part of the menu (Num. 11:5). Jacob used lentils in his famous stew (Gen. 25:34).

The Significance of Eating

Eating and drinking together among the people of Bible lands signified a bond of friendship that was highly respected. When they ate together, there was bread and salt between them and they were no longer strangers to each other, no matter what their previous relationship might have been. To share bread and salt was to forget all previous grievances. This made eating almost a sacred affair. Thus God required salt as a sign of an indissoluble covenant to accompany all meal offerings given to Him (Lev. 2:13; Num. 18:19).

VOCATIONS

The Hebrew craftsmen showed remarkable skill in using the simple tools at their disposal. The father's occupation was generally adopted by his son from one generation to the next. Some families took great pride in their work and developed trade secrets that were closely guarded.

The Shepherd

Sheep were very common in the Holy Land; thus sheepherding was one of the first occupations assumed by the Palestinians. The chief responsibility of the shepherd was to provide green grass and water for his flock. When the pools and streams were dry, the sheep were watered from a well.

The shepherd's staff was a cane, five or six feet in length. It served as a walking stick. Sometimes it was in the form as a crook. A sling was used against lurking enemies. It was made of two cords with a leather pouch between to hold a stone. This sling was swung around the head and then discharged by letting go of one of the strings.

The shepherd's pipe was a flute of reed. The strange sounds which came from this instrument aroused the attention of the sheep.

The sheepfold was a fence or corral built of tangled thorn bushes, branches of trees, logs, or rocks. This served as a shelter for the sheep at night.

The Farmer

When the nomadic Hebrews became a settled people, the science of farming was developed. The ground was broken by crude wooden plows pulled by oxen. Those who had no oxen used the mattock or pickaxe (I Sam. 13:20–21) to break up the soil and prepare the seed bed. The seeds were sown by hand as described in the parable of the "Four Soils" (Mark 4:3–8). The ripened grain was cut with a sickle. In early times sickles were made of flints inserted as blades in a wooden stock or a leg bone, but in later periods iron was used.

A primitive method of threshing the grain was to pound it out with a flail. This was a flat, wooden, broomlike instrument. In the story of Ruth we read that she "beat out what she had gleaned" (Ruth 2:17). A wooden sledge with sharp bits of metal on the underside and pulled by oxen was more commonly used to thresh the grain. Isaiah described such a threshing instrument: "Behold, I will make you a threshing sledge, new, sharp, and having teeth" (Is. 41:15).

The grain was separated from the straw with a winnowing fork. During a breeze, the grain was thrown up into the air so that the light chaff would be blown to one side and the heavier ripe grain fall directly to the ground (Ps. 1:4).

The Vinedresser

Vine culture was an important occupation of the Hebrew people. They planted their vineyards on the hillsides. Each vine was trained as a separate stock, pruned back each season to the main stem, and propped up to keep the grapes from the soil.

Every vineyard had a watchtower built of field stones. Here the owner or vinedresser stayed during the harvest season to guard the grapes. There was also a winepress in each vineyard. This was hollowed out of solid limestone in the ground. The ripened grapes were placed in it and the juice was trodden out by bare feet (Is. 63:2–3). The juice ran down into a vat cut out on a lower level and was allowed to settle there; then the clear liquid was stored as wine in jars of clay or goatskin bottles (Jer. 13:12; 48:11).

The Carpenter

The carpenter worked at his bench. Isaiah mentions four tools which were used by this artisan. "The carpenter stretches a line, he marks it out with a pencil; he fashions it with planes, and marks it with a compass" (Is. 44:13). The line was no doubt a crude ruler to measure lengths. The pencil was probably a simple stylus used in making marks on clay tablets. The plane smoothed the lumber and the compass was used in making circles.

In Deuteronomy we read of the axe which was used to cut down the trees (Deut. 19:5). The awl was in common usage (Ex. 21:6). Before the days of Saul the Israelites must have used a saw made from flint stones. By the time of the prophets, saws were made of thin pieces of metal (Is. 10:15). Jeremiah referred to the use of hammer and nails (Jer. 10:4).

The Day Laborer

In every city there were many people who worked by the day. They gathered in the public market places to seek employment (Mat. 20:3–4). Some of these people served as porters, who carried heavy loads from place to place. Others were masons' assistants, who carried the stones from the quarry to the building site (Neh. 4:10). A few carried their pickaxe and hoe with them, ready to till the soil for those who needed help. Many were willing to cut wood for the ovens. If there was no employment, they and their families went hungry. The Law of Moses required the employer to pay them at the end of each day (Lev. 19:13; Deut. 24:15; Jas. 5:4).

The Merchant

The marketplace was important in the lives of the people. Here the merchants carried on their trade. These marketplaces were usually near the city gate or in open squares at the center of the city. Often streets were set aside for some trade or particular kind of merchandise. Jeremiah spoke about the "bakers' street" (Jer. 37:21). The word "streets" is used in the sense of "bazaar" in I Kings 20:34 when Ben-hadad gave King Ahab the right to establish trading posts in Damascus.

Often goods were bartered rather than being sold for money. Before coins began to be introduced in the seventh century B.C., metals were weighed out in payment of a commodity; thus, Abraham "weighed to Ephron the silver" that had been agreed on for the purchase of the cave of Machpelah (Gen. 23:16). Often there was no set price for an article, so there was much argument and haggling.

The Fisherman

Fishing was an important vocation of the Bible lands. The Sea of Galilee and the Mediterranean Sea furnished much fishing for those who lived along their coasts.

Hooks were sometimes used for catching fish. Peter used a hook to catch the fish in whose mouth he found the coin to pay the temple tax (Mat. 17:27). Another method of catching fish was referred to by Job: "Canst thou fill his skin with barbed irons? or his head with fish spears?" (Job 41:7). A third means of catching fish was with nets. Peter and Andrew were casting nets into the sea when Jesus met them (Mat. 4:18–20).

The Potter

The making of pottery was one of the most important trades in Palestine. Large jars were needed to carry water and to store oil, honey, and meal or grain. Vessels of copper and bronze were very expensive and leather was unsatisfactory. Thus, there was a real demand for clay pottery; moreover, since clay jars broke easily, it was frequently necessary to replace them.

The clay used in pottery was mixed with water and trodden under foot until it was the right consistency. Isaiah spoke of treading the clay (Is. 41:25). The potter's wheel consisted of two flat, wooden wheels placed horizontally, one above the other. The upper one was supported on an axle or wooden pole standing up from the center of the lower disk. The lower wheel was put in motion by the foot. This is turn spun the upper wheel. A small lump of clay was put on this revolving upper wheel. As the wheel turned, the soft clay was shaped into whatever vessel the potter desired to make. The thumb was used to make a hole in the top of the whirling clay. This opening was widened until it was the desired size. A small piece of wood held in the right hand was used to smooth the outside of the pottery.

The finished vessels were put on a shelf, protected from the sun but open to the wind, so that they would slowly set in shape. When a sufficient number of jars were finished, they were placed in a small circular kiln or oven. The fire hardened the clay to make it fairly strong.

The Mason

Masonry was always an important occupation among the people of the Bible lands. The first task of a mason was to dig a deep, wide trench. Into this, stone and lime were packed for the foundation. Jesus told of the mason who "dug deep, and laid the foundation upon rock" (Luke 6:48). When the first layer of stone was laid upon the foundation, a large square stone was set at each corner to bind the walls together (Job 38:4–6). Thus, Jesus was referred to as the stone which the builders rejected, yet He became the chief cornerstone (Mat. 21:42).

The Metal Worker

Workers with metal appeared very early in the Scriptures. Tubal-cain, "the forger of all instruments of bronze and iron," is mentioned prior to Noah's Flood (Gen. 4:22).

In the days of King Saul, the Philistines placed a ban on Hebrew blacksmiths, "Now there was no smith to be found throughout all the land of Israel, for the Philistines said, 'Lest the Hebrews make themselves swords or spears' " (I Sam. 13:19).

Jewish blacksmiths were active in the days of Isaiah, for he referred to the blacksmith's anvil, which was a cube of iron fixed upon a block of wood (Is. 41:7).

The Tanner

While he was at Joppa, Peter stayed in the house of Simon, a tanner (Acts 9:43). The tanning of skins was an important industry among the people of Palestine. Goatskins were used as vessels to carry water, to hold new wine, to store milk, and to churn butter. Jesus spoke of the wine bag or "bottle" in connection with his denunciation of the Pharisees (Mark 2:22). Sheepskin was used in making sandals and other articles of clothing.

The Dyer

Dyeing was another common industry of the Hebrews. Purple dye, made from a secretion in the throat of a shellfish gathered along the coast of Phoenicia, was very valuable since only one drop was secured from each one. Thus purple became the "royal" color for kings and their nobles (Luke 16:19). Blue or violet was likewise obtained from the shellfish, but a less costly blue dye came from the leaves of the herb known as woad. The dye for brilliant crimson came from a grub which fed on the oak tree.

The various colored dyes were put in stone jars, and cloth or yarn was soaked in the solution. When it was sufficiently colored, the dyer would wring out the surplus dye; then the color was set by soaking the material for a time in a lime mixture.

The Tentmaker

Because of the general use of tents by the Hebrew people, the making of tents was an important industry. The material for making the tent came from the coarse, black hair of goats. Priscilla and Aquilla were tentmakers; Paul worked with them in Corinth (Acts 18:1-3).

The Money Changer

The money changer was a familiar sight in every village and city. He would sit by a table in a conspicuous place to change the people's money from one to another of the many types of currency in use throughout the world of that time. The fee for this transaction was sometimes very high and unfair; according to the Hebrew *Talmud*, a rate of about 12 per cent was charged. This business was unscrupulous and was held in very low esteem by the people.

In the Temple the money changers were busy because the Temple tax, which was required of every Jewish male over twenty-one years of age, had to be paid in the Hebrew coin called the half shekel. Many of the worshippers came from distant lands, where a different coinage system was used. And even in Palestine, Roman coins were commonly used for everyday transactions. Thus is was necessary to get the right and accepted Hebrew coin for use in the Temple.

The Tax Collector

The tax collector, sometimes called a publican, was not a very popular person. His task was legitimate enough, since taxes had to be paid in order to run the government; however, the resentment came because he collected taxes for the hated Roman government. Roman officials employed Hebrews who were willing to profit at the expense of their own countrymen. There was much graft in connection with the collecting of the tax money.

The Scribe

Aside from the religious scribe, who interpreted the law of Moses, there were also public scribes, who sat in front of government buildings or on important street corners with their inkhorns and parchment (Ezek. 9:2–3). Their principal task was to write letters for those who could not read or write. Baruch wrote down God's words for Jeremiah (Jer. 36:1–4, 17–18, 32). The scribe drew up contracts and prepared legal documents.

CLOTHING

The clothing worn by the people of Palestine was determined largely by the climate, their financial circumstances, and the outdoor life they lived. The primitive nomads wore garments made from the skins of their flocks and herds. The dress of the poor was always simple. The development of spinning, weaving, and embroidery added color and design to the clothing made principally from wool and flax (Prov. 31:13). The people discovered that loose garments permitted the circulation of air. The evenings in Palestine are usually cold and required heavier clothing to keep warm. A cloth over the head protected the scalp from the burning rays of the sun. Sandals soothed the feet of the weary travelers.

The Waistcloth

The simplest article of male attire was the loincloth, waistcloth, or kilt, worn next to the skin. It has been distinguished from the longer tunic in Egyptian tomb paintings and Assyrian sculptures representing Palestinian captives or visitors to the royal court. Soldiers (Is. 5:27) and slaves (Job 12:18) and some of the prophets, such as Elijah (II Ki. 1:8) and John the Baptist (Mat. 3:4) wore a waistcloth, usually made of leather.

The Tunic

The tunic was a kimono-like garment, fitting close to the neck (cf. Job 30:18), that was worn next to the skin. It was made of leather, haircloth, wool, linen, or cotton. Tunics were made with or without sleeves and often reached only to the knees. Among the poorer people the tunic was often the only garment worn in warm weather. People of higher rank used the tunic in the privacy of their homes, but ordinarily did not appear in public without an outer garment (cf. Mat. 5:40; Luke 15:22; 20:46). In the Bible the word "naked" may refer in some cases to those who wore only their tunic (Is. 20:2). Joseph's "coat of many colors" was a long tunic or robe (Gen. 37:3). It was fitted with long, wide sleeves and reached to the palms and soles. The use of such a garment was ordinarily restricted to the prominent, wealthier classes —as in the case of the royal princess Tamar (II Sam. 13:18)—and undoubtedly indicated to his brothers that their father had placed young Joseph in a highly favored position.

The Girdle

The tunic was held close to the body by a girdle. Ordinarily the girdle was simply a long strip of cloth that was wrapped about the waist and fastened in a knot, with a clasp, or else simply by twisting it around itself. Those who loved fine clothing wore girdles made of broad bands of silk, linen, or heavily embroidered material (Ex. 28:4; Rev. 1:13; 15:6). The girdle served as a means of carrying the sword, the purse, and the lunch bag. The scribe carried his inkhorn in his girdle.

The Cloak

The cloak is mentioned many times in the Scriptures. It was often referred to as the robe or mantle. The cloak was similar to the tunic in many ways, but it was heavier, looser, and longer. It had no sleeves since at night it was used as a blanket. Hannah made a little cloak and brought it to her son every year (I Sam. 2:19). David upon finding King Saul in the cave, cut off a part of the king's cloak (I Sam. 24:4).

Sandals

Sandals were the most common footwear of Palestine. They consisted of a sole of wood or leather which was fastened to the foot by thongs (Gen. 14:23). The sandal was removed before entering a house or a sacred place. It was the task of the humblest servant to wash the dust from the feet of a person who came in from a long journey. John the Baptist felt that he was not even worthy to perform the task of untying the sandal, let alone wash the feet of Jesus (John 1:26–27). Jesus was willing to act in the capacity of a servant by washing the disciples' feet (John 13:3–5).

The Turban

When in public the Hebrews usually wore a turban. The intense heat of the sun in Palestine made it dangerous to expose the head to its direct rays. The shepherds, like the Bedouin today, preferred a head cloth to a turban since it was cooler and afforded more freedom to catch the movement of any cooling breeze. This head cloth was kept in place by a black coil of camel's hair.

The Hair

The Hebrew people gave much attention to their hair. They loved to wear it long and were proud of their thick, heavy, curly hair (II Sam. 14:25–26). Barbers are mentioned only once in the Old Testament (Ezek. 5:1), but razors are mentioned often. The men took pride in their well-trimmed beards (cf. II Sam. 19:24) since it was a mark of manly dignity. Little is known about the hairdress of women except that braids or plaits are referred to in I Timothy 2:9 and 1 Peter 3:3.

The Dress of Women

The Law of Moses forbade men to wear women's clothing or women to dress like men (Deut. 22:5). The difference in dress between the two was in the detail rather than the kind of clothing. Like the men, the women perhaps wore a linen shirt as an undergarment, and certainly the tunic as a dress, and the cloak for warmth; but they embroidered their garments more copiously in needlework of gaily colored yarns. To give an added feminine touch, the woman's cloak was often of the shawl variety, draped from head to foot. Women's garments were longer than those usually worn by the men.

The Prayer Shawl

From the writings of Judaism we know that Jewish men and boys wore a prayer shawl when they went to the synagogue on the Sabbath. It was a large oblong cloth, three feet wide and five feet long, made of a fine material, often in broad black and white stripes. At each corner of the prayer shawl hung a tassel of eight threads, twisted together in five knots. Tradition prescribed the color of the thread to be used, the way the thread was to be twisted, and the number of knots permitted.

The Phylactery

The phylactery was a case of black calfskin containing a rolled-up strip of parchment upon which was written, with a special ink, the passage from Deuteronomy 6:4–9, which became the basic creed of Judaism. It was attached to a heavier piece of leather and worn on the left arm at the elbow. Sometimes the phylacteries were worn on the forehead, fastened by a band of leather around the head. In some homes the phylacteries were hung on the doorposts. The Pharisees wore these at all times, but the ordinary people used them only during the hours of prayer. Women were not permitted to wear phylacteries.

Accessories

The men often carried a staff or a cane, which might be simply a plain stick of wood or might be elaborately carved and ornamented. The staff served as a support while walking and as a protection from robbers and wild beasts.

Men also wore signet rings or seals used to sign letters and legal documents (Is. 15:22). When this signet ring was stamped on wet clay or soft sealing wax it left an imprint which served as the official signature of the person. Pharaoh gave Joseph such a ring (Gen. 41:42).

The women wore bracelets, anklets, and armlets to adorn themselves. Abraham's servant had two bracelets to give Rebekah (Gen. 24:22). Earrings were worn by the women of Jacob's family (Gen. 35:4). In the wilderness the Hebrew women gave their earrings to make the golden calf (Ex. 32:2–3).

PLANTS AND ANIMALS OF THE BIBLE

Earle L. Core

PLANTS OF THE BIBLE

ALMOND, *shaqedh* (Gen. 43:11; Ex. 25:33–36; Eccles. 12:5; Jer. 1:11). *Amygdalus communis*, a native of Persia, common in Palestine as early as the time of Jacob. The Israelites selected the almond flowers with their knops (sepals) and flowers (petals) as models for the cups of the golden candlesticks (lampstands). *Shaqedh* means "the wakeful tree," the first to bloom in spring.

ALOES (OT), *ahalim*, *ahaloth* (Ps. 45:8; Prov. 7:17; Song of Sol. 4:14). *Aquilaria agallocha*, eaglewood, a tall tree, member of the mezereon family, native to the Malay region, with fragrant wood.

APPLE, *tappuah* (Prov. 25:11; Song 2:3, 5; Joel 1:12). A great deal of discussion has taken place over the "apple" of the Bible. It is now generally considered to have been the apricot (*Prunus armeniaca*), since the apple does not thrive in Palestine.

BALM, *tsori* (Ezek. 27:17). Perhaps *Commiphora opobalsamum*, the true balm of Gilead. The false balm of Gilead (*Balanites aegyptiaca*) is thought to be referred to in other places (e.g., Gen. 37:25; Jer. 8:22, 46:11). This plant yields a healing gum.

BARLEY, *se'orim* (Ex. 9:31; Deut. 8:8; Judg. 7:13; Ruth 2:17, 23; 3:2, 15–17; Hos. 3:2). A widely cultivated grain in Palestine. Three forms were grown: common barley (*Hordeum distichon*), winter barley (*H. hexastichon*), and spring barley (*H. vulgare*).

BITTER HERBS, *merorim* (Ex. 12:8; Num. 9:11). Salad plants, mostly weedy herbs common in Egypt and Palestine, including: endive (*Cichorium endivia*), chicory (*C. intybus*), lettuce (*Lactuca sativa*), sorrel (*Rumex acetosella*), watercress (*Nasturtium officinale*), and dandelion (*Taraxacum officinale*).

BULRUSH, *gome* (Ex. 2:3, 5). Papyrus (*Cyperus papyrus*), a tall sedge with three-sided stems, was formerly abundant along the Nile River, and also in marshes around Lake Huleh. It provided the earliest known material for making paper, which gets its name from the Greek word for the plant.

CEDAR OF LEBANON, *erez* (I Kings, 4:33). This is *Cedrus libani*, the famous cedar of Lebanon, the largest trees with which the Israelites

25

were acquainted, growing to heights of 120 feet. It was used in the construction of Solomon's temple.

CUMMIN, *cammon;* Greek *kuminon* (Isa. 28:25, 27; Matt. 23:23). An annual plant of the carrot family (*Cuminum cyminum*), the aromatic seeds of which are used as a condiment.

FIG, *te'enah* (Gen. 3:7; I Kings 4:25; and many other places). *Ficus carica*, the first tree to be mentioned in the Bible. The fruits were very valuable as fresh and dried food.

FLAX, *pishtah* (Ex. 9:31; Prov. 31:13). The oldest known of textile fiber plants, the source of linen. Flax (*Linum usitatissimum*) and linen are mentioned scores of times in the Bible.

FRANKINCENSE, *levonah* (Lev. 2:1, 2, 15, 16; Matt. 2:11, and many other references). A clear yellow resin, the product of frankincense trees (*Boswellia thurifera*, *B. carteri*, *B. papyrifera*). Not native to Palestine but imported from Arabia, Ethiopia, and other lands.

GALL, *rosh* (Job 16:13; Matt. 27:34). The origin of gall is most uncertain. Some authorities believe it was produced by the colocynth (*Citrullus colocynthis*), which may also have been the "vine of Sodom." Others think in the Matthew reference it may have been the juice of the opium poppy (*Papaver somniferum*).

HYSSOP, *ezobh;* Greek *hyssopus* (Ex. 12:22; Lev. 14:4, 6, 52; Num. 19:6, 18; I Kings 4:33; Ps. 51:7; Heb. 9:19). One of the most puzzling and controversial of all the botanical terms in the Bible; probably reference is made to several different species. It is definitely not the garden hyssop (*Hyssopus officinalis*), which is not a native of Palestine. Dozens of species have been suggested, with the Syrian marjoram (*Origanum maru*) and the common caper (*Capparis sicula*) as the most likely.

LILY OF THE FIELD, Greek *krinon* (Matt. 6:28). Most authorities regard the anemone or windflower (*Anemone coroharia*) as the famous "lily of the field," which surpassed "Solomon in all his glory." It is one of the most conspicuous and brilliantly colored herbs of the fields.

MANDRAKE, *dudhay* (Gen. 30:14–16; Song 7:13). The true mandrake (*Mandragora officinarum*), a plant long held in superstitious awe. It was supposed to contain certain properties that encourage fertility.

MYRRH, *mor* (Ex. 30:23; Esther 2:12; Ps. 45:8; Matt. 2:11; John 19:39, etc.). One of the most valuable of gum resins, produced by the true myrrh (*Commiphora myrrha*).

OAK, *allon* (Gen. 35:8, Zech. 11:2, and many other passages). Oaks were symbols of strength and long life. Four or more species are native to Palestine (*Quercus aegilops*, probably the oak of Bashan; *Q. coccifera*, *Q. ilex*, and *Q. lusitanica*).

OLIVE, *zayith* (Gen. 8:11, the first reference in the Bible, and scores of other passages). The olive (*Olea europaea*), the most valuable tree of ancient Palestine, provided edible fruit, oil for medicinal purposes and for lamps, and timber for cabinet work.

PALM TREE, *tamar* (Ex. 15:27; Lev. 23:40; John 12:13, and many other references). The date palm (*Phoenix dactylifera*), cultivated in the Near East for at least 5,000 years for its edible fruit, etc. The name "Phoenicia" has been interpreted to mean "land of palms," although evidence points to the meaning "maker of purple."

POMEGRANATE, *rimmon* (Ex. 28:34; 39:26, and many other passages). A large shrub or small tree producing a pleasantly acid fruit, the common pomegranate (*Punica granatum*).

SYCAMORE, *shikmah* (I Kings 10:27; I Chr. 27:28; II Chr. 1:15; 9:27; Amos 7:14; Luke 19:4, etc.). The sycamore-fig or fig mulberry (*Ficus sycomorus*), an evergreen tree 30 to 40 feet tall, producing a fruit resembling but much inferior to the common fig.

VINE, *gephen* (Gen. 40:9–11; Deut. 32:23; Ps. 128:3; Zech. 3:10, and scores of other references). The grape (*Vitis vinifera*), the first plant in Biblical history recorded as cultivated. It was a symbol of fruitfulness and its harvest season was a time of joyous festivity.

ANIMALS OF THE BIBLE

ADDER, *pethen* (Ps. 58:4). The Bible contains numerous references to serpents, but no single species can be identified with certainty. Tristram lists 33 species, among them several poisonous varieties. The Hebrew words *tsiph'oni* and *tseph'a* (Prov. 23:32) are also sometimes translated as adder, but sometimes as asp or cockatrice. The viper or adder (*Vipera euphratica*) is common in the region.

ASS, *hamor, athon, pere, etc.* (Gen. 42:27; Ex. 4:20; Num. 22:21; Hos. 8:9). More than 150 passages of the Bible refer to the ass (*Equus asinus*), and the animal is mentioned in the earliest Hebrew literature. Distinction is made betweeen *hamor*, the male animal, the ordinary beast of burden; *athon*, the she-ass, a favorite for riding; and *ayir*, or ass's colt. The possessor of a large herd of asses was a rich man. There are also passages referring to the wild ass (*pere, arodh*), several species of which occur in the area; they are untamable.

BEE, *debhorah* (Deut. 1:44). Culture of the honeybee (*Apis sp.*) may have been known to the Israelites, but wild bees were abundant and their honey was collected.

BEHEMOTH, *behemoth* (Job 40:15). Thought to be the hippopotamus (*Hippopotamus amphibius*), the "river horse" of Africa.

CAMEL, *gamal* (Gen. 12:16; Judg. 6:5; Job 1:3). The camel (*Camelus spp.*), the typical beast of burden in desert regions, is mentioned about 65 times in the Bible. The dromedary, the one-humped species (*C. dromedarius*), was the Palestinian animal.

CATTLE, *miqneh* ("property," compare modern "chattel"). Cattle are the domesticated descendants of ancient species of *Bos*. The Bible refers to *abbir*, bull; *par*, bullock; *baqar*, bullock, ox; *eghel*, calf; *shor*, cow; *eglah*, heifer; *eleph*, ox, etc. Much of the wealth of the ancient Israelites was in their herds of cattle, and their valuable products, milk, butter, cheese, and leather, are frequently mentioned. Sheep were also often included under *miqneh*.

DOG, *kelebh* (Ex. 11:7; Job 30:1; Prov. 26:11). Dogs (*Canis familiaris*) were perhaps the first animals domesticated by man. About 40 Biblical passages refer to these animals, which were sometimes used to guard flocks but more often ran loose and were despised outcasts.

DOVE, *yonah* (Gen. 8:8; Matt. 3:16). A generic term, probably referring to both wild and domesticated pigeons (*Columba spp.*).

EAGLE, *nesher* (Lev. 11:13; Deut. 32:11; Job 9:26). Numerous species of hawk-like birds seem to be intended, even including vultures. They are symbols of strength, speed, pride, and indomitable spirit.

FISHES. The Bible contains numerous references to fish, but no particular species can be identified.

GOAT, *ez, attudh, sa'ir*, etc. (Gen. 37:31; Lev. 4:24; Num. 7:16). Both wild and tame goats are mentioned in the Bible. Goats (*Capra hircus*) were domesticated before 3000 B.C. and were an important element of wealth in the time of the early patriarchs. More than 130 passages refer to goats and about 50 to kids (*gelhi*), or young goats.

HORSE, *sus, parash, rekheoh* (Gen. 47:17, etc.). More than 150 passages refer to the horse (*Equus caballus*), domesticated in the patriarchal age. They were used for riding and for drawing chariots.

LEOPARD, *namer, pardalus* (Song 4:8; Isa. 11:6; Jer. 13:23; Rev. 13:2). The leopard (*Felis leopardus*), a savage and treacherous animal found in Palestine in ancient times and inhabiting areas east of the Jordan in modern times.

LEVIATHAN, *liwyathan* (Job 41:1; Ps. 74:14; Isa. 27:1. A mythological monster, the great devourer. But in Job the reference is to the crocodile (*Crocodilus niloticus*) of Egypt and of the Jordan Valley.

LOCUST. At least 10 Hebrew words are translated as locust, bald locust (Lev. 11:22), or grasshopper (Lev. 11:22). Some of these were edible and regarded as very palatable. But they were very destructive and caused great plagues (Ex. 10:4–6), so that they became a symbol of destruction (Rev. 9:3–11). Words translated as caterpillar (Ps. 78:46), cankerworm (Nah. 3:15) and palmerworm (Joel 1:4) are also thought to refer to locusts.

QUAIL, *selaw* (Ex. 16:13; Num. 11:31). A ground-dwelling bird (*Coturnix vulgaris*); not the quail or bobwhite of America.

SCORPION, *aqrabh* (Deut. 8:15). A small animal related to spiders, of the order Scorpionida, phylum Arthropoda.

SERPENT. The Bible contains numerous references to serpents, often implying poisonous species, but few can be identified with certainty. The serpent is used as a symbol of evil.

SHEEP. Numerous Hebrew words are used for sheep, as *rahel*, ewe; *kesebh*, lamb; *ayil*, *tsaphir*, ram. Sheep (*Ovis aries*) were domesticated as early as 3000 B.C., before cattle, and receive more attention in the Bible than any other animal.

UNICORN, *re'em* (Num. 23:22; 24:8; Job 39:9, etc.). The unicorn is a mythological animal with a single horn. The name as used in the Bible probably refers to the wild ox (*Bos primigenius*, the German *aurochs*), now extinct.

WOLF, *ze'ebh* (Gen. 49:27; Matt. 7:15) (*Canis lupus*).

MONEY, WEIGHTS, AND MEASURES

E. Leslie Carlson

Coined money, apparently an invention of the Greeks, was unknown before 700 B.C., and none was used by the Hebrews until the post-Exilic Period when they began to make widespread use of this practice which they had learned in the Babylonian Exile (Ezra 2:69; Haggai 1:6). Prior to this time trading was done by the bartering of animals and agricultural products and by the exchange of metals. Often these practices existed side-by-side just as they do in some parts of the world today. The earliest mention of a sale of property in the Bible is Abraham's purchase of a burial cave at Machpelah for which he *weighed* four hundred shekels of silver as payment (Gen. 23:16).

When trade moved beyond the stage of animal and agricultural barter it was necessary to develop a standard system of weights and measures. This process had begun long before the appearance of the Hebrews in Palestine. It was difficult to achieve an agreed-upon standard since a change of government almost invariably meant a change in standards. But the attempt was made, and it is known, for example, that the Assyrians and the Babylonians had a standard system of weights in the form of bulls, ducks, and lions, each inscribed with the royal seal and the officially determined weight.

It is generally conceded that the Biblical system is based upon methods from the Mesopotamian Valley, and that there is little Egyptian influence. A possible exception may be that the Egyptians influenced the Hebrews in their use of the decimal system since a decimal system is found mixed with the sexagesimal system which was used in Mesopotamia.

MONEY

BEKA. A Hebrew weight equivalent to ½ shekel or 0.20 grams (Ex. 38:26).

DENARIUS. A Roman coin equivalent to the Hebrew shekel in weight, but its value as money varied. Equivalent of a day's wages and therefore of a higher value than its weight. It was worth less in the 2nd century A.D. (Matt. 20:2–13; Luke 10:35; John 6:7, 12:5).

DRACHMA. A Greek silver coin used in the Hellenistic world after 330 B.C. and about the value of the Hebrew shekel.

DARIC. Persian gold coin used among the Jews after their return from the Babylonian exile. It weighed 128.4 grams and its value was about $5.30 (Ezra 2:69; I Chr. 29:7; Neh. 7:70).

GERAH. The smallest weight, ½₀ of a shekel. (See Weights.) Used as money but not as a coin. Its value depended upon what was being weighed. Usually worth about three cents (Lev. 27:25; Num. 3:47; Ezek. 45:12).

PENNY. Equivalent to the Roman silver denarius. (Luke 12:6).

PIECE OF GOLD. The equivalent to the gold shekel. Its value depended upon the content of gold (II Kings 5:5). (See Weights.)

PIECES OF SILVER. Equivalent of the silver shekel. Its value depended upon its weight (Ex. 21:32; Hos. 3:2). (See Weights.)

POUND. Equal to 100 silver drachma. Its value was about $17.00 (Luke 19:13–25).

SHEKEL. A Hebrew weight and used as such until coinage was adopted about 400 B.C. The gold shekel was valued at $5.50, and the silver shekel at about 75 cents (Matt. 17:27).

TALENT. Largest weight used for metals by the Hebrews. Gold weighing a talent was valued at $30,000 and that of silver at $2,000 (II Kings 23:33). In the New Testament period when used as coins, silver talents were valued at $560.00 (Matt. 25:14–30).

WEIGHT MEASURES

Since coins were not used by the Hebrews until after their return from the Babylonian exile, buying and selling were done by bartering or weighing out metals such as gold or iron. Even stones were sometimes used. The basic weight was the:

SHEKEL (Heb., "to weigh out") Jer. 32:9. This weight was used from the Exodus period. Before this it is evident that Egyptian weights were used. There were three standards of the shekel: (1) The temple shekel of 10 grams (approx. 0.35 ounce); (2) the common or commercial shekel of about 11½ grams (approx. 0.40 ounce); (3) the heavy shekel of about 13 grams (approx. 0.45 ounce), (Gen. 23:16; II Sam. 14:26;

II Kings 15:20; Ezek. 45:12, etc.). The half-shekel weight was ordered by God to be paid as a ransom of the individual Hebrew's soul (Ex. 30:13).

GERAH. The smallest Hebrew weight equivalent to $\frac{1}{20}$ of a shekel (8.71 grams), (Ex. 30:13; Ezek. 45:12, etc.).

DARIC. Less than $\frac{3}{10}$ of a shekel (I Chr. 29:7; Ezra. 2:69; 8:27; Neh. 7:70).

BEKA. Equal to $\frac{1}{2}$ shekel or 0.20 ounce (Ex. 38:26).

PIM. Equal to about $\frac{2}{3}$ of a shekel or 0.268 ounce (I Sam. 13:19–21).

MINA. Equal to 50 holy shekels, about 1.26 pounds (I Kings 10:17; Ezra 2:69).

TALENT. The largest Hebrew weight and defined as the full weight for an able man to carry. Equals 3,000 shekels or 60 minas. Value was dependent upon whether it was of gold, silver, copper, etc. Usual weight was equivalent to 76.5 pounds (U.S. Standard).

DRY MEASURES

HANDFUL. Natural capacity of the human hand (Lev. 2:2; 5:12).

KAB. Equivalent to $2\frac{2}{3}$ dry pints (II Kings 6:25).

TENTH. A tenth part of a homer, about $2\frac{1}{2}$ pecks (Ex. 29:40; Num. 28:13).

OMER. About $1\frac{4}{5}$ kabs or 4 U.S. dry pints (Ex. 16:16–36).

MEASURE. About $\frac{1}{3}$ of an ephah or about $\frac{1}{5}$ U.S. bushel (I Sam. 25:18; II Kings 7:16, 18).

EPHAH. Contains 10 omers or $\frac{3}{5}$ U.S. bushel (Ex. 16:36; Judg. 6:19).

LETHECH, or ONE HALF HOMER. Contains 5 ephahs or $3\frac{1}{8}$ bushels (Hos. 3:2).

HOMER. The largest measure and contains 10 ephahs or about $6\frac{1}{4}$ U.S. bushels (Lev. 27:16; Num. 11:32; Ezek. 45:11).

LIQUID MEASURE

1. LOG—Originally signified a basin which held about a pint. However, the accepted measure is $\frac{2}{3}$ liquid pint (Lev. 14:10).

2. POT—A cup or pitcher which held about one pint (Mark 7:4).

3. HIN—It is of Egyptian origin and equals 12 logs, equivalent to 3.86 U.S. quarts (Ex. 29:40; 30:24; Num. 15:4–9; Ezek. 4:11).

4. BATH—It is among the larger of the liquid measures, equal to 6 hins and equivalent to about 5.8 U.S. gallons (Ezek. 45:11).

5. COR—Equals 10 baths and is equivalent to about 58 U.S. gallons and is reckoned about the same as a homer (Ezek. 45:14).

6. POUND—About 12 ounces of liquid (Luke 19:13 ff.).

LINEAL MEASURE

1. FINGER—The smallest measure of the Hebrews, equal to the breadth of a man's finger of about .73 inch (Jer. 52.21).

2. HANDBREADTH—The width of 4 fingers tightly pressed together, equal to 2.9 inches based on the common cubit of 17.5 inches. (Ex. 37:12; I Kings 7:26; II Chr. 4:5; Ps. 39:5).

3. SPAN—The width from the end of the thumb to the end of the little finger measuring about 9 inches (Ex. 28:16; 39:9; I Sam. 17:4).

4. CUBIT—An important and fixed measure among the Hebrews. The length of the arm from the point of the elbow to the end of the middle finger or about 17.5 inches (Ex. 25:10; I Kings 7:24). In Ezekiel the long cubit of 20.44 inches is used (Ezek. 40:5).

5. PACE—The equivalent of a yard (II Sam. 6:13). The Roman "pace" was 2½ feet.

6. FATHOM—Equivalent to 6 feet (Acts 27:28).

7. MEASURING REED—Translated "rod" in Rev. 11:1. Properly, a sweet cane stalk measuring 8 feet 9 inches on the 17.5 cubit as a basis. Following the long cubit used in Ezekiel it measures 10 feet 2.4 inches (Ezek. 40:3, 5). The cubit of the New Testament was the same as the Roman cubit, 17.5 inches.

8. LINE—Equivalent to 146 feet (Ezek. 40:3).

9. FURLONG—This Greek "stadion" was adopted by the Jews. It measured 600 Greek feet, 606½ Roman feet and 606⅜ English feet (Matt. 14:24).

10. MILE—The Roman mile was 8 furlongs and hence 4852 feet (Matt. 5:41).

11. SABBATH DAY'S JOURNEY—Exact distance is uncertain for apparently there was some elasticity in this distance. Josephus states that it is 5 or 6 stadia (furlongs), 3000 or 3600 feet which is about the distance from Jerusalem to the Mount of Olives (Acts 1:12).

12. DAY'S JOURNEY—In Bible times the distance was usually measured by the length of time necessary to travel: e.g. "three day's journey" (Gen. 30:36). In New Testament times the distance was measured in furlongs or Roman miles (Matt. 14:24; Luke 24:13).

AREA MEASURE

Area measure is the *Acre*, an area that a team of oxen can plow in one day, about ½ a U.S. acre. Estimates vary from ⅔ acre to ⅝ acre (I Sam. 14:14; Isa. 5:10).

YOUNG READER'S

DICTIONARY-CONCORDANCE

for the REVISED STANDARD VERSION of the

HOLY BIBLE

by

Martha Pounds Weaver

Consultants:

Iris V. Cully, Ph.D., Associate Professor of Christian
Education, The Divinity School, Yale University
Kendig Brubaker Cully, Ph.D., Dean and Professor of Christian
Education, New York Theological Seminary

In the pages that follow there are two Bible reading helps combined
in one. First, there is a Bible dictionary, giving you the special meanings of words as used in the Bible and as generally understood in church
usage. Then there is a concordance, listing the important Bible passages
where a particular word, like "love," is found. Some words have both
a definition and a concordance listing, some have only one or the other,
as needed. References to Bible passages containing the words defined
are included in definitions where this will help you understand the
meanings.

Suppose you want to know what "baptism" means. In the dictionary-
concordance you will find a definition of what it is usually taken to mean
in church usage. Following the definition you will find references to
passages in the Bible on which the understanding of baptism is based.
Look up such a word as "heaven" and see how much you learn that you
didn't know before, even though the word is familiar to you.

Indeed, the dictionary-concordance provides an interesting way to explore the Bible. You will, for example, find guides to stories, miracles, and parables of the Bible under those headings. Or you can simply leaf through, following up the references given for a word or the name of a Biblical character. The dictionary-concordance will be most helpful in your Bible reading and, especially, in church school work. The words it contains were selected because they are frequently encountered in church school.

KEY TO PRONUNCIATION

Pronunciation of difficult or unfamiliar words is shown in parentheses immediately following the boldface entry word. The pronunciation marks used are the simplest practical, those familiar to most readers. The syllable receiving most emphasis in a word is indicated with an accent mark (').

a *as in* hat	oi *as in* oil
ä *as in* ah, arm, father	oo *as in* fool
ā *as in* tame	oo *as in* foot
â *as in* fare	ou *as in* foul
e *as in* met, second	à *as in* abet, protect
ē *as in* mete	ch *as in* chair
ī *as in* fine	th *as in* thin
i *as in* him, plentiful	th *as in* then
o *as in* lot	j *as in* joy
ō *as in* alone	k *as in* kind, character
ô *as in* nor	s *as in* sea, celestial
u *as in* us	sh *as in* shame, delicious, attraction
ü *as in* rude	z *as in* dizzy, his
ũ *as in* turner	zh *as in* adhesion

ABBREVIATIONS USED FOR THE BOOKS OF THE BIBLE are the same as those shown on Page xi in the front of this Bible.

DIRECT QUOTATIONS FROM THE BIBLE TEXT in concordance listings are shown in italics, the entry word indicated with its initial letter: **ask**, a. *in prayer*. In the reference the abbreviation of the Bible book comes first, followed by the chapter and then the verse(s), thus: Mt 21.22.

A

Aaron (â'ron), Moses' brother.
Lord said to A. Ex 4.27
to Moses and A. Ex 6.13

Abba, father.
he said, "A. Father . . ." Mk 14.36
we cry, "A. Father . . ." Rom 8.15

Abednego (à-bed'nē-gō), Hebrew
boy taken hostage in war.
in the king's palace Dan 1
in fiery furnace Dan 3.19–30

Abel (ā'bel), Adam's second son.
A. was a keeper of Gen 4.2
By faith A. offered Heb 11.4

abide, live or last.
a. in me and I in you Jn 15.4
faith, . . . love a. I Cor 13.13

Abraham or **Abram,** father of the
Hebrew nation.
moves to a new land Gen 12.1–9
moves again Gen 12.10–19
gives Lot a choice Gen 13.5ff
is promised a land Gen 17.8
is promised a son Gen 18.9–10
tries to save city Gen 18.23ff
told to sacrifice son Gen 22.2
finds wife for son Gen 24.1ff

Adam, [Hebrew: man] first man.
God created A. Gen 1.27
named animals Gen 2.19–20
given a wife Gen 2.21–23
disobeys God Gen 3.1–6
A. and Eve punished Gen 3.17ff
sons of A. Gen 4.1–2, 25

adultery, mating between a man
and woman not married to each
other.
shall not commit a. Ex 20.14

Advent, period of time beginning
four Sundays before Christmas,
when Christians prepare to celebrate the coming of Jesus.

Ahab (ā-hab'), king of Israel who
was led astray by Jezebel, his wife.
A. did evil I Kings 16.30
A. married Jezebel I Kings 16.31
A. and Elijah I Kings 18.17ff

alms, money, food, or clothing
given to needy persons.
when you give a. Mt 6.2

giving a. brings treasure in heaven
Lk 12.33
one who sat for a. Acts 3.10

alpha (al'fà), first letter of Greek
alphabet; beginning (Rev 1.8).

STONE ALTAR

altar, a raised stone or table used
as a place of sacrifice and offerings.
Noah built an a. Gen 8.20
Abraham built an a. Gen 22.9
Moses built an a. Ex 17.15
Gideon built an a. Judg 6.24
an a. of bronze II Chron 4.1
erected a. to Baals II Chron 33.3
gift at the a. Mt 5.23
a. to unknown god Acts 17.23

Amos (ā'mòs), Old Testament book
named for shepherd prophet.
God called A. Amos 7.14–15
visions of A. Amos 7, 8, 9

Ananias (an-à-nī'às), 1. a man who
lied to Peter about money
(Acts 5.1ff). 2. a man who helped
Saul become a Christian (Acts
9.10–13). 3. a high priest who
tried Paul (Acts 23.1–5).

Andrew, one of the twelve dis-
ciples of Jesus.
A. was a fisherman Mk 1.16–17
A. brought his brother Jn 1.41
A. found boy with loaves and fish
Jn 6.8–9

angel, [Greek: messenger] a heavenly spirit who works for God.
a. on Jacob's ladder Gen 28.12

a. guard you Ps 91.11
a. talked to Joseph Mt 1.20, 2.13
a. *said to women* Mt 28.5
like a. in heaven Mk 12.25
a. talked to Zechariah Lk 1.11
a. talked to Mary Lk 1.26–38
work of a. Heb 1.13–14

anger,
Moses' a. at calf Ex 32.19
harsh words and a. Prov 15.1
a. with brother Mt 5.22
sun go down on a. Eph 4.26
be slow to a. Jas 1.19

anoint, to put oil or ointment on
head or body.
wash and a. yourself Ruth 3.3
a. *my head with oil* Ps 23.5
go and a. him Mk 16.1

answer,
consider and a. Ps 13.3
the Lord a. *you* Ps 20.1
a soft a. *turns* Prov 15.1
a. *to many prayers* II Cor 1.11

anxious,
do not be a. Mt 6.25
a. *and troubled* Lk 10.41

Apostle, one sent out by Jesus to
spread his teachings: originally
twelve (Mt 10.1); others added
(Lk 10.1).
names of twelve a. Mt 10.2
God appointed a. I Cor 12.28

Aquilla (ak'wi-là), Paul's friend
and helper.
Priscilla and A. Acts 18.2
church in A's house I Cor 16.19

ark, 1. the large boat in which Noah,
his family, and two of every kind
of animal lived during the great
flood (Gen 6.14ff). 2. a decorated
chest for keeping the tablets of
the Law (Ex 25.10).
capture of the a. I Sam 5.1
put the holy a. II Chron 35.3
description of a. Heb 9.4–5

Ascension, the act of Jesus leaving
earth forty days after Easter
(Acts 1.9).

ask,
a. *in prayer* Mt 21.22
a. *and it will be* Lk 11.9
a. *in my name* Jn 14.13
a. *anything according to his will* I
Jn 5.14

asleep,
Jesus a. in boat Mt 8.24
Simon, are you a. Mk 14.37
Lazarus . . . fallen a. Jn 11.11

Athens, city in Greece.
Men of A. Acts 17.22
left behind at A. I Thess 3.1

atonement, Day of, a Jewish holy
day for cleansing people of their
sins (Lev 23.27).

B

Baal, a god worshipped by some
people in Canaan, but proved
powerless by Elijah in the famous
altar test (I Kings 18.20–40).

baby,
famous twin b. Gen 25.24–26
b. in a basket Ex 2
b. given to God I Sam 1.20–28
b. claimed by two women I Kings
3.16ff
b. laid in manger Lk 2

Babylon (bab'i-lon'), nation east of
Palestine that conquered Judah.
exile into B. II Chron 36.20
by the waters of B. Ps 137.1

Is this not great B. Dan 4.30

baptism, a sacrament by which a
person is admitted into the Christian church, the water used signi-
fying the washing away of sins
(Mark 1.4) and participation in
the death and resurrection of
Jesus (Romans 6.3–4).
b. of Jesus Mt 3.13–17; Mk 1.9
Jesus asks disciples to b. Mt 28.19
Peter urges b. Acts 2.38
b. into death of Christ Rom 6.4
one b. Eph 4.5

Barabbas (bàr-ab'às), prisoner
freed instead of Jesus (Mk 15.6ff).

barn,
nor gather into b. Mt 6.26
wheat into the b. Mt 13.30
Barnabas (bär′nȧ-bȧs), teacher
who worked with Paul (Acts 13.2).
Bartholomew (bär-thol′o-mū),
one of Jesus' disciples (Mt 10.3).
Baruch (bâr′ȧk), secretary and
friend of Jeremiah (Jer 36, 45).
basket,
cakes in a b. Gen 40.16ff
baby Moses in a b. Ex 2.3
b. of summer fruit Amos 8.1
Paul in a b. II Cor 11.33
bear, 1. give or tell.
not b. *false witness* Ex 20.16
2. another name for Big Dipper.
made the B. *and Orion* Job 9.9
3. give birth.
b. *a son* Mt 1.23
4. carry.
b. *his own cross* Jn 19.17
Beatitudes (bē-at′ȧ-tōōdz), a
group of sayings of Jesus, all beginning with "blessed," in which
he describes those to whom God
gives joy (Mt 5.3–12).
beautiful,
everything b *in its* Eccles 3.11
how b. *are the feet* Is 52.7
done a b. *thing* Mt 26.10
gate called B. Acts 3.2
believe,
repent and b. Mk 1.15
b. *in God,* b. *also in me* Jn 14.1
b. *in the Lord Jesus* Acts 16.31
b. *all things, hopes* I Cor 13.7
b. *that Jesus is the* I Jn 5.1
benediction, a blessing on others,
such as is spoken by the minister
at close of a service.
Bible b. are found: Gen 31.49;
Numbers 6.24–26; Jude 24
Benjamin, Jacob's youngest son
(Gen 35.17–18).
Bethany (beth′ȧ-nē), village near
Jerusalem where Jesus visited
friends (Mt 26.6).
Bethlehem, town where Jesus was
born (Mt 2.5; Lk 2.4).
better,
men b. than sheep Mt 12.12
count others b. *than* Phil 2.3

Bible, the Scriptures; sixty-six
books written with God's help, to
tell us about him and his plan
for us. Includes books on law,
poetry, history, and prophecy; in
two main divisions or testaments.
He opened the book Lk 4.17
in all the scriptures Lk 24.27
All scripture is inspired II Tim
3.16–17
birds,
God created b. Gen 1.20
Jesus talks about b. Mt 6.26, 8.20,
13.4; Lk 9.58, 12.24, 13.19
birthright, oldest son's right to
become head of the family (Gen
25.31, 43.33).
bless, 1. to ask God's favor upon;
for God to bestow favor upon.
The Lord b. *you and* Num 6.24
b. *those who curse you* Lk 6.28
2. to praise, honor, adore.
I will b. *the Lord* Ps 34.1
B. *the Lord O my soul* Ps 103.1
blessed, having the joy or happiness that comes from God's favor.
B. *is the man who* Ps 1.1
B. *are the pure* Mt 5.8
more b. *to give* Acts 21.35
boast,
b. *of the Lord* I Cor 1.31
do not b. *and be* Jas 3.14
body,
this is my b. Mk 14.22
did not find the b. Lk 24.3
present you b. Rom 12.1

BOOTH

booth, a room built of branches of
trees and often used at festival

time (Sukkoth) to remind the Hebrews of the days God cared for them while they traveled in the wilderness (Deut 16.13).

born,
unto us a child is b. Is 9.6
when Jesus was b. *in* Mt 2.1
unless one is b. *anew* Jn 3.3

bread,
shall eat unleavened b. Ex 12.20
b. *from heaven* Ex 16.4
cannot live by b. Mt 4.4
and he took b. Lk 22.19

I am the b. *of* Jn 6.35

build,
Solomon plans to b. God's house I Kings 5.5
b. *the wall again* Neh 2.17
unless the Lord b. *the* Ps 127.1
b. *his house on sand* Mt 7.26
on this rock I will b. Mt 16.18
if you b. *count the cost* Lk 14.28

burnt offerings, best animals from a flock, burnt on an altar as an offering to God (Lev 1.3).
better than b. o. Mk 12.33

C

Caesar, Roman Emperor.
taxes to C., *or not?* Mk 12.14
I appeal to C. Acts 25.11

Cain, son of Adam (Gen 4.2ff).

calf,
a golden c. Ex 32.4
the fatted c. Lk 15.23

camel,
easier for a c *to go* Mt 19.24
swallowing a c. Mt 23.24

Canaan (kā′năn), land promised to Hebrew people by God (Gen 12.5).

caravan, group of travelers riding or walking together (Gen 37.25).

carpenter,
the c.'s *son* Mt 13.55
is this not the c. Mk 6.3

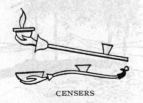

CENSERS

censer, an ornamental metal container in which incense is burned.

centurion, a Roman officer in charge of 100 soldiers.

a c. *came to him* Mt 8.5
Paul said to the c. Acts 22.25

chaff, husks remaining after the grain has been taken out.
but are like c. Ps 1.4
the c. *he will burn* Mt 3.12

chariot, two-wheeled cart pulled by horses.
c. *of fire and horses* II Kings 2.11
seated in his c. Acts 8.28

child,
a c. *is known by his* Prov 20.11
train up a c. Prov 22.6
to us a c. *is born* Is 9.6
a c. *shall lead them* Is 11.6
when I was a c. I Cor 13.11

children,
Let the c. *come* Mt 19.14
c., *obey your parents* Eph 6.1

choose,
c. *this day* Josh 24.15
c. *what is right* Job 34.4
c. *the good* Is 7.15

Christ, [Greek: the anointed one] see Jesus (Mt 16.16).

Christians, followers of Jesus Christ.
first called C. *at* Acts 11.26
suffers as C. I Pet 4.16

church, place of worship; a group of worshippers.
on this rock I will build my c. Mt 16.18

beginning of Christian c. or Pentecost Acts 2

a great number join c. Acts 2.41

early c. lived and worked together Acts 2.44–47

Saul laid waste the c. Acts 8.3

work in the c. I Cor 12.27ff

Christ loved the c. Eph 5.25

church, meeting places for:

on a mountain Mt 5.1

in a house Acts 12.12

at the riverside Acts 16.13

church, other names for:

tent of meeting Ex 33.7

tabernacle Ex 39.32

house of God I Chron 6.48

house of the Lord Ps 122.1

synagogue Mt 12.9

house of prayer Mk 11.17

temple Lk 21.37

my Father's house Jn 2.16

body of Christ I Cor 12.27

circumcision, a ceremony in which Jewish baby boys are marked as a sign of the agreement between God and Israel (Acts 7.8).

not necessary I Cor 7.17–19

clean, 1. a term applied to the animals Jews were permitted to eat (Gen 8.20).

Jesus said all foods were c. Mk 7.19

2. having done those things required for worship under the laws found in Leviticus.

3. having no leprosy or other unusual body conditions.

priest shall pronounce him c. Lev 13.23

he who has c. *hands* Ps 24.4

create in me a c. *heart* Ps 51.10

coat,

Joseph's c. Gen 37.3

a man takes your c. Mt 5.40

he who has two c. Lk 3.11

coins, see money.

they brought him a c. Mt 22.19

put in two copper c. Mk 12.42

if she loses one c. Lk 15.8

colt,

a prophecy that their king would come riding on a c. Zech 9.9

find a c. *tied* Mk 11.2

commandment, rule; law; order.

Ten c. given to Moses Ex 20

teaching the c. Mt 5.19

Jesus' last c. Mt 28.19–20

A new c. *I give* Jn 13.34

If you love me . . . keep my c. Jn 14.15

communion, sharing or doing something together. *Holy Communion* is a sacrament or special act of the Christian church when bread and wine (or juice) are shared as (or as symbols of) the body and blood of Christ. (Also see Lord's Supper and Last Supper)

confess, 1. admit or tell (a sin).

If we c. *our sins* I Jn 1.9

2. tell others something we believe.

c. *that Jesus is Lord* Phil 2.11

confirmation, a ceremony in which one who has received instruction, baptism, and the gift of the Holy Spirit confesses his faith and is fully received into the church.

conversion, a turning from sin or lack of faith to belief in God.

Paul's c. Acts 9.3ff

the c. of the Gentiles Acts 15.3

covenant, an agreement between God and his people.

God's c. with Noah Gen 6.18ff

c. with Abraham Gen 17.2–8

c. with Jacob Gen 28.13–14

c. with David II Sam 23.5

New Testament c. Jn 3.16; Heb 9.15

covet, to desire something another person has (Ex 20.11).

created,

in the beginning God c. Gen 1

God c. *man in his own image* Gen 1.27

Has not one God c. Mal 2.10

cross, a symbol used by the Christian church because of Jesus' death on a cross.

take up his c. Mt 10.38

Simon carried the c. Mt 27.32

bearing his own c. Jn 19.17

standing by the c. Jn 19.25
endured the c. Heb 12.2

crowd, Jesus and the
speaking to the c. Mt 5.1ff;
Lk 8.4ff
feeding the c. Mt 15.38; Mk 8
honored by the c. Mk 11.7–10
escaping the c. Lk 4.29–30
condemned by the c. Jn 19.6

crucified, put to death by nailing
or tying on a cross.
Jesus was c. Mt 27.32ff; Mk
15.21ff; Lk 23.26ff; Jn 19.17

two robbers were c. Mt 27.38
you c. *and killed* Acts 2.23

cubit, a measure equal to the
length of a man's arm from the
end of the middle finger to the
elbow (Gen 6.15); in New Testament probably meant "small
amount" (Mt 6.27).

cup,
Joseph's silver c. Gen 44.2
my c. *overflows* Ps 23.5
a c. *of cold water* Mt 10.42
and he took a c. Mt 26.27

D

Daniel, a prophet whose faith in God
saved him from a den of lions.
D. captured by enemy Dan 1.3ff
D. refused rich food Dan 1.8ff
a plot against D. Dan 6.1ff
D. prayed often Dan 6.10
D. in lion's den Dan 6.16ff

darkness,
d. *was upon the earth* Gen 1.2
d. *is as light* Ps 139.12
who walked in d. Is 9.2
the sixth hour there was d. Lk 23.44
loved d. *rather than* Jn 3.19
in him is no d. *at all* I Jn 1.5

David, shepherd boy, fighter, king
of Israel.
D. keeping the sheep I Sam 16.11
Saul anoints D. I Sam 16.13
D. *took the lyre* I Sam 16.23
D. fights Goliath I Sam 17
D. and Jonathan I Sam 19.1ff
D. in danger I Sam 19.1
D. made king II Sam 2.4
D. and war II Sam 5–9
D. in trouble II Sam 11, 12
D. tells Solomon to build temple
I Chron 22.6

day,
called the light d. Gen 1.5
this is the d. *which* Ps 118.24
neither the d. *nor the* Mt 25.13

death, the end of life as we know
it, but Christians believe that

God's love and plan for us do not
end with death.
d. of Jesus (see crucified)
d. of a rich man Lk 16.19–31
a promise about d. Jn 3.16
from d. *to life* Jn 5.24
d. of a grain of wheat Jn 12.24
Jesus' promise of a place after d.
Jn 14.2
after Jesus' d. he went to be with
God Jn 16.28
d. of Stephen Acts 7.54
wages of sin is d. Rom 6.23
d. and resurrection I Cor 15.12ff
sting of d. *is sin* I Cor 15.56
d. *shall be no more* Rev 21.4

Deborah, woman judge who settled
quarrels for Hebrews.
D. judges Israel Judg 4.4–5
D. helps in war Judg 4.6ff

Delilah (di-lī′là), woman who
betrayed Samson (Judg 16.6).

demon, evil spirit thought to
cause illness and injury.
d. went into pigs Mt 8.28–33
he has a d. Mt 11.18
the d. *came out* Mt 17.18

devil, the chief evil spirit; enemy
of God and man. (Satan, Serpent,
evil one)
tempted by the d. Mt 4.1
enemy is the d. Mt 13.39
d. *is a murderer* Jn 8.44

d. has no truth in him Jn 8.44
d. *has sinned* I Jn 3.8
d. is thrown out of heaven Rev 12.7–12
disciple, follower; believer in teachings of someone.
all the d. . . . *fled* Mt 26.56
d. sent out by twos Mk 6.7–13
d. of Jesus Mt 10.2–4; Lk 6.14
d. of John the Baptist Jn 1.35
Jesus washed the d.'s feet Jn 13.4ff
d. who betrayed Jesus Jn 18.2
d. *whom Jesus loved* Jn 19.26
d. *first called Christians* Acts 11.26
divine, holy, coming from God.
have d. power II Cor 10.4
door,
I am the d. Jn 10.9
d. *were shut but Jesus came* Jn 20.26
prison d. *were open* Acts 16.27

a d. *was opened for me* II Cor 2.12
stand at the d. Rev 3.20
Dorcas, also called Tabitha, a woman who sewed for the needy (Acts 9.36–37).
dream, images, thoughts and feelings occurring during sleep, sometimes given special meaning.
Jacob's ladder d. Gen 28.12
Joseph's d. about greatness Gen 37.5
d. of butler and baker Gen 40
Pharaoh's d. about cows Gen 41
Nebuchadnezzar's d. Dan 2
angel comes to Joseph in a d. Mt 2.13
Pilate's wife's d. Mt 27.19
dwell, make one's home, live.
d. *in the house of the* Ps 23.6
Christ may d. *in us* Eph 3.17

E

ears,
who has e. *to hear* Mt 11.15
cut off his e. Mt 26.51
first the blade then the e. Mk 4.28
have itching e. II Tim 4.3
earth,
while the e. *remains* Gen 8.22
inherit the e. Mt 5.5
on e. *as it is in heaven* Mt 6.10
treasures on e. Mt 6.19
peace on e. Lk 2.14
witness . . . to the end of the e. Acts 1.8
not on things that are on e. Col 3.2
east,
as far as e. *is from* Ps 103.12
wise men from the e. Mt 2.1
Easter, a Sunday in Spring when Christians celebrate Jesus' resurrection (see Jesus, his life).
eat,
e. *the king's rich food* Dan 1.13
what shall you e. Mt 6.25
e. *with tax collectors and* Mt 9.11
Take e., *this is my* Mt 26.26

eat, drink, and be merry Lk 12.19
Egypt (ē'jipt), country in northeast Africa, near the Holy Land.
Abraham goes to E. Gen 12.10
Joseph sold into E. Gen 37.36
Hebrews leave E. Ex 13.17ff
Baby Jesus taken to E. Mt 2.13
Eli, the high priest who trained Samuel (I Sam 1–3).
Elijah, a Hebrew prophet.
E. fed by ravens I Kings 17.5ff
E. helped a boy I Kings 17.21ff
E. proved God greater than Baal I Kings 18.20ff
E. taken to heaven II Kings 2.11
Elisha, a Hebrew prophet after Elijah.
E. sees Elijah go II Kings 2.9ff
E. and the vessels II Kings 4.1ff
a room for E. II Kings 4.8ff
E. restores boy II Kings 4.18
his name shall be called E. Mt 1.23
enemies,
love your e. Mt 5.44
if your e. *hungers* Rom 12.20

enrollment, a counting of the people in the tribes to which they belonged (Lk 2.2).

enter,
E. *his gates with* Ps 100.4
e. *the kingdom of* Mt 5.20
e. . . . *into temptation* Mt 26.41
can he e. *a second time* Jn 3.4

Epiphany (ē-pif′à-nē), a church festival (Jan. 6) celebrating the visit of the wise men to Jesus.

Esau (ē′saw), twin brother of Jacob.
E. *was a hunter* Gen 25.27
E. *is a hairy man* Gen 27.11
E. *and the birthright* Gen 25.34
E. lost his blessing Gen 27
Jacob and E. meet again Gen 33

eternal, lasting forever.
have e. *life* Jn 3.16
this is e. *life, that* Jn 17.3
gift of God is e. *life* Rom 6.23

evangelist, a person who preaches the gospel, often traveling from place to place.
Philip the e. Acts 21.8
some e., *some pastors* Eph 4.11
the work of an e. II Tim 4.5

Eve, Adam's wife; first woman.
serpent deceived E. Gen 3.1ff
his wife's name E. Gen 3.20

everlasting,
the e. *covenant* Gen 9.16
from e. *to* e. *thou art God* Ps 90.2
God, E. *Father* Is 9.6
with an e. *love* Jer 31.3

evil, bad or wrong, done on purpose.
hate e., *and love good* Amos 5.15
e. *against you falsely* Mt 5.11
deliver us from e. Mt 6.13

exile, one forced to leave his own country and live in another.
Hebrews taken into e. II Chron 36.20
Moses . . . became an e. Acts 7.29

Exodus, the going out of the Israelites from Egypt; Old Testament book about this.

eye,
e. *of the Lord are* Ps 34.15; I Pet 3.12
the seeing e. . . . . Prov 20.12
an e. *for an* e. Mt 5.38
e. *is the lamp of the body* Lk 11.34
if the whole body were an e. I Cor 12.17

F

face,
The Lord make his f. *to shine* Num 6.25
but then f. *to* f. I Cor 13.12
own f. *in a mirror* Jas 1.23

faith, believing and trusting.
Have f. *in God* Mk 11.22
f. *has made you well* Lk 8.48
good fight of f. I Tim 6.12
examples of f. Heb 11
f. *without works* Jas 2.17

false,
not bear f. *witness* Ex 20.16
hate every f. *way* Ps 119.104

famine, a lack of food, causing starvation.
seven years of f. Gen 41.27

a great f. *over all* Lk 4.25
or f., *or nakedness* Rom 8.35

fast, to stop eating food for a time.
Moses f. forty days Ex 35.28
David f. when child was ill II Sam 12.17–23
Elijah f. before reaching the mount I Kings 19.8
Jesus f. forty days Mt 4.2

father,
Honor your f. *and* Ex 20.12
makes a glad f. Prov 10.1
have we not all one f. Mal 2.10

fear,
f. *not; for I am with* Gen 26.24
do not f., *only believe* Mk 5.36
perfect love casts out f. I Jn 4.18

feasts and **festivals,** times of remembering anniversaries of important happenings with special food, celebration, and worship.

PASSOVER, celebration in remembrance of the time when God helped the Hebrews escape from slavery: their homes were passed over while Egyptian first-born sons were killed (Ex 12.27).

FEAST OF UNLEAVENED BREAD, feast celebrating the escape from Egypt (see Passover).

PENTECOST, festival 50 days after Passover to celebrate close of spring harvest (Ex 34.22); Christians celebrate it as the day the Holy Spirit came upon the Apostles (Acts 2.1ff).

FEAST OF BOOTHS or TABERNACLES (Sukkoth), a celebration in remembrance of the time when the Hebrews wandered in the wilderness and lived in booths (Lev 23.34).

feet,
a lamp to my f. Ps 119.105
beautiful are the f. Is 52.7
wet his f. *with her* Lk 7.38
wash the disciples' f. Jn 13.5

fire,
bush burned with f. Ex 3.2
f. *of the Lord fell* I Kings 18.38
tongues of f. Acts 2.3

firmament, sky or heavens.
God made the f. Gen 1.7

fish,
f. *in Nile died* Ex 7.21
f. *to swallow ... Jonah* Jon 1.17
five loaves and two f. Mt 14.17
f. with money in mouth Mt 17.27

FLAGON

flagon, an earthenware container for liquids.

flood,
story of great f. Gen 6ff
Lord ... over the f. Ps 29.10

fool,
f. *says in his heart* Ps 14.1
"F., *this night your ...* " Lk 12.20

forgive,
f. *us our debts* Mt 6.12
if you do not f. Mt 6.15
how often to f. Mt 18.21-??
"*Father,* f. *them ...* " Lk 23.34

forty,
rained f. days Gen 7ff
ate manna f. years Ex 16.35
Moses on mount f. days Ex 24.18
f. years in wilderness Num 14.33
Jesus fasted f. days Mt 4.2

frankincense, oily gum with spicy smell used in temple worship (Ex 30.34; Mt 2.11).

friend,
a f. *loves ... all times* Prov 17.17
f. *sticks closer than* Prov 18.24
Jesus talks about f. Jn 15.12–17

G

Gabriel (gā′brē-ál), an angel.
I am G. Lk 1.19

Galilee (gal′à-lē), a lake; region in Northern Palestine.

gall, a bitter liquid.
offered to Jesus Mt 27.34

garden,
g. *in Eden* Gen 2.8
g. *where Jesus prayed* Mt 26.36

garment, piece of clothing.

John's g. *of camel's hair* Mt 3.4
his g. became white Mt 17.2
divided his g. Mt 27.35
g. at feet of Saul Acts 7.58

GATEKEEPER AT GATE

gate,
enter his g. with thanksgiving Ps 100.4
by the narrow g. Mt 7.13
Gentiles, people who are not Jews.
even the G. do the same Mt 5.47
door of faith to . . . G. Acts 14.27
God of the G. Rom 3.29
Gideon (gid'ē-àn), a hero of Israel who led his people in battle against the Midianites.
angel speaks to G. Judg 6.11ff
G. and fleece Judg 6.36ff
G. against Midianites Judg 7
gift,
offering your g. Mt 5.23
to give good g. Lk 11.13
the g. of God Jn 4.10
every good and perfect g. Jas 1.17
gird, 1. to put on as a belt. 2. to get ready, as for action.
a towel with which he g. Jn 13.3-4
having g. . . . with truth Eph 6.14
give,
g. to him that begs Mt 5.42
measure you g. Lk 6.38
more blessed to g. Acts 20.35
glad,
I was g. when they Ps 122.1
make merry and be g. Lk 15.32
glean, gathering of grain by the needy after the harvest by the regular workers.
God's command to allow g. Lev 19.9-10
Ruth goes to g. Ruth 2.2ff
God, he who made and rules the universe and is worshipped by man; Creator; Father; Lord; the Almighty; Holy One; Yahweh (see Jesus, Holy Spirit, Trinity).
G. *created* Gen 1, Jn 1.3
Hannah's prayer about G. 1 Sam 2.1-10
why G. is hard to understand Job 11.7-9, 33.14; Is 55.8-9; Jn 4.24
G. *is . . . judge* Ps 7.11
G. *is my rock and* Ps 18.2
G. hears our cries Ps 40.1
G. *is our refuge* Ps 46.1-2
G. will be our guide Ps 48.14
the everlasting G. Ps 90.2; Is 40.28
G. is good and faithful Ps 100.5
G. is very great Ps 104.1
G. is good Ps 118.1, 136.1
G. made me Ps 119.73
G. will keep you from evil Ps 121.7
G. knows all our ways Ps 139.1-3
G. sees all Prov 15.3
G. loves justice, hates wrong Is 61.8; Jer 9.24
G. is perfect Mt 5.48
G. is our Father Mt 6.9
G. knows your needs Mt 6.32
G. forgives sins Mk 2.7
no one has seen G. Jn 1.18
G. *so loved the world* Jn 3.16
G. *is true* Jn 3.33
G. *is Spirit* Jn 4.24
G. in Jesus and Jesus in G. Jn 14.10
G. *shows no partiality* Acts 10.34
G. is seen in things he made Rom 1.19-20
if G. *is for us* Rom 8.31
G. lives in us I Cor 3.16
one G. and Father for all Eph 4.6
G. helps us do all Phil 4.13
the invisible G. Col 1.15
G. *cannot be tempted* Jas 1.13
God and I
if he is G. follow him I Kings 18.21

believe in G. II Chron 20.20; Jn 14.1
trust G. Ps 56.3–4
praise G. Ps 67.5, 150
thank G. Ps 100.4
fear G. Eccles 12.13
what G. requires Mic 6.8; Mal 3.8
love G. with heart, soul, and mind Mt 22.36–37
love others as a way of loving G. Mt 25.34–46
Have faith in G. Mk 11.22
pray to G. Lk 18.1
we must obey G. Acts 5.29
you are G.'s *temple* I Cor 3.16
put on G.'s armor Eph 6.10ff
G. asks us to confess sin I Jn 1.9

gods, beings or objects of worship, supposed to have special powers.
have no other g. *before me* Ex 20.3
make for us g. Acts 7.40
g. *made . . . are not* g. Acts 19.26

gold,
took g. and made calf Ex 32.4
made an image of g. Dan 3.1
g., *frankincense, and myrrh* Mt 2.11
no silver and g. Acts 3.6

golden rule, Jesus' command to do to others as you wish them to do to you (Mt 7.12; Lk 6.31).

Goliath (gȧ-lī'ȧth), a giant killed by David (I Sam 17).

good,
showed . . . what is g. Mic 6.8
fell on g. *soil* Mt 13.8
g. *and faithful* Mt 25.21
no one g. *but* God Mk 10.18
good Samaritan Lk 10.29–36
I am the g. *shepherd* Jn 10.11
Fight the g. *fight* I Tim 6.12

Good Friday, Friday before Easter; day of Jesus' death.

Gospel, good news; name given to the first four books in the New Testament, telling the story of Jesus.

grace, 1. the unearned love and favor given to man through God's goodness.
G. *to you and peace* Rom 1.7
by g. *you have been saved* Eph 2.5
partakers of g. Phil 1.7
2. a short prayer asking a blessing or giving thanks for a meal.
Samuel said g. I Sam 9.11–13
Jesus said g. Mt 14.19
Paul said g. Acts 27.35

graven, carved or cut out.
not make . . . g. *image* Ex 20.4

great,
of you a g. *nation* Gen 12.2
g. *is your reward* Mt 5.12
g. *in kingdom of heaven* Mt 5.19
g. *and first commandment* Mt 22.38

GRAVEN IMAGE

H

Hades, supposed to be a place where the spirits of dead go (see hell).
brought down to H. Mt 11.23

hair,
Samson and his h. Judg 16.17ff
Absalom and his h. II Sam 18.9

h. *of your head* Mt 10.30
wiped Jesus' feet with her h. Lk 7.36–44

hallowed, holy.
h. the Sabbath day Ex 20.11
h. *be thy name* Mt 6.9

hands,
he who has clean h. Ps 24.4
your h. *find to do* Eccles 9.10
the laying on of the apostles' h.
  Acts 8.18

happy,
h. *is he whose help is God* Ps 146.5
h. *is the man that* Prov 3.13
h. when you are kind to poor Prov
  14.21
ways to find happiness or joy Mt
  5.1–12

harlot, a woman who mates with
  men for money.
the spies and the h. Josh 2.1
tax collectors and h. Mt 21.31

hate,
those who h. *evil* Ps 97.10
h. *evil . . . love good* Amos 5.15
good to those who h. Mt 5.44
I do . . . thing I h. Rom 7.15

head,
lift up your h., *O gates* Ps 24.7
coals of fire on . . . h. Prov 25.22
h. *of John the Baptist* Mt 14.8
Christ is h. of all I Cor 11.3

heal, see miracles, diseases.
h. *the brokenhearted* Ps 147.3
h. *the sick, raise* Mt 10.8
lawful to h. *on Sabbath* Mt 12.10

hear,
H. *O Israel, the Lord* Deut 6.4
h. *and* h., *but do not* Is 6.9
everyone who h. Mt 7.24
has ears to h. Mt 11.15

heart,
with all your h. Deut 6.5; Mt 22.37
in me a clean h. Ps 51.10
search . . . know my h. Ps 139.23
pure in h. Mt 5.8
will your h. *be also* Mt 6.21
your h. *be troubled* Jn 14.1
believes with his h. Rom 10.10

heaven, 1. space in which sun,
  moon and stars move in the sky.
called the firmament, H. Gen 1.8
h. *. . . telling glory of God* Ps 19.1
  2. the place where God, angels
  and saints are thought to live.
h. *is my throne* Is 66.1
which is in h. Mt 6.9
more joy in h. Lk 15.7
ascended into h. Jn 3.13

3. kingdom of heaven, kingdom
of God; a special place or way of
life established by God in which
perfect happiness is found under
his rule; many believe it is
entered in the life after death.
reward . . . in h. Mt. 5.12
least and great in h. Mt 5.19;
  Mt 18.4
is compared to man sowing Mt
  13.24
is like a grain of mustard seed Mt
  13.31
is like leaven Mt 13.33
is like hidden treasure Mt 13.44
is like man looking for pearls Mt
  13.45
is like a net Mt 13.47
good news of kingdom Lk 8.1
For the kingdom of God Rom 14.17

hell, a place or way of punishment
  for those who turn against God;
  Hades; Sheol; Outer Darkness.
will not leave soul in h. Ps 16.10;
  Acts 2.27
in h. . . . thou art there Ps 139.8
a story about h. Lk 16.19ff

help,
he is our h. *and shield* Ps 33.20
my h. *comes from* Ps 121.2
Fear not, I will h. Is 41.13
h. *my unbelief* Mk 9.24
h. the weak I Thess 5.14

Herod, king of Judea at the time
  Jesus was born (Mt 2.7).

high priest, the chief priest.

HIGH PRIEST

Led to Caiaphas the h. p. Mt 26.57
We have a h. p. Heb 4.14

hills,
my eyes to the h. Ps 121.1
before the h. *I was* Prov 8.25
into the h. *to pray* Mt 14.23

hold,
God will h. your hand Ex 3.5
h. *fast to what is good* Rom 12.9

holy, set apart for special use by
or for God; pure and sinless.
standing on h. *ground* Ex 3.5
Sabbath day . . . keep it h. Ex 20.8
in his h. *temple* Ps 11.4
h., h., h., *is the Lord God of hosts*
Is 6.3
the h. *scriptures* Rom 1.2

Holy Spirit or **Holy Ghost,** the
spirit of God, the third person in
The Trinity, God with us but unseen.
take not thy H. S. *from me* Ps 51.11
with Jesus at baptism Mt 3.16
H. S. *will teach you* Jn 14.26
filled with H. S. Acts 2.4
gift of H. S. Acts 2.38
through the H. S. Rom 5.5

honor,
h. *your father and mother* Ex 20.12

hope,
h. *that is seen is not* h. Rom 8.24
faith, h., love I Cor 13.13

house,
dwell in the h. *of the Lord* Ps 23.6
my h. . . . *called* h. *of prayer* Is 56.7
h. *upon the rock* Mt 7.24
in my father's h. Lk 2.49; Jn 14.2

hunger,
Blessed are those that h. Mt 5.6
comes to me shall not h. Jn 6.35
if your enemy is h. Rom 12.20

husband,
wife is crown of her h. Prov 12.4
her h. *Joseph, being a just man* Mt
1.19
h. *love your wives as Christ loved*
Eph 5.25

hypocrite, a person who pretends
to be good but isn't.
as the h. *do* Mt 6.2
You h., *first take the log out of your
own eye* Mt 7.5
scribes and Pharisees, h. Mt
23.15

I

idol, an image or model of a god
that is worshipped.
the gods of the people are i. Ps 96.5
an i. *has no real existence* I Cor 8.4

image, a drawing, picture, or
statue of something; a copy or
something very much like another
thing.
created man in his own i. Gen 1.27
not make a graven i. Ex 20.4

incarnation, God's taking human
form in Jesus.
being found in human form Phil 2.8

incense, a substance made of
spices and gum, burned for its
sweet smell.
an altar to burn i. *on* Ex 30.1

inherit, to receive from another,
often from one who has died.
meek, for they shall i. Mt 5.5

i. *the kingdom* Mt 25.34

iniquity, see sin.
forgives all your i. Ps 103.3
you are full of i. Mt 23.28

inn, a place providing rooms and
food for travelers.
no place in the i. Lk 2.7

Isaac, son of Abraham, father of
Jacob.
called his son . . . I. Gen 21.3
almost sacrificed Gen 22.1–13
married Rebekah Gen 25.20
had twin sons Gen 25.24–26

Israel, 1. a Hebrew kingdom.
restore the kingdom of I. Acts 1.6
2. the name given to Jacob (Gen
35.10). 3. the Jewish people (Ps
59.5).

Israelites, people of Israel; Jews
(Ex 9.7).

J

Jacob, Israel, son of Isaac, father of those from whom came the twelve tribes of Israel.
J. born Gen 25.24–26
J. *was a quiet man* Gen 25.27
birthright and pottage Gen 25.29ff
J. blessed by Isaac Gen 27
J. goes away Gen 28.1–5
J. has a dream Gen 28.11–16
J. finds relatives Gen 29
J. and his wives Gen 29.15ff
J. and Esau meet Gen 33
J. has twelve sons Gen 35.22–23

James, 1. disciple, brother of John (Mk 1.19). 2. disciple, son of Alphaeus (Mk 3.18). 3. brother of Jesus (Mt 13.55). 4. father of Judas (Lk 6.16). 5. New Testament book.

Jeremiah (jer-à-mī′à), Hebrew prophet; Old Testament book.
God appointed J. Jer 1.4–10
visions of J. Jer 1.11–19
J. speaks to Israel Jer 2ff
J. speaks to Judah Jer 7ff
J. and the scroll Jer 36
J. in prison Jer 37.15
J. in cistern Jer 38.6ff

Jerusalem, capital of Judah, where Solomon's temple was built.
conquered by David II Sam 5.7
Solomon . . . build in J. I Kings 9.19
and all J. *with him* Mt 2.3
boy Jesus in J. Lk 2.42ff
be my witnesses in J. Acts 1.8

Jesus, Son of God; second person in The Trinity; Christ; the Messiah; Savior; Immanuel; God in human form.
HIS LIFE:
birth of J. Mt 2; Lk 2
boy J. at Temple Lk 2.41–52
J. baptized by John Mt 3.13ff
J. tempted by devil Mt 4.1–11
J. chose disciples Mt 4.18–22, 9.9; Mk 1.16–20, 2.14

J. teaches Mt 5, 6; Mk 1.21–22
Jesus teaches with stories (see Stories of Jesus)
J. heals (see Miracles of Jesus)
J. blesses children Mk 10.13–16
J. sent disciples out Lk 9.1–6
some criticize J. Mk 2.7, 15–17, 18, 24, 3.2
J. and prayer Mt 6.5–13, 14.23; Lk 3.21, 6.12, 9.28, 22.44, 23.46; Jn 11.41–42, 12.27–88
J. transfigured Mt 17; Mk 9
LAST WEEK:
J. rides into city Mt 21.1–11; Mk 11.1–11; Lk 19.29–44; Jn 12.12–19
J. in the temple Mt 21.12–17; Mk 11.15–19; Lk 19.45–48
J. teaches and answers Mt 21.18–25.46; Mk 12; Lk 20, 21
the Last Supper (Passover) Mt 26.17–29; Mk 14.12–25; Lk 22.7–38; Jn 13
J. in the garden Mt 26.36–56; Mk 14.32–52; Lk 22.39–54
J. trial Mk 15.2–20
J. is crucified Mk 15.21–41
J. arose Mt 28; Mk 16; Lk 24; Jn 20
Ascension Lk 24.50–51; Acts 1.9
OTHER VERSES ABOUT JESUS:
my beloved Son Mt 3.17
You are the Christ Mt 16.16
the Holy One of God Mk 1.24
God gave his only Son Jn 3.16
I am the light Jn 8.12
I am the good shepherd Jn 10.11
I go to prepare a place Jn 14.3–4
I am the way . . . truth . . . life Jn 14.6
because I live, you will live Jn 14.19
J. will come again Acts 1.11

Jews, people tracing their beginning to Abraham; Hebrews; Israelites.

Job, a man in the Old Testament book of that name who kept his faith in God even after many troubles.

John, 1. one of the twelve apostles. 2. the Baptist, cousin of Jesus. 3. New Testament Gospel.

Jonah, 1. Hebrew prophet sent by God to warn Nineveh to repent; swallowed by big fish. 2. Old Testament book.

Jonathan, son of Saul; friend of David.

Saul, and J. his son I Sam 13.16

J. *made a covenant with David* I Sam 18.3

Joseph, 1. Jacob's favorite son. He was sold into slavery in Egypt by his brothers.

J. quarrels with brothers Gen 37.2–4

J. and dreams Gen 37.5–11

J. sold as slave Gen 37.12ff

J. serves Potiphar Gen 39.1–20

J. in prison Gen 39.21–41.14

J. explains dreams Gen 40.5ff, 41.14ff

Pharaoh appoints J. Gen 41.41

J. helps his brothers Gen 42–46

2. husband of Mary, mother of Jesus (Lk 2). 3. of Arimathaea (Mt 27.57).

Josiah, a boy king (II Kings 22).

journey,

a man going on a long j. Mt 25.14

went a day's j. Lk 2.44

j. *into a far country* Lk 15.13

joy,

j. *of the Lord is* Neh 8.10

put more j. *in my heart* Ps 4.7

the j. *of thy salvation* Ps 51.12

hills sing for j. Ps 98.8

exceedingly great j. Mt 2.10

the seventy returned with j. Lk 10.17

that my j. *may be in you* Jn 15.11

sorrow will turn . . . to j. Jn 16.20

j. *that was set before* Heb 12.2

count it all j. Jas 1.2

j. *may be complete* I Jn 1.4

Judas (jü′dás), 1. disciple, son of James (Lk 6.16). 2. J. Iscariot, disciple who betrayed Jesus (Lk 6.16). 3. brother of Jesus (Mt 13.55; Mk 6.3).

Judea (jü-dē′á), a part of southern Palestine, where Bethlehem is located (Mt 2.1).

judge, 1. tribal ruler in Israel (see Judges). 2. to hear cases and decide what is right and true.

God is a righteous j. Ps 7.11

he will j. *the world* Ps 98.9

j. *not that you be not* Mt 7.1

K

keep,

Lord bless and k. you Num. 6.24

k. *your tongue from evil* Ps 34.13

k. *him in perfect peace* Is 26.3

all the earth k. *silence* Hab 2.20

k. *your hearts and minds* Phil 4.7

kill,

you shall not k. Ex 20.13

you have heard, you shall not k., but I say Mt 5.21–22

do not fear those who k. *the body* Mt 10.28

kin, relatives or family.

among his own k. Mk 6.4

kind,

love is . . . and k. I Cor 13.4

be k. *to one another* Eph 4.32

kingdom, a country or region ruled by a king (for kingdom of God, kingdom of heaven, see heaven 3).

Thy k. *come* Mt 6.10

Seek first his k. Mt 6.33

preaching the gospel of the k. Mt 9.35

the secrets of the k. Mt 13.11

kings, some well-known:

SAUL, first king of Israel I Sam 9–31

DAVID, I and II Sam

SOLOMON, who built temple I Kings 1–12

AHAB, married to Jezebel I Kings 16–18

JOSIAH, boy king II Kings 22, 23

NEBUCHADNEZZAR, king of Babylon II Kings 24; Dan 1–4

kneading bowl, a shallow, open container in which dough is kneaded for baking.

know,
Be still and k. that Ps 46.10
and k. my heart Ps 139.23
you will k. the truth Jn 8.32

KNEADING BOWL

L

labor,
six days you shall l. Ex 20.9
come . . . all who l. Mt 11.28

lamb, 1. young sheep, often used as a sacrifice.
Passover l. killed Ex 12
2. name for Jesus because he gave his life as a sacrifice.
like that of a l. without spot I Pet 1.19
the L. of God Jn 1.29

lamp, a dishlike vessel holding oil and a wick, used to give light.
Thy word is a l. Ps 119.105
light a l. and put it under a Mt 5.15
the foolish took their l. Mt 25.3

last,
l. who will be first Lk 13.30

Last Supper, the meal Jesus shared with his disciples before he was crucified (Mt 26) (see Jesus' last week).

law, the rules for living given by God to the Hebrews; first five books of the Old Testament.
table of l. Ex 24.12
l. of the Lord is perfect Ps 19.7
put my l. within them Jer 31.33
Jesus and the l. Mt 5.17ff
love fulfills l. Rom 13.10

lawful, permitted, allowed.
Is it l. . . . on Sabbath Mt 12.10
l. for me I Cor 6.12

Lazarus (laz′å-räs), 1. poor man in Jesus' story (Lk 16.19ff). 2. brother of Mary and Martha (Jn 11).

lead,
l. me beside still waters Ps 23.2
l. me in the way Ps 139.24
l. us not into temptation Mt 6.13

leaven, yeast or substance to make dough rise, and make bread light (full of tiny airholes).
kingdom of heaven is like l. Mt 13.33

legion, a large number.
twelve l. of angels Mt 26.53
man whose name was L. Lk 8.30

leper, person having leprosy (see leprosy).
a l. came to him Mt 8.2
he was met by ten l. Lk 17.12

leprosy, a disease causing sores, scabs, crippling, and loss of feeling. People with it were said to be "unclean."
rules about l. Lev 13
Miriam's l. Num 12.10
Naaman's l. II Kings 5

Levites, members of the tribe of

Levi, who worked in temple with priests (Deut 21.5; Jn 1.19).

liberty, freedom, as not being slave or prisoner.
proclaim l. Lev 25.10
to set at l. *those* Lk 4.18

life,
the breath of l. Gen. 2.7
anxious about your l. Mt 6.25
loses his l. *for my sake* Mt 10.39
have eternal l. Jn 3.16
passed from death to l. Jn 5.24
the bread of l. Jn 6.35
spirit that gives l. Jn 6.63
resurrection and the l. Jn 11.25
lay down his l. *for* Jn 15.13

light,
lift up the l. *of thy* Ps 4.6
have seen a great l. Mt 4.16
the l. *of the world* Mt 5.14
a l. *from heaven* Acts 26.13

lion,
Samson and the l. Judg 14.5ff
David and the l. I Sam 17.34
Daniel and the l. Dan 6.16

live,
not l. *by bread alone* Mt 4.4
in him we l. *and move* Acts 17.28

loaves,
stones . . . become l. *of bread* Mt 4.3
five l. *and two fish* Mt 14.17
lend me three l. Lk 11.5

Lord, God, Jesus
the L. *our God is one* L. Deut 6.4
this is the L.'s *doing* Ps 118.23
We have seen the L. Jn 20.25
one L., *one faith,* Eph 4.5
King of kings and L. *of lords* Rev 19.16

Lord's Day, first day of the week, celebrated by Christians in remembrance of Christ's resurrection (Rev 1.10).

Lord's Prayer, prayer Jesus taught his disciples (Mt 6.9ff; Lk 11.2–4).

Lord's Supper, the symbolic meal shared by Christians in keeping with Jesus' command (I Cor 11.23–26); Holy Communion.

Lot, Abraham's nephew.
L. *with him* Gen 13.1
Abraham and L. settle a quarrel Gen 13.8ff
L. in Sodom Gen 19

Lot's wife, the woman who was turned into a pillar of salt (Gen 19.26).

love,
l. *your neighbor* Lev 19.18; Mt 19.19
l. *the Lord your God* Deut 6.5; Mt 22.37
a friend l. *at all times* Prov 17.17
hate evil, l. *good* Amos 5.15
l. *kindness* Mic 6.8
l. *your enemies* Mt 5.44
if you l. *me* Jn 14.15
l. *one another* Jn 15.12; I Jn 4.7
greater l. *has no man* Jn 15.13
shows his l. *for us* Rom 5.8
the l. *of Christ* Rom 8.35
l. *does no wrong* Rom 13.10
a chapter about l. I Cor 13
make l. *your aim* I Cor 14.1
l. *of money* I Tim 6.10
God is l. I Jn 4.8, 16
perfect l. *casts out fear* I Jn 4.18
he who l. *God, should* l. I Jn 4.21

Luke, doctor, companion of Paul, who probably wrote Acts and the Gospel named Luke (Col 4.14).

Lydia, Christian friend of Paul who sold purple dye and cloth (Acts 16.14ff).

M

Macedonia (mas-à-dō'nē-à), a conquered Greek territory, province of Rome; one of the places Paul visited (Acts 16.9).

Magdalene (mag'dà-lēn), one of the Marys, so called because she came from Magdala (Lk 8.2).

Magi (mā'jī), wise men who brought gifts to Jesus.

maidens, girls or young women.
ten m. who took lamps Mt 25.1

man,
God is greater than m. Job 33.12
Blessed is the m. Ps 1.1
what is m. *that thou art* Ps 8.4
what sort of m. *is this* Mt 8.27
obey God rather than m. Acts 5.29

manna, food which God gave the Israelites in wilderness, white flakes, tasting like honey (Ex.16).

Mark, follower of Jesus, Paul's helper, writer of New Testament Gospel by that name.

marriage, the joining of man and woman as husband and wife; a ceremony or sacrament of the Christian church.

Martha, friend of Jesus, sister of Mary and Lazarus.
served Jesus and wanted Mary to help Lk 10.38ff
M.'s brother restored to life Jn 11.1ff

Mary, 1. Mother of Jesus.
M. and family call on Jesus Mk 3.31ff
angel Gabriel visits M. Lk 1.26ff
M. visits Elizabeth Lk 1.39ff
M. gives birth to son Lk 2
M. at a marriage feast Jn 2.1
Jesus asked disciple to care for M. Jn 19.27
2. friend of Jesus, sister of Martha and Lazarus.
M. sat at Jesus' feet Lk 10.39
M. at time of brother's death Jn 11.1ff
M. anointed Jesus' feet Jn 12
3. M. Magdalene, follower of Jesus (Mt 27.56, 28.1).

master, one who rules others.
no man can serve two m. Mt 6.24
you have one m. Mt 23.10
Is it I, M. Mt 26.25
Hail, M! Mt 26.49

Matthew, 1. disciple of Jesus; 2. New Testament Gospel.

Matthias, new Apostle chosen to replace Judas (Acts 1.25–26).

Maundy Thursday, Thursday be-

fore Easter, day in remembrance of Jesus' washing his disciples' feet at the Last Supper (Jn 13.4–10); name comes from Latin *mandatum*, "commandment," referring to Jesus' commandment to the disciples to love one another (Jn 13.34).

meal, 1. ground-up grain.
only a handful of m. I Kings 17.12
hid leaven in m. Mt 13.33
2. a time of eating food.
sold birthright for a m. Heb 12.16

meek, patient, gentle.
m. *shall possess the land* Ps 37.11
Blessed are the m. Mt 5.5

merciful, having kindness and being able to forgive.
The Lord is m. Ps 103.8
Blessed are the m. Mt 5.7

Messiah (mà-sī'à), [Hebrew: the anointed one] one sent by God to save his people; a name given to Jesus.
I have found the M. Jn 1.41
the M. *is coming* Jn 4.25

mezuzah (me-zōō'zà), a small metal case attached to a Jewish doorpost, holding a parchment with Deut 6.4–9 and 11.13–21 written on one side and the name of God on the other.

Michael, one of the chief angels of God (Jude 9; Rev 12.7).

might, strength, power.
with all your m. Deut 6.5
not by m., *nor by power* Zech 4.6

millstone, large flat stone used for grinding grain (Mt 18.6).

mind,
m. *stayed on thee* Is 26.3
with all your m. Mt 22.37

minister, 1. spiritual head of a church who may preach, conduct worship, celebrate sacraments.
I was made a m. Eph 3.7
a good m. *of Christ* I Tim 4.6
2. to serve, give help.
angels came and m. *to him* Mt 4.11
did not m. *to thee* Mt 25.44

miracle, a happening which seems to be against the laws of nature or science, which only God can perform or explain; a mighty work of God.

miracles, New Testament

1. of Jesus (healing)

a leper Mt 8.2–4

paralyzed servant Mt 8.5–13

woman who touched his coat Mt 9.20–22

dumb demoniac Mt 9.32

dumb and blind Mt 12.22

unclean spirit Mk 1.23

girl with demon Mk 7.29

hearing and speech Mk 7.32

high fever Lk 4.38

man on a bed Lk 5.18

withered hand Lk 6.6

twelve-year-old girl Lk 8.42

official's son Jn 4.46

ill for 38 years Jn 5.5

one born blind Jn 9.1

Lazarus to life Jn 11

2. of Jesus (other than healing)

walking on the sea Mt 14.25

feeding 4000 Mt 15.32ff

money from a fish Mt 17.27

stopping a storm Mk 4.35ff

escaping the mob Lk 4.28ff

nets full of fish Lk 5.1ff

wine from water Jn 2.1ff

feeding 5000 Jn 6.5ff

3. through the Apostles

hearing in own language Acts 2.7–8

cripple at the gate Acts 3.1ff

many signs and wonders Acts 5.12–16

prison doors open Acts 5.19

conversion of Paul Acts 9

bedridden for 8 years Acts 9.32ff

Dorcas to life Acts 9.36ff

cripple from birth Acts 14.8

young man who fell Acts 20.7ff

miracles, Old Testament:

ten plagues of Egypt Ex 7ff

Red Sea parts Ex 14.21ff

manna sent for food Ex 16.14

widow's oil and meal II Kings 4

Naaman's leprosy II Kings 5

young men in fiery furnace Dan 3.19

Daniel in lion's den Dan 6.16

Jonah in the fish Jon 1.17ff

Miriam, sister of Moses.

M. saves baby Moses Ex 2.1–10

And M. sang to them Ex 15.20

behold M. was leprous Num 12.10

missionary, one sent out by the church to teach, preach, and aid others.

Philip was m. to Samaria Acts 8.5ff

Paul and Barnabas sent out as m. Acts 13.2–3

Jesus' command to be m. Mt 28.19–20

money-changer, one who changed money of other countries into the kind needed for temple offerings or taxes (Mt 21.12).

money used in Bible,

DENARIUS, gold or silver coin worth 10 to 16 cents (Mt 20.2).

PENNY, same as denarius (Mt 10.20).

SHEKEL, gold or silver coin worth 14 to 42 cents (Mt 17.27).

TALENT, coin worth from 1000 to 40,000 dollars (Mt 25.15).

mortar, mud or clay used to hold bricks together in building.

Israelites use m. and brick Ex 1.14

Moses, leader and law-giver of the Israelites.

when M. was a baby Ex 2

God speaks to M. Ex 3, 4

M. and Pharaoh Ex 5–12

M. leads people out Ex 14

M. gets laws Ex 19, 20

M. builds tabernacle Ex 25–31

M. dies Deut 34.5–8

myrrh, a sticky substance with a sweet smell used in incense.

gold, frankincense and m. Mt 2.11

mystery,

no one can reveal m. but God Dan 2.27–28

of the m. *of God* I Cor 4.1

m. *of the gospel* Eph 6.19

Great . . . is the m. I Tim 3.16

N

name,
a good n. *is better* Eccles 7.1
Hallowed be thy n. Mt 6.9
prophesy in your n. Mt 7.22
two or three are gathered in my n. Mt 18.20
you ask in my n. Jn 14.13
above every n. Eph 1.21

Naomi, mother-in-law of Ruth (Ruth 1).

narrow,
enter by the n. *gate* Mt 7.13

Nazareth, town in northern Palestine where Jesus lived as a child (Lk 1.26).

Nebuchadnezzar, see Kings.

needle,
the eye of a n. Mt 19.24

Nehemiah, rebuilt the walls of Jerusalem; Old Testament book.
N.'s prayer for help Neh 1
N. returns to Jerusalem. Neh 2
the people help rebuild Neh 3ff

neighbor,
love your n. *as yourself* Mt 19.19
who is my n. Lk 10.29

nettle, a weed with stinging hairs (Is 34.13; Hos 9.6).

Nicodemus (nik-ȯ-dē'mŭs), a Pharisee who was interested in Jesus (Jn 3.1–21).

Noah, man who built an ark to save his family during flood.
God tells N. to build ark Gen 6.11ff
N. takes animals and family into the ark Gen 7.1–5
the flood comes Gen 7.11ff
God's covenant and the rainbow Gen 9.8–17

NETTLE

O

obey,
if you will o. *my commandments* Deut 11.13
even the winds and sea o. Mt 8.27
o. *God rather than* Acts 5.29
children o. . . . . *parents* Col 3.20

offering, a gift offered to God.
Cain's o. Gen 4.3
Abel's o. Gen 4.4
o. of cattle Lev 1.2
if o. is a burnt o. Lev 1.3
cereal o. Lev 2.1
peace o. Lev 3.1
love better than burnt o. Hos 6.6
tithes and o. Mal 3.8

more than o. *and sacrifices* Mk 12.33
Christ's o. *for us* Eph 5.2

oil, a greasy liquid, as from olives.
o. used in offerings Lev 2.4
o. used for anointing new king I Sam 10.1

ointment, an oily cream rubbed on the body to heal, make soft, or to perfume.
woman put o. *on Jesus* Mt 26.6
prepared spices and o. Lk 23.56

overcome,
I have o. *the world* Jn 16.33
o. *evil with good* Rom 12.21

P

Palestine, country where most of the Bible events took place; Holy Land; Canaan; Land of Israel.

pallet, a straw bed or mattress.
let down the p. Mk 2.4
take up your p. *and walk* Mk 2.9

Palm Sunday, Sunday before Easter when Christians remember the entry of Jesus into Jerusalem.

parable, a short story that teaches a religious truth (Mk 4.33–34).

parables, New Testament (of Jesus)
speck and log Mt 7.3–5
house on rock Mt 7.24–27
where the seeds fell Mt 13.1–9
weeds in the field Mt 13.24–30
lost sheep Mt 18.12–14
unforgiving servant Mt 18.23–34
workers in vineyard Mt 20.1–16
father and two sons Mt 21.28–32
wise and foolish maidens Mt 25.1–13
talents Mt 25.14–30
sheep and goats Mt 25.31–46
growing seeds Mk 4.26–29
mustard seed Mk 4.31–32
watching Mk 13.34–36
two debtors Lk 7.41–50
good Samaritan Lk 10.25–35
friend at midnight Lk 11.5–8
rich fool Lk 12.16–21
fig tree Lk 13.6–9
great banquet Lk 14.16–24
lost coin Lk 15.8–10
the prodigal son Lk 15.11–32
rich man and Lazarus Lk 16.19–31
widow and judge Lk 18.1–8
Pharisee and publican Lk 18.9–14
pounds Lk 19.12–27

parables, Old Testament
poor man's one lamb II Sam 12.1–6
the wild grapes Is 5.1–6

Passover, see feasts and festivals.

patriarch, father and ruler of family or tribe; especially one of the founders of the Hebrew family such as Abraham, Isaac, and Jacob (Acts 2.29).

Paul, also called Saul, an apostle of Jewish family and Roman citizenship; missionary; tentmaker; his letters to churches became books of New Testament.
P. see a stoning Acts 7.58–8.1
P. hates Christians Acts 8.3
P. changes after a strange experience Acts 9.1–22
a narrow escape Acts 9.21–22
first missionary journey Acts 13–14
P. stoned and left Acts 14.19
P. and the Jerusalem Council Acts 15.1–35
second journey Acts 15.36–18.22
P. finds Timothy Acts 16.1ff
P. helps a slave girl and is put in prison Acts 16.16–24
earthquake opens prison Acts 16.25ff
third journey Acts 18.23–21.19
young man fell out window Acts 20.7–12
P.'s arrest, hearings, defense Acts 21.27–26.32
fourth journey or trip to Rome Acts 27.1ff
storm and shipwreck Acts 27.14ff
escape to an island Acts 28.1
P. bitten by viper Acts 28.3
P. preaches in prison Acts 28.23

peace,
Prince of P. Is 9.6
him in perfect p. Is 26.3
on earth p. *among men* Lk 2.14

pearl,
do not throw p. *before swine* Mt 7.6
finding one p. *of great* Mt 13.46

penance, something done as self-punishment to show sorrow for and repentance of sin.

Pentecost, see feasts and festivals.

perfect,
law of Lord is p. Ps 19.7
you . . . must be p. Mt 5.48
every p. *gift is from* Jas 1.17
p. *love casts out fear* I Jn 4.18

persecute, to treat in a cruel way,

especially for holding certain beliefs.

and p. you and utter Mt 5.11

Saul, why do you p. Acts 9.4

Bless those who p. you Rom 12.14

Peter, also called Simon, an Apostle; two letters or books in New Testament are named for him.

P. was a fisherman Mt 4.18

P. walked on water Mt 14.28ff

P. blessed by Jesus Mt 16.17ff

Jesus chose P. to watch Mt 26.37

P. denies he knew Jesus Mt 26.69ff

P. on Easter morning Jn 20.2ff

P. talks to Jesus one morning after a fishing trip Jn 21

the sermon that brought 3000 people into the church Acts 2.14–41

P. and John give a man something better than gold Acts 3.1ff

man and woman lie to P. Acts 5.1ff

even P.'s shadow had power (with God's help) Acts 5.15

P. raises Dorcas from the dead Acts 9.36ff

P. had a vision when hungry Acts 10.9ff

P. decides God loves all Acts 10.34

P. rescued from prison Acts 12

Pharaoh, name for rulers of Egypt.

Joseph said to P. Gen 41.25

When P. *let the people go* Ex 13.17

Pharisee, a Jew belonging to a group that strictly obeyed the law of Moses.

Jesus talked about P. Mt 23.1ff

Philip, 1. apostle (Jn 1.43–46). 2. a member of early church who preached and served (Acts 6.1–6, 8.4–40).

Philistine, a neighboring seacoast people and enemies of Israelites (I Sam 17).

phylacteries (fil-ak′tȧ-rēz), small leather cases holding slips of parchment on which were written selected passages from one law of Moses, worn on foreheads or arms.

Pilate, Pontius, the Roman governor of Judea (Mk 15.1; Lk 3.1).

plague, something bringing suffering or trouble to large numbers of people, as a disease; any of the disasters sent down on the Egyptians by God (Ex 7ff).

poor,

Blessed are the p. *in* Mt 5.3

sell and give to the p. Mt 19.21

good news to the p. Lk 4.18

praetorium, where a governor lived.

took Jesus into the p. Mt 27.27

praise, to worship and show love for; many psalms p. God, such as 135, 136, 146, 147, 148, 149, 150.

pray, communicate with God (asking, thanking, praising, confessing).

PRAY WHEN: evening, morning, noon Ps 55.17

Daniel . . . three times a day Dan 6.10

when facing trouble Mt 26.39

Jesus p. all night Lk 6.12

p. *at all times* Eph 6.18

when suffering, sick, or sinful Jas 5.13–16

PRAY HOW:

falling to the ground Num 16.22

with my whole heart Ps 9.1

with hands uplifted Ps 28.2

kneel before the Lord Ps 95.6

p. *like this: Our Father* Mt 6.9ff

you stand praying Mk 11.25

with help of God's spirit Rom 8.26–27

PRAY WHERE:

before altar I Kings 8.22

out of doors Ps 121.1

in one's room Mt 6.6

PHYLACTERY

in every place I Tim 2.8

PRAY WHY:
for God's help Ps 121.2
to praise God Ps 147.1
to help people who harm us Mt 5.44
to ask for food Mt 6.11
to be forgiven Mt 6.12
to keep us strong Mt 6.13
Jesus thanked God Lk 10.21
so we won't be anxious Phil 4.6
to help suffering Jas 5.13
because we have sinned Jas 5.16

OTHER HELPS IN PRAYER:
The Lord will answer Ps 20.1
wait for the Lord Ps 27.14
God hears us p. Ps 65.2
will receive if you have faith Mt 21.22
ask, seek, and knock Lk 11.9
ask in Jesus' name Jn 14.13
don't ask wrongly Jas 4.3

prayer,
p. often used to close a worship service Num 24.6
p. of David I Chron 29.10–13
the Lord's P. Mt 6.9–13
Paul's p. Col 1.9–12

priest, a person who performs religious ceremonies in a house of worship.
show yourself to the p. Mt 8.4
by chance a p. *was going* Lk 10.31

prison,
Joseph in p. Gen 39–41
John the Baptist in p. Mk 6.17
Peter in p. Acts 12.3
Paul in p. Acts 16.23, 21.34

prize,
toward the goal for the p. Phil 3.14

prodigal, wasteful and reckless with money.

the p. son Lk 15.11–32

prophecy, word of God spoken by a prophet.

prophet, one who speaks for God, as Isaiah, Jeremiah, Ezekial, Hosea, Amos, Micah.

Proverbs, Old Testament book of wise sayings.

PRUNING HOOK

pruning hook, tool with a sharp curved blade for pruning grapevines (Is 2.4).

Psalms, Old Testament book of hymns of praise used in worship.

purple, purple dye was very expensive; garments dyed with it were worn by kings and rich people (Acts 16.14).
p. garments worn by kings Judg 8.26
clothed in p. Lk 16.19

Q

queens,
BATHSHEBA, mother of Solomon by King David (II Sam 11).

BERNICE, wife of King Agrippa who felt Paul was innocent (Acts 25.23, 26.30).

ESTHER, Jewish wife of Persian king who saved her people; Old Testament book.

JEZEBEL, the wicked wife of King Ahab of Israel (I Kings 16.31, 18.17, 19.1; II Kings 9.30–37).

SHEBA, Queen of, ruler of Sheba who visited King Solomon (I Kings 10.1–13).

R

rabbi, a teacher of Jewish law; title of respect; master.
they love being called r. Mt 23.7
R. (*which means Teacher*) Jn 1.38
Rabboni (ra-bō′nī), my master, a high title of respect for a teacher or rabbi (Jn 20.16).
raiment, clothing (Mt 28.3).
rain,
r. for forty days Gen 7.4
r. *on just and unjust* Mt 5.45
r. *fell, floods came* Mt 7.25
rainbow, see Noah.
ransom, price paid for freeing a slave or captive.
give his life as a r. Mt 20.28
reap, cut and gather ripe grain.
neither sow nor r. Mt 6.26
Rebekah, wife of Isaac, mother of Jacob (Gen 24.15ff).
redeemer, one who sets free or rescues, as from sin; said of Jesus.
I know my R. *lives* Job 19.25
Holy One . . . your R. Is 54.5–8
Christ gave self to redeem Tit 2.13–14
rejoice, be or make glad, happy.
let us r. *and be glad* Ps 118.24
r. . . . *for your reward is* Mt 5.12
love does not r. *at wrong* I Cor 13.6
r. *in the Lord always* Phil 4.4
repent, to feel sorry for having done wrong (Ezek 14.6; Acts 2.38).
repentance, a change in one's life because he is sorry for having done wrong.
I baptize you . . . for r. Mt 3.11
resurrection, a rising from the dead.

I am the r. *and the life* Jn 11.25
Jesus and the r. Acts 17.18
with him in a r. *like* I Cor 15.13
revelation, a showing or revealing of something that had not been known (Gal 1.12).
revile, to call bad names, say harsh things about.
men r. *you and persecute* Mt 5.11
reward,
great is your r. Mt 5.12
they have their r. Mt 6.2
rich,
hard for a r. man Mt 19.24
be r. *in good deeds* I Tim 6.18
righteous, doing what is right, fair, and just.
suppose there are fifty r. Gen 18.24
knows the way of the r. Ps 1.6
separate evil from r. Mt 13.49
ninety-nine r. *persons* Lk 15.7
robber,
make it a den of r. Mt 21.13
two r. *were crucified* Mt 27.38
Barabbas was a r. Jn 18.40
robe,
a long r. *with sleeves* Gen 37.3
thorns and a purple r. Jn 19.5
rock,
Moses gets water from r. Ex 17.6
Lord is my r. Ps 18.2
house on a r. Mt 7.25
on this r. . . . *build my church* Mt 16.18
seed fell on r. Lk 8.6
Ruth, Moabite woman who left her own people to go with Naomi and became an Israelite; Old Testament book about her.

S

Sabbath, 1. seventh day of week, set aside for rest and worship by the Jews. 2. see Sunday.
Remember the S. Ex 20.8
is it lawful on S. Mt 12.12
S. made for men Mk 2.27

SACKCLOTH GARMENT

sackcloth, coarse cloth worn to show trouble or sorrow.
Jacob put on s. Gen 37.34
Job put on s. Job 16.15

sacrament, a holy rite performed in the Christian church as commanded by Jesus, such as baptism (Mt 28.19) and the Lord's Supper (I Cor 11.24–26).

sacrifice, something of value given as an offering to God; the act of giving it (see offering).
a son almost given for a s. Gen 22
the law of s. Lev 7.11ff
your bodies a living s. Rom 12.1
the s. *of himself* Heb 9.26

Sadducees (saj′ü-sēz), group of Jews who were strict in keeping the law of Moses, but who did not believe in angels, in life after death, or in the traditional laws handed down orally.
beware of teaching of S. Mt 16.12

saint, 1. a person who has lived a very good and holy life.

with all his s. I Thess 3.13
2. a sincere follower of Jesus Christ.
called to be s. I Cor 1.2
Peter came . . . to the s. Acts 9.32

salt,
Lot's wife turned to s. Gen 19.26
the s. *of the earth* Mt 5.13

salvation, saving of the soul from sin and death; healing.
God is our s. Ps 68.19
Today, s. *has come* Lk 19.9
s. *in no one else* Acts 4.12

Samaritans (sà-mâr′i-tàns), people in Samaria; in Jesus' time, related to but greatly despised by the Jews.
the Good S. Lk 10.25–37
S. gave thanks Lk 17.16
woman of Samaria Jn 4.7ff
no dealings with S. Jn 4.9

Samson, a judge in Israel remembered for his great strength.
his life Judg 13–16

sanctuary (sank′chōō-âr-ē), a holy place set aside for worship (Num 3.38).

Sanhedrin (san′he-drin), council of Jewish religious leaders in Jerusalem to whom the Roman ruler gave authority over their people (Lk 22.66).

Sarah, wife of Abraham, mother of Isaac (Gen 17.15).

Satan, see devil.

Saul, 1. see Paul. 2. first king of Israel (I Sam 9–31).

save,
he will s. *his people* Mt 1.21
whoever would s. *his life* Mt 16.25
seek and s. *the lost* Lk 19.10

Savior, 1. title given to Jesus as sent by God to save the world (Jn 3.16–17).
born this day . . . a S. Lk 2.11
2. God.
Holy One . . . your S. Is 43.3

scribe, a teacher of Jewish law; a

secretary who copied the law.
Baruch the s. Jer 36.32
the s. and Pharisees Mt 23.2
scripture, holy writing, Bible.
all s. is inspired by God II Tim 3.16
scroll, roll of parchment with writing on it (Jer 36.2)
seek, search for.
s. *the Lord your God* Deut 4.29
s. *first his kingdom* Mt 6.33
s. *and you will find* Lk 11.9
sepulchre (sep′ul-ker), grave or tomb; place for burial (Mt 28.1).
sermon, a speech on religious themes.
Jesus′ s. on mount Mt 5–7
Peter′s s. on Pentecost Acts 2

SHEEPFOLD

sheepfold, a yard or enclosure for sheep.
shekel, see money.
Shema, words of faith and confession repeated by the Jews; found in Deut 6.4–9, 11.13–21; Num 15.37–41.
shepherd, one who cares for sheep.
the Lord is my s. Ps 23.1
I am the good s. Jn 10.14
Simon, 1. Peter, the disciple (Mt 4.18). 2. the Zealot, disciple (Lk 6.15). 3. of Cyrene, who carried cross (Mt 27.32).
sin, disobeying God′s commandments; falling short of what God would have us be and do.
I am sorry for my s. Ps 38.18
wages of s. *is death* Rom 6.23
if we confess our s. I Jn 1.9
Sodom and Gomorrah (sod′om,

gà-môr′à), cities destroyed by fire (Gen 13–18).
Solomon, a king of Israel who was said to be very wise.
birth of S. II Sam 12.24
David chooses S. to be king I Kings 1.29ff
S. prays for understanding I Kings 3.6–9
Queen of Sheba visits S. I Kings 10
S. was a builder I Kings 5–8
S. was a judge I Kings 3.16ff
son,
This is my beloved S. Mt 3.17
gave his only S. Jn 3.16
soul, the center of our thinking, feeling, loving, and responding to God.
love God with all your s. Deut 6.5
destroy both s. *and body* Mt 10.28
my s. *magnifies the Lord* Lk 1.46
able to save your s. Jas 1.21
sow, to plant seed (Mt 6.26).
spirit, 1. a being not of the natural world, like an angel: God is often thought of as spirit. 2. the part of oneself that is not body; soul. 3. the part of God that dwells in persons.
God is s. Jn 4.24
s. *gives life* Jn 6.63
flesh and s. Rom 8.2–17
God′s S. *dwells in you* I Cor 3.16
steal,
You shall not s. Ex 20.15
where thieves break in and s. Mt 6.19
Stephen, first Christian known to have died for his faith (Acts 7.59)
stone,
tables of s. (laws) Ex 24.12
with a sling and s. I Sam 17.50
ask for loaf . . . give s. Mt 7.9
rolled back the s. Mt 28.2
command this s. *to become bread* Lk 4.3
stories about Jesus, see Jesus, his life.
stories Jesus told, see Parables.
stories, New Testament, see Peter, Paul, Stephen, Philip.
stories, Old Testament
the beginning Gen 1 and 2

Adam and Eve disobey Gen 3
Cain kills brother Gen 4
great flood Gen 6–9
Abraham gives Lot first choice Gen 13
God tests Abraham Gen 22
Jacob and Esau Gen 25.24ff
Jacob works for wives Gen 29ff
Joseph, the dreamer Gen 37ff
baby Moses in a basket Ex 2
burning bush Ex 3
Moses saves his people Ex 4ff
the golden calf Ex 32
the ass that talked Num 22.21ff
the woman saves lives of spies Josh 2
the woman who saved Israel Judg 4
the man who wouldn't believe God until he saw the fleece Judg 6, 7
the man whose strength was in his hair Judg 16
Ruth goes with Naomi to a new home Book of Ruth
child who was given to God I Sam 3
David and his slingshot I Sam 17
two women claim one baby I Kings 3.16
Elijah proves God greater I Kings 18
a room on the roof II Kings 4.8
slave girl helps Naaman II Kings 5
book of law found in temple II Kings 22
boys refuse king's food Dan 1
fiery furnace Dan 3
Daniel in lion's den Dan 6
a queen saves her people Esther 7
Job, the man who lost all Job 1
Jonah, saved by huge fish Jon 1

Sukkoth, see Feasts of Booths or Tabernacles.

Sunday, the Christian Sabbath, observed the first day of the week because of Jesus' resurrection on that day.

swaddling, long bands of cloth wrapped around a new baby (Lk 2.7).

synagogue, meeting place for Jewish worship and study.

T

tabernacle, tent in which Hebrews worshipped in the presence of God, taken with them on their journeys in the wilderness; a meeting place for worshipping God.

talent, see money.

taskmasters, overseers or bosses (Ex 5.14).

temple, a building for worship (Mt 21.12).
you are God's t. I Cor 3.16

temptation, chance or opportunity to do wrong (Mt 6.13).

testament, a will or promise.

Testament, New, last 27 books of the Bible, regarded by Christians as part of the Scriptures; the name means "new covenant," the agreement with God centering on Christ as man's redeemer (Heb 7.22–25).

Testament, Old, first 39 books of the Bible, accepted as holy Scriptures by both Jews and Christians; the name, not used by Jews, means "old covenant," referring to the agreement between God and the Israelites (Ex 24.7).

thanks,
O give t. to the Lord Ps 106.1
having given t. he Mt 15.36
T. be to God for II Cor 9.15

Thomas, disciple of Jesus (Mt 10.3).
doubted resurrection Jn 20.24ff

threshing, separating grain from straw and chaff (Ruth 3.14).

TIMBREL

timbrel, musical instrument similar to a tambourine (Ps 150.4).

time, B.C. (before Christ) the years before Jesus' birth; includes the Old Testament years. A.D. (Anno Domini, year of our Lord) time from year in which Jesus was believed to have been born; includes all but earliest New Testament events.

Timothy, Paul's young friend; two books in New Testament written as letters to Timothy.

T., *the son of a Jewish woman* Acts 16.1

tithe, one tenth of one's income paid to support the church (Mal 3.10).
all the t. of the land Lev 27.30

toil, to work hard, labor.
they neither t. nor spin Mt 6.28
t. all night and took nothing Lk 5.5

transfiguration, a change in Jesus' appearance on the mountain (Mt 17).

transgression, sin, wrongdoing.
whose t. is forgiven Ps 32.1
wounded for our t. Is 53.5

treasure
where your t. is, there will Mt 6.21
have t. in heaven Mt 19.21

Trinity, the Christian Church's belief that God is one, yet known three ways, as Father, Son, and Holy Spirit.

truth,
worship in spirit and in t. Jn 4.24
t. will make you free Jn 8.32
the t. is not in us I Jn 1.8

U

uncircumcised, not bearing the mark of a member of Israel.

unclean, not clean (see clean).

unleavened, describing a kind of bread or cake that has no leaven or yeast in it (Ex 12.15).

unrighteous, wicked or sinful.
the u. man his thoughts Is 55.7
cleanse us from all u. I Jn 1.9

upper room, a room on the second floor or on the roof, used for guests and special times; especially the upper room where Jesus and the apostles ate their last supper together.
a large u. r. furnished Mk 14.15

uttermost, farthest away.
dwell in the u. parts Ps 139.9
salvation to the u. Acts 13.47

V

vain, without success (Mt 15.9); without respect or honor (Ex 30.7).

veil, 1. light fabric worn over the face (Gen 24.65). 2. curtain in the tabernacle which closed off the most holy place (Lev 16.2).

vessel, container such as pan or tub.
put the good into v. Mt 13.48
treasure in earthen v. II Cor 4.7

vineyard, a piece of land where grapes are grown (Mt 20.1).

virgin, a woman who has never mated with a man.
Behold a v. *shall conceive* Mt 1.23
a v. *betrothed to a man* Lk 1.27

vision, something seen that is not of the real world, as in a dream or trance, or like Peter's vision of the animals (Acts 10.9–16).
to Daniel in a v. Dan 2.19
he had seen a v. Lk 1.22
v. *appeared to Paul* Acts 16.9

voice,
a still small v. I Kings 19.12
v. *of one crying in the* Mt 3.3
lo, a v. *from heaven* Mt 3.17
the sheep hear his v. Jn 10.3

vow, a serious promise to God.
Jacob made a . saying Gen 28.20
Hannah's v. I Sam 1.11
Make your v. *to the Lord* Ps 76.11

W

wait,
w. *for the Lord* Prov 20.22
they who w. *for the Lord* Is 40.31

watch,
w. *therefore, for you do* Mt 24.42
w. *and pray that you may* Mt 26.41

WATCHTOWER

watchtower, a fortified structure on the wall or above the gate of a city from which watch is kept for enemies (Is 21.8).

water,
opened the rock and w. *gushed* Ps 105.41
baptize you with w. Mt 3.11
walked on the w. Mt 14.29

w. *now became wine* Jn 2.9
get that living w. Jn 4.11

way,
Teach me thy w., *O Lord* Ps 27.11
This is the w., *walk in it* Is 30.21
I am the w. . . . *the truth,* Jn 14.6

white,
I shall be w. *than snow* Ps 51.7
his garments became w. Mt 17.2

wicked,
if there be any w. *way* Ps 139.24
Let the w. *forsake his* Is 55.7

wife,
man . . . cleaves to his w. Gen 2.24
verses about a good w. Prov 31.10ff

will, something wished or desired.
Thy w. *be done* Mt 6.10
he who does the w. *of* Mt 7.21

wind,
even w. *and sea obey* Mt 8.27
comparing w. and spirit Jn 3.8
and tossed by the w. Jas 1.6

window,
opened the w. *of the ark* Gen 8.6
by a rope through the w. Josh 2.15
young man sitting in the w. Acts 20.9
in a basket through a w. II Cor 11.33

wisdom, the quality of being wise, judging rightly.
God gave Solomon w. I Kings 4.29

about w. of Jesus Mt 13.54; Lk 2.52
But the w. from above Jas 3.17

wise men, men who studied the stars and prophecies (Mt 2).

witness, a person who saw or can give a first-hand account of something.
shall bear false w. Ex 20.16
shall be my w. Acts 1.8
w. to his resurrection Acts 1.22

woman,
shall be called w. because Gen 2.23
w. of Samaria Jn 4.7

word, the, 1. the word of God; 2. the Bible; the written record of man's relationship with God.
Thy w. is a lamp to my Ps 119.105
In the beginning was the w. Jn 1.1
the W. became flesh and Jn 1.14
Let the w. . . . dwell in you Col 3.16

w. of the Lord abides I Pet 1.25

works,
great are thy w., O Lord Ps 92.5
see your good w. and give Mt 5.16
faith apart from w. is Jas 2.26

world,
the light of the w. Mt 5.14; Jn 8.12
God so loved the w. Jn 3.16
If the w. hates you Jn 15.18

worship, to show love, devotion, and honor to God (or a god), usually by a gathering of people, as in a church service, joining in prayer, music, offerings, etc.
if you w. other gods Deut 30.17
O come, let us w. and Ps 95.6
you shall w. the Lord Mt 4.10
which is your spiritual w. Rom 12.1

wrong,
Paul talks about doing w. Rom 7.15–25
Love does no w. to a Rom 13.10

Y

years,
For a thousand y. in thy Ps 90.4
bound him for a thousand y. Rev 20.2

Z

Zacchaeus (za-kē′ás), a tax collector who climbed a tree to see Jesus.
Jesus meets Z. Lk 19.2–10

Zealot, members of a group of Jews who wanted to get rid of Roman rule in their land.
who was called the Z. Lk 6.15

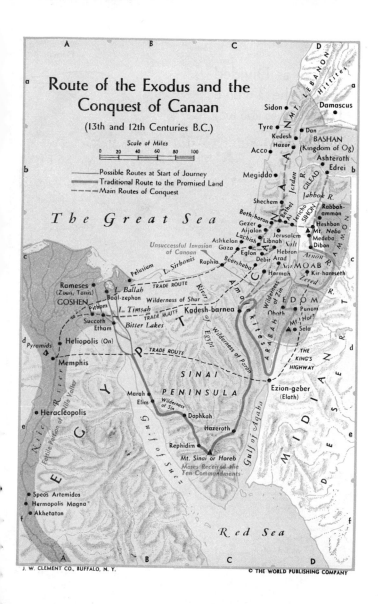

Route of the Exodus and the Conquest of Canaan

(13th and 12th Centuries B.C.)

Scale of Miles
0   20   40   60   80   100

—— Possible Routes at Start of Journey
══ Traditional Route to the Promised Land
- - - Main Routes of Conquest

The Great Sea

Sidon • Damascus
Tyre • Kedesh • Dan BASHAN (Kingdom of Og)
Acco • Hazor Ashteroth
Megiddo • Edrei
Shechem • Jabbok R.
Beth-horon • Bethel Ai Jericho SIHON Rabbah-ammon
Gezer • Heshbon
Aijalon • Jerusalem Mt. Nebo
Ashkelon • Lachish Libnah Salt Medeba
Gaza • Eglon Hebron Dibon
Debir Arad AMMON
Beersheba • Hermah MOAB
Raphia Kir-hareseth
Unsuccessful Invasion of Canaan Zered
Pelusium L. Sirbonis EDOM
TRADE ROUTE Oboth Punon
Rameses (Zoan, Tanis) L. Ballah Baal-zephon Wilderness of Shur Mt. Hor
GOSHEN Pithom L. Timsah Kadesh-barnea Sela
Succoth Bitter Lakes TRADE ROUTE
Etham THE KING'S HIGHWAY
Heliopolis (On)
Pyramids TRADE ROUTE Ezion-geber (Elath)
Memphis
SINAI
PENINSULA
Marah • Heracleopolis
Elim Wilderness of Sin
Dophkah
Hazeroth
Rephidim
Mt. Sinai or Horeb
Moses Received the Ten Commandments
Speos Artemidos
Hermopolis Magna
Akhetaton

Red Sea

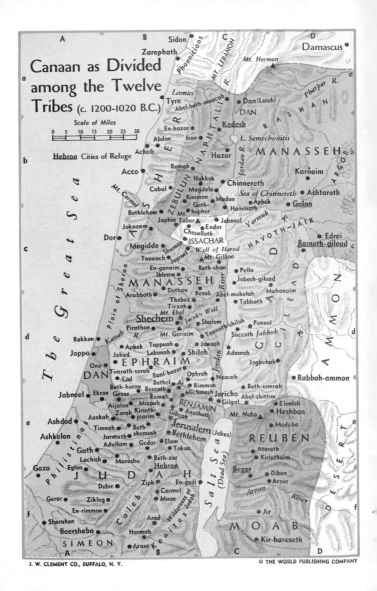

Canaan as Divided among the Twelve Tribes (c. 1200-1020 B.C.)

Scale of Miles
0 5 10 15 20 25 30

Hebron Cities of Refuge

Sidon
Zarephath
Damascus
Leontes
Tyre
Abel-beth-maacah
Mt. Lebanon
Mt. Hermon
Phoenicians
Dan (Laish)
DAN
Kedesh
En-hazor
Iron
BASHAN
Abdon
Hazor
L. Semechonitis
MANASSEH
Achzib
Ramah
Karnaim
Acco
Hukkok
Chinnereth
Cabul
Magdala
Rimmon
Madon
Sea of Chinnereth
Ashtaroth
Gath-hepher
Aphek
Golan
Bethlehem
Hammath
Jokneam
Japhia
Tabor
Jabneel
Jabneel
Dor
Endor
Chesulloth
Yarmuk
Megiddo
ISSACHAR
Well of Herod
HAVOTH-JAIR
Edrei
Shunem
Mt. Gilboa
Ramoth-gilead
Taanach
Jezreel
Beth-shan
Pella
En-gannim
Jabesh-gilead
Ibleam
Arubboth
Dothan
Bezek
Abel-meholah
Mahanaim
Thebez
Tabbath
Tirzah
Mt. Ebal
Jacob's Well
GILEAD
Shechem
Shalem
Pirathon
Mt. Gerizim
Taanath-shiloh
Penuel
Rakkon
Tappuah
Lebonah
Janoah
Succoth
Jabbok
AMMON
Joppa
Aphek
Shiloh
Jordan
Adamah
Jogbehah
Ono
EPHRAIM
Jehud
Timrath-serah
Baal-hazor
Ophrah
Nearah
Rabbah-ammon
DAN
Lod
Bethel
Ai
Rimmon
Beth-nimrah
Jabneel
Ekron
Gezer
Beeroth
Michmash
Jericho
Abel-shittim
Aijalon
Ramah
Gilgal
Ashdod
Azekah
Mizpah
Gibeon
Anathoth
Mt. Nebo
Elealeh
Heshbon
Zorah
Kiriath-jearim
JERUSALEM (Jebus)
Ashkelon
Timnah
Beth-shemesh
Bethlehem
Medeba
REUBEN
Jarmuth
Elam
Gath
Adullam
Gedor
Tekoa
Ataroth
Lachish
Maresha
Beth-zur
Kiriathaim
Gaza
Eglon
Hebron
Bezer
Dibon
Ziph
En-gedi
Aroer
Dobir
Arnon
Gerar
Carmel
Arad
Maon
MOAB
Ziklag
Wilderness of Judah
En-rimmon
JUDAH
Caleb
Ar
Sharuhen
Hormah
Kenites
Kir-haresheth
Beersheba
SIMEON
Aroer
Salt Sea (Dead Sea)

ASHER
NAPHTALI
ZEBULUN
Mt. Carmel
BENJAMIN
Plain of Sharon
Kanah R.
Philistia
The Great Sea
Jordan R.
Pharpar R.
ARGOB
DESERT

J. W. CLEMENT CO., BUFFALO, N. Y.

© THE WORLD PUBLISHING COMPANY

The Empire of David and Solomon

(Tenth Century B.C.)

Scale of Miles
0 20 40 60 80

Territory conquered by David

CYPRUS

Arvad

Hamath — ARAM OR

HAMATH

Emesa — SYRIA

Kadesh

Tadmor (Palmyra)

Riblah Zedad

Byblos (Gebal)

Chun — Hazar-enan

Baalbek (Heliopolis)

Berothai

ZOBAH

May have been under Solomon's control

Helbon

Sidon

Damascus

Aramaeans

Leontes R. — Ijon

Tyre — Abel Dan — Mt. Hermon

Kadesh — MAACAH

Sea of Chinnereth

Acco — GESHUR — Ashtaroth

ARGOB

Cabul — Aphek — Kenath

Dor — Beth-shan

Megiddo — Jabesh-gilead — Edrei — Bosrah (Bostra)

Jezreel — Ramoth-gilead — Salecah

Tirzah — Mahanaim

Shechem — Jordan R.

ISRAEL — AMMON

Joppa — Adamah

Shiloh — GILEAD

Bethel — Rabbah-ammon

Ekron — Jerusalem — Heshbon

Ashdod — Bethlehem — Medeba

Ashkelon — Gath — Dibon

Gaza — Lachish — Hebron

Gerar — JUDAH — Ar

Raphia — MOAB

Beersheba — Kir-hareseth

Wilderness of Judah

R. of Egypt

GREAT DESERT

Kadesh-barnea — Bozrah

Punom

EDOM

ARABAH — Sela

Teman

Wilderness of Paran

David reigned over Judah 7 years and 6 months, over Judah and Israel 33 years. Solomon's reign was noted for cultural and economic growth

Ezion-geber (Elath)

The Great Sea

PHOENICIA

LEBANON

PHILISTIA

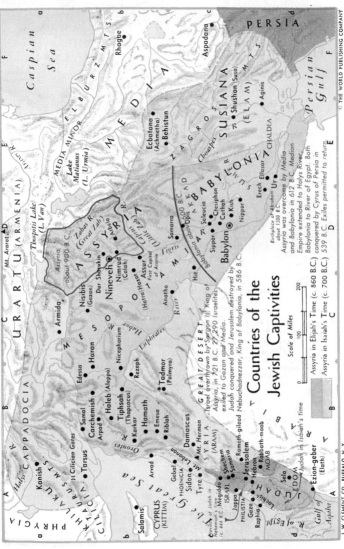

Countries of the Jewish Captivities

PERSIA

Caspian Sea

Rhagae

Aspadana

ELBURZ MTS.

MEDIA MINOR

MEDIA

ZAGROS MTS.

Lake Matianus (L. Urmia)

Ecbatana (Achmetha) •Behistun

SUSIANA

Shushan (Susa) (ELAM)

Aginis

Choaspes

Persian Gulf

© THE WORLD PUBLISHING COMPANY

Mt. Ararat

URARTU (ARMENIA)

Thospitis Lake (L. Van)

Zabus R. (Great Zab)

Armida

Caprus R. (Little Zab)

Assyria about 900 B.C.

ASSYRIA

Arbela

Nisibis (Gozan)

Dur Sharukin

Nineveh •Nimrud (Calah)

Assur
First Capital of Assyria

Erech Ellasar Ur

CHALDEA

Birthplace of Abram about 1300 B.C.

Babylonia about 600 B.C.

A K K A D

Seleucia Ctesiphon

Sippar Cuthah Kish

Babylon

Nippur

M I S O P O T A M I A

Hit

Sumarra

(Hatra) Hatra

Anatho

Tigris R.

Assyria was overcome by Media and Babylonia in 612 B.C. Median Empire extended to Halys River, Babylonia to River of Egypt. Both Babylonia and Persia conquered by Cyrus of Persia in 539 B.C. Exiles permitted to return.

Judah conquered and Jerusalem destroyed by Nebuchadnezzar, King of Babylonia, in 586 B.C.

Israel overthrown by Sargon II, King of Assyria, in 721 B.C. 27,290 Israelites exiled to Gozan and Media.

GREAT DESERT

Edessa

Haran

Euphrates River

Nicephorium

Rezeph

Tadmor (Palmyra)

Kanish

PHRYGIA

CAPPADOCIA

TAURUS MTS.

Cilician Gates

Tarsus

CILICIA

Samal

Carchemish

Arpad

Haleb (Aleppo)

Tiphsah (Thapsacus)

Karkar

Hamath

Riblah

Orontes R.

Emesa

Damascus

SYRIA (ARAM)

Mt. Hermon

Lebanon

Ramoth-gilead

Rabbath-moab

MOAB

EDOM

Sela

Ezion-geber (Elath)

Gulf of Aqaba

Salamis

CYPRUS (KITTIM)

Great Sea

Arvad

Gebal

Sidon

Tyre

PHOENICIA

Joppa

Gaza

Raphia

PHILISTIA

ISRAEL

Shechem Samaria

Jerusalem

Hebron

Lachish

JUDAH

Megiddo

Captivity of Israel in Nehemiah's Time (c. 444 B.C.)

Judah in Isaiah's time

River of Egypt

Scale of Miles

0   50   100   200

Assyria in Elijah's Time (c. 860 B.C.)

Assyria in Isaiah's Time (c. 700 B.C.)

J. W. CLEMENT CO. BUFFALO, N. Y.

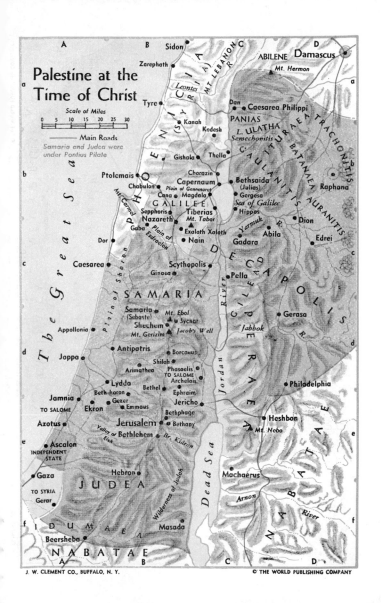

Palestine at the Time of Christ

Scale of Miles

0 5 10 15 20 25 30

— Main Roads

Samaria and Judea were under Pontius Pilate

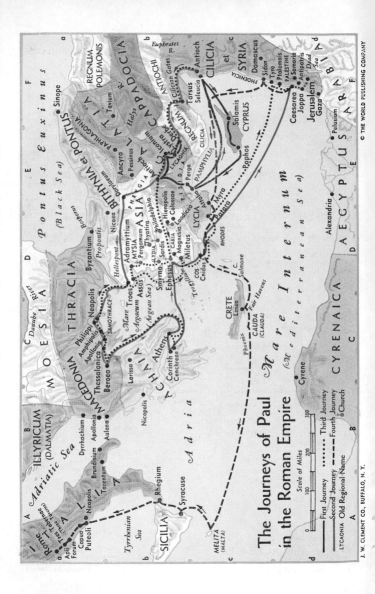

The Journeys of Paul
in the Roman Empire

Scale of Miles

0   100   200   300

First Journey
Second Journey
Third Journey ··········
Fourth Journey ----
LYCAONIA Old Regional Name   ● Church

Modern Jerusalem

Scale of Feet

0 500 1000 1500 2000

MT. SCOPUS

German Hospital

MOUNT OF OLIVES

Church of the Ascension

Carmelite Convent

Church of the Prophets

Vir Gallilei Chapel

Church of the Tomb of the Virgin

Russian Church

Gethsemane Church

Tomb of Absalom

Tomb of Zechariah

JERICHO ROAD

MOUNT OF OFFENCE

Stork's Tower

Pool of Bethesda

Church of St. Anne

St. Mary's

Church Sitti Mariam

Birket Israel

St. Stephen's Gate

Golden Gate

Tomb of the Virgin

Museum

American School of Oriental Research

American Colony

Gordon's Calvary

Jeremiah's Grotto

Herod's Gate

VIA DOLOROSA

HARAM ESH-SHARIF

Dome of the Rock

Aksa Mosque

"Solomon's Stables"

KIDRON VALLEY

Silwan

NO MAN'S LAND
(Under United Nations Protection)

Aceldama, Field of Blood

SALADIN RD.

Ecole Biblique

St. Étienne

Damascus Gate

JERICHO RD.

MOHAMMEDAN QUARTER

OLD CITY

Wailing Wall

JEWISH QUARTER

Dung Gate

Virgin's Fountain

Pool of Siloam

Hezekiah's Aqueduct

MT. OPHEL

Old Pool

NABLUS

JORDAN

ISRAEL

New Gate

Notre Dame de France

CHRISTIAN QUARTER

Church of the Holy Sepulchre

David's Tower

Protestant Church

Cathedral of St. James

ARMENIAN QUARTER

Zion Gate

David's Tomb

Cenaculum

Dormition Church

Necrosterion

MT. ZION

JORDAN

ISRAEL

Tombs of the Kings

St. George's Cathedral

Mandelbaum Gate

St. George's RD.

Italian Hospital

Abyssinian Church

Hospitals

Immigration Office

Cathedral

Russian Compound

Post Office

ST. PAUL'S RD.

French Hospital

Jaffa Gate

The Citadel

Herod's Palace

David's Tower

Hazekiah's Pool

New Pool

VALLEY OF HINNOM

BETHLEHEM RD.

VALLEY

MEA SHEARIM STREET

STREET OF THE PROPHETS

TEL AVIV-JAFFA STREET

American Consulate

French Consulate

King David Hotel

Y.M.C.A.

Birket es Sultan (Sultan's Pool)

KING DAVID RD.

Pilate's Aqueduct

Railroad Station

Museum

Ratisbonne Monastery and School

Jerusalem Girls College

Rehavia

Jewish Agency

Terra Sancta

Marillah Pool

Moslem Cemetery

Stad um

MAMILLAH RD.

KING GEORGE AVE.

GAZA ROAD

Talbiya

© THE WORLD PUBLISHING COMPANY

J. W. CLEMENT CO., BUFFALO, N. Y.

The Holy Land Today

Scale of Miles
0 5 10 15 20 25 30

—— Railroads
—— Main Roads
• Ancient Sites

Mediterranean Sea

A — **B** — **C** — **D**

Saydā (Sidon)
Aṣ Ṣarafand (Zarephath)
Rāshayyā
Dimashq (Damascus)
Qatanā
Kiswah
Ḥāṣbayyā
Mt. Hermon
'Awaj R.

Ṣūr (Tyre) (Kanah)
Litani
An Nāqūrah
Qānā
Metulla
Baniyas (Caesarea Philippi)
Ghaghghib
Dan
Tibnin
Bint Jubayl
Al Quanaytirah
Aṣ Ṣanamayn

Nahariyya
Kedesh
Hazor
Meiron
Na'rān
Al Khushnīyah
Nawa
Izra

Acre (Acco, Ptolemais)
Shefar'am
Safad
Rama
Chorazin
Kefar Ata
Migdal (Magadan)
Capernaum
Shaykh Miskīn
Haifa
Tsippori
Cana
Tiberias
Sea of Galilee
Fiq (Aphek)
Tafas
Tirat Karmel
Nazareth
Deganya
Susita (Hippos)
'Atlit
Mt. Tabor
Umm Qays (Gadara)
Dar'ā (Edret)
Jabir
Dor
'Afula
Yarmuk R.
Zikhron Ya'aqov
Megiddo (Armageddon)
Beit Hashitta
Irbid (Arbela)
Caesarea
Pardes Hanna
Mt. Gilboa
Al Husn
Hadera
Arrabāh
Beit Shean
Tabaqat Fahl (Pella)
Al Mafraq
Natanya
Tūl Karm
Dothan
Tubās
Ajlun
Jarash (Gerasa)
Even Yehuda
Kefar Sava
Sabastiyah (Samaria)
Ra'anana
Qalqilyah
Nābulus (Shechem)
Penuel
Zarqā (Jabbok)
Herzliya
Antipatris
Jacob's Well
Ramat Gan
Benei Beraq
Petah Tiqva
Shiloh
Dāmiyā (Adamah)
As Salt
Az Zarqā
Tel Aviv-Jaffa (Joppa)
Bat Yam
Holon
Phasaelis
Suwaylih
Amman (Rabbah-ammon) (Philadelphia)
Rishon le Zion
Shuqba
Nī'lin
Baytin (Bethel)
Na'ūr
Sahab
Ramle
Rām Allah
Gibeah
Al Bīrah
Arīhā (Jericho)
Al Yadūdah
Rehovot
Imwas
(Ekron) 'Eqron
Gezer
Gederah
NO MAN'S LAND
Al 'Ayzarīyah (Bethany)
Heshbon
Mt. Nebo
Zuwayzā
(Azotus) Ashdod
Ashkelon
Bayt Jālā
Jerusalem
Khirbat Qumran *Dead Sea Scrolls found here*
Ma'daba
New Ashkelon
Anata
Bayt Laḥm (Bethlehem)
Tekoa
Beth-zur
Machaerus
Dab'ah
Gaza
Lachish
Al Khalil (Hebron)
Wilderness of Judah
En-gedi
Dhiban (Dibon)
Khān az Zabīb
Eglon
Debir
Gerar
Wadi Su'aydah (R. Arnon)
U.A.R. (EGYPT)
Masada
Al Mazra
Al Qatranah
Beersheba
Arad
Sodom
Al Karak
Mu'tah
Al Manzil

LEBANON
MT. LEBANON
PHOENICIA
GALILEE
SYRIA
Mt. Carmel
Plain of Sharon
Plain of Esdraelon
SAMARIA
TRANSJORDAN
Jordan R.
PHILISTIA
JUDEA
MOAB
IDUMEA
NEGEV
Dead Sea